COMICS VALUES ANNUAL: 1998 EDITION
The Comics Books Price Guide

by Alex G. Malloy

edited by Stuart Wells III

Antique Trader Books
Dubuque, Iowa

Copyright © 1997 by Alex G. Malloy & Stuart W. Wells III
All Rights Reserved
Published by Antique Trader Books, Dubuque, Iowa

No part of this book may be reproduced, transmitted, or stored
in any form or by any means, electronic or mechanical,
without prior written permission from the publisher.

Designed by Stuart W. Wells III

Manufactured in the United States of America

ISBN: 0–930625–85–4
ISSN: 1062–4503

**Other books and magazines published by
Antique Trader Publications:**
The Antique Trader Weekly
Collector Magazine & Price Guide
Toy Trader Magazine
Postcard Collector Magazine
DISCoveries Magazine
Big Reel Magazine
Military Trader Magazine
Baby Boomer Collectibles Magazine
Antique Trader Books

**To order additional copies of this book or
other publications listed above, contact:**
Antique Trader Publications
P.O. Box 1050
Dubuque, Iowa 52004
1-800-334-7165

Contents

PREFACE

By Alex G. Malloy

As perhaps could be expected, this past year has proven to be yet another full of tumultuous changes within the comic book industry; and not all of them good. Last year's trends of plummeting sales of individual titles continues, as virtually every company has experienced a sharp drop off in sales. Comic book stores across the country continue to close their doors even as other shops open for the first time, and sales of back issues continue to be soft.

Perhaps the biggest news of the past year was the plummeting value (or lack thereof), of Marvel's Stock. Early in the year the company went into Chapter 11 to protect its assets, and reorganize. This has caused the company's stock to drop, and as the Fall of '97 approached, the company (which once traded for $60.00 a share), was listed at $1.75 per share, less than its comics, which sell for $1.99. As the year closed out, the mainstream press reported apparent success in Marvel's last–ditch efforts to salvage the company and prevent it from slipping into Chapter 7, where the assets would simply be auctioned off to the highest bidder. If the verbal deal can be reduced to writing, Marvel would be able to deal with the crushing debt load it incurred in buying trading card manufacturers Fleer and Skybox, in part by selling off Panini, which mostly makes stickers.

Meanwhile there were all sorts of reports of in–fighting between owner Ronald O. Perlman, and the stockholders who were attempting to wrest control of the company away from Perlman. These stories (most filtering down to the comic–buying public in the forms of rumors and snippets of half–truths, and misinformation), ran from having Perlman selling off the various characters to numerous different publishers (from DC to Image), to the triumphant return of Jim Shooter to the editor–in–chief position. Only time will tell which were/are true.

Naturally enough, the smaller houses have also had to scale back their operations, Chaos!, Crusade, and numerous other smaller publishers continue to exist, but command a smaller, and smaller percentage of the audience. Which is not to say that Independents are dying out, as every month there seems to be a whole new graduating class of indie comics that are being produced. As a cottage industry, the indies are here to stay, and will continue to become a more

significant part of the market in years to come.

Then, of course, there are the deaths in the family, some (perhaps) expected, some not. Curt Swan, long–time Superman artist passed away, as did Marvel Executive Editor, Mark Gruenwald. Gruenwald's ashes were added to the ink used to reprint a bound volume of the *Squadron Supreme*, as per his will.

Still, all the news out there isn't bad.

Acclaim comics, managed to resuscitate itself with a new management team, and several revamped titles. Marvel kicked off a year–long *Heroes Reborn* saga with its most popular titles (*Captain America*, *The Avengers*, *Iron Man*, and *The Fantastic Four*), that was creatively directed and implemented by several of the ex–Marvel/current Image founders. Several comic book movies hit the big screen (*Batman & Robin*, *Men in Black*, *Spawn*, *Steel*), with mixed results (*B&R* was slammed; *MIB* proved to be a certifiable blockbuster; *Spawn* was praised; while *Steel* was generally overlooked).

The Acclaim re–rebirth was kicked off with brand–new incarnations of several of their characters, including Turok, XO-Manowar, Solar, Magnus, Eternal Warrior, Ninjack, and others. While these new incarnations proved to be somewhat jarring to those fans who had followed the original incarnations, the books have garnered a new following, and hence, a new lease on life. To these new/old characters, several new titles were added—*Quantum and Woody*, *Troublemakers*, *Trinity Angels*—to name a few.

Marvel's Heroes Reborn kicked off with Jim Lee handling the rebirth, and retelling of the origins of the FF and Iron Man, and Rob Liefeld in charge of Cap. America and the Avengers. The plan was for these two creators to re–introduce and re–tell the first year or so of the origins of this group of characters. While the project was kicked off with a bang, about half–way through it seemed to run into rough waters. First of all, Liefeld and Jim Valentino (who was writing *The Avengers*), had a falling out (more later), then Marvel gave Liefeld the heave–ho (and turned his two titles over to Lee to complete).

Liefeld, no stranger to controversy himself, had his hands full this year. He was ousted (or quit, depending on who's story you believe), from Image, and, with his two new partners: Scott Rosenberg—the former head of Malibu, and the man who brought Men in Black to the Silver Screen (who had just resigned from Marvel), and Jeph Loeb (*Batman*, *Cable*, *X–Force*, *Captain America: Heroes Reborn*), formed Awesome Entertainment, and began to produce *The Coven*, *Kaboom*, *Supreme*, and *The Fighting American*.

Yes, that Fighting American. In a story that was as exciting as it was controversial, Liefeld left *Cap. America*, and announced that he was planning on issuing his own patriotic character Agent America, this was followed by an announcement that he had cut a deal with Joe Simon and Roz Kirby to produce

the Simon/Kirby character, The Fighting American. Needless to say this was followed by the usual saber rattling from Marvel who attempted a lawsuit, only to have it shot down in the court system (see Jeph Loeb interview).

All–in–all, during the calendar year of 1997, the world of comics had—once again—proven to be volatile, thrilling, and exciting. People (both fans and foes), predicted the imminent demise of not only several of the major (and minor), players in the field. There were no major failures of any of publishing houses. Comics continue to publish, magazines about comics continue to publish, and movies, toys, videogames, and other collectibles relating to comic books continue to be licensed and produced.

Is the end of this industry in sight? Who knows? Certainly not us. However, the participants in this industry show every sign of refusing to go quietly into that dark night, and for every nay–sayer, there is at least one individual who still makes the weekly trek to their favorite comic shop to purchase the newest installment of their favorite four–color action hero. Who will win out? Tune in next week, same Bat–time, same Bat–channel.

Special thanks to Kevin Halstead, John A. Wilcox, Shelly Robertson, Mark Haverty, Don Bouchard, Jeremy Shorr, Mark Brown, Howard Harris, Stephen Passarelli, Carl Bridgers, John Pearce, Steve Sorbo, Bryan Ash, John Dacey, Michael Shippey, Don Bettis, Pat Callanan, Mike Salvo, Castle Comics and Tim Fredrick for their assistance in producing this book.

I must also mention Harry Rinker, Robert J. Sodaro, Jeph Loeb, Mike Gold, Rich Spears and Allan Miller for guidance and talent in making this annual possible.

Last, but not least, to all the writers, artists, letterers, colorists, editors, and all at DC, Marvel, Dark Horse, Image, Malibu, Acclaim-Valiant, Entity Comics, Topps, Warp Graphics, Teckno Comics and Continuity... Hearty Thanks!

THE RISE AND FALL OF ATLAS COMICS

(According to Jeff Rovin)
as told to Robert J. Sodaro

Way back in 1991, seven hot young artists laboring in the vineyards of comics determined that they had had enough with the industry's corporate structure, as well as the work-for-hire contracts under which they had been toiling, and—very vocally—split with the established comic publishing houses. These seven intrepid souls then went off on their own, and did what they wanted to do, which was create and own their own line of comics. These seven were the founding fathers of Image Comics. Two years later history—after a fashion—repeated itself; not once, but twice. Frank Miller, John Byrne and some friends founded Legend, an imprint of creator-owned comics that was distributed through Dark Horse Comics, and Malibu Comics began a line of creator-owned comics entitled Bravura with Walt Simonson, Jim Starlin, Howard Chaykin, and others.

In the interim, Legend and Bravura have ceased to exist (Malibu was sold to Marvel, and while Dark Horse still publishes several of the Legend creators, the "Easter Island" logo no longer appears on the covers). At the time of their foundations, both Miller and Simonson publicly acknowledged their debt and lineage to Image, yet there was another company—out of print since the mid-'70s—that is little known by much of today's comic-buying audience which—in retrospect—is actually a much earlier ancestor of all three companies. That company was Atlas Comics. While the company lasted barely a full year, and none of its books were published for more than five or six issues, the effects of Atlas are still echoing throughout the industry today, more than 20 years after its demise.

Destructor #2, © Atlas Comics

The Line-Up

According to Jeff Rovin, co-editor of the line (along with Stan Lee's brother, Larry Lieber), stated that save for the

lack of a Direct Market, "...I think we would have been Image Comics." Considering the array of talent that contributed to Atlas, this is no idle boast. A partial list of contributors includes Howard Chaykin, Walt Simonson, Alex Toth, Mike Kaluta, Al Milgrom, Sal Amendola, Steve Ditko, Wally Wood, Neil Adams, Pat Broderick, Marshall Rogers, Pat Boyette, Mike Sikeowski, Pablo Marcus, John Severin, Russ Heath, Frank Thorne, Ernie Colon, Jim Mooney, Larry Hama, Michael Fleisher, Archie Goodwin, John Albano, and Rick Meyers.

Iron Jaw #2, © Atlas Comics

According to Rovin, Atlas was founded in 1974 by Martin Goodman, former publisher of Marvel. "I went to work at Atlas in June of '74. At the time, Martin Goodman, who is of course, the founder of Marvel Comics, wanted to publish five color comics, and two black-and-white comics. Even before we started, it became apparent to him that in order to get the rack space we needed, we had to publish more titles than that. We ended up with 20-odd monthly magazines. I was doing about six plus black-and-whites, and Larry Lieber was doing four color books."

Apparently part of the deal when Goodman had sold Marvel Comics to Magazine Management Corporation, was that his son, Chip, would still work there. "It was never clear whether Chip quit, or was fired," Rovin stated, "But when he became unemployed, Martin started Seaboard Periodicals. We also published romance magazines, puzzle books, and a mystery magazine, which was pretty interesting. I don't think Chip's heart was ever into comic books."

In the Beginning

Given the presence of a direct market and the plethora of comic book publishers in 1997, it may be hard to understand that it wasn't always this way. In fact, for quite a significant period of time, there were almost virtually just three comic book publishers, DC, Marvel, and Archie. Between these three giants, they had all but cornered the U. S. market. It was in this atmosphere, that Martin Goodman ventured back into the market after selling off Marvel. Speaking from this historical perspective, Rovin related Atlas' auspicious beginnings; "When we started, there were only two other comic book companies of any significance [producing superheroes], DC and Marvel. There was Gold Key, of course, but

they had their niche. Charlton was around, they had their niche. Mike Friedrich was doing his comic books [Star*Reach]."

Other comic companies at the time that were producing non-superhero titles included Warren (where Rovin had been working when he jumped to Atlas), which stuck to black-and-white magazines; Archie, which all but owned the teenage humor market; and Harvey another kiddy/humor publisher. Needless to say, DC, Marvel, and Archie were the Big Three; commanding the lion's share of the market, with all other publishers comprising the bottom 10% or so.

"Word went out, that anybody who worked for Atlas would not be permitted to work for DC. It scared a lot of artists off." The memo—direct from the office of then VP and editor-in-chief of DC, Carmine Infantino—indicated that a number of benefits would be forthcoming to all freelance writers, artists, colorists, and letterers. These included bonuses, returned artwork and color proofs, rate increases, and reprint rates. However, implicit in the memo, was the restriction that said freelancers were working solely for DC.

Morlock 2001 #1, © Atlas Comics

Infantino's reason for doing this was plainly obvious to Rovin. "At the time, there was a rather limited pool of talent to draw from. Justifiably he was afraid of loosing writers and artists." Marvel's reaction to the impending birth of Atlas was not as overt. "They had to be careful because of Martin's former relationship there. Also, Stan Lee was very gracious. He made a call very early on, saying he felt there was room for everybody. I don't think it was Stan who decided to flood the market with reprints at that time, and grab up the rack space, but none-the-less that's how Marvel responded."

Needless to say, starting up a new color line of Code-approved superhero comics in 1974 was going to be an up-hill battle. Yet, in spite of the odds stacked against them, the Goodmans determined to give it a try. "We had a lot of writers come over and make inquiries," Rovin revealed. "But I think we were used as a lever to get better deals elsewhere." According to Rovin the tide really turned when he managed to convince Howard Chaykin to come on board. "The first

artist who joined us was Howie Chaykin. His courage in so doing, was enormous."

Planet of the Vampires #1,
© Atlas Comics

Rovin—who was still working for Warren at the time—approached Chaykin (who had just dropped off a job at the Warren offices), and informed him of the new company. "Howie had just turned in a job that I liked a lot," Rovin related. "I followed him into the elevator and explained to him what was happening. He said, 'Count me in.' He didn't hesitate for a second. I told him we wanted him to do a monthly book, and that he would have complete freedom to do what he wanted to after we hammered out the initial concepts."

Much of Rovin's admiration and regard for Chaykin is a direct result of Chaykin's complete willingness to sign up with the company, given the state of the industry at the time. "He was the first Name we got, period. The fact that he came along and had all this enthusiasm fired up a lot of people. Which I think and I don't want to speak for him, even though I think I'm accurate, I think his levels of enthusiasm are proportionate to his bitterness now about some of it. Because he was so excited. Because it was so free and open, the disappointment we all felt was proportionate to that. I think he certainly took it on the chin that way."

Rovin went so far as to liken the effect of signing Chaykin to work for Atlas to the effect of signing Brando to act in the first Superman movie: it immediate gave Atlas untold credibility with the artistic community, which soon became apparent when Chaykin's contemporaries began to contract for work shortly afterwards. "Walt [Simonson] was with him [in the elevator] at the time, or Bernie Wrightson I forget who. Then Walt came immediately thereafter. He didn't want to do a monthly book. He just wanted to do black-and-white. Whatever else we could come up with. We gave him one story, Gorgo vs. Rodan. We were negotiating with ToHo at the time to do their monsters. However, unfortunately for Atlas, Marvel moved in and bought that out from under them. That was kind of frustrating. We had lots of deals. We had deals to do movie stuff that Chip backed out on, now that I think of it. We were suppose to do *Planet of the Vampires: the Movie.*"

The Atlas Effect

As indicated by the reactions of both Marvel and DC, it was apparent that they were running scared at the birth of Atlas, and to combat the threat of a new publisher of four-color superhero comics, they began to scramble to secure their stranglehold on the marketplace. "We were paying, in some cases, better rates. Certainly to get talent who was reluctant to work with us, we had to pay better rates. Guys like Neil Adams weren't cheap." Among the long-term contributions to the field, that came about as a direct result of Atlas Comics were better working conditions for creators (in the form of returned work and better pay), as well as the beginnings of creator-rights.

"We were single-handedly responsible for artists getting their work back from DC, and for royalties being paid. If you look at Carmine's document, you will see August 13, 1974 in National Periodicals' new program for a broad-range of added benefits, sending out bonus checks, increased rates, artists got their originals back, etc. This was a direct result of our coming into the field, and the fact we were doing that."

Marvel also began to wake up and smell the coffee, although it took a while longer. "Marvel [didn't come around] until Jim Shooter got in there and duked it out. Jim Warren had to do the same things. Artists, I won't say became spoiled, because we weren't around long enough, but they saw it could be different. So they rallied behind people like Neil Adams and became something of a force for creator's rights. Neil was, of course, very active in that at the time. We talked on many occasions on how we could do things better."

One of the other things that Rovin managed to acquire for his team of creators was a partial ownership of the characters on which they worked. "One of the things I had negotiated with Martin, was a partial ownership of all characters, and royalty set-up for the writers and artists. At the time you had to publish three issues before you got sales reports, so I was not around when the sales reports came in, but I subsequently learned that the titles did very well, before they were altered. Theoretically everyone should have been entitled to royalties. We have documents to that effect."

"Unfortunately, not everyone got to sign those documents. Howie, Michael Fleisher, Ernie Colon, and one or two others were the only ones who ever got to sign them. I have a copy of those here. Martin is dead. We can't really confirm what he agreed to with me. It was understood, that if we took these characters and did other things with them, that he would get a percentage of the money. It was a large percent, like 75%, but we would be free to market them elsewhere in other formats. Novelizations, a cartoon series, whatever."

Martin Goodman, who was only interested in the publishing end of things, was apparently not interested in any ancillary rights, So he told Rovin to go ahead

Scorpion #2, © Atlas Comics

Wulf the Barbarian #1, © Atlas Comics

Brute #1, © Atlas Comics

Grim Ghost #1, © Atlas Comics

and let the creators run with those things. He did, however want the lion's share of the money. "In terms of today's market, 75% corporate ownership is an outrageous sum. In 1974 it was an unprecedented freedom to have.

The Beginning of the End

The seeds of Atlas' destruction were, unfortunately, sown at its birth, for in spite of the major strides the company had initially made, the end was not far off. The fact of the matter is that Chip simply lost interest. I only edited two issues of most of the books before I left. I left in January of 1975, which was not a long time after starting. I'd only done two *Scorpions*, two *Wulf the Barbarian*, two *Brutes*, and two *Grim Ghosts*.

When Martin and Chip saw what Rovin was doing with his books, they got nervous, because they didn't look like Marvel books. It was then that they made a demand. "They demanded that all the books, look, read, and sound like Marvel Comics. They started hiring on their own, all the talent. Some of them were under contract with Marvel and were paid under the table, and worked anonymously. "Without my consent they would redo covers to make them look more like Marvel. *Wulf the Barbarian* #2 was a beautiful cover, until they cut in some demon woman that didn't belong there."

It soon became apparent to all involved that what had begun as a haven for creators was turning into a third-rate, hack publisher. "I'll tell you what Chip was thinking. The difference in budgeting five titles and budgeting 20-odd titles is considerable. As the money was going out, he started to panic. He started to panic before the sales reports came in, and he just decided to lay the ax to the group, and stop spending. That meant killing the titles." It also meant that writers and artists who had completed work weren't getting paid.

Wolf the Barbarian #2, © Atlas Comics

Rovin complained that not only did the Goodmans hire people who were not going to be true to the storylines set-up. They were famous for firing artists they didn't like. "Chip would take home finished material over weekends. Read it, not like it, and not want to pay for it. "That put me in a miserable position. I think Walt might have missed out getting paid on something. It was unbearable to be

in that position." Chip even required Rovin to fire art director Steve Mitchell. "Chip never liked him. Chip wanted me to fire him, and I did. Steve is my friend, still, and I have made amends for what I did."

Rovin felt that in order to be able to salvage his relationship with Chip, such as it was—this was in December, towards the end of Rovin's tenure—he had to remove this impediment (Mitchell), which he did. However, Rovin attempted to make an end-run around letting his friend go. "The only way I was able to fire him, was to make sure that he would have enough freelance stuff to make up for the loss of income. Chip agreed to that. Then, Chip started rejecting stories."

Other people that got screwed included Ernie Colon, who, according to Rovin "Got screwed royally..." and since has become one of Rovin's best friends. "Larry Hama's mother was dying. We had to get his book done. I put pressure on him, however tactfully applied, it was still pressure. I've since talked to him about it."

Phoenix #1, © Atlas Comics

Chip even asked Rovin to ask Dick Giordano do redo a cover. "The first *Phoenix* cover, because disaster stories were big, he wanted to have a city falling down in the background. We went ahead and did that. That was the first sign that we had to watch out for publisher interference. We figured it was an aberration, and let it go." In an effort to save money, Atlas began purchasing artwork from overseas artists, which angered Jim Warren because that practice cut into his talent pool. "That pissed off Jim Warren enormously, and I don't blame him. We were cutting into his market; using some of his artists. It was something that I deeply regret doing. In retrospect, we shouldn't have done the black-and-white magazines. Jim was something of a mentor. He was another one of the people that I would have treated differently in retrospect."

Unable to effect any changes, and unable to produce the kind of comics that he desired to, Rovin left the company early in 1975. As for what became of Atlas/Seaboard—the comic book publisher that could have been a contender—after that; Rovin adds this postscript. "Sometime 1974, Chip bought *Swank*, the sex magazine. That became his primary focus. That is all that survived in 1975. I don't remember how many years he

stayed with that. He has recently been publishing a UFO magazine, and other things."

The Dust at the End of the Trail

When asked about the viability of the line if Chip Goodman had stuck with it a little longer, and allowed Rovin and Lieber to preside over the comics, letting the various creators produce the kind of comics they had set out to produce, he responded in this fashion. "If Chip had just stuck with the original concepts of the characters, I have no doubt that it would have worked." Rovin left the company before the first sales reports became available, but he states that he had gotten word that the books were selling well, and probably would have improved had the editors been free of publisher interference.

Martin had us put "All new! No reprint!" on the cover. "Marvel was charging 20–25¢ for reprints, and we were charging 25¢ for all-new material. I think Chip got fed up with a lot of the artists. He didn't understand the mentality. He didn't understand why Mike Sikowski felt the need to write 5H17 on the wing of a plane, so it would reproduce to look like the word 'shit', because he didn't like what he was doing. None of us liked *The Brute*. It was Martin's idea. He wanted to do a character like the Hulk, so we came up with this. He didn't understand why Howard Nostrand, who was a remarkably talented man, would come in and grab Rick [Marshall] by the lapels, and throw him out the door, or over the desk, I forget which." (Apparently Nostrand did this simply because it amused him: Rovin and Lieber allowed the practice to continue so long as it was Marshall and not one of them.)

Tiger-Man 1, © Atlas Comics

In spite of all the hardships and aggravation, Rovin remembered the good times. "From June to November, when we were on our own, and just running free, it was magical, and we had a lot of fun." However much Rovin feels that—had they been left alone the line would still be on-going—he likewise feels that there is no way to go back and recreate that magic. "Those characters are very much of the time. I remember, for example, the Grim Ghost, and the Tarantula, both of which were nasty characters. Michael Fleisher really pushed the

limits of the Comics Code on that. We had a superhero, or a character (the Tarantula) that was eating people. Pat Boyette, who drew it, brought a real quirky style to color comics."

Rovin felt that there was a whole *Saturday Night Live* sense of irreverence, and yet affection that was very much of the '70s, for the line. "If you did it now, it would just be more of the escapades of the Grim Ghost, or more adventures of the Scorpion." Rovin attributes this feeling of magic to the dedication, and drive of the creators involved. "We had the kind of dedication from people that was unparalleled in the field. Artists and writers were really busting their backs to do the best work that they could. Walt and Archie Goodwin did an incredible samurai story. New talent was coming to us. Sal Amendola, who had never gotten to do a superhero thing the way he wanted to was getting to do them. Oh yeah, if they had left us alone, we definitely would have been viable."

"Further, in the works were all kinds of comic, and non-comic-related deals; We would have been in on the beginning of the direct market. Plus, I had already signed some book contracts with Citadel Press, and was developing contacts in other fields. We were talking to Otto Preminger—who was around the corner—about motion pictures. All of these things were just getting started when I left, and consequently they died."

Savage Combat Tales #1,
© Atlas Comics

These sentiments were echoed in a letter that Ernie Colon had sent to the comic book magazine *Amazing Heroes* after the magazine had run an article about Atlas. The letter read in part: "About your *Atlas Reconsidered* article in AH #81, I was surprised at the omission of Jeff Rovin's name... It was his judgment which was mainly responsible for the team of artists who gravitated to Atlas—partly for better rates, partly because they were offered an artistic freedom unknown in the field... It was the tone that Jeff set that gave rise to the creativity that, had top management been more astute, would today have still been viable. Many of the characters birthed during his tenure are still with us, as you noted, under different names... Left to Jeff Rovin and under the fine team he inspired to put out some of the best work they've ever done, Atlas would still be here giving

Marvel and DC a damn good run for their money."

Rovin said that, towards the end, his office often seemed the only safe place in the building. "We felt like my office was the Alamo towards the end. We just felt so embattled. So many of the things we wanted to do never got done. It's so heart-breaking to look back. Yet, the record needs to be set straight."

Monkey in the Middle

Rovin indicated that working in a position that requires a person to act as an intermediary between the creators that produce the work, and the Suits that fund it, is often untenable. "I think when somebody is an intermediary between money people and creative people, they're gonna get chewed up. It happened to Bill DuBay [at Warren]. It happened to Jim Shooter [at Marvel], It happened to me [at Atlas]. Both of those people are nothing, nothing, like they've been made out to be, by so many people in the creative community. They are not the beasts and monsters they've been made out to be."

Rovin feels that such people wind up looking two-faced because they are required to play both ends against the middle. "They have to go to the creators and say, 'Yeah okay, I'll take care of your ego,' and then go suck up to the suits and say, 'It's okay. I've got them in line. ' I lunched with Jim [Shooter] about a month ago. We were discussing this very issue. It is simply impossible to please everyone."

What is especially galling to Rovin, is that the stories that circulate always seem to be about atrocities committed by these people and rarely—if ever—are about the enormous good they do. "You don't hear about at Atlas, the artist who was incredibly ill, and had no money, who we advanced money against the job. You don't hear about the other artist who needed a down-payment for his house, so I vouchered stories that he hadn't done yet, knowing that he would, so he could make the down-payment. I did not do any of these without Chip's approval, but I still had to vouch that the work would come in."

Rovin lamented the disparity of this. "You don't hear about Alex Toth being so depressed and having to be nursemaided through the stories. You don't hear about how Bill DuBay and Jim Warren did the same thing with Rick Crandel or Russ Heath You rarely see letters in print from these guys. Somehow people just assume that Larry Lieber did it all, and that Martin Goodman waved his wand, and talented people just came over, which wasn't the case."

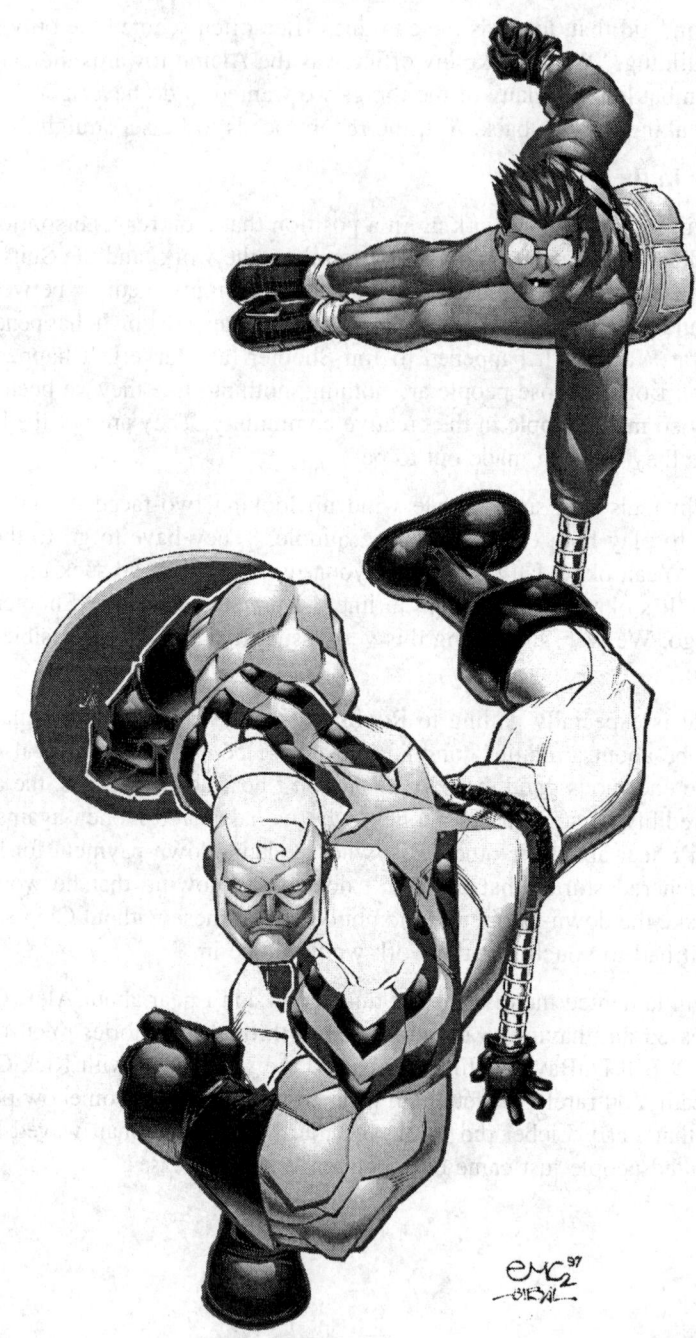

© *Awesome Entertainment*

JEPH LOEB INTERVIEW

As if the comic book industry didn't have enough scandal this year, Headlines were made when Rob Liefeld, one of the most vocal of the infamous "Image Seven" made a very vocal split with his former partners and co-founders. This announcement was (almost immediately),m followed up by another announcement that he had teamed with Scott Rosenberg and Jeph Loeb to form Awesome Entertainment. Now, virtually everybody in the filed had heard of both Rob and Scott (Rob is...well Rob, and Scott, of course, founded Malibu), so that left people with the question, exactly who is this Jeph Loeb character, and how did he hook up with the other two?

For anyone who still doesn't know who the talented Mr. Loeb is, **CVA** *managed to catch up with him shortly after the release of three of their titles (***The Fighting American***,* **The Coven** *and* **Supreme***), and he graciously filled us in on his bonafides, as well as the background of the founding of Awesome, as well as some of their future plans*

****

CVA: So, who are you anyway, and what makes you think you know anything about comics?

Loeb: I'm the mystery guy. (Laughter) Actually, for a long time the primary way I made my living was as a screenwriter and as a producer. I made movies like **Teen Wolf** with Michael J. Fox and **Commando** with Schwarzenegger, and I worked again with Schwarzenegger on a little made–for–HBO movie called **Christmas in Connecticut**. I also have a movie coming out this spring called **Firestorm** with Howie Long.

CVA: Is that based on the comic book character?

Loeb: No. I've been collecting comics since 1970, and I have this massive collection that my wife wishes was somewhere other than in this house. (Laughter) I just sort of by fluke, being a screenwriter, got an opportunity to write an annual that was then called **The Batman Halloween Special**, and I thought there was only going to be one of them. Then we did three years, and DC came to us—Tim Sale and I—and asked if we'd take over Batman for a year and so we've been doing this Batman thing. Which brings me all the way back to they asked me to do my bio in the back of

Coven © Awesome Entertainment

the last issue, and for my bio I said I was looking forward to working on *Superman*, the comic not the movie, and I was looking forward to the release of my feature film, *Firestorm*, the movie, not the comic. That tells you how my two lives collide. I, as a producer, was involved with setting up motion picture and television properties based on comic books. *Reid Flemming, the World's Toughest Milkman*, which is a small, independent comic book that is hilarious.

CVA: I Love Reid Flemming! Is that becoming a movie finally?

JL: We're doing our best. It's at Warner Bros. It has a terrific script, and we're just waiting to hear what they have to say.

CVA: Is he still publishing as a comic book?

JL: Actually, David Boswell is self–publishing as an independent out of Vancouver. Actually, he just started again, he had not been publishing for about five or six years.

CVA: I have to find him. I think his is close to the best comic ever published.

JL: Yes, it is so wonderful. So there was that, and there was a little comic called *Model by Day* that Kevin Taylor was self–publishing out of New York City, and we bought the rights to that and made it into a two–hour pilot with the Bond girl from the last Bond movie, who went on to make a lot of different movies. I worked with Jerry Jones and Will Jacobs on a project called *Trouble with Girls*, because I love *Girls...Girls*, the book...and it just sort of started, more and more, the two worlds, were overlapping on each other. I was looking for an opportunity to find financing in order to start a new company that was to very different from the way other companies were run. Scott Rosenberg was looking to finance a new company, and Rob Liefeld was looking to expand beyond where he had gone with Extreme. It purely was more serendipity than anything else. I can't really explain it, there are so many places where the worlds intercept each other.

CVA: What other comics have you worked on?

JL: I went to go work at Marvel Comics, and the two books I worked on were *Cable* and *X–Force*, which were Rob's creations. I ran into Rob about a year–and–a–half ago at the Oakland WonderCon, and I had no idea whether or not he knew who I was, and second of all, I had no idea whether or not he was going to say to me "So, you're the bastard who's been killing Cable." Quite the contrary, he was very complimentary to me and we just hit it off. He, at the time, was just about to begin *Captain America; Heroes Reborn*, and I so wanted to be part of that project. I knew it was going to be the biggest story of the year, and I knew it was

going to become exactly what it became; which was extremely controversial, but at the same time very, very successful. One night about a month later I got a call from Rob, and he wanted to know whether or not I wanted to come on board. What I love, is what he said is "How would you like to join *Waterworld*?" and I asked him what he meant, and he said "We're the most despised, worst reviewed comic book and no one has ever seen a page of it. Referring to fact that everyone hated *Waterworld* even before it came out.

CVA: I thought that *Waterworld* was not an incredibly awful film, and was in fact a decent film. In fact, I think that it is incredibly ballsy of Acclaim to publish a comic based on a movie that was so universally reviled.

JL: And yet, I'm sure that there were people out there who saw it and liked it. And, that was sort of the attitude I took I had admired what Rob had accomplished and wanted to see what it was like. We sort of both agreed that if it was a disaster after the first issue we would—at the end—both shake hands, and go our ways. After the first issue I not only wanted to do that, I wanted to do the *Avengers*. He and Jim Valentino had a parting of the ways [and he offered me the book]. The next six months was about the most fun and most aggravating experience that either one of us had ever had. We were having a great time making these comics and working with some of the most talented people in the business; from Richard Starkings who did the lettering to all the people who worked at Extreme Color, to Ian Churchill, Rob, and all these people who were having just a great time. We were having a good time. Marvel was all of a sudden...it was like dad came home and pulled the plug. You know, "You're now supposed to be watching television after 11:00. It was really very, very strange. The books were selling very well, and aside from the fact that it was clearly so embarrassing for the people at Marvel because we were these bandits out there on the range, making better comics that they were making. I think that someone had to put an end to it, and they did. So, there we were without really much idea to what we were going to do, it all sort of very quickly came together. Scott completed his sale of Malibu to Marvel, and he and I had been talking, and he and Rob sat down again, and the next thing we knew, this is what we were going to do. It was always going to be that Rob was going to work with Scott on finding a larger partner to fully integrate the company and to fully finance the company, and we sort of expected that at the end of the first year. Six weeks after we opened our doors, a company called Crossroads, which does film, software, and music financing called and wanted to be in the publishing business. The next thing we knew we were sold. We were fully financed and we had a really top-flight, brilliant man by the name John Hyde, and Ann Jacobus, who's our general councilor, and den

Kaboom © Awesome Entertainment

mother. We all just became this new family. What happened with Scott, is that Scott profited enormously, as he is wont to do, and Scott still maintains a consultant basis with the company and is involved in the motion picture end of things. He just put together *Men In Black* and a movie that will be out in two years that is called *Cowboys and Aliens*. So here we were, married to a new company, that completely believed in the philosophy that we had set out to do. That philosophy is that we want to make the best comics that we can. But we also see that, given the current environment, comics cannot exist publishing by themselves, or, you'll go under. It's been proven time and time again, by the young start–up companies. The answer as wee see it, is to create properties that make really good movies, and really good toys, and really good television shows, but is still very, very respectful of the comic book industry. So that if, there are those purists out there who believe that comic books shouldn't be made into movies—to them we say, "Well then, buy our comics, have a good time, and don't go to the movies."

CVA: And there have been so many silly movies based on comic books that have been made over the years.

JL: Right, and my attitude—and its funny, because I was just having this conversation the today—and they were saying that there are so many terrible movies, why don't you just concentrate on making comic books. My response to them was very simple. I said, "Look, you don't have to go to the movies." That's the first thing, You always have the comic books, no one is going to take them away. The question I want to put forward is, when was the last time that you heard that a comic book got canceled because of a bad movie? I said, actually, more often than not, an awful lot of comic books get a second lease on life simply because there is a movie based upon them. I don't think that Dark Horse—and I don't know this for a fact—but my guess is that Dark Horse would not have continued to publish *The Mask*, had it not been such a phenomenally successful movie. I think that *The Crow* is another example of that. No one had any interest in *Men in Black*, and now there's a tremendous interest in doing a *Men in Black* comic book. I do think that it is a double–edged sword...

CVA: ...And certainly Captain America and the Punisher didn't cease being comic books because they were turned into a pair of ghod–awful movies.

JL: No, Punisher sort of ran out of steam on its own. I think that a lot of it has to do with execution, and a lot of it has to do with the people that are involved. One of the things that make our company fairly unique, is that when you think of all of the people in the comic book business, the person who has been the most successful at translating properties into

motion picture properties, is Rob, and while a number of the things that he has worked on, have not seen screen yet, when they do, it will come fast and furious, and people will start going "Wow!" In terms of understanding the business, and in terms of creating new material, and in terms of having unbridled enthusiasm—that part about Rob I really admire. It is always so funny, because whoever I talk to, eventually they do come around to it. They say, "No matter what else you think of Rob..." as if I partnered with some sort of serial killer. (Laughter) "Oh yeah, there was those 10 people in Dallas, but other

Coven #1, © Awesome Entertainment

than that...and he really hasn't killed anybody in a long time." The funny part about it is that I've never had any of the experiences that people have claimed to have had; and I've been with this man for the better part of a year and a half. If we have not been together, we have spoken every day, and I keep waiting to see this "other person" that everyone keeps describing to me. Either this person existed prior to my being involved in his life, or it simply is a side of his that I've never seen of him. The only thing that I know is that we have a company that is built on three premises—aside from the idea that we are looking for properties that will work in other media. The first is that we are all sort of have been abused in some way, at some point in the system, and are looking to have the artistic and editorial freedom to do what we want to do, and to make the mistakes that we want to make. It is sort of funny that we have sort of found each other in that way. I think it is well documented Alan Moore's unhappiness with the various companies that he's worked with, and he finds a very happy home with us. We're extremely fortunate to have him. Look at the two young artists that we have working for us now, Ian Churchill, who does **The Coven** for us, and Jeff Matsuda, who does **Kaboom** for us. Both of whom were at Marvel for a long time, and both of whom were looking for a new place to go.

CVA: So, what's it like working over in the Awesome offices?

JL: It is just sort of a repeated kind of place to go, and have fun, and behave silly. I don't want to say in any way that it is comparable, but it is—in reading the early Marvels—I really strongly remember those Marie Severin drawings of Stan and Jack jumping over tables at each other wearing Galactus helmets and throwing fireballs at each other while Roy Thomas was hiding under the table and someone was running down the hall screaming and yelling because something else was on fire. That's sort of the way our office runs. We just sort of have this great time running around screaming and yelling and trying to think, well, why not do that? What is the down side of doing that? We're such a small operation, that there is no committee, and there's no "Well, we have to do a P&L and see whether or not that works and…" just sort of look at things and just run things by the seat of our pants. For that, I think that that spirit of entrepreneuralism and that spirit of go by the seat of your pants is what Rob infuses in the company. I tend to be much more conservative in my thinking and what I would do, and Rob is a great believer in, "Just light the match, and see what happens." So we make a very good team: he is extraordinary at being able to come up with concepts, and I'm pretty damn good at execution. Between the two of us we've been able to put out only a few books here at the beginning, but we're very proud of the work that we've done and—I think—a number of people are surprised by it. That to me was always the thing I found surprising was that when ***The***

Supreme #51, © Awesome Entertainment

Coven came out, the number of, and I mean literally hundreds of letters and phone calls, mostly calling to say, "This is such a beautiful book. How did you do it?" Rob and I look at each other and say, this is what we want to do. We just haven't had either the financing or the patience, or the wherewithal, or someone as talented as Ian who could do. It was one of the other things that was important to us when we started the company. Rob was very, very lucky in the five years at Extreme to have a number of young artists to come through the system. Rob believed in that system, and believed very strongly in the idea of giving somebody that had never had a chance before whether it was Anthony Winn or Chap Yaep or Matsuda or Chris Lightner, or a number of people

along the way who passed through the halls of Extreme; who then went on to greater glory working at the Marvel offices. Particularly in the X--Men office, especially in the X–Men office you know how particular they are up there.

CVA: Let's talk a little about *The Fighting American* if we could.

JL: We were terminated off *Captain America* for low sales, which—to me—is sort of like saying to a cow "I am no longer going to use you because give milk." But, such is the nature of the business and that's fine, and so Rob came to me and we started talking about what we were going to do next and Rob had actually planned on doing another project which is a project that I think we're going to do next year. He just kept drawing, and he kept drawing this patriotic figure. He kept saying, "I'm looking around me and seeing the success of *Independence Day*, and the success of *Air Force One*, I'm looking at the success of all these movies where patriotism has such a very strong theme and. I don't see any reason why we shouldn't be able to our own character." It may not have been the best idea, but some of the best ideas have sometimes come out of the not so good ideas. The idea was to try to create a new character not unlike the Superpatriot, The Shield, or USA. There have been a lot of patriotic characters out there, so why shouldn't Rob have a patriotic character? So Rob created a character called Agent America, and almost immediately people with torches came to the house, and said, "You can do a lot of things in this world, but that's not something that you can do." One of the parties that came to the door interestingly enough was Joe Simon, who called and said, "I really like what it is that you guys have in mind, why don't you guys do the Fighting American?" We were so stunned. It was as if we decided to do a story about a guy who could fly, was impervious to bullets, and could leap over buildings and all of a sudden we got a call from Jerry Siegel and Joe Shuster saying, "You know, instead of doing Superduper, why not do whatever the heck they called were calling Superman before he was Superman. In this particular case we actually had a character that had been in existence since 1954. He actually co–existed with Captain America, which really made it very interesting from our point of view.

CVA: So, how has it been working with Joe?

JL: Joe is great, he was aggressive, funny, and bright. He's however years old and he coordinated with Roz Kirby, who is in charge of Jack's estate. The next thing we know, we took most of the ideas that were Agent America, and abandoned them and started over again. We were happily going our own way, and a week before publishing we got served [by Marvel]. Marvel had decided that they would sue us for copyright infringement.

Fighting American #1 & Fighting American #1, © Awesome Entertainment

We sort of said that they took an awful lot of time to do this, but this is the decision that they wanted to do. Their first step was to try and get a temporary restraining order, and we showed up in court to contest it, they withdrew. They then decided that what they wanted to do was get a preliminary injunction which would have stopped us from publishing. The judge heard a number of arguments and the judge decided there was no basis for this, but left open the door that Marvel could go to trial. The concept that Marvel would continue was beyond me particularly for a company that is such financial bad shape. The enormous amount of money that it would take to go to trail, but if that's what they are going to do, that's what they are going to do. In the mean time we're going to continue to publish *The Fighting American*.

CVA: You must obviously be pleased that it went in your favor then.

JL: Of course that was an enormous relief to have someone outside of ourselves to look at the material and say that there does not seem to be confusion and these two characters have peacefully existed for 43 years, it seems to the State of New York that Marvel you don't have a case and you guys can publish your book. So we did. I just found out today that we sold out. The book only came out on Thursday. And Again, I know

---

that there is an awful lot of people out there who say its not possible, or whatever, and I can just assure them that my mom, and Rob's mom have not bought all tne copies and hidden them in the house. (Laughter) What we set out to do is do a book that is great fun. A book that was the adventures of a patriotic figure who had no direct affiliation with anyone else. Captain America came with a lot of baggage. He was so identified with the government and being the symbol of America; whereas the Fighting American was just a guy who was a fighting American. Which meant that he could get away with a lot more than Captain America could.

CVA: What did you do—if anything—to bring him into the '90s?

JL: He had had a sidekick named Speedboy; we decided to update that to a sidekick named Spice, who is a state–of–the–art android that is capable of…as she refers to herself, she's a state–of–the–art weapon of mass destruction. They have a very antagonistic relationship to each other, which we also thought was interesting, between a 13 year–old girl, and a 20–something/30–something man who—at this point in his life, would rather just be left alone. He had been the Fighting American in the 1950s something happened, which is sort of the mystery of his life—he decided that he didn't want to be the Fighting American any longer. Now his main villain has come back and has created such massive destruction that he had to come back too, and has been assigned by the government this robot sidekick, who he would just a soon see disassembled and moved out of the way. They have a very *Paper Moon* kind of relationship with each other.

CVA: Who are the creative personnel on the book?

JL: Rob is doing the first two issues, and then we're going to be doing four–issue arcs. The next four–issue arc is going to be by Ed McGuinness who was doing *Deadpool* for Marvel, and left Marvel to work for us; and Stephen Platt who had his heart broken, because he really wanted to draw *Captain America* more than anything else in the world, and did not get that opportunity because Marvel pulled the plug is going to do the next arc, and then I think we'll go back to McGuinness again and we'll trade back and forth between McGuinness and Plat. Both of them have very different styles which, I think, will make the book even more interesting to look at. That's what we have planned for *The Fighting American*.

CVA GRADING GUIDE

In David Brin's science fiction–fantasy novel, *The Practice Effect*, things improve with use. You start with a crudely made tool and keep using it until it becomes a fine instrument. If our world worked that way, you could read your golden age comics as often as you liked and they would just get better looking each time. Unfortunately, our world does not work that way, and reading your comics (along with just about everything else) causes comics to deteriorate.

Even if you could protect your comics from external light, heat, cold, moisture, pressure and everything else, you couldn't protect them from their own paper. Most comic books were printed on pulp paper, which has a high acid content. This means that the paper slowly turns brittle with age, no matter what you do to it, short of special museum-style preservation.

Very old, well-preserved comics are coveted collector's items. In most cases, people did not save their comic books for future generations. They read them and discarded them. Comic books were considered harmless ephemera for children. When these children outgrew their comics, their parents often threw them away. If everybody kept all of their comics, comics would not be valuable because everybody would have them scattered about the house!

The value of any comic depends on scarcity, popularity and condition. Scarcity increases with age and popularity depends on the whim of the public — only condition automatically decreases with age. Newer comics are generally available in near-mint condition, so newer comics in lesser condition have little collector potential. However, older comics are scarce, so they are still collectible in less than near-mint condition, but the value is obviously less. This is a basic tenet of all collectibles. A car is more valuable with its original paint. A baseball card is more valuable if it has not been marred by bicycle spokes. Coke bottles, stamps, coins, and toys in good condition are all more valuable than their abused counterparts. Comic books are no exception.

New comic book collectors should learn how to assess the prospective value of a comic in order to protect themselves from being fleeced by unscrupulous dealers or hucksters. Yet, a majority of dealers, especially store owners, can be considered reliable judges of comic grade. Because comic retail may be their primary source of income, certain dealers are particularly adept at noticing comic book imperfections, especially in issues they intend to purchase. As such, hobbyists and collectors must understand that dealers need to make a minimum

profit on their investments. Buying collectible comics entails certain risks. Therefore, dealers must scrutinize a comic to determine if the particular book will stand a chance of resale. Well-preserved comics are invariably more desirable to dealers because they are more desirable to collectors.

There are eight standard comic grades: mint, near mint, very fine, fine, very good, good, fair, and poor. Clearly, these eight grades could be split into even finer categories when haggling over an exceptionally rare or coveted Golden Age comic. In most cases, however, comic books can be evaluated using these eight standard grades. The values listed in *Comics Values Annual* are all for comics in "Near Mint" condition. The grading/price chart given at the back of this book should be used to adjust this price for comics in different grades.

Mint

Finding new comics in true mint condition can be difficult. Finding old comics in mint condition is almost impossible. Mint condition comics usually fetch prices higher than price guide listings. Mint comics can sell for 120% or more of *Comics Values Annual* listed prices. The reason for this is the strict criteria reserved for mint comics.

Mint comics are perfect comics and allow no room for imperfections. Pages and covers must be free of discoloration, wear, and wrinkles. A mint comic is one that looks like it just rolled off the press. Staples and spine must meet perfectly without cover "rollover." The cover must be crisp, bright, and trimmed perfectly. The staples must not be rusted and the cover should not have any visible creases.

The interior pages of a mint comic are equally crisp and new. A mint comic must not show any signs of age or decay. Because of the paper stock used on many older comics, acid and oxygen cause interior pages to yellow and flake. It is much harder to find pre-1970 mint comics because of inferior storage techniques and materials. In the early days of collecting, few people anticipated that the very boxes and bags in which they stored their comics were contributing to decay. Acid from bags, backing boards, and boxes ate away at many comics.

Near Mint

A near mint comic and a mint comic are close siblings, with their differences slight, even to an experienced eye. Most of the new comics on the shelf of the local comic shop are in near mint condition. These are comics that have been handled gingerly to preserve the original luster of the book.

Near mint comics are bright, clean copies with no major or minor defects. Slight stress lines near the staples and perhaps a very minor printing defect are permissible. Corners must still be sharp and devoid of creases. Interior pages of newsprint stock should show almost no discernible yellowing. Near mint comics usually trade for 100% of the suggested *Comics Values Annual* listed prices.

Very Fine

A very fine comic is one that is routinely found on the shelves and back issue bins of most good direct market comic shops. This grade comic has few defects, none of them major. Stress around the staples of a very fine comic are visible but not yet radical enough to create wrinkles. Both the cover and interior pages should still be crisp and sharp, devoid of flaking and creases. Interior pages may be slightly yellowed from age.

Most high-quality older comics graded as very fine can obtain 80-90% of *Comics Values Annual* listed prices. Newer comics graded as very fine get about 70-85% because many near mint copies probably exist. Despite that, very fine comics are desirable for most collectors.

Fine

Fine comics are often issues that may have been stored carefully under a bed or on a shelf by a meticulous collector. This grade of comic is also very desirable because it shows little wear and retains much of its original sharpness. The cover may be slightly off center from rollover. The cover retains less of its original gloss and may even possess a chip or wrinkle. The comers should be sharp but may also have a slight crease. Yellowing begins to creep into the interior pages of a comic graded as fine.

Fine comics are respectable additions to collections and sell for about 40-60% of the listed prices.

Very Good

A very good comic may have been an issue passed around or read frequently. This grade is the common condition of older books. Its cover will probably have lost some luster and may have two or three creases around the staples or edges. The corners of the book may begin to show the beginnings of minor rounding and chipping, but it is by no means a damaged or defaced comic. Comics in very good condition sell for about 30-40% of *Comics Values Annual* listed prices.

Good

A good comic is one that has been well read and is beginning to show its age. Although both front and back covers are still attached, a good grade comic may have a number of serious wrinkles and chips. The corners and edges of this grade comic may show clear signs of rounding and flaking. There should be no major tears in a good comic nor should any pages be clipped out or missing. Interior pages may be fairly yellowed and brittle. Good comics sell for about 15-25% of the *Comics Values Annual* listed prices.

Fair

A fair comic is one that has definitely seen better days and has considerably limited resale value for most collectors. This comic may be soiled and damaged on the cover and interior. Fair comics should be completely intact and may only

be useful as a comic to lend to friends. Fair comics sell for about 10-20% of the *Comics Values Annual* listed prices.

Poor

Comics in poor condition are generally unsuitable for collecting or reading because they range from damaged to unrecognizable. Poor comics may have been water damaged, attacked by a small child, or worse, perhaps, gnawed on by the family pet! Interior and exterior pages may be cut apart or missing entirely. A poor comic sells for about 5-15% of the *Comics Values Annual* listed price.

Sniffing Out Grades

Despite everything that is mentioned about comic grading, the process remains relative to the situation. A comic that seems to be in very good condition may actually be a restored copy. A restored copy is generally considered to be in between the grade it was previous to restoration and the grade it has become. Many collectors avoid restored comics entirely.

Each collector builds his collection around what he believes is important. Some want every issue of a particular series or company. Others want every issue of a favorite artist or writer. Because of this, many collectors will purchase lower-grade comics to fill out a series or to try out a new series. Mint and near mint comics are usually much more desirable to hard-core collectors. Hobbyists and readers may find the effort and cost of collecting only high-grade comics financially prohibitive.

Getting artists or writers to autograph comics has also become a source of major dispute. Some collectors enjoy signed comics and others consider those very comics defaced! The current trends indicate that most collectors do enjoy signed comics. A signature does not usually change the grade of the comic.

As mentioned, comic grading is a subjective process that must be agreed upon by the buyer and seller. Buyers will often be quick to note minor defects in order to negotiate a better price. Sellers are sometimes selectively blind to their comic's defects. *Comics Values Annual: 1998* provides this grading guide as a protection for both parties.

Name	Abbreviation
Abel, Jack	**JA**
Abell, Dusty	DAb
Abnett, Dan	DAn
Abrams, Paul	PlA
Adams, Art	AAd
Adams, Neal	NA
Addeo, Stephen	StA
Adkins, Dan	DA
Adlard, Charlie	CAd
Albano, John	JAo
Albrecht, Jeff	JAl
Alcala, Alfredo	AA
Alcazar, Vincent	VAz
Alexander, Chris	CAx
Alibaster, Jo	JoA
Allred, Michael	MiA
Alstaetter, Karl	KlA
Althorp, Brian	BAp
Amaro, Gary	GyA
Amendola, Sal	Sal
Ammerman, David	DvA
Anderson, Bill	BAn
Anderson, Brent	BA
Anderson, Murphy	MA
Andriola, Alfred	AlA
Andru, Ross	RA
Aparo, Jim	JAp
Aragones, Sergio	SA
Arcudi, John	JAr
Artis, Tom	TAr
Ashe, Edd	EA
Augustyn, Brian	BAu
Austin, Terry	TA
Avison, Al	AAv
Ayers, Dick	DAy
Bachalo, Chris	**CBa**
Badger, Mark	MBg
Bagley, Mark	MBa
Baikie, Jim	JBa
Bailey, Bernard	BBa
Bair, Michael	MlB
Baker, Kyle	KB
Baker, Matt	MB
Balent, Jim	JBa
Banks, Darryl	DBk
Barks, Carl	CB
Baron, Mike	MBn
Barr, Mike	MiB
Barras, John	DBs
Barreiro, Mike	MkB
Barreto, Ed	EB
Barry, Dan	DBa
Batista, Chris	CsB
Battlefield, D.	DB
Beatty, John	JhB
Beatty, Terry	TBe
Beauvais, Denis	DB
Beeston, John	JBe
Belardinelli, M.	MBe
Bell, Bob Boze	BBB
Bell, George	GBl
Bell, Julie	JuB
Benefiel, Scott	ScB
Benes, Ed	EBe
Benitez, Joe	JBz
Benjamin, Ryan	RBn
Bennett, Joe	JoB
Bennett, Richard	RiB
Benson, Scott	StB
Berger, Charles	ChB
Bernado, Ramon	RBe
Bernstein, Robert	RbB
Bierbaum, Mary	MBm
Bierbaum, Tom	TBm
Biggs, Geoffrey	GB
Binder, Jack	JaB
Bingham, Jerry	JBi
Birch, JJ	JJB
Biro, Charles	CBi
Bisley, Simon	SBs
Bissette, Stephen	SBi
Blaisdell, Tex	TeB
Blasco, Jesus	JBl
Blevins, Bret	BBl
Blum, Alex	AB
Bode, Vaughn	VB
Bogdanove, Jon	JBg
Bolland, Brian	BB
Bolle, Frank	FBe
Boller, David	DdB
Bolton, John	JBo
Bond, Philip	PBd
Booth, Brett	BBh
Boring, Wayne	WB
Bossart, William	WmB
Boxell, Tim	TB
Bradstreet, Tim	TBd
Braithwaite, Doug	DBw
Brasfield, Craig	CrB
Braun, Russell	RsB
Breeding, Brett	BBr
Brereton, Daniel	DlB
Brewster, Ann	ABr
Breyfogle, Norm	NBy
Bridwell, E. Nelson	ENB
Briefer, Dick	DBr
Bright, Mark	MBr
Brigman, June	JBr
Broderick, Pat	PB
Brodsky, Allyn	AyB
Broom, John	JBm
Broome, Matt	MtB
Brothers, Hernandez	HB
Brown, Bob	BbB
Browne, Dick	DkB
Brunner, Frank	FB
Bryant, Rick	RkB
Buckingham, Mark	MBu
Buckler, Rich	RB
Budget, Greg	GBu
Bugro, Carl	CBu
Bulanadi, Danny	DBl
Burchett, Rick	RBr
Burgard, Tim	TmB
Burke, Fred	FBk
Burns, John	JBn
Burns, Robert	RBu
Burroughs, W.	WBu
Buscema, John	JB
Buscema, Sal	SB
Busiek, Kurt	KBk
Butler, Jeff	JBt
Butler, Steve	SBt
Buzz	Buzz
Byrd, Mitch	MBy
Byrne, John	JBy
Calafiore, Jim	**JCf**
Caldes, Charles	CCa
Callahan, Jim	JiC
Calnan, John	JCa
Cameron, Don	DCn
Cameron, Lou	LC
Campbell, Eddie	ECa
Campbell, J. Scott	JSC
Campbell, Stan	StC
Campenella, Robert	RbC
Campos, Marc	MCa
Capullo, Greg	GCa
Cardy, Nick	NC
Carey, Mike	MCy
Cariello, Sergio	SCi
Carlin, Mike	MCr
Carpenter, Brent D	BDC
Carralero, Ricky	RCl
Carrasco, Dario	DoC
Carter, Joe	JCt
Case, Richard	RCa
Castellaneta, Dan	DaC
Castellini, Claudio	CCt
Chadwick, Paul	PC
Chan, Ernie	ECh
Chang, Bernard	BCh
Charest, Travis	TC
Chase, Bobbie	BCe
Chaykin, Howard	HC
Check, Sid	SC
Chen, Mike	MCh
Chen, Sean	SCh
Chestney, Lillian	LCh
Chiarello, Mark	MCo
Chichester, D.G.	DGC
Chiodo, Joe	JCh
Choi, Brandon	BCi
Chriscross	Ccs
Christopher, Tom	TmC
Chua, Ernie	Chu
Chun, Anthony	ACh
Churchhill, Ian	IaC
Cirocco, Frank	FC
Citron, Sam	SmC
Claremont, Chris	CCl
Clark, Mike	MCl
Clark, Scott	ScC
Cockrum, Dave	DC
Cohn, Gary	GCh
Coker, Tomm	TCk
Colan, Gene	GC
Colby, Simon	SCy
Cole, Jack	JCo
Cole, Leonard B.	LbC
Colletta, Vince	ViC
Collins, Max Allan	MCn
Collins, Mike	MC
Collins, Nancy	NyC
Colon, Ernie	EC
Conner, Amanda	ACo
Conway, Gerry	GyC
Cooper, Dave	DvC
Cooper, John	JCp
Corben, Richard	RCo
Costanza, Peter	PrC
Cowan, Denys	DCw
Cox, Jeromy	JCx
Craig, Johnny	JCr
Crandall, Reed	RC
Crespo, Steve	SCr
Crilley, Mark	MCi
Crumb, Robert	RCr
Cruz, E. R.	ERC
Cruz, Jerry	JCz
Cruz, Roger	RCz
Culdera, Chuck	CCu
Cullins, Paris	PCu
Currie, Andrew	ACe
Damaggio, Rodolfo	RDm
Daniel, Tony	**TnD**
Danner, Paul	PuD
Darrow, Geof	GfD
David, Peter	PDd
Davis, Alan	AD
Davis, Dan	DDv
Davis, Guy	GyD
Davis, Jack	JDa
Davis, Malcolm	MDa
Davison, Al	ADv
Day, Dan	Day
Day, Gene	GD
DeFalco, Tom	TDF
Deitch, Kim	KDe
Delano, Jamie	JaD
DeLaRosa, Sam	SDR
Delgado, Richard	DRd
Dell, John	JhD
DeMatteis, J. M.	JMD
DeMulder, Kim	KDM
Deodato, Jr., Mike	MD2
Derenick, Tom	TDr
DeZago, Todd	TDz
DeZuniga, M.	MDb
DeZuniga, Tony	TD
Diaz, Paco	PaD
Dillin, Dick	DD
Dillon, Glyn	GlD
Dillon, Steve	SDi
Dini, Paul	PDi
Ditko, Steve	SD
Dixon, Chuck	CDi
Dixon, John	JDx
Dobbyn, Nigel	ND
Dodson, Terry	TyD
Doherty, Peter	PD
Dominguez, Luis	LDz
Doran, Colleen	CDo
Dorey, Mike	MDo
Dorkin, Evan	EDo
Dorman, Dave	DvD
Doucet, Julie	JDo
Drake, Stan	SDr
Dresser, Larry	LDr
Dringenberg, Mike	MDr
Drucker, Mort	MD
DuBerkr, Randy	RDB
Duffy, Jo	JDy
Dumm, Gary	GDu
Dunn, Ben	BDn
Duranona, Leo	LDu
Duursema, Jan	JD
Dwyer, Kieron	KD
Eastman, Kevin	KEa
Eaton, Scott	**SEa**
Edginton, Ian	IEd
Edlund, Ben	BEd

Egeland, Marty	MEg	Giacuia, Frank	FrG	Hempel, Mark	MaH	Karounos, Paris T.	PaK
Eisner, Will	WE	Giarrano, Vince	VGi	Henry, Flint	FH	Katz, Jack	JKz
Elder, Bill	BE	Gibbons, Dave	DGb	Herman, Jack	JH	Kavanagh, Terry	TKa
Eldred, Tim	TEl	Gibson, Ian	IG	Hernandez, Gilbert	GHe	Kelly, Walt	WK
Elias, Lee	LE	Giella, Joe	JoG	Hernandez, Jaime	JHr	Kennedy, Cam	CK
Elliot, D.	DE	Giffen, Keith	KG	Herrera,Ben	BHr	Keown, Dale	DK
Ellis, Warren	WEl	Gilbert, Michael T.	MGi	Hester, Phil	PhH	Kerschl, Karl	KlK
Ellison, Harlan	HaE	Giordano, Dick	DG	Hewlett, Jamie	JHw	Kesel, Babara	BKs
Emberlin, Randy	RyE	Glanzman, Sam	SG	Hibbard, E.E.	EHi	Kesel, Karl	KK
Englehart, Steve	SEt	Golden, Michael	MGo	Hicklenton, John	JHk	Kieth, Sam	SK
Ennis, Garth	GEn	Gonzalez, Jorge	JGz	Higgins, Graham	GHi	King, Hannibal	HbK
Epting, Steve	SEp	Goodman, Till	TGo	Higgins, John	JHi	Kinsler, Everett R.	EK
Erskine, Gary	GEr	Goodwin, Archie	AGw	Higgins, Michael	MHi	Kirby, Jack	JK
Erwin, Steve	StE	Gordon, Al	AG	Hitch, Bryan	BHi	Kisniro, Yukito	YuK
Esposito, Mike	ME	Gottfredson, Floyd	FG	Hobbs, Bill	BlH	Kitson, Barry	BKi
Estes, John	JEs	Gould, Chester	ChG	Hoberg, Rick	RHo	Kobasic, Kevin	KoK
Estrada, Ric	RE	Grant, Alan	AlG	Hoffer, Mike	MkH	Kolins, Scott	ScK
Evans, George	GE	Grant, Steve	StG	Hogarth, Burne	BHg	Krause, Peter	PKr
Everett, Bill	BEv	Grau, Peter	PGr	Holcomb, Art	AHo	Krenkel, Roy	RKu
Ewins, Brett	BEw	Gray, Mick	MGy	Holdredge, John	JHo	Krigstein, Bernie	BK
Ezquerra, Carlos	CE	Green, Dan	DGr	Hoover, Dave	DHv	Kristiansen, Teddy H.	TKr
Fabry, Glenn	**GF**	Green, Randy	RGr	Hopgood, Kevin	KHd	Kruse, Brandon	BKr
Fago, Al	AFa	Greene, Sid	SGe	Horie, Richard	RHe	Kubert, Adam	AKu
Farmer, Mark	MFm	Grell, Mike	MGr	Hotz, Kyle	KHt	Kubert, Andy	NKu
Fegredo, Duncan	DFg	Griffith, Bill	BG	Howarth, Matt	MHo	Kubert, Joe	JKu
Feldstein, Al	AF	Griffiths, Martin	MGs	Howell, Rich	RHo	Kupperberg, Paul	PuK
Ferry, Pascual	PFe	Grindberg, Tom	TGb	Hudnall, James	JHl	Kurtzman, Harvey	HK
Fine, Lou	LF	Gross, Daerick	DkG	Hughes, Adam	AH	Kwitney, Alisa	AaK
Fingeroth, Danny	DFr	Gross, Peter	PrG	Hund, Dave	DeH	LaBan, Terry	TLa
Finnocchiaro, Sal	SF	Grossman, R.	RGs	Hunt, Chad	CH	**Lago, Ray**	**RyL**
Fleisher, Michael	MFl	Gruenwald, Mark	MGu	**Immonen, Stuart**	**SI**	Laird, Peter	PLa
Fleming, Robert	RFl	Grummett, Tom	TG	Infantino, Carmine	CI	Lanning, Andy	ALa
Flemming, Homer	HFl	Guardineer, Frank	FG	Ingles, Graham	GrI	Lansdale, Joe	JLd
Foreman, Dick	DiF	Guay, Rebecca	RGu	Iorio, Medio	MI	Lapham, Dave	DL
Forte, John	JF	Guice, Jackson	JG	Isherwood, Geoff	GI	Lark, Michael	MLr
Forton, Gerald	GFo	Guichet, Yvel	YG	Ivie, Larry	LI	Larkin, Bob	BLr
Fosco, Frank	FFo	Guinan, Paul	PGn	Ivy, Chris	CIv	LaRocque, Greg	GrL
Foster, Alan Dean	ADF	Gulacy, Paul	PG	Jackson, Julius	JJn	Larroca, Salvador	SvL
Fox, Gardner	GaF	Gustovich, Mike	MG	Janke, Dennis	DJa	Larsen, Erik	EL
Fox, Gill	GFx	**Ha, Gene**	**GeH**	Janson, Klaus	KJ	Lash, Batton	BLs
Fox, Matt	MF	Haley, Matt	MHy	Javinen, Kirk	KJa	Lashley, Ken	KeL
Fraga, Dan	DaF	Hall, Bob	BH	Jenkins, Paul	PJe	Lavery, Jim	JLv
Franchesco	Fso	Halsted, Ted	TeH	Jenney, Robert	RJ	Lawlis, Dan	DLw
Frank, Gary	GFr	Hama, Larry	LHa	Jensen, Dennis	DJ	Lawrence, Terral	TLw
Frazetta, Frank	FF	Hamilton, Tim	TH	Jimenez, Leonardo	LJi	Lawson, Jim	JmL
Freeman, John	JFr	Hamner, Cully	CHm	Jimminiz, Phil	PJ	Layton, Bob	BL
Freeman, Simon	SFr	Hampton, Bo	BHa	Johnson, Dave	DvJ	Leach, Garry	GL
Frenz, Ron	RF	Hampton, Scott	SHp	Johnson, Jeff	JJ	Leach, Rick	RkL
Friedman, Michael Jan	MFr	Hanna, Scott	SHa	Johnson, Paul	PuJ	Lee, Elaine	ELe
Friedrich, Mike	MkF	Hannigan, Ed	EH	Johnson, Todd	TJn	Lee, Jae	JaL
Frolechlich, A.	AgF	Hanson, Neil	NHa	Jones, Casey	CJ	Lee, Jim	JLe
Fry III, James	JFy	Harras, Bob	BHs	Jones, Gerard	GJ	Lee, Patrick	PtL
Fujitani(Fuje), Bob	BF	Harris, N. Steven	NSH	Jones, J.B.	JJo	Lee, Scott	ScL
Furman, Simon	SFu	Harris, Tim	THa	Jones, Jeff	JeJ	Lee, Stan	StL
Gaiman, Neil	**NGa**	Harris, Tony	TyH	Jones, Kelley	KJo	Leeke, Mike	MLe
Galan, Manny	MaG	Harrison, Lou	LuH	Jones, Malcolm	MJ	Leialoha, Steve	SL
Gallant, Shannon	ShG	Harrison, Simon	SHn	Jones, R.A.	RAJ	Leon, John Paul	JPL
Gammill, Kerry	KGa	Hart, Ernest	EhH	Jones, Robert	RJn	Leonardi, Rick	RL
Garcia, Dave	DaG	Hartsoe, Everette	EHr	Jones, Robert	RJn	Levins, Rik	RLe
Garner, Alex	AGo	Hathaway, Kurt	KtH	Jurgens, Dan	DJu	Lieber, Larry	LLi
Garney, Ron	RG	Hawkins, Matt	MHw	Jusko, Joe	JJu	Liefeld, Rob	RLd
Garzon, Carlos	CG	Hayes, Drew	DHa	**Kaluta, Mike**	**MK**	Lightle, Steve	SLi
Gascoine, Phil	PGa	Haynes, Hugh	HH	Kamen, Jack	JKa	Lim, Ron	RLm
Gaughan, Jack	JGa	Hazlewood, Douglas	DHz	Kaminski, Len	LKa	Linsner, Joseph M.	JLi
Gecko, Gabe	GG	Heath, Russ	RH	Kane & Romita	K&R	Livingstone, R.	RLv
Geggan	Ggn	Hebbard, Robert	RtH	Kane, Bob	Bka	Lloyd, David	DvL
Gerard, Ruben	RGd	Heck, Don	DH	Kane, Gil	GK	Lobdell, Scott	SLo
Gerber, Steve	SvG	Heisler, Mike	MHs	Kaniger, Bob	BbK	Locke, Vince	VcL
				Kaniuga, Trent	TKn		

Name	Abbr.	Name	Abbr.	Name	Abbr.	Name	Abbr.
Loeb, Jeph	JLb	Medley, Linda	LiM	O'Neill, Kevin	KON	Quinones, Peter	PQ
Lopez, Jose	JL	Mercadoocasio, Harvey	HMo	**Olbrich, Dave**	**DO**	**Raboy, Mac**	**MRa**
Lopresti, Aaron	AaL	Meskin, Mort	MMe	Olivetti, Ariel	AOl	Ramos, Humberto	HuR
Louapre, Dave	DLp	Messner-Loebs, Bill	BML	Olliffe, Patrick	PO	Ramos, Rodney	RyR
Lowe, John	Low	Michelinie, David	DvM	One, Dark	DOe	Randall, Ron	RoR
Lubbers, Bob	BLb	Miehm, Grant	GtM	Ordway, Jerry	JOy	Raney, Tom	TR
Lustbader, Eric Van	ELu	Mighten, Duke	DMn	Orlando, Joe	JO	Rankin, Rich	RRa
Luzniak, Greg	GLz	Mignola, Michael	MMi	Ortiz, Jose	JOt	Rapmund, Norm	NRd
Lyle, Tom	TL	Miki, Danny	DaM	Oskner, Bob	BO	Raymond, Alex	AR
Macchio, Ralph	**RMc**	Milgrom, Al	AM	Ostrander, John	JOs	Redondo, Nestor	NR
Mack, David	DMk	Millar, Mark	MMr	Owen, James	JOn	Reed, David	DvR
Mackie, Howard	HMe	Miller, Frank	FM	Ozkan, Tayyar	TOz	Reeves-Stevens, Judith	JRv
Madan, Dev	DeM	Miller, Mike S.	MsM	Pace, Richard	RPc	Reinhold, Bill	BR
Madureira, Joe	JMd	Miller, Steve	SM	**Pacella, Mark**	**MPa**	Richards, Ted	TR
Maggin, Elliot S.	ESM	Milligan, Peter	PrM	Pacheco, Carlos	CPa	Richardson, Mike	MRi
Maguire, Kevin	KM	Mills, Pat	PMs	Palais, Rudy	RP	Ricketts, Mark	MRc
Magyar, Rick	RM	Minor, Jason	JnM	Palmer, Tom	TP	Rico, Don	DRi
Mahlstedt, Larry	LMa	Mitchel, Barry	BM	Palmiotti, Jimmy	JP	Ridgeway, John	JRy
Mahnke, Doug	DoM	Moder, Lee	LMd	Pamai, Gene	GPi	Rieber, John Ney	JNR
Mandrake, Tom	TMd	Moebius	Moe	Panalign, Noly	NPi	Riley, John	JnR
Maneely, Joe	JMn	Moeller, Chris	CsM	Paniccia, Mark	MPc	Riply	Rip
Manley, Mike	MM	Moench, Doug	DgM	Panosian, Dan	DPs	Robbins, Frank	FR
Mann, Roland	RMn	Montano, Steve	SeM	Parkhouse, Annie	APh	Robbins, Trina	TrR
Mann, Roland	Man	Mooney, Jim	JM	Parkhouse, Steve	SvP	Robertson,Darrick	DaR
Manning, Russ	RsM	Moore, Alan	AMo	Parobeck, Mike	MeP	Robinson, James	JeR
Marais, Raymond	RdM	Moore, Jeff	JMr	Pascoe, James	JmP	Rodier, Denis	DRo
Mariotte, Jeff	JMi	Moore, Jerome	JeM	Pasko, Martin	MPk	Rogers, Marshall	MR
Maroto, Esteban	EM	Moore, John Francis	JFM	Patterson, Bruce	BrP	Romita, John	JR
Marrinan, Chris	ChM	Moore, Terry	TMr	Pearson, Jason	JPn	Romita, John Jr.	JR2
Marrs, Lee	LMr	Morales, Rags	RgM	Pelletier, Paul	PaP	Rosenberger, J.	JRo
Martin, Gary	GyM	Moretti, Mark	MMo	Pence, Eric	ErP	Ross, Alex	AxR
Martin, Joe	JMt	Morgan, Tom	TMo	Pennington, Mark	MPn	Ross, David	DR
Martinbrough, Shawn	SMa	Morisi, Pete	PMo	Pensa, Shea Anton	SAP	Ross, John	JRs
Martinez, Henry	HMz	Morosco, Vincent	VMo	Perez, George	GP	Ross, Luke	LRs
Martinez, Roy Allan	RMr	Morrison, Grant	GMo	Perham, James	JPh	Roth, Werner	WR
Marz, Ron	RMz	Morrow, Gray	GM	Perlin, Don	DP	Royle, Jim	JRl
Marzan, Jose	JMz	Mortimer, Win	WMo	Perryman, Edmund	EP	Royle, John	JRe
Mason, Tom	TMs	Motter, Dean	DMt	Peterson, Brandon	BPe	Rozum, John	JRz
Massengill, Nathan	NMa	Moy, Jeffrey	JMy	Peterson, Jonathan	JPe	Rubi, Melvin	MvR
Matsuda, Jeff	JMs	Murray, Brian	BrM	Petrucha, Stefan	SPr	Rubinstein, Joe	JRu
Mattsson, Steve	SMt	Musial, Joe	JoM	Peyer, Tom	TPe	Rude, Steve	SR
Maus, Bill	BMs	Muth, Jon J.	JMu	Phillips, Joe	JoP	Ruffner, Sean	SRf
Mayer, Sheldon	ShM	Mychaels, Marat	MMy	Phillips, Scott	SPl	Russell, P. Craig	CR
Mayerik, Val	VMk	**Naifeh, Ted**	**TNa**	Phillips, Sean	SeP	Russell, Vince	VRu
Mazzucchelli, David	DM	Napolitano, Nick	NNa	Pini, Richard	RPi	Ryan, Matt	MRy
McCarthy, Brendon	BMy	Napton, Bob	BNa	Pini, Wendy	WP	Ryan, Paul	PR
McCloud, Scott	SMl	Nauck, Todd	TNu	Platt, Stephen	SPa	Ryder, Tom	TmR
McCorkindale, B	BMC	Neary, Paul	PNe	Pleece, Warren	WaP	Sakai, Stan	SS
McCraw, Tom	TMw	Nebres, Rudy	RN	Ploog, Mike	MP	Sale, Tim	TSe
McCrea, John	JMC	Nelson	Nel	Plunkett, Kilian	KPl	Salmons, Tony	TSa
McDaniel, Scott	SMc	Netzer, Mike	MN	Pollack, Rachel	RaP	Saltares, Javier	JS
McDaniel, Walter	WMc	Newton, Don	DN	Pollard, Keith	KP	Sanders, Jim III	JS3
McDonnell, Luke	LMc	Nguyen, Hoang	HNg	Pollina, Adam	AdP	Sasso, Mark	MSo
McDuffie, Dwayne	DMD	Nichols, Art	ANi	Pope, Paul	PPo	Saviuk, Alex	AS
McFarlane, Todd	TM	Nicieza, Fabian	FaN	Porch, David	DPo	Schaffenberger, Kurt	KS
McGregor, Don	DMG	Nino, Alex	AN	Portacio, Whilce	WPo	Schane, Tristan	TnS
McKean, Dave	DMc	Nocenti, Ann	ANo	Porter, Howard	HPo	Schiller, Fred	FdS
McKeever, Ted	TMK	Nocon, Cedric	CNn	Post, Howard	HwP	Schmitz, Mark	MaS
McKenna, Mike	MkK	Nodell, Martin	MnN	Potts, Carl	CP	Schultz, Mark	MSh
McKie, Angus	AMK	Nolan, Graham	GN	Powell, Bob	BP	Scoffield, Sean	SSc
McKone, Mike	MMK	Nord, Cary	CNr	Power, Dermot	DPw	Scott, Jeffery	JSc
McLaughlin, Frank	FMc	Norem, Earl	EN	Pratt, George	GgP	Scott, Trevor	TvS
McLaughlin, Sean	SML	Nostrand, Howard	HN	Prosser, Jerry	JeP	Seagle, Steven T.	SSe
McLeod, Bob	BMc	Novick, Irv	IN	Pugh, Steve	StP	Sears, Bart	BS
McMahon, M.	MMc	Nowlan, Kevin	KN	Pulido, Brian	BnP	Sekowsky, Mike	MSy
McManus, Shawn	SwM	Nutman, Philip	PNu	Queen, Randy	RQu	Semeiks, Val	VS
McWilliams, Al	AMc	O'Barr, James	JOb	**Quesada, Joe**	**JQ**	Senior, Geoff	GSr
Medina, Angel	AMe	O'Neil, Denny	DON	Quinn, David	DQ	Serpe, Jerry	JyS

GENERAL ABBREVIATIONS FOR COMICS LISTINGS

Abbreviation	Name
3RW	Robert Washington 3
AA	Alfredo Alcala
AAd	Art Adams
AaK	Alisa Kwitney
AaL	Aaron Lopresti
AAv	Al Avison
AB	Alex Blum
ABr	Ann Brewster
ACe	Andrew Currie
ACh	Anthony Chun
ACo	Amanda Conner
AD	Alan Davis
ADF	Alan Dean Foster
AdP	Adam Pollina
ADv	Al Davison
AdW	Andrew Wendel
AF	Al Feldstein
AFa	Al Fago
AG	Al Gordon
AgF	A. Frolechlich
AGo	Alex Garner
AGw	Archie Goodwin
AH	Adam Hughes
AHo	Art Holcomb
AIA	Alfred Andriola
AKu	Adam Kubert
ALa	Andy Lanning
AlG	Alan Grant
AM	Al Milgrom
AMc	Al McWilliams
AMe	Angel Medina
AMK	Angus McKie
AMo	Alan Moore
AN	Alex Nino
ANi	Art Nichols
ANo	Ann Nocenti
AOl	Ariel Olivetti
APh	Annie Parkhouse
AR	Alex Raymond
AS	Alex Saviuk
ASm	Andy Smith
ASp	Art Spiegelman
AT	Angelo Torres
ATh	Alex Toth
ATi	Art Thibert
AV	Al Vey
AVs	Andrew Vachss
AW	Al Williamson
AWi	Anthony Williams
AWs	Aron Wiesenfeld
AxR	Alex Ross
AyB	Allyn Brodsky
BA	**Brent Anderson**
BAn	Bill Anderson
BAp	Brian Althorp
BAu	Brian Augustyn
BB	Brian Bolland
BBa	Bernard Bailey
BbB	Bob Brown
BBB	Bob Boze Bell
BBh	Brett Booth
BbK	Bob Kanigher
BBl	Bret Blevins
BBr	Brett Breeding
BCe	Bobbie Chase
BCh	Bernard Chang
BCi	Brandon Choi
BDC	Brent D Carpenter
BDn	Ben Dunn
BE	Bill Elder
BEd	Ben Edlund
BEv	Bill Everett
BEw	Brett Ewins
BF	Bob Fujitani(Fuje)
BG	Bill Griffith
BH	Bob Hall
BHa	Bo Hampton
BHg	Burne Hogarth
BHi	Bryan Hitch
BHr	Ben Herrera
BHs	Bob Harras
BiT	Bill Tucci
BK	Bernie Krigstein
Bka	Bob Kane
BKi	Barry Kitson
BKr	Brandon Kruse
BKs	Babara Kesel
BL	Bob Layton
BLb	Bob Lubbers
BlH	Bill Hobbs
BLr	Bob Larkin
BLs	Batton Lash
BM	Barry Mitchel
BMc	Bob McLeod
BMC	B. McCorkindale
BML	Bill Messner-Loebs
BMs	Bill Maus
BMy	Brendon McCarthy
BNa	Bob Napton
BnP	Brian Pulido
BO	Bob Oskner
BoW	Bob Wood
BP	Bob Powell
BPe	Brandon Peterson
BR	Bill Reinhold
BrM	Brian Murray
BrP	Bruce Patterson
BS	Bart Sears
BSf	Brian Stelfreeze
BSt	Beau Smith
BSz	Bill Sienkiewicz
BT	Bryan Talbot
BTn	Billy Tan
Buzz	Buzz
BV	Boris Vallejo
BVa	Brad Vancata
BW	Basil Wolverton
BWa	Bill Ward
BWg	Bill Willingham
BWi	Bob Wiacek
BWo	Bill Woggin
BWr	Berni Wrightson
BWS	Barry Windsor-Smith
BZ	Bruce Zick
CAd	**Charlie Adlard**
CaS	Cam Smith
CAx	Chris Alexander
CB	Carl Barks
CBa	Chris Bachalo
CBi	Charles Biro
CBu	Carl Bugro
CCa	Charles Caldes
CCl	Chris Claremont
Ccs	Chriscross
CCt	Claudio Castellini
CCu	Chuck Culdera
CDi	Chuck Dixon
CDo	Colleen Doran
CE	Carlos Ezquerra
CG	Carlos Garzon
CH	Chad Hunt
ChB	Charles Berger
ChG	Chester Gould
ChM	Chris Marrinan
CHm	Cully Hamner
ChT	Chas Truog
Chu	Ernie Chua
CI	Carmine Infantino
CIv	Chris Ivy
CJ	Casey Jones
CK	Cam Kennedy
CNn	Cedric Nocon
CNr	Cary Nord
CP	Carl Potts
CPa	Carlos Pacheco
CR	P. Craig Russell
CrB	Craig Brasfield
CS	Curt Swan
CsB	Chris Batista
CsM	Chris Moeller
CSp	Chris Sprouse
CU	Chris Ulm
CV	Charles Vess
CW	Chris Warner
CWf	Chance Wolf
CWi	Colin Wilson
CWn	Chris Weston
CYp	Chap Yaep
DA	**Dan Adkins**
DAb	Dusty Abell
DaC	Dan Castellaneta
DaF	Dan Fraga
DaG	Dave Garcia
DaM	Danny Miki
DAn	Dan Abnett
DaR	Darrick Robertson
DaW	Damon Willis
Day	Dan Day
DAy	Dick Ayers
DB	D. Battlefield
DB	Denis Beauvais
DBa	Dan Barry
DBk	Darryl Banks
DBl	Danny Bulanadi
DBr	Dick Briefer
DBs	John Barras
DBw	Doug Braithwaite
DC	Dave Cockrum
DCn	Don Cameron
DCw	Denys Cowan
DD	Dick Dillin
DdB	David Boller
DDv	Dan Davis
DdW	David Williams
DE	D. Elliot
DeH	Dave Hund
DeM	Dev Madan
DeT	Derek Thomason
DFg	Duncan Fregredo
DFr	Danny Fingeroth
DG	Dick Giordano
DGb	Dave Gibbons
DGC	D.G. Chichester
DgM	Doug Moench
DGr	Dan Green
DH	Don Heck
DHa	Drew Hayes
DHv	Dave Hoover
DHz	Douglas Hazlewood
DiF	Dick Foreman
DJ	Dennis Jensen
DJa	Dennis Janke
DJu	Dan Jurgens
DK	Dale Keown
DkB	Dick Browne
DkG	Daerick Gross
DL	Dave Lapham
DlB	Daniel Brereton
DLp	Dave Louapre
DLw	Dan Lawlis
DM	David Mazzucchelli
DMc	Dave McKean
DMD	Dwayne McDuffie
DMG	Don McGregor
DMk	David Mack
DMn	Duke Mighten
DMt	Dean Motter
DN	Don Newton
DnS	Dan Steffan
DO	Dave Olbrich
DoC	Dario Carrasco
DOe	Dark One
DoM	Doug Mahnke
DON	O'Neil, Denny
DP	Don Perlin
DPo	Porch, David
DPs	Dan Panosian
DPw	Power, Dermot
DQ	David Quinn
DR	Ross, David
DRd	Richard Delgado
DRi	Don Rico
DRo	Denis Rodier
DS	Dave Sim
DSp	Dan Spiegle
DSs	Don Simpson
DSt	Dave Stevens
DSw	Dan Sweetman
DT	Dwayne Turner
DTs	Dann Thomas
DTy	David Taylor
DvA	David Ammerman
DVa	Dan Vado
DvC	Dave Cooper
DvD	Dave Dorman
DvJ	Dave Johnson
DvL	David Lloyd
DvM	David Michelinie
DvR	David Reed
DW	Doug Wildey
DWe	David Wenzel
DZ	Dean Zachary
EA	**Edd Ashe**
EB	Ed Barreto
EBe	Ed Benes
EC	Ernie Colon
ECa	Eddie Campbell
ECh	Ernie Chan
EcS	Eric Silvestri
EDo	Evan Dorkin
EH	Ed Hannigan
EhH	Ernest Hart

EHi — E.E. Hibbard	GPi — Gene Pamai	JD — Jan Duursema	JoM — Joe Musial
EHr — Everette Hartsoe	GrI — Graham Ingles	JDa — Jack Davis	JOn — James Owen
EiS — Eric Shanower	GrL — Greg LaRocque	JDo — Julie Doucet	JoP — Joe Phillips
EK — Everett R. Kinsler	GSh — Gerry Shamray	JDx — John Dixon	JoS — Joe Shuster
EL — Erik Larsen	GSr — Geoff Senior	JDy — Jo Duffy	JOs — John Ostrander
ELe — Elaine Lee	GT — George Tuska	JeJ — Jeff Jones	JOt — Jose Ortiz
ELu — Eric Van Lustbader	GtM — Grant Miehm	JeM — Jerome Moore	JOy — Jerry Ordway
EM — Esteban Maroto	GW — Gahan Wilson	JeP — Jerry Prosser	JP — Jimmy Palmiotti
EN — Earl Norem	GWt — Greg Wright	JeR — James Robinson	JPe — Jonathan Peterson
ENB — E. Nelson Bridwell	GyA — Gary Amaro	JEs — John Estes	JPh — James Perham
EP — Edmund Perryman	GyC — Gerry Conway	JF — John Forte	JPi — Joe St.Pierre
ERC — E.R. Cruz	GyD — Guy Davis	JFM — John Francis Moore	JPL — John Paul Leon
ErP — Eric Pence	GyM — Gary Martin	JFr — John Freeman	JPn — Jason Pearson
ErS — Eric Stephenson	**HaE — Harlan Ellison**	JFy — James Fry III	JQ — Joe Quesada
ESM — Elliot S. Maggin	HB — Hernandez Brothers	JG — Jackson Guice	JR — John Romita
FaN — Fabian Nicieza	HbK — Hannibal King	JGa — Jack Gaughan	JR2 — John Romita, Jr.
FB — Frank Brunner	HC — Howard Chaykin	JGz — Jorge Gonzalez	JRe — John Royle
FBe — Frank Bolle	HFl — Homer Flemming	JH — Jack Herman	JRl — Jim Royle
FBk — Fred Burke	HH — Hugh Haynes	JhB — John Beatty	JRo — J. Rosenberger
FC — Frank Cirocco	HK — Harvey Kurtzman	JhD — John Dell	JRs — John Ross
FdS — Fred Schiller	HMe — Howard Mackie	JHi — John Higgins	JRu — Joe Rubinstein
FF — Frank Frazetta	HMo — Harvey Mercadoocasio	JHk — John Hicklenton	JRv — Judith Reeves-Stevens
FFo — Frank Fosco	HMz — Henry Martinez	JHl — James Hudnall	JRy — John Ridgeway
FG — Frank Guardineer	HN — Howard Nostrand	JHo — John Holdredge	JRz — John Rozum
FG — Floyd Gottfredson	HNg — Hoang Nguyen	JHr — Jaime Hernandez	JS — Javier Saltares
FH — Flint Henry	HPo — Howard Porter	JHw — Jamie Hewlett	JS3 — Jim Sanders III
FM — Frank Miller	HSm — Howard Shum	JiC — Jim Callahan	JSb — Jonathan Sibal
FMc — Frank McLaughlin	HSn — Howard Simpson	JiS — Jim Shooter	JSc — Jeffery Scott
FR — Frank Robbins	HT — Herb Trimpe	JJ — Jeff Johnson	JSC — J. Scott Campbell
FrG — Frank Giacoia	HuR — Humberto Ramos	JJB — JJ Birch	JSe — John Severin
FrS — Frank Spinks	HWe — Howard Weinstein	JJn — Julius Jackson	JSh — Jim Sherman
FS — Frank Springer	HwP — Howard Post	JJo — J.B. Jones	JSi — Jeff Smith
Fso — Franchesco	**IaC — Ian Churchhill**	JJu — Joe Jusko	JSm — Joe Simon
FT — Frank Thorne	IEd — Ian Edginton	JK — Jack Kirby	JSn — Jim Starlin
FTa — Francis Takenaga	IG — Ian Gibson	JKa — Jack Kamen	JSo — Jim Steranko
GaF — Gardner Fox	IN — Irv Novick	JkS — Jack Sparling	JSon — Joe Staton
GB — Geoffrey Biggs	IV — Ivan Velez, Jr.	JKu — Joe Kubert	JSP — Joe St. Pierre
GBl — George Bell	**JA — Jack Abel**	JKz — Jack Katz	JSt — Joe Sinnott
GBu — Greg Budget	JaB — Jack Binder	JL — Jose Lopez	JTo — John Totleben
GC — Gene Colan	JaD — Jamie Delano	JLb — Jeph Loeb	JuB — Julie Bell
GCa — Greg Capullo	JaL — Jae Lee	JLd — Joe Lansdale	JV — Jim Valentino
GCh — Gary Cohn	JAl — Jeff Albrecht	JLe — Jim Lee	JVF — John Van Fleet
GD — Gene Day	JAo — John Albano	JLi — Joseph M. Linsner	JWf — Joseph Wolfe
GDu — Gary Dumm	JAp — Jim Aparo	JIT — Jill Thompson	JWi — J.H. Williams
GE — George Evans	JAr — John Arcudi	JLv — Jim Lavery	JWk — John Watkiss
GeH — Gene Ha	JB — John Buscema	JM — Jim Mooney	JWo — Jim Woodring
GEn — Garth Ennis	JBa — Jim Baikie	JMC — John McCrea	JWp — Jason Waltrip
GEr — Gary Erskine	JBa — Jim Balent	JMd — Joe Madureira	JWt — John Waltrip
GF — Glenn Fabry	JBe — John Beeston	JMD — J.M. DeMatteis	JyS — Jerry Serpe
GfD — Geof Darrow	JBg — Jon Bogdanove	JMi — Jeff Mariotte	JZ — Jorge Zaffino
GFo — Gerald Forton	JBi — Jerry Bingham	JmL — Jim Lawson	JZe — Joe Zabel
GFr — Gary Frank	JBl — Jesus Blasco	JMn — Joe Maneely	JZy — Joseph Zyskowski
GFx — Gill Fox	JBm — John Broom	JmP — James Pascoe	**K&R — Kane & Romita**
GG — Gabe Gecko	JBn — John Burns	JMr — Jeff Moore	KB — Kyle Baker
Ggn — Geggan	JBo — John Bolton	JMs — Jeff Matsuda	KBk — Kurt Busiek
GgP — George Pratt	JBr — June Brigman	JMt — Joe Martin	KD — Kieron Dwyer
GHe — Gilbert Hernandez	JBt — Jeff Butler	JMu — Jon J. Muth	KDe — Kim Deitch
GHi — Graham Higgins	JBy — John Byrne	JMy — Jeffrey Moy	KDM — Kim DeMulder
GI — Geoff Isherwood	JBz — Joe Benitez	JMz — Jose Marzan	KEa — Kevin Eastman
GJ — Gerard Jones	JCa — John Calnan	JnM — Jason Minor	KeL — Ken Lashley
GK — Gil Kane	JCf — Jim Calafiore	JnR — John Riley	KeW — Kevin Walker
GL — Garry Leach	JCh — Joe Chiodo	JNR — John Ney Rieber	KG — Keith Giffen
GlD — Glyn Dillon	JCo — Jack Cole	JnS — John Smith	KGa — Kerry Gammill
GLz — Greg Luzniak	JCp — John Cooper	JO — Joe Orlando	KHd — Kevin Hopgood
GM — Gray Morrow	JCr — Johnny Craig	JoA — Jo Alibaster	KHt — Kyle Hotz
GMo — Grant Morrison	JCt — Joe Carter	JoB — Joe Bennett	KJ — Klaus Janson
GN — Graham Nolan	JCx — Jeromy Cox	JOb — James O'Barr	KJa — Kirk Javinen
GP — George Perez	JCz — Jerry Cruz	JoG — Joe Giella	KJo — Kelley Jones

Abbr.	Name
KK	Karl Kesel
KIA	Karl Alstaetter
KIK	Karl Kerschl
KIS	Karl Story
KM	Kevin Maguire
KN	Kevin Nowlan
KoK	Kevin Kobasic
KON	Kevin O'Neill
KP	Keith Pollard
KPI	Kilian Plunkett
KS	Kurt Schaffenberger
KSW	Keith S. Wilson
KSy	Ken Steacy
KtH	Kurt Hathaway
KVH	Kevin VanHook
KW	Kent Williams
KWe	Kevin West
KWi	Keith Williams
KWo	Kirk Van Wormer
LbC	**Leonard B. Cole**
LC	Lou Cameron
LCh	Lillian Chestney
LDr	Larry Dresser
LDu	Leo Duranona
LDz	Luis Dominguez
LE	Lee Elias
LeS	Len Strazewski
LF	Lou Fine
LHa	Larry Hama
LI	Larry Ivie
LiM	Linda Medley
LJi	Leonardo Jimenez
LKa	Len Kaminski
LLi	Larry Lieber
LMa	Larry Mahlstedt
LMc	Luke McDonnell
LMd	Lee Moder
LMr	Lee Marrs
Low	John Lowe
LRs	Luke Ross
LS	Lee Sullivan
LSh	Liam Sharp
LSi	Louise Simonson
LSn	Larry Stroman
LSt	Leonard Starr
LuH	Lou Harrison
LW	Lee Weeks
LWn	Len Wein
LyW	Larry Welch
MA	**Murphy Anderson**
MaG	Manny Galan
MaH	Mark Hempel
Man	Roland Mann
MaS	Mark Schmitz
MaT	Mark Tenney
MB	Matt Baker
MBa	Mark Bagley
MBe	M. Belardinelli
MBg	Mark Badger
MBm	Mary Bierbaum
MBn	Mike Baron
MBr	Mark Bright
MBu	Mark Buckingham
MBy	Mitch Byrd
MC	Mike Collins
MCa	Marc Campos
MCh	Mike Chen
MCi	Mark Crilley
MCl	Mike Clark
MCn	Max Allan Collins
MCo	Mark Chiarello
MCr	Mike Carlin
MCW	M.C. Wyman
MCy	Mike Carey
MD	Mort Drucker
MD2	Mike Deodato, Jr.
MDa	Malcolm Davis
MDb	M. DeZuniga
MDo	Mike Dorey
MDr	Mike Dringenberg
ME	Mike Esposito
MEg	Marty Egeland
MeP	Mike Parobeck
MeW	Mike Weringo
MF	Matt Fox
MFl	Michael Fleisher
MFm	Mark Farmer
MFr	Michael Jan Friedman
MG	Mike Gustovich
MGi	Michael T. Gilbert
MGo	Michael Golden
MGr	Mike Grell
MGs	Martin Griffiths
MGu	Mark Gruenwald
MGy	Mick Gray
MHi	Michael Higgins
MHo	Matt Howarth
MHs	Mike Heisler
MHw	Matt Hawkins
MHy	Matt Haley
MI	Medio Iorio
MiA	Michael Allred
MiB	Mike Barr
MJ	Malcolm Jones
MK	Mike Kaluta
MkB	Mike Barreiro
MkF	Mike Friedrich
MkH	Mike Hoffer
MkK	Mike McKenna
MkW	Mark Wheatley
MlB	Michael Bair
MLe	Mike Leeke
MLr	Michael Lark
MM	Mike Manley
MMc	M. McMahon
MMe	Mort Meskin
MMi	Michael Mignola
MMK	Mike McKone
MMo	Mark Moretti
MMr	Mark Millar
MMy	Marat Mychaels
MN	Mike Netzer
MnN	Martin Nodell
Moe	Moebius
MP	Mike Ploog
MPa	Mark Pacella
MPc	Mark Paniccia
MPk	Martin Pasko
MPn	Mark Pennington
MR	Marshall Rogers
MRa	Mac Raboy
MRc	Mark Ricketts
MRi	Mike Richardson
MRy	Matt Ryan
MS	Mark Silvestri
MSh	Mark Schultz
MsM	Mike S. Miller
MSo	Mark Sasso
MSt	Malcolm Smith
MSy	Mike Sekowsky
MT	Mark Texeira
MtB	Matt Broome
MTk	Masashi Tanaka
MV	Mike Vosburg
MvR	Melvin Rubi
MW	Mary Wilshire
MWa	Mark Waid
MWg	Matt Wagner
MWn	Marv Wolfman
MZ	Mike Zeck
MZi	Michael Zulli
NA	**Neal Adams**
NBy	Norm Breyfogle
NC	Nick Cardy
ND	Nigel Dobbyn
Nel	Nelson
NGa	Neil Gaiman
NHa	Neil Hanson
NKu	Andy Kubert
NMa	Nathan Massengill
NNa	Nick Napolitano
NPl	Noly Panalign
NR	Nestor Redondo
NRd	Norm Rapmund
NSH	N. Steven Harris
NV	Neil Vokes
NyC	Nancy Collins
OW	**Ogden Whitney**
PaD	**Paco Diaz**
PaK	Paris T. Karounos
PaP	Paul Pelletier
PB	Pat Broderick
PBd	Philip Bond
PC	Paul Chadwick
PCu	Paris Cullins
PD	Peter Doherty
PDd	Peter David
PDi	Paul Dini
PFe	Pascual Ferry
PG	Paul Gulacy
PGa	Phil Gascoine
PGn	Paul Guinan
PGr	Peter Grau
PhH	Phil Hester
PJ	Phil Jimminiz
PJe	Paul Jenkins
PKr	Peter Krause
PlA	Paul Abrams
PLa	Peter Laird
PMo	Pete Morisi
PMs	Pat Mills
PNe	Paul Neary
PNu	Philip Nutman
PO	Patrick Olliffe
PPo	Paul Pope
PQ	Peter Quinones
PR	Paul Ryan
PrC	Peter Costanza
PrG	Peter Gross
PrM	Peter Milligan
PS	Paul Smith
PSj	Peter Snejbjerg
PtL	Patrick Lee
PuD	Paul Danner
PuJ	Paul Johnson
PuK	Paul Kupperberg
RA	**Ross Andru**
RAJ	R.A. Jones
RaP	Rachel Pollack
RB	Rich Buckler
RbB	Robert Bernstein
RbC	Robert Campenella
RBe	Ramon Bernado
RBn	Ryan Benjamin
RBr	Rick Burchett
RBu	Robert Burns
RC	Reed Crandall
RCa	Richard Case
RCl	Ricky Carralero
RCo	Richard Corben
RCr	Robert Crumb
RCz	Roger Cruz
RDB	Randy DuBerkr
RdM	Raymond Marais
RDm	Rodolfo Damaggio
RE	Ric Estrada
RF	Ron Frenz
RFl	Robert Fleming
RG	Ron Garney
RGd	Ruben Gerard
RgM	Rags Morales
RGr	Randy Green
RGs	R. Grossman
RGT	R.G. Taylor
RGu	Rebecca Guay
RH	Russ Heath
RHe	Richard Horie
RHo	Rick Hoberg
RHo	Rich Howell
RiB	Richard Bennett
Rip	Riply
RJ	Robert Jenney
RJn	Robert Jones
RkB	Rick Bryant
RkL	Rick Leach
RKu	Roy Krenkel
RL	Rick Leonardi
RLd	Rob Liefeld
RLe	Rik Levins
RLm	Ron Lim
RLv	R. Livingstone
RM	Rick Magyar
RMc	Ralph Macchio
RMn	Roland Mann
RMr	Roy Allan Martinez
RMz	Ron Marz
RN	Rudy Nebres
RnT	Ron Tinker
RoR	Ron Randall
RoW	on Wagner
RP	Rudy Palais
RPc	Richard Pace
RPi	Richard Pini
RQu	Randy Queen
RRa	Rich Rankin
RS	Ron Smith
RsB	Russell Braun
RSd	Randy Stradley
RsM	Russ Manning
RSm	Robin Smith
RSt	Roger Stern
RT	Romeo Tanghal

RtH . . . . . . Robert Hebbard	SK . . . . Sam Kieth	TC . . . . Travis Charest	TSg . . . . Tom Sniegoski
RTs . . . . Roy Thomas	SL . . . . Steve Leialoha	TCk . . . . Tomm Coker	TSr . . . . . Terry Shoemaker
RV . . . . Rick Veitch	SLi . . . . Steve Lightle	TD . . . . Tony DeZuniga	TT . . . . . . Timothy Truman
RyE . . . . . . Randy Emberlin	SLo . . . . Scott Lobdell	TDF . . . . Tom DeFalco	TTg . . . . . . Tom Taggart
RyL . . . . Ray Lago	SM . . . . Steve Miller	TDr . . . . Tom Derenick	TTn . . . . . . Ty Templeton
RyR . . . . . . Rodney Ramos	SMa . . . . Shawn Martinbrough	TDz . . . . Todd DeZago	TV . . . . Tim Vigil
S&K . . . . . Simon & Kirby	SmC . . . . Sam Citron	TeB . . . . Tex Blaisdell	TVE . . . . Trevor Von Eeden
S&S . . . . . Siegel & Shuster	SMc . . . . . . Scott McDaniel	TeH . . . . Ted Halsted	TvS . . . . Trevor Scott
SA . . . . . Sergio Aragones	SMl . . . . . . Scott McCloud	TEl . . . . Tim Eldred	TWo . . . . . Teri Sue Wood
Sal . . . . Sal Amendola	SML . . . . . Sean McLaughlin	TG . . . . Tom Grummett	TY . . . . Tom Yeates
SAP . . . . Shea Anton Pensa	SMt . . . . . Steve Mattsson	TGb . . . . . . Tom Grindberg	TyD . . . . . Terry Dodson
SaV . . . . Sal Velluto	SnW . . . . Stan Woch	TGo . . . . . . Till Goodman	TyH . . . . . . Tony Harris
SB . . . . Sal Buscema	SPa . . . . . . Stephen Platt	TH . . . . Tim Hamilton	TyT . . . . . Tony Tallarico
SBi . . . . . Stephen Bissette	Spk . . . . Spark	THa . . . . Tim Harris	**VAz . . . . . Vincent Alcazar**
SBs . . . . Simon Bisley	SPl . . . . . . Scott Phillips	TJn . . . . . . Todd Johnson	VB . . . . Vaughn Bode
SBt . . . . Steve Butler	SPr . . . . . Stefan Petrucha	TKa . . . . . Terry Kavanagh	VcL . . . . Vince Locke
SC . . . . Sid Check	SR . . . . Steve Rude	TKn . . . . Trent Kaniuga	VGi . . . . . Vince Giarrano
ScB . . . . . Scott Benefiel	SRf . . . . . . Sean Ruffner	TKr . . . Teddy H. Kristiansen	ViC . . . . . Vince Colletta
ScC . . . . Scott Clark	SS . . . . Stan Sakai	TL . . . . Tom Lyle	VMk . . . . . . Val Mayerik
SCh . . . . Sean Chen	SSc . . . . . . Sean Scoffield	TLa . . . . Terry LaBan	VMo . . . . Vincent Morosco
SCi . . . . . . Sergio Cariello	SSe . . . . . Steven T. Seagle	TLw . . . . . Terral Lawrence	VRu . . . . . Vince Russell
ScK . . . . Scott Kolins	SSh . . . . . Sean Shaw	TM . . . . . Todd McFarlane	VS . . . . Val Semeiks
ScL . . . . Scott Lee	SSr . . . . . Steve Skroce	TmB . . . . . Tim Burgard	VV . . . . . Vagner Vargas
SCr . . . . Steve Crespo	SSt . . . . Steve Stern	TmC . . . . Tom Christopher	**WaP . . . . . Warren Pleece**
SCy . . . . Simon Colby	StA . . . . . Stephen Addeo	TMd . . . . Tom Mandrake	WB . . . . . . Wayne Boring
SD . . . . Steve Ditko	StB . . . . Scott Benson	TMK . . . . Ted McKeever	WBu . . . . . . W. Burroughs
SDi . . . . Steve Dillon	StC . . . . . . Stan Campbell	TMo . . . . . Tom Morgan	WE . . . . Will Eisner
SDr . . . . Stan Drake	StE . . . . Steve Erwin	TmR . . . . . . Tom Ryder	WEl . . . . . . Warren Ellis
SDR . . . Sam DeLaRosa	StG . . . . . Steve Grant	TMr . . . . . Terry Moore	WiS . . . . . William Stout
SEa . . . . Scott Eaton	StL . . . . . . Stan Lee	TMs . . . . . Tom Mason	WK . . . . Walt Kelly
SeM . . . . . Steve Montano	StP . . . . Steve Pugh	TmT . . . . . . Tom Teney	Wld . . . . Andrew Wildman
SeP . . . . . . Sean Phillips	SvG . . . . . Steve Gerber	TMw . . . . Tom McCraw	WmB . . . . William Bossart
SEp . . . . . . Steve Epting	SvL . . . . Salvador Larroca	TNa . . . . . Ted Naifeh	WMc . . . . Walter McDaniel
SeT . . . . . . Steve Tappin	SvP . . . . Steve Parkhouse	TnD . . . . . Tony Daniel	WMo . . . . . Win Mortimer
SEt . . . . . Steve Englehart	SvS . . . . . Steve Stiles	TnS . . . . . Tristan Schane	Woj . . . . Chuck Wojtkiewicz
SF . . . . . Sal Finnocchiaro	SW . . . . . Scott Williams	TNu . . . . . Todd Nauck	WP . . . . . . Wendy Pini
SFr . . . . . . Simon Freeman	SWi . . . . Skip Williamson	ToT . . . . . Tony Takezaki	WPo . . . . Whilce Portacio
SFu . . . . . . Simon Furman	SwM . . . . Shawn McManus	TOz . . . . . Tayyar Ozkan	WR . . . . Werner Roth
SG . . . . . . Sam Glanzman	SY . . . . . Steve Yeowell	TP . . . . Tom Palmer	WS . . . . . Walt Simonson
SGe . . . . Sid Greene	SZ . . . . Steven Zyskowski	TPe . . . . . . Tom Peyer	WSm . . . . . Will Simpson
SHa . . . . Scott Hanna	**TA . . . . Terry Austin**	TR . . . . Tom Raney	WW . . . . . . Wally Wood
ShG . . . . . Shannon Gallant	TAr . . . . Tom Artis	TR . . . . . Ted Richards	**YG . . . . Yvel Guichet**
ShM . . . . . Sheldon Mayer	TB . . . . Tim Boxell	TRt . . . . . Trina Robbins	YuK . . . . . . Yukito Kisniro
SHn . . . . . Simon Harrison	TBd . . . . . Tim Bradstreet	TS . . . . . . Tom Sutton	
SHp . . . . . . Scott Hampton	TBe . . . . . . Terry Beatty	TSa . . . . . Tony Salmons	
SI . . . . Stuart Immonen	TBm . . . . . Tom Bierbaum	TSe . . . . Tim Sale	

GENERAL ABBREVIATIONS FOR COMICS LISTINGS

A: . . . . Appearance of	GAm . . . . . . Graphic Album	Prev. . . . . Preview
(a) . . . . Artist	GNv . . . . . . Graphic Novel	pt. . . . . Part
Adapt. . . . . Adaptation	G-Size . . . . Giant Size	rep. . . . . . . Reprinted issue
Anniv. . . . . Anniversary	HC . . . . Hardcover	R: . . . . . . Return/Revival of
Ann.# . . . . Annual	I: . . . . Introduction of	rtd. . . . . Retold
(a&pl) . . . . Art & Plot	(i) . . . . Inks by	(s) . . . . Scripted/Written By
(a&s) . . . . Art & Script	IR: . . . . . Idenity Revealed	S.A. . . . . Silver Age
B: . . . . Beginning of	J: . . . . Joins of	SC . . . . Softcover
b: . . . . Birth	K-Size . . . . King Size	(s&i) . . . . . Script & inks
BU: . . . . . . Back-Up Story	L: . . . . Leaving of	Spec. . . . . Special
C: . . . . Cameo by	N: . . . . New Costume	TPB . . . . Trade Paperback
(c) . . . . Cover	N# . . . No issue Number	T.U. . . . . Team Up
(c&s) . . . . Cover and Script	O: . . . . Origin of	V: . . . . Versus
D: . . . . Death/Destruction of	P(c) . . . . . . Painted Cover	W: . . . . Wedding of
Ed. . . . . Edition	(p) . . . . Pencils by	w/ . . . . With
E: . . . . Ending of	PF . . . . . Prestige Format	w/o . . . . Without
F: . . . . Features	Ph(c) . . . . Photographic cover	x-over . . . Crossover with
G.A. . . . . Golden Age	(pl) . . . . Plotter	

DC COMICS

Action Comics #27 © DC Comics, Inc.

Action Comics #75 © DC Comics, Inc.

All comics prices listed are for *Near Mint* condition.   **CVA Page 1**

DC COMICS

123 V:Skid Russell 375.00
124 Superman becomes
   radioactive 400.00
125 V:Lex Luthor 400.00
126 V:Chameleon 375.00
127 JKu,Superman on Truth or
   Consequences 400.00
128 V:'Aces' Deucey 375.00
129 Meets Gob-Gob 375.00
130 V:Captain Kidder 375.00
131 V:Lex Luthor 375.00
132 Superman meets George
   Washington 375.00
133 V:Emma Blotz 375.00
134 V:Paul Strong 375.00
135 V:John Morton 375.00
136 Superman Show-Off! 375.00
137 Meets Percival Winter ... 375.00
138 Meets Herbert Hinkle 375.00
139 Clark Kent...Daredevil! ... 375.00
140 Superman becomes Hermit 375.00
141 V:Lex Luthor 375.00
142 V:Dan the Dip 375.00
143 Dates Nikki Larve 375.00
144 O:Clark Kent reporting for
   Daily Planet 425.00
145 Meets Merton Gloop 375.00
146 V:Luthor 375.00
147 V:'Cheeks' Ross 375.00
148 Superman, Indian Chief .. 375.00
149 The Courtship on Krypton! . 375.00
150 V:Morko 375.00
151 V:Mr.Mxyzptlk,Lex Luthor
   and Prankster 375.00
152 I:Metropolis Shutterbug
   Society 375.00

Action Comics #250 © DC Comics, Inc.

153 V:Kingpin 375.00
154 V:Harry Reed 375.00
155 V:Andrew Arvin 375.00
156 Lois Lane becomes Superwoman,V:Lex Luthor 375.00
157 V:Joe Striker 375.00
158 V:Kane Korrell
   O:Superman (retold) 850.00
159 Meets Oswald Whimple .. 350.00
160 I:Minerva Kent 350.00
161 Meets Antara 350.00
162 V:'IT!' 300.00

163 Meets Susan Semple 300.00
164 Meets Stefan Andriessen . 300.00
165 V:Crime Czar 300.00
166 V:Lex Luthor 300.00
167 V:Prof. Nero 300.00
168 O:Olaf 300.00
169 Caveman Clark Kent! 300.00
170 V:Mad Artist of Metropolis . 300.00
171 The Secrets of Superman . 300.00
172 Lois Lane..Witch! 300.00
173 V:Dragon Lang 300.00
174 V:Miracle Twine Gang ... 300.00
175 V:John Vinden 300.00
176 V:Billion Dollar Marvin
   Gang 300.00
177 V:General 300.00
178 V:Prof. Sands 300.00
179 Superman in Mapleville ... 300.00
180 V:Syndicate of Five 275.00
181 V:Diamond Dave Delaney . 275.00
182 The Return from Planet
   Krypton 275.00
183 V:Lex Luthor 275.00
184 Meets Donald Whitmore .. 275.00
185 V:Issah Pendleton 275.00
186 The Haunted Superman .. 275.00
187 V:Silver 275.00
188 V:Cushions Raymond gang 275.00
189 Meets Mr.&Mrs. John
   Vandeveir 275.00
190 V:Mr. Mxyzptlk 275.00
191 V:Vic Vordan 275.00
192 Meets Vic Vordan 275.00
193 V:Beetles Brogan 275.00
194 V:Maln 275.00
195 V:Tiger Woman 275.00
196 Superman becomes Mental
   Man 275.00
197 V:Stanley Stark 275.00
198 The Six Lives of Lois Lane 275.00
199 V:Lex Luthor 275.00
200 V:Morwatha 275.00
201 V:Benny the Brute 275.00
202 Lois Lane's X-Ray Vision . 275.00
203 Meets Pietro Paresca ... 275.00
204 Meets Sam Spulby 275.00
205 Sergeant Superman 275.00
206 Imaginary story featuring
   Lois Lane 275.00
207 Four Superman Medals! .. 275.00
208 V:Mr. Mxyzptlk 275.00
209 V:'Doc' Winters 275.00
210 V:Lex Luthor,I:Superman
   Land 275.00
211 Superman Spectaculars .. 250.00
212 V:Thorne Varden 250.00
213 V:Paul Paxton 250.00
214 Superman,Sup.Destroyer! . 250.00
215 I:Superman of 2956 ..... 250.00
216 A:Jor-El 250.00
217 Meets Mr&Mrs.Roger Bliss 250.00
218 I:Super-Ape from Krypton . 250.00
219 V:Art Shaler 250.00
220 The Interplanetary
   Olympics 250.00
221 V:Jay Vorrell 200.00
222 The Duplicate Superman . 200.00
223 A:Jor-El 200.00
224 I:Superman Island 200.00
225 The Death of Superman .. 225.00
226 V:Lex Luthor 200.00
227 The Man with the Triple
   X-Ray Eyes 200.00
228 A:Superman Museum 200.00
229 V:Dr. John Haley 200.00

230 V:Bart Wellins 200.00
231 Sir Jimmy Olsen, Knight of
   Metropolis 200.00
232 Meets Johnny Kirk 200.00
233 V:Torm 200.00
234 Meets Golto 200.00
235 B:Congo Bill,
   B:Tommy Tomorrow 200.00
236 A:Lex Luthor 200.00
237 V:Nebula Gang 200.00
238 I:King Krypton,the Gorilla . 200.00
239 'Superman's New Face' .. 200.00
240 V:Superman Sphinx 200.00
241 WB,A:Batman,Fortress of
   Solitude (Fort Superman) . 175.00
242 I&O:Brainiac 1,100.00
243 Lady and the Lion 175.00
244 CS,A:Vul-Kor,Lya-La 175.00
245 WB,V:Kak-Kul 175.00
246 WB,A:Krypton Island 175.00
247 WB,Superman Lost Parents 175.00
248 B&I:Congorilla 175.00
249 AP,A:Lex Luthor 175.00
250 WB,'The Eye of Metropolis' 175.00
251 AP,E:Tommy Tomorrow . 175.00
252 I&O:Supergirl 1,200.00
253 B:Supergirl 275.00
254 I:Adult Bizarro 300.00
255 I:Bizarro Lois 175.00
256 'Superman of the Future' . 125.00
257 WB,JM,V:Lex Luthor 125.00
258 A:Cosmic Man 125.00
259 A:Lex Luthor,Superboy .. 125.00
260 A:Mighty Maid 125.00
261 I:Streaky,E:Congorilla 125.00

Action Comics #265 © DC Comics, Inc.

262 A:Bizarro 100.00
263 O:Bizarro World 125.00
264 V:Bizarro 90.00
265 A:Hyper-Man 90.00
266 A:Streaky,Krypto 90.00
267 JM,3rd A:Legion,I:Invisible
   Kid 400.00
268 WB,A:Hercules 100.00
269 A:Jerro 100.00
270 CS,JM,A:Batman 110.00
271 A:Lex Luthor 100.00
272 A:Aquaman 100.00

DC COMICS

273 A:Mr.Mxyzptlk 100.00	341 CS,V:Vakox,A:Batman 13.00	387 CS,A:Legion,Even	
274 A:Superwoman 100.00	342 WB,JM,V:Brainiac 13.00	Supermen Die 9.00	
275 WB,JM,V:Braimiac 100.00	343 WB,V:Eterno 13.00	388 CS,A:Legion,Puzzle of	
276 JM,6th A:Legion,I:Brainiac 5,	344 WB,JM,A:Batman 13.00	The Wild Word 9.00	
Triplicate Girl,Bouncing Boy 175.00	345 CS(c),A:Allen Funt 13.00	389 A:Legion,The Kid Who	
277 CS,JM,V:Lex Luthor 80.00	346 WB,JM 13.00	Struck Out Superman 9.00	
278 CS,Perry White Becomes	347 CS(c),A:Supergirl, 80pgs. . . 25.00	390 CS,'Self-Destruct Superman' . 9.00	
Master Man 80.00	348 WB,JM,V:Acid Master 12.00	391 CS,Punishment of	
279 JM,V:Hercules,Samson 80.00	349 WB,JM,V:Dr.Kryptonite 12.00	Superman's Son 9.00	
280 CS,JM,V:Braniac,	350 A:JLA 12.00	392 CS,E:Legion 9.00	
A:Congorilla 80.00	351 WB,I:Zha-Vam 12.00	393 CS,MA,RA,A:Super Houdini . 9.00	
281 JM,A:Krypto 80.00	352 WB,V:Zha-Vam 12.00	394 CS,MA 9.00	
282 JM,V:Mxyzptlk 80.00	353 WB,JM,V:Zha-Vam 12.00	395 CS,MA,A:Althera 9.00	
283 CS,JM,A:Legion of Super	354 JM,A:Captain Incredible . . . 12.00	396 CS,MA 9.00	
Outlaws 100.00	355 WB,JM,V:Lex Luthor 12.00	397 CS,MA,Imaginary Story 9.00	
284 A:Krypto,Jerro 90.00	356 WB,JM,V:Jr. Annihilitor 12.00	398 NA(c),CS,MA,I:Morgan Edge . 9.00	
285 JM,Supergirl Existence Revealed,	357 WB,JM,V:Annihilitor 12.00	399 NA(c),CS,MA,A:Superbaby . . 9.00	
C:Legion (12th app.) 100.00	358 NA(c),CS,JM,A:Superboy . . 12.00	400 NA(c),CS,MA,Kandor Story . 10.00	
286 CS,JM,V:Lex Luthor 50.00	359 NA(c),CS,KS,C:Batman . . . 12.00	401 CS,MA,V:Indians 8.00	
287 JM,A:Legion 50.00	360 CS(c),A:Supergirl, 80pgs. . . 25.00	402 NA(c),CS,MA,V:Indians 8.00	
288 JM,A:Mon-El 50.00	361 NA(c),A:Parasite 10.00	403 CS,MA,Vigilante rep. 8.00	
289 JM,A:Adult Legion 50.00	362 RA,KS,V:Lex Luthor 10.00	404 CS,MA,Aquaman rep 8.00	
290 JM,C:Phantom Girl 50.00		405 CS,MA,Vigilante rep. 8.00	
291 JM,V:Mxyzptlk 45.00		406 CS,MA,Atom & Flash rep. . . . 8.00	
292 JM,I:Superhorse 50.00		407 CS,MA,V:Lex Luthor 8.00	
293 JM,O:Comet-Superhorse . . . 80.00		408 CS,MA,Atom rep. 8.00	
294 JM,V:Lex Luthor 45.00		409 CS,MA,T.Tommorrow rep. . . . 8.00	
295 CS,JM,O:Lex Luthor 48.00		410 CS,MA,T.Tommorrow rep. . . . 8.00	
296 V:Super Ants 45.00		411 CS,MA,O:Eclipso rep. 9.00	
297 CS,JM,A:Mon-El 45.00		412 CS,MA,Eclipso rep. 8.00	
298 CS,JM,V:Lex Luthor 45.00		413 CS,MA,V:Brainiac 8.00	
299 O:Superman Robots 45.00		414 CS,MA,B:Metamorpho 8.00	
300 JM,A:Mxyzptlk 60.00		415 CS,MA,V:Metroplis Monster . 8.00	
301 CS(c),JM,O:Superhorse . . . 25.00		416 CS,MA 8.00	
302 CS(c),JM,O:Superhorse . . . 25.00		417 CS,MA,V:Luthor 8.00	
303 CS(c),Red Kryptonite story . 20.00		418 CS,MA,V:Luthor,	
304 CS,JM,I&O:Black Flame . . . 30.00		E:Metamorpho 8.00	
305 CS(c),O:Supergirl 20.00		419 CS,MA,CI,DG,I:HumanTarget 9.00	
306 JM,C:Mon-El,Brainiac 5 . . . 20.00		420 CS,MA,DG,V:Towbee 8.00	
307 CS,JM,A:Saturn Girl 20.00		421 CS,MA,B:Green Arrow 8.00	
308 CS(c),V:Hercules 20.00		422 CS,DG,O:Human Target 7.00	
309 CS,A:Batman,JFK,Legion . . 25.00		423 CS,MA,DG,A:Lex Luthor . . . 7.00	
310 CS,JM,I:Jewel Kryptonite . . 22.00		424 CS,MA,Green Arrow 8.00	
311 CS,JM,O:Superhorse 20.00		425 CS,DD,NA,DG,B:Atom 17.00	
312 CS,JM,V:Metallo-Superman 20.00		426 CS,MA,Green Arrow 7.00	
313 JM,A:Supergirl,Lex Luthor,		427 CS,MA,DD,DG,Atom 7.00	
Batman 20.00		428 CS,MA,DG,Luthor 7.00	
314 JM,A:Justice League 20.00		429 CS,BO,DG,C:JLA 7.00	
315 JM,V:Zigi,Zag 20.00		430 CS,MA,DD,DG,Atom 7.00	
316 JM,A:Zigi,Zag,Zyra 20.00		431 CS,MA,Green Arrow 7.00	
317 JM,V:Lex Luthor 20.00		432 CS,MA,DG,Toyman 7.00	
318 CS,JM,A:Brainiac 20.00		433 CS,BO,DD,DG,A:Atom 7.00	
319 CS,JM,A:Legion,V:L.Luthor . 20.00		434 CS,DD,Green Arrow 7.00	
320 CS,JM,V:Atlas,Hercules . . . 20.00		435 FM(c),CS,DD,DG,Atom 7.00	
321 CS,JM,A:Superhorse 20.00		436 CS,DD,Green Arrow 7.00	
322 JM,'Coward of Steel' 20.00		437 CS,DG,Green Arrow	
323 JM,A:Superhorse 20.00		(100 page giant) 15.00	
324 JM,A:Abdul 20.00		438 CS,BO,DD,Atom 7.00	
325 CS,JM,SkyscraperSuperman 20.00		439 CS,BO,DD,Atom 7.00	
326 CS,JM,V:Legion of Super		440 1st MGr Green Arrow 7.50	
Creatures 20.00	363 RA,KS,V:Lex Luthor 10.00	441 CS,BO,MGr,A:Green Arrow,	
327 JM,C:Brainiac 20.00	364 RA,KS,V:Lex Luthor 10.00	Flash,R:Krypto 6.00	
328 JM,Hands of Doom 20.00	365 A:Legion & J.L.A. 10.00	442 CS,MS,MGr,Atom 3.50	
329 JM,V:Drang 20.00	366 RA,KS,A:J.L.A. 10.00	443 CS,A:JLA(100 pg.giant) 9.00	
330 CS,JM,Krypto 20.00	367 NA(c),CS,KS,A:Supergirl . . . 10.00	444 MGr,Green Arrow 4.50	
331 CS,V:Dr.Supernatural 20.00	368 CS,KS,V:Mxyzptlk 10.00	445 MGr,Green Arrow 4.50	
332 CS,A:Brainiac 20.00	369 CS,KS,Superman's Greatest	446 MGr,Green Arrow 4.50	
333 CS(c),A:Lex Luthor 20.00	Blunder 10.00	447 CS,BO,RB,KJ,Atom 3.50	
334 JM(c),A:Lex Luthor,80pgs . . 40.00	370 NA(c),CS,KS 10.00	448 CS,BO,DD,JL,Atom 3.50	
335 CS,V:Lex Luthor 15.00	371 NA(c),CS,KS 10.00	449 CS,BO 3.50	
336 CS,O:Akvar 15.00	372 NA(c),CS,KS 10.00	450 MGr,Green Arrow 4.00	
337 CS,V:Tiger Gang 15.00	373 A:Supergirl,(giant size) 25.00	451 MGr,Green Arrow 4.00	
338 CS,JM,V:Muto 15.00	374 NA(c),CS,KS,V:Super Thief . 9.00	452 CS,MGr,Green Arrow 4.00	
339 CS,V:Muto,Brainiac 15.00	375 CS,KS,The Big Forget 9.00	453 CS,Atom 3.50	
340 JM,I:Parasite 18.00	376 CS,KS,E:Supergirl 9.00	454 CS,E:Atom 3.50	
	377 CS,KS,B:Legion 9.00		
	378 CS,KS,V:Marauder 9.00		
	379 CS,JA,MA,V:Eliminator 9.00		
	380 KS,Confessions of Superman 9.00		
	381 CS,Dictators of Earth 9.00		
	382 CS,Clark Kent-Magician 9.00		
	383 CS,The Killer Costume 9.00		
	384 CS,The Forbidden Costume . 9.00		
	385 CS,The Mortal Superman . . . 9.00		
	386 CS,Home For Old Supermen 9.00		

Action Comics #309 © DC Comics, Inc.

DC COMICS

455 CS,Green Arrow	4.00
456 CS,MGr,Green Arrow	4.00
457 CS,MGr,Green Arrow	4.00
458 CS,MGr,I:Black Rock	4.00
459 CS,BO,Blackrock	3.50
460 CS,I:Karb-Brak	3.50
461 CS,V:Karb-Brak	3.50
462 CS,V:Karb-Brak	3.50
463 CS,V:Karb-Brak	3.50
464 CS,KS,V:Pile-Driver	3.50
465 CS,FMc,Luthor	3.50
466 NA(c),CS,V:Luthor	3.50
467 CS,V:Mzyzptlk	3.50
468 NA(c),CS,FMc,V:Terra-Man	3.50
469 CS,TerraMan	3.50
470 CS,Flash Green Lantern	3.50
471 CS,V:Phantom Zone Female	3.50
472 CS,V:Faora Hu-Ul	3.50
473 NA(c),CS,Phantom Zone	
Villians	3.50
474 KS,V:Doctor Light	3.50
475 KS,V:Karb-Brak,A:Vartox	3.50
476 KS,V:Vartox	3.50
477 CS,DD,Land Lords of Earth	3.50
478 CS,Earth's Last	3.50
479 CS	3.50
480 CS,A:JLA,V:Amazo	3.50
481 CS,A:JLA,V:Amazo	3.50
482 CS,Amazo	3.50
483 CS,Amazo,JLA	3.50
484 CS,W:Earth 2 Superman	
& Lois Lane	3.75
485 NA(c),CS,rep.Superman#233	4.00
486 GT,KS,V:Lex Luthor	3.50
487 CS,AS,O:Atom	4.00
488 CS,AS,A:Air Wave	3.50
489 CS,AS,A:JLA,Atom	3.50
490 CS,Brainiac	3.50
491 CS,A:Hawkman	3.50
492 CS,'Superman's After Life'	3.50
493 CS,A:UFO	3.50
494 CS	3.50
495 CS	3.50
496 CS,A:Kandor	3.50
497 CS	3.50
498 CS,Vartox	3.50
499 CS,Vartox	3.50
500 CS,Superman's Life Story	
A:Legion	6.00
501 KS	2.50
502 CS,A:Supergirl,Gal.Golem	2.50
503 CS,'A Save in Time'	2.50
504 CS,'The Power and Choice'	2.50
505 CS	2.50
506 CS	2.50
507 CS,A:Jonathan Kent	2.50
508 CS,A:Jonathan Kent	2.50
509 CS,JSn,DG	2.75
510 CS,Luthor	2.50
511 CS,AS,V:Terraman,	
A:Air Wave	2.50
512 CS,RT,V:Luthor,A:Air Wave	2.50
513 CS,RT,V:Krell,A:Air Wave	2.50
514 CS,RT,V:Brainiac,A:Atom	2.50
515 CS,AS,A:Atom	2.50
516 CS,AS,V:Luthor,A:Atom	2.50
517 CS,DH,A:Aquaman	2.50
518 CS,DH,A:Aquaman	2.50
519 CS,DH,A:Aquaman	2.50
520 CS,DH,A:Aquaman	2.50
521 CS,AS,I:Vixen,A:Atom	2.50
522 CS,AS,A:Atom	2.50
523 CS,AS,A:Atom	2.50
524 CS,AS,A:Atom	2.50
525 JSon,FMc,AS,I:Neutron	

A:Air Wave	2.50
526 JSon,AS,V:Neutron	2.50
527 CS,AS,I:Satanis,A:Aquaman	3.00
528 CS,AS,V:Brainiac,A:Aq'man	2.50
529 GP(c),CS,DA,AS,A:Aquaman,	
V:Brainiac	2.50
530 CS,DA,Brainiac	2.50
531 JSon,FMc,AS,A:Atom	2.50
532 CS,C:New Teen Titans	2.50
533 CS,V:The.	2.50
534 CS,AS,V:Satanis,A:Air Wave	2.50
535 GK(c),JSon,AS,	
A:Omega Men	2.50
536 JSon,AS,FMc,A:Omega Men	2.50
537 IN,CS,AS,V:Satanis	
A:Aquaman	2.50
538 IN,AS,FMc,V:Satanis,	
A:Aquaman	2.50
539 KG(c),GK,AS,DA,A:Flash,	
Atom,Aquaman	2.50
540 GK,AS,V:Satanis	2.50
541 GK,V:Satanis	2.50
542 AS,V:Vandal Savage	2.50
543 CS,V:Vandal Savage	2.50
544 CS,MA,GK,GP,45th Anniv.	
D:Ardora,Lexor	3.50
545 GK,Brainiac	2.50
546 GK,A:JLA,New Teen Titans	2.50
547 GK(c),CS	2.50
548 GK(c),AS,Phantom Zone	2.50
549 GK(c),AS	2.50
550 AS(c),GT	2.50
551 GK,Starfire becomes	
Red Star	2.50
552 GK,Forgotten Heroes	
(inc.Animal Man)	6.00
553 GK,Forgotten Heroes(inc.	
Animal Man)	6.00
554 GK(a&c)	2.00
555 CS,A:Parasite (X-over	
Supergirl #20)	2.00
556 CS,KS,C:Batman	2.00
557 CS,Terra-man	2.00
558 KS	2.00
559 KS,AS	2.00
560 AS,KG,BO,A:Ambush Bug	2.00
561 KS,WB,Toyman	2.00
562 KS,Queen Bee	2.00
563 AS,KG,BO,A:Ambush Bug	2.00
564 AS,V:Master Jailer	2.00
565 KG,KS,BO,A:Ambush Bug	2.00
566 BO(i),MR	2.00
567 KS,AS,PB	2.00
568 CS,AW,AN	2.00
569 IN	2.00
570 KS	2.00
571 BB(c),AS,A:Thresh 222	2.00
572 WB,BO	2.00
573 KS,BO,AS	2.00
574 KS	2.00
575 KS,V:Intellax	2.00
576 KS,Earth's Sister Planet	2.00
577 KG,BO,V:Caitiff	2.00
578 KS,Parasite	2.00
579 KG,BO,Asterix Parody	2.00
580 GK(c),KS,Superman's Failure	2.00
581 DCw(c),KS,Superman	
Requires Legal aid	2.00
582 AS,Superman's Parents	
Alive	2.00
583 CS,KS,AMo(s),Last Pre	
Crisis Superman	8.00
584 JBy,DG,A:NewTeenTitans,	
I:Modern Age Superman.	3.00
585 JBy,DG,Phantom Stranger	2.50

586 JBy,DG,Legends,V:New	
Gods,Darkseid	2.50
587 JBy,DG,Demon	2.50
588 JBy,DG,Hawkman	2.50
589 JBy,DG,Gr.Lant.Corp.	2.50
590 JBy,DG,Metal Men	2.50
591 JBy,V:Superboy,A:Legion	2.50
592 JBy,Big Barda	2.50
593 JBy,Mr. Miracle	2.50
594 JBy,A:Booster Gold	2.50
595 JBy,A:M.Manhunter,	
I:Silver Banshee	2.50
596 JBy,A:Spectre,Millenium	2.50
597 JBy,L.Starr(i),Lois V:Lana	2.50
598 JBy,TyT,I:Checkmate	3.50
599 RA,JBy(i),A:MetalMen,	
BonusBook	2.50
600 JBy,GP,KS,JOy,DG,CS,MA,	
MMi,A:Wonder Woman;	
Man-Bat,V:Darkseid	6.00

Action Comics #469 © DC Comics, Inc.

Becomes:
ACTION WEEKLY
1988–89

601 GK,DSp,CS,DJu,TD,	
B:Superman,Gr.Lantern,	
Blackhawk,Deadman,Secret	
Six,Wilddog	2.00
602 GP(c),GK,DSp,CS,DJu,TD	1.75
603 GK,CS,DsP,DJu,TD	1.75
604 GK,DSp,CS,DJu,TD	1.75
605 NKu/AKu(c),GK,DSp,CS,	
DJu,TD	1.75
606 DSp,CS,DJu,TD	1.75
607 SLi(c),TD,DSp,CS,DJu	1.75
608 DSp,CS,DJu,TD,E:Blackhawk	1.75
609 BB(c),DSp,DJu,TD,CS,	
E:Wild Dog,B:Black Canary	1.75
610 KB,DJu,CS,DSp,TD,CS	
A:Phantom Stranger	2.00
611 AN(c),DJu,DSp,CS,BKi,	
BKi,B:Catwoman	3.00
612 PG(c),DSp,CS,BKi,TD,	
E:Secret Six,Deadman	2.50
613 MK(c),BKi,CS,MA,TGr,	
Nightwing,B:Phantom Stranger	2.50
614 TG,CS,Phantom Stranger	

DC COMICS

E:Catwoman 2.50
615 MMi(c),CS,MA,BKi,TGr,
   Blackhawk,B:Wild Dog 1.75
616 ATh(c),CS,MA,E:Bl.Canary . . 1.75
617 CS,MA,JO,A:Ph.Stranger . . . 1.75
618 JBg(c),CS,MA,JKo,TD,
   B:Deadman,E:Nightwing 1.75
619 CS,MA,FS,FMc,KJo,TD,FMc,
   B:Sinister Six. 1.75
620 CS,MA,FS,FMc,KJo,TD 1.75
621 JO(c),CS,MA,FS,FMc,KJo,
   TD,MBr,E:Deadman 1.75
622 RF(c),MBr,TL,CS,MA,FS,
   FMc,A:Starman,E:Wild
   Dog,Blackhawk 1.75
623 MBr,TD,CS,MA,FS,FMc,JL,
   JKo,A:Ph.Stranger,
   B:Deadman,Shazam 1.75
624 AD(c),MBr,FS,FMc,CS,MA,
   TD,B:Black Canary 1.75
625 MBr,FS,FMc,CS,MA,
   TD,FMc 1.50
626 MBr,FS,FMc,CS,MA,JKo,TD,
   E:Shazam,Deadman 1.50
627 GK(c),MBr,RT,FS,FMc,CS,
   MA,TMd,B:Nightwing,Speedy . 1.75
628 TY(c),MBr,RT,TMd,CS,MA,
   FS,FMc,B:Blackhawk 1.50
629 CS,MA,MBr,RT,FS,FMc,TMd . 1.50
630 CS,MA,MBr,RT,FS,FMc,TMd,
   E:Secret Six 1.50
631 JS(c),CS,MA,MBr,RT,TMd,
   B:Phantom Stranger 1.50
632 TGr(c),CS,MA,MBr,RT,TMd . 1.50
633 CS,MA,MBr,RT,TMd 1.50
634 CS,MA,MBr,RT,TMd,E:Ph.Stranger,
   Nightwing,Speedy,Bl.hawk . . 1.50
635 CS,MA,MBr,RT,EB,E:Black
   Canary,Green Lantern 1.50
636 DG(c),CS,MA,NKu,MPa,FMc,
   B:Demon,Wild Dog,Ph.Lady,
   Speedy,A:Phantom Stranger . 1.75
637 CS,MA,KS,FMc,MPa,
   B:Hero Hotline 1.50
638 JK(c),CS,MA,KS,FMc,MPa . 1.50
639 CS,MA,KS,FMc,MPa 1.50
640 CS,KS,MA,FS,FMc,MPa,
   E:Speedy,Hero Hotline 1.50
641 CS,MA,JL,DG,MPa,E:Demon,
   Phant.Lady,Superman,Wild Dog,
   A:Ph.Stranger,Hum.Target . . 1.75
642 GK,SD,ATi,CS,JAp,JM,CI,KN,
   Green Lantern,Superman 1.50

Becomes:

ACTION COMICS
1989–97
643 B:RSt(s),GP,BBr,V:Intergang . 2.50
644 GP,BBr,V:Matrix 2.00
645 GP,BBr,I:Maxima 2.00
646 KG,V:Alien Creature,
   A:Brainiac 2.50
647 GP,KGa,BBr,V:Brainiac 2.00
648 GP,KGa,BBr,V:Brainiac 2.00
649 GP,KGa,BBr,V:Brainiac 2.00
650 JOy,BBr,CS,BMc,GP,KGa,
   ATi,DJu,A:JLA,C:Lobo 3.00
651 GP,KGa,BBr,Day of Krypton
   Man #3,V:Maxima 3.00
652 GP,KGa,BBr,Day of Krypton
   Man #6,V:Eradicator 3.00
653 BMc,BBr,D:Amanda 2.00
654 BMc,BBr,A:Batman Pt.3 . . . 2.50
655 BMc,BBr,V:Morrisson,Ma
   Kent's Photo Album 2.00
656 BMc,BBr,Soul Search #1,

V:Blaze 2.00
657 KGa,BBr,V:Toyman 2.00
658 CS,Sinbad Contract #3 . . . . 2.00
659 BMc,BBr,K.Krimson
   Kryptonite #3 . . . . 3.50
660 BMc,BBr,D:Lex Luthor 3.00
661 BMc,BBr,A:Plastic Man 2.00
662 JOy,JM,TG,BMc,V:Silver
   Banshee,Clark tells
   Lois his identity 4.00
662a 2nd printing 2.00
663 BMc,Time & Time Again,pt.2,
   A:JSA,Legion 2.00
664 BMc,Time & Time Again,pt.5 . 2.00
665 TG,V:Baron Sunday 2.00
666 EH,Red Glass Trilogy,pt.3 . . . 2.00
667 JOy,JM,TG,ATi,DJu,Revenge
   of the Krypton Man,pt.4 . . . . . 2.25
668 BMc,Luthor confirmed dead . 2.00
669 BMc,V:Intergang,A:Thorn . . . 2.00
670 BMc,A:Waverider,JLA,JLE . . 2.00
671 KD,Blackout,pt.2 . . . . 2.00
672 BMc,Superman Meets Lex
   Luthor II 2.00
673 BMc,V:Hellgramite 2.00
674 BMc,Panic in the Sky (Prologue)
   R:Supergirl(Matrix) 3.50
675 BMc,Panic in the Sky #4,
   V:Brainiac 1.75
676 B:KK(s),JG,A:Supergirl,Lex
   Luthor II 1.75
677 JG,Supergirl V:Superman . . . 1.75
678 JG,O:Lex Luthor II 1.75
679 JG,I:Shellshock 1.75
680 JG,Blaze/Satanus War,pt.2 . . 1.75
681 JG,V:Hellgramite 1.75
682 DAb,TA,V:Hi-Tech 1.75
683 JG,I:Jackal,C:Doomsday 3.00
683a 2nd printing 1.50
684 JG,Doomsday Pt.4. . . . . 4.00
684a 2nd printing 1.75
685 JG,Funeral for a Friend#2 . . 3.00

Action Comics #662 © DC Comics, Inc.

686 JG,Funeral for a Friend#6 . . . 3.00
687 JG,Reign of Superman #1,Direct
   Sales,Die-Cut(c),Mini-Poster,
   F:Last Son of Krypton 2.50
687a newsstand Ed. 1.75
688 JG,V:Guy Gardner 2.00

689 JG,V:Man of Steel,A:Superboy,
   Supergirl,R:Real Superman . . . 3.50
690 JG,Cyborg Vs. Superboy 2.50
691 JG,A:All Supermen,V:Cyborg
   Superman,Mongul 3.50
692 JG,A:Superboy,Man of Steel . 1.75
693 JG,A:Last Son of Krypton . . . 1.75
694 JG,Spilled Blood#2,V:Hi-Tech . 1.75
695 JG,Foil(c),I:Cauldron,A:Lobo . 2.50
695a Newsstand Ed. 1.75
697 JG,Bizarro's World#3,
   V:Bizarro 1.75
698 JG,A:Lex Luthor 1.75
699 JG,A:Project Cadmus 1.75
700 JG,Fall of Metropolis#1 . . . . . 3.00
700a Platinum Edition 15.00
701 JG,Fall of Metropolis#5,
   V:Luthor 3.00
702 JG,DvM,B:DyM(s),R:Bloodsport1.75
703 JG,DvM,Zero Hour 1.75
704 JG,DvM,Eradicator 1.50
705 JG,DvM,Supes real? 1.50
706 JG,DvM,A:Supergirl 1.50
707 JG,DvM,V:Shado Dragon . . . 1.50
708 JG,DvM,R:Deathtrap 1.50
709 JG,DvM,A:Guy Gardner,
   Warrior 1.50
710 JG,DvM,Death of Clark Kent,pt.3
   [new Miraweb format begins] . . 1.95
711 JG,DvM,Death of Clark
   Kent,pt.7 . . . . 1.95
712 Rescue Jimmy Olsen 1.95
713 . . . . 1.95
714 R:The Joker 1.95
715 DvM,DaR,V:Parasite 1.95
716 DvM,DaR,Trial of Superman . 1.95
717 DvM,DaR,Trial of Superman . 1.95
718 DvM,DRo,mystery of Demolitia 1.95
719 DvM,DRo 1.95
720 DvM,DRo,Lois ends
   engagement 1.95
721 DvM,DRo,lottery fever 1.95
722 DvM,DaR,Tornados in
   Smallville 1.95
723 V:Brainiac 1.95
724 V:STAR.labs monster 1.95
725 Tolos 1.95
726 DvM(s),TMo,DRo,Krisis of the
   Krimson Kryptonite follow-up . . 1.95
727 DvM(s),TMo,DRo,brutal weather
   in Metropolis, Final Night tie-in . 1.95
728 DvM(s),TG,DRo, Some
   Honeymoon! 1.95
729 DvM(s),TG,DRo, in Fortress of
   Solitude 1.95
730 DvM(s),TG,Ro,. 1.95
731 DvM(s),TG,DRo, R:Cauldron . 1.95
732 DvM(s),TG,DRo, Atomic Skull
   rampages through Metropolis . 1.95
733 DvM(s),TG,DRo, V:Matallo,
   A:Ray 1.95
734 DvM(s),TG,DRo, Superman &
   Atom in Kandor 1.95
735 DvM(s),TG,DRo, V:Savior . . . 1.95
736 DvM(s),TG,DRo 1.95
736 MWa(s),TG,DRo, Luthor gets
   day in court 1.95
Ann.#1 AAd,DG,A:Batman 8.00
Ann.#2 MMi,CS,GP,JOy,DJu,BBr,
   V:Mongul 4.00
Ann.#3 TG,Armageddon X-over . . 3.00
Ann.#4 Eclipso,A:Captain
   Marvel 3.00
Ann.#5 MZ(c),Bloodlines, I:Loose

All comics prices listed are for *Near Mint* condition.

DC COMICS

Cannon 2.75
Ann.#6 Elseworlds,JBy(a&S) 3.00
Ann.#7 Year One Annual 3.95
Ann.#8 DvM,"Legends of the Dead
 Earth" 2.95
Ann.#9 Pulp Heroes (Macabre) . . 3.95
Gold.Ann.rep.#1 . . . . 1.50
#0 Peer Pressure,pt.4 (1994) 2.00

ADAM STRANGE
1990
1 NKu,A.Strange on Rann 5.00
2 NKu,Wanted:Adam Strange . . . 4.50
3 NKu,final issue 4.50

ADVANCED
DUNGEONS & DRAGONS
1988–91
1 JD,I:Onyx,Priam,Timoth,
 Cybriana,Vajra,Luna 8.00
2 JD,V:Imgig Zu,I:Conner 6.00
3 JD,V:Imgig Zu 7.00
4 JD,V:Imgig Zu,I:Kyriani 5.00
5 JD,Spirit of Myrrth I 5.00
6 JD,Spirit of Myrrth II 5.00
7 JD,Spirit of Myrrth III 4.50
8 JD,Spirit of Myrrth IV 4.50
9 JD,Catspawn Quartet I 4.50
10 JD,Catspawn Quartet II 4.00
11 JD,Catspawn Quartet III 4.00
12 JD,Catspawn Quartet IV 4.00
13 JD,Spell Games I 4.00
14 JD,Spell Games II 4.00
15 JD,Spell Games III 3.00
16 JD,Spell Games IV 3.00
17 JD,RM,Kyriani's Story I 3.00
18 JD,RM,Kyriani's Story II 3.00
19 JD,RM,Luna I 3.00
20 JD,RM,Luna II 3.00
21 JD,RM,Luna III 3.00
22 JD,RM,Luna IV 3.00
23 TMd,RM,Siege Dragons I . . . 3.00
24 Scavengers 2.50
25 JD,RM,Centaur Village 2.00
26 JD,Timoth the Centaur 2.00
27 JD,Kyriani,Dragons Eye #1 . . 2.00
28 JD,Dragons Eye #2 . . . . 2.00
29 JD,RM,Dragons Eye #3 . . . . . 2.00
30 JD,RM,Carril's Killer
 Revealed 2.00
31 TMd,Onyx'Father,pt.1 . . . . . . 2.00
32 TMd,Onyx'Father,pt.2 . . . . . . 2.00
33 JD,Waterdeep,pt.1 . . . . 2.00
34 JD,Waterdeep,pt.2 . . . . 2.00
35 JD,RM,Waterdeep,pt.3 . . . . . 2.00
36 JD,RM,final issue 2.00
Ann.#1 JD,RM,Tmd 5.50

ADVENTURE COMICS
Nov. 1938–83
[Prev: New Comics]
32 CF(c) 3,000.00
33 . . . . 1,200.00
34 FG(c) 1,200.00
35 FG(c) 1,200.00
36 Giant Snake(c) 1,200.00
37 Rampaging Elephant(c) . . . 1,200.00
38 Tiger(c) 1,200.00
39 Male Bondage(c) 1,300.00
40 CF(c),1st app. Sandman . 32,000.00
41 Killer Shark(c) 4,000.00
42 CF,Sandman(c) 5,000.00
43 CF(c) 2,400.00
44 CF,Sandman(c) 4,500.00

45 FG(c) 2,200.00
46 CF,Sandman(c) 3,500.00
47 Sandman (c) 3,200.00
48 1st app.& B:Hourman . . 20,000.00
49 . . . . 1,500.00

Adventure Comics #51
© DC Comics, Inc.

50 Hourman(c) 1,700.00
51 BBa(c),Sandman(c) 2,000.00
52 BBa(c),Hourman(c) 1,800.00
53 BBa(c),1st app. Minuteman 1,300.00
54 BBa(c),Hourman(c) 1,300.00
55 BBa(c),same 1,300.00
56 BBa(c),same 1,300.00
57 BBa(c),same 1,300.00
58 BBa(c),same 1,300.00
59 BBa(c),same 1,300.00
60 Sandman(c) 2,000.00
61 CF(c),JBu,Starman(c) . . . 11,000.00
62 JBu(c),JBu,Starman(c) . . . 1,200.00
63 JBu(c),JBu,same 1,200.00
64 JBu(c),JBu,same 1,200.00
65 JBu(c),JBu,same 1,200.00
66 JBu(c),JBu,O:Shining Knight,
 Starman(c) 1,300.00
67 JBu(c),JBu,O:Mist 1,200.00
68 JBu(c),JBu,same 1,200.00
69 JBu(c),JBu,1st app. Sandy,
 Starman(c) 1,300.00
70 JBu(c),JBu,Starman(c) . . . 1,200.00
71 JBu(c),JBu,same 1,000.00
72 JBu(c),S&K,JBu,Sandman 10,000.00
73 S&K(c),S&K,I:Manhunter . 11,000.00
74 S&K(c),S&K,You can't Escape
 your Fate-The Sandman . 1,500.00
75 S&K(c),S&K,Sandman and
 Sandy Battle Thor in
 'Villian from Valhalla' 1,500.00
76 S&K(c),Sandman(c),S&K . 1,500.00
77 S&K,(c),S&K,same 1,500.00
78 S&K(c),S&K,same 1,500.00
79 S&K(c),S&K,Manhunter in
 'Cobras of the Deep' 1,500.00
80 S&K(c),Sandman(c),S&K . 1,500.00
81 S&K(c),MMe,S&K,same . . 900.00
82 S&K(c),S&K,Sandman
 X-Mas story 900.00
83 S&K(c),S&K,Sandman
 Boxing(c),E:Hourman 900.00
84 S&K(c),S&K 900.00
85 S&K(c),S&K,Sandman in

'The Amazing Dreams of
 Gentleman Jack' 900.00
86 S&K(c),Sandman(c) 900.00
87 S&K(c),same 900.00
88 S&K(c),same 900.00
89 S&K(c),same 900.00
90 S&K(c),same 900.00
91 S&K(c),JK 850.00
92 S&K(c) 750.00
93 S&K(c),Sandman in 'Sleep
 for Sale' 750.00
94 S&K(c),Sandman(c) 750.00
95 S&K(c),same 750.00
96 S&K(c),same 750.00
97 S&K(c),same 750.00
98 JK(c),Sandman in 'Hero
 of Dreams' 750.00
99 JK(c) 750.00
100 . . . . 1,000.00
101 S&K(c) 750.00
102 S&K(c) 750.00
103 B:Superboy stories,(c),BU:
 Johnny Quick,Aquaman,Shining
 Knight,Green Arrow . . 2,500.00
104 S&S,ToyTown USA 800.00
105 S&S,Palace of Fantasy . . 550.00
106 S&S,Weather Hurricane . 550.00
107 S&S,The Sky is the Limit . 550.00
108 S&S,Proof of the Proverbs 550.00
109 S&S,You Can't Lose 550.00
110 S&S,The Farmer Takes
 it Easy 550.00
111 S&S,The Whiz Quiz Club . 500.00
112 S&S,Super Safety First . . 500.00
113 S&S,The 33rd Christmas . 450.00
114 S&S,Superboy Spells
 Danger 450.00
115 S&S,The Adventure of
 Jaguar Boy 450.00
116 S&S,JBu,Superboy Toy
 Tester 450.00
117 S&S,JBu,Miracle Plane . . 450.00
118 S&S,JBu,The Quiz Biz
 Broadcast 450.00
119 WMo,JBu,Superboy
 Meets Girls 450.00
120 S&S,JBu,A:Perry White;
 I:Ringmaster 500.00
121 S&S,Great Hobby Contest 425.00
122 S&S,Superboy-Super-
 Magician 425.00
123 S&S,Lesson For a Bully . . 425.00
124 S&S,Barbed Wire Boys
 Town 425.00
125 S&S,The Weight Before
 Christmas 425.00
126 S&S,Superboy:Crime
 Fighting Poet 425.00
127 MMe,O:Shining Knight;
 Super Bellboy 425.00
128 WMo,How Clark Kent Met
 Lois Lane' 425.00
129 WMo,Pupils of the Past . . 425.00
130 WMo,Superboy Super
 Salesman 425.00
131 WMo,The Million Dollar
 Athlete 375.00
132 WMo,Superboy Super
 Cowboy 375.00
133 WMo,Superboy's Report
 Card 375.00
134 WMo,Silver Gloves Sellout 375.00
135 WMo,The Most Amazing
 of All Boys 375.00
136 WMo,My Pal Superboy . . 375.00

DC COMICS

137 WMo,Treasure of Tondimo 375.00
138 WMo,Around the World in
　Eighty Minutes 375.00
139 WMo,Telegraph Boy 375.00
140 Journey to the Moon 375.00

Adventure Comics #63
© DC Comics, Inc.

141 WMo,When Superboy Lost
　His Powers 375.00
142 WMo,The Man Who Walked
　With Trouble 400.00
143 WMo,The Superboy Savings
　Bank,A:Wooden Head Jones 400.00
144 WMo,The Way to Stop
　Superboy 400.00
145 WMo,Holiday Hijackers ... 400.00
146 The Substitute Superboy .. 400.00
147 Clark Kent,Orphan 400.00
148 Superboy Meets Mummies . 400.00
149 Fake Superboys 400.00
150 FF,Superboy's Initiation .. 450.00
151 FF,No Hunting(c) 450.00
152 Superboy Hunts For a Job . 400.00
153 FF,Clark Kent,Boy Hobo .. 450.00
154 The Carnival Boat Crimes . 300.00
155 FF,Superboy-Hollywood
　Actor 400.00
156 The Flying Peril 300.00
157 FF,The Worst Boy in
　Smallville 400.00
158 The Impossible Task 300.00
159 FF,Superboy Millionaire? . 400.00
160 Superboy's Phoney Father 300.00
161 FF 400.00
162 'The Super-Coach of
　Smallville High!' 300.00
163 FF,'Superboy's Phoney
　Father' 400.00
164 Discovers the Secret of
　a Lost Indian Tribe! 300.00
165 'Superboy's School for
　Stunt Men!' 300.00
166 'The Town That Stole
　Superboy' 300.00
167 'Lana Lang, Super-Girl!' .. 300.00
168 'The Boy Who Out Smarted
　Superboy' 300.00
169 'Clark Kent's Private
　Butler' 300.00
170 'Lana Lang's Big Crush' .. 275.00
171 'Superboy's Toughest

Tasks!' 275.00
172 'Laws that Backfired' 275.00
173 'Superboy's School of
　Hard Knocks' 275.00
174 'The New Lana Lang!' 275.00
175 'Duel of the Superboys' ... 275.00
176 'Superboy's New Parents!' . 275.00
177 'Hot-Rod Chariot Race!' .. 275.00
178 'Boy in the Lead Mask' ... 275.00

Adventure Comics #293
© DC Comics, Inc.

179 'The World's Whackiest
　Inventors' 275.00
180 Grand Prize o/t Underworld 275.00
181 'Mask for a Hero' 275.00
182 The Super Hick from
　Smallville' 250.00
183 'Superboy and Cleopatra' . 250.00
184 'The Shutterbugs of
　Smallville' 250.00
185 'The Mythical Monster' ... 250.00
186 .... 250.00
187 '25th Century Superboy' .. 250.00
188 'The Bull Fighter from
　Smallville' 250.00
189 Girl of Steel(Lana Lang) .. 250.00
190 The Two Clark Kents 250.00
191 .... 250.00
192 'The Coronation of
　Queen Lana Lang' 250.00
193 'Superboy's Lost Costume' 250.00
194 'Super-Charged Superboy' 250.00
195 'Lana Lang's Romance
　on Mars!' 250.00
196 'Superboy vs. King Gorilla' 250.00
197 V:Juvenile Gangs 250.00
198 'The Super-Carnival
　from Space' 250.00
199 'Superboy meets Superlad' 250.00
200 'Superboy and the Apes!' . 400.00
201 'Safari in Smallville!' 275.00
202 'Superboy City, U.S.A.' ... 275.00
203 'Uncle Superboy!' 325.00
204 'The Super-Brat of
　Smallville' 275.00
205 'The Journey of the
　Second Superboy!' 275.00

206 'The Impossible Creatures' 275.00
207 'Smallville's Worst
　Athlete' 275.00
208 'Rip Van Winkle of
　Smallville?' 275.00
209 'Superboy Week!' 275.00
210 I:Krypto,'The Superdog
　from Krypton' 3,000.00
211 'Superboy's Most
　Amazing Dream!' 250.00
212 'Superboy's Robot Twin' .. 250.00
213 'The Junior Jury of
　Smallville!' 250.00
214 A:Krypto 500.00
215 'The Super-Hobby of
　Superboy' 250.00
216 'The Wizard City' 250.00
217 'Superboy's Farewell
　to Smallville' 250.00
218 'The Two World's of
　Superboy' 250.00
219 The Rip Van Wrinkle of
　Smallville 250.00
220 The Greatest Show on Earth
　A:Krypto 250.00
221 'The Babe of Steel' 200.00
222 'Superboy's Repeat
　Performance' 200.00
223 'Hercules Junior' 200.00
224 'Pa Kent Superman' 200.00
225 'The Bird with
　Super-Powers' 200.00
226 'Superboy's Super Rival!' . 200.00
227 'Good Samaritan of
　Smallville' 200.00
228 'Clark Kent's Body Guard' . 200.00
229 .... 200.00
230 'The Secret of the
　Flying Horse' 200.00
231 'The Super-Feats of
　Super-Baby!' 200.00
232 'The House where
　Superboy was Born' 200.00
233 'Joe Smith, Man of Steel!' . 200.00
234 'The 1,001 Rides of
　Superboy!' 200.00
235 'The Confessions of
　Superboy!' 200.00
236 'Clark Kent's Super-Dad!' . 200.00
237 Robot War of Smallville! .. 200.00
238 'The Secret Past of
　Superboy's Father' 200.00
239 'The Super-Tricks of
　the Dog of Steel' 200.00
240 'The Super Teacher
　From Krypton' 200.00
241 'The Super-Outlaw of
　Smallville' 200.00
242 'The Kid From Krypton' ... 200.00
243 'The Super Toys From
　Krypton' 200.00
244 'The Poorest Family in
　Smallville' 200.00
245 'The Mystery of Monster X' 200.00
246 'The Girl Who Trapped
　Superboy!' 200.00
247 I&O:Legion 4,200.00
248 Green Arrow 150.00
249 CS,Green Arrow 150.00
250 JK,Green Arrow 150.00
251 JK,Green Arrow 150.00
252 JK,Green Arrow 150.00
253 JK,1st Superboy &
　Robin T.U 225.00
254 JK,Green Arrow 165.00

DC COMICS

255 JK,Green Arrow 165.00	320 A:Dev-Em 60.00	362 I:Dr.Mantis Morto 12.00
256 JK,O:Green Arrow 575.00	321 I:Time Trapper 75.00	363 V:Dr.Mantis Morlo 12.00
257 CS,LE,A:Hercules,Samson . 135.00	322 JF,A:Legion of Super Pets . 50.00	364 A:Legion of Super Pets 12.00
258 LE,Aquaman,Superboy . . . 135.00	323 JF,BU:Kypto 50.00	365 CS,I:Shadow Lass,
259 I:Crimson Archer 135.00	324 JF,I:Legion of	V:Fatal Five 12.00
260 1st S.A. O:Aquaman 625.00	Super Outlaws 50.00	366 CS,J:Shadow Lass 10.00
261 GA,A:Lois Lane 100.00	325 JF,V:Lex Luthor 50.00	367 N:Legion H.Q.,I:Dark Circle . 12.00
262 O:Speedy 100.00	326 BU:Superboy 50.00	368 CS 10.00
263 GA,Aquaman,Superboy . 100.00	327 I&J:Timber Wolf 50.00	369 CS,JAb,I:Mordru 10.00
264 GA,A:Robin Hood 100.00	328 Legion 50.00	370 CS,JAb,V:Mordru 10.00
265 GA,Aquaman,Superboy . 100.00	329 I:Legion of Super Bizarros . . 50.00	371 CS,JAb,I:Chemical King . . . 12.00
266 GA,I:Aquagirl 100.00	330 Legion 50.00	372 CS,JAb,J:Timber Wolf,
267 N:Legion(2nd app.) 800.00	331 Legion 40.00	Chemical King 12.00
268 I:Aquaboy 100.00	332 Legion 40.00	373 I:Tornado Twins 10.00
269 I:Aqualad,E:Green Arrow . 200.00	333 Legion 40.00	374 WM,I:Black Mace 10.00
270 2nd A:Aqualad,B:Congorilla 100.00	334 Legion 40.00	375 I:Wanderers 10.00
271 O:Lex Luthor rtd 225.00	335 Legion 40.00	376 Execution of Cham.Boy . . . 10.00
272 I:Human Flying Fish 85.00	336 Legion 40.00	377 Heroes for Hire 10.00
273 Aquaman,Superboy 85.00	337 Legion 40.00	378 Twelve Hours to Live 10.00
274 Aquaman,Superboy 85.00	338 Legion 40.00	379 Burial In Space 10.00
275 O:Superman/Batman	339 Legion 40.00	380 The Amazing Space Odyssey
T.U. rtd 200.00	340 I:Computo 40.00	of the Legion,E:Legion 10.00
276 Superboy,3rd A:Metallo 90.00		381 The Supergirl Gang
277 Aquaman,Superboy 90.00		C:Batgirl,B:Supergirl 30.00
278 Aquaman,Superboy 90.00		382 NA(c),The Superteams Split
279 CS,Aquaman,Superboy 90.00		Up,A:Superman 5.00
280 CS,A:Lori Lemaris 90.00		383 NA(c),Please Stop my Funeral,
281 Aquaman,Superboy		A:Superman,Comet,Streaky . . 6.00
E:Congorilla 90.00		384 KS,The Heroine Haters,
282 5th A:Legion,I:Starboy . . . 175.00		A:Superman 5.00
283 I:Phantom Zone 150.00		385 Supergirl's Big Sister 5.00
284 CS,JM,Aquaman,Superboy . 90.00		386 The Beast That Loved
285 WB,B:Bizarro World 125.00		Supergirl 5.00
286 I:Bizarro Mxyzptlk 125.00		387 Wolfgirl of Stanhope;
287 I:Dev-Em,Bizarro Perry White,		A:Superman;V:Lex Luthor 5.00
Jimmy Olsen 85.00		388 Kindergarten Criminal;
288 A:Dev-Em 85.00		V:Luthor,Brainiac 5.00
289 Superboy 75.00		389 A:Supergirl's Parents,
290 8th A:Legion,O&J:Sunboy,		V:Brainiac 5.00
I:Brainiac 5 . . . . 150.00		390 Linda Danvers Superstar
291 A:Lex Luthor 65.00		(80 page giant) 15.00
292 Superboy,I:Bizarro Lucy Lane,		391 The Super Cheat;A:Comet . . 4.50
Lana Lang 65.00		392 Supergirls Lost Costume . . . 4.50
293 CS,O&I:Marv-El,I:Bizarro		393 KS,Unwanted Supergirl 4.50
Luthor 100.00		394 KS,Heartbreak Prison 4.50
294 I:Bizarro M.Monroe,JFK . . 100.00		395 Heroine in Haunted House . . 4.50
295 I:Bizarro Titano 65.00		396 Mystery o/t Super Orphan . . 4.50
296 A:Ben Franklin,George		397 Now Comes Zod,N:Supergirl,
Washington 65.00		V:Luthor 4.50
297 Lana Lang Superboy Sister . 65.00		398 Maid of Doom,A:Superman,
298 The Fat Superboy 65.00		Streaky,Krypto,Comet 4.50
299 I:Gold Kryptonite 65.00		399 CI,Johnny Dee,Hero Bum . . 4.50
300 B:Legion,J:Mon-El,		400 MSy,35th Anniv.,Return of the
E:Bizarro World 400.00		Black Flame 5.00
301 CS,O:Bouncing Boy 125.00	341 CS,D:Triplicate Girl (becomes	401 MSy,JAb,The Frightened
302 CS,Legion 90.00	Duo Damsel) 32.00	Supergirl,V:Lex Luthor 6.00
303 I:Matter Eater Lad 90.00	342 CS,Star Boy expelled 30.00	402 MSy,JAb,TD,I:Starfire,
304 D:Lightning Lad 90.00	343 CS,V:Lords of Luck 30.00	Dr.Kangle 6.00
305 A:Chameleon Boy 90.00	344 CS,Super Stalag,pt.1 . . . . . 30.00	403 68 page giant 15.00
306 I:Legion of Sub.Heroes . . . 80.00	345 CS,Super Stalag,pt.2 . . . . . 30.00	404 MSy,JAb,V:Starfire 5.00
307 I:Element Lad 90.00	346 CS,I&J:Karate Kid,Princess	405 V:Starfire,Dr.Kangle 5.00
308 I:Light Lass 90.00	Projectra,I:Nemesis Kid 30.00	406 MSy,JAb,Suspicion 5.00
309 I:Legion of Super Monsters . 80.00	347 CS,Legion 18.00	407 MSy,JAb,Suspicion Confirmed
310 A:Mxyzptlk 80.00	348 I:Dr.Regulus 20.00	N:Supergirl 5.00
311 CS,V:Legion of Substitue	349 CS,I:Rond Vidar 18.00	408 The Face at the Window 5.00
Heroes 70.00	350 CS,I:White Witch 20.00	409 MSy,DG,Legion rep. 5.00
312 R:Lightning Lad 80.00	351 CS,R:Star Boy 18.00	410 N:Supergirl 5.00
313 CS,J:Supergirl 70.00	352 CS,I:Fatal Fire 18.00	411 CI,N:Supergirl 5.00
314 A:Hitler 70.00	353 CS,D:Ferro Lad 25.00	412 rep.Strange Adventures #180
315 A:Legion of Substitute	354 CS,Adult Legion 15.00	(I:Animal Man). 7.00
Heroes 70.00	355 CS,J:Insect Queen 15.00	413 GM,JKu,rep.Hawkman 2.25
316 O:Legion 60.00	356 CS,Five Legion Orphans . . . 12.00	414 Animal Man rep. 4.00
317 I&J:Dreamgirl 60.00	357 CS,I:Controller 12.00	415 BO,GM,CI,Animal Man rep. . . 3.00
318 Legion 60.00	358 I:Hunter 12.00	416 CI,All women issue,giantsize . 5.00
319 Legion 60.00	359 CS,Outlawed Legion,pt.1 . . 12.00	417 GM,inc.rep.Adventure #161,
	360 CS,Outlawed Legion,pt.2 . . 12.00	
	361 I:Dominators (30th century) . 14.00	

Adventure Comics #420
© DC Comics, Inc.

DC COMICS

Frazetta art. 2.25
418 ATh,Black Canary 2.25
419 ATh,Black Canary 2.25
420 Animal Man rep. 3.25
421 MSy,Supergirl 2.25
422 MSy,Supergirl 2.25
423 MSy,Supergirl 2.25
424 MSy,E:Supergirl,A:JLA 2.25
425 AN,ATh,I:Captain Fear 4.00
426 MSy,DG,JAp,Vigilante 2.25
427 TD 3.00
428 TD,I:Black Orchid 12.00
429 TD,AN,Black Orchid 7.00
430 A:Black Orchid 7.00
431 JAp,ATh,B:Spectre 12.00
432 JAp,AN,A:Spectre,Capt.Fear . 6.00
433 JAp,AN 6.00
434 JAp 6.00
435 MGr(1st work),JAp,Aquaman . 6.00
436 JAp,MGr,Aquaman 6.00
437 JAp,MGr,Aquaman 6.00
438 JAp,HC,DD,7 Soldiers 6.00
439 JAp 6.00

Adventure Comics #426
© DC Comics, Inc.

440 JAp,O:New Spectre 6.00
441 JAp,B:Aquaman 2.00
442 JAp,A:Aquaman 2.00
443 JAp 2.00
444 JAp 2.00
445 JAp,RE,JSon,Creeper 2.00
446 JAp,RE,JSon,Creeper 2.00
447 JAp,RE,JSon,Creeper 2.00
448 JAp,Aquaman 2.00
449 JAp,MN,TA,Jonn J'onz 1.75
450 JAp,MN,TA,Supergirl 1.75
451 JAp,MN,TA,Hawkman 1.75
452 JAp,Aquaman 1.75
453 MA,CP,JRu,B:Superboy
& Aqualad 1.75
454 CP,DG,A:Kryptonite Kid 1.75
455 CP,DG,A:Kryptonite Kid
E:Aqualad 1.75
456 JSon,JA 1.75
457 JSon,JA,JO,B:Eclipso 3.50
458 JSon,JAp,JO,BL,E:Superboy
& Eclipso 3.00
459 IN,FMc,JAp,JSon,DN,JA,A:Wond.
Woman,New Gods,Green Lantern,
Flash,Deadman,(giant size) . . . 8.00

460 IN,FMc,JAp,DN,DA,JSon,JA,
D:Darkseid 8.00
461 IN,FMc,JAp,JSon,DN,JA,
B:JSA & Aquaman 4.00
462 IN,FMc,DH,JL,DG,JA,
D:Earth 2,Batman 4.00
463 DH,JL,JSon,FMc 1.50
464 DH,JAp,JSon,DN,DA,
Deadman 1.75
465 DN,JSon,DG,JL 1.50
466 MN,JL,JSon,DN,DA 1.50
467 JSon,SD,RT,I:Starman
B:Plastic Man 10.00
468 SD,JSon 1.50
469 SD,JSon,O:Starman 1.50
470 SD,JSon,O:Starman 1.50
471 SD,JSon,I:Brickface 1.50
472 SD,RT,JSon 1.50
473 SD,RT,JSon 1.50
474 SD,RT,JSon 1.50
475 BB(c),SD,RT,JSon,DG,
B:Aquaman 1.50
476 SD,RT,JSon,DG 1.50
477 SD,RT,JSon,DG 1.50
478 SD,RT,JSon,DG 1.50
479 CI,DG,JSon,Dial H For Hero,
E:Starman and Aquaman 1.50
480 CI,DJ,B:Dial H for Hero 1.50
481 CI,DJ 1.50
482 CI,DJ,DH 1.50
483 CI,DJ,DH 1.50
484 GP(c),CI,DJ,DH 1.50
485 GP(c),CI,DJ 1.50
486 GP(c),DH,RT,TVE 1.50
487 CI,DJ,DH 1.50
488 CI,DJ,TVE 1.50
489 CI,FMc,TVE 1.50
490 GP(c),CI,E:Dial H for Hero . . 1.50
491 KG(c),DigestSize,DN,
Shazam,rep.other material . . . 1.50
492 KG(c),DN,E:Shazam 1.50
493 KG(c),GT,B:Challengers of
the Unknown,reprints 1.50
494 KG(c),GT,Challengers,
reprints 1.50
495 ATh,reprints,Challengers . . . 1.75
496 GK(c),ATh,reprints,
Challengers 1.75
497 ATh,DA,reps.,E:Challengers . 1.75
498 GK(c),reprints,Rep.Legion . . 1.50
499 GK(c),reprints,Rep 1.50
500 KG(c),Legion reprints,Rep . . 2.00
501 reprints,Rep 1.50
502 reprints,Rep 1.50
503 reprints,final issue 1.50

ADVENTURES IN
THE DC UNIVERSE
March 1997

1 F:New JLA 1.75
2 F:The Flash,Catwoman 1.75
3 Wonder Woman vs. Cheetah;
Poison Ivy vs. Batman 1.75
4 F:Green Lantern vs. Glorious
Godfrey; Mister Miracle 1.75
5 F:Martian Manhunter, all alien
issue 1.75
6 F:Ocean Master, Power Girl . . 1.75

ADVENTURES OF
ALAN LADD
1949–51

1 Ph(c) 700.00
2 Ph(c) 400.00

Adventures of Alan Ladd #5
© DC Comics, Inc.

3 Ph(c) 300.00
4 Ph(c) 300.00
5 Ph(c),inc.Destination Danger . 225.00
6 Ph(c) 225.00
7 . . . . 225.00
8 Grand Duchess takes over . 225.00
9 Deadlien in Rapula 225.00

ADVENTURES OF
BOB HOPE
1951–68

1 Ph(c) 1,200.00
2 Ph(c) 600.00
3 Ph(c) 325.00
4 Ph(c) 300.00
5 thru 10 . . . . @275.00
11 thru 20 . . . . @150.00
21 thru 40 . . . . @100.00
41 thru 90 . . . . @75.00
91 thru 93 . . . . @25.00
94 C:Aquaman 30.00
95 thru 105 . . . . @22.00
106 NA 40.00
107 NA 40.00
108 NA 40.00
109 NA 40.00

ADVENTURES OF
DEAN MARTIN AND
JERRY LEWIS
1952–57

1 . . . . 600.00
2 . . . . 300.00
3 thru 10 . . . . @150.00
11 thru 20 . . . . @100.00
21 thru 40 . . . . @75.00
Becomes:
ADVENTURES OF
JERRY LEWIS
1957–71

41 thru 55 . . . . @50.00
56 thru 69 . . . . @35.00
70 thru 87 . . . . @25.00
88 A:Bob Hope 30.00
89 thru 91 . . . . @20.00
92 C:Superman 30.00

DC COMICS

93 thru 96	@20.00
97 A:Batman & Joker	35.00
98 thru 100	@20.00
101 thru 104 NA	@35.00
105 A:Superman	25.00
106 thru 111	@10.00
112 A:Flash	20.00
113 thru 116	@10.00
117 A:Wonder Woman	15.00
118 thru 124	@8.00

ADVENTURES OF FORD FAIRLANE
1990

1 DH,DG	1.50
2 DH	1.50
3 DH	1.50
4 DH	1.50

ADVENTURES OF THE OUTSIDERS
(see BATMAN & THE OUTSIDERS)

ADVENTURES OF OZZIE AND HARRIET
1949–50

1 Ph(c)	650.00
2	350.00
3	300.00
4	300.00
5	300.00

ADVENTURES OF REX, THE WONDERDOG
1952–59

1 ATh	800.00
2 ATh	400.00
3 ATh	300.00
4	250.00
5	250.00
6 thru 11	@150.00
12 thru 20	@100.00
21 thru 46	@75.00

ADVENTURES OF SUPERBOY
(See: SUPERBOY)

ADVENTURES OF SUPERMAN
(See: SUPERMAN)

AGENT LIBERTY SPECIAL
1992

1 DAb,O:Agent Liberty	2.00

ALIEN NATION
1988

1 JBi,movie adaption	2.50

ALL-AMERICAN COMICS
1939–48

1 B:Hop Harrigan,Scribbly,Mutt&Jeff, Red,White&Blue,Bobby Thatcher, Skippy,Daiseybelle,Mystery Men of Mars,Toonerville	5,500.00
2 B:Ripley's Believe It or Not	1,500.00
3 Hop Harrigan (c)	1,000.00
4 Flag(c)	1,000.00

5 B:The American Way	1,000.00
6 ShM(c),Fredric Marchin in 'The American Way'	850.00
7 E:Bobby Thatcher,C.H. Claudy's 'A Thousand Years in a Minute'	850.00
8 B:Ultra Man	1,300.00
9	800.00
10 ShM(c),E:The American Way, Santa-X-Mas(c)	750.00
11 Ultra Man(c)	750.00
12 E:Toonerville Folks	750.00
13 'The Infra Red Des'Royers'	750.00
14	750.00
15 E:Tippie and Reg'lar Fellars	750.00
16 O&1st App:Green Lantern, B:Lantern(c)	62,000.00
17 SMo(c)	12,500.00
18 SMo(c)	8,500.00
19 SMo(c),O&I: Atom, E:Ultra Man	12,000.00
20 I:Atom's costume,Hunkle becomes Red Tornado	3,500.00

All-American Comics #53
© DC Comics, Inc.

21 E:Wiley of West Point & Skippy	2,000.00
22	1,500.00
23 E:Daieybelle	1,800.00
24 E:Ripley's Believe It or Not	2,200.00
25 O&I:Dr. Mid-Nite	8,200.00
26 O&I:Sargon the Sorcerer	3,000.00
27 I:Doiby Dickles	3,200.00
28	1,200.00
29 ShM(c)	1,200.00
30 ShM(c)	1,200.00
31 Adventures of the underfed orphans	1,200.00
32	900.00
33	900.00
34	900.00
35 Doiby discovers Lantern's ID	900.00
36	900.00
37	900.00
38	900.00
39	900.00
40	900.00
41	750.00
42	750.00
43	750.00
44 'I Accuse the Green Lantern!	750.00

45	750.00
46	750.00
47 Hop Harrigan meets the Enemy,(c)	750.00
48	750.00
49	750.00
50 E:Sargon	750.00
51 'Murder Under the Stars'	650.00
52	650.00
53 Green Lantern delivers the Mail	650.00
54	650.00
55 'The Riddle of the Runaway Trolley'	650.00
56 V:Elegant Esmond	650.00
57 V:The Melancholy Men	650.00
58	650.00
59 'The Story of the Man Who Couldn't Tell The Truth'	650.00
60	650.00
61 O:Soloman Grundy,'Fighters Never Quit'	3,500.00
62 'Da Distrik Attorney'	600.00
63	600.00
64 'A Bag of Assorted Nuts!'	600.00
65 'The Man Who Lost Wednesday'	600.00
66 'The Soles of Manhattan!'	600.00
67 V:King Shark	600.00
68 Meets Napoleon&Joe Safeen	600.00
69 'Backwards Man!'	600.00
70 JKu,I:Maximillian O'Leary, V:Colley, the Leprechaun	600.00
71 E:Red,White&Blue,'The Human Bomb'	550.00
72 B:Black Pirate	550.00
73 B:Winkey,Blinky&Noddy, 'Mountain Music Mayhem'	550.00
74	550.00
75	550.00
76 'Spring Time for Doiby'	550.00
77 Hop Harrigan(c)	550.00
78	550.00
79 Mutt & Jeff	550.00
80	550.00
81	550.00
82	550.00
83 Mutt & Jeff	550.00
84 'The Adventure of the Man with Two Faces'	550.00
85	500.00
86 V:Crime of the Month Club	500.00
87 'The Strange Case of Professor Nobody'	500.00
88 'Canvas of Crime'	500.00
89 O:Harlequin	500.00
90 O:Icicle	500.00
91 'Wedding of the Harlequin'	550.00
92 'The Icicle goes South'	550.00
93 'The Double Crossing Decoy'	550.00
94 A:Harlequin	550.00
95 'The Unmasking of the Harlequin'	550.00
96 ATh(c),'Solve the Mystery of the Emerald Necklaces!'	550.00
97 ATh(c),'The Country Fair Crimes'	550.00
98 ATh,ATh(c),'End of Sports!'	550.00
99 ATh,ATh(c),E:Hop Harrigan	550.00
100 ATh,I:Johnny Thunder	1,200.00
101 ATh,ATh(c),E:Mutt and Jeff	900.00
102 ATh,ATh(c),E:GrnLantern	1,500.00

Becomes:

ALL-AMERICAN WESTERN
1948–52

103 A:Johnny Thunder,'The City Without Guns,'All Johnny Thunder stories	350.00
104 ATh(c),'Unseen Allies'	350.00
105 ATh(c),'Hidden Guns'	200.00
106 ATh(c),'Snow Mountain Ambush'	150.00
107 ATh(c),'Cheyenne Justice'	200.00
108 ATh(c),'Vengeance of the Silver Bullet'	150.00
109 ATh(c),'Secret of Crazy River'	150.00
110 ATh(c),'Ambush at Scarecrow Hills'	150.00
111 ATh(c),'Gun-Shy Sheriff'	150.00
112 ATh(c),'Double Danger'	150.00
113 ATh(c),'Johnny Thunder Indian Chief'	175.00
114 ATh(c),'The End of Johnny Thunder'	150.00
115 ATh(c),'Cheyenne Mystery'	150.00
116 ATh(c),'Buffalo Raiders of the Mesa'	150.00
117 ATh(c),V:Black Lightnin	125.00
118 ATh(c),'Challenge of the Aztecs'	125.00
119 GK(c),'The Vanishing Gold Mine'	125.00
120 GK(c),'Ambush at Painted Mountain'	125.00
121 ATh(c),'The Unmasking of Johnny Thunder'	125.00
122 ATh(c),'The Real Johnny Thunder'	125.00
123 GK(c),'Johnny Thunder's Strange Rival'	125.00
124 ATh(c),'The Iron Horse's Last Run'	125.00
125 ATh(c),'Johnny Thunder's Last Roundup'	125.00
126 ATh(c),'Phantoms of the Desert'	125.00

Becomes:

ALL-AMERICAN MEN OF WAR
1952–66

127 (0)	700.00
128 (1)	500.00
2 JGr(c),Killer Bait	400.00
3 Pied Piper of Pyong-Yang	400.00
4 JGr(c),The Hills of Hate	400.00
5 One Second to Zero	300.00
6 IN(c),Jungle Killers	300.00
7 IN(c),Beach to Hold	300.00
8 IN(c),Sgt. Storm Cloud	300.00
9	300.00
10	300.00
11 JGr(c),Dragon's Teeth	300.00
12	250.00
13 JGr(c),Lost Patrol	250.00
14 IN(c),Pigeon Boss	250.00
15 JGr(c),Flying Roadblock	250.00
16 JGr(c),The Flying Jeep	250.00
17 JGr(c),Booby Trap Ridge	250.00
18 JKu(c),The Ballad of Battling Bells	250.00
19 JGr(c),IN,Torpedo Track	175.00
20 JGr(c),JKu,Lifenet to Beach Road	175.00
21 JGr(c),IN,RH,The Coldest War	175.00
22 JGr(c),IN,JKu,Snipers Nest	175.00
23 JGr(c),The Silent War	175.00
24 JGr(c),The Thin Line	175.00
25 JGr(c),IN,For Rent-One Foxhole	175.00
26	175.00
27 JGr(c),RH,Fighting Pigeon	175.00
28 JGr(c),RA,JKu,Medal for A Dog	175.00
29 IN(c),JKu,Battle Bridges	200.00
30 JGr(c),RH,Frogman Hunt	175.00
31 JGr(c),Battle Seat	200.00
32 JGr(c),RH,Battle Station	200.00
33 JGr(c),IN,Sky Ambush	175.00
34 JGr(c),JKu,No Man's Alley	175.00
35 JGr(c),IN, Battle Call	150.00
36 JGr(c),JKu,Battle Window	150.00
37 JGr(c),JKu,The Big Stretch	150.00
38 JGr(c),RH,JKu,The Floating Sentinel	150.00
39 JGr(c),JKu,The Four Faces of Sgt. Fay	150.00

All-American Western #116
© DC Comics, Inc.

40 JGr(c),IN,Walking Helmet	150.00
41 JKu(c),RH,JKu,The 50-50 War	100.00
42 JGr(c),JKu,Battle Arm	100.00
43 JGr(c),JKu,Command Post	100.00
44 JKu(c),The Flying Frogman	100.00
45 JGr(c),RH,Combat Waterboy	100.00
46 JGr(c),IN,RH,Tank Busters	100.00
47 JGr(c),JKu,MD,Battle Freight	100.00
48 JGr(c),JKu,MD,Roadblock	100.00
49 JGr(c),Walking Target	100.00
50 IN,RH,Bodyguard For A Sub	100.00
51 JGr(c),RH,Bomber's Moon	75.00
52 JKu(c),RH,MD,Back Seat Driver	75.00
53 JKu(c),JKu,Night Attack	75.00
54 JKu(c),IN,Diary of a Fighter Pilot	75.00
55 JKu(c),RH,Split-Second Target	75.00
56 JKu,IN,RH,Frogman Jinx	75.00
57 Pick-Up for Easy Co.	75.00
58 JKu(c),RH,MD,A Piece of Sky	75.00
59 JGr(c),JKu,The Hand of War	75.00
60 JGr(c),The Time Table	75.00
61 JGr(c),IN,MD,Blind Target	75.00
62 JGr(c),RH,RA,No(c)	75.00

63 JGr(c),JKu,Frogman Carrier	75.00
64 JKu(c),JKu,RH,The Other Man's War	75.00
65 JGr(c),JKu,MD,Same Old Sarge	75.00
66 JGr(c),The Walking Fort	75.00
67 JGr(c),RH,A:Gunner&Sarge, The Cover Man	250.00
68 JKu(c),Gunner&Sarge, The Man & The Gun	75.00
69 JGr(c),A:Tank Killer, Bazooka Hill	75.00
70 JKu(c),IN,Pigeon Without Wings	75.00
71 JGr(c),A:Tank Killer,Target For An Ammo Boy	75.00
72 JGr(c),A:Tank Killer,T.N.T. Broom	75.00
73 JGr(c),JKu,No Detour	75.00
74 The Minute Commandos	75.00
75 JKu(c),Sink That Flattop	75.00
76 JKu(c),A:Tank Killer, Just One More Tank	75.00
77 JKu(c),IN,MD,Big Fish-little Fish	75.00
78 JGr(c),Tin Hat for an Iron Man	75.00
79 JKu(c),RA,Showdown Soldier	75.00
80 JGr(c),RA,The Medal Men	75.00
81 JGr(c),IN,Ghost Ship of Two Wars	60.00
82 IN(c),B:Johnny Cloud, The Flying Chief	60.00
83 IN(c),Fighting Blind	60.00
84 IN(c),Death Dive	60.00
85 RH(c),Battle Eagle	60.00
86 JGr(c),Top-Gun Ace	60.00
87 JGr(c),Broken Ace	60.00
88 JGr(c),The Ace of Vengeance	60.00
89 JGr(c),The Star Jockey	60.00
90 JGr(c),Wingmate of Doom	60.00
91 RH(c),Two Missions To Doom	60.00
92 JGr(c),The Battle Hawk	60.00
93 RH(c),The Silent Rider	60.00
94 RH(c),Be Brave-Be Silent	60.00
95 RH(c),Second Sight For a Pilot	60.00
96 RH(c),The Last Flight	

All-American Men of War #13
© DC Comics, Inc.

DC COMICS

DC COMICS

of Lt. Moon 60.00
97 IN(c),A 'Target' Called
Johnny 60.00
98 The Time-Bomb Ace 60.00
99 IN(c),The Empty Cockpit 60.00
100 RH(c),Battle o/t Sky Chiefs . 60.00
101 RH(c),Death Ship of
Three Wars 25.00
102 JKu(c),Blind Eagle-Hungry
Hawk 25.00
103 IN(c),Battle Ship-
Battle Heart 25.00
104 JKu(c),The Last Target 25.00
105 IN(c),Killer Horse-Ship 25.00
106 IN(c),Death Song For
A Battle Hawk 25.00
107 IN(c),Flame in the Sky 25.00
108 IN(c),Death-Dive of the Aces 25.00
109 IN(c),The Killer Slot 25.00
110 RH(c),The Co-Pilot was
Death 25.00
111 RH(c),E:Johnny Cloud, Tag–
You're Dead 25.00
112 RH(c),B:Balloon Buster,Lt.
Steve Savage-Balloon Buster 25.00
113 JKu(c),The Ace of
Sudden Death 25.00
114 JKu(c),The Ace Who
Died Twice 25.00
115 IN(c),A:Johnny Cloud,
Deliver One Enemy Ace-
Handle With Care 25.00
116 JKu(c),A:Baloon Buster,
Circle of Death 25.00
117 Sept.–Oct., 1966 . . . . 25.00

All-Flash #13 © DC Comics, Inc.

ALL-FLASH
1941–47
1 EHi,O:Flash,I:The Monocle 12,000.00
2 EHi,The Adventure of Roy
Revenge 2,300.00
3 EHi,The Adventure of
Misplaced Faces 1,200.00
4 EHi,Tale o/t Time Capsule . 1,100.00
5 EHi,The Case of the Patsy
Colt! Last Quarterly 900.00
6 EHi,The Ray that Changed
Men's Souls 750.00
7 EHi,Adventures of a Writers

Fantasy, House of Horrors . 750.00
8 EHi,Formula to Fairyland! . . 750.00
9 EHi,Adventure of the Stolen
Telescope 750.00
10 EHi,Case of the Curious Cat 750.00
11 EHi,Troubles come
in Doubles 650.00
12 EHi,Tumble INN to Trouble,
Becomes Quarterly on orders
from War Production Board
O:The Thinker 650.00
13 EHi,I:The King 650.00
14 EHi,I:Winky,Blinky & Noddy
Green Lantern (c) 750.00
15 EHi,Secrets of a Stranger . . 550.00
16 EHi,A:The Sinister 550.00
17 Tales of the Three Wishes . 500.00
18 A:Winky,Blinky&Noddy
B:Mutt & Jeff reprints 500.00
19 No Rest at the Rest Home . 500.00
20 A:Winky, Blinky & Noddy . . 500.00
21 I:Turtle 450.00
22 The Money Doubler,E:Mutt
& Jeff reprints 450.00
23 The Bad Men of Bar Nothing 450.00
24 I:Worry Wart,3 Court
Clowns Get Caught 450.00
25 I:Slapsy Simmons,
Flash Jitterbugs 450.00
26 I:The Chef,The Boss,Shrimp
Coogan,A:Winky, Blinky &
Noddy 500.00
27 A:The Thinker,Gangplank
Gus story 450.00
28 A:Shrimp Coogan,Winky,
Blinky & Noddy 450.00
29 The Thousand-Year Old Terror,
A:Winky,Blinky & Noddy . . 450.00
30 The Vanishing Snowman . . 450.00
31 A:Black Hat,The Planet
of Sport 450.00
32 I:Fiddler,A:Thinker 650.00

ALL FUNNY COMICS
1943–48
1 Genius Jones 375.00
2 same 150.00
3 same 100.00
4 same 100.00
5 thru 10 . . . . @100.00
11 Genius Jones 75.00
12 same 50.00
13 same 75.00
14 . . . . 60.00
15 . . . . 75.00
16 A:DC Superheroes 200.00
17 . . . . 75.00
18 . . . . 75.00
19 . . . . 75.00
20 . . . . 75.00
21 . . . . 75.00
22 . . . . 75.00
23 . . . . 75.00

ALL-STAR COMICS
Summer, 1940–51
1 B:Flash,Hawkman,Hourman,Sandman,
Spectre,Red White & Blue 12,000.00
2 B:Green Lantern and Johnny
Thunder 5,000.00
3 First meeting of Justice Society
with Flash as Chairman . 35,000.00
4 First mission of JSA 4,200.00
5 V:Mr. X,I:Hawkgirl 4,000.00
6 Flash leaves 2,900.00

All-Star Comics #5 © DC Comics, Inc.

7 Green Lantern becomes Chairman,
L:Hourman, C:Superman,
Batman & Flash 3,000.00
8 I:Wonder Women;Starman and
Dr. Mid-Nite join,Hawkman
becomes chairman 25,000.00
9 JSA in Latin America 2,400.00
10 C:Flash & Green Lantern,
JSA Time Travel story . . . 2,200.00
11 Wonder Women joins;
I:Justice Battalion 2,100.00
12 V:Black Dragon society . . . 2,100.00
13 V:Hitler 2,000.00
14 JSA in occupied Europe . . 2,000.00
15 I:Brain Wave,A:JSA's
Girl Friends 2,000.00
16 Propaganda/relevance issue 1,600.00
17 V:Brain Wave 1,600.00
18 I:King Bee 1,700.00
19 Hunt for Hawkman 1,600.00
20 I:Monster 1,600.00
21 Time travel story 1,500.00
22 Sandman and Dr. Fate leave,
I:Conscience, Good Fairy . 1,500.00
23 I:Psycho-Pirate 1,500.00
24 Propaganda/relevance issue,
A:Conscience&Wildcat,Mr.Terrific;
L:Starman & Spectre; Flash
& Green Lantern return . . 1,500.00
25 JSA whodunit issue 1,300.00
26 V:Metal Men from Jupiter . 1,300.00
27 Handicap issue,A:Wildcat . 1,300.00
28 Ancient curse comes to life 1,100.00
29 I:Landor from 25th century 1,100.00
30 V:Brain Wave 1,100.00
31 V:Zor 1,100.00
32 V:Psycho-Pirate 1,100.00
33 V:Soloman Grundy,A:Doiby
Dickles, Last appearance
Thunderbolt 2,300.00
34 I:Wizard 1,000.00
35 I:Per Degaton 1,000.00
36 A:Superman and Batman . 2,300.00
37 I:Injustice Society of
the World 1,300.00
38 V:Villians of History,
A:Black Canary 1,500.00
39 JSA in magic world,
Johnny Thunder leaves . . . 1,000.00

All-Star Comics #28 © DC Comics, Inc.

40 A:Black Canary,Junior Justice
  Society of America 1,000.00
41 Black Canary joins,A:Harlequin,
  V:Injustice Society
  of the World 1,000.00
42 I:Alchemist 900.00
43 V:Interdimensional gold men 900.00
44 I:Evil Star 900.00
45 Crooks develop stellar
  JSA powers 850.00
46 Comedy issue 850.00
47 V:Billy the Kid 850.00
48 Time Travel story 850.00
49 V:Comet-being invaders . . . 850.00
50 V:College classmate of Flash 900.00
51 V:Diamond men from center
  of the Earth 850.00
52 JSA disappears from
  Earth for years 850.00
53 Time Travel issue 850.00
54 Circus issue 850.00
55 JSA fly to Jupiter 850.00
56 V:Chameleons from
  31st Century 850.00
57 I:Key 1,100.00
Becomes:

ALL STAR WESTERN
April-May 1951
58 Trigger Twins 300.00
59 . . . . 150.00
60 . . . . 150.00
61 thru 64 ATh 125.00
65 . . . . 125.00
66 . . . . 125.00
67 GK,B:Johnny Thunder 150.00
68 thru 81 . . . . @75.00
82 thru 98 . . . . @60.00
99 FF 75.00
100 . . . . 60.00
101 thru 104 . . . . @45.00
105 O:JSA, March, 1987 . . . . . 45.00
106 and 107 . . . . @45.00
108 O:Johnny Thunder 125.00
109 thru 116 . . . . @45.00
117 CI,O:Super-Chief 60.00
118 . . . . 45.00
119 . . . . 40.00

ALL-STAR COMICS
1976–78
58 RE,WW,R:JSA,I:Power Girl . . . 2.50
59 RE,WW,Brain Wave 2.25
60 KG,WW,I:Vulcan 2.25
61 KG,WW,V:Vulcan 2.25
62 KG,WW,A:E-2 Superman . . . 2.25
63 KG,WW,A:E-2 Superman,
  Solomon Grundy 2.25
64 WW,Shining Knight 2.25
65 KG,WW,E-2 Superman,
  Vandal Savage 2.25
66 JSon,BL,Injustice Society . . . 2.25
67 JSon,BL 2.25
68 JSon,BL 2.25
69 JSon,BL,A:E-2 Superman,
  Starman,Dr.Mid-Nite 2.25
70 JSon,BL,Huntress 2.25
71 JSon,BL 2.00
72 JSon,A:Golden.Age Huntress . 2.00
73 JSon 2.00
74 JSon 2.00

ALL STAR SQUADRON
1981–87
1 RB,JOy,JSa,I:Degaton 1.75
2 RB,JOy,Robotman 1.50
3 RB,JOy,Robotman 1.50
4 RB,JOy,Robotman 1.50
5 RB/JOy,I:Firebrand(Dannette) . 1.50
6 JOy,Hawkgirl 1.50
7 JOy,Hawkgirl 1.50
8 DH/JOy,A:Steel 1.50
9 DH/JOy,A:Steel 1.50
10 JOy,V:Binary Brotherhood . . . 1.50
11 JOy,V:Binary Brotherhood . . . 1.50
12 JOy,R:Dr.Hastor O:Hawkman . 1.50
13 JOy,photo(c) 1.50
14 JOy,JLA crossover 1.50
15 JOy,JLA crossover 1.50
16 I&D:Nuclear 1.50
17 Trial of Robotman 1.50
18 V:Thor 1.50
19 V:Brainwave 1.50
20 JOy,V:Brainwave 1.50
21 JOy,I:Cyclotron (1st JOy
  Superman) 1.75
22 JOy,V:Deathbolt,Cyclotron . . . 1.50
23 JOy,I:Amazing-Man 1.50
24 JOy,I:Brainwave,Jr. 3.50
25 JOy,I:Infinity Inc. 3.00
26 JOy,Infinity Inc. 2.50
27 Spectre 1.50
28 JOy,Spectre 1.50
29 JOy,retold story 1.50
30 V:Black Dragons 1.50
31 All-Star gathering 1.50
32 O:Freedom Fighters 1.50
33 Freedom Fighters,I:Tsunami . . 1.50
34 Freedom Fighters 1.50
35 RB,Shazam family 1.50
36 Shazam family 1.50
37 A:Shazam Family 1.50
38 V:The Real American 1.50
39 V:The Real American 1.50
40 D:The Real American 1.50
41 O:Starman 1.50
42 V:Tsunami,Kung 1.50
43 V:Tsunami,Kung 1.50
44 I:Night & Fog 1.50
45 I:Zyklon 1.50
46 V:Baron Blitzkrieg 1.50
47 TM,O:Dr.Fate 3.50
48 A:Blackhawk 1.50
49 A:Dr.Occult 1.50

All-Star Squadron #65
© DC Comics, Inc.

50 Crisis 2.00
51 AA,Crisis 1.50
52 Crisis 1.50
53 Crisis,A:The Dummy 1.50
54 Crisis,V:The Dummy 1.50
55 Crisis,V:Anti-Monitor 1.50
56 Crisis 1.50
57 A:Dr.Occult 1.50
58 I:Mekanique 1.50
59 A:Mekanique,Spectre 1.50
60 Crisis 1942, conclusion 1.50
61 O:Liberty Belle 1.50
62 O:The Shining Knight 1.50
63 O:Robotman 1.50
64 WB/TD,V:Funny Face 1.50
65 DH/TD,O:Johnny Quick 1.50
66 TD,O:Tarantula 1.50
67 TD,Last Issue,O:JSA 1.50
Ann.#1 JOy,O:G.A.,Atom 1.50
Ann.#2 JOy,Infinity Inc. 1.50
Ann.#3 WB,JOy,KG,GP,DN 1.50

ALL STAR WESTERN
(see WEIRD WESTERN TALES)

ALPHA CENTURION
1996
Spec.#1 . . . . 3.00

AMBER:
THE GUNS OF AVALON
Aug. 1996
1 (of 3) adapt. of Roger Zelazny
  classic 6.95
2 and 3 conclusion . . . . @6.95

AMBUSH BUG
1985
1 KG,I:Cheeks 1.25
2 KG thru 4 . . . . @1.00
AMBUSH BUG: STOCKING STUFFER 1986
1 KG,R:Cheeks 1.25
AMBUSH BUG: NOTHING SPECIAL 1992
1 KG,A:Sandman,Death 2.50

All comics prices listed are for *Near Mint* condition.

DC COMICS

DC COMICS

AMERICA vs. JUSTICE SOCIETY
Jan.–April, 1985
1 AA,R,Thomas Script		1.50
2 AA		1.25
3 AA		1.25
4 AA,		1.25

AMERICAN FREAK: A TALE OF THE UN-MEN
Vertigo 1994
1 B:DLp,(s),VcL,R:Un-Men		2.25
2 VcL,A:Crassus		2.25
3 VcL,A:Scylla		2.25
4 VcL,A:Scylla		2.25
5 VcL,Final Issue		2.25

AMETHYST
[Limited Series] 1983–84
[PRINCESS OF GEMWORLD]
1 Origin		1.25
2 thru 7 EC		@1.00
8 EC,O:Gemworld		1.00
9 EC		1.00
10 EC		1.00
11 EC		1.00
12 EC		1.00
Spec.#1 KG		1.25
[Regular Series]
1985–86
1 thru 12 EC		@1.00
13 EC,Crisis,A:Dr.Fate		1.00
14 EC		1.00
15 EC,Castle Amethyst Destroyed		1.00
16 EC		1.00
Spec.#1 EM		1.25
[Mini-Series]
1987–88
1 EM		1.25
2 EM		1.25
3 EM		1.25
4 EM,O:Mordru		1.25

ANARKY
March 1997
1 AlG(s),NBy,JRu,Anarky vs. Etrigan		2.50
2 AlG(s),NBy,JRu,V:Darkseid		2.50
3 AlG(s),NBy,JRu,A:Batman		2.50
4 AlG(s),NBy,JRu,A:Batman,concl.		2.50

ANGEL & THE APE
1991
1 Apes of Wrath,pt.1		1.00
2 Apes of Wrath,pt.2, A:G.Gardner		1.00
3 Apes of Wrath,pt.3, A: Inferior Five		1.00
4 Apes of Wrath,pt.4, A: Inferior Five, final issue		1.00

ANIMA
Vertigo 1994–95
1 R:Anima		2.00
2 V:Scarecrow		2.00
3 V:Scarecrow		2.00
4 A:Nameless one		2.00
5 CI,V:Arkana		2.00
6 CI,V:Arkana		2.00
7 Zero Hour		2.00
8 Nameless One		2.00
9 Superboy & Nameless One		2.00

10 A:Superboy		2.00
11 V:Nameless One		2.00
12 A:Hawkman,V:Shrike		1.95
13 A:Hawkman,Shrike		1.95
14 Return to Gotham City		1.95
15 V:Psychic Vampire, final issue		2.25

ANIMAL ANTICS
1946–49
1		275.00
2		150.00
3 thru 10		@90.00
11 thru 23		@65.00

Animal Man #60 © DC Comics, Inc.

ANIMAL-MAN
1988–95
1 BB(c),B:GMo(s),ChT,DHz, B:Animal Rights,I:Dr.Myers		8.00
2 BB(c),ChT,DHz,A:Superman		6.00
3 BB(c),ChT,DHz,A:B'wana Beast		3.00
4 BB(c),ChT,DHz,V:B'wana Beast, E:Animal Rights		3.00
5 BB(c),ChT,DHz, I&D:Crafty Coyote		3.50
6 BB(c),ChT,DHz,A:Hawkman		3.00
7 BB(c),ChT,DHz,D:Red Mask		3.00
8 BB(c),ChT,DHz,V:Mirror Master		3.00
9 BB(c),DHz,TG,A:Martian Manhunter		3.00
10 BB(c),ChT,DHz,A:Vixen, B:O:Animal Man		3.00
11 BB(c),ChT,DHz,I:Hamed Ali, Tabu,A:Vixen		3.00
12 BB(c),D:Hamed Ali,A:Vixen, B'wanaBeast		3.00
13 BB(c),I:Dominic Mndawe,R:B'wana Beast,Apartheid		3.00
14 BB(c),TG,SeM,A:Future Animal Man,I:Lennox		3.00
15 BB(c),ChT,DHz,A:Dolphin		3.00
16 BB(c),ChT,DHz,A:JLA.		3.00
17 BB(c),ChT,DHz,A:Mirr.Master		3.00
18 BB(c),ChT,DHz,A:Lennox		3.00
19 BB(c),ChT,DHz,D:Ellen, Cliff,Maxine		3.00
20 BB(c),ChT,DHz,I:Bug-Man		3.00
21 BB(c),ChT,DHz,N&V:Bug-Man		3.00

22 BB(c),PCu,SeM,A:Rip Hunter		3.00
23 BB(c),A:Phantom Stranger		2.50
24 BB(c),V:Psycho Pirate		2.50
25 BB(c),ChT,MFm,I:Comic Book Limbo		2.50
26 BB(c),E:GMo(s),ChT,MFm, A:Grant Morrison		2.50
27 BB(c),B:PMi(s),ChT,MFm		2.50
28 BB(c),ChT,MFm,I:Nowhere Man, I&D:Front Page		2.50
29 ChT,SDi,V:National Man		2.50
30 BB(c),ChT,MFm,V:Angel Mob		2.50
31 BB(c),ChT,MFm		2.50
32 BB(c),E:PMi(s),ChT,MFm		2.50
33 BB(c),B:TV(s),SDi,A:Travis Cody		2.50
34 BB(c),SDi,Requiem		2.50
35 BB(c),SDi,V:Radioactive Dogs		2.50
36 BB(c),SDi,A:Mr.Rainbow		2.50
37 BB(c),SDi,Animal/Lizard Man		2.50
38 BB(c),SDi,A:Mr.Rainbow		2.50
39 BB(c),TMd,SDi,Wolfpack in San Diego		2.00
40 BB(c),SDi,War of the Gods x-over		2.00
41 BB(c),SDi,V:Star Labs Renegades,I:Winky		2.00
42 BB(c),SDi,V:Star Labs Renegades		2.00
43 BB(c),SDi,I:Tristess,A:Vixen		2.00
44 BB(c),SDi,A:Vixen		2.00
45 BB(c),StP,SDi,I:L.Decker		2.00
46 BB(c),SDi,I:Frank Baker		2.00
47 BB(c),SDi,I:Shining Man, (B'wana Beast)		2.00
48 BB(c),SDi,V:Antagon		2.00
49 BB(c),SDi,V:Antagon		2.00
50 BB(c),E:TV(s),SDi,I:Metaman		3.50
51 BB(c),B:JaD(s),StP,B:Flesh and Blood		2.50
52 BB(c),StP,Homecoming		2.50
53 BB(c),StP,Flesh and Blood		2.50
54 BB(c),StP,Flesh and Blood		2.50
55 BB(c),StP,Flesh and Blood		2.50
56 BB(c),StP,E:Flesh and Blood, Double-sized		3.00

Vertigo
57 BB(c),StP,B:Recreation, Ellen in NY		2.50
58 BB(c),StP,Wild Side		2.50
59 BB(c),RsB,GHi(i),Wild Town		2.50
60 RsB,GHi(i),Wild life		2.50
61 BB(c),StP,Tooth and Claw#1		2.50
62 BB(c),StP,Tooth and Claw#2		2.50
63 BB(c),V:Leviathan		2.50
64 DlB(c),WSm,DnS(i), Breath of God		2.50
65 RDB(c),WSm, Perfumed Garden		2.25
66 A:Kindred Spirit		2.25
67 StP,Mysterious Ways #1		2.25
68 StP,Mysterious Ways #2		2.25
69 Animal Man's Family		2.25
70 GgP(c),StP		2.25
71 GgP(c),StP,Maxine Alive?		2.25
72 StP		2.25
73 StP,Power Life Church		2.25
74 StP,Power Life Church		2.25
75 StP,Power Life Church		2.25
76 StP,Pilgrimage problems		2.00
77 Cliff shot		2.00
78 StP,Animal Man poisoned		2.00
79 New Direction		2.00
80 New Direction		2.00
81 Wild Type,pt.1		2.00

DC COMICS

82 Wild Type,pt.2 . . . . 2.00
83 Wild Type,pt.3 . . . . 2.00
84 F:Maxine,SupernaturalDreams 2.00
85 Animal Mundi,pt.1 . . . . 2.25
86 Animal Mundi,pt.2 . . . . 2.25
87 Animal Mundi,pt.3 . . . . 2.25
88 Morphogenetic Fields 2.25
89 final issue 2.25
Ann.#1 BB(c),JaD,TS(i),RIB(i),
    Children Crusade,F:Maxine . . . 4.25
TPB Rep.#1 thru #10 . . . . 19.95

Animaniacs #16 © DC Comics, Inc.

ANIMANIACS
Warner Bros./DC May 1995

1 F:Yakko,Wakko,Dot 1.50
2 Health Spa 1.50
3 Travel back in time 1.50
4 . . . . 1.50
5 . . . . 1.50
6 V:Cleopatra 1.50
7 Scratchinsniff Replaced 1.50
8 Disputin win Newton 1.50
9 thru 12 . . . . @1.50
13 thru 17 . . . . @1.75
18 visit to France 1.75
19 "The Y Files" 1.75
20 "Rebels Just Because" 1.75
21 x-mas issue,A:Santa 1.75
22 . . . . 1.75
23 F:Hellow Nurse 1.75
24 F:The Goodfeathers,A:Pinky and
    the Brain 1.75
25 F:Slappy Squirrel 1.75
26 "Haunted House of Pancakes" 1.75
27 "Plane for Keeps" 1.75
28 "Science Issue" 1.75
29 "The Return of Hello Nurse,
    Agent of H.U.B.B.A." 1.75
Christmas Spec. 1.50

ANTHRO
1968–69

1 HwP 26.00
2 HwP 18.00
3 thru 5 HwP . . . . @18.00
6 HwP,WW(c&a) 18.00

Aquaman #61 © DC Comics, Inc.

AQUAMAN
[1st Regular Series] 1962–78

1 NC,I:Quisp 575.00
2 NC,V:Captain Sykes 250.00
3 NC,Aquaman from Atlantis . 150.00
4 NC,A:Quisp 90.00
5 NC,The Haunted Sea 85.00
6 NC,A:Quisp 75.00
7 NC,Sea Beasts of Atlantis . . 75.00
8 NC,Plot to Steal the Seas . . . 75.00
9 NC,V:King Neptune 75.00
10 NC,A:Quisp 75.00
11 I: Mera 60.00
12 NC,The Cosmic Gladiators . . 55.00
13 NC,Invasion of the Giant
    Reptiles 55.00
14 NC,AquamanSecretPowers . . 55.00
15 NC,Menace of the Man-Fish . 55.00
16 NC,Duel of the Sea Queens . 50.00
17 NC,Man Who Vanquished
    Aquaman 50.00
18 W:Aquaman & Mera 52.00
19 NC,Atlanteans for Sale 45.00
20 NC,Sea King's DoubleDoom . 45.00
21 NC,I:Fisherman 35.00
22 NC,The Trap of the Sinister
    Sea Nymphs 35.00
23 NC,I:Aquababy 35.00
24 NC,O:Black Manta 28.00
25 NC,Revolt of Aquaboy 28.00
26 NC,I:O.G.R.E. 28.00
27 NC,Battle of the Rival
    Aquamen' 28.00
28 NC,Hail Aquababy,King of
    Atlantis 28.00
29 I:Ocean Master 29.00
30 NC,C:JLA 22.00
31 NC,V:O.G.R.E. 22.00
32 NC,V:Tryton 22.00
33 NC,I:Aquagirl 45.00
34 NC,I:Aquabeast 25.00
35 I:Black Manta 25.00
36 NC,What Seeks the
    Awesome Threesome? 25.00
37 I:Scavenger 25.00
38 NC,I:Liquidator 25.00
39 NC,How to Kill a Sea King . . 25.00

40 JAp,Sorcerers from the Sea . 22.00
41 JAp,Quest for Mera,pt.1 . . . . 14.00
42 JAp,Quest for Mera,pt.2 . . . . 14.00
43 JAp,Quest for Mera,pt.3 . . . . 14.00
44 JAp,Quest for Mera,pt.4 . . . . 14.00
45 JAp,Quest for Mera,pt.5 . . . . 14.00
46 JAp,Quest for Mera concl. . . . 14.00
47 JAp,Revolution in Atlantis #1
    rep.Adventure #268 . . . . 12.00
48 JAp,Revolution in Atlantis #2
    rep.Adventure #260 . . . . 17.00
49 JAp,As the Seas Die 12.00
50 JAp,NA,A:Deadman 25.00
51 JAp,NA,A:Deadman 25.00
52 JAp,NA,A:Deadman 25.00
53 JAp,Is California Sinking? 8.00
54 JAp,Crime Wave 8.00
55 JAp,Return of the Alien 8.00
56 JAp,I&O:Crusader (1970) 8.00
57 JAp,V:Black Manta (1977) 8.00
58 JAp,O:Aquaman rtd 9.00
59 JAp,V:Scavenger 8.00
60 DN,V:Scavenger 8.00
61 DN,BMc,A:Batman 8.00
62 DN,A:Ocean Master 7.00
63 DN,V:Ocean Master,
    final issue 7.00

*Aquaman (2nd Series) #5
© DC Comics, Inc.*

[2nd Regular Series] 1991–92
1 Poseidonis Under Attack,
    C:J'onn J'onzz,Blue Beetle . . . 2.25
2 V:Oumland 2.00
3 I:Iqula 2.00
4 V:Iqula,A:Queequeg 1.50
5 A:Aqualad,Titans,M.Manhunter,
    R:Manta 1.50
6 V: Manta 1.50
7 R:Mera 1.50
8 A:Batman,V:NKV Demon 1.50
9 Eco-Wars#1,A:Sea Devils 1.50
10 Eco-Wars#2,A:Sea Devils 1.50
11 V:Gigantic Dinosaur 1.50
12 A:Iaula 1.50
13 V:The Scavenger 1.50
14 V:The Scavenger 1.50

[3rd Regular Series] 1994–97
0 B:PDd(s),Paternal secret 2.00

DC COMICS

1 PDd(s),R:Aqualad,I:Charybdis . 2.50
2 V:Charybdis 4.00
3 B:PDd(s),Superboy 2.00
4 B:PDd(s),Lobo 2.00
5 New Costume 2.00
6 V:The Deep Six 2.00
7 Kako's Metamorphosis 2.00
8 V:Corona and Naiad 2.00
9 JSP(c&a),V:Deadline,A:Koryak . 1.75
10 A:Green Lantern,Koryak 1.75
11 R:Mera 1.75
12 F:Mera 1.75
13 V:Thanatos 1.75
14 PDd,V:Major Disaster,Underworld
   Unleashed tie-in 1.75
15 PDd,V:Tiamat 1.75
16 PDd,A:Justice League 1.75
17 PDd,V:underwater gargoyles . . 1.75
18 . . . . 1.75
19 PDd,V:Ocean Master 1.75
20 PDd,V:Ocean Master 1.75
21 PDd,JCf,A:Dolphin,
   V:ThiernaNaOge 1.75
22 PDd(s) 1.75
23 PDd(s),I:Deep Blue (Neptune
   Perkins) 1.75
24 PDd(s),A:Neptune Perkins . . . 1.75
25 PDd(s),MEg,HSm,Atlantis united,
   Aquaman routed? 1.75
26 PDd(s),MEg,HSm,Oceans
   threatened, Final Night tie-in . . 1.75
27 PDd(s),MEg,HSm,V:Demon
   Gate, dolphin killer 1.75
28 PDd(s),JCf,JP,A:J'Onn J'Onzz 1.75
29 PDd(s),MEg,HSm, ... 1.75
30 PDd(s),MEg,HSm,"The Pit" . . . 1.75
31 PDd(s),V:The Shark, mind-
   controlled aquatic army 1.75
32 PDd(s),A:Swamp Thing 1.75
33 PDd(s),Aquaman's dark powers
   affect him physically 1.75
34 PDd(s),V:Triton 1.75
35 PDd(s),JCf,I:Gamesman,
   A:Animal Man 1.75
35 PDd(s),JCf,R:Poseidonis,
   Tempest,Vulko 1.75
Ann.#1 Year One Annual, V:Triton,
   A:Superman,Mera 3.50
Ann.#2 Legends o/t Dead Earth . 2.95
Ann.#3 Pulp Heroes (Hard Boiled) 3.95

AQUAMAN
[1st Limited Series] 1986
1 V:Ocean Master 5.00
2 V:Ocean Master 3.00
3 V:Ocean Master 3.00
4 V:Ocean Master 3.00
[2nd Limited Series] 1989
1 CS,Atlantis Under Siege 3.00
2 CS,V:Invaders 1.75
3 CS,Mera turned Psychotic 1.50
4 CS,Poseidonis Under Siege . . 1.50
5 CS,Last Stand,final issue 1.50
Spec#1 MPa,Legend o/Aquaman . 2.00

AQUAMAN: TIME & TIDE
1993–94
1 PDd(s),O:Aquaman 2.50
2 and 3 PDd(s),O:Aquaman
   contd. . . . . @2.00
4 PDd(s),O:Aquaman,final issue. 1.75
TPB rep.#1–4 . . . . 9.95

ARAK
1981–85
1 EC,O:Ara 1.50
2 EC 1.00
3 EC,I:Valda 1.00
4 thru 10 EC . . . . @1.00
11 EC,AA 1.00
12 EC,AA,I:Satyricus 1.00
13 thru 19 AA . . . . @1.00
20 AA,O:Angelica 1.00
21 thru 23 AA 1.00
24 Double size 1.50
25 thru 30 . . . . @1.00
31 D Arak,becomes shaman . . . 1.00
32 thru 48 . . . . @1.00
49 Cl/TD 1.00
50 TD 1.25
Ann.#1 . . . . 1.00

ARCANA: THE BOOKS
OF MAGIC
Vertigo 1994
Ann.#1 JBo(c),JNR(s),PrG,Children's
   Crusade,R:Tim Hunter,
   A:Free Country 6.00

ARGUS
[Mini-Series] 1995
1 R:Argus,I:Raver 1.50
2 Blinded by metahuman hitmen . 1.75
3 Spy Satellite 1.75
4 The Watcher 1.75
5 Data Highways 1.75
6 Restored Sight 1.75

Arion, Lord of Atlantis #7
© DC Comics, Inc.

ARION,
LORD OF ATLANTIS
1982–85
1 JDu 1.50
2 JDu 1.00
3 JDu 1.00
4 JDu,O:Arion 1.00
5 JDu 1.00
6 JDu 1.00
7 thru 12 . . . . @1.00

13 JDu 1.00
14 JDu 1.00
15 JDu 1.00
16 thru 35 . . . . @1.00
Spec. 1.25

ARION THE IMMORTAL
1 RWi,R:Arion 1.75
2 RWi,V:Garffon 1.50
3 RWi,V:Garn Daanuth 1.50
4 RWi,V:Garn Daanuth 1.50
5 RWi,Darkworlet 1.50
6 RWi,MG,A:Power Girl 1.50

ARMAGEDDON 2001
May 1991
1 DJu,DG,I&O:Waverider 4.00
1a 2nd printing 2.00
1b 3rd printing (silver) 1.75
2 DJu,ATi,Monarch revealed as Hawk,
   D:Dove,L:Capt Atom(JLE) 2.00
Spec.#1 MR 1.75

ARMAGEDDON 2001
ARMAGEDDON:
THE ALIEN AGENDA
1991–92
1 DJu,JOy,A:Monarch,Capt.Atom 1.75
2 V:Ancient Romans 1.25
3 JRu(i),The Old West 1.25
4 DG,GP,V:Nazi's,last issue 1.25

ARMAGEDDON:
INFERNO
1992
1 TMd,LMc,A:Creeper,Batman,
   Firestorm 1.75
2 AAd,LMc,WS,I:Abraxis,A:Lobo . 1.50
3 AAd,WS,LMc,TMd,MN,R:Justice
   Society 1.50
4 AAd,WS,LMc,TMd,MN,DG,
   V:Abraxis,A:Justice Society . . . 1.50

ARTEMIS: REQUIEM
1996
1 BML(s) (of 6) 1.75
2 thru 6 BML(s),EBe, ... @1.75

ATARI FORCE
1984–85
1 JL,I:TempestDart 1.50
2 JL 1.00
3 JL 1.00
4 RA/JL/JO 1.00
5 RA/JL/JO 1.00
6 thru 12 JL . . . . @1.00
13 KG 1.00
14 thru 21 EB . . . . @1.00

ATLANTIS CHRONICLES
1990
1 EM,Atlantis 50,000 years ago . 3.50
2 EM,Atlantis Sunk 3.25
3 EM,Twin Cities of Poseidonis
   & Tritonis 3.25
4 EM,King Orin's Daughter
   Cora Assumes Throne 3.25
5 EM,Orin vs. Shalako 3.25
6 EM,Contact with Surface
   Dwellers 3.25
7 EM,Queen Atlanna gives Birth to
   son(Aquaman)48 pg.final issue 3.25

Atom #33 © DC Comics, Inc.

ATOM, THE
1962–68

1 MA,GK,I:Plant Master	750.00
2 MA,GK,V:Plant Master	325.00
3 MA,GK,I:Chronos	225.00
4 MA,GK,Snapper Carr	150.00
5 MA,GK	150.00
6 MA,GK	150.00
7 MA,GK,1st Atom & Hawkman team-up	250.00
8 MA,GK,A:JLA,V:Doctor Light	125.00
9 MA,GK	125.00
10 MA,GK	125.00
11 MA,GK	100.00
12 MA,GK	100.00
13 MA,GK	100.00
14 MA,GK	100.00
15 MA,GK	100.00
16 MA,GK	75.00
17 MA,GK	75.00
18 MA,GK	75.00
19 MA,GK,A:Zatanna	75.00
20 MA,GK	75.00
21 MA,GK	50.00
22 MA,GK	50.00
23 MA,GK	50.00
24 MA,GK,V:Jason Woodrue	50.00
25 MA,GK	50.00
26 GK	45.00
27 GK	45.00
28 GK	45.00
29 GK,A:E-2 Atom,Thinker.	150.00
30 GK	50.00
31 GK,A:Hawkman	45.00
32 GK	45.00
33 GK	45.00
34 GK,V:Big Head	45.00
35 GK	45.00
36 GK,A:Golden Age Atom	65.00
37 GK,I:Major Mynah	45.00
38 "Sinister stopover Earth"	45.00

Becomes:

ATOM & HAWKMAN
1968–69

39 MA, V:Tekla	50.00
40 DD,JKu,MA	40.00
41 DD,JKu,MA	40.00
42 MA,V:Brama	40.00
43 MA,I:Gentleman Ghost	40.00
44 DD	40.00
45 DD	40.00

ATOM SPECIAL
1 SDi,V:Chronos (1993)	3.00
2 Zero Hour Atom (1994)	3.00

AVATAR
1991
1 A:Midnight & Allies	8.00
2 Search for Tablets	6.00
3 V:Cyric, Myrkul, final issue	6.00

AZRAEL
1994
1 I:New Azreal,Brian Bryan	6.00
2 A:Batman,New Azreal	4.50
3 V:Order of St. Dumas	3.50
4 The System	3.00
5 BKi(c&a),R:Ra's al Ghul,Talia [new Miraweb format begins]	3.00
6 BKi(c&a),Ra's al Ghul,Talia	2.50
7 Sister Lily's Transformation	2.50
8 System Secret	2.25
9 Jean Paul Vanishes	2.25
10 DON,BKi,JmP,F:Neron, Underworld Unleashed tie-in	2.00
11 DON,BKi,JmP,A:Batman	2.00
12 DON,BKi,JmP,Azreal looks for Shondra	2.00
13 DON,BKi,Demon Time,pt.1	2.00
14 DON,BKi,Demon Time,pt.2	2.00
15 DON,BKi,Contagion,pt.5	2.00
16 DON,BKi,Contagion,pt.10	2.00
17 DON,BKi,JmP,A:Dr.Orchid	2.00
18 DON,BKi,JmP,A:Dr.Orchid	2.00
19 DON(s)	2.00
20 DON(s)	2.00
21 DON(s)	2.00
22 DON(s),BKi,JmP,"Angel in Hiding," pt.2 (of 3)	2.00
23 DON(s),BKi,JmP,"Angel in Hiding," pt.3	2.00
24 DON(s),BKi,JmP,The Order's return	2.00
25 DON(s),BKi,JmP,V:Brother Rollo	2.00
26	2.00
27 DON(s),BKi,JmP,"Angel Insane, "pt.1	2.00
28 DON(s),BKi,JmP,Joker, Riddler & Two-Face escape from Arkham Asylum	2.00
29 DON(s),DBw,JmP, F:Rä's Al Ghül, pt.1	2.00
30 DON(s),DBw,JmP, F:Rä's Al Ghül, pt.2	2.00
31 DON(s),JmP "Angel and the Monster Maker" pt.1 (of 3)	2.00
32 DON(s),JmP "Angel and the Monster Maker" pt.2	2.00
33 DON(s),JmP "Angel and the Monster Maker" pt.3 concl.	2.00
Ann.#1 Year One Annual	4.00
Ann.#2 Legends o/t Dead Earth	3.00
Ann.#3 Pulp Heroes (Hard Boiled)	4.00

AZRAEL/ASH
March 1997
1 one-shot DON(s),JQ,V:Surtr, A:Batman, x-over	4.95

AZRAEL PLUS
Oct. 1996
1 one-shot, DON(s),VGi,F:Vic Sage, The Question	2.95

AZTEK: THE ULTIMATE MAN
1996–97
1 GMo&MMr(s),NSH,I:Aztek & Synth	2.50
2 GMo&MMr(s),NSH,A:Green Lantern	2.00
3 GMo&MMr(s),NSH,V:Doll-Face	2.00
4 GMo&MMr(s),NSH,I:Lizard King, Vanity	2.00
5 GMo&MMr(s),NSH,O:Aztek, V:Lizard King	1.75
6 GMo&MMr(s),NSH, V:Vanity, A: Joker	1.75
7 GMo&MMr(s),NSH,A:Batman	1.75
8 GMo&MMr(s),NSH,return to Brother-hood of Zuetzatcoatl,A:Raptor	1.75
9 GMo&MMr(s),NSH,V:Parasite, A:Superman	1.75
10 GMo&MMr(s),NSH,A:Justice League, final issue	1.75

BABYLON 5
1995
1 From TV series	11.00
2 From TV series	7.00
3 Mysterious Assassin	6.00
4 V:Mysterious Assassin	6.00
5 Shadows of the Present,pt.1	6.00
6 Shadows of the Present,pt.2	6.00
7 Shadows of the Present,pt.3	5.00
8 Laser-Mirror Starweb,pt.1	5.00
9 Laser-Mirror Starweb,pt.2	5.00
10 Laser-Mirror-Starweb,pt.3	5.00
11 final issue	5.00

BATGIRL
1988
Spec.#1 V: Cormorant,I:Slash	8.00

BATMAN
Spring,1940
1 I:Joker,Cat(Catwoman),V:Hugo Strange	60,000.00
2 V:Joker/Catwoman team	10,000.00
3 V:Catwoman	7,000.00
4 V:Joker	5,500.00
5 V:Joker	4,200.00
6 V:'Clock Maker'	3,500.00
7 V:Joker	3,500.00
8 V:Joker	3,500.00
9 V:Joker	3,500.00
10 V:Catwoman	3,500.00
11 V:Joker,Penguin	5,000.00
12 V:Joker	2,200.00
13 V:Joker	2,100.00
14 V:Penguin;Propaganda sty	2,500.00
15 V:Catwoman	2,100.00
16 I:Alfred,V:Joker	4,500.00
17 V:Penguin	1,300.00
18 V:Tweedledum & Tweedledee	1,300.00
19 V:Joker	1,300.00
20 V:Joker	1,300.00
21 V:Penguin	1,100.00
22 V:Catwoman,Cavalier	1,100.00
23 V:Joker	1,600.00
24 I:Carter Nichols, V:Tweedledum	

DC COMICS

DC COMICS

Batman #11 © DC Comics, Inc.

Batman #56 © DC Comics, Inc.

69 I:King of the Cats, A:Catwoman	600.00
70 V:Penguin	550.00
71 V:Mr. Cipher	550.00
72 'The Jungle Batman'	550.00
73 V:Joker,A:Vicki Vale	650.00
74 V:Joker	550.00
75 I:The Gorilla Boss	550.00
76 V:Penguin	550.00
77 'The Crime Predictor'	550.00
78 'The Manhunter from Mars'	650.00
79 A:Vicki Vale	550.00
80 V:Joker	550.00
81 V:Two-Face	550.00
82 'The Flying Batman'	450.00
83 V:'Fish' Frye	450.00
84 V:Catwoman	500.00
85 V:Joker	450.00
86 V:Joker	450.00
87 V:Joker	450.00
88 V:Mr. Mystery	450.00
89 I:Aunt Agatha	450.00
90 I:Batboy	350.00
91 V:Blinky Grosset	350.00
92 I:Ace, the Bat-Hound	350.00
93 'The Caveman Batman'	350.00
94 Alfred has Amnesia	350.00
95 'The Bat-Train'	350.00
96 'Batman's College Days'	350.00
97 V:Joker	350.00
98 A:Carter Nichols,Jules Verne	350.00
99 V:Penguin,A:Carter Nichols, Bat Masterson	350.00
100 'Great Batman Contest'	2,000.00
101 'The Great Bat-Cape Hunt'	375.00
102 V:Mayne Mallok	375.00
103 A:Ace, the Bat-Hound	375.00
104 V:Devoe	375.00
105 A:Batwoman	450.00
106 V:Keene Harper gang	350.00
107 V:Daredevils	350.00
108 Bat-cave story	350.00
109 'The 1,000 Inventions of Batman'	350.00
110 V:Joker	375.00
111	300.00
112 I:Signalman	300.00
113 I:Fatman	300.00
114	300.00
115	300.00
116	300.00
117	300.00
118	300.00
119	300.00
120	300.00
121 I:Mr.Freeze	200.00
122	210.00
123 A:Joker	200.00
124 "Mystery Seed from Space"	200.00
125	200.00
126	200.00
127 A:Superman & Joker	225.00
128	200.00
129 O:Robin(Retold)	265.00
130	200.00
131 I:2nd Batman	150.00
132 'Lair of the Sea-Fox'	150.00
133	150.00
134	150.00
135	150.00
136 A:Joker,Bat-Mite	175.00
137 V:Mr.Marvel,The Brand	150.00
138 A:Bat-Mite	150.00
139 I:Old Batgirl	165.00
140 A:Joker	165.00

& Tweedledee	1,200.00
25 V:Joker/Penguin team	1,500.00
26 V:Cavalier	1,000.00
27 V:Penguin	1,000.00
28 V:Joker	1,100.00
29 V:Scuttler	1,000.00
30 V:Penguin,I:Ally Babble	1,000.00
31 I:Punch and Judy	800.00
32 O:Robin,V:Joker	850.00
33 V:Penguin,Jackall	900.00
34 A:Ally Babble	800.00
35 V:Catwoman	800.00
36 V:Penguin,A:King Arthur	800.00
37 V:Joker	800.00
38 V:Penguin	800.00
39 V:Catwoman,Christmas Story	800.00
40 V:Joker	900.00
41 V:Penguin	650.00
42 V:Catwoman	650.00
43 V:Penguin	650.00
44 V:Joker,A:Carter Nichols,Meets ancester Silas Wayne	1,000.00
45 V:Catwoman	650.00
46 V:Joker,A:Carter Nichols, Leonardo Da Vinci	600.00
47 O:Batman,V:Catwoman	2,500.00
48 V:Penguin, Bat-Cave story	750.00
49 I:Mad Hatter & Vicki Vale	1,200.00
50 V:Two-Face,A:Vicki Vale	700.00
51 V:Penguin	650.00
52 V:Joker	700.00
53 V:Joker	700.00
54 V:'The Treasure Hunter'	650.00
55 V:Joker	700.00
56 V:Penguin	650.00
57 V:Joker	700.00
58 V:Penguin	650.00
59 I:Deadshot	650.00
60 V:'Shark' Marlin	650.00
61 V:Penguin	800.00
62 O:Catwoman,I:Knight & Squire	850.00
63 V:Joker	600.00
64 V:Killer Moth	600.00
65 I:Wingman,V:Catwoman	625.00
66 V:Joker	625.00
67 V:Joker	625.00
68 V:Two-Face,Alfred story	550.00

141 V:Clockmaster	150.00
142 Batman robot story	150.00
143 A:Bathound	150.00
144 A:Joker,Bat-Mite,Bat-Girl	150.00
145 V:Mr.50,Joker	165.00
146 A:Bat-Mite,Joker	125.00
147 Batman becomes Bat-Baby	125.00
148 A:Joker	150.00
149 V:Maestro	125.00
150 V:Biff Warner,Jack Pine	125.00
151 V:Harris Boys	100.00
152 A:Joker	110.00
153 Other Dimension story	100.00
154 V:Dr. Dorn	100.00
155 1st S.A. Penguin	450.00
156 V:Gorilla Gang	100.00
157 V:Mirror Man	100.00
158 A:Bathound,Bat-Mite	100.00
159 A:Joker,Clayface	110.00
160 V:Bart Cullen	100.00
161 A:Bat-Mite	100.00
162 F:Robin	100.00
163 A:Joker	100.00
164 CI,A:Mystery Analysts,new Batmobile	90.00
165 V:The Mutated Man	90.00
166 Escape story	90.00
167 V:Karabi & Hydra, the Crime Cartel	90.00
168 V:Mr. Mammoth	90.00
169 A:Penguin	125.00
170 V:Getaway Genius	90.00
171 CI,1st S.A. Riddler	450.00
172 V:Flower Gang	65.00
173 V:Elwood Pearson	65.00
174 V:Big Game Hunter	65.00
175 V:Eddie Repp	65.00
176 Giant rep.A:Joker,Catwom.	75.00
177 BK,A:Elongated Man,Atom	65.00
178 CI	65.00
179 CI,2nd Riddler(Silver)	135.00
180 BK,A:Death-Man	65.00
181 CI,I:Poison Ivy	90.00
182 A:Joker,(giant size rep).	65.00
183 CI,A:Poison Ivy	75.00
184 CI,Mystery of the Missing Manhunters	60.00
185 Giant rep.	65.00

DC COMICS

186 A:Joker 50 00
187 Giant rep.A:Joker 65.00
188 CI,A:Eraser 35.00
189 CI,A:Scarecrow 55.00
190 CI,A:Penguin 45.00
191 CI,The Day Batman Soldout 35.00
192 CI,The Crystal ball that
    betrayed Batman 35.00
193 Giant rep. 45.00
194 MSy,BK,A:Blockbuster,Mystery
    Analysts of Gotham City 35.00
195 CI 35.00
196 BK,Psychic Super-Sleuth . . 35.00
197 MSy,A:Bat Girl,Catwoman . . 75.00
198 A:Joker,Penguin,Catwoman,
    O:Batman rtd,(G-Size rep) . . 75.00
199 CI,'Peril o/t Poison Rings' . . 35.00
200 NA(c),O:rtd,A:Joker,Pengiun,
    Scarecrow 175.00
201 A:Batman Villians 30.00
202 BU:Robin 18.00
203 NA(c),(giant size) 25.00
204 FR(s),IN,JG 16.00
205 FR(s),IN,JG 16.00
206 FR(s),IN,JG 16.00
207 FR(s),IN,JG 16.00
208 GK,new O:Batman,
    A:Catwoman 35.00
209 FR(s),IN,JG 18.00
210 A:Catwoman 20.00
211 FR(s),IN,JG 18.00
212 FR(s),IN,JG 18.00
213 RA,30th Anniv.Batman,new O:
    Robin,rep.O:Alfred,Joker 60.00
214 IN,A:Batgirl 15.00
215 IN,DG 15.00
216 IN,DG,I:DaphnePennyworth 15.00
217 NA(c) 16.00
218 NA(c),giant 35.00
219 NA,IN,DG,Batman Xmas . . 35.00
220 NA(c),IN 15.00
221 IN,DG 15.00
222 IN,Rock'n Roll story 30.00
223 NA(c),giant 30.00
224 NA(c) 14.00
225 NA(c),IN,DG 14.00
226 IN,DG I:10-Eyed Man 14.00
227 IN,DG,A:Daphne
    Pennyworth 14.00
228 giant Deadly Traps rep. . . . 30.00
229 IN 14.00
230 NA(c),Robin 14.00
231 F:Ten-Eyed Man 14.00
232 DON(s),NA,DG,
    I:Ras al Ghul 75.00
233 giant Bruce Wayne iss. 30.00
234 NA,DG,IN,1stS.A.Two-Face 110.00
235 CI,V:Spook 13.00
236 NA 16.00
237 NA 35.00
238 NA,JC,JKu,giant 16.00
239 NA,RB 14.00
240 NA(c),RB,giant,R-Ghul 12.00
241 IN,DG,RB,A:Kid Flash 12.00
242 RB,MK 12.00
243 NA,DG,Ras al Ghul 24.00
244 NA,Ras al Ghul 24.00
245 NA,IN,DG,FMc,Ras al Ghul . 22.00
246 . . . . 12.00
247 Deadly New Year 12.00
248 . . . . 12.00
249 'Citidel of Crime' 12.00
250 IN,DG 12.00
251 NA,V:Joker 40.00
252 . . . . 12.00

253 AN,DG,A:Shadow 12.00
254 NA,GK,B:100 page issues . . 18.00
255 GK,CI,NA,DG,I:CrazyQuilt . . 22.00
256 Catwoman 14.00
257 IN,DG,V:Penguin 15.00
258 IN,DG 13.00
259 GK,IN,DG,A:Shadow 13.00
260 IN,DG,Joker 35.00
261 CI,GK,E:100 page issues . . 12.00
262 A:Scarecrow 9.00
263 DG(i),A:Riddler 12.00
264 DON(s),DG,A:Devil Dayre . . 8.00
265 RB,BWr 9.00
266 DG,Catwoman(old Costume) 10.00
267 DG 8.00
268 DON(s),IN,TeB,V:Sheikh . . . 8.00
269 A:Riddler 9.00
270 B:DvR(s) 8.00
271 IN,FMc 8.00
272 JL 8.00
273 V:Underworld Olympics/76 . . 8.00
274 . . . . 8.00
275 . . . . 8.00

Batman #132 © DC Comics, Inc.

276 . . . . 8.00
277 . . . . 8.00
278 . . . . 8.00
279 A:Riddler 9.00
280 . . . . 8.00
281 . . . . 8.00
282 . . . . 8.00
283 V:Camouflage 8.00
284 JA,R:Dr.Tzin Tzin 8.00
285 . . . . 7.00
286 V:Joker 9.00
287 BWi,MGr,Penguin 8.00
288 BWi,MGr,Penguin 8.00
289 MGr, V:Skull 7.00
290 MGr,V:Skull Dagger 7.00
291 B:Underworld Olympics #1,
    A:Catwoman 8.00
292 A:Riddler 8.00
293 A:Superman & Luthor 8.00
294 E:DvR(s),E:Underworld
    Olympics,A:Joker 9.00
295 GyC(s),MGo,JyS,V:Hamton . 8.00
296 B:DvR(s),V:Scarecrow 8.00
297 RB,Mad Hatter 8.00
298 JCA,DG,V:Baxter Bains 8.00

299 DG 8.00
300 WS,DG,A:Batman E-2,
    Robin E-2 . . . . 14.00
301 JCa,TeB 9.00
302 JCa,DG,V:Human Dynamo . 9.00
303 JCa,DG 9.00
304 E:DvR(s),V:Spook 9.00
305 GyC,JCa,DeH,V:Thanatos . . 10.00
306 JCa,DeH,DN,V:Black Spider 10.00
307 B:LWn(s),JCa,DG,
    I:Limehouse Jack 10.00
308 JCa,DG,V:Mr.Freeze 10.00
309 E:LWn(s),JCa,FMc,
    V:Blockbuster 10.00
310 IN,DG,A:Gentleman Ghost . 10.00
311 SEt,FMc,IN,Batgirl,
    V:Dr.Phosphorus 10.00
312 WS,DG,Calenderman 10.00
313 IN,FMc,VTwo-Face 10.00
314 IN,FMc,V:Two-Face 10.00
315 IN,FMc,V:Kiteman 10.00
316 IN,FMc,F:Robin,
    V:Crazy Quilt 10.00
317 IN,FMc,V:Riddler 11.00
318 IN,I:Fire Bug 10.00
319 JKu(c),IN,DG,A:Gentleman
    Ghost,E:Catwoman 10.00
320 BWr(c) 10.00
321 DG,WS,A:Joker,Catwoman . 11.00
322 V:Cap.Boomerang,Catwoman 10.00
323 IN,A:Catwoman 10.00
324 IN,A:Catwoman 10.00
325 . . . . 10.00
326 A:Catwoman 10.00
327 IN,A:Proffesor.Milo 10.00
328 A:Two-Face 10.00
329 IN,A:Two-Face 10.00
330 . . . . 10.00
331 DN,FMc,V:Electrocutioner . . 10.00
332 IN,DN,Ras al Ghul.1st solo
    Catwoman story 11.00
333 IN,DN,A:Catwoman,
    Ras al Ghul 10.00
334 FMc,Ras al Ghul,Catwoman 10.00
335 IN,FMc,Catwoman,Ras al
    Ghul 10.00
336 JL,FMc,Loser Villains 7.50
337 DN,V:Snow Man 7.50
338 DN,Deathsport 7.50
339 A:Poison Ivy 7.50
340 GC,A:Mole 7.50
341 A:Man Bat 7.50
342 V:Man Bat 7.50
343 GC,KJ,I:The Dagger 7.50
344 GC,KJ,Poison Ivy 7.50
345 I:New Dr.Death,A:Catwoman . 7.50
346 DN,V:Two Face 7.50
347 A:Alfred 7.50
348 GC,KJ,Man-Bat,A:Catwoman 8.00
349 GC,AA,A:Catwoman 8.00
350 GC,TD,A:Catwoman 8.00
351 GC,TD,A:Catwoman 8.00
352 Col Blimp 7.50
353 JL,DN,DA,A:Joker 9.00
354 DN,AA,V:HugoStrange,A:
    Catwoman 7.50
355 DN,AA:A:Catwoman 7.50
356 DG,DN,Hugo Strange 7.50
357 DN,AA,I:Jason Todd 9.00
358 A:King Croc 7.50
359 DG,O:King Croc,Joker 9.00
360 I:Savage Skull 7.00
361 DN,Man-Bat,I:Harvey Bullock 7.00
362 V:Riddler 7.00
363 V:Nocturna 7.00

All comics prices listed are for *Near Mint* condition.

DC COMICS

364 DN,AA,J.Todd 1st full solo
  story (cont'd Detective #531) . . 7.00
365 DN,AA,C:Joker 7.00
366 DN,AA,Joker,J.Todd in
  Robin Costume 25.00
367 DN,AA,I:Dr.Fang,V:Deadshot 7.00
368 DN,AA,I:2nd Robin
  (Jason Todd) 20.00
369 DN,AA,I:Dr.Fang,V:Deadshot 7.00
370 DN,AA 7.00
371 DN,AA,V:Catman 4.50
372 DN,AA,V:Dr.Fang 4.00
373 DN,AA,V:Scarecrow 4.00
374 GC,AA,V:Penguin 5.00
375 GC,AA,V:Dr.Freeze 4.00
376 DN,Halloween issue 4.00
377 DN,AA,V:Nocturna 4.00
378 V:Mad Hatter 4.00
379 V:Mad Hatter 4.00
380 AA,V:Nocturna 4.00
381 V:Batman 4.00
382 A:Catwoman 4.50
383 GC 4.00

Batman #409 © DC Comics, Inc.

384 V:Calender Man 4.00
385 V:Calender Man 4.00
386 I:Black Mask 4.00
387 V:Black Mask 4.00
388 V:Capt.Boomerang & Mirror
  Master 4.00
389 V:Nocturna,Catwoman 4.50
390 V:Nocturna,Catwoman 4.50
391 V:Nocturna,Catwoman 4.50
392 A:Catwoman 4.50
393 PG,V:Cossack 3.50
394 PG,V:Cossack 3.50
395 V:Film Freak 3.50
396 V:Film Freak 3.50
397 V:Two-Face,Catwoman 4.00
398 V:Two-Face,Catwoman 4.00
399 HaE(s),Two-Face 3.50
400 BSz,AAd,GP,BB,A:Joker . . . 22.00
401 JBy(c),TVE,Legends,
  A:Magpie 3.50
402 JSn,Fake Batman 3.50
403 DCw,Batcave discovered . . . 3.50
404 DM,FM(s),B:Year 1,I:Modern
  Age Catwoman 17.00
405 FM,DM,Year 1 . . . . 8.00

406 FM,DM,Year 1 . . . . 8.00
407 FM,DM,E:Year 1 . . . . 8.00
408 CW,V:Joker,
  new O:Jason Todd 5.00
408a 2nd printing 1.00
409 DG,RA,V:Crime School 4.00
409a 2nd printing 1.00
410 DC,Jason Todd 4.00
411 DC,DH,V:Two Face 3.00
412 DC,DH,I:Mime 3.00
413 DC,DH 3.00
414 JAp,Slasher 3.00
415 JAp,Millenium Week #2 . . . . 3.00
416 JAp,1st Batman/Nightwing
  T.U. 3.00
417 JAp,B:10 Nights,I:KGBeast 11.00
418 JAp,V:KGBeast 10.00
419 JAp,V:KGBeast 10.00
420 JAp,E:10 Nights,D:KGBeast 10.00
421 DG 3.50
422 MBr,V:Dumpster Slayer 3.00
423 TM(c),DC,Who is Batman . . . 3.00
424 MBr,Robin 3.00
425 MBr,Gordon Kidnapped 3.00
426 JAp,B:Death in the Family,
  V:Joker 11.00
427 JAp,V:Joker 9.00
428 JAp,D:2nd Robin 8.00
429 JAp,A:Superman,
  E:Death in the Family 5.00
430 JAp,JSn,V:Madman 4.00
431 JAp,Murder Investigation . . . 2.75
432 JAp 2.75
433 JBy,JAp,Many Deaths of the
  Batman #1 . . . . 5.00
434 JBy,JAp,Many Deaths #2 . . 4.00
435 JBy,Many Deaths #3 . . . . . 4.00
436 PB,B:Year#3,A:Nightwing,I:Tim
  Drake as child 8.00
436a 2ndPrint(green DC logo) . . 2.00
437 PB,year#3 . . . . 3.00
438 PB,year#3 . . . . 2.50
439 PB,year#3 . . . . 2.50
440 JAp,Lonely Place of Dying #1,
  A:Tim Drake (face not shown) . 4.00
441 JAp,Lonely Place Dying 4.00
442 JAp,I:3rd Robin(Tim Drake) . 6.00
443 JAp,I:Crimesmith 2.00
444 JAp,V:Crimesmith 2.00
445 JAp,I:K.G.Beast Demon . . . 2.00
446 JAp,V:K.G.Beast Demon . . . 2.00
447 JAp,D:K.G.Beast Demon . . . 2.00
448 JAp,A:Penguin#1 . . . . 2.50
449 MBr,A:Penguin#3 . . . . 2.50
450 JAp,I:Joker II 2.00
451 JAp,V:Joker II 2.00
452 KD,Dark Knight Dark City#1 2.00
453 KD,Dark Knight Dark City#2 . 2.00
454 KD,Dark Knight Dark City#3 . 2.00
455 Identity Crisis#1,
  A:Scarecrow 3.00
456 IdentityCrisis#2 . . . . 4.00
457 V:Scarecrow,A:Robin,
  New Costume 6.00
457a 2nd printing 2.00
458 R:Sarah Essen 2.00
459 A:Sarah Essen 2.00
460 Sisters in Arms,pt.1
  A:Catwoman 3.00
461 Sisters in Arms,pt.2
  Catwoman V:Sarah.Essen . . 3.00
462 Batman in San Francisco . . 1.75
463 Death Valley 1.75
464 V:Two-Hearts 1.75
465 Batman/Robin T.U. 3.00

466 Robin Trapped 2.00
467 Shadowbox #1(sequel to
  Robin Mini-Series) 2.50
468 Shadowbox #2 . . . . 2.00
469 Shadowbox #3 . . . . 2.00
470 War of the Gods x-over 1.75
471 V:Killer Croc 1.75
472 The Idiot Root,pt.1 . . . . 1.75
473 The Idiot Root,pt.3 . . . . 1.75
474 Destroyer,pt.1 (LOTDK#27) . 2.25
475 R:Scarface,A:VickiVale . . . 1.75
476 A:Scarface 1.75
477 Ph(c),Gotham Tale,pt.1 . . . 1.75
478 Ph(c),Gotham Tale,pt.2 . . . 1.75
479 TMd,I:Pagan 1.75
480 JAp,To the father I never
  knew 1.75
481 JAp,V:Maxie Zeus 1.75
482 JAp,V:Maxie Zeus 1.75
483 JAp,I:Crash & Burn 1.75
484 JAp,R:Black Mask 1.75
485 TGr,V:Black Mask 1.75
486 JAp,I:Metalhead 1.75

Batman #484 © DC Comics, Inc.

487 JAp,V:Headhunter 1.75
488 JAp,N:Azrael 10.00
489 JAp,Bane vs Killer Croc,
  I:Azrael as Batman 9.00
489a 2nd Printing 2.00
490 JAp,Bane vs.Riddler 7.00
490a 2nd Printing 1.75
490b 3rd Printing 1.50
491 JAp,V:Joker,A:Bane 6.00
491a 2nd Printing 1.50
492 B:DgM(s),NB,Knightfall#1,
  V:Mad Hatter,A:Bane 9.00
492a Platinum Ed. 25.00
492b 2nd Printing 1.50
493 NB,Knightfall,#3,Mr.Zsasz . . 5.00
494 JAp,TMd,Knightfall #5,A:Bane,
  V:Cornelius,Stirk,Joker 4.00
495 NB,Knightfall#7,V:Poison
  Ivy,A:Bane 3.50
496 JAp,JRu,Knightfall#9,V:Joker,
  Scarecrow,A:Bane 3.50
497 JAp,DG,Knightfall#11,V:Bane,
  Batman gets back broken 7.50
497a 2nd Printing 1.75
498 JAp,JRu,Knightfall#15,A:Bane,

Catwoman,Azrael Becomes	
Batman	2.50
499 JAp,SHa,Knightfall#17,	
A:Bane,Catwoman	2.50
500 JQ(c),JAp,MM,Die Cut(c),	
Direct Market,Knightfall#19,	
V:Bane,N:Batman	5.00
500a KJo(c),Newstand Ed.	3.50
501 MM,I:Mekros	2.00
502 MM,V:Mekros	2.00
503 MM,V:Catwoman	2.00
504 MM,V:Catwoman	2.00
505 MM,V:Canibal	2.00
506 KJo(c),MM,A:Ballistic	2.00
507 KJo(c),MM,A:Ballistic	2.00
508 KJo(c),MM,V:Abattior	2.00
509 KJo(c),MM,KnightsEnd#1,	
A:Shiva	4.00
510 KJo(c),MM,Knights End #7,	
V:Azrael	2.00
511 Zero Hour, A:Batgirl	2.00
512 Killer Croc sewer battles	2.00
513 Two-Face and convicts	2.00
514 Identity Crisis	2.00
515 KJo,Return of Bruce Wayne,	
Troika,pt.1	2.00
515 Collector's Edition	3.50
516 V:The Sleeper	2.00
517 V:The Sleeper	2.00
518 V:The Black Spider	2.00
519 KJo,V:The Black Spider	
[new Miraweb format begins] ..	2.00
520 EB,A:James Gordon	2.00
521 R:Killer Croc	2.00
522 R:Scarecrow	2.00
523 V:Scarecrow	2.00
524 DgM,KJo,V:Scarecrow	2.00
525 DgM,KJo,Underworld	
Unleashed tie-in	2.00
526 DgM,A:Alfred,Nightwing,Robin	2.00
527 DgM,V:Two-Face,I:Schism ..	2.00
528	2.00
529 DgM,KJo,Contagion,pt.6 ...	3.00
530 DgM,KJo,The Aztec	
Connection,pt.1	2.50
530a collector's edition	2.50
531 DgM,KJo,The Aztec	
Connection,pt.2	2.00
531a collectors edition	2.50
532 DgM(s),KJo,"The Aztec Connec-	
tion," pt.3, A:Deadman	2.00
532a card stock cover	2.50
533 DgM(s),KJo,Legacy prelude .	2.00
534 DgM(s),KJo,Legacy, pt.5 ...	2.00
535 DgM(s),KJo,JhB,I:The Ogre,	
double size	4.00
535a Collector's edition,	
gatefold cover	3.95
536 DgM(s),KJo,JhB,V:Man-Bat,	
Final Night tie-in	2.00
537 DgM(s),KJo,JhB,A:Man-Bat,	
pt.2	2.00
538 DgM(s),KJo,JhB,A:Man-Bat,	
pt.3	2.00
539	2.00
540 DgM(s),KJo,JhB,A:Spectre,pt.1	2.00
541 DgM(s),KJo,JhB,A:Spectre,pt.2	2.00
542 DgM(s),KJo,JhB,V:Faceless,	
pt. 1	2.00
543 DgM(s),KJo,JhB,pt. 2	2.00
544 DgM(s),KJo,JhB, F:Joker,pt.1	2.00
545 DgM(s),KJo, F:Joker, Demon,	
pt.2	2.00
545 DgM(s),KJo,JhB,F:Joker,	
Demon, pt.3 concl.	2.00

Batman Annual #2 © DC Comics, Inc.

Ann.#1 CS	450.00
Ann.#2	220.00
Ann.#3 A:Joker	200.00
Ann.#4	100.00
Ann.#5	100.00
Ann.#6	80.00
Ann.#7	80.00
Ann.#8 TVE,A:Ras al Ghul ..	8.00
Ann.#9 JOy,AN,PS	7.00
Ann.#10 DCw,DG,V:HugoStrange	7.00
Ann.#11 JBy(c),AMo(s),V:Penguin	8.00
Ann.#12 RA,V:Killer	5.00
Ann.#13 A:Two-Face	6.00
Ann.#14 O:Two-Face	4.00
Ann.#15 Armageddon,pt.3	6.00
Ann.#15a 2nd printing(silver)	2.50
Ann.#16 SK(c),Eclipso,V:Joker ...	3.00
Ann.#17 EB,Bloodline#8,	
I:Decimator	3.00
Ann.#18 Elseworld Story	3.50
Ann.#19 Year One, O:Scarecrow .	4.00
Ann.#20 Legends o/t Dead Earth .	2.95
Ann.#21 Pulp Heroes (Weird	
Mystery) DgM(s)	3.95
PF Batman Returns:Movie Adaption,	
SE,JL	6.00
Newsstand Format	4.00
Spec.#0 (1994)	3.00
Spec.#1 MGo,I:Wrath	4.00
TPB Batman: The Last Arkham .	12.95
TPB, Many Deaths of the Batman;	
rep. #433-#435	3.95
TPB, Death in the Family;reprints	
Batman #426-#429	6.50
2nd printing	4.00
3rd printing	4.00
TPB Batman: Knight's End, rep.	
Batman #509-#510, Shadow of the	
Bat #29-#30, Detective #676-#677,	
Legends #62-#63, Catwoman #12,	
Robin #8-#9	14.95
TPB Knightfall rep. #1-#11	12.95
TPB Knightfall rep. #12-#19	12.95
TPB Legacy, sequel to Contagion,	
rep.	17.95
TPB The Movies, (all 4)	19.95
TPB Ten Knights of the Beast ..	5.95
TPB Venom	9.95
TPB Year One FM(s)	12.95

TPB Year Two	9.95
Batman JOy,Movie adaptation ...	3.00
Perfect Bound	6.00
Batman Archives Vol.3	39.95
Batman: Arkham Asylum,DMc ..	28.00
Batman: Blind Justice	7.50
Batman: Bloodstorm,KJo,V:Joker,	
Vampires, (sequel to Red Rain)	
HC	24.95
TPB	12.95
Batman: The Blue,The Grey,and	
The Bat;JL (Elseworlds)	5.95
Batman: Bride of the Demon,TGr,	
V:Rä's Al Ghul	21.00
Batman: Brotherhood of the Bat	
1-shot Elseworlds story	5.95
Batman: Castle of the Bat,	
Elseworlds Story	5.95
Batman: Crime and Punishment ..	4.95
Batman: Dark Allegiances GN HC	5.95
Batman: Dark Joker KJo	26.00
Batman/Houdini: The Devil's	
Workshop	6.50
Batman: Digital Justice	26.00
Batman Forever Movie Adaptation	5.95
Newsstand version	3.95
Batman: Full Circle AD,A:Reaper .	7.00
Batman Gallery,collection of past	
(c),posters,pin-ups,JQ(c)	4.00
Batman: Gotham By Gaslight,MMi,	
V:Jack the Ripper	6.00
Batman: Holy Terror	6.50
Batman: In Darkest Knight	
MiB(s),JBi	5.50
Batman/Judge Dredd: Judgement on	
Gotham,SBs,V:Scarecrow,Judge	
Death	9.00
Batman: The Killing Joke,BB,AMo(s),	
O:Joker,Batgirl paralyzed ...	18.00
2nd thru 6th Printings	@5.00
Batman Knightgallery	3.50
Batman: The Last Angel, F:Catwoman	
V:Aztec bat-god	12.95
Batman: Master of the Future,EB,	
Sequel to Goth.by Gaslight ...	6.00
Batman: Night Cries,SHa	30.00
Batman/Dracula:Red Rain KJo,MJ,	
Batman becomes Vampire,	
HC, Elseworlds Story	50.00
SC	12.00
Batman: The Riddle Factory ...	4.95
Batman: Seduction of the Gun,	
V:Illegal Gun Control	3.00
Batman: Son of the Demon,JBi,	
HC	55.00
SC	17.00
2nd thru 4th printings	@8.95
Two-Face Strikes Twice#1	5.25
Two-Face Strikes Twice#2	5.25
Batman: Vengeance of Bane,	
GN,I:Bane	30.00
2nd Printing	5.00
Batman: Vengeance of Bane II ..	3.95
Batman: Year One Rep. Batman	
#404-#407	14.00
2nd Printing	9.95
3rd Printing	9.95
Batman: The Ultimate Evil:	
1 Novel adaptation (of 2)	5.95
2 Novel adaptation, finale	5.95

BATMAN ADVENTURES
1992–95
(Based on TV cartoon series)

1 MeP,V:Penguin	6.00

DC COMICS

All comics prices listed are for *Near Mint* condition.

Batman Adventures #3
© DC Comics, Inc.

Batman and the Outsiders #20
© DC Comics, Inc.

2 MeP,V:Catwoman	5.00
3 MeP,V:Joker	4.00
4 MeP,V:Scarecrow	4.00
5 MeP,V:Scarecrow	4.00
6 MeP,A:Robin	4.00
7 MeP,V:Killer Croc,w/card	8.00
8 MeP,Larceny my Sweet	3.00
9 MeP,V:Two Face	3.00
10 MeP,V:Riddler	4.00
11 MeP,V:Man-Bat	2.50
12 MeP,F:Batgirl	2.50
13 MeP,V:Talia	2.50
14 MeP,F:Robin	2.00
15 MeP,F:Commissioner Gordon	2.00
16 MeP,V:Joker	2.00
17 MeP,V:Talia	2.00
18 MeP,R:Batgirl	1.75
19 MeP,V:Scarecrow	1.75
20 MeP,V:Mastermind,Mr.Nice, Perfessor	1.75
21 MeP,V:Man-Bat,Tygrus	1.75
22 MeP,V:Two-Face	1.75
23 MEP,V:Poison Ivy	1.75
24 MeP,I:Kyodi Ken	1.75
25 MeP,dbl.size,Superman	2.50
26 MeP,A:Robin,Batgirl	1.75
27 MeP,I:Doppleganger	1.75
28 Joker	1.75
29 A:Talia	1.50
30 O:Mastermind, Mr. Nice	1.50
31 I:Anarcky	1.50
32 Criminals dressed as Napoleonic Soldiers	1.75
33 Bruce and date mugged	1.75
34 V:Dr. Hugo Strange	1.75
35 A:Catwoman	1.75
36 V:Joker, Final issue	1.75
Ann.#1 Roxy Rocket	3.00
Ann.#2 JBa,BBl,DG,TG,SHa,MM, GN,JRu,V:Demon,Ra's al Ghul,Etrigan	3.50
Holiday Special	2.95
Spec. Mad Love	3.95
TPB Collected Adventures #1	5.95
TPB Collected Adventures #2	5.95

BATMAN AND THE OUTSIDERS
Aug., 1983

1 B:MiB(s),JAp,O:Outsiders, O:Geo Force	3.00
2 JAp,V:Baron Bedlam	2.50
3 JAp,V:Agent Orange	2.00
4 JAp,V:Fearsome Five	2.00
5 JAp,A:New Teen Titans	2.50
6 JAp,V:Cryonic Man	1.50
7 JAp,V:Cryonic Man	1.50
8 JAp,A:Phantom Stranger	1.50
9 JAp,I:Master of Disaster	1.50
10 JAp,A:Master of Disaster	1.50
11 JAp,V:Takeo	1.50
12 JAp,DG,O:Katana	1.50
13 JAp,Day,O:Batman	1.50
14 BWg,Olympics,V:Maxi Zeus	1.50
15 TVE,Olympics,V:Maxi Zeus	1.50
16 JAp,L:Halo	1.50
17 JAp,V:Ahk-Ton	1.50
18 JAp,V:Ahk-Ton	1.50
19 JAp,A:Superman	1.50
20 JAp,V:Syonide,R:Halo	1.50
21 TVE,JeM,Solo Stories	1.50
22 AD,O:Halo,I:Aurakles	1.50
23 AD,O:Halo,V:Aurakles	1.50
24 AD,C:Kobra	1.50
25 AD,V:Kobra	1.50
26 AD	1.50
27 AD,V:Kobra	1.50
28 AD,I:Lia Briggs(Looker)	1.50
29 AD,V:Metamorpho	1.50
30 AD,C:Looker	1.50
31 AD,I&J:Looker	1.50
32 AD,L:Batman	1.50
Ann.#1 JA N:Geo-Force, I:Force of July	1.75
Ann.#2 V:Tremayne,W:Metamorpho & Sapphire Stagg	1.50

Becomes:

ADVENTURES OF THE OUTSIDERS
May, 1986

33 AD,V:Baron Bedlam	1.50

34 AD,Masters of Disaster	1.50
35 AD,V:Adolph Hitler	1.50
36 AD,A:Masters of Disaster	1.50
37	1.50
38	1.50
39 thru 47 JAp,reprints Outsiders #1-#9	@1.50

BATMAN AND ROBIN ADVENTURES, THE
Nov. 1995

1 TTn	2.00
2 TTn,V:Two-Face	1.75
3 TTn,V:The Riddler	1.75
4 TTn,V:The Penguin	1.75
5 TTn	1.75
6 TTn,Robin Fired?	1.75
7 TTn,V:Scarface	1.75
8 TTn(s)	1.75
9 TTn(s),F:Batgirl & Talia	1.75
10 TTn(s),F:Ra's Al Ghul	1.75
11 TTn(s),Alfred & Robin look for monster in Batcave	1.75
12 TTn(s),BKr,RBr, sequel to "Bane" TV episode	1.75
13 TTn(s),BKr,RBr,V:Scarecrow	1.75
14 TTn(s),BKr,RBr,young criminal turns to Batman for help	1.75
15 TTn(s)	1.75
16 TTn(s),V:Catman,A:Catwoman	1.75
17 PDi&TTn(s),JSon,RBr,Mad Hatter dies in Arkham	1.75
18 TTn(s),BKr,TBe,A:Joker, Harley Quinn	1.75
19 TTn(s),BKr,TBe,The Huntress	1.75
20 TTn(s),BKr,TBe, office pool	1.75
21 TTn(s),JSon,Riddler kidnaps Commissioner Gordon	1.75
22 TTn(s),BKr,TBe,V:Two-Face	1.75
Ann.#1 PDi(s),TTn, sequel to Batman: Mask of the Phantasm	3.00
Sub-Zero one-shot, F:Mr. Freeze, Nora, 64pg.	3.95

BATMAN AND ROBIN
May 1997

GN DON(s),Movie Adaptation	3.95
GN collector's edition,	5.95

BATMAN: BANE
1997

GN BSz(c) movie tie-in	4.95

BATMAN: BATGIRL
1997

GN BSz(c) movie tie-in	4.95

BATMAN BLACK & WHITE
1996

1 JLe(c) numerous artists (of 4)	3.50
2 thru 4	@3.00

BATMAN: BLACKGATE
Nov. 1996

1 one-shot, CDi(s),JSon,in Blackgate prison,	4.50

BATMAN: BLOODSTORM

GN V:Dracula	24.95
SC	12.95

DC COMICS

DC COMICS

BATMAN CHRONICLES
1995
1 CDi,LW,BSz, multiple stories	. .	3.00
2 V:Feedback	. . . .	3.00
3 All villains issue	. . . .	3.00
4 F:Hitman	. . . .	3.00
5 Oracle, Year One story	. . . . .	3.00
6 Rā's Al Ghūl	. . . .	3.00
7 JOy,LW, woman on death row	.	3.00
8 Talia goes to Gotham to		
eliminate Batman	. . . .	3.00
9 CDi(s),F:Batgirl, Mr. Freeze,		
Poison Ivy	. . . .	3.00
Gallery #1, Pin-ups	. . . .	3.50
GN The Gauntlet	. . . .	4.95

BATMAN: THE CULT
1988
1 JSn,BWr,V:Deacon Blackfire	. .	9.00
2 JSn,BWr,V:Deacon Blackfire	. .	7.00
3 JSn,BWr,V:Deacon Blackfire	. .	7.00
4 JSn,BWr,V:Deacon Blackfire	. .	6.00
TPB Rep.#1-#4	. . . .	14.95

BATMAN: THE DARK KNIGHT RETURNS
1986
1 FM,KJ,V:Two-Face	. . . .	20.00
1a 2nd printing	. . . .	5.00
1b 3rd printing	. . . .	3.00
2 FM,KJ,V:Sons of the Batman	. .	9.00
2a 2nd printing	. . . .	3.00
2b 3rd printing	. . . .	2.50
3 FM,KJ,D:Joker	. . . .	7.00
3a 2nd printing	. . . .	3.00
4 FM,KJ,Batman vs.Superman,		
A:Green Arrow,D:Alfred	. . . . .	5.00
HC	. . . .	50.00
Paperback book	. . . .	20.00
Warner paperback	. . . .	17.00
HC,sign/num.	. . . .	270.00
2nd–8th printing	. . . .	12.95
TPB 10th Anniv. Spec, 224 pg.	. .	14.95

BATMAN/DEADMAN
TPB Death and Glory, JeR(s),JEs	12.95

BATMAN: A DEATH IN THE FAMILY
1 rep. Batman #426-429	. . . .	8.00
1a 2nd printing	. . . .	5.00
1b 3rd printing	. . . .	4.00

BATMAN: DEATH OF INNOCENTS
Oct. 1996
1 one-shot DON(s),JSt,BSz, Land		
mine victims	. . . .	4.00

BATMAN FAMILY
Sept.–Oct., 1975
1 MGr,NA(rep.) Batgirl &		
Robin begins,giant	. . . .	7.50
2 V:Clue Master	. . . .	4.50
3 Batgirl & Robin reveal ID	. . . . .	5.00
4	. . . .	4.50
5	. . . .	4.50
6 Joker Daughter	. . . .	6.00
7 CS,A:Sportsmaster,		
G.A.Huntress	. . . .	3.50
8 First solo Robin story,		
C:Joker's Daughter	. . . .	3.00

9 Joker's Daughter	. . . .	5.50
10 R:B'woman,1st solo Batgirl sty		4.00
11 MR,Man-Bat begins	. . . .	5.00
12 MR	. . . .	5.00
13 MR,DN,BWi	. . . .	5.00
14 HC/JRu,Man-Bat	. . . .	4.00
15 MGo,Man-Bat	. . . .	3.00
16 MGo,Man-Bat	. . . .	3.00
17 JA,DH,MG,Batman, B:Huntress		
A:Demon,MK(c),A:Catwoman	.	6.00
18 MGo,JSon,BL,Huntress,BM	. .	3.00
19 MGo,JSon,BL,Huntress,BM	. .	3.00
20 MGo,JSon,DH,A:Ragman,		
ElongatedMan, Oct.–Nov.,1978	4.00

Batman: GCPD #4 © DC Comics, Inc.

BATMAN: GCPD
[Mini-Series] Aug. 1996
1 CDi(s),JAp,BSz	. . . .	2.25
2 CDi(s),JAp,BSz	. . . .	2.25
3 CDi(s), JAp,BSz,F:Montoya,		
Kitch & Bullock	. . . .	2.25
4 CDi(s), JAp,BSz, finale	. . . . . .	2.25

BATMAN: GORDON'S LAW
October 1996
1 CDi(s),KJ,Gordon looks for		
bad cops	. . . .	2.00
2 CDi(s),KJ,Gordon combats		
corruption	. . . .	2.00
3 CDi(s),KJ,	. . . .	2.00
4 (of 4) CDi(s),KJ, concl.	. . . . . .	2.00

BATMAN: GOTHAM NIGHTS
1 Gotham City Mini-series	. . . . .	2.00
2 Lives of Gotham Citizens	. . . .	2.00
3 Lives of Gotham Citizens	. . . .	2.00
4 Lives of Gotham Citizens	. . . .	2.00

BATMAN: GOTHAM NIGHTS II
1995
1 Sequel to Gotham Nights	. . . .	1.95
2 F:Carmine Sansone	. . . .	1.95

3 Fire	. . . .	1.95
4 JQ(c) Decisions	. . . .	1.95

BATMAN: JAZZ
[Mini-Series] 1995
1 I:Blue Byrd	. . . .	2.50
2 V:Brotherhood of Bop	. . . . . .	2.50
3 F:Blue Byrd	. . . .	2.50

BATMAN: LEGENDS OF THE DARK KNIGHT 1989
1 EH,Shaman of Gotham,pt.1,		
Yellow(c)	. . . .	7.00
1a Blue,Orange or Pink(c)	. . . . .	7.00
2 EH,Shaman of Gotham,pt.2	. . .	5.00
3 EH,Shaman of Gotham,pt.3	. .	4.00
4 EH,Shaman of Gotham,pt.4	. .	4.00
5 EH,Shaman of Gotham,pt.5	. .	4.00
6 KJ,Gothic,pt.1	. . . .	4.50
7 KJ,Gothic,pt.2	. . . .	4.00
8 KJ,Gothic,pt.3	. . . .	4.00
9 KJ,Gothic,pt.4	. . . .	4.00
10 KJ,Gothic,pt.5	. . . .	4.00
11 PG,TA,Prey,pt.1	. . . .	5.00
12 PG,TA,Prey,pt.2	. . . .	4.00
13 PG,TA,Prey,pt.3	. . . .	4.00
14 PG,TA,Prey,pt.4	. . . .	4.00
15 PG,TA,Prey,pt.5	. . . .	4.00
16 TVE,Venom,pt.1	. . . .	7.00
17 TVE,JL,Venom,pt.2	. . . .	7.00
18 TVE,JL,Venom,pt.3	. . . .	7.00
19 TVE,JL,Venom,pt.4	. . . .	7.00
20 TVE,JL,Venom,pt.5	. . . .	7.00
21 BS,Faith,pt.1	. . . .	2.50
22 BS,Faith,pt.2	. . . .	2.50
23 BS,Faith,pt.3	. . . .	2.50
24 GK,Flyer,pt.1	. . . .	2.50
25 GK,Flyer,pt.2	. . . .	2.50
26 GK,Flyer,pt.3	. . . .	2.50
27 Destroyer,pt.2 (Batman#474)	.	3.00
28 MWg,Faces,pt.1,V:Two-Face	.	4.00
29 MWg,Faces,pt.2,V:Two-Face	.	4.00
30 MWg,Faces,pt.3,V:Two-Face	.	4.00
31 BA,Family	. . . .	2.50
32 Blades,pt.1	. . . .	2.50
33 Blades,pt.2	. . . .	2.50
34 Blades,pt.3	. . . .	2.50
35 BHa,Destiny Pt.1	. . . .	2.50
36 BHa,Destiny Pt.2	. . . .	2.50
37 I:Mercy,V:The Cossack	. . . . .	2.50
38 KON,R:Bat-Mite	. . . .	2.50
39 BT,Mask#1	. . . .	2.50
40 BT,Mask#2	. . . .	2.50
41 Sunset	. . . .	2.25
42 CR,Hothouse #1	. . . .	2.25
43 CR,Hothouse #2,V:Poison Ivy	.	2.25
44 SMc,Turf #1	. . . .	2.25
45 Turf#2	. . . .	2.25
46 RH,A:Catwoman,V:Catman	. . .	2.50
47 RH,A:Catwoman,V:Catman	. . .	2.50
48 RH,A:Catwoman,V:Catman	. . .	2.50
49 RH,A:Catwoman,V:Catman	. . .	2.50
50 BBl,JLe,KN,KM,WS,MZ,BB,		
V:Joker	. . . .	6.00
51 JKu,A:Ragman	. . . .	2.25
52 Tao #1,V:Dragon	. . . .	2.25
53 Tao #2,V:Dragon	. . . .	2.25
54 MMi	. . . .	2.00
55 B:Watchtower	. . . .	2.00
56 CDi(s),V:Battle Guards	. . . . . .	2.00
57 CDi(s),E:Watchtower	. . . .	2.00
58 Storm	. . . .	2.50
59 DON(s),RoW,B:Qarry	. . . .	2.50
60 RoW,V:Asp	. . . .	2.50

All comics prices listed are for *Near Mint* condition.

DC COMICS

Batman: Legends of the Dark
Knight #18 © DC Comics, Inc.

61 RoW,V:Asp 2.50
62 RoW,KnightsEnd#4,A:Shiva,
　Nightwing 3.50
63 Knights End #10,V:Azrael 2.00
64 CBa 1.95
65 Joker 1.95
66 Joker 1.95
67 Going Sane,pt.3 .... 1.95
68 Going Sane,pt.4 .... 1.95
69 Criminals,pt.1 .... 1.95
70 Criminals,pt.2 .... 1.95
71 Werewolf,pt.1 .... 1.95
72 JWk(c&a),Werewolf,pt.2
　[new Miraweb format begins] .. 1.95
73 JWk(c&a),Werewolf,pt.3 ..... 1.95
74 Engins,pt.1 .... 1.95
75 Engins,pt.2 .... 1.95
76 The Sleeping,pt.1 .... 1.95
77 The Sleeping,pt.2 .... 1.95
78 The Sleeping,pt.3 .... 1.95
79 Favorite Things 1.95
80 Idols,pt.1 .... 1.95
81 Idols,pt.2 .... 1.95
82 Idols, climax 1.95
83 new villain 1.95
84 WEI(s) 1.95
85 JeR(s) 1.95
86 DgM,JWi,MGy,"Conspiracy,"
　pt.1 (of 3) 1.95
87 DgM,JWi,MGy,"Conspiracy,"pt.2 1.95
88 DgM,JWi,MGy,"Conspiracy,"pt.3 1.95
89 AlG(s),"Clay," pt. 1 .... 1.95
90 AlG(s),"Clay," pt. 2 .... 1.95
91 "Freakout," pt.1 .... 1.95
92 GEn(s),WSm,"Freakout," pt.2 . 1.95
93 GEn(s),WSm,"Freakout," pt.3 . 1.95
94 MGi(s),Saul Fisher's story 1.95
95 DAn&ALa(s),AWi,ALa,"Dirty
　Tricks" pt.1 .... 1.95
96 DAn&ALa(s),AWi,ALa,"Dirty
　Tricks" pt.2 .... 1.95
97 DAn&ALa(s),AWi,ALa,"Dirty
　Tricks" concl. 1.95
98 PJe(s),SeP,"Steps," pt.1 ..... 1.95
Ann.#1 JAp,KG,DSp,TL,JRu,
　MGo,JQ,'Duel',C:Joker 5.50
Ann.#2 MN,LMc,W:Gordn&Essen . 4.00

Ann.#3 MM,I:Cardinal Sin 3.75
Ann.#4 JSon(c),Elseworlds Story . 3.75
Ann.#5 CDi(s)Year One Annuals,
　O:Man-Bat 3.95
Ann.#6 Legends o/t Dead Earth .. 2.95
Ann.#7 Pulp Heroes (War) 3.95
Halloween Spec.I 6.95
Halloween Spec.II 4.95
Ghosts, Halloween Special 4.95
TPB Batman: Gothic, rep.Legends of
　the Dark Knight #6-#10 ..... 12.95
TPB Prey,rep.Legends of the Dark
　Knight #11–#15 .... 12.95
Collected Legends of the Dark Knight
　BB(c),rep.#32-#34,#38,
　#42-#43 .... 12.95
TPB Shaman rep.#1-#5 ...... 12.95

BATMAN:
THE LONG HALLOWEEN
October 1996

1 (of 13) JLb,TSe,Who is Holiday?
　F: usual suspects 2.95
2 JLb(s),TSe,V:Holiday,A:Solomon
　Grundy 2.95
3 JLb,TSe, ... 2.95
4 JLb(s),TSe,"New Year's Eve" .. 2.95
5 JLb(s),TSe,F:Poison Ivy, Search
　for Holiday 2.95
6 JLb(s),TSe,F:Poison Ivy,
　Catwoman 2.95
7 JLb(s),TSe,V:The Riddler 2.95
8 JLb(s),TSe,V:Scarecrow 2.95
9 JLb(s),TSe,A:Holiday,Scarecrow 2.95
10 JLb(s),TSe,V:Scarecrow,Mad
　Hatter 2.95
TPB Haunted Knight, rep. Fears,
　Madness & Ghosts 12.95

BATMAN: MAN-BAT
1995

1 R:Man-Bat, painted series ... 4.95
2 F:Marilyn Muno 4.95
3 JBo,Elseworlds story, concl. ... 4.95
TPB rep. mini-series 14.95

BATMAN: MASK OF
THE PHANTASM

1 Movie Adapt. 5.25
1a Newstand Ed. 3.25

BATMAN: MASQUE
Elseworlds

GN MGr,in turn of the century
　Gotham City 5.95

BATMAN: MR. FREEZE
1997

GN BSz(c) movie tie-in 4.95

BATMAN: MITEFALL

1 V:Bane Mite 4.95

BATMAN: POISON IVY
1997

GN BSz(c) movie tie-in 4.95

BATMAN RECORD
COMIC
1966

1 .... 1.00

BATMAN: RUN,
RIDDLER RUN
1992

1 MBg,Batman V:Riddler 5.50
2 MBg,Batman V:Riddler 5.25
3 MBg,V:Perfect Securities 5.25

BATMAN: SHADOW OF
THE BAT
1992–97

1 NB,Last Arkham Pt.1 .... 3.50
1a Collector set,w/posters,pop-up 5.50
2 NB,Last Arkham Pt.2 .... 3.00
3 NB,Last Arkham Pt.3 .... 3.00
4 NB,Last Arkham Pt.4 .... 3.00
5 NB,A:Black Spider 2.50
6 NB,I:Chancer 2.50
7 Misfits Pt.1 .... 2.50
8 Misfits Pt.2 .... 2.50
9 Misfits Pt.3 .... 2.50
10 MC,V:Mad Thane of Gotham . 2.00
11 V:Kadaver 2.00
12 V:Kadaver,A:Human Flea 2.00
13 NB,'The Nobody' 2.00
14 NB,Gotham Freaks#1 ...... 2.00
15 NB,Gotham Freaks#2 ...... 2.00
16 BBI,MM,A:Anarchy,Scarecrow . 2.00
17 BBI,V:Scarecrow 2.00
18 BBI,A:Anarchy,Scarecrow ... 2.00
19 BBI,Knightquest:The Crusade,pt.2,
　V:Gotham criminals 2.00
20 VGi,Knightquest:The Crusade,
　V:Tally Man 2.00
21 BBI,Knightquest:The Search,
　V:Mr.Asp 2.00
22 BBI,Knightquest:The Search,
　In London 2.00
23 BBI,Knightquest:The Search .. 2.00
24 BBI,Knightquest:The Crusade . 2.00
25 BSf(c),BBI,Knightquest: Crusade,
　A:Joe Public,V:Corrosive Man . 2.00
26 BSf(c),BBI,Knightquest: Crusade,
　V:Clayface 2.00
27 BSf(c),BBI,Knightquest: Crusade,
　I:Clayface Baby 2.00
28 BSf(c),BBI 2.00
29 BSf(c),BBI,KnightsEnd#2,
　A:Nightwing 3.50
30 BSf(c),BBI,KnightsEnd#8,
　V:Azrael 2.25
31 Zero Hour, V:Butler 1.95
32 Ventriloquist,Two-Face 1.95
33 Two-Face 1.95
34 V:Tally Man 1.95
35 BKi,Return of Bruce Wayne,
　Troika,pt.2 .... 1.95
35a Collectors Edition 2.95
36 Black Canary 1.95
37 Joker Hunt 1.95
38 V:The Joker 1.95
39 BSf(c),R:Solomon Grundy
　[new Miraweb format begins] .. 1.95
40 BSf(c), F:Anarky 1.95
41 Explosive Dirigible 1.95
42 .... 1.95
43 Secret of the Universe,pt1 ... 1.95
44 AlG,BSz(c) Secret of the
　Universe,pt.3 .... 1.95
45 AlG,BSz(c) 100 year old corpse 1.95
46 AlG,BSz(c) V:Cornelius Stirk .. 1.95
47 AlG,BSz(c) V:Cornelius Stirk .. 1.95
48 AlG 1.95
49 AlG,Contagion,pt.7 .... 1.95
50 AlG,Nightmare on Gotham,pt.1 1.95

51 AIG,DTy, Nightmare on
Gotham,pt.2 (of 3) 1.95
52 AIG(s),"Nightmare on Gotham,"
pt.3 . . . . 1.95
53 AIG(s),Legacy, prelude 1.95
54 AIG(s),Legacy, pt. 4, x-over . . 1.95
55 AIG(s),RBr,KJ,Bruce Wayne a
murderer? A:Nightwing 1.95
56 AIG(s),DTy,SnW,"Leaves of
Grass,pt.1,V:Poison Ivy 1.95
57 AIG(s),DTy,SnW,"Leaves of
Grass,pt.2 . . . . 1.95
58 AIG(s),DTy,SnW,"Leaves of
Grass,pt.3 . . . . 1.95
59 AIG(s),DTy,SnW,"Killer,"
Killer," pt.1 . . . . 1.95
60 AIG(s),DTy,SnW,"Killer,
Killer," pt.2 . . . . 1.95
61 AIG(s),JAp,SnW,night of
second chances 1.95
62 AIG(s),DTy,SnW,Two-Face, pt.1 1.95
63 AIG(s),DTy,SnW,Two-Face, pt.2 1.95
64 AIG(s),DTy,SnW,A:Jason Blood 1.95
65 AIG(s),NBy,JRu, A:Oracle, pt.1 1.95
66 AIG(s),NBy,JRu, V:Thinker,
Cheat, pt.2 . . . . 1.95
Ann.#1 TVE,DG,Bloodlines#3,
I:Joe Public 3.75
Ann.#2 Elseworlds story 3.95
Ann.#3 Year One Annual 3.95
Ann.#4 Legends of the Dead
Earth 2.95
Ann.#5 Pulp Heroes (Romance) . . 3.95

BATMAN: SWORD OF AZRAEL
1992–93
1 JQ,KN,I:Azrael 22.00
2 JQ,KN,A:Azrael 12.00
3 JQ,KN,V:Biis,A:Azrael 12.00
4 JQ,KN,V:Biis,A:Azrael 12.00
TPB rep.#1-#4 . . . . 11.00
TPB Platinum 25.00

BATMAN/ GREEN ARROW: THE POISON TOMORROW
1 MN,JRu,V:Poison Ivy 6.25

BATMAN/GRENDEL: DEVIL'S MASQUE & DEVIL'S RIDDLE
1 MWg,Batman meets Grendel . . 5.25
2 MWg,Batman Vs. Grendel 5.25

BATMAN/JUDGE DREDD: VENDETTA IN GOTHAM
1 AIG(s),V:Ventriliquist 5.25

BATMAN/PUNISHER LAKE OF FIRE
1 DON(s),BKi,A:Punisher,
V:Jigsaw 5.25

BATMAN/SPAWN: WAR DEVIL
1 DgM,CDi,AIG(s),KJ,V:Croatoan 6.00
GN CDi,AIG 4.95

BATMAN: THE ULTIMATE EVIL
1 V:Child Abuse 5.95

BATMAN: VENOM
TPB TVE 9.95

Batman vs. Predator #3
© DC Comics, Inc.

BATMAN vs. PREDATOR
DC/Dark Horse 1991–92
1 NKu,AKu,inc.8 trading cards
bound in (Prestige) 6.00
1a Newsstand 5.00
2 NKu,AKu,Inc. pinups (prestige) 5.00
2a Newsstand 4.00
3 NKu,AKu,conclusion,inc.
8 trading cards (Prestige) 5.00
3a Newsstand 4.00
TPB,rep.#1-#3 . . . . 5.95

BATMAN vs. PREDATOR II BLOODMATCH
1994–95
1 R:Predators 2.75
2 A:Huntress 2.50
3 Assassins 2.50
4 V:Head Hunters 2.50
TPB Rep.#1-#4 . . . . 6.95

BATMAN/WILDCAT
Feb. 1997
1 (of 3) CDi&BSt(s),SCi,ATi,
Batman and Robin discover
Secret Ring of combat 2.25
2 CDi&BSt(s),SCi,V:KGBeast,
Willis Danko 2.25
3 CDi&BSt(s),SCi, Batman vs.
Wildcat, concl. 2.25

BATTLE CLASSICS
Sept.–Oct., 1978
1 JKu, reprints 1.50

BEAUTIFUL STORIES FOR UGLY CHILDREN
Piranha Press 1989–91
1 thru 11 . . . . @2.00
12 thru 14 . . . . @2.50
15 Blood Day 2.50
16 thru 23 . . . . @2.50

BEOWOLF
April-May, 1975
1 thru 5 . . . . @1.00
6 Feb.–March, 1976 . . . . 1.00

BEST OF THE BRAVE & THE BOLD
1 JL(c),NA,rep.B&B #85. . . . . . . 2.50
2 JL(c),NA,rep.B&B #81 . . . . 2.50
3 JL(c),NA,rep.B&B #82 . . . . 2.50
4 JL(c),NA,rep.B&B #80 . . . . 2.50
5 JL(c),NA,rep.B&B #93 . . . . 2.50
6 JL(c),NA,rep.B&B #83 . . . . 2.50

BEWARE THE CREEPER
1968–69
1 . . . . 12.00
2 thru 6 . . . . @7.50

BIG ALL-AMERICAN COMIC BOOK
Dec., 1944
1 JKu 11,000.00

BIG BOOK OF FUN COMICS
Spring, 1936
1 . . . . 12,000.00

BIG BOOK OF CONSPIRACIES, THE
DC/Paradox Press B&W 1995
TPB 12.95

BIG BOOK OF DEATH, THE
DC/Paradox Press B&W 1994
TPB 12.95

BIG BOOK OF HOAXES, THE
DC/Paradox Press B&W Sept. 1996
TPB 14.95

BIG BOOK OF LITTLE CRIMINALS, THE
DC/Paradox Press B&W 1996
TPB 14.95

BIG BOOK OF LOSERS, THE
DC/Paradox Press B&W
TPB by Paul Kirchner 14.95

BIG BOOK OF THUGS, THE
DC/Paradox B&W Oct. 1996
TPB 14.95

DC COMICS

BIG BOOK OF THE UNEXPLAINED
DC/Paradox B&W April 1997
GN DgM(s),strange phenomena . 14.95

BIG BOOK OF URBAN LEGENDS, THE
DC/Paradox B&W 1994
TPB 12.95

BIG BOOK OF WEIRDOS, THE
DC/Paradox Press B&W 1995
TPB 12.95

BIRDS OF PREY: MANHUNT
1996
1 CDi(s),MHy,F:Black Canary,
  Oracle 1.95
2 CDi(s),MHy,V,Archer Braun,
  A:Catwoman 1.95
3 CDi(s),MHy,V:Catwoman,
  Huntress 1.95
4 CDi(s),MHy,V:Lady Shiva 1.95

BIRDS OF PREY: REVOLUTION
one-shot CDi(s),BMc 2.95

Black Canary #7 © DC Comics, Inc.

BLACK CANARY
[Limited Series] 1991–92
1 TVE/DG,New Wings,pt.1 . . . . . . 2.25
2 TVE/DG,New Wings,pt.2 . . . . . 2.00
3 TVE/DG,New Wings,pt.3 . . . . . 2.00
4 TVE/DG,New Wings,pt.4,Conc . 2.00
[Regular Series] 1993
1 TVE,Hero Worship,pt.1 . . . . . . 2.25
2 TVE,Hero Worship,pt.2 . . . . . 2.00
3 TVE,Hero Worship,pt.3 . . . . . 2.00
4 TVE,V:Whorrsman 2.00
5 . . . . 2.00
6 Blynde Woman's Bluff 2.00
7 TVE,V:Maniacal Killer 2.00

8 . . . . 1.75
9 A:Huntress 1.75
10 TVE,A:Nightwing,Huntress . . . 1.75
11 TVE,A:Nightwing 1.75
12 final issue 1.75

BLACK CANARY/ORACLE: BIRDS OF PREY
1996
1-shot DDi, double size 3.95

BLACK CONDOR
1992–93
1 I&O:Black Condor 1.25
2 V:Sky Pirate 1.25
3 V:Sky Pirate 1.25
4 V:The Shark 1.25
5 V:Mind Force 1.25
6 V:Mind Force 1.25
7 Forest Fire 1.25
8 MG,In Jail 1.25
9 A:The Ray 1.25
10 . . . . 1.25
11 O:Black Condor 1.25

BLACKHAWK
Prev: Golden Age
1957–1984
108 DD,CCu,DD&CCu(c),The
   Threat from the Abyss
   A:Blaisie 450.00
109 DD,CCu,DD&CCu(c),The
   Avalance Kid 125.00
110 DD,CCu,DD&CCu(c),Mystery
   of Tigress Island 125.00
111 DD,CCu,DD&CCu(c),Menace
   of the Machines 125.00
112 DD,CCu,DD(c),The Doomed
   Dog Fight 125.00
113 DD,CCu,CCu(c),Volunteers
   of Doom 125.00
114 DD,CCu,DD&CCu(c),Gladiators
   of Blackhawk Island 125.00
115 DD,CCu,DD&CCu(c),The
   Tyrant's Return 125.00
116 DD,CCu,DD&CCu(c),Prisoners
   of the Black Island 125.00
117 DD,CCu,DD&CCu(c),Menace
   of the Dragon Boat 125.00
118 DD,CCu,DD&SMo(c),FF,The
   Bandit With 1,000 Nets . . . 135.00
119 DD,CCu,DD&SMo(c),
   V:Chief Blackhawk 75.00
120 DD,CCu,DD&SMo(c),The
   Challenge of the Wizard . . . 75.00
121 DD,CCu,DD&CCu(c),Secret
   Weapon of the Archer 75.00
122 DD,CCu,DD&CCu(c),The
   Movie That Backfired 75.00
123 DD,CCu,DD&CCu(c),The
   Underseas Gold Fort 75.00
124 DD,CCu,DD&CCu(c),Thieves
   With A Thousand Faces 75.00
125 DD,CCu,DD&CCu(c),Secrets
   o/t Blackhawk Time Capsule . 75.00
126 DD,CCu,DD&CCu(c),Secret
   of the Glass Fort 75.00
127 DD,CCu,DD&CCu(c),Blackie-
   The Winged Sky Fighter 75.00
128 DD,CCu,DD&CCu(c),The
   Vengeful Bowman 75.00
129 DD,CCu,DD&CCu(c),The
   Cavemen From 3,000 B.C. . . . 75.00
130 DD,CCu,DD&SMo(c),The

Mystery Missle From Space . 75.00
131 DD,CCu,DD&CCu(c),The
   Return of the Rocketeers . . . 60.00
132 DD,CCu,DD&CCu(c),Raid
   of the Rocketeers 60.00
133 DD,CCu,DD&CCu(c),Human
   Dynamo 60.00
134 DD,CC,DD&CC(c),The
   Sinister Snowman 60.00
135 DD,CCu,DD&CCu(c),The
   Underworld Supermarket . . . 60.00
136 DD,CCu,DD&CCu(c),The
   Menace of the Smoke-Master 60.00
137 DD,CCu,DD&CCu(c),The
   Weapons That Backfired 60.00
138 DD,CCu,DD&SMo(c),The
   Menace of the Blob 60.00
139 DD,CCu,DD&CCu(c),The
   Secret Blackhawk 60.00
140 DD,CCu,DD&CCu(c),The
   Space Age Marauders 60.00
141 DD,CCu,DD&CCu(c),Crimes
   of the Captive Masterminds . . 50.00
142 DD,CCu,DD&CCu(c),Alien
   Blackhawk Chief 50.00
143 DD,SMo,DD&CCu(c),Lady
   Blackhawk's Rival 50.00
144 DD,CCu,DD&CCu(c),The
   Underworld Sportsmen 50.00
145 DD,CCu,DD&CCu(c),The
   Deadly Lensman 50.00
146 DD,CCu,DD&CCu(c),The
   Fantastic Fables of Blackhawk 50.00
147 DD,SMo,DD&CCu(c),The
   Blackhawk Movie Queen 50.00
148 DD,CCu,DD&CCu(c),Four
   Dooms For The Blackhawks . 50.00
149 DD,CCu,DD&CCu(c),Masks
   of Doom 50.00
150 DD,CCu,DD&SMo(c),
   Blackhawk Mascot from Space 35.00
151 DD,CCu,DD&CCu(c),Lost City 35.00
152 DD,CCu,DD&SMo(c),Noah's
   Ark From Space 35.00
153 DD,CCu,DD&SMo(c),
   Boomerang Master 35.00
154 DD,CCu,DD&SMo(c),The
   Beast Time Forgot 35.00
155 DD,CCu,DD&CCu(c),Killer
   Shark's Land Armada 35.00
156 DD,CCu,DD&SMo(c),Peril of
   the Plutonian Raider 35.00
157 DD,CCu,DD&SMo(c),Secret
   of the Blackhawk Sphinx 35.00
158 DD,CCu,DD&SMo(c),Bandit
   Birds From Space 35.00
159 DD,CCu,DD&SMo(c),Master
   of the Puppet Men 35.00
160 DD,CCu,DD&CCu(c),The
   Phantom Spy 35.00
161 DD,SMo,DD&SMo(c),Lady
   Blackhawk's Crime Chief . . . 35.00
162 DD,CCu,DD&CCu(c),The
   Invisible Blackhawk 35.00
163 DD,CCu,DD&SMo(c),
   Fisherman of Crime 35.00
164 DD,O:Blackhawk retold 40.00
165 DD,V:League of Anti
   Blackhawks 30.00
166 DD,A:Lady Blackhawk 30.00
167 DD,The Blackhawk Bandits . 30.00
168 DD,Blackhawk Time
   Travelers 25.00
169 DD,Sinister Hunts of Mr.
   Safari 25.00

DC COMICS

170 DD,A:Lady Blackhawk,V:Killer
  Shark 25.00
171 DD,Secret of Alien Island . . 25.00
172 DD,Challenge of the
  GasMaster 20.00
173 DD,The Super Jungle Man . 20.00
174 DD,Andre's Impossible
  World 20.00
175 DD,The Creature with
  Blackhawk's Brain 20.00
176 DD,Stone Age Blackhawks . . 15.00
177 DD,Town that time Forgot . . 15.00
178 DD,Return of the Scorpions . 15.00
179 DD,Invisible Dr.Dunbar 14.00
180 DD,Son of Blackhawk 15.00
181 DD,I:Tom Thumb Blackhawk . 10.00
182 DD,A:Lady Blackhawk 10.00
183 DD,V:Killer Shark 10.00
184 DD,Island of Super
  Monkeys 10.00
185 DD,Last 7 days of the
  Blackhawks 10.00
186 DD,A:Lady Blackhawk 10.00
187 DD,V:Porcupine 11.00
188 DD,A:Lady Blackhawk 11.00
189 DD:O:rtd 11.00
190 DD,FantasticHumanStarfish . 12.00
191 DD,A:Lady Blackhawk 10.00
192 DD,V:King Condor 9.00
193 DD,The Jailer's Revenge . . . 9.00
194 DD,The Outlaw Blackhawk . . 9.00
195 DD,A:Tom Thumb Blackhawk . 9.00
196 DD,Blackhawk WWII Combat
  Diary story 9.00
197 DD:new look 9.00
198 DD:O:rtd 11.00
199 DD,Attack with the Mummy
  Insects 10.00
200 DD,A:Lady Blackhawk,
  I:Queen Killer Shark 10.00
201 DD,Blackhawk Detached Diary
  Story,F:Hendrickson 10.00
202 DD,Combat Diary,F:Andre . . 10.00
203 DD:O:Chop-Chop 10.00
204 DD,A:Queen Killer Shark . . 10.00
205 DD,Combat Diary story 10.00
206 DD,Combat Diary, F:Olaf . . . 10.00
207 DD,Blackhawk Devil Dolls . . 10.00
208 DD,Detached service diary
  F:Chuck 10.00
209 DD,V:King Condor 10.00
210 DD,Danger..Blackhawk Bait
  rep.Blackhawk #139. . . . . 6.00
211 DD,GC,Detached service
  diary 7.00
212 DD,Combat Diary,
  F:Chop-Chop 7.00
213 DD,Blackhawk goes
  Hollywood 7.00
214 DD,Team of Traitors 7.00
215 DD,Detached service diary
  F:Olaf 7.00
216 DD,A:Queen Killer Shark . . 7.00
217 DD,Detached service diary
  F:Stanislaus 7.00
218 DD,7 against Planet Peril . . 7.00
219 DD,El Blackhawk Peligroso . 7.00
220 DD,The Revolt of the
  Assembled Man 7.00
221 DD,Detach service diary
  F:Hendrickson 6.00
222 DD,The Man from E=MC2 . . 6.00
223 DD,V:Mr.Quick CHange 6.00
224 DD,Combat Diary,
  F:Stanislaus 6.00

Blackhawk 3rd Series #11
© DC Comics, Inc.

225 DD,A:Queen Killer Shark . . . 6.00
226 DD,Secret Monster of
  Blackhawk Island 6.00
227 DD,Detached Service diary
  F:Chop-Chop 6.00
228 DD (1st art on JLA characters)
  Blackhawks become super-heroes,
  Junk-Heap heroes #1(C:JLA) . 6.00
229 DD,Junk-Heap Heroes #2
  (C:JLA) 6.00
230 DD,Junk-Heap Heroes concl.
  (C:JLA) 6.00
231 DD,A:Lady Blackhawk 6.00
232 DD,A:Lady Blackhawk 6.00
233 DD,Too Late,The Leaper . . . 6.00
234 DD,The Terrible Twins 6.00
235 DD,A Coffin for
  a Blackhawk 6.00
236 DD,Melt,Mutant, Melt 6.00
237 DD,Magnificent 7 Assassins . 6.00
238 DD,Walking Booby-Traps . . . 6.00
239 DD,The Killer That Time
  Forgot 6.00
240 DD,He Who Must Die 6.00
241 DD,A Blackhawk a Day 6.00
242 Blackhawks back in blue &
  black costumes 6.00
243 Mission Incredible (1968) . . . 6.00
244 GE,new costumes,Blackhawks
  become mercenaries (1976) . . . 2.00
245 GE,Death's Double Deal 2.00
246 RE,GE,Death's Deadly Dawn . 2.00
247 RE,AM,Operation:Over Kill . . 2.00
248 JSh,Vengeance is Mine!..
  Sayeth the Cyborg 2.00
249 RE,GE,V:Sky-Skull 2.00
250 RE,GE,FS,D:Chuck(1977) . . 2.00
251 DSp,Back to WWII(1982) . . . 2.00
252 thru 258 DSp . . . . @2.00
259 . . . . 2.00
260 HC,ATh 2.00
261 thru 271 DSp . . . . @2.00
272 . . . . 2.00
273 DSp 2.00
274 DSp 2.00

[2nd Series]
1 HC Mini-series,Blackhawk accused

of communism 4.50
2 HC,visits Soviet Union 3.50
3 HC,Atom Bomb threat to N.Y. . 3.50

[3rd Series]
1 All in color for a Crime,pt.1
  I:The Real Lady Blackhawk . . . 1.50
2 All in color for a Crime,pt.2 . . . 1.50
3 Agent Rescue Attempt in Rome 1.50
4 Blackhawk's girlfriend murdered 1.50
5 I:Circus Organization 1.50
6 Blackhawks on false mission . . 1.50
7 V:Circus,A:Suicide Squad, rep.
  1st Blackhawk story 2.50
8 Project: Assimilation 1.50
9 V:Grundfest 1.50
10 Blackhawks Attacked 1.50
11 Master plan revealed 1.50
12 Raid on BlackhawkAirwaysHQ . 1.75
13 Team Member Accused of . . . 1.75
14 Blackhawk test pilots 1.75
15 Plans for independence 1.75
16 Independence, final issue 1.75
Ann.#1 Hawks in Albania 2.95
Spec.#1 Assassination of JFK
  to Saigon,1975 . . . . 3.50

BLACK HOOD
Impact 1991–92
1 O:Black Hood 1.25
2 Nick Cray becomes Black Hood 1.00
3 New Year's Eve,A:Creeptures . 1.00
4 Nate Cray become Black Hood,
  Dr.M.Harvey becomes Ozone . 1.00
5 E:Nate Cray as Black Hood
  V:Ozone 1.00
6 New Black Hood 1.00
7 History of Seaside City 1.25
8 V:Hit Coffee 1.25
9 V:Hit Coffee 1.25
10 Slime of Your Life #1 . . . . 1.25
11 Slime of Your Life #2 . . . . 1.25
12 Final Issue 1.25
Ann#1 Earthquest,w/trading card . 2.50

BLACK LAMB, THE
DC/Helix Sept. 1996
1 TT,Vampire saga 2.50
2 TT,war between werewolf clans 2.50
3 TT,O:Black Lamb,V:Lykaon . . . 2.50
4 TT thru 6 . . . . @2.50

BLACK LIGHTNING
1977–78
1 TVE/FS,I&O:Black Lightning . . 3.50
2 TVE/FS,A:Talia 2.00
3 TVE,I:Tobias Whale 2.00
4 TVE,A:Jimmy Olsen 2.00
5 TVE,A:Superman 2.00
6 TVE,I:Syonide 2.00
7 TVE,V:Syonide 2.00
8 TVE,V:Tobias Whale 2.00
9 TVE,V:Annihilist 2.00
10 TVE,V:Trickster 2.00
11 TVE,BU:The Ray 2.50
[2nd Series] 1995–96
1 He's Back 1.95
2 V:Painkiller 1.95
3 V:Painkiller 1.95
4 V:Painkiller,Royal Family 1.95
5 Flashbacks of Past 1.95
6 V:Gangbuster 2.25
7 V:Gangbuster 2.25
8 V:Tobias Whale 2.25
9 I&V:Demolition 2.25

DC COMICS

DC COMICS

10 Jefferson Pierce becomes Black
    Lightning full time 2.25
11 Hunt for Sick Nick 2.25
12 V:Sick Nick's death squad . . 2.25
13 final issue 2.25

BLACK MASK
1993–94
1 I:Black Mask 5.00
2 V:Underworld 5.00
3 V:Valentine 5.00

BLACK ORCHID
1993–95
1 DMc,O:Black Orchid,
    A:Batman,Luthor,Poison Ivy . 7.50
2 DMc,O:cont,Arkham Asylum . . 9.00
3 DMc,A:SwampThing,conc. 7.00
TPB rep. #1 thru #3 . . . . 20.00
Vertigo
1 DMc(c),B:DiF(s),JIT,SnW,I:Sherilyn
    Somers,I:Logos,F:Walt Brody . 2.50
1a Platinum Ed. 12.00
2 JIT,SnW,Uprooting,V:Logos . . . 2.25
3 JIT,SnW,Tainted Zone,
    V:Fungus 2.25
4 JIT,SnW,I:Nick & Orthia 2.25
5 DMc(c),JIT,SnW,
    A:Swamp Thing 2.25
6 JIT,BMc(i),God in the Cage . . . 2.25
7 JIT,RGu,SnW,
    Upon the Threshold 2.25
8 DMc(c),RGu,A:Silent People . . 2.25
9 DMc(c),RGu 2.25
10 DMc(c),RGu 2.25
11 DMc(c),RGu,In Tennessee . . . 2.25
12 DMc(c),RGu 2.25
13 DMc(c),RGu,F:Walt Brody 2.25
14 DMc(c),RGu,Black Annis 1.95
15 DMc(c),RGu,Kobolds 1.95
16 DMc(c),RGu,Suzy,Junkin . . . 1.95
17 Twisted Season,pt.1 . . . . 1.95
18 Twisted Season,pt.2 . . . . 1.95
19 Twisted Season,pt.3 . . . . 1.95
20 Twisted Season,pt.4 . . . . 1.95
21 Twisted Season,pt.5 . . . . 1.95
22 Twisted Season,pt.6, final iss. . 2.25
Ann.#1 DMc(c),DiF(s),GyA,JnM,F:Suzy,
    Childrens Crusade,BU:retells
    Adventure Comics#430 . . . . . . 4.25

BLASTERS SPECIAL
1989
1 A:Snapper Carr, Spider Guild . 2.00

BLOOD: A TALE
DC/Vertigo Sept. 1996
[Mini-series,
re-release of Marvel Epic]
1 JMD(s),KW, quest for truth
    begins 2.95
2 JMD(s),KW, Blood falls in love . 2.95
3 JMD(s),KW, companion dies . . 2.95
4 JMD(s),KW, finale 2.95

BLOOD & SHADOWS
(Vertigo) 1996
1 . . . . 5.95
2 Journal of Justice Jones 5.95
3 Chet Daley flung into
    21st century 5.95
4 V:God of the Razor, finale 5.95

BLOODBATH
1993
1 A:Superman 3.75
2 A:New Heroes 3.75

BLOODPACK
[Mini-Series] 1995
1 I:Blood Pack, V:Demolition . . . 1.50
2 A:Superboy 1.50
3 Loira's Corpse 1.50
4 Real Heroes Final Issue 1.50

Blood Syndicate #1 © DC Comics, Inc.

BLOOD SYNDICATE
(Milestone) 1993–96
1 I:Blood Syndicate,Rob Chaplick,
    Dir.Mark.Ed.,w/B puzzle piece,
    Skybox card,Poster 3.50
1a Newstand Ed. 2.00
2 I:Boogieman,Tech-9 Vs.
    Holocaust 1.75
3 V:S.Y.S.T.E.M.,I:Mom,D:Tech-9 1.75
4 V:S.Y.S.T.E.M. 1.75
5 I:John Wing,Kwai,Demon Fox . 1.75
6 V:John Wing 1.75
7 I:Edmund,Cornelia 1.75
8 V:Demon Fox 1.75
9 O:Blood Syndicate,I:Templo . . 1.75
10 WS(c),Ccs,Shadow War,I:Iota,
    Sideshow,Rainsaw,Slag,Ash,
    Bad Betty,Oro 2.25
11 IV(s),Ccs,A:Aquamaria 1.75
12 IV(s),Ccs,V:Dinosaur 1.75
13 IV(s),Ccs,B:Roach War 1.75
14 IV(s),Ccs,V:Roaches 1.75
15 IV(s),Ccs,E:Roach War 1.75
16 IV(s),Ccs,Worlds Collide#6,
    A:Superman 1.75
17 Ccs,Worlds Collide#13,V:Rift . . 1.75
18 Ccs,V:S.Y.S.T.E.M. 1.75
19 . . . . 1.75
20 . . . . 1.75
21 . . . . 1.75
22 . . . . 1.75
23 F:Boogieman 1.75
24 L:Third Rail,Brickhouse 1.75
25 R:Tech-9 . . . . 2.95
26 Return of the Dead 1.75

27 R:Masquerade 1.75
28 Tech-9 takes control 2.50
29 Reader's Choice 0.99
30 Long Hot Summer 2.50
31 V:New Threat 2.50
32 MC(c),V:Soulbreaker 2.50
33 Kwai returns to paris Island . . . 0.99
34 Visit to Kwen Lun 2.50
35 final issue 3.50

BLOODY MARY
DC/Helix Aug. 1996
1 (of 4) GEn(s),CE, near-
    future war 2.25
2 thru 4 GEn(s),CE, near-future
    war, concl. . . . . @2.25

BLOODY MARY:
LADY LIBERTY
DC/Helix July 1996
1 (of 4) GEn(s),CE, ... 2.50

BLUE BEETLE
1986–88
1 O:Blue Beetle 1.50
2 V:Fire Fist 1.00
3 V:Madmen 1.00
4 V:Doctor Alchemy 1.00
5 A:Question 1.00
6 V:Question 1.00
7 A:Question 1.00
8 A:Chronos 1.00
9 A:Chronos 1.00
10 Legends, V:Chronos 1.00
11 A:New Teen Titans 1.00
12 A:New Teen Titans 1.00
13 A:New Teen Titans 1.00
14 Pago Island,I:Catalyst 1.00
15 RA:V:Carapax 1.00
16 RA,Chicago Murders 1.00
17 R:Dan Garrett/Blue Beetle . . . 1.00
18 D:Dan Garrett 1.00
19 RA,R:Dr. Cyber 1.00
20 RA,Millennium,A:JLI 1.00
21 RA,A:Mr.Miracle,
    Millennium tie in 1.00
22 RA,Prehistoric Chicago 1.00

Blue Beetle #14 © DC Comics, Inc.

DC COMICS

23 DH,V:The Madmen 1.00
24 DH,final issue 1.00

BLUE DEVIL
1984–86
1 O:Blue Devil 2.00
2 . . . . 1.50
3 A:Superman 1.50
4 A:JLA 1.50
5 . . . . 1.50
6 EC,I:Bolt 1.00
7 KG 1.00
8 GV 1.00
9 thru 16 . . . . @1.00
17 Crisis 1.25
18 Crisis 1.25
19 . . . . 1.00
20 RM,Halloween 1.00
21 RM,I:Roadmaster 1.00
22 RM,A:Jorj & Lehni 1.00
23 A:Jorj & Lehni 1.00
24 V:Blue Devil Toys 1.00
25 Mary Frances Cassidy 1.00
26 Special Baseball issue 1.00
27 Godfrey Goose 1.00
28 real live fan guest star 1.00
29 . . . . 1.00
30 Double sized 1.25
31 BSz,V:Seraph 1.25
Ann.#1 . . . . 1.50

BOB, THE GALACTIC BUM
[Mini-Series] 1995
1 A:Lobo 2.00
2 Planet Gnulp,A:Lobo 2.00
3 V:Khunds 2.00
4 Rando's Coronation 2.00

BOMBA, THE JUNGLE BOY
1967–68
1 CI,MA,I:Bomba 15.00
2 thru 7 . . . . @10.00

BOOK OF FATE, THE
1 KG(s),RoW,BR, ... 2.25
2 KG(s),RoW,BR,"The Chaos-
　Order War," pt.1 (of 4) 2.25
3 KG(s),RoW,BR,"The Chaos-
　Order War," pt.2 . . . . 2.25
4 KG(s),RoW,BR,"The Chaos-
　Order War," pt.3, A:Two-Face . 2.25
5 KG(s),RoW,BR,"The Chaos-
　Order War," pt.4 . . . . 2.25
6 KG(s),RoW,BR,Convergence,"
　pt.1 x-over 2.25
7 KG(s),RoW,BR, Signs, pt.1 . . . 2.25
8 KG(s),RoW,BR, Signs, pt.2 . . . 2.25

BOOKS OF FAERIE, THE
DC/Vertigo Jan. 1997
1 PrG,F:Titania and Auberon . . . 2.50
2 PrG, ... 2.50
3 (of 3) PrG 2.50

BOOKS OF MAGIC
[Limited Series] 1990–91
1 B:NGa(s),JBo,F:Phantom Stranger,
　A:J.Constantine,Tim Hunter,
　Doctor Occult,Mister E 12.00
2 SHp,F:J.Constantine,A:Spectre,
　Dr.Fate,Demon,Zatanna 12.00
3 CV,F:Doctor Occult,

A:Sandman 10.00
4 E:NGa(s),PuJ,F:Mr.E,A:Death 10.00
TPB rep.#1-#4 . . . . 20.00

[Regular Series]
Vertigo 1994–97
1 MkB,B:Bindings,R:Tim Hunter . 6.00
1a Platinum Edition 15.00
2 CV(c),MkB,V:Manticore 5.00
3 CV(c),MkB,E:Bindings 5.00
4 CV(c),MkB,A:Death 6.00
5 CV(c),I:Khara 4.00
6 Sacrifices,pt.I 4.00
7 Sacrifices,pt.II 4.00
8 Tim vs. evil Tim 4.00
9 Artificial Heart,pt.1 . . . . 3.50
10 Artificial Heart,pt.2 . . . . 3.50
11 Artificial Heart,pt.3 . . . . 3.50
12 Small Glass Worlds,pt.1 . . . . 3.50
13 Small Glass Worlds,pt.2 . . . . 3.50
14 CV(c),A:The Wobbly 3.00
15 Hell and Back,pt.1 . . . . 3.00
16 Hall and Back,pt.2 . . . . 3.00
17 Playgrounds,pt.1 . . . . 3.00
18 JNR,PrG,Playgrounds,cont. . . 3.00
19 JNR,PrG,Playgrounds,concl. . . 3.00
20 Barabatos gives the orders . . 3.00
21 JNR,PrG,Molly seeks Mayra . . 3.00
22 . . . . 3.00
23 JNR,V:Margraves Strafenkinder 3.00
24 JNR,PrG,F:Molly vs. Amadan . 3.00
25 JNR,PrG,Death and the Endless 3.00
26 JNR,PrG,Rites of Passage, pt.1 3.00
27 JNR,PrG,Rites of Passage, pt.2 3.00
28 JNR,PrG,Rites of Passage, pt.3,
　Cupid & Psyche 3.00
29 JNR,PrG,"Rite of Passage" . . 2.50
30 JNR,PrG,"Rite of Passage" . . 2.50
31 JNR,PrG,"Rite of Passage" . . 2.50
32 JNR(s),PSj,"Rites of Passage" 2.50
33 JNR(s),PSj,"Rites of Passage" 2.50
34 JNR(s),PSj,"Rites of Passage" 2.50
35 JNR(s),PrG,"Rites of Passage" 2.50
36 JNR,"Rites of Passage" cont . . 2.50
37 JNR,"Rites of Passage" cont. . 2.50
38 JNR,"Rites of Passage" concl. . 2.50
39 PrG, at Sphinx casino 2.50
40 JNR(s),F:Tim & Molly 2.50
TPB Rep. #5-#13 & Rave #1 . . . 12.95
TPB Reckonings, 192pg.
　rep. #14–#20 . . . . 12.95

BOOSTER GOLD
1986–88
1 DJ,V:Blackguard 3.00
2 DJ,V:Minddancer 2.50
3 DJ,V:Minddancer 2.00
4 DJ,V:Minddancer 1.50
5 DJ,V:Fascinator 1.50
6 DJ,A:Superman 1.00
7 DJ,A:Superman 1.00
8 DJ,A:Braniac 5,Cham.Boy,
　Ultra Boy,pt.1 . . . . 1.25
9 DJ,A:Braniac 5,Cham.Boy,
　Ultra Boy,pt.2 . . . . 1.25
10 DJ,V:1000 . . . . 1.00
11 DJ,V:Shockwave 1.00
12 DJ,Booster Weakening 1.00
13 DJ,I:Rip Hunter(modern) 1.00
14 DJ,Rip Hunter 1.00
15 DJ,Rip Hunter 1.00
16 DJ,Boosters new company . . . 1.00
17 DJ,A:Cheshire & Hawk 1.00
18 DJ,V:Broderick 1.00
19 DJ,V:Rainbow Raider 1.00
20 DJ,V:Rainbow Raider 1.00

Booster Gold #24 © DC Comics, Inc.

21 DJ,Goldstar captured by aliens 1.00
22 DJ,A:J.L.I.,D:Goldstar 1.00
23 DJ,A:Superman & Luthor 1.25
24 DJ,Millenium 1.00
25 DJ,last issue 1.00

BOY COMMANDOS
Winter, 1942–43
1 S&K,O:Liberty Belle;Sandman
　& Newsboy Legion 4,200.00
2 S&K 1,100.00
3 S&K 700.00
4 . . . . 500.00
5 . . . . 500.00
6 S&K 450.00
7 S&K 350.00
8 S&K 350.00
9 . . . . 350.00
10 S&K 350.00
11 Infinity(c) 350.00
12 thru 16 . . . . @175.00
17 Science Fiction(c) 225.00
18 . . . . 175.00
19 . . . . 175.00
20 . . . . 200.00
21 . . . . 150.00
22 . . . . 150.00
23 S&K,S&K,(c) 175.00
24 . . . . 160.00
25 . . . . 160.00
26 Science Fiction(c) 200.00
27 . . . . 150.00
28 . . . . 150.00
29 S&K story 160.00
30 Baseball Storm 160.00
31 . . . . 150.00
32 A:Dale Evans(c) 160.00
33 . . . . 150.00
34 I:Wolf 150.00
35 . . . . 150.00
36 Nov.–Dec., 1949 . . . . 225.00

BRAVE AND THE BOLD
Aug.–Sept., 1955
1 JKu,RH,IN,I:VikingPrince,Golden
　Gladiator,Silent Knight . . . 2,500.00
2 F:Viking Prince 1,200.00

DC COMICS

3 F:Viking Prince	600.00
4 F:Viking Prince	600.00
5 B:Robin Hood	650.00
6 JKu,F:Robin Hood,E:Golden Gladiator	450.00
7 JKu,F:Robin Hood	450.00
8 JKu,F:Robin Hood	450.00
9 JKu,F:Robin Hood	450.00
10 JKu,F:Robin Hood	450.00
11 JKu,F:Viking Prince	325.00
12 JKu,F:Viking Prince	325.00
13 JKu,F:Viking Prince	325.00
14 JKu,F:Viking Prince	300.00
15 JKu,F:Viking Prince	300.00
16 JKu,F:Viking Prince	300.00
17 JKu,F:Viking Prince	300.00
18 JKu,F:Viking Prince	300.00
19 JKu,F:Viking Prince	300.00
20 JKu,F:Viking Prince	300.00
21 JKu,F:Viking Prince	300.00
22 JKu,F:Viking Prince	300.00
23 JKu,O:Viking Prince	450.00
24 JKu,E:Viking Prince,Silent Knight	300.00
25 RA,I&B:Suicide Squad	400.00
26 F:Suicide Squad	300.00
27 Creature of Ghost Lake	275.00
28 I:Justice League of America,O:Snapper Carr	5,000.00
29 F:Justice League	2,400.00
30 F:Justice League	2,000.00
31 F:Cave Carson	350.00
32 F:Cave Carson	250.00
33 F:Cave Carson	250.00
34 JKu,I&O:S.A. Hawkman	2,000.00
35 JKu:F:Hawkman	500.00
36 JKu:F:Hawkman	500.00
37 F:Suicide Squad	450.00
38 F:Suicide Squad	225.00
39 F:Suicide Squad	225.00
40 JKu,F:Cave Carson	150.00
41 F:Cave Carson	150.00
42 JKu,F:Hawkman	300.00
43 JKu,O:Hawkman	350.00
44 JKu,F:Hawkman	250.00
45 CI,F:Strange Sports	75.00
46 CI,F:Strange Sports	75.00
47 CI,F:Strange Sports	75.00
48 CI,F:Strange Sports	75.00
49 CI,F:Strange Sports	75.00
50 F:GreenArrow & JonnJ'onzz	175.00
51 F:Aquaman & Hawkman	250.00
52 JKu,F:Sgt.Rock	125.00
53 ATh,F:Atom & Flash	75.00
54 I&O:Teen Titans	275.00
55 F:Metal Man & Atom	50.00
56 F:Flash & J'onn J'onzz	50.00
57 I&O:Metamorpho	150.00
58 F:Metamorpho	75.00
59 F:Batman & Green Lantern	100.00
60 A:Teen Titans,I:Wonder Girl	100.00
61 MA,O:Starman,BlackCanary	125.00
62 MA,O:Starman,BlackCanary	125.00
63 F:Supergirl&WonderWoman	40.00
64 F:Batman,V:Eclipso	60.00
65 DG,FMc,F:Flash & Doom Patrol	25.00
66 F:Metamorpho & Metal Men	25.00
67 CI,F:Batman & Flash	50.00
68 F:Batman,Metamorpho,Joker, Riddler,Penguin	65.00
69 F:Batman & Green Lantern	30.00
70 F:Batman & Hawkman	30.00
71 F:Batman & Green Arrow	30.00
72 CI,F:Spectre & Flash	30.00

73 F:Aquaman & Atom	25.00
74 B:Batman T.U.,A:Metal Men	25.00
75 F:Spectre	25.00
76 F:Plastic Man	25.00
77 F:Atom	25.00
78 F:Wonder Woman	25.00
79 NA,F:Deadman	50.00
80 NA,DG,F:Creeper	40.00
81 NA,F:Flash	40.00
82 NA,F:Aquaman,O:Ocean Master	40.00
83 NA,F:Teen Titans	50.00
84 NA,F:Sgt.Rock	40.00
85 NA,F:Green Arrow	40.00
86 NA,F:Deadman	40.00
87 F:Wonder Woman	25.00
88 F:Wildcat	25.00
89 RA,F:Phantom Stranger	25.00
90 F:Adam Strange	25.00
91 F:Black Canary	25.00
92 F:Bat Squad	25.00
93 NA,House of Mystery	35.00
94 NC,F:Teen Titans	18.00

Brave and the Bold #72
© *DC Comics, Inc.*

95 F:Plastic Man	15.00
96 F:Sgt.Rock	15.00
97 NC(i),F:Wildcat	15.00
98 JAp,F:Phantom Stranger	15.00
99 NC,F:Flash	15.00
100 NA,F:Green Arrow	40.00
101 JA,F:Metamorpho	7.00
102 NA,JA,F:Teen Titans	12.00
103 FMc,F:Metal Men	7.00
104 JAp,F:Deadman	7.00
105 JAp,F:Wonder Woman	7.00
106 JAp,F:Green Arrow	7.00
107 JAp,F:Black Canary	7.00
108 JAp,F:Sgt.Rock	7.00
109 JAp,F:Demon	7.00
110 JAp,F:Wildcat	7.00
111 JAp,F:Joker	12.50
112 JAp,F:Mr.Miracle	9.00
113 JAp,F:Metal Men	9.00
114 JAp,F:Aquaman	9.00
115 JAp,O:Viking Prince	9.00
116 JAp,F:Spectre	9.00
117 JAp,F:Sgt.Rock	9.00

118 JAp,F:Wildcat,V:Joker	14.00
119 JAp,F:Man-Bat	5.00
120 JAp,F:Kamandi	5.00
121 JAp,F:Metal Men	5.00
122 JAp,F:Swamp Thing	5.00
123 JAp,F:Plastic Man	5.00
124 JAp,F:Sgt.Rock	5.00
125 JAp,F:Flash	5.00
126 JAp,F:Aquaman	5.00
127 JAp,F:Wildcat	5.00
128 JAp,F:Mr.Miracle	5.00
129 F:Green Arrow,V:Joker	13.00
130 F:Green Arrow,V:Joker	13.00
131 JAp,F:WonderWoman, A:Catwoman	8.00
132 JAp,F:King Fu Foom	5.00
133 JAp,F:Deadman	5.00
134 JAp,F:Green Lantern	5.00
135 JAp,F:Metal Men	5.00
136 JAp,F:Metal Men,Green Arr.	5.00
137 F:Demon	5.00
138 JAp,F:Mr.Miracle	5.00
139 JAp,F:Hawkman	5.00
140 JAp,F:Wonder Woman.	5.00
141 JAp,F:Bl.Canary,A:Joker	12.00
142 JAp,F:Aquaman	4.00
143 O:Human Target	4.00
144 JAp,F:Green Arrow	4.00
145 JAp,F:Phantom Stranger	4.00
146 JAp,F:E-2 Batman	4.00
147 JAp,A:Supergirl	4.00
148 JSon,JAp,F:Plastic Man	4.00
149 JAp,F:Teen Titans	4.50
150 JAp,F:Superman	4.00
151 JAp,F:Flash	4.50
152 JAp,F:Atom	4.00
153 DN,F:Red Tornado	4.00
154 JAp,F:Metamorpho	4.00
155 JAp,F:Green Lantern	4.00
156 DN,F:Dr.Fate	4.00
157 JAp,F:Kamandi	4.00
158 JAp,F:Wonder Woman	4.00
159 JAp,A:Ras al Ghul	4.00
160 JAp,F:Supergirl	4.00
161 JAp,F:Adam Strange	4.00
162 JAp,F:Sgt.Rock	4.00
163 DG,F:Black Lightning	4.00
164 JL,F:Hawkman	4.00
165 DN,F:Man-bat	4.00
166 DG,TA,DSp,F:Black Canary A:Penguin,I:Nemesis	4.00
167 DC,DA,F:Blackhawk	4.00
168 JAp,DSp,F:Green Arrow	4.25
169 JAp,DSp,F:Zatanna	4.00
170 JA,F:Nemesis	4.00
171 JL,DSp,V:Scalphunter	4.00
172 CI,F:Firestorm	4.00
173 JAp,F:Guardians	4.00
174 JAp,F:Green Lantern	4.00
175 JAp,A:Lois Lane	4.00
176 JAp,F:Swamp Thing	4.00
177 JAp,F:Elongated Man	4.00
178 JAp,F:Creeper	4.00
179 EC,F:Legion o/Superheroes	4.00
180 JAp,F:Spectre,Nemesis	4.00
181 JAp,F:Hawk & Dove	4.00
182 JAp,F:E-2 Robin	4.00
183 CI,V:Riddler	4.50
184 JAp,A:Catwoman	5.00
185 F:Green Arrow	4.25
186 JAp,F:Hawkman	4.00
187 JAp,F:Metal Men	4.00
188 JAp,F:Rose & Thorn	4.00
189 JAp,A:Thorn	4.00
190 JAp,F:Adam Strange	4.00

DC COMICS

Brave and the Bold #149
© DC Comics, Inc.

191 JAp,V:Joker,Penguin	9.00
192 JAp,F:Superboy	4.00
193 JAp,D:Nemesis	4.00
194 Cl,F:Flash	4.00
195 JA,I:Vampire	4.00
196 JAp,F:Ragman	4.00
197 JSon,W:Earth II Batman & Catwoman	5.00
198 F:Karate Kid	4.00
199 RA,F:Spectre	4.00
200 DGb,JAp,A:Earth-2 Batman,I: Outsiders (GeoForce,Katana,Halo), E:Batman T.U.,final issue	12.00

[Limited Series]

1 SAP,Green Arrow/Butcher T.U.	2.00
2 SAP,A:Black Canary,Question	2.00
3 SAP,Green Arrow/Butcher	2.00
4 SAP,GA on Trial;A:Black Canary	2.00
5 SAP,V:Native Canadians,I.R.A.	2.00

BREATHTAKER
1990

1 I:Breathtaker(Chase Darrow)	6.00
2 Chase Darrow captured	6.00
3 O:Breathtaker	6.00
4 V:The Man, final issue	4.95

BRAINBANX
DC/Helix Jan. 1997

1 ELe(s),"Down Upon the Darkness"	2.50
2 ELe(s),Anna flees to the Sheol	2.50
3 Ele(s),Anna stranded	2.50
4 ELe(s),Anna & Logan	2.50
5 ELe(s),"To Enter the Kingdom"	2.50
6 (of 6)	2.50

BROTHER POWER, THE GEEK
Sept.–Oct., 1968

1	25.00
2 Nov.–Dec., 1968	20.00

BUGS BUNNY
1990

1 A:Bugs,Daffy,Search for Fudd Statues	1.00
2 Search for Statues cont. V:WitchHazel	1.00
3 Bugs&Co.in outer space, final	1.50

Butcher #1 © DC Comics

BUTCHER, THE
[Limited Series] 1990

1 MB,I:John Butcher	5.00
2 MB,in San Francisco	3.50
3 MB,V:Corporation	3.00
4 MB,A:Green Arrow	2.50
5 MB,A:Corvus,final issue	2.25

BUZZY
1944–58

1	165.00
2	75.00
3 thru 5	@40.00
6 thru 10	@35.00
11 thru 15	@25.00
16 thru 25	@25.00
26 thru 35	@20.00
36 thru 45	@15.00
46 thru 77	@15.00

CAMELOT 3000
Dec., 1982

1 BB,O:Arthur,Merlin	4.50
2 BB,A:Morgan LeFay	3.50
3 BB,J:New Knights	3.50
4 BB,V:McAllister	3.50
5 BB,O:Morgan Le Fay	3.50
6 BB,TA,W:Arthur	3.50
7 BB,TA,R:Isolde	3.50
8 BB,TA,D:Sir Kay	3.50
9 BB,TA,L:Sir Percival	3.50
10 BB,TA,V:Morgan Le Fay	3.50
11 BB,TA,V:Morgan Le Fay	3.50
12 BB,TA,D:Arthur	3.50

CAPTAIN ACTION
[Based on toy] Oct.–Nov., 1968

1 WW,I:Captain Action,Action	

Boy,A:Superman	80.00
2 GK,WW, V:Krellik	35.00
3 GK,I:Dr.Evil	35.00
4 GK,A:Dr.Evil	35.00
5 GK,WW,A:Matthew Blackwell, last issue	35.00

CAPTAIN ATOM
March, 1987

1 PB,O:Captain Atom	2.50
2 PB,C:Batman	2.00
3 PB,O:Captain Atom	1.75
4 PB,A:Firestorm	1.75
5 PB,A:Firestorm	1.75
6 PB,Dr.Spectro	1.75
7 R:Plastique	1.75
8 PB,Capt.Atom/Plastique	1.75
9 V:Bolt	1.75
10 PB,A:JLI	2.00
11 PB,A:Firestorm	1.50
12 PB,I:Major Force	1.50
13 PB,Christmas issue	1.50
14 PB,A:Nightshade	1.50
15 PB,Dr.Spectro, Major Force	1.50
16 PB,A:JLI,V:Red Tornado	1.75
17 V:Red Tornado;A:Swamp Thing,JLI	1.75
18 PB,A:Major Force	1.50
19 PB,Drug War	1.50
20 FMc,BlueBeetle	1.50
21 PB,A:Plastique,Nightshade	1.50
22 PB,A:MaxLord,Nightshade, Plastique	1.50
23 PB,V:The Ghost	1.50
24 PB,Invasion X-over	1.50
25 PB,Invvasion X-over	1.50
26 A:JLA,Top Secret,pt.1	1.75
27 A:JLA,Top Secret,pt.2	1.75
28 V:Ghost, Top Secret,pt.3	1.50
29 RT,Captain Atom cleared (new direction)	1.50
30 Janus Directive #11,V:Black Manta	1.50
31 RT,Capt.Atom's Powers, A:Rocket Red	1.50
32 Loses Powers	1.50
33 A:Batman	2.00
34 C:JLE	1.50
35 RT,Secret o/t Silver Shield, A:Major Force	1.50
36 RT,Las Vegas Battle,A:Major Force	1.50
37 I:New Atomic Skull	1.25
38 RT,A:Red Tornado, Black Racer	1.25
39 RT,A:Red Tornado	1.25
40 RT,V:Kobra	1.25
41 RT,A:Black Racer, Red Tornado	1.25
42 RT,A:Phantom Stranger,Red Tornado,Black Racer, Death from Sandman	1.25
43 RT,V:Nekron	1.25
44 RT,V:Plastique	1.25
45 RT,A:The Ghost,I:Ironfire	1.25
46 RT,A:Superman	1.25
47 RT,A:SupermanV:Ghost	1.25
48 RT,R:Red Tornado	1.25
49 RT,Plastique on trial	1.25
50 RT,V:The Ghost,DoubleSize	2.50
51 RT	1.25
52 RT,Terror on RTE.91'	1.25
53 RT,A:Aquaman	1.25
54 RT,A:Rasputin,Shadowstorm	1.25
55 RT,Inside Quantum Field	1.25

DC COMICS

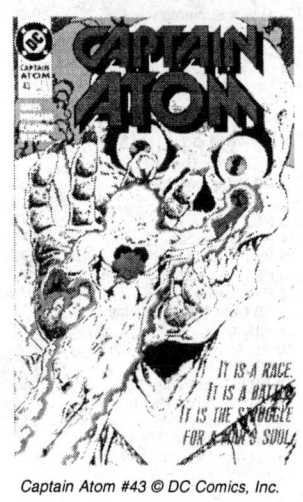

Captain Atom #43 © DC Comics, Inc.

56 RT,Quantum Field cont. 1.25
57 RT,V:ShadowStorm,
    Quantum.Field 1.25
Ann.#1 I:Maj.Force 1.50
Ann.#2 A:RocketRed,Maj.Force . . 1.50

CAPTAIN CARROT
March, 1982
1 RA,A:Superman,Starro 1.25
2 AA 1.00
3 thru 19 . . . . @1.00
20 A:Changeling,Nov., 1983 . . . . 1.00

CAPTAIN STORM
May-June, 1964
1 IN(c),Killer Hunt 20.00
2 IN(c),First Shot-Last Shot . . 15.00
3 JKu,Death of a PT Boat 15.00
4 IN(c),First Command-Last
    Command 15.00
5 IN(c), Killer Torpedo 15.00
6 JKu,IN(c),Medals For An Ocean15.00
7 IN(c),A Bullet For The General 15.00
8 IN(c),Death of A Sub 15.00
9 IN(c),Sink That Flattop 15.00
10 IN(c),Only The Last Man Lives 15.00
11 IN(c),Ride a Hot Torpedo . . . 15.00
12 JKu(c),T.N.T. Tea Party Abroad
    PT 47 . . . . 15.00
13 JKu,Yankee Banzai 15.00
14 RH(c),Sink Capt. Storm 15.00
15 IN(c),My Enemy-My Friend . . 15.00
16 IN(c),Battle of the Stinging
    Mosquito 15.00
17 IN(c),First Shot for a Dead Man15.00
18 March-April, 1967 . . . . 15.00

CARTOON NETWORK PRESENTS
Warner Bros./DC June 1997
1: Dexter's Laboratory 1.75
2: Space Ghost coast-to-coast . . 1.75

CATWOMAN
[Limited Series] 1989
1 O:Catwoman 13.00

2 Catwoman'sSister kidnapped . . 9.00
3 Battle 6.00
4 Final,V:Batman 6.00
[Regular Series] 1993–97
0 JBa,O:Catwoman 1.50
1 B:JDy(s),JBa,DG,A:Bane . . . 6.00
2 JBa,DG,A:Bane 3.00
3 JBa,DG,at Santa Prisca 2.75
4 JBa,DG,Bane's Secret 2.50
5 JBa,V:Ninjas 2.25
6 JBa,A:Batman 2.25
7 JBa,A:Batman 2.25
8 JBa,V:Zephyr 2.25
9 JBa,V:Zephyr 2.25
10 JBa,V:Arms Dealer 2.25
11 JBa 2.25
12 JBa,Knights End #6,A:Batman 5.00
13 JBa,Knights End,Aftermath#2 . 2.00
14 JBa,Zero Hour 2.00
15 JBa,new path 2.00
16 JBa,Island forterss 2.00
17 . . . . 2.00
18 . . . . 2.00
19 Amazonia 2.00
20 Hollywood 2.00
21 JBa(c&a)V:Movie Monster
    [new Miraweb format begins] . . 2.00
22 JBa(c&a) Family Ties,pt.1 . . . . 2.00
23 Family Ties,pt.2 . . . . 2.00
24 . . . . 2.00
25 A:Robin,Psyba-Rats 2.50
26 AIG,JBa,The Secret of the
    Universe,pt.2 (of 3) 2.00
27 CDi,Underworld Unleashed tie-in2.00
28 CDi,Catwoman enlists help . . . 2.00
29 CDi,A:Penguin 2.00
30 . . . . 2.00
31 . . . . 3.00
32 CDi,JBa,Contagion,pt.9 . . . . . 3.00
33 CDi,JBa,Hellhound,pt.1 . . . . . 2.00
34 CDi,JBa,Hellbound,pt.2 (of 3) . 2.50
35 CDi,JBa 2.50
36 CDi,JBa, Legacy, pt.2 x-over . . 2.00
37 CDi,JBa, Panara, the Leopard
    Woman 2.00
38 DgM(s),JBa,MPn,"Catwoman,
    Year One," pt.1 (of 3) 2.00
39 DgM(s),JBa,MPn,"Catwoman,
    Year One," pt. 2 . . . . 2.00
40 DgM(s),JBa,MPn,"Catwoman,
    Year One," pt. 3 . . . . 2.00
41 DgM(s),JBa,I:MorelandMcShane 2.00
42 DgM(s),JBa,"Red Fang and
    Claw," pt.1 . . . . 2.00
43 DgM(s),JBa,"Red Fang and
    Claw," pt.2 . . . . 2.00
44 DgM(s),JBa,"Red Fang and
    Claw," pt.3 . . . . 2.00
45 DgM(s),JBa,"Nine Deaths of
    the Cat" 2.00
46 DgM(s),JBa,F:Two Face, pt.1 . 1.95
47 DgM(s),JBa,F:Two Face, pt.2 . 1.95
48 DgM(s),JBa,V:Morella, pt.1 . . 1.95
49 DgM(s),JBa,V:Morella, pt. 2 . . 1.95
Ann.#1 Elseworlds Story,A:Ra's Al
    Ghul 2.95
Ann.#2 JBa(c&a) Year One Annuals,
    Young Selina Kyle 3.95
Ann.#3 Legends o/t Dead Earth . . 2.95
Ann.#4 Pulp Heroes (Macabre) . . 3.95

CATWOMAN DEFIANT
1 TGr,DG,V:Mr.Handsome 6.00

CENTURIONS
June, 1987
1 DH,V:Doc Terror 1.00
2 DH,O:Centurions 1.00
3 DH,V:Doc Terror 1.00
4 DH,Sept., 1987 . . . . 1.00

CHAIN GANG WAR
1993–94
1 I:Chain Gang 2.50
2 V:8-Ball 1.75
3 C:Deathstroke 1.75
4 C:Deathstroke 1.75
5 Embossed(c),A:Deathstroke . . 2.50
6 A:Deathstroke,Batman 1.75
7 V:Crooked Man 1.75
8 B:Crooked Man 1.75
9 V:Crooked Man 1.75
10 A:Deathstroke,C:Batman 1.75
11 A:Batman 1.75
12 E:Crooked Man,D:Chain Gang,
    Final Issue 1.75

CHALLENGERS OF THE UNKNOWN
1958–78
1 JK&JK(c),The Man Who
    Tampered With Infinity . . 2,100.00
2 JK&JK(c),The Monster Maker 800.00
3 JK&JK(c),The Secret of the
    Sorcerer's Mirror 650.00
4 JK,WW,JK(c),The Wizard of
    Time 550.00
5 JK,WW&JK(c),The Riddle of
    the Star-Stone 550.00
6 JK,WW,JK(c),Captives of
    the Space Circus 550.00
7 JK,WW,JK(c),The Isle of
    No Return 550.00
8 JK,WW,JK&WW(c),The
    Prisoners of the Robot Planet 550.00
9 The Plot To Destroy Earth . . 250.00
10 The Four Faces of Doom . . 250.00
11 The Creatures From The
    Forbidden World 175.00
12 The Three Clues To Sorcery 175.00
13 The Prisoner of the
    Tiny Space Ball 175.00
14 O: Multi Man 175.00
15 Lady Giant and the Beast . . 175.00
16 Prisoners of the Mirage World 150.00
17 The Secret of the
    Space Capsules 150.00
18 Menace of Mystery Island . . 150.00
19 The Alien Who Stole a Planet 150.00
20 Multi-Man Strikes Back 150.00
21 Weird World That Didn't Exist 150.00
22 The Thing In
    Challenger Mountain 150.00
23 The Island In The Sky 90.00
24 The Challengers Die At Dawn 90.00
25 Captives of the Alien Hunter . 90.00
26 Death Crowns The
    Challenge King 90.00
27 Master of the Volcano Men . . 90.00
28 The Riddle of the
    Faceless Man 90.00
29 Four Roads to Doomsday . . . 90.00
30 Multi-Man...Villain Turned
    Hero 90.00
31 O:Challengers 90.00
32 One Challenger Must Die . . . 40.00
33 Challengers Meet Their Master 40.00
34 Beachhead, USA 40.00

DC COMICS

35 War Against The Moon Beast	40.00
36 Giant In Challenger Mountain	40.00
37 Triple Terror of Mr. Dimension	40.00
38 Menace the Challengers Made	40.00
39 Phantom of the Fair	40.00
40 Super-Powers of the Challengers	40.00
41 The Challenger Who Quit	20.00
42 The League of Challenger-Haters	20.00
43 New look begins	20.00
44 The Curse of the Evil Eye	20.00
45 Queen of the Challenger-Haters	20.00
46 Strange Schemes of the Gargoyle	20.00
47 The Sinister Sponge	20.00
48 A:Doom Patrol	20.00
49 Tyrant Who Owned the World	20.00
50 Final Hours for the Challengers	20.00
51 A:Sea Devil	20.00
52 Two Are Dead - Two To Go	20.00
53 Who is the Traitor Among Us?	20.00
54 War of the Sub-Humans	20.00
55 D:Red Ryan	20.00
56 License To Kill	20.00
57 Kook And The Kilowatt Killer	20.00
58 Live Till Tomorrow	20.00
59 Seekeenakee - The Petrified Giant	20.00
60 R:Red Ryan	20.00
61 Robot Hounds of Chang	20.00
62 Legion of the Weird	20.00
63 None Shall Escape the Walking Evil	20.00
64 JKu(c),Invitation to a Hanging	20.00
65 The Devil's Circus	10.00
66 JKu(c),Rendezvous With Revenge	10.00
67 NA(c),The Dream Killers	10.00
68 NA(c),One of Us is a Madman	10.00
69 JKu(c),I:Corinna	10.00
70 NA(c),Scream of Yesterdays	10.00
71 NC(c),When Evil Calls	10.00
72 NA(c),A Plague of Darkness	10.00
73 NC(c),Curse of the Killer Time Forgot	10.00
74 GT&NA(c),A:Deadman	22.00
75 JK(c),Ultivac Is Loose	7.00
76 JKu(c),The Traitorous Challenger	7.00
77 JK(c),Menace of the Ancient Vials	7.00
78 JK(c),The Island of No Return	5.00
79 JKu(c),The Monster Maker	5.00
80 NC(c),The Day The Earth Blew Up	5.00
81 MN&NA(c),Multi-Man's Master Plan	5.00
82 MN&NA(c),Swamp Thing	5.00
83 Seven Doorways to Destiny	5.00
84 To Save A Monster	5.00
85 The Creature From The End Of Time	5.00
86 The War At Time's End	5.00
87 final issue, July, 1978	5.00

CHALLENGERS OF THE UNKNOWN
1991

1 BB(c) In The Spotlight	1.75
2	1.75
3 Challengers 'Split Up'	1.75
4 'Separate Ways'	1.75

5 Moffet	1.75
6 GK(c),Challengers reunited	1.75
7 AAd(c),June pregnant	1.75
8 final issue	1.75

CHALLENGERS OF THE UNKNOWN

1 StG(s),JPL	2.25
2 StG(s),LKa,JPL,SMa,Zombies	2.25
3 StG(s),JPL,death of Challenger	2.25
4 StG&LKa(s),JPL,SMa, O:Challengers	2.25
5 StG&LKa(s)JPL,SMa, V:The Fearslayer	2.25
6 StG(s),JPL,SMa,"Convergence" pt. 3 x-over	2.25
7 StG(s),JPL,"Past Perfect" pt.1 (of 3)	2.25
8 StG(s),JPL,"Past Perfect" pt.2	2.25

Checkmate #3 © DC Comics, Inc.

CHECKMATE
April, 1988

1 From Vigilante & Action Comics	3.00
2 Chicago Bombings cont.	2.00
3 V:Terrorist Right	1.50
4 V:Crime Lords Abroad,B.U.Story 'Training of a Knight' begins	1.50
5 Renegade nation of Quarac	1.50
6 Secret Arms Deal	1.50
7 Checkmate Invades Quarac	1.50
8 Consequences-Quarac Invasion	1.50
9 Checkmate's security in doubt	1.50
10 V:Counterfeiting Ring	1.50
11 Invasion X-over	1.50
12 Invasion Aftermath extra	1.50
13 CommanderH.Stein's vacation	1.50
14 R:Blackthorn	1.50
15 Janus Directive #1	1.50
16 Janus Directive #3	1.50
17 Janus Directive #6	1.50
18 Janus Directive #9	1.50
19 Reorganization of Group	1.50
20 'Shadow of Bishop' A:Peacemaker,pt.1	1.50
21 Peacemaker behind Iron Curtain,pt.2	1.50
22 Mystery of Bishop Cont.,pt.3	1.50

23 European Scientists Suicides,pt.4	1.50
24 Bishop Mystery cont.,pt.5	1.50
25 Bishop's Identity Revealed	1.50
26 Mazarin kidnaps H.Stein's kids	1.50
27 Stein rescue attempt,I:Cypher	1.50
28 A:Cypher, Bishop-Robots	1.50
29 A:Cypher,Blackthorn	1.50
30 Irish Knight W.O'Donnell/British Knight L.Hawkins team-up	1.50
31 V:Cypher International	2.00
32 V:Cypher International	2.00
33 final issue (32 pages)	2.00

CHIAROSCURO: THE PRIVATE LIVES OF LEONARDO DaVINCI
Vertigo 1995–96

1 Biographical, Adult	2.50
2 Two of Da Vinci Sisters	2.50
3	2.50
4 F:Salari	2.95
5 Crazy Leonardo	2.95
6 Salai schemes,O:Mona Lisa	2.95
7 V:Borgia & Machiavelli	2.95
8 daVinci returns to Florence	2.95
9	2.95
10 finale	2.95

CHILDREN'S CRUSADE
Vertigo 1993–94

1 NGa(s),CBa,MkB(i),F:Rowland, Payne (From Sandman)	4.75
2 NGa(s),AaK(s),JaD(s),PSj,A:Tim Hunter,Suzy,Maxine,final issue	4.50

CHRISTMAS WITH THE SUPER-HEROES
1988–89

1 JBy(c)	2.95
2 PC,GM,JBy,NKu,DG A:Batman Superman,Deadman,(last Supergirl appearance)	2.95

CINDER & ASHE
March, 1988

1 JL,I:Cinder & Ashe	2.00
2 JL,Viet Nam Flashbacks	2.00
3 JL,Truth About Lacey revealed	2.00
4 JL,final issue, June, 1988	2.00

CLASH
1991

1 AKu,I:Joe McLash(b/w)	4.95
2 AKu,Panja-Rise to Power	4.95
3 AKu,V:Archons,conclusion	4.95

CLAW THE UNCONQUERED
May-June, 1975

1	2.00
2	1.50
3 Nudity panel	1.25
4	1.00
5	1.00
6	1.00
7	1.00
8 KG	1.00
9 KG/BL,Origin	1.00
10 KG	1.00
11 KG	1.00
12 KG/BL,Aug.–Sept., 1978	1.00

DC COMICS

The Comet #16 © DC Comics, Inc.

COMET, THE
Impact 1991–92

1 TL,I&O:Comet I:Applejack, Victoria Johnson, Ben Lee	1.50
2 TL,A:Applejack,Lance Perry	1.25
3 TL,V:Anti-nuclear terrorists	1.25
4 TL,I&V:Black Hood,I:Inferno	1.25
5 V:Cyborg Soldier	1.25
6 TL,I:The Hangman	1.25
7 'Press Problems'	1.25
8 TL,Comet ID discovered	1.25
9 TL,'Bad Judgment'	1.25
10 Fly/Comet T.U.,V:Dolphus	1.25
11 V:Inferno	1.25
12 V:Inferno	1.25
13 O:Comet's Powers	1.25
14 O:Comet's Powers Pt.2	1.25
15 Rob finds his mother	1.25
16 V:Aliens	1.25
17 "Shocking Truth"	1.25
18 Last Issue	1.25
Ann.#1 Earthquest,w/trading card	1.75

COMIC CAVALCADE
1942–43

1 Green Lantern, Flash, Wildcat, Wonder Woman, Black Pirate	8,000.00
2 ShM,B:Mutt & Jeff	1,700.00
3 ShM,B:HotHarrigan,Sorcerer	1,200.00
4 Gay Ghost, A:Scribby, A:Red Tornado	1,100.00
5 Green Lantern, Flash Wonder Woman	1000.00
6 Flash, Wonder Woman Green Lantern	800.00
7 A:Red Tornado, E:Scribby	800.00
8 Flash, Wonder Woman Green Lantern	800.00
9 Flash, Wonder Woman Green Lantern	800.00
10 Flash, Wonder Woman Green Lantern	800.00
11 Flash, Wonder Woman Green Lantern	700.00
12 E:Red, White & Blue	700.00
13 A:Solomon Grundy	1,100.00

14 Flash, Wonder Woman, Green Lantern	700.00
15 B:Johnny Peril	700.00
16 Flash, Wonder Woman, Green Lantern	700.00
17 Flash, Wonder Woman, Green Lantern	700.00
18 Flash, Wonder Woman, Green Lantern	700.00
19 Flash, Wonder Woman, Green Lantern	700.00
20 Flash, Wonder Woman, Green Lantern	700.00
21 Flash, Wonder Woman, Green Lantern	700.00
22 A:Atom	700.00
23 A:Atom	700.00
24 A:Solomon Grundy	800.00
25 A:Black Canary	500.00
26 ATh, E:Mutt & Jeff	500.00
27 ATh,ATh(c)	500.00
28 ATh E:Flash, Wonder Woman Green Lantern	500.00
29 E:Johnny Peril	550.00
30 RG,B:Fox & Crow	350.00
31 thru 39 RG	@175.00
40 RG,ShM	150.00
41 thru 49 RG,ShM	@125.00
50 thru 62 RG,ShM	@150.00
63 RG,ShM, July 1954	250.00

CONGO BILL
Aug.–Sept., 1954

1	600.00
2	500.00
3 thru 6	450.00
7 Aug.–Sept.,1955	@500.00

CONGORILLA
1992–93

1 R:Congo Bill	2.00
2 BB(c),V:Congo Bill	1.75
3 BB(c),V:Congo Bill	1.75
4 BB(c),V:Congo Bill	1.75

CONQUEROR OF THE BARREN EARTH
1985

1 thru 4	@1.00

COOL WORLD
1992

1 Prequel to Movie	1.75
2 Movie Adapt.	1.75
3 Movie Adapt.	1.75
4	1.75

COPS
1988–89

1 PB,O:Cops,double-size	2.00
2 PB,V:Big Boss	1.50
3 PB,RT,V:Dr.Bad Vibes	1.25
4 BS,A:Sheriff Sundown	1.25
5 PB,Blitz the Robo-Dog	1.25
6 PB,A:Ms.Demeaner	1.25
7 PB,A:Tramplor	1.25
8 PB,V:BigBoss & Ally	1.25
9 PB,Cops Trapped	1.25
10 PB,Dr.Bad Vibes becomes Dr.Goodvibes	1.25
11 PB,V:Big Boss	1.25
12 PB,V:Dr.Badvibe's T.H.U.G.S	1.25
13 Berserko/Ms.Demeanor	

marriage proposal	1.25
14 A:Buttons McBoom-Boom	1.25
15 Cops vs. Crooks, final issue	1.25

COSMIC BOY
Dec., 1986

1 KG,EC,Legends tie-in	2.00
2 KG,EC,'Is History Destiny'	1.25
3 KG,EC,'Past,Present,Future'	1.25
4 KG,EC,Legends	1.25

COSMIC ODYSSEY
1988

1 MMi,A:Superman,Batman,John Stewart,Starfire,J'onnJ'onzz, NewGods,Demon,JSn story	5.50
2 MMi,'Disaster'(low dist)	6.50
3 MMi,Return to New Genesis	5.00
4 MMi,A:Dr.Fate, final	4.00

CRIMSON AVENGER
1988

1 Mini-series	1.00
2 V:Black Cross	1.00
3 'V:Killers of the Dark Cross'	1.00
4 'V:Dark Cross,final issue	1.00

CRISIS ON INFINITE EARTHS
April, 1985

1 B:MWn(s),GP,DG,I:Pariah,I&O:Alex Luthor,D:Crime Syndicate	10.00
2 GP,DG,V:Psycho Pirate, A:Joker,Batman	8.00
3 GP,DG,D:Losers	6.00
4 GP,D:Monitor,I:2nd Dr.Light	6.00
5 GP,JOy,I:Anti-Monitor	6.00
6 GP,JOy,I:2nd Wildcat,A:Fawcett, Quality & Charlton heroes	6.00
7 GP,JOy,DG,D:Supergirl	9.00
8 GP,JOy,D:1st Flash	11.00
9 GP,JOy,D:Aquagirl	6.00
10 GP,JOy,D:Psimon,A:Spectre	6.00
11 GP,JOy,D:Angle Man	7.00
12 E:MWn(s),GP,JOy,D:Huntress,Kole, Kid Flash becomes 2nd Flash, D:Earth 2	7.00

CRUCIBLE
Impact 1993

1 JQ,F:The Comet	1.25
2 JQ,A:Black Hood,Comet	1.50
3 JQ,Comet Vs.Black Hood	1.50
4 JQ,V:Tomorrow Men	1.50
5 JQ,Black Hod vs Shield	1.25
6 JQ,V:The Crucible	1.25

CRUSADERS
Impact May, 1992

1 DJu(c),I:Crusaders,inc Trading cards	1.25
2 V:Kalathar	1.00
3 V:Kalathar	1.00
4 Crusaders form as group	1.00
5 V:Cyber-Punks	1.25
6 V:Cyborg Villains	1.25
7 Woj,Low,F:Fireball	1.25
8 Last Issue	1.25

CYBERELLA
DC/Helix Sept. 1996

1 HC(s),DCn,	2.25

DC COMICS

2 HC(s),DCn,Secret history
　revealed 2.25
3 HC(s),DCn,Sunny goes on
　rampage 2.25
4 HC(s),DCn,Attack on MacroCorp 2.25
5 HC(s),DCn,V:Army of
　Necronauts 2.25
6 HC(s),DCn, ... 2.25
7 HC(s),DCn,Trip to Hell 2.25
8 HC(s),DCn,V:BTIII, concl. 2.50
9 DCn, The Informers 2.25
10 HC(s),DCn,Wuvzums,
　Digitina,pt.1 . . . . 2.25
11 HC(s),DCn,Wuvzums,pt.2 . . . 2.25
12 HC(s),final issue 2.50

DALE EVANS COMICS
1948–52
1 Ph(c),ATh,B:Sierra Smith . . . 700.00
2 Ph(c),ATh 350.00
3 ATh 225.00
4 thru 11 . . . . @200.00
12 thru 24 . . . . @100.00

Damage #6 © DC Comics, Inc.

DAMAGE
1994–96
1 I:Damage,V:Metallo 2.00
2 V:Symbolix 2.00
3 V:Troll 2.00
4 V:Troll 2.00
5 A:New Titans,V:Baron 2.25
6 Zero Hour,A:New Titans 2.25
7 Trial 1.95
8 Fragments,pt.1 . . . . 1.95
9 Fragments,pt.2 . . . . 1.95
10 Fragments,pt.3 . . . . 1.95
11 Fragments,pt.4 . . . . 1.95
12 Fragments,pt.5 . . . . 1.95
13 Picking Up The Pieces,pt.1 . . . 2.25
14 Picking Up The Pieces,pt.2
　A:The Ray 2.25
15 Picking Up the Pieces,pt.3 . . . 2.25
16 . . . . 2.25
17 V:Bounty 2.25
18 Underworld Unleashed tie-in . . 2.25
19 Underworld Unleashed tie-in . . 2.25
20 final issue 2.25

DANGER TRAIL
July–Aug., 1950
1 CI,Ath,I:King For A Day 800.00
2 ATh 600.00
3 ATh 900.00
4 ATh 500.00
5 March-April, 1951 . . . . 500.00

DANGER TRAIL
1 thru 4 CI,FMc,F:King Faraday
　V:Cobra 2.00

DARK MANSION OF FORBIDDEN LOVE, THE
Sept.–Oct., 1971
1 . . . . 6.00
2 and 4 March-April, 1972 . . . @3.50

DARKSEID VS. GALACTUS THE HUNGER
1 Orion vs. Silver Surfer 4.95

DARKSTARS
1992–96
0 History 2.00
1 TC(c),LSn,I:Darkstars 3.50
2 TC(c),LSn,F:Ferin Colos 2.50
3 LSn,J:Mo,Flint,V:Evil Star 2.00
4 TC,V:Evilstar 3.00
5 TC,A:Hawkman,Hawkwoman . . 3.00
6 TC,A:Hawkman 2.50
7 TC,V:K'llash 2.00
8 F:Ferris Colos 2.00
9 Colos vs K'lassh 2.00
10 V:Con Artists 2.00
11 TC,Trinity#4,A:Green Lantern,
　L.E.G.I.O.N. 2.00
12 TC(c),Trinity#7,A:Green Lantern,
　L.E.G.I.O.N. 2.00
13 TC(c),V:Alien Underworld 2.00
14 I:Annihilator 2.00
15 V:Annihilator 2.00
16 V:Annihilator 2.00
17 Murders 2.00
18 B:Eve of Destruction 2.00
19 A:Flash 2.00
20 E:Eve of Destruction 2.00
21 A:John Stewart,Donna Troy . . 2.00
22 A:Controllers 2.25
23 Donna Troy is new Darkstar . . 2.25
24 Zero Hour,V:HalJordan,Entropy 2.25
25 Stewart 2.25
26 Alien criminals 2.25
27 and 28 . . . . @2.00
29 V:Alien Syndicate 2.00
30 A:Green Lantern 2.00
31 V:Darkseid 2.25
32 Crimelord/Syndicate War,pt.3,
　A:New Titans,Supergirl,
　Deathstroke 2.25
33 V:Jeddigan 2.25
34 . . . . 2.25
35 A:Flash 2.25
36 MkF,MC,A:Flash 2.25
37 MkF,MC,Colos vs. Warrior . . . 2.25
38 final issue 2.25

DC CHALLENGE
Nov., 1985
1 GC,Batman 4.00
2 Superman 1.50
3 CI,Adam Strange 1.50
4 GK/KJ,Aquaman 1.50

5 DGb,Dr.Fate,Capt.Marvel 1.50
6 Dr. 13 . . . . 1.50
7 Gorilla Grodd 1.50
8 DG,Outsiders, New Gods 1.50
9 New Teen Titans,JLA 1.50
10 CS,New Teen Titans,JLA 1.50
11 KG,Outsiders 1.50
12 DCw,TMd,DSp,New Teen Titans,
　Oct., 1986 . . . . 2.50

DC COMICS PRESENTS
July–Aug., 1978
[all have Superman]
1 JL,DA,F:Flash 3.00
2 JL,DA,F:Flash 2.00
3 JL,F:Adam Strange 1.75
4 JL,F:Metal Men,A:Mr.IQ 1.75
5 MA,F:Aquaman 1.75
6 CS,F:Green Lantern 1.75
7 DD,F:Red Tornado 1.75
8 MA,F:Swamp Thing 1.75
9 JSon,JA,RH,F:Wonder Woman 1.75
10 JSon,JA,F:Sgt.Rock 1.75
11 JSon,F:Hawkman 1.75
12 RB,DG,F:Mr.Miracle 1.75
13 DD,DG,F:Legion 2.00
14 DD,DG,F:Superboy 1.50
15 JSon,F:Atom,C:Batman 1.50
16 JSon,F:Black Lightning 1.50
17 JL,F:Firestorm 1.50
18 DD,F:Zatanna 1.50
19 JSon,F:Batgirl 2.00
20 JL,F:Green Arrow 1.50
21 JSon,JSa,F:Elongated Man . . . 1.50
22 DD,FMc,F:Captain Comet 1.50
23 JSon,F:Dr.Fate 1.50
24 JL,F:Deadman 1.50
25 DD,FMc,F:Phantom Stranger . 1.50
26 GP,DG,JSn,I:New Teen Titans,
　Cyborg,Raven,Starfire
　A:Green Lantern 10.00
27 JSn,RT,I:Mongul 3.00
28 JSn,RT,GK,F:Mongul 2.00
29 JSn,RT,AS,F:Spectre 2.00
30 CS,AS,F:Black Canary 1.50
31 JL,DG,AS,F:Robin 1.50
32 KS,AS,F:Wonder Woman 1.50

DC Comics Presents #35
© DC Comics, Inc.

DC COMICS

33 RB,DG,AS,F:Captain Marvel . . 1.50
34 RB,DG,F:Marvel Family 1.50
35 CS,GK,F:Man-bat 1.50
36 JSn,F:Starman 2.00
37 JSn,AS,F:Hawkgirl 1.50
38 GP(c),DH,AS,DG,D:Crimson
    Avenger,F:Flash 1.50
39 JSon,AS,F:PlasticMan,Toyman 1.50
40 IN,FMc,AS,F:Metamorpho . . . 1.50
41 JL,FMc,GC,RT,I:New Wonder
    Woman,A:Joker 8.00
42 IN,FMc,F:Unknown Soldier . . . 1.50
43 BB(c),CS,F:Legion 1.50
44 IN,FMc,F:Dial H for Hero 2.00
45 RB,F:Firestorm 1.50
46 AS,I:Global Guardians 1.50
47 CS,I:Masters of Universe. 1.50
48 GK(c),AA,IN,FMc,F:Aquaman . 1.50
49 RB,F:Shazam!,V:Black Adam . 1.50
50 CS,CS,F:Clark Kent 1.50
51 AS,FMc,CS,F:Atom,Masters
    of the Universe 1.50
52 KG,F:Doom Patrol,
    I:Ambush Bug 1.50
53 CS,TD,RA,DG,I:Atari Force . . 1.50
54 DN,DA,F:Gr.Arrow,Bl.Canary . 1.50
55 AS,F:Air Wave,A:Superboy . . 1.50
56 GK(c),F:Power Girl 1.50
57 AS,FMc,F:Atomic Knights . . . 1.50
58 GK(c),AS,F:Robin,Elongated
    Man 1.50
59 KG,KS,F:Ambush Bug 1.50
60 GK(c),IN,TD,F:Guardians 1.50
61 GP,F:Omac 1.50
62 GK(c),IN,F:Freedom Fighters . 1.50
63 AS,EC,F:Amethyst 1.50
64 GK(c),AS,FMc,F:Kamandi . . . 1.50
65 GM,F:Madame Xanadu 1.50
66 JKu,F:Demon 1.50
67 CS,MA,F:Santa Claus 1.50
68 GK(c),CS,MA,F:Vixen 1.50
69 IN,DJ,F:Blackhawk 1.50
70 AS,TD,F:Metal Men 1.50
71 CS,F:Bizarro 1.50
72 AS,DG,F:Phant.Stranger,Joker 3.50
73 CI,F:Flash 1.50
74 AS,RT,F:Hawkman 1.50
75 TMd,F:Arion 1.50
76 EB,F:Wonder Woman 1.50
77 CS,F:Forgotten Heroes 3.50
78 CS,F:Forgotten Villains 3.50
79 CS,AW,F:Legion 1.50
80 CS,F:Clark Kent 1.50
81 KG,BO,F:Ambush Bug 1.50
82 KJ,F:Adam Strange 1.50
83 IN,F:Batman/Outsiders. 1.50
84 JK,ATh,MA,F:Challengers . . . 1.50
85 RV,AW,AMo(s),
    F:Swamp Thing 4.00
86 Crisis,F:Supergirl 1.50
87 CS,AW,Crisis,I:Earth Prime
    Superboy 1.75
88 KG,Crisis,F:Creeper 1.50
89 MMi(c),AS,F:Omega Men 1.50
90 DCw,F:Firestorm,Capt.Atom . 1.50
91 CS,F:Captain Comet 1.50
92 CS,F:Vigilante 1.50
93 JSn(c),AS,KS,F:Elastic Four . 1.50
94 GP(c),TMd,DH,Crisis,F:Lady
    Quark,Pariah,Harbinger 1.50
95 MA(i),F:Hawkman 1.50
96 JSon,KS,F:Blue Devil 1.50
97 RV,F:Phantom Zone Villians,
    final issue,double-sized 1.50
Ann.#1,RB,F:Earth 2 Superman . 1.50

Ann.#2 GK(c),KP,I:Superwoman . 1.25
Ann.#3 GK,F:Captain Marvel 1.25
Ann.#4 EB,JOy,F:Superwoman . . 1.25

DC/MARVEL: ALL ACCESS
October 1996
sequel to DC Versus Marvel
1 (of 4) RMz(s),JG,JRu, crossover
    crisis again, 48pg 4.00
2 RMz(s),JG,JRu,F:Jubilee,Robin,
    Daredevil,Two-Face 3.00
3 RMz(s),JG,JRu,F:Doctor
    Strange, X-Men 3.00
4 RMz(s),JG,JRu,48pg 3.50

DC/MARVEL CROSSOVER CLASSICS
TPB, rep. all x-overs 17.95

DC GRAPHIC NOVEL
Nov., 1983
1 JL,Star Raiders 6.00
2 Warlords 6.00
3 EC,Medusa Chain 6.00
4 JK,Hunger Dogs 6.00
5 Me and Joe Priest 7.00
6 Space Clusters 7.00

DC SCIENCE FICTION GRAPHIC NOVEL
1985–87
1 KG,Hell on Earth 6.00
2 Nightwings 6.00
3 Frost and Fire 6.00
4 Merchants of Venus 6.00
5 Metalzoic 6.00
6 MR,Demon-Glass Hand 6.00
7 Sandkings 6.00

DC SPECIAL
Oct.–Dec., 1968
[All reprint]
1 CI,F:Flash,Batman,Adam Strange,
    (#1 thru #21 reps) 11.00
2 F:Teen Titans 8.00
3 GA,F:Black Canary 7.00
4 Mystery 7.00
5 JKu,F:Viking Prince/Sgt.Rock . . 7.00
6 Wild Frontier 7.00
7 F:Strange Sports 7.00
8 Wanted 7.00
9 . . . . 7.00
10 LAW 7.00
11 NA,BWr,F:Monsters 7.00
12 JKu,F:Viking Prince 7.00
13 F:Strange Sports 7.00
14 Wanted,F:Penguin/Joker 7.00
15 GA,F:Plastic Man 10.00
16 F:Super Heroes & Gorillas . . . 5.00
17 F:Green Lantern 5.00
18 Earth Shaking Stories 5.00
19 F:War Against Gianta 5.00
20 Green Lantern 5.00
21 F:War Against Monsters 5.00
22 Three Musketeers 5.00
23 Three Musketeers 5.00
24 Three Musketeers 5.00
25 Three Musketeers 5.00
26 F:Enemy Ace(rep) 5.00
27 RB,JR,F:Captain Comet 5.00
28 DN,DA,Earth disasters 5.00
29 JSon,BL,O:JSA 6.00

DC SPECIAL SERIES
Sept., 1977
1 MN,DD,IN,FMc,JSon,JA,BMc,
    JRu,F:Batman,Flash,Green
    Lantern,Atom,Aquaman 5.00
2 BWr(c),BWr,F:Swamp Thing rep. 4.00
3 JKu(c),F:Sgt.Rock 3.00
4 AN,RT,Unexpected Annual . . . 3.00
5 CS,F:Superman 3.25
6 BMc(i),Secret Society Vs.JLA . 3.00
7 AN,F:Ghosts 3.00
8 RE,DG,F:Brave&Bold,Deadman 3.50
9 SD,RH,DAy,F:Wonder Woman . 3.00
10 JSon,MN,DN,TA,Secret Origins,
    O:Dr.Fate 3.00
11 JL,KS,MA,IN,WW,AS,F:Flash . 3.50
12 MK(c),RT,RH,TS,Secrets of
    Haunted House 3.00
13 JKu(c),RT,SBi,RE,F:Sgt.Rock . 3.00
14 BWr(c),F:Swamp Thing rep. . . 3.50
15 MN,JRu,MR,DG,MGo,
    F:Batman 4.50
16 RH,D:Jonah Hex 3.25
17 F:Swamp Thing rep. 3.50
18 JK(c),digest,F:Sgt.Rock rep. . . 3.00
19 digest,Secret Origins
    O:Wonder Woman 3.50
20 BWr(c),F:Swamp Thing rep. . . 3.50
21 FM,JL,DG,RT,DA,F:Batman,
    Legion 18.00
22 JKu(c),F:G.I.Combat 3.25
23 digest size,F:Flash 3.25
24 F:Worlds Finest 3.25
25 F:Superman II,Photo Album . . 3.50
26 RA,F:Superman's Fortress . . . 4.00
27 JL,DG,F:Batman vs.Hulk 7.50

DC Super-Stars #11 © DC Comics, Inc.

DC SUPER-STARS
1976–78
1 F:Teen Titans rep. 4.00
2 F:DC Super-Stars of Space . . . 1.50
3 CS,F:Superman,Legion 2.50
4 DC,MA,F:Super-Stars of Space 1.50
5 CI,F:Flash rep. 1.50
6 MA,F:Super-Stars of Space . . . 1.50
7 F:Aquaman rep. 1.50
8 CI,MA,F:Adam Strange 4.00

DC COMICS

9 F:Superman rep. 1.50
10 DD,FMc,F:Superhero Baseball
　Special,A:Joker 5.50
11 GM,Super-Stars of Magic 1.50
12 CS,MA,F:Superboy 1.50
13 SA 1.50
14 RB,BL,JA,JRu,Secret Origins . 1.50
15 JKu(c),RB,RT(i),War Heroes . . 1.50
16 DN,BL,I:Star Hunters 1.50
17 JSon,MGr,BL,I&O:Huntress,O:Gr.
　Arrow,D:EarthII Catwoman . . 3.50
18 RT,DG,BL,F:Deadman,Phantom
　Stranger 2.50

DC UNIVERSE HOLIDAY BASH
1 one shot, yuletide tales 3.95

DC UNIVERSE: TRINITY
1993
1 TC,GeH,BKi,F:Darkstars,Green
　Lantern,L.E.G.I.O.N.,V:Triarch . 3.50
2 BKi,SHa,F:Darkstars,Green Lantern,
　L.E.G.I.O.N.,V:Triarch 3.50

DC VS. MARVEL
1996
1 RMz 5.50
1 2nd printing 4.00
2 & 3 see Marvel
4 PDa 5.00

DEADMAN
May, 1985
1 Cl,NA,rep 4.00
2 NA,rep. 3.00
3 NA,rep. 2.50
4 NA,rep. 2.50
5 NA,rep. 2.50
6 NA,rep. 2.50
7 NA,rep.Nov., 1985. . . . . 2.50
[Mini-Series] 1986
1 JL,A:Batman 2.50
2 JL,V:Sensei,A:Batman 2.00
3 JL,D:Sensei 2.00
4 JL,V:Jonah, final issue 2.00

DEADMAN: EXORCISM
[Limited-Series] 1992
1 KJo,A:Phantom Stranger 5.25
2 KJo,A:Phantom Stranger 5.25

DEADMAN: LOST SOULS
TPB Mike Baron, Kelly Jones . . 19.95

DEADMAN: LOVE AFTER DEATH
1989–90
1 KJo,Circus of Monsters 4.25
2 KJo,Circus of Monsters 4.25

DEADSHOT
1988–89
1 LMc,From Suicide Squad 2.00
2 LMc,Search for Son 2.00
3 LMc,V:Pantha 1.50
4 LMc,final issue 1.50

DEATH GALLERY
Vertigo
1 DMc(c),NGa Death Sketch
　Various Pinups 3.50

DEATH: THE HIGH COST OF LIVING
Vertigo 1993
1 B:NGa(s),CBa,MBu(i),Death
　becomes Human,A:Hettie 9.00
1a Platinum Ed. 18.00
2 CBa,MBu(i),V:Eremite,A:Hettie . 4.50
3 E:NGa(s),CBa,MBu(i),V:Eremite,
　A:Hettie 3.50
3a Error Copy 7.00
HC 19.95
TPB w/Tori Amos Intro 12.95

DEATH: THE TIME OF YOUR LIFE
Vertigo 1995
1 NGa,MBu,four-issue miniseries . 2.95
2 NGa,MBu,F:Foxglove 2.95
3 NGa,MBu,conclusion 2.95
HC NGa(s),rep. #1–#4 . . . . . . 19.95

Deathstroke: The Terminator #17
© DC Comics, Inc.

DEATHSTROKE: THE TERMINATOR
1991–94
1 MZ(c),(from New Teen Titans)
　SE,I:2nd Ravager 5.00
1a Second Printing,Gold 3.00
2 MZ(c),SE,Qurac Agents 3.50
3 SE,V:Ravager 3.00
4 SE,D:2ndRavager(Jackel) 3.00
5 Winter Green Rescue Attempt . 3.00
6 MZ(c),SE,B:City of Assassins,
　A:Batman 3.00
7 MZ(c),SE,A:Batman 2.50
8 MZ(c),SE,A:Batman 2.00
9 MZ(c),SE,E:City of Assassins,
　A:Batman;I:2nd Vigilante 2.00
10 MZ(c),ANi,GP,A:2nd Vigilante . 2.00
11 MZ(c),ANi,GP,A:2nd Vigilante . 2.00
12 MGo,Short Stories re:Slade . . 2.00
13 SE,V:Gr.Lant.,Flash,Aquaman . 2.00
14 ANi,Total Chaos#1,A:New Titans,
　Team Titans,V:Nightwing 2.00
15 ANi,Total Chaos#4,A:New Titans,
　Team Titans,I:Sweet Lili 2.00

16 ANi,Total Chaos#7 . . . . 2.00
17 SE,Titans Sell-Out #2
　A:Brotherhood of Evil 2.00
18 SE,V:Cheshire,R:Speedy 2.00
19 SE,V:Broth.of Evil,A:Speedy . 2.00
20 SE,MZ(c),V:Checkmate 2.00
21 SE,MZ(c),A:Checkmate 2.00
22 MZ(c),Quality of Mercy#1 . . . 2.00
23 MZ(c),Quality of Mercy#2 . . . 2.00
24 MZ(c),V:The Black Dome . . . 2.00
25 MZ(c),V:The Black Dome . . . 2.00
26 MZ(c),SE,in Kenya 2.00
27 MZ(c),SE,B:World Tour,
　in Germany 2.00
28 MZ(c),SE,in France 2.00
29 KM(c),SE,in Hong Kong 2.00
30 SE,A:Vigilante 2.00
31 SE,in Milwaukie 2.00
32 SE,in Africa 2.00
33 SE,I:Fleur de Lis 2.00
34 SE,E:World Tour 2.00
35 V:Mercenaries 2.00
36 V:British General 2.00
37 V:Assassin 2.00
38 A:Vigilante 2.25
39 A:Vigilante 2.25
40 Wedding in Red 2.25
Ann.#1 Eclipso,A:Vigilante 3.75
Ann.#2 SE,I:Gunfire 4.00
Ann.#3 Elseworlds Story 4.25
TPB Full Circle rep#1–#4,
　New Titans#70 . . . . 12.95
Becomes:

DEATHSTROKE: THE HUNTED
1994–95
0 Slade 2.50
41 Bronze Tiger 2.25
42 Wounded 2.25
43 . . . . 1.95
44 . . . . 1.95
45 A:New Titans 1.95
Becomes:

DEATHSTROKE
1995–96
46 Checkmate,Wintergreen 1.95
47 I:New Vigilante 1.95
48 Crimelord/Syndicate War,pt.1 . 2.25
49 Crimelord/Syndicate War,pt.4
　A:Supergirl, New Titans, Hawkman
　Blood Pack 2.25
50 A:Titans,Outsiders,Steel 3.50
51 No Fate or Future,pt.1 . . . . . . 2.25
52 No Fate or Future,pt.2 . . . . . . 2.25
53 The Borgia Plague,pt.1 . . . . . . 2.25
54 The Borgia Plague,pt.2 . . . . . . 2.25
55 MWn,Rebirth? 2.25
56 MWn,Night of the Karrion,pt.2 . 2.25
57 . . . . 2.25
58 MWn,V:The Joker 2.25
59 MWn,F:Hellriders 2.25
60 MWn,final issue 2.25

DEATHWISH
1994–95
1 New mini-series 1.75
2 F:Rahme 2.50
3 . . . . 2.50
4 V:Boots 2.50

DEMOLITION MAN
1993–94
1 thru 4 Movie Adapt 1.75

DC COMICS

Demon #7
© DC Comics, Inc.

DEMON
[1st Regular Series] 1972–74
1 JK,I:Demon	25.00
2 JK	10.00
3 JK	9.00
4 JK	9.00
5 JK	9.00
6 JK	7.00
7 JK	7.00
8 JK	7.00
9 JK	7.00
10 JK	7.00
11 JK	7.00
12 JK	7.00
13 JK	7.00
14 JK	7.00
15 JK	7.00
16 JK	7.00

[Limited Series] 1987
1 MWg,B:Jason Blood's Case	3.00
2 MWg,Fight to Save Gotham	2.00
3 MWg,Fight to Save Gotham	2.00
4 MWg,final issue	2.00

[2nd Regular Series] 1990–95
0 Relationships	1.95
1 VS,A:Etrigan (32 pages)	4.00
2 VS,V:TheCrone	2.50
3 VS,A:Batman	2.25
4 VS,A:Batman	2.25
5 VS,ThePit	2.25
6 VS,In Hell	2.25
7 VS,Etrigan-King of Hell	2.25
8 VS,Klarion the Witch Boy	2.25
9 VS,Jason Leaves Gotham	2.25
10 VS,A:PhantomStranger	2.25
11 VS,A:Klarion,C:Lobo	2.50
12 VS,Etrigan Vs. Lobo	2.50
13 VS,Etrigan Vs. Lobo	2.50
14 VS,V:Odd Squad,A:Lobo	2.50
15 VS,Etrigan Vs.Lobo	2.50
16 VS,Etrigan & Jason Blood switch bodies	2.00
17 VS, War of the Gods x-over	2.00
18 VS,V:Wotan,A:Scape Goat	2.00
19 VS,O:Demon,Demon/Lobo	

pin-up	3.00
20 VS,V:Golden Knight	2.00
21 VS,Etrigan/Jason, A:Lobo,Glenda	2.00
22 MWg,V:Mojo & Hayden	2.25
23 VS,A:Robin	2.00
24 VS,A:Robin	2.00
25 VS,V:Gideon Ryme	2.00
26 VS,B:America Rules	2.00
27 VS,A:Superman	2.00
28 VS,A:Superman	2.00
29 VS,E:America Rules	2.00
30 R:Asteroth	2.00
31 VS(c),A:Lobo	2.00
32 VS(c),A:Lobo,W.Woman	2.00
33 VS(c),A:Lobo,V:Asteroth	2.00
34 A:Lobo	2.00
35 A:Lobo,V:Belial	2.00
36 A:Lobo,V:Belial	2.00
37 A:Lobo,Morax	2.00
38 A:Lobo,Morax	2.00
39 A:Lobo	2.00
40 New Direction,B:GEn(s)	3.50
41 V:Mad Bishop	2.50
42 V:Demons	2.25
43 A:Hitman	10.00
44 V:Gotho-Demon,A:Hitman	9.00
45 V:Gotho-Demon,A:Hitman	9.00
46 R:Haunted Tank	2.50
47 V:Zombie Nazis	2.00
48 A:Haunted Tank,V:Zombie Nazis	2.00
49 b:Demon's Son,A:Joe Gun	1.95
50 GEn(s)	3.00
51 GEn(s),Son & Lovers	2.25
52 Etrigan & son–Hitman	4.00
53 Glenda & child–Hitman	4.00
54 Suffer the Children	1.95
55 Rebellion	1.95
56 F:Etrigan	1.95
57 Last Stand	1.95
58 Last issue	1.95
Ann.#1 Eclipso,V:Klarion	3.25
Ann.#2 I:Hitman	15.00

DETECTIVE COMICS
March, 1937
1 I:Slam Bradley	65,000.00
2 JoS	15,000.00
3 JoS	10,000.00
4 JoS	6,500.00
5 JoS	6,000.00
6 JoS	4,500.00
7 JoS	4,500.00
8 JoS,Mr. Chang(c)	7,000.00
9 JoS	4,500.00
10	4,500.00
11	4,500.00
12	3,500.00
13	3,500.00
14	3,500.00
15	3,500.00
16	3,500.00
17 I:Fu Manchu	3,500.00
18 Fu Manchu(c)	5,000.00
19	3,000.00
20 I:Crimson Avenger	5,500.00
21	3,000.00
22	3,500.00
23	3,000.00
24	3,000.00
25	3,000.00
26	3,000.00
27 BK,I:Batman	155,000.00
28 BK,V:Frenchy Blake	15,000.00

Detective Comics #11
© DC Comics, Inc.

29 BK,I:Doctor Death	25,000.00
30 BK,V:Dr. Death	5,000.00
31 BK,I:Monk	25,000.00
32 BK,V:Monk	5,000.00
33 O:Batman,V:Scarlet Horde	35,000.00
34 V:Due D'Orterre	4,000.00
35 V:Sheldon Lenox	7,000.00
36 I:Hugo Strange	5,000.00
37 V:Count Grutt, last Batman solo	4,800.00
38 I:Robin, the Boy Wonder	30,000.00
39 V:Green Dragon	4,600.00
40 I:Clayface (Basil Karlo)	5,800.00
41 V:Graves	2,800.00
42 V:Pierre Antal	1,800.00
43 V:Harliss Greer	1,800.00
44 Robin Dream Story	1,800.00
45 V:Joker	2,800.00
46 V:Hugo Strange	1,600.00
47 Meets Harvey Midas	1,600.00
48 Meets Henry Lewis	1,600.00
49 V:Clayface	1,600.00
50 V:Three Devils	1,600.00
51 V:Mindy Gang	1,200.00
52 V:Loo Chung	1,200.00
53 V:Toothy Hare gang	1,200.00
54 V:Hook Morgan	1,200.00
55 V:Dr. Death	1,200.00
56 V:Mad Mack	1,200.00
57 Meet Richard Sneed	1,200.00
58 I:Penguin	3,300.00
59 V:Penguin	1,400.00
60 V:Joker,I:Air Wave	1,400.00
61 The Three Racketeers	1,200.00
62 V:Joker	1,800.00
63 I:Mr. Baffle	1,200.00
64 I:Boy Commandos,V:Joker	3,300.00
65 Meet Tom Bolton	2,400.00
66 I:Two-Face	2,400.00
67 V:Penguin	1,700.00
68 V:Two-Face	1,400.00
69 V:Joker	1,400.00
70 Meet the Amazing Carlo	900.00
71 V:Joker	1,000.00
72 V:Larry the Judge	800.00
73 V:Scarecrow	900.00
74 I:Tweedledum & Tweedledee	800.00

Detective Comics #67
© DC Comics, Inc.

75 V:Robber Baron	800.00
76 V:Joker	1,300.00
77 V:Dr. Matthew Thorne	900.00
78 V:Baron Von Luger	900.00
79 'Destiny's' Auction	900.00
80 V:Two-Face	1,000.00
81 I:Cavalier	750.00
82 V:Blackee Blondeen	750.00
83 V:Dr. Goodwin	775.00
84 V:Ivan Krafft	750.00
85 V:Joker	900.00
86 V:Gentleman Jim Jewell	700.00
87 V:Penguin	750.00
88 V:Big Hearted John	700.00
89 V:Cavalier	700.00
90 V:Capt. Ben	700.00
91 V:Joker	900.00
92 V:Braing Bulow	600.00
93 V:'Tiger' Ragland	600.00
94 V:Lefty Goran	600.00
95 V:The Blaze	600.00
96 F:Alfred	600.00
97 V:Nick Petri	600.00
98 Meets Casper Thurbridge	600.00
99 V:Penguin	900.00
100 V:Digger	950.00
101 V:Joe Bart	600.00
102 V:Joker	850.00
103 Meet Dean Gray	600.00
104 V:Fat Frank gang	600.00
105 V:Simon Gurlan	600.00
106 V:Todd Torrey	600.00
107 V:Bugs Scarpis	600.00
108 Meet Ed Gregory	600.00
109 V:Joker	750.00
110 V:Prof. Moriarty	600.00
111 'Coaltown, USA'	600.00
112 'Case Without A Crime'	600.00
113 V:Blackhand	600.00
114 V:Joker	750.00
115 V:Basil Grimes	600.00
116 A:Carter Nichols, Robin Hood	600.00
117 'Steeplejack's Slowdown'	600.00
118 V:Joker	750.00
119 V:Wiley Derek	600.00
120 V:Penguin	1,200.00

121 F:Commissioner Gordon	600.00
122 V:Catwoman	950.00
123 V:Shiner	600.00
124 V:Joker	700.00
125 V:Thinker	575.00
126 V:Penguin	575.00
127 V:Dr. Agar	575.00
128 V:Joker	700.00
129 V:Diamond Dan mob	575.00
130	575.00
131 V:'Trigger Joe'	450.00
132 V:Human Key	450.00
133 Meets Arthur Loom	450.00
134 V:Penguin	475.00
135 A:Baron Frankenstein, Carter Nichols	450.00
136 A:Carter Nichols	450.00
137 V:Joker	550.00
138 V:Joker,O:Robotman	900.00
139 V:Nick Bailey	450.00
140 I:Riddler	3,500.00
141 V:'Blackie' Nason	500.00
142 V:Riddler	900.00
143 V:Pied Piper	525.00
144 A:Kay Kyser (radio personality)	525.00
145 V:Yellow Mask mob	525.00
146 V:J.J. Jason	525.00
147 V:Tiger Shark	525.00
148 V:Prof. Zero	525.00
149 V:Joker	800.00
150 V:Dr. Paul Visio	525.00
151 I&O:Pow Wow Smith	550.00
152 V:Goblin	550.00
153 V:Slits Danton	550.00
154 V:Hatch Marlin	550.00
155 A:Vicki Vale	550.00
156 'The Batmobile of 1950'	550.00
157 V:Bart Gillis	500.00
158 V:Dr. Doom	500.00
159 V:T. Worthington Chubb	500.00
160 V:Globe-Trotter	500.00
161 V:Bill Waters	525.00
162 Batman on railroad	525.00
163 V:Slippery Jim Elgin	525.00
164 Bat-signal story	525.00
165 'The Strange Costumes of Batman'	525.00
166 Meets John Gillen	525.00
167 A:Carter Nichols, Cleopatra	525.00
168 O:Joker	3,000.00
169 V:'Squint' Tolmar	525.00
170 Batman teams with Navy and Coast Guard	525.00
171 V:Penguin	700.00
172 V:Paul Gregorian	500.00
173 V:Killer Moth	500.00
174 V:Dagger	500.00
175 V:Kangaroo Kiley	500.00
176 V:Mr. Velvet	500.00
177 Bat-Cave story	400.00
178 V:Baron Swane	400.00
179 'Mayor Bruce Wayne'	400.00
180 V:Joker	425.00
181 V:Human Magnet	400.00
182 V:Maestro Dorn	400.00
183 V:John Cook	400.00
184 I:Firefly(Garfield Lynns)	400.00
185 I:'Secret's of Batman's Utility Belt'	400.00
186 'The Flying Bat-Cave'	400.00
187 V:Two-Face	425.00
188 V:William Milden	400.00
189 V:Styx	400.00
190 Meets Dr. Sampson,	

Detective Comics #147
© DC Comics, Inc.

O:Batman	575.00
191 V:Executioner	375.00
192 V: Nails Riley	375.00
193 V:Joker	425.00
194 V:Sammy Sabre	375.00
195 Meets Hugo Marmon	375.00
196 V:Frank Lumardi	375.00
197 V:Wrecker	375.00
198 Batman in Scotland	375.00
199 V:Jack Baker	375.00
200 V:Brand Keldon	500.00
201 Meet Human Target	375.00
202 V:Jolly Roger	375.00
203 V:Catwoman	400.00
204 V:Odo Neral	375.00
205 O:Bat-Cave	525.00
206 V:Trapper	375.00
207 Meets Merko the Great	375.00
208 V:Groff	375.00
209 V:Inventor	375.00
210 V:'Brain' Hobson	375.00
211 V:Catwoman	375.00
212 Meets Jonathan Bard	375.00
213 V:Mirror-Man	450.00
214 'The Batman Encyclopedia'	350.00
215 I:Ranger, Legionairy, Gaucho & Musketeer,A:Knight & Squire (See World's Finest 89)	350.00
216 A:Brane Taylor	350.00
217 Meets Barney Barrows	350.00
218 V:Dr. Richard Marston	350.00
219 V:Marty Mantee	350.00
220 A:Roger Bacon, historical scientist/philosopher	350.00
221 V:Paul King	350.00
222 V:'Big Jim' Jarrell	350.00
223 V:'Blast' Varner	350.00
224	350.00
225 I&O:Martian Manhunter (J'onn J'onzz)	5,000.00
226 O:Robin's costume, A:J'onn J'onzz	1,200.00
227 A:Roy Raymond, J'onn J'onzz	450.00
228 A:Roy Raymond, J'onnJ'onz	425.00
229 A:Roy Raymond,	

DC COMICS

DC COMICS

J'onnJ'onz	425.00
230 A:Martian Manhunter,I:Mad Hatter	500.00
231 A:Batman,Jr.,Roy Raymond J'onn J'onzz	325.00
232 A:J'onn J'onzz	300.00
233 I&O:Batwoman	1,200.00
234 V:Jay Caird	300.00
235 O:Batman's Costume	550.00
236 V:Wallace Walby	350.00
237 F:Robin	300.00
238 V:Checkmate(villain)	300.00
239 Batman robot story	300.00
240 V:Burt Weaver	300.00
241 The Rainbow Batman	300.00
242 Batcave story	250.00
243 V:Jay Vanney	250.00
244 O:Batarang	250.00
245 F:Comm.Gordon	250.00
246	250.00
247 I:Professor Milo	250.00
248	250.00
249 V:Collector	250.00

Detective Comics #277
© DC Comics, Inc.

250 V:John Stannor	250.00
251 V:Brand Ballard	225.00
252 Batman in a movie	225.00
253 I:Terrible Trio	225.00
254 A:Bathound	225.00
255 V:Fingers Nolan	225.00
256 Batman outer-space story	225.00
257 Batman sci-fi story	225.00
258 Batman robot story	225.00
259 I:Calendar Man	225.00
260 Batman outer space story	225.00
261 I:Dr. Double X	200.00
262 V:Jackal-Head	200.00
263 V:The Professor	200.00
264	200.00
265 O:Batman retold	300.00
266 V:Astro	200.00
267 I&O:Bat-Mite	225.00
268 V:"Big Joe" Foster	200.00
269 V:Director	200.00
270 Batman sci-fi story	210.00
271 V:Crimson Knight,O:Martian Manhunter(retold)	210.00
272 V:Crystal Creature	210.00

273 A:Dragon Society	150.00
274 V:Nails Lewin	150.00
275 A:Zebra-Man	150.00
276 A:Batmite	150.00
277 Batman Monster story	150.00
278 A:Professor Simms	150.00
279 Batman robot story	150.00
280 A:Atomic Man	150.00
281 Batman robot story	125.00
282 Batman sci-fi story	125.00
283 V:Phantom of Gotham City	125.00
284 V:Hal Durgan	125.00
285 V:Harbin	125.00
286 A:Batwoman	125.00
287 A:Bathound	125.00
288 V:Multicreature	125.00
289 A:Bat-Mite	125.00
290 Batman's robot story	125.00
291 Batman sci-fi story	125.00
292 Last Roy Raymond	125.00
293 A:Aquaman,J'onnJ'onzz	125.00
294 V:Elemental Men, A:Aquaman	125.00
295 A:Aquaman	125.00
296 A:Aquaman	125.00
297 A:Aquaman	125.00
298 I:Clayface(Matt Hagen)	250.00
299 Batman sci-fi stories	90.00
300 I:Mr.Polka-dot,E:Aquaman	100.00
301 A:J'onn'onzz	90.00
302 A:J'onnJ'onnz	80.00
303 A:J'onnJ'onnz	80.00
304 A:Clayface,J'onnJ'onz	80.00
305 Batman sci-fi story	80.00
306 A:J'onnJ'onnz	80.00
307 A:J'onnJ'onnz	80.00
308 A:J'onnJ'onnz	80.00
309 A:J'onnJ'onnz	80.00
310 A:Bat-Mite,J'onnJ'onnz	80.00
311 I:Cat-Man,Zook	90.00
312 A:Clayface,J'onnJ'onnz	70.00
313 A:J'onnJ'onnz	70.00
314 A:J'onnJ'onnz	70.00
315 I:Jungle Man	70.00
316 A:Dr.DoubleX,J'onnJ'onz	70.00
317 A:J'onnJ'onnz	70.00
318 A:Cat-Man,J'onnJ'onnz	70.00
319 A:J'onnJ'onnz	70.00
320 A:Vicki Vale	70.00
321 I:Terrible Trio	75.00
322 A:J'onnJ'onnz	65.00
323 I:Zodiac Master, A:J'onn J'onnz	65.00
324 A:Mad Hatter,J'onnJ'onnz	65.00
325 A:Cat-Man,J'onnJ'onnz	65.00
326 Batman sci-fi story	65.00
327 CI,25th ann,symbol change	125.00
328 D:Alfred,I:WayneFoundation	125.00
329 A:Elongated Man	65.00
330 "Fallen Idol of Gotham"	65.00
331 A:Elongated Man	65.00
332 A:Joker	50.00
333 A:Gorla	50.00
334	50.00
335	50.00
336	50.00
337 "Deep Freeze Menace	50.00
338	50.00
339	50.00
340	50.00
341 A:Joker	60.00
342	50.00
343 BK,CI,Elongated Man	50.00
344	50.00
345 CI,I:Blockbuster	50.00

346	50.00
347 CI,Elongated Man	50.00
348 Elongated Man	50.00
349 BK(c),CI,Blockbuster	50.00
350 Elongated Man	50.00
351 CI,A:Elongated Man, I:Cluemaster	50.00
352 BK,Elongated Man	50.00
353	50.00
354 BK,Elongated Man,I:Dr. Tzin-Tzin	50.00
355 CI,Elongated Man	50.00
356 BK,Outsider,Alfred	50.00
357	50.00
358 BK,Elongated Man	50.00
359 I:new Batgirl	100.00
360	50.00
361 CI	50.00
362 CI,Elongated Man	50.00
363 CI,Elongated Man	50.00
364 BK,Elongated Man	50.00
365 A:Joker	60.00
366 Elongated Man	50.00

Detective Comics #417
© DC Comics, Inc.

367 Elongated Man	50.00
368 BK,Elongated Man	50.00
369 CA,Elongated Man, Catwoman	60.00
370 BK,Elongated Man	55.00
371 BK,Elongated Man	50.00
372 BK,Elongated Man	35.00
373 BK,Elongated Man	35.00
374 BK,Elongated Man	35.00
375 CI,Elongated Man	35.00
376	35.00
377 MA,Elongated Man, V:Riddler	35.00
378 Elongated Man	35.00
379 CI,Elongated Man	35.00
380 Elongated Man	35.00
381 GaF,Marital Bliss Miss	35.00
382 FR(s),BbB,JoG,GaF(s),SGe	35.00
383 FR(s),BbB,JoG,GaF(s),SGe	35.00
384 FR(s),BbB,JoG,GaF(s),SGe, BU:Batgirl	35.00
385 E:FR(s),BbB,JoG,NA(c),GK,MA, MkF,BU:Batgirl	35.00
386 BbK,MkF,BbB,JoG,	

BU:Batgirl 35.00
387 RA,rep.Detective #27 . . . . . 75.00
388 JBr(s),BbB,JoG,
   GK,MA,FR(s) 50.00
389 FR(s),BbB,JoG,GK,MA 35.00
390 FR(s),BbB,JoG,GK,MA,
   A:Masquerader 35.00
391 FR(s),NA(c),BbB,
   JoG,GK,MA 20.00
392 FR(s),BbB,JoG,I:Jason Bard 20.00
393 FR(s),BbB,JoG,GK,MA 20.00
394 FR(s),BbB,JoG,GK,MA 20.00
395 FR(s),NA,DG,GK,MA 30.00
396 FR(s),BbB,JoG,GK,MA 20.00
397 DON(s),NA,DG,GK,MA 30.00
398 FR(s),BbB,JoG,GK,ViC 20.00
399 NA(c),DON(s),BbB,JoG,
   GK,ViC,Robin 22.00
400 FR(s),NA,DG,GK,I:Man-Bat . 60.00
401 NA(c),FR(s),JoG,
   BbB,JoG,GK,ViC 14.00
402 FR(s),NA,DG,V:Man-Bat . . . 30.00
403 FR(s),BbB,JoG,NA(c),GK,ViC,
   BU:Robin 20.00
404 NA,GC,GK,A:Enemy Ace . . 30.00
405 IN,GK,I:League of Assassins 20.00
406 DON(s),BbB,FrG 20.00
407 FR(s),NA,DG,V:Man-bat . . . 30.00
408 MWn(s),LWn(s),NA,DG,
   V:DrTzin Tzin 30.00
409 B:FR(s),BbB,FrG,DH,DG . . . 20.00
410 DON(s),FR(s),NA,DG,DH . . 30.00
411 NA(c),DON(s),BbB,DG,DH . . 18.00
412 NA(c),BbB,DG,DH 18.00
413 NA(c),BbB,DG,DH 18.00
414 DON(s),IN,DG,DH 18.00
415 BbB,DG,DH 18.00
416 DH 18.00
417 BbB,DG,DH,BU:Batgirl 18.00
418 DON(s),DH,IN,DG,A:Creeper 18.00
419 DON(s),DH 18.00
420 DH 18.00
421 DON(s),BbB,DG,DH,A:Batgirl 15.00
422 BbB,DG,DH,Batgirl 15.00
423 BbB,DG,DH 15.00
424 BbB,DG,DH,Batgirl 15.00
425 BWr(c),DON(s),IN,DG,DH . . 15.00
426 LWn(s),DG,A:Elongated Man 15.00
427 IN,DG,DH,BU:Batgirl 15.00
428 BbB,DG,ENB(s),DD,JoG,
   BU:Hawkman 15.00
429 DG,JoG,V:Man-Bat 15.00
430 BbB,NC,ENS(s),DG,
   A:Elongated Man 15.00
431 DON(s),IN,MA 15.00
432 MA,A:Atom 15.00
433 DD,DG,MA 15.00
434 IN,DG,ENB(s),RB,DG 15.00
435 E:FR(s),DG,IN 15.00
436 MA,(i),DG,A:Elongated Man 15.00
437 JA,WS,I:Manhunter 20.00
438 JA,WS,Manhunter 30.00
439 DG,WS,O:Manhunter,Kid
   Eternity rep. 30.00
440 JAp,WS 30.00
441 HC,WS 20.00
442 ATh,WS 30.00
443 WS,D:Manhunter 30.00
444 JAp,B:Bat-Murderer,
   A:Ra's Al Ghul 30.00
445 JAp,MGr,A:Talia 30.00
446 JAp,last giant 9.00
447 DG(i),A:Creeper 8.00
448 DG(i),E:Bat-Murderer,
   A:Creeper,Ra's Al Ghul 8.00

449 'Midnight Rustler in Gotham' . 9.00
450 WS 10.00
451 . . . . 8.00
452 . . . . 8.00
453 . . . . 8.00
454 . . . . 8.00
455 MGr,A:Hawkman,V:Vampire . 7.50
456 V:Ulysses Vulcan 7.50
457 O:Batman rtd 10.00
458 A:Man Bat 7.50
459 A:Man Bat 7.50
460 . . . . 7.50
461 V:Capt.Stingaree 7.50
462 V:Capt.Stingaree,A:Flash . . 7.50
463 MGr,Atom,I:Calc.,Bl.Spider . 7.50
464 MGr,TA,BlackCanary 7.50
465 TA,Elongated Man 7.50
466 MR,TA,V:Signalman 15.00
467 MR,TA 15.00
468 MR,TA,A:JLA 15.00
469 WS,I:Dr.Phosphorus 7.50
470 WS,AM,V:Dr.Phosphorus . . 7.50
471 MR,TA,A:Hugo Strange . . . 15.00

Detective Comics #422
© DC Comics, Inc.

472 MR,TA,A:Hugo Strange . . . 15.00
473 MR,TA,R:Deadshot 15.00
474 MR,TA,A:Penguin,
   N:Deadshot 16.00
475 MR,TA,A:Joker 28.00
476 MR,TA,A:Joker 28.00
477 MR,DG,rep.NA 20.00
478 MR,DG,I:3rd Clayface 15.00
479 MR,DG,A:3rd Clayface 15.00
480 DN,MA 8.00
481 JSt,CR,DN,DA,MR,
   A:ManBat 15.00
482 HC,MGo,DG,A:Demon 8.00
483 DN,DA,SD,A:Demon,
   40 Anniv. 12.00
484 DN,DA,Demon,O:1st Robin . 6.00
485 DN,DA,D:Batwoman,A:Demon
   A:Ras al Ghul 5.00
486 DN,DA,DG,I:Odd Man,
   V:Scarecrow 5.00
487 DN,DA,A:Ras Al Ghul 5.00
488 DN,V:Spook,Catwoman . . . 6.50
489 IN,DH,DN,DA,Ras Al Ghul . . 5.00
490 DN,DA,PB,FMc,A:Black

Lightning;A:Ras Al Ghul 5.00
491 DN,DA,PB,FMc,A:Black
   Lightning;V:Maxie Zeus 5.00
492 DN,DA,A:Penguin 6.50
493 DN,DA,A:Riddler 6.00
494 DN,DA,V:Crime Doctor 5.00
495 DN,DA,V:Crime Doctor 5.00
496 DN,DA,A:Clayface I 5.00
497 DN,DA 5.00
498 DN,DA,V:Blockbuster 5.00
499 DN,DA,V:Blockbuster 5.00
500 DG,CI,WS,TY,JKu,Dead-
   man,Hawkman,Robin 12.00
501 DN,DA 5.00
502 DN,DA 5.00
503 DN,DA,Batgirl,Robin,
   V:Scarecrow 5.00
504 DN,DA,Joker 7.00
505 DN,DA 5.00
506 DN,DA 5.00
507 DN,DA 5.00
508 DN,DA,V:Catwoman 7.00
509 DN,DA,V:Catman,Catwoman . 7.00
510 DN,DA,V:Madhatter 5.00
511 DN,DA,I:Mirage 5.00
512 GC,45th Anniv. 5.00
513 V:Two-Face 6.50
514 . . . . 5.00
515 . . . . 5.00
516 . . . . 5.00
517 . . . . 5.00
518 V:Deadshot 5.00
519 . . . . 5.00
520 A:Hugo Strange,Catwoman . 6.00
521 IN,TVE,A:Catwoman,B:BU:Green
   Arrow 6.50
522 D:Snowman 5.00
523 V:Solomon Grundy 5.00
524 2nd A:J.Todd 6.00
525 J.Todd 5.00
526 DN,AA,A:Joker,Catwoman
   500th A:Batman 20.00
527 V:Man Bat 4.00
528 Green Arrow,Ozone 4.00
529 I:Night Slayer,Nocturna 4.00
530 V:Nocturna 4.00
531 GC,AA,Chimera,J.Todd (see
   Batman #364) 4.00
532 GC,Joker 7.00
533 . . . . 4.00
534 GC,A:Gr.Arrow,V:Poisonivy . 4.00
535 GC,A:Gr.Arrow,V:Crazy Quitt
   2nd A:New Robin 6.00
536 GC,A:Gr.Arrow,V:Deadshot . 4.00
537 GC,A:Gr.Arrow 4.00
538 GC,A:Gr.Arrow,V:Catman . . 4.00
539 GC,A:Gr.Arrow 4.00
540 GC,A:Gr.Arrow,V:Scarecrow . 4.00
541 GC,A:Gr.Arrow,V:Penguin . . 5.50
542 GC,A:Gr.Arrow 4.00
543 GC,A:Gr.Arrow,V:Nightslayer . 4.00
544 GC,A:Gr.Arrow,V:Nightslayer
   Nocturna 4.00
545 . . . . 4.00
546 . . . . 4.00
547 . . . . 4.00
548 PB 4.00
549 PB,KJ,AMo(s),Gr.Arrow . . . 4.50
550 KJ,AMo(s),Gr.Arrow 4.50
551 PB,V:Calendar Man 4.00
552 V:Black Mask 4.00
553 V:Black Mask 4.00
554 KJ,N:Black Canary 4.00
555 GC,DD,GreenArrow 4.00
556 GC,Gr.Arrow,V:Nightslayer . . 4.00

DC COMICS

All comics prices listed are for *Near Mint* condition.

DC COMICS

Detective Comics #532
© DC Comics, Inc.

557 V:Nightslayer	4.00
558 GC,Green Arrow	4.00
559 GC,Green Arrow	4.00
560 GC,A:Green Arrow	4.00
561	4.00
562 GC,V:Film Freak	4.00
563 V:Two Face	4.00
564 V:Two Face	4.00
565 GC,A:Catwoman	5.50
566 GC,Joker	6.00
567 GC,HarlanEllison	5.00
568 KJ,Legends tie-in,A:Penguin	5.50
569 AD,V:Joker	7.00
570 AD,EvilCatwoman,A:Joker	7.00
571 AD,V:Scarecrow	5.00
572 AD,CI,A:Elongated Man,Sherlock	
Holmes,SlamBradley,50thAnn	5.00
573 AD,V:Mad Hatter	5.00
574 AD,End old J.Todd/Robin sty	5.00
575 AD,Year 2,pt.1,I:Reaper	15.00
576 TM,AA,Year 2,pt.2,	
R:Joe Chill	12.00
577 TM,AA,Year 2,pt.3,V:Reaper	12.00
578 TM,AA,Year 2,pt.4,	
D:Joe Chill	12.00
579 I:NewCrimeDoctor	3.00
580 V:Two Face	3.00
581 V:Two Face	3.00
582 Millenium X-over	3.00
583 I:Ventriloquist	3.00
584 V:Ventriloquist	3.00
585 I:Rat Catcher	3.00
586 V:Rat Catcher	3.00
587 NB,V:Corrosive Man	3.00
588 NB,V:Corrosive Man	3.00
589 Bonus Book #5	4.00
590 NB,V:Hassan	3.00
591 NB,V:Rollo	3.00
592 V:Psychic Vampire	3.00
593 NB,V:Stirh	3.00
594 NB,A:Mr.Potato	3.00
595 IN,bonus book #11	3.00
596 V:Sladek	3.00
597 V:Sladek	3.00
598 DCw,BSz,Blind Justice #1	7.00
599 DCw,BSz,Blind Justice #2	4.00
600 DCw,BSz,Blind Justice #3,	

50th Anniv.(double size)	5.00
601 NB,I:Tulpa	3.00
602 NB,A:Jason Blood	2.50
603 NB,A:Demon	2.50
604 NB,MudPack #1,V:Clayface,	
poster insert	2.50
605 NB,MudPack #2,V:Clayface	2.50
606 NB,MudPack #3,V:Clayface	2.50
607 NB,MudPack #4,V:Clayface,	
poster insert	2.50
608 NB,I:Anarky	2.00
609 NB,V:Anarky	2.00
610 NB,V:Penguin	3.00
611 NB,V:Catwoman,Catman	3.00
612 NB,A:Vicki Vale	1.75
613 Search for Poisoner	1.75
614 V:Street Demons	1.75
615 NB,Return Penguin #2 (see	
Batman #448-#449)	2.75
616 NB	1.75
617 A:Joker	1.75
618 NB,DG,A:Tim Drake	1.75
619 NB,V:Moneyspider	1.75
620 NB,V:Obeah,Man	1.75
621 NB,SM,Obeah,Man	1.75
622 Demon Within,pt.1	2.00
623 Demon Within,pt.2	2.00
624 Demon Within,pt.3	2.00
625 JAp,I:Abattior	1.75
626 JAp,A:Electrocutioner	1.75
627 600th issue w/Batman,rep.	
Detective #27	4.00
628 JAp,A:Abattoir	1.75
629 JAp,'The Hungry Grass'	1.75
630 JAp,I:Stiletto	1.75
631 JAp,V:Neo-Nazi Gangs	1.75
632 JAp,V:Creature	1.75
633 TMd,Fake Batman?	1.75
634 'The Third Man'	1.75
635 Video Game,pt.1	1.75
636 Video Game,pt.2	1.75
637 Video Game,pt.3	1.75
638 JAp,Walking Time Bomb	1.75
639 JAp,The Idiot Root,pt.2	1.75
640 JAp,The Idiot Root,pt.4	1.75
641 JAp,Destroyer,pt.3	
(see LOTDK#27)	2.00
642 JAp,Faces,pt.2	1.75
643 JAp,'Librarian of Souls'	1.75
644 TL,Electric City,pt.1	
A:Electrocutioner	1.75
645 TL,Electric City,pt.2	1.75
646 TL,Electric City,pt.3	1.75
647 TL,V:Cluemaster	1.75
648 MWg(c),TL,V:Cluemaster	1.75
649 MWg(c),TL,V:Cluemaster	1.75
650 TL,A:Harold,Ace	1.75
651 TL,'A Bullet for Bullock'	1.75
652 GN,R:Huntress	1.75
653 GN,A:Huntress	1.75
654 MN,The General,pt.1	1.75
655 MN,The General,pt.2	2.00
656 MN,The General,pt.3,C:Bane	6.00
657 MN,A:Azrael,I:Cypher	10.00
658 MN,A:Azrael	8.00
659 MN,Knightfall#2,	
V:Ventriloquist,A:Bane	7.50
660 Knightfall#4,Bane Vs.	
Killer Croc	5.00
661 GN,Knightfall#6,V:Firefly,	
Joker,A:Bane	4.00
662 GN,Knightfall#8,V:Firefly,	
Joker,A:Huntress,Bane	3.50
663 GN,Knightfall#10,V:Trogg,	
Zombie,Bird,A:Bane	3.00

Detective Comics #639
© DC Comics, Inc.

664 GN,Knightfall#12,A:Azrael	3.00
665 GN,Knightfall#16,A:Azrael	3.00
666 GN,SHa,A:Azrael,Trogg,	
Zombie,Bird	2.25
667 GN,SHa,Knightquest:Crusade,	
V:Trigger Twins	2.00
668 GN,SHa,Knightquest:Crusade,	
Robin locked out of Batcave	2.00
669 GN,SHa,Knightquest:Crusade,	
V:Trigger Twins	2.00
670 GN,SHa,Knightquest:Crusade,	
F:Rene Montoya	2.00
671 GN,SHa,V:Joker	2.00
672 KJ(c),GN,SHa,Knightquest:	
Crusade,V:Joker	2.00
673 KJ(c),GN,SHa,Knightquest:	
Crusade,V:Joker	2.00
674 KJ(c),GN,SHa,Knightquest:	
Crusade	2.00
675 Foil(c),KJ(c),GN,SHa,Knightquest:	
Crusade,V:Gunhawk,foil(c)	3.25
675a Newsstand ed.	1.75
675b Platinum edition	20.00
676 KJ(c),GN,SHa,Knights End #3,	
A:Nightwing	4.00
677 KJ(c),GN,SHa,Knights End #9	
V:Azrael	3.00
678 GN,SHa,Zero Hour	2.00
679 Ratcatcher	2.00
680 Batman,Two-Face	1.75
681 CDi,GN,KJ,Jean-Paul Valley	1.75
682 CDi,GN,SHa,Return of Bruce	
Wayne,Troika,pt.3	1.75
682a Collector's Edition	2.50
683 R:Penguin,I:Actuary	1.75
684 Daylight Heist	1.75
685 Chinatown War	1.75
686 V:King Snake,Lynx	2.00
687 CDi,SHa,V:River Pirate	2.00
688 V:Captian Fear	2.00
689 F:Black Mask,Firefly	2.00
690 F:Black Mask,Firefly	2.00
691 V:Spellbinder	2.00
692 CDi,SHa,Underworld	
Unleashed tie-in	2.00
693 CDi,SHa,V:Poison Ivy	
& Agent Orange	2.00

DC COMICS

694 CDi,find plant-killer 2.00
695 CDi 3.00
696 CDi,GN,SHa,Contagion,pt.8 . 3.00
697 CDi,GN,SHa,pt.1 (of 3)
   V:Lock-up 2.00
698 CDi(s),A:Two-Face 2.00
699 CDi(s), ... 2.00
700 double size, Legacy, pt.1
   x-over, R:Bane 3.50
700a cardstock cover 5.00
701 Legacy, pt. 6 x-over, V:Bane . 1.95
702 CDi(s),GN,SHa,Legacy
   aftermath 1.95
703 CDi(s),GN,SHa, riots in Gotham
   City, Final Night tie-in 1.95
704 CDi(s),GN,TP,V:Al Gabone . . 1.95
705 CDi(s),GN,Riddler & Cluemaster
   clash 1.95
706 CDi(s),GN 1.95
707 CDi(s),GN,Riddler/Cluemaster
   concl. 1.95
708 CDi(s),GN,BSz,F:Deathstroke,
   R:Gunhawk,pt.1 (of 3) . . . 1.95
709 CDi(s),GN,BSz,F:Deathstroke,
   Gunhawk,pt.2 . . . . 1.95
710 CDi(s),GN,BSz,F:Deathstroke,
   Gunhawk,pt.3 . . . . 1.95
711 CDi(s),GN,CaS,Bruce Wayne
   fights crime 1.95
712 CDi(s),GN,I:Gearhead 1.95
713 CDi(s),GN,V:Gearhead,pt.2 . 1.95
Ann.#1 KJ,TD,A:Question,Talia,
   V:Penguin 6.00
Ann.#2 VS,A:Harvey Harris 6.00
Ann.#3 DJu,DG,Batman in Japan . 3.50
Ann.#4 Armageddon,pt.10 . . . . . 3.00
Ann.#5 SK(c),TMd,Eclipso,V:The
   Ventriloquist,Joker 3.00
Ann.#6 JBa,I:Geist 2.75
Ann.#7 CDi,Elseworlds Story . . . 3.25
Ann.#8 CDi,KD(c) Year One Annual
   O:The Riddler 3.95
Ann.#9 Legends o/t Dead Earth . . 2.95
Ann.#10 Pulp Heroes (War) CDi(s),
   SB,KJ 3.95

DETENTION COMICS
Aug. 1996
one-shot DON(s) 64pg, 3 stories . 3.50

DHAMPIRE: STILLBORN
DC/Vertigo Sept. 1996
GN Nancy A. Collins adaptation . . 5.95

DOC SAVAGE
1987–88
1 AKu/NKu,D:Orig. Doc Savage . 3.00
2 AKu/NKu,V:Nazi's 2.50
3 AKu/NKu,V:Nazi's 2.50
4 AKu/NKu,V:Heinz 2.50
[2nd Series] 1988–90
1 'Five in the Sky'(painted cov.) . 3.00
2 Chip Lost in Himalayas 2.25
3 Doc declares war on USSR . . . 2.25
4 DocSavage/Russian team-up . . 2.25
5 V:The Erisians 2.25
6 U.S.,USSR,China Alliance
   vs. Erisians 2.25
7 Mind Molder,pt.1, I:Pat Savage . 2.25
8 . . . . 2.25
9 In Hidalgo 2.25
10 V:Forces of the Golden God . . 2.25
11 Sunlight Rising,pt.1 . . . . 2.25
12 Sunlight Rising,pt.2 . . . . 2.25

Doc Savage (2nd Series) #3
© DC Comics, Inc.

13 Sunlight Rising,pt.3 . . . . 2.25
14 Sunlight Rising,pt.4 . . . . 2.25
15 SeaBaron #1 . . . . 2.25
16 EB,Shadow & Doc Savage . . 2.25
17 EB,Shadow & Doc Savage . . 2.25
18 EB,Shadow/DocSavage conc. . 2.25
19 All new 1930's story 2.25
20 V:Airlord a his Black Zepplin . 2.25
21 Airlord (30's story conc.) 2.25
22 Doc Savages Past,pt.1 . . . . . 2.25
23 Doc Savages Past,pt.2 . . . . . 2.25
24 Doc Savages Past,pt.3 (final) . 2.25
Ann.#1 1956 Olympic Games . . . 4.50

DOCTOR FATE
July, 1987
1 KG,V:Lords of Chaos 3.00
2 KG,New Dr. Fate 2.50
3 KG,A:JLI 2.50
4 KG,V:Lords of Chaos Champion 2.50
[2nd Series] 1988–92
1 New Dr.Fate,V:Demons 2.50
2 A:Andrew Bennett(I,Vampire) . . 2.00
3 A:Andrew Bennett(I,Vampire) . . 2.00
4 V:I,Vampire 2.00
5 Dr.Fate & I,Vampire in Europe . 2.00
6 A:Petey 2.00
7 Petey returns home dimension . 2.00
8 Linda become Dr.Fate again . . 2.00
9 Eric's Mother's Ghost,
   A:Deadman 2.00
10 Death of Innocence,pt.1 . . . . 2.00
11 Return of Darkseid, Death of
   Innocence,pt.2 . . . . 2.00
12 Two Dr.Fates Vs.Darkseid,
   Death of Innocence,pt.3 . . . . 2.00
13 Linda in the Astral Realm,
   Death of Innocence,pt.4 . . . . 2.00
14 Kent & Petey vs. Wotan 2.00
15 V:Wotan,A:JLI 2.00
16 Flashback-novice Dr.Fate . . . 1.75
17 Eric's Journey thru afterlife . . 1.75
18 Search for Eric 1.75
19 A:Dr.Benjamine Stoner, Lords of
   Chaos, Phantom Stranger,
   Search for Eric continued 1.75

20 V:Lords of Chaos,Dr.Stoner,
   A:Phantom Stranger 1.75
21 V:Chaos,A:PhantomStranger . . 1.75
22 A:Chaos and Order 1.75
23 Spirits of Kent & Inza Nelson . 1.75
24 L:Dr.Fate Characters 1.75
25 I:New Dr. Fate 1.75
26 Dr.Fate vs. Orig.Dr.Fate 1.75
27 New York Crime 1.75
28 'Diabolism' 1.75
29 Kent Nelson 1.75
30 'Resurrection' 1.75
31 'Resurrection' contd. 1.75
32 War of the Gods x-over 1.75
33 War of the Gods x-over 1.75
34 A:T'Gilian 1.75
35 Kent Nelson in N.Y. 1.75
36 Search For Inza,A:Shat-Ru . . 1.75
37 Fate Helmet Powers revealed . 1.75
38 'The Spirit Motor,'Flashback . . 1.75
39 U.S.Senate Hearing 1.75
40 A:Wonder Woman 1.75
41 O:Chaos and Order,last issue . 1.75
Ann.#1 TS,R:Eric's dead mother . 2.95

DOOM FORCE
Spec.#1 MMi(c),RCa,WS,PCu,KSy,
   I:Doom Force 2.75

DOOM PATROL
[1st series]
(see MY GREATEST ADVENTURE)

DOOM PATROL
[2nd Regular Series]
Oct., 1987
1 SLi,R:Doom Patrol,plus Who's Who
   background of team, I:Kalki . . . 2.50
2 SLi,V:Kalki 1.75
3 SLi,I:Lodestone 1.75
4 SLi,I:Karma 1.75
5 SLi,R:Chief 1.75
6 B:PuK(s),EL,GyM(i),
   I:Scott Fischer 2.00
7 EL,GyM(i),V:Shrapnel 1.75
8 EL,GyM(i),V:Shrapnel 1.75
9 E:PuK(s),EL,GyM(i),V:Garguax,
   & Bonus Book 1.75
10 EL,A:Superman 2.00
11 EL,R:Garguax 1.75
12 EL,A:Garguax 1.75
13 EL,A:Power Girl 1.75
14 EL,A:Power Girl 1.75
15 EL,Animal-Veg-.Mineral Man . 1.75
16 V:GenImmotus,Animal-Veg.-
   Mineral Man 1.75
17 D:Celsius,A:Aquaman & Sea
   Devils, Invasion tie-in 3.00
18 Invasion 1.50
19 B:GMo(s),New Direction,
   I:Crazy Jane 5.00
20 I:Rebis(new Negative-Being),
   A:CrazyJane,Scissormen 4.00
21 V:Scissormen 3.50
22 City of Bone,V:Scissormen . . . 3.50
23 A:RedJack,Lodestone kidnap . 3.50
24 V:Red Jack 3.50
25 Secrets of New Doom Patrol . 3.50
26 I:Brotherhood of Dada 3.00
27 V:Brotherhood of Dada 3.00
28 Trapped in nightmare,V:Dada . 3.00
29 Trapped in painting,
   A:Superman 3.00
30 SBs(c),V:Brotherhood of Dada 3.00

DC COMICS

Doom Patrol #9 © DC Comics, Inc.

31 SBs(c),A:The Pale Police		3.00
32 SBs(c),V:Cult of Unwritten Book		3.00
33 SBs(c),V:Cult,A:Anti-God the DeCreator		3.00
34 SBs(c),Robotman vs. his brain, R:The Brain & Mr.Mallah		3.00
35 SBs(c),A:Men from N.O.W.H.E.R.E.		3.00
36 SBs(c),V:Men from N.O.W.H.E.R.E.		3.25
37 SBs(c),Rhea Jones Story		2.50
38 SBs(c),V:Aliens		2.50
39 SBs(c),V:Aliens		2.50
40 SBs(c),Aliens		2.50
41 SBS(c),Aliens		2.50
42 O:Flex Mentallo		2.50
43 SBs(c),V:N.O.W.H.E.R.E.		2.50
44 SBs(c),V:N.O.W.H.E.R.E.		2.50
45		2.50
46 SBs(c),RCa,MkK,A:Crazy Jane, Dr.Silence		2.50
47 Scarlet Harlot (Crazy Jane)		2.50
48 V:Mr.Evans		2.50
49 TTg(c),RCa,MGb,I:Mr.Nobody		2.50
50 SBs(c),V:Brotherhood of Dada & bonus artists portfolio		3.00
51 SBs(c),Mr.Nobody Runs for President		2.50
52 SBs(c),Mr.Nobody saga conc		2.50
53 SBs(c),Parody Issue,A:Phantom Stranger,Hellblazer,Mr.E		2.50
54 Rebis'Transformation		2.50
55 SBs(c),V:Crazy Jane, Candle Maker		2.50
56 SBs(c),RCa,V:Candle Maker		2.50
57 SBs(c),RCa,V:Candle Maker, O:Team,Double-sized		3.00
58 SBs(c),V:Candle Maker		2.25
59 TTg(c),RCa,SnW(i),A:Candlemaker D:Larry Trainor		2.25
60 JHw(c),RCa,SnW(i), V:Candlemaker,A:Magnus		2.25
61 TTg(c),RCa,SnW(i),A:Magnus D:Candlemaker		2.25
62 DFg(c),RCa,SnW(i), V:Nanomachines		2.25
63 E:GMo(s),RCa,R:Crazy Jane,		

V:Keysmiths,BU:Sliding from the Wreckage		2.25
Vertigo 1993		
64 BB(c),B:RaP(s),RCa,SnW(i), B:Sliding from the Wreckage, R:Niles Caulder		2.25
65 TTg(c),RCa,SnW(i),Nannos		2.25
66 RCa,E:Sliding from the Wreckage		2.25
67 TTg(c),LiM,GHi(i),New HQ,I:Charlie, George,Marion,V:Wild Girl		2.25
68 TTg(c),LiM,GHi(i),I:Indentity Addict		2.25
69 TTg(c),LiM,GHi(i),V:Identity Addict		2.25
70 TTg(c),SEa,TS(i),I:Coagula, V:Codpiece		2.25
71 TTg(c),LiM,TS(i),Fox & Crow		2.25
72 TTg(c),LiM,TS(i),Fox vs Crow		2.25
73 LiM,GPi(i),Head's Nightmare		2.25
74 LiM,TS(i),Bootleg Steele		2.25
75 BB(c),TMK,Teiresias Wars#1, Double size		2.25
76 Teiresias Wars#2		2.25
77 BB(c),TMK,N:Cliff		2.25
78 BB(c),V:Tower of Babel		2.25
79 BB(c),E:Teiresias Wars		2.25
80 V:Yapping Dogs		2.25
81 B:Masquerade		2.25
82 E:Masquerade		2.25
83 False Memory		1.95
84 The Healers		1.95
85 Charlie the Doll		1.95
86 Imagine Ari's Friends		1.95
87 KB(c),Imagine Ari's Friends,pt.4,final issue		1.95
Ann.#1 A:Lex Luthor		2.00
Ann.#2 RaP(s),MkW,Children's Crusade,F:Dorothy,A:Maxine		4.25
Doom Patrol/Suicide Squad #1 EL, D:Mr.104,Thinker,Psi,Weasel		2.50
TPB Crawling From the Wreckage, SBs(c),rep.#19-#25		19.95

DOOMSDAY

Ann.#1 Year One annuals		3.95

DOORWAY TO NIGHTMARE
1978

1 I:Madame Xanadu		1.00
2		1.00
3		1.00
4 JCr		1.00
5		1.00

DOUBLE ACTION COMICS
Jan., 1940

2 Pre-Hero DC		10,000.00

DRAGONLANCE
1988–91

1 Krynn's Companion's advent.		5.00
2 Vandar&Riva vs.Riba's brother		4.00
3 V:Takhesis,Queen of Darkness		3.50
4 V:Lord Soth & Kitiara		3.50
5 V:Queen of Darkness		3.50
6 Gnatch vs. Kalthanan		3.50
7 Raistlin's Evil contd.		3.50
8 Raistlin's Evil concl.		2.00
9 Journey to land o/t Minotaurs A:Tanis, Kitiara		2.00

Dragonlance #28 © DC Comics, Inc.

10 Blood Sea,'Arena of Istar'		2.00
11 Cataclysm of Krynn Revealed 'Arena of Istar' contd.		2.00
12 Horak vs.Koraf, Arena contd.		2.00
13 Test of High Sorcery #1		2.00
14 Test of High Sorcery #2		2.00
15 Test of High Sorcery #3		2.00
16 Test of High Sorcery #4		2.00
17 Winter'sKnight:DragonkillPt.1		2.00
18 Winter'sKnight:DragonkillPt.1		2.00
19 Winter'sKnight:DragonkillPt.1		2.00
20 Winter'sKnight:DragonkillPt.1		2.00
21 Move to New World		2.00
22 Taladas,pt.1,A:Myrella		2.00
23 Taladas,pt.2,Riva vs. Dragon		2.00
24 Taladas,pt.3,V:Minotaur Lord		2.00
25 Taladas,pt.4,V:Axantheas		2.00
26 Rune Discovery,V:Agents of Eristem		2.00
27 V:Agents of Eristem		2.00
28 Riva continued.		2.00
29 Riva continued		2.00
30 Dwarf War,pt.1		1.75
31 Dwarf War,pt.2		1.75
32 Dwarf War,pt.3		1.75
33 Dwarf War,pt.4		1.75
34 conc., last issue		1.75
Ann.#1 Myrella of the Robed Wizards		2.95

DREAMING, THE
DC/Vertigo June 1996

1 TLa(s),PSj,"The Goldie Factor,"pt.1		2.50
2 TLa(s),PSj,"The Goldie Factor,"pt.2		2.50
3 TLa(s),PSj,"The Goldie Factor,"pt.3		2.50
4 SvP,"The Lost Boy," pt.1 (of 4)		2.50
5 SvP,"The Lost Boy," pt.2		2.50
6 SvP,"The Lost Boy," pt.3		2.50
7 SvP,"The Lost Boy," pt.4		2.50
8 AaK(s),MZi, visitor from Cain's past		2.50
9 BT(s),PD,TOz,"Weird Romance," pt.1 (of 4)		2.50
10 BT(s),PD,TOz,"Weird Romance,"		

pt.2	2 50
11 BT(s),PD,TOz,"Weird Romance,"	
pt.3	2.50
12 BT(s),PD,TOz,"Weird Romance,"	
pt.4	2.50
13 TLa,JIT,"Coyote's Kiss," pt. 1	2.50
14 TLa,JIT,"Coyote's Kiss," pt. 2	2.50
15	2.50
16 GyA,F:Nuala	2.50

DYNAMIC CLASSICS
Sept.-Oct. 1978
1 Rep. Detective 395 & 438 . . . . 3.00

Eclipso #5 © DC Comics, Inc.

ECLIPSO
1992–94
1 BS,MPn,V:South American	
Drug Dealers	2.50
2 BS,MPn,A:Bruce Gordon	2.00
3 BS,MPn,R:Amanda Waller . . .	2.00
4 BS,A:Creeper,Cave Carson . .	3.00
5 A:Creeper,Cave Carson	3.00
6 LMc,V:Bruce Gordon	3.00
7 London,1891	3.50
8 A:Sherlock Holmes	1.50
9 I:Johnny Peril	1.50
10 CDo,V:Darkseid	1.50
11 A:Creeper,Peacemaker,Steel	1.50
12 V:Shadow Fighters	1.50
13 D:Manhunter,Commander Steel,	
Major Victory,Peacemaker,	
Wildcat,Dr.Midnight,Creeper	1.75
14 A:JLA	1.50
15 A:Amanda Waller	1.50
16 V:US Army	1.50
17 A:Amanda Waller,Martian	
Manhunter,Wonder Woman,Flash,	
Bloodwynd,Booster Gold . .	1.75
18 A:Spectre,JLA,final issue . . .	2.00
Ann.#1 I:Prism	2.50

ECLIPSO: THE
DARKNESS WITHIN
1992
1 BS,Direct w/purple diamond,	
A:Superman,Creeper	4.00
1a BS,Newstand w/out diamond	3.00

2 BS,MPn,DC heroes V:Eclipso,	
D:Starman	3.00

EGYPT
1995–96
1 College Experiments	2.50
2 College Experiments	2.50
3 New York Haunt	2.50
4 V:Seth,Isis	2.50
5 V: The Priests	2.50
6	2.50
7 finale	2.50

80 PAGE GIANTS
Aug., 1964
1 Superman	450.00
2 Jimmy Olsen	250.00
3 Lois Lane	200.00
4 Golden Age-Flash	210.00
5 Batman	210.00
6 Superman	150.00
7 JKu&JKu(c),Sgt. Rock's Prize	
Battle Tales	150.00
8 Secret Origins,O:JLA,Aquaman,	
Robin,Atom, Superman . . .	350.00
9 Flash	150.00
10 Superboy	135.00
11 Superman,A:Lex Luthor . . .	135.00
12 Batman	135.00
13 Jimmy Olsen	150.00
14 Lois Lane	150.00
15 Superman & Batman	160.00
16 JLA #39	75.00
17 Batman #176	40.00
18 Superman #183	18.00
19 Our Army at War #164	10.00
20 Action #334	16.00
21 Flash #160	30.00
22 Superboy #129	7.00
23 Superman #187	13.00
24 Batman #182	26.00
25 Jimmy Olsen #95	10.00
26 Lois Lane #68	10.00
27 Batman #185	35.00
28 World's Finest #161	11.00
29 JLA #48	16.00
30 Batman #187	35.00
31 Superman #193	13.00
32 Our Army at War #177	8.00
33 Action #347	11.00
34 Flash #169	30.00
35 Superboy #138	6.00
36 Superman #197	12.00
37 Batman #193	16.00
38 Jimmy Olsen #104	5.00
39 Lois Lane #77	6.00
40 World's Finest #170	10.00
41 JLA #58	12.00
42 Superman #202	12.00
43 Batman #198	24.00
44 Our Army at War #190	5.00
45 Action #360	8.00
46 Flash #178	18.00
47 Superboy #147	7.00
48 Superman #207	12.00
49 Batman #203	14.00
50 Jimmy Olsen #113	5.00
51 Lois Lane #86	6.00
52 World's Finest #179	6.00
53 JLA #67	8.00
54 Superman #212	12.00
55 Batman #208	13.00
56 Our Army at War #203	5.00
57 Action #373	8.00
58 Flash #187	13.00

59 Superboy #156	6.00
60 Superman #217	10.00
61 Batman #213	35.00
62 Jimmy Olsen #122	5.00
63 Lois Lane #95	5.00
64 World's Finest #188	6.00
65 JLA #76	7.00
66 Superman #222	10.00
67 Batman #218	13.00
68 Our Army at War #216	5.00
69 Adventure #390	6.00
70 Flash #196	12.00
71 Superboy #165	6.00
72 Superman #227	10.00
73 Batman #223	14.00
74 Jimmy Olsen #131	5.00
75 Lois Lane #104	4.00
76 World's Finest #197	5.00
77 JLA #85	6.00
78 Superman #232	10.00
79 Batman #228	12.00
80 Our Army at War #229	5.00
81 Adventure #403	6.00
82 Flash #205	9.00
83 Superboy #174	5.00
84 Superman #239	10.00
85 Batman #233	12.00
86 Jimmy Olsen #140	5.00
87 Lois Lane #113	4.00
88 World's Finest #206	5.00
89 JLA #93	6.00

EL DIABLO
1989–91
1 I:El Diablo, double-size	2.50
2 V:Crime Lord Benny Contreras	2.00
3 'Day of the Dead' Celebration	2.00
4 Storm #1	2.25
5 Storm #2	2.25
6 Storm #3	2.25
7 Storm #4	2.25
8 V:Car-Theft Ring	2.00
9 V:Crime Lord of Dos Rios . . .	2.00
10 The Franchise #1	2.00
11 The Franchise #2	2.00
12 A:Greg Sanders (golden age)	2.00
13 The River #1	2.00
14 The River #2	2.00
15 The River #3	2.00
16 Final Issue	2.00

ELECTRIC WARRIOR
1986–87
1 SF series,I:Electric Warriors . . .	2.50
2 'Bloodstalker Mode'	2.00
3 Rogue Warrior vs. Z-Primes .	2.00
4 Primmies vs. Electric Warriors	2.00
5 Lek 0-03 Rebels	2.00
6 Lek 0-03 vs. Masters	1.75
7 Lek'sFate,Derek Two-Shadows	1.75
8 Derek Two-Shadows Betrayed	1.75
9 Fate of Derek Two-Shadows .	1.75
10 Two-Shadows as one	1.75
11 Rebellion	1.75
12 Rebellion continued	1.75
13 V:Prime One	1.75
14 Mutants Join Rebellion	1.75
15 Invaders Arrival	1.75
16 Unified Warriors vs. Invaders	1.75
17 V:Terrans, O:Electric Warriors	1.75
18 Origin continued, final issue . .	1.75

All comics prices listed are for *Near Mint* condition.

DC COMICS

DC COMICS

Elongated Man #2 © DC Comics, Inc.

ELONGATED MAN
1992

1 A:Copperhead	1.00
2 Modora,A:Flash,I:Sonar	1.00
3 A:Flash,V:Wurst Gang	1.00

ELVIRA
1986–87

1 DSp,BB(c)	3.25
2 thru 9	@1.00
10	2.00
11 DSt(c)Find Cain	2.50

ENIGMA
Vertigo 1993

1 B:PrM(s),DFg,I:Enigma,Michael Smith,V:The Head	3.50
2 DFg,I:The Truth	3.25
3 DFg,V:The Truth,I:Envelope Girl, Titus Bird	3.00
4 DFg,D:The Truth,I:Interior League	3.00
5 DFg,I:Enigma's Mother	3.00
6 DFg,V:Envelope Girl	3.00
7 DFg,V:Enigma's Mother,D:Envelope Girl,O:Enigma	3.00
8 E:PrM(s),DFg,final issue	3.00
TPB Rep. #1-#8	19.95

ERADICATOR
1996

1 IV,Low,	1.75
2 IV,Low,	1.75
3 IV,Low,"Reign of the Superman" concl.A:Superboy	1.75

ESSENTIAL VERTIGO: SWAMP THING
DC/Vertigo Sept. 1996
B&W reprints

1 AMo(s), rep. Saga of the Swamp Thing #21.	2.50
2 thru 11 AMo(s), rep. Saga of the Swamp Thing #22–#31.	@1.95

ESSENTIAL VERTIGO: THE SANDMAN
DC/Vertigo 1996

3 NGa(s),SK,MDr,rep.	1.95
4 NGa(s),SK,MDr,rep. F:Etrigan the Demon	1.95
5 NGa(s),SK,MJ,F:Morpheus, John Dee	1.95
6 NGa(s),SK,MJ,V:Dr. Destiny	1.95
7	1.95
8 NGa(s),MDr,MJ,"The Sound of Her Wings"	1.95
9 NGa(s),MDr,MJ,"The Doll's House" F:Nada	1.95
10 NGa(s),MDr,MJ,"The Doll's House"	1.95
11 NGa(s),MDr,RT	1.95
12 NGa(s),CBa,MJ,"The Doll's House," pt.3	1.95
13 NGa,rep. "Doll's House", pt.4	1.95
14 NGa,rep. "Doll's House", pt.5	1.95

EXTREME JUSTICE
1995–96

O New Group	1.50
1 V:Captain Atom	1.50
2 V:War Cyborgs	1.50
3 V:Synge	1.50
4 R:Firestorm the Nuclear Man	1.50
5 Firestorm & Elementals	1.75
6 Monarch,Captain Atom, Booster Gold, Maxima	1.75
7 F:Monarch,Captain Atom	1.75
8	1.75
9 F:Firestorm	1.75
10 Underworld Unleashed tie-in	1.75
11 Underworld Unleashed tie-in	1.75
12 Monarch's scheme revealed	1.75
13 Monarch vs. Captain Atom	1.75
14	1.75
15 TMo,V:The Slavemaster from the Stars	1.75
16 TMo,V:Legion of Doom	1.75
17 TMo,V:Legion of Doom	1.75

EXTREMIST
Vertigo 1993

1 B:PrM(s),TMK,I:The Order, Extremist(Judy Tanner)	2.50
1a Platinum Ed.	12.00
2 TMK,D:Extremist(Jack Tanner)	2.25
3 TMK,V:Patrick	2.25
4 E:PrM(s),TMK,D:Tony Murphy	2.25

FACE, THE

GN DFg,PrM	4.95

FAMILY MAN
Paradox 1995

1 I:Family Man	4.95
2 V:Brother Charles	4.95
3 Escape	4.95

FAREWELL MOONSHADOW
DC/Vertigo

GN JMD(s),JMu, prose & pictures	7.95

FATE
1994–96

1 Dr. Fate	2.50
2 Nabu,Astral plane	2.25

3 Bloodstain	1.95
4 Decisions	1.95
5 Judged by Enclave	1.95
6 V:Grimoire	1.95
7 V:Dark Agent	1.95
8 V:Dark Agent	2.25
9 Tries to change his destiny	2.25
10 A:Zatanna	2.25
11	2.25
12 A:Sentinel	2.25
13 V:Blaze	2.25
14 LKa,ALa,AWi,Underworld Unleashed tie-in	2.25
15 LKa,ALa,AWi,V:Charnelle	2.25
16 LKa,ALa,AWi,canibal drug-cult	2.25
17 LKa,ALa,AWi	2.25
18 LKa,ALa,AWi,V:Charnelle	2.25
19 LKa,ALa,AWi,V:men in black	2.25

FAULT LINES
DC/Vertigo March 1997
Mini-series

1 LMr(s),F:Tracey Farrand	2.50
2 LMr(s)	2.50
3 LMr(s)	2.50
4 LMr(s)	2.50
5 (of 6) LMr(s)	2.50

FIGHTING AMERICAN
1994

1 GrL,R:Fighting American	1.75
2 GrL,Media Circus	1.75
3 GrL,I&V:Gross Nation Product, Def Iffit	1.75
4 GrL,V:Gross Nation Product, Def Iffit	1.75
5 GrL,PhorOptor	1.75
6 Final Issue	1.75

FINAL NIGHT, THE
Sept. 1996
[Cross-Over Series]

1 KK(s),SI,JMz, Alien crash lands on Earth	1.95
2 KK(s),SI,JMz, Earth's sun extinguished	1.95
3 KK(s),SI,JMz, Attempts to stave off inevitable	1.95
4 KK(s),SI,JMz, Can they save the world, and at what price?	1.95

FIREBRAND
1995

1 SaV,Alex Sanchez becomes Firebrand	1.75
2 SaV	1.75
3 SaV,Generation Prime case climax	1.75
4 SaV,Young gang member	1.75
5 SaV,V;serial killer(s)	1.75
6 BAu,SaV	1.75
7	1.75
8	1.75
9 final issue	1.75

FIRESTORM
March, 1978

1 AM,JRu,I&O:Firestorm	4.00
2 AM,BMc,A:Superman	2.50
3 AM,I:Killer Froat	2.50
4 AM,BMc,I:Hyena	2.50
5 AM,BMc,Hyena	2.50

FIRESTORM, THE NUCLEAR MAN
(see FURY OF FIRESTORM)

First Issue Special #4
© DC Comics, Inc.

FIRST ISSUE SPECIAL
April, 1975

1	JK,Atlas	3.00
2	Green Team	2.50
3	Metamorpho	2.50
4	Lady Cop	2.50
5	JK,Manhunter	2.75
6	JK,Dingbats	2.50
7	SD,Creeper	2.50
8	MGr,Warlord	15.00
9	WS,Dr.Fate	3.00
10	Outsiders(not Batman team)	2.50
11	NR,AM Code:Assassin	2.50
12	new Starman	2.50
13	return of New Gods	3.50

FLASH COMICS
Jan., 1940

1	SMo,SMo(c),O:Flash,Hawkman,The Whip & Johnny Thunder,B:Cliff Cornwall,Minute Movies	60,000.00
2	B:Rod Rain	6,000.00
3	SMo,SMo(c),B:The King	4,500.00
4	SMo,SMo(c),F:The Whip	3,500.00
5	SMo,SMo(c),F:The King	3,000.00
6	F:Flash	4,000.00
7	Hawkman(c)	3,400.00
8	Male bondage(c)	2,200.00
9	Hawkman(c)	2,200.00
10	SMo,SMo(c),Flash(c)	2,200.00
11	SMo,SMo(c)	1,500.00
12	SMo,SMo(c),B:Les Watts	1,500.00
13	SMo,SMo(c)	1,400.00
14	SMo,SMo(c)	1,500.00
15	SMo,SMo(c)	1,400.00
16	SMo,SMo(c)	1,400.00
17	SMo,SMo(c),E:CliffCornwall	1,400.00
18	SMo,SMo(c)	1,400.00
19	SMo,SMo(c)	1,400.00
20	SMo,SMo(c)	1,400.00
21	SMo(c)	1,200.00
22	SMo,SMo(c)	1,200.00
23	SMo,SMo(c)	1,200.00
24	SMo,SMo(c),Flash V:Spider-Men of Mars,A:Hawkgirl	1,500.00
25	SMo,SMo(c)	800.00
26	SMo,SMo(c)	800.00
27	SMo,SMo(c)	800.00
28	SMo,SMo(c),Flash goes to Hollywood	800.00
29	SMo,SMo(c)	800.00
30	SMo,SMo(c),Flash in'Adventure of the Curiosity Ray!'	800.00
31	SMo,SMo(c),Hawkman(c)	750.00
32	SM(c),Flash in'Adventure of the Fictious Villians'	735.00
33	SMo,SMo(c)	725.00
34	SMo,SMo(c),Flash in 'The Robbers of the Round Table'	725.00
35	SMo,SMo(c)	725.00
36	SMo,SMo(c),Flash in'The Mystery of the Doll Who Walks Like A Man'	725.00
37	SMo,SMo(c)	725.00
38	SMo,SMo(c)	725.00
39	SMo,SMo(c)	725.00
40	SMo,SMo(c),Flash in 'The Man Who Could Read Man's Souls!'	725.00
41	SMo,SMo(c)	700.00
42	SMo,SMo(c),Flash V:The Gangsters Baby!'	700.00
43	SMo,SMo(c)	700.00
44	SMo,SMo(c),Flash V:The Liars Club	700.00
45	SMo,SMo(c),F:Hawkman,Big Butch Makes Hall of Fame	700.00
46	SMo,SMo(c)	700.00
47	SMo,SMo(c),Hawkman in 'Crime Canned for the Duration'	700.00
48	SMo,SMo(c)	700.00
49	SMo,SMo(c)	700.00
50	SMo,SMo(c),Hawkman in 'Tale o/t 1,000 Dollar Bill'	700.00
51	SMo,SMo(c)	600.00
52	SMo,SMo(c),Flash in 'Case of the Machine that Thinks Like A Man'	600.00
53	SMo,SMo(c),Hawkman in 'Simple Simon Met the Hawkman'	600.00
54	SMo,SMo(c),Flash in 'Mysterious Bottle from the Sea'	600.00
55	SMo,SMo(c),Hawkman in 'The Riddle of the Stolen Statuette! 3	600.00
56	SMo,SMo(c)	600.00
57	SMo,SMo(c),Hawkman in 'Adventure of the Gangster and the Ghost'	600.00
58	SMo,SMo(c),'Merman meets the Flash'	600.00
59	SMo,SMo(c),Hawkman V:Pied Piper	600.00
60	SMo,SMo(c),Flash V:The Wind Master	600.00
61	SMo,SMo(c),Hawkman V:The Beanstalk	600.00
62	JKu,Flash in 'High Jinks on the Rinks'	750.00
63	JKu(c),Hawkman in 'The Tale of the Mystic Urn'	575.00
64		575.00
65	JKu(c),Hawkman in 'Return of the Simple Simon'	575.00
66		575.00
67	JKu(c)	575.00
68	Flash in 'The Radio that Ran Wild'	575.00
69		575.00
70	JKu(c)	575.00
71	JKu(c),Hawkman in 'Battle of the Birdmen'	575.00
72	JKu	575.00
73	JKu(c)	575.00
74	JKu(c)	575.00
75	JKu(c),Hawkman in 'Magic at the Mardi Gras'	575.00
76	A:Worry Wart	575.00
77	Hawkman in 'The Case of the Curious Casket'	575.00
78		575.00
79	Hawkman in 'The Battle of the Birds'	575.00
80	Flash in 'The Story of the Boy Genius'	575.00
81	JKu(c),Hawkman's Voyage to Venus	575.00
82	A:Walter Jordan	575.00
83	JKu,JKu(c),Hawkman in 'Destined for Disaster'	575.00
84	Flash V:'The Changeling'	575.00
85	JKu,JKu(c),Hawkman in Hollywood	575.00
86	JKu,1st Black Canary,Flash V:Stone Age Menace	1,800.00
87	Hawkman meets the Foil	850.00
88	JKu,Flash in 'The Case of the Vanished Year!'	850.00
89	I:The Thorn	850.00
90	Flash in 'Nine Empty Uniforms'	850.00
91	Hawkman V:The Phantom Menace	1,000.00
92	1st full-length Black Canary story	2,400.00
93	Flash V:Violin of Villainy	1,000.00
94	JKu(c)	1,000.00
95		1,000.00
96		1,000.00
97	Flash in 'The Dream that Didn't Vanish'	1,000.00
98	JKu(c),Hawkman in 'Crime Costume!'	1,000.00

Flash Comics #11 © DC Comics, Inc.

DC COMICS

DC COMICS

99 Flash in 'The Star Prize
  of the Year' 1,000.00
100 Hawkman in 'The Human
  -Fly Bandits!' 2,400.00
101 . . . . 1,800.00
102 Hawkman in 'The Flying
  Darkness' 1,800.00
103 . . . . 2,400.00
104 JKu,Hawkman in 'Flaming
  Darkness' Feb., 1949 . . 6,000.00

FLASH
Feb.–March, 1959

105 CI,O:Flash,I:Mirror
  Master 5,000.00
106 CI,I&O:Gorilla Grodd,
  O:Pied Piper 1,300.00
107 CI,A:Grodd 700.00
108 CI,A:Grodd 600.00
109 CI,A:Mirror Master 500.00
110 CI,MA,I:Kid Flash,
  Weather Wizard 1,350.00
111 CI,A:Kid Flash,The Invasion
  Of the Cloud Creatures 350.00
112 CI,I&O:Elongated Man,
  A:Kid Flash 400.00
113 CI,I&O:Trickster 375.00
114 CI,A:Captain Cold 275.00
115 CI,A:Grodd 250.00
116 CI,A:Kid Flash,The Man
  Who Stole Central City 250.00
117 CI,MA,I:Capt.Boomerang . 300.00
118 CI,MA 200.00
119 CI,W:Elongated Man 200.00
120 CI,A:Kid Flash,Land of
  Golden Giants 200.00
121 CI,A:Trickster 150.00
122 CI,I&O:The Top 150.00
123 I:Earth 2,R:G.A.Flash 900.00
124 CI,A:Capt.Boomerang 150.00
125 CI,A:Kid Flash,The
  Conquerors of Time 125.00
126 CI,A:Mirror Master 125.00
127 CI,A:Grodd 125.00
128 CI,O:Abra Kadabra 125.00
129 CI,A:Capt.Cold,Trickster,A:Gold.
  Age Flash,C:JLA (flashback) 300.00
130 CI,A:Mirror Master,
  Weather Wizard 125.00
131 CI,A:Green Lantern 120.00
132 CI,A:Daphne Dean 120.00
133 CI,A:Abra Kadabra 120.00
134 CI,A:Captain Cold 120.00
135 CI,N:Kid Flash 120.00
136 CI,A:Mirror Master 120.00
137 CI,Vandal Savage,R:JSA,
  A:G.A.Flash 400.00
138 CI,A:Pied Piper 120.00
139 CI,I&O:Prof.Zoom(Reverse
  Flash) 150.00
140 CI,O:Heat Wave 120.00
141 CI,A:Top 80.00
142 CI,A:Trickster 80.00
143 CI,A:Green Lantern 80.00
144 CI,A:Man Missile,Kid Flash . 80.00
145 CI,A:Weather Wizard 80.00
146 CI,A:Mirror Master 75.00
147 CI,A:Mr.Element,A:Reverse
  Flash 75.00
148 CI,A:Capt.Boomerang 75.00
149 CI,A:Abra Kadabra 75.00
150 CI,A:Captain Cold 75.00
151 CI,A:Earth II Flash,
  The Shade 125.00
152 CI,V:Trickster 75.00

153 CI,A:Mr.Element,Rev.Flash . 75.00
154 CI,The Day Flash Ran Away
  with Himself 75.00
155 CI,A:MirrorMaster,Capt.Cold,Top
  Capt. Boomerang,Grodd 75.00
156 CI,A:Kid Flash,The Super Hero
  who Betrayed the World 75.00
157 CI,A:Doralla Kon,The Top . . 75.00
158 CI,V:The Breakaway Bandit
  A:The Justice League 75.00
159 CI,A:Kid Flash 75.00
160 CI,giant 85.00
161 CI,A:Mirror Master 50.00
162 CI,Who Haunts the Corridor
  of Chills 50.00
163 CI,A:Abra kadabra 50.00
164 CI,V:Pied Piper,A:KidFLash . 50.00
165 CI,W:Flash,Iris West 60.00
166 CI,A:Captain Cold 50.00
167 CI,O:Flash,I:Mopee 50.00
168 CI,A:Green Lantern 50.00
169 CI,O:Flash rtd,giant 80.00
170 CI,A:Abra Kadabra,
  G.A.Flash 50.00

Flash Comics #204 © DC Comics, Inc.

171 CI,A:Dexter Myles,Justice
  League,Atom;V:Dr Light 45.00
172 CI,A:Grodd 45.00
173 CI,A:Kid Flash,EarthII Flash
  V:Golden Man 45.00
174 CI,A:Mirror Master,Top
  Captain Cold 45.00
175 2nd Superman/Flash race,
  C:Justice League o/America . 150.00
176 giant-size 40.00
177 RA,V:The Trickster 50.00
178 CI,(giant size) 55.00
179 RA,Fact or Fiction 50.00
180 RA,V:Baron Katana 50.00
181 RA,V;Baron Katana 30.00
182 A:Abra Kadabra 30.00
183 RA,V:The Frog 30.00
184 RA,V:Dr Yom 30.00
185 RA,Threat of the High Rise
  Buildings 30.00
186 RA,A:Sargon 30.00
187 CI,AbraKadabra,giant 50.00
188 A:Mirror Master 30.00
189 JKu(c),RA,A:Kid Flash 30.00

190 JKu(c),RA,A:Dexter Myles . . 30.00
191 JKu(c),RA,A:Green Lantern . 30.00
192 RA,V:Captain Vulcan 30.00
193 A:Captain Cold 30.00
194 . . . . 30.00
195 GK,MA 30.00
196 CI,giant 50.00
197 GK 30.00
198 GK 30.00
199 GK 30.00
200 IN,MA 30.00
201 IN,MA,A:G.A. Flash 15.00
202 IN,MA,A:Kid Flash 15.00
203 IN 15.00
204 . . . . 15.00
205 giant 30.00
206 A:Mirror Master 15.00
207 . . . . 15.00
208 . . . . 15.00
209 A:Capt.Boomerang,Grodd
  Trickster 15.00
210 CI 15.00
211 O:Flash 16.00
212 A:Abra Kadabra 15.00
213 CI 15.00
214 CI,rep.Showcase #37
  (O:Metal Men),giant size. . . 20.00
215 IN,FMc,rep.Showcase #14 . 20.00
216 A:Mr.Element 15.00
217 NA,A:Gr.Lant,Gr.Arrow 20.00
218 NA,A:Gr.Lant,Gr.Arrow 20.00
219 NA,L:Greeen Arrow 20.00
220 IN,DG,A:KidFlash,Gr.Lantern 10.00
221 IN 10.00
222 IN 10.00
223 DG,Green Lantern 10.00
224 IN,DG,A:Green Lantern 10.00
225 IN,DG,A:Gr.Lant,Rev.Flash . 11.00
226 NA,A:Capt. Cold 15.00
227 IN,FMc,DG,Capt.Boomerang,
  Green Lantern 9.00
228 IN 9.00
229 IN,FMc,A:Green Arrow,
  V:Rag Doll (giant size) 12.00
230 A:VandalSavage,Dr.Alchemy . 9.00
231 FMc 9.00
232 giant 16.00
233 giant 16.00
234 V:Reverse Flash 5.00
235 . . . . 4.00
236 MGr 4.00
237 IN,FMc,MGr,A:Prof Zoom,
  Green Lantern 4.50
238 MGr 4.00
239 . . . . 4.00
240 MGr 4.00
241 A:Mirror Master 4.00
242 MGr,D:Top 4.00
243 IN,FMc,MGr,TA,O:Top,
  A:Green Lantern 4.00
244 IN,FMc,A:Rogue's Gallery . . . 4.00
245 IN,FMc,DD,TA,I:PlantMaster . 4.00
246 IN,FMc,DD,TA,I:PlantMaster . 4.00
247 . . . . 4.00
248 FMc,IN,I:Master 4.00
249 FMc,IN,V:Master 4.00
250 IN,FMc,I:Golden Glider 4.00
251 FMc,IN,V:Golden Glider 3.50
252 FMc,IN,I:Molder 3.50
253 FMc,IN,V:Molder 3.50
254 FMc 3.50
255 FMc,A:MirrorMaster 3.50
256 FMc,V:Top 3.50
257 FMc,A:Green Glider 3.50
258 FMc,A:Black Hand 3.50

259 FMc,IN 3.50
260 FMc,IN 3.50
261 FMc,IN,V:Golden Glider 3.50
262 FMc,IN,V:Golden Glider 3.50
263 FMc,IN,V:Golden Glider 3.50
264 FMc,IN,V:Golden Glider 3.50
265 FMc,IN 3.50
266 FMc,IN,V:Heat Wave 3.50
267 FMc,IN,V:Heat Wave 3.50
268 FMc,IN,A:E2 Flash 3.50
269 FMc,IN,A:Kid Flash 3.50
270 FMc,IN,V:Clown 3.50
271 RB,V:Clown 3.50
272 RB,V:Clown 3.50
273 RB 3.50
274 RB 3.50
275 AS,D:Iris West,PCP story ... 4.00
276 AS,A:JLA 3.50
277 AS,FMc,A:JLA,
　V:MirrorMaster 3.50
278 A:Captain.Boomerang
　& Heatwave 3.50
279 A:Captain.Boomerang
　& Heatwave 3.50
280 DH 3.50
281 DH,V:Reverse Flash 4.00
282 DH,V:Reverse Flash 4.00
283 DH,V:Reverse Flash 4.00
284 DH,Flash's life story
　I:Limbo Lord 3.50
285 DH,V:Trickster 3.50
286 DH,I:Rainbow Raider 3.50
287 DH,V:Dr.Alchemy 3.50
288 DH,V:Dr.Alchemy 3.50
289 DH,GP,1st GP DC art; V:Dr.
　Alchemy;B:B.U.Firestorm ... 8.00
290 GP 3.00
291 GP,DH,V:Sabretooth 3.00
292 GP,DH,V:Mirror Master 3.00
293 GP,DH,V:Pied Piper 3.00
294 GP,DH,V:Grodd 3.00
295 CI,JSn,V:Grodd 3.00
296 JSn,A:Elongated Man 3.00
297 CI,A:Captain Cold 3.00
298 CI,V:Shade,Rainbowraider .. 3.00
299 CI,V:Shade,Rainbowraider .. 3.00
300 A:New Teen Titans 5.00
301 CI,A:Firestorm 3.00
302 CI,V:Golden Glider 3.00
303 CI,V:Golden Glider 3.00
304 CI,PB,I:Col.Computron;E:B.U.
　Firestorm 3.00
305 KG,CI,A:G.A.Flash,B:Dr.Fate . 4.00
306 CI,KG,V:Mirror Master 4.00
307 CI,KG,V:Pied Piper 3.00
308 CI,KG 4.00
309 CI,KG 4.00
310 CI,KG,V:Capt.Boomerang ... 3.00
311 CI,KG,V:Capt.Boomerang .. 3.00
312 CI,A:Heatwave 3.00
313 KG,A:Psylon,E:Dr.Fate 3.00
314 CI,I:Eradicator 3.00
315 CI,V:Gold Face 3.00
316 CI,V:Gold Face 3.00
317 CI,V:Gold Face 3.00
318 CI,DGb,V:Eradicator;B:
　B.U.Creeper 3.00
319 CI,DGb,V:Eradicator 3.00
320 CI,V:Eradicator 3.00
321 CI,D:Eradicator 3.00
322 CI,V:Reverse Flash 3.00
323 CI,V:Reverse Flash;E:
　B.U.Creeper 3.00
324 CI,D:Reverse Flash 4.00
325 CI,A:Rogues Gallery 3.00

326 CI,A:Weather Wizard 3.00
327 CI,A:JLA,G.Grodd 3.00
328 CI 3.00
329 CI,A:J.L.A.,G.Grodd 3.00
330 CI,FMc,V:G.Grodd 3.00
331 CI,FMc,V:G.Grodd 3.00
332 CI,FMc,V:Rainbow Raider ... 3.00
333 CI,FMc,V:Pied Piper 3.00
334 CI,FMc,V:Pied Piper 3.00
335 CI,FMc,V:Pied Piper 3.00
336 CI,FMc,V:Pied Piper 3.00
337 CI,FMc,V:Pied Piper 3.00
338 CI,FMc,I:Big Sir 3.00
339 CI,FMc,A:Big Sir 3.00
340 CI,FMc,Trial,A:Big Sir 3.00
341 CI,FMc,Trial,A:Big Sir 3.00
342 CI,FMc,Trial,V:RogueGallery . 3.00
343 CI,FMc,Trial,A:GoldFace 3.00
344 CI,O:Kid Flash,Trial 3.00
345 CI,A:Kid Flash,Trial 3.00
346 CI,FMc,Trial,V:AbraKadabra . 3.00
347 CI,FMc,Trial,V:AbraKadabra . 3.00
348 CI,FMc,Trial,V:AbraKadabra . 3.00
349 CI,FMc,Trial,V:AbraKadabra . 3.00
350 CI,FMc,Trial,V:AbraKadabra . 7.00
Ann.#1 O:ElongatedMan,
　G.Grodd 325.00

Flash Comics (2nd Series) #80
© DC Comics, Inc.

FLASH
[2nd Series] Oct., 1985
1 JG,Legends,C:Vandal Savage 11.00
2 JG,V:Vandal Savage 6.00
3 JG,I:Kilgore 5.00
4 JG,A:Cyborg 4.00
5 JG,V:Speed Demon 4.00
6 JG,V:Speed Demon 4.00
7 JG,V:Red Trinity 4.00
8 JG,V:BlueTrinity,Millenium .. 4.00
9 JG,I:Chunk,Millenium 4.00
10 V:Chunk,Chunks World 3.00
11 Return to Earth 3.00
12 Velocity 9 .... 3.00
13 Vandal Savage,V:Velocity 9
　Adicts 3.00
14 V:Vandal Savage 3.00
15 A:Velocity 9 Junkies 3.00

16 C:V.Savage,SpeedMcGeePt.1 . 3.00
17 GLa,Speed McGee,pt.2 ..... 3.00
18 GLa,SpeedMcGeePt.3,
　V:V.Savage 2.25
19 JM:+bonus book,R:Rogue
　Gallery,O:Blue/Red Trinity 2.25
20 A:Durlan 2.25
21 A:Manhunter,Invasion x-over .. 2.25
22 A:Manhunter,Invasion x-over .. 2.25
23 V:Abrakadabra 2.25
24 GLa,FlashRegainsSpeed,
　A:L.Lane 2.25
25 GLa,Search for Flash 2.25
26 GLa,I:Porcupine Man 2.25
27 GLa,Porcupine Man as Flash . 2.25
28 GLa,A:Golden Glider,
　Capt.Cold 2.25
29 A:New Phantom Lady 2.25
30 GLa,Turtle Saga,pt.1 ...... 2.25
31 GLa,Turtle Saga,pt.2 ...... 2.00
32 GLa,Turtle Saga,pt.3,
　R:G.A.Turtle 2.00
33 GLa,Turtle Saga,pt.4 ...... 2.00
34 GLa,Turtle Saga,pt.5 ...... 2.00
35 GLa,Turtle Saga,pt.6,
　D:G.A.Turtle 2.00
36 GLa,V:Cult 2.00
37 GLa,V:Cult 2.00
38 GLa,V:Cult 2.00
39 GLa,V:Cult 2.00
40 GLa,A:Dr.Alchemy 2.00
41 GLa,A:Dr.Alchemy 2.00
42 GLa,MechanicalTroubles ... 2.00
43 GLa,V:Kilgore 2.00
44 GLa,V:Velocity 2.00
45 V:Gorilla Grod 2.00
46 V:Gorilla Grod 2.00
47 V:Gorilla Grod 2.00
48 .... 2.00
49 A:Vandal Savage 2.00
50 N:Flash (double sz)V:Savage . 5.00
51 I:Proletariat 2.00
52 I.R.S. Mission 1.75
53 A:Superman,Race to Save
　Jimmy Olsen 1.75
54 Terrorist Airline Attack 1.75
55 War of the Gods x-over 1.75
56 The Way of a Will,pt.1 ...... 1.75
57 The Way of a Will,pt.2 ...... 1.75
58 Meta Gene-activated Homeless 1.75
59 The Last Resort 1.75
60 Love Song of the Chunk 1.75
61 Wally's Mother's Wedding Day 1.75
62 GLa,Year 1,pt.1 .... 2.25
63 GLa,Year 1,pt.2 .... 1.75
64 GLa,Year 1,pt.3 .... 1.75
65 GLa,Year 1,pt.4 .... 1.75
66 A:Aq'man,V:Marine Marauder . 1.75
67 GLa,V:Abra Kadabra 1.75
68 GLa,V:Abra Kadabra 1.75
69 GLa,Gorilla Warfare#2 ..... 1.75
70 Gorilla Warfare#4 .... 1.75
71 GLa,V:Dr.Alchemy 1.75
72 GLa,V:Dr.Alchemy,C:Barry
　Allen 2.50
73 GLa,Xmas Issue,R:Barry Allen 4.50
74 GLa,A:Barry Allen? 3.00
75 GLa,A:Reverse Flash,V:Mob
　Violence 3.50
76 GLa,A:Reverse Flash 2.25
77 GLa,G.A.Flash vs
　Reverse Flash 2.25
78 GLa,V:Reverse Flash 2.25
79 GLa,V:Reverse Flash,48 pgs. . 3.25
80 AD(c),V:Frances Kane 3.00

DC COMICS

DC COMICS

80a Newstand Ed 2.00
81 AD(c) 2.00
82 AD(c),A:Nightwing 2.00
83 AD(c),A:Nightwing,Starfire 2.00
84 AD(c),I:Razer 2.00
85 AD(c),V:Razer 2.00
86 AD(c),A:Argus 2.00
86 V:Santa Claus 2.00
87 Christmas issue 2.00
88 . . . . 2.00
89 On Trial 2.00
90 On Trial#2 . . . . 2.00
91 Out of Time 5.00
92 I:3rd Flash 12.00
93 A:Impulse 5.00
94 Zero Hour 5.00
95 Terminal Velocity,pt.1 . . . . . . 4.00
96 Terminal Velocity,pt.2 . . . . . . 4.00
97 Terminal Velocity,pt.3 . . . . . . 2.00
98 Terminal Velocity,pt.4 . . . . . . 2.00
99 Terminal Velocity,pt.5 . . . . . . 2.00
100 I:New Flash 5.00
100a Collector's Edition 2.50
101 Velocity Aftermath 1.50
102 V:Mongul 1.75
103 Supernatural threat from
   Linda's Past Secret 1.75
104 Exorcise Demons 1.75
105 . . . . 1.75
106 R:Magenta 1.75
107 MWa,Underworld Unleashed
   tie-in 1.75
108 MWa,Dead Heat,pt.1 . . . . . . 1.75
109 MWa,Dead Heat,pt.2 . . . . . . 1.75
110 MWa,Dead Heat,pt.4 . . . . . . 1.75
111 MWa,Dead Heat,pt.6 . . . . . . 1.75
112 MWa,New Flash in town 1.75
113 MWa,F:Linda 1.75
114 MWa,V:Chillblaine 1.75
115 thru 117 . . . . @1.75
118 MWa&BAu(s),Flash returns
   from the future 1.75
119 MWa&BAu(s),PR,Final Night
   tie-in 1.75
120 MWa&BAu(s),PR,"Presidential
   Race," pt.1 . . . . 1.75
121 MWa&BAu(s),PR,"Presidential
   Race," pt.2 . . . . 1.75
122 MWa&BAu(s),PR, ... 1.75
123 MWa&BAu(s),PR,Flash moves
   to Santa Marta 1.75
124 MWa&BAu(s),PR,Wally doesn't
   know reality from illusion 1.75
125 MWa&BAu(s),PR,California,
   V:Major Disaster 1.75
126 MWa&BAu(s),PR,V:Major
   Disaster 1.75
127 MWa&Bau(s),PR,"Hell to Pay,"
   pt. 1 (of 3) 1.75
128 MWa&BAu(s),PR,"Hell to Pay"
   pt. 2, A:JLA 1.75
129 MWa&BAu(s),PR,"Hell to Pay"
   pt. 3, concl. 1.75
Ann.#1 JG,The Deathtouch 4.00
Ann.#2 A:Wally's Father 3.00
Ann.#3 Roots 2.50
Ann.#4 Armageddon,pt7 . . . . 2.50
Ann.#5 TC(1st Full Work),Eclipso,
   V:Rogue's Gallery 8.00
Ann.#6 Bloodlines#4,I:Argus 2.75
Ann.#7 Elseworlds story 2.95
Ann.#8 Year One story 3.00
Ann.#9 Legends o/t Dead Earth . . 2.95
Ann.#10 Pulp Heroes (Romance) . 3.95
Spec #1,IN,DG,CI,50th Anniv.,

Three Flash's 4.50
T.V. Spec.#1,JS,w/episode guide . 4.25
TPB Terminal Velocity 12.95

THE FLASH PLUS
Nov. 1996
1 MWa(s),F:Wally West, Dick
   Grayson 2.95

FLASH GORDON
1988
1 DJu,I:New Flash Gordon 2.50
2 DJu,A:Lion-Men,Shark-Men . . . 2.00
3 DJu,V:Shark-Men 1.50
4 DJu,Dale Kidnapped by Voltan 1.50
5 DJu,Alliance Against Ming 1.50
6 DJu,Arctic City 1.50
7 DJu,Alliance vs. Ming 1.50
8 DJu,Alliance vs. Ming 1.50
9 DJu,V:Ming, final issue 1.50

FLINTSTONES AND THE JETSONS, THE
Warner Bros./DC
1 Ancestors and Descendents meet 1.75
2 Dino wins a contest, Bay
   Watchdog 1.75

The Fly #12 © DC Comics, Inc.

FLY, THE
Impact 1991–92
1 I&O:Fly I:Arachnus,Chromium . 1.50
2 V:Chromium 1.25
3 O:Arachnus, I:Lt.Walker Odell . 1.00
4 A:Black Hood, V:Arachnus 1.00
5 V:Arachnus 1.00
6 I:Blackjack 1.00
7 Oceanworld,V:Dolphus 1.00
8 A:Comet,Dolphus 1.00
9 F:Fireball, with trading card . . . 1.00
10 V:General Mechanix 1.00
11 Suicide Issue 1.25
12 V:Agent from WEB 1.25
13 I:Tremor 1.25
14 V:Domino 1.25
15 V:Domino 1.25
16 V:Arachnus 1.25

17 Final Issue 1.25
Ann.#1 Earthquest,pt.4,w/card . . 2.25

FORBIDDEN TALES OF DARK MANSION
May-June, 1972
5 thru 15 Feb.–March, 1974 . . @1.50

FOREVER PEOPLE, THE
1971–72
1 I:Forever People,A:Superman,
   A:Darkseid 50.00
2 A:Darkseid 30.00
3 A:Darkseid 30.00
4 A:Darkseid 30.00
5 . . . . 25.00
6 thru 11 . . . . @12.50

FOREVER PEOPLE
1988
1 Return of Forever People 1.75
2 'Return of Yesterday' 1.25
3 A:Mark Moonrider 1.25
4 The Dark controlls M.Moonrider 1.25
5 R:MotherBox,Infinity Man 1.25
6 Donny's Fate, final issue 1.25

FORGOTTEN REALMS
1989–91
1 A:RealmsMaster,PriamAgrivar . 8.00
2 Mystic Hand of Vaprak,
   A:Ogre Mage 6.00
3 Mystic Hand of Vaprak contd. . 5.50
4 Ogre Mage vs.Omen the Wizard 5.50
5 Dragon Reach #1 . . . . 5.50
6 Dragon Reach #2 . . . . 4.50
7 Dragon Reach #3 . . . . 3.50
8 Dragon Reach #4 . . . . 3.00
9 V:Giant Squid 2.50
10 'Head Cheese' 2.50
11 Triangles #1 . . . . 2.50
12 Triangles #2 . . . . 2.50
13 Triangles #3 . . . . 2.50
14 A:Lich Viranton the Mage 2.00
15 Avatar Comics tie-in 2.00
16 Mad Gods and Paladins,pt.1 . 2.00
17 Mad Gods and Paladins,pt.2 . 2.00
18 Mad Gods and Paladins,pt.3 . 2.00
19 Mad Gods and Paladins,pt.4 . 2.00
20 Realms Master Crew captured 2.00
21 Catewere Tribe 2.00
22 V:The Akri 1.75
23 A:Sandusk the Leprechaun . . . 1.75
24 'Everybody wants to rule
   the realms' 1.75
25 The Wake, final issue 1.75
Ann.#1 V:Advanced D&D crew . . 2.95

FOUR STAR BATTLE TALES
1973
1 thru 5 . . . . @1.50

FOUR STAR SPECTACULAR
March-April, 1976
1 . . . . 1.50
2 thru 6 . . . . @1.25

FOURTH WORLD GALLERY
1-shot pin-up collection (1996) . . 3.50

DC COMICS

FOX AND THE CROW
Dec.–Jan., 1951

1	750.00
2	350.00
3	225.00
4	225.00
5	225.00
6 thru 10	@150.00
11 thru 20	@125.00
21 thru 40	@125.00
41 thru 60	@50.00
61 thru 80	@35.00
81 thru 94	@25.00
95	30.00
96 thru 99	@15.00
100	18.00
101 thru 108	@15.00

Becomes:

STANLEY & HIS MONSTER

109 thru 112 Oct.Nov.,1968	@10.00

FREEDOM FIGHTERS
March-April, 1976

1 Freedom Fighters go to Earth 1	1.50
2	1.25
3	1.25
4	1.25
5 A:Wonder Woman	1.25
6	1.25
7	1.25
8	1.25
9	1.25
10 O:Doll Man	1.25
11 O:Ray	1.25
12 O:Firebrand	1.25
13 O:Black Condor	1.25
14 A:Batgirl	1.25
15 O:Phantom Lady	1.25

FROM BEYOND THE UNKNOWN
Oct.–Nov., 1969

1 JKu,CI	70.00
2 MA(c),CI,ATh	18.00
3 NA(c),CI	15.00

From Beyond The Unknown #19
© DC Comics, Inc.

4 MA(c),CI	15.00
5 MA(c),CI	15.00
6 NA(c),I:Glen Merrit	18.00
7 CI,JKu(c)	15.00
8 NA(c),CI	18.00
9 NA(c),CI	18.00
10 MA(c),CI	15.00
11 MA(c),CI	12.00
12 JKu(c),CI	15.00
13 JKu(c),CI,WW	20.00
14 JKu(c),CI	15.00
15 MA(c),CI	12.00
16 MA(c),CI	12.00
17 MA(c),CI	12.00
18 MK(c),CI	10.00
19 MK(c),CI	10.00
20	10.00
21	10.00
22 MA(c)	12.00
23 CI,Space Museum	10.00
24 CI	10.00

FUNNY STOCKING STUFFER
March, 1985

1	1.00

FUNNY STUFF
Summer, 1944

1 B:3 Mousketeer Terrific Whatzit	650.00
2	350.00
3	200.00
4	175.00
5	175.00
6 thru 10	@150.00
11 thru 20	@125.00
21	75.00
22 C:Superman	300.00
23 thru 30	@75.00
31 thru 78	@50.00
79 July-Aug., 1954	50.00

FURY OF FIRESTORM
June, 1982

1 PB,I:Black Bison	3.00
2 PB,V:Black Bison	2.00
3 PB,V:Pied Piper, Killer Frost	2.00
4 PB,A:JLA,Killer Frost	2.00
5 PB,V:Pied Piper	2.00
6 V:Pied Piper	2.00
7 I:Plastique	2.00
8 V:Typhoon	2.00
9 V:Typhoon	2.00
10 V:Hyena	2.00
11 V:Hyena	2.00
12 PB,V:Hyena	2.00
13	2.00
14 PB,I:Enforcer,A:Multiplex	2.00
15 V:Multiplex	2.00
16 V:Multiplex	2.00
17 I:2000 Committee,Firehawk	2.00
18 I:Tokamak,A:Multiplex	2.00
19 GC,V:Goldenrod	2.00
20 A:Killer Frost	2.00
21 D:Killer Frost	2.50
22 O:Firestorm	2.50
23 I:Bug & Byte	2.00
24 I:Blue Devil,Bug & Byte	2.50
25 I:Silver Deer	2.00
26 V:Black Bison	2.00
27 V:Black Bison	2.00
28 I:Slipknot	2.00
29 I:2000 C'tee,I:Breathtaker	2.00

30 V:2000 Committee	2.00
31 V:2000 Committee	2.00
32 Phantom Stranger	2.00
33 A:Plastique	2.00
34 I:Killer Frost 2	2.00
35 V:K.Frost/Plastique,I:Weasel	2.00
36 V:Killer Frost & Plastique	2.00
37	2.00
38 V:Weasel	2.00
39 V:Weasel	2.00
40	2.00
41 Crisis	2.00
42 Crisis,A:Firehawk	2.00
43 V:Typhoon	2.00
44 V:Typhoon	2.00
45 V:Multiplex	2.00
46 A:Blue Devil	2.00
47 A:Blue Devil	2.00
48 I:Moonbow	2.00
49 V:Moonbow	2.00
50 W:Ed Raymond	2.00
51 A:King Crusher	2.00
52 A:King Crusher	2.00
53 V:Steel Shadow	2.00
54 I:Lava	2.00
55 Legends,V:World's Luckiest Man	2.00
56 Legends,A:Hawk	2.00
57	2.00
58 I:Parasite II	2.00
59	2.00
60 Secret behind Hugo's accident	2.00
61 V:Typhoon	2.00
61a Superman Logo	55.00
62 A:Russian 'Firestorm'	2.00
63 A:Capt.Atom	2.00
64 A:Suicide Squad	2.00
Ann.#1 EC,A:Firehawk, V:Tokamak	2.25
Ann.#2	2.25
Ann.#3	2.25
Ann.#4 KG,CS,GC,DG	2.25

Becomes:

FIRESTORM, THE NUCLEAR MAN
Nov., 1987

65 A:New Firestorm	2.00

Firestorm, The Nuclear Man #78
© DC Comics, Inc.

All comics prices listed are for _Near Mint_ condition.

DC COMICS

66 A:Green Lantern 2.00
67 Millenium, Week 1 . . . . 2.00
68 Millenium 2.00
69 V:Zuggernaut,Stalnivolk USA . 2.00
70 V:Flying Dutchman 2.00
71 Trapped in the Timestream . . . 2.00
72 V:Zuggernaut 2.00
73 V:Stalnivolk & Zuggernaut 2.00
74 Quest for Martin Stein 2.00
75 Return of Martin Stein 2.00
76 Firestorm & Firehawk
    vs Brimstone 2.00
77 Firestorm & Firehawk in Africa 2.00
78 'Exile From Eden',pt.1 . . . . . . 2.00
79 'Exile From Eden',pt.2 . . . . . . 2.00
80 A:Power Girl,Starman,Invasion
    x-over 2.00
81 A:Soyuz,Invasion aftermath . . . 2.00
82 Invasion Aftermath 2.00
83 V:Svarozhich 2.00
84 . . . . 2.00
85 Soul of Fire,N:Firestorm 2.00
86 TMd,Janus Directive #7 . . . . . 2.00
87 TMd 2.00
88 TMd,E:Air Wave B:Maser 2.00
89 TMd,V:Firehawk,Vandermeer
    Steel 2.00
90 TMd,Elemental War #1 . . . . . . 2.00
91 TMd,Elemental War #2 . . . . . . 2.00
92 TMd,Elemental War #3 . . . . . . 2.00
93 TMd,Elemental War concl. 2.00
94 TMd,A:Killer Frost 2.00
95 TMd,V:Captains of Industry . . . 2.00
96 TMd,A:Shango,African God &
    Obatala,Lord o/t White Cloth . . 2.00
97 TMd,A:Obatala,V:Shango 2.00
98 TMd,A:Masar 2.00
99 TMd,A:Brimstone,PlasmaGiant 2.00
100 TMd,AM,V:Brimstone (Firestorm
    back-up story) final issue 3.00
Ann.#5 JLI,Suicide Squad
    I:New Firestorm 2.50

GAMMARAUDERS
1989
1 I:Animal-Warrior Bioborgs 2.00
2 V:The Slugnoids 2.00
3 V:Slugnoids,I:Squawk the
    Penguinoid 2.00
4 V:Slugnoids 1.50
5 V:Bioborg/Podnoid 1.50
6 Slash vs.Sassin,A:RadicalDebs 1.50
7 Jok findsSword that was broken 2.00
8 Jok's search for KirkwardDerby 2.00
9 Jok the Congressman 2.00
10 The Big Nada, final issue 2.00

GANG BUSTERS
1947–58
1 . . . . 600.00
2 . . . . 275.00
3 . . . . 200.00
4 . . . . 200.00
5 . . . . 200.00
6 . . . . 200.00
7 . . . . 200.00
8 . . . . 200.00
9 Ph(c) 150.00
10 Ph(c) 150.00
11 Ph(c) 125.00
12 Ph(c) 125.00
13 Ph(c) 125.00
14 Ph(c),FF 250.00
15 . . . . 90.00
16 . . . . 90.00

17 . . . . 225.00
18 . . . . 80.00
19 . . . . 80.00
20 . . . . 80.00
21 thru 25 . . . . @75.00
26 JK 70.00
27 thru 40 . . . . @65.00
41 thru 44 . . . . @50.00
45 Comics Code 50.00
46 thru 50 . . . . 50.00
51 MD 55.00
52 thru 67 . . . . @55.00

GEMINI BLOOD
DC/Helix
1 . . . . 2.25
2 . . . . 2.25
3 Royal Caste 2.50
4 V:Shraddhan 2.25
5 WSi(c),V:Rolk 2.25
6 . . . . 2.50
7 BSz, Gillian's secret revealed . 2.50
8 Loothka 2.50
9 Nick captured by Loothka,
    final issue 2.50

GHOSTDANCING
Vertigo 1995
[Mini-Series]
1 I:Snake,Ghost Dancing 1.95
2 Secrets 1.95
3 I:Father Craft 2.50
4 Coyote prisoner 2.50
5 F:Snot Boy 2.50

Ghosts #97 © DC Comics, Inc.

GHOSTS
Sept.–Oct., 1971
1 JAp,NC(c),Death's Bridegroom! 20.00
2 WW,NC(c),Mission
    Supernatural 10.00
3 TD,NC(c),Death is my Mother . 6.00
4 GT,NC(c),The Crimson Claw . . 6.00
5 NC(c),Death, The Pale
    Horseman 6.00
6 NC(c),A Specter Poured
    The Potion 4.00
7 MK(c),Death's Finger Points . . 4.00

8 NC(c),The Cadaver In
    The Clock 4.00
9 AA,NC(c),The Last Ride
    Of Rosie The Wrecker 4.00
10 NC(c),A Specter Stalks Saigon 4.00
11 NC(c),The Devils Lake 4.00
12 NC(c),The Macabre Mummy
    Of Takhem-Ahtem 4.00
13 NC(c),Hell Is One Mile High . . 4.00
14 NC(c),The Bride Wore
    A Shroud 4.00
15 AA,NC(c),The Ghost That
    Wouldn't Die 4.00
16 NC(c),Death's Grinning Face . 4.00
17 NC(c),Death Held the
    Lantern High 4.00
18 AA,NC(c),Graveyard of
    Vengeance 4.00
19 AA,NC(c),The Dead Live On . 4.00
20 NC(c),The Haunting Hussar
    Of West Point 4.00
21 NC(c),The Ghost In The
    Devil's Chair 3.50
22 NC(c),The Haunted Horns
    Of Death 3.50
23 NC(c),Dead Is My Darling! . . . 3.50
24 AA,NC(c),You Too, Will Die . . 3.50
25 AA,NC(c),Three Skulls On
    The Zambezi 3.50
26 DP,NC(c),The Freaky Phantom
    Of Watkins Glen 3.50
27 NC(c),Conversation With
    A Corpse 3.50
28 DP,NC(c),Flight Of The
    Lost Phantom 3.50
29 NC(c),The Haunted Lady
    Of Death 3.50
30 NC(c),The Fangs of
    the Phantom 3.50
31 NC(c),Blood On The Moon . . 3.50
32 NC(c),Phantom Laughed Last . 3.50
33 NC(c),The Hangman of
    Haunted Island 3.50
34 NC(c),Wrath of the Ghost Apes 3.50
35 NC(c),Feud with a Phantom . . 3.50
36 NC(c),The Boy Who Returned
    From The Gave 3.50
37 LD(c),Fear On Ice 3.50
38 LD(c),Specter In The Surf . . . 3.50
39 LD(c),The Haunting Hitchhiker 3.50
40 LD(c),The Nightmare That
    Haunted The World 3.50
41 LD(c),Ship of Specters 3.50
42 LD(c),The Spectral Sentries . 3.50
43 LD(c),3 Corpses On A Rope . . 3.50
44 LD(c),The Case of the
    Murdering Specters 3.50
45 LD(c),Bray of the
    Phantom Beast 3.50
46 LD(c),The World's Most
    Famous Phantom 3.50
47 LD(c),Wrath of the
    Restless Specters 3.50
48 DP,LD(c),The Phantom Head . 3.50
49 The Ghost in the Cellar 3.50
50 Home Is Where The Grave Is . 3.50
51 The Ghost Who Would Not Die 3.50
52 LD(c),The Thunderhead
    Phantom 3.50
53 LD(c),Whose Spirit Invades Me 3.50
54 LD(c),The Deadly Dreams
    Of Ernie Caruso 3.50
55 LD(c),The House That Was
    Built For Haunting 3.50
56 LD(c),The Triumph Of The

DC COMICS

Teen-Age Phantom 3 50
57 LD(c),The Flaming Phantoms
  of Oradour 3.50
58 LD(c),The Corpse in the Closet 3.50
59 LD(c),That Demon Within Me . 3.50
60 LD(c),The Spectral Smile
  of Death 3.50
61 LD(c),When Will I Die Again . . 3.00
62 LD(c),The Phantom Hoaxer! . . 3.00
63 LD(c),The Burning Bride 3.00
64 LD(c),Dead Men Do Tell Tales 3.00
65 LD(c),The Imprisoned Phantom 3.00
66 LD(c),Conversation With A
  Corpse 3.00
67 LD(c),The Spectral Sword 3.00
68 LD(c),The Phantom of the
  Class of '76 . . . . 3.00
69 LD(c),The Haunted Gondola . . 3.00
70 LD(c),Haunted Honeymoon . . . 3.00
71 LD(c),The Ghost Nobody Knew 3.00
72 LD(c),The Ghost of
  Washington Monument 3.00
73 LD(c),The Specter Of The
  Haunted Highway 3.00
74 LD(c),The Gem That Haunted
  the World! 3.00
75 LD(c),The Legend Of The
  Lottie Lowry 3.00
76 LD(c),Two Ghosts of
  Death Row 3.00
77 LD(c),Ghost, Where Do
  You Hide? 3.00
78 LD(c),The World's Most
  Famous Phantom 3.00
79 LD(c),Lure of the Specter 3.00
80 JO(c),The Winged Specter . . . 3.00
81 LD(c),Unburied Phantom 3.00
82 LD(c),The Ghost Who
  Wouldn't Die 3.00
83 LD(c),Escape From the Haunt
  of the Amazon Specter 3.00
84 LD(c),Torment of the
  Phantom Face 3.00
85 LD(c),The Fiery Phantom
  of Faracutin 3.00
86 LD(c),The Ghostly Garden . . . 3.00
87 LD(c),The Phantom Freak 3.00
88 LD(c),Harem In Hell 3.00
89 JKu(c),Came The Specter
  Shrouded In Seaweed 3.00
90 The Ghost Galleon 3.00
91 LD(c),The Haunted Wheelchair 3.00
92 DH(c),Double Vision 3.00
93 MK(c),The Flaming Phantoms
  of Nightmare Alley 3.00
94 LD(c),Great Caesar's Ghost . . 3.00
95 All The Stage Is A Haunt 3.00
96 DH(c),Dread of the
  Deadly Domestic 3.00
97 JAp(c),A Very Special Spirit
  A:Spectre 8.00
98 JAp(c),The Death of a Ghost
  A:Spectre 8.00
99 EC(c),Till Death Do Us Join
  A:Spectre 8.00
100 EC&DG(c),The Phantom's
  Final Debt 2.00
101 MK(c),The Haunted Hospital . 2.00
102 RB&DG(c),The Fine Art
  Of Haunting 2.00
103 RB&DG(c),Visions and
  Vengeance 2.00
104 LD(c),The First Ghost 2.00
105 JKu(c) 2.00
106 JKu(c) 2.00

107 JKu(c) 2.00
108 JKu(c) 2.00
109 EC(c) 2.00
110 EC&DG(c) 2.00
111 JKu(c) 2.00
112 May, 1982 . . . . 2.00

G.I.Combat #167 © DC Comics, Inc.

G.I. COMBAT
Jan., 1957
Prev: Golden Age

44 RH,JKu,The Eagle and
  the Wolves 400.00
45 RH,JKu,Fireworks Hill 225.00
46 JKu,The Long Walk
  To Wansan 150.00
47 RH, The Walking Weapon . 150.00
48 No Fence For A Jet 150.00
49 Frying Pan Seat 150.00
50 Foxhole Pilot 150.00
51 RH,The Walking Grenade . . 125.00
52 Jku,JKu(c),Call For A Tank . 125.00
53 JKu,The Paper Trap 125.00
54 RH,JKu,Sky Tank 125.00
55 Call For A Gunner 125.00
56 JKu,JKu(c),The D.I.-And the
  Sand Fleas 125.00
57 RH,Live Wire For Easy 125.00
58 JKu(c),Flying Saddle 125.00
59 JKu,Hot Corner 125.00
60 RH,Bazooka Crossroads . . . 125.00
61 JKu(c),The Big Run 75.00
62 RH,JKu,Drop An Inch 75.00
63 MD,JKu(c),Last Stand 75.00
64 MD,RH,JKu,JKu(c),The
  Silent Jet 75.00
65 JKu,Battle Parade 75.00
66 MD,The Eagle of Easy
  Company 75.00
67 JKu(c),I:Tank Killer 100.00
68 JKu,RH,The Rock 75.00
69 JKu,RH,The Steel Ribbon . . 75.00
70 JKu,Bull's-Eye Bridge 75.00
71 MD,JKu(c),Last Stand 70.00
72 MD,JKu(c),Ground Fire 70.00
73 RH,JKu(c),Window War 70.00
74 RH,A Flag For Joey 70.00
75 RH,Dogtag Hill 70.00
76 MD,RH,JKu,Bazooka For

A Mouse 70.00
77 RH,JKu,H-Hour For A Gunner 70.00
78 MD,RH,JKu(c),Who Cares
  About The Infantry 70.00
79 JKu,RH,Big Gun-Little Gun . . 70.00
80 JKu,RH(c),Flying Horsemen . 70.00
81 Jump For Glory 60.00
82 IN,Get Off My Back 60.00
83 Too Tired To Fight 65.00
84 JKu(c),Dog Company
  Is Holding 60.00
85 IN,JKu(c),The T.N.T. Trio . . . 60.00
86 JKu,RH(c),Not Return 60.00
87 RH(c),I:Haunted Tank 200.00
88 RH,JKu(c),Haunted Tank Vs.
  Ghost Tank 60.00
89 JA,RH,IN,Tank With Wings . . 60.00
90 JA,IN,RH,Tank Raiders 60.00
91 IN,RH,The Tank and the Turtle 50.00
92 JA,IN,The Tank of Doom . . . 50.00
93 RH(c),JA,No-Return Mission . 50.00
94 IN,RH(c),Haunted Tank Vs.
  The Killer Tank 50.00
95 JA,RH(c),The Ghost of
  the Haunted Tank 50.00
96 JA,RH(c),The Lonesome Tank 50.00
97 IN,RH(c),The Decoy Tank . . . 50.00
98 JA,RH(c),Trap of Dragon's
  Teeth 50.00
99 JA,JKu,RH(c),Battle of the
  Thirsty Tanks 50.00
100 JA,JKu,Return of the
  Ghost Tank 50.00
101 JA,The Haunted Tank Vs.
  Attila's Battle Tiger 45.00
102 JKu(c),Haunted Tank
  Battle Window 45.00
103 JKu,JA,RH(c),Rabbit Punch
  For A Tiger 45.00
104 JA,JKu,RH(c),Blind
  Man's Radar 45.00
105 JA,JKu(c),Time Bomb Tank . 45.00
106 JA,JKu(c),Two-Sided War . . 45.00
107 JKu(c),The Ghost Pipers . . . 45.00
108 JKu(c),The Wounded
  Won't Wait,I:Sgt.Rock 48.00
109 JKu(c),Battle of the Tank
  Graveyard 45.00
110 IN,JKu(c),Choose Your War 45.00
111 JA,RH(c),Death Trap 45.00
112 JA,JKu(c),Ghost Ace 40.00
113 JKu,RH(c),Tank Fight In
  Death Town 40.00
114 JA,RH(c),O:Haunted Tank . . 75.00
115 JA,RH(c),MedalsForMayhem 25.00
116 IN,JA,JKu(c),Battle Cry
  For A Dead Man 25.00
117 JA,RH,JKu(c),Tank In
  The Ice Box 25.00
118 IN,JA,RH(c),My Buddy-
  My Enemy 25.00
119 IN,RH(c),Target For
  A Firing Squad 25.00
120 IN,JA,RH(c),Pull ATiger'sTail 25.00
121 RH(c),Battle of Two Wars . . 25.00
122 JA,JKu(c),Who Dies Next? . 25.00
123 IN,RH(c),The Target of Terro 25.00
124 IN,RH(c),Scratch That Tank . 25.00
125 RH(c),Stay Alive-Until Dark . 25.00
126 JA,RH(c),Tank Umbrella . . . 25.00
127 JA,JKu(c),Mission-Sudden
  Death 25.00
128 RH(c),The Ghost of
  the Haunted Tank 25.00
129 JA,RH(c),Hold That Town

All comics prices listed are for *Near Mint* condition. **CVA Page 53**

DC COMICS

For A Dead Man	25.00
130 RH(c),Battle of the Generals	25.00
131 JKu&RH(c),Devil For Dinner	25.00
132 JA,JKu(c),The Executioner	25.00
133 JKu(c),Operation:Death Trap	25.00
134 MD,JKu(c),Desert Holocaust	25.00
135 GE,JKu(c),Death is the Joker	25.00
136 JKu(c),Kill Now-Pay Later	25.00
137 JKu(c),We Can't See	25.00
138 JKu(c),I:The Losers	30.00
139 JKu(c),Corner of Hell	25.00
140 RH,MD,JKu(c),The LastTank	25.00
141 MD,JKu(c),Let Me Live..	
Let Me Die	7.00
142 RH,JKu(c),Checkpoint-Death	7.00
143 RH,JKu(c),The Iron Horseman	7.00
144 RH,MD,JKu(c),Every	
Man A Fort	7.00
145 MD,JKu(c),Sand,Sun	
and Death	7.00
146 JKu(c),Move the World	7.00
147 JKu(c),Rebel Tank	7.00
148 IN,JKu(c),The Gold-Plated	
General	7.00
149 JKu(c),Leave The	
Fighting To Us	7.00
150 JKu(c),The Death of the	
Haunted Tank	7.00
151 JKu(c),A Strong Right Arm	7.00
152 JKu(c),Decoy Tank	7.00
153 JKu(c),The Armored Ark	7.00
154 JKu(c),Battle Prize	7.00
155 JKu(c),The Long Journey	7.00
156 JKu(c),Beyond Hell	7.00
157 JKu(c),The Fountain	7.00
158 What Price War	7.00
159 JKu(c),Mission Dead End	7.00
160 JKu(c),Battle Ghost	7.00
161 JKu(c),The Day of the Goth	7.00
162 JKu(c),The Final Victor	7.00
163 A Crew Divided	7.00
164 Siren Song	7.00
165 JKu(c),Truce,Pathfinder	7.00
166 Enemy From Yesterday	7.00
167 JKu(c),The Finish Line	7.00
168 NA(c),The Breaking Point	7.00
169 WS(c),The Death of the	
Haunted Tank	7.00
170 Chain of Vengeance	7.00
171 JKu(c),The Man Who	
Killed Jeb Stuart	7.00
172 RH(c),At The Mercy of	
My Foes	7.00
173 JKu(c),The Final Crash	7.00
174 JKu(c),Vow To A Dead Foe	7.00
175 JKu(c),The Captive Tank	7.00
176 JKu(c),A Star Can Cry	7.00
177 JKu(c),The Tank That	
Missed D-Day	7.00
178 JKu(c),A Tank Is Born	7.00
179 JKu(c),One Last Charge	7.00
180 JKu(c),The Saints Go	
Riding On	7.00
181 JKu(c),The Kidnapped Tank	7.00
182 JKu(c),Combat Clock	7.00
183 JKu(c),6 Stallions To	
Hell- And Back	7.00
184 JKu(c),Battlefield Bundle	7.00
185 JKu(c),No Taps For A Tank	7.00
186 JKu(c),Souvenir	
From A Headhunter	7.00
187 JKu(c),The General	
Died Twice	7.00
188 The Devil's Pipers	7.00
189 The Gunner is a Gorilla	7.00

190 The Tiger and The Terrier	7.00
191 Decoy For Death	7.00
192 The General Has Two Faces	7.00
193 JKu(c),The War That	
Had To Wait	7.00
194 GE(c),Blitzkrieg Brain	7.00
195 JKu(c),The War That	
Time Forgot	7.00
196 JKu(c),Dead Men Patrol	7.00
197 JKu(c),Battle Ark	7.00
198 JKu(c),The Devil	
Rides A Panzer	7.00
199 JKu(c),A Medal From A Ghost	7.00
200 JKu(c),The Tank That Died	7.00
201 NA&RH(c),The Rocking	
Chair Soldiers	3.50
202 NA&RH(c),Walking Wounded	
Don't Cry	3.50
203 JKu(c),To Trap A Tiger	3.50
204 JKu(c),A Winter In Hell	3.50
205 JKu(c),A Gift From	
The Emperor	3.50
206 JKu(c),A Tomb For A Tank	3.50

G.I. Combat #288 © DC Comics, Inc.

207 JKu(c),Foxhole for a Sherman	3.50
208 JKu(c),Sink That Tank	3.50
209 JKu(c),Ring Of Blood	3.50
210 JKu(c),Tankers Also Bleed	3.50
211 JKu(c),A Nice Day For Killing	3.50
212 JKu(c),Clay Pigeon Crew	3.50
213 JKu(c),Back Door To War	3.50
214 JKu(c),The Tanker Who	
Couldn't Die	3.50
215 JKu(c),Last Stand For Losers	3.50
216 JKu(c),Ghost Squadron	3.50
217 JKu(c), The Pigeon Spies	3.50
218 JKu(c), 48 Hours to Die	3.50
219	3.50
220	3.50
221 thru 288	@3.50

GILGAMESH II
1989

1 JSn,O:Gilgamesh	5.00
2 JSn,V:Nightshadow	4.50
3 JSn,V:Robotic Ninja	4.50
4 JSn,final issue	4.00

GODDESS
Vertigo 1995–96
[Mini-Series]

1 I:Rosie Nolan	2.95
2 Rosie arrested	2.95
3 I:Jenny	2.95
4 CIA Chase	2.95
5 V:Agent Hooks	2.95
6 V:Harry Hooks	2.95
7 Mudhawks Past	2.95
8 finale	2.95

GOLDEN AGE
Elseworld 1993–94

1 PS,F:JSA,All-Star Squadron	10.00
2 PS,I:Dynaman	8.00
3 PS,IR:Mr. Terrific is	
Ultra-Humanite	8.00
4 PS,D:Dynaman,Mr. Terrific	6.00

GON
DC/Paradox 1996

1	5.95
2	5.95
3 (of 4) MTk,Here Today, Gon	
Tomorrow	5.95
4 MTk,Going, Going Gon	5.95

GREATEST STORIES EVER TOLD

Greatest Superman Stories Ever Told:

HC	75.00
SC	15.95

Greatest Batman Stories Ever Told:

HC	60.00
SC	16.00
Vol.#2 Catwoman & Penguin	16.95

Greatest Joker Stories Ever Told:

HC	45.00
SC BBo(c)	15.00

Greatest Flash Stories Ever Told:

HC	30.00
SC	15.00

Greatest Golden Age Stories Ever Told:

HC	25.00
SC	15.00

Greatest Fifties Stories Ever Told:

HC	30.00
SC	15.00

Greatest Team-Up Stories Ever Told:

HC	25.00
SC	15.00

GREEN ARROW
[Limited Series] 1983

1 TVE,DG,O:Green Arrow	5.00
2 TVE,DG,A:Vertigo	3.50
3 TVE,DG,A:Vertigo	3.50
4 TVE,DG,A:Black Canary	3.50
#### [Regular Series] 1988–97	
1 EH,DG,V:Muncie	5.00
2 EH,DG,V:Muncie	4.00
3 EH,DG,FMc,V:Fyres	4.00
4 EH,DG,FMc,V:Fryes	4.00
5 EH,DG,FMc,Gauntlet	4.00
6 EH,DG,FMc,Gauntlet	4.00
7 EB,DG,A:Black Canary	4.00
8 DG,Alaska	3.50
9 EH,DG,FMc,R:Shado	3.50
10 EH,DG,FMc,A:Shado	3.50
11 EH,DG,FMc,A:Shado	3.50
12 EH,DG,FMc,A:Shado	3.00

13 DJu,DG,FMc,Moving Target . . 3.00	59 Predator,pt.1 . . . . 2.00	Species" pt.2 . . . . 2.25
14 EH,DG,FMc 3.00	60 Predator,pt.2 . . . . 2.00	120 CDi(s),RbC,at grandfather's
15 EH,DG,FMc,Seattle And Die . . 3.00	61 FS,F:Draft Dodgers 2.00	ranch 2.25
16 EH,DG,FMc,Seattle And Die . . 3.00	62 FS 2.00	121 CDi(s),RbC,V:The Silver
17 DJu,DG,FMc,The Horse Man . 2.50	63 FS,B:Hunt for Red Dragon . . . 2.00	Monkey 2.25
18 DJu,DG,FMc,The Horse Man . 2.50	64 FS,Hunt for Red Dragon 2.00	122 CDi(s),RbC, at Idaho ranch . . 2.25
19 EH,DG,FMc,A:Hal Jordan 2.50	65 MGr(c),Hunt for Red Dragon . . 2.00	123 CDi(s),JAp,KJ,"The
20 EH,DG,FMc,A:Hal Jordan 2.50	66 MGr(c),E:Hunt for Red Dragon 2.00	Stormbringers" concl. 2.25
21 DJu,DG,B:Blood of Dragon,	67 MGr(c),FS,V:Rockband Killer . 2.00	124 CDi(s),RbC,V:Milo Armitage . 2.25
A:Shado 2.50	68 MGr(c),FS,BumRap 2.00	Ann.#1 A:Question,FablesII 3.50
22 DJu,DG,A:Shado 2.50	69 MGr(c),Reunion Tour #1 . . . . . 2.00	Ann.#2 EH,DG,FMc,A:Question . . 3.00
23 DJu,DG,A:Shado 2.50	70 Reunion Tour #2 . . . . 2.00	Ann.#3 A:Question 2.25
24 DJu,DG,E:Blood of Dragon . . . 2.50	71 Wild in the Streets #1 . . . . . . 2.00	Ann.#4 'The Black Alchemist' . . . 3.25
25 TVE,Witch Hunt #1 . . . . 2.25	72 MGr(c),Wild in the Streets#2 . 2.00	Ann.#5 TVE,Eclipso,Batman . . . 3.25
26 Witch Hunt #2 . . . . 2.25	73 MGr(c),F:Vietnam Vet 2.00	Ann.#6 JBa(c),I:Hook 3.50
27 DJu,DG,FMc,R:Warlord 2.25	74 SAP,MGr(c),V:Sniper 2.00	Ann.#7 CDi, Year One 3.95
28 DJu,DG,FMc,A:Warlord 2.25	75 MGr(c),A:Speedy Shado,	Spec. #0 Return 2.00
29 DJu,DG,FMc,Coyote Tears . . 2.25	Black Canary 3.00	
30 DJu,DG,FMc,Coyote Tears . . 2.25	76 MGr(c),R:Eddie Fyers 2.00	**GREEN ARROW**
31 FMc,V:Drug Dealers 2.25	77 MGr(c),A:Eddie Fyers 2.00	**LONGBOW HUNTERS**
32 FMc,V:Drug Dealers 2.25	78 MGr(c),V:CIA 2.00	**Aug., 1987**
33 DJu,FMc,Psychology Issue . . 2.25	79 MGr(c),V:CIA 2.00	1 MGr,N:GreenArrow,I:Shado . . . 5.00
34 DJu,DG,A:Fryes,Arrested . . . 2.25	80 MGr(c),E:MGr(s),V:CIA 2.00	1a 2nd printing 2.50
	81 B:CDi(s),JAp,V:Shrapnel,	2 MGr,'Shadow' Revealed 4.00
	Nuklon 2.00	2a 2nd printing 2.50
	82 JAp,I:Rival 2.00	3 MGr,Tracking Snow 4.00
	83 JAp,V:Yakuza 2.00	TPB, rep. #1-#3 . . . . 12.95
	84 E:CDi(s),JAp,In Las Vegas . . . 2.00	
	85 AlG(s),JAp,A:Deathstroke 2.00	**GREEN ARROW:**
	86 DgM(s),JAp,A:Catwoman 2.00	**THE WONDER YEARS**
	87 JAp,V:Factory Owner 2.00	**1993**
	88 JAp,A:M.Manhunter,Bl.Beetle . 2.00	1 MGr,GM,B:New O:Green Arrow 2.50
	89 JAp,A:Anarky 2.25	2 MGr,GM,I:Brianna Stone 2.00
	90 Zero Hour 2.25	3 MGr,GM,A:Brianna Stone 2.00
	91 Hitman 2.25	4 MGr,GM,Conclusion 2.00
	92 Partner attacked 2.25	
	93 Secrets of Red File 2.25	**GREEN CANDLES**
	94 I:Camo Rouge 2.25	**1995**
	95 V:Camo Rouge 2.25	1 Paradox Mystery,F:John Halting 5.95
	96 I:Slyfox,A:Hal Jordan 1.95	2 F:John Halting 5.95
	97 Where Angels Fear to	3 finale 5.95
	Tread,pt.2 . . . . 2.25	TPB B&W rep. #1–#3 . . . . 9.95
	98 Where Angels Fear to	
	Tread,pt.3, A:Arsenal 2.25	**GREEN LANTERN**
	99 Where Angels Fear to Tread . . 2.25	**Autumn, 1941**
	100 . . . . 2.25	1 O:Green Lantern, V:Master of
	101 A:Superman,Black Canary . . 2.25	Light, Arson in the Slums 25,000.00
	102 CDi,RbC,Underworld	2 V:Baldy,Tycoon's Legacy . . 6,000.00
	Unleashed tie-in 2.25	3 . . . . 4,000.00
	103 CDi,RbC,Underworld	4 Doiby and Green Lantern
	Unleashed tie-in 2.25	join the Army 3,000.00
	104 CDi,RbC,A:Green Lantern . . . 2.25	5 V:Nazis and Black
	105 CDi,RbC,A:Robin 2.25	Prophet,A:General Prophet 2,000.00
	106 . . . . 2.25	6 V:Nordo & Hordes of War Hungry
	107 CDi,RbC,protects child-king . . 2.25	Henchmen,Exhile of Exiles,
	108 CDi,A:Thorn 2.25	A:Shiloh 1,500.00
	109 CDi,JAp,BSz,in Metropolis . . 2.25	7 The Wizard of Odds 1,650.00
	110 CDi(s),RbC,I:Hatchet, Green	8 The Lady and Her Jewels,
	Lantern x-over 2.25	A:Hop Harrigan 1,500.00
	111 CDi(s),RbC,I:Hatchet, Green	9 V:The Whistler, The School
	Lantern x-over 2.25	for Vandals 1,400.00
	112 CDi(s),RbC, ... 2.25	10 V:Vandal Savage,The Man Who
	113 CDi(s),RbC,In the Mongolian	Wanted the World,O:Vandal
	wastes 2.25	Savage 1,400.00
	114 CDi(s) RbC,airplane downed,	11 The Distardly Designs of
	Final Night tie-in 2.25	Doiby Dickles' Pals 1,100.00
	115 CDi(s),RbC,"The Iron Death,"	12 O:The Gambler 1,100.00
	pt.1 . . . . 2.25	13 A:Angela Van Enters 1,100.00
	116 CDi(s),RbC,"The Iron Death,"	14 Case of the Crooked Cook 1,100.00
	pt.2 . . . . 2.25	15 V:Albert Zero, One...Two...
	117 CDi(s),RbC,"The Iron Death,"	Three...Stop Thinking . . . 1,100.00
	pt.3, concl. 2.25	16 V:The Lizard 1,100.00
	118 CDi(s),DBw,RbC,"Endangered	17 V:Kid Triangle, Reward for
	Species" pt.1 . . . . 2.25	
	119 CDi(s),DBw,RbC,"Endangered	

Green Arrow #77 © DC Comics, Inc.

35 B:Black Arrow Saga,A:Shade . 2.25	
36 Black Arrow Saga,A:Shade . . . 2.25	
37 Black Arrow Saga,A:Shade . . . 2.25	
38 E:Black Arrow Saga,A:Shade . 2.25	
39 DCw,Leaves Seattle 2.25	
40 MGr,Spirit Quest,A:	
Indian Shaman 2.25	
41 DCw,I.R.A 2.25	
42 DCw,I.R.A 2.25	
43 DCw,I.R.A 2.25	
44 DCw,Rock'n'Runes,pt.1 . . . . . 2.25	
45 Rock'n'Runes,pt.2 . . . . 2.25	
46 DCw,Africa 2.25	
47 DCw,V:Trappers 2.25	
48 DCw,V:Trappers 2.25	
49 V:Trappers 2.25	
50 MGr(c),50th Anniv.,R:Seattle . 3.00	
51 Tanetti's Murder,pt.1 . . . . 2.00	
52 Tanetti's Murder,pt.2 . . . . 2.00	
53 The List,pt.1,A:Fyres 2.00	
54 The List,pt.2,A:Fyres 2.00	
55 Longbow Hunters tie-in 2.00	
56 A:Lt. Cameron 2.00	
57 And Not A Drop to Drink,pt.1 . 2.00	
58 And Not A Drop to Drink,pt.2 . 2.00	

Green Lantern 1,100.00
18 V:The Dandy,The Connoisseur of
    crime,X-mas(c) 1,200.00
19 V:Harpies, Sing a Song of
    Disaster A:Fate 1,000.00
20 A:Gambler 1,000.00
21 V:The Woodman,The Good
    Humor Man 1,000.00
22 A:Dapper Dan Crocker ... 1,000.00
23 Doiby Dickles Movie
    Ajax Pictures 1,000.00
24 A:Mike Mattson,OnceA Cop 1,000.00
25 The Diamond Magnet 1,000.00
26 The Scourge of the Sea .. 1,000.00
27 V:Sky Pirate 1,000.00
28 The Tricks of the
    Sports Master 1,000.00
29 Meets the Challange of
    the Harlequin 1,000.00
30 I:Streak the Wonder Dog . 1,000.00
31 The Terror of the Talismans   800.00
32 The Case of the
    Astonishing Juggler 800.00
33 Crime goes West 800.00
34 Streak meets the Princess . 800.00
35 V:The Three-in-One Criminal 800.00
36 The Mystery of the
    Missing Messanger 1,000.00
37 A:Sargon 1,000.00
38 DoublePlay,May-June,1949 1,000.00

Green Lantern #10 © DC Comics, Inc.

GREEN LANTERN
1960–72, 1976–86

1 GK,O:Green Lantern 2,700.00
2 GK,I:Qward,Pieface 750.00
3 GK,V:Qward 450.00
4 GK,Secret of GL Mask 350.00
5 GK,I:Hector Hammond 350.00
6 GK,I:Tomar-Re 325.00
7 GK,I&O:Sinestro 275.00
8 GK,1st Story in 5700 A.D. .. 275.00
9 GK,A:Sinestro 275.00
10 GK,O:Green Lantern's Oath 275.00
11 GK,V:Sinestro 175.00
12 GK,Sinestro,I:Dr.Polaris . 175.00
13 GK,A:Flash,Sinestro 200.00
14 GK,I&O:Sonar,1st Jordan

Brothers story 165.00
15 GK,Zero Hour story 150.00
16 GK,MA,I:Star Saphire,
    O:Abin Sur 175.00
17 GK,V:Sinestro 150.00
18 GK 150.00
19 GK,A:Sonar 150.00
20 GK,A:Flash 165.00
21 GK,O:Dr.Polaris 140.00
22 GK,A:Hector Hammond,Jordan
    Brothers story 140.00
23 GK,I:Tattooed Man 140.00
24 GK,O:Shark 140.00
25 GK,V:Sonar,HectorHammond 140.00
26 GK,A:Star Sapphire 140.00
27 GK 140.00
28 GK,I:Goldface 140.00
29 GK,I:Black Hand 145.00
30 GK,I:Katma Tui 140.00
31 GK,Jordan brothers story . 120.00
32 GK 120.00
33 GK,V:Dr. Light 120.00
34 GK,V:Hector Hammond ... 120.00
35 GK,I:Aerialist 120.00
36 GK 120.00
37 GK,I:Evil Star 120.00
38 GK,A:Tomar-Re 120.00
39 GK,V:Black Hand 120.00
40 GK,O:Guardians,A:Golden
    Age Green Lantern 550.00
41 GK,A:Star Sapphire 75.00
42 GK,A:Zatanna 75.00
43 GK,A:Major Disaster 75.00
44 GK,A:Evil Star 75.00
45 GK,I:Prince Peril,A:Golden
    Age Green Lantern 125.00
46 GK,V:Dr.Polaris 75.00
47 GK,5700 A.D. V:Dr.Polaris .. 75.00
48 GK,I:Goldface 75.00
49 GK,I:Dazzler 75.00
50 GK,V:Thraxon the Powerful .. 75.00
51 GK,Green Lantern's Evil
    Alter-ego 55.00
52 GK,A:Golden Age Green
    Lantern Sinestro 80.00
53 GK,CI,Jordon brothers story . 55.00
54 GK,Menace in the Iron Lung . 55.00
55 GK,Cosmic Enemy #1 ..... 55.00
56 GK 55.00
57 GK,V:Major Disaster 55.00
58 GK,Perils of the Powerless
    Green Lantern 55.00
59 GK,I:Guy Gardner(imaginary
    story) 225.00
60 GK,I:Lamplighter 50.00
61 GK,A:Gold.Age Gr.Lantern . 55.00
62 Steel Small,Rob Big 50.00
63 NA(c),This is the Way the
    World Ends 50.00
64 MSy,We Vow Death to Green
    Lantern 50.00
65 MSy,Dry up and Die 50.00
66 MSy,5700 AD story 50.00
67 DD,The First Green Lantern . 50.00
68 GK,I Wonder where the
    Yellow Went? 50.00
69 GK,WW,If Earth Fails the
    Test.. It Means War 50.00
70 GK,A Funny Thing Happened
    on the way to Earth 50.00
71 GK,DD,MA,Jordan brothers .. 25.00
72 GK,Phantom o/t SpaceOpera 25.00
73 GK,MA,A:Star Sapphire
    Sinestro 25.00
74 GK,MA,A:Star Sapphire,

Sinestro 25.00
75 GK,Qward 25.00
76 NA,Gr.Lantern & Gr.Arrow
    team-up begins 165.00
77 NA,Journey to Desolation ... 50.00
78 NA,A:Black Canary,A Kind of
    Loving..A Way to Death 50.00
79 NA,DA,A:Black Canary,Ulysses
    Star is Still Alive 40.00
80 NA,DG,Even an Immortal
    can die 40.00
81 NA,DG,A:Black Canary,Death
    be my Destiny 35.00
82 NA,DG,A:Black Canary,
    V:Sinestro,(BWr 1 page) 35.00
83 NA,DG,A:BlackCanary,Gr.Lantern
    reveals I.D. to Carol Ferris .. 35.00
84 NA,BWr,V:Black Hand 35.00
85 NA,Speedy on Drugs,pt.1,
    rep.Green Lantern #1 ...... 60.00
86 NA,DG,Speedy on Drugs,pt.2,
    ATh(rep)Golden Age G.L. ... 60.00
87 NA,DG,I:John Stewart,
    2nd Guy Gardner app. 32.00
88 all reprints............... 9.00
89 NA,And Through Him Save
    the World 27.00
90 MGr,New Gr.Lantern rings ... 7.00
91 MGr,V:Sinestro 6.00
92 MGr,V:Sinestro 6.00
93 MGr,TA,War Against the
    World Builders 5.00
94 MGr,TA,DG,Green Arrow
    Assassin,pt.1 .... 5.00
95 MGr,Gr.Arrow Assassin,pt.2 .. 5.00
96 MGr,A:Katma Tui 5.00
97 MGr,V:Mocker 5.00
98 MGr,V:Mocker 5.00
99 MGr,V:Mocker 5.00
100 MGr,AS,I:Air Wave 9.00
101 MGr,A:Green Arrow 5.50
102 AS,A:Green Arrow 4.50
103 AS,Earth-Asylum for an Alien 3.50
104 AS,A:Air Wave 5.00
105 AS,Thunder Doom 5.00
106 MGr,Panic..In High Places
    & Low 5.00
107 AS,Green Lantern Corp.story 5.00
108 MGr,BU:G.A.Green Lantern,
    V:Replikon 6.00
109 MGr,Replicon#2,GA.GL.#2 .. 5.00
110 MGr,GA.GL.#3 .... 5.00
111 AS,O:Green Lantern,
    A:G.A.Green Lantern 6.00
112 AS,O&A:G.A. Green Lantern . 8.00
113 AS,Christmas story 4.00
114 AS,I:Crumbler 4.00
115 AS,V:Crumbler 4.00
116 Guy Gardner as Gr.Lantern . 26.00
117 JSon,I:KariLimbo,V:Prof.Ojo . 4.00
118 AS,V:Prof.Ojo 4.00
119 AS,G.L.& G.A.solo storys ... 3.50
120 DH,A:Kari,V:El Espectro 3.50
121 DH,V:El Espectro 3.50
122 DH,A:Guy Gardner,Superman 6.00
123 JSon,DG,E:Green Lantern/Green
    Arrow T.U.,A:G.Gardner,
    V:Sinestro 7.00
124 JSon,V:Sinestro 3.50
125 JSon,FMc,V:Sinestro 3.50
126 JSon,FMc,V:Shark 3.50
127 JSon,FMc,V:Goldface 3.50
128 JSon,V:Goldface 3.50
129 JSon,V:Star Sapphire 3.50
130 JSon,FMc,A:Sonar,B:Tales of the

DC COMICS

DC COMICS

Green Lantern Corps 3.00
131 JSon,AS,V:Evil Star 3.00
132 JSon,AS,E:Tales of GL Corps
    B:B.U.Adam Strange 3.00
133 JSon,V:Dr.Polaris 2.50
134 JSon,V:Dr.Polaris 2.50
135 JSon,V:Dr.Polaris 2.50
136 JSon,A:Space Ranger,
    Adam Strange 2.50
137 JSon,CI,MA,I:Citadel,A:Space
    Ranger,A.Strange 2.50
138 JSon,A&O:Eclipso 4.00
139 JSon,V:Eclipso 3.00
140 JSon,I:Congressman Block
    Adam Strange 2.50
141 JSon,I:OmegaMen 6.00
142 JSon,A:OmegaMen 4.00
143 JSon,A:OmegaMen 4.00
144 JSon,D:Tattooed Man,Adam
    Strange 2.50
145 JSon,V:Goldface 2.50
146 JSon,CI,V:Goldface
    E:B.U.Adam Strange 2.50

Green Lantern #25 © DC Comics, Inc.

147 JSon,CI,V:Goldface 2.50
148 JSon,DN,DA,V:Quardians . . . 2.50
149 JSon,A:GL.Corps 2.50
150 JSon,anniversary 3.50
151 JSon,GL.Exiled in space 2.50
152 JSon,CI,GL Exile #2 . . . . . . 2.50
153 JSon,CI,Gr.Lantern Exile #3 . 2.50
154 JSon,Gr.Lantern Exile #4 . . . 2.50
155 JSon,Gr.Lantern Exile #5 . . . 2.50
156 GK,Gr.Lantern Exile #6 . . . . 2.50
157 KP,IN,Gr.Lantern Exile #7 . . 2.50
158 KP,IN,Gr.Lantern Exile #8 . . 2.50
159 KP,Gr.Lantern Exile #9 . . . . 2.50
160 KP,Gr.Lantern Exile #10 . . . 2.50
161 KP,A:Omega Men,Exile #11 . 2.50
162 KP,Gr.Lantern Exile #12 . . . 2.50
163 KP,Gr.Lantern Exile #13 . . . 2.50
164 KP,A:Myrwhidden,Exile #14 . 2.50
165 KP,A:John Stewart & Gr.Arrow
    Green Lantern Exile #15 . . . . 2.00
166 GT,FMc,DGi,Exile #16 . . . . 2.00
167 GT,FMc,G.L.Exile #17 . . . . 2.00
168 GT,FMc,G.L. Exile #18 . . . . 2.00
169 Green Lantern Exile #19 . . . 2.00
170 GT,MSy,GreenLanternCorps . 2.00

171 ATh,TA,DGb,Green Lantern
    Exile #20 . . . . 2.00
172 DGb,E:Gr.Lant.Exile 2.00
173 DGb,I:Javelin,A:Congressman
    Bloch 2.00
174 DGb,V:Javelin 2.00
175 DGb,A:Flash 2.25
176 DGb,V:The Shark 2.00
177 DGb,rep. Gr.Lant #128 . . . . 2.00
178 DGb,A:Monitor,V:Demolition
    Team 2.00
179 DGb,I:Predator 2.00
180 DGb,A:JLA 2.00
181 DGi,Hal Jordan quits as GL . 2.75
182 DGi,John Stewart taks over
    V:Major Disaster 2.50
183 DGi,V:Major Disaster 2.50
184 DGb,Rep. Gr.Lant. #59 . . . . 3.50
185 DGi,DH,V:Eclipso 4.00
186 DGi,V:Eclipso 4.00
187 BWi,John Stewart meets
    Katma Tui 2.25
188 JSon,C:GrArrow,V:Sonar,John
    Stewart reveals I.D. to world . . 3.50
189 JSon,V:Sonar 2.00
190 JSon,A:Green Arrow/Black
    Canary,Guy Gardner 2.00
191 JSon,IR:Predator is Star
    Sapphire 2.00
192 JSon,O:Star Sapphire 2.00
193 JSon,V:Replikon,
    A:G.Gardner 2.50
194 JSon,Crisis,R:G.Gardner 5.00
195 JSon,Guy Gardner as Green
    Lantern,develops attitude . . . 10.00
196 JSon,V:Shark,Hal Jordan
    regains ring 3.00
197 JSon,V:Shark,Sonar,
    Goldface 3.00
198 JSon,D:Tomar-Re,Hal returns as
    Green Lantern,(double size) . . 3.00
199 JSon,V:Star Sapphire 2.00
200 JSon,final Gr.Lantern issue . . 2.50
Becomes:

GREEN LANTERN CORPS
1986–88
201 JSon,I:NewGr.LantCorps,V:Star
    Sapphire, Sonar, Dr.Polaris . . 2.00
202 JSon,set up headquarters . . . 2.00
203 JSon,tribute to Disney 2.00
204 JSon,Arisia reaches puberty . . 2.00
205 JSon,V:Black Hand 2.00
206 JSon,V:Black Hand 2.00
207 JSon, Legneds crossover . . . 2.00
208 JSon,I:Rocket Red Brigade,
    Green Lanterns in Russia#1 . . 2.00
209 JSon,In Russia #2 . . . . 2.00
210 JSon,In Russia #3 . . . . 2.00
211 JSon,John Stewart proposes
    to Katma Tui 1.75
212 JSon,W:J.Stewart&KatmaTui . 1.75
213 Json,For Want of a Male 1.75
214 IG,5700 A.D. Story 1.75
215 IG,Salaak and Chip quit 1.75
216 IG,V:Carl 1.75
217 JSon,V:Sinestro 1.75
218 BWg,V:Sinestro 1.75
219 BWg,V:Sinestro 1.75
220 JSon,Millenium,pt.3 . . . . 1.75
221 JSon,Millenium 1.75
222 JSon,V:Sinestro 1.75
223 GK,V:Sinestro 1.75
224 GK,V:Sinestro 2.00

Ann.#1 GK 2.00
Ann.#2 JSa,BWg,S:AnM 2.50
Ann.#3 JBy,JL,JR 2.00
Spec.#1 A:Superman 2.00
Spec.#2 MBr,RT,V:Seeker 2.00
TPB rep.#84-#87,#89,Flash
    #217-#219 . . . . 12.95
TPB rep. reprints of #1-#7 . . . . . 8.95

*Green Lantern (2nd Series) #220
© DC Comics, Inc.*

GREEN LANTERN
[2nd Regular Series] 1990–97
1 PB,A:Hal Jordan,John Stuart,
    Guy Gardner 5.00
2 PB,A:Tattooed Man 3.00
3 PB,Jordan vs.Gardner 4.00
4 PB,Vanishing Cities 2.00
5 PB Return to OA 2.00
6 PB 3GL'sCaptive 2.00
7 PB R:Guardians 2.00
8 PB R:Guardians 2.00
9 JSon,G.Gardner,pt.1 . . . . 3.00
10 JSon,G.Gardner,pt.2 . . . . 3.00
11 JSon,G.Gardner,pt.3 . . . . 3.00
12 JSon,G.Gardner,pt.4 . . . . 3.00
13 Jordan,Gardner,Stuart(giant) . . 2.50
14 PB,Mosaic,pt.1 . . . . 2.00
15 RT,Mosaic,pt.2 . . . . 2.00
16 MBr,RT,Mosaic,pt.3 . . . . 2.00
17 MBr,RT,Mosaic,pt.4 . . . . 2.00
18 JSon,JRu,G.Gardner,
    A:Goldface 2.00
19 MBr,PB,JSon,A:All Four G.L.'s,
    O:Alan Scott,A:Doiby Dickles
    (D.Size-50th Ann.Iss.) 3.00
20 PB,RT,Hal Jordan G.L. Corp
    story begins, A:Flicker 1.75
21 PB,RT,G.L. Corp.,pt.2,
    V:Flicker 1.75
22 PB,RT,G.L. Corp.,pt.3,
    R:Star Sapphire 1.75
23 PB,RT,V:Star Sapphire,
    A:John Stuart 1.75
24 PB,RT,V:Star Sapphire 1.75
25 MBr,JSon,RT,Hal Vs.Guy,
    A:JLA 2.75
26 MBr,V:Evil Star,Starlings 1.50

27 MBr,V:Evil Star,Starlings 1.50
28 MBr,V:Evil Star,Starlings 1.50
29 MBr,RT,R:Olivia Reynolds 1.50
30 MBr,RT,Gorilla Warfare#1 . . . . 1.50
31 MBr,RT,Gorilla Warfare#3 . . . . 1.50
32 RT(i),A:Floro,Arisia 1.50
33 MBr,RT,Third Law#1,
   A;New Guardians 1.50
34 MBr,RT,Third Law#2,I:Entropy 1.50
35 MBr,RT,Third Law#3,V;Entropy 1.50
36 V:Dr.Light 1.50
37 MBg,RT,A:Guy Gardner 1.50
38 MBr,RT,A:Adam Strange 1.50
39 MBr,RT,A:Adam Strange 1.50
40 RT(i),A:Darkstar,
   V:Reverse Flash 1.75
41 MBr,RT,V:Predator,
   C:Deathstroke 1.50
42 MBr,RT,V:Predator,
   Deathstroke 1.50
43 RT(i),A:Itty 1.50
44 RT(i),Trinity#2,A:L.E.G.I.O.N . . 1.75
45 GeH,Trinity#5,A:L.E.G.I.O.N.,
   Darkstars 1.75
46 MBr,A:All Supermen,
   V:Mongul 8.00
47 A:Green Arrow 6.00
48 KM(c),B:Emerald Twilight,I:Kyle
   Rayner (Last Green Lantern) . . 7.00
49 KM(c),GJ(s),A:Sinestro 6.00
50 KM(c),GJ(s),D:Sinestro,Kiliwog,
   Guardians,I:Last Green
   Lantern (in Costume) 8.00
51 V:Ohm,A:Mongul 3.00
52 V:Mongul 2.00
53 A:Superman,V:Mongul 2.00
54 D:Alex,V:Major Force 2.00
55 Zero Hour,A:Alan Scott,
   V:Major Force 2.25
56 Green Lantern and ring 2.00
57 Psimon 2.00
58 Donna Troy,Felix Faust 2.00
59 V:Dr. Polaris 2.00
60 Capital Punishment,pt.3 . . . . . 2.00
61 V:Kalibak,A:Darkstar 2.00
62 V:Duality,R:Ganthet 2.00
63 Parallax View: The Resurrection
   of Hal Jordan,pt.1 . . . . 2.00
64 Parallax View,pt.2,A:Superman,
   Flash,V:Parallax 2.00
65 Siege of ZiCharan,pt.2 . . . . . 2.00
66 V:Sonar 2.00
67 A:Flash,V:Sonar 2.00
68 RMz,RT,Underworld
   Unleashed tie-in 2.00
69 RMz,RT,Underworld
   Unleashed tie-in 2.00
70 RMz,RT,A:Supergirl 2.00
71 RMz,RT,Hero Quest,pt.1 . . . . . 2.00
72 RMz,RT,Hero Quest,pt.2 . . . . . 2.00
73 RMz,RT,Hero Quest,pt.3 . . . . . 2.00
74 RMz,RT,A:Adam Strange,
   V:Grayven 2.00
75 A:Adam Strange 2.00
76 Green Arrow x-over 2.00
77 Green Arrow x-over 2.00
78 . . . . 2.00
79 V:Sonar 2.00
80 RMz(s),JWi,MGy,V:Dr. Light,
   Final Night tie-in 2.00
81 RMz(s),DBk,RT,Memorial for
   Hal Jordan 4.00
81a deluxe edition + extra stories,
   foil cover on cardstock 6.00
82 RMz(s),TGb,RT,F:Kyle Rayner,

Alan Scott, Guy Gardner &
   John Stewart 1.75
83 . . . . 1.75
84 "Retribution," pt.2 . . . . 1.75
85 "Retribution," concl. 1.75
86 RMz,JJ,RT,A:Jade, V:Obsidian 1.75
87 RMz,TGb,RT,A:Martian
   Manhunter, vs. alien invasion . 1.75
88 RMz(s),DBk,TA,A:Donna Troy,
   visit Kyle's mom 1.75
89 RM(s),TA,V:Machine Messiah . 1.75
90 RM(s),Why did Kyle Rayner
   become Green Lantern 1.75
Ann.#1 Eclipso,V:Star Sapphire . 2.75
Ann.#2 Bloodlines#7,I:Nightblade . 2.50
Ann.#3 Elseworlds Story 2.95
Ann.#4 Year One story 3.00
Ann.#5 Legends o/t Dead Earth . . 2.95
Ann.#6 Pulp Heroes (High-
   Adventure) 3.95
TPB Emerald Twilight 6.25

GREEN LANTERN CORPS QUARTERLY
1992–94

1 DAb,JSon,FH,PG,MBr,F:Alan
   Scott G'nort 3.00
2 DAb,JSon,PG,AG,Alan Scott . . 2.75
3 DAb,RT,F:Alan Scott,G'Nort . . . 2.75
4 TA,AG(i),F:H.Jordan,G'Nort . . . 2.75
5 F:Alan Scott,I:Adam 2.75
6 JBa,TC,F:Alan Scott 3.25
7 Halloween Issue 3.25
8 GeH,SHa,final issue 3.25

Green Lantern: Emerald Dawn II #6
© DC Comics, Inc.

GREEN LANTERN: EMERALD DAWN
[1st Limited Series] 1989–90

1 MBr,RT,I:Mod.Age.Gr.Lantern . 7.00
2 MBr,RT,I:Legion (not group) . . 5.00
3 MBr,RT,V:Legion 4.00
4 MBr,RT,A:Green Lantern Corps 3.50
5 MBr,RT,V:Legion 3.00
6 MBr,RT,V:Legion 3.00
TPB rep#1-#6 . . . . 5.50

[2nd Limited Series] 1991
1 MBr,A:Sinestro,Guy Gardner . . 2.50
2 MBr,RT,V:Alien Aliance 1.75
3 MBr,RT,Sinestro's Home Planet 1.75
4 MBr,RT,Korugar Revolt 1.75
5 MBr,RT,A:G.Gardner 1.75
6 MBr,RT,Trial of Sinestro 1.75

GREEN LANTERN GALLERY
1 one-shot life in pictures 3.50

GREEN LANTERN: GANTHET'S TALE
1 JBy,O:Guardians 7.00

GREEN LANTERN/ GREEN ARROW
1983–84
1 NA rep. 5.00
2 NA,DG rep. 4.00
3 NA,DG rep. 4.00
4 NA,DG rep. 4.00
5 NA,DG rep. 4.00
6 NA,DG rep. 4.00
7 NA,DG rep. 4.00
TPB Roadback 8.95
TPB Traveling Heroes, Vol.1 . . . 12.95
TPB Traveling Heroes, Vol.2 . . . 12.95

GREEN LANTERN: MOSAIC
1992–93
1 F:John Stewart 2.00
2 D:Ch'p 1.75
3 V:Sinestro 1.50
4 F:The Children on Oa 1.50
5 V:Hal Jordan 1.50
6 A:Kilowog 1.50
7 V:Alien Faction 1.50
8 V:Ethereal Creatures 1.50
9 Christmas issue 1.50
10 V:Guardians 1.50
11 R:Ch'p 1.50
12 V:KKK 1.50
13 V:KKK,Racism 1.50
14 A:Salaak,Ch'p 1.50
15 A:Katma Tui,Ch'p 1.50
16 LMc,A:JLA,Green Lantern . . . 1.50
17 A:JLA 1.50
18 final issue 1.50

GREEN LANTERN PLUS
1 one-shot RMz(s), F:The Ray,
   V:Dr. Polaris 2.95

GREEN LANTERN/ SILVER SURFER
1-shot DC/Marvel RMz,TA
   A:Thanos vs. Parallax 4.95

GREGORY III
Bookshelf Ed. 4.95
Platinum Ed. 12.00

GRIFFIN
1991–92
1 I:Matt Williams as Griffin 5.50
2 V:Carson 5.25
3 A:Mary Wayne 5.25
4 A:Mary Wayne 5.25

DC COMICS

5 Face to Face with Himself 5.25	
6 Final Issue 5.25	

GROSS POINT
July 1997
1 MWa&BAu(s) parody 2.50
2 Independence Day picnic 2.50

GUARDIANS OF METROPOLIS
Nov. 1994
1 Kirby characters 1.50
2 Donovan's creations 1.50
3 . . . . 1.50
4 Female Furies 1.50

GUNFIRE
1994–95
1 B:LWn(s),StE,I:Ricochet 2.00
2 StE,V:Ricochet 2.00
3 StE,I:Purge 2.00
4 StE,V:Maraud 3 . . . . 2.00
5 StE,I:Exomorphic Man 1.95
6 New costume 1.95
7 Ragnarok 1.95
8 V:Tattoo 1.95
9 V:Ragnarock 1.95
10 V:Yakuza 1.95
11 V:Yakuza 1.95
12 I:New Weapon 1.95
13 A:JLA,V:Ragnarok, final issue . 2.25

Guy Gardner #12 © DC Comics, Inc.

GUY GARDNER
1992–94
1 JSon,A:JLA,JLE 2.00
2 JSon,A:Kilowog 1.50
3 JSon,V:Big,Ugly Alien 1.50
4 JSon,G.Gardner vs Ice 1.50
5 JSon,A:Hal Jordan,V:Goldface . 1.50
6 JSon,A:Hal Jordan,V:Goldface . 1.50
7 JSon,V:Goldface 1.50
8 JSon,V:Lobo 1.50
9 JSon,Boodikka 1.50
10 JSon,V:Boodikka 1.50
11 JSon,B:Year One 1.50
12 JSon,V:Batman,Flash,Green

Lantern 1.50	
13 JSon,Year One#3 . . . . 1.50	
14 JSon,E:Year One 1.50	
15 V:Bad Guy Gardner 1.50	
16 B:CDi(s),MaT,V:Guy's Brother . 1.75	

Becomes:

GUY GARDNER: WARRIOR
1994–96
17 V:Militia 2.00
18 B:Emerald Fallout,N:Guy Gardner,
   V:Militia 4.00
19 A:G.A.Green Lantern,V:Militia . 4.00
20 A:JLA,Darkstars 2.00
21 E:Emerald Fallout,V:H.Jordan . 2.00
22 I:Dementor 1.75
23 A:Buck Wargo 1.75
24 Zero Hour 1.50
25 A:Buck Wargo 2.50
26 Zero Hour 1.50
27 Capital Punishment 1.50
28 Capital Punishment,pt.2 . . . . . 1.50
29 I:Warriors Bar 1.50
29a Collector's Edition 2.95
30 V:Superman,Supergirl 1.50
31 A:Sentinel,Supergirl,
   V:Dementor 1.75
32 Way of the Warrior,pt.1,A:JLA . 1.75
33 Way of the Warrior,pt.4 . . . . . . 1.75
34 . . . . 1.75
35 Return of an Old Foe 1.75
36 Underworld Unleashed tie-in . . 1.75
37 Underworld Unleashed tie-in . . 1.75
38 A new woman 1.75
39 guest stars galore 1.75
40 . . . . 1.75
41 V:Dungeon 1.75
42 Martika revealed as Seductress 1.75
43 V:5 foes 1.75
Ann.#1 Year One Annual, Leechun
   vs. Vuldarians 3.50

GUY GARDNER: REBORN
1992
1 JSon,JRu,V:Goldface,C:Lobo . . 6.00
2 JSon,JRu,A:Lobo,V:Weaponers
   of Qward 5.50
3 JSon,JRu,A:Lobo,N:G.Gardner
   V:Qwardians 5.50

HACKER FILES
1992–93
1 TS,Soft Wars#1,I:Jack Marshall 2.25
2 TS,Soft Wars#2 . . . . 1.95
3 TS,Soft Wars#3 . . . . 1.95
4 TS,Soft Wars#4 . . . . 1.95
5 TS,A:Oracle(Batgirl) 1.95
6 TS,A:Oracle,Green Lantern . . . 1.95
7 TS,V:Digitronix 1.95
8 TS,V:Digitronix 1.95
9 TS,V:Digitronix 1.75
10 V:Digitronix 1.95
11 TS,A:JLE 1.95
12 TS,V:Digitronix,final issue . . . 1.95

HAMMER LOCKE
1992–93
1 I:Hammerlocke 2.50
2 V:Tharn the Iron Spider 1.75
3 V:Tharn the Iron Spider 1.75
4 O:Hammerlocke 1.75
5 V:Sahara Skyhawk 1.75
6 V:Tharn the Iron Spider 1.75

7 V:Tharn 1.75	
8 CSp,V:Iron Spider 1.75	

Hardware #41 © DC Comics, Inc.

HARDWARE
(Milestone) 1993–96
1 DCw,I:Hardware,Edwin Alva,Reprise,
   Dir.Mark.Ed.,w/A puzzle piece,
   Skybox Card,Poster 4.00
1a NewsstandEd. 2.00
1b Platinum Ed. 6.00
2 DCw,V:Reprise,I:Barraki Young 2.00
3 DCw,O:EDwin Alva,
   I:S.Y.S.T.E.M. 2.00
4 DCw,V:S.Y.S.T.E.M. 2.00
5 DCw,I:Deathwish 2.00
6 DCw,V:Deathwish 1.75
7 DCw,O:Deathwish 1.75
8 DCw(c),O:Hardware 1.75
9 DCw(c),I:Technique 1.75
10 DCw(c),I:Harm,Transit 1.75
11 WS(c),DCw,Shadow War,
   I:Iron Butterfly,Dharma 1.75
12 RB,V:Harm 1.75
13 DCw,A:Reprise 1.75
14 DCw 1.75
15 DCw(c),HuR,V:Alva 1.75
16 Die-Cut(c),JBy(c),DCw,
   N:Hardware 4.25
16a Newsstand ED. 2.25
17 Worlds Collide,pt.2,A:Steel . . . 1.75
18 Worlds Collide,pt.9,V:Rift 2.00
19 I:Evan,Tetras 1.75
20 . . . . 1.75
21 Arcana,Helga 1.75
22 Curt & Assistant 1.75
23 . . . . 1.75
24 . . . . 1.75
25 V:Death Row, Sanction 2.95
26 Hunt For Deathwish,pt.1 . . . . . 1.75
27 Hunt For Deathwish,pt.2 . . . . . 1.75
28 Hunt For Deathwish,pt.3 . . . . . 1.75
29 Long Hot Summer, A:The Blood
   Syndicate, spec.low price . . . 0.99
30 Long Hot Summer 2.50
31 . . . . 2.50
32 Control of Alva 2.50
33 HC(c), Cyborg 2.50

All comics prices listed are for *Near Mint* condition.

DC COMICS

34 V:Huaca Aires 2.50	
35 A:Sanction 2.50	
36 A:Sanction 2.50	
37 . . . . 2.50	
38 V:Malleus, without armor 2.50	
39 F:Sabrina Alva 2.50	
40 V:Top Dog 2.50	
41 . . . . 2.50	
42 . . . . 2.50	
43 . . . . 2.50	
44 A:Heroes 2.50	

45 DGC(s),Hardware & Hard
Company go back to basics . . 2.50
46 DGC(s),discovery of Edwin
Alva's artificial intelligence . . 2.50
47 DGC(s),the truth behind a
brutal murder 2.50
48 . . . . 2.50
49 DGC(s),Moe(c),V:Tyrant 2.50
50 DGC(s), 48pg. anniversary issue3.95
51 DMc(s) final issue 2.50

HAWK & DOVE
[1st Regular Series] 1968–69
1 SD 50.00
2 SD 40.00
3 GK 35.00
4 GK 35.00
5 GK,C:Teen Titans 40.00
6 GK 35.00
[Limited Series] 1988–89
1 RLd,I:New Dove 6.00
2 RLd,V:Kestrel 5.00
3 RLd,V:Kestrel 4.50
4 RLd,V:Kestrel 4.50
5 RLd,V:Kestrel,O:New Dove . . 4.50
TPB rep. #1–#5 . . . . 9.95
[2nd Regular Series] 1989–91
1 A:Superman,Green Lantern
Hawkman 2.00
2 V:Aztec Goddess 1.75
3 V:Aztec Goddess 1.75
4 I:The Untouchables 1.50
5 I:Sudden Death, A:1st Dove's
Ghost 1.50
6 A:Barter,Secrets o/Hawk&Dove 1.50
7 A:Barter,V:Count St.Germain . . 1.50
8 V:Count St.Germain 1.50
9 A:Copperhead 1.50
10 V:Gauntlet & Andromeda 1.50
11 A:New Titans,V:M.A.C.,
Andromeda Gauntlet 1.50
12 A:New Titans,V:Scarab 1.50
13 1960's,I:Shellshock 1.50
14 Prelue to O:Hawk & Dove,
V:Kestrel 1.50
15 O:Hawk & Dove begins 1.50
16 HawkV:Dove,V:Lord of Chaos . 1.50
17 V:Lords-Order & Chaos 1.50
18 The Creeper #1 . . . . 1.50
19 The Creeper #2 . . . . 1.50
20 KM,DG,Christmas Story 1.50
21 Dove 1.50
22 V:Sudden Death 1.50
23 A:Velv.Tiger,SuddenDeath . . . 1.50
24 A:Velv.Tiger,SuddenDeath . . . 1.50
25 Recap 1st 2 yrs.(48 pg) 2.00
26 Dove's past 1.50
27 The Hunt for Hawk 1.50
28 War of the Gods,A:Wildebeest
A:Uncle Sam,final issue,
double size 2.00
Ann.#1 In Hell 2.00
Ann.#2 CS,KGa,ArmageddonPt.5 . 2.00

TPB RLd 9.95

HAWKMAN
1964–68
[1st Regular Series]
1 MA,V:Chac 550.00
2 MA,V:Tralls 200.00
3 MA,V:Sky Raiders 135.00
4 MA,I&O:Zatanna 150.00
5 MA 135.00
6 MA 125.00
7 MA,V:I.Q. 125.00
8 MA 125.00
9 MA,V:Matter Master 125.00
10 MA,V:Caw 125.00
11 MA 75.00
12 MA 75.00
13 MA 75.00
14 GaF,MA,V:Caw 75.00
15 GaF,MA,V:Makkar 75.00
16 GaF,MA,V:Ruthvol 75.00
17 GaF,MA,V:Raven 75.00
18 GaF,MA,A:Adam Strange . . . 50.00
19 GaF,MA,A:Adam Strange . . . 50.00
20 GaF,MA,V:Lionmane 45.00
21 GaF,MA,V:Lionmane 45.00
22 V:Falcon 45.00
23 V:Dr.Malevolo 45.00
24 Robot Raiders from
Planet Midnight 45.00
25 DD,V:Medusa,G.A.Hawkman . 45.00
26 RdM,CCu,DD 45.00
27 DD,JKu(c),V:Yeti 45.00

Hawkman (2nd Series) #1
© DC Comics, Inc.

[2nd Regular Series] 1986–87
1 DH,A:Shadow Thief 3.00
2 DH,V:Shadow Thief 2.00
3 DH,V:Shadow Thief 1.50
4 DH A:Zatanna 1.50
5 DH,V:Lionmane 1.50
6 DH,V:Gentleman Ghost,
Lionmane 1.50
7 DH,Honor Wings 1.50
8 DH,Shadow War contd. 1.50
9 DH,Shadow War contd. 1.50
10 JBy(c),D:Hyatis Corp 1.50
11 End of Shadow War 1.50

12 Hawks on Thanagar 1.50
13 DH,Murder Case 1.50
14 DH,Mystery o/Haunted Masks . 1.50
15 DH,Murderer Revealed 1.50
16 DH,Hawkwoman lost 1.50
17 EH,DH,final issue 1.50
TPB rep.Brave & Bold apps. . . . 19.95
[3rd Regular Series] 1993–96
1 B:JOs(s),JD,R:Hawkman,
V:Deadline 4.00
2 JD,A:Gr.Lantern,V:Meta-Tech . 2.50
3 JD,I:Airstryke 2.25
4 JD,RM 2.00
5 JD(c),V:Count Viper 2.00
6 JD(c),A:Eradicator 2.00
7 JD(c),PuK(s),LMc,B:King of the
Netherworld 2.00
8 LMc,E:King of the Netherworld . 2.00
9 BML(s) 2.00
10 I:Badblood 2.00
11 V:Badblood 2.00
12 V:Hawkgod 2.25
13 V:Hawkgod 2.25
14 New abilities,pt.1 . . . . 1.95
15 New abilities,pt.2 . . . . 1.95
16 Eyes of the Hawk,pt.3 . . . . . 1.95
17 Eyes of the Hawk,pt.4 . . . . . 1.95
18 Seagle,Ellis, Pepoy 1.95
19 F:Hawkman 1.95
21 RLm,V:Shadow Thief,
Gentleman Ghost 2.25
22 Way of the Warrior,pt.3
A:Warrior,JLA 2.25
23 Way of the Warrior,pt.6 . . . . . 2.25
24 . . . . 2.25
25 V:Lionmane,painted(c) 2.25
26 WML,Underworld
Unleashed tie-in 2.25
27 WML,Underworld
Unleashed tie-in 2.25
28 WML,V:Doctor Polaris 2.25
29 HC(c),V:Vandal Savage 2.25
30 . . . . 2.25
31 serial killer has Tangarian
technology 2.25
32 MC,Search for serial killer . . . 2.25
Ann.#1 JD,I:Mongrel 3.75
Ann.#2 Year One Annual 3.95

HAWKWORLD
1989
1 TT,Hawkman, Origin retold . . . 6.00
2 TT,Katar tried for treason 4.00
3 TT,Hawkgirl's debut 4.00
[1st Regular Series] 1990–93
1 GN,Byth on Earth,R:Kanjar Ro . 3.50
2 GN,Katar & Shayera in Chicago 2.50
3 GN,V:Chicago Crime 2.00
4 GN,Byth's Control Tightens . . . 2.00
5 GN,Return of Shadow Thief . . . 2.00
6 GN,Stolen Thanagarian Ship . . 2.00
7 GN,V:Byth 2.00
8 GN,Hawkman vs. Hawkwoman 2.00
9 GN,Hawkwoman in Prison 2.00
10 Shayera returns to Thanagar . 2.00
11 GN,Blackhawk,Express 2.00
12 GN,Princess Treska 2.00
13 TMd,A:Firehawk,V:Marauder . 2.00
14 GN,Shayera's Father 2.00
15 GN,War of the Gods X-over . 2.00
16 GN War of the Gods X-over . 2.00
17 GN,Train Terrorists 2.00
18 GN,V:Atilla 2.00
19 GN,V:Atilla 2.00
20 V:Smir'Beau 2.00

DC COMICS

Hawkworld #19 © DC Comics, Inc.

21 GN,Thanagar Pt.1,
A:J.S.A. Hawkman 2.00
22 GN,Thanagar Pt.2 . . . . 2.00
23 GN,Thanagar Pt.3 . . . . 2.00
24 GN,Thanagar Pt.4 . . . . 2.00
25 GN,Thanagar Pt.5 . . . . 2.00
26 GN,V:Attilla battle armor 2.00
27 JD,B:Flight's End 2.00
28 JD,Flight's End #2 . . . . 2.00
29 TT(c),JDu,Flight's End #3 . . 2.00
30 TT,Flight's End #4 . . . . 2.00
31 TT,Flight's End #5 . . . . 2.00
32 TT,V:Count Viper,final issue . 2.50
Ann.#1 A:Flash 4.50
Ann.#2 Armageddon,pt.6 . . . . . . 4.00
Ann.#2a reprint (Silver) 3.50
Ann.#3 Eclipso tie-in 3.25

HAYWIRE
1988–89
1 . . . . 1.50
2 . . . . 1.25
3 thru 13 . . . . 1.00

HEARTLAND
DC/Vertigo Jan. 1997
1 GEn(s),SDi,Kit faces childhood
memories 4.95

HEART OF THE BEAST
GNv SeP 19.95

HECKLER, THE
1992–93
1 KG,MJ,I:The Heckler 1.25
2 KG,MJ,V:The Generic Man . . 1.25
3 KG,MJ,V:Cosmic Clown 1.25
4 KG,V:Bushwacker 1.25
5 KG,Theater Date 1.25
6 KG,I:Lex Concord 1.25
7 KG,V:Cuttin'Edge 1.25

HELLBLAZER
Jan., 1988
1 B:JaD(s),JRy,F:John
Constantine 25.00

2 JRy,I:Papa Midnight 15.00
3 JRy,I:Blathoxi 12.00
4 JRy,I:Resurrection Crusade,
Gemma 10.00
5 JRy,F:Pyramid of Fear 10.00
6 JRy,V:Resurrection Crusade,
I:Nergal 8.00
7 JRy,V:Resurrection Crusade,
I:Richie Simpson 7.00
8 JRy,AA,Constantine receives
demon blood,V:Nergal 8.00
9 JRy,A:Swamp Thing 7.00
10 JRy,V:Nergal 7.00
11 MBu,Newcastle Incident,pt.1 . . 6.00
12 JRy,D:Nergal 6.00
13 JRy,John has a Nightmare . . . 5.00
14 JRy,B:The Fear Machine,
I:Mercury,Marj,Eddie 5.00
15 JRy,Shepard's Warning. 5.00
16 JRy,Rough Justice 5.00
17 MkH,I:Mr. Wester 5.00
18 JRy,R:Zed 5.00
19 JRy,I:Simon Hughes 10.00
20 JRy,F:Mr.Webster 6.00
21 JRy,I:Jallakuntilliokan 6.00
22 JRy,E:The Fear Machine. . . . 6.00
23 I&D:Jerry O'Flynn 5.00
24 E:JaD(s),I:Sammy Morris . . . 5.00
25 GMo(s),DvL,Early Warning . . 5.00
26 GMo(s) 5.00
27 NGa(s),DMc,Hold Me 11.00
28 B:JaD(s),RnT,KeW,F:S.Morris . 5.00
29 RnT,KeW,V:Sammy Morris . . 5.00
30 RnT,KeW,D:Sammy Morris . . 5.00
31 E:JaD(s),SeP,Constantine's
Father's Funeral 5.00
32 DiF(s),StP,I&D:Drummond . . 4.50
33 B:JaD(s),MPn,I:Pat McDonell . 4.50
34 SeP,R:Mercury,Marj 4.50
35 SeP,Constantine's Past 4.50
36 Future Death,(preview of
World Without End) 4.50
37 Journey to England's Secret
Mystics 4.50
38 Constantine's Journey contd. . 4.50
39 Journey to Discovery 4.50
40 DMc,I:2nd Kid Eternity 6.00
41 B:GEn(s),WSm,MPn,Dangerous
Habits 10.00
42 Dangerous Habits 6.00
43 I:Chantinelle 6.00
44 Dangerous Habits 6.00
45 Dangerous Habits 6.00
46 Dangerous Habits epilogue,
I:Kit(John's girlfriend) 6.00
47 SnW(i),Pub Where I Was Born 5.00
48 Love Kills 5.00
49 X-mas issue,Lord o/t Dance . . 5.00
50 WSm,Remarkable Lives,A:Lord of
Vampires (48pgs) 5.00
51 JnS,SeP,Laundromat-
Possession 3.00
52 GF(c),WSm, Royal Blood 3.00
53 GF(c),WSm, Royal Blood 3.00
54 GF(c),WSm, Royal Blood 3.00
55 GF(c),WSm, Royal Blood 3.00
56 GF(c),B:GEn(s),DvL,
V:Danny Drake 3.00
57 GF(c),SDi,Mortal Clay#1,
V:Dr. Amis 3.00
58 GF(c),SDi,Mortal Clay#2,
V:Dr. Amis 3.00
59 GF(c),WSm,MkB(i),KDM,B:Guys &
Dolls 3.00
60 GF(c),WSm,MkB(i),F:Tali,

Chantinelle 7.50
61 GF(c),WSm,MkB(i),E:Guys & Dolls,
V:First of the Fallen 5.00
62 GF(c),SDi,End of the Line,I:Gemma,
AIDS storyline insert w/Death . 3.25
Vertigo
63 GF(c),SDi,C:Swamp Thing,Zatanna
Phantom Stranger 2.50
64 GF(c),SDi,B:Fear & Loathing,
A:Gabriel (Racism) 2.75
65 GF(c),SDi,D:Dez 2.50
66 GF(c),SDi,E:Fear and Loathing 2.50
67 GF(c),SDi,Kit leaves John . . . 2.50
68 GF(c),SDi,F:Lord of Vampires,
Darius,Mary 2.50
69 GF(c),SDi,D:Lord of Vampires . 2.25
70 GF(c),SDi,Kit in Ireland 2.25
71 GF(c),SDi,A:WWII Fighter Pilot 2.25
72 GF(c),SDi,B:Damnation's
Flame,A:Papa Midnight 2.25
73 GF(c),SDi,Nightmare NY,
A:JFK 2.25
74 GF(c),SDi,I:Cedella,A:JFK . . . 2.25
75 GF(c),SDi,E:Damnation'sFlame 2.25
76 GF(c),SDi,R:Brendan 2.25
77 Returns to England 2.25
78 GF(c),SDi,B:Rake at the
Gates of Hell 2.25
79 GF(c),SDi,In Hell 2.25
80 GF(c),SDi,In London 2.25
81 GF(c),SDi 2.25
82 Kit 2.25
83 Rake,Gates of Hell 2.25
84 John's past 2.25
85 Warped Notions,pt.1 . . . . 2.25
86 Warped Notions,pt.2 . . . . 2.25
87 Warped Notions,pt.3 . . . . 2.25
88 Warped Notions,pt.4 . . . . 2.25
89 Dreamtime 2.25
90 Dreamtime,pt.2 . . . . 2.25
91 Visits Battlefield 2.25
92 Critical Mass,pt.1 . . . . 2.25
93 Critical Mass,pt.2 . . . . 2.25
94 Critical Mass,pt.3 . . . . 2.25
95 SeP,Critical Mass,pt.4 . . . . . 2.25
96 SeP,Critical Mass,pt.5 . . . . . 2.25
97 SeP,Critical Mass epilogue . . . 2.25
98 SeP, helps neighbor 2.25
99 SeP 2.25
100 SeP, In a coma 3.50
101 SeP,deal with a demon 2.25
102 SeP,Difficult Beginnings,
pt.1 (of 3) 2.25
103 SeP,"Difficult Beginnings, pt.2" 2.25
104 SeP,"Difficult Beginnings, pt.3" 2.25
105 . . . . 2.25
106 PJe(s),SEp,"In the Line of
Fire," pt.1 (of 2) 2.25
107 PJe(s),SEp,"In the Line of
Fire," pt. 2 . . . . 2.25
108 PJe(s),SeP,a Bacchic
celebration 2.25
109 PJe(s),SeP,cattle mutilations
in Northern England 2.25
110 PJe(s),SeP,"Last Man
Standing," pt.1 . . . . 2.25
111 PJe(s),SeP,"Last Man
Standing," pt.2 . . . . 2.25
112 PJe(s),SeP,"Last Man
Standing," pt.3 . . . . 2.25
113 PJe(s),SeP,"Last Man
Standing," pt.4 . . . . 2.25
114 PJe(s),SeP,"Last Man
Standing," pt.5 . . . . 2.25
115 PJe(s),SeP(s),Dani's ex-

DC COMICS

boyfriend 2.25
116 SeP, "Widdershins" pt.1 (of 2) 2.25
117 SeP, "Widdershins" pt.2 . . . . 2.25
Ann.#1 JaD(s),BT,Raven Scar . . . 7.00
Spec.#1 GF(c),GEn(s),SDi,John
  Constantine's teenage years . . 4.50
TPB Original Sins,rep.#1–#9 . 19.95
TPB Dangerous Habits,
  rep.#41–#46 . . . . 14.95
TPB Fear and Loathing 14.95

HERCULES UNBOUND
Oct.–Nov., 1975
1 thru 11 . . . . @1.25
12 Aug.–Sept., 1977 . . . . 1.25

HEROES
Milestone 1996
1 Six heroes join 2.50
2 battle royale 2.50
3 . . . . 2.50
4 . . . . 2.50
5 . . . . 2.50
6 final issue 2.50

HEROES AGAINST HUNGER
1 NA,DG,JBy,CS,AA,BWr,BS,
  Superman,Batman 3.50

HERO HOTLINE
1 thru 6, Mini-series . . . . @1.75

HEX
Sept., 1985
1 MT,I:Hex 2.50
2 MT 2.00
3 MT,V:Conglomerate 2.00
4 MT,V:Conglomerate 2.00
5 MT,A:Chainsaw Killer 2.00
6 MT,V:Conglomerate 2.00
7 MT,Tries to Return to own era . 2.00
8 MT,The Future 2.50
9 MT,Future Killer Cyborgs 1.50
10 MT,V:Death Cult 1.50
11 MT,V:The Batman 3.00
12 MT,A:Batman,V:Terminators . . 3.00
13 MT,I:New Supergroup 2.50
14 MT,A:The Dogs of War 1.50
15 KG,V:Chainsaw Killer 1.50
16 KG,V:Dogs of War 1.50
17 KG,Hex/Dogs of War T.U.
  V:XXGG 1.50
18 KGr,Confronting the Past,final
  Issue 1.50

HISTORY OF DC UNIVERSE
Sept., 1986
1 GP, From start to WWII 5.00
2 GP, From WWII to present . . . 5.00

A HISTORY OF VIOLENCE
DC/Paradox Press March 1997
GN B&W 9.95

HITCHHIKER'S GUIDE TO THE GALAXY
1 Based on the book 7.00
2 Based on the book 6.50
3 Based on the book 6.50

GN from Douglas Adams book . 14.95

HITMAN
1996–97
1 GEn, F:Tommy Monaghan 7.00
2 GEn, Attempt to kill Joker 5.00
3 GEn(s),JMC, Mawzin & The
  Arkanonne 4.50
4 GEn(s),JMC, ... 3.00
5 GEn(s),JMC, ... 3.00
6 GEn(s),JMC,A:Johnny Navarone,
  Natt the Hatt 3.00
7 GEn(s),JMC, Pat's dead, Hitman
  wants revenge 3.00
8 GEn(s),JMC,barricaded in
  Noonan's Bar, Final Night tie-in 3.00
9 GEn(s),JMC,A:Six-Pack 3.00
10 GEn(s),JMC,A:Green Lantern . 3.00
11 . . . . 2.25
12 GEn(s),JMC,"Local Heroes,
  "A:Green Lantern 2.25
13 . . . . 2.25
14 GEn(s),JMC, "Zombie Night at
  the Aquarium," concl. 2.25
15 GEn(s),JMC, "Ace of
  Killers," pt.1, V:Mawzir 2.25
16 GEn(s),JMC, "Ace of
  Killers," pt.2 . . . . 2.25
17 GEn(s),JMC, "Ace of Killers,"
  pt.3,A:Catwoman, Demon
  Etrigan 2.25
18 GEn(s),JMC, "Ace of Killers,"
  pt.4,A:Demon Etrigan, Baytor . 2.25
Ann.#1 Pulp Heroes (Western) . 3.95

HOPALONG CASSIDY
Feb., 1954
86 GC,Ph(c):William Boyd & Topper,
  'The Secret of the Tattooed
  Burro' 250.00
87 GC,Ph(c),'The Tenderfoot
  Outlaw' 135.00
88 Ph(c),GC,'15 Robbers of Rimfire
  Ridge' 100.00
89 GC,Ph(c),'One-Day
  Boom Town' 100.00
90 GC,Ph(c),'Cowboy Clown
  Robberies' 75.00
91 GC,Ph(c),'The Riddle of
  the Roaring R Ranch' 85.00
92 GC,Ph(c),'The Sky-Riding
  Outlaws' 85.00
93 GC,Ph(c),'The Silver Badge
  of Courage' 85.00
94 GC,Ph(c),'Mystery of the
  Masquerading Lion' 85.00
95 GC,Ph(c),'Showdown at the
  Post-Hole Bank' 85.00
96 GC,Ph(c),'Knights of
  the Range' 85.00
97 GC,Ph(c),'The Mystery of
  the Three-Eyed Cowboy' 85.00
98 GC,Ph(c),'Hopalong's
  Unlucky Day' 85.00
99 GC,Ph(c),'Partners in Peril' . . 85.00
100 GC,Ph(c),'The Secrets
  of a Sheriff' 100.00
101 GC,Ph(c),'Way Out West
  Where The East Begins' 60.00
102 GC,Ph(c),'Secret of the
  Buffalo Hat' 60.00
103 GC,Ph(c),'The Train-Rustlers
  of Avalance Valley' 60.00
104 GC,Ph(c),'Secret of the
  Surrendering Outlaws' 60.00

105 GC,Ph(c),'Three Signs
  to Danger' 60.00
106 GC,Ph(c),'The Secret of
  the Stolen Signature' 60.00
107 GC,Ph(c),'The Mystery Trail
  to Stagecoach Town' 60.00
108 GC,Ph(c),'The Mystery
  Stage From Burro Bend' 60.00
109 GC,'The Big Gun on Saddletop
  Mountain' 60.00
110 GC,'The Dangerous Stunts
  of Hopalong Cassidy' 50.00
111 GC,'Sheriff Cassidy's
  Mystery Clue' 50.00
112 GC,'Treasure Trail to
  Thunderbolt Ridge 50.00
113 GC,'The Shadow of the
  Toy Soldier 50.00
114 GC,'Ambush at
  Natural Bridge' 50.00
115 GC,'The Empty-Handed
  Robberies' 50.00
116 GC,'Mystery of the
  Vanishing Cabin' 50.00
117 GC,'School for Sheriffs' 50.00
118 GC,'The Hero of
  Comanche Ridge' 50.00
119 GC,'The Dream Sheriff of
  Twin Rivers' 50.00
120 GC,'Salute to a Star-Wearer' 50.00
121 GC,'The Secret of the
  Golden Caravan' 50.00
122 GC,'The Rocking
  Horse Bandits' 50.00
123 GK,'Mystery of the
  One-Dollar Bank Robbery' . . 50.00
124 GK,'Mystery of the
  Double-X Brand' 50.00
125 GK,'Hopalong Cassidy's
  Secret Brother' 50.00
126 GK,'Trail of the
  Telltale Clues' 50.00
127 GK,'Hopalong Cassidy's
  Golden Riddle' 50.00
128 GK,'The House That
  Hated Outlaws' 50.00
129 GK,'Hopalong Cassidy's
  Indian Sign' 50.00
130 GK,'The Return of the
  Canine Sheriff' 50.00
131 GK&GK(c),'The Amazing
  Sheriff of Double Creek' 50.00
132 GK,'Track of the
  Invisible Indians' 50.00
133 GK,'The Golden Trail
  to Danger' 50.00
134 GK,'Case of the
  Three Crack-Shots' 50.00
135 GK,May-June, 1959 . . . . . . 50.00

HORRORIST
(Vertigo) 1995
1 I:Horrorist 5.95
2 conclusion 5.95

HOT WHEELS
March-April, 1970
1 ATh 25.00
2 thru 5 ATh . . . . @20.00
6 NA 30.00

HOUSE OF MYSTERY
Dec.–Jan., 1952
1 I Fell In LoveWithA Monster 1,600.00

DC COMICS

2 The Mark of X 700.00
3 . . . . 500.00
4 The Man With the Evil Eye . 400.00
5 The Man With the Strangler
　　Hands! 400.00
6 The Monster in Clay! 300.00
7 Nine Lives of Alger Denham! 300.00
8 . . . . 300.00
9 . . . . 300.00
10 The Wishes of Doom 300.00
11 Deadly Game of G-H-O-S-T 250.00
12 The Devil's Chessboard . . . 250.00
13 The Theater Of A
　　Thousand Thrills! 250.00
14 . . . . 250.00
15 The Man Who Could Change
　　the World 250.00
16 Dead Men Tell No Tales! . . 200.00
17 . . . . 175.00
18 . . . . 175.00
19 . . . . 175.00
20 The Beast Of Bristol 175.00
21 Man Who Could See Death 175.00

House of Mystery #27
© DC Comics, Inc.

22 The Phantom's Return 175.00
23 . . . . 175.00
24 Kill The Black Cat 175.00
25 The Man With Three Eyes! . 175.00
26 . . . . 125.00
27 Fate Held Four Aces! 125.00
28 The Wings Of Mr. Milo! . . . 125.00
29 . . . . 125.00
30 . . . . 125.00
31 The Incredible Illusions! . . . 125.00
32 Pied Piper of the Sea 125.00
33 Mr. Misfortune! 125.00
34 The Hundred Year Duel . . . 125.00
35 . . . . 125.00
36 The Treasure of Montezuma! 110.00
37 MD,The Statue That
　　Came to Life 110.00
38 The Voyage Of No Return . 110.00
39 . . . . 110.00
40 The Coins That Came To Life 110.00
41 The Impossible Tricks! 110.00
42 The Stranger From Out There 110.00
43 . . . . 110.00
44 The Secret Of Hill 14 . . . . . 110.00

45 . . . . 110.00
46 The Bird of Fate 110.00
47 The Robot Named Think . . . 110.00
48 The Man Marooned On Earth 110.00
49 The Mysterious Mr. Omen . 110.00
50 . . . . 100.00
51 Man Who Stole Teardrops . 90.00
52 The Man With The Golden
　　Shoes 90.00
53 The Man Who Hated Mirrors . 90.00
54 The Woman Who Lived Twice 90.00
55 I Turned Back Time 90.00
56 The Thing In The Black Box . 90.00
57 The Untamed 90.00
58 . . . . 90.00
59 The Tomb Of Ramfis 90.00
60 The Prisoner On Canvas . . 90.00
61 JK,Superstition Day 90.00
62 The Haunting Scarecrow . . . 75.00
63 JK,The Lady and The Creature 90.00
64 The Golden Doom 75.00
65 JK,The Magic Lantern 90.00
66 JK,Sinister Shadow 90.00
67 The Wizard Of Water 75.00
68 The Book That Bewitched . . 75.00
69 The Miniature Disasters . . . 75.00
70 JK,The Man With Nine Lives . 90.00
71 The Menace o/t Mole Man . . 75.00
72 JK,Dark Journey 90.00
73 Museum That Came to Life . 65.00
74 Museum That Came To Life . 65.00
75 Assignment Unknown! 65.00
76 JK,Prisoners Of The Tiny
　　Universe 80.00
77 The Eyes That Went Berserk 60.00
78 JK(c),The 13th Hour 75.00
79 JK(c),The Fantastic Sky
　　Puzzle 75.00
80 Man With Countless Faces! . 65.00
81 The Man Who Made Utopia . 65.00
82 The Riddle of the Earth's
　　Second Moon 65.00
83 The Mystery of the
　　Martian Eye 65.00
84 JK,BK,The 100-Century Doom 75.00
85 JK(c),Earth's Strangest
　　Salesman 70.00
86 The Baffling Bargains 65.00
87 The Human Diamond 65.00
88 Return of the Animal Man . . 65.00
89 The Cosmic Plant! 65.00
90 The Invasion Of The Energy
　　Creatures! 65.00
91 DD&SMo(c),The Riddle of the
　　Alien Satellite 65.00
92 DD(c),Menace of the
　　Golden Globule 65.00
93 NC(c),I Fought The
　　Molten Monster 65.00
94 DD&SMo(c),The Creature
　　In Echo Lake 65.00
95 The Wizard's Gift 65.00
96 The Amazing 70-Ton Man . . 65.00
97 The Alien Who Change
　　History 65.00
98 DD&SMo(c),The Midnight
　　Creature 65.00
99 The Secret of the
　　Leopard God 65.00
100 The Beast Beneath Earth . . 75.00
101 The Magnificent Monster . . 55.00
102 Cellmate to a Monster 55.00
103 Hail the Conquering Aliens . 55.00
104 I was the Seeing-Eye Man . 55.00
105 Case of the Creature X-14 . 55.00

106 Invaders from the Doomed
　　Dimension 55.00
107 Captives o/t Alien
　　Fisherman 55.00
108 RMo,Four Faces of Frank
　　Forbes 55.00
109 ATh,JKu,Secret of the Hybrid
　　Creatures 55.00
110 Beast Who Stalked Through
　　Time 55.00
111 Operation Beast Slayer 55.00
112 Menace of Craven's
　　Creatures 55.00
113 RMo,Prisoners of Beast
　　Asteroid 55.00
114 The Movies from Nowhere . 55.00
115 Prisoner o/t Golden Mask . . 55.00
116 RMo,Return of the
　　Barsfo Beast 55.00
117 Menace of the Fire Furies . . 50.00
118 RMo,Secret o/SuperGorillas 50.00
119 Deadly Gift from the Stars . 50.00
120 ATh,Catman of KarynPeale . 55.00
121 RMo,Beam that Transformed
　　Men 50.00
122 Menace fo the Alien Hero . . 50.00
123 RMo,Lure o/t Decoy
　　Creature 50.00
124 Secret of Mr. Doom 50.00
125 Fantastic Camera Creature . 50.00
126 The Human Totem Poles . . 50.00
127 RMo,Cosmic Game o/Doom 50.00
128 NC,The Sorcerer's Snares . 50.00
129 Man in the Nuclear Trap . . 50.00
130 The Alien Creature Hunt . . . 50.00
131 Vengeance o/t GeyserGod . 45.00
132 MMe,Beware My Invisible
　　Master 45.00
133 MMe,Captive Queen of
　　Beast Island 45.00
134 MMe,Secret Prisoner of
　　Darkmore Dungeon 45.00
135 MMe,Alien Body Thief 45.00
136 MMe,Secret o/t StolenFace . 45.00
137 MMe,Tunnel to Disaster . . . 45.00
138 MMe,Creature Must Die . . . 45.00
139 MMe,Creatures of
　　Vengeful Eye 45.00
140 I&Only app.:Astro 45.00
141 MMe,The Alien Gladiator . . 45.00
142 MMe,The Wax Demons . . . 45.00
143 J'onn J'onzz begins 250.00
144 J'onn J'onzz on Weird
　　World of Gilgana 150.00
145 J'onn J'onzz app 100.00
146 BP,J'onn J'onzz 100.00
147 J'onn J'onzz 100.00
148 J'onn J'onzz 100.00
149 ATh,J'onn J'onzz 100.00
150 MMe,J'onn J'onzz 100.00
151 J'onn J'onzz 100.00
152 MMe,J'onn J'onzz 100.00
153 J'onn J'onzz 100.00
154 J'onn J'onzz 100.00
155 J'onn J'onzz 100.00
156 JM,I:Dial H for Hero (Giantboy
　　Cometeer,Mole)J.J'onzz sty 125.00
157 JM,Dial H for Hero (Human
　　Bullet,Super Charge,Radar
　　Sonar Man) J'onn J'onzz sty 100.00
158 JM,Dial H for Hero (Quake
　　MasterSquid)J'onn J'onzz sty 90.00
159 JM,Dial H for Hero (Human
　　Starfish,Hypno Man,Mighty
　　Moppet) J'onn J'onzz sty . . . 90.00

DC COMICS

160 JM,Dial H for Hero (King Kandy A:Plastic Man,I:Marco Xavier (J'onn J'onzz new secret I.D.) 125.00
161 JM,Dial H for Hero (Magneto, Hornet Man,Shadow Man) . . 75.00
162 JM,Dial H for Hero (Mr.Echo, Future Man) J'onnJ'onzz sty . 75.00
163 JM,Dial H for Hero(Castor&Pollux, King Coil) J'onnJ'onzz sty . . 75.00
164 JM,Dial H for Hero (Super Nova Zip Tide) J'onnJ'onzz sty . . 75.00
165 JM,Dial H for Hero (Whoozis, Whatsis,Howzis) J'onn J'onzz story 75.00
166 JM,Dial H for Hero (Yankee Doodle Kid,Chief Mighty Arrow) J'onn J'onzz sty 75.00
167 JM,Dial H for Hero (Balloon Boy, Muscle Man,Radar Sonar Man) J'onn J'onzz sty 75.00
168 JM,Dial H for Hero (Thunderbolt, Mole,Cometeer,Hoopster) J'onn J'onzz sty 75.00
169 JM,I:Gem Girl in Dial H for Hero,J'onnJ'onzz sty 75.00
170 JM,Dial H for Hero (Baron BuzzSaw,Don Juan,Sphinx Man) J'onn J'onzz sty 75.00
171 JM,Dial H for Hero (King Viking Whirl-I-Gig) J'onnJ'onzz sty . . 65.00
172 JM,Dial H for Hero 65.00
173 E:Dial H for Hero,F:J'onn Jonzz 65.00
174 New direction,SA pg.13 . . . 25.00
175 I:Cain 25.00
176 SA,Cain's Game Room 25.00
177 Curse of the Car 25.00
178 NA,The Game 30.00
179 BWr,NA,O,Widow'sWalk . . 65.00
180 GK,WW,BWr,SA,Room 13 . . 20.00
181 BWr,The Siren of Satan . . . 20.00
182 ATh,The Devil's Doorway . . 18.00
183 BWr,WW(i),DeadCanKill . . 22.00
184 ATh,GK,WW,Eye o/Basilisk . 18.00
185 AW,The Beautiful Beast . . . 22.00
186 BWr,NA,Nightmare 25.00
187 ATh,Mask of the Red Fox . . 9.00
188 TD,BWr,House of Madness . 15.00
189 WW(i),Eyes of the Cat 8.00
190 ATh,Fright 11.00
191 BWr,TD,Christmas Story,. . . 11.00
192 JAp,GM,DH,Garnener of Eden 8.00
193 BWr 13.00
194 ATh,NR,RH(rep)JK(rep) Born Loser 9.00
195 NR,BWr,ThingsOld..Things Forgotten 25.00
196 GM,GK,ATh(rep)A Girl & Her Dog 8.00
197 DD,NR,House of Horrors . . . 8.00
198 MSy,NC,Day of the Demon . 8.00
199 WW,RB,Sno'Fun 9.00
200 MK,TD,The Beast's Revenge 8.00
201 JAp,The Demon Within 8.00
202 MSy,GC(rep),SA,The Poster Plague,John Prentice? 8.00
203 NR,Tower of Prey 8.00
204 BWr,AN,All in the Family . . . 12.00
205 The Coffin Creature 8.00
206 MSy,TP,The Burning 8.00
207 JSn,The Spell 10.00
208 Creator of Evil 8.00
209 AA,JAp,Tomorrow I Hang . . 10.00
210 The Immortal 8.00

211 NR,Deliver Us From Evil . . . 10.00
212 MA,AN,Ever After 8.00
213 AN,Back from the Realm of the Damned 10.00
214 NR,The Shaggy Dog 10.00
215 The Man Who Wanted Power over Women 8.00
216 TD,Look into My Eyes & Kill . 8.00
217 NR,AA,Swamp God 10.00
218 FT,An Ice Place to Visit 8.00
219 AA,NR,Pledge to Satan 8.00
220 AA,AN,They Hunt Butterflies Don't They? 8.00
221 FT,BWr,MK,He Who Laughs Last 10.00
222 AA,Night of the Teddy Bear . 8.00
223 Demon From the Deep 8.00
224 FR,AA,SheerFear,B:100pg . 11.00
225 AA,FT,AN,See No Evil 9.00
226 AA,FR,NR,SA,Monster in House Tour of House of Mystery . . . 10.00
227 NR,AA,The Carriage Man . . . 9.00
228 FR,NA(i),The Rebel 9.00

House of Mystery #269
© DC Comics, Inc.

229 NR,Nightmare Castle, last 100 page 9.00
230 Experiment In Fear 8.00
231 Cold,Cold Heart 9.00
232 Last Tango in Hell 8.00
233 FR,Cake! 8.00
234 AM,Lafferty's Luck 8.00
235 NR,Wings of Black Death . . . 8.00
236 SD,NA(i)Death Played a Sideshow 10.00
237 FT,Night of the Chameleon . . 8.00
238 . . . . 8.00
239 Day of the Witch 8.00
240 The Murderer 8.00
241 FR,NR,DeathPulls theStrings 8.00
242 FR,The Balloon Vendor 8.00
243 Brother Bear 8.00
244 FT,Kronos..Zagros-Eborak . 8.00
245 AN,Check the J.C.Demon Catalogue Under...Death 8.00
246 DeathVault of Eskimo Kings . 8.00
247 SD,Death Rides the Waves . . 8.00
248 NightJamieGaveUp theGhost 8.00
249 Hit Parade of Death 8.00

250 AN,Voyage to Hell 8.00
251 WW,AA,theCollector,68 pgs 10.00
252 DP,RT,AA,FR,AN,ManKillers 10.00
253 TD,AN,GK,KJ,Beware the Demon Child 7.00
254 SD,AN,MR,TheDevil's Place . 8.00
255 RE,GM,SometimesLeopards 10.00
256 DAy,AN,Museum of Murders 10.00
257 RE,MGo,TD(i),MBr,Xmas iss. 8.00
258 SD,RB,BMc,DG(i),The Demon and His Boy 8.00
259 RE,RT,MGo,DN,BL,'Hair Today, Gone Tomorrow,last giant 9.00
260 Go to Hades 8.00
261 The Husker 8.00
262 FreedFrom Infernos of Hell . . 8.00
263 JCr,Is There Vengeance After Death? 8.00
264 Halloween Issue 8.00
265 The Perfect Host 8.00
266 The Demon Blade 8.00
267 A Strange Way to Die 8.00
269 Blood on the Grooves 8.00
270 JSh,JRu,JBi,Black Moss 8.00
271 TS,HellHound of Brackenmoor 8.00
272 DN,DA,theSorcerer's Castle . 8.00
273 The Rites of Inheritance 8.00
274 MR,JBi,Hell Park 8.00
275 JCr,'Final Installment' 8.00
276 SD,MN,'Epode' 8.00
277 HC,AMi,'LimitedEngagement' 8.00
278 'TV or Not TV' 8.00
279 AS,Trial by Fury 8.00
280 VMK,DAy,Hungry Jaws of Death 8.00
281 Now Dying in this Corner . . . 8.00
282 JSw,DG,Superman/Radio Shack ins 8.00
283 RT,AN'Kill Me Gently' 8.00
284 KG,King and the Dragon 8.00
285 Cold Storage 8.00
286 Long Arm of the Law 8.00
287 NR,AS,BL,Legend o/t Lost . . 8.00
288 DSp,Piper at Gates of Hell . . 8.00
289 Brother Bobby's Home for Wayward Girls & Boys 8.00
290 TS,I:I..Vampire 8.00
291 TS,DAy,I..Vampire #2 . . . . . . 8.00
292 TS,MS,TD,RE,DSp,Wendigo . 8.00
293 GT,TS,A:I..Vampire #3 . . . . . 8.00
294 CI,TY,GT,TD,The Darkness . 8.00
295 TS,TVE,JCr,I..Vampire #4 . . . 8.00
296 CI,BH,Night Women 8.00
297 TS,DCw,TD,I..Vampire #5 . . . 8.00
298 TS,'Stalker on a Starless Night' 8.00
299 TS,DSp,I..Vampire #6 . . . . . . 8.00
300 GK,DA,JSon,JCr,DSp,Anniv. . 8.00
301 JDu,TVE,KG,TY '...Virginia' . 8.00
302 TS,NR,DSp,I..Vampire #7 . . . 8.00
303 TS,DSp,I..Vampire #8 . . . . . . 8.00
304 EC,RE,I..Vampire #9 . . . . . . 8.00
305 TVE,EC,I..Vampire #10 . . . . . 8.00
306 TS,TD,I..Vampire #11, A:Jack the Ripper 8.00
307 TS,I..Vampire #12 . . . . 8.00
308 TS,MT,NR,I..Vampire #13 . . . 8.00
309 TS,I..Vampire #14 . . . . 8.00
310 TS(i),I..Vampire #15 . . . . 8.00
311 I..Vampire #16 . . . . 8.00
312 TS(i),I..Vampire #17 . . . . 8.00
313 TS(i),CI,I..Vampire #18 . . . . . 8.00
314 TS,I..Vampire #19 . . . . 8.00
315 TS(i),TY,I..Vampire #20 . . . . . 8.00

DC COMICS

316 TS(i),GT,TVE,I..Vampire #21	8.00
317 TS(i),I..Vampire #22	8.00
318 TS(i),I..Vampire #23	8.00
319 TS,JOy,I..Vampire conc.	8.00
320 GM,Project: Inferior	8.00
321 final issue	8.00

HOUSE OF SECRETS
Nov.–Dec., 1956

1 MD,JM,The Hand of Doom	1,000.00
2 JPr,RMo,NC,Mask of Fear	450.00
3 JM,JK,MMe,The Three Prophecies	375.00
4 JM,JK,MMe,Master of Unknown	275.00
5 MMe,The Man Who Hated Fear	175.00
6 NC,MMe,Experiment 1000	175.00
7 RMo,Island o/t Enchantress	175.00
8 JK,RMo,The Electrified Man	225.00
9 JM,JSt,The Jigsaw Creatures	175.00
10 JSt,NC,I was a Prisoner of the Sea	175.00
11 KJ(c),NC,The Man who couldn't stop growing	175.00
12 JK,The Hole in the Sky	185.00
13 The Face in the Mist	125.00
14 MMe,The Man who Stole Air	125.00
15 The Creature in the Camera	125.00
16 NC,We matched wits with a Gorilla genius	100.00
17 DW,Lady in the Moon	100.00
18 MMe,The Fantastic Typewriter	100.00
19 MMe,NC,Lair of the Dragonfly	100.00
20 Incredible FireballCreatures	100.00
21 Girl from 50,000 Fathoms	100.00
22 MMe,Thing from Beyond	100.00
23 MMe,I&O:Mark Merlin	110.00
24 NC,Mark Merlin story	100.00
25 MMe,Mark Merlin story	90.00
26 NC,MMe, Mark Merlin story	90.00
27 MMe,Mark Merlin	90.00
28 MMe,Mark Merlin	90.00
29 NC,MMe,Mark Merlin	90.00
30 JKu,MMe,Mark Merlin	90.00
31 DD,MMe,RH,Mark Merlin	75.00
32 MMe,Mark Merlin	75.00
33 MMe,Mark Merlin	75.00
34 MMe,Mark Merlin	75.00
35 MMe,Mark Merlin	75.00
36 MMe,Mark Merlin	75.00
37 MMe,Mark Merlin	75.00
38 MMe,Mark Merlin	75.00
39 JKu,MMe,Mark Merlin	75.00
40 NC,MMe,Mark Merlin	75.00
41 MMe,Mark Merlin	75.00
42 MMe,Mark Merlin	75.00
43 RMo,MMe,CI,Mark Merlin	75.00
44 MMe,Mark Merlin	75.00
45 MMe,Mark Merlin	75.00
46 MMe,Mark Merlin	75.00
47 MMe,Mark Merlin	75.00
48 ATh,MMe,Mark Merlin	75.00
49 MMe,Mark Merlin	75.00
50 MMe,Mark Merlin	75.00
51 MMe,Mark Merlin	65.00
52 MMe,Mark Merlin	65.00
53 CI,Mark Merlin	65.00
54 RMo,MMe,Mark Merlin	65.00
55 MMe,Mark Merlin	65.00
56 MMe,Mark Merlin	65.00
57 MMe,Mark Merlin	65.00
58 MMe,O:Mark Merlin	65.00

59 MMe,Mark Merlin	65.00
60 MMe,Mark Merlin	65.00
61 I:Eclipso,A:Mark Merlin	175.00
62 MMe,Eclipso,Mark Merlin	100.00
63 GC,ATh,Eclipso,Mark Merlin	70.00
64 MMe,ATh,M Merlin,Eclipso	70.00
65 MMe,ATh,M Merlin,Eclipso	70.00
66 MMe,ATh,M Merlin,Eclipso	110.00
67 MMe,ATh,M Merlin,Eclipso	75.00
68 MMe,Mark Merlin,Eclipso	55.00
69 MMe,Mark Merlin,Eclipso	55.00
70 MMe,Mark Merlin,Eclipso	55.00
71 MMe,Mark Merlin,Eclipso	55.00
72 MMe,Mark Merlin,Eclipso	55.00
73 MMe,D:Mark Merlin,I:Prince Ra-Man; Eclipso	55.00
74 MMe,Prince Ra-Man,Eclipso	55.00
75 MMe,Prince Ra-Man,Eclipso	55.00
76 MMe,Prince Ra-Man,Eclipso	55.00
77 MMe,Prince Ra-Man,Eclipso	55.00
78 MMe,Prince Ra-Man,Eclipso	55.00
79 MMe,Prince Ra-Man,Eclipso	55.00
80 MMe,Prince Ra-Man,Eclipso	55.00

House of Secrets #43
© DC Comics, Inc.

81 I:Abel, new mystery format Don't Move It	12.00
82 DD,NA,One & only, fully guaranteed super-permanent 100%	11.00
83 ATh,The Stuff that Dreams are Made of	10.00
84 DD,If I had but world enough and time	10.00
85 DH,GK,NA,Second Chance	11.00
86 GT,GM,Strain	10.00
87 DD,DG,RA,MK,The Coming of Ghaglan	11.00
88 DD,The Morning Ghost	10.00
89 GM,DH,Where Dead MenWalk	10.00
90 GT,RB,NA,GM,The Symbionts	14.00
91 WW,MA,The Eagle's Talon	12.00
92 BWr,TD(i),I:Swamp Thing (Alex Olson)	450.00
93 JAp,TD,ATh(rep.)Lonely in Death	7.50
94 TD,ATh(rep.)Hyde.and go Seek	7.50
95 DH,NR,The Bride of Death	7.00
96 DD,JAb,WW, the Monster	8.00

97 JAp,Divide and Murder	7.00
98 MK,ATh(rep),Born Losers	7.50
99 NR,TD(i),Beyond His Imagination	7.50
100 TP,TD,AA,Rest in Peace	7.50
101 AN,Small Invasion	7.00
102 NR,A Lonely Monstrosity	7.00
103 AN,Village on Edge o/Forever	6.00
104 NR,AA,GT,Ghosts Don't Bother Me...But...	5.00
105 JAp,AA,An Axe to Grind	5.00
106 AN,AA,This Will Kill You	6.00
107 AA,The Night of the Nebbish	6.00
108 A New Kid on the Block	5.00
109 AA,AN...And in Death, there is no Escape	5.00
110 Safes Have Secrets, Too	3.50
111 TD,Hair-I-Kari	3.50
112 Case of the Demon Spawn	3.50
113 MSy,NC,NR,Spawns of Satan	3.50
114 FBe,Night Game	3.50
115 AA,AN,Nobody Hurts My Brother	3.50
116 NR,Like Father,Like Son	3.50
117 AA,AN,Revenge for the Deadly Dummy	3.50
118 GE,Very Last Picture Show	3.50
119 A Carnival of Dwarves	3.50
120 TD,AA,The Lion's Share	3.50
121 Ms.Vampire Killer	3.50
122 AA,Requiem for Igor	3.50
123 ATh,A Connecticut Ice Cream Man in King Arthur's Court	4.00
124 Last of the Frankensteins	3.50
125 AA,FR,Instant Re-Kill	3.50
126 AN,On Borrowed Time	3.50
127 MSy,A Test of Innocence	3.50
128 AN,Freak Out!	3.50
129 Almost Human	3.50
130 All Dolled Up!	3.50
131 AN,Point of No Return	3.50
132 Killer Instinct	3.50
133 Portraits of Death	3.50
134 NR,Inheritance of Blood	3.50
135 The Vegitable Garden	4.00
136 Last Voyage of Lady Luck	3.50
137 The Harder They Fall	3.50
138 Where Dreams are Born	4.00
139 SD,NR,A Real Crazy Kid	3.50
140 NR,O:Patchwork Man	4.00
141 You Can't Beat the Devil	4.00
142 Playmate	3.50
143 The Evil Side	3.50
144 The Vampire of Broadway	3.50
145 Operation wasSuccessful,But	3.50
146 Snake's Alive	3.50
147 AN,The See-Through Thief	3.50
148 SD,Sorcerer's Apprentice	3.50
149 The Evil One	3.50
150 A:PhantomStranger & Dr.13	3.50
151 MGo,Nightmare	3.50
152 Sister Witch	3.50
153 VM,AN,Don't Look Now	3.50
154 JL,Last issue	3.50

HOUSE OF SECRETS
DC/Vertigo Aug. 1996

1 SSe(s),TKr, judgments on your darkest secrets	2.50
2 SSe(s),TKr, F:Rain	2.50
3 SSe(s),TKr,Seattle's citizens secrets	2.50
4 SSe(s),TKr,Eric's secrets exposed	2.50

DC COMICS

5 . . . . 2.50
6 SSe(s),DFg,Other rooms:
"Meeting" 2.50
7 SSe(s),TKr,"Blueprint:
Elevation A" 2.50
8 SSe(s),TKr,"The Road to
You," pt.1 . . . . 2.50
9 SSe(s),TKr,"The Road to
You," pt.2 . . . . 2.50
10 SSe(s),TKr,"The Road to
You," pt.3, concl 2.50
11 "The Book of Law" pt.1 (of 5) . 2.50
12 "The Book of Law" pt.2 . . . . . 2.50
TPB Foundation, rep.#1–#5 . . . . 14.95

HUMAN TARGET SPECIAL

1 DG(i),Prequel to T.V. Series . . 2.00

HUNTER'S HEART
1995

1 Cops vs. Serial Killer 4.95
2 . . . . 4.95
3 F:Lieutenant Slidell 4.95

The Huntress #11 © DC Comics, Inc.

HUNTRESS, THE
1989–90

1 JSon/DG 2.00
2 JSon,Search for Family's
Murderer 2.00
3 JSon,A:La Bruja 1.50
4 JSon,Little Italy/Chinatown
Gangs 1.50
5 JSon,V:Doctor Mandragora . . . 1.50
6 JSon,Huntress'secrets revealed 1.50
7 JSon,V:Serial Killer 1.50
8 JSon,V:Serial Killer 1.50
9 JSon,V:Serial Killer 1.50
10 JSon,Nuclear Terrorists in NY . 1.50
11 JSon,V:Wyvern,Nuclear
Terrorists contd. 1.50
12 JSon,V:Nuclear Terrorists cont 1.50
13 JSon,Violence in NY 1.50
14 JSon,Violence contd.,New
Mob boss 1.50
15 JSon,I:Waterfront Warrior 1.50
16 JSon,Secret of Waterfront

Warrior revealed 1.50
17 JSon,Batman+Huntress#1 . . . 1.25
18 JSon,Batman+Huntress#2 . . . 1.25
19 JSon,Batman+Huntress#3,final
issue 1.25

HUNTRESS
[Limited Series] 1994

1 CDi(s),MN,V:Redzone 1.75
2 MN,V:Redzone 1.50
3 MN,V:Redzone 1.75
4 MN,V:Spano,Redzone 1.50

ICON
Milestone 1993–96

1 Direct Market Ed.,MBr,MG,I:Icon,
Rocket,S.H.R.E.D.,w/poster,
card,C puzzle piece 3.25
1a Newsstand Ed. 2.00
2 MBr,MG,I:Payback 1.75
3 MBr,MG,V:Payback 1.75
4 MBr,MG,Teen Pregnancy Issue 1.75
5 MBr,MG,V:Blood Syndicate . . . 1.75
6 MBr,MG,V:Blood Syndicate . . . 1.75
7 MBr,MG 1.75
8 MBr,MG,O:Icon 1.75
9 WS(c),MBr,MG,Shadow War,
I:Donner,Blitzen 1.75
10 MBr,MG,V:Holocaust 1.75
11 MBr,Hero Worship 1.75
12 Sanctimony 1.75
13 MBr,Rocket & Static T.U. 1.75
14 JBy(c) 1.75
15 Worlds Collide,pt.4,A:Superboy 1.75
16 Worlds Collide,pt.11,
V:Superman,Rift 1.75
17 Mothership Connection 1.75
18 Mothership Connection,pt.2 . . 1.75
19 Mothership Connection,pt.3 . . 1.75
20 Rocket 1.75
21 . . . . 1.75
22 . . . . 1.75
23 New Rocket 1.75
24 F:Buck Wild 1.75
25 V:Oblivion 3.00
26 V:Oblivion 1.75
27 Move to Paris Island projects . 2.50
28 Long Hot Summer 2.50
29 Long Hot Summer 2.50
30 Icon Leaves Earth 2.50
31 HC(c) Readers Choice comic . 1.00
32 Rocket, Galactic Corporate . . . 2.50
33 V:Rocket 2.50
34 V:Cooperative 2.50
35 . . . . 2.50
36 Rocket returns to Earth 2.50
37 MBr,RT,F:Rocket 2.50
38 DMD(s),RT 2.50
39 DMD(s),RT,V:Holocaust & Blood
Syndicate 2.50
40 DMD(s),RT, V:Holocaust 2.50
41 DMD(s),RT, V:Blood Syndicate 2.50
42 DMD(s),RT 2.50
43 DMD(s),RT,"Blood Reign" concl. 2.50
44 DMD(s),RT,V:Smurphs 2.50
45 DMD(s),RT, final issue 2.50
TPB A Hero's Welcome 12.95

IMMORTAL DR. FATE
1995

1 WS,KG,rep. 1.75
2 KG,rep. 1.25
3 KG,rep. 1.25

IMPACT WINTER SPECIAL
Impact 1991

1 CI/MR/TL,A:All Impact Heros,
President Kidnapped 2.50

IMPULSE
1995–97

1 Young Flash Adventures 2.75
2 V:Terrorists 2.00
3 In School 2.00
4 V:White Lightning 1.75
5 V:White Lightning 1.75
6 . . . . 1.75
7 V:Gridlock 1.75
8 MWa,Underworld
Unleashed tie-in 1.75
9 MWa,F:XS, ... 1.75
10 MWa,Dead Heat,pt.3 . . . . . . 1.75
11 MWa,Dead Heat,pt.5 . . . . . . 1.75
12 . . . . 1.75
13 MWa,new daredevil in town . . 1.75
14 AWi,A:White Lightning 1.75
15 . . . . 1.75
16 . . . . 1.75
17 . . . . 1.75
18 MPk(s),AWi,Virtual reality
nightmare 1.75
19 MWa(s),HuR, Bart's dreams . . 1.75
20 MWa(s),HuR, baseball 1.75
21 MWa(s),F:Legion of Super-
Heroes 1.75
22 MWa(s) 1.75
23 MWa(s),HuR,Mercury at a
crossroads 1.75
24 MWa(s),HuR,Impulse's mother
comes from the future 1.75
25 MWa(s),HuR,Impulse & his mom
in 30th century 1.75
26 MWa(s),Bart Allen back in the
20th century 1.75
27 MWa(s) 1.75
28 . . . . 1.75
29 BML,Bart searches for Max
Mercury 1.75
Ann.#2 Pulp Heroes (Western) . . 3.95
TPB Reckless Youth MWa(s) rep.
Flash #92–#94 . . . . 14.95

IMPULSE PLUS
July 1997

1 48pg. with Grossout, ... 2.95

INDUSTRIAL GOTHIC
Vertigo 1995

1 Jail Break Plans 2.50
2 thru 5 Jail Break Plans . . . . @2.50

INFERIOR FIVE
March-April, 1967

1 MSy 40.00
2 MSy,A:Plastic Man 20.00
3 . . . . 15.00
4 . . . . 15.00
5 . . . . 15.00
6 . . . . 15.00
7 . . . . 15.00
8 . . . . 15.00
9 . . . . 15.00
10 A:Superman 15.00
11 JO(c&a) 15.00
12 JO(c&a) 15.00

Infinity, Inc. #37 © DC Comics, Inc.

INFINITY, INC.
March, 1984

1 JOy,O:Infinity Inc.		4.00
2 JOy,End of Origin		3.00
3 JOy,O:Jade		2.50
4 JOy,V:JSA		2.50
5 JOy,V:JSA		2.50
6 JOy,V:JSA		2.50
7 JOy,V:JSA		2.50
8 JOy,V:Ultra Humanite		2.50
9 JOy,V:Ultra Humanite		2.50
10 JOy,V:Ultra Humanite		2.00
11 DN,GT,O:Infinity Inc.		2.00
12 Infinity Unmasks,I:Yolanda Montez (New Wildcat)		2.00
13 DN,V:Rose & Thorn		2.00
14 1st TM DC art,V:Chroma		4.00
15 TM,V:Chroma		3.00
16 TM,I:Helix (Mr. Bones)		3.00
17 TM,V:Helix		3.00
18 TM,Crisis		3.00
19 TM,JSA,JLA x-over, I:Mekanique		3.00
20 TM,Crisis		3.00
21 TM,Crisis,I:HourmanII, Dr.Midnight		3.00
22 TM,Crisis		3.00
23 TM,Crisis		3.00
24 TM,Crisis		3.00
25 TM,Crisis,JSA		3.00
26 TM,V:Carcharo		3.00
27 TM,V:Carcharo		3.00
28 TM,V:Carcharo		3.00
29 TM,V:Helix		3.00
30 TM,Mourning of JSA		3.00
31 TM,V:Psycho Pirate		3.00
32 TM,V:Psycho Pirate		3.00
33 TM,O:Obsidian		3.00
34 TM,A: Global Guardians		3.00
35 TM,V:Infinitors		3.00
36 TM,V:Injustice Unl.		3.00
37 TM,TD,O:Northwind		3.00
38 Helix on Trial		1.75
39 O:Solomon Grundy		1.75
40 V:Thunderbolt		1.75
41 Jonni Thunder		1.75
42 TD,V:Hastor,L:Fury		1.75

43 TD,V:Hastor,Silver Scarab		1.75
44 TD,D:Silver Scarab		1.75
45 MGu,A:New Teen Titans, V:Ultra-Humanite		1.75
46 TD,Millenium,V:Floronic Man		1.75
47 TD,Millenium,V:Harlequin		1.75
48 TD,O:Nuklon		1.75
49 Silver Scarab becomes Sandman		2.00
50 TD,V:The Wizard,O:Sandman		2.50
51 W:Fury & Sandman,D:Skyman		1.75
52 V:Helix		1.75
53 V:Justice Unlimited,last issue		1.75
Ann.#1 TM,V:Thorn		4.00
Ann.#2 V:Degaton,x-over Young All-Stars Annual #1		2.00
Spec.#1 TD,A:Outsiders,V:Psycho Pirate		1.75

INVASION!
1988–89

1 TM,I:Vril Dox,Dominators (20th century)		4.00
2 TM,KG,DG,I:L.E.G.I.O.N.		3.00
3 BS,DG,I:Blasters		3.00
Daily Planet-Invasion! 16p		2.00

INVISIBLES
Vertigo 1994–96

1 GMo(s)		3.50
2 GMo(s),Down & Out,pt.1		2.50
3 GMo(s),Down & Out,pt.2		2.50
4 GMo(s),Down & Out,pt.3		2.50
5 Arcadia,pt.1		2.25
6 Arcadia,pt.2		2.25
7 Arcadia,pt.3		2.25
8 Arcadia,pt.4		2.25
9 SeP(c),L:Dane		2.50
10 SeP(c),CWn,Jim Crow v. Zombies		2.50
11 V:New Breed of Hunter		2.50
12		2.50
13 GMO,Sheman,pt.1		2.50
14 GMo,SeP,Sheman,pt.2		2.50
15 GMo,Sheman,pt.3		2.50
16 GMo,An offer from Sir Miles		2.50
17 GMo,Entropy in the U.K.,pt.1		2.50
18 GMo,Entropy in the U.K.,pt.2		2.50
19 GMo,Entropy in the U.K.,pt.3		2.50
20 GMo,F:RaggedRobin,Dane,Boy		2.50
21 GMo,PuJ,F:Dane		2.50
22 GMo(s),MBu,MPn		2.50
23 GMo(s),MBu,MPn		2.50
24 GMo(s),MBu,MPn		2.50
25 GMo(s),MBu,MPn,final issue Aug. 1996		2.50

[Volume 2]
DC/Vertigo 1996

1 GMo(s),PJ,"Black Science," pt.1		2.50
2 GMo(s),PJ,"Black Science," pt.2		2.50
3 GMo(s),PJ,"Black Science," pt.3		2.50
4 GMo(s),PJ,"Black Science," pt.4		2.50
5 GMo(s),PJ,In SanFrancisco,pt.1		2.50
6 GMo(s),PJ,In SanFrancisco,pt.2		2.50
7 GMo(s),PJ,BB(c) "Time Machine Go" concl.		2.50
8 GMo(s),PJ,BB(c) "Sensitive Criminals," pt.1.		2.50

IRONWOLF
1986

1 HC,rep.		2.00

IRONWOLF: FIRES OF THE REVOLUTION
1992

Hardcov.GN MMi,CR,R:Ironwolf	29.95

ISIS
Oct.–Nov., 1976

1 RE/WW		5.00
2 MN		1.25
3		1.25
4		1.25
5		1.25
6		1.25
7 O:Isis		1.25
8 Dec.–Jan., 1977–78		1.25

IT'S GAMETIME
Sept.–Oct., 1955

1		400.00
2		350.00
3		350.00
4 March-April, 1956		350.00

JACKIE GLEASON AND THE HONEYMOONERS
June-July, 1956

1 Based on TV show		650.00
2		450.00
3		350.00
4		350.00
5		350.00
6		350.00
7		350.00
8		350.00
9		350.00
10		350.00
11		350.00
12 April-May, 1958		400.00

JACK KIRBY'S FOURTH WORLD
Jan. 1997

1 JBy,Worlds of New Genesis & Apokolips become one		1.95
2 JBy,F:Big Barda vs. Thor		1.95
3 JBy,at Wall of the Source		1.95
4 JBy,Can Highfather save his son		1.95
5 JBy,conflict between the gods		1.95
6 JBy,Cause of Orion's transformation		1.95
6 JBy,Orion taught lesson		1.95

JAGUAR
Impact

1 I&O:Jaguar I: Timon De Guzman, Maxx 13,Prof.Ruiz, Luiza Timmerman		1.25
2 Development of Powers		1.25
3 A:Maxx-13		1.25
4 A:Black Hood		1.25
5 V:Void,The Living Black Hole		1.25
6 'The Doomster,'A:Maxx-13		1.25
7 Jaguar Secret Discovered, V:Void		1.25
8 V:Aryan League		1.25
9 I:Moonlighter(w/trading cards)		1.25
10 V:Invisible Terror		1.25
11 Defending Comedienne		1.25
12 V:The Bodyguard		1.25
13 V:Purge		1.25
14 'Frightmare in Rio',last iss.		1.25
Ann.#1 Earthquest,w/trading card		2.50

DC COMICS

All comics prices listed are for *Near Mint* condition.

DC COMICS

JEMM, SON OF SATURN
Sept., 1984
1 GC/KJ mini-series	1.50
2 GC	1.25
3 GC,Origin	1.25
4 A:Superman	1.25
5 Kin	1.25
6 thru 12 GC, Aug. 1985 . . . . @	1.25

JIMMY WAKELY
Sept.–Oct., 1949
1 Ph(c),ATh,The Cowboy Swordsman	750.00
2 Ph(c),ATh,The Prize Pony . .	350.00
3 Ph(c),ATh,The Return of Tulsa Tom	350.00
4 Ph(c),ATh,FF,HK,Where's There'sSmokeThere'sGunfire	375.00
5 ATh,The Return of the Conquistadores	275.00
6 ATh,Two Lives of Jimmy Wakely	275.00
7 The Secret of Hairpin Canyon	275.00
8 ATh,The Lost City of Blue Valley	275.00
9 ATh,The Return of the Western Firebrands	250.00
10 ATh,Secret of Lantikin'sLight	250.00
11 ATh,Trail o/a Thousand Hoofs	250.00
12 ATh,JKU,The King of Sierra Valley	250.00
13 ATh,The Raiders of Treasure Mountain	250.00
14 ATh(c),JKu,The Badmen of Roaring Flame Valley . . .	250.00
15 GK(c),Tommyguns on the Range	250.00
16 GK(c),The Bad Luck Boots .	225.00
17 GK(c),Terror atThunderBasin	225.00
18 July-Aug., 1952	250.00

JLA
Nov. 1996
1 GMo(s),HPo,JhD,V:Hyperclan .	8.00
2	8.00
3 GMo(s),HPo,JhD,"War of the Worlds"	4.00
4 GMo(s),HPo,JhD,battle of the super-heroes, conc.	2.00
5 GMo(s),HPo,JhD "Woman of Tomorrow"	2.00
6 GMo(s),HPo,JhD, "Fire in theSky"	1.95
7 GMo(s),HPo,JhD, "Heaven on Earth"	1.95
8 GMo(s),HPo,JhD, "Imaginary Stories" F:Green Arrow	1.95
9 GMo(s),V:The Key	1.95
10 GMo(s),HPo,JhD,R:Injustice Gang, pt.1 (of 6)	1.95
Ann.#1 Pulp Heroes (Hard Boiled)	3.95
GN New World Order GMo(s),HPo, JhD, rep. #1–#4	4.95
Spec.#1 GN Secret Files	4.95

JLA/WILDC.A.T.S
GMo(s),VS,x-over	5.95

JOHNNY THUNDER
Feb.–March, 1973
1 ATh	5.00
2 GK,MD	4.00
3 ATh,GK,MD,July-Aug., 1973 . .	4.00

The Joker #4 © DC Comics, Inc.

JOKER, THE
1975–76
1 IN,DG,A:TwoFace	22.00
2 IN,JL WillieTheWeeper	13.00
3 JL,A:Creeper	12.00
4 JL,A:GreenArrow	10.00
5	10.00
6 V:Sherlock Holmes	10.00
7 IN,A:Luthor	10.00
8	10.00
9 A:Catwoman	12.00
Greatest Joker Stories Ever Told:	
1 HC	45.00
1a SC	16.00
The Devil's Advocate HC GN . .	24.95
GN	12.95

JONAH HEX
1977–85
1 'Vengeance For A Fallen Gladiator'	42.00
2 'The Lair of the Parrot'	20.00
3 'The Fugitive'	14.00
4 'The Day of Chameleon'	14.00
5 'Welcome to Paradise'	14.00
6 'The Lawman'	10.00
7 'Son of the Apache'	10.00
8 O:Jonah Hex	9.00
9 BWr(c)	9.00
10 GM(c),'Violence at Vera Cruz' .	9.00
11 'The Holdout'	7.00
12 JS(c)	7.00
13 'The Railroad Blaster'	7.00
14 'The Sin Killer'	7.00
15 'Saw Dust and Slow Death' . . .	7.00
16 'The Wyandott Verdict!'	5.00
17	5.00
18	5.00
19 'The Duke of Zarkania!'	5.00
20 'Phantom Stage to William Bend'	5.00
21 'The Buryin'!'	5.00
22 'Requiem For A Pack Rat' . . .	5.00
23 'The Massacre of the Celestials!'	5.00
24 'Minister of the Lord'	5.00
25 'The Widow Maker'	5.00

26 'Death Race to Cholera Bend!'	4.00
27 'The Wooden Six Gun!'	4.00
28 'Night of the Savage'	4.00
29 'The Innocent'	4.00
30 O:Jonah Hex	4.50
31 A:Arbee Stoneham	4.00
32 A:Arbee Stoneham	4.00
33 'The Crusador'	4.00
34 'Christmas in an Outlaw Town'	4.00
35 'The Fort Charlotte Brigade' . .	4.00
36 'Return to Fort Charlotte' . . .	4.00
37 DAy,A:Stonewall Jackson . . .	4.00
38	4.00
39 'The Vow of a Samurai!'	4.00
40 DAy	4.00
41 DAy,'Two for the Hangman!' . .	4.00
42 'Wanted for Murder'	4.00
43 JKu(c)	4.00
44 JKu(c),DAy	4.00
45 DAy,Jonah gets married	4.00
46 JKu(c),DAy	4.00
47 DAy,'Doom Rides the Sundown Town'	4.00
48 DAy,A:El Diablo	4.00
49 DAy	4.00
50 DAy,'The Hunter'	4.00
51 DAy,'The Comforter'	3.50
52 DAy,'Rescue!'	3.50
53 DAy	3.50
54	3.50
55 'Trail of Blood'	3.50
56 DAy,'The Asylum'	3.50
57 B:El Diablo backup story	3.50
58 DAy,'The Treasure of Catfish Pond'	3.50
59 DAy,'Night of the White Lotus' .	3.50
60 DAy,'Domain of the Warlord' .	3.50
61 DAy,'In the Lair of the Manchus!'	3.50
62 DAy,'The Belly of the Malay Tiger!'	3.50
63 DAy	3.50
64 DAy,'The Pearl!'	3.50
65 DAy,'The Vendetta!'	3.50
66 DAy'Requiem for a Coward' . .	3.50
67 DAy,'Deadman's Hand!'	3.50
68 DAy,'Gunfight at Gravesboro!' .	3.50
69 DAy,'The Gauntlet!'	3.50
70 DAy	3.50
71 DAy,'The Masquerades'	3.50
72 DAy,'Tarantula'	3.50
73 DAy,Jonah in a wheel chair . .	3.50
74 DAy,A:Railroad Bill	3.50
75 DAy,JAp,A:Railroad Bill	3.50
76 DAy,Jonah goes to Jail	3.00
77 DAy,'Over the Wall'	3.00
78 DAy,Me Ling returns	3.00
79 DAy,'Duel in the Sand'	3.00
80 A:Turnbull	3.00
81 thru 89 DAy . . . . @	3.00
90 thru 92 . . . . @	3.00

JONAH HEX AND OTHER WESTERN TALES
Sept.–Oct., 1979
1	2.00
2 NA,ATh,SA,GK	3.00
3 Jan.–Feb., 1980	1.75

JONAH HEX: RIDERS OF THE WORM AND SUCH
Vertigo 1995
[Mini-Series]
1 R:Ronah Hex	2.95
2 At Wildes West Ranch	2.95

DC COMICS

3 History Lesson 2.95
4 I:Autumn Brothers 2.95
5 V:Big worm, final issue 2.95

JONAH HEX: TWO-GUN MOJO
Vertigo 1993
1 B:JLd(s),TT,SG(i),R:Jonah Hex,
  I:Slow Go Smith 8.00
1a Platinum Ed. 20.00
2 TT,SG(i),D:Slow Go Smith,I:Doc
  Williams,Wild Bill Hickok 6.00
3 TT,SG(i),Jonah captured 5.00
4 TT,SG(i),O:Doc Williams 5.00
5 TT,SG(i),V::Doc Williams 5.00

JONNI THUNDER
Feb., 1985
1 DG,origin issue 1.25
2 DG 1.25
3 DG 1.25

JUDGE DREDD
1994–96
1 R:Judge Dredd 2.50
2 Silicon Dreams 2.25
3 Terrorists 2.50
4 Mega-City One crisis 2.25
5 Solitary Dredd 2.25
6 V:Richard Magg 2.25
7 . . . . 2.25
8 V:Ministry of Fear 2.25
9 V:Mister Synn 2.25
10 D:Judge Dredd 2.25
11 Mega-City One Chaos 2.25
12 V:Wally Squad 2.25
13 Block Wars,pt.1 . . . . 2.25
14 Block Wars,pt.2 . . . . 2.25
15 Block Wars,pt.3 . . . . 2.25
16 R:Judge with a Grudge 2.25
17 F:Judge Cadet Lewis,
  Nova Scotia 2.25
18 final issue 2.25
Movie Adaptation 5.95

JUDGE DREDD: LEGENDS OF THE LAW
1994–95
1 Organ Donor,pt.1 . . . . 2.50
2 Organ Donor,pt.2 . . . . 2.25
3 Organ Donor,pt.3 . . . . 2.25
4 Organ Donor,pt.4 . . . . 2.25
5 Trial By Gunfire,pt.1 . . . . 2.25
6 Trial By Gunfire,pt.2 . . . . 2.25
7 JHi(c),Trial By Gunfire,pt.3 . . . . 2.25
8 JBy(s),Fall From Grace,pt.1 . . . 2.25
9 Fall From Grace,pt.2 . . . . 2.25
10 Fall From Grace,pt.3 . . . . 2.25
11 Dredd of Night,pt.1 . . . . 2.25
12 Dredd of Night,pt.2 . . . . 2.25
13 Dredd of Night,pt.3,final issue . 2.25

JUNK CULTURE
DC/Vertigo May 1997
1 (of 2) TMK 2.50
2 (of 2) TMK "Deuces Wild" 2.50

JUSTICE, INC.
May-June, 1975
1 AMc,JKu(c),O:Avenger 3.00
2 JK 1.25
3 JK 1.25

4 JK,JKu(c),Nov.–Dec.,
  1975 . . . . 1.25
[Mini-Series] 1989
1 PerfectBound 'Trust & Betrayal' 3.95
2 PerfectBound 3.95

JUSTICE LEAGUE AMERICA
(see JUSTICE LEAGUE INTERNATIONAL)

Justice League Europe #11
© DC Comics, Inc.

JUSTICE LEAGUE EUROPE
1989–93
1 BS,A:Wonder Woman 4.00
2 BS,Search for Nazi-Killer 3.00
3 BS,A:Jack O'Lantern,
  Queen Bee 2.50
4 BS,V:Queen Bee 2.50
5 JRu,BS,Metamorpho's Baby,
  A:Sapphire Starr 2.50
6 BS,V:Injustice League 2.00
7 BS,Teasdale Imperative#2,
  A:JLA 2.00
8 BS,Teasdale Imperative#4,
  A:JLA 2.00
9 BS,ANi,A:Superman 2.00
10 BS,V:Crimson Fox 2.00
11 BS,C:DocMagnus&Metal Men . 2.00
12 BS,A:Metal Men 2.00
13 BS,V:One-Eyed Cat, contd
  from JLA #37 . . . . 2.00
14 I:VCR 2.00
15 BS,B:Extremists Vector saga,
  V:One-Eyed Cat,A:BlueJay . . . 2.00
16 BS,A:Rocket Reds, Blue Jay . . 2.25
17 BS,JLI in Another Dimension . . 2.25
18 BS,Extremists Homeworld 2.25
19 BS,E:Extremist Vector Saga . . 2.25
20 MR,I:Beefeater,V:Kilowog 1.75
21 MR,JRu,New JLE embassy in
  London,A:Kilowog 1.50
22 MR,JLE's Cat stolen 1.50
23 BS,O:Crimson Fox 1.50
24 BS,Worms in London 1.50

25 BS,V:Worms 1.50
26 BS,V:Starro 1.50
27 BS,JLE V:JLE,A:JLA,V:Starro . 1.50
28 BS, JLE V:JLE,A:J'onnJ'onzz,
  V:Starro 1.50
29 BS,Breakdowns #2,V:Global
  Guardians 1.75
30 Breakdowns#4,V:J.O'Lantern . 1.50
31 Breakdowns #6,War of the
  Gods tie-in 1.50
32 Breakdowns #8,A:Chief(Doom
  Patrol) 1.50
33 Breakdowns #10,Lobo vs.
  Despero 1.50
34 Breakdowns #12,Lobo
  vs.Despero 1.50
35 Breakdowns #14,V:Extremists,
  D:Silver Sorceress 1.50
36 Breakdowns #16,All Quit 1.50
37 B:New JLE,I:Deconstructo . . . 1.75
38 V:Deconstructo,A:Batman . . . 1.50
39 V:Deconstructo,A:Batman . . . 1.50
40 J:Hal Jordan,A:Metamorpho . . 1.50
41 A:Metamorpho,Wond.Woman . 1.50
42 A:Wonder Woman,V:Echidna . 1.50
43 V:Amos Fortune 1.50
44 V:Amos Fortune 1.50
45 Red Winter#1,V:Rocket Reds . 1.50
46 Red Winter#2 . . . . 1.50
47 Red Winter#3,V:Sonar 1.50
48 Red Winter#4,V:Sonar 1.50
49 Red Winter #5,V:Sonar 1.50
50 Red Winter#6,Double-sized,
  V:Sonar,J:Metamorpho 3.25
Ann.#1 A:Global Guardians 2.00
Ann.#2 MR,CS,ArmageddonPt.7 . 3.00
Ann.#3 RT(i),Eclipso tie-in 2.75
Justice League Spectacular JLE(c)
  New Direction 1.50

Becomes: Justice League International [2nd Series]

JUSTICE LEAGUE [INTERNATIONAL]
[1st Series] 1987
1 KM,TA,New Team,I:Max. Lord . 6.00
2 KM,AG,A:BlueJay & Silver
  Sorceress 4.00
3 KM,AG,J:Booster Gold, V:Rocket
  Lords 3.00
3a Superman Logo 75.00
4 KM,AG,V:Royal Flush 3.00
5 KM,AG,A:The Creeper 3.00
6 KM,AG,A:The Creeper 3.00
Becomes:

JUSTICE LEAGUE INTERNATIONAL
1988–89
7 KM,AG,L:Dr.Fate,Capt.Marvel,
  J:Rocket Red,Capt.Atom
  (Double size) 3.00
8 KM,AG,KG,Move to Paris Embassy,
  I:C.Cobert,B.U.Glob.Guardians. 2.50
9 KM,AG,KG,Millenium,Rocket
  Red-Traitor 2.50
10 KG,KM,AG,A:G.L.Corps,
  Superman,I:G'Nort 2.50
11 KM,AG,V:Construct,C:Metron . 2.50
12 KG,KM,AG,O:Max Lord 2.50
13 KG,AG,A:Suicide Squad 2.50
14 SL,AG,J:Fire&Ice,L:Ron,
  I:Manga Kahn 2.50

DC COMICS

15 SL,AG,V:Magna Kahn 2.00
16 KM,AG,I:Queen Bee 2.00
17 KM,AG,V:Queen Bee 2.00
18 KM,AG,MPn,A:Lobo,Guy Gardner
   (bonus book) 3.00
19 KM,JRu,A:Lobo vs.Guy Gardner,
   J:Hawkman & Hawkwoman . . . 3.00
20 KM,JRu(i),A:Lobo,G.Gardner . . 2.00
21 KM,JRu(i),A:Lobo vs.Guy
   Gardner 2.00
22 KM,JRu,Imskian Soldiers 2.00
23 KM,JRu,I:Injustice League . . . 2.00
24 KM,JRu,DoubleSize + Bonus
   Bk#13,I:JusticeLeagueEurope . 4.00
25 KM(c),JRu(i),Vampire story . . . 2.00
Ann.#1 BWg,DG,CR 2.00
Ann.#2 BWg,JRu,A:Joker 3.00
Ann.#3 KM(c),JRu,JLI Embassies 2.50
Spec.#1 Mr.Miracle 2.00
Spec.#2,The Huntress 2.95
TPB new beginning,rep.#1-#7 . . 12.95
TPB The Secret Gospel of Maxwell
   Lord Rep. #8-#12, Ann.#1 . . . 12.95
Becomes:

JUSTICE LEAGUE
AMERICA
1989–96

26 KM(c),JRu(i),Possessed Blue
   Beetle 2.50
27 KM(c),JRu,DG(i),'Exorcist',
   (c)tribute 2.00
28 KM(c),JRu(i), A:Black Hand . . 2.00
29 KM(c),JRu(i),V:Mega-Death . . 2.00
30 KM(c),BWg,JRu,J:Huntress,
   D:Mega-Death 2.00
31 ANi,AH,JRu,Teasdale Imperative
   #1,N:Fire,Ice,A:JLE 3.00
32 ANi,AH,Teasdale Imperative
   #3, A:JLE 3.00
33 ANi,AH,GuyGardner vs.Kilowog 2.50
34 ANi,AH,'Club JLI,'A:Aquaman . 2.50
35 ANi,JRu,AH,A:Aquaman 2.50
36 Gnort vs. Scarlet Skier 2.00
37 ANi,AH,L:Booster Gold 2.00
38 JRu,AH,R:Desparo,D:Steel . . 2.00
39 JRu,AH,V:Desparo,D:Mr.Miracle,
   Robot 2.00
40 AH,Mr.Miracle Funeral 2.00
41 MMc,MaxForce 2.00
42 MMc,J:L-Ron 2.00
43 AH,KG,The Man Who Knew Too
   Much #1 . . . . 2.00
44 AH,Man Knew Too Much #2 . . 2.00
45 AH,MJ,JRu,Guy & Ice's 2nd
   date 2.00
46 Glory Bound #1,I:Gen.Glory . . 2.00
47 Glory Bound #2,J:Gen.Glory . . 2.00
48 Glory Bound #3,V:DosUberbot 2.00
49 Glory Bound #4 . . . . 2.00
50 Glory Bound #5 (double size) . 2.50
51 JRu,AH,V:BlackHand,
   R:Booster Gold 2.00
52 TVE,Blue Beetle Vs. Guy Gardner
   A:Batman 2.00
53 Breakdowns #1, A:JLE 2.00
54 Breakdowns #3, A:JLE 2.00
55 Breakdowns #5,V:Global
   Guardians 2.00
56 Breakdowns #7, U.N. revokes
   JLA charter 2.00
57 Breakdowns #9,A:Lobo,
   V:Despero 2.00
58 BS,Breakdowns #11,Lobo
   Vs.Despero 2.00

Justice League America #65
© DC Comics, Inc.

59 BS,Breakdowns #13,
   V:Extremists 2.00
60 KM,TA,Breakdowns #15,
   End of J.L.A. 2.00
61 DJu,I:Weapons Master,B:New
   JLA Line-up,I:Bloodwynd 3.00
62 DJu,V:Weapons Master 2.00
63 DJu,V:Starbreaker 2.00
64 DJu,V:Starbreaker 2.00
65 DJu,V:Starbreaker 2.00
66 DJu,Superman V:Guy Gardner 2.00
67 DJu,Bloodwynd mystery 2.00
68 DJu,V:Alien Land Baron 2.00
69 DJu, Doomsday Pt.1-A 10.00
69a 2nd printing 2.00
70 DJu,Funeral for a Friend#1 . . 6.00
70a 2nd printing 2.00
71 DJu,J:Agent Liberty,Black Condor,
   The Ray,Wonder Woman 5.00
71a Newsstand ed. 2.00
71b 2nd Printing 1.50
72 DJu,A:Green Arrow,Black
   Canary,Atom,B:Destiny's Hand 4.00
73 DJu,Destiny's Hand #2 . . . . . 3.00
74 DJu,Destiny's Hand #3 . . . . . 2.00
75 DJu,E:Destiny's Hand #4,Martian
   Manhunter as Bloodwynd 2.00
76 DJu,Blood Secrets#1,
   V:Weaponmaster 1.50
77 DJu,Blood Secrets#2,
   V:Weaponmaster 1.50
78 MC,V:The Extremists 1.50
79 MC,V:The Extremists 1.50
80 KWe,N:Booster Gold 1.50
81 KWe,A:Captain Atom 1.50
82 KWe,A:Captain Atom 1.50
83 KWe,V:Guy Gardner 1.50
84 KWe,A:Ice 1.75
85 KWe,V:Frost Giants 1.75
86 B:Cults of the Machine 1.75
87 N:Booster Gold 1.75
88 E:Cults of the Machine 1.75
89 Judgement Day#1,
   V:Overmaster 1.75
90 Judgement Day#4 . . . . 1.50
91 Aftershocks #1 . . . . 1.75
92 Zero Hour,I:Triumph 1.75

93 Power Girl and child 1.50
94 Scarabus 1.50
95 . . . . 1.50
96 Funeral 1.50
97 I:Judgment 1.50
98 J:Blue Devil, Ice Maiden 1.50
99 V:New Metahumes 1.50
100 GJ,Woj,V:Lord Havok,dbl.size 3.00
100a Collector's Edition 4.00
101 GJ,Woj,Way of the
   Warrior,pt.2 . . . . 1.75
102 Way of the Warrior,pt.5 . . . . . 1.75
103 . . . . 1.75
104 F:Metamorpho 1.75
105 GJ,Woj,Underworld
   Unleashed tie-in 1.75
106 GJ,Woj,Underworld
   Unleashed tie-in 1.75
107 GJ,Woj,secret of Power
   Girl's son 1.75
108 GJ,Woj,The Arcana revealed . 1.75
109 . . . . 1.75
110 GJ,Woj,V:El Diablo 1.75
111 GJ,Woj,The Purge,pt.1 (of 3) . 1.75
112 GJ,Woj,The Purge,pt.2 (of 3) . 1.75
113 GJ,Woj,The Purge,pt.3 (of 3) . 1.75
Ann.#4 KM(c),I:JL Antartica 3.00
Ann.#5 MR,KM,DJu,Armageddon 3.00
Ann.#5a 2nd Printing,silver 2.00
Ann.#6 DC,Eclipso 2.75
Ann.#7 I:Terrorsmith 2.75
Ann.#8 Elseworlds Story 3.25
Ann.#9 Year One Annual 3.50
Ann.#10 CPr(s),SCi,NNa,"Legends
   of the Dead Earth" 2.95
Justice League Spectacular DJu,
   JLA(c) New Direction 2.00

JUSTICE LEAGUE
INTERNATIONAL
[2nd Regular Series] 1993–94
Prev: Justice League Europe

51 Aztec Cult 1.50
52 V:Aztec Cult 1.50
53 R:Fox's Husband 1.50
54 RoR,I:Creator 1.50
55 RoR,A:Creator 1.50
56 RoR,V:Terrorists 1.50
57 RoR,V:Terrorists 1.50
58 RoR,V:Aliens 1.50
59 RoR,A:Guy Gardner 1.50
60 GJ(s),RoR 1.75
61 GJ(s),V:Godfrey 1.75
62 GJ(s),N:Metamorpho,V:Godfrey 1.75
63 GJ(s),In Africa 1.75
64 GJ(s),V:Cadre 1.75
65 JudgmentDay#3,V:Overmaster 1.75
66 JudgmentDay#6,V:Overmaster 1.75
67 Aftershock #3 . . . . 1.75
68 Zero Hour, Final Issue 1.50
Ann.#4 Bloodlines#9,I:Lionheart . 2.75
Ann.#5 . . . . 3.25
Ann.#6 Elseworlds Story 2.95

JUSTICE LEAGUE
[INTERNATIONAL]
QUARTERLY
1990–94

1 I:Conglomerate 4.00
2 MJ(i),R:Mr.Nebula 3.50
3 V:Extremists,C:Original JLA . . 3.50
4 KM(c),MR,CR,A:Injustice
   League. 3.00

DC COMICS

5 KM(c),Superhero Attacks 3.00
6 EB,Elongated Man,B.U.Global
   Guardians,Powergirl,B.Beetle . 3.00
7 EB,DH,MR.Global Guardians . . 3.00
8 . . . . 3.00
9 DC,F:Power Girl,Booster Gold . 3.50
10 F:Flash,Fire & Ice 3.50
11 F:JL Women 3.50
12 F:Conglomerate 3.50
13 V:Ultraa 12.00
14 MMi(c),PuK(s),F:Captain Atom,Blue
   Beetle,Nightshade,Thunderbolt 3.75
15 F:Praxis 3.50
16 F:Gen Glory 3.50
17 Final Issue 3.50

JUSTICE LEAGUE: A MIDSUMMER'S NIGHTMARE
1996

1 (of 3) MWa(s),FaN,JJ,DaR, . . . 5.00
2 MWa(s),FaN,JJ,DaR,Batman &
   Superman attempt to free
   other heroes 4.00
3 MWa&FaN(s), Know-Man's plot
   revealed, finale . . . . @4.00
TPB Rep. 3 issues 8.95

Justice League of America #11
© DC Comics, Inc.

JUSTICE LEAGUE OF AMERICA
Oct.–Nov., 1960

1 MSy,I&O:Despero 3,000.00
2 MSy,A:Merlin 750.00
3 MSy,I&O:Kanjar Ro 600.00
4 MSy,J:Green Arrow 425.00
5 MSy,I&O:Dr.Destiny 350.00
6 MSy,Prof. Fortune 300.00
7 MSy,Cosmic Fun-House 300.00
8 MSy,For Sale-Justice League 300.00
9 MSy,O:JLA 450.00
10 MSy,I:Felix Faust 300.00
11 MSy,A:Felix Faust 225.00
12 MSy,I&O:Dr Light 225.00
13 MSy,A:Speedy 225.00
14 MSy,J:Atom 225.00

15 MSy,V:Untouchable Aliens . 175.00
16 MSy,I:Maestro 150.00
17 MSy,A:Tornado Tyrant 150.00
18 MSy,V:Terrane,Ocana 150.00
19 MSy,A:Dr.Destiny 150.00
20 MSy,V:Metal Being 150.00
21 MSy,R:JSA,1st S.A Hourman,
   Dr.Fate 350.00
22 MSy,R:JSA 325.00
23 MSy,I:Queen Bee 90.00
24 MSy,A:Adam Strange 90.00
25 MSy,I:Draad,the Conqueror . 90.00
26 MSy,A:Despero 90.00
27 MSy,V:I,A:Amazo 90.00
28 MSy,I:Headmaster Mind,
   A:Robin 90.00
29 MSy,I:Crime Syndicate,A:JSA,
   1st S.A. Starman 140.00
30 MSy,V:Crime Syndicate,
   A:JSA 100.00
31 MSy,J:Hawkman 75.00
32 MSy,I&O:Brain Storm 70.00
33 MSy,I:Endless One 60.00
34 MSy,A:Dr.Destiny,Joker 65.00
35 MSy,A:Three Demons 60.00
36 MSy,A:Brain Storm,
   Handicap story 60.00
37 MSy,A:JSA,x-over,
   1st S.A.Mr.Terrific 75.00
38 MSy,A:JSA,Mr.Terrific 75.00
39 Giant 100.00
40 MSy,A:Shark,Penguin 60.00
41 MSy,I:Key 60.00
42 MSy,A:Metamorpho 50.00
43 MSy,I:Royal Flush Gang 50.00
44 MSy,A:Unimaginable 50.00
45 MSy,I:Shaggy Man 50.00
46 MSy,A:JSA,Blockbuster,Solomon
   Grundy,1st S.A.Sandman . . 110.00
47 MSy,A:JSA,Blockbuster,
   Solomon Grundy 50.00
48 Giant 60.00
49 MSy,A:Felix Faust 35.00
50 MSy,A:Robin 35.00
51 MSy,A:Zatanna,Elong.Man . . 35.00
52 MSy,A:Robin,Lord of Time . . 35.00
53 MSy,A:Hawkgirl 35.00
54 MSy,A:Royal Flush Gang . . . 35.00
55 MSy,A:JSA,E-2 Robin 60.00
56 MSy,A:JSA,E-2 Robin 40.00
57 MSy,Brotherhood 35.00
58 Reprint(giant size). 40.00
59 MSy,V:Impossibles 35.00
60 MSy,A:Queen Bee,Batgirl . . . 35.00
61 MSy,A:Lex Luthor,Penguin . . 35.00
62 MSy,V:Bulleteers 25.00
63 MSy,A:Key 25.00
64 DD,I:Red Tornado,A:JSA . . . 30.00
65 DD,A:JSA 30.00
66 DD,A:Demmy Gog 25.00
67 MSy,Giant reprints 32.00
68 DD,V:Choas Maker 28.00
69 DD,L:Wonder Woman 25.00
70 DD,A:Creeper 20.00
71 DD,L:J'onn J'onnz 20.00
72 DD,A:Hawkgirl 20.00
73 DD,A:JSA 20.00
74 DD,D:Larry Lance,A:JSA . . . 20.00
75 DD,J:Black Canary 20.00
76 Giant,MA,two page pin-up . . . 14.00
77 DD,A:Joker,L:Snapper Carr . . 10.00
78 DD,R:Vigilante 10.00
79 DD,A:Vigilante 10.00
80 DD,A:Tomar-Re,Guardians . . 10.00
81 DD,V:Jest-Master 10.00

82 DD,A:JSA 8.00
83 DD,A:JSA,Spectre 8.00
84 DD,Devil in Paradise 7.50
85 Giant reprint 17.00
86 DD,V:Zapper 8.00
87 DD,A:Zatanna,I:Silver
   Sorceress,Blue Jay 9.00
88 DD,A:Mera 8.00
89 DD,A:Harlequin Ellis,
   (i.e. Harlan Ellison) 8.00
90 CI(c),MA(ci),DD,V:Pale People 8.00
91 DD,A:JSA,V:Solomon Grundy . 8.00
92 DD,A:JSA,V:Solomon Grundy . 9.00
93 DD:A:JSA,(giant size) 17.00
94 DD,NA,O:Sandman,rep.
   Adventure #40 . . . . 35.00
95 DD,rep.More Fun Comics #67,
   All American Comics #25 . . . 14.00
96 DD,I:Starbreaker 10.00
97 DD,MS,O:JLA 8.00
98 DD,A:Sargon,Gold.Age reps . . 8.00
99 DD,G.A. reps.. . . . . 8.00
100 DD,A:JSA,Metamorpho,
   R:7 Soldiers of Victory 9.00
101 DD,A:JSA,7 Soldiers 7.00
102 DD,DG,A:JSA,7 Soldiers
   D:Red Tornado 7.00
103 DD,DG,Halloween issue,
   A:Phantom Stranger 5.00

Justice League of America #90
© DC Comics, Inc.

104 DD,DG,A:Shaggy Man,
   Hector Hammond 5.00
105 DD,DG,J:ElongatedMan 5.00
106 DD,DG,J:RedTornado 5.00
107 DD,DG,I:Freedom Fighters,
   A:JSA 9.00
108 DD,DG,A:JSA,
   Freedom Fighters 7.00
109 DD,DG,L:Hawkman 5.00
110 DD,DG,A:John Stewart,
   Phantom Stranger 5.00
111 DD,DG,I:Injustice Gang 5.00
112 DD,DG,A:Amazo 5.00
113 DD,DG,A:JSA 6.00
114 DD,DG,A:SnapperCarr 5.00
115 DD,FMc,A:J'onnJ'onnz 5.00
116 DD,FMc,I:Golden Eagle 5.00
117 DD,FMc,R:Hawkman 3.50

All comics prices listed are for *Near Mint* condition.

Justice League of America #207
© DC Comics, Inc.

118 DD,FMc		3.50
119 DD,FMc,A:Hawkgirl		3.50
120 DD,FMc,A:Adam Strange		3.50
121 DD,FMc,W:Adam Strange		3.50
122 DD,FMc,JLA casebook story		
V:Dr.Light		3.50
123 DD,FMc,A:JSA		5.50
124 DD,FMc,A: JSA		5.50
125 DD,FMc,A:Two-Face		3.50
126 DD,FMc,A:Two-Face		3.50
127 DD,FMc,V:Anarchist		3.50
128 DD,FMc,J:W.Woman		3.50
129 DD,FMC,D:RedTornado		3.00
130 DD,FMc,O:JLASatellite		3.00
131 DD,FMc,V:Queen Bee,Sonar		3.00
132 DD,FMc,A:Supergirl		3.00
133 DD,FMc,A:Supergirl		3.00
134 DD,FMc,A:Supergirl		3.00
135 DD,FMc,A:Squad.of Justice		3.00
136 DD,FMc,A:E-2Joker		3.50
137 DD,FMc,Superman vs.		
Capt. Marvel		4.00
138 NA(c),DD,FMc,A:Adam		
Strange		3.00
139 NA(c),DD,FMc,A:AdamStrange,		
Phantom Stranger,doub.size		3.50
140 DD,FMc,Manhunters		3.00
141 DD,FMc,Manhunters		3.00
142 DD,FMc,F:Aquaman,Atom,		
Elongated Man		3.00
143 DD,FMc,V:Injustice Gang		3.50
144 DD,FMc,O:JLA		3.00
145 DD,FMc,A:Phant.Stranger		3.00
146 J:Red Tornado,Hawkgirl		3.00
147 DD,FMc,A:Legion		3.00
148 DD,FMc,A:Legion		3.00
149 DD,FMc,A:Dr.Light		3.00
150 DD,FMc,A:Dr.Light		3.00
151 DD,FMc,A:Amos Fortune		2.50
152 DD,FMc		2.50
153 GT,FMc,I:Ultraa		2.50
154 MK(c),DD,FMc		2.50
155 DD,FMc		2.50
156 DD,FMc		2.50
157 DD,FMc,W:Atom		2.50
158 DD,FMc,A:Ultraa		2.50
159 DD,FMc,A:JSA,Jonah Hex,		

Enemy Ace		3.00
160 DD,FMc,A:JSA,Jonah Hex,		
Enemy Ace		3.00
161 DD,FMc,J:Zatanna		2.50
162 DD,FMc		2.50
163 DD,FMc,V:Mad Maestro		2.50
164 DD,FMc,V:Mad Maestro		2.50
165 DD,FMc		2.50
166 DD,FMc,V:Secret Society		2.50
167 DD,FMc,V:Secret Society		2.50
168 DD,FMc,V:Secret Society		2.50
169 DD,FMc,A:Ultraa		2.50
170 DD,FMc,A:Ultraa		2.50
171 DD,FMc,A:JSA,D:Mr.Terrific		2.50
172 DD,FMc,A:JSA,D:Mr.Terrific		2.50
173 DD,FMc,A:Black Lightning		2.50
174 DD,FMc,A:Black Lightning		2.50
175 DD,FMc,V:Dr.Destiny		2.50
176 DD,FMc,V:Dr.Destiny		2.00
177 DD,FMc,V:Desparo		2.00
178 JSn(c),DD,FMc,V:Desparo		2.00
179 JSn(c),DD,FMc,J:Firestorm		2.50
180 JSn(c),DD,FMc,V:Satin Satan		2.00
181 DD,FMc,L:Gr.Arrow,V:Star		3.50
182 DD,FMc,A:Green Arrow,		
V:Felix Faust		3.00
183 JSn(c),DD,FMc,A:JSA,		
NewGods		3.00
184 GP,FMc,A:JSA,NewGods		3.00
185 JSn(c),GP,FMc,A:JSA,		
New Gods		3.00
186 FMc,GP,V:Shaggy Man		2.00
187 DH,FMc,N:Zatanna		2.00
188 DH,FMc,V:Proteus		2.00
189 BB(c),RB,FMc,V:Starro		2.00
190 BB(c),RB,LMa,V:Starro		2.00
191 RB,V:Amazo		2.00
192 GP,O:Red Tornado		2.00
193 GP,RB,JOy,I:AllStarSquad		2.50
194 GP,V:Amos Fortune		2.00
195 GP,A:JSA,V:Secret Society		3.00
196 GP,RT,A:JSA,V:Secret Soc.		3.00
197 GP,RT,KP,A:JSA,V:Secret		
Society		3.00
198 GP,DH,A:J.Hex,BatLash		2.00
199 GP(c),DH,BBr,A:Jonah Hex,		
BatLash		2.00
200 GP,DG,BB (1st Batman),PB,TA,		
BBr,GK,CI,JAp,JKu,Anniv.,A:Adam		
Strange,Phantom Stranger,		
J:Green Arrow		4.50
201 GP(c),DH,A:Ultraa		2.00
202 GP(c),DH,BBr,JLA in Space		2.00
203 GP(c),DH,RT,V:Royal		
Flush Gang		2.00
204 GP(c),DH,RT,V:R.FlushGang		2.00
205 GP(c),DH,RT,V:R.FlushGang		2.00
206 DH,RT,A:Demons 3		2.00
207 GP(c),DH,RT,A:All Star		
Squadron,JSA		2.50
208 GP(c),DH,RT,A:All Star		
Squadron,JSA		2.50
209 GP(c),DH,RT,A:All Star		
Squadron,JSA		2.50
210 RB,RT,JLA casebook #1		2.00
211 RB,RT,JLA casebook #2		2.00
212 GP(c),RB,PCu,RT,c.book #3		2.00
213 GP(c),DH,RT		2.00
214 GP(c),DH,RT,I:Siren Sist.h'd		2.00
215 GP(c),DH,RT		2.00
216 DH		2.00
217 GP(c),RT(i)		2.00
218 RT(i),A:Prof.Ivo		2.00
219 GP(c),RT(i),A:JSA		2.25
220 GP(c),RT,O:Bl.Canary,A:JSA		2.25

221 Beasts #1		2.00
222 RT(i),Beasts #2		2.00
223 RT(i),Beasts #3		2.00
224 DG(i),V:Paragon		2.00
225 V:Hellrazor		2.00
226 FMc(i),V:Hellrazor		2.00
227 V:Hellrazor,I:Lord Claw		2.00
228 GT,AN,R:J'onnJonzz,War of		
the Worlds,pt.1		2.00
229 War of the Worlds,pt.2		2.00
230 War of the Worlds conc.		2.00
231 RB(i),A:JSA,Supergirl		2.25
232 A:JSA Supergirl		2.25
233 New JLA takes over book,		
B:Rebirth,F:Vibe		2.00
234 F:Vixen		2.00
235 F:Steel		2.00
236 E:Rebirth,F:Gypsy		2.00
237 A:Superman,Flash,WWoman		2.00
238 A:Superman,Flash,WWoman		2.00
239 V:Ox		2.00
240 MSy,TMd		2.00
241 GT,V:Amazo		2.00
242 GT,V:Amazo,Mask(Toy tie-in)		
insert		2.00
243 GT,L:Aquaman,V:Amazo		2.00
244 JSon,Crisis,A:InfinityInc,JSA		2.00
245 LMc,Crisis,N:Steel		2.00
246 LMc,JLA leaves Detroit		2.00
247 LMc,JLA returns to old HQ		2.00
248 LMc,F:J'onn J'onzz		2.00
249 LMc,Lead-in to Anniv.		2.00
250 LMc,Anniv.,A:Superman,		
Green Lantern,Green Arrow,		
Black Canary,R:Batman		2.75
251 LMc,V:Despero		1.75
252 LMc,V:Despero,N:Elongated		
Man		1.75
253 LMc,V:Despero		1.75
254 LMc,V:Despero		1.75
255 LMc,O:Gypsy		1.75
256 LMc,Gypsy		1.75
257 LMc,A:Adam,L:Zatanna		1.75
258 LMc,Legends x-over,D:Vibe		1.75
259 LMc,Legends x-over		1.75
260 LMc,Legends x-over,D:Steel		1.75
261 LMc,Legends,final issue		4.00
Ann.#1 DG(i),A:Sandman		3.00
Ann.#2 I:NewJLA		2.00
Ann.#3 MG(i),Crisis		2.00

JUSTICE LEAGUE TASK FORCE
1993–96

1 F:Mart.Manhunter,Nightwing,		
Aquaman,Flash,Gr.Lantern		2.50
2 V:Count Glass,Blitz		1.75
3 V:Blitz,Count Glass		1.75
4 DG,F:Gypsy,A:Lady Shiva		1.75
5 JAI,Knightquest:Crusade,F:Bronze		
Tiger,Green Arrow,Gypsy		2.00
6 JAI,Knightquest:Search,F:Bronze		
Tiger,Green Arrow,Gypsy		1.75
7 PDd(s),F:Maxima,Wonder Woman,		
Dolphin,Gypsy,Vixen,V:Luta		1.75
8 PDd(s),SaV,V:Amazons		1.75
9 GrL,V:Wildman		1.75
10 Purification Plague#1		1.75
11 Purification Plague#2		1.75
12 Purification Plague#3		1.75
13 Jugedment Day#2,		
V:Overmaster		1.75
14 Jugedment Day#5,		
V:Overmaster		1.75
15 Aftershocks #2		1.75

DC COMICS

Justice League Task Force #12
© DC Comics, Inc.

16 Zero Hour,A:Triumph 1.75
17 Savage 1.50
18 Savage 1.50
19 Martian Manhunter 1.50
20 Savage Legacy,pt.4 .... 1.50
21 F:Martian Manhunter 1.50
22 F:Triumph 1.50
23 V:Vampire 1.50
24 F:Von Mauler, Gypsy 1.50
25 A:Impulse & Damage, V:Mystek 1.75
26 Cut Day 1.75
27 F:L-Ron 1.75
28 Triumph vs. Manhunter 1.75
29 A:Glenn Gammeron 1.75
30 Underworld Unleashed tie-in . 1.75
31 Despero on trial 1.75
32 Despero vs. terrorists 1.75
33 .... 1.75
34 On Earth, or Skartaris? 1.75
35 A:Warlord Travis Morgan 1.75

JUSTICE SOCIETY OF AMERICA
[Limited Series]
April–Nov., 1991
1 B:Veng.From Stars,A:Flash ... 2.00
2 A:BlackCanary,V:Solomon Grundy,
   C:G.A.Green Lantern. 1.75
3 A:G.A.Green Lantern,Black Canary,
   V:Sol.Grundy 1.75
4 A:G.A.Hawkman,C:G.A.Flash ... 1.75
5 A:G.A.Hawkman,Flash 1.75
6 FM:c(i),A:Bl.Canary,G.A.Gr.Lantern,
   V:Sol.Grundy,V:Savage 1.75
7 JSA united,V:Vandal Savage .. 1.75
8 E:Veng.FromStar,V:V.Savage,
   Solomon Grundy 1.75
Spec.#1 DR,MG,End of JSA 2.00
[Regular Series] 1992–93
1 V:The New Order 1.75
2 V:Ultra Gen 1.50
3 R:Ultra-Humanite 1.50
4 V:Ultra-Humanite 1.50
5 V:Ultra-Humanite 1.50
6 F:Johnny Thunderbolt 1.50
7 ..Or give me Liberty 1.50

8 Pyramid Scheme 1.50
9 V:Kulak 1.50
10 V:Kulak,final issue 1.50

KAMANDI, THE LAST BOY ON EARTH
Oct.–Nov., 1972
1 JK,O:Kamandi 27.00
2 JK 15.00
3 JK 8.00
4 JK,I:Prince Tuftan 8.00
5 JK 8.00
6 JK 8.00
7 JK 7.00
8 JK 7.00
9 JK 7.00
10 JK 7.00
11 JK 7.00
12 JK 7.00
13 thru 24 JK .... @6.00
25 thru 28 JK .... @3.00
29 A:Superman 3.00
30 JK 3.00
31 .... 3.00
32 Double size 4.00
33 thru 57 .... @3.00
58 A:Karate Kid 3.00
59 JSn,A:Omac, Sept.–Oct,1978 . 5.00

Kamandi: At Earth's End #2
© DC Comics, Inc.

KAMANDI: AT EARTH'S END
[Mini-Series] 1993
1 R:Kamandi 2.00
2 V:Kingpin,Big Q 2.00
3 A:Sleeper Zom,Saphira 2.00
4 A:Superman 2.00
5 A:Superman,V:Ben Boxer 2.00
6 final issue 2.00

KARATE KID
March-April, 1976
1 I:Iris Jacobs,A:Legion 1.50
2 A:Major Disaster 1.25
3 thru 10 .... @1.25
11 A:Superboy/Legion 1.25

12 A:Superboy/Legion 1.25
13 A:Superboy/Legion 1.25
14 A:Robin 1.25
15 July-Aug., 1978 .... 1.25

KENTS, THE
1997
1 (of 12) JOs(s),TT,MiB 2.50
2 JOs(s),TT,MiB, tragedy strikes . 2.50

KID ETERNITY
1991
1 GMo(s),DFg,O:Kid Eternity ... 5.50
2 GMo(s),DFg,A:Mr.Keeper 5.50
3 GMo(s),DFg,True Origin revealed,
   final issue. 5.50

KID ETERNITY
Vertigo 1993–94
1 B:ANo(s),SeP,R:Kid Eternity,
   A:Mdm.Blavatsky,Hemlock ... 2.75
2 SeP,A:Sigmund Freud,Carl Jung,
   A:Malocchio 2.50
3 SeP,A:Malocchio,I:Dr.Pathos . 2.25
4 SeP,A:Neal Cassady 2.25
5 SeP,In Cyberspace 2.25
6 SeP,A:Dr.Pathos,Marilyn
   Monroe 2.25
7 SeP,I:Infinity 2.25
8 SeP,In Insane Asylum 2.25
9 SeP,Asylum,A:Dr.Pathos 2.25
10 SeP,Small Wages 2.25
11 ANi(s),I:Slap 2.25
12 SeP,A:Slap 2.25
13 SeP,Date in Hell,pt.1 ...... 2.25
14 SeP,Date in Hell,pt.2 ...... 2.25
15 SeP,Date in Hell,pt.3 ...... 2.25
16 SeP,The Zone 2.25

KILL YOUR BOYFRIEND
Vertigo 1995
GNv PBd(c) 4.95

KINGDOM COME
Elseworlds 1996
1 MWa,AxR 9.00
2 MWa,AxR,R:JLA 8.00
3 MWa,AxR,A:Capt. Marvel 8.00
4 MWa,AxR, final issue 8.00
HC Elseworlds rep. 29.95

KISSYFUR
1989
1 .... 2.00

KOBALT
Milestone 1994–95
1 JBy(c),I:Kobalt,Richard Page .. 2.25
2 .... 2.00
3 I:Slick,Volt,Red Light 2.00
4 I:Slick,Volt,Red Light 2.00
5 Richard Page 1.75
6 Volt 1.75
7 Static 1.75
8 A:Hardward 1.75
9 .... 1.75
10 A:Harvest 1.75
11 V:St.Cloud 1.75
12 V:Rabid 1.75
13 V:Harvester 1.75
14 Long Hot Summer, V:Harvester 2.50
15 Long Hot Summer 2.50

KOBRA
1976–77
1 JK,I:Kobra & Jason Burr 2.00
2 I:Solaris 1.50
3 KG/DG,TA,V:Solaris 1.75
4 V:Servitor 1.25
5 RB/FMc,A:Jonny Double 1.25
6 MN/JRu,A:Jonny Double 1.25
7 MN/JRu,A:Jonny Double last iss 1.25

KONG THE UNTAMED
June-July, 1975
1 thru 4 . . . . @1.25
5 Feb.–March, 1976 . . . . 1.25

Korak, Son of Tarzan #46
© DC Comics, Inc.

KORAK, SON OF TARZAN
1975
(Previously published by Gold Key)
46 B:Carson of Venus, 1972 . . . . 4.00
47 . . . . 3.50
48 thru 59, 1975 . . . . 3.00
Becomes: TARZAN FAMILY

KRYPTON CHRONICLES
1981
1 CS,A:Superman 1.50
2 CS,A:Black Flame 1.25
3 CS,O:Name of Kal-El 1.25

LAST DAYS OF THE
JUSTICE SOCIETY
1986
1 . . . . 3.00

LAST ONE
Vertigo 1993
1 B:JMD(s),DSw,I:Myrwann,Patrick
   Maguire's Story 3.25
2 DSw,Pat's Addiction to Drugs . 3.00
3 DSw,Pat goes into Coma 3.00
4 DSw,In Victorian age 3.00
5 DSw,Myrwann Memories 3.00
6 E:JMD(s),DSw,final Issue 3.00

LEADING COMICS
Winter, 1941–42
1 O:Seven Soldiers of Victory,
   B:Crimson Avenger,Green Arrow
   & Speedy,Shining Knight,
   A:The Dummy 3,300.00
2 MMe,V:Black Star 1,100.00
3 V:Dr. Doome 900.00
4 'Seven Steps to Conquest',
   V:The Sixth Sense 700.00
5 'The Miracles that Money
   Couldn't Buy' 700.00
6 'The Treasure that Time
   Forgot' 600.00
7 The Wizard of Wisstark 600.00
8 Seven Soldiers Go back
   through the Centuries 600.00
9 V:Mr. X,'Chameleon of Crime' 600.00
10 King of the Hundred Isles . . 600.00
11 'The Hard Luck Hat!' 400.00
12 'The Million Dollar
   Challenge!' 400.00
13 'The Trophies of Crime' . . . 400.00
14 Bandits from the Book' 400.00
15 (fa) 175.00
16 thru 22 (fa) . . . . @75.00
23 (fa),I:Peter Porkchops 150.00
24 thru 30 (fa) . . . . @60.00
31 (fa) 50.00
32 (fa) 50.00
33 (fa) 60.00
34 thru 40 (fa) . . . . @50.00
41 (fa),Feb.–March, 1950 . . . . 50.00

LEAGUE OF JUSTICE
1996
1 (of 2) Elseworlds 5.95
2 (of 2) Elseworlds 5.95

LEAVE IT TO BINKY
Feb.–March, 1948
1 . . . . 175.00
2 . . . . 70.00
3 . . . . 60.00
4 . . . . 60.00
5 thru 14 . . . . @30.00
15 SM,Scribbly 40.00
16 thru 60 . . . . @15.00
61 thru 71 . . . . @7.50

LEGEND OF
THE SHIELD
Impact 1991–92
1 I:Shield,V:Mann-X,I:Big Daddy,
   Lt.Devon Hall,Arvell Hauser,Mary
   Masterson-Higgins 1.50
2 Shield in Middle East 1.25
3 Shield Goes A.W.O.L. 1.25
4 Hunt for Shield 1.25
5 A:Shield's Partner Dusty 1.25
6 O:Shield, V:The Jewels 1.25
7 Shield/Fly team-up 1.25
8 V:Weapon 1.25
9 Father Vs. Son 1.25
10 Arvell Hauser 1.25
11 inc,Trading cards 1.25
12 . . . . 1.25
13 Shield court martialed 1.25
14 Mike Barnes becomes Shield . 1.25
15 Shield becomes a Crusader . . 1.25
16 V:Soviets,final issue 1.25
Ann.#1 Earthquest,w/trading card . 2.25

LEGEND OF
WONDER WOMAN
1986
1 Return of Atomia 1.25
2 A:Queens Solalia & Leila 1.25
3 Escape from Atomia 1.25
4 conclusion 1.25

Legends #3 © DC Comics, Inc.

LEGENDS
1986–87
1 JBy,V:Darkseid 3.00
2 JBy,A:Superman 2.00
3 JBy,I:Suicide Squad 2.00
4 JBy,V:Darkseid 2.00
5 JBy,A:Dr. Fate 2.00
6 JBy,I:Justice League 5.00
TPB rep.#1-#6 JBy(c) 9.95

LEGENDS OF
DANIEL BOONE, THE
Oct., 1955–Jan., 1957
1 . . . . 450.00
2 . . . . 300.00
3 thru 8 . . . . 250.00

LEGENDS OF
THE DARK KNIGHT
(see BATMAN)

LEGENDS OF THE
WORLD FINEST
1994
1 WS(s),DIB,V:Silver Banshee,Blaze,
   Tullus,Foil(c) 5.25
2 WS(s),DIB,V:Silver Banshee,Blaze,
   Tullus,Foil(c) 5.25
3 WS(s),DIB,V:Silver Banshee,Blaze,
   Tullus,Foil(c) 5.25
TPB 14.95

L.E.G.I.O.N. '89-94
1989–94
1 BKi,V:Computer Tyrants 4.00
2 BKi,V:Computer Tyrants 3.00
3 BKi,V:Computer Tyrants,

DC COMICS

DC COMICS

A:Lobo	3.00
4 BKi,V: Lobo	3.00
5 BKi,J:Lobo(in the rest of the	
series),V:Konis-Biz	3.00
6 BKi,V:Konis-Biz	3.00
7 BKi,Stealth vs. Dox	3.00
8 BKi,R:Dox	3.00
9 BKi,J:Phase (Phantom Girl)	2.50
10 BKi,Stealth vs Lobo	2.50
11 BKi,V:Mr.Stoorr	2.50
12 BKi,V:Emerald Eye	2.50
13 BKi,V:Emerald Eye	2.50
14 BKi,V:Pirates	2.50
15 BKi,V:Emerald Eye	2.50
16 BKi,J:LarGand	2.50
17 BKi,V:Dragon-Ro	2.50
18 BKi,V:Dragon-Ro	2.50
19 V:Lydea,L:Stealth	2.50
20 Aftermath	2.50
21 D:Lyrissa Mallor,V:Mr.Starr	2.50
22 V:Mr.Starr	2.50
23 O:R.J.Brande(double sized)	3.50
24 BKi,V:Khunds	2.50
25 BKi,V:Khunds	2.50
26 BKi,V:Khunds	2.50
27 BKi,J:Lydea Mallor	2.50
28 KG,Birth of Stealth's Babies	2.50
29 BKi,J:Capt.Comet,Marij'n Bek	2.50
30 BKi,R:Stealth	2.50
31 Lobo vs.Capt.Marvel	3.50
32 V:Space Biker Gang	2.00
33 A:Ice-Man	2.00
34 MPn,V:Ice Man	2.00
35 Legion Disbanded	2.00
36 Dox proposes to Ignea	2.00
37 V:Intergalactic Ninjas	2.00
38 BKi,Lobo V:Ice Man	2.00
39 BKi,D:G'odd,V:G'oddSquad	2.00
40 BKi,V:Kyaltic Space Station	2.00
41 BKi,A:Stealth'sBaby	2.00
42 BKi,V:Yeltsin-Beta	2.00
43 BKi,V:Yeltsin-Beta	2.00
44 V:Yeltsin-Beta,C:Gr.Lantern	2.00
45	2.00
46 BKi,A:Hal Jordan	2.00
47 BKi,Lobo vs Hal Jordan	2.00
48 BKi,R:Ig'nea	2.00
49 BKi,V:Ig'nea	2.00
50 BKi,V:Ig'nea,A:Legion'67	3.75
51 F:Lobo,Telepath	2.00
52 BKi,V:Cyborg Skull of Darius	2.00
53 BKi,V:Shadow Creature	2.00
54 BKi,V:Shadow Creature	2.00
55 BKi,V:Shadow Beast	2.00
56 BKi,A:Masked Avenger	2.00
57 BKi,Trinity,V:Green Lantern	2.00
58 BKi,Trinity#6,A:Green Lantern,	
Darkstar	2.00
59 F:Phase	2.00
60 V:Phantom Riders	2.00
61 Little Party	2.00
62 A:R.E.C.R.U.I.T.S.	2.00
63 A:Superman	2.00
64 BKi(c),V:Mr.B	2.00
65 BKi(c),V:Brain Bandit	2.00
66 Stealth and Dox name child	2.00
67 F:Telepath	2.00
68	1.75
69	2.00
70 Zero Hour, last issue	2.50
Ann.#1 A:Superman,V:Braniac	5.50
Ann.#2 Armageddon 2001	3.50
Ann.#3 Eclipso tie-in	2.00
Ann.#4 SHa(i),I:Pax	3.75
Ann.#5 Elseworlds story	3.50

LEGION OF SUBSTITUTE HEROES
1985

Spec.#1 KG	1.50

LEGION OF SUPER-HEROES
[Reprint Series] 1973

1 rep. Tommy Tomorrow	11.00
2 rep. Tommy Tomorrow	7.00
3 rep. Tommy Tomorrow	7.00
4 rep. Tommy Tomorrow	7.00

[1st Regular Series] 1980–84
Prev: SUPERBOY (& LEGION)

259 JSon,L:Superboy	5.00
260 RE,I:Circus of Death	3.50
261 RE,V:Circus of Death	3.50
262 JSh,V:Engineer	3.50
263 V:Dagon the Avenger	3.50
264 V:Dagon the Avenger	3.50
265 JSn,DG,Superman/Radio Shack	
insert	3.50

Legion of Super-Heroes #282
© DC Comics, Inc.

266 R:Bouncing Boy,Duo Damsel	3.00
267 SD,V:Kantuu	3.00
268 SD,BWi,V:Dr.Mayavale	3.00
269 V:Fatal Five	3.00
270 V:Fatal Five	3.00
271 V:Tharok (Dark Man)	2.50
272 CI,SD,O:J:Blok, I:New	
Dial 'H' for Hero	2.50
273 V:Stargrave	2.50
274 SD,V:Captain Frake	2.50
275 V:Captain Frake	2.50
276 SD,V:Mordru	2.50
277 A:Reflecto(Superboy)	2.50
278 A:Reflecto(Superboy)	2.50
279 A:Reflecto(Superboy)	2.50
280 R:Superboy	2.50
281 SD,V:Time Trapper	2.50
282 V:Time Trapper	2.50
283 O:Wildfire	2.50
284 PB,V:Organleggor	2.50
285 PB,KG(1st Legion)V:Khunds	3.00
286 PB,KG,V:Khunds	3.00
287 KG,V:Kharlak	4.00

288 KG,V:Kharlak	3.00
289 KG,Stranded	3.00
290 KG,B:Great Darkness Saga,	
J:Invisible Kid II	3.00
291 KG,V:Darkseid's Minions	2.00
292 KG,V:Darkseid's Minions	2.00
293 KG,Daxam destroyed	2.00
294 KG,E:Great Darkness Saga,	
V:Darkseid,A:Auron,Superboy	2.00
295 KG,A:Green Lantern Corps	1.75
296 KG,D:Cosmic Boys family	1.75
297 KG,O:Legion,A:Cosmic Boy	1.75
298 KG,EC,I:Amethyst	1.75
299 KG,R:Invisible Kid I	1.75
300 KG,CS,JSon,DC,KS,DG	2.00
301 KG,R:Chameleon Boy	1.75
302 KG,A:Chameleon Boy	1.75
303 KG,V:Fatal Five	1.75
304 KG,V:Fatal Five	1.75
305 KG,V:Micro Lad	1.75
306 KG,CS,RT,O:Star Boy	1.75
307 KG,GT,Omen	1.75
308 KG,V:Omen	1.75
309 KG,V:Omen	1.75
310 KG,V:Omen	1.75
311 KG,GC,New Headquarters	1.75
312 KG,V:Khunds	1.75
313 KG,V:Khunds	1.75
Ann.#1 IT,KG,I:Invisible Kid	3.50
Ann.#2 DGb,W:Karate Kid and	
Princess Projectra	2.00
Ann.#3 CS,RT,A:Darkseid	2.00
Ann.#4 reprint	2.00
Ann.#5 reprint	1.75
Legion Archives Vol 1 HC	39.95
Legion Archives Vol 2 HC	39.95
Legion Archives Vol 3 HC	39.95
Legion Archives Vol 4 HC	39.95

Becomes:

TALES OF LEGION OF SUPER HEROES

LEGION OF SUPER-HEROES
[3rd Regular Series] 1984–89

1 KG,V:Legion of Super-Villians	3.00
2 KG,V:Legion of Super-Villians	2.50
3 KG,V:Legion of Super-Villians	2.50
4 KG,D:Karate Kid	2.50
5 KG,D:Nemesis Kid	2.50
6 JO,F:Lightning Lass	2.25
7 SLi,A:Controller	2.25
8 SLi,V:Controller	2.25
9 SLi,V:Sklarians	2.25
10 V:Khunds	2.25
11 EC,KG,I:Orig 3 members	2.00
12 SLi,EC,A:Superboy	2.00
13 SLi,V:Lythyls,F:TimberWolf	2.00
14 SLi,J:Sensor Girl (Princess	
Projectra),Quislet,Tellus,Polar	
Boy,Magnetic Kid	2.00
15 GLa,V:Dr. Regulus	2.00
16 SLi,Crisis tie-in,F:Braniac5	2.00
17 GLa,O:Legion	2.00
18 GLa,Crisis tie-in,V:InfiniteMan	2.00
19 GLa,V:Controller	2.00
20 GLa,V:Tyr	2.00
21 GLa,V:Emerald Empress	1.75
22 GLa,V:Restorer,A:Universo	1.75
23 SLi,GLa,A:Superboy,	
Jonah Hex	1.75
24 GLa,NBi,A:Fatal Five	1.75
25 GLa,V:FatalFive	1.75
26 GLa,V:FatalFive,O:SensorGirl	1.75

DC COMICS

Legion of Super-Heroes (3rd Series) #27 © DC Comics, Inc.

Legion of Super-Heroes (4th Series) #11 © DC Comics, Inc.

27 GLa,GC,A:Mordru 1.75
28 GLa,L:StarBoy 1.75
29 GLa,V:Starfinger 1.75
30 GLa,A:Universo 1.75
31 GLa,A:Ferro Lad,Karate Kid . . 1.75
32 GLa,V:Universo,I:Atmos 1.75
33 GLa,V:Universo 1.75
34 GLa,V:Universo 1.75
35 GLa,V:Universo,R:Saturn Girl . . 1.75
36 GLa,R:Cosmic Boy 1.75
37 GLa,V:Universo,I:Superboy
    (Earth Prime) 5.00
38 GLa,V:TimeTrapper,
    D:Superboy 9.00
39 CS,RT,O:Colossal Boy 1.75
40 GLa,I:New Starfinger 1.75
41 GLa,V:Starfinger 1.75
42 GLa,Millenium,V:Laurel Kent . . 1.75
43 GLa,Millenium,V:Laurel Kent . . 1.75
44 GLa,O:Quislet 1.75
45 GLa,CS,MGr,DC,30th Ann. . . . 3.00
46 GLa,Conspiracy 1.75
47 GLa,PB,V:Starfinger 1.75
48 GLa,Conspiracy,A:Starfinger . . 1.75
49 PB,Conspiracy,A:Starfinger . . 1.75
50 KG,V:Time Trapper,A:Infinite
    Man,E:Conspiracy 3.00
51 KG,V:Gorak,L:Brainiac5 . . . . . 1.75
52 KG,V:Gil'Dishpan 1.75
53 KG,V:Gil'Dishpan 1.75
54 KG,V:Gorak 1.75
55 KG,EC,JL,EL,N:Legion 1.75
56 EB,V:Inquisitor 1.75
57 KG,V:Emerald Empress 1.75
58 KG,V:Emerald Empress 1.75
59 KG,MBr,F:Invisible Kid 1.75
60 KG,B:Magic Wars 1.75
61 KG,Magic Wars 1.75
62 KG,D:Magnetic Lad 1.75
63 KG,E:Magic Wars #4,final iss. . 1.75
Ann.#1 KG,Murder Mystery 2.50
Ann.#2 KG,CS,O:Validus,
    A:Darkseid 3.00
Ann.#3 GLa,I:2nd Karate Kid 2.50
Ann.#4 BKi,V:Starfinger 2.50
Ann #5 I:2nd Legion Sub.Heroes . 2.50

[4th Regular Series] 1989–97
1 KG,R:Cosmic Boy, Chameleon . 3.00
2 KG,R:Ultra Boy,I:Kono 2.50
3 KG,D:Block,V:Roxxas 2.50
4 KG,V:Time Trapper 2.50
5 KG,V:Mordru,A:Glorith 2.50
6 KG,I:Laurel Gand 2.50
7 KG,V:Mordru 2.25
8 KG,O:Legion 2.25
9 KG,O:Laurel Gand 2.25
10 KG,V:Roxxas 2.25
11 KG,V:Roxxas 2.00
12 KG,I:Kent Shakespeare 2.00
13 KG,V:Dominators,posters 2.00
14 KG,J:Tenzil Kem 2.00
15 KG,Khund Invasion 2.00
16 KG,V:Khunds 2.00
17 KG,V:Khunds 2.00
18 KG,V:Khunds 2.00
19 KG,cont.from Adv.of Superman
    #478,A:Original Dr. Fate 2.25
20 KG,V:Dominators 2.00
21 KG,B:Quiet Darkness,
    A:Lobo,Darkseid 3.00
22 KG,A:Lobo,Darkseid 2.50
23 KG,A:Lobo,Darkseid 2.50
24 KG,E:Quiet Darkness,A:Lobo,
    Darkseid,C:Legionairres 2.75
25 DAb,I:Legionairres 3.00
26 JPn,B:Terra Mosaic,V:B.I.O.N . 2.00
27 JPn,V:B.I.O.N. 2.00
28 JPn,O:Sun Boy 2.00
29 JPn,I:Monica Sade 2.00
30 JPn,V:Dominators 2.00
31 CS,AG,F:Shvaughn as man . . 2.00
32 JPn,D:Karate Kid,Prin.Projectra,
    Chameleon Boy(Legionaires) . 2.00
33 R:Kid Quantum 2.00
34 R:Sun Boy 2.00
35 JPN,V:Dominators 2.00
36 JPn,E:Terra Mosaic 2.00
37 JBr,R:Star Boy,Dream Girl . . . 2.00
38 JPn,Earth is destroyed 5.00
39 SI,A:Legionaires 2.00
40 SI,Legion meets Legionaires . . 2.00
41 SI,F:The Legionaires 2.25
42 SI,V:Glorith 2.00

43 SI,B:Mordru Arises 2.00
44 SI,R:Karate Kid 2.00
45 SI,R:Roxxas 2.00
46 SI, ... 2.00
47 SI, ... 2.00
48 SI,E:Mordru Arises 2.00
49 F:Matter Eater Lad 2.00
50 W:Tenzil & Saturn Queen,
    R:Wildfire,V:B.I.O.N. 3.75
51 R:Kent,Celeste,Ivy,V:Grimbor . 2.00
52 F:Timber Wolf 2.00
53 SI,V:Glorith 2.25
54 SI,Foil,Die-Cut(c),
    N:L.E.G.I.O.N. 3.25
55 SI,On Rimbor 2.50
56 SI,R:Espionage Squad 2.00
57 SI,R:Khund Legionnaires 2.00
58 SI,D:Laurel Gand 2.00
59 SI,R:Valor,Dawnstar 2.25
60 SI,End of an Era#3 . . . . 2.25
61 SI,End of an Era#6 . . . . 2.25
62 I:New Team 1.95
63 Alien Attack 1.95
64 . . . . 1.95
65 . . . . 1.95
66 I:New Team Members 1.95
67 F:Leviathan 1.95
68 F:Leviathan 1.95
69 V:Durlan 2.25
70 A:Andromeda, Brainiac 5 . . . . 2.25
71 Planet Trom 2.25
72 . . . . 2.25
73 Sibling Rivalry,pt.1 . . . . 2.25
74 Future Tense,pt2 . . . . 2.25
75 Two Timer,pt.1 (of 2) 2.25
76 F:Valor & Triad 2.25
77 F:Brainiac 5 . . . . 2.25
78 . . . . 2.25
79 Fatal Five attacks 2.25
80 V:Fatal Five 2.25
81 R:Dirk Morgna 2.25
82 . . . . 2.25
83 . . . . 2.25
84 . . . . 2.25
85 TPe&TMw(s),LMd,A:Superman,
    back in 20th century 2.25
86 TPe&TMw(s),LMd,Final Night
    tie-in 2.25
87 TPe&TMw(s),LMd,F:Deadman   2.25
88 TPe&TMw(s),LMd,A:Impulse . . 2.25
89 TPe&TMw(s),LMd, ... 2.25
90 TPe&TMw(s),LMd,V:Dr. Psycho 2.25
91 TPe&TMw(s),LMd,Legion back
    together, but trapped in
    timestream 2.25
92 TPe&TMs(s),LMd,"Displaced
    in Time" 2.25
93 TPe&TMw(s),MC, All-tragedy
    issue 2.25
94 TPe&TMw(s),LMd,"22 short
    pages about the Legion of
    Super-Heroes" 2.25
95 MFm,F:Brainiac 5 . . . . 2.25
96 MFm,wedding 2.25
Ann.#1 O:Ultra Boy,V:Glorith 3.50
Ann.#2 O:Valor 3.50
Ann.#3 N:Timberwolf 4.00
Ann.#4 I:Jamm 3.50
Ann.#5 SI(c),CDo,MFm,TMc,
    Elseworlds Story 3.75
Ann.#6 Year One Annual + pin-ups 3.95
Ann.#7 TPe(s),MC,MFm,"Legends
    of the Dead Earth" 3.50
HC Archives, Vol. 6 rep.Adventure
    #350–358 . . . . 49.95

TPB Great Darkness Saga 17.95
TPB Legion Archives, rep.#1-#3 . 39.95
TPB Legion Archives, rep.#4 . . . 49.95

Legionnaires #1 © DC Comics, Inc.

LEGIONNAIRES
1992–97
1 CSp,V:Mano and the Hand,Bagged
 w/SkyBox promo card 3.50
1a w/out card 2.50
2 CSp,V:Mano 2.00
3 CSp,I:2nd Emerald Empress . . 2.00
4 CSp,R:Fatal Five 2.00
5 CSp,V:Fatal Five 2.00
6 CSp,V:Fatal Five 1.75
7 AH,V:Devil Fish 1.75
8 CDo,F:Brainiac 5 . . . . 1.75
9 CSp,A:Kid Quantum 1.75
10 CSp,A:Kono,I:2nd Kid Pyscho . 1.75
11 CSp,J:2nd Kid Pyscho 1.75
12 CSp,A:2nd Kid Pyscho 1.75
13 FFo,V:Grimbor 1.75
14 V:Grimbor 1.75
15 V:Grimbor 1.75
16 In Time 1.75
17 End of An Era #1 . . . . 1.75
18 Zero Hour, LSH 1.75
19 Problems 1.50
20 Moon Battle 1.50
21 and 22 . . . . @1.50
23 Saturday Night 1.50
24 F:Triad 1.50
25 F:Chameleon 1.50
26 F:Apparition, Ultra Boy 1.75
27 V:The Daxamites 2.25
28 V:Daxamites 2.25
29 . . . . 2.25
30 Silbing Rivalry,pt.2 . . . . 2.25
31 Future Tense,pt.3 . . . . 2.25
32 Two Timer, pt.2 . . . . 2.25
33 deadly new villain 2.25
34 Shrinking Violet killed? 2.25
35 . . . . 2.25
36 RSt,V:Fatal Five 2.25
37 RSt,A:Kinetix,The Empress . . 2.25
38 . . . . 2.25
39 . . . . 2.25
40 . . . . 2.25
41 RSt&TMw(s),JMy,Legion of

Super-Heroes #84 aftermath . . 2.25
42 RSt&TMw(s),JMy,Mysa vs.
 Kinetix 2.25
43 RSt&TMw(s),JMy,Legionnaire
 try-outs 2.25
44 TPe&TMw(s),JMy,revenge by
 rejected applicants 2.25
45 . . . . 2.25
46 RSt&TMw(s),JMy,M'Onel's life
 hangs by a thread 2.25
47 TPe&TMw(s),JMy,Brainiac 5 has
 plan to return Legionnaires to
 the future 2.25
48 RSt&TMw(s),JMy,"Dawn of the
 Dark Lord," pt.1 . . . . 2.25
49 RSt&TMw(s),JMy,"Dawn of the
 Dark Lord," pt.2 . . . . 2.25
50 RSt&TMw(s),JMy,"The Bride of
 Mordru" 48pg, with poster 3.95
51 "Picking Up the Pieces" 2.25
52 RSt&TMw(s),JMy,"LeVlathan" . 2.25
Ann.#1 Elseworlds Story 2.95
Ann.#2 Year One Story 3.00
Ann.#3 RSt&TMw(s) Legends of the
 Dead Earth 3.50

LEGIONAIRRES THREE
1986
1 EC,Saturn Girl,Cosmic Boy . . . 4.00
2 EC,V:Time Trapper,pt.1 . . . . . . 3.00
3 EC,V:Time Trapper,pt.2 . . . . . . 3.00
4 EC,V:Time Trapper,pt.3 . . . . . . 2.75

LIFE, THE UNIVERSE AND EVERYTHING
1996
1 thru 3 Doug Adams adapt. . . . @6.95

LIMITED COLLECTORS EDITION
Summer, 1973
21 Shazam 10.00
22 Tarzan 8.00
23 House of Mystery 8.00
24 Rudolph, the Red-nosed
 Reindeer 4.00
25 NA,NA(c),Batman 10.00
27 Shazam 7.00
29 Tarzan 4.00
31 NA,O:Superman 9.00
32 Ghosts 4.00
33 Rudolph 3.00
34 X-Mas with Superheroes 7.00
35 Shazam 5.00
36 The Bible 4.00
37 Batman 10.00
38 Superman 8.00
39 Secret Origins 8.00
40 Dick Tracy 4.00
41 ATh,Super Friends 7.00
42 Rudolph 3.00
43 X-mas with Super-Heroes 9.00
44 NA,Batman 10.00
45 Secret Origins-Super Villians . . 6.00
46 ATh,JLA 7.00
47 Superman 5.00
48 Superman-Flash Race 5.00
49 Superboy & Legion of
 Super-Heroes 5.00
50 Rudolph 3.00
51 NA,NA(c),Batman 10.00
52 NA,NA(c),The Best of DC 9.00
57 Welcome Back Kotter 4.00
59 NA,BWr,Batman,1978 . . . . . . 12.00

LITTLE SHOP OF HORRORS
1 GC 2.50

Lobo #3 © DC Comics, Inc.

LOBO
[1st Limited Series] 1990–91
1 SBs,Last Czarnian #1 . . . . 4.00
1a 2nd Printing 2.00
2 SBs,Last Czarnian #2 . . . . 3.00
3 SBs,Last Czarnian #3 . . . . 3.00
4 SBs,Last Czarnian #4 . . . . 3.00
Ann.#1 Bloodlines#1,I:Layla 3.75
Lobo Paramilitary X-Mas SBs . . . 5.50
Lobo:Blazing Chain of Love,DCw . 1.50
TPB Last Czarnian,rep.#1-#4 . . . . 9.95
TPB Lobo's Greatest Hits 12.95
[Regular Series] 1993–97
1 VS,Foil(c),V:Dead Boys 3.25
2 VS 4.00
3 VS 2.75
4 VS,Quigly Affair 2.75
5 V:Bludhound 2.00
6 I:Bim Simms 2.00
7 A:Losers 2.25
8 A:Losers 2.25
9 V:Lobo 2.25
10 Preacher 1.95
11 Goldstar vs. Rev.Bo 1.95
12 . . . . 1.95
13 . . . . 1.95
14 Lobo, P.I. 1.95
15 Lobo, P.I.,pt.2 . . . . 1.95
16 Lobo, P.I.,pt.3 . . . . 1.95
17 Lobo, P.I.,pt.4 . . . . 2.25
18 Lobo, P.I.,pt.5 . . . . 2.25
19 . . . . 2.25
20 Toilot Fight 2.25
21 AIG,KON,R:Space Cabby . . . 2.25
22 AIG,Underworld Unleashed tie-in2.25
23 AIG,Stargaze Rally,pt.1 . . . . . 2.25
24 AIG,Stargaze Rally,pt.2 . . . . . 2.25
25 AIG 2.25
26 AIG,V:Erik the Khund 2.25
27 AIG,V:Billy Krono 2.25
28 AIG,A:Great Big Fat Bastiches 2.25
29 . . . . 2.25

DC COMICS

DC COMICS

30 . . . . 2.25
31 . . . . 2.25
32 AIG(s),Lobo attends a seance,
   frags himself 2.25
33 AIG(s),Lobo returns from spirit
   world 2.25
34 AIG(s),vs. Japan, whaling, . . . 2.25
35 AIG(s) "Deathtrek" 2.25
36 . . . . 2.25
37 AIG(s),BKi,Lobo's Guide to Girls 2.25
38 AIG(s),Bomandi The Last Boy
   on Earth 2.25
39 AIG(s),"In the Belly of the
   Behemoth,"pt. 1 . . . . 2.25
40 AIG(s),"In the Belly of the
   Behemoth,"pt. 2 . . . . 2.25
41 AIG(s),roommates 2.25
42 AIG(s),A:Perfidia 2.25
43 AIG(s),A:Jonas 2.25
Ann.#1 Bloodlines 4.00
Ann.#2 Elseworlds Story 3.50
Ann.#3 AIG Year One 4.95

LOBO'S BIG BABE SPRING BREAK SPECIAL
1 Miss Voluptuous Contest 1.95

LOBO: BLAZING CHAINS OF LOVE
1 . . . . 1.50

LOBO BOUNTY HUNTING FOR FUN AND PROFIT
1 F:Fanboy 4.95

LOBO: CHAINED
March 1997
one-shot AIG(s), Lobo in prison . . 1.95

LOBO: A CONTRACT ON GAWD
1994
1 AIG(s),KD 2.00
2 AIG(s),KD,A:Dave 2.00
3 AIG(s),KD 1.75
4 AIG(s),KD,Final Issue 1.75

LOBO CONVENTION SPECIAL
1 Lobo at Comic Convention . . . 2.00

LOBO'S BACK
1992
1 SBs,w/3(c) inside,V:Loo 3.50
1a 2nd printing 1.50
2 SBs,Lobo becomes a woman . 3.00
3 SBs,V:Heaven 2.50
4 SBs,V:Heaven 2.50
TPB GF(c),rep.#1-#4 . . . . 9.95

LOBO: DEATH & TAXES
Aug. 1996
[Mini-series]
1 (of 4) KG&AIG(s) 2.25
2 KG&AIG(s),Interstellar Revenue
   learns Lobo doesn't pay taxes . 2.25
3 KG&AIG(s),Lobo walks into
   IRS trap 2.25
4 KG&AIG(s),Lobo destroys IRS . 2.25

LOBO/DEMON: HELLOWE'EN
1 AIG(s),VGi,perils of helping
   a dragon destroy earth 2.25

LOBO: INFANTICIDE
1992–93
1 KG,V:Su,Lobo Bastards 2.00
2 Lobo at Boot Camp 1.75
3 KG,Lobo Vs.his offspring 1.75
4 KG,V:Lobo Bastards 1.75

LOBO IN THE CHAIR
1 AIG(s) 2.25

LOBO/MASK
1 AIG&JAr(s),DoM,Kwi, humorous
   x-over 5.95
2 AIG&JAr(s),DoM,Kwi, concl. . . . 5.95

LOBO: I QUIT
1 AIG,nicotine withdrawal 2.25

LOBO/JUDGE DREDD: PSYCHO BIKERS VS. MUTANTS FROM HELL
1-shot 4.95

LOBO: PORTRAIT OF A VICTIM
1 VS,I:John Doe 2.00

LOBO: UNAMERICAN GLADIATORS
1993
1 CK,V:Satan's Brothers 2.00
2 CK,V:Jonny Caesar 2.00
3 CK,MMi(c),V:Satan Brothers . 2.00
4 CK,MMi(c),V:Jonny Caeser . . 2.00

LOBOCOP
1 StG(s) 2.25

LOIS AND CLARK: THE NEW ADVENTURES OF SUPERMAN
TPB 9.95

LOIS LANE
Aug., 1986
1 and 2 GM . . . . @1.50

LONG HOT SUMMER, THE
Milestone 1995
[Mini-Series]
1 Blood Syndicate v. G.R.I.N.D. . 2.95
2 A:Icon,Xombi,Hardware 2.50

LOONEY TUNES MAG.
1 thru 6 . . . . @1.95

LOONEY TUNES
1994
1 thru 6 Warner Bros. cartoons @1.75
7 thru 11 Warner Bros. . . . . . . @1.75
12 The Cotton Tail Club 1.50
13 F:Tasmanian Devil 1.50
14 Football Season 1.50

15 Jewel Thief 1.50
16 F:Yosemite Sam,Speedy
   Gonzales 1.50
17 F:Sylvester 1.50
18 . . . . 1.50
19 Ben Hur Spoof 1.50
20 F:Sylvester 1.50
21 thru 23 . . . . @1.50
24 thru 32 . . . . @1.75

LOOSE CANNON
[Mini-Series] 1995
1 AdP,V:Bounty Hunters 1.75
2 V:Bounty Hunters & The
   Eradicator 1.75
3 A:Eradicator 1.75

LORDS OF THE ULTRAREALM
1986
1 PB 3.50
2 PB 2.00
3 PB 1.50
4 PB 1.50
5 PB 1.50
6 PB 1.50
Spec.#1 PB,DG,Oneshot 2.25

LOSERS SPECIAL
1985
1 Crisis,D:Losers 1.25

MADAME XANADU
1981
1 MR/BB 2.00

MAJOR BUMMER
June 1997
1 JAr(s),DoM,I:Major Bummer . . . 2.50
2 JAr(s),DoM,Major Bummer gets
   new costume 2.50

MAN-BAT
1975–76
1 SD,AM,A:Batman 8.00
2 V:The Ten-Eyed Man 7.00

Man-Bat #1 © DC Comics, Inc.

Reprint NA(c) 4.00

MAN-BAT
1996
1 CDi,terrorizes city 2.25
2 . . . . 2.25
3 CDi,V:Steeljacket, finale 2.25

MAN-BAT vs. BATMAN
1 NA,DG,reprint 4.00

A MAN CALLED A•X
May 1997
1 MWn(s),SwM, A•X joins DC
   Universe 2.50

MANHUNTER
1988–90
1 from Millenium-Suicide Squad . 1.50
2 in Tokyo,A:Dumas 1.25
3 The Yakuza,V:Dumas 1.25
4 Secrets Revealed-Manhunter,
   Dumas & Olivia 1.25
5 A:Silvia Kandery 1.25
6 A:Argent,contd.Suicide Squad
   Annual #1 . . . . 1.25
7 Vlatavia, V:Count Vertigo 1.25
8 FS,A:Flash,Invasion x-over . . . 1.25
9 FS,Invasion Aftermath extra
   (contd from Flash #22) 1.25
10 Salvage,pt.1 . . . . 1.25
11 Salvage,pt.2 . . . . 1.25
12 . . . . 1.25
13 V:Catman 1.25
14 Janus Directive #5 . . . . 1.25
15 I:Mirage 1.25
16 V:Outlaw 1.25
17 In Gotham,A:Batman 1.50
18 Saints & Sinners,pt.1,R:Dumas 1.25
19 Saints & Sinners,pt.2,V:Dumas 1.25
20 Saints & Sinners,pt.3,V:Dumas 1.25
21 Saints & Sinners,pt.4,
   A:Manhunter Grandmaster . . . 1.25
22 Saints & Sinners,pt.5,
   A:Manhunter Grandmaster . . . 1.25
23 Saints & Sinners,pt.6,V:Dumas 1.25
24 DG,Showdown, final issue . . . 1.25
[2nd Series] 1994–95
0 . . . . 1.95
1 . . . . 1.95
2 N:Wild Huntsman 1.95
3 V:Malig 1.95
4 Necrodyne 1.95
5 V:Skin Walker 1.95
6 V:Barbarian,Incarnate 1.95
7 V:Incarnate,A:White Lotus
   & Capt. Atom 2.25
8 V:Butcher Boys 2.25
9 V:Butcher Boys 2.25
10 V:Necrodyne 2.25
11 Return of Old Enemy 2.25
12 Underworld Unleashed, finale . 2.25

MAN OF STEEL
1986
1 JBy,DG,I:Modern Superman . . 5.00
1a 2nd edition 3.00
2 JBy,DG,R:Lois Lane 3.50
3 JBy,DG,A:Batman 3.00
4 JBy,DG,V:Lex Luther 3.00
5 JBy,DG,I:Modern Bizarro 3.00
6 JBy,DG,A:Lana Lang 3.00
TPB rep. Man of Steel #1–#6 . . 12.95

TPBa 2nd printing 7.95

MANY LOVES OF DOBIE GILLIS
May-June, 1960
1 . . . . 150.00
2 . . . . 75.00
3 . . . . 65.00
4 . . . . 65.00
5 thru 9 . . . . @40.00
10 thru 25 . . . . @28.00
26 Oct., 1964 . . . . 28.00

MARTIAN MANHUNTER
1988
1 A:JLI 1.75
2 A:JLI,V:Death God 1.50
3 V:Death God,A:Dr.Erdel 1.50
4 A:JLI,final issue 1.50
[Mini-Series]
1 EB,American Secrets #1 . . . . . 5.25
2 EB,American Secrets #2 . . . . . 4.95
3 EB,American Secrets #3 . . . . . 4.95

Mask (2nd Series) #6
© DC Comics, Inc.

MASK
Dec., 1985
1 HC(c),TV tie-in,I:Mask Team . . 2.00
2 HC(c),In Egypt,V:Venom 1.75
3 HC(c),'Anarchy in the U.K.' . . . 1.75
4 HC(c),V:Venom,final issue,
   March, 1986 . . . . 1.00
[2nd Series]
Feb., 1987
1 CS/KS,reg.series 1.25
2 CS/KS,V:Venom 1.00
3 CS/KS,V:Venom 1.00
4 CS/KS,V:Venom 1.00
5 CS/KS,Mask operatives hostage 1.00
6 CS/KS,I:Jacana 1.00
7 CS/KS,Mask gone bad? 1.00
8 CS/KS,Matt Trakker,V:Venom . 1.00
9 CS/KS,V:Venom, last issue,
   Oct., 1987 . . . . 1.00

MASTERS OF THE UNIVERSE
May, 1986
1 GT,AA,O:He-Man 1.50
2 GT,AA,V:Skeletor 1.25
3 GT,V:Skeletor 1.25

MASTERWORKS SERIES OF GREAT COMIC BOOK ARTISTS
May, 1983
1 . . . . 2.50
2 . . . . 2.50
3 Dec., 1983 . . . . 2.50

'MAZING MAN
Jan., 1986
1 I:Maze 1.00
2 . . . . 1.00
3 . . . . 1.00
4 . . . . 1.00
5 . . . . 1.00
6 Shea Stadium 1.00
7 Shea Stadium 1.00
8 Cat-Sitting 1.00
9 Bank Hold-up 1.00
10 . . . . 1.00
11 Jones Beach 1.00
12 FM(c),last issue, Dec., 1986 . . 1.00
Spec.#1 . . . . 2.25
Spec.#2 . . . . 2.25
Spec.#3 KB/TM 2.25

MEN OF WAR
Aug., 1977
1 I:Gravedigger,Code Name:
   Gravedigger,I:Enemy Ace 1.50
2 JKu(c),The Five-Walled War . . 1.25
3 JKu(c),The Suicide Strategem . 1.25
4 JKu(c),Trail by Fire 1.25
5 JKu(c),Valley of the Shadow . . 1.25
6 JKu(c),A Choice of Deaths . . . 1.25
7 JKu(c),Milkrun 1.25
8 JKu(c),Death-Stroke 1.25
9 JKu(c),Gravedigger-R.I.P. 1.25
10 JKu(c),Crossroads 1.25
11 JKu(c),Berkstaten 1.25
12 JKu(c),Where Is Gravedigger? 1.25
13 JKu(c),Project Gravedigger -
   Plus One 1.25
14 JKu(c),The Swirling
   Sands of Death 1.25
15 JKu(c),The Man With the
   Opened Eye 1.25
16 JKu(c),Hide and Seek The Spy 1.25
17 JKu(c),The River of Death . . . 1.25
18 JKu(c),The Amiens Assault . . . 1.25
19 JKu(c),An Angel Named Marie 1.25
20 JKu(c),Cry:Jerico 1.25
21 JKu(c),Home-Is Where
   The Hell Is 1.25
22 JKu(c),Blackout On
   The Boardwalk 1.25
23 JKu(c),Mission: Six Feet Under 1.25
24 JKu&DG(c),The Presidential
   Peril 1.25
25 GE(c),Save the President . . . 1.25
26 March, 1980 . . . . 1.25

MENZ INSANA
DC/Vertigo
GN 7.95

DC COMICS

All comics prices listed are for *Near Mint* condition.

DC COMICS

MERCY
Vertigo
Graphic Novel I:Mercy 8.00

METAL MEN
1965–78
[1st Regular Series]
1 RA,I:Missile Men	450.00
2 RA,Robot of Terror	185.00
3 RA,Moon's Invisible Army . .	100.00
4 RA,Bracelet of Doomed Hero	100.00
5 RA,Menace of the Mammoth	
Robots	100.00
6 RA,I:Gas Gang	85.00
7 RA,V:Solar Brain	55.00
8 RA,Playground of Terror	55.00
9 RA,A:Billy	55.00
10 RA,A:Gas Gang	55.00
11 RA,The Floating Furies	50.00
12 RA,A:Missle Men	40.00
13 RA,I:Nameless	40.00
14 RA,A:Chemo	40.00

Metal Men #15 © DC Comics, Inc.

15 RA,V:B.O.L.T.S.	40.00
16 RA,Robots for Sale	40.00
17 JKu(c),RA,V:Bl.Widow Robot	40.00
18 JKu(c),RA	40.00
19 RA,V:Man-Horse of Hades . .	40.00
20 RA,V:Dr.Yes	40.00
21 RA,C:Batman & Robin,Flash	
Wonder Woman	25.00
22 RA,A:Chemo	25.00
23 RA,A:Sizzler	25.00
24 RA,V:Balloonman	25.00
25 RA,V:Chemo	25.00
26 RA,V:Metal Mods	25.00
27 RA,O:Metal Men,rtd	50.00
28 RA	25.00
29 RA,V:Robot Eater	25.00
30 RA,GK,in the Forbidden Zone	25.00
31 RA,GK	23.00
32 RA,Robot Amazon Blues . . .	18.00
33 MS,The Hunted Metal Men . .	18.00
34 MS	18.00
35 MS	18.00
36 MS,The Cruel Clowns	18.00
37 MS,To walk among Men	18.00
38 MS	18.00

39 MS,Beauty of the Beast	18.00
40 MS	18.00
41 MS	18.00
42 RA,reprint	10.00
43 RA,reprint	10.00
44 RA,reprint,V:Missile Men	10.00
45 WS	10.00
46 WS,V:Chemo	10.00
47 WS,V:Plutonium Man	10.00
48 WS,A:Eclipso	15.00
49 WS,A:Eclipso	15.00
50 WS,JSa	10.00
51 JSn,V:Vox	10.00
52 JSn,V:Brain Children	10.00
53 JA(c),V:Brain Children	10.00
54 JSn,A:Green Lantern	10.00
55 JSn,A:Green Lantern	10.00
56 JSn,V:Inheritor	10.00
[Limited Series] 1993–94	
1 DJu,BBr,Foil(c)	7.00
2 DJu,BBr,O:Metal Men	5.00
3 DJu,BBr,V:Missile Men	3.50
4 DJu,BBr,final issue	3.00

METAMORPHO
July-Aug., 1965
[Regular Series]
1 A:Kurt Vornok	100.00
2 Terror from the Telstar	60.00
3 Who stole the USA	60.00
4 V:Cha-Cha Chaves	40.00
5 V:Bulark	40.00
6	40.00
7 thru 9	@35.00
10 I:Element Girl	45.00
11 thru 17 March-April, 1968 .	@20.00
[Limited Series]	
1 GN,V:The Orb of Ra	1.75
2 GN,A:Metamorpho's Son	1.75
3 GN,V:Elemental Man	1.75
4 GN,final Issue	1.75

METROPOLIS S.C.U.
Nov. 1994
1 Special Police unit	1.50
2 Eco-terror in Metropolis	1.50
3 Superman	1.50
4 final issue	1.50

MILLENIUM
Jan., 1988
1 JSa,SEt, The Plan	1.75
2 JSa,SEt, The Chosen	1.75
3 JSa,SEt, Reagen/Manhunters .	1.75
4 JSa,SEt, Mark Shaw/Batman . .	1.75
5 JSa,SEt, The CHosen	1.75
6 JSa,SEt, Superman	1.75
7 JSa,SEt, Boster Gold	1.75
8 JSa,SEt,I:New Guardians	1.75

MILLENNIUM FEVER
1995–96
1 Young Love	2.50
2 Nightmares Worsen	2.50
3 Worst Nightmare	2.50
4	2.50

MISTER E
1991
1 (From Books of Magic)	1.75
2 A:The Shadower	1.75
3 A:The Shadower	1.75
4 A:Tim Hunter, Dr. Fate, Phantom	

Stranger, final issue	1.75

MISTER MIRACLE
1971–78
1 JK,I:Mr.Miracle	35.00
2 JK,I:Granny Goodness	20.00
3 JK,'Paraniod Pill'	11.00
4 JK,I:Barda	10.00
5 JK,I:Vermin Vundabar	10.00
6 JK,I:Female Furies	10.00
7 JK,V:Kanto	10.00
8 JK,V:Lump	10.00
9 JK,O:Mr.Miracle,C:Darkseid . . .	8.00
10 JK,A:Female Furies	6.00
11 JK,V:Doctor Bedlum	6.00
12 JK	6.00
13 JK	6.00
14 JK	6.00
15 JK,O:Shilo Norman	6.00

Mister Miracle #17
© DC Comics, Inc.

16 JK	6.00
17 JK	6.00
18 JK,W:Mr.Miracle & Barda	6.00
19 MR,NA,DG,TA,JRu,AM	6.00
20 MR	4.00
21 MR	4.00
22 MR	4.00
23 MG	4.00
24 MG,RH	4.00
25 MG,RH	4.00
Spec.#1 SR	2.50
[2nd Series] 1989–91	
1 IG	2.50
2 IG	1.75
3 IG,A:Highfather,Forever People	1.50
4 IG,A:The Dark,Forever People .	1.50
5 IG,V:TheDark,A:ForeverPeople	1.50
6 A:G.L. Gnort	1.25
7 A:Blue Beetle,Booster Gold . . .	1.25
8 RM,A:Blue Beetle,Booster Gold	1.25
9 I:Maxi-Man	1.25
10 V:Maxi-Man	1.25
11	1.25
12	1.25
13 Manga Khan Saga begins,	
A:L-Ron,A:Lobo	2.50
14 A:Lobo	2.00

DC COMICS

15 Manga Khan contd	1 25
16 MangaKhan cont.,JLA#39tie-in	1.25
17 On Apokolips,A:Darkseid	1.25
18 On Apokolips	1.25
19 Return to Earth, contd from JLA#42	1.25
20 IG,Oberon	1.25
21 Return of Shilo	1.25
22 New Mr.Miracle revealed	1.25
23 Secrets of the 2 Mr. Miracles revealed, A:Mother Box	1.25
24	1.25
25	1.25
26 Monster Party,pt.1	1.25
27 Monster Party,pt.2, A:Justice League	1.25
28 final issue	1.25

MISTER MIRACLE
1996

1 JK, new mythology	1.95
2 V:Justice League	1.95
2 How can Scott Free save Big Barda	1.95
3 accepts his powers	1.95
4 corruption throughout the cosmos	1.95
5 SCr	1.95
6 SCr	1.95
7 final issue	1.95

MR. DISTRICT ATTORNEY
Jan.–Feb., 1948

1 The Innocent Forger	750.00
2 The Richest Man In Prison	350.00
3 The Honest Convicts	250.00
4 The Merchant of Death	250.00
5 The Booby-Trap Killer	250.00
6 The D.A. Meets Scotland Yard	200.00
7 The People vs. Killer Kane	200.00
8 The Rise and Fall of 'Lucky' Lynn	200.00
9 The Case of the Living Counterfeit	200.00
10 The D.A. Takes a Vacation	150.00
11 The Game That Has No Winners	150.00
12 Fake Accident Racket	150.00
13 The Execution of Caesar Larsen	150.00
14 The Innocent Man In Murderers' Row	150.00
15 Prison Train	150.00
16 The Wire Tap Crimes	150.00
17 The Bachelor of Crime	150.00
18 The Case of the Twelve O'Clock Killer	150.00
19 The Four King's Of Crime	150.00
20 You Catch a Killer	150.00
21 I Was A Killer's Bodyguard	100.00
22 The Marksman of Crime	100.00
23 Diary of a Criminal	100.00
24 The Killer In The Iron Mask	100.00
25 I Hired My Killer	100.00
26 The Case of the Wanted Criminals	100.00
27 The Case of the Secret Six	100.00
28 Beware the Bogus Beggars	100.00
29 The Crimes of Mr. Jumbo	100.00
30 Man of a Thousand Faces	100.00
31 The Hot Money Gang	100.00
32 The Case o/t Bad Luck Clues	100.00
33 A Crime Is Born	100.00
34 The Amazing Crimes of Mr. X	100.00

35 This Crime For Hire	100.00
36 The Chameleon of Crime	100.00
37 Miss Miller's Big Case	100.00
38 The Puzzle Shop For Crime	100.00
39 Man Who Killed Daredevils	100.00
40 The Human Vultures	100.00
41 The Great Token Take	100.00
42 Super-Market Sleuth	100.00
43 Hotel Detective	100.00
44 S.S. Justice,B:Comics Code	75.00
45 Miss Miller, Widow	75.00
46 Mr. District Attorney, Public Defender	75.00
47 The Missing Persons Racket	75.00
48 Manhunt With the Mounties	75.00
49 The TV Dragnet	75.00
50 The Case of Frank Bragan, Little Shot	75.00
51 The Big Heist	75.00
52 Crooked Wheels of Fortune	75.00
53 The Courtroom Patrol	75.00
54 The Underworld Spy Squad	75.00
55 The Flying Saucer Mystery	75.00
56 The Underworld Oracle	75.00
57 The Underworld Employment Agency	75.00
58 The Great Bomb Scare	75.00
59 Great Underworld Spy Plot	75.00
60 The D.A.'s TV Rival	75.00
61 SMo(c),Architect of Crime	75.00
62 A-Bombs For Sale	75.00
63 The Flying Prison	75.00
64 SMo(c),The Underworld Treasure Hunt	75.00
65 SMo(c),World Wide Dragnet	75.00
66 SMo(c),The Secret of the D.A.'s Diary	75.00
67 Jan.–Feb., 1959	75.00

MR. PUNCH
HC DMc,NGa;Nightmarish

tale, 1994	24.95

MOBFIRE
1994–95

1 WaP,Gangsters in London	2.50
2 WaP	2.50
3 WaP,The Bocor	2.50
4 WaP,V:Bocor	2.50
5 WaP,Voice in My Head	2.50
6 WaP,Genetic Babies, final issue	2.50

MODESTY BLAISE

1 DG,V:Gabriel	4.95
2 DG,V:Gabriel	4.95
GN Spy Thriller	19.95

MOONSHADOW
Vertigo 1994–95

1 JMD(s),JMu,rep.	2.25
2 thru 4 JMD	@2.25
5 fully painted	2.25
6	2.25
7 F:Shady Lady	2.25
8 Rep. Search for Ira	2.25
9 JMD,JMu,A:Tittletat Twins	2.25
10 JMD,JMu,Interplanetary Prostitutes	2.25
11 JMu,Ira's life story	2.25
12 Rep. w/6pg new material	2.95

MORE FUN COMICS
(See: NEW FUN COMICS)

MOVIE COMICS
April, 1939

1 'Gunga Din'	2,700.00
2 Stagecoach	1,800.00
3 East Side of Heaven	1,400.00
4 Captain Fury,B:Oregon Trail	1,100.00
5 Man in the Iron Mask	1,100.00
6 Sept., 1939	1,400.00

MS. TREE QUARTERLY

1 MGr,A:Batman	3.50
2 A:Butcher	2.95
3 A:Butcher	2.95
4 'Paper Midnight'	3.95
5 Murder/Rape Investigation	3.95
6 Gothic House	3.95
7	3.95
8 CI,FMc,Ms Tree Pregnant(c), B.U. King Faraday	3.95
9 Child Kidnapped	3.95
10 V:International Mob	3.50

MUTT AND JEFF
1939

1	1,200.00
2	650.00
3	500.00
4 and 5	@450.00
6 thru 10	@200.00
11 thru 20	@125.00
21 thru 30	@85.00
31 thru 50	@60.00
51 thru 70	@40.00
71 thru 80	@35.00
81 thru 99	@30.00
100	35.00
101 thru 103	@30.00
104 thru 148	@20.00

MY GREATEST ADVENTURE
Jan.–Feb., 1955

1 LSt,I Was King Of Danger Island	1,200.00
2 My Million Dollar Dive	600.00
3 I Found Captain	

My Greatest Adventure #40
© DC Comics, Inc.

Kidd's Treasure 375.00
4 I Had A Date With Doom ... 375.00
5 I Escaped From Castle Morte 350.00
6 I Had To Spend A Million .. 350.00
7 I Was A Prisoner On Island X 325.00
8 The Day They Stole My Face 325.00
9 I Walked Through The Doors
   of Destiny 325.00
10 We Found A World Of
   Tiny Cavemen 325.00
11 LSt(c),My Friend, Madcap
   Manning 250.00
12 MMe(c),I Hunted Big Game
   in Outer Space 250.00
13 LSt(c),I Hunted Goliath
   The Robot 250.00
14 LSt,I Had the Midas
   Touch of Gold 250.00
15 JK, I Hunted the Worlds
   Wildest Animals 250.00
16 JK,I Died a Thousand Times 250.00
17 JK,I Doomed The World ... 250.00
18 JK(c),We Discovered The
   Edge of the World 250.00
19 I Caught Earth's
   Strangest Criminal 250.00
20 JK,I Was Big-Game
   on Neptune 250.00
21 JK,We Were Doomed By
   The Metal-Eating Monster .. 250.00
22 I Was Trapped In The
   Magic Mountains 200.00
23 I Was A Captive In
   Space Prison 200.00
24 NC(c),I Was The Robinson
   Crusoe of Space 200.00
25 I Led Earth's Strangest
   Safari! 200.00
26 NC(c),We Battled The
   Sand Creature 200.00
27 I Was the Earth's First Exile 200.00
28 I Stalked the Camouflage
   Creatures 250.00
29 I Tracked the
   Forbidden Powers 150.00
30 We Cruised Into the
   Supernatural! 150.00
31 I Was A Modern Hercules .. 100.00
32 We Were Trapped In A Freak
   Valley! 100.00
33 I Was Pursued by
   the Elements 100.00
34 DD,We Unleashed The Cloud
   Creatures 100.00
35 I Solved the Mystery of
   Volcano Valley 100.00
36 I Was Bewitched
   By Lady Doom 100.00
37 DD&SMo(c),I Hunted the
   Legendary Creatures! 100.00
38 DD&SMo(c),I Was the Slave
   of the Dream-Master 100.00
39 DD&SMo(c),We were Trapped
   in the Valley of no Return .. 100.00
40 We Battled the Storm Creature 100.00
41 DD&SMo(c),I Was Tried
   by a Robot Court 75.00
42 DD&SMo(c),My Brother
   Was a Robot 75.00
43 DD&SMo(c),I Fought the
   Sonar Creatures 75.00
44 DD&SMo(c),We Fought the
   Beasts of Petrified Island .. 75.00
45 DD&SMo(c),We Battled the
   Black Narwahl 75.00

46 DD&SMo(c),We Were Prisoners
   of the Sundial of Doom 75.00
47 We Became Partners of the
   Beast Brigade 75.00
48 DD&SMo(c),I Was Marooned
   On Earth 75.00
49 DD&SMo(c),I Was An Ally
   Of A Criminal Creature 75.00
50 DD&SMo(c),I Fought the
   Idol King 75.00
51 DD&SMo(c),We Unleashed
   the Demon of the Dungeon .. 70.00
52 DD&SMo(c),I Was A
   Stand-In For an Alien 70.00
53 DD&SMo(c),I, Creature Slayer 70.00
54 I Was Cursed With
   an Alien Pal 70.00
55 DD&SMo(c),I Beacame The
   Wonder-Man of Space 70.00
56 DD&SMo(c),My Brother-The
   Alien 70.00
57 DD&SMo(c),Don't Touch Me
   Or You'll Die 70.00
58 DD&SMo(c),ATh,I was Trapped
   in the Land of L'Oz 75.00
59 DD&SMo(c),Listen Earth-I
   Am Still Alive 75.00
60 DD&SMo(c),ATh,I Lived in
   Two Worlds 75.00
61 DD&SMo(c),ATh,I Battled For
   the Doom-Stone 75.00
62 DD&SMo(c),I Fought For
   An Alien Enemy 50.00
63 DD&SMo(c),We Braved the
   Trail of the Ancient Warrior .. 50.00
64 DD&SMo(c),They Crowned My
   Fiance Their King! 50.00
65 DD&SMo(c),I Lost the Life
   or Death Secret 50.00
66 DD&SMo(c),I Dueled with
   the Super Spirits 50.00
67 I Protected the Idols
   of Idoro! 50.00
68 DD&SMo(c),My Deadly Island
   of Space 50.00
69 DD&SMo(c),I Was A Courier
   From the Past 50.00
70 DD&SMo(c),We Tracked the
   Fabled Fish-Man! 50.00
71 We Dared to open the Door
   of Danger Dungeon 50.00
72 The Haunted Beach 50.00
73 I Defeiller Mountain 50.00
74 GC(c),We Were Challenged
   By The River Spirit 50.00
75 GC(c),Castaway Cave-Men
   of 1950 .... 50.00
76 MMe(c),We Battled the
   Micro-Monster 50.00
77 ATh,We Found the Super-
   Tribes of Tomorrow 55.00
78 Destination-'Dead Man's Alley' 50.00
79 Countdown in Dinosaur Valley 50.00
80 BP,I:Doom Patrol 400.00
81 BP,ATh,I:Dr. Janus 160.00
82 BP,F:Doom Patrol 150.00
83 BP,F:Doom Patrol 150.00
84 BP,V:General Immortus ... 150.00
85 BP,ATh,F:Doom Patrol 150.00

Becomes:

DOOM PATROL
March, 1964

86 BP,I:Brogherhood of Evil ... 125.00
87 BP,O:Negative Man 90.00
88 BP,O:Chief 80.00

89 BP,I:Animal-Veg.-MineralMan 80.00
90 BP,A:Brotherhood of Evil ... 80.00
91 BP,I:Manto, Gargvax 80.00
92 BP,I:Dr.Tyme, A:Mento 80.00
93 BP,A:Brotherhood of Evil ... 80.00
94 BP,I:Dr.Radich, The Claw ... 80.00
95 BP,A:Animal-Vegetable
   -Mineral Man 80.00
96 BP,A:General Immortus,
   Brotherhood of Evil 75.00
97 BP,A:General Immortus,
   Brotherhood of Evil 75.00
98 BP,I:Mr.103 .... 75.00
99 I:Beast Boy 80.00
100 BP,O:Beast Boy,Robotman 100.00
101 BP,A:Beast Boy 50.00
102 BP,A:Beast Boy,Challengers
    of the Unknown 45.00
103 BP,A:Beast Boy 45.00
104 BP,W:Elasti-Girl,Mento,
    C:JLA,Teen Titans 45.00
105 BP,A:Beast Boy 45.00
106 BP,O:Negative Man 45.00
107 BP,A:Beast Boy, I:Dr.Death . 45.00
108 BP,A:Brotherhood of Evil .. 45.00
109 BP,I:Mandred 45.00
110 BP,A:Garguax,Mandred,
    Brotherhood of Evil 40.00
111 BP,I:Zarox-13,A:Brotherhood
    of Evil 40.00
112 BP,O:Beast Boy,Madame
    Rouge 40.00
113 BP,A:Beast Boy,Mento 40.00
114 BP,A:Beast Boy 40.00
115 BP,A:Beast Boy 40.00
116 BP,A:Madame Rouge 40.00
117 BP,I:Black Vulture 40.00
118 BP,A:Beast Boy 40.00
119 BP,A:Madam Rouge 40.00
120 I:Wrecker 40.00
121 JO,D:Doom Patrol 100.00
122 rep.Doom Patrol #89 ..... 5.00
123 rep.Doom Patrol #95 ..... 5.00
124 rep.Doom Patrol #90 ..... 5.00

[2nd Series]
See: DOOM PATROL

MY NAME IS CHAOS
1992

1 JRy,Song Laid Waste to Earth . 4.95
2 JRy,Colonization of Mars 4.95
3 JRy,Search for Eternal Beings . 4.95
4 JRy,final issue 4.95

MY NAME IS HOLOCAUST
Milestone 1995
[Mini-Series]

1 F:Holocaust (Blood Syndicate) . 1.75
2 V:Cantano 1.75
3 A:Blood Syndicate 1.75

MYSTERY IN SPACE
April-May, 1951

1 CI&FrG(c),FF,B:Knights of the
   Galaxy,Nine Worlds to
   Conquer 2,800.00
2 CI(c),MA,A:Knights of the
   Galaxy, Jesse James-
   Highwayman of Space ... 1,100.00
3 CI(c),A:Knights of the
   Galaxy, Duel of the Planets . 850.00
4 CI(c),S&K,MA,A:Knights of the
   Galaxy, Master of Doom ... 750.00
5 CI(c),A:Knights of the Galaxy,

DC COMICS

Mystery in Space #28
© *DC Comics, Inc.*

Outcast of the Lost World . . 750.00
6 CI(c),A:Knights of the Galaxy,
  The Day the World Melted . 550.00
7 GK(c),ATh,A:Knights of the Galaxy,
  Challenge o/t Robot Knight . 550.00
8 MA,It's a Women's World . . 550.00
9 MA(c),The Seven Wonders
  of Space 550.00
10 MA(c),The Last Time I
  Saw Earth 550.00
11 GK(c),Unknown Spaceman . 400.00
12 MA,The Sword in the Sky . 400.00
13 MA(c),MD,Signboard
  in Space 400.00
14 MA,GK(c),Hollywood
  in Space 400.00
15 MA(c),Doom from Station X 400.00
16 MA(c),Honeymoon in Space 400.00
17 MA(c),The Last Mile of Space 400.00
18 MA(c),GK,Chain Gang
  of Space 400.00
19 MA(c),The Great
  Space-Train Robbery 375.00
20 MA(c),The Man in the
  Martian Mask 350.00
21 MA(c),Interplanetary
  Merry- Go-Round 350.00
22 MA(c),The Square Earth . . . 350.00
23 MA(c),Monkey-Rocket
  to Mars 350.00
24 MA(c),A:Space Cabby,
  Hitchhiker of Space 350.00
25 MA(c),Station Mars on the Air 325.00
26 GK(c),Earth is the Target . . 325.00
27 The Human Fishbowl 325.00
28 The Radio Planet 325.00
29 GK(c),Space-Enemy
  Number One 325.00
30 GK(c),The Impossible
  World Named Earth 325.00
31 GK(c),The Day the Earth
  Split in Two 300.00
32 GK(c),Riddle of the
  Vanishing Earthmen 300.00
33 The Wooden World War . . . 300.00
34 GK(c),The Man Who
  Moved the World 300.00

35 The Counterfeit Earth 300.00
36 GK(c),Secret of the
  Moon Sphinx 300.00
37 GK(c),Secret of the
  Masked Martians 300.00
38 GK(c),The Canals of Earth . 300.00
39 GK(c),Sorcerers of Space . . 300.00
40 GK(c),Riddle of the
  Runaway Earth 300.00
41 GK(c),The Miser of Space . 250.00
42 GK(c),The Secret of the
  Skyscraper Spaceship 250.00
43 GK(c),Invaders From the
  Space Satellites 250.00
44 GK(c),Amazing Space Flight
  of North America 250.00
45 GK(c),MA,Flying Saucers
  Over Mars 250.00
46 GK(c),MA,Mystery of the
  Moon Sniper 250.00
47 GK(c),MA,Interplanetary Tug
  of War 250.00
48 GK(c),MA,Secret of the
  Scarecrow World 250.00
49 GK(c),The Sky-High Man . . 250.00
50 GK(c),The Runaway
  Space-Train 250.00
51 GK(c),MA,Battle of the
  Moon Monsters 250.00
52 GK(c),MSy,Mirror Menace
  of Mars 250.00
53 GK(c),B:Adam Strange stories,
  Menace o/t Robot Raiders 1,700.00
54 GK(c),Invaders of the
  Underground World 400.00
55 GK(c),The Beast From
  the Runaway World 300.00
56 GK(c),The Menace of
  the Super-Atom 200.00
57 GK(c),Mystery of the
  Giant Footsteps 200.00
58 GK(c),Chariot in the Sky . 200.00
59 GK(c),The Duel of the
  Two Adam Stranges 200.00
60 GK(c),The Attack of the
  Tentacle World 200.00
61 CI&MA(c),Threat of the
  Tornado Tyrant 150.00
62 CI&MA(c),The Beast with
  the Sizzling Blue Eyes 150.00
63 The Weapon that
  Swallowed Men 150.00
64 The Radioactive Menace . . 150.00
65 Mechanical Masters of Rann 150.00
66 Space-Island of Peril 150.00
67 Challenge of the
  Giant Fireflies 150.00
68 CI&MA(c),Fadeaway Doom . 150.00
69 CI&MA(c),Menace of the
  Aqua-Ray Weapon 150.00
70 CI&MA(c),Vengeance of
  the Dust Devil 150.00
71 CI&MA(c),The Challenge of
  the Crystal Conquerors 150.00
72 The Multiple Menace Weapon 100.00
73 CI&MA(c),The Invisible
  Invaders of Rann 100.00
74 CI&MA(c),The Spaceman
  Who Fought Himself 100.00
75 CI&MA(c),The Planet That
  Came to a Standstill 225.00
76 CI&MA(c),Challenge of
  the Rival Starman 100.00
77 CI&MA(c),Ray-Gun in the Sky 100.00
78 CI&MA(c),Shadow People

Mystery in Space #51
© *DC Comics, Inc.*

  of the Eclipse 100.00
79 CI&MA(c),The Metal
  Conqueror of Rann 100.00
80 CI&MA(c),The Deadly
  Shadows of Adam Strange . 100.00
81 CI&MA(c),The Cloud-Creature
  That Menaced Two Worlds . . 75.00
82 CI&MA(c),World War on
  Earth and Rann 75.00
83 CI&MA(c),The Emotion-Master
  of Space 75.00
84 CI&MA(c),The Powerless
  Weapons of Adam Strange . . 75.00
85 CI&MA(c),Riddle of the
  Runaway Rockets 75.00
86 CI&MA(c),Attack of the
  Underworld Giants 75.00
87 MA(c),The Super-Brain of
  Adam Strange,B:Hawkman . 200.00
88 CI&MA(c),The Robot Wraith
  of Rann 175.00
89 MA(c),Siren o/t Space Ark . 175.00
90 CI&MA(c),Planets and
  Peril, E:Hawkman 175.00
91 CI&MA(c),Puzzle of
  the Perilous Prisons 35.00
92 DD&SMo(c),The Alien Invasion
  From Earth,B:Space Ranger . 40.00
93 DD&SMo(c),The Convict
  Twins of Space 40.00
94 DD&SMo(c),The Adam
  Strange Story 40.00
95 The Hydra-Head From
  Outer Space 40.00
96 The Coins That Doomed
  Two Planets 40.00
97 The Day Adam Strange
  Vanished 40.00
98 The Wizard of the Cosmos . . 40.00
99 DD&SMo(c),The World-
  Destroyer From Space 40.00
100 DD&SMo(c),GK,The Death
  of Alanna 40.00
101 GK(c),The Valley of
  1,000 Dooms 40.00
102 GK,The Robot World of Rann 40.00
103 The Billion-Dollar Time-

DC COMICS

Capsule(Space Ranger),I:Ultra
the Multi-Agent 40.00
104 thru 109 . . . . @15.00
110 Sept. 1966 . . . . 15.00
111 JAp,SD,MR,DSp,Sept. 1980 15.00
112 JAp,TS,JKu(c) 15.00
113 JKu(c),MGo 15.00
114 JKu(c),JCr,SD,DSp 15.00
115 JKu(c),SD,GT,BB 15.00
116 JSn(c),JCr,SD 15.00
117 DN,GT,March, 1981 . . . . . . 15.00

MYSTERY PLAY
Vertigo
HC GMo(s),JMu 19.95

MYTHOS:
THE FINAL TOUR
DC/Vertigo Oct. 1996
1 JNR(s),GyA,PrG,F:Rock Star
Adam Case 5.95
2 JNR(s),PSj,F:Rock Star Adam
Case 5.95
3 JNR(s), finale 5.95

NATHANIEL DUSK
Feb., 1984
1 GC(p) 1.50
2 GC(p) 1.25
3 GC(p) 1.25
4 GC(p), May 1984 . . . . 1.25

NATHANIEL DUSK II
Oct., 1985
1 thru 4 GC,Jan., 1986 . . . . . . @2.00

NAZZ, THE
1990–91
1 Michael'sBook 5.50
2 Johnny'sBook 4.95
3 Search for Michael Nazareth . . 4.95
4 V:Retaliators,final issue 4.95

NEW ADVENTURES
OF SUPERBOY
(See: SUPERBOY)

NEW BOOK OF COMICS
1937
1 Dr.Occult 11,000.00
2 Dr.Occult 7,000.00

NEW COMICS
1935
1 . . . . 15,000.00
2 . . . . 5,500.00
3 thru 6 . . . . @4,000.00
7 thru 11 . . . . @2,500.00
Becomes:

NEW ADVENTURE
COMICS
Jan., 1937
12 S&S 3,000.00
13 thru 20 . . . . @2,600.00
21 . . . . 2,600.00
22 thru 31 . . . . @2,200.00
Becomes:
ADVENTURE COMICS

NEW FUN COMICS
Feb., 1935
1 B:Oswald the Rabbit,
Jack Woods 40,000.00
2 . . . . 17,000.00
3 . . . . 8,000.00
4 . . . . 8,000.00
5 . . . . 8,000.00
6 S&S,B:Dr.Occult,
Henri Duval 20,000.00
Becomes:

MORE FUN COMICS
7 S&S,WK 5,200.00
8 S&S,WK 5,000.00
9 S&S,E:Henri Duval 6,000.00
10 S&S 3,500.00
11 S&S,B:Calling all Girls . . . 3,200.00
12 S&S 2,800.00
13 S&S 2,800.00
14 S&S,Color,Dr.Occult 13,000.00
15 S&S 4,800.00
16 S&S,Christmas(c) 4,800.00
17 S&S 4,500.00
18 S&S 2,000.00
19 S&S 2,000.00
20 HcK,S&S 2,000.00
21 S&S 1,900.00
22 S&S 1,900.00
23 S&S 1,900.00
24 S&S 1,900.00
25 S&S 1,700.00
26 S&S 1,700.00
27 S&S 1,700.00
28 S&S 1,700.00
29 S&S 1,700.00
30 S&S 1,700.00
31 S&S 1,700.00
32 S&S,E:Dr. Occult 1,700.00
33 . . . . 1,700.00
34 . . . . 1,700.00
35 . . . . 1,700.00
36 B:Masked Ranger 1,700.00
37 thru 40 . . . . @1,700.00
41 E:Masked Ranger 1,200.00
42 thru 50 . . . . @1,200.00
51 I:The Spectre 4,500.00
52 O:The Spectre,pt.1,
E:Wing Brady 50,000.00
53 O:The Spectre,pt.2,
B:Capt.Desmo 35,000.00
54 E:King Carter,Spectre(c) . . 9,000.00
55 I:Dr.Fate,E:Bulldog Martin,
Spectre(c) 12,000.00
56 B:Congo Bill,Dr.Fate(c) . . . 4,500.00
57 Spectre(c) 2,800.00
58 Spectre(c) 2,800.00
59 A:Spectre 2,500.00
60 Spectre(c) 2,800.00
61 Spectre(c) 2,200.00
62 Spectre(c) 2,200.00
63 Spectre(c),E:St.Bob Neal . 2,200.00
64 Spectre(c),B:Lance Larkin . 2,200.00
65 Spectre(c) 2,200.00
66 Spectre(c) 2,200.00
67 Spectre(c),O:Dr. Fate,
E:Congo Bill,Biff Bronson . 6,500.00
68 Dr.Fate(c),B:Clip Carson . 1,800.00
69 Dr.Fate(c) 1,800.00
70 Dr.Fate(c),E:Lance Larkin . 1,800.00
71 Dr.Fate(c),I:Johnny Quick . 5,000.00
72 Dr. Fate has Smaller Helmet,
E:Sgt. Carey,Sgt.O'Malley . 1,500.00
73 Dr.Fate(c),I:Aquaman,Green
Arrow,Speedy 12,000.00

More Fun Comics #41
© DC Comics, Inc.

74 Dr.Fate(c),A:Aquaman . . . 2,000.00
75 Dr.Fate(c) 1,700.00
76 Dr.Fate(c),MMe,E:Clip Carson,
B:Johnny Quick 1,700.00
77 MMe,Green Arrow(c) 1,700.00
78 MMe,Green Arrow(c) 1,700.00
79 MMe,Green Arrow(c) 1,700.00
80 MMe,Green Arrow(c) 1,700.00
81 MMe,Green Arrow(c) 1,000.00
82 MMe,Green Arrow(c) 1,000.00
83 MMe,Green Arrow(c) 1,000.00
84 MMe,Green Arrow(c) 1,000.00
85 MMe,Green Arrow(c) 1,000.00
86 MMe 1,000.00
87 MMe,E:Radio Squad 1,000.00
88 MMe,Green Arrow(c) 1,000.00
89 MMe,O:Gr.Arrow&Speedy . 1,200.00
90 MMe,Green Arrow(c) 800.00
91 MMe,Green Arrow(c) 750.00
92 MMe,Green Arrow(c) 750.00
93 MMe,B:Dover & Clover 750.00
94 MMe,Green Arrow(c) 750.00
95 MMe,Green Arrow(c) 750.00
96 MMe,Green Arrow(c) 750.00
97 MMe,JKu,E:Johnny Quick . 750.00
98 E:Dr. Fate 750.00
99 Green Arrow(c) 750.00
100 Anniversary Issue 1,000.00
101 O&I:Superboy,
E:The Spectre 7,500.00
102 A:Superboy 1,000.00
103 A:Superboy 800.00
104 Superboy(c) 650.00
105 Superboy(c) 650.00
106 . . . . 650.00
107 E:Superboy 650.00
108 A:Genius Jones,'Genius
Meets Genius' 150.00
109 A:Genius Jones, The
Disappearing Deposits 150.00
110 A:Genius Jones, Birds,
Brains and Burglary 150.00
111 A:Genius Jones, Jeepers
Creepers 150.00
112 A:Genius Jones, The
Tell-Tale Tornado 150.00
113 A:Genius Jones, Clocks

and Shocks 150.00
114 A:Genius Jones, The
  Milky Way 150.00
115 A:Genius Jones,Foolish
  Questions 150.00
116 A:Genius Jones,Palette
  For Plunder 150.00
117 A:Genius Jones,Battle of
  the Pretzel Benders 150.00
118 A:Genius Jones,The
  Sinister Siren 150.00
119 A:Genius Jones,A
  Perpetual Jackpot 150.00
120 A:Genius Jones,The Man
  in the Moon 150.00
121 A:Genius Jones,The
  Mayor Goes Haywire 150.00
122 A:Genius Jones,When Thug-
  Hood Was In Floor 125.00
123 A:Genius Jones,Hi Diddle
  Diddle, the Cat and the Fiddle 125.00
124 A:Genius Jones,
  The Zany Zoo 125.00
125 Genius Jones,
  Impossible But True 575.00
126 A:Genius Jones,The Case
  of the Gravy Spots 125.00
127 Nov.–Dec., 1947 . . . . . . 225.00

NEW GODS, THE
Feb.–March, 1971

1 JK,I:Orion 35.00
2 JK 17.00
3 JK 14.00
4 JK,O:Manhunter, rep. 14.00
5 JK,I:Fastbak & Black Racer . . 14.00
6 JK 14.00
7 JK,O:Orion 14.00
8 JK 14.00
9 JK,I:Forager 14.00
10 JK 14.00
11 JK 14.00
12 DN,DA,R:New Gods 5.00
13 DN,DA 5.00
14 DN,DA 5.00
15 RB,BMc 5.00
16 DN,DA 5.00
17 DN,DA 5.00
18 DN,DA 5.00
19 DN,DA 4.00

NEW GODS
(Reprints) 1984

1 JK reprint 2.25
2 JK reprint 2.00
3 JK reprint 2.00
4 JK reprint 2.00
5 JK reprint 2.00
6 JK rep.+NewMaterial 2.00

NEW GODS
[2nd Series] 1989

1 From Cosmic Odyssey 2.00
2 A:Orion of New Genesis 1.50
3 A:Orion 1.50
4 Renegade Apokolyptian Insect
  Colony 1.50
5 Orion vs. Forager 1.50
6 A:Eve Donner, Darkseid 1.50
7 Bloodline #1 . . . . 1.50
8 Bloodline #2 . . . . 1.50
9 Bloodline #3 . . . . 1.50
10 Bloodline #4 . . . . 1.50
11 Bloodline #5 . . . . 1.50

New Gods #3 © DC Comics, Inc.

12 Bloodlines #6 . . . . 1.50
13 Back on Earth 1.50
14 I:Reflektor 1.50
15 V:Serial Killer 1.50
16 A:Fastbak & Metron 1.50
17 A:Darkseid, Metron 1.50
18 A:YugaKhan,Darkseid,
  Moniters 1.50
19 V:Yuga Khan 1.50
20 Darkseid Dethroned,
  V:Yuga Khan 1.50
21 A:Orion 1.50
22 A:Metron 1.50
23 A:Forever People 1.50
24 A:Forever People 1.50
25 The Pact #1,R:Infinity Man . . . 1.50
26 The Pact #2 . . . . 1.50
27 Asault on Apokolips,Pact#3 . . 1.50
28 Pact #4, final issue 1.50

[3rd Series] 1995–97

1 F:Orion vs. Darkseid 1.95
2 RaP,Underworld Unleashed tie-in 1.95
3 RaP,Darkseid destroyed 1.95
4 RaP,F:Lightray 1.95
5 RaP,F:Orion 1.95
6 . . . . 1.95
7 RaP,R:Darkseid 1.95
8 RaP,DZ,F:Highfather,Darkseid . 1.95
9 thru 11 . . . . @1.95
12 JBy,BWi,F:Metron 99
13 JBy,BWi,Orion reappears
  on Earth 1.95
14 JBy,BWi,A:Forever People,
  Lightray 1.95

NEW GUARDIANS
1988–89

1 JSon,from Millenium series . . . 2.50
2 JSon,Colombian Drug Cartel . . 1.75
3 JSon,in South Africa,
  V:Janwillem's Army 1.25
4 JSon,V:Neo-Nazi Skinheads
  in California 1.25
5 JSon,Tegra Kidnapped 1.25
6 JSon, In China, Invasion x-over 1.25
7 JSon, Guardians Return Home 1.25
8 JSon, V:Janwillem 1.25

9 JSon, A:Tome Kalmaku,
  V:Janwillem 1.25
10 JSon, A:Tome Kalmaku 1.25
11 PB,Janwillem's secret 1.25
12 PB,New Guardians Future
  revealed, final issue 1.25

*New Teen Titans #19
© DC Comics, Inc.*

NEW TEEN TITANS
Nov., 1980

1 GP,RT,V:Gordanians (see DC
  Comics Presents #26 . . . . . . 14.00
2 GP,RT,I:Deathstroke the
  Terminator, I&D:Ravager . . . 14.00
3 GP,I:Fearsome Five 4.00
4 GP,RT,A:JLA,O:Starfire 5.00
5 CS,RT,O:Raven,I:Trigon 5.00
6 GP,V:Trigon,O:Raven 3.00
7 GP,RT,O:Cyborg 4.00
8 GP,RT,A Day in the Life 3.00
9 GP,RT,A:Terminator,
  V:Puppeteer 4.00
10 GP,RT,A:Terminator 8.00
11 GP,RT,V:Hyperion 3.00
12 GP,RT,V:Titans of Myth 3.00
13 GP,RT,R:Robotman 3.00
14 GP,RT,I:New Brotherhood of
  Evil,V:Zahl and Rouge 3.00
15 GP,RT,D:Madame Rouge 3.00
16 GP,RT,I:Captain Carrot 3.00
17 GP,RT,I:Frances Kane 3.00
18 GP,RT,A:Orig.Starfire 3.00
19 GP,RT,A:Hawkman 3.00
20 GP,RT,V:Disruptor 3.00
21 GP,RT,GC,I:Brother Blood,
  Night Force 3.00
22 GP,RT,V:Brother Blood 2.50
23 GP,RT,I:Blackfire 2.50
24 GP,RT,A:Omega Men,I:X-hal . 2.50
25 GP,RT,A:Omega Men 2.50
26 GP,RT,I:Terra,Runaway #1 . . . 2.50
27 GP,RT,A:Speedy,Runaway #2 2.50
28 GP,RT,V:Terra 3.00
29 GP,RT,V:Broth.of Evil 2.00
30 GP,RT,V:Broth.of Evil,J:Terra . 2.00
31 GP,RT,V:Broth.of Evil 1.50
32 GP,RT,I:Thunder & Lightning . 1.50

DC COMICS

33 GP,I:Trident 1.50	
34 GP,V:The Terminator 3.00	
35 KP,RT,V:Mark Wright 1.50	
36 KP,RT,A:Thunder & Lightning . 1.50	
37 GP,RT,A:Batman/Outsiders(x-over	
BATO#5),V:Fearsome Five . . . 2.00	
38 GP,O:Wonder Girl 1.50	
39 GP,Grayson quits as Robin . . 5.00	
40 GP,A:Brother Blood 1.50	
Ann.#1 GP,RT,Blackfire 3.50	
Ann.#2 GP,I:Vigilante 3.00	
Ann.#3 GP,DG,D:Terra,A:Deathstroke	
V:The H.I.V.E. 3.50	
Ann.#4 rep.Direct Ann.#1 . . . . . . 1.25	
TPB Judas Contract rep.#39-#44,	
Ann.#3,new GP(c) 14.95	

[Special Issues]

Keebler:GP,DG,Drugs 2.50	
Beverage:Drugs,RA 2.50	
IBM:Drugs 3.00	

Becomes:

TALES OF THE TEEN TITANS
1984–88

41 GP,A:Brother Blood 2.00	
42 GP,DG,V:Deathstroke 5.00	
43 GP,DG,V:Deathstroke 5.00	
44 GP,DG,I:Nightwing,O:Deathstroke	
Joe Wilson becomes Jericho . . 8.00	
45 GP,A:Aqualad,V:The H.I.V.E. . 2.00	
46 GP,A:Aqualad,V:The H.I.V.E. . 2.00	
47 GP,A:Aqualad,V:The H.I.V.E. . 2.00	
48 SR,V:The Recombatants 2.00	
49 GP,CI,V:Dr.Light,A:Flash 2.00	
50 GP/DG W:Wonder Girl &	
Terry Long,C:Batman,	
Wonder Woman 2.50	
51 RB,A:Cheshire 2.00	
52 RB,A:Cheshire 2.00	
53 RB,I:Ariel,A:Terminator 2.50	
54 RB,A:Terminator 2.50	
55 A:Terminator 2.50	
56 A:Fearsome Five 1.75	
57 A:Fearsome Five 1.75	
58 E:MWn(s),A:Fearsome Five . . 1.75	
59 rep. DC presennts #26 . . . . . . 1.50	
60 thru 91 rep. . . . . @1.50	

[Limited Series]

1 GP,O:Cyborg 2.00	
2 GP,O:Raven 2.00	
3 GD,O:Changling 2.00	
4 GP/EC,O:Starfire 2.00	

NEW TEEN TITANS
[Direct sales series]
Aug., 1984

1 B:MWn(s),GP,L:Raven 4.00	
2 GP,D:Azareth,A:Trigon 3.00	
3 GP,V:Raven 3.00	
4 GP,V:Trigon,Raven 3.00	
5 GP,D:Trigon,Raven disappears 3.00	
6 GP,A:Superman,Batman 2.50	
7 JL,V:Titans of Myth 2.50	
8 JL,V:Titans of Myth 2.50	
9 JL,V:Titans of Myth,I:Kole . . . 2.50	
10 JL,O:Kole 2.50	
11 JL,O:Kole 2.50	
12 JL,Ghost story 2.50	
13 EB,Crisis 2.25	
14 EB,Crisis 2.25	
15 EB,A:Raven 2.25	
16 EB,A:OmegaMen 2.25	
17 EB,V:Blackfire 2.25	

18 E:MWn(s),EB,V:Blackfire 2.25	
19 EB,V:Mento 2.25	
20 GP(c),EB,V:Cheshire,J.Todd . 2.25	
21 GP(c),EB,V:Cheshire,J.Todd . 2.25	
22 GP(c),EB,V:Blackfire,Mento,	
Brother Blood 2.25	
23 GP(c),V:Blackfire 2.25	
24 CB,V:Hybrid 2.25	
25 EB,RT,V:Hybrid,Mento,A:Flash 2.25	
26 KGa,V:Mento 2.25	
27 KGa,Church of Br.Blood 2.00	
28 EB,RT,V:BrotherBlood,A:Flash 2.00	
29 EB,RT,V:Brother Blood,	
A:Flash,Robin 2.00	
30 EB,Batman,Superman 2.25	
31 EB,RT,V:Brother Blood,A:Flash	
Batman,Robin,Gr.Lantern Corps	
Superman 2.00	
32 EB,RT,Murder Weekend 2.00	
33 EB,V:Terrorists 2.00	
34 EB,RT,V:Mento,Hybrid 2.00	
35 PB,RT,V:Arthur & Eve 2.00	
36 EB,RT,I:Wildebeest 2.50	
37 EB,RT,V:Wildebeest 2.00	
38 EB,RT,A:Infinity 2.00	
39 EB,RT,F:Raven 2.00	
40 EB,RT,V:Gentleman Ghost . . . 2.00	
41 EB,V:Wildebeest,A:Puppeteer,	
Trident,Wildebeest 2.00	
42 EB,RT,V:Puppeteer,Gizmo,	
Trident,Wildebeest 2.00	
43 CS,RT,V:Phobia 2.00	
44 RT,V:Godiva 2.00	
45 EB,RT,A:Dial H for Hero 2.00	
46 EB,RT,A:Dial H for Hero 2.00	
47 O:Titans,C:Wildebeest 2.00	
48 EB,RT,A:Red Star 2.00	
49 EB,RT,A:Red Star 2.00	
Ann.#1 A:Superman,V:Brainiac . . 2.50	
Ann.#2 JBy,JL,O:Brother Blood . . 3.00	
Ann.#3 I:Danny Chase 2.50	
Ann.#4 V:Godiva 2.50	

Becomes:

NEW TITANS
1988–96

50 B:MWn(s),GP,BMc,B:Who is	
Wonder Girl? 4.00	
51 GP,BMc 3.00	
52 GP,BMc 3.00	
53 GP,RT 3.00	
54 GP,RT,E:Who is Wonder Girl? 3.00	
55 GP,RT,I:Troia 3.00	
56 MBr,RT,Tale of Middle Titans . 2.50	
57 GP,BMc,V:Wildebeast 2.50	
58 GP,TG,BMc,V:Wildebeast 2.50	
59 GP,TG,BMc,V:Wildebeast 2.50	
60 GP,TG,BMc,3rd A:Tim Drake	
(Face Revealed),Batman 5.00	
61 GP,TG,BMc,A:Tim Drake,	
Batman 5.00	
62 TG,AV,A:Deathstroke 3.00	
63 TG,AV,A:Deathstroke 3.00	
64 TG,AV,A:Deathstroke 3.00	
65 TG,AV,A:Deathstroke,Tim Drake,	
Batman 3.00	
66 TG,AV,V:Eric Forrester 2.50	
67 TG,AV,V:Eric Forrester 2.50	
68 SE,V:Royal Flush Gang 2.50	
69 SE,V:Royal Flush Gang 2.50	
70 SE,A:Deathstroke 3.00	
71 TG,AV,B:Deathstroke,	
B:Titans Hunt 5.00	
72 TG,AV,D:Golden Eagle 4.00	
73 TG,AV,I:Phantasm 4.00	
74 TG,AV,I:Pantha 3.00	

75 TG,AV,IR:Jericho/Wildebeest . 3.00	
76 TG,AV,V:Wildebeests 2.50	
77 TG,AV,A:Red Star,N:Cyborg . . 2.50	
78 TG,AV,V:Cyborg 2.50	
79 TG,AV,I:Team Titans 3.00	
80 KGa,PC,A:Team Titans 2.50	
81 CS,AV,War of the Gods 2.50	
82 TG,AV,V:Wildebeests 2.50	
83 TG,AV,D:Jericho 3.00	
84 TG,AV,E:Titans Hunt 2.50	
85 TG,AV,I:Baby Wildebeest 2.50	
86 CS,AV,E:Deathstroke. 2.50	
87 TG,AV,A:Team Titans 2.50	
88 TG,AV,CS,V:Team Titans 2.50	
89 JBr,I:Lord Chaos 2.50	
90 TG,AV,Total Chaos#2,A:Team	
Titans,D'stroke,V:Lord Chaos . 2.00	
91 TG,AV,Total Chaos#5,A:Team	
Titans,D'stroke,V:Lord Chaos . 2.00	
92 E:MWn(s),TG,AV,Total Chaos#8,	
A:Team Titans,V:Lord Chaos . 2.00	
93 TG,AV,Titans Sell-Out#3 . . . . . 2.00	
94 PJ,F:Red Star & Cyborg 2.00	

New Titans #82 © DC Comics, Inc.

95 PJ,Red Star gains new powers 2.00	
96 PJ,I:Solar Flare,	
V:Konstantine 2.00	
97 TG,AV,B:The Darkening,R:Speedy	
V:Brotherhood of Evil 2.00	
98 TG,AV,V:Brotherhood of Evil . . 2.00	
99 TG,AV,I:Arsenal (Speedy) 2.00	
100 TG,AV,W:Nightwing&Starfire,	
V:Deathwing,Raven,A:Flash,Team	
Titans,Hologram(c) 4.00	
101 AV(i),L:Nightwing 2.00	
102 AV(i),A:Prester John 2.00	
103 AV(i),V:Bro. of Evil 2.00	
104 Terminus #1 . . . . 2.00	
105 Terminus #2 . . . . 2.00	
106 Terminus #3 . . . . 2.00	
107 Terminus #4 . . . . 2.00	
108 A:Supergirl,Flash 2.00	
109 F:Starfire 2.00	
110 A:Flash,Serg.Steele 2.00	
111 A:Checkmate 2.00	
112 A:Checkmate 2.00	
113 F:Nightwing 2.25	
114 L:Starfire, Nightwing,Panthra,	
Wildebeest 1.95	

DC COMICS

115 A:Trigon 1.95
116 Changling 1.95
117 V:Psimon 1.95
118 V:Raven + Brotherhood 1.95
119 Suffer the Children,pt.1 . . . . . 1.95
120 Forever Evil,pt.2 . . . . 1.95
121 Forever Evil,pt.3 . . . . 1.95
122 Crimelord/Syndicate War,pt.2
   J:Supergirl 2.25
123 MWn(s),RRa,O:Minion 2.25
124 The Siege of Zi Charan 2.25
125 The Siege of Zi Charan 3.00
126 Meltdown,pt.1 . . . . 2.25
127 MWn,Meltdown, cont. 2.25
128 MWn,Meltdown, cont. 2.25
129 MWn,Meltdown, cont. 2.25
130 MWn,Meltdown,final issue . . . 2.25
Ann.#5 V:Children of the Sun . . . 3.00
Ann.#6 CS,F:Starfire 3.00
Ann.#7 Armageddon 2001,I:Future
   Teen Titans 4.00
Ann.#8 PJ,Eclipso,V:Deathstroke . 3.75
Ann.#9 Bloodlines#5,I:Anima 3.75
Ann.#10 Elseworlds story 3.75
Ann.#11 Year One Annual 3.95
#0 Spec. Zero Hour,new team . . . 1.95

NEW TITANS SELL-OUT SPECIAL
1 SE,AV,AH,I:Teeny Titans,
   w/Nightwing poster 3.75

NEW YORK WORLD'S FAIR
1 1939 . . . . 24,000.00
2 1940 . . . . 14,000.00

NIGHT FORCE
Aug., 1982
1 GC,1:Night Force 1.25
2 thru 13 GC . . . . @1.25
14 GC,Sept.,1983 . . . . 1.25

NIGHT FORCE
Oct. 1996
1 MWn(s),BA,Baron Winters leads 2.25
2 MWn(s) 2.25
3 MWn(s) 2.25
4 MWn(s),EB,"Hell Seems a
   Heaven" 2.25
5 MWn(s),Low,SMa,"Dreamers of
   Dreams" pt.1 . . . . 2.25
6 MWn(s),Low,SMa,"Dreamers of
   Dreams" pt.2 . . . . 2.25
7 MWn(s),Low,SMa,"Dreamers of
   Dreams" pt.3 . . . . 2.25
8 MWn(s),"Convergence," x-over 2.25
9 MWn(s),Low,Sma,"The Eleventh
   Man" pt.1 (of 3) 2.25
10 MWn(s),"Eleventh Man" pt.2 . 2.50

NIGHTWING
1995
1 R:Nightwing 3.50
2 N:Nightwing 3.00
3 visit to Kravia (of 4) 3.00
4 conclusion 3.00

NIGHTWING
Aug. 1996
1 CDi(s),SMc,KIS,Nightwing goes
   to Blühaven 4.00
2 CDi(s),SMc,KIS,V:smugglers . . 2.50

---

3 CDi(s),SMc,KIS,run-down bank
   "held up" 2.25
4 CDi(s),SMc,KIS,V:Lady Vick . . 2.25
5 CDi(s),SMc,KIS, ... 2.25
6 CDi(s),SMc,KIS,A:Tim Drake . . 2.25
7 CDi(s),SMc,KIS,"Rough Justice" 2.25
8 CDi(s),SMc,KIS,V: the kingpin
   of Blühaven 1.95
9 CDi(s),SMc,KIS,kidnapping, pt.1 1.95
10 CDi(s),SMc,KIS,nightmare
   or dream? 1.95
11 CDi(s),SMc,V:Soames,
   Blockbuster 1.95
12 CDi(s),SMc,Mutt 1.95
Ann.#1 Pulp Heroes (Romance) . 3.95
TPB The Ties That Bind 12.95

NIGHTWING: ALFRED'S RETURN
1 . . . . 3.50

NUTSY SQUIRREL
Sept.–Oct., 1954
61 SM 40.00
62 thru 71 . . . . @25.00
72 Nov., 1957 . . . . 25.00

OMAC
Sept.–Oct., 1974
1 JK,I&O:Omac 10.00
2 JK,I:Mr.Big 6.00
3 JK,100,000 foes 6.00
4 JK,V:Kafka 6.00
5 JK,New Bodies for Old 6.00
6 JK,The Body Bank 6.00
7 JK,The Ocean Stealers 6.00
8 JK,Last issue 6.00
[2nd Series] 1991
1 JBy,B&W prestige 5.00
2 JBy,The Great Depression era . 4.50
3 JBy,'To Kill Adolf Hitler' 4.50
4 JBy,D:Mr.Big 4.50

OMEGA MEN
Dec., 1982
1 KG,V:Citadel 2.50
2 KG,O:Broot 2.00
3 KG,I:Lobo 7.00
4 KG,D:Demonia,I:Felicity 1.50
5 KG,V:Lobo 4.00
6 KG,V:Citadel,D:Gepsen 2.00
7 O:Citadel,L:Auron 2.00
8 R:Nimbus,I:H.Hokum 2.00
9 V:HarryHokum,A:Lobo 3.00
10 A:Lobo (First Full Story) 6.00
11 V:Blackfire 1.50
12 R:Broots Wife 1.50
13 A:Broots Wife 1.50
14 Karna 1.50
15 Primus Goes Mad 1.50
16 Spotlight Issue 1.50
17 V:Psions 1.50
18 V:Psions 1.50
19 V:Psions,C:Lobo 2.00
20 V:Psions,A:Lobo 3.00
21 Spotlight Issue 1.50
22 Nimbus 1.50
23 Nimbus 1.50
24 Okaara 1.50
25 Kalista 1.50
26 V:Spiderguild 1.50
27 V:Psions 1.50
28 V:Psions 1.50

Omega Men #13 © DC Comics, Inc.

DC COMICS

29 V:Psions 1.50
30 R:Primus,I:Artin 1.50
31 Crisis tie-in 1.50
32 Felicity 1.50
33 Regufe World 1.50
34 A:New Teen Titans 1.50
35 A:New Teen Titans 1.50
36 Last Days of Broot 1.50
37 V:Spiderguild,A:Lobo 3.00
38 A:Tweener Network 1.25
Ann.#1 KG,R:Harpis 2.25
Ann.#2 KG,O:Primus 2.25

100% TRUE?
DC/Paradox Press B&W 1996
1 rep. from Paradox Press books 3.50

OUR ARMY AT WAR
Aug., 1952
1 CI(c),Dig Your FoxholeDeep 1,100.00
2 CI(c),Champ 600.00
3 GK(c),No Exit 400.00
4 IN(c),Last Man 400.00
5 IN(c),T.N.T. Bouquet 350.00
6 IN(c),Battle Flag 350.00
7 IN(c),Dive Bomber 350.00
8 IN(c),One Man Army 350.00
9 GC(c),Undersea Raider . . . 350.00
10 IN(c),Soldiers on the
   High Wire 350.00
11 IN(c),Scratch One Meatball . 350.00
12 IN(c),The Big Drop 250.00
13 BK(c),Ghost Ace 250.00
14 Drummer of Waterloo 250.00
15 IN(c),Thunder in the Skies . 250.00
16 IN(c),A Million To One Shot 250.00
17 IN(c),The White Death 250.00
18 IN(c),Frontier Fighter 250.00
19 IN(c),The Big Ditch 250.00
20 IN(c),Abandon Ship 250.00
21 IN(c),Dairy of a Flattop . . . 175.00
22 JGr(c),Ranger Raid 175.00
23 IN(c),Jungle Navy 175.00
24 IN(c),Suprise Landing 175.00
25 JGr(c),Take 'Er Down 175.00
26 JGr(c),Sky Duel 175.00
27 IN(c),Diary of a Frogman . . 175.00

DC COMICS

28 JGr(c),Detour-War 175.00
29 IN(c),Grounded Fighter 175.00
30 JGr(c),Torpedo Raft 175.00
31 IN(c),Howitzer Hill 175.00
32 IN(c),Battle Mirror 150.00
33 JGr(c),Fighting Gunner 150.00
34 JGr(c),Point-Blank War 150.00
35 JGr(c),Frontline Tackle 150.00
36 JGr(c),Foxhole Mascot 150.00
37 JGr(c),Walking Battle Pin . . 150.00
38 JGr(c),Floating Pillbox 150.00
39 JGr(c),Trench Trap 150.00
40 RH(c),Tank Hunter 150.00
41 JGr(c),Jungle Target 150.00
42 IN(c),Shadow Targets 125.00
43 JGr(c),A Bridge For Billy . . 125.00
44 JGr(c),Thunder In The Desert 125.00
45 JGr(c),Diary of a Fighter Pilot 125.00
46 JGr(c),Prize Package 125.00
47 JGr(c),Flying Jeep 125.00
48 JGr(c),Front Seat 125.00
49 JKu(c),Landing Postponed . 125.00
50 JGr(c),Mop-Up Squad 125.00
51 JGr(c),Battle Tag 110.00
52 JGr(c),Pony Express Pilot . 110.00
53 JGr(c),One Ringside-For War 110.00
54 JKu(c),No-Man Secret 110.00
55 JGr(c),No Rest For A Raider . 110.00
56 JKu(c),You're Next 110.00
57 JGr(c),Ten-Minute Break . . 110.00
58 JKu(c),The Fighting SnowBird 110.00
59 JGr(c),The Mustang Had
    My Number 110.00
60 JGr(c),Ranger Raid 110.00
61 JGr(c),A Pigeon For Easy Co.100.00
62 JKu(c),Trigger Man 100.00
63 JGr(c),The Big Toss 100.00
64 JGr(c),Tank Rider 100.00
65 JGr(c),Scramble-War Upstairs 100.00
66 RH(c),Gunner Wanted 100.00
67 JKu(c),Boiling Point 100.00
68 JKu(c),End of the Line 100.00
69 JGr(c),Combat Cage 100.00
70 JGr(c),Torpedo Tank 100.00
71 JGr(c),Flying Mosquitoes . . 100.00
72 JGr(c),No. 1 Pigeon 100.00
73 JKu(c),Shooting Gallery . . . 100.00
74 JGr(c),Ace Without Guns . . 100.00
75 JGr(c),Blind Night Fighter . . 100.00
76 JKu(c),Clipped Hellcat 100.00
77 JGr(c),Jets Don't Dream . . . 100.00
78 IN(c),Battle Nurse 100.00
79 JGr(c),What's the Price
    of a B-17? 100.00
80 JGr(c),The Sparrow And
    The...Hawk 100.00
81 JGr(c),Sgt. Rock in The
    Rock of Easy Co. 2,100.00
82 JGr(c),Gun Jockey 450.00
83 JGr(c),B:Sgt.Rock Stories,
    The Rock and the Wall 750.00
84 JKu(c),Laughter On
    Snakehead Hill 175.00
85 JGr(c),Ice Cream Soldier . . 250.00
86 RH(c),Tank 711 . . . . 175.00
87 RH(c),Calling Easy Co. 175.00
88 JKu(c),The Hard Way 175.00
89 RH(c),No Shoot From Easy . 175.00
90 JKu(c),3 Stripes Hill 175.00
91 JGr(c),No Answer from Sarge 175.00
92 JGr(c),Luck of Easy 125.00
93 JGr(c),Deliver One Airfield . 125.00
94 JKu(c),Target-Easy Company 125.00
95 JKu(c),Battle Of The Stripes . 125.00
96 JGr(c),Last Stand For Easy . 125.00

97 JKu(c),What Makes A
    Sergeant Run? 125.00
98 JKu(c),Soldiers Never Die . . 125.00
99 JKu(c),Easy's Hardest Battle 125.00
100 JKu(c),No Exit For Easy . . 125.00
101 JKu(c),End Of Easy 75.00
102 JKu(c),The Big Star 75.00
103 RH(c),Easy's Had It 75.00
104 JKu(c),A New Kind Of War . 75.00
105 JKu(c),T.N.T. Birthday 75.00
106 JKu(c),Meet Lt. Rock 75.00
107 JKu(c),Doom Over Easy . . 75.00
108 JGr(c),Unknown Sergeant . 75.00
109 JKu(c),Roll Call For Heroes 75.00
110 JKu(c),That's An Order . . . 75.00
111 JKu(c),What's The Price
    Of A Dog Tag 75.00
112 JKu(c),Battle Shadow 75.00
113 JKu(c),Eyes Of A
    Blind Gunner 75.00
114 JKu(c),Killer Sergeant 75.00
115 JKu(c),Rock's Battle Family . 75.00
116 JKu(c),S.O.S. Sgt. Rock . . . 75.00

Our Army at War #7 © DC Comics, Inc.

117 JKu(c),Snafu Squad 60.00
118 RH(c),The Tank Vs. The
    Tin Soldier 60.00
119 JKu(c),A Bazooka For
    Babyface 60.00
120 JGr(c),Battle Tags
    For Easy Co. 50.00
121 JKu(c),New Boy In Easy . . 50.00
122 JKu(c),Battle of the
    Pajama Commandoes 50.00
123 JGr(c),Battle Brass Ring . . 50.00
124 JKu(c),Target-Sgt. Rock . . 50.00
125 JKu(c),Hold-At All Costs . . 50.00
126 RH(c),The End Of
    Easy Company 50.00
127 JKu(c),4 Faces of Sgt. Rock 50.00
128 JKu(c),O:Sgt. Rock 185.00
129 JKu(c),Heroes Need Cowards 50.00
130 JKu(c),No Hill For Easy . . . 50.00
131 JKu(c),One Pair of
    Dogtags For Sale 50.00
132 JKu(c),Young Soldiers
    Never Cry 50.00
133 JKu(c),Yesterday's Hero . . 50.00
134 JKu(c),The T.N.T. Book . . . 50.00

135 JKu(c),Battlefield Double . . . 50.00
136 JKu(c),Make Me A Hero . . . 50.00
137 JKu(c),Too Many Sergeants 50.00
138 JKu(c),Easy's Lost Sparrow 50.00
139 JKu(c),A Firing Squad
    For Easy 50.00
140 JKu(c),Brass Sergeant 50.00
141 JKu(c),Dead Man's Trigger . 50.00
142 JKu(c),Easy's New Topkick . 50.00
143 JKu(c),Easy's T.N.T. Crop . . 50.00
144 JKu(c),The Sparrow And
    The Tiger 50.00
145 JKu(c),A Feather For
    Little Sure Shot 50.00
146 JKu(c),The Fighting Guns
    For Easy 50.00
147 JKu(c),Book One:Generals
    Don't Die 50.00
148 JKu(c),Book Two:Generals
    Don't Die:Generals Are
    Sergeants With Stars 50.00
149 JKu(c),Surrender Ticket . . . 50.00
150 JKu(c),Flytrap Hill 50.00
151 JKu(c),War Party,
    I:Enemy Ace 300.00
152 JKu(c),Last Man-Last Shot 100.00
153 JKu(c),Easy's Last Stand . . 75.00
154 JKu(c),Boobytrap Mascot . . 50.00
155 JKu(c),No Stripes For Me . . 50.00
156 JKu(c),The Human Tank Trap 50.00
157 JKu(c),Nothin's Ever
    Lost In War 50.00
158 JKu(c),Iron Major-Rock
    Sergeant 50.00
159 JKu(c),The Blind Gun 50.00
160 JKu(c),What's The Color
    Of Your Blood 50.00
161 JKu(c),Dead End
    For A Dogface 50.00
162 JKu(c),The Price and
    The Sergeant 50.00
163 JKu(c),Kill Me-Kill Me 50.00
164 JKu(c),No Exit For Easy,
    reprint from #100 . . . . 60.00
165 JKu(c),The Return of the
    Iron Major 40.00
166 JKu(c),Half A Sergeant . . . 40.00
167 JKu(c),Kill One-Save One . . 40.00
168 JKu(c),I Knew The
    Unknown Soldier 40.00
169 JKu(c),Nazi On My Back . . . 40.00
170 JKu(c),Buzzard Bait Hill . . . 40.00
171 JKu(c),The Sergeant Must Die 30.00
172 JKu(c),A Slug For A Sergeant 30.00
173 JKu(c),Easy's Hardest Battle,
    reprint from #99 . . . . 30.00
174 JKu(c),One Kill Too Many . . 30.00
175 JKu(c),T.N.T. Letter 30.00
176 JKu(c),Give Me Your Stripes 30.00
177 JKu(c),Target-Easy Company,
    reprint from #94 . . . . 30.00
178 JKu(c),Only One Medal
    For Easy 30.00
179 JKu(c),A Penny Jackie
    Johnson 30.00
180 JKu(c),You Can't
    Kill A General 30.00
181 RH(c),Monday's Coward-
    Tuesday's Hero 30.00
182 NA,RH(c),The Desert Rats
    of Easy 35.00
183 NA,JKu(c),Sergeants Don't
    Stay Dead 35.00
184 JKu(c),Candidate For A
    Firing Squad 25.00

DC COMICS

185 JKu(c),Battle Flag For A G.I. 25 00
186 NA,JKu(c),3 Stripes Hill
   reprint from #90 . . . . 35.00
187 JKu(c),Shadow of a Sergeant 25.00
188 JKu(c),Death Comes for Easy 25.00
189 JKu(c),The Mission Was
   Murder 25.00
190 JKu(c),What Make's A
   Sergeant Run?, reprint
   from #97 . . . . 25.00
191 JKu(c),Death Flies High,
   A:Johnny Cloud 25.00
192 JKu(c),A Firing Squad
   For A Sergeant 25.00
193 JKu(c),Blood In the Desert . 25.00
194 JKu(c),Time For Vengeance 25.00
195 JKu(c),Dead Town 25.00
196 JKu(c),Stop The War-I Want
   To Get Off 25.00
197 JKu(c),Last Exit For Easy . . 25.00
198 JKu(c),Plugged Nickel 25.00
199 JKu(c),Nazi Ghost Wolf 25.00
200 JKu(c),The Troubadour 30.00
201 JKu(c),The Graffiti Writer . . 25.00
202 JKu(c),The Sarge Is Dead . . . 8.00
203 JKu(c),Easy's Had It,
   reprint from # 103 . . . . 15.00
204 JKu(c) 8.00
205 JKu(c) 8.00
206 JKu(c),There's A War On . . 8.00
207 JKu(c),A Sparrow's Prayer . . 8.00
208 JKu(c),A Piece of Rag...And
   A Hank of Hair 8.00
209 JKu(c),I'm Still Alive 8.00
210 JKu(c),I'm Kilroy 8.00
211 JKu(c),The Treasure of
   St. Daniel 8.00
212 JKu(c),The Quiet War 8.00
213 JKu(c),A Letter For Bulldozer 8.00
214 JKu(c),Where Are You? 8.00
215 JKu(c),Pied Piper of Peril . . 8.00
216 JKu(c),Doom Over Easy,
   reprint from # 107 . . . . 15.00
217 JKu(c),Surprise Party 6.00
218 JKu(c),Medic! 6.00
219 JKu(c),Yesterday's Hero 6.00
220 JKu(c),Stone-Age War 6.00
221 JKu(c),Hang-Up 6.00
222 JKu(c),Dig In, Easy 6.00
223 JKu(c),On Time 6.00
224 JKu(c),One For The Money . . 6.00
225 JKu(c),Face Front 6.00
226 JKu(c),Death Stop 6.00
227 JKu(c),Traitor's Blood 6.00
228 JKu(c),It's A Dirty War 6.00
229 JKu(c),The Battle of the
   Sergeants, reprint from #128 . 15.00
230 JKu(c),Home Is The Hunter . 6.00
231 JKu(c),My Brother's Keeper . 6.00
232 JKu(c),3 Men In A Tub 6.00
233 JKu(c),Head Count 6.00
234 JKu(c),Summer In Salerno . 6.00
235 JKu(c),Pressure Point 6.00
236 JKu(c),Face The Devil 6.00
237 JKu(c),Nobody Cares 6.00
238 JKu(c),I Kid You Not 6.00
239 JKu(c),The Soldier 6.00
240 JKu(c),NA 8.00
241 JKu(c),War Story 6.00
242 JKu(c),Infantry 6.00
243 JKu(c),24 Hour Pass 7.50
244 JKu(c),Easy's First Tiger 6.00
245 JKu(c),The Prisoner 6.00
246 JKu(c),Naked Combat 6.00
247 JKu(c),The Vision 6.00

248 JKu(c),The Firing Squad 6.00
249 JKu(c),The Luck of Easy,WW . 8.00
250 JKu(c),90 Day Wonder 6.00
251 JKu(c),The Iron Major 6.00
252 JKu(c),The Iron Hand 6.00
253 JKu(c),Rock and Iron 6.00
254 JKu(c),The Town 6.00
255 JKu(c),What's It Like 6.00
256 JKu(c),School For Sergeants . 6.00
257 JKu(c),The Castaway 6.00
258 JKu(c),The Survivors 6.00
259 JKu(c),Lost Paradise 6.00
260 JKu(c),Hell's Island 6.00
261 JKu(c),The Medal That
   Nobody Wanted 6.00
262 JKu(c),The Return 6.00
263 JKu(c),The Cage 6.00
264 JKu(c),The Hunt 6.00
265 JKu(c),The Brother 6.00
266 JKu(c),The Evacuees 6.00
267 JKu(c),A Bakers Dozen 6.00
268 JKu(c),The Elite 6.00
269 JKu(c) 6.00
270 JKu(c),Spawn of the Devil . . . 6.00
271 JKu(c),Brittle Harvest 6.00
272 JKu(c),The Bloody Flag 6.00
273 JKu(c),The Arena 6.00
274 JKu(c),Home Is The Hero . . . 6.00
275 JKu(c),Graveyard Battlefield . 6.00
276 JKu(c),A Bullet For Rock 6.00
277 JKu(c),Gashouse Gang 6.00
278 JKu(c),Rearguard Action 6.00
279 JKu(c),Mined City 6.00
280 JKu(c),Mercy Mission 6.00
281 JKu(c),Dead Man's Eyes 6.00
282 JKu(c),Pieces of Time 6.00
283 JKu(c),Dropouts 6.00
284 JKu(c),Linkup 6.00
285 JKu(c),Bring Him Back 6.00
286 JKu(c),Firebird 6.00
287 JKu(c),The Fifth Dimension . . 6.00
288 JKu(c),Defend-Or Destroy . . . 6.00
289 JKu(c),The Line 6.00
290 JKu(c),Super-Soldiers 6.00
291 JKu(c),Death Squad 6.00
292 JKu(c),A Lesson In Blood . . . 6.00
293 JKu(c),It Figures 6.00
294 JKu(c),Coffin For Easy 6.00
295 JKu(c),The Devil in Paradise . 6.00
296 JKu(c),Combat Soldier 6.00
297 JKu(c),Percentages 6.00
298 JKu(c),Return to Chartres . . . 6.00
299 JKu(c),Three Soldiers 6.00
300 JKu(c),300th Hill 6.00
301 JKu(c),The Farm 6.00
Becomes:

SGT. ROCK
1977–88
302 JKu(c),Anzio-The Bloodbath,
   part I 8.00
303 JKu(c),Anzio, part II 6.00
304 JKu(c),Anzio, part III 6.00
305 JKu(c),Dead Man's Trigger,
   reprint from #141 . . . . 6.00
306 JKu(c),The Last Soldier 6.00
307 JKu(c),I'm Easy 6.00
308 JKu(c),One Short Step 6.00
309 JKu(c),Battle Clowns 6.00
310 JKu(c),Hitler's Wolf Children . 6.00
311 JKu(c),The Sergeant and
   the Lady 6.00
312 JKu(c),No Name Hill 6.00
313 JKu(c),A Jeep For Joey 6.00
314 JKu(c),Gimme Sky 6.00
315 JKu(c),Combat Antenna 6.00

316 JKu(c),Another Hill... . . . . . . 6.00
317 JKu(c),Hell's Oven 6.00
318 JKu(c),Stone-Age War 6.00
319 JKu(c),To Kill a Sergeant . . . 6.00
320 JKu(c),Never Salute a
   Sergeant 6.00
321 JKu(c),It's Murder Out Here . 5.00
322 JKu(c),The Killer 5.00
323 JKu(c),Monday's Hero 5.00
324 JKu(c),Ghost of a Tank 5.00
325 JKu(c),Future Kill, part I 5.00
326 JKu(c),Future Kill, part II 5.00
327 JKu(c),Death Express 5.00
328 JKu(c),Waiting For Rock 5.00
329 JKu(c),Dead Heat 5.00
330 JKu(c),G.I. Trophy 5.00
331 JKu(c),The Sons of War 5.00
332 JKu(c),Pyramid of Death 5.00
333 JKu(c),Ask The Dead 5.00
334 JKu(c),What's Holding Up
   The War 5.00
335 JKu(c),Killer Compass 5.00
336 JKu(c),The Red Maple Leaf . 5.00
337 JKu(c),A Bridge Called Charlie 5.00
338 JKu(c),No Escape From
   the Front 5.00
339 JKu(c),I Was Here Before . . . 5.00
340 JKu(c),How To Win A War . . . 5.00
341 JKu(c),High-Flyer 5.00
342 JKu(c),The 6 sides of
   Sgt. Rock 5.00
343 thru 350 . . . . @5.00
351 thru 422 . . . . @2.00

Our Fighting Fources #8
© DC Comics, Inc.

OUR FIGHTING FORCES
Oct.–Nov., 1954
1 IN,JGr(c),Human Booby Trap 650.00
2 RH,IN,IN(c),Mile-Long Step . 350.00
3 RA,JKu(c),Winter Ambush . . 300.00
4 RA,JGr(c),The Hot Seat . . . 250.00
5 IN,RA,JGr(c),The Iron Punch . 250.00
6 IN,RA,JGr(c),The Sitting Tank 200.00
7 RA,JKu,JGr(c),Battle Fist . . . 200.00
8 IN,RA,JGr(c),No War
   For A Gunner 200.00
9 JKu,RH,JGr(c),Crash-

All comics prices listed are for *Near Mint* condition.

Landing At Dawn 200.00	Hunter 50.00	117 JKu(c),Colder Than Death . . 10.00
10 WW,RA,JGr(c),Grenade	64 JK,RH,JGr(c),A Lifeline	118 JKu(c),Hell Underwater 10.00
Pitcher 225.00	For Sarge 50.00	119 JKu(c),Bedlam In Berlin . . . 10.00
11 JKu,JGr(c),Diary of a Sub . . 150.00	65 IN,JA,JGr(c),Dogtag Patrol . . 50.00	120 JKu(c),Devil In The Dark . . 10.00
12 IN,JKu,JGr(c),Jump Seat . . 150.00	66 JKu,JA,JGr(c),Trail of the	121 JKu(c),Take My Place 10.00
13 RA,JGr(c),Beach Party 150.00	Ghost Bomber 50.00	122 JKu(c),24 Hours To Die . . . 10.00
14 JA,RA,IN,JGr(c),Unseen War 150.00	67 IN,JA,JGr(c),Purple Heart	123 JKu(c),B:Born Losers,No
15 RH,JKu,JGr(c),Target For	For Pooch 50.00	Medals No Graves 10.00
A Lame Duck 150.00	68 JA,JGr(c),Col. Hakawa's	124 JKu(c),Losers Take All 10.00
16 RH,JGr(c),Night Fighter . . . 150.00	Birthday Party 50.00	125 Daughters of Death 10.00
17 RA,JGr(c),Anchored Frogman 150.00	69 JA,JKu,JGr(c),	126 JKu(c),Lost Town 10.00
18 RH,JKu,JGr(c),Cockpit Seat . 150.00	Destination Doom 50.00	127 JKu(c),Angels Over Hell's
19 RA,JKu(c),Straighten ThatLine150.00	70 JA,JKu(c),The Last Holdout . 50.00	Corner 10.00
20 RA,MD,JGr(c),The	71 JA,JGr(c),End of the Marines . 22.00	128 JKu(c),7 11 War 10.00
Floating Pilot 150.00	72 JA,JGr(c),Four-Footed Spy . . 18.00	129 JKu(c),Ride The Nightmare . 10.00
21 RA,JKu(c),The Bouncing	73 IN,JGr(c),The Hero Maker . . . 18.00	130 JKu(c),Nameless Target . . . 10.00
Baby of Company B 100.00	74 IN,JGr(c),Three On A T.N.T.	131 JKu(c),Half A Man 10.00
22 JKu,JA,JGr(c),3 Doorways	Bull's-Eye 18.00	132 JKu(c),Pooch, The Winner . 10.00
To War 100.00	75 JKu(c),Purple Heart Patrol . . 18.00	133 JKu(c),Heads or Tails 10.00
23 RA,IN,JA,JGr(c),Tin Fish Pilot 100.00	76 JKu(c),The T.N.T. Seat 18.00	134 JKu(c),The Real Losers . . . 10.00
24 RA,RH,JGr(c),Frogman Duel 100.00	77 JKu(c),No Foxhole-No Home . 18.00	135 JKu(c),Death Picks A Loser 10.00
25 RA,JKu(c),Dead End 100.00	78 JGr(c),The Last Medal 18.00	136 JKu(c),Decoy For Death . . . 10.00
26 IN,RH,JKu(c),Tag Day 100.00	79 JA,JGr(c),Backs to the Sea . . 18.00	137 JKu(c),God Of The Losers . 10.00
27 MD,RA,JKu(c),TNT Escort . 100.00	80 JA,JGr(c),Don't Come Back . 18.00	138 JKu(c),The Targets 10.00
28 RH,MD,JKu(c),All Quiet at C.P.100.00	81 JA,JGr(c),Battle of	139 JKu(c),The Pirate 10.00
29 JKu,JKu(c),Listen To A Jet . 100.00	the Mud Marines 18.00	140 JKu(c),Lost...One Loser . . . 10.00
30 IN,RA,JKu(c),Fort	82 JA,JGr(c),Battle of the	141 JKu(c),Bad Penny, The 10.00
For A Gunner 100.00	Empty Helmets 18.00	142 JKu(c), 1/2 A Man 10.00
31 MD,RA,JKu(c),Silent Sub . . 90.00	83 RA,JKu(c),Any Marine	143 JKu(c),Diamonds Are
32 RH,MD,RH(c),PaperWorkWar 90.00	Can Do It 18.00	For Never 10.00
33 RH,JKu,JKu(c),Frogman	84 JA,JKu(c),The Gun of Shame 18.00	144 JKu(c),The Lost Mission . . . 10.00
In A Net 90.00	85 JA,JKu(c),The TNT Pin-Points 18.00	145 JKu(c),A Flag For Losers . . 10.00
34 JA,JGr,JKu(c),Calling U-217 . 90.00	86 JKu(c),3 Faces of Combat . . 18.00	146 JKu(c),The Forever Walk . . . 10.00
35 JA,JGr,JKu(c),Mask of	87 JKu(c),Battle o/t Boobytraps . 18.00	147 NA(c),The Glory Road 10.00
a Frogman 90.00	88 GC,JKu(c),Devil Dog Patrol . . 18.00	148 JKu(c),The Last Charge . . . 10.00
36 MD,JA,JKu(c),Steel Soldier . 90.00	89 JKu(c),TNT Toothache 18.00	149 FT(c),A Bullet For
37 JA,JGr,JGr(c),Frogman	90 JKu(c),Stop the War 18.00	A Traitor 10.00
In A Bottle 90.00	91 JKu(c),The Human Shooting	150 JKu(c),Mark Our Graves . . . 10.00
38 RH,RA,JA,JGr(c),Sub Sinker . 90.00	Gallery 15.00	151 JKu(c),Kill Me With Wagner 10.00
39 JA,RH,RH(c),Last Torpedo . . 90.00	92 JA,JKu(c),The Bomb That	152 JK(c),A Small Place In Hell . 10.00
40 JGr,JA,JKu,JKu(c),The	Stopped The War 15.00	153 JK(c),Big Max 10.00
Silent Ones 90.00	93 IN,JKu(c),The Human Sharks 15.00	154 JK(c),Bushido,Live By The
41 JGr,RH,JA,JKu(c),Battle	94 RH(c),E:Gunner,Sarge & Pooch,	Code, Die By The Code 10.00
Mustang 125.00	The Human Blockbusters . . 15.00	155 JK(c),The Partisans 10.00
42 RH,MD,JGr(c),Sorry-	95 GC,RH(c),B:The Fighting Devil	156 JK(c),Good-Bye Broadway . 10.00
Wrong Hill 75.00	Dog, Lt. Rock, The	157 JK(c),Panama Fattie 10.00
43 MD,JKu,JGr(c),Inside Battle . 75.00	Fighting Devil Dog 15.00	158 JK(c),Bombing Out On
44 MD,RH,RA,JGr(c),Big Job	96 JA,RH(c),Battle of Fire 15.00	The Panama Canal 10.00
For Baker 75.00	97 IN(c),Invitation To A	159 JK(c),Mile-A-Minute Jones . 10.00
45 RH,RA,JGr(c),B:Gunner and	Firing Squad 15.00	160 JKu(c),Ivan 10.00
Sarge, Mop-Up Squad 250.00	98 IN(c),E:The Fighting Devil	161 JKu(c),The Major's Dream . 10.00
46 RH,RA,JGr(c),Gunner'sSquad 125.00	Dog, Death Wore A Grin 15.00	162 Gung-Ho 10.00
47 RH,JKu(c),TNT Birthday 75.00	99 JA,JKu(c),B:Capt. Hunter,	163 JKu(c),The Unmarked Graves 10.00
48 JA,RH,JGr(c),A Statue	No Mercy in Vietnam 15.00	164 JKu(c),A Town Full Of Losers 10.00
For Sarge 60.00	100 GC,IN(c),Death Also	165 LD(c),The Rowboat Fleet . . 10.00
49 MD,RH,JGr(c),Blind Gunner . 80.00	Stalks the Hunter 10.00	166 LD(c),Sword of Flame 10.00
50 JA,RH,JGr(c),I:Pooch,My	101 JA,RH(c),Killer of Vietnam . . 10.00	167 LD(c),A Front Seat In Hell . . 10.00
Pal, The Pooch 60.00	102 RH,JKu(c),Cold Steel	168 LD(c),A Cold Day To Die . . 10.00
51 RA,JA,RH(c),Underwater	For A Hot War 10.00	169 JKu(c),Welcome Home-And
Gunner 50.00	103 JKu(c),The Tunnels of Death 10.00	Die 10.00
52 MD,JKu,JKu(c),The Gunner	104 JKu(c),Night Raid In Vietnam 10.00	170 JKu(c),A Bullet For
and the Nurse 50.00	105 JKu(c),Blood Loyality 10.00	The General 10.00
53 JA,RA,JGr(c),An Egg	106 IN(c),Trail By Fury 10.00	171 JKu(c),A Long Day...
For Sarge 50.00	107 IN(c),Raid Of The Hellcats . 10.00	A Long War 10.00
54 . . . . 50.00	108 IN(c),Kill The Wolf Pack . . . 10.00	172 JKu(c),The Two-Headed Spy 10.00
55 MD,JKu(c),The Last Patrol 50.00	109 IN(c),Burn, Raiders, Burn . . 10.00	173 JKu(c),An Appointment
56 RH,RA,JGr(c),Bridge of Bullets 50.00	110 IN(c),Mountains Full of Death 10.00	With A Direct Hit 10.00
57 JA,IN,JGr(c),A Tank For Sarge 50.00	111 IN(c),Train of Terror 10.00	174 JKu(c),Winner Takes-Death 10.00
58 JA,JGr(c),Return of the Pooch 50.00	112 IN(c),What's In It For	175 JKu(c),Death Warrant 10.00
59 RH,JA,JGr(c),Pooch-Patrol	The Hellcats? 10.00	176 JKu(c),The Loser Is A
Leader 50.00	113 IN(c),Operation-Survival . . . 10.00	Teen-Ager 10.00
60 RH,JA,JGr(c),Tank Target . . . 50.00	114 JKu(c),No Loot For The	177 JKu(c),This Loser Must Die . 10.00
61 JA,JGr(c),Pass to Peril 50.00	Hellcats 10.00	178 JKu(c),Last Drop For Losers 10.00
62 JA,JGr(c),The Flying Pooch . 50.00	115 JKu(c),Death In The Desert . 10.00	179 JKu(c),The Last Loser 10.00
63 JA,RH,JGr(c),Pooch-Tank	116 JKu(c),Peril From the Casbah 10.00	180 JKu(c),Hot Seat In A

DC COMICS

DC COMICS

Cold War 10.00
181 JKu(c),Sept.–Oct., 1978 . . . 10.00

OUTCASTS
Oct., 1987

1 . . . . 2.00
2 thru 11 . . . . @1.75

Outlaws #5 © DC Comics, Inc.

OUTLAWS
1991

1 LMc,I:Hood 1.95
2 LMc,O:Hood 1.95
3 LMc,V:Evil King 1.95
4 LMc,V:Lord Conductor 1.95
5 LMc,Archery contest 1.95
6 LMc,Raid on King's Castle . . . 1.95
7 LMc,Refuge, V:Lord Conductor 1.95

OUTSIDERS, THE
Nov., 1985
[1st Regular Series]

1 JAp,I:Looker 3.00
2 JAp,V:Nuclear Family 2.50
3 JAp,V:Force of July 2.00
4 JAp,V:Force of July 2.00
5 JAp,Christmas Issue 2.00
6 JAp,V:Duke of Oil 2.00
7 JAp,V:Duke of Oil 2.00
8 JAp,Japan 2.00
9 JAp/SD/JOp,Bik Lightning 2.00
10 JAp,I:Peoples Heroes 2.00
11 JAp,Imprisoned in death camp 1.75
12 JAp,Imprisoned in death camp 1.75
13 JAp,desert island 1.75
14 JAp,Looker/murder story 1.75
15 DJu,V:Bio-hazard 1.75
16 Halo vs.Firefly 1.75
17 JAp,J:Batman 1.75
18 JAp,BB,V:Eclipso 2.00
19 JAp,V:Windfall 1.75
20 JAp,Masters of Disaster 1.75
21 JAp,V:Kobra,I:Clayface IV . . . 1.75
22 JAp,V:Strike Force Kobra 1.75
23 Return of People's Heroes . . . 1.75
24 TVE,JAp,V:Skull,A:Duke of Oil 1.75
25 JAp,V:Skull 1.75
26 JAp,in Markovia 1.75

27 EL,Millenium 1.75
28 EL,Millenium,final issue 1.75
Ann.#1,KN,V:Skull,A:Batman 2.50
Spec.#1,A:Infinity,Inc 1.75
[2nd Regular Series] 1993–95
1 Alpha,TC(c),B:MiB(s),PaP,
　I:Technocrat,Faust,Wylde . . . 3.00
1a Omega,TC(c),PaP,V:Vampires 3.00
2 PaP,V:Sanction 2.00
3 PaP,V:Eradicator 2.00
4 PaP,A:Eradicator 2.00
5 PaP,V:Atomic Knight,A:Jihad . . 2.00
6 PaP,V:Jihad 2.00
7 PaP,C:Batman 2.00
8 PaP,V:Batman,I:Halo 2.00
9 PaP,V:Batman 2.00
10 PaP,B:Final Blood, R:Looker . . 2.25
11 PaP,Zero Hour,E:Final Blood . 1.95
12 PaP 1.95
13 New base 1.95
14 Martial Arts Spectacular 1.95
15 V:New Year's Evil 1.95
16 R:Windfall 1.95
17 A:Green Lantern 1.95
18 Sins of the Father 1.95
19 Sins of the Father, pt.2 . . . . . 2.25
20 DvA,V:Metamorpho 2.25
21 A:Apokolips 2.25
22 Alien Assassin 2.25
23 V:Defilers 2.25
24 finale 2.25

PARALLAX:
EMERALD NIGHT
1 RMz(s),MMK,MkK, pivotal tie-in
　to Final Night 4.50

Peacemaker #2 © DC Comics, Inc.

PEACEMAKER
Jan., 1988

1 A:Dr.Tzin-Tzin 1.25
2 The Wages of Tzin 1.25
3 and 4 . . . . @1.25

PENGUIN
TRIUMPHANT
1 JSon,A:Batman,Wall Street . . . 6.00

PETER CANNON:
THUNDERBOLT
1992–93

1 thru 6 MC . . . . @1.50
7 MC,'Battleground' 1.50
8 MC,Cairo Kidnapped 1.50
9 MC 1.50
10 MC,A:JLA 1.50
11 MC,V:Havoc,A:Checkmate . . . 1.50
12 MC,final Issue 1.25

PETER PANDA
Aug.–Sept., 1953

1 . . . . 165.00
2 . . . . 95.00
3 thru 9 . . . . @60.00
10 Aug.–Sept., 1958 . . . . 60.00

*Peter Porkchops #9
© DC Comics, Inc.*

PETER PORKCHOPS
Nov.–Dec., 1949

1 . . . . 250.00
2 . . . . 125.00
3 thru 10 . . . . @100.00
11 thru 30 . . . . @75.00
31 thru 61 . . . . @50.00
62 Oct.–Dec., 1960 . . . . 50.00

PHANTOM, THE
Oct., 1987

1 JO,A:Modern Phantom,13th
　Phantom 2.00
2 JO,Murder Trial in Manhattan . 1.50
3 JO,A:Chessman 1.50
4 JO,V:Chessman,final issue . . . 1.50

PHANTOM, THE
1989–90

1 LMc,V:Gun Runners 2.50
2 LMc,V:Gun Runners 2.00
3 LMc,V:Drug Smugglers 1.75
4 LMc,In America,A:Diana Palner 1.75
5 LMc,Racial Riots 1.50
6 LMc,in Africa,Toxic Waste
　Problem 1.50
7 LMc,'Gold Rush' 1.50
8 LMc,'Train Surfing' 1.50

All comics prices listed are for *Near Mint* condition.　　　**CVA Page 91**

DC COMICS

9 LMc,'The Slave Trade' 1.50
10 LMc,Famine in Khagana 1.50
11 LMc,Phantom/Diana Wedding
 proposal 1.50
12 LMc,Phantom framed for
 murder 1.50
13 W:Phantom & Diana Palner
 C:Mandrake last issue 1.50

PHANTOM STRANGER
Aug.–Sept., 1952
1 . . . . 1,400.00
2 . . . . 900.00
3 . . . . 750.00
4 . . . . 750.00
5 . . . . 750.00
6, June-July, 1953 . . . . 750.00

Phantom Stranger #37
© DC Comics, Inc.

PHANTOM STRANGER
May-June, 1969
1 CI rep.&new material 65.00
2 CI rep.&new material 25.00
3 CI rep.&new material 23.00
4 NA,I:Tala,1st All-new issue . . 30.00
5 MSy,MA,A:Dr.13 . . . . 20.00
6 MSy,A:Dr.13 . . . . 20.00
7 JAp,V:Tala 20.00
8 JAp,A:Dr.13 . . . . 20.00
9 JAp,A:Dr.13 . . . . 20.00
10 JAp,I:Tannarak 20.00
11 JAp,V:Tannarak 15.00
12 JAp,TD,Dr.13 solo story 15.00
13 JAp,TD,Dr.13 solo 15.00
14 JAp,TD,Dr.13 solo 15.00
15 JAp,ATh(rep),TD,Iron Messiah 10.00
16 JAp,TD,MMes(rep)Dr.13 solo 10.00
17 JAp,I:Cassandra Craft 10.00
18 TD,Dr.13 solo 10.00
19 JAp,TD,Dr.13 solo 10.00
20 JAp,'And A Child
 Shall Lead Them' 10.00
21 JAp,TD,Dr.13 solo 6.00
22 JAp,TD,I:Dark Circle 6.00
23 JAp,MK,I:Spawn-Frankenstein . 6.00
24 JAp,MA,Spawn Frankenstein . 6.50
25 JAp,MA,Spawn Frankenstein . 6.00

26 JAp,A:Frankenstein 6.00
27 V:Dr. Zorn 6.00
28 BU:Spawn of Frankenstein . . 6.00
29 V:Dr.Zorn,BU:Frankenstein . . 6.00
30 E:Spawn of Frankenstein 6.00
31 B:BU:Black Orchid 7.00
32 NR,BU:Black Orchid 7.00
33 MGr,A:Deadman 6.50
34 BU:Black Orchid 7.00
35 BU:Black Orchid 7.00
36 BU:Black Orchid 7.00
37 "Crimson Gold,"BU:BlackOrchid 7.00
38 "Images of the Dead" 7.00
39 A:Deadman 6.00
40 A:Deadman 6.00
41 A:Deadman 6.00

PHANTOM STRANGER
Oct., 1987
1 MMi,CR,V:Eclipso 3.00
2 MMi,CR,V:Eclipso 2.25
3 MMi,CR,V:Eclipso 2.25
4 MMi,CR,V:Eclipso, Jan. 1988 . . 2.25

PHANTOM ZONE, THE
Jan., 1982
1 GD/TD,A:Jax-Ur 1.25
2 GC/TD,A:JLA 1.25
3 GC/TD,A:Mon-El 1.25
4 GC/TD 1.25

PICTURE STORIES
FROM THE BIBLE
Autumn, 1942–43
1 thru 4 Old Testament . . . @150.00
1 thru 3 New Testament . . . @175.00

PINKY AND THE BRAIN
Warner Bros./DC
1 thru 4 . . . . @1.75
5 Oklahoma crud 1.75
6 "Plan Brain From Outer Space" 1.75
7 Yuletide tale 1.75
8 . . . . 1.75
9 SML(s) back to school 1.75
10 V:Melmouse 1.75
11 "Narftasia" 1.75
12 "Beach Blanket Brain" 1.75
13 "Ali Brain and the Forty Thieves"1.75
14 "Brainlet" 1.75
15 "Biker Mamas from Heck" 1.75

PLASTIC MAN
[1st Series]
Nov.–Dec., 1966
1 GK,I:Dr.Drome(1966 series
 begins) 60.00
2 V:The Spider 20.00
3 V:Whed 20.00
4 V:Dr.Dome 20.00
5 1,001 Plassassins 20.00
6 V:Dr.Dome 20.00
7 O:Plastic Man Jr.,A:Original
 Plastic Man,Woozy Winks . . 20.00
8 V:The Weasel 12.00
9 V:Joe the Killer Pro 12.00
10 V:Doll Maker(series ends) . . 12.00
11 (1976 series begins) 6.00
12 I:Carrot-Man 6.00
13 A:Robby Reed 6.00
14 V:Meat By-Product & Sludge . . 6.00
15 I:Snuffer,V:Carrot-Man 6.00
16 V:Kolonel Kool 6.00

17 O:Plastic Man 6.00
18 V:Professor Klean 6.00
19 I&Only App.Marty Meeker 6.00
20 V:Snooping Sneetches
 Oct.–Nov., 1977 . . . . 6.00

PLASTIC MAN
1988–89
1 Mini-series,Origin retold 1.25
2 V:The Ooze Brothers 1.25
3 In Los Angeles 1.25
4 End-series,A:Superman 1.25

PLOP!
Sept.–Oct., 1973
1 SA-AA,GE,ShM 5.00
2 AA,SA 4.00
3 AA,SA 4.00
4 BW,SA 4.00
5 MA,MSy,SA 4.00
6 MSy,SA 4.00
7 SA 3.50
8 SA 3.50
9 SA 3.50
10 SA 3.50
11 ATh,SA 4.00
12 SA 3.50
13 WW(c),SA 5.00
14 WW,SA 5.00
15 WW(c),SA 5.00
16 SD,WW,SA 5.00
17 SA 3.50
18 SD,WW,SA 5.00
19 WW,SA 5.00
20 SA,WW 5.00
21 JO,WW 5.00
22 JO,WW,BW 5.00
23 BW,WW 3.00
24 SA,WW,Nov.–Dec., 1976 . . . . 2.00

POWER GIRL
[Mini-Series] 1988
1 . . . . 1.00
2 A:The Weaver, mongo Krebs . . 1.00
3 V:The Weaver 1.00
4 V:Weaver, final issue 1.00

POWER OF SHAZAM!
1995–97
1 R:Captain Marvel 2.00
2 V:Arson Fiend 1.50
3 V:Ibac 1.50
4 JOy,R:Mary Marvel,Tawky,
 Tawny 1.75
5 JOy(c&a),F:Mary Marvel,
 V:Black Adam 1.75
6 R:Captain Marvel 1.75
7 V:Captain Nazi 1.75
8 R:Captain Marvel,Jr. 1.75
9 JOy,MM,V:Black Adam 1.75
10 JOy,MM,V:Seven Deadly
 Enemies of Man 1.75
11 JOy,MM,R:Ibis as Captain Marvel1.75
12 JOy,MM,How Billy Batson's
 father met Shazam 1.75
13 JOy,MM 1.75
14 JOy,GK,MM,F:CaptainMarvelJr 1.75
15 JOy,MM,V:Mr.Mind 1.75
16 thru 18 . . . . @1.75
19 JOy(s),GK,MM,Captain Marvel
 Jr. V:Captain Nazi 1.75
20 JOy(s),PKr,MM,A:Superman . . 1.75
21 JOy(s),PKr,MM,V:Liquidator . . 1.75
22 JOy(s),PKr,MM,A:Batman 1.75

DC COMICS

23 JOy(s),PKr,MM, ... 1.75
24 JOy(s),PKr,MM,V:Baron Blitz-
krieg, prelude to new family . . 1.75
25 JOy(s),PKr,MM,The Marvel
Family '97 . . . . 1.75
26 JOy(s),PKr,MM,new Capt.
Marvel framed for murder 1.75
27 JOy(s),PKr,MM,D:Captain
Marvel 1.75
28 JOy(s),DG, V:Patty Patty
Bang Bang 1.75
29 JOy(c),DG,F:Hoppy 1.75
30 JOy(c),PKr,DG,V:Mr. Finish . . 1.75
Ann.#1 JOy(s),MM,"Legends of
the Dead Earth" 2.95
HC JOy(a&s),O:Captain Marvel . 22.00
GNv JOy(a&s),O:Captain Marvel . 9.95

Power of the Atom #2
© DC Comics, Inc.

POWER OF THE ATOM
1988–89
1 1st Issue, Origin retold 1.25
2 Return of Powers 1.25
3 I:Strobe 1.25
4 A:Hawkman+bonus book #8 . . 1.25
5 DT,A:Elongated Man 1.25
6 JBy,V:Chronos 1.25
7 GN,Invasion,V:Khunds,Chronos 1.25
8 GN,Invasion,V:Chronos 1.25
9 GN,A:Justice League 1.25
10 GN,I:Humbug 1.25
11 GN,V:Paul Hoben 1.25
12 GN,V:Edg.the Destroyer 1.25
13 GN,Blood Stream Journey . . . 1.25
14 GN,V:Humbug 1.25
15 GN,V:Humbug 1.25
16 GN,V:The CIA 1.25
17 GN,V:The Sting 1.25
18 GN,V:The CIA, last issue 1.25

PREACHER
Vertigo 1995–97
1 I:Jesse Custer, Genesis 50.00
2 Saint of Killers 45.00
3 GF(c),I:Angels 40.00
4 GF(c),V:Saint of Killers 30.00
5 Naked City,pt.1 . . . . 25.00

6 Naked City,pt.2 . . . . 20.00
7 Naked City,pt.3 . . . . 15.00
8 GEn,SDi,All in the Family,pt.1 . 9.00
9 GEn,SDi,All in the Family,pt.2 . 9.00
10 GEn,SDi,All in the Family,pt.3 . 8.00
11 GEn,SDi,All in the Family,pt.4 . 8.00
12 GEn,SDi,All in the Family,pt.5 . 10.00
13 GEn,SDi,Hunters,pt.1 . . . . 5.00
14 GEn,SDi,Hunters,pt.2 (of 4) . . 4.00
15 and 16 . . . . @4.00
17 Star captures Cassidy 3.00
18 GEn(s),SDi,secret of Jesse
Custer's cigarette lighter 3.00
19 GEn(s),SDi,"Crusaders," pt.1 . . 2.50
20 GEn(s),SDi,"Crusaders," pt.2 . . 2.50
21 GEn(s),SDi,"Crusaders," pt.3 . . 2.50
22 GEn(s),SDi,"Crusaders," pt.4 . . 2.50
23 GEn(s),SDi,"Crusaders," pt.5 . . 2.50
24 GEn(s),SDi,"Crusaders" concl. . 2.50
25 GEn(s),SDi,"Cry Blood, Cry
Erin" 2.50
26 GEn(s),SDi,"To the Streets of
Manhattan I Wandered Away" . 2.50
27 GEn(s),SDi, Jessie & Tulip in
New York, pt.1 . . . . 2.50
28 GEn(s),SDi, Jessie & Tulip in
New York, pt.2 . . . . 2.50
29 GEn(s),SDi, south to New
Orleans 2.50

PREACHER SPECIAL: SAINT OF KILLERS
DC/Vertigo 1996
1 GEn(s),StP 5.00
2 GEn(s),StP 3.50
3 GEn(s),StP 3.00
4 GEn(s),StP 2.50

PREACHER SPECIAL: THE GOOD OLD BOYS
DC/Vertigo
Spec. pardoy 5.50

PREACHER SPECIAL: THE STORY OF YOU-KNOW-WHO
DC/Vertigo Oct. 1996
1 one-shot, GEn(s),RCa,
O:Arseface 4.95

PREZ
Aug.–Sept., 1973
1 I:Prez (from Sandman #54) . . 12.00
2 thru 4 F:Prez 8.00

PRIDE & JOY
DC/Vertigo May 1997
[Mini-series]
1 (of 4) GEn(s),JHi, ... 2.50
2 GEn(s),JHi 2.50
3 GEn(s),JHi 2.50

PRIMAL FORCE
1994–95
O New Team 1.95
1 Claw 1.95
2 Cataclysm 1.95
3 . . . . 1.95
4 Claw 1.95
5 V:Demons 1.95
6 V:The Four Beasts 1.95

7 Trip to the Past 1.95
8 N.Choles(p),I:New Team 2.25
9 Maltis worsens, Tornado speaks 2.25
10 V:August 2.25
11 . . . . 2.25
12 Black Condor vs. August 2.25
13 Underworld Unleashed tie-in . . 2.25
14 final issue 2.25

PRINCE
Piranha Press
1 DCw,KW,based on rock star . 10.00
1a Second printing 2.50
1b 3rd printing 2.00

PRISONER, THE
1988–89
1 Based on TV series 5.00
2 'By Hook or by Crook' 5.00
3 'Confrontation' 5.00
4 'Departure' final issue 5.00

PSYBA-RATS, THE
[Mini-Series] 1995
1 CDi,A:Robin 2.50
2 CDi,A:Robin 1.50
3 CDi,F:Razorsharp,final issue . . 1.50

PSYCHO
1 I:Psycho 12.00
2 Sonya Rescue 10.00
3 'Psycho against the World' . . . 7.00

QUESTION, THE
Feb., 1987
1 DCw,R:Question,I:Myra,A:Shiva 3.00
2 DCw,A:Batman,Shiva 2.00
3 DCw,I:Mayor Firman 2.00
4 DCw,V:Hatch 2.00
5 DCw,Hub City fall Apart 2.00
6 DCw,Abuse story 2.00
7 DCw,V:Mr.Volk 2.00
8 DCw,I:Mikado 2.00
9 DCw,O:Rodor 2.00
10 DCw,O:Rodor cont. 2.00
11 DCw,Transformation 2.00
12 DCw,Poisoned Ground 2.00
13 DCw,V:The Spartans 2.00
14 DCw,V:The Spartans 2.00
15 DCw,The Klan in Hub City . . . 2.00
16 DCw,'Butch Cassidy &
Sundance Kid' 2.00
17 DCw,A:Green Arrow 2.50
18 DCw,A:Green Arrow 2.50
19 DCw,V:Terrorists 2.00
20 DCw,Travelling Circus 2.00
21 DCw,V:Junior Musto 2.00
22 DCw,Election Night 2.00
23 DCw,Election Night contd 2.00
24 DCw,Election Night contd 2.00
25 DCw,Myra Critically Ill 2.00
26 A:Riddler 2.00
27 DCw 2.00
28 DCw,A:Lady Shiva 2.00
29 DCw,V:Lady Shiva 2.00
30 DCw,A:Lady Shiva 2.00
31 DCw,Hub City Chaos contd . . 2.00
32 DCw,Identity Crisis 2.00
33 DCw,Identity Crisis contd 2.00
34 DCw,Identity Crisis contd 2.00
35 DCw,Fate of Hub City 2.00
36 DCw,final issue (contd.G.A.Ann#3
Question Quarterly #1) 2.00

DC COMICS

Ann.#1 DCw,A:Batman,G.A. 3.00
Ann.#2 A:Green Arrow 4.00

QUESTION QUARTERLY
1 DCw 4.50
2 DCw 3.95
3 DCw(c) Film 2.95
4 DCw,MM,'Waiting for Phil' 2.95
5 DCw,MMi,MM,last issue 2.95

RAGMAN
[1st Limited Series] 1976–77
1 I&O:Ragman 5.00
2 I:Opal 3.50
3 V:Mr. Big 3.00
4 JKu(1st interior on character) . . 3.00
5 JKu,O:Ragman,final issue 3.00
[2nd Limited Series] 1991–92
1 PB,O:Ragman 3.00
2 PB,O:Ragman Powers 3.00
3 PB,Original Ragman 2.75
4 PB,Gang War 2.75
5 PB,V:Golem 2.75
6 PB,V:Golem,A:Batman 2.75
7 PB,V:Golem,A:Batman 2.75
8 PB,V:Golem,A:Batman 2.75

RAGMAN: CRY OF THE DEAD
1993–94
1 JKu(c),R:Ragman 2.00
2 JKu(c),A:Marinette 2.00
3 JKu(c),V:Marinette 2.00
4 JKu(c),Exorcism 2.00
5 JKu(c),V:Marinette 2.00
6 JKu(c),final issue 2.00

THE RAY
[Limited Series] 1992
1 JQ,ANi,I&O:Ray(Ray Torril) . . 11.00
2 JQ,ANi,I:G.A. Ray 7.00
3 JQ,ANi,A:G.A. Ray 5.00
4 JQ,ANi,V:Dr.Polaris 8.00
5 JQ,ANi,V:Dr.Polaris 4.00
6 JQ,ANi,C:Lobo,final issue 4.00
TPB In A Blaze of Power 9.95
[Regular Series] 1994–96
1 JQ(c),RPr,V:Brinestone,
  A:Superboy 3.50
1a Newsstand Ed. 1.75
2 RPr,V:Brinestone,A:Superboy . . 1.75
3 RPr,I:Death Masque 2.00
4 JQ(c),RPr,I:Death Masque,
  Dr. Polarus 2.00
5 JQ,RPr,V:G.A.Ray 1.95
6 JQ(c),RPr,V:Black Canary 1.95
7 JQ(c),RPr,V:Canary/Ray 1.95
8 V:Lobo,Black Canary 1.95
9 Ray Undoes the past 1.95
10 F:Happy Terril 1.95
11 30 years in future 1.95
12 V:Mystech 1.95
13 V:Death Masque 2.25
14 The Ray needs help, V:Death
  Masque 2.25
15 F:Vandal Savage 2.25
16 D:Happy Terrill 2.25
17 I:Josh Terrill,V:Atomic Skull . . 2.25
18 Underworld Unleashed tie-in . . 2.25
19 Underworld Unleashed tie-in . . 2.25
20 F:Black Condor 2.25
21 Black Condor captured 2.25
22 . . . . 2.25

The Ray #13 © DC Comics, Inc.

23 V:Death Masque 2.25
24 . . . . 2.25
25 double size 3.50
26 . . . . 2.25
27 . . . . 2.25
28 CPr,final issue 2.25
Ann.#1 Year One Annual 3.95

REAL FACT COMICS
March-April, 1946
1 S&K,Harry Houdini story . . . 500.00
2 S&K, Rin-Tin-Tin story 350.00
3 H.G. Wells story 300.00
4 Jimmy Stewart story,B:Just
  Imagine 350.00
5 Batman & Robin(c) 1,500.00
6 O:Tommy Tomorrow 1,000.00
7 'The Flying White House' . . . 150.00
8 VF,A:Tommy Tomorrow 500.00
9 S&K,Glen Miller story 250.00
10 'The Vigilante' by MMe 250.00
11 EK,'How the G-Men Capture
  Public Enemies!' 150.00
12 'How G-Men are Trained' . . 150.00
13 Dale Evans story 450.00
14 Will Rogers story,'Diary of
  Death' 125.00
15 A:The Master Magician-
  Thurston 125.00
16 A:Four Reno Brothers,
  T.Tommorrow 400.00
17'I Guard an Armored Car' . . . 125.00
18 'The Mystery Man of
  Tombstone' 125.00
19 'The Weapon that Won the
  West' 125.00
20 JKu 150.00
21 JKu,July-Aug., 1949 . . . . . . 125.00

REAL SCREEN COMICS
Spring, 1945
1 B:Fox & the Crow,Flippity
  & Flop 850.00
2 (fa) 400.00
3 (fa) 200.00
4 thru 7 (fa) . . . . @150.00
8 thru 11 (fa) . . . . @125.00

12 thru 20 (fa) . . . . @90.00
21 thru 30 (fa) . . . . @75.00
31 thru 40 (fa) . . . . @50.00
41 thru 128 (fa) . . . . @35.00
Becomes:

TV SCREEN CARTOONS
129 thru 137 . . . . @40.00
138 Jan.–Feb., 1961 . . . . 40.00

R.E.B.E.L.S '94
0 New team 1.95
1 L.E.G.I.O.N.,Green Lantern . . . 1.95
2 Dissent 1.95
3 . . . . 1.95
4 Ship goes Insane 1.95

R.E.B.E.L.S '95
5 F:Dox 1.95
6 Dox Defeated 1.95
7 John Sin 1.95
8 V:Galactic Bank 2.25
9 F:Dox,Ignea,Garv,Strata 2.25
10 V:World Bank 2.25
11 . . . . 2.25
12 F:Iceman Assassin 2.25
13 Underworld Unleashed tie-in . . 2.25
14 F:Lyrl Dox 2.25

R.E.B.E.L.S. '96
15 V:Lyrl Dox 2.25
16 V:Lyrl Dox's satellite 2.25

RED TORNADO
1985
1 CI/FMc 1.25
2 CI/FMc,A:Superman 1.25
3 CI/FMc 1.25
4 CI/FMc 1.25

RESTAURANT AT THE END OF THE UNIVERSE
1994
1 Adapt. 2nd book in Hitchhikers'
  Guide to the Galaxy,
  I:The Restaurant 5.95
2 V:The Meal 6.95
3 Final issue 6.95

RESURRECTION MAN
March 1997
1 DAn(s),JG,lenticular death's
  head cover 2.50
2 DAn(s),JG,V:Amazo 2.50
3 DAn(s),JG,"Scorpion Memories"
  pt.1 (of 3) 2.50
4 DAn(s),JG,"Scorpion Memories"
  pt.2 . . . . 2.50
5 DAn(s),JG,"Scorpion Memories"
  pt.3 concl. 2.50

RICHARD DRAGON, KUNG FU FIGHTER
April-May, 1975
1 O:Richard Dragon 1.50
2 JSn/AM 1.50
3 JK 1.25
4 RE/WW 1.25
5 RE/WW 1.25
6 RE/WW 1.25
7 RE/WW 1.25
8 RE/WW 1.25
9 RE 1.25
10 RE 1.25
11 RE 1.25

12 RE 1.25
13 thru 17 RE . . . . @1.25
18 Nov.–Dec., 1977 . . . . 1.25

Rima, The Jungle Girl #1
© DC Comics, Inc.

RIMA, THE JUNGLE GIRL
April–May, 1974

1 NR,I:Rima,O:Pt. 1 . . . . 2.00
2 NR,O:Pt.2 . . . . 1.50
3 NR,O:Pt.3 . . . . 1.25
4 NR,O:Pt.4 . . . . 1.25
5 NR 1.25
6 NR 1.25
7 April–May, 1975 . . . . 1.25

RING, THE

1 GK,Opera Adaption 12.00
2 GK,Sigfried's Father's Sword . . 7.00
3 GK,to save Brunhilde 6.00
4 GK, final issue 6.00
TPB rep.#1 thru #4 . . . . 19.95

RIP HUNTER, TIME MASTER
March–April, 1961

1 . . . . 500.00
2 . . . . 225.00
3 thru 5 . . . . @125.00
6 and 7 Ath . . . . @125.00
8 thru 15 . . . . @75.00
16 thru 20 . . . . @75.00
21 thru 28 . . . . @75.00
29 Nov.–Dec., 1965 . . . . 75.00

ROBIN
[1st Limited Series] 1991

1 TL,BB(c),Trial,pt.1(&Poster) . . . 5.00
1a 2nd printing 2.50
1b 3rd printing 1.50
2 TL,BB(c) Trial,pt.2 . . . . 2.50
2a 2nd printing 1.50
3 TL,BB(c) Trial,pt.3 . . . . 2.00
4 TL,Trial,pt.4 . . . . 2.00
5 TL,Final issue,A:Batman 2.00
TPB BB(c),rep.#1–#5,Batman

#455–#457 . . . . 7.95

[2nd Limited Series] 1991
[ROBIN II: THE JOKER'S WILD]

1 Direct,Hologram(c)Joker face . . 2.00
1a (c)Joker straightjacket 2.00
1b (c)Joker standing 2.00
1c (c)Batman 2.00
1d Newsstand(no hologram) 1.00
1e collectors set,extra holo. 5.00
2 Direct,Hologram(c) Robin/Joker
   Knife 1.50
2a (c)Joker/Robin-Dartboard 1.50
2b (c)Robin/Joker-Hammer 1.50
2c Newsstand(no hologram) 1.00
2d collectors set,extra holo. 5.00
3 Direct,Holo(c)Robin standing . . 1.50
3a (c)Robin swinging 1.50
3b Newsstand(no hologram) 1.50
3c collectors set,extra holo. 3.00
4 Direct,Hologram 1.50
4a Newsstand (no hologram) . . . 1.25
4b collectors set,extra holo. 2.00
Collectors set (#1 thru #4) 30.00

[3rd Limited Series] 1992–93
[ROBIN III: CRY OF THE HUNTRESS]

1 TL,A:Huntress,Collector's Ed.
   movable(c),poster 3.00
1a MZ(c),Newsstand Ed. 1.50
2 TL,V:KGBeast,A:Huntress 2.75
2a MZ(c),Newsstand Ed 1.50
3 TL,V:KGBeast,A:Huntress 2.75
3a MZ(c),newsstand Ed. 1.50
4 TL,V:KGBeast,A:Huntress 2.75
4a MZ(c),newsstand Ed. 1.50
5 TL,V:KGBeast,A:Huntress 2.75
5a MZ(c),newsstand Ed. 1.50
6 TL,V:KGBeast,King Snake,
   A:Huntress. 2.75
6a MZ(c),Newsstand Ed. 1.50

[Regular Series] 1993–97

1 B:CDi(s),TG,SHa,V:Speedboyz . 4.00
1a Newstand Ed. 2.00
2 TG,V:Speedboyz 2.00
3 TG,V:Cluemaster,
   Electrocutioner 1.75
4 TG,V:Cluemaster,Czonk,
   Electrocutioner 1.75
5 TG,V:Cluemaster,Czonk,
   Electrocutioner 1.75
6 TG,A:Huntress 1.75
7 TG,R:Robin's Father 2.00
8 TG,KnightsEnd#5,A:Shiva 3.00
9 TG,Knights End:Aftermath 2.25
10 TG,Zero Hour,V:Weasel 1.50
11 New Batman 1.50
12 Robin vs. thugs 1.50
13 V:Steeljacket 1.50
14 CDi(s),TG,Return of Bruce
   Wayne,Troika,pt.4 . . . . 1.50
14a Collector's edition 2.50
15 Cluemaster Mystery 1.50
16 F:Spoiler 1.50
17 I:Silver Monkey,V:King Snake,Lynx
   [New Miraweb format begins] . 1.95
18 Gotham City sabotaged 1.95
19 V:The General 1.95
20 F:Robin 1.95
21 Ninja Camp,pt.1 . . . . 1.95
22 CDi,TG,Ninja Camp,pt.2 . . . . . 1.95
23 CDi,Underworld Unleashed tie-in 1.95
24 CDi,V:Charaxes 1.95
25 CDi,F:Green Arrow 1.95
26 . . . . 1.95
27 . . . . 1.95
28 CDi,Contagion: conclusion . . . 1.95

Robin (Regular Series) #1
© DC Comics, Inc.

29 CDi,FFo,SnW,A:Maxie Zeus . . 1.95
30 CDi,FFo,SnW,A:Maxie Zeus . . 1.95
31 CDi(s),A:Wildcat 1.95
32 CDi(s),Legacy, pt. 3 x-over . . . 1.95
33 CDi(s),Legacy, pt. 7 x-over . . . 1.95
34 CDi(s),JhD,action at a
   Shakespear play 1.95
35 CDi(s),Robin & Spoiler, Final
   Night tie-in 1.95
36 CDi(s),V:Toyman, The General 1.95
37 CDi(s),V:The General, Toyman 1.95
38 CDi(s), ... 1.95
39 CDi(s), pt.2 . . . . 1.95
40 CDi(s), ... 1.95
41 CDi(s),F:Tim and Ariana 1.95
42 CDi(s),F:Crocky the Crocodile . 1.95
43 CDi(s),A:Spoiler 1.95
44 CDi(s) Pt.2 (of 2) 1.95
45 CDi(s) Tim Drake grounded . . 1.95
Ann.#1 TL,Eclipso tie-in,V:Anarky 3.00
Ann.#2 KD,JL,Bloodlines#10,
   I:Razorsharp 2.75
Ann.#3 Elseworlds Story 3.25
Ann.#4 Year One Annual 2.95
Ann.#5 CDi,Legends of the Dead
   Earth 2.95
Ann.#5 Legends o/t Dead Earth . 2.95
Ann.#6 Pulp Heroes (Western),
   CDi(s) 3.95
TPB A Hero Reborn,JAp,TL 4.95
TPB Tragedy and Triumph,
   TL,NBy 9.95

ROBIN PLUS

1 MWa&BAu(s), F:Bart Allen, skiing
   rips, V:Mystral 2.95

ROBIN 3000

1 CR,Elseworlds,V:Skulpt 5.25
2 CR,Elseworlds,V:Skulpt 5.25

ROBIN HOOD TALES
Jan.–Feb., 1957–Mar.–Apr., 1958

7 . . . . 120.00
8 thru 14 . . . . @120.00

All comics prices listed are for *Near Mint* condition.

DC COMICS

ROBOTECH DEFENDERS
1 MA,mini-series 3.50
2 MA 3.00

ROGAN GOSH
Vertigo 1994
1 PF PrM(s) (From Revolver) . . . 7.25

RONIN
July, 1983
1 FM,1:Billy 7.00
2 FM,I:Casey 6.00
3 FM,V:Agat 6.00
4 FM,V:Agat 6.00
5 FM,V:Agat 7.00
6 FM,D:Billy 9.00
Paperback, FM inc. Gatefold . . . 12.00

ROOTS OF THE SWAMP THING
July, 1986
1 BWr,rep.SwampThing#1&#2 . . 3.00
2 BWr,rep.SwampThing#3&#4 . . 3.00
3 BWr,rep.SwampThing#5&#6 . . 3.00
4 BWr,rep.SwampThing#7&#8 . . 3.00
5 BWr,rep.SwampThing#9&#10,
   H.O.S. #92, final issue 3.00

RUDOLPH THE RED -NOSED REINDEER
Dec., 1950
1950 . . . . 50.00
1951 thru 1954 . . . . @35.00
1955 thru 1962 Winter . . . . . @20.00

SAGA OF RĀS AL GHŪL
1988
1 NA,DG,reprints 5.00
2 rep. 4.00
3 rep.Batman #242&#243 . . . . . 4.00
4 rep.Batman #244&#245,
   Detective #410 . . . . 4.00
TPB reps. 17.95

SAGA OF THE SWAMP THING
1982–85
1 JmP(s),TY,DSp,O:Swamp Thing,
   BU:PhantomStranger 4.00
2 Ph(c),TY,DSp,I:Grasp 2.00
3 TY,DSp,V:Vampires 2.00
4 TY,TD,V:Demon 2.00
5 TY 2.00
6 TY,I:General Sunderland 2.00
7 TY 2.00
8 TY 2.00
9 TY 2.00
10 TY 2.00
11 TY,I:Golem 2.00
12 LWn(s),TY 2.00
13 TY,D:Grasp 2.00
14 A:Phantom Stranger 2.00
15 . . . . 2.00
16 SBi,JTo 2.00
17 I:Matthew Cable 4.00
18 JmP(s),LWn(s),SBi,JTo,BWr,
   R:Arcane 2.00
19 JmP(s),SBi,JTo,V:Arcane . . . 2.00
20 B:AMo(s),Day,JTo(i),D:Arcane

(Original incarnation) 17.00
21 SBi,JTo,O:Swamp Thing,I:Floronic
   Man,D:General Sunderland . . 15.00
22 SBi,JTo,O:Floronic Man 10.00
23 SBi,JTo,V:Floronic Man 10.00
24 SBi,JTo,V:Floronic Man,A:JLA,
   In Arkham 10.00
25 SBi,A:Jason Blood,I:Kamara . . 8.00
26 SBi,A:Demon,
   D:Matthew Cable 8.00
27 SBi,D:Kamara,A:Demon 7.00
28 SwM,Burial of Alec Holland . . . 7.00
29 SBi,JTo,R:Arcane 7.00
30 SBi,AA,D:Abby,C:Joker,
   V:Arcane 9.00
31 RV,JTo,D:Arcane 6.00
32 SwM,Tribute to WK Pogo strip   6.00
33 rep.H.O.S.#92,A:Cain & Abel . 6.00
34 SBi,JTo,Swamp Thing & Abby
   Fall in Love 8.00
35 SBi,JTo,Nukeface,pt.1 . . . . . . 5.00
36 SBi,JTo,Nukeface,pt.2 . . . . . . 5.00
37 RV,JTo,I:John Constantine,
   American Gothic,pt.1 . . . . . . 18.00
38 SnW,JTo,V:Water-Vampires
   (Pt.1) A:J.Constantine 7.00
39 SBi,JTo,V:Water-Vampires
   (Pt.2) A:J.Constantine 6.00
40 SBi,JTo,C:J.Constantine,
   The Curse 5.00
41 SBi,AA,Voodoo Zombies #1 . . 3.00
42 SBi,JTo,RoR,
   Voodoo Zombies #2 . . . . 3.00
43 SnW,RoR,Windfall,
   I:Chester Williams 3.00
44 SBi,JTo,RoR,V:Serial Killer,
   C:Batman,Constantine,Mento . 5.00
45 SnW,AA,Ghost Dance 3.00
Ann.#1 MT,TD,Movie Adaption . . 2.00
Ann.#2 AMo(s),E:Arcane,A:Deadman,
   Phantom Stranger,Spectre,
   Demon,Resurrection of Abby . . 7.00
Ann.#3 AMo(s),Ape issue 4.00
TPB rep.#21-#27 . . . . 12.95
TPB rep.#28-#34,Ann.#2 . . . . 14.95
Becomes:

SWAMP THING

SANDMAN
[1st Regular Series] 1974–75
1 JK,I&O:Sandman,I:General
   Electric 10.00
2 V:Dr.Spider 5.00
3 Brain that Blanked
   out the Bronx 5.00
4 JK,Panic in the Dream Stream . 5.00
5 JK,Invasion of the Frog Men . . 5.00
6 JK,WW,V:Dr.Spider 6.00
[2nd Regular Series] 1989–93
1 B:NGa(s),SK,I:2nd Sandman . 85.00
2 SK,A:Cain,Abel 55.00
3 SK,A:John Constantine 45.00
4 SK,A:Demon 40.00
5 SK,A:Mr.Miracle,J'onnJ'onzz . 40.00
6 V:Doctor Destiny 35.00
7 V:Doctor Destiny 30.00
8 Sound of her wings,F:Death . 60.00
8a Guest Ed.Pin-Up Cover . . . 175.00
9 Tales in the Sand,Doll's House
   prologue 18.00
10 B:Doll's House,A:Desire
   & Despair,I:Brut & Glob 17.00
11 MovingIn,A:2ndS-man 17.00
12 Play House,D;2ndS'man 17.00

Sandman #1 © DC Comics, Inc.

13 Men of Good Fortune,A:Death,
   Lady Constantine 17.00
14 Collectors,D:Corinthian 19.00
15 Into' Night,DreamVortex 13.00
16 E:Doll's House,Lost Hearts . . 13.00
17 Calliope 11.00
18 Dream of a 1000 Cats 11.00
18a error pg.1 . . . . 50.00
19 Midsummer Nights Dream . . 10.00
19a error copy 55.00
20 Strange Death Element Girl,
   A:Death 10.00
21 Family Reunion,B:Season
   of Mists 12.00
22 Season of Mists,I:Daniel Hall   28.00
23 Season of Mists 11.00
24 Season of Mists 11.00
25 Season of Mists 11.00
26 Season of Mists 9.00
27 E:Season of Mists 9.00
28 Ownership of Hell 9.00
29 A:Lady J.Constantine 9.00
30 Ancient Rome,A:Death,Desire . 8.00
31 Ancient Rome,pt.2 . . . . 7.00
32 B:The Game of You 8.00
33 The Game of You 7.00
34 The Game of You 6.00
35 The Game of You 6.00
36 The Game of You,48pgs 7.00
37 The Game of You,Epilogue . . 6.00
38 Convergence 6.00
39 Convergence,A:Marco Polo . . 5.00
40 Convergence,A:Cain,Abel,Eve,
   Matthew the Raven 5.00
41 JIT,VcL,(i),B:Brief Lives,
   F:Endless 6.00
42 JIT,VcL,(i),F:Delirium,Dream . 5.00
43 JIT,VcL,(i),A:Death,Etain 5.00
44 JIT,VcL,(i),R:Corinthian,
   Destruction 4.50
45 JIT,VcL,(i),F:Tiffany,
   Ishtar(Belli) 4.50
46 JIT,VcL,(i),F:Morpheus/Bast,A:AIDS
   insert story,F:Death 5.50
Vertigo 1994–96
47 JIT,VcL,(i),A:Endless 3.50
48 JIT,VcL,(i),L:Destruction 3.50
49 JIT,VcL,(i),E:Brief Lives,

DC COMICS

F:Orpheus 3.50
50 DMc(c),CR,Tales of Baghdad,
  pin-upsby TM,DMc,MK 4.00
50a Gold Ed. 40.00
51 BT,MBu(i),B:Inn at the end of the
  World,Gaheris' tale 3.50
52 BT,MBu(i),JWk,Cluracan's
  Story 3.50
53 BT,DG,MBu(i),MZi,Hob's
  Leviathan 3.50
54 BT,MiA,MBu(i),R:Prez 3.50
55 SAp,VcL,BT,MBu(i),F:Klaproth,
  Cerements's Story 3.50
56 BT,MBu(i),DG(i),SLi(i),GyA,TyH(i),
  E:Inn at the end of the World,
  C:Endless 3.50
57 MaH,B:Kindly Ones,Inc.American
  Freak Preview 4.50
58 MaH,Kindly Ones,pt.2,
  A:Lucifer 3.00
59 MaH,Kindly Ones,pt.3,R:Fury . 2.50
60 MaH,Kindly Ones,pt.4 . . . . . 2.50
61 MaH,Kindly Ones,pt.5 . . . . . 2.50
62 Kindly Ones,pt.6,Murder 2.50
63 MaH,Kindly Ones,pt.7,
  A:Rose Walker 2.50
64 Kindly Ones,pt.8 . . . . 2.50
65 MaH,Kindly Ones,pt.9,Dream
  Kingdom 2.50
66 MaH,Kindly Ones,pt.10 . . . . 2.50
67 MaH,Kindly Ones,pt.11 . . . . 2.50
68 MaH,Kindly Ones,pt.12 . . . . 2.50
69 MaH,Kindly Ones finale 4.00
70 The Wake,pt.1 . . . . 2.50
71 The Wake,pt.2 . . . . 2.50
72 NGa,DMc,The Wake,pt.3 . . . . 2.50
73 NGa,Sunday Mourning 2.50
74 NGa,V:Lord of Dreams 2.50
TPB Dream Country,Rep.#17-#20 15.00
TPB The Dolls House,Rep.#8-#16 15.00
Fables and Reflections,HC,rep. . 29.95
TPB Preludes & Nocturnes,
  Rep.#1-#8 . . . . 15.00
Season of Mists,HC,rep.#21-#28 40.00
Season of Mists,SC 19.95
Spec.BT,Glow in the Dark(c),The
  Legend of Orpheus,
  (inc. Portrait Gallery) 6.00
HC A Game of You,rep.#32-#37 32.00
HC Brief Lives 29.95
TPB Brief Lives 19.95
TPB Sandman:A Game of You . 19.95
TPB Fables & Reflections 19.95
TPB World's End DMc(c) 19.95
HC The Doll's House 29.95

SANDMAN MYSTERY THEATRE
Vertigo 1993–97

1 B:MWg(s),GyD,R:G.A.Sandman,
  B:Tarantula,I:Mr.Belmont,
  Dian Belmont 3.50
2 GyD,V:Tarantula 3.00
3 GyD,V:Tarantula 2.50
4 GyD,E:Tarantula 2.50
5 JWk,B:The Face 2.25
6 JWk,The Face #2 . . . . 2.25
7 JWk,The Face #3 . . . . 2.25
8 JWk,E:The Face 2.25
9 RGT,B:The Brute,I:Rocket
  Ramsey 2.25
10 RGT,The Brute#2 . . . . 2.25
11 RGT,The Brute#3 . . . . 2.25
12 RGT,E:The Brute 2.25

13 GyD,B:The Vamp 2.25
14 GyD,The Vamp#2 . . . . 2.25
15 GyD,The Vamp#3 . . . . 2.25
16 GyD,E:The Vamp 2.25
17 GyD,B:The Scorpion 2.25
18 GyD,The Scorpion,pt.2 . . . . 2.25
19 GyD,The Scorpion,pt.3 . . . . 2.25
20 GyD,The Scorpion,pt.4 . . . . 2.25
21 Dr. Death 2.25
22 Dr. Death,pt.2 . . . . 2.25
23 Dr. Death,pt.3 . . . . 2.25
24 Dr. Death,pt.4 . . . . 2.25
25 The Butcher,pt.1 . . . . 2.25
26 The Butcher,pt.2 . . . . 2.25
27 The Butcher,pt.3 . . . . 2.25
28 The Butcher,pt.4 . . . . 2.25
29 The Hourman,pt.1 . . . . 2.25
30 The Hourman,pt.2 . . . . 2.25
31 The Hourman,pt.3 . . . . 2.25
32 The Hourman,pt.4 . . . . 2.25
33 The Python,pt.1 . . . . 2.25
34 The Python,pt.2 . . . . 2.25
35 The Python,pt.3 . . . . 2.25
36 The Python,pt.4 . . . . 2.25
37 The Mist,pt.1 . . . . 2.25
38 The Mist,pt.2 . . . . 2.25
39 The Mist,pt.3 (of 4) 2.25
40 . . . . 2.50
41 MWg&SSe(s),GyD, Phantom of
  the Fair pt. 1 . . . . 2.50
42 MWg&SSe(s),GyD, Phantom of
  the Fair pt. 2 . . . . 2.50
43 MWg&SSe(s),GyD, Phantom of
  the Fair pt. 3 . . . . 2.50
44 MWg&SSe(s),GyD, Phantom of
  the Fair pt. 4 . . . . 2.50
45 MWg&SSe(s),"The Blackhawk,"
  pt.1 . . . . 2.50
46 MWg&SSe(s),"The Blackhawk,"
  pt.2 . . . . 2.50
47 MWg&SSe(s),"The Blackhawk,"
  pt.3 . . . . 2.50
48 MWg&SSe(s),RCa,"The
  Blackhawk" concl. 2.50
49 MWg&SSe(s),"The Scarlet
  Ghost," pt.1 . . . . 2.50
50 MWg&SSe(s),"The Scarlet
  Ghost," pt.2, 48pg 3.50
51 MWg&SSe(s),"The Scarlet
  Ghost," pt.3 . . . . 2.50
52 MWg&SSe(s),"The Scarlet
  Ghost," pt.4 . . . . 2.50
53 MWg&SSe(s),"The Crone" pt.1 2.50
53 MWg&SSe(s),"The Crone" pt.2 2.50
Ann.#1 . . . . 3.95
TPB The Tarantula 14.95

SANDMAN: THE WAKE
DC/Vertigo

HC Rep. Sandman #70–#75 . . . 29.95

SCARAB
Vertigo 1993–94

1 GF(c),B:JnS(s),SEa,MkB(i),
  R&O:Scarab,V:Halaku-umid . . 2.25
2 GF(c),SEa,MkB(i),A:Phantom
  Stranger 2.25
3 GF(c),SEa,MkB(i),in North
  Carolina 2.25
4 GF(c),SEa,MkB(i),V:Rathoroch . 2.25
5 GF(c),SEa,MkB(i) 2.25
6 GF(c),SEa,MkB(i),V:Gloryboys . 2.25
7 GF(c),SEa,MkB(i),V:Scientists . 2.25
8 GF(c),SEa,MkB(i),Final Issue . . 2.25

SCARE TACTICS
Oct. 1996

1 LKa(s),AWi,ALa,monsters of
  the MTV age 2.25
2 LKa(s),AWi,ALa,I:Scaremobile . 2.25
3 LKa(s),AWi,ALa, ... 2.25
4 LKa(s),AWi,ALa, "Big For His
  Age," O:Grossout 2.25
5 LKa(s),AWi,ALa, Valentine's Day
  issue 2.25
6 LKa(s),AWi,Ala, F:Fang 2.25
7 LKa(s),AWi,ALa, F:The Children
  of the Beast 2.25
8 LKa(s),AWi,ALa, Convergence,
  x-over, concl. 2.25
9 LKa(s),AWi,ALa,"Snake Oil"
  concl. 2.25

Scarlett #4 © DC Comics, Inc.

SCARLETT
1993–94

1 I:Scarlett,Blood of the Innocent 3.50
2 Blood of the Innocent cont. . . . 1.75
3 Blood of the Innocent cont. . . . 1.75
4 V:The Nomads 1.75
5 GM,O:Nomads 1.75
6 thru 8 GM,Blood of the Damned 1.75
9 GM,V:Undead 1.75
10 B:Blood of the City 1.75
11 I:Afterburn 1.75
12 V:Sligoth 1.75
13 V:Gearsman 1.75
14 final issue 1.75

SCRIBBLY
Aug.–Sept., 1948

1 SM 600.00
2 . . . . 400.00
3 . . . . 300.00
4 . . . . 300.00
5 . . . . 300.00
6 thru 10 . . . . @250.00
11 thru 15, Dec-Jan.1951–52 @200.00

SCOOBY-DOO
Warner Bros./DC June 1997

1 . . . . 1.75
2 . . . . 1.75

SEA DEVILS
Sept.–Oct., 1961

1 RH		500.00
2 RH		250.00
3 RH		175.00
4 RH		150.00
5 RH		150.00
6 thru 10 RH		@85.00
11		65.00
12		65.00
13 JKu,GC,RA		65.00
14 thru 20		@65.00
21 I:Capt X,Man Fish		40.00
22 thru 35, May-June, 1967		@40.00

SEBASTIAN O
Vertigo 1993

1 GMo(s),SY,I:Sebastian O,A:Lord
Lavender,Roaring Boys 2.50
2 GMo(s),SY,V:Roaring Boys,
Assassins,A:Abbe 2.50
3 GMo(s),SY,D:Lord Lavender . . 2.50

SECRET HEARTS
Sept.–Oct., 1949

1 'Make Believe Sweetheart'		400.00
2 ATh,'Love Is Not A Dream'		175.00
3 'Sing Me A Love Song'		150.00
4 ATh		150.00
5 ATh		150.00
6		150.00
7		200.00
8		125.00
9		125.00
10 thru 20		@125.00
21 thru 26		@75.00
27 B:Comics Code		50.00
28 thru 30		@50.00
31 thru 70		@45.00
71 thru 110		@25.00
111 thru 120		@20.00
121 thru 150		@10.00
151 thru 153, July 1971		@5.00

SECRET ORIGINS
Feb.–March, 1973

1 O:Superman,Batman,Ghost,
Flash 8.00
2 O:Green Lantern,Atom,
Supergirl 5.00
3 O:Wonder Woman,Wildcat 4.00
4 O:Vigilante by MMe 4.00
5 O:The Spectre 3.00
6 O:Blackhawk,Legion of Super
Heroes 3.00
7 O:Robin, Aquaman,Oct.–
Nov., 1974 . . . . 3.00

SECRET ORIGINS
April, 1986

1 JOy,WB,F:Superman 4.00
2 GK,F:Blue Beetle 3.50
3 JBi,F:Captain Marvel 3.00
4 GT,F:Firestorm 2.75
5 GC,F:Crimson Aventer 3.00
6 DG,MR,F:Batman 5.00
7 F:Sandman,Guy Gardner 3.50
8 MA,F:Shadow Lass,Dollman . . 2.50
9 GT,F:Skyman,Flash 2.50
10 JL,JO,JA,F:Phantom Stranger . 2.25
11 LMc,TD,F:Hawkman,Powergirl 2.00
12 F:Challengers of the Unknown
I:G.A. Fury 2.00

13 EL,F:Nightwing		3.00
14 F:Suicide Squad		2.25
15 KMo,DG,F:Deadman,Spectre		2.25
16 AKu,F:Hourman,Warlord		2.00
17 KGi,F:Green Lantern		2.25
18		2.00
19 JM(c),MA		2.00
20 RL,DG,F:Batgirl		3.00
21 GM,MA,F:Jonah Hex		2.00
22 F:Manhunter,Millenium tie-in		2.00
23 F:Manhunter,Millenium tie-in		2.00
24 F:Dr.Fate,Blue Devil		2.00
25 F:The Legion		2.00
26 F:Black Lightning		2.00
27 F:Zatanna,Zatara		1.75
28 RLd,GK,F:Nightshade,Midnight		1.75
29 F:Atom,Red Tornado		1.75
30 F:Elongated Man		1.75
31 F:Justice Society of America.		1.75
32 F:Justice League America.		3.00
33 F:Justice League Inter..		2.00
34 F:Justice League Inter.		2.00
35 KSu,F:Justice League Inter.		2.00

Secret Origin #5
© *DC Comics, Inc.*

36 F:Green Lantern		3.00
37 F:Legion of Subst. Heroes		2.00
38 F:Green Arrow,Speedy		2.00
39 F:Batman,Animal Man		3.50
40 F:Gorilla City		2.00
41 F:Flash Villains		2.50
42 DC,F:Phantom Girl		2.00
43 TVE,TT,F:Hawk & Dove		2.00
44 F:Batman,Clayface tie-in		3.00
45 F:Blackhawk,El Diablo		2.00
46 CS,F:All Headquarters		2.00
47 CS,F:The Legion		2.00
48 KG,F:Ambush Bug		2.00
49 F: The Cadmus Project		2.50
50 GP,CI,DG,F:Batman,Robin, Flash,Black Canary		4.00
Ann.#1 JBy,F:Doom Patrol		3.00
Ann.#2 CI,MA,F:Flash		2.00
Ann.#3 F:The Teen Titans		3.00
Spec.#1 SK,PB,DG,F:Batman's worst Villians,A:Penguin		4.00
TPB DG,New Origin Batman		4.50

SECRET SOCIETY OF SUPER-VILLAINS
May-June, 1976

1 A:Capt.Boomerang, Grodd,
Sinestro 2.50
2 R:Capt.Comet,A:Green Lantern 2.50
3 A:Mantis, Darkseid 2.00
4 A:Kalibak,Darkseid,Gr.Lantern . 2.00
5 RB,D:Manhunter,A:JLA 2.00
6 RB/BL,A:Black Canary 1.50
7 RB/BL,A:Hawkgirl,Lex Luthor . . 1.50
8 RB/BL,A:Kid Flash 1.50
9 RB/BMc,A:Kid Flash, Creeper . 1.50
10 DAy/JAb,A:Creeper 1.25
11 JO,N:Wizard 1.25
12 BMc,A:Blockbuster 1.25
13 A:Crime Syndicate of America . 1.00
14 A:Crime Syndicate of America . 1.00
15 A:G.A.Atom, Dr. Mid Nite . . . 1.25

SECRETS OF HAUNTED HOUSE
April-May, 1975

1 LD(c),Dead Heat 2.00
2 ECh(c),A Dead Man 1.50
3 ECh(c),Pathway To Purgatory . 1.50
4 LD(c),The Face of Death 1.50
5 BWr(c),Gunslinger! 1.50
6 JAp(c),Deadly Allegiance 1.50
7 JAp(c),It'll Grow On You 1.50
8 MK(c),Raising The Devil 1.50
9 LD(c),The Man Who Didn't
Believe in Ghosts 1.50
10 MK(c),Ask Me No Questions . . 1.50
11 MK(c),Picasso Fever! 1.25
12 JO&DG(c),Yorick's Skull 1.25
13 JO&DG(c),The Cry of the
Warewolf 1.25
14 MK(c),Selina 1.25
15 LD(c),Over Your Own Dead
Body 1.25
16 MK(c),Water, Water Every Fear 1.25
17 LD(c),Papa Don 1.25
18 LD(c),No Sleep For The Dying 1.25
19 LD(c),The Manner of Execution 1.25
20 JO(c),The Talisman of the
Serpent 1.25
21 LD(c),The Death's Head
Scorpion 1.25
22 LD(c),See How They Die 1.25
23 LD(c),The Creeping Red Death 1.25
24 LD(c),Second Chance To Die . 1.25
25 LD(c),The Man Who Cheated
Destiny 1.25
26 MR(c),Elevator to Eternity 1.25
27 DH(c),Souls For the Master . . 1.25
28 DH(c),Demon Rum 1.25
29 MK(c),Duel of Darkness 1.25
30 JO(c),For the Love of Arlo . . . 1.25
31 I:Mister E 2.00
32 The Legend of the Tiger's Paw 1.25
33 In The Attic Dwells Dark Seth . 1.25
34 Double Your Pleasure 1.25
35 Deathwing, Lord of Darkness . 1.25
36 RB&DG(c),Sister Sinister 1.25
37 RB&DG(c),The Third Wish Is
Death 1.25
38 RB&DG(c),Slaves of Satan . . 1.25
39 RB&DG(c),The Witch-Hounds
of Salem 1.25
40 RB&DG(c),The Were-Witch
of Boston 1.25
41 JKu(c),House at Devil's Tail . . 1.25
42 JKu(c),Mystic Murder 1.25

DC COMICS

43 JO(c),Mother of Invention 1.25
44 BWr(c),Halloween God 1.25
45 EC&JO(c),Star-Trakker 1.25
46 March, 1982 .... 1.25

SINISTER HOUSE OF SECRET LOVE
Oct.–Nov., 1971

1 .... 1.50
2 JJ(c) 1.50
3 ATh 1.25
4 April-May, 1972 .... 1.25
Becomes:

SECRETS OF SINISTER HOUSE
June-July, 1972

5 .... 2.00
6 .... 1.25
7 NR 1.25
8 .... 1.25
9 .... 1.25
10 NA(i) 4.00
11 .... 1.25
12 .... 1.25
13 .... 1.25
14 .... 1.25
15 .... 1.25
16 .... 1.25
17 DBa 1.25
18 June-July, 1974 .... 1.25

SECRETS OF THE LEGION OF SUPER-HEROES
Jan., 1981

1 O:Legion 1.50
2 O:Brainiac 5 .... 1.00
3 March, 1981,O:Karate Kid 1.00

SEEKERS
Vertigo

1 & 2 .... @2.50

SEEKERS INTO THE MYSTERY

1 .... 2.50
2 .... 2.50
3 .... 2.50
4 JMD,Lucas Hart spirit
   resurrected 2.50
5 JMD,JMu, ... 2.50
6 .... 2.50
7 .... 2.50
8 .... 2.50
9 JMD(s),MZi,"Falling Down from
   Heaven," pt.4 concl. 2.50
10 JMD(s),JMu,F:Charlie Limbo .. 2.50
11 JMD(s),JIT,"God's Shadow" pt.1 2.50
12 JMD(s),JIT,"God's Shadow" pt.2 2.50
13 JMD(s),JIT,"God's Shadow" pt.3 2.50
14 JMD(s),JIT,"In God's Shadow,"
   concl. 2.50
15 JMD(s),JMu,Hart meets
   Magician, final issue 2.95

SENSATION COMICS
1942–52

1 I:Wonder Woman,Wildcat 22,000.00
2 I:Etta Candy & the Holiday
   Girls, Dr. Poison 3,500.00
3 Diana Price joins Military

Intelligence 2,000.00
4 I:Baroness PaulaVonGunther1 ,500.00
5 V:Axis Spies 1,200.00
6 Wonder Woman receives magic
   lasso,V:Baroness Gunther . 1,200.00
7 V:Baroness Gunther 750.00
8 Meets Gloria Bullfinch 750.00
9 A:The Real Diana Prince ... 750.00
10 V:Ishti 750.00
11 I:Queen Desira 750.00
12 V:Baroness Gunther 650.00
13 V:Olga,Hitler(c) 900.00
14 .... 650.00
15 V:Simon Slikery 650.00
16 V:Karl Schultz 650.00
17 V:Princess Yasmini 650.00
18 V:Quito 650.00
19 Wonder Woman goes
   berserk 650.00
20 V:Stoffer 650.00
21 V:American Adolf 600.00
22 V:Cheetah 600.00
23 'War Laugh Mania' 600.00
24 I:Wonder Woman's
   mental radio 600.00
25 .... 600.00
26 A:Queen Hippolyte 600.00
27 V:Ely Close 600.00
28 V:Mayor Prude 600.00
29 V:Mimi Mendez 600.00
30 V:Anton Unreal 600.00
31 'Grow Down Land' 400.00
32 V:Crime Chief 400.00
33 Meets Percy Pringle 400.00
34 I:Sargon 450.00
35 V:Sontag Henya in Atlantis . 350.00
36 V:Bedwin Footh 350.00
37 A:Mala((1st app. All-Star #8) 350.00
38 V:The Gyp 350.00
39 V:Nero 350.00
40 I:Countess Draska Nishki .. 350.00
41 V:Creeper Jackson 300.00
42 V:Countess Nishki 300.00
43 Meets Joel Heyday 300.00
44 V:Lt. Sturm 300.00
45 V:Jose Perez 300.00
46 V:Lawbreakers Protective
   League 300.00
47 V:Unknown 300.00
48 V:Topso and Teena 300.00
49 V:Zavia 300.00
50 V:'Ears' Fellock 300.00
51 V:Boss Brekel 250.00
52 Meets Prof. Toxino 250.00
53 V:Wanta Wynn 250.00
54 V:Dr. Fiendo 250.00
55 V:Bughumans 250.00
56 V:Dr. Novel 250.00
57 V:Syonide 250.00
58 Meets Olive Norton 250.00
59 V:Snow Man 250.00
60 V:Bifton Jones 250.00
61 V:Bluff Robust 250.00
62 V:Black Robert of Dogwood 250.00
63 V:Prof. Vibrate 250.00
64 V:Cloudmen 250.00
65 V:Lim Slait 250.00
66 V:Slick Skeener 250.00
67 V:Daredevil Dix 250.00
68 'Secret of the Menacing
   Octopus' 275.00
69 V:Darcy Wells 250.00
70 Unconquerable Woman of
   Cocha Bamba 250.00
71 V:Queen Flaming 250.00

Sensation Comics #16
© DC Comics, Inc.

72 V:Blue Seal Gang 250.00
73 Wonder Woman time
   travel story. 250.00
74 V:Spug Spangle 250.00
75 V:Shark 250.00
76 V:King Diamond 250.00
77 V:Boss Brekel 250.00
78 V:Furiosa 250.00
79 Meets Leila and Solala 250.00
80 V:Don Enrago 250.00
81 V:Dr. Frenzi 275.00
82 V:King Lunar 200.00
83 V:Prowd 200.00
84 V:Duke Daxo 200.00
85 Meets Leslie M. Gresham .. 200.00
86 'Secret of the Amazing
   Bracelets' 200.00
87 In Twin Peaks(in Old West) 200.00
88 Wonder Woman in Holywood 200.00
89 V:Abacus Rackeett gang .. 200.00
90 'The Secret of the Modern
   Sphinx' 200.00
91 .... 200.00
92 V:Duke of Deceptions 200.00
93 V:Talbot 200.00
94 Girl Isue 300.00
95 .... 275.00
96 .... 275.00
97 .... 275.00
98 'Strange Mission' 275.00
99 I:Astra 275.00
100 .... 400.00
101 'Battle for the Atom World' 275.00
102 'Queen of the South Seas' 275.00
103 V:Robot Archers 275.00
104 'The End of Paradise
   Island' 275.00
105 'Secret of the Giant Forest' 275.00
106 E:Wonder Woman 275.00
107 ATh,Mystery issue 450.00
108 ATh,I:Johnny Peril 400.00
109 Ath,A:Johnny Peril 450.00
Becomes:

SENSATION MYSTERY
1952–53

110 B:Johnny Peril 275.00

DC COMICS

111 'Spectre in the Flame' . . . 250.00
112 'Death has 5 Guesses' . . . 250.00
113 . . . . 250.00
114 GC,'The Haunted Diamond' 250.00
115 'The Phantom Castle' 250.00
116 'The Toy Assassins',
   July-Aug., 1953 . . . . 250.00

SERGEANT BILKO
May-June, 1957
1 Based on TV show 500.00
2 . . . . 275.00
3 . . . . 250.00
4 . . . . 200.00
5 . . . . 200.00
6 thru 17 . . . . @175.00
18 March-April, 1960 . . . . 175.00

SERGEANT BILKO'S PVT. DOBERMAN
June-July, 1958
1 . . . . 300.00
2 . . . . 175.00
3 . . . . 125.00
4 . . . . 125.00
5 . . . . 125.00
6 thru 10 . . . . @100.00
11 Feb.–March, 1960 . . . . 100.00

SGT. ROCK
(See: OUR ARMY AT WAR)

SGT. ROCK SPECIAL
Oct., 1988
#1 rep.Our Army at War#162-#63 2.00
#2 rep.Brave & Bold #52 . . . . . . 2.00
#3 rep.Showcase #45 . . . . 2.00
#4 rep.Our Army at War#147-#48 2.00
#5 rep.Our Army at War#81&#103 2.00
#6 rep.Our Army at War #160 . . . 2.00
#7 rep.Our Army at War #85 . . . . 2.00
#8 rep. 2.00
#9 thru #20 reprints. . . . . @2.00

SGT. ROCK'S PRIZE BATTLE TALES
Winter, 1964
1 . . . . 225.00

SGT. ROCK SPECIAL
1 TT,MGo,JKu,CR,(new stories) . 2.95

SHADE
June-July, 1977
[1st Regular Series]
1 SD,I&O: Shade 4.00
2 SD,V:Form 3.25
3 SD,V:The Cloak 2.75
4 SD,Return to Meta-Zone 2.75
5 SD,V:Supreme Decider 2.75
6 SD,V:Khaos 2.75
7 SD,V:Dr.Z.Z. 2.75
8 SD,last issue 2.75

SHADE, THE
Feb. 1997
1 (of 4) JeR(s),GeH,A:Ludlows . 2.25
2 JeR(s),JWi,MGy,poisoned by love
   of his life 2.25
3 JeR(s),BBl,Golden Age Flash Jay
   Garrick retiring 2.25
4 JeR(s),MZi,V:last of the Ludlows 2.25

Shade, The Changing Man #2
© DC Comics, Inc.

SHADE, THE CHANGING MAN
July, 1990
1 B:PrM(s),CBa,MPn,I:Kathy George,
   I&D:Troy Grezer 6.00
2 CBa,MPn,Who Shot JFK#1 . . 4.00
3 CBa,MPn,Who Shot JFK#2 . . 3.00
4 CBa,MPn,V:American Scream . 3.00
5 CBa,MPn,V:Hollywood
   Monsters 3.00
6 CBa,MPn,V:Ed Loot 3.00
7 CBa,MPn,I:Arnold Major 3.00
8 CBa,Mpn,I:Lenny 3.00
9 CBa,MPn,V:Arnold Major 3.00
10 CBa,MPn,Paranioa 2.75
11 CBa,MPn,R:Troy Grezer 2.50
12 CBa,MPn,V:Troy Grezer 2.50
13 CBa,MPn,I:Fish Priest 2.50
14 CBa,MPn,V:Godfather of Guilt . 2.50
15 CBa,MPn,I:Spirit 2.50
16 CBa,MPn,V:American Scream . 2.50
17 RkB(i),V:Rohug 2.50
18 MPn,E:American Scream 2.50
19 MPn,V:Dave Messiah Seeker . 2.50
20 JD,CBa,MPn,RkB,R:Roger . . . 2.50
21 MPn,The Road,A:Stringer . . . 2.25
22 The Road,Childhood 2.25
23 The Road 2.25
24 The Road 2.25
25 The Road 2.25
26 MPn(i),F:Lenny 2.25
27 MPn(i),Shade becomes female 2.25
28 MPn(i),Changing Woman#2 . . 2.25
29 MPn(i),Changing Woman#3 . . 2.25
30 Another Life 2.25
31 Ernest & Jim#1 . . . . 2.25
32 Ernest & Jim#2 . . . . 2.25
Vertigo
33 CBa,B:Birth Pains 2.25
34 CBa,RkB(i),GID(i),A:Brian Juno,
   Garden of Pain 2.25
35 CBa,RkB(i),E:Birth Pains,
   I:Juno 2.25
36 CBa,PrG(i),RkB(i),B:Passion child,
   I:Miles Laimling 2.25
37 CBa,RkB(i),Shade/Kathy 2.25

38 CBa,RkB(i),Great American
   Novel 2.25
39 CBa,SEa,RkB(i),Pond Life . . . 2.25
40 PBd,at Hotel Shade 2.25
41 GID,Pandora's Story,Kathy is
   pregnant 2.25
42 CBa,RkB(i),SY,B:History Lesson,
   A:John Constantine 2.50
43 CBa,RkB(i),PBd,Trial of William
   Matthieson,A:J.Constantine . . 2.50
44 CBa,RkB(i),E:History Lesson,
   D:William Matthieson,A:John
   Constantine 2.50
45 CBa,B:A Season in Hell 2.25
46 CBa(c),GID,Season in Hell#2 . 2.25
47 CBa(c),GID,A:Lenny 2.25
48 CBa(c),GID 2.25
49 CBa(c),GID,Kathy's Past 2.25
50 GID,BBl,MiA,pin-up gallery . . . 3.25
51 GID,BBl,MiA,Masks,pt.1 . . . . 1.95
52 GID,BBl,MiA,Masks,pt.2 . . . . 1.95
53 GID,BBl,MiA,Masks,pt.3 . . . . 1.95
54 Meeting 1.95
55 . . . . 1.95
56 . . . . 1.95
57 MBu,PrM,F:George 1.95
58 PrM,Michael Lark 1.95
59 MBu,PrM,Nasty Infections,pt.1 2.25
60 MBu,PrM,Nasty Infections,pt.2 2.25
61 MBu,PrM,Nasty Infections,pt.3 2.25
62 Nasty Infections,pt.4 . . . . . . 2.25
63 Nasty Infections,finale 2.25
64 The Madness 2.25
65 The Roots of Madness,pt.1 . . 2.25
66 The Roots of Madness,pt.2 . . 2.25
67 The Roots of Madness,pt.3 . . 2.25
68 After Kathy,pt.1 . . . . 2.25
69 After Kathy,pt.2 . . . . 2.25
70 After Kathy,pt.3, final issue . . . 2.25

SHADO, SONG OF THE DRAGON
1992
1 GM(i),From G.A. Longbow
   Hunters 5.50
2 GM(i),V:Yakuza 4.95
3 GM(i),V:Yakuza 4.95
4 GM(i),V:Yakuza 4.95

SHADOW, THE
1973–75
[1st Regular Series]
1 MK,The Doom Puzzle 30.00
2 MK,V:Freak Show Killer 22.00
3 MK,BWr 24.00
4 MK,Ninja Story 22.00
5 FR 12.00
6 MK 22.00
7 FR 11.00
8 FR 11.00
9 FR 11.00
10 . . . . 11.00
11 A:Avenger 11.00
12 . . . . 11.00
[Limited Series] 1986
1 HC,R:Shadow 6.00
2 HC,O:Shadow 4.00
3 HC,V:Preston Mayrock 3.00
4 HC,V:Preston Mayrock 3.00
TPB rep. #1 thru #4 . . . . 12.95
[2nd Regular Series] 1987–89
1 BSz,Shadows & Light,pt.1 . . . . 3.50
2 BSz,Shadows & Light,pt.2 . . . . 3.50
3 BSz,Shadows & Light,pt.3 . . . . 3.50

DC COMICS

4 BSz,Shadows & Light,pt.4	3.50
5 BSz,Shadows & Light,pt.5	3.50
6 BSz,Shadows & Light,pt.6	3.50
7 MR,KB,Harold Goes to Washington	2.00
8 KB,Seven Deadly Finns,pt.1	2.00
9 KB,Seven Deadly Finns,pt.2	2.00
10 KB,Seven Deadly Finns,pt.3	2.00
11 KB,Seven Deadly Finns,pt.4	2.00
12 KB,Seven Deadly Finns,pt.5	2.00
13 KB,Seven Deadly Finns,pt.6	2.00
14 KB,Body And Soul,pt.1	2.00
15 KB,Body And Soul,pt.2	2.00
16 KB,Body And Soul,pt.3	2.00
17 KB,Body And Soul,pt.4	2.00
18 KB,Body And Soul,pt.5	2.00
19 KB,Body And Soul,pt.6	2.00
Ann.#1 JO,AA,Shadows & Light prologue	3.00
Ann.#2 KB,Agents	2.50

SHADOW CABINET
Milestone 1994–95

0 WS(c),3RL,Shadow War,Foil(c),A:All Milestone characters	3.00
1 JBy(c),3RW,I&D:Corpsickle	3.00
2 3RW,V:Arcadian League	1.75
3 3RW,F:Sideshow	2.00
4 3RW,F:Sideshow	2.00
5	1.75
6	1.75
7	1.75
8 New Cabinet	1.75
9 R:Old Cabinet	1.75
10 V:Red Dog	1.75
11 Death Issue	1.75
12 SYSTEM	1.75
13 A:Hardware,Starlight	1.75
14 Long Hot Summer, Iron Butterfly Starlight	2.50
15 Long Hot Summer	2.50
16 Changing of the Guard	2.50
17 V:Dharma,final issue	2.50

SHADOWDRAGON ANNUAL
1995

Ann.#1 Year One Annual	3.50

SHADOW OF BATMAN

1 reprints of Detective Comics	10.00
2	7.50
3	7.50
4	7.50

SHADOW OF THE BATMAN
1985–86

1 WS,AM,MR,rep.	8.00
2 MR,TA,rep.A:Hugo Strange	5.00
3 MR,TA,rep.A:Penguin	5.00
4 MR,TA,rep.A:Joker	6.00
5 MR,DG,rep.	5.00

SHADOW'S FALL
1994–95

1 JVF,Voyage of self-discovery	2.95
2 JVF,More of tale	2.95
3 JVF,Shen confronts shadow	2.95
4 JVF,Gale wounded	2.95
5 JVF,Shadow goes Berserk	2.95
6 JVF,F:Warren Gale,final issue	2.95

SHADOW STRIKES!, THE
1989–92

1 EB,Death's Head	3.00
2 EB,EB,PoliticalKiller,V:Rasputin	2.50
3 EB,V:Mad Monk,V:Rasputin	2.50
4 EB,D:Mad Monk,V:Rasputin	2.50
5 EB,Shadow & Doc Savage#1	2.50
6 Shadow & Doc Savage #3	2.50
7 RM,A:Wunderkind,O:Shadow's Radio Show	2.50
8 EB,A:Shiwan Khan	2.50
9 Fireworks#2	2.50
10 EB,Fireworks#3	2.50
11 EB,O:Margo Lane	2.50
12 EB,V:Chicago Mob	2.50
13 EB,V:Chicago Mob	2.50
14 EB,V:Chicago Mob	2.50
15 EB,V:Chicago Mob	2.50
16 Assassins,pt.1	2.50
17 Assassins,pt.2	2.50
18 Shrevvie	2.50
19 NY,NJ Tunnel	2.50
20 Shadow+Margo Vs.Nazis	2.50
21 V:Shiwan Khan	2.50
22 V:Shiwan Khan	2.50
23 V:Shiwan Khan	2.50
24 Search for Margo Lane	2.50
25 In China	2.50
26 V:Shiwan Khan	2.50
27 V:Shiwan Khan,Margo Rescued	2.50
28 SL,In Hawaii	2.50
29 DSp,'Valhalla',V:Nazis	2.50
30 The Shadow Year One,pt.1	2.50
31 The Shadow Year One,pt.2	2.50
Ann.#1 DSp 'Crimson Dreams'	4.00

SHADOW WAR OF HAWKMAN
May, 1985

1 AA,V:Thangarians	1.50
2 AA,V:Thangarians	1.25
3 AA,V:Thangarians,A:Aquaman, Elong.Man	1.25
4 AA,V:Thangarians	1.25
Spec.#1 V:Thangarians	1.25

SHAZAM!
1973–78
[1st Regular Series]

1 B:DON(s),CCB,O:Capt.Marvel	5.00
2 CCB,A:Mr.Mind	4.00
3 CCB,V:Shagg Naste	3.00
4 E:DON(s),CCB,V:Ibac	3.00
5 B:ESM(s),CCB,A:Leprechaun	3.00
6 B:DON(s),CCB,Dr.Sivana	3.00
7 CCB,A:Capt Marvel Jr.	3.00
8 CCB,O:Marvel Family	3.50
9 E:DON(S)DC,CCB,A:Mr.Mind, Captain Marvel Jr.	3.00
10 ESM(s)CCB,BO	3.00
11 ViCKS,BO,rep.	3.00
12 BO,DG	3.50
13 BO,KS,A:Luthor	3.50
14 KS,A:Monster Society	3.50
15 KS,BO,Luther	3.50
16 KS,BO	3.50
17 KS,BO	3.00
18 KS,BO	3.00
19 KS,BO,Mary Marvel	3.00
20 KS,A:Marvel Family	3.00
21 reprint	3.00
22 reprint	3.00
23 reprint	3.00

Shazam! #1 © DC Comics, Inc.

24 reprint	3.00
25 KS,DG,I&O:Isis	3.00
26 KS	3.00
27 KS,A:Kid ternity	3.50
28 KS	3.00
29 KS	3.00
30 KS	3.00
31 KS,A:MinuteMan	3.00
32 KS	3.00
33 KS	3.00
34 O:Capt.Marvel Jr.	3.00
35 DN,KS,A:Marvel Family	3.00

SHAZAM ARCHIVES

1 Rep.Whiz Comics#2-#15	49.95

SHAZAM, THE NEW BEGINNING
April, 1987

1 O:Shazam & Capt.Marvel	1.50
2 V:Black Adam	1.25
3 V:Black Adam	1.25
4 V:Black Adam	1.25

SHERLOCK HOLMES
Sept.–Oct., 1975

1	1.00

SHOWCASE
1956–70, 1977–78

1 F:Fire Fighters	3,000.00
2 JKu,F:Kings of Wild	800.00
3 F:Frogmen	775.00
4 CI,JKu,I&O:S.A. Flash (Barry Allen)	26,000.00
5 F:Manhunters	1,000.00
6 JK,I&O:Challengers of the Unknown	3,500.00
7 JK,F:Challengers	1,700.00
8 CI,F:Flash,I:Capt.Cold	8,500.00
9 F:Lois Lane	5,000.00
10 F:Lois Lane	2,400.00
11 JK(c),F:Challengers	1,500.00
12 JK(c),F:Challengers	1,500.00
13 CI,F:Flash,Mr.Element	3,500.00
14 CI,F:Flash,Mr.Element	4,500.00

All comics prices listed are for *Near Mint* condition.

DC COMICS

DC Showcase #78 © DC Comics, Inc.

15 I:Space Ranger 1,700.00
16 F:Space Ranger 1,000.00
17 GK(c),I:Adam Strange . . . 2,000.00
18 GK(c),F:Adam Strange . . . 1,100.00
19 GK(c),F:Adam Strange . . . 1,200.00
20 I:Rip Hunter 900.00
21 F:Rip Hunter 500.00
22 GK,I&O:S.A. Green Lantern
   (Hal Jordan) 4,800.00
23 GK,F:Green Lantern 1,600.00
24 GK,F:Green Lantern 1,600.00
25 JKu,F:Rip Hunter 300.00
26 JKu,F:Rip Hunter 300.00
27 RH,I:Sea Devils 800.00
28 RH,F:Sea Devils 400.00
29 RH,F:Sea Devils 400.00
30 O:Aquaman 750.00
31 GK(c),F:Aquaman 400.00
32 F:Aquaman 400.00
33 F:Aquaman 450.00
34 GK,MA,I&O:S.A. Atom . . . 1,400.00
35 GK,MA,F:Atom 800.00
36 GK,MA,F:Atom 600.00
37 RA,I:Metal Man 550.00
38 RA,F:Metal Man 450.00
39 RA,F:Metal Man 350.00
40 RA,F:Metal Man 325.00
41 F:Tommy Tomorrow 175.00
42 F:Tommy Tomorrow 175.00
43 F:Dr.No(James Bond 007) . 400.00
44 F:Tommy Tomorrow 125.00
45 JKu,O:Sgt.Rock 225.00
46 F:Tommy Tomorrow 100.00
47 F:Tommy Tomorrow 100.00
48 F:Cave Carson 75.00
49 F:Cave Carson 75.00
50 MA,CI,F:I Spy 75.00
51 MA,CI,F:I Spy 75.00
52 F:Cave Carson 75.00
53 JKu(c),RH,F:G.I.Joe 75.00
54 JKu(c),RH,F:G.I.Joe 75.00
55 MA,F:Dr.Fate,Spectre,1st S.A.
   Green Lantern,Solomon
   Grundy 260.00
56 MA,F:Dr.Fate 75.00
57 JKu,F:Enemy Ace 150.00
58 JKu,F:Enemy Ace 125.00
59 F:Teen Titans 100.00

60 MA,F:Spectre 250.00
61 MA,F:Spectre 150.00
62 JO,I:Inferior 5 . . . . 75.00
63 JO,F:Inferior 5 . . . . 50.00
64 MA,F:Spectre 150.00
65 F:Inferior 5 . . . . 50.00
66 I:B'wana Beast 30.00
67 F:B'wana Beast 30.00
68 I:Maniaks 30.00
69 F:Maniaks 30.00
70 I:Binky 30.00
71 F:Maniaks 30.00
72 JKu,ATh,F:Top Gun 30.00
73 SD,I&O:Creeper 125.00
74 I:Anthro 75.00
75 SD,I:Hawk & Dove 100.00
76 NC,I:Bat Lash 50.00
77 BO,I:Angel & Ape 50.00
78 I:Jonny Double 30.00
79 I:Dolphin 50.00
80 NA(c),F:Phantom Stranger . . 25.00
81 I:Windy & Willy 25.00
82 I:Nightmaster 60.00
83 BWr,MK,F:Nightmaster 50.00

DC Showcase #98 © DC Comics, Inc.

84 BWr,MK,F:Nightmaster 50.00
85 JKu,F:Firehair 18.00
86 JKu,F:Firehair 18.00
87 JKu,F:Firehair 18.00
88 F:Jason's Quest 7.00
89 F:Jason's Quest 7.00
90 F:Manhunter 6.00
91 F:Manhunter 6.00
92 F:Manhunter 6.00
93 F:Manhunter 6.00
94 JA,JSon,I&O:2nd
   Doom Patrol 10.00
95 JA,JSon,F:2nd Doom Patrol . . 9.00
96 JA,JSon,F:2nd Doom Patrol . . 9.00
97 JO,JSon,O:Power Girl 5.00
98 JSon,DG,Power Girl 5.00
99 JSon,DG,Power Girl 5.00
100 JSon,all star issue 6.00
101 JKu(c),AM,MA,Hawkman . . . 5.00
102 JKu(c),AM,MA,Hawkman . . . 5.00
103 JKu(c),AM,MA,Hawkman . . . 5.00
104 RE,OSS Spies 5.00
TPB Rep.1956–59 . . . . 19.95

SHOWCASE' 93

1 AAd(c),EH,AV,F:Catwoman,
   Blue Devil,Cyborg 5.00
2 KM(c),EH,AV,F:Catwoman,
   Blue Devil,Cyborg 3.50
3 KM(c),EH,TC,F:Catwoman,
   Blue Devil,Flash 3.00
4 F:Catwoman,Blue Devil,
   Geo-Force 2.50
5 F:KD,DG,BHi,F:Robin,Blue
   Devil,Geo-Force 2.50
6 MZ(c),KD,DG,F:Robin,Blue
   Devil,Deathstroke 2.50
7 BSz(c),KJ,Knightfall#13,F:Two-
   Face,Jade&Obsidian 5.00
8 KJ,Knightfall#14,F:Two-Face,
   Peacemaker,Fire and Ice . . . 4.00
9 F:Huntress,Peacemaker,Shining
   Knight 2.50
10 BWg,SI,F:Huntress,Batman,
   Dr.Light,Peacemaker,Deathstroke,
   Katana,M.Manhunter 2.50
11 GP(c),F:Robin,Nightwing,
   Peacemaker,Deathstroke,Deadshot,
   Katana,Dr.Light,Won.Woman . 2.50
12 AD(c),BMc,F:Robin,Nightwing,
   Green Lantern,Creeper 2.50

SHOWCASE '94

1 KN,F:Joker,Gunfire,Orion,Metro 2.25
2 KON(c),E:Joker,B:Blue Beetle . 2.25
3 MMi(c),B:Razorsharpe 2.25
4 AIG(s),DG,F:Arkham Asylum inmates
   E:Razorsharpe,Blue Bettle . . . 2.25
5 WS(c),CDi(s),PJ,B:Robin & Huntress,
   F:Bloodwynd,Loose Cannon . . 2.25
6 PJ,KK(s),F:Robin & Huntress . . 2.25
7 JaL(c),PDd(s),F:Comm. Gordon 2.25
8 AIG(s),O:Scarface,Ventriloquist,
   F:Monarch,1st Wildcat 3.00
9 AIG(s),DJ,O:Scarface,Ventriloquist,
   F:Monarch,Waverider 2.75
10 JQ(c),AIG(s),F:Azrael,Zero Hour,
   B:Black Condor 3.00
11 Black Condor, Man-Bat 2.25
12 Barbara Gordon 2.00

SHOWCASE '95

1 Supergirl 2.50
2 . . . . 2.50
3 F:Eradicator,Claw 2.25
4 A:Catwoman,Hawke 3.00
5 F:Thorne,Firehawk 3.00
6 DRo(c&a),F:Lobo,Bibbo 3.00
7 F:Mongul 3.00
8 . . . . 3.00
9 F:Lois Lane 3.00
10 F:Gangbuster 3.00
11 F:Agent Liberty 3.00
12 F:Supergirl,Maitresse 3.00

SHOWCASE '96

1 F:Steel & Warrior 3.00
2 F:Steel and Warrior 3.00
3 . . . . 3.00
4 F:Firebrand 3.00
5 F:Green Arrow & Thorn 3.00
6 F:Superboy, Animated Series . 3.00
7 F:Mary Marvel 3.00
8 F:Superman, Superboy &
   Supergirl 4.00
9 F:Lady Shiva & Shadowdragon,
   Martian Manhunter 3.00
10 F:Ultra Boy, Captain Comet . . 3.00

11 Legion of Super-Heroes 3.00
12 "10,000 Brainiacs" 3.00

SILVER AGE DC CLASSICS

Action #252(rep) 1.50
Adventure #247(rep) 1.50
Brave and Bold #28 (rep) 1.50
Detective #225 (rep) 1.50
Detective #327 (rep) 1.50
Green Lantern #76 (rep) 1.50
House of Secrets #92 (rep) 2.00
Showcase #4 (rep) 1.75
Showcase #22 (rep) 1.50
Sugar & Spike #99(1st printing) . . 1.50

Silver Blade #2 © DC Comics, Inc.

SILVER BLADE
Sept., 1987

1 KJ,GC,maxi-series 1.50
2 thru 12 GC . . . . @1.50

SKIN GRAFT
Vertigo 1993

1 B:JeP(s),WaP,I:John Oakes,
  A:Tattooed Man(Tarrant) 3.25
2 WaP,V:Assassins 3.00
3 WaP,In Kyoto,I:Mizoguchi Kenji 3.00
4 E:JeP(s),WaP,V:Tarrant,Kenji . 3.00

SKREEMER
May, 1989

1 . . . . 1.50
2 thru 6 . . . . @2.00

SKULL AND BONES
1992

1 EH,I&O:Skull & Bones 4.95
2 EH,V:KGB 4.95
3 EH,V:KGB 4.95

SLASH MARAUD
Nov., 1987

1 PG 2.25
2 PG 2.00
3 thru 10 PG . . . . @2.00

SONIC DISRUPTORS
1987–88

1 thru 10 . . . . @1.75

SON OF AMBUSH BUG
July, 1986

1 . . . . 1.00
2 thru 6 KG . . . . @1.00

SOVEREIGN SEVEN
1995–97

1 CCI(s),DT,I:Sovereign Seven,
  V:Female Furies,A:Darkseid . . 1.95
2 I:Nike,Kratos,Zelus,Bia 1.95
3 V:Nike,Kratos,Zelus,Bia 1.95
4 I:Skin Dance 1.95
5 CCI,DT,V:Skin Dance 1.95
6 CCI,DT,V:Force Majeure 1.95
7 CCI,DT,Wild Hunt,pt.2 . . . . . . 1.95
8 CCI,DT,Clv,Wild Hunt,pt.3 . . . . 1.95
9 CCI,DT,Clv 1.95
10 CCI,DT,Clv,Road Trip,pt.1 . . . 1.95
11 CCI,DT,Clv,Road Trip,pt.2 (of 3) 1.95
12 CCI(s) 1.95
13 CCI(s) 1.95
14 CCI(s) 1.95
15 CCI,DT,Clv,Sovereign team
  betrayed 1.95
16 CCI,DT,Clv,Network betrays
  Sovereigns, Final Night tie-in . . 1.95
17 CCI(s),RLm,Clv,V:Network . . . 1.95
18 CCI(s),RLm,Clv,V:Network and
  Kim 1.95
19 CCI(s) 1.95
20 CCI(s),VGi,Finale trapped in
  Forest Fire 1.95
21 CCI(s),RLm,DC,Clv,Danae's
  secret 1.95
22 CCI(s),RLm,DC,Clv,Indigo &
  Rampart fall 1.95
23 CCI(s),RLm,DC,Clv,Finale
  hallucinates 1.95
24 CCI(s),RLm,Clv,A:Superman . . 1.95
25 CCI(s),RLm,Clv,V:Power Girl . . 1.95
26 CCI(s),RLm,Clv,A:Hitman 1.95
Ann.#1 CCI, Year One Annual . . . 3.95
Ann.#2 CCI(s),RL,KJ,Legends of
  the Dead Earth 2.95
TPB CCI(s),DT, rep.#1–#5 . . . . . 12.95

SOVEREIGN SEVEN PLUS

1 one-shot 2.95

SPACE JAM
Warner Bros./DC Oct. 1996
one-shot comic adaptation of movie 5.95

SPANNER'S GALAXY
Dec., 1984

1 mini-series 1.50
2 thru 6 . . . . @1.00

SPECTRE, THE
1967–69

1 MA,V:Captain Skull 100.00
2 NA,V:Dirk Rawley 75.00
3 NA,A:Wildcat 70.00
4 NA 70.00
5 NA 70.00
6 MA 45.00
7 MA,BU:Hourman 45.00
8 MA,Parchment of Power
  Perilous 45.00

9 BWr(2nd BWr Art) 50.00
10 MA 45.00

Spectre (2nd Series) #28
© DC Comics, Inc.

[2nd Regular Series] 1987–89

1 GC,O:Spectre 3.50
2 GC,Cult of BRM 3.00
3 GC,Fashion Model Murders . . . 2.00
4 GC 2.00
5 GC,Spectre's Murderer 2.00
6 GC,Spectre/Corrigan separated 2.00
7 A:Zatanna,Wotan 2.00
8 A:Zatanna,Wotan 2.00
9 GM,Spectre's Revenge 2.00
10 GM,A:Batman,Millenium 2.25
11 GM,Millenium 2.00
12 GM,The Talisman,pt.1 . . . . . . 2.00
13 GM,The Talisman,pt.2 . . . . . . 2.00
14 GM,The Talisman,pt.3 . . . . . . 2.00
15 GM,The Talisman,pt.4 . . . . . . 2.00
16 Jim Corrigan Accused 2.00
17 New Direction,'Final Destiny' . . 2.00
18 Search for Host Body 2.00
19 'Dead Again' 2.00
20 Corrigan Detective Agency . . . 2.00
21 A:Zoran 1.75
22 BS,Sea of Darkness,A:Zoran . 1.75
23 A:Lords of Order,
  Invasion x-over 1.75
24 BWg,Ghosts i/t Machine#1 . . . 1.75
25 Ghosts in the Machine #2 . . . . 1.75
26 Ghosts in the Machine #3 . . . . 1.75
27 Ghosts in the Machine #4 . . . . 1.75
28 Ghosts in the Machine #5 . . . . 1.75
29 Ghosts in the Machine #6 . . . . 1.75
30 Possession 1.75
31 Spectre possessed, final issue 1.75
Ann.#1, A:Deadman 2.75

[3rd Regular Series] 1992–97

1 B:JOs(s),TMd,R:Spectre,
  Glow in the dark(c) 9.00
2 TMd,Murder Mystery 10.00
3 TMd,O:Spectre 5.00
4 TMd,O:Spectre 4.00
5 TMd,BB(c),V:Kidnappers 3.50
6 TMd,Spectre prevents evil 3.50
7 TMd 3.50
8 TMd,Glow in the dark(c) 5.00

All comics prices listed are for *Near Mint* condition.

DC COMICS

DC COMICS

9 TMd,MWg(c),V:The Reaver . . . 3.00
10 TMd,V:Michael 3.00
11 TMd,V:Azmodeus 3.00
12 V:Reaver 3.00
13 TMd,V:Count Vertigo,
   Glow in the Dark(c) 3.00
14 JoP,A:Phantom Stranger 2.00
15 TMd,A:Phantom Stranger,Demon,
   Doctor Fate,John Constantine . 2.00
16 JAp,V:I.R.A. 2.00
17 TT(c),TMd,V:Eclipso 2.00
18 TMd,D:Eclipso 2.00
19 TMd,V:Hate 2.00
20 A:Lucien 2.00
21 V:Naiad,C:Superman 3.00
22 A:Superman 2.25
23 Book of Judgment, pt.1 . . . . . 2.00
24 Book of Judgment, pt.2 . . . . . 2.00
25 Book of Judgment, pt.3 . . . . . 2.00
26 . . . . 2.00
27 R:Azmodus 2.00
28 V:Azmodus 2.00
29 V:Azmodus 2.00
30 V:Azmodus 2.00
31 Descent into Pandemonium . . 2.25
32 V:Killo 2.25
33 . . . . 2.25
34 Power of the Undead 2.25
35 JOs,TMd,Underworld
   Unleashed tie-in 2.25
36 JOs,TMd,Underworld
   Unleashed tie-in 2.25
37 JOs,TMd,The Haunting of
   America,pt.1 . . . . 2.25
38 JOs,TMd,The Haunting of
   America,pt.2 . . . . 2.25
39 JOs,TMd,The Haunting of
   America,pt.3 . . . . 2.25
40 JOs,TMd,The Haunting of
   America,pt.4 . . . . 2.25
41 JOs,TMd,The Haunting of
   America,pt.5 . . . . 2.25
42 JOs,TMd,The Haunting of
   America,pt.6 . . . . 2.25
43 Witchcraft 2.25
44 Madame Xanadu 2.25
45 . . . . 2.25
46 JOs(s),TMd,discovery of the
   Spear of Destiny 2.25
47 JOs(s),TMd,"The Haunting of
   America" Final Night tie-in . . 2.25
48 JOs(s),TMd,"The Haunting of
   America" 2.25
49 JOs(s),TMd,"The Haunting of
   America" 2.25
50 JOs(s),TMd, ... 2.25
51 JOs(s),TMd,A:Batman,Joker . . 2.25
52 JOs(s),TMd,Nate Kane discovers
   murder evidence 2.25
53 JOs(s),TMd,"Haunting of Jim
   Corrigan" cont. 2.25
54 JOs(s),TMd,hunt for murderer of
   Mister Terrific 2.25
55 JOs(s),TMd,Corrigan implicated
   in murder 2.25
56 JOs(s),TMd,JTo "Haunting if Jim
   Corrigan" 2.50
57 JOs(s),TMd,Spectre & Jim
   Corrigan in Heaven 2.50
Ann.#1 JOs,TMd,Year One 3.95
TPB Punishment and Crimes . . . 9.95

SPELLJAMMER
Sept., 1990
1 RogueShip#1 . . . . 3.00

2 RogueShip#2 . . . . 2.50
3 RogueShip#3 . . . . 2.00
4 RogueShip#4 . . . . 2.00
5 New Planet 1.75
6 Tember, Planet contd 1.75
7 Planet contd 1.75
8 conclusion 1.75
9 Meredith Possessed 1.75
10 Tie-in w/Dragonlance #33&34 . 1.75
11 Dwarf Citidel 1.75
12 Kirstig Vs. Meredith 1.75
13 Tember to the Rescue 1.75
14 Meredith's Son #1 . . . . 1.75
15 Meredith's Son #2 . . . . 1.75

STALKER
1975–1976
1 O&I:Stalker 5.00
2 thru 4 . . . . @2.50

STANLEY & HIS MONSTER
(see FOX AND THE CROW)

STANLEY & HIS MONSTER
1 R:Stanley 1.25
2 I:Demon Hunter 1.25
3 A:Ambrose Bierce 1.25
4 final issue 1.25

S.T.A.R. CORPS
1 A:Superman 2.00
2 I:Fusion,A:Rampage 1.75
3 I:Brainstorm 1.75
4 I:Ndoki 1.75
5 I:Trauma 1.75
6 I:Mindgame 1.75

STAR CROSSED
DC/Helix April 1997
1 (of 3) MHo,Dyltah's romance
   with Saa 2.50
2 MHo,"Love During Wartime" . 2.50
3 . . . . 2.50

Starfire #3 © DC Comics, Inc.

STARFIRE
1976–77
1 . . . . 1.50
2 thru 8 . . . . @1.00

STAR HUNTERS
Oct.–Nov., 1977
1 DN&BL 1.00
2 LH&BL 1.00
3 MN&BL,D:Donovan Flint 1.00
4 thru 7 . . . . @1.00

STARMAN
1988–92
1 TL,I&O:New Starman 5.00
2 TL,V:Serial Killer,C:Bolt 4.00
3 TL,V:Bolt 4.00
4 TL,V:Power Elite 3.50
5 TL,Invasion,A:PowerGirl,
   Firestorm 3.50
6 TL,Invasion,A:G.L.,Atom 3.00
7 TL,Soul Searching Issue 3.00
8 TL,V:LadyQuark 3.00
9 TL,A:Batman,V:Blockbuster . . 2.50
10 TL,A:Batman,V:Blockbuster . . 2.50
11 TL,V:Power Elite 2.25
12 TL,V:Power Elite,A:Superman . 2.25
13 TL,V:Rampage 2.25
14 TL,A:A:Superman,V:Parasite . . 2.25
15 TL,V:Deadline 2.00
16 TL,O:Starman 2.00
17 TL,V:Dr.Polaris,A:PowerGirl . . 2.00
18 TL,V:Dr.Polaris,A:PowerGirl . . 2.00
19 TL,V:Artillery 2.00
20 TL,FireFighting 2.00
21 TL,Starman Quits 2.00
22 TL,V:Khunds 2.00
23 TL,A:Deadline 2.00
24 TL,A:Deadline 2.00
25 TL,V:Deadline 2.00
26 V:The Mist 2.00
27 V:The Mist 2.00
28 A:Superman 7.00
29 V:Plasmax 2.00
30 Seduction of Starman #1 . . . . 2.00
31 Seduction of Starman #2 . . . . 2.00
32 Seduction of Starman #3 . . . . 2.00

Starman #2 © DC Comics, Inc.

33 Seduction of Starman #4 .... 2.00	R.A.F.,Star Spangled Kid,	45 7th War Loan (c) 350.00
34 A:Batman 2.00	Armstrong of the Army ... 3,500.00	46 .... 350.00
35 A:Valor,Mr.Nebula,ScarletSkier 2.00	2 V:Dr. Weerd 1,200.00	47 .... 350.00
36 A:Les Mille Yeux 2.00	3 .... 750.00	48 .... 350.00
37 A:Les Mille Yeux 2.00	4 V:The Needle 750.00	49 .... 350.00
38 War of the Gods X-over 2.00	5 V:Dr. Weerd 750.00	50 .... 350.00
39 V:Plasmax 2.00	6 E:Armstrong 500.00	51 A:Robot Robber 350.00
40 V:Las Vegas 2.00	7 S&K,O&1st app:The Guardian,	52 'Rehearsal for Crime' 350.00
41 V:Maaldor 2.00	B:Robotman,The Newsboy	53 'The Poet of Suicide Slum' . 350.00
42 Star Shadows,pt.1,A:Eclipso .. 3.00	Legion, TNT 5,800.00	54 'Dead-Shot Dade's Revenge' 350.00
43 Star Shadows,pt.2,A:Lobo,	8 O:TNT & Dan the Dyna-Mite 1,700.00	55 'Gabby Strikes a Gusher' .. 350.00
Eclipso 2.50	9 .... 1,400.00	56 'The Treasuer of Araby' 350.00
44 Star Shadows,pt.3,A:Eclipso	10 .... 1,400.00	57 'Recruit for the Legion' 350.00
V:Lobo 2.50	11 .... 1,100.00	58 'Matadors of Suicide Slum' . 350.00
45 Star Shadows,pt.4, V:Eclipso 2.50	12 Newsboy Legion stories,	59 .... 350.00
2nd Series 1994–97	'Prevue of Peril!' 1,100.00	60 .... 350.00
0 New Starman 6.00	13 'Kill Dat Story!' 1,100.00	61 .... 350.00
1 Threat of the Mist 6.00	14 'Meanest Man on Earth' .. 1,100.00	62 'Prevue of Tomorrow' 350.00
2 .... 3.00	15 'Playmates of Peril' 1,100.00	63 .... 350.00
3 V:Son of the Mist 3.00	16 'Playboy of Suicide Slum!' . 1,100.00	64 'Criminal Cruise' 350.00
4 .... 3.00	17 V:Rafferty Mob 1,100.00	65 B:Robin,(c) & stories ... 1,100.00
5 V:Starman 3.00	18 O:Star Spangled Kid 1,300.00	66 V:No Face 700.00
6 Times Past Features 3.00	19 E:Tarantula 1,000.00	67 'The Castle of Doom' 550.00
7 Sinister Circus 2.50		68 .... 550.00
8 TyH(c),Sinister Circus 2.50		69 'The Stolen Atom Bomb' ... 850.00
9 TyH(c),Mist's daughter breaks		70 V:The Clock 550.00
out of prison 2.25		71 'Perils of the Stone Age' ... 550.00
10 Sins of the Chile,prelude 2.25		72 'Robin Crusoe' 550.00
11 .... 2.25		73 V:The Black Magician 550.00
12 JeR,TyH,Sins of the Child,pt.1 2.25		74 V:The Clock 550.00
13 JeR,TyH,Sins of the Child,pt.2 2.25		75 The State vs. Robin 550.00
14 JeR,TyH,Sins of the Child,pt.3 2.25		76 V:The Fence 550.00
15 JeR,TyH,Sins of the Child,pt.4 2.25		77 'The Boy who Wanted Robin
16 JeR,TyH,Sins of the Child,pt.5 2.25		for Christmas' 550.00
17 JeR,TyH 2.25		78 "Rajah Robin" 550.00
18 JeR,TyH,Orig.Starman		79 'V:The Clock,'The Tick-Tock
vs.The Mist 2.25		Crimes' 550.00
19 JeR,TyH,Talking with David 2 . 2.25		80 'The Boy Disc Jockey' 550.00
20 JeR(s),TyH,GyD,"Sand and		81 'The Seeing-Eye Dog Crimes' 450.00
Stars," pt.1 .... 2.25		82 'The Boy who Hated Robin' 450.00
21 JeR(s),TyH,GyD,"Sand and		83 'Who is Mr. Mystery',B:Captain
Stars," pt.2 .... 2.25		Compass backup story 450.00
22 JeR(s),TyH,GyD,"Sand and		84 How can we Fight Juvenile
Stars," pt.3 .... 2.25		Delinquency? 650.00
23 JeR(s),TyH,GyD,"Sand and		85 'Peril at the Pole' 450.00
Stars," pt.4 concl 2.25		86 .... 475.00
24 JeR(s),TyH,"Hell & Back," pt.1 2.25		87 V:Sinister Knight 650.00
25 JeR(s),TyH,"Hell & Back," pt.2 2.25		88 Robin Declares War on
26 JeR(s),TyH,"Hell & Back," pt.3 2.25		Batman, B:Batman app. .. 525.00
27 .... 2.25	*Star Spangled Comics #7*	89 'Batman's Utility Belt?' 525.00
28 JeR(s)Superfreaks and	*© DC Comics, Inc.*	90 'Rancho Fear!' 525.00
Backstabbers 2.25		91 'Cops 'n' Robbers?' 525.00
29 JeR(s),TyH,GyD,V:The Shade,	20 B:Liberty Belle 1,000.00	92 'Movie Hero No. 1?' 525.00
Starman history 2.25	21 .... 800.00	93 .... 525.00
30 JeR(s),TyH,"Infernal Devices"	22 'Brains for Sale' 800.00	94 'Underworld Playhouse' ... 525.00
pt.1 (of 6) 2.25	23 'Art for Scrapper's Sake' ... 800.00	95 'The Man with the Midas Touch',
31 JeR(s),TyH,"Infernal Devices"	24 .... 800.00	E:Robin(c),Batman story ... 525.00
pt.2 .... 2.25	25 'Victuals for Victory' 800.00	96 B:Tomahawk(c) & stories .. 350.00
32 JeR(s),TyH,"Infernal Devices"	26 'Louie the Lug goes Literary' 800.00	97 'The 4 Bold Warriors' 300.00
pt.3 .... 2.25	27 'Turn on the Heat!' 800.00	98 .... 300.00
33 JeR(s),TyH,"Infernal Devices"	28 'Poor Man's Rich Man' .. 800.00	99 'The Second Pocahontas' .. 300.00
pt.4,A:Batman, Sentinel 2.25	29 'Cabbages and Comics' .. 800.00	100 'The Frontier Phantom' ... 300.00
34 JeR(s),TyH,A:Batman, Sentinel,	30 .... 400.00	101 Peril on the High Seas ... 250.00
Floronic Man 2.25	31 'Questions Please!' 400.00	102 .... 250.00
Ann.#1 Legends o/t Dead Earth .. 3.50	32 .... 400.00	103 'Tomahawk's Death Duell' . 250.00
Ann.#2 Pulp Heroes (Romance) .. 3.95	33 .... 400.00	104 'Race with Death!' 250.00
TPB Sins of the Father,rep.#0–#5 12.95	34 'From Rags to Run!' 400.00	105 'The Unhappy Hunting
TPB Night and Day, rep. stories	35 'The Proud Poppas' 400.00	Grounds' 250.00
from #7–#16 .... 14.95	36 'Cowboy of Suicide Slum' .. 400.00	106 'Traitor in the War Paint' .. 250.00
	37 .... 400.00	107 'The Brave who Hunted
STAR SPANGLED	38 .... 400.00	Tomahawk' 250.00
COMICS	39 'Two Guardians are a Crowd' 400.00	108 'The Ghost called Moccasin
Oct., 1941	40 .... 400.00	Foot!' 250.00
1 O:Tarantula,B:Captain X of the	41 Back the 6th War Loan(c) .. 350.00	109 'The Land Pirates of
	42 .... 350.00	Jolly Roger Hilll' 250.00
	43 American Red Cross(c) ... 350.00	
	44 .... 350.00	

All comics prices listed are for *Near Mint* condition.

DC COMICS

110 'Sally Raines Frontier Girl'	275.00
111 'The Death Map of Thunder Hill'	275.00
112	300.00
113 FF,V:'The Black Cougar'	325.00
114 'Return of the Black Cougar'	350.00
115 'Journey of a Thousand Deaths'	300.00
116 'The Battle of Junction Fort'	300.00
117 'Siege?'	300.00
118 V:Outlaw Indians	250.00
119 'The Doomed Stockade?'	225.00
120 'Revenge of Raven Heart!'	225.00
121 'Adventure in New York!'	225.00
122 'I:Ghost Breaker,(c)& stories	250.00
123 'The Dolls of Doom'	200.00
124 'Suicide Tower'	200.00
125 The Hermit's Ghost Dog!'	200.00
126 'The Phantom of Paris!'	200.00
127 'The Supernatural Alibi!'	200.00
128 C:Batman,'The Girl who lived 5,000 Years!'	200.00
129 'The Human Orchids'	250.00
130 'The Haunted Town', July, 1952	275.00

Becomes:

STAR SPANGLED WAR STORIES
Aug., 1952

131 CS&StK(c),I Was A Jap Prisoner of War	750.00
132 CS&StK(c),The G.I. With The Million-Dollar Arm	550.00
133 CS&StK(c),Mission-San Marino	500.00
3 CS&StK(c),Hundred-Mission Mitchell	275.00
4 CS&StK(c),The Hot Rod Tank	275.00
5 LSt(c),Jet Pilot	275.00
6 CS(c),Operation Davy Jones	275.00
7 CS(c),Rookie Ranger,The	200.00
8 CS(c),I Was A Holywood Soldier	200.00
9 CS&StK(c),Sad Sack Squad	200.00
10 CS,The G.I. & The Gambler	200.00
11 LSt(c),The Lucky Squad	200.00
12 CS(c),The Four Horseman of Barricade Hill	200.00
13 No Escape	200.00
14 LSt(c),Pitchfork Army	200.00
15 The Big Fish	200.00
16 The Yellow Ribbon	200.00
17 IN(c),Prize Target	200.00
18 IN(c),The Gladiator	200.00
19 IN(c),The Big Lift	200.00
20 JGr(c),The Battle of the Frogmen	200.00
21 JGr(c),Dead Man's Bridge	150.00
22 JGr(c),Death Hurdle	150.00
23 JGr(c),The Silent Frogman	150.00
24 JGr(c),Death Slide	150.00
25 JGr(c),S.S. Liferaft	150.00
26 JGr(c),Bazooka Man	150.00
27 JGr(c),Taps for a Tail Gunner	150.00
28 JGr(c),Tank Duel	150.00
29 JGr(c),A Gun Called Slugger	150.00
30 JGr(c),The Thunderbolt Tank	150.00
31 IN(c),Tank Block	100.00
32 JGr(c),Bridge to Battle	100.00
33 JGr(c),Pocket War	100.00
34 JGr(c),Fighting...Snowbirds	100.00
35 JGr(c),Zero Hour	100.00
36 JGr(c),A G.I. Passed Here	100.00

37 JGr(c),A Handful of T.N.T.	100.00
38 RH(c),One-Man Army	100.00
39 JGr(c),Flying Cowboy	100.00
40 JGr(c),Desert Duel	100.00
41 IN(c),A Gunner's Hands	85.00
42 JGr(c),Sniper Alley	85.00
43 JGr(c),Top Kick Brother	85.00
44 JGr(c),Tank 711 Doesn't Answer	85.00
45 JGr(c),Flying Heels	85.00
46 JGr(c),Gunner's Seat	85.00
47 JGr(c),Sidekick	85.00
48 JGr(c),Battle Hills	85.00
49 JGr(c),Payload	85.00
50 JGr(c),Combat Dust	85.00
51 JGr(c),Battle Pigeon	70.00
52 JGr(c),Cannon-Man	70.00
53 JGr(c),Combat Close-Ups	70.00
54 JGr(c),Flying Exit	70.00
55 JKu(c),The Burning Desert	70.00
56 JKu(c),The Walking Sub	70.00
57 JGr(c),Call For a Frogman	70.00
58 JGr(c),MD,Waist Punch	70.00
59 JGr(c),Kick In The Door	70.00
60 JGr(c),Hotbox	70.00
61 JGr(c),MD,Tow Pilot	70.00
62 JGr(c),The Three GIs	70.00
63 JGr(c),Flying Range Rider	70.00
64 JGr(c),MD,Frogman Ambush	70.00
65 JGr(c),JSe,Frogman Block	70.00
66 JGr(c),Flattop Pigeon	70.00
67 RH(c),MD,Ashcan Alley	70.00
68 JGr(c),The Long Step	70.00
69 JKu(c),Floating Tank, The'	70.00
70 JKu(c),No Medal For Frogman	65.00
71 JKu(c),Shooting Star	65.00
72 JGr(c),Silent Fish	65.00
73 JGr(c),MD,The Mouse & the Tiger	65.00
74 JGr(c),MD,Frogman Bait	65.00
75 JGr(c),MD,Paratroop Mousketeers	65.00
76 MD,JKu(c),Odd Man	65.00
77 MD,JKu(c),Room to Fight	65.00
78 MD,JGr(c),Fighting Wingman	65.00
79 MD,JKu(c),Zero Box	65.00
80 MD,JGr(c),Top Gunner	65.00
81 MD,RH(c),Khaki Mosquito	65.00
82 MD,JKu(c),Ground Flier	65.00
83 MD,JGr(c),Jet On My Shoulder	65.00
84 MD,IN(c),O:Mademoiselle Marie	150.00
85 IN(c),A Medal For Marie	80.00
86 JGr(c),A Medal For Marie	80.00
87 JGr(c),T.N.T. Spotlight	75.00
88 JGr(c),The Steel Trap	75.00
89 IN(c),Trail of the Terror	75.00
90 RA(c),Island of Armored Giants	350.00
91 JGr(c),The Train of Terror	55.00
92 Last Battle of the Dinosaur Age	125.00
93 Goliath of the Western Front	55.00
94 JKu(c),The Frogman and the Dinosaur	125.00
95 Guinea Pig Patrol,Dinosaurs	125.00
96 Mission X,Dinosaur	125.00
97 The Sub-Crusher, Dinosaur	125.00
98 Island of Thunder, Dinosaur	125.00
99 The Circus of Monsters, Dinosaur	125.00
100 The Volcano of Monsters, Dinosaur	150.00

101 The Robot and the Dinosaur	125.00
102 Punchboard War,Dinosaur	125.00
103 Doom at Dinosaur Island, Dinosaur	125.00
104 The Tree of Terror, Dinosaurs	125.00
105 The War of Dinosaur Island	125.00
106 The Nightmare War, Dinosaurs	125.00
107 Battle of the Dinosaur Aquarium	125.00
108 Dinosaur D-Day	125.00
109 The Last Soldiers	125.00
110 thru 133	@125.00
134 NA	100.00
135	75.00
136	75.00
137 Dinosaur	75.00
138 Enemy Ace	100.00
139 O:Enemy Ace	90.00
140	65.00
141	65.00
142	50.00
143	50.00
144 NA,JKu	60.00
145	50.00
146	50.00
147	50.00
148	50.00
149	50.00
150 JKu,Viking Prince	50.00
151 I:Unknown Soldier	50.00
152	15.00
153	15.00
154 O:Unknown Soldier	40.00
155	10.00
156 I:Battle Album	8.00
157 thru 160	6.00
161 E:Enemy Ace	6.00
162 thru 170	@10.00
171 thru 200	@8.00
201 thru 204	@2.50

Becomes:

UNKNOWN SOLDIER
April-May, 1977

205 thru 247	@1.25
248 and 249 O:Unknown Soldier	@1.25
250	1.25
251 B:Enemy Ace	1.25
252 thru 268	@1.25

STAR TREK
1984–88
[1st Regular Series]

1 TS,The Wormhole Connection	15.00
2 TS,The Only Good Klingon	8.00
3 TS,Errand of War	7.00
4 TS,Deadly Allies	7.00
5 TS,Mortal Gods	7.00
6 TS,Who is Enigma?	6.00
7 EB,O:Saavik	6.00
8 TS,Blood Fever	6.00
9 TS,Mirror Universe Saga #1	6.00
10 TS,Mirror Universe Saga #2	6.00
11 TS,Mirror Universe Saga #3	6.00
12 TS,Mirror Universe Saga #4	6.00
13 TS,Mirror Universe Saga #5	5.00
14 TS,Mirror Universe Saga #6	5.00
15 TS,Mirror Universe Saga #7	5.00
16 TS,Mirror Universe Saga end	5.00
17 TS,The D'Artagnan Three	5.00
18 TS,Rest & Recreation	5.00
19 DSp,W.Koenig story	5.00
20 TS,Girl	5.00

DC COMICS

Star Trek #45 © DC Comics, Inc.

21 TS,Dreamworld		5.00
22 TS,The Wolf #1		5.00
23 TS,The Wolf #2		4.00
24 TS,Double Blind #1		4.00
25 TS,Double Blind #2.		4.00
26 TSV:Romulans		4.00
27 TS,Day in the Life		4.00
28 GM,The Last Word		4.00
29 Trouble with Bearclaw		4.00
30 CI,F:Uhura		4.00
31 TS,Maggie's World		4.00
32 TS,Judgment Day		4.00
33 TS,20th Anniv.		4.50
34 V:Romulans		2.50
35 GM,Excelsior		2.50
36 GM,StarTrek IV tie-in		2.50
37 StarTrek IV tie-in		2.50
38 AKu,The Argon Affair		2.50
39 TS,A:Harry Mudd		2.50
40 TS,A:Harry Mudd		2.50
41 TS,V:Orions		2.50
42 TS,The Corbomite Effect		2.50
43 TS,Paradise Lost #1		2.50
44 TS,Paradise Lost #2		2.50
45 TS,Paradise Lost #3		2.50
46 TS,Getaway		2.50
47 TS,Idol Threats		2.50
48 TS,The Stars in Secret		
Influence		2.50
49 TS,Aspiring to be Angels		2.50
50 TS,Anniv.		3.50
51 TS,Haunted Honeymoon		2.50
52 TS,'Hell in a Hand Basket'		2.50
53 'You're Dead,Jim'		2.50
54 Old Loyalties		2.50
55 TS,Finnegan's Wake		2.50
56 GM,Took place during 5 year		
Mission		2.50
Ann.#1 All Those Years Ago		4.00
Ann.#2 DJw,The Final Voyage		3.00
Ann.#3 CS,F:Scotty		3.00
Star Trek III Adapt.TS		2.50
Star Trek IV Adapt. TS		2.50
StarTrek V Adapt.		2.50

[2nd Regular Series]
1989–96

1 The Return		10.00
2 The Sentence		5.00
3 Death Before Dishonor		4.00
4 Reproccussions		4.00
5 Fast Friends		4.00
6 Cure All		4.00
7 Not Sweeney!		4.00
8 Going,Going		3.50
9 ...Gone		3.50
10 Trial of James Kirk #1		3.50
11 Trial of James Kirk #2		3.50
12 Trial of James Kirk #3		3.50
13 Return of Worthy #1		3.50
14 Return of Worthy #2		3.50
15 Return of Worthy #3		3.50
16 Worldsinger		3.00
17 Partners? #1		3.00
18 Partners? #2		3.00
19 Once A Hero		3.00
20		3.00
21 Kirk Trapped		3.00
22 A:Harry Mudd		3.00
23 The Nasgul,A:Harry Mudd		3.00
24 25th Anniv.,A:Harry Mudd		3.50
25 Starfleet Officers Reunion		2.50
26 Pilkor 3		2.50
27 Kirk Betrayed		2.50
28 V:Romulans		2.50
29 Mediators		2.50
30 Veritas #1		2.50
31 Veritas #2		2.50
32 Veritas #3		2.50
33 Veritas #4		2.50
34 JD,F:Kirk,Spock,McCoy		2.50
35 Tabukan Syndrome#1		2.50
36 Tabukan Syndrome#2		2.50
37 Tabukan Syndrome#3		2.50
38 Tabukan Syndrome#4		2.50
39 Tabukan Syndrome#5		2.50
40 Tabukan Syndrome#6		2.50
41 Runaway		2.50
42 Helping Hand		2.50
43 V:Binzalans		2.50
44 Acceptable Risk		2.50
45 V:Trelane		2.50
46 V:Captain Klaa		2.50
47 F:Spock & Saavik		2.50
48 The Neutral Zone		2.50
49 weapon from Genesis		2.50
50 "The Peacemaker"		3.75
51 "The Price"		2.00
52 V:Klingons		2.00
53 Timecrime #1		2.00
54 Timecrime #2		2.00
55 Timecrime #3		2.00
56 Timecrime #4		2.00
57 Timecrime #5		2.00
58 F:Chekov		2.00
59 Uprising		2.00
60 Hostages		2.00
61 On Talos IV		2.25
62 Alone,pt.1, V:aliens		2.25
63 Alone,pt.2		2.25
64 Kirk		2.25
65 Kirk in Space		2.25
66 Spock		2.25
67 Ambassador Stonn		2.25
68		2.25
69 Wolf in Cheap Clothing,pt.1		2.25
70 Wolf in Cheap Clothing,pt.2		2.25
71 Wolf in Cheap Clothing,pt.3		2.50
72 Wolf in Cheap Clothing,pt.4		2.50
73 Star-crossed,pt.1		2.50
74 Star-crossed,pt.2		2.25
75		2.25
76 Tendar		2.25
77 to the Romulan Neutral Zone		2.50

78 The Chosen,pt.1 (of 3)		2.50
79 The Chosen,pt.2		2.50
80 The Chosen,pt.3		2.50
Ann.#1 GM,sty by G.Takei(Sulu)		4.00
Ann.#2 Kirks 1st Yr At Star		
Fleet Academy		4.00
Ann #3 KD,F:Ambassador Sarek		3.50
Ann.#4 F:Spock on Pike's ship		3.50
Ann.#6 Convergence,pt.1		3.95
Spec.#1 PDd(s),BSz		3.75
Spec.#2 The Defiant		3.95
Spec.#3 V:Orion pirates		3.95
Debt of Honor,AH,CCI(s),HC		27.00
Debt of Honor SC		14.95
Spec. 25th Anniv.		6.95
Star Trek VI,movie adapt(direct)		5.95
Star Trek VI,movie(newsstand)		2.95
TPB Best of Star Trek reps.		19.95
TPB Who Killed Captain Kirk?,		
rep.Star Trek#49-#55		16.95
TPB The Ashes of Eden, Shatner		
novel adapt.		14.95

STAR TREK:
THE ASHES OF EDEN
1995

TPB adaptation of novel		14.95

STAR TREK: THE
MODALA IMPERATIVE
1991

1 Planet Modula		6.00
2 Modula's Rebels		4.50
3 Spock/McCoy rescue Attempt		4.00
4 Rebel Victory		4.00
TPB reprints both minis		19.95

STAR TREK: THE
NEXT GENERATION
Feb., 1988
[1st Regular Series]

1 based on TV series,Where No		
Man Has Gone Before		15.00
2 Spirit in the Sky		10.00
3 Factor Q		8.00
4 Q's Day		8.00
5 Q's Effects		8.00
6 Here Today		8.00

[2nd Regular Series] 1989–95

1 Return to Raimon		15.00
2 Murder Most Foul		9.00
3 Derelict		7.50
4 The Hero Factor		7.50
5 Serafin's Survivors		6.00
6 Shadows in the Garden		6.00
7 The Pilot		5.00
8 The Battle Within		5.00
9 The Pay Off		5.00
10 The Noise of Justice		5.00
11 The Imposter		4.00
12 Whoever Fights Monsters		4.00
13 The Hand of the Assassin		4.00
14 Holiday on Ice		4.00
15 Prisoners of the Ferengi		3.50
16 I Have Heard the Mermaids		
Singing		3.50
17 The Weapon		3.50
18 MM,Forbidden Fruit		3.50
19 The Lesson		3.50
20 Lost Shuttle		3.50
21 Lost Shuttle cont.		3.50
22 Lost Shuttle cont.		3.50
23 Lost Shuttle cont.		3.50

DC COMICS

24 Lost Shuttle conc.	3.50	
25 Okona S.O.S.	3.50	
26 Search for Okona	3.50	
27 Worf,Data,Troi,Okona trapped on world	3.50	
28 Worf/K'Ehleyr story	3.50	
29 Rift,pt.1	3.50	
30 Rift,pt.2	3.50	
31 Rift conclusion	3.50	
32	3.50	
33 R:Mischievous Q	3.50	
34 V:Aliens,F:Mischievous Q	3.50	
35 Way of the Warrior	3.50	
36 Shore Leave in Shanzibar#1	3.25	
37 Shore Leave in Shanzibar#2	3.25	
38 Shore Leave in Shanzibar#3	3.25	
39 Divergence #1	3.25	
40 Divergence #2	3.25	
41 V:Strazzan Warships	3.25	
42 V:Strazzans	3.25	
43 V:Strazzans	3.25	
44 Disrupted Lives	3.25	
45 F:Enterprise Surgical Team	3.25	

Star Trek The Next Generation #63
© DC Comics, Inc.

46 Deadly Labyrinth	3.25
47 Worst of Both World's#1	3.00
48 Worst of Both World's#2	3.00
49 Worst of Both World's#3	3.00
50 Double Sized,V:Borg	4.00
51 V:Energy Beings	3.00
52 in the 1940's	3.00
53 F:Picard	3.00
54 F:Picard	3.00
55 Data on Trial	3.00
56 Abduction	3.00
57 Body Switch	3.00
58 Body Switch	3.00
59 B:Children in Chaos	3.00
60 Children in Chaos#2	3.00
61 E:Children in Chaos	3.00
62 V:Stalker	3.00
63 A:Romulans	3.00
64 Geordie	3.00
65 Geordie	3.00
66	3.00
67 Friends/Strangers	3.00
68 Friends/Strangers,pt.2	3.00
69 Friends/Strangers,pt.3	3.00

70 Friends/Strangers,pt.4	3.00
71 War of Madness,pt.1	2.50
72 War of Madness,pt.2	2.50
73 War of Madness,pt.3	2.50
74 War of Madness,pt.4	2.50
75	2.50
76 F:Geordi	2.50
77 Gateway, pt.1	2.50
78 Gateway, pt.2	2.50
79 Crew transformed into androids	2.50
80 Mysterious illness	2.50
Ann.#1 A:Mischievous Q	4.50
Ann.#2 BP,V:Parasitic Creatures	4.00
Ann.#3	2.50
Ann.#4 MiB(s),F:Dr.Crusher	4.00
Ann.#6 Convergence,pt.2	3.95
Series Finale	4.25
Spec.#1	3.75
Spec.#2 CCi(s)	4.00
Star Trek N.G.:Sparticus	5.00
TPB Beginnings, BSz(c) rep.	19.95

STAR TREK: THE NEXT GENERATION — BEGINNINGS

TPB 160pg.	19.95

STAR TREK: THE NEXT GENERATION DEEP SPACE NINE
1994–95

1 Crossover with Malibu	2.50
2	2.50

STAR TREK: THE NEXT GENERATION ILL WIND
1995–96

1 Solar-sailing race	2.50
2 Explosion Investigated	2.50
3 A bomb aboard ship	2.50
4 finale	2.50

STAR TREK THE NEXT GENERATION MODALA IMPERATIVE
1991

1 A:Spock,McCoy	6.00
2 Modula Overrun by Ferengi	5.00
3 Picard,Spock,McCoy & Troi trapped	4.00
4 final issue	4.00

STAR TREK THE NEXT GENERATION SHADOWHEART
1994–95

1 thru 3	@2.25
4 Worf Confront Nikolai	2.25

STAR TREK: REVISITATIONS

TPB rep. #22–#24,F:Gary Seven, #49–#50,F:Harry Mudd, 176pg	19.95

STATIC
Milestone 1993–96

1 JPL,I:Static,Hotstreak,Frieda Goren, w/poster,card,D puzzle piece	4.00

1a Newstand Ed.	2.00
1b Platinum Ed.	8.00
2 JPL,V:Hotstreak,I:Tarmack	2.00
3 JPL,V:Tarmack	1.75
4 JPL,A:Holocaust,I:Don Cornelius	1.75
5 JPL,I:Commando X	1.75
6 JPL,V:Commando X	1.75
7 3RW,V:Commando X	1.75
8 WS(c),3RW,Shadow War,I:Plus	1.75
9 3RW,I:Virus	1.75
10 3RW,I:Puff,Coil	1.75
11 3RW,V:Puff,Coil	1.75
12 3RW,I:Joyride	1.75
13 I:Shape Changer	1.75
14 Worlds Collide,V:Rift	2.75
15 V:Paris Bloods	1.75
16 Revelations	1.75
17 Palisade	1.75
18 Princess Nightmare	1.75
19	1.75
20	1.75
21 A:Blood Syndicate	1.75
22 V:Rabis	1.75
23 A:Boogieman	1.75
24 A:Dusk	1.75
25 Long Hot Summer, V:Dusk, 48pgs	3.95
26 Long Hot Summer	2.50
27	2.50
28 Drug Raid	2.50
29 HC(c), Friend Drug Dealer	2.50
30 Deals with Friend's Death	2.50
31 GK	2.50
32 V:Swarm	2.50
33	2.50
34 V:Ruberband Man	2.50
35 new Prometheus	2.50
36 JP,V:Sinister Botanist	2.50
37	2.50
38	2.50
39	2.50
40 JMr	2.50
41 Virgil's relationship with Daisy	2.50
42 V:six enemies	2.50
43 A:Brickhouse, V:Frieda Goren	2.50
44	2.50
45 MBr(s),JMr,Static lays a trap for Laserjet	2.50
46 MBr(s),JMr	2.50
47 DMD(s),JMr, final issue	2.50

STEEL
1994–97

1 JBg(c),B:LSi(s),CsB,N:Steel	3.00
2 JBg(c),CsB,V:Toastmaster	2.00
3 JBg(c),CsB,V:Amertek	2.00
4 JBg(c),CsB	2.00
5 JBg(c),CsB,V:Sister's Attacker	2.00
6 JBg(c),CsB,Worlds Collide,pt.5	2.00
7 Worlds Collide,pt.6	1.75
8 Zero Hour,I:Hazard	1.75
9 F:Steel	1.50
10 F:Steel	1.50
11	1.50
12	1.50
13 A:Maxima	1.50
14 A:Superman	1.50
15 R:White Rabbit	1.50
16 V:White Rabbit [new Miraweb format begins]	1.95
17 Steel controls armor powers	1.95
18 Abduction	1.95
19	1.95
20 Body Rejects Armor	1.95
21 LSi,Underworld Unleashed tie-in	1.95

Steel #3 © DC Comics, Inc.

22 Steel separated from Superboy 1.95
23 Steel attacked 1.95
24 V:Hazard's 1.95
25 . . . . 1.95
26 Natasha gains superpowers . . 1.95
27 LSi,V:Hazard 1.95
28 . . . . 1.95
29 . . . . 1.95
30 . . . . 1.95
31 LSi(s),V:Armorbeast 1.95
32 V:Blockbuster 1.95
33 JAp,DG,Natasha's drug abuse 1.95
34 CPr(s),DCw,TP,A:Natasha, in
Jersey City 1.95
35 CPr(s),DCw,TP, ... 1.95
36 CPr(s),DCw,TP,Combing the
sewers of Jersey City 1.95
37 CPr(s),DCw,TP,John Irons,
Amanda Quick & Skorpio a
romantic triangle 1.95
38 CPr(s),DCw,TP,A:The Question 1.95
39 CPr(s),DCw,TP,V:Crash 1.95
40 CPr(s),VGi,Steel tries out
new hammer 1.95
41 CPr(s),DCw,TMo, John Irons
guilty of murder? 1.95
42 CPr(s),DCw,TP,Irons and
Amanda assaulted 1.95
Ann.#1 Elseworlds story 2.95
TPB THe Forging of a Hero LSi(s) 19.95

STEEL, THE
INDESTRUCTIBLE MAN
March, 1978

1 DH,I:Steel 1.00
2 DH 1.00
3 DH 1.00
4 DH 1.00
5 Oct.–Nov., 1978 . . . . 1.00

STRANGE ADVENTURES
1950–74

1 The Menace of the Green
Nebula 2,300.00
2 S&K,JM(c),Doom From
Planet X 1,000.00
3 The Metal World 650.00

4 BP,The Invaders From the
Nth Dimension 650.00
5 The World Inside the Atom . 600.00
6 The Confessions of a Martian 600.00
7 The World of Giant Ants . . . 600.00
8 MA,ATh,Evolution Plus 600.00
9 MA,B:Captain Comet,The
Origin of Captain Comet . . 1,400.00
10 MA,CI,The Air Bandits
From Space 600.00
11 MA,CI,Day the Past
Came Back 450.00
12 MA,CI,GK(c),The Girl From
the Diamond Planet 450.00
13 MA,CI,GK(c),When the Earth
was Kidnapped 450.00
14 MA,CI,GK(c),Destination
Doom 450.00
15 MA,CI,GK(c),Captain Comet-
Enemy of Earth 425.00
16 MA,CI,GK(c),The Ghost of
Captain Comet 425.00
17 MA,CI,GK(c),Beware the
Synthetic Men 425.00
18 CI,MA(c),World of Flying Men 425.00
19 CI,MA(c),Secret of the
Twelve Eternals 425.00
20 CI,Slaves of the Sea Master 425.00
21 CI,MA(c),Eyes of the
Other Worlds 350.00
22 CI,The Guardians of the
Clockwork Universe 350.00
23 CI,MA(c),The Brain Pirates
of Planet X 350.00
24 CI,MA(c),Doomsday on Earth 350.00
25 CI,GK(c),The Day
That Vanished 350.00
26 CI,Captain Vs. Miss Universe 350.00
27 CI,MA(c),The Counterfeit
Captain Comet 350.00
28 CI,Devil's Island in Space . . 350.00
29 CI,The Time Capsule From
1,000,000 B.C. 350.00
30 CI,MA(c),Menace From the
World of Make-Believe 325.00
31 CI,Lights Camera Action . . . 325.00
32 CI,MA(c),The Challenge of
Man-Ape the Mighty 325.00
33 CI,MA(c),The Human Beehive 325.00
34 CI,MA(c) 325.00
35 CI,MA(c),Cosmic Chessboard 325.00
36 CI,MA(c),The Grab-Bag
Planet 325.00
37 CI,MA(c),The Invaders From
the Golden Atom 325.00
38 CI,MA(c),Seeing-Eye Humans 325.00
39 CI,MA(c),The Guilty Gorilla . 350.00
40 CI,MA(c),The Mind Monster 300.00
41 CI,MA(c),The Beast From Out
of Time 300.00
42 CI,MD,MA(c),The Planet of
Ancient Children 300.00
43 CI,MD,MA(c),The Phantom
Prize Fighter 300.00
44 CI,MA(c),The Planet That
Plotted Murder 300.00
45 CI,MD,MA(c),Gorilla World . 300.00
46 CI,MA(c),E:Captain Comet
Interplanetary War Base . . . 300.00
47 CI,MA(c),The Man Who Sold
the Earth 300.00
48 CI,MA(c),Human Phantom . 300.00
49 CI,MA(c),The Invasion
from Indiana 300.00
50 CI,MA(c),The World Wrecker 250.00

Strange Adventures #5
© DC Comics, Inc.

51 CI,MA(c),The Man Who
Stole Air 250.00
52 CI,MA(c),Prisoner of the
Parakeets 250.00
53 CI,MA(c),The Human Icicle . 250.00
54 CI,MA(c),The Electric Man . 175.00
55 CI,MA(c),The Gorilla Who
Challanged the World,pt.I . . 175.00
56 CI,The Jungle Emperor,pt.II 175.00
57 CI,The Spy from Saturn . . . 175.00
58 CI,I Hunted the Radium Man 175.00
59 CI,The Ark From Planet X . . 175.00
60 CI,Across the Ages 175.00
61 CI,The Mirages From Space 175.00
62 CI,The Fireproof Man 175.00
63 CI,I Was the Man in the Moon 175.00
64 CI,GK(c),Gorillas In Space . 175.00
65 CI,GK(c),Prisoner From Pluto 175.00
66 CI,GK(c),The Human Battery 175.00
67 CI,GK(c),Martian Masquerader 175.00
68 CI,The Man Who Couldn't
Drown 175.00
69 CI,Gorilla Conquest of Earth 175.00
70 CI,Triple Life of Dr. Pluto . . 175.00
71 CI,MSy,Zero Hour For Earth 150.00
72 CI,The Skyscraper That Came
to Life 150.00
73 CI,Amazing Rain of Gems . 150.00
74 CI,The Invisible Invader
From Dimension X 150.00
75 CI,Secret of the Man-Ape . . 150.00
76 CI,B:Darwin Jones,The Robot
From Atlantis 150.00
77 CI,A:Darwin Jones,The World
That Slipped Out of Space . 150.00
78 CI,The Secret of the Tom
Thumb Spaceman 150.00
79 CI,A:Darwin Jones,Invaders
from the Ice World 150.00
80 CI,Mind Robbers of Venus . 150.00
81 CI,The Secret of the
Shrinking Twins 150.00
82 CI,Giants of the Cosmic Ray 150.00
83 CI,Assignment in Eternity . . 125.00
84 CI,Prisoners of the Atom
Universe 125.00
85 CI,The Amazing Human Race 125.00
86 CI,The Dog That Saved the

DC COMICS

Earth 125.00
87 CI,New Faces For Old 125.00
88 CI,A:Darwin Jones,The Gorilla
   War Against Earth 125.00
89 CI,Earth For Sale 125.00
90 CI,The Day I Became a
   Martian 125.00
91 CI,Midget Earthmen of Jupiter 125.00
92 CI,GK(c),The Amazing Ray
   of Knowledge 125.00
93 CI,GK(c),A:Darwin Jones,
   Space-Rescue By Proxy . . . 125.00
94 MA,CI,GK(c),Fisherman of
   Space 125.00
95 CI,The World at my Doorstep 125.00
96 CI,MA(c),The Menace of
   Saturn's Rings 125.00
97 CI,MA(c),MSy,Secret of the
   Space-Giant 125.00
98 CI,GK(c),MSy,Attack on Fort
   Satellite 125.00
99 CI,MSy,GK(c),Big Jump Into
   Space 125.00
100 CI,MSy,The Amazing Trial
   of John (Gorilla) Doe 135.00
101 CI,MSy,GK(c),Giant From
   Beyond 80.00
102 MSy,GK(c),The Three Faces
   of Barry Morrell 80.00
103 GK(c),The Man Who
   Harpooned Worlds 80.00
104 MSy,GK(c),World of Doomed
   Spacemen 80.00
105 MSy,GK(c),Fisherman From
   the Sea 80.00
106 MSy,CI,GK(c),Genie in the
   Flying Saucer 80.00
107 MSy,CI,GK(c),War of the
   Jovian Bubble-Men 80.00
108 MSy,CI,GK(c),The Human
   Pet of Gorilla Land 80.00
109 MSy,CI,GK(c),The Man Who
   Weighted 100 Tons 80.00
110 MSy,CI,GK(c),Hand From
   Beyond 80.00
111 MSy,CI,GK(c),Secret of
   the Last Earth-Man 80.00
112 MSy,CI,GK(c),Menace of
   the Size-Changing Spaceman 80.00
113 MSy,CI,GK(c),Deluge From
   Space 80.00
114 MSy,CI,GK(c),Secret of the
   Flying Buzz Saw 80.00
115 MSy,CI,GK(c),The Great
   Space-Tiger Hunt 80.00
116 MSy,CI,RH,GK(c),Invasion
   of the Water Warriors 80.00
117 MSy,CI,GK(c),I:Atomic
   Knights 600.00
118 MSy,CI,The Turtle-Men of
   Space 125.00
119 MSy,CI,MA(c),Raiders
   From the Giant World 100.00
120 MSy,CI,MA,Attack of the Oil
   Demons 250.00
121 MSy,CI,MA(c),Invasion of the
   Flying Reptiles 65.00
122 MSy,CI,MA(c),David and the
   Space-Goliath 65.00
123 MSy,CI,MA(c),Secret of the
   Rocket-Destroyer 65.00
124 MSy,CI,MA(c),The Face-Hunter
   From Saturn 65.00
125 MSy,CI,The Flying Gorilla
   Menace 65.00

126 MSy,CI,MA(c),Return of the
   Neanderthal Man 65.00
127 MSy,CI,MA(c),Menace
   From the Earth-Globe 65.00
128 MSy,CI,MA(c),The Man
   With the Electronic Brain 65.00
129 MSy,CI,MA(c),The Giant
   Who Stole Mountains 65.00
130 MSy,CI,MA.War With the
   Giant Frogs 65.00
131 MSy,CI,MA(c),Emperor
   of the Earth 65.00
132 MSy,CI,MA(c),The Dreams
   of Doom 65.00
133 MSy,CI,MA(c),The Invisible
   Dinosaur 65.00
134 MSy,CI,MA(c), The Aliens
   Who Raided New York 65.00
135 MSy,CI,MA(c),Fishing Hole
   in the Sky 65.00
136 MSy,CI,MA(c),The Robot
   Who Lost Its Head 50.00
137 MSy,CI,MA(c),Parade of the
   Space-Toys 50.00

Strange Adventures #243
© DC Comics, Inc.

138 MSy,CI,MA(c),Secret of the
   Dinosaur Skeleton 65.00
139 MSy,CI,MA(c),Space-Roots
   of Evil 50.00
140 MSy,CI,MA(c),Prisoner of
   the Space-Patch 50.00
141 MSy,CI,MA(c),Battle Between
   the Two Earths 65.00
142 MSy,CI,MA(c),The Return of
   the Faceless Creature 50.00
143 MSy,CI,MA(c),The Face in
   the Atom-Bomb Cloud 50.00
144 MSy,CI,MA(c),A:Atomic
   Knights, When the Earth
   Blacked Out 55.00
145 MSy,CI,MA,The Man Who
   Lived Forever 50.00
146 MSy,CI,MA(c),Perilous Pet
   of Space 50.00
147 MSy,CI,MA(c),The Dawn-
   World Menace 55.00
148 MSy,CI,MA(c),Earth Hero,
   Number One 50.00

149 MSy,CI,MA(c),Raid of
   the Rogue Star 50.00
150 MSy,CI,MA(c),When Earth
   Turned into a Comet 55.00
151 MSy,CI,MA(c),Invasion Via
   Radio-Telescope 50.00
152 MSy,MA(c),The Martian
   Emperor of Earth 50.00
153 MSy,MA(c),Threat of the
   Faceless Creature 50.00
154 CI,MSy,MA,GK(c),Earth's
   Friendly Invaders 50.00
155 MSy,MA,GK(c),Prisoner
   of the Undersea World 50.00
156 MSy,CI,MA(c),The Man
   With the Head of Saturn 50.00
157 MSy,CI,MA(c),Plight of
   the Human Cocoons 50.00
158 MSy,CI,MA(c),The Mind
   Masters of Space 50.00
159 MSy,CI,MA(c),The Maze
   of Time 50.00
160 MSy,CI,MA(c),A:Atomic
   Knights, Here Comes the
   Wild Ones 50.00
161 MSy,CI,MA(c),Earth's Frozen
   Heat Wave,E:Space Museum 35.00
162 CI,MA(c),Mystery of the
   12 O'Clock Man 35.00
163 MA(c),The Creature in
   the Black Light 35.00
164 DD&SMo(c),I Became
   a Robot 35.00
165 DD&SMo(c),I Broke the
   Supernatural Barrier 35.00
166 DD&SMo(c),I Lived in
   Two Bodies 35.00
167 JkS(c),The Team That
   Conqured Time 35.00
168 JkS(c),I Hunted Toki
   the Terrible 35.00
169 DD&SMo(c),The Prisoner
   of the Hour Glass 35.00
170 DD&SMo(c),The Creature
   From Strange Adventures . . . 35.00
171 The Diary o/t 9-Planet Man? 35.00
172 DD&SMo(c),I Became
   the Juggernaut Man 35.00
173 The Secret of the
   Fantasy Films 35.00
174 JkS(c),The Ten Ton Man . . 35.00
175 Danger: This Town is
   Shrinking 35.00
176 DD&SMo(c),The Case of
   the Cosmonik Quartet 35.00
177 I Lived a Hundred Lives,
   O:Immortal Man 35.00
178 JkS(c),The Runaway Comet 35.00
179 JkS(c),I Buried Myself Alive . 35.00
180 CI,I:Animal Man,'I Was the
   Man With Animal Powers . . 250.00
181 The Man of Two Worlds . . 15.00
182 JkS(c),The Case of the
   Blonde Bombshell 15.00
183 JM(c),The Plot to Destroy
   the Earth 15.00
184 GK(c),A:Animal Man,The
   Return of the Man With
   Animal Powers 150.00
185 JkS(c),Ilda-Gangsters Inc. . . 15.00
186 Beware the Gorilla Witch . . 15.00
187 JkS(c),O:The Enchantress . 20.00
188 SD,JkS(c),I Was the
   Four Seasons 15.00
189 SD,JkS(c),The Way-Out

DC COMICS

Worlds of Bertram Tilley	15.00
190 CI,A:Animal Man,A-Man-the Hero with Animal Powers	150.00
191 JkS(c),Beauty vs. the Beast	15.00
192 Freak Island	15.00
193 The Villian Maker	15.00
194 JkS(c),The Menace of the Super- Gloves	15.00
195 JkS(c),Secret of the Three Earth Dooms,A:Animal Man	100.00
196 JkS(c),Mystery of the Orbit Creatures	15.00
197 The Hostile Hamlet	12.00
198 JkS(c),Danger! Earth is Doomed	12.00
199 Robots of the Round Table	12.00
200	12.00
201 JkS,Animal Man	50.00
202	12.00
203	12.00
204	12.00
205 CI,I&O:Deadman	75.00
206 NA,MSy	60.00
207 NA	45.00
208 NA	45.00
209 NA	45.00
210 NA	45.00
211 NA	45.00
212 NA	45.00
213 NA	45.00
214 NA	45.00
215 NA	45.00
216 NA	45.00
217 MA,MSy,A:Adam Strange	11.00
218 MA,CI,MSy	10.00
219 CI,JKu	10.00
220 CI,JKu	10.00
221 CI	10.00
222 MA,New Adam Strange	12.00
223 MA,CI	10.00
224 MA,CI	10.00
225 MA,JKu	10.00
226 MA,JKu,New Adam Strange	12.00
227 JKu	10.00
228 NA(c)	25.00
229	10.00
230 GM(c)	10.00
231 E:Atomic Knights	10.00
232 JKu	8.00
233 JKu	8.00
234 JKu	8.00
235 NA(c)	20.00
236	8.00
237	8.00
238 MK(c)	8.00
239	8.00
240 MK(c)	8.00
241	8.00
242 MA	8.00
243 F:Adam Strange	8.00
244 Oct.–Nov., 1974	8.00

STRANGE SPORTS STORIES
Sept.–Oct. 1973

1 CS,DG	10.00
2 thru 6	@6.00

STREETS
1993

1 Tenderloin	4.95
2 Procurement	4.95
3	4.95

SUGAR & SPIKE
April-May, 1956

1 SM	1,000.00
2 SM	500.00
3 SM	400.00
4 SM	350.00
5 SM	350.00
6 thru 10 SM	@250.00
11 thru 20 SM	@200.00
21 thru 29 SM	@100.00
30 SM,A:Scribbly	125.00
31 thru 50 SM	@100.00
51 thru 70 SM	@70.00
71 thru 79 SM	@50.00
80 SM,I:Bernie the Brain	50.00
81 thru 97 SM	@30.00
98 SM,Oct.–Nov., 1971	30.00

STUCK RUBBER BABY SOFTCOVER
DC/Paradox Press

GN by Howard Cruise	14.00

Suicide Squad #41 © DC Comics, Inc.

SUICIDE SQUAD
1987–91

1 LMc,Legends,I:Jihad	2.50
2 LMc,V:The Jihad	2.00
3 LMc,V:Female Furies	1.75
4 LMc,V:William Hell	1.75
5 LM,A:Penguin	2.50
6 LM,A:Penguin	2.50
7 LMc,V:Peoples Hero	1.50
8 LMc,O:SquadMembers	1.50
9 LMc,Millenium	1.50
10 LMc,A:Batman	1.50
11 LMc,A:Vixen,Speedy	1.50
12 LMc,Enchantress, V:Nightshade	1.50
13 LMc,X-over,JLI#13	2.00
14 Nightshade Odyssey #1	1.50
15 Nightshade Odyssey #2	1.50
16 R:Shade	3.00
17 LMc,V:The Jihad	1.25
18 LMc,V:Jihad	1.25
19 LMc,Personal Files 1988	1.25
20 LMc,V:Mirror Master	1.25
21 LMc,bonus book #10	1.25
22 LMc,D:Senator Cray	1.25
23 LMc,Invasion	1.25
24 LMc,V:Guerillas	1.25
25 L:Nightshade	1.25
26 D:Rick Flag,Jihad	1.25
27 Janus Directive #2	1.25
28 Janus Directive #4	1.25
29 Janus Directive #8	1.25
30 Janus Directive #10	1.25
31 Personal Files 1989	1.25
32 V:Female Furies	1.25
33 GI,V:Female Furies	1.25
34 GI,V:Granny Goodness	1.25
35 LMc,GI,V:Female Furies	1.25
36 GI,D:Original Dr.Light	1.25
37 GI,A:Shade,The Changing Man,V:Loa	1.50
38 LMc,GI,O:Bronze Tiger	1.25
39 GI,D:Loa	1.25
40 Phoenix Gambit #1,A:Batman Int. Poster	1.50
41 Phoenix Gambit #2	1.25
42 Phoenix Gambit,A:Batman	1.25
43 Phoenix Gambit,A:Batman	1.25
44 I:New Atom,O:Captain Boomerang	1.25
45 A:Kobra	1.00
46 A:Kobra	1.00
47 GI,A:Kobra,D:Ravan	1.00
48 GI,New Thinker	1.00
49 GI,New Thinker	1.00
50 GI,50 Years of S.Squad	2.00
51 A:Deadshot	1.00
52 R:Docter Light	1.00
53 GI,The Dragon's Horde #1	1.00
54 GI,The Dragon's Horde #2	1.00
55 GI,The Dragon's Horde #3	1.00
56 GI,The Dragon's Horde #4	1.00
57 GI,The Dragon's Horde conc.	1.00
58 GI,War of the Gods x-over	1.00
59 GI,A:Superman, Batman, Aquaman,A:Jihad, Hayoth	1.25
60 GI,A:Superman,Batman, Aquaman,Jihad,The Hayoth	1.25
61 GI,A:Superman,Batman, Aquaman,V:Jihad	1.25
62 GI,R:Ray Palmer,A:Batman Superman,Aquaman	1.25
63 GI,I:Gvede, Lord of Death	1.25
64 GI,A:Task Force X	1.25
65 GI,Bronze Tiger	1.25
66 GI,Final Iss.E:Suicide Squad	1.25
Ann.#1 GN,V:Argent,A:Manhunter	1.75

SUPERBOY
1949–76

1 Superman (c)	6,500.00
2 'Superboy Day'	1,500.00
3	1,100.00
4 The Oracle of Smallville	800.00
5 Superboy meets Supergirl, Pre-Adventure #252	750.00
6 I:Humpty Dumpty,the Hobby Robber	700.00
7 WB,V:Humpty Dumpty	700.00
8 CS,I:Superbaby,V:Humpty Dumpty	650.00
9 V:Humpty Dumpty	650.00
10 CS,I:Lana Lang	650.00
11 CS,2nd Lang,V:Humpty Dumpty	500.00
12 CS,The Heroes Club	500.00
13 CS,Scout of Smallville	500.00
14 CS,I:Marsboy	500.00

All comics prices listed are for *Near Mint* condition.

Superboy #19 © DC Comics, Inc.

15 CS,A:Superman 500.00
16 CS,A:Marsboy 375.00
17 CS,Superboy's Double 375.00
18 CS,Lana Lang-Hollywood
   Star 375.00
19 CS,The Death of Young
   Clark Kent 375.00
20 CS,The Ghost that Haunted
   Smallville 375.00
21 CS,Lana Lang-Magician . . . 275.00
22 CS,The New Clark Kent . . . 275.00
23 CS,The Super Superboy . . . 275.00
24 CS,The Super Fat Boy of
   Steel 275.00
25 CS,Cinderella of Smallville . 275.00
26 CS,A:Superbaby 275.00
27 CS,Clark Kent-Runaway. . . 275.00
28 CS,The Man Who Defeated
   Superboy 275.00
29 CS,The Puppet Superboy . . 275.00
30 CS,I:Tommy Tuttle 200.00
31 CS,The Amazing Elephant
   Boy From Smallville 200.00
32 CS,His Majesty King
   Superboy 200.00
33 CS,The Crazy Costumes of
   the Boy of Steel 200.00
34 CS,Hep Cats o/Smallville . . 200.00
35 CS,The Five Superboys . . . 200.00
36 . . . . 200.00
37 CS,I:Thaddeus Lang 200.00
38 CS,Public Chimp #1 . . . . . . 200.00
39 CS,Boy w/Superboy Powers 200.00
40 CS,The Magic Necklace . . . 175.00
41 CS,Superboy Meets
   Superbrave 175.00
42 CS,Gaucho of Smallville . . 175.00
43 CS,Super-Farmer o/Smallville 175.00
44 The Amazing Adventure of
   Superboy's Costume 175.00
45 A Trap For Superboy 175.00
46 The Battle of Fort Smallville 175.00
47 CS,A:Superman 175.00
48 CS,Boy Without Super-Suit . 175.00
49 I:Metallo (Jor-El's Robot) . . 200.00
50 The Super-Giant of Smallville 175.00
51 I:Krypto 150.00
52 CS,The Powerboy from Earth 150.00

53 CS,A:Superman 150.00
54 CS,The Silent Superboy . . . 150.00
55 CS,A:Jimmy Olson 150.00
56 CS,A:Krypto 150.00
57 CS,One-Man Baseball Team 150.00
58 CS,The Great Kryptonite
   Mystery 150.00
59 CS,A:Superbaby 150.00
60 The 100,000 Cowboy 150.00
61 The School For Superboys . 125.00
62 I:Gloria Kent 125.00
63 CS,The Two Boys of Steel . 125.00
64 CS,A:Krypto 125.00
65 Superboy's Moonlight Spell . 125.00
66 The Family with X-Ray Eyes 125.00
67 I:Klax-Ar 125.00
68 O&I:Bizarro 500.00
69 How Superboy Learned
   To Fly 100.00
70 O:Superboy's Glasses 100.00
71 A:Superbaby 100.00
72 The Flying Girl of Smallville 100.00
73 CS,A:Superbaby 100.00
74 A:Jor-El & Lara 100.00
75 A:Superbaby 100.00
76 I:Super Monkey 100.00
77 Superboy's Best Friend . . . 100.00
78 O:Mr.Mzyzptlk 150.00
79 A:Jar-El & Lara 85.00
80 Superboy meets Supergirl . 125.00
81 The Weakling From Earth . . 75.00
82 A:Bizarro Krypto 75.00
83 I:Kryptonite Kid 75.00
84 A:William Tell 75.00
85 Secret of Mighty Boy 75.00
86 I:PeteRoss,A:Legion 150.00
87 I:Scarlet Jungle of Krypton . 80.00
88 The Invader from Earth 80.00
89 I:Mon-El 250.00
90 A:Pete Ross 75.00
91 CS,Superboy in Civil War . . 75.00
92 CS,I:Destructo,A:Lex Luthor . 75.00
93 A:Legion 65.00
94 I:Superboy Revenge Squad,
   A:Pete Ross 50.00
95 Imaginary Story,The Super
   Family From Krypton 50.00
96 A:Pete Ross,Lex Luther 50.00
97 Krypto Story 40.00
98 Legion,I&O:Ultraboy 55.00
99 O: The Kryptonite Kid 45.00
100 I:Phantom Zone 175.00
101 The Handsome Hound
   of Steel 35.00
102 O:Scarlet Jungle of Krypton 35.00
103 CS,A:King Arthur,Jesse James
   Red Kryptonite 35.00
104 O:Phantom Zone 35.00
105 CS,'The Simpleton of Steel' 35.00
106 CS,A:Brainiac 35.00
107 CS,I:Superboy Club of
   Smallville 40.00
108 The Kent's First Super Son . 35.00
109 The Super Youth of Bronze . 35.00
110 A:Jor-El 35.00
111 Red Kryptonite Story 35.00
112 CS,A:Superbaby 35.00
113 'The Boyhood of Dad Kent'. 35.00
114 A:Phantom Zone,
   Mr.Mxyzptlk 35.00
115 A:Phantom Zone,Lex Luthor 35.00
116 'The Wolfboy of Smallville'. 35.00
117 A:Legion 35.00
118 CS,'The War Between
   Superboy and Krypto' 35.00

Superboy #141 © DC Comics, Inc.

119 V:Android Double 30.00
120 A:Mr.Mxyzptlk 30.00
121 CS,A:Jor-El,Lex Luthor 30.00
122 Red Kryptonite Story 30.00
123 CS,The Curse of the
   Superboy Mummy 30.00
124 I:Insect Queen 30.00
125 O:Kid Psycho 30.00
126 O:Krypto 30.00
127 A:Insect Queen 32.00
128 A:Phantom Zone,Kryptonite
   Kid,Dev En 32.00
129 rep.A:Mon-El,SuperBaby . . . 35.00
130 . . . . 20.00
131 A:Lex Luthor,Mr.Mxyzptlk,I:
   Space Canine Patrol Agents . 20.00
132, CS,A:Space Canine
   Patrol Agents 20.00
133 A:Robin, repr. 20.00
134 'The Scoundrel of Steel' . . . 20.00
135 A:Lex Luthor 20.00
136 A:Space Canine Agents . . . 20.00
137 Mysterious Mighty Mites . . . 20.00
138 giant, Superboy's Most
   Terrific Battles 35.00
139 'The Samson of Smallville' . 15.00
140 V:The Gambler 15.00
141 No Mercy for a Hero 15.00
142 A:Super Monkey 15.00
143 NA(c),'The Big Fall' 15.00
144 'Superboy's Stolen Identity' . 15.00
145 NA(c)Kents become young . 15.00
146 NA(c),CS,'The Runaway' . . . 15.00
147 giant O:Legion 22.00
148 NA(c),CS,C:PolarBoy 14.00
149 NA(c),A:Bonnie & Clyde . . . 14.00
150 JAb,V:Mr.Cipher 14.00
151 NA(c),A:Kryptonite Kid 14.00
152 NA(c),WW 14.00
153 NA(c),WW,A:Prof Mesmer . . 12.00
154 WW(i),A:Jor-El & Lara
   'Blackout For Superboy' 12.00
155 NA(c),WW,'Revolt of the
   Teenage Robots' 12.00
156 giant 15.00
157 WW 12.00
158 WW,A:Jor-El & Lara 12.00
159 WW(i),A:Lex Luthor 12.00

DC COMICS

Superboy #147 © DC Comics, Inc.

Superboy #173 © DC Comics, Inc.

Superboy #212 © DC Comics, Inc.

160 WW,'I Chose Eternal Exile' . 12.00
161 WW,'The Strange Death of
  Superboy' 12.00
162 A:Phantom Zone 12.00
163 NA(c),'Reform School Rebel' 12.00
164 NA(c),'Your Death Will
  Destroy Me' 12.00
165 giant 15.00
166 NA(c),A:Lex Luthor 12.00
167 NA(c),MA,A:Superbaby 12.00
168 NA(c),MA,Hitler 12.00
169 MA,A:Lex Luthor 12.00
170 MA,A:Genghis Khan 12.00
171 MA,A:Aquaboy 12.00
172 MA(i),GT,A:Legion,
  O:Lightning Lad,Yango 13.00
173 NA(c),GT,DG,O:CosmicBoy 12.00
174 giant 15.00
175 NA(c),MA,Rejuvenation of
  Ma & Pa Kent 12.00
176 NA(c),MA,GT,WW,A:Legion 12.00
177 MA,A:Lex Luthor . . . 6.00
178 NA(c),MA,Legion Reprint . . . 6.00
179 MA,A:Lex Luthor 6.00
180 MA,O:Bouncing Boy 6.00
181 MA 6.00
182 MA,A:Bruce Wayne 6.00
183 MA,GT,CS(rep),A:Legion . . 6.00
184 MA,WW,O:Dial H rep. 6.00
185 A:Legion 10.00
186 MA 2.50
187 MA 2.50
188 MA,DC,O:Karkan,A:Legn . . 2.50
189 MA 2.50
190 MA,WW 3.00
191 MA,DC O:SunBoy retold . . . 2.50
192 MA 2.50
193 MA,WW,N:Chameleon Boy,
  Shrinking Violet 3.00
194 MA 2.50
195 MA,WW,I:Wildfire,
  N:Phantom Girl 3.00
196 last Superboy solo 2.50
197 DC,Legion begins, New
  Costumes,I:Tyr 9.00
198 DC N:Element Lad,
  Princess Projects 3.00
199 DC,A:Tyr, Otto Orion 3.00

200 DC,M:Bouncing Boy
  & Duo Damsel 8.00
201 DC,Wildfire returns 3.00
202 N:Light Lass 3.00
203 MGr,D:Invisible Kid 3.00
204 MGr,A:Supergirl 3.00
205 MGr,CG,100 pages 4.00
206 MGr,A:Ferro Lad 3.00
207 MGr,O:Lightning Lad 3.00
208 MGr,CS,68pp,Legion of
  Super Villains 3.00
209 MGr,N:Karate Kid 3.00
210 MGr,O:Karate Kid 3.00
211 MGr 2.50
212 MGr,L:Matter Eater Lad . . . 2.50
213 MGr,V:Benn Pares 2.50
214 MGr,V:Overseer 2.50
215 MGr,A:Emerald Empress . . 2.50
216 MGr,I:Tyroc 2.50
217 MGr,I:Laurel Kent 2.50
218 J:Tyroc,A:Fatal Five 2.50
219 MGr,A:Fatal Five 2.50
220 MGi,BWi 2.50
221 MGr,BWi,I:Grimbor 2.50
222 MGr,BWi,MN,BL,A:Tyroc . . 2.50
223 MGr,BWi 2.50
224 MGr,BWi,V:Pulsar Stargrave . 2.50
225 MGr(c),BWi,JSh,MN 2.50
226 MGr(c),MN,JSh,JA,
  I:Dawnstar 2.75
227 MGr(c),JSon,JA,V:Stargrave . 2.00
228 MGr(c),JSh,JA,
  D:Chemical King 2.50
229 MGr(c),JSh,JA,V:Deregon . . 2.00
230 MGr(c),JSh,V:Sden 2.00
Becomes:

SUPERBOY & THE LEGION OF SUPER-HEROES
1976–79
231 MGr(c),JSh,MN,JA,doub.size
  begins,V:Fatal Five 2.00
232 MGr(c),JSh,RE,JA,V:
  Dr.Regulus 2.00
233 MGr(c),JSh,BWi,MN,BL,
  I:Infinite Man 2.00
234 MGr(c),RE,JA,V:Composite
  Creature 2.00

235 MGr,GT 2.00
236 MGr(c),BMc,JSh,MN,JRu,
  V:Khunds 2.00
237 MGr(c),WS,JA 2.50
238 JSn(c),reprint 2.00
239 MGR(c),JSn,JRu,Ultra Boy
  accused 2.50
240 MGr(c),HC,BWi,JSh,BMc,
  O:Dawnstar;V:Grimbor 2.00
241 JSh,BMc,A:Ontir 2.00
242 JSh,BMc,E:Double Size . . . 2.00
243 MGr(c),JA,JSon 2.00
244 JSon,V:Dark Circle 2.00
245 MA,JSon,V:Mordu 2.00
246 MGr(c),JSon,DG,MA,
  V:Fatal Five 2.00
247 JSon,JA,anniv.issue. 2.00
248 JSon 2.00
249 JSon,JA 2.00
250 JSn,V:Omega 2.50
251 JSn,Brainiac 5 goes insane . . 2.50
252 JSon,V:Starburst bandits . . 2.00
253 JSon,I:Blok,League of
  Super Assassins 2.00
254 JSon,V:League of Super
  Assassins 2.00
255 JSon,A:Jor-El 2.00
256 JSon 2.00
257 SD,JSon,DA,V:Psycho
  Warrior 2.00
258 JSon,V:Psycho Warrior 2.00
Becomes:

Legion of Super Heroes
[2nd Series]

[NEW ADVENTURES OF] SUPERBOY
Jan., 1980
1 KS 1.50
2 KS 1.25
3 KS 1.25
4 KS 1.25
5 KS 1.25
6 KS 1.25
7 KS,JSa 1.25
8 thru 33 KS . . . . @1.25
34 KS,I:Yellow Peri 1.25

DC COMICS

DC COMICS

35 thru 44 KS	@1.25
45 KS,I:Sunburst	1.25
46 KS,A:Sunburst	1.25
47 KS,A:Sunburst	1.25
48 KS	1.25
49 KS,A:Zatara	1.25
50 KS,KG,A:Legion	1.50
51 KS,FM(c)In Between Years	1.25
52 KS	1.25
53 KS	1.25
54 KS	1.25

SUPERBOY
1990–91

1 TV Tie-in,JM,photo(c)	1.25
2 JM,T.J.White Abducted	1.25
3 JM,'Fountain of Youth'	1.25
4 JM,'Big Man on Campus'	1.25
5 JM,Legion Homage	1.25
6 JM,Luthor	1.25
7 JM,Super Boy Arrested	1.25
8 JM,AAd(i),Bizarro	1.25
9 JM/CS,PhantomZone#1	1.25
10 JM/CS,PhantomZone#2	1.25
11 CS	1.25
12 CS,X-Mas in Smallville	1.25

Becomes:
ADVENTURES OF SUPERBOY
1991

13 A:Mr.Mxyzptlk	1.75
14 CS,A:Brimstone	1.25
15 CS,Legion Homage	1.25
16 CS,Into the Future	1.25
17 CS,A:Luthor	1.25
18 JM,'At the Movies'	1.25
19 JM,Blood Transfusion	1.25
20 JM,O:Nicknack,(G.Gottfried script)	1.25
21 V:Frost Monster	1.25
22	1.25
Spec.#1 CS,A:Ma Kent	1.75

SUPERBOY
[2nd Series]
1994–97

1 B:KK(s),TG,DHz,V:Sidearm	3.00
2 TG,DHz,I:Knockout	2.50
3 TG,DHz,I:Scavenger	2.00
4 TG,DHz,MeP,I:Lock n' Load	2.00
5 TG,DHz,I:Silver Sword	2.00
6 TG,DHz,Worlds Collide,pt.3 C:Rocket	1.75
7 Worlds Collide, pt.8,V:Rift	1.75
8 Zero Hour,A:Superboy	1.50
9 Silican Dragon	1.50
10 Monster	1.50
11 Techno	1.50
12 Copperhead	1.50
13 Watery Grave,pt.1	1.50
14 Watery Grave,pt.2	1.50
15 Watery Grave,pt.3	1.50
16 TG,DHz,KK,V:Loose Cannon [New Miraweb format begins]	1.95
17 TG,DHz,KK Looking for Roxy Leech	1.95
18 V:Valor	1.95
19	1.95
20 R:Scavenger	1.95
21 KK,TG,DHz,Future Tense,Pt.1	1.95
22 KK,TG,DHz,Underworld Unleashed x-over	1.95
23 KK,TG,DHz,V:Technician	1.95
24 KK,TG,DHz,V:Silversword	1.95

Superboy (2nd Series) #32
© DC Comics, Inc.

25	1.95
26 KK,DHz,Losin'it,pt.2	1.95
27 KK,DHz,Losin'it,pt.3	1.95
28 KK,DHz,Losin'it,pt.4 (of 6)	1.95
29	1.95
30	1.95
31	1.95
32 RMz(s),RBe,DHz,V:King Shark	1.95
33 RMz(s),RBe,DHz, survivors flee to Hawaii, Final Night tie-in	1.95
34 RMz(s),RBe,DHz, V:Dubbilex	1.95
35 RMz(s),RBe,DHz, Superboy abducted	1.95
36 RMz(s),RBe,DHz,V:King SHark	1.95
37 RMz(s),SB,V:Sledge	1.95
38 RMz(s),RBe,DHz,"Meltdown," pt.1 (of 3)	1.95
39 RMz(s),RBe,DHz,"Meltdown," pt.2	1.95
40 RMz(s),RBe,DHz,"Meltdown," pt.2 x-over	1.95
41 RMz(s),RBe,DHz,"Meltdown," pt.3 concl.	1.95
42 SB	1.95
43 SB,Lanie & Ken	1.95
Ann.#1 Elseworlds Story	3.25
Ann.#2 KK,BKs, Year One	3.95
Ann.#3 Legends o/t Dead Earth	2.95
Ann.#4 Pulp Heroes (High-Adventure)	3.95

SUPERBOY & THE RAVERS

1 KK&SMt(s),PaP,DDv,	2.00
2 KK&SMt(s),PaP,DDv,InterC.E.P.T. pursues Superboy and Kaliber	2.00
3 KK&SMT(s),PaP,DDv,teleported to Rann,V:Half-Life	2.00
4 KK&SMt(s),PaP,DDv,A:Adam Strange	2.00
5 KK&SMt(s),PaP,DDv,O:Hero	2.00
6 KK&SMt(s),PaP,DDv,	2.00
7 KK&SMt(s),PaP,DDv, "Road Trip," pt.1,A:Impulse	2.00
8 KK&SMt(s),PaP,DDv, "Road Trip," pt.2,A:Guy Gardner	2.00

9 KK&SMt(s),PaP,DDv, "Road Trip," pt.3,A:Aura	2.00
10 KK&SMt(s),DDv, "Meltdown," pt. 4	2.00
11 KK&SMt(s),PaP,DDv, Superboy presumed dead	2.00
12 KK(s),AaL,	2.00
13 KK(s),SMt,F:Hero,Sparx	2.00

SUPERBOY PLUS
Nov. 1996

1 RMz(s),ASm,F:Captain Marvel Jr.	2.95

SUPER DC GIANT
1970–71, 1976

S-13 Binky	12.00
S-14 Top Guns of the West	5.00
S-15 Western Comics	5.00
S-16 Best of the Brave & the Bold	5.00
S-17 Love 1970	5.00
S-18 Three Mouseketeers	5.00
S-19 Jerry Lewis	5.00
S-20 House of Mystery	7.50
S-21 Love 1971	5.00
S-22 Top Guns of the West	5.00
S-23 The Unexpected	7.50
S-24 Supergirl	6.00
S-25 Challengers of the Unknown	5.00
S-26 Aquaman	5.00
S-27 Strange Flying Saucer Advengures (1976)	5.00

SUPER FRIENDS
Nov., 1976

1 ECh(c),JO,RE,'Fury of the Superfoes',A:Penguin	2.50
2 RE,A:Penguin	1.50
3 RF(c),RF,A:JLA	1.50
4 RF,V:Riddler,I:Skyrocket	1.50
5 RF(c),RF,V:Greenback	1.50
6 RF(c),RF,A:Atom	1.50
7 RF(c),RF,I:Zan & Jana, A:Seraph	1.50
8 RF(c),RF,A:JLA	1.50
9 RF(c),RF,A:JLA,I:Iron Maiden	1.50
10 RF(c),RF'TheMonkeyMenace'	1.50
11 RF(c),RF	1.50
12 RF(c),RF,A:TNT	1.50
13 RF(c),RF	1.50
14 RF(c),RF	1.50
15 RF(c),RF, A:The Elementals	1.50
16 RF(c),RF,V:The Cvags	1.50
17 RF(c),RF,A:Queen Hippolyte	1.50
18 KS(c),V:Tuantra,Time Trapper	1.50
19 RF(c),RF,V:Menagerie Man	1.50
20 KS(c),KS,V:Frownin' Fritz	1.50
21 RF(c),RF,V:Evil Superfriends Doubles	1.50
22 RF(c),RF,V:Matador Mob	1.50
23 FR(c),RF,V:Mirror Master	1.50
24 RF(c),RF,V:Exorians	1.50
25 RF(c),RF,V:Overlord, A:Green Lantern, Mera	1.50
26 RF(c),RF,A:Johnny Jones	1.50
27 RF(c),RF,'The Spaceman Who Stole the Stars	1.50
28 RF(c),RF,A:Felix Faust	1.50
29 RF(c),RF,B.U.KS,'Scholar From the Stars	1.50
30 RF(c),RF,V:Grodd & Giganta	1.50
31 RF(c),RF,A:Black Orchid	1.50
32 KS(c),KS,A:Scarecrow	1.50
33 RF(c),RF,V:Menagerie Man	1.50

DC COMICS

34 RF(c)RF,'The Creature That
Slept a Million Years' 1.50
35 RT,'Circus o/t Super Stars .. 1.50
36 RF(c),RF,A:Plastic Man
& Woozy 1.50
37 RF(c),RF,A:Supergirl;
B.U. A:Jack O'Lantern 1.50
38 RF(c),RF,V:Grax;
B.U. A:Serpah 1.50
39 RF(c),RF,A:Overlord;
B.U. A:Wonder Twins 1.50
40 RF(c),RF,V:The Monacle;
B.U. Jack O'Lantern 1.50
41 RF(c),RF,V:Toyman;
B.U. A:Seraph 1.50
42 RT,A:Flora,V:Flame; B.U.Wonder
Twins' Christmas Special 1.50
43 KS(c),RT,V:Futuro; B.U.JSon
A:Plastic Man 1.50
44 KS(c),RT,'Peril o/t Forgotten
Identities'; B.U.Jack O'Lantern . 1.50
45 KS(c),RT,A:Bushmaster,
Godiva, Rising Sun, Olympian,
Little Mermaid, Wild Huntsman;
B.U. Plastic Man,V: Sinestro .. 1.50
46 RT,V:The Conqueror;
B.U. BO,Seraph 1.50
47 KS(c),RT,A:Green Fury
Aug. 1981 .... 1.50

SUPERGIRL
[1st Regular Series]
Nov., 1972—Sept. 1974
1 'Trail of the Madman';
Superfashions From Fans;
B:B.U. DG,Zatanna 2.50
2 BO(c)A:Prof.Allan,Bottle
City of Kandor 1.50
3 BO(c),'The Garden of Death' .. 1.50
4 V:Super Scavanger 1.50
5 BO(c),A:Superman,V:Chakat; B.U.
MA:Rep.Hawkman #4 ...... 1.50
6 BO(c),'Love & War' 1.50
7 BO(c),A:Zatanna 1.50
8 BO(c),A:Superman,Green Lantern
Hawkman 1.50
9 BO(c),V:Sharkman 1.50
10 A:Prey,V:Master Killer 1.50

[DARING NEW ADVENTURES OF] SUPERGIRL
[2nd Regular Series]
Nov. 1982
1 CI,BO,I:Psi; B:B.U.Lois Lane .. 1.50
2 CI,BO,C:Decay 1.50
3 CI,BO,V:Decay,'Decay Day' .. 1.50
4 CI,BO,V:The Gang 1.50
5 CI,BO,V:The Gang 1.50
6 CI,BO,V:The Gang 1.50
7 CI,BO,V:The Gang 1.50
8 CI,BO,A:Doom Patrol 1.50
9 CI,BO,V:Reactron
A:Doom Patrol 1.50
10 CI,BO,'Radiation Fever' 1.50
11 CI,BO,V:Chairman 1.50
12 CI,BO,V:Chairmann 1.50
13 CI,BO,N:Supergirl,A:Superman
V:Blackstarr 1.50
Becomes:
SUPERGIRL
Dec., 1983–Sept. 1984
14 GK(c),CI,BO,V:Blackstarr

A:Rabbi Nathan Zuber 1.50
15 CI,BO,V:Blackstarr,
A:Blackstarr's Mom 1.50
16 KG/BO(c),CI,BO,
A:Ambush Bug 1.50
17 CI/DG(c),CI,BO,V:Matrix
Prime 1.50
18 DG(c),CI,BO, V:Kraken 1.50
19 EB/BO(c),CI,BO,'Who Stole
Supergirl's Life' 1.50
20 CI,BO,C:JLA,Teen Titans:
Teh Parasite 1.50
21 EB/BO(c),EB,Kryptonite Man .. 1.50
22 EB(c),CI,BO,'I Have Seen the
Future & it is Me' 1.50
23 EB(c),CI,BO,'The Future
Begins Today 1.50
Spec.#1 JL/DG(c),GM,Movie Adapt.1.50
Spec.#1 AT,Honda give-away ... 1.50

*Supergirl Limited Series #4
© DC Comics, Inc.*

[Limited Series] 1994
1 KGa(c),B:RSt(s),JBr,O:Supergirl 5.00
2 KGa(c),JBr 4.00
3 KGa(c),JBr,D:Clones 3.00
4 KGa(c),RSt(s),JBr,final Issue .. 3.00

SUPERGIRL
Sept. 1996
1 PDd(s),GFr,CaS, ... 5.00
2 PDd(s),GFr,CaS,V:Chakat 4.00
3 PDd(s),GFr,CaS,V:Grodd, Final
Night tie-in 3.00
4 PDd(s),GFr,CaS,transformed into
savage 2.50
5 PDd(s),GFr,CaS,Supergirl visits
the Kents,V:Chemo 2.50
6 PDd(s),GFr,CaS, ... 2.25
7 PDd(s),GFr,CaS,Supergirl learns
about Linda Danvers 2.25
8 PDd(s),GFr,CaS,Buzz gets date
with Supergirl 2.00
9 PDd(s),GFr,CaS,V:Tempus ... 2.00
10 PDd(s),Linda tries to relax .. 1.95
11 PDd(s),CaS,V:Silver Banshee . 1.95
12 PDd(s),Mattie possessed by
Silver Banshee 1.95
13 CaS, 3 girls dreams invaded by

incubus 1.95
Ann.#1 Legends o/t Dead Earth .. 2.95
Ann.#2 Pulp Heroes (Romance) .. 3.95

SUPERGIRL/LEX LUTHOR SPECIAL
1993
1 JBr,F:Supergirl,Lex Luthor 4.00

SUPER HEROES BATTLE SUPER GORILLA
Winter, 1976
1 Superman Flash rep......... 1.00

Superman #15 © DC Comics, Inc.

SUPERMAN
1939–86
1 JoS,O:Superman,reprints Action
Comics #1-#4 .... 110,000.00
2 JoS,I:George Taylor 9,500.00
3 JoS,V:Superintendent
Lyman 6,500.00
4 JoS,V:Lex Luthor 5,000.00
5 JoS,V:Lex Luthor 3,500.00
6 JoS,V:'Brute' Bashby 2,500.00
7 JoS,I:Perry White 2,400.00
8 JoS,V:Jackal 2,100.00
9 JoS,V:Joe Gatson 2,100.00
10 JoS,V:Lex Luthor 2,000.00
11 JoS,V:Rolf Zimba 1,500.00
12 JoS,V:Lex Luthor 1,500.00
13 JoS,I:Jimmy Olsen,V:Lex
Luthor,'The Archer' 1,500.00
14 JoS,I:Lightning Master ... 1,500.00
15 JoS,V:The Evolution King . 1,400.00
16 JoS,V:Mr. Sinus 1,300.00
17 JoS,V:Lex Luthor,Lois Lane first
suspects Clark is Superman 1,300.00
18 JoS,V:Lex Luthor 1,300.00
19 JoS,V:Funnyface,
1st Imaginary story 1,200.00
20 JoS,V:Puzzler,Leopard ... 1,200.00
21 JoS,V:Sir Gauntlet 1,000.00
22 JoS,V:Prankster 1,000.00
23 JoS,Propaganda story ... 1,000.00
24 V:Cobra King 1,100.00
25 Propaganda story 1,000.00

Superman #28 © DC Comics, Inc.

26 I:J.Wilbur Wolfingham,
  A:Mercury 1,000.00
27 V:Toyman 1,000.00
28 V:J.Wilbur Wolfingham,
  A:Hercules 1,000.00
29 V:Prankster 1,000.00
30 I&O:Mr. Mxyztplk 1,400.00
31 V:Lex Luthor 900.00
32 V:Toyman 900.00
33 V:Mr. Mxyztplk 900.00
34 V:Lex Luthor 900.00
35 V:J.Wilbur Wolfingham ... 900.00
36 V:Mr. Mxyztplk 900.00
37 V:Prankster,A:Sinbad 900.00
38 V:Lex Luthor 900.00
39 V:J.Wilbur Wolfingham ... 900.00
40 V:Mr. Mxyztplk,A:Susie
  Thompkins 900.00
41 V:Prankster 600.00
42 V:J.Wilbur Wolfingham ... 600.00
43 V:Lex Luthor 600.00
44 V:Toyman,A:Shakespeare .. 600.00
45 A:Hocus & Pocus,Lois Lane
  as Superwoman 600.00
46 V:Mr. Mxyztplk,Lex Luthor,
  Superboy flashback 600.00
47 V:Toyman 600.00
48 V:Lex Luthor 600.00
49 V:Toyman 600.00
50 V:Prankster 600.00
51 V:Mr. Mxyztplk 500.00
52 V:Prankster 500.00
53 WB,O:Superman 2,000.00
54 V:Wrecker 500.00
55 V:Prankster 500.00
56 V:Prankster 500.00
57 V:Lex Luthor 500.00
58 V:Tiny Trix 500.00
59 V:Mr.Mxyztplk 500.00
60 V:Toyman 500.00
61 I:Kryptonite,V:Prankster .. 1,000.00
62 V:Mr.Mxyztplk,A:Orson
  Welles 500.00
63 V:Toyman 500.00
64 V:Prankster 500.00
65 V:Mala,Kizo and U-Ban ... 500.00
66 V:Prankster 500.00
67 A:Perry Como,I:Brane
  Taylor 500.00

68 V:Lex Luthor 500.00
69 V:Prankster,A:Inspector
  Erskine Hawkins 500.00
70 V:Prankster 500.00
71 V:Lex Luthor 450.00
72 V:Prankster 450.00
72a giveaway 750.00
73 Flashback story 450.00
74 V:Lex Luthor 450.00
75 V:Prankster 450.00
76 A:Batman (Superman &
  Batman revel each other's
  identities) 1,200.00
77 A:Pocahontas 425.00
78 V:Kryptonian snagriff,
  A:Lana Lang 425.00
79 V:Lex Luthor,A:Inspector
  Erskine Hawkins 425.00
80 A:Halk Kar 425.00
81 V:Lex Luthor 425.00
82 V:Mr. Mxyzptlk 400.00
83 V:'The Brain' 400.00
84 Time-travel story 400.00
85 V:Lex Luthor 400.00
86 V:Mr.Mxyzptlk 400.00
87 WB,V:The Thing from
  40,000 AD' 400.00
88 WB,V:Lex Luthor,Toyman,
  Prankster team 425.00
89 V:Lex Luthor 400.00
90 V:Lex Luthor 425.00
91 'The Superman Stamp' ... 400.00
92 Goes back to 12th Century
  England 400.00
93 V:'The Thinker' 400.00
94 'Clark Kent's Hillbilly Bride' . 400.00
95 A:Susie Thompkins 400.00
96 V:Mr. Mxyzptlk 350.00
97 'Superboy's Last Day In
  Smallville' 350.00
98 'Clark Kent, Outlaw!' 350.00
99 V:Midnite gang 350.00
100 F:Superman-Substitute
  Schoolteacher 1,600.00
101 A:Lex Luthor 275.00
102 I:Superman Stock
  Company 275.00
103 A:Mr.Mxyzptlk 275.00
104 F:Clark Kent,Jailbird 275.00
105 A:Mr.Mxyzptlk 275.00
106 A:Lex Luthor 300.00
107 F:Superman In 30th century
  (pre-Legion) 250.00
108 I:Perry White Jr. 250.00
109 I:Abner Hokum 250.00
110 A:Lex Luthor 250.00
111 Becomes Mysto the Great . 225.00
112 A:Lex Luthor 225.00
113 A:Jor-El 225.00
114 V:The Great Mento 225.00
115 V:The Organizer 225.00
116 Return to Smallville 225.00
117 A:Lex Luthor 225.00
118 F:Jimmy Olsen 225.00
119 A:Zoll Orr 225.00
120 V:Gadget Grim 225.00
121 I:XL-49 (Futureman) 200.00
122 In the White House 200.00
123 CS,pre-Supergirl tryout
  A:Jor-El & Lara 225.00
124 F:Lois Lane 200.00
125 F:Superman College Story 200.00
126 F:Lois Lane 200.00
127 WB,I&O:Titano 225.00
128 V:Vard & Boka 200.00

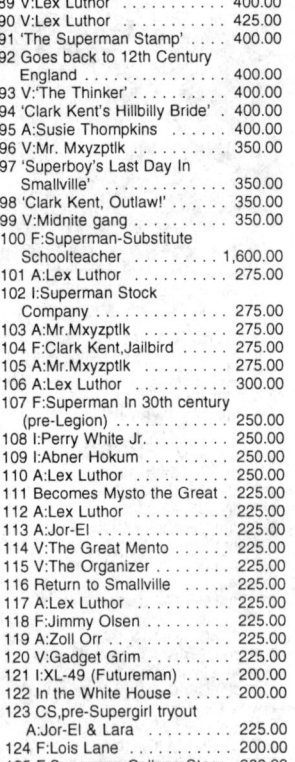

Superman #227 © DC Comics, Inc.

129 WB,I&O:Lori Lemaris 225.00
130 A:Krypto,the Superdog .. 200.00
131 A:Mr. Mxyzptlk 150.00
132 A:Batman & Robin 150.00
133 F:Superman Joins Army .. 150.00
134 A:Supergirl & Krypto 150.00
135 A:Lori Lemaris,Mr.Mxyzptlk 150.00
136 O:Discovery Kryptonite ... 150.00
137 CS,I:Super-Menace 150.00
138 A:Titano,Lori Lemaris 150.00
139 CS,O:Red Kryptonite 150.00
140 WB,I:Bizarro Jr,Bizarro
  Supergirl,Blue Kryptonite. .. 165.00
141 I:Lyla Lerrol,A:Jor-EL
  & Lara 125.00
142 WB,CS,A:Al Capone 125.00
143 WB,F:Bizarro meets
  Frankenstein 125.00
144 O:Superboy's 1st Public
  Appearance 125.00
145 F:April Fool's Issue 125.00
146 F:Superman's life story ... 175.00
147 CS,I:Adult Legion 150.00
148 CS,V:Mxyzptlk 150.00
149 CS:A:Luthor,C:JLA 150.00
150 CS,KS,V:Mxyzptlk 75.00
151 CS 75.00
152 A:Legion 75.00
153 CS 75.00
154 CS,V:Mzyzptlk 75.00
155 WB,CS,V:Cosmic Man ... 75.00
156 CS,A:Legion,Batman 75.00
157 CS,I:Gold kryptonite 80.00
158 CS,I:Nightwing&Flamebird .. 75.00
159 CS,Imaginary Tale
  F:Lois Lane 75.00
160 CS,F:Perry White 75.00
161 D:Ma & Pa Kent 80.00
162 A:Legion 80.00
163 CS 55.00
164 CS,Luthor,I:Lexor 55.00
165 CS,A:Saturn Woman 55.00
166 CS 55.00
167 CS,I:Ardora,Brainiac 85.00
168 CS 55.00
169 Great DC Contest 55.00
170 CS,A:J.F.Kennedy,Luthor .. 55.00
171 CS,Mxyzptlk 55.00

DC COMICS

172 CS,Luthor,Brainiac 55.00	233 CS,MA,I:Quarrum 25.00	280 CS,BO 3.00
173 CS,A:Batman 55.00	234 NA(c),CS,MA 25.00	281 CS,BO,I:Vartox 3.00
174 Mxyzptlk 55.00	235 CS,MA 25.00	282 CS,KS,N:Luthor 3.00
175 CS,Luthor 55.00	236 CS,MA,DG,A:Green Arrow . 25.00	283 CS,BO,Mxyzptlk 3.00
176 CS,Green Kryptonite 55.00	237 NA(c),CS,MA 25.00	284 CS,BO,100p reprint 8.00
177 Fortress of Solitude 55.00	238 CS,MA,GM 25.00	285 CS,BO 3.00
178 CS, Red Kryptonite 55.00	239 giant 35.00	286 CS,BO 3.00
179 CS,Clark Kent in Marines . . 55.00	240 CS,DG,MK,A:I-Ching 11.00	287 CS,BO,R:Krypto 3.00
180 CS 55.00	241 CS,MA,A:Wonder Woman . . 9.00	288 CS,BO 3.00
181 Superman 2965 . . . . 55.00	242 CS,MA,A:Wonder Woman . . 10.00	289 CS,BO,JL 3.00
182 CS,Toyman 55.00	243 CS,MA 9.00	290 CS,V:Mxyzptlk 3.00
183 giant 55.00	244 CS,MA 9.00	291 CS,BO 3.00
184 Secrets of the Fortress 50.00	245 100 pg reprints 15.00	292 CS,BO,AM,O:Luthor 3.00
185 JM,Superman's Achilles	246 CS,MA,RB,I:S.T.A.R. Labs . . 8.00	293 CS,BO 3.00
Heel 50.00	247 CS,MA,Guardians o/Universe 8.00	294 CS,JL,A:Brain Storm 3.00
186 CS,The Two Ghosts of	248 CS,MA,A:Luthor,I:Galactic	295 CS,BO 3.00
Superman 50.00	Golem 8.00	296 CS,BO,Identity Crisis #1 . . . 3.00
187 giant 50.00	249 CS,MA,DD,NA,I:Terra-Man . 12.00	297 CS,BO,Identity Crisis #2 . . . 3.00
188 V:Zunial,The Murder Man . . 55.00	250 CS,MA,Terraman 8.00	298 CS,BO,Identity Crisis #3 . . . 3.00
189 WB,The Mystery of Krypton's	251 CS,MA,RB 8.00	299 CS,BO,Identity Crisis #4
Second Doom 50.00	252 NA(c),rep.100pgs 15.00	A:Luthor,Brainiac,Bizarro . . . 3.00
190 WB,I:Amalak 50.00	253 CS,MA 6.00	300 CS,BO,2001,anniversary . . . 10.00
191 The Prisoner of Demon . . . 50.00	254 CS,MA,NA 7.50	301 BO,JL,V:Solomon Grundy . . . 3.00
192 CS,Imaginary Story,		302 JL,BO,V:Luthor,A:Atom 3.00
I:Superman Jr. 50.00		303 CS,BO,I:Thunder&Lightning . 3.00
193 giant 50.00		304 CS,BO,V:Parasite 3.00
194 CS,Imaginary,A:Supes Jr. . . 40.00		305 CS,BO,V:Toyman 3.00
195 CS,V:Amalak 40.00		306 CS,BO,V:Bizarro 3.00
196 WB,reprint 40.00		307 NA(c),JL,FS,A:Supergirl 3.00
197 giant 50.00		308 NA(c),JL,FS,A:Supergirl 3.00
198 CS,F:The Real Clark Kent . . 40.00		309 JL,FS,A:Supergirl 2.50
199 CS,F:Superman/Flash race,		310 CS,V:Metallo 2.50
A:JLA 200.00		311 CS,FS,A:Flash 2.50
200 WB,A:Brainiac 40.00		312 CS,FS,A:Supergirl 2.50
201 CS,F:Clark Kent Abandons		313 NA(c),CS,DA,A:Supergirl . . . 2.50
Superman 30.00		314 NA(c),CS,DA,A:Gr.Lantern . . 2.50
202 A:Bizarro,(giant size) 35.00		315 CS,DA,V:Blackrock 2.50
203 F:When Superman Killed His		316 CS,DA,V:Metallo 2.50
Friends 30.00		317 NA(c),CS,DA,V:Metallo 2.50
204 NA(c),RA,A:Lori Lemaris . . . 30.00	*Superman #256 © DC Comics, Inc.*	318 CS 3.00
205 NA(c),I:Black Zero 30.00	255 CS,MA,DG 3.50	319 CS,V:Solomon Grundy 3.00
206 NA(c),F:The Day Superman	256 CS,MA 3.50	320 CS,V:Solomon Grundy 3.00
Became An Assistant 30.00	257 CS,MA,DD,DG,A:Tomar-Re . 3.50	321 CS,V:Parasite 3.00
207 CS,F:The Case Of the	258 CS,MA,DC 3.50	322 CS,V:Solomon Grundy 3.00
Collared Crimefighter 35.00	259 CS,MA,A:Terra-Man 3.50	323 CS,DA,I:Atomic Skull 3.00
208 NA(c),CS 30.00	260 CS,DC,I:Valdemar 3.50	324 CS,A:Atomic Skull 3.00
209 CS,F:The Clark Kent Monster 30.00	261 CS,MA,V:Star Sapphire 3.50	325 CS 3.00
210 CS,F:Clark Kent's Last Rites 30.00	262 CS,MA 3.50	326 CS,V:Blackrock 3.00
211 CS,RA 30.00	263 CS,MA,DD,FMc 3.50	327 CS,KS,V:Kobra,C:JLA 3.00
212 giant 40.00	264 DC,CS,I:SteveLombard 3.50	328 CS,KS,V:Kobra 3.00
213 CS,JA,V:Luthor,C:Brainiac 5 30.00	265 CS,MA 3.50	329 KS,CS 3.00
214 CS,JA,A:F:The Ghosts	266 CS,MA,DD,V:Snowman 3.50	330 CS,F:glasses explained 3.00
That Haunted Superman 25.00	267 CS,MA,BO 3.50	331 CS,I:Master Jailer 3.00
215 NA(c),CS,JA,V:Luthor,	268 CS,BO,DD,MA,A:Batgirl . . . 3.50	332 CS,V:Master Jailer 3.00
Imaginary Story 25.00	269 CS,MA 3.50	333 CS,V:Bizarro 3.00
216 JKu(c),RA,Superman in Nam 25.00	270 CS,MA,V:Valdemar 3.50	334 CS 3.00
217 CS,A:Mr.Mxyzptlk 30.00	271 CS,BO,DG,V:Brainiac 3.50	335 CS,W:Mxyzptlk 3.00
218 CS,JA,A:Mr.Mxyzptlk 25.00	272 100pg.reprints 12.00	336 CS,V:Rose And Thorn 3.00
219 CS,F:Clark Kent-Hero,	273 CS,DG 3.00	337 CS,A:Brainiac,Bizarro 3.00
Superman Public Enemy 25.00	274 CS 3.00	338 CS,F:Kandor enlarged 3.00
220 CS,A:Flash 25.00	275 CS,DG,FMc 3.00	339 CS,I:N.R.G.X 3.00
221 CS,F:The Two Ton Superman 25.00	276 CS,BO,I&O:Captain Thunder . 3.00	340 CS,V:N.R.G.X 3.00
222 giant 40.00	277 CS 3.00	341 CS,F:Major Disaster 3.00
223 CS,A:Supergirl 25.00	278 CS,BO,Terraman,100page . 10.00	342 CS,V:Chemo 3.00
224 CS,Imaginary Story 25.00	279 CS,Batgirl,Batman 3.00	343 CS 3.00
225 CS,F:The Secret of the		344 CS,A:Phantom Stranger 3.00
Super Imposter 25.00		345 CS,'When time ran backward' 3.00
226 CS,F:When Superman Became		346 CS,'Streak of Bad Luck' 3.00
King Kong 25.00		347 JL 3.00
227 Krypton,(giant) 30.00		348 CS 3.00
228 CS,DA 25.00		349 CS,V:Mxyzptlk 3.00
229 WB,CS 25.00		350 CS,'Clark Kent's Vanishing
230 CS,DA,Luthor 25.00		Classmate' 3.00
231 CS,DA,Luthor 25.00		351 CS,JL,A:Mxyzptlk 3.00
232 F:Krypton,(giant) 30.00		352 CS,RB 3.00

All comics prices listed are for *Near Mint* condition.

DC COMICS

353 CS,origin 3.00
354 CS,JSon,I:Superman 2020 . . 3.00
355 CS,JSon,F:Superman 2020 . . 3.00
356 CS,V:Vartox 3.00
357 CS,DCw,F:Superman 2020 . . 3.00
358 CS,DG,DCw 3.00
359 CS 3.00
360 CS,AS,F:World of Krypton . . . 3.00
361 CS,AS 3.00
362 CS,KS,DA 3.00
363 CS,RB,C:Luthor 3.00
364 GP(c),RB,AS 3.00
365 CS,KS 3.00
366 CS,KS 3.00
367 CS,GK,F:World of Krypton . . 3.00
368 CS,AS 3.00
369 RB,FMc,V:Parasite 3.00
370 CS,KS,FMc,A:Chemo 3.00
371 CS 3.00
372 CS,GK,F:Superman 2021 . . . 3.00
373 CS,V:Vartox 3.00
374 GK(c),CS,DA,KS,V:Vartox . . . 3.00
375 CS,DA,GK,V:Vartox 3.00
376 CS,DA,CI,BO,SupergirlPrev. . 2.75
377 GK(c),CS,V:Terra-Man 2.75
378 CS 2.75
379 CS,V:Bizarro 2.75
380 CS 2.75
381 GK(c),CS 2.75
382 GK(c),CS 2.75
383 CS 2.75
384 GK(c),CS 2.75
385 GK(c),CS,V:Luthor 2.75
386 GK(c),CS,V:Luthor 2.75
387 GK(c),CS 2.75
388 GK(c),CS 2.75
389 GK(c),CS 2.75
390 GK(c),CS,V:Vartox 2.75
391 GK(c),CS,V:Vartox 2.75
392 GK(c),CS,V:Vartox 2.75
393 IN,DG,V:Master Jailer 2.75
394 CS,V:Valdemar 2.75
395 CS,V:Valdemar 2.75
396 CS 2.75
397 EB,V:Kryptonite Man 2.75
398 CS,AS,DJ 2.75
399 CS,BO,EB 2.75
400 HC(c),FM,AW,JO,JSo,MR,
    TA,WP,MK,KJ,giant 6.00
401 CS,BO,V:Luthor 2.75
402 CS,BO,WB 2.75
403 CS,BO,AS 2.75
404 CI,BO,V:Luthor 2.75
405 KS,KK,AS,F:Super-Batman . . 2.75
406 IN,AS,KK 2.75
407 IN,V:Mxyzptlk 2.75
408 CS,AW,JRu,F:Nuclear
    Holocaust 2.75
409 CS,AW,KS 2.75
410 CS,AW,V:Luthor 2.75
411 CS,MA,F:End Earth-Prime . . 2.75
412 CS,AW,V:Luthor 2.75
413 CS,AW,V:Luthor 2.75
414 CS,AW,Crisis tie-in 3.00
415 CS,AW,Crisis,W:Super Girl . . 3.00
416 CS,AW,Luthor 2.75
417 CS,V:Martians 2.75
418 CS,V:Metallo 2.75
419 CS,V:Iago 2.75
420 CS,F:Nightmares 2.75
421 CS,V:Mxyzptlk 2.75
422 BB(c),CS,TY,LMa,V:Werewolf 2.75
423 AMo(s),CS,GP,F:Last
    Superman 2.75
Ann.#1 I:Supergirl Rep 900.00

Superman Annual #11
© DC Comics, Inc.

Ann.#2 I&O:Titano 400.00
Ann.#3 I:Legion 300.00
Ann.#4 O:Legion 250.00
Ann.#5 A:Krypton 200.00
Ann.#6 A:Legion 200.00
Ann.#7 O:Superman,Silver Anniv.150.00
Ann.#8 F:Secret origins 125.00
Ann.#9 GK(c),ATh,TA,CS,
    A:Batman 6.00
Ann.#10 CS,MA,F:Sword of
    Superman 5.00
Ann.#11 AMo(s),DGb,A:Batman,
    Robin,Wonder Woman 6.00
Ann.#12 BB(c),AS,A:Lex Luthor,
    Last War Suit 3.00
Game Give-away 10.00
Giveaway CS,AT 2.00
Pizza Hut 1977 . . . . 6.00
Radio Shack 1980 JSw,DG 5.00
Radio Shack 1981 CS 5.00
Radio Shack 1982 CS 5.00
Spec.#1 GK 3.50
Spec.#2 GK,V:Brainiac 3.50
Spec.#3 IN,V:Amazo 3.50
Superman III Movie,CS 1.50
Superman IV Movie,DH,DG,FMc . 1.50

Becomes:

ADVENTURES OF
SUPERMAN
1987

424 JOy,I:Man O'War 2.50
425 JOy,Man O'War 2.25
426 JOy,Legends,V:Apokolips . . . 2.25
427 JOy,V:Qurac 2.25
428 JOy,V:Qurac,I:JerryWhite . . . 2.25
429 JOy,V:Concussion 2.25
430 JOy,V:Fearsome Five 2.25
431 JOy,A:Combattor 2.00
432 JOy,I:Jose Delgado 2.00
433 JOy,V:Lex Luthor 2.00
434 JOy,I:Gang Buster 2.50
435 JOy,A:Charger 2.00
436 JOy,Millenium X-over 2.00
437 JOy,Millenium X-over 2.00
438 JOy,N:Brainiac 2.50
439 JOy,R:Superman Robot 2.00

The Adventures of Superman #494
© DC Comics, Inc.

440 JOy,A:Batman,Wond.Woman 2.00
441 JOy,V:Mr.Mxyzptlk 2.00
442 JOy,V:Dreadnaught,A:JLI . . . 2.00
443 JOy,DHz,I:Husque 2.00
444 JOy,Supergirl SagaPt.2 . . . . . 2.00
445 JOy,V:Brainiac 2.00
446 JOy,A:Gangbuster,
    A:Luthor's Old Costume 2.00
447 JOy,A:Gangbuster 2.00
448 JOy,I:Dubbilex,A:Gangbuster . 2.00
449 JOy,Invasion X-over 2.00
450 JOy,Invasion X-over 2.00
451 JOy,'Superman in Space' 2.00
452 DJu,V:Wordbringer 2.00
453 JOy,DJu,A:Gangbuster 2.00
454 JOy,DJu,I:New Mongul 2.50
455 DJu,ATb,A:Eradicator 3.50
456 DJu,ATb,V:Turmoil 2.00
457 DJu,V:Intergang 2.00
458 DJu,KJ,R:Elastic Lad
    (Jimmy Olsen) 2.00
459 DJu,V:Eradicator 3.00
460 DJu,NKu,V:Eradicator 3.00
461 DJu,GP,V:Eradicator 3.00
462 DJu,ATb,Homeless
    Christmas Story 2.00
463 DJu,ATb,Superman Races
    Flash 3.00
464 DJu,ATb,Day of Krypton
    Man #2,A:Lobo 3.50
465 DJu,ATb,Day of Krypton
    Man #5,V:Draaga 3.00
466 DJu,DG,V:Team Excalibur
    Astronauts,I:Hank Henshaw
    (becomes Cyborg Superman) . 4.50
467 DJu,ATb,A:Batman 2.50
468 DJu,ATb,Man Of Steel's
    Journal,V:Hank Henshaw 3.00
469 DJu,ATb,V:Dreadnaught 2.00
470 DJu,ATb,Soul Search #3,
    D:Jerry White 2.00
471 CS,Sinbad Contract #2 . . . . . 2.00
472 DJu,ATb,Krisis of Krimson
    Kryptonite #2 . . . . 3.00
473 DJu,ATb,A:Green Lantern,
    Guy Gardner 2.00
474 DJu,ATb,Drunk Driving issue . 2.00

DC COMICS

475 DJu,ATb,V:Kilgrave,Sleez . . 2 00
476 DJu,BBr,Time & Time Again,pt.1,
　A:Booster Gold,Legion 2.00
477 DJu,BBr,T & T Again,pt.4,
　A:Legion 2.00
478 DJu,BBr,T & T Again,pt.7,
　A:Legion,Linear Man 2.00
479 EH,Red Glass Trilogy#2 . . . 2.00
480 JOy,DJu,BMc,TG,BBr,CS,
　Revenge of the Krypton
　Man,pt.3 . . . . 3.00
481 1st TG Supes,DHz,V:Parasite 2.00
482 TG,DHz,V:Parasite 2.00
483 TG,DHz,V:Blindspot 2.00
484 TG,Blackout #1,V:Mr.Z 2.00
485 TG,DHz,Blackout #5,A:Mr.Z . 2.00
486 TG,V:Purge 2.00
487 TG,DHz,X-mas,A:Agent
　Liberty 2.00
488 TG,Panic in the Sky,pt.3,
　V:Brainiac 3.00
489 TG,Panic in the Sky,Epiloge . 2.50
490 TG,A:Agent Liberty,Husque . 1.75
491 TG,DHz,V:Cerberus,Metallo . 1.75
492 WS(c),V:Sons of Liberty,
　A:Agent Liberty 1.75
493 TG,Blaze/Satanus War,pt.1 . 1.75
494 TG,DHz,I:Kismet 1.75
495 TG,DHz,A:Forever People,
　Darkseid 1.75
496 V:Mr.Mxyzptlk,C:Doomsday . . 2.00
496a 2nd printing 1.50
497 TG,Doomsday Pt.3,A:Maxima,
　Bloodwynd 5.00
497a 2nd printing 1.75
498 TG,Funeral for a Friend#1 . . . 3.00
498a 2nd Printing 1.25
499 TG,DHz,Funeral for a
　Friend#5 . . . . 3.50
500 JOy(c),B:KK(s),TG,DJu,JBg,JG,
　BBr,Bagged,Superman in limbo,
　I:Four Supermen,Direct Sales . 3.50
500a Newsstand Ed. 3.00
500b Platinum Ed. 15.00
501 TG,Reign of Supermen#2,Direct
　Sales,Die-Cut(c),Mini-poster
　F:Superboy 2.50
501a Newstand Ed. 2.00
502 TG,A:Supergirl,V:Stinger 2.00
503 TG,Cyborg Superman Vs.
　Superboy 2.50
504 TG,DHz,A:All Supermen,
　V:Mongul 2.50
505 TG,DHz,Superman returns to
　Metropolis,Holografx(c) 2.50
505a Newstand Ed. 2.00
506 TG,DHz,A:Guardian 1.75
507 Spilled Blood#1,V:Bloodsport 1.75
508 BKi,A:Challengers of the
　Unknown 1.75
509 BKi,A:Auron 1.75
510 BKi,Bizarro's World#2,
　V:Bizarro 1.75
511 BKi,A:Guardian 1.75
512 BKi,V:Parasite 1.75
513 BKi,Battle for Metropolis #4 . 1.75
514 BKi,Fall of Metropolis #4 . . . 1.75
515 BKi,Massacre in Metropolis . 1.75
516 BKi,Zero Hour,I:Alpha
　Centurion 1.50
517 BKi,deathtrap 1.50
518 BKi 1.50
519 KK,BKi,Secret of Superman's
　Tomb 1.50
520 SI,KK,JMz,100 crimes at

midnight 1.50
521 SI,KK,R:Thorn 1.50
522 SI,KKIdentity known 1.50
523 SI,KK,Death of C.Kent,pt.2 . . 1.50
524 SI,KK,Death of C.Kent,pt.6
　[New Miraweb format begins] . 1.95
525 SI,KK 1.95
526 Bloodsport vs. Bloodsport . . . 1.95
527 . . . . 1.95
528 Trial of Superman,prelude . . . 1.95
529 Trial of Superman 1.95
530 KK,SI,JMz,Trial of Superman 1.95
531 KK,SI,JMz,Trial of Superman,
　concl. 1.95
532 KK,SI,JMz, return of Lori
　Lemaris 1.95
533 KK,SI,JMz 1.95
534 KK,SI,JMz,V:Lord Satannus . 1.95
535 KK,SI,JMz,Lois & LoriLemaris 1.95
536 . . . . 1.95
537 . . . . 1.95
538 . . . . 1.95

Adventures of Superman #502
© DC Comics, Inc.

539 F:Guardian and the Newsboy
　Legion 1.95
540 KK(s),TyD,KIS,A:Ferro, Final
　Night tie-in 1.95
541 KK(s),SI,JMz,on Honeymoon,
　A:Superboy,Tana Moon,Kekona 1.95
542 KK&JOy(s),PR,JMz,V:Misa . . 1.95
543 . . . . 1.95
544 KK(s),SI,JMz,"Who Killed Clark
　Kent in braod daylight? 1.95
545 KK(s),SEa,JMz,Return of the
　Atomic Skull,new blue costume 1.95
546 KK(s),SI,JMz,V:Metallo, uses
　new powers 1.95
547 KK(s),SI,JMz,Superman goes
　to Kandor,A:The Atom 1.95
548 KK(s),SI,JMz,V:Lex Luthor . . 1.95
549 KK(s),SI,JMz,F:Jimmy Olsen . 1.95
550 KK(s),SI,TGu,JMz,DRo, 48pg 3.50
Ann.#1 JSn(c),DJu,I:Word Bringer 3.00
Ann.#2 CS/JBy,KGa/DG,BMc,
　A:L.E.G.I.O.N.'90 (Lobo) 4.00
Ann.#3 BHi,JRu,DG,
　Armageddon 2001. . . . . 3.00
Ann.#4 BMc,A:Lobo,Guy Gardner,

Eclipso tie-in 3.00
Ann.#5 TG,I:Sparx 2.75
Ann.#6 MMi(c),Elseworlds Story . . 3.00
Ann.#7 Year One Story 4.00
Ann.#8 Legends o/t Dead Earth . . 2.95
Ann.#9 Pulp Heroes (Western) . . 3.95
Spec.#0 PeerPressure,pt.3 (1994) 2.00
Superman Archives HC rep 39.95

SUPERMAN ADVENTURES
Sept. 1996
1 PDi(s),RBr,TA, from animated
　TV show 1.75
2 SMI,RBr,TA,V:Metallo 1.75
3 SMI(s),RBr,TA,V:Brainiac 1.75
4 SMI(s), ... 1.75
5 SMI(s),BBI,TA,V:Livewire 1.75
6 SMI(s),RBr,TA,Metropolis
　in ruins 1.75
7 SMI(s),RBr,TA,V:Jax-Ur, Mala . 1.75
8 SMI(s),RBr,TA,V:Jax-Ur 1.75
9 SMI(s),MM,TA,"Return of
　the Hero" 1.75
10 SMI(s),RBr,TA,V:Toyman . . . 1.75
11 SMI(s),RBr,TA,struck down
　by strange malady 1.75

SUPERMAN'S BUDDY
1954
1 w/costume 1,000.00
1 w/out costume 400.00

SUPERMAN'S
CHRISTMAS ADVENTURE
1 (1940) 3,500.00
2 (1944) 800.00

SUPERMAN AND THE
GREAT CLEVELAND FIRE
1948
1 for Hospital Fund 450.00

SUPERMAN (miniature)
1942
1 Py-Co-Pay Tooth Powder
　Give- Away 600.00
2 CS,Superman Time Capsule 400.00
3 CS,Duel in Space 300.00
4 CS,Super Show in Metropolis 300.00

SUPERMAN RECORD
COMIC
1966
1 w/record 100.00
1 w/out record 35.00

SUPERMAN-TIM
STORE PAMPHLETS
1942
Superman-Tim store Monthly
　Membership Pamphlet, 16
　pages of stories, games,
　puzzles (1942), each 100.00
Superman-Tim store Monthly
　Membership Pamphlet, 16
　pages of stories, games,
　puzzles (1943), each 100.00
Superman-Tim store Monthly
　Membership Pamphlet, 16
　pages of stories, games,
　puzzles (1944), each 100.00
Superman-Tim store Monthly

Membership Pamphlet, 16 pages of stories, games, puzzles (1945), each	100.00
Superman-Tim store Monthly Membership Pamphlet, 14-16 pages of stories, games, puzzles, 5"x8" color(c), (1946), each	100.00
Superman-Tim stamp album, 1946	150.00
Superman-Tim store Monthly Membership Pamphlet, 14-16 pages of stories, games, puzzles, 5"x8" color(c), (1947), each	100.00
Superman-Tim stamp album, Superman story, 1947	175.00
Superman-Tim store Monthly Membership Pamphlet, 14-16 pages of stories, games, puzzles, 5"x8" color(c),(1948), each	100.00
Superman-Tim stamp album, 1948	125.00
Superman-Tim store Monthly Membership Pamphlet, 14-16 pages of stories, games, puzzles, 5"x8" color(c), (1949), each	100.00
Superman-Tim store Monthly Membership Pamphlet, 14-16 pages of stories, games, puzzles, 5"x8" color(c) (1950), each	100.00

Superman (2nd Regular Series) #1
© DC Comics, Inc.

SUPERMAN
[2nd Regular Series] 1987–97

1 JBy,TA,I:Metallo	5.00
2 JBy,TA,V:Luthor	3.00
3 JBy,TA,Legends tie-in	2.50
4 JBy,KK,V:Bloodsport	2.25
5 JBy,KK,V:Host	2.00
6 JBy,KK,A:Prankster	2.00
7 JBy,KK,V:Rampage	2.00
8 JBy,KK,A:Superboy,Legion	2.00
9 JBy,KK,V:Joker	4.00

10 JBy,KK,V:Rampage	2.00
11 JBy,KK,V:Mr.Mxyzptlk	2.00
12 JBy,KK,A:Lori Lemerias	2.00
13 JBy,KK,Millenium	2.00
14 JBy,KK,A:Green Lantern	2.00
15 JBy,KK,I:New Prankster	2.00
16 JBy,KK,A:Prankster	2.00
17 JBy,KK,O:Silver Banshee	2.00
18 MMi,KK,A:Hawkman	2.00
19 JBy,V:Skyhook	2.00
20 JBy,KK,A:Doom Patrol	2.50
21 JBy,A:Supergirl	2.00
22 JBy,A:Supergirl	2.00
23 MMi,CR,O:Silver Banshee	2.00
24 KGa,V:Rampage	2.00
25 KGa,V:Brainiac	2.00
26 KGa,BBr,V:Baron Sunday	2.00
27 KGa,BBr,V:Guardian	2.00
28 KGa,BBr,Supes Leaves Earth	2.00
29 DJu,BBr,V:Word Bringer	2.00
30 KGa,DJu,A:Lex Luthor	2.00
31 DJu,PCu,V:Mxyzptlk	2.00
32 KGa,V:Mongul	2.00
33 KGa,A:Cleric	2.00
34 KGa,V:Skyhook	2.00
35 CS,KGa,A:Brainiac	2.00
36 JOy,V:Prankster	2.00
37 JOy,A:Guardian	2.00
38 JOy,Jimmy Olsen Vanished	2.00
39 JOy,KGa,V:Husque	2.00
40 JOy,V:Four Armed Terror	2.00
41 JOy,Day of Krypton Man #1, A:Lobo	3.50
42 JOy,Day of Krypton Man #4, V:Draaga	3.50
43 JOy,V:Krypton Man	2.00
44 JOy,A:Batman	2.00
45 JOy,F:Jimmy Olsen's Dairy	2.00
46 DJu,JOy,A:Jade,Obsidian, I:New Terra-Man	2.00
47 JOy,Soul Search #2,V:Blaze	2.00
48 CS,Sinbad Contract #1	2.00
49 JOy,Krisis of K.Kryptonite#1	3.00
50 JBy,KGa,DJu,JOy,BBr,CS,Krisis of Krimson Kryptonite #4, Clark Proposes To Lois	6.00
50a 2nd printing	1.50
51 JOy,I:Mr.Z	1.75
52 KGa,V:Terra-Man	1.75
53 JOy,Superman reveals i.d.	3.50
53a 2nd Printing	1.25
54 JOy,KK,Time & Time Again#3	1.75
55 JOy,KK,Time & Time Again#6	1.75
56 EH,KK,Red Glass Trilogy#1	1.75
57 JOy,DJu,BBr,ATi,JBg,BMc,TG, Revenge o/t Krypton Man #2	3.50
58 DJu,BBr,I:Bloodhounds	1.75
59 DJu,BBr,A:Linear Men	1.75
60 DJu,EB,I:Agent Liberty, V:Intergang	2.00
61 DJu,BBr,A:Waverider, V:Linear Men	1.75
62 DJu,BBr,Blackout #4,A:Mr.Z	1.75
63 DJu,A:Aquaman	1.75
64 JG,Christmas issue	1.75
65 DJu,Panic in the Sky#2, I:New Justice League	3.50
66 DJu,Panic in the Sky#6, V:Brainiac	8.00
67 DJu,Aftermath	1.75
68 DJu,V:Deathstroke	1.75
69 WS(c),DJu,A:Agent Liberty	1.75
70 DJu,BBr,A:Robin,V:Vampires	1.75
71 DJu,Blaze/Satanus War	1.75
72 DJu,Crisis at Hand#2	1.75

73 DJu,A:Waverider,V:Linear Men,C:Doomsday	4.00
73a 2nd printing	1.50
74 DJu,V:Doomsday,A:JLA	7.00
74a 2nd printing	1.75
75 DJu,V:Doomsday,D:Superman, Collectors Ed.	15.00
75a newstand Ed.	9.00
75b 2nd printing	4.00
75c 3rd printing	1.50
75d 4th Printing	1.50
75e Platinum Ed.	60.00
76 DJu,BBr,Funeral for Friend#4	3.00
77 DJu,BBr,Funeral for Friend#8	3.00
78 DJu,BBr,Reign of Supermen#3, Die-Cut(c),Mini poster,F:Cyborg Supes,A:Doomsday	2.50
78a Newsstand Ed.	2.00
79 DJu,BBr,Memorial Service for Clark	2.00
80 DJu,BBr,Coast City Blows up, V:Mongul	4.00
81 DJu,O:Cyborg Superman	3.50
82 DJu,Chromium(c),A:All Supermen, V:Cyborg Superman	5.00
82a Newstand Ed.	2.25
83 DJu,A:Batman	1.75
84 DJu,V:Toyman	1.75
85 DJu,V:Toyman	1.75
86 DJu,A:Sun Devils	1.75
87 DJu(c&s),SI,JRu,Bizzaro's World#1 R:Bizarro	1.75
88 DJu(c&s),SI,JRu,Bizzaro's World#5 D:Bizarro	1.75
89 DJu(c&s),V:Cadmus Project	1.75
90 DJu(c&s),Battle for Metropolis#3	1.75
91 DJu(c&s),Fall of Metropolis#3	1.75
92 Massacre in Metropolis	1.75
93 Zero Hour,A:Batman	1.75
94 Conduit	1.75
95 Brainiac	1.75
96 Virtual Reality	1.75
97 Shadow Dragon	1.75
98 R:Shadow Strike	1.75
99 R:Agent Liberty	1.75
100 BBr,DJu,Death of C.Kent,pt.1	2.95
100a Collectors Edition	3.95
101 Death of Clark Kent,pt.5 [New Miraweb format begins]	1.95
102 DJu,A:Captain Marvel	1.95
103 O:Arclight	1.95
104	1.95
105 A:Green Lantern	1.95
106 DJu,RF,The Trial of Superman	1.95
107 DJu,RF,The Trial of Superman	1.95
108 DJu,RF,The Trial of Superman	1.95
109 DJu,RF,V:Kill Fee	1.95
110	1.95
111 DJu,RF,Cat Grant in charge	1.95
112 DJu,RF,Lois & Clark	1.95
113 DJu(s),RF,JRu,	1.95
114 DJu(s),RF,JRu,A:Brainiac	1.95
115 DJu(s),RF,JRu,Lois leaves Metropolis	1.95
116 DJu(s),RF,JRu,battle city siga concl., V:Daxamite,B.U. Teen Titans preview	1.95
117 DJu(s),RF,JRu,V: his own robots, Final Night tie-in	1.95
118 DJu(s),RF,JRu,F:time-lost Legion of Super Heroes	1.95
119 DJu(s),RF,JRu,A:Legion of Super Heroes	1.95
120 DJu(s),RF,JRu,	1.95

DC COMICS

121 DJu(s),RF,JRu,"They Call it
  Suicide Slum" 1.95
122 DJu(s),RF,JRu,Lois visits
  Fortress of Solitude 1.95
123 DJu(s),RF,Jru,Superman gets
  New Costume 1.95
123a collector's edition, glow-in-
  the-dark cover, ... 1.95
124 DJu(s),RF,JRu,A:Scorn, prince
  of Kandor 1.95
125 DJu(s),RF,JRu,Kandor and
  Metropolis,A:Atom 1.95
126 DJu(s),RF,JRu,A:Batman . . . 1.95
127 DJu(s),RF,JRu,F:Jimmy Olsen 1.95
Ann.#1 RF,BBr,A:Titano 2.00
Ann.#2 RF,BBr,R:Newsboy Legion
  & Guardian 3.00
Ann.#3 DAb(1st Work),TA,DG,
  Armageddon 2001. . . . . 9.00
Ann.#3a 2nd printing(silver) 2.00
Ann.#4 Eclipso 2.75
Ann.#5 Bloodlines#6,DL,I:Myriad . 2.75
Ann.#6 Elseworlds Story 2.95
Ann.#7 WS(c),Year One Annual
  A:Dr. Occult 3.95
Ann.#8 Legends o/t Dead Earth . 2.95
Ann.#9 Pulp Heroes (High-
  Adventure) DJu 3.95
Earth Day 1991 KGa 5.50
Earth Stealers JBy,CS,JOy 2.95
Greatest Superman Stories Ever Told:
  HC 75.00
  TPB 15.95
Legacy of Superman#1 WS,JG,F:
  Guardian,Waverider,Sinbad . . 4.00
Newstime-The Life and Death of
  the Man of Steel-Magazine,
  DJu,BBr,JOy,JG,JBg 3.25
Spec#1 WS,V:L.Luthor,'Sandman' 6.00
Speeding Bullets EB 8.00
Under a Yellow Sun KGa,EB 5.95
TPB Panic in the Sky rep.
  Panic in the Sky 9.95
TPB Return of Superman rep.Reign
  of Superman 14.95
TPB Time and Time Again 7.50
TPB World Without Superman . . . 7.50
TPB Krisis of the Krimson Kryptonite
  rep. Superman #49-#50, Adven-
  tures of Superman #472-#473,
  Action Comics #659-#660 and
  Starman #28 . . . . 12.95
Superman: The Wedding Album,
  96pg. special 4.95
Superman: The Wedding Album,
  collector's edition, cardstock
  cover 4.95

SUPERMAN: THE DEATH
OF CLARK KENT

TPB Rep. Superman:Man of Steel #43-
  #46, Superman #99-#102, Action
  Comics #709-#711, Adventures of
  Superman #523-#525, Superman:
  Man of Tomorrow #1 . . . . . . 19.95

SUPERMAN,
EARTH DAY 1991

1 KGa,Metropolis 'Clean-Up' 5.50

Superman/Doomsday #3
© DC Comics, Inc.

SUPERMAN/DOOMSDAY:
HUNTER/PREY
1994

1 DJu(a&s),BBr,R:Doomsday,R:Cyborg
  Superman,A:Darkseid 5.50
2 DJu(a&s),BBr,V:Doomsday,Cyborg
  Superman,A:Darkseid 5.25
3 DJu(a&s),BBr,V:Doomsday . . . 5.25
TPB Rep. #1-#3 . . . . 14.95

SUPERMAN FAMILY
**Prev: Superman's Pal,
Jimmy Olsen
1974-82**

164 KS,NC(c),Jimmy Olsen:'Death
  Bites with Fangs of Stone' . . . 5.00
165 KS,NC(c),Supergirl:'Princess
  of the Golden Sun' 3.00
166 KS,NC(c),Lois Lane:'The
  Murdering Arm of Metropolis' . 3.00
167 KS,NC(c),Jimmy Olsen:'A
  Deep Death for Mr. Action' . . . 3.00
168 NC(c),Supergirl:'The Girl
  with the See-Through Mind' . . 3.00
169 NC(c),Lois Lane:'Target of
  the Tarantula' 3.00
170 KS(c),Jimmy Olsen:'The Kid
  Who Adopted Jimmy Olsen' . . 3.00
171 ECh(c),Supergirl:'Cleopatra-
  Queen of America' 3.00
172 KS(c),Lois Lane:'The Cheat
  the Whole World Cheered' . . . 3.00
173 KS(c),Jimmy Olsen:'Menace
  of the Micro-Monster' 3.00
174 KS(c),Supergirl:'Eyes of
  the Serpent' 3.00
175 KS(c),Lois Lane:'Fadeout
  For Lois' 3.00
176 KS(c),Jimmy
  Olsen:'Nashville, Super-Star' . 3.00
177 KS(c),Supergirl:'Bride
  of the Stars' 2.50
178 KS(c),Lois Lane:'The Girl
  With the Heart of Steel' 2.50
179 KS(c),Jimmy Olsen:'I Scared
  Superman to Death' 2.50

180 KS,Supergirl:'The Secret of
  the Spell-Bound Supergirl' . . . 2.50
181 ECh(c),Lois Lane:'The Secret
  Lois Lane Could Never Tell' . . 2.50
182 CS&NA(c),Jimmy Olsen:
  'Death on Ice' 2.50
183 NA(c),Supergirl:'Shadows
  of Phantoms' 2.50
184 NA(c),Supergirl:'The
  Visitors From The Void' 2.50
185 NA(c),Jimmy Olsen: The
  Fantastic Fists and Fury
  Feet of Jimmy Olsen' 2.50
186 JL&DG(c),Jimmy Olsen:
  'The Bug Lady' 2.50
187 JL(c),Jimmy Olsen:'The
  Dealers of Death' 2.50
188 JL&DG(c),Jimmy Olsen:
  'Crisis in Kandor' 2.50
189 JL(c),Jimmy Olsen:'The
  Night of the Looter' 2.50
190 Jimmy Olsen:'Somebody
  Stole My Town' 2.50
191 Superboy:'The Incredible
  Shrinking Town' 2.50
192 RA&DG(c),Superboy:'This
  Town For Plunder' 2.50
193 RA&DG(c),Superboy:'Menace
  of the Mechanical Monster' . . . 2.50
194 MR,Superboy:'When
  the Sorcerer Strikes' 2.50
195 RA&DG(c),Superboy:'The Curse
  of the Un-Secret Identity' 2.50
196 JL&DG(c),Superboy:'The
  Shadow of Jor-El' 2.50
197 JL(c),Superboy:'Superboy's
  Split Personality' 2.50
198 JL(c),Superboy:'Challenge
  of the Green K-Tastrophe' 2.50
199 RA&DG(c),Supergirl:'The
  Case of Cape Caper' 2.50
200 RA&DG(c),Lois Lane:
  'Unhappy Anniversary' 2.50
201 RA&DG(c),Supergirl:'The
  Face on Cloud 9' 2.50
202 RA&DG(c),Supergirl:'The
  Dynamic Duel' 2.50
203 RA&DG(c),Supergirl:'The
  Supergirl From Planet Earth' . . 2.50
204 RA&DG(c),Supergirl:'The
  Earth-quake Enchantment' . . . 2.50
205 RA&DG(c),Supergirl:'Magic
  Over Miami' 2.50
206 RA&DG(c),Supergirl:'Strangers
  at the Heart's Core' 2.50
207 RA&DG(c),Supergirl:'Look
  Homeward, Argonian' 2.50
208 RA&DG(c),Supergirl:'The
  Super-Switch to New York' . . . 2.50
209 Supergirl:'Strike Three-
  You're Out' 2.50
210 Supergirl:'The Spoil Sport
  of New York' 2.50
211 RA&DG(c):Supergirl:'The Man
  With the Explosive Mind' 2.50
212 RA&DG(c):Supergirl:'Payment
  on Demand' 2.50
213 . . . . 2.50
214 . . . . 2.50
215 . . . . 2.50
216 thru 222 . . . . @2.50

SUPERMAN: KAL

1 Medieval Superman 5.95

Superman: The Man of Steel #16
© DC Comics, Inc.

SUPERMAN:
THE MAN OF STEEL
1991–97

1 B:LSi(s),DJu,BMc,JOy,BBr,TG,
  Revenge o/t Krypton Man#1 . . 5.00
2 JBg,V:Cerberus 3.00
3 JBg,War of the Gods X-over . . 2.50
4 JBg,V:Angstrom 2.50
5 JBg,CS,V:Atomic Skull 2.50
6 JBg,Blackout#3,A:Mr.Z 2.50
7 JBg,V:Cerberus 2.50
8 KD,V:Jolt,Blockhouse 2.50
9 JBg,Panic in the Sky#1,
  V:Brainiac. 3.00
10 JBg,Panic in the Sky#5,
  D:Draaga 2.50
11 JBg,V:Flashpoint 2.00
12 JBg,V:Warwolves 2.00
13 JBg,V:Cerberus 2.00
14 JBg,A:Robin,V:Vampires 2.00
15 JBg,KGa,Blaze/Satanus War . . 2.00
16 JBg,Crisis at Hand#1 . . . . 2.00
17 JBg,V:Underworld,
  C:Doomsday 6.00
17a 2nd printing 1.50
18 JBg,I:Doomsday,V:Underworld 8.00
18a 2nd printing 4.00
18b 3rd printing 2.00
19 JBg,Doomsday,pt.5 . . . . 5.00
19a 2nd printing 2.00
20 JBg,Funeral for a Friend#3 . . . 3.00
21 JBg,Funeral for a Friend#7 . . . 3.00
22 JBg,Reign of Supermen#4,Direct
  Sales,Die-Cut(c),mini-poster,
  F:Man of Steel 2.50
22a Newsstand Ed. 1.75
23 JBg,V:Superboy 2.00
24 JBg,V:White Rabbit,A:Mongul . 2.00
25 JBg,A:Real Superman 3.00
26 JBg,A:All Supermen,V:Mongul,
  Cyborg Superman 2.50
27 JBg,A:Superboy,Lex Luthor . . . 2.00
28 JBg(c),A:Steel 1.75
29 LSi(s),JBg,Spilled Blood#3,
  V:Hi-Tech,Blood Thirst 1.75
30 LSi(s),JBg,V:Lobo,Vinyl(c) . . . 2.50

30a Newstand Ed. 1.75
31 MBr,A:Guardian 1.75
32 MBr,Bizarro's World#4,
  V:Bizarro 1.75
33 MBr,V:Parasite 1.75
34 JBg,A:Lex Men,Dubbile Men . . 1.75
35 JBg,Worlds Collide#1,
  I:Fred Bentson 1.75
36 JBf,Worlds Collide,pt.10,V:Rift
  A:Icon 1.75
37 JBg,Zero Hour,A:Batman 1.75
38 Mystery 1.50
39 JBg,Luthor 1.50
40 . . . . 1.50
41 Locke 1.50
42 F:Locke 1.50
43 V:Deathtrap 1.50
44 Prologue to Death 1.50
45 JGb,DJa,Death of Clark Kent,pt.4
  [New Miraweb format begins] . 1.95
46 JBg,DJa,A:Shadowdragon . . . 1.95
47 O:Bloodsport 1.95
48 . . . . 1.95
49 Skyhook 1.95
50 JBg,DJa,The Trial of
  Superman, 48pg 2.95
51 JBg,DJa,The Trial of Superman 1.95
52 JBg,The Trial of Superman . . . 1.95
53 JBg,DRo,A:Lex Luthor,Contessa 1.95
54 JBg 1.95
55 JBg,DJa, Clark dates Lori
  Lemaris 1.95
56 JBg,DJa, manipulator revealed 1.95
57 RSt,JBg,DJa, more twisters . . 1.95
58 LSi(s),JBg,DJa,A:Supergirl . . . 1.95
59 LSi(s),JBg,DJa,Parasite, Steel . 1.95
60 LSi(s),JBg,DJa,R:Bottled City
  of Kandor 1.95
61 LSi(s),JBg,DJa,V:Riot 1.95
62 LSi(s),JBg,DJa, Superman
  looses powers, Final Night tie-in 1.95
63 LSi(s),JBg,DJa,Clark is
  kidnapped & revealed identity . 1.95
64 LSi(s),JBg,DJa,Superman tries to
  restore his powers 1.95
65 LSi(s),SB,DJa,V:Superman
  Revenge Squad 1.95
66 LSi(s),JBg,DJa,V:Rajiv 1.95
67 LSi(s),JBg,DJa,New powers
  prequel 1.95
68 LSi(s),JBg,DJa,V:Metallo 1.95
69 KK&LSi(s),SEa,DJa,A:Atom,
  in Kandor 1.95
70 LSi(s),SEa,DJa,V:Saviour 1.95
71 LSi(s),SEa,DJa,V:Mainframe,
  Superman Revenge Squad . . . 1.95
Ann.#1 Eclipso tie-in,A:Starman . . 2.75
Ann.#2 Bloodlines#2,I:Edge 2.75
Ann.#3 MBr,Elseworlds Story . . . 2.95
Ann.#4 Year One Annual 2.95
Ann.#5 Legends o/t Dead Earth . . 2.95
Ann.#6 Pulp Heroes (Hard Boiled)
  LSi(s),DJa 3.95
Gallery 1 . . . . 3.50

SUPERMAN:
THE MAN OF TOMORROW
1995–96

1 TGu,BBr,RSt(s),V:Lex Luthor . . 2.00
2 v:Parasite 2.00
3 TG,BBr, The Trial of Superman 2.00
4 RSt(s),PR,BBr,A:Shazam 2.00
5 RSt(s),PR,BBr,Wedding of Lex
  Luthor 2.00
6 RSt(s),PR,BBr,Superman V:

Jackal again 2.00
7 RSt(s),PR,BBr, ... 2.00
8 RSt(s),PR,BBr,V:Carbide 2.00
9 RSt(s),PR,BBr,Ma and Pa Kent
  open their album 2.00

Superman's Girl Friend Lois Lane #119
© DC Comics, Inc.

SUPERMAN'S GIRL
FRIEND, LOIS LANE
1958–74

1 CS,KS 2,700.00
2 CS,KS 750.00
3 CS,KS,spanking panel shown 500.00
4 CS,KS 400.00
5 CS,KS 375.00
6 CS,KS 300.00
7 CS,KS 300.00
8 CS,KS 250.00
9 CS,KS, A:Pat Boone 250.00
10 CS,KS 250.00
11 CS,KS 200.00
12 CS,KS 200.00
13 CS,KS 175.00
14 KS,'Three Nights in the
  Fortress of Solitude' 150.00
15 KS,I:Van-Zee 150.00
16 KS, Lois' Signal-Watch 150.00
17 KS,CS,A:Brainiac 150.00
18 KS,A:Astounding Man 150.00
19 KS,'Superman of the Past' . . 125.00
20 KS,A:Superman 125.00
21 KS,A:Van-Zee 125.00
22 KS,A:Robin Hood 125.00
23 KS,A:Elastic Lass, Supergirl 125.00
24 KS,A:Van-Zee, Bizarro 125.00
25 KS,'Lois Lane's
  Darkest Secret' 110.00
26 KS,A:Jor-El 110.00
27 KS,CS,A:Bizarro 110.00
28 KS,A:Luthor 110.00
29 CS,A:Aquaman,Batman,Green
  Arrow 110.00
30 KS,A:Krypto,Aquaman 65.00
31 KS,A:Lori Lemaris 60.00
32 KS,CS,A:Bizarro 60.00
33 KS,CS,A:Phantom Zone,Lori
  Lemaris, Mon-El 65.00

Superman's Girl Friend, Lois Lane #123
© DC Comics, Inc.

34 KS,A:Luthor,Supergirl 60.00
35 KS,CS,A:Supergirl 60.00
36 KS,CS,Red Kryptonite Story . 60.00
37 KS,CS,'The Forbidden Box' . 60.00
38 KS,CS,A:Prof.Potter,
   Supergirl 60.00
39 KS,CS,A:Supergirl,Jor-El,
   Krypto, Lori Lemaris 60.00
40 KS,'Lois Lane, Hag!' 60.00
41 KS,CS,'The Devil and
   Lois Lane' 60.00
42 KS,A:Lori Lemaris 60.00
43 KS,A:Luthor 60.00
44 KS,A:Lori Lemaris,Braniac,
   Prof. Potter 60.00
45 KS,CS,'The Superman-Lois
   Hit Record' 60.00
46 KS,A:Luthor 60.00
47 KS,'The Incredible Delusion' . 60.00
48 KS,A:Mr. Mxyzptlk 60.00
49 KS,The Unknown Superman . 60.00
50 KS,A:Legion 60.00
51 KS,A:Van-Zee & Lori Lemaris 40.00
52 KS,'Truce Between Lois
   Lane and Lana Lang' 40.00
53 KS,A:Lydia Lawrence 40.00
54 KS,CS,'The Monster That
   Loved Lois Lane' 40.00
55 KS,A:Superigrl 40.00
56 KS,'Lois Lane's
   Super-Gamble!' 42.00
57 KS,'The Camera From
   Outer Space' 40.00
58 KS,'The Captive Princess' . . . 40.00
59 KS,CS,A:Jor-El & Batman . . . 40.00
60 KS,'Get Lost,Superman!' 40.00
61 KS,A:Mxyzptlk 40.00
62 KS,A:Mxyzptlk 40.00
63 KS,'The Satanic Schemes
   of S.K.U.L.' 40.00
64 KS,A:Luthor 40.00
65 KS,A:Luthor 40.00
66 KS,'They Call Me the Cat!' . . 40.00
67 KS,'The Bombshell of
   the Boulevards' 40.00
68 giant size 45.00
69 KS,Lois Lane's Last Chance . 40.00

70 KS,I:Silver Age Catwoman,
   A:Batman,Robin,Penguin . . 225.00
71 KS,A:Catwoman,Batman,
   Robin,Penguin 130.00
72 KS,CS,A:Ina Lemaris 25.00
73 KS,'The Dummy and
   the Damsell' 25.00
74 KS,A:Justice League & Bizarro
   World,I:Bizarro Flash 35.00
75 KS,'The Lady Dictator' 25.00
76 KS,A:Hap-El 25.00
77 giant size 25.00
78 KS,Courtship,Kryptonian Style 25.00
79 KS,B:NA(c) 12.00
80 KS,'Get Out of My Life,
   Superman' 9.00
81 KS,'No Witnessesin
   Outerspace' 9.00
82 GT,A:Brainiac&Justice League 9.00
83 GT,'Witch on Wheels' 9.00
84 GT,KS,'Who is Lois Lane?' . . 9.00
85 GT,KS,A:Kandorians 9.00
86 giant size 15.00
87 GT,KS,A:Cor-Lar 9.00
88 GT,KS,'Through a Murderer's
   Eyes' 9.00
89 CS,A:Batman & Batman Jr. . . 10.00
90 GT,A:Dahr-nel 8.00
91 GT,A:Superlass 8.00
92 GT,A:Superhorse 8.00
93 GT,A:Wonder Woman 8.00
94 GT,KS,A:Jor 8.00
95 giant size 15.00
96 GT,A:Jor 6.00
97 GT,KS,A:Lori Lemaris,
   Luma Lynai,Lyla Lerrol 6.00
98 GT,A:Phantom Zone 6.00
99 GT,KS,A:Batman 7.00
100 GT,A:Batman 7.00
101 GT,KS,'The Super-Reckless
   Lois Lane' 6.00
102 GT,KS,When You're Dead,
   You're Dead 6.00
103 GT,KS,A:Supergirl 6.00
104 giant size 11.00
105 RA,I&O:Rose & Thorn 12.00
106 WR,'I am Curious Black!' . . . 5.00
107 WR,The Snow-Woman Wept . 5.00
108 WR,The Spectre Suitor 5.00
109 WR,'I'll Never Fall
   in Love Again' 5.00
110 WR,'Indian Death Charge!' . . 5.00
111 WR,A:Justice League 5.00
112 WR,KS,A:Lori Lemaris 3.00
113 giant size 7.00
114 WR,KS,A:Rose & Thorn 3.00
115 WR,A:The Black Racer 3.00
116 WR,A:Darkseid & Desaad . . 3.00
117 WR,'S.O.S From Tomorrow!' . 3.00
118 WR,A:Darkseid & Desaad . . 3.00
119 WR,A:Darkseid & Lucy Lane . 3.00
120 WR,'Who Killed Lucy Lane?' . 3.00
121 WR,A:The Thorn 3.00
122 WR,A:The Thorn 3.00
123 JRo,'Ten Deadly Division
   of the 100' 3.00
124 JRo,'The Hunters' 3.00
125 JRo,'Death Rides Wheels!' . . 3.00
126 JRo,'The Brain Busters' 3.00
127 JRo,'Curse of the Flame' . . . 3.00
128 JRo,A:Batman & Aquaman . . 3.00
129 JRo,'Serpent in Paradise' . . . 3.00
130 JRo,'The Mental Murster' . . . 3.00
131 JRo,Superman–Marry Me!' . 3.00
132 JRo,Zatanna B.U. 3.00

133 JRo,'The Lady is a Bomb' . . . 3.00
134 JRo,A:Kandor 3.00
135 JRo,'Amazing After-Life
   of Lois Lane' 3.00
136 JRo,A:Wonder Woman 3.00
137 JRo,'The Stolen Subway' . . . 4.00
Ann.#1 . . . . 175.00
Ann.#2 . . . . 125.00

SUPERMAN'S PAL, JIMMY OLSEN
1954–74
1 CS,'The Boy of 100 Faces!' 4,200.00
2 CS,The Flying Jimmy Olsen 1,100.00
3 CS,'The Man Who Collected
   Excitement 650.00
4 CS,'King For A Day!' 450.00
5 CS,'The Story of Superman's
   Souvenirs 425.00
6 CS,Kryptonite story 300.00
7 CS,'The King of Marbles' . . . 300.00
8 CS,'Jimmy Olsen, Crooner' . . 275.00
9 CS,'The Missile of Steel' . . . 275.00
10 CS,'Jungle Jimmy Olsen' . . . 275.00
11 CS,'TNT.Olsen,The Champ' . 225.00
12 CS,'Invisible Jimmy Olsen' . 225.00
13 CS,'Jimmy Olsen's
   Super Issue' 200.00
14 CS,'The Boy Superman' . . . 200.00
15 CS,'Jimmy Olsen,Speed
   Demon' 200.00
16 CS,'The Boy Superman' . . . 200.00
17 CS,J.Olsen as cartoonist . . 200.00
18 CS,A:Superboy 200.00
19 CS,'Supermam's Kid Brother 175.00
20 CS,'Merman of Metropolis' . 175.00
21 CS,'The Wedding of Jimmy
   Olsen' 150.00
22 CS,'The Super Brain of
   Jimmy Olsen' 150.00
23 CS,'The Adventure of
   Private Olsen' 150.00
24 CS,'The Gorilla Reporter' . . 150.00
25 CS,'The Day There Was
   No Jimmy Olsen 150.00
26 CS,'Bird Boy of Metropolis' . 125.00
27 CS,'The Outlaw Jimmy Olsen'125.00
28 CS,'The Boy Who Killed
   Superman' 125.00
29 CS,A:Krypto 125.00
30 CS,'The Son of Superman' . 125.00
31 CS,I:Elastic Lad 100.00
32 CS,A:Prof.Potter 100.00
33 CS,'Human Flame Thrower' 100.00
34 CS,'Superman's Pal of Steel' 100.00
35 CS,'Superman's Enemy' . . . 100.00
36 CS,I:Lois Lane,O:Jimmy Olsen
   as Superman's Pal 100.00
37 CS,O:Jimmy Olsen's SignalWatch,
   A:Elastic Lad(Jimmy Olsen) 100.00
38 CS,'Olsen's Super-Supper' . 100.00
39 CS,'The Super-Lad of Space' 100.00
40 CS,A:Supergirl,Hank White
   (Perry White's son) 100.00
41 CS,'The Human Octopus' . . . 75.00
42 CS,'Jimmy The Genie' 75.00
43 WB,CS,'Jimmy Olsen's Private
   Monster' 75.00
44 CS,'Miss Jimmy Olsen' 75.00
45 CS,A:Kandor 75.00
46 CS,A:Supergirl,Elastic Lad . . 75.00
47 CS,'Monsters From Earth!' . . 75.00
48 CS,I:Superman Emergency
   Squad 75.00
49 CS,A:Congorilla & Congo Bill 75.00

DC COMICS

Superman's Pal, Jimmy Olsen #149
© DC Comics, Inc.

50 CS,A:Supergirl,Krypto,Bizarro 75.00
51 CS,A:Supergirl 60.00
52 CS,A:Mr. Mxyzptlk,
   Miss Gzptlsnz 60.00
53 CS,A:Kandor,Lori Lemaris,
   Mr.Mxyzltk 60.00
54 CS,A:Elastic Lad 60.00
55 CS,A:Aquaman,Thor 60.00
56 KS,Imaginary story 60.00
57 KS,A:Supergirl,Imaginary story 35.00
58 CS,C:Batman 35.00
59 CS,A:Titano 35.00
60 CS,'The Fantastic Army of
   General Olsen' 35.00
61 CS,Prof. Potter 35.00
62 CS,A:Elastic Lad,Phantom
   Zone 35.00
63 CS,A:Supergirl,Kandor 40.00
64 CS,'Jimmy Olsen's
   Super-Romance 30.00
65 CS,A:Miss Gzptlsnz 30.00
66 CS,KS,A:Mr. Mxyzptlk 30.00
67 CS,'The Dummy That Haunted
   Jimmy Olsen' 30.00
68 CS,'The Helmet of Hate' 30.00
69 CS,A:Nightwing,Flamebird . 30.00
70 A:Supergirl,Lori Lemaris,
   Element Lad 30.00
71 CS,A:Mr. Mxyzptlk 25.00
72 CS,A:Legion of Super-Heroes,
   Jimmy Olsen becomes honorary
   member 30.00
73 A:Kandor 30.00
74 CS,A:Mr. Mxyzptlk,Lex Luthor 30.00
75 CS,A:Supergirl 25.00
76 CS,A:Legion of Super-Heroes 25.00
77 CS,Jimmy Olsen becomes
   Colossal Boy, A:Titano 25.00
78 CS,A:Aqualad 25.00
79 CS,'The Red-Headed Beetle
   of 1,000 B.C.' 25.00
80 CS,A:Bizarro 25.00
81 CS,KS,A:Lori Lemaris,I&O
   only A:Mighty Eagle 25.00
82 CS,'The Unbeatable Jimmy
   Olsen' 25.00
83 CS,A:Kandor 25.00

84 CS,A:Titano 25.00
85 CS,C:Legion of Super-Heroes 30.00
86 CS,A:Congorilla,Braniac 25.00
87 A:Lex Luthor,Brainiac,Legion
   of Super-Villians 30.00
88 C:Legion of Super-Heroes . . 25.00
89 I:Agent Double-Five,C:John F.
   Kennedy 25.00
90 CS,A:Mr. Mxyzptlk 25.00
91 CS,C:Batman & Robin 25.00
92 JM,A:Batman,Robin,Supergirl 25.00
93 'The Batman-Superman of
   Earth-X!' 25.00
94 O:Insect Queen retold 25.00
95 Giant 30.00
96 I:Tempus 22.00
97 A:Fortress of Solitude 22.00
98 'The Bride of Jungle Jimmy' . 22.00
99 A:Legion of Super-Heroes . . 22.00
100 A:Legion of Super-Heroes . . 25.00
101 A:Jor-El and Lara 12.00
102 'Superman's Greatest Double
   Cross!' 12.00
103 'The Murder of Clark Kent!' . 10.00
104 Giant 25.00
105 V:Tempus 10.00
106 CS,A:Legion of Super-Heroes 10.00
107 A:Krypto 10.00
108 CS,'The Midas of Metropolis' 10.00
109 A:Lex Luthor 10.00
110 CS,'Jimmy Olsen's Blackest
   Deeds!' 10.00
111 . . . . 10.00
112 . . . . 10.00
113 V:Magnaman 22.00
114 'The Wrong Superman!' 10.00
115 A:Aquaman 10.00
116 A:Brainiac 10.00
117 'Planet of the Capes' 10.00
118 A:Lex Luthor 10.00
119 'Nine Lives Like a Cat!' 10.00
120 V:Climate King 10.00
121 thru 125 . . . . @10.00
126 CS,Riddle of Kryptonite Plus 10.00
127 CS,Jimmy in Revolutionary
   War 10.00
128 I:Mark Olsen(Jimmy's Father) 10.00
129 MA,A:Mark Olsen 10.00
130 MA,A:Robin,Brainiac 10.00
131 . . . . 20.00
132 MA,When Olsen Sold out
   Superman 10.00
133 JK,B:New Newsboy Legion,
   I:Morgan Edge 30.00
134 JK,I:Darkseid 45.00
135 JK,I:New Guardian 18.00
136 JK,O:New Guardian,
   I:Dubbilex 8.00
137 JK,I:Four Armed Terror 8.00
138 JK,V:Four Armed Terror 8.00
139 JK,A:Don Rickles,I:Ugly
   Mannheim 8.00
140 . . . . 8.00
141 JK,A:Don Rickles,Lightray
   B:Newsboy Legion rep 8.00
142 JK,I:Count Dragorian 8.00
143 JK,V:Count Dragorian 8.00
144 JK,A Big Thing in a Deep
   Scottish Lake 8.00
145 JK,Brigadoon 8.00
146 JK,Homo Disastrous 8.00
147 JK,Superman on New
   Genesis,A:High Father,
   I:Victor Volcanium 8.00
148 JK,V:Victor Volcanium,

   E:Newsboy Legion rep 8.00
149 BO(i),The Unseen Enemy,
   B:Plastic Man rep 7.00
150 BO(i) A Bad Act to Follow . . 7.00
151 BO(i),A:Green Lantern 7.00
152 MSy,BO,I:Real Morgan Edge 7.00
153 MSy,Murder in Metropolis . . 7.00
154 KS,The Girl Who Was Made
   of Money 7.00
155 KS,Downfall of Judas Olsen . 7.00
156 KS,Last Jump for
   a Skyjacker 7.00
157 KS,Jimmy as Marco Polo . . . 7.00
158 KS,A:Lena Lawrence
   (Lucy Lane) 7.00
159 KS,Jimmy as Spartacus . . . 7.00
160 KS,A:Lena Lawrence
   (Lucy Lane) 7.00
161 KS,V:Lucy Lane 7.00
162 KS,A:Lex Luthor 7.00
163 KS,Jimmy as Marco Polo . . . 7.00

SUPERMAN'S METROPOLIS

Elseworlds Nov. 1996
GN RLo&RTs(s),TMK, in Fritz
   Lang's Metropolis 5.95

SUPERMAN SPECTACULAR

1982
1 A:Luthor & Terra-Man 2.50

SUPERMAN, THE SECRET YEARS

Feb., 1985
1 CS,KS,FM(c) 1.50
2 CS,KS,FM(c) 1.25
3 CS,KS,FM(c) 1.25
4 CS,KS,FM(c), May 1985 . . . . 1.25

SUPERMAN VS. AMAZING SPIDER-MAN

April, 1976
1 RA/DG,oversized 25.00
1a 2nd printing, signed 50.00

SUPERMAN/ WONDER WOMAN: WHOM GODS DESTROY

Elseworlds Oct. 1996
Mini-series
1 CCI(s),DAb, Lois becomes the
   immortal Wonder Woman . . . 4.95
2 CCI(s),DAb, search for Lana
   Lang 4.95
3 . . . . 4.95
4 CCI(s),DAb, romance of the
   century, concl. 4.95

SUPERMAN WORKBOOK

1945
1 rep. Superman #14 . . . . 1,000.00

SUPER POWERS

1984
[Kenner Action Figures]
1 A:Batman & Joker 1.75
2 A:Batman & Joker 1.25
3 A:Batman & Joker 1.00
4 A:Batman & Joker 1.00

DC COMICS

Super Powers #2 © DC Comics, Inc.

5 JK(c),JK,A:Batman & Joker ... 1.25
[2nd Series] 1985–86
1 JK,'Seeds of Doom' 1.00
2 JK,'When Past & Present Meet' 1.00
3 JK,'Time Upon Time' 1.00
4 JK,There's No Place Like Rome 1.00
5 JK,'Once Upon a Tomorrow' .. 1.00
6 JK,'Darkkseid o/t Moon' 1.00
[3rd Series] 1986
1 CI,'Threshold' 1.00
2 CI,'Escape' 1.00
3 CI,'Machinations' .... .75
4 CI,'A World Divided' .... .75

SUPER-TEAM FAMILY
1975–78
1 rep. 2.50
2 Creeper/Wildcat 2.00
3 RE/WW,Flash & Hawkman ... 2.00
4 .... 2.00
5 .... 2.00
6 .... 2.00
7 .... 2.00
8 JSh,Challengers 2.00
9 JSh,Challengers 2.00
10 JSh,Challengers 2.00
11 Supergirl,Flash,Atom 2.00
12 Green Lantern,Hawkman 2.00
13 Aquaman, Capt. Comet 2.00
14 Wonder Woman,Atom 2.00
15 Flash & New Gods 2.00

SWAMP THING
[1st Regular Series]
Oct.–Nov., 1972
1 B:LWn(s),BWr,O:Swamp Thing 80.00
2 BWr,I:Arcane 35.00
3 BWr,I:Patchwork Man 20.00
4 BWr 20.00
5 BWr 18.00
6 BWr 18.00
7 BWr,A:Batman 25.00
8 BWr,Lurker in Tunnel 13 ... 14.00
9 BWr 14.00
10 E:BWr,A;Arcane 14.00
11 thru 22 NR .... @6.00
23 NR,reverts to Dr.Holland 6.00

24 NR 6.00
TPB rep.#1-#10,House of Secrets
#92, Dark Genesis Saga 19.95

Swamp Thing #66 © DC Comics, Inc.

SWAMP THING
1986–96
Previously:
SAGA OF THE SWAMP THING
46 B:AMo(s) cont'd,SBi,JTo,Crisis,
A:John Constantine,Phantom
Stranger 4.00
47 SBi,Parliment of Trees,Full
origin,A:Constantine 3.00
48 SBi,JTo,V:Brujeria,
A:Constantine. 3.00
49 SBi,AA,A:Constantine,Demon,Ph.
Stranger,Spectre,Deadman ... 3.00
50 SBi,RV,JTo,concl.American
Gothic,D:Zatara&Sargon,
Double Size 6.00
51 RV,AA,L:Constantine 3.00
52 RV,AA,Arkham Asylum,A:Flor.
Man,Lex Luthor,C:Joker,
2-Face,Batman 4.00
53 JTo,V:Batman,Swamp Thing
Banished to Space 4.00
54 JTo script,RV,AA,C:Batman . 3.00
55 RV,AA,JTo,A:Batman,. 3.00
56 RV,AA,My Blue Heaven 3.00
57 RV,AA,A:Adam Strange 3.00
58 RV,AA,A:Adam Strange,GC,
Spectre preview 3.00
59 JTo,RV,AA,D:Patchwork Man . 3.00
Direct Sales Only
60 JTo,Loving the Alien 3.00
61 RV,AA,All Flesh is Grass
G.L.Corps X-over 3.00
62 RV(&script),AA,Wavelength,
A:Metron,Darkseid 3.00
63 RV,AA,Loose Ends(reprise) .. 3.00
64 E:AMo(s),SBi,TY,RV,AA,
Return of the Good Gumbo ... 3.00
65 RV,JTo,A:Constantine 3.50
66 RV,Elemental Energy 2.50
67 RV,V:Solomon Grundy,
Hellblazer preview 4.00
68 RV,O:Swamp Thing 2.50

69 RV,O:Swamp Thing 2.50
70 RV,AA,Quest for SwampThing 2.50
71 RV,AA,Fear of Flying 2.50
72 RV,AA,Creation 2.50
73 RV,AA,A:John Constantine ... 3.00
74 RV,AA,Abbys Secret 2.50
75 RV,AA,Plant Elementals 2.50
76 RV,AA,A:John Constantine ... 3.00
77 TMd,AA,A:John Constantine . 3.00
78 TMd,AA,Phantom Pregnancy . 2.50
79 RV,AA,A:Superman,Luthor ... 2.50
80 RV,AA,V:Aliends 2.50
81 RV,AA,Invasion x-over 2.50
82 RV,AA,A:Sgt.Rock & Easy Co. 2.50
83 RV,AA,A:Enemy Ace 2.50
84 RV,AA,A:Sandman 10.00
85 RV,TY,Time Travel contd..... 2.50
86 RV,TY,A:Tomahawk 2.50
87 RV,TY,Camelot,A:Demon 2.50
88 RV,TY,A:Demon,Golden
Gladiator 2.50
89 MM,AA,The Dinosaur Age ... 2.50
90 BP,AA,Birth of Abbys Child
(Tefe) 2.75
91 PB,AA,Abbys Child (New
Elemental) 2.50
92 PB,AA,Ghosts of the Bayou .. 2.50
93 PB,AA,New Power 2.50
94 PB,AA,Ax-Murderer 2.50
95 PB,AA,Toxic Waste Dumpers . 2.50
96 PB,AA,Tefes Powers 2.50
97 PB,AA,Tefe,V:Nergal,
A:Arcane 2.50
98 PB,AA,Tefe,in Hell 2.50
99 PB,AA,Tefe,A:Mantago,
John Constantine 3.00
100 PB,AA,V:Angels of Eden,
(48 pages) 3.50
101 AA,A:Tefe 2.50
102 V:Mantagos Zombies,inc. prev.
of Worlds Without End 2.50
103 Green vs. Grey 2.50
104 Quest for Elementals,pt.1 ... 2.50
105 Quest for Elementals,pt.2 ... 2.50
106 Quest for Elementals,pt.3 ... 2.50
107 Quest for Elementals,pt.4 ... 2.50
108 Quest for Elementals,pt.5 ... 2.50
109 Quest for Elementals,pt.6 ... 2.50
110 TMd,A:Father Tocsin 2.50
111 V:Ghostly Zydeco Musician .. 2.50
112 TMd,B:Swamp Thing
for Governor 2.50
113 E:Swamp Thing for Governor 2.50
114 TMd,Hellblazer 2.75
115 TMd,A:Hellblazer,V:Dark
Conrad 2.75
116 From Body of Swamp Thing . 2.25
117 JD,The Lord of Misrule,
Mardi Gras 2.25
118 A Childs Garden,A:Matthew
the Raven 2.25
119 A:Les Perdu 2.25
120 F:Lady Jane 2.25
121 V:Sunderland Corporation ... 2.25
122 I:The Needleman 2.25
123 V:The Needleman 2.25
124 In Central America 2.25
125 V:Anton Arcane,20th Anniv. . 3.75
126 Mescalito 2.25
127 Project Proteus #1 .... 2.25
128 Project proteus #2 .... 2.25
Vertigo
129 CV(c),B:NyC(s),SEa,KDM(i),
Sw.Thing's Deterioration 2.25
130 CV(c),SEa,KDM(i),A:John

Constantine,V:Doctor Polygon . 2.25
131 CV(c),SEa,KDM(i),I:Swamp
Thing's,Doppleganger,
F:The Folk 2.25
132 CV(c),SEa,KDM(i),
V:Doppleganger 2.25
133 CV(c),SEa,KDM(i),R:General
Sunderland,V:Thunder Petal . . 2.25
134 CV(c),SEa,KDM(i),Abby Leaves,
C:John Constantine 2.25
135 CV(c),SEa,KDM(i),A:J.Constantine,
Swamp Thing Lady Jane meld 2.25
136 CV(c),RsB,KDM(i),A:Lady Jane,
Dr.Polygon,John Constantine . 2.25
137 CV(c),E:NyC(s),RsB,KDM(i),
IR:Sunderland is Anton Arcane,
A:J.Constantine 2.25
138 CV(c),DiF(s),RGu,KDM,B:Mind
Fields 2.25
139 CV(c),DiF(s),RGu,KDM,A:Black
Orchid,In Swamp Thing's mind,
cont'd fr.Black Orchid #5 . . . . 2.25
140 B:Bad Gumbo 2.50
140a Platinum Ed. 10.00
141 A:Abigail Arcane 2.25
142 Bad Gumbo#3 . . . . 2.25
143 E:Bad Gumbo 2.25
144 In New York City 2.25
145 In Amsterdam 2.25
146 V:Nelson Strong 2.25
147 Hunter 1.95
148 Sargon 1.95
149 Sargon 1.95
150 V:Sargon 1.95
151 . . . . 1.95
152 River Run,pt.1 . . . . 1.95
153 River Run 1.95
154 River Run 2.25
155 River Run 2.25
156 PJ,River Run 2.25
157 . . . . 2.25
158 . . . . 2.25
159 Swamp Dog 2.25
160 PhH,KDM,Atmospheres 2.25
161 Atmospheres 2.25
162 Atmospheres 2.25
163 Atmospheres 2.25
164 . . . . 2.25
165 CS,KDM,F:Chester Williams . 2.25
166 PhH,KDM,Trial by Fire,pt.1 . . 2.25
167 PhH,KDM,Trial by Fire,pt.2 . . 2.25
168 MMr(s),PhH,KDM,Trial by Fire,
pt.3 . . . . 2.25
169 MMr(s),PhH,KDM,Trial by Fire,
pt.4 . . . . 2.25
170 MMr(s),PhH,KDM,Trial by Fire,
pt.5 . . . . 2.25
171 MMr(s),PhH,KDM,"Trial by Fire,"
pt.6 last issue 2.25
Ann.#4 PB/AA,A:Batman 2.75
Ann.#5 A:BrotherPower Geek . . . 3.25
Ann.#6 Houma 3.50
Ann.#7 CV(c),NyC(s),MBu(i),Childrens
Crusade,F:Tefe,A:Maxine:BU:
Beautyand the Beast 4.25

SWORD OF SORCERY
Feb.–March, 1973
1 MK(c),HC 10.00
2 BWv,NA,Hc 15.00
3 BWv,HC,MK,WS 10.00
4 HC,WS 5.00
5 Nov.–Dec., 1973 . . . . 5.50

SWORD OF THE ATOM
Sept., 1983
1 GK 1.50
2 GK 1.25
3 GK 1.25
4 GK 1.25
Spec.#1 GK 1.25
Spec.#2 GK 1.25
Spec.#3 PB 1.50

SYSTEM, THE
DC/Vertigo 1996
TPB by Peter Kuper 12.95

Tailgunner Jo #4 © DC Comics, Inc.

TAILGUNNER JO
Sept., 1988
1 . . . . 1.25
2 . . . . 1.25
3 . . . . 1.25
4 . . . . 1.25
5 . . . . 1.25
6 . . . . 1.25

TAKION
1996
1 PuK,AaL,Josh Sanders
becomes Takion 1.75
2 . . . . 1.75
3 . . . . 1.75
4 . . . . 1.75
5 PuK,AaL,Adventures of Source
Elemental" cont. 1.75
6 PuK,AaL,Final Night tie-in 1.75
7 PuK,AaL,Arzaz trains Takion,
final issue 1.75

TALES OF THE GREEN
LANTERN CORPS
May, 1981
1 JSon,FMc,O:Green Lantern . . . 1.50
2 JSon,FMc 1.25
3 JSon,FMc 1.25

*Tales of the Legion of Super
Heroes #352 © DC Comics, Inc.*

TALES OF THE LEGION
OF SUPER HEROES
Aug., 1984
(Previously:
Legion of Super Heroes)
314 KG,V:Ontiir 1.50
315 KG(i),V:Dark Circle 1.50
316 KG(i),O:White Witch 1.50
317 KG(i),V:Dream Demon 1.50
318 KG(i),V:Persuader 1.50
319 KG(i),V:Persuader,
A:Superboy 1.50
320 DJu,V:Magpie 1.50
321 DJu,Exile,V:Kol 1.50
322 DJu,Exile,V:Kol 1.50
323 DJu,Exile,V:Kol 1.50
324 DJu,EC,V:Dev-Em 1.50
325 DJu,V:Dark Circle 1.50
326 reprint of Baxter #1 . . . . 1.00
327 reprint of Baxter #2 . . . . 1.00
328 reprint of Baxter #3 . . . . 1.00
329 reprint of Baxter #4 . . . . 1.00
330 reprint of Baxter #5 . . . . 1.00
331 reprint of Baxter #6 . . . . 1.00
332 reprint of Baxter #7 . . . . 1.00
333 reprint of Baxter #8 . . . . 1.00
334 reprint of Baxter #9 . . . . 1.00
335 reprint of Baxter #10 . . . . . . 1.00
336 reprint of Baxter #11 . . . . . . 1.00
337 reprint of Baxter #12 . . . . . . 1.00
338 reprint of Baxter #13 . . . . . . 1.00
339 reprint of Baxter #14 . . . . . . 1.00
340 reprint of Baxter #15 . . . . . . 1.00
341 reprint of Baxter #16 . . . . . . 1.00
342 reprint of Baxter #17 . . . . . . 1.00
343 reprint of Baxter #19 . . . . . . 1.00
344 reprint of Baxter #19 . . . . . . 1.00
345 reprint of Baxter #20 . . . . . . 1.00
346 reprint of Baxter #21 . . . . . . 1.00
347 reprint of Baxter #22 . . . . . . 1.00
348 reprint of Baxter #23 . . . . . . 1.00
349 reprint of Baxter #24 . . . . . . 1.00
350 reprint of Baxter #25 . . . . . . 1.00
351 reprint of Baxter #26 . . . . . . 1.00
352 reprint of Baxter #27 . . . . . . 1.00
353 reprint of Baxter #28 . . . . . . 1.00

DC COMICS

354 reprint of Baxter #29 . . . . . . 1.00
Ann.#4 rep. Baxter Ann.#1 . . . . . 1.00
Ann.#5 rep. Baxter Ann.#2 . . . . . 1.00

TALES OF THE
NEW TEEN TITANS
June, 1982

1 GP, O:Cyborg 2.00
2 GP, O:Raven 2.00
3 GD, O:Changling 2.00
4 GP/EC,O:Starfire 2.00

TALES OF THE
TEEN TITANS
(see NEW TEEN TITANS)

Tales of the Unexpected #6
© DC Comics, Inc.

TALES OF THE
UNEXPECTED
1956–68

1 The Out-Of-The-World Club 1,000.00
2 . . . . 500.00
3 . . . . 375.00
4 Seven Steps to the Unknown 375.00
5 . . . . 375.00
6 'The Girl in the Bottle' 275.00
7 NC(c),Pen That Never Lied . 275.00
8 . . . . 275.00
9 LSt(c),The Amazing Cube . . 275.00
10 MMe(c),The Strangest Show
   On Earth 275.00
11 LSt(c),Who Am I? 175.00
12 JK,Four Threads of Doom . . 200.00
13 JK(c),Weapons of Destiny . . 200.00
14 SMo(c),The Forbidden Game 175.00
15 JK,MMe,Three Wishes
   to Doom 200.00
16 JK,The Magic Hammer 200.00
17 JK,Who Is Mr. Ashtar? 200.00
18 JK(c),MMe,A Man Without A
   World 200.00
19 NC,Man From Two Worlds . 150.00
20 NC(c),The Earth Gladiator . 150.00
21 JK,The Living Phantoms . . . 200.00
22 JK(c),The Man From Robot
   Island 200.00

23 JK,The Invitation From Mars! 200.00
24 LC,The Secret Of Planetoid
   Zero! 175.00
25 The Sorcerer's Asteroid! . . . 175.00
26 MMe,The Frozem City 175.00
27 MMe,The Prison In Space . . 175.00
28 The Melting Planet 175.00
29 The Phantom Raider 175.00
30 The Jinxed Planet 175.00
31 RH,Keep Off Our Planet . . . 125.00
32 Great Space Cruise Mystery 125.00
33 The Man Of 1,000 Planets . 125.00
34 Ambush In Outer Space . . . 125.00
35 MMe,I was a Space Refugee 125.00
36 The Curse Of The
   Galactic Goodess 125.00
37 The Secret Prisoners
   Of Planet 13 . . . . 125.00
38 The Stunt Man Of Space . . 125.00
39 The Creatures From The
   Space Globe 125.00
40 B:Space Ranger,The Last
   Days Of Planet Mars! 900.00
41 SMo(c),The Destroyers From
   The Stars! 300.00
42 The Secret Of The
   Martian Helmet 300.00
43 The Riddle Of The Burning
   Treasures,I:Space Ranger . 700.00
44 DD&SMo(c),The Menace Of
   The Indian Aliens 225.00
45 DD&SMo(c),The Sheriff
   From Jupiter 225.00
46 DD&SMo(c),The
   Duplicate Doom! 225.00
47 DD(c),The Man Who Stole
   The Solar System 150.00
48 Bring 'Em Back Alive-
   Space 150.00
49 RH,The Fantastic Lunar-Land 150.00
50 MA,King Barney The Ape . . 150.00
51 Planet Earth For Sale 125.00
52 Prisoner On Pluto 125.00
53 InterplanetaryTroubleShooter 125.00
54 The Ugly Sleeper Of Klanth,
   Dinosaur 150.00
55 The Interplanetary
   Creature Trainer 125.00
56 B:Spaceman At Work,Invaders
   From Earth 125.00
57 The Jungle Beasts Of Jupiter 125.00
58 The Boss Of The
   Saturnian Legion 125.00
59 The Man Who Won A World 125.00
60 School For Space Sleuths . 125.00
61 The Mystery Of The
   Mythical Monsters 100.00
62 The Menace Of The Red
   Snow Crystals 100.00
63 Death To Planet Earth 100.00
64 Boy Usurper Of Planet Zonn 100.00
65 The Creature That
   Couldn't Exist 100.00
66 MMe,Trap Of The Space
   Convict 100.00
67 The Giant That
   Devoured A Village 100.00
68 Braggart From Planet Brax . 75.00
69 Doom On Holiday Asteroid . . 75.00
70 The Hermit Of Planetoid X . . 75.00
71 Manhunt In Galaxy G-2! . . . 75.00
72 The Creature Of 1,000 Dooms 75.00
73 The Convict Defenders
   Of Space! 75.00
74 Prison Camp On Asteroid X-3! 75.00

75 The Hobo Jungle Of Space . . 75.00
76 The Warrior Of Two Worlds! . 75.00
77 Dateline-Outer Space 75.00
78 The Siren Of Space 75.00
79 Big Show On Planet Earth! . . 75.00
80 The Creature Tamer! 75.00
81 His Alien Master! 75.00
82 Give Us Back Our Earth!,
   E:Space Ranger 75.00
83 DD&SMo(c),The Anti-Hex
   Merchant! 45.00
84 DD&SMo(c),The Menace Of
   The 50-Fathom Men 45.00
85 JkS(c),The Man Who Stole My
   Powers,B:Green Glob 45.00
86 DD&SMo(c),They'll Never
   Take Me Alive! 40.00
87 JkS(c),The Manhunt Through
   Two Worlds 40.00
88 DD&SMo(c),GK,The Fear
   Master 40.00
89 DD,SMo(c),Nightmare on Mars 40.00
90 JkS(c),The Hero Of 5,000 BC 40.00
91 JkS(c),The Prophetic Mirages,
   I:Automan 40.00
92 The Man Who Dared To Die! 40.00
93 JkS(c),Prisoners Of Hate
   Island 40.00
94 The Monster Mayor - USA . . 40.00
95 The Secret Of Chameleo-Man 40.00
96 Wanted For Murder...1966...
   6966 . . . . 40.00
97 One Month To Die 40.00
98 Half-Man/Half Machine 40.00
99 JkS(c),Nuclear Super-Hero! . 40.00
100 Judy Blonde, Secret Agent! . 40.00
101 The Man in The Liquid Mask! 35.00
102 Bang!Bang! You're Dead . . 35.00
103 JA,ABC To Disaster 35.00
104 NA(c),Master Of The
   Voodoo Machine 35.00

Becomes:

UNEXPECTED, THE
1968–82

105 The Night I Watched
   Myself Die 25.00
106 B:Johnny Peril,The Doorway
   Into Time 18.00
107 MD,JkS(c),The Whip Of Fear! 20.00
108 JkS(c),Journey To
   A Nightmare 18.00
109 JkS(c),Baptism By Starfire! . 18.00
110 NA(c),Death Town, U.S.A.! . 25.00
111 NC(c),Mission Into Eternity . 15.00
112 NA(c),The Brain Robbers! . . 15.00
113 NA(c),The Shriek Of
   Vengeance 25.00
114 NA(c),My Self-My Enemy! . . 25.00
115 BWr,NA(c),Diary Of
   A Madman 25.00
116 NC(c),Express Train
   To Nowhere! 15.00
117 NC(c),Midnight Summons
   The Executioner! 15.00
118 NA(c),A:Judge Gallows,Play
   A Tune For Treachery 18.00
119 BWr,NC(c),Mirror,Mirror
   On The Wall 15.00
120 NC(c),Rambeau's Revenge . 12.00
121 BWr,NA(c),Daddy's
   Gone-A-Hunting 20.00
122 WW,DG(c),The Phantom
   Of The Woodstock Festival . . 15.00
123 NC(c),Death Watch! 12.00
124 NA(c),These Walls Shall

Be Your Grave 18.00
125 NC(c),Screech Of Guilt! . . . 10.00
126 ATh,NC(c),You Are Cordially
Invited To Die! 12.00
127 GT,JK,ATh,NC(c),Follow The
Piper To Your Grave 12.00
128 DW,BWr,NC(c),Where Only
The Dead Are Free! 15.00
129 NC(c),Farewell To A
Fading Star 10.00
130 NC(c),One False Step 10.00
131 NC(c),Run For Your Death! . 10.00
132 MD,GT,NC(c),The Edge Of
Madness 10.00
133 WW,JkS(c),A:Judge Gallows,
Agnes Doesn't Haunt Here
Anymore! 12.00
134 GT,NC(c),The Restless Dead 10.00
135 NC(c),Death, Come
Walk With Me! 8.00
136 SMo,GT,NC(c),An Incident
of Violence 10.00
137 WW,NC(c),Dark Vengeance! 12.00
138 WW,NC(c),Strange Secret of
the Huan Shan Idol 12.00
139 GT,NC(c),The 2 Brains of
Beast Bracken! 10.00
140 JkS(c),The Anatomy of Hate . 8.00
141 NC(c),Just What Did Eric See? 8.00
142 NC(c),Let The Dead Sleep! . . 8.00
143 NC(c),Fear is a Nameless
Voice 8.00
144 NC(c),The Dark Pit of
Dr. Hanley 8.00
145 NC(c),Grave of Glass 6.00
146 NC(c),The Monstrosity! 6.00
147 NC(c),The Daughter of
Dr. Jekyll 6.00
148 NC(c),Baby Wants Me Dead! 6.00
149 NC(c),To Wake the Dead . . . 6.00
150 NC(c),No One Escapes From
Gallows Island 6.00
151 NC(c),Sorry, I'm Not Ready
To Die! 6.00
152 GT,NC(c),Death Wears Many
Faces 8.00
153 NC(c),Who's That Sleeping
In My Grave? 6.00
154 NC(c),Murder By Madness . . 6.00
155 NC(c),Non-Stop Journey
Into Fear 6.00
156 NC(c),A Lunatic Is Loose
Among Us! 6.00
157 NC(c),The House of
the Executioner 6.00
158 NC(c),Reserved for Madmen
Only 6.00
159 NC(c),A Cry in the Night 6.00
160 NC(c),Death of an Exorcist . . 6.00
161 BWr,NC(c),Has Anyone
Seen My Killer 10.00
162 JK,NC(c),I'll Bug You
To Your Grave 7.00
163 DD,LD(c),Room For Dying . . 5.00
164 House of the Sinister Sands . 5.00
165 LD(c),Slayride in July 5.00
166 LD(c),The Evil Eyes of Night . 5.00
167 LD(c),Scared Stiff 5.00
168 LD(c),Freak Accident 5.00
169 LD(c),What Can Be Worse
Than Dying? 5.00
170 LD(c),Flee To Your Grave . . 5.00
171 LD(c),I.O.U. One Corpse 5.00
172 LD(c),Strangler in Paradise . . 5.00
173 LD(c),What Scared Sally? . . 5.00

174 LD(c),Gauntlet of Fear 5.00
175 LD(c),The Haunted Mountain 5.00
176 JkS(c),Having A
Wonderful Crime 5.00
177 ECh(c),Reward for the Wicked 5.00
178 LD(c),Fit To Kill! 5.00
179 LD(c),My Son, The Mortician . 5.00
180 GT,LD(c),The Loathsome
Lodger of Nightmare Inn 7.00
181 LD(c),Hum of the Haunted . . 5.00
182 LD(c),Sorry, This Coffin
is Occupied 5.00
183 LD(c),The Dead Don't
Always Die 5.00
184 LD(c),Wheel of Misfortune! . . 5.00
185 LD(c),Monsters from a
Thousand Fathoms 5.00
186 LD(c),To Catch a Corpse . . . 5.00
187 LD(c),Mangled in Madness . . 5.00
188 LD(c),Verdict From The Grave 5.00
189 SD,LD(c),Escape From the
Grave 6.00
190 LD(c),The Jigsaw Corpse . . . 4.00
191 MR,JO(c),Night of the Voodoo
Curse 6.00
192 LD(c),A Killer Cold & Clammy 4.00
193 DW,LD(c),Don't Monkey the
Murder 4.00
194 LD(c),Have I Got a Ghoul
For You 4.00
195 JCr,LD(c),Whose Face is at
My Window 6.00
196 LD(c),The Fear of Number 13 4.00
197 LD(c),Last Laugh of a Corpse 4.00
198 JSn(c),Rage of the
Phantom Brain 4.00
199 LD(c),Dracula's Daughter . . 4.00
200 GT,RA&DG(c),A:Johnny Peril,
House on the Edge of Eternity 6.00
201 Do Unto Others 4.00
202 JO,LD(c),Death Trap 4.00
203 MK(c),Hang Down Your
Head, Joe Mundy 4.00
204 DN,JKu(c),Twinkle, Twinkle
Little Star 4.00
205 JkS,A:Johnny Peril,The Second
Possession of Angela Lake . . 4.00
206 JkS,A:Johnny Peril,The
Ultimate Assassin 4.00
207 JkS,A:Johnny Peril,Secret of
the Second Star 4.00
208 JkS,A:Johnny Peril,Factory
of Fear 4.00
209 JkS,Game for the Ghastly . . . 4.00
210 Vampire of the Apes,Time
Warp 4.00
211 A:Johnny Peril,The Temple
of the 7 Stars 4.00
212 JkS,MK(c),A:Johnny Peril,The
Adventure of the Angel's Smile 4.00
213 A:Johnny Peril,The Woman
Who Died Forever 4.00
214 JKu(c),Slaughterhouse Arena 4.00
215 JKu(c),Is Someone
Stalking Sandra 4.00
216 GP,JKu(c),Samurai Nightmare 4.00
217 ShM,DSp,EC(c),Dear Senator 4.00
218 KG,ECh&DG(c),I'll Remember
You Yesterday 4.00
219 JKu(c),A Wild Tale 4.00
220 ShM,JKu(c),The Strange
Guide 4.00
221 SD,ShM,JKu(c),Em the
Energy Monster 4.00
222 KG,SD(c) 4.00

TALES OF THE WILDERNESS
1 GK,special 2.00

TALOS OF THE WILDERNESS SEA
Aug. 1987
1-shot GK 2.00

TANK GIRL
1995
1 Movie Adaptation 5.95

TANK GIRL: APOCALYPSE
1995–96
1 AIG,BBo(c) 2.25
2 AIG,BBo(c)Tank Girl Pregnant . 2.25
3 AIG,BBo(c) 2.25
4 AIG, finale 2.25

TANK GIRL: THE ODYSSEY
Vertigo 1995
1 New Limited Series 2.25
2 BBo(c),Land of Milk & Honey . . 2.25
3 I:The Sirens 2.25

Tarzan #212 © DC Comics, Inc.

TARZAN
April, 1972
(Previously published by Gold Key)
207 JKu,O:Tarzan,pt.1 . . . . 5.00
208 thru 210 JKu,O:Tarzan,pt.2–4 3.00
211 thru 258 Feb., 1977 . . . . . @2.00

TARZAN FAMILY
Nov.–Dec., 1975
(Previously: Korak, Son of Tarzan)
60 B:Korak 1.25
61 thru 66 Nov.–Dec.,1976 . . . @1.25

TEAM TITANS
1992–94
1 KM,Total Chaos#3,A:New Titans,

DC COMICS

Deathstroke,V:Lord Chaos,
  BU:KGa,Killowat 2.50
1a BU:AV(i),Mirage 2.50
1b BU:MN,GP,Nightrider 2.50
1c BU:AH,Redwing 2.50
1d BU:GP(i),Terra 2.50
2 KM,Total Chaos#6,A:New
  Titans, V:Chaos,C:Battalion . . . 2.00
3 KM,Total Chaos#9,V:Lord
  Chaos, A:New Titans 2.00
4 KM,Titans Sell-Out#4,
  J:Battalion, Troia 2.00
5 KM,A:Battalion 2.00
6 ANi,A:Battalion 2.00
7 PJ,I:Nightwing of 2001 . . . . . 2.00
8 PJ,A:Raven 2.00
9 PJ,V:Bloodwing 2.00
10 PJ,V:Vampiric Creatures 2.00
11 PJ,F:Battalion 2.00
12 PJ,F:Battalion 2.00
13 PJ,New Direction 2.00
14 PJ,V:Clock King,Chronos,Calander
  Man,Time Commander 2.00
15 PJ 2.00
16 PJ,F:Nightrider 2.00
17 PJ,A:Deathwing 2.00
18 IR:Leader 2.00
19 V:Leader 2.00
20 PJ,V:Lazarium 2.00
21 PJ,V:US Government 2.00
22 PJ,A:Chimera 2.25
23 PJ,I:Warhawk(Redwing) 2.25
24 PJ,Zero Hour,R.Kole,last issue 2.25
Ann.#1 I:Chimera 3.50
Ann.#2 PJ,Elseworlds Story 3.75

TEEN BEAT
Nov.–Dec., 1967
1 Monkees photo 17.00
Becomes:
TEEN BEAM
2 Monkees 14.00

TEEN TITANS
[1st Series]
Jan., 1966
1 NC,Titans join Peace Corps . 200.00
2 NC,I:Garn Akaru 100.00
3 NC,I:Ding Dong Daddy 50.00
4 NC,A:Speedy 50.00
5 NC,I:Ant 50.00
6 NC,A:Beast Boy 45.00
7 NC,I:Mad Mod 35.00
8 IN/JAb,I:Titans Copter 35.00
9 NC,A:Teen Titan Sweatshirts . 35.00
10 NC,I:Bat-Bike 35.00
11 IN/NC A:Speedy 30.00
12 NC,in Spaceville 35.00
13 NC,Christmas story 25.00
14 NC,I:Gargoyle 25.00
15 NC,I:Capt. Rumble 25.00
16 NC,I:Dimension X 25.00
17 NC,A:Mad Mod 25.00
18 NC,1:Starfire (Russian) 30.00
19 GK,WW,J:Speedy 21.00
20 NA,NC J:Joshua 23.00
21 NA,NC,A:Hawk,Dove 23.00
22 NA,NC,O:Wondergirl 23.00
23 GK,NC,N:Wondergirl 12.00
24 GK,NC 12.00
25 NC,I:Lilith,A:J.L.A 12.00
26 NC,I:Mal 14.00
27 NC 12.00
28 NC,A:Ocean Master 12.00

Teen Titans (1st Series) #9
© DC Comics, Inc.

29 NC,A:Ocean Master 12.00
30 NC,A:Aquagirl 12.00
31 NC,GT,A:Hawk,Dove 12.00
32 NC,I:Gnarrk 9.00
33 GT,NS,A:Gnarrk 9.00
34 GT,NC 9.00
35 GT,NC,O:Mal 9.00
36 GT,NC,JAp,V:Hunchback 9.00
37 GT,NC 9.00
38 GT,NC 9.00
39 GT,NC,Rep.Hawk & Dove . . . 9.00
40 NC,A:Aqualad 9.00
41 NC,DC,Lilith Mystery 9.00
42 NC 9.00
43 NC,Inherit the Howling Night . . 9.00
44 C:Flash 9.00
45 IN,V:Fiddler 9.00
46 IN,A:Fiddler 12.00
47 C:Two-Face 6.00
48 I:Bumblebee,Harlequin,
  A:Two-Face 11.00
49 R:Mal As Guardian 6.00
50 DH,I:Teen Titans West 10.00
51 DH,A:Teen Titans West 6.00
52 DH,A:Teen Titans West 6.00
53 O:Teen Titans, A:JLA 8.00

TEEN TITANS, THE
Aug. 1996
1 DJu(s),GP,"Titan's Children,"
  pt.1 (of 3) 4.00
2 DJu(s),GP,"Titan's Children,"
  pt.2,V:Prysm 3.00
3 DJu(s),GP,"Titan's Children,"
  pt.3 . . . . 2.50
4 DJu(s),GP,"Coming Out," pt.1,
  A:Robin 2.00
5 DJu(s),GP,"Coming Out," pt.2 . 2.00
6 DJu(s),DJu,GP,F:Risk 2.00
7 DJu(s),DJu,GP,The Atom quits
  team 2.00
8 DJu(s),DJu,GP,J:Atom,V:Dark
  Nemesis 2.00
9 DJu(s),DJu,GP,"Lost World of
  Skartaris," pt.1 . . . . 2.00
10 DJu(s),DJu,GP,"Lost World of

Skartaris," pt.2 . . . . 2.00
11 DJu(s),DJu,GP,"Lost World of
  Skartaris" concl.,A:Warlord, . . 2.00
12 DJu(s),DJu,GP,Original Titans,
  pt.1 (of 4) 48pg 2.95
Ann.#1 Pulp Heroes (High-
  Adventure) 3.95

TEEN TITANS SPOTLIGHT
Aug., 1986
1 DCw,DG,Starfire "Apartheid" . 1.50
2 DCw,DG,Starfire Apartheid#2 . 1.00
3 RA,Jericho 1.00
4 RA,Jericho 1.00
5 RA,Jericho 1.00
6 RA,Jericho 1.00
7 JG,Hawk 1.50
8 JG,Hawk 1.00
9 Changeling 1.00
10 EL,Aqualad And Mento 1.50
11 JO,Brotherhood of Evil 1.00
12 EC,Wondergirl 1.00
13 Cyborg 1.00
14 1stNightwing/Batman
  Team-up 2.50
15 EL,Omega Men 1.50
16 Thunder And Lightning 1.00
17 DH,Magennta 1.00
18 ATi,Aqualad,A:Aquaman 1.50
19 Starfire,A:Harbinger,Millenium
  X-over 1.00
20 RT(i),Cyborg 1.00
21 DSp,Flashback sty w/orig.Teen
  Titans 1.25

TEMPEST
Sept. 1996
Mini-series
1 (of 4) from Aquaman 1.75
2 new costume 1.75
3 O:Tempest 1.75
4 finale 1.75

TEMPUS FUGITIVE
1990
1 KSy,Time Travel,I:Ray 27 . . . 4.95
2 KSy,Viet Nam 4.95
3 KSy,World War I 4.95
4 KSy,final issue 4.95

TERMINAL CITY
DC/Vertigo 1996–97
1 thru 3 DMt(s),MLr, ... @2.50
4 DMt(s),MLr,I:Kid Gloves 2.50
5 DMt(s),MLr,Missing link on
  the loose 2.50
6 DMt(s),MLr, ... 2.50
7 DMt(s),MLr,A:Lady in Red . . . 2.50
8 DMt(s),MLr, ... 2.50
9 (of 9) DMt(s),MLr,finale 2.50

3-D BATMAN
1953, 1966
1 rep.Batman #42 & #48 . . . . 700.00
1a A:Tommy Tomorrow (1966) 250.00

THRILLER
Nov., 1983
1 TVE 1.75
2 TVE,O:Thriller 1.50
3 TVE 1.50
4 TVE 1.50

---

5 TVE,DG,Elvis satire 1.50
6 TVE,Elvis satire 1.50
7 TVE 1.50
8 TVE 1.50
9 TVE 1.50
10 TVE 1.50
11 AN 1.50
12 AN 1.50

THRILLKILLER
Elseworlds
1 HC(s),DIB,F:Robin and Batgirl . 3.50
2 HC(s),DIB, ... 3.00
3 HC(s),DIB,conl. 3.00

TIMBER WOLF
1992–93
1 AG(i),V:Thrust 2.00
2 V:Captain Flag 1.50
3 AG(i),V:Creeper 1.50
4 AG(i),V:Captain Flag 1.50
5 AG(i),V:Dominators,Capt.Flag . 1.50

TIME BREAKERS
DC/Helix
1 (of 5) RaP(s),CWn,time
  paradoxes created 2.50
2 RaP(s),CWn, ... 2.50
3 RaP(s),CWn,expedition to 20th
  century England 2.50
4 RaP(s),CWn,Angela travels back
  in time 2.50
5 RaP(s),CWn,final issue 2.50

TIME MASTERS
Feb., 1990
1 ATi,O:Rip Hunter,A:JLA 2.50
2 ATi,A:Superman 2.00
3 ATi,A:Jonah Hex, Cave Carson 2.00
4 ATi,Animal Man #22 x-over ... 2.00
5 ATi,A:Viking Prince 2.00
6 ATi,A:Dr.Fate 2.00
7 ATi,A:GrLantern,Arion 2.00
8 ATi,V:Vandal Savage 2.00

TITANS: SCISSORS, PAPER, STONE
Elseworlds March 1997
1 Manga style 4.95

TITANS SELL-OUT SPECIAL
1 SE,AV,I:Teeny Titans,
  w/Nightwing poster 3.75

TIME WARP
Oct.–Nov., 1979
1 JAp,RB,SD,MK(c),DN,TS 15.00
2 DN,JO,TS,HC,SD,MK(c),GK . 10.00
3 DN,SD,MK(c),TS 10.00
4 MN,SD,MK(c),DN 10.00
5 DN,MK(c),July 1980 .... 1.00

TOMAHAWK
1950–72
1 Prisoner Called Tomahawk 1,200.00
2 FF(4pgs),Four Boys
  Against the Frontier 450.00
3 Warpath 325.00
4 Tomahawk Wanted: Dead
  or Alive 325.00
5 The Girl Who Was Chief ... 325.00
6 Tomahawk-King of the Aztecs 250.00

7 Punishment of Tomahawk . . 250.00
8 The King's Messenger 250.00
9 The Five Doomed Men 250.00
10 Frontied Sabotage 250.00
11 Girl Who Hated Tomahawk . 200.00
12 Man From Magic Mountain . 200.00
13 Dan Hunter's Rival 200.00
14 The Frontier Tinker 200.00
15 The Wild Men of
  Wigwam Mountain 200.00
16 Treasure of the Angelique . . 200.00
17 Short-Cut to Danger 200.00
18 Bring In M'Sieur Pierre 200.00
19 The Lafayette Volunteers . . 200.00
20 NC(c),The Retreat of
  Tomahawk 200.00
21 NC(c),The Terror of the
  Wrathful Spirit 125.00
22 CS(c),Admiral Tomahawk . . 125.00
23 CS(c),The Indian Chief
  From Oxford 125.00
24 NC(c),Adventure In the
  Everglades 125.00
25 NC(c),The Star-Gazer of
  Freemont 125.00
26 NC(c),Ten Wagons For
  Tomahawk 125.00
27 NC(c),Frontier Outcast 125.00
28 I:Lord Shilling 150.00
29 The Conspiracy of Wounded
  Bear 175.00
30 The King of the Thieves ... 125.00
31 NC(c),The Buffalo Brave
  From Misty Mountain 100.00
32 NC(c),The Clocks That
  Went to War 100.00
33 The Paleface Tribe 100.00
34 The Capture of General
  Washington 100.00
35 Frontier Feud 100.00
36 NC(c),A Cannon for Fort
  Reckless 100.00
37 NC(c),Feathered Warriors . . 100.00
38 The Frontier Zoo 100.00
39 The Redcoat Trickster 100.00
40 Fearless Fettle-Daredevil ... 100.00
41 The Captured Chieftain 100.00
42 The Prisoner Tribe 100.00
43 Tomahawk's Little Brother . . 100.00
44 The Brave Named Tomahawk 100.00
45 The Last Days of Chief Tory 100.00
46 The Chief With 1,000 Faces . 75.00
47 The Frontier Rain-Maker 75.00
48 Indian Twin Trouble 75.00
49 The Unknown Warrior 75.00
50 The Brave Who Was Jinxed . 75.00
51 General Tomahawk 75.00
52 Tom Thumb of the Frontier . . 75.00
53 The Four-Footed Renegade . 75.00
54 Mystery of the 13th Arrows . . 75.00
55 Prisoners of the Choctaw ... 75.00
56 The Riddle of the
  Five Little Indians 75.00
57 The Strange Fight
  at Fort Bravo 100.00
58 Track of the Mask 50.00
59 The Mystery Prisoner of
  Lost Island 50.00
60 The Amazing Walking Fort . . 50.00
61 Tomahawk's Secret Weapons 50.00
62 Strongest Man in the World . 50.00
63 The Frontier Super Men 50.00
64 The Outcast Brave 50.00
65 Boy Who Wouldn't Be Chief . 50.00
66 DD&SMo(c),A Trap For

Tomahawk 50.00
67 DD&SMo(c),Frontier Sorcerer 50.00
68 DD&SMo(c),Tomahawk's
  Strange Ally 50.00
69 DD&SMo(c),Tracker-King
  of the Wolves 50.00
70 DD&SMo(c),Three Tasks
  for Tomahawk 50.00
71 DD&SMo(c),The Boy Who
  Betrayed His Country 50.00
72 DD&SMo(c),The Frontier Pupil 50.00
73 DD&SMo(c),The Secret of
  the Indian Sorceress 50.00
74 DD&SMo(c),The Great
  Paleface Masquerade 50.00
75 DD&SMo(c),The Ghost of
  Lord Shilling 50.00
76 DD&SMo(c),The Totem-Pole
  Trail 50.00
77 DD&SMo(c),The Raids of
  the One-Man Tribe 50.00
78 DD&SMo(c),The Menace
  of the Mask 50.00
79 DD&SMo(c),Eagle Eye's
  Debt of Honor 50.00
80 DD&SMo(c),The Adventures
  of Tracker 35.00
81 The Strange Omens of
  the Indian Seer 35.00
82 The Son of the Tracker 35.00
83 B:Tomahawk Rangers,
  Against the Tribe 35.00
84 There's a Coward Among
  the Rangers 35.00
85 The Wispering War 35.00
86 Rangers vs. King Colossus . . 20.00
87 The Secrets of Sgt.
  Witch Doctor 20.00
88 The Rangers Who Held
  Back the Earth 20.00
89 The Terrible Tree-Man 20.00
90 The Prisoner In The Pit 20.00
91 The Tribe Below the Earth ... 20.00
92 The Petrified Sentry of
  Peaceful Valley 20.00
93 The Return of King Colosso . 20.00
94 Rip Van Ranger 20.00
95 The Tribe Beneath the Sea .. 20.00
96 The Ranger Killers 20.00
97 The Prisoner Behind the
  Bull's-Eye 20.00
98 The Pied Piper Rangers 20.00
99 The Rangers vs.ChiefCobweb 20.00
100 The Weird Water-Tomahawk 20.00
101 Tomahawk, Enemy Spy ... 15.00
102 The Dragon Killers 15.00
103 The Frontier Frankenstein . 15.00
104 The Fearful Freak of
  Dunham's Dungeon 15.00
105 The Attack of the Gator God 15.00
106 The Ghost of Tomahawk ... 15.00
107 Double-Cross of the
  Gorilla Ranger 15.00
108 New Boss For the Rangers . 15.00
109 The Caveman Ranger 15.00
110 Tomahawk Must Die 15.00
111 Vengeance of the Devil-Dogs 8.00
112 The Rangers vs. Tomahawk . 8.00
113 The Mad Miser of
  Carlisle Castle 8.00
114 The Terrible Power of
  Chief Iron Hands 8.00
115 The Deadly Flaming Ranger . 8.00
116 NA(c),The Last Mile of
  Massacre Trail 8.00

DC COMICS

DC COMICS

117 NA(c),Rangers'Last Stand . . . 8.00
118 NA(c),Tomahawk, Guilty
    of Murder 8.00
119 NA(c),Bait For a Buzzard . . . 8.00
120 NC(c),The Coward Who
    Lived Forever 8.00
121 NA(c),To Kill a Ranger 8.00
122 IN(c),Must the Brave Die . . . 8.00
123 NA(c),The Stallions of Death . 8.00
124 NA(c),The Valley of
    No Return 8.00
125 NA(c),A Chief's Feather
    For Little Bear 8.00
126 NA(c),The Baron of
    Gallows Hill 8.00
127 NA(c),The Devil is Waiting . . 8.00
128 NA(c),Rangers-Your 9
    Lives For Mine 8.00
129 NA(c),Treachery at
    Thunder Ridge 8.00
130 NA(c),Deathwatch at
    Desolation Valley 8.00
131 JKu(c),B:Son of Tomahawk,
    Hang Him High 8.00
132 JKu(c),Small Eagle...Brother
    Hawk 6.00
133 JKu(c),Scalp Hunter 6.00
134 JKu(c),The Rusty Ranger . . . 6.00
135 JKu(c),Death on Ghost
    Mountain 6.00
136 JKu(c),A Piece of Sky 6.00
137 JKu(c),Night of the Knife . . . 6.00
138 JKu(c),A Different Kind
    of Christmas 6.00
139 JKu(c),Death Council 6.00
140 Jku(c),The Rescue 6.00

TOR
May-June, 1975
1 JKu,O:Tor 1.25
2 thru 6, Tor reprints . . . . @1.25

TOTAL JUSTICE
Sept. 1996
1 thru 3 CPr(s),RBe,DG, toy
    line tie-in . . . . @2.25

Tor #1 © DC Comics, Inc.

TOTAL RECALL
1990
1 Movie Adaption 3.00

TRANSMETROPOLITAN
DC/Helix July 1997
1 WEI,DaR,JeM, gonzo journalism
    in 21st century 2.50

TRIUMPH
[Mini-Series] 1995
1 From Zero Hour 1.75
2 Teamates Peril 1.75
3 V:Mind Readers 1.75

TSR WORLDS
TSR 1990
1 I:SpellJammer 4.50

TV SCREEN CARTOONS
(see REAL SCREEN COMICS)

2020 VISIONS
DC/Vertigo April 1997
1 (of 12) the Disunited States
    of America 2.25
2 JaD(s), ... 2.25
3 JaD(s), ... 2.25
4 JaD(s),WaP, "La Tormenta"
    pt.1 (of 3) 2.25
5 JaD(s),WaP, "La Tormenta" pt.2 2.25

TWILIGHT
1990–91
1 JL,Last Frontier 5.50
2 JL,K.SorensenVs.T.Tomorrow . 4.95
3 JL,K.SorensenVs.T.Tomorrow
    (Conclusion) 4.95

UNAUTHORIZED BIO OF LEX LUTHOR
1 EB 3.95

UNDERWORLD
Dec., 1987
1 EC,New Yorks Finest 1.25
2 EC,A:Black Racer 1.25
3 EC,V:Black Racer 1.25
4 EC,final issue 1.25

UNDERWORLD UNLEASHED
1995–96
1 PWa,F:Neron 2.95
2 PWa,Neron Vs.Green Lantern . 2.95
3 PWa,conclusion 2.95
Abyss—Hell's Sentinel 1-shot . . 2.95
Apokolips-Dark Uprising 1-shot . 2.95
Batman—Devil's Asylum 1-shot
    AIG,BSz 2.95
Patterns of Fear 1-shot 2.95

UNEXPECTED, THE
(see TALES OF THE UNEXPECTED)

UNKNOWN SOLDIER
(see STAR SPANGLED)

UNKNOWN SOLDIER
April, 1977
1 True Origin revealed,Viet
    Nam 1970 . . . . 1.50
2 Origin contd.,Iran 1977 . . . . . 1.50
3 Origin contd.Afghanistan1982 . 1.50
4 Nicaragua 1.50
5 Nicaragua contd. 1.50
6 . . . . 1.50
7 Libia 1.50
8 Siberia, U.S.S.R. 1.75
9 North Korea 1952 . . . . 1.75
10 C.I.A. 1.75
11 C.I.A., Army Intelligence 1.75
12 final issue,Oct.1982 . . . . 1.75

UNKNOWN SOLDIER
DC/Vertigo Feb. 1997
1 (of 4) GEn(s),KPI,F:maverick
    CIA agent 2.50
2 GEn(s),KPI,search for Unknown
    Soldier continues 2.50
3 GEn(s),KPI,search for Unknown
    Soldier continues 2.50
4 GEn(s),KPI,intrigue, finale 2.50

UNTOLD LEGEND OF BATMAN
July, 1980
1 JA,JBy,(1st DC work)O:Batman 6.00
2 JA,O:Joker&Robin 4.50
3 JA,O:Batgirl 4.50

V
(TV Adaptation)
Feb., 1985
1 CI/TD 1.35
2 CI/TD 1.25
3 CI/TD 1.25
4 CI/TD 1.25
5 CI/TD 1.25
6 CI/TD 1.25
7 CI/TD 1.25
8 CI/TD 1.25
9 CI/TD 1.25
10 CI/TD 1.25
11 CI/TD 1.25
12 CI/TD 1.25
13 CI/TD 1.25
14 CI/TD 1.25
15 CI/TD 1.25
16 CI/TD 1.25
17 DG 1.25
18 DG 1.25

VALOR
1992–94
1 N:Valor,A:Lex Luthor Jr 2.00
2 MBr,AG,V:Supergirl 1.50
3 MBr,AG,V:Lobo 1.50
4 MBr,AG,V:Lobo 1.50
5 MBr,A:Blasters 1.50
6 A:Blasters,V:Kanjar Ru 1.50
7 A:Blasters 1.50
8 AH(c),V:The Unimaginable . . . 1.50
9 AH(c),PCu,A:Darkstar 1.50
10 AH(c),V:Unimaginable 1.50
11 A:Legionnaires 1.50
12 AH(c),B:D.O.A. 3.00
13 AH(c),D:Valor's Mom 3.00
14 AH(c),A:JLA,Legionnaires 2.50
15 SI(c),D.O.A #4. . . . . 2.00
16 CDo,D.O.A #5. . . . . 2.00

Valor #13 © DC Comics, Inc.

17 CDo,LMc,D:Valor	1.75
18 A:Legionnaires	1.75
19 CDo,A:Legionnaires,V:Glorith	1.75
20 CDo,A:Wave Rider	1.75
21	1.75
22 End of an Era,pt.2	1.75
23 Zero Hour	2.50

VAMPS
Vertigo 1994–95

1 BB(c)	3.00
2 BB(c)	2.50
3 thru 5 BB(c)	@2.25
6 BB(c),last issue	2.25
TPB	9.95

VAMPS:
HOLLYWOOD & VEIN
Vertigo 1996

1 F:Mink	2.25
2	2.25
3 I:Maggot	2.25
4 F:Mink,Screech	2.25
5 off to rescue Hugh Evans (of 6)	2.25
6	2.25

VERMILLION
DC/Helix Aug. 1996

1 ADv,MKu(c) Lucius Shepard story	2.50
2 ADv,MKu(c) Jonathan Cave's cover blown	2.50
3 ADv,riot aboard space ship, Ildiko's tale	2.50
4 ADv,Starship's engines run wild	2.50
5 ADv	2.50
6 ADv,Creation of Vermillion	2.50
7 ADv,Jonathan Cave discovers hiding place of enemy	2.50
8 ADv,"Joyland"	2.50
9 GEr, the library in Kaia Mortai	2.50
10 GEr, "Lord Iron and Lady Manganese, pt.2	2.50
11 GEr,"Lord Iron and Lady Manganese" concl.	2.50
12 final issue	2.50

V FOR VENDETTA
Sept., 1988

1 Reps.Warrior Mag(U.K.),I:V, A:M.Storm (Moore scripts)	5.00
2 Murder Spree	3.50
3 Govt. Investigators close in	3.00
4 T.V. Broadcast take-over	3.00
5 Govt.Corruption Expose	3.00
6 Evey in Prison	3.00
7 Evey released	2.50
8 Search for V,A:Finch	2.50
9 V:Finch	2.50
10 D:V	2.50
TPB 1990	14.95

VERTIGO GALLERY:
DREAMS AND
NIGHTMARES
1995

1 Various artists	3.50

VERTIGO JAM
1993

1 GF(c),NGa(s),ANo(s),PrM(s),GEn(s), JaD(s),KN,SDi,SEa,NyC(s),EiS,PhH, KDM(i),SeP,MiA,RaP(s),MPn(i), Vertigo Short Stories	4.50

VERTIGO PREVIEW
1992

Preview of new Vertigo titles, new Sandman story	1.75

VERTIGO VERITE:
THE SYSTEM

1 thru 3	@2.95
GN Seven Miles a Second	7.95

VERTIGO VERITE:
THE UNSEEN HAND
DC/Vertigo 1996

1 thru 3 TLa	@2.50
4 TLa, final issue	2.50

VERTIGO VISIONS:
DR. OCCULT

1 F:Dr. Occult	3.95

VERTIGO VISIONS:
THE GEEK
1993

1 RaP(s),MiA,V:Dr.Abuse	4.25

VERTIGO VISIONS:
PHANTOM STRANGER
1993

1 AaK(s),GyD,The Infernal House	3.75

VERTIGO VISIONS:
THE EATERS
1995

1 I:The Quills	4.95

VIGILANTE
Oct., 1983

1 KP,DG,F:Adrian Chase	3.50
2 KP	3.00
3 KP,Cyborg	2.50
4 DN,V:Exterminator	2.50

Vigilante #33 © DC Comics, Inc.

5 KP	2.50
6 O:Vigilante	3.00
7 O:Vigilante	3.00
8 RA,V:Electrocutioner	2.50
9 RA,V:Electrocutioner	2.50
10 RA,DG,avenges J.J.	2.50
11 RA,V:Controller	2.00
12 GK,"Journal"	2.00
13 GK,"Locke Room Murder"	2.00
14 RA,V:Hammer	2.00
15 RA,V:Electrocutioner	2.00
16 RA	2.00
17 Moore	3.00
18 Moore	3.00
19 RA	2.00
20 A:Nightwing	2.50
21 A:Nightwing	2.50
22	2.00
23 V:Electrocutioner	2.00
24 "Mother's Day"	2.00
25 RM,V:Police Torturers	2.00
26 V:Electrocutioner	2.00
27 V:Electrocutioner	2.00
28 New Vigilante	2.00
29 RM,New Vigilante	2.00
30 RM,D:Glitz Jefferson	2.00
31 RM,New York Violence	2.00
32 RM,New York Violence	2.00
33 RM,V:Rapist	2.00
34	2.00
35 JBy(c),O:MadBomber	2.00
36 MGr(c),V:Peacemaker	2.25
37 MGr,RM,V:Peacemaker	2.25
38 MGr,PeaceMaker	2.25
39 White Slavery	2.00
40 HC(c),White Slavery	2.00
41	2.00
42 A:Peacemaker,V:Terrorists	2.00
43 V:PeaceMaker	2.00
44 DC,V:Qurac	2.00
45 I:Black Thorn	2.00
46 Viigilante in Jail	2.00
47 A:Batman	2.50
48 I:Homeless Avenger	2.00
49	2.00
50 KSy(c)D:Vigilante	2.50
Ann.#1	3.00
Ann.#2 V:Cannon	2.50

DC COMICS

VIGILANTE: CITY LIGHTS, PRAIRIE JUSTICE
1995–96
1 JeR,MCo,(of 4) 2.50
2 JeR,V:Bugsy Siegel 2.50
3 JeR 2.50
4 finale 2.50

VIPER
1994
1 Based on the TV Show 2.25
2 . . . . 2.00
3 . . . . 1.95
4 final issue 1.95

WANDERERS
June, 1988
1 I:New Team 1.25
2 V:The Performer 1.25
3 A:Legion of Superheroes 1.25
4 V:Controller Hunters 1.25
5 O:Wanderers 1.25
6 V:Terrorists 1.25
7 V:Medtorians 1.25
8 O:Psyche 1.25
9 O:Psyche 1.25
10 F:Quantum Queen 1.25
11 F:Quantum Queen 1.25
12 V:Aliens 1.25
13 V:Dinosaurs 1.25

WANTED: THE WORLD'S MOST DANGEROUS VILLIANS
July-Aug., 1972
1 rep. Batman,Green Lantern . . . 4.00
2 Batman/Joker/Penguin 5.00
3 . . . . 3.00
4 . . . . 3.00
5 . . . . 3.00
6 . . . . 3.00
7 . . . . 3.00
8 . . . . 3.00
9 . . . . 3.00

WARLORD
Jan., 1976
1 MGr,O:Warlord 14.00
2 MGr,I:Machiste 8.00
3 MGr,'War Gods of Skartaris' . . 6.00
4 MGr,'Duel of the Titans' 6.00
5 MGr,'The Secret of Skartaris' . . 6.00
6 MGr,I:Mariah,Stryker 5.00
7 MGr,O:Machiste 5.00
8 MGr,A:Skyra 5.00
9 MGr,N:Warlord 5.00
10 MGr,I:Ashiya 5.00
11 MGr,rep.1st Issue special #8 . . 4.00
12 MGr,I:Aton 4.00
13 MGr,D:Stryker 4.00
14 MGr,V:Death 4.00
15 MGr,I:Joshua 4.00
16 MGr,I:Saaba 4.00
17 MGr,'Citadel of Death' 4.00
18 MGr,I:Shadow 4.00
19 MGr,'Wolves of the Steppes' . . 4.00
20 MGr,I:Joshua clone 5.00
21 MGr,D:Joshua clone,Shadow . . 3.00
22 MGr'Beast in the Tower' 3.00
23 MGr,'Children of Ba'al' 3.00
24 MGr,I:Iigia 3.00
25 MGr,I:Ahir 3.00
26 MGr,'The Challenge' 3.00
27 MGr,'Atlantis Dying' 3.00
28 MGr,I:Wizard World' 3.00
29 MGr,I:Mongo Ironhand' 3.00
30 MGr,C:Joshua 3.00
31 MGr,'Wing over Shamballah' . . 3.00
32 MGr,I:Shakira 3.00
33 MGr,Birds of Prey,A:Shakira . . 3.00
34 MGr,Sword of the Sorceror,
   I:Hellfire 3.00
35 MGr,C:Mike Grell 3.00
36 MGr,'Interlude' 3.00
37 MGr,JSn,I:Firewing,B:Omac . . 6.00
38 MGr,I:Jennifer,A:Omac 3.00
39 MGr,JSn,'Feast of Agravar' . . . 4.00
40 MGr,N:Warlord 3.00
41 MGr,A:Askir 2.50
42 MGr,JSn,A:Tara,Omac 3.50
43 MGr,JSn,'Berserk'A:Omac . . . 3.50
44 MGr,'The Gamble' 3.00
45 MGr,'Nightmare in Vista
   Vision',A:Omac 3.00
46 MGr,D:Shakira 3.00
47 MGr,I:Mikola,E:Omac 3.00
48 MGr,EC,TY,I:Arak,Claw(B) . . . 3.00
49 MGr,TY,A:Shakira,E:Claw 2.50
50 MGr,'By Fire and Ice' 2.50
51 MGr,TY,rep.#1,
   I(B):Dragonsword 2.00
52 MGr,TY,'Back in the U.S.S.R. . . 2.50
53 MT,TY,'Sorcerer's Apprentice' . 2.00
54 MT,'Sorceress Supreme',
   E:Dragonsword 2.00
55 MT,'Have a Nice Day' 2.00
56 MT,JD,I:Gregmore,(B:)Arion . . 2.00
57 MT,'The Two Faces of
   Travis Morgan' 2.00
58 MT,O:Greamore 2.00
59 MGr,A:Joshua 2.00
60 JD,'Death Dual' 2.00
61 JD,A:Greamore 2.00
62 JD,TMd,A:Mikola,E:Arion 2.00
63 JD,RR,I(B):Barren Earth 2.00
64 DJu,RR'Elsewhere' 2.00
65 DJu,RR,A:Wizard World,
   No Barren Earth 2.00
66 DJu'Wizard World',
   No Barren Earth 2.00
67 DJu,RR,'The Mark' 2.00
68 DJu,RR 2.00
69 DJu,RR 2.00
70 DJu,'Outback' 2.00
71 DJu/DA,'The Journey Back'
   No Barren Earth 2.00
72 DJu,DA,I:Scarhart,No Barren
   Earth 2.00
73 DJ,DA,'Cry Plague' 2.00
74 DJu,No Barren Earth 2.00
75 DJu,'All Dreams Must Pass'
   No Barren Earth 2.00
76 DJu,DA,RR,A:Sarga 2.00
77 DJu,DA,RR,Let My People Go 2.00
78 DJu,RR,'Doom's Mouth' 2.00
79 PB,RM,'Paradox',No Barren
   Earth 2.00
80 DJu,DA,RR,'Future Trek' 2.00
81 DJu,DA,RR,'Thief's Magic' . . . 2.00
82 DJu,DA,RR,'Revolution' 2.00
83 DJu,RR,'All the President's
   Men' 2.00
84 DJu,DA,RR,'Hail to the Chief' . 2.00
85 DJu,RR,'The Price of Change' . 2.00
86 DJ,DA,No Barren Earth 2.00
87 DJu,RB,RR,I:Hawk 2.00

Warlord #72 © DC Comics, Inc.

88 DJu,RB,RR,I:Patch,E:Barren
   Earth 2.00
89 RB,I:Sabertooth 2.00
90 RB,'Demon's of the Past' 2.00
91 DJu,DA,I:Maddox,O:Warlord
   O:Jennifer 1.75
92 NKu,'Evil in Ebony' 2.00
93 RR,A:Sabertooth 1.75
94 'Assassin's Prey' 1.75
95 AKu,'Dragon's Doom' 2.00
96 'Nightmare Prelude' 1.75
97 RB,A:Saaba,D:Scarhart 1.75
98 NKu,Crisis tie-in 2.00
99 NKu'Fire and Sword' 2.00
100 AKu,D:Greamore,Sabertooth . 2.00
101 MGr,'Temple of Demi-god' . . . 1.75
102 I:Zuppara,Error-Machiste
   with two hands 1.75
103 JBi,'Moon Beast' 1.75
104 RR,'Dragon Skinner' 1.75
105 RR,'Stalifers of Skinner' 1.75
106 RR,I:Daimon 1.75
107 RR,'Bride of Yano' 1.75
108 RR,I:Mortella 1.75
109 RR,A:Mortella 1.75
110 RR,A:Skyra III 1.75
111 RR,'Tearing o/t Island Sea' . . 1.75
112 RR,'Obsession' 1.75
113 RR,'Through Fiends
   Destroy Me' 1.75
114 RR,'Phenalegeno Dies' 1.75
115 RR,'Citadel of Fear' 1.75
116 RR,'Revenge of the Warlord' . 1.75
117 RR,A:Power Girl 1.75
118 RR,A:Power Girl 1.75
119 RR,A:Power Girl 1.75
120 ATb,A:Power Girl 1.75
121 ATb,A:Power Girl 1.75
122 ATb,A:Power Girl 1.75
123 JD,TMd,N:Warlord 1.75
124 JD,TMd,I:Scavenger 1.75
125 JD,TMd,D:Tara 1.75
126 JD,TMd,A:Machiste 1.75
127 JD,'The Last Dragon' 1.75
128 JD,I:Agife 1.75
129 JD,Vision of Quest 1.75
130 JD,A:Maddox 1.75
131 JD,RLd,'Vengeful Legacies' . . 3.00

DC COMICS

132 'A New Beginning' 1.75
133 JD,final issue (44pg) 2.00
Ann.#1 MGr,A:Shakira 3.00
Ann.#2 I:Krystovar 1.75
Ann.#3 DJu,'Full Circle' 1.75
Ann.#4 A:New Gods,
  Legends tie-in 1.75
Ann.#5 AKu,Hellfire 1.75
Ann.#6 F:New Gods 1.50
TPB Warlord:Savage Empire,
  Rep.#1–#10,#12,Special #8 . . 19.95

[Limited Series]
1 Travis Morgan retrospective . . . 1.75
2 Fate of T. Morgan revealed . . . 1.75
3 Return of Deimos 1.75
4 V:Deimos 1.75
5 MGr(c),Skartaros at War 1.75
6 finale 1.75

WAR OF THE GODS
1 GP,A:Lobo,Misc.Heroes,Circe
  (direct) 1.75
2 GP,A:Misc.Heroes,V:Circe,
  w/poster 1.75
2a (Newsstand) 1.75
3 GP,A:Misc.Heroes,V:Circe,
  w/poster 1.75
3a Newsstand 1.75
4 GP,A:Misc.Heroes,V:Circe,
  w/poster 1.75
4a Newsstand 1.75

WASTELAND
Dec., 1987
1 Selection of Horror stories 1.75
2 . . . . 1.75
3 . . . . 1.75
4 . . . . 1.75
5 'The big crossover story' 1.75
6 . . . . 1.75
7 'Great St.Louis Electrical
  Giraffe Caper' 1.75
8 'Dead Detective' 1.75
9 . . . . 1.75
10 TT,African Folk Tale 1.75
11 'Revenge o/t Swamp Creature' 1.75
12 JO,'After the Dead Detective' . 1.75
13 TT(c),JO 2.00
14 JO,RM,'Whistling Past the
  Graveyard' 2.00
15 JO,RM 2.00
16 JO 2.00
17 JO 2.00
18 JO,RM,final issue 2.00

WATCHMEN
Sept., 1986
1 B:AMo,DGb,D:Comedian 7.50
2 DGb,Funeral for Comedian . . . 5.00
3 DGb,F:Dr.Manhattan 5.00
4 DGb,O:Dr.Manhattan 5.00
5 DGb,F:Rorschach 5.00
6 DGb,O:Rorschach 5.00
7 DGb,F:Nite Owl 5.00
8 DGb,F:Silk Spectre 5.00
9 DGb,O:Silk Spectre 5.00
10 DGb,A:Rorschach 5.00
11 DGb,O:Ozymandius 5.00
12 DGb,D:Rorsharch 5.00
TPB rep.#1–#12 . . . . 14.95

WEB, THE
Impact 1991–92
1 I:Gunny, Bill Grady, Templar . 1.25

2 O:The Web, I:Brew, Jump,
  Sunshine Kid 1.00
3 Minions of Meridian, I:St.James 1.00
4 Agent Jump vs. UFO 1.00
5 Agent Buster/Fly team-up
  V:Meridian 1.00
6 I:Posse,A:Templar 1.00
7 V:Meridian's Forces 1.00
8 R: Studs 1.00
9 Earthquest,pt.1 . . . . 2.50
10 V:Templar 1.25
11 V:Templar 1.25
12 "The Gauntlet",A:Shield 1.25
13 Frenzy#1 . . . . 1.25
14 Frenzy#2 . . . . 1.25
Ann.#1 Earthquest,w/trading card . 2.50

The Weird #2 © DC Comics, Inc.

WEIRD, THE
April, 1988
1 BWr,A:JLI 4.00
2 BWr,A:JLI 3.00
3 BWr,V:Jason 3.00
4 final issue 2.50

WEIRD
DC/Paradox Press 1997
1 B&W magazine 2.99

WEIRD WAR TALES
Sept.–Oct., 1971
1 JKu(c),JKu,RH,Fort which
  Did Not Return 6.00
2 JKu,MD,Military Madness 5.00
3 JKu(c),RA,The Pool 5.00
4 JKu(c),Ghost of Two Wars . . . 4.00
5 JKu(c),RH,Slave 4.00
6 JKu(c),Pawns, The Sounds
  of War 4.00
7 JKu(c),JKu,RH,Flying Blind . . . 4.00
8 NA(c), The Avenging Grave . . . 6.00
9 NC(c),The Promise 4.00
10 NC(c),Who is Haunting
  the Haunted Chateau 4.00
11 NC(c),ShM,Oct. 30, 1918:
  The German Trenches, WWI . . 3.00
12 MK(c),God of Vengeance 2.00
13 LD(c),The Die-Hards 2.00

14 LD(c),ShM,The Ghost of
  McBride's Woman 2.00
15 LD(c),Ace King Just Flew
  In From Hell 2.00
16 LD(c),More Dead Than Alive . 2.00
17 GE(c),Dead Man's Hands 3.00
18 GE(c),Captain Dracula 3.00
19 LD(c),The Platoon That
  Wouldn't Die 2.00
20 LD(c),Operation Voodoo 2.00
21 LD(c),One Hour To Kill 2.00
22 LD(c),Wings of Death 2.00
23 LD(c),The Bird of Death 2.00
24 LD(c),The Invisible Enemy . . . 2.00
25 LD(c),Black Magic...White
  Death 2.00
26 LD(c),Jump Into Hell 2.00
27 LD(c),Survival of the
  Fittest 2.00
28 LD(c),Isle of Forgotten
  Warriors 2.00
29 LD(c),Breaking Point 2.00
30 LD(c),The Elements of Death . 2.00
31 LD(c),Death Waits Twice 2.00
32 LD(c),The Enemy, The Stars . . 2.00
33 LD(c),Pride of the Master
  Race 2.00
34 LD(c),The Common Enemy . . . 2.00
35 LD(c),The Invaders 2.00
36 JKu(c),Escape 2.00
37 LD(c),The Three Wars of
  Don Q 2.00
38 JKu(c),Born To Die 2.00
39 JKu(c),The Spoils of War 2.00
40 ECh(c),Back From The Dead . 2.00
41 JL(c), The Dead Draftees of
  Regiment Six 2.00
42 JKu(c),Old Soldiers Never
  Die 2.00
43 ECh(c),Bulletproof 2.00
44 JKu(c),ShM,The Emperor
  Weehawken 2.00
45 JKu(c),The Battle of Bloody
  Valley 2.00
46 Kill Or Be Killed 2.00
47 JKu(c),Bloodbath of the Toy
  Soldiers 2.00
48 JL(c),Ultimate Destiny 2.00
49 The Face Of The Enemy 2.00
50 ECh(c),-An Appointment With
  Destiny 2.00
51 JKu(c),Secret Weapon 2.00
52 JKu(c),The Devil Is A
  Souvenir Hunter 2.00
53 JAp(c), Deadly Dominoes 2.00
54 GM(c),Soldier of Satan 2.00
55 JKu(c),A Rebel Shall Rise
  From The Grave 2.00
56 AM(c),The Headless Courier . . 2.00
57 RT(c),Trial By Combat 2.00
58 JKu(c),Death Has A Hundred
  Eyes 2.00
59 The Old One 2.00
60 JKu(c),Night Flight 2.00
61 HC(c),Mind War 2.00
62 JKu(c),The Grubbers 2.00
63 JKu(c),Battleground 2.00
64 JKu(c),Deliver Me For D-Day . 2.00
65 JKu(c),The Last Cavalry
  Charge 2.00
66 JKu(c),The Iron Star 2.00
67 JKu(c),The Attack of the
  Undead 2.00
68 FM,JKu(c),The Life and Death of
  Charlie Golem 2.00

DC COMICS

69 JKu(c),The Day After Doomsday	2.00
70 LD(c),The Blood Boat	2.00
71 LD(c),False Prophet	2.00
72 JKu(c),Death Camp	2.00
73 GE(c),The Curse of Zopyrus	2.00
74 GE(c),March of the Mammoth	2.00
75 JKu(c),The Forgery	2.00
76 JKu(c),The Fire Bug	2.00
77 JKu(c),Triad	2.00
78 JKu(c),Indian War In Space	2.00
79 JKu(c),The Gods Themselves	2.00
80 JKu(c),An Old Man's Profession	2.00
81 JKu(c),It Takes Brains To Be A Killer	2.00
82 GE(c),Funeral Fire	2.00
83 GE(c),Prison of the Mind	2.00
84 JKu(c),Devil's Due	2.00
85 thru 124 June 1983	@2.00

WEIRD WAR TALES
DC/Vertigo April 1997

1 (of 4) anthology	2.50
2 MK(c)	2.50
3	2.50
4	2.50

All Star Western #3 © DC Comics, Inc.

ALL-STAR WESTERN
Aug.–Sept. 1970

1 NA(c),CI	12.00
2 NA(c),GM,B:Outlaw	5.00
3 NA(c),GK,O:El Diablo	4.00
4 NA(c),GK,JKu,GM	4.00
5 NA(c),JAp,E:Outlaw	4.00
6 GK,B:Billy the Kid	4.00
7	4.00
8 E:Billy the Kid	4.00
9 FF	6.00
10 GM,I:Jonah Hex	110.00
11 GM,A:Jonah Hex	50.00

Becomes:

WEIRD WESTERN TALES
June–July, 1972

12 NA,BWr,JKu	6.00
13	6.00
14 ATh	3.00
15 NA(c),GK	6.00
16 thru 28	@2.00

29 O:Jonah Hex	8.00
30	2.00
31 thru 38	@2.00
39 I&O:Scalphunter	2.00
40 thru 70	@2.00

WEIRD WORLDS
Aug.–Sept., 1971

1 JO,MA,John Carter	10.00
2 NA,JO(c),MA,BWr	15.00
3 MA,NA	12.00
4 MK(c),MK	5.00
5 MK(c),MK	5.00
6 MK(c),MK	5.00
7 John Carter ends	5.00
8 HC,I:Iron Wolf	4.00
9 and 10 HC	@4.00

WESTERN COMICS
Jan.–Feb., 1948

1 MMe,B:Vigilante,Podeo Rick, WyomingKid,CowboyMarshal	550.00
2 MMe,Vigilante vs. Dirk Bigger	300.00
3 MMe,Vigilante vs. Pecos Kid	225.00
4 MMe,Vigilante as Pecos Kid	225.00
5 I:Nighthawk	200.00
6 Wyoming Kid vs. 'The Murder Mustang'	175.00
7 Wyoming Kid in 'The Town That Was Never Robbed'	175.00
8 O:Wyoming Kid	200.00
9 Wyoming Kid vs. Jack Slaughter	150.00
10 Nighthawk in 'Tunnel ofTerror'	150.00
11 Wyoming Kid vs. Mayor Brock	125.00
12 Wyoming Kid vs. Baldy Ryan	125.00
13 I:Running Eagle	125.00
14 Wyoming Kid in 'The Siege of Praire City	125.00
15 Nighthawk in 'Silver, Salt and Pepper	125.00
16 Wyoming Kid vs. Smilin' Jim	125.00
17 BP,Wyoming Kid vs. Prof. Penny	125.00
18 LSt on Nighthawk,WyomingKid in 'Challenge of the Chiefs'	125.00
19 LSt,Nighthawk in 'The Invisible Rustlers	125.00
20 LSt,Nighthawk in 'The Mystery Mail From Defender Dip'	100.00
21 LSt,Nighthawk in 'Rattlesnake Hollow'	100.00
22 LSt,I:Jim Pegton	100.00
23 LSt,Nighthawk reveals ID to Jim	100.00
24 The $100,000 Impersonation	100.00
25 V:Souix Invaders	100.00
26 The Storming of the Sante Fe Trail	100.00
27 The Looters of Lost Valley	100.00
28 The Thunder Creek Rebellion	100.00
29 Six Guns of the Wyoming Kid	100.00
30 V:Green Haired Killer	100.00
31 The Sky Riding Lawman	100.00
32 Death Rides the Stage Coach	100.00
33	100.00
34 Prescription For Killers	100.00
35 The River of Rogues	100.00
36 Nighthawk(c),Duel in the Dark	75.00
37 The Death Dancer	75.00
38 Warpath in the Sky	75.00
39 Death to Fort Danger	75.00
40 Blind Man's Bluff	75.00
41 thru 60	@75.00
61 thru 85	@50.00

WHERE IN THE WORLD IS CARMEN SANDIEGO?
DC/Helix 1996

1 thru 3	@1.75
4	1.75

WHO'S WHO
1985–87

1	2.00
2 thru 9	@1.50
10 inc.	1.25
11 inc. Infinity Inc.	1.25
12 inc. Kamandi	1.25
13 inc. Legion of Super Heroes/ Villains	1.25
14 inc.	1.25
15 inc. Metal Men	1.25
16 inc. New Gods	1.25
17 inc. Outsiders	1.25
18 inc. Power Girl	1.25
19 inc. Robin	1.25
20 inc.	1.25
21 inc. The Spectre	1.25
22 inc. Superman	1.25
23 inc. Teen Titans	1.25
24 inc. Unknown Soldier	1.25
25 inc.	1.25
26 inc.	1.25

WHO'S WHO
(PACKET)

1 inc. Superman	6.00
1a 2nd printing	5.50
2 inc. Flash	5.50
2a 2nd printing	5.00
3 inc. Green Lantern	5.50
4 inc. Wonder Woman	5.50
5 inc. Batman.	5.50
6 inc. Hawkman	5.50
7 inc. Shade	5.50
8 inc. Lobo	6.00
9 inc. Legion of Super-Heroes	5.50
10 inc. Robin	5.50
11 inc. L.E.G.I.O.N. '91	5.50
12 inc. Aquaman	5.50
13 Villains issue, inc. Joker	6.00
14 inc. New Titans	5.50
15 inc. Doom Patrol	5.50
16 inc. Catwoman,final issue	5.00

WHO'S WHO IN IMPACT

1 Shield	4.95
2 Black Hood	4.95

WHO'S WHO IN THE LEGION
1987–88

1 History/Bio of Legionnaires	1.25
2 inc. Dream Girl	1.25
3 inc. Karate Kid	1.25
4 inc. Lightning Lad	1.25
5 inc. Phantom Girl	1.25
6 inc. Timber Wolf	1.25
7 wraparound(c)	1.25

WHO'S WHO IN STAR TREK
1987

1 HC(c)	1.50
2 HC(c)	1.50

DC COMICS

WHO'S WHO UPDATE '87

1 inc. Blue Beetle	1.50
2 inc. Catwoman	1.25
3 inc. Justice League	1.25
4	1.25
5 inc. Superboy	1.25

WHO'S WHO UPDATE '88

1 inc. Brainiac	1.25
2 inc. JusticeLeagueInternational	1.25
3 inc. Shado	1.25
4 inc. Zatanna	1.25

WHO'S WHO UPDATE '93

1 F:Eclipso,Azrael	5.25

WILD DOG
Sept., 1987

1 mini series DG(i),I:Wild Dog	1.00
2 DG(i),V:Terrorists	1.00
3 DG(i)	1.00
4 DG(i),O:Wild Dog, final issue	1.00
Spec.#1	2.50

WINDY & WILLY
May-June, 1969

1 thru 4	@1.00

WISE SON: THE WHITE WOLF
DC/Milestone Sept. 1996

1 by Ho Che Anderson	2.50
2 thru 4	@2.50

Witchcraft #1
© DC Comics, Inc.

WITCHCRAFT
Vertigo 1994

1 CV(c),Three Witches from Sandman	4.00
2 F:Mildred	3.50
3 Final issue	3.25
TPB rep. mini-series	14.95

WONDER WOMAN
1942–86

1 O:Wonder Woman,A:Paula Von Gunther	17,000.00
2 I:Earl of Greed,Duke of Deception and Lord Conquest, A:Mars	2,000.00
3 Paula Von Gunther reforms	1,400.00
4 A:Paula Von Gunther	1,200.00
5 I:Dr. Psycho,A:Mars	1,200.00
6 I:Cheetah	1,000.00
7	1,000.00
8 I:Queen Clea	1,000.00
9 I:Giganto	1,000.00
10 I:Duke Mephisto Saturno	1,000.00
11 I:Hypnoto	700.00
12 I:Queen Desira	700.00
13 V:King Rigor & the Seal Men	700.00
14 I:Gentleman Killer	700.00
15 I:Solo	700.00
16 I:King Pluto	700.00
17 Wonder Woman goes to Ancient Rome	700.00
18 V:Dr. Psycho	700.00
19 V:Blitz	700.00
20 V:Nifty and the Air Pirates	700.00
21 I:Queen Atomia	600.00
22 V:Saturno	600.00
23 V:Odin and the Valkyries	600.00
24 I:Mask	600.00
25 V:Purple Priestess	600.00
26 I:Queen Celerita	600.00
27 V:Pik Socket	600.00
28 V:Cheetah,Clea,Dr. Poison, Giganta,Hypnata,Snowman, Zara (Villainy,Inc.)	550.00
29 V:Paddy Gypso	550.00
30 'The Secret of the Limestone Caves'	550.00
31 V:Solo	400.00
32 V:Uvo	400.00
33 V:Inventa	400.00
34 V:Duke of Deception	400.00
35 'Jaxo,Master of Thoughts'	400.00
36 V:Lord Cruello	400.00
37 A:Circe	400.00
38 V:Brutex	400.00
39 'The Unmasking of Wonder Woman'	400.00
40 'Hollywood Goes To Paradise Island'	400.00
41 'Wonder Woman,Romance Editor'	275.00
42 V:General Vertigo	275.00
43 'The Amazing Spy Ring Mystery'	275.00
44 V:Master Destroyer	275.00
45 'The Amazon and the Leprachaun'	575.00
46 V:Prof. Turgo	275.00
47 V:Duke of Deception	275.00
48 V:Robot Woman	275.00
49 V:Boss	275.00
50 V:Gen. Voro	275.00
51 V:Garo	175.00
52 V:Stroggo	175.00
53 V:Crime Master of Time	175.00
54 A:Merlin	175.00
55 'The Chessmen of Doom'	175.00
56 V:Plotter Gang	175.00
57 V:Mole Men	175.00
58 V:Brain	175.00
59 V:Duke Dozan	175.00
60 A:Paula Von Gunther	175.00
61 'Earth's Last Hour'	150.00

Wonder Woman #10
© DC Comics, Inc.

62 V:Angles Andrews	150.00
63 V:Duke of Deception	150.00
64 V:Thought Master	150.00
65 V:Duke of Deception	150.00
66 V:Duke of Deception	150.00
67 'Confessions of a Spy'	150.00
68 'Landing of the Flying Saucers'	150.00
69 A:Johann Gutenberg,Chris. Columbus, Paul Revere and the Wright Brothers	150.00
70 I:Angle Man	150.00
71 'One-Woman Circus'	135.00
72 V:Mole Goldings	125.00
73 V:Prairie Pirates	125.00
74 'The Carnival of Peril'	125.00
75 V:Angler	125.00
76	125.00
77 V:Smokescreen gang	125.00
78 V:Angle Man	125.00
79 V:Spider	125.00
80 V:Machino	125.00
81 V:Duke of Deception, Angle Man	125.00
82 A:Robin Hood	125.00
83 'The Boy From Nowhere'	125.00
84 V:Duke of Deception, Angle Man	125.00
85 V:Capt. Virago	125.00
86 V:Snatcher	125.00
87 'The Day the Clocks Stopped'	125.00
88 V:Duke of Deception	125.00
89 'The Triple Heroine'	125.00
90 Wonder Woman on Jupiter	125.00
91 'The Interplanetary Olympics'	100.00
92 V:Angle Man	100.00
93 V:Duke of Deception	100.00
94 V:Duke of Deception, A:Robin Hood	100.00
95 O:Wonder Woman's tiara	110.00
96 V:Angle Man	100.00
97 'The Runaway Time Express'	100.00
98	100.00
99 V:Silicons	100.00
100 Anniversary Issue	125.00
101 V:Time Master	90.00
102 F:Steve Trevor	90.00
103 V:Gadget-Maker	90.00

DC COMICS

104 A:Duke of Deception	90.00
105 O,I:Wonder Woman	500.00
106 W.Woman space adventure	90.00
107 Battles space cowboys	90.00
108 Honored by U.S. Post Off.	90.00
109 V:Slicker	90.00
110 I:Princess 1003	90.00
111 I:Prof. Menace	90.00
112 V:Chest of Monsters	75.00
113 A:Queen Mikra	75.00
114 V:Flying Saucers	75.00
115 A:Angle Man	75.00
116 A:Professor Andro	75.00
117 A:Etta Candy	75.00
118 A:Merman	75.00
119 A:Mer Boy	75.00
120 A:Hot & Cold Alien	75.00
121 A:Wonder Woman Family	50.00
122 I:Wonder Tot	50.00
123 A:Wonder Girl,Wonder Tot	50.00
124 A:Wonder Girl,Wonder Tot	50.00
125 WW-Battle Prize	50.00
126 I:Mr.Genie	50.00

Wonder Woman #36
© DC Comics, Inc.

127 Suprise Honeymoon	40.00
128 O:InvisiblePlane	30.00
129 A:WonderGirl,WonderTot	30.00
130 A:Angle Man	30.00
131	30.00
132 V:Flying Saucer	30.00
133 A:Miss X	30.00
134 V:Image-Maker	30.00
135 V:Multiple Man	30.00
136 V:Machine Men	30.00
137 V:Robot Wonder Woman	30.00
138 V:Multiple Man	30.00
139 Amnesia revels Identity	30.00
140 A:Morpheus,Mr.Genie	30.00
141 A:Angle Man	30.00
142 A:Mirage Giants	30.00
143 A:Queen Hippolyte	30.00
144 I:Bird Boy	30.00
145 V:Phantom Sea Beast	30.00
146 $1,000 Dollar Stories	30.00
147 Wonder Girl becomes Bird Girl and Fish Girl	30.00
148 A:Duke of Deception	30.00
149 Last Day of the Amazons	30.00
150 V:Phantome Fish Bird	30.00

151 F:1st Full Wonder Girl story	25.00
152 F:Wonder Girl	25.00
153 V:Duke of Deception	25.00
154 V:Boiling Man	25.00
155 I married a monster	25.00
156 V:Brain Pirate	25.00
157 A:Egg Fu,the First	25.00
158 A:Egg Fu,the First	25.00
159 Origin	35.00
160 A:Cheetah,Dr. Psycho	25.00
161 A:Angle Man	25.00
162 O:Diana Prince	25.00
163 A:Giganta	25.00
164 A:Angle Man	25.00
165 A:Paper Man,Dr.Psycho	25.00
166 A:Egg Fu,The Fifth	25.00
167 A:Crimson Centipede	25.00
168 RA,ME,V:Giganta	25.00
169 RA,ME,Crimson Centipede	25.00
170 RA,ME,V:Dr.Psycho	25.00
171 A:Mouse Man	15.00
172 IN,A:Android Wonder Woman	15.00
173 A:Tonia	15.00
174 A:Angle Man	15.00
175 V:Evil Twin	15.00
176 A:Star Brothers	15.00
177 A:Super Girl	15.00
178 MSy,DG,I:New Wonder Woman	15.00
179 D:Steve Trevor,I:Ching	10.00
180 MSy,DG,wears no costume I:Tim Trench	10.00
181 MSy,DG,A:Dr.Cyber	10.00
182 MSy,DG	10.00
183 MSy,DG,V:War	10.00
184 MSy,DG,A:Queen Hippolyte	10.00
185 MSy,DG,V:Them	10.00
186 MSy,DG,I:Morgana	10.00
187 MSy,DG,A:Dr.Cyber	10.00
188 MSy,DG,A:Dr.Cyber	10.00
189 MSy,DG	10.00
190 MSy,DG	10.00
191 MSy,DG	10.00
192 MSy,DG	10.00
193 MSy,DG	10.00
194 MSy,DG	10.00
195 MSy,WW	11.00
196 MSy,DG,giant,Origin rep.	12.00
197 MSy,DG	10.00
198 MSy,DG	10.00
199 JJ(c),DG	11.00
200 JJ(c),DG	11.00
201 DG,A:Catwoman	7.00
202 DG,A:Catwoman,I:Fafhrd & the Gray Mouser	7.00
203 DG,Womens lib	7.00
204 DH,BO,rewears costume	2.00
205 DH,BO	2.00
206 DH,O:Wonder Woman	2.50
207 RE	2.50
208 RE	2.50
209 RE	2.50
210 RE	2.50
211 RE,giant	3.00
212 CS,A:Superman,tries to rejoin JLA	2.50
213 IN,A:Flash	2.50
214 CS,giant,A:Green Lantern	3.00
215 A:Aquaman	2.50
216 A:Black Canary	2.50
217 DD,A:Green Arrow	2.75
218 KS,Red Tornado	2.50
219 CS,A:Elongated Man	2.50
220 DG,NA,A:Atom	2.75
221 CS,A:Hawkman	2.50

222 A:Batman	2.75
223 R:Steve Trevor	2.50
224	2.50
225	2.50
226	2.50
227	2.50
228 B:War stories	2.50
229	2.50
230 V:Cheetah	2.50
231	2.50
232 MN,A:JSA	2.50
233 GM	2.50
234	2.50
235	2.50
236	2.50
237 RB(c),O:Wonder Woman	3.00
238 RB(c)	2.50
239 RB(c)	2.50
240	2.50
241 JSon,DG,A:Spectre	2.50
242	1.50
243	1.50
244	1.50

Wonder Woman #122
© DC Comics, Inc.

245	1.50
246	1.50
247	1.50
248 D:Steve Trevor	1.50
249 A:Hawkgirl	1.50
250 I:Orana	1.50
251 O:Orana	1.50
252	1.50
253	1.50
254	1.50
255 V:Bushmaster	1.50
256 V:Royal Flush Gang	1.50
257	1.50
258	1.50
259	1.50
260	1.50
261	1.50
262 RE,A:Bushmaster	1.50
263	1.50
264	1.50
265	1.50
266	1.50
267 R:Animal Man	12.00
268 A:Animal Man	10.00

DC COMICS

Wonder Woman #288
© DC Comics, Inc.

269 WW(i),Rebirth of Wonder
   Woman,pt.1 . . . . 1.50
270 Rebirth,pt.2 . . . . 1.50
271 JSon,B:Huntress,Rebirth,pt.3 . 1.50
272 JSon 1.50
273 JSon,A:Angle Man 1.50
274 JSon,I:Cheetah II 1.50
275 JSon,V:Cheetah II 1.50
276 JSon,V:Kobra 1.50
277 JSon,V:Kobra 1.50
278 JSon,V:Kobra 1.50
279 JSon,A:Demon,Catwoman . . 2.50
280 JSon,A:Demon,Catwoman . . 2.50
281 JSon,Earth 2 Joker 3.50
282 JSon,Earth 2 Joker 3.50
283 Earth 2 Joker 3.50
284 . . . . 1.50
285 JSon,V:Red Dragon 1.50
286 . . . . 1.50
287 DH,RT,JSon,Teen Titans . . . 2.25
288 GC,RT,New Wonder Woman 1.50
289 GC,RT,JSon,New W.Woman . 1.50
290 GC,RT,JSon,New W.Woman . 1.50
291 GC,FMc,A:Zatanna 1.50
292 GC,FMc,RT,Supergirl 1.50
293 GC,FMc,Starfire,Raven 1.50
294 GC,FMc,JSon,V:Blockbuster . 1.50
295 GC,FMc,JSon,Huntress 1.50
296 GC,Fmc,JSon 1.50
297 MK(c),GC,FMc,JSon 1.50
298 GC,FMc,JSon 1.50
299 GC,FMc,JSon 1.50
300 GC,FMc,RA,DG,KP,RB,KG
   C:New Teen Titans 3.25
301 GC,FMc 1.50
302 GC,FMc,V:Artemis 1.50
303 GC,FMc,Huntress 1.50
304 GC,FMc,Huntress 1.50
305 GC,Huntress,I:Circe 5.00
306 DH,Huntress 1.50
307 DH,Huntress,Black Canary . . 1.50
308 DH,Huntress,Black Canary . . 1.50
309 DH,Huntress 1.50
310 DH,Huntress 1.50
311 DH,Huntress 1.50
312 DH,DSp,A:Gremlins 1.50
313 DH,V:Circe 1.50

314 DH,Huntress 1.50
315 DH,Huntress 1.50
316 DH,Huntress 1.50
317 DH,V:Cereberus 1.50
318 DH,V:Space Aliens 1.50
319 DH,V:Dr.Cyber 1.50
320 DH 1.50
321 DH,Huntress 1.50
322 IN 1.50
323 DH,A:Cheetah, Angle Man . . 1.50
324 DH 1.50
325 DH 1.50
326 DH 1.50
327 DH,Crisis 1.50
328 DH,Crisis 1.50
329 DH,Crisis, giant 2.00

WONDER WOMAN
[2nd Regular Series] 1987–97
1 GP,O:Amazons,Wonder Woman 4.00
2 GP,I:Steve Trevor 3.00
3 GP,I:Julia Vanessa 2.50
4 GP,V:Decay 2.00
5 GP,V:Deimos,Phobos 2.00
6 GP,V:Ares 1.50
7 GP,I:Myndi Mayer 1.50
8 GP,O:Legends,A:JLA,Flash . 1.50
9 GP,I:New Cheetah 1.50
10 GP,V:Seven Headed Hydra,
   Challenge of the Gods,pt.1,
   gatefold(c) 1.50
10a regular(c) 1.50
11 GP,V:Echidna,Challenge
   of the Gods,pt.3 . . . . 1.50
12 GP,Millenium,V:Pan, Challenge
   of the Gods,pt.3,
   Millenium x-over 1.50
13 GP,Millenium,A:Ares,Challenge
   of the Gods,pt.4 . . . . 1.50
14 GP,A:Hercules 1.50
15 GP,I:New Silver Swan 1.50
16 GP,V:Silver Swan 1.50
17 GP,DG,V:Circe 1.50
18 GP,DG,V:Circe,+Bonus bk#4 1.50
19 GP,FMc,V:Circe 1.50
20 GP,BMc,D:Myndi Mayer 1.50
21 GP,BMc,L:Greek Gods,
   Destruction of Olympus 1.50
22 GP,BMc,F:Julia, Vanessa . . . 1.50
23 GP,R:Hermes,V:Phobos,
   Prelude to New Titans #50 . . . 1.50
24 GP,V:Ixion, Phobos 1.50
25 CMa,Invasion,A:JLA 1.25
26 CMa,Invasion,V:Capt.Atom . . 1.25
27 CMa,V:Khunds,A:Cheetah . . 1.25
28 CMa,V:Cheetah 1.25
29 CMa,V:Cheetah 1.25
30 CMa,V:Cheetah 1.25
31 CMa,V:Cheetah 1.25
32 TG,V:Amazons,A:Hermes . . . 1.25
33 CMa,V:Amazons,Cheetah . . . 1.25
34 CMa,I:Shim'Tar 1.25
35 CMa,V:Shim'Tar 1.25
36 CMa,A:Hermes 1.25
37 CMa,V:Discord,A:Superman . 1.25
38 CMa,V:Eris 1.25
39 CMa,V:Eris,A:Lois Lane 1.25
40 CMa,V:Eris,A:Lois Lane 1.25
41 CMa,RT,F:Julia,Ties that Bind . 1.25
42 CMa,RT,V:Silver Swan 1.25
43 CMA,RT,V:Silver Swan 1.25
44 CMa,RT,V:SilverSwan 1.25
45 CM,RT,Pandora's Box 1.25
46 RT,Suicide Issue,D:Lucy 1.50
47 RT,A:Troia 1.25

Wonder Woman (2nd Regular
Series) #1 © DC Comics, Inc.

48 RTP,A:Troia 1.25
49 recap of 1st four years 1.25
50 RT,SA,BB,AH,CM,KN,PCR,MW
   A:JLA,Superman 2.00
51 RT,V:Mercury 1.25
52 CM,KN,Shards,V:Dr.Psycho . 1.25
53 RT,A:Pariah 1.25
54 RT,V:Dr.Psycho 1.25
55 RT,V:Dr.Psycho 1.25
56 RT,A:Comm.Gordon 1.25
57 RT,A:Clark Kent,Bruce Wayne 1.25
58 RT,War of the Gods,V:Atlas . . 2.00
59 RT,War of the Gods,
   A:Batman Robin 2.00
60 RT,War of the Gods,
   A:Batman, Lobo 2.00
61 RT,War of the Gods,V:Circe . . 2.00
62 War o/t Gods,Epilogue. 1.50
63 BB(c)A:Deathstroke,Cheetah . 1.75
64 BB(c),Kidnapped Child 1.50
65 BB(c),PCu,V:Dr.Psycho 1.50
66 BB(c),PCu,Exodus In Space#1 1.50
67 BB(c),PCu,Exodus In Space#2 1.50
68 BB(c),PCu,Exodus In Space#3 1.50
69 PCu, Exodus In Space#4 . . . . 1.50
70 PCu,Exodus In Space#5 . . . . . 1.50
71 BB(c),DC,RT,Return fr.space . 1.50
72 BB(c),O:retold 1.75
73 BB(c),Diana gets a job 1.50
74 BB(c),V:White Magician 1.50
75 BB(c),A:The White Magician . . 1.50
76 BB(c),A:Doctor Fate 1.50
77 BB(c) 1.50
78 BB(c),A:Flash 1.50
79 BB(c),V:Mayfly,A:Flash 1.50
80 BB(c),V:Ares Buchanan 1.50
81 BB(c),V:Ares Buchanan 1.50
82 BB(c),V:Ares Buchanan 1.50
83 BB(c),V:Ares Buchanan 1.50
84 BB(c),V:Ares Buchanan 1.75
85 BB(c) 15.00
86 BB(c),Turning Point 2.50
87 BB(c),No Quarter,NoSanctuary 2.50
88 BB(c),A:Superman 12.00
89 BB(c),A:Circle 11.00
90 New Direction 15.00
91 Choosing Wonder Woman . . . 8.00

92 New Wonder Woman	8.00
93 New Wonder Woman	6.00
94	3.00
95 V:Cheetah	3.00
96 V:The Joker	3.00
97 V:The Joker	3.00
98 BB(c),F:Artemis	3.00
99 BB(c),A:White Magician	3.00
100 BB(c) White Magician defeats Artemis	6.00
100a Collector's ed., holo(c)	3.95
101 V:White Magician	3.00
102 V:Metron,Darkseid	2.25
103 JBy,A:Darkseid	2.00
104 JBy,Diana takes crown?	2.00
105 JBy,Grecian artifact comes to life	2.00
106 JBy,A:The Demon,Phantom Stranger	2.00
107	2.00
108 JBy,F:The Demon,Arion,The Phantom Stranger	2.00
109 JBy,V:The Flash,I:Champion	2.00
110 JBy,V:Sinestro	2.00
111 JBy,I:New Wonder Girl, V:Doomsday	2.00
112 JBy,V:Doomsday,A:Superman	2.50
113 JBy,Wonder Girl vs. Decay	2.00
114 JBy,V:Doctor Psycho	2.00
115 JBy,beneath the Arctic ice	2.00
116 JBy,beneath the Arctic ice	2.00
117 JBy,V:Earth Moovers	2.00
118 JBy	2.00
119 JBy,fight to regain Cheetah's humanity, cont.	2.00
120 JBy,48pg., pin-ups	3.00
121 JBy,Wonder Woman reverting to clay	1.95
122 JBy,Gods of Olympus are back	1.95
123 JBy,R:Artemis	1.95
124 JBy,A:Demon	1.95
125 JBy,A:Donna Troy & JLA	1.95
Ann.#1,GP,AAd,RA,BB,JBo,JL,CS Tales of Paradise Island	2.00
Ann.#2 CM,F:Mayer Agency	2.50
Ann.#3 Eclipso tie-in	2.50
Ann.#4 Year One Annual	3.50
Ann.#5 JBy,DC,NBy,Legends of the Dead Earth	2.95
Ann.#6 Pulp Heroes (Macabre)	3.95
Spec #1 A:Deathstroke,Cheetah	2.95
Spec.#0 History of Amazons	7.00
TPB The Contest, rep. #90,#0 #91-#93	9.95
TPB The Challenge of Artemas	9.95
TPB Second Genesis JBy, rep. #101–#105	9.95

WONDER WOMAN PLUS
Nov. 1996

1 CPr(s),MC,TP,Jesse Quick and Wonderwoman	2.95

WORLD OF KRYPTON
July, 1979

1 HC/MA.O:Jor-El	1.50
2 HC/MA,A:Superman	1.00
3 HC	1.00
[2nd Series] 1987–88	
1 MMi,John Byrne script	1.00
2 MMi,John Byrne script	1.00
3 MMi,John Byrne script	1.00
4 MMi,A:Superman	1.00

WORLD OF METROPOLIS
1988

1 DG(i),O:Perry White	1.00
2 DG(i),O:Lois Lane	1.00
3 DG(i),Clark Kent	1.00
4 DG(i),O:Jimmy Olsen	1.00

World of Smallville #3
© DC Comics, Inc.

WORLD OF SMALLVILLE
1988

1 KS/AA,Secrets of Ma&Pa Kent	1.25
2 KS/AA,'Stolen Moments'	1.25
3 KS/AA,Lana Lang/Manhunter	1.25
4 KS/AA,final issue	1.25

WORLDS COLLIDE
1994

1 MBr(c),3RW,CsB,Ccs,DCw, TG,A:Blood Syndicate,Icon, Hardware,Static,Superboy, Superman,Steel,Vinyl Cling(c)	4.25
1a Newsstand Ed.	2.75

WORLD'S BEST COMICS
Spring, 1941

1 Superman vs. the Rainmaker, Batman vs. Wright	12,000.00

Becomes:

WORLD'S FINEST COMICS
1941–86

2 Superman V:'The Unknown X', Batman V:Ambrose Taylor	3,500.00
3 I&O:Scarecrow	2,700.00
4 Superman V:Dan Brandon, Batman V:Ghost Gang	2,000.00
5 Superman V:Lemuel P.Potts, Batman V:Brains Kelly	2,000.00
6 Superman V:Metalo,Batman meets Scoop Scanlon	1,400.00
7 Superman V:Jenkins,Batman V:Snow Man Bandits	1,400.00
8 Superman:'Talent Unlimited' Batman V:Little Nap Boyd, B:Boy Commandos	1,300.00
9 Superman:'One Second to Live',Batman V:Bramwell B. Bramwell	1,300.00
10 Superman V:The Insect Master, Batman reforms Oliver Hunt	1,100.00
11 Superman V:Charlie Frost, Batman V:Rob Calendar	1,000.00
12 Superman V:Lynx,Batman: 'Alfred Gets His Man'	1,000.00
13 Superman V:Dice Dimant, Batman,V:Swami Pravhoz	1,000.00
14 Superman V:Al Bandar,Batman V:Jib Buckler	1,000.00
15 Superman V:Derby Bowser, Batman V:Mennekin	1,000.00
16 Superman:'Music for the Masses, Batman V:Nocky Johnson	1,000.00
17 Superman:'The Great Godini', Batman V:Dr.Dreemo	950.00
18 Superman:'The Junior Reporters, Batman V:Prof.Brane	900.00
19 A:The Joker	900.00
20 A:Toyman	900.00
21 Superman:'Swindle in Sweethearts!'	600.00
22 Batman V:Nails Finney	600.00
23 Superman:'The Colossus of Metropolis	600.00
24	600.00
25 Superman V:Ed Rook,Batman: 'The Famous First Crimes'	600.00
26 'Confessions of Superman'	600.00
27 'The Man Who Out-Supered Superman	600.00
28 A:Lex Luther,Batman V:Glass Man	600.00
29 Superman:'The Books that couldn't be Bound'	600.00
30 Superman:'Sheriff Clark Kent', Batman V:Joe Coyne	600.00
31 'Superman's Super-Rival',Batman: 'Man with the X-Ray Eyes'	550.00
32 Superman visits Ancient Egypt	550.00
33 'Superman Press, Inc.', Batman V:James Harmon	550.00
34 'The Un-Super Superman'	550.00
35 Daddy Superman,A:Penguin	550.00
36 Lois Lane,Sleeping Beauty	550.00
37 'The Superman Story',Batman V:T-Gun Jones	550.00
38 If There were No Superman	550.00
39 Superman V:Big Jim Martin, Batman V:J.J.Jason	550.00
40 Superman V:Check,Batman:'4 Killers Against Fate!'	550.00
41 I:Supermanium, E:Boy Commandos	400.00
42 Superman goes to Uranus, A:Marco Polo & Kubla Khan	400.00
43 A:J.Wilbur Wolfingham	400.00
44 Superman:'The Revolt of the Thought Machine'	400.00
45 Superman:'Lois Lane and Clark Kent,Private Detectives	400.00
46 Superman V:Mr. 7	400.00
47 Superman:'The Girl Who Hated Reporters	400.00
48 A:Joker	400.00
49 Superman meets the Metropolis Shutterbug Society, A:Penguin	400.00
50 'Superman Super Wrecker'	400.00
51 Superman:'The Amazing Talents of Lois Lane'	400.00
52 A:J.Wilbur Wolfingham	400.00

DC COMICS

All comics prices listed are for *Near Mint* condition.

DC COMICS

World's Finest Comics #14
© DC Comics, Inc.

53 Superman V:Elias Toomey . 400.00
54 'The Superman Who Avoided
  Danger!' 400.00
55 A:Penguin 400.00
56 Superman V:Dr.Vallin,Batman
  V:Big Dan Hooker 400.00
57 'The Artificial Superman' . . . 400.00
58 Superman V:Mr.Fenton 400.00
59 A:Lex Luthor,Joker 400.00
60 A:J.Wilbur Wolfingham 400.00
61 A:Joker,'Superman's
  Blackout' 250.00
62 A:Lex Luthor 250.00
63 Superman:'Clark Kent,
  Gangster' 250.00
64 Superman:'The Death of Lois
  Lane,Batman:'Bruce Wayne...
  Amateur Detective' 250.00
65 'The Confessions of Superman',
  Batman V:The Blaster 550.00
66 'Superman,Ex-Crimebuster;
  Batman V:Brass Haley 400.00
67 Superman:'Metropolis-Crime
  Center!' 400.00
68 Batman V:The Crimesmith . 400.00
69 A:Jor-El,Batman
  V:Tom Becket 400.00
70 'The Two Faces of Superman',
  Batman:'Crime Consultant' . 400.00
71 B:Superman/Batman
  team-ups 750.00
72 V:Heavy Weapon gang 550.00
73 V:Fang 575.00
74 'The Contest of Heroes' . . . 450.00
75 V:The Purple Mask Mob . . . 400.00
76 'When Gotham City
  Challenged Metropolis 300.00
77 V:Prof.Pender 300.00
78 V:Varrel mob 300.00
79 A:Aladdin 300.00
80 V:Mole 300.00
81 Meet Ka Thar from future . . 225.00
82 A:Three Musketeers 225.00
83 'The Case of the Mother
  Goose Mystery' 225.00
84 V:Thad Linnis gang 225.00
85 Meet Princess Varina 225.00
86 V:Henry Bartle 225.00

87 V:Elton Craig 225.00
88 1st team-up Luthor & Joker . 250.00
89 I:Club of Heroes 225.00
90 A:Batwoman 225.00
91 V:Rohtul,descendent of Lex
  Luthor 175.00
92 Ist & only A:Skyboy 150.00
93 V:Victor Danning 175.00
94 O:Superman/Batman team,
  A:Lex Luthor 525.00
95 'Battle o/t Super Heroes' . . . 150.00
96 'Super-Foes from Planet X' . 150.00
97 V:Condor Gang 150.00
98 I:Moonman 150.00
99 JK,V:Carl Verril 150.00
100 A:Kandor, Lex Luthor 300.00
101 A:Atom Master 125.00
102 V:Jo-Jo Groff gang,
  B:Tommy Tomorrow 125.00
103 'The Secrets of the
  Sorcerer's Treasure 125.00
104 A:Lex Luthor 125.00
105 V:Khalex 125.00
106 V:Duplicate Man 125.00
107 'The Secret of the Time
  Creature' 125.00
108 'The Star Creatures' 125.00
109 V:Fangan 125.00
110 'The Alien Who Doomed
  Robin!' 125.00
111 V:Floyd Frisby 125.00
112 . . . . 125.00
113 1st Bat-Mite/Mr.Mxyzptlk
  team-up 125.00
114 'Captives o/t Space Globes' 125.00
115 The Curse That Doomed
  Superman 100.00
116 V:Vance Collins 100.00
117 A:Batwoman,Lex Luthor . . 100.00
118 V:Vath-Gar 100.00
119 V:General Grambly 100.00
120 V:Faceless Creature 100.00
121 I:Miss Arrowette 100.00
122 V:Klor 50.00
123 A:Bat-Mite & Mr. Mxyzptlk . . 50.00
124 V:Hroguth,E:Tommy
  Tomorrow 50.00
125 V:Jundy,B:Aquaman 50.00
126 A:Lex Luthor 50.00
127 V:Zerno 50.00
128 V:Moose Morans 50.00
129 Joker/Luthor T.U. 60.00
130 . . . . 45.00
131 V:Octopus 45.00
132 V:Denny Kale, Shorty Biggs . 45.00
133 . . . . 45.00
134 V:Band of Super-Villians . . . 45.00
135 V:The Future Man 45.00
136 The Batman Nobody
  Remembered 45.00
137 A:Lex Luthor 45.00
138 V:General Grote 45.00
139 V:Sphinx Gang,E:Aquaman . 45.00
140 CS,V:Clayface 45.00
141 CS,A:Jimmy Olsen 45.00
142 CS,O:Composite Man 45.00
143 CS,A:Kandor,I:Mailbag 40.00
144 CS,A:Clayface,Brainiac 40.00
145 CS,Prison for Heroes 40.00
146 CS,Batman,Son of Krypton . 40.00
147 CS,A:Jimmy Olsen 40.00
148 CS,A:Lex Luthor,Clayface . . 40.00
149 CS,The Game of the
  Secret Identities 40.00
150 CS,V:Rokk and Sorban 35.00

World's Finest Comics #148
© DC Comics, Inc.

151 CS,A:Krypto,BU:Congorilla . 35.00
152 CS,A:The Colossal Kids,Bat-
  mite,V:Mr.Mxyzptlk 30.00
153 CS,V:Lex Luthor 30.00
154 CS,The Sons of Batman &
  Superman(Imaginary) 30.00
155 CS,The 1000th Exploit of
  Batman & Superman 30.00
156 CS,I:BizarroBatman,V:Joker 100.00
157 CS,The Abominable Brats
  (Imaginary story) 30.00
158 CS,V:Brainiac 30.00
159 CS,A:Many Major villians,I:Jim
  Gordon as Anti-Batman & Perry
  White as Anti-Superman . . . 30.00
160 V:Dr Zodiac. 30.00
161 CS,80 page giant 35.00
162 V:The Jousting Master 25.00
163 CS,The Court of No Hope . . 25.00
164 CS,I:Genia,V:Brainiac 25.00
165 CS,The Crown of Crime . . . 25.00
166 CS,V:Muto & Genia 28.00
167 CS,The New Superman &
  Batman(Imaginary) V:Luthor . 25.00
168 CS,R:Composite Superman 25.00
169 The Supergirl/Batgirl Plot;
  V:Batmite,Mr.Mxyzptlk 25.00
170 80 page giant,reprint 25.00
171 CS,V:The Executioners 25.00
172 CS,Superman & Batman
  Brothers (Imaginary) 25.00
173 CS,The Jekyll-Hyde Heroes 25.00
174 CS,Secrets of the Double
  Death Wish 25.00
175 NA(1st Batman),C:Flash . . . 20.00
176 NA,A:Supergirl & Batgirl . . . 20.00
177 V:Joker & Luthor 22.00
178 CS,The Has-Been Superman 10.00
179 CS,giant 18.00
180 RA,ME,Supermans Perfect
  Crime 10.00
181 RA,ME 10.00
182 RA,ME,The Mad Manhunter . 10.00
183 RA,ME,Supermans Crimes
  of the Ages 10.00
184 RA,ME,A:JLA,Robin 10.00
185 CS,The Galactic Gamblers . 10.00

186 RA,ME,The Bat Witch	10.00
187 RA,ME,Demon Superman	10.00
188 giant,reprint	18.00
189 RA,ME,V:Lex Luthor	10.00
190 RA,V:Lex Luthor	8.00
191 RA,A:Jor-El,Lara	8.00
192 RA,The Prison of No Escape	8.00
193 The Breaking of Batman and Superman	8.00
194 RA,ME,Inside the Mafia	8.00
195 RA,ME,Dig Now-Die Later	8.00
196 CS,The Kryptonite Express, E:Batman	8.00
197 giant	18.00
198 DD,B:Superman T.U., A:Flash	90.00
199 DD,Superman & Flash race	90.00
200 NA(c),DD,Prisoners of the Immortal World; A:Robin	8.00
201 NA(c),DD,A Prize of Peril, A:Green Lantern,Dr. Fate	7.00
202 NA(c),DD,Vengeance of the Tomb Thing,A:Batman	7.00
203 NA(c),DD,Who's Minding the Earth,A:Quamar	7.00
204 NA(c),DD,Journey to the End of Hope,A:Wonder Woman	7.00
205 NA(c),DD,The Computer that Captured a Town,Frazetta Ad, A:Teen Titans	8.00
206 DD,giant reprint	11.00
207 DD,Superman,A:Batman, V:Dr.Light	7.00
208 NA(c),DD,A:Dr Fate	7.00
209 NA(c),DD,A:Green Arrow, Hawkman,I&V:The Temper	7.00
210 NA(c),DD,A:Batman	7.00
211 NA(c),DD,A:Batman	7.00
212 CS(c),And So My World Begins,A:Martian Manhunter	7.00
213 DD,Peril in a Very Small Place,A:The Atom	7.00
214 DD,A:Vigilante	7.00
215 DD,Saga of the Super Sons (Imaginary story)	7.00
216 DD,R:Super Sons,Little Town with a Big Secret	7.00
217 DD,MA,Heroes with Dirty Hands	7.00
218 DD,DC,A:Batman, BU:Metamorpho	7.00
219 DD,Prisoner of Rogues Rock; A:Batman	7.00
220 DD,MA,Let No Man Write My Epitaph,BU:Metamorpho	7.00
221 DD,Cry Not For My Forsaken Son; R:Super Sons	7.00
222 DD,Evil In Paradise	7.00
223 DD,giant,A:Deadman,Aquaman Robotman	9.00
224 DD,giant,A:Super Sons, Metamorpho,Johnny Quick	9.00
225 giant,A:Rip Hunter,Vigilante, Black Canary,Robin	7.00
226 A:Sandman,Metamorpho, Deadman,Martian Manhunter	8.00
227 MGr,BWi,A:The Demonic Duo, Vigilante,Rip Hunter,Deadman, I:Stargrave	7.00
228 ATh,A:Super Sons,Aquaman, Robin,Vigilante	7.00
229 I:Powerman,A:Metamorpho	7.00
230 A:Super-Sons,Deadman, Aquaman	7.00
231 A:Green Arrow,Flash	7.00

232 DD,The Dream Bomb	7.00
233 A:Super-Sons	7.00
234 CS,Family That Fled Earth	7.00
235 DD,V:Sagitaurus	7.00
236 DD,A:The Atom	7.00
237 Intruder from a Dead World	7.00
238 DD,V:Luthor,A:Super-Sons	7.00
239 CS,A:Gold(from Metal Men)	7.00
240 DD,A:Kandor	5.00
241 Make Way For a New World	5.00
242 EC,A:Super-Sons	5.00
243 CS,AM,A:Robin	5.00
244 NA(c),JL,MA,MN,TA,giant B:Green Arrow	6.00
245 NA(C),CS,MA,MN,TA, GM,JSh,BWi,giant	6.00
246 NA(c),KS,MA,MN,TA,GM, DH,A:JLA	5.00
247 KS,GM,giant	6.00
248 KS,GM,DG,TVE,A:Sgt.Rock	5.00
249 KS,SD,TVE,A:Phantom Stranger,B:Creeper	6.00

World's Finest Comics #210
© DC Comics, Inc.

250 GT,SD,Superman,Batman, Wonder Woman,Green Arrow, Black Canary,team-up	3.00
251 GT,SD,JBi,BL,TVE,RE, JA,A:Poison Ivy,Speedy, I:CountVertigo	3.00
252 GT,TVE,SD,JA,giant	3.00
253 KS,DN,TVE,SD,B:Shazam	3.00
254 GT,DN,TVE,SD,giant	3.00
255 JL,DA,TVE,SD,DN,KS, E:Creeper	3.00
256 MA,DN,KS,DD,Hawkman,Black Lightning,giant	3.00
257 DD,FMc,DN,KS,GT,RB, RT,giant	3.00
258 NA(c),RB,JL,DG,DN,KS,RT, giant	3.00
259 RB,DG,MR,MN,DN,KS	3.00
260 RB,DG,MN,DN	2.50
261 RB,DG,AS,RT,EB,DN, A:Penguin, Terra Man	4.00
262 DG,DN,DA,JSon,RT, Aquaman	2.50
263 RB,DG,DN,TVE,JSh,Aquaman, Adam Strange	2.50

264 RB,DG,TVE,DN,Aquaman	2.50
265 RB,DN,RE,TVE	2.50
266 RB,TVE,DN	2.50
267 RB,DG,TVE,AS,DN, A:Challengers of the Unknown	2.50
268 DN,TVE,BBr,RT,AS	2.50
269 RB,FMc,TVE,BBr,AS,DN,DA	2.50
270 NA(c),RB,RT,TVE,AS, DN,LMa	2.50
271 GP(c),RB,FMc,O:Superman/ Batman T.U.	2.75
272 RB,DN,TVE,BBr,AS	2.50
273 TVE,LMa,JSon,AS,DN,DA, A:Plastic Man	2.50
274 TVE,LMa,BBr,GC,AS,DN, Green Arrow	2.50
275 RB,FMc,TVE,LMa,DSp,AS, DN,DA,A:Mr.Freeze	2.50
276 GP(c),RB,TVE,LMa,DSp,CI, DN,DA	2.50
277 GP(c),RT,TVE,DSp,AS,DN, DH,V:Dr.Double X	2.50
278 GP(c),RB,TVE,LMa,DSp,DN	2.50
279 KP,TVE,LMa,AS,DN, B:Kid Eternity	2.50
280 RB,TVE,LMa,AS,DN	2.50
281 GK(c),IN,TVE,LMa,AS,DN	2.50
282 IN,FMc,GK,CI,last giant E:Kid Eternity	2.50
283 GT,FMc,GK	2.25
284 GT,DSp,A:Legion,E:G.Arrow	2.50
285 FM(c),RB,A:Zatanna	2.25
286 RB,A:Flash	2.50
287 TVE,A:Flash	2.50
288 A:JLA	2.25
289 GK(c),Kryll way of Dying	2.25
290 TD(i),I:Stalagron	2.25
291 WS(c),TD(i),V:Stalagron	2.25
292	2.25
293	2.25
294	2.25
295 FMc(i)	2.25
296 RA	2.25
297 GC,V:Pantheon	2.25
298 V:Pantheon	2.25
299 GC,V:Pantheon	2.25
300 RA,GP,KJ,MT,FMc,A:JLA	3.50
301 Rampage	2.25
302 DM,NA(rep)	2.25
303 Plague	2.25
304 SLi,O:Null&Void	2.25
305 TVE,V:Null&Void	2.25
306 SLi,I:Swordfish & Barracuda	2.25
307 TVE,V:Null&Void	2.25
308 GT,Night and Day	2.25
309 MT,AA,V:Quantum	2.25
310 I:Sonik	2.25
311 A:Monitor	2.25
312 AA,I:Network	2.25
313 AA(i),V:Network	2.25
314 AA(i),V:Executrix	2.25
315 V:Cathode	2.25
316 LSn,I:Cheapjack	2.25
317 LSn,V:Cheapjack	2.25
318 AA(i),A:Sonik	2.25
319 AA(i),I:REM	2.25
320 AA(i),V:REM	2.25
321 AA,V:Chronos	2.25
322 KG,The Search	2.25
323 AA(i),final issue	2.25

WORLD'S FINEST
[Limited Series] 1990

1 SR,KK,Worlds Apart	8.00
2 SR,KK,Worlds Collide	6.00

DC COMICS

DC COMICS

World's Finest (Ltd. Series) #1
© DC Comics, Inc.

3 SR,KK,Worlds At War		6.00
TPB rep.#1-#3		19.95

WORLD'S FINEST: SUPERBOY/ROBIN
Oct. 1996

1 (of 2) CDi&KK(s),TG,SHa, V:Poison Ivy, Metallo	4.95
2 CDi&KK(s),TG,SHa, V:Poison Ivy, Metallo	4.95

WORLD'S GREATEST SUPER-HEROES
1977

1 A:Batman,Robin	2.50

WORLD WITHOUT END
1990

1 The Host, I:Brother Bones	5.00
2 A:Brother Bones	3.50
3	3.50
4 House of Fams	2.50
5 Female Fury	2.50
6 conclusion	2.50

WRATH OF THE SPECTRE
May, 1988

1 JAp,rep.Adventure #431-#433	2.50
2 JAp,rep.Adventure #434-#436	2.50
3 JAp,rep.Adventure #437-#440	2.50
4 JAp,reps.,final issue	2.50

XENOBROOD
1994–95

0 New team	1.50
1 Battles	1.50
2 Bestiary	1.50
3 A:Superman	1.50
4 V:Bestiary	1.50
5 V:Vimian	1.50
6 final issue	1.50

XERØ
March 1997

1 Cpr(s),Ccs,Trane Walker/Xero	1.75
2 CPr(s),Ccs,"The Rookie"	1.75
3 Cpr(s),Ccs,"The Beast"	1.75
4 CPr(s)	1.75

Xombi #4 © DC Comics, Inc.

XOMBI
Milestone 1994–96

0 WS(c),DCw,Shadow War,Foil(c), I:Xombi,Twilight	2.50
1 JBy(c),B:Silent Cathedrals	2.00
1a Platinum ed.	15.00
2 I:Rabbi Simmowitz,Golms,Liam Knight of the Spoken Fire	1.75
3 A:Liam	2.00
4 Silent Cathedrals	2.00
5 Silent Cathedrals	1.75
6 Silent Cathedrals	1.75
7 School of Anguish	1.75
8 School of Anguish,pt.2	1.75
9 School of Anguish,pt.3	1.75
10 School of Anguish,pt.4	1.75
11 School of Anguish,pt.5	1.75
12 Truth and Surprises	1.75
13 V:Kinderessen	1.75
14 Long Hot Summer, A:Cheryl Saltz	2.50
15 Long Hot Summer	2.50
16 Long Hot Summer	2.50
17 Reader's Choice	2.50
18 Serpent's Tail	2.50
19 Mister Missy, Bellhop	2.50
20	2.50
21 final issue	3.50

YOUNG ALL STARS
June, 1987

1 I:IronMunro&FlyingFox,D:TNT	4.50
2 V:Axis Amerika	2.50
3 V:Axis Amerika	2.00
4 I:The Tigress	1.50
5 I:Dyna-mite,O:Iron Munro	1.50
6	1.50
7 Baseball Game,A:Tigress	1.25
8 Millenium	1.25
9 Millenium	1.25

10 Hugo Danner	1.25
11 'Birth of Iron Munro'	1.25
12 'Secret of Hugo Danner'	1.25
13 'V:Deathbolt,Ultra-Humanite	1.25
14 Fury+Ultra Humanite	1.25
15 IronMunro At high school	1.25
16 Ozyan Inheritance	1.25
17 Ozyan Inheritance	1.25
18 Ozyan Inheritance	1.25
19 Ozyan	1.50
20 O:Flying Fox	1.50
21 Atom & Evil#1	1.50
22 Atom & Evil#2	1.50
23 Atom & Evil#3	1.50
24 Atom & Evil#4	1.50
25	1.50
26 End of the All Stars?	1.75
27 'Sons of Dawn' begins	1.75
28 Search for Hugo Danner	1.75
29 A:Hugo Danner	1.75
30 V:Sons of Dawn	1.75
31 V:Sons of Dawn,last issue	1.75
Ann.#1 MG,V:Mekanique	2.25

YOUNG HEROES IN LOVE
April 1997

1 DeM,F:Hard Drive	1.75
2 DeM,sex, lies and superheroics	1.75
3 A:Superman	1.75
4 F:Hard Drive	1.75

YOUNG LOVE
Sept.–Oct., 1963

39	8.00
40 thru 50	@5.00
51 thru 70	@4.00
71 thru 80	@3.00
81 thru 126	@1.50

ZATANNA
1987

1 R:Zatanna	2.25
2 N:Zatanna	2.25
3 Come Together	2.25
4 V:Xaos	2.25

ZERO HOUR: CRISIS IN TIME
1994

4 DJu(a&s),JOy,A:All DC Heroes, D;2nd Flash	1.50
3 DJu(a&s),JOy,D:G.A.Sandman, G:A.Atom,Dr.Fate,1st Wildcat IR:Time Trapper is Rokk Krinn, Hawkmen merged	1.50
2 DJu(a&s),Joy	1.50
1 DJu(a&s),JOy,b:Power Gir's Child	1.50
0 DJu(A&s),JOy,Gatefold(c),Extant vs. Spectre	1.50

DC COMICS

AMAZON
DC (1996–97)
1 JBy,TA 3.00
1 one-shot JBy,Princess Ororo
  is Wonder Woman 1.95

ASSASSINS
DC (1996–97)
1 DGC,SMc 3.00
1 one-shot DGC(s),SMc,F:Dare
  and Catsai 1.95

BAT-THING
DC (1997)
1 one-shot LHa(s),RDm,BSz,
  V:motorcycle gang 1.95

Bruce Wayne, Agent of S.H.I.E.L.D. #1
© DC/Marvel

BRUCE WAYNE:
AGENT OF S.H.I.E.L.D.
Marvel Comics (1996)
1 CDi, ... 3.00

BULLETS & BRACELETS
Marvel Comics (1996)
1 JOs,GFr,CaS 3.00

CHALLENGERS OF
THE FANTASTIC
Marvel (1997)
1 KK,TGu,AV 1.95

DARK CLAW
ADVENTURES, THE
DC (1997)
1 one-shot TTy,RBr,V:Ladia Talia 1.95

DC VERSUS MARVEL
MARVEL VERSUS DC
1 (DC)DJu 6.00
1a 2nd printing 4.00
2 (Marvel)PDd,DJu 5.00
2a 2nd printing 4.00

3 (Marvel)DJu 4.00
4 (DC)PDd,DJu 4.00
TPB rep. mini series #1–#4 . . . . 12.95

DOCTOR STRANGEFATE
DC Comics (1996–97)
1 RMz,KN . . . .
1 one-shot RMz(s),JL,KN,Supreme
  Lord of Order 1.95

EXCITING X-PATROL
Marvel (1997)
1 BKs,BHi 1.95

Generation Hex #1
© DC/Marvel

GENERATION HEX
DC (1997)
1 one-shot,PrM(s),AdP,F:Jono Hex,
  Madam Banshee 1.95

IRON LANTERN
Marvel (1997)
1 KB,PSm,AW 1.95

JLX
DC Comics (1996–97)
1 MWa,GJ, ... 3.00
1 one-shot,MWa(s),GJ,HPo,JhD . 1.95

JLX UNLEASHED
DC (1997)
1 one-shot, CPr,"The Inextinguish-
  able Flame" 1.95

LEGENDS OF
THE DARK CLAW
DC Comics (1996–97)
1 LHa,JBa, ... 3.00
1 one-shot LHa(s),JBa, ... 1.95
1 2nd printing 1.95

LOBO THE DUCK
DC (1997)
1 one-shot, AlG,VS, ... 1.95

MAGNETO &
THE MAGNETIC MEN
Marvel Comics (1996)
1 MWa,GJ,JMs,ATi 3.00

MAGNETIC MEN
FEATURING MAGNETO
Marvel (1997)
1 TPe,BKi,DPs 1.95

SPEED DEMON
Marvel Comics (1996)
1 HMe,SvL,AM 3.00

SPIDER-BOY
Marvel Comics (1996)
1 KK,MeW 3.00

SPIDER-BOY TEAM-UP
Marvel Comics (1997)
1 KK,RSt 1.95

Super Soldier: Man of War #1
© DC/Marvel

SUPER-SOLDIER
DC Comics (1996–97)
1 MWa,DGb 3.00
1-shot MWa(s),DGb,V:Ultra-
  Metallo, Green Skull, Hydra . . 1.95

SUPER SOLDIER:
MAN OF WAR
DC (1997)
1 one-shot MWa(s),DGb,JP,
  V:Nazis 1.95

THORION OF
THE NEW ASGODS
Marvel (1997)
1 KG,JR2 . . . . 1.95

X-PATROL
Marvel Comics (1996)
1 KK,BKs, ... 3.00

All comics prices listed are for *Near Mint* condition.

MARVEL

ABOMINATIONS
1996
1 (of 3) IV,AMe, Future Imperfect
  spin-off 1.50
2 IV,AMe, ... 1.50
3 IV,AMe, ... 1.50

ABRAHAM STONE
1995
1 JKu, Early 20th century 6.95
2 Wandering Man in the 20s 6.95

ACTION FORCE
March, 1987
1 U.K. G.I. Joe Series 1.50
2 thru 39 . . . . @1.00
40 1988 . . . . 1.00

ACTUAL CONFESSIONS
See: LOVE ADVENTURES

ACTUAL ROMANCES
Oct., 1949
1 . . . . 45.00
2 Photo Cover 25.00

ADVENTURE INTO FEAR
See: FEAR

ADVENTURE INTO MYSTERY
Atlas 1956–57
1 BEv(c),Future Tense 235.00
2 Man on the 13th Floor 125.00
3 Next Stop Eternity 100.00
4 AW, The Hex 125.00
5 BEv,The People Who Weren't 100.00
6 The Wax Man 100.00
7 . . . . 100.00

ADVENTURES INTO TERROR
See: JOKER COMICS

ADVENTURES INTO WEIRD WORLDS
Jan., 1952–June 1954
1 RH,GT,The Walking Death . 350.00
2 The Thing In the Bottle 225.00
3 The Thing That Waited 150.00
4 BEv,RH,TheVillageGraveyard 150.00
5 BEv,I Crawl Thru Graves . . . 150.00
6 The Ghost Still Walks 150.00
7 Monsters In Disguise 150.00
8 Nightmares 150.00
9 Do Not Feed 150.00
10 BEv,Down In The Cellar . . . 150.00
11 Phantom 125.00
12 Lost In the Graveyard 125.00
13 Where Dead Men Walk 125.00
14 A Shriek In the Night 125.00
15 Terror In Our Town 125.00
16 The Kiss of Death 125.00
17 RH,He Walks With A Ghost 125.00
18 Ivan & Petroff 125.00
19 It Happened One Night 125.00

20 The Doubting Thomas 125.00
21 What Happened In the Cave 135.00
22 RH,The Vampire's Partner . 100.00
23 The Kiss of Death 75.00
24 Halfway Home 75.00
25 BEv,JSt,The Mad Mamba . . . 75.00
26 Good-Bye Earth 100.00
27 The Dwarf of Horror Moor . . 200.00
28 DW,Monsters From the Grave 125.00
29 Bone Dry 85.00
30 JSt,The Impatient Ghost . . . 85.00

ADVENTURES OF CAPTAIN AMERICA
Sept., 1991
1 KM,JRu,O:Capt. America 5.75
2 KM,KWe,TA,O:Capt.America . . 5.50
3 KM,KWe,JRu,D:Lt.Col.Fletcher 5.50
4 KWe,JRu,V:Red Skull 5.50

ADVENTURES OF CYCLOPS & PHOENIX
1994
1 SLo(s),GeH,AV,O:Cable 4.00
2 SLo(s),GeH,AV,O:Cable 3.50
3 SLo(s),GeH,AV,O:Cable 3.50
4 SLo(s),GeH,AV,O:Cable 3.50
TPB Rep. #1-#4 . . . . 14.95

ADVENTURES OF HOMER GHOST
Atlas June–Aug., 1957
1 . . . . 30.00
2 . . . . 25.00

ADVENTURES OF PINKY LEE
Atlas July, 1955
1 . . . . 125.00
2 . . . . 65.00
3 thru 5 . . . . @54.00

ADVENTURES OF SNAKE PLISSKIN
1997
1-shot LKa, Escape From L.A.
  movie adapt. 3.00

ADVENTURES OF SPIDER-MAN
1996
1 from animated TV show 1.00
2 V:Hammerhead 1.00
3 thru 8 . . . . 1.00
8 AS,V:Kingpin 1.00
9 MHi,A:Dr. Strange, ... 1.00
10 AS,V:The Beetle 1.00
11 AS,V:Doctor Octopus, Venom . 1.00
12 AS,V:Doctor Octopus, Venom . 1.00

ADVENTURES OF THE UNCANNY X-MEN
1995
1 Rep. 1.00

Adventures of the X-Men #12
© Marvel Entertainment Group

ADVENTURES OF THE X-MEN
1996–97
1 from animated TV show 1.00
2 X-Factor vs. X-Men 1.00
3 thru 7 . . . . 1.00
8 RMc,BHr,GyM,Gambit back in
  New Orleans 1.00
9 RMc,GyM,F:Storm 1.00
10 RMc,A:Vanisher 1.00
11 RMc,V:Man-Thing 1.00
12 RMc,Age of Apocalypse 1.00

ADVENTURES ON THE PLANET OF THE APES
Oct., 1975
1 GT,Planet of the Apes Movie
  Adaptation 2.50
2 GT,Humans Captured 2.50
3 GT,Man Hunt 2.50
4 GT,Trial By Fear 2.50
5 GT, Fury in the
  Forbidden Zone 2.50
6 GT,The Forbidden Zone,Cont'd 2.50
7 AA,Man Hunt Cont'd 2.50
8 AA,Brent & Nova Enslaved . . . 2.50
9 AA,Mankind's Demise 2.50
10 AA,When Falls the Lawgiver . 2.50
11 AA,The Final Chapter;
  Dec., 1976 . . . . 2.50

ADVENTURES OF THE THING
April–July 1992
1 rep. Marvel 2 in 1 #50 . . . . . . 2.50
2 rep. Marvel 2 in 1 #80
  B.U. Ghost Rider 1.50
3 rep. Marvel 2 in 1 #51 . . . . . . 1.50
4 rep. Marvel 2 in 1 #77 . . . . . . 1.50

     All comics prices listed are for *Near Mint* condition.

AGE OF INNOCENCE
1995
1-shot Timeslid aftermath 2.50

AIRTIGHT GARAGE
Epic July–Oct. 1993
1 thru 4 rep.Moebius GNv ... @2.50

AKIRA
Epic Sept., 1988
1 The Highway,I:Kaneda,Tetsuo,
　Koy,Ryu,Colonel,Takaski ... 20.00
1a 2nd printing 3.00
2 Pursuit,I:Number27,(Masaru) . 10.00
2a 2nd printing 4.50
3 Number 41,V:Clown Gang 9.00
4 King of Clowns,V:Colonel ... 10.00
5 Cycle Wars,V:Clown Gang 9.00
6 D:Yamagota 8.00
7 Prisoners and Players,I:Miyo .. 8.00
8 Weapon of Vengeance 8.00
9 Stalkers 8.00
10 The Awakening 8.00
11 Akira Rising 7.00
12 Enter Sakaki 7.00
13 Desperation 7.00
14 Caught in the Middle 7.00
15 Psychic Duel 7.00
16 Akira Unleashed 7.00
17 Emperor of Chaos 7.00
18 Amid the Ruins 6.00
19 To Save the Children 6.00
20 Revelations 6.00
21 .... 6.00
22 .... 6.00
23 .... 6.00
24 Clown Gang 6.00
25 Search For Kay 6.00
26 Juvenile A Project 6.00
27 Kay and Kaneda 6.00
28 Tetsuo 6.00
29 Tetsuo 6.00
30 Tetsuo,Kay,Kaneda 6.00
31 D:Kaori,Kaneda,Vs.Tetsuo . 6.00
32 Tetsuo'sForces vs.U.S.Forces . 6.00
33 Tetsuo V:Kaneda 6.00
TPB Akira:Reprints#1-#3 ..... 13.95
TPB Akira:Reprints#4-#6 ..... 13.95
TPB Akira:Reprints#7-#9 ..... 13.95
TPB Akira:Reprints#10-#12 ... 14.95
TPB Akira:Reprints#13-#15 ... 14.95
TPB Akira:Reprints#16-#18 ... 14.95
TPB Akira:Reprints#19-#21 ... 16.95
TPB Akira:Reprints#22-#24 ... 16.95
TPB Akira:Reprints#25-#27 ... 16.95
TPB Akira:Reprints#28-#30 ... 17.95
34 64pt. R:Otomo 5.00
35 Leads toward final battle 6.95
36 Lady Miyako 6.95
37 ghost of Tetsuo 6.95
38 conclusion 6.95

ALADDIN
1 .... 1.50
2 .... 1.50
3 .... 1.50
4 .... 1.50
5 A:Queen Tatiana 1.50
6 A:Zena 1.50
7 Genie Convention 1.50
8 Body Switch 1.50
9 Archery Contest 1.50
10 Genie winds back his powers . 1.50
11 Magic Carpet Grand Prix 1.50

12 F:Iago 1.50

Alf #5 © Marvel Entertainment Group

ALF
Star March, 1988
1 Photo Cover 1.50
1a 2nd printing 1.00
2 Alf Causes trouble 1.50
3 More adventures 1.50
4 Willie on Melmac 1.50
5 I:Alf's evil twin 1.50
6 Photo Cover 1.50
7 Pygm-Alien 1.50
8 Ochmoneks' Garage 1.25
9 Alf's Independence Day 1.25
10 Alf goes to College 1.25
11 Halloween special 1.00
12 Alf loses memory 1.00
13 Racetrack of my Tears 1.00
14 Night of the Living Bread ... 1.25
15 Alf on the Road 1.00
16 More Adventures 1.00
17 Future vision 1.00
18 More Adventures 1.00
19 The Alf-strologer 1.00
20 Alf the Baby Sitter,pt.1 .... 1.00
21 Alf the Baby Sitter,pt.2 .... 1.00
22 X-Men parody 1.00
23 Alf visits Australia 1.00
24 Rhonda visits Earth 1.00
25 More Adventures 1.00
26 Alf gets a job 1.00
27 Alf lost 1.00
28 Alf's Amnesia 1.00
29 Alf/Brian reporters 1.00
30 Shakespeare Baby 1.00
31 Alf's Summer Camp 1.00
32 Arnold Schwarzemeimac .. 1.00
33 Dungeons & Dragons Spoof .. 1.00
34 Alf-Red & Alf-Blue(2 Alfs) 1.00
35 Gone with the Wind 1.00
36 More Adventures 1.00
37 Melmacian Gothic 1.00
38 Boundtree Hunters 1.00
39 Pizarro Alf 1.00
40 A:Zoreo 1.00
41 TV 1.00
42 V:Alf 1.00
43 House Break-in 1.00
44 A:Fantastic Fur 1.00

45 Melmenopaus 1.00
46 Goes to Center of Earth ... 1.00
47 Meteor Bye-Products,pt.1 .... 1.00
48 Meteor Bye-Products,pt.2 .... 1.00
49 1st Rhonda solo story 1.00
50 Final Issue, giant size 1.75
Ann.#1 Evol.War 3.00
Ann.#2 .... 1.75
Spring Spec.#1 .... 1.75
Holiday Spec.#2 .... 2.00

ALIEN LEGION
Epic April, 1984
1 FC,TA,I:Sarigar,Montroc 4.00
2 FC,TA,CP,V:Harkilons 3.50
3 FC,TA,CW,V:Kroyzo 3.00
4 FC,TA,CW,F:Skob 3.00
5 FC,CW,D:Skob 3.00
6 FC,CW,WPo,V:Harkilons 3.00
7 CW,WPo,I:Lora 2.50
8 CW,WPo,V:Harkilons 2.50
9 CW,V:Harkilons 2.50
10 CW,LSn,V:Harkilons 2.50
11 CW,LSn,V:Harkilons 2.50
12 LSn,A:Aob-Sin 2.50
13 LSn,F:Montroc 2.50
14 LSn,V:Cordar 2.50
15 LSn,V:Alphor,Betro,&Gamoid . 2.50
16 LSn,J:Tomaro 2.50
17 LSn,Durge on Drugs 2.50
18 LSn,V:Dun 2.50
19 LSn,A:GalarcyScientist 2.50
20 LSn,L:Skilene 2.50

[2nd Series] Aug. 1987
1 LSn,I:Guy Montroc 3.00
2 LSn,V:Quallians 2.50
3 LSn,Hellscope 2.50
4 LSn,V:Harkillons 2.50
5 LSn,F:JuggerGrimrod 2.50
6 LSn,F:JuggerGrimrod 2.50
7 LSn,A:Guy Montroc 2.50
8 LSn,I:Nakhira 2.50
9 LSn,V:Harkilons 2.50
10 LSn,V:Harkilons 2.50
11 LSn,V:Harkilons 2.50
12 LSn,Tamara Pregnant 2.50
13 LSn,V:MomojianKndrel 2.50
14 LSn,J:Saravil 2.50
15 LSn,J:Spellik 2.50
16 LSn,D:Jugger's Father 2.50
17 LSn,O:JuggerGrimrod 2.50
18 LSn,O:JuggerGrimrod 2.50
GN Grimrod 5.95

ALIEN LEGION: BINARY DEEP
Epic 1993
1-shot with trading card 3.50

ALIEN LEGION: JUGGER GRIMROD
Epic Aug. 1992
Book One 5.95

ALIEN LEGION: ONE PLANET AT A TIME
Epic May 1993
1 HNg,CDi,One Planet at a Time 4.95
2 HNg,CDi 4.95
3 HNg,CDi 4.95

MARVEL

MARVEL

ALIEN LEGION: ON THE EDGE
Epic Nov. 1990
1 LSn,V:B'Be No N'ngth 4.95
2 LSn,V:B'Be No N'ngth 4.95
3 LSn,V:B'Be No N'ngth 4.95
4 LSn,V:B'Be No N'ngth 4.95

ALIEN LEGION: TENANTS OF HELL
Epic 1991
1 LSn,Nomad Squad On
   Combine IV 4.50
2 LSn,L:Torie Montroc,I:Stagg . . 4.50
TPB Alien Legion:Slaughterworld . 9.95

ALL-SELECT COMICS
Fall, 1943
Timely (Daring Comics)
1 B:Capt.America,Sub-Mariner,
   Human Torch;WWII 7,500.00
2 A:Red Skull,V:Axis Powers 2,500.00
3 B:Whizzer,V:Axis 1,500.00
4 V: Axis 1,300.00
5 E:Sub-Mariner,V:Axis 1,200.00
6 A:The Destroyer,V:Axis 900.00
7 E:Whizzer,V:Axis 900.00
8 V:Axis Powers 900.00
9 V:Axis Powers 900.00
10 E:Capt.America,Human Torch;
   A:The Destroyer 900.00
11 I:Blonde Phantom,A:Miss
   America 1,500.00
Becomes:

BLONDE PHANTOM
12 B:Miss America;The Devil's
   Playground 1,000.00
13 B:Sub-Mariner;Horror In
   Hollywood 650.00
14 E:Miss America;Horror At
   Haunetd Castle 600.00
15 The Man Who Deserved
   To Die 600.00
16 A:Capt.America,Bucky;
   Modeled For Murder 800.00
17 Torture & Rescue 550.00
18 Jealously,Hate & Cruelty . . . 550.00
19 Killer In the Hospital 550.00
20 Blonde Phantom's Big Fall . 550.00
21 Murder At the Carnival 550.00
22 V: Crime Bosses 550.00
Becomes:

LOVERS
23 Love Stories 50.00
24 My Dearly Beloved 25.00
25 The Man I Love 30.00
26 thru 29 . . . . @15.00
30 . . . . 30.00
31 thru 36 . . . . @15.00
37 . . . . 34.00
38 . . . . 34.00
39 . . . . 14.00
40 . . . . 14.00
41 . . . . 14.00
42 thru 65 . . . . @14.00
66 . . . . 12.00
67 ATh 35.00
68 thru 86 Aug. 1957 . . . . . @12.00

ALL SURPRISE
Timely Fall, 1943
1 (fa),F:Super Rabbit,Gandy,

Sourpuss 150.00
2 . . . . 75.00
3 . . . . 50.00
4 thru 10 . . . . @50.00
11 HK 75.00
12 Winter, 1946 . . . . 50.00

ALL-TRUE CRIME
See: OFFICIAL TRUE CRIME CASES

All Winners #13
© Marvel Entertainment Group

ALL WINNERS COMICS
Summer, 1941
1 S&K,BEv,B:Capt.America & Bucky,
   Human Torch & Toro,Sub-Mariner
   A:The Angel,Black Marvel 15,000.00
2 S&K,B:Destroyer,Whizzer . 4,000.00
3 BEv,Bucky & Toro Captured 2,400.00
4 BEv,Battle For Victory
   For America 2,500.00
5 V:Nazi Invasion Fleet 1,500.00
6 V:Axis Powers,A:
   Black Avenger 1,600.00
7 V:Axis Powers 1,200.00
8 V:Axis Powers 1,100.00
9 V:Nazi Submarine Fleet . . . 1,100.00
10 V:Nazi Submarine Fleet . . 1,200.00
11 V: Nazis 1,000.00
12 A:Red Skull,E:Destroyer;
   Jap P.O.W. Camp 1,200.00
13 V:Japanese Fleet 1,000.00
14 V:Japanese Fleet 1,000.00
15 Japanese Supply Train . . . 1,000.00
16 In Alaska V:Gangsters . . . 1,000.00
17 V:Gansters;Atomic
   Research Department 1,000.00
18 V:Robbers;Internal Revenue
   Department 1,100.00
19 I:All Winners Squad,
   Fall, 1946 . . . . 3,000.00
21 A:All-Winners Squad;Riddle
   of the Demented Dwarf . . . 2,500.00
Becomes:

ALL TEEN COMICS
20 F:Georgie,Willie,
   Mitzi,Patsy Walker 50.00

Becomes:

TEEN COMICS
21 A:George,Willie,Mitzi,
   Patsy Walker 55.00
22 A:George,Willie,Margie,
   Patsy Walker 30.00
23 A:Patsy Walker,Cindy,George 30.00
24 . . . . 45.00
25 . . . . 30.00
26 . . . . 40.00
27 . . . . 30.00
28 . . . . 45.00
29 . . . . 30.00
30 . . . . 45.00
31 thru 34 . . . . @30.00
35 May, 1950 . . . . 30.00
Becomes:

JOURNEY INTO UNKNOWN WORLDS
Atlas Sept. 1950
36(1) RH,End of the Earth . . 1,500.00
37(2) BEv,GC,When Worlds
   Collide 700.00
38(3) GT,Land of Missing Men 550.00
4 MS,RH,Train to Nowhere . . . 375.00
5 MS,Trapped in Space 375.00
6 GC,RH,World Below
   the Atlantic 375.00
7 BW,RH,House That Wasn't . 600.00
8 RH,The Stone Thing 375.00
9 MS,JSt,The People Who
   Couldn't Exist 450.00
10 THe Undertaker 375.00
11 BEv,Frankie Was Afraid . . . 275.00
12 The Last Voice You Hear . . 275.00
13 The Witch Woman 200.00
14 BW,BEv,CondemnedBuilding 450.00
15 They Crawl By Night 450.00
16 Scared to Death 225.00
17 BEv,GC,RH,The Ice
   Monster Cometh 225.00
18 The Broth Needs Somebody 250.00
19 GC,The Long Wait 250.00
20 GC,RH,The Race That
   Vanished 200.00
21 thru 25 . . . . @150.00
26 thru 35 . . . . @125.00
36 thru 44 . . . . @100.00
45 AW,SD 110.00
46 . . . . 85.00
47 . . . . 85.00
48 GW 85.00
49 . . . . 85.00
50 JDa,RC 100.00
51 WW,SD,JSe 100.00
52 . . . . 85.00
53 RC,BP 100.00
54 AT,BP 100.00
55 AW,RC,BEv 100.00
56 BEv 100.00
57 JO 85.00
58 MO 85.00
59 AW,August, 1957 . . . . . . 100.00

ALL WINNERS COMICS
[2nd Series] August, 1948
1 F:Blonde Phantom,A:Capt.America
   Sub-Mariner,Human Torch 1,600.00
Becomes:

ALL WESTERN WINNERS
2 B,I&O:Black Rider,B:Two-Gun
   Kid, Kid-Colt 400.00

3 Black Rider V: Satan 200.00	9 JBy,O:Aurora,A:Wolverine,	43 DR,WPo,V:Mesmero,Sentinels 2.25
4 Black Rider Unmasked 200.00	Super Skrull 2.00	44 DR,WPo,D:Snowbird,
Becomes:	10 JBy,O:Northstar,V:SuperSkrull . 2.00	A:Pestilence 2.25

WESTERN WINNERS

5 I Challenge the Army 200.00	11 JBy,I:Omega Flight,Wild Child	45 JBr,WPo,R:Sasquatch,
6 The Mountain Mystery 175.00	O:Sasquatch 2.00	L:Shaman 2.25
7 Ph(c) Randolph Scott 175.00	12 JBy,D:Guardian,V:Omega	46 JBr,WPo,I:2nd Box 2.25
Becomes:	Flight 2.00	47 MMi,WPo,TA,Vindicator solo . 2.25

BLACK RIDER

8 Ph(c),B:Black Rider;Valley	13 JBy,C:Wolverine,Nightmare . . . 3.00	48 SL(i),I:Omega 2.25
of Giants 275.00	14 JBy,V:Genocide 2.00	49 JBr,WPo,I:Manikin,D:Omega . . 2.25
9 Wrath of the Redskin 125.00	15 JBy,R:Master 2.00	50 WS(c),JBr,WPo,L:Northstar,Puck,
10 O:Black Rider 150.00	16 JBy,BWi,V:Master,C:Wolverine	Aurora,A:Loki,Double size 2.50
11 Redmen on the Warpath 75.00	I:Madison Jeffries 2.25	51 JLe(1st Marv),WPo(i),V:Cody . 6.00
12 GT,The Town That Vanished . . 75.00	17 JBy,BWi,A:Wolverine,X-Men . . 3.00	52 JBr,WPo(i),I:Bedlam,
13 The Terrified Tribe 75.00	18 JBy,BWi,J:Heather,I:Ranaq . . . 2.00	A:Wolverine 3.00
14 The Tyrant of Texas 75.00	19 JBy,I:Talisman,V:Ranaq 2.00	53 JLe,WPo(i),I:Derangers,Goblyn
15 Revolt of the Redskins 60.00	20 JBy,I:Gilded Lily,N:Aurora . . . 2.00	D&V:Bedlam,A:Wolverine . . . 3.00
16 . . . . 60.00	21 JBy,BWi,O:Gilded Lily,Diablo . 2.00	54 WPo(i),O&J:Goblyn 2.00
17 . . . . 60.00	22 JBy,BWi,I:Pink Pearl 2.00	55 JLe,TD,V:Tundra 2.50
18 . . . . 60.00	23 JBy,BWi,D:Sasquatch,	56 JLe,TD,V:Bedlamites 2.50
19 SSh,GT,A:Two-Gun Kid 60.00	I:Tanaraq 2.00	57 JLe,TD,V:Crystals,
20 GT 75.00	24 JBy,BWi,V:Great Beasts,J:Box 2.00	C:Dreamqueen 2.50
21 SSh,GT,A:Two-Gun Kid 65.00	25 JBy,BWi,V:Omega Flight	58 JLe,AM,V:Dreamqueen 2.50
22 SSh,A:Two-Gun Kid 65.00	I:Dark Guardian 2.00	59 JLe,AM,I:Jade Dragon,R:Puck . 2.50
23 SSh,A:Two-Gun Kid 65.00		60 JLe,AM,V:J.Dragon,D.Queen . 2.50
24 SSh,JSt 65.00		61 JLe,AM,on Trial
25 SSh,JSt,A:Arrowhead 65.00		(1st JLe X-Men) 2.50
26 SSh,A:Kid-Colt 65.00		62 JLe,AM,V:Purple Man 2.50
27 SSh,A:Kid-Colt 70.00		63 MG,V:U.S.Air Force 2.00
Becomes:		64 JLe,AM,V:Great Beasts 2.50

WESTERN TALES OF BLACK RIDER

28 JSe,D:Spider 80.00		65 JLe(c),AM(i),Dream Issue . . . 2.00
29 . . . . 60.00		66 JLe(c),I:China Force 2.00
30 . . . . 60.00		67 JLe(c),O:Dream Queen 2.00
31 . . . . 60.00		68 JLe(c),V:Dream Queen 2.00
Becomes:		69 JLe(c),V:Dream Queen 2.00

GUNSMOKE WESTERN

32 F:Kid Colt,Billy Buckskin 60.00		70 MM(i),V:Dream Queen 2.00
33 . . . . 57.00		71 MM(i),I:Sorcerer 2.00
34 . . . . 28.00		72 V:Sorcerer 2.00
35 . . . . 57.00		73 MM(i),V:Sorcerer 2.00
36 . . . . 57.00		74 MM(i),Alternate Earth 2.00
37 . . . . 30.00		75 JLe(c),MMi(i),Double Size . . . 3.00
38 . . . . 23.00		76 MM(i),V:Sorcerer. 2.00
39 . . . . 23.00		77 MM(i),V:Kingpin 2.00
40 . . . . 40.00		78 MM(i),A:Dr.Strange,Master . . . 2.00
41 . . . . 20.00		79 MM(i),AofV,V:Scorpion,Nekra . 2.00
42 . . . . 20.00		80 MM(i),AofV,V:Scorpion,Nekra . 2.00
43 . . . . 20.00		81 JBy(c),MM(i),B:R:Northstar . . 2.00
44 . . . . 23.00		82 JBy(c),MM(i),E:R:Northstar . . 2.00
45 . . . . 23.00		83 JSh 2.00
46 thru 55 . . . . @20.00		84 MM(i),Northstar 2.00
56 . . . . 23.00		85 MM(i) 2.00
57 thru 76 . . . . @18.00		86 MBa,MM,V:Sorcerer 2.00
77 July, 1963 . . . . 16.00		87 JLe(c),MM(i),A:Wolverine 4.00
	26 JBy,BWi,A:Omega Flight,Dark	88 JLe(c),MM(i),A:Wolverine 3.50
	Guardian 2.00	89 JLe(c),MM(i),R:Guardian,A:

ALPHA FLIGHT

August, 1983

1 JBy,I:Puck,Marrina,Tundra 3.00	27 JBy,V:Omega Flight 2.00	Wolverine 3.50
2 JBy,I:Master,Vindicator Becomes	28 JBy,Secret Wars II,V:Omega	90 JLe(c),MM(i),A:Wolverine 3.50
Guardian,B:O:Marrina 2.00	Flight,D:Dark Guardian 2.00	91 MM(i),A:Dr.Doom 2.00
3 JBy,O:Master,A:Namor,Invisible	29 MMi,V:Hulk,A:Box 2.00	92 Guardian vs.Vindicator 2.00
Girl, ... 2.00	30 MMi,I&O:Scramble,R:Deadly	93 MM(i),A:Fant.Four,I:Headlok . . 2.00
4 JBy,A:Namor,Invisible Girl,	Ernest 2.00	94 MM(i),V:Fant.Four,Headlok . . . 2.00
E:O:Marrina,A:Master 2.00	31 MMi,D:Deadly Ernest,	95 MM(i),Lifelines 2.00
5 JBy,B:O:Shaman,F:Puck 2.00	O:Nemesis 2.00	96 MM(i),A:Master 2.00
6 JBy,E:O:Shaman,I:Kolomag . . 2.00	32 MMi(c),JBg,O:Puck,I:2nd	97 B:Final Option,A:Her 2.00
7 JBy,B,O:Snowbird,I:Delphine	Vindicator 2.00	98 A:Avengers 2.00
Courtney & Deadly Ernest 2.00	33 MMi(c),SB,X-Men,I:Deathstrike . 3.00	99 A:Avengers 2.00
8 JBy,E:O:Snowbird,O:Deadly	34 MMi(c),SB,Wolverine,V:	100 JBr,TMo,DR,LMa,E:Final Option
Ernest,I:Nemesis 2.00	Deathstrike 3.00	A:Galactus,Avengers,D:
	35 DR,R:Shaman 2.00	Guardian,G-Size 2.50
	36 MMi(c),DR,A:Dr.Strange 2.00	101 TMo,Final Option Epilogue,
	37 DR,O:Pestilence,N:Aurora . . . 2.00	A:Dr.Strange,Avengers 2.00
	38 DR,A:Namor,V:Pestilence . . . 2.00	102 TMo,I:Weapon Omega, ... 2.00
	39 MMi(c),DR,WPo,A:Avengers . . 2.25	103 TMo,V:Diablo,U.S.Agent . . . 2.00
	40 DR,WPo,W:Namor & Marrina . 2.25	104 TMo,N:Alpha Flight,Weapon
	41 DR,WPo,I:Purple Girl,	Omega is Wild Child 2.00
	J:Madison Jeffries 2.25	105 TMo,V:Pink Pearl 2.00
	42 DR,WPo,I:Auctioneer,J:Purple Girl,	
	A: Beta Flight 2.25	

Alpha Flight #5
© Marvel Entertainment Group

MARVEL

MARVEL

Alpha Flight Special #4
© Marvel Entertainment Group

106 MPa,Aids issue,Northstar
  acknowledges homosexuality . 3.00
106a 2nd printing 2.50
107 A:X-Factor,V:Autopsy 2.00
108 A:Soviet Super Soldiers 2.00
109 V:Peoples Protectorate 2.00
110 PB,Infinity War,I:2nd Omega
  Flight,A:Wolverine 2.00
111 PB,Infinity War,V:Omega
  Flight,A:Wolverine 2.00
112 PB,Infinity War,V:Master 2.00
113 V:Mauler 2.00
114 A:Weapon X 2.00
115 PB,I:Wyre,A:Weapon X 2.00
116 PB,I:Rok,V:Wyre 2.00
117 PB,V:Wyre 2.00
118 PB,V:Thunderball 2.00
119 PB,V:Wrecking Crew 2.00
120 PB,10th Anniv.,V:Hardliners,
  w/poster 2.50
121 PCu,V:Brass Bishop,A:Spider-
  Man,Wolverine,C:X-Men 2.00
122 PB,BKi,Inf.Crusade 2.00
123 PB,BKi,Infinity Crusade 2.00
124 PB,BKi,Infinity Crusade 2.00
125 PB,V:Carcass 2.00
126 V:Carcass 2.00
127 SFu(s),Infinity Crusade 2.00
128 B:No Future 2.00
129 C:Omega Flight 2.00
130 E:No Future,last issue,
  Double Sized 2.50
Ann.#1 LSn,V:Diablo,Gilded Lily . 3.00
Ann.#2 JBr,BMc 2.00
Spec.#1 PB,A:Wolverine,
  O:First Team,V:Egghead 3.75
Spec.#1–#3 Newsstand versions
  of #97–#99 . . . . @1.50
Spec.#4 Newsstand ver.of #100 . . 2.00

ALPHA FLIGHT
1997

1 SSe,ScC,former team kidnapped,
  I:Murmur, Radius,Flex,Guardian 2.00
2 SSe,ScC 2.00

2 variant cover 2.00
Spec. #1 SSe,"In the Beginning,"
  Flashback, A:Wolverine 1.95

ALPHA FLIGHT SPECIAL
1991

1 thru 4 reprints . . . . @1.50

Amazing Adventures #6
© Marvel Entertainment Group

AMAZING ADVENTURES
June, 1961

1 JK,SD,O&B:Dr.Droom;Torr 1,200.00
2 JK,SD,This is Manoo 500.00
3 JK,SD,Trapped in the
  Twilight World 450.00
4 JK,SD, I Am X 400.00
5 JK,SD, Monsteroso 400.00
6 JK,SD,E:Dr.Droom; Sserpo . 450.00
Becomes:

AMAZING ADULT FANTASY
Dec., 1961

7 SD,Last Man on Earth 575.00
8 SD,The Coming of the Krills . 450.00
9 SD,The Terror of Tim Boo Ba 400.00
10 SD,Those Who Change . . . 400.00
11 SD,In Human Form 400.00
12 SD,Living Statues 400.00
13 SD,At the Stroke of Midnight 400.00
14 SD,Beware of the Giants . . 425.00
Becomes:

AMAZING FANTASY
August, 1962

15 JK(c),SD,I&O:Spider-Man,I:Aunt
  May, Flash Thompson, Burglar,
  I&D:Uncle Ben 28,000.00
[Second Series] 1995
15a gold Rep. (1995) 25.00
16 KBk, O:Spider-Man,painted . . 4.00
17 KBk, More early adventures . . 4.00
18 KBk,conclusion 4.00

AMAZING ADVENTURES
August, 1970
[1st Regular Series]

1 JK,JB,B:Inhumans,Bl.Widow . 17.00

2 JK,JB,A:Fantastic Four 11.00
3 JK,GC,BEv,V:Mandarin 10.00
4 JK,GC,BEv,V:Mandarin 10.00
5 NA,TP,DH,BEv,V:Astrologer . 12.00
6 NA,DH,SB,V:Maximus 10.00
7 NA,DH,BEv 10.00
8 NA,DH,BEv,E:Black Widow,
  A:Thor,(see Avengers #95) . . 10.00
9 MSy,BEv,V:Magneto 12.00
10 GK(c),MSy,V:Magneto,
  E:Inhumans 12.00
11 GK(c),TS,B:O:New Beast,
  A:X-Men 17.00
12 GK(c),TS,MP,A:Iron Man . . . 10.00
13 JR(c),TS,V:New Br'hood
  Evil Mutants,I:Buzz Baxter
  (Mad Dog) 10.00
14 GK(c),TS,JM,V:Quasimodo . . 10.00
15 JSn(c),TS,A:X-Men,V:Griffin . 10.00
16 JSn(c),FMc(i),V:Juggernaut . . 10.00
17 JSn,A:X-Men,E:Beast 10.00
18 HC,NA,B:Killraven 10.00
19 HC,Sirens on 7th Avenues . . 6.00
20 Coming of the Warlords 6.00
21 Cry Killraven 6.00
22 Killraven 6.00
23 Killraven 6.00
24 New Year Nightmare-2019AD . 6.00
25 RB,V:Skar 6.00
26 GC,V:Ptson-Rage Vigilante . . 6.00
27 CR,JSn,V:Death Breeders . . . 6.00
28 JSn,CR,V:Death Breeders . . . 6.00
29 CR,Killraven 6.00
30 CR,Killraven 6.00
31 CR,Killraven 6.00
32 CR,Killraven 6.00
33 CR,Killraven 6.00
34 CR,D:Hawk 6.00
35 KG,Killraven Continued 6.00
36 CR,Killraven Continued 6.00
37 CR,O:Old Skull 6.00
38 CR,Killraven Continued. 6.00
39 CR,E:Killraven 6.00
[2nd Regular Series]
1 rep.X-Men#1,38,Professor X . . 7.00
2 rep.X-Men#1,39,O:Cyclops . . . 6.00
3 rep.X-Men#2,40,O:Cyclops . . . 6.00
4 rep.X-Men#2,41,O:Cyclops . . . 6.00
5 rep.X-Men#3,42,O:Cyclops . . . 6.00
6 JBy(c),rep.X-Men#3,43,Cyclops 6.00
7 rep.X-Men#4,44,O:Iceman . . . 6.00
8 rep.X-Men#4,45,O:Iceman . . . 6.00
9 JBy(c),X-Men#5,46,O:Iceman . 6.00
10 rep.X-Men#5,47,O:Iceman . . . 6.00
11 rep-X-Men#6,48,Beast 6.00
12 rep-X-Men#6,Str.Tales#168 . . 6.00
13 rep.X-Men #7 . . . . 6.00
14 rep.X-Men #8 . . . . 6.00

AMAZING COMICS
Timely Comics Fall, 1944
1 F:Young Allies,Destroyer,
  Whizzer, Sergeant Dix . . . 1,500.00
Becomes:
COMPLETE COMICS
2 F:Young Allies,Destroyer,Whizzer
  Sergeant Dix; Winter'44-5 . . 700.00

AMAZING DETECTIVE CASES
Atlas Nov., 1950
3 Detective/Horror Stories . . . 150.00
4 Death of a Big Shot 75.00

MARVEL

5	75.00
6 Danger in the City	75.00
7	55.00
8	55.00
9 GC, The Man Who Wasn't	55.00
10 GT	55.00
11 The Black Shadow	90.00
12 MS,BK, Harrigan's Wake	90.00
13 BEv,JSt,	150.00
14 Hands Off; Sept., 1952	90.00

AMAZING HIGH ADVENTURE
August, 1984

1 BSz,JSo,JS	3.00
2 PS,AW,BSz,TA,MMi,BBl,CP,CW	2.50
3 MMi,VM,JS	2.50
4 JBo,JS,SBi	2.50
5 JBo; Oct., 1986	2.50

AMAZING SCARLET SPIDER

1 MBa,LMa,VirtualMortality,pt.2	1.95
2 TDF,MBa,CyberWar,pt.2	1.95

AMAZING SPIDER-MAN
March, 1963

1 JK(c),SED,I:Chameleon,J.Jonah & John Jameson,A:F.Four	20,000.00
2 SD,I:Vulture,Tinkerer C:Mysterio(disguised)	2,800.00
3 SD,I&O:Dr.Octopus	2,000.00
4 SD,I&O:Sandman,I:Betty Brant,Liz Allen	1,700.00
5 SD,V:Dr.Doom,C:Fant.Four	1,500.00
6 SD,I&O:Lizard,The Connors	1,200.00
7 SD,V:Vulture	800.00
8 SD,JK,I:Big Brain,V:Human Torch,A:Fantastic Four	750.00
9 SD,I&O:Electro	900.00
10 SD,I:Enforcers,Big Man	800.00
11 SD,V:Dr.Octopus, D:Bennett Brant	500.00
12 SD,V:Dr.Octopus	450.00
13 SD,I:Mysterio	650.00
14 SD,I:Green Goblin, V:Enforcers, Hulk	1,500.00
15 SD,I:Kraven,A:Chameleon	600.00
16 SD,A:Daredevil, V:Ringmaster	400.00
17 SD,2nd A:Green Goblin, A:Human Torch	600.00
18 SD,V:Sandman,Enforcers, C:Avengers,F.F.,Daredevil	400.00
19 SD,V:Sandman,I:Ned Leeds A:Human Torch	300.00
20 SD,I&O:Scorpion	400.00
21 SD,A:Beetle,Human Torch	250.00
22 SD,V:The Clown,Masters of Menace	225.00
23 SD,V:GreenGoblin(3rd App.)	350.00
24 SD,V:Mysterio	185.00
25 SD,I:Spider Slayer,Spencer Smythe,C:Mary Jane	250.00
26 SD,I:CrimeMaster,V:Green Goblin	275.00
27 SD,V:CrimeMaster, Green Goblin	250.00
28 SD,I:Molten Man,Peter Parker Graduates High School,rare in near-mint condition	350.00
29 SD,V:Scorpion	150.00
30 SD,I:Cat Burglar	150.00
31 SD,I:Gwen Stacy,Harry Osborn	

Amazing Spider-Man #3
© Marvel Entertainment Group

Prof.Warren,V:Dr.Octopus	175.00
32 SD,V:Dr.Octopus	150.00
33 SD,V:Dr.Octopus	150.00
34 SD,V:Kraven	150.00
35 SD,V:Molten Man	150.00
36 SD,I:The Looter	150.00
37 SD,V:Professor Stromm, I:Norman Osborn	160.00
38 SD,V:Joe Smith(Boxer)	150.00
39 JR,IR:Green Goblin is Norman Osborn	225.00
40 JR,O:Green Goblin	325.00
41 JR,I:Rhino,C:Mary Jane	160.00
42 JR,V:John Jameson,I:Mary Jane (Face Revealed)	150.00
43 JR,O:Rhino	100.00
44 JR,V:Lizard(2nd App.)	100.00
45 JR,V:Lizard	100.00
46 JR,I&O:Shocker	110.00
47 JR,V:Kraven	100.00
48 JR,I:Fake Vulture,A:Vulture	100.00
49 JR,V:Fake Vulture,Kraven	100.00
50 JR,I:Kingpin,Spidey Quits, C:Johnny Carson	400.00
51 JR,V:Kingpin	150.00
52 JR,V:Kingpin,I:Robbie Robertson,D:Fred Foswell	85.00
53 JR,V:Dr.Octopus	75.00
54 JR,V:Dr.Octopus	70.00
55 JR,V:Dr.Octopus	70.00
56 JR,V:Dr.Octopus,I:Capt.Stacy	75.00
57 JR,DH,A:Kazar	70.00
58 JR,DH,V:Spencer Smythe, Spider Slayer	70.00
59 JR,DH,V:Kingpin	75.00
60 JR,DH,V:Kingpin	75.00
61 JR,DH,V:Kingpin	75.00
62 JR,DH,V:Medusa	55.00
63 JR,DH,V:1st & 2nd Vulture	55.00
64 JR,DH,V:Vulture	55.00
65 JR,JM,V:Prisoners	55.00
66 JR,DH,V:Mysterio	55.00
67 JR,JM,V:Mysterio,I:Randy Robertson	55.00
68 JR,JM,V:Kingpin	60.00

69 JR,JM,V:Kingpin	60.00
70 JR,JM,V:Kingpin	60.00
71 JR,JM,V:Quicksilver,C:Scarlet Witch,Toad,A:Kingpin	50.00
72 JR,JB,JM,V:Shocker	50.00
73 JR,JB,JM,I:Man Mountain Marko, Silvermane	50.00
74 JR,JM,V:Silvermane	45.00
75 JR,JM,V:Silvermane,A:Lizard	45.00
76 JR,JM,V:Lizard,A:H.Torch	45.00
77 JR,JM,V:Lizard,A:H.Torch	45.00
78 JR,JM,I&O:Prowler	50.00
79 JR,JM,V:Prowler	45.00
80 JR,JB,JM,V:Chameleon	45.00
81 JR,JB,JM,I:Kangaroo	45.00
82 JR,JM,V:Electro	45.00
83 JR,I:Richard Fisk(as Schemer), Vanessa(Kingpin's wife) V:Kingpin	50.00
84 JR,JB,JM,V:Schemer,Kingpin	45.00
85 JR,JB,JM,V:Schemer,Kingpin	45.00
86 JR,JM,V:Black Widow, C:Iron Man, Hawkeye	45.00
87 JR,JM,Reveals ID to his friends,changes mind	45.00
88 JR,JM,V:Dr.Octopus	45.00
89 GK,JR,V:Dr.Octopus	45.00
90 GK,JR,V:Dr.Octopus D:Capt.Stacy	60.00
91 GK,JR,I:Bullit	45.00
92 GK,JR,V:Bullit,A:Iceman	45.00
93 JR,V:Prowler	45.00
94 JR,SB,V:Beetle,O:Spider-Man	70.00
95 JR,SB,London,V:Terrorists	45.00
96 GK,JR,A:Green Goblin,Drug Mention,No Comic Code	90.00
97 GK,V:Green Goblin,Drugs	85.00
98 GK,V:Green Goblin,Drugs	85.00
99 GK,Prison Riot,A:Carson	50.00
100 JR(c),GK,Spidey gets four arms from serum	200.00
101 JR(c),GK,I:Morbius,the Living Vampire,A:Lizard	175.00
101a Reprint,Metallic ink	2.50
102 JR(c),GK,O:Morbius, V:Lizard	135.00
103 GK,V:Kraven,A:Kazar	30.00
104 GK,V:Kraven,A:Kazar	30.00
105 GK,V:Spenser Smythe, Spider Slayer	30.00
106 JR,V:Spenser Smythe, Spider Slayer	27.00
107 JR,V:Spenser Smythe, Spider Slayer	27.00
108 JR,R:Flash Thompson, I:Sha-Shan,V:Vietnamese	27.00
109 JR,A:Dr.Strange, V:Vietnamese	27.00
110 JR,I:The Gibbon	27.00
111 JR,V:The Gibbon,Kraven	27.00
112 JR,Spidey gets an Ulcer	27.00
113 JSn,JR,I:Hammerhead V:Dr.Octopus	30.00
114 JSn,JR,V:Hammerhead,Dr. Octopus,I:Jonas Harrow	30.00
115 JR,V:Hammerhead, Dr.Octopus	30.00
116 JR,JM,V:The Smasher	27.00
117 JR,JM,V:Smasher,Disruptor	27.00
118 JR,JM,V:Smasher,Disruptor	27.00
119 JR,A:Hulk	45.00
120 GK,JR,V:Hulk	45.00
121 GK,JR,V:Green Goblin D:Gwen Stacy,Drugs	125.00
122 GK,JR,D:Green Goblin	150.00

Amazing Spider-Man #42
© Marvel Entertainment Group

123 GK,JR,A:Powerman 25.00
124 GK,JR,I:Man-Wolf 26.00
125 RA,JR,O:Man-Wolf 25.00
126 JM(c),RA,JM,V:Kangaroo,
    A: Human Torch 25.00
127 JR(c),RA,V:3rd Vulture,
    A:Human Torch 25.00
128 JR(c),RA,V:3rd Vulture 25.00
129 K&R(c),RA,I:Punisher,
    Jackal 250.00
129a reprint,Marv.Milestone . . 2.95
130 JR(c),RA,V:Hammerhead,
    Dr.Octopus,I:Spider-Mobile . . 22.00
131 GK(c),RA,V:Hammerhead,
    Dr.Octopus 22.00
132 GK(c),JR,V:Molten Man . . 20.00
133 JR(c),RA,V:Molten Man . . 20.00
134 JR(c),RA,I:Tarantula,C:
    Punisher(2nd App.) 27.00
135 JR(c),RA,V:Tarantula,
    A:Punisher 60.00
136 JR(c),RA,I:2nd GreenGoblin 40.00
137 GK(c),RA,V:Green Goblin . . 35.00
138 K&R(c),RA,I:Mindworm 25.00
139 K&R(c),RA,I:Grizzly,V:Jackal 25.00
140 GK(c),RA,I:Gloria Grant,
    V:Grizzly,Jackal 25.00
141 JR(c),RA,V:Mysterio 25.00
142 JR(c),RA,V:Mysterio 25.00
143 K&R(c),RA,I:Cyclone 25.00
144 K&R(c),RA,V:Cyclone 25.00
145 K&R(c),RA,V:Scorpion 25.00
146 RA,JR,V:Scorpion 25.00
147 JR(c),RA,V:Tarantula 25.00
148 GK(c),RA,V:Tarantula,IR:Jackal
    is Prof.Warren 30.00
149 K&R(c),RA,D:Jackal 100.00
150 GK(c),RA,V:SpenserSmythe 55.00
151 RA,JR,V:Shocker 45.00
152 K&R(c),RA,V:Shocker 17.00
153 K&R(c),RA,V:Paine 17.00
154 JR(c),SB,V:Sandman 17.00
155 JR(c),SB,V:Computer 16.00
156 JR(c),RA,I:Mirage,W:Ned
    Leeds & Betty Brant 16.00
157 JR(c),RA,V:Dr.Octopus . . . 16.00
158 JR(c),RA,V:Dr.Octopus 16.00
159 JR(c),RA,V:Dr.Octopus 16.00

160 K&R(c),RA,V:Tinkerer 16.00
161 K&R(c),RA,A:Nightcrawler,
    C:Punisher 18.00
162 JR(c),RA,Nightcrawler,
    Punisher,I:Jigsaw 17.00
163 JR(c),RA,Kingpin 11.00
164 JR(c),RA,Kingpin 11.00
165 JR(c),RA,Lizard 11.00
166 JR(c),RA,Lizard 11.00
167 JR(c),RA,V:Spiderslayer,
    I:Will-o-the Wisp 11.00
168 JR(c),KP,V:Will-o-the Wisp . 14.00
169 RA,V:Dr.Faustas 11.00
170 RA,V:Dr.Faustas 11.00
171 RA,A:Nova 12.00
172 RA,V:Molten Man 11.00
173 JR(c),RA,JM,V:Molten Man . 11.00
174 RA,TD,JM,A:Punisher 16.00
175 RA,JM,A:Punisher,D:Hitman 16.00
176 RA,TD,V:Green Goblin 16.00
177 RA,V:Green Goblin 16.00
178 RA,JM,V:Green Goblin 16.00
179 RA,V:Green Goblin 16.00
180 RA,IR&V:Green Goblin is Bart
    Hamilton) 16.00
181 GK(c),SB,O:Spider-Man.. . 10.00
182 RA,A:Rocket Racer 9.00
183 RA,BMc,V:Rocket Racer . . . 9.00
184 RA,V:White Tiger 9.00
185 RA,V:White Tiger 9.00
186 KP,A:Chameleon,Spidy
    cleared by police of charges . . 9.00
187 JSn,BMc,A:Captain
    America,V:Electro 10.00
188 KP,A:Jigsaw 9.00
189 JBy,JM,A:Man-Wolf 10.00
190 JBy,JM,A:Man-Wolf 10.00
191 KP,V:Spiderslayer 8.00
192 KP,JM,V:The Fly 8.00
193 KP,JM,V:The Fly 8.00
194 KP,I:Black Cat 16.00
195 KP,AM,JM,O:Black Cat 9.00
196 AM,JM,D:Aunt May,A:Kingpin 8.00
197 KP,JM,V:Kingpin 8.00
198 SB,JM,V:Mysterio 8.00
199 SB,JM,V:Mysterio 8.00
200 JR(c),KP,JM,D:Burglar,Aunt May
    alive,O:Spider-Man 30.00
201 KP,JM,A:Punisher 15.00
202 KP,JM,A:Punisher 15.00
203 FM(c),KP,A:Dazzler 9.00
204 JR2(c),KP,V:Black Cat 8.00
205 KP,JM,V:Black Cat 8.00
206 JBy,GD,V:Jonas Harrow . . . 10.00
207 JM,V:Mesmero 8.00
208 JR2,AM,BBr,V:Fusion(1stJR2
    SpM art),I:Lance Bannon . . . 11.00
209 KJ,BMc,JRu,BWi,AM,
    I:Calypso, V:Kraven 9.00
210 JR2,JSt,I:Madame Web . . . 9.00
211 JR2,JM,A:Sub-mariner 7.50
212 JR2,JM,I:Hydro-Man 7.50
213 JR2,JM,V:Wizard 7.50
214 JR2,JM,V:Frightful Four,
    A: Namor,Llyra 7.50
215 JR2,JM,V:Frightful Four,
    A: Namor,Llyra 7.50
216 JR2,JM,A:Madame Web . . . 7.50
217 JR2,JM,V:Sandman,
    Hydro-Man 7.50
218 FM(c),JR2,JM,AM,V:Sandman
    Hydro-Man 7.50
219 FM(c),LMc,JM,V:Grey
    Gargoyle,A:Matt Murdock . . . 7.50
220 BMc,A:Moon Knight 7.50

Amazing Spider-Man #71
© Marvel Entertainment Group

221 JM(i),A:Ramrod 7.00
222 WS(c),BH,JM,I:SpeedDemon 7.00
223 JR2,AM,A:Red Ghost 7.00
224 JR2,V:Vulture 7.00
225 JR2,BWi,V:Foolkiller 7.00
226 JR2,JM,A:Black Cat 7.00
227 JR2,JM,A:Black Cat 7.00
228 RL,Murder Mystery 7.00
229 JR2,JM,V:Juggernaut 8.50
230 JR2,JM,V:Juggernaut 8.50
231 JR2,AM,V:Cobra 7.00
232 JR2,JM,V:Mr.Hyde 7.00
233 JR2,JM,V:Tarantula 7.00
234 JR2,DGr,V:Tarantula 7.00
235 JR2,V:Tarantula,C:Deathlok
    O:Will-o-the Wisp 7.00
236 JR2,D:Tarantula 7.00
237 BH,A:Stilt Man 7.00
238 JR2,JR,I:Hobgoblin (inc.
    Tattoo transfer) 75.00
238a w/out Tattoo 22.00
239 JR2,V:Hobgoblin 45.00
240 JR2,BL,Vulture 7.00
241 JR2,O:Vulture 7.00
242 JR2,Mad Thinker 7.00
243 JR2,Peter Quits School 7.00
244 JR2,KJ,V:Hobgoblin 12.00
245 JR2,V:Hobgoblin 17.00
246 JR2,DGr,Daydreams issue . . 7.00
247 JR2,JR,V:Thunderball 7.00
248 JR2,BBr,RF,TA,V:Thunderball,
    Kid who Collects Spider-Man . 7.00
249 JR2,DGr,V:Hobgoblin,
    A:Kingpin 14.00
250 JR2,KJ,V:Hobgoblin 14.00
251 RF,KJ,V:Hobgoblin,Spidey
    Leaves for Secret Wars 15.00
252 RF,BBr,returns from Secret
    Wars,N:Spider-Man 35.00
253 RL,I:Rose 10.00
254 RL,JRu,V:Jack O'Lantern . . . 7.00
255 RF,JRu,Red Ghost 7.00
256 RF,JRu,I:Puma,A:Black Cat . 8.00
257 RF,JRu,V:Puma,
    A:Hobgoblin 10.00
258 RF,JRu,A:Black Cat,Fant.Four,
    Hobgoblin,V:Black Costume . 15.00
259 RF,JRu,A:Hobgoblin,O:

Amazing Spider-Man #129
© Marvel Entertainment Group

Mary Jane 17.00
260 RF,JRu,A:Hobgoblin . . . 12.00
261 CV(c),RF,JRu,V:Hobgoblin . 12.00
262 Ph(c),BL,Spidey Unmasked . 10.00
263 RF,BBr,I:Spider-Kid 5.00
264 Paty,V:Red Nine 5.00
265 RF,JRu,V:Black Fox,
    I:Silver Sable 15.00
265a 2nd printing 1.50
266 RF,JRu,I:Misfits,Toad 5.00
267 BMc,PDd(s),A:Human Torch . 5.00
268 JBy(c),RF,JRu,Secret WarsII . 5.00
269 RF,JRu,V:Firelord 5.00
270 RF,BMc,V:Firelord,
    A:Avengers,I:Kate Cushing . . . 5.00
271 RF,JRu,A:Crusher Hogan,
    V:Manslaughter 5.00
272 SB,KB,I&O:Slyde 5.00
273 RF,JRu,Secret Wars II,
    A:Puma 5.00
274 TMo,JR,Secret Wars II,
    Beyonder V:Mephisto,A:1st
    Ghost Rider 10.00
275 RF,JRu,V:Hobgoblin,O:Spidey
    (From Amaz.Fantasy#15) . . . 13.00
276 RF,BBr,V:Hobgoblin 10.00
277 RF,BL,CV,A:Daredevil,
    Kingpin 8.00
278 A:Hobgoblin,V:Scourge,
    D:Wraith 6.00
279 RL,A:Jack O'Lantern,
    2nd A:Silver Sable 7.00
280 RF,BBr,V:Sinister Syndicate,
    A:Silver Sable,Hobgoblin,
    Jack O'Lantern 6.00
281 RF,BBr,V:Sinister Syndicate,
    A:Silver Sable,Hobgoblin,
    Jack O'Lantern 11.00
282 RL,BL,A:X-Factor 5.50
283 RF,BL,V:Titania,Absorbing
    Man,C:Mongoose 6.50
284 RF,BBr,JRu,B:Gang War,
    A: Punisher,Hobgoblin 9.00
285 MZ(c),A:Punisher,Hobgoblin . 13.00
286 ANi(i),V:Hobgoblin,A:Rose . 10.00

287 EL,ANi,A:Daredevl,Hobgoblin . 8.00
288 E:Gang War,A:Punisher,
    Falcon,Hobgoblin,Daredevil,
    Black Cat, Kingpin 9.00
289 TMo,IR:Hobgoblin is Ned Leeds,
    I:2nd Hobgoblin (Jack O'
    Lantern) 22.00
290 JR2,Peter Proposes 7.00
291 JR2,V:Spiderslayer 7.00
292 AS,V:Spiderslayer,Mary
    Jane Accepts proposal 7.00
293 MZ,BMc,V:Kraven 12.00
294 MZ,BMc,D:Kraven 12.00
295 BSz(c),KB(i),Mad Dog,pt.#2 . 7.00
296 JBy(c),AS,V:Dr.Octopus 6.00
297 AS,V:Dr.Octopus 6.00
298 TM,BMc,V:Chance,C:Venom
    (not in costume) 40.00
299 TM,BMc,V:Chance,I:Venom . 30.00
300 TM,O:Venom 75.00
301 TM,A:Silver Sable 18.00
302 TM,V:Nero,A:Silver Sable . 18.00
303 TM,A:Silver Sable,Sandman . 18.00
304 TM,JRu,V:Black Fox,Prowler
    I:Jonathan Caesar 16.00
305 TM,JRu,V:BlackFox,Prowler . 16.00
306 TM,V:Humbug,Chameleon . 13.00
307 TM,O:Chameleon 13.00
308 TM,V:Taskmaster,J.Caesar . 13.00
309 TM,I:Styx & Stone 13.00
310 TM,V:Killershrike 13.00
311 TM,Inferno,V:Mysterio 13.00
312 TM,Inferno,Hobgoblin V:
    Green Goblin 16.00
313 TM,Inferno,V:Lizard 12.00
314 TM,X-mas issue,V:J.Caesar . 12.00
315 TM,V:Venom,Hydro-Man . . . 20.00
316 TM,V:Venom 20.00
317 TM,V:Venom,A:Thing 20.00
318 TM,V:Scorpion 10.00
319 TM,V:Scorpion,Rhino 10.00
320 TM,B:Assassin Nation Plot
    A:Paladin,Silver Sable 10.00
321 TM,A:Paladin,Silver Sable . . 8.00
322 TM,A:Silver Sable,Paladin . . . 8.00
323 TM,A:Silver Sable,Paladin,
    Captain America 8.00
324 TM(c),EL,AG,V:Sabretooth,A:
    Capt.America,Silver Sable . 15.00
325 TM,E:Assassin Nation Plot,
    V:Red Skull,Captain America,
    Silver Sable 8.00
326 V:Graviton,A of V. 5.00
327 EL,AG,V:Magneto,A of V. . . . 6.00
328 TM,V:Hulk,A of V. 12.00
329 EL,V:Tri-Sentinel 6.00
330 EL,A:Punisher,Black Cat . . . 6.00
331 EL,A:Punisher,C:Venom 8.00
332 EL,V:Venom,Styx & Stone . 12.00
333 EL,V:Venom,Styx & Stone . 12.00
334 EL,B:Sinister Six,A:Iron Man . 6.00
335 EL,TA,A:Captain America . . . 6.00
336 EL,D:Nathan Lubensky,
    A:Dr.Strange,Chance 5.00
337 WS(c),EL,TA,A:Nova 5.00
338 EL,A:Jonathan Caesar 5.00
339 EL,JR,E:Sinister Six,A:Thor
    D:Jonathan Caesar 5.00
340 EL,V:Femme Fatales 4.00
341 EL,V:Tarantula,Powers Lost . 4.00
342 EL,A:Blackcat,V:Scorpion . . . 4.00
343 EL,Powers Restored,
    C:Cardiac,V:Chameleon 4.00
344 EL,V:Rhino,I:Cardiac,Cletus
    Kassady(Carnage),A:Venom . 10.00

Amazing Spider-Man #301
© Marvel Entertainment Group

345 MBa,V:Boomerang,C:Venom,
    A:Cletus Kassady(infected w/
    Venom-Spawn) 15.00
346 EL,V:Venom 10.00
347 EL,V:Venom 10.00
348 EL,A:Avengers 4.00
349 EL,A:Black Fox 4.00
350 EL,V:Doctor Doom,Black Fox . 5.00
351 MBa,A:Nova,V:Tri-Sentinal . . 5.00
352 MBa,A:Nova,V:Tri-Sentinal . . 4.00
353 MBa,B:Round Robin:The Side
    Kick's Revenge,A:Punisher,
    Nova,Moon Knight,Darkhawk . 4.00
354 MBa,A:Nova,Punisher,
    Darkhawk,Moon Knight 4.00
355 MBa,A:Nova,Punisher,
    Darkhawk,Moon Knight 4.00
356 MBa,A:Moon Knight,
    Punisher,Nova 4.00
357 MBa,A:Moon Knight,
    Punisher,Darkhawk,Nova 4.00
358 MBa,E:Round Robin:The Side
    Kick's Revenge,A:Darkhawk,
    Moon Knight,Punisher,Nova,
    Gatefold(c) 4.00
359 CMa,A:Cardiac,C:Cletus
    Kasady (Carnage) 6.00
360 CMa,V:Cardiac,C:Carnage . . 7.00
361 MBa,I:Carnage 15.00
361a 2nd printing 3.00
362 MBa,V:Carnage,Venom . . . 11.00
362a 2nd printing 3.00
363 MBa,V:Carnage,Venom, . . . 9.00
364 MBa,V:Shocker 3.00
365 MBa,JR,V:Lizard,30th Anniv.,
    Hologram(c),w/poster,Prev.of
    Spider-Man 2099 by RL 6.00
366 JBi,A:Red Skull,Taskmaster . 3.00
367 JBi,A:Red Skull,Taskmaster . 3.00
368 MBa,B:Invasion of the Spider
    Slayers #1,BU:Jonah Jameson . 2.50
369 MBa,V:Electro,BU:Green
    Goblin 2.50
370 MBa,V:Scorpion,BU:A.May . . 2.00
371 MBa,V:Spider-Slayer,
    BU:Black Cat 2.50

All comics prices listed are for *Near Mint* condition.

372 MBa,V:Spider-Slayer 2.50
373 MBa,V:Sp.-Slayer,BU:Venom 3.00
374 MBa,V:Venom 3.00
375 MBa,V:Venom,30th Anniv.,Holo
  graphx(c) 5.00
376 V:Styx&Stone,A:Cardiac 2.00
377 V:Cardiac,O:Styx&Stone 2.00
378 MBa,Total Carnage#3,V:Shriek,
  Carnage,A:Venom,Cloak 2.00
379 MBa,Total Carnage#7,
  V:Carnage,A:Venom 2.00
380 MBa,Maximum Carnage#11 . 2.00
381 MBa,V:Dr.Samson,A:Hulk . . . 1.75
382 MBa,V:Hulk,A:Dr.Samson . . . 1.75
383 MBa,V:Jury 1.75
384 MBa,AM,V:Jury 1.75
385 B:DvM(s),MBa,RyE,V:Jury . 1.50
386 MBa,RyE,B:Lifetheft,V:Vulture 4.00
387 MBa,RyE,V:Vulture 4.00
388 Blue Foil(c),MBa,RyE,RLm,TP,
  E:Lifetheft,D:Peter's Synthetic
  Parents,BU:Venom,Cardiac,
  Chance, ... 4.00
388a Newsstand Ed. 3.00
389 MBa,RyE,E:Pursuit,
  V:Chameleon, ... 1.75
390 MBa,RyE,B:Shrieking,
  A:Shriek,w/cel 3.25
390a Newsstand Ed. 1.75
391 MBa,RyE,V:Shriek,Carrion . . 1.75
392 MBa,RyE,V:Shriek,Carrion . . 1.75
393 MBa,RyE,E:Shrieking,
  V:Shriek,Carrion 1.75
394 MBa,RyE,Power & Responsibility,
  pt.2,V:Judas Traveller, ... 5.00
394a w/flip book,2 covers 3.00
395 MBa,RyE,R:Puma 1.75
396 MBa,RyE,A:Daredevil,
  V:Vulture, Owl 1.75
397 MBa,Web of Death,pt.1,V:Stunner,
  Doc Ock 1.75
398 MBa,Web of Death,pt.3 . . . . . 1.75
399 MBa,Smoke and Mirrors,pt.2 . 1.75
400 MBa,Death of a Parker 6.00
400a die-cut cover 3.25
401 MBa,The Mark of Kaine,pt.2 . 1.50
402 MBa,R:Judas Travellor 1.50
403 MBa,JMD,LMa The Trial of
  Peter Parker, pt.2 . . . . 1.50
404 Maximum Clonage 1.50
405 JMD,DaR,LMa,Exiled,pt.2, . . 1.50
406 I:New Doc Ock 1.50
407 TDF,MBa,LMa,Return of
  Spider-Man,pt.2 . . . . 1.50
408 TDF,MBa,LMa,Media
  Blizzard,pt.2 . . . . 1.50
409 . . . . 1.50
410 . . . . 1.50
411 TDF,MBa,LMa,Blood
  Brothers,pt.2 . . . . 1.50
412 . . . . 1.50
413 . . . . 1.50
414 A:The Rose 1.50
415 Onslaught saga,V:Sentinels . 1.50
416 Onslaught epilogue 1.50
417 TDF,RG,secrets of Scrier &
  Judas Traveler 1.50
418 Revelations,pt.3, R:Norman
  Osborn 1.50
419 TDF,SSr,V:Black Tarantula . 1.50
420 TDF,SSr,X-Man x-over,pt.1 . . 1.50
421 TDF,SSr,I:Dragonfly; Electro
  Kidnapped 1.50
422 TDF,SSr,V:Electro,Tarantula . 1.50
423 TDF,V:Electro 1.50

424 TDF,JoB,V:Black Tarantula, The
  Hand, Dragonfly, Delilah,
  The Rose, Elektra 1.50
425 TDF,SSr, V:Electro,double size 2.50
426 TDF,SSr,V:Doctor Octopus . . 1.50
Minus 1 Spec., TDF,JBe, flashback,
  early Kingpin 1.95
Ann.#1 SD,I:Sinister Six 600.00

Amazing Spider-Man #361
© *Marvel Entertainment Group*

Ann.#2 SD,A:Dr.Strange 250.00
Ann.#3 JR,DH,A:Avengers 100.00
Ann.#4 A:H.Torch,V:Mysterio,
  Wizard 90.00
Ann.#5 JR(c),A:Red Skull,I:Peter
  Parker's Parents 100.00
Ann.#6 JR(c),Rep.Ann.#1,Fant.
  Four Ann.#1,SpM #8 . . . . . 30.00
Ann.#7 JR(c),Rep.#1,#2,#38 . . 25.00
Ann.#8 Rep.#46,#50 . . . . 25.00
Ann.#9 JR(c),Rep.Spec.SpM #2 . 28.00
Ann.#10 JR(c),GK,V:Human Fly . 15.00
Ann.#11 GK(c),DP,JM,JR2,AM, . 15.00
Ann.#12 JBy(c),KP,Rep.#119,
  #120 . . . . 15.00
Ann.#13 JBy,TA,V:Dr.Octopus . . 15.00
Ann.#14 FM,TP,A:Dr.Strange,
  V:Dr.Doom,Dormammu 17.00
Ann.#15 FM,KJ,BL,Punisher . . . 20.00
Ann.#16 JR2,JR,I:New Captain
  Marvel,A:Thing 9.00
Ann.#17 EH,JM,V:Kingpin 7.00
Ann.#18 RF,BL,JG,V:Scorpion . . 7.00
Ann.#19 JR(c),MW,V:Spiderslayer 7.00
Ann.#20 BWi(i),V:Iron Man 2020 . 7.00
Ann.#21 JR(c),PR,W:SpM,direct 16.00
Ann.#21a W:SpM,news stand . 15.00
Ann.#22 JR(c),MBa(1stSpM),SD,
  JG,RLm,TD,Evolutionary War,
  I:Speedball,New Men 9.00
Ann.#23 JBy(c),RLd,MBa,RF,
  AtlantisAttacks#4,A:She-Hulk . 9.00
Ann.#24 GK,SD,MZ,DGr,
  A:Ant Man 5.00
Ann.#25 EL(c),SB,PCu,SD,
  Vibranium Vendetta#1,Venom . 6.00
Ann.#26 Hero Killers#1,A:New
  Warriors,BU:Venom,Solo 6.00

Ann.#27 TL,I:Annex,w/card 3.50
Ann.#28 SBt(s),V:Carnage,BU:Cloak &
  Dagger,Rhino 3.25
Ann. '96 two new stories, 48pg, . 3.00
Ann. '97 RSt,TL,RJn, 48pg, ... 3.00
G-Size Superheroes #1 GK,
  A:Morbius,Man-Wolf 55.00
G-Size #1 JR(c),RA,DH,
  A:Dracula 25.00
G-Size #2 K&R(c),RA,AM,
  A:Master of Kung Fu 18.00
G-Size #3 GK(c),RA,DocSavage 18.00
G-Size #4 GK(c),RA,Punisher . 35.00
G-Size #5 GK(c),RA,V:Magnum . 15.00
G-Size #6 Rep.Ann.#4 . . . . 10.00
G-Size Spec.#1 O:Symbiotes . . . 3.95
GNv Fear Itself RA,A:S.Sable . . 12.95
GNv Spirits of the Earth CV,Scotland,
  V:Hellfire Club 25.00
Milestone rep.#149 . . . . 2.95
TPB Assassination Plot,
  rep.#320-325 . . . . 14.95
TPB Carnage,rep.#361-363 . . . . 6.95
TPB Cosmic Adventures rep.
  Amaz.SpM #327-329,Web #59
  61,Spec.SpM #158-160 . . . . 19.95
TPB Kraven's Last Hunt. Reps. AS
  #293,294,Web.#31,32,P.Parker
  #131,132,SC 15.95
  HC 19.95
TPB Origin of the Hobgoblin rep.#238,
  239,244,245,249-251 . . . . . . 14.95
TPB Saga of the Alien Costume,reps.
  #252-259 . . . . 9.95
TPB Spider-Man Vs. Venom,reps.
  A.SpM#298-300,315-317 . . . 10.00
TPB Venom Returns rep.Amaz.SpM.
  #331-333,344-347 . . . . 12.95
TPB The Wedding,Reps.A.S.
  #290-292,Ann#21 . . . . 12.95
Nothing Can Stop the Juggernaut,
  reps.#229,230 . . . . 3.95
Sensational Spider-Man,reps.
  Ann.#14,15; 4.95
Skating on Thin Ice(Canadian) . 15.00
Skating on Thin Ice(US) 1.50
Soul of the Hunter MZ,BMc,
  R:Kraven 7.00
Unicef:Trial of Venom,
  A:Daredevil,V:Venom 50.00
See Also:
PETER PARKER;
SPECTACULAR SPIDER-MAN;
WEB OF SPIDER-MAN

AMAZING SPIDER-MAN INDEX
SEE: OFFICIAL MARVEL INDEX TO THE AMAZING SPIDER-MAN

AMAZING SPIDER-MAN COLLECTION
1 Mark Bagley card set 2.95
2 and 3 MBa, from card set . . . @2.95

AMAZING X-MEN, THE
March–June 1995
1 X-Men after Xavier 6.00
2 Exodus,Dazzler,V:Abyss 3.50
3 F:Bishop 3.00
4 V:Apocalypse 2.50
TPB Rep. #1-#4 . . . . 8.95

MARVEL

AMERICAN TAIL II
Dec., 1991
1 movie adaption 1.00
2 movie adaption 1.00

ANIMAX
Star Comics Dec., 1986
1 Based on Toy Line 1.00
2 . . . . 1.00
3 . . . . 1.00
4 June, 1987 . . . . 1.00

ANNEX
Aug.–Nov. 1994
1 WMc,I:Brace, Crucible of Power 2.00
2 WMc,V:Brace, Crucible, pt.2 . . 1.75
3 Crucible of Power, pt.3 . . . . . 1.75
4 Crucible of Power, pt.4 . . . . . 1.95

ANNIE
(Treasury Edition)
Oct., 1982
1 Movie Adaptation 1.25
2 Nov., 1982 . . . . 1.25

ANNIE OAKLEY
Atlas Spring, 1948
1 A:Hedy Devine 250.00
2 CCB,I:Lana,A:Hedy Devine . 150.00
3 . . . . 125.00
4 . . . . 125.00
5 . . . . 75.00
6 . . . . 60.00
7 . . . . 60.00
8 . . . . 60.00
9 AW, ... 60.00
10 . . . . 50.00
11 June, 1956 . . . . 50.00

A-1
1 The Edge 5.95
2 Cheeky,Wee Budgie Boy 5.95
3 King Leon 5.95
4 King Leon 5.95

APOCALYPSE STRIKEFILES
1 After Xavier special 2.50

ARCHANGEL
1-shot B&W 2.50

ARIZONA KID
Atlas March, 1951
1 RH,Coming of the Arizons Kid 125.00
2 RH,Code of the Gunman . . . 50.00
3 RH(c) 42.00
4 . . . . 42.00
5 . . . . 40.00
6 Jan., 1952 . . . . 40.00

ARRGH!
Dec., 1974
Satire
1 Vampire Rats 3.75
2 . . . . 2.00
3 Beauty And the Big Foot 2.00
4 The Night Gawker 2.00
5 Sept., 1975 . . . . 2.00

ARROWHEAD
April, 1954
1 Indian Warrior Stories 75.00
2 . . . . 50.00
3 . . . . 50.00
4 Nov., 1954 . . . . 50.00

ASTONISHING
See: MARVEL BOY

Astonishing Tales #30
© *Marvel Entertainment Group*

ASTONISHING TALES
August, 1970
1 BEv(c),JK,WW,KaZar,Dr.Doom 25.00
2 JK,WW,Ka-Zar,Dr.Doom 14.00
3 BWS,WW,Ka-Zar,Dr.Doom . . 18.00
4 BWS,WW,Ka-Zar,Dr.Doom . . 18.00
5 BWS,GT,Ka-Zar,Dr.Doom . . . 18.00
6 BWS,BEv,GT,I:Bobbi Morse . 18.00
7 HT,GC,Ka-Zar,Dr.Doom 12.00
8 HT,TS,GT,GC,TP,Ka-Zar . . . 12.00
9 GK(c),JB,Ka-Zar,Dr.Doom . . . 7.00
10 GK(c),BWS,SB,Ka-Zar 10.00
11 GK,O:Kazar 7.00
12 JB,DA,NA,V:Man Thing 8.00
13 JB,RB,DA,V:Man Thing 3.00
14 GK(c),rep. Kazar 3.00
15 GK,TS,Kazar 3.00
16 RB,AM,A:Kazar 3.00
17 DA,V:Gemini 3.00
18 JR(c),DA,A:Kazar 3.00
19 JR(c),DA,JSn,JA,I:Victorious . . 3.00
20 JR(c),A:Kazar 3.00
21 RTs(s),DAy,B:It 3.00
22 RTs(s),DAy,V:Granitor 3.00
23 RTs(s),DAy,A:Fin Fang Foom . 3.00
24 RTs(s),DAy,E:It 3.00
25 RB(a&s),B:I&O:Deathlok,
　 GP(1st art) 35.00
26 RB(a&s),I:Warwolf 11.00
27 RB(a&s),V:Warwolf 10.00
28 RB(a&s),V:Warwolf 10.00
29 rep.Marv.Super Heroes #18 . 13.00
30 RB(a&s),KP, ... 10.00
31 RB(a&s),BW,KP,V:Ryker . . . 10.00
32 RB(a&s),KP,V:Ryker 9.00
33 RB(a&s),KJ,I:Hellinger 9.00
34 RB(a&s),KJ,V:Ryker 9.00

35 RB(a&s),KJ,I:Doomsday-Mech　9.00
36 RB(a&s),KP,E:Deathlok,
　 I:Godwulf 11.00

ASTONISHING X-MEN, THE
March–June 1995
1 Uncanny X-Men 5.00
2 V:Holocaust 3.50
3 V:Abyss 3.00
4 V:Beast,Infinities 2.50
TPB Rep. #1-#4 . . . . 8.95

A-TEAM
March, 1984
1 . . . . 1.00
2 . . . . 1.00
3 May, 1984 . . . . 1.00

ATOMIC AGE
Epic Nov., 1990
1 AW 4.50
2 AW 4.50
3 AW,Feb., 1991 . . . . 4.50

AVENGERS
Sept., 1963
1 JK,O:Avengers,V:Loki 2,500.00
1a rep.Marvel Milestone 2.95
2 JK,V:Space Phantom 625.00
3 JK,V:Hulk,Sub-Mariner 400.00
4 JK,R&J:Captain America . . 1,500.00
5 JK,L:Hulk,V:Lava Men 250.00
6 JK,I:Masters of Evil 180.00
7 JK,V:Baron Zemo,
　 Enchantress 180.00
8 JK,I:Kang 190.00
9 JK(c),DH,I&D:Wonder Man . 215.00
10 JK(c),DH,I:Immortus 175.00
11 JK(c),DH,A:Spider-Man,
　 V:Kang 200.00
12 JK(c),DH,V:Moleman,
　 Red Ghost 100.00
13 JK(c),DH,I:Count Nefaria . . 100.00
14 JK(c),DH,V:Count Nefaria . . . 95.00
15 JK,DH,D:Baron Zemo 80.00
16 JK,J:Hawkeye,Scarlet Witch,
　 Quicksilver 80.00
16a Marvel Milestone 2.95
17 JK(c),DH,V:Mole Man,A:Hulk　85.00
18 JK(c),DH,V:The Commisar . . 85.00
19 JK(c),DH,I&O:Swordsman,
　 O:Hawkeye 90.00
20 JK(c),DH,WW,V:Swordsman,
　 Mandarin 60.00
21 JK(c),DH,WW,V:Power Man
　 (not L.Cage),Enchantress . . . 60.00
22 JK(c),DH,WW,V:Power Man . 60.00
23 JK(c),DH,JR,V:Kang 40.00
24 JK(c),DH,JR,V:Kang 40.00
25 JK(c),DH,V:Dr.Doom 50.00
26 DH,V:Attuma 40.00
27 DH,V:Attuma,Beetle 40.00
28 JK(c),DH,I:1st Goliath,
　 I:Collector 42.00
29 DH,V:Power Man,Swordsman 40.00
30 JK(c),DH,V:Swordsman 40.00
31 DH,V:Keeper of the Flame . . 40.00
32 DH,I:Bill Foster 35.00
33 DH,V:Sons of the Serpent
　 A:Bill Foster 35.00
34 DH,V:Living Laser 35.00
35 DH,V:Mandarin 35.00
36 DH,V:The Ultroids 35.00
37 GK(c),DH,V:Ultroids 35.00

MARVEL

38 GK(c),DH,V:Enchantress,
 Ares,J:Hercules 35.00
39 DH,V:Mad Thinker 35.00
40 DH,V:Sub-Mariner 35.00
41 JB,V:Dragon Man,Diablo 25.00
42 JB,V:Dragon Man,Diablo 25.00
43 JB,V:Red Guardian 25.00
44 JB,V:Red Guardian,
 O:Black.Widow 25.00
45 JB,V:Super Adoptoid 25.00
46 JB,V:Whirlwind 25.00
47 JB,GT,V:Magneto 30.00
48 GT,I&O:New Black Knight . . . 30.00
49 JB,V:Magneto 30.00
50 JB,V:Typhon 25.00
51 JB,GT,R:Iron Man,Thor
 V:Collector 25.00
52 JB,J:Black Panther,
 I:Grim Reaper 30.00

Avengers #8
© Marvel Entertainment Group

53 JB,GT,A:X-Men; x-over
 X-Men #45 . . . . 40.00
54 JB,GT,V:Masters of Evil
 I:Crimson Cowl(Ultron) 25.00
55 JB,I:Ultron,V:Masters of Evil . 20.00
56 JB,D:Bucky retold,
 V:Baron Zemo 20.00
57 JB,I:Vision,V:Ultron 70.00
58 JB,O&J:Vision 45.00
59 JB,I:Yellowjacket 20.00
60 JB,W:Yellowjacket & Wasp . . 18.00
61 JB,A:Dr.Strange,x-over
 Dr. Strange #178 . . . . 17.00
62 JB,I:Man-Ape,A:Dr.Strange . . 17.00
63 GC,I&O:2nd Goliath(Hawkeye)
 V:Egghead 16.00
64 GC,V:Egghead,O:Hawkeye . . 16.00
65 GC,V:Swordsman,Egghead . . 16.00
66 BWS,I:Ultron 6,Adamantium . 17.00
67 BWS,V:Ultron 6 . . . . 17.00
68 SB,V:Ultron 13.00
69 SB,I:Nighthawk,Grandmaster,
 Squadron Supreme, V:Kang . 15.00
70 SB,O:Squadron Supreme
 V:Kang 13.00
71 SB,I:Invaders,V:Kang 25.00
72 SB,A:Captain Marvel,
 I:Zodiac 14.00
73 HT(i),V:Sons of Serpent 14.00

74 JB,TP,V:Sons of Serpent,
 IR:Black Panther on TV 14.00
75 JB,TP,I:Arkon 15.00
76 JB,TP,V:Arkon 14.00
77 JB,TP,V:Split-Second Squad . 14.00
78 SB,TP,V:Lethal Legion 14.00
79 JB,TP,V:Lethal Legion 14.00
80 JB,TP,I&O:Red Wolf 15.00
81 JB,TP,A:Red Wolf 14.00
82 JB,TP,V:Ares,A:Daredevil . . . 14.00
83 JB,TP,I:Valkyrie,
 V:Masters of Evil 15.00
84 JB,TP,V:Enchantress,Arkon . . 14.00
85 JB,V:Squadron Supreme . . . 14.00
86 JB,JM,A:Squad Supreme . . . 14.00
87 SB(i),O:Black Panther,
 V: A.I.M. 30.00
88 SB,JM,V:Psyklop,A:Hulk,
 Professor.X 14.00
89 SB,B:Kree/Skrull War 14.00
90 SB,V:Sentry #459,Ronan,
 Skrulls 14.00
91 SB,V:Sentry #459,Ronan,
 Skrulls 14.00
92 SB,V:Super Skrull,Ronan, . . . 14.00
93 NA,TP,V:Super-Skrull,G-Size . 55.00
94 NA,JB,TP,V:Super-Skrull,
 I:Mandroids 35.00
95 NA,TP,V:Maximus,Skrulls,
 A:Inhumans,O:Black Bolt . . . 35.00
96 NA,TP,V:Skrulls,Ronan 35.00
97 GK&BEv(c),JB,TP,E:Kree-Skrull
 War,V:Annihilus,Ronan,Skrulls,
 A:Golden Age Heroes 20.00
98 BWS,SB,V:Ares,R:Hercules,
 R&N:Hawkeye 25.00
99 BWS,TS,V:Ares 25.00
100 BWS,JSr,V:Ares & Kratos . . 75.00
101 RB,DA,A:Watcher 9.00
102 RB,JSt,V:Grim Reaper,
 Sentinels 9.00
103 RB,JSt,V:Sentinels 9.00
104 RB,JSt,V:Sentinels 9.00
105 JB,JM,V:Savage Land
 Mutates; A:Black Panther . . . 9.00
106 GT,DC,RB,V:Space Phantom 9.00
107 GT,DC,JSn,V:Space
 Phantom, Grim Reaper 11.00
108 DH,DC,JSt,V:Space
 Phantom,Grim Reaper 9.00
109 DH,FMc,V:Champion,
 L:Hawkeye 9.00
110 DH,V:Magneto,A:X-Men . . . 19.00
111 DH,J:Bl.Widow,A:Daredevil,
 X-Men,V:Magneto 19.00
112 DH,I:Mantis,V:Lion-God,
 L:Black Widow 10.00
113 FBe(i),V:The Living Bombs . 8.00
114 JR(c),V:Lion-God,J:Mantis,
 Swordsman 8.00
115 JR(c),A:Defenders,V:Loki,
 Dormammu 10.00
116 JR(c),A:Defenders,S.Surfer
 V:Loki,Dormammu 10.00
117 JR(c),FMc(i),A:Defenders,Silv.
 Surfer,V:Loki,Dormammu . . . 10.00
118 JR(c),A:Defenders,S.Surfer
 V:Loki,Dormammu 10.00
119 JR(c),DH(i),V:Collector 7.50
120 JSn(c),DH(i),V:Zodiac 7.50
121 JR&JSn(c),JB,DH,V:Zodiac . 7.50
122 K&R(c),V:Zodiac 7.50
123 JR(c),DH(i),O:Mantis 7.50
124 JR(c),JB,DC,V:Kree,O:Mantis 7.50
125 JR(c),JB,DC,V:Thanos 14.00

126 DC(i),V:Klaw,Solarr 10.00
127 GK(c),SB,JSon,A:Inhumans,
 V:Ultron,Maximus 10.00
128 K&R(c),SB,JSon,V:Kang . . . 7.50
129 SB,JSon,V:Kang 7.50
130 GK(c),SB,JSon,V:Slasher,
 Titanic Three 7.50
131 GK(c),SB,JSon,V:Kang,
 Legion of the Unliving 7.00
132 SB,JSon,Kang,Legion
 of the Unliving 7.00
133 GK(c),SB,JSon,O:Vision . . . 7.00
134 K&R(c),SB,JSon,O:Vision . . 7.00
135 JSn&JR(c),GT,O:Mantis,
 Vision,C:Thanos 8.00
136 K&R(c),rep Amazing Adv#12 . 7.00
137 JR(c),GT,J:Beast,
 Moondragon 8.50
138 GK(c),GT,V:Toad 7.00

Avengers #100
© Marvel Entertainment Group

139 K&R(c),GT,V:Whirlwind 7.00
140 K&R(c),GT,V:Whirlwind 7.00
141 GK(c),GP,V:Squad.Sinister . . 6.00
142 K&R(c),GP,V:Squadron
 Sinister,Kang 6.00
143 GK(c),GP,V:Squadron
 Sinister,Kang 6.00
144 GP,GK(c),V:Squad.Sinister,
 O&J:Hellcat,O:Buzz Baxter . . 6.00
145 GK(c),DH,V:Assassin 6.00
146 GK(c),DH,KP,V:Assassin . . . 6.00
147 GP,V:Squadron Supreme . . . 6.00
148 JK(c),GP,V:Squad.Supreme . 6.00
149 GP,V:Orka 6.00
150 GP,JK,rep.Avengers #16 . . . 6.00
151 GP,new line-up,
 R:Wonder Man 5.50
152 JB,JSt,I:New Black Talon . . . 6.00
153 JB,JSt,V:L.Laser,Whizzer . . . 5.50
154 GP,V:Attuma 5.50
155 SB,V:Dr.Doom,Attuma 5.50
156 SB,I:Tyrak,V:Attuma 5.50
157 DH,V:Stone Black Knight . . . 5.50
158 JK(c),SB,I&O:Graviton, ... 5.50
159 JK(c),SB,V:Graviton, ... 5.50
160 GP,V:Grim Reaper 5.50

161 GP,V:Ultron,A:Ant-Man	5 50	
162 GP,V:Ultron,I:Jocasta	5.50	
163 GT,A:Champions,V:Typhon . .	5.50	
164 JBy,V:Lethal Legion	6.00	
165 JBy,V:Count Nefario	6.00	
166 JBy,V:Count Nefario	6.00	
167 GP,A:Guardians,A:Nighthawk,		
Korvac,V:Porcupine	5.00	
168 GP,A:Guardians,V:Korvac,		
I:Gyrich	5.00	
169 SB,I:Eternity Man	5.00	
170 GP,R:Jocasta,C:Ultron,		
A:Guardians	5.00	
171 GP,V:Ultron,A:Guardians,		
Ms Marvel	5.00	
172 SB,KJ,V:Tyrak	5.00	
173 SB,V:Collector	5.00	
174 GP(c),V:Collector	5.00	
175 V&O:Korvac,A:Guardians . . .	5.00	
176 V:Korvac,A:Guardians	5.00	
177 DC(c),D:Korvac,A:Guardians	5.00	
178 CI,V:Manipulator	5.00	
179 JM,AG,V:Stinger,Bloodhawk .	5.00	
180 JM,V:Monolith,Stinger,		
D:Bloodhawk	5.00	
181 JBy,GD,I:Scott Lang	6.50	
182 JBy,KJ,V:Maximoff	5.50	
183 JBy,KJ,J:Ms.Marvel	5.50	
184 JBy,KJ,J:Falcon,		
V:Absorbing Man	5.50	
185 JBy,DGr,O:Quicksilver & Scarlet		
Witch,I:Bova,V:Modred	5.50	
186 JBy,DGr,V:Modred,Chthon . .	5.50	
187 JBy,DGr,V:Chthon,Modred . .	5.50	
188 JBy,DGr,V:The Elements . . .	5.50	
189 JBy,DGr,V:Deathbird	5.50	
190 JBy,DGr,V:Grey Gargoyle,		
A:Daredevil	5.50	
191 JBy,DGr,V:Grey Gargoyle,		
A:Daredevil	5.50	
192 I:Inferno	3.50	
193 FM(c),SB,DGr,O:Inferno . . .	3.50	
194 GP,JRu,J:Wonder Man	3.50	
195 GP,JRu,A:Antman,		
I&C:Taskmaster	4.00	
196 GP,JA,A:Antman,		
V:Taskmaster, ...	3.50	
197 CI,JAb,V:Red Ronin	3.50	
198 GP,DGr,V:Red Ronan	3.50	
199 GP,DGr,V:Red Ronan	3.50	
200 GP,DGr,V:Marcus,		
L:Ms.Marvel	5.00	
201 GP,DGr,F:Jarvis	4.00	
202 GP,V:Ultron	4.00	
203 CI,V:Crawlers,F:Wonderman .	3.50	
204 DN,DGr,V:Yellow Claw	3.50	
205 DGr,V:Yellow Claw	3.50	
206 GC,DGr,V:Pyron	3.50	
207 GC,DGr,V:Shadowlord	3.50	
208 GC,DGr,V:Berserker	3.50	
209 DGr,A:Mr.Fantastic,V:Skrull .	3.50	
210 GC,DGr,V:Weathermen	3.50	
211 GC,DGr,Moon Knight,J:Tigra	3.50	
212 DGr,V:Elfqueen	3.50	
213 BH,DGr,L:Yellowjacket	3.50	
214 BH,DGr,V:Gh.Rider,A:Angel	4.00	
215 DGr,A:Silver Surfer,		
V:Molecule Man	3.00	
216 DGr,A:Silver Surfer,		
V:Molecule Man	3.00	
217 BH,DGr,V:Egghead,		
R:Yellowjacket,Wasp3	3.00	
218 DP,V:M.Hardy	3.00	
219 BH,A:Moondragon,Drax	3.50	
220 BH,DGr,D:Drax,V:MnDragon .	3.50	

221 J:She Hulk	3.00	
222 V:Masters of Evil	3.00	
223 A:Antman	3.00	
224 AM,A:Antman	3.00	
225 A:Black Knight	3.00	
226 A:Black Knight	3.00	
227 J:2nd Captain Marvel,		
O:Avengers	3.00	
228 V:Masters of Evil	3.00	
229 JSt,V:Masters of Evil	3.00	
230 A:Cap.Marvel,L:Yellowjacke .	3.00	
231 AM,JSi,J:2nd Captain Marvel,		
Starfox	2.50	
232 AM,JSi	2.50	
233 JBy,V:Annihilus	2.50	
234 AM,JSi,O:ScarletWitch	2.50	
235 AM,JSi,V:Wizard	2.50	
236 AM,JSi,A:SpM,V:Lava Men .	2.50	
237 AM,JSi,A:SpM,V:Lava Men . .	2.50	
238 AM,JSi,V:Moonstone,		
O:Blackout	3.00	
239 AM,JSi,A:David Letterman . .	3.50	

Avengers #215
© Marvel Entertainment Group

240 AM,JSi,A:Dr.Strange	2.50	
241 AM,JSi,V:Morgan LeFey	2.50	
242 AM,JSi,Secret Wars	2.50	
243 AM,JSi,Secret Wars	2.50	
244 AM,JSi,V:Dire Wraiths	2.50	
245 AM,JSi,V:Dire Wraiths	2.50	
246 AM,JSi,V:Eternals	2.50	
247 AM,JSi,A:Eternals,V:Deviants	2.50	
248 AM,JSi,A:Eternals,V:Deviants	2.50	
249 AM,JSi,A:Maelstrom	2.50	
250 AM,JSi,A:W.C.A.		
V:Maelstrom	3.50	
251 BH,JSi,A:Paladin	2.50	
252 BH,JSi,J:Hercules		
V:Blood Brothers	2.50	
253 BH,JSi,J:Black Knight	2.50	
254 BH,JSi,A:W.C.A.	2.50	
255 TP,p(c),JB,Legacy of		
Thanos/Sanctuary II	2.50	
256 JB,TP,A:Kazar	2.50	
257 JB,TP,D:Savage Land,		
I:Nebula	3.00	
258 JB,TP,A:SpM,Firelord,Nebula	2.50	

259 JB,TP,V:Nebula	2.50	
260 JB,TP,SecretWarsII,		
IR:Nebula is Thanos' Grand		
daughter	2.50	
261 JB,TP,Secret Wars II	2.50	
262 JB,TP,J:Submariner	2.50	
263 JB,TP,X-Factor tie-in,		
Rebirth,Marvel Girl,pt.1	6.00	
264 JB,TP,I:2nd Yellow Jacket . . .	2.50	
265 JB,TP,Secret Wars II	2.50	
266 JB,TP,Secret Wars II,A:		
Silver Surfer	2.50	
267 JB,TP,V:Kang	2.50	
268 JB,TP,V:Kang	2.50	
269 JB,TP,V:Kang,A:Immortus . .	2.50	
270 JB,TP,V:Moonstone	2.50	
271 JB,TP,V:Masters of Evil	2.50	
272 JB,TP,A:Alpha Flight	2.50	
273 JB,TP,V:Masters of Evil	2.50	
274 JB,TP,V:Masters of Evil	2.50	
275 JB,TP,V:Masters of Evil	2.50	
276 JB,TP,V:Masters of Evil	2.50	
277 JB,TP,V:Masters of Evil	2.50	
278 JB,TP,V:Tyrok,J:Dr.Druid . . .	2.50	
279 JB,TP,new leader	2.50	
280 BH,KB,O:Jarvis	2.50	
281 JB,TP,V:Olympian Gods . . .	2.50	
282 JB,TP,V:Cerberus	2.50	
283 JB,TP,V:Olympian Gods . . .	2.50	
284 JB,TP,V:Olympian Gods . . .	2.50	
285 JB,TP,V:Zeus	2.50	
286 JB,TP,V:Fixer	2.50	
287 JB,TP,V:Fixer	2.50	
288 JB,TP,V:Sentry 459	2.50	
289 JB,TP,J:Marrina	2.50	
290 JB,TP,V:Adaptoid	2.50	
291 JB,TP,V:Marrina	2.50	
292 JB,TP,V:Leviathon	2.50	
293 JB,TP,V:Leviathon	2.50	
294 JB,TP,V:Nebula	2.50	
295 JB,TP,V:Nebula	2.50	
296 JB,TP,V:Nebula	2.50	
297 JB,TP,V:Nebula	2.50	
298 JB,TP,Inferno,Edwin Jarvis . .	2.50	
299 JB,TP,Inferno,V:Orphan		
Maker,R:Gilgemesh	2.50	
300 JB,TP,WS,Inferno,V:Kang,		
O:Avengers,J:Gilgemesh,		
Mr.Fantastic,Invis.Woman . . .	4.00	
301 BH,DH,A:SuperNova	2.25	
302 RB,TP,V:SuperNova,		
A:Quasar	2.25	
303 RB,TP,V:SuperNova,A:FF . . .	2.00	
304 RB,TP,V:U-Foes,Puma	2.00	
305 PR,TP,V:Lava Men	2.25	
306 PR,TP,O:Lava Men	2.00	
307 PR,TP,V:Lava Men	2.00	
308 PR,TP,A:Eternals,J:Sersi . . .	2.00	
309 PR,TP,V:Blastaar	2.00	
310 PR,TP,V:Blastaar	2.00	
311 PR,TP,Acts of Veng.,V:Loki . .	2.50	
312 PR,TP,Acts of Vengeance,		
V:Freedom Force	2.50	
313 PR,TP,Acts of Vengeance,		
V:Mandarin,Wizard	2.50	
314 PR,TP,J:Sersi,A:Spider-Man,		
V:Nebula	3.00	
315 PR,TP,A:SpM,V:Nebula	2.50	
316 PR,TP,J:Spider-Man	2.50	
317 PR,TP,A:SpM,V:Nebula	2.50	
318 PR,TP,A:SpM,V:Nebula	2.50	
319 PR,B:Crossing Line	2.00	
320 PR,TP,A:Alpha Flight	2.00	
321 PR,Crossing Line#3	2.00	
322 PR,TP,Crossing Line#4	2.00	

323 PR,TP,Crossing Line#5 . . . . . 2.00
324 PR,TP,E:Crossing Line 2.00
325 V:MotherSuperior,
Machinesmith 2.00
326 TP,I:Rage 5.50
327 TP,V:Monsters 2.00
328 TP,O:Rage 4.00
329 TP,J:Sandman,Rage 2.75
330 TP,V:Tetrarch of Entropy . . . 2.00
331 TP,J:Rage,Sandman 2.00
332 TP,V:Dr.Doom 2.00
333 HT,V:Dr.Doom 2.00
334 NKu,TP,B:Collector,
A:Inhumans 2.00
335 RLm(c),SEp,TP,V:Thane
Ector,A:Collector, ... 1.75
336 RLm(c),SEp,TP 1.75
337 RLm(c),SEp,TP,V:ThaneEctor 1.75
338 RLm(c),SEp,TP,A:Beast, ... 1.75
339 RLm(c),SEp,TP,E:Collector . . 1.75
340 RLm(c),F:Capt.Amer.,Wasp . . 1.75
341 SEp,TP,A:New Warriors,V:Sons
of Serpents 1.75
342 SEP,TP,A:New Warriors,
V:Hatemonger 1.75
343 SEp,TP,J:Crystal,C&I:2nd
Swordsman,Magdalene 2.00
344 SEp,TP,I:Proctor 2.00
345 SEp,TP,Oper. Galactic Storm
Pt.5,V:Kree,Shiar 1.75
346 SEp,TP,Oper. Galactic Storm
Pt.12,I:Star Force 1.75
347 SEp,TP,Oper. Galactic Storm
Pt.19,D:Kree Race,Conclusion 2.00
348 SEp,TP,F:Vision 1.75
349 SEp,TP,V:Ares 1.75
350 SEp,TP,rep.Avengers#53,A:Prof.
X,Cyclops,V:StarJammers 3.00
351 KWe,V:Star Jammers 1.75
352 V:Grim Reaper 1.75
353 V:Grim Reaper 1.75
354 V:Grim Reaper 1.75
355 BHs(s),SEp,I:Gatherers,
Coal Tiger 2.00
356 B:BHs(s),SEp,TP,A:Bl.Panther
D:Coal Tiger 1.75
357 SEp,TP,A:Watcher 1.75
358 SEp,TP,V:Arkon 1.75
359 SEp,TP,A:Arkon 1.75
360 SEp,TP,V:Proctor,double-size,
bronze foil(c) 5.00
361 SEp,I:Alternate Vision 1.50
362 SEp,TP,V:Proctor 1.50
363 SEp,TP,V:Proctor,D:Alternate
Vision,C:Deathcry,Silver Foil(c),
30th Anniv., ... 4.00
364 SEp,TP,I:Deathcry,V:Kree . . . 1.50
365 SEp,TP,V:Kree 1.50
366 SEp,TP,V:Kree,N:Dr.Pym,Gold
Foil(c) 4.50
367 F:Vision 2.00
368 SEp,TP,Bloodties#1,
A:X-Men 4.00
369 SEp,TP,E:BHs(s),Bloodties#5,
D:Cortez,V:Exodus,Platinum
Foil(c) 3.50
370 SEp(c),TP(c),GI,V:Deviants,
A:Kro,I:Delta Force 1.50
371 GM,TP,V:Deviants,A:Kro 1.50
372 B:BHs(s),SEp,TP,I:2nd
Gatherers,A:Proctor 1.50
373 SEp,TP,I:Alternate Jocasta,
V:Sersi 1.50
374 SEp,TP,O&I:Proctor is Alternate
Black Knight 1.50

375 SEp,TP,Double Sized,D:Proctor,
L:Sersi,Black Knight 3.25
376 F:Crystal,I:Terrigen 1.75
377 F:Quicksilver 1.50
378 TP,I:Butcher 1.50
379 TP,Hercules,V:Hera 1.50
379a Avengers Double Feature #1
flip-book with Giant-Man #1 . . 2.50
380 Hera 4.00
380a Avengers Double Feature #2
flip-book with Giant Man #2 . . 2.50
381 Quicksilvr, Scarlet Witch 1.50
381a Avengers Double Feature #3
flip-book with Giant Man #3 . . 2.50
382 Wundagore 1.50
382a Avengers Double Feature #4

Avengers #400
© *Marvel Entertainment Group*

flip-book with Giant Man #4 . . . 2.50
383 A:Fantastic Force,V:Arides . . . 1.50
384 Hercules Vs. Stepmom 5.00
385 V:Red Skull 4.00
386 F:Black Widow 2.00
387 Taking A.I.M.,pt.2 . . . . 4.00
388 Taking A.I.M.,pt.4 . . . . 4.00
389 B:Mike Deodato 4.00
390 BHs,TP,The Crossing, prelude 4.00
391 BHs,Cont. From Avg. Crossing 4.00
392 BHs,TP,The Crossing 2.25
393 BHs,TP,The Crossing 2.25
394 BHs,TP,The Crossing 2.25
395 BHs,TP,Timeslide concludes . 2.00
396 . . . . 2.00
397 TP,Incred.Hulk #440 x-over . . 2.00
398 TP,V:Unknown foe 2.00
399 . . . . 2.00
400 MeW,MWa,double size 4.50
401 MeW,MWa,Onslaught saga . . 2.50
402 MWa,MD2,Onslaught, finale . 2.50
Ann.#1 DH,V:Mandarin,
Masters of Evil 60.00
Ann.#2 DH,JB,V:Scar.Centurion . 35.00
Ann.#3 rep.#4,T.ofSusp.#66-68 . 25.00
Ann.#4 rep.#5,#6 . . . . 15.00
Ann.#5 JK(c),rep.#8,#11 . . . . . . 15.00
Ann.#6 GP,HT,V:Laser,Nuklo,
Whirlwind 10.00
Ann.#7 JSn,JRu,V:Thanos,A:Captain
Marvel,D:Warlock(2nd) 20.00
Ann.#8 GP,V:Dr.Spectrum 6.00

Ann.#9 DN,V:Arsenal 5.00
Ann.#10 MGo,A:X-Men,Spid.Woman,
I:Rogue,V:Br.o/Evil Mutants . . 30.00
Ann.#11 DP,V:Defenders 5.00
Ann.#12 JG,V:Inhumans,Maximus 4.00
Ann.#13 JBy,V:Armin Zola 4.00
Ann.#14 JBy,KB,V:Skrulls 4.00
Ann.#15 SD,KJ,V:Freedom Force 4.00
Ann.#16 RF,BH,TP,JR2,BSz,KP,AW,
MR,BL,BWi,JG,KN,A:Silver
Surfer,Rebirth Grandmaster . . 4.50
Ann.#17 MBr,MG,Evol.Wars,J:2nd
Yellow Jacket 4.00
Ann.#18 MBa,MG,Atlan.Attack#8,
J:Quasar 3.00
Ann.#19 HT,Terminus Factor 2.50
Ann.#20 Subterran.Odyssey#1 . . 2.50
Ann.#21 Citizen Kang#4 . . . . 2.50
Ann.#22 I:Bloodwraith,w/card 3.25
Ann.#23 JB 3.25
G-Size#1 JR(c),RB,DA,I:Nuklo . . . 6.00
G-Size#2 JR(c),DC,O:Kang,
D:Swordsman,O:Rama-Tut . . . 5.00
G-Size#3 GK(c),DC,V:Kang,Legion
of the Unliving 5.00
G-Size#4 K&R(c),DH,W:Scarlet Witch
&Vision,O:Mantis,Moondragon 5.00
G-Size#5 rep,Annual #1. . . . . . . 3.00
GNv Death Trap:The Vault RLm,
A:Venom 20.00
Milestone #1,Rep.#1 . . . . 2.95
Milestone #2 rep.#16 . . . . 2.95
TPB Greatest Battles of the
Avengers 15.95
TPB Korvac Saga,rep.#167-177 . 12.95
TPB Yesterday Quest,Rep.#181,182
185-187 . . . . 6.95

AVENGERS
(Nov. 1996)
1 RLd,JV,CYp,JSb,Heroes Reborn,
F:Thor, Captain America,
V:Loki 6.00
1A Variant cover 7.50
1 gold signature edition, bagged 40.00
2 RLd,JV,CYp,JSb,V:Kang 2.50
3 RLd,JV,CYp,JSb,V:Kang,A:Nick
Fury 2.50
4 RLd,JLb,CYp,JSb 2.50
4A variant cover 2.50
5 RLd,CYp,JSb,V:Hulk,concl. . . . 2.00
6 RLd,JLb,CYp,JSb,"Industrial
Revolution", pt.1 x-over 2.00
7 RLd,JLb,IaC,JSb, ... 2.00
8 RLd,JLb,IaC,JSb,F:Simon
Williams (Wonder Man),V:Ultron,
Lethal Legion 2.00
9 JLb,RLd,IaC,F:Vision, Wonder
Man 1.95
10 WS, ... 1.95
Minus 1 Spec., JLb,RLd,IaC,JSb,
flashback 1.95

AVENGERS INDEX
**SEE: OFFICIAL MARVEL
INDEX TO THE AVENGERS**

AVENGERS LOG
1 GP(c),History of the Avengers . 2.25

AVENGERS SPOTLIGHT
**August, 1989
Formerly: Solo Avengers**
21 AM,DH,TMo,JRu,Hawkeye,

Starfox 1.25
22 AM,DH,Hawkeye,O:Swordsman 1.25
23 AM,DH,KD,Hawkeye,Vision . . . 1.25
24 AM,DH,Hawkeye,O:Espirita . . . 1.25
25 AM,TMo,Hawkeye,Rick Jones . . 1.25
26 A of V,Hawkeye,Iron Man 1.25
27 A of V,AM,DH,DT,Hawkeye,
    Avengers 1.25
28 A of V,AM,DH,DT,Hawkeye,
    Wonder Man,Wasp 1.25
29 A of V,DT,Hawkeye,Iron Man . 1.25
30 AM,DH,Hawkeye,New Costume 1.25
31 AM,DH,KW,Hawkeye,US.Agent 1.25
32 AM,KW,Hawkeye,U.S.Agent . . 1.25
33 AM,DH,KW,Hawkeye,US.Agent 1.25
34 AM,DH,KW,SLi(c),Hawkeye
    U.S.Agent 1.25
35 JV,Gilgamesh 1.25
36 AM,DH,Hawkeye 1.25
37 BH,Dr.Druid 1.25
38 JBr,Tigra 1.25
39 GCo,Black Knight 1.25
40 Vision,Last Issue 1.25

AVENGERS STRIKEFILE

1 BHa(s),Avengers Pin-ups 2.00

AVENGERS:
THE CROSSING

1 BHs,Death of an Avenger,
    chromium cover,48pg. 6.00

AVENGERS: THE
TERMINATRIX OBJECTIVE

1 B:MGu(s),MG,Holografx(c),
    V:Terminatrix 2.75
2 MG,V:Terminatrix,A:Kangs 2.00
3 MG,V:Terminatrix,A:Kangs 2.00
4 MG,Last issue 2.00

AVENGERS: TIMESLIDE

1 BHs,TKa,End of the Crossing
    Megallic chrome cover 4.95

AVENGERS/ULTRAFORCE

1 V:Malibu's Ultraforce 3.95

AVENGERS UNLEASHED

1 V:Count Nefarious 1.00
Becomes:
AVENGERS UNPLUGGED
1996
2 Crushed by Graviton 1.00
3 x-over with FF Unplugged 1.00
4 . . . . 1.00
5 . . . . 1.00

AVENGERS WEST COAST
Sept., 1989
Prev: West Coast Avengers
47 JBy,V:J.Random 2.00
48 JBy,V:J.Random 2.00
49 JBy,V:J.Random,W.Man 2.00
50 JBy,R:G.A.Human Torch 2.00
51 JBy,R:Iron Man 2.00
52 JBy,V:MasterPandmonum 2.00
53 JBy,Acts ofVeng.,V:U-Foes . . . 2.00
54 JBy,Acts ofVeng.,V:MoleMan . 2.00
55 JBy,Acts ofVeng.finale,V:Loki
    Magneto kidnaps Sc.Witch . . . 2.50
56 JBy,V:Magneto 2.50
57 JBy,V:Magneto 2.50

Avengers West Coast #96
© Marvel Entertainment Group

58 V:Vibro, ... 2.00
59 TMo,V:Hydro-Man,A:Immortus 2.00
60 PR,V:Immortus, ... 2.00
61 PR,V:Immortus 2.00
62 V:Immortus 2.00
63 PR,I:Living Lightning 2.00
64 F:G.A.Human Torch 2.00
65 PR,V:Ultron,Grim Reaper 2.00
66 PR,V:Ultron,Grim Reaper 2.00
67 PR,V:Ultron,Grim Reaper 2.00
68 PR,V:Ultron 2.00
69 PR,USAgent vs Hawkeye,
    I:Pacific Overlords 2.50
70 DR,V:Pacific Overlords 1.75
71 DR,V:Pacific Overlords 1.75
72 DR,V:Pacific Overlords 1.75
73 DR,V:Pacific Overlords 1.75
74 DR,J:Living Lightning,Spider
    Woman,V:Pacific Overlords. . . 1.75
75 HT,A:F.F,V:Arkon,double 2.00
76 DR,Night Shift,I:Man-Demon . . 1.50
77 DR,A:Satannish & Nightshift . . 1.50
78 DR,V:Satannish & Nightshift . . 1.50
79 DR,A:Dr.Strange,V:Satannish . 1.50
80 DR,Galactic Storm,pt.2 . . . . . 1.50
81 DR,Galactic Storm,pt.9 . . . . . 1.50
82 DR,Galactic Storm,pt.16
    A:Lilandra 1.50
83 V:Hyena 1.50
84 DR,I:Deathweb,A:SpM,
    O:Spider-Woman 1.75
85 DR,A:SpM,V:Death Web 1.50
86 DR,A:SpM,V:Death Web 1.50
87 DR,A:Wolverine,V:Bogatyri . . . 1.75
88 DR,A:Wolverine,V:Bogatyri . . . 1.75
89 DR,V:Ultron 1.50
90 DR,A:Vision,V:Ultron 1.50
91 DR,V:Ultron,I:War Toy 1.50
92 DR,V:Goliath(Power Man) 1.50
93 DR,V:Doctor Demonicus 1.50
94 DR,J:War Machine 1.75
95 DR,A:Darkhawk,V:Doctor
    Demonicus 1.50
96 DR,Inf.Crusade x-over 1.50
97 ACe,Inf.Crusade,V:Power
    Platoon 1.50
98 DR,I:4th Lethal Legion 1.50
99 DR,V:4th Lethal Legion 1.50

100 DR,D:Mockingbird,V:4th Lethal
    Legion,Red Foil(c) 3.50
101 DR,Bloodties#3,V:Exodus . . . 4.00
102 DR,L:Iron Man,Spider-Woman,
    US Agent,Scarlet Witch,War
    Machine,last issue 4.00
Ann.#4 JBy,TA,MBa,Atlan.Attacks
    #12,V:Seven Brides of Set . . . 4.00
Ann.#5 Terminus Factor 3.50
Ann.#6 Subterranean Odyssey#5 . 2.50
Ann.#7 Assault on Armor City#4 . 2.25
Ann.#8 DR,I:Raptor w/card 3.25

BALDER THE BRAVE
Nov., 1985
1 WS,SB,V:Frost Giants 1.50
2 WS,SB,V:Frost Giants 1.25
3 WS,SB,V:Frost Giants 1.25
4 WS,SB,V:Frost Giants;Feb,1986 1.25

BARBIE
Jan., 1991
1 polybagged with Credit Card . . 3.00
2 . . . . 1.50
3 . . . . 1.50
4 Ice Skating 1.50
5 Sea Cruise 1.50
6 Sun Runner Story 1.50
7 Travel issue 1.50
8 TV Commercial 1.50
9 Music Tour Van 1.50
10 Barbie in Italy 1.50
11 Haunted Castles 1.50
12 Monkey Bandit 1.50
13 MW,A:Skipper,Ken 1.50
14 Country Fair 1.50
15 Barbie in Egypt,pt.1 . . . . 1.50
16 Barbie in Egypt,pt.2 . . . . 1.50
17 Weightwatchers/Art issue . . . 1.50
18 V:heavy Metal Band 1.50
19 A:Surfer Pal 1.50
20 Skipper at Special Olympics . . 1.25
21 I:Whitney,female fire fighter . . 1.25
22 Barbie in Greece 1.25
23 thru 27 . . . . @1.25
28 Valentine's Day Issue 1.25
29 Skipper babysits 1.25
30 Cowgirls on the Range 1.25
31 Rest and Relaxation 1.25
32 A:Dandy the Gorilla 1.25
33 thru 41 . . . . @1.25
42 thru 49 . . . . @1.50
50 Anniv. issue, Disney World(c) . 2.25
51 Vet's assistant 1.50
52 Valentines Day Special 1.50
53 Marooned 1.50
54 Female Inventors 1.50
55 in Nashville 1.50
56 Sherlock Barbie 1.50
57 Nashville 1.50
58 Barbie Teaches Skating 1.50
59 Famous Females 1.50
60 Halloween Hero 1.50
61 Alaska Gold Rush 1.50
62 Christmas/Nutcracker 1.50
63 . . . . 1.50
64 . . . . 1.50
65 Under Antarctica 1.50

BARBIE FASHION
Jan., 1991
1 polybagged with dorknob hanger 2.00
2 thru 55 . . . . @1.25

MARVEL

MARVEL

BATTLE
Atlas March, 1951
1 They called Him a Coward	175.00
2 The War Department Secrets	75.00
3 The Beast of the Bataan	50.00
4 I:Buck Private O'Toole	50.00
5 Death Trap Of Gen. Wu.	50.00
6 RH	50.00
7 Enemy Sniper	50.00
8 A Time to Die	50.00
9 RH	45.00
10	40.00
11 thru 20	@30.00
21	40.00
22	30.00
23	40.00
24	30.00
25	30.00
26 JR	30.00
27	30.00
28 JSe	30.00
29	30.00
30	30.00
31 RH	32.00
32 JSe,GT	30.00
33 GC,JSe,JSt	30.00
34 JSe	30.00
35	30.00
36 BEv	32.00
37 RA,JSt	30.00
38	25.00
39	25.00
40	25.00
41	28.00
42 thru 46	@25.00
47 JO	25.00
48	25.00
49	25.00
50 BEv	25.00
51	25.00
52 GWb	25.00
53	25.00
54	25.00
55 GC	40.00
56	25.00
57	28.00
58	25.00
59	25.00
60 A:Combat Kelly	25.00
61 A:Combat Kelly	25.00
62 A:Combat Kelly	25.00
63	30.00
64	30.00
65	30.00
66 JSe,JK	35.00
67 JSe,JK	35.00
68 JSe,JK	28.00
69 RH,JSe,JK	28.00
70 BEv,SD; June, 1960	28.00

BATTLE ACTION
Atlas Feb., 1952
1	125.00
2	50.00
3	30.00
4	30.00
5	28.00
6	30.00
7	40.00
8	40.00
9	30.00
10	30.00
11 thru 15	@25.00
16 thru 26	@20.00

27	30.00
28	20.00
29	20.00
30 August, 1957	30.00

BATTLE BRADY
See: MEN IN ACTION

BATTLEFIELD
Atlas April, 1952
1 RH, Slaughter on Suicide Ridge	100.00
2	50.00
3 Ambush Patrol	50.00
4	50.00
5 Into the Jaws of Death	50.00
6 thru 10	@22.00
11 GC,May, 1953	22.00

BATTLEFRONT
Atlas June, 1952
1 RH(c),Operation Killer	150.00
2	70.00
3 Spearhead	50.00
4 Death Trap of General Chun	50.00
5 Terror of the Tank Men	40.00
6 A:Combat Kelly	40.00
7 A:Combat Kelly	40.00
8 A:Combat Kelly	40.00
9 A:Combat Kelly	40.00
10 A:Combat Kelly	40.00
11 thru 20	@25.00
21 thru 39	@18.00
40 AW	40.00
15	20.00
16 AW	40.00
43 thru 48 August,1957	@20.00

BATTLEGROUND
Atlas Sept., 1954
1	100.00
2 JKz	50.00
3 thru 8	@35.00
9	40.00
10	35.00
11	40.00
12	25.00
13	40.00
14	35.00
15	25.00
16	25.00
17	25.00
18	40.00
19	25.00
20 August, 1957	25.00

BATTLESTAR GALACTICA
March, 1979
1 EC,B:TV Adaptation; Annihalation	3.00
2 EC,Exodus	2.50
3 EC,Deathtrap	2.50
4 WS,Dogfight	2.50
5 WS,E:TV Adaptation;Ambush	2.50
6 Nightmare	2.00
7 Commander Adama Trapped	2.00
8 Last Stand	2.00
9 Space Mimic	2.00
10 This Planet Hungers	2.00
11 WS,Starbuck's Dilemma	2.00
12 WS,Memory Ends	2.00
13 WS,All Out Attack	2.00

14 Radiation Threat	2.00
15 Ship of Crawling Death	2.00
16	2.00
17 Animal on the Loose	2.00
18 Battle For the Forbidden Fruit	2.00
19 Starbuck's Back	2.00
20 Duel to the Death	2.00
21 To Slay a Monster..To Deatroy a World	2.00
22 WS,A Love Story?	2.00
23 Dec., 1981	2.00

BATTLETIDE
1 thru 4 F: Death's Head II and Killpower	@1.75

BATTLETIDE II
1 Foil embossed cover	2.95
2 thru 8 F: Death's Head II and Killpower	@1.75

BEAST
(March 1997)
1 (of 3) KG,CNn,F:Karma, Cannonball, V:Viper & Spiral	2.50
2 KG,CNn,V:Spiral	2.50
3 KG,CNn, concl.	2.50

Beauty and the Beast #3
© *Marvel Entertainment Group*

BEAUTY AND THE BEAST
Jan., 1985
1 DP,Beast & Dazzler,direct	3.00
1a DP,Beast & Dazzler,UPC	2.00
2 DP,Beast & Dazzler	2.00
3 DP,Beast & Dazzler	2.00
4 DP,Beast & Dazzler	2.00

BEAUTY AND THE BEAST
1	1.50
2 Wardrobe's birthday party	1.50
3	1.50
4	1.50
5	1.50
6 Lumiere takes Cogsworth's job	1.50
7 Belle & Chip caught in snow	1.50
8	1.50
9 Can Beast prove his love?	1.50

10 Chip & Belle have a snow ball 1.50
11 History of Beast's Castle 1.50
12 . . . . 1.50
13 The Dessert Disaster 1.50

BEAVIS & BUTT-HEAD
March 1994
1 Based on the MTV Show 5.00
1a 2nd Printing 2.50
2 Dead from the Neck up 3.50
3 Break out at Burger World 3.00
4 Tattoo Parlor 2.25
5 Field Day 2.25
6 Revulsion 2.25
7 Oldies bot 2.25
8 Be a clown 2.25
9 Makin' movies 2.25
10 Halloween 2.25
11 . . . . 2.00
12 . . . . 2.00
13 . . . . 2.00
14 Join Biker Gang 2.00
15 Spring Break 2.00
16 Capture The Flag 2.00
17 with video camera 2.00
18 Woodsuck 2.00
19 break-up? 2.00
20 Solar Eclipse 2.00
21 Male Cheerleaders 2.00
22 Antics at theme park 2.00
23 Witless 2.00
24 Holiday suck-tacular 2.00
25 . . . . 1.95
26 . . . . 1.95
27 Easter spirit 1.95
TPB Greatest Hits, rep.#1–#4 . 12.95
TPB Holidazed and Confused . . 12.95

BEST OF MARVEL '96
TPB 224pg. 19.95

BEST WESTERN
June, 1949
58 A:KidColt,BlackRider,Two-Gun
   Kid;Million DollarTrainRobbery110.00
59 A:BlackRider,KidColt,Two-Gun
   Kid;The Black Rider Strikes . . 90.00
Becomes:
WESTERN OUTLAWS
& SHERIFFS
60 PH(c),Hawk Gaither 100.00
61 Ph(c),Pepper Lawson 75.00
62 Murder at Roaring
   House Bridge 75.00
63 thru 65 . . . . @75.00
66 . . . . 50.00
67 . . . . 70.00
68 thru 72 . . . . @50.00
73 June, 1952 . . . . 40.00

BEWARE
March, 1973
1 Reprints 4.50
2 thru 8 . . . . @2.50
Becomes:
TOMB OF DARKNESS
9 Reprints 2.00
10 thru 22 . . . . @1.00
23 November, 1976 . . . . 2.00

BIKER MICE FROM MARS
1 I:Biker Mice 1.50

2 thru 3 . . . . 1.50

BILL & TED'S
BOGUS JOURNEY
Nov., 1991
1 Movie Adaption 3.25

BILL & TED'S
EXCELLENT COMICS
Dec., 1991
1 From Movie; Wedding Reception 1.25
2 Death Takes a Vacation 1.25
3 'Daze in the Lives' 1.25
4 Station Plague 1.25
5 Bill & Ted on Trial 1.25
6 Time Trial 1.25
7 Time Trial, Concl 1.25
8 History Final 1.25
9 I:Morty(new Death) 1.25
10 'Hyperworld' 1.25
11 Lincoln assassination 1.25
12 Last issue 1.25

BILLY BUCKSKIN
WESTERN
Atlas Nov., 1955
1 MD,Tales of the Wild Frontier . 70.00
2 MD,Ambush 45.00
3 MD,AW, Thieves in the Night . 45.00
Becomes:
2-GUN KID
4 SD,A: Apache Kid 60.00
Becomes:
TWO-GUN WESTERN
5 B:Apache Kid,Doc Holiday,
   Kid Colt Outlaw 60.00
6 . . . . 30.00
7 . . . . 30.00
8 RC 40.00
9 AW 40.00
10 . . . . 30.00
11 AW 40.00
12 Sept., 1957,RC 40.00

BISHOP
1 Mountjoy, foil cover 4.50
2 foil stamped cover 4.00
3 JOs 3.50
4 V:Mountjoy 3.50

BIZARRE ADVENTURES
See: MARVEL PREVIEW

BLACK AXE
1 JR2(c),A:Death's Head II 2.00
2 JR2(2),A:Sunfire,V:The Hand . 2.00
3 A:Death's Head II,V:Mesphisto . 2.00
4 in ancient Egypt 2.00
5 KJ(c),In Wakanda 2.00
6 KJ(c),A:Black Panther 2.00
7 KJ(c),A:Black Panther 1.75
8 thru 13 . . . . @1.75

BLACK CAT
Limited Series]
1 Wld,A:Spider-Man,V:Cardiac,
   I:Faze 1.75
2 Wld,V:Faze 1.50
3 Wld,Cardiac 1.50
4 Wld,V:Scar 1.50

Black Knight #4
© Marvel Entertainment Group

BLACK DRAGON
Epic May 1985
1 JBo 6.00
2 JBo 4.00
3 JBo 3.00
4 JBo 3.00
5 JBo 3.00
6 JBo 3.00

BLACK GOLIATH
Feb., 1976—Nov., 1976
1 GT,O:Black Goliath,Cont's
   From Powerman #24 . . . . . . 5.00
2 GT,V:Warhawk 4.00
3 GT,D:Atom-Smasher 4.00
4 KP,V:Stilt-Man 4.00
5 D:Mortag 4.00

BLACK KNIGHT, THE
Atlas May, 1955—April, 1956
1 O: Crusader;The Black Knight
   Rides 650.00
2 Siege on Camelot 500.00
3 Blacknight Unmasked 400.00
4 Betrayed 400.00
5 SSh,The Invincible Tartar . . 400.00

BLACK KNIGHT
June, 1990—Sept., 1990
1 TD,R:Original Black Knight . . . 2.00
2 TD,A:Dreadknight 1.75
3 RB,A:Dr.Strange 1.75
4 RB,TD,A:Dr Strange, Valkyrie . 1.75

BLACK KNIGHT
Exodus R:Black Knight,A:Sersi,
   O:Exodus 2.50

BLACK PANTHER
[1st Series]
Jan., 1977—May, 1979
1 JK,V:Collectors 9.00
2 JK,V:Six Million Year Man . . . 5.00
3 JK,V:Ogar 3.50
4 JK,V:Collectors 3.50
5 JK,V:Yeti 3.50

6 JK,V:Ronin	3.50
7 JK,V:Mister Little	3.50
8 JK,D:Black Panther	3.50
9 JK,V:Jakarra	3.50
10 JK,V:Jakarra	3.50
11 JK,V:Kilber the Cruel	3.50
12 JK,V:Kilber the Cruel	3.50
13 JK,V:Kilber the Cruel	3.50
14 JK,A:Avengers,V:Klaw	3.50
15 JK,A:Avengers,V:Klaw	3.50

BLACK PANTHER
July 1988—Oct. 1988
[1st Mini-Series]

1 I:Panther Spirit	2.50
2 V:Supremacists	2.50
3 A:Malaika	2.50
4 V:Panther Spirit	2.50

[2nd Mini-Series]
PANTHER'S PREY
May, 1991

1 DT,A:W'Kabi,V:Solomon Prey	4.95
2 DT,V:Solomon Prey	4.95
3 DT,V:Solomon Prey	4.95
4 DT,V:Solomon Prey	4.95

BLACK RIDER
See: ALL WINNERS COMICS

BLACK RIDER RIDES AGAIN
Atlas Sept., 1957

1 JK,Treachery at Hangman's Ridge	150.00

BLACKSTONE, THE MAGICIAN
May, 1948—Sept., 1948

2 B:Blonde Phantom	400.00
3	275.00
4 Bondage(c)	300.00

BLACKWULF

1 AMe,Embossied(c),I:Mammoth, Touchstone,Toxin,D:Pelops, V:Tantalus,	2.75
2 AMe,I:Sparrow,Wildwind	1.75
3 AMe,I:Scratch	1.50
4 AMe,I:Giant-man	1.50
5 AMe	1.50
6 AMe,Tantalus	1.50
7 AMe,V:Tantalus	1.50
8 AMe	1.50
9 Seven Worlds of Tantalus,pt.1 A:Daredevil	1.50
10 Seven Worlds of Tantalus,pt.2, last issue	1.50

BLADE, THE VAMPIRE HUNTER

1 Foil(c),Clv(i),R:Dracula	3.25
2 Clv(i),V:Dracula	1.95
3 Clv(i)	1.95
4 Clv(i)	1.95
5 Clv(i)	1.95
6 Clv(i)	1.95
7 Clv(i)	1.95
8 Bible John, Morbius	1.95
9	1.95
10 R:Dracula	1.95
11 Dracula Untombed,pt.2	1.95

Blade, The Vampire Hunter #6
© *Marvel Entertainment Group*

BLADE RUNNER
Oct., 1982

1 AW, Movie Adaption	1.50
2 AW,	1.50

BLAZE
[Limited Series]

1 HMe(s),RoW,A:Clara Menninger	2.00
2 HMe(s),RoW,I:Initiate	2.00
3 HMe(s),RoW,	2.00
4 HMe(s),RoW,D:Initiate,Last issue	2.00

[Regular Series] Aug. 1994

1 HMz,LHa,foil (c)	3.25
2 HMz,LHa,I:Man-Thing	2.25
3 HMz,LHa,V:Ice Box Bob	1.95
4 HMz,LHa,Apache Autumn,pt.1	1.95
5 HMz,LHa,Apache Autumn,pt.2	1.95
6 Apache Autumn,pt.3	1.95
7 Carnivale Quintano	1.95
8 A:Arcae	1.95
9 Clara's Eyeballs	1.95
10 Undead M.C.	1.95
11 A:Punisher	1.95
12 reunited with children, final iss.	1.95

BLAZE CARSON
Sept., 1948

1 SSh(c),Fight,Lawman or Crawl	135.00
2 Guns Roar on Boot Hill	75.00
3 A:Tex Morgan	85.00
4 A:Two-Gun Kid	75.00
5 A:Tex Taylor	75.00

Becomes:
REX HART

6 CCB,Ph(c),B:Rex Hart, A:Black Rider	125.00
7 Ph(c),Mystery at Bar-2 Ranch	100.00
8 Ph(c),The Hombre Who Killed His Friends	100.00

Becomes:
WHIP WILSON

9 Ph(c),B:Whip Wilson,O:Bullet; Duel to the Death	350.00
10 Ph(c),Wanted for Murder	250.00

11 Ph(c)	250.00

Becomes:
GUNHAWK, THE

12 The Redskin's Revenge	75.00
13 GT,The Man Who Murdered Gunhawk	60.00
14	60.00
15	60.00
16	60.00
17	60.00
18 Dec., 1951	60.00

BLAZE, THE WONDER COLLIE
Oct., 1949

2 Ph(c),Blaze-Son of Fury	125.00
3 Ph(c), Lonely Boy;Feb.,1950	100.00

BLONDE PHANTOM
See: ALL-SELECT COMICS

BLOOD
Feb., 1988—April, 1988

1	6.00
2 thru 4	@5.00

BLOOD & GLORY

1 KJ Cap & the Punisher	5.95
2 KJ Cap & the Punisher	5.95
3 KJ Cap & the Punisher	5.95

BLOODLINES
Epic

1 F:Kathy Grant-Peace Corps	5.95

BLOODSEED

1 LSh,I:Bloodseed	2.25
2 LSh,V:Female Bloodseed	2.25

BOOK OF THE DEAD

1 thru 4 Horror rep	@2.00
5 and 6	@1.75

BOZZ CHRONICLES, THE
Epic Dec., 1985

1 thru 5	@1.75
6 May, 1986	1.75

BRATS BIZARRE
Epic

1	3.25
2 thru 4	@2.50

BREAK THE CHAIN

1 KB,KRS-One,w/audio tape	7.00

BRUTE FORCE
August, 1990

1 JD/JSt	1.00
2	1.00
3	1.00
4 November, 1990	1.00

BUCK DUCK
Atlas June, 1953

1 (fa)stories	40.00
2 and 3	@22.00
4 Dec., 1953	22.00

MARVEL

BUCKAROO BANZAI
Dec., 1984
1 Movie Adaption 3.00
2 Conclusion, Feb., 1985 . . . . . . 2.00

BUG
1997
1-shot 48pg 3.00

BULLWINKLE & ROCKY
Star Nov., 1987
1 EC&AM,Based on 1960's TV
  Series 3.00
2 EC&AM, ... 2.00
3 EC&AM,Rumpled Mudluck
  Thyme Mag 2.00
4 EC&AM,Boris and Natasha . . . 2.00
5 EC&AM, ... 2.00
6 EC&AM,Wassamatta Me 2.00
7 EC&AM,Politics,Moose V:Boris 2.00
8 EC&AM,Superhero, March,1989 2.00
9 EC 2.00

BULLWINKLE &
ROCKY COLLECTION
TPB, AM,early stories 4.95

Cable #39
© Marvel Entertainment Group

CABLE
[Limited Series]
1 JR2,DGr,V:Mutant Liberation
  Front,A:Weapon X 4.00
2 JR2,DGr,V:Stryfe,O:Weapon X 3.00
[Regular Series]
1 B:FaN(s),ATi,O:Cable,V:New
  Canaanites,A:Stryfe,foil(c) 5.00
2 ATi,V:Stryfe 2.50
3 ATi,A:Six Pack 2.25
4 ATi,A:Six Pack 2.25
5 DaR,V:Sinsear 2.25
6 DT,A:Tyler,Zero,Askani,
  Mr.Sinister,C:X-Men 2.50
7 V:Tyler,A:Askani,X-Men,Domino 2.50
8 O:Cable,V:Tyler,A:X-Men,Cable is
  Nathan Summers 2.50
9 MCW,B:Killing Field,A:Excalibur,

V:Omega Red 2.25
10 MCW,A:Acolytes,Omega Red . 2.25
11 MCW,E:Killing Field,D:Katu . . . 2.25
12 SLo(s),B:Fear & Loathing,
  V:Senyaka 2.25
13 V:D'Spayre 2.00
14 V:S'yM 2.25
15 A:Thorn 2.25
16 Foil(c),Dbl-size,A:Jean,Scott
  Logan,V:Phalanx 7.00
16a Newsstand ed. 2.50
17 Deluxe ed. 2.25
17a Newsstand ed. 1.50
18 Deluxe ed. 2.25
18a Newsstand ed. 1.50
19 Deluxe ed. 2.25
19a Newsstand ed. 1.50
20 V:Legion, Deluxe ed. w/card . . 4.00
20a Newsstand ed. 1.50
21 Cable makes tough decisions,
  A:Domino 2.25
22 V:Fortress 2.25
23 IaC,A:Domino 2.25
24 F:Blaquesmith 1.95
25 IaC,SHa,F:Cable's Wife,foil(c) 5.00
26 Tries to return to X-Mansion . . 1.95
27 IaC, A:Domino 1.95
28 IaC,SHa,concl. war in Genosha 1.95
29 . . . . 1.95
30 . . . . 1.95
31 IaC, cont.X-Men/Cable war . . 1.95
32 Onslaught saga 3.00
33 Onslaught saga 3.00
34 Onslaught saga 3.00
35 Onslaught saga 2.00
36 . . . . 1.95
37 JLb,IaC,SHa,V:Askani'son,Kane 1.95
38 JLb,IaC,SHa,V:Psycho-Man,
  A:Kane 1.95
39 JLb,IaC,SHa,V:Psycho-Man . . 1.95
40 TDz,IaC,SHa,A:Renee Majcomb 1.95
41 TDz,SHa,F:Bishop 1.95
42 TDz,RGr,SHa,"The Prophecy
  of the Twelve" 1.95
43 TDz,RGr,Images of Nathan's
  past 1.95
44 TDz,RGr,SHa,A:Madelyne Pryor
  (Cable's mom) 1.95
45 JeR,RGr,Zero Tolerance,
  "No Escape,"pt.2 . . . . 1.95
46 JeR,RGr,SHa,Zero Tolerance,
  "No Escape," pt.2 (of 3) 1.95
Cable & X-Force '95 Spec. 3.95
Minus 1 Spec., TDz,JeR, flashback 1.95
TPB Cable,rep.New Mutants
  #87-94 . . . . 15.95

CABLE & X-FORCE '96
1 48pg. 3.00

CABLE & X-FORCE '97
(April 1997)
1 JFM,CJ,V:Malekith,48pg. 3.00

CADILLACS &
DINOSAURS
Epic Nov., 1990
1 Rep.Xenozoic Tales 3.00
2 Rep.Xenozoic Tales 2.50
3 Rep.Xenozoic Tales 2.50
4 Rep.Xenozoic Tales 2.50
5 Rep.Xenozoic Tales 2.50
6 Rep.Xenozoic Tales, April,1991 2.50

CAGE
1 DT,R:Luke Cage,I:Hardcore, . . 2.50
2 DT,V:Hammer 1.50
3 DT,A:Punisher,V:Untouchables 1.50
4 DT,A:Punisher,V:Untouchables 1.50
5 DT,I:New Power Man 1.50
6 DT,V:New Power Man 1.50
7 DT,A:Avengers West Coast . . . 1.50
8 DT,V:Steele,Wonder Man 1.50
9 V:Rhino,A:Hulk 1.50
10 DT,V:Hulk,Rhino 1.50
11 DT,V:Rapidfire 1.50
12 A:Iron Fist,double size 2.00
13 V:The Thinker 1.50
14 PCu,I:Coldfire 1.50
15 DT,For Love Nor Money#2,
  A:Silver Sable,Terror 1.50
16 DT,For Love Nor Money#5,
  A:Silver Sable,Terror 1.50
17 DT,Infinty Crusade 1.50
18 A:Dred,V:Creed 1.50
19 A:Dakota North 1.50
20 Last issue 1.50

CAMP CANDY
May, 1990
1 thru 6, Oct. 1990 . . . . @1.00

CAPTAIN AMERICA
COMICS
Timely/Atlas May, 1941
1 S&K,Hitler(c),I&O:Capt.America &
  Bucky,A:Red Skull,B:Hurricane,
  Tuk the Caveboy . . 55,000.00
2 S&K,RC,AAv,Hitler(c),
  I:Circular Shield;Trapped
  in the Nazi Stronghold . . 10,000.00
3 S&K,RC,AAv,Stan Lee's 1st Text,
  A:Red Skull,Bondage(c) . 8,500.00
4 S&K,AAv,Horror Hospital . 5,000.00
5 S&K,AAv,Ringmaster's
  Wheel of Death 4,500.00
6 S&K,AAv,O:Father Time,
  E:Tuk 4,000.00
7 S&K,A: Red Skull 4,000.00
8 S&K, The Tomb 3,500.00
9 S&K,RC,V:Black Talon . . . 3,200.00
10 S&K,RC,Chamber
  of Horrors 3,200.00
11 AAv,E:Hurricane;Feuding
  Mountaneers 3,000.00
12 AAv,B:Imp,E:Father Time;
  Pygmie's Terror 2,800.00
13 AAv,O:Secret Stamp;All Out
  For America 3,000.00
14 AAv,V:Japs;Pearl Harbor
  Symbol cover 2,800.00
15 AAv,Den of Doom 2,800.00
16 AAv,R.Skull;CapA
  Unmasked 3,400.00
17 AAv,I:Fighting Fool;
  Graveyard 2,500.00
18 AAv,V:Japanese 2,200.00
19 AAv,V:Ghouls,
  B:Human Torch 1,800.00
20 AAv,A:Sub-Mariner,V:Nazis 1,800.00
21 SSh(c),Bucky Captured . . 1,700.00
22 SSh(c),V:Japanese 1,700.00
23 SSh(c),V:Nazis 1,700.00
24 SSh(c),V:Black
  Dragon Society 1,700.00
25 SSh(c),V:Japs;Drug Story . 1,700.00
26 ASh(c),V:Nazi Fleet 1,600.00
27 ASh(c)CapA&Russians

MARVEL

V:Nazis, E:Secret Stamp . . 1,600.00
28 ASh(c),NaziTortureChamber1,600.00
29 ASh(c),V:Nazis;French
    Underground 1,600.00
30 ASh(c),Bucky Captured . . 1,600.00
31 ASh(c),Bondage(c) 1,500.00
32 SSh(c),V: Japanese Airforce1,500.00
33 ASh(c),V:Nazis;BrennerPass1,500.00
34 SSh(c),Bondage(c) 1,500.00
35 SSh(c),CapA in Japan . . . 1,500.00
36 SSh(c),V:Nazis;Hitler(c) . . 2,000.00
37 ASh(c),CapA in Berlin,
    A:Red Skull 1,600.00
38 ASh(c),V:Japs;Bondage(c) 1,400.00
39 ASh(c),V:Japs;Boulder Dam1,400.00
40 SSh(c),V:Japs;Ammo Depot 1,400.00
41 ASh(c),FinalJapaneseWar(c)1,300.00
42 ASh(c),V:Bank Robbers . . 1,300.00
43 ASh(c),V:Gangsters 1,300.00
44 ASh(c),V:Gangsters 1,300.00
45 ASh(c),V:Bank Robbers . . 1,300.00
46 ASh(c),Holocaust(c) 1,300.00
47 ASh(c),Final Nazi War(c) . 1,300.00
48 ASh(c),V:Robbers 1,200.00
49 ASh(c),V:Sabatuers 1,200.00
50 ASh(c),V:Gorilla Gang . . . 1,300.00
51 ASh(c),V:Gangsters 1,200.00
52 ASh(c),V:AtomBombThieves1,200.00
53 ASh(c),V:Burglars 1,200.00
54 ASh(c),TV Studio,
    V:Gangsters 1,200.00
55 V:Counterfeiters 1,200.00
56 SSh(c),V:Art Theives 1,200.00
57 Symbolic CapA(c) 1,200.00
58 ASh(c),V:Bank Robbers . . 1,200.00
59 SSh(c)O:CapA Retold;Private
    Life of Captain America . . 2,500.00
60 V:The Human Fly 1,200.00
61 SSh(c),V:Red Skull;
    Bondage(c) 1,900.00
62 SSh(c),Kingdom of Terror . 1,200.00
63 SSh(c),I&O:Asbestos Lady;
    The Parrot Strikes 1,300.00
64 Diamonds Spell Doom . . . 1,200.00
65 When Friends Turn Foes . 1,200.00
66 O:Golden Girl;Bucky Shot . 1,400.00
67 E:Toro(in Human Torch);
    Golden Girl Team-Up 1,200.00
68 A:Golden Girl;Riddle of
    the Living Dolls 1,200.00
69 Weird Tales of the Wee
    Males, A:Sun Girl 1,200.00
70 A:Golden Girl,Sub-Mariner,
    Namora;Worlds at War . . . 1,200.00
71 A:Golden Girl; Trapped . . 1,200.00
72 Murder in the Mind 1,200.00
73 The Outcast of Time 1,200.00
74 A:Red Skull;Capt.America's
    Weird Tales 3,500.00
75 Thing in the Chest 1,200.00
76 JR(c),CapACommieSmasher1,200.00
77 CapA Commie Smasher . . . 750.00
78 JR(c),V:Communists;
    Sept., 1954 . . . . 800.00

CAPTAIN AMERICA
Prev: **Tales of Suspense**
          April, 1968
100 JK,A:Avengers 325.00
101 JK,I:4th Sleeper 90.00
102 JK,V:Red Skull,4th Sleeper . 45.00
103 JK,V:Red Skull 45.00
104 JK,DA,JSo,V:Red Skull . . . 45.00
105 JK,DA,A:Batroc 45.00
106 JK,Cap.Goes Wild 45.00

107 JK,Red Skull 45.00
108 JK,Trapster 45.00
109 JK,O:Captain America 55.00
110 JSo,JSt,A:Hulk,Rick Jones
    in Bucky Costume 60.00
111 JSo,JSt,I:Man Killer 65.00
112 JK,GT,Album 40.00
113 JSo,TP,Avengers,
    D:Madame Hydra 65.00
114 JR,SB,C:Avengers 25.00
115 JB,SB,A:Red Skull 25.00
116 GC,JSt,A:Avengers 25.00
117 JR(c),GC,JSt,I:Falcon 60.00
118 JR(c),GC,JSt,A:Falcon 20.00
119 GC,JSt,O:Falcon 20.00
120 GC,JSt,A:Falcon 20.00
121 GC,JSt,V:Man Brute 18.00
122 GC,JSt,Scorpion 15.00
123 GC,JSt,A:NickFury,
    V:Suprema 15.00

Captain America #135
© Marvel Entertainment Group

124 GC,JSt,I:Cyborg 15.00
125 GC,Mandarin 15.00
126 JK&BEv(c),GC,A:Falcon . . 15.00
127 GC,WW,A:Nick Fury 15.00
128 GC,V:Satan's Angels 15.00
129 GC,Red Skull 15.00
130 GC,I:Batroc 17.00
131 GC,V:Hood 13.00
132 GC,A:Bucky Barnes 13.00
133 GC,O:Modok,B:Capt.America/
    Falcon Partnership 13.00
134 GC,V:Stone Face 13.00
135 JR(c),GC,TP,A:Nick Fury . . 13.00
136 GC,BEv,V:Tyrannus 13.00
137 GC,BEv,A:Spider-Man 15.00
138 JR,A:Spider-Man 14.00
139 JR,Falcon solo 10.00
140 JR,O:Grey Gargoyle 10.00
141 JR,JSt,V:Grey Gargoyle 8.00
142 JR,JSt,Nick Fury 8.00
143 JR,Red Skull 8.00
144 GM,JR,N:Falcon,V:Hydra . . . 8.00
145 GK,JR,V:Hydra 8.00
146 JR(c),SB,V:Hydra 7.00
147 GK(c),SB,V:Hydra 7.00
148 SB,JR,Red Skull 7.00

149 GK(c),SB,JM,V:Batroc 7.00
150 K&R(c),SB,V:The Stranger . . 7.00
151 SB,V:Mr.Hyde 7.00
152 SB,V:Scorpion,Mr.Hyde 7.00
153 SB,JM,V:50's Cap 7.00
154 SB,V:50's Cap 7.00
155 SB,FMc,O:50's Cap 7.00
156 SB,FMc,V:50's Cap 7.00
157 SB,I:The Viper 7.00
158 SB,V:The Viper 6.00
159 SB,V:PlantMan,Porcupine . . . 6.00
160 SB,FMc,V:Solarr 6.00
161 SB,V:Dr.Faustus 6.00
162 JSn(c),SB,V:Dr.Faustus 6.00
163 SB,I:Serpent Squad 7.00
164 JR(c),I:Nightshade 7.00
165 SB,FMc,V:Yellow Claw 6.00
166 SB,FMc,V:Yellow Claw 6.00
167 SB,V:Yellow Claw 6.00
168 SB,I&O:Phoenix
    (2nd Baron Zemo) 7.00

Captain America #144
© Marvel Entertainment Group

169 SB,FMc,C:Black Panther 6.00
170 K&R(c),SB,C:Black Panther . . 6.00
171 JR(c),SB,A:Black Panther . . . 6.00
172 GK(c),SB,C:X-Men 16.00
173 GK(c),SB,A:X-Men 17.00
174 GK(c),SB,A:X-Men 17.00
175 SB,A:X-Men 17.00
176 JR(c),SB,O:Capt.America . . . 9.00
177 JR(c),SB,A:Lucifer,Beast 7.00
178 SB,A:Lucifer 7.00
179 SB,A:Hawkeye 7.00
180 GK(c),SB,I:1st Nomad(Cap) . 10.00
181 GK(c),SB,I&O:New Cap 7.00
182 FR,Madam Hydra 7.00
183 GK(c),FR,R:Cap,D:New Cap . 10.00
184 K&R(c),HT,A:Red Skull 7.00
185 GK(c),SB,FR,V:Red Skull . . . 7.00
186 GK(c),FR,O:Falcon 8.00
187 K&R(c),FR,V:Druid 6.00
188 GK(c),SB,V:Druid 6.00
189 GK(c),FR,V:Nightshade 6.00
190 GK(c),FR,A:Nightshade 6.00
191 FR,A:Stilt Man,N.Fury 6.00
192 JR(c),FR,A:Dr.Faustus 6.00
193 JR(c),JK,'Mad Bomb' 6.00
194 JK,I:Gen.Heshin 6.00
195 JK,1984 . . . . 6.00

MARVEL

196 JK,Madbomb	6.00	
197 JK,Madbomb	6.00	
198 JK,Madbomb	6.00	
199 JK,Madbomb	6.00	
200 JK,Madbomb	7.00	
201 JK,Epilogue	5.00	
202 JK,Night People	5.00	
203 JK,Night People	5.00	
204 JK,I:Argon	5.00	
205 JK,V:Argon	5.00	
206 JK,I:Swine	5.00	
207 JK,V:Swine	5.00	
208 JK,I:Arnim Zola,D:Swine	5.00	
209 JK,O:Arnim Zola,I:Primus	5.00	
210 JK,A:Red Skull	5.00	
211 JK,A:Red Skull	5.00	
212 JK,A:Red Skull	5.00	
213 JK,I:Night Flyer	5.00	
214 JK,D:Night Flyer	5.00	
215 GT,Redwing	5.00	
216 Reprint,JK	5.00	
217 JB, I:Quasar(Marvel Boy) I:Vamp	6.00	
218 SB,A:Iron Man	5.00	
219 SB,JSt,V:TheCorporation	5.00	
220 SB,D:L.Dekker	5.00	
221 SB,Ameridroid	5.00	
222 SB,I:Animus(Vamp)	5.00	
223 SB,Animus	5.00	
224 MZ,V:Animus	5.00	
225 SB,A:Nick Fury	5.00	
226 SB,A:Nick Fury	5.00	
227 SB,A:Nick Fury	5.00	
228 SB,Constrictor	5.00	
229 SB,R:SuperAgents of Shield	5.00	
230 SB,A:Hulk	5.00	
231 SB,DP,A:Grand Director	5.00	
232 SB,DP,V:Grand Director	5.00	
233 SB,DP,D:Sharon Carter	5.00	
234 SB,DP,A:Daredevil	5.50	
235 SB,FM,A:Daredevil	5.50	
236 SB,V:Dr.Faustus	5.00	
237 SB,'From the Ashes'	5.00	
238 SB,V:Hawk Riders	5.00	
239 JBy(c),SB,V:Hawk Riders	5.00	
240 SB,V:A Guy Named Joe	5.00	
241 A:Punisher	18.00	
242 JSt,A:Avengers	4.00	
243 GP(c),RB,V:Adonis	4.00	
244 TS,'A Monster Berserk'	4.00	
245 CI,JRn,Nazi Hunter	4.00	
246 GP(c),JBi,V:Joe	4.00	
247 JBy,V:BaronStrucker	5.00	
248 JBy,JRu,Dragon Man	5.00	
249 JBy,O:Machinesmith, A:Air-Walker	5.00	
250 JBy,Cap for Pres	5.00	
251 JBy,V:Mr.Hyde	5.00	
252 JBy,V:Batrok	5.00	
253 JBy,V:Baron Blood	5.00	
254 JBy,D:B.Blood,UnionJack,I:3rd Union Jack	5.00	
255 JBy,40th Anniv.,O:Cap	5.00	
256 GC,V:Demon Druid	3.50	
257 A:Hulk	3.50	
258 MZ,V:Blockbuster	3.50	
259 MZ,V:Dr. Octopus	3.50	
260 AM,In Jail	3.50	
261 MZ,A:Nomad	4.00	
262 MZ,V:Ameridroid	3.50	
263 MZ,V:Red Skull	3.50	
264 MZ,X-Men	3.50	
265 MZ,A:Spider-Man,N.Fury	4.00	
266 MZ,A:Spider-Man	4.00	
267 MZ,V:Everyman	3.50	

268 MZ,A:Defenders(x-over from Def.#106)	3.50	
269 MZ,A:Team America	3.50	
270 MZ,V:Tess-One	3.50	
271 MZ,V:Mr.X	3.50	
272 MZ,I:Vermin	4.50	
273 MZ,A:Nick Fury	3.50	
274 MZ,D:SamSawyer	3.50	
275 MZ,V:Neo-Nazis	3.50	
276 MZ,V:Baron Zemo	3.50	
277 MZ,V:Baron Zemo	3.50	
278 MZ,V:Baron Zemo	3.50	
279 MZ,V:Primus	3.50	
280 MZ,V:Scarecrow	3.50	
281 MZ,A:Spider Woman, R:'50's Bucky	3.50	
282 MZ,I:2nd Nomad	8.00	
282a (second printing)	2.00	
283 MZ,A:Viper	4.00	
284 SB,Nomad	3.50	
285 MZ,V:Porcupine	3.50	
286 MZ,V:Deathlok	5.00	

Captain America #275
© *Marvel Entertainment Group*

287 MZ,V:Deathlok	5.00	
288 MZ,V:Deathlok,D:Hellinger	5.00	
289 MZ,A:Red Skull	3.50	
290 JBy(c),RF,A:Falcon	3.50	
291 JBy(c),HT,V:Tumbler	3.50	
292 I&O:Black Crow	3.50	
293 V:Mother Superior	3.50	
294 R:Nomad	3.50	
295 V:Sisters of Sin	3.50	
296 V:Baron Zemo	3.50	
297 O:Red Skull	3.50	
298 V:Red Skull	3.50	
299 V:Red Skull	3.50	
300 D:Red Skull	5.00	
301 PNe,A:Avengers	3.00	
302 PNe,I:Machete,V:Batroc	3.00	
303 PNe,V:Batroc	3.00	
304 PNe,V:Stane Armor	3.00	
305 PNe,A:Capt.Britain,V:Modred	3.00	
306 PNe,A:Capt.Britain,V:Modred	3.00	
307 PNe,I:Madcap	3.00	
308 PNe,I:Armadillo, Secret WarsII	3.00	
309 PNe,V:Madcap	3.00	
310 PNe,V:Serpent Society,I:Cotton Mouth,Diamondback	3.50	

311 PNe,V:Awesome Android	3.00	
312 PNe,I:Flag Smasher	3.00	
313 PNe,D:Modok	3.00	
314 PNe,A:Nighthawk	3.00	
315 PNe,V:Serpent Society	3.00	
316 PNe,A:Hawkeye	3.00	
317 PNe,I:Death-Throws	3.00	
318 PNe,V&D:Blue Streak	3.00	
319 PNe,V:Scourge,D:Vamp	3.00	
320 PNe,V:Scourge	3.00	
321 PNe,V:Flagsmasher, I:Ultimatum	3.00	
322 PNe,V:Flagsmasher	3.00	
323 PNe,I:Super Patriot (US Agent)	5.00	
324 PNe,V:Whirlwind,Trapster	2.50	
325 I:Slug,A:Nomad	2.50	
326 V:Dr.Faustus	2.50	
327 MZ(c)V:SuperPatriot	4.00	
328 MZ(c),I:Demolition Man	2.50	
329 MZ(c),A:Demolition Man	2.50	
330 A:Night Shift,Shroud	2.50	
331 A:Night Shift,Shroud	2.50	
332 BMc,Rogers resigns	10.00	
333 B:John Walker Becomes 6th Captain America	7.00	
334 I:4th Bucky	5.00	
335 V:Watchdogs	4.00	
336 A:Falcon	3.50	
337 TMo,I:The Captain	3.50	
338 KD,AM,V:Professor Power	3.50	
339 KD,TD,Fall of Mutants, V:Famine	3.50	
340 KD,AM,A:Iron Man,	3.00	
341 KD,AM,I:Battlestar,A:Viper	2.50	
342 KD,AM,A:D-Man,Falcon, Nomad,Viper	2.50	
343 KD,AM,A:D-Man,Falcon, Nomad	2.50	
344 KD,AM,A:D-Man,Nomad	3.00	
345 KD,AM,V:Watchdogs	2.50	
346 KD,AM,V:Resistants	2.50	
347 KD,AM,V:RWinger&LWinger	2.50	
348 KD,AM,V:Flag Smasher	2.50	
349 KD,AM,V:Flag Smasher	2.50	
350 KD,AM,doub-size,Rogers Ret. as Captain Am,V:Red Skull, E:6th Cap	5.00	
351 KD,AM,A:Nick Fury	2.50	
352 KD,AM,I:Supreme Soviets	2.50	
353 KD,AM,V:Supreme Soviets	2.50	
354 KD,AM,I:USAgent, V:Machinesmith	4.00	
355 RB,AM,A:Falcon,Battlestar	2.50	
356 AM,V:Sisters of Sin	2.50	
357 KD,AM,V:Sisters of Sin Baron Zemo,Batroc	2.50	
358 KD,B:Blood Stone Hunt	2.50	
359 KD,V:Zemo,C:Crossbones	2.00	
360 KD,I:Crossbones	2.75	
361 KD,V:Zemo,Batroc	2.00	
362 KD,V:Zemo,Crossbones	2.00	
363 KD,E:Blood Stone Hunt, V:Crossbones,C:Wolverine	2.00	
364 KD,V:Crossbones	2.00	
365 KD,Acts of Vengeance, V:SubMariner,Red Skull	2.00	
366 1st RLm Capt.Amer.,Acts of Vengeance,V:Controller	2.50	
367 KD,Acts of Vengeance, Magneto Vs. Red Skull	3.00	
368 RLm,V:Machinesmith	2.00	
369 RLm,I:Skeleton Crew	2.00	
370 RLm,V:Skeleton Crew	2.00	
371 RLm,V:Trump,Poundcakes	2.00	

MARVEL

MARVEL

372 RLm,B:Streets of Poison,
   Cap on Drugs,C:Bullseye 2.50
373 RLm,V:Bullseye,A:Bl.Widow . 2.00
374 RLm,V:Bullseye,A:Daredevil . 2.00
375 RLm,V:Daredevil 2.00
376 RLm,A:Daredevil 2.00
377 RLm,V:Crossbones,Bullseye . 2.00
378 RLm,E:Streets of Poison,Red
   Skull vs Kingpin,V:Crossbones 2.00
379 RLm(c),V:Serpent Society . . . 2.00
380 RLm,V:Serpent Society 2.00
381 RLm,V:Serpent Society 2.00
382 RLm,V:Serpent Society 2.00
383 RLm(c),RLm,50th Anniv.
   64Pages 5.00
384 RLm,A:Jack Frost 2.00
385 RLm,A:USAgent 2.00
386 RLm,Cap./USAgent T.U. . . . 2.00
387 B:Superia Strategem 2.00
388 A:Paladin 2.00
389 Superia Strategem #3 . . . . . 2.00
390 Superia Strategem #4 . . . . . 2.00
391 Superia Strategem #5 . . . . . 2.00
392 E:Superia Strategem 2.00
393 V:Captain Germany 2.00
394 A:Red Skull,Diamondback . . 2.00
395 A:Red Skull,Crossbones . . . 2.00
396 I:2nd Jack O'Lantern 2.00
397 V:Red Skull,X-Bones,Viper . 1.75
398 Operation:Galactic Storm
   Pt.1,V:Warstar 2.00
399 Operation Galactic Storm
   Pt.8,V:Kree Empire 2.00
400 Operation Galactic Storm
   Pt.15,BU:rep.Avengers #4 . . 4.00
401 R:D-Man,A:Avengers 2.00
402 RLe,B:Man & Wolf,
   A:Wolverine 2.00
403 RLe,A:Wolverine 2.00
404 RLe,A:Wolverine 2.00
405 RLe,A:Wolverine 2.00
406 RLe,A:Wolverine 2.00
407 RLe,A:Wolverine,Cable 2.00
408 RLe,E:Man & Wolf 1.75
409 RLe,V:Skeleton Crew 1.50
410 RLe,V:Crossbones,Skel.Crew 1.50
411 RLe,V:Snapdragon 1.50
412 RLe,V:Batroc,A:Shang-Chi . . 1.50
413 A:Shang-Chi,V:Superia 1.50
414 RLe,A:Kazar,Black Panther . 1.50
415 Rle,A:Black Panther,Kazar . 1.50
416 RLe,Savage Land Mutates,
   A:Black.Panther,Kazar 1.50
417 RLe,A:Black Panther,Kazar,
   V:AIM 1.50
418 RLe,V:Night People 1.50
419 RLe,V:Viper 1.50
420 RLe,I:2nd Blazing Skull,
   A:Nightshift 3.00
421 RLe,V:Nomad 1.50
422 RLe,I:Blistik 1.50
423 RTs(s),MCW,V:Namor 1.50
424 MGv(s),A:Sidewinder 1.50
425 B:MGu(s),DHv,Embossed(c),I:2nd
   Super Patriot,Dead Ringer . . 3.50
426 DHv,A:Super Patriot,Dead Ringer,
   V:Resistants 1.50
427 DHv,V:Super Patriot,Dead
   Ringer 1.75
428 DHv,I:Americop 1.75
429 DHv,V:Kono 1.50
430 Daemon Dran, Americop . . . 1.75
431 DHv,I:Free Spirit 1.50
432 DHv,Fighting Chance 1.50
433 DHv,Baron Zemo 1.50

434 DHv,A:Fighting Spirit,
   V:King Cobra 1.50
435 DHv,Fighting Chance 1.50
436 V:King Cobra, Mister Hyde,
   Fighting Chance conclusion . . 1.50
437 Cap in a Coma 1.50
438 I:New Body Armor 1.50
439 Dawn's Early Light,pt.2 . . . . . 1.50
440 Taking A.I.M.,pt.1 . . . . 1.50
441 Taking A.I.M.,pt.3 . . . . 1.50
442 Batroc, Cap,V:Zeitgeist 1.50
443 MGu,24 hours to live 1.50
444 MWa,RG,President Kidnapped 5.00
445 MWa,RG,R:Captain America . 3.00
446 MWa,RG,Operation
   Rebirth,pt.2 . . . . 3.00
447 MWa,RG,Op.Rebirth,pt.3 . . . 3.00
448 MWa,RG,Operation
   Rebirth,pt.4,double size 5.00
449 . . . . 2.50
450 . . . . 1.50
451 RG,DRo,Man Without
   A Country,pt.2,new costume . . 2.00
Ann.#1 rep. 22.00
Ann.#2 rep. 11.00
Ann.#3 JK, ... 5.00
Ann.#4 JK,V:Magneto,I:Mutant
   Force 10.00
Ann.#5 'Deathwatcher' 4.00
Ann.#6 A:Contemplator 4.00
Ann.#7 O:Shaper of Worlds 4.00
Ann.#8 MZ,A:Wolverine 40.00
Ann.#9 MBa,SD,Terminus Factor
   #1,N:Nomad 4.50
Ann.#10 MM,Baron Strucker,pt.3
   (see Punisher Ann.#4) 2.50
Ann.#11 Citizen Kang#1 . . . . . . 2.50
Ann.#12 I:Bantam,w/card 3.25
Ann.#13 RTs(s),MCW, ... 3.25
Drug Wars PDd(s),SaV,A:New
   Warriors 2.00
G-Size#1 GK(c),rep.O:Cap.Amer. 12.00
HC vol.Slipcase Rep.#1
   thru #10 (From 1940's) 75.00
Medusa Effect RTs(s),MCW,RB,
   V:Master Man 2.95
Movie Adapt 2.00
Spec.#1 Rep.Cap.A #110,#111 . 2.00
Spec.#2 Rep.Cap.A #113
   & Strange Tales #169 . . . . . 2.00
TPB Bloodstone Hunt,rep.
   #357-364 . . . . 15.95
TPB Streets of Poison,
   rep. #372–#377
TPB War and Remembrance,
   rep. #247–#255 . . . . 12.95
Collector's Preview 1.95
Ashcan 75

CAPTAIN AMERICA
(Nov. 1996)
1 RLd,CDi,JSb, Heroes Reborn,
   I:Nick Fury,48pg. 5.00
1A Stars and stripes background
   variant cover 7.50
1b gold signature edition,
   cardstock cover 30.00
1c San Diego Con edition 35.00
2 RLd,JLb,JSb,Falcon & Red Skull 3.00
3 RLd,JLb,JSb,A:Hulk,V:Red Skull
   & Master Man 2.50
4 RLd,JLb,JSb,F:Prince Namor, . 2.50
5 RLd,JLb,JSb,V:Crossbones . . 2.50
6 RLd,JLb,JSb,"Industrial
   Revolution," epilogue,A:Cable . 2.50

7 RLd,JLb,DaF, ... 1.95
8 RLd,JLb,SPa,A:Nick Fury,
   WWII story 1.95
9 JLb,RLd,SPa,WWII story. . . . 1.95
10 JLb,RLd,SPa,WWII story, concl. 1.95
11 JeR,JoB,Odyssey across
   America, pt.4, concl. 1.95
Ashcan, ComicCon 5.00

CAPTAIN BRITAIN CLASSICS
1 AD rep. 2.50

CAPTAIN CONFEDERACY
Epic Nov., 1991
1 I:Capt.Confederacy,Kid Dixie . . 2.25
2 Meeting of Superhero Reps . . . 2.25
3 Framed for Murder 2.25
4 Superhero conference,final iss. 2.25

CAPTAIN JUSTICE
March, 1988
1 Based on TV Series 1.00
2 April, 1988 . . . . 1.00

Captain Marvel #44
© Marvel Entertainment Group

CAPTAIN MARVEL
May, 1968
1 GC,O:retold,V:Sentry#459 . . . 90.00
2 GC,V:Super Skrull 30.00
3 GC,V:Super Skrull 25.00
4 GC,Sub-Mariner 20.00
5 DH,I:Metazoid 20.00
6 DH,I:Solam 15.00
7 JR(c),DH,V:Quasimodo 15.00
8 DH,I:Cuberex 15.00
9 DH,D:Cuberex 15.00
10 DH,V:Number 1 . . . . 12.00
11 BWS(c),I:ZO 12.00
12 K&R(c),I:Man-Slayer 10.00
13 FS,V:Man-Slayer 10.00
14 FS,Iron Man 10.00
15 TS,DA,Z0 . . . . 9.00
16 DH,Ronan 9.00
17 GK,DA,O:R.Jones ret,N:Capt.
   Marvel 10.00
18 GK,JB,DA,I:Mandroid 9.00

19 GK,DA,Master.of.MM 9.00
20 GK,DA,I:Rat Pack 9.00
21 GK,DA,Hulk 9.00
22 GK(c),WB,V:Megaton 9.00
23 GK(c),WB,FMc,V:Megaton . . . 9.00
24 GK(c),WB,ECh,I:L.Mynde 9.00
25 1st JSn,Cap.Marvel,Cosmic
   Cube Saga Begins 20.00
26 JSn,DC,Thanos(2ndApp.)
   A:Thing 25.00
27 JSn,V:Thanos,A:Mentor,
   Starfox, I:Death 15.00
28 JSn,DGr,Thanos Vs.Drax,
   A:Avengers 15.00
29 JSn,AM,O:Zeus,C:Thanos
   I:Eon,O:Mentor 9.00
30 JSn,AM,Controller,C:Thanos . . 9.00
31 JSn,AM,Avengers,
   Thanos,Drax,Mentor 9.00
32 JSn,AM,DGr,O:Drax,
   Moondragon,A:Thanos 10.00
33 JSn,KJ,E:Cosmic Cube Saga
   1st D:Thanos 15.00
34 JSn,JA,V:Nitro(leads to
   his Death) 8.00
35 GK(c),AA,Ant Man 5.00
36 AM,Watcher,Rep.CM#1 . . . . . 6.00
37 AM,KJ,Nimrod 5.00
38 AM,KJ,Watcher 5.00
39 AM,KJ,Watcher 5.00
40 AM,AMc,Watcher 5.00
41 AM,BWr,CR,BMc,TA,Kree 4.50
42 AM,V:Stranger,C:Drax 4.00
43 AM,V:Drax 4.50
44 GK(c),AM,V:Drax 4.50
45 AM,I:Rambu 4.00
46 AM,TA,D:Fawn 4.00
47 AM,TA,A:Human Torch 4.00
48 AM,TA,I:Chetah 4.00
49 AM,V:Ronan,A:Cheetah 4.00
50 AM,TA,Avengers,
   V:Super Adaptiod 4.00
51 AM,TA,V:Mercurio,4-D Man . . 4.00
52 AM,TA,V:Phae-dor 4.00
53 AM,TA,A:Inhumans 4.00
54 PB,V:Nitro 4.00
55 PB,V:Death-grip 4.00
56 PB,V:Death-grip 4.00
57 PB,V:Thor,A:Thanos 6.00
58 PB,Drax/Titan 4.00
59 PB,Drax/Titan,I:Stellarax 4.00
60 PB,Drax/Titan 4.00
61 PB,V:Chaos 4.00
62 PB,V:Stellarax 4.00
G-Size #1 reprints 8.00

CAPTAIN MARVEL
1989
1 MBr,I:Powerkeg,V:Moonstone . 3.00
1 DyM(s),MBr,V:Skinhead(1993) . 2.00
PF Death of Captain Marvel . . . 7.95
TPB Life of Captain Marvel,JSn . 14.95

CAPTAIN MARVEL
1995
1 FaN,R:Captain Marvel(son of) . 1.95
2 FaN,V:X-Treme,Erik the Red . . 1.95
3 FaN,V:X-treme 1.95
4 thru 6 FaN . . . . @1.95

CAPTAIN PLANET
Oct., 1991
1 I&O:Captain Planet 1.00
2 V:Dr.Blights' Smog Monster . . . 1.00

---

3 V:Looten Plunder 1.00
4 'Pollutionland' 1.25
5 V:Duke Nukem 1.25
6 A:Capt.Pollution,Eco-Villains . 1.25
7 thru 9 . . . . @1.25
10 V:Litterbug 1.25
11 BHi,V:Greedly 1.25
12 V:Looten Plunder,last issue . . 1.25

CAPT. SAVAGE & HIS LEATHERNECK RAIDERS
Jan., 1968
1 SSh(c),C:Sgt Fury;The Last
   Bansai 12.50
2 SSh(c),O:Hydra;Return of Baron
   Strucker 6.00
3 SSh,Two Against Hydra 6.00
4 SSh,V:Hydra;The Fateful Finale 6.00
5 SSh,The Invincible Enemy . . . 6.00
6 Mission;Save a Howler 6.00
7 SSh,Objective:Ben Grimm . . . 6.50
8 Mission:Foul Ball 6.00
Becomes:

CAPT. SAVAGE & HIS BATTLEFIELD RAIDERS
9 . . . . 6.00
10 To the Last Man 5.00
11 A:Sergeant Fury 5.00
12 V:The Japanese 3.75
13 The Junk Heap Juggernauts . . 5.00
14 Savage's First Mission 5.00
15 Within the Temple Waits Death 5.00
16 V:The Axis Powers 5.00
17 V:The Axis Powers 5.00
18 V:The Axis Powers 5.00
19 March, 1970 . . . . 5.00

CARE BEARS
Star Nov., 1985
1 . . . . 1.50
2 thru 14 . . . . @1.00
Marvel
15 thru 20 . . . . @1.00

CARNAGE: MINDBOMB
1-shot foil cover 2.95

CARTOON KIDS
Atlas 1957
1 A:Dexter the Demon,Little
   Zelda,Willie,Wise Guy 35.00

CAR WARRIORS
Epic 1990
1 Based on Roll Playing Game . . 2.25
2 Big Race Preparations 2.25
3 Ft.Delorean-Lansing Race begin 2.25
4 Race End, Final issue 2.25

CASEY–CRIME PHOTOGRAPHER
August, 1949
1 Ph(c),Girl on the Docks . . . 100.00
2 Ph(c),Staats Cotsworth 60.00
3 Ph(c),He Walked With Danger . 60.00
4 Ph(c),Lend Me Your Life . . . 60.00
Becomes:

TWO GUN WESTERN
[1st Series]
5 JB,B,I&O:Apache Kid 125.00
6 The Outcast 75.00

---

7 Human Sacrifice 75.00
8 JR,DW,A:Kid Colt,Texas Kid,
   Doc Holiday 75.00
9 A:Kid Colt,Marshall"Frosty"
   Bennet Texas Kid 75.00
10 . . . . 75.00
11 thru 14 June, 1952 . . . . . @60.00

CASPER
1996
1 From Animated TV show 1.50
2 visit to Harvey Castle 1.50

CAT, THE
Nov., 1972—June 1973
1 JM,I&O:The Cat 12.00
2 JM,V:The Owl 7.00
3 BEv,V:Kraken 7.00
4 JSn,V:Man-Bull 7.00

CENTURY: DISTANT SONS
1-shot DAn,48pg. 2.95

CHAMBER OF CHILLS
Nov., 1972
1 SSh,A Dragon Stalks By
   Night,(H.Ellison Adapt.) 6.00
2 FB,BEv,SD,Monster From the
   Mound,(RE Howard Adapt.) . . 3.00
3 FB,BEv,SD, Thing on the Roof . 3.00
4 FB,BEv,SD, Opener of the
   Crypt,(J.Jakes,E.A.Poe Adapt) . 3.00
5 FB,BEv,SD, Devils Dowry 3.00
6 FB,BEv,SD, Mud Monster 3.00
7 thru 24 FB,BEv,SD . . . . . . @3.00
25 FB,BEv,SD November, 1976 . . 3.00

Chamber of Darkness #5
© Marvel Entertainment Group

CHAMBER OF DARKNESS
Oct., 1969
1 JB, Tales of Maddening Magic 35.00
2 NA(script),Enter the Red Death 13.00
3 JK,BWS,JB, Something Lurks
   on Shadow Mountain 15.00
4 JK Monster Man Came Walking,
   BU:BWS 42.00

MARVEL

5 JK,SD, And Fear Shall Follow
   plus Lovecraft adapt. 7.00
6 SD 7.00
7 SD,JK,BWr, Night of the
   Gargoyle 20.00
8 DA,BEv, Beast that Walks Like
   a Man Special, 5 Tales of
   Maddening Magic,Jan. 1972 . 7.00
Becomes:

MONSTERS ON THE PROWL

9 SAD,BWS,Monster Stories
   Inc,Gorgilla 7.50
10 JK,Roc 5.00
11 JK,A Titan Walks the Land . . . 5.00
12 HT,JK,Gomdulla The Living
   Pharoah 5.00
13 HT,JK,Tragg 5.00
14 JK,SD,Return of the Titan 5.00
15 FrG,JK,The Thing Called It . . . 5.00
16 JSe,SD,JK, Serpent God of
   Lost Swamp,A:King Kull 5.00
17 JK,SD,The Coming of Colossus 5.00
18 JK,SD,Bruttu 5.00
19 JK,SD,Creature From the
   Black Bog 5.00
20 JK,SD,Oog Lives Again 5.00
21 JK,SD,A Martian Stalks
   the City 5.00
22 JK,SD,Monster Runs Amok . . . 3.00
23 JK,The Return of Grogg 3.00
24 JK,SD, Magnetor 3.00
25 JK,Colossus Lives Again 3.00
26 JK,SD,The Two Headed Thing 3.00
27 JK,Sserpo 3.00
28 JK,The Coming of Monsteroso 3.00
29 JK,SD Monster at my Window . 3.00
30 JK,Diablo Demon from the 5th
   Dimension, Oct., 1974 . . . . . . 3.00

CHAMPIONS
June, 1986

1 GK(c),DH,I&O:Champions . . . 20.00
2 DH,O:Champions 14.00
3 GT,Assault on Olympus 13.00
4 GT,'Murder at Malibu' 12.00
5 DH,I:Rampage 12.00
6 JK(c),GT,V:Rampage 12.00
7 GT,O:Black Widow,I:Darkstar . 12.00
8 BH,O:Black Widow 12.00
9 BH,BL,V:Crimson Dynamo . . 12.00
10 BH,BL,V:Crimson Dynamo . . 12.00
11 JBy,A:Black Goliath,Hawkeye 13.00
12 JBy,BL,V:Stranger 13.00
13 JBy,BL,V:Kamo Tharn 13.00
14 JBy,I:Swarm 13.00
15 JBy,V:Swarm 13.00
16 BH,A:Magneto,Dr.Doom,
   Beast 12.00
17 GT,JBy,V:Sentinels,last issue 13.00

CHILDREN OF THE VOYAGE

1 F:Sam Wantling 3.25
2 Counterfeit Man 2.25
3 V:Voyager 2.25
4 Last Issue 2.25

CHILI
May, 1969

1 . . . . 18.00
2 . . . . 10.00
3 . . . . 9.00

Chilli #8
© Marvel Entertainment Group

4 . . . . 9.00
5 . . . . 9.00
6 thru 15 . . . . @7.00
16 thru 20 . . . . @6.00
21 thru 25 . . . . @5.00
26 Dec., 1973 . . . . 5.00
Spec.#1,1971 . . . . 10.00

CHUCK NORRIS
Star Jan.–Sept., 1987

1 SD 1.00
2 thru 5 . . . . @1.00

CINDY COMICS
See: KRAZY COMICS

CLANDESTINE

Preview issue, Intro 1.50
1 MFm,AD,foil(c) 3.25
2 . . . . 2.50
3 I:Argent,Kimera 2.50
4 R:Adam 2.50
5 MFm,AD,O:Adam Destine . . . 2.50
6 A:Spider-Man 2.50
7 A:Spider-Man 2.50
8 A:Dr.Strange 2.50
9 Training Time 2.50
10 A:Britanic 2.50
11 V:Modan 2.50
12 Aftermath 2.50
13 Who Will Lead 2.50
14 Vincent Vs. Adam 2.50

CLASSIC CONAN
See: CONAN SAGA

CLASSIC X-MEN
See: X-MEN

CLIVE BARKER'S BOOK OF THE DAMNED
Epic Nov., 1991

1 JBo,Hellraiser companion . . . 4.95
2 MPa,Hellraiser Companion . . 4.95

CLIVE BARKER'S HELLRAISER
Epic

1 BWr,DSp 7.00
2 . . . . 6.00
3 . . . . 6.50
4 . . . . 4.50
5 . . . . 4.50
6 . . . . 4.50
7 The Devil's Brigade #1 . . . . . 4.50
8 The Devil's Brigade #2&3 . . . . 4.50
9 The Devil's Brigade #4&5 . . . . 4.50
10 The Devil's Brigade #6&7
   foil Cover 5.00
11 The Devil's Brigade #8&9 . . . . 4.50
12 The Devil's Brigade #10-12 . . 4.50
13 MMi,RH,Devil's Brigade #13 . . 4.50
14 The Devil's Brigade #14 . . . . 4.95
15 The Devil's Brigade #15 . . . . 4.95
16 E:Devil's Brigade 4.95
17 BHa,DR,The Harrowing 4.95
18 O:Harrowers 4.95
19 A:Harrowers 4.95
20 NGa(s),DMc,Last Laugh 4.95
Dark Holiday Spec.#1 . . . . 4.95

CLOAK & DAGGER
(Limited Series)
Oct., 1983

1 RL,TA,I:Det.O'Reilly,
   Father Delgado 2.50
2 RL,TA,V:Duane Hellman 2.00
3 RL,TA,V:Street Gang 2.00
4 RL,TA,O:Cloak & Dagger, ... 2.00

CLOAK & DAGGER
[1st Regular Series]
July 1985

1 RL,Pornography 2.00
2 RL,Dagger's mother 1.50
3 RL,A:Spider-Man 2.00
4 RL,Secret Wars II 1.50
5 RL,I:Mayhem 1.50
6 RL,A:Mayhem 1.50
7 RL,A:Mayhem 1.50
8 TA, Drugs 1.50
9 AAd,TA,A:Mayhem 2.50
10 BBI,TA,V:Dr. Doom 1.50
11 BBI,TA,Last Issue 1.50

[Mutant Misadventures of] CLOAK & DAGGER
[2nd Regular Series]
Oct., 1988

1 CR(i),A:X-Factor 3.00
2 CR(i),C:X-Factor,V:Gromitz . . . 2.50
3 SW(i),JLe(c),A:Gromitz 2.00
4 TA(i),Inferno,R:Mayhem 2.00
5 TA(i),R:Mayhem 2.00
6 TA(i),A:Mayhem 1.75
7 A:Crimson Daffodil,V:Ecstacy . 1.75
8 Acts of Vengeance prelude . . . 1.75
9 Acts of Vengeance 2.00
10 Acts of Vengeance,"X-Force"
   name used,Dr.Doom 2.00
11 . . . . 1.50
12 A:Dr.Doom 1.50
13 A:Dr.Doom 1.50
14 RL 1.50
15 RL 1.50
16 RL,A:Spider-Man 2.00
17 A:Spider-Man, ... 2.00
18 Inf.Gauntlet X-over,

A:Spider-Man, Ghost Rider . . . 2.50
19 O:Cloak & Dagger,final issue . 2.50
GNv Predator and Prey 14.95

A CLUELESS VALENTINE
1 characters from movie, 48pg . . 2.50

CODENAME: GENETIX
1 PGa,A:Wolverine 2.00
2 PGa,V:Prime EvilA:Wolverine . 2.00
3 . . . . 2.00
4 A:Wolverine,Kazar 2.00

CODE OF HONOR
1996
1 (of 4) CDi,TnS,I:Jeff Piper,
  fully painted 5.95
2 thru 4 CDi, ... @5.95

CODE NAME: SPITFIRE
See: SPITFIRE AND
THE TROUBLESHOOTERS

COLOSSUS: GOD'S COUNTRY
PF V:Cold Warriors 6.95

COMBAT
Atlas June, 1952
1 War Stories, Bare Bayonets . 125.00
2 Break Thru,(Dedicated to US
  Infantry) 65.00
3 . . . . 35.00
4 . . . . 50.00
5 thru 10 . . . . @35.00
11 April, 1953 . . . . 35.00

COMBAT CASEY
See: WAR COMBAT

COMBAT KELLY AND THE DEADLY DOZEN
Atlas Nov., 1951
1 RH,Korean war stories 150.00
2 Big Push 75.00
3 The Volunteer 45.00
4 V:Communists 45.00
5 OW,V:Communists 45.00
6 V:Communists 45.00
7 V: Communists 45.00
8 Death to the Reds 45.00
9 . . . . 45.00
10 . . . . 45.00
11 . . . . 35.00
12 thru 16 . . . . @35.00
17 A:Combat Casey 60.00
18 A:Battle Brady 25.00
19 V:Communists 25.00
20 V:Communists 25.00
21 Transvestite Cover 35.00
22 thru 40 . . . . @25.00
41 thru 44 August, 1957 . . . . @25.00

COMBAT KELLY
June, 1972
1 JM, Stop the Luftwaffe 3.00
2 The Big Breakout 2.00
3 O:Combat Kelly 2.00
4 Mutiny,A:Sgt.Fury and the
  Howling Commandoes 2.00
5 Escape or Die 2.00

6 The Fortress of Doom 2.00
7 Nun Hostage,V:Nazis 2.00
8 V:Nazis 2.00
9 Oct., 1973 . . . . 2.00

COMET MAN
Feb., 1987
1 BSz(c),I:Comet Man 1.50
2 BSz(c),A:Mr.Fantastic 1.00
3 BSz(c),A:Hulk 1.00
4 BSz(c),A:Fantastic Four 1.00
5 BSz(c),A:Fantastic Four 1.00
6 BSz(c),Last issue, July,1987 . . 1.00

COMIX BOOK
(black & white magazine)
1974
1 . . . . 7.50
2 . . . . 4.50
3 . . . . 5.00
4 . . . . 3.75
5 1976 . . . . 3.75

COMIX ZONE
1 video game tie-in 2.50
2 video game tie-in 2.50

COMMANDO ADVENTURES
Atlas June, 1957
1 Seek, Find and Destroy 45.00
2 MD, Hit 'em and Hit 'em
  Hard, August,1957 . . . . 40.00

COMPLETE COMICS
See: AMAZING COMICS

COMPLETE MYSTERY
August, 1948
1 Seven Dead Men 325.00
2 Jigsaw of Doom 300.00
3 Fear in the Night 300.00
4 A Squealer Dies Fast 300.00
Becomes:

TRUE COMPLETE MYSTERY
5 Rice Mancini,
  The Deadly Dude 150.00
6 Ph(c),Frame-up that Failed . 100.00
7 Ph(c),Caught 100.00
8 Ph(c),The Downfall of Mr.
  Anderson, Oct., 1949 . . . . . 100.00

CONAN
1 Pit Fighter 2.95
2 LHa,Hyborean tortue factory . . 2.95
3 V:Cannibals 2.95
4 LHa,JP,Rune Conan Prelude . . 2.95
5 LHa,V:yeti 2.95
6 LHa, the plague 2.95
7 LHa,BBl,V:The Iron Man 2.95
8 . . . . 2.95
9 . . . . 2.95
10 Conan kidnapped by Amazons 2.95

CONAN THE ADVENTURER
1 RT(s),RK,Red Foil(c) 3.00
2 RT(s),RK 1.75
3 RT(s),RK 1.50
4 . . . . 1.50

5 . . . . 1.50
6 . . . . 1.50
7 . . . . 1.50
8 . . . . 1.50
9 . . . . 1.50
10 . . . . 1.50
11 Torture Chamber 1.50
12 Abominations of Yondo 1.50
13 Seven Warriors 1.50
14 RTs,Young Conan,last issue . . 1.50

CONAN THE BARBARIAN
Oct., 1979
1 BWS/DA,O:Conan,A:Kull . . . 250.00
2 BWS/SB,Lair o/t Beast-Men . . 95.00
3 BWS,SB,Grey God Passes . 150.00
4 BWS,SB,Tower o/t Elephant . 60.00
5 BWS,Zukala's Daughter 60.00
6 BWS,SB,Devil Wings Over
  Shadizar 40.00
7 BWS,SB,DA,C:Thoth-Amon,
  I:Set 40.00
8 BWS,TS,TP,Keepers o/t Crypt 40.00
9 BWS,SB,Garden of Fear 40.00
10 BWS,SB,JSe,Beware Wrath of
  Anu;BU:Kull 50.00
11 BWS,SB,Talons of Thak 50.00
12 BWS,GK,Dweller in the Dark,
  Blood of the Dragon B.U. . . . 30.00
13 BWS,SB,Web o/t Spider-God . 28.00
14 BWS,SB,Green Empress of
  Melnibone 45.00
15 BWS,SB 45.00
16 BWS,Frost Giant's Daughter . 30.00
17 GK,Gods of Bal-Sagoth,
  A:Fafnir 13.00
18 GK,DA,Thing in the Temple,
  A:Fafnir 13.00
19 BWS,DA,Hawks from
  the Sea 28.00
20 BWS,DA,Black Hound of
  Vengeance,A:Fafnir 28.00
21 BWS,CR,VM,DA,SB, Monster
  of the Monoliths 25.00
22 BWS,DA,rep.Conan #1 . . . . . 28.00
23 BWS,DA,Shadow of the
  Vulture,I:Red Sonja 35.00

Conan the Barbarian #8
© Marvel Entertainment Group

MARVEL

24 BWS,Song of Red Sonja . . . 32.00
25 JB,SB,JSe,Mirrors of Kharam
   Akkad,A:Kull 12.00
26 JB,Hour of the Griffin 7.00
27 JB,Blood of Bel-Hissar 6.00
28 JB,Moon of Zembabwei 6.00
29 JB,Two Against Turan 6.00
30 JB,The Hand of Nergal 6.00
31 JB,Shadow in the Tomb 5.00
32 JB,Flame Winds of Lost Khitai 5.00
33 JB,Death & 7 Wizards 5.00
34 JB,Temptress in the Tower
   of Flame 5.00
35 JB,Hell-Spawn of Kara-Shehr . 5.00
36 JB,Beware of Hyrkanians
   bearing Gifts 5.00
37 NA,Curse of the Golden Skull . 8.00
38 JB,Warrior & Were-Woman . . . 3.50
39 JB,Dragon from the
   Inland Sea 3.50
40 RB,Fiend from Forgotten City . 3.50
41 JB,Garden of Death & Life . . 3.50

Conan the Barbarian #44
© Marvel Entertainment Group

42 JB,Night of the Gargoyle 3.50
43 JB,Tower o/Blood,A:RedSonja 3.50
44 JB,Flame&Fiend,A:RedSonja . 5.00
45 JB,Last Ballad of Laza-Lanti . . 5.00
46 JB,JSt,Curse of the Conjurer . 3.50
47 JB,DA,Goblins in the
   Moonlight 3.50
48 JB,DG,DA,Rats Dance at Raven
   gard,BU:Red Sonja 3.50
49 JB,DG,Wolf-Woman 3.50
50 JB,DG,Dweller in the Pool . . . 3.50
51 JB,DG,Man Born of Demon . . 3.00
52 JB,TP,Altar and the Scorpion . 3.00
53 JB,FS,Brothers of the Blade . . 3.00
54 JB,TP,Oracle of Ophir 3.00
55 JB,TP,Shadow on the Land . . 3.00
56 JB,High Tower in the Mist . . . 3.00
57 MP,Incident in Argos 3.00
58 JB,Queen o/tBlackCoast,
   2nd A:Belit 4.00
59 JB,Ballad of Belit,O:Belit 3.00
60 JB,Riders o/t River Dragons . . 3.00
61 JB,She-Pirate,I:Amra 2.50

62 JB,Lord of the Lions,O:Amra . . 2.50
63 JB,Death Among Ruins,
   V&D:Amra 2.50
64 JSon,AM,rep.Savage Tales#5 . 2.50
65 JB,Fiend o/tFeatheredSerpent . 2.50
66 JB,Daggers & Death Gods,
   C:Red Sonja 2.50
67 JB,Talons of the Man-Tiger,
   A:Red Sonja 2.50
68 JB,Of Once & Future Kings,
   V:KingKull,A:Belit,Red Sonja . 2.50
69 VM,Demon Out of the Deep . . 2.50
70 JB,City in the Storm 2.50
71 JB,Secret of Ashtoreth 2.50
72 JB,Vengeance in Asgalun 2.50
73 JB,..In the Well of Skelos 2.50
74 JB,Battle at the Black Walls
   C:Thoth-Amon 2.50
75 JB,Hawk-Riders of Harakht . . . 2.50
76 JB,Swordless in Stygia 2.50
77 JB,When Giants Walk
   the Earth 2.50
78 JB,rep.Savage Sword #1,
   A:Red Sonja 2.50
79 HC,Lost Valley of Iskander . . . 2.50
80 HC,Trial By Combat 2.50
81 HC,The Eye of the Serpent . . 2.00
82 HC,The Sorceress o/t Swamp . 2.00
83 HC,The Dance of the Skull . . . 2.00
84 JB,Two Against the Hawk-City,
   I:Zula 2.00
85 JB,Of Swordsmen & Sorcerers,
   O:Zulu 2.00
86 JB,Devourer of the Dead 2.00
87 TD, rep. Savage Sword #3. . . . 2.00
88 JB,Queen and the Corsairs . . 2.00
89 JB,Sword & the Serpent,
   A:Thoth-Amon 2.00
90 JB,Diadem of the Giant-Kings . 2.00
91 JB,Savage Doings in Shem . . 2.00
92 JB,The Thing in the Crypt . . . 2.00
93 JB,Of Rage & Revenge 2.00
94 JB,BeastKing ofAbombi,L:Zulu 2.00
95 JB,The Return of Amra 2.00
96 JB,Long Night of Fang
   & Talon,pt.1 . . . . 2.00
97 JB,Long Night of Fang
   & Talon,pt.2 . . . . 2.00
98 JB,Sea-Woman 2.00
99 JB,Devil Crabs o/t Dark Cliffs 2.00
100 JB,Death on the Black Coast,
    D:Belit (double size) 3.50
101 JB,The Devil has many Legs . 1.75
102 JB,The Men Who
    Drink Blood 1.75
103 JB,Bride of the Vampire 1.75
104 JB,The Vale of Lost Women . 1.75
105 JB,Whispering Shadows 1.75
106 JB,Chaos in Kush 1.75
107 JB,Demon of the Night 1.75
108 JB,Moon-Eaters of Darfar . . . 1.75
109 JB,Sons o/t Bear God 1.75
110 JB,Beward t/Bear o/Heaven . 1.75
111 JB,Cimmerian Against a City . 1.75
112 JB,Buryat Besieged 1.75
113 JB,A Devil in the Family 1.75
114 JB,The Shadow of the Beast . 1.75
115 JB,A War of Wizards, A:Red
    Sonja Double size 10th Anniv.
    (L:Roy Thomas script) 2.50
116 JB,NA,Crawler in the Mist . . . 1.75
117 JB,Corridor of Mullah-Kajar . . 1.75
118 JB,Valley of Forever Night . . . 1.75
119 JB,Voice of One Long Gone . 1.75
120 JB,The Hand of Erlik 1.75

121 JB,BMc,Price of Perfection . . 1.75
122 JB,BMc,The City Where Time
    Stood Still 1.75
123 JB,BMc,Horror Beneath the
    Hills 1.75
124 JB,BMc,the Eternity War 1.75
125 JB,BMc,the Witches ofNexxx . 1.75
126 JB,BMc,Blood Red Eye
    of Truth 1.75
127 GK,Snow Haired Woman
    of the Wastes 1.75
128 GK,And Life Sprang Forth
    From These 1.75
129 GK,The Creation Quest 1.75
130 GK,The Quest Ends 1.75
131 GK,The Ring of Rhax 1.75
132 GK,Games of Gharn 1.75
133 GK,The Witch of Widnsor . . . 1.75
134 GK,A Hitch in Time 1.75
135 MS,JRu,The Forest o/t Night . 1.75
136 JB,The River of Death 1.75
137 AA,Titans Gambit 1.75
138 VM,Isle of the Dead 1.75
139 VM,In the Lair of
    the Damned 1.75

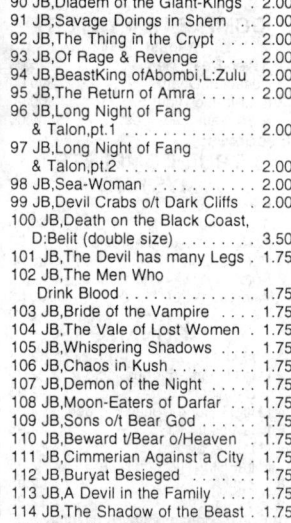
Conan the Barbarian #55
© Marvel Entertainment Group

140 JB,Spider Isle 1.75
141 JB,The Web Tightens 1.75
142 JB,The Maze,the Man,
    the Monster 1.75
143 JB,Life Among the Dead 1.75
144 JB,The Blade & the Beast . . . 1.75
145 Son of Cimmeria 1.75
146 JB,Night o/t Three Sisters . . . 1.75
147 JB,Tower of Mitra 1.75
148 JB,The Plague of Forlek 1.75
149 JB,Deathmark 1.75
150 JB,Tower of Flame 1.75
151 JB,Vale of Death 1.50
152 JB,Dark Blade of
    Jergal Zadh 1.50
153 JB,Bird Men of Akah Ma'at . . 1.50
154 JB,the Man-Bats of
    Ur-Xanarrh 1.50
155 JB,SL,The Anger of Conan . . 1.50
156 JB,The Curse 1.50
157 JB,The Wizard 1.50
158 JB,Night of the Wolf 1.50
159 JB,Cauldron of the Doomed . 1.50

160 Veil of Darkness	1.50
161 JB,House of Skulls,A:Fafnir	1.50
162 JB,Destroyer in the Flame, A:Fafnir	1.50
163 JB,Cavern of the Vines of Doom,A:Fafnir	1.50
164 The Jeweled Sword of Tem	1.50
165 JB,V:Nadine	1.50
166 JB,GI,Blood o/t Titan,A:Fafnir	1.50
167 JB,Creature From Time's Dawn,A:Fafnir	1.50
168 JB,Bird Woman & the Beast	1.50
169 JB,Tomb of the Scarlet Mage	1.50
170 JB,Dominion of the Dead, A&D:Fafnir	1.50
171 JB,Barbarian Death Song	1.50
172 JB,Reavers in Borderland	1.50
173 JB,Honor Among Thieves	1.50
174 JB,V:Tetra	1.50
175 JB,V:Spectre ofDeath	1.50
176 JB,Argos Rain	1.50
177 JB,V:Nostume	1.50
178 JB,A:Tetra,Well of Souls	1.50
179 JB,End of all there is,A:Kiev	1.50
180 JBV:AnitRenrut	1.50
181 JB,V:KingMaddoc II	1.50
182 JB,V:King of Shem	1.50
183 JB,V:Imhotep	1.50
184 JB,V:Madoc	1.50
185 JB,R:Tetra	1.50
186 JB,The Crimson Brotherhood	1.50
187 JB,V:Council of Seven	1.50
188 JB,V:Devourer-Souls	1.50
189 JB,V:Devourer-Souls	1.50
190 JB,Devourer-Souls	1.50
191 Deliverance	1.50
192 JB,V:TheKeeper	1.50
193 Devourer-Souls	1.50
194 V:Devourer-Souls	1.50
195 Blood of Ages	1.50
196 V:Beast	1.50
197 A:Red Sonja	1.50
198 A:Red Sonja	1.50
199 O:Kaleb	1.50
200 JB,D.sizeV:Dev-Souls	2.00
201 NKu,GI,Thulsa Doom	1.50
202	1.50
203 V:Thulsa Doom	1.50
204 VS,GI,A:Red Sonja,I:Strakkus	1.50
205 A:Red Sonja	1.50
206 VS,GI,Heku trilogy,pt.1	1.50
207 VS,GI,Heku,pt.2,O:Kote	1.50
208 VS,GI,Heku,pt.3	1.50
209 VS,GI,Heku epilogue	1.50
210 VS,GI,V:Sevante	1.50
211 VS,GI,V:Sevante	1.50
212 EC,GI	1.50
213 V:Ghamud Assassins	1.50
214 AA	1.50
215 VS,AA,Conan Enslaved	1.50
216 V:Blade of Zed	1.50
217 JLe(c),V:Blade of Zed	1.50
218 JLe(c),V:Picts	1.50
219 JLe(c),V:Forgotten Beasts	1.50
220 Conan the Pirate	1.50
221 Conan the Pirate	1.50
222 AA,DP,Revenge	1.50
223 AA,Religious Cult	1.50
224 AA,Cannibalism	1.50
225 AA,Conan Blinded	1.50
226 AA,Quest for Mystic Jewel	1.50
227 AA,Mystic Jewel,pt.2	1.50
228 AA,Cannibalism,pt.1	1.50
229 AA,Cannibalism,pt.2	1.50
230 FS,SDr,Citadel,pt.1	1.50

Conan The Barbarian #178
© Marvel Entertainment Group

231 FS,DP,Citadel,pt.2	1.50
232 RLm,Birth of Conan	3.00
233 RLm,DA,B:Conan as youth	2.00
234 RLm,DA	2.00
235 RLm,DA	2.00
236 RLm,DA	2.00
237 DA,V:Jormma	1.50
238 DA,D:Conan	1.50
239 Conan Possessed	1.50
240 Conan Possessed	1.50
241 TM(c),R:RoyThomasScript	3.50
242 JLe(c),A:Red Sonja	2.50
243 WPo(c),V:Zukala,	2.00
244 A:Red Sonja,Zula	1.50
245 A:Red Sonja,V:King of Vampires	1.50
246 A:Red Sonja,V:MistMonster	1.50
247 A:Red Sonja,Zula	1.50
248 V:Zulu	1.50
249 A:Red Sonja,Zula	1.50
250 A:RedSonja,Zula,V:Zug double size	2.00
251 Cimmeria,V:Shumu Gorath	1.50
252 ECh	1.50
253 ECh,V:Kulan-Goth(X-Men Villain)	1.50
254 ECh,V:Shuma-Gorath (Dr. Strange Villain)	1.50
255 ECh,V:Shuma-Gorath	1.50
256 ECh,D:Nemedia's King	1.50
257 ECh,V:Queen Vammator	1.50
258 AA(i),A:Kulan Gath	1.50
259 V:Shuma-Gorath	1.50
260 AA(i),V:Queen Vammatar	1.50
261 V:Cult of the Death Goddess	1.50
262 V:The Panther	1.50
263 V:Malaq	1.50
264 V:Kralic	1.50
265 V:Karlik	1.50
266 Conan the Renegade(adapt)	1.50
267 adaption of Tor	1.50
268 adaption of Tor	1.50
269 V:Agohoth,Prince Borin	1.50
270 Devourer of the Dead	1.50
271 V:Devourer of Souls	1.50

272 V:Devourer	1.50
273 V:Purple Lotus	1.50
274 V:She-Bat	1.50
275 RTs(s),Last Issue cont. in Savage Sword of Conan	5.00
G-Size#1 GK,TS,Hour of the Dragon, inc.rep.Conan#3, I:Belit	8.00
G-Size#2 GK,TS,Conan Bound, inc. rep Conan #5	5.00
G-Size#3 GK,TS,To Tarantia & the Tower,inc.rep.Conan#6	5.00
G-Size#4,GK,FS,Swords of the South,inc.rep.Conan #7	5.00
G-Size#5 rep.Conan #14,#15 & Back-up story #12	5.00
KingSz.#1 rep.Conan #2,#4	13.00
Ann.#2 BWS,Phoenix on the Sword A:Thoth-Amon	4.00
Ann.#3 JB,HC,Mountain of the Moon God, B.U.Kull story	2.00
Ann.#4 JB,Return of the Conqueror,A:Zenobia	2.00
Ann.#5 JB,W:Conan/Zenobia	2.00
Ann.#6 GK,King of the Forgotten People	2.00
Ann.#7 JB,Red Shadows & Black Kraken	1.50
Ann.#8 VM,Dark Night of the White Queen	1.50
Ann.#9	1.50
Ann.#10 Scorched Earth (Conan #176 x-over)	1.50
Ann.#11	1.50
Conan-Barbarian Movie Spec.#1	1.25
Conan-Barbarian Movie Spec.#2	1.25
Conan-Destroyer Movie Spec.#1	1.25
Red Nails Special Ed.BWS	4.00
Conan & Ravagers Out of Time	9.95
Conan the Reaver	9.95
Conan the Rogue, JB,V:Romm	9.95
Horn of Azroth	9.95
Skull of Set	9.95

CLASSIC CONAN
June, 1987

1 BWS,rep.	2.00
2 BWS,rep.	2.00
3 BWS,rep.	2.00

Becomes:

CONAN SAGA

4 rep.	3.00
5 rep.	3.00
6 rep.	3.00
7 rep.	3.00
8 rep.	3.00
9 rep.	3.00
10 rep.	3.00
11 rep.	2.50
12 rep.	2.50
13 rep.	2.50
14 rep.Savage Sword #5	2.50
15 rep.Savage Sword #7	2.50
16 rep.Savage Sword #12	2.50
17 rep.Savage Sword	2.50
18 rep.Savage Sword	2.50
19 rep.Savage Sword #28	2.50
20 rep.Savage Sword #25	2.50
21 rep.Savage Sword	2.50
22 rep.Giant Size Conan #1&2	2.50
23 rep.Hour of the Dragon	2.50
24 rep.Hour of the Dragon	2.50
25 rep.Savage Sword	2.50
26 rep.Savage Sword #11	2.50

All comics prices listed are for *Near Mint* condition.

MARVEL

27 rep.Savage Sword #15	2.50
28 rep.Savage Sword #16	2.25
29 rep.Savage Sword #17	2.25
30 rep.Savage Sword #18	2.25
31 rep.Savage Sword #19	2.25
32 rep.Savage Sword #5	2.25
33 rep.Savage Sword #5	2.25
34 rep.Savage Sword #	2.25
35 rep.Savage Sword #32	2.25
36 rep.Savage Sword #12	2.25
37 rep.Savage Sword #34	2.25
38 rep.Conan #94&#95	2.25
39 rep.Conan #96&#97	2.25
40 rep.Savage Sword #26	2.25
41 rep.Savage Sword #27	2.25
42 rep.Savage Sword #40	2.25
43 rep.Savage Sword #41	2.25
44 rep.Savage Sword #42	2.25
45 rep.Savage Sword #43	2.25
46 rep.Savage Sword #15	2.25
47 rep.Savage Sword #22	2.25
48 rep.Savage Sword #23	2.25
49 rep.Sav.Sword Super Spec#2	2.25
50 rep.Conan #58	2.25
51 rep.Conan #59&#60	2.25
52 rep.Conan #61	2.25
53 thru 63 rep.Savage Sword	@2.25
64 thru 94 rep.	@2.25
95 D:Belit	2.25
96	2.25
97 Red Sonja rep.	2.25
98 rep. #106–#108	2.25

CONAN CLASSICS

1 rep. Conan #1	2.00
2 rep. Conan #2	2.00
3 rep. Conan #3	1.75
4 rep. Conan #4	1.50
5 rep. Conan #5	1.50
6 rep. Conan #6	1.50
7 rep. Conan #7	1.50
8 rep.	1.50
9 Garden of Fear	1.50
10 V:Anu	1.50
11 New Sword Manuever	1.50

CONAN/RUNE

1 BWS,Conan Vs. Rune	3.50

CONAN

1 CCt,	
2 CCt,V:Sorcerer	
3 (of 3) CCt,	

KING CONAN
March, 1980

1 JB/ECh,I:Conn,V:Thoth-Amon	3.00
2 JB,Black Sphinx of Nebthu	2.50
3 JB,Dragon Wings Over Zembabwei	2.50
4 JB,V:Thoth-Amon	2.50
5 JB,The Sorcerer in the Realm of Madness	2.50
6 JB,The Lady's Name Is..Trouble	2.50
7 PS,JB	2.75
8 A:Queen Reclaimed	2.75
9 JB,V:Medusa Monster	2.25
10 V:Sea Monster	2.25
11 V:Giant Totem Monster	1.75
12 V:Monster	1.75
13 V:Monster	1.75
14 V:Demon	1.75
15 V:Sea Monster	1.75
16 Conan Into Battle	1.75

King Conan #1
© *Marvel Entertainment Group*

17 A:Conn	1.75
18 King of the Freaks?	1.75
19 MK(c),Skull & X-Bones cover	1.75

Becomes:

CONAN THE KING

20 MS,The Prince is Dead	2.00
21 MS,Shadows	2.00
22 GI/MS,The Black Dragons,Prince Conan II back-up story begins	2.00
23 MS/GI,Ordeal	2.00
24 GI/MS,Fragments:A Witch'sTale	2.00
25 MS/GI,Daggers	2.00
26 MS/GI,PrinceConanII B.U.ends	2.00
27 MS/GI,A Death in Stygia	2.00
28 MS/GI,Call of the Wild, A:Red Sonja	2.00
29 MS,The Sleeping Lion	2.00
30 GI,Revenge on the Black River	2.00
31 GI,Force of Arms	2.00
32 GI,Juggernaut	2.00
33	2.00
34	2.00
35	2.00
36	2.00
37 AW,Sack of Belverus	2.00
38 MM,A:Taurus,Leora	2.00
39 The Tower	2.00
40	2.00
41 V:Leora	2.00
42 Thee Armada,A:Conn	2.00
43	2.00
44	2.00
45 V:Caliastros	2.00
46 V:Caliastros	2.00
47 TD,V:Caliastros	2.00
48	2.00
49	2.00
50 GI,50th Anniversary issue	2.00
51 GI,Death of Prince Conn	2.00
52 GI,Prince Conn story contd	2.00
53 GI,A:Thoth-Amon	2.00
54 GI,V:Thoth-Amon	2.00
55 GI,Sorcerers Ring,final issue	2.00

CONAN THE SAVAGE

1 New Series	2.95

2 CDi,Conan a gladiator	2.95
3 V:Monster	2.95
4 CDi,Conan vs. Rune	2.95
5 MBn,VMk,Ice age tale	2.95
6 Bros.Hildebrandt(c),V:FallenIdol	2.95
7 CDi,F:Iron Maidens	2.95
8	2.95
9	2.95
10 JB story, 48pg.	2.95

CONEHEADS

1 Based SNL	2.00
2 Based SNL	2.00
3 Based SNL	1.75

CONTEST OF CHAMPIONS
June, 1982

1 JR2,Grandmaster vs. Mistress Death, A:Alpha Flight	7.00
2 JR2,Grandmaster vs. Mistress Death, A:X-Men	5.00
3 JR2,D:Grandmaster, Rebirth Collector, A:X-Men	5.00

COPS: THE JOB

1 MGo(c),V:Serial killer	1.50
2 MGo(c)	1.25
3 MGo(c),V:Eviscerator	1.25
4 MGo(c),D:Eviscerator,Nick	1.25

COSMIC POWERS

1 RMz(s),RLm,JP,F:Thanos	2.75
2 RMz(s),JMr,F:Terrax	2.75
3 RMz(s),F:Jack of Hearts	2.75
4 RMz(s),RLm,F:Legacy	2.75
5 RMz(s),F&O:Morg	2.75
6 RMz(s),F&O:Tyrant	2.75

COSMIC POWERS UNLIMITED

1 Surfer vs. Thanos	3.95
2 Jack of Hearts vs. Jakar	3.95
3 GWt,JB,F:Lunatik,64pg.	3.95
4 GWt,SEa,cont.StarMasters#3	3.95
5 GWt,SEa,R:Captain Universe	3.95

COUNT DUCKULA
Star Nov., 1988

1 O:CountDuckula,B:DangerMouse	1.25
2 A:Danger Mouse	1.00
3 thru 15	@1.00

COWBOY ACTION
See: WESTERN THRILLERS

COWBOY ROMANCES
Oct., 1949

1 Ph(c),Outlaw and the Lady	125.00
2 Ph(c),William Holden/Mona Freeman,Streets of Laredo	75.00
3 Phc,Romance in Roaring Valley	50.00

Becomes:

YOUNG MEN

4 A Kid Names Shorty	85.00
5 Jaws of Death	55.00
6 Man-Size	55.00
7 The Last Laugh	55.00
8 Adventure stories continued	55.00
9 Draft Dodging story	55.00
10 US Draft Story	55.00

MARVEL

MARVEL

11 Adventure stories continued . 40.00
12 B:On the Battlefield,
inc.Spearhead 40.00
13 RH,Break-through 40.00
14 RH,Fox Hole 40.00
15 Battlefield stories cont, ... 40.00
16 Sniper Patrol 40.00
17 Battlefield stories cont, ... 40.00
18 BEv,Warlord 40.00
19 BEv 40.00
20 BEv,E:On the Battlefield . . . 40.00
21 B:Flash Foster and his High
Gear Hot Shots 40.00
22 Screaming Tires 40.00
23 E:Flash Foster and his High
Gear Hot Shots 40.00
24 BEv,B:Capt. America,Human
Torch,Sub-Mariner,O:Capt.
America,Red Skull 450.00
25 BEv,JR, Human Torch,Capt.
America,Sub-Mariner 350.00
26 BEv,Human Torch, Capt.
America,Sub Mariner 350.00
27 Bev, Human Torch/Toro
V:Hypnotist 350.00
28 E:Human Torch, Capt.America,
Sub Mariner,June, 1954 . . . 350.00

COWGIRL ROMANCES
See: DARING MYSTERY

COYOTE
Epic June, 1983
1 SL, ... 1.50
2 SL 1.50
3 BG 1.50
4 SL 1.50
5 SL 1.50
6 SL 1.50
7 SL,SD 1.50
8 SL 1.50
9 SL,SD 1.50
10 SL 1.50
11 FS,1st TM art,O:Slash 4.00
12 TM 2.00
13 TM 2.00
14 FS,TM,A:Badger 2.00
15 SL 1.50
16 SL,A:Reagan,Gorbachev . . . 1.50

CRASH RYAN
Epic Oct., 1984
1 War Story 1.75
2 Doomsday 1.50
3 Fortress Japan 1.50
4 Jan., 1985 . . . . 1.50

CRAZY
Atlas Dec., 1953
1 BEv,satire, Frank N.Steins
Castle 150.00
2 BEv,Beast from 1000 Fathoms125.00
3 Bev,Madame Knockwurst's
Whacks Museum 100.00
4 BEv,I Love Lucy satire 100.00
5 BEv,Censorship satire 100.00
6 BEv,satire 100.00
7 BEv,satire,July, 1954 . . . . . 100.00

CRAZY
Feb., 1973
1 Not Brand Echh reps,
Forbushman 4.00

2 Big,Batty Love and Hisses issue 3.00
3 Stupor-Man,A:Fantastical
Four, June 1973 . . . . 3.00

CRAZY
(Black and white magazine)
Oct., 1973
1 Satire,parody 3.50
2 . . . . 2.00
3 thru 81 . . . . @1.50
82 X-Men(c) 1.50
83 thru 93 . . . . @1.00

CREATURES ON THE LOOSE
See: TOWER OF SHADOWS

CRIME CAN'T WIN
See: KRAZY COMICS

CRIME FIGHTERS
April, 1948—Nov., 1949
1 Police Stories 125.00
2 Jewelry robbery 50.00
3 The Nine who were Doomed . . 50.00
4 Human Beast at Bay 40.00
5 V:Gangsters 40.00
6 Pickpockets 40.00
7 True Cases, Crime Can't Win . 40.00
8 True Cases, Crime Can't Win . 40.00
9 Ph(c),It Happened at Night . . . 40.00
10 Ph(c),Killer at Large 40.00
Atlas Sept., 1954—Jan., 1955
11 V:Gangsters 35.00
12 V:Gangsters 35.00
13 Clay Pidgeon 35.00

CRITICAL MASS
Epic Jan.–July, 1990
1 KS,GM,BSzF:ShadowlineSaga . 4.95
2 . . . . 4.95
3 GM,SDr,JRy 4.95
4 . . . . 4.95
5 JZ 4.95
6 . . . . 4.95
7 July, 1990 . . . . 4.95

CROSSOVER CLASSICS
TPB Marvel and D.C. GP(c),reprints
both Spider-Man/Superman,the
Batman/Hulk and the X-Men/New
Teen Titans Battles 17.95

CRYPT OF SHADOWS
Jan., 1973
1 BW,RH,Midnight on Black
Mountain 5.50
2 Monster at the Door 2.50
3 Dead Man's Hand 2.50
4 CI,Secret in the Vault 2.50
5 JM,The Graveyard Ghoul 2.50
6 BEv,Don't Bury Me Deep 2.50
7 JSt,The Haunting of Bluebeard . 2.50
8 How Deep my Grave 2.50
9 Beyond Death 2.50
10 A Scream in the Dark 2.50
11 The Ghouls in my Grave 2.00
12 Behind the Locked Door 2.00
13 SD,Back From the Dead 2.00
14 The Thing that Creeps 2.00
15 My Coffin is Crowded 2.00
16 . . . . 2.00

17 In the Hands of Shandu 2.00
18 SD,Face of Fear 2.00
19 SD,Colossus that Challenged
the World 2.00
20 A Monster walks Among Us . . 2.00
21 SD,Death Will Be Mine,
Nov. 1975 . . . . 2.00

CUPID
Dec., 1949
1 Ph(c),Cora Dod's Amazing
Decision 60.00
2 Ph(c),Betty Page, Mar. 1950 125.00

CURSE OF THE WEIRD
1 thru 4 SD,rep. 50's Sci-Fi . . . 1.50

CUTTING EDGE
1 WML,F:Hulk,Ghosts of the
Future tie-in 2.95

CYBERSPACE 3000
1 A:Dark Angel,Galactus,V:Badoon,
Glow in the dark(c) 3.00
2 SeT,A:Galactus,Dark Angel . . . 2.00
3 SeT,A:Galactus,Keeper 2.00
4 SeT,A:Keeper 2.00
5 SeT,A:Keeper 2.00
6 SeT,A:Warlock 2.00
7 SeT,I:Gamble 2.00
8 SeT,A:Warlock 2.00
9 SeT 1.75
10 SeT 1.75
11 SeT 1.75

DAILY BUGLE
B&W 1996
1 (of 3) KIK,GA 2.50
2 KIK,GA 2.50
3 KIK,GA 2.50

DAKOTA NORTH
1986
1 (Now in Cage) 1.50
2 . . . . 1.25
3 . . . . 1.25
4 . . . . 1.25
5 Feb., 1987 . . . . 1.25

DAMAGE CONTROL
May, 1989
1 EC/BWi;A:Spider-Man 2.50
2 EC/BWi;A:Fant.Four 2.00
3 EC/BWi;A:Iron Man 2.00
4 EC/BWi;A:X-Men 2.00
[2nd Series]
1 EC,A:Capt.America&Thor 3.00
2 EC,A:Punisher 2.50
3 EC 2.00
4 EC,Punisher 2.00
[3rd Series]
1 Clean-up Crew Returns 1.50
2 A:Hulk,New Warriors 1.50
3 A:Avengers W.C.,Wonder Man,
Silver Surfer 1.50
4 A:SilverSurfer & others 1.50

DANCES WITH DEMONS
1 CAd 2.95
2 CAd,V:Manitou 1.95
3 CAd,V:Manitou 1.95
4 CAd,last issue 1.95

---

5 Okay, there's more! 1.95
6 . . . . 1.95

Daredevil #18
© *Marvel Entertainment Group*

DAREDEVIL
April, 1964

1 B:StL(s),JK(c),BEv,I&O:Daredevil,
  I:Karen Page,Foggy Nelson 1,700.00
2 JK(c),JO,V:Electro 500.00
3 JK(c),JO,I&O:The Owl 350.00
4 JK(c),JO,I&O:Killgrave 325.00
5 JK(c),WW,V:Masked Matador 225.00
6 WW,I&O Original Mr. Fear . . 150.00
7 WW,I:Red Costume,V:Namor 275.00
8 WW,I&O:Stiltman 150.00
9 WW(i),Killers Castle 150.00
10 WW(i),V:Catman 150.00
11 WW(i),R:Cat 125.00
12 JK,JR,2nd A:Ka-Zar 125.00
13 JK,JR,O:Ka-Zar 75.00
14 JR,If This Be Justice 75.00
15 JR,A:Ox 75.00
16 JR,A:Spider-Man,
   I:Masked Marauder 100.00
17 JR,A:Spider-Man 90.00
18 DON(s),JR,I:Gladiator 60.00
19 JR,V:Gladiator 60.00
20 JR(c),GC,V:Owl 50.00
21 GC,BEv,V:Owl 40.00
22 GC,V:Tri-man 40.00
23 GC,V:Tri-man 40.00
24 GC,A:Ka-Zar 40.00
25 GC,V:Leapfrog 32.00
26 GC,V:Stiltman 32.00
27 GC,Spider-Man 35.00
28 GC,V:Aliens 30.00
29 GC,V:The Boss 30.00
30 BEv(c),GC,A:Thor 30.00
31 GC,V:Cobra 28.00
32 GC,V:Cobra 28.00
33 GC,V:Beetle 28.00
34 BEv(c),GC,O:Beetle 28.00
35 BEv(c),GC,A:Susan Richards 28.00
36 GC,A:FF 28.00
37 GC,V:Dr.Doom 28.00
38 GC,A:FF 28.00
39 GC,GT,V:Unholy Three 28.00

40 GC,V:Unholy Three 28.00
41 GC,D:Mike Murdock 25.00
42 GC,DA,I:Jester 25.00
43 JK(c),GC,A:Capt.America . . . 24.00
44 JSo(c),GC,V:Jester 20.00
45 GC,V:Jester 20.00
46 GC,V:Jester 20.00
47 GC,'Brother Take My Hand' . 20.00
48 GC,V:Stiltman 20.00
49 GC,V:Robot,I:Starr Saxon . . 20.00
50 JR(c),BWS,JCr,V:Robot 25.00
51 B:RTs(s),BWS,V:Robot 25.00
52 BWS,JCr,A:Black Panther . . . 25.00
53 GC,O:Daredevil. 27.00
54 GC,V:Mr.Fear,A:Spidey 20.00
55 GC,V:Mr.Fear 15.00
56 GC,V:Death Head 15.00
57 GC,V:Death Head 15.00
58 GC,V:Stunt Master 14.00
59 GC,V:Torpedo 14.00
60 GC,V:Crime Wave 14.00
61 GC,V:Cobra 14.00
62 GC,O:Night Hawk 14.00
63 GC,V:Gladiator 14.00
64 GC,A:Stuntmaster 14.00
65 GC,V:BrotherBrimstone 14.00
66 GC,V:BrotherBrimstone 14.00
67 BEv(c),GC,Stiltman 14.00
68 AC,V:Kragg Blackmailer,
   a:Bl.Panther,DD'sID Rev. . . 14.00
69 E:RTs(s),GC,V:Thunderbolts,
   A:Bl.Panther(DD's ID Rev) . 14.00
70 GC,V:Terrorists 14.00
71 RTs(s),GC,V:Terrorists 14.00
72 GyC(s),GC,Tagak,V:Quother . 12.00
73 GC,V:Zodiac 12.00
74 B:GyC(s),GC,I:Smasher 12.00
75 GC,V:El Condor 12.00
76 GC,TP,V:El Condor 12.00
77 GC,TP,V:Manbull 12.00
78 GC,TP,V:Manbull 12.00
79 GC,TP,V:Manbull 12.00
80 GK(c),GC,TP,V:Owl 12.00
81 GK(c),GC,JA,A:Black Widow . 12.00
82 GK(c),GC,JA,V:Scorpion . . . 12.00
83 JR(c),BWS,BEv,V:Mr.Hyde . . 14.00
84 GK(c),GC,Assassin 10.00
85 GK(c),GC,A:Black Widow . . . 10.00
86 GC,TP,V:Ox 10.00
87 GC,TP,V:Electro 10.00
88 GK(c),GC,TP,O:Black Widow . 10.00
89 GC,TP,A:Black Widow 10.00
90 E:StL(s),GK(c),GC,TP,V:Ox . . 10.00
91 GK(c),GC,TP,I:Mr. Fear III . . 10.00
92 GK(c),GC,TP,A:BlackPanther . 11.00
93 GK(c),GC,TP,A:Black Widow . 10.00
94 GK(c),GC,TP,V:Damon Dran . 10.00
95 GK(c),GC,TP,V:Manbull 10.00
96 GK(c),GC,ECh,V:Manbull . . . 10.00
97 GK(c),V:Dark Messiah 10.00
98 E:GyC(s),GC,ECh,V:Dark
   Messiah 10.00
99 B:SvG(s),JR(c),V:Hawkeye . . 10.00
100 GC,V:Angar the Screamer . 25.00
101 RB,A:Angar the Screamer . . 9.00
102 A:Black Widow 7.00
103 JR(c),DH,A:Spider-Man . . . 7.00
104 GK(c),DH,V:Kraven 7.00
105 DH,JSn,DP,C:Thanos 9.00
106 JR(c),DH,A:Black Widow . . . 7.00
107 JSn(c),JB(i),A:Capt.Marvel . 7.00
108 K&R(c),PG(i),V:Beetle 7.00
109 GK(c),DH(i),V:Beetle 7.00
110 JR(c),GC,A:Thing,O:Nekra . 7.00
111 JM(i),I:Silver Samurai 8.50

112 GK(c),GC,V:Mandrill 7.00
113 JR(c),V:Gladiator 7.00
114 GK(c),I:Death Stalker 7.00
115 V:Death Stalker 6.00
116 GK(c),GC,V:Owl 6.00
117 E:SvG(s),K&R(c),V:Owl 6.00
118 JR(c),DH,I:Blackwing 6.00
119 GK(c),DH(i),V:Crusher 6.00
120 GK(c),V:Hydra,I:El Jaguar . . 6.00
121 GK(c),A:Shield 5.00
122 GK(c),V:Blackwing 5.00
123 V:Silvermane,I:Jackhammer . 5.00
124 B:MWn(s),GK(c),GC,KJ,
   I:Copperhead 5.00
125 GK(c),KJ(i),V:Copperhead . . 5.00
126 GK(c),KJ(i),D: 2nd Torpedo . 5.00
127 GK(c),KJ(i),V:3rd Torpedo . . 5.00
128 GK(c),KJ(i),V:Death Stalker . 5.00
129 KJ(i),V:Man Bull 5.00
130 KJ(i),V:Brother Zed 5.00
131 KJ(i),I&O:2nd Bullseye 20.00
132 KJ(i),V:Bullseye 6.00
133 JM(i),GK(c),V:Jester 4.00
134 JM(i),V:Chamelon 4.00
135 JM(i),V:Jester 4.00
136 JB,JM,V:Jester 4.00
137 JB,V:Jester 4.00
138 JBy,A:Ghost Rider 5.00
139 SB,V:A Bomber 4.00
140 SB,V:Gladiator 4.00
141 GC,Bullseye 4.00
142 GC,V:Cobra 4.00
143 E:MWn(s),GC,V:Cobra 4.00
144 GT,V:Manbull 4.00
145 GT,V:Owl 4.00
146 GC,V:Bullseye 5.00
147 GC,V:Killgrave 3.50
148 GC,V:Deathstalker 3.50
149 KI,V:Smasher 3.50
150 GC,KJ,I:Paladin 4.00
151 GC,Daredevil Unmasked . . . 3.50
152 KJ,V:Paladin 3.50
153 GC,V:Cobra 3.50
154 GC,V:Mr. Hyde 3.50
155 V:Avengers 3.50
156 GC,V:Death Stalker 3.50
157 GC,V:Death Stalker 3.50
158 FM,V:Death Stalker 55.00
159 FM,V:Bullseye 25.00
160 FM,Bullseye 20.00
161 FM,V:Bullseye 20.00
162 SD,JRu,'Requiem' 3.50
163 FM,V:Hulk,I:Ben Urich . . . 12.00
164 FM,KJ,A:Avengers 12.00
165 FM,KJ,V:Dr.Octopus 12.00
166 FM,KJ,V:Gladiator 12.00
167 FM,KJ,V:Mauler 12.00
168 FM,KJ,I&O:Elektra 45.00
169 FM,KJ,V:Bullseye 15.00
170 FM,KJ,V:Bullseye 15.00
171 FM,KJ,V:Kingpin 8.00
172 FM,KJ,V:Gliador 8.00
173 FM,KJ,V:Gliador 8.00
174 FM,KJ,A:Gladiator 8.00
175 FM,KJ,A:Elektra,V:Hand . . 10.00
176 FM,KJ,A:Elektra 8.00
177 FM,KJ,A:Stick 9.00
178 FM,KJ,A:PowerMan&I.Fist . 9.00
179 FM,KJ,V:Elektra 9.00
180 FM,KJ,V:Kingpin 8.00
181 FM,KJ,V:Bullseye,D:Elektra,
   A:Punisher 12.00
182 FM,KJ,A:Punisher 7.00
183 FM,KJ,V:PunisherDrug 7.00
184 FM,KJ,V:PunisherDrug 7.00

MARVEL

Daredevil #52
© *Marvel Entertainment Group*

185 FM,KJ,V:King Pin	5.00
186 FM,KJ,V:Stiltman	5.00
187 FM,KJ,A:Stick	5.00
188 FM,KJ,A:Black Widow	5.00
189 FM,KJ,A:Stick,A:BlackWidow	5.00
190 FM,KJ,R:Elektra	6.00
191 FM,TA,A:Bullseye	5.00
192 KJ,V:Kingpin	3.50
193 KJ,Betsy	3.50
194 KJ,V:Kingpin	3.50
195 KJ,Tarkington Brown	3.50
196 KJ,A:Wolverine	12.00
197 V:Bullseye	3.00
198 V:Dark Wind	3.00
199 V:Dark Wind	3.00
200 JBy(c),V:Bullseye	3.50
201 JBy(c),A:Black Widow	2.50
202 I:Micah Synn	2.50
203 JBy(c),I:Trump	2.50
204 BSz(c),V:Micah Synn	2.50
205 I:Gael	2.50
206 V:Micah Synn	2.50
207 BSz(c),A:Black Widow	2.50
208 Harlan Ellison	3.00
209 Harlan Ellison	3.00
210 DM,V:Micah Synn	2.50
211 DM,V:Micah Synn	2.50
212 DM,V:Micah Synn	2.50
213 DM,V:Micah Synn	2.50
214 DM,V:Micah Synn	2.50
215 DM,A:Two-Gun Kid	2.50
216 DM,V:Gael	2.50
217 BS(c),V:Gael	2.50
218 KP,V:Jester	2.50
219 FM,JB	3.00
220 DM,D:Heather Glenn	2.50
221 DM,Venice	2.50
222 DM,A:Black Widow	2.50
223 DM,Secret Wars II	2.50
224 DM,V:Sunturion	2.50
225 DM,V:Vulture	2.50
226 FM(plot),V:Gladiator	3.00
227 FM,Kingpin,Kar.Page	8.00
228 FM,DM,V:Kingpin	5.00
229 FM,Kingpin,Turk	5.00

230 R:Matt's Mother	5.00
231 FM,DM,V:Kingpin	5.00
232 FM,V:Kingpin,Nuke	5.00
233 FM,Kingpin,Nuke,Capt.Am.	5.00
234 SD,KJ,V:Madcap	2.00
235 SD,KJ,V:Mr. Hyde	2.00
236 BWS,A:Black Widow	5.00
237 AW(i),V:Klaw	2.00
238 SB,SL,AAd(c)V:Sabretooth	7.00
239 AAd(c),AW,Gl(i),V:Rotgut	2.00
240 AW,V:Rotgut	2.00
241 MZ(c),TM,V:Trixter	4.00
242 KP,V:Caviar Killer	2.00
243 AW,V:Nameless One	2.00
244 TD(i),V:Nameless One	2.00
245 TD(i),A:Black Panther	2.00
246 TD(i),V:Chance	2.00
247 KG,A:Black Widow	2.00
248 RL,AW,A:Wolverine, V:Bushwhacker	7.00
249 RL,AW,V:Wolverine, Bushwhacker	7.00
250 JR2,AW,I:Bullet	3.50
251 JR2,AW,V:Bullet	3.00
252 JR2,AW,Fall o/Mutants	4.50
253 JR2,AW,V:Kingpin	3.00
254 JR2,AW,I:Typhoid Mary	15.00
255 JR2,AW,A:Kingpin,TMary	7.00
256 JR2,AW,A:Kingpin,TMary	7.00
257 JR2,AW,A:Punisher	7.00
258 RLm,V:Bengal	3.50
259 JR2,AW,V:TyphoidMary	4.00
260 JR2,AW,V:T.Mary,K.pin	4.00
261 JR2,AW,HumanTorch	2.50
262 JR2,AW,Inferno	2.50
263 JR2,AW,Inferno	2.50
264 SD,AW,MM,V:The Owl	2.50
265 JR2,AW,Inferno	2.50
266 JR2,AW,V:Mephisto	2.50
267 JR2,AW,V:Bullet	2.50
268 JR2,AW,V:TheMob	2.50
269 JR2,AW,V:Pyro&Blob	2.50
270 JR2,AW,A:Spider-Man, I:Blackheart	3.00
271 JR2,AW,I:Number9	2.50
272 JR2,AW,I:Shotgun	3.00
273 JR2,AW,V:Shotgun	2.50
274 JR2,AW,V:Inhumans	2.50
275 JR2,AW,ActsOfVen.,V:Ultron	2.50
276 JR2,AW,ActsOfVen.,V:Ultorn	2.50
277 RL,AW,Vivian's Story	2.00
278 JR2,AW,V:Blackheart, A:Inhumans	2.50
279 JR2,AW,V:Mephisto, A:Inhumans	2.50
280 JR2,AW,V:Mephisto, A:Inhumans	2.50
281 JR2,AW,V:Mephisto, A:Inhumans	2.50
282 JR2,AW,V:Mephisto, A:Silver Surfer, Inhumans	2.50
283 MBa,AW,A:Captain America	2.00
284 LW,AW,R:Bullseye	2.00
285 LW,AW,B:Bullseye become DD#1	2.00
286 LW,AW,GCa,Fake Daredevil #2	2.00
287 LW,AW,Fake Daredevil #3	2.00
288 LW,AW,A:Kingpin	2.00
289 LW,AW,A:Kingpin	2.00
290 LW,AW,E:Fake Daredevil	2.00
291 LW,AW,V:Bullet	2.00
292 LW,A:Punisher,V:Tombstone	2.00
293 LW,A:Punisher,V:Tombstone	2.00
294 LW,V:The Hand.	1.75

295 LW,V:The Hand, A:GhostRider.	1.75
296 LW,AW,V:The Hand	1.75
297 B:DGC(s),LW,AW,B:Last Rites, V:Typhoid Mary,A:Kingpin	3.50
298 LW,AW,A:Nick Fury,Kingpin	2.50
299 LW,AW,A:Nick Fury,Kingpin	2.50
300 LW,AW,E:Last Rites,	4.50
301 V:The Owl	1.75
302 V:The Owl	1.75
303 V:The Owl.	1.75
304 AW,Non-action issue	1.75
305 AW,A:Spider-Man	1.75
306 AW,A:Spider-Man	1.75
307 1st SMc DD,Dead Man's Hand #1, A:Nomad	3.00
308 SMc,Dead Man's Hand #5, A:Punisher,V:Silvermane	2.00
309 SMc,Dead Man's Hand#7, A:Nomad,Punisher	2.00
310 SMc,Inf.War,V:Calipso	2.00
311 SMc,V:Calypso	2.00
312 Firefighting issue	1.75
313 SMc,V:Pyromaniac	2.00
314 SMc,V:Mr.Fear,I:Shock	2.00
315 SMc,V:Mr.Fear	2.00
316 Goes Underground	1.75
317 SMc,Comedy Issue	2.00
318 SMc,V:Taskmaster	2.00
319 SMc,Fall from Grace Prologue, A:Silver Sable,Garrett,Hand	6.00
319a 2nd Printing	5.00
320 SMc,B:Fall from Grace, V:Crippler,S.Sable,A:Stone	5.00
321 SMc,N:Daredevil,A:Venom, Garret, V:Hellspawn,Glow in the Dark(c)	3.00
321a Newsstand Ed.	3.00
322 SMc,A:Venom,Garret,Siege	3.00
323 SMc,V:Venom,A:Siege,Garret, I:Erynys	2.50
324 SMc,A:Garret,R:Elektra, A:Stone, Morbius	2.50
325 SMc,E:Fall from Grace, A:Garret, Siege,Elektra,Morbius,V:Hand, D:Hellspawn,Double size	3.00
326 SMc,B:Tree of Knowledge, I:Killobyte,A:Capt.America	2.00
327 E:DGC(s),SMc,A:Capt.Amer.	2.00
328 GtW(s),V:Wirehead,A:Captain America,S.Sable,Wild Pack	1.75
329 B:DGC(s),SMc,A:Captain America, S.Sable,Iron Fist	1.75
330 SMc,A:Gambit	1.75
331 SMc,A:Captain America, VLHydra	1.75
332 A:Captain America,Gambit	1.75
333 TGb,GWt	1.75
334 TGb,GWt	1.75
335	1.75
336	1.50
337 V:Kingpin,A:Blackwulf	1.50
338 Wages of Sin,pt.1	1.50
339 Wages of Sin,pt.2	1.50
340 R:Kingpin	1.50
341 Kingpin	1.50
342 DGc,KP,V:Kingpin	1.50
343 Without Costume	1.50
344 Identity Crisis,pt.1	1.95
345 Identity Crisis,pt.2	1.95
346 V:Sir	1.95
347 V:mystery man	1.95
348 In NY City	1.95
349 Retreats to the Chaste	1.95
350 Double size	2.95

MARVEL

Daredevil #309
© Marvel Entertainment Group

351 . . . . 1.95
352 Return of Matt Murdock 1.95
353 KK,CNr,A:Mr. Hyde 1.95
354 KK,CNr,A:Spider-Man 1.50
355 KK,CNr,A:Pyro 1.50
356 KK,CNr, ... 1.50
357 KK,CNr, ... 1.50
358 KK,CNr,MRy,A:Mysterio . . . 1.50
359 KK,CNr,A:Absorbing Man . . . 1.50
360 KK,CNr,MRy,V:Onslaught . . . 1.50
361 KK,CNr,MRy,A:Black Widow . 1.50
362 KK,CNr,Romance 1.95
363 KK,GC,CaS,V:Insomnia 1.95
364 KK,CNr,MRy,V:Insomnia . . . 1.95
365 CNr,MRy,V:Mr. Fear,
   A:Molten Man 1.95
366 GC,V:Gladiator 1.95
367 GC,V:Gladiator, concl. 1.95
Minus 1 Spec., GC, flashback . . . 1.95
Ann.#1 GC 30.00
Ann.#2 reprints 8.00
Ann.#3 reprints 8.00
Ann.#4 (1976)GT,A:Black
   Panther,Namor 6.00
Ann.#5 (1989)MBa,JLe,JR2,KJ,
   WPo,AM,Atlantis Attacks,
   A:Spider-Man 5.00
Ann.#6 TS,Lifeform#2,A:Typhoid
   Mary 2.75
Ann.#7 JG,JBr,Von Strucker
   Gambit,pt.1,A:Nick Fury 2.50
Ann.#8 Sys.Bytes#2,A:Deathlok . . 2.75
Ann.#9 MPa,I:Devourer,w/card,tie-in
   to "Fall From Grace" 5.00
Ann.#10 I:Ghostmaker,A:Shang
   Chi, Elektra 3.25
G-Size #1 GK(c),reprints 12.00
TPB Born Again,rep.#227-#233 . 10.95
TPB Fall of the Kingpin,
   rep.#297-300 . . . . 15.95
TPB Gangwar,Reprints
   #169-#172,#180 . . . . 12.95
TPB Marked for Death,reps#159-
   161,163,164 . . . . 9.95
Daredevil/Punisher:Child's Play
   reprints#182-#184 . . . . 7.00

DAREDEVIL/BATMAN
1997
Spec. DGC,SMc, 48pg 6.00

DAREDEVIL/ DEADPOOL '97
Spec, BCh, JHo, Two annuals in
one, 48pg 5.00

DAREDEVIL/SHI SHI/DAREDEVIL
Marvel/Crusade 1996
1 (Daredevil/Shi) TSg,AW,
   x-over,pt.1 . . . . 2.95
1 (Shi/Daredevil)x-over, pt.2 . . . 2.95

DAREDEVIL: THE MAN WITHOUT FEAR
1 B:FM(s),JR2,AW,O:Daredevil,
   A:Stick,D:Daredevil's Father . . 7.00
2 JR2,AW,A:Stick,Stone,Elektra . 6.00
3 JR2,AW,A:Elektra,Kingpin . . . 5.00
4 JR2,AW,A:Kingpin,I:Mickey . . 5.00
5 JR2,AW,A:Mickey,Last Issue . 5.00
TPB rep.#1#5 . . . . 15.95

DARING MYSTERY COMICS
Timely Jan., 1940
1 ASh(c),JSm,O:Fiery Mask,
   A:Monako John Steele,Doc Doyle,
   Flash FosterBarney Mullen,
   Sea Rover, Bondage (c) . 16,000.00
2 ASh(c),JSm,O:Phantom Bullet
   A:Zephyr Jones & K4,Laughing
   Mask Mr.E,B:Trojak 5,500.00
3 ASh(c),JSm,A:Phantom
   Reporter,Marvex,Breeze
   Barton, B:Purple Mask . . 3,500.00
4 ASh(c),A:G-Man Ace,K4,Monako,
   Marvex,E:Purple Mask,
   B:Whirlwind Carter 2,200.00
5 JSm,B:Falcon,A:Fiery Mask,K4,
   Little Hercules,Bondage(c) 2,200.00
6 S&K,O:Marvel Boy,A:Fiery
   Mask, Flying Fame,Dynaman,
   Stuporman,E:Trojak 2,900.00
7 S&K,O:Blue Diamond,A:The Fin,
   Challenger,Captain Daring,
   Silver Scorpion,Thunderer . 2,500.00
8 S&K,O:Citizen V,A:Thunderer,
   Fin Silver Scorpion,Captain
   Daring Blue Diamond . . . 2,000.00
Becomes:

DARING COMICS
9 ASh(c),B:Human Torch,Toro,
   Sub Mariner 850.00
10 ASh(c),A:The Angel 750.00
11 ASh(c),A:The Destroyer . . 750.00
12 E:Human Torch,Toro,Sub-
   Mariner, Fall, 1945 . . . . . . 750.00
Becomes:

JEANIE COMICS
13 B:Jeanie,Queen of the
   Teens Mitzi,Willie 70.00
14 Baseball(c) 40.00
15 Schoolbus(c) 40.00
16 Swimsuit(c) 56.00
17 HK,Fancy dress party(c),
   Hey Look 37.00
18 HK,Jeanie'sDate(c),Hey Look 37.00

19 Ice-Boat(c),Hey Look 37.00
20 Jukebox(c) 30.00
21 . . . . 30.00
22 HK,Hey Look 37.00
23 . . . . 30.00
24 . . . . 30.00
25 . . . . 30.00
26 . . . . 30.00
27 E:Jeanie,Queen of Teens . . . 30.00
Becomes:

COWGIRL ROMANCES
28 Ph(c),Mona Freeman/MacDonald
   Carey,Copper Canyon 125.00

DARK ANGEL
See: HELL'S ANGEL

DARK CRYSTAL
April, 1983
1 movie adaption 1.00
2 movie adaption,May 1983 . . . . 1.00

DARK GUARD
1 A:All UK Heroes 2.95
2 A:All UK Heroes 1.75
3 V:Leader,MyS-Tech 1.75
4 V:MyS-Tech 1.75
5 . . . . 1.75
6 and 7 . . . . @1.75

DARKHAWK
March, 1991
1 MM,I&O:Darkhawk,
   A:Hobgoblin 4.00
2 MM,A:Spider-Man,V:Hobgoblin 2.50
3 MM,A:Spider-Man,V:Hobgoblin 2.50
4 MM,I:Savage Steel 2.50
5 MM,I:Portal 2.50
6 MM,A:Cap.Am,D.D.,Portal,
   V:U-Foes 2.50
7 MM,I:Lodestone 2.00
8 MM,V:Lodestone 2.00
9 MM,A:Punisher,V:Savage Steel 2.00
10 MM,A&N:Tombstone 2.00
11 MM,V:Tombstone 2.00
12 MM,V:Tombstone,R:Dark
   Hawks'Father 2.00
13 MM,V:Venom 3.00
14 MM,V:Venom,D:Dark
   Hawks Father 3.00
15 MM,Heart of the Hawk,concl . . 2.00
16 MM,V:Terrorists 2.00
17 MM,I:Peristrike Force 2.00
18 MM,V:Mindwolf 2.00
19 MM,R:Portal,A:Spider-Man,V:The
   Brotherhood of Evil Mutants . 2.00
20 MM,A:Spider-Man,Sleepwalker,
   V:Brotherhood of Evil Mutants . 2.00
21 MM,B:Return to Forever 1.75
22 MM,A:Ghost Rider 1.75
23 MM,I:Evilhawk 1.75
24 V:Evilhawk 1.50
25 MM,O:Darkhawk,V:Evilhawk,
   Holo-graphx(c) 2.50
26 A:New Warriors 1.50
27 A:New Warriors,V:Zarrko . . . 1.50
28 A:New Warriors,Zarrko 1.50
29 A:New Warriors 1.50
30 I:Purity 1.50
31 Infinity Crusade 1.50
32 R:Savage Steel 1.50
33 I:Cuda 1.50
34 V:Cuda 1.50

MARVEL

35 DFr(s),V:Venom 1.50
36 DFr(s),V:Scokers,A:Venom . . . 1.50
37 DFr(s),V:Venom 1.50
38 DFr(s),N:Darkhawk 1.50
39 DFr(s) 1.50
40 DFr(s) 1.75
41 DFr(s) 1.75
42 DFr(s), V:Portal,I:Shaper 1.75
43 DFr(s) 1.75
44 DFr(s) 1.75
45 DFr(s),A:Portal 1.75
46 DFr(s) 1.75
47 . . . . 1.50
48 R:Darkhawk,V:Mahari 1.50
49 V:Overhawk 1.50
50 V:Overhawk 2.50
Ann.#1 MM,Assault on ArmorCity . 3.00
Ann.#2 GC,AW,I:Dreamkiller,
   w/Trading card 3.00
Ann.#3 I:Damek 3.00

DARKHOLD
1 RCa,I:Redeemers,Polybagged
   w/poster,A:Gh.Rider,Blaze . . . 3.00
2 RCa,R:Modred 2.50
3 A:Modred,Scarlet Witch 2.00
4 V:Sabretooth,N'Garai 2.00
5 A:Punisher, Ghost Rider 2.00
6 RCa,V:Dr.Strange 2.00
7 A:Dr.Strange,V:Japanese Army 2.00
8 Betrayal #1 . . . . 2.00
9 Diabolique 2.00
10 V:Darkholders 2.00
11 Midnight Massacre#3,D:Modred,
   Vicki 2.50
12 V:Chthon 2.00
13 V:Missing Link 2.00
14 Vicki's Secret revealed 2.00
15 Siege of Darkness,pt.#4 . . . . . 2.00
16 Siege of Darkness,pt.#12 . . . . 2.00

DARK MAN
MOVIE ADAPTION
Sept., 1990
1 BH/MT/TD 2.00
2 BH/TD 1.50
3 BH/TD,final issue 1.50

DARKMAN
Sept., 1990
1 JS,R:Darkman 3.50
2 JS,V:Witchfinder 2.95
3 JS,Witchfinder 2.95
4 JS,V:Dr.West 2.95
5 JS,Durant 2.95
6 JS,V:Durant 2.95

DATE WITH MILLIE
Atlas Oct., 1956
[1st Series]
1 . . . . 110.00
2 . . . . 60.00
3 thru 7 . . . . @40.00
[2nd Series]
Oct., 1959
1 . . . . 50.00
2 thru 7 . . . . @30.00
Becomes:

LIFE WITH MILLIE
8 . . . . 30.00
9 . . . . 23.00
10 . . . . 23.00
11 thru 20 . . . . @19.00

Becomes:
MODELING WITH MILLIE
21 . . . . 30.00
22 thru 54 June, 1967 . . . . . @17.00

DATE WITH PATSY
Sept., 1957
1 A:Patsy Walker 35.00

DAYDREAMERS
Aug., 1997
1 (of 3) JMD,MEg,HSm 2.50
2 JMD,MEg,HSm, ... 2.50

Dazzler #22
© Marvel Entertainment Group

DAZZLER
March, 1981
1 AA,JR2,A:X-Men,Spm,
   O:Dazzler 2.50
2 WS,JR2,AA,X-Men,A:SpM 2.00
3 JR2,Dr.Doom 1.50
4 FS,Dr.Doom 1.50
5 FS,I:Blue Shield 1.50
6 FS,Hulk 1.50
7 FS,Hulk 1.50
8 FS,Quasar 1.50
9 FS,D:Klaw 1.50
10 FS,Galactus 1.50
11 FS,Galactus 1.50
12 FS,The Light That Failed 1.50
13 FS,V:Grapplers 1.50
14 FS,She Hulk 1.50
15 FS,BSz,Spider Women 1.50
16 FS,BSz,Enchantress 1.50
17 FS,Angel,V:Doc Octopus 1.50
18 FS,BSz,A:Fantastic Four,Angel,
   V:Absorbing Man 1.50
19 FS,Blue Bolt,V:Absorbing Man 1.50
20 FS,V:Jazz and Horn 1.50
21 FS,A:Avengers,F.F.,C:X-Men,
   (double size) 1.50
22 FS,V:Rogue,Mystique 2.00
23 FS,V:Rogue,A:Powerman,
   Iron Fist 2.00
24 FS,V:Rogue,A:Powerman,

Iron Fist 1.75
25 FS,'The Jagged Edge' 1.50
26 FS,Lois London 1.50
27 FS,Fugitive 1.50
28 FS,V:Rogue 2.00
29 FS,Roman Nekoboh 1.50
30 FS,Moves to California 1.50
31 FS,The Last Wave 1.50
32 FS,A:Inhumans 1.50
33 Chiller 1.50
34 FS,Disappearance 1.50
35 FS,V:Racine Ramjets 1.50
36 JBy(c),FS,V:Tatterdemalion . . 1.50
37 JBy(c),FS 1.50
38 PC,JG,X-Men 5.00
39 PC,JG,Caught in the grip of
   death 1.50
40 PC,JG,Secret Wars II 1.75
41 PC,JG,A:Beast 1.50
42 PC,JG,A:Beast,last issue 2.00

DEADLIEST HEROES
OF KUNG FU
(magazine)
Summer, 1975
1 . . . . 3.50

DEADLY FOES
OF SPIDER-MAN
May, 1991
1 AM,KGa,V:Sinister Syndicate . . 4.00
2 AM,Boomerang on Trial 3.00
3 AM,Deadly Foes Split 3.00
4 AM,Conclusion 3.00
TPB rep. #1–#4 . . . . 12.95

DEADLY HANDS
OF KUNG FU
April, 1974
1 NA(c),JSa,JSon,O:Sons of
   the Tiger, B:Shang-Chi,
   Bruce Lee Pin-up 5.00
2 NA(c),JSa 2.50
3 NA(c),JSon,A:Sons of the Tiger 2.50
4 NA(Bruce Lee)(c),JSon,Bruce
   Lee biography 4.00
5 . . . . 3.00
6 GP,JSon,A:Sons of the Tiger . 3.00
7 GP,JSon,A:Sons of the Tiger . 3.00
8 GP,JSon,A:Sons of the Tiger . 3.00
9 GP,JSon,A:Sons of the Tiger . 3.00
10 GP,JSon,A:Sons of the Tiger . 3.00
11 NA(c),GP,JSon,A:Sons
   of the Tiger 3.00
12 NA(c),GP,JSon,A:Sons
   of the Tiger 3.00
13 GP,JSon,A:Sons of the Tiger . 3.00
14 NA(c),GP,JSon,A:Sons
   of the Tiger 3.00
15 JSa,Annual #1 . . . . 5.00
16 JSon,A:Sons of the Tiger 2.00
17 NA9c),JSon,KG,A:Sons
   of the Tiger 2.00
18 JSon,A:Sons of the Tiger 2.00
19 JSon,I:White Tiger 2.00
20 GP,O:White Tiger 3.00
21 . . . . 2.00
22 KG 2.00
23 GK 2.00
24 KG 2.00
25 . . . . 2.00
26 . . . . 2.00
27 . . . . 2.00

All comics prices listed are for *Near Mint* condition.

28 JSon,O:Jack of Hearts	4.00
29	2.00
30	2.00
31 JSon	2.00
32 MR,JSon	2.00
33 MR,Feb., 1977	2.00
Spec. Album Ed.,NA, Sum.1974	3.00

DEAD OF NIGHT
Dec., 1973

1 JSt,Horror reprints,A Haunted House is not a Home	5.00
2 BEv(c),House that Fear Built	3.00
3 They Lurk Below	3.00
4 Warewolf Beware	3.00
5 Deep Down	3.00
6 Jack the Ripper	3.00
7 SD,The Thirteenth Floor	3.00
8 Midnight Brings Dark Madness	3.00
9 Deathride	3.00
10 SD,I Dream of Doom	3.00
11 GK/BWr(c),I:Scarecrow, Fires of Rebirth,Fires of Death August, 1975	3.00

Deadpool #3
© Marvel Entertainment Group

DEADPOOL

1 B:FaN(s),JMd,MFm(i), V:Slayback,Nyko	4.00
2 JMd,MFm(i),V:Black Tom Cassidy,Juggernaut	3.00
3 JMd,MFm(i),I:Comcast, Makeshift,Rive,A:Slayback	2.50
4 E:FaN(s),JMd,MFm(i), A:Slayback,Kane	2.50

[2nd Limited Series]

1 A:Banshee,Syrin,Juggernaut Black Tom	2.00
2 A:Banshee,Syrin,V:Juggernaut	2.00
3 A:Syrin,Juggernaut	2.00
4 Final issue	2.00

DEADPOOL
1996

1 NMa,V:Sasquatch,48pg,	2.95
2 NMa,A:Copycat	1.95
3 NMa,A:Siryn	1.95
4 NMa,Will Hulk cure him?	1.95

5 NMa,A:Siryn,T-Ray	1.95
6 NMa,I:	1.95
7 AaL,A:Typhoid Mary	1.95
8 NMa, cont. from Daredevil/ Deadpool '97,A:Gerry	1.95
Minus 1 Spec., ALo, flashback, O:Deadpool	1.95
TPB MWa,IaC,Sins of the Past, rep. limited series	
TPB Circle Chase,FaN,JMd,MFm,	12.95

DEATH³

1 I:Death Metal,Death Wreck	2.95
2 V:Ghost Rider	1.75
3 A:Hulk,Cable,Storm,Thing	1.75
4 Last issue	1.75

DEATHLOK
July, 1990
[Limited Series]

1 JC,SW,I:Michael Colins (2nd Deathlok)	3.00
2 JC,SW,V:Wajler	2.00
3 DCw,SW,V:Cyberants	2.00
4 DCw,SW,V:Sunfire,final issue	2.00

[Regular Series]

1 DCw,MM,V:Warwolf	2.50
2 DCw,MM,A:Dr.Doom,Machine Man, Forge	2.50
3 DCw,MM,V:Dr.Doom, A:Mr.Fantastic	2.50
4 DCw,MM,A:X-Men,F.F.,Vision, O:Mechadoom	2.50
5 DCw,MM,V:Mechadoom, A:X-Men,Fantastic Four	2.50
6 DCw,MM,A:Punisher, V:Silvermane	2.50
7 DCw,MM,A:Punisher, V:Silvermane	2.50
8 A:Main Frame,Ben Jacobs	2.00
9 DCw,MM,A:Ghost Rider, V:Nightmare	2.50
10 DCw,MM,A:GhR,V:Nightmare	2.50
11 DCw,MM,V:Moses Magnum	2.00
12 DCw,MM,Biohazard Agenda	2.00
13 DCw,MM,Biohazard Agenda	2.00
14 DCw,MM,Biohazard Agenda	2.00
15 DCw,MM,Biohazard Agenda	2.00
16 DCw,MM,Inf.War,V:Evilok	2.00
17 WMc,MM,B:Cyberwar	2.00
18 WMc,A:Silver Sable	2.00
18a Newstand Ed.	1.75
19 SMc,Cyberwar#3	2.00
20 SMc,Cyberwar#4	2.00
21 E:Cyberwar,A:Cold Blood Nick Fury	2.00
22 V:MosesMagnum,A:Bl.Panther	2.00
23 A:Bl.Panther,V:Phreak,Stroke	2.00
24 V:MosesMagnum,A:Bl.Panther	2.00
25 WMc,V:MosesMagnum,A:Black Panther,holo-grafx(c)	2.50
26 V:Hobgoblin	2.00
27 R:Siege	2.00
28 Infinty Crusade	2.00
29 Inner Fears	2.00
30 KHd,V:Hydra	2.00
31 GWt(s),KoK,B:Cyberstrike, R:1st Deathlok	2.00
32 GWt(s),KoK,A:Siege	2.00
33 GWt(s),KoK,V:Justice Peace	2.00
34 GWt(s),KoK,E:Cyberstrike,V:Justice Peace,final issue	2.00
Ann.#1 JG,I:Timestream	2.75
Ann.#2 I:Tracer,w/card	2.95

DEATHLOK SPECIAL

1 Rep.MiniSeries	2.50
2 Rep.MiniSeries	2.50
3 Rep.MiniSeries	2.50
4 Rep.MiniSeries, final issue	2.50

DEATH METAL

1 JRe,I:Argon,C:Alpha Flight	1.95
2 JRe,V:Alpha Flight	1.95
3 JRe,I:Soulslug	1.95
4 Re,Last Issue	1.95

DEATH METAL VS. GENETIX

1 PaD,w/card	2.95
2 PaD,w/card	2.95

DEATH'S HEAD
Dec., 1988

1 V:Backbreaker	5.00
2 A:Dragons Claws	4.00
3	4.00
4 V:Plague Dog	3.00
5 V:Big Shot	3.00
6 V:Big Shot	3.00
7	3.00
8	3.00
9 A:Fantastic Four	3.50
10 A:Iron Man	3.50
TPB Reprints#1-#10	12.95

DEATH'S HEAD
[Limited Series]

1 A:'Old' Death's Head	1.95

DEATH'S HEAD II
March, 1992
[Limited Series]

1 LSh,I:2nd Death's Head, D:1st Death's Head	5.00
1a 2nd printing,Silver	3.00
2 LSh,A:Fantastic Four	3.00
2a 2nd printing,Silver	3.50
3 LSh,I:Tuck	3.50
4 LSh,A:Wolverine,Spider-Man, Punisher	3.50

[Regular Series]

1 LSh,A:X-Men,I:Wraithchilde	3.00
2 LSh,A:X-Men	2.25
3 LSh,A:X-Men,V:Raptors	2.25
4 LSh,A:X-Men,V:Wraithchilde	2.25
5 V:UnDeath's Head II, A:Warheads	2.25
6 R:Tuck,V:Major Oak	2.25
7 V:Major Oak	2.25
8 V:Wizard Methinx	2.25
9 BHi,V:Cybernetic Centaurs	2.25
10 DBw,A:Necker	2.25
11 SCy,R:Charnel	2.25
12 DAn(s),SvL,V:Charnel	2.25
13 SvL,A:Liger	2.25
14 SvL,Brain Dead Cold,Blue Foil(c)	3.25
15 SvL,V:Duplicates	2.25
16 SvL,DAn	2.25
17 SvL,DAn	1.95
18 SvL,DAn	1.95
Spec. Gold Ed. LSh(a&s)	3.95

DEATH'S HEAD II/DIE CUT

1 I:Die Cut	3.25
2 O:Die Cut	1.75

DEATH'S HEAD II/ KILLPOWER: BATTLETIDE
[1st Limited Series]
1 GSr,A:Wolverine 2.50
2 thru 4 GSr,A:Wolverine . . . @2.00
[2nd Limited Series]
1 A:Hulk 3.25
2 V:Hulk 1.75
3 A:Hulk 1.75
4 last issue 1.75

DEATH-WRECK
1 A:Death's Head II 1.95
2 V:Gangsters 1.95
3 A:Dr.Necker 1.95
4 last issue 1.95

DEEP, THE
Nov., 1977
1 CI,Movie Adaption 2.00

Defenders #11
© *Marvel Entertainment Group*

DEFENDERS
August, 1972
1 SB,I&D:Necrodames 65.00
2 SB,V:Calizuma 30.00
3 GK(c),SB,JM,V:UndyingOne . 25.00
4 SB,FMc,Bl.Knight,V:Valkyrie . 25.00
5 SB,FMc,D:Omegatron 25.00
6 SB,FMc,V:Cyrus Black 20.00
7 SB,FBe,A:Hawkeye 20.00
8 SB,FBe,Avengers,SilverSurfer 20.00
9 SB,FMc,Avengers 20.00
10 SB,FBe,Thor vs. Hulk 25.00
11 SB,FBe,A:Avengers 12.00
12 SB,JA,Xemnu 10.00
13 GK(c),SB,KJ,J:Night Hawk . . 10.00
14 SB,DGr,O:Hyperion 10.00
15 SB,KJ,A:Professor X,V:Magneto,
Savage Land Mutates 18.00
16 GK(c),SB,Professor X,V:Magneto,
Savage Land Mutates 18.00
17 SB,DGr,Power Man 8.00
18 GK(c),SB,DGr,A:Power Man . 8.00
19 GK(c),SB,KJ,A:Power Man . . 8.00
20 K&R(c),SB,A:Thing 8.00
21 GK(c),SB,O:Valkyrie 7.00

22 GK(c),SB,V:Sons o/t Serpent . 7.00
23 GK(c),SB,A:Yellow Jacket 7.00
24 GK(c),SB,BMc,A:Daredevil . . . 7.00
25 GK(c),SB,JA,A:Daredevil 7.00
26 K&R(c),SB,A:Guardians 12.00
27 K&R(c),SB,A:Guardians
C:Starhawk 12.00
28 K&R(c),SB,A:Guardians
I:Starhawk 11.00
29 K&R(c),SB,A:Guardians . . . 11.00
30 JA(i),A:Wong 5.00
31 GK(c),SB,JM,Nighthawk 5.00
32 GK(c),SB,JM,O:Nighthawk . . . 5.00
33 GK(c),SB,JM,V:Headmen . . . 5.00
34 SB,JM,V:Nebulon 5.00
35 GK(c),SB,KJ,I:Red Guardian . 5.00
36 GK(c),SB,KJ,A:Red Guardian . 5.00
37 GK(c),SB,KJ,J:Luke Cage . . . 5.00
38 SB,KJ,V:Nebulon 5.00
39 SB,KJ,V:Felicia 5.00
40 SB,KJ,V:Assassin 5.00
41 KG,KJ,Nighthawk 5.00
42 KG,KJ,V:Rhino 5.00
43 KG,KJ,Cobalt Man,Egghead . 5.00
44 KG,KJ,J:Hellcat,V:Red Rajah . 5.00
45 KG,KJ,Valkyrie V:Hulk 5.00
46 KG,KJ,L:DrStrange,LukeCage . 5.00
47 KG,KJ,Moon Knight 5.00
48 KG,A:Wonder Man 5.00
49 KG,O:Scorpio 5.00
50 KG,Zodiac,D:Scorpio 5.00
51 KG,Moon Knight 5.00
52 KG,Hulk,V:Sub Mariner 5.00
53 KG,DC,MG,TA,C&I:Lunatik . . 4.50
54 MG,Nigh Fury 4.50
55 CI,O:Red Guardian 4.50
56 CI,KJ,Hellcat,V:Lunatik 4.50
57 DC,Ms.Marvel 4.50
58 Return of Dr.Strange 4.50
59 I:Belathauzer 4.50
60 V:Vera Gemini 4.50
61 Spider-Man,A:Lunatik 4.00
62 Hercules,C:Polaris 4.00
63 Mutli Heroes 4.00
64 Mutli Heroes 4.00
65 Red Guardian 4.00
66 JB,Valkyrie I 4.00
67 Valkyrie II 4.00
68 HT,When Falls the Mountain . . 4.00
69 HT,A:The Anything Man 4.00
70 HT,A:Lunatik 4.00
71 HT,O:Lunatik 4.00
72 HT,V:Lunatik 4.00
73 HT,Foolkiller,V:WizardKing . . 6.00
74 HT,Foolkiller,L:Nighthawk . . . 6.00
75 HT,Foolkiller 5.00
76 HT,O:Omega 3.00
77 HT,Moon Dragon 3.00
78 HT,Yellow Jacket 3.00
79 HT,Tunnel World 3.00
80 HT,DGr,Nighthawk 3.00
81 HT,Tunnel World 3.00
82 DP,JSt,Tunnel World 3.00
83 DP,JSt,Tunnel World 3.00
84 DP,JSt,Black Panther 3.00
85 DP,JSt,Black Panther 3.00
86 DP,JSt,Black Panther 3.00
87 DP,JSt,V:Mutant Force 3.00
88 DP,JSt,Matt Mardock 3.00
89 DP,JSt,D:Hellcat's
Mother, O:Mad-Dog 3.00
90 DP,JSt,Daredevil 3.00
91 DP,JSt,Daredevil 3.00
92 DP,JSt,A:Eternity,
Son of Satan 4.00

93 DP,JSt,Son of Satan 4.00
94 DP,JSt,I:Gargoyle 3.00
95 DP,JSt,V:Dracula,O:Gargoyle . 3.00
96 DP,JSt,Ghost Rider 4.00
97 DP,JSt,False Messiah 3.00
98 DP,JSt,A:Man Thing 3.00
99 DP,JSt,Conflict 3.00
100 DP,JSt,DoubleSize,V:Satan . . 4.00
101 DP,JSt,Silver Surfer 3.00
102 DP,JSt,Nighthawk 3.00
103 DP,JSt,I:Null 3.00
104 DP,JSt,Devilslayer,J:Beast . . 3.00
105 DP,JSt,V:Satan 3.00
106 DP,Daredevil,D:Nighthawk . . 3.00
107 DP,JSt,Enchantress,A:D.D. . . 3.00
108 DP,A:Enchantress 3.00
109 DP,A:Spider-Man 3.50
110 DP,A:Devilslayer 3.00
111 DP,A:Hellcat 3.00
112 DP,A:SquadronSupreme . . . 3.00
113 DP,A:SquadronSupreme 3.00
114 DP,A:SquadronSupreme 3.00

Defenders #129
© *Marvel Entertainment Group*

115 DP,A:Submariner 3.00
116 DP,Gargoyle 3.00
117 DP,Valkyrie 3.00
118 DP,V:Miracleman 3.00
119 DP,V:Miracleman 3.00
120 DP,V:Miracleman 3.00
121 DP,V:Miracleman 3.00
122 DP,A:Iceman 3.00
123 DP,I:Cloud,V:Secret Empire . 3.00
124 DP,V:Elf 3.00
125 DP,New Line-up:Gargoyle,Moon
dragon,Valkyrie,Iceman,Beast,
Angel,W:Son of Satan & Hellcat
I:Mad Dog 4.00
126 DP,A:Nick Fury 3.00
127 DP,V:Professor Power 3.00
128 DP,V:Professor Power 3.00
129 DP,V:Professor Power,New
Mutants X-over 3.00
130 DP,V:Professor Power 3.00
131 DP,V:Walrus,A:Frogman 3.00
132 DP,V:Spore Monster 3.00
133 DP,V:Spore Monster 3.00
134 DP,I:Manslaughter 3.00
135 DP,V:Blowtorch Brand 3.00
136 DP,V:Gargoyle 3.00

MARVEL

137 DP,V:Gargoyle 3.00
138 DP,O:Moondragon 3.00
139 DP,A:Red Wolf,V:Trolls 3.00
140 DP,V:Asgardian Trolls 3.00
141 DP,All Flesh is Grass 3.00
142 DP,V:M.O.N.S.T.E.R. 3.00
143 DP,I:Andromeda,Runner 3.00
144 DP,V:Moondragon 3.00
145 DP,V:Moondragon 3.00
146 DP,Cloud 3.00
147 DP,A:Andromeda,I:Interloper . 3.00
148 DP,A:Nick Fury 3.00
149 DP,V:Manslaughter,O:Cloud . 3.00
150 DP,O:Cloud,double-size 3.50
151 DP,A:Interloper 3.00
152 DP,Secret Wars II,D:Moon-
  dragon,Valkyrie,Gargoyle 4.00
G-Size#1 GK(c),JSn,AM,O:Hulk . 12.00
G-Size#2 GK,KJ,Son of Satan . . . 8.00
G-Size#3 JSn,DA,JM,DN,A:D.D.. . 6.00
G-Size#4 GK(c),DH,A:YellowJack 6.00
G-Size#5 K&R(c),DH,A:Guardians 6.00
Ann.#1 SB,KJ 6.00

DEFENDERS OF
DYNATRON CITY
1 FC,I:Defenders of Dynatron City
  (from video game & TV ser.) . . 1.25
2 FC,O:Defender of D.City 1.25
3 FC,A:Dr Mayhem 1.25
4 FC 1.25
5 FC,V:Intelligent Fleas 1.25
6 FC,V:Dr.Mayhem 1.25

DEFENDERS OF
THE EARTH
Jan., 1987—Sept., 1984
1 AS,Flash Gordon & Mandrake . 2.00
2 AS,Flash Gordon & Mandrake . 2.00
3 AS,O:Phantom 2.00
4 AS,O:Mandrake 2.00

DELLA VISION
Atlas April, 1955
1 The Television Queen 80.00
2 . . . . 55.00
3 . . . . 55.00
Becomes:
PATTY POWERS
4 . . . . 35.00
5 . . . . 22.00
6 . . . . 22.00
7 Oct., 1956 . . . . 22.00

DENNIS THE MENACE
Nov., 1981
1 . . . . 1.25
2 thru 12 . . . . @1.00
13 November, 1982 . . . . 1.00

DESTROYER, THE
Nov., 1989
1 Black & White Mag. 3.50
2 thru 9 . . . . @2.25
10 June 1990 . . . . 2.25
TPB rep. B/w mag(color) 9.95

THE DESTROYER:
TERROR
Dec., 1991
1 V:Nuihc 1.95

Destroyer #1
© Marvel Entertainment Group

2 V:Nuihc 1.95
3 GM,V:Nuihc 1.95
4 DC,'The Last Dinosaur' 1.95

DEVIL DINOSAUR
April, 1978—Dec., 1978
1 JK,I:Devil Dinosaur,Moon Boy . 4.00
2 JK,War With the Spider God . . 3.00
3 JK,Giant 3.00
4 JK,Objects From the Sky 3.00
5 JK,The Kingdom of the Ants . . 3.00
6 JK.The Fall 3.00
7 JK,Prisoner of the Demon Tree 3.00
8 JK,V:Dino Riders 3.00
9 JK,Lizards That Stand 3.00

DEVIL DINOSAUR
SPRING FLING
Spec. F:Devil Dinosaur,
  Moon-Boy, 48pg 2.99

DEVIL-DOG DUGAN
Atlas July, 1956
1 War Stories 75.00
2 . . . . 50.00
3 . . . . 35.00
Becomes:
TALE OF THE MARINES
4 BP,War Stories 40.00
Becomes:
MARINES AT WAR
5 War Stories 30.00
6 . . . . 30.00
7 The Big Push,August, 1957 . . 30.00

DEXTER THE DEMON
See: MELVIN THE MONSTER

DIE-CUT
1 A:Beast 2.50
2 V:X-Beast 1.75
3 A:Beast,Prof.X 1.75

4 V:Red Skull 1.75

DIE-CUT VS. G-FORCE
1 SFr(s),LSh(c),I:G-Force 2.75
2 SFr(s),LSh(c),Last issue 2.75

DIGITEK
1 DPw,I:Digitek,C:Deathlok 2.25
2 DPw,A:Deathlok,V:Bacillicons . 2.25
3 DPw,A:Deathlok,V:Bacillicons . 2.25
4 DPw,V:Bacillicons 2.25

DINO RIDERS
Feb., 1989
1 Based on Toys 1.00
2 . . . . 1.00
3 May, 1989 . . . . 1.00

DINOSAURS: A
CELEBRATION
Epic
Horns and Heavy Armor 4.95
Bone-Heads and Duck-Bills 4.95
Terrible Claws and Tyrants 4.95
Egg Stealers and Earth Shakers . 4.95
TPB 192pg 12.95

DISNEY AFTERNOON
1 DarkwingDuck vs.FearsomeFive 1.50
2 . . . . 1.50
3 . . . . 1.50
4 DarkwingDuck:Gum w/t Wind . . 1.50
5 F:Baloo, Mrs. Cunningham . . . 1.50
6 . . . . 1.50
7 F:Darkwing Duck 1.50
8 . . . . 1.50
9 DarkwingDuck:Borsht to Death 1.50
10 F:Scrooge & Mrs. Beakley . . 1.50

DISNEY COMIC HITS
1 . . . . 1.50
2 F:Lion King 1.50
3 F:Pocahontas 1.50
4 F:Toy Story 1.50
5 Holiday 1.50
6 Aladdin 1.50
7 . . . . 1.50
8 Lion King story 1.50
9 thru 13 . . . . @1.50
14 F:Toy Story characters 1.50
15 101 Dalmations 1.50
16 101 Dalmatians 1.50
17 final issue 1.50

DISNEY PRESENTS
1 F:Aladdin 1.50
2 F:Timon & Pummba 1.50
3 . . . . 1.50

DOC SAMSON
1 From The Incredible Hulk 1.95
2 A:She-Hulk 1.95
3 & 4 . . . . @1.95

DOC SAVAGE
Oct., 1972
1 JM,Pulp Adapts,Death Eighty
  Stories High 8.50
2 JSo(c),The Feathered Serpent
  Strikes 6.00
3 JSo(c),Silver Death's Head . . . 6.00
4 JSo(c),The Hell Diver 5.00

MARVEL

5 GK(c),Night of the Monsters . .	5.00
6 JSo(c),Where Giants Walk	5.00
7 JSo(c),Brand of the Werewolfs .	5.00
8 In the Lair of the Werewolf	
Jan., 1974	5.00
G-Size#1 thru #2 Reprints	4.50

DOC SAVAGE
August, 1975
(black & white magazine)

1 JB,Ph(c),Ron Ely	5.75
2 JB	3.25
3 JB	3.25
4	3.25
5 thru 7	@3.25
8 Spring 1977	3.25

DR. STRANGE
[1st Series]
Prev: **Strange Tales**
June, 1968

169 DA,O:Dr.Strange	125.00
170 DA,A:Ancient One	50.00
171 TP,DA,V:Dormammu	40.00
172 GC,TP,V:Dormammu	40.00
173 GC,TP,V:Dormammu	40.00
174 GC,TP,I:Satannish	40.00
175 GC,TP,I:Asmodeus	40.00
176 GC,TP,V:Asmodeus	40.00
177 GC,TP,D:Asmodeus,	
N:Dr.Strange	40.00
178 GC,TP,A:Black Knight	40.00
179 BWS(c),rep.Amazing Spider-	
Man Ann.#2	40.00
180 GC,TP,V:Nightmare	40.00
181 FB(c),GC,TP,I:Demons of	
Despair	40.00
182 GC,TP,V:Juggernaut	45.00
183 BEv(c),GC,TP,	
I:Undying Ones	45.00

[2nd Regular Series]

1 FB,DG,I:Silver Dagger	28.00
2 FB,DG,I:Soul Eater	15.00
3 FB,A:Dormammu	7.00
4 FB,DG,V:Death	6.00
5 FB,DG,A:Silver Dagger	6.00
6 FB(c),GC,KJ,A:Umar,I:Gaea . .	5.00
7 GC,JR,A:Dormammu	5.00
8 GK(c),GC,TP,O:Clea	5.00
9 GK(c),GC,A:Dormammu,O:Clea	5.00
10 B:MWn(s),GK(c),GC,A:Eternity	5.00
11 JR(c),GC,TP,A:Eternity	4.50
12 GC,TP,A:Eternity	4.50
13 GC,TP,A:Eternity	4.50
14 GC,TP,A:Dracula	4.50
15 GC,TP,A:Devil	4.50
16 GC,TP,A:Devil	4.50
17 GC,TP,A:Styggro	4.50
18 GC,A:Styggro	4.50
19 GC,AA,I:Xander	4.50
20 A:Xander	4.50
21 DA,O:Dr.Strange	4.00
22 I:Apalla	4.00
23 E:MWn(s),JSn,A:Wormworld . .	4.00
24 JSn,A:Apalla,I:Visamajoris . .	4.00
25 AM,V:Dr.Strange Yet	4.00
26 JSn,A:The Ancient One	4.00
27 TS,A:Stygyro,Sphinx	4.00
28 TS,A:Ghost Rider,	
V:In-Betweener	5.00
29 TS,A:Nighthawk	4.00
30 I:Dweller	3.50
31 TS,A:Sub Mariner	3.50
32 A:Sub Mariner	3.50

Doctor Strange (2nd Series) #24
© Marvel Entertainment Group

33 TS,A:The Dreamweaver	3.50
34 TS,A:Nightmare,D:CyrusBlack .	3.50
35 TS,V:Dweller,I:Ludi	3.50
36 Thunder of the Soul	3.50
37 Fear,the Final Victor	3.50
38 GC,DG,A:Baron Mordo	3.50
39 GC,DG,A:Baron Mordo	3.50
40 GC,A:Asrael	3.50
41 GC,A:Man Thing	3.00
42 GC,A:Black Mirror	3.00
43 V:Shadow Queen	3.00
44 GC,A:Princess Shialmar	3.00
45 GC,A:Demon in the Dark	3.00
46 FM,A:Sibylis	3.00
47 MR,TA,I:Ikonn	3.00
48 MR,TA,Brother Voodoo	3.00
49 MR,TA,A:Baron Mordo	3.00
50 MR,TA,A:Baron Mordo	3.00
51 MR,TA,A:Sgt. Fury,	
V:Baron Mordo	3.00
52 MR,TA,A:Nightmare	2.50
53 MR,TA,A:Nightmare,Fantastic	
Four,V:Rama-Tut	2.50
54 PS,V:Tiboro	2.50
55 MGa,TA,V:Madness	2.50
56 PS,TA,O:Dr.Strange	4.00
57 KN,TA,A:Dr.Doom	2.50
58 DGr,TA,V:Dracula	2.50
59 DGr,TA,V:Dracula	2.50
60 DGr,TA,Scarlet Witch	2.50
61 DGr,TA,V:Dracula	2.50
62 SL,V:Dracula	2.50
63 CP,V:Topaz	2.50
64 TSa,'Art Rage'	2.50
65 PS,Charlatan	2.50
66 PS,'The Cosen One'	2.50
67 SL,A:Jessica Drew,Shroud . .	2.50
68 PS,A:Black Knight	2.25
69 PS,A:Black Knight	2.25
70 BBI,V:Umar	2.25
71 DGr,O:Dormammu	2.25
72 PS,V:Umar	2.25
73 PS,V:Umar	2.25
74 MBg,Secret Wars II	2.25
75 A:Fantastic Four	2.25
76 A:Fantastic Four	2.25
77 A:Topaz	2.25
78 A:Cloak,I:Ecstacy	3.00

79 A:Morganna	2.00
80 A:Morganna,C:Rintah	2.00
81 V:Urthona,I:Rintah	2.00
Ann.#1 CR,'Doomworld'	4.50
G-Size#1 K&R(c),reps Strange	
Tales#164-#168	6.00

[3rd Regular Series]

1 V:Dorammu	4.00
2 V:Dorammu	3.00
3 I:Dragon Force	3.00
4 EL(c),A:Dragon Force	3.00
5 JG,V:Baron Mordo	3.50
6 JG,I:Mephista	3.00
7 JG,V:Agamotto,Mephisto	3.00
8 JG,V:Mephisto & Satanish . . .	3.00
9 JG,O:Dr.Strange	3.00
10 JG,V:Morbius	3.50
11 JG,A of V,V:Hobgoblin,	
C:Morbius	4.00
12 JG,A of V,V:Enchantress . . .	2.75
13 JG,A of V,V:Arkon	2.75
14 JG,B:Vampiric Verses,	
A:Morbius	3.50
15 JG,A:Morbius,Amy Grant(C) .	5.00
16 JG,A:Morbius,Brother Voodoo .	3.50
17 JV,TD,A:Morbius,Br.Voodoo . .	3.50
18 JG,E:Vampiric Verses,A:Morbius,	
Brother Voodoo,R:Varnae	3.50
19 GC,A:Azrael	2.50
20 JG,TD,A:Morbius,V:Zom	3.50
21 JG,TD,B:Dark Wars,	
R:Dormammu	2.50
22 JG,TD,LW,V:Dormammu	2.50
23 JG,LW,V:Dormammu	2.50
24 JG,E:Dark Wars,V:Dormammu	2.50
25 RLm,A:Red Wolf, Black Crow .	2.50
26 GI,V:Werewolf By Night	2.50
27 GI,V:Werewolf By Night	2.50
28 X-over Ghost Rider #12,	
V:Zodiac	3.00
29 A:Baron Blood	2.50
30 Topaz' Fate	2.50
31 TD,Inf.Gauntlet,A:Silver Surfer	3.00
32 Inf.Gauntlet,A:Warlock,Silver	
Surfer,V:Silver Dagger	2.50
33 Inf.Gauntlet,V:Thanos,	
Zota,A:Pip	2.50
34 Inf.Gauntlet,V:Dr.Doom,	
A:Pip,Scarlet Witch	2.50
35 Inf.Gauntlet,A:Thor,Pip,	
Scarlet Witch	2.50
36 Inf.Gauntlet,A:Warlock(leads	
into Warlock&Inf.Watch#1) . . .	3.00
37 GI,V:Frankensurfer	2.00
38 GI,Great Fear #1	2.00
39 GI,Great Fear #2	2.00
40 GI,Great Fear #3,A:Daredevil .	3.00
41 GI,A:Wolverine	2.25
42 GI,Infinity War,V:Galactus,A:	
Silver Surfer	2.25
43 GI,Infinity War,Galactus Vs.	
Agamotto,A:Silver Surfer	2.00
44 GI,Infinity War,V:Juggernaut . .	2.00
45 GI,Inf.War,O:Doctor Strange . .	2.00
46 GI,Inf.War,R:old costume . . .	2.00
47 GI,Inf.War,V:doppleganger . . .	2.00
48 GI,V:The Vishanti	2.00
49 GI,R:Dormammu	2.00
50 GI:Hulk,Ghost Rider,Silver	
Surfer,V:Dormammu(leads into	
Secret Defenders)holo-grafx(c)	3.50
51 GI,V:Religious Cult	2.00
52 GI,A:Morbius	2.00
53 GI,Closes Mansion,L:Wong . .	2.00
54 GI,Infinity Crusade	2.00

Doctor Strange (3rd Series) #79
© Marvel Entertainment Group

55 GI,Inf.Crusade 2.00
56 GI,Inf.Crusade 2.00
57 A:Kyllian,Urthona 2.00
58 V:Urthona 2.00
59 GI,V:Iskelior 2.00
60 B:DQ(s),Siege of
   Darkness,pt.#7 . . . . 4.00
61 Siege of Darkness,pt.#15 . . . 3.25
62 V:Dr.Doom 2.25
63 JJ(c),V:Morbius 2.00
64 MvR,V:Namor 2.00
65 MvR,V:Namor,Vengeance 2.25
66 A:Wong 2.25
67 R:Clea 2.25
68 MvR 1.95
69 MvR 1.95
70 A:Hulk 1.95
71 V:Hulk 1.95
72 Metallic(c),Last Rites,pt.1 . . . . 1.95
73 Last Rites,pt.2 . . . . 1.95
74 SY,DQ,Last Rites,pt.3 . . . . . . 1.95
75 Prismatic cover 3.50
76 I:New Costume 1.95
77 Mob Clean-up 1.95
78 R:Chton 1.95
79 Doc's new Asylum 1.95
80 Missing for four months? 1.95
81 A:Nick Fury 1.95
82 A:Hellstorm 1.95
83 V:Tempo Mob,Dormammu 1.95
84 The Homecoming,pt.1 . . . . . . 1.95
85 The Homecoming,pt.2 . . . . . . 1.95
86 The Homecoming,pt.3 . . . . . . 1.95
87 The Homecoming,pt.4 . . . . . . 1.95
88 The Fall of the Tempo,pt.1 . . . 1.95
89 The Fall of the Tempo,pt.2 . . . 1.95
Ann #2 Return of Defenders,Pt4 . 5.00
Ann #3 GI,I:Killiam,w/card 3.25
Ann.#4 V:Salome 2.95
GNv Triumph and Torment MBg,
   F:Dr. Strange & Dr.Doom 9.95
   HC 14.95
Ash Can .75

DR. STRANGE CLASSICS
March, 1984
1 SD,Reprints 1.75

2 . . . . 1.75
3 . . . . 1.75
4 June, 1984 . . . . 1.75

DR. STRANGE
VS. DRACULA
1 rep. MWn(s),GC 2.00

DR. STRANGE/GHOST
RIDER SPECIAL
1 Newsstand vers. of Dr.Str.#28 . 6.00

DOCTOR WHO
1984–86
1 BBC TV Series,UK reprints,
   Return of the Daleks 4.50
2 Star Beast 3.00
3 Transformation 3.00
4 A:K-9,Daleks 3.00
5 V:Time Witch,Colin Baker
   interview 3.00
6 B:Ancient Claw saga 3.00
7 . . . . 3.00
8 The Collector 3.00
9 The Life Bringer 3.00
10 This is your Life 3.00
11 The Deal 3.00
12 End of the Line 3.00
13 V:The Cybermen 3.00
14 Clash of the Neutron Knight . 3.00
15 B:Peter Davison-Dr. Who 3.00
16 Into the Realm of Satan, ... 3.00
17 Peter Davison Interview 3.00
18 A:Four Dr.Who's 3.00
19 A:The Sontarans 3.00
20 The Stockbridge Horror 3.00
21 The Stockbridge Horror 3.00
22 The Stockbridge Horror 3.00
23 The Unearthly Child 3.00

DR. ZERO
Epic April, 1988
1 BSz,DCw,I:Dr.Zero 2.00
2 BSz,DCw 1.50
3 BSz,DCw 1.50
4 thru 6 . . . . @1.50
7 DSp 1.50
8 End series, August, 1989 . . . . 1.50

DOLLY DILL
1945
1 Newsstand 80.00

DOMINO
1996
1 thru 3 . . . . @1.95

DOOM 2099
1 PB,I:Doom 2099,V:Tiger Wylde,
   foil(c) 3.00
2 I:Rook Seven 2.00
3 PB,V:Tiger Wylde 2.00
4 PB,V:Tiger Wylde 2.00
5 PB,I:Fever 2.00
6 I:Duke Stratosphear 2.00
7 PB,I:Paloma,V:Duke,Fever Haze 2.00
8 PB,C:Ravage 2.00
9 EC,V:Jack the Ripper 2.00
10 PB,w/Poster 2.00
11 PB,I:Thandaza 1.75
12 PB,V:Thandaza 1.75
13 PB(c),JFm(s),V:Necrotek 1.75

14 RLm(c),PB,Fall o/t Hammer#4 . 1.75
15 PB,I:Radian 1.75
16 EC(a&s), ... 1.75
17 PB,V:Radian,w/card 1.75
18 PB, ... 1.75
19 PB,C:Bloodhawk 1.75
20 PB,A:Bloodhawk 1.75
21 PB,Shadow King 1.75
22 PB,R:Duke Stratosphere 1.50
23 PB,R:Tyger Wylde 1.50
24 PB 1.50
25 PB 2.50
25a foil cover 3.25
26 . . . . 1.50
27 Revolution 1.50
28 Prologue to D-Day 1.50
Becomes:
DOOM 2099 A.D.
29 Doom Invades America 1.95
29a Chromium Cover 3.50
30 D:Corporate Head 1.95
31 PB,One Nation Under Doom . . 1.95
32 Ravage Aftermath 1.95
33 . . . . 1.95
34 I:Anthony Herod 1.95
35 E:One Nation Under Doom . . . 1.95
36 . . . . 1.95
37 . . . . 1.95
38 . . . . 1.95
39 . . . . 1.95
40 Rage Against Time,pt.1 . . . . . 1.95
41 Rage Against Time,pt.2 . . . . . 1.95

DOPEY DUCK COMICS
Timely Fall, 1945
1 A:Casper Cat,Krazy Krow . . . 75.00
2 A:Casper Cat,Krazy Krow . . . 72.00
Becomes:
WACKY DUCK
3 Paperchase(c) 65.00
4 Wacky Duck(c) 90.00
5 Duck & Devil(c) 57.00
6 Cliffhanger(c) 57.00
1 Baketball(c) 40.00
2 Traffic Light(c) 40.00
Becomes: JUSTICE COMICS

DOUBLE DRAGON
July, 1991
1 I:Billy&Jimmy Lee 1.00
2 Dragon Statue Stolen,V:Stelth . 1.00
3 Billy Vs. Jimmy 1.00
4 Dragon Force out of control . . . 1.00
5 V:Stealth 1.00
6 V:Nightfall, final issue 1.00

DOUBLE EDGE
Alpha Punisher vs. Nick Fury 4.95
Omega D:Major Character 4.95

D.P. 7
Nov., 1986
1 O:DP7 . . . . 1.00
2 V:Headhunter 1.00
3 RT,Headhunters 1.00
4 RT,V:Wompus 1.00
5 RT,Exorcist 1.00
6 RT,I:The Sweat Shop 1.00
7 RT,V:Clinic 1.00
8 RT,V:Clinic 1.00
9 RT,AW,I:New Paranormals 1.00
10 RT,I:Mysterious People 1.00
11 AW(i)V:Regulator 1.00

MARVEL

12 O:Randy 1.00
13 O:Charly 1.00
14 AW 1.00
15 . . . . 1.00
16 V:BlackPower 1.00
17 . . . . 1.00
18 Pitt tie-in 1.00
19 . . . . 1.25
20 Spitfire 1.25
21 . . . . 1.25
22 . . . . 1.25
23 A:PsiForce 1.25
24 A:Mastodon 1.25
25 V:Famileech 1.50
26 V:Famileech 1.50
27 The Pitt 1.50
28 V:The Candidate 1.25
29 Deadweight 1.50
30 V:Para-troop 1.25
31 A:Chrome 1.50
32 I:The Cure,last issue,
    June 1989 . . . . 1.50
Ann.#1,I:Witness 1.00

DRACULA LIVES
B&W Magazine, 1973—75
1 . . . . 10.00
2 O:Dracula 7.50
3 . . . . 6.00
4 MP 5.00
5 thru 13 . . . . @4.00

DRAFT, THE
1988
1 Sequel to The Pit 3.75

DRAGON LINES
[1st Limited Series]
1 RLm,V:Terrorist on Moon,
    Embossed(c) 3.00
2 RLm,V:Kuei Emperor 2.25
3 RLm,V:Spirit Boxer 2.25
4 RLm,K:Kuei Emperor 2.25
    [Regular Series]
1 B:PQ(s),RLm,I:Tao 2.50
2 RLm, ... 2.50

DRAGONSLAYER
Oct.–Nov., 1981
1 Movie adapt. 1.25
2 Movie adapt. 1.25

DRAGON STRIKE
1 Based on TSR Game 1.50

DRAGON'S TEETH/
DRAGON'S CLAWS
July, 1988
1 GSr,I:Mercy Dragon,
    Scavenger,Digit Steel 1.75
2 GSr,V:Evil Dead 1.50
3 GSr,Go Home 1.50
4 GSr 1.50
5 GSr,I:Death's Head 18.00
6 thru 10 GSr . . . . @1.75

DREADLANDS
Epic
1 Post-Apocalyptic Mini-series . 3.95
2 Trapped in Prehistoric Past . . 3.95
3 V:Alien Time Travelers 3.95
4 Final Issue 3.95

Dreadstar #23
© Marvel Entertainment Group

DREADSTAR
Epic Nov., 1982
1 JSn,I:Lord Papal 4.00
2 JSn,O:Willow 2.50
3 JSn,V:Lord Papal 2.25
4 JSn,I:Z 2.25
5 JSn,V:Teutun 2.25
6 JSn,BWr,Interstellar Toybox . . . 2.25
7 JSn,BWr,V:Dr.Mezlo 2.25
8 JSn,V:Z 2.25
9 JSn,V:Z 2.25
10 JSn,V:Z 2.25
11 JSn,O:Lord Papal 2.00
12 JSn,I:Dr.Delphi 2.00
13 JSn,V:Infra Red & Ultra Violet . 2.00
14 JSn,V:Lord Papal 2.00
15 JSn,new powers 2.00
16 JSn,V:Lord Papal 2.00
17 JSn,V:Willows father 2.00
18 JSn,V:Dr.Mezlo 2.00
19 JSn,V:Dr Mezlo 2.00
20 JSn,D:Oedi 2.00
21 JSn,D:Dr.Delphi 2.00
22 JSn,V:Lord Papal 2.00
23 JSn,V:Lord Papal 2.00
24 JSn,JS,V:Lord Papal 2.00
25 JSn,V:Lord Papal 2.00
26 JSn,R:Oedi 2.00
Ann.#1 JSn,The Price 2.50
See OTHER PUB. section

DREADSTAR & COMPANY
July, 1985
1 JSo,reprint 1.25
2 JSo,rep. 1.00
3 JSo,rep. 1.00
4 JSo,rep. 1.00
5 JSo,rep,Dec., 1985. . . . . 1.00

DROIDS
Star April, 1986
1 JR 3.00
2 AW 3.00
3 JR/AW 3.00

4 AW 3.00
5 AW 3.00
6 EC/AW,A:Luke Skywalker . . . 3.00
7 EC/AW,A:Luke Skywalker . . . 3.00
8 EC/AW,A:Luke Skywalker 3.00

DRUID
1 R:Dr. Druid Surprise!!! 2.50
2 F:Nekra 1.95
3 deranged canibal wisemen . . . 1.95
4 Why Must He Die? 1.95

DUNE
April, 1985
1 Movie Adapt,Rep. Marvel
    Super Spec,BSz 1.50
2 Movie Adapt,BSz 1.50
3 Movie Adapt,BSz,June, 1985 . 1.50

DYNOMUTT
Nov., 1977
1 Based on TV series 1.00
2 thru 5 . . . . @1.00
6 Sept., 1978 . . . . 1.00

EARTHWORM JIM
1 I:Earthworm Jim 2.25
2 Cow tipping 2.25
3 V:Lawyers,conclusion 2.25

ECTOKID
Razorline
1 I:Dex Mungo,BU:Hokum & Hex 2.75
2 O:Dex 2.00
3 I:Ectosphere 2.00
4 I:Brothers Augustine 2.00
5 A:Saint Sinner 2.00
6 Highway 61 Revisited 2.00
7 . . . . 2.00
8 V:Ice Augustine 1.75
9 Love is like a Bullet 1.95
10 . . . . 1.95
Ectokid Unleashed 2.95

ELECTRIC UNDERTOW
Dec., 1989
1 MBa,Strike Force 3.95
2 MBa, Will Deguchis 3.95
3 MBa, Alien Invaders 3.95
4 MBa,Attack on Beijing 3.95
5 MBa, Morituri defeated,March,
1990 . . . . 3.95

ELEKTRA
(Nov. 1996)
1 PrM,MD2, ... 2.95
1A variant (c) 4.00
2 PrM,MD2,V:Bullseye, round two 1.95
3 PrM,MD2, ... 1.95
4 PrM,MD2 . . . . 1.95
5 PrM,MD2, ... 1.95
6 PrM,MD2 . . . . 1.95
7 PrM,MD2,A:Konrad,The Architect 1.95
8 PrM,MD2,V:The Architect 1.95
9 PrM,MD2,V:The Four Winds . . 1.95
10 PrM,MD2,V:Daredevil,"American
    Samurai," pt.1 . . . . 1.95
Minus 1 Spec., PMg,MD2, flashback 1.95

ELEKTRA: ASSASSIN
August, 1986
1 FM,BSz,V:Shield 6.00
2 FM,BSz,I:Garrett 5.00

MARVEL

MARVEL

3 FM,BSz,V:Shield,A:Garrett 5.00
4 FM,BSz,V:Shield,A:Garrett 5.00
5 FM,BSz,I:Chastity,A:Garrett . . . 5.00
6 FM,BSz,A:Nick Fury,Garrett . . . 5.00
7 FM,BSz,V:Ken Wind,A:Garrett . 5.00
8 FM,BSz,V:Ken Wind,A:Garrett . 6.00
TPB Rep #1-8 . . . . 12.95

ELEKTRA LIVES AGAIN
Graphic Novel FM,R:Elektra,A:Matt
   Murdock,V:The Hand 30.00
TPB FM, rep. of HC, 80pg. 6.95

ELEKTRA: ROOT OF EVIL
1 V:Snakeroot 2.95
2 V:Snakeroot 2.95
3 Elektra's Brother 2.95
4 V:The Hand 2.95

ELEKTRA: SAGA
Feb., 1984
1 FM,rep.Daredevil 7.00
2 FM,rep.Daredevil 7.00
3 FM,rep.Daredevil 7.00
4 FM,rep.Daredevil 7.00
TPB Reprints#1-#4 . . . . 16.95
GN Book One FM,KJ, rep. from
   Daredevil, 96pg. 3.95
GN Book Two FM,KJ, rep. from
   Daredevil, 96pg. 3.95

ELEKTRA/WITCHBLADE
1-shot "Devil's Reign,"
   pt.6, x-over 2.95

ELFQUEST
August, 1985
1 WP,reprints 4.00
2 WP 2.50
3 WP 2.50
4 WP 2.50
5 WP 2.50
6 WP,Young Cutter V:Mad Coil . . 2.50
7 WP,Young Cutter V:Mad Coil . . 2.25
8 WP 2.25
9 WP 2.25
10 WP,A:Cutter, Skywise 2.25
11 WP,I:Two Edge 2.25
12 WP,The Mysterious Forest . . . 2.25
13 WP,The Forest, A:Leetah 2.25
14 WP,A:The Bone Woman 2.25
15 WP,The Forest, continued . . . 2.25
16 WP,Forbidden Grove 2.00
17 WP,Blue Mountain 2.00
18 WP,Secrets 2.00
19 WP,Twisted Gifts 2.00
20 WP,Twisted Gifts 2.00
21 WP 2.00
22 WP,A:Winnowill 2.00
23 WP,Blue Mountain,A:Winnowill 2.00
24 WP,The Quest Usurped 2.00
25 WP,Northern Wastelands 2.00
26 WP,Rayeks Story 2.00
27 WP,Battle Preparations 2.00
28 WP,Elves vs. Trolls 2.00
29 WP,Battle Beneath Blue
   Mountain 2.00
30 and 31 WP . . . . @2.00
32 WP,Conclusion, March 1988 . . 2.00

ELSEWHERE PRINCE
Epic May–Oct., 1990
1 thru 6 . . . . @2.00

ELVIRA
Oct., 1988
Spec.Black & White,Movie Adapt. 2.00

EPIC
1 Wildcards,Hellraiser 4.95
2 Nightbreed,Wildcards 4.95
3 DBw,MFm,Alien Legion 4.95
4 Stalkers,Metropol,Wildcards . . . 4.95

EPIC GRAPHIC NOVEL
Moebius 1: Upon a Star 10.00
Moebius 2: Arzach 10.00
Moebius 3: Airtight Garage 10.00
Moebius 4: Long Tomorrow 10.00
Moebius 5: 10.00
Moebius 6: Pharadonesia 10.00
Last of Dragons 7.00
The Incal 1 Moebius 11.00
The Incal 2 Moebius 11.00
The Incal 3 Moebius 11.00
JBo,Someplace Strange 7.00
MZ,Punisher 16.95

EPIC ILLUSTRATED
Spring, 1980
1 Black and White/Color Mag. . . 6.00
2 thru 10 . . . . @4.50
11 thru 15 . . . . @3.50
16 . . . . 4.00
17 thru 20 . . . . @3.00
21 thru 25 . . . . @3.00
26 thru 34, March, 1986 . . . . . @5.50

EPIC LITE
Epic Nov., 1991
One-shot short stories 3.95

ESSENTIAL SPIDER-MAN
Vol. 1 StL,SD, rep. Amaz. Fant. #15,
   Amaz Sp.-M #1–#20, Ann. #1 . .
Vol. 2 StL,SD, rep. Amaz. Sp.-M
   #21–#43, Ann.#2&#3 . . . .

ETERNALS
[1st Series]
July, 1976
1 JK,I:Ikaris 4.50
2 JK,I:Ajak 3.50
3 JK,I:Sersi 5.00
4 JK,Night of the Demons 2.50
5 JK,I:Makarri,Zuras Thena,Domo 2.50
6 JK,Gods & Men at City College 2.50
7 JK,V:Celestials 2.50
8 JK,I:Karkas, Reject 2.50
9 JK,I:Sprite,Reject vs. Karkas . 2.50
10 JK,V:Celestials 2.50
11 JK,I:Kingo Sunen 2.50
12 JK,I:Uni-Mind 2.50
13 JK,I:FOrgottenOne(Gilgamesh) 2.50
14 JK,V:Hulk 2.50
15 JK,V:Hulk 2.50
16 JK,I:Dromedan 2.50
17 JK,I:Sigmar 2.50
18 JK,I:Nerve Beast 2.50
19 JK,Secret o/t Pyramid 2.50
Ann.#1 JK,V:Timekillers 3.00

ETERNALS, THE
[2nd Series]
Oct., 1985
1 SB,I:Cybele 1.50

Eternals (Second Series) #1
© Marvel Entertainment Group

2 SB,V:Deviants 1.50
3 SB,V:Deviants 1.50
4 SB,V:Deviants 1.50
5 SB,V:Deviants 1.50
6 SB,V:Deviants 1.50
7 SB,V:Deviants 1.50
8 WS,SB,V:Deviants 1.50
9 WS,SB,V:Deviants 1.50
10 WS,SB,V:Deviants 1.50
11 WS,KP,V:Deviants 1.50
12 WS,KP,V:Deviants 1.50

ETERNALS:
HEROD FACTOR
Nov., 1991
1 MT/BMc,A:Sersi (giant size) . . . 2.50

EVERYMAN
Epic
One Shot.Supernatural Story
   (Animated Cel Artwork) 4.50

EWOKS
Star June, 1985—Sept., 1987
1 Based on TV Series 3.00
2 . . . . 2.50
3 . . . . 2.50
4 A:Foonars 2.50
5 Wicket vs. Ice Demon. 2.50
6 Mount Sorrow, A:Teebo 2.50
7 A:Logray,V:Morag 2.50
8 . . . . 2.50
9 Lost in Time 2.50
10 Lost in Time 1.50
11 Kneesaa Shrunk,A:Fleebogs . 1.50
12 . . . . 1.50
13 . . . . 1.50
14 Teebo- King for a Day 1.50
15 . . . . 1.50

EXCALIBUR
April, 1988
1 AD,Special,O:Excalibur,
   V:Technet 6.00

1a 2nd Printing	2.50	
1b 3rd Printing	2.00	
2 AAd,Mojo Mayhem,A:X-Babies	2.50	
3 Air Apparent Spec.RLm,KJ,JG,TP,		
RL,EL,JRu,A:Coldblood	3.00	
[Regular Series]		
1 B:CCI(s),AD,V:Warwolves,		
I:Widget	5.00	
2 AD,V:Warwolves,I:Kylun	4.00	
3 AD,V:Juggernaut	3.00	
4 AD,V:Arcade,Crazy Gang	3.00	
5 AD,V:Arcade	3.00	
6 AD,Inferno,I:Alistaire Stuart	3.00	
7 AD,Inferno	3.00	
8 RLm,JRu,A:New Mutants	3.00	
9 AD,I:Nazi-Excalibur	3.00	
10 MR,V:Nazi-Excalibur	3.00	
11 MR,V:Nazi-Excalibur	3.00	
12 AD,Fairy Tale Dimension	3.00	
13 AD,The Prince,N:Capt.Britian	3.00	
14 AD,Too Many Heroes	2.50	
15 AD,I:US James Braddock	2.50	
16 AD,V:Anjulie	2.50	
17 AD,C:Prof.X,Starjammers	2.50	
18 DJ,DA,V:Jamie Braddock	2.50	
19 RL,TA,AM,V:Jamie Braddock	2.50	
20 RLm,JRu,V:Demon Druid	2.50	
21 I:Crusader X	2.50	
22 V:Crusader X	2.50	
23 AD,V:Magik	2.50	
24 AD,Return Home,C:Galactus	2.50	
25 E:CCI(s),AM,A:Galactus,Death,		
Watcher	2.50	
26 RLm,JRu,V:Mastermind	2.50	
27 BWS,BSz,A:Nth Man	3.00	
28 BBI,Night at Bar	2.50	
29 JRu,V:Nightmare,A:PowerPack	2.50	
30 DR,AM,A:Doctor Strange	2.50	
31 DR,AM,V:Son of Krakoa	2.50	
32 V:Mesmero	2.50	
33 V:Mesmero	2.50	
34 V:Mesmero	2.50	
35 AM,Missing Child	2.50	
36 AM,V:Silv.Sable,Sandman	2.50	
37 A:Avengers W.C.,Dr.Doom	2.50	
38 A:Avengers W.C.,Dr.Doom	2.50	
39 A:Avengers W.C.,Dr.Doom	2.50	
40 O:Excalibur,Trial-Lockheed	2.50	
41 V:Warwolves,C:Cable	3.00	
42 AD,Team Broken Up	3.00	
43 AD,Nightcrawler,V:Capt.Brit	3.00	
44 AD,Capt.Britain On Trial	3.00	
45 AD,I:N-Men	3.00	
46 AD,Return of Kylun,C:Cerise	3.00	
47 AD,I:Cerise	3.00	
48 AD,A:Anti-Phoenix	3.00	
49 AD,MFm,V:Necrom,R:Merlyn	3.00	
50 AD,Phoenix,V:Necrom,Merlyn	4.00	
51 V:Giant Dinosaurs	2.00	
52 O:Phoenix,A:Prof X,MarvGirl	2.00	
53 A:Spider-Man,V:The Litter	2.00	
54 AD,MFm,V:Crazy Gang	2.50	
55 AD,MFm,A:Psylocke	2.50	
56 AD,MFm,A:Psylocke,		
V:Saturyne,Jamie Braddock	2.50	
57 A:X-Men,Alchemy,V:Trolls	2.75	
58 A:X-Men,Alchemy,V:Trolls	2.75	
59 A:Avengers	2.25	
60 A:Avengers	2.25	
61 AD,MFm,Phoenix Vs.Galactus	2.25	
62 AD,MFm,A:Galactus	2.25	
63 AD,MFm,V:Warpies	2.25	
64 AD,MFm,V:RCX,R:Rachel	2.25	
65 AD,MFm,R:Dark Phoenix	2.25	
66 AD,MFm,V:Ahab,Sentinels,		

O:Widget	2.25	
67 AD,MFm,V:Ahab,Sentinels	2.25	
68 V:Starjammers	2.00	
69 A:Starjammers	2.00	
70 A:Starjammers	2.00	
71 DaR,Hologram(c),N:Excalibur	6.00	
72 KeL,V:Siena Blaze	2.00	
73 TSr,V:Siena Blaze	2.00	
74 InC,A:Mr.Sinster,Siena Blaze	2.00	
75 SLo(s),KeL,I:Daytripper(Amanda		
Sefton),Britannic(Capt.Britain),		
BU:Nightcrawler	3.50	
75a Newstand Ed.	2.25	
76 KeL,V:D'spayre	2.00	
77 KeL,R:Doug Ramsey	2.00	
78 A:Zero,Doug Ramsey	2.25	
79 A:Zero,Doug Ramsey	2.25	
80 A:Zero,Doug Ramsey	2.25	
81 Doug Ramsey	2.25	
82	2.50	
82a foil(c)	3.50	
83 regular ed.	1.50	
83a Deluxe ed. Kitty,Nightcrawler	2.25	
84 regular ed.	1.50	
84a Deluxe ed.	2.25	
85 regular ed.	1.50	
85a Deluxe ed.	2.25	
86 regular ed.	1.50	
86a Deluxe ed.	2.25	
87 KeL,Secrets of the Genoshan		
Mutate Technology	1.95	
88 Dream Nails,pt.1	1.95	
89 Dream Nails,pt.2	1.95	
90 Between Uncreated,Phalanx	2.95	
91 F:Colossus	1.95	
92 F:Colossus	1.95	
93 F:Wolfsbane	1.95	
94 A:Karma & Psylocke	1.95	
95	1.95	
96	1.95	
97 BWi,B.Braddock's secrets told	1.95	
98	1.95	
99 European Hellfire Club,		
Onslaught	1.95	
100 Onslaught saga, double size	2.95	
101	1.95	
102	1.95	
103 WEl,F:Colossus,Kitty &		
Nichtcrawler	1.95	
104 JAr,BHi,PNe,Douglock's		
dark side	1.95	
105 JAr,BHi,PNe,V:Moonstar	1.95	
106	1.95	
107 SvL,New direction	1.95	
108 Dragons of the Crimson Dawn	1.95	
109 V:Spiral,A:Captain Britain	1.95	
110 V:The Dragons of the		
Crimson Dawn	1.95	
111 F:Shadowcat,R:Rory Cambell		
(Ahab?)	1.95	
112 Quicksilver tie-in	1.95	
Minus 1 Spec., flashback,		
F:Nightcrawler	1.95	
Ann.#1 I:Khaos,w/card	3.25	
Spec #1 The Possession	4.00	
Spec #2 RLm,DT,JG,RL,		
A:Original X-Men	2.75	
PF Cold Blood	4.95	
GN Weird War III	9.95	
TPB Wild, Wild Life	5.95	

FACTOR X

1 After Xavier	4.00	
2 Scott vs. Alex Summers	3.00	
3 Cyclops vs. Havok	2.50	

4 Jean & Scott	2.50	
TPB Rep. #1-#4	8.95	

FAFHRD AND THE GRAY MOUSER
Epic Oct., 1990

1 MMi	5.00	
2 & 3 MMi	@5.00	
4 MMi, Feb. 1991	5.00	

FAITHFUL
Nov., 1949

1 Ph(c),I Take This Man	65.00	
2 Ph(c),Love Thief,Feb.,1950	50.00	

FALCON
Nov., 1983

1 PS,V:Nemesis	2.00	
2 V:Sentinels	1.50	
3 V:Electro	1.50	
4 A:Capt.America, Feb., 1984	1.50	

FALLEN ANGELS
April, 1987

1 KGa,TP,A:Sunspot,Warlock	3.00	
2 KGa,TP,I:Gomi,Fallen Angels	2.50	
3 KGa,TP,A:X-Factor	2.50	
4 KGa,TP,A:Moon Boy, Devil		
Dinosaur	2.50	
5 JSon,D:Angel,Don	2.50	
6 JSon,Coconut Grove	2.50	
7 KGa,Captured in CoconutGrove	2.50	
8 KGa,L:Sunspot,Warlock	2.50	

FANTASTIC FORCE

1 Foil stamped cover	2.50	
2 Moses	2.25	
3	2.25	
4 A:Captain America	2.25	
5 I:Dreadface	2.25	
6 F:Vibraxis	1.75	
7 V:Doom	1.75	
8 V:Crimson Cadre	1.75	
9 Atlantis Rising	1.75	
10 A:Human Torch	1.75	
11 A:Black Panther	1.75	
12 V:Vanguard	1.75	
13 J:She-Hulk	1.75	
14 V:Wakanda	1.75	
15 End of the Fantastic Force?	1.75	
16 End of the Fantastic Force?	1.75	
17	1.75	
18	1.75	

FANTASTIC FOUR
Nov., 1961

1 JK,I&O:Mr.Fantastic,Thing		
Invisible Girl,Human Torch		
Mole Man	18,000.00	
2 JK,I:Skrulls	3,200.00	
3 JK,I:Miracleman	2,200.00	
4 JK,R:Submariner	2,600.00	
5 JK,JSt,I&O:Doctor Doom	2,800.00	
6 JK,V:Doctor Doom	1,500.00	
7 JK,I:Kurrgo	850.00	
8 JK,I:Alicia Masters,I&O:		
Puppet Master	850.00	
9 JK,V:Submariner	800.00	
10 JK,V:Doctor Doom,I:Ovoids	800.00	
11 JK,I:Impossible Man	650.00	
12 JK,V:Hulk	1,100.00	
13 JK,SD,I&O:Red Ghost,		
I:Watcher	500.00	

MARVEL

Fantastic Four #13
© Marvel Entertainment Group

14 JK,SD,V:Submariner	300.00
15 JK,I:Mad Thinker	300.00
16 JK,V:Doctor Doom	300.00
17 JK,V:Doctor Doom	300.00
18 JK,I:Super Skrull	300.00
19 JK,I&O:Rama Tut	300.00
20 JK,I:Molecule Man	300.00
21 JK,I:Hate Monger	250.00
22 JK,V:Mole Man	250.00
23 JK,V:Doctor Doom	250.00
24 JK,I:Infant Terrible	250.00
25 JK,Thing vs.Hulk	400.00
26 JK,V:Hulk,A:Avengers	375.00
27 JK,A:Doctor Strange	175.00
28 JK,1st X-Men x-over	250.00
29 JK,V:Red Ghost	125.00
30 JK,I&O:Diablo	125.00
31 JK,V:Mole Man	100.00
32 JK,V:Superskrull	100.00
33 JK,I:Attuma	100.00
34 JK,I:Gideon	100.00
35 JK,I:Dragon Man,A:Diablo	100.00
36 JK,I:Medusa,Frightful Four	100.00
37 JK,V:Skrulls	90.00
38 JK,V:Frightful Four,I:Trapster	90.00
39 JK,WW,A:Daredevil	90.00
40 JK,A:Daredevil,Dr.Doom	90.00
41 JK,V:Fright.Four,A:Medusa	76.00
42 JK,V:Frightful Four	76.00
43 JK,V:Frightful Four	76.00
44 JK,JSt,I:Gorgon, V:Dragon Man	80.00
45 JK,JSt,I:Inhumans(Black Bolt, Triton,Lockjaw,Crystal, Karnak)	90.00
46 JK,JSt,V:Seeker	74.00
47 JK,JSt,I:Maximus,Attilan, Alpha Primitives	65.00
48 JK,JSt,I:Silver Surfer, C:Galactus	850.00
49 JK,JSt,A:Silver Surfer, V:Galactus	225.00
50 JK,JSt,V:Galactus,Silver Surfer,I:Wyatt Wingfoot	250.00
51 JK,JSt,I:Negative Zone	65.00
52 JK,JSt,I:Black Panther	100.00
53 JK,JSt,I:Klaw,Vibranium	100.00
54 JK,JSt,I:Prester John	60.00

55 JK,JSt,A:Silver Surfer	85.00
56 JK,JSt,O:Klaw,A:Inhumans, C:Silver Surfer	70.00
57 JK,JSt,V:Doc Doom, A:Silver Surfer	70.00
58 JK,JSt,V:Doc Doom, A:Silver Surfer	70.00
59 JK,JSt,V:Doc Doom, A:Silver Surfer	70.00
60 JK,JSt,V:Doc Doom, A:Silver Surfer	70.00
61 JK,JSt,V:Sandman, A:Silver Surfer	70.00
62 JK,JSt,I:Blastaar	45.00
63 JK,JSt,V:Blastaar	50.00
64 JK,JSt,I:The Kree,Sentry	50.00
65 JK,JSt,I:Ronan,Supreme Intelligence	50.00
66 JK,JSt,O:Him,A:Crystal	100.00
67 JK,JSt,I:Him	125.00
68 JK,JSt,V:Mad Thinker	60.00
69 JK,JSt,V:Mad Thinker	50.00
70 JK,JSt,V:Mad Thinker	50.00
71 JK,JSt,V:Mad Thinker	50.00
72 JK,JSt,A:Watcher,S.Surfer	50.00
73 JK,JSt,A:SpM,DD,Thor	35.00
74 JK,JSt,A:Silver Surfer	45.00
75 JK,JSt,A:Silver Surfer	45.00
76 JK,JSt,V:Psycho Man,S.Surf	40.00
77 JK,JSt,V:Galactus,S.Surfer	40.00
78 JK,JSt,V:Wizard	35.00
79 JK,JSt,A:Crystall,V:Mad Thinker	35.00
80 JK,JSt,A:Crystal	35.00
81 JK,JSt,J:Crystal,V:Wizard	35.00
82 JK,JSt,V:Maximus	35.00
83 JK,JSt,V:Maximus	35.00
84 JK,JSt,V:Doctor Doom	25.00
85 JK,JSt,V:Doctor Doom	25.00
86 JK,JSt,V:Doctor Doom	25.00
87 JK,JSt,V:Doctor Doom	25.00
88 JK,JSt,V:Mole Man	25.00
89 JK,JSt,V:Mole Man	25.00
90 JK,JSt,V:Skrulls	22.00
91 JK,JSt,V:Skrulls,I:Torgo	22.00
92 JK,JSt,V:Torgo,Skrulls	22.00
93 JK,V:Torgo,Skrulls	22.00
94 JK,JSt,I:Agatha Harkness	22.00
95 JK,JSt,I:Monocle	22.00
96 JK,JSt,V:Mad Thinker	20.00
97 JK,JSt,V:Monster from Lost Lagoon	20.00
98 JK,JSt,V:Kree Sentry	20.00
99 JK,JSt,A:Inhumans	20.00
100 JK,JSt,V:Puppetmaster	75.00
101 JK,JSt,V:Maggia	20.00
102 JK,JSt,V:Magneto	22.00
103 JR,V:Magneto	22.00
104 JR,V:Magneto	22.00
105 JR,L:Crystal	20.00
106 JR,JSt,'Monster's Secret'	20.00
107 JB,JSt,V:Annihilus	20.00
108 JK,JB,JR,JSt, V:Annihilus	20.00
109 JB,JSt,V:Annihilus	20.00
110 JB,JSt,V:Annihilus	20.00
111 JB,JSt,A:Hulk	20.00
112 JB,JSt,Thing vs. Hulk	50.00
113 JB,JSt,I:Overmind	15.00
114 JR(c),JB,V:Overmind	15.00
115 JR(c),JB,JSt,I:Eternals	15.00
116 JB,JSt,O:Stranger	15.00
117 JB,JSt,V:Diablo	11.00
118 JR(c),JB,JM,V:Diablo	11.00
119 JB,JSt,V:Klaw	11.00
120 JB,JSt,I:Gabriel(Airwalker)	

Fantastic Four #47
© Marvel Entertainment Group

(Robot)	11.00
121 JB,JSt,V:Silver Surfer,D: Gabriel Destroyer	15.00
122 JR(c),JB,JSt,V:Galactus, A:Silver Surfer	15.00
123 JB,JSt,V:Galactus, A:Silver Surfer	14.00
124 JB,JSt,V:Monster	10.00
125 E:StL(s),JB,JSt,V:Monster	10.00
126 B:RTs(s),JB,JSt, O:FF,MoleMan	10.00
127 JB,JSt,V:Mole Man	10.00
128 JB,JSt,V:Mole Man	12.00
129 JB,JSt,I:Thundra, V:Frightful Four	9.00
130 JSo(c),JB,JSt,V:Frightful Four	8.00
131 JSo(c),JB,JSt,V:QuickSilver	8.00
132 JB,JSt,J:Medusa	8.00
133 JSt(i),V:Thundra	8.00
134 JB,JSt,V:Dragon Man	8.00
135 JB,JSt,V:Gideon	8.00
136 JB,JSt,A:Shaper	8.00
137 JB,JSt,A:Shaper	8.00
138 JB,JSt,O:Miracle Man	8.00
139 JB,V:Miracle Man	8.00
140 JB,JSt,O:Annihilus	8.00
141 JR(c),JB,JSt,V:Annihilus	8.00
142 RB,JSt,A:Doc Doom	8.00
143 GK(c),RB,V:Doc Doom	8.00
144 RB,JSt,V:Doc Doom	8.00
145 JSt&GK(c),RA,I:Ternak	8.00
146 RA,JSt,V:Ternak	8.00
147 RB,JSt,V:Subby	8.00
148 RB,JSt,V:Frightful Four	8.00
149 RB,JSt,V:Sub-Mariner	8.00
150 GK(c),RB,JSt,W:Crystal & Quicksilver,V:Ultron	9.00
151 RB,JSt,O:Thundra	5.00
152 JR(c),RB,JM,A:Thundra	5.00
153 GK(c),RB,JSt,A:Thundra	5.00
154 GK(c),rep.Str.Tales #127	5.00
155 RB,JSt,A:Surfer	8.00
156 RB,JSt,A:Surfer,V:Doom	8.00
157 RB,JSt,A:Surfer	8.00
158 RB,JSt,V:Xemu	5.00
159 RB,JSt,V:Xemu	5.00
160 K&R(c),JB,V:Arkon	4.50

MARVEL

Fantastic Four #67
© Marvel Entertainment Group

161 RB,JSt,V:Arkon 4.50
162 RB,DA,JSt,V:Arkon 4.50
163 RB,JSt,V:Arkon 4.50
164 JK(c),GP,JSt,V:Crusader,R:
   Marvel Boy,I:Frankie Raye . . 4.50
165 GP,JSt,O:Crusader,
   O&D:Marvel Boy 4.50
166 GP,V:Hulk 6.00
167 JK(c),GP,JSt,V:Hulk 6.00
168 RB,JSt,J:Luke Cage 5.00
169 RB,JSt,V:Puppetmaster 5.00
170 GP,JSt,L:Luke Cage 5.00
171 JK(c),RB,GP,JSt,I:Gor 4.00
172 JK(c),GP,JSt,V:Destroyer . . 5.00
173 JB,JSt,V:Galactus,O:Heralds . 5.00
174 JB,V:Galactus 5.00
175 JB,A:High Evolutionary 4.00
176 GP,JSt,V:Impossible Man . . 4.00
177 JP,JS,A:Frightful Four
   I:Texas Twister,Capt.Ultra 3.50
178 GP,V:Frightful Four,Brute . . 3.50
179 JSt,V:Annihilus 3.50
180 reprint #101 . . . . 3.50
181 E:RTs(s),JSt,V:Brute,
   Annihilus 3.50
182 SB,JSt,V:Brute,Annihilus 3.50
183 SB,JSt,V:Brute,Annihilus 3.50
184 GP,JSt,V:Eliminator 3.50
185 GP,JSt,V:Nich.Scratch 3.50
186 GP,JSi,I:Salem's Seven 3.50
187 GP,JSt,V:Klaw,Molecule Man 3.50
188 GP,JSt,V:Molecule Man 3.50
189 reprint FF Annual #4 . . . . . . 3.50
190 SB,O:Fantastic Four 4.00
191 GP,JSt,V:Plunderer,
   Team Breaks Up 3.50
192 GP,JSt,V:Texas Twister 3.50
193 KP,JSt,V:Darkoth,Diablo 3.50
194 KP,V:Darkoth,Diablo 3.50
195 KP,A:Sub-Mariner 3.50
196 KP,V:Invincible Man (Reed),
   A:Dr.Doom,Team Reunited . . . 3.50
197 KP,JSt,Red Ghost 3.50
198 KP,JSt,V:Doc Doom 3.50
199 KP,JSt,V:Doc Doom 3.50
200 KP,JSt,V:Doc Doom 6.00

201 KP,JSt,FF's Machinery 3.00
202 KP,JSt,V:Quasimodo 3.00
203 KP,JSt,V:Mutant 3.00
204 KP,JSt,V:Skrulls 3.00
205 KP,JSt,V:Skrulls 3.00
206 KP,JSt,V:Skrulls,A:Nova . . . 3.00
207 SB,JSt,V:Monocle,A:SpM . . . 4.00
208 SB,V:Sphinx,A:Nova 2.50
209 JBy,JSt,I:Herbie,A:Nova . . . 5.00
210 JBy,JS,A:Galactus 4.00
211 JBy,JS,I:Terrax,A:Galactus . . 5.00
212 JBy,JSt,V:Galactus,Sphinx . 4.00
213 JBy,JSt,V:Terrax,Galactus
   Sphinx 4.00
214 JBy,JSt,V:Skrull 4.00
215 JBy,JSt,V:Blastaar 4.00
216 JBy,V:Blastaar 4.00
217 JBy,JSt,A:Dazzler 4.50
218 JBy,JSt,V:FrightfulFour,
   A:Spider-Man 5.00
219 BSz,JSt,A:Sub-Mariner 3.00
220 JBy,JSt,A:Vindicator 3.50
221 JBy,JSt,V:Vindicator 3.50
222 BSz,JSt,V:Nicholas Scratch . . 2.75
223 BSz,JSt,V:Salem's Seven . . . 2.75
224 BSz,A:Thor 2.75
225 BSz,A:Thor 2.75
226 BSz,A:Shogun 2.75
227 BSz,JSt,V:Ego-Spawn 2.75
228 BSz,JSt,V:Ego-Spawn 2.75
229 BSz,JSt,I:Firefrost,Ebon
   Seeker 3.00
230 BSz,JSt,A:Avengers,
   O:Firefrost & Ebon Seeker . . 2.75
231 BSz,JSt,V:Stygorr 2.75
232 JBy,New Direction,V:Diablo . 5.00
233 JBy,V:Hammerhead 3.50
234 JBy,V:Ego 3.50
235 JBy,O:Ego 3.50
236 JBy,V:Dr.Doom,A:Puppet
   Master, 20th Anniv. 4.50
237 JBy,V:Solons 3.50
238 JBy,O:Frankie Raye,
   new Torch 3.50
239 JBy,I:Aunt Petunia,
   Uncle Jake 4.50
240 JBy,A:Inhumans,b:Luna . . . 3.50
241 JBy,A:Black Panther 3.50
242 JBy,A:Daredevil,Thor,Iron Man
   Spider-Man,V:Terrax 3.50
243 JBy,A:Daredevil,Dr.Strange,
   Spider-Man,Avengers,V:Galactus,
   Terrax 4.00
244 JBy,A:Avengers,Dr.Strange,
   Galactus, Frankie Raye
   Becomes Nova 5.00
245 JBy,V:Franklin Richards 3.50
246 JBy,V:Dr.Doom,
   A:Puppet Master 3.50
247 JBy,A:Dr.Doom,I:Kristoff,
   D:Zorba 3.50
248 JBy,A:Inhumans 3.50
249 JBy,V:Gladiator 3.50
250 JBy,A:Capt.America,SpM
   V:Gladiator 4.00
251 JBy,V:Annihilus 3.00
252 JBy,1st sideways issue,V:
   Ootah,A:Annihilus,w/tattoo . . 4.50
252a w/o tattoo 2.00
253 JBy,V:Kestorans,A:Annihilus . 3.00
254 JBy,V:Mantracora,
   A:She-Hulk,Wasp 3.00
255 JBy,A:Daredevil,Annihilus,
   V:Mantracora 3.00
256 JBy,A:Avengers,Galactus,

Fantastic Four #100
© Marvel Entertainment Group

   V:Annihilus,New Costumes . . . 3.00
257 JBy,A:Galactus,Death,Nova,
   Scarlet Witch 3.50
258 JBy,A:Dr.Doom,D:Hauptmann 3.00
259 JBy,V:Terrax,Dr.Doom,
   C:Silver Silver 3.00
260 JBy,V:Terrax, Dr.Doom,
   A:Silver Surfer,Sub-Mariner . . 5.00
261 JBy,A:Sub-Mariner,Marrina,
   Silver Surfer,Sc.Witch,Lilandra 5.00
262 JBy,O:Galactus,A:Odin,
   (J.Byrne in story) 3.50
263 JBy,V:Messiah,A:Mole Man . . 3.00
264 JBy,V:Messiah,A:Mole Man . . 3.00
265 JBy,A:Trapster,Avengers,
   J:She-Hulk,Secret Wars 4.50
266 KGa,JBy,A:Hulk,Sasquatch,
   V:Karisma 3.00
267 JBy,A:Hulk,Sasquatch,Morbius,
   V:Dr.Octopus,Sue miscarries . . 4.00
268 JBy,V:Doom's Mask 3.00
269 JBy,R:Wyatt Wingfoot,
   I:Terminus 3.00
270 JBy,V:Terminus 3.00
271 JBy,V:Gormuu 3.00
272 JBy,I:Warlord (Nathaniel
   Richards) 3.00
273 JBy,V:Warlord 3.00
274 JBy,AG,cont.from Thing#19,
   A:Spider-Man's Black Costume 3.00
275 JBy,A:V:T.J.Vance 3.00
276 JBy,JOy,V:Mephisto,
   A:Dr.Strange 3.00
277 JBy,JOy,V:Mephisto,
   A:Dr.Strange,R:Thing 3.00
278 JBy,JOy,O:Dr.Doom,A:Kristoff
   (as Doom) 3.00
279 JBy,JOy,V:Dr.Doom(Kristoff),
   I:New Hate-Monger 3.00
280 JBy,JOy,I:Malice,
   V:Hate-Monger 3.00
281 JBy,JOy,A:Daredevil,V:Hate
   Monger,Malice 3.00
282 JBy,JOy,A:Power Pack,Psycho
   Man,Secret Wars II 3.00

MARVEL

283 JBy,JOy,V:Psycho-Man 3.00
284 JBy,JOy,V:Psycho-Man 3.00
285 JBy,JOy,Secret Wars II
   A:Beyonder 3.00
286 JBy,TA,R:Jean Grey,
   A:Hercules Capt.America . . 4.50
287 JBy,JSt,A:Wasp,V:Dr.Doom . 3.00
288 JBy,JSt,V:Dr.Doom,Secret
   Wars II 3.00
289 JBy,AG,D:Basilisk,V:Blastaar,
   R:Annihilus 3.00
290 JBy,AG,V:Annihilus 3.00
291 JBy,CR,A:Nick Fury 3.00
292 JBy,AG,A:Nick Fury,V:Hitler . 3.00
293 JBy,AG,A:Avengers.W.C. . . . 3.00
294 JOy,AG,V:FutureCentralCity . 2.50
295 JOy,AG,V:Fut.Central City . . . 2.50
296 BWS,KGa,RF,BWi,AM,KJ,JB,
   SL,MS,JRu,JOy,JSt,25th
   Anniv.,V:MoleMan 3.00
297 JB,SB,V:Umbra-Sprite 2.50
298 JB,SB,V:Umbra-Sprite 2.50
299 JB,SB,She-Hulk,V:Thing,
   A:Spider-Man,L:She-Hulk . . 2.50
300 JB,SB,W:Torch & Fake Alicia
   (Lyja),A:Puppet-Master,Wizard,
   Mad Thinker,Dr.Doom 3.00
301 JB,SB,V:Wizard,MadThinker . 2.25
302 JB,SB,V:Project Survival . . . 2.25
303 JB,RT,A:Thundra,V:Machus . 2.25
304 JB,JSt,V:Quicksilver,
   A:Kristoff 2.25
305 JB,JSt,V:Quicksilver,
   J:Crystal,A:Dr.Doom 2.25
306 JB,JSt,A:Capt.America,
   J:Ms.Marvel,V:Diablo 2.25
307 JB,JSt,L:Reed&Sue,V:Diablo . 2.25
308 JB,JSt,I:Fasaud 2.25
309 JB,JSt,V:Fasaud 2.25
310 KP,JSt,V:Fasaud,N:Thing
   & Ms.Marvel 2.25
311 KP,JSt,A:Black Panther,
   Dr.Doom,V:THRob 2.25
312 KP,JSt,A:Black Panther,
   Dr.Doom,X-Factor 2.25
313 SB,JSt,V:Lava Men,
   A:Moleman 2.00
314 KP,JSt,V:Belasco 2.00
315 KP,JSt,V:Mast.Pandem. 2.00
316 KP,JSt,A:CometMan 2.00
317 KP,JSt,L:Crystal 2.00
318 KP,JSt,V:Dr.Doom 2.00
319 KP,JSt,G-Size,O:Beyonder . . 2.25
320 KP,JSt,Hulk vs Thing 2.50
321 RLm,RT,A:She-Hulk 2.00
322 KP,JSt,Inferno,V:Graviton . . . 2.00
323 KP,JSt,RT,Inferno A:Mantis . . 2.00
324 KP,JSt,RT,A:Mantis 2.00
325 RB,RT,A:Silver Surfer,
   D:Mantis 2.50
326 KP,RT,I:New Frightful Four . . 2.00
327 KP,RT,V:Frightful Four 2.00
328 KP,RT,V:Frightful Four 2.00
329 RB,RT,V:Mole Man 2.00
330 RB,RT,V:Dr.Doom 2.00
331 RB,RT,V:Ultron 2.00
332 RB,RT,V:Aron 2.00
333 RB,RT,V:Aron,Frightful Four . 2.00
334 RB,Acts of Vengeance 2.00
335 RB,RT,Acts of Vengeance . . . 2.00
336 RLm,Acts of Vengeance, . . . 2.00
337 WS,A:Thor,Iron Man,
   B:Timestream saga 5.00
338 WS,V:Deathshead,A:Thor,
   Iron Man 2.50

Fantastic Four #292
© *Marvel Entertainment Group*

339 WS,V:Gladiator 2.50
340 WS,V:Black Celestial 2.50
341 WS,A:Thor,Iron Man 2.50
342 A:Rusty,C:Spider-Man 2.50
343 WS,V:Stalin 2.50
344 WS,V:Stalin 2.50
345 WS,V:Dinosaurs 2.50
346 WS,V:Dinosaurs 2.50
347 AAd,ATi(i)A:Spider-Man,
   GhostRider,Wolverine,Hulk . . 5.50
347a 2nd printing 4.50
348 AAd,ATi(i)A:Spider-Man,
   GhostRider,Wolverine,Hulk . . 5.50
348a 2nd printing 4.00
349 AAd,ATi(i),AM(i)A:Spider-Man,
   Wolverine,GhostRider,Hulk,
   C:Punisher 5.00
350 WS,Am(i),R:Ben Grimm as
   Thing,(48p) 3.00
351 MBa,Kubic 2.50
352 WS,Reed Vs.Dr.Doom 2.50
353 WS,E:Timestream Saga,
   A:Avengers, ... 2.50
354 WS,Secrets of the Time
   Variance Authority 2.50
355 AM,V:Wrecking Crew 2.00
356 B:TDF(s),PR,A:New Warriors,
   V:Puppet Master 2.00
357 PR,V:Mad Thinker,
   Puppetmaster, ... 2.00
358 PR,AAd,30th Anniv.,1st Marv. Die
   Cut(c),D:Lyja,V:Paibok,BU:
   Dr.Doom 4.00
359 PR,I:Devos the Devastator . . 2.00
360 PR,V:Dreadface 2.00
361 PR,V:Dr.Doom,X-masIssue . . 2.00
362 PR,A:Spider-Man,
   I:WildBlood 2.00
363 PR,I:Occulus,A:Devos 2.00
364 PR,V:Occulus 2.00
365 PR,V:Occulus 2.00
366 PR,Infinity War,R:Lyja 2.00
367 PR,Inf.War,A:Wolverine 2.00
368 PR,V:Infinity War X-Men 2.00
369 PR,Inf.War,R:Malice, ...

A:Thanos 2.00
370 PR,Inf.War,V:Mr.Fantastic
   Doppleganger 2.00
371 PR,V:Lyja,foil(c) 5.00
371a 2nd Printing 3.00
372 PR,A:Spider-Man,Silver
   Sable 2.00
373 PR,V:Aron,Silver sable 2.00
374 PR,V:Secret Defenders 2.00
375 V:Dr.Doom,A:Inhumans,Lyja,
   Holo-Grafix(c) 4.00
376 PR,A:Nathan Richards,V:Paibok,
   Devos,w/Dirt Magazine 3.75
376a w/out Dirt Magazine 2.00
377 PR,V:Paibok,Devos,Klaw,
   I:Huntara 2.00
378 PR,A:Sandman,SpM,DD . . . 2.00
379 PR,V:Ms.Marvel 2.00
380 PR,A:Dr.Doom,V:Hunger . . . 2.00
381 PR,D:Dr.Doom,Mr.Fantastic,
   V:Hunger 7.00
382 PR,V:Paibok,Devos,Huntara . 3.00
383 PR,V:Paibok,Devos,Huntara . 2.00
384 PR,A:Ant-Man,V:Franklin
   Richards 2.00
385 PR,A:Triton,Tiger Shark,
   Starblast#7 . . . . 2.00
386 PR,Starblast#11,A:Namor,Triton,
   b:Johnny & Lyja child 1.75
387 Die-Cut & Foil (c),PR,N:Invisible
   Woman,J:Ant-Man,A:Namor . . 3.25
387a Newsstand Ed. 1.75
388 PR,I:Dark Raider,V:FF,
   Avengers,w/cards 2.00
389 PR,I:Raphael Suarez,A:Watcher,
   V:Collector 2.00
390 PR,A:Galactus 2.00
391 PR,I:Vibraxas 1.75
392 Dark Raider 1.75
393 . . . . 1.75
394 Neon(c) w/insert print 2.95
394a Newsstand ed.,no bag/inserts 1.75
395 Thing V:Wolverine 1.75
396 . . . . 1.75
397 Resurrection,pt.1 . . . . 1.75
398 regular edition 1.50
398a Enhanced cover 2.75
399 Watcher's Lie 1.75
399a Foil stamped cover 2.50
400 Watcher's Lie,pt.3 . . . . 3.95
401 V:Tantalus 1.50
402 Atlantis Rising,Namor
   vs. Black Bolt 1.50
403 TDF,PR,DBi,F:Thing,Medusa 1.50
404 R:Namor,I:New Villian 1.50
405 J:Namor 1.50
406 TDF,PR,DBi,R:Dr. Doom,
   I:Hyperstorm 1.50
407 TDF,PR,DBi,Return of
   Reed Richards 1.50
408 TDF,PR,DBi,Original FF unite 1.50
409 TDF,PR,DBi,All new line-up . 1.50
410 . . . . 1.50
411 . . . . 1.50
412 TDF,PR,DBi,Mr.Fantastic
   vs. Sub-Mariner 1.50
413 . . . . 1.50
414 Galactus vs. Hyperstorm . . . 1.50
415 Onslaught saga, A:X-Men . . . 2.50
416 Onslaught saga, A:Dr. Doom,
   double size, finale 2.50
Ann.#1 JK,SD,I:Atlantis,Dorma,
   Krang,V:Namor,O:FF 500.00
Ann.#2 JK,JSt,O:Dr.Doom 350.00
Ann.#3 JK,W:Reed and Sue . . 145.00

Ann.#4 JK,JSt,I:Quasimodo 75.00
Ann.#5 JK,JSt,A:Inhumans,Silver
  Surfer,Black Panther,
  I:Psycho Man 120.00
Ann.#6 JK,JSt,I:Annihilus,
  Franklin Richards 50.00
Ann.#7 JK(c),reprints 23.00
Ann.#8 JR(c),reprints 12.00
Ann.#9 JK(c),reprints 12.00
Ann.#10 reprints Ann.#3 . . . . . . 12.00
Ann.#11 JK(c),JB,A:The Invaders . 8.00
Ann.#12 A:The Invaders 7.00
Ann.#13 V:The Mole Man 7.00
Ann.#14 GP,V:Salem's Seven . . . 7.00
Ann.#15 GP,V:Dr.Doom,Skrulls . . 5.00
Ann.#16 V:Dragonlord 5.00
Ann.#17 JBy,V:Skrulls 5.00
Ann.#18 KGa,V:Skrulls,W:Black
  Bolt and Medusa,A:Inhumans . 5.00
Ann.#19 JBy,V:Skrulls 5.00
Ann.#20 TD(i),V:Dr.Doom 4.00
Ann.#21 JG,JSt,Evol.Wars 4.00
Ann.#22 RB,Atlantis Attacks,
  A:Avengers 4.00
Ann.#23 JG,GCa,Days of Future
  Present #1 . . . . 5.00
Ann.#24 JG,AM,Korvac Quest #1,
  A:Guardians of the Galaxy . . . 3.00
Ann.#25 Citizen Kang #3 . . . . . . 2.50
Ann.#26 HT,I:Wildstreak,
  V:Dreadface,w/card 3.25
Ann.#27 MGu,V:Justice Peace . . . 3.25
G-Size#1 RB,Thing/Hulk 15.00
G-Size#2 K&R(c),JB,Time to Kill . 9.00
G-Size#3 RB,JSt,Four Horseman . 9.00
G-Size#4 JB,JSt,I:Madrox 10.00
G-Size#5 JK(c),V:Psycho Man,
  Molecule Man 7.00
G-Size#6 V:Annihilus 7.00
Spec.#1 Rep.Ann.#1 JBy(c) 2.00
TPB Rep.#347-349 . . . . 5.95
TPB Nobody Gets Out Alive, rep.
  Fant.Four #387–#392 + new. 15.95
TPB Trial of Galactus,reprints
  #242-244,#257-262 . . . . 9.95
Milestone rep. #1 . . . . 2.95
Ashcan .75
Spec. The Origin of Galactus 2.50
  Series Three (Nov. 1996)
1 JLe,BCi,SW, 48pg 5.00
1A Mole Man cover 12.00
1B Gold signature, bagged,
  limited 38.00
2 JLe,BCi,V:Namor 3.50
3 JLe,BCi,SW,A:Avengers 3.00
4 JLe,BCi,SW,I:Black Panther . . . 2.50
4A x-mas cover 2.50
5 JLe,BCi,SW,V:Dr. Doom 2.50
6 JLe,BCi,SW,Industrial Revolution
  prologue 2.25
7 JLe,BCi,BBh,V:Blastaar 1.95
8 JLe,BCi,BBh,V:Inhumans 1.95
9 JLe,BCi,BBh,V:Inhumans 1.95
10 JLe,BCi,BBh,A:Silver Surfer,
  Tyrax 1.95
11 JLe,BCi,BBh,A:Silver Surfer,
  Firelord, Terrax 1.95
Ashcan, signed, numbered 10.00

FANTASTIC FOUR:
ATLANTIS RISING
1 B:Atlantis Rising 3.95
2 TDF,MCW,finale, acetate(c) . . . 3.95

FANTASTIC FOUR INDEX
SEE: OFFICIAL MARVEL
INDEX TO THE
FANTASTIC FOUR

FANTASTIC FOUR ROAST
1 FH/MG/FM/JB/MA/TA,May,1982 5.00

FANTASTIC FOUR 2099
1 Cont. from 2099 Genesis 3.95
2 V:Stark/Fujikawa elite guard . . 1.95
3 . . . . 1.95
4 . . . . 1.95
5 A:Spider-Man 2099 . . . . 1.95

FANTASTIC FOUR
UNLIMITED
1 HT,A:Bl.Panther,V:Klaw . . . 4.50
2 HT,JQ(c),A:Inhumans 4.25
3 HT,V:Blastaar,Annihilus 4.25
4 RTs(s),HT,V:Mole Man,A:Hulk . 4.25
5 RTs(s),HT,V:Frightful Four . . . 4.25
6 RTs(s),HT,V:Namor 3.95
7 HT,V:Monsters 3.95
8 . . . . 3.95
9 A:Antman 3.95
10 RTs,HT,V:Maelstrom,A:Eternals 3.95
11 RTs,HT,Atlantis Rising fallout . 3.95
12 RTs,TDF,V:Hyperstorm 3.95
13 . . . . 3.95

FANTASTIC FOUR
UNPLUGGED
1 comic for a buck 1.00
2 Reed Richard's Will 1.00
3 F:Mr. Fantastic 1.00
4 . . . . 1.00
5 Back in NY,V:Blastaar 1.00

FANTASTIC FOUR
VS. X-MEN
Feb., 1987
1 JBg,TA,V:Dr.Doom 5.00
2 JBg,TA,V:Dr.Doom 3.00
3 JBg,TA,V:Dr.Doom 3.00
4 JBg,TA,V:Dr.Doom, June 1987 3.00
TPB Reprints Mini-series 12.95

FANTASTIC WORLD OF
HANNA-BARBERA
Dec., 1977
1 . . . . 1.00
2 . . . . 1.00
3 June, 1978 . . . . 1.00

FANTASY MASTERPIECES
Feb., 1966
1 JK/DH/SD,reprints 45.00
2 JK,SD,DH,Fin Fang Foom . . . 25.00
3 GC,DH,JK,SD,Capt.A rep. . . . 20.00
4 JK,Capt.America rep. 20.00
5 JK,Capt.America rep. 20.00
6 JK,Capt.America rep. 20.00
7 SD,Sub Mariner rep. 20.00
8 H.Torch & Sub M.rep. 25.00
9 SD,MF,O:Human Torch Rep . 25.00
10 rep.All Winners #19 . . . . 20.00
11 JK,(rep),O:Toro 20.00
Becomes:
MARVEL SUPER-HEROES

Fantasy Masterpieces #11
© Marvel Entertainment Group

FANTASY MASTERPIECES
[Volume 2]
Dec., 1979
1 JB,JSt,Silver Surfer rep. 5.00
2 JB,JSt,Silver Surfer rep. 5.00
3 JB,JSt,Silver Surfer rep. 5.00
4 JB,JSt,Silver Surfer rep. 5.00
5 JB,JSt,Silver Surfer rep. 5.00
6 JB,JSt,Silver Surfer rep. 5.00
7 JB,JSt,Silver Surfer rep. 5.00
8 JB/JSn,Warlock rep.Strange
  Tales #178 . . . . 4.00
9 JB,JSn,rep.StrangeTales#179 . 4.00
10 JB,JSn,rep.StrangeTales#180 . 4.00
11 JB,JSn,rep.StrangeTales#181 . 4.00
12 JB,JSn,rep.Warlock #9 . . . . . . 4.00
13 JB,JSn,rep.Warlock #10 . . . . . 4.00
14 JB,JSn,rep.Warlock #11 . . . . . 4.00

FAREWELL TO WEAPONS
1 DirtBag,W/Nirvana Tape 3.50

FEAR
Nov., 1970
1 1950's Monster rep. B:I Found
  Monstrum,The Dweller
  in the Black Swamp 9.00
2 X The Thing That Lived 5.00
3 Zzutak, The Thing That
  Shouldn't Exist 5.00
4 I Turned Into a Martian 5.00
5 I Am the Gorilla Man 4.00
6 The Midnight Monster 4.00
7 I Dream of Doom 4.00
8 It Crawls By Night! 4.00
9 Dead Man's Escape 4.00
Becomes:
ADVENTURE INTO FEAR
1972
10 GM,B:Man-Thing 7.00
11 RB,I:Jennifer Kale,Thog 5.00
12 JSn,RB 5.00
13 VM,Where World's Collide . . . 3.00
14 VM,Plague o/t Demon Cult . . . 3.00
15 VM,Lord o/t Dark Domain 3.00

MARVEL

16 VM,ManThing in Everglades . . 3.00
17 VM,I:Wundarr(Aquarian) 3.00
18 VM 3.00
19 VM,FMc,I:Howard the Duck,
   E:Man-Thing 12.00
20 PG,B:Morbius 20.00
21 GK,V:Uncanny Caretaker . . . 12.00
22 RB,V:Cat-Demond 10.00
23 1st CR art,A World He
   Never Made 10.00
24 CR,V:Blade, The Vampire
   Slayer 10.00
25 You Always Kill the One
   You Love 9.00
26 V:Uncanny Caretaker 9.00
27 V:Simon Stroud 9.00
28 Doorway Down into Hell 9.00
29 Death has a Thousand Eyes . . 9.00
30 Bloody Sacrifice 9.00
31 last issue,Dec. 1975 . . . . 9.00

FEUD
Epic
1 I:Skids,Stokes,Kite 2.50
2 V:Grunts,Skide,Stockers 2.25
3 . . . . 2.25
4 . . . . 2.25

FIGHT MAN
1 I:Fight Man 2.00

FIRESTAR
March, 1986
1 MW,SL,O:Firestar,A:X-Men,
   New Mutants 4.00
2 MW,BWI,A:New Mutants 5.00
3 AAd&BSz(c),MW,SL,
   A:White Queen 3.00
4 MW,SL,V:White Queen 3.00

FISH POLICE
1 V:S.Q.U.I.D,Hook 1.25
2 V:Hook 1.25
3 V:Hook 1.25
4 V:Hook 1.25
5 V:Goldie Prawn 1.25
6 Shark Bait #1 . . . . 1.25

FLASH GORDON
1 R:Flash Gordon 2.00
2 AW,V:Ming, final issue 2.95

FLINTSTONE KIDS
Star Comics August, 1987
1 thru 10 . . . . @1.00
11 April, 1989 . . . . 1.00

FLINTSTONES
Oct., 1977–Feb. 1979
1 From TV Series 1.50
2 . . . . 1.25
3 . . . . 1.25
4 A:Jetsons 1.25
5 thru 7 . . . . @1.25

FLYING HERO BARBIE
1 Super Hero Barbie 1.50

FOOLKILLER
Oct., 1990
1 I:Kurt Gerhardt
   (Foolkiller III) 3.50

Foolkiller #4
© Marvel Entertainment Group

2 O:Foolkiller I & II 3.00
3 Old Costume 3.00
4 N:Foolkiller 2.50
5 Body Count 2.50
6 Fools Paradise 2.00
7 Who the Fools Are 2.00
8 Sane Must Inherit Earth,A:SpM 2.00
9 D:Darren Waite 2.00
10 New Identity, July 1991 . . . . 2.00

FOORFUR
Star Comics August, 1987
1 thru 6 . . . . @1.00

FORCE WORKS
1 TmT,Pop-up(c),I:Century,V:Kree,
   N:US Agent 4.75
2 TmT,V:Scatter 1.75
3 TmT,V:Scatter 1.50
4 Civil War 1.50
5 regular cover 1.50
5a Neon(c),bagged w/print 2.95
6 Hands of the Mandarin,pt.1 . . 1.50
7 Hands of the Mandarin,pt.2 . . 1.50
8 DAn,ALa,Christmas Party . . . 1.50
9 I:Dream Guard 1.50
10 V:Dream Guard 1.50
11 F:War Machine 1.50
12 V:Recorder 2.50
13 DAn,ALa,A:Avengers 1.50
14 . . . . 1.50
15 DAn,ALa,O:Century 1.50
16 . . . . 1.50
17 DAn,ALa,The Crossing 1.50
18 DAn,ALa,The Crossing 1.50
19 DAn,ALa,The Crossing 1.50
20 DAn,cont.Avengers:Timeslide . 1.50

FOR YOUR EYES ONLY
1 HC,James Bond rep. 2.00
2 HC,James Bond rep. 2.00

FRAGGLE ROCK
1 thru 8 . . . . @1.00
[Volume 2]

1 thru 5 . . . . @1.00
6 Sept., 1988 . . . . 1.00

FRANCIS, BROTHER
OF THE UNIVERSE
(one shot) 1980
1 . . . . 2.50

FRANKENSTEIN
See: MONSTER OF
FRANKENSTEIN

FRED HEMBECK
DESTROYS THE
MARVEL UNIVERSE
1 . . . . 2.00

FRIGHT
June, 1975
1 . . . . 1.50

FRONTIER WESTERN
Feb., 1956
1 RH, ... 100.00
2 AW,GT 65.00
3 MD 65.00
4 MD 40.00
5 RC 50.00
6 AW, ... 60.00
7 JR 30.00
8 RC 30.00
9 . . . . 30.00
10 August, 1957 . . . . 30.00

FUNNY FROLICS
Summer, 1945
1 (fa) 86.00
2 . . . . 46.00
3 . . . . 38.00
4 . . . . 38.00
5 HK 45.00

FURTHER ADVENTURES
OF CYCLOPS
AND PHOENIX
1 thru 4 . . . . 1.95
TPB PrM,JPL,O:Mr. Sinister, ...

FURY
1 MCW,O:Fury,A:S.A. Heroes . . . 3.25

FURY OF S.H.I.E.L.D.
1 Foil etched cover 2.50
2 A:Iron Man 1.95
3 J:Hydra 1.95
4 w/decoder card 2.50

GALACTIC GUARDIANS
1 KWe,C:Woden 1.75
2 KWe,I:Hazmat,Savant,Ganglia . 1.50
3 KWe 1.50
4 KWe,final issue 1.50

GAMBIT
1 HMe(c),LW,KJ,Embossed(c),D:Henri
   LeBeau,V:Assassin's Guild . . . 6.50
1a Gold Ed. 25.00
2 LW,KJ,C:Gideon,A:Rogue 5.00
3 LW,KJ,A:Candra,Rogue,

D:Gambit's Father 4.50
4 LW,KJ,A:Candra,Rogue,D:Tithe
  Collector 4.00
TPB Rep.#1-#4 . . . . 8.95

GAMBIT
1 (of 4) HMe,KJ,In Miami 2.50

GAMBIT AND THE X-TERNALS
1 X-Force after Xavier 3.50
2 V:Deathbird,Starjammers 2.50
3 V:Imperial Guard 2.25
4 Charles Kidnapped 2.25

GARGOYLE
June, 1985
1 BWr(c),from 'Defenders' 2.00
2 . . . . 1.50
3 . . . . 1.50
4 . . . . 1.50

GARGOYLES
1 TV Series 2.50
2 TV Series 1.50
3 F:Broadway 1.50
4 V:Statues 1.50
5 Humanoid Gargoyles 1.50
6 Medusa Project concl. 1.50
7 Demona & Triad 1.50
8 I:The Pack 1.50
9 V:Demonia,Triad 1.50
10 Demonia gains magical powers 1.50
11 Elisa turns to Xanatos 1.50
12 Sorceress traps Gargoyles . . . 1.50
13 Behind Enemy Lines 1.50
14 . . . . 1.50
15 . . . . 1.50
16 Hammer of Fear 1.50

Gene Dogs #1
© Marvel Entertainment Group

GENE DOGS
1 I:Gene DOGS,w/cards 2.75
2 V:Genetix 2.00
3 V:Hurricane 2.00
4 last issue 1.75

GENERATION NEXT
1 Generation X AX 3.50
2 Genetic Slave Pens 2.50
3 V:Sugar Man 2.25
4 V:Sugar Man 2.25

GENERATION X
1 CBa,Banshee & White Queen . 6.50
2 CBa,SLo 2.00
2a Deluxe edition 4.00
3 CBa 2.00
3a Deluxe edition 3.50
4 CBa,V:Nanny,Orphanmaker . . . 2.00
4a Deluxe edition 3.00
5 SLo,CBa,MBu,two new young
  mutants at the Academy 2.25
6 A:Wolverine 2.25
7 SLo,F:Banshee,A:White Queen 2.25
8 F:Banshee 2.00
9 SLo,TG,Chamber in a kilt 2.00
10 SLo,TG,MBu,Banshee vs.
  OmegaRed 2.00
11 SLo,TG,V:Omega Red 2.00
12 SLo,TG,V:Emplate 2.00
13 . . . . 2.00
14 . . . . 2.00
15 SLo,MBu,Synch goes psycho . 2.00
16 . . . . 2.00
17 SLo,CBa,Onslaught saga,
  X-Cutioner vs. Skin 2.00
18 SLo,CBa,Onslaught saga 2.00
19 SLo,CBa, ... 2.00
20 SLo,CBa, ... 2.00
21 SLo,CBa,MBu,F:Skin & Chamber,
  A:Beverly Switzer, Howard
  the Duck 1.95
22 SLo,CBa, ... 1.95
23 SLo,CBa,V:Black Tom Cassidy 1.95
24 SLo,MBy,F:Monet,Emplate . . . 1.95
25 SLo,CBa,double size 2.95
26 SLo,CBa,Shot down over the
  Atlantic 1.95
27 SLo,CBa,on nuclear sub. 1.95
28 SLo,CBa,No Exit prelude 1.95
29 JeR,CBa, V:Sentinels 1.95
30 JeR,CBa, V:Zero Tolerance . . . 1.95
Minus 1 Spec., JeR,CBa, flashback,
  F:Banshee 1.95

GENERATION X '95
1 SLo,J:Mondo,V:Hellfire Club . . 3.95

GENERATION X '96
GN MGo,JJ,DPs,V:Fenris 2.95

GENERIC COMIC
1 . . . . 1.50

GENETIX
1 B:ALa(s),w/cards 2.75
2 I:Tektos 2.00
3 V:Tektos 1.75
4 PGa,V:MyS-Tech 1.75
5 PGa,V:MyS-Tech 1.75
6 V:Tektos 1.95

GEORGIE COMICS
Spring, 1945
1 Georgie stories begin 120.00
2 Pet Shop (c) 55.00
3 Georgie/Judy(c) 40.00
4 Wedding Dress(c) 40.00
5 Monty/Policeman(c) 40.00

6 Classroom(c) 40.00
7 Fishing(c) 45.00
8 Soda Jerk(c) 35.00
9 Georgie/Judy(c),HK,Hey Look 45.00
10 Georgie/Girls(c),HK,Hey Look 45.00
11 Table Tennis(c),A:Margie,Millie 30.00
12 Camping(c) 30.00
13 Life Guard(c),HK,Hey Look . . 40.00
14 Classroom(c),HK,Hey Look . . 45.00
15 Winter Sports(c) 25.00
16 . . . . 25.00
17 HK,Hey Look 25.00
18 . . . . 25.00
19 Baseball(c) 25.00
20 Title change to Georgie
  & Judy Comics 25.00
21 Title change to Georgie
  & Judy Comics 20.00
22 Georgie comics 20.00
23 . . . . 20.00
24 . . . . 20.00
25 . . . . 40.00
26 . . . . 20.00
27 . . . . 20.00
28 . . . . 20.00
29 . . . . 35.00
30 thru 38 . . . . @20.00
39 Oct., 1952 . . . . 20.00

GETALONG GANG
May, 1985—March, 1986
1 thru 6 . . . . @1.00

GHOST RIDER
[1st Regular Series]
Sept., 1973
1 GK,JSt,C:Son of Satan 45.00
2 GK,I:Son of Satan,A:Witch
  Woman 15.00
3 JR,D:Big Daddy Dawson,
  new Cycle 12.00
4 GK,A:Dude Jensen 12.00
5 GK,JR,I:Roulette 12.00
6 JR,O:Ghost Rider 11.00
7 JR,A:Stunt Master 11.00
8 GK,A:Satan,I:Inferno 10.00
9 GK,TP,O:Johnny Blaze 11.00
10 JSt,A:Hulk 11.00
11 GK,KJ,SB,A:Hulk 10.00
12 GK,KJ,FR,A:Phantom Eagle . 8.00
13 GK,JS,GT,A:Trapster 8.00
14 GT,A:The Orb 8.00
15 SB,O:The Orb 8.00
16 DC,GT,Blood in the Water . . . 8.00
17 RB,FR,I:Challenger 8.00
18 RB,FR,A:Challenger,
  Spider-Man 9.00
19 GK,FR,A:Challenger 8.00
20 GK,KJ,JBy,A:Daredevil 10.00
21 A:Gladiator,D:Eel 5.00
22 AM,DH,KP,JR,A:Enforcer 5.00
23 JK,DH,DN,I:Water Wiz. 5.00
24 GK,DC,DH,A:Enforcer 5.00
25 GK,DH,A:Stunt Master 5.00
26 GK,DP,A:Dr. Druid 5.00
27 SB,DP,A:Hawkeye 5.00
28 DP,A:The Orb 5.00
29 RB,DP,A:Dormammu 5.00
30 DP,A:Dr.Strange 5.00
31 FR,DP,BL,A:Bounty Hunt. . . . 5.00
32 KP,BL,DP,A:Bounty Hunt. . . . 5.00
33 DP,I:Dark Riders 5.00
34 DP,C:Cyclops 5.00
35 JSn,AM,A:Death 6.00

MARVEL

Ghost Rider #5
© Marvel Entertainment Group

36 DP,Drug Mention 5.00
37 DP,I:Dick Varden 5.00
38 DP,A:Death Cult 5.00
39 DP,A:Death Cult 5.00
40 DP,I:Nuclear Man 5.00
41 DP,A:Jackal Gang 5.00
42 DP,A:Jackal Gang 5.00
43 CI:Crimson Mage 5.00
44 JAb,CI,A:Crimson Mage 5.00
45 DP,I:Flagg Fargo 5.00
46 DP,A:Flagg Fargo 5.00
47 AM,DP 5.00
48 BMc,DP 5.00
49 DP,I:The Manitou 5.00
50 DP,A:Night Rider 6.00
51 AM,PD,A:Cycle Gang 4.00
52 AM,DP 4.00
53 DP,I:Lord Asmodeus 4.00
54 DP,A:The Orb 4.00
55 DP,A:Werewolf By Night 4.00
56 DP,A:Moondark,I:Night Rider . 4.00
57 AM,DP,I:The Apparition 4.00
58 DP,FM,A:Water Wizard 4.00
59 V:Water Wizard,Moon Dark . . . 4.00
60 DP,HT,A:Black Juju 4.00
61 A:Arabian Knight 4.00
62 KJ,A:Arabian Knight 4.00
63 LMc,A:The Orb 4.00
64 BA,A:Azmodeus 4.00
65 A:Fowler 4.00
66 BL,A:Clothilde 4.00
67 DP,A:Sally Stantop 4.00
68 O:Ghost Rider 4.00
69 . . . . 4.00
70 I:Jeremy 4.00
71 DP,I:Adam Henderson 4.00
72 A:Circus of Crime 4.00
73 A:Circus of Crime 4.00
74 A:Centurions 4.00
75 I:Steel Wind 4.00
76 DP,A:Mephisto,I:Saturnine . . . 4.00
77 O:Ghost Rider's Dream 4.00
78 A:Nightmare 4.00
79 A:Man Cycles 4.00
80 A:Centurions 4.00

81 D:Ghost Rider 9.00
[2nd Regular Series]
1 JS,MT,I:2nd Ghost Rider,
   Deathwatch 6.00
1a 2nd printing 2.00
2 JS,MT,I:Blackout 4.00
3 JS,MT,A:Kingpin,V:Blackout,
   Deathwatch 3.50
4 JS,MT,V:Mr.Hyde 3.50
5 JLe(c),JS,MT,A:Punisher 3.50
5a rep.Gold 3.00
6 JS,MT,A:Punisher 3.50
7 MT,V:Scarecrow 3.50
8 JS,MT,V:H.E.A.R.T 3.50
9 JS,MT,A:Morlocks,X-Factor . . . 3.00
10 JS,MT,V:Zodiac 3.00
11 LSn,MT,V:Nightmare,
   A:Dr.Strange 3.00
12 JS,MT,A:Dr.Strange 3.00
13 MT,V:Snow Blind,R:J.Blaze . . 3.00
14 MT,Blaze Vs.Ghost Rider. . . . 3.00
15 MT,A:Blaze,V:Blackout
   Glow in Dark(c) 4.00
15a 2nd printing (gold) 3.00
16 MT,A:Blaze,Spider-Man,
   V:Hobgoblin 3.00
17 MT,A:Spider-Man,Blaze,
   V:Hobgoblin 3.00
18 MT,V:Reverend Styge 2.25
19 MT,A:Mephisto 2.25
20 MT(i),O:Zodiac 2.25
21 MT(i),V:Snowblind,
   A:Deathwatch 2.25
22 MT,A:Deathwatch,Ninjas 2.25
23 MT,I:Hag & Troll,A:Deathwatch 2.25
24 MT,V:Deathwatch,D:Snowblind,
   C:Johnny Blaze 2.25
25 V:Blackout (w/Center spread
   pop-up) 2.50
26 A:X-Men,V:The Brood 2.50
27 A:X-Men,V:The Brood 2.50
28 NKu,JKu,Rise of the Midnight
   Sons#1,V:Lilith,w/poster . . . 2.50
29 NKu,JKu,A:Wolverine,Beast . 2.50
30 NKu,JKu,V:Nightmare 2.25
31 NKu,JKu,Rise o/t Midnight
   Sons#6, A:Dr.Strange,Morbius,
   Nightstalkers,Redeemers,
   V:Lilith,w/poster 2.25
32 BBi,A:Dr.Strange 2.00
33 BBi,AW,V:Madcap (inc.Superman
   tribute on letters page) 2.00
34 BBi,V:Deathwatchs' ninja . . . 2.00
35 BBi,AW,A:Heart Attack 2.00
36 BBi,V:Mr.Hyde,A:Daredevil . . 2.00
37 BBi,A:Archangel,V:HeartAttack 2.00
38 MM,V:Scarecrow 2.00
39 V:Vengeance 2.00
40 Midnight Massacre#2,
   D:Demogblin 2.50
41 Road to Vengeance#1 . . . . . 2.00
42 Road to Vengeance#2 . . . . . 2.00
43 Road to Vengeance#3 . . . . . 2.00
44 Siege of Darkness,pt.#2 . . . . 2.00
45 Siege of Darkness,pt.#10 . . . 2.00
46 HMe(s),New Beginning 2.00
47 HMe(s),RG 2.00
48 HMe(s),RG,A:Spider-Man 2.00
49 HMe(s),RG,A:Hulk,w/card . . . 2.25
50 Red Foil(c),AKu,SMc,A:Blaze,
   R:2nd Ghost Rider 3.25
50a Newsstand Ed. 2.75
51 SvL 2.25
52 SvL 1.95
53 SvL,V:Blackout 1.95

54 SvL,V:Blackout 1.95
55 V:Mr. Hyde 1.95
56 The Next Wave 1.95
57 A:Wolverine 1.95
58 HMe,SvL,Betrayal,pt.1 . . . . . 1.95
59 Betrayal,pt.2 . . . . 1.95
60 Betrayal,pt.3 . . . . 1.95
61 Betrayal,pt.4 . . . . 1.95
62 EventInChains,pt.1,A:Fury . . . 1.95
63 EventInChains,pt.2 . . . . 1.95
64 EventInChains,pt.3 . . . . 1.95
65 EventInChains,pt.4,R:Blackout 1.95
66 V:Blackout 1.95
67 A:Gambit,V:Brood 1.95
68 A:Gambit,Wolverine,V:Brood . 1.95
69 Domestic Violence 1.95
70 New Home in Bronx 1.95
71 . . . . 1.95
72 . . . . 1.95
73 John Blaze is back 1.95
74 A:Blaze, Vengeance 1.95
75 . . . . 1.50
76 V:Vengeance 1.50
77 A:Dr. Strange 1.50
78 new costume, A:Dr. Strange . . 1.50
79 IV,New costume, A:Valkyrie, . 1.50
80 IV,V:Furies,Valkyrie,
   A:Black Rose 1.50
81 IV,A:Howard the Duck,
   Devil Dinosaur 1.50
82 IV,A:Devil Dinosaur, ... 1.50
83 IV,A:Scarecrow,Lilith 1.50
84 IV,A:Scarecrow, Lilith 1.95
85 IV,V:Lilith, Scarecrow 1.95
86 IV,rampage through the Bronx 1.95
87 IV,KIK,AM, ... 1.95
88 IV, V:Pao Fu,Blackheart 1.95
Ann.#1 I:Night Terror,w/card 3.25
Ann.#2 F:Scarecrow 2.95
TPB Midnight Sons,rep.GhR#28,31,
   Morbius#1,Darkhold#1,Spirirts of
   Vengeance#1,Nightstalkers#1 19.95
TPB Resurrected rep.#1-#7 . . 12.95
TPB Ghost Rider/Wolverine/Punisher:
   Dark Design 5.95
   Hearts of Darkness 4.95
Poster Book 4.95
Spec. Crossroads 3.95
Minus 1 Spec., IV,JS, flashback . . 1.95

**GHOST RIDER/BLAZE
SPIRITS OF VENGEANCE**
1 AKu,polybagged w/poster,V:Lilith,
   Rise of the Midnight Sons#2 . . 3.50
2 AKu,V:Steel Wind 2.50
3 AKu,CW,V:The Lilin 2.50
4 AKu,V:Hag & Troll,C:Venom . . 3.00
5 AKu,BR,Spirits of Venom#2,
   A:Venom,Spidey,Hobgoblin . . 5.00
6 AKu,Spirits of Venom#4,A:Venom,
   Spider-Man,Hobgoblin 3.50
7 AKu,V:Steel Vengeance 2.00
8 V:Mephisto 2.00
9 I:Brimstone 2.00
10 AKu,V:Vengeance 2.00
11 V:Human Spider Creature . . . 2.00
12 AKu,BR,Vengeance,glow in the
   dark(c) 3.25
13 AKu,Midnight Massacre#5 . . 2.50
14 Missing Link#2 . . . . 2.00
15 Missing Link#3 . . . . 2.00
16 V:Zarathos,Lilith 2.00
17 HMe(s),Siege/Darkness,pt.8 . 2.00
18 HMe(s),Siege/Darkness,pt.13 . 2.00
19 HMe(s),HMz,V:Vampire 2.00

Ghost Rider/Blaze: Spirits of Vengeance
#2 © Marvel Entertainment Group

20 HMe(s),A:Steel Wind 2.00
21 HMe(s),HMz,V:Werewolves . . . 2.00
22 HMe(s),HMz,V:Cardiac 2.25
23 HMe(s),HMz,A:Steel Wind . . . 2.25

GHOST RIDER/BALLISTIC
Marvel/Top Cow 1996
1-shot WEI,BTn,"Devil's
Reign," pt.3, x-over 2.95

GHOST RIDER/CAPTAIN
AMERICA: FEAR
1 GN, AW, V:Scarecrow 6.25

GHOST RIDER/CYBLADE
Marvel/Top Cow 1996
1-shot IV,ACh,"Devil's Reign,"
pt.2, x-over 2.95

GHOST RIDER 2099
1 Holografx(c),LKa,CBa,MBu,I:Ghost
Rider 2099,w/card 2.75
1a Newsstand Ed. 1.75
2 LKa,CBa,MBu, ... 1.75
3 LKa,CBa,MBu,I:Warewolf 1.75
4 LKa,CBa,MBu,V:Warewolf 1.75
5 LKa,CBa,MBu 1.75
6 LKa,CBa,MBu 1.75
7 LKa,CBa,MBu 1.75
8 LKa,CBa,MBu 1.75
9 . . . . 1.50
10 . . . . 1.50
11 V:Bloodsport Society 1.50
12 I:Coda 1.50
Becomes:
GHOST RIDER 2099 A.D.
13 F:Doom 1.95
14 Deputized by Doom 1.95
15 One Nation Under Doom 1.95
16 V:Max Synergy 1.95
17 . . . . 1.95
18 V:L-Cipher 1.95
19 V:L-Cipher 1.95
20 . . . . 1.95
21 V:Vengeance 2099 . . . . 1.95

22 V:Vengeance 2099 . . . . 1.95
23 . . . . 1.95
24 . . . . 1.95
25 Double size final issue 2.95

GIANT-SIZE CHILLERS
1975
1 AA, ... 4.00
2 . . . . 3.00
3 BWr,Night of the Gargoyle 4.00

GIANT-SIZE CHILLERS
1974
1 I&O:Lilith,F:Curse of Dracula . . 5.00
Becomes:
GIANT-SIZE DRACULA
2 Vengeance of the Elder Gods . 5.00
3 rep. Uncanny Tales #6 . . . . . . 4.00
4 SD,Demon of Devil's Lake 3.00
5 JBy, 1st Marvel art 6.00

G.I. JOE:
A REAL AMERICAN HERO
June, 1982
1 HT,BMc,Baxter paper 4.00
2 DP,JAb,North Pole 5.00
3 HT,JAb,Trojan Robot 2.00
4 HT,JAb,Wingfield 2.00
5 DP,Central Park 2.00
6 HT,V:Cobra 2.00
7 HT,Walls of Death 2.00
8 HT,Sea Strike 2.00
9 The Diplomat 2.00
10 Springfield 2.00
11 Alaska Pipeline 2.00
12 V:Snake Eyes 2.50
13 Rio Lindo 2.00
14 V:Destro 2.00
15 A:Red Eye 2.00
16 V:Cobra 2.00
17 Loose Ends 2.00
18 V:Destro 2.00
19 D:General Kwinn 2.00
20 JBy(c),GI,Clutch 2.00
21 SL(i),Silent Interlude 2.00
22 V:Destro 2.00
23 I:Duke 1.75
24 RH,I:Storm Shadow 2.00
25 FS,I:Zartan 2.00
26 SL(i),O:Snake Eyes 2.50
27 FS,O:Snake Eyes 2.00
28 Swampfire 2.00
29 FS,V:Destro 2.00
30 JBy(c),FS,V:Dreddnoks 2.00
31 V:Destro 1.75
32 FS,V:Dreddnoks 2.00
33 FS,Celebration 1.75
34 Shakedown 1.75
35 JBy(c),MBr,V:Dreddnoks 1.75
36 MBr,Shipwar 1.75
2a to 36a 2nd printings . . . . @1.00
37 FS,Twin Brothers,I:Flint 2.00
38 V:Destro 2.00
39 Jungle 2.00
40 Hydrofoil 2.00
41 . . . . 2.00
42 A:Stormshadow 2.00
43 Death Issue,New Joe 2.00
44 V:Cobra 2.00
45 V:Cobra 2.00
46 V:Cobra 2.00
47 V:Cobra,D:Stormshadow 2.00
48 V:Cobra 2.00

G.I. Joe #44
© Marvel Entertainment Group

49 V:Cobra,I:Serpentor 2.00
50 I:G.I.Joe Missions,R:S'shadow 2.25
51 V:Cobra Emperor 1.50
52 V:Stormshadow 1.50
53 Hawk V:Cobra 1.50
54 V:Destro 1.50
55 The Pit 1.50
56 V:Serpentor 1.50
57 V:Destro 1.50
58 V:Cobra 1.50
59 Armor 1.50
60 TM,I:Zanzibar 2.50
61 MR,D:Cobra Commander 1.25
62 Trial 1.25
63 A:GI Joe Snow Job 1.25
64 V:Baroness 1.25
65 V:Cobra 1.25
66 Stalker Rescued 1.25
67 . . . . 1.25
68 I:Battleforce 2000 . . . . 1.25
69 TSa 1.25
70 V:Destro 1.25
71 . . . . 1.25
72 . . . . 1.25
73 . . . . 1.25
74 . . . . 1.25
75 MR 1.25
76 D:Serpentor 1.25
77 MR,V:Cobra 1.25
78 V:Cobra 1.25
79 MR,V:Dreadnoks 1.25
80 V:Cobra 1.25
81 MR,V:Dreadnoks 1.00
82 MR,V:Cobra 1.00
83 I:RoadPig 1.00
84 MR,O:Zartan 1.00
85 Storm Shadow,Vs.Zartan 1.00
86 MR,25th Anniv. 1.00
87 TSa,V:Cobra 1.00
88 TSa,V:Python Patrol 1.00
89 MBr,V:Road Pig 1.00
90 MBr,R:Red Ninjas 1.00
91 TSa,V:Red Ninjas,D:Blind
Masters 1.00
92 MBr,V:Cobra Condor 1.00

MARVEL

93 MBr,V:Baroness 1.00
94 MBr,A:Snake Eyes 1.00
95 MBr,A:Snake Eyes 1.00
96 MBr,A:Snake Eyes 1.00
97 . . . . 1.00
98 MBr,R:Cobra Commander 1.00
99 HT 1.00
100 MBr 1.50
101 MBr 1.00
102 MBr 1.00
103 MBr,A:Snake Eyes 1.00
104 MBr,A:Snake Eyes 1.00
105 MBr,A:Snake Eyes 1.00
106 MBr,StormShadowStalker . . . 1.00
107 . . . . 1.00
108 I:G.I.Joe Dossiers 1.00
109 Death Issue 1.00
110 Mid-East Crisis 1.00
111 A:Team Ninjas 1.00
112 A:Team Ninjas 1.00
113 V:Cobra 1.00
114 V:Cobra 1.00
115 Story Concl.Dusty Dossier . . 1.00
116 Destro:Search&Destroy #1 . . 1.00
117 Destro:Search&Destroy #2 . . 1.00
118 Destro:Search&Destroy #3 . . 1.00
119 HT,Android Dopplegangers . . 1.00
120 V:Red Ninjas,Slice & Dice . . . 1.00
121 V:Slice & Dice 1.25
122 V:Slice & Dice 1.25
123 I:Eco-Warriors,A:Big Man . . . 1.25
124 V:Headman 1.25
125 V:Headhunters 1.25
126 R:Firefly 1.25
127 R:Original G.I.Joe 1.25
128 V:Firefly 1.25
129 V:Cobra Commander 1.25
130 V:Cobra Commander 1.25
131 V:Cobra Commander 1.25
132 V:Cobra 1.25
133 V:Cobra 1.25
134 V:Red Ninjas, Firefly,
　　Hostilities 1.25
135 V:Cobra Ninja w/card 1.75
136 w/Trading Card 1.75
137 V:Night Creepers,w/card . . . 1.75
138 V:Night Creepers,w/card 1.75
139 R:Transformers,V:Cobra . . . 1.25
140 A:Transformers 1.25
141 A:Transformers 1.25
142 A:Transformers 1.25
143 F:Scarlet 1.25
144 O:Snake Eyes 1.25
145 V:Cobra 1.25
146 F:Star Brigade 1.25
147 F:Star Brigade 1.25
148 F:Star Brigade 1.25
149 . . . . 1.25
150 Cobra Commander vs.
　　Snake Eyes 2.00
151 V:Cobra 1.50
152 First G.I. Joe 1.50
153 V:Cobra 1.50
154 . . . . 1.50
155 final issue 1.50
SC GI Joe and the Transformers . 4.95
Spec. TM rep.#61 . . . . 1.50
Ann.#1 . . . . 3.00
Ann.#2 . . . . 2.00
Ann.#3 . . . . 2.00
Ann.#4 . . . . 2.00
Ann.#5 . . . . 2.00

G.I. JOE
EUROPEAN MISSIONS
June, 1988
1 British rep. 1.25
2 . . . . 1.50
3 . . . . 1.50
4 . . . . 1.50
5 thru 15 . . . . @1.75

G.I. Joe Special Missions #9
© Marvel Entertainment Group

G.I. JOE
SPECIAL MISSIONS
Oct., 1986
1 HT,New G.I. Joe 1.75
2 HT 1.50
3 HT 1.50
4 HT 1.50
5 HT 1.50
6 HT,Iron Curtain 1.50
7 HT 1.50
8 HT 1.50
9 HT 1.50
10 thru 21 HT . . . . @1.00
22 . . . . 1.00
23 HT 1.00
24 . . . . 1.00
25 HT 1.00
26 HT 1.00
27 . . . . 1.00
28 HT,final 1.00

G.I. JOE AND
THE TRANSFORMERS
1 HT,mini-series 1.75
2 HT,Cobra 1.50
3 HT,Cobra,Deceptions 1.00
4 HT,Cobra,Deceptions 1.00

G.I. JOE UNIVERSE
1 Biographies rep.#1 . . . . 2.50
2 . . . . 2.00
3 MZ(c) 2.00
4 . . . . 1.25

G.I. JOE YEARBOOK
1 Biographies 2.50

2 MG 2.00
3 MZ(c) 2.00
4 . . . . 2.00

G.I. TALES
See: SERGEANT BARNEY
BARKER

GIRL COMICS
Atlas Nov., 1949
1 Ph(c),True love stories,I Could
　　Escape From Love 125.00
2 Ph(c),JKu,Blind Date 65.00
3 BEv,Ph(c),Liz Taylor 90.00
4 PH(c),Borrowed Love 45.00
5 Love stories 45.00
6 same 45.00
7 same 45.00
8 same 45.00
9 same 45.00
10 The Deadly Double-Cross . . . 45.00
11 Love stories 45.00
12 BK,The Dark Hallway 50.00
Becomes:
GIRL CONFESSIONS
13 . . . . 50.00
14 . . . . 30.00
15 . . . . 30.00
16 BEv 35.00
17 BEv 35.00
18 BEv 35.00
19 . . . . 25.00
20 . . . . 25.00
21 thru 34 . . . . @17.00
35 August, 1954 . . . . 17.00

GIRLS' LIFE
Atlas Jan., 1954
1 . . . . 50.00
2 . . . . 25.00
3 . . . . 20.00
4 . . . . 20.00
5 . . . . 20.00
6 November, 1954 . . . . 20.00

GLADIATOR/SUPREME
1997
1 KG,ASm,x-over 5.00

GODZILLA
August, 1977
1 HT,JM,Based on Movie Series　 8.00
2 HT,FrG,GT,Seattle Under Seige　 6.00
3 HT,TD,A;Champions 4.00
4 TS,TD,V;Batragon 4.00
5 TS,KJ,Isle of the Living
　　Demons 6.00
6 HT,A Monster Enslaved 6.00
7 V:Red Ronin 6.00
8 V:Red Ronin 6.00
9 Las Gamble in Las Vegas . . . 6.00
10 V:Yetrigar 6.00
11 V:Red Ronin,Yetrigar 4.00
12 Star Sinister 4.00
13 V:Mega-Monster 4.00
14 V:Super-Beasts 4.00
15 Stampede 4.00
16 Jaws of Fear 4.00
17 Godzilla Shrunk 4.00
18 Battle Beneath Eighth Avenue . 4.00
19 Panic on the Pier 4.00
20 A;Fantastic Four 4.50
21 V;Devil Dinosaur 4.00

22 V:Devil Dinosaur	4.00
23 A;Avengers	4.50
24 July, 1979	4.00

GOLDEN AGE OF MARVEL
TPB RyL . . . .

GREATEST SPIDER-MAN & DAREDEVIL TEAM-UPS
TPB 175pg . . . .

GREEN GOBLIN

1 I:New Green Goblin	2.95
2 TDF,SMc,V:Rhino	1.95
3 TDF,SMc,CyberWar tie-in	1.95
4 TDF,SMc,V:Hobgoblin	1.95
5 TDF,V:Hobgoblin	1.95
6	1.95
7	1.95
8 TDF,SMc,I:Angelface	1.95
9	1.95
10	1.95
11	1.95
12 Onslaught saga	1.95
13 Onslaught saga	1.95

GROO CHRONICLES
Epic 1989

1 SA	5.00
2 SA	4.00
3 SA	4.00
4 SA	4.00
5 SA	4.00
6 SA	3.50

Groo The Wanderer #18
© Marvel Entertainment Group

[SERGIO ARAGONE'S]
GROO, THE WANDERER
(see Pacific, Eclipse)
Epic

1 SA,I:Minstrel	10.00
2 SA,A:Minstrel	6.00
3 SA,Medallions	5.00
4 SA,Airship	4.00
5 SA,Slavers	4.00

6 SA,The Eye of the Kabala	4.00
7 SA,A:Sage	4.00
8 SA,A:Taranto	4.00
9 SA,A:Sage	4.00
10 SA,I:Arcadio	4.00
11 SA,A:Arcadio	4.00
12 SA,Groo Meets the Thespians	4.00
13 SA,A:Sage	4.00
14 SA	4.00
15 SA,Monks	4.00
16 SA,A:Taranto	4.00
17 SA,Pirannas	4.00
18 SA,I:Groo Ella	4.00
19 SA,A:Groo Ella	3.00
20 SA,A:Groo Ella	3.00
21 SA,I:Arba,Dakarba	3.00
22 SA,Ambassador	3.00
23 SA,I:Pal,Drumm	3.00
24 SA,Arcadio's	3.00
25 SA,Taranto	3.00
26 SA,A:Arba,Taranto	3.00
27 SA,A:Minstrel,Sage	3.00
28 SA	3.00
29 SA,I:Ruferto	4.00
30 SA,A:Ruferto	3.00
31 SA,A:Pal,Drumm	2.00
32 SA,C:Sage	2.00
33 SA,Pirates	2.00
34 SA,Wizard's amulet	2.00
35 SA,A:Everybody	2.00
36 SA,A:Everybody	2.00
37 SA,A:Ruferto	2.00
38 SA,Dognappers	2.00
39 SA,A:Pal,Drumm	2.00
40 SA	2.00
41 SA,I:Granny Groo	2.00
42 SA,A:Granny Groo	2.00
43 SA,A:Granny Groo	2.00
44 SA,A:Ruferto	2.00
45 SA	2.00
46 SA,New Clothes	2.00
47 SA,A:Everybody	2.00
48 SA,A:Ruferto	2.00
49 SA,C:Chakaal	2.00
50 SA,double size	3.00
51 SA,A:Chakaal	2.00
52 SA,A:Chakaal	2.00
53 SA,A:Chakaal	2.00
54 SA,A:Ahak	2.00
55 SA,A:Ruferto	2.00
56 SA,A:Minstrael	2.00
57 SA,A:Ruferto	2.00
58 SA,A:Idol	2.00
59 SA	2.00
60 SA,A:Ruferto	2.00
61 SA,A:Horse	2.00
62 SA,A:Horse	1.75
63 SA,A:Drumm	1.75
64 SA,A:Artist	1.75
65 SA	1.75
66 SA	1.75
67 SA	1.75
68 SA	1.75
69 SA	1.75
70 SA	1.50
71 SA	1.50
72 SA	1.50
73 SA,Amnesia,pt1	1.50
74 SA,Amnesia,pt2	1.50
75 SA,Memory Returns	1.50
76 SA	1.50
77 SA	1.50
78 SA,R:Weaver,Scribe	1.50
79 SA,Groo the Assassin	1.50
80 SA,I:Thaiis,pt.1	1.50

81 SA,Thaiis,pt.2	1.50
82 SA,Thaiis,pt.3	1.50
83 SA,Thaiis,pt.4	1.50
84 SA,Thaiis Conclusion	1.50
85 SA,Groo turns invisible	1.50
86 SA,Invisible Groo	1.50
87 SA,Groo's Army	1.50
88 SA,V:Cattlemen,B.U. Sage	2.50
89 SA,New Deluxe Format	2.25
90 SA,Worlds 1st Lawyers	2.25
91 SA,Bonus Pages	2.25
92 SA,Groo Becomes Kid Groo	2.25
93 SA,Groo destroys glacier	2.25
94 SA	2.25
95 SA,Endangered Species	2.25
96 SA,Wager of the Gods#1	2.25
97 SA,Wager of the Gods#2	2.25
98 SA,Wager of the Gods#3	2.25
99 SA,E:Wager of the Gods	2.25
100 SA,Groo gets extra IQ points	2.75
101 SA,Groo loses intelligence	2.25
102 SA,F:Newly literate Groo	2.25
103 SA,General Monk	2.25
104 SA,F:Oso,Ruferto	2.25
105 SA,V:Minotaurs	2.25
106 SA,B:Man of the People	2.25
107 SA,Man of the People#2	2.25
108 SA,Man of the People#3	2.25
109 SA,E:Man of the People	2.25
110 SA,Mummies	2.25
111 SA,The Man who Killed Groo	2.25
112 SA,Rufferto Avenged	2.25
113 SA	2.25
114 SA,V:Vultures	2.25
115 SA	2.25
116 SA,Early unto Morning	2.25
117 SA	2.25
118 SA	2.25
119 SA	2.25
120 Groo hangs up swords	2.25
GNv Death of Groo	8.00
GNv 2nd print	8.00
TPB Groo Adventures	8.95
TPB Groo Carnival	8.95
TPB Groo Expose	8.95
TPB GRoo Festival	8.95
TPB Groo Garden	10.95

GROOVY
March, 1968—July, 1968

1 Monkeys,Ringo Starr,Photos	50.00
2 Cartoons,Gags,Jokes	40.00
3	40.00

GUARDIANS OF THE GALAXY
June, 1990

1 B:JV(a&s),I:Taserface,R:Aleta	4.00
2 MZ(c),JV,V:Stark,C:Firelord	3.00
3 JV,V:Stark,I:Force,C:Firelord	3.00
4 JV,V:Stark,A:Force,Firelord	3.00
5 JV,TM(c),V:Force,I:Mainframe (Vision)	3.00
6 JV,V:Force,Vance Possesses Capt.America Shield	3.00
7 GP(c),JV,I:Malevolence, O:Starhawk	3.50
8 SLi(c),JV,V:Yondu,C:Rancor	3.50
9 RLd(c),JV,I:Replica,Rancor	3.50
10 JLe(c),JV,V:Rancor,The Nine I&C:Overkill(Taserface)	3.50
11 BWi(c),JV,V:Rancor,I:Phoenix	3.50
12 ATb(c),JV,V:Overkill A:Firelord	2.50

Guardians of the Galaxy #1
© Marvel Entertainment Group

13 JV,A:Ghost Rider,Force,
　Malevolence 3.00
14 JS(c),JV,A:Ghost Rider,Force,
　Malevolence 3.00
15 JSn(c),JV,I:Protege,V:Force . . 2.50
16 JV,V:Force,A:Protege,
　Malevolence,L:Vance Astro . . . 2.50
17 JV,V:Punishers(Street Army),
　L:Martinex,N:Charlie-27, ... 2.50
18 JV,V:Punishers,I&C:Talon,A:
　Crazy Nate 3.00
19 JV,V:Punishers,A:Talon 2.50
20 JV,I:Major Victory (Vance Astro)
　J:Talon & Krugarr 2.50
21 JV,V:Rancor 2.50
22 JV,V:Rancor 2.50
23 MT,V:Rancor,C:Silver Surfer . . 2.50
24 JV,A:Silver Surfer 3.00
25 JV, Prismatic Foil(c)
　V:Galactus,A:SilverSurfer 3.50
25a 2nd printing,Silver 2.50
26 JV,O:Guardians (retold) 2.00
27 JV,Infinity War,O:Talon,
　A:Inhumans 2.00
28 JV,Inf.War,V:Various Villians . . 2.00
29 HT,Inf.War,V:Various Villians . 2.00
30 KWe,A:Captain America 2.00
31 KWe,V:Badoon,A:Capt.A. 1.75
32 KWe,V:Badoon Gladiator 1.75
33 KWe,A:Dr.Strange,R:Aleta . . . 1.50
34 KWe,J:Yellowjacket II 1.50
35 KWe,A:Galatic Guardians,
　V:Bubonicus 1.50
36 KWe,A:Galatic Guardians,
　V:Dormammu 1.50
37 KWe,V:Dormammu,A:Galatic
　Guardians 1.50
38 KWe,N:Y.jacket,A:Beyonder . . 1.50
39 KWe,Rancor Vs. Dr.Doom,Holo-
　grafx(c) 3.25
40 KWe,V:Loki,Composite 1.50
41 KWe,V:Loki,A:Thor 1.50
42 KWe,I:Woden 1.50
43 KWe,A:Woden,V:Loki 1.50
44 KWe,R:Yondu 1.50
45 KWe,O:Starhawk 1.50
46 KWe,N:Major Victory 1.50
47 KWe,A:Beyonder,Protoge,

Overkill 1.50
48 KWe,V:Overkill 1.75
49 KWe,A:Celestial 1.75
50 Foil(c),R:Yondu,Starhawk sep-
　arated,BU:O:Guardians 3.25
51 KWe,A:Irish Wolfhound 1.50
52 KWe,A:Drax 1.50
53 KWe,V:Drax 1.50
54 KWe,V:Sentinels 1.50
55 KWe,Ripjack 1.50
56 Ripjack 1.50
57 R:Keeper 1.50
58 . . . . 1.50
59 A:Keeper 1.50
60 F:Starhawk 1.50
61 F:Starhawk 1.50
62 Guardians Stop War of the Worlds
　last issue 1.50
Ann.#1 Korvac Quest #4,I:Krugarr 3.00
Ann.#2 HT,I:Galactic Guardians,
　System Bytes #4 . . . . 3.00
Ann.#3 CDo,I:Irish Wolfhound,
　w/Trading card 3.25
Ann.#4 V:Nine 3.25
TPB rep #1 thru #6 . . . . 12.95

GUNHAWK, THE
See: BLAZE CARSON

GUNHAWKS
Oct., 1972
1 SSh,B:Reno Jones & Kid
　Cassidy Two Rode Together . . 4.00
2 Ride out for Revenge 2.75
3 Indian Massacre 2.75
4 Trial by Ordeal 2.75
5 The Reverend Mr. Graves 2.75
6 E:Reno Jones & Kid Cassidy
　D:Kid Cassidy 2.75
7 A Gunhawks Last Stand
　A;Reno Jones, Oct., 1973 . . . 2.75

GUNRUNNER
1 I:Gunrunner,w/trading cards . . . 2.95
2 A:Ghost Rider 2.00
3 V:Cynodd 2.00
4 . . . . 2.00
5 A:Enhanced 2.00
6 final issue 1.75

GUNSLINGER
See: TEX DAWSON,
GUNSLINGER

GUNSMOKE WESTERN
See: ALL WINNERS COMICS

HARROWERS
1 MSt(s),GC,F:Pinhead 3.25
2 GC,AW(i), ... 2.75
3 GC,AW(i), ... 2.75
4 GC,AW(i), ... 2.75
5 GC,AW(i),Devil's Pawn#1 . . . . 2.75
6 GC,AW(i),Devil's Pawn#2 . . . . 2.75

HARVEY
Oct., 1970
1 . . . . 6.00
2 thru 5 . . . . @4.00
6 Dec., 1972 . . . . 4.00

HARVEY PRESENTS:
CASPER
1 . . . . 1.50

HAVOK & WOLVERINE
Epic March, 1988
1 JMu,KW,V:KGB,Dr.Neutron . . . 5.00
2 JMu,KW,V:KGB,Dr.Neutron . . . 4.00
3 JMu,KW,V:Meltdown 4.00
4 JMu,KW,V:Meltdown,Oct.1989 . 4.00
TPB rep.#1-4 . . . . 16.95

HAWKEYE
Sept., 1983
[1st Limited Series]
1 A:Mockingbird 3.00
2 I:Silencer 2.50
3 I:Bombshell,Oddball 2.00
4 V:Crossfire,W:Hawkeye &
　Mockingbird, (Dec. 1983) 2.00
[2nd Limited Series]
1 B:CDi(s),ScK,V:Trickshot,
　I:Javelynn,Rover 2.00
2 ScK,V:Viper 2.00
3 ScK,A:War Machine,N:Hawkeye,
　V:Secret Empire 2.00
4 E:CDi(s),ScK,V:Trickshot,Viper,
　Javelynn 2.00

HEADMASTERS
STAR July, 1987
1 FS,Transformers 1.25
2 and 3 . . . . @1.00
4 Jan., 1988 75

HEARTS OF DARKNESS
One Shot JR2/KJ,F:Ghost Rider,
　Punisher,Wolverine,V:Blackheart,
　(double Gatefold Cover) 5.50

HEATHCLIFF
Star April, 1985
1 thru 16 . . . . @1.00
17 Masked Moocher 1.00
18 thru 49 . . . . @1.00
50 Double-size 1.00
51 thru 55 . . . . @1.00

HEATHCLIFF'S
FUNHOUSE
Star May, 1987
1 thru 9 . . . . @1.00
10 1988 . . . . 1.00

HEAVY HITTERS
Ann.#1 . . . . 4.00

HEDY DEVINE COMICS
Aug., 1947—Sept., 1952
22 I:Hedy Devine 70.00
23 BW,Beauty and the Beach,
　HK,Hey Look 75.00
24 High Jinx in Hollywood,
　HK, Hey Look 75.00
25 Hedy/Bull(c),HK,Hey Look . . . 80.00
26 Skating(c),HK,Giggles&Grins . 60.00
27 Hedy at Show(c),HK,Hey Look 70.00
28 Hedy/Charlie(c),HK,Hey Look . 70.00
29 Tennis(c),HK,Hey Look 70.00
30 . . . . 70.00
31 thru 34 . . . . @40.00

35 thru 50 . . . . @40.00

HEDY WOLFE
Atlas August, 1957
1 Patsy Walker's Rival 40.00

HELLHOUND
1 Hellhound on my Trial 2.50
2 Love in Vain 2.50
3 Last Fair Deal Gone Down . . . 2.25

HELLRAISER
**See: CLIVE BARKER'S
HELLRAISER**

HELLRAISER III
HELL ON EARTH
1 Movie Adaptation,(prestige) . . 4.95
1a Movie Adapt.(magazine) 2.95

HELLSTORM,
PRINCE OF LIES
1993
1 R:Daimon Hellstrom,
  Parchment(c) 3.50
2 A:Dr.Strange,Gargoyle 3.00
3 O:Hellstorm. 2.75
4 V:Ghost Rider 2.75
5 MB, ... 2.50
6 MB,V:Dead Daughter 2.50
7 A:Armaziel 2.50
8 Hell is where the heart is 2.25
9 LKa(s),Highway to Heaven . . . 2.25
10 LKa(s),Heaven's Gate 2.25
11 LKa(s),PrG,Life in Hell 2.25
12 Red Miracles 2.25
13 Red Miracles Sidewalking 2.25
14 Red Miracles Murder is Easy . 2.25
15 Cigarette Dawn 2.75
16 Down Here 2.25
17 The Saint of the Pit 2.00
18 . . . . 2.00
19 . . . . 2.00
20 . . . . 2.00
21 final issue 2.00

HELL'S ANGEL
1 GSr,A:X-Men,O:Hell's Angel . . 3.00
2 GSr,A:X-Men,V:Psycho Warriors 2.50
3 GSr,A:X-Men,V:MyS-Tech 2.00
4 GSr,A:X-Men,V:MyS-Tech 2.00
5 GSr,A:X-Men,V:MyS-Tech 2.00
6 Gfr,A:X-Men,V:MyS-Tech 2.00
7 DMn,A:Psylocke,V:MyS-Tech . . 2.00
Becomes:

DARK ANGEL
8 DMn,A:Psylocke 2.00
9 A:Punisher 2.00
10 MyS-Tech Wars tie-in 2.00
11 A:X-Men,MyS-Tech wars tie-in 2.00
12 A:X-Men 2.00
13 A:X-Men,Death's Head II 2.00
14 Aftermath#2 . . . . 1.75
15 Aftermath#3 . . . . 1.75
16 SvL,E:Aftermath,last issue . . 1.75

HERCULES AND THE
HEART OF CHAOS
Limited Series Aug., 1997
1 (of 3) TDF,RF,PO, ... 2.50
2 TDF,RF,PO, ... 2.50

HERCULES PRINCE
OF POWER
Sept., 1982
1 BL,I:Recorder 3.00
2 BL,I:Layana Sweetwater 2.00
3 BL,V:The Brothers,C:Galactus . 2.00
4 BL,A:Galactus 2.00
[2nd Series]
March, 1984
1 BL,I:Skyypi 2.50
2 BL,A:Red Wolf 1.50
3 BL,A:Starfox 1.50
4 BL,D:Zeus, June, 1984 . . . . . 1.50
TPB BL rep. Vol.1 #1–#4 and
  Vol.2 #1–#4 . . . .

HERO
May, 1990
1 . . . . 2.50
2 . . . . 2.00
3 . . . . 1.50
4 RH 1.50
5 RH 1.50
6 Oct., 1990 . . . . 1.50

Hero For Hire #2
© Marvel Entertainment Group

HERO FOR HIRE
June, 1972
1 GT,JR,I&O:Power Man 30.00
2 GT,A:Diamond Back 13.00
3 GT,I:Mace 11.00
4 V:Phantom of 42nd St. 11.00
5 GT,A:Black Mariah 11.00
6 V:Assassin 7.00
7 GT,Nuclear Bomb issue 7.00
8 GT,A:Dr.Doom 7.00
9 GT,A:Dr.Doom,Fant.Four 7.00
10 GT,A:Dr.Death,Fant.Four . . . 7.00
11 GT,A:Dr.Death 6.00
12 GT,C:Spider-Man 6.00
13 A:Lion Fang 6.00
14 V:Big Ben 6.00
15 Cage Goes Wild 6.00
16 O:Stilletto,D:Rackham 6.00
Becomes: POWER MAN

HEROES FOR HIRE
July, 1997
1 JOs,PFe,F:Iron Fist 1.99
2 JOs,PFe,V:Nitro 1.99
2A Variant PFe cover 1.99
3 JOs,PFe,V:Nitro 1.99

HEROES FOR HOPE
1 TA/JBy/HC/RCo/BWr,A:XMen . 7.00

HEROES REBORN
Marvel/Wizard 1996
½ prequel 7.50

HOKUM & HEX
Razorline
1 BU:Saint Sinner 2.75
2 I:Analyzer 2.00
3 I:Wrath 2.00
4 I:Z-Man 2.00
5 V:Hyperkind 2.00
6 B:Bloodshed 2.00
7 V:Bloodshed 2.00
8 V:Bloodshed 2.00
9 E:Bloodshed,final issue 2.25

HOLIDAY COMICS
Jan., 1951
1 LbC(c),Christmas(c) 145.00
2 LbC(c),Easter Parade(c) . . . 150.00
3 LbC(c),4th of July(c) 100.00
4 LbC(c),Summer Vacation 75.00
5 LbC(c),Christmas(c) 80.00
6 LbC(c),Birthday(c) 90.00
7 LbC(c),Rodeo (c) 75.00
8 LbC(c),Christmas(c)
  Oct., 1952 . . . . 75.00

HOLLYWOOD
SUPERSTARS
Epic Nov., 1990
1 DSp 2.00
2 thru 5 DSp, March, 1991 . . . @2.25

HOMER, THE HAPPY
GHOST
March, 1955
1 . . . . 45.00
2 . . . . 25.00
3 . . . . 16.00
4 thru 15 . . . . @16.00
16 thru 22 . . . . @14.00
[2nd Series]
Nov., 1969
1 . . . . 8.00
2 thru 5 . . . . @7.50

HOOK
1 JRy,GM,movie adaption 1.00
2 JRy,Return to Never Land 1.00
3 Peter Pans Magic 1.00
4 conclusion 1.00
Hook Super Spec.#1 . . . . 2.95

HORRORS, THE
Jan., 1953—April, 1954
11 LbC(c),The Spirit of War . . . 150.00
12 LbC(c),Under Fire 100.00
13 LbC(c),Terror Castle 100.00
14 LbC(c),Underworld Terror . . 100.00
15 LbC(c),The Mad Bandit 100.00

MARVEL

All comics prices listed are for *Near Mint* condition.

HOT SHOTS
AVENGERS
1 Painted Pin-ups 2.95
SPIDER-MAN
1 Painted pin-ups 2.95
X-MEN
1 Painted pin-ups 2.95

HOUSE II
1 1987, Movie Adapt. 2.00

HOWARD THE DUCK
Jan., 1976
1 FB,SL,A:Spider-Man,I:Beverly . 7.00
2 FB,V:TurnipMan&Kidney Lady . 2.00
3 JB,Learns Quack Fu 1.50
4 GC,V:Winky Man 1.50
5 GC,Becomes Wrestler 1.50
6 GC,V:Gingerbread Man 1.50
7 GC,V:Gingerbread Man 1.50
8 GC,A:Dr.Strange,ran for Pres. . 1.50
9 GC,V:Le Beaver 1.25
10 GC,A:Spider-Man 2.00
11 GC,V:Kidney Lady 1.25
12 GC,I:Kiss 4.00
13 GC,A:Kiss 4.00
14 GC,Howard as Son of Satan . . 2.00
15 GC,A:Dr.Strange,A:Dr.Bong . . 1.25
16 GC,DC,JB,DG,TA,
       V:Incredible Creator 1.25
17 GC,D:Dr.Bong 1.25
18 GC,Howard the Human #1 . . . 1.25
19 GC,Howard the Human #2 . . . 1.25
20 GC,V:Sudd 1.25
21 GC,V:Soofi 1.25
22 A:ManThing,StarWars Parody . 1.25
23 A:ManThing,StarWars Parody . 1.25
24 GC,NightAfter..SavedUniverse 1.25
25 GC,V:Circus of Crime 1.25
26 GC,V:Circus of Crime 1.25
27 GC,V:Circus of Crime 1.25
28 GC,Cooking With Gas 1.25
29 Duck-Itis Poster Child 1978 . . 1.25
30 Iron Duck,V:Dr. Bong 1.25
31 Iron Duck,V:Dr. Bong 1.25
32 V:Gopher 1.25
33 BB(c),The Material Duck 1.25
Ann.#1, V:Caliph of Bagmom . . . 1.25
Holiday Spec. LHa,ATi,PFe (1996) .

HOWARD THE DUCK MAGAZINE
Oct., 1979
(black & white)
1 . . . . 2.50
2 . . . . 1.50
3 . . . . 1.50
4 Beatles,Elvis,Kiss 5.00
5 . . . . 1.50
6 . . . . 1.50
7 . . . . 2.00
8 . . . . 1.50
9 March, 1981 . . . . 1.50

HUGGA BUNCH
Star Oct., 1986—Aug., 1987
1 . . . . 1.25
2 thru 6 . . . . @1.00

HULK 2099
1 GJ,Foil(c),V:Draco 2.50
2 GJ,V:Draco 1.50

3 I:Golden Boy 1.50
4 . . . . 1.50
5 Ultra Hulk 1.50
Becomes:

HULK 2099 A.D.
6 Gamma Ray Scientist 1.50
7 A:Doom,Dr.Apollo 1.95
8 One Nation Under Doom 1.95
9 California Quake 1.95

HUMAN FLY
July, 1987
1 I&O:Human Fly,A:Spider-Man . 5.00
2 A:Ghost Rider 7.50
3 DC,JSt(c),DP,'Fortress of Fear' 1.75
4 JB/TA(c),'David Drier' 1.75
5 V:Makik 1.75
6 Fear in Funland 1.75
7 ME,Fury in the Wind 1.75
8 V:White Tiger 1.75
9 JB/TA(c),ME,V:Copperhead,A:
       White Tiger,Daredevil 1.75
10 ME,Dark as a Dungeon 1.75
11 ME,A:Daredevil 1.75
12 ME,Suicide Sky-Dive 1.75
13 BLb/BMc(c),FS,V:Carl Braden . 1.75
14 BLb/BMc(c),SL,Fear Over
       Fifth Avenue 1.75
15 BLb/BMc(c),War in the
       Washington Monument 1.75
16 BLb/BMc(c),V:Blaze Kendall . . 1.75
17 BLb,DP,Murder on the Midway 1.75
18 V:Harmony Whyte 1.75
19 BL(c),V:Jacopo Belbo
       March, 1979 . . . . 1.75

RED RAVEN COMICS
Timely Comics August, 1940
1 JK,O:Red Raven,I:Magar,A:Comet
       Pierce & Mercury,Human Top,
       Eternal Brain 11,000.00
Becomes:

HUMAN TORCH
Fall, 1940
2 (#1)ASh(c),BEv,B:Sub-Mariner
    A:Fiery Mask,Falcon,Mantor,
    Microman 20,000.00
3 (#2)Ash(c),BEv,V:Sub-
    Mariner,Bondage(c) 4,500.00
4 (#3)ASh(c),BEv,O:Patriot . . 3,500.00
5 (#4)V:Nazis,A:Patriot,Angel
    crossover 2,500.00
5a(#5)ASh(c),V:Sub-Mariner . 3,500.00
6 ASh(c),Doom Dungeon . . . 1,500.00
7 ASh(c),V:Japanese 1,600.00
8 ASh(c),BW,V:Sub-Mariner . 2,500.00
9 ASh(c),V:General Rommel . 1,500.00
10 ASh(c),BW,V:Sub-Mariner . 2,000.00
11 ASh(c),Nazi Oil Refinery . . 1,200.00
12 ASh(c),V:Japanese.
       Bondage(c) 1,600.00
13 ASh(c),V:Japanese,
       Bondage(c) 1,300.00
14 ASh(c),V:Nazis 1,300.00
15 ASh(c),Toro Trapped 1,300.00
16 ASh(c),V:Japanese 850.00
17 ASh(c),V:Japanese 850.00
18 ASh(c),V:Japanese,
       MacArthurs HQ 850.00
19 ASh(c),Bondage(c) 850.00
20 ASh(c),Last War Issue 850.00
21 ASh(c),V:Organized Crime . 850.00
22 ASh(c),V:Smugglers 850.00

23 ASh(c),V:Giant Robot 850.00
24 V:Mobsters 850.00
25 The Masked Monster 850.00
26 Her Diary of Terror 850.00
27 SSh(c),BEv,V:The Asbestos
       Lady 850.00
28 BEv,The Twins Who Weren't 850.00
29 You'll Die Laughing 850.00
30 BEv,The Stranger,A:Namora 800.00
31 A:Namora 650.00
32 A:Sungirl,Namora 650.00
33 Capt.America crossover . . . 700.00
34 The Flat of the Land 650.00
35 A:Captain America,Sungirl . 700.00
36 A:Submariner 650.00
37 BEv,A:Submariner 650.00
38 BEv,A:Submariner,
       Final Issue,August, 1954 . . 650.00

HUMAN TORCH
Sept., 1974
1 JK,rep.StrangeTales #101 . . . . 6.00
2 rep.Strange Tales #102 . . . . . . 4.00
3 rep.Strange Tales #103 . . . . . . 4.00
4 rep.Strange Tales #104 . . . . . . 4.00
5 rep.Strange Tales #105 . . . . . . 4.00
6 rep.Strange Tales #106 . . . . . . 4.00
7 rep.Strange Tales #107 . . . . . . 4.00
8 rep.Strange Tales #108 . . . . . . 4.00

Hyperkind #7
© Marvel Entertainment Group

HYPERKIND
Razorline
1 I:Hyperkind,BU:EctoKid 2.75
2 I:Bliss 2.00
3 V:Living Void 2.00
4 FBk(s),I:Paragon John 2.00
5 V:Paragon John 2.00
6 Vetus Unleashed 2.00
7 Ambertrance 2.00
8 I:Tempest 2.00
9 I:Lazurex,w/card 2.25

HYPERKIND UNLEASHED
1 BU,V:Thermakk 2.95

MARVEL

Iceman #1
© Marvel Entertainment Group

ICEMAN
Dec., 1984

1 DP,mini-series	2.00
2 DP,V:Kali	1.50
3 DP,A;Original X-Men,Defenders Champions	1.50
4 DP,Oblivion,June, 1985	1.50

IDEAL
Timely July, 1948

1 Antony and Cleopatra	225.00
2 The Corpses of Dr.Sacotti .	200.00
3 Joan of Arc	175.00
4 Richard the Lionhearted A:The Witness	300.00
5 Phc,Love and Romance	125.00

Becomes:

LOVE ROMANCES

6 Phc,I Loved a Scoundrel . . .	40.00
7	30.00
8	35.00
9 thru 20 . . . . @20.00
21	35.00
22	20.00
23	20.00
24	35.00
25	35.00
26 thru 34 . . . . @18.00
35	18.00
36	30.00
37	18.00
38	30.00
39	18.00
40 thru 44 . . . . @16.00
45	19.00
46	15.00
47	15.00
48	10.00
49	29.00
50	10.00
51	10.00
52	10.00
53	29.00
54	10.00
55	10.00
56	10.00
57	19.00

58 thru 74 . . . . @10.00
75	18.00
76	10.00
77	10.00
78	18.00
79	10.00
80	10.00
81	10.00
82 JK(c)	18.00
83	10.00
84 JK	20.00
85	23.00
86 thru 95 . . . . @8.00
96 JK	18.00
97	10.00
98 JK	30.00
99 JK	18.00
100	10.00
101	10.00
102	10.00
103	10.00
104	10.00
105 JK	18.00
106 JKJuly, 1963	18.00

IDEAL COMICS
Timely Fall, 1944

1 B:Super Rabbit,Giant Super Rabbit V:Axis(c)	125.00
2 Super Rabbit at Fair(c)	75.00
3 Beach Party(c)	65.00
4 How to Catch Robbers	65.00

Becomes:

WILLIE COMICS

5 B:Willie,George,Margie,Nellie Football(c)	60.00
6 Record Player(c)	30.00
7 Soda Fountain(c),HK,Hey Look	42.00
8 Fancy Dress(c)	30.00
9	30.00
10 HK,Hey Look	40.00
11 HK,Hey Look	40.00
12	25.00
13	35.00
14 thru 18 . . . . @24.00
19	35.00
20 Li'L Willie Comics	24.00
21 Li'L Willie Comics	24.00
22	24.00
23 May, 1950	24.00

IDOL
Epic

1 I:Idol	2.95
2 Phantom o/t Set	2.95
3 Conclusion	2.95

ILLUMINATOR
1993

1	5.00
2	5.00
3	3.00
4	3.00

IMMORTALIS

1 A:Dr.Strange	1.95
2 A:Dr.Strange	1.95
3 A:Dr.Strange,V:Vampires . . .	1.95
4 Mephisto, final issue	1.75

IMPERIAL GUARD
[Limited Series] 1997

1 (of 3) BAu,Woj, ...	2.00

2 and 3 BAu,Woj . . . . @2.00

IMPOSSIBLE MAN SUMMER VACATION

1 GCa,DP	2.50
2	2.00
Summer Fun Spec. TPe, Vacation on Earth	2.50

INCAL, THE
Epic Nov., 1988

1 Moebius,Adult	2.50
2 Moebius,Adult	2.00
3 Moebius,Adult, Jan., 1989 . .	2.00

INCOMPLETE DEATH'S HEAD

1 thru 10 rep.Death's Head #1 thru #10 . . . . @2.00
11 rep.Death's Head #11	1.75

INCREDIBLE HULK
May, 1962

1 JK,I:Hulk(Grey Skin),Rick Jones, Thunderbolt Ross,Betty Ross, Gremlin,Gamma Base . .	11,000.00
2 JK,SD,O:Hulk,(Green skin)	2,500.00
3 JK,O:rtd.,I:Ring Master, Circus of Crime	1,600.00
4 JK,V:Mongu	1,400.00
5 JK,I:General Fang	1,400.00
6 SD,I:Metal Master	2,000.00

See: Tales to Astonish #59–#101
April, 1968

102 MSe,GT,O:Retold	185.00
103 MSe,I:Space Parasite	90.00
104 MSe,O&N:Rhino	75.00
105 MSe,GT,I:Missing Link	55.00
106 MSe,HT,GT	50.00
107 HT,V:Mandarin	50.00
108 HT,JMe,A:Nick Fury	50.00
109 HT,JMe,A:Ka-Zar	50.00
110 HT,JMe,A:Ka-Zar	50.00
111 HT,DA,I:Galaxy Master . . .	30.00
112 HT,DA,O:Galaxy Master . . .	30.00
113 HT,DA,V:Sandman	30.00
114 HT,DA	30.00
115 HT,DA,A:Leader	30.00
116 HT,DA,V:Super Humanoid .	30.00
117 HT,DA,A:Leader	30.00
118 HT,V:Sub-Mariner	30.00
119 HT,V:Maximus	18.00
120 HT,V:Maximus	16.00
121 HT,I:The Glob	18.00
122 HT,V:Thing	30.00
123 HT,V:Leader	18.00
124 HT,SB,V:Rhino,Leader	18.00
125 HT,V:Absorbing Man	18.00
126 HT,A:Dr.Strange	18.00
127 HT,Moleman vs.Tyrannus I:Mogol	12.00
128 HT,A:Avengers	12.00
129 HT,V:Glob	12.00
130 HT,Banner Vs Hulk	12.00
131 HT,A:Iron Man	10.00
132 HT,JSe,V:Hydra	10.00
133 HT,JSe,I:Draxon	10.00
134 HT,SB,I:Golem	10.00
135 HT,SB,V:Kang	10.00
136 HT,SB,I:Xeron	10.00
137 HT,V:Abomination	10.00
138 HT,V:Sandman	10.00
139 HT,V:Leader	10.00

MARVEL

All comics prices listed are for *Near Mint* condition.

Incredible Hulk #107
© Marvel Entertainment Group

140 HT,V:Psyklop 10.00
141 HT,JSe,I&O:Doc Samson . . 11.00
142 HT,JSe,V:Valkyrie,A:Doc
   Samson 7.50
143 DA,JSe,V:Dr.Doom 7.50
144 DA,JSe,V:Dr.Doom 7.50
145 HT,JSe,O:Retold 9.00
146 HT,JSe,Leader 7.00
147 HT,JSe,Doc Samson loses
   Powers 7.00
148 HT,JSe,I:Fialan 7.00
149 HT,JSe,I:Inheritor 7.00
150 HT,JSe,I:Viking,A:Havoc . . . 10.00
151 HT,JSe,C:Ant Man 7.00
152 HT,DA,Many Cameos 7.00
153 HT,JSe,C:Capt.America . . . 7.00
154 HT,JSe,A:Ant Man,
   V:Chameleon 7.00
155 HT,JSe,I:Shaper of Worlds . 7.00
156 HT,V:Hulk 7.00
157 HT,I:Omnivac,Rhino 7.00
158 HT,C:Warlock,V:Rhino 7.00
159 HT,V:Abomination,Rhino . . . 7.00
160 HT,V:Tiger Shark 6.00
161 HT,V:Beast 8.00
162 HT,I:Wendigo I 9.50
163 HT,I:Gremlin 6.00
164 HT,I:Capt.Omen 6.00
165 HT,I:Aquon 6.00
166 HT,I:Zzzax 6.00
167 HT,JAb,V:Modok 6.00
168 HT,JAb,I:Harpy 6.00
169 HT,JAb,I:Bi-Beast 6.00
170 HT,JAb,V:Volcano 6.00
171 HT,JAb,A:Abomination,Rhino 6.00
172 HT,JAb,X:X-Men 10.00
173 HT,V:Cobolt Man 6.00
174 HT,V:Cobolt Man 6.00
175 JAb,V:Inhumans 6.00
176 HT,JAb,A:Man-Beast,C:Warlock
   Crisis on Counter-Earth 14.00
177 HT,JAb,D:Warlock 15.00
178 HT,JAb,Warlock Lives 15.00
179 HT,JAb, ... 6.00
180 HT,JAb,I:Wolverine
   V:Wendigo I 110.00
181 HT,JAb,A:Wolverine (1st
   Full Story),V:Wendigo II . . . 425.00

182 HT,JAb,I&D:Crackajack
   Jackson,C:Wolverine 65.00
183 HT,V:Zzzaz 5.00
184 HT,V:Living Shadow 5.00
185 HT,V:General Ross 5.00
186 HT,I:Devastator 5.00
187 HT,JSt,V:Gremlin 5.00
188 HT,JSt,I:Droog 5.00
189 HT,JSt,I:Datrine 5.00
190 HT,MSe,Toadman 5.00
191 HT,JSt,Toadman,I:Glorian . . . 5.00
192 HT,V:The Lurker 5.00
193 HT,JSt,Doc.Samson regains
   Powers 5.00
194 SB,JSt,V:Locust 5.00
195 SB,JSt,V:Abomination 5.00
196 SB,JSt,V:Army 5.00
197 BWr(c),SB,JSt,A:Man-Thing . 5.00
198 SB,JSt,A:Man-Thing 5.00
199 SB,JSt,V:Shield,Doc Samson 5.00
200 SB,JSt,Multi,Hulk in Glenn
   Talbots Brain 33.00
201 SB,JSt,V:Fake Conan 4.00
202 SB,JSt,A:Jarella 4.00
203 SB,JSt,A:Jarella 4.00
204 SB,JStI:Kronus 4.00
205 SB,JSt,D:Jarella 4.00
206 SB,JSt,C:Dr.Strange 4.00
207 SB,JSt,A:Dr.Strange 4.00
208 SB,JSt,V:Absorbing Man . . . 4.00
209 SB,JSt,V:Absorbing Man . . . 4.00
210 SB,A:Dr.Druid,O:Merlin II . . . 4.00
211 SB,A:Dr.Druid 4.00
212 SB,I:Constrictor 4.50
213 SB,TP,I:Quintronic Man 4.00
214 SB,Jack of Hearts 4.00
215 SB,V:Bi-Beast 3.50
216 SB,Gen.Ross 3.50
217 SB,I:Stilts,A:Ringmaster . . . 3.50
218 SB,KP,Doc Samson versus
   Rhino 3.50
219 SB,V:Capt.Barravuda 3.50
220 SB,Robinson Crusoe 3.50
221 SB,AA,A:Sting Ray 3.50
222 JSn,AA,Cavern of Bones . . . 3.50
223 SB,V:Leader 3.50
224 SB,V:The Leader 3.50
225 SB,V:Leader,A:Doc Samson . 3.50
226 SB,JSt,A:Doc Samson 3.50
227 SB,JK,A:Doc Samson 3.50
228 SB,BMc,I:Moonstone,V:Doc
   Samson 3.50
229 SB,O:Moonstone,V:Doc
   Samson 3.50
230 JM,BL,A:Bug Thing 3.50
231 SB,I:Fred Sloan 3.50
232 SB,A:Capt.America 3.50
233 SB,A:Marvel Man 3.50
234 SB,Marvel Man Changes name
   to Quasar 3.50
235 SB,A:Machine Man 3.50
236 SB,A:Machine Man 3.50
237 SB,A:Machine Man 3.50
238 SB,JAb,Jimmy Carter 3.50
239 SB,I:Gold Bug 3.50
240 SB,Eldorado 3.50
241 SB,A:Tyrannus 3.00
242 SB,Eldorado 3.00
243 SB,A:Gammernon 3.00
244 SB,A:It 3.00
245 SB,A:Super Mandroid 3.00
246 SB,V:Capt.Marvel 3.00
247 SB,A:Bat Dragon 3.00
248 SB,V:Gardener 3.00
249 SD,R:Jack Frost 3.00

Incredible Hulk #175
© Marvel Entertainment Group

250 SB,A:Silver Surfer 12.00
251 MG,A:3-D Man 3.00
252 SB,A:Woodgod 3.00
253 SB,A:Woodgod 3.00
254 SB,I:U-Foes 3.00
255 SB,V:Thor 3.00
256 SB,I&O:Sabra 3.00
257 SB,I&O:Arabian Knight 3.00
258 I:Soviet Super Soldiers 3.00
259 SB,A:Soviet Super-Soldiers
   O:Darkstar 3.00
260 SB,Sugata 3.00
261 SB,V:Absorbing Man 3.00
262 SB,I:Glazer 3.00
263 SB,Avalanche 3.00
264 SB,A:Corruptor 3.00
265 SB,I:Rangers 3.50
266 SB,V:High Evolutionary 2.50
267 SB,V:Rainbow,O:Glorian . . . 2.50
268 SB,I:Pariah 2.50
269 SB,I:Bereet 2.50
270 SB,A:Abomination 2.50
271 SB,I:Rocket Raccoon,
   20th Anniv. 2.50
272 SB,C:X-Men,I:Wendigo III . . 5.00
273 SB,A:Alpha Flight 4.00
274 SB,Beroct 2.50
275 SB,JSt,I:Megalith 2.50
276 SB,JSt,V:U-Foes 2.50
277 SB,JSt,U-Foes 2.50
278 SB,JSt,C:X-Men,
   Avengers,Fantastic Four 2.50
279 SB,JSt,C:X-Men,
   Avengers,Fantastic Four 2.50
280 SB,JSt,Jack Daw 2.50
281 SB,JSt,Trapped in Space . . . 2.50
282 SB,JSt,A:She Hulk 2.50
283 SB,JSt,A:Avengers 2.50
284 SB,A:Avengers 2.50
285 SB,JSt,Northwind,V:Zzzax . . 2.50
286 SB,JSt,V:Soldier 2.50
287 SB,JSt,V:Soldier 2.50
288 SB,JSt,V:Abomination 2.50
289 SB,JSt,V:Modok 2.50
290 SB,JSt,V:Modok 2.50

MARVEL

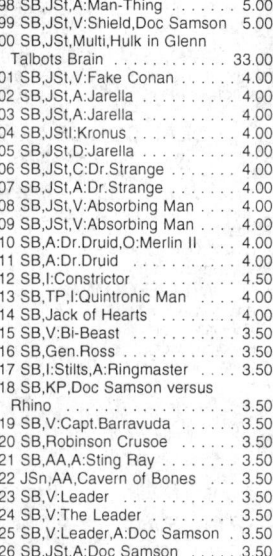

291 SB,JSt,V:Thunderbolt Ross . . 2.50
292 SB,JSt,V:Dragon Man 2.50
293 SB,V:Nightmare 2.50
294 SB,V:Boomerang 2.50
295 SB,V:Boomerang 2.50
296 SB,A:Rom 2.50
297 SB,V:Nightmare 2.50
298 KN(c),SB,V:Nightmare 2.50
299 SB,A:Shield 2.50
300 SB,A:Spider-Man,Avengers
   Doctor Strange 6.00
301 SB,Crossroads 2.50
302 SB,Crossroads 2.50
303 SB,V:The Knights 2.50
304 SB,V:U-Foes 2.50
305 SB,V:U-Foes 2.50
306 SB,V:Klaatu 2.50
307 SB,V:Klaatu 2.50
308 SB,V:Puffball Collective 2.50
309 SB,V:Goblin & Glow 2.50
310 Crossroads 2.50
311 Crossroads 2.50
312 Secret Wars II,O:Bruce 3.50
313 A:Alpha Flight 2.50
314 JBy,V:Doc Samson 5.00
315 JBy,A:Doc Samson,Banner
   & Hulk Separated 3.00
316 JBy,A:Avengers,N:Doc
   Samson 3.00
317 JBy,I:Hulkbusters,A:Doc
   Samson 3.00
318 JBy,A:Doc Samson 3.00
319 JBy,W:Bruce & Betty 5.00
320 AM,A:Doc Samson 2.50
321 AM,A:Avengers 2.50
322 AM,A:Avengers 2.50
323 AM,A:Avengers 2.50
324 AM,R:Grey Hulk(1st since #1),
   A:Doc Samson 10.00
325 AM,Rick Jones as Hulk 3.50
326 A:Rick Jones,New Hulk 6.00
327 AM,F:General Ross 2.50
328 AM,1st PDd(s),Outcasts 7.00
329 AM,V:Enigma 5.00
330 1st TM Hulk,D:T-bolt Ross . 15.00
331 TM,V:Leader 11.00
332 TM,V:Leader 7.00
333 TM,V:Leader 7.00
334 TM,I:Half-life 7.00
335 HorrorIssue 4.00
336 TM,A:X-Factor 5.00
337 TM,A:X-Factor,
   A:Doc Samson 5.00
338 TM,I:Mercy,V:Shield 5.00
339 TM,A:RickJones 5.00
340 TM,Hulk vs Wolverine 30.00
341 TM,V:Man Bull 4.00
342 TM,V:Leader 4.00
343 TM,V:Leader 4.00
344 TM,V:Leader 4.00
345 TM,V:Leader,Double-Size . . 7.00
346 TM,EL,L:Rick Jones 6.00
347 In Las Vegas,I:Marlo Chandler,
   V:Absorbing Man 4.00
348 V:Absorbing Man 3.00
349 A:Spider-Man 3.50
350 Hulk vs Thing,A:Beast
   V:Dr.Doom 4.00
351 R:Jarella's World 3.00
352 V:Inquisitor 3.00
353 R:Bruce Banner 3.00
354 V:Maggia 3.00
355 V:Glorian 3.00
356 V:Glorian,Cloot 3.00
357 V:Glorian,Cloot 3.00

358 V:Glorian,Cloot 3.00
359 JBy(c),C:Wolverine(illusion) . . 4.00
360 V:Nightmare & Dyspare 3.00
361 A:Iron Man,V:Maggia 3.00
362 V:Werewolf By Night 3.00
363 Acts of Vengeance 3.00
364 A:Abomination,B:Countdown . 3.00
365 A:Fantastic Four 3.00
366 A:Leader,I:Riot Squad 3.00
367 1st DK Hulk,I:Madman(Leader's
   brother),E:Countdown 8.00
368 SK,V:Mr.Hyde 4.00
369 DK,V:Freedom Force 3.00
370 DK,R:Original Defenders 3.00
371 DK,BMc,A:Orig.Defenders . . 3.00
372 DK,R:Green Hulk 9.00
373 DK,Green Hulk & Grey Hulk . 4.00
374 DK,BMc,Skrulls,
   R:Rick Jones 4.00
375 DK,BMc,V:Super Skrull 4.00
376 DK,BMc,Green Hulk,Grey
   Hulk & Banner fight 5.00

Incredible Hulk #340
© Marvel Entertainment Group

377 DK,BMc,New Green Hulk,
   combination of green,grey, and
   Bruce Banner,A:Ringmaster . 11.00
377a 2nd printing (gold) 5.00
378 V:Rhino,Christmas Issue 3.00
379 DK,MFm,I:Pantheon 4.00
380 A:Nick Fury,D:Crazy-8 . . . . . 3.00
381 DK,MFm,Hulk J:Pantheon . . . 4.00
382 DK,MFm,A:Pantheon 4.00
383 DK,MFm,Infinity Gauntlet . . . 4.00
384 DK,MFm,Infinity Gauntlet . . . 4.00
385 DK,MFm,Infinity Gauntlet . . . 4.00
386 DK,MFm,V:Sabra,A:Achilles . 4.00
387 DK,MFm,V:Sabra,A:Achilles . 4.00
388 DK,MFm,I:Speed Freak,Jim
   Wilson,revealed to have AIDS . 5.00
389 1st Comic art By Gary Barker
   (Garfield),A:Man-Thing,Glob . 4.00
390 DK,MFm,B:War & Pieces,
   C:X-Factor 4.00
391 DK,MFm,V:X-Factor 4.00
392 DK,MFm,E:War & Pieces,
   A:X:Factor 4.00
393 DK,MFm,R:Igor,A:Soviet Super Soldiers,30th Anniv..Green foil(c) . 5.00

393a 2nd printing,Silver 2.50
394 MFm(i),F:Atalanta,I:Trauma . . 3.00
395 DK,MFm,A:Punisher,
   I:Mr.Frost 3.00
396 DK,MFm,A:Punisher,
   V:Mr.Frost 3.00
397 DK,MFm,B:Ghost of the
   Past,V:U-Foes,A:Leader 3.00
398 DK,MFm,D:Marlo,V:Leader . . 3.00
399 JD,A:FF,Dr.Strange 3.00
400 JD,MFm,E:Ghost of the Past,
   V:Leader,1st Holo-grafx(c),1st
   GFr Hulk(pin-up) 3.50
400a 2nd Printing 2.50
401 JDu,O:Agememnon 2.00
402 JDu,V:Juggernaut 2.00
403 GFr,V:Red Skull,A:Avengers . 3.00
404 GFr,V:Red Skull,Juggernaut,
   A:Avengers 3.50
405 GFr,Ajax Vs. Achilles 2.75
406 GFr,V:Captain America 2.00
407 GFr,I:Piecemeal,A:Madman,
   B:O:Ulysses 2.00
408 GFr,V:Madman,Piecemeal,
   D:Perseus,A:Motormouth,
   Killpower 1.75
409 GFr,A:Motormouth,Killpower,
   V:Madman 1.75
410 GFr,A:Nick Fury,S.H.I.E.L.D.,
   Margo agrees to marry Rick . . 1.75
411 GFr,V:Nick Fury,S.H.I.E.L.D. . 1.75
412 PaP,V:Bi-Beast,A:She-Hulk . . 1.75
413 GFr,CaS,B:Troyjan War,
   I:Cassiopea,Armageddon,
   V:Trauma 1.75
414 GFr,CaS,V:Trauma,C:S.Surfer 1.75
415 GFr,CaS,V:Trauma,A:Silver
   Surfer,Starjammers 1.75
416 GFr,CaS,E:Troyjan War,D:Trauma,
   A:S.Surfer,Starjammers 1.75
417 GFr,CaS,Rick's/Marlo's Bachelor/
   Bachelorette Party 1.75
418 GFr,CaS,W:Rick & Marlo,
   A:Various Marvel persons,
   Die Cut(c) 2.75
418a Newsstand Ed. 1.75
419 CaS,V:Talos 1.75
420 GFr,CaS,AIDS Story,
   D: Jim Wilson 1.75
421 CaS,B:Myth Conceptions . . . 1.75
422 GFr,Myth Conceptions,pt.2 . . 1.75
423 GFr,CaS,MythConcept.,pt.3 . 1.50
424 B:Fall of the Hammer 1.50
425 Enhanced cover 3.50
426 PDa,LSh,R:Mercy 1.50
426a deluxe edition 1.95
427 A:Man-Thing 1.50
427a deluxe edition 1.95
428 Suffer The Children 1.95
429 Abortion Issue 1.95
430 A:Speed Freak 1.95
431 PDa,LSh R:Abomination 1.95
432 V:Abomination 1.95
433 PDd,V:Abomination 1.95
434 Funeral of the Year 1.95
435 Hulk Vs. Rhino baseball 2.50
436 PDd,Ame,Ghosts of the
   Future,pt.1 . . . . 1.95
437 PDd,AMe,Ghosts of the
   Future,pt.2 . . . . 1.95
438 PDd,AMe,Ghosts of the
   Future,pt.3 . . . . 1.95
439 PDd,AMe,Ghosts of the
   Future,pt.4 . . . . 1.95
440 PDd,AMe, ... 1.95

All comics prices listed are for *Near Mint* condition. **CVA Page 199**

441 PDd,AMe,A:She-Hulk 1.95
442 A:Molecule Man, She-Hulk ... 1.95
443 Janis 1.50
444 Onslaught saga, V:Cable ... 1.50
445 Onslaught saga 1.50
446 blamed for loss of Fantastic Four
and Avengers 1.50
447 PDd,MD2,F:The Unleashed
Hulk 1.50
447A Variant Tank Smashing cover 5.00
448 PDd,MD2,V:The Pantheon .. 1.50
449 PDd,MD2,I:Thunderbolts 1.50
450 PDd,MD2,F:Doctor Strange,
56pg. 2.95
451 PDd,MD2, ... 1.50
452 PDd,MD2, ... 1.50
453 PDd,MD2,V:Future Hulk ... 1.50
454 PDd,AKu,MFm,A God,
in Savage Land 1.50
455 PDd,AKu,MFm,in X-Mansion . 1.50
456 PDd,AKu,MFm,A:Apocalypse 1.50
Spec.#1,A:Inhumans 60.00
Spec.#2 rep.O:Hulk,A:Leader .. 35.00
Spec.#3 rep.A:Leader 10.00
Spec.#4 IR:Hulk/Banner 8.00
Ann.#5 V:Xemnu,Diablo 6.00
Ann.#6 HT,A:Dr.Strange,I:Paragon
(Her) 4.00
Ann.#7 JBy,BL,A:Angel,Iceman
A:Doc Samson 7.00
Ann.#8 Alpha Flight 6.00
Ann.#9 Checkmate 3.00
Ann.#10,A:Captain Universe ... 3.00
Ann.#11 RB,JSt,A:Spider-Man,
Avengers,V:Unis 4.00
Ann.#12 .... 3.00
Ann.#13 .... 3.00
Ann.#14 JBy,SB 3.00
Ann.#15 V:Abomitation 3.00
Ann.#16 HT,Life Form #3,
A:Mercy 3.00
Ann.#17 Subterran.Odyssey #2 .. 3.00
Ann #18 KM,TA,TC(1st Work),Return
of the Defenders,Part 1 .... 7.00
Ann.#19 I:Lazarus,w/card 3.25
Ann.#20 SvL,SI 1.75
G-Size#1 rep.Greatest Foes ... 10.00
TPB Ground Zero rep.#340-345 . 12.95
TPB Future Imperfect, PDd,GP, 96pg
TPB Ghosts of the Past,
Rep. #396–#400 ....
Minus 1 Spec., PDd,AKu,MFm,
flashback 1.95
TPB Transformations, 176pg. ....

INCREDIBLE HULK '97
Spec. 1 Onslaught aftermath 2.99

INCREDIBLE HULK:
FUTURE IMPERFECT
1 GP,V:Maestro 10.00
2 GP,V:Maestro 8.00
TPB Rep. 12.95

INCREDIBLE HULK
MEGAZINE
TPB six stories, 96pg 3.95

INCREDIBLE HULK/PITT
1997
Spec. PDd,DK,x-over 6.00

INCREDIBLE HULK
VS. WOLVERINE
Oct., 1986
1 HT,rep #181 B:,V:Wolverine. . 12.00

INDEPENDENCE DAY
1996
0 .... 1.50
1 .... 1.50
2 .... 1.50
TPB rep. #0–#2, 96pg 6.95

[Further Adventures of]
INDIANA JONES
Jan., 1983
1 JBy/TA 2.00
2 JBy/TA 1.50
3 .... 1.50
4 KGa 1.50
5 KGa 1.50
6 HC/TA 1.50
7 thru 24 KGa .... @1.50
25 SD,What Lurks Within the Tomb 1.50
26 SD 1.50
27 SD 1.50
28 SD 1.50
29 SD 1.50
30 SD 1.50
31 SD,The Summit Meeting 1.50
32 SD,Fly the Friendly Skies ... 1.50
33 SD 1.50
34 SD, March, 1986 .... 1.50

INDIANA JONES AND
THE LAST CRUSADE
1 B&W,Mag.,movie adapt, 1989. . 2.95
[Mini-Series]
1 Rep,Movie adapt, 1989. ..... 1.25
2 Rep,Movie adapt. 1.25
3 Rep,Movie adapt 1.25
4 Rep,Movie adapt. 1.25

INDIANA JONES AND
THE TEMPLE OF DOOM
1 Movie adapt, 1984 .... 1.25
2 Movie adapt. 1.25
3 Movie adapt. 1.25

INFINITY CRUSADE
1 RLm,AM,I:Goddess,A:Marvel
Heroes,foil(c) 4.00
2 RLm,AM,V:Goddess 3.00
3 RLm,AM,V:Goddess,Mephisto . 3.00
4 RLm,AM,V:Goddess,A:Magnus 3.00
5 RLm,AM,V:Goddess 3.00
6 RLm,AM,V:Goddess 3.00

INFINITY GAUNTLET
July, 1991
1 GP,O:Infinity Gauntlet 5.00
2 GP,JRu,2ndRebirth:Warlock .. 4.00
3 GP,JRu,I:Terraxia 4.00
4 GP,JRu,RLm,V:Thanos 4.00
5 JRu,RLm,V:Thanos,D:Terraxia . 4.00
6 RLm,JRu,V:Nebula 4.00
TPB rep. #1 thru 6 .... 24.95

INFINITY WAR
1 RLm,AM,R:Magus,Thanos 5.00
2 RLm,AM,V:Magus,A:Everyone . 3.00
3 RLm,AM,V:Magus,A:Everyone . 2.50

Infinity War #1
© *Marvel Entertainment Group*

4 RLm,AM,Magus gets Gauntlet . 2.50
5 RLm,AM,V:Magus 2.50
6 RLm,AM,V:Magus 2.50

INHUMANOIDS
Star Jan.–July, 1987
1 Hasbro Toy 1.25
2 O:Inhumanoids 1.25
3 V:D'Compose 1.25
4 A:Sandra Shore 1.25

INHUMANS
Oct., 1975
1 GP,V:Blastaar 4.00
2 GP,V:Blastaar 2.50
3 GP,I:Kree S 2.00
4 GK,Maximus 2.00
5 GK,V:Maximus 2.00
6 GK,Maximus 2.00
7 GK,DP,I:Skornn 2.00
8 GP,DP,Skornn 2.00
9 reprint,V:Mor-Tog 2.00
10 KP,D:Warkon 2.00
11 KP,JM,I:Pursuer 2.00
12 KP,Hulk 2.00
Spec#1(The Untold Saga),
O:Inhumans 2.00
Spec. Atlantis Rising story 2.95

INTERFACE
Epic Dec., 1989
1 ESP 2.50
2 thru 7 .... @2.00
8 .... 2.25

INVADERS
August, 1975
1 FR,JR(c),A:Invaders,
A:Mastermind 10.00
2 FR,JR(c)I:Brain Drain 7.00
3 FR,JR(c),I:U-Man 6.00
4 FR,O&V:U-Man 5.00
5 RB,JM,V:Red Skull 5.00
6 FR,V:Liberty Legion 5.00

7 FR,I:Baron Blood,
  1st Union Jack 5.00
8 FR,FS,J:Union Jack 5.00
9 FR,FS,O:Baron Blood 5.00
10 FR,FS,rep.Captain
   America Comics#22 . . . . 5.00
11 FR,FS,I:Blue Bullet 4.00
12 FR,FS,I:Spitfire 4.00
13 FR,FS,GK(c),I:Golem,
   Half Face 4.00
14 FR,FS,JK(c),I:Crusaders 4.00
15 FR,FS,JK(c),V:Crusaders . . . 4.00
16 FR,JK(c),V:Master Man 4.00
17 FR,FS,GK(c),I:Warrior Woman . 4.00
18 FR,FS,GK(c),R:1st Destroyer . 4.00
19 FR,FS,V:Adolph Hitler 4.00
20 FR,FS,GK(c),I&J:2nd Union Jack
   BU:rep.Marvel Comics #1 . . . 7.50
21 FR,FS,GK(c),BU:rep.Marvel
   Mystery #10 . . . . 5.50
22 FR,FS,GK(c),O:Toro 3.00
23 FR,FS,GK(c),I:Scarlet Scarab . 3.00
24 FR,FS,GK(c),rep.Marvel
   Mystery #17 . . . . 4.00
25 FR,FS,GK(c),V:Scarlet Scarab . 3.00
26 FR,FS,GK(c),V:Axis Agent . . . 3.00
27 FR,FS,GK(c),V:Axis Agent . . . 3.00
28 FR,FS,I:2nd Human Top,
   Golden Girl,Kid Commandos . 3.00
29 FR,FS,I:Teutonic Knight 3.00
30 FR,FS,V:Teutonic Knight 3.00
31 FR,FS,V:Frankenstein 3.00
32 FR,FS,JK(c),A:Thor 4.50
33 FR,FS,JK(c),A:Thor 4.50
34 FR,FS,V:Master Man 3.00
35 FR,FS,I:Iron Cross 3.00
36 FR,FS,O:Iron Cross 3.00
37 FR,FS,V:Iron Cross 3.00
38 FR,FS,V:Lady Lotus 3.00
39 FR,FS,O:Lady Lotus 3.00
40 FR,FS,V:Baron Blood 3.00
41 E:RTs(s)FR,FS,V:Super Axis,
   double-size 5.00
Ann.#1 A:Avengers,R:Shark 5.00
G-Size#1 FR,rep.Submariner#1 . . 5.00

[Limited Series]

1 R:Invaders 2.00
2 V:Battle Axis 2.00
3 R:Original Vison (1950's) 2.00
4 V:The Axis 2.00

IRON FIST
Nov., 1975

1 JBy,A:Iron Man 45.00
2 JBy,V:H'rythl 17.00
3 JBy,KP,KJ,V:Ravager 14.00
4 JBy,V:Radion 14.00
5 JBy,V:Scimitar 14.00
6 JBy,O:Misty Knight 12.50
7 JBy,V:Khimbala Bey 12.50
8 JBy,V:Chaka 12.50
9 JBy,V:Chaka 12.50
10 JBy,DGr,A:Chaka 12.50
11 JBy,V:Wrecking Crew 12.50
12 JBy,DGr,V:Captain America . 12.50
13 JBy,A:Boomerang 12.50
14 JBy,I:Sabretooth 150.00
14a reprint,Marv.Milestone 4.00
15 JBy,A&N:Wolverine,A:X-Men
   Sept. 1977 . . . . 35.00

IRON MAN
May, 1968

1 B:StL,AGw(s),JCr,GC,

I:Mordius 400.00
2 JCr,I:Demolisher 125.00
3 JCr,V:The Freak 100.00
4 JCr,A:Unicorn 80.00
5 JCr,GT,I:Cerebos 65.00
6 JCr,GT,V:Crusher 75.00
7 JCr,GT,V:Gladiator 50.00
8 JCr,GT,O:Whitney Frost 45.00
9 JCr,GT,A:Mandarin 42.00
10 JCr,GT,V:Mandarin 42.00
11 JCr,GT,V:Mandarin 37.00
12 JCr,GT,I:Controller 37.00
13 JCr,GT,A:Nick Fury 37.00
14 JCr,V:Night Phantom 37.00
15 JCr,GT,A:Red Ghost 37.00
16 JCr,GT,V:Unicorn 27.00
17 JCr,GT,I:Madam Masque,
   Midas 29.00
18 JCr,GT,V:Madame Masque . . 27.00
19 JCr,GT,V:Madame Masque . . 27.00
20 JCr,I:Charlie Gray 27.00
21 JCr,I:Eddie 22.00
22 JCr,D:Janice Cord 22.00
23 JCr,I:Mercenary 24.00
24 JCr,GT,V:Madame Masque . . 22.00
25 JCr,A:Sub-Mariner 24.00
26 JCr,DH,J:Val-Larr 20.00
27 JCr,DH,I:Firebrand 20.00
28 E:AGw(s),JCr,DH,
   V:Controller 20.00
29 B:StL,AyB(s),DH,V:Myrmidon 22.00
30 DH,I:Monster Master 22.00
31 DH,I:Mastermind 18.00
32 GT,I:Mechanoid 17.00
33 DH,I:Spy Master 17.00
34 DH,A:Spy Master 17.00
35 DH,A:Daredevil,Spymaster . . 17.00
36 E:AyB(s),DH,I:RamRod 17.00
37 DH,A:Ramrod 17.00
38 GT,Jonah 17.00
39 HT,I:White Dragon 15.00
40 GT,A:White Dragon 15.00
41 GT,JM,I:Slasher 15.00
42 GT,I:Mikas 15.00
43 GT,JM,A:Mikas,I:Guardsmen 15.00
44 GT,A:Capt.America 15.00
45 GT,A:Guardsman 15.00
46 GT,D:Guardsman 15.00
47 BS,JM,O:Iron Man 22.00
48 GT,V:Firebrand 14.00
49 GT,V:Adaptoid 14.00
50 B:RTs(s),GT,V:Prin.Python . 14.00
51 GT,C:Capt.America 14.00
52 GT,I:Raga 14.00
53 GT,JSn,I:BlackLama 12.00
54 GT,BEv,Sub-Mariner,I:Madame
   MacEvil (Moondragon) 14.00
55 JSn,I:Destroyer,Thanos,Mentor
   Starfox(Eros),Blood Bros. . . 45.00
55a reprint,Marv.Milestone 2.95
56 JSn,I:Fangor 15.00
57 GT,R:Mandarin 10.00
58 GT,V:Mandarin 10.00
59 GT,A:Firebrand 10.00
60 GT,C:Daredevil 10.00
61 GT,Marauder 10.00
62 whiplash 10.00
63 GT,A:Dr.Spectrum 10.00
64 GT,I:Rokk 10.00
65 GT,O:Dr.Spectrum 10.00
66 GT,V:Thor 10.00
67 GT,V:Freak 10.00
68 GT,O:Iron Man 12.00
69 GT,V:Mandarin 9.00
70 GT,A:Sunfire 9.00

71 GT,V:Yellow Claw 7.50
72 E:RTs(s),GT,V:Black Lama . . . 7.50
73 B:LWn(s),KP,JM,V:Titanic
   Three 7.50
74 KP,V:Modok 7.50
75 V:Black Lama 7.50
76 Rep,A:Hulk 7.50
77 V:Thinker 7.50
78 GT,V:Viet Cong 7.50
79 GT,I:Quasar(not Current one) . 7.50
80 JK(c),O:Black Lama 7.50
81 A:Black Lama 6.00
82 MSe,A:Red Ghost 6.00
83 E:LWn(s),HT,MSe,Red Ghost . 6.00
84 HT,A:Dr.Ritter 6.00
85 HT,MSe,A:Freak 6.00
86 B:MWn(s),GT,V:Blizzard . . . 7.00
87 GT,V:Blizzard 6.00
88 E:MWn(s),GT,
   V:Blood Brothers 6.00
89 GT,A:D.D.,Blood Bros. 6.00
90 JK(c),GT,Controller,A:Thanos . 7.50
91 GT,BL,A:Controller 6.00
92 JK(c),GT,V:Melter 6.00

Iron Man #11
© Marvel Entertainment Group

93 JK(c),HT,V:Kraken 6.00
94 JK(c),HT,V:Kraken 6.00
95 JK(c),GT,PP,V:Ultimo 6.00
96 GT,DP,V:Ultimo 6.00
97 GT,DP,I:Guardsman II 6.00
98 GT,DP,A:Sunfire 6.00
99 GT,V:Mandarin 6.00
100 JSn(c),GT,V:Mandarin 14.00
101 GT,I:Dread Knight 5.00
102 GT,O:Dread Knight 5.00
103 GT,V:Jack of Hearts 5.00
104 GT,V:Midas 5.00
105 GT,V:Midas 5.00
106 GT,V:Midas 5.00
107 KP,V:Midas 5.00
108 CI,A:Growing Man 5.00
109 JBy(c),CI,V:Van Guard 5.00
110 KP,I:C.Arcturus 5.00
111 KP,O:Rigellians 5.00
112 AA,KP,V:Punisher from
   Beyond 5.00
113 KP,HT,V:Unicorn,Spymaster . 5.50
114 KG,I:Arsenal 5.00
115 JR2,O:Unicorn,V:Ani-men . . . 5.00

116 JR2,BL,V:MadameMasque . . 5.00
117 BL,JR2,1st Romita Jr 6.00
118 JBy,BL,A:Nick Fury 8.00
119 BL,JR2,Alcholic Plot 6.00
120 JR2,BL,A:Sub-Mariner,
   I:Rhodey(becomes War Machine),
   Justin Hammer 6.00
121 BL,JR2,A:Submariner 5.00
122 DC,CI,BL,O:Iron Man 5.00
123 BL,JR2,V:Blizzard 5.00
124 BL,JR2,A:Capt.America 4.00
125 BL,JR2,A:Ant-Man 4.00
126 BL,JR2,V:Hammer 4.00
127 BL,JR2,Battlefield 4.00
128 BL,JR2,Alcohol 6.00
129 SB,A:Dread Night 3.50
130 BL,V:Digital Devil 3.50
131 BL,V:Hulk 3.50
132 BL,V:Hulk 3.50
133 BL,A:Hulk,Ant-Man 3.50
134 BL,V:Titanium Man 3.50
135 BL,V:Titanium Man 3.50
136 V:Endotherm 3.50
137 BL,Fights oil rig fire 3.50
138 BL,Dreadnought,Spymaster . 3.50
139 BL,Dreadnought,Spymaster . 3.50
140 BL,V:Force 3.50
141 BL,JR2,V:Force 3.50
142 BL,JR2,Space Armor 3.50
143 BL,JR2,V:Sunturion 3.50
144 BL,JR2,Sunturion,O:Rhodey . 3.50
145 BL,JR2,A:Raiders 3.50
146 BL,JR2,I:Black Lash 3.50
147 BL,JR2,V:Black Lash 3.00
148 BL,JR2,V:Terrorists 3.00
149 BL,JR2,V:Dr.Doom 3.00
150 BL,JR2,V:Dr.Doom,Dble 5.00
151 TA,BL,A:Antman 3.00
152 BL,JR2,New Armor 3.00
153 BL,JR2,V:Living Laser 3.00
154 BL,JR2,V:Unicorn 3.00
155 JR2,V:Back-Getters 3.00
156 JR2,I:Mauler 3.25
157 V:Spores 3.00
158 CI,AM,Iron Man Drowning . . . 3.00
159 PS,V:Diablo 3.00
160 SD,V:Serpent'sSquad 3.00
161 A:Moon Knight 3.00
162 V:Space Ships 3.00
163 V:Chessmen 3.00
164 LMc,A:Bishop 3.00
165 LMc,Meltdown 3.00
166 LMc,V:Melter 2.50
167 LMc,Alcholic Issue 2.50
168 LMc,A:Machine Man 2.50
169 LMc,B:Rhodey as 2nd
   Ironman 11.00
170 LMc,2nd Ironman 10.00
171 LMc,2nd Ironman 3.00
172 LMc,V:Firebrand 3.00
173 LMc,Stane International 3.00
174 LMc,Alcoholism 3.50
175 LMc,Alcoholism 3.50
176 LMc,Alcoholism 3.50
177 LMc,Alcoholism 3.00
178 LMc,V:Wizard 3.00
179 LMc,V:Mandarin 3.00
180 LMc,V:Mandarin 3.00
181 LMc,V:Mandarin 3.00
182 LMc,Secret Wars 3.00
183 LMc,Turning Point 3.00
184 LMc,Moves to California 3.00
185 LMc,V:Zodiac Field 3.00
186 LMc,I:Vibro 3.00
187 LMc,V:Vibro 3.00

Iron Man #78
© Marvel Entertainment Group

188 LMc,I:New Brother's Grimm . 3.00
189 LMc,I:Termite 3.00
190 LMc,O:Termite,A:Scar.Witch . 3.00
191 LMc,New Grey Armor 5.00
192 LMc,V:Iron Man(Tony Stark) . 5.00
193 LMc,V:Dr.Demonicus 3.00
194 LMc,I:Scourge,A:West Coast
   Avengers 3.00
195 LMc,A:Shaman 3.00
196 LMc,V:Dr.Demonicus 3.00
197 LMc,Secret Wars II 3.00
198 SB,V:Circuit Breaker 3.00
199 LMc,E:Rhodey as 2nd Ironman,
   V:Obadiah Stone 3.00
200 LMc,D:Obadiah Stone 6.00
201 MBr,V:Madam Masque 2.00
202 A:Kazar 2.00
203 MBr,A:Hank Pym 2.00
204 MBr,V:Madame Masque 2.00
205 MBr,V:A.I.M. 2.00
206 MBr,V:Goliath 2.00
207 MBr,When t/Sky Rains Fire . 2.00
208 MBr,V:A.I.M. 2.00
209 V:Living Laser 2.00
210 MBr,V:Morgan Le Fey 2.00
211 AS,V:Living Laser 2.00
212 DT,V:Iron Monger 2.00
213 A:Dominic Fortune 2.00
214 A:Spider-Woman 2.00
215 BL,AIM 2.00
216 BL,MBr,D:Clymenstra 2.00
217 BL,MRr,V:Hammer 2.00
218 BL,MBr,Titanic 2.00
219 BL,V:The Ghost 2.00
220 BL,MBr,V:The Ghost,
   D:Spymaster 2.00
221 BL,MBr,V:The Ghost 2.00
222 BL,MBr,R:Abrogast 2.00
223 BL,MBr,V:Blizzard,Beetle . . . 2.00
224 BL,V:Justin Hammer,Force . . 2.00
225 BL,MBr,B:Armor Wars 5.00
226 BL,MBr,V:Stingray 4.50
227 BL,MBr,V:Mandroids 4.00
228 BL,MBr,V:Guardsmen 4.00
229 BL,D:Titanium Man 4.00
230 V:Firepower 4.00
231 V:Firepower,N:Iron Man 4.00
232 BWS,Nightmares,E:Armor

Wars 4.50
233 JG,BL,A:AntMan 2.00
234 JG,BL,A:Spider-Man 3.00
235 JG,BL,V:Grey Gargoyle 2.00
236 JG,BL,V:Grey Gargoyle 2.00
237 JG,BL,V:SDI Monster 2.00
238 JG,BL,V:Rhino,D:M.Masque . 2.00
239 JG,BL,R:Ghost 2.00
240 JG,BL,V:Ghost 2.00
241 BL,V:Mandarin 2.00
242 BL,BWS,V:Mandarin 3.00
243 BL,BWS,Stark Paralyzed . . . 4.00
244 BL,V:Fixer,A:Force(D.Size) . . 5.00
245 BL(c),V:Dreadnaughts 2.00
246 BL,HT,V:A.I.M.,Maggia 2.00
247 BL,A:Hulk 2.25
248 BL,Tony Stark Cured 2.25
249 BL,V:Dr.Doom 2.00
250 BL,V:Dr.Doom,A of V 2.00
251 HT,AM,V:Wrecker,A of V . . . 2.00
252 HT,AM,V:Chemistro,A of V . . 2.00
253 BL,V:Slagmire 2.00
254 BL,V:Spymaster 2.00
255 HT,V:Devestator
   I:2nd Spymaster 2.00
256 JR2,V:Space Station 2.00
257 V:Samurai Steel 2.00
258 JR2,BWi,B:Armor Wars II,V:
   Titanium Man 2.25
259 JR2,BWi,V:Titanium Man . . . 2.00
260 JR2,BWi,V:Living Laser 2.00
261 JR2,BWi,A:Mandarin 1.75
262 JR2,BWi,A:Mandarin 1.75
263 JR2,BWi,A:Wonderman,
   V:Living Laser 1.75
264 JR2,BWi,A:Mandarin 1.75
265 JR2,BWi,V:Dewitt 1.50
266 JR2,BWi,E:Armor Wars II . . . 1.50
267 PR,BWi,B:New O:Iron Man,
   Mandarin,V:Vibro 1.75
268 PR,BWi,E:New O:Iron Man. . . 1.75
269 PR,BWi,A:Black Widow 1.75
270 PR,BWi,V:Fin Fang Foom . . . 1.75
271 PR,BWi,V:Fin Fang Foom . . . 1.75
272 PR,BWi,O:Mandarin 1.75
273 PR,BWi,V:Mandarin 1.75
274 MBr,BWi,V:Mandarin 1.75
275 PR,BWi,A:Mandarin,Fin Fang
   Foom (Double size) 2.00
276 PR,BWi,A:Black Widow 1.75
277 PR,BWi,A:Black Widow 1.75
278 BWi,Galactic Storm,pt.6
   A:Capt.America,V:Shatterax . . 1.75
279 BWi,Galactic Storm,pt.13,
   V:Ronan,A:Avengers 1.75
280 KHd,V:The Stark 1.75
281 KHd,I&V:Masters of Silence,
   C:War Machine Armor 3.50
282 KHd,I:War Machine Armor,
   V:Masters of Silence 3.50
283 KHd,V:Masters of Silence . . . 2.50
284 KHd,Stark put under Cryogenic
   Freeze,B:Rhodey as Iron Man . 3.00
285 KHd,BWi(i),Tony's Funeral . . 2.00
286 KHd,V:Avengers West Coast . 1.75
287 KHd,I:New Atom Smasher . . 1.75
288 KHd,30th Anniv.,V:Atom
   Smasher,foil(c) 4.50
289 KHd,V:Living Laser,
   R:Tony Stark 1.50
290 KHd,30th Anniv.,N:Iron Man,
   Gold foil(c) 4.50
291 KHd,E:Rhodey as Iron Man,
   Becomes War Machine 2.00
292 KHd,Tony reveals he is alive . 1.50

Iron Man #232
© Marvel Entertainment Group

293 KHd,V:Controller 1.50
294 KHd,Infinity Crusade 1.50
295 KHd,Infinity Crusade 1.50
296 KHd,V:Modam,A:Omega Red   1.50
297 KHd,V:Modam,Omega Red . . 1.50
298 KHd(c),I:Earth Mover 1.50
299 KHd(c),R:Ultimo 1.50
300 KHd,TMo,N:Iron Man,I:Iron Legion,
    Foil(c),A:W.Machine,V:Ultimo . 4.25
300a Newstand Ed. 2.75
301 KHd,B:Crash and Burn,
    A:Deathlok,C:Venom 1.50
302 KHd,V:Venom 1.75
303 KHd,V:New Warriors,
    C:Thundrstrike 1.75
304 KHd,C:Hulk,V:New Warriors,
    Thundrstrike,N:Iron Man 1.75
305 KHd,V:Hulk, ... 1.75
306 KHd,E:Stark Enterprise 1.75
307 TMo,I:Vor/Tex,R:Mandarin . . 1.50
308 TMo,Vor/Tex 1.50
309 TMo,Vor/Tex 1.50
310 regular 1.50
310a Neon(c),with insert print . . . 2.95
311 V:Mandarin 1.50
312 . . . . 1.50
313 LKa,TMo,AA Meeting 1.50
314 LKa,TMo,new villain 1.50
315 A:Black Widow 1.50
316 I:Slag,A:Crimson Dynamo . . 1.50
317 In Dynamos Armor 1.50
318 LKa,TMo,V:Slag 1.50
319 LKa,TMo,New Space Armor . 1.50
320 F:Hawkeye 1.50
321 Cont. From Avg. Crossing . . . 1.50
322 TKa,TheCrossing,V:JackFrost 1.50
323 TKa,V:Avengers 1.50
324 TKa,The Crossing 1.50
325 TKa,Avengers:Timeslide after 1.50
326 . . . . 1.50
327 . . . . 1.50
328 TKa, Tony Stark at Columbia U1.50
329 thru 332 . . . . 1.95
G-Size#1 Reprints 8.00
Ann.#1 rep.Iron Man #25 . . . . . . 20.00
Ann.#2 rep.Iron Man #6 . . . . 10.00
Ann.#3 SB,Manthing 6.00

Ann.#4 DP,GT,V:Modok,
    A:Champions 4.00
Ann.#5 JBr,A:Black Panther 2.50
Ann.#6 A:Eternals,V:Brother
    Tode 2.50
Ann.#7 LMc,A:West Coast
    Avengers, I:New Goliath 2.50
Ann.#8 A:X-Factor 3.00
Ann.#9 V:Stratosfire,A:Sunturion . 2.50
Ann.#10 PS,BL,Atlantis Attacks #2
    A:Sub-Mariner 3.00
Ann.#11 SD,Terminus Factor #2 . 2.00
Ann.#12 Subterran.Odyssey #4 . . 2.00
Ann.#13 GC,AW,Assault on Armor
    City,A:Darkhawk 2.50
Ann.#14 TMo,I:Face Theif,w/card,
    BU:War Machine 3.25
Ann.#15 GC,V:Controller 3.25
Spec.#1 rep. 20.00
Spec.#2 rep. 8.00
PB Iron Man 2020 . . . . 5.95
TPB Armor Wars rep.#225-#232 12.95
TPB Many Armors of Iron Man . 15.95
TPB Power of Iron Man 9.95
TPB JR2,BL,Iron Man vs. Dr. Doom
    rep.#149-#150,#249-#250 . . 12.95
Iron Manual BSz(c),guide to Iron
    Man's technology 2.00

IRON MAN
(Nov. 1996)
1 JLe,SLo,WPo,SW,A:Bruce
    Banner, New O:Hulk,48pg., . . . 4.00
1A variant Hulk showing cover . . 7.00
1 gold signature edition, bagged 35.00
2 JLe,SLo,WPo,SW 3.50
3 JLe,SLo,WPo,SW,Heroes brawl 2.50
4 JLe,SLo,WPo,SW,V:Laser 2.25
4A X-mas cover 4.00
5 JLe,SLo,WPo,SW, Whirlwind . . 1.95
6 JLe,SLo,WPo,SW,"Industrial
    Revolution," pt.2 x-over 1.95
7 JLe,SLo,WPo,SW,A:Pepper
    Potts,Villain revealed 1.95
8 JLe,SLo,RBn,fate of Rebel 1.95
9 JLe,SLo,RBn,V:Mandarin 1.95
10 JLe,SLo,RBn,F:The Hulk 1.95
11 JLb,RBn,V:Dr. Doom,A:Hydra . 1.95

IRON MAN:
AGE OF INNOCENCE
1-shot Avengers:Timeslide 2.50

IRON MAN/
FORCE WORKS
COLLECTORS' PREVIEW
1 Neon wrap-around(c), double
    size, X-over preview 1.95

IRON MAN &
SUBMARINER
1 GC,April, 1968 . . . . 225.00

IRON MANUAL
1 BSz(c),Guide to Iron Man's
    technology 1.75

ISLAND OF DR. MOREAU
Oct., 1977
1 GK(c),movie adapt. 2.00

IT'S A DUCK'S LIFE
Feb., 1950
1 F;Buck Duck,Super Rabbit . . 60.00
2 . . . . 30.00
3 thru 10 . . . . @20.00
11 Feb., 1952 . . . . 20.00

JACK OF HEARTS
Jan., 1984
1 Mini series 1.50
2 O:Jack of Hearts 1.00
3 . . . . 1.00
4 Final issue,April 1984 . . . . 1.00

JAMES BOND JR.
1 I&O:JamesBondJr.(TVseries) . . 3.00
2 Adventures Contd. 1.50
3 V:Goldfinger,Odd Job 1.50
4 thru 6 . . . . @1.50
V:Scumlord 1.50
8 V:Goldfinger,Walter D.Plank . . 1.50
9 V:Dr.No in Switzerland 1.50
10 V:Robot,Dr.DeRange 1.50
11 V:S.C.U.M. 1.50
12 V:Goldfinger,Jaws 1.50

JANN OF THE JUNGLE
See: JUNGLE TALES

JEANIE COMICS
See: DARING MYSTERY

JIHAD
Epic
1 Cenobites vs. Nightbreed 4.50
2 E:Cenobites vs. Nightbreed . . 4.50

JOHN CARTER,
WARLORD OF MARS
June, 1977
1 GK,DC,O:John Carter,Created
    by Edgar Rice Burroughs 5.00
2 GK/DC(c),GK,RN, White Apes
    of Mars 3.00
3 GK,RN,Requiem for a Warlord . 3.00
4 GK,RN, Raiding Party 3.00
5 GK,RN,Giant Battle Issue 3.00
6 GK/DC(c),GK,Alone Against a
    World 3.00
7 GK,TS,Showdown 3.00
8 GK,RN,Beast With Touch of
    Stone 3.00
9 GK,RN,Giant Battle Issue 3.00
10 GK,The Death of Barsoom? . . 3.00
11 RN,O:Dejah Thoris 2.00
12 RN,City of the Dead 2.00
13 RN,March of the Dead 2.00
14 RN,The Day Helium Died 2.00
15 RN,GK,Prince of Helium
    Returns 2.00
16 RN,John Carters Dilemna 2.00
17 BL,What Price Victory 5.00
18 FM,Tars Tarkas Battles Alone . 1.50
19 RN(c),War With the Wing Men 1.50
20 RN(c),Battle at the Bottom
    of the World 1.50
21 RN(c),The Claws of the Banth 1.50
22 RN(c),The Canyon of Death . . 1.50
23 Murder on Mars 1.50
24 GP/TA(c),Betrayal 1.50
25 Inferno 1.50
26 Death Cries the Guild of

MARVEL

MARVEL

Assassins	1.50
27 Death Marathon	1.50
28 Guardians of the Lost	
City Oct., 1979	2.50
Ann.#1 RN(c),GK,Battle story	2.00
Ann.#2 RN(c),GK,Outnumbered	2.00
Ann.#3 RN(c),GK,Battle story	2.00

JOKER COMICS
Timely April, 1942

1 BW,I&B:Powerhouse Pepper, A:Stuporman	1,600.00
2 BW,I:Tessie the Typist	650.00
3 BW,A:Tessie the Typist, Squat Car Squad	450.00
4 BW,Squat Car (c)	450.00
5 BW,same	450.00
6 BW,	250.00
7 BW	250.00
8 BW	250.00
9 BW	250.00
10 BW,Shooting Gallery (c)	250.00
11 BW	200.00
12 BW	200.00
13 BW	200.00
14 BW	200.00
15 BW	200.00
16 BW	200.00
17 BW	200.00
18 BW	200.00
19 BW	200.00
20 BW	200.00
21 BW	175.00
22 BW	175.00
23 BW,HK,'Hey Look'	175.00
24 BW,HK,'Laff Favorites'	175.00
25 BW,HK,same	175.00
26 BW,HK,same	175.00
27 BW	175.00
28	50.00
29 BW	175.00
30 BW	175.00
31 BW	125.00
32 B:Millie,Hedy	50.00
33 HK	50.00
34	35.00
35 HK	50.00
36 HK	50.00
37	35.00
38	35.00
39	35.00
40	35.00
41 A:Nellie the Nurse	35.00
42 I:Patty Pin-up	50.00

Becomes:

ADVENTURES INTO TERROR

43(1)AH,B:Horror Stories	450.00
44(2)AH,'Won't You Step Into My Palor'	325.00
3 GC,'I Stalk By Night'	160.00
4 DR,'The Torture Room'	160.00
5 GC,DR,'The Hitchhiker'	175.00
6 RH,'The Dark Room'	150.00
7 GT(c),BW,'Where Monsters Dwell'	375.00
8 JSt,'Enter... the Lizard'	150.00
9 RH(c),JSt,'The Dark Dungeon'	165.00
10 'When the Vampire Calls'	165.00
11 JSt,'Dead Man's Escape'	100.00
12 BK,'The Man Who Cried Ghost'	150.00
13 BEv(c),'The Hands of Death'	100.00

14 GC,'The Hands'	100.00
15 'Trapped by the Tarantula'	100.00
16 RH(c),'Her Name Is Death'	100.00
17 'I Die Too Often',Bondage(c)	100.00
18 'He's Trying To Kill Me'	100.00
19 'The Girl Who Couldn't Die'	100.00
20	100.00
21	90.00
22	90.00
23	90.00
24 MF,GC	100.00
25 thru 30	@75.00
31 May, 1954	75.00

Journey Into Mystery #123
© *Marvel Entertainment Group*

JOURNEY INTO MYSTERY
June, 1952

1 RH(c),B:Mystery/Horror stories	2,500.00
2 'Don't Look'	700.00
3 'I Didn't See Anything'	500.00
4 RH,BEv(c),'I'm Drowning,' severed hand (c)	500.00
5 RH,BEv(c),'Fright'	350.00
6 BEv(c),'Till Death Do Us Part'	350.00
7 BEv(c),'Ghost Guard'	350.00
8 'He Who Hesitates'	350.00
9 BEv(c),'I Made A Monster'	350.00
10 'The Assassin of Paris'	350.00
11 RH,GT,'Meet the Dead'	325.00
12 'A Night At Dragmoor Castle'	275.00
13 'The Living and the Dead'	275.00
14 DAy,RH,'The Man Who Owned A World'	275.00
15 RH(c),'Till Death Do Us Part'	275.00
16 DW,'Vampire Tale'	275.00
17 SC,'Midnight On Black Mountain'	275.00
18 'He Wouldn't Stay Dead'	275.00
19 JF,'The Little Things'	275.00
20 BEv,BP,'After Man, What'	275.00
21 JKu,'The Man With No Past'	275.00
22 'Haunted House'	275.00
23 GC,'Gone, But Not Forgotten'	175.00

24 'The Locked Drawer'	175.00
25 'The Man Who Lost Himself'	175.00
26 'The Man From Out There'	175.00
27 'BP,JSe,'Masterpiece'	175.00
28 'The Survivor'	175.00
29 'Three Frightened People'	175.00
30 JO,'The Lady Who Vanished'	175.00
31 'The Man Who Had No Fear'	175.00
32 'Elevator In The Sky'	175.00
33 SD,AW,'There'll Be Some Changes Made'	200.00
34 BP,BK,'The Of The Mystic Ring'	175.00
35 LC,JF,'Turn Back The Clock'	175.00
36 'I, The Pharaoh'	175.00
37 BEv(c),'The Volcano'	175.00
38 SD,'Those Who Vanish'	175.00
39 BEv(c),DAy,WW,'The Forbidden Room'	175.00
40 BEv(c),JF,'The Strange Secret Of Henry Hill'	175.00
41 BEv(c),GM,RC,'I Switched Bodies'	150.00
42 BEv(c),GM,'What Was Farley's Other Face	150.00
43 AW,'Ghost Ship'	150.00
44 thru 50 SD,JK	@150.00
51 thru 55 SD,JK	@150.00
56 thru 61 SD,JK	@150.00
62 SD,JK,I:Xemnu	200.00
63 thru 68 SD,JK	@150.00
69 thru 82	@150.00
83 JK,SD,I&O:Thor	4,500.00
84 JK,SD,DH,I:Executioner	1,000.00
85 JK,SD,I:Loki,Heimdall,Balder, Tyr,Odin,Asgard	600.00
86 JK,SD,DH,V:Tomorrow Man	375.00
87 JK,SD,V:Communists	300.00
88 JK,SD,V:Loki	300.00
89 JK,SD,O:Thor(rep)	300.00
90 SD,I:Carbon Copy	150.00
91 JSt,SD,I:Sandu	125.00
92 JSt,SD,V:Loki,I:Frigga	125.00
93 DAy,JK,SD,I:Radioactive Man	150.00
94 JSt,SD,V:Loki	135.00
95 JSt,SD,I:Duplicator	135.00
96 JSt,SD,I:Merlin II	125.00
97 JK,I:Lava Man,O:Odin	150.00
98 DH,JK,I&O:Cobra	125.00
99 DH,JK,I:Mr.Hyde,Surtur	125.00
100 DH,JK,V:Mr.Hyde	125.00
101 JK,V:Tomorrow Man	85.00
102 JK,I:Sif,Hela	90.00
103 JK,I:Enchantress, Executioner	90.00
104 JK,Giants	85.00
105 JK,V:Hyde,Cobra	85.00
106 JK,O:Balder	85.00
107 JK,I:Grey Gargoyle,Karnilla	85.00
108 JK,A:Dr.Strange	75.00
109 JK,V:Magneto	125.00
110 JK,V:Hyde,Cobra,Loki	75.00
111 JK,V:Hyde,Cobra,Loki	75.00
112 JK,V:Hulk,O:Loki	175.00
113 JK,V:Grey Gargoyle	75.00
114 JK,I&O:Absorbing Man	75.00
115 JK,O:Loki,V:Absorbing Man	100.00
116 JK,V:Loki,C:Daredevil	75.00
117 JK,V:Loki	75.00
118 JK,I:Destroyer	75.00
119 JK,V:Destroyer,I:Hogun, Fandrall,Volstagg	75.00
120 JK,A:Avengers,Absorbing Man	75.00

121 JK,V:Absorbing Man	75.00
122 JK,V:Absorbing Man	75.00
123 JK,V:Absorbing Man	75.00
124 JK,A:Hercules	75.00
125 JK,A:Hercules	75.00
Annual #1, JK,I:Hercules	160.00

Becomes: THOR

JOURNEY INTO MYSTERY
[2nd series] Oct., 1972

1 GK,TP,MP,'Dig Me No Grave'	8.00
2 GK,'Jack the Ripper'	4.00
3 JSn,TP,'Shambler From the Stars'	4.00
4 GC,DA,'Haunter of the Dark', H.P. Lovecraft adaptation	4.00
5 RB,FrG,'Shadow From the Steeple',R. Bloch adaptation	4.00
6 Mystery Stories	3.00
7 thru 19	@3.00

JOURNEY INTO UNKNOWN WORLDS
See: ALL WINNERS COMICS

JUGGERNAUT
1997

1-shot 48pg.	2.99

JUNGLE ACTION
Atlas Oct., 1954

1 JMn,JMn(c),B:Leopard Girl	200.00
2 JMn,JMn(c)	250.00
3 JMn,JMn(c)	150.00
4 JMn,JMn(c)	150.00
5 JMn,JMn(c)	150.00
6 JMn,JMn(c),August, 1955	150.00

Jungle Action #1
© Marvel Entertainment Group

JUNGLE ACTION
Oct., 1972—Nov., 1976

1 JB(c),Lorna,Tharn,Jann reprints	8.50
2 GK(c),same	4.50
3 JSn(c),same	4.50

4 GK(c),same	4.50
5 JR(c),JB,B:Black Panther, V:Man-Ape	7.50
6 RB/FrG(c),RB,V:Kill-Monger	4.50
7 RB/KJ(c),RB,V:Venomn	4.50
8 RB/KJ(c),RB,GK, O:Black Panther	4.50
9 GK/KJ(c),RB,V:Baron Macabre	4.50
10 GK/FrG(c),V:King Cadaver	4.50
11 GK(c),V:Baron Macabre,Lord Karnaj	4.50
12 RB/KJ(c),V:Kill Monger	4.00
13 GK/JK(c),V:White Gorilla, Sombre	4.00
14 GK(c),V:Prehistoric Monsters	4.00
15 GK(c),V:Prehistoric Monsters	4.00
16 GK(c),V:Venomm	4.00
17 GK(c),V:Kill Monger	4.00
18 JKu(c),V:Madame Slay	4.00
19 GK(c),V:KKK,'Sacrifice of Blood'	4.00
20 V:KKK,'Slaughter In The Streets'	4.00
21 V:KKK,'Cross Of Fire, Cross Of Death'	3.50
22 JB(c),V:KKK,Soul Stranger	3.50
23 JBy(c),V:KKK	3.50
24 GK(c),I:Wind Eagle	3.50

JUNGLE TALES
Atlas Sept., 1954

1 B:Jann of the Jungle,Cliff Mason,Waku	225.00
2 GT,Jann Stories cont.	175.00
3 Cliff Mason,White Hunter, Waku Unknown Jungle	150.00
4 Cliff Mason,Waku,Unknown Jungle	150.00
5 RH(c),SSh,Cliff Mason,Waku, Unknown Jungle	150.00
6 DH,SSh,Cliff Mason,Waku, Unknown Jungle	150.00
7 DH,SSh,Cliff Mason,Waku, Unknown Jungle	150.00

Becomes:

JANN OF THE JUNGLE

8 SH,SSh,'The Jungle Outlaw'	175.00
9 'With Fang and Talons'	100.00
10 AW,'The Jackal's Lair'	110.00
11 'Bottonless Pit'	80.00
12 'The Lost Safari'	80.00
13 'When the Trap Closed'	80.00
14 V:Hunters	80.00
15 BEv(c),DH,V:Hunters	80.00
16 BEv(c),AW,'Jungle Vengeance'	125.00
17 BEv(c),DH,AW,June, 1957	125.00

JUSTICE
Nov., 1986

1 I:Justice	1.25
2	1.00
3 Yakuza Assassin	1.00
4	1.00
5	1.00
6	1.00
7	1.00
8	1.00
9 KG	1.00
10 thru 18	@1.00
19 thru 31	@1.25
32 Last issue,A:Joker	1.50

JUSTICE COMICS
Atlas Fall, 1947

7(1) B:FBI in Action,'Mystery of White Death'	175.00
8(2),HK,'Crime is For Suckers'	125.00
9(3),FBI Raid	100.00
4 Bank Robbery	100.00
5 Subway(c)	85.00
6 E:FBI In Action	85.00
7 Symbolic(c)	85.00
8 Funeral(c)	85.00
9 B:'True Cases Proving Crime Can't Win'	85.00
10 Ph(c),Bank Hold Up	85.00
11 Ph(c),Behind Bars	85.00
12 Ph(c),The Crime of Martin Blaine	60.00
13 Ph(c),The Cautiouc Crook	75.00
14 Ph(c)	75.00
15 Ph(c)	60.00
16 F:"Ears"Karpik-Mobster	50.00
17 'The Ragged Stranger'	50.00
18 'Criss-Cross'	50.00
19 'Death Of A Spy'	50.00
20 'Miami Mob'	50.00
21 'Trap'	50.00
22 'The Big Break'	50.00
23 thru 51	@45.00
52 'Flare Up'	50.00

Becomes:

TALES OF JUSTICE
May, 1955—Aug., 1957

53 BEv,'Keeper Of The Keys'	125.00
54 thru 57	@85.00
58 BK	95.00
59 BK	95.00
60 thru 63	@50.00
64 RC,DW,JSe	75.00
65 RC	75.00
66 JO,AT	75.00
67 DW	75.00

JUSTICE: FOUR BALANCE

1 A:Thing, Yancy Street Gang	1.75
2 V:Hate Monger	1.75
3 the story continues...	1.75
4 ...to its conclusion	1.75

KATHY
Atlas Oct., 1959—Feb., 1964

1 'Teenage Tornado'	35.00
2	20.00
3 thru 15	@15.00
16 thru 27	@8.00

KA-ZAR
[Reprint Series] Aug., 1970

1 X-Men ID	14.00
2 Daredevil 12, 13	10.00
3 DDH,Spider-Man,March, 1971	10.00

[1st Series] Jan., 1974

1 O:Savage Land	3.50
2 DH,JA,A:Shanna The She-Devil	2.50
3 DH,V:Man-God,A:El Tigre	2.50
4 DH,V:Man-God	2.50
5 DH,D:El-Tigre	2.50
6 JB/AA,V:Bahemoth	2.00
7 JB/BMc'Revenge of the River-Gods'	2.00
8 JB/AA,'Volcano of Molten Death'	2.00
9 JB,'Man Who Hunted Dinosaur'	2.00

All comics prices listed are for *Near Mint* condition.

MARVEL *(vertical side tab)*

MARVEL

10 JB,'Dark City of Death'	2.00
11 DH/FS,'Devil-God of Sylitha'	1.50
12 RH,'Wizard of Forgotten Death'	1.50
13 V:Lizard Men	1.50
14 JAb,V:Klaw	1.50
15 VM,V:Klaw,'Hellbird'	1.50
16 VM,V:Klaw	1.50
17 VM,V:Klaw	1.50
18 VM,V:Klaw,Makrum	1.50
19 VM,V:Klaw,Raknor the Slayer	1.50
20 VM,V:Klaw,'Fortress of Fear'	1.50

Ka-Zar (2nd Series) #1
© Marvel Entertainment Group

[2nd Series] Apr. 1981

1 BA,O:Ka-Zar	2.00
2 thru 7 BA	@1.50
8 BA,Kazar Father	1.50
9 BA	1.50
10 BA,Direct D	1.50
11 BA/GK,Zabu	1.50
12 BA,Panel Missing	1.50
12a Scarce Reprint	2.00
13 BA	2.00
14 BA/GK,Zabu	1.50
15 BA	1.50
16	1.50
17 Detective	1.50
18	1.50
19	1.50
20 A:Spider-Man	2.00
21	2.00
22 A:Spider-Man	2.00
23 A:Spider-Man	2.00
24 A:Spider-Man	2.00
25 A:Spider-Man	2.00
26 A:Spider-Man	2.00
27 A:Buth	1.50
28 Pangea	1.50
29 W:Kazar & Shanna, Doub.Size	2.00
30 V:Pterons	1.50
31 PangeaWarII	1.50
32 V:Plunderer	1.50
33 V:Plunderer	1.50
34 Last Issue Doub.Size	2.00

KA-ZAR
1997

1 MWa,NKu,Ka-Zar, Shanna, Zabu,

V:Gregor, 40pg	1.95
2 MWa,NKu,V:Gregor	1.95
2A NKu variant cover	1.95
3 MWa,NKu,Ka-Zar's son dead?	1.95
4 MWa,NKu,in New York City	1.95
5 MWa,NKu,	1.95

KA-ZAR OF THE SAVAGE LAND
1996

1-shot CDi,V:Sauron, 48pg. prelude to series

KA-ZAR: SIBLING RIVALRY

1 MWa,TDz, Flashback 1.95

KELLYS, THE
See: KID KOMICS

KENT BLAKE OF THE SECRET SERVICE
May, 1951—July, 1953

1 U.S. Govt. Secret Agent stories,Bondage cover	100.00
2 JSt,Drug issue,'Man with out A Face	75.00
3 'Trapped By The Chinese Reds'	45.00
4 Secret Service Stories	45.00
5 RH(c),'Condemned To Death'	45.00
6 Cases from Kent Blake files	45.00
7 RH(c),Behind Enemy Lines	45.00
8 V:Communists	45.00
9 thru 14	@45.00

KICKERS INC.
Nov., 1986

1 SB,O:Kickers	1.25
2 SB	1.00
3 RF,Witches	1.00
4 RF,FIST	1.00
5 RF,A:D.P.7	1.00
6 RF	1.00
7 RF	1.00
8 RF	1.00
9	1.00
10 TD	1.00
11	1.00
12 Oct., 1987	1.00

KID & PLAY

1 Based on Rap Group	1.25
2 Drug Issue	1.25
3 At your Friends Expense	1.25
4	1.25
5	1.25
6 Record Contract	1.25
7 Fraternity Pledging	1.25
8 Kid and Cindy become an item	1.25
9 C:Marvel Heroes	1.25

KID COLT OUTLAW
Atlas **Aug., 1948**

1 B:Kid Colt,A:Two-Gun Kid	600.00
2 'Gun-Fighter and the Girl'	300.00
3 'Colt-Quick Killers For Hire'	250.00
4 'Wanted',A:Tex Taylor	250.00
5 'Mystery of the Misssing Mine',A:Blaze Carson	250.00
6 A:Tex Taylor,'Valley of	

the Warewolf'	150.00
7 B:Nimo the Lion	150.00
8	150.00
9	135.00
10 'The Whip Strikes',E:Nimo the Lion'	160.00
11 O:Kid Colt	150.00
12	125.00
13 DRi	125.00
14	125.00
15 'Gun Whipped in Shotgun City'	125.00
16	125.00
17	125.00
18 DRi	125.00
19	100.00
20 'The Outlaw'	100.00
21 thru 30	@100.00
31	75.00
32	75.00
33 thru 45 A:Black Rider	@60.00
46 RH(c)	50.00
47 DW	50.00
48 RH(c),JKu	50.00
49	50.00
50	50.00
51 thru 56	@45.00
57 AW	50.00
58 AW	50.00
59 AW	50.00
60 AW	50.00
61	25.00
62	25.00
63	25.00
64	30.00
65	30.00
66 thru 78	@25.00
79 Origin Retold	30.00
80 thru 86	@25.00
87 JDa(reprint)	30.00
88 AW	35.00
89 AW,Matt Slade	35.00
90 thru 99	@15.00
100	25.00
101	20.00
102	15.00
103 'The Great Train Robbery'	15.00
104 JKu(c),DH,'Trail of Kid Colt'	15.00
105 DH,V:Dakota Dixon	15.00
106 JKu(c),'The Circus of Crime'	15.00
107	15.00
108 BEv	15.00
109 DAy,V:The Barracuda	15.00
110 GC,V:Iron Mask	15.00
111 JKu(c),V:Sam Hawk, The Man Hunter	15.00
112 JKu(c),V:Mr. Brown	15.00
113 JKu(c),GC,V:Bull Barton	15.00
114 JKu(c),Return of Iron Mask	15.00
115 JKu(c),V:The Scorpion	15.00
116 JKu(c),GC,V:Dr. Danger & Invisible Gunman	15.00
117 JKu(c),GC,V:The Fatman & His Boomerang	15.00
118 V:Scorpion,Bull Barton, Dr. Danger	15.00
119 DAy(c),JK,V:Bassett The Badman	15.00
120 'Cragsons Ride Again'	15.00
121 A:Rawhide Kid,Iron Mask	10.00
122 V:Rattler Ruxton	10.00
123 V:Ringo Barker	10.00
124 A:Phantom Raider	10.00

MARVEL

125 A:Two-Gun Kid	10.00
126 V:Wes Hardin	7.50
127 thru 129	@7.50
130 O:Kid Colt	7.50
131 thru 150	@7.50
151 thru 200 reprints	@5.00
201 thru 228 reprints	@2.50
229 April, 1979	2.50

KID FROM DODGE CITY
Atlas July, 1957—Sept., 1957
1	50.00
2	25.00

KID FROM TEXAS
Atlas June, 1957—Aug., 1957
1	50.00
2	25.00

KID KOMICS
Timely Feb., 1943
1 SSh(c),BW,O:Captain Wonder & Tim Mulrooney I:Whitewash, Knuckles,Trixie Trouble, Pinto Pete Subbie	3,000.00
2 AsH(c),F:Captain Wonder Subbie, B:Young Allies, B:Red Hawk,Tommy Tyme	1,400.00
3 ASh(c),A:The Vision & Daredevils	1,000.00
4 ASh(c),B:Destroyer,A:Sub-Mariner, E:Red Hawk,Tommy Tyme	900.00
5 ASh(c),V:Nazis	650.00
6 ASh(c),V:Japanese	650.00
7 ASh(c),B;Whizzer	600.00
8 ASh(c),V:Train Robbers	600.00
9 ASh(c),V:Elves	600.00
10 ASh(c),E:Young Allies, The Destoyer,The Whizzer	600.00
Becomes:	

KID MOVIE KOMICS
11 F:Silly Seal,Ziggy Pig HK,Hey Look	175.00
Becomes:	

RUSTY COMICS
12 F:Rusty,A:Mitzi	85.00
13 Do not Disturb(c)	50.00
14 Beach(c),BW,HK,Hey Look	75.00
15 Picnic(c),HK,Hey Look	60.00
16 Juniors Grades,HK,HeyLook	60.00
17 John in Trouble,HK,HeyLook	60.00
18 John Fired	35.00
19 Fridge raid(c),HK	35.00
20 And Her Family,HK	65.00
21 And Her Family,HK	100.00
22	100.00
Becomes:	

KELLYS, THE
23 F:The Kelly Family(Pop, Mom,Mike,Pat & Goliath)	60.00
24 Mike's Date,A;Margie	40.00
25 Wrestling(c)	40.00
Becomes:	

SPY CASES
26(#1) Spy stories	150.00
27(#2) BEv,Bondage(c)	100.00
28(#3) Sabotage,A:Douglas Grant Secret Agent	100.00
4 The Secret Invasion	75.00
5 The Vengeance of Comrade de Casto	75.00
6 A:Secret Agent Doug Grant	75.00

7 GT,A:Doug Grant	75.00
8 Atom Bomb(c),Frozen Horror	70.00
9 Undeclared War	60.00
10 Battlefield Adventures	45.00
11 Battlefield Adventures	40.00
12 Battlefield Adventures	40.00
13 Battlefield Adventures	40.00
14 Battlefield Adventures	40.00
15 Doug Grant	40.00
16 Doug Grant	40.00
17 Doug Grant	40.00
18 Contact in Ankara	40.00
19 Final Issue,Oct., 1953	40.00

KID SLADE GUNFIGHTER
See: MATT SLADE

KILLFRENZY
1	1.95
2 Castle Madspike	1.95

KILLPOWER: THE EARLY YEARS
1 B:MiB,Goes on Rampage	3.25
2 thru 3 O:Killpower	2.00
4 E:MiB,last issue	2.00

KING ARTHUR & THE KNIGHTS OF JUSTICE
1 Based on Cartoon	1.25
2 Based on Cartoon	1.25
3 Based on Cartoon	1.25

KING CONAN:
See: CONAN THE KING

KISSNATION
1997
1 Rock & Roll, A:X-Men	10.00

KITTY PRIDE & WOLVERINE
Nov., 1984
1 AM,V:Ogun	6.00
2 AM,V:Ogun	4.00
3 thru 5 AM,V:Ogun	@4.00
6 AM,D:Ogun, April, 1985	3.00

KNIGHTS OF PENDRAGON
July, 1990
[1st Regular Series]
1 GEr	2.75
2 thru 7	@2.25
8 inc.SBI Poster	2.25
9 V:Bane Fisherman	2.25
10 Cap.Britain/Union Jack	2.25
11 A:Iron Man	2.25
12 A:Iron Man,Union Jack	2.25
13 O:Pendragon	2.25
14 A:Mr.Fantastic,Invisible Woman Black Panther	2.25
15 BlackPanther/Union Jack T.U.	2.25
16 A:Black Panther	2.25
17 D:Albion, Union Jack, A:Black Panther	2.25
18 A:Iron Man,Black Panther	2.25
[2nd Regular Series]	
1 GEr,A:Iron Man,R:Knights of Pendragon,V:MyS-TECH	2.25

Knights of Pendragon #6
© Marvel Entertainment Group

2 A:Iron Man,Black Knight	2.00
3 PGa,A:Iron Man,Black Knight	2.00
4 Gawain Vs. Bane	2.00
5 JRe,V:Magpie	2.00
6 A:Spider-Man	2.00
7 A:Spider-Man,V:Warheads	2.00
8 JRe,A:Spider-Man	2.00
9 A:Spider-Man,Warheads	2.00
10 V:Baron Blood	2.00
11	2.00
12 MyS-TECH Wars,V:Skire	2.00
13 A:Death's Head II	2.00
14 A:Death's Head II	2.00
15 D:Adam,A:Death's Head II	2.00

KRAZY KOMICS
Timely July, 1942
1 B:Ziggy Pig,Silly Seal	350.00
2 Toughy Tomcat(c)	150.00
3 Toughy Tomcat/Bunny(c)	100.00
4 Toughy Tomcat/Ziggy(c)	100.00
5 Ziggy/Buzz Saw(c)	100.00
6 Toughy/Cannon(c)	100.00
7 Cigar Store Indian(c)	100.00
8 Toughy/Hammock(c)	100.00
9 Hitler(c)	100.00
10 Newspaper(c)	125.00
11 Canoe(c)	75.00
12 Circus(c)	100.00
13 Pirate Treasure(c)	75.00
14 Fishing(c)	75.00
15 Ski-Jump(c)	75.00
16 Airplane(c)	60.00
17 Street corner(c)	60.00
18 Mallet/Bell(c)	60.00
19 Bicycle(c)	60.00
20 Ziggy(c)	60.00
21 Toughy's date(c)	60.00
22 Crystal Ball(c)	60.00
23 Sharks in bathtub(c)	60.00
24 Baseball(c)	60.00
25 HK,Krazy Krow(c)	75.00
26 Super Rabbit(c)	60.00
Becomes:	

CINDY COMICS
27 HK,B:Margie,Oscar	80.00
28 HK,Snow sled(c)	50.00

29	50.00
30	50.00
31 HK	50.00
32	30.00
33 A;Georgie	30.00
34 thru 40	@30.00

Becomes:

CRIME CAN'T WIN

41 Crime stories	110.00
42	50.00
43 GT,Horror story	65.00
4 thru 11	@40.00
12 Sept., 1953	40.00

KRAZY KOMICS
Timely
[2nd Series] Aug., 1948

1 BW,HK,B:Eustice Hayseed	300.00
2 BW,O:Powerhouse Pepper	
November, 1948	225.00

KRAZY KROW
Summer, 1945

1 B:Krazy Krow	92.00
2	55.00
3 Winter, 1945-46	55.00

KREE-SKRULL WAR
Sept., 1983

1 JB,NA,reprints	5.00
2 JB,NA,Oct., 1983	5.00

KRULL
Nov., 1983

1 Ph(c),BBI,movie adapt	1.00
2 BBI,reprint,Marvel Super	
Special,Dec., 1983	1.00

KULL THE CONQUEROR
[1st Series] June, 1971

1 MSe,RA,WW,A King Comes	
Riding,O:Kull	10.00
2 MSe,JSe,Shadow Kingdom	5.00
3 MSe,JSe,Death Dance of	
Thulsa Doom	5.00
4 MSe,JSe,Night o/t Red Slayers	3.00
5 MSe,JSe,Kingdom By the Sea	3.00
6 MSe,JSe,Lurker Beneath	
the Sea	2.00
7 MSe,JSe,Delcardes'Cat,	
A:Thulsa Doom	2.00
8 MSe,JSe,Wolfshead	2.00
9 MSe,JSe,The Scorpion God	2.00
10 MSe,Swords o/t White Queen	2.00
11 MP,King Kull Must Die, O:Kull	
cont.,A:Thulsa Doom	2.00
12 MP,SB,Moon of Blood,V:Thulsa	
Doom,B:SD,B.U.stories	2.00
13 MP,AM,Torches From Hell,	
V:Thulsa Doom	2.00
14 MP,JA,The Black Belfry,	
A:Thulsa Doom	2.00
15 MP,Wings o/t Night-Beast,	
E:SD,B.U.stories	2.00
16 EH,Tiger in the Moon,	
A:Thulsa Doom	2.00
17 AA,EH,Thing from Emerald	
Darkness	2.00
18 EH,AA,Keeper of Flame	
& Frost	2.00
19 EH,AA,The Crystal Menace	2.00
20 EH,AA,Hell Beneath Atlantis	2.00
21 City of the Crawling Dead	1.75

Kull The Conqueror #5
© Marvel Entertainment Group

22 Talons of the Devil-Birds	1.75
23 Demon Shade	1.75
24 Screams in the Dark	1.75
25 A Lizard's Throne	1.75
26 Into Death's Dimension	1.75
27 The World Within	1.75
28 Creature and the Crown,	
A:Thulsa Doom	1.75
29 To Sit the Topaz Throne,	
V:Thulsa Doom, final issue	1.75

[2nd Series]

1 JB,Brule	2.50
2 Misareenia	2.00

[3rd Series]
1983–85

1 JB,BWi,DG,Iraina	1.50
2 JB,Battle to the Death	1.25
3 JB	1.00
4 JB	1.00
5 JB	1.00
6 JB	1.00
7 JB,Masquerade Death	1.00
8 JB	1.00
9 JB	1.00
10 JB	1.00

KULL AND THE BARBARIANS
May, 1975

1 NA,GK,reprint Kull #1	5.00
2 BBI,reprint,Dec., 1983	2.00
3 NA,HC,O:Red Sonja	3.00

LABRYNTH
1986–87

1 Movie adapt	2.00
2	1.50
3	1.50

LAFF-A-LYMPICS
1978–79

1 F;Hanna Barbera	2.00
2 thru 5	@1.50
6 thru 13	@1.00

LANA
August, 1948

1 F:Lana Lane The Show Girl,	
A:Rusty,B:Millie	100.00
2 HK,Hey Look,A:Rusty	50.00
3 Show(c),B:Nellie	30.00
4 Ship(c)	30.00
5 Audition(c)	30.00
6 Stop sign(c)	30.00
7 Beach(c)	30.00

Becomes:

LITTLE LANA

8 Little Lana(c)	26.00
9 Final Issue,March, 1950	26.00

LANCE BARNES: POST NUKE DICK

1 I:Lance Barnes	2.50
2 Cigarettes	2.50
3 Warring Mall Tribe	2.50
4 V:Ex-bankers,last issue	2.50

LAST AMERICAN
Epic 1990–91

1	3.50
2	3.00
3	2.50
4 Final issue.	2.25

THE LAST AVENGERS STORY

1 PDd, Alterverse,Future world	5.95
2 PDd, Final fate,fully painted	5.95
TPB PDd,AOl, rep. Alterniverse	
story, 96pg.	12.95

LAST STARFIGHTER, THE
Oct.–Dec., 1984

1 JG(c),BBI,Movie adapt.	1.00
2 Movie adapt	1.00
3 BBI	1.00

LAWBREAKERS ALWAYS LOSE!
Spring, 1948–Oct. 1949

1 Partial Ph(c),Adam and Eve,	
HK,Giggles and Grins	200.00
2 FBI V:Fur Theives	100.00
3	75.00
4 Asylum(c)	75.00
5	75.00
6 Pawnbroker(c)	65.00
7 Crime at Midnight	125.00
8 Prison Break	50.00
9 Ph(c),He Prowled at Night	50.00
10 Phc(c),I Met My Murderer	50.00

LAWDOG

1 B:CDi(s),FH,I:Lawdog	2.50
2 FH,V:Vocal-yokel Cultist	2.25
3 FH,Manical Nazis	2.25
4 FH,V:Zombies	2.25
5 FH	2.25
6 FH	2.25
7 FH,V:Zombies	2.25
8 FH,w/card	2.25
9 FH,w/card	2.25
10 last issue, w/card	2.25

MARVEL

LAWDOG & GRIMROD: TERROR AT THE CROSSROADS

1 . . . . 3.50

LEGION OF MONSTERS
Sept., 1975
(black & white magazine)
1 NA(c),GM,I&O:Legion of
Monsters,O:Manphibian 30.00

LEGION OF NIGHT
Oct., 1991
1 WPo/SW,A:Fin Fang Foom . . . 5.50
2 WPo,V:Fin Fang Foom 5.50

LETHAL FOES OF SPIDER-MAN
1 B:DFr(s),SMc,R:Stegron 2.00
2 SMc,A:Stegron 2.00
3 SMc,V:Spider-Man 2.00
4 E:DFr(s),SMc,Last Issue 2.00

LIFE OF CAPTAIN MARVEL
August, 1985
1 rep.Iron Man #55,
Capt.Marvel #25,26 . . . . 9.00
2 rep.Capt.Marvel#26-28 . . . . . 6.50
3 rep.Capt.Marvel#28-30
Marvel Feature #12 . . . . . . 6.00
4 rep.Marvel Feature #12,Capt.
Marvel #31,32,Daredevil#105 . 6.00
5 rep.Capt.Marvel #32-#34 . . . . 6.00

LIFE OF CHRIST
1 Birth of Christ 3.00
2 MW,The Easter Story 3.00

LIFE OF POPE JOHN-PAUL II
1 JSt, Jan., 1983 . . . . 5.00
1a Special reprint 3.00

LIFE WITH MILLIE
See: DATE WITH MILLIE

LIGHT AND DARKNESS WAR
Epic Oct., 1988
1 . . . . 4.00
2 . . . . 3.00
3 thru 6 Dec., 1989 . . . . @2.50

LINDA CARTER, STUDENT NURSE
Atlas Sept., 1961
1 . . . . 24.00
2 thru 9, Jan., 1963 . . . . . . @15.00

LION KING
1 based on Movie 2.75

LI'L KIDS
August, 1970
1 . . . . 7.50
2 thru 11 . . . . @4.50
12 June, 1973 . . . . 4.50

Li'l Kids #1
© Marvel Entertainment Group

LI'L PALS
Sept., 1972
1 . . . . 2.50
2 thru 5, May, 1973 . . . . @2.50

LITTLE ASPRIN
July, 1949
1 HK,A;Oscar 70.00
2 HK 40.00
3 Dec., 1949 . . . . 25.00

LITTLE LANA
See: LANA

LITTLE LENNY
June, 1949
1 . . . . 40.00
2 . . . . 22.00
3 November, 1949 . . . . 22.00

LITTLE LIZZIE
June, 1949
1 Roller Skating(c) 44.00
2 Soda(c) 25.00
3 Movies(c) 25.00
4 Lizzie(c) 25.00
5 Lizzie/Swing(c) April,1950 . . . 25.00
[2nd Series]
Sept., 1953
1 . . . . 30.00
2 . . . . 20.00
3 Jan., 1954 . . . . 20.00

LITTLE MERMAID, THE
1 . . . . 1.50
2 Reception for Pacifica royalty . . 1.50
3 TrR,Ariel joins fish club 1.50
4 . . . . 1.50
5 . . . . 1.50
6 TrR,Ariel decorates coral"tree" . 1.50
7 TrR,Flogglefish banished 1.50
8 . . . . 1.50
9 Annual Sea Horse Tournament 1.50
10 TrR,AnnualBlowfishTournament 1.50
11 TrR,Sharkeena,King Triton . . . 1.50
12 . . . . 1.50

13 Lobster Monster 1.50

LOGAN
1-shot HMe,48pg 5.95

LOGAN: PATH OF THE WARRIOR
1996
1-shot 5.00

LOGAN: SHADOW SOCIETY
1996
1-shot HMe,TCk Early life of
Wolverine 5.00

LOGAN'S RUN
Jan., 1977
1 GP,From Movie 3.00
2 GP,Cathedral Kill 2.00
3 GP,Lair of Laser Death 2.00
4 GP,Dread Sanctuary 2.00
5 GP,End Run 2.00
6 MZ,B.U.Thanos/Drax 7.00
7 TS,Cathedral Prime 2.00

LONGSHOT
Sept., 1985
1 AAd,WPo(i),BA,I:Longshot 8.00
2 AAd,WPo(i),I:RicoshetRita 6.00
3 AAd,WPo(i),I:Mojo,Spiral 6.00
4 AAd,WPo(i),A:Spider-Man 6.00
5 AAd,WPo(i),A:Dr. Strange 6.00
6 AAd,WPo(i),A:Dr. Strange 6.00
TPB Reprints #1–#6 . . . . 16.95

LOOSE CANNONS
1 DAn 2.50
2 DAn 2.50
3 DAn 2.75

LORNA, THE JUNGLE GIRL
Atlas 1953–57
1 Terrors of the Jungle,O:Lorna 200.00
2 Headhunter's Strike
I:Greg Knight 100.00
3 . . . . 85.00
4 . . . . 85.00
5 . . . . 85.00
6 RH(c),GT 75.00
7 RH(c) 75.00
8 Jungle Queen Strikes Again . 75.00
9 . . . . 75.00
10 White Fang 75.00
11 Death From the Skies 75.00
12 Day of Doom 50.00
13 thru 17 . . . . @50.00
18 AW(c) 60.00
19 thru 26 . . . . @50.00

LOVE ADVENTURES
Atlas Oct., 1949
1 Ph(c) 75.00
2 Ph(c),Tyrone Power/Gene
Tierney 75.00
3 thru 12 . . . . @40.00
Becomes:
ACTUAL CONFESSIONS
13 . . . . 16.00
14 Dec., 1952 . . . . 16.00

MARVEL

LOVE DRAMAS
Oct., 1949
1 Ph(c),JKa 75.00
2 Jan., 1950 . . . . 50.00

LOVE ROMANCES
See: IDEAL

LOVERS
See: ALL-SELECT COMICS

LOVE SECRETS
Oct., 1949
1 . . . . 70.00
2 Jan., 1950 . . . . 40.00

LUNATIK
1995
1 KG 1.95
2 V:The Avengers 1.95
3 conclusion 1.95

Machine Man #10
© Marvel Entertainment Group

MACHINE MAN
April, 1978
1 JK,From 2001 . . . . 3.00
2 JK 2.50
3 JK,V:Ten-For,The Mean
   Machine 2.50
4 JK,V:Ten-For,Battle on A
   Busy Street 2.50
5 JK,V:Ten-For,Day of the
   Non-Hero 2.50
6 JK,V:Ten-For 2.50
7 JK,With A Nation Against Him . 2.50
8 JK,Escape:Impossible 2.50
9 JK,In Final Battle 2.50
10 SD,Birth of A Super-Hero . . . 2.50
11 SD,V:Binary Bug 2.50
12 SD,"Where walk the Gods" . . . 2.50
13 SD,Xanadu 2.50
14 SD,V:Machine Man 2.50
15 SD,A:Thing,Human Torch 2.50
16 SD,I:Baron Brimstone And the
   Satan Squad 2.50
17 SD,Madam Menace 2.50

18 A:Alpha Flight 3.50
19 I:Jack o'Lantern 16.00

MACHINE MAN
[Limited-Series]
Oct., 1984
1 HT,BWS,V:Baintronics 3.00
2 HT,BWS,C:Iron Man of 2020 . . 3.00
3 HT,BWS,I:Iron Man of 2020 . . . 3.50
4 HT,BWS,V:Iron Man of 2020 . . 3.00
TPB rep.#1-4 . . . . 5.95

MACHINE MAN 2020
1 rep. limited series #1–#2 . . . . 2.00
2 rep. limited series #3–#4 . . . . 2.00

MAD ABOUT MILLIE
April, 1969
1 . . . . 23.00
2 thru 16 . . . . @12.50
17 Dec., 1970 . . . . 12.50
Ann.#1 . . . . 10.00

MADBALLS
Star Sept., 1986
1 Based on Toys 1.25
2 thru 9 . . . . @1.00
10 June, 1988 . . . . 1.00

MAD DOG
1 from Bob TV Show 1.50
2 V:Trans World Trust Corp. 1.25
3 V:Cigarette Criminals 1.25
4 V:Dogs of War 1.25
5 thru 6 . . . . @1.95

MAGIK
Dec., 1983
1 JB,TP,F:Storm and Illyana . . . 3.50
2 JB,TP,A:Belasco,Sym 3.00
3 TP,A:New Mutants,Belasco . . . 3.00
4 TP,V:Belasco,A:Sym 3.00

MAGNETO
1993
0 JD,JBo,rep. origin stories. . . . 4.00
0a Gold ed. 15.00
0b Platinum ed. 18.00

MAGNETO
1996
1 (of 4) PrM,KJo,JhB, Joseph . . 1.95
2 PrM,KJo,JhB, Joseph's search for
   his past life 1.95
3 PrM,KJo,JhB 1.95
4 PrM,KJo,JhB, concl. 1.95

MAN COMICS
Atlas 1949–53
1 GT, Revenge 140.00
2 GT, Fury in his Fists 75.00
3 Mantrap 50.00
4 The Fallen Hero 50.00
5 Laugh,Fool,Laugh 50.00
6 Black Hate 40.00
7 The Killer 40.00
8 BEv,An Eye For an Eye 45.00
9 B:War Issues,Here Comes
   Sergeant Smith 30.00
10 Korean Communism 30.00
11 RH,Cannon Fodder 30.00
12 The Black Hate 30.00

13 GC,RH,Beach Head 30.00
14 GT,No Prisoners 40.00
15 . . . . 30.00
16 . . . . 25.00
17 RH 25.00
18 thru 20 . . . . @25.00
21 GC 25.00
22 BEv,BK,JSt 60.00
23 thru 26 . . . . @25.00
27 E:War Issues 25.00
28 Where Mummies Prowl 25.00

MANDRAKE
1 fully painted series 2.95
2 V:Octon 2.95
3 final issue 2.95

MAN FROM ATLANTIS
Feb., 1978
1 TS,From TV Series,O:Mark
   Harris 1.50
2 FR,FS,The Bermuda Triangle
   Trap 1.25
3 FR,FS,Undersea Shadow 1.25
4 FR,FS,Beware the Killer
   Spores 1.25
5 FR,FS,The Ray of the
   Red Death 1.25
6 FR,FS,Bait for the Behemoth . 1.25
7 FR,FS,Behold the Land
   Forgotten, August, 1978 . . . . 1.25

Man Thing #7
© Marvel Entertainment Group

MAN-THING
[1st Series]
Jan., 1974
1 FB,JM,A:Howard the Duck . . . 14.00
2 VM,ST,Hell Hath No Fury 7.00
3 VM,JA,I:Original Foolkiller 6.00
4 VM,JA,O&D:Foolkiller 4.00
5 MP,Night o/t Laughing Dead . . 4.00
6 MP,V:Soul-Slayers,Drug Issue . 4.00
7 MP,A Monster Stalks Swamp . . 4.00
8 MP,Man Into Monster 4.00
9 MP,Deathwatch 4.00
10 MP,Nobody Dies Forever 4.00
11 MP,Dance to the Murder 4.00

MARVEL

12 KJ,Death-Cry of a Dead Man . 4.00
13 TS,V:Captain Fate 4.00
14 AA,V:Captain Fate 4.00
15 A Candle for Saint Cloud 4.00
16 JB,TP,Death of a Legend 4.00
17 JM,Book Burns in Citrusville . . 4.00
18 JM,Chaos on the Campus 4.00
19 JM,FS,I:Scavenger 4.00
20 JM,A:Spider-Man,Daredevil,
   Shang-Chi,Thing 4.50
21 JM,O:Scavenger,Man Thing . . 4.00
22 JM,C:Howard the Duck 4.00
G-Size #1 MP,SD,JK,rep.TheGlob 5.00
G-Size #2 JB,KJ,The
   Monster Runs Wild 4.00
G-Size #3 AA,A World He
   Never Made 4.00
G-Size #4 FS,EH,inc.Howard the
   Duck vs.Gorko 4.00
G-Size #5 DA,EH,inc.Howard the
   Duck vs.Vampire 6.00

MAN-THING
[2nd Series]
Nov., 1979—July, 1981
1 JM,BWi 2.00
2 BWi,JM,Himalayan Nightmare . 1.50
3 BWi,JM,V:Snowman 1.50
4 BWi,DP,V:Mordo,A:Dr Strange . 1.50
5 DP,BWi,This Girl is Terrified . . 1.50
6 DP,BWi,Fraternity Rites 1.25
7 BWi,DP Return of Captain Fate 1.25
8 BWi,DP,V:Captain Fate 1.25
9 BWi(c),Save the Life of My
   Own Child 1.25
10 BWi,DP,Swampfire 1.25
11 Final issue 1.25

MARINES AT WAR
See: DEVIL-DOG DUGAN

MARINES IN ACTION
Atlas June, 1955
1 B:Rock Murdock,Boot Camp
   Brady 50.00
2 thru 13 . . . . @30.00
14 Sept., 1957 . . . . 30.00

MARINES IN BATTLE
Atlas Aug., 1954
1 RH,B:Iron Mike McGraw . . . 100.00
2 . . . . 50.00
3 thru 6 . . . . @35.00
7 . . . . 45.00
8 . . . . 35.00
9 . . . . 35.00
10 . . . . 35.00
11 thru 16 . . . . @30.00
17 . . . . 50.00
18 thru 22 . . . . @30.00
23 . . . . 50.00
24 . . . . 30.00
25 Sept., 1958 . . . . 35.00

MARK HAZZARD: MERC
Nov., 1986
1 GM,O:Mark Hazzard 1.50
2 GM 1.00
3 M,Arab Terrorists 1.00
4 GM 1.00
5 GM 1.00
6 GM 1.00
7 GM 1.00

Mark Hazzard: Merc #1
© Marvel Entertainment Group

8 GM 1.00
9 NKu/AKu 1.00
10 . . . . 1.00
11 . . . . 1.00
12 Oct., 1987 . . . . 1.00
Ann.#1 D:Merc 1.25

MARSHALL LAW
Epic 1987–89
1 . . . . 4.50
2 . . . . 3.00
3 thru 6 . . . . @2.50

MARVEL ACTION HOUR:
FANTASTIC FOUR
1 regular 1.50
1a bagged with insert print from
   animated series 3.00
2 V:Puppet Master 1.50
3 . . . . 1.50
4 V:Sub-Mariner 1.50
5 . . . . 1.50
6 R:Skrulls 1.50
7 V:Doctor Doom 1.50
8 Wanted by the Law 1.50

MARVEL ACTION HOUR:
IRON MAN
1 regular 1.50
1a bagged with insert print from
   animated series 3.25
2 V:War Machine 1.50
3 V:Ultimo 1.50
4 A:Force Works, Hawkeye,
   War Machine 1.50
5 O:Iron Man 1.50
6 V:Fing Fang Foom 1.50
7 V:Mandarin 1.50
8 V:Robots 1.50

MARVEL ACTION
UNIVERSE
TV Tie-in, Jan., 1989
1 Rep.Spider-Man & Friends . . 2.50

MARVEL ADVENTURES
STARRING DAREDEVIL
Dec., 1975–Oct. 1976
1 Rep,Daredevil #22 . . . . 2.00
2 thru 5, Rep,Daredevil #23-26 . @1.25
6 DD #27 . . . . 1.25

MARVEL ADVENTURES
Feb. 1997
1 RMc,F:The Hulk 1.50
2 RMc,F:Spider-Man 1.50
3 RMc,F:Quicksilver & Scarlet
   Witch 1.50
4 RMc,BHr,F:Hulk,V:Brotherhood
   of Evil Mutants 1.50
5 RMc,BHr,F:Spider-Man, The
   X-Men 1.50
6 RMc,BHr,A:Spider-Man,Invisible
   Woman, Human Torch 1.50

MARVEL &
DC PRESENTS
Nov., 1982
1 WS,TA,X-Men & Titans,A:Darkseid,
   Deathstroke(3rd App.), ... 18.00

MARVEL BOY
Dec., 1950
1 RH,O:Marvel Boy,Lost World 650.00
2 BEv,The Zero Hour 550.00
Becomes:
ASTONISHING
3 BEv,Marvel Boy,V:Mr Death 650.00
4 BEv,Stan Lee,The
   Screaming Tomb 450.00
5 BEv,Horro in the Caves of
   Doom 450.00
6 BEv,My Coffin is Waiting
   E:Marvel Boy 450.00
7 JR,Nightmare 175.00
8 RH,Behind the Wall 175.00
9 RH(c),The Little Black Box . . 175.00
10 BEv,Walking Dead 175.00
11 BF,JSt.Mr Mordeau 150.00
12 GC,BEv,Horror Show 150.00
13 BK,MSy,Ghouls Gold 150.00
14 BK,The Long Jump Down . . 150.00
15 BEv(c),Grounds for Death . . 125.00
16 BEv(c),DAy,SSh,Don't Make
   a Ghoul of Yourself 150.00
17 Who Was the Wilmach
   Werewolf? 125.00
18 BEv(c),JR,Vampire at my
   Window 175.00
19 BK,Back From the Grave . . 150.00
20 GC,Mystery at Midnight . . . 125.00
21 Manhunter 100.00
22 RH(c),Man Against Werewolf 100.00
23 The Woman in Black 125.00
24 JR,The Stone Face 100.00
25 RC,I Married a Zombie 125.00
26 RH(c),I Died Too Often 100.00
27 . . . . 100.00
28 No Evidence 100.00
29 BEv(c),GC,Decapitation(c) . 100.00
30 Tentacled eyeball story . . . 150.00
31 . . . . 100.00
32 A Vampire Takes a Wife . . . 100.00
33 SMo 100.00
34 Transformation 100.00
35 . . . . 100.00
36 Pithecanthrope Giant 100.00
37 BEv,Poor Pierre 100.00

All comics prices listed are for *Near Mint* condition.

MARVEL

38 The Man Who Didn't Belong .	75.00
39	75.00
40	75.00
41	75.00
42	75.00
43	75.00
44 RC	90.00
45 BK	90.00
46	75.00
47 BK	90.00
48	75.00
49	75.00
50	75.00
51	75.00
52	75.00
53	90.00
54	90.00
55	100.00
56	75.00
57	125.00
58	70.00
59	70.00
60	80.00
61	70.00
62	80.00
63 August, 1957	80.00

MARVEL CHILLERS
Oct., 1975

1 GK(c),I:Mordred the Mystic . . . 4.00
2 E:Mordred 2.50
3 HC/BWr(c),B:Tigra,The Were
  Woman 2.50
4 V:Kraven The Hunter 2.50
5 V:Rat Pack,A:Red Wolf 2.50
6 RB(c),JBy,V:Red Wolf 2.50
7 JK(c),GT,V:Super Skrull
  E:Tigra,Oct., 1976 . . . . 2.50
GN MGu(s),LSh,F:The Hulk . . 2.99
GN LHa(s) F:Wolverine 2.99

MARVEL CHRISTMAS SPECIAL

1 DC/AAd/KJ/SB/RLm,A:Ghost Rider
  X-Men,Spider-Man 2.25

MARVEL CLASSICS COMICS
1976–78

1 GK/DA(c),B:Reprints from
  Pendulum Illustrated Comics
  Dr.Jekyll & Mr. Hyde 5.00
2 GK(c),AN,Time Machine 3.50
3 GK/KJ(c) The Hunchback of
  Notre Dame 3.50
4 GK/DA(c),20,000 Leagues–
  Beneath the Sea by Verne . . 3.50
5 GK(c),RN,Black Beauty 3.50
6 GK(c),Gullivers Travels 3.50
7 GK(c),Tom Sawyer 3.50
8 GK(c),AN,Moby Dick 3.50
9 GK(c),NR,Dracula 3.50
10 GK(c),Red Badge of Courage . 3.50
11 GK(c),Mysterious Island 3.50
12 GK/DA(c),AN,Three Musketeers 3.50
13 GK(c),Last of the Mohicans . . . 3.50
14 GK(c),War of the Worlds 3.50
15 GK(c),Treasure Island 3.50
16 GK(c),Ivanhoe 3.00
17 JB/ECh(c),The Count of
  Monte Cristo 3.00
18 ECh(c),The Odsyssey 3.00
19 JB(c),Robinson Crusoe 3.00
20 Frankenstein 3.00

Marvel Classics Comics #11
© Marvel Entertainment Group

21 GK(c),Master of the World . . . 3.00
22 GK(c),Food of the Gods 3.00
23 Moonstone by Wilkie Collins . . 3.00
24 GK/RN(c),She 3.00
25 The Invisible Man by H.G.Wells 3.00
26 JB(c),The Illiad by Homer 3.00
27 Kidnapped 3.00
28 MGo(1st art) The Pit and
  the Pendulum 10.00
29 The Prisoner of Zenda 3.00
30 The Arabian Nights 3.00
31 The First Men in the Moon . . . 3.00
32 GK(c),White Fang 3.00
33 The Prince and the Pauper . . . 3.00
34 AA,Robin Hood 3.00
35 FBe,Alice in Wonderland 3.00
36 A Christmas Carol 3.00

MARVEL COLLECTORS ITEM CLASSICS
Feb., 1965

1 SD,JK,reprint FF #2 . . . . 46.00
2 SD,JK,reprint FF #3 . . . . 25.00
3 SD,JK,reprint FF #4 . . . . 25.00
4 SD,JK,reprint FF #7 . . . . 25.00
5 SD,JK,reprint FF #8 . . . . 12.00
6 SD,JK,reprint FF #9 . . . . 12.00
7 SD,JK,reprint FF #13 . . . . . . 12.00
8 SD,JK,reprint FF #10 . . . . . . 12.00
9 SD,JK,reprint FF #14 . . . . . . 12.00
10 SD,JK,reprint FF #15 . . . . . . 12.00
11 SD,JK,reprint FF #16 . . . . . . 10.00
12 SD,JK,reprint FF #17 . . . . . . 10.00
13 SD,JK,reprint FF #18 . . . . . . 10.00
14 SD,JK,reprint FF #20 . . . . . . 10.00
15 SD,JK,reprint FF #21 . . . . . . 10.00
16 SD,JK,reprint FF #22 . . . . . . 10.00
17 SD,JK,reprint FF #23 . . . . . . 10.00
18 SD,JK,reprint FF #24 . . . . . . 10.00
19 SD,JK,reprint FF #27 . . . . . . 10.00
20 SD,JK,reprint FF #28 . . . . . . 10.00
21 SD,JK,reprint FF #29 . . . . . . 10.00
22 SD,JK,reprint FF #30 . . . . . . 10.00
Becomes:

MARVEL'S GREATEST COMICS

23 SD,JK,reprint FF#31 . . . . 4.00

24 SD,JK,reprint FF#32	4.00
25 SD,JK,reprint FF#33	4.00
26 SD,JK,reprint FF#34	4.00
27 SD,JK,reprint FF#35	4.00
28 SD,JK,reprint FF#36	4.00
29 JK,reprint FF#37	4.00
30 JK,reprint FF#38	4.00
31 JK,reprint FF#40	4.00
32 JK,reprint FF#42	4.00
33 JK,reprint FF#44	4.00
34 JK,reprint FF#47	4.00
35 JK,reprint FF#48	8.50
36 JK,reprint FF#49	7.00
37 JK,reprint FF#50	7.00
38 JK,reprint FF#51	3.00
39 JK,reprint FF#52	3.00
40 JK,reprint FF#53	3.00
41 JK,reprint FF#54	3.00
42 JK,reprint FF#55	3.00
43 JK,reprint FF#56	3.00
44 JK,reprint FF#61	3.00
45 JK,reprint FF#62	3.00
46 JK,reprint FF#63	3.00
47 JK,reprint FF#64	3.00
48 JK,reprint FF#65	3.00
49 JK,reprint FF#66	6.00
50 JK,reprint FF#67	6.00
51 thru 75 JK,reprint FF	@1.75
76 thru 82 JK,reprint FF	@1.25
83 thru 95 Reprint FF	@1.25
96 Reprint FF#, Jan., 1981	1.25

MARVEL COMICS
Oct.-Nov., 1939

1 FP(c),BEv,CBu,O:Sub-Mariner
  I&B:The Angel,A:Human Torch,
  Kazar,Jungle Terror,
  B:The Masked Raider . 100,000.00
Becomes:

MARVEL MYSTERY COMICS

2 CSM(c),BEv,CBu,PGn,
  B:American, Ace,Human
  Torch,Sub-Mariner,Kazar 20,000.00
3 ASh(c),BEv,CBu,PGn,
  E:American Ace 8,600.00
4 ASh(c),BEv,CBu,PGn,
  I&B:Electro,The Ferret,
  Mystery Detective 7,000.00
5 ASh(c),BEv,CBu,PGn,
  Human Torch(c) 15,000.00
6 ASh(c),BEv,CBu,PGn,
  Angel(c) 5,000.00
7 ASh(c),BEv,CBu,PGn,
  Bondage(c) 5,000.00
8 ASh(c),BEv,CBu,PGn,Human
  TorchV:Sub-Mariner . . . 7,000.00
9 ASh(c),BEv,CBu,PGn,Human
  Torch V:Sub-Mariner(c) . 15,000.00
10 ASh(c),BEv,CBu,PGn,B:Terry
  Vance Boy Detective . 5,000.00
11 ASh(c),BEv,CBu,PGn,
  Human Torch V:Nazis(c) . . 2,500.00
12 ASh(c),BEv,CBu,
  PGn,Angel(c) 3,000.00
13 ASh(c),BEv,CBu,PGn,S&K,
  I&B:The Vision 3,500.00
14 ASh(c),BEv,CBu,PGn,S&K,
  Sub-Mariner V:Nazis 1,700.00
15 ASh(c),BEv,CBu,PGn,S&K,
  Sub-Mariner(c) 1,800.00
16 ASh(c),BEv,CBu,PGn,S&K,Human
  Torch/Nazi Airbase (c) . . . 1,700.00
17 ASh(c),BEv,CBu,PGn,S&K

MARVEL

Human Torch/Sub-Mariner 1,900.00
18 ASh(c),BEv,CBu,PGn,S&K,
 Human Torch & Toro(c) . . 1,500.00
19 ASh(c),BEv,CBu,PGn,S&K,
 O:Toro,E:Electro 1,700.00
20 ASh(c),BEv,CBu,PGn,S&K,
 O:The Angel 1,800.00
21 ASh(c),BEv,CBu,PGn,S&K,
 I&B:The Patriot 1,500.00
22 ASh(c),BEv,CBu,PGn,S&K,
 Toro/Bomb(c) 1,300.00
23 ASh(c),BEv,CBu,PGn,S&K,
 O:Vision,E:The Angel 1,300.00
24 ASh(c),BEv,CBu,S&K,
 Human Torch(c) 1,300.00
25 BEv,CBu,S&K,ASh Nazi(c) 1,300.00
26 ASh(c),BEv,CBu,S&K,
 Sub-Mariner(c) 1,200.00
27 ASh(c),BEv,CBu,
 S&K,E:Kazar 1,200.00
28 ASh(c),BEv,CBu,S&K,Bondage
 (c),B:Jimmy Jupiter 1,200.00
29 ASh(c),BEv,CBu,Bondage(c)1,200.00

Marvel Mystery Comics #10
© Marvel Entertainment Group

30 BEv,CBu,Pearl Harbor(c) . 1,200.00
31 BEv,CBu,HUman Torch(c) 1,000.00
32 CBu,I:The Boboes 1,000.00
33 ASHc(c),CBu,Japanese(c) 1,000.00
34 ASh(c),CBu,V:Hitler 1,200.00
35 ASh(c),Beach Assault(c) . . 1,000.00
36 ASh(c),Nazi Invasion of
 New York(c) 1,000.00
37 SSh(c),Nazi(c) 1,000.00
38 SSh(c),Battlefield(c) 1,000.00
39 ASh(c),Nazis/U.S(c) 1,000.00
40 ASh(c),Zeppelin(c) 1,000.00
41 ASh(c),JapaneseCommand(c)900.00
42 ASh(c),Japanese Sub(c) . . . 900.00
43 ASh(c),Destroyed Bridge(c) . 900.00
44 ASh(c),Nazi Super Plane(c) 900.00
45 ASh(c),Nazi(c) 900.00
46 ASh(c),Hitler Bondage(c) . . 900.00
47 ASh(c),Ruhr Valley Dam(c) . 900.00
48 ASh(c),E:Jimmy Jupiter,
 Vision,Allied Invasion(c) . . . 900.00
49 SSh(c),O:Miss America,
 Bondage(c) 1,200.00
50 ASh(c),Bondage(c),Miss
 Patriot 1,000.00

51 ASh(c),Nazi Torture(c) 900.00
52 ASh(c),Bondage(c) 900.00
53 ASh(c),Bondage(c) 900.00
54 ASh(c),Bondage(c) 900.00
55 ASh(c),Bondage(c) 900.00
56 ASh(c),Bondage(c) 900.00
57 ASh(c),Torture/Bondage(c) . 900.00
58 ASh(c),Torture(c) 900.00
59 ASh(c),Testing Room(c) . . . 900.00
60 ASh(c),Japanese Gun(c) . . 900.00
61 Torturer Chamber(c) 900.00
62 ASh(c),Violent(c) 900.00
63 ASh(c),NaziHighCommand(c) 900.00
64 ASh(c),Last Nazi(c) 900.00
65 ASh(c),Bondage(c) 900.00
66 ASh(c),Last Japanese(c) . . . 900.00
67 ASh(c),Treasury raid(c) 800.00
68 ASh(c),Torture Chamber(c) . 800.00
69 ASh(c),Torture Chamber(c) . 800.00
70 Cops & Robbers(c) 800.00
71 ASh(c),Egyptian(c) 800.00
72 Police(c) 800.00
73 Werewolf Headlines(c) 800.00
74 ASh(c),Robbery(c),E:The
 Patriot 800.00
75 Tavern(c),B:Young Allies . . 800.00
76 ASh(c),Shoot-out(c),B:Miss
 America 800.00
77 Human Torch/Sub-Mariner(c) 800.00
78 Safe Robbery(c) 800.00
79 Super Villians(c),E:The
 Angel 800.00
80 I:Capt.America(in Marvel) 1,000.00
81 Mystery o/t Crimson Terror . 850.00
82 I:Sub-Mariner/Namora Team-up
 O:Namora,A:Capt.America 1,500.00
83 The Photo Phantom,E:Young
 Allies 750.00
84 BEv,B:The Blonde Phantom 1,000.00
85 BEv,A:Blonde Phantom,
 E:Miss America 750.00
86 BEv,Blonde Phantom ID
 Revealed,E:Bucky 850.00
87 BEv,I:Capt.America/Golden
 Girl Team-up 900.00
88 BEv,E:Toro 800.00
89 BEv,I:Human Torch/Sun Girl
 Team-up 850.00
90 BEv,Giant of the Mountains 850.00
91 BEv,I:Venus,E:Blonde
 Phantom,Sub-Mariner 850.00
92 BEv,How the Human Torch was
 Born,D:Professor Horton,I:The
 Witness,A:Capt.America . . 1,800.00
92a Marvel #33(c)rare,reprints10,000.00
Becomes:

MARVEL TALES
August, 1949

93 The Ghoul Strikes 1,000.00
94 BEv,The Haunted Love 650.00
95 The Living Death 475.00
96 MSy,The Monster Returns . 475.00
97 DRi,MSy,The Wooden Horror 475.00
98 BEv,BK,MSy,The Curse of
 the Black Cat 475.00
99 DRi,The Secret of the Wax
 Museum 475.00
100 The Eyes of Doom 475.00
101 The Man Who Died Twice . 475.00
102 BW,A Witch Among Us . . . 650.00
103 RA,A Touch of Death 475.00
104 RH(c),BW,BEv,The Thing
 in the Mirror 600.00
105 RH(c),GC,JSt,The Spider . 475.00
106 RH(c),BK,BEv,In The Dead of

the Night 400.00
107 GC,OW,BK,The Thing in the
 Sewer 400.00
108 RH(c),BEv,JR,Horror in the
 Moonlight 250.00
109 BEv(c),Sight for Sore Eyes 250.00
110 RH,SSh,A Coffin for Carlos 250.00
111 BEv,Horror Under the Earth 250.00
112 The House That Death Built 250.00
113 RH,Terror Tale 250.00
114 BEv(c),GT,JM,2 for Zombie 250.00
115 The Man With No Face . . . 250.00
116 JSt 250.00
117 BEv(c),GK,Terror in the
 North 250.00
118 RH,DBr,GC,A World
 Goes Mad 250.00
119 RH,They Gave Him A Grave 250.00
120 GC,Graveyard(c) 250.00
121 GC,Graveyard(c) 250.00
122 JKu,Missing One Body . . . 250.00
123 No Way Out 250.00
124 He Waits at the Tombstone 250.00
125 JF,Horror House 250.00
126 DW,It Came From Nowhere 175.00
127 BEv(c),GC,MD,Gone is the
 Gargoyle 175.00
128 Emily,Flying Saucer(c) . . . 175.00
129 You Can't Touch Bottom . . 175.00
130 RH(c),JF,The Giant Killer . 175.00
131 GC,BEv,Five Fingers 175.00
132 . . . . 125.00
133 . . . . 125.00
134 BK,JKu,Flying Saucer(c) . . 150.00
135 thru 141 . . . . @100.00
142 . . . . 100.00
143 . . . . 100.00
144 . . . . 110.00
145 . . . . 100.00
146 . . . . 75.00
147 . . . . 100.00
148 . . . . 75.00
149 . . . . 75.00
150 . . . . 75.00
151 . . . . 75.00
152 . . . . 100.00
153 . . . . 110.00
154 . . . . 75.00
155 . . . . 75.00
156 . . . . 75.00
157 . . . . 100.00
158 . . . . 75.00
159 August, 1957 . . . . 100.00

MARVEL COMICS PRESENTS
Sept., 1988

1 WS(c),B:Wolverine(JB,KJ),Master
 of Kung Fu(TS),Man-Thing(TGr,DC)
 F:Silver Surfer(AM) 10.00
2 F:The Captain(AM) 5.00
3 JR2(c),F:The Thing(AM) 4.00
4 F:Thor(AM) 4.00
5 F:Daredevil(DT,MG) 4.00
6 F:Hulk 4.00
7 F:Submariner(SD) 4.00
8 CV(c),E:Master of Kung Fu,F:
 Iron Man(JS) 4.00
9 F:Cloak,El Aquila 4.00
10 E:Wolverine,B:Colossus(RL,CR),
 F:Machine Man(SD,DC) 4.00
11 F:Ant-Man(BL),Slag(RWi) . . . 3.00
12 E:Man-Thing,F:Hercules(DH),
 Namorita(FS) 3.00
13 B:Black Panther(GC,TP),F:

MARVEL

Shanna,Mr.Fantastic &
  Invisible Woman 3.00
14 F:Nomad(CP),Speedball(SD) . 3.00
15 F:Marvel Girl(DT,MG),Red
  Wolf(JS) 3.00
16 F:Kazar(JM),Longshot(AA) . . 3.00
17 E:Colossus,B:Cyclops(RLm),
  F:Watcher(TS) 4.00
18 F:She-Hulk(JBy,BWi),Willie
  Lumpkin(JSt) 3.00
19 RLd(c)B:Dr.Strange(MBg),
  I:Damage Control(EC,AW) . . 3.00
20 E:Dr.Strange,F:Clea(RLm) . . 3.00
21 F:Thing,Paladin(RWi,DA) . . . 3.00
22 F:Starfox(DC),Wolfsbane &
  Mirage 3.00
23 F:Falcon(DC),Wheels(RWi) . . 3.00
24 F:Cyclops(JS),Havok(RB,JRu),
  F:Shamrock(DJ,DA) 3.00
25 F:Ursa Major,I:Nth Man 4.00
26 B&I:Coldblood(PG),F:Hulk . . 2.50
27 F:American Eagle(RWi) 2.50
28 F:Triton(JS) 2.50
29 F:Quasar(PR) 2.50
30 F:Leir(TMo) 2.50
31 TM,E:Havok,B:Excalibur
  (EL,TA) 4.00
32 TM(c),F:Sunfire(DH,DC) 3.00
33 F:Namor(JLe) 4.00
34 F:Captain America(JsP) 3.00
35 E:Coldblood,F:Her(EL,AG) . . 4.00
36 BSz(c),F:Hellcat(JBr) 4.00
37 E:Bl.Panther,F:Devil-Slayer . . 3.00
38 E:Excalibur,B:Wonderman(JS),
  Wolverine(JB),F:Hulk(MR,DA) . 4.00
39 F:Hercules(BL),Spider-Man . . . 3.50
40 F:Hercules(BL),Overmind(DH) . 3.50
41 F:Daughters of the Dragon(DA),
  Union Jack(KD) 3.50
42 F:Iron Man(MBa),Siryn(LSn) . . 3.50
43 F:Iron Man(MBa),Siryn(LSn) . . 3.50
44 F:Puma(BWi),Dr.Strange 3.50
45 E:Wonderman,F:Hulk(HT),
  Shooting Star 3.50
46 RLd(c),B:Devil-Slayer,F:Namor,
  Aquarian 3.50
47 JBy(c),E:Wolverine,F:Captain
  America,Arabian Knight(DP) . . 3.50
48 F:Wolverine&Spider-Man(EL),
  F:Wasp,Storm&Dr.Doom 5.00
49 E:Devil-Slayer,F:Daredevil(RWi),
  Gladiator(DH) 4.50
50 E:Wolverine&Spider-Man,B:Comet
  Man(KJo),F:Captain Ultra(DJ),
  Silver Surfer(JkS) 4.50
51 B:Wolverine(RLd),F:Iron Man
  (MBr,DH),Le Peregrine 4.00
52 F:Rick Jones,Hulk(RWi,TMo) . 4.00
53 E:Wolverine,Comet Man,F:
  Silver Sable&Black Widow
  (RLd,BWi),B:Stingray 4.00
54 B:Wolverine&Hulk(DR),
  Werewolf,F:Shroud(SD,BWi) . . 6.00
55 F:Collective Man(GLa) 6.00
56 E:Stingray,F:Speedball(SD) . . 6.00
57 DK(c),B:Submariner(MC,MFm),
  Black Cat(JRu) 6.00
58 F:Iron Man(SD) 6.00
59 E:Submariner,Werewolf,
  F:Punisher 6.00
60 B:Poison,Scarlet Witch,
  F:Captain America(TL) 6.00
61 E:Wolverine&Hulk,
  F:Dr.Strange 6.00
62 F:Wolverine(PR),Deathlok(JG) . 6.00

63 F:Wolverine(PR),E:Scarlet
  Witch,Thor(DH) 4.00
64 B:Wolverine&Ghost Rider(MT),
  Fantastic Four(TMo),F:Blade . . 4.00
65 F:Starfox(ECh) 3.50
66 F:Volstagg 3.50
67 E:Poison,F:Spider-Man(MG) . . 3.50
68 B:Shanna(PG),E:Fantastic Four
  F:Lockjaw(JA,AM) 3.50
69 B:Daredevil(DT),F:Silver Surfer 3.50
70 F:BlackWidow&Darkstar(AM) . 3.50
71 E:Wolverine&Ghost Rider,F:
  Warlock(New Mutants)(SMc) . 3.50
72 B:Weapon X(BWS),E:Daredevil,
  F:Red Wolf(JS) 7.00
73 F:Black Knight(DC),
  Namor(JLe) 5.00
74 F:Constrictor(SMc),Iceman &
  Human Torch(JSon,DA) 5.00
75 F:Meggan & Shadowcat,
  Dr.Doom(DC) 5.00
76 F:Death's Head(BHi,MFm),
  A:Woodgod(DC) 5.00

Marvel Comics Presents #163
© Marvel Entertainment Group

77 E:Shanna,B:Sgt.Fury&Dracula
  (TL,JRu),F:Namor 4.50
78 F:Iron Man(KSy),Hulk&Selene . 4.50
79 E:Sgt.Fury&Dracula,F:Dr.Strange,
  Sunspot(JBy) 4.50
80 F:Daughters of the Dragon,Mister
  Fantastic(DJ),Captain America
  (SD,TA) 4.50
81 F:Captain America(SD,TA),
  Daredevil(MR,AW),Ant-Man . . 4.00
82 B:Firestar(DT),F:Iron Man(SL),
  Power Man 4.00
83 F:Hawkeye,Hum.Torch(SD,EL) 4.00
84 E:Weapon X 5.00
85 B:Wolverine(SK),Beast(RLd,JaL-
  1st Work),F:Speedball(RWi),
  I:Cyber 7.00
86 F:PaladinE:RLd on Beast 5.00
87 F:Firestar,F:Shroud(RWi) 5.00
88 F:Solo,Volcana(BWi) 5.00
89 F:Spitfire(JSn),Mojo(JMa) . . . 5.00
90 B:Ghost Rider & Cable,F:
  Nightmare 4.50
91 F:Impossible Man 3.50
92 E:Wolverine,Beast,

  F:Northstar(JMa) 3.50
93 SK(c),B:Wolverine,Nova,
  F:Daredevil 3.00
94 F:Gabriel 3.00
95 SK(c),E:Wolverine,F:Hulk 3.00
96 B:Wolverine(TT),E:Nova,
  F:Speedball 3.00
97 F:Chameleon,Two-Gun Kid,
  E:Ghost Rider/Cable 3.00
98 E:Wolverine,F:Ghost Rider,
  Werewolf by Night 2.50
99 F:Wolverine,Ghost Rider,
  Mary Jane,Captain America. . . 2.50
100 SK,F:Ghost Rider,Wolverine,
  Dr.Doom,Nightmare 3.00
101 SK(c),B:Ghost Rider&Doctor
  Strange,Young Gods,Wolverine
  &Nightcrawler,F:Bar With
  No Name 2.00
102 RL,GC,AW,F:Speedball 2.00
103 RL,GC,AW,F:Puck 2.00
104 RL,GC,AW,F:Lockheed 2.00
105 RL,GC,AW,F:Nightmare 2.00
106 RL,GC,AW,F:Gabriel,E:Ghost
  Rider&Dr.Strange 2.00
107 GC,AW,TS,B:Ghost Rider&
  Werewolf 2.00
108 GC,AW,TS,SMc,E:Wolverine&
  Nightcrawler,B:Thanos 2.00
109 SLi,TS,SMc,B:Wolverine&
  Typhoid Mary,E:Young Gods . 2.00
110 SLi,SMc,F:Nightcrawler 2.00
111 SK(c),SLi,RWi,F:Dr.Strange,
  E:Thanos 2.00
112 SK(c),SLi,F:Pip,Wonder Man,
  E:Ghost Rider&Werewolf 2.00
113 SK(c),SLi,B:Giant Man,
  Ghost Rider&Iron Fist 1.75
114 SK(c),SLi,F:Arabian Knight . . 1.75
115 SK(c),SLi,F:Cloak&Dagger . . 1.75
116 SK(c),SLi,E:Wolverine &
  Typhoid Mary 1.75
117 SK,PR,B:Wolverine&Venom,
  I:Ravage 2099 . . . . 4.00
118 SK,PB,RWi,E:Giant Man,
  I:Doom 2099 . . . . 3.00
119 SK,GC,B:Constrictor,E:Ghost
  Rider&Iron Fist,F:Wonder Man 3.00
120 SK,GC,E:Constrictor,B:Ghost
  Rider/Cloak & Dagger,
  F:Spider-Man 2.50
121 SK,GC,F:Mirage,Andromeda . 2.50
122 SK(c),GK,E:Wolverine&Venom,
  Ghost Rider&Cloak&Dagger,F:
  Speedball&Rage,Two-Gun Kid 2.50
123 SK(c),DJ,SLi,B:Wolverine&Lynx,
  Ghost Rider&Typhoid Mary,
  She-Hulk,F:Master Man 1.75
124 SK(c),DJ,MBa,SLi,F:Solo . . . 1.75
125 SLi,SMc,DJ,B:Iron Fist 1.75
126 SLi,DJ,E:She-Hulk 1.75
127 SLi,DJ,DP,F:Speedball 1.75
128 SLi,DJ,RWi,F:American Eagle 1.75
129 SLi,DJ,F:Ant Man 1.75
130 DJ,SLi,RWi,E:Wolverine&Lynx,
  Ghost Rider&Typhoid Mary,Iron
  Fist,F:American Eagle 1.75
131 MFm,B:Wolverine,Ghost Rider&
  Cage,Iron Fist&Sabretooth,
  F:Shadowcat 1.75
132 KM(c),F:Iron Man 1.75
133 F:Cloak & Dagger 1.75
134 SLi,F:Vance Astro 1.75
135 SLi,F:Daredevil 1.75
136 B:Gh.Rider&Masters of Silence,

MARVEL

F:Iron Fist,Daredevil 1 75	
137 F:Ant Man 1.75	
138 B:Wolverine,Spellbound . . . 1.75	
139 F:Foreigner 1.75	
140 F:Captain Universe 1.75	
141 BCe(s),F:Iron Fist 1.75	
142 E:Gh.Rider&Masters of Silence,	
F:Mr.Fantastic 1.75	
143 Siege of Darkness,pt.#3,	
B:Werewolf,Scarlet Witch,	
E:Spellbound 2.00	
144 Siege of Darkness,pt.#6,	
B:Morbius, ... 2.00	
145 Siege of Darkness,pt.#11 . . . 2.00	
146 Siege of Darkness,pt.#14 . . . 1.75	
147 B:Vengeance,F:Falcon,Masters of	
Silence,American Eagle 1.75	
148 E:Vengeance,F:Capt.Universe,	
Black Panther 1.75	
149 F:Daughter o/t Dragon,Namor,	
Vengeance,Starjammers 1.75	
150 ANo(s),SLi,F:Typhoid Mary,DD,	
Vengeance,Wolverine 1.75	
151 ANo(s),F:Typhoid Mary,DD,	
Vengeance 1.75	
152 CDi(s),PR,B:Vengeance,Wolverine,	
War Machine,Moon Knight . . . 1.75	
153 CDi(s),A:Vengeance,Wolverine,	
War Machine,Moon Knight . . . 1.75	
154 CDi(s),E:Vengeance,Wolverine,	
War Machine,Moon Knight . . . 1.75	
155 CDi(s),B:Vengeance,Wolverine,	
War Machine,Kymaera 1.75	
156 B:Shang Chi,F:Destroyer . . . 1.50	
157 F:Nick Fury 1.50	
158 AD,I:Clan Destine,E:Kymaera,	
Shang Chi,Vengeance 1.75	
159 B:Hawkeye, New Warriors,	
F:Fun,E:Vengeance 1.75	
160 B:Vengeance,Mace 2.00	
161 E:Hawkeye 1.75	
162 B:Tigra,E:Mace 1.75	
163 E:New Warriors 1.75	
164 Tigra, Vengeance 1.75	
165 Tigra, Vengeance 1.75	
166 Turbo, Vengeance 1.75	
167 Turbo, Vengeance 1.75	
168 Thing, Vengeance 1.75	
169 Mandarin, Vengeance 1.75	
170 Force, Vengeance 1.75	
171 Nick Fury 1.75	
172 Lunatik 1.75	
173 . . . . 1.75	
174 . . . . 1.75	
175 . . . . 1.75	
TPB Ghost Rider & Cable,rep	
#90-97 . . . . 3.95	
TPB Save the Tyger,rep.Wolverine	
story from #1-10 . . . . 3.95	

MARVEL COMICS SUPER SPECIAL
[Magazine, 1977]

1 JB,WS,Kiss,Features &Photos 65.00
2 JB,Conan(1978) 6.00
3 WS,Close Encounters 5.00
4 GP,KJ,Beatles story 15.00
Becomes:
MARVEL SUPER SPECIAL
5 Kiss 1978 . . . . 35.00
6 GC,Jaws II 3.00
7 Does Not Exist
8 Battlestar Galactica(Tabloid) . . 3.00
9 Conan 4.00

10 GC,Starlord 3.00	
11 JB,RN,Weirdworld, ... 3.00	
12 JB,Weirdworld, ... 3.00	
13 JB,Weirdworld, ... 3.00	
14 GC,Meteor,adapt 3.00	
15 Star Trek 6.00	
15a Star Trek 9.00	
16 AW,B:Movie Adapts,Empire	
Strikes Back 7.00	
17 Xanadu 2.00	
18 HC(c),JB,Raiders of the Lost	
Ark 2.00	
19 HC,For Your Eyes Only 5.00	
20 Dragonslayer 2.50	
21 JB,Conan 1.00	
22 JSo(c),AW,Bladerunner 2.00	
23 Annie 2.00	
24 Dark Crystal 2.00	
25 Rock and Rule 2.00	
26 Octopussy 2.50	
27 AW,Return of the Jedi 6.00	
28 PH(c),Krull 2.00	
29 DSp,Tarzan of the Apes 2.00	
30 Indiana Jones and the Temple	
of Doom 2.50	
31 The Last Star Fighter 2.00	
32 Muppets Take Manhattan 2.00	
33 Buckaroo Banzai 2.00	
34 GM,Sheena 2.00	
35 JB,Conan The Destroyer 2.00	
36 Dune 2.00	
37 2010 . . . . 2.00	
38 Red Sonja 2.00	
39 Santa Claus 2.00	
40 JB,Labrynth 2.00	
41 Howard the Duck,Nov.,1986 . . 2.00	

MARVEL DOUBLE FEATURE
Dec., 1973

1 JK,GC,B:Tales of Suspense
Reprints,Capt.America,
Iron-Man 4.00
2 JK,GC ,A:Nick Fury 2.50
3 JK,GC 2.50
4 JK,GC,Cosmic Cube 2.50
5 JK,GC,V:Red Skull 2.50
6 JK,GC,V:Adaptoid 2.50
7 JK,GC,V:Tumbler 2.50
8 JK,GC,V:Super Adaptoid 2.50
9 GC,V:Batroc 2.50
10 GC 2.50
11 GC,Capt.America Wanted . . . 2.50
12 GC,V:Powerman,Swordsman . 2.50
13 GC,A:Bucky 2.50
14 GC,V:Red Skull 2.50
15 GK,GC,V:Red Skull 2.50
16 GC,V:Assassin 2.50
17 JK,GC,V:Aim,Iron Man &
Sub-Mariner #1 . . . . 4.00
18 JK,GC,V:Modok,Iron Man #1 . . 5.00
19 JK,GC,E:Capt.America 5.00
20 JK(c) 2.50
21 Capt.America,Black Panther
March, 1977 . . . . 2.50

MARVEL FANFARE
March, 1972

1 MG,TA,PS,F:Spider-Man,
Daredevil,Angel 7.00
2 MG,SM,FF,TVe,F:SpM,Ka-Zar . 5.00
3 DC,F:X-Men 5.00
4 PS,TA,MG,F:X-Men,Deathlok . . 5.00
5 MR,F:Dr.Strange 4.00

Marvel Fanfare #15
© *Marvel Entertainment Group*

6 F:Spider-Man,Scarlet Witch . . . 4.50
7 F:Hulk/Daredevil 3.00
8 CI,TA,GK,F:Dr.Strange 3.00
9 GM,F:Man Thing 3.00
10 GP,B:Black Widow 3.50
11 GP,D:M.Corcoran 3.50
12 GP,V:Snapdragon 3.50
13 GP,E:B.Widow,V:Snapdragon . 3.50
14 F:Fantastic Four,Vision 2.75
15 BWS,F:Thing,Human Torch . . 3.00
16 DC,JSt,F:Skywolf 2.50
17 DC,JSt,F:Skywolf 2.50
18 FM,JRu,F:Captain America . . . 3.00
19 RL,F:Cloak and Dagger 2.50
20 JSn,F:Thing&Dr.Strange 3.00
21 JSn,F:Thing And Hulk 3.00
22 KSy,F:Iron Man 2.50
23 KSy,F:Iron Man 2.50
24 F:Weird World 3.00
25 F:Weird World 2.50
26 F:Weird World 2.50
27 F:Daredevil 2.50
28 KSy,F:Alpha Flight 2.50
29 JBy,F:Hulk 3.00
30 BA,AW,F:Moon Knight 2.50
31 KGa,F:Capt.America,
Yellow Claw 2.50
32 KGa,PS,F:Capt.America,
Yellow Claw 2.50
33 JBr,F:X-Men 5.00
34 CV,F:Warriors Three 2.50
35 CV,F:Warriors Three 2.50
36 CV,F:Warriors Three 2.50
37 CV,F:Warriors Three 2.50
38 F:Captain America 2.50
39 JSon,F:Hawkeye,Moon Knight . 2.50
40 DM,F:Angel,Storm,Mystique . . 3.00
41 DGb,F:Dr.Strange 2.50
42 F:Spider-Man 3.00
43 F:Sub-Mariner,Human Torch . . 2.50
44 KSy,F:Iron Man vs.Dr.Doom . . 2.50
45 All Pin-up Issue,WS,AAd,MZ,
JOy,BSz,KJ,HC,PS,JBy 3.00
46 F:Fantastic Four 2.50
47 MG,F:Spider-Man,Hulk 3.00

48 KGa,F:She-Hulk 2.50
49 F:Dr.Strange 2.50
50 JSon,JRu,F:Angel 3.00
51 JB,JA,GC,AW,F:Silver Surfer . 4.00
52 F:Fantastic Four 2.50
53 GC,AW,F:Bl.Knight,Dr.Strange 2.50
54 F:Black Knight,Wolverine 3.50
55 F:Powerpack,Wolverine 3.50
56 CI,DH,F:Shanna t/She-Devil . . 2.50
57 BBI,AM,F:Shanna,Cap.Marvel . 2.50
58 BBI,F:Shanna,Vision/Sc.Witch . 2.50
59 BBI,F:Shanna,Hellcat 2.50
60 PS,F:Daredevil,Capt.Marvel . . 2.50

MARVEL FANFARE
Second Series 1996
1 Captain America, Falcon 1.00
2 New Fantastic Four 1.00
3 BbB,F:Spider-Man, Ghost Rider, 1.00
4 F:Longshot 1.00
5 F:Longshot 1.00
6 F:Power Man & Iron Fist V.
   Sabretooth 1.00

MARVEL FEATURE
[1st Regular Series]
Dec., 1971
1 RA,BE,NA,I&O:Defenders &
   Omegatron 85.00
2 BEv,F:The Defenders 50.00
3 BEv,F:The Defenders 45.00
4 F:Ant-Man 15.00
5 F:Ant-Man 11.00
6 F:Ant-Man 10.00
7 CR,F:Ant-Man 10.00
8 JSc,CR,F:Ant-Man,O:Wasp . . 10.00
9 CR,F:Ant-Man 10.00
10 CR,F:Ant-Man 10.00
11 JSn,JSt,F:Thing & Hulk 15.00
12 JSn,JSt,F:Thing,Iron Man,
   Thanos,Blood Brothers 12.00
[2nd Regular Series]
(All issues feature Red Sonja)
1 DG,The Temple of Abomination 5.00
2 FT,Blood of the Hunter 2.00
3 FT,Balek Lives 2.00
4 FT.Eyes of the Gorgon 2.00

Marvel Feature #5
© Marvel Entertainment Group

5 FT,The Bear God Walks 2.00
6 FT,C:Conan,Belit 2.00
7 FT,V:Conan,A:Belit,Conan#68 . 2.00

MARVEL FRONTIER COMICS SPECIAL
1 All Frontier Characters 3.25
1994 . . . . 2.95

MARVEL FUMETTI BOOK
April, 1984
1 NA(c),Stan Lee, All photos . . . 1.25

MARVEL GRAPHIC NOVEL
1982
1 JSn,D:Captain Marvel,A:Most
   Marvel Characters 30.00
1a 2nd printing 10.00
1b 3rd-5th printing 7.00
2 F:Elric,Dreaming City 12.00
2a 2nd printing 7.00
3 JSn,F:Dreadstar 12.00
3a 2nd-3rd printing 7.00
4 BMc,I:New Mutants,Cannonball
   Sunspot,Psyche,Wolfsbane . . 22.00
4a 2nd printing 10.00
4b 3rd-4th printing 8.00
5 BA,F:X-Men 17.00
5a 2nd printing 9.00
5b 3rd-5th printing 7.00
6 WS,F:Starslammers 10.00
6a 2nd printing 7.00
7 CR,F:Killraven 7.00
8 RWi,AG,F:Super Boxers 8.00
8a 2nd printing 7.00
9 DC,F:Futurians 12.00
9a 2nd printing 7.00
10 RV,F:Heartburst 8.00
10a 2nd printing 6.00
11 VM,F:Void Indigo 12.00
12 F:Dazzler the Movie 10.00
12a 2nd printing 6.00
13 MK,F:Starstruck 7.00
14 JG,F:SwordsofSwashbucklers . 6.00
15 CV,F:Raven Banner 6.00
16 GLa,F:Alladin Effect 6.00
17 MS,F:Living Monolith 7.00
18 JBy,F:She-Hulk 9.00
18 later printings 8.00
19 F:Conan 6.00
20 F:Greenberg the Vampire . . . 6.00
21 JBo,F:Marada the She-wolf . . 6.00
22 BWr,Hooky,F:Spider-Man . . . 12.00
23 DGr,F:Dr.Strange 6.00
24 FM,BSz,F:Daredevil 10.00
25 F:Dracula 8.00
26 FC,TA,F:Alien Legion 6.00
27 BH,F:Avengers 6.00
28 JSe,F:Conan the Reaver 6.50
29 BWr,F:Thing & Hulk 8.00
30 F:A Sailor's Story 6.00
31 F:Wolf Pack 6.00
32 SA,F:Death of Groo 15.00
33 F:Thor 6.00
34 AW,F:Cloak & Dagger 6.00
35 MK/RH,F:The Shadow 12.00
36 F:Willow movie adaption 7.00
37 BL,F:Hercules 7.00
38 JB,F:Silver Surfer 15.00
39 F:Iron Man,Crash 14.50
40 JZ,F:The Punisher 12.00
41 F:Roger Rabbit 7.00
42 F:Conan of the Isles 9.00
43 EC,F:Ax 6.00

44 BJ,F:Arena 6.00
45 JRy,F:Dr.Who 9.00
46 TD,F:Kull 7.00
47 GM,F:Dreamwalker 7.00
48 F:Sailor's Storm II 7.00
49 MBd,F:Dr.Strange&Dr.Doom . 16.00
50 F:Spider-Man,Parallel Lives . . 9.00
51 F:Punisher,Intruder 10.00
52 DSp,F:Roger Rabbit 9.00
53 PG,F:Conan 6.95
54 HC,F:Wolverine & Nick Fury . 17.00

MARVEL HEROES
1 StL,FaN,Mega-Jam,48pg 2.95

MARVEL HOLIDAY SPECIAL
1 StG(s),PDd(s),SLo(s),RLm,PB, 3.25
1-shot MWa,KK 2.95

MARVEL MASTERPIECES COLLECTION
1 Joe Jusko Masterpiece Cards . 3.25
2 F:Wolverine,Thanos,Apocalypse 3.00
3 F:Gambit,Venom,Hulk 3.00
4 F:Wolverine Vs. Sabretooth . . . 3.00

MARVEL MASTERPIECES II COLLECTION
1 thru 3 w/cards . . . . @3.00

MARVEL MILESTONE EDITION
1 X-Men #1 rep. 2.95
2 Fantastic Four #1, Rep. 2.95
3 Amazing Fantasy #15 rep. 2.95
4 Incredible Hulk #1 . . . . 2.95
5 Amazing Spider-Man #1 . . . . . 2.95

MARVEL MINI-BOOKS
1966
(black & white)
1 F:Capt.America,Spider-Man,Hulk
   Thor,Sgt.Fury 12.00
2 F:Capt.America,Spider-Man,Hulk
   Thor,Sgt.Fury 12.00
3 F:Capt.America,Spider-Man,Hulk
   Thor,Sgt.Fury 12.00
4 thru 6 F:Capt.America,Spider-Man,
   Hulk,Thor,Sgt.Fury . . . . @12.00

MARVEL MOVIE PREMIERE
1975
(black & white magazine)
1 Land That Time Forgot,
   Burroughs adapt 5.00

MARVEL MOVIE SHOWCASE FEATURING STAR WARS
Nov., 1982
1 Rep,Stars Wars #1-6 . . . . 4.00
2 Dec., 1982 . . . . 4.00

MARVEL MOVIE SPOTLIGHT FEATURING RAIDERS OF THE LOST ARK

Nov., 1982
1 Rep,Raiders of Lost Ark#1-3 . . 3.00

MARVEL MYSTERY COMICS
See: MARVEL COMICS

MARVEL NO-PRIZE BOOK
Jan., 1983
1 MGo(c),Stan Lee as
Dr Doom(c) 3.00

MARVEL: PORTRAITS OF A UNIVERSE
1 Fully painted moments 2.95
2 Fully painted moments 2.95
3 F:Death of Elektra 2.95
4 final issue 2.95

Marvel Premiere #24
© Marvel Entertainment Group

MARVEL PREMIERE
April, 1972
1 GK,O:Warlock,Receives Soul Gem,
Creation of Counter Earth . . . 40.00
2 GK,JK,F:Warlock 25.00
3 BWS,F:Dr.Strange 28.00
4 FB,BWS,F:Dr.Strange 14.00
5 MP,CR,F:Dr.Strange,I:Sligguth 10.00
6 MP,FB,F:Dr.Strange 10.00
7 MP,CR,F:Dr.Strange,I:Dagoth 10.00
8 JSn,F:Dr.Strange 10.00
9 NA,FB,F:Dr.Strange 10.00
10 FB,F:Dr.Strange,
D:Ancient One 10.00
11 NA,FB,F:Dr.Strange,I:Shuma 10.00
12 NA,FB,F:Dr.Strange 10.00
13 NA,FB,F:Dr.Strange 10.00
14 NA,FB,F:Dr.Strange 10.00
15 GK,DG,I&O:Iron Fist,pt.1 . . . 50.00
16 DG,O:Iron Fist,pt.2,V:Scythe . 25.00
17 DG,'Citadel on the
Edge of Vengeance' 15.00
18 DG,V:Triple Irons 15.00
19 DG,A:Ninja 13.00
20 I:Misty Knight 13.00
21 V:Living Goddess 13.00
22 V:Ninja 13.00

23 PB,V:Warhawk 13.00
24 PB,V:Monstroid 13.00
25 1st JBy,AMc,E:Iron Fist 18.00
26 JK,GT,F:Hercules 7.00
27 F:Satana 7.00
28 F:Legion Of Monsters,A:Ghost
Rider,Morbius,Werewolf. . . . 15.00
29 JK,I:Liberty Legion,
O:Red Raven 5.00
30 JK,F:Liberty Legion 5.00
31 JK,I:Woodgod 5.00
32 HC,F:Monark 5.00
33 HC,F:Solomon Kane 5.00
34 HC,F:Solomon Kane 5.00
35 I&O:Silver Age 3-D Man 5.00
36 F:3-D Man 5.00
37 F:3-D Man 5.00
38 AN,MP,I:Weird World 5.00
39 AM,I:Torpedo(1st solo) 5.00
40 AM,F:Torpedo 5.00
41 TS,F:Seeker 3000 . . . . 5.00
42 F:Tigra 5.00
43 F:Paladin 5.00
44 KG,F:Jack of Hearts(1stSolo) . 5.00
45 GP,F:Manwolf 5.00
46 GP,F:Manwolf 5.00
47 JBy,I:2nd Antman(Scott Lang) . 5.00
48 JBy,F:2nd Antman 4.00
49 F:The Falcon 4.00
50 TS,TA,F:Alice Cooper 7.00
51 JBi,F:Black Panther,V:Klan . . . 3.00
52 JBi,F:B.Panther,V:Klan 3.00
53 JBi,F:B.Panther,V:Klan 3.00
54 GD,TD,I:Hammer 3.00
55 JSt,F:Wonderman(1st solo) . . . 4.00
56 HC,TA,F:Dominic Fortune . . . 2.50
57 WS(c),I:Dr.Who 3.50
58 TA(c),FM,F:Dr.Who 3.00
59 F:Dr.Who 3.00
60 WS(c),DGb,F:Dr.Who 3.00
61 TS,F:Starlord 3.00

MARVEL PRESENTS
Oct., 1975
1 BMc,F:Bloodstone 7.50
2 BMc,O:Bloodstone 6.00
3 AM,B:Guardians/Galaxy 16.00
4 AM,I:Nikki 12.00
5 AM,'Planet o/t Absurd' 12.00
6 AM,V:Karanada 12.00
7 AM,'Embrace the Void' 12.00
8 AM,JB,JSt,reprint.S.Surfer#2 . 15.00
9 AM,O:Starhawk 12.00
10 AM,O:Starhawk 12.00
11 AM,D:Starhawk's Children . . 12.00
12 AM,E:Guardians o/t Galaxy . 12.00

MARVEL PREVIEW
Feb., 1975
(black & white magazine)
1 NA,AN,Man Gods From
Beyond the Stars 5.00
2 GM(c),O:Punisher 150.00
3 GM(c),Blade the Vampire Slayer 3.00
4 GM(c),I&O:Starlord 4.00
5 Sherlock Holmes 3.00
6 Sherlock Holmes 3.00
7 KG,Satana,A:Sword in the Star 4.00
8 GM,MP,Legion of Monsters . . 9.00
9 Man-God,O:Starhawk 3.00
10 JSn,Thor the Mighty 4.00
11 JBy,I:Starlord 5.00
12 MK,Haunt of Horror 3.50
13 JSn(c),Starhawk 5.00
14 JSn(c),Starhawk 5.00

15 MK(c),Starhawk 3.50
16 GC,Detectives 3.00
17 GK,Black Mask 3.00
18 GC,Starlord 3.00
19 Kull 3.00
20 HC,NA,GP,Bizarre Adventures 4.00
21 SD,Moonlight 4.00
22 JB,King Arthur 3.00
23 JB,GC,FM,Bizarre Adventures . 5.00
24 Debut Paradox 3.00
Becomes:

BIZARRE ADVENTURES
25 MG,TA,MR,Lethal Ladies 3.00
26 JB(c),King Kull 3.00
27 JB,AA,GP,Phoenix,A:Ice-Man . 6.00
28 MG,TA,FM,NA,The Unlikely
Heroes,Elektra 4.00
29 JB,WS,Horror 3.50
30 JB,Tomorrow 3.00
31 JBy,After the Violence Stops . . 3.50
32 Gods 3.00
33 Ph(c),Horror 3.00
34 PS,Christmas Spec,Son of Santa
Howard the Duck,Feb.,1983 . . 3.50

MARVEL PREVIEW 1993
Preview of 1993 . . . . 3.95

MARVEL SAGA
Dec., 1985
1 JBy,Fantastic Four,Wolv. 2.50
2 Hulk 1.50
3 Spider-Man 2.50
4 X-Men 2.50
5 Thor 1.50
6 Fantastic Four 1.50
7 Avengers 1.50
8 X-Men 2.00
9 Angel 1.50
10 X-Men 2.00
11 X-Men 2.00
12 O:Capt. America 1.50
13 O:Daredevil,Elektra 1.50
14 O:Green Goblin 2.00

Marvel Saga #5
© Marvel Entertainment Group

MARVEL

15 Avengers	1.50
16 Daredevil,X-Men	2.00
17 Kazar,X-Men	2.00
18 Hawkeye-Quicksilver	1.50
19 SpM,Thor,Daredevil	2.00
20 Daredevil,Giant Man	1.50
21 FF,V:Frightful Four	1.50
22 Wedding	1.50
23	1.50
24	1.50
25 O:Silver Surfer,Dec.,1987	2.25

MARVEL SPECTACULAR
August, 1973

1 JK,rep Thor #128	2.50
2 JK,rep Thor #129	2.00
3 JK,rep Thor #130	2.00
4 JK,rep Thor #133	2.00
5 JK,rep Thor #134	2.00
6 JK,rep Thor #135	1.75
7 JK,rep Thor #136	1.75
8 JK,rep Thor #137	1.75
9 JK,rep Thor #138	1.75
10 JK,rep Thor #139	1.75
11 JK,rep Thor #140	1.75
12 JK,rep Thor #141	1.75
13 JK,rep Thor #142	1.75
14 JK,rep Thor #143	1.75
15 JK,rep Thor #144	1.75
16 JK,rep Thor #145	1.75
17 JK,rep Thor #146	1.75
18 JK,rep Thor #147	1.75
19 JK,rep Thor#148,Nov.,1975	1.75

Marvel Spotlight #3
© Marvel Entertainment Group

MARVEL SPOTLIGHT
Nov., 1971
[1st Regular Series]

1 NA(c)WW,F:Red Wolf	25.00
2 MP,BEv,NA,I&O:Werewolf	40.00
3 MP,F:Werewolf	18.00
4 SD,MP,F:Werewolf	18.00
5 SD,MP,I&O:Ghost Rider	60.00
6 MP,TS,F:Ghost Rider	20.00
7 MP,TS,F:Ghost Rider	20.00
8 JM,MB,F:Ghost Rider	20.00

9 TA,F:Ghost Rider	14.00
10 SD,JM,F:Ghost Rider	20.00
11 SD,F:Ghost Rider	20.00
12 SD,2nd A:Son of Satan	18.00
13 F:Son of Satan	10.00
14 JM,F:Son of Satan,I:Ikthalon	10.00
15 JM, F:Son of Satan, I:Baphomet	7.00
16 JM,F:Son of Satan	7.00
17 JM,F:Son of Satan	7.00
18 F:Son of Satan, I:Allatou	7.00
19 F:Son of Satan	7.00
20 F:Son of Satan	7.00
21 F:Son of Satan	7.00
22 F:Son of Satan, Ghost Rider	8.00
23 F:Son of Satan	7.00
24 JM,F:Son of Satan	7.00
25 GT,F:Sinbad	4.00
26 F:The Scarecrow	4.00
27 F:The Sub-Mariner	4.00
28 F:Moon Knight (1st full solo)	11.00
29 F:Moon Knight	10.00
30 JSt,JB,F:Warriors Three	5.00
31 HC,JSn,F:Nick Fury	5.00
32 I:Spiderwoman, Jessica Drew	9.00
33 F:Deathlok, I:Devilslayer	6.00

MARVEL SPOTLIGHT
[2nd Regualar Series]
July, 1979

1 PB,F:Captain Marvel	2.50
1a No'1' on Cover	4.00
2 FM(c),F:Captain Marvel,A:Eon	2.00
3 PB,F:Captain Marvel	2.00
4 PB,F:Captain Marvel	2.00
5 FM(c),SD,F:Dragon Lord	2.00
6 F:Star Lord	2.00
7 FM(c),F:StarLord	2.50
8 FM,F:Captain Marvel	2.50
9 FM(c),SD,F:Captain Universe	2.00
10 SD,F:Captain Universe	2.00
11 SD,F:Captain Universe	2.00

MARVEL SPOTLIGHT ON CAPTAIN AMERICA

1 thru 4, Captain America rep. @2.95

MARVEL SPOTLIGHT ON DR. STRANGE

1 thru 4, Dr. Strange, rep. @2.95

MARVEL SPOTLIGHT ON SILVER SURFER

1 thru 4, Silver Surfer, rep. @2.95

MARVEL SUPER ACTION
(One-Shot)
Jan., 1976

1 TD,GE,FS,MP,HC,F:Punisher, Weirdworld,Dominic Fortune, I:Huntress(Mockingbird)	65.00

MARVEL SUPER ACTION
May, 1977

1 JK,reprint,Capt.America #100	3.50
2 JK,reprint,Capt.America #101	2.00
3 JK,reprint,Capt.America #102	2.00
4 BEv,RH,reprint,Marvel Boy #1	2.00
5 JK,reprint,Capt.America #103	2.00
6 JK,reprint,Capt.America #104	2.00
7 JK,reprint,Capt.America #105	2.00
8 JK,reprint,Capt.America #106	2.00

9 JK,reprint,Capt.America #107	2.00
10 JK,reprint,Capt.America #108	2.00
11 JK,reprint,Capt.America #109	2.00
12 JSo,reprint,Capt.America #110	2.00
13 JSo,reprint,Capt.America #111	2.00
14 JB,reprint,Avengers #55	2.00
15 JB,reprint,Avengers #56	2.00
16 Reprint,Avengers,annual #2	2.00
17 Reprint,Avengers #	2.00
18 JB(c),reprint,Avengers #57	2.00
19 JB(c),reprint,Avengers #58	2.00
20 JB(c),reprint,Avengers #59	2.00
21 Reprint,Avengers #60	1.50
22 JB(c),reprint,Avengers #61	1.50
23 Reprint,Avengers #63	1.50
24 Reprint,Avengers #64	1.50
25 Reprint,Avengers #65	1.50
26 Reprint,Avengers #66	1.50
27 BWS,Reprint,Avengers #67	1.50
28 BWS,Reprint,Avengers #68	1.50
29 Reprint,Avengers #69	1.50
30 Reprint,Avengers #70	1.50
31 Reprint,Avengers #71	1.50
32 Reprint,Avengers #72	1.50
33 Reprint,Avengers #73	1.50
34 Reprint,Avengers #74	1.50
35 JB(c),Reprint,Avengers #75	1.50
36 JB(c),Reprint,Avengers #75	1.50
37 JB(c),Reprint,Avengers #76 November, 1981	1.50

MARVEL SUPERHEROES
Oct., 1966
(One-Shot)

1 Rep. D.D. #1, Avengers #2, Marvel Mystery #8	75.00

MARVEL SUPER-HEROES
[1st Regular Series]
(Prev.: Fantasy Masterpieces)

12 GC,I&O:Captain Marvel	125.00
13 GC,2nd A:Captain Marvel	65.00
14 F:Spider-Man	110.00
15 GC,F:Medusa	20.00
16 I:Phantom Eagle	20.00
17 O:Black Knight	20.00
18 GC,I:Guardians o/t Galaxy	50.00
19 F:Kazar	15.00
20 F:Dr.Doom,Diablo	15.00
21 thru 31 reprints	@10.00
32 thru 55 rep. Hulk/Submariner from Tales to Astonish	@2.00
56 reprints Hulk #102	3.50
57 thru 105 reps.Hulk issues	@2.00

MARVEL SUPERHEROES
May, 1990
[2nd Regular Series]

1 RLm,F:Hercules,Moon Knight, Magik,Bl.Panther,Speedball	4.00
2	3.50
3 F:Captain America,Hulk,Wasp	4.00
4 AD,F:SpM,N.Fury,D.D.,Speedball Wond.Man,Spitfire,Bl.Knight	3.50
5 F:Thor,Thing,Speedball, Dr.Strange	3.50
6 RB,SD,F:X-Men,Power Pack, Speedball,Sabra	3.00
7 RB,F:X-Men,Cloak & Dagger	2.75
8 F:X-Men,Iron Man,Namor	2.50
9 F:Avengers W.C,Thor,Iron Man	3.00
10 DH,F:Namor,Fantastic Four, Ms.Marvel#24	3.50
11 F:Namor,Ms.Marvel#25	3.00

12 F:Dr.Strange,Falcon,Iron Man . 3.00	
13 F:Iron Man 2.75	
14 BMc,RWi,F:Iron Man,	
Speedball, Dr.Strange 2.75	
15 KP,DH,F:Thor,Iron Man,Hulk . . 2.75	
Holiday Spec.#1 AAd,DC,JRu,F:FF,	
X-Men,Spider-Man,Punisher . . 3.25	
Holiday Spec.#2 AAd(c),SK,MGo,	
RLm,SLi,F:Hulk,Wolverine,	
Thanos,Spider-Man 3.25	
Fall Spec.RB,A:X-Men,Shroud,	
Marvel Boy,Cloak & Dagger . . 2.25	

MARVEL SUPERHEROES MEGAZINE
1 thru 6 rep. . . . . @2.95

MARVEL SUPER SPECIAL
See: MARVEL COMICS

MARVEL SWIMSUIT
1 Schwing Break 4.95

MARVEL TAILS
Nov., 1983
1 ST,Peter Porker 2.00

Marvel Tales #15
© Marvel Entertainment Group

MARVEL TALES
1964
1 All reprints,O:Spider-Man . . . 250.00	
2 rep.Avengers #1,X-Men #1,	
Hulk #3 . . . . 80.00	
3 rep.Amaz.SpM.#6 . . . . 40.00	
4 rep.Amaz.SpM.#7 . . . . 20.00	
5 rep.Amaz.SpM.#8 . . . . 20.00	
6 rep.Amaz.SpM.#9 . . . . 20.00	
7 rep.Amaz.SpM.#10 . . . . 20.00	
8 rep.Amaz.SpM.#13 . . . . 15.00	
9 rep.Amaz.SpM.#14 . . . . 18.00	
10 rep.Amaz.SpM.#15 . . . . 18.00	
11 rep.Amaz.SpM.#16 . . . . 18.00	
12 rep.Amaz.SpM.#18 . . . . 18.00	
13 rep.Amaz.SpM.#18	
rep.1950's Marvel Boy 12.00	
14 rep.Amaz.SpM.#19,	
reps.Marvel Boy 7.50	

15 rep.Amaz.SpM.#20,	
reps.Marvel Boy 7.50	
16 rep.Amaz.SpM.#21,	
reps.Marvel Boy 7.50	
17 thru 22 rep.Amaz.SpM.	
#22-#27 . . . . @5.50	
23 thru 27 rep.Amaz.SpM.	
#30-#34 . . . . @5.50	
28 rep.Amaz.SpM.#35&36 . . . . . 5.00	
29 rep.Amaz.SpM.#39&40 . . . . . 5.00	
30 rep.Amaz.SpM.#58&41 . . . . . 5.00	
31 rep.Amaz.SpM.#42 . . . . 5.00	
32 rep.Amaz.SpM.#43&44 . . . . . 5.00	
33 rep.Amaz.SpM.#45&47 . . . . . 5.00	
34 rep.Amaz.SpM.#48 . . . . 4.00	
35 rep.Amaz.SpM.#49 . . . . 4.00	
36 thru 41 rep.	
Amaz.SpM#51-#56 . . . . @4.00	
42 thru 53 rep.	
Amaz.SpM#59-#70 . . . . @4.00	
54 thru 80 rep.	
Amaz.SpM#73-#99 . . . . @4.00	
81 rep.Amaz.SpM.#103 . . . . . . 4.00	
82 rep.Amaz.SpM.#103-4 . . . . . 4.50	
83 thru 97 rep.	
Amaz.SpM.#104-#118 . . . . . @4.00	
98 rep.Amaz.SpM.#121 . . . . . . 4.00	
99 rep.Amaz.SpM.#122 . . . . . . 4.50	
100 rep.Amaz.SpM.#123,BU:Two	
Gun Kid,Giant-Size 3.50	
101 thru 105 rep.Amaz.	
SpM.#124-#128 . . . . @3.00	
106 rep.Amaz.SpM.#129,	
(I:Punisher) 4.00	
107 thur 110 rep.Amaz.	
SpM.#130-133 . . . . @2.00	
111 Amaz.SpM#134,A:Punisher . . 4.00	
112 Amaz.SpM#135,A:Punisher . . 3.00	
113 thru 125 rep.Amaz.Spider	
Man #136-#148 . . . . @2.00	
126 rep.Amaz.Spider-Man#149 . . 4.00	
127 rep.Amaz.Spider-Man#150 . . 4.00	
128 rep.Amaz.Spider-Man#151 . . 4.00	
129 thru 136 rep.Amaz.Spider	
Man #152-#159 . . . . @2.50	
137 rep.Amaz.Fantasy#15 . . . . . 7.00	
138 rep.Amaz.SpM.#1 . . . . 7.00	
139 thru 149 rep.	
AmazSpM#2-#12 . . . . @2.50	
150 rep.AmazSpM Ann#1 . . . . . 2.50	
151 rep.AmazSpM#13 . . . . 2.50	
152 rep.AmazSpM#14 . . . . 4.00	
153 thru 190	
rep.AmazSpM#15-52 . . . . . @2.00	
191 rep. #96-98 . . . . 2.25	
192 rep. #121-122 . . . . 2.25	
193 thru 198 rep.Marv.Team	
Up#59-64 . . . . @2.00	
199 . . . . 2.00	
200 rep. SpM Annual 14 . . . . . . 2.00	
201 thru 206 rep.Marv.	
Team Up#65-70 . . . . @2.00	
207 . . . . 2.00	
208 . . . . 2.00	
209 MZ(c),rep.SpM#129,Punisher 3.00	
210 MZ(c),rep.SpM#134 . . . . . . 4.00	
211 MZ(c),rep.SpM#135 . . . . . . 4.00	
212 MZ(c),rep.Giant-Size#4 . . . . 4.00	
213 MZ(c),rep.Giant-Size#4 . . . . 4.00	
214 MZ(c),rep.SpM#161 . . . . . . 4.00	
215 MZ(c),rep.SpM#162 . . . . . . 3.00	
216 MZ(c),rep.SpM#174 . . . . . . 3.00	
217 MZ(c),rep.SpM#175 . . . . . . 3.00	
218 MZ(c),rep.SpM#201 . . . . . . 3.00	
219 MZ(c),rep.SpM#202 . . . . . . 3.00	

220 MZ(c),rep.Spec.SpM #81 . . . 3.00	
221 MZ(c),rep.Spec.SpM #82 . . . 3.00	
222 MZ(c),rep.Spec.SpM #83 . . . 2.00	
223 thru 227 TM(c),rep.	
SpM #88-92 . . . . @2.25	
228 TM(c),rep.Spec.SpM.#17 . . . 2.00	
229 TM(c),rep.Spec.SpM.#18 . . . 2.00	
230 TM(c),rep.SpM #203 . . . . . . 2.00	
231 TM(c),rep.Team-Up#108 . . . 2.00	
232 TM(c),rep. 2.00	
233 TM(c),rep. X-Men 2.00	
234 TM(c),rep. X-Men 2.00	
235 TM(c),rep. X-Men 2.00	
236 TM(c),rep. X-Men 2.00	
237 TM(c),rep. 2.00	
238 TM(c),rep. 2.00	
239 TM(c),rep.SpM,Beast 2.00	
240 rep.SpM,Beast,MTU#90 . . . . 1.50	
241 rep.MTU#124 . . . . 1.50	
242 rep.MTU#89,Nightcrawler . . 1.50	
243 rep.MTU#117,SpM,Wolverine 1.50	
244 MR(c),rep. 1.50	
245 MR(c),rep. 1.50	
246 MR(c),rep. 1.50	
247 MR(c),rep.MTU Annual #6 . . 1.50	
248 MR(c),rep. 1.50	
249 MR(c),rep.MTU #14 . . . . . . 1.50	
250 MR(c),rep.MTU #100 . . . . . 1.50	
251 rep.Amaz.SpM.#100 . . . . . . 1.50	
252 rep.Amaz.SpM.#101 . . . . . . 3.50	
253 rep.Amaz.SpM.#102 . . . . . . 3.00	
254 rep.MTU #15,inc.2 Ghost	
Rider pin-ups by JaL 3.00	
255 SK(c),rep.MTU #58,	
BU:Ghost Rider 1.75	
256 rep. MTU 1.50	
257 rep.Amaz.SpM.#238 . . . . . . 1.50	
258 rep.Amaz.SpM.#239 . . . . . . 1.50	
259 thru 261 rep.Amaz.SpM.#249	
thru 251 . . . . 1.50	
262 rep Marvel Team-Up #53 . . . 1.25	
263 rep Marvel Team-Up #54 . . . 1.25	
264 rep.B:Amaz.SpM.Ann.#5 . . . 1.25	
265 rep.E:Amaz.SpM.Ann.#5 . . . 1.25	
266 thru 274 rep.Amaz.SpM#252	
thru #260 . . . . @1.25	
275 rep.Amaz.SpM.#261 . . . . . . 1.25	
276 rep.Amaz.SpM.#263 . . . . . . 1.25	
277 rep.Amaz.SpM.#265 . . . . . . 1.25	
278 thru 282 rep.Amaz.SpM#268	
thru 272 . . . . 1.25	
283 rep.Amaz.SpM.#273 . . . . . . 1.25	
284 rep.Amaz.SpM.#275 . . . . . . 1.25	
285 rep.Amaz.SpM.#276 . . . . . . 1.25	
286 rep.Amaz.SpM.#277 . . . . . . 1.25	
287 rep.Amaz.SpM.#278 . . . . . . 1.25	
288 rep.Amaz.SpM.#280 . . . . . . 1.50	
289 rep.Amaz.SpM.#281 . . . . . . 1.50	
290 rep.Amaz.SpM 1.50	
291 rep.Amaz–SpM 1.50	

MARVEL TALES
See: MARVEL COMICS

MARVEL TEAM-UP
March, 1972
(Spider-Man in all,unless *)
1 RA,F:Hum.Torch,V:Sandman . 80.00	
2 RA,F:Hum.Torch,V:Sandman . 28.00	
3 F:Human Torch,V:Morbius . . 50.00	
4 GK,F:X-Men,A:Morbius 50.00	
5 GK,F:Vision 11.00	
6 GK,F:Thing,O:Puppet Master,	
V:Mad Thinker 11.00	

MARVEL

All comics prices listed are for *Near Mint* condition.

7 RA,F:Thor	11.00	
8 JM,F:The Cat	11.00	
9 RA,F:Iron Man	11.00	
10 JM,F:Human Torch	11.00	
11 JM,F:The Inhumans	10.00	
12 RA,F:Werewolf	11.00	
13 GK,F:Captain America	8.00	
14 GK,F:Sub-Mariner	8.00	
15 RA,F:Ghostrider	8.00	
16 GK,JM,F:Captain Marvel	7.00	

7 RA,F:Thor 11.00
8 JM,F:The Cat 11.00
9 RA,F:Iron Man 11.00
10 JM,F:Human Torch 11.00
11 JM,F:The Inhumans 10.00
12 RA,F:Werewolf 11.00
13 GK,F:Captain America ... 8.00
14 GK,F:Sub-Mariner 8.00
15 RA,F:Ghostrider 8.00
16 GK,JM,F:Captain Marvel . 7.00
17 GK,F:Mr.Fantastic,
   A:Capt.Marvel 7.00
18 *F:Hulk,Human Torch 7.00
19 SB,F:Ka-Zar 7.00
20 SB,F:Black Panther 8.00
21 SB,F:Dr.Strange 5.00
22 SB,F:Hawkeye 5.00
23 *F:Human Torch,Iceman,
   C:Spider-Man,X-Men 6.00
24 JM,F:Brother Voodoo 5.00
25 JM,F:Daredevil 5.00
26 *F:H.Torch,Thor,V:Lavamen . 5.00
27 JM,F:The Hulk 5.00
28 JM,F:Hercules 5.00
29 *F:Human Torch,Iron Man ... 5.00
30 JM,F:The Falcon 5.00
31 JM,F:Iron Fist 5.00
32 *F:Hum.Torch,Son of Satan . 5.00
33 SB,F:Nighthawk 5.00
34 SB,F:Valkyrie 5.00
35 SB,*F:H.Torch,Dr.Strange ... 5.00
36 SB,F:Frankenstein 6.00
37 SB,F:Man-Wolf 6.00
38 SB,F:Beast 5.00
39 SB,F:H.Torch,I:Jean Dewolff .. 5.00
40 SB,F:Sons of the Tiger .. 5.00
41 SB,F:Scarlet Witch 5.00
42 SB,F:Scarlet Witch,Vision . 5.00
43 SB,F:Dr.Doom 5.00
44 SB,F:Moon Dragon 5.00
45 SB,F:Killraven 6.00
46 SB,F:Deathlok 6.00
47 F:The Thing 5.00
48 SB,F:Iron Man,I:Wraith ... 5.00
49 SB,F:Iron Man 5.00
50 SB,F:Dr.Strange 5.00
51 SB,F:Iron Man 4.00
52 SB,F:Captain America ... 4.00
53 1st JBy New X-Men,F:Hulk . 15.00
54 JBy,F:Hulk,V:Woodgod ... 6.00
55 JBy,F:Warlock,I:Gardener .. 8.00
56 SB,F:Daredevil 4.00
57 SB,F:Black Widow 4.00
58 SB,F:Ghost Rider,V:Trapster . 5.00
59 JBy,F:Yellowjacket,V:Equinox . 5.00
60 JBy,F:Wasp,V:Equinox ... 5.00
61 JBy,F:Human Torch 5.00
62 JBy,F:Ms.Marvel 5.00
63 JBy,F:Iron Fist 5.50
64 JBy,F:Daughters o/t Dragon . 5.00
65 JBy,I:Captain Britain(U.S.)
   I:Arcade 7.50
66 JBy,F:Captain Britain ... 6.00
67 JBy,F:Tigra,V:Kraven ... 5.00
68 JBy,F:Man-Thing,I:D'Spayre . 5.00
69 JBy,F:Havok 6.00
70 JBy,F:Thor 5.00
71 F:The Falcon,V:Plantman ... 4.00
72 F:Iron Man 4.00
73 F:Daredevil 4.00
74 BH,F:Not ready for prime time
   players(Saturday Night Live) . 5.00
75 JBy,F:Power Man 4.00
76 HC,F:Dr.Strange 4.00
77 HC,F:Ms.Marvel 4.00

78 DP,F:Wonderman 4.00
79 JBy,TA,F:Red Sonja 5.00
80 SpM,F:Dr.Strange,Clea ... 4.00
81 F:Satana 4.00
82 SB,F:Black Widow 5.00
83 SB,F:Nick Fury 5.00
84 SB,F:Master of Kung Fu .. 5.00
85 SB,F:Bl.Widow,Nick Fury .. 5.00
86 BMc,F:Guardians o/t Galaxy . 4.00
87 GC,F:Black Panther 4.00
88 SB,F:Invisible Girl 4.00
89 RB,F:Nightcrawler 4.50
90 BMc,F:The Beast 4.00
91 F:Ghost Rider 4.00
92 CI,F:Hawkeye,I:Mr.Fear IV . 3.50
93 CI,F:Werewolf
   I:Tatterdemalion (named) ... 4.00
94 MZ,F:Shroud 3.50
95 I:Mockingbird(Huntress) ... 4.00
96 F:Howard the Duck 3.50
97 *F:Hulk,Spiderwoman ... 3.50
98 F:Black Widow 3.50
99 F:Machine Man 3.50

Marvel Team-Up #25
© Marvel Entertainment Group

100 FM,JBy,F:F.F.,I:Karma,
    BU:Storm & Bl.Panther 12.00
101 F:Nighthawk 3.00
102 F:Doc Samson,Rhino ... 3.00
103 F:Antman 3.00
104 *F:Hulk,Ka-zar 3.00
105 *F:Powerman,Iron Fist,Hulk . 3.00
106 HT,F:Captain America .. 3.00
107 HT,F:She-Hulk 3.00
108 HT,F:Paladin 3.00
109 HT,F:Dazzler 3.00
110 HT,F:Iron Man 3.00
111 HT,F:Devil Slayer 3.00
112 HT,F:King Kull 3.00
113 HT,F:Quasar,V:Lightmaster . 3.00
114 HT,F:Falcon 3.00
115 HT,F:Thor 3.00
116 HT,F:Valkyrie 3.00
117 HT,F:Wolv,V:Prof Power . 15.00
118 HT,F:Professor X 4.00
119 KGa,F:Gargoyle 3.00
120 KGa,F:Dominic Fortune . 3.00

121 KGa,F:Human Torch,I:Leap
    Frog(Frog Man) 3.00
122 KGa,F:Man-Thing 3.00
123 KGa,F:Daredevil 3.00
124 KGa,F:Beast 3.50
125 KGa,F:Tigra 3.00
126 BH,F:Hulk 3.00
127 KGa,F:Watcher,X-mas issue . 3.00
128 Ph(c)KGa,F:Capt.America. . 3.00
129 KGa,F:The Vision 3.00
130 KGa,F:The Scarlet Witch ... 3.00
131 KGa,F:Leap Frog 3.00
132 KGa,F:Mr.Fantastic ... 3.00
133 KGa,F:Fantastic Four ... 3.00
134 F:Jack of Hearts 3.00
135 F:Kitty Pryde 3.00
136 F:Wonder Man 3.00
137 *F:Aunt May & F.Richards ... 3.00
138 F:Sandman,I:New Enforcers . 3.00
139 F:Sandman,Nick Fury ... 3.00
140 F:Black Widow 3.00
141 SpM(2nd App Black Costume)
    F:Daredevil 4.00
142 F:Captain Marvel(2nd one) .. 3.00
143 F:Starfox 3.00
144 F:M.Knight,V:WhiteDragon . 3.00
145 F:Iron Man 3.00
146 F:Nomad 3.50
147 F:Human Torch 3.00
148 F:Thor 3.00
149 F:Cannonball 3.50
150 F:X-Men,V:Juggernaut .. 5.50
Ann.#1 SB,F:New X-Men ... 16.00
Ann.#2 F:The Hulk 5.00
Ann.#3 F:Hulk,PowerMan ... 4.00
Ann.#4 F:Daredevil,Moon Knight . 3.00
Ann.#5 F:Thing,Scarlet Witch,
    Quasar,Dr.Strange 3.00
Ann.#6 F:New Mutants,Cloak &
    Dagger(cont.New Mutants#22) . 4.00
Ann.#7 F:Alpha Flight 3.00

MARVEL TEAM-UP INDEX
SEE: OFFICIAL MARVEL
INDEX TO
MARVEL TEAM-UP

MARVEL TEAM-UP
1 TPe,PO,AW, F:Spider-Man,
  Generation X 1.99

MARVEL
Treasury Edition
Sept., 1974
1 SD,Spider-Man,I:Contemplator . 9.00
2 JK,F:Fant.Four,Silver Surfer ... 6.00
3 F:Thor 4.00
4 BWS,F:Conan 6.00
5 O:Hulk 5.00
6 GC,FB,SD,F:Dr.Strange .. 5.00
7 JB,JK,F:The Avengers ... 6.00
8 F:X-Mas stories 7.00
9 F:Super-Hero Team-Up ... 5.00
10 F:Thor 4.50
11 F:Fantastic Four 4.50
12 F:Howard the Duck 4.50
13 F:X-Mas stories 4.50
14 F:Spider-Man 5.00
15 BWS,F:Conan,Red Sonja . 6.00
16 F:Defenders 4.50
17 F:The Hulk 4.50
18 F:Spider Man,X-Men ... 6.00
19 F:Conan 5.00
20 F:Hulk 4.00

21 F:Fantastic Four	4.00
22 F:Spider-Man	4.50
23 F:Conan	4.00
24 F:The Hulk	4.00
25 F:Spider-Man,Hulk	4.00
26 GP,F:Hulk,Wolverine,Hercules	8.00
27 HT,F:Hulk,Spider-Man	5.00
28 JB,JSt,F:SpM/Superman	14.00

MARVEL TREASURY OF OZ
1975
(oversized)

1 JB,movie adapt.	4.00

MARVEL TREASURY SPECIAL

1 Vol. I Spider-Man,1974	4.00
2 Vol. II Capt. America,1976	3.50

MARVEL TRIPLE ACTION
Feb., 1972

1 Rep.	4.00
2 thru 47 rep.	@1.50
G-Size#1 F:Avengers	3.00
G-Size#2 F:Avengers	3.00

MARVEL TWO-IN-ONE
Jan., 1974
(Thing in all, unless *)

1 GK,F:Man-Thing	25.00
2 GK,JSt,F:Namor,Namorita	10.00
3 F:Daredevil	10.00
4 F:Capt.America,Namorita	10.00
5 F:Guardians of the Galaxy	12.00
6 F:Dr.Strange	10.00
7 F:Valkyrie	6.00
8 F:Ghost Rider	7.00
9 F:Thor	5.00
10 KJ,F:Black Widow	5.00
11 F:Golem	4.00
12 F:Iron Man	4.00
13 F:Power Man	4.00
14 F:Son of Satan	5.00
15 F:Morbius	5.00
16 F:Ka-zar	4.00
17 F:Spider-Man	4.50
18 F:Spider-Man	4.50
19 F:Tigra	4.00
20 F:The Liberty Legion	4.00
21 F:Doc Savage	3.50
22 F:Thor,Human Torch	3.50
23 F:Thor,Human Torch	3.50
24 SB,F:Black Goliath	3.50
25 F:Iron Fist	4.00
26 F:Nick Fury	3.00
27 F:Deathlok	4.00
28 F:Sub-Mariner	3.00
29 F:Master of Kung Fu	3.00
30 JB,F:Spiderwoman	4.00
31 F:Spiderwoman	3.00
32 F:Invisible girl	3.00
33 F:Modred the Mystic	3.00
34 F:Nighthawk,C:Deathlok	3.50
35 F:Skull the Slayer	3.00
36 F:Mr.Fantastic	3.00
37 F:Matt Murdock	3.00
38 F:Daredevil	3.00
39 F:The Vision	3.00
40 F:Black Panther	3.00
41 F:Brother Voodoo	3.00
42 F:Captain America	3.00
43 JBy,F:Man-Thing	5.00

Marvel Two-In-One #4
© Marvel Entertainment Group

44 GD,F:Hercules	3.00
45 GD,F:Captain Marvel	4.50
46 F:The Hulk	5.00
47 GD,F:Yancy Street Gang, I:Machinesmith	3.00
48 F:Jack of Hearts	3.00
49 GD,F:Dr.Strange	3.00
50 JBy,JS,F:Thing & Thing	3.50
51 FM,BMc,F:Wonderman,Nick Fury, Ms.Marvel	4.00
52 F:Moon Knight,I:Crossfire	3.00
53 JBy,JS,F:Quasar,C:Deathlok	3.50
54 JBy,JS,D:Deathlok, I:Grapplers	3.00
55 JBy,JS,I:New Giant Man	3.00
56 GP,GD,F:Thundra	2.50
57 GP,GD,F:Wundarr	2.50
58 GP,GD,I:Aquarian,A:Quasar	2.50
59 F:Human Torch	2.50
60 GP,GD,F:Impossible Man, I:Impossible Woman	2.50
61 GD,F:Starhawk,I&O:Her	3.00
62 GD,F:Moondragon	3.00
63 GD,F:Warlock	3.00
64 DP,GD,F:Stingray, I:Serpent Squad	2.50
65 GP,GD,F:Triton	2.50
66 GD,F:Scarlet Witch, V:Arcade	2.50
67 F:Hyperion,Thundra	2.50
68 F:Angel,V:Arcade	2.50
69 GD,F:Guardians o/t Galaxy	2.50
70 F:The Inhumans	2.50
71 F:Mr.Fantastic,I:Deathurge, Maelstrom	2.50
72 F:Stingray	2.50
73 F:Quasar	2.50
74 F:Puppet Master,Modred	2.50
75 F:The Avengers,O:Blastaar	2.50
76 F:Iceman,O:Ringmaster	2.50
77 F:Man-Thing	2.50
78 F:Wonder Man	2.50
79 F:Blue Diamond,I:Star Dancer	2.50
80 F:Ghost Rider	2.00
81 F:Sub-Mariner	2.00
82 F:Captain America	2.00
83 F:Sasquatch	3.00
84 F:Alpha Flight	3.00

85 F:Giant-Man	2.00
86 O:Sandman	2.25
87 F:Ant-Man	2.00
88 F:She-Hulk	2.00
89 F:Human Torch	2.00
90 F:Spider-Man	2.25
91 V:Sphinx	2.00
92 F:Jocasta,V:Ultron	2.00
93 F:Machine Man,D:Jocasta	2.25
94 F:Power Man,Iron Fist	2.00
95 F:Living Mummy	2.00
96 F:Sandman,C:Marvel Heroes	2.00
97 F:Iron Man	2.00
98 F:Franklin Richards	2.00
99 JBy(c),F:Rom	2.00
100 F:Ben Grimm	2.50
Ann.#1 SB,F:Liberty Legion	5.00
Ann.#2 JSn,2nd D:Thanos,A:Spider Man,Avengers,Capt.Marvel, I:Lord Chaos,Master Order	12.00
Ann.#3 F:Nova	4.00
Ann.#4 F:Black Bolt	3.50
Ann.#5 F:Hulk,V:Pluto	3.00
Ann.#6 I:American Eagle	3.00
Ann.#7 I:Champion,A:Hulk,Thor, DocSamson,Colossus,Sasquatch, WonderMan	3.50

OFFICIAL HANDBOOK OF THE MARVEL UNIVERSE
Jan., 1983

1 Abomination-Avengers' Quintet	7.50
2 BaronMordo-Collect.Man	6.00
3 Collector-Dracula	5.00
4 Dragon Man-Gypsy Moth	5.00
5 Hangman-Juggernaut	5.00
6 K-L	4.00
7 Mandarin-Mystique	4.00
8 Na,oria-Pyro	4.00
9 Quasar to She-Hulk	4.00
10 Shiar-Sub-Mariner	4.00
11 Subteraneans-Ursa Major	4.00
12 Valkyrie-Zzzax	4.00
13 Book of the Dead	4.00
14 Book of the Dead	4.00
15 Weaponry	4.00

[2nd Series]

1 Abomination-Batroc	5.00
2 Beast-Clea	4.00
3 Cloak & D.-Dr.Strange	4.00
4 Dr.Strange-Galactus	4.00
5 Gardener-Hulk	4.00
6 Human Torch-Ka-Zar	3.25
7 Kraven-Magneto	3.25
8 Magneto-Moleman	3.25
9 Moleman-Owl	3.25
10	3.25
11	2.50
12 S-T	2.50
13	2.50
14 V-Z	2.50
15	2.50
16 Book of the Dead	2.50
17 Handbook of the Dead,inc. JLe illus.	2.50
18	2.50
19	2.50
20 Inc.RLd illus.	2.50

Marvel Universe Update

1 thru 8	@1.75

Marvel Universe Packet

1 inc. Spider-Man	5.50
2 inc. Captain America	4.50

MARVEL

MARVEL

3 inc. Ghost Rider	5.00
4 inc. Wolverine	4.50
5 inc. Punisher	4.25
6 inc. She-Hulk	3.95
7 inc. Daredevil	3.95
8 inc. Hulk	3.95
9 inc. Moon Knight	3.95
10 inc. Captain Britain	3.95
11 inc. Storm	3.95
12 inc. Silver Surfer	3.95
13 inc. Ice Man	4.50
14 inc. Thor	4.50
15 thru 22	@4.50
23 inc. Cage	4.50
24 inc. Iron Fist	4.50
25 inc.Deadpool,Night Thrasher	4.50
26 inc. Wonderman	4.95
27 inc.Beta Ray Bill,Pip	4.95
28 inc.X-Men	4.95
29 inc.Carnage	4.95
30 thru 36	@4.95

MARVEL X-MEN COLLECTION

1 thru 3 JL from the 1st series X-Men Cards	3.25

MARVEL UNIVERSE
1996

1 Post Onslaught	2.95

MARVEL VALENTINE'S SPECIAL
1997

1-shot MWa,TDF, 48pg	2.99

MARVEL: SHADOWS & LIGHT
B&W 1996

1-shot MGo,JPL,KJ,48pg.	2.95

MARVELS

1 B:KBk(s),AxR,I:Phil Sheldon, A:G.A.Heroes,Human Torch Vs Namor	8.00
2 AxR,A:S.A.Avengers,FF,X-Men	6.00
3 AxR,FF vs Galactus	5.00
4 AxR,Final issue	5.00
HC rep.#1-#4	34.95

MARVIN MOUSE
Atlas Sept., 1957

1 BEv,F:Marvin Mouse	30.00

MASTER OF KUNG FU, SPECIAL MARVEL ED.
April, 1974
Prev: SPECIAL MARVEL EDITION

17 JSn,I:Black Jack Tarr	20.00
18 PG,1st Gulacy Art	14.00
19 PG,A:Man-Thing	10.00
20 GK(c),PG,AM,V:Samurai	10.00
21 AM,Season of Vengeance.. Moment of Death	9.00
22 PG,DA,Death	9.00
23 AM,KJ,River of Death	9.00
24 JSn,WS,AM,ST,Night of the Assassin	8.00
25 JSt(c),PG,ST,Fists Fury... Rites of Death	8.00
26 KP,ST,A:Daughter of	

Fu Manchu	7.00
27 SB,FS,A:Fu Manchu	7.00
28 EH,ST,Death of a Spirit	7.00
29 PG,V:Razor-Fist	7.00
30 PG,DA,Pit of Lions	7.00
31 GK&DA(c),PG,DA,Snowbuster	7.00
32 GK&ME(c),SB,ME,Assault on an Angry Sea	7.00
33 PG,Messenger of Madness, I:Leiko Wu	7.00
34 PG,Captive in A Madman's Crown	7.00
35 PG,V:Death Hand	7.00
36 The Night of the Ninja's	7.00
37 V:Darkstrider & Warlords of the Web	5.00
38 GK(c),PG,A:The Cat	5.00
39 GK(c),PG,A:The Cat	5.00
40 PG,The Murder Agency	5.00
41	5.00
42 GK(c),PG,TS,V:Shockwave	5.00
43 PG,V:Shockwave	5.00
44 SB(c),PG,V:Fu Manchu	5.00

Master of Kung Fu #17
© Marvel Entertainment Group

45 GK(c),PG,Death Seed	5.00
46 PG,V:Sumo	5.00
47 PG,The Cold White Mantle of Death	5.00
48 PG,Bridge of a 1,000 Dooms	5.00
49 PG,V:Shaka Kharn,The Demon Warrior	5.00
50 PG,V:Fu Manchu	5.00
51 PG(c),To End...To Begin	5.00
52 Mayhem in Morocco	4.00
53	4.00
54 JSn(c),Death Wears Three Faces	4.00
55 PG(c),The Ages of Death	4.00
56 V:The Black Ninja	4.00
57 V:Red Baron	4.00
58 Behold the Final Mask	4.00
59 GK(c),B:Phoenix Gambit, Behold the Angel of Doom	4.00
60 A:Dr.Doom,Doom Came	4.00
61 V:Skull Crusher	3.50
62 Coast of Death	3.50

63 GK&TA(c),Doom Wears Three Faces	3.50
64 PG(c),To Challenge a Dragon	3.50
65 V:Pavane	3.50
66 V:Kogar	3.50
67 PG(c),Dark Encounters	3.50
68 Final Combats,V:The Cat	3.50
69	3.50
70 A:Black Jack Tarr,Murder Mansion	3.50
71 PG(c),Ying & Yang (c)	3.50
72 V:Shockwave	3.50
73 RN(c),V:Behemoths	3.50
74 TA(c),A:Shockwave	3.50
75 Where Monsters Dwell	3.50
76 GD,Battle on the Waterfront	3.75
77 GD,I:Zaran	3.75
78 GD,Moving Targets	3.75
79 GD,This Side of Death	3.75
80 GD,V:Leopard Men	3.75
81 GD,V:Leopard Men	3.75
82 GD,Flight into Fear	3.75
83 GD,	3.75
84 GD,V:Fu Manchu	3.75
85 GD,V:Fu Manchu	3.75
86 GD,V:Fu Manchu	3.75
87 GD,V:Zaran	3.75
88 GD,V:Fu Manchu	3.75
89 GD,D:Fu Manchu	3.75
90 MZ,Death in Chinatown	3.75
91 GD,Gang War,drugs	4.00
92 GD,Shadows of the Past	3.75
93 GD,Cult of Death	3.75
94 GD,V:Agent Synergon	3.75
95 GD,Raid	3.75
96 GD,I:Rufus Carter	3.75
97 GD,V:Kung Fu's Dark Side	3.75
98 GD,Fight to the Finish	3.75
99 GD,Death Boat	3.75
100 GD,Doublesize	5.00
101 GD,Not Smoke,Nor Beads, Nor Blood	3.75
102 GD,Assassins,1st GD(p)	4.00
103 GD,V:Assassins	3.75
104 GD,Fight without Reason, C:Cerberus	3.75
105 GD,I:Razor Fist	3.75
106 GD,C:Velcro	3.75
107 GD,A:Sata	3.75
108 GD	3.75
109 GD,Death is a Dark Agent	3.75
110 GD,Perilous Reign	3.75
111 GD	3.75
112 GD(c),Commit and Destroy	3.75
113 GD(c),V:Panthers	3.75
114 Fantasy o/t Autumn Moon	3.75
115 GD	3.75
116 GD	3.75
117 GD,Devil Deeds Done in Darkness	3.75
118 GD,D:Fu Manchu,double	3.75
119 GD	3.75
120 GD,Dweller o/t Dark Stream	3.75
121 Death in the City of Lights'	2.00
122	2.00
123 V:Ninjas	2.00
124	2.00
125	2.00
G-Size#1,CR,PG	3.00
G-Size#2 PG,V:Yellow Claw	2.00
G-Size#3	2.00
G-Size#4 JK,V:Yellow Claw	2.00
Spec.#1 Bleeding Black	3.25

MASTER OF KUNG FU: BLEEDING BLACK
1 V:ShadowHand,1991 . . . . 2.95

MASTERS OF TERROR
July, 1975
1 GM(c),FB,BWS,JSn,NA 3.00
2 JSn(c),GK,VM,Sept., 1975 . . . 2.00

MASTERS OF THE UNIVERSE
Star May, 1986—March, 1988
1 I:Hordak 1.50
2 thru 12 . . . . @1.00
Movie #1 GT 2.00

Matt Slade, Gunfighter #1
© Marvel Entertainment Group

MATT SLADE, GUNFIGHTER
Atlas May, 1956
1 AW,AT,F:Matt Slade,Crimson
Avenger 80.00
2 AW,A:Crimson Avenger 50.00
3 A:Crimson Avenger 35.00
4 A:Crimson Avenger 35.00
Becomes:
KID SLADE GUNFIGHTER
5 F:Kid Slade 40.00
6 . . . . 21.00
7 AW,Duel in the Night 45.00
8 July, 1957 . . . . 21.00

MAVERICK
1 JGz,F:Christopher Nord/David
North/Maverick, 48pg 2.99
1-shot LHa, V:Sabretooth,48pg . . 2.95

MELVIN THE MONSTER
Atlas July, 1956
1 . . . . 60.00
2 thru 6 . . . . @40.00
Becomes:
DEXTER THE DEMON
Sept., 1957
7 . . . . 25.00

MEMORIES
Epic
1 Space Adventures 2.50

MENACE
Atlas May, 1953
1 RH,BEv,GT,One Head Too
Many 350.00
2 RH,BEv,GT,JSt,Burton's Blood 250.00
3 BEv,RH,JR,The Werewolf . . 200.00
4 BEv,RH,The Four Armed Man 200.00
5 BEv,RH,GC,GT,I&O:Zombie . 300.00
6 BEv,RH,JR,The Graymoor
Ghost 150.00
7 JSt,RH,Fresh out of Flesh . . 125.00
8 RH,The Lizard Man 125.00
9 BEv,The Walking Dead 135.00
10 RH(c),Half Man,Half... . . . . 125.00
11 JKz,JR,Locked In,May, 1954 125.00

MEN IN ACTION
Atlas April, 1952
1 Sweating it Out 60.00
2 US Infantry stories 30.00
3 RH 20.00
4 War stories 20.00
5 Squad Charge 20.00
6 War stories 20.00
7 RH(c),BK,No Risk Too Great . 40.00
8 JRo(c),They Strike By Night . 20.00
9 SSh(c),Rangers Strike Back . 20.00
Becomes:
BATTLE BRADY
10 SSh(c),F:Battle Brady 50.00
11 SSh(c) 28.00
12 SSh(c),Death to the Reds . . 20.00
13 . . . . 20.00
14 Final Issue,June, 1953 . . . . 20.00

MEN IN BLACK
1 ANi, prequel to movie . . . .

MEN IN BLACK: THE MOVIE
Spec. Movie Adaptation . . . .

MEN'S ADVENTURES
See: TRUE WESTERN

MEPHISTO vs. FOUR HEROES
April–July, 1987
1 JB,BWi,A:Fantastic Four 2.50
2 JB,BWi,A:X-Factor 2.25
3 JB,AM,A:X-Men 2.25
4 JB,BWi,A:Avengers 2.00

METEOR MAN
1 R:Meteor Man 1.25
2 V:GhostStrike,Malefactor,Simon 1.25
3 A:Spider-Man 1.25
4 A:Night Thrasher 1.25
5 Exocet 1.25
6 final issue 1.25

[TED McKEEVER'S} METROPOL
Epic
1 Ted McKeever 2.95
2 . . . . 2.95

3 . . . . 2.95
4 . . . . 2.95
5 . . . . 2.95
6 . . . . 2.95
7 . . . . 2.95
8 Return of Eddy Current 2.95
9 'Wings of Silence' 2.95
10 'Rotting Metal,Rusted Flesh' . 2.95
11 'Diagram of the Heart' 2.95
12 . . . . 2.95

METROPOL A.D.
Epic
1 R:The Angels 3.50
2 V:Demons 3.50
3 V:Nuclear Arsenal 3.50

Micronauts #58
© Marvel Entertainment Group

MICRONAUTS
[1st Series]
Jan., 1979
1 MGo,JRu,O:Micronauts 3.00
2 MGo,JRu,Earth 2.50
3 MGo,JRu 2.00
4 MGo 2.00
5 MGo,V:Prometheus 2.00
6 MGo 2.00
7 MGo,A:Man Thing 2.00
8 MGo,BMc,I:Capt. Univ. 2.50
9 MGo,I:Cilicia 2.00
10 MGo 2.00
11 MGo 2.00
12 MGo 2.00
13 HC,F:Bug 1.50
14 HC,V:Wartstaff 1.50
15 HC,AM,A:Fantastic Four 1.50
16 HC,AM,A:Fantastic Four 1.50
17 HC,AM,A:Fantastic Four 1.50
18 HC,Haunted House Issue . . . 1.50
19 PB,V:Odd John 1.50
20 PB,A:Antman 1.50
21 PB,I:Microverse 1.50
22 PB 1.50
23 PB,V:Molecule Man 1.50
24 MGo,V:Computrex 1.50
25 PB,A:Mentallo 1.50
26 PB,A:Baronkarza 1.25
27 PB,V:Hydra,A:Shield 1.25

MARVEL

All comics prices listed are for *Near Mint* condition.   **CVA Page 223**

MARVEL

28 PB,V:Hydra,A:Shield	1.25
29 PB,Doc Samson	1.25
30 PB,A:Shield	1.25
31 PB,A:Dr.Strange	1.25
32 PB,A:Dr.Strange	1.25
33 PB,A:Devil of Tropica	1.25
34 PB,A:Dr.Strange	1.25
35 O:Microverse	1.50
36 KG,Dr.Strange	1.50
37 KG,Nightcrawler	3.50
38 GK,1st direct	2.50
39 SD	1.75
40 GK,A:FF	1.75
41 GK,Dr.Doom	1.25
42 GK	1.25
43	1.25
44	1.25
45 Arcade	1.25
46	1.25
47	1.25
48 JG	2.00
49 JG,V:BaronKarza	1.50
50 JG,V:BaronKarza	1.50
51 JG	1.50
52 JG	1.50
53 JG,V:Untouchables	1.50
54 JG,V:Tribunal	1.50
55 JG,V:KarzaWorld	1.50
56 JG,Kaliklak	1.50
57 JG,V:BaronKarza	1.50
58 JG,V:BaronKarza	1.50
59 JG,V:TheMakers	1.50
Ann.#1,SD	2.00
#2 SD	1.50

[2nd Series]

1 V:The Makers	1.50
2 AAd(c),V:The Makers	1.50
3 Huntarr'sEgg	1.00
4 V:The Makers	1.00
5 The Spiral Path	1.00
6 L:Bug	1.00
7 Acroyear	1.00
8 V:Scion	1.00
9 R:Devil	1.00
10 V:Enigma Force	1.00
11 V:Scion	1.00
12 V:Scion	1.00
13 V:Dark Armada	1.00
14 V:Keys of the Zodiac	1.00
15 O:Marionette	1.00
16 Secret Wars II	1.50
17 V:Scion	1.00
18 Acroyear	1.00
19 R:Baron Karza	1.00
20 Last Issue	1.25

MICRONAUTS
(Special Edition)
Dec., 1983

1 MGo/JRu,rep.	2.00
2 MGo/JRu,rep.	2.00
3 Rep.MG/JRu	2.00
4 Rep.MG/JRu	2.00
5 Rep.MG/JRu,April, 1984	2.00

MIDNIGHT MEN

1 HC,I:Midnight Men	2.75
2 HC,J:Barnett	2.25
3 HC,Pasternak is Midnight Man	2.25
4 HC,Last issue	2.25

MIDNIGHT SONS UNLIMITED

1 JQ,JBi,MT(c),A:Midnight Sons	4.25

2 BSz(c),F:Midnight Sons	4.25
3 JR2(c),JS,A:Spider-Man	4.25
4 Siege of Darkness #17, D:2nd Ghost Rider	4.25
5 DQ(s),F:Mordred,Vengeance, Morbius,Werewolf,Blaze, I:Wildpride	4.25
6 DQ(s),F:Dr.Strange	3.95
7 DQ(s),F:Man-Thing	3.95
8	3.95
9 J:Mighty Destroyer	3.95

MIGHTY MARVEL WESTERN
Oct., 1968

1 JK,All reprints,B:Rawhide Kid Kid Colt,Two-Gun Kids	7.50
2 JK,DAy,Beware of the Barker Brothers	5.00
3 HT(c),JK,DAy,Walking Death	5.00
4 HT(c),DAy	5.00
5 HT(c),DAy,Ambush	5.00
6 HT(c),DAy Doom in the Desert	5.00
7 DAy,V:Murderous Masquerader	5.00
8 HT(c),DAy,Rustler's on the Range	5.00
9 JSe(c),JK,DAy,V:Dr Danger	5.00
10 OW,DH,Cougar	5.00
11 V:The Enforcers	2.00
12 JK,V:Blackjack Bordon	2.00
13 V:Grizzly	2.00
14 JK.V:The Enforcers	2.00
15 Massacre at Medicine Bend	2.00
16 JK,Mine of Death	2.00
17 Ambush at Blacksnake Mesa	2.00
18 Six-Gun Thunderer	2.00
19 Reprints cont	2.00
20 same	2.00
21 same	1.50
22	1.50
23 same	1.50
24 JDa,E:Kid Colt	1.50
25 B:Matt Slade	1.50
26 thru 31 Reprints	@1.50
32 JK,AW,Ringo Kid #23	1.25
33 thru 36 Reprints	@1.25
37 JK,AW Two-Gun #51	1.25
38 thru 45 Reprints	@1.25
46 same,Sept., 1976	1.25

SABAN'S MIGHTY MORPHIN POWER RANGERS

1 SLo,FaN,New ongoing series	2.25
2 FaN,RLm,JP,more	1.75
3 FaN,RLm,JP,more adventures	1.75
4 LSn,JP,V:Glob monster	1.75
5	1.75
6	1.75
7 Close Encounter with Alien	1.75
Photo Adaptation	2.95

SABAN'S MIGHTY MORPHIN POWER RANGERS: NINJA RANGERS/ VR TROOPERS

1 FaN,RLm,JP,flip book	1.75
2 JP,flip book	1.75
3 New outfits	1.75
4	1.75

5	1.75
6	1.75

MIGHTY MOUSE
Fall, 1946
[1st Series]

1 Terytoons Presents	750.00
2	350.00
3	250.00
4 Summer, 1947	250.00

Mighty Mouse #3
© Marvel Entertainment Group

MIGHTY MOUSE
Oct., 1990

1 EC,Dark Mite Returns	3.00
2 EC,V:The Glove	2.00
3 EC/JBr(c)Prince Say More	1.50
4 EC/GP(c)Alt.Universe #1	1.50
5 EC,Alt.Universe #2	1.50
6 'Ferment',A:MacFurline'	1.50
7 EC,V:Viral Worm	1.25
8 EC,BAT-BAT:Year One, O:Bug Wonder	1.25
9 EC,BAT-BAT:Year One, V:Smoker	1.25
10 'Night o/t Rating Lunatics'	1.25

MILLIE THE MODEL
Winter, 1945

1 O:Millie the Model, Bowling(c)	400.00
2 Totem Pole(c)	250.00
3 Anti-Noise(c)	125.00
4 Bathing Suit(c)	125.00
5 Blame it on Fame	125.00
6 Beauty and the Beast	125.00
7 Bathing Suit(c)	125.00
8 Fancy Dress(c),HK,Hey Look	125.00
9 Paris(c),BW	135.00
10 Jewelry(c),HK,Hey Look	125.00
11 HK,Giggles and Grins	75.00
12 HK,Hedy Devine	65.00
13 A;Hedy Devine,HK,Hey Look	75.00
14 HK,Hey Look	75.00
15 HK,Hey Look	45.00
16	75.00
17 thru 20	@60.00
21 thru 30	@50.00

31 thru 75	@30.00
76 thru 99	@20.00
100	22.00
101 thru 126	@15.00
127 Millie/Clicker	20.00
128 A:Scarlet Mayfair	15.00
129 The Truth about Agnes	15.00
130 thru 153	@15.00
154 B:New Millie	15.00
155 thru 206	@15.00
207 Dec., 1973	15.00
Ann.#1 How Millie Became a Model	125.00
Ann.#2 Millies Guide to the world of Modeling	75.00
Ann.#3 Many Lives of Millie	50.00
Ann.#4 Many Lives of Millie	30.00

MISS AMERICA COMICS
1944
1 Miss America(c),pin-ups	900.00

MISS AMERICA MAGAZINE
Nov., 1944—Nov. 1958
2 Ph(c),Miss America costume I;Patsy Walker,Buzz Baxter, Hedy Wolfe	850.00
3 Ph(c),A:Patsy Walker,Miss America	300.00
4 Ph(c),Betty Page,A:Patsy Walker,Miss America	300.00
5 Ph(c),A:Patsy Walker,Miss America	300.00
6 Ph(c),A:Patsy Walker	50.00
7 Patsy Walker stories	30.00
8 same	30.00
9 same	30.00
10 same	30.00
11 same	30.00
12 same	30.00
13 thru 18	@30.00
21	35.00
22 thru 45	@25.00
46 thru 93	@20.00

MISS FURY COMICS
Timely Winter, 1942-43
1 Newspaper strip reprints, ASh(c) O:Miss Fury	2,000.00
2 V:Nazis(c)	1,000.00
3 Hitler/Nazi Flag(c)	800.00
4 ASh(c),Japanese(c)	600.00
5 ASh(c),Gangster(c)	600.00
6 Gangster(c)	600.00
7 Gangster(c)	600.00
8 Atom-Bomb Secrets(c) Winter, 1946	600.00

MISTY
Star Dec., 1985
1 F:Millie the Models Niece	1.50
2 thru 5	@1.00
6 May, 1986	1.00

MITZI COMICS
Timely Spring, 1948
1 HK:Hey Look,Giggles and Grins	75.00
Becomes:
MITZI'S BOYFRIEND
2 F:Chip,Mitzi/Chip(c)	33.00

3 Chips adventures	25.00
4 thru 7 same	@25.00
Becomes:
MITZI'S ROMANCES
8 Mitzi/Chip(c)	32.00
9	25.00
10 Dec., 1949	25.00

MODELING WITH MILLIE
See: DATE WITH MILLIE

MOEBIUS
Epic Oct., 1987
1	12.00
2	12.00
3	15.00
4	12.00
5	12.00
6 1988	12.00

MOEBIUS: FUSION
1 128pg Sketchbook	19.95

MOLLY MANTON'S ROMANCES
Sept., 1949
1 Ph(c),Dare Not Marry	50.00
2 Ph(c),Romances of	35.00
Becomes:
ROMANTIC AFFAIRS
3 Ph(c)	27.00

MONSTER MENACE
1 thru 4 SD,rep.	@1.25

MONSTER OF FRANKENSTEIN
Jan., 1973
1 MP,Frankenstein's Monster	18.00
2 MP,Bride of the Monster	9.00
3 MP,Revenge	9.00
4 MP,Monster's Death	9.00
5 MP,The Monster Walks Among Us	9.00
Becomes:
FRANKENSTEIN
1973–75
6 MP,Last of the Frankensteins	5.00
7 JB,The Fiend and the Fury	5.00
8 JB,A:Dracula	10.00
9 JB,A:Dracula	10.00
10 JB,Death Strikes Frankenstein	5.00
11 Carnage at Castle Frankenstein	3.75
12 Frankenstein's Monster today	3.75
13 Undying Fiend	3.75
14 Fury of the Night Creature	3.75
15 Trapped in a Nightmare	3.75
16 The Brute and the Berserker	3.75
17 Phoenix Aflame	3.75
18 Children of the Damned Sept., 1975	3.75

MONSTERS ON THE PROWL
See: CHAMBER OF DARKNESS

MONSTERS UNLEASHED
July, 1973
1 GM(c),GC,DW,Black&White Mag	6.00

2 JB,FB,BEv,B:Frankenstein	8.00
3 NA(c),GK,GM,GT,B:Man-Thing	4.00
4 JB,GC,BK,I:Satana	4.00
5 JB	5.00
6 MP	4.00
7 AW	4.00
8 GP,NA	4.00
9 A:Wendigo	5.00
10 O:Tigra	4.00
11 FB(C),April, 1975	4.00
Ann.#1 GK	4.00

MOON KNIGHT
[1st Regular Series]
Nov., 1980
1 BSz,O:Moon Knight	6.00
2 BSz,V:Slasher	4.00
3 BSz,V:Midnight Man	3.50
4 BSz,V:Committee of 5	3.50
5 BSz,V:Red Hunter	3.50
6 BSz,V:White Angels	3.50
7 BSz,V:Moon Kings	3.50
8 BSz,V:Moon Kings, Drug	3.00
9 BSz,V:Midnight Man	3.00
10 BSz,V:Midnight Man	3.00
11 BSz,V:Creed (Angel Dust)	3.00
12 BSz,V:Morpheus	3.00
13 BSz,A:Daredevil & Jester	3.00
14 BSz,V:Stained Glass Scarlet	3.00
15 FM(c),BSz,1st Direct	4.00
16 V:Blacksmith	3.00
17 BSz,V:Master Sniper	3.00
18 BSz,V:Slayers Elite	3.00
19 BSz,V:Arsenal	3.00
20 BSz,V:Arsenal	3.00
21 A:Bother Voodoo	2.25
22 BSz,V:Morpheus	2.50
23 BSz,V:Morpheus	2.50
24 BSz,V:Stained Glass Scarlet	2.50
25 BSz,Black Specter	2.50
26 KP,V:Cabbie Killer	2.00
27 A:Kingpin	2.00
28 BSz,"Spirits in the Sands"	2.00
29 BSz,V:Werewolf	3.00
30 BSz,V:Werewolf	2.00
31 TA,V:Savage Studs	2.00
32 KN,Druid Walsh	2.00
33 KN,V:Druid Walsh	2.00

Moon Knight (2nd Series) #39
© Marvel Entertainment Group

34 KN,Marc Spector	2.00
35 KN,X-Men,FF,V:The Fly DoubleSized	3.00
36 A:Dr.Strange	2.00
37 V:Zohar	2.00
38 V:Zohar	2.00

[2nd Regular Series]

1 O:Moon Knight,DoubleSize	2.50
2 Yucatan	2.00
3 V:Morpheus	2.00
4 A:Countess	2.00
5 V:Lt.Flint	2.00
6 GI,LastIssue	2.00

[3rd Regular Series]

1 V:Bushmaster	5.00
2 A:Spider-Man	4.00
3 V:Bushmaster	2.50
4 RH,A:Midnight,Black Cat	2.50
5 V:Midnight,BlackCat	2.50
6 A:BrotherVoodoo	2.50
7 A:BrotherVoodoo	2.50
8 TP,A:Punisher,A of V	4.00
9 TP,A:Punisher,A of V	4.00
10 V:Killer Shrike,A of V	2.00
11 TP,V:Arsenal	2.00
12 TP,V:Bushman,A:Arsenal	2.00
13 TP,V:Bushman	2.00
14 TP,V:Bushman	2.00
15 TP,Trial o/Marc Spector #1,A: Silv.Sable,Sandman,Paladin	3.00
16 TP,Trial o/Marc Spector #2,A: Silv.Sable,Sandman,Paladin	3.00
17 TP,Trial o/Marc Spector #3	3.00
18 TP,Trial o/Marc Spector #4	3.00
19 RLd(c),TP,SpM,Punisher	3.50
20 TP,A:Spider-Man,Punisher	3.00
21 TP,Spider-Man,Punisher	3.00
22 I:Harbinger	2.00
23 Confrontation	2.00
24 A:Midnight	2.00
25 MBa,TP,A:Ghost Rider	3.00
26 BSz(c),TP,B:Scarlet Redemption V:Stained Glass Scarlet	2.00
27 TP,V:Stained Glass Scarlet	2.00
28 TP,V:Stained Glass Scarlet	2.00
29 TP,V:Stained Glass Scarlet	2.00
30 TP,V:Stained Glass Scarlet	2.00
31 TP,E:Scarlet Redemption, A:Hobgoblin	2.50
32 TP,V:Hobgoblin,SpM(in Black)	3.00
33 TP,V:Hobgoblin,A:Spider-Man	3.00
34 V:Killer Shrike	2.00
35 TP,Return of Randall Spector Pt.1,A:Punisher	2.00
36 TP,A:Punisher,Randall	2.00
37 TP,A:Punisher,Randall	2.00
38 TP,A:Punisher,Randall	2.00
39 TP,N:Moon Knight,A:Dr.Doom	2.00
40 TP,V:Dr.Doom	2.00
41 TP,Infinity War,I:Moonshade	2.00
42 TP,Infinity War,V:Moonshade	2.00
43 TP(i),Infinity War	2.00
44 Inf.War,A:Dr.Strange.FF	2.00
45 V:Demogoblin	2.00
46 V:Demogoblin	2.00
47 Legacy Quest Scenario	2.00
48 I:Deadzone	2.00
49 V:Deadzone	2.00
50 A:Avengers,I:Hellbent, Die-cut(c)	3.50
51 A:Gambit,V:Hellbent	2.00
52 A:Gambit,Werewolf	2.00
53 "Pang"	2.00
54	2.00
55 SPa,V:Sunstreak	9.00

56 SPa,V:Seth	7.00
57 SPa,Inf.Crusade	6.00
58 SPa(c),A:Hellbent	3.00
59 SPa(c),	3.00
60 E:TKa(s),SPa,D:Moonknight	5.00
Spec.#1 ANi,A:Shang-Chi	2.50

MOON KNIGHT
(Special Edition)
Nov., 1983

1 BSz,reprints	2.00
2 BSz,reprints	2.00
3 BSz,reprints,Jan., 1984	2.00

MOON KNIGHT:
DIVIDED WE FALL

1 DCw,V:Bushman	4.95

MOONSHADOW
Epic May, 1985

1 JMu,O:Moonshadow	6.00
2 JMu,Into Space	4.00
3 JMu,The Looney Bin	3.50
4 JMu,Fights Ira	3.50
5 JMu,Prisoner	3.50
6 JMu,Hero of War	3.50
7 JMu,UnkshussFamily	3.50
8 JMu,Social Outcast	3.50
9 JMu,Search For Ira	3.50
10 JMu,Internat.House of T	3.50
11 JMu,UnkshussFamily	3.50
12 JMu,UnkshussFamily,Feb.1987	3.50

MORBIUS

1 V:Lilith,Lilin,A:Blaze,Gh.Rider, Rise o/t Midnight Sons #3, polybagged w/poster	4.00
2 V:Simon Stroud	2.50
3 A:Spider-Man	2.00
4 I:Dr.Paine,C:Spider-Man	2.00
5 V:Basilisk,(inc Superman tribute on letters page)	2.00
6 V:Basilisk	2.00
7 V:Vic Slaughter	2.00
8 V:Nightmare	2.00
9 V:Nightmare	2.00
10 Two Tales	2.00
11 A:Nightstalkers	2.00
12 Midnight Massacre#4	2.50
13 R:Martine,A:Lilith	2.00
14 RoW,V:Nightmare,A:Werewolf	2.00
15 A:Ghost Rider,Werewolf	2.00
16 GWt(s),Siege of Darkness#5	2.00
17 GWt(s),Siege of Darkness#17	2.00
18 GWt(s),A:Deathlok	2.00
19 GWt(s),A:Deathlok	2.00
20 GWt(s),I:Bloodthirst	2.00
21 B:Dance of the Hunter,A:SpM	2.25
22 A:Spider-Man	2.25
23 E:Dance of the Hunter,A:SpM	2.25
24 Return of the Dragon	2.25
25 RoW	2.50
26	1.95
27	1.95
28 A:Werewolf	1.95
29	1.95
30 New Morbius	1.95
31 A:Mortine	1.95
32 Another Kill	1.95

MORBIUS REVISITED

1 WMc,rep.Fear #20	1.95
2 WMc,rep.Fear #28	1.95

3 WMc,rep.Fear #29	1.95
4 WMc,rep.Fear #30	1.95
5 WMc,rep.Fear #31	1.95

MORT THE DEAD
TEENAGER

1 LHa(s),I:Mort	1.75
2 thru 4 LHa(s),	1.75

MOTHER TERESA
1984

1 Mother Teresa Story	2.00

Motor Mouth & Killpower #9
© Marvel Entertainment Group

MOTOR MOUTH
& KILLPOWER

1 GFr,A:Nick Fury,I:Motor Mouth,Killpower	3.00
2 GFr,A:Nick Fury,	2.00
3 GFr,V:Killpower,A:Punisher	2.00
4 GFr,A:Nick Fury,Warheads, Hell's Angel,O:Killpower	2.00
5 GFr,A:Excalibur,Archangel	2.00
6 GFr,A:Cable,Punisher	2.00
7 EP,A:Cable,Nick Fury	2.00
8 JFr,A:Cable,Nick Fury	2.00
9 JFr,A:Cable,N.Fury,V:Harpies	2.00
10 V:Red Sonja	2.00
11 V:Zachary Sorrow	2.00
12 A:Death's Head II	2.00
13 A:Death's Head II	2.00

MS. MARVEL
Jan., 1977

1 JB,O:Ms Marvel	5.00
2 JB,JSt,V:Scorpion	4.00
3 JB,JSt,V:Doomsday Man	3.00
4 JM,JSt,V:Destructor	3.00
5 JM,JSt,A:V:Vision	3.00
6 JM,JSt,V:Grotesk	3.00
7 JM,JSt,V:Modok	3.00
8 JM,JSt,V:Grotesk	3.00
9 KP,JSt,I:Deathbird	5.00
10 JB,TP,V:Deathbird,Modok	3.00
11 V:Elementals	2.00
12 V:Hecate	2.00
13 Bedlam in Boston	2.00

MARVEL

14 V:Steeplejack	2.00
15 V:Tigershark	2.00
16 V:Tigershark,A:Beast	2.00
17	2.00
18 I:Mystique,A;Avengers	6.50
19 A:Captain Marvel	3.00
20 V:Lethal Lizards,N:Ms.Marvel	2.00
21 V:Lethal Lizards	2.00
22 V:Deathbirds	2.00
23 The Woman who Fell to Earth April, 1979	2.00

MUPPET BABIES
Star August, 1984

1 thru 10	@1.00
11 thru 20	@1.00
21 thru 25 July, 1989	@1.00

MUPPETS TAKE MANHATTAN

1 movie adapt,November, 1984	1.00
2 movie adapt	1.00
3 movie adapt,Jan., 1985	1.00

MUTANTS: THE AMAZING X-MEN

1 X-Men After Xavier	3.50
2 Exodus, Dazzler,V:Abyss	2.25
3 F:Bishop	1.95
4 V:Apocalypse	1.95

MUTANTS: THE ASTONISHING X-MEN

1 Uncanny X-Men	3.50
2 V:Holocaust	2.25
3 V:Abyss	1.95
4 V:Beast,Infinities	1.95

MUTANTS: GENERATION NEXT

1 Generation X Ax	3.50
2 Genetic Slave Pens	2.25
3 V:Sugar Man	1.95
4 V:Sugar Man	1.95

MUTATIS
Epic

1 I:Mutatis	2.25
2 O:Mutatis	2.25
3 A:Mutatis	2.25

MY DIARY
Dec., 1949

1 Ph(c),The Man I Love	50.00
2 Ph(c),I Was Anybody's Girl March, 1950	45.00

MY LOVE
July, 1949

1 Ph(c),One Heart to Give	50.00
2 Ph(c),Hate in My Heart	30.00
3 Ph(c),	30.00
4 Ph(c),Betty Page, April, 1950	115.00

MY LOVE
Sept., 1969

1 Love story reprints	7.50
2 thru 9	@4.00
10	5.00
11 thru 38	@3.00
39 March, 1976	3.00

MY ROMANCE
Sept., 1948

1 Romance Stories	50.00
2	27.00
3	27.00

Becomes:

MY OWN ROMANCE

4 Romance Stories Continue	47.00
5 thru 10	@25.00
11 thru 20	@18.00
21 thru 50	@15.00
51 thru 54	@11.00
55	30.00
56 thru 60	@11.00
61 thru 70	@6.00
71	55.00
72 thru 76	@10.00

Becomes:

TEENAGE ROMANCE

77 Romance Stories Continue	10.00
78 thru 85	@10.00
86 March, 1962	10.00

MYS-TECH WARS

1 BHi,A:FF,X-Men,Avengers	2.00
2 A:FF,X-Men,X-Force	2.00
3 BHi,A:X-Men,X-Force	2.00
4 A:Death's Head II	2.00

MYSTERY TALES
Atlas March, 1952

1 GC,Horror Strikes at Midnight	550.00
2 BK,BEv,OW,The Corpse is Mine	300.00
3 RH,GC,JM, The Vampire Strikes	225.00
4 Funeral of Horror	225.00
5 Blackout at Midnight	225.00
6	225.00
7 JRo,The Ghost Hunter	225.00
8 BEv	225.00
9 BEv(c),the Man in the Morgue	225.00
10 BEV(c),GT,What Happened to Harry	225.00
11 BEv(c)	175.00
12 GT,MF	175.00
13	150.00
14 BEv(c),GT	150.00
15 RH(c),EK	150.00
16	150.00
17 RH(c)	150.00
18 AW,DAy,GC	165.00
19	135.00
20 Electric Chair	135.00
21 JF,MF,Decapitation	150.00
22 JF,MF	150.00
23 thru 27	@125.00
28	100.00
29 thru 32	@110.00
33 BEv	100.00
34	100.00
35 BEv	100.00
36	110.00
37 DW	100.00
38	110.00
39 BK	110.00
40	110.00
41 thru 43	@100.00
44 AW	120.00
45 SD	110.00
46 RC,SD,JP	120.00
47 DAy	120.00
48	100.00

49 GM,AT	100.00
50 JO,AW	120.00
51 DAy	120.00
52	100.00
53	100.00
54 RC,August, 1957	125.00

MYSTICAL TALES
Atlas June, 1956

1 BEv,BP,JO,Say the Magical Words	300.00
2 BEv(c),JO,Black Blob	175.00
3 BEv(c),RC,Four Doors To	165.00
4 BEv(c).The Condemned	150.00
5 AW,Meeting at Midnight	150.00
6 BK,AT,He Hides in the Tower	100.00
7 BEv,JF,JO,AT,FBe,The Haunted Tower	100.00
8 BK,SC, Stone Walls Can't Stop Him,August, 1957	100.00

MYSTIC COMICS
Timely March, 1940
[1st Series]

1 ASh(c),O;The Blue Blaze,Dynamic Man,Flexo,B:Dakor the Magician A:Zephyr Jones,3X's,Deep Sea Demon,Bondage(c)	12,000.00
2 ASh(c),B:The Invisible Man Mastermind,	3,000.00
3 ASh(c),O:Hercules	2,500.00
4 ASh(c),O:Thin Man,Black Widow E:Hercules,Blue Blazes,Dynamic Man,Flexo,Invisible Man	2,800.00
5 ASh(c)O:The Black Marvel, Blazing Skull,Super Slave Terror,Sub-Earth Man	2,300.00
6 ASh(c),O:The Challenger, B:The Destroyer	2,600.00
7 S&K(c),B:The Witness,O:Davey and the Demon,E;The Black Widow,Hitler(c)	2,900.00
8 Bondage(c)	1,500.00
9 MSy,DRi,Hitler/Bondage(c)	1,500.00
10 E:Challenger,Terror	1,500.00

[2nd Series] Oct., 1944

1 B:The Angel,Human Torch, Destroyer,Terry Vance, Tommy Tyme,Bondage(c)	1,650.00
2 E:Human Torch,Terry Vance,Bondage(c)	1,000.00
3 E:The Angel,Tommy Tyme Bondage(c)	900.00
4 ASh(c),A:Young Allies Winter, 1944-45	800.00

MYSTIC
[3rd Series] March, 1951

1 MSy,Strange Tree	550.00
2 MSy,Dark Dungeon	300.00
3 GC,Jaws of Creeping Death	250.00
4 BW,MSy,The Den of the Devil Bird	500.00
5 MSy,Face	175.00
6 BW,She Wouldn't Stay Dead	500.00
7 GC,Untold Horror waits in the Tomb	175.00
8 DAy(c),BEv,GK,A Monster Among Us	175.00
9 BEv	175.00
10 GC	175.00
11 JR,The Black Gloves	150.00
12 GC	150.00
13 In the Dark	150.00

All comics prices listed are for _Near Mint_ condition.

MARVEL

14 The Corpse and I	150.00
15 GT,JR,House of Horror	150.00
16 A Scream in the Dark	150.00
17 BEv,Behold the Vampire	150.00
18 BEv(c),The Russian Devil	150.00
19 Swamp Girl	150.00
20 RH(c)	150.00
21 BEv(c),GC	125.00
22 RH(c)	125.00
23 RH(c),RA,Chilling Tales	125.00
24 GK,How Many Times Can You Die	125.00
25 RH(c),RA,E.C.Swipe	125.00
26 Severed Head(c)	150.00
27 Who Walks with a Zombie	135.00
28 DW,Not Enough Dead	135.00
29 SMo,The Unseen	135.00
30 RH(c),DW	135.00
31 SC,JKz	135.00
32 The Survivor	135.00
33 thru 36	@135.00
37 thru 51	@100.00
52	110.00
53 thru 57	@100.00
58 thru 60	@110.00
61	100.00

The 'Nam #1
© Marvel Entertainment Group

'NAM, THE
Dec., 1986

1 MGo,Vietnam War	3.00
1a 2nd printing	1.50
2 MGo,Dust Off	2.50
3 MGo,Three Day Pass	2.00
4 MGo,TV newscrew	2.00
5 MGo,Top Sgt.	2.00
6 MGo,Monsoon	2.00
7 MGo,Cedar Falls	2.00
8 MGo,5th to the 1st	2.00
9 MGo,ActionIssue	2.00
10 MGo,Saigon	2.00
11 MGo,Christmas	1.75
12 MGo,AgentOrange	1.75
13 MGo	1.75
14	1.75
15 ReturningVets	1.75

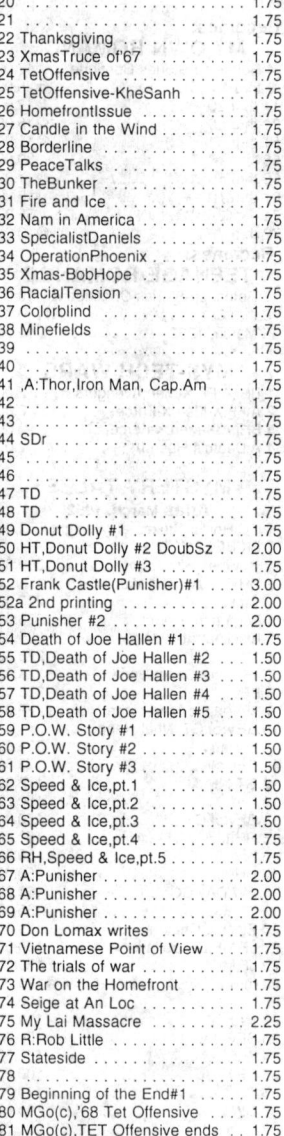

16	1.75
17 Vietcong	1.75
18	1.75
19	1.75
20	1.75
21	1.75
22 Thanksgiving	1.75
23 XmasTruce of'67	1.75
24 TetOffensive	1.75
25 TetOffensive-KheSanh	1.75
26 HomefrontIssue	1.75
27 Candle in the Wind	1.75
28 Borderline	1.75
29 PeaceTalks	1.75
30 TheBunker	1.75
31 Fire and Ice	1.75
32 Nam in America	1.75
33 SpecialistDaniels	1.75
34 OperationPhoenix	1.75
35 Xmas-BobHope	1.75
36 RacialTension	1.75
37 Colorblind	1.75
38 Minefields	1.75
39	1.75
40	1.75
41 ,A:Thor,Iron Man, Cap.Am	1.75
42	1.75
43	1.75
44 SDr	1.75
45	1.75
46	1.75
47 TD	1.75
48 TD	1.75
49 Donut Dolly #1	1.75
50 HT,Donut Dolly #2 DoubSz	2.00
51 HT,Donut Dolly #3	1.75
52 Frank Castle(Punisher)#1	3.00
52a 2nd printing	2.00
53 Punisher #2	2.00
54 Death of Joe Hallen #1	1.75
55 TD,Death of Joe Hallen #2	1.50
56 TD,Death of Joe Hallen #3	1.50
57 TD,Death of Joe Hallen #4	1.50
58 TD,Death of Joe Hallen #5	1.50
59 P.O.W. Story #1	1.50
60 P.O.W. Story #2	1.50
61 P.O.W. Story #3	1.50
62 Speed & Ice,pt.1	1.50
63 Speed & Ice,pt.2	1.50
64 Speed & Ice,pt.3	1.50
65 Speed & Ice,pt.4	1.75
66 RH,Speed & Ice,pt.5	1.75
67 A:Punisher	2.00
68 A:Punisher	2.00
69 A:Punisher	2.00
70 Don Lomax writes	1.75
71 Vietnamese Point of View	1.75
72 The trials of war	1.75
73 War on the Homefront	1.75
74 Seige at An Loc	1.75
75 My Lai Massacre	2.25
76 R:Rob Little	1.75
77 Stateside	1.75
78	1.75
79 Beginning of the End#1	1.75
80 MGo(c),'68 Tet Offensive	1.75
81 MGo(c),TET Offensive ends	1.75
82 TET Offensive	1.75
83 thru 84 Last issue	1.75

'NAM MAGAZINE, THE
August, 1988
(black & white)

1 Reprints	3.00
2 thru 9	@2.50

10 May, 1989	2.50

NAMORA
Fall, 1948

1 BEv,DR	1,200.00
2 BEv,A:Sub-Mariner,Blonde Phantom	1,000.00
3 BEv,A:Sub-Mariner,Dec.,1948	950.00

NAMOR THE SUB-MARINER
April, 1990

1 JBy,BWi,I:Desmond & Phoebe Marrs	3.50
2 JBy,BWi,V:Griffin	2.50
3 JBy,BWi,V:Griffin	2.50
4 JBy,A:Reed & Sue Richards, Tony Stark	2.50
5 JBy,A:FF,IronMan,C:Speedball	2.50
6 JBy,V:Sluj	2.50
7 JBy,V:Sluj	2.50
8 JBy,V:Headhunter,R:D.Rand	2.50
9 JBy,V:Headhunter	2.50
10 JBy,V:Master Man,Warrior Woman	2.00
11 JBy,V:Mast.Man,War.Woman	2.00
12 JBy,R:Invaders,Spitfire	2.00
13 JBy,Namor on Trial,A:Fantastic Four,Captain America,Thor	2.00
14 JBy,R:Lady Dorma,A:Kazar Griffin	2.00
15 JBy,A:Iron Fist	2.00
16 JBy,A:Punisher,V:Iron Fist	2.00
17 JBy,V:Super Skrull(Iron Fist)	2.00
18 JBy,V:SuperSkrull,A:Punisher	2.00
19 JBy,V:Super Skrull,D:D.Marrs	2.00
20 JBy,Search for Iron Fist, O:Namorita	2.00
21 JBy,Visit to K'un Lun	2.00
22 JBy,Fate of Iron Fist, C:Wolverine	2.00
23 JBy,BWi,Iron Fist Contd., C:Wolverine	2.00
24 JBy,BWi,V:Wolverine	2.50
25 JBy,BWi,V:Master Khan	2.00
26 JaL,BWi,Search For Namor	5.00
27 JaL,BWi,V:Namorita	4.00
28 JaL,BWi,A:Iron Fist	3.00
29 JaL,BWi,After explosion	2.50
30 JaL,A:Doctor Doom	2.50
31 JaL,V:Doctor Doom	2.50
32 JaL,V:Doctor Doom, Namor regains memory	2.50
33 JaL,V:Master Khan	2.00
34 JaL,R:Atlantis	2.00
35 JaL,V:Tiger Shark	2.00
36 JaL,I:Suma-Ket,A:Tiger Shark	2.00
37 JaL,Blue Holo-Grafix,Altantean Civil War,N:Namor	2.50
38 JaL,O:Suma-Ket	2.00
39 A:Tigershark,V:Suma-Ket	1.50
40 V:Suma-Ket	1.50
41 V:War Machine	1.50
42 MCW,A:Stingray,V:Dorcas	1.50
43 MCW,V:Orka,Dorcas	1.50
44 I:Albatross	1.50
45 GI,A:Sunfire,V:Attuma	1.50
46 GI,	1.50
47 GI,Starblast #2	1.50
48 GI,Starblast #9,A:FF	1.50
49 GI,A:Ms. Marrs	1.50
50 GI,Holo-grafx(c),A:FF	3.00
50a Newsstand Ed.	2.00
51 AaL,	1.75

Namor, The Sub-Mariner #57
© Marvel Entertainment Group

52 GI,I:Sea Leopard	1.75
53 GI,V:Sea Leopard	1.75
54 GI,I:Llyron	1.50
55 GI,V:Llyron	1.50
56 GI,V:Llyron	1.50
57 A:Capt. America, V:Llyron	1.50
58	1.50
59 GI,V:Abomination	1.50
60 A:Morgan Le Fay	1.50
61 Atlantis Rising	1.50
62 V:Triton	1.50
Ann.#1 Subterran.Odyssey #3	2.00
Ann.#2 Return o/Defenders,pt.3	4.00
Ann.#3 I:Assassin,A:Iron Fist, w/Trading card	3.25
Ann.#4 V:Hydra	3.25

NAVY ACTION
August, 1954

1 US Navy War Stories	100.00
2 Navy(c)	50.00
3 thru 17	@30.00
18 August, 1957	30.00

NAVY COMBAT
Atlas June, 1955

1 DH,B;Torpedo Taylor	100.00
2 DH	50.00
3 DH	35.00
4 DH	35.00
5 DH	35.00
6 A:Battleship Burke	35.00
7 thru 10	@35.00
11 MD	30.00
12 RC	45.00
13	25.00
14	30.00
15	25.00
16	25.00
17 AW	50.00
18	25.00
19	25.00
20 Oct., 1958	25.00

NAVY TALES
Atlas Jan., 1957

1 BEv(c),BP,Torpedoes	75.00

2 AW,RC,One Hour to Live	65.00
3 JSe(c)	50.00
4 JSe(c),GC,JSt,RC,July, 1957	50.00

NELLIE THE NURSE
Atlas 1945

1 Beach(c)	175.00
2 Nellie's Date(c)	85.00
3 Swimming Pool(c)	60.00
4 Roller Coaster(c)	60.00
5 Hospital(c),HK,Hey Look	65.00
6 Bedside Manner(c)	45.00
7 Comic book(c)A:Georgie	45.00
8 Hospital(c),A:Georgie	45.00
9 BW,Nellie/Swing(c)A:Millie	55.00
10 Bathing Suit(c),A:Millie	40.00
11 HK,Hey Look	60.00
12 HK,Giggles 'n' Grins	40.00
13 HK	35.00
14 HK	60.00
15 HK	60.00
16 HK	60.00
17 HK.A:Annie Oakley	35.00
18 HK	55.00
19	35.00
20	35.00
21	30.00
22	30.00
23	30.00
24	30.00
25	30.00
26	30.00
27	30.00
28 HK,Rusty Reprint	32.00
29 thru 35	@25.00
36 Oct., 1952	25.00

NEW ADVENTURES OF CHOLLY & FLYTRAP
Epic

1	4.95
2	3.95
3	3.95

NEW MUTANTS, THE
March, 1983

1 BMc,MG,O:New Mutants	10.00
2 BMc,MG,V:Sentinels	6.00
2a Ltd.Test Cover 75c	30.00
3 BMc,MG,V:Brood Alien	5.00
4 SB,BMc,A:Peter Bristow	4.00
5 SB,BMc,A:Dark Rider	4.00
6 SB,AG,V:Viper	4.00
7 SB,BMc,V:Axe	4.00
8 SB,BMc,I:Amara Aquilla	4.00
9 SB,TMd,I:Selene	4.00
10 SB,BMc,C:Magma	4.00
11 SB,TMd,I:Magma	4.00
12 SB,TMd,J:Magma	4.00
13 SB,TMd,I:Cypher(Doug Ramsey) A:Kitty Pryde,Lilandra	5.00
14 SB,TMd,J:Magik,A:X-Men	4.00
15 SB,TMd,Mass.Academy	4.00
16 SB,TMd,V:Hellions,I:Warpath I:Jetstream	6.00
17 SB,TMd,V:Hellions,A:Warpath	5.00
18 BSz,V:Demon Bear,I:New Warlock,Magus	8.00
19 BSz,V:Demon Bear	4.00
20 BSz,V:Demon Bear	4.00
21 BSz,O&J:Warlock,doub.sz	9.00
22 BSz,A:X-Men	4.50
23 BSz,Sunspot,Cloak & Dagger	4.00
24 BSz,A:Cloak & Dagger	4.00

25 BSz,A:Cloak & Dagger	11.00
26 BSz,I:Legion(Prof.X's son)	14.00
27 BSz,V:Legion	13.00
28 BSz,O:Legion	9.00
29 BSz,V:Gladiators,I:Guido (Strong Guy)	5.00
30 BSz,A:Dazzler	4.00
31 BSz,A:Shadowcat	4.00
32 SL,V:Karma	3.50
33 SL,V:Karma	3.50
34 SL,V:Amahl Farouk	3.50
35 BSz,J:Magneto	4.00
36 BSz,A:Beyonder	3.50
37 BSz,D:New Mutants	3.50
38 BSz,A:Hellions	3.50
39 BSz,A:White Queen	3.50
40 JG,KB,V:Avengers	3.50
41 JG,TA,Mirage	3.50
42 JG,KB,A:Dazzler	3.50
43 SP,V:Empath,A:Warpath	3.50
44 JG,V:Legion	9.00
45 JG,A:Larry Bodine	3.50
46 JG,KB,Mutant Massacre	4.00
47 JG,KB,V:Magnus	3.50
48 JG,CR,Future	3.50
49 VM,Future	3.50
50 JG,V:Magus,R:Prof.X	4.00
51 KN,A:Star Jammers	3.50
52 RL,DGr,Limbo	3.50
53 RL,TA,V:Hellions	3.50
54 SB,TA,N:New Mutants	3.50
55 BBI,TA,V:Aliens	3.00
56 JBr,TA,V:Hellions,A:Warpath	3.00
57 BBI,TA,I&J:Bird-Boy	3.00
58 BBI,TA,Bird-Boy	4.00
59 BBI,TA,Fall of Mutants, V:Dr.Animus	4.00
60 BBI,TA,F.of M.,D:Cypher	4.00
61 BBI,TA,Fall of Mutants	4.00
62 JMu,A:Magma,Hellions	3.00
63 BHa,JRu,Magik	3.50
64 BBI,TA,R:Cypher	3.00
65 BBI,TA,V:FreedomForce	3.00
66 BBI,TA,V:Forge	3.00
67 BBI,I:Gosamyr	3.00
68 BBI,V:Gosamyr	3.00
69 BBI,AW,I:Spyder	3.00
70 TSh,AM,V:Spyder	3.00
71 BBI,AW,V:N'Astirh	3.50
72 BBI,A,Inferno	3.50
73 BBI,W,A:Colossus	3.50
74 BBI,W,A:X-Terminators	3.00
75 JBy,Mc,Black King,V:Magneto	4.50
76 RB,TP,J:X-Terminators	3.00
77 RB,V:Mirage	3.00
78 RL,AW,V:FreedomForce	3.00
79 BBI,AW,V:Hela	3.00
80 BBI,AW,Asgard	3.00
81 LW,TSh,JRu,A:Hercules	3.00
82 BBI,AW,Asgard	3.00
83 BBI,Asgard	3.00
84 TSh,AM,A:QueenUla	3.00
85 RLd&TMc(c),BBI,V:Mirage	3.00
86 RLd,BWi,V:Vulture,C:Cable	10.00
87 RLd,BWi,I:Mutant Liberation Front,Cable	30.00
87a 2nd Printing	2.00
88 RLd,2nd Cable,V:Freedom Force	12.00
89 RLd,V:Freedom Force	8.00
90 RLd,A:Caliban,V:Sabretooth	8.00
91 RLd,A:Caliban,Masque, V:Sabretooth	8.00
92 RLd(c),BH,V:Skrulls	5.00
93 RLd,A:Wolverine,Sunfire,	

MARVEL

New Mutants #34
© Marvel Entertainment Group

V:Mutant Liberation Front 8.00
94 RLd,A:Wolverine,Sunfire,
  V:Mutant Liberation Front 7.00
95 RLd,Extinction Agenda,V:Hodge
  A:X-Men,X-Factor,D:Warlock . . 7.00
95a 2nd printing(gold) 5.00
96 RLd,ATb,JRu,Extinction Agenda
  V:Hodge,A:X-Men,X-Factor . . 7.00
97 E:LSi(s),RLd(c),JRu,Extinction
  Agenda,V:Hodge 7.00
98 FaN(s),RLd,I:Deadpool,Domino,
  Gideon,L:Rictor 9.00
99 FaN(s),RLd,I:Feral,Shatterstar,
  L:Sunspot,J:Warpath 7.00
100 FaN(s),RLd,J:Feral,Shatterstar,
  I:X-Force,V:Masque,Imperial
  Protectorate,A:MLF 10.00
100a 2nd Printing(Gold) 7.00
100b 3rd Printing(Silver) 3.50
Ann.#1 BMc,TP,L.Cheney 7.00
Ann.#2 AD,V:Mojo,I:Psylocke,Meggan
  (American App.) 7.00
Ann.#3 AD,PN,V:Impossible Man . 3.00
Ann.#4 JBr,BMc,Evol.Wars 6.00
Ann.#5 RLd,JBg,MBa,KWi,Atlantis
  Attacks,A:Namorita,I:Surf . . . 15.00
Ann.#6 RLd(c),Days o/Future Present
  V:FranklinRichards,(Pin-ups) . . 6.00
Ann.#7 JRu,RLd,Kings of Pain,
  I:Piecemeal & Harness,
  Pin-ups X-Force 5.00
Spec #1,AAd,TA,Asgard War 6.00
Summer Spec.#1 BBl,Megapolis . 3.50
TPB Demon Bear,rep.#18-21 . . . . 9.00

NEW MUTANTS: DEMON BEAR
CCl/BSz,Rep.DemonBear 8.95

NEW WARRIORS
July, 1990
1 B:FaN(s),MBa,AW,V:Terrax,
  O:New Warriors 6.00
1a Gold rep. 2.50
2 FaN(s),MBa,AW,I:Midnight's Fire,

Silhouette 5.00
3 MBa,LMa(i),V:Mad Thinker . . . 4.00
4 MBa,LMa(i),I:Psionex 3.50
5 MBa,LMa(i),V:Star Thief,
  C:White Queen 3.50
6 MBa,LMa(i),V:StarThief,
  A:Inhumans 3.50
7 MBa,LMa(i),V:Bengal,
  C:Punisher 3.50
8 MBa,LMa(i),V:Punisher,
  I:Force of Nature 4.00
9 MBa,LMa(i),V:Punisher,Bengal,
  Force of Nature 3.50
10 MBa,LMa(i),V:Hellions,White
  Queen,I:New Sphinx 3.50
11 MBa,LMa(i),V:Sphinx,
  B:Forever Yesterday 2.50
12 MBa,LMa(i),V:Sphinx 2.50
13 MBa,LMa(i),V:Sphinx,
  E:Forever Yesterday 2.50
14 MBa,LMa(i),A:Namor,
  Darkhawk 2.50
15 MBa,LMa(i),V:Psionex,
  R:Terrax,N:Nova 2.50
16 MBa,LMa(i),A:Psionex,
  V:Terrax 2.50
17 MBa,LMa(i),A:Silver Surfer,Fant.
  Four,V:Terrax,I:Left Hand . . . 2.50
18 MBa,LMa(i),O:Night Thrasher . 2.00
19 MBa,LMa(i),V:Gideon 2.00
20 MBa,LMa(i),V:Clan Yashida,
  Marvel Boy kills his father . . . 2.00
21 MBa,LMa(i),I:Folding Circle . . 2.00
22 MBa,LMa(i),A:Darkhawk,Rage . 2.00
23 MBa,LMa(i),V:Folding Circle . . 2.00
24 LMa(i),V:Folding Circle 2.00
25 MBa,LMa(i),Die-Cut(c),Marvel Boy
  found guilty of murder,D:Tai,
  O:Folding Circle 2.50
26 DaR,LMa(i),V:Guardsmen . . . 2.00
27 DaR,LMa(i),Inf.War,Speedball Vs.
  his doppelganger,N:Rage 2.00
28 DaR,LMa(i),I:Turbo,Cardinal . . 2.00
29 DaR,LMa(i),V:Trans-Sabal . . . 2.00
30 DaR,LMa(i),V:Trans Sabal . . . 2.00
31 DaR,LMa(i)A:Cannonball,Warpath,
  Magma,O&N:Firestar 2.00
32 DaR,LMa(i),B:Forces of Darkness,
  Forces of Light,A:Spider-Man,
  Archangel,Dr.Strange 1.75
33 DaR,LMa(i),A:Cloak & Dagger,
  Turbo,Darkhawk 1.75
34 DaR,LMa(i),A:Avengers,SpM,
  Thing,Torch,Darkhawk,
  C:Darkling 1.75
35 DaR,LMa(i),A:Turbo 1.75
36 DaR,LMa(i),A:Turbo 1.75
37 F:Marvel Boy,V:Wizard 1.75
38 DaR,LMa(i),D:Rage's granny,
  V:Poison Memories 1.75
39 DaR,LMa(i),L:Namorita 1.75
40 DaR,LMa(i),B:Starlost,
  V:Supernova 2.50
40a Newsstand Ed. 1.50
41 DaR,LMa(i),V:Supernova 1.75
42 DaR,LMa(i),E:Starlost,N:Nova,
  V:Supernova 1.75
43 DaR,LMa(i),N&I:Justice
  (Marvel Boy) 1.75
44 Ph(c),DaR,LMa(i),N&I:Kymaera
  (Namorita) 1.75
45 DaR,LMa(i),Child's Play#2,
  N:Silhouette,Speedball,
  V:Upstarts 1.75
46 DaR,LMa(i),Child's Play#4,

V:Upstarts 1.75
47 DaR,LMa(i),Time&TimeAgain,pt.1,
  A:Sphinx,I:Powerpax 1.75
48 DaR,LMa(i),Time&TimeAgain,pt.4,
  J:Cloak&Dagger,Darkhawk,Turbo,
  Powerpax,Bandit 1.75
49 DaR,LMa(i),Time&TimeAgain,pt.8
  V:Sphinx 1.75
50 reg. (c) 2.00
50a Glow-in-the-dark(c),V:Sphinx . 3.25
51 revamp 1.50
52 R:Psionex 1.50
53 V:Psionex 1.50
54 V:Speedball 1.50
55 V:Soldiers of Misfortune 1.50
56 V:Soldiers 1.50
57 A:Namor 1.50
58 F:Sabra 1.50
59 F:Speedball 1.50
60 Nova Omega,pt.2 . . . . 2.50
61 J:Scarlet Spider,Maximum
  Clonage prologue 1.50
62 F:Scarlet Spider,Maximum
  Clonage tie-in 1.50
63 F:Firestar 1.50
64 I:Psionix 1.50
65 F:Scarlet Spider,V:Kymaera . . 1.50
66 F:Speedball 1.50
67 Nightmare in Scarlet,pt.2 . . . 1.50
68 Future Shock,pt.1 . . . . 1.50
69 . . . . 1.50
70 . . . . 1.50
71 Future Shock,pt.4 . . . . 1.50
Ann.#1 MBa,A:X-Force,V:Harness,
  Piecemeal,Kings of Pain #2 . . 4.00
Ann.#2 Hero Killers #4,V:Sphinx . 2.75
Ann.#3 LMa(i),E:Forces of Light,
  Forces of Darkness,I:Darkling
  w/card 3.25
Ann.#4 DaR(s),V:Psionex 3.25
TPB New Beginnings rep.Thor #411,
  412,New Warriors #1-#4 . . . . 12.95

NFL SUPERPRO
1 . . . . 7.00
Spec.#1 reprints 2.00
(Regular Series)
Oct., 1991
1 A:Spider-Man,I:Sanzionaire . . . 2.50
2 V:Quickkick 1.25
3 I:Instant Replay 1.00
4 V:Sanction 1.00
5 A:Real NFL Player 1.25
6 Racism Iss.,recalled by Marvel . 6.00
7 thru 11 . . . . @1.25
12 V:Nefarious forces of evil 1.25

NICK FURY, AGENT OF S.H.I.E.L.D.
June, 1968
[1st Regular Series]
1 JSo/JSt,I:Scorpio 35.00
2 JSo,A:Centaurius 22.00
3 JSo,DA,V:Hell Hounds 18.00
4 FS,O:Nick Fury 17.00
5 JSo,V:Scorpio 20.00
6 FS,"Doom must Fall" 11.00
7 FS,V:S.H.I.E.L.D. 11.00
8 FS,Hate Monger 6.00
9 FS,Hate Monger 6.00
10 FS,JCr,Hate Monger 6.00
11 BS(c),FS,Hate Monger 6.00
12 BS 8.00
13 . . . . 5.00

MARVEL

14	4.00
15 I:Bullseye	24.00
16 JK,rep.	4.00
17 JK,rep.	4.00
18 JK,rep.	4.00

[Limited Series]

1 JSo,rep.	3.00
2 JSo,rep.	2.00

Nick Fury, Agent of S.H.I.E.L.D. #1
© Marvel Entertainment Group

[2nd Regular Series]

1 BH,I:New Shield,V:Death's Head(not British hero)	3.00
2 KP,V:Death's Head	2.00
3 KP,V:Death's Head	1.50
4 KP,V:Death's Head	1.50
5 KP,V:Death's Head	1.50
6 KP,V:Death's Head	1.50
7 KP,Chaos Serpent #1	1.50
8 KP,Chaos Serpent #2	1.50
9 KP,Chaos Serpent #3	1.50
10 KP,Chaos Serpent ends, A:Capt.America	1.50
11 D:Murdo MacKay	1.50
12 Hydra Affair #1	1.50
13 Hydra Affair #2	1.50
14 Hydra Affair #3	1.50
15 Apogee of Disaster #1	1.50
16 Apogee of Disaster #2	1.50
17 Apogee of Disaster #3	1.50
18 Apogee of Disaster #4	1.50
19 Apogee of Disaster #5	1.50
20 JG,A:Red Skull	2.50
21 JG,R:Baron Strucker	2.00
22 JG,A:Baron Strucker,R:Hydra	2.00
23 JG,V:Hydra	2.00
24 A:Capt.Am,Thing,V:Mandarin	1.75
25 JG,Shield Vs. Hydra	2.00
26 JG,A:Baron Strucker, C:Wolverine	2.50
27 JG,V:Hydra,A:Wolverine	2.50
28 V:Hydra,A:Wolverine	2.50
29 V:Hydra,A:Wolverine	2.50
30 R:Leviathan,A:Deathlok	2.00
31 A:Deathlok,V:Leviathan	2.00
32 V:Leviathan	2.00
33 Super-Powered Agents	2.00
34 A:Bridge(X-Force),V:Balance of Terror	2.00

35 A:Cage,V:Constrictor	2.00
36	2.00
37	2.00
38 Cold War of Nick Fury #1	2.00
39 Cold War of Nick Fury #2	2.00
40 Cold War of Nick Fury #3	2.00
41 Cold War of Nick Fury #4	2.00
42 I:Strike Force Shield	2.00
43 R:Clay Quatermain	2.00
44 A:Captain America	2.00
45 A:Bridge	2.00
46 V:Gideon,Hydra	2.00
47 V:Baron Strucker,last issue	2.00
TPB Death Duty V:Night Raven	5.95
TPB Captain America	5.95
TPB Scorpion Connection	7.95
Ashcan	.75

NICK FURY, VERSUS S.H.I.E.L.D.
June, 1988

1 JSo(c),D:Quartermail	8.00
2 BSz(c),Into The Depths	9.00
3 Uneasy Allies	5.00
4 V:Hydra	4.00
5 V:Hydra	4.00
6 V:Hydra, Dec., 1988	4.00
TPB Reprints #1-#6	15.95

NIGHTBREED
Epic April, 1990

1	5.00
2	3.00
3	2.50
4	2.50
5 JG	2.50
6 BBl,Blasphemers,pt.1	2.50
7 JG,Blasphemers,pt.2	2.50
8 BBl,MM,Blasphemers,pt.3	2.50
9 BBl,Blasphemers,pt.4	2.50
10 BBl,Blasphemers,pt.5	2.50
11 South America,pt.1	2.25
12 South America,pt.2	2.25
13 Emissaries o/Algernon Kinder	2.25
14 Rawhead Rex Story	2.25
15 Rawhead Rex	2.25
16 Rawhead Rex	2.25
17 KN(i),V:Werewolves	2.25
18 V:Werewolves	2.25
19 V:Werewolves	2.25
20 Trapped in the Forest	2.25
21 V:Ozymandias	2.50
22 V:Ozymandias	2.50
23 F:Peloquin	2.50
24 Search for New Midian	2.50
25 Search for New Midian	2.50
Nightbreed:Genesis, Rep.#1-#4	9.95

NIGHTCAT

1 DCw,I&O:Night Cat	4.50

NIGHTCRAWLER
Nov., 1985

1 DC,A;Bamfs	4.00
2 DC	3.00
3 DC,A:Other Dimensional X-Men	3.00
4 DC,A:Lockheed,V:Dark Bamf Feb., 1986	3.00

NIGHTMARE

1 ANo	1.95
2 ANo	1.95
3 ANo	1.95

NIGHTMARE CIRCUS

1 video-game tie-in	2.50
2 video-game tie-in	2.50

NIGHTMARE ON ELM STREET
Oct., 1989

1 RB/TD/AA.,Movie adapt	3.00
2 AA,Movie adapt,Dec., 1989	2.25

NIGHTMASK
Nov., 1986

1 O:Night Mask	1.25
2 V:Gnome	1.00
3 V:Mistress Twilight	1.00
4 EC,D:Mistress Twilight	1.00
5 EC,Nightmare	1.00
6 EC	1.00
7 EC	1.00
8 EC	1.00
9	1.00
10 Lucian	1.00
11	1.00
12 Oct. 1987	1.00

NIGHT NURSE
Nov., 1972

1 The Making of a Nurse	4.00
2 Moment of Truth	2.50
3	2.00
4 Final Issue,May, 1973	2.00

NIGHT RIDER
Oct., 1974

1 Reprint Ghost Rider #1	3.00
2 Reprint Ghost Rider #2	3.00
3 Reprint Ghost Rider #3	2.00
4 Reprint Ghost Rider #4	2.00
5 Reprint Ghost Rider #5	2.00
6 Reprint Ghost Rider #6 August, 1975	2.00

NIGHTSTALKERS

1 TP(i),Rise o/t Midnight Sons#5 A:GR,J.Blaze,I:Meatmarket, polybagged w/poster	3.00
2 TP(i),V:Hydra	2.50
3 TP(i),V:Dead on Arrival	2.00
4 TP(i),V:Hydra	2.00
5 TP(i),A:Punisher	2.00
6 TP(i),A:Punisher	2.00
7 TP(i),A:Ghost Rider	2.00
8 Hannibal King vs Morbius	2.00
9 MPa,A:Morbius	2.00
10 Midnight Massacre#1,D:Johnny Blaze,Hannibal King	2.50
11 O:Blade	2.00
12 V:Vampires	2.00
13 V:Vampires	2.00
14 Wld,Siege of Darkness#1	2.00
15 Wld,Siege of Darkness#9	2.00
16 V:Dreadnought	2.00
17 F:Blade	2.00
18 D:Hannibal King,Frank Drake, last issue	2.00

NIGHT THRASHER
[Limited Series]

1 B:FaN(s),DHv,N:Night Thrasher, V:Bengal	2.50
2 DHv,I:Tantrium	2.25
3 DHv,V:Gideon	2.25
4 E:FaN(s),DHv,A:Silhoutte	2.25

MARVEL

MARVEL

Night Thrasher #5
© Marvel Entertainment Group

[Regular Series]
1 B:FaN(s),MBa,JS,V:Poison
  Memories 3.25
2 JS,V:Concrete Dragons 2.00
3 JS(c),I:Aardwolf,A:Folding Circle 2.00
4 JS(c),V:Aardwolf,I:Air Force . . . 2.00
5 JS,V:Air Force 2.00
6 Face Value,A:Rage 2.00
7 DdB,V:Bandit 2.00
8 DdB,V:Bandit 2.00
9 DdB,A:Tantrum 2.00
10 DdB,A:Iron Man,w/card 2.25
11 DdB,Time & Time Again,pt.2 . . 2.25
12 DdB,Time & Time Again,pt.5 . . 2.25
13 Lost in the Shadows,pt.1 . . . . 1.95
14 Lost in the Shadows,pt.2 . . . . 1.95
15 Money Don't Buy,pt.1 . . . . 1.95
16 A:Prowler 1.95
17 . . . . 1.95
18 . . . . 1.95
19 V:Tantrum 1.95
20 . . . . 1.95
21 Rage vs. Grind 1.95

NIGHTWATCH
1 RLm,I:Salvo,Warforce Holo(c) . 3.00
1a Newsstand ed. 1.75
2 RLm,AM,I:Flashpoint 1.50
3 RLm,AM,V:Flashpoint 1.50
4 RLm,A:Warrent,V:Gauntlet . . . 1.75
5 I:Sunstreak,A:Venom 1.50
6 V:Venom 1.50
7 I:Cardiaxe 1.50
8 V:Cardiaxe 1.50
9 origins 1.50
10 . . . . 1.50
11 . . . . 1.50
12 . . . . 1.50

NOCTURNE
1 DAn, in London 1.50
2 DAn,O:Nocturne 1.50
3 Interview with Amy 1.50
4 V:Dragon 1.50

NO ESCAPE
1 & 2 Movie adaptation . . . . . @1.50

Nomad #1
© Marvel Entertainment Group

NOMAD
Nov., 1990
[Limited Series]
1 B:FaN(s),A:Capt.America 3.00
2 A:Capt.America 2.50
3 A:Capt.America 2.50
4 A:Capt.America, final issue,
  Feb. 1989 . . . . 2.50

[Regular Series]
1 B:FaN(s),R:Nomad,[Gatetfold(c),
  map] 3.00
2 V:Road Kill Club 2.50
3 V:U.S.Agent 2.00
4 DeadMan's Hand#2,V:Deadpool 2.00
5 DeadMan's Hand#4,V:Punisher 2.00
6 DeadMan's Hand#8,A:Punisher,
  Daredevil 2.00
7 Infinity War,V:Gambit,
  Doppleganger 2.00
8 L.A.Riots 2.00
9 I:Ebbtide 2.00
10 A:Red Wolf 2.00
11 in Albuquerque 2.00
12 In Texas 2.00
13 AIDS issue 2.00
14 Hidden in View 2.00
15 Hidden in View 2.00
16 A:Gambit 2.00
17 Bucky Kidnapped 2.00
18 A:Captain America,Slug 2.00
19 FaN(s),Faustus Affair 2.00
20 A:Six Pack 2.00
21 A:Man-Thing 2.00
22 American Dreamers#1,V:Zaran 2.00
23 American Dreamers#2 . . . . 2.00
24 American Dreamers#3 . . . . . . 2.00
25 American Dreamers#4, finale . 2.00

NORTHSTAR
1 SFr,DoC,V:Weapon:P.R.I.M.E. . 2.00
2 SFr,DoC,V:Arcade 2.00
3 SFr,DoC,V:Arcade 2.00
4 SFr,DoC,final issue 2.00
N Presents James O'Barr 2.50

NOT BRAND ECHH
August, 1967
1 JK(c),BEv,Forbush Man(c) . . 35.00
2 MSe,FrG,Spidey-Man,Gnat-Man
  & Rotten 20.00
3 MSe(C),JK,FrG,O:Charlie
  America 20.00
4 GC,JTg,TS,Scaredevil,
  ECHHs-Men 20.00
5 JK,TS,GC,I&O:Forbush Man . 20.00
6 MSe(c),GC,TS,W:Human Torch 20.00
7 MSe(c),GC,TS,O:Fantastical
  Four,Stupor Man 20.00
8 MSe(c),GC,TS,C:Beatles . . . 22.00
9 Bulk V:Sunk-Mariner 22.00
10 JK,The Worst of... . . . . 22.00
11 King Konk 22.00
12 Frankenstein,A:Revengers . . . 22.00
13 Stamp Out Trading Cards(c) . 22.00

NOTHING CAN STOP
THE JUGGERNAUT
1989
1 JR2,rep.SpM#229&#230 . . . . . 3.95

NOVA
Sept., 1976
[1st Regular Series]
1 B:MWn(s),JB,JSt,I&O:Nova . . . 7.00
2 JB,JSt,I:Condor,Powerhouse . . 4.00
3 JB,JSt,I:Diamondhead 3.00
4 SB,TP,A:Thor,I:Corruptor 3.00
5 SB,V:Earthshaker 3.00
6 SB,V:Condor,Powerhouse,
  Diamondhead,I:Sphinx 3.00
7 SB,War in Space,O:Sphinx . . . 3.00
8 V:Megaman 3.00
9 V:Megaman 3.00
10 V:Condor,Powerhouse,
  Diamond-head Sphinx 3.00
11 V:Sphinx 2.50
12 A:Spider-Man 3.00
13 I:Crimebuster,A:Sandman 2.50
14 A:Sandman 2.00
15 CI,C:Spider-Man, Hulk 2.00
16 CI,A:Yellow Claw 2.00
17 A:Yellow Claw 2.00
18 A:Yellow Claw, Nick Fury 2.00
19 CI,TP,I:Blackout 2.00
20 What is Project X? 2.00
21 JB,BMc,JRu 2.00
22 CI,I:Comet 2.00
23 CI,V:Dr.Sun 2.00
24 CI,I:New Champions,V:Sphinx . 2.00
25 E:MWn(s),CI,A:Champions,
  V:Sphinx 2.00
[2nd Regular Series]
1 B:FaN(s),ChM,V:Gladiator,Foil
  Embossed(c) 3.00
2 ChM,V:Tail Hook Rape 2.00
3 ChM,A:Spider-Man,Corruptor . . 2.00
4 ChM,I:NovaO:O 2.00
5 ChM,R:Condor,w/card 2.25
6 ChM,Time & Time Again,pt.3 . . 2.25
7 ChM,Time & Time Again,pt.6 . . 2.25
8 ChM,I:Shatterforce 2.25
9 ChM,V:Shatterforce 1.95
10 ChM,V:Diamondhead 1.95
11 ChM,V:Diamondhead 1.95
12 ChM,A:Inhumans 1.95
13 ChM,A:Inhumans 1.95
14 A:Condor 1.95
15 V:Brethern of Zorr 1.95
16 Countdown Conclusion 1.95

17 Nova Loses Powers 1.96
18 Nova Omega,pt.1 . . . . 1.95

Nth MAN
August, 1989
1 . . . . 2.00
2 . . . . 1.00
3 . . . . 1.00
4 . . . . 1.00
5 thru 7 . . . . @1.00
8 DK 2.00
9 thru 16, finale, Sept., 1990 . @1.00

OBNOXIO THE CLOWN
April, 1983
1 X-Men 2.00

OFFCASTES
1 I:Offcastes 2.50
2 V:Kaoro 1.95
3 Last Issue 1.95

Official Marvel Index to Amazing Spider-Man #8 © Marvel Entertainment Group

OFFICIAL MARVEL INDEX:
1985–88
TO THE AMAZING SPIDER-MAN
Index 1 . . . . 3.00
Index 2 thru 9 . . . . @2.50
TO THE AVENGERS
Index 1 thru 7 . . . . @2.50
TO THE FANTASTIC FOUR
Index 1 thru 12 . . . . @2.25
TO MARVEL TEAM-UP
Index 1 thru 6 . . . . @1.75
TO THE X-MEN
Index 1 thru 7 . . . . @2.95
[Vol. 2] 1994
Index 1 thru 5 . . . . @1.95

OFFICIAL MARVEL TIMELINE
1-shot, 48pg 5.95

OFFICIAL TRUE CRIME CASES
Fall, 1947
24 (1)SSh(c),The Grinning Killer 150.00
25 (2)She Made Me a Killer,HK   110.00
Becomes:
ALL-TRUE CRIME
26 SSh(c),The True Story of Wilbur
   Underhill 135.00
27 Electric Chair(c),Robert Mais . 80.00
28 Cops V:Gangsters(c) 35.00
29 Cops V:Gangsters(c) 35.00
30 He Picked a Murderous Mind . 35.00
31 Hitchiking Thugs(c) 35.00
32 Jewel Thieves(c) 35.00
33 The True Story of Dinton
   Phillips 35.00
34 Case of the Killers Revenge . 35.00
35 Ph(c),Date with Danger 35.00
36 Ph(c) 35.00
37 Ph(c),Story of Robert Marone 35.00
38 Murder Weapon,Nick Maxim . 35.00
39 Story of Vince Vanderee 35.00
40 . . . . 35.00
41 Lou "Lucky" Raven 35.00
42 BK,Baby Face Nelson 45.00
43 Doc Channing Paulson 30.00
44 Murder in the Big House 30.00
45 While the City Sleeps 30.00
46 . . . . 30.00
47 Gangster Terry Craig 30.00
48 GT,They Vanish By Night . . . 30.00
49 BK,Squeeze Play 45.00
50 Shoot to Kill 30.00
51 Panic in the Big House 30.00
52 Prison Break, Sept., 1952 . . . 30.00

OLYMPIANS
Epic July, 1991
1 Spoof Series 3.95
2 Conclusion 3.95

OMEGA THE UNKNOWN
March, 1976
1 JM,I:Omega 4.00
2 JM,A:Hulk 2.50
3 JM,A:Electro 2.00
4 JM,V:Yellow Claw 2.00
5 JM,V:The Wrench 2.00
6 JM,V:Blockbuster 2.00
7 JM,V:Blockbuster 2.00
8 JM,C:New Foolkiller,V:Nitro . . . 5.00
9 JM,A:New Foolkiller,
   D:Blockbuster 7.00
10 JM,D:Omega the Unknown . . . 2.00

ONE, THE
Epic July, 1985
1 thru 5 . . . . @1.75
6 Feb., 1986 . . . . 1.75

101 WAYS TO END THE CLONE SAGA
1-shot 2.50

ONSLAUGHT
Marvel Universe: AKu,SLo,MWd, Marvel
   Heroes vs. Onslaught 7.00
Marvel Universe: Gold edition . 35.00
X-Men: AKu,SLo,MWd, ... 6.00
X-Men: Gold editon 35.00
Onslaught: Epilogue 3.00

TPB Book 1, rep. X-Men #53 & #54,
   Uncanny X-Men 322 & 334
   and Onslaught X-Men 12.95
TPB Book 2, rep. X-Man #18 & #19
   and X-Force #57 & 58 . . . . . . 9.95
TPB Book 3, rep. Uncanny X-Men
   #335, Avengers #401, FF #415,
   X-Men #55 . . . . 9.95
TPB Book 4, rep. Inc.Hulk #444
   & #445, Cable #34 & #35 . . . 9.95
TPB Book 5, rep. X-Factor #125,
   Punisher #11, Green Goblin #12,
   Amaz. Sp.-M. #415, Sp.-M. #72 9.95
TPB Book 6, rep. Uncanny X-Men
   #336, X-Men #56, Avengers #402,
   FF #416 & Onslaught: Marvel
   Universe 12.95

ONYX OVERLORD
Epic
1 JBi,Sequel to Airtight Garage . . 3.00
2 JBi,The Joule 2.75
3 JBi,V:Overlord 2.75
4 V:Starbilliard 2.75

OPEN SPACE
Dec., 1989–Aug. 1990
1 . . . . 6.00
2 thru 4 . . . . @5.25

ORIGINAL GHOST RIDER
1 MT(c),rep Marvel Spotlight#5 . . 2.25
2 rep.Marvel Spotlight#6 . . . . . . 2.00
3 rep.Marvel Spotlight#7 . . . . . . 2.00
4 JQ(c),rep.Marvel Spotlight#8 . . 2.00
5 KM(c),rep.Marvel spotlight#9 . . 2.00
6 rep.Marvel Spotlight#10 . . . . . 2.00
7 rep.Marvel Spotlight#11 . . . . . 2.00
8 rep.Ghost Rider#1 . . . . 2.00
9 rep.Ghost Rider#2 . . . . 2.00
10 rep.Marvel Spotlight#12 . . . . . 2.00
11 rep.Ghost Rider#3 . . . . 2.00
12 rep.Ghost Rider#4 . . . . 2.00
13 rep.Ghost Rider#38 . . . . 2.00
14 rep.Ghost Rider#6 . . . . 1.75
15 rep.Ghost Rider#7 . . . . 1.75
15 rep.Ghost Rider#8 . . . . 1.75
18 rep.Ghost Rider#9 . . . . 1.75
18 rep.Ghost Rider#10 . . . . 1.75
19 rep.Ghost Rider#11 . . . . 1.75
20 rep.Ghost Rider#12 . . . . 1.75
21 rep.Ghost Rider#13 . . . . 1.75
22 rep.Ghost Rider#14 . . . . 1.75
23 rep.Ghost Rider#15 . . . . 1.95

ORIGINAL GHOST RIDER RIDES AGAIN
July, 1991
1 rep.GR#68+#69(O:JohnnyBlaze) 3.00
2 rep.G.R. #70,#71 . . . . 2.00
3 rep.G.R. #72,#73 . . . . 2.00
4 rep.G.R. #74,#75 . . . . 2.00
5 rep.G.R. #76,#77 . . . . 2.00
6 rep.G.R. #78,#79 . . . . 2.00
7 rep.G.R. #80,#81 . . . . 2.00

ORIGINS OF MARVEL COMICS
TPB StL,JK,SD reprinting, 260pg 25.00

OSBORN JOURNALS, THE
1-shot KHt,F:Norman Osborn . . . .

MARVEL

MARVEL

OUR LOVE
Sept., 1949
1 Ph(c),The Guilt of Nancy Crane 55.00
2 Ph(c),My Kisses Were Cheap . 35.00
Becomes:

TRUE SECRETS
3 Love Stories,continued 50.00
4 . . . . 24.00
5 . . . . 24.00
6 BEv 30.00
7 . . . . 24.00
8 . . . . 24.00
9 . . . . 24.00
10 . . . . 24.00
11 thru 21 . . . . @18.00
22 BEv 30.00
23 thru 39 . . . . @12.00
40 Sept., 1956 . . . . 12.00

OUR LOVE STORY
Oct., 1969
1 . . . . 7.50
2 . . . . 5.00
3 . . . . 5.00
4 . . . . 5.00
5 JSo 15.00
6 thru 13 . . . . @5.00
14 Gary Friedrich &Tarpe Mills . 7.50
15 thru 37 . . . . @2.00
38 Feb., 1976 . . . . 2.00

OUTLAW FIGHTERS
Atlas August, 1954
1 GT,Western Tales 55.00
2 GT 35.00
3 . . . . 35.00
4 A;Patch Hawk 35.00
5 RH, Final Issue,April, 1955 . . 35.00

OUTLAW KID
Atlas Sept., 1954
1 SSh,DW,B&O:Outlaw Kid,A;Black
  Rider 135.00
2 DW,A:Black Rider 60.00
3 DW,AW,GWb 55.00
4 DW(c),Death Rattle 40.00
5 . . . . 40.00
6 . . . . 40.00
7 . . . . 40.00
8 AW,DW 45.00
9 . . . . 35.00
10 . . . . 45.00
11 thru 17 . . . . @25.00
18 AW 40.00
19 Sept., 1957 . . . . 25.00
[2nd series]
August, 1970
1 JSe(c),DW,Jo,Showdown,rep . 5.00
2 DW,One Kid Too Many 5.00
3 HT(c),DW,Six Gun Double
  Cross 3.00
4 DW 2.00
5 DW 2.00
6 DW 2.00
7 HT(c),DW,Treachery on
  the Trail 2.00
8 HT(c),DW,RC,Six Gun Pay Off 2.00
9 JSe(c),DW,GWb,The Kids
  Last Stand 3.00
10 GK(c),DAy,NewO:Outlaw Kid . 1.50
11 GK(c),Thunder Along the
  Big Iron 1.50
12 The Man Called Bounty Hawk . 1.50

13 The Last Rebel 1.50
14 The Kid Gunslingers of
  Calibre City 1.50
15 GK(c),V:Madman of Monster
  Mountain 1.50
16 The End of the Trail 1.50
17 thru 29 . . . . @1.50
30 Oct., 1975 . . . . 1.50

OVER THE EDGE
AND UNDER A BUCK
1 F:Daredevil vs. Mr. Fear 0.99
2 F:Doctor Strange 0.99
3 F:Hulk 0.99
4 in Cypress Hills 0.99
5 . . . . 0.99
6 F:Daredevil 0.99
7 Doc & Nightmare 0.99

PARAGON
1 I:Paragon,Nightfire 5.00

PATSY & HEDY
Atlas Feb., 1952
1 B:Patsy Walker&Hedy Wolfe . 75.00
2 Skating(c) 35.00
3 Boyfriend Trouble 30.00
4 Swimsuit(c) 30.00
5 Patsy's Date(c) 30.00
6 Swimsuit/Picnic(c) 30.00
7 Double-Date(c) 30.00
8 The Dance 30.00
9 . . . . 30.00
10 . . . . 30.00
11 thru 25 . . . . @20.00
26 thru 50 . . . . @15.00
51 thru 60 . . . . @10.00
61 thru 109 . . . . @6.00
110 Feb., 1967 . . . . 6.00

PATSY & HER PALS
May, 1953
1 MWs(c),F:Patsay Walker . . . 60.00
2 MWs(c),Swimsuit(c) 30.00
3 MWs(c),Classroom(c) 22.00
4 MWs(c),Golfcourse(c) 22.00
5 MWs(c).Patsy/Buzz(c) 22.00
6 thru 10 . . . . @22.00
11 thru 28 . . . . @15.00
29 August, 1957 . . . . 15.00

PATSY WALKER
1945
1 F:Patsy Walker Adventures . 275.00
2 Patsy/Car(c) 125.00
3 Skating(c) 75.00
4 Perfume(c) 75.00
5 Archery Lesson(c) 75.00
6 Bus(c) 75.00
7 Charity Drive(c) 75.00
8 Organ Driver Monkey(c) 75.00
9 Date(c) 75.00
10 Skating(c),Wedding Bells . . . 75.00
11 Date with a Dream 50.00
12 Love in Bloom,Artist(c) 50.00
13 Swimsuit(c),There Goes My
  Heart;HK,Hey Look 60.00
14 An Affair of the Heart,
  HK,Hey Look 60.00
15 Dance(c) 50.00
16 Skating(c) 50.00
17 Patsy's Diary(c),HK,Hey Look 60.00
18 Autograph(c) 50.00

19 HK,Hey Look 60.00
20 HK,Hey Look 60.00
21 HK,Hey Look 60.00
22 HK,Hey Look 60.00
23 . . . . 40.00
24 . . . . 40.00
25 HK,Rusty 65.00
26 . . . . 30.00
27 . . . . 30.00
28 . . . . 30.00
29 . . . . 30.00
30 HK,Egghead Double 45.00
31 . . . . 30.00
32 thru 57 . . . . @20.00
58 thru 99 . . . . @15.00
100 . . . . 15.00
101 thru 123 . . . . @8.00
124 Dec., 1965 . . . . 8.00
Fashion Parade #1 . . . . 40.00

Peter Parker #5
© Marvel Entertainment Group

PETER PARKER, THE SPECTACULAR SPIDER-MAN
Dec., 1976
1 SB,V:Tarantula 55.00
2 SB,V:Kraven,Tarantula 20.00
3 SB,I:Lightmaster 15.00
4 SB,V:Vulture,Hitman 15.00
5 SB,V:Hitman,Vulture 15.00
6 SB,V:Morbius,rep.M.T.U.#3 . . 18.00
7 SB,V:Morbius,A:Human Torch 25.00
8 SB,V:Morbius 20.00
9 SB,I:White Tiger 10.00
10 SB,A:White Tiger 10.00
11 JM,V:Medusa 8.00
12 SB,V:Brother Power 8.00
13 SB,V:Brother Power 8.00
14 SB,V:Brother Power 8.00
15 SB,V:Brother Power 8.00
16 SB,V:The Beetle 8.00
17 SB,A:Angel & Iceman
  Champions disbanded 9.00
18 SB,A:Angel & Iceman 9.00
19 SB,V:The Enforcers 8.00

MARVEL

20 SB,V:Lightmaster	8.00
21 JM,V:Scorpion	8.00
22 MZ,A:Moon Knight,V:Cyclone	8.00
23 A:Moon Knight,V:Cyclone	8.00
24 FS,A:Hypno-Hustler	6.00
25 JM,FS,I:Carrion	8.00
26 JM,A:Daredevil,V:Carrion	7.00
27 DC,FM,I:Miller Daredevil, V:Carrion	20.00
28 FM,A:Daredevil,V:Carrion	18.00
29 JM,FS,V:Carrion	7.00
30 JM,FS,V:Carrion	7.00
31 JM,FS,D:Carrion	7.00
32 BL,JM,FS,V:Iguana	5.50
33 JM,FS,O:Iguana	5.50
34 JM,FS,V:Iguana,Lizard	5.50
35 V:Mutant Mindworm	5.50
36 JM,V:Swarm	5.50
37 DC,MN,V:Swarm	5.50
38 SB,V:Morbius	8.00
39 JM,JR2,V:Schizoid Man	5.50
40 FS,V:Schizoid Man	5.50
41 JM,V:Meteor Man,A:GiantMan	5.00
42 JM,A:Fant.Four,V:Frightful 4	5.00
43 JBy(c),MZ,V:The Ringer, V:Belladonna	5.00
44 JM,V:The Vulture	5.00
45 MSe,V:The Vulture	5.00
46 FM(c),MZ,V:Cobra	5.00
47 MSe,A:Prowler II	5.00
48 MSe,A:Prowler II	5.00
49 MSe,I:Smuggler	5.00
50 JR2,JM,V:Mysterio	5.00
51 MSe&FM(c),V:Mysterio	5.00
52 FM(c),D:White Tiger	5.00
53 JM,FS,V:Terrible Tinkerer	5.00
54 FM,WS,MSe,V:Silver Samurai	5.00
55 LMc,JM,V:Nitro	5.00
56 FM,JM,V:Jack-o-lantern	13.00
57 JM,V:Will-o-the Wisp	5.00
58 JBy,V:Ringer,A:Beetle	6.00
59 JM,V:Beetle	5.00
60 JM&FM(c),O:Spider-Man, V:Beetle	5.50
61 JM,V:Moonstone	4.50
62 JM,V:Goldbug	4.50
63 JM,V:Molten Man	4.50
64 JM,I:Cloak&Dagger	10.00
65 BH,JM,V:Kraven,Calypso	4.50
66 JM,V:Electro	4.00
67 AMb,V:Boomerang	4.00
68 LMc,JM,V:Robot of Mendell Stromm	4.00
69 AM,A:Cloak & Dagger	8.00
70 A:Cloak & Dagger	8.00
71 JM,Gun Control issue	4.00
72 AM,V:Dr.Octopus	4.00
73 AM,JM,V:Dr.Octopus,A:Owl	4.00
74 AM,JM,V:Dr.Octopus,R:Bl.Cat	4.00
75 AM,JM,V:Owl,Dr.Octopus	4.50
76 AM,Black Cat on deathbed	3.50
77 AM,V:Gladiator,Dr.Octopus	3.50
78 AM,V:Dr.Octopus,C:Punisher	3.50
79 AM,V:Dr.Octopus,A:Punisher	4.00
80 AM,F:J.Jonah Jameson	3.50
81 A:Punisher	7.00
82 A:Punisher	7.00
83 A:Punisher	7.00
84 AM,F:Black Cat	3.50
85 AM,O:Hobgoblin powers (Ned Leeds)	20.00
86 FH,V:Fly	3.50
87 AM,Reveals I.D.to Black Cat	3.50
88 AM,V:Cobra,Mr.Hyde	3.50
89 AM,Secret Wars,A:Kingpin	4.00

90 AM,Secret Wars	5.00
91 AM,V:Blob	3.50
92 AM,I:Answer	3.50
93 AM,V:Answer	3.50
94 AM,A:Cloak & Dagger,V: Silver Mane	3.50
95 AM,A:Cloak & Dagger,V: Silvermane	3.50
96 AM,A:Cloak & Dagger,V: Silvermane	3.50
97 HT,JM,A:Black Cat	3.50
98 HT,JM,I:Spot	3.50
99 HT,JM,V:Spot	3.50
100 AM,V:Kingpin,C:Bl.Costume	6.00
101 JBy(c),AM,V:Killer Shrike	3.00
102 JBy(c),AM,V:Backlash	3.00
103 AM,V:Blaze;Not John Blaze	3.00
104 JBy(c),AM,V:Rocket Racer	3.00
105 AM,A:Wasp	3.00
106 AM,A:Wasp	3.00
107 RB,D:Jean DeWolf,I:SinEater	5.00
108 RB,A:Daredevil,V:Sin-Eater	4.00
109 RB,A:Daredevil,V:Sin-Eater	4.00

Peter Parker #25
© *Marvel Entertainment Group*

110 RB,A:Daredevil,V:Sin-Eater	4.00
111 RB,Secret Wars II	3.00
112 RB,A:Santa Claus,Black Cat	3.00
113 RB,Burglars,A:Black Cat	3.00
114 BMc,V:Lock Picker	3.00
115 BMc,A:Black Cat,Dr.Strange, I:Foreigner	3.50
116 A:Dr.Strange, Foreigner, Black Cat, Sabretooth	7.00
117 DT,C:Sabretooth,A:Foreigner, Black Cat,Dr.Strange	5.00
118 MZ,D:Alexander,V:SHIELD	3.00
119 RB,BMc,V:Sabretooth, A:Foreigner,Black Cat	7.00
120 KG	3.00
121 RB,BMc,V:Mauler	3.00
122 V:Mauler	3.00
123 V:Foreigner,Black Cat	3.00
124 V:Dr.Octopus	3.00
125 V:Wr.Crew,A:Spiderwoman	3.00
126 JM,A:Sp.woman,V:Wrecker	3.00
127 AM,V:Lizard	3.00
128 C:DDevil,A:Bl.Cat,Foreigner	3.50
129 A:Black Cat,V:Foreigner	3.00
130 A:Hobgoblin	6.00

131 MZ,BMc,V:Kraven	9.00
132 MZ,BMc,V:Kraven	9.00
133 BSz(c),Mad Dog,pt.3	8.00
Ann.#1 RB,JM,V:Dr.Octopus	5.00
Ann.#2 JM,I&O:Rapier	4.50
Ann.#3 JM,V:Manwolf	4.50
Ann.#4 AM,O:Aunt May,A:Bl.Cat	5.00
Ann.#5 I:Ace,Joy Mercado	4.50
Ann.#6 V:Ace	4.50
Ann.#7 Honeymoon iss,A:Puma	4.50

Becomes:
SPECTACULAR SPIDER-MAN

PETER PORKER
Star **May, 1985**

1 Parody	2.50
2	1.50
3	1.50
4	1.50
5 V:Senior Simians	1.50
6 A Blitz in Time	1.50
7	1.50
8 Kimono My House	1.25
9 Uncouth my Tooth	1.25
10 Lost Temple of the Golden Retriever	1.25
11 Dog Dame Afternoon	1.25
12 The Gouda,Bad & Ugly	1.25
13 Halloween issue	1.25
14 Heavy Metal Issue	1.25
15	1.25
16 Porker Fried Rice,Final Issue	1.25
17 Sept., 1987	1.25

PETER, THE LITTLE PEST
Nov., 1969

1 F:Peter	6.00
2 Rep,Dexter & Melvin	5.00
3 Rep,Dexter & Melvin	5.00
4 Rep,Dexter & Melvin, May, 1970	5.00

PHANTOM

1 Lee Falk's Phantom	4.00
2 V:General Babalar	4.00
3 final issue	4.00

Phantom 2040 #3
© *Marvel Entertainment Group*

MARVEL

PHANTOM 2040
1 Based on cartoon	2.50
2 V:Alloy	2.50
3 MPa,V:Crime Syndicate	2.50
4 Vision Quest	2.50

PHOENIX
(UNTOLD STORY)
April, 1984
1 JBy,O:Phoenix (R.Summers)	12.00

PILGRIM'S PROGRESS
1 adapts John Bunyans novel	10.00

PINHEAD
1 Red Foil(c),from Hellraiser	2.95
2 DGC(s),V:Cenobites	2.50
3 DGC(s),V:Cenobites	2.50
4 DGC(s),V:Cenobites	2.50
5 DGC(s),Devil in Disguise	2.50
6 DGC(s),	2.50

PINHEAD VS.
MARSHALL LAW
1 KON,In Hell	2.95
2 KON	2.95

PINOCHIO & THE
EMPEROR OF THE NIGHT
March, 1988
1 Movie adapt.	1.25

PIRATES OF
DARK WATERS
Nov., 1991
1 based on T.V. series	1.00
2 Search for 13 Treasures	1.00
3 V:Albino Warriors,Konk	1.00
4 A:Monkey Birds	1.25
5 Tula Steals 1st Treasuer	1.25
6 thru 9	@1.25

PITT, THE
March, 1988
1 SB,SDr,A:Spitfire	4.50

PLANET OF THE APES
August, 1974
(black & white magazine)
1 MP	6.00
2 MP	4.00
3	3.00
4	5.00
5	5.00
6 thru 10	@2.50
11 thru 20	@2.00
21 thru 28	@1.50
29 Feb., 1977	1.50

PLANET TERRY
Star April, 1985
1 thru 11	@1.00
12 March, 1986	1.00

PLASMER
1 A:Captain America	3.50
2 A:Captain Britain,Black Knight	2.25
3 A:Captain Britain	2.25
4 A:Captain Britain	2.25
5 thru 7	1.95

PLASTIC FORKS
Epic 1990
1	5.50
2 thru 5	@5.25

POLICE ACADEMY
Nov., 1989
1 Based on TV Cartoon	1.25
2	1.00
3	1.00
4 and 5	@1.00
6 Feb., 1990	1.00

POLICE ACTION
Jan., 1954
1 JF,GC,Riot Squad	125.00
2 JF,Over the Wall	55.00
3	45.00
4 DAy	45.00
5 DAy	45.00
6	45.00
7 BPNov., 1954	45.00

POLICE BADGE
See: SPY THRILLERS

POPPLES
Star Dec., 1986
1 Based on Toys	1.00
2	1.00
3	1.00
4	1.00
5 August, 1987	1.00

POWDERED TOAST-MAN
Spec. F:Powder Toast-Man	3.25

POWERHOUSE PEPPER
COMICS
1943—Nov., 1948
1 BW,Movie Auditions(c)	1,100.00
2 BW,Dinner(c)	600.00
3 BW,Boxing Ring(c)	500.00
4 BW,Subway(c)	500.00
5 BW,Bankrobbers(c)	700.00

POWER LINE
Epic May, 1988
1 BMc(i)	2.25
2 Aw(i)	2.00
3 A:Dr Zero	2.00
4	2.00
5 thru 7 GM	@2.00
8 GM Sept., 1989	2.00

POWER MAN
Prev: Hero for Hire
Feb., 1974
17 GT,A:Iron Man	10.00
18 GT,V:Steeplejack	7.00
19 GT,V:Cottonmouth	7.00
20 GT,Heroin Story	7.00
21 V:Original Power Man	5.00
22 V:Stiletto & Discus	5.00
23 V:Security City	5.00
24 GT,I:BlackGoliath(BillFoster)	5.00
25 A:Circus of Crime	5.00
26 GT,V:Night Shocker	5.00
27 GP,AMc,V:Man Called X	5.00
28 V:Cockroach	5.00
29 V:Mr.Fish	5.00

30 RB,KJ,KP,I:Piranha	5.00
31 SB,NA(i),V:Piranha	5.00
32 JSt,FR,A:Wildfire	3.50
33 FR,A:Spear	3.50
34 FR,A:Spear,Mangler	3.50
35 DA,A:Spear,Mangler	3.50
36 V:Chemistro	3.50
37 V:Chemistro	3.50
38 V:Chemistro	3.50
39 KJ,V:Chemistro,Baron	3.50
40 V:Baron	3.50
41 TP,V:Thunderbolt,Goldbug	3.50
42 V:Thunderbolt,Goldbug	3.50
43 AN,V:Mace	3.50
44 TP,A:Mace	3.50
45 JSn,A:Mace	4.00
46 GT,I:Zzzax(recreated)	3.50
47 BS,A:Zzzax	4.00
48 JBy,A:Iron Fist	4.00
49 JBy,A:Iron Fist	4.00

Power Man and Iron Fist #104
© Marvel Entertainment Group

Becomes:
POWER MAN & IRON FIST
50 JBy,I:Team-up with Iron Fist	3.00
51 MZ,Night on the Town	2.50
52 MZ,V:Death Machines	2.50
53 SB,O:Nightshade	2.50
54 TR,O:Iron Fist	3.50
55 Chaos at the Coliseum	2.50
56 Mayhem in the Museum	2.50
57 X-Men,V:Living Monolith	7.00
58 1st El Aguila(Drug)	2.00
59 BL(c),TVE,V:Big Apple	
Bomber	1.75
60 BL(c),V:Terrorists	1.75
61 BL(c),V:The Maggia	1.75
62 BL(c),KGa,V:Man Mountain	
D:Thunerbolt	1.75
63 BL(c),Cage Fights Fire	1.75
64 DGr&BL(c),V:Suetre,Muerte	1.75
65 BL(c),A:El Aquila,	1.75
66 FM(c),Sabretooth(2nd App.)	25.00
67 V:Bushmaster	1.75
68 FM(c),V:Athur Nagan	2.00
69 V:Soldier	2.00
70 FM(c)V:El Supremo	1.75
71 FM(c),I:Montenegro	1.75
72 FM(c),V:Chako	1.75

73 FM(c),V:Rom 1.75
74 FM(c),V:Ninja 1.75
75 KGa,O:IronFist 2.50
76 KGa,V:Warhawk 2.50
77 KGa,A:Daredevil 2.50
78 KGa,A:El Aguila,Sabretooth
 (Slasher)(3rd App.) 18.00
79 V:Dredlox 1.75
80 KJ(c),V:Montenegro 1.75
81 V:Black Tiger 1.75
82 V:Black Tiger 1.75
83 V:Warhawk 1.75
84 V:Constrictor,A:Sabertooth
 (4th App.) 18.00
85 KP,V:Mole Man 1.75
86 A:Moon Knight 1.75
87 A:Moon Knight 1.75
88 V:Scimtar 1.75
89 V:Terrorists 1.75
90 V:Unus BS(c) 1.75
91 "Paths and Angles" 1.75
92 V:Hammeread,I:New Eel 1.75
93 A:Chemistro 1.75
94 V:Chemistro 1.75
95 Danny Rand 1.75
96 V,Chemistro 1.75
97 K'unlun,A:Fera 1.75
98 V:Shades & Commanche 1.75
99 R:Daught.of Dragon 1.75
100 O:K'unlun,DoubleSize 1.75
101 A:Karnak 1.75
102 V:Doombringer 1.75
103 O:Doombringer 1.75
104 V:Dr.Octopus,Lizard 1.75
105 F:Crime Buster 1.75
106 Luke Gets Shot 1.75
107 JBy(c),Terror issue 1.75
108 V:Inhuman Monster 1.75
109 V:The Reaper 1.75
110 V:Nightshade,Eel 1.75
111 I:Captain Hero 1.75
112 JBy(c),V:Control7 . . . . 1.75
113 JBy(c),A:Capt.Hero 1.75
114 JBy(c),V:Control7 . . . . 1.75
115 JBy(c),V:Stanley 1.75
116 JBy(c),V:Stanley 1.75
117 R:K'unlun 1.75
118 A:Colleen Wing 1.75
119 A:Daught.of Dragon 1.75
120 V:Chiantang 1.75
121 Secret Wars II 1.75
122 V:Dragonkin 1.75
123 V:Race Killer 1.75
124 V:Yellowclaw 1.75
125 MBr,LastIssue;D:Iron Fist . . 3.00
G-Size#1 reprints 4.00
Ann.#1 Earth Shock 5.00

POWER PACHYDERMS
Sept., 1989
1 Elephant Superheroes 1.50

POWER PACK
August, 1984
1 JBr,BWi,I&O:Power Pack,
 I:Snarks 2.50
2 JBr,BWi,V:Snarks 2.00
3 JBr,BWi,V:Snarks 2.00
4 JBr,BWi,V:Snarks 2.00
5 JBr,BWi,V:Bogeyman 2.00
6 JBr,BWi,A:Spider-Man 2.00
7 JBr,BWi,A:Cloak & Dagger . . . 2.00
8 JBr,BWi,A:Cloak & Dagger . . . 2.00
9 BA,BWi,A:Marrina 1.50
10 BA,BWi,A:Marrina 1.50

11 JBr,BWi,V:Morlocks 2.00
12 JBr,BWi,A:X-Men,V:Morlocks . 3.00
13 BA,BWi,Baseball issue 1.50
14 JBr,BWi,V:Bogeyman 1.50
15 JBr,BWi,A:Beta Ray Bill 1.50
16 JBr,BWi,I&O:Kofi,J:Tattletale
 (Franklin Richards) 2.00
17 JBr,BWi,V:Snarks 1.50
18 BA,SW,Secret Wars II,
 V:Kurse 2.00
19 BA,SW,Doub.size,Wolverine . 4.00
20 BMc,A:NewMutants 1.50
21 BA,TA,C:Spider-Man 1.50
22 JBg,BWi,V:Snarks 1.50
23 JBg,BWi,V:Snarks,C:FF 1.50
24 JBg,BWi,V:Snarks,C:Cloak . . 2.00
25 JBg,BWi,A:FF,V:Snarks 1.25
26 JBg,BWi,A:Cloak & Dagger . . 1.25
27 JBg,AG,A:Wolverine,X-Factor,
 V:Sabretooth 4.00
28 A:Fantastic Four,Hercules . . . 1.25
29 JBg,DGr,A:SpM,V:Hobgoblin . . 2.00
30 VM,Crack 1.25

Power Pack #2
© *Marvel Entertainment Group*

31 JBg,I:Trash 1.25
32 JBg,V:Trash 1.25
33 JBg,A:Sunspot,Warlock,
 C:Spider-Man 1.75
34 TD,V:Madcap 1.25
35 JBg,A:X-Factor,D:Plague 1.75
36 JBg,V:Master Mold 1.25
37 SDr(i),I:Light-Tracker 1.25
38 SDr(i),V:Molecula 1.25
39 V:Bogeyman 1.25
40 A:New Mutants,V:Bogeyman . . 1.75
41 SDr(i),V:The Gunrunners 1.25
42 JBg,SDr,Inferno,V:Bogeyman . 2.00
43 JBg,SDr,AW,Inferno,
 V:Bogeyman 2.00
44 JBr,Inferno,A:New Mutants . . 2.25
45 JBr,End battle w/Bogeyman . . 1.50
46 WPo,A:Punisher,Dakota North . 2.00
47 JBg,I:Bossko 1.50
48 JBg,Toxic Waste #1 . . . . 1.50
49 JBg,JSh,Toxic Waste #2 . . . . 1.50
50 AW(i),V:Snarks 1.50
51 GM,I:Numinus 1.50
52 AW(i),V:Snarks,A:Numinus . . 1.50
53 EC,A of V,A:Typhoid Mary . . 1.50

54 JBg,V:Mad Thinker 1.50
55 DSp,V:Mysterio 1.50
56 TMo,A:Fant.Four,Nova 1.50
57 TMo,A:Nova,V:Star Stalker . . 1.50
58 TMo,A:Galactus,Mr.Fantastic . 1.50
59 TMo,V:Ringmaster 1.50
60 TMo,V:Puppetmaster 1.50
61 TMo,V:Red Ghost & Apes 1.50
62 V:Red Ghost & Apes
 (last issue) 1.50
Holiday Spec.JBr,Small Changes . 2.25

PRINCE NAMOR, THE SUB-MARINER
Sept., 1984
1 I:Dragonrider, Dara 2.50
2 I:Proteus 1.50
3 . . . . 1.25
4 Dec., 1984 . . . . 1.25

PRINCE VALIANT
1 JRy,CV,Thule, Camelot
 and the Misty Isles 4.00
2 JRy,CV 4.00
3 JRy,CV 4.00
4 JRy,CV, final issue 4.00

PRIVATE EYE
Atlas Jan., 1951
1 . . . . 85.00
2 . . . . 55.00
3 GT 55.00
4 . . . . 40.00
5 . . . . 40.00
6 JSt 40.00
7 . . . . 40.00
8 March, 1952 . . . . 40.00

PROFESSOR XAVIER AND THE X-MEN
1 1st Year Together 1.00
2 V:The Vanisher 1.00
3 FaN,F:The Blob 1.00
4 V:Magneto & Brotherhood 1.00
5 . . . . 1.00
6 . . . . 1.00
7 FdS,Sub-Mariner 1.00
8 thru 12 . . . . 1.00
13 AHo,F:Juggernaut 1.00
14 JGz,V:Juggernaut, ... 1.00
15 JGz,F:Quicksilver & Scarlet
 Witch 1.00
16 . . . . 1.00
17 JGz,V:Sentinels,F:Beast 1.00
18 JGz,X-Men vs. Sentinels,
 final issue 1.00

PROWLER, THE
1 Creatures of the Night, pt.1 . . 1.75
2 V:Nightcreeper, Creatures, pt.2 1.75
3 Creatures of the Night, pt.3 . . 1.75
4 V:Vulture, Creatures, pt.4 . . . 1.75

PSI FORCE
Nov., 1986
1 MT,O:PSI Force 1.25
2 MT 1.00
3 MT,CIA 1.00
4 MT,J:Network 1.00
5 MT 1.00
6 MT(c) 1.00
7 MT(c) 1.00
8 MT 1.00

MARVEL

Psi Force #28
© Marvel Entertainment Group

9 MT(c)	1.00
10 PSI Hawk	1.00
11	1.00
12 MT(c)	1.00
13	1.00
14 AW	1.00
15	1.00
16 RLm	1.25
17 RLm	1.25
18 RLm	1.25
19 RLm	1.25
20 RLm,V:Medusa Web;Rodstvow	1.50
21 RLm	1.50
22 RLm,A:Nightmask	1.50
23 A:D.P.7	1.50
24	1.50
25	1.25
26	1.25
27 thru 31	@1.50
32 June, 1989	1.50
Ann.#1	1.25

PSYCHONAUTS
Epic

1 thru 4 War in the Future	4.95

PSYLOCKE & ANGEL:
CRIMSON DAWN

1 SvL,ATi,V:Obsideon	
2 (of 4) SvL,ATi,	

PUNISHER
Jan., 1986
[Limited Series]

1 MZ,Circle of Blood,double size	15.00
2 MZ,Back to the War	8.00
3 MZ,V:The Right	6.00
4 MZ,V:The Right	5.00
5 V:Jigsaw,end Mini-Series	5.00

[Regular Series]

1 KJ,V:Wilfred Sobel,Drugs	8.00
2 KJ,V:General Trahn,Bolivia	4.00
3 KJ,V:Colonel Fryer	3.50
4 KJ,I:The Rev,Microchip Jr.	3.50
5 KJ,V:The Rev	3.50
6 DR,KN,V:The Rosettis	3.50

7 DR,V:Ahmad,D:Rose	3.50
8 WPo,SW(1st Punisher), V:Sigo & Roky	6.00
9 WPo,SW,D:MicrochipJr,V:Sigo	5.00
10 WPo,SW,A:Daredevil (x-over w/Daredevil #257)	6.00
11 WPo,SW,O:Punisher	3.00
12 WPo,SW,V:Gary Saunders	3.00
13 WPo,SW,V:Lydia Spoto	3.00
14 WPo,SW,I:McDowell,Brooks	3.00
15 WPo,SW,V:Kingpin	3.00
16 WPo,SW,V:Kingpin	3.00
17 WPo,SW,V:Kingpin	3.00
18 WPo,SW,V:Kingpin,C:X-Men	3.00
19 LSn,In Australia	3.00
20 WPo(c),In Las Vegas	3.00
21 EL,SW,Boxing Issue	3.00
22 EL,SW,I:Saracen	3.00
23 EL,SW,V:Scully	3.00
24 EL,SW,A:Shadowmasters	3.00
25 EL,AW,A:Shadowmasters	3.00
26 RH,Oper.Whistle Blower#1	2.50
27 RH,Oper.Whistle Blower#2	2.50
28 BR,A:Dr.Doom,A of Veng.	2.50
29 BR,A:Dr.Doom,A of Veng.	2.50
30 BR,V:Geltrate	2.50
31 BR,V:Bikers #1	2.50
32 BR,V:Bikers #2	2.50
33 BR,V:The Reavers	2.50
34 BR,V:The Reavers	2.50
35 BR,MF,Jigsaw Puzzle #1	2.50
36 MT,MF,Jigsaw Puzzle #2	2.50
37 MT,Jigsaw Puzzle #3	2.50
38 BR,MF,Jigsaw Puzzle #4	2.50
39 JSh,Jigsaw Puzzle #5	2.50
40 BR,JSh,Jigsaw Puzzle #6	2.50
41 BR,TD,V:Terrorists	2.50
42 MT,V:Corrupt Mili. School	2.50
43 BR,Border Run	2.00
44 Flag Burner	2.00
45 One Way Fare	2.00
46 HH,Cold Cache	2.00
47 HH,Middle East #1	2.00
48 HH,Mid.East #2,V:Saracen	2.00
49 HH,Punisher Hunted	2.00
50 RH,MGo(c),I:Yo Yo Ng	3.00
51 Chinese Mafia	2.00
52 Baby Snatchers	2.00
53 HH,in Prison	2.50
54 HH,in Prison	2.50
55 HH,in Prison	2.50
56 HH,in Prison	2.50
57 HH,in Prison	2.50
58 V:Kingpin's Gang,A:Micro	3.00
59 MT(c),V:Kingpin	2.00
60 VM,AW,Black Punisher, A:Luke Cage	2.00
61 VM,A:Luke Cage	2.00
62 VM,AW,A:Luke Cage	1.50
63 MT(c),VM,V:Thieves	1.50
64 Eurohit #1	1.50
65 thru 70 Eurohit	@1.50
71 AW(i)	1.50
72 AW(i)	1.50
73 AW(i),Police Action #1	1.50
74 AW(i),Police Action #2	1.50
75 AW(i),Police Action #3,foil(c), double size	3.25
76 LSn,in Hawaii	1.50
77 VM,Survive#1	1.50
78 VM,Survive#2	1.50
79 VM,Survive#3	1.50
80 Goes to Church	1.50
81 V:Crooked Cops	1.50
82 B:Firefight	1.50

83 Firefight#2	1.50
84 E:Firefight	1.50
85 Suicide Run	2.00
86 Suicide Run#3,Foil(c),	3.25
87 Suicide Run#6	1.50
88 LSh(c),Suicide Run#9	1.50
89	1.75
90 Hammered	1.75
91 Silk Noose	1.75
92 Razor's Edge	1.75
93 Killing Streets	1.75
94 B:No Rules	1.50
95 No Rules	1.50
96	1.50
97 CDi	1.50
98	1.50
99	1.50
100 New Punisher	2.95
100a Enhanced ed.	3.95
101 CC,Raid's Franks Tomb	1.50
102 A:Bullseye	1.50
103 Countdown 4	1.50
104 CDi,Countdown 1, V:Kingpin, final issue	1.50
Ann.#1 MT,A:Eliminators, Evolutionary War.	5.00
Ann.#2 JLe,Atlantis Attacks #5, A:Moon Knight	3.50
Ann.#3 LS,MT,Lifeform #1	3.00
Ann.#4 Baron Strucker,pt.2 (see D.D.Annual #7)	3.00
Ann.#5 System Bytes #1	2.50
Ann.#6 I:Eradikator,w/card	3.25
GNv	5.00
Summer Spec #1 VM,MT	3.50
Summer Spec #2 SBs(c)	2.50
Summer Spec #3 V:Carjackers	2.50
Summer Spec #4	3.25
Punisher:No Escape A:USAgent, Paladin	5.00
Movie Spec.BA	5.95
Punisher: The Prize	5.50
Punisher:Bloodlines DC	6.25
Punisher:Blood on the Moors	16.95
Punisher:G-Force	5.25
Punisher:Origin of Mirco Chip #1, O:Mirco Chip	2.00
Punisher:Origin of Mirco Chip #2 V:The Professor	2.00
Classic Punisher rep early B/w magazines	7.00
Punisher:Back To School Spec. #1 JRy,short stories	3.25
#2 BSz	2.95
Punisher:Die Hard in the Big Easy Mardi Gras	5.25
Holiday Spec.#1 V:Young Mob Capo	3.25
Holiday Spec #2	2.95
Punisher:Ghosts of the Innocent#1 TGr, V:Kingpin's Dead Men	5.95
Punisher:Ghosts of the Innocent#2 TGr, V:Kingpin,Snake	5.95
TPB Punisher: Eye For An Eye	9.95

[2nd Regular Series] 1995

1 JOs,TL,Punisher sent to the Electric Chair, foil(c)	2.95
2 JOs,TL,Clv,Crime family boss	1.95
3 JOs,TL,Clv,V:Hatchetman	1.95
4 JOs,TL,Clv,A:Daredevil,Jigsaw	1.95
5	1.95
6	1.95
7 JOs,TL,Clv,V:Son of Nick Fury	1.95
8	1.50
9	1.50

MARVEL

10 .... 1.50	
11 Onslaught saga 1.50	
12 A:X-Cutioner 3.00	
13 JOs,TL, Working for S.H.I.E.L.D.?,	
A:X-Cutioner 1.50	
14 .... 1.50	
15 JOs,TL, X-Cutioner 1.50	
16 JOS,TL, concl.? 1.50	
17 JOS,TL,A:Daredevil,Doc Samson,	
Spider-Man 1.50	
18 JOS,TL,Frank Castle amnesia? 1.95	
19 JOS,TL,V:Taskmaster 1.95	
20 JOS,TL, fugitive Punisher 1.95	

PUNISHER ARMORY
July, 1990

1 JLe(c) 5.00	
2 JLe(c) 3.00	
3 .... 2.50	
4 thru 6 .... @2.25	
7 thru 10 .... @2.00	

PUNISHER/BATMAN
Spec. CDi,JR2, 48pg 5.00

PUNISHER/ CAPTAIN AMERICA: BLOOD AND GLORY
1 thru 3 KJ,V:Drug Dealers ... @6.25

CLASSIC PUNISHER
1 TDz 4.95

PUNISHER/DAREDEVIL
1 Rep.Daredevil 6.00

PUNISHER KILLS THE MARVEL UNIVERSE
1-shot Alterniverse 5.95

PUNISHER MAGAZINE
Oct., 1989

1 MZ,rep.,Punisher #1 .... 2.50	
2 MZ,rep 2.25	
3 thru 13 KJ,rep. .... @2.25	
14 rep. PWJ #1&#2 .... 2.25	
15 rep. PWJ 2.25	
16 rep.,1990 .... 2.25	

PUNISHER MEETS ARCHIE

1 JB 4.25	
1a newsstand ed. 3.25	

PUNISHER MOVIE COMIC
Nov., 1989

1 Movie adapt. 1.50	
2 Movie adapt. 1.50	
3 Movie adapt,Dec., 1989 .... 1.50	

PUNISHER MOVIE SPECIAL
1 Movie Adapt.BA,1989 ...... 5.95

PUNISHER: NO ESCAPE
OneShot A:USAgent,Paladin,1990 5.50

PUNISHER P.O.V.
July, 1991
1 BWr,Punisher/Nick Fury 5.50

2 BWr,A:Nick Fury,Kingpin 5.50	
3 BWr,V:Mutant Monster,	
A:Vampire Slayer 5.50	
4 BWr,A:Nick Fury 5.25	

PUNISHER: THE PRIZE
1 1990 .... 4.95

Punisher 2099 #12
© Marvel Entertainment Group

PUNISHER 2099

1 TMo,Jake Gallows family	
Killed, foil(c) 2.50	
2 TMo,I:Fearmaster,Kron,Multi	
Factor 2.25	
3 TMo,V:Frightening Cult 2.25	
4 TMo,V:Cyber Nostra 1.75	
5 TMo,V:Cyber Nostra,Fearmaster 1.75	
6 TMo,V:Multi-Factor 1.75	
7 TMo,Love and Bullets#1 ..... 1.75	
8 TMo,Love and Bullets#2 ..... 1.75	
9 TMo,Love and Bullets#3 ..... 1.75	
10 TMo,I:Jigsaw 1.50	
11 TMo,V:Jigsaw 1.50	
12 TMo,A:Spider-Man 2099 ..... 1.50	
13 TMo,Fall of the Hammer#5 ... 1.50	
14 WSm, ... 1.50	
15 TMo,V:Fearmaster,	
I:Public Enemy 1.50	
16 TMo,V:Fearmaster,	
Public Enemy 1.75	
17 TMo,V:Public Enemy 1.75	
18 TMo,I:Goldheart 1.75	
19 TMo,I:Vendetta 1.50	
20 .... 1.50	
21 .... 1.50	
22 V:Hotwire 1.50	
23 I:Synchron,V:Hotwire 1.50	
24 V:Synchron 1.50	
25 Enhanced cover 2.95	
25a newsstand ed. 2.25	
26 V:Techno-Shaman 1.50	
27 R:Blue Max 1.50	

Becomes:

PUNISHER 2099 A.D.

28 Minister of Punishment 1.95	
29 Minister of Punishment 1.95	
30 One Nation Under Doom 1.95	
31 .... 1.95	

32 Out of Ammo 1.95	
33 Counddown to final issue 1.95	
34 final issue 1.95	

PUNISHER WAR JOURNAL
Nov., 1988

1 CP,JLe,O:Punisher 4.00	
2 CP,JLe,A:Daredevil 3.00	
3 CP,JLe,A:Daredevil 2.50	
4 CP,JLeV:The Sniper 2.50	
5 CP,JLe,V:The Sniper 2.50	
6 CP,JLe,A:Wolverine 3.00	
7 CP,JLe,A:Wolverine 3.00	
8 JLe,I:Shadowmasters 2.50	
9 JLe,A:Black Widow 2.50	
10 JLe,V:Sniper 2.50	
11 JLe,Shock Treatment 2.50	
12 JLe,AM,V:Bushwacker 2.50	
13 JLe(c),V:Bushwacker 2.50	
14 JLe(c),DR,RH,A:Spider-Man . 2.50	
15 JLe(c),DR,RH,A:Spider-Man . 2.50	
16 MT(i),Texas Massacre 2.25	
17 JLe,AM,Hawaii 2.50	
18 JLe,AM,Kahuna,Hawaii 2.50	
19 JLe,AM,Traume in Paradise . . 2.50	
20 AM 2.00	
21 TSm,AM 2.00	
22 TSm,AM,Ruins #1 .... 2.00	
23 TSm,AM,Ruins #2 .... 2.00	
24 .... 2.00	
25 MT 2.00	
26 MT,A:Saracen 2.00	
27 MT,A:Saracen 2.00	
28 MT 2.00	
29 MT,A:Ghostrider 2.00	
30 MT,A:Ghostrider 2.00	
31 NKu,Kamchatkan	
Konspiracy#1 .... 2.00	
32 Kamchatkan Konspiracy #2 . . . 2.00	
33 Kamchatkan Konspiracy #3 . . . 2.00	
34 V:Psycho 2.00	
35 Movie Stuntman 2.00	
36 Radio Talk Show #1 .... 2.00	
37 Radio Talk Show #2 .... 2.00	
38 .... 2.00	
39 DGr,V:Serial Killer 2.00	
40 MWg 1.75	
41 Armageddon Express 1.75	
42 Mob run-out 1.75	
43 JR2(c) 1.75	
44 Organ Donor Crimes 1.75	
45 Dead Man's Hand #3,V:Viper . 2.00	
46 Dead Man's Hand #6,V:Chainsaw	
and the Praetorians 1.75	
47 Dead Man's Hand #7,A:Nomad,	
D.D,V:Hydra,Secret Empire . . . 1.75	
48 B:Payback 1.75	
49 JR2(c),V:Corrupt Cop 1.75	
50 MT,V:Highjackers,I:Punisher	
2099 .... 2.00	
51 E:Payback 1.75	
52 A:Ice(from The'Nam) 1.75	
53 A:Ice(from the Nam) 1.75	
54 Hyper#1 .... 1.75	
55 Hyper#2 .... 1.75	
56 Hyper#3 .... 1.75	
57 A:Ghost Rider,Daredevil 1.75	
58 A:Ghost Rider,Daredevil 1.75	
59 F:Max the Dog 1.75	
60 CDi(s),F:Max the Dog 1.75	
61 CDi(s),Suicide Run#1,Foil(c) . . 3.00	
62 CDi(s),Suicide Run#4 ...... 2.00	
63 CDi(s),Suicide Run#7 ...... 2.00	
64 CDi(s),Suicide Run#10 ...... 3.00	

All comics prices listed are for *Near Mint* condition. | **CVA Page 239**

MARVEL

64a Newsstand Ed.	2.50
65 B:Pariah	2.00
66 A:Captain America	2.25
67 Pariah#3	2.25
68 A:Spider-Man	2.25
69 E:Pariah	1.95
70	1.95
71	1.95
72 V:Fake Punisher	1.95
73 E:Frank Castle	1.95
74	1.95
75 MT(c)	2.50
76 First Entry	1.95
77 R:Stone COld	1.95
78 V:Payback,Heathen	1.95
79 Countdown 3	1.95
80 Countdown 0, A:Nick Fury,	
V:Bullseye, final issue	1.95
TPB reprints #6,7	4.95

Punisher War Zone #1
© Marvel Entertainment Group

PUNISHER WAR ZONE

1 JR2,KJ,Punisher As Johnny Tower	
Die-Cut Bullet Hole(c)	3.00
2 JR2,KJ,Mafia Career	2.50
3 JR2,KJ,Punisher/Mafia,contd	2.50
4 JR2,KJ,Cover gets Blown	2.50
5 JR2,KJ,A:Shotgun	2.50
6 JR2,KJ,A:Shotgun	2.50
7 JR2,V:Rapist in Central Park	2.00
8 JR2,V:Rapist in Central Park	2.00
9 JR2,V:Magnificent Seven	2.00
10 JR2,V:Magnificent Seven	2.00
11 JR2,MM,V:Magnificent Seven	2.00
12 Punisher Married	2.00
13 Self-Realization	2.00
14 Psychoville#3	2.00
15 Psychoville#4	2.00
16 Psychoville#5	2.00
17 Industrial Esponiage	2.00
18 Jerico Syndrome#2	2.00
19 Jerico Syndrome#3	2.00
20 B:2 Mean 2 Die	2.00
21 2 Mean 2 Die#2	2.00
22 A:Tyger Tyger	2.00
23 Suicide Run#2,Foil(c)	3.25

24 Suicide Run#5,	2.00
25 Suicide Run#8,	2.50
26 CDi(s),JB,Pirates	2.00
27 CDi(s),JB,	2.25
28 CDi(s),JB,Sweet Revenge	2.25
29 CDi(s),JB,The Swine	2.25
30 CDi(s),JB	1.95
31 CDi(s),JB,River of Blood,pt.1	1.95
32 CDi(s),JB,River of Blood,pt.2	1.95
33 CDi(s),JB,River of Blood,pt.3	1.95
34 CDi(s),JB,River of Blood,pt.4	1.95
35 River of Blood,pt.5	1.95
36 River of Blood,pt.6	1.95
37 O:Max	1.95
38 Dark Judgment,pt.1	1.95
39 Dark Judgment,pt.2	1.95
40 In Court	1.95
41 CDi,Countdown 2, final issue	1.95
Ann.#1 Jb,MGo,(c),I:Phalanx,	
w/Trading card	3.25
Ann.#2 CDi(s),DR	2.95

PUNISHER: YEAR ONE

1 O:Punisher	2.50
2 O:Punisher	2.50
3 O:Punisher	2.50
4 finale	2.50

PUSSYCAT
Oct., 1968
(black & white magazine)

1 BEv,BWa,WW	125.00

QUASAR
Oct., 1989

1 O:Quasar	2.50
2 V:Deathurge,A:Eon	2.00
3 A:Human Torch,V:The Angler	2.00
4 Acts of Vengeance,A:Aquarian	2.00
5 A of Veng,V:Absorbing Man	2.00
6 V:Klaw,Living Laser,Venom,	
Red Ghost	3.00
7 MM,A:Cosmic SpM,V:Terminus	2.50
8 MM,A:New Mutants,BlueShield	2.00
9 MM,A:Modam	2.00
10 MM,A:Dr.Minerva	2.00
11 MM,A:Excalibur,A:Modred	2.00
12 MM,A:Makhari,Blood Bros.	1.75
13 JLe(c)MM,J.into Mystery #1	1.75
14 TM(c)MM,J.into Mystery #2	2.00
15 MM,Journey into Mystery #3	1.75
16 MM,Double sized	2.00
17 MM,Race,A:Makkari,Whizzer,	
Quicksilver,Capt.Marv,Super	
Sabre,Barry Allen Spoof	2.25
18 GCa,N:Quasar	1.75
19 GCa,B:Cosmos in Collision,	
C:Thanos	2.00
20 GCa,A:Fantastic Four	2.00
21 GCa,V:Jack of Hearts	2.00
22 GCa,D:Quasar,A:Ghost Rider	2.00
23 GCa,A:Ghost Rider	2.00
24 GCa,A:Thanos,Galactus,	
D:Maelstrom	2.00
25 GCa,A:Eternity & Infinity,N:Quasar,	
E:Cosmos Collision	2.00
26 GCa,Inf.Gauntlet,A:Thanos	2.50
27 GCa,Infinity Gauntlet,I:Epoch	2.00
28 GCa,A:Moondragon,Her,	
X-Men	2.00
29 GCa,A:Moondragon,Her	1.50
30 GCa,What If? tie-in	1.50
31 GCa,R:New Universe	1.50
32 GCa,Op.GalacticStorm,pt.3	1.50

33 GCa,Op.GalacticStorm,pt.10	1.50
34 GCa,Op.GalacticStorm,pt.17	1.50
35 GCa,Binary V:Her	1.50
36 GCa,V:Soul Eater	1.50
37 GCa,V:Soul Eater	1.50
38 GCa,Inf.War,V:Warlock	1.50
39 SLi,Inf.War,V:Deathurge	1.50
40 SLi,Inf.War,V:Deathurge	1.50
41 R:Marvel Boy	1.50
42 V:Blue Marvel	1.50
43 V:Blue Marvel	1.50
44 V:Quagmire	1.50
45 V:Quagmire,Antibody	1.50
46 Neutron,Presence	1.50
47 1st Full Thunderstrike Story	1.50
48 A:Thunderstrike	1.50
49 Kalya Vs. Kismet	1.50
50 A:Man-Thing,Prism(c)	3.25
51 V:Angler,A:S.Supreme	1.50
52 V:Geometer	1.50
53	1.50
54 MGu(s),Starblast #2	1.50
55 MGu(s),A:Stranger	1.50
56 MGu(s),Starblast #10	1.50
57 MGu(s),A:Kismet	1.50
58	1.50
59 A:Thanos,Starfox	1.50
60 final issue	1.50

QUESTPROBE
August, 1984

1 JR,A:Hulk,I:Chief Examiner	2.00
2 AM,JM,A:Spider-Man	1.75
3 JSt,A:Thing & Torch	1.50

QUICK-TRIGGER WESTERN
See: WESTERN THRILLERS

RAIDERS OF THE LOST ARK
Sept., 1981

1 JB/KJ,movie adaption	2.00
2 JB/KJ,	1.75
3 JB/KJ,Nov.,1981	1.75

Raiders of the Lost Ark #2
© Marvel Entertainment Group

RAVAGE 2099

1 PR,I:Ravage	2.50
2 PR,V:Deathstryk	2.00
3 PR,V:Mutroids	2.00
4 PR,V:Mutroids	1.50
5 PR,Hellrock	1.50
6 PR,N:Ravage	1.50
7 PR,new Powers	1.50
8 V:Deathstryke	1.50
9 PR,N:Ravage	1.50
10 V:Alchemax	1.50
11 A:Avatarr	1.50
12 Ravage Transforms	1.50
13 V:Fearmaster	1.50
14 V:Punisher 2099	1.50
15 Fall of the Hammer #2	1.50
16 I:Throwback	1.50
17 GtM,V:Throwback,O:X-11	1.50
18 GtM,w/card	1.75
19 GtM,	1.75
20 GtM,V:Hunter	1.50
21 Savage on the Loose	1.50
22 Exodus	1.50
23 Blind Justice	1.50
24 Unleashed	1.50
25 Flame Bearer	2.25
25a Deluxe ed.	2.95
26 V:Megastruck	1.50
27 V:Deathstryke	1.50
28 R:Hela	1.50
29 V:Deathstryke	1.50
30 King Ravage	1.50

Becomes:

RAVAGE 2099 A.D.

31 V:Doom	1.95
32 One Nation Under Doom	1.95
33 Final issue	1.95

RAWHIDE KID

Atlas March, 1955–May, 1979

1 B:Rawhide Kid & Randy, A:Wyatt Earp	500.00
2 Shoot-out(c)	175.00
3 V:Hustler	100.00
4 Rh(c)	100.00
5 GC	100.00
6 Six-Gun Lesson	75.00
7 AW	75.00
8	75.00
9	75.00
10 thru 16	@60.00
17 JK,O:Rawhide Kid	60.00
18 thru 20	@50.00
21	40.00
22	40.00
23 JK,O:Rawhide Kid Retold	85.00
24 thru 30	@40.00
31 JK,DAy,No Law in Mesa	35.00
32 JK,DAy,Beware of the Parker Brothers	35.00
33 JK(c),JDa,V:Jesse James	40.00
34 JDa,JK,V:Mister Lightning	40.00
35 JK(c),GC,JDa,I&D:The Raven	40.00
36 DAy,A Prisoner in Outlaw Town	35.00
37 JK(c),DAy,GC,V:The Rattler	35.00
38 DAy,V:The Red Raven	35.00
39 DAy	35.00
40 JK(c),DAy,A:Two Gun Kid	35.00
41 JK(c),The Tyrant of Tombstone Valley	35.00
42 JK	35.00
43 JK	35.00
44 JK(c),V:The Masked Maverick	35.00

45 JK(c),O:Rawhide Kid Retold	40.00
46 JK(c),ATh	30.00
47 JK(c),The Riverboat Raiders	25.00
48 GC,V:Marko the Manhunter	22.00
49 The Masquerader	22.00
50 A;Kid Colt,V:Masquerader	22.00
51 DAy,Trapped in the Valley of Doom	22.00
52 DAy,Revenge at Rustler's Roost	22.00
53 Guns of the Wild North	22.00
54 DH,BEv,The Last Showdown	22.00
55	22.00
56 DH,JTgV:The Peacemaker	22.00
57 V:The Scorpion	22.00
58 DAy	22.00
59 V:Drako	22.00
60 DAy,HT,Massacre at Medicine Bend	22.00
61 DAy,TS,A:Wild Bill Hickok	20.00
62 Gun Town,V:Drako	20.00
63 Shootout at Mesa City	20.00
64 HT,Duel of the Desparadoes	20.00
65 JTg,HT,BE	20.00
66 JTg,BEv,Death of a Gunfighter	20.00
67 Hostage of Hungry Hills	20.00
68 JB,V:The Cougar	20.00
69 JTg,The Executioner	20.00
70 JTg,The Night of the Betrayers	15.00
71 JTg,The Last Warrior	15.00
72 JTg,The Menace of Mystery Valley	15.00
73 JTg,The Manhunt	15.00
74 JTg,The Apaches Attack	15.00
75 JTg,The Man Who Killed The Kid	15.00
76 JTg,V:The Lynx	15.00
77 JTg,The Reckoning	15.00
78 JTg	15.00
79 JTg,AW,The Legion of the Lost	15.00
80 Fall of a Hero	15.00
81 thru 85	@15.00
86 JK,O:Rawhide Kid retold	15.00
87 thru 99	@9.00
100 O:Rawhide Kid retold	12.00
101 thru 135	@10.00
126 thru 151	@8.00

RAWHIDE KID

August, 1985

1 JSe,mini-series	1.50
2 thru 4	@1.25

RAZORLINE FIRST CUT

Razorline

1 Intro Razorline	1.00

REAL EXPERIENCES

See: TESSIE THE TYPIST

RED RAVEN

See: HUMAN TORCH

RED SONJA

[1st Series] Jan., 1977

1 FT,O:Red Sonja,'Blood of the Unicorn'	3.50
2 FT,'Demon of the Maze'	2.50
3 FT,'The Games of Gita'	2.00
4 FT,'The Lake of the Unknown'	2.00
5 FT,'Master of the Bells'	2.00
6 FT,'The Singing Tower'	1.25
7 FT,'Throne of Blood'	1.25

8 FT,Vengeance o/t Golden Circle	1.25
9 FT,'Chariot o/t Fire-Stallions'	1.25
10 FT,Red Lace,pt.1	1.25
11 FT,Red Lace,pt.2	1.25
12 JB/JRu,'Ashes & Emblems'	1.25
13 JB/AM,'Shall Skranos Fall'	1.25
14 SB/AM,'Evening on the Border'	1.25
15 JB/TD,'Tomb of 3 Dead Kings' May, 1979	1.25

Red Sonja #1
© Marvel Entertainment Group

[2nd Series]
Feb., 1983

1 TD,GC, The Blood That Binds	1.25
2 GC, March,1983	1.00

[3rd Series]
August, 1983

1	1.25
2 thru 13	@1.25
1 movie adaption, 1985	1.25
2 movie adaption, 1985	1.25

RED SONJA

1-shot Bros.Hildebrandt(c),48pg	2.95

RED WARRIOR

Atlas Jan.–Dec., 1951

1 GT,Indian Tales	100.00
2 GT(c),The Trail of the Outcast	65.00
3 The Great Spirit Speaks	50.00
4 O:White Wing	50.00
5	50.00
6 Final Issue	50.00

RED WOLF

May, 1972–Sept. 1973

1 SSh(c),GK,JSe,F:Red Wolf & Lobo	5.50
2 GK(c),SSh,Day of the Dynamite Doom	3.00
3 SSh,War of the Wolf Brothers	3.00
4 SSh,V:Man-Bear	3.00
5 GK(c),SSh	3.00
6 SSh,JA,V;Devil Rider	3.00
7 SSh,JA,Echoes from a Golden Grave	3.00
8 SSh,Hell on Wheels	3.00
9 DAy,To Die Again,O:Lobo	3.00

MARVEL

REN AND STIMPY SHOW

1 Polybagged w/Air Fowlers, Ren(c)	5.00
1a Stimpy(c)	4.00
1b 2nd Printing	3.00
1c 3rd Printing	2.00
2 Frankenstimpy	3.00
2a 2nd Printing	2.00
3 Christmas issue	3.00
3a 2nd Printing	2.00
4 Where's Stimpy?	3.00
5 Teacher Bingo	3.00
6 A:SpM,V:Powdered Toast Man	3.00
7 F:Offical Yak Shaving Day	3.00
8 F:Bun Boy Burger Bunny	3.00
9 Untamed World	3.00
10 Bug Out	3.00
11 Ren's Peaceful Place	3.00
12 Teacher Bingo	3.00
13 Halloween issue	2.50
14 Mars needs Vecro	2.50
15 Christmas Spec.	2.25
16	2.25
17 This Year's Model	2.25
18 U.S. Ohhhhh No!	2.25
19 Minimalist issue	2.25
20 F:Muddy Mudskipper	2.25
21 I'm The Cat	2.25
22 Badtime Stories	1.95
23 Athletics	1.95
24 Halloween	1.95
25 regular (c)	1.95
25a die-cut(c),A new addition	2.95
26	1.95
27	1.95
28 Filthy the Monkey	1.95
29 Loch Ness Mess	1.95
30 Pinata game	1.95
31 Sausage Castle	1.95
32 Join Circus, UFO Abduction	1.95
33 Bowling	1.95
34 lottery ticket	1.95
35 Pasta Monster	1.95
36 Ren Cabby Driver	1.95
37 Medical experiment	1.95
38 Cat who Knew too Much	1.95
39 Mad Computer	1.95
40	1.95
41	1.95
42 at Cap'n Salty Wet World	1.95
Spec.#1	3.25
Spec.#2	3.25
Spec.#3 Powder Toast Man	2.95
Spec.#4	2.95
Spec.#5 Virtual Stupidity	2.95
Spec.#6 History of Music	2.95
Holiday Special	2.95
Spec. Radio Dazed & Confused	1.95
Spec. Around the World in a Daze	2.95
TPB Running Joke,rep.#1-4,w/new material	13.25
TPB Pick of the Litter	13.25
TPB Tastes Like Chicken	13.25
TPB Your Pals	12.95
TPB Seech Little Monkeys	12.95

RETURN OF THE JEDI

1 AW,movie adapt	3.00
2 AW,movie adapt	3.00
3 AW,movie adapt	3.00
4 AW,movie adapt	3.00

REX HART
See: BLAZE CARSON

RICHIE RICH

1 Movie Adaptation	2.95

RINGO KID
Jan., 1970
[2nd Series]

1 AW,Reprints	3.00
2 JSe,Man Trap	2.00
3 JR,the Man From the Panhandle	1.50
4 HT(c),The Golden Spur	2.00
5 JMn,Ambush	2.00
6 Capture or Death	2.00
7 HT(c),JSe,JA,Terrible Treasure of Vista Del Oro	2.00
8 The End of the Trail	2.00
9 JSe,Mystery of the Black Sunset	2.00
10 Bad day at Black Creek	2.00
11 Bullet for a Bandit	1.50
12 A Badge to Die For	1.50
13 DW,Hostage at Fort Cheyenne	1.50
14 Showdown in the Silver Cartwheel	1.50
15 Fang,Claw, and Six-Gun	1.50
16 Battle of Cattleman's Bank	1.50
17 Gundown at the Hacienda	1.50
18	1.50
19 Thunder From the West	1.50
20 AW	1.50
21 thru 29	@1.50
30 Nov., 1973	1.50

RINGO KID WESTERN
Atlas August, 1954

1 JSt,O:Ringo Kid,B:Ringo Kid	185.00
2 I&O:Arab,A:Black Rider	85.00
3	50.00
4	50.00
5	50.00
6	55.00
7	55.00
8 JSe	55.00
9	30.00
10 JSe(c),AW	40.00
11 JSe(c)	30.00
12 JO	30.00
13 AW	40.00
14 thru 20	@30.00
21 Sept., 1957	30.00

ROBOCOP
March, 1990

1 LS,I:Nixcops	9.00
2 LS,V:Nixcops	5.00
3 LS	3.50
4 LS	3.00
5 LS,WarzonePt1	3.00
6 LS,WarzonePt2	3.00
7 LS	2.50
8 LS,V:Gang-5	2.50
9 LS,V:Vigilantes	2.50
10 LS	2.50
11 HT	2.50
12 LS,Robocop Army #1	2.00
13 LS,Robocop Army #2	2.00
14 LS,Robocop Army #3	2.00
15 LS,Robocop Army #4	2.00
16 TV take over	2.00
17 LS,V:The Wraith	2.00
18 LS,Mindbomb #1	2.00
19 LS,Mindbomb #2	2.00
20 In Detroit	2.00
21 LS,Beyond the Law,pt.1	2.00
22 LS,Beyond the Law,pt.2	2.00

23 LS,Beyond the Law,pt.3,final	2.00
Robocop Movie Adapt	4.95
Robocop II Movie Adapt	4.95

ROBOCOP II
August, 1990

1 MBa,rep.Movie Adapt	2.00
2 and 3 MBa,rep.Movie adapt	@1.50

ROBOTIX
Feb., 1986

1 Based on toys	1.00

ROCKET RACCOON
May, 1985—Aug., 1985

1 thru 4 MM	@1.50

ROCKO'S MODERN LIFE

1 and 2	@2.25
3 and 4	@1.95

ROGUE

1 Enhanced cover	4.50
2 A:Gambit	4.00
3 Gamtit or Rogue?	2.95
4 final issue	2.95

Rom #12
© *Marvel Entertainment Group*

ROM
Dec., 1979

1 SB,I&O:Rom	3.00
2 FM(c),SB,V:Dire Wraiths	2.50
3 FM(c),SB,I:Firefall	2.50
4 SB,A:Firefall	2.00
5 SB,A:Dr.Strange	2.00
6 SB,V:Black Nebula	1.50
7 SB,V:Dark Nebula	1.50
8 SB,V:Dire Wraiths	1.50
9 SB,V:Serpentyne	1.50
10 SB,V:U.S.Air Force	1.50
11 SB,V:Dire Wraiths	1.50
12 SB,A:Jack O' Hearts	1.75
13 SB,V:Plunderer	1.25
14 SB,V:Mad Thinker	1.25
15 SB,W:Brandy and Dire Wraith	1.25

16 SB,V:Watchwraith 1.25
17 SB,A:X-Men 3.00
18 SB,A:X-Men 3.00
19 SB,JSt,C:X-Men 1.50
20 SB,JSt,A:Starshine 1.25
21 SB,JSt,A:Torpedo 1.25
22 SB,JSt,A:Torpedo 1.25
23 SB,JSt,A:Powerman,Iron Fist. . 1.25
24 SB,JSt,A:Nova 1.25
25 SB,JSt,Double-Sized 1.50
26 SB,JSt,V:Galactus 1.00
27 SB,JSt,V:Galactus 1.00
28 SB,JSt,D:Starshine 1.00
29 SB,Down in the Mines 1.00
30 SB,JSt,A:Torpedo 1.00
31 SB,JSt,V:Evil Mutants,Rogue . 2.00
32 SB,JSt,V:Evil Mutants 2.00
33 SB,V:Sybil 1.00
34 SB,A:Sub-Mariner 1.00
35 SB,A:Sub-Mariner 1.00
36 SB,V:Scarecrow 1.00
37 SB,A:Starshine 1.00
38 BSA,A:Master of Kung Fu 1.00
39 SB,A:Master of Kung Fu 1.00
40 SB,A:Torpedo 1.00
41 SB,A:Dr.Strange 1.00
42 SB,A:Dr.Strange 1.00
43 SB,Rom Becomes Human . . . 1.00
44 SB,A:Starshine,O:Gremlin . . . 1.00
45 SB,V:Soviet Super Soldiers . . . 1.00
46 SB,V:Direwraiths 1.00
47 SB,New Look for Wraiths 1.00
48 SB,V:Dire Wraiths 1.00
49 SB,V:Dire Wraiths 1.00
50 SB,D:Torpedo,V:Skrulls 1.25
51 SB,F:Starshine 1.00
52 BSz(c),SB,V:Dire Wraiths 1.00
53 SB,BSz,V:Dire Wraiths 1.00
54 V:Dire Wraiths 1.00
55 V:Dire Wraihs 1.00
56 A:Alpha Flight 2.00
57 A:Alpha Flight 2.00
58 JG(c),A:Antman 1.00
59 SD,BL,V:Microbe Menace 1.00
60 SD,TP,V:Dire Wraiths 1.00
61 SD,V:Wraith-Realm 1.00
62 SD,A:Forge 1.25
63 SD,V:Dire Wraiths 1.00
64 SD,V:Dire Wraiths 1.00
65 SD,A:X-Men,Avengers 1.25
66 SD,Rom leaves Earth 1.25
67 SD,V:Scorpion 1.00
68 BSz(c)SD,Man & Machine . . . 1.00
69 SD,V:Ego 1.00
70 SD 1.00
71 SD,V:Raak 1.00
72 SD,Secret Wars II 1.25
73 SD,JSt 1.00
74 SD,JBy,Code of Honor 1.00
75 SD,CR,Doublesize,last issue . . 1.50
Ann.#1 PB,A:Stardust 1.50
Ann.#2 I:Knights of Galador 1.25
Ann.#3 A:New Mutants 2.00
Ann.#4 V:Gladiator 1.25

ROMANCE DIARY
Dec., 1949
1 . . . . 65.00
2 March, 1950 . . . . 60.00

ROMANCES OF
THE WEST
Nov., 1949
1 Ph(c),Calamity Jane,

Sam Bass 100.00
2 March, 1950 . . . . 65.00

ROMANCE TALES
Oct., 1949
(no #1 thru 6)
7 . . . . 65.00
8 . . . . 35.00
9 March, 1950 . . . . 30.00

ROMANTIC AFFAIRS
See: MOLLY MANTON'S
ROMANCES

ROYAL ROY
Star May, 1985
1 thru 5 . . . . @1.00
6 March, 1986 . . . . 1.00

RUGGED ACTION
Atlas Dec., 1954
1 Man-Eater 55.00
2 JSe,DAy.Manta-Ray 35.00
3 DAy 35.00
4 . . . . 35.00
Becomes:

STRANGE STORIES
OF SUSPENSE
5 RH,The Little Black Box . . . 250.00
6 BEv,The Illusion 125.00
7 JSe(c),BEv,Old John's House 150.00
8 AW,BP,TYhumbs Down . . . 150.00
9 BEv(c),Nightmare 125.00
10 RC,MME,AT 150.00
11 . . . . 100.00
12 . . . . 100.00
13 . . . . 90.00
14 AW 100.00
15 BK 90.00
16 August, 1957 . . . . 90.00

RUINS
1 Marvel's Alterverse 4.95
2 Fully painted, 32pg 4.95

RUSTY COMICS
See: KID KOMICS

SABRETOOTH
[Limited Series]
1 B:LHa(s),MT,A:Wolverine 5.00
2 MT,A:Mystique,C:Wolverine . . . 4.00
3 MT,A:Mystique,Wolverine . . . 3.50
4 E:LHa(s),MT,D:Birdy 3.00
TPB rep. #1-#4 . . . . 12.95

SABRETOOTH CLASSICS
1 rep. Power Man/Iron Fist #66 . . 1.75
2 rep. Power Man/Iron Fist #78 . . 1.75
3 rep. Power Man/Iron Fist #84 . . 1.75
4 rep. Spider-Man #116 . . . . . . 1.75
5 rep. Spider-Man #119 . . . . . . 1.50
6 reprints 1.50
7 reprints 1.50
8 reprints 1.50
9 reprints 1.50
10 Morlock Massacre 1.50
11 rep. Daredevil #238 . . . . . . 1.50
12 rep. V:Wolverine 1.50
13 rep. 1.50
14 A:Mauraders 1.50

15 Mutant Massacre, rep.
   Uncanny X-Men #221 . . . . 1.50

SABRETOOTH
Spec.#1 FaN, cont.from X-Men#48 4.95

SABRETOOTH
& MYSTIQUE
1 JGz,AOl, ... 1.95
2 thru 4 JGz,AOl . . . . @1.95

SACHS & VIOLENS
Epic
1 GP,PDd(s) 3.00
2 GP,PDd(s),V:Killer 2.50
3 GP,PDd(s),V:White Slavers . . . 2.50
4 GP,PDd(s),D:Moloch 2.25

SAGA OF CRYSTAR
May, 1983
1 O:Crystar 2.25
2 A:Ika 1.50
3 A:Dr.Strange 1.50
4 . . . . 1.50
5 . . . . 1.50
6 A:Nightcrawler 2.00
7 I:Malachon 1.50
8 . . . . 1.50
9 . . . . 1.50
10 Chaos 1.50
11 Alpha Flight,Feb., 1985 . . . . 2.00

SAGA OF ORIGINAL
HUMAN TORCH
1 RB,O:Original Human Torch . . 3.00
2 RB,A:Toro 2.50
3 RB,V:Adolph Hitler 2.50
4 RB,Torch vs. Toro 2.50

ST. GEORGE
Epic June, 1988
1 KJ,Shadow Line 1.25
2 KJ,I:Shrek 1.25
3 KJ 1.50
4 KJ 1.50
5 . . . . 1.50
6 . . . . 1.50
7 DSp 1.50
8 Oct., 1989 . . . . 1.50

SAINT SINNER
Razorline
1 I:Phillip Fetter 2.75
2 F:Phillip Fetter 2.00
3 in Vertesque 2.00
4 . . . . 2.00
5 Arcadia 2.00
6 . . . . 2.00
7 The Child Stealer 2.00
8 . . . . 1.95

SAM & MAX
GO TO THE MOON
1 Dirtbag Special,w/Nirvana Tape 4.00
[Regular Series]
1 MMi,AAd,F:Skull Boy 3.25
2 AAd,MMi 2.95
3 . . . . 2.95

SAMURAI CAT
Epic

MARVEL

---

1 I:MiaowaraTomokato 2.25
2 I:Con-Ed,V:Thpaghetti-Thoth . . 2.25
3 EmpireStateStrikesBack 2.25

Savage Sword of Conan #10
© Marvel Entertainment Group

SAVAGE SWORD
OF CONAN
August, 1974
(black & white magazine)
1 BWS,JB,NA,GK,O:Blackmark,
   3rdA:Red Sonja,Boris(c) 75.00
2 NA(c),HC,GK,'Black Colossus,'
   B.U.King Kull;B.U.Blackmark . 35.00
3 JB,BWS,GK,'At The Mountain
   of the Moon God;B.U.s:
   Kull;Blackmark 30.00
4 JB,RCo,GKIron Shadows in the
   Moon B.U.Blackmark,Boris(c) . 15.00
5 JB,A WitchShall beBorn,Boris(c)15.00
6 AN,'Sleeper 'Neath the Sands' 12.50
7 JB,Citadel at the Center
   of Time Boris(c) 12.50
8 inc.GK,'Corsairs against Stygia 12.50
9 Curse of the Cat-Goddess,
   Boris(c),B.U.King Kull 12.50
10 JB,'Sacred Serpent of Set'
   Boris(c) 10.00
11 JB,'The Abode of the Damned' 10.00
12 JB,Haunters of Castle Crimson
   Boris(c) 10.00
13 GK,The Thing in the Temple,
   B.U. Solomon Kane 10.00
14 NA,Shadow of Zamboula,
   B.U.Solomon Kane 10.00
15 JB,Boris(c),'Devil in Iron' 10.00
16 JB,BWS,People of the Black
   Circle,B.U.Bran Mak Morn . . . 10.00
17 JB,'On to Yimsha!,
   B.U.Bran Mak Morn 10.00
18 JB,'The Battle of the Towers'
   B.U. Solomon Kane 10.00
19 JB,'Vengeance in Vendhya'
   B.U. Solomon Kane 10.00
20 JB,'The Slithering Shadow'
   B.U. Solomon Kane 10.00
21 JB,'Horror in the Red Tower' . 10.00
22 JB,'Pool o/t Black One'
   B.U. Solomon Kane 10.00

23 JB,FT,'Torrent of Doom'
   B.U. Solomon Kane 10.00
24 JB,BWS,'Tower of the
   Elephant'B.U.Cimmeria 10.00
25 DG,SG,Jewels of Gwahlur,
   B.U.Solomon Kane. 10.00
26 JB,TD,Beyond the Black River,
   B.U.Solomon Kane 8.00
27 JB/TD,Children of Jhebbal Sag 8.00
28 JB/AA,Blood of the Gods 8.00
29 ECh,FT,Child of Sorcery,
   B.U. Red Sonja 8.00
30 FB,The Scarlet Citadel 8.00
31 JB/TD,The Flaming Knife,pt.1 . 8.00
32 JB/TD,Ghouls of Yanaldar,pt.2 8.00
33 GC,Curse of the Monolith,
   B.U.Solomon Kane 8.00
34 CI/AA,MP,Lair o/t Ice Worm;B.U.
   Solomon Kane,B.U.King Kull . . 8.00
35 ECh,Black Tears 8.00
36 JB,AA,Hawks over Shem 8.00
37 SB,Sons of the White Wolf
   B.U. Solomon Kane 8.00
38 JB/TD,The Road of the Eagles 8.00
39 SB/TD,The Legions of the Dead,
   B.U.Solomon Kane concl. 8.00
40 JB/TD,A Dream of Blood 8.00
41 JB/TD,Quest for the Cobra Crown
   A:Thoth-Amon,B.U.Sol.Kane . . 8.00
42 JB/TD,Devil-Tree of Gamburu,
   A:Thoth-Amon,B.U.Sol.Kane . . 8.00
43 JB/TD,King Thoth-Amon,
   B.U.King Kull 8.00
44 SB/TD,The Star of Khorala . . . 8.00
45 JB/TD,The Gem in the Tower,
   B.U. Red Sonja 8.00
46 EC/TD,Moon of Blood,
   B.U. Hyborian Tale 8.00
47 GK/JB/JRu,Treasure of Tranicos
   C:Thoth-Amon 8.00
48 JB/KJ,A Wind Blows from Stygia
   C:Thoth-Amon 8.00
49 JB/TD,When Madness Wears the
   Crown, B.U.Hyborian Tale 6.00
50 JB/TD,Swords Across the
   Alimane 6.00
51 JB/TD,Satyrs' Blood 6.00
52 JB/TD,Conan the Liberator . . . 6.00
53 JB,The Sorcerer and the Soul,
   B.U. Solomon Kane 6.00
54 JB,The Stalker Amid the Sands,
   B.U. Solomon Kane 6.00
55 JB,Black Lotus & Yellow Death
   B.U. King Kull 6.00
56 JB/TD,The Sword of Skelos . . 6.00
57 JB/TD,Zamboula 6.00
58 JB/TD,KGa,For the Throne of
   Zamboula,B.U.OlgerdVladislav 6.00
59 AA,ECh,City ofSkulls,B.U.Gault 6.00
60 JB,The Ivory Goddess 6.00
61 JB,Wizard Fiend of Zingara . . . 6.00
62 JB/ECh,Temple of the Tiger,
   B.U. Solomon Kane 6.00
63 JB/ECh,TP/BMc,GK,Moat of Blood
   I:Chane of the Elder Earth . . . 6.00
64 JB/ECh,GK,Children of Rhan,
   B.U. Chane 6.00
65 GK,JB,Fangs of the Serpent,
   B.U. Bront 6.00
66 thru 75 . . . . @6.00
76 thru 80 . . . . @5.00
81 JB/ECh,Palace of Pleasure,
   B.U. Bront 5.00
82 AA,BWS,Devil in the Dark.Pt.1
   B.U.repConan#24,Swamp Gas 5.00

83 AA,MW,NA,ECh,Devil in the Dark
   Pt.2,B.U. Red Sonja,Sol.Kane . 5.00
84 VM,Darksome Demon of
   Rabba Than 5.00
85 GK,Daughter of the God King . 5.00
86 GK,Revenge of the Sorcerer . . 5.00
87 . . . . 5.00
88 JB,Isle of the Hunter 5.00
89 AA,MW,Gamesman of Asgalun,
   B.U. Rite of Blood 5.00
90 JB,Devourer of Souls 5.00
91 JB,VM,Forest of Friends,
   B.U. The Beast,The Chain . . . 5.00
92 JB,The Jeweled Bird 5.00
93 JB/ECh,WorldBeyond the Mists 5.00
94 thru 101 . . . . @5.00
102 GD,B.U.Bran Mac Morn 4.00
103 GD,White Tiger of Vendhya,
   B.U. Bran Mac Morn 4.00
104 . . . . 4.00
105 . . . .'. . . . 4.00
106 Feud of Blood 4.00
107 thru 118 . . . . @4.00
119 ECh,A:Conan's Sister 4.00
120 Star of Thama-Zhu 4.00
121 . . . . 4.00
122 . . . . 4.00
123 ECh,Secret of the GreatStone 4.00
124 ECh,Secret of the Stone 4.00
125 Altar of the Goat God 4.00
126 The Mercenary 4.00
127 Reunion in Scarlet,Return
   of Valeria 4.00
128 . . . . 4.00
129 . . . . 4.00
130 Reavers of the Steppes 4.00
131 GI,Autumn of the Witch 4.00
132 ECh,Masters o/t Broadsword . 4.00
133 . . . . 4.00
134 Conan the Pirate 4.00
135 Conan the Pirate 4.00
136 NKu,Stranded on DesertIsland 4.00
137 ECh,The Lost Legion 4.00
138 ECh,Clan o/t Lizard God 4.00
139 ECh,A:Valeria 4.00
140 ECh,The Ghost's Revenge . . 4.00
141 ECh 4.00
142 ECh,V:Warlord 4.00
143 ECh 4.00
144 ECh 4.00
145 ECh 4.00
146 ECh 4.00
147 ECh 4.00
148 BMc 4.00
149 TGr,BMc,Conan Enslaved . . . 4.00
150 ECh 4.00
151 ECh 4.00
152 ECh,Valley Beyond the Stars 4.00
153 Blood on the Sand,Pt.1 . . . . . 4.00
154 Blood on the Sand,Pt.2 . . . . . 4.00
155 ECh,V:Vampires 4.00
156 V:Corinthian Army 4.00
157 V:Hyborians 4.00
158 ECh,The Talisman-Gem 4.00
159 Conan Enslaved 4.00
160 . . . . 4.00
161 V:Magician/Monsters 4.00
162 AW,Horned God,B.U.Sol.Kane 3.00
163 V:Picts 3.00
164 Conan's Revenge 3.00
165 B.U. King Kull 3.00
166 ECh,Conan in New World,Pt.1 3.00
167 ECh,Conan in New World,Pt.2 3.00
168 ECh,Conan in New
   World,concl 3.00

MARVEL

169 . . . . 3.00
170 AW,A:Red Sonja,Valeria
   B.U. Solomon Kane 3.00
171 TD,Conan Youth Story 2.50
172 JS,JRu,Haunted Swamp,
   B.U.King Kull,Valeria,
   Red Sonja 2.50
173 ECh,Under Siege 2.50
174 AA,Red Stones of
   Rantha Karn 2.50
175 The Demonslayer Sword 2.50
176 FH,TT,V:Wizard,B.U. Witch
   Queen,Dagon,Ghouls 2.50
177 LMc,TD,ECh,Conan the Prey,
   B.U.King Conan,Red Sonja . . . 2.50
178 AA,The Dinosaur God 2.50
179 ECh,A:Red Sonja,Valeria,
   B.U.Conan 2.50
180 ECh,Sky-God Bardisattva,
   B.U. King Kull 2.50
181 TD,Conan the Pagan God?,
   B.U. Voodoo Tribe 2.50
182 RB/RT,V:Killer Ants 2.50

Savage Sword of Conan #90
© Marvel Entertainment Group

183 ECh,V:Kah-Tah-Dhen,
   B.U.King Kull 2.50
184 AA,Return of Sennan 2.50
185 The Ring of Molub 2.50
186 AW,A:Thulsa Doom 2.50
187 ECh,A:Conan's Brother? . . . 2.50
188 V:Kharban the Sorcerer 2.50
189 A:Search Zukala for Gem . . . 2.50
190 JB/TD,Skull on the Seas,pt.1 . 2.25
191 JB/ECh,Skull on the Seas,pt.2
   Thulsa Doom Vs.Thoth-Amon . 2.25
192 JB/ECh,Skull on the Seas,pt.3
   B.U. King Kull 2.25
193 JB/ECh,Skull on the Seas concl.
   V:Thulsa Doom & Thoth-Amon 2.25
194 JB/ECh,Wanted for Murder,
   B.U. Li-Zya 2.25
195 JB/ECh,V:Yamatains,
   Giant Tortoise 2.25
196 JB/ECh,Treasure of the Stygian
   Prince-Toth-Mekri,A:Valeria . 2.25
197 RTs,JB,EC,Red Hand 2.25
198 RTs,JB,EC,Red Hand 2.25
199 RTs,JB,EC,V:Black Zarona . . 2.25
200 RTs,JB,ECh,JJu(c),The Barbarian

from Cross Plains 2.25
201 RTs,MCW,return to Tarantia . 2.25
202 RTs,JB,ECh,Conan in the City
   of Magicians,pt.1 . . . . 2.25
203 RTs,JB,ECh,Conan in the City
   of Magicians,pt.2 . . . . 2.25
204 RTs,JB,ECh,Conan in the City
   of Magicians,pt.3 . . . . 2.25
205 RTs,JB,ECh,Conan in the City
   of Magicians,pt.4 . . . . 2.25
206 RTs,JB,ECh,BLr(c),Conan in the
   City of Magicians,concl. 2.25
207 RTs,JB,ECh,MK(c), Conan and
   the Spider God, pt.1 . . . . 2.25
208 RTs,JB,ECh, Conan and the
   Spider God, pt.2 . . . . 2.25
209 RTs,JB,Conan and the
   Spider God,pt.3 . . . . 2.25
210 RTs,Conan and the
   Spider God,pt.4 . . . . 2.25
211 RTs,Conan and the Gods of
   the Mountain,pt.1 . . . . 2.25
212 RTs,Conand and the Gos of
   the Mountain,pt.2 . . . . 2.25
213 RTs,Conan and the Gods of
   the Mountain,pt.3 . . . . 2.25
214 RTs,Conan and the Gods of
   the Mountain,pt.4 . . . . 2.25
215 RTs,JuB(c),Conan and the Gods
   of the Mountain,concl. 2.25
216 RTs,AA,Vengeance of Nitocris 2.25
217 RTs,Conan theMercenary,pt.1 2.25
218 RTs,Conan theMercenary,pt.2 2.25
219 RTs,A:Solomon Kane 2.25
220 RTs,V:Skull Out of Time 2.25
221 RTs,C.L.Moore story adapt. . 2.25
222 RTs,The Haunter of the Towers
   B.U,JB,Conan Barbarian #1 . . 2.25
223 RTs,A:Tuzune Thune 2.25
224 RTs,JWk,The Dwellers Under the
   Tombs,adapt. B.U.V:Dinosaurs 2.25
225 . . . . 2.25
226 RTs,EN(c),The Four Ages
   of Conan, A:Red Sonja 2.25
227 RTs,JBu, besieged in a lost
   city, B.U. Kull,Red Sonja 2.25
228 RTs,AN,Conan in chains! . . . 2.25
229 RTs 2.25
230 RTs, Acheron falls, Ring of
   Tkrubu,pt.2, R:Kull 2.25
231 RTs, V:Tuzoun Thune. B.U.
   EM,Red Sonja 2.25
232 RTs 2.25
233 A:Juma the Black, Kull 2.25
234 RTs,JBu, A:Nefartari;
   A:Red Sonja, Zula 2.25
235 RTs,JBu,The Daughter of
   Raktauanishi, final issue 2.25
Ann.#1 SB,BWS,inc.'Beware the
   Wrath of Anu',B.U. King
   Kull Vs.Thulsa Doom 2.25

SAVAGE TALES
May, 1971
(black & white magazine)
1 GM,BWS,JR,I&O:Man-Thing,
   B:Conan,Femizons,A:Kazar 150.00
2 GM,FB,BWS,AW,BWr,A:King
   Kull rep,Creatures on
   the Loose #10 . . . . 50.00
3 FB,BWS,AW,JSo 35.00
4 NA(c),E:Conan 20.00
5 JSn,JB,B:Brak the Barbarian 20.00
6 NA(c),JB,AW,B:Kazar 8.00
7 GM,NA 6.00

8 JB,A:Shanna,E:Brak 5.00
9 MK,A:Shanna 5.00
10 RH,NA,AW,A:Shanna 5.00
11 RH 5.00
12 Summer, 1975 . . . . 5.00
Ann.#1 GM,GK,BWS,O:Kazar . . . 6.00

SAVAGE TALES
Nov., 1985
(black & white magazine)
1 MGo,I:The 'Nam 2.00
2 MGo 4.00
3 MGo 4.00
4 MGo 4.00
5 MGo 4.00
6 MGo 3.00
7 MGo 3.00
8 MGo 3.00
9 MGo,March, 1987 . . . . 3.00

SCARLET SPIDER
1 HMe,GK,TP,VirtualMortality,pt.3 1.95
2 HMe,JR2,AW,CyberWar,pt.3 . . 1.95

SCARLET SPIDER UNLIMITED
1 True Origin,64pg 3.95

SCARLET WITCH
1 ALa(s),DAn(s),JH,I:Gargan,
   C:Master Pandemonium 2.00
2 C:Avengers West Coast 2.00
3 A:Avengers West Coast 2.00
4 V:Lore,last issue 2.00

SCOOBY-DOO
Oct., 1977
1 B:DynoMutt 1.50
2 thru 8 . . . . @1.00
9 Feb., 1979 . . . . 1.00

SECRET DEFENDERS
1 F:Dr.Strange(in all),Spider
   Woman,Nomad,Darkhawk,
   Wolverine,V:Macabre 3.25
2 F:Spider Woman,Nomad,Darkhawk,
   Wolverine,V:Macabre 2.50
3 F:Spider Woman,Nomad,Darkhawk,
   Wolverine,V:Macabre 2.00
4 F:Namorita,Punisher,
   Sleepwalker,V:Roadkill 2.00
5 F:Naromita,Punisher,
   Sleepwalker, V:Roadkill 2.00
6 F:Spider-Man,Scarlet Witch,Captain
   America,V:Suicide Pack 2.00
7 F:Captain America,Scarlet Witch,
   Spider-Man 2.00
8 F:Captain America,Scarlet Witch,
   Spider-Man 2.00
9 F:War Machine,Thunderstrike,
   Silver Surfer 2.00
10 F:War Machine,Thunderstrike,
   Silver Surfer 2.00
11 TGb,F:Hulk,Nova,Northstar . . 2.00
12 RMz(s),TGb,F:Thanos 2.75
13 RMz(s),TGb,F:Thanos,Super Skrull,
   Rhino,Nitro,Titanium Man 2.00
14 RMz(s),TGb,F:Thanos,Super Skrull,
   Rhino,Nitro,Titanium Man,
   A:Silver Surfer 2.00
15 F:Dr.Druid,Cage,Deadpool . . 2.25
16 F:Dr.Druid,Cage,Deadpool . . 2.25
17 F:Dr.Druid,Cage,Deadpool . . 2.25

MARVEL

Secret Defenders #22
© Marvel Entertainment Group

18 F:Iron Fist,Giant Man	2.25
19 F:Dr.Druid,Cadaver,	
Shadowoman	1.95
20 V:Venom	1.95
21 V:Slaymaker	1.95
22 Final Defense,pt.1	1.95
23 Final Defense,pt.2	1.95
24 Final Defense,pt.3	1.95
25 V:Dr.Druid	1.95

SECRET WARS
May, 1984

1 MZ,A:X-Men,Fant.Four,Avengers,	
Hulk,SpM in All,I:Beyonder	4.00
2 MZ,V:Magneto	3.00
3 MZ,I:Titania & Volcana	3.00
4 BL,V:Molecule Man	3.00
5 BL,F:X-Men	3.00
6 MZ,V:Doctor Doom	3.00
7 MZ,I:New Spiderwoman	3.50
8 MZ,I:Alien Black Costume	
(for Spider-Man)	12.00
9 MZ,V:Galactus	2.00
10 MZ,V:Dr.Doom	2.00
11 MZ,V:Dr.Doom	2.00
12 MZ,Beyonder Vs. Dr.Doom	2.50
TPB rep #1-#12	19.95

SECRET WARS II
July, 1985

1 AM,SL,A:X-Men,New Mutants	2.00
2 AM,SL,A:Fantastic Four	1.50
3 AM,SL,A:Daredevil	1.50
4 AM,I:Kurse	1.50
5 AM,SL,I:Boom Boom	2.50
6 AM,SL,A:Mephisto	1.50
7 AM,SL,A:Thing	1.50
8 AM,SL,A:Hulk	1.50
9 AM,SL,A:Everyone,double-size	2.00

SECTAURS
June, 1985

1 Based on toys	1.50
2	1.00
3	1.00
4	1.00
5 thru 10 1986	@1.00

SEMPER FI
Dec., 1988

1 JSe	2.00
2 JSe	1.50
3 JSe	1.50
4 JSe	1.50
5 JSe	1.50
6	1.50
7	1.00
8	1.00
9 August, 1989,final issue	1.00

SENSATIONAL SPIDER-MAN

1 KM/TP/KJ,Rep.	5.95

SENSATIONAL SPIDER-MAN
(Jan. 1996)

0 DJu,KJ,Return of Spider-Man,pt.1	
Lenticular cover	5.00
1 DJu,KJ,Media Blizzard,pt.1,	
V:New Mysterio	1.95
2 DJu,KJ,Return of Kaine,pt.2	1.95
3 DJu,KJ,Web of Carnage,pt.1	1.95
4 DJu,KJ,Blood Brothers,pt.1	1.95
5 DJu	1.95
6 DJu	1.95
7 TDz,A:Onslaught	1.95
8 TDz,The Looter	1.95
9 TDz,Onslaught tie-in	1.95
10 TDz,RCa,V:Swarm	1.95
11 TDz,Revelations, pt.2	1.95
11A bagged with card, etc.	5.00
12 TDz,SwM, V:Trapster	1.95
13 TDz,RCa,A:Ka-zar, Shanna	1.95
14 TDz,RCa,Savage Land saga	1.95
15 TDz,RCa,Savage Land saga	1.95
16 TDz,RCa,R:Black Cat,	
V:Prowler,Vulture	1.95
17 TDz,RCa,V:Black Cat,	
Prowler,Vulture	1.95
18 TDz,RCa,V:Vulture	1.95
19 TDz,RCa,R:Living Monolith	1.95
Minus 1 Spec.,TDz,RCa, flashback	1.95
TPB In the Savage Land	
rep.#13-#15	
Wizard mini-comic	1.00

SENSATIONAL SPIDER-MAN '96

TPB JMD,SwM, seq. to Kraven's	
Last Hunt, 64pg.	2.95

SERGEANT BARNEY BARKER
August, 1956

1 JSe,Comedy	70.00
2 JSe,Army Inspection(c)	50.00
3 JSe,Tank(c)	50.00
Becomes:	

G.I. TALES

4 JSe,At Grips with the Enemy	35.00
5	20.00
6 JO,BP,GWb, July, 1957	25.00

SGT. FURY & HIS HOWLING COMMANDOS
May, 1963–Dec. 1981

1 Seven Against the Nazis	1,000.00
2 JK,Seven Doomed Men	300.00
3 JK,Midnight on Massacre	
Mountain	175.00
4 JK,V:Lord Ha-Ha,D:Junior	
Juniper	175.00
5 JK,V:Baron Strucker	175.00
6 JK,The Fangs of the Fox	125.00
7 JK,Fury Court Martial	125.00
8 JK,V:Dr Zemo,I:Percival	
Pinkerton	125.00
9 DAy,V:Hitler	125.00
10 DAy,On to Okinwawa,I:Capt.	
Savage	125.00
11 DAy,V:Capt.Flint	75.00
12 DAy,Howler deserts	75.00
13 DAy,JK,A;Capt.America	275.00
14 DAy,V:Baron Strucker	75.00
15 DAy,SD,Too Small to Fight	
Too Young to Die	75.00
16 DAy,In The Desert a Fortress	
Stands	75.00
17 DAy,While the Jungle Sleeps	75.00
18 DAy,Killed in Action	75.00
19 DAy,An Eye for an Eye	75.00
20 DAy,V:the Blitz Squad	75.00
21 DAy,To Free a Hostage	50.00
22 DAy,V:Bull McGiveney	50.00
23 DAy,The Man who Failed	50.00
24 DAy,When the Howlers Hit	
the Home Front	50.00
25 DAy,Every Man my Enemy	50.00
26 DAy,Dum Dum Does it the	
Hard Way	50.00
27 DAy,O:Fury's Eyepatch	50.00
28 DAy,Not a Man Shall Remain	
Alive	50.00
29 DAy,V:Baron Strucker	50.00
30 DAy,Incident in Italy	50.00
31 Day,Into the Jaws of Death	25.00
32 DAy,A Traitor in Our Midst	25.00
33 DAy,The Grandeur That was	
Greece	25.00
34 DAy,O:Howling Commandoes	25.00
35 DAy,Berlin Breakout,J:Eric	
Koenig	25.00
36 DAy,My Brother My Enemy	25.00
37 DAy,In the Desert to Die	25.00
38 This Ones For Dino	25.00
39 Into the Fortress of Fear	25.00
40 That France Might be Free	25.00
41 V:The Blitzers	25.00
42 Three Were AWOL	25.00
43 Scourge of the Sahara,A:Bob	
Hope,Glen Miller	25.00
44 JSe,The Howlers First Mission	25.00
45 JSe,I:The War Lover	25.00
46 JSe,They Also Serve	25.00
47 Tea and Sabotage	25.00
48 A:Blitz Squad	25.00
49 On to Tarawa	25.00
50 The Invasion Begins	25.00
51 The Assassin	25.00
52 Triumph at Treblinka	25.00
53 To the Bastions of Bavaria	25.00
54 Izzy Shoots the Works	25.00
55 Cry of Battle, Kiss of Death	20.00
56 Gabriel Blow Your Horn	20.00
57 TS,The Informer	20.00
58 Second Front	20.00
59 D-Day for Dum Dum	20.00
60 Authorised Personnel Only	20.00
61 The Big Breakout	20.00
62 The Basic Training of Fury	20.00
63 V:Nazi Tanks	20.00
64 The Peacemonger,A:Capt	
Savage	20.00

MARVEL

65 Eric Koenig,Traitor 20 00
66 Liberty Rides the Underground 20.00
67 With a Little Help From My
Friends 20.00
68 Welcome Home Soldier 20.00
69 While the City Sleeps 20.00
70 The Missouri Marauders . . . 20.00
71 Burn,Bridge,Burn 20.00
72 Battle in the Sahara 20.00
73 Rampage on the
Russian Front 20.00
74 Each Man Alone 20.00
75 The Deserter 15.00
76 He Fought the Red Baron . . . 15.00
77 A Traitor's Trap,A:Eric Koenig 15.00
78 Escape or Die 15.00
79 Death in the High Castle 15.00
80 To Free a Hostage 15.00
81 The All American 15.00
82 Howlers Hit The
Home Front,rep 15.00
83 Dum DumV:Man-Mountain
McCoy 15.00

Sgt. Fury #69
© *Marvel Entertainment Group*

84 The Devil's Disciple 15.00
85 Fury V:The Howlers 15.00
86 Germ Warfare 15.00
87 Dum Dum does it...rep 15.00
88 Save General Patton 15.00
89 O:Fury's eyepatch,rep 15.00
90 The Chain That Binds 15.00
91 Not A Man...rep 12.00
92 Some Die Slowly 12.00
93 A Traitor...rep 12.00
94 GK(c),Who'll Stop the Bombs 12.00
95 7 Doomed Men, rep 12.00
96 GK(c),Dum-Dum Sees it
Through 12.00
97 Till the Last Man Shall Fail . . 12.00
98 A:Deadly Dozen 12.00
99 Guerillas in Greece 12.00
100 When a Howler Falls 12.00
101 Pearl Harbor 7.00
102 Death For A Dollar 7.00
103 Berlin Breakout 7.00
104 The Tanks Are Coming 7.00
105 My Brother,My Enemy 7.00
106 Death on the Rhine 7.00
107 Death-Duel in the Desert . . . 7.00

108 Slaughter From the Skies . . . 7.00
109 This Ones For Dino,rep 7.00
110 JSe(c),The Reserve 7.00
111 V:Colonel Klaw 7.00
112 V:Baron Strucker 7.00
113 That France Might
Be Free,rep 7.00
114 Jungle Bust Out 7.00
115 V:Baron Strucker 7.00
116 End of the Road 7.00
117 Blitz Over Britain 7.00
118 War Machine 7.00
118 War Machine 7.00
119 They Strike by Machine 7.00
120 Trapped in the Compound of
Death 7.00
121 An Eye for an Eye 5.00
122 A;The Blitz Squad 5.00
123 To Free a Hostage 5.00
124 A:Bull McGiveney 5.00
125 The Man Who Failed 5.00
126 When the Howlers Hit Home.. 5.00
127 Everyman My Enemy,rep . . . 5.00
128 Dum Dum does it...rep 5.00
129 O:Fury's Eyepatch 5.00
130 A:Baron Strucker 5.00
131 Armageddon 5.00
132 Incident in Italy 5.00
133 thru 140 . . . . @5.00
141 thru 150 . . . . @5.00
151 thru 160 . . . . @4.00
161 thru 167 . . . . @4.00
Ann.#1 Korea #4,#5 . . . . 90.00
Ann.#2 This was D-Day 50.00
Ann.#3 Vietnam 30.00
Ann.#4 Battle of the Bulge 15.00
Ann.#5 Desert Fox 7.50
Ann.#6 Blaze of Battle 7.50
Ann.#7 Armageddon 7.50

SERGIO ARAGONES
MASSACRES MARVEL
1-shot Parody 4.95

SEVEN BLOCK
Epic 1990
1 . . . . 2.50

SHADOWMASTERS
Oct., 1989–Jan. 1990
1 RH 11.00
2 . . . . 7.00
3 . . . . 6.00
4 . . . . 5.00

SHADOWRIDERS
1 I:Shadowriders,A:Cable,
Ghost Rider 2.00
2 A:Ghost Rider 2.00
3 A:Cable 2.00
4 A:Cable 2.00

SHANNA, THE SHE-DEVIL
Dec., 1972–Aug. 1973
1 GT,F:Shanna 7.50
2 RA,The Dungeon of Doom . . . 5.00
3 RA,The Hour of the Bull 3.00
4 RA,Mandrill 3.00
5 JR(c),RA,V:Nekra 3.00

SHEENA
Dec., 1984–Feb. 1985
1 and 2 Movie adapt . . . . @1.00

She-Hulk #18
© *Marvel Entertainment Group*

SHE-HULK
Feb., 1980
[1st Regular Series]
1 JB,BWi,I&O:She-Hulk 4.00
2 BWi,D:She-Hulk's best friend . . 2.50
3 BWi,Wanted for Murder 2.50
4 BWi,V:Her Father 2.50
5 BWi,V:Silver Serpent 2.50
6 A:Iron Man 2.00
7 BWi,A:Manthing 2.00
8 BWi,A:Manthing 2.00
9 BWi,Identity Crisis 2.00
10 V:The Word 2.00
11 BWi,V:Dr.Morbius 2.00
12 V:Gemini 2.00
13 V:Man-Wolf 1.50
14 V:Hellcat 1.50
15 V:Lady Kills 1.50
16 She Hulk Goes Berserk 1.50
17 V:Man-Elephant 1.50
18 V:Grappler 1.50
19 V:Her Father 1.50
20 A:Zapper 1.50
21 V:Seeker 1.50
22 V:Radius 1.50
23 V:Radius 1.50
24 V:Zapper 1.50
25 Double-sized,last issue 2.00
[2nd Regular Series]
1 JBy,V:Ringmaster 2.50
2 JBy 2.25
3 JBy,A:Spider-Man 2.25
4 JBy,I:Blond Phantom 2.25
5 JBy 2.25
6 JBy,A:U.S.1,Razorback 2.25
7 JBy,A:U.S.1,Razarback 2.25
8 JBy,A:Saint Nicholas 2.25
9 AM(i) 2.00
10 AM(i) 2.00
11 . . . . 2.00
12 . . . . 2.00
13 SK(c) 2.00
14 MT(c),A:Howard the Duck 2.00
15 SK(c) 2.00
16 SK(c) 2.00
17 SK(c),V:Dr.Angst 2.00

MARVEL

18 SK(c) 2.00
19 SK(c),V:Nosferata 2.00
20 SK(c),Darkham Asylum 2.00
21 SK(c),V:Blonde Phantom 2.00
22 SK(c),V:Blonde Phantom,A:All
   Winners Squad 2.00
23 V:Blonde Phantom 2.00
24 V:Deaths'Head 4.00
25 A:Hercules,Thor 2.00
26 A:Excalibur 2.00
27 Cartoons in N.Y. 2.00
28 Game Hunter Stalks She-Hulk   2.00
29 A:Wolv.,Hulk,SpM,Venom . . . 2.50
30 MZ(c),A:Silver Surfer,Thor
   Human Torch 2.25
31 JBy,V:Spragg the Living Hill . . 2.50
32 JBy,A:Moleman,V:Spragg 2.00
33 JBy,A:Moleman,V:Spragg 2.00
34 JBy,Returns to New York 2.00
35 JBy,V:X-Humed Men 2.00
36 JBy,X-mas issue (#8 tie-in) . . . 2.00
37 JBy,V:Living Eraser 2.00
38 JBy,V:Mahkizmo 2.00
39 JBy,V:Mahkizmo 2.00
40 JBy,V:Spraggs,Xemnu 2.00
41 JBy,V:Xemnu 2.00
42 JBy,V:USArcher 2.00
43 JBy,V:Xemnu 2.00
44 JBy,R:Rocket Raccoon 2.00
45 JBy,A:Razorback 2.00
46 JBy,A:Rocket Raccoon 2.00
47 V:D'Bari 2.00
48 JBy,A:Rocket Raccoon 2.00
49 V:Skrulls,D'Bari 2.00
50 JBy,WS,TA,DGb,AH,HC,
   D:She-Hulk 4.00
51 TMo,V:Savage She-Hulk 2.00
52 D:She-Hulk,A:Thing,Mr.Fantastic,
   I:Rumbler,V:Titania 2.00
53 AH(c),A:Zapper 2.00
54 MGo(c),A:Wonder Man 2.00
55 V:Rumbler 2.00
56 A:War Zone 2.00
57 A:Hulk 2.00
58 V:Electro 2.00
59 V:Various Villains 2.00
60 last issue 2.00
TPB rep. #1-#8 . . . . 12.95

SHE HULK: CEREMONY
1 JBr/SDr 4.00
2 JBr/FS 4.00

SHIELD
Feb., 1973
1 . . . . 4.00
2 . . . . 3.00
3 . . . . 3.00
4 . . . . 3.00
5 Oct., 1973 . . . . 3.00

SHOGUN WARRIORS
Feb., 1979
1 HT,DGr,F:Raydeen, Combatra,
   Dangard Ace 4.00
2 HT,DGr,V:Elementals of Evil . . 2.50
3 AM(c),HT,DGr,V:Elementals
   of Evil 2.50
4 HT,DGr,'Menace of the
   Mech Monsters' 2.50
5 HT,DGr,'Into The Lair
   of Demons' 2.50
6 HT,ME 2.00
7 HT,ME 2.00

8 HT,ME 2.00
9 'War Beneath The Waves' . . . 2.00
10 'Five Heads of Doom' 2.00
11 TA(c) 2.00
12 WS(c) 2.00
13 'Demons on the Moon' 2.00
14 V:Dr. Demonicus 2.00
15 . . . . 2.00
16 . . . . 2.00
17 . . . . 2.00
18 . . . . 2.00
19 A:Fantastic Four 2.50
20 Sept., 1980 . . . . 2.00

SHROUD
Limited Series
1 B:MiB(s),MCW,A:Spider-Man,
   V:Scorpion 2.00
2 MCW,A:Spider-Man,V:Scorpion 2.00
3 MCW,I:Kali 2.00
4 MCW,Final Issue 2.00

SILVERHAWKS
August, 1987
1 thru 5 . . . . @1.00
6 June, 1988 . . . . 1.00

SILVER SABLE
1 Foil stamped(c),A:Sandman,
   Spider-Man 3.00
2 I:Gattling 2.00
3 V:Gattling,Foreigner 1.75
4 Infinity War,V:Doctor Doom . . 1.75
5 Infinity War,V:Doctor Doom . . 1.50
6 A:Deathlok 1.50
7 A:Deathlok 1.50
8 V:Hydra 1.50
9 O:Silver Sable 1.50
10 A:Punisher,Leviathan 1.50
11 Cyber Warriors,Hydra 1.50
12 V:Cyberwarriorss,R:Sandman . 1.50
13 For Love Nor Money#3,
   A:Cage,Terror 1.50
14 For Love Nor Money#6,
   A:Cage,Terror 1.50
15 V:Viper,A:Captain America . . . 1.50
16 SBt,Infinty Crusade 1.50
17 Infinity Crusade 1.50
18 A:Venom 1.50
19 Siege of Darkness x-over 1.50
20 GWt(s),StB,BU:Sandman,Fin . 1.50
21 Gang War 1.50
22 . . . . 1.50
23 GWt(s),A:Deadpool,Daredevil,
   BU:Sandman 1.50
24 GWt(s),BU:Crippler,w/card . . 1.75
25 V:Hydra 2.25
26 F:Sandman 1.75
27 A:Code Blue 1.50
28 F:Chen 1.50
29 A:Wild Pack 1.50
30 problems with law 1.50
31 V:terrorists 1.50
32 A:The Foreigner 1.50
33 V:Hammerhead 1.50
34 . . . . 1.50
35 Li'l Silvie Tale 1.50

SILVER SURFER
[1st Series]
August, 1968
1 B:StL(s),JB,JSr,GC,O:Silver Surfer,
   O:Watcher,I:Shala Bal 450.00
2 JB,JSr,GC,A:Watcher 165.00

3 JB,JSr,GC,I:Mephisto 135.00
4 JB,A:Thor,low distribution
   scarce 425.00
5 JB,A:Fant.Four,V:Stranger . . . 85.00
6 JB,FB,A:Watcher 100.00
7 JB,A:Watcher,I:Frankenstein's
   Monster 85.00
8 JB,DA,A:Mephisto,I:Ghost . . . 60.00
9 JB,DA,A:Mephisto,A:Ghost . . 60.00
10 JB,DA,South America 60.00
11 JB,DA 50.00
12 JB,DA,V:The Abomination . . . 50.00
13 JB,DA,V:Doomsday Man 50.00
14 JB,DA,A:Spider-Man 70.00
15 JB,DA,A:Human Torch 50.00
16 JB,V:Mephisto 50.00
17 JB,V:Mephisto 50.00
18 E:StL(s),JK,V:Inhumans 50.00
[2nd Regular Series]
1 JBy,TP,Direct Only,V:Mephisto 10.00
[3rd Regular Series]
1 MR,JRu,A:Fantastic Four,
   Galactus,V:Champion 12.00
2 MR,A:Shalla Bal,V:Skrulls 8.00
3 MR,V:Collector & Runner 7.00
4 MR,JRu,A:Elders,I:Obliterator . 7.00
5 MR,JRu,V:Obliterator 6.00
6 MR,JRu,O:Obliterator,A:Kree,
   Skrulls 6.00
7 MR,JRu,V:Supremor,Elders/
   Soul Gems 5.00
8 MR,JRu,V:Supremor 5.00
9 MR,Elders Vs.Galactus 5.00
10 MR,A:Galactus,Eternity 5.00
11 JSon,JRu,V:Reptyl 4.50
12 MR,JRu,V:Reptyl,A:Nova 4.50
13 JSon,DC,V:Ronan 4.50
14 JSon,JRu,V:Skrull Surfer 4.50
15 RLm,JRu,A:Fantastic Four . . . 8.00
16 RLm,Inbetweener possesses
   Soul Gem,A:Fantastic Four . . 5.00
17 RLm,A:Inbetweener,Galactus,
   Fantastic Four,D:Trader,
   Possessor,Astronomer 5.00
18 RLm,Galactus V:Inbetweener . 5.00
19 RLm,MR,V:Firelord 4.50
20 RLm,A:Superskrull,Galactus . . 4.50
21 MR,DC,V:Obliterator 4.50

Silver Surfer (3rd Series) #13
© Marvel Entertainment Group

---

22 RLm,V:Ego 4.50
23 RLm,V:Dragon 4.50
24 RLm,V:G.I.G.O. 4.50
25 RLm,V:Ronan,Kree Skrull War . 4.50
26 RLm,V:Nenora 4.50
27 RLm,V:Stranger 4.50
28 RLm,D:Super Skrull,V:Reptyl . 4.50
29 RLm,V:Midnight Sun 4.50
30 RLm,V:Midnight Sun 4.50
31 RLm,O:Living Tribunal &
   Stranger (double size) 5.50
32 RF,JSt,A:Mephisto 4.50
33 Rlm,V:Impossible Man 4.50
34 RLm,(1stJSn),2nd R:Thanos . . 7.00
35 RLm,A:Thanos,R:Drax 5.00
36 RLm,V:Impossible Man,A:Warlock
   Capt.Marvel,C:Thanos 3.00
37 RLm,V:Drax,A:Mentor 3.00
38 RLm,V:Thanos(continued in
   Thanos Quest) 4.00
39 JSh,V:Algol 3.50
40 RLm,V:Dynamo City 3.00
41 RLm,V:Dynamo City,A:Thanos 3.00

Silver Surfer (3rd Series) #65
© Marvel Entertainment Group

42 RLm,V:Dynamo City,A:Drax . . 3.00
43 RLm,V:DynamoCity 3.00
44 RLm,R:Thanos,Drax,
   O:Inf.Gems 3.00
45 RLm,Thanos vs. Mephisto . . . 4.00
46 RLm,R:Warlock,A:Thanos 5.00
47 RLm,Warlock V:Drax,
   A:Thanos 4.00
48 RLm,A:Galactus,Thanos 4.00
49 RLm,V:Thanos Monster 3.00
50 RLm,Silver Stamp(D.size),
   V:Thanos Monster 8.00
50a 2nd printing 2.50
50b 3rd printing 2.50
51 RLm,Infinity Gauntlet x-over . . 3.00
52 RLm,Infinity Gauntlet x-over . 3.00
53 RLm,Infinity Gauntlet x-over . 2.00
54 RLm,I.Gauntlet x-over,V:Rhino 2.50
55 RLm,I.Gauntlet x-over,Universe
   According to Thanos,pt.1 . . . . 2.50
56 RLm,I.Gauntlet x-over,Universe
   According to Thanos,pt.2 . . . . 2.50

57 RLm,Infinity Gauntlet x-over . . 2.50
58 RLm,(c),Infinity Gauntlet x-over,
   A:Hulk,Namor,Dr.Strange 2.50
59 RLm,(c),TR,Infinity Gauntlet,
   Thanos V:Silver Surfer 2.50
60 RLm,V:Midnight Sun,
   A:Inhumans 2.00
61 RLm,I:Collection.Agency 2.00
62 RLm,O:Collection Agency 2.00
63 RLm,A:Captain Marvel 2.00
64 RLm,V:Dark Silver Surfer 2.00
65 RLm,R:Reptyl,I:Princess
   Alaisa 2.00
66 RLm,I:Avatar,Love & Hate . . . 2.00
67 RLm,(c),KWe,Inf.War,V:Galactus
   A:DrStrange 2.00
68 RLm,(c),KWe,Inf.War,O:Nova . 2.00
69 RLm,(c),KWe,Infinity War,
   A:Galactus 2.00
70 RLm,(c),Herald War#1,I:Morg . 2.00
71 RLm,(c),Herald War#2,V:Morg . 2.00
72 RLm,(c),Herald War#3,R:Nova . 2.00
73 RLm,R:Airwalker 2.00
74 RLm,V:Terrax 2.00
75 RLm,E:Herald Ordeal,V:Morg,
   D:Nova 3.00
76 RLm,A:Jack of Hearts 1.50
77 RLm,A:Jack of Hearts 1.50
78 RLm,R:Morg,V:Nebula 1.50
79 RLm,V:Captain Atlas 1.50
80 RLm,I:Ganymede,Terrax
   Vs.Morg 1.50
81 RLm,O:Ganymede,I:Tyrant . . . 1.50
82 RLm,V:Tyrant,double sized . . . 2.50
83 Infinity Crusade 1.50
84 RLm,(c),Infinity Crusade 1.50
85 RLm,(c),Infinity Crusade 2.50
86 RLm,(c), Blood & Thunder,pt.2
   V:Thor,A:Beta Ray Bill 1.50
87 RLm,(c),Blood & Thunder,pt.7 . 1.50
88 RLm,(c),Blood & Thunder,pt.10 . 1.50
89 RLm,(c),CDo,C:Legacy 1.50
90 RLm,(c),A:Legacy,C:Avatar . . . 1.50
91 RLm 1.50
92 RLm,V:Avatar 1.75
93 V:Human Torch 1.75
94 A:Fantastic Four, Warlock 1.75
95 SEa,A:Fantastic Four 1.50
96 A:Fantastic Four,Hulk 1.50
97 A:Fantastic Four,R:Nova 1.50
98 R:Champion 1.50
99 A:Nova 1.50
100 V:Mephisto 2.25
100a enhanced ed. 3.95
101 RMz,JoP,A:Shalla Bal 1.50
102 V:Galactus 1.50
103 I:Death quad 1.50
104 Surfer Rampage 1.50
105 V:Super Skrull 1.50
106 A:Legacy,Morg 1.50
107 TGb,BAn,A:Galactus,Morg,
   Tyrant 1.50
108 Galactus Vs. Tyrant 1.50
109 Morg has Ultimate Nulifier . . . 1.50
110 JB,F:Nebula 1.50
111 GP,TGb,BAn,to Other Side
   of Galaxy 1.95
112 GP,TGb,BAn, ... 1.95
113 GP,TGb,BAn,V:Blackbody . . . 1.95
114 . . . . 1.95
115 GP,TGb,BAn,Surfer in pieces 1.95
116 GP,TGb,BAn,Pieces cause
   trouble 1.95
117 . . . . 1.95
118 . . . . 1.50

119 . . . . 1.50
120 . . . . 1.50
121 A:Quasar, Beta Ray Bill 1.50
122 GP,SEa, returns to Marvel
   Universe 1.50
123 GP,RG 1.50
124 GP,RG 1.50
125 RG,V:Hulk, double size 2.50
126 JMD,RG,BWi,A:Dr. Strange . . 1.50
127 JMD,RG,BWi,A:Alicia Masters 1.50
128 JMD,RG,BWi,V:Puppet Master 1.50
129 JMD,RG,BWi,back in time,
   late 1940s 1.50
130 JMD,CNr,BWi, trapped in past 1.50
131 JMD,RG,BWi, ... 1.50
Minus 1 Spec., JMD,RG,BWi,
   flashback, first human contact . 1.95
Ann.#1 RLm,JSon,Evolution War . 7.00
Ann.#2 RLm,Atlantis Attacks 5.00
Ann.#3 RLm,Lifeform #4 . . . . 4.00
Ann.#4 RLm,Korvac Quest #3,A:
   Guardians of Galaxy 3.00
Ann.#5 RLm,Ret.o/Defenders #3 . 2.50
Ann.#6 RLm,(c),I:Legacy,w/card . 3.75
GNv The Enslavers,KP 16.95
GNv Homecoming,
   A:Moondragon 12.95
TPB Rebirth of Thanos,reprints
   #34-38 . . . . 12.95
Ashcan .75

SILVER SURFER '97
1 JMD,VS,KJ,V:Scrier, 48pg 2.00

SILVER SURFER
Epic Dec., 1988
1 Moebius,V:Galactus 3.00
2 Moebius,V:Galactus 3.00
Graphic Novel 14.95

SILVER SURFER:
DANGEROUS ARTIFACTS
1-shot RMz,Galactus, Thanos . . . 3.95

SILVER SURFER
THE ENSLAVERS
1 KP 16.95

SILVER SURFER/
SUPERMAN
Marvel/DC 1996
Spec. GP,RLm,TA, x-over 5.95

SILVER SURFER VS.
DRACULA
1 rep,MWn(s),GC,TP 1.75

SILVER SURFER/
WARLOCK:
RESURRECTION
1 JSn,V:Mephisto,Death 3.50
2 JSn,TA,V:Death 3.00
3 JSn,TA,V:Mephisto 3.00
4 JSn,TA,V:Mephisto 3.00

SILVER SURFER/
WEAPON ZERO
Marvel/Top Cow 1996
1-shot Devil's Reign, pt.8 . . . . . . 4.00

MARVEL

MARVEL

SISTERHOOD OF STEEL
Epic Dec., 1984

1 I:Sisterhood		2.00
2		2.00
3		2.00
4 thru 8		@1.50

SIX FROM SIRIUS
Epic July, 1984

1 PG,limited series		3.00
2 PG		2.00
3 PG		2.00
4 PG		2.00

SIX FROM SIRIUS II
Epic Feb., 1986

1 PG		1.75

SIX-GUN WESTERN
Atlas Jan., 1957

1 JSe(c),RC,JR,'Kid Yukon Gunslinger'		100.00
2 SSh,AW,DAy,JO,'His Guns Hang Low'		75.00
3 AW,BP,DAy		75.00
4 JSe(c),JR,GWb		50.00

SKELETON WARRIORS

1 based on cartoon		1.50
2 Legion of Light		1.50
3 V:Grimstar		1.50
4 Grimskull abandons Legion of Light		1.50

SKRULL KILL CREW

1 I:Kill Crew		2.95
2 V:Hydra		2.95
3 V:Captain America		2.95
4 V:Fantastic Four		2.95
5 Conclusion		2.95

SKULL, THE SLAYER
August, 1975

1 GK(c),O:Skull the Slayer		2.50
2 GK(c),'Man Against Gods'		1.50
3 'Trapped in the Tower of Time'		1.50
4 'Peril of the Pyramids', A:Black Knight		1.50
5 A:Black Knight		1.50
6 'The Savage Sea'		1.50
7 'Dungeon of Blood'		1.50
8 JK(c),Nov., 1976		1.50

SLAPSTICK

1 TA(i),I:Slapstick		1.50
2 TA(i),A:Spider-Man,V:Overkill		1.25
3 V:Dr.Denton		1.25
4 A:GR,DD,FF,Cap.America		1.25

SLEDGE HAMMER
Feb., 1988

1		1.25
2 March, 1988		1.00

SLEEPWALKER
June, 1991

1 BBl,I:Rick Sheridan,C:8-Ball		3.00
2 BBl,V:8-Ball		2.00
3 BBl,A:Avengers,X-Men,X-Factor, FF,I:Cobweb,O:Sleepwalker		1.75

Sleepwalker #31
© Marvel Entertainment Group

4 RL,I:Bookworm		1.75
5 BBl,A:SpM,K.Pin,V:Ringleader		1.75
6 BBl,A:SpM,Inf.Gauntlet x-over		1.75
7 BBl,Infinity Gauntlet x-over, V:Chain Gang		1.75
8 BBl,A:Deathlok		1.50
9 BBl,I:Lullaby		1.50
10 BBl,MM,I:Dream-Team		1.50
11 BBl,V:Ghost Rider		1.50
12 JQ,A:Nightmare		2.50
13 BBl,MM,I:Spectra		1.50
14 BBl,MM,V:Spectra		1.50
15 BBl,MM,I:Thought Police		1.50
16 BBl,MM,A:Mr.Fantastic,Thing		1.50
17 BBl,A:Spider-Man,Darkhawk, V:Brotherhood o/Evil Mutants		1.50
18 JQ(c),Inf.War,A:Prof.X		1.50
19 V:Cobweb,w/pop out Halloween Mask		2.00
20 V:Chain Gang,Cobweb		1.50
21 V:Hobgoblin		1.50
22 V:Hobgoblin,8-Ball		1.50
23 V:Cobweb,Chain Gang		1.50
24 Mindfield#6		1.50
25 O:Sleepwalker,Holo-grafx(c)		3.50
26 V:Mindspawn		1.50
27 A:Avengers		1.50
28 I:Psyko		1.50
29 DG,V:Psyko		1.50
30 V:Psyko		1.50
31 DG(ci),A:Spectra		1.50
32 V:Psyko		1.50
33 V:Mindspawn,Last issue		1.50
Holiday Spec.#1 JQ(c)		2.25

SLEEZE BROTHERS
August, 1989

1 Private Eyes		1.75
2		1.75
3		1.75
4		1.75
5		1.75
6		1.75

SMURFS
Dec., 1982

1		1.00

2		1.00
3		1.00
Treasury Edition		2.50

SOLARMAN
Jan., 1989

1 JM		1.25
2 MZ/NR,A:Dr.Doom, May, 1990		1.25

SOLO
[Limited Series]

1 RoR,I:Cygnus		1.75
2 RoR,V:A.R.E.S.		1.75
3 RoR,V:Spidey		1.75
4 final issue		1.75

SOLO AVENGERS
Dec., 1987

1 MBr,JRu,JLe,AW,Hawkeye; Mockingbird		4.00
2 MBr,JRu,KD,BMc,Hawkeye; Capt.Marvel		1.50
3 MBr,JRu,BH,SDr,Hawkeye; Moon Knight		1.50
4 RLm,JRu,PR,BL,Hawkeye; Black Knight		2.00
5 MBr,JRu,JRy,Hawkeye; Scarlet Witch		1.50
6 MBr,JRu,TGr,Hawkeye;Falcon		1.25
7 MBr,JG,BL,Hawkeye;Bl.Widow		1.25
8 MBr,Hawkeye;Dr.Pym		1.25
9 MBr,JBr,SDr,Hawkeye;Hellcat		1.25
10 MBr,LW,Hawkeye;Dr.Druid		1.25
11 MBr,JG,BL,Hawkeye;Hercules		1.25
12 RLm,SDr,Hawkeye; New Yellow Jacket		2.00
13 RLm,JG,Hawkeye;WonderMan		2.00
14 AM,AD,JRu,Hawkeye;She-Hulk		1.25
15 AM,Hawkeye;Wasp		1.25
16 AM,DP,JA,Hawkeye; Moondragon		1.25
17 AM,DH,DC,Hawkeye; Sub-Mariner		1.25
18 RW,DH,Hawkeye;Moondragon		1.25
19 RW,DH,Hawkeye,BlackPanther		1.25
20 RW,DH,Hawkeye;Moondragon		1.25

Becomes:
AVENGERS SPOTLIGHT

SOLOMON KANE
Sept., 1985

1 F:Solomon Kane		1.50
2		1.00
3 BBl,'Blades of the Brotherhood'		1.00
4 MMi		1.00
5 'Hills of the Dead'		1.00
6		1.00

SON OF SATAN
Dec., 1975

1 GK(c),JM,F:Daimon Hellstrom		10.00
2 Demon War,O:Possessor		8.00
3		6.00
4 The Faces of Fear		6.00
5 V:Mind Star		6.00
6 A World Gone Mad		6.00
7 Mirror of Judgement		6.00
8 RH,To End in Nightmare Feb., 1977		6.00

SOVIET SUPER SOLDIERS

1 AMe,JS,I:Redmont 4		2.00

SPACEMAN
Atlas Sept., 1953
1 BEv(c),F:Speed Carter and the Space Sentinals	450.00
2 JMn,'Trapped in Space'	300.00
3 BEv(c),JMn,V:Ice Monster	250.00
4 JMn	250.00
5 GT	250.00
6 JMn,'The Thing From Outer Space',Oct., 1954	250.00

SPACE SQUADRON
Atlas June, 1951
1 F:Capt. Jet Dixon,Blast,Dawn, Revere,Rusty Blake	450.00
2 GT(c),	400.00
3 'Planet of Madness',GT	300.00
4	300.00
5	300.00

Becomes:
SPACE WORLDS
April, 1952
6 'Midnight Horror'	300.00

SPECIAL COLLECTOR'S EDITION
Dec., 1975
1 Kung-Fu,Iron Fist	6.00

SPECIAL MARVEL EDITION
Jan., 1971
1 JK,B:Thor,B:Reprints	6.00
2 JK,V:Absorbing Man	5.00
3 JK,'While a Universe Trembles'	5.00
4 JK,'Hammer and the Holocaust', E:Thor	5.00
5 JSe(c),JK,DAy,B:Sgt. Fury	5.00
6 HT(c),DAy,'Death Ray of Dr. Zemo'	4.00
7 DAy,V:Baron Strucker	4.00
8 JSe(c),DAy'On To Okinawa'	4.00
9 DAy,'Crackdown of Captain Flint	4.00
10 DAy	4.00
11 JK,DAy,A:Captaim America & Bucky	4.00
12 DAy,V:Baron Strucker	4.00
13 JK/DAy(c),DAy,SD,'Too Small to Fight, Too Young To Die'	4.00
14 DAy,E:Reprints,Sgt. Fury	4.00
15 JSn,AM,I:Shang-Chi & Master of Kung Fu,I&O:Nayland Smith, Dr. Petrie	35.00
16 JSn,AM,I&O:Midnight	20.00
KingSz.Ann.#1 A:Iron Fist	7.00

Becomes:
MASTER OF KUNG FU

SPECTACULAR SCARLET SPIDER
1 SB,BSz,Virtual Morality,pt.4	1.95
2 SB,BSz,CyberWar,pt.4	1.95

SPECTACULAR SPIDER-MAN
July, 1968
(magazine)
1	65.00
2 V:Green Goblin,Nov.1968	110.00

SPECTACULAR SPIDER-MAN
Dec., 1976
Prev: Peter Parker
134 SB,A:Sin-Eater,V:Electro	4.00
135 SB,A:Sin-Eater,V:Electro	3.00
136 SB,D:Sin-Eater,V:Electro	3.00
137 SB,I:Tarantula II	3.00
138 SB,A:Capt.A.,V:TarantulaII	3.00
139 SB,O:Tombstone	4.00
140 SB,A:Punisher,V:Tombstone	3.00
141 SB,A:Punisher,V:Tombstone	3.00
142 SB,A:Punisher,V:Tombstone	3.00
143 SB,A:Punisher,D:Persuader, I:Lobo Brothers.	3.00
144 SB,V:Boomerang	3.00
145 SB,A:Boomerang	3.00
146 SB,R:Green Goblin	5.00
147 SB,V:Hobgoblin (Demonic Power)	15.00
148 SB,Inferno	3.00
149 SB,V:Carrion II	5.00
150 SB,A:Tombstone,Trial J.Robertson	3.00
151 SB,V:Tombstone	3.00
152 SB,O:Lobo Bros.,A:Punisher, Tombstone	4.00
153 SB,V:Hammerhead,A: Tombstone	3.00
154 SB,V:Lobo Bros.,Puma	3.00
155 SB,V:Tombstone	3.00
156 SB,V:Banjo,A:Tombstone	3.00
157 SB,V:Shocker,Electro, A:Tombstone	3.00
158 SB,Super Spider Spec., I:Cosmic Spider-Man	10.00
159 Cosmic Powers,V:Brothers Grimm	7.00
160 SB,A:Hydro Man,Shocker, Rhino,Dr.Doom	6.00
161 SB,V:Hobgoblin,Hammerhead, Tombstone	3.00
162 SB,V:Hobgoblin,Carrion II	3.00
163 SB,V:Hobgoblin,D:Carrion II	3.00
164 SB,V:Beetle	2.50
165 SB,SDr,D:Arranger,I:Knight & Fogg	2.50
166 SB,O:Knight & Fogg	2.50
167 SB,D:Knight & Fogg	2.50
168 SB,A:Kingpin,Puma, Avengers	2.50
169 SB,I:Outlaws,A:R.Racer, Prowler,Puma,Sandman	2.50
170 SB,A:Avengers,Outlaws	2.50
171 SB,V:Puma	2.50
172 SB,V:Puma	2.50
173 SB,V:Puma	2.50
174 SB,A:Dr.Octopus	2.50
175 SB,A:Dr.Octopus	2.50
176 SB,I:Karona	2.50
177 SB,V:Karona,A:Mr.Fantastic	2.50
178 SB,B:Child Within,V:Green Goblin, A:Vermin	3.50
179 SB,V:Green Goblin,Vermin	3.00
180 SB,V:Green Goblin,Vermin	3.00
181 SB,V:Green Goblin	3.00
182 SB,V:Green Goblin	3.00
183 SB,V:Green Goblin	3.00
184 SB,E:Child Within,V:Green Goblin	3.00
185 SB,A:Frogman,White Rabbit	2.00
186 SB,B:FuneralArrangements V:Vulture	2.00
187 SB,V:Vulture	2.00

188 SB,E:Funeral Arrangements V:Vulture	2.00
189 SB,30th Ann.,Hologram(c), V:Green Goblin	7.00
189a Gold 2nd printing	3.25
190 SB,V:Rhino,Harry Osborn	2.00
191 SB,Eye of the Puma	1.75
192 SB,Eye of the Puma	1.75
193 SB,Eye of the Puma	1.75
194 SB,Death of Vermin#1	1.75
195 SB,Death of Vermin#2	1.75
195a Dirtbag Spec,w/Dirt#2 tape	2.50
196 SB,Death of Vermin#3	1.75
197 SB,A:X-Men,V:Prof.Power	1.75
198 SB,A:X-Men,V:Prof.Power	1.75
199 SB,A:X-Men,Green Goblin	2.00
200 SB,V:Green Goblin,D:Harry Osborn,Holografx(c)	5.00
201 SB,Total Carnage,V:Carnage, Shriek,A:Black Cat,Venom	1.75
202 SB,Total Carnage#9,A:Venom, V:Carnage	1.75
203 SB,Maximum Carnage#13	1.75

Spectacular Spider-Man #198
© Marvel Entertainment Group

204 SB,A:Tombstone	1.75
205 StG(s),SB,V:Tombstone, A:Black Cat	1.75
206 SB,V:Tombstone	1.75
207 SB,A:The Shroud	1.50
208 SB,A:The Shroud	1.50
209 StB,SB,I:Dead Aim, BU:Black Cat	1.50
210 StB,SB,V:Dead Aim, BU:Black Cat	1.50
211 Pursuit#2,V:Tracer	1.50
212	
213 ANo(s),V:Typhiod Mary,w/cel	3.25
213a Newsstand Ed.	1.75
214 V:Bloody Mary	1.75
215 V:Scorpion	1.75
216 V:Scorpion	1.75
217 V:Judas Traveller,clone	2.00
217a Foil(c),bonus stuff	5.00
218 V:Puma	1.75
219 Back from the Edge,pt.2	2.00
220 Web of Death,pt.3	2.50
221 Web of Death,finale	3.00
222 The Price of Truth	1.50
223 Aftershocks,pt.4	4.00

MARVEL

223a enhanced cover 1.95
224 The Mark of Kaine,pt.4 . . . . . 2.50
225 SB,TDF,BSz,I:New Green
   Goblin, 48pg.s 2.95
225a 3-D HoloDisk Cover 5.00
226 SB,BSz,The Trial of Peter
   Parker,pt.4, identity revealed . . 2.25
227 TDF,SB,BSz,Maximum
   Clonage,pt.5 . . . . 1.50
228 Timebomb,pt.1 . . . . 1.50
229 Greatest Responsibility,pt.3 . . 2.50
229a Special cover 3.95
230 SB,Return of Spider-Man,pt.4 1.50
231 SB,Return of Kaine,pt.1 . . . . 1.50
232 . . . . 1.50
233 SB,JP,Web of Carnage,pt.4 . 1.50
234 SB,Blood Brothers,pt.4 . . . . . 1.50
235 . . . . 1.50
236 . . . . 1.50
237 V:Lizard 1.50
238 V:Lizard 1.50
239 V:Lizard 1.50
240 TDz,LRs,"Book of Revelations,"
   pt.1 (of 4) 1.50
241 Revelations epilogue 1.50
242 JMD,LRs,R:Chameleon,
   A:Kangaroo 1.50
243 JMD,LRs,R:Chameleon 1.50
244 JMD,LRs,V:Chameleon 1.50
245 JMD,LRs,V:Chameleon,
   A:Kangaroo 1.50
246 JMD,LRs,V:Kangaroo,Grizzly 1.50
247 JMD,LRs,F:Jack O'Lantern, pt.11 1.50
248 JMD,LRs,DGr,F:Jack O'
   Lantern, pt.2 . . . . 1.50
249 JMD,LRs,DGr, Last Temptation of
   Flash Thompson 1.50
Ann.#8 MBa,RLm,TD,Evolutionary
   Wars,O:Gwen Stacy Clone . . . 5.00
Ann.#9 DR,MG,DJu,MBa,Atlantis
   Attacks 4.00
Ann.#10 SLi(c),RB,MM,TM,RA . . . 6.00
Ann.#11 EL(c),RWi,Vib.Vendetta . 2.50
Ann.#12 Hero Killers#2,A:New
   Warriors,BU:Venom 4.50
Ann.#13 I:Noctune,w/Card 3.25
Ann.#14 V:Green Goblin 2.95
Super-Size Spec.#1 Planet of the
   Symbiotes,pt.4,64pg flip-book . 3.95
Minus 1 Spec., JMD,LRs,DGr,
   flashback, F:Flash Thompson . 1.95

SPEEDBALL
Sept., 1988
1 SD,JG,O:Speedball 2.00
2 SD,JG,V:Sticker,Graffiti Gorillas 1.50
3 SD,V:Leaper Logan 1.25
4 SD,DA,Ghost Springdale High . 1.25
5 SD,V:Basher 1.25
6 SD,V:Bug-Eyed Voice 1.25
7 SD,V:Harlequin Hit Man 1.25
8 SD,V:Bonehead Gang 1.25
9 SD,V:Nathan Boder 1.25
10 SD,V:Mutated Pigs,Killer
   Chickens, last issue 1.25

SPELLBOUND
Atlas March, 1952
1 'Step into my Coffin' 450.00
2 BEv,RH,'Horror Story',
   A:Edgar A. Poe 225.00
3 RH(c),OW 200.00
4 RH,Decapitation story 200.00
5 BEv,JM,'Its in the Bag' 200.00

6 BK,'The Man Who Couldn't
   be Killed' 200.00
7 BEv,JMn,'Don't Close
   the Door' 150.00
8 BEv(c),RH,JSt,DAy,
   'The Operation' 150.00
9 BEv(c),RH,'The Death of
   Agatha Slurl' 150.00
10 JMn(c),BEv,RH,'The Living
   Mummy' 150.00
11 'The Empty Coffin' 100.00
12 RH,'My Friend the Ghost' . 100.00
13 JM,'The Dead Men' 100.00
14 BEv(c),RH,JMn,'Close Shave' 100.00
15 'Get Out of my Graveyard' . 100.00
16 RH,BEv,JF,JSt,'Behind
   the Door' 100.00
17 BEv(c),GC,BK,'Goodbye
   Forever' 125.00
18 BEv(c),JM 125.00
19 BEv(c),BP,'Witch Doctor' . . 125.00
20 RH(c),BP 125.00
21 RH(c) 100.00
22 . . . . 100.00
23 . . . . 100.00
24 JMn(c),JR 75.00
25 JO,'Look into my Eyes' 75.00
26 JR,'The Things in the Box' . . 75.00
27 JMn,JR,'Trap in the Mirage' . 75.00
28 BEv 75.00
29 JSe(c),SD 100.00
30 BEv(c) 75.00
31 . . . . 75.00
32 BP,'Almost Human' 75.00
33 AT 75.00
34 June, 1957 . . . . 75.00

SPELLBOUND
Jan., 1988
1 thru 3 . . . . @1.50
4 A:New Mutants 2.00
5 . . . . 1.50
6 double-size 2.25

SPIDER-MAN
August, 1990
1 TM Purple Web(c),V:Lizard,
   A:Calypso,B:Torment 5.00
1a Silver Web(c) 7.00
1b Bag,Purple Web 8.00
1c Bag,Silver Web 10.00
1d 2nd print,Gold(c) 5.00
1e 2nd print Gold UPC(rare) . . 15.00
1f Platinum Ed. 150.00
2 TM,V:Lizard,A:Calypso 5.00
3 TM,V:Lizard,A:Calypso 5.00
4 TM,V:Lizard,A:Calypso 5.00
5 TM,V:Lizard,A:Calypso,
   E:Torment 5.00
6 TM,A:Ghost Rider,V:Hobgoblin 5.00
7 TM,A:Ghost Rider,V:Hobgoblin 5.00
8 TM,B:Perceptions,A:Wolverine
   I:Wendigo IV 5.00
9 TM,A:Wolverine,Wendigo . . . 4.00
10 TM,RLd,SW,JLe(i),A:Wolv. . . 4.00
11 TM,A:Wolverine,Wendigo. . . . 4.00
12 TM,E:Perceptions,A:Wolv.. . . 4.00
13 TM,V:Morbius,R:Black Cost. . 5.00
14 TM,V:Morbius,A:Black Cost. . 5.00
15 EL,A:Beast 3.50
16 TM,RLd,A:X-Force,V:Juggernaut,
   Black Tom,cont.in X-Force#4 . 4.00
17 RL,AW,A:Thanos,Death 3.50
18 EL,B:Return of the Sinister Six,
   A:Hulk 3.00

Spider-Man #28
© Marvel Entertainment Group

19 EL,A:Hulk,Deathlok 3.00
20 EL,A:Nova 2.50
21 EL,A:Hulk,Deathlok,Solo 2.50
22 EL,A:Ghost Rider,Hulk 2.50
23 EL,E:Return of the Sinister Six,
   A:Hulk,G.Rider,Deathlok,FF . . 2.50
24 Infinity War,V:Hobgoblin,
   Demogoblin 2.25
25 CMa,A:Excalibur,V:Arcade . . 2.25
26 RF,MBa,Hologram(c),30th Anniv.
   I:New Burglar 4.00
27 MR,Handgun issue 2.25
28 MR,Handgun issue 2.25
29 CMa,Ret.to Mad Dog Ward#1 . 2.25
30 CMa,Ret.to Mad Dog Ward#2 . 2.25
31 CMa,Ret.to Mad Dog Ward#3 . 2.25
32 BMc,A:Punisher,V:Master of
   Vengeance 2.25
33 BMc,A:Punisher,V:Master of
   Vengeance. 2.25
34 BMc,A:Punisher,V:Master of
   Vengeance 2.25
35 TL,Total Carnage#4,V:Carnage,
   Shriek,A:Venom,Black Cat . . . 2.25
36 TL,Total Carnage#8,V:Carnage,
   A:Venom,Morbius 2.25
37 TL,Total Carnage#12,
   V:Carnage 2.25
38 thru 40 KJ,V:Electro 2.25
41 TKa(s),JaL,I:Platoon,
   A:Iron Fist 2.25
42 TKa(s),JaL,V:Platoon,
   A:Iron Fist 2.25
43 TKa(s),JaL,V:Platoon,
   A:Iron Fist 2.25
44 HMe(s),TL,V:Hobgoblin 2.25
45 HMe(s),TL,SHa,Pursuit#1,
   V:Chameleon 2.25
46 HMe(s),TL,V:Hobgoblin,w/cel . 3.25
46a Newsstand Ed. 1.75
47 TL,SHa,V:Demogoblin 2.25
48 TL,SHa,V:Hobgoblin,
   D:Demogoblin 2.25
49 TL,SHa,I:Coldheart 2.25
50 TL,SHa,I:Grim Hunter,foil(c) . 4.25
50a newsstand ed. 2.50
51 TL,SHa,Power,pt.3,foil(c) . . . 4.00

51a newsstand ed. 2.25
52 TL,SHa,Spide-clone,V:Venom . 2.25
53 TL,SHa,Clone,V:Venom 2.25
54 Web of Life,pt.3 . . . . 2.25
55 Web of Life,finale 2.25
56 Smoke and Mirrors 2.00
57 Aftershocks,pt.1 . . . . 2.50
57a enhanced cover 3.00
58 The Mark of Kaine,pt.3 . . . . . . 2.00
59 F:Travellor,Host 2.00
60 TL,SHa,HMa,The Trial of
    Peter Parker,pt.3 . . . . 2.00
61 TL,Maximum Clonage,pt.4 . . . 2.00
62 HMe,TL,Exiled,pt.3 . . . . 2.00
63 HMe,TL,Greatest
    Responsibility,pt.2 . . . . 2.00
64 HMe,JR2,Return of
    Spider-Man,pt.3 . . . . 2.00
65 HMe,JR2,AW,Media
    Blizzard,pt.3 . . . . 2.00
66 HMe,JR2,Return of Kaine,pt.4 . 2.00
67 HMe,JR2,Web of Carnage,pt.3 2.00
68 HMe,JR2,AW,Blood
    Brothers,pt.3 . . . . 2.00
69 HMe,JR2,Blood Brothers
    aftermath 2.00
70 HMe,JR2,A:Onslaught 3.00
71 HMe,JR2, ... 1.95
72 HMe,JR2,Onslaught saga 1.95
73 HMe,JR2 . . . . 1.95
74 HMe,JR2,AW,A:Daredevil,
    V:Fortunato 1.95
75 HMe,JR2,Revelations, pt.4 . . 3.00
76 HMe,JR2,SHa,Post-Onslaught
    world,I:Shoc 1.95
77 HMe,JR2,SHa,V:Morbius 1.95
Becomes:

PETER PARKER,
SPIDER-MAN

78 HMe,JR2,SHa,F:Mary Jane
    Parker 1.95
79 HMe,JR2,SHa,V:Hydra,A:Captain
    Arthur Stacy 1.95
80 HMe,JR2,SHa,V:S.H.O.C. . . . 1.95
81 HMe,JR2,SHa,V:Shang-Chi,pt.1 1.95
82 HMe,JR2,SHa,Anti-Mutant
    Movement 1.95
83 HMe,JR2,SHa,V:Morbius 1.95
Minus 1 Spec., HMe,JR2,SHa,
    flashback, A:Stacys 1.95
GN Fear Itself 12.95
GN Nothing Stops Juggernaut . . 3.95
GN Parallel Lives 8.95
GN JMD,MZ,Soul of the Hunter . 5.95
HC Kraven's Last Hunt 19.95
HC CV,Spirits of the Earth 18.95
Spec. Chaos in Calgary 1.50
Spec. Double Trouble 1.50
Spec. Hit and Run, Canadian . . . 1.50
Spec. Skating on Thin Ice 1.50
Spec. Trial of Venom,UNICEF . 15.00
Sup.Sz.Spec#1 Planet of the
    Symbiotes, pt.2;
    flipbook F:Scarlet Spider 3.95
TPB Assasination Plot 14.95
TPB Carnage 6.95
TPB Cosmic Adventures 19.95
TPB Hooky 6.95
TPB Maximum Carnage 24.95
TPB Origin of the Hobgoblin . . . 14.95
TPB Return of the Sinister Six . . 15.95
TPB Round Robin 15.95
TPB Saga of the Alien Costume 14.00
    2nd printing 12.95

TPB Spider-Man vs. Venom 9.95
TPB Torment Rep.#1-#5 . . . . . 12.95
TPB Venom Returns 12.95
TPB Very Best of Spider-Man . 15.95
TPB The Wedding 12.95
TPB Invasion Spider Slayers . . 15.95
TPB Clone Genesis 16.95
TPB V:Green Goblin 15.95
TPB Spider-Man'sGreatestVillains 15.95
Holiday Spec.'95 . . . . 2.95

PETER PARKER,
SPIDER-MAN '97

1 Simon Garth—Zombie 2.95

SPIDER-MAN
ADVENTURES

1 From animated series 1.50
1a foil (c) 2.95
2 Animated Adventures 1.50
3 V:Spider-Slayer 1.50
4 Animated Adventures 1.50
5 V:Mysterio 1.50
6 V:Kraven 1.50
7 V:Doctor Octopus 1.50
8 O:Venom,pt.1 . . . . 1.50
9 O:Venom,pt.2 . . . . 1.50
10 V:Venom 1.50
11 V:Hobgoblin 1.50
12 V:Hobgoblin 1.50
13 V:Chameleon 1.50
14 V:Doc Octopus 1.50
15 Doc Conners 1.50
TPB Rep.#1-#5, 112pg 8.95

SPIDER-MAN
& AMAZING FRIENDS
Dec., 1981

1 DSp,A:Iceman,I:Firestar 5.50

SPIDER-MAN/BADROCK
Marvel/Maximum Press 1997

1 x-over, pt.1 . . . . 2.99
2 x-over, pt. 2 . . . . 2.99

SPIDER-MAN/BATMAN

1 JMD,MBa,MFm,V:Carnage,Joker 5.95

SPIDER-MAN CLASSICS

1 rep.Amazing Fantasy#15 . . . . . 1.75
2 thru 11 rep.Amaz.SpM#1-#10 @1.75
12 rep.Amaz.SpM#11 . . . . 1.50
13 rep.Amaz.SpM#12 . . . . 1.50
14 rep.Amaz.SpM#13 . . . . 1.50
15 rep.Amaz.SpM#14,w/cel 3.25
15a Newsstand Ed. 1.50

SPIDER-MAN
COMICS MAGAZINE
Jan., 1987

1 . . . . 2.50
2 thru 13 . . . . @1.50

SPIDER-MAN:
DEAD MAN'S HAND

1-shot, RSt,DaR,JeM,V:Carrion . . 2.99

SPIDER-MAN:
THE FINAL ADVENTURE

1 FaN,DaR,Clv,I:Tendril 2.95

2 FaN,DaR,JAl,V:Tendril 2.95
3 FaN,DaR,JAl,V:Tendril 2.95
4 FaN,DaR,JAl,V:Tendril,concl. . . 2.95

SPIDER-MAN:
FRIENDS AND ENEMIES

1 V:Metahumes 1.95
2 A:Nova,Darkhawk,Speedball . . 1.95
3 V:Metahumes 1.95
4 F:Metahumes 1.95

SPIDER-MEN: FUNERAL
FOR AN OCTOPUS

1 Doc Oc Dead 1.95
2 A:Sinister Six 1.50
3 Final Issue 1.50

SPIDER-MAN/GEN[13]
Marvel/Wildstorm 1996

1-shot PDd,SI,CaS x-over 4.95

SPIDER-MAN:
HOBGOBLIN LIVES

1 (of 3) RSt,RF,GP 2.50
2 RSt,RF,GP,Who was the original
    Hobgoblin? 2.50
3 RSt,RF,GP,Original identity
    revealed 2.50

SPIDER-MAN:
MAXIMUM CLONAGE

Alpha Maximum Clonage,pt.1 . . 5.50
Omega TL,Maximum Clonage,pt.6 4.95

SPIDER-MAN MEGAZINE

1 rep. 2.95
2 rep. 2.95
3 and 4 rep. . . . . @.95
5 Vision rep. 2.95
6 V:Thing & Torch, rep. 2.95

SPIDER-MAN:
MUTANT AGENDA

0 thru 2 Paste in Book . . . . . . @1.50
3 Paste in Book 1.50

Spider-Man Mutant Agenda #1
© Marvel Entertainment Group

MARVEL

SPIDER-MAN: POWER OF TERROR
1 R:Silvermane,A:Deathlok 1.95
2 V:Silvermane 1.95
3 New Scorpion 1.95
4 V:Silvermane 1.95

SPIDER-MAN/PUNISHER
Part 1 TL,A:Tombstone 2.95
Part 2 TL,A:Tombstone 2.95

SPIDER-MAN/PUNISHER/ SABERTOOTH: DESIGNER GENES
1 SMc,Foil(c) 9.50

SPIDER-MAN: REDEMPTION
1 thru 4 JMD,MZ,BMc, Mary Jane
   arrested for Murder . . . . @1.50

SPIDER-MAN SAGA
Nov., 1991
1 SLi(c),History from Amazing
   Fantasy #15-Amaz.SpM#100 . 3.25
2 SLi(c),Amaz.SpM#101-#175 . . 3.25
3 Amaz.SpM#176-#238 . . . . . . 3.25
4 Amaz.SpM #239-#300 . . . . . . 3.25

SPIDER-MAN SUPER SIZE SPECIAL
1 Planet of the Symbiotes,pt.2 . 3.95

SPIDER-MAN TEAM-UP
1 MWa,KeL,V:Hellfire Club 2.95
2 thru 4 . . . . 2.95
5 SvG,DaR,JFr,F:Gambit,
   Howard the Duck 3.00
6 JMD,LHa,F:Hulk & Doctor
   Strange 3.00
7 KBk,SB,F:Thunderbolts 3.00

SPIDER-MAN: THE ARACHNIS PROJECT
1 Wld, beginnings 1.75
2 Wld,V:Diggers 1.75
3 Wld,V:Jury 1.75
4 Wld,V:Life Foundation 1.75
5 Wld,V:Jury 1.75

SPIDER-MAN: THE CLONE JOURNALS
One-shot 1.95

SPIDER-MAN: THE JACKAL FILES
1 Files of the Jackal 1.95

SPIDER-MAN: THE LOST YEARS
0 JMD,JR2,LSh,64pg,rep. 3.95
1 History of Kaine,Ben 2.95
2 JMD,JR2,KJ,Kaine & Ben . . . 2.95
3 Ben vs. Kaine 2.95

SPIDER-MAN: THE PARKER YEARS
1 JR2,JSP,F:The real Clone 2.50

SPIDER-MAN 2099
1 RL,AW,I:Spider-Man 2099 . . . . 5.50
2 RL,AW,O:Spider-Man 2099 . . . 5.00
3 RL,AW,V:Venture 3.00
4 RL,AW,I:Specialist,
   A:Doom 2099 . . . . 2.00
5 RL,AW,V:Specialist 2.00
6 RL,AW,I:New Vulture 2.00
7 RL,AW,Vulture of 2099 . . . . . . 2.00
8 RL,AW,V:New Vulture 2.00
9 KJo,V:Alchemax 2.00
10 RL,AW,O:Wellvale Home 2.00
11 RL,AW,V:S.I.E.G.E. 2.00
12 RL,AW,w/poster 2.00
13 RL,AW,V:Thanatos 1.75
14 PDd(s),RL(c),TGb,Downtown . 1.75
15 PDd(s),RL,I:Thor 2099,
   Heimdall 2099 . . . . 1.75
16 PDd(s),RL,Fall of the
   Hammer#1 . . . . 1.75
17 PDd(s),RL,V:Bloodsword 1.75
18 PDd(s),RLm,V:Lyla 1.75
19 PDd(s),RL,w/card 1.75
20 PDd(s),RL,Crash & Burn 1.75
21 V:Gangs 1.75
22 V:Gangs 1.75
23 RL,I:Risque 3.00
24 Kasey 1.75
25 A:Hulk 2099, dbl-size,foil(c) . . 3.25
25a Newsstand ed. 2.25
26 V:Headhunter, Travesty 1.50
27 V:Travesty 1.50
28 V:Travesty 1.50
29 V:Foragers 1.50
30 V:Flipside 1.50
31 I:Dash 1.50
Becomes:

SPIDER-MAN 2099 A.D.
32 I:Morgue 1.95
33 One Nation Under Doom 1.95
34 V:Alchemex 1.95
35 . . . . 1.95
36a Spider-Man 2099(c) 1.95
36b Venom 2099(c) 1.95
37a Venom 2099 . . . . 1.95
37b variant cover 1.95
38 . . . . 1.95
39 A:Venom 2099 . . . . 1.95
40 V:Goblin 2099 . . . . 1.95
41 . . . . 1.95
42 . . . . 1.95
43 V:Sub-Mariner 2099 . . . . 1.95
Ann.#1 PDd(s),RL 2.95
Spec.#1 I:3 new villains 3.95

SPIDER-MAN UNLIMITED
1 RLm,Maximun Carnage#1,I:Shriek,
   R:Carnage 5.00
2 RLm,Maximum Carnage#14 . . 4.50
3 RLm,O:Doctor Octopus 4.50
4 RLm,V:Mysrterio,Rhino 4.25
5 RLm,A:Human Torch,
   I:Steel Spider 4.25
6 RLm,A:Thunderstrike 3.95
7 RLm,A:Clone 3.95
8 Tom Lyle 3.95
9 The Mark of Kaine,pt.5 . . . . . . 3.95
10 SwM,Exiled,pt.4 . . . . 3.95
11 FaN,V:Black Cat 3.95
12 Blood Brother tie-in 3.95
13 . . . . 3.00
14 JoB, an ally dies 3.00
15 TDF,JoB,F:Puma 3.00

16 cont. from X-Force #64 . . . . . . 3.00
17 JoB, Revelations, sequel 3.00

SPIDER-MAN UNMASKED
1-shot 64pg information source . . .

SPIDER-MAN VS. DRACULA
1 rep. 1.75

SPIDER-MAN vs. VENOM
1990
1 TM(c) 8.95

SPIDER-MAN vs. WOLVERINE
1990
1 MBr,AW,D:Ned Leeds(the original
   Hobgoblin),V:Charlie 22.00
1a reprint 5.00

SPIDER-MAN: WEB OF DOOM
1 3-part series 1.75
2 Spidey falsely accused 1.75
3 conclusion 1.75

SPIDER-MAN & X-FACTOR: SHADOW GAMES
1 PB,I:Shadowforce 2.25
2 PB,V:Shadowforce 2.25
3 PB,V:Shadowforce, final issue . 2.25

Spider-Woman #25
© Marvel Entertainment Group

SPIDER-WOMAN
April, 1978
1 CI,TD,O:Spiderwoman 6.00
2 CI,TD,I:Morgan Le Fey 2.00
3 CI,TD,I:Brother's Grimm 2.00
4 CI,TD,V:Hangman 2.00
5 CI,TD,Nightmares 2.00
6 CI,A:Werewolf By Night 2.00
7 CI,SL,AG,V:Magnus 2.00
8 CI,AG,"Man who would not die" 2.00

---

9 CI,AG,A:Needle,Magnus	2.00
10 CI,AG,I:Gypsy Moth	2.00
11 CI,AG,V:Brothers Grimm	1.50
12 CI,AG,V:Brothers Grimm	1.50
13 CI,AG,A:Shroud	1.50
14 BSz(c),CI,AG,A:Shroud	1.50
15 BSz(c),CI,AG,A:Shroud	1.50
16 BSz(c),CI,AG,V:Nekra	1.50
17 CI,Deathplunge	1.50
18 CI,A:Flesh	1.50
19 CI,A:Werewolf By Night, V:Enforcer	1.75
20 FS,A:Spider-Man	1.50
21 FS,A:Bounty Hunter	1.50
22 FS,A:Killer Clown	1.50
23 TVE,V:The Gamesmen	1.50
24 TVE,V:The Gamesmen	1.50
25 SL,Two Spiderwomen	1.50
26 JBy(c),SL,V:White Gardenia	1.50
27 BSz(c),JBi,A:Enforcer	1.50
28 BSz(c),SL,A:Enforcer,Spidey	1.50
29 JR2(c),ECh,FS,A:Enforcer, Spider-Man	1.50
30 FM(c),SL,JM,I:Dr.Karl Malus	1.50
31 FM(c),SL,JM,A:Hornet	1.50
32 FM(c),SL,JM,A:Werewolf	1.75
33 SL,V:Yesterday's Villian	1.50
34 SL,AM,V:Hammer and Anvil	1.50
35 SL,AG,V:Angar the Screamer	1.50
36 SL,Spiderwoman Shot	1.50
37 SL,TA,BWi,AM,FS,A:X-Men,I: Siryn,V:Black Tom	3.50
38 SL,BWi,A:X-Men,Siryn	3.00
39 SL,BWi,Shadows	1.50
40 SL,BWi,V:The Flying Tiger	1.50
41 SL,BWi,V:Morgan LeFay	1.50
42 SL,BWi,V:Silver Samurai	1.50
43 SL,V:Silver Samurai	1.50
44 SL,V:Morgan LeFay	1.50
45 SL,Spider-Man Thief Cover	1.50
46 SL,V:Mandroids,A:Kingpin	1.50
47 V:Daddy Longlegs	1.50
48 O:Gypsy Moth	1.50
49 A:Tigra	1.50
50 PH(c),D:Spiderwoman	3.50

[Limited Series]

1 V:Therak	2.00
2 O:Spider-Woman	2.00
3 V:Deathweb	2.00
4 V:Deathweb,Last issue	2.00

SPIDEY SUPER STORIES
Oct., 1974

1 Younger reader's series in association with the Electric Company,O:Spider-Man	4.00
2 A:Kraven	3.00
3 A:Ringleader	3.00
4 A:Medusa	3.00
5 A:Shocker	3.00
6 A:Iceman	3.00
7 A:Lizard, Vanisher	3.00
8 A:Dr. Octopus	3.00
9 A:Dr. Doom	3.25
10 A:Green Goblin	3.00
11 A:Dr. Octopus	3.00
12 A:The Cat,V:The Owl	3.00
13 A:Falcon	3.00
14 A:Shanna	3.00
15 A:Storm	3.25
16	2.50
17 A:Captain America	2.50
18 A:Kingpin	2.50

19 A:Silver Surfer,Dr. Doom	3.25
20 A;Human Torch,Invisible Girl	2.50
21 A:Dr. Octopus	2.50
22 A:Ms. Marvel,The Beetle	2.50
23 A:Green Goblin	3.00
24 A:Thundra	2.50
25 A:Dr. Doom	2.50
26 A:Sandman	2.50
27 A:Thor,Loki	2.50
28 A:Medusa	2.50
29 A:Kingpin	2.50
30 A:Kang	2.50
31 A:Moondragon,Dr. Doom	2.50
32 A:Spider-Woman,Dr. Octopus	2.50
33	2.50
34 A:Sub-Mariner	2.50
35	2.50
36 A:Lizard	2.50
37 A:White Tiger	2.50
38 A:Fantastic Four	2.50
39 A:Hellcat,Thanos	6.00
40 A:Hawkeye	2.00
41 A:Nova,Dr. Octopus	2.00
42 A:Kingpin	2.00
43 A:Daredevil,Ringmaster	2.00
44 A:Vision	2.00
45 A:Silver Surfer,Dr. Doom	3.25
46 A:Mysterio	2.00
47 A:Spider-Woman,Stilt-Man	2.00
48 A:Green Goblin	2.25
49 Spidey for President	2.00
50 A:She-Hulk	2.00
51	2.00
52	2.00
53 A:Dr. Doom	2.00
54 'Attack of the Bird-Man'	2.00
55 A:Kingpin	2.00
56 A:Captain Britain, Jack O'Lantern	3.00
57 March, 1982	2.00

SPITFIRE AND THE TROUBLESHOOTERS
Oct., 1986

1 HT/JSt	1.00
2 HT	1.00
3 HT,Macs Armor	1.00
4 TM/BMc(Early TM work)	3.00
5 HT/TD,A:StarBrand	1.00
6 HT,Trial	1.00
7 HT	1.00
8 HT,New Armor	1.00
9	1.00

Becomes:
CODE NAME: SPITFIRE

10 MR/TD	1.00
11 thru 13	@1.00

SPOOF
Oct., 1970

1 MSe	3.00
2 MSe,'Brawl in the Family'	2.00
3 MSe,Richard Nixon cover	2.00
4 MSe,'Blechhula'	2.00
5 MSe,May, 1973	4.00

SPORT STARS
Nov., 1949

1 The Life of Knute Rockne	250.00

Becomes:
SPORTS ACTION

2 BP(c),Life of George Gipp	225.00
3 BEv,Hack Wilson	150.00

4 Art Houtteman	125.00
5 Nile Kinnick	125.00
6 Warren Gun	125.00
7 Jim Konstanty	125.00
8 Ralph Kiner	135.00
9 Ed "Strangler" Lewis	125.00
10 JMn,'The Yella-Belly'	125.00
11 'The Killers'	125.00
12 'Man Behind the Mask'	125.00
13 Lew Andrews	125.00
14 MWs,Ken Roper,Sept.,1952	100.00

SPOTLIGHT
Sept., 1978

1 F:Huckleberry Hound, Yogi Bear	1.25
2 Quick Draw McDraw	1.00
3 The Jetsons	1.00
4 Magilla Gorilla, March, 1979	1.00

SPUMCO COMIC BOOK

1 I:Jimmy the Hapless Boy	6.95
2	6.95
3 64pgs of sick humor	6.95
4 More sick humor	6.95
TPB	24.95

SPY CASES
See: KID KOMICS

SPY FIGHTERS
March, 1951

1 GT	150.00
2 GT	75.00
3	65.00
4 thru 13	@60.00
14 thru 15 July, 1953	@65.00

SPYKE
Epic

1 BR,I:Spyke	2.75
2 V:Conita	2.75
3 thru 4 BR	@1.95

SPY THRILLERS
Atlas Nov., 1954

1 'The Tickling Death'	125.00

Squadron Supreme #4
© Marvel Entertainment Group

MARVEL

2 V:Communists	75.00
3	50.00
4	50.00

Becomes:

POLICE BADGE

5 Sept., 1955	30.00

SQUADRON SUPREME
Sept., 1985

1 BH,L:Nighthawk	3.00
2 BH,F:Nuke,A:Scarlet Centurion	2.50
3 BH,D:Nuke	2.50
4 BH,L:Archer	2.00
5 BH,L:Amphibian	2.00
6 PR,J:Institute of Evil	2.00
7 JB,JG,V:Hyperion	2.00
8 BH,V:Hyperion	2.00
9 BSz(c),PR,D:Tom Thumb	2.00
10 PR,V:Quagmire	2.00
11 PR,V:Redeemers	2.00
12 PR,D:Nighthawk,Foxfire,	
Black Archer	2.50
GN Death of a Universe	9.95

STALKERS
Epic April, 1990

1 MT	1.50
2 MT	1.50
3 MT	1.50
4 MT	1.50
5 MT	1.50
6 VM,MT	1.50
7 VM,MT	1.50
8 VM,MT	1.50
9 VM	1.50
10 VM	1.50
11 VM	1.50
12 VM, 1991	1.50

STARBLAST

1 MGu(s),HT,After the Starbrand	2.25
2 MGu(s),HT,After the Starbrand	2.00
3 MGu(s),HT,After the Starbrand	2.00
4 MGu(s),HT,Final Issue	2.00

STARBRAND
Oct., 1986

1 JR2,O:Starbrand	1.50
2 JR2/AW	1.00
3 JR2/AW	1.00
4 JR2/AW	1.00
5 JR2/AW	1.00
6 JR2/AW	1.00
7 JR2/AW	1.00
8 JR2/AW	1.00
9 KG/BWi,A:Nightmask	1.00
10	1.00
11 JR2,TP	1.00
12 JR2,TP,X-Men X-over	1.25
13 JR2,TP	1.25
14 JR2,TP	1.25
15	1.25
16	1.25
17 JBy,TP,New Starbrand	1.50
18 JBy/TP	1.50
19 JBy/TP	1.50
Ann.#1	1.25

STAR COMICS MAGAZINE
Dec., 1986 (digest size)

1 F:Heathcliff,Muppet Babies,	
Ewoks	1.50

2 thru 13 1988	@1.50

STARJAMMERS

1 I:The Uncreated	2.95
2 War For the Shi'ar	2.95
3 stuck in deep space	2.95
4 conclusion	2.95

STAR-LORD, SPECIAL EDITION
Feb., 1982

1 JBy reprints	6.00

STARLORD
Mini-Series 1996

1 (of 3) DLw,	2.50
2 DLw	2.50
3 DLw,V:Damyish	2.50

STARLORD MEGAZINE

TPB CCI,JBy,TA, rep., 64pg	2.95

STAR MASTER

1 MGu,Cosmic Avengers assemble	1.95
2 MGu,Worldengine saga	1.95
3 MGu,Cauldron of Conversion	

STARRIORS
August, 1984

1	1.50
2	1.25
3	1.25
4 Feb., 1982	1.25

STARSTRUCK
March, 1985

1 MK	2.00
2 MK	1.75
3 thru 8 MK, Feb. 1986	@1.50

STAR TREK
April, 1980

1 DC,KJ,rep.1st movie Adapt.	8.00
2 DC,KJ,rep.1st movie Adapt.	6.00
3 DC,KJ,rep.1st movie Adapt.	5.00

Star Trek #5
© *Marvel Entertainment Group*

4 DC,KJ,The Weirdest Voyage	5.00
5 DC,KJ,Dr.McCoy..Killer	5.00
6 DC,KJ,A:Ambassador Phlu	5.00
7 MN,KJ,Kirk/Spock(c)	5.00
8 DC(p),F:Spock	5.00
9 DC,FS,Trapped in a Web of	
Ghostly Vengeance	5.00
10 KJ(i),Spock the Barbarian	5.00
11 TP(i),Like A Woman Scorned	5.00
12 TP(i),Trapped in a Starship	
Gone Mad	5.00
13 TP(i),A:Barbara McCoy	5.00
14 LM,GD,We Are Dying,	
Egypt,Dying	5.00
15 GK,The Quality of Mercy	5.00
16 LM,There's no Space	
like Gnomes	5.00
17 EH,TP,The Long Nights Dawn	5.00
18 A Thousand Deaths,last issue	5.00

STAR TREK: DEEP SPACE NINE
1996

1 HWe(s),TGb,AM,DS9 in the	
Gamma Quadrant,pt.1 (of 2)	1.95
2 DS9 in Gamma Quadrant,pt.2	1.95
3 TGb,AM,pt.1 (of 2)	1.95
4 TGb,AM,pt.2	1.95
5 AM,terrorist attack	1.95
6 HWe(s),TGb,AM,Shirn sentence	
Sisko to Death, "Risk," pt.1	1.95
7 HWe(s),TGb,"Risk,"pt.2	1.95
8 TGb,AM,V:Maquis & Romulans	1.95
9 TGb,AM,V:Maquis & Romulans,	
pt.2	1.95
10 HWe,TGb, trapped in the	
holosuite	1.95
11 HWe,TGb,	1.95

STAR TREK: EARLY VOYAGES
(Dec. 1996)

1 DAn,IEd,Captain Pike's crew,	
double size premier	2.95
2 DAn,IEd,distress signal	1.95
3 DAn,IEd,on Rigel 7, prologue to	
"The Cage"	1.95
4 DAn,IEd, prologue to "The Cage"	1.95
5 DAn,IEd, V:Vulcans	1.95
6 DAn,IEd, Cloak & Dagger concl.	1.95
7 DAn,IEd, The wrath of Kaaj	1.95
8 DAn,IEd,F:Dr. Boyce	1.95

STAR TREK: FIRST CONTACT

GN Movie Adapt.	5.95

STAR TREK: MIRROR, MIRROR
1996

1-shot continuation of famous	
classic episode	3.95

STAR TREK: OPERATION ASSIMILATION

1-shot Borg story	2.95

STAR TREK: STARFLEET ACADEMY
1996

1 Cadets vs. Gorns	1.95

MARVEL

2 ALa, R&R in Australia	1.95
3 F:Decker	1.95
4 V:Klingon Bird-of-prey	1.95
5 V:Klingons	1.95
6 Funeral of Kamilah	
Goldstein,I:Edam Astrun	1.95
7 ALa,F:Edam Astrun,Nog	1.95
8 ALa, Return of Charlie X	1.95
9 ALa, on Talos, V:Jem'Hadar	1.95
10 ALa,F:Captain Pike, Jem'Hadar	1.95

STAR TREK: UNLIMITED
1996

1 DAn,IEd,MBu,JeM,AW, Classic series & TNG	2.95
2 DAn,IEd,MBu,	2.95
3 DAn,IEd,MBu,	2.95
4 DAn,IEd,MBu,AW, 2 classic tales	2.95
5 DAn,IEd,TMo,RoR,AW,ANi, 48pg	2.95

STAR TREK: VOYAGER
1996

1 F:Neelix & Talaxians, pt.1	1.95
2 F:Neelix & Talaxians, pt.2	1.95
3 F:Neelix & Talaxians, pt.3	1.95
4 HWe(s),"Homeostasis", pt.1	1.95
5 HWe(s),"Homeostasis", pt.2	1.95
6 HWe(s),"Homeostasis", pt.3	1.95
7 Ancient Relic	1.95
8 Mysterious Relic encountered	1.95
9 DAn,IEd,AM, rescue mission	1.95
10 The Borg are back	1.95

STAR TREK/X-MEN

1-shot SLo,MS, 64pg.	5.00

Star Wars #37
© Marvel Entertainment Group

STAR WARS
July, 1977

1 HC,30 Cent,movie adaption.	65.00
1a HC,35 Cent(square Box)	400.00
1b "Reprint"	7.50
2 HC,movie adaptation	25.00
2b "Reprint"	4.00
3 HC,movie adaptation	25.00
3b "Reprint"	4.00
4 HC,SL,movie adapt.(low dist.)	20.00
4b "Reprint"	4.00
5 HC,SL,movie adaptation	20.00
5b "Reprint"	3.00
6 HC,DSt,E:movie adaption	20.00
6b "Reprint"	3.00
7 HC,FS,F:Luke&Chewbacca	18.00
7b "Reprint"	2.50
8 HC,TD,Eight against a World	18.00
8b "Reprint"	2.50
9 HC,TP,V:Cloud Riders	18.00
9b "Reprint"	2.50
10 HC,TP,Behemoth fr.Below	18.00
11 CI,TP,Fate o/Luke Skywalker	15.00
12 TA,CI,Doomworld	15.00
13 TA,JBy,CI,Deadly Reunion	15.00
14 TA,CI	15.00
15 CI,V:Crimson Jack	15.00
16 WS,V:The Hunter	15.00
17 Crucible, Low Dist.	16.00
18 CI,Empire Strikes(Low Dist).	16.00
19 CI,Ultimate Gamble(Low Dist)	16.00
20 CI,Death Game(Scarce)	16.00
21 TA,CI,Shadow of a Dark Lord(Scarce)	16.00
22 CI,Han Solo vs.Chewbacca	12.00
23 CI,Flight Into Fury	12.00
24 CI,Ben Kenobi Story	12.00
25 CI,Siege at Yavin	12.00
26 CI,Doom Mission	10.00
27 CI,V:The Hunter	10.00
28 CI,Cavern o/t Crawling Death	10.00
29 CI,Dark Encounter	10.00
30 CI,A Princess Alone	10.00
31 CI,Return to Tatooine	10.00
32 CI,The Jawa Express	10.00
33 CI,GD,V:Baron Tagge	10.00
34 CI,Thunder in the Stars	10.00
35 CI,V:Darth Vader	10.00
36 CI,V:Darth Vader	10.00
37 CI,V:Darth Vader	10.00
38 TA,MG,Riders in the Void	10.00
39 AW,B:Empire Strikes Back	15.00
40 AW,Battleground Hoth	14.00
41 AW,Imperial Pursuit	14.00
42 AW,Bounty Hunters	14.00
43 AW,Betrayal at Bespin	14.00
44 AW,E:Empire Strikes Back	14.00
45 CI,GD,Death Probe	10.00
46 CI,TP,V:Dreamnaut Devourer	10.00
47 CI,GD,Droid World	10.00
48 CI,Leia vs.Darth Vader	10.00
49 SW,TP,The Last Jedi	10.00
50 WS,AW,TP,G-Size issue	12.00
51 WS,TP,Resurrection of Evil	9.00
52 WS,TP	9.00
53 CI,WS	9.00
54 CI,WS	9.00
55 thru 66 WS,TP	@9.00
67 TP	9.00
68 GD,TP	9.00
69 GD,TP	9.00
70 A:Han Solo	9.00
71 A:Han Solo	7.00
72	7.00
73 Secret of Planet Lansbane	7.00
74 thru 91	@7.00
92 BSz(c)	7.00
93 thru 97	@7.00
98 AW	7.00
99	7.00
100 Painted(c),double-size	15.00
101 BSz	12.00
102 KRo's Back	12.00
103 thru 106	@12.00
107 WPo(i),last issue	30.00
Ann.#1 WS(c),V:Winged Warlords	10.00
Ann.#2 RN	8.00
Ann.#3 RN,Darth Vader(c)	8.00

STEELGRIP STARKEY
Epic July, 1986

1	1.75
2	1.75
3	1.75
4	1.75
5	1.75
6 June, 1987	1.75

STEELTOWN ROCKERS
April, 1990—Sept., 1990

1 SL	1.50
2 thru 6 SL	@1.50

STORM

1 TyD,KIS,V:Candra	2.95
2	2.95
3	2.95
4 TyD,KIS, conclusion,foil cover	2.95

STRANGE COMBAT TALES

1 thru 2	2.75
3 Tiger by the Tail	2.50
4 Midnight Crusade	2.50

STRANGE STORIES OF SUSPENSE
See: RUGGED ACTION

STRANGE TALES
June, 1951
[1st Regular Series]

1 'The Room'	2,500.00
2 'Trapped In A Tomb'	800.00
3 JMn,'Man Who Never Was'	600.00
4 BEv,'Terror in the Morgue'	650.00
5 'A Room Without A Door'	650.00
6 RH(c),'The Ugly Man'	450.00
7 'Who Stands Alone'	450.00
8 BEv(c),'Something in the Fog'	450.00
9 'Drink Deep Vampire'	450.00
10 BK,'Hidden Head'	475.00
11 BEv(c),GC,'O'Malley's Friend'	275.00
12 'Graveyard At Midnight'	275.00
13 BEv(c),'Death Makes A Deal'	275.00
14 GT,'Horrible Herman'	275.00
15 BK,'Don't Look Down'	300.00
16 Decapitation cover	275.00
17 DBr,JRo,'Death Feud'	275.00
18 'Witch Hunt'	275.00
19 RH(c),'The Rag Doll'	275.00
20 RH(c),GC,SMo,'Lost World'	275.00
21 BEv	225.00
22 BK,JF	225.00
23 'The Strangest Tale in the World'	225.00
24 'The Thing in the Coffin'	225.00
25	225.00
26	225.00
27 JF,'The Garden of Death'	225.00
28 'Come into my Coffin'	250.00
29 'Witch-Craft'	225.00
30 'The Thing in the Box'	225.00
31 'The Man Who Played with Blocks'	225.00
32	225.00
33 JMn(c),'Step Lively Please'	225.00
34 'Flesh and Blood'	200.00

Strange Tales #89
© Marvel Entertainment Group

35 'The Man in the Bottle' 175.00
36 .... 175.00
37 'Out of the Storm' 175.00
38 .... 175.00
39 'Karnoff's Plan' 175.00
40 BEv,'The Man Who Caught a
    Mermaid' 175.00
41 BEv,'Riddle of the Skull' ... 200.00
42 DW,BEv,JMn,'Faceless One' 200.00
43 JF,'The Mysterious Machine' 175.00
44 .... 175.00
45 JKa,'Land of the
    Vanishing Men' 200.00
46 thru 57 .... @175.00
58 AW 175.00
59 BK 175.00
60 .... 150.00
61 BK 175.00
62 .... 150.00
63 .... 175.00
64 AW 150.00
65 .... 150.00
66 .... 150.00
67 thru 78 .... @175.00
79 SD,JK,Dr.Strange Prototype 175.00
80 thru 83 SD,JK .... @150.00
84 SD,JK,Magneto Prototype .. 175.00
85 SD,JK 150.00
86 SD,JK,'I Who
    Created Mechano' 150.00
87 SD,JK,'Return of Grogg' ... 150.00
88 SD,JK,'Zzutak' 150.00
89 SD,JK,'Fin Fang Foom' 400.00
90 SD,JK,'Orrgo the
    Unconquerable' 150.00
91 SD,JK,'The Sacrifice' 150.00
92 SD,JK,'The Thing That Waits
    For Me' 150.00
93 SD,JK,'The Wax People' ... 150.00
94 SD,JK,'Pildorr the Plunderer' 150.00
95 SD,JK,'Two-Headed Thing' . 150.00
96 SD,JK,'I Dream of Doom' .. 150.00
97 SD,JK,'When A Planet Dies' 350.00
98 SD,JK,'No Human Can
    Beat Me' 125.00
99 SD,JK,'Mister Morgan's
    Monster' 125.00
100 SD,JK,'I Was Trapped

    in the Crazy Maze' 125.00
101 B:StL(s),SD,JK,
    B:Human Torch 900.00
102 SD,JK,I:Wizard 300.00
103 SD,JK,I:Zemu 250.00
104 SD,JK,I:The Trapster 250.00
105 SD,JK,V:Wizard 250.00
106 SD,A:Fantastic Four 175.00
107 SD,V:Sub-Mariner 200.00
108 SD,JK,A:FF,I:The Painter . 175.00
109 SD,JK,I:Sorcerer 175.00
110 SD,I&B:Dr.Strange,
    Nightmare 1,300.00
111 SD,I:Asbestos,
    Baron Mordo 350.00
112 SD,I:The Eel 125.00
113 SD,I:Plant Man 125.00
114 SD,JK,A:Captain America . 400.00
115 SD,O:Dr.Strange 500.00
116 SD,V:Thing 125.00
117 SD,V:The Eel 100.00
118 SD,V:The Wizard 125.00
119 SD,C:Spider-Man 125.00
120 SD,1st Iceman/Torch T.U. . 135.00
121 SD,V:Plantman 75.00
122 SD,V:Dr.Doom 65.00
123 SD,A:Thor,I:Beetle 65.00
124 SD,I:Zota 65.00
125 SD,V:Sub-Mariner 65.00
126 SD,I:Dormammu,Clea ... 65.00
127 SD,V:Dormammu 60.00
128 SD,I:Demon 60.00
129 SD,I:Tiboro 60.00
130 SD,C:Beatles 65.00
131 SD,I:Dr.Vega 55.00
132 SD,I:Orini 55.00
133 SD,I:Shazana 55.00
134 SD,E:Torch,I:Merlin ... 55.00
135 SD,JK:I:Shield & Hydra
    B:Nick Fury 100.00
136 SD,JK,V:Dormammu 50.00
137 SD,JK,A:Ancient One ... 60.00
138 SD,JK,I:Eternity 45.00
139 SD,JK,V:Dormammu 45.00
140 SD,JK,V:Dormammu 45.00
141 SD,JK,I:Fixer,Mentallo . 45.00
142 SD,JK,I:THEM,V:Hydra .. 45.00
143 SD,JK,V:Hydra 45.00
144 SD,JK,V:Druid,I:Jasper
    Sitwell 45.00
145 SD,JK,I:Mr.Rasputin ... 45.00
146 SD,JK,V:Dormammu,I:AIM . 45.00
147 BEv,JK,F:Wong 45.00
148 BEv,JK,O:Ancient One ... 75.00
149 BEv,JK,V:Kaluu 45.00
150 BEv,JK,JB(1st Marvel Art)
    I:Baron Strucker,Umar .. 45.00
151 JK,JSo(1st Marvel Art),
    I:Umar 60.00
152 BEv,JK,JSo,V:Umar 40.00
153 JK,JSo,MSe,V:Hydra ... 40.00
154 JSo,MSe,I:Dreadnought . 40.00
155 JSo,MSe,A:L.B.Johnson . 40.00
156 JSo,MSe,I:Zom 40.00
157 JSo,MSe,A:Zom,C:Living
    Tribunal 40.00
158 JSo,MSe,A:Zom,I:Living
    Tribunal(full story) 45.00
159 JSo,MSe,O:Nick Fury,A:Capt.
    America,I:Val Fontaine ... 50.00
160 JSo,MSe,A:Captain America
    I:Jimmy Woo 40.00
161 JSo,I:Yellow Claw 40.00
162 JSo,DA,A:Captain America . 40.00
163 JSo,DA,V:Yellow Claw ... 40.00

Strange Tales #167
© Marvel Entertainment Group

164 JSo,DA,V:Yellow Claw ... 40.00
165 JSo,DA,V:Yellow Claw 40.00
166 DA,GT,JSo,A:AncientOne .. 40.00
167 JSo,DA,V:Doctor Doom .. 50.00
168 JSo,DA,E:Doctor Strange,Nick
    Fury,V:Yandroth 40.00
169 JSo,I&O:Brother Voodoo .. 5.00
170 JSo,O:Brother Voodoo 5.00
171 GC,V:Baron Samed 4.00
172 GC,DG,V:Dark Lord 4.00
173 GC,DG,I:Black Talon 4.00
174 JB,JM,O:Golem 4.00
175 SD,R:Torr 4.00
176 F:Golem 4.00
177 FB,F:Golem 4.00
178 JSn,B&O:Warlock,I:Magus . 27.00
179 JSn,I:Pip,I&D:Capt.Autolycus 18.00
180 JSn,I:Gamora,Kray-tor 18.00
181 JSn,E:Warlock 18.00
182 SD,GK,rep Str.Tales
    #123,124 .... 3.00
183 SD,rep Str.Tales #130,131 .. 3.00
184 SD,rep Str.Tales #132,133 .. 3.00
185 SD,rep Str.Tales #134,135 .. 3.00
186 SD,rep Str.Tales #136,137 .. 3.00
187 SD,rep Str.Tales #138,139 .. 3.00
188 SD,rep Str.Tales #140,141 .. 3.00
Ann.#1 V:Grottu,Diablo 450.00
Ann.#2 A:Spider-Man 500.00
[2nd Regular Series]
1 BB!,CW,B:Cloak&Dagger,Dr.
    Strange,V:Lord of Light 1.50
2 BBI,CW,V:Lord of Light,Demon 1.25
3 BBI,AW,CW,A:Nightmare,Khat . 1.25
4 BBI,CW,V:Nightmare 1.25
5 BBI,V:Rodent,A:Defenders 1.25
6 BBI,BWi,V:Erlik Khan,
    A:Defenders 1.25
7 V:Nightmare,A:Defenders 1.25
8 BBI,BWi,V:Kaluu 1.25
9 BBI,BWi,A:Dazzler,I:Mr.Jip,
    V:Kaluu 1.25
10 BBI,BWi,RCa,A:Black Cat,
    V:Mr.Jip,Kaluu 1.25
11 RCa,BWi,V:Mr.Jip,Kaluu 1.25

MARVEL

12 WPo,BWi,A:Punisher,V:Mr.Jip	2.00
13 JBr,BWi,RCa,Punisher, Power Pack	2.00
14 JBr,BWi,RCa,Punisher,P.Pack	2.00
15 RCa,BMc,A:Mayhem	1.25
16 RCa,BWi,V:Mr.Jip	1.25
17 RCa,BWi,V:Night	1.25
18 RCa,KN,A:X-Factor',V:Night	1.50
19 MMi(c),EL,TA,RCa,A:Thing	1.25
TPB Fully painted	6.95

STRANGE TALES OF THE UNUSUAL
Dec., 1955—Aug., 1957

1 JMn(c),BP,DH,JR,'Man Lost'	300.00
2 BEv,'Man Afraid'	150.00
3 AW,'The Invaders'	175.00
4 'The Long Wait'	100.00
5 RC,SD,'The Threat'	125.00
6 BEv	100.00
7 JK,JO	110.00
8	100.00
9 BEv(c),BK	125.00
10 GM,AT	100.00
11 BEv(c),August, 1957	100.00

STRANGE WORLDS
Dec., 1958

1 JK,SD	600.00
2 SD	350.00
3 JK	250.00
4 AW	225.00
5 SD	200.00

STRAWBERRY SHORTCAKE
Star June, 1985—April, 1986

1	1.25
2 thru 7	@1.00

STRAY TOASTERS
Epic Jan., 1988

1 BSz	5.00
2 BSz	4.50
3 and 4 BSz	@4.00

STRIKEFORCE MORITURI
Dec., 1986

1 BA,SW,WPo(1st pencils-3 pages),I:Blackwatch	2.50
2 BA,SW,V:The Horde	1.50
3 BA,SW,V:The Horde	1.50
4 BA,SW,WPo,V:The Horde	2.00
5 BA,SW,V:The Horde	1.50
6 BA,SW,V:The Horde	1.25
7 BA,SW,V:The Horde	1.25
8 BA,SW,V:The Horde	1.25
9 BA,SW,V:The Horde	1.25
10 WPo,(1st pencils-full story), SW,R:Black Watch,O:Horde	3.00
11 BA,SW,V:The Horde	1.25
12 BA,SW,D:Jelene	1.25
13 BA,SW,Old V:NewTeam	1.25
14 BA,AW,V:The Horde	1.25
15 BA,AW,V:The Horde	1.25
16 WPo,SW,V:The Horde	2.50
17 WPo(c),SW,V:The Horde	1.25
18 BA,SW,V:Hammersmith	1.25
19 BA,SW,V:THe Horde,D:Pilar	1.25
20 BA,SW,V:The Horde	1.25
21 MMi(c),TD(i),V:The Horde	1.25

22 TD(i),V:The Horde	1.25
23 MBa,VM,V:The Horde	1.50
24 VM(i),I:Vax,V:The Horde	1.75
25 TD(i),V:The Horde	1.75
26 MBa,VM,V:The Horde	1.75
27 MBa,VM,O:MorituriMaster	1.75
28 MBa,V:The Tiger	1.75
29 MBa,V:Zakir Shastri	1.75
30 MBa,V:Andre Lamont,The Wind	1.75
31 MBa(c),V:The Wind,last issue	1.75

STRONG GUY REBORN
Spec. TDz,ASm,ATi,

STRYFE'S STRIKE FILE

1 LSn,NKu,GCa,BP,C:Siena Blaze,Holocaust	4.00
1a 2nd Printing	1.75

Sub-Mariner #12
© Marvel Entertainment Group

SUB-MARINER
May, 1968

1 JB,O:Sub-Mariner	125.00
2 JB,A:Triton	50.00
3 JB,A:Triton	35.00
4 JB,V:Attuma	35.00
5 JB,I&O:Tiger Shark	35.00
6 JB,DA,V:Tiger Shark	35.00
7 JB,I:Ikthon	35.00
8 JB,V:Thing	35.00
9 MSe,DA,A:Lady Dorma	35.00
10 GC,DA,O:Lemuria	35.00
11 GC,V:Capt.Barracuda	25.00
12 MSe,I:Lyna	25.00
13 MSe,JS,A:Lady Dorma	25.00
14 MSe,V:Fake Human Torch	30.00
15 MSe,V:Dragon Man	25.00
16 MSe,I:Nekaret,Thakos	15.00
17 MSe,I:Stalker,Kormok	15.00
18 MSe,A:Triton	15.00
19 MSe,I:Stingray	17.00
20 JB,V:Dr.Doom	15.00
21 MSe,D:Lord Seth	15.00
22 MSe,A:Dr.Strange	15.00
23 MSe,I:Orka	10.00
24 JB,JM,V:Tiger Shark	10.00
25 SB,JM,O:Atlantis	10.00

26 SB,A:Red Raven	10.00
27 SB,I:Commander Kraken	11.00
28 SB,V:Brutivae	10.00
29 SB,V:Hercules	9.00
30 SB,A:Captain Marvel	10.00
31 SB,A:Triton	9.00
32 SB,JM,I&O:Llyra	9.00
33 SB,JM,I:Namora	9.00
34 SB,JM,AK,1st Defenders	18.00
35 SB,JM,A:Silver Surfer	18.00
36 BWr,SB,W:Lady Dorma	10.00
37 RA,D:Lady Dorma	9.00
38 RA,JSe,O:Rec,I:Thakorr,Fen	9.00
39 RA,JM,V:Llyra	9.00
40 GC,I:Turalla,A:Spidey	10.00
41 GT,V:Rock	6.00
42 GT,JM,V:House Named Death	6.00
43 GC,V:Tunal	6.00
44 MSe,JM,V:Human Torch	7.00
45 MSe,JM,V:Tiger Shark	6.00
46 GC,D:Namor's Father	6.00
47 GC,A:Stingray,V:Dr.Doom	6.00
48 GC,V:Dr.Doom	6.00
49 GC,V:Dr.Doom	6.00
50 BEv,I:Namorita	9.00
51 BEv,O:Namorita,C:Namora	7.00
52 GK,V:Sunfire	6.00
53 BEv,V:Sunfire	6.00
54 BEv,AW,V:Sunfire,I:Lorvex	6.00
55 BEv,V:Torg	6.00
56 DA,I:Coral	6.00
57 BEv,I:Venus	6.00
58 BEv,I:Tamara	6.00
59 BEv,V:Tamara	6.00
60 BEv,V:Tamara	6.00
61 BEv,JM,V:Dr.Hydro	6.00
62 HC,JSt,I:Tales of Atlantis	6.00
63 HC,JSt,V:Dr.Hydro,I:Arkus	6.00
64 HC,JSe,I:Maddox	6.00
65 DH,DP,V:She-Devil,inc.BEv Eulogy Pin-up	6.00
66 DH,V:Orka,I:Raman	6.00
67 DH,A:FF,V:Triton,N:Namor I&O:Force	6.00
68 DH,O:Force	6.00
69 GT,V:Spider-Man	7.00
70 GT,I:Piranha	6.00
71 GT,V:Piranha	6.00
72 DA,V:Slime/Thing	6.00
Spec.#1 Rep. Tales to Astonish #70-#73	8.25
Spec.#2 Rep. Tales to Astonish #74-#76	8.25

[Limited Series]

1 RB,BMc,Namor's Birth	2.50
2 RB,BMc,Namor Kills Humans	2.00
3 RB,BMc,V:Surface Dwellers	2.00
4 RB,BMc,V:Human Torch	2.00
5 RB,BMc,A:Invaders	2.00
6 RB,BMc,V:Destiny	2.00
7 RB,BMc,A:Fantastic Four	2.00
8 RB,BMc,A:Hulk,Avengers	2.00
9 RB,BMc,A:X-Men,Magneto	2.00
10 RB,BMc,V:Thing	2.00
11 RB,BMc,A:Namorita,Defenders	2.00
12 RB,BMc,A:Dr.Doom, AlphaFlight	2.00

(SAGA OF THE) SUB-MARINER
[Mini-Series] Nov., 1988

1 RB,BMc,Namor's Birth	2.50
2 RB,BMc,Namor Kills Humans	1.50
3 RB,BMc,V:Surface Dwellers	1.50

MARVEL

MARVEL

MARVEL

4 RB,BMc,V:Human Torch 1.50
5 RB,BMc,A:Invaders 1.50
6 RB,BMc,V:Destiny 1.50
7 RB,BMc,A:Fantastic Four 1.50
8 RB,BMc,A:Hulk,Avengers 1.50
9 RB,BMc,A:X-Men,Magneto . . . 2.00
10 RB,BMc,V:Thing 1.50
11 RB,BMc,A:Namorita,Defenders 1.50
12 RB,BMc,A:Dr.Doom,Alp.Flight . 1.50

SUB-MARINER COMICS
Timely Spring, 1941

1 ASh(c),BEv,PGn,B:Sub-
Mariner, The Angel 20,000.00
2 ASh(c),BEv,Nazi
Submarine (c) 4,500.00
3 ASh(c),BEv 3,000.00
4 ASh(c),BEv,BW 2,500.00
5 . . . . 1,800.00
6 ASh(c) 1,400.00
7 . . . . 1,400.00
8 ASh(c) 1,400.00
9 ASh(c),BW 1,400.00
10 ASh(c) 1,400.00
11 ASh(c) 1,100.00
12 ASh(c) 1,100.00
13 ASh(c) 1,100.00
14 ASh(c) 1,100.00
15 ASh(c) 1,100.00
16 ASh(c) 1,100.00
17 ASh(c) 1,100.00
18 ASh(c) 1,100.00
19 . . . . 1,100.00
20 ASh(c) 1,100.00
21 SSh(c),BEv 750.00
22 SSh(c),BEv 750.00
23 SSh(c),BEv 750.00
24 MSy(c),BEv,A:Namora,
bondage cover 750.00
25 MSy(c),HK,B:The Blonde
Phantom, A:Namora,
bondage(c) 1,000.00
26 BEv,A:Namora 725.00
27 DRi(c),BEv,A:Namora 725.00
28 DRi(c),BEv,A:Namora 725.00
29 BEv,A:Namora,Human Torch 725.00
30 DRi(c),BEv,'Slaves Under
the Sea' 725.00
31 BEv,'The Man Who Grew',
A:Capt. America,E:Blonde
Phantom 725.00
32 BEv,O:Sub-Mariner . . . 1,300.00
33 BEv,O:Sub-Mariner,A:Human
Torch,B:Namora 700.00
34 BEv,A:Human Torch,bondage
cover 550.00
35 BEv,A:Human Torch 550.00
36 BEv 550.00
37 JMn(c),BEv 550.00
38 SSh(c),BEv,JMn 650.00
39 JMn(c),BEv 550.00
40 JMn(c),BEv 550.00
41 JMn(c),BEv 550.00
42 BEv,Oct., 1955 . . . . 650.00

SUBURBAN JERSEY NINJA SHE-DEVILS

1 I:Ninja She-Devils 1.50

SUPERNATURAL THRILLERS
Dec., 1972

1 JSo(c),JSe,FrG,IT! 1.50

2 VM,DA,The Invisible Man 1.50
3 GK,The Valley of the Worm . . 1.25
4 Dr. Jekyll and Mr. Hyde 1.25
5 RB,The Living Mummy 1.25
6 GT,JA,The Headless Horseman 1.25
7 VM,B:The Living Mummy,'
Back From The Tomb' 1.25
8 VM,'He Stalks Two Worlds' . . 1.25
9 GK/AM(c),VM,DA,'Pyramid of
the Watery Doom' 1.25
10 VM,'A Choice of Dooms' 1.25
11 VM,'When Strikes the ASP' . . 1.25
12 VM,KJ,'The War That Shook
the World' 1.25
13 VM,DGr,'The Tomb of the
Stalking Dead' 1.25
14 VM,AMc,'All These Deadly
Pawns' 1.25
15 TS, E:The Living Mummy,'Night
of Armageddon',Oct., 1975 . . . 1.25

SUPER SOLDIERS

1 I:Super Soldier,A:USAgent 2.75
2 A:USAgent 2.00
3 A:USAgent 2.00
4 A:USAgent,Avengers 2.00
5 A:Captain America,AWC 2.00
6 O:Super Soldiers 2.00
7 in Savage Land 2.00

SUPER-VILLAIN CLASSICS
May, 1983

1 O:Galactus 3.50

Super-Villain Team-Up #1
© Marvel Entertainment Group

SUPER-VILLAIN TEAM-UP
August, 1975

1 GT/BEv(c),B:Dr.Doom/Sub-
Mariner,A:Attuma,Tiger Shark 6.00
2 SB,A:Tiger Shark, Attuma . . . 4.00
3 EH(c),JA,V:Attuma 4.00
4 HT,JM,Dr.Doom vs. Namor . . . 4.00
5 RB/JSt(c),HT,DP,A:Fantastic

Four,I:Shroud 4.00
6 HT,JA,A:Shroud,Fantastic Four 3.00
7 RB/KJ(c),HT,O:Shroud 3.00
8 KG,V:Ringmaster 3.00
9 ST,A:Avengers,Iron Man 3.00
10 BH,DP,A:Capt.America,
V:Attuma,Red Skull 3.00
11 DC/JSt(c),BH,DP,B:Dr. Doom,
Red Skull,A:Capt. America . . . 3.00
12 DC/AM(c),BH,DP,Dr.Doom vs.
Red Skull 3.00
13 KG,DP,Namor vs. Krang 3.00
14 JBy/TA(c),BH,DP,V:Magneto,
X-over with Champions #15 . . 5.00
15 GT,ME,A:Red Skull 3.00
16 CI,A:Dr. Doom 3.00
17 KP(c),Red Skull Vs.Hatemonger
June 1976 . . . . 3.00
G-Size#1 F:Namor, Dr.Doom 3.00
G-Size#2 F:Namor, Dr.Doom 3.00

SUSPENSE
Atlas Dec., 1949

1 BP,Ph(c),Sidney Greenstreet/
Peter Lorne (Maltese Falcon) 400.00
2 Ph(c),Dennis O'Keefe/Gale
Storm (Abandoned) 200.00
3 B:Horror stories,'The Black
Pit' 200.00
4 'Thing In Black' 150.00
5 BEv,GT,RH,BK,DBr,'Hangman's
House' 160.00
6 BEv,GT,PAM,RH,'Madness
of Scott Mannion' 150.00
7 DBr,GT,DR,'Murder' 150.00
8 GC,DRi,RH,'Don't Open
the Door' 150.00
9 GC,DRi,'Back From The Dead'150.00
10 JMn(c),WIP,RH,'Trapped
In Time' 150.00
11 MSy,'The Suitcase' 125.00
12 GT,'Dark Road' 125.00
13 JMn(c),'Strange Man',
bondage cover 125.00
14 RH,'Death And Doctor Parker'125.00
15 JMn(c),OW,'The Machine' . . 125.00
16 OW,'Horror Backstage' 125.00
17 'Night Of Terror' 125.00
18 BK,'The Cozy Coffin' 125.00
19 BEv,RH 100.00
20 . . . . 100.00
21 BEv(c) 100.00
22 BEv(c),BK,OW 100.00
23 BEv 100.00
24 RH,GT 125.00
25 'I Died At Midnight' 125.00
26 BEv(c) 100.00
27 DBr 110.00
28 BEv 100.00
29 JMn,BF,JRo,April, 1953 . . . 100.00

SWORDS OF THE SWASHBUCKLERS

1 JG,Adult theme 2.25
2 JG 1.75
3 JG 1.75
4 JG 1.50
5 JG 1.50
6 JG 1.50
7 JG 1.50
8 thru 12, June 1987 . . . . @1.50

TALE OF THE MARINES
See: DEVIL-DOG DUGAN

All comics prices listed are for *Near Mint* condition.

TALES OF ASGARD
Oct., 1968
1 . . . . 35.00
Vol.2 #1 Feb,1984 . . . . 2.00

TALES OF G.I. JOE
Jan., 1988
1 reprints,#1 . . . . 2.00
2 #2 . . . . 1.50
3 #3 . . . . 1.50
4 #4 . . . . 1.50
5 #5 . . . . 1.50
6 #6 . . . . 1.50
7 rep. #7 - #16 . . . . 1.50

TALES OF JUSTICE
See: JUSTICE COMICS

TALES OF THE AGE OF APOCALYPSE
1996
One shot SLo,JoB,Age of Apocalypse
stories 5.00

TALES OF THE MARVELS: BLOCKBUSTER
Fully Painted 5.95

TALES OF THE MARVELS: INNER DEMONS
Fully painted, 48pg. 5.95

TALES OF THE MARVELS: WONDER YEARS
1 & 2 DAb . . . . @4.95

TALES OF SUSPENSE
Jan., 1959
1 DH(c),AW,'The Unknown
Emptiness' 1,300.00
2 SK,'Robot in Hiding' 500.00
3 SD,JK,'The Aliens Who
Captured Earth' 400.00
4 JK,AW,'One Of Us
Is A Martian' 450.00
5 JF,'Trapped in the Tunnel
To Nowhere' 275.00
6 JK(c),'Howl in the Swamp' . 275.00
7 SD,JK,'The Molten Man-Thing'275.00
8 BEv,'Monstro' 275.00
9 JK(c),JF,'Diablo' 300.00
10 RH,'I Bought Cyclops Back
To Life' 275.00
11 JK(c),'I Created Sporr' . . . 200.00
12 RC,'Gorkill The Living Demon'200.00
13 'Elektro' 200.00
14 JK(c),'I Created Colossus' . . 200.00
15 JK/DAy(c),'Behold...Goom' . 200.00
16 JK/DAy(c),'The Thing Called
Metallo' 250.00
17 JK/DAy(c),'Goo Gam, Son
of Goom' 200.00
18 JK/DAy(c),'Kraa the Inhuman' 200.00
19 JK,DAy,SD,'The Green Thing' 200.00
20 JK,DAy,SD,'Colossus Lives
Again' 200.00
21 JK/DAy(c),SD,'This Is Klagg' 150.00
22 JK/DAy(c),SD,'Beware
Of Bruttu' 150.00
23 JK,DAy,SD,'The Creature
in the Black Bog' 150.00

Tales of Suspense #73
© Marvel Entertainment Group

24 JK,DAy,SD,'Insect Man' . . . 150.00
25 JK,DAy,SD,'The Death of
Monstrollo' 150.00
26 JK,DAy,SD,'The Thing That
Crawled By Night' 150.00
27 JK,DAy,SD,'When Oog Lives
Again' 150.00
28 JK,DAy,SD,'Back From
the Dead' 150.00
29 JK,DAy,SD,DH,'The Martian
Who Stole A City' 125.00
30 JK,DAy,SD,DH,'The Haunted
Roller Coaster' 125.00
31 JK,DAy,SD,DH,'The Monster
in the Iron Mask' 125.00
32 JK,DAy,SD,DH,'The Man in
the Bee-Hive' 135.00
33 JK,DAy,SD,DH,'Chamber of
Fear' 125.00
34 JK,DAy,SD,DH,'Inside The
Blue Glass Bottle' 125.00
35 JK,DAy,SD,DH,'The Challenge
of Zarkorr' 125.00
36 SD,'Meet Mr. Meek' 125.00
37 DH,SD,'Hagg' 125.00
38 'The Teenager who ruled
the World 125.00
39 JK,O&I:Iron Man 3,100.00
39a rep.#39,Marvel Milestone . . . 2.95
40 JK,C:Iron Man 1,200.00
41 JK 600.00
42 DH,SD,I:Red Pharoah 260.00
43 JK,DH,I:Kala,A:Iron Man . . . 260.00
44 DH,SD,V:Mad Pharoah 250.00
45 DH,V:Jack Frost 250.00
46 DH,CR,I:Crimson Dynamo . 160.00
47 SD,V:Melter 160.00
48 SD,N:Iron Man 175.00
49 SD,A:Angel 150.00
50 DH,I:Manderin 100.00
51 DH,I:Scarecrow 80.00
52 DH,I:Black Widow 110.00
53 DH,O:Watcher 100.00
54 DH,V:Mandarin 60.00
55 DH,V:Mandarin 60.00
56 DH,I:Unicorn 60.00

57 DH,I&O:Hawkeye 135.00
58 DH,B:Captain America 230.00
59 DH,1st S.A. Solo Captain America,
I:Jarvis 230.00
60 DH,JK,V:Assassins 110.00
61 DH,JK,V:Mandarin 60.00
62 DH,JK,O:Mandarin 60.00
63 JK,O:Captain America 175.00
64 DH,JK,A:Black Widow,
Hawkeye 70.00
65 DH,JK,I:Red Skull 100.00
66 DH,JK,O:Red Skull 100.00
67 DH,JK,V:Adolph Hitler 40.00
68 DH,JK,V:Red Skull 40.00
69 DH,JK,I:Titanium Man 40.00
70 DH,JK,V:Titanium Man 35.00
71 DH,JK,WW,V:Titanium Man . 35.00
72 DH,JK,V:The Sleeper 35.00
73 JK,GT,A:Black Knight 35.00
74 JK,GT,V:The Sleeper 35.00
75 JK,I:Batroc,Sharon Carter . . . 35.00
76 JR,V:Mandarin 40.00
77 JK,JR,V:Ultimo,I:Peggy
Carter 35.00
78 GC,JK,V:Ultimo 35.00
79 GC,JK,V:Red Skull,
I:Cosmic Cube 55.00
80 GC,JK,V:Red Skull 60.00
81 GC,JK,V:Red Skull 40.00
82 GC,JK,V:The Adaptoid 40.00
83 GC,JK,V:The Adaptoid 40.00
84 GC,JK,V:Mandarin 40.00
85 GC,JK,V:Batroc 40.00
86 GC,JK,V:Mandarin 40.00
87 GC,V:Mole Man 40.00
88 JK,GC,V:Power Man 40.00
89 JK,GC,V:Red Skull 40.00
90 DH,GC,V:Red Skull 40.00
91 GC,JK,V:Crusher 40.00
92 GC,JK,A:Nick Fury 40.00
93 GC,JK,V:Titanium Man 40.00
94 GC,JK,I:Modok 40.00
95 GC,JK,V:Grey Gargoyle,IR:Cap.
America 40.00
96 GC,JK,V:Grey Gargoyle . . . 40.00
97 GC,JK,I:Whiplash,
A:Black Panther 40.00
98 GC,JK,I:Whitney Frost
A:Black Panther 60.00
99 GC,JK,A:Black Panther 65.00
Becomes:
CAPTAIN AMERICA

TALES OF SUSPENSE MARVEL MILESTONE
1 Metallic(c) rep. Tales 2.95

TALES OF THE MARVELS: WONDER YEARS
1 F:Wonder Man 4.95
2 F:Wonder Man 4.95

TALES OF THE ZOMBIE
August, 1973
(black & white magazine)
1 Reprint Menace #5,O:Zombie 18.00
2 GC,GT 10.00
3 . . . . 10.00
4 'Live and Let Die' 10.00
5 BH 10.00
6 . . . . 10.00
7 thru 9 AA . . . . @10.00
10 March, 1975 . . . . 10.00

MARVEL

Tales to Astonish #38
© Marvel Entertainment Group

TALES TO ASTONISH
[1st Series]
Jan., 1959

1 JDa,'Ninth Wonder o/t World'1,500.00
2 SD,'Capture A Martian' 600.00
3 SD,JK,'The Giant From
  Outer Space' 400.00
4 SD,JK,'The Day The
  Martians Struck' 400.00
5 SD,AW,'The Things on
  Easter Island' 425.00
6 SD,JK,'Invasion of the
  Stone Men' 375.00
7 SD,JK,'The Thing on Bald
  Mountain' 350.00
8 SD,JK,'Mummex, King of
  the Mummies' 350.00
9 JK(c),SD,'Droom, the
  Living Lizard' 350.00
10 JK,SD,'Titano' 350.00
11 JK,SD,'Monstrom, the Dweller
  in the Black Swamp' 225.00
12 JK/DAy(c),SD,'Gorgilla' 225.00
13 JK,SD,'Groot, the Monster
  From Planet X' 225.00
14 JK,SD,'Krang' 225.00
15 JK/DAy,'The Blip' 275.00
16 JK,SD,'Thorr' 250.00
17 JK,SD,'Vandoom' 225.00
18 JK,SD,'Gorgilla Strikes Again' 225.00
19 JK,SD,'Rommbu' 225.00
20 JK,SD,'X, The Thing
  That Lived' 225.00
21 JK,SD,'Trull the Inhuman' . . 225.00
22 JK,SD,'The Crawling
  Creature' 175.00
23 JK,SD,'Moomba is Here' . . . 175.00
24 JK,SD,'The Abominable
  Snowman' 175.00
25 JK,SD,'The Creature From
  Krogarr' 175.00
26 JK,SD,'Four-Armed Things' . 175.00
27 StL(s),SD,JK,I:Antman . . 3,300.00
28 JK,SD,I Am the Gorilla Man . 150.00
29 JK,SD,When the Space
  Beasts Attack 150.00
30 JK,SD,Thing From the

Hidden Swamp 150.00
31 JK,SD,The Mummy's Secret . 150.00
32 JK,SD,Quicksand 150.00
33 JK,SD,Dead Storage 150.00
34 JK,SD,Monster at Window . 150.00
35 StL(s),JK,SD, B:Ant Man
  (2nd App.) 1,500.00
36 JK,SD,V:Comrade X 550.00
37 JK,SD,V:The Protector 350.00
38 JK,SD,Betrayed By the Ants 350.00
39 JK,DH,V:Scarlet Beetle 350.00
40 JK,SD,DH,The Day Ant-Man
  Failed 350.00
41 DH,St,SD,V:Kulla 225.00
42 DH,JSe,SD,Voice of Doom . 225.00
43 DH,SD,Master of Time 225.00
44 JK,SD,I&O:Wasp 250.00
45 DH,SD,V:Egghead 150.00
46 DH,SD,I:Cyclops(robot) 150.00
47 DH,SD,V:Trago 150.00
48 DH,SD,I:Porcupine 150.00
49 JK,DH,AM,Ant-Man Becomes
  Giant-Man 175.00
50 JK,SD,I&O:Human Top 100.00
51 JK,V:Human Top 100.00
52 I&O:Black Knight 100.00
53 DH,V:Porcupine 100.00
54 DH,I:El Toro 100.00
55 V:Human Top 100.00
56 V:The Magician 100.00
57 A:Spider-Man 150.00
58 V:Colossus(not X-Men one) . 100.00
59 V:Hulk,Black Knight 150.00
60 SD,B:Hulk,Giant Man 200.00
61 SD,I:Glenn Talbot,
  V:Egghead 75.00
62 I:Leader,N:Wasp 75.00
63 SD,O:Leader(1st full story) . . 75.00
64 SD,V:Leader 75.00
65 DH,SD,N:Giant-Man,. 75.00
66 JK,SD,V:Leader,Chameleon . 75.00
67 JK,SD,I:Kanga Khan 75.00
68 JK,N:Human Top,V:Leader . . 75.00
69 JK,V:Human Top,Leader,
  E:Giant-Man 75.00
70 JK,B:Sub-Mariner/Hulk,I:
  Neptune 100.00
71 JK,V:Leader,I:Vashti 60.00
72 JK,V:Leader 60.00
73 JK,V:Leader,A:Watcher 60.00
74 JK,V:Leader,A:Watcher 60.00
75 JK,A:Watcher 60.00
76 JK,Atlantis 60.00
77 JK,V:Executioner 60.00
78 GC,JK,Prince and the Puppet 60.00
79 JK,Hulk vs.Hercules 60.00
80 GC,JK,Moleman vs Tyrannus 60.00
81 GC,JK,I:Boomerang,Secret Empire,
  Moleman vs Tyrannus 60.00
82 GC,JK,V:Iron Man 75.00
83 JK,V:Boomerang 50.00
84 GC,JK,Like a Beast at Bay . . 50.00
85 GC,JB,Missile & the Monster . 50.00
86 JB,V:Warlord Krang 50.00
87 BEv,IR:Hulk 50.00
88 BEv,GK,V:Boomerang 50.00
89 BEv,GK,V:Stranger 50.00
90 JK,I:Abomination 50.00
91 BEv,DA,V:Abomination 50.00
92 MSe,C:Silver Surfer x-over . . 62.00
93 MSe,Silver Surfer x-over . . . 60.00
94 BEv,MSe,V:Dragorr,High
  Evolutionary. 50.00
95 BEv,MSe,V:High Evolutionary 50.00
96 MSe,Skull Island,High Evol. . 50.00

Tales to Astonish #62
© Marvel Entertainment Group

97 MSe,C:Kazar,X-Men 55.00
98 DA,MSe,I:Legion of the Living
  Lightning,I:Seth 50.00
99 DA,MSe,V:Legion of the Living
  Lighting 50.00
100 MSe,DA,Hulk v.SubMariner . 60.00
101 MSe,GC,V:Loki 85.00
Becomes: INCREDIBLE HULK

TALES TO ASTONISH
[2nd Series]
Dec., 1979

1 JB,rep.Sub-Mariner#1 . . . . . . 1.75
2 JB,rep.Sub-Mariner#2 . . . . . . 1.25
3 JB,rep.Sub-Mariner#3 . . . . . . 1.25
4 JB,rep.Sub-Mariner#4 . . . . . . 1.25
5 JB,rep.Sub-Mariner#5 . . . . . . 1.25
6 JB,rep.Sub-Mariner#6 . . . . . . 1.25
7 JB,rep.Sub-Mariner#7 . . . . . . 1.25
8 JB,rep.Sub-Mariner#8 . . . . . . 1.25
9 JB,rep.Sub-Mariner#9 . . . . . . 1.25
10 JB,rep.Sub-Mariner#10 . . . . . 1.25
11 JB,rep.Sub-Mariner#11 . . . . . 1.25
12 JB,rep.Sub-Mariner#12 . . . . . 1.25
13 JB,rep.Sub-Mariner#13 . . . . . 1.25
14 JB,rep.Sub-Mariner#14 . . . . . 1.25

TARZAN
June, 1977

1 JB,Edgar Rice Burroughs Adapt. 4.00
2 JB,O:Tarzan 2.50
3 JB,'The Alter of the Flaming
  God',I:LA 2.00
4 JB,TD,V:Leopards 2.00
5 JB,TD,'Vengeance',A:LA 2.00
6 JB,TD,'Rage of Tantor,A:LA . . 2.00
7 JB,TD,'Tarzan Rescues The
  Moon' 2.00
8 JB,'Battle For The Jewel Of
  Opar' 2.00
9 JB,'Histah, the Serpent' 2.00
10 JB,'The Deadly Peril of
  Jane Clayton' 2.00
11 JB 2.00
12 JB,'Fangs of Death' 2.00
13 JB,'Lion-God' 2.00
14 JB,'The Fury of Fang and Claw' 2.00

MARVEL

Tarzan #16
© Marvel Entertainment Group

15 JB,'Sword of the Slaver' 2.00
16 JB,'Death Rides the Jungle
    Winds' 2.00
17 JB,'The Entrance to the
    Earths Core' 2.00
18 JB,'Corsairs of the Earths Core' 2.00
19 'Pursuit' 2.00
20 'Blood Bond' 2.00
21 'Dark and Bloody Sky' 2.00
22 JM,RN,'War In Pellucidar' 2.00
23 'To the Death' 2.00
24 'The Jungle Lord Returns' 2.00
25 RB(c),V:Poachers 2.00
26 RB(c),'Caged' 2.00
27 RB(c),'Chaos in the Caberet' .. 2.00
28 'A Savage Against A City' 2.00
29 Oct., 1979 .... 2.00
Ann.#1 JB 2.50
Ann.#2 'Drums of the
    Death-Dancers' 2.00
Ann.#3 'Ant-Men and the
    She-Devils' 2.00

TARZAN OF THE APES
July, 1984
1 (movie adapt.) 1.25
2 .... 1.25

TEAM AMERICA
June, 1982
1 O:Team America 2.00
2 V:Marauder 1.25
3 LMc,V:Mr.Mayhem 1.25
4 Lmc,V:Arcade Assassins 1.25
5 A:Marauder 1.25
6 A:R.U. Ready 1.25
7 LMc,V:Emperor of Texas 1.25
8 DP,V:Hydra 1.25
9 A:Iron Man 1.25
10 V:Minister Ashe 1.00
11 A:Marauder,V:GhostRider 3.00
12 DP,Marauder unmasked,
    May, 1983 .... 2.50

TEAM HELIX
1 A:Wolverine 2.00
2 A:Wolverine 2.00

TEAM X/TEAM 7
1-shot LHa,SEp,MRy 4.95

TEEN COMICS
See: ALL WINNERS COMICS

TEENAGE ROMANCE
See: MY ROMANCE

TERMINATOR 2
Sept., 1991
1 KJ,movie adaption 1.25
2 KJ,movie adaption 1.25
3 KJ,movie adaption 1.25
Terminator II (bookshelf format) .. 4.95
Terminator II (B&W mag. size) ... 2.25

TERRARISTS
Epic
1 thru 4 w/card .... @2.50
5 thru 7 .... @2.50

TERROR INC.
1 JZ,I:Hellfire 3.00
2 JZ,I:Bezeel,Hellfire 2.50
3 JZ,A:Hellfire 2.00
4 JZ,A:Hellfire,V:Barbatos 2.00
5 JZ,V:Hellfire,A:Dr Strange ... 2.00
6 JZ,MT,A:Punisher 2.00
7 JZ,V:Punisher 2.00
8 Christmas issue 2.00
9 JZ,V:Wolverine 2.25
10 V:Wolverine 2.25
11 A:Silver Sable,Cage 2.00
12 For Love Nor Money#4,A:Cage,
    Silver Sable 2.00
13 Inf.Crusade,A:Gh.Rider 2.00

TESSIE THE TYPIST
Timely Summer, 1944
1 BW,'Doc Rockblock' 325.00
2 BW,'Powerhouse Pepper' .. 225.00
3 Football cover 75.00
4 BW 125.00
5 BW 125.00
6 BW,HK,'Hey Look' 125.00
7 BW 125.00
8 BW 125.00
9 BW,HK,'Powerhouse Pepper' 135.00
10 BW,A:Rusty 135.00
11 BW,A:Rusty 135.00
12 BW,HK 135.00
13 BW,A:Millie The Model,Rusty 110.00
14 BW 80.00
15 HK,A:Millie,Rusty 80.00
16 HK 55.00
17 HK,A:Millie, Rusty 55.00
18 HK 55.00
19 Annie Oakley story 50.00
20 .... 45.00
21 A:Lana, Millie 45.00
22 .... 45.00
23 .... 45.00
Becomes:
TINY TESSIE
24 .... 35.00
Becomes:
REAL EXPERIENCES
25 Ph(c),Jan., 1950 .... 25.00

TEXAS KID
Atlas Jan., 1951
1 GT,JMn,O:Texas Kid 125.00
2 JMn 60.00
3 JMn,'Man Who Didn't Exist' . 50.00
4 JMn 50.00
5 JMn 50.00
6 JMn 50.00
7 JMn 50.00
8 JMn 50.00
9 JMn 50.00
10 JMn,July, 1952 .... 50.00

TEX DAWSON, GUNSLINGER
Jan., 1973
1 JSo(c) 2.00
Becomes:
GUNSLINGER
2 .... 1.25
3 June, 1973 .... 1.25

TEX MORGAN
August, 1948
1 .... 165.00
2 'Boot Hill Welcome For A
    Bad Man' 125.00
3 .... 100.00
4 'Trapped in the Outlaws Den',
    A:Arizona Annie 75.00
5 'Valley of Missing Cowboys' . 75.00
6 'Never Say Murder',
    A:Tex Taylor 75.00
7 CCB,Ph(c),'Captain Tootsie',
    A:Tex Taylor 100.00
8 Ph(c),'Terror Of Rimrock
    Valley', A:Diablo 100.00
9 Ph(c),'Death to Tex Taylor'
    Feb., 1950 .... 100.00

TEX TAYLOR
Sept., 1948
1 'Boot Hill Showdown' 175.00
2 'When Two-Gun Terror Rides
    the Range' 100.00
3 'Thundering Hooves and Blazing
    Guns' 80.00
4 Ph(c),'Draw or Die Cowpoke' 100.00
5 Ph(c),'The Juggler of Yellow
    Valley',A:Blaze Carson ... 100.00
6 Ph(c),'Mystery of Howling Gap' 80.00
7 Ph(c),'Trapped in Times' Lost
    Land',A:Diablo 120.00
8 Ph(c),'The Mystery of Devil-Tree
    Plateau',A:Diablo 120.00
9 Ph(c),'Guns Along the Border',
    A:Nimo,March, 1950 ..... 120.00

THANOS QUEST
1990
1 JSn,RLm,V:Elders,
    for Soul Gems 6.00
1a 2nd printing 3.00
2 JSn,RLm,O:SoulGems,I:
    Infinity Gauntlet (story
    cont.in SilverSurfer #44) 5.00
2a 2nd printing 3.00

THING, THE
July, 1983
1 JBy,O:Thing 2.50
2 JBy,Woman from past 1.75

3 JBy,A:Inhumans	1.50
4 JBy,A:Lockjaw	1.50
5 JBy,A:Spider-Man,She-Hulk	1.50
6 JBy,V:Puppet Master	1.25
7 JBy,V:Goody Two Shoes	1.25
8 JBy,V:Egyptian Curse	1.25
9 JBy,F:Alicia Masters	1.25
10 JBy,Secret Wars	1.25
11 JBy,B:Rocky Grimm	1.25
12 JBy,F:Rocky Grimm	1.25
13 JBy,F:Rocky Grimm	1.25
14 F:Rocky Grimm	1.25
15 F:Rocky Grimm	1.25
16 F:Rocky Grimm	1.25
17 F:Rocky Grimm	1.25
18 F:Rocky Grimm	1.25
19 F:Rocky Grimm	1.25
20 F:Rocky Grimm	1.25
21 V:Ultron	1.25
22 V:Ultron	1.25
23 R:Thing to Earth,A:Fant.Four	1.25
24 V:Rhino,A:Miracle Man	1.25
25 V:Shamrock	1.25

Thing #27
© Marvel Entertainment Group

26 A:Vance Astro	1.50
27 I:Sharon Ventura	1.25
28 A:Vance Astro	1.25
29 A:Vance Astro	1.25
30 Secret Wars II,A:Vance Astro	1.25
31 A:Vance Astro	1.25
32 A:Vance Astro	1.25
33 A:Vance Astro,I:NewGrapplers	1.25
34 V:Titania,Sphinx	1.25
35 I:New Ms.Marvel,PowerBroker	1.25
36 Last Issue,A:She-Hulk	1.25

[Mini-Series]

1 rep.Marvel Two-in-One #50	1.75
2 rep Marvel Two-in-One,V:GR	1.75
3 rep Marvel Two-in-One #51	1.25
4 rep Marvel Two-in-One #43	1.25

THOR, THE MIGHTY
Prev: Journey Into Mystery
March, 1966

126 JK,V:Hercules	135.00
127 JK,I:Pluto,Volla	55.00
128 JK,V:Pluto,A:Hercules	55.00

129 JK,V:Pluto,I:Ares	55.00
130 JK,V:Pluto,A:Hercules	55.00
131 JK,I:Colonizers	55.00
132 JK,A:Colonizers,I:Ego	55.00
133 JK,A:Colonizers,A:Ego	55.00
134 JK,I:High Evolutionary, Man-Beast	60.00
135 JK,O:High Evolutionary	50.00
136 JK,F:Odin	45.00
137 JK,I:Ulik	45.00
138 JK,V:Ulik,A:Sif	45.00
139 JK,V:Ulik	45.00
140 JK,V:Growing Man	45.00
141 JK,V:Replicus	35.00
142 JK,V:Super Skrull	35.00
143 JK,BEv,V:Talisman	35.00
144 JK,V:Talisman	35.00
145 JK,V:Ringmaster	35.00
146 JK,O:Inhumans Part 1	45.00
147 JK,O:Inhumans Part 2	40.00
148 JK,I:Wrecker,O:Black Bolt	40.00
149 JK,O:Black Bolt,Medusa	40.00
150 JK,A:Triton	35.00
151 JK,V:Destroyer	35.00
152 JK,V:Destroyer	35.00
153 JK,F:Dr.Blake	35.00
154 JK,I:Mangog	35.00
155 JK,V:Mangog	35.00
156 JK,V:Mangog	35.00
157 JK,D:Mangog	35.00
158 JK,O:Don Blake Part 1	75.00
159 JK,O:Don Blake Part 2	35.00
160 JK,I:Travrians	32.00
161 JK,Shall a God Prevail	32.00
162 JK,O:Galactus	45.00
163 JK,I:Mutates,A:Pluto	25.00
164 JK,A:Pluto,V:Greek Gods	25.00
165 JK,V:Him/Warlock	45.00
166 JK,V:Him/Warlock	45.00
167 JK,F:Sif	23.00
168 JK,O:Galactus	42.00
169 JK,O:Galactus	42.00
170 JK,BEv,V:Thermal Man	21.00
171 JK,BEv,V:Wrecker	21.00
172 JK,BEv,V:Ulik	21.00
173 JK,BEv,V:Ulik,Ringmaster	21.00
174 JK,BEv,V:Crypto-Man	21.00
175 JK,Fall of Asgard,V:Surtur	21.00
176 JK,V:Surtur	21.00
177 JK,I:Igon,V:Surtur	21.00
178 JK,C:Silver Surfer	24.00
179 JK,MSe,C:Galactus	21.00
180 NA,JSi,V:Loki	15.00
181 NA,JSi,V:Loki	15.00
182 JB,V:Dr.Doom	7.50
183 JB,V:Dr.Doom	7.50
184 JB,I:The Guardian	7.50
185 JB,JSt,V:Silent One	7.50
186 JB,JSt,V:Hela	7.50
187 JB,JSt,V:Odin	7.50
188 JB,JM,F:Odin	7.50
189 JB,JSt,V:Hela	7.50
190 JB,I:Durok	7.50
191 JB,JSt,V:Loki	7.50
192 JB	7.50
193 JB,SB,V:Silver Surfer	45.00
194 JB,SB,V:Loki	7.50
195 JB,JR,V:Mangog	7.50
196 JB,NR,V:Kartag	7.50
197 JB,V:Mangog	7.50
198 JB,V:Pluto	7.50
199 JB,V:Pluto,Hela	7.50
200 JB,Ragnarok	9.00
201 JB,JM,Odin resurrected.	6.00
202 JB,V:Ego-Prime	6.00

The Mighty Thor #148
© Marvel Entertainment Group

203 JB,V:Ego-Prime	6.00
204 JB,JM,Demon from t/Depths	6.00
205 JB,V:Mephisto	6.00
206 JB,V:Absorbing Man	5.00
207 JB,V:Absorbing Man	5.00
208 JB,V:Mercurio	5.00
209 JB,I:Druid	5.00
210 JB,DP,I:Ulla,V:Ulik	5.00
211 JB,DP,V:Ulik	4.00
212 JB,JSt,V:Sssthgar	4.00
213 JB,DP,I:Gregor	4.00
214 SB,JM,V:Dark Nebula	4.00
215 JB,JM,J:Xorr	4.00
216 JB,JM,V:4D-Man	4.00
217 JB,SB,I:Krista,V:Odin	4.00
218 JB,JM,A:Colonizers	4.00
219 JB,I:Protector	4.00
220 JB,V:Avalon	4.00
221 JB,V:Olympus	4.00
222 JB,JSe,A:Hercules,V:Pluto	4.00
223 JB,A:Hercules,V:Pluto	4.00
224 JB,V:Destroyer	4.00
225 JB,JSi,I:Fire Lord	8.00
226 JB,A:Watcher,Galactus	4.00
227 JB,JSi,V:Ego	4.00
228 JB,JSi,A:Galactus,D:Ego	4.00
229 JB,JSi,A:Hercules,I:Dweller	4.00
230 JB,A:Hercules	4.00
231 JB,DG,V:Armak	4.00
232 JB,JSi,A:Firelord	4.00
233 JB,Asgard Invades Earth	4.00
234 JB,V:Loki	4.00
235 JB,JSi,I:Possessor (Kamo Tharnn)	4.00
236 JB,JSi,V:Absorbing Man	3.50
237 JB,JSi,V:Ulik	3.50
238 JB,JSi,V:Ulik	3.50
239 JB,JSi,V:Ulik	3.50
240 SB,KJ,V:Seth	3.50
241 JB,JGi,I:Geb	3.50
242 JB,JSi,V:Servitor	3.50
243 JB,JSt,V:Servitor	3.50
244 JB,V:Servitor	3.50
245 JB,JSt,V:Servitor	3.50
246 JB,JSt,A:Firelord	3.50
247 JB,JSt,A:Firelord	3.50
248 JB,V:Storm Giant	3.50
249 JB,V:Odin	3.50

All comics prices listed are for *Near Mint* condition.

250 JB,D:Igron,V:Mangog 3.50	321 I:Menagerie 2.50	366 WS,A:Thunder Frog 2.25
251 JB,A:Sif 3.50	322 V:Heimdall 2.50	367 WS,D:Malekith,A:Kurse 2.25
252 JB,V:Ulik 3.50	323 V:Death 2.50	368 WS,F:Balder t/Brave,Kurse . . 2.25
253 JB,I:Trogg 3.50	324 V:Graviton 2.50	369 WS,F:Balder the Brave 2.25
254 JK,O:Dr.Blake rep 3.50	325 JM,O:Darkoth,V:Mephisto . . 2.75	370 JB,V:Loki 2.25
255 Stone Men of Saturn Rep. . . 3.50	326 I:New Scarlet Scarab 2.75	371 SB,I:Justice Peace,V:Zaniac . 2.25
256 JB,I:Sporr 3.50	327 V:Loki & Tyr 2.50	372 SB,V:Justice Peace 2.25
257 JK,JB,I:Fee-Lon 3.50	328 I:Megatak 2.75	373 SB,A:X-Factor,(Mut.Mass) . . . 5.00
258 JK,JB,V:Grey Gargoyle . . . 3.50	329 HT,V:Hrungnir 2.50	374 WS,SB,A:X-Factor,(Mut.Mass)
259 JB,A:Spider-Man 4.00	330 BH,I:Crusader 2.50	A:Sabretooth 7.00
260 WS,I:Doomsday Star 4.00	331 Threshold of Death 2.50	375 WS,SB,N:Thor(Exoskeleton) . 2.25
261 WS,I:Soul Survivors 3.00	332 V:Dracula 2.75	376 WS,SB,V:Absorbing Man . . . 2.25
262 WS,Odin Found,I:Odin Force 3.00	333 BH,V:Dracula 2.75	377 WS,SB,N:Thor,A:Ice Man . . . 2.25
263 WS,V:Loki 3.00	334 Quest For Rune Staff 2.50	378 WS,SB,V:Frost Giants 2.25
264 WS,V:Loki 3.00	335 V:Possessor 2.50	379 WS,V:Midgard Serpent 2.25
265 WS,V:Destroyer 3.00	336 A:Captain Ultra 2.75	380 WS,V:Midgard Serpent 2.25
266 WS,Odin Quest 3.00	337 WS,I:Beta Ray Bill,A:Surtur . 8.50	381 WE,SB,A:Avengers 2.50
267 WS,F:Odin 3.00	338 WS,O:Beta Ray Bill,I:Lorelei . 5.00	382 WS,SB,V:Frost Giants,Loki . . 2.50
268 WS,V:Damocles 3.00	339 WS,V:Beta Ray Bill 3.50	383 BBr,Secret Wars story 2.50
269 WS,V:Stilt-Man 3.00	340 WS,A:Beta Ray Bill 3.00	384 RF,BBr,I:Future Thor(Dargo) . 5.00
270 WS,V:Blastaar 3.00	341 WS,V:Fafnir 2.25	385 EL,V:Hulk 2.00
271 Avengers,Iron Man x-over . . . 3.00	342 WS,V:Fafnir,I:Eilif 2.25	386 RF,BBr,I:Leir 2.00
272 JB,Day the Thunder Failed . . 3.00	343 WS,V:Fafnir 2.25	387 RF,BBr,V:Celestials 2.00
273 JB,V:Midgard Serpent 3.00		388 RF,BBr,V:Celestials 2.00
274 JB,D:Balder,I:Hermod,Hoder . 3.00		389 RF,BBr,V:Celestials 2.00
275 JB,V:Loki,I:Sigyn 3.00		390 RF,BBr,A:Avengers,V:Seth . . 2.00
276 JB,Trial of Loki 3.00		391 RF,BBr,I:Mongoose,Eric
277 JB,V:Fake Thor 3.00		Masterson,A:Spider-Man 5.00
278 JB,V:Fake Thor 3.00		392 RF,I:Quicksand 2.00
279 A:Pluto,V:Ulik 3.00		393 RF,BBr,V:Quicksand,A:DD . . 2.00
280 V:Hyperion 3.00		394 RF,BBr,V:Earth Force 2.00
281 O:Space Phantom 3.00		395 RF,V:Earth Force 2.00
282 V:Immortus,I:Tempus 3.00		396 RF,A:Black Knight 2.00
283 JB,V:Celestials 3.00		397 RF,A:Loki 2.00
284 JB,V:Gammenon 3.00		398 RF,DH,R:Odin,V:Seth 2.00
285 JB,R:Karkas 3.00		399 RF,RT,R:Surtur,V:Seth 2.00
286 KP,KRo,D:Kro,I:Dragona . . 3.00		400 RF,JSt,CV,V:Surtur,Seth . . . 5.00
287 KP,2nd App & O:Forgotten		401 V:Loki 2.00
One(Hero) 3.00		402 RF,JSt,V:Quicksand 2.00
288 KP,V:Forgotten One 3.00		403 RF,JSt,V:Executioner 2.00
289 KP,V:Destroyer 3.00		404 RF,JSt,TD,V:Annihilus 2.00
290 I:Red Bull(Toro Rojo) 3.00		405 RF,JSt,TD,V:Annihilus 2.00
291 KP,A:Eternals,Zeus 3.00		406 RF,JSt,TD,V:Wundagore . . . 2.00
292 KP,V:Odin 3.00		407 RF,JSt,R:Hercules,High Evol. 2.00
293 KP,Door to Minds Eye 3.00		408 RF,JSt,I:Eric Masterson/Thor
294 KP,O:Odin & Asgard,I:Frey . . 3.00		V:Mongoose 3.50
295 KP,I:Fafnir,V:Storm Giants . . 3.00		409 RF,JSt,V:Dr.Doom 2.00
296 KP,D:Siegmund 3.00		410 RF,JSt,V:Dr.Doom,She-Hulk . 2.00
297 KP,V:Sword of Siegfried . . . 3.00		411 RF,JSt,C:New Warriors
298 KP,V:Dragon(Fafnir) 3.00		V:Juggernaut,A of V 6.00
299 KP,V:Valkyrie,I:Hagen 3.00		412 RF,JSt,I:New Warriors
300 KP,giant,O:Odin & Destroyer,		V:Juggernaut,A of V 10.00
Rindgold Ring Quest ends,D:Uni-		413 RF,JSt,A:Dr.Strange 1.75
Mind,I:Mother Earth 6.00		414 RF,JSt,V:Ulik 1.75
301 KP,O:Mother Earth,V:Apollo . 3.00	344 WS,Balder Vs.Loki,I:Malekith . 2.25	415 HT,O:Thor 1.75
302 KP,V:Locus 3.00	345 WS,V:Malekith 2.25	416 RF,JSt,A:Hercules 1.75
303 Whatever Gods There Be . . . 3.00	346 WS,V:Malekith 2.25	417 RF,JSt,A:High Evolutionary . . 1.75
304 KP,V:Wrecker 3.00	347 WS,V:Malekith,I:Algrim	418 RF,JSt,V:Wrecking Crew . . . 1.75
305 KP,R:Gabriel(Air Walker) . . . 3.00	(Kurse) 2.25	419 RF,JSt,B:Black Galaxy
306 KP,O&V:Firelord,O:AirWalker 3.00	348 WS,V:Malekith 2.25	Saga,I:Stellaris 1.75
307 KP,I:Dream Demon 3.00	349 WS,R:Beta Ray Bill,O:Odin,	420 RF,JSt,A:Avengers,V:Stellaris 1.75
308 KP,V:Snow Giants 3.00	I&O:Vili & Ve(Odin's brothers) . 2.50	421 RF,JSt,V:Stellaris 1.75
309 V:Bomnardiers 3.00	350 WS,V:Surtur 2.25	422 RF,JSt,V:High Evol.,Nobilus . 1.75
310 KP,V:Mephisto 3.00	351 WS,V:Surtur 2.25	423 RF,JSt,A:High Evol.,Celestials
311 KP,GD,A:Valkyrie 3.00	352 WS,V:Surtur 2.25	Count Tagar 1.75
312 KP,V:Tyr 3.00	353 WS,V:Surtur,D:Odin 2.25	424 RF,JSt,V:Celestials,E:Black
313 KP,Thor Trial 3.00	354 WS,V:Hela 2.25	Galaxy Saga 1.75
314 KP,A:Drax,Moondragon . . . 3.00	355 WS,SB,A:Thor's Great	425 RF,AM,V:Surtur,Ymir 1.75
315 KP,O:Bi-Beast 3.00	Grandfather 2.25	426 RF,JSt,HT,O:Earth Force . . . 1.50
316 KP,A:Iron Man,Man Thing,	356 BL,BG,V:Hercules 2.25	427 RF,JSt,A:Excalibur 1.50
V:Man-Beast 3.00	357 WS,A:Beta Ray Bill 2.50	428 RF,JSt,A:Excalibur 1.50
317 KP,V:Man-Beast 3.00	358 WS,A:Beta Ray Bill 2.50	429 RF,JSt,A:Ghost Rider 2.00
318 GK,V:Fafnir 3.00	359 WS,V:Loki 2.25	430 RF,AM,A:Mephisto,Gh.Rider . 1.75
319 KP,I&D:Zaniac 3.00	360 WS,V:Hela 2.25	431 HT,AM,V:Ulik,Loki 1.75
320 KP,V:Rimthursar 2.75	361 WS,V:Hela 2.25	432 RF,D:Loki,Thor Banished,Eric
	362 WS,V:Hela 2.25	
	363 WS,Secret Wars II,V:Kurse . 2.50	
	364 WS,I:Thunder Frog 2.25	
	365 WS,A:Thunder Frog 2.25	

MARVEL COMICS GROUP

25¢ 233

THE MIGHTY THOR

ASGARD and EARTH!

THUNDER GOD

The Mighty Thor #233
© Marvel Entertainment Group

MARVEL

All comics prices listed are for *Near Mint* condition.   **CVA Page 265**

MARVEL

Masterson becomes 2nd Thor . 4.00
433 RF,V:Ulik 5.00
434 RF,AM,V:Warriors Three 2.50
435 RF,AM,V:Annihilus 2.50
436 RF,AM,V:Titania,Absorbing
   Man,A:Hercules 1.50
437 RF,AM,V:Quasar 1.50
438 RF,JSt,A:Future Thor(Dargo) . 1.50
439 RF,JSt,A:Drago 1.50
440 RF,AM,I:Thor Corps 2.50
441 RF,AM,Celestials vs.Ego . . . 2.50
442 RF,AM,Don Blake,Beta Ray
   Bill,Mephisto 1.50
443 RF,AM,A:Dr.Strange,Silver
   Surfer,V:Mephisto 1.50
444 RF,AM,Special X-mas tale . . 1.50
445 AM,Galactic Storm,pt.7
   V:Gladiator 1.50
446 AM,Galactic Storm,pt.14
   A:Avengers 1.50
447 RF,AM,V:Absorbing Man
   A:Spider-Man 1.50
448 RF,AM,V:Titania,A:SpM 1.50

The Mighty Thor #338
© Marvel Entertainment Group

449 RF,AM,V:Ulik 1.50
450 RF,AM,V:Heimdall,A:Code Blue
   Double-Sized,Gatefold(c),rep.
   Journey Into Mystery#87 . . . . 3.00
451 RF,AM,I:Bloodaxe 1.50
452 RF,AM,V:Bloodaxe 1.50
453 RF,AM,V:Mephisto 1.50
454 RF,AM,V:Mephisto,Loki,
   Karnilla 1.50
455 AM(i),V:Loki,Karnilla,R:Odin,
   A:Dr.Strange 1.50
456 RF,AM,V:Bloodaxe 1.50
457 RF,AM,R:1st Thor 1.50
458 RF,AM,Thor vs Eric 1.50
459 RF,AM,C&I:Thunderstrike(Eric
   Masterson) 2.00
460 I:New Valkyrie 1.50
461 V:Beta Ray Bill 1.50
462 A:New Valkyrie 1.50
463 Infinity Crusade 1.50
464 Inf.Crusade,V:Loki 1.50
465 Infinity Crusade 1.50
466 Infinity Crusade 1.50
467 Infinity Crusade 1.50
468 RMz(s),Blood & Thunder#1 . . 3.00

469 RMz(s),Blood & Thunder#5 . . 1.50
470 MCW,Blood & Thunder#9 . . . 1.50
471 MCW,E:Blood & Thunder . . . 1.50
472 B:RTs(s),MCW,I:Godling,C:High
   Evolutionary 1.50
473 MCW,V:Godling,High Evolutionary
   I&C:Karnivore(Man-Beast) 1.75
474 MCW,C:High Evolutionary . . . 1.50
475 MCW,Foil(c),A:Donald Blake,
   N:Thor 3.00
475a Newsstand Ed. 2.00
476 V:Destroyer 1.75
477 V:Destroyer,A:Thunderstrike . 1.75
478 V:Norvell Thor 1.75
479 V:Norvell Thor 1.75
480 V:High Evolutionary 1.50
481 V:Grotesk 1.50
482 Don Blake construct 1.50
483 RTs,MCW,V:Loki 1.50
484 Badoy and Soul 1.50
485 V:The Thing 1.50
486 High Evolutionary,Godpack . . 1.50
487 V:Kurse 1.50
488 RTs,MCW,Kurse Saga concl. . 1.50
489 RTs,V:Kurse,A:Hulk 1.50
490 TDF,Thunderstrike post-mortem 1.50
491 N:Thor 7.50
492 Worldengine's Secrets 5.00
493 Worldengine trigers Ragnarok . 3.00
494 Worldengine saga conclusion . 3.00
495 BML,Avengers:Timeslide 2.50
496 MD2,BML 2.50
497 MD2,BML 2.50
498 BML,V:Absorbing Man 2.00
499 MD2,BML, ... 2.00
500 MD2,BML,double size,A:Dr.
   Strange 3.00
501 MD2,BML,I:Red Norvell 2.00
502 MD2,BML,Onslaught tie-in, A:Red
   Norvell, Jane Foster, Hela 2.00
Becomes:

JOURNEY INTO MYSTERY
Third Series (Nov. 1996)
503 TDF,MD2, The Lost Gods, New
   Norse gods? 1.50
504 TDF,Golden Realm in ruins,
   V:Ulik the Troll 1.50
505 TDF,MD2, V:Wrecker,
   A:Spider-Man 1.50
506 TDF,MD2, R:Heimdall 1.50
507 TDF,Odin kidnapped 1.50
508 TDF, ... 1.95
509 TDF,Battle for the Future
   of Asgard 1.95
510 TDF,Return of Loki,A:Seth . . 1.95
511 TDF,EBe,Lost Gods reunited
   with Odin 1.95
512 EBe, Odin vs. Seth 1.95
Ann.#2 JK,V:Destroyer 50.00
Ann.#3 JK,rep,Grey Gargoyle. . . 13.00
Ann.#4 JK,rep,TheLivingPlanet. . 11.00
Ann.#5 JK,JB,Hercules,O:Odin . 10.00
Ann.#6 JK,JB,A:Guardians of the
   Galaxy,V:Korvac 10.00
Ann.#7 WS,Eternals 9.00
Ann.#8 JB,V:Zeus 8.00
Ann.#9 LMc,Dormammu 7.00
Ann.#10 O:Chthon,Gaea,A:Pluto . 6.00
Ann.#11 O:Odin 6.00
Ann.#12 BH,I:Vidar(Odin's son) . . 6.00
Ann.#13 JB,V:Mephisto 6.00
Ann.#14 AM,DH,Atlantis Attacks . 5.00
Ann.#15 HT,Terminus Factor #3 . 4.00
Ann.#16 Korvac Quest,pt.2,
   Guardians of Galaxy 2.50

Ann.#17 Citizen Kang#2 . . . . 2.50
Ann.#18 TGr,I:The Flame,w/card . 3.25
Ann.#19 V:Flame 3.25
G-Size.#1 Battles,A:Hercules . . . 14.00
TPB Alone Against the Celestials,
   rep.Thor#387-389 . . . . 5.95
TPB Ballad of Beta Ray Bill,rep.
   Thor#337-340 . . . . 8.95
Minus 1 Spec., TDF,EBe,flashback 1.95

THOR CORPS
[Limited Series]
1 TDF(s),PO,V:Demonstaff 2.00
2 TDF(s),PO,A:Invaders 2.00
3 TDF(s),PO,A:Spider-Man 2099 . 2.00
4 TDF(s),PO,Last Issue 2.00

THREE MUSKETEERS
1 thru 2 movie adapt. 1.25

THUNDERBOLTS
(Feb. 1997)
1 KBk,MBa,VRu,Post-onslaught new
   team:Citizen V, Meteorite, Techno,
   Songbird, Atlas & Mach-1, . . . 2.99
2 KBk,MBa,VRu,V:Mad Thinker . . 1.95
2a variant cover by MBa&VRu . . 1.95
3 KBk,MBa,VRu,Headquarters at
   Freedom's Plaza 1.95
4 KBk,MBa,VRu,I:Jolt 1.95
5 KBk,MBa,VRu,V:Elements of
   Doom 1.95
6 KBk,MBa,VRu,V:Elements of
   Doom 1.95

THUNDERBOLTS '97
Spec. KBk,MBa,TGu,GP,
   O:Thunderbolts, 48pg 2.95

THUNDERBOLTS:
DISTANT RUMBLINGS
1 KBk,SEp,Flashback,F:Citizen V .

THUNDERCATS
Star Dec., 1985
1 JM,TV tie-in 2.00

Thundercats #1
© Marvel Entertainment Group

1a 2nd printing 1.00	
2 JM,A:Berbils,V:Mumm-Ra 1.50	
3 . . . . 1.50	
4 JM,I:Lynxana 1.50	
5 JM 1.50	
6 JM 1.50	
7 Return to Thundera 1.50	
8 V:Monkiang 1.50	
9 V:Pekmen 1.00	
10 . . . . 1.00	
11 I:The Molemen 1.00	
12 'The Protectors' 1.00	
13 EC/AW,V:Safari Joe 1.00	
14 V:Snaf 1.00	
15 JM,A:Spidera 1.00	
16 'Time Capsula' 1.00	
17 . . . . 1.00	
18 EC/AW,'Doom Gaze' 1.00	
19 . . . . 1.00	
20 EC/AW 1.00	
21 JM,A:Hercules Baby 1.00	
22 I:Devious Duploids 1.00	
23 V:Devious Duploids 1.00	
24 June, 1988 . . . . 1.00	

THUNDERSTRIKE

1 B:TDF(s),RF,Holografx(c),
  V:Bloodaxe,I:Car Jack 3.25
2 RF,V:Juggernaut 1.50
3 RF,I:Sangre 1.50
4 RF,A:Spider-Man,I:Pandora . . . 1.50
5 RF,A:Spider-Man,V:Pandora . . 1.50
6 RF,I:Blackwulf,Bristle,Schizo,Lord
  Lucian,A:SpM,Code:Blue,Stellaris,
  V:SHIELD,Pandora,C:Tantalus 1.50
7 KP,V:Tantalus,D:Jackson . . . 1.75
8 RF,I&V:Officer ZERO 1.75
9 RF,V:Bloodaxe 1.75
10 RF,A:Thor 1.75
11 RF,A:Wildstreak 1.50
12 RF,A:Whyte Out 1.50
13 RF,Inferno 42 . . . . 1.50
13a Double Feature flip book
  with Code Blue #1 . . . . 2.50
14 RF, Inferno 42 . . . . 1.50
14a Double Feature flip book
  with Code Blue #2 . . . . 2.50
15 RF,V:Methisto 1.50
15a Double Feature flip book
  with Code Blue #3 . . . . 2.50
16 . . . . 1.50
17 V:Bloodaxe 1.50
18 V:New Villain 1.50
19 Shopping Network 1.50
20 A: Black Panther 1.50
21 A:War Machine,V:Loki 1.50
22 TDF,AM,RF,Mystery of Bloodaxe
  blows open 1.50
23 TDF,A:Avengers 1.50
24 TDF,V:Bloodaxe, final issue . . 1.50

TIMESPIRITS
Epic Jan., 1985

1 TY 2.00
2 . . . . 1.75
3 . . . . 1.75
4 AW 1.50
5 . . . . 1.50
6 . . . . 1.50
7 . . . . 1.50
8 March, 1986 . . . . 1.50

TIMESTRYKE

1 . . . . 1.95

---

2 . . . . 1.95

TINY TESSIE
See: TESSIE THE TYPIST

TOMB OF DARKNESS
See: BEWARE

TOMB OF DRACULA
April, 1972

1 GC,Night of the Vampire 85.00
2 GC,Who Stole My Coffin? . . . 50.00
3 GC,TP,I:Rachel Van Helsing . 30.00
4 GC,TP,Bride of Dracula! 30.00
5 GC,TP,To Slay A Vampire . . . 30.00
6 GC,TP,Monster of the Moors . 25.00
7 GC,TP,Child is Slayer of
  the Man 25.00
8 GC(p),The Hell-Crawlers 25.00
9 The Fire Cross 25.00
10 GC,I:Blade Vampire Slayer . 28.00

Tomb of Dracula #18
© Marvel Entertainment Group

11 GC,TP,Master of the Undead
  Strikes Again! 15.00
12 GC,TP,House that Screams . 15.00
13 GC,TP,O:Blade 18.00
14 GC,TP,Vampire has Risen
  from the Grave 15.00
15 GC,TP,Stay Dead 15.00
16 GC,TP,Back from the Grave . 15.00
17 GC,TP,A Vampire Rides This
  Train! 15.00
18 GC,TP,A:Werewolf By Night . 18.00
19 GC,TP,Snowbound in Hell . . 15.00
20 GC,TP,ManhuntForAVampire 15.00
21 GC,TP,A:Blade 13.00
22 GC,TP,V:Gorna 11.00
23 GC,TP,Shadow over Haunted
  Castle 11.00
24 GC,TP,I am your Death 11.00
25 GC,TP,Blood Stalkers of Count
  Dracula 11.00
26 GC,TP,A Vampire Stalks the
  Night 11.00
27 GC,TP,...And the Moon Spews
  Death! 11.00
28 GC,TP,Five came to Kill a
  Vampire' 11.00

---

29 GC,TP,Vampire goes Mad? . 11.00
30 GC,TP,A:Blade 11.00
31 GC,TP,Child of Blood 11.00
32 GC,TP,The Vampire Walks
  Among Us 11.00
33 GC,TP,Blood on My Hands . . 11.00
34 GC,TP,Bloody Showdown . . . 11.00
35 GC,TP,A:Brother Voodoo . . . 11.00
36 GC,TP,Dracula in America . . 11.00
37 GC,TP,The Vampire Walks
  Among Us 7.00
38 GC,TP,Bloodlust for a Dying
  Vampire 11.00
39 GC,TP,Final Death of Dracula 11.00
40 GC,TP,Triumph of Dr.Sun . . 11.00
41 GC,TP,A:Blade 8.00
42 GC,TP,V:Dr.Sun 7.00
43 GC,TP,A:NewYear'sNightmare 7.00
44 GC,TP,A:Dr.Strange 7.00
45 GC,TP,A:Hannibal King 8.00
46 GC,TP,W:Dracula & Domini . . 7.00
47 GC,TP,Death-Bites 7.00
48 GC,TP,A:Hannibal King 8.00
49 GC,TP,A:Robin Hood,
  Frankenstein's Monster 7.00
50 GC,TP,A:Silver Surfer 15.00
51 GC,TP,A:Blade 7.50
52 GC,TP,V:Demon 6.50
53 GC,TP,A:Hannibal King,Blade . 7.50
54 GC,TP,Twas the Night Before
  Christmas 6.50
55 GC,TP,Requiem for a Vampire 6.50
56 GC,TP,A:Harold H. Harold . . 6.50
57 GC,TP,The Forever Man 6.50
58 GC,TP,A:Blade 7.00
59 GC,TP,The Last Traitor 6.50
60 GC,TP,The Wrath of Dracula . 6.50
61 GC,TP,Resurrection 6.50
62 GC,TP,What Lurks Beneath . . 6.50
63 GC,TP,A:Janus 6.50
64 GC,TP,A:Satan 6.50
65 GC,TP,Where No Vampire
  Has Gone Before 6.50
66 GC,TP,Marked for Death 6.50
67 GC,TP,A:Lilith 6.50
68 GC,TP,Dracula turns Human . 6.50
69 GC,TP,Cross of Fire 6.50
70 GC,TP,double size,last issue . 8.50
Savage Return of Dracula. rep.
  Tomb of Dracula #1,#2 . . . . . 2.00
Wedding of Dracula. rep.Tomb
  of Dracula #30,#45,#46 . . . . 2.00
Requiem for Dracula. rep.Tomb
  of Dracula #69,70 . . . . 2.00

TOMB OF DRACULA
[Mini-Series]
Nov., 1991

1 GC,AW,Day of Blood 6.00
2 GC,AW,Dracula in DC 5.50
3 GC,AW,A:Blade 5.50
4 GC,AW,D:Dracula 5.50

TOMB OF DRACULA
Nov., 1979
(black & white magazine)

1 . . . . 3.50
2 SD 5.00
3 FM 5.00
4 . . . . 3.00
5 . . . . 3.00
6 Sept., 1980 . . . . 3.00

MARVEL

MARVEL

TOMB OF DRACULA MEGAZINE
TPB Halloween, MWn,GC,TP . . . 3.95

TOMORROW KNIGHTS
Epic June, 1990
1	1.95
2	1.50
3	1.50
4 Origin	1.50
5	2.25
6	2.25

TOP DOG
Star Comics April, 1985
1	1.25
2 thru 14, June 1987	@1.00

TOR
1 JKu,R:Tor,Magazine Format	6.25
2 JKu	6.25
3 JKu,V:The Iduard Ring	6.25

TOUGH KID SQUAD COMICS
Timely March, 1942
1 O:The Human Top,Tough Kid
Squad,A:The Flying Flame,
V:Doctor Klutch 7,500.00

TOWER OF SHADOWS
Sept., 1969
1 JR(c),JSo,JCr,'At The Stroke
of Midnight' 30.00
2 JR(c),DH,DA,NA,'The Hungry
One' 15.00
3 GC,BWs,GT,'Midnight in the Wax
Museum' 16.00
4 DH,'Within The Witching Circle' 8.00
5 DA,BWS,WW,'Demon That Stalks
Hollywood' 9.00
6 WW,SD,'Pray For the Man in the
Rat-Hole 12.00
7 BWS,WW,'Titano' 12.00
8 WW,SD,'Demons of
Dragon-Henge' 9.00
9 BWr(c),TP,Lovecraft story 8.00
Becomes:

CREATURES ON THE LOOSE
March, 1971
10 BWr,A:King Kull 35.00
11 DAy,rep Moomba is Here 4.00
12 JK,'I Was Captured By Korilla' 4.00
13 RC,'The Creature
From Krogarr' 4.00
14 MSe,'Dead Storage' 4.00
15 SD,'Spragg the Living Mountain' 2.25
16 GK,BEv,GK,B&O:Gullivar Jones,
Warrior of Mars 4.00
17 GK,'Slaves o/t Spider Swarm' . 2.25
18 RA,'The Fury of Phra' 4.00
19 WB,JM,GK,'Red Barbarian
of Mars' 4.00
20 GK(c),GM,SD,'The Monster...
And the Maiden 4.00
21 JSo(c),GM,'Two Worlds To
Win',E:Guilliver 4.00
22 JSo(c),SD,VM,B:Thongor,
Warrior of Lost Lemuria . . . 4.00
23 VM,'The Man-Monster Strikes' 4.00

24 VM,'Attack of the Lizard-Hawks' 2.25
25 VM,GK(c),'Wizard of Lemuria' . 4.00
26 VM,'Doom of the Serpent Gods' 1.75
27 VM,SD,'Demons Dwell in the
Crypts of Yamath' 3.50
28 SD,'The Hordes of Hell' 3.50
29 GK(c),'Day of the Dragon Wings',
E:Thongor,Warrior of Lost
Lemuria 3.50
30 B:Man-Wolf,'Full Moon, Dark
Fear' 3.50
31 GT,'The Beast Within' 3.50
32 GT,V:Kraven the Hunter 3.50
33 GK(c),GP,'The Name of the
Game is Death' 3.50
34 GP,'Nightflight to Fear' 3.50
35 GK(c),GP 3.50
36 GK(c),GP,'Murder by Moonlight' 1.75
37 GP,Sept., 1975 . . . . 3.50

The Toxic Aventer #1
© Marvel Entertainment Group

TOXIC AVENGER
March, 1991
1 VM(i)I&O:Toxic Avenger 1.50
2 VM(i) 1.50
3 VM(i)'Night of LivingH.bodies . . 1.50
4 Legend of Sludgeface 1.50
5 I:Biohazard 1.50
6 V:Biohazard 1.50
7 'Sewer of Souviaki' 1.50
8 'Sewer of Souviaki' conc. 1.50
9 Abducted by Aliens 1.50
10 'Die,Yuppie Scum',pt.1 . . . . . 1.50

TOXIC CRUSADERS
1 F:Toxic Avengers & Crusaders 1.50
2 SK(c),V:Custard-Thing 1.25
3 SK(c),V:Custard-Thing 1.25
4 V:Giant Mutant Rats 1.25
5 V:Dr.Killemoff 1.25
6 V:Dr.Killemoff 1.25
7 F:Yvonne 1.25
8 V:Psycho 1.25
(2nd Series)
1 . . . . 1.25
2 . . . . 1.25

TRANSFORMERS
Sept., 1984
[1st Regular Series]
1 FS,Toy Comic 2.50
2 FS,OptimusPrime V:Megatron . 1.75
3 FS.A:Spider-Man 1.75
4 MT(c),FS 1.50
5 Transformers Dead? 1.50
6 Autobots vs.Decepticons 1.50
7 KB,V:Megatron 1.50
8 KB,A:Dinobots 1.50
9 MM,A:Circuit Breaker 1.50
10 Dawn of the Devastator 1.50
11 HT 1.50
12 HT,V:Shockwave 1.50
13 DP,Return of Megatron 1.50
14 DP,V:Decepticons 1.50
15 DP 1.50
16 KN,A:Bumblebee 1.50
17 DP,I:New Transformers,pt.1 . . 1.50
18 DP,I:New Transformers,pt.2 . . 1.50
19 DP,I:Omega Supreme 1.50
20 HT,Skid vs.Ravage 1.50
21 DP,I:Aerialbots 1.25
22 DP,I:Stuntacons(Menasor) . . . 1.25
23 DP,Return of Circuit Breaker . . 1.25
24 DP,D:Optimus Prime 1.25
25 DP,Decpticons (full story) 1.25
26 DP 1.25
27 DP,V:Head Hunter 1.25
28 DP 1.25
29 DP,I:Scraplets, Triplechangers 1.25
30 DP,V:Scraplets 1.25
31 DP,Humans vs. Decepticons . . 1.25
32 DP,'Autobots for Sale' 1.25
33 DP,Autobots vs.Decepticons . . 1.25
34 V:Sky Lynx 1.25
35 JRy,I:UK.version Transformers 1.25
36 . . . . 1.00
37 . . . . 1.00
38 . . . . 1.00
39 . . . . 1.00
40 Autobots' New Leader 1.00
41 . . . . 1.00
42 Return of Optimus Prime 1.00
43 Optimus Prime,Goldbug 1.00
44 FF,Return of Circuit Breaker . . 1.00
45 V:The Jammers 1.00
46 I:New Transformers 1.00
47 B:Underbase saga,I:Seacons . 1.00
48 Optimus Prime/Megatron
(past story) 1.00
49 Underbase saga Contd. 1.00
50 E:Underbase saga,I:New
Characters 1.00
51 I:Pretender Decepticon Beasts 1.00
52 I:Mecannibles,pt.1 . . . . 1.00
53 Mecannibles,pt.2 . . . . 1.00
54 I:Micromasters 1.00
55 MG 1.00
56 Return of Megatron 1.00
57 Optimus Prime vs.Scrapanok . 1.00
58 V:Megatron 1.00
59 A:Megatron,D:Ratchet 1.00
60 Battle on Cybertron 1.00
61 O:Transformers 1.00
62 B:Matrix Quest,pt.1 . . . . 1.00
63 . . . . 1.00
64 I:The Klud 1.00
65 GSr 1.00
66 E:Matrix Quest,pt.5 . . . . 1.00
67 V:Unicorn,Also Alternative
World 1.00
68 I:Neoknights 1.00
69 Fate of Ratchet & Megatron

Transformers #10
© *Marvel Entertainment Group*

revealed 1.00
70 Megatron/Ratchet fused
together 1.00
71 Autobots Surrender to
Decepticons 1.00
72 Decepticon Civil War,
I:Gravitron 1.00
73 I:Unicron,A:Neoknights 1.00
74 A:Unicron&Brothers of Chaos . 1.00
75 V:Thunderwing & Dark Matrix . 1.00
76 Aftermath of War 1.00
77 Unholy Alliance 1.00
78 Galvatron vs.Megatron 1.00
79 Decepticons Invade Earth . . . 1.00
80 Return of Optimus Prime,final . 1.00
[2nd Regular Series]
1 Split Foil(c),A:Dinobots 3.00
2 A:G.I.Joe,Cobra 2.00
3 . . . . 2.00
4 MaG,V:Jhiaxus 2.00
5 . . . . 2.00
6 V:Megatron 2.00
7 V:Darkwing 2.00
8 V:Darkwing 2.00
9 . . . . 2.00
10 Total War 2.00
11 . . . . 1.75

TRANSFORMERS COMICS MAGAZINE
1986–88
1 Digest Size 1.50
2 thru 11 . . . . @1.50

TRANSFORMERS, THE MOVIE
Dec., 1986–Feb. 1987
1 thru 3 Animated Movie adapt. . @1.25

TRANSFORMERS UNIVERSE
Dec., 1986
1 . . . . 1.25

---

2 . . . . 1.25
3 . . . . 1.25
4 March, 1987 . . . . 1.25

TRANSMUTATION OF IKE GARAUDA
Epic
1 JSh,I:IkeGaruda 3.95
2 JSh,conclusion 3.95

TROUBLE WITH GIRLS
1 BBl,AW,R:Lester Girls 2.75
2 BBl,AW,V:Lizard Lady 2.25
3 BBl,AW,V:Lizard Lady 2.25
4 BBl,AW,last issue 2.25

TRUE COMPLETE MYSTERY
See: COMPLETE MYSTERY

TRUE SECRETS
See: OUR LOVE

TRUE WESTERN
Dec., 1949
1 Ph(c),Billy the Kid 100.00
2 Ph(c),Alan Ladd,Badmen vs.
Lawmen 100.00
Becomes:
TRUE ADVENTURES
3 BP,MSy,Boss of Black Devil . 75.00
Becomes:
MEN'S ADVENTURES
4 He Called me a Coward . . . 175.00
5 Brother Act 120.00
6 Heat of Battle 85.00
7 The Walking Death 85.00
8 RH,Journey Into Death 85.00
9 Bullets,Blades and Death . . . 60.00
10 BEv,The Education of Thomas
Dillon 60.00
11 Death of A Soldier 60.00
12 Firing Squad 60.00
13 RH(c),The Three Stripes . . . 60.00
14 GC,BEv,Steel Coffin 60.00
15 JMn(c) 60.00
16 . . . . 60.00
17 . . . . 60.00
18 . . . . 60.00
19 JRo 60.00
20 RH(c) 60.00
21 BEv(c),JSt,The Eye of Man . . 75.00
22 BEv,JR,Mark of the Witch . . . 75.00
23 BEv(c),RC,The Wrong Body . . 75.00
24 RH,JMn,GT,Torture Master . . 75.00
25 SSh(c),Who Shrinks My Head 75.00
26 Midnight in the Morgue 75.00
27 CBu(c),A:Capt.America,Human
Torch,Sub-Mariner 750.00
28 BEv,A:Capt.America,Human Torch,
Sub-Mariner,July, 1954 . . . . 700.00

TRY-OUT WINNER BOOK
March, 1988
1 Spider-Man vs. Doc Octopus . 15.00

TV STARS
August, 1978
1 A:Great Grape Ape 1.25
2 . . . . 1.00
3 . . . . 1.00

---

4 A:Top Cat,Feb., 1979 . . . . . . 1.00

2-GUN KID
See: BILLY BUCKSKIN

TWO-GUN KID
Atlas March, 1948—April, 1977
1 B:Two-Gun Kid,The Sheriff . 700.00
2 Killers of Outlaw City 275.00
3 RH,A:Annie Oakley 225.00
4 RH,A:Black Rider 225.00
5 . . . . 275.00
6 . . . . 175.00
7 RH,Brand of a Killer 175.00
8 The Secret of the Castle of
Slaves 175.00
9 JSe,Trapped in Hidden Valley
A:Black Rider 175.00
10 JK(c),The Horrible Hermit
of Hidden Mesa 175.00
11 JMn(c),GT,A:Black Rider . . 125.00
12 JMn(c),GT,A:Black Rider . . 125.00
13 thru 24 . . . . @100.00
25 AW 100.00
26 . . . . 90.00
27 . . . . 90.00
28 . . . . 90.00
29 . . . . 90.00
30 AW 100.00
31 thru 44 . . . . 50.00
45 . . . . 55.00
46 . . . . 55.00
47 . . . . 35.00
48 . . . . 40.00
49 . . . . 35.00
50 . . . . 30.00
51 . . . . 40.00
52 thru 59 . . . . @20.00
60 DAy,New O:Two Gun Kid . . 20.00
61 JK,DAy,The Killer and The Kid 20.00
62 JK,DAy,At the Mercy of Moose
Morgan 20.00
63 DAy,The Guns of Wild Bill
Taggert 10.00
64 DAy,Trapped by Grizzly
Gordon 10.00
65 DAy,Nothing Can Save Fort
Henry 10.00
66 DAy,Ringo's Raiders 10.00
67 DAy,The Fangs of the Fox . . 10.00
68 DAy,The Purple Phantom . . . 10.00
69 DAy,Badman Called Goliath . 10.00
70 DAy,Hurricane 10.00
71 DAy,V:Jesse James 10.00
72 DAy,V:Geronimo 10.00
73 Guns of the Galloway Gang . 10.00
74 Dakota Thompson 10.00
75 JK,Remember the Alamo . . . 10.00
76 JK,Trapped on the Doom . . . 10.00
77 JK,V:The Panther 10.00
78 V:Jesse James 10.00
79 The River Rats 10.00
80 V:The Billy Kid 10.00
81 The Hidden Gun 5.00
82 BEv,Here Comes the Conchos 5.00
83 Durango,Two-Gun
Kid Unmasked 5.00
84 Gunslammer 5.00
85 Fury at Falcon Flats,
A:Rawhide Kids 5.00
86 V:Cole Younger 5.00
87 OW,The Sidewinder and the
Stallion 5.00
88 thru 100 . . . . @5.00

MARVEL

All comics prices listed are for *Near Mint* condition.

Two-Gun Kid #109
© Marvel Entertainment Group

101	. . . .	5.00
102 thru 136	. . . .	@2.00

TWO-GUN KID: SUNSET RIDERS

1 FaN,R:Two-Gun Kid,64pgs	. . .	6.95
2 FaN,concl. 64pgs.	. . . .	6.95

TWO GUN WESTERN
See: CASEY–CRIME PHOTOGRAPHER

TWO-GUN WESTERN
See: BILLY BUCKSKIN

2001: A SPACE ODYSSEY
Oct., 1976

1 JK,FRg,Based on Movie	. . . . .	3.00

2001: A SPACE ODYSSEY
Dec., 1976—Sept., 1977

1 JK,Based on Movie	. . . .	2.50
2 JK,Vira the She-Demon	. . . . .	1.50
3 JK,Marak the Merciless	. . . . .	1.50
4 JK,Wheels of Death	. . . .	1.50
5 JK,Norton of New York	. . . . .	1.50
6 JK,Immortality ...Death	. . . . .	1.50
7 JK,The New Seed	. . . .	1.50
8 JK,Capture of X-51,I&O:Mr. Machine(Machine-Man)	. . . . .	4.00
9 JK,A:Mr Machine	. . . .	1.50
10 Hotline to Hades,A:Mr Machine	1.50

2010
April, 1985

1 TP,movie adapt	. . . .	1.00
2 TP,movie adapt,May, 1985	. . .	1.00

2099 A.D.

1 Chromium cover	. . . .	3.95

2099 GENESIS

1 Chromium Cover	. . . .	4.95

2099 SPECIAL: THE WORLD OF DOOM

1 The World of Doom	. . . .	2.25

2099 UNLIMITED

1 DT,I:Hulk 2099,A:Spider-Man 2099, I:Mutagen	. . . .	4.50
2 DT,F:Hulk 2099,Spider-Man 2099, I:R-Gang	. . . .	4.25
3 GJ(s),JJB,F:Hulk & SpM 2099	.	4.25
4 PR(c),GJ(s),JJB,I:Metalscream 2099,Lachryma 2099	. . . . . .	4.25
5 GJ(s),I:Vulx,F:Hazarrd 2099	. . .	3.95
6	. . . .	3.95

Becomes:
2099 A.D. UNLIMITED

7	. . . .	3.95
8 F:Public Enemy	. . . .	3.95
9 One Nation Under Doom	. . . . .	3.95
10 V:Chameleon 2099	. . . .	3.95
Spec. #1 The World of Doom	. . .	2.25

2099: WORLD OF TOMORROW
(Sept. 1996)

1	. . . .	2.50
2	. . . .	2.50
3 MMk,MsM,ATi,F:Spider-Man, X-Men	. . . .	2.50
4 ATi,X-Men 2099 discover secret	2.50
5 ATi	. . . .	2.50
6 PFe&ATi(c),Phalanx's final assault	. . . .	2.50
7 Spider-Man 2099 searches for his brother: Green Goblin	. . . . .	2.50
8 Phalanx invasion aftermath	. . .	2.50
9 Humanity vs. Lunatika	. . . . . .	2.50

TYPHOID

1 ANo,JVF,Painted series	. . . . .	3.95
2 ANo,JVF,Hunt for serial killer	. .	3.95
3 ANo,JVF,sex,blood & videotapes	3.95
4 ANo,JVF,conclusion	. . . .	3.95

ULTIMATE AGE OF APOCALYPSE
Rep. #1–#4 Age of Apocalypse stories:

Ultimate Amazing X-Men	. . . . . .	8.95
Ultimate Astonishing X-Men	. . . .	8.95
Ultimate Factor X	. . . .	8.95
Ultimate Gambit and the X-Ternals	8.95
Ultimate Generation Next	. . . . .	8.95
Ultimate Weapon X	. . . .	8.95
Ultimate X-Calibre	. . . .	8.95
Ultimate X-Man	. . . .	8.95

ULTRAFORCE/AVENGERS

1 V:Loki,A:Malibu's Ultraforce	. . .	3.95

ULTRA GIRL
Mini-Series 1996

1 BKs,I&O:Ultra Girl	. . . .	1.50
2 BKs,	. . . .	1.50
3 BKs,R:New Warriors	. . . .	1.50

ULTRA X-MEN COLLECTION

1 Metallic(c), art from cards	. . . .	2.95
2 thru 5 art from cards	. . . . . .	@2.95

ULTRA X-MEN III

Preview	. . . .	2.95

Uncanny Origins #2
© Marvel Entertainment Group

UNCANNY ORIGINS
(Sept. 1996)

1 F:Cyclops	. . . .	1.00
2 F:Quicksilver	. . . .	1.00
3 DHv,BAn,F:Archangel	. . . . . .	1.00
4 F:Firelord	. . . .	1.00
5 MHi,F:Hulk	. . . .	1.00
6 F:Beast	. . . .	1.00
7 F:Venom	. . . .	1.00
8 F:Nightcrawler	. . . .	1.00
9 F:Storm	. . . .	1.00
10 F:Black Cat	. . . .	1.00
11 F:Luke Cage	. . . .	1.00
12 F:Black Knight	. . . .	1.00
13 LWn,MCa,F:Doctor Strange	. .	1.00

UNCANNY TALES
Atlas June, 1952

1 RH,While the City Sleeps	. .	500.00
2 JMn,BEv	. . . .	300.00
3 Escape to What	. . . .	250.00
4 JMn,Nobody's Fool	. . . . . .	250.00
5 Fear	. . . .	250.00
6 He Lurks in the Shadows	. .	250.00
7 BEv,Kill,Clown,Kill	. . . . . .	200.00
8 JMn,Bring Back My Face	. . .	200.00
9 RC,The Executioner	. . . . .	200.00
10 RH(c),JR,The Man Who Came Back To Life	. . . .	200.00
11 GC,The Man Who Changed	175.00
12 BP,BEv,Bertha Gets Buried	175.00
13 RH,Scared Out of His Skin	.	175.00
14 RH,The Victims of Vonntor	.	175.00
15 JSt,The Man Who Saw Death	175.00
16 JMn,GC,Zombie at Large	. .	175.00
17 GC,I Live With Corpses	. . .	175.00
18 JF,BP,Clock Face(c)	. . . . .	175.00
19 DBr,RKr,The Man Who Died Again	. . . .	175.00
20 DBr,Ted's Head	. . . .	175.00
21 thru 27	. . . .	@125.00
28	. . . .	135.00
29 thru 41	. . . .	@85.00
42	. . . .	95.00

MARVEL

43 thru 49 . . . . @75.00	4 FS,ME 1.00	

VALKYRIE
1996
1-shot JMD, ... 2.50

43 thru 49 . . . . @75.00
50 . . . . 80.00
51 . . . . 100.00
52 . . . . 75.00
53 . . . . 75.00
54 . . . . 85.00
55 . . . . 75.00
56 Sept., 1957 . . . . 85.00

UNCANNY TALES FROM THE GRAVE
Dec., 1973—Oct., 1975
1 RC,Room of no Return 3.00
2 DAy,Out of the Swamp 2.00
3 No Way Out 2.00
4 JR,SD,Vampire 2.00
5 GK,GT,Don't Go in the Cellar . . 2.00
6 JR,SD,The Last Kkrul 2.00
7 RH,SD,Never Dance With a Vampire 2.00
8 SD,Escape Into Hell 2.00
9 JA,The Nightmare Men 2.00
10 SD,DH,Beware the Power of Khan 2.00
11 SD,JF,RH,Dead Don't Sleep . . 2.00
12 SD,Final Issue 2.00

UNCANNY X-MEN
SEE: X-MEN

UNKNOWN WORLDS OF SCIENCE FICTION
Jan., 1975
(black & white magazine)
1 AW,RKr,AT,FF,GC 4.00
2 FB,GP 3.25
3 GM,AN,GP,GC 3.25
4 . . . . 3.25
5 GM,NC,GC 3.25
6 FB,AN,GC,Nov., 1975 . . . . . . 3.25
Spec.#1 AN,NR,JB 3.50

U.S.A. COMICS
Timely Aug., 1941
1 S&K(c),BW,Bondage(c),The Defender(c) 9,500.00
2 S&K(c),BW,Capt.Terror(c) . 2,800.00
3 S&K(c),Capt.Terror(c) 2,100.00
4 . . . . 1,600.00
5 Hitler(c),O:American Avenger 1,700.00
6 ASh(c),Capt.America(c) . . . 1,800.00
7 BW,O:Marvel Boy 1,700.00
8 Capt.America (c) 1,400.00
9 Bondage(c), Capt.America . 1,400.00
10 SSh(c),Bondage(c), Capt. America 1,400.00
11 SSh(c),Bondage(c), Capt. America 1,100.00
12 ASh(c),Capt.America 1,100.00
13 ASh(c),Capt.America 1,100.00
14 Capt.America 900.00
15 Capt.America 900.00
16 ASh(c),Bondage(c), Capt.America 900.00
17 Bondage(c),Capt.America . . 900.00

U.S. 1
May, 1983
1 AM(c),HT,Trucking Down the Highway 1.25
2 HT,Midnight 1.00
3 FS,ME,Rhyme of the Ancient Highwayman 1.00

4 FS,ME 1.00
5 FS,ME,Facing The Maze 1.00
6 FS,ME 1.00
7 FS,ME 1.00
8 FS,ME 1.00
9 FS,ME,Iron Mike-King of the Bike 1.00
10 FS,ME 1.00
11 FS,ME 1.00
12 FS,ME,Final Issue,Oct.,1984 . . 1.00

U.S. AGENT
1 V:Scourge,O:U.S.Agent 2.00
2 V:Scourge 2.00
3 V:Scourge 2.00
4 last issue 2.00

UNTAMED
1 I:Griffen Palmer 2.75
2 V:Kosansui 2.25
3 V:Kosansui 2.25

UNTOLD LEGEND OF CAPTAIN MARVEL, THE
1997
1 (of 3) Early days of Captain Marvel 2.50
2 Early days of Captain Marvel . . 2.50
3 V:Kree 2.50

UNTOLD TALES OF SPIDER-MAN
1 F:Young Spider-Man 3.00
2 V:Batwing 1.50
3 V:Sandman 1.00
4 V:J.Jonah Jameson 1.00
5 V:Vulture 1.00
6 A:Human Torch 1.00
7 . . . . 1.00
8 . . . . 1.00
9 A:Batwing,Lizard 1.00
10 KBk,PO,I:Commanda 1.00
11 KBk,PO, ... 1.00
12 KBk,PO, ... 1.00
13 KBk,PO, ... 1.00
14 KBk,PO, ... 1.00
15 KBk,PO,AV,Gordon's plan to control the Bugle 1.00
16 Re-I:Mary Jane Watson 1.00
17 KBk,PO,AV,V:Hawkeye 1.00
18 KBk,PO,AV,A:Green Goblin, Headsman 1.00
19 KBk,PO,AW,F:Doctor Octopus . 1.00
20 KBk,PO,AW,V:Vulture 1.00
21 KBk,PO,AW,V:Menace,A:Original X-Men 1.00
22 KBk,PO,AW,V:Scarecrow, ... 1.00
23 KBk,PO,AW,V:Crime Master, A:Green Goblin 1.00
24 KBk,PO,BMc, Fate of Batwing . 1.00
Minus 1 Spec., RSt,JR, flashback, Peter's parents 1.95
TPB rep. #1–#8 . . . . 17.00

UNTOLD TALES OF SPIDER-MAN '96
1 KBk,MiA,JSt,A date with Invisible Girl? 1.95

UNTOLD TALES OF SPIDER-MAN '97
1 KBk,TL,A:everyone, 48pg 2.95

VAMPIRE TALES
August, 1973
(black & white magazine)
1 BEv,B:Morbius the Living Vampire 25.00
2 JSo,I:Satana 10.00
3 A:Satana 15.00
4 GK 15.00
5 GK,O:Morbius the Living Vampire 18.00
6 AA,I:Lilith 15.00
7 HC,PG 15.00
8 AA,A:Blade The Vampire Slayer 15.00
9 RH,AA 15.00
10 . . . . 15.00
11 June, 1975 . . . . 15.00
Ann.#1 . . . . 15.00

Vault of Evil #8
© *Marvel Entertainment Group*

VAULT OF EVIL
Feb., 1973—Nov., 1975
1 B:1950's reps,Come Midnight, Come Monster 5.00
2 The Hour of the Witch 3.00
3 The Woman Who Wasn't 3.00
4 Face that Follows 3.00
5 Ghost 3.00
6 The Thing at the Window 3.00
7 Monsters 3.00
8 The Vampire is my Brother . . . 3.00
9 Giant Killer 3.00
10 The Lurkers in the Caves 3.00
11 Two Feasts For a Vampire . . . 3.00
12 Midnight in the Haunted Mansion 3.00
13 Hot as the Devil 3.00
14 Midnight in the Haunted Manor 3.00
15 Don't Shake Hands with the Devil 3.00
16 A Grave Honeymoon 3.00
17 Grave Undertaking 3.00
18 The Deadly Edge 3.00
19 Vengeance of Ahman Ra 3.00

MARVEL

20	3.00
21 Victim of Valotorr	3.00
22	3.00
23 Black Magician Lives Again . .	3.00

VENOM

1 MBa,A:Spider-Man.holo-grafx(c)	5.00
1a Gold Ed..	8.00
1b Black Ed..	20.00
2 MBa,A:Spider-Man	3.50
3 MBa,Families of Venom's victims	3.50
4 RLm,A:Spider-Man,V:Life Foundation	3.50
5 RLm,V:Five Symbiotes,A:SpM	3.50
6 RLm,V:Spider-Man	3.50
Super Size Spec.#1 Planet of the Symbiotes,pt.3	3.95
Venom:Deathtrap:The Vault,RLm, A:Avengers,Freedom Force . . .	6.95
TPB Lethal Protector RLm,DvM .	15.95

VENOM: ALONG CAME A SPIDER

1 LHA,GLz,V:New Spider-Man . .	3.00
2 LHa,JSP,V:New Spider-Man . .	3.00
3	3.00
4 conclusion, 48pg	3.00

VENOM: CARNAGE UNLEASHED

1 Venom vs. Carnage	3.00
2 Venom vs. Carnage	3.00
3 No Spider-Help	3.00
4 JRu,Wld,LHa,cardstock(c)	3.00

VENOM: ENEMY WITHIN

1 BMc,Glow-in-the-dark(C), A:Demogoblin,Morbius	3.25
2 BMc,A:Demogoblin,Morbius . .	3.25
3 BMc,V:Demogoblin,A:Morbius .	3.25

VENOM: FUNERAL PYRE

1 TL,JRu,A:Punisher	3.50
2 TL,JRu,AM,V:Gangs	3.50
3 TL,JRu,Last issue	3.50

VENOM: THE HUNGER
1996

1 thru 4 LKa,TeH,V:Dr. Paine .	@2.00

VENOM: THE HUNTED

1 LHa,3 part mini-series	3.00

VENOM: LICENSE TO KILL

1 (of 3) LHa,KHt, sequel to Venom on trial	2.00
2 LHa,V:Dr. Yes	2.00
3 LHa,V:Dr. Yes	2.00

VENOM: THE MACE

1 Embossed(c),CP(s),LSh,I:Mace	3.25
2 CP(s),LSh,V:Mace	3.25
3 CP(s),LSh,V:Mace,final issue . .	3.25

VENOM: THE MADNESS

1 B:ANi(s),KJo,V:Juggernaut . .	3.50
2 KJo,V:Juggernaut	3.25
3 E:ANi(s),KJo,V:Juggernaut . . .	3.25

VENOM: NIGHTS OF VENGEANCE

1 RLm,I:Stalkers,A:Vengeance . .	3.25
2 RLm,A:Vengeance,V:Stalkers .	3.25
3 RLm,V:Stalkers	3.25
4 RLm,final issue	3.25

VENOM: ON TRIAL
(Jan. 1997)

1 LHa,Tries to break out	2.00
2 LHa,Defended by Matt Murdock (Daredevil),A:Spider-Man . .	2.00
3 LHa,A:Spider-Man, Carnage, Daredevil	2.00

VENOM: SEED OF DARKNESS

1 LKa,JFy,Flashback, early Eddie Brock	2.00

VENOM: SEPARATION ANXIETY

1 Embossed(c)	3.00
2 V:Symbiotes	3.00
3	3.00
4	3.00
TPB Rep.#1-#4 HMe,RoR,SDR . .	9.95

VENOM: SIGN OF THE BOSS

1 (of 2) IV,TDr,V:Ghost Rider . . .	2.00

VENOM: SINNER TAKES ALL

1 LHa,GLz,I:New Sin-Eater	3.00
2 V:Sineater	3.00
3 Wrong Man	3.00
4 LHa,GLz,V:Sin-Eater	3.00
5 LHa, finale	3.00

VENOM: TOOTH AND CLAW
1996

1 (of 3) LHa,JSP,AM, Dirtnap usurps Venom's body	2.00
2 LHa,JSP,AM,V:Wolverine	2.00
3 LHa,JSP,AM,V:Wolverine, Chimera	2.00

VENUS
Atlas August, 1948

1 B:Venus,Hedy Devine,HK,Hey Look	850.00
2 Venus(c)	500.00
3 Carnival(c)	400.00
4 Cupid(c).HK,Hey Look	425.00
5 Serenade(c)	425.00
6 Wrath of a Goddess,A:Loki . .	400.00
7 The Romance That Could Not Be	400.00
8 The Love Trap	400.00
9 Whom the Gods Destroy . .	400.00
10 B:Scince Fiction/Horror, Trapped On the Moon	400.00
11 The End of the World	550.00
12 GC,The Lost World	300.00
13 BEv,King of the Living Dead	500.00
14 BEv,The Fountain of Death .	500.00
15 BEv,The Empty Grave . . .	500.00
16 BEv,Where Gargoyles Dwell	500.00
17 BEv,Tower of Death,	

Bondage(c)	500.00
18 BEv,Terror in the Tunnel . . .	500.00
19 BEv,THe Kiss Of Death . . .	500.00

VERY BEST OF MARVEL COMICS
One Shot reps Marvel Artists

Favorite Stories	12.95

VIDEO JACK
Nov., 1987

1 KGi,O:Video Jack	2.50
2 KGi	2.00
3 KGi	1.75
4 KGi	1.75
5 KGi	1.75
6 KGi,NA,BWr,AW	1.25

VISION, THE

1 BHs,mini-series	1.75
2 BHs	1.75
3 BHs	1.75

VISION & SCARLET WITCH
[1st Series]
Nov., 1982

1 RL,V:Halloween	2.00
2 RL,V:Isbisa,D:Whizzer	1.50
3 RL,A:Wonderman,V:GrimReaper	1.50
4 RL,A:Magneto,Inhumans	1.50
#### [2nd Series]	
1 V:Grim Reaper	2.00
2 V:Lethal Legion,D:Grim Reaper	1.75
3 V:Salem's Seven	1.75
4 I:Glamor & Illusion	1.75
5 A:Glamor & Illusion	1.75
6 A:Magneto	1.75
7 V:Toad	1.75
8 A:Powerman	1.75
9 V:Enchantress	1.75
10 A:Inhumans	1.75
11 A:Spider-Man	1.75
12 Birth of V&S's Child	1.25

VISIONARIES
Star Nov., 1987

1 thru 5	@1.00
6 Sept., 1988	1.00

VOID INDIGO
Epic Nov., 1984

1 VM,Epic Comics	2.00
2 VM,Epic Comics,March, 1985 .	2.00

WACKY DUCK
See: DOPEY DUCK

WALLY THE WIZARD
Star April, 1985

1	1.25
2 thru 11	@1.00
12 March, 1986	1.00

WAR, THE
1989

1 Sequel to The Draft & The Pit .	3.50
2	3.50
3	3.50
4 1990	3.50

MARVEL

WAR ACTION
Atlas April, 1952
1 JMn,RH,War Stories, Six Dead
  Men 100.00
2 . . . . 60.00
3 Invasion in Korea 40.00
4 thru 10 . . . . @40.00
11 . . . . 50.00
12 . . . . 50.00
13 BK 50.00
14 Rangers Strike,June, 1953 . . 45.00

WAR ADVENTURES
Atlas Jan., 1952
1 GT,Battle Fatigue 100.00
2 The Story of a Slaughter . . 50.00
3 JRo 35.00
4 RH(c) 35.00
5 RH,Violent(c) 35.00
6 Stand or Die 35.00
7 JMn(c) 35.00
8 BK 50.00
9 RH(c) 30.00
10 JRo(c),Attack at Dawn 30.00
11 Red Trap 30.00
12 . . . . 30.00
13 RH(c),The Commies Strike
  Feb., 1953 . . . . 30.00

WAR COMBAT
Atlas March, 1952
1 JMn,Death of a Platoon Leader 75.00
2 . . . . 40.00
3 JMn(c) 30.00
4 JMn(c) 30.00
5 The Red Hordes 30.00
Becomes:
COMBAT CASEY
6 BEv,Combat Casey cont . . . 50.00
7 . . . . 35.00
8 JMn(c) 28.00
9 . . . . 25.00
10 RH(c) 35.00
11 . . . . 20.00
12 . . . . 20.00
13 thru 19 . . . . @35.00
20 . . . . 20.00
21 thru 33 . . . . @15.00
34 July, 1957 . . . . 15.00

WAR COMICS
Atlas Dec., 1950
1 You Only Die Twice 140.00
2 Infantry's War 75.00
3 . . . . 50.00
4 GC,The General Said Nuts . . 50.00
5 . . . . 50.00
6 The Deadly Decision of
  General Kwang 50.00
7 RH 50.00
8 RH,No Survivors 50.00
9 RH 50.00
10 . . . . 50.00
11 thru 21 . . . . @40.00
22 . . . . 65.00
23 thru 37 . . . . @30.00
38 JKu 45.00
39 . . . . 30.00
40 . . . . 30.00
41 . . . . 30.00
42 . . . . 30.00
43 AT 40.00
44 . . . . 30.00

45 . . . . 30.00
46 RC 45.00
47 . . . . 30.00
48 . . . . 30.00
49 Sept., 1957 . . . . 45.00

WARHEADS
1 GEr,I:Warheads,A:Wolverine, . . 2.25
2 GEr,V:Nick Fury 2.00
3 DTy,A:Iron Man 2.00
4 SCy,A:X-Force 2.00
5 A:X-Force,C:Deaths'Head II . 2.00
6 SCy,A:Death's Head II 2.00
7 SCy,A:Death's Head II,S.Surfer 2.00
8 SCy,V:Mephisto 2.00
9 SCy,V:Mephisto 2.00
10 JCz,V:Mephisto 2.00
11 A:Death's Head II 2.00
12 V:Mechanix 2.00
13 Xenophiles Reptiles 2.00
14 last issue 2.00

WARHEADS: BLACK DAWN
1 A:Gh.Rider,Morbius 3.25
2 V:Dracula 2.00

WAR IS HELL
Jan., 1973—Oct., 1975
1 B:Reprints,Decision at Dawn . 2.00
2 Anytime,Anyplace,War is Hell . 1.50
3 Retreat or Die 1.50
4 Live Grenade 1.50
5 Trapped Platoon 1.50
6 We Die at Dawn 1.50
7 While the Jungle Sleeps,A:Sgt
  Fury 1.50
8 Killed in Action,A:Sgt Fury . . 1.50
9 B:Supernatural,War Stories . . 1.50
10 Death is a 30 Ton Tank 1.50
11 thru 15 . . . . @1.50

WARLOCK
[1st Regular Series]
August, 1972
1 GK,I:Counter Earth,A:High
  Evolutionary 20.00
2 JB,TS,V:Man Beast 9.00
3 GK,TS,V:Apollo 8.00
4 JK,TS,V:Triax 7.00
5 GK,TS,V:Dr.Doom 7.00
6 TS(i),O:Brute 7.00
7 TS(i),V:Brute,D:Dr.Doom . . . 7.00
8 TS(i),R:Man-Beast(cont
  in Hulk #176) 7.00
9 JSn,1st'Rebirth'Thanos,O:Magnus,
  N:Warlock,I:In-Betweener 9.00
10 JSn,SL,O:Thanos,V:Magus,
  A:In-Betweener 11.00
11 JSn,SL,D:Magus,A:Thanos,
  In-Betweener 10.00
12 JSn,SL,O:Pip,V:Pro-Boscis
  A:Starfox 6.00
13 JSn,SL,I&O:Star-Thief 6.00
14 JSn,SL,V:Star-Thief 6.00
15 JSn,A:Thanos,V:Soul-Gem . . 15.00
[2nd Regular Series]
1 JSn,rep.Strange Tales #178-180
  Baxter Paper 3.00
2 JSn,rep.Strange Tales #180
  & Warlock #9 . . . . 2.50
3 JSn,rep.Warlock #10-#12 . . . 2.50
4 JSn,rep.Warlock #13-#15 . . . 2.50

5 JSn,rep.Warlock #15 . . . . 2.50
6 JSn,rep. 2.50

WARLOCK
(Limited Series)
1 Rep.Warlock Series 3.50
2 Rep.Warlock Series 3.00
3 Rep.Warlock Series 3.00
4 Rep.Warlock Series 3.00
5 Rep.Warlock Series 3.00
6 Rep.Warlock Series 3.00

Warlock & The Infinity Watch #9
© Marvel Entertainment Group

WARLOCK AND THE INFINITY WATCH
1 AMe,Trial of the Gods(from
  Infinity Gauntlet) 4.00
2 AMe,I:Infinity Watch(Gamora,Pip,
  Moondragon,Drax & 1 other) . . 3.00
3 RL,TA,A:High Evolutionary,
  Nobilus,I:Omega 3.00
4 RL,TA,V:Omega 2.50
5 AMe,TA,V:Omega 2.50
6 AMe,V:Omega(Man-Beast) . . . 2.50
7 TR,TA,V:Mole Man,A:Thanos . . 2.50
8 TR,TA,Infinity War,A:Thanos . . 2.25
9 AMe,TA,Inf.War,O:Gamora . . . 2.00
10 AMe,Inf.War,Thanos vs
  Doppleganger 2.50
11 O:Pip,Gamora,Drax,M'dragon . 2.00
12 TR,Drax Vs.Hulk 2.00
13 TR,Drax vs Hulk 2.00
14 AMe,V:United Nations 2.00
15 AMe,Magnus,Him 2.00
16 TGr,I:Count Abyss 2.00
17 TGr,I:Maxam 2.00
18 AMe,Inf.Crusade,N:Pip 2.00
19 TGr,A:Hulk,Wolverine,Infinity
  Crusade 2.00
20 AMe,Inf.Crusade 2.00
21 V:Thor 2.00
22 AMe,Infinity Crusade 2.00
23 JSn(s),TGb,Blood &
  Thunder#4 . . . . 2.00
24 JSn(s),TGb,V:Geirrodur 2.00
25 JSn(s),AMe,Die-Cut(c),Blood &
  Thunder #12 . . . . 3.25

MARVEL

26 A:Avengers	2.00
27 TGb,V:Avengers	2.00
28 TGb,V:Man-Beast	2.00
29 A:Maya	2.25
30 PO	2.25
31	1.95
32 Heart & Soul	1.95
33 V:Count Abyss	1.95
34 V:Count Abyss	1.95
35 V:Tyrannus	1.95
36	1.95
37 A:Zaharius	1.95
38	1.95
39 V:Domitron	1.95
40 A:Thanos	1.95
41 Monster Island	1.95
42 Warlock vs. Maxam, Atlantis Rising, final issue	1.95

WARLOCK CHRONICLES

1 TR,F:Adam Warlock,holo-grafx(c), I:Darklore,Meer'lyn	3.25
2 TR,Infinity Crusade,Thanos revealed to have the Reality Gem	2.25
3 TR,A:Mephisto	2.25
4 TR,A:Magnus	2.25
5 TR(c),Inf.Crusade	2.25
6 TR,Blood & Thunder,pt.#3	2.25
7 TR,Blood & Thunder,pt.#7	2.25
8 TR,Blood & Thunder,pt.#11	2.25
9 TR	2.00
10 TR	2.00
11 TR	2.00

WAR MACHINE

1 GG,Foil Embossed(c),B:LKa&StB, O:War Machine,V:Cable, C:Deathlok	3.25
1a Newstand Ed.	2.25
2 GG,V:Cable,Deathlok,w/card	1.75
3 GG,V:Cable,Deathlok	1.75
4 GG,C:Force Works	1.75
5 GG,I:Deachtoll	1.50
6 GG,V:Deathtoll	1.50
7 GG,A:Hawkeye	1.50
8 reg ed.	1.50
8a neon(c),w/insert print	3.00
9 Hands of Mandarin,pt.2	1.50
10 Hands of Mandarin,pt.5	1.50
11 X-Mas Party	1.50
12 V:Terror Device	1.50
13 V:The Rush Team	1.50
14 A:Force Works	1.50
15 In The Past of WWII	2.50
16 DAn,A:Rick Fury,Cap.America	1.50
17 The Man Who Won WWII	1.50
18 DAn,N:War Machine	1.50
19 DAn,A:Hawkeye	1.50
20 DAn,The Crossing	1.50
21 DAn,The Crossing	1.50
22 DAn,V:Iron Man	1.50
23 DAn,Avengers:Timeslide	1.50

WAR MAN
Epic

1 thru 2 CDi(s)	2.50

WEAPON X

1 Wolverine After Xavier	4.00
2 Full Scale War	2.25
3 Jean Leaves	1.95
4 F:Gateway	1.95
TPB Rep.#1-#4	8.95

WEAVEWORLD
Epic

1 MM, Clive Barker adaptation	4.95
2 MM,'Into the Weave'	4.95
3 MM	4.95

WEB OF SCARLET SPIDER

1 TDF,Virtual Mortality,pt.1	1.95
2 TDF,CyberWar,pt.2	1.95
3 Nightmare in Scarlet,pt.1	1.95
4 Nightmare in Scarlet,pt.3	1.95

Web of Spider-Man #4
© *Marvel Entertainment Group*

WEB OF SPIDER-MAN
April, 1985

1 JM,V:New Costume	22.00
2 JM,V:Vulture	8.00
3 JM,V:Vulture	7.00
4 JM,JBy,V:Dr.Octopus	6.00
5 JM,JBy,V:Dr.Octopus	6.00
6 MZ,BL,JM,Secret Wars II	6.00
7 SB,A:Hulk,V:Nightmare, C:Wolverine	6.00
8 V:Smithville Thunder	6.00
9 V:Smithville Thunder	6.00
10 JM,A:Dominic Fortune, V:Shocker	6.00
11 BMc,V:Thugs	6.00
12 BMc,SB,V:Thugs	6.00
13 BMc,V:J.JonahJameson	6.00
14 KB,V:Black Fox	6.00
15 V:Black Fox,I:Chance	7.00
16 MS,KB,V:Magma	5.00
17 MS,V:Magma	5.00
18 MS,KB,Where is Spider-Man?	7.00
19 MS,BMc,I:Solo,Humbug	5.50
20 MS,V:Terrorists	5.00
21 V:Fake Spider-Man	5.00
22 MS,V:Terrorists	5.00
23 V:Slyde	5.00
24 SB,V:Vulture,Hobgoblin	6.00
25 V:Aliens	5.00
26 V:Thugs	5.00
27 V:Headhunter	5.00
28 BL,V:Thugs	5.00
29 A:Wolverine,2nd App:New Hobgoblin	16.00
30 KB,O:Rose,C:Daredevil,Capt. America,Wolverine,Punisher	13.00
31 MZ,BMc,V:Kraven	11.00
32 MZ,BMc,V:Kraven	10.00
33 BSz(c),SL,V:Kingpin,Mad Dog Ward,pt.#1	5.00
34 SB,A:Watcher	5.00
35 AS,V:Living Brain	5.00
36 AS,V:Phreak Out,I:Tombstone	6.00
37 V:Slasher	5.00
38 AS,A:Tombstone,V:Hobgoblin	6.00
39 AS,V:Looter(Meteor Man)	4.00
40 AS,V:Cult of Love	4.00
41 AS,V:Cult of Love	4.00
42 AS,V:Cult of Love	4.00
43 AS,V:Cult of Love	4.00
44 AS,V:Warzone,A:Hulk	3.00
45 AS,V:Vulture	3.00
46 A:Dr.Pym,V:Nekra	3.00
47 AS,V:Hobgoblin	5.00
48 AS,O:New Hobgoblin's Demonic Power	13.00
49 VM,V:Drugs	4.00
50 AS,V:Chameleon(double size)	6.00
51 MBa,V:Chameleon,Lobo Bros.	4.00
52 FS,JR,O:J.Jonah Jameson V:Chameleon	4.00
53 MBa,V:Lobo Bros.,C:Punisher A:Chameleon	4.50
54 AS,V:Chameleon,V:Lobo Bros.	4.00
55 AS,V:Chameleon,Hammerhead, V:Lobo Bros.	4.00
56 AS,I&O:Skin Head, A:Rocket Racer	3.50
57 AS,D:SkinHead, A:Rocket Racer	3.00
58 AS,V:Grizzly	3.00
59 AS,Acts of Vengeance,V:Titania A:Puma,Cosmic Spider-Man	8.00
60 AS,A of V,V:Goliath	5.00
61 AS,A of V,V:Dragon Man	5.00
62 AS,V:Molten Man	3.00
63 AS,V:Mister Fear	3.00
64 AS,V:Graviton,Titania,Trapster	3.00
65 AS,V:Goliath,Trapster,Graviton	3.00
66 AS,V:Tombstone,A:G.Goblin	4.00
67 AS,A:GreenGoblin, V:Tombstone	4.00
68 AS,A:GreenGoblin, V:Tombstone	3.50
69 AS,V:Hulk	5.00
70 AS,I:The Spider/Hulk	3.00
71 A:Silver Sable	2.50
72 AM,A:Silver Sable	2.50
73 AS,A:Human Torch, Colossus,Namor	2.50
74 AS,I:Spark,V:Bora	2.50
75 AS,C:New Warriors	2.50
76 AS,Spidey in Ice	2.50
77 AS,V:Firebrand,Inheritor	2.50
78 AS,A:Firebrand,Cloak&Dagger	2.50
79 AS,V:Silvermane	2.50
80 AS,V:Silvermane	2.50
81 I:Bloodshed	2.25
82 V:Man Mountain Marko	2.25
83 V:A.I.M. Supersuit	2.25
84 AS,B:Name of the Rose	3.00
85 AS,Name of the Rose	2.50
86 AS,I:Demogoblin	3.50
87 AS,I:Praetorian Guard	2.50
88 AS,Name of the Rose	2.50
89 AS,E:Name of the Rose, I:Bloodrose	2.50
90 AS,30th Ann.,w/hologram,	

Web of Spider-Man #93
© Marvel Entertainment Group

polybagged,V:Mysterio . . . 6.00
90a Gold 2nd printing 3.25
91 AS,V:Whisper And Pulse . . 2.00
92 AS,V:Foreigner 2.00
93 AS,BMc,V:Hobgoblin,A:Moon
Knight,Foreigner 2.00
94 AS,V:Hobgoblin,A:MoonKnight 2.00
95 AS,Spirits of Venom#1,A:Venom,
J.Blaze,GR,V:Hag & Troll . . . 4.00
96 AS,Spirits of Venom#3, A:G.R,
J.Blaze,Venom,Hobgoblin 3.00
97 AS,I:Dr.Trench,V:Bloodrose . . 1.75
98 AS,V:Bloodrose,Foreigner 1.75
99 I:Night Watch,V:New Enforcer . 1.75
100 AS,JRu,V:Enforcers,Bloodrose,
Kingpin(Alfredo),I:Spider Armor,
O:Night Watch,Holografx(c) . . . 4.00
101 AS,Total Carnage,V:Carnage,
Shriek,A:Cloak and Dagger,
Venom 1.75
102 Total Carnage#6,V:Carnage,
A:Venom,Morbius 1.75
103 AS,Maximum Carnage#10,
V:Carnage 1.50
104 AS,Infinity Crusade 1.50
105 AS,Infinity Crusade 1.50
106 AS,Infinity Crusade 1.50
107 AS,A:Sandman,Quicksand . . 1.50
108 B:TKa(s),AS,I:Sandstorm,
BU:Cardiac 1.50
109 AS,V:Shocker,A:Night Thrasher,
BU:D:Calypso 1.50
110 AS,I:Warrant,A:Lizard 1.50
111 AS,V:Warrant,Lizard 1.50
112 AS,Pursuit#3,V:Chameleon,
w/card 1.75
113 AS,A:Gambit,Black Cat,w/cel . 3.50
113a Newsstand Ed. 1.75
114 AS 1.75
115 AS,V:Facade 1.75
116 AS,V:Facade 1.75
117 Foil(c), flip book with
Power & Responsibility #1 . . . 5.50
117a Newsstand ed. 2.50
118 Spider-clone, V:Venom 3.00
119 Clone,V:Venom 2.25
119a bagged with Milestone rep.
Amazing Sp-Man #150,checklist 6.50

120 Web of Life,pt.1 . . . . 2.50
121 Web of Life,pt.3 . . . . 2.50
122 Smoke and Mirrors,pt.1 . . . . . 2.50
123 The Price of Truth,pt.2 . . . . . 1.50
124 The Mark of Kaine,pt.1 . . . . . 1.50
125 R:Gwen Stacy 2.95
125a 3-D Holodisk cover 4.25
126 The Trial of Peter Parker,pt.1 1.50
127 Maximum Clonage,pt.2 . . . . . 1.50
128 TDF,Exiled,pt.1 . . . . 1.50
129 Timebomb,pt.2 . . . . 1.50
Ann.#1 V:Future Max 6.00
Ann.#2 AAd,MMi,A:Warlock 8.00
Ann.#3 AS,DP,JRu,JM,BL 4.50
Ann.#4 AS,TM,RLm,Evolutionary
Wars,A:Man Thing,V:Slug 5.00
Ann.#5 AS,SD,JS,Atlantis
Attacks,A:Fantastic Four 3.50
Ann.#6 SD,JBr,SB,A:Punisher . . . 4.50
Ann.#7 Vibranium Vendetta #3 . . 2.50
Ann.#8 Hero Killers#3,A:New
Warriors,BU:Venom,Black Cat . 3.00
Ann.#9 CMa,I:Cadre,w/card 3.25
Ann.#10 V:Shriek 3.75
Super Size Spec.#1 Planet of
the Symbiotes,pt.5 . . . . 3.95

Weird Wonder Tales #20
© Marvel Entertainment Group

WEIRD WONDERTALES
Dec., 1973
1 B:Reprints 5.00
2 I Was Kidnapped by a Flying
Saucer 2.50
3 The Thing in the Bog 2.50
4 It Lurks Behind the Wall 2.50
5 . . . . 2.50
6 The Man Who Owned a Ghost 2.50
7 The Apes That Walked
like Men 2.50
8 Reap A Deadly Harvest 2.50
9 The Murder Mirror 2.50
10 Mister Morgans Monster 2.50
11 Slaughter in Shrangri-La 2.50
12 The Stars Scream Murder 2.50
13 The Totem Strikes 2.50
14 Witching Circle 2.50
15 . . . . 2.50
16 The Shark 2.50

17 Creature From Krogarr 2.50
18 Krang 2.50
19 A:Dr Druid 2.50
20 The Madness 2.50
21 A:Dr Druid 2.50
22 The World Below,May, 1975 . . 2.50

WEREWOLF BY NIGHT
Sept., 1972
1 MP(cont from Marvel Spotlight)
FullMoonRise..WerewolfKill . . 50.00
2 MP,Like a Wild Beast at Bay . 20.00
3 MP,Mystery of the Mad Monk 13.00
4 MP,The Danger Game 13.00
5 MP,A Life for a Death 13.00
6 MP,Carnival of Fear 10.00
7 MP,JM,Ritual of Blood 8.00
8 MP,Krogg,Lurker from Beyond . 8.00
9 TS,V:Tatterdemalion 8.00
10 TS,bondage cover 8.00
11 GK,TS,Full Moon..Fear Moon . 6.00
12 GK,Cry Monster 6.00
13 MP,ManMonsterCalledTaboo . 5.00
14 MP,Lo,the Monster Strikes . . . 5.00
15 MP,(new)O:Werewolf,
V:Dracula 6.00
16 MP,TS,A:Hunchback of Notre
Dame 5.00
17 Behold the Behemoth 5.00
18 War of the Werewolves 5.00
19 V:Dracula 7.00
20 The Monster Breaks Free 5.00
21 GK(c),To Cure a Werewolf . . . 4.00
22 GK(c),Face of a Friend 4.00
23 Silver Bullet for a Werewolf . . . 4.00
24 GK(c),V:The Brute 4.00
25 GK(c),Eclipse of Evil 4.00
26 GK(c),A Crusade of Murder . . 4.00
27 GK(c),Scourge o/t Soul-Beast . 4.00
28 GK(c),V:Dr.Glitternight 4.00
29 GK(c),V:Dr.Glitternight 4.00
30 GK(c),Red Slash across
Midnight 4.00
31 Death in White 4.00
32 I&O:Moon Knight 65.00
33 Were-Beast..Moon Knight
A:Moon Knight(2nd App) 30.00
34 GK(c),TS,House of Evil..House
of Death 4.00
35 TS,JS,BWi,Jack Russell vs.
Werewolf 4.00
36 Images of Death 4.00
37 BWr(c),BW,A:Moon Knight,
Hangman,Dr.Glitternight 7.00
38 . . . . 3.50
39 V:Brother Voodoo 3.50
40 A:Brother Voodoo,V:Dr.
Glitternight 3.50
41 V:Fire Eyes 3.50
42 A:IronMan,Birth of a Monster . 3.50
43 Tri-Animal Lives,A:Iron Man . . 3.50
G-Size#2,SD,A:Frankenstein
Monster (reprint) 3.00
G-Size#3 GK(c),Transylvania . . 3.50
G-Size#4 GK(c),A:Morbius 10.00
G-Size#5 GK(c),Peril of
Paingloss 3.00

WEST COAST AVENGERS
[Limited Series]
Sept., 1984
1 BH,A:Shroud,J:Hawkeye,IronMan,
WonderMan,Mockingbird,Tigra 4.00
2 BH,V:Blank 3.00

MARVEL

West Coast Avengers #1
© Marvel Entertainment Group

3 BH,V:Graviton 2.00
4 BH,V:Graviton 2.00
[Regular Series]
1 AM,JSt,V:Lethal Legion 4.00
2 AM,JSt,V:Lethal Legion 3.00
3 AM,JSt,V:Kraven 3.00
4 AM,JSt,A:Firebird,Thing,I:Master
  Pandemonium 3.00
5 AM,JSt,A:Werewolf,Thing 3.00
6 AM,KB,A:Thing 3.00
7 AM,JSt,V:Ultron 3.00
8 AM,JSt,V:Rangers,A:Thing . . . 3.00
9 AM,JSt,V:Master Pandemonium 3.00
10 AM,JSt,V:Headlok,Griffen . . . 3.00
11 AM,JSt,A:Nick Fury 2.50
12 AM,JSt,V:Graviton 2.50
13 AM,JSt,V:Graviton 2.50
14 AM,JSt,V:Pandemonium 2.50
15 AM,JSt,A:Hellcat 2.50
16 AM,JSt,V:Tiger Shark,
  Whirlwind 2.50
17 AM,JSt,V:Dominus' Minions . . 2.50
18 AM,JSt,V:The Wild West 2.50
19 AM,JSt,A:Two Gun Kid 2.50
20 AM,JSt,A:Rawhide Kid 2.50
21 AM,JSt,A:Dr.Pym,Moon Knight 2.50
22 AM,JSt,A:Fant.Four,Dr.Strange,
  Night Rider 2.00
23 AM,RT,A:Phantom Rider 2.00
24 AM,V:Dominus 2.00
25 AM,V:Abomination 2.00
26 AM,V:Zodiac 2.00
27 AM,V:Zodiac 1.75
28 AM,V:Zodiac 1.75
29 AM,V:Taurus,A:Shroud 1.75
30 AM,C:Composite Avenger . . . 1.75
31 AM,V:Arkon 1.75
32 AM,TD,V:Yetrigar,J:Wasp . . . 1.75
33 AM,O:Ant-Man,Wasp;
  V:Madam X,El Toro 1.75
34 AM,V:Quicksilver,J:Vision &
  Scarlet Witch 1.75
35 AM,V:Dr.Doom,Quicksilver . . 1.75
36 AM,V:The Voice 1.75
37 V:The Voice,A:Mantis 1.75
38 AM,TMo,V:Defiler 1.50
39 AM,V:Swordsman 1.50
40 AM,MGu,V:NightShift,

A:Shroud 1.50
41 TMo,I:New Phantom Rider,
  L:Moon Knight 1.50
42 JBy,Visionquest#1,V:Ultron . . 2.50
43 JBy,Visionquest#2, ... 2.25
44 JBy,Visionquest#3,J:USAgent . 2.00
45 JBy,Visionquest#4,
  I:New Vision 2.25
46 JBy,I:Great Lakes Avengers . . 2.00
Ann. #1 MBr,GI,V:Zodiak 2.25
Ann. #2 AM,A:SilverSurfer,V:Death,
  Collector,R:Grandmaster 2.00
Ann. #3 AM,RLm,TD,Evolutionary
  Wars,R:Giant Man 3.50
Becomes:
AVENGERS WEST COAST

WESTERN GUNFIGHTERS
August, 1970
[2nd series]
1 JK,JB,DAy,B:Ghost Rider
  A:Fort Rango,The Renegades
  Gunhawk 6.00
2 HT(c),DAy,JMn,O:Nightwind,
  V:Tarantula 3.50
3 DAy,V:Hurricane(reprint) 3.50
4 HT(c),DAy,TS,B:Gunhawk,
  Apache Kid,A:Renegades 3.50
5 DAy,FrG,A:Renegades 3.50
6 HT(c),DAy,SSh,Death of
  Ghost Rider 4.00
7 HT(c),DAy,SSh,O:Ghost Rider
  retold,E:Ghost Rider,Gunhawk 5.00
8 DAy,SSh,B:Black Rider,Outlaw
  Kid(rep) 3.00
9 DW,Revenge rides the Range . 3.00
10 JK,JMn,O:Black Rider,B:Matt
  Slade,E:Outlaw Kid 3.00
11 JK,Duel at Dawn 3.00
12 JMn,O:Matt Slade 3.00
13 Save the Gold Coast Expires . 3.00
14 JSo(c),Outlaw Town 3.00
15 E:Matt Slade,Showdown in
  Outlaw Canyon 3.00
16 B:Kid Colt,Shoot-out in Silver
  City 3.00
17 thru 20 . . . . @3.00
21 thru 24 . . . . @2.50
25 . . . . 2.50
26 F:Kid Colt,Gun-Slinger,Apache
  Kid 2.50
27 thru 32 . . . . @2.50
33 Nov., 1975 . . . . 2.50

WESTERN KID
Dec., 1954
[1st Series]
1 JR,B:Western Kid,O:Western Kid
  (Tex Dawson) 100.00
2 JMn,JR,Western Adventure . . 50.00
3 JMn(c),JR,Gunfight(c) 40.00
4 JMn(c),JR,The Badlands 40.00
5 JR 40.00
6 JR 40.00
7 JR 40.00
8 JR 40.00
9 JR,AW 50.00
10 JR,AW,Man in the Middle . . . 50.00
11 thru 16 . . . . @30.00
17 August, 1957 . . . . 30.00
[2nd Series] Dec., 1971–Aug. 1972
1 Reprints 4.00
2 . . . . 3.00
3 . . . . 3.00

4 . . . . 3.00
5 . . . . 3.00

WESTERN OUTLAWS
Atlas Feb., 1954—Aug., 1957
1 JMn(c),RH,BP,The Greenville
  Gallows,Hanging(c) 125.00
2 . . . . 65.00
3 thru 10 . . . . @50.00
11 AW 50.00
12 . . . . 45.00
13 MB 50.00
14 AW 55.00
15 AT,GT 50.00
16 BP 40.00
17 . . . . 45.00
18 . . . . 40.00
19 . . . . 50.00
20 and 21 . . . . @45.00

WESTERN OUTLAWS
& SHERIFFS
See: BEST WESTERN

WESTERN TALES
OF BLACK RIDER
See: ALL WINNERS COMICS

WESTERN TEAM-UP
Nov., 1973
1 Rawhide Kid/Dakota Kid 2.00

WESTERN THRILLERS
Nov., 1954
1 JMn,Western tales 75.00
2 . . . . 40.00
3 . . . . 40.00
4 . . . . 40.00
Becomes:
COWBOY ACTION
5 JMn(c),The Prairie Kid 45.00
6 . . . . 30.00
7 . . . . 30.00
9 . . . . 30.00
10 . . . . 30.00
11 MN,AW,Ther Manhunter March,
  1956 . . . . 45.00
Becomes:
QUICK-TRIGGER
WESTERN
12 Bill Larson Strikes 55.00
13 The Man From Cheyenne . . . 60.00
14 BEv,RH(c) 50.00
15 AT 40.00
16 JK 35.00
17 GT 35.00
18 GM 35.00
19 JSe 30.00

WESTERN WINNERS
See: ALL WINNERS COMICS

WHAT IF?
[1st Regular Series]
Feb., 1977
1 Spider-Man joined Fant.Four . 18.00
2 GK(c),Hulk had Banner brain . . 9.00
3 GK,KJ,F:Avengers 6.00
4 GK(c),F:Invaders 6.00
5 F:Captain America 6.00

MARVEL

6 F:Fantastic Four 6 00
7 GK(c),F:Spider-Man 6.00
8 GK(c),F:Daredevil 5.50
9 JK(c),F:Avengers of the '50s . . 6.00
10 JB,F:Thor 5.00
11 JK,F:FantasticFour 5.00
12 F:Hulk 5.00
13 JB,Conan Alive Today 6.00
14 F:Sgt. Fury 5.00
15 CI,F:Nova 5.00
16 F:Master of Kung Fu 5.00
17 CI,F:Ghost Rider 5.00
18 TS,F:Dr.Strange 4.00
19 PB,F:Spider-Man 5.00
20 F:Avengers 4.00
21 GC,F:Sub-Mariner 4.00
22 F:Dr.Doom 4.00
23 JB,F:Hulk 4.00
24 GK,RB,Gwen Stacy had lived . 5.00
25 F:Thor,Avengers,O:Mentor . . . 4.00
26 JBy(c),F:Captain America 4.00
27 FM(c),Phoenix hadn't died . . . 7.00
28 FM,F:Daredevil,Ghost Rider. . . 6.00
29 MG(c),F:Avengers 4.00

What If? #13
© *Marvel Entertainment Group*

30 RB,F:Spider-Man 10.00
31 Wolverine killed the Hulk . . . 15.00
32 Avengers lost to Korvac 3.50
33 BL,Dazzler herald of Galactus . 3.50
34 FH,FM,JBy,BSz:Humor issue . 3.50
35 FM,Elektra had lived 6.00
36 JBy,Fant.Four had no powers . 3.00
37 F:Thing,Beast,Silver Surfer . . 3.50
38 F:Daredevil,Captain America . . 3.00
39 Thor had fought Conan 3.00
40 F:Dr.Strange 3.00
41 F:Sub-Mariner 3.50
42 F:Fantastic Four 3.00
43 F:Conan 3.00
44 F:Captain America 3.00
45 F:Hulk,Berserk 3.50
46 Uncle Ben had lived 5.00
47 F:Thor,Loki 3.00
Spec.#1 F:Iron Man,Avengers . . 4.00
Best of What IF? rep.#1,#24,
   #27,#28 . . . . 12.95
[2nd Regular Series]
1 RWi,MG,The Avengers had lost
   the Evolutionary War 5.00

2 GCa,Daredevil Killed Kingpin,
   A:Hobgoblin, The Rose 4.00
3 Capt.America Hadn't Given Up
   Costume,A:Avengers 3.50
4 MBa,Spider-Man kept Black
   Costume,A:Avengers,Hulk . . . 4.50
5 Vision Destroyed Avengers,
   A:Wonder Man 3.50
6 RLm,X-Men Lost Inferno,
   A:Dr.Strange 6.00
7 RLd,Wolverine Joined Shield,
   A:Nick Fury,Black Widow 7.00
8 Iron Man Lost The Armor Wars,
   A:Ant Man 3.50
9 RB,New X-Men Died 6.00
10 MZ(c),BMc,Punisher's Family
   Didn't Die,A:Kingpin 3.00
11 TM(c),JV,SM,Fant.Four had the
   Same Powers,A:Nick Fury . . . 3.50
12 JV,X-Men Stayed in Asgard,
   A:Thor,Hela 3.00
13 JLe(c),Prof.X Became
   Juggernaut,A:X-Men 3.50
14 RLm(c),Capt.Marvel didn't die
   A:Silver Surfer 3.00
15 GCa,Fant.Four Lost Trial of
   Galactus,A:Gladiator 3.00
16 Wolverine Battled Conan,
   A:X-Men,Red Sonja 5.00
17 Kraven Killed Spider-Man,
   A:Daredevil,Captain America . . 3.00
18 LMc,Fant.Four fought Dr.Doom
   before they gained powers . . . 2.50
19 RW,Vision took over Earth,
   A:Avengers,Dr.Doom 2.50
20 Spider-Man didn't marry Mary
   Jane,A:Venom,Kraven 3.00
21 Spider-Man married Black Cat,
   A:Vulture,Silver Sable 2.50
22 RLm,Silver Surfer didn't escape
   Earth,A:F.F,Mephisto,Thanos . 4.00
23 New X-Men never existed,
   A:Eric the Red,Lilandra 2.50
24 Wolverine Became Lord of
   Vampires,A:Punisher 3.00
25 Marvel Heroes lost Atlantis
   Attacks,double size 3.25
26 LMc,Punisher Killed Daredevil,
   A:Spider-Man 2.50
27 Submariner Joined Fantastic
   Four,A:Dr. Doom 2.00
28 RW,Capt.America led Army of
   Super-Soldiers,A:Submariner . 2.00
29 RW,Capt.America formed the
   Avengers 2.00
30 Inv.Woman's 2nd Child had
   lived,A:Fantastic Four 2.00
31 Spider-Man/Captain Universe
   Powers 2.00
32 Phoenix Rose Again,pt.1 . . . . 2.00
33 Phoenix Rose Again,pt.2 . . . . 2.00
34 Humor Issue 1.75
35 B:Time Quake,F.F. vs.Dr.Doom
   & Annihilus 1.75
36 Cosmic Avengers,V:Guardians
   of the Galaxy 1.75
37 X-Vampires,V:Dormammu . . . 1.75
38 Thor was prisoner of Set 1.75
39 E:Time Quake,Watcher saved the
   Universe 1.75
40 Storm remained A thief? 1.75
41 JV,Avengers fought Galactus . 2.00
42 KWe,Spidey kept extra arms . . 1.75
43 Wolverine married Mariko 1.75
44 Punisher possessed by Venom . 1.75

45 Barbara Ketch became G.R. . . 1.75
46 Cable Killed Prof.X,Cyclops &
   Jean Grey 1.75
47 Magneto took over USA 1.75
48 Daredevil Saved Nuke 1.50
49 Silver Surfer had Inf.Gauntlet? . 4.00
50 Hulk killed Wolverine 4.00
51 PCu,Punisher is Capt.America . 1.50
52 BHi,Wolverine led Alpha Flight . 2.00
53 F:Iron Man,Hulk 1.50
54 F:Death's Head 1.50
55 LKa(s),Avengers lose G.Storm . 1.50
56 Avengers lose G.Storm#2 . . . . 1.50
57 Punisher a member of SHIELD . 1.50
58 Punisher kills SpM 1.50
59 Wolverine lead Alpha Flight . . 2.00
60 RoR,Scott & Jean's Wedding . 1.50
61 Spider-Man's Parents 1.95
62 Woverine vs Weapon X 2.25
63 F:War Machine,Iron Man 1.95
64 Iron Man sold out 2.25
65 Archangel fell from Grace 1.50
66 Rogue and Thor 1.50
67 Cap.America returns 1.50
68 Captain America story 1.50
69 Stryfe Killed X-Men 1.50
70 Silver Surfer 1.50
71 The Hulk 1.50
72 Parker Killed Burglar 1.50
73 Daredevil,Kingpin 1.50
74 Sinister Formed X-Men 1.50
75 Gen-X's Blink had lived 1.50
76 Flash Thompson Spider-Man . 1.50
77 Legion had killed Magneto . . . 1.50
78 FF had stayed together 1.50
79 Storm had Phoenix's Power . . 1.50
80 KGa,Hulk was Cured 1.50
81 Age of Apocalypse didn't end . 1.50
82 WML,J.JonahJameson
   adopted Spider-Man 1.50
83 . . . . 1.50
84 . . . . 1.50
85 Magneto Ruled all mutants . . . 1.50
86 . . . . 1.50
87 . . . . 1.50
88 . . . . 1.50
89 . . . . 1.50
90 . . . . 1.50
91 F:Hulk, nice guy, Banner violent 1.50
92 F:Cannonball,Husk 1.50
93 F:Wolverine 1.50
94 JGz,F:Juggernaut 1.50
95 IV,F:Ghost Rider 1.50
96 CWo,F:Quicksilver, ... 1.95
97 F:Black Knight 1.95
98 F:Nightcrawler & Rogue 1.95
99 F:Black Cat 1.95
100 IV,KJ,F:Gambit & Rogue, 48pg 2.99
Minus 1 Spec., AOI, flashback,
   F:Bishop 1.95
TPB Best of What If? 12.95

WHAT THE -?!
[Parodies]
August, 1988

1 . . . . 5.00
2 JBy,JOy,AW, ... 4.00
3 TM, ... 5.00
4 . . . . 3.00
5 EL,JLe,WPo,Wolverine 5.00
6 Wolverine,Punisher 3.00
7 . . . . 2.50
8 DK 2.50
9 . . . . 1.75
10 JBy,X-Men,Dr.Doom, Cap.

All comics prices listed are for *Near Mint* condition.

MARVEL

What The-?! #6
© *Marvel Entertainment Group*

8 The Four-Armed Men	3.50
9 Bumbu	3.50
10 Monster That Walks Like A Man	3.50
11 Gruto	3.00
12 Orogo	3.00
13 The Thing That Crawl	3.00
14 The Green Thing	3.00
15 Kraa- The Inhuman	3.00
16 Beware the Son Of Goom	3.00
17 The Hidden Vampires	3.00
18 The Mask of Morghum	3.00
19 The Insect Man	3.00
20 Klagg	3.00
21 Fin Fang Foom	3.00
22 Elektro	3.00
23 The Monster Waits For Me	3.00
24 The Things on Easter Island	3.00
25 The Ruler of the Earth	3.00
26	3.00
27	3.00
28 Droom,The Living Lizard	3.00
29 thru 37 Reprints	@3.00
38 Reprints,Oct., 1975	3.00

America	1.75
11 DK,RLd(part)	2.00
12 Conan, F.F.,Wolverine.	1.50
13 Silver Burper,F.F.,Wolverine.	1.50
14 Spittle-Man	1.50
15 Capt.Ultra,Wolverina	1.50
16 Ant Man,Watcher	1.25
17 Wulverean/Pulverizer,Hoagj/ Spider-Ham,SleepGawker,F.F.	1.25
18	1.25
19	1.25
20 Infinity Wart Crossover	1.25
21 Weapon XX,Toast Rider	1.25
22 F:Echs Farce	1.25
23	1.25
24 Halloween issue	1.25
25	1.25
26 Spider-Ham 2099	1.25
Summer Spec.	2.50
Fall Spec.	2.50

WHERE CREATURES ROAM
July, 1970—Sept., 1971

1 JK,SD,DAy,B:Reprints The Brute That Walks	4.50
2 JK,SD,Midnight/Monster	2.50
3 JK,SD,DAy,Thorg	2.50
4 JK,SD,Vandoom	2.50
5 JK,SD,Gorgilla	2.50
6 JK,SD,Zog	2.50
7 SD	2.50
8 The Mummy's Secret,E:Reprints	2.50

WHERE MONSTERS DWELL
Jan., 1970

1 B:Reprints,Cyclops	5.00
2 Sporr	3.50
3 Grottu	3.50
4	3.50
5 Taboo	3.50
6 Groot	3.50
7 Rommbu	3.50

WHIP WILSON
See: BLAZE CARSON

WILD
Atlas Feb., 1954

1 BEv,JMn,Charlie Chan Parody	165.00
2 BEv,RH,JMn,Witches(c)	100.00
3 CBu(c),BEv,RH,JMn,	75.00
4 GC,Didja Ever See a Cannon Brawl	75.00
5 RH,JMn,August, 1954	75.00

WILD CARDS
Epic Sept., 1990

1 JG	5.50
2 JG,V:Jokers	4.50
3 A:Turtle	4.50

WILD THING

1 A:Virtual Reality Venom and Carnage	3.00
2 A:VR Venom and Carnage	2.00
3 A:Shield	2.00
4	2.00
5 Virtual Reality Gangs	2.00
6 Virtual Reality Villians	2.00
7 V:Trask	2.00
8	1.75
9	1.75
10	1.75
11	1.75
12	1.75
13	1.75

WILD WEST
Spring, 1948

1 SSh(c),B:Two Gun Kids,Tex Taylor,Arizona Annie	175.00
2 SSh(c),CCb, Captain Tootsie	135.00

Becomes:

WILD WESTERN

3 SSh(c),B:Tex Morgan,Two Gun Kid,Tex Taylor,Arizona Annie	175.00
4 Rh,SSh,CCB,Capt. Tootsie. A:Kid Colt,E:Arizona Annie	125.00
5 RH,CCB,Captain Tootsie A;Black Rider,Blaze Carson	125.00

6 A:Blaze Carson,Kid Colt	75.00
7	75.00
8 RH	75.00
9 Ph(c),B:Black Rider	100.00
10 Ph(c)	125.00
11	75.00
12	60.00
13	60.00
14	60.00
15	65.00
16 thru 20	@55.00
21 thru 29	@50.00
30 JKa	55.00
31 thru 40	@35.00
41 thru 47	@25.00
48	35.00
49 thru 53	@25.00
54 AW	45.00
55 AW	45.00
56	25.00
57 Sept., 1957	25.00

William Shatner's Tek World #12
© *Marvel Entertainment Group*

WILLIAM SHATNER'S TEK WORLD

1 LS,Novel adapt.	2.25
2 LS,Novel adapt.cont.	2.00
3 LS,Novel adapt.cont.	2.00
4 LS,Novel adapt.cont.	2.00
5 LS,Novel adapt.concludes	2.00
6 LS,V:TekLords	2.00
7 E:The Angel	2.00
8	2.00
9	2.00
10	2.00
11 thru 17	2.00
18	2.00
19 Sims of the Father#1	1.75
20 Sims of the Father#2	1.75
21 Who aren't in Heaven	1.75
22 Father and Guns	1.75
23 We'll be Right Back	2.00
24	1.75

WILLIE COMICS
See: IDEAL COMICS

MARVEL

WILLOW
August, 1988
1 Movie adapt. 1.00
2 Movie adapt. 1.00
3 Movie adapt,Oct., 1988. . . . . . 1.00

WITNESS, THE
Sept., 1948
1 . . . . 450.00

WOLFPACK
August, 1988
1 I:Wolfpack 1.00
2 thru 11 . . . . @1.00
12 July, 1988 . . . . 1.00

Wolverine #1
© Marvel Entertainment Group

WOLVERINE
Sept., 1982
[Limited Series]
1 B:CCl(s),FM,JRu,A:Mariko,
  I:Shingen 42.00
2 FM,JRu,A:Mariko,I:Yukio . . . 30.00
3 FM,JRu,A:Mariko,Yukio 30.00
4 B:CCl(s),FM,JRu,A:Mariko,
  D:Shingen 32.00
[Regular Series]
1 JB,AW,V:Banipur 40.00
2 JB,KJ,V:Silver Samurai 20.00
3 JB,AW,V:Silver Samurai 15.00
4 JB,AW,I:Roughouse,
  Bloodsport 14.00
5 JB,AW,V:Roughouse,
  Bloodsport 14.00
6 JB,AW,V:Roughouse,
  Bloodsport 13.00
7 JB,A:Hulk 12.00
8 JB,A:Hulk 12.00
9 GC,Old Wolverine Story 12.00
10 JB,BSz,V:Sabretooth
  (1st battle) 37.00
11 JB,BSz,B:Gehenna Stone 8.00
12 JB,BSz,Gehenna Stone 8.00
13 JB,BSz,Gehenna Stone 8.00
14 JB,BSz,Gehenna Stone 8.00
15 JB,BSz,Gehenna Stone 8.00
16 JB,BSz,E:Gehenna Stone 8.00

17 JBy,KJ,V:Roughouse 7.00
18 JBy,KJ,V:Roughouse 7.00
19 JBy,KJ,A of V,I:La Bandera . . . 7.00
20 JBy,KJ,A of V,V:Tigershark . . . 6.00
21 JBy,KJ,V:Geist 6.00
22 JBy,KJ,V:Geist,Spore 6.00
23 JBy,KJ,V:Geist,Spore 6.00
24 GC,'Snow Blind' 5.00
25 JB,O:Wolverine(part) 5.00
26 KJ,Return to Japan 4.50
27 thru 30 Lazarus Project 4.50
31 MS,DGr,A:Prince o'Mandripoor 4.50
32 MS,DGr,V:Ninjas 4.50
33 MS,Wolverine in Japan 4.50
34 MS,DGr,Wolverine in Canada . 4.50
35 MS,DGr,A:Puck 4.50
36 MS,DGr,A:Puck,Lady D'strike . . 4.50
37 MS,DGr,V:Lady Deathstrike . . 4.50
38 MS,DGr,A:Storm,I:Elsie Dee . . 4.50
39 MS,DGr,Wolverine Vs. Clone . 4.50
40 MS,DGr,Wolverine Vs. Clone . 4.50
41 MS,DGr,R:Sabretooth,
  A:Cable 12.00
41a 2nd printing 2.25
42 MS,DGr,A:Sabretooth,Cable . . 7.00
42a 2nd printing 2.25
43 MS,DGr,A:Sabretooth,C:Cable 5.00
44 LSn,DGr 4.00
45 MS,DGr,A:Sabretooth 5.00
46 MS,DGr,A:Sabretooth 4.50
47 V:Tracy 4.00
48 LHa(s),MS,DGr,B:Shiva
  Scenario 4.00
49 LHa(s),MS,DGr, ... 4.00
50 LHa(s),MS,DGr,A:X-Men,Nick Fury,
  I:Shiva,Slash-Die Cut(c) 8.00
51 MS,DGr,A:Mystique,X-Men . . 3.50
52 MS,DGr,A:Mystique,V:Spiral . . 3.50
53 MS,A:Mystique,V:Spiral,Mojo . 3.50
54 A:Shatterstar 3.50
55 MS,V:Cylla,A:Gambit,Sunfire . 3.50
56 MS,A:Gambit,Sunfire,V:Hand,
  Hydra 3.50
57 MS,D:Lady Mariko,A:Gambit . . 4.00
58 A:Terror 3.00
59 A:Terror 3.00
60 Sabretooth vs.Shiva,
  I:John Wraith 3.50
61 MT,History of Wolverine and
  Sabretooth,A:John Wraith 3.50
62 MT,A:Sabretooth,Silver Fox . . 3.00
63 MT,V:Ferro,D:Silver Fox 3.00
64 MPa,V:Ferro,Sabretooth 3.00
65 MT,A:Professor X 3.00
66 MT,A:X-Men 3.00
67 MT,A:X-Men 3.00
68 MT,V:Epsilon Red 3.00
69 DT,A:Rogue,V:Sauron,tie-in to
  X-Men#300 . . . . 2.75
70 DT,Sauron,A:Rogue,Jubilee . . 2.75
71 DT,V:Sauron,Brain Child,A:Rogue,
  Jubilee 2.75
72 DT,Sentinels 2.75
73 DT,V:Sentinels 2.75
74 ANi,V:Sentinels 2.50
75 AKu,Hologram(c),Wolv.has Bone
  Claws,leaves X-Men 10.00
76 DT(c),B:LHa(s),A:Deathstrike,
  Vindicator,C:Puck 2.25
77 AKu,A:Vindicator,Puck,V:Lady
  Deathstrike 2.25
78 AKu,V:Cylla,Bloodscream . . . 2.25
79 AKu,V:Cyber,I:Zoe Culloden . 2.25
80 IaC,V:Cyber, ... 2.25
81 IaC,V:Cyber,A:Excalibur 2.25

82 AKu,BMc,A:Yukio,Silver
  Samurai 2.25
83 AKu,A:Alpha Flight 2.25
84 A:Alpha Flight 1.95
85 Phalanx Covenant, Final Sanction,
  V:Phalanx,holografx(c) 4.50
85a newsstand ed. 2.50
86 AKu,V:Bloodscream 2.50
87 AKu,deluxe,V:Juggernaut . . . 3.25
87a newsstand ed. 1.50
88 AKu,deluxe ed. 3.25
88a newsstand ed. 1.50
89 deluxe ed. 3.25
89a newsstand ed. 1.50
90 V:Sabretooth, deluxe ed. . . . 3.00
90a newsstand ed. 1.50
91 LHa,Logan's future unravels . 4.00
92 LHa,AKu,DGr,A:Sabretooth . . 4.00
93 R:Cyber 4.00
94 Feral Wolverine 4.00
95 LHa,AKu,DGr,V:Dark Riders . 4.00
96 LHa,Aku,DGr,Death of Cyber . 4.00
97 LHa,AKu,DGr,A:Genesis 3.50
98 LHa,AKu,F:Genesis 3.50
99 . . . . 3.50
100 LHa,AKu,DG,A:Elektra;double-
  size, Foil Hologram cover . . . 12.00
100a regular edition 6.00
101 LHa,AKu,A:Elektra 4.00
102 LHa 3.50
103 LHa,Elektra,A:Onslaught 5.00
104 LHa,Gateway, Onslaught . . . 2.50
105 LHa,Gateway, Elektra 2.25
106 LHa 2.25
107 LHa,VS,prologue to Elektra#1 2.25
108 LHa,back to Tokyo,A:Yukio . . 2.25
109 LHa,DG, ... 2.25
110 LHa,DG,Who's spying on
  Logan 2.25
111 LHa,DG,Logan moves to NYC 2.25
112 LHa,DG,Logan in NYC 2.25
113 LHa,R:Ogun,A:Lady Deathstrike &
  Spiral 1.95
114 LHa,back in costume,V:Cyborg
  Donald Pierce 1.95
115 LHa, Zero Tolerance, V:Bastion 1.95
116 LHa, Zero Tolerance, ... 1.95
TPB Wolverine rep Marvel Comics
  Presents #1-#10 . . . . 2.95
Jungle Adventure MMi,(Deluxe) . 5.50
SC Acts of Vengeance, rep. . . . 6.95
Bloodlust (one shot),AD
  V:Siberian Were-Creatures . . . 6.00
Global Jeapordy,PDd(s) 2.95
Killing, KSW,JNR 5.95
Rahne of Terror, C:Cable 8.00
Save the Tiger,rep. 2.95
GNv Bloody ChoicesJB,A:N.Fury 12.95
Typhoid's Kiss,rep. 6.95
Inner Fury,BSz,V:Nanotech
  Machines 6.25
GN Scorpio Rising, T.U.Fury . . . 5.95
HC Weapon X 19.95
Spec. '95 LHa,F:Nightcrawler . . 3.95
Minus 1 Spec., LHa,CNn, flashback,
  F:Weapon X 1.95
TPB Triumphs & Tragedies . . . 16.95

WOLVERINE & PUNISHER:
DAMAGING EVIDENCE
1 B:CP(s),GEr,A:Kingpin 2.25
2 GEr,A:Kingpin,Sniper 2.25
3 GEr,Last issue 2.25

MARVEL

WOLVERINE ENCYCLOPEDIA
Vol. 1 AKu(c) 48pg. 5.95
Vol. 2 48pg 5.95
Vol. 3 48pg 5.95

WOLVERINE/GAMBIT: VICTIMS
1 Takes Place in London 2.95
2 Is Wolverine the Killer? 2.95
3 V:Mastermind 2.95
4 conclusion 2.95

WOLVERINE SAGA
Sept., 1989
1 RLd(c), ... 6.50
2 . . . . 5.00
3 . . . . 5.00
4 Dec., 1989 . . . . 5.00

WONDER DUCK
Sept., 1949
1 Whale(c) 50.00
2 . . . . 33.00
3 March, 1950 . . . . 33.00

WONDERMAN
March, 1986
1 KGa,one-shot special 3.00

Wonder Man Annual #2
© Marvel Entertainment Group

WONDER MAN
Sept., 1991
1 B:GJ(s),JJ,V:Goliath 2.50
2 JJ,A:West Coast Avengers . . . 1.50
3 JJ,V:Abominatrix,I:Spider 1.50
4 JJ,I:Splice,A:Spider 1.50
5 JJ,A:Beast,V:Rampage 1.50
6 JJ,A:Beast,V:Rampage 1.50
7 JJ,Galactic Storm,pt.4,
   A:Hulk & Rich Jones 1.50
8 JJ,GalacticStorm,pt.11,A:Vision 1.50
9 JJ,GalacticStorm,pt.18,A:Vision 1.50
10 JJ,V:Khmer Rouge 1.50
11 V:Angkor 1.50
12 V:Angkor 1.50

13 Infinity War 1.50
14 Infinity War,V:Warlock 1.50
15 Inf.War,V:Doppleganger 1.50
16 JJ,I:Armed Response,
   A:Avengers West Coast 1.50
17 JJ,A:Avengers West Coast . . . 1.50
18 V:Avengers West Coast 1.50
19 . . . . 1.50
20 V:Splice,Rampage 1.50
21 V:Splice,Rampage 1.50
22 JJ,V:Realm of Death 1.50
23 JJ,A:Grim Reaper,Mephisto . . . 1.50
24 JJ,V:Grim Reaper,Goliath 1.50
25 JJ,N:Wonder Man,D:Grim Reaper,
   V:Mephisto 3.25
26 A:Hulk,C:Furor,Plan Master . . . 1.50
27 A:Hulk 1.50
28 RoR,A:Spider-Man 1.50
29 RoR,A:Spider-Man 1.50
30 V:Hate Monger 1.25
31 . . . . 1.25
32 . . . . 1.25
33 . . . . 1.25
Spec.#1 (1985),KGa 3.00
Ann.#1 System Bytes #3 . . . . . 2.25
Ann.#2 I:Hit-Maker,w/card 2.95

WORLD CHAMPIONSHIP WRESTLING
1 F:Lex Luger,Sting 1.50
2 . . . . 1.25
3 . . . . 1.25
4 Luger Vs El Gigante 1.25
5 Rick Rude Vs. Sting 1.25
6 F:Dangerous Alliance,R.Rude . 1.25
7 F:Steiner Brothers 1.25
8 F:Sting,Dangerous Alliance . . . 1.25
9 Bunkhouse Brawl 1.25
10 Halloween Havoc 1.25
11 Sting vs Grapplers 1.25
12 F:Ron Simmons 1.25

WORLD OF FANTASY
Atlas May, 1956
1 The Secret of the Mountain . . 300.00
2 AW,Inside the Tunnel 175.00
3 DAy,SC, The Man in the Cave 160.00
4 BEv(c),Back to the Lost City . 125.00
5 BEv(c),BP,In the Swamp . . . 125.00
6 BEv(c),The Strange Wife of
   Henry Johnson 125.00
7 BEv(c),GM,Man in Grey . . . 125.00
8 GM,JO,MF,The Secret of the
   Black Cloud 135.00
9 BEv,BK 110.00
10 . . . . 100.00
11 AT 110.00
12 BEv(c) 100.00
13 BEv,JO 100.00
14 JMn(c),GM,JO 100.00
15 JK(c) 100.00
16 AW,SD,JK 125.00
17 JK(c),SD 120.00
18 JK(c) 120.00
19 JK(c),SD,August, 1959 . . . . 120.00

WORLD OF MYSTERY
Atlas June, 1956
1 BEv(c),AT,JO,The Long Wait 275.00
2 BEv(c),The Man From
   Nowhere 100.00
3 SD,AT,JDa, The Bugs 125.00
4 SD(c),BP,What Happened in the
   Basement 125.00

5 JO,She Stands in the Shadows100.00
6 AW,SD,Sinking Man 150.00
7 Pick A Door July, 1957 . . . . 100.00

WORLD OF SUSPENSE
Atlas April, 1956
1 JO,BEv,A Stranger Among Us 225.00
2 SD,When Walks the Scarecrow 125.00
3 AW,The Man Who Couldn't
   Be Touched 135.00
4 Something is in This House . 100.00
5 BEv,DH,JO 100.00
6 BEv(c),BP 100.00
7 AW,The Face 110.00
8 The Prisoner of the Ghost Ship100.00

WORLDS UNKNOWN
May, 1973
1 GK,AT,The Coming of the
   Martians,Reprints 3.00
2 GK,TS,A Gun For A Dinosaur . 2.00
3 The Day the Earth Stood
   Still 2.00
4 JB,Arena 2.00
5 DA,JM,Black Destroyer 2.00
6 GK(c),The Thing Called It 2.00
7 GT,The Golden Voyage of
   Sinbad,Part 1 . . . . 2.00
8 The Golden Voyage of
   Sinbad,Part 2, August, 1974 . 2.00

WYATT EARP
Atlas Nov., 1955
1 JMn,F:Wyatt Earp 100.00
2 AW,Saloon(c) 60.00
3 JMn(c),The Showdown,
   A:Black Bart 50.00
4 Ph(c),Hugh O'Brian,JSe,
   India Sundown 50.00
5 Ph(c),Hugh O'Brian,DW,
   Gun Wild Fever 50.00
6 . . . . 50.00
7 AW 60.00
8 . . . . 50.00
9 and 10 . . . . @50.00
11 . . . . 60.00
12 AW 50.00
13 thru 20 . . . . @35.00
21 JDa(c) 30.00
22 thru 29 . . . . @25.00
30 Reprints 2.50
31 thru 33 Reprints . . . . @1.25
34 June, 1973 . . . . 1.25

XAVIER INSTITUTE ALUMNI YEARBOOK
GN 48pg 5.95

X-CALIBRE
1 Excaliber After Xavier 5.00
2 V:Callisto & Morlock Crew 3.50
3 D:Juggernaut 3.00
4 Secret Weapon 3.00
TPB Rep.#1-#4 . . . . 8.95

X-FACTOR
Feb., 1986
1 WS(c),JG,BL,JRu,I:X-Factor,
   Rusty 12.00
2 JG,BL,I:Tower 6.00
3 JG,BL,V:Tower 5.00
4 KP,JRu,V:Frenzy 5.00
5 JG,JRu,I:Alliance of Evil,

WAR ACTION
Atlas April, 1952
1 JMn,RH,War Stories, Six Dead
  Men 100.00
2 .... 60.00
3 Invasion in Korea 40.00
4 thru 10 .... @40.00
11 .... 50.00
12 .... 50.00
13 BK 50.00
14 Rangers Strike,June, 1953 .. 45.00

WAR ADVENTURES
Atlas Jan., 1952
1 GT,Battle Fatigue 100.00
2 The Story of a Slaughter .. 50.00
3 JRo 35.00
4 RH(c) 35.00
5 RH,Violent(c) 35.00
6 Stand or Die 35.00
7 JMn(c) 35.00
8 BK 50.00
9 RH(c) 30.00
10 JRo(c),Attack at Dawn 30.00
11 Red Trap 30.00
12 .... 30.00
13 RH(c),The Commies Strike
  Feb., 1953 .... 30.00

WAR COMBAT
Atlas March, 1952
1 JMn,Death of a Platoon Leader 75.00
2 .... 40.00
3 JMn(c) 30.00
4 JMn(c) 30.00
5 The Red Hordes 30.00
Becomes:
COMBAT CASEY
6 BEv,Combat Casey cont .. 50.00
7 .... 35.00
8 JMn(c) 28.00
9 .... 25.00
10 RH(c) 35.00
11 .... 20.00
12 .... 20.00
13 thru 19 .... @35.00
20 .... 20.00
21 thru 33 .... @15.00
34 July, 1957 .... 15.00

WAR COMICS
Atlas Dec., 1950
1 You Only Die Twice 140.00
2 Infantry's War 75.00
3 .... 50.00
4 GC,The General Said Nuts .. 50.00
5 .... 50.00
6 The Deadly Decision of
  General Kwang 50.00
7 RH 50.00
8 RH,No Survivors 50.00
9 RH 50.00
10 .... 50.00
11 thru 21 .... @40.00
22 .... 65.00
23 thru 37 .... @30.00
38 JKu 45.00
39 .... 30.00
40 .... 30.00
41 .... 30.00
42 .... 30.00
43 AT 40.00
44 .... 30.00

45 .... 30.00
46 RC 45.00
47 .... 30.00
48 .... 30.00
49 Sept., 1957 .... 45.00

WARHEADS
1 GEr,I:Warheads,A:Wolverine, .. 2.25
2 GEr,V:Nick Fury 2.00
3 DTy,A:Iron Man 2.00
4 SCy,A:X-Force 2.00
5 A:X-Force,C:Deaths'Head II .. 2.00
6 SCy,A:Death's Head II 2.00
7 SCy,A:Death's Head II,S.Surfer 2.00
8 SCy,V:Mephisto 2.00
9 SCy,V:Mephisto 2.00
10 JCz,V:Mephisto 2.00
11 A:Death's Head II 2.00
12 V:Mechanix 2.00
13 Xenophiles Reptiles 2.00
14 last issue 2.00

WARHEADS: BLACK DAWN
1 A:Gh.Rider,Morbius 3.25
2 V:Dracula 2.00

WAR IS HELL
Jan., 1973—Oct., 1975
1 B:Reprints,Decision at Dawn . 2.00
2 Anytime,Anyplace,War is Hell . 1.50
3 Retreat or Die 1.50
4 Live Grenade 1.50
5 Trapped Platoon 1.50
6 We Die at Dawn 1.50
7 While the Jungle Sleeps,A:Sgt
  Fury 1.50
8 Killed in Action,A;Sgt Fury .. 1.50
9 B:Supernatural,War Stories .. 1.50
10 Death is a 30 Ton Tank 1.50
11 thru 15 .... @1.50

WARLOCK
[1st Regular Series]
August, 1972
1 GK,I:Counter Earth,A:High
  Evolutionary 20.00
2 JB,TS,V:Man Beast 9.00
3 GK,TS,V:Apollo 8.00
4 JK,TS,V:Triax 7.00
5 GK,TS,V:Dr.Doom 7.00
6 TS(i),O:Brute 7.00
7 TS(i),V:Brute,D:Dr.Doom 7.00
8 TS(i),R:Man-Beast(cont
  in Hulk #176) 7.00
9 JSn,1st'Rebirth'Thanos,O:Magnus,
  N:Warlock,I:In-Betweener 9.00
10 JSn,SL,O:Thanos,V:Magus,
  A:In-Betweener 11.00
11 JSn,SL,D:Magus,A:Thanos,
  In-Betweener 10.00
12 JSn,SL,O:Pip,V:Pro-Boscis
  A:Starfox 6.00
13 JSn,SL,I&O:Star-Thief 6.00
14 JSn,SL,V:Star-Thief 6.00
15 JSn,A:Thanos,V:Soul-Gem ... 15.00
[2nd Regular Series]
1 JSn,rep.Strange Tales #178-180
  Baxter Paper 3.00
2 JSn,rep.Strange Tales #180
  & Warlock #9 .... 2.50
3 JSn,rep.Warlock #10-#12 .... 2.50
4 JSn,rep.Warlock #13-#15 .... 2.50

5 JSn,rep.Warlock #15 .... 2.50
6 JSn,rep. 2.50

WARLOCK
(Limited Series)
1 Rep.Warlock Series 3.50
2 Rep.Warlock Series 3.00
3 Rep.Warlock Series 3.00
4 Rep.Warlock Series 3.00
5 Rep.Warlock Series 3.00
6 Rep.Warlock Series 3.00

Warlock & The Infinity Watch #9
© Marvel Entertainment Group

WARLOCK AND THE INFINITY WATCH
1 AMe,Trial of the Gods(from
  Infinity Gauntlet) 4.00
2 AMe,I:Infinity Watch(Gamora,Pip,
  Moondragon,Drax & 1 other) .. 3.00
3 RL,TA,A:High Evolutionary,
  Nobilus,I:Omega 3.00
4 RL,TA,V:Omega 2.50
5 AMe,TA,V:Omega 2.50
6 AMe,V:Omega(Man-Beast) ... 2.50
7 TR,TA,V:Mole Man,A:Thanos .. 2.50
8 TR,TA,Infinity War,A:Thanos .. 2.25
9 AMe,TA,Inf.War,O:Gamora ... 2.00
10 AMe,Inf.War,Thanos vs
  Doppleganger 2.50
11 O:Pip,Gamora,Drax,M'dragon . 2.00
12 TR,Drax Vs.Hulk 2.00
13 TR,Drax vs Hulk 2.00
14 AMe,V:United Nations 2.00
15 AMe,Magnus,Him 2.00
16 TGr,I:Count Abyss 2.00
17 TGr,I:Maxam 2.00
18 AMe,Inf.Crusade,N:Pip 2.00
19 TGr,A:Hulk,Wolverine,Infinity
  Crusade 2.00
20 AMe,Inf.Crusade 2.00
21 V:Thor 2.00
22 AMe,Infinity Crusade 2.00
23 JSn(s),TGb,Blood &
  Thunder#4 .... 2.00
24 JSn(s),TGb,V:Geirrodur 2.00
25 JSn(s),AMe,Die-Cut(c),Blood &
  Thunder #12 .... 3.25

MARVEL

26 A:Avengers	2.00
27 TGb,V:Avengers	2.00
28 TGb,V:Man-Beast	2.00
29 A:Maya	2.25
30 PO	2.25
31	1.95
32 Heart & Soul	1.95
33 V:Count Abyss	1.95
34 V:Count Abyss	1.95
35 V:Tyrannus	1.95
36	1.95
37 A:Zaharius	1.95
38	1.95
39 V:Domitron	1.95
40 A:Thanos	1.95
41 Monster Island	1.95
42 Warlock vs. Maxam, Atlantis Rising, final issue	1.95

WARLOCK CHRONICLES

1 TR,F:Adam Warlock,holo-grafx(c), I:Darklore,Meer'lyn	3.25
2 TR,Infinity Crusade,Thanos revealed to have the Reality Gem	2.25
3 TR,A:Mephisto	2.25
4 TR,A:Magnus	2.25
5 TR(c),Inf.Crusade	2.25
6 TR,Blood & Thunder,pt.#3	2.25
7 TR,Blood & Thunder,pt.#7	2.25
8 TR,Blood & Thunder,pt.#11	2.25
9 TR	2.00
10 TR	2.00
11 TR	2.00

WAR MACHINE

1 GG,Foil Embossed(c),B:LKa&StB, O:War Machine,V:Cable, C:Deathlok	3.25
1a Newstand Ed.	2.25
2 GG,V:Cable,Deathlok,w/card	1.75
3 GG,V:Cable,Deathlok	1.75
4 GG,C:Force Works	1.75
5 GG,I:Deachtoll	1.50
6 GG,V:Deathtoll	1.50
7 GG,A:Hawkeye	1.50
8 reg ed.	1.50
8a neon(c),w/insert print	3.00
9 Hands of Mandarin,pt.2	1.50
10 Hands of Mandarin,pt.5	1.50
11 X-Mas Party	1.50
12 V:Terror Device	1.50
13 V:The Rush Team	1.50
14 A:Force Works	1.50
15 In The Past of WWII	2.50
16 DAn,A:Rick Fury,Cap.America	1.50
17 The Man Who Won WWII	1.50
18 DAn,N:War Machine	1.50
19 DAn,A:Hawkeye	1.50
20 DAn,The Crossing	1.50
21 DAn,The Crossing	1.50
22 DAn,V:Iron Man	1.50
23 DAn,Avengers:Timeslide	1.50

WAR MAN
Epic

1 thru 2 CDi(s)	2.50

WEAPON X

1 Wolverine After Xavier	4.00
2 Full Scale War	2.25
3 Jean Leaves	1.95
4 F:Gateway	1.95
TPB Rep.#1-#4	8.95

WEAVEWORLD
Epic

1 MM, Clive Barker adaptation	4.95
2 MM,'Into the Weave'	4.95
3 MM	4.95

WEB OF SCARLET SPIDER

1 TDF,Virtual Mortality,pt.1	1.95
2 TDF,CyberWar,pt.2	1.95
3 Nightmare in Scarlet,pt.1	1.95
4 Nightmare in Scarlet,pt.3	1.95

Web of Spider-Man #4
© Marvel Entertainment Group

WEB OF SPIDER-MAN
April, 1985

1 JM,V:New Costume	22.00
2 JM,V:Vulture	8.00
3 JM,V:Vulture	7.00
4 JM,JBy,V:Dr.Octopus	6.00
5 JM,JBy,V:Dr.Octopus	6.00
6 MZ,BL,JM,Secret Wars II	6.00
7 SB,A:Hulk,V:Nightmare, C:Wolverine	6.00
8 V:Smithville Thunder	6.00
9 V:Smithville Thunder	6.00
10 JM,A:Dominic Fortune, V:Shocker	6.00
11 BMc,V:Thugs	6.00
12 BMc,SB,V:Thugs	6.00
13 BMc,V:J.JonahJameson	6.00
14 KB,V:Black Fox	6.00
15 V:Black Fox,I:Chance	7.00
16 MS,KB,V:Magma	5.00
17 MS,V:Magma	5.00
18 MS,KB,Where is Spider-Man?	7.00
19 MS,BMc,I:Solo,Humbug	5.50
20 MS,V:Terrorists	5.00
21 V:Fake Spider-Man	5.00
22 MS,V:Terrorists	5.00
23 V:Slyde	5.00
24 SB,V:Vulture,Hobgoblin	6.00
25 V:Aliens	5.00
26 V:Thugs	5.00
27 V:Headhunter	5.00
28 BL,V:Thugs	5.00
29 A:Wolverine,2nd App:New	

Hobgoblin	16.00
30 KB,O:Rose,C:Daredevil,Capt. America,Wolverine,Punisher	13.00
31 MZ,BMc,V:Kraven	11.00
32 MZ,BMc,V:Kraven	10.00
33 BSz(c),SL,V:Kingpin,Mad Dog Ward,pt.#1	5.00
34 SB,A:Watcher	5.00
35 AS,V:Living Brain	5.00
36 AS,V:Phreak Out,I:Tombstone	6.00
37 V:Slasher	5.00
38 AS,A:Tombstone,V:Hobgoblin	6.00
39 AS,V:Looter(Meteor Man)	4.00
40 AS,V:Cult of Love	4.00
41 AS,V:Cult of Love	4.00
42 AS,V:Cult of Love	4.00
43 AS,V:Cult of Love	4.00
44 AS,V:Warzone,A:Hulk	3.00
45 AS,V:Vulture	3.00
46 A:Dr.Pym,V:Nekra	3.00
47 AS,V:Hobgoblin	5.00
48 AS,O:New Hobgoblin's Demonic Power	13.00
49 VM,V:Drugs	4.00
50 AS,V:Chameleon(double size)	6.00
51 MBa,V:Chameleon,Lobo Bros.	4.00
52 FS,JR,O:J.Jonah Jameson V:Chameleon	4.00
53 MBa,V:Lobo Bros.,C:Punisher A:Chameleon	4.50
54 AS,V:Chameleon,V:Lobo Bros.	4.00
55 AS,V:Chameleon,Hammerhead, V:Lobo Bros.	4.00
56 AS,I&O:Skin Head, A:Rocket Racer	3.50
57 AS,D:SkinHead, A:Rocket Racer	3.00
58 AS,V:Grizzly	3.00
59 AS,Acts of Vengeance,V:Titania A:Puma,Cosmic Spider-Man	8.00
60 AS,A of V,V:Goliath	5.00
61 AS,A of V,V:Dragon Man	5.00
62 AS,V:Molten Man	3.00
63 AS,V:Mister Fear	3.00
64 AS,V:Graviton,Titania,Trapster	3.00
65 AS,V:Goliath,Trapster,Graviton	3.00
66 AS,V:Tombstone,A:G.Goblin	4.00
67 AS,A:GreenGoblin, V:Tombstone	4.00
68 AS,A:GreenGoblin, V:Tombstone	3.50
69 AS,V:Hulk	5.00
70 AS,I:The Spider/Hulk	3.00
71 A:Silver Sable	2.50
72 AM,A:Silver Sable	2.50
73 AS,A:Human Torch, Colossus,Namor	2.50
74 AS,I:Spark,V:Bora	2.50
75 AS,C:New Warriors	2.50
76 AS,Spidey in Ice	2.50
77 AS,V:Firebrand,Inheritor	2.50
78 AS,A:Firebrand,Cloak&Dagger	2.50
79 AS,V:Silvermane	2.50
80 AS,V:Silvermane	2.50
81 I:Bloodshed	2.25
82 V:Man Mountain Marko	2.25
83 V:A.I.M. Supersuit	2.25
84 AS,B:Name of the Rose	3.00
85 AS,Name of the Rose	2.50
86 AS,I:Demogoblin	3.50
87 AS,I:Praetorian Guard	2.50
88 AS,Name of the Rose	2.50
89 AS,E:Name of the Rose, I:Bloodrose	2.50
90 AS,30th Ann.,w/hologram,	

MARVEL

Web of Spider-Man #93
© *Marvel Entertainment Group*

120 Web of Life,pt.1 . . . . 2.50
121 Web of Life,pt.3 . . . . 2.50
122 Smoke and Mirrors,pt.1 . . . . 2.50
123 The Price of Truth,pt.2 . . . . 1.50
124 The Mark of Kaine,pt.1 . . . . 1.50
125 R:Gwen Stacy 2.95
125a 3-D Holodisk cover 4.25
126 The Trial of Peter Parker,pt.1 1.50
127 Maximum Clonage,pt.2 . . . . 1.50
128 TDF,Exiled,pt.1 . . . . 1.50
129 Timebomb,pt.2 . . . . 1.50
Ann.#1 V:Future Max 6.00
Ann.#2 AAd,MMi,A:Warlock 8.00
Ann.#3 AS,DP,JRu,JM,BL 4.50
Ann.#4 AS,TM,RLm,Evolutionary
   Wars,A:Man Thing,V:Slug . . . 5.00
Ann.#5 AS,SD,JS,Atlantis
   Attacks,A:Fantastic Four . . . 3.50
Ann.#6 SD,JBr,SB,A:Punisher . . 4.50
Ann.#7 Vibranium Vendetta #3 . . 2.50
Ann.#8 Hero Killers#3,A:New
   Warriors,BU:Venom,Black Cat . 3.00
Ann.#9 CMa,I:Cadre,w/card 3.25
Ann.#10 V:Shriek 3.75
Super Size Spec.#1 Planet of
   the Symbiotes,pt.5 . . . . 3.95

Weird Wonder Tales #20
© *Marvel Entertainment Group*

WEIRD WONDERTALES
Dec., 1973
1 B:Reprints 5.00
2 I Was Kidnapped by a Flying
   Saucer 2.50
3 The Thing in the Bog 2.50
4 It Lurks Behind the Wall 2.50
5 . . . . 2.50
6 The Man Who Owned a Ghost 2.50
7 The Apes That Walked
   like Men 2.50
8 Reap A Deadly Harvest 2.50
9 The Murder Mirror 2.50
10 Mister Morgans Monster 2.50
11 Slaughter in Shrangri-La 2.50
12 The Stars Scream Murder . . . 2.50
13 The Totem Strikes 2.50
14 Witching Circle 2.50
15 . . . . 2.50
16 The Shark 2.50

polybagged,V:Mysterio . . . 6.00
90a Gold 2nd printing 3.25
91 AS,V:Whisper And Pulse . . . 2.00
92 AS,V:Foreigner 2.00
93 AS,BMc,V:Hobgoblin,A:Moon
   Knight,Foreigner 2.00
94 AS,V:Hobgoblin,A:MoonKnight 2.00
95 AS,Spirits of Venom#1,A:Venom,
   J.Blaze,GR,V:Hag & Troll . . . 4.00
96 AS,Spirits of Venom#3, A:G.R,
   J.Blaze,Venom,Hobgoblin . . . 3.00
97 AS,I:Dr.Trench,V:Bloodrose . . 1.75
98 AS,V:Bloodrose,Foreigner . . . 1.75
99 I:Night Watch,V:New Enforcer . 1.75
100 AS,JRu,V:Enforcers,Bloodrose,
   Kingpin(Alfredo),I:Spider Armor,
   O:Night Watch,Holografx(c) . . 4.00
101 AS,Total Carnage,V:Carnage,
   Shriek,A:Cloak and Dagger,
   Venom 1.75
102 Total Carnage#6,V:Carnage,
   A:Venom,Morbius 1.75
103 AS,Maximum Carnage#10,
   V:Carnage 1.50
104 AS,Infinity Crusade 1.50
105 AS,Infinity Crusade 1.50
106 AS,Infinity Crusade 1.50
107 AS,A:Sandman,Quicksand . . 1.50
108 B:TKa(s),AS,I:Sandstorm,
   BU:Cardiac 1.50
109 AS,V:Shocker,A:Night Thrasher,
   BU:D:Calypso 1.50
110 AS,I:Warrant,A:Lizard 1.50
111 AS,V:Warrant,Lizard 1.50
112 AS,Pursuit#3,V:Chameleon,
   w/card 1.75
113 AS,A:Gambit,Black Cat,w/cel . 3.50
113a Newsstand Ed. 1.75
114 AS 1.75
115 AS,V:Facade 1.75
116 AS,V:Facade 1.75
117 Foil(c), flip book with
   Power & Responsibility #1 . . 5.50
117a Newsstand ed. 2.50
118 Spider-clone, V:Venom 3.00
119 Clone,V:Venom 2.25
119a bagged with Milestone rep.
   Amazing Sp-Man #150,checklist 6.50

17 Creature From Krogarr 2.50
18 Krang 2.50
19 A:Dr Druid 2.50
20 The Madness 2.50
21 A:Dr Druid 2.50
22 The World Below,May, 1975 . . 2.50

WEREWOLF BY NIGHT
Sept., 1972
1 MP(cont from Marvel Spotlight)
   FullMoonRise..WerewolfKill . . 50.00
2 MP,Like a Wild Beast at Bay . 20.00
3 MP,Mystery of the Mad Monk . 13.00
4 MP,The Danger Game 13.00
5 MP,A Life for a Death 13.00
6 MP,Carnival of Fear 10.00
7 MP,JM,Ritual of Blood 8.00
8 MP,Krogg,Lurker from Beyond . 8.00
9 TS,V:Tatterdemalion 8.00
10 TS,bondage cover 8.00
11 GK,TS,Full Moon..Fear Moon . 6.00
12 GK,Cry Monster 6.00
13 MP,ManMonsterCalledTaboo . 5.00
14 MP,Lo,the Monster Strikes . . . 5.00
15 MP,(new)O:Werewolf,
   V:Dracula 6.00
16 MP,TS,A:Hunchback of Notre
   Dame 5.00
17 Behold the Behemoth 5.00
18 War of the Werewolves 5.00
19 V:Dracula 7.00
20 The Monster Breaks Free . . . 5.00
21 GK(c),To Cure a Werewolf . . . 4.00
22 GK(c),Face of a Friend 4.00
23 Silver Bullet for a Werewolf . . 4.00
24 GK(c),V:The Brute 4.00
25 GK(c),Eclipse of Evil 4.00
26 GK(c),A Crusade of Murder . . 4.00
27 GK(c),Scourge o/t Soul-Beast . 4.00
28 GK(c),V:Dr.Glitternight 4.00
29 GK(c),V:Dr.Glitternight 4.00
30 GK(c),Red Slash across
   Midnight 4.00
31 Death in White 4.00
32 I&O:Moon Knight 65.00
33 Were-Beast..Moon Knight
   A:Moon Knight(2nd App) 30.00
34 GK(c),TS,House of Evil..House
   of Death 4.00
35 TS,JS,BWi,Jack Russell vs.
   Werewolf 4.00
36 Images of Death 4.00
37 BWr(c),BW,A:Moon Knight,
   Hangman,Dr.Glitternight 7.00
38 . . . . 3.50
39 V:Brother Voodoo 3.50
40 A:Brother Voodoo,V:Dr.
   Glitternight 3.50
41 V:Fire Eyes 3.50
42 A:IronMan,Birth of a Monster . 3.50
43 Tri-Animal Lives,A:Iron Man . . 3.50
G-Size#2,SD,A:Frankenstein
   Monster (reprint) 3.00
G-Size#3 GK(c),Transylvania . . 3.50
G-Size#4 GK(c),A:Morbius 10.00
G-Size#5 GK(c),Peril of
   Paingloss 3.00

WEST COAST AVENGERS
[Limited Series]
Sept., 1984
1 BH,A:Shroud,J:Hawkeye,IronMan,
   WonderMan,Mockingbird,Tigra 4.00
2 BH,V:Blank 3.00

All comics prices listed are for *Near Mint* condition.

West Coast Avengers #1
© Marvel Entertainment Group

3 BH,V:Graviton 2.00
4 BH,V:Graviton 2.00
[Regular Series]
1 AM,JSt,V:Lethal Legion 4.00
2 AM,JSt,V:Lethal Legion 3.00
3 AM,JSt,V:Kraven 3.00
4 AM,JSt,A:Firebird,Thing,I:Master
   Pandemonium 3.00
5 AM,JSt,A:Werewolf,Thing 3.00
6 AM,KB,A:Thing 3.00
7 AM,JSt,V:Ultron 3.00
8 AM,JSt,V:Rangers,A:Thing . . . 3.00
9 AM,JSt,V:Master Pandemonium 3.00
10 AM,JSt,V:Headlok,Griffen 3.00
11 AM,JSt,A:Nick Fury 2.50
12 AM,JSt,V:Graviton 2.50
13 AM,JSt,V:Graviton 2.50
14 AM,JSt,V:Pandemonium 2.50
15 AM,JSt,A:Hellcat 2.50
16 AM,JSt,V:Tiger Shark,
   Whirlwind 2.50
17 AM,JSt,V:Dominus' Minions . . 2.50
18 AM,JSt,V:The Wild West 2.50
19 AM,JSt,A:Two Gun Kid 2.50
20 AM,JSt,A:Rawhide Kid 2.50
21 AM,JSt,A:Dr.Pym,Moon Knight 2.50
22 AM,JSt,A:Fant.Four,Dr.Strange,
   Night Rider 2.00
23 AM,RT,A:Phantom Rider 2.00
24 AM,V:Dominus 2.00
25 AM,V:Abomination 2.00
26 AM,V:Zodiac 2.00
27 AM,V:Zodiac 1.75
28 AM,V:Zodiac 1.75
29 AM,V:Taurus,A:Shroud 1.75
30 AM,C:Composite Avenger 1.75
31 AM,V:Arkon 1.75
32 AM,TD,V:Yetrigar,J:Wasp . . . 1.75
33 AM,O:Ant-Man,Wasp;
   V:Madam X,El Toro 1.75
34 AM,V:Quicksilver,J:Vision &
   Scarlet Witch 1.75
35 AM,V:Dr.Doom,Quicksilver . . . 1.75
36 AM,V:The Voice 1.75
37 V:The Voice,A:Mantis 1.75
38 AM,TMo,V:Defiler 1.50
39 AM,V:Swordsman 1.50
40 AM,MGu,V:NightShift,

A:Shroud 1.50
41 TMo,I:New Phantom Rider,
   L:Moon Knight 1.50
42 JBy,Visionquest#1,V:Ultron . . . 2.50
43 JBy,Visionquest#2, ... 2.25
44 JBy,Visionquest#3,J:USAgent . 2.00
45 JBy,Visionquest#4,
   I:New Vision 2.25
46 JBy,I:Great Lakes Avengers . . 2.00
Ann. #1 MBr,GI,V:Zodiac 2.25
Ann. #2 AM,A:SilverSurfer,V:Death,
   Collector,R:Grandmaster 2.00
Ann. #3 AM,RLm,TD,Evolutionary
   Wars,R:Giant Man 3.50
Becomes:
AVENGERS WEST COAST

WESTERN GUNFIGHTERS
August, 1970
[2nd series]
1 JK,JB,DAy,B:Ghost Rider
   A:Fort Rango,The Renegades
   Gunhawk 6.00
2 HT(c),DAy,JMn,O:Nightwind,
   V:Tarantula 3.50
3 DAy,V:Hurricane(reprint) 3.50
4 HT(c),DAy,TS,B:Gunhawk,
   Apache Kid,A;Renegades 3.50
5 DAy,FrG,A:Renegades 3.50
6 HT(c),DAy,SSh,Death of
   Ghost Rider 4.00
7 HT(c),DAy,SSh,O:Ghost Rider
   retold,E:Ghost Rider,Gunhawk 5.00
8 DAy,SSh,B:Black Rider,Outlaw
   Kid(rep) 3.00
9 DW,Revenge rides the Range . 3.00
10 JK,JMn,O:Black Rider,B:Matt
   Slade,E:Outlaw Kid 3.00
11 JK,Duel at Dawn 3.00
12 JMn,O:Matt Slade 3.00
13 Save the Gold Coast Expires . 3.00
14 JSo(c),Outlaw Town 3.00
15 E:Matt Slade,Showdown in
   Outlaw Canyon 3.00
16 B:Kid Colt,Shoot-out in Silver
   City 3.00
17 thru 20 . . . . @3.00
21 thru 24 . . . . @2.50
25 . . . . 2.50
26 F:Kid Colt,Gun-Slinger,Apache
   Kid 2.50
27 thru 32 . . . . @2.50
33 Nov., 1975 . . . . 2.50

WESTERN KID
Dec., 1954
[1st Series]
1 JR,B:Western Kid,O:Western Kid
   (Tex Dawson) 100.00
2 JMn,JR,Western Adventure . . 50.00
3 JMn(c),JR,Gunfight(c) 40.00
4 JMn(c),JR,The Badlands 40.00
5 JR 40.00
6 JR 40.00
7 JR 40.00
8 JR 40.00
9 JR,AW 50.00
10 JR,AW,Man in the Middle . . . 50.00
11 thru 16 . . . . @30.00
17 August, 1957 . . . . 30.00
[2nd Series] Dec., 1971–Aug. 1972
1 Reprints 4.00
2 . . . . 3.00
3 . . . . 3.00

4 . . . . 3.00
5 . . . . 3.00

WESTERN OUTLAWS
Atlas Feb., 1954—Aug., 1957
1 JMn(c),RH,BP,The Greenville
   Gallows,Hanging(c) 125.00
2 . . . . 65.00
3 thru 10 . . . . @50.00
11 AW 50.00
12 . . . . 45.00
13 MB 50.00
14 AW 55.00
15 AT,GT 50.00
16 BP 40.00
17 . . . . 45.00
18 . . . . 40.00
19 . . . . 50.00
20 and 21 . . . . @45.00

WESTERN OUTLAWS
& SHERIFFS
See: BEST WESTERN

WESTERN TALES
OF BLACK RIDER
See: ALL WINNERS COMICS

WESTERN TEAM-UP
Nov., 1973
1 Rawhide Kid/Dakota Kid 2.00

WESTERN THRILLERS
Nov., 1954
1 JMn,Western tales 75.00
2 . . . . 40.00
3 . . . . 40.00
4 . . . . 40.00
Becomes:
COWBOY ACTION
5 JMn(c),The Prairie Kid 45.00
6 . . . . 30.00
7 . . . . 30.00
9 . . . . 30.00
10 . . . . 30.00
11 MN,AW,Ther Manhunter March,
   1956 . . . . 45.00
Becomes:
QUICK-TRIGGER
WESTERN
12 Bill Larson Strikes 55.00
13 The Man From Cheyenne . . . 60.00
14 BEv,RH(c) 50.00
15 AT 40.00
16 JK 35.00
17 GT 35.00
18 GM 35.00
19 JSe 30.00

WESTERN WINNERS
See: ALL WINNERS COMICS

WHAT IF?
[1st Regular Series]
Feb., 1977
1 Spider-Man joined Fant.Four . 18.00
2 GK(c),Hulk had Banner brain . . 9.00
3 GK,KJ,F:Avengers 6.00
4 GK(c),F:Invaders 6.00
5 F:Captain America 6.00

MARVEL

6 F:Fantastic Four 6 00	
7 GK(c),F:Spider-Man 6.00	
8 GK(c),F:Daredevil 5.50	
9 JK(c),F:Avengers of the '50s . . 6.00	
10 JB,F:Thor 5.00	
11 JK,F:FantasticFour 5.00	
12 F:Hulk 5.00	
13 JB,Conan Alive Today 6.00	
14 F:Sgt. Fury 5.00	
15 CI,F:Nova 5.00	
16 F:Master of Kung Fu 5.00	
17 CI,F:Ghost Rider 5.00	
18 TS,F:Dr.Strange 4.00	
19 PB,F:Spider-Man 5.00	
20 F:Avengers 4.00	
21 GC,F:Sub-Mariner 4.00	
22 F:Dr.Doom 4.00	
23 JB,F:Hulk 4.00	
24 GK,RB,Gwen Stacy had lived . 5.00	
25 F:Thor,Avengers,O:Mentor . . . 4.00	
26 JBy(c),F:Captain America 4.00	
27 FM(c),Phoenix hadn't died . . . 7.00	
28 FM,F:Daredevil,Ghost Rider. . . 6.00	
29 MG(c),F:Avengers 4.00	

What If? #13
© Marvel Entertainment Group

30 RB,F:Spider-Man 10.00	
31 Wolverine killed the Hulk . . . 15.00	
32 Avengers lost to Korvac 3.50	
33 BL,Dazzler herald of Galactus . 3.50	
34 FH,FM,JBy,BSz:Humor issue . . 3.50	
35 FM,Elektra had lived 6.00	
36 JBy,Fant.Four had no powers . 3.00	
37 F:Thing,Beast,Silver Surfer . . 3.50	
38 F:Daredevil,Captain America . . 3.00	
39 Thor had fought Conan 3.00	
40 F:Dr.Strange 3.00	
41 F:Sub-Mariner 3.50	
42 F:Fantastic Four 3.00	
43 F:Conan 3.00	
44 F:Captain America 3.00	
45 F:Hulk,Berserk 3.50	
46 Uncle Ben had lived 5.00	
47 F:Thor,Loki 3.00	
Spec.#1 F:Iron Man,Avengers . . . 4.00	
Best of What IF? rep.#1,#24,	
#27,#28 . . . . 12.95	
[2nd Regular Series]	
1 RWi,MG,The Avengers had lost	
the Evolutionary War 5.00	

2 GCa,Daredevil Killed Kingpin,	
A:Hobgoblin, The Rose 4.00	
3 Capt.America Hadn't Given Up	
Costume,A:Avengers 3.50	
4 MBa,Spider-Man kept Black	
Costume,A:Avengers,Hulk . . . 4.50	
5 Vision Destroyed Avengers,	
A:Wonder Man 3.50	
6 RLm,X-Men Lost Inferno,	
A:Dr.Strange 6.00	
7 RLd,Wolverine Joined Shield,	
A:Nick Fury,Black Widow . . . 7.00	
8 Iron Man Lost The Armor Wars,	
A:Ant Man 3.50	
9 RB,New X-Men Died 6.00	
10 MZ(c),BMc,Punisher's Family	
Didn't Die,A:Kingpin 3.00	
11 TM(c),JV,SM,Fant.Four had the	
Same Powers,A:Nick Fury . . . 3.50	
12 JV,X-Men Stayed in Asgard,	
A:Thor,Hela 3.00	
13 JLe(c),Prof.X Became	
Juggernaut,A:X-Men 3.50	
14 RLm(c),Capt.Marvel didn't die	
A:Silver Surfer 3.00	
15 GCa,Fant.Four Lost Trial of	
Galactus,A:Gladiator 3.00	
16 Wolverine Battled Conan,	
A:X-Men,Red Sonja 5.00	
17 Kraven Killed Spider-Man,	
A:Daredevil,Captain America . . 3.00	
18 LMc,Fant.Four fought Dr.Doom	
before they gained powers . . . 2.50	
19 RW,Vision took over Earth,	
A:Avengers,Dr.Doom 2.50	
20 Spider-Man didn't marry Mary	
Jane,A:Venom,Kraven 3.00	
21 Spider-Man married Black Cat,	
A:Vulture,Silver Sable 2.50	
22 RLm,Silver Surfer didn't escape	
Earth,A:F.F,Mephisto,Thanos . 4.00	
23 New X-Men never existed,	
A:Eric the Red,Lilandra 2.50	
24 Wolverine Became Lord of	
Vampires,A:Punisher 3.00	
25 Marvel Heroes lost Atlantis	
Attacks,double size 3.25	
26 LMc,Punisher Killed Daredevil,	
A:Spider-Man 2.50	
27 Submariner Joined Fantastic	
Four,A:Dr. Doom 2.00	
28 RW,Capt.America led Army of	
Super-Soldiers,A:Submariner . 2.00	
29 RW,Capt.America formed the	
Avengers 2.00	
30 Inv.Woman's 2nd Child had	
lived,A:Fantastic Four 2.00	
31 Spider-Man/Captain Universe	
Powers 2.00	
32 Phoenix Rose Again,pt.1 . . . . 2.00	
33 Phoenix Rose Again,pt.2 . . . . 2.00	
34 Humor Issue 1.75	
35 B:Time Quake,F.F. vs.Dr.Doom	
& Annihilus 1.75	
36 Cosmic Avengers,V:Guardians	
of the Galaxy 1.75	
37 X-Vampires,V:Dormammu 1.75	
38 Thor was prisoner of Set 1.75	
39 E:Time Quake,Watcher saved the	
Universe 1.75	
40 Storm remained A thief? 1.75	
41 JV,Avengers fought Galactus . 2.00	
42 KWe,Spidey kept extra arms . . 1.75	
43 Wolverine married Mariko 1.75	
44 Punisher possessedby Venom . 1.75	

45 Barbara Ketch became G.R. . . 1.75	
46 Cable Killed Prof.X,Cyclops &	
Jean Grey 1.75	
47 Magneto took over USA 1.75	
48 Daredevil Saved Nuke 1.50	
49 Silver Surfer had Inf.Gauntlet? 1.50	
50 Hulk killed Wolverine 4.00	
51 PCu,Punisher is Capt.America 1.50	
52 BHi,Wolverine led Alpha Flight 2.00	
53 F:Iron Man,Hulk 1.50	
54 F:Death's Head 1.50	
55 LKa(s),Avengers lose G.Storm 1.50	
56 Avengers lose G.Storm#2 . . . 1.50	
57 Punisher a member of SHIELD 1.50	
58 Punisher kills SpM 1.50	
59 Wolverine lead Alpha Flight . . 2.00	
60 RoR,Scott & Jean's Wedding . 1.50	
61 Spider-Man's Parents 1.95	
62 Woverine vs Weapon X 2.25	
63 F:War Machine,Iron Man 1.95	
64 Iron Man sold out 2.25	
65 Archangel fell from Grace 1.50	
66 Rogue and Thor 1.50	
67 Cap.America returns 1.50	
68 Captain America story 1.50	
69 Stryfe Killed X-Men 1.50	
70 Silver Surfer 1.50	
71 The Hulk 1.50	
72 Parker Killed Burglar 1.50	
73 Daredevil,Kingpin 1.50	
74 Sinister Formed X-Men 1.50	
75 Gen-X's Blink had lived 1.50	
76 Flash Thompson Spider-Man . 1.50	
77 Legion had killed Magneto . . . 1.50	
78 FF had stayed together 1.50	
79 Storm had Phoenix's Power . . 1.50	
80 KGa,Hulk was Cured 1.50	
81 Age of Apocalypse didn't end . 1.50	
82 WML,J.JonahJameson	
adopted Spider-Man 1.50	
83 . . . . 1.50	
84 . . . . 1.50	
85 Magneto Ruled all mutants . . . 1.50	
86 . . . . 1.50	
87 . . . . 1.50	
88 . . . . 1.50	
89 . . . . 1.50	
90 . . . . 1.50	
91 F:Hulk, nice guy, Banner violent 1.50	
92 F:Cannonball,Husk 1.50	
93 F:Wolverine 1.50	
94 JGz,F:Juggernaut 1.50	
95 IV,F:Ghost Rider 1.50	
96 CWo,F:Quicksilver, ... 1.95	
97 F:Black Knight 1.95	
98 F:Nightcrawler & Rogue 1.95	
99 F:Black Cat 1.95	
100 IV,KJ,F:Gambit & Rogue, 48pg 2.99	
Minus 1 Spec., AOI, flashback,	
F:Bishop 1.95	
TPB Best of What If? 12.95	

WHAT THE -?!
[Parodies]
August, 1988

1 . . . . 5.00	
2 JBy,JOy,AW, ... 4.00	
3 TM, ... 5.00	
4 . . . . 3.00	
5 EL,JLe,WPo,Wolverine 5.00	
6 Wolverine,Punisher 3.00	
7 . . . . 2.50	
8 DK 2.50	
9 . . . . 1.75	
10 JBy,X-Men,Dr.Doom, Cap.	

MARVEL

MARVEL

What The-?! #6
© *Marvel Entertainment Group*

America	1.75
11 DK,RLd(part)	2.00
12 Conan, F.F.,Wolverine.	1.50
13 Silver Burper,F.F.,Wolverine. .	1.50
14 Spittle-Man	1.50
15 Capt.Ultra,Wolverina	1.50
16 Ant Man,Watcher	1.25
17 Wulverean/Pulverizer,Hoagg/	
Spider-Ham,SleepGawker,F.F.	1.25
18	1.25
19	1.25
20 Infinity Wart Crossover	1.25
21 Weapon XX,Toast Rider	1.25
22 F:Echs Farce	1.25
23	1.25
24 Halloween issue	1.25
25	1.25
26 Spider-Ham 2099	1.25
Summer Spec.	2.50
Fall Spec.	2.50

WHERE CREATURES ROAM
July, 1970—Sept., 1971

1 JK,SD,DAy,B:Reprints	
The Brute That Walks	4.50
2 JK,SD,Midnight/Monster	2.50
3 JK,SD,DAy,Thorg	2.50
4 JK,SD,Vandoom	2.50
5 JK,SD,Gorgilla	2.50
6 JK,SD,Zog	2.50
7 SD	2.50
8 The Mummy's Secret,E:Reprints	2.50

WHERE MONSTERS DWELL
Jan., 1970

1 B:Reprints,Cyclops	5.00
2 Sporr	3.50
3 Grottu	3.50
4	3.50
5 Taboo	3.50
6 Groot	3.50
7 Rommbu	3.50

8 The Four-Armed Men	3.50
9 Bumbu	3.50
10 Monster That Walks	
Like A Man	3.50
11 Gruto	3.00
12 Orogo	3.00
13 The Thing That Crawl	3.00
14 The Green Thing	3.00
15 Kraa- The Inhuman	3.00
16 Beware the Son Of Goom . . .	3.00
17 The Hidden Vampires	3.00
18 The Mask of Morghum	3.00
19 The Insect Man	3.00
20 Klagg	3.00
21 Fin Fang Foom	3.00
22 Elektro	3.00
23 The Monster Waits For Me . . .	3.00
24 The Things on Easter Island . .	3.00
25 The Ruler of the Earth	3.00
26	3.00
27	3.00
28 Droom,The Living Lizard	3.00
29 thru 37 Reprints	@3.00
38 Reprints,Oct., 1975	3.00

WHIP WILSON
See: BLAZE CARSON

WILD
Atlas Feb., 1954

1 BEv,JMn,Charlie Chan	
Parody	165.00
2 BEv,RH,JMn,Witches(c) . . .	100.00
3 CBu(c),BEv,RH,JMn.	75.00
4 GC,Didja Ever See a Cannon	
Brawl	75.00
5 RH,JMn,August, 1954	75.00

WILD CARDS
Epic Sept., 1990

1 JG	5.50
2 JG,V:Jokers	4.50
3 A:Turtle	4.50

WILD THING

1 A:Virtual Reality Venom and	
Carnage	3.00
2 A:VR Venom and Carnage . . .	2.00
3 A:Shield	2.00
4	2.00
5 Virtual Reality Gangs	2.00
6 Virtual Reality Villians	2.00
7 V:Trask	2.00
8	1.75
9	1.75
10	1.75
11	1.75
12	1.75
13	1.75

WILD WEST
Spring, 1948

1 SSh(c),B:Two Gun Kids,Tex	
Taylor,Arizona Annie	175.00
2 SSh(c),CCb, Captain Tootsie	135.00

Becomes:

WILD WESTERN

3 SSh(c),B:Tex Morgan,Two Gun	
Kid,Tex Taylor,Arizona Annie	175.00
4 Rh,SSh,CCB,Capt. Tootsie.	
A:Kid Colt,E:Arizona Annie .	125.00
5 RH,CCB,Captain Tootsie	
A;Black Rider,Blaze Carson	125.00

6 A:Blaze Carson,Kid Colt	75.00
7	75.00
8 RH	75.00
9 Ph(c),B:Black Rider	100.00
10 Ph(c)	125.00
11	75.00
12	60.00
13	60.00
14	60.00
15	65.00
16 thru 20	@55.00
21 thru 29	@50.00
30 JKa	55.00
31 thru 40	@35.00
41 thru 47	@25.00
48	35.00
49 thru 53	@25.00
54 AW	45.00
55 AW	45.00
56	25.00
57 Sept., 1957	25.00

William Shatner's Tek World #12
© *Marvel Entertainment Group*

WILLIAM SHATNER'S TEK WORLD

1 LS,Novel adapt.	2.25
2 LS,Novel adapt.cont.	2.00
3 LS,Novel adapt.cont.	2.00
4 LS,Novel adapt.cont.	2.00
5 LS,Novel adapt.concludes	2.00
6 LS,V:TekLords	2.00
7 E:The Angel	2.00
8	2.00
9	2.00
10	2.00
11 thru 17	2.00
18	2.00
19 Sims of the Father#1	1.75
20 Sims of the Father#2	1.75
21 Who aren't in Heaven	1.75
22 Father and Guns	2.00
23 We'll be Right Back	2.00
24	1.75

WILLIE COMICS
See: IDEAL COMICS

X-Factor #18
© *Marvel Entertainment Group*

C:Apocalypse 6.00
6 JG,BMc,I:Apocalypse 18.00
7 JG,JRu,V:Morlocks,I:Skids . . 5.00
8 MS,JRu,V:Freedom Force 5.00
9 JRu(i),V:Freedom Force
(Mutant Massacre) 6.00
10 WS,BWi,V:Marauders(Mut.Mass),
A:Sabretooth 7.00
11 WS,BWi,A:Thor(Mutant Mass) . 6.00
12 MS,BWi,V:Vanisher 5.00
13 WS,DGr,V:Mastermold 5.00
14 WS,BWi,V:Mastermold 5.00
15 WS,BWi,D:Angel 6.00
16 DM,JRu,V:Masque 5.00
17 WS,BWi,I:Rictor 6.00
18 WS,BWi,V:Apocalypse 5.00
19 WS,BWi,V:Horsemen of
Apocalypse 4.00
20 JBr,A:X-Terminators 3.00
21 WS,BWi,V:The Right 3.00
22 SB,BWi,V:The Right 3.00
23 WS,BWi,C:Archangel 11.00
24 WS,BWi,Fall of Mutants,
I:Archangel 16.00
25 WS,BWi,Fall of Mutants 4.00
26 WS,BWi,Fall of Mutants,
N:X-Factor 4.00
27 WS,BWi,Christmas Issue 3.50
28 WS,BWi,V:Ship 3.00
29 WS,BWi,V:Infectia 3.00
30 WS,BWi,V:Infectia,Free.Force . 3.00
31 WS,BWi,V:Infectia,Free.Force . 3.00
32 SLi,A:Avengers 3.00
33 WS,BWi,V:Tower & Frenzy,
R:Furry Beast 3.00
34 WS,BWi,I:Nanny,
Orphan Maker 3.00
35 JRu(i),WS(c),V:Nanny,
Orphan Maker 3.00
36 WS,BWi,Inferno,V:Nastirh . . . 3.50
37 WS,BWi,Inferno,V:Gob.Queen . 3.50
38 WS,AM,Inferno,A:X-Men,D:
MadelynePryor(GoblinQueen) . 3.50
39 WS,AM,Inferno,A:X-Men,
V:Mr.Sinister 3.50
40 RLd,AM,O:Nanny,Orphan Maker
1st Liefeld Marvel work 8.00
41 AAd,AM,I:Alchemy 3.50

42 AAd,AM,A:Alchemy 3.50
43 PS,AM,V:Celestials 3.00
44 PS,AM,V:Rejects 2.50
45 PS,AM,V:Rask 2.50
46 PS,AM,V:Rejects 2.50
47 KD,AM,V:Father 2.50
48 thru 49 PS,AM,V:Rejects 2.50
50 RLd&TM(c),RB,AM,A:Prof.X
(double sized),BU:Apocalypse . 4.00
51 AM,V:Sabretooth,Caliban . . . 5.00
52 RLd(c),AM,V:Sabretooth,
Caliban 4.00
53 AM,V:Sabretooth,Caliban 4.00
54 MS,AM,A:Colossus,I:Crimson . 2.00
55 MMi(c),CDo,AM,V:Mesmero . . 2.00
56 AM,V:Crimson 2.00
57 NKu,V:Crimson 2.00
58 JBg,AM,V:Crimson 2.00
59 AM,V:Press Gang 2.00
60 JBg,AM,X-Tinction Agenda#3 . 4.00
60a 2nd printing(gold) 3.00
61 JBg,AM,X-Tinction Agenda#6 . 4.00
62 JBg,AM,JLe(c),E:X-Agenda . . 5.00
63 WPo,I:Cyberpunks 5.00
64 WPo,ATb,V:Cyberpunks 5.00
65 WPo,ATb,V:Apocalypse 4.00
66 WPo,ATb,I:Askani,
V:Apocalypse 4.00
67 WPo,ATb,V:Apocalypse,I:Shinobi
Shaw,D:Sebastian Shaw 3.00
68 WPo,ATb,JLe(c),V:Apocalypse,
L:Nathan,(taken into future) . . 5.00
69 WPo,V:Shadow King 3.00
70 MMi(c),JRu,Last old team 3.00
71 LSn,AM,New Team 4.00
71a 2nd printing 1.50
72 LSn,AM,Who shot Madrox
revealed 3.00
73 LSn,AM,Mob Chaos in D.C. . . 3.00
74 LSn,AM,I:Slab 2.50
75 LSn,AM,I:Nasty Boys(doub.sz) . 3.25
76 LSn,AM,A:Hulk,Pantheon 2.50
77 LSn,AM,V:Mutant Lib. Front . . 2.25
78 LSn,AM,V:Mutant Lib. Front . . 2.25
79 LSn,AM,V:Helle's Belles 2.25
80 LSn,AM,V:Helle's Belles,
C:Cyber 2.25
81 LSn,AM,V:Helle's Belles,Cyber . 2.25
82 JQ(c),LSn,V:Brotherhood of Evil
Mutants,I:X-iles 2.25
83 MPa,A:X-Force,X-iles 2.25
84 JaL,X-Cutioners Song #2,
V:X-Force,A:X-Men 4.00
85 JaL,X-Cutioners Song #6,
Wolv.& Bishop,V:Cable 4.00
86 JaL,AM,X-Cutioner's Song#10,
A:X-Men,X-Force,V:Stryfe 4.00
87 JQ,X-Cutioners Song
Aftermath 3.00
88 JQ,AM,V:2nd Genegineer,
I:Random 4.00
89 JQ,V:Mutates,Genosha 2.00
90 JQ,AM,Genosha vs. Aznia . . . 2.00
91 AM,V:Armageddon 1.75
92 JQ,AM,V:Fabian Cortez,
Acolytes,hologram(c) 5.00
93 Magneto Protocols 3.00
94 PR,J:Forge 3.00
95 B:JMD(s),AM,Polaris
Vs. Random 1.75
96 A:Random 1.75
97 JD,I:Haven,A:Random 1.75
98 GLz,A:Haven,A:Random 1.50
99 JD,A:Haven,Wolfsbane returns
to human 1.50

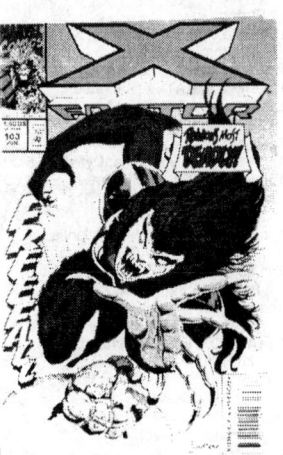

X-Factor #103
© *Marvel Entertainment Group*

100 JD,Red Foil(c),V:Haven,
D:Madrox 3.25
100a Newstand Ed. 2.00
101 JD,AM,Aftermath 1.50
102 JD,AM,V:Crimson Commando,
Avalanche 1.50
103 JD,AM,A:Malice 1.75
104 JD,AM,V:Malice,
C:Mr. Sinister 1.75
105 JD,AM,V:Malice 1.75
106 Phalanx Covenant,Life Signs
Holografx(c) 3.25
106a newsstand ed 2.00
107 A:Strong Guy 1.75
108 A:Mystique, deluxe ed. 2.50
108a newsstand ed. 1.50
109 A:Mystique,V:Legion, deluxe . 1.95
109a newsstand ed. 1.50
110 Invasion 1.95
110a deluxe ed. 1.95
111 Invasion 1.50
111a deluxe ed. 1.95
112 AM,JFM,SEp,F:Guido,Havok . 1.95
113 A:Mystique 1.95
114 AM,Wild Child & Mystique . . . 1.95
115 F:Wild Child,Havok 1.95
116 F:Wild Child 1.95
117 HMe,AM,F:Cyclops 1.95
118 HMe,AM,A:Random,Shard . . . 1.95
119 HMe,AM,F:Sabretooth 1.95
120 . . . . 1.95
121 . . . . 1.95
122 HMe,SEp,AM,J:Sabretooth . . 1.95
123 . . . . 1.95
124 A:Onslaught 2.50
125 Onslaught saga, double size . 3.00
126 Beast vs. Dark Beast 1.95
127 Mystique 1.95
128 HMe,JMs,AM,Hound Program 1.95
129 HMe,JMs,AM,Graydon Creed's
campaign 1.95
130 HMe,JMs,AM,Assassination of
Graydon Creed 1.95
131 HMe,JMs,ATi,Havok strikes
back 1.95
132 HMe,JMs,ATi,Break away from
government 1.95
133 HMe,JMs,ATi,A:Multiple Man &

MARVEL

MARVEL

Strong Guy 1.95
134 HMe,JMs,Ati,"Operation X-Factor
   Underground," cont. 1.95
135 HMe,JMs,Strong Guy awakes 1.95
136 HMe,JMs,ATi, A:Sabretooth . 1.95
137 HMe,JMs,ATi, Final fate of
   Shard and Polaris 1.95
Spec #1 JG,Prisoner of Love 5.00
Ann.#1 BL,BBr,V:CrimsonDynamo 5.00
Ann.#2 TGr,JRu,A:Inhumans 4.00
Ann.#3 WS(c),AM,JRu,PC,TD,
   Evolutionary War 3.50
Ann.#4 JBy,WS,JRu,MBa,Atlantis
   Attacks,BU:Doom & Magneto . 3.50
Ann.#6 Flesh Tears Saga,pt.4,
   A:X-Force, New Warriors 4.00
Ann #7 JQ,JRu,Shattershot,pt.3 . . 4.00
Ann.#8 I:Charon,w/card 3.25
Ann.#9 JMD(s),MtB,V:Prof.Power,
   A:Prof.X,O:Haven 3.25
Minus 1 Spec., HMe,JMs,ATi,
   flashback,F:Havok 1.95

X-Force #1
© Marvel Entertainment Group

X-FORCE
August, 1991
1 RLd,V:Stryfe,Mutant Liberation
   Front,bagged, white on black graphics
   with X-Force Card 5.00
1a with Shattershot Card 4.00
1b with Deadpool Card 4.00
1c with Sunspot & Gideon Card . 4.00
1d with Cable Card 5.00
1e Unbagged Copy 1.75
1f 2nd Printing 1.75
2 RLd,I:New Weapon X,V:
   Deadpool 4.50
3 RLd,C:Spider-Man,
   V:Juggernaut,Black Tom 3.00
4 RLd,SpM/X-Force team-up,
   V:Juggernaut(cont.from SpM#16)
   Sideways format 3.00
5 RLd,A:Brotherhood Evil Mutants 3.00
6 RLd,V:Bro'hood Evil Mutants . . 3.00
7 RLd,V:Bro'hood Evil Mutants . . 3.00
8 MMi,O:Cable(Part) 3.00

9 RLd,D:Sauron,Masque 3.00
10 MPa,V:Mutant Liberation Front 2.00
11 MPa,Deadpool Vs Domino . . . 2.00
12 MPa,A:Weapon Prime,Gideon . 2.00
13 MPa,V:Weapon Prime 2.00
14 TSr,V:Weapon Prime,Krule . . . 2.00
15 GCa,V:Krule,Deadpool 2.00
16 GCa,X-Cutioners Song #4,
   X-Factor V:X-Force 3.00
17 GCa,X-Cutioners Song#8,
   Apocalypse V:Stryfe 3.00
18 GCa,X-Cutioners Song#12,
   Cable vs Stryfe 3.00
19 GCa,X-Cutioners Song
   Aftermath,N:X-Force 2.00
20 GCa,O:Graymalkin 2.00
21 GCa,V:War Machine,SHIELD . 2.00
22 GCa,V:Externals 2.00
23 GCa,V:Saul,Gigeon,A:Six Pack 2.00
24 GCa,A:Six Pack,A:Deadpool . . 1.50
25 GCa,A:Mageneto,Exodus,
   R:Cable 5.00
26 GCa(c),MtB,I:Reignfire 1.50
27 GCa(c),MtB,V:Reignfire,MLF,
   I:Moonstar,Locus 1.50
28 MtB,V:Reignfire,MLF 1.50
29 MtB,V:Arcade,C:X-Treme 1.50
30 TnD,V:Arcade,A:X-Treme 1.50
31 F:Siryn 1.50
32 Child's Play#1,A:New Warriors . 1.50
33 Child's Play#3,A:New Warriors,
   V:Upstarts 1.50
34 F:Rictor,Domino,Cable 3.50
35 TnD,R:Nimrod 1.50
36 TnD,V:Nimrod 1.75
37 PaP,I&D:Absalom 1.50
38 TaD,Life Signs,pt.2,
   I:Generation X, foil(c) 3.50
38a newsstand ed. 2.00
39 TaD 1.50
40 TaD, deluxe 2.00
40a newsstand ed. 1.50
41 TaD,O:feral,deluxe 2.00
41a newsstand ed. 1.50
42 Emma Frost, deluxe 2.00
42a newsstand ed. 1.50
43 Home is Where Heart 1.50
43a deluxe ed. 2.00
44 AdP,Prof.X,X-Mansion 2.00
45 AdP,Caliban vs. Sabretooth . . 2.00
46 R:The Mimic 3.25
47 A:Deadpool 2.00
48 AdP,Siryn Takes Charge 2.00
49 ADp,MBu,Holocaust is here . . 2.00
50 AdP,MPn,F:Sebastian Shaw . . 2.00
50a prismatic foil cover 4.00
51 AdP,MPn,V:Risque 2.00
52 A:Onslaught 3.00
53 . . . . 2.00
54 AdP, Can X-Force
   protect X-Ternals? 2.00
55 . . . . 2.00
56 Deadpool, A:Onslaught 3.00
57 Onslaught saga 2.50
58 Onslaught saga 2.50
59 . . . . 1.95
60 JLb,,F:Shattershot,A:Long Shot 1.95
61 JLb,R:Longshot,O:Shattershot . 1.95
62 JLb,F:Sunspot 1.95
63 JFM,AdP,F:Risque,Cannonball 1.95
64 JFM,AdP,In Latveria, searching
   for Doctor Doom's weapons . . 1.95
65 JFM,AdP,Warpath follows Risque
   to Florida 1.95
66 JFM,AdP,A:Risque,James

Proudstar 1.95
67 JFM,AdP,F:Warpath, Risque . . 1.95
68 JFM,AdP,Zero Tolerance 1.95
69 JFM,AdP,Zero Tolerance
   aftermath 1.95
Ann.#1 Shattershot,pt1 . . . . 2.75
Ann.#2 JaL,LSn,I:X-Treme,w/card 3.25
Ann.#3 . . . . 2.95
Minus 1 Spec., JFM,AdP, flashback,
   F:John Proudstar 1.95

X-FORCE & SPIDER-MAN: SABOTAGE
TPB rep.X-Force #3 & #4 and
   Spider-Man #16 . . . . 6.95

X-FORCE MEGAZINE
TPB LSi,RLd, rep. New Mutants
   #99–#100 . . . . 3.95

X-MAN
1 Cable after Xavier 7.50
2 Sinister's Plan 4.00
3 V:Domino 3.00
4 V:Sinister 3.00
5 Into this World 3.00
6 V:X-Men 2.50
7 Evil from Age of Apocalypse . . 2.25
8 Crossover Adventure 2.00
9 F:Nate's Past 2.00
10 Nate's Past 2.00
11 Young Nate seeks out X-Men . 2.00
12 F:Excalibur 2.00
13 . . . . 2.00
14 . . . . 2.00
15 JOs,X-Men/Cable war aftermath 2.00
16 Holocaust,A:Onslaught 5.00
17 Holocaust,Quicksilver,Scarlet
   Witch, A:Onslaught 4.00
18 Onslaught saga 2.50
19 Onslaught saga 2.50
20 . . . . 1.95
21 TKa,RCz,F:Nate 1.95
22 TKa,RCz,F:Threnody,A:Madelyne
   Pryor 1.95
23 TKa,RCz,F:Bishop 1.95
24 TKa,RCz,Spider-Man vs. Nate 1.95
25 TKa,RCz,Madelyne Pryor,
   double size 2.95
26 TKa,RCz,Nate limps to Muir
   Isle,A:Moira Mactaggert 1.95
27 TKa,RCz,Hellfire Club, concl. . 1.95
28 TKa,RCz,Dark Beast's offer . . 1.95
29 TKa,RCz,Back in New York, . . 1.95
30 TKa,RCz,F:Nate Grey 1.95
Minus 1 Spec., TKa,RCz,
   flashback,O:Nate Grey 1.95

X-MAN '96
1-shot 2.95

X-MEN
Sept., 1963
1 JK,O:X-Men,I:Professor X,Beast
   Cyclops,Marvel Girl,Iceman
   Angel,Magneto 5,200.00
2 JK,I:Vanisher 1,500.00
3 JK,I:Blob 600.00
4 JK,I:Quicksilver,Scarlet Witch
   Mastermind,Toad 600.00
5 JK,V:Broth. of Evil Mutants . 400.00
6 JK,V:Sub-Mariner 350.00
7 JK,V:Broth. of Evil Mutants,

X-Men #14
© Marvel Entertainment Group

Scarlet Witch,O:Iceman	55.00
46 DH,V:Juggernaut,O:Iceman	50.00
47 DH,I:Maha Yogi	50.00
48 DH,JR,V:Quasimodo	50.00
49 JSo,DH,C:Magneto,I:Polaris,	
Mesmero,O:Beast	60.00
50 JSo,V:Magneto,O:Beast	55.00
51 JSo,V:Magneto,Polaris,	
Erik the Red,O:Beast	55.00
52 DH,MSe,JSt,O:Lorna Dane	
V:Magneto,O:Beast	50.00
53 1st BWS,O:Beast	65.00
54 BWS,DH,I:Havok,O:Angel	70.00
55 BWS,DH,O:Havok,Angel	60.00
56 NA,V:LivingMonolith,O:Angel	60.00
57 NA,V:Sentinels,A:Havok	56.00
58 NA,A:Havoc,V:Sentinels	70.00
59 NA,V:Sentinels,A:Havoc	56.00
60 NA,I:Sauron	60.00
61 NA,V:Sauron	56.00
62 NA,A:Kazar,Sauron,Magneto	56.00
63 A:Ka-Zar,V:Magneto	56.00
64 DH,A:Havok,I:Sunfire	47.00
65 NA,MSe,A:Havok,Shield,	
Return of Prof.X	56.00
66 SB,MSe,V:Hulk,A:Havok	40.00
67 rep.X-Men #12,#13	25.00
68 rep.X-Men #14,#15	25.00
69 rep.X-Men #16,#19	25.00
70 rep.X-Men #17,#18	25.00
71 rep.X-Men #20	25.00
72 rep.X-Men #21,#24	25.00
73 thru 93 rep.X-Men #25-45	@25.00
94 GK(c),B:CCl(s),DC,BMc,B:2nd	
X-Men,V:Count Nefaria	425.00
95 GK(c),DC,V:Count Nefaria,	
Ani-Men,D:Thunderbird	80.00
96 DC,I:Moira McTaggert,	
Kierrok	65.00
97 DC,V:Havok,Polaris,Eric	
the Red,I:Lilandra	55.00
98 DC,V:Sentinels,Stephen Lang	55.00
99 DC,V:Sentinels,S.Lang	60.00
100 DC,V:Stephen Lang	65.00
101 DC,I:Phoenix,Black Tom,	
A:Juggernaut	65.00
102 DC,O:Storm,V:Juggernaut,	
Black Tom	30.00
103 DC,V:Juggernaut,Bl.Tom	40.00
104 DC,V:Magneto,I:Star	
Jammers,A:Lilandra	30.00
105 DC,BL,V:Firelord	30.00
106 DC,TS,V:Firelord	30.00
107 DC,DGr,I:Imperial Guard,Star	
Jammers,Gladiator,Corsair	40.00
108 JBy,TA,A:Star Jammers,	
C:Fantastic Four,Avengers.	75.00
109 JBy,TA,I:Vindicator	45.00
110 TD,DC,V:Warhawk	28.00
111 JBy,TA,V:Mesmero,A:Beast,	
Magneto	28.00
112 GP(c),JBy,TA,V:Magneto,	
A:Beast	28.00
113 JBy,TA,V:Magneto,A:Beast	28.00
114 JBy,TA,A:Beast,R:Sauron	28.00
115 JBy,TA,V:Sauron,Garokk,	
A:Kazar,I:Zaladane	26.00
116 JBy,TA,V:Sauron,Garokk,	
A:Kazar	26.00
117 JBy,TA,O:Prof.X,I:Amahl	
Farouk (Shadow King)	32.00
118 JBy,I:Moses Magnum,A:Sunfire	
C:Iron Fist,I:Mariko	26.00
119 JBy,TA,V:Moses Magnum,	
A:Sunfire	26.00

Blob	275.00
8 JK,I:Unus,1st Ice covered	
Iceman	275.00
9 JK,A:Avengers,I:Lucifer	275.00
10 JK,I:Modern Kazar	275.00
11 JK,I:Stranger	225.00
12 JK,O:Prof.X,I:Juggernaut	325.00
13 JK,JSt,V:Juggernaut	225.00
14 JK,I:Sentinels	225.00
15 JK,O:Beast,V:Sentinels	225.00
16 JK,V:Mastermold,Sentinels	225.00
17 JK,V:Magneto	125.00
18 V:Magneto	125.00
19 I:Mimic	125.00
20 V:Lucifer	125.00
21 V:Lucifer,Dominus	100.00
22 V:Maggia	100.00
23 V:Maggia	100.00
24 I:Locust(Prof.Hopper)	100.00
25 JK,I:El Tigre	100.00
26 V:El Tigre	85.00
27 C:Fant.Four,V:Puppet Master	85.00
28 I:Banshee	130.00
29 V:Super-Apaptoid	80.00
30 JK,I:The Warlock	80.00
31 JK,I:Cobalt Man	67.00
32 V:Juggernaut	67.00
33 GK,A:Dr.Strange,Juggernaut	67.00
34 V:Tyrannus,Mole Man	67.00
35 JK,A:Spider-Man,Banshee	75.00
36 V:Mekano	58.00
37 DH,V:Blob,Unus	58.00
38 DH,A:Banshee,O:Cyclops	75.00
39 DH,GT,A:Banshee,V:Mutant	
Master,O:Cyclops	58.00
40 DH,GT,V:Frankenstein,	
O:Cyclops	58.00
41 DH,GT,I:Grotesk,O:Cyclops	50.00
42 DH,GT,JB,V:Grotesk,	
O:Cyclops,D:Prof.X	50.00
43 GT,JB,V:Magneto,Quicksilver,	
Scarlet Witch,C:Avengers	55.00
44 V:Magneto,Quicksilver,Sc.Witch,	
R:Red Raven,O:Iceman	55.00
45 PH,JB,V:Magneto,Quicksilver,	

X-Men #58
© Marvel Entertainment Group

120 JBy,TA,I:AlphaFlight (Shaman,	
Sasquatch,Northstar,Snowbird,	
Aurora)	38.00
121 JBy,TA,V:Alpha Flight	45.00
122 JBy,TA,A:Juggernaut,Black	
Tom,Arcade,Power Man	24.00
123 JBy,TA,V:Arcade,A:SpM	22.00
124 JBy,TA,V:Arcade	22.00
125 JBy,TA,A:Beast,Madrox the	
Multiple Man,Havok,Polaris	22.00
126 JBy,TA,I:Proteus,	
A:Havok,Madrox	22.00
127 JBy,TA,V:Proteus,A:Havok,	
Madrox	22.00
128 GP(c),JBy,TA,V:Proteus,	
A:Havok,Madrox	22.00
129 JBy,TA,I:Shadow Cat,White	
Queen,C:Hellfire Club	28.00
130 JR2(c),JBy,TA,I:Dazzler	
V:White Queen	24.00
131 JBy,TA,V:White Queen,	
A:Dazzler	20.00
132 JBy,TA,I:Hellfire Club,	
V:Mastermind	20.00
133 JBy,TA,V:Hellfire Club,	
Mastermind,F:Wolverine	20.00
134 JBy,TA,V:Hellfire Club,Master	
mind,I:Dark Phoenix,A:Beast	20.00
135 JBy,TA,V:Dark Phoenix,C:SpM,	
Fant.Four,Silver Surfer	20.00
136 JBy,TA,V:Dark Phoenix,	
A:Beast	20.00
137 JBy,TA,D:Phoenix,V:Imperial	
Guard,A:Beast	26.00
138 JBy,TA,History of X-Men,	
L:Cyclops,C:Shadow Cat	22.00
139 JBy,TA,A:Alpha Flight,R:Wendigo,	
N:Wolverine,J:Shadowcat	35.00
140 JBy,TA,V:Wendigo,A:Alpha	
Flight	25.00
141 JBy,TA,I:2nd Brotherhood of Evil	
Mutants,I:Rachel (Phoenix II)	35.00
Becomes: UNCANNY X-MEN	
142 JBy,TA,V:Evil Mutants,	
A:Rachel (Phoenix II)	25.00

MARVEL

Uncanny X-Men #121
© Marvel Entertainment Group

177 JR2,JR,V:Brotherhood of
  Evil Mutants 6.00
178 JR2,BWi,BBr,V:Brotherhood
  of Evil Mutants 6.00
179 JR2,DGr,V:Morlocks 6.00
180 JR2,DGr,BWi,Secret Wars . . 6.00
181 JR2,DGr,A:Sunfire 6.00
182 JR2,DGr,V:S.H.I.E.L.D. 6.00
183 JR2,DGr,V:Juggernaut 6.00
184 JR2,DGr,V:Selene,I:Forge . . . 8.00
185 JR2,DGr,V:Shield,U.S.
  Govt.,Storm loses powers 6.00
186 BWS,TA,Lifedeath,
  V:Dire Wraiths 7.00
187 JR2,DGr,V:Dire Wraiths 6.00
188 JR2,DGr,V:Dire Wraiths 6.00
189 JR2,SL,V:Selene,A:Magma . . 6.00
190 JR2,DGr,V:Kulan Gath,A:SpM,
  Avengers,New Mutants 6.00
191 JR2,DGr,A:Avengers,Spider-Man,
  New Mutants,I:Nimrod 6.00
192 JR2,DGr,V:Magus 6.00
193 JR2,DGr,V:Hellions,I:Firestar
  Warpath,20th Anniv. 8.00
194 JR2,DGr,SL,V:Nimrod 6.00
195 BSz(c),JR2,DGr,A:Power
  Pack,V:Morlocks 6.00
196 JR2,DGr,J:Magneto 7.00
197 JR2,DGr,V:Arcade 6.00
198 BWS,F:Storm,'Lifedeath II' . . 6.00
199 JR2,DGr,I:Freedom Force,
  Rachel becomes 2nd Phoenix . 6.00
200 JR2,DGr,A:Magneto,I:Fenris 11.00
201 RL,WPo(i),I:Nathan
  Christopher (Cyclops son) . . . 15.00
202 JR2,AW,Secret Wars II 7.00
203 JR2,AW,Secret Wars II 7.00
204 JBr,WPo,V:Arcade 8.00
205 BWS,A:Lady Deathstrike . . . 18.00
206 JR2,DGr,V:Freedom Force . . 7.00
207 JR2,DGr,V:Selene 7.00
208 JR2,DGr,V:Nimrod,
  A:Hellfire Club 7.00
209 JR2,CR,V:Nimrod,A:Spiral . . . 7.00
210 JR2,DGr,I:Marauders,
  (Mutant Massacre) 20.00
211 JR2,BBI,AW,V:Marauders,
  (Mutant Massacre) 20.00
212 RL,DGr,V:Sabretooth,
  (Mutant Massacre) 24.00
213 AD,V:Sabretooth (Mut.Mass) 24.00
214 BWS,BWi,V:Malice,A:Dazzler 6.00
215 AD,DGr,I:Stonewall,Super
  Sabre,Crimson Commando . . . 6.00
216 BWS(c),JG,DGr,V:Stonewall . 6.00
217 WS(c),JG,SL,V:Juggernaut . . 6.00
218 AAD(c),MS,DGr,V:Juggernaut 6.00
219 BBI,DGr,V:Marauders,Polaris
  becomes Malice,A:Sabertooth . 7.00
220 MS,DGr,A:Naze 6.00
221 MS,DGr,I:Mr.Sinister,
  V:Marauders 15.00
222 MS,DGr,V:Marauders,Eye
  Killers,A:Sabertoom 17.00
223 KGa,DGr,A:Freedom Force . . 6.00
224 MS,DGr,V:Adversary 6.00
225 MS,DGr,Fall of Mutants
  I:1st US App Roma 9.00
226 MS,DGr,Fall of Mutants 9.00
227 MS,DGr,Fall of Mutants 9.00
228 RL,TA,A:OZ Chase 6.00
229 MS,DGr,I:Reavers,Gateway . 6.00
230 RL,DGr,Xmas Issue 6.00
231 RL,DGr,V:Limbo 6.00
232 MS,DGr,V:Brood 6.00

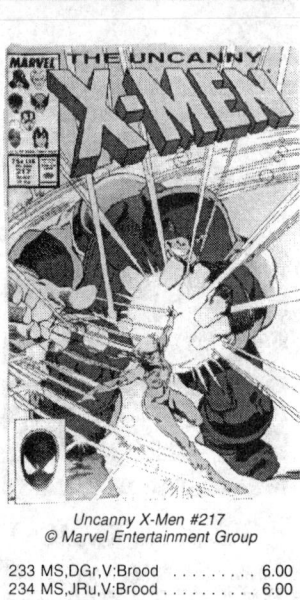

Uncanny X-Men #217
© Marvel Entertainment Group

233 MS,DGr,V:Brood 6.00
234 MS,JRu,V:Brood 6.00
235 RL,CR,V:Magistrates 6.00
236 MS,DGr,V:Magistrates 6.00
237 RL,TA,V:Magistrates 6.00
238 MS,DGr,V:Magistrates 6.00
239 MS,DGr,Inferno,A:Mr.Sinister . 7.00
240 MS,DGr,Inferno,V:Marauders . 7.50
241 MS,DGr,Inferno,O:Madeline
  Pryor,V:Marauders 7.50
242 MS,DGr,Inferno,D:N'Astirh,
  A:X-Factor,Double-sized 7.50
243 MS,Inferno,A:X-Factor. 7.50
244 MS,DGr,I:Jubilee 25.00
245 RLd,DGr,Invasion Parody . . . 6.00
246 MS,DGr,V:Mastermold,
  A:Nimrod 6.00
247 MS,DGr,V:Mastermold 5.00
248 JLe(1st X-Men Art),DGr,
  V:Nanny & Orphan Maker . . . 28.00
248a 2nd printing 2.00
249 MS,DGr,C:Zaladane,
  V:Savage Land Mutates. 5.00
250 MS,SL,I:Zaladane. 5.00
251 MS,DGr,V:Reavers 5.00
252 JLe,BSz(c),RL,SW,V:Reavers 5.00
253 MS,SL,V:Amahl Farouk 5.00
254 JLe(c),MS,DGr,V:Reavers . . . 5.00
255 MS,DGr,V:Reavers,D:Destiny 5.00
256 JLe,SW,Acts of Vengeance,
  V:Manderin,A:Psylocke 16.00
257 JLe,JRu,AofV,V:Manderin . . 14.00
258 JLe,SW,AofV,V:Manderin . . . 15.00
259 MS,DGr,V:Magistrates 7.00
260 JLe(c),MS,DGr,A:Dazzler . . . 5.50
261 JLe(c),MS,DGr,V:Hardcase &
  Harriers 5.50
262 KD,JRu,V:Masque,Morlocks . 5.50
263 JRu(i),O:Forge,V:Morlocks . . 5.50
264 JLe(c),MC,JRu,V:Magistrate . 5.50
265 JRu(i),V:Shadowking 5.50
266 NKu(c),MC,JRu,I:Gambit . . . 40.00
267 JLe,WPo,SW,V:Shadowking 16.00
268 JLe,SW,A:Captain America,
  Black Widow,V:The Hand,

143 JBy,TA,V:N'Garai,I:Lee
  Forrester 10.00
144 BA,JRu,A:Man-Thing,
  O:Havok, V:D'Spayre 9.00
145 DC,JRu,V:Arcade,A:DrDoom . 9.00
146 DC,JRu,V:Dr.Doom,Arcade . . 9.00
147 DC,JRu,V:Dr.Doom,Arcade . . 9.00
148 DC,JRu,I:Caliban,A:Dazzler
  Spiderwoman 9.00
149 DC,JRu,A:Magneto 9.00
150 DC,JRu,BWi,V:Magneto . . . 11.00
151 JSh,BMc,JRu,V:Sentinels . . . 7.00
152 BMc,JRu,V:White Queen . . . 7.00
153 DC,JRu,I:Bamf 7.00
154 DC,JRu,BWi,I:Sidrian Hunters
  A:Corsair,O:Cyclops(part) 7.00
155 DC,BWi,V:Deathbird,I:Brood . 7.00
156 DC,BWi,V:Death Bird,
  A:Tigra, Star Jammers 7.00
157 DC,BWi,V:Deathbird 7.00
158 DC,BWi,2nd A:Rogue,
  Mystique 10.00
159 BSz,BWi,V:Dracula 7.00
160 BA,BWi,V:Belasco,I:Magik . . . 7.00
161 DC,BWi,I:Gabrielle Haller,
  O:Magneto,Professor X 8.00
162 DC,BWi,V:Brood 11.00
163 DC,BWi,V:Brood 7.00
164 DC,BWi,V:Brood,I:Binary 7.00
165 PS,BWi,V:Brood 7.00
166 PS,BWi,V:Brood,A:Binary,
  I:Lockheed 8.00
167 PS,BWi,V:Brood,A:N.Mutants 8.00
168 PS,BWi,I:Madelyne Pryor . . . 7.00
169 PS,BWi,I:Morlocks 7.00
170 PS,BWi,A:Angel,V:Morlocks . 7.00
171 WS,BWi,J:Rogue,V:Binary . 11.00
172 PS,BWi,V:Viper,Silver
  Samurai, ... 8.00
173 PS,BWi,V:Viper,Silver
  Samurai, ... 6.00
174 PS,BWi,A:Mastermind 6.00
175 PS,JR2,BWi,W:Cyclops and
  Madelyne,V:Mastermind 9.00
176 JR2,BWi,I:Val Cooper 6.00

MARVEL

Baron Strucker 24.00
269 JLe,ATi,Rogue V:Ms.Marvel . 9.00
270 JLe,ATi,SW,X-Tinction Agenda
#1, A:Cable,New Mutants . . . 13.00
270a 2nd printing(Gold) 4.00
271 JLe,SW,X-Tinction Agenda
#4,A:Cable,New Mutants 9.00
272 JLe,SW,X-Tinction Agenda
#7,A:Cable,New Mutants 9.00
273 JLe,WPo,JBy,KJ,RL,MS,MGo,
LSn,SW,A:Cable,N.Mutants . . . 8.50
274 JLe,SW,V:Zaladane,A:Magneto,
Nick Fury,Kazar 7.00
275 JLe,SW,R:Professor X,A:Star
Jammers,Imperial Guard 11.00
275a 2nd Printing (Gold) 3.00
276 JLe,SW,V:Skrulls,Shi'ar 6.00
277 JLe,SW,V:Skrulls,Shi'ar 6.00
278 PS,Professor X Returns to
Earth,V:Shadowking 4.00
279 NKu,SW,V:Shadowking 4.00
280 E:CCl(s),NKu,A:X-Factor,
D:Shadowking,Prof.X Crippled . 4.00
281 WPo,ATi,new team (From X-Men
#1),D:Pierce,Hellions,V:Sentinels,
I:Trevor Fitzroy,Upstarts 10.00
281a 2nd printing,red(c) 1.25
282 WPo,ATi,V:Fitzroy,C:Bishop 15.00
282a 2nd printing,gold(c) of #281
inside 1.25
283 WPo,ATi,I:Bishop,Malcolm,
Randall 15.00
284 WPo,ATi,SOS from USSR. . . 4.00
285 WPo,I:Mikhail(Colossus'
brother from Russia) 3.25
286 JLe,WPo,ATi,A:Mikhail 3.25
287 JR2,O:Bishop,
D:Malcolm,Randall 5.00
288 NKu,BSz,A:Bishop 3.00
289 WPo,ATi,Forge proposes
to Storm 3.00
290 WPo,SW,V:Cyberpunks,
L:Forge 3.00
291 TR,V:Morlocks 2.50
292 TR,V:Morlocks 2.50
293 TR,D:Morlocks,Mikhail 2.50
294 BP,TA,X-Cutioner's Song#1,
Stryfe shoots Prof.X,A:X-Force,
X-Factor,polybag.w/ProfX card 4.00
295 BP,TA,X-Cutioners Song #5,
V:Apocalypse 3.00
296 BP,TA,X-Cutioners Song #9,
A:X-Force,X-Factor,V:Stryfe . . 3.00
297 BP,X-Cutioners Song
Aftermath 2.00
298 BP,TA,V:Acolytes 2.00
299 BP,A:Forge,Acolytes,I:Graydon
Creed (Sabretooth's son) 2.00
300 JR2,DGr,BP,V:Acolytes,A:Forge,
Nightcrawler,Holografx(c) 6.00
301 JR2,DGr,I:Sienna Blaze,
V:Fitzroy 2.00
302 JR2,V:Fitzroy 2.00
303 JR2,V:Upstarts,D:Illyana 2.00
304 JR2,JaL,PS,L:Colossus,
V:Magneto,Holo-grafx(c) 6.50
305 JD,F:Rogue,Bishop 2.00
306 JR2,V:Hodge 2.00
307 JR2,Bloodties#4,A:Avengers,
V:Exodus,Cortez 2.00
308 JR2,Scott & Jean announce
impending marriage 2.00
309 JR2,O:Professor X & Amelia . 2.00
310 JR2,DG,A:Cable,V:X-Cutioner,
w/card 5.00

311 JR2,DG,AV,V:Sabretooth,
C:Phalanx 2.00
312 JMd,DG,A:Yukio,I:Phalanx,
w/card 2.00
313 JMd,DG,V:Phalanx 2.00
314 LW,BSz,R:White Quen 2.00
315 F:Acolytes 2.00
316 V:Phalanx,I:M,Phalanx Covenant
Generation Next,pt.1, holo(c) . . 5.00
316a newsstand ed. 2.00
317 JMd,V:Phalanx,prism(c) 5.00
317a newsstand ed. 2.00
318 JMd,L:Jubilee, deluxe 2.25
318a newsstand ed. 2.00
319 R:Legion, deluxe 2.25
319a newsstand ed. 2.00
320 deluxe ed. 4.00
320 newsstand ed. 2.00
321 R:Lilandra, deluxe ed. 2.25
321 newsstand ed. 2.00
322 SLo,TGu,Rogue,Iceman run from
Gambit's Secret 6.00
323 I:Onslaught 2.25

X-Men #281
© Marvel Entertainment Group

324 SLo,F:Cannonball 2.25
325 R:Colossus 4.00
326 SLo,JMd,F:Gambit,Sabretooth 2.00
327 SLo,JMd,Magneto's Fate . . . 2.00
328 SLo,JMd,Sabretooth freed . . 2.00
329 SLo,JMd,A:Doctor Strange . . 2.00
330 . . . . 2.00
331 . . . . 2.00
332 SLo,JMd, cont from
Wolverine #100 . . . . 2.00
333 SLo,JMd, Operation: Zero
Tolerance, Onslaught saga . . . 3.00
334 SLo,JMd, Onslaught saga . . . 3.00
335 SLo,JMd, Onslaught saga . . . 3.00
336 Apocalypse vs. Onslaught . . . 2.50
337 Operation: Zero Tolerance . . . 2.00
338 SLo,JMd,R:Angel 1.95
339 SLo,JMd,F:Cyclops, J.J.
Jameson, Havok 1.95
340 SLo,JMd,F:Iceman 1.95
341 SLo,JMd,Rogue gets gift . . . 1.95
342 SLo,JMd, Shi'ar Empire,pt.1 . 1.95
342a Rogue cover 9.00

343 SLo,JMd, Shi'ar Empire, pt.2 . 1.95
344 SLo,JMd, Shi'ar Empire, pt.3 . 1.95
345 SLo,JMd, trip home, A:Akron . 1.95
346 SLo,JMd,Zero Tolerance,
A:Spider-Man 1.95
347 SLo,JMd,Zero Tolerance 1.95
Ann.#1 rep.#9,#11 . . . . 75.00
Ann.#2 rep.#22,#23 . . . . 65.00
Ann.#3 GK(c),GP,TA,A:Arkon . . 19.00
Ann.#4 JR2,BMc,A:Dr.Strange . . 12.00
Ann.#5 BA,BMc,A:F.F. 10.00
Ann.#6 BSz,BWi,Dracula 11.00
Ann.#7 MGo,TMd,BWi,TA,BBr,BA,JRu,
BBI,SL,AM,V:Impossible Man . 8.00
Ann.#8 SL,Kitty's story 8.00
Ann.#9 AAd,AG,MMi,Asgard,V:Loki,
Enchantress,A:New Mutants . 15.00
Ann.#10 AAd,TA,V:Mojo,
J:Longshot,A:New Mutants . . 13.00
Ann.#11 AD,V:Horde,A:CaptBrit . . 6.00
Ann.#12 AAd,BWi,RLm,TD,Evol.
War,V:Terminus,Savage Land . 6.00
Ann.#13 MBa,JRu,Atlantis Attacks 5.00
Ann.#14 AAd,DGr,BWi,AM,ATi,
V:Ahab,A:X-Factor. 14.00
Ann.#15,TR,JRu,MMi(c),Flesh Tears,
Pt.3,A:X-Force,New Warriors . 4.50
Ann.#16 JaL,JRu,Shattershot
Part.2 . . . . 8.00
Ann.#17 JPe,MFm,I:X-Cutioner,
D:Mastermind,w/card 4.00
Ann.#18 JR2,V:Caliban,
BU:Bishop 3.25
Unc.X-Men 95' F:Husk 3.95
G-Size #1,GK,DC,I:New X-Men
(Colossus,Storm,Nightcrawler,
Thunderbird,3rd A:Wolv.) . . 450.00
G-Size #2,rep.#57-59 . . . . 50.00
GNv Pryde of the X-Men 10.95
PF God Loves, Man Kills 6.95
TPB Asgardian Wars 15.95
TPB Bloodties V:Exodus 15.95
TPB Coming of Bishop 12.95
TPB Dark Phoenix Saga 12.95
TPB Day of Future Present 14.95
TPB Days of Future Past 4.95
TPB Fatal Attractions 17.95
TPB From the Ashes 16.95
TPB Greatest Battles 15.95
TPB Savage Land 9.95
TPB X-Cutioner's Song 24.95
TPB X-Tinction Agenda 19.95
X-Men Survival Guide to the
Mansion, NKu(c) 6.95
Uncanny X-Men '95 Spe. 3.95
Minus 1 Spec., SLo,JMd,, flashback,
discovery of mutants 1.95
TPB Essential X-Men
collection, rep. 12.95

X-MEN
[2nd Regular Series]
Oct., 1991

1A(c);Storm,Beast,B:CCl(s),JLe,SW
I:Fabian Cortez,Acolytes,
V:Magneto 2.50
1B(c);Colossus,Psylocke 2.50
1C(c);Cyclops,Wolverine 2.50
1D(c);Magneto 2.50
1E(c);Gatefold w/pin-ups 5.00
2 JLe,SW,V:Magneto Contd. 5.00
3 E:CCl(s),JLe,SW,V:Magneto . . . 4.00
4 JBy(s),JLe,SW,I:Omega Red,
V:Hand 6.00
5 B:SLo(s),JLe,SW,V:Hand,

Uncanny X-Men (2nd Series) #8
© Marvel Entertainment Group

Omega Red,I:Maverick 6.00
6 JLe,SW,V:Omega Red, Hand,
  Sabretooth 5.00
7 JLe,SW,V:Omega Red,Hand,
  Sabretooth 5.00
8 JLe,SW,Bishop vs. Gambit . 5.00
9 JLe,SW,A:Ghost Rider,V:Brood 5.00
10 JLe,SW,MT,Longshot Vs. Mojo,
  BU:Maverick 5.00
11 E:SLo(s)JLe,MT,V:Mojo,
  BU:Maverick 4.00
12 B:FaN(s),ATb,BWi,I:Hazard . . . 3.00
13 ATb,BWi,V:Hazard 3.00
14 NKu,X-Cutioners Song#3,A:X-Fact.
  X-Force,V:Four Horsemen . . . 3.00
15 NKu,X-Cutioners Song #7,
  V:Mutant Liberation Front 3.00
16 NKu,MPn,X-Cutioners Song #11,
  A:X-Force,X-Factor,V:Dark Riders,
  Apocalypse Vs.Archangel,IR:Stryfe
  is Nathan Summers 3.00
17 NKu,MPn,R:Illyana,A:Darkstar . 2.50
18 NKu,MPn,R:Omega Red,V:Soul
  Skinner 2.50
19 NKu,MPn,V:Soul Skinner,
  Omega Red 2.00
20 NKu,MPn,J.Grey vs Psylocke . 2.00
21 NKu,V:Silver Samurai,Shinobi . 2.00
22 BPe,V:Silver Samurai,Shinobi . 2.00
23 NKu,MPn,V:Dark Riders,
  Mr.Sinister 2.00
24 NKu,BSz,A Day in the Life . . . 2.00
25 NKu,Hologram(c),V:Magneto,Wolv.'s
  Adamantium skel. pulled out . . 11.00
26 NKu,Bloodties#2,A:Avengers,
  I:Unforgiven 3.00
27 RiB,I:Threnody 2.50
28 NKu,MRy,F:Sabretooth 2.50
29 NKu,MRy,V:Shinobi 2.50
30 NKu,MRy,W:Cyclops&Jean Grey,
  w/card 6.00
31 NKu,MRy,A:Spiral,Matsuo,
  D:Kwannon 2.25
32 NKu,MRy,A:Spiral,Matsuo 2.25
33 NKu,MRy,F:Gambit &
  Sabretooth 2.25

34 NKu,MRy,A:Riptide 2.25
35 LSh,A:Nick Fury 2.25
36 NKu,MRy,I:Synch, Phalanx Covenant
  Generation Next,pt.2, deluxe . . 4.00
36a Newsstand ed. 1.75
37 NKu,MRy,Generation Next,pt.3
  foil(c) 4.00
37a newsstand ed. 1.75
38 NKu,MRy,F:Psylocke 2.50
38a newsstand ed. 1.50
39 X-Treme, deluxe 2.50
39a newsstand ed. 1.50
40 deluxe 3.00
40a newsstand ed. 1.50
41 V:Legion, deluxe 2.50
41a newsstand ed. 1.50
42 PS,PaN,Mysterious Visitor 2.00
43 Rogue and Iceman 2.00
44 FaN,Mystery of Magneto 2.00
45 20th Anniv.pt.2 . . . . 3.50
46 FaN,Aku,V:Comcast 2.00
47 SLo,AKu,CaS,F:Dazzler 2.00
48 SLo,AKu,CaS,F:Sabretooth . . . 2.00
49 SLo,AKu,Bishop wanted 5.00
50 Onslaught(c) 8.00
50a regular edition 5.00
51 MWa,Onslaught 3.00
52 MWa,AKu,CaS,V:Sinister 3.00
53 Onslaught saga 7.00
54 Onslaught saga 4.00
55 Onslaught saga 4.00
56 Onslaught saga 3.00
57 Operation: Zero Tolerence . . . 2.00
58 SLo,NKu 2.00
59 . . . . 2.00
60 SLo,NKu,F:Ororo, V:Candra . . 2.00
61 SLo,CNn,F:Storm, V:Candra . . 2.00
62 SLo,CPa,F:Sebastian Shaw,
  Shang Chi 2.00
62A variant Storm/Wolverine cover 5.00
63 SLo,CPa,ATi,A:Sebastian Shaw,
  Inner Circle 1.95
64 SLo,CPa,ATi,V:Hellfire Club . . 1.95
65 SLo,CPa,ATi, No Exit prelude . 1.95
66 SLo,CPa,ATi, Zero Tolerance,
  A:Bastion 1.95
67 SLo,CPa,ATi, Zero Tolerance,
  F:Iceman, Cecilia Reyes 1.95
Ann.#1 JLe,Shattershot,pt.1,
  I:Mojo II 3.00
Ann.#2 I:Empyrean,w/card 3.25
Ann.#3 F:Storm 3.50
TPB Magneto Returns 15.95
TPB Dawn of the Age of
  Apocalypse, gold foil cover . . 8.95
TPB Twilight of the Age of
  Apocalypse, gold foil cover . . 8.95
TPB Legion Quest 8.95
Minus 1 Spec., SLo,CPa,ATi,
  flashback,F:Magneto 1.95

X-MEN ADVENTURES
[1st Season]
1 V:Sentinals, Based on TV
  Cartoon 6.00
2 V:Sentinals,D:Morph 5.00
3 V:Magneto,A:Sabretooth 4.00
4 V:Magneto 4.00
5 V:Morlocks 4.00
6 V:Sabretooth 3.50
7 V:Cable,Genosha,Sentinels . . . 3.00
8 A:Colossus,A:Juggernaut 3.00
9 I:Colossus(on cartoon),
  V:Juggernaut 3.00
10 A:Angel,V:Mystique 3.00

11 I:Archangel(on cartoon) . . . 2.00
12 V:Horsemen of Apocalypse . . . 2.00
13 RMc(s),I:Bishop(on cartoon) . . 2.00
14 V:Brotherhood of Evil Mutants . 2.00
TPB Vol.1 . . . . 4.95
TPB Vol.2 . . . . 4.95
TPB Vol.3 . . . . 5.95
TPB Vol.4 rep. Days of Future Past
  and Final Conflict 6.95
[2nd Season]
1 R:Morph,I:Mr. Sinister
  (on cartoon) 3.00
2 I:Nasty Boys (on cartoon) 2.00
3 I:Shadow King (on cartoon) . . . 2.00
4 I:Omega Red (on cartoon) 2.00
5 I:Alpha Flight (on cartoon) . . . 2.00
6 F:Gambit 2.00
7 A:Cable,Bishop,Apocalypse . . 1.25
8 A:Cable,Bisihp,Apocalypse . . . 1.50
9 O:Rogue 1.50
10 . . . . 1.50
11 F:Mojo,Longshot 1.50
12 Reunions,pt.1 . . . . 1.50
13 Reunions,pt.1 . . . . 1.50
[3rd Season]
1 Out of the Past,pt.1 . . . . 3.00
2 V:Spirit Drinker 1.75
3 Phoenix Saga,pt.1 . . . . 1.75
4 Phoenix Saga,pt.2 . . . . 1.75
5 Phoenix Saga,pt.3 . . . . 1.75
6 Phoenix Saga,pt.4 . . . . 1.75
7 Phoenix Saga,pt.5 . . . . 1.50
8 War in The Savage Land 1.50
9 F:Ka-Zar 1.50
10 Dark Phoenix,Saga,pt.1 . . . . . 1.50
11 Dark Phoenix Saga,pt.2 . . . . . 1.50
12 Dark Phoenix Saga,pt.3 . . . . . 1.50
13 Dark Phoenix Saga,pt.4 . . . . . 1.50

X-MEN: ALPHA
1 double size 10.00
1a gold edition, 48pp 50.00

X-MEN/ALPHA FLIGHT
Jan., 1986
1 PS,BWi,V:Loki 5.00

X-Men/Alpha Flight #1
© Marvel Entertainment Group

2 PS,BWi,V:Loki 4.00

X-MEN/ ANIMATION SPECIAL
TV Screenplay Adapt 10.95

X-MEN ARCHIVES: CAPTAIN BRITAIN
1 AMo,AD,Secret History 3.00
2 AMo,AD,F:Captain Britain 3.00
3 AMo,AD,Trial of Captain Britain 3.00
4 AMo,AD,Trial cont. 3.00
5 AD,AMo,F:Captain Britain 3.00
6 AMo,AD,Final Apocalypse? . . . 3.00
7 AMo,AD,conclusion 3.00

X-MEN: ASKANI'SON
1 SLo,GeH,sequel to Adventures of
   Cyclops & Phoenix 3.00
2 SLo,GeH,A:Stryfe 3.00
3 SLo,GeH 3.00
4 SLo,GeH,conclusion 3.00
Books of Askani, portraits 3.00

X-MEN AT STATE FAIR
1 KGa,Dallas Times Herald . . . 40.00

X-MEN CHRONICLES
1 X-Men Unlimited AX 3.95
2 V:Abbatoir 3.95

X-MEN/CLANDESTINE
1996
1 & 2 AD,MFm,48pg . . . . . . @2.95

X-MEN CLASSICS
Dec., 1983
1 NA,rep. 3.50
2 NA,rep. 3.50
3 NA,rep. 3.50

X-MEN: EARLY YEARS
1 rep. X-Men (first series) #1 . . . 1.75
2 rep. X-Men (first series) #2 . . . 1.75
3 rep. X-Men (first series) #3 . . . 1.75
4 thru 16 rep. X-Men (first series)
   #4 to #16 . . . . @1.50
17 Rep. X-Men #17 & #18 . . . . . . 2.50

CLASSIC X-MEN
Sept., 1986
1 AAd(c),JBo,New stories, rep.
   giant size X-Men 1 . . . . 10.00
2 rep.#94,JBo/AAd(c),BU:
   Storm & Marvel Girl 7.00
3 rep.#95,JBo/AAd(c),BU:
   I:Thunderbird II 5.00
4 rep.#96,JBo/AAd(c),BU:
   Wolverine & N.Crawler 4.50
5 rep.#97,JBo/AAd(c),BU:
   Colossus 4.00
6 rep.#98,JBo/AAd(c),BU:
   JeanGrey,I:Seb.Shaw 4.00
7 rep.#99,JBo/AAd(c),BU:
   HellfireClub,W.Queen 4.00
8 rep.#100,JBo/AAd(c),BU:
   O:Jean Grey/Phoenix 4.00
9 rep.#101,JBo/AAd(c),BU:
   Nightcrawler 4.00
10 rep.#102,JBo/AAd(c),BU:
   Wolverine,A:Sabretooth 9.00
11 rep.#103,JBo/BL(c),BU:Storm . 3.50

12 rep.#104,JBo/AAd(c),BU:
   O:Magneto 8.00
13 rep.#105,JBo/AAd(c),BU:
   JeanGrey & Misty Knight 3.50
14 rep.#107,JBo/AAd(c),BU:
   Lilandra 3.50
15 rep.#108,JBo/AAd(c),BU:
   O:Starjammers 3.50
16 rep.#109,JBo/AAd(c),BU:
   Banshee 3.50
17 rep.#111,JBo/TA(c),BU:
   Mesmero 6.00
18 rep.#112,JBo/AAd(c),BU:
   Phoenix 5.00
19 rep.#113,JBo/AAd(c),BU:
   Magnetoo 5.00
20 rep.#114,JBo/AAd(c),
   BU:Storm 4.00
21 rep.#115,JBo/AAd(c),
   BU:Colossus. 4.00
22 rep.#116,JBo/AAd(c),
   BU:Storm 4.00
23 rep.#117,JBo/KGa(c),BU:
   Nightcrawler 4.00

Classic X-Men #9
© Marvel Entertainment Group

24 rep.#118,JBo/KGa(c),BU:
   Phoenix 4.00
25 rep.#119,JBo/KGa(c),BU:Wolv. 4.00
26 rep.#120,JBo/AAd(c),BU:Wolv. 5.50
27 rep.#121,JBo/KD(c),BU:
   Wolverine & Phoenix 3.00
28 rep.#122,JBo/KD(c),BU:X-Men 3.00
29 rep.#123,JBo/KD(c),BU:
   Colossus 3.00
30 rep.#124,JBo/SLi(c),BU:
   O:Arcade 3.00
31 rep.#125,JBo/SLi(c),BU:
   Professor.X 3.00
32 rep.#126,JBo/SLi(c),BU:
   Wolverine. 3.00
33 rep.#127,JBo/SLi(c),BU:
   Havok 3.00
34 rep.#128,JBo/SLi(c),BU:
   W.Queen,M.Mind 3.00
35 rep.#129,JBo/SLi(c),BU:
   K.Pryde 3.00
36 rep.#130,MBr/SLi(c),BU:
   Banshee & Moira 3.00
37 rep.#131,RL/SLi(c),BU:

Dazzler 3.00
38 rep.#132,KB/SLi(c),BU:
   Dazzler 3.00
39 rep.#133,2nd JLe X-Men/SLi(c),
   BU:Storm 11.00
40 rep.#134,SLi(c),BU:N.Crawler . 2.00
41 rep.#135,SLi(c),BU:
   Mr. Sinister,Cyclops 2.00
42 rep.#136,SLi(c),BU:
   Mr. Sinister,Cyclops 2.00
43 rep.#137,JBy(c),BU:
   Phoenix,Death 2.50
Becomes:

X-MEN CLASSICS
44 rep.#138,KD/SLi(c) 2.00
45 thru 49 rep.#139–#145,SLi(c) @2.00
50 thru 69 rep.#146–#165 . . . . @1.50
70 rep.#166 . . . . 1.75
71 thru 99 rep.#167–#195 . . . . @1.50
100 thru 105 rep. #196–#201 . . @1.50
106 Phoenix vs. Beyonder 1.50
107 F:Rogue 1.50
108 F:Nightcrawler 1.50
109 Rep. Uncanny X-Men #205 . . 1.50
110 Rep. Uncanny X-Men #206 . . 1.50

X-MEN: DAYS OF FUTURE PAST
1 Rep. X-Men #141-142 . . . . . . 4.00

X-MEN: DAYS OF FUTURE PRESENT
1 MMi(c),Rep.F.F.Ann.#23,X-Men
   Ann.#14,X-Factor Ann.#5,
   New Mutant Ann.#10 . . . . . . 14.95

X-MEN FIRSTS
1-shot Rep. I:Wolverinek,Rogue
   Gambit & Mr. Sinister 5.00

X-MEN INDEX
SEE: OFFICIAL MARVEL
INDEX TO THE X-MEN

X-MEN: INFERNO
TPB 352pg 19.95

X-MEN: LOST TALES
1 CCI,JBo,rep. from Classic X-Men2.99
2 CCI,JBo,rep. from Classic X-Men2.99

X-MEN MEGAZINE
TPB CCI,JLe,rep. Uncanny X-Men
   #273–#275 . . . . 3.95

X-MEN/MICRONAUTS
Jan., 1984
1 JG,BWi,Limited Series 3.50
2 JG,BWi,KJo,V:Baron Karza . . . 2.50
3 JG,BWi,V:Baron Karza 2.50
4 JG,BWi,V:Baron Karza,Apr.1984 2.50

X-MEN: MUTANT MASSACRE
TPB rep. 256pg. 24.95

X-MEN '95
1 F:Mister Sinister 3.95

X-MEN '96

MARVEL

All comics prices listed are for *Near Mint* condition.

MARVEL

GN LHa, 64pg., F:Gambit, Rogue,
Magneto, Jubilee & Wolverine . 2.95
GN TKa,AD,MFm, Age of
Apocalypse 2.95

X-MEN '97
1-shot JFM,SEp,F:Gambit,
Joesph & Phoenix 2.99

X-MEN OMEGA
1 FaN,Slo,After Xavier, concl. . . 10.00
1a Gold ed. Chromium(c) 48pg. . 50.00

X-MEN PRIME
1 SLo,FaN,BHi,major plotlines for
all X books begin, chromium(c) 10.00

X-MEN: PRYDE & WISDOM
1 WEI,TyD,KIS 1.95
2 & 3 WEI,TyD,KIS . . . . @1.95

X-MEN RARITIES
1 F:Classic Stories 5.95

X-MEN: THE RISE OF APOCALYPSE
1 TKa,AdP, ancient history of
X-Men 1.95
2 thru 4 TKa,AdP, ... @1.95

X-MEN SPOTLIGHT ON STARJAMMERS
1990
1 DC,F:Starjammers,A:Prof.X . . 5.00
2 DC,F:Starjammers,A:Prof.X . . 5.00

X-MEN 2099
1 B:JFM(s),RLm,JP,I:X-Men 2099 5.00
1a Gold Ed. 12.00
2 RLm,JP,V:Rat Pack 3.00
3 RLm,JP,D:Serpentina 2.50
4 RLm,JP,I:Theatre of Pain 2.00
5 RLm,JP,Fall of the Hammer#3 . 2.00
6 RLm,JP,I:Freakshow 2.00
7 RLm,JP,V:Freakshow 2.00
8 RLm(c),JS3,JP,N;Metalhead,
I:2nd X-Men 2099 . . . . 1.75
9 RLm,JP,V:2nd X-Men 2099 . . 1.75
10 RLm,JP,A:La Lunatica 1.75
11 RLm,JP,V:2nd X-Men 2099 . . 1.75
12 RLm,JP,A:Junkpile 1.75
13 RLm,JP 1.75
14 RLm,JP,R:Loki 1.75
15 RLm,JP,F:Loki,I:Haloween Jack 1.50
16 . . . . 1.50
17 X'ian 1.50
18 Haloween Jack 1.50
19 Conclusion Halloween Jack . . 1.50
Becomes:

X-MEN 2099 A.D.
20 F:Bloodhawk 1.95
21 Doom Factor 1.95
22 One Nation Under Doom 1.95
23 V:Junkpile 1.95
24 . . . . 1.95
25 X-Men Reunited 2.50
25a variant cover 4.25
26 V:Graverobber 1.95
27 . . . . 1.95
28 X-Nation x-over 1.95
29 X-Nation x-over 1.95
30 . . . . 1.95

31 . . . . 1.95
32 V:Foolkiller 1.95
Spec.#1 Bros.Hildebrandt(c) . . . 3.95

X-MEN UNLIMITED
1 CBa,BP,O:Siena Blaze 8.00
2 JD,O:Magneto 7.00
3 FaN(s),BSz(c),MMK,Sabretooth
joins X-Men,A:Maverick 8.00
4 SLo(s),RiB,O:Nightcrawler,Rogue,
Mystique,IR:Mystique is
Nightcrawler's mother 6.00
5 JFM(s),LSh,After Shi'ar/
Kree War 5.00
6 JFM(s),PS,Sauron 5.00
7 JR2,HMe,O:Storm 5.00
8 Legacy Virus Victim 3.95
9 LHa,Wolverine & Psylocke . . . 3.95
10 MWa,Dark Beast,Beast,
double-size 10.00
11 Rogue & Magneto, double-size 10.00
12 Onslaught x-over,A:Juggernaut 3.95
13 GP,Binary gone berserk 3.95
14 TKa, Onslaught fallout 3.95
15 HMe,F:Wolverine, Iceman &
Maverick 3.95
16 MvR,F:Banshee, White Queen,
I:Primal 3.95

X-MEN VS. AVENGERS
April, 1987
1 MS,JRu,V:Soviet SuperSoldiers 5.00
2 MS,JRu,V:Sov.Super Soldiers . 4.50
3 MS,JRu,V:Sov.Super Soldiers . 4.50
4 KP,JRu,BMc,AW,AM,V:Magneto
July 1987 . . . . 4.00
TPB 12.95

X-MEN VS. DRACULA
1 rep. X-Men Ann.#6 . . . . 2.00

X-MEN: X-TINCTION AGENDA
TPB,rep.X-Men #270-272,X-Factor
#60-62,New Mutants #95-97 . 19.95

X-MEN: WRATH OF APOCALYPSE
1-shot Rep.X-Factor#65-#68 . . . . 4.95

X-NATION 2099
1 . . . . 1.95
2 . . . . 1.95
3 At Herod's Themepark 1.95

X.S.E.
Mini-Series 1996
1 (of 4) JOs,Bishop & Shard's
secrets 1.95
2 JOs, How did Shard die 1.95
3 JOs, How Shard died 1.95
4 JOs, conclusion 1.95

X-TERMINATORS
Oct., 1988—Jan., 1989
1 JBg,AW,AM,I:N'astirh 4.50
2 JBg,AM,V:N'astirh 3.50
3 JBg,AM,V:N'astirh 3.00
4 JBg,AM,A:New Mutants 3.00

X-UNIVERSE
1 The Other Heroes 3.50

2 F:Ben Grimm,Tony Stark 3.50

YOGI BEAR
Nov., 1977
1 A:Flintstones 1.25
2 . . . . 1.25
3 . . . . 1.25
4 . . . . 1.25
5 . . . . 1.25
6 . . . . 1.25
7 . . . . 1.25
8 . . . . 1.25
9 March, 1979 . . . . 1.25

YOUNG ALLIES COMICS
Timely
Summer, 1941—Oct., 1946
1 S&K,Hitler(c),I&O:Young Allies
1st meeting Capt. America &
Human Torch,A:Red Skull 9,500.00
2 S&K,A;Capt.America,Human
Torch 2,500.00
3 Remember Pearl Harbor(c) 1,700.00
4 A:Capt. America,Torch,Red Skull
ASh(c),Horror In Hollywood
A:Capt.America,Torch 2,800.00
5 ASh(c) 1,100.00
6 ASh(c) 750.00
7 ASh(c) 750.00
8 ASh(c) 750.00
9 ASh(c),Axis leaders(c),B:Tommy
Type 750.00
10 ASh(c) 750.00
11 ASh(c) 650.00
12 ASh(c) 650.00
13 ASh(c) 650.00
14 . . . . 650.00
15 ASh(c) 650.00
16 ASh(c) 650.00
17 ASh(c) 650.00
18 ASh(c) 650.00
19 ASh(c),E:Tommy Type 650.00
20 . . . . 650.00

YOUNG HEARTS
Nov., 1949—Feb., 1950
1 . . . . 37.50
2 Feb., 1950 . . . . 22.00

YOUNG MEN
See: COWBOY ROMANCES

YUPPIES FROM HELL
1989
1 Satire 2.95
2 . . . . 2.95
3 . . . . 2.95

ZORRO
Marvel United Kingdom
1990
1 Don Diego 1.00
2 thru 12 . . . . @1.00

GOLDEN AGE

A-1 COMICS
Magazine Enterprises
1944

N# F:Kerry Drake,BU:Johnny
Devildog & Streamer Kelly . 175.00
1 A:Dotty Driple,Mr. EX,Bush
Berry and Lew Loyal 90.00
2 A:Texas Slim & Dirty Dalton,
The Corsair,Teddy Rich, Dotty
Dripple,Inca Dinca,Tommy Tinker
Little Mexico and Tugboat . . . 50.00
3 same 30.00
4 same 30.00
5 same 30.00
6 same 28.00
7 same 25.00

A-1 Comics #120
© Magazine Enterprises

8 same 25.00
9 Texas Slim Issue 28.00
10 Same characters as
issues #2–#8 . . . . 25.00
11 Teena 40.00
12 Teena 30.00
13 JCr,Guns of Fact and Fiction,
narcotics & junkies featured 150.00
14 Tim Holt WesternAdventures 375.00
15 Teena 35.00
16 Vacation Comics 28.00
17 Jim Holt #2, E:A-1 on cover 200.00
18 Jimmy Durante, Ph(c) 175.00
19 Tim Holt #3 . . . . 150.00
20 Jimmy Durante Ph(c) 150.00
21 OW,Joan of Arc movie adapt. 135.00
22 Dick Powell (1949) 150.00
23 Cowboys N' Indians #6 . . . . . 35.00
24 FF(c),LbC,Trail Colt #2 . . . . 250.00
25 Fibber McGee & Molly (1949) 45.00
26 LbC, Trail Colt #2 . . . . 185.00
27 Ghost Rider#1,O:GhostRider 500.00
28 Christmas (Koko & Kola) . . . 20.00
29 FF(c), Ghost Rider #2 . . . . . 450.00
30 BP, Jet Powers #1 . . . . 225.00
31 FF,Ghost Rider#3,O:Ghost

Rider 450.00
32 AW,GE,Jet Powers #2 . . . 165.00
33 Muggsy Mouse #2 . . . . 28.00
34 FF(c),Ghost Rider #4 . . . . . 425.00
35 AW,Jet Powers 250.00
36 Muggsy Mouse 35.00
37 FF(c),Ghost Rider 450.00
38 AW,WW,Jet Powers 275.00
39 Muggsy Mouse 20.00
40 Dogface Dooley 28.00
41 Cowboys N' Indians 22.00
42 BP,Best of the West 300.00
43 Dogface Dooley 20.00
44 Ghost Rider 175.00
45 American Air Forces 25.00
46 Best of the West 125.00
47 FF,Thunda 900.00
48 Cowboys N' Indians 22.00
49 Dogface Dooley 15.00
50 BP,Danger Is Their Busines . 50.00
51 Ghost Rider 175.00
52 Best of the West 100.00
53 Dogface Dooley 15.00
54 BP,American Air Forces 25.00
55 BP,U.S. Marines 25.00
56 BP,Thunda 130.00
57 Ghost Rider 150.00
58 American Air Forces 25.00
59 Best of the West 100.00
60 The U.S. Marines 25.00
61 Space Ace 350.00
62 Starr Flagg 250.00
63 Manhunt 175.00
64 Dogface Dooley 15.00
65 BP,American Air Forces 25.00
66 Best of the West 100.00
67 American Air Forces 25.00
68 U.S. Marines 25.00
69 Ghost Rider 160.00
70 Best of the West 75.00
71 Ghost Rider 150.00
72 U.S. Marines 25.00
73 BP,Thunda 75.00
74 BP,American Air Forces 20.00
75 Ghost Rider 150.00
76 Best of the West 75.00
77 Manhunt 110.00
78 BP,Thunda 80.00
79 American Air Forces 28.00
80 Ghost Rider 150.00
81 Best of the West 75.00
82 BP,Cave Girl 275.00
83 BP,Thunda 75.00
84 Ghost Rider 150.00
85 Best of the West 75.00
86 BP,Thunda 70.00
87 Best of the West 75.00
88 Bobby Benson's B-Bar-B . . 45.00
89 BP,Home Run,Stan Musial . 175.00
90 Red Hawk 60.00
91 BP,American Air Forces 20.00
92 Dream Book of Romance . . . 30.00
93 BP,Great Western 100.00
94 FF,White Indian 150.00
95 BP,Muggsy Mouse 15.00
96 BP,Cave Girl 200.00
97 Best of the West 70.00
98 Undercover Girl 275.00
99 Muggsy Mouse 12.00
100 Badmen of the West 125.00

101 FF,White Indian 135.00
101(a) FG, Dream Book of
Romance, Marlon Brando . . 100.00
103 BP,Best of the West 75.00
104 FF,White Indian 125.00
105 Great Western 60.00
106 Dream Book of Love 40.00
107 Hot Dog 25.00
108 BP,BC,Red Fox 75.00
109 Dream Book of Romance . . 25.00
110 Dream Book of Romance . . 25.00
111 I'm a Cop 65.00
112 Ghost Rider 110.00
113 BP,Great Western 60.00
114 Dream Book of Love 40.00
115 Hot Dog 18.00
116 BP,Cave Girl 170.00
117 White Indian 55.00
118 BP(c),Undercover Girl 250.00
119 Straight Arrow's Fury 75.00
120 Badmen of the West 75.00
121 Mysteries of the
Scotland Yard 75.00
122 Black Phantom 275.00
123 Dream Book of Love 25.00
124 Hot Dog 18.00
125 BP,Cave Girl 175.00
126 BP,I'm a Cop 55.00
127 BP,Great Western 60.00
128 BP,I'm a Cop 50.00
129 The Avenger 200.00
130 BP,Strongman 100.00
131 BP,The Avenger 150.00
132 Strongman 80.00
133 BP,The Avenger 150.00
134 Strongman 75.00
135 White Indian 50.00
136 Hot Dog 15.00
137 BP,Africa 125.00
138 BP,Avenger 150.00
139 BP,Strongman, 1955 . . . . . 85.00

ABBIE AN' SLATS
United Features Syndicate
March–Aug., 1948

1 RvB(c) 125.00
2 RvB(c) 100.00
3 RvB(c) 75.00
4 August, 1948 . . . . 50.00
N# 1940,Earlier Issue 275.00
N# 225.00

ABBOTT AND COSTELLO
St. John Publishing Co.
February, 1948

1 PP(c), Waltz Time 375.00
2 Jungle Girl and Snake(c) . . . 175.00
3 Outer Space cover 125.00
4 MD, Circus cover 90.00
5 MD,Bull Fighting cover 90.00
6 MD,Harem cover 90.00
7 MD,Opera cover 90.00
8 MD,Pirates cover 90.00
9 MD,Polar Bear cover 90.00
10 MD,PP(c),Son of Sinbad tale 170.00
11 MD 75.00
12 PP(c), Movie issue 70.00
13 Fire fighters cover 70.00
14 Bomb cover 70.00

All comics prices listed are for *Near Mint* condition.

GOLDEN AGE

15 Bubble Bath cover	70.00
16 thru 29 MD	@60.00
30 thru 39 MD	@50.00
40 MD,September, 1956	50.00
3-D #1, Nov. 1953	230.00

ACE COMICS
David McKay Publications
April, 1937

1 JM, F:Katzenjammer Kids	2,500.00
2 JM, A:Blondie	725.00
3 JM, A:Believe It Or Not	500.00
4 JM, F:Katzenjammer Kids	475.00
5 JM, A:Believe It Or Not	475.00
6 JM, A:Blondie	365.00
7 JM, A:Believe It Or Not	365.00
8 JM, A:Jungle Jim	365.00
9 JM, A:Blondie	365.00
10 JM, F:Katzenjammer Kids	285.00
11 I:The Phantom series	500.00
12 A:Blondie, Jungle Jim	265.00
13 A:Ripley's Believe It Or Not	240.00
14 A:Blondie, Jungle Jim	240.00
15 A:Blondie	235.00
16 F:Katzenjammer Kids	235.00
17 A:Blondie	235.00
18 A:Ripley's Believe It Or N8t	235.00
19 F:Katzenjammer Kids	225.00
20 A:Jungle Jim	225.00
21 A:Blondie	200.00
22 A:Jungle Jim	200.00
23 F:Katzenjammer Kids	200.00
24 A:Blondie	200.00
25	200.00
26 O:Prince Valiant	650.00
27 thru 36	@200.00
37 Krazy Kat Ends	130.00
38 thru 49	@100.00
50 thru 59	@90.00
60 thru 69	@85.00
70 thru 79	@80.00
80 thru 89	@75.00
90 thru 99	@60.00
100	75.00
101 thru 109	@60.00
110 thru 119	@52.00
120 thru 143	@50.00
144 Beginning of Phantom covers	80.00
145 thru 150	@70.00
151 October-November, 1949	75.00

ACES HIGH
E.C. Comics
March-April, 1955

1 GE(c)	200.00
2 GE(c)	125.00
3 GE(c)	100.00
4 GE(c)	100.00
5 GE(c)Nov.-Dec., 1955	100.00

ADVENTURES INTO DARKNESS
Standard Publications
August, 1952

5 JK(c), ATh	175.00
6 GT, JK	125.00
7 JK(c)	100.00
8 ATh	110.00
9 JK,ATh	140.00
10 JK,ATh,MSy	110.00
11 JK,ATh,MSy	110.00
12 JK,ATh,MYs	110.00
13 Cannibalism feature	125.00

Adventures into Darkness #10
© Standard Publ.

14	85.00

ADVENTURES INTO THE UNKNOWN!
American Comics Group
Fall 1948

1 FG, Haunted House cover	1,400.00
2 Haunted Island cover	550.00
3 AF, Sarcophagus cover	600.00
4 Monsters cover	250.00
5 Monsters cover	250.00
6 Giant Hands cover	185.00
7 Skeleton Pirate cover	175.00
8 Horror	175.00
9 Snow Monster	175.00
10 Red Bats	175.00
11 Death Shadow	175.00
12 OW(c)	125.00
13 OW(c),Dinosaur	150.00
14 OW(c),Cave	150.00
15 Red Demons	150.00
16	125.00
17 OW(c),The Thing Type	200.00
18 OW(c),Wolves	150.00
19 OW(c),Graveyard	125.00
20 OW(c),Graveyard	125.00
21 Bats and Dracula	125.00
22 Death	125.00
23 Bats	120.00
24	120.00
25	120.00
26	120.00
27 AW	200.00
28 thru 39	@100.00
40 thru 49	@90.00
50	85.00
51 Lazarus	200.00
52 Lazarus	200.00
53	175.00
54	175.00
55	175.00
56 Lazarus	175.00
57	175.00
58 Lazurus	175.00
59	150.00
60	65.00
61	65.00

62 thru 69	@60.00
70 thru 79	@35.00
80 thru 89	@30.00
90 thru 99	@35.00
100	32.00
101 thru 115	@30.00
116 AW,AT	28.00
117 thru 127	@25.00
128 AW,Forbidden Worlds	30.00
129 thru 152	@25.00
153 A:Magic Agent	25.00
154 O:Nemesis	30.00
155	20.00
156 A:Magic Agent	22.00
157 thru 174, Aug. 1967	@20.00

ADVENTURES IN WONDERLAND
Lev Gleason Publications
April, 1955

1	40.00
2	30.00
3	25.00
4	25.00
5	28.00

Adventures of Mighty Mouse #2
© St. John Publishing Co.

ADVENTURES OF MIGHTY MOUSE
St. John Publishing Co.
November, 1951

1 Mighty Mouse Adventures	175.00
2 Menace of the Deep	135.00
3 Storm Clouds of Mystery	100.00
4 Thought Control Machine	85.00
5 Jungle Peril	75.00
6 'The Vine of Destruction'	65.00
7 Space Ship(c)	65.00
8 Charging Alien(c)	65.00
9 Meteor(c)	55.00
10 Revolt at the Zoo"	55.00
11 Jungle(c)	55.00
12 A:Freezing Terror	55.00
13 A:Visitor from Outer Space	55.00
14 V:Cat	50.00
15	50.00

GOLDEN AGE

16	50.00
17	50.00
18 May, 1955	50.00

AGGIE MACK
Four Star Comics/
Superior Comics
January, 1948

1 AF,HR(c)	200.00
2 JK(c)	100.00
3 AF,JK(c)	90.00
4 AF	125.00
5 AF,JK(c)	100.00
6 AF,JK(c)	90.00
7 AF,Burt Lancaster on cover .	100.00
8 AF,JK(c), August 1949	80.00

BILL BARNES,
AMERICA'S AIR ACE
Street and Smith Publications
July, 1940

1 (Bill Barnes Comics)	650.00
2 Second Battle Valley Forge .	350.00
3 A:Aviation Cadets	300.00
4 Shotdown(c)	275.00
5 A:Air Warden, Danny Hawk .	225.00
6 A:Danny Hawk,RocketRodney	200.00
7 How to defeat the Japanese	200.00
8 Ghost Ship	200.00
9 Flying Tigers, John Wayne .	210.00
10 I:Roane Waring	200.00
11 Flying Tigers	200.00
12 War Workers	200.00

Becomes:

AIR ACE

2-1 Invades Germany	135.00
2-2 Jungle Warfare	90.00
2-3 A:The Four Musketeers . .	75.00
2-4 A:Russell Swann	75.00
2-5 A:The Four Musketeers . .	75.00
2-6 Raft(c)	60.00
2-7 BP, What's New In Science	60.00
2-8 XP-59	60.00
2-9 The Northrop P-61	60.00
2-10 NCG-14	60.00
2-11 Whip Lanch	60.00
2-12 PP(c)	60.00
3-1	45.00
3-2 Atom and It's Future	45.00
3-3 Flying in the Future	45.00
3-4 How Fast Can We Fly . . .	45.00
3-5 REv(c)	45.00
3-6 V:Wolves	45.00
3-7 BP(c), Vortex of Atom Bomb	125.00
3-8 February-March, 1947 . . .	50.00

AIRBOY
(see AIR FIGHTERS
COMICS)

AIR FIGHTERS COMICS
Hillman Periodicals
November, 1941

1 I:BlackCommander	
(only App)	1,500.00
2 O:Airboy A:Sky Wolf	2,500.00
3 O:Sky Wolf and Heap	1,200.00
4 A:Black Angel, Iron Ace . .	800.00
5 A:Sky Wolf and Iron Ace . .	650.00
6 Airboy's Bird Plane	600.00
7 Airboy battles Kultur	550.00
8 A:Skinny McGinty	525.00

Air Fighters #14 (2/2)
© *Hillman Periodicals*

9 A:Black Prince, Hatchet Man	500.00
10 I:The Stinger	500.00
11 Kida(c)	475.00
12 A:Misery	475.00
2-1 A:Flying Dutchman	475.00
2-2 I:Valkyrie	600.00
2-3 Story Panels cover	475.00
2-4 V:Japanese	475.00
2-5 Air Boy in Tokyo	475.00
2-6 'Dance of Death'	475.00
2-7 A:Valkyrie	475.00
2-8 Airboy Battles Japanese .	475.00
2-9 Airboy Battles Japanese .	475.00
2-10 O:Skywolf	550.00

Becomes:

AIRBOY

2-11	550.00
2-12 A:Valkyrie	350.00
3-1	300.00
3-2	225.00
3-3 Never published	
3-4 I:The Heap	250.00
3-5 Airboy	225.00
3-6 A:Valkyrie	225.00
3-7 AMc,Witch Hunt	225.00
3-8 A:Condor	235.00
3-9 O:The Heap	250.00
3-10	200.00
3-11	200.00
3-12 Airboy missing	250.00
4-1 Elephant in chains cover .	235.00
4-2 I:Rackman	150.00
4-3 Airboy profits on name . . .	150.00
4-4 S&K	160.00
4-5 S&K,The American Miracle	180.00
4-6 S&K,A:Heap and	
Flying Fool	180.00
4-7 S&K	180.00
4-8 S&K,Girlfriend captured . .	180.00
4-9 S&K,Airboy in quick sand .	180.00
4-10 S&K,A:Valkyrie	180.00
4-11 S&K,A:Frenchy	180.00
4-12 FBe	200.00
5-1 LSt	125.00
5-2 I:Wild Horse of Calabra . .	125.00
5-3	125.00

5-4 CI	125.00
5-5 Skull on cover	125.00
5-6	125.00
5-7	125.00
5-8 Bondage Cover	150.00
5-9 Zoi,Row	125.00
5-10 A:Valkrie,O:The Heap . .	135.00
5-11 Airboy vs. The Rats	125.00
5-12 BK,Rat Army captures	
Airboy	125.00
6-1	125.00
6-2	125.00
6-3	125.00
6-4 Airboy boxes	135.00
6-5 A:The Ice People	125.00
6-6	125.00
6-7 Airboy vs. Chemical Giant	125.00
6-8 O:The Heap	150.00
6-9	125.00
6-10	125.00
6-11	125.00
6-12	125.00
7-1	120.00
7-2 BP	120.00
7-3 BP	120.00
7-4 I:Monsters of the Ice	120.00
7-5 V:Monsters of the Ice	120.00
7-6	120.00
7-7 Mystery of the Sargasso	
Sea	120.00
7-8 A:Centaur	120.00
7-9 I:Men of the StarlightRobot	120.00
7-10 O:The Heap	120.00
7-11	120.00
7-12 Airboy visits India	120.00
8-1 BP,A:Outcast and Polo	
Bandits	100.00
8-2 BP,Suicide Dive cover . . .	100.00
8-3 I:The Living Fuse	100.00
8-4 A:Death Merchants o/t Air .	120.00
8-5 A:Great Plane from Nowhere	100.00
8-6	100.00
8-7	100.00
8-8	100.00
8-9	100.00
8-10 A:Mystery Walkers	100.00
8-11	100.00
8-12	120.00
9-1	100.00
9-2 A:Valkyrie	90.00
9-3 A:Heap (cover)	90.00
9-4 A:Water Beast, Frog Headed	
Riders	100.00
9-5 A:Heap vs.Man of Moonlight	90.00
9-6 Heap cover	90.00
9-7 Heap cover	90.00
9-8 Heap cover	100.00
9-9	100.00
9-10 Space cover	100.00
9-11	90.00
9-12 Heap cover	90.00
10-1 Heap cover	90.00
10-2 Ships on Space	90.00
10-3	90.00
10-4 May, 1953	90.00

AL CAPP'S
DOG PATCH COMICS
Toby Press
June, 1949

1	175.00
2 A:Daisy	125.00
3	110.00
4 December, 1949	110.00

AL CAPP'S SHMOO
Toby Press
July, 1949
1 100 Trillion Schmoos 250.00
2 Super Shmoo(c) 175.00
3 . . . . 175.00
4 . . . . 150.00
5 April, 1950 . . . . 150.00

AL CAPP'S WOLF GAL
Toby Press
1951
1 Pin-Up 225.00
2 1952 . . . . 200.00

ALL-FAMOUS CRIME
Star Publications
May, 1951
8 LbC(c) 75.00
9 LbC(c) 125.00
10 LbC(c) 60.00
4 LbC(c) 60.00
5 LbC(c) 60.00
Becomes:

ALL-FAMOUS POLICE CASES
6 LbC(c) 75.00
7 LbC(c) 65.00
8 LbC(c) 60.00
9 LbC(c) 55.00
10 thru 15 LbC(c) . . . . @50.00
16 September, 1954 . . . . 60.00

ALL GOOD COMICS
R. W. Voight/Fox Publ. /St. John Publ.
1 1944 . . . . 125.00
1 1946 . . . . 100.00
N# 1949 . . . . 450.00

ALL GREAT COMICS
(see DAGGER, DESERT HAWK)

ALL HERO COMICS
Fawcett Publications
March, 1943
1 A:Capt. Marvel Jr.,Capt. Midnight,Ibis, Golden Arrow and Spy Smasher 1,200.00

ALL HUMOR COMICS
Comic Favorites, Inc. (Quality Comics)
Spring 1946
1 . . . . 125.00
2 PG 65.00
3 I:Kelly Poole 30.00
4 thru 7 . . . . @25.00
8 PG 30.00
9 . . . . 30.00
10 . . . . 30.00
11 thru 17 . . . . @22.00

ALL LOVE ROMANCES
(see SCREAM COMICS)

ALL NEGRO COMICS
1 . . . . 2,500.00

All-New Comics #3
© Family Comics/Harvey Publ.

ALL-NEW COMICS
Family Comics (Harvey Publ.)
January, 1943
1 A:Steve Case, Johnny Rebel I:Detective Shane 1,800.00
2 JKu,O:Scarlet Phantom 700.00
3 . . . . 550.00
4 AdH 550.00
5 Flash Gordon 500.00
6 I:Boy Heroes and Red Blazer 500.00
7 JKu,AS(c),A:Black Cat & Zebra 500.00
8 JKu,A:Shock Gibson 500.00
9 JKu,A:Black Cat 500.00
10 JKu,A:Zebra 450.00
11 A:Man in Black, Girl Commandos 450.00
12 JKu 450.00
13 Stuntman by S&K, A:Green Hornet&cover 475.00
14 A:Green Hornet 450.00
15 Smaller size, Distributed by Mail, March-April, 1947 . 400.00

ALL TOP COMICS
William H. Wise Co.
1944
N# 132pgs.,A:Capt. V,Red Robbins 225.00

ALL TOP COMICS
Fox Features Syndicate
Spring 1946
1 A:Cosmo Cat, Flash Rabbit . 100.00
2 . . . . 50.00
3 . . . . 40.00
4 . . . . 40.00
5 . . . . 40.00
6 . . . . 40.00
7 . . . . 40.00
7a 85.00
8 JKa(c),I:BlueBeetle 1,300.00
9 JKa(c),A:Rulah 700.00
10 JKa(c),A:Rulah 750.00
11 A:Rulah,Blue Beetle 600.00

12 A:Rulah,Jo Jo,Blue Beetle . 600.00
13 A:Rulah 550.00
14 A:Rulah,Blue Beetle 700.00
15 A:Rulah 550.00
16 A:Rulah,Blue Beetle 500.00
17 A:Rulah,Blue Beetle 500.00
18 A:Dagar,Jo Jo 400.00
Green Publ.
6 1957 . . . . 20.00
6 1958 . . . . 20.00
6 1959 . . . . 20.00
6 1959 . . . . 20.00
6 Supermouse cover 20.00

ALLEY OOP
Argo Publications
November, 1955
1 . . . . 100.00
2 . . . . 75.00
3 March, 1956 . . . . 75.00

AMAZING ADVENTURES
Ziff-Davis Publ. Co.
1950
1 WW, Asteroid Witch 500.00
2 Masters of Living Flame . . . 225.00
3 The Evil Men Do 225.00
4 Invasion of the Love Robots 225.00
5 Secret of the Crater-Men . . . 225.00
6 Man Who Killed a World . . . 250.00

AMAZING GHOST STORIES
(See: WEIRD HORRORS)

AMAZING-MAN COMICS
Centaur Publications
September, 1939
5 BEv,O:Amazing Man 15,000.00
6 BEv,B:The Shark 2,500.00
7 BEv,I:Magician From Mars . 1,500.00
8 BEv 1,200.00
9 BEv 1,200.00
10 BEv 1,000.00
11 BEv,I:Zardi 900.00
12 SG(c) 900.00
13 SG(c) 900.00
14 B:Reef Kinkaid, Dr. Hypo . 700.00
15 A:Zardi 550.00
16 Mighty Man's powers revealed 600.00
17 A:Dr. Hypo 550.00
18 BLb(a),SG(c) 550.00
19 BLb(a),SG(c) 550.00
20 BLb(a),SG(c) 550.00
21 O:Dash Dartwell 565.00
22 A:Silver Streak, The Voice . 550.00
23 I&O:Tommy the Amazing Kid 600.00
24 B:King of Darkness,Blue Lady 550.00
25 A:Meteor Marvin 900.00
26 A:Meteor Marvin,Electric Ray February, 1942 . . . . 750.00

AMAZING MYSTERY FUNNIES
Centaur Publications
1938
1 Skyrocket Steele in the Year X 2,700.00
2 WE,Skyrocket Steele 1,300.00
3 . . . . 500.00
(#4) WE,bondage (c) 700.00

GOLDEN AGE

Amazing Mystery Funnies #16
© Centaur Publications

2-1(#5) 650.00
2-2(#6) Drug use 550.00
2-3(#7) Air Sub DX 550.00
2-4(#8) 550.00
2-5(#9) 700.00
2-6(#10) 550.00
2-7(#11) scarce 2,700.00
2-8(#12) Speed Centaur 1,000.00
2-9(#13) 600.00
2-10(#14) 600.00
2-11(#15) 600.00
2-12(#16) BW,I:Space Patrol . 1,400.00
3-1(#17) I:Bullet 500.00
18 . . . . 500.00
19 BW,Space Patrol 750.00
20 . . . . 500.00
21 BW,Space Patrol 750.00
22 BW,Space Patrol 750.00
23 BW,Space Patrol 750.00
24 BW,Space Patrol 750.00

AMAZING WILLIE MAYS
Famous Funnies
1954
1 Willie Mays(c) 550.00

AMERICAN LIBRARY
David McKay Publ.
1943
(#1) Thirty Seconds Over
 Tokyo, movie adapt. 250.00
(#2) Guadalcanal Diary 175.00
3 Look to the Mountain 100.00
4 The Case of the Crooked
 Candle (Perry Mason) 100.00
5 Duel in the Sun 100.00
6 Wingate's Raiders 110.00

AMERICA'S BEST
COMICS
Nedor/Better/Standard
Publications
February 1942
1 B:Black Terror, Captain Future,
 The Liberator,Doc Strange 1,500.00
2 O:American Eagle 600.00

3 B:Pyroman 500.00
4 A:Doc Strange, Jimmy Cole . 350.00
5 A:Lone Eagle, Capt. Future . 325.00
6 A:American Crusader 300.00
7 A:Hitler,Hirohito 450.00
8 The Liberator ends 325.00
9 ASh(c) 350.00
10 ASh(c) 300.00
11 ASh(c) 300.00
12 Red Cross cover 300.00
13 . . . . 300.00
14 Last American Eagle app . . 300.00
15 ASh(c) 275.00
16 ASh(c) 285.00
17 Doc Strange carries football 275.00
18 Bondage cover 275.00
19 ASh(c) 275.00
20 vs. the Black Market 275.00
21 Infinity cover 250.00
22 A:Captain Future 250.00
23 B:Miss Masque 325.00
24 Bondage cover 325.00
25 A:Sea Eagle 250.00
26 A:The Phantom Detective . . 250.00
27 ASh(c) 250.00
28 A:Commando Cubs,
 Black Terror 250.00
29 A:Doc Strange 250.00
30 ASh(c) 250.00
31 July, 1949 . . . . 250.00

AMERICA'S BIGGEST
COMICS BOOK
William H. Wise
1944
1 196 pgs. A:Grim Reaper, Zudo,
 Silver Knight, Thunderhoof,
 Jocko and Socko,Barnaby
 Beep,Commando Cubs 300.00

AMERICA'S GREATEST
COMICS
Fawcett Publications
Fall 1941
1 MRa(c),A:Capt. Marvel,
 Bulletman,Spy Smasher and
 Minute Man 2,200.00
2 F:Capt. Marvel 1,200.00
3 F:Capt. Marvel 800.00
4 B:Commando Yank 600.00
5 Capt.Marvel in "Lost Lighting" 600.00
6 Capt.Marvel fires Machine
 Gun 500.00
7 A:Balbo the Boy Magician . . 500.00
8 A:Capt.Marvel Jr.,Golden
 Arrow,Summer 1943 . . . . . . 500.00

AMERICA IN ACTION
Dell Publishing Co.
1942
1 . . . . 100.00

ANDY COMICS
(see SCREAM COMICS)

ANGEL
Dell Publishing Co.
August, 1954
(1) *see Dell Four Color #576*
2 . . . . 15.00
3 thru 16 . . . . @12.00

ANIMAL ANTICS
Dell Publishing Co.
1946
1 B:Racoon Kids 275.00
2 . . . . 150.00
3 thru 10 . . . . @90.00
11 thru 23 . . . . @50.00

ANIMAL COMICS
Dell Publishing Co.
1942
1 WK,Pogo 1,000.00
2 Uncle Wiggily(c),A:Pogo . . 450.00
3 Muggin's Mouse(c),A:Pogo . 325.00
4 Uncle Wiggily(c) 250.00
5 Uncle Wiggily(c) 325.00
6 Uncle Wiggily 200.00
7 Uncle Wiggily 200.00
8 Pogo 250.00
9 War Bonds(c),A:Pogo 250.00
10 Pogo 250.00
11 Pogo 175.00
12 Pogo 175.00
13 Pogo 175.00
14 Pogo 175.00
15 Pogo 175.00
16 Uncle Wiggily 100.00
17 Pogo(c) 125.00
18 Pogo(c) 125.00
19 Pogo(c) 125.00
20 Pogo 100.00
21 Pogo(c) 125.00
22 Pogo 75.00
23 Pogo 75.00
24 Pogo(c) 85.00
25 Pogo(c) 85.00
26 Pogo(c) 85.00
27 Pogo(c) 65.00
28 Pogo(c) 65.00
29 Pogo(c) 65.00
30 Pogo(c) 65.00

ANIMAL FABLES
E.C. Comics
July-August 1946
1 B:Korky Kangaroo,Freddy Firefly
 Petey Pig and Danny Demon 275.00
2 B:Aesop Fables 150.00
3 . . . . 125.00
4 . . . . 125.00
5 Firefly vs. Red Ants 125.00
6 . . . . 125.00
7 O:Moon Girls,Nov.-Dec.1947 425.00

ANIMAL FAIR
Fawcett Publications
March 1946
1 B:Captain Marvel Bunny,
 Sir Spot 150.00
2 A:Droopy, Colonel Walrus . . 75.00
3 . . . . 35.00
4 A:Kid Gloves, Cub Reporter . 35.00
5 thru 7 . . . . 35.00
8 . . . . 25.00
9 . . . . 25.00
10 . . . . 25.00
11 February 1947 . . . . 25.00

ANNIE OAKLEY & TAGG
Dell Publishing Co.
1953
(1) *see Dell Four Color #438*
(2) *see Dell Four Color #481*

GOLDEN AGE

(3) *see Dell Four Color #575*

4	125.00
5	90.00
6 thru 10	@75.00
11 thru 18	@50.00

Archie Comics #28
© Archie Publications

ARCHIE COMICS
MLJ Magazines
Winter, 1942-43

1 I:Jughead & Veronica	9,000.00
2	2,000.00
3	1,500.00
4	900.00
5	850.00
6	650.00
7 thru 11	@600.00
12 thru 15	@450.00
16 thru 19	@400.00

Archie Publications

20	400.00
21	300.00
22 thru 31	@275.00
32 thru 42	@150.00
43 thru 50	@100.00
51 thru 60	@75.00
61 thru 70	@50.00
71 thru 80	@40.00
81 thru 99	@30.00
100	50.00
101	25.00
102 thru 115	@15.00
116 thru 130	@12.00
131 thru 145	@10.00
146 thru 160	@7.50
161 thru 180	@5.00
181 thru 200	@4.00
201 thru 250	@3.00
251 thru 280	@2.00
281 thru 389	@1.50

ARCHIE'S GIANT SERIES MAGAZINE
Archie Publications
1954

1	900.00
2	550.00

3	400.00
4	350.00
5	350.00
6 thru 10	@250.00
11 thru 20	@200.00
21 thru 29	@125.00
30 thru 35	@45.00
136 thru 141	@45.00
142	32.00
143 thru 160	@12.00
161 thru 199	@8.00
200	5.00
201 thru 250	@2.50
251 thru 299	@1.50
300 thru 500	@1.00

ARCHIE'S GIRLS BETTY AND VERONICA
Archie Publications
1950

1	1,100.00
2	500.00
3	350.00
4	250.00
5	240.00
6 thru 10	@200.00
11 thru 15	@150.00
16 thru 20	@100.00
21	90.00
22 thru 29	@85.00
30 thru 40	@60.00
41 thru 50	@50.00
51 thru 60	@40.00
61 thru 70	@35.00
71 thru 80	@30.00
81 thru 90	@25.00
91 thru 99	@20.00
100	25.00
101 thru 120	@12.00
121 thru 140	@10.00
141 thru 160	@7.00
161 thru 180	@3.00
181 thru 199	@2.00
200	3.00
201 thru 220	@2.00
221 thru 240	@1.50
241 thru 347	@1.00

ARCHIE'S JOKE BOOK MAGAZINE
Archie Publications
1953

1	650.00
2	350.00
3	250.00
15 thru 19	@165.00
20 thru 25	@120.00
26 thru 35	@90.00
36 thru 40	@60.00
41 1st NA art	125.00
42 & 43	60.00
44 thru 48 NA	@70.00
49 thru 60	@20.00
61 thru 70	@15.00
71 thru 80	@10.00
81 thru 100	@5.00
101 thru 200	@2.50
201 thru 288	@1.00

ARCHIE'S MECHANICS
Archie Publications
September, 1954

1	550.00

2	400.00
3	300.00

ARCHIE'S PAL, JUGHEAD
Archie Publications
1949

1	900.00
2	450.00
3	275.00
4	250.00
5	250.00
6	200.00
7 thru 10	@175.00
11 thru 15	@125.00
16 thru 20	@85.00
21 thru 30	@65.00
31 thru 39	@50.00
40 thru 50	@35.00
51 thru 60	@30.00
61 thru 70	@25.00
71 thru 80	@20.00
81 thru 99	@15.00
100	17.00
101 thru 126	@10.00

Archie's Pals 'N' Gals #3
© Archie Publications

ARCHIE'S PALS 'N' GALS
Archie Publications
1952 thru 53

1	550.00
2	300.00
3	200.00
4	135.00
5	135.00
6	80.00
7	80.00
8 thru 10	@75.00
11 thru 15	@50.00
16 thru 20	@35.00
21 thru 30	@20.00
31 thru 40	@20.00
41 thru 50	@12.00
51 thru 60	@10.00
61 thru 70	@7.00
71 thru 80	@5.00
81 thru 99	@2.50

GOLDEN AGE

100 . . . . 3.00	
101 thru 120 . . . . @2.00	
121 thru 160 . . . . @1.50	
161 thru 224 . . . . @1.00	

ARCHIE'S RIVAL REGGIE
Archie Publications
1950

1 . . . . 550.00	
2 . . . . 275.00	
3 . . . . 200.00	
4 . . . . 175.00	
5 . . . . 175.00	
6 . . . . 150.00	
7 thru 10 . . . . @125.00	
11 thru 13 . . . . @75.00	
14 thru 15 . . . . @65.00	
16 August, 1954 . . . . 70.00	

ARMY & NAVY COMICS
(see SUPERSNIPE COMICS)

ARROW, THE
Centaur Publications
October 1940

1 B:Arrow 2,200.00
2 BLB(c) 900.00
3 O:Dash Dartwell,Human
  Meteor, Rainbow, Bondage
  cover, October, 1941 . . . . . 800.00

ATOMAN
Spark Publications
February 1946

1 JRo,MMe,O:Atoman,A:Kid
  Crusaders 350.00
2 JRo,MMe 250.00

ATOMIC COMICS
Green Publishing Co.
January, 1946

1 S&S,A:Radio Squad, Barry
  O'Neal 1,000.00
2 MB,A:Inspector Dayton, Kid
  Kane 450.00
3 MB,A:Zero Ghost Detective   300.00
4 JKa(c), July-August, 1946 . . 275.00

ATOMIC COMICS
Daniels Publications
1946 (Reprints)

1 A:Rocketman,Yankee Boy,
  Bondage cover,rep. 225.00

ATOMIC MOUSE
**Capital Stories/
Charlton Comics**
March, 1953

1 AFa,O:Atomic Mouse 125.00
2 AFa,Ice Cream cover 50.00
3 AFa,Genie and Magic
  Carpet cover 35.00
4 AFa 35.00
5 AFa,A:Timmy the Timid Ghost 35.00
6 thru 10 Funny Animal . . . . @32.00
11 thru 14 Funny Animal . . . . @20.00
15 A:Happy the Marvel Bunny . . 25.00
16 Funny Animal,Giant 27.00
17 thru 30 Funny Animal . . . . @20.00
31 thru 36 Funny Animal . . . . @15.00
37 A:Atom the Cat 15.00

38 thru 40 Funny Animal . . . . @12.00	
41 thru 53 Funny Animal . . . . @10.00	
54 June, 1963 . . . . 10.00	

ATOMIC THUNDER BOLT, THE
Regor Company
February, 1946

1 I:Atomic Thunderbolt,
  Mr. Murdo 375.00

AUTHENTIC POLICE CASES
St. John Publ. Co.
1948

1 Hale the Magician 275.00
2 Lady Satan, Johnny Rebel . . 150.00
3 A:Avenger 300.00
4 Masked Black Jack 175.00
5 JCo 175.00
6 JCo,MB(c) 300.00
7 thru 10 . . . . @125.00
11 thru 15 . . . . @100.00
16 thru 23 . . . . @75.00
24 thru 28 . . . . @125.00
29 thru 38 . . . . @45.00

AVIATION AND MODEL BUILDING
(see TRUE AVIATION PICTURE STORIES)

AVON ONE-SHOTS
Avon Periodicals
1949-1953
{Listed in Alphabetical Order}

1 Atomic Spy Cases 200.00
N# WW,Attack on Planet Mars . 550.00
1 Batcholer's Diary 150.00
1 Badmen of the West 200.00
N# Badmen of Tombstone 75.00
1 Behind Prison Bars 150.00
2 Betty and Her Steady 35.00
N# Blackhawk Indian
  Tomahawk War 75.00
1 Blazing Sixguns 75.00
1 Butch Cassidy 80.00
N# Chief Crazy Horse 100.00
N# FF,Chief Victorio's
  Apache Massacre 300.00
N# City of the Living Dead 275.00
1 Complete Romance 150.00
N# Custer's Last Fight 75.00
1 Dalton Boys 70.00
N# Davy Crockett 70.00
N# The Dead Who Walk 275.00
1 Diary of Horror,Bondage(c) . 275.00
N# WW,An Earth Man on Venus 900.00
1 Eerie, bondage (c) 650.00
1 Escape from Devil's Island . 150.00
N# Fighting Daniel Boone 80.00
N# For a Night of Love 125.00
1 WW,Flying Saucers 450.00
N# Flying Saucers. 400.00
1 Going Steady with Betty 60.00
N# Hooded Menace 275.00
N# King of the Badmen
  of Deadwood 80.00
1 King Solomon's Mines 200.00
N# Kit Carson &
  Blackfeet Warriors 50.00
N# Last of the Comanches 75.00

Avon One-Shots (Batchelor's Diary) #1
© Avon Periodicals

N# Masked Bandit 75.00
1 WW,Mask of Dr. Fu Manchu 600.00
N# Night of Mystery 175.00
1 Outlaws of the Wild West . . 150.00
1 Out of this World 475.00
N# Pancho Villa 125.00
1 Phantom Witch Doctor 200.00
1 Pixie Puzzle Rocket
  to Adventureland 50.00
1 Prison Riot,drugs 150.00
N# Red Mountain Featuring
  Quantrell's Raiders 125.00
N# Reform School Girl 800.00
1 Robotmen of the Lost Planet 700.00
N# WW(c),Rocket to the Moon . 750.00
N# JKu,Secret Diary of
  Eerie Adventures 1,100.00
1 Sheriff Bob Dixon's
  Chuck Wagon 65.00
1 Sideshow 135.00
1 JKu,Sparkling Love 80.00
N# Speedy Rabbit 30.00
1 Teddy Roosevelt &
  His Rough Riders 110.00
N# The Underworld Story 125.00
N# The Unknown Man 130.00
1 War Dogs of the U.S. Army . . 75.00
N# White Chief of the
  Pawnee Indians 65.00
N# Women to Love 150.00

BABE
Prize/Headline Feature
June-July 1948

1 BRo,A;Boddy Rogers 120.00
2 BRo,same 75.00
3 Bro,same 50.00
4 thru 9 BRo,same . . . . @35.00

BABE RUTH SPORTS COMICS
Harvey Publications
April, 1949

1 BP 350.00
2 BP 250.00
3 BP,Joe Dimaggio(c) 200.00
4 BP,Bob Feller(c) 175.00

GOLDEN AGE

5 BP,Football(c)	175.00
6 BP,Basketball(c)	175.00
7 BP	175.00
8 BP	175.00
9 BP, Stan Musial(c)	150.00
11 February, 1951	150.00

BANNER COMICS
Ace Magazines
September, 1941

3 B:Captain Courageous, Lone Warrior	750.00
4 JM(c),Flag(c)	500.00
5	450.00

Becomes:
CAPTAIN COURAGEOUS COMICS

6 I:The Sword	450.00

BARNYARD COMICS
Animated Cartoons
June, 1944

1 (fa)	80.00
2 (fa)	40.00
3 (fa)	25.00
4 (fa)	25.00
5 (fa)	25.00
6 thru 12 (fa)	@22.00
13 FF(ti)	30.00
14 FF(ti)	30.00
15 FF(ti)	30.00
16	35.00
17 FF(ti)	30.00
18 FF,FF(ti)	75.00
19 FF,FF(ti)	75.00
20 FF,FF(ti)	75.00
21 FF(ti)	30.00
22 FF,FF(ti)	75.00
23 FF(ti)	30.00
24 FF,FF(ti)	75.00
25 FF,FF(ti)	75.00
26 FF(ti)	30.00
27 FF(ti)	30.00
28	20.00
29 FF(ti)	30.00
30 and 31	@20.00

Becomes:
DIZZY DUCK

32 thru 39	@15.00

BASEBALL COMICS
Will Eisner Productions
Spring, 1949

1 A:Rube Rocky	600.00

BASEBALL HEROS
Fawcett Publications
1952

N# Babe Ruth cover	650.00

BASEBALL THRILLS
Ziff-Davis Publ. Co.
Summer 1951

10 Bob Feller Predicts Pennant Winners	300.00
2 BP, Yogi Berra story	200.00
3 EK, Joe DiMaggio story, Summer 1952	250.00

BATTLEFIELD ACTION
(see DYNAMITE)

BEANY & CECIL
Dell Publishing Co.
January, 1952

1	140.00
2	100.00
3	100.00
4	100.00
5	100.00

BEN BOWIE & HIS MOUNTAIN MEN
Dell Publishing Co.
1952

(1) see Dell Four Color #443
(2 thru 6) see Dell Four Color

7	15.00
8 thru 10	@15.00
11 I:Yellow Hair	17.00
12	12.00
13	12.00
14	12.00
15	12.00
16	12.00
17	12.00

BEST COMICS
Better Publications
November, 1939

1 B:Red Mask	550.00
2 A:Red Mask, Silly Willie	350.00
3 A:Red Mask	350.00
4 Cannibalism story, February, 1940	400.00

BEWARE
(see CAPTAIN SCIENCE)

BIG CHIEF WAHOO
Eastern Color Printing
July, 1942

1	300.00
2 BWa(c),Three Ring Circus	150.00
3 BWa(c)	100.00
4 BWa(c)	100.00
5 BWa(c),Wild West Rodeo	100.00
6 A:Minnie-Ha-Cha	75.00
7	50.00
8	50.00
9	50.00
10	60.00
11 thru 22	@40.00
23 1943	40.00

BIG SHOT COMICS
Columbia Comics Group
May, 1940

1 MBi,OW,Skyman,B:The Face, Joe Palooka, Rocky Ryan	1,500.00
2 MBi,OW,Marvelo cover	550.00
3 MBi,Skyman cover	450.00
4 MBi,OW,Joe Palooka cover	400.00
5 MBi,Joe Palooka cover	375.00
6 MBi,Joe Palooka cover	325.00
7 MBi,Elect Joe Palooka and Skyman	300.00
8 MBi,Joe Palooka and Skyman dress as Santa	300.00
9 MBi,Skyman	325.00
10 MBi,Skyman	325.00
11 MBi	250.00
12 MBi,OW	250.00
13 MBi,OW	250.00

Big Shot Comics #20
© Columbia Comics Group

14 MBi,OW,O:Sparky Watts	250.00
15 MBi,OW,O:The Cloak	300.00
16 MBi,OW	200.00
17 MBi(c),OW	200.00
18 MBi,OW	200.00
19 MBi,OW,The Face cover	210.00
20 MBi,OW,OW(c),Skyman cov.	210.00
21 MBi,OW,A:Raja the Arabian Knight	175.00
22 MBi,OW,Joe Palooka cover	175.00
23 MBi,OW,Sparky Watts cover	150.00
24 MBi,OW,Uncle Sam cover	175.00
25 MBi,OW,Sparky Watts cover	150.00
26 MBi,OW,Devildog cover	175.00
27 MBi,OW,Skyman cover	185.00
28 MBi,OW,Hitler cover	225.00
29 MBi,OW,I:Captain Yank	185.00
30 MBi,OW,Santa cover	150.00
31 MBi,OW,Sparky Watts cover	125.00
32 MBi,OW,B:Vic Jordan newspaper reps	150.00
33 MBi,OW,Sparky Watts cover	110.00
34 MBi,OW	125.00
35 MBi,OW	125.00
36 MBi,OW,Sparky Watts cover	110.00
37 MBi,OW	125.00
38 MBi,Uncle Slap Happy cover	110.00
39 MBi,Uncle Slap Happy cover	110.00
40 MBi,Joe Palooka Happy cover	110.00
41 MBi,Joe Palooka	100.00
42 MBi,Joe Palooka parachutes	100.00
43 MBi,V:Hitler	110.00
44 MBi,Slap Happy cover	100.00
45 MBi,Slap Happy cover	100.00
46 MBi,Uncle Sam cover,V:Hitler	110.00
47 MBi,Uncle Slap Happy cover	100.00
48 MBi	100.00
49 MBi	75.00
50 MBi,O:The Face	75.00
51 MBi	75.00
52 MBi,E:Vic Jordan (Hitler cov) newspaper reps	100.00
53 MBi,Uncle Slap Happy cover	75.00
54 MBi,Uncle Slap Happy cover	75.00
55 MBi,Happy Easter cover	75.00
56 MBi	75.00
57 MBi	75.00
58 MBi	75.00

All comics prices listed are for *Near Mint* condition.

59 MBi,Slap Happy	75.00
60 MBi,Joe Palooka	60.00
61 MBi	55.00
62 MBi	55.00
63 MBi	55.00
64 MBi,Slap Happy	50.00
65 MBi,Slap Happy	50.00
66 MBi,Slap Happy	50.00
67 MBi	50.00
68 MBi,Joe Palooka	50.00
69 MBi	50.00
70 MBi,OW,Joe Palooka cover	50.00
71 MBi,OW	55.00
72 MBi,OW	55.00
73 MBi,OW,The Face cover	55.00
74 MBi,OW	55.00
75 MBi,OW,Polar Bear swim club cover	55.00
76 thru 80 MBi,OW	@45.00
81 thru 84 MBi,OW	@40.00
85 MBi,OW,Dixie Dugan cover	42.00
86 thru 95 MBi,OW	@40.00
96 MBi,OW,X-Mas cover	40.00
97 thru 99 MBi,OW	@40.00
100 MBi,OW,Special issue	45.00
101 thru 103 MBi,OW	@40.00
104 MBi, August, 1949	45.00

BIG-3
Fox Features Syndicate
Fall 1940

1 B:BlueBeetle,Flame,Samson	1,500.00
2 A:BlueBeetle,Flame,Samson	650.00
3 same	500.00
4 same	450.00
5 same	450.00
6 E:Samson, bondage cover	350.00
7 A:V-Man, January, 1942	325.00

BILL BARNES, AMERICA'S AIR ACE
(see AIR ACE)

BILL BOYD WESTERN
Fawcett Publications
February, 1950

1 B:Bill Boyd, MidnitePh(c)	375.00
2 P(c)	200.00
3 B:Ph(c)	150.00
4	100.00
5	100.00
6	100.00
7	75.00
8	75.00
9	75.00
10	75.00
11	70.00
12	70.00
13	70.00
14	70.00
15 thru 21	@65.00
22 E:Ph(c)	65.00
23 June, 1952	75.00

BILL STERN'S SPORTS BOOK
Approved Comics
Spring-Summer, 1951

1 Ewell Blackwell	150.00
2	100.00
2-2 EK Giant	125.00

BILLY THE KID ADVENTURE MAGAZINE
Toby Press
October, 1950

1 AW,FF,AW(c),FF(c)	225.00
2 Photo cover	50.00
3 AW,FF	250.00
4	30.00
5	30.00
6 FF,Photo cover	60.00
7 Photo cover	30.00
8	30.00
9 HK Pot-Shot Pete	60.00
10	30.00
11	30.00
12	30.00
13 HK	35.00
14 AW,FF	60.00
15 thru 21	@25.00
22 AW,FF	30.00
23 thru 29	@22.00
30 1955	25.00

BINGO COMICS
Howard Publications
1945

1	125.00

Black Cat #5 © Harvey Publications

BLACK CAT COMICS
Harvey Publications
(Home Comics)
June-July, 1946

1 JKu	450.00
2 JKu,JSm(c)	250.00
3 JSm(c)	200.00
4 B:Red Demon	175.00
5 S&K	250.00
6 S&K,A:Scarlet Arrow, O:Red Demon	250.00
7 S&K	250.00
8 S&K,B:Kerry Drake	200.00
9 S&K,O:Stuntman	250.00
10 JK,JSm	150.00
11	150.00
12 "Ghost Town Terror"	150.00
13 thru 16 LEI	@125.00
17 A:Mary Worth, Invisible	

Scarlet	125.00
18 LEI	125.00
19 LEI	125.00
20 A:Invisible Scarlet	125.00
21 LEI	125.00
22 LEI thru 26	@125.00
27 X-Mas issue	150.00
28 I:Kit,A:Crimson Raider	150.00
29 Black Cat bondage cover	150.00

Becomes:
BLACK CAT MYSTERY

30 RP,Black Cat(c)	150.00
31 RP	100.00
32 BP,RP,Bondage cover	120.00
33 BP,RP,Electrocution cover	135.00
34 BP,RP	100.00
35 BP,RP,OK, Atomic Storm	125.00
36 RP	150.00
37 RP	100.00
38 RP	100.00
39 RP	125.00
40 RP	100.00
41	100.00
42	100.00
43 BP	100.00
44 BP,HN,JkS,Oil Burning cover	125.00
45 BP,HN,Classic cover	150.00
46 BP,HN	110.00
47 BP,HN	110.00
48 BP,HN	110.00
49 BP,HN	110.00
50 BP,Rotting Face	200.00
51 BP,HN,MMe	110.00
52 BP	75.00
53 BP	75.00

Becomes:
BLACK CAT WESTERN

54 A:Black Cat & Story	100.00
55 A:Black Cat	75.00
56 same	75.00

Becomes:
BLACK CAT MYSTIC

58 JK,Starts Comic Code	90.00
59 KB	85.00
60 JK	85.00
61 HN	75.00
62	50.00
63 JK	50.00
64 JK	65.00
65 April, 1963	65.00

BLACK DIAMOND WESTERN
(see DESPERADO)

UNCLE SAM QUARTERLY
Quality Comics Group
Fall, 1941

1 BE,LF(c),JCo	2,500.00
2 LG(c),BE	1,000.00
3 GT,GT(c)	700.00
4 GT,GF(c)	600.00
5 RC,GT	550.00
6 GT	500.00
7 Hitler, Tojo, Mussolini	650.00
8	@525.00

Becomes:
BLACKHAWK
Comic Magazines
Winter, 1944

9 Bait for a Death Trap	2,500.00
10 RC	850.00

All comics prices listed are for *Near Mint* condition.

11 RC 600.00
12 Flies to thrilling adventure . . 500.00
13 Blackhawk Stalks Danger . . 500.00
14 BWa 475.00
15 Patrols the Universe 475.00
16 RC,BWa,Huddles for Action 450.00
17 BWa,Prepares for Action . . 450.00
18 RC,RC(c),BWa,One for All
    and All for One 425.00
19 RC,RC(c),BWa,Calls
    for Action 425.00
20 RC,RC(c),BWa,Smashes
    Rugoth the ruthless God . . . 425.00
21 BWa,Battles Destiny
    Written n Blood 350.00
22 RC,RC(c),BWa,Fear battles
    Death and Destruction 350.00
23 RC,RC(c),BWa,Batters
    Down Oppression 350.00
24 RC,RC(c),BWa 350.00
25 RC,RC(c),BWa,V:The Evil
    of Mung 350.00

Blackhawk #14 © Comic Magazines

26 RC,RC(c),V:Menace of a
    Sunken World 325.00
27 BWa,Destroys a War-Mad
    Munitions Magnate 325.00
28 BWa,Defies Destruction in the
    Battle of the Test Tube 325.00
29 BWa,Tale of the Basilisk
    Supreme Chief 325.00
30 BWa,RC,RC(c),The Menace
    of the Meteors 325.00
31 BWa,RC,RC(c),JCo,Treachery
    among the Blackhawks 250.00
32 BWa,RC,RC(c),A:Delya,
    Flying Fish 250.00
33 RC,RC(c),BWa,
    A:The Mockers 250.00
34 BWa,A:Tana,Mavis 250.00
35 BWa,I:Atlo,Strongest Man
    on Earth 250.00
36 RC,RC(c),BWa,V:Tarya . . . 225.00
37 RC,RC(c),BWa,V:Sari,The
    Rajah of Ramastan 225.00
38 BWa 225.00
39 RC,RC(c),BWa,V:Lilith 225.00
40 RC,RC(c),BWa,Valley of
    Yesterday 225.00
41 RC,RC(c),BWa 200.00

42 RC,RC(c),BWa,
    V:Iron Emperor 200.00
43 RC,RC(c),BWa,Terror
    from the Catacombs 200.00
44 RC,RC(c),BWa,The King
    of Winds 200.00
45 BWa,The Island of Death . . 200.00
46 RC,RC(c),BWa,V:DeathPatrol 200.00
47 RC,RC(c),BWa,War! 200.00
48 RC,RC(c),BWa,A:Hawks of
    Horror,Port of Missing Ships 200.00
49 RC,RC(c),BWa,A:Valkyrie,
    Waters of Terrible Peace . . 200.00
50 RC,RC(c),BWa,I:Killer Shark,
    Flying Octopus 225.00
51 BWa,V:The Whip, Whip of
    Nontelon 175.00
52 RC,RC(c),BWa,Traitor in
    the Ranks 175.00
53 RC,RC(c),BWa,V:Golden
    Mummy 175.00
54 RC,RC(c),BWa,V:Dr. Deroski,
    Circles of Suicide 175.00
55 RC,RC(c),BWa,V:Rocketmen 175.00
56 RC,RC(c),BWa,V:The Instructor,
    School for Sabotage 175.00
57 RC,RC(c),BWa,Paralyzed City
    of Armored Men 175.00
58 RC,RC(c),BWa,V:King Cobra,
    The Spider of Delanza 175.00
59 BWa,V:Sea Devil 175.00
60 RC,RC(c),BWa,V:Dr. Mole and
    His Devils Squadron 175.00
61 V:John Smith, Stalin's
    Ambassador of Murder 165.00
62 V:General X, Return of
    Genghis Kahn 165.00
63 RC,RC(c),The Flying
    Buzz-Saws 165.00
64 RC,RC(c),V:Zoltan Korvas,
    Legion of the Damned 165.00
65 Olaf as a Prisoner in Dungeon
    of Fear 165.00
66 RC,RC(c),V:The Red
    Executioner, Crawler 165.00
67 RC,RC(c),V:Future Fuehrer . 165.00
68 V:Killers of the Kremlin 150.00
69 V:King of the Iron Men,
    Conference of the Dictators . 150.00
70 V:Killer Shark 150.00
71 V:Von Tepp, The Man Who
    could Defeat Blackhawk
    O:Blackhawk 200.00
72 V:Death Legion 150.00
73 V:Hangman,The Tyrannical
    Freaks 150.00
74 Plan of Death 150.00
75 V:The Mad Doctor Baroc,
    The Z Bomb Menace 150.00
76 The King of Blackhawk Island 150.00
77 V:The Fiendish
    Electronic Brain 150.00
78 V:The Killer Vulture,
    Phantom Raider 150.00
79 V:Herman Goering, The
    Human Bomb 150.00
80 V:Fang, the Merciless,
    Dr. Death 150.00
81 A:Killer Shark, The Sea
    Monsters of Killer Shark . . . 150.00
82 V:Sabo Teur, the Ruthless
    Commie Agent 150.00
83 I:Hammmer & Sickle, V:Madam
    Double Cross 150.00
84 V:Death Eye,Dr. Genius,

The Dreaded Brain Beam . . 150.00
85 V:The Fiendish Impersonator 150.00
86 V:The Human Torpedoes . . 150.00
87 A:Red Agent Sovietta,V:Sea
    Wolf, Le Sabre,Comics Code 100.00
88 V:Thunder the Indestructible,
    The Phantom Sniper 100.00
89 V:The Super Communists . . 100.00
90 V:The Storm King, Villainess
    who smashed the Blackhawk
    team 100.00
91 Treason in the Underground 100.00
92 V:The World Traitor 100.00
93 V:Garg the Destroyer,
    O:Blackhawk 125.00
94 V:Black Widow, Darkk the
    Destroyer 100.00
95 V:Madam Fury, Queen of the
    Pirates 100.00
96 Doom in the Deep 100.00
97 Revolt of the Slave Workers 100.00
98 Temple of Doom 100.00
99 The War That Never Ended 100.00
100 The Delphian Machine 110.00
101 Satan's Paymaster 100.00
102 The Doom Cloud 100.00
103 The Super Race 100.00
104 The Jet Menace 100.00
105 The Red Kamikaze Terror 100.00
106 The Flying Tank Platoon . 100.00
107 The Winged Menace 100.00
    (Please see DC Listings)

BLACK HOOD
(see LAUGH COMICS)

BLACK TERROR
Better Publications/
Standard
Winter, 1942-43
1 Bombing cover 1,700.00
2 V:Arabs,Bondage(c) 700.00
3 V:Nazis,Bondage(c) 500.00
4 V:Sub Nazis 400.00
5 V:Japanese 400.00
6 Air Battle 350.00
7 Air Battle,V:Japanese,
    A:Ghost 350.00
8 V:Nazis 350.00
9 V:Japanese,Bondage(c) 400.00
10 V:Nazis 350.00
11 thru 16 . . . . @275.00
17 Bondage(c) 300.00
18 ASh 275.00
19 ASh 275.00
20 ASh 275.00
21 ASh 300.00
22 FF,ASh 275.00
23 ASh 275.00
24 Bondgae(c) 300.00
25 ASh 275.00
26 GT,ASh 275.00
27 MME,GT,ASh 275.00

BLAZING COMICS
Enwil Associates/Rural Home
June, 1944
1 B:Green Turtle, Red Hawk,
    Black Buccaneer 350.00
2 Green Turtle cover 250.00
3 Green Turtle cover 225.00
4 Green Turtle cover 225.00
5 March, 1945 . . . . 225.00
5a Black Buccaneer(c),1955 . . . 75.00

6 Indian-Japanese(c), 1955 . . . 75.00

BLONDIE COMICS
David McKay
Spring, 1947

1	150.00
2	75.00
3	50.00
4	50.00
5	50.00
6 thru 10	@30.00
11 thru 15	@20.00

Harvey Publications

16	25.00
17 thru 20	@15.00
21 thru 30	@12.00
31 thru 50	@10.00
51 thru 80	@7.50
81 thru 99	@6.00
100	7.50
101 thru 124	@6.00
125 Giant	7.00
126 thru 135	@6.00
136 thru 140	@5.00
141 thru 163	@7.00

King Publications

164 thru 167	@7.00
168 thru 174	@3.00

Charlton Comics

175 thru 200	@2.00
201 thru 220	@1.50

Blue Beetle #54
© Fox Features/Holyoke Publ.

BLUE BEETLE, THE
Fox Features Syndicate/
Holyoke Publ.
Winter 1939

1 O:Blue Beetle,A:Master Magician	3,500.00
2	1,100.00
3 JSm(c)	750.00
4 Mentions marijuana	500.00
5 A:Zanzibar the Magician	450.00
6 B:Dynamite Thor, O:Blue Beetle	450.00
7 A:Dynamo	400.00
8 E:Thor,A:Dynamo	400.00

9 A:Black Bird,Gorilla	400.00
10 A:Black Bird, bondage cover	400.00
11 A:Gladiator	350.00
12 A:Black Fury	350.00
13 B:V-Man	400.00
14 JKu,I:Sparky	400.00
15 JKu	400.00
16	300.00
17 A:Mimic	275.00
18 E:V-Man,A:Red Knight	275.00
19 JKu,A:Dascomb Dinsmore	300.00
20 I&O:The Flying Tiger Squadron	325.00
21	200.00
22 A:Ali-Baba	225.00
23 A:Jimmy DooLittle	225.00
24 I:The Halo	225.00
25	225.00
26 General Patton story	235.00
27 A:Tamoa	200.00
28	175.00
29	175.00
30 L:Holyoke	175.00
31 F:Fox	150.00
32 Hitler cover	200.00
33 Fight for Freedom	150.00
34 A:Black Terror,Menace of K-4	150.00
35	150.00
36 The Runaway House	150.00
37 Inside the House	150.00
38 Revolt of the Zombies	150.00
39	150.00
40	150.00
41 A:O'Brine Twins	125.00
42	125.00
43	125.00
44	125.00
45	125.00
46 A:Puppeteer	150.00
47 JKa,V:Junior Crime Club	800.00
48 JKa,A:Black Lace	650.00
49 JKa	650.00
50 JKa,The Ambitious Bride	550.00
51 JKa, Shady Lady	525.00
52 JKa(c),Bondage cover	800.00
53 JKa,A:Jack "Legs" Diamond,Bondage(c)	550.00
54 JKa,The Vanishing Nude	900.00
55 JKa	550.00
56 JKa,Tri-State Terror	550.00
57 JKa,The Feagle Bros.	550.00
58	100.00
59	100.00
60 August, 1960	100.00

BLUE BEETLE
(see THING!, THE)

BLUE BOLT
Funnies, Inc./Novelty Press/
Premium Service Co
June, 1940

1 JSm,PG,O:Blue Bolt	2,300.00
2 JSm	1,000.00
3 S&K,A:Space Hawk	900.00
4 PG	800.00
5 BEv,B:Sub Zero	750.00
6 JK,JSm	750.00
7 S&K,BEv	800.00
8 S&K(c)	750.00
9	700.00
10 S&K(c)	700.00
11 BEv(c)	750.00
12	750.00

2-1 BEv(c),PG,O:Dick Cole & V:Simba	225.00
2-2 BEv(c),PG	200.00
2-3 PG,Cole vs Simba	175.00
2-4 BD	175.00
2-5 I:Freezum	175.00
2-6 O:Sgt.Spook, Dick Cole	125.00
2-7 BD	100.00
2-8 BD	100.00
2-9 JW	100.00
2-10 JW	100.00
2-11 JW	100.00
2-12 E:Twister	100.00
3-1 A:115th Infantry	80.00
3-2 A:Phantom Sub	80.00
3-3	80.00
3-4 JW(c)	60.00
3-5 Jor	60.00
3-6 Jor	60.00
3-7 X-Mas cover	60.00
3-8	60.00
3-9 A:Phantom Sub	60.00
3-10 DBa	60.00
3-11 April Fools cover	60.00
3-12	60.00
4-1 Hitler,Tojo,Mussolini cover	100.00
4-2 Liberty Bell cover	50.00
4-3 What are You Doing for Your Country	50.00
4-4 I Fly for Vengence	50.00
4-5 TFH(c)	50.00
4-6 HcK	50.00

Blue Bolt #7
© Funnies, Inc./Novelty Press

4-7 JWi(c)	50.00
4-8 E:Sub Zero	50.00
4-9	50.00
4-10	50.00
4-11	50.00
4-12	50.00
5-1 thru 5-12	@45.00
6-1	45.00
6-2 War Bonds (c)	50.00
6-3	40.00
6-4 Racist(c)	60.00
6-5 Soccer cover	40.00
6-6 thru 6-12	@40.00
7-1 thru 7-12	@40.00
8-1 Baseball cover	45.00
8-2 JHa	40.00

GOLDEN AGE

GOLDEN AGE

8-3 JHe	40.00
8-4 JHa	40.00
8-5 JHe	40.00
8-6 JDo	40.00
8-7 LbC(c).	60.00
8-8	40.00
8-9 AMc(c)	40.00
8-10	40.00
8-11 Basketball cover	45.00
8-12	40.00
9-1 AMc,Baseball cover	35.00
9-2 AMc	30.00
9-3	30.00
9-4 JHe	30.00
9-5 JHe	30.00
9-6 LbC(c),Football cover	60.00
9-7 JHe	30.00
9-8 Hockey cover	40.00
9-9 LbC(c),3-D effect	70.00
9-10	32.00
9-11	32.00
9-12	32.00
10-1 Baseball cover,3-D effect	50.00
10-2 3-D effect	45.00

Star Publications

102 LbC(c),Chameleon	200.00
103 LbC(c),same	175.00
104 LbC(c),same	175.00
105 LbC(c),O:Blue Bolt Space, Drug Story	350.00
106 S&K,LbC(c),A;Space Hawk	300.00
107 S&K,LbC(c),A;Space Hawk	300.00
108 S&K,LbC(c),A:Blue Bolt	300.00
109 BW,LbC(c)	300.00
110 B:Horror covers,A:Target	300.00
111 Weird Tales of Horror, A:Red Rocket	300.00
112 JyD,WiP	275.00
113 BW,JyD,A:Space Hawk	275.00
114 LbC(c),JyD	275.00
115 LbC(c),JyD,A:Sgt.Spook	300.00
116 LbC(c),JyD,A:Jungle Joe	300.00
117 LbC(c),A:Blue Bolt,Jo-Jo	300.00
118 WW,LbC(c),A:White Spirit	300.00
119 LbC(c)	300.00

Becomes:

GHOSTLY WEIRD STORIES
Star Publications
September, 1953

120 LbC,A:Jo-Jo	200.00
121 LbC,A:Jo-Jo	175.00
122 LbC,A:The Mask	175.00
123 LbC,A:Jo-Jo	175.00
124 LbC, September, 1954	175.00

BLUE CIRCLE COMICS
Enwil Associates/Rural Home
June, 1944

1 B:Blue Circle,O:Steel Fist	150.00
2	100.00
3 Hitler parody cover	110.00
4	65.00
5 E:Steel Fist,A:Driftwood Davey	65.00
6	65.00

BLUE RIBBON COMICS
MLJ Magazines
November, 1939

1 JCo,B:Dan Hastings, Richy-Amazing Boy	2,500.00
2 JCo,B:Bob Phantom, Silver Fox	950.00

3 JCo,A:Phantom,Silver Fox	650.00
4 O:Fox,Ty Gor,B:Doc Strong, Hercules	700.00
5 Gattling Gun cover	500.00
6 Amazing Boy Richy cover	475.00
7 A:Fox cover,Corporal Collins V:Nazis	475.00
8 E:Hercules	475.00
9 O&I:Mr. Justice	2,000.00
10 Mr. Justice cover	750.00
11 SCp(c)	750.00
12 E:Doc Strong	750.00
13 B:Inferno	750.00
14 A:Inferno	650.00
15 A:Inferno,E:Green Falcon	650.00
16 O:Captain Flag	1,400.00
17 Captain Flag V:Black Hand	675.00
18 Captain Flag-Black Hand	650.00
19 Captain Flag cover	650.00
20 Captain Flag V:Nazis cover	700.00
21 Captain Flag V:Death	650.00
22 Circus Cover, March, 1942	650.00

BLUE RIBBON COMICS
St. John Publications
February, 1949

1 Heckle & Jeckle	40.00
2 MB(c),Diary Secrets	55.00
3 MB,MB(c),Heckle & Jeckle	35.00
4 Teen-age Diary Secrets	55.00
5 MB,Teen-age Diary Secrets	65.00
6 Dinky Duck	12.00

BO
Charlton Comics
June, 1955

1	35.00
2	30.00
3 October, 1955	30.00

BOB COLT
Fawcett Publications
November, 1950

1 B:Bob Colt,Buck Skin	275.00
2 Death Round Train	175.00
3 Mysterious Black Knight of the Prairie	135.00
4 Death Goes Downstream	135.00
5 The Mesa of Mystery	135.00
6 The Mysterious Visitors	135.00
7 Dragon of Disaster	100.00
8 Redman's Revenge	100.00
9 Hidden Hacienda	100.00
10 Fiend from Vulture Mountain	100.00

BOLD STORIES
Kirby Publishing Co.
March, 1950

1 WW,Near nudity cover	900.00
2 GI,Cobra's Kiss	750.00
3 WW,Orge of Paris,July, 1950	650.00
4 Case of the Winking Buddha	300.00
5 It Rhymes with Lust	300.00
6 Candid Tales, April 1950	300.00

BOMBER COMICS
Elliot Publishing Co.
March, 1944

1 B:Wonder Boy,Kismet, Eagle Evans	400.00
2 Wonder Boy cover	250.00
3 Wonder Boy-Kismet cover	250.00

4 Hitler,Tojo, Mussolini cover	300.00

BOOK OF ALL COMICS
William H. Wise
1945

1 A:Green Mask,Puppeteer	250.00

BOOK OF COMICS, THE
William H. Wise
1945

N# A:Captain V	250.00

Boy Comics #12 © Lev Gleason Publ.

BOY COMICS
Comic House, Inc.
(Lev Gleason Publ.)
April, 1942

3 O:Crimebuster,Bombshell,Young Robin, B:Yankee Longago, Swoop Storm	2,200.00
4 Hitler,Tojo,Mussolini cover	900.00
5 Crimebuster saves day cover	700.00
6 O:Iron Jaw & Death of Son, B:Little Dynamite	1,700.00
7 Hitler,Tojo,Mussolini cover	650.00
8 D:Iron Jaw	675.00
9 I:He-She	600.00
10 Iron Jaw returns	900.00
11 Iron Jaw falls in love	550.00
12 Crimebuster V:Japanese	500.00
13 V:New,more terrible Iron Jaw	500.00
14 V:Iron Jaw	500.00
15 I:Rodent,D:Iron Jaw	550.00
16 Crimebuster V:Knight	250.00
17 Flag cover,Crimebuster V:Moth	265.00
18 Smashed car cover	225.00
19 Express train cover	225.00
20 Coffin cover	225.00
21 Boxing cover	175.00
22 Under Sea cover	175.00
23 Golf cover	175.00
24 County insane asylum cover	175.00
25 52 pgs	175.00
26 68 pgs	175.00
27 Express train cover	200.00
28 E:Yankee Longago	200.00

29 Prison break cover	200.00
30 O:Crimebuster,Murder cover	225.00
31 68 pgs	175.00
32 E:Young Robin Hood	175.00
33	175.00
34 Suicide cover & story	135.00
35	125.00
36	125.00
37	125.00
38	125.00
39 E:Little Dynamite	125.00
40	125.00
41 thru 50	@110.00
51 thru 56	@100.00
57 B:Dilly Duncan	125.00
58	100.00
59	100.00
60 Iron Jaw returns	125.00
61 O:Iron Jaw,Crimebuster	135.00
62 A:Iron Jaw	125.00
63 thru 70	@75.00
71 E:Dilly Duncan	75.00
72	75.00
73	75.00
74 thru 79	@75.00
80 I:Rocky X	60.00
81 thru 88	@60.00
89 A:The Claw	65.00
90 same	65.00
91 same	65.00
92 same	65.00
93 The Claw(c),A:Rocky X	65.00
94	55.00
95	55.00
96	55.00
97	55.00
98 A:Rocky X	65.00
99	55.00
100	65.00
101	65.00
102	65.00
103 thru 118	@65.00
119 March, 1956	65.00

BOY EXPLORERS
(see TERRY AND
THE PIRATES)

BRENDA STARR
Four Star Comics Corp./
Superior Comics Ltd.
September, 1947

13(1)	600.00
14(2) JKa,Bondage cover	650.00
2-3	500.00
2-4 JKa,Operating table cover	600.00
2-5 Swimsuit cover	500.00
2-6	500.00
2-7	500.00
2-8 Cosmetic cover	500.00
2-9 Giant Starr cover	500.00
2-10 Wedding cover	500.00
2-11	500.00
2-12	500.00

BRICK BRADFORD
Best Books
(Standard Comics)
July, 1949

5	100.00
6 Robot cover	125.00
7 AS	80.00
8	80.00

BROADWAY ROMANCES
Quality Comics Group
January, 1950

1 PG,BWa&(c)	200.00
2 BWa,Glittering Desire	150.00
3 BL,Stole My Love	50.00
4 Enslaved by My Past	60.00
5 Flame of Passion,Sept.,1950	60.00

BRONCHO BILL
Visual Editions
(Standard Comics)
January, 1948

5	60.00
6 AS(c)	35.00
7 AS(c)	28.00
8 ASh	28.00
9 AS(c)	28.00
10 AS(c)	28.00
11 AS(c)	22.00
12 AS(c)	22.00
13 AS(c)	22.00
14 ASh	22.00
15 ASh	22.00
16 AS(c)	22.00

BRUCE GENTRY
Four Star Publ./
Visual Editions/
Superior
January, 1948

1 B:Ray Bailey reprints	300.00
2 Plane crash cover	225.00
3 E:Ray Bailey reprints	200.00
4 Tiger attack cover	150.00
5	150.00
6 Help message cover	150.00
7	150.00
8 End of Marriage cover, July, 1949	150.00

BUCCANEERS
(see KID ETERNITY)

BUCK JONES
Dell Publishing Co.
October, 1950

1	150.00
2	75.00
3	50.00
4	50.00
5	50.00
6	50.00
7	50.00
8	50.00

BUCK ROGERS
Eastern Color Printing
Winter 1940

1 Partial Painted(c)	2,700.00
2	1,000.00
3 Living Corpse from Crimson Coffin	800.00
4 One man army of greased lightning	700.00
5 Sky Roads	725.00
6 September, 1943	725.00

Toby Press

100 Flying Saucers	175.00
101	150.00
9	150.00

BUG MOVIES
Dell Publishing Co.
1931

1	100.00

Bugs Bunny Christmas Funnies #2
© Dell Publishing Co.

BUGS BUNNY
DELL GIANT EDITIONS
Dell Publishing Co.
Christmas

1 Christmas Funnies (1950)	300.00
2 Christmas Funnies (1951)	250.00
3 Christmas Funnies (1952)	200.00
4 Christmas Funnies (1953)	200.00
5 Christmas Funnies (1954)	200.00
6 Christmas Party (1955)	175.00
7 Christmas Party (1956)	185.00
8 Christmas Funnies (1957)	185.00
9 Christmas Funnies (1958)	185.00
1 County Fair (1957)	200.00

Halloween

1 Halloween Parade (1953)	200.00
2 Halloween Parade (1954)	175.00
3 Trick 'N' Treat Halloween Fun (1955)	185.00
4 Trick 'N' Treat Halloween Fun (1956)	185.00

Vacation

1 Vacation Funnies (1951)	300.00
2 Vacation Funnies (1952)	275.00
3 Vacation Funnies (1953)	250.00
4 Vacation Funnies (1954)	200.00
5 Vacation Funnies (1955)	200.00
6 Vacation Funnies (1956)	175.00
7 Vacation Funnies (1957)	175.00
8 Vacation Funnies (1958)	175.00
9 Vacation Funnies (1959)	175.00

BUGS BUNNY
Dell Publishing Co.
1942
see Four Color for early years

28 thru 30	@40.00
31 thru 50	@30.00
51 thru 70	@25.00
71 thru 85	@20.00
86 Giant-Show Time	75.00

All comics prices listed are for *Near Mint* condition.

87 thru 100	@10.00
101 thru 120	@7.00
121 thru 140	@5.00
141 thru 190	@4.00
191 thru 245	@3.00

BULLETMAN
Fawcett Publications
Summer, 1941

1 I:Bulletman & Bulletgirl	2,700.00
2 MRa(c)	1,200.00
3 MRa(c)	850.00
4 V:Headless Horror, Guillotine cover	800.00
5 Riddle of Dr. Riddle	700.00
6 V:Japanese	650.00
7 V:Revenge Syndicate	600.00
8 V:Mr. Ego	575.00
9 V:Canine Criminals	575.00
10 I:Bullet Dog	600.00
11 V:Fiendish Fiddler	550.00
12	500.00
13	500.00
14 V:Death the Comedian	500.00
15 V:Professor D	500.00
16 VanishingElephant,Fall 1946	500.00

Buster Crabbe #6 © Famous Funnies

BUSTER CRABBE
Famous Funnies
November, 1951

1 The Arrow of Death	225.00
2 AW&GE(c)	250.00
3 AW&GE(c)	275.00
4 FF(c)	300.00
5 AW,FF,FF,(c)	800.00
6 Sharks cover	100.00
7 FF	125.00
8 Gorilla cover	100.00
9 FF	100.00
10	100.00
11 Snakes cover	65.00
12 September, 1953	65.00

BUSTER CRABBE
Lev Gleason Pub. 1953

1 Ph(c)	125.00
2 ATh	150.00
3 ATh	150.00

4 F. Gordon(c)	125.00

BUZ SAWYER
Standard Comics
June, 1948

1	120.00
2 I:Sweeney	75.00
3	50.00
4	50.00
5 June, 1949	50.00

CALLING ALL BOYS
Parents Magazine Institute
January, 1946

1 Skiing	65.00
2	30.00
3 Peril Out Post	25.00
4 Model Airplane	25.00
5 Fishing	25.00
6 Swimming	25.00
7 Baseball	25.00
8 School	25.00
9 The Miracle Quarterback	25.00
10 Gary Cooper cover	35.00
11 Rin-Tin-Tin cover	25.00
12 Bob Hope cover	50.00
13 Bing Cosby cover	40.00
14 J. Edgar Hoover cover	25.00
15 Tex Granger cover	18.00
16	18.00
17 Tex Granger cover, May, 1948	18.00

Becomes:
TEX GRANGER

18 Bandits of the Badlands	55.00
19 The Seven Secret Cities	45.00
20 Davey Crockett's Last Fight	35.00
21 Canyon Ambush	35.00
22 V:Hooded Terror	35.00
23 V:Billy the Kid	35.00
24 A:Hector, September, 1949	40.00

CALLING ALL GIRLS
Parent Magazine Press, Inc.
September, 1941

1	85.00
2 Virginia Weidler cover	40.00
3 Shirley Temple cover	55.00
4 Darla Hood cover	25.00
5 Gloria Hood cover	25.00
6	18.00
7	18.00
8	18.00
9 Flag cover	20.00
10	18.00
11 thru 20	@15.00
21 thru 39	@10.00
40 Liz Taylor	55.00
41	7.00
42	7.00
43 October, 1945	7.00

CALLING ALL KIDS
Quality Comics, Inc.
December/January, 1946

1 Funny Animal stories	35.00
2	20.00
3	12.00
4	10.00
5	10.00
6	10.00
7	10.00
8	10.00

9	10.00
10	10.00
11 thru 25	@6.00
26 August, 1949	6.00

CAMERA COMICS
U.S. Camera Publishing Corp.
July-September, 1944

1 Airfighter,Grey Comet	125.00
2 How to Set Up a Darkroom	75.00
3 Linda Lens V:Nazi cover	80.00
4 Linda Lens cover	60.00
5 Diving cover	60.00
6 Jim Lane cover	60.00
7 Linda Lens cover	60.00
8 Linda Lens cover	60.00
9 Summer, 1946	60.00

CAMP COMICS
Dell Publishing Co.
February, 1942

1 Ph(c),WK,A:Bugs Bunny	400.00
2 Ph(c),WK,A:Bugs Bunny	300.00
3 Ph(c),Wk	400.00

CAPTAIN AERO COMICS
Holyoke Publishing Co.
December, 1941

1 B:Flag-Man,Master of Magic Captain Aero, Captain Stone	1,200.00
2 A:Pals of Freedom	550.00
3 JKu,B:Alias X,A:Pals of Freedom	550.00
4 JKu,O:Gargoyle,	

Captain Aero #7 © Holyoke Publishing

Parachute jump	550.00
5 JKu	450.00
6 JKu,Flagman,A:Miss Victory	400.00
7 Alias X	250.00
8 O:Red Cross,A:Miss Victory	250.00
9 A:Miss Victory,Alias X	200.00
10 A:Miss Victory,Red Cross	150.00
11 A:Miss Victory	125.00
12 same	125.00
13 same	125.00
14 same	125.00
15 AS(c),A:Miss Liberty	125.00
16 AS(c),Leather Face	100.00

---

17 LbC(c) 200 00
21 LbC(c) 200.00
22 LbC(c),I:Mighty Mite 200.00
23 LbC(c) 200.00
24 LbC(c) American Planes Dive
Bomb Japan 225.00
25 LbC(c),Science Fiction(c) . . 225.00
26 LbC(c) 200.00

CAPTAIN BATTLE
New Friday Publ./
Magazine Press
Summer, 1941
1 B:Captain Battle,O:Blackout   850.00
2 Pirate Ship cover 600.00
3 Dungeon cover 550.00
4 . . . . 400.00
5 V:Japanese, Summer, 1943   400.00

CAPTAIN BATTLE, Jr.
Comic House
Fall, 1943
1 Claw V:Ghost, A:Sniffer . . . 850.00
2 Man who didn't believe
in Ghosts 600.00

CAPTAIN COURAGEOUS
(see BANNER COMICS)

CAPTAIN EASY
Standard Comics
1939
N# Swash Buckler 750.00
10 . . . . 80.00
11 . . . . 50.00
12 . . . . 50.00
13 ASh(c) 50.00
14 . . . . 50.00
15 . . . . 50.00
16 ASh(c) 50.00
17 September, 1949 . . . . 50.00

CAPTAIN FEARLESS
COMICS
Helnit Publishing Co.
August, 1941
1 O:Mr. Miracle,Alias X,Captain
Fearless Citizen Smith,
A:Miss Victory 600.00
2 A:Border Patrol, Sept.,1941 . 400.00

CAPTAIN FLASH
Sterling Comics
November, 1954
1 O:Captain Flash 250.00
2 V:Black Knight 150.00
3 Beasts from 1,000,000 BC . 150.00
4 Flying Saucer Invasion 150.00

CAPTAIN FLEET
Approved Comics
Fall, 1952
1 Storm and Mutiny ...Typhoon 100.00

CAPTAIN FLIGHT
COMICS
Four Star Publications
March, 1944
N# B:Captain Flight,Ace Reynolds
Dashthe Avenger,Professor X 250.00
2 . . . . 125.00

3 . . . . 100.00
4 B:Rock Raymond Salutes
America's Wartime Heroines 120.00
5 Bondage cover,B:Red Rocket
A:The Grenade 250.00
6 Girl tied at the stake 100.00
7 Dog Fight cover 150.00
8 B:Yankee Girl,A:Torpedoman 200.00
9 Dog Fight cover 200.00
10 Bondage cover 225.00
11 LBc(c),Future(c),
Feb-March, 1947 . . . . 225.00

CAPTAIN GALLANT
Charlton Comics
1955
1 Ph(c),Buster Crabbe 55.00
2 . . . . 45.00
3 . . . . 45.00
4 September, 1956 . . . . 45.00

CAPTAIN JET
Four Star Publ.
May, 1952
1 Factory bombing cover 100.00
2 Parachute jump cover 75.00
3 Tank bombing cover 50.00
4 Parachute cover 50.00
5 . . . . 50.00

CAPTAIN KIDD
(see ALL GREAT COMICS)

CAPTAIN MARVEL
ADVENTURES
Fawcett Publications
Spring, 1941
N# JK, B:Captain Marvel &
Sivana 27,500.00
2 GT,JK(c),Billy Batson (c) . 3,000.00
3 JK(c),Thunderbolt (c) . . . 2,000.00
4 Shazam(c) 1,300.00
5 V:Nazis 1,000.00
6 Solomon, Hercules, Atlas, Zeus,
Achilles & Mercury cover . . 800.00
7 Ghost of the White Room . . 800.00
8 Forward America 800.00
9 A:Ibac the Monster, Nippo
the Nipponese, Relm of
the Subconscious 800.00
10 V:Japanese 800.00
11 V:Japanese and Nazis 650.00
12 Joins the Army 650.00
13 V:Diamond-Eyed Idol of
Doom 650.00
14 Nippo meets his Nemesis . . 650.00
15 Big "Paste the Axis" contest 650.00
16 Uncle Sam cover, Paste
the Axis 650.00
17 P(c), Paste the Axis 600.00
18 P(c), O:Mary Marvel 1,300.00
19 Mary Marvel & Santa cover . 500.00
20 Mark of the Black
Swastika 3,000.00
21 Hitler cover 2,800.00
22 B:Mr. Mind serial,
Shipyard Sabotage 650.00
23 A:Steamboat 450.00
24 Minneapolis Mystery 450.00
25 Sinister Faces cover 450.00
26 Flag cover 450.00
27 Joins Navy 350.00
28 Uncle Sam cover 375.00

29 Battle at the China Wall . . 350.00
30 Modern Robinson Crusoe . . 350.00
31 Fights his own Conscience . 350.00
32 V:Mole Men, Dallas 350.00
33 Mt. Rushmore parody
cover, Omaha 325.00
34 Oklahoma City 325.00
35 O:Radar the International
Policeman, Indianapolis . . . 300.00
36 Missing face contest,
St. Louis 300.00
37 V:Block Busting Bubbles,
Cincinnati 300.00
38 V:Chattanooga Ghost,
Rock Garden City 300.00
39 V:Mr. Mind's Death Ray,
Pittsburgh 300.00
40 V:Ghost of the Tower,Boston 300.00
41 Runs for President, Dayton . 250.00
42 Christmas special, St. Paul . 250.00
43 V:Mr. Mind,I:Uncle Marvel,
Chicago 250.00
44 OtherWorlds,Washington,D.C.250.00

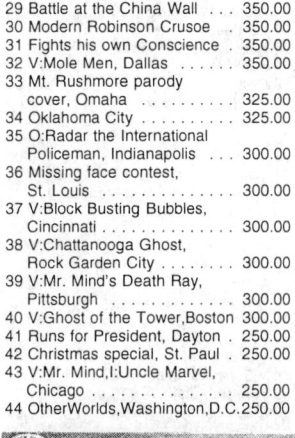

Captain Marvel #22
© *Fawcett Publications*

45 V:Blood Bank Robbers 250.00
46 E: Mr. Mind Serial, Tall
Stories of Jonah Joggins . . . 250.00
47 . . . . 235.00
48 Signs Autographs cover . . . 225.00
49 V: An Unknown Killer 225.00
50 Twisted Powers 225.00
51 Last of the Batsons 175.00
52 O&I:Sivana Jr.,V:Giant
Earth Dreamer 200.00
53 Gets promoted 175.00
54 Marooned in the Future,
Kansas City 200.00
55 Endless String, Columbus . 175.00
56 Goes Crazy, Mobile 175.00
57 A:Haunted Girl, Rochester . 175.00
58 V:Sivana 175.00
59 . . . . 175.00
60 Man who made Earthquakes 175.00
61 I&V: Oggar, the Worlds
Mightiest Immortal 225.00
62 The Great Harness Race . . 175.00
63 Stuntman 175.00
64 . . . . 175.00
65 V:Invaders from Outer Space 175.00

66 Atomic War cover	200.00
67 Hartford	175.00
68 Scenes from the Past, Baltimore	175.00
69 Gets Knighted	175.00
70 Horror in the Box	175.00
71 Wheel of Death	175.00
72	175.00
73 Becomes a Petrophile	175.00
74 Who is the 13th Guest	175.00
75 V:Astonishing Yeast Menace	175.00
76 A:Atom Ambassador	175.00
77 The Secret Life	175.00
78 O:Mr. Tawny	200.00
79 O:Atom,A:World's Worst Actor	250.00
80 Twice told story	350.00
81 A:Mr. Atom	150.00
82 A:Mr. Tawny	150.00
83 Indian Chief	150.00
84 V:Surrealist Imp	150.00
85 Freedom Train	185.00
86 A:Mr. Tawny	150.00
87 V:Electron Thief	150.00
88 Billy Batson's Boyhood	150.00
89 V:Sivana	150.00
90 A:Mr. Tawny	150.00
91 A:Chameleon Stone	150.00
92 The Land of Limbo	150.00
93 Book of all Knowledge	150.00
94 Battle of Electricity	150.00
95 The Great Ice Cap	150.00
96 V:Automatic Weapon	150.00
97 Wiped Out	150.00
98 United Worlds	150.00
99 Rain of Terror	150.00
100 V:Sivana,Plot against the Universe	300.00
101 Invisibility Trap	150.00
102 Magic Mix-up	150.00
103 Ice Covered World of 1,000,000 AD	150.00
104 Mr. Tawny's Masquerade	150.00
105 The Dog Catcher	150.00
106 V:Menace of the Moon	150.00
107 V:Space Hunter	150.00
108 V:Terrible Termites	150.00
109 The Invention Inventor	150.00
110 V:Sivana	150.00
111 The Eighth Sea	150.00
112	150.00
113 Captain Marvel's Feud	150.00
114 V:The Ogre	150.00
115	150.00
116 Flying Saucer	175.00
117	135.00
118 V:Weird Water Man	150.00
119	150.00
120	150.00
121	150.00
122	150.00
123	150.00
124 V:Discarded Instincts	150.00
125 V:Ancient Villain	150.00
126 thru 130	@150.00
131	150.00
132 V:Flood	150.00
133	150.00
134	150.00
135 Perplexing Past Puzzle	150.00
136	150.00
137	150.00
138 V:Haunted Horror	150.00
139	150.00
140 Hand of Horror	150.00

141 Horror	150.00
142	150.00
143 Great Stone Face on the Moon	150.00
144 thru 147	@150.00
148 V:The World	150.00
149	150.00
150 Captains Marvel's Wedding, November, 1953	200.00

Captain Marvel Jr. #3
© Fawcett Publications

CAPTAIN MARVEL JR.
Fawcett Publications
November, 1952

1 O:Captain Marvel, Jr., A:Capt. Nazi	4,200.00
2 O:Capt.Nippon,V:Capt. Nazi	1,400.00
3 Parade to Excitement	800.00
4 V:Invisible Nazi	800.00
5 V:Capt. Nazi	700.00
6 Adventure of Sabbac	600.00
7 City under the Sea	600.00
8 Dangerous Double	550.00
9 Independence cover	550.00
10 Hitler cover	575.00
11	450.00
12 Scuttles the Axis Isle in the Sky	500.00
13 V:The Axis,Hitler,cover	475.00
14 X-Mas cover, Santa wears Capt. Marvel uniform	400.00
15	450.00
16 A:Capt. Marvel, Sivana, Pogo	400.00
17 Meets his Future self	400.00
18 V:Birds of Doom	400.00
19 A:Capt. Nazi & Capt. Nippon	400.00
20 Goes on the Warpath	375.00
21 Buy War Stamps	300.00
22 Rides World's oldest steamboat	300.00
23	300.00
24 V:Weather Man	300.00
25 Flag cover	300.00
26 Happy New Year	300.00
27 Jungle Thrills	300.00
28 V:Sivana's Crumbling Crimes	300.00
29 Blazes a Wilderness Trail	300.00
30	300.00

31	200.00
32 Keeper of the Lonely Rock	200.00
33	200.00
34/35 I&O:Sivana Jr.	200.00
36 Underworld Tournament	200.00
37 FreddyFreeman'sNews-stand	200.00
38 A:Arabian Knight	200.00
39 V:Sivana Jr., Headline Stealer	200.00
40 Faces Grave Situation	200.00
41 I:The Acrobat	150.00
42 V:Sivana Jr.	150.00
43 V:Beasts on Broadway	150.00
44 Key to the Mystery	150.00
45 A:Icy Fingers	150.00
46	150.00
47 V:Giant of the Beanstalk	150.00
48 Whale of a Fish Story	150.00
49 V:Dream Recorder	150.00
50 Wanted: Freddy Freeman	150.00
51 The Island Riddle	125.00
52 A:Flying Postman	125.00
53 Atomic Bomb on the Loose	175.00
54 V:Man with 100 Heads	150.00
55 Pyramid of Eternity	150.00
56 Blue Boy's Black Eye	150.00
57 Magic Ladder	150.00
58 Amazing Mirror Maze	150.00
59	150.00
60 V:Space Menace	150.00
61 V:Himself	125.00
62	125.00
63 V:Witch of Winter	125.00
64 thru 70	@125.00
71 thru 74	@125.00
75 V:Outlaw of Crooked Creek	125.00
76 thru 85	@125.00
86 Defenders of time	125.00
87 thru 89	@125.00
90 The Magic Trunk	100.00
91 thru 99	@100.00
100 V:Sivana Jr	125.00
101 thru 106	@100.00
107 The Horror Dimension	100.00
108 thru 118	@100.00
119 Condemned to Die, June, 1953	100.00

CAPTAIN MIDNIGHT
Fawcett Publications
September, 1942

1 O:Captain Midnight, Capt. Marvel cover	2,200.00
2 Smashes Jap Juggernaut	1,000.00
3 Battles the Phantom Bomber	700.00
4 Grapples the Gremlins	600.00
5 Double Trouble in Tokyo	600.00
6 Blasts the Black Mikado	500.00
7 Newspaper headline cover	500.00
8 Flying Torpedoes Berlin-Bound	500.00
9 MRa(c), Subs in Mississippi	500.00
10 MRa(c), Flag cover	500.00
11 MRa(c), Murder in Mexico	375.00
12 V:Sinister Angels	375.00
13 Non-stop Flight around the World	375.00
14 V:King of the Villains	375.00
15 V:Kimberley Killer	375.00
16 Hitler's Fortress Breached	375.00
17 MRa(c), Hello Adolf	350.00
18 Death from the Skies	350.00
19 Hour of Doom for the Axis	350.00
20 Brain and Brawn against Axis	350.00
21 Trades with Japanese	300.00

All comics prices listed are for *Near Mint* condition.

GOLDEN AGE

Captain Midnight #1
© Fawcett Publications

22 Plea for War Stamps 300.00
23 Japanese Prison cover 300.00
24 Rising Sun Flag cover 300.00
25 Amusement Park Murder . . 300.00
26 Hotel of Horror 300.00
27 Death Knell for Tyranny . . . 300.00
28 Gliderchuting to Glory 300.00
29 Bomb over Nippon 300.00
30 . . . . 300.00
31 . . . . 200.00
32 . . . . 200.00
33 V:Shark 200.00
34 . . . . 200.00
35 thru 40 . . . . @200.00
41 thru 50 . . . . @150.00
51 thru 63 . . . . @150.00
64 V:XOG, Ruler of Saturn . . . 150.00
65 . . . . 150.00
66 V:XOG 150.00
67 Fall, 1948 . . . . 150.00
Becomes:

SWEET HEART

68 Robert Mitchum 65.00
69 thru 118 . . . . @20.00
111 Ronald Reagan story 30.00
119 Marilyn Monroe 150.00
120 Atomic Bomb story . . . . . @35.00
121 . . . . 15.00
122 1954 . . . . 12.00

CAPTAIN SCIENCE
Youthful Magazines
November, 1950
1 WW,O:Captain Science,
  V:Monster God of Rogor . . . 600.00
2 WW,V:Cat Men of Phoebus,
  Space Pirates 300.00
3 Ghosts from the Underworld 300.00
4 WW,Vampires 600.00
5 WW,V:Shark Pirates of Pisces 600.00
6 WW,V:Invisible Tyrants,
  bondage cover 500.00
7 WW,Bondage(c) Dec., 1951 500.00
Becomes:

FANTASTIC

8 Isle of Madness 200.00

---

9 Octopus cover 150.00
Becomes:

BEWARE

10 SHn,Doll of Death 200.00
11 SHn,Horror Head 175.00
12 SHn,Body Snatchers 150.00
Becomes:

CHILLING TALES

13 MF,Screaming Skull 300.00
14 SHn,Smell of Death 175.00
15 SHn,Curse of the Tomb . . . 175.00
16 HcK,Mark of the Beast
   Bondage(c) 175.00
17 MFc(c),Wandering Willie,
   Oct.,1953 . . . . 200.00

CAPTAIN STEVE SAVAGE
[1st Series]
Avon Periodicals
1950
N# WW 275.00
2 EK(c),The Death Gamble . . 125.00
3 EK(c),Crash Landing in
  Manchuria 50.00
4 EK(c),V:Red Raiders from
  Siang-Po 40.00
5 EK(c),Rockets of Death 40.00
6 Operation Destruction 40.00
7 EK(c),Flight to Kill 40.00
8 EK(c),V:Red Mystery Jet . . . 40.00
9 EK(c) 40.00
10 . . . . 40.00
11 EK(c) 45.00
12 WW 75.00
13 . . . . 50.00

[2nd Series]
September/October, 1954
5 . . . . 35.00
6 WW 50.00
7 thru 13 . . . . @20.00

CAPTAIN VIDEO
Fawcett Publications
February, 1951
1 GE,Ph(c) 800.00
2 Time when Men could not
  Walk 550.00
3 GE,Indestructible Antagonist 450.00
4 GE,School of Spies 450.00
5 GE,Missiles of Doom,
  Photo cover 450.00
6 GE,Island of Conquerors,
  Photo cover; Dec. 1951 . . . 450.00

CASPER, THE
FRIENDLY GHOST
St. John Publishing
September, 1949
1 O:Baby Huey 1,200.00
2 . . . . 500.00
3 . . . . 450.00
4 . . . . 350.00
5 . . . . 350.00
Harvey Publications
7 . . . . 275.00
8 thru 9 . . . . @150.00
10 I:Spooky 175.00
11 A:Spooky 100.00
12 thru 18 . . . . @75.00
19 I:Nightmare 85.00
20 I:Wendy the Witch 85.00
21 thru 30 . . . . @50.00

Casper, The Friendly Ghost #10
© St. John Publishing

31 thru 40 . . . . @40.00
41 thru 50 . . . . @30.00
51 thru 60 . . . . @25.00
61 thru 69 . . . . @20.00
70 July, 1958 . . . . 22.00

CAT MAN COMICS
Helnit Publ. Co./
Holyoke Publ. Co./
Continental Magazine
May, 1941
1 O:Deacon&Sidekick Mickey,
  Dr. Diamond & Ragman,A:Black
  Widow, B:Blaze Baylor . . . 2,500.00
2 Ragman 800.00
3 B:Pied Piper 600.00
4 CQ 550.00
5 I&O: The Kitten 500.00
6 CQ 450.00
7 CQ 450.00
8 JKa, I:Volton 600.00
9 JKa 400.00
10 JKa,O:Blackout,
   B:Phantom Falcon 375.00
11 JKa,DRi,BF 410.00
12 . . . . 350.00
13 . . . . 350.00
14 CQ 350.00
15 Rajah of Destruction 350.00
16 Bye-Bye Axis 425.00
17 Buy Bonds and Stamps . . . 400.00
18 Buy Bonds and Stamps . . . 400.00
19 CQ,Hitler,Tojo and
   Mussolini cover 425.00
20 CQ,Hitler,Tojo and
   Mussolini cover 425.00
21 CQ 300.00
22 CQ 300.00
23 CQ 300.00
N# V:Japanese,Bondage(c) . . . 310.00
N# V:Demon 300.00
N# A:Leather Face 300.00
27 LbC(c),Flag cover,O:Kitten . 500.00
28 LbC(c),Horror cover 500.00
29 LbC(c),BF 500.00
30 LbC(c),Bondage(c) 550.00
31 LbC(c) 500.00

GOLDEN AGE

---

32 August, 1946 . . . . 400.00

CHALLENGER, THE
Interfaith Publications
1945

N# O:The Challenger Club . . 225.00
2 JKa 200.00
3 JKa 200.00
4 JKa,BF 200.00

Chamber of Chills #23
© Harvey Publications

CHAMBER OF CHILLS
Harvey Publications/
Witches Tales
June, 1951

21 . . . . 250.00
22 . . . . 150.00
23 Eyes Ripped Out 150.00
24 Bondage cover 175.00
5 Shrunken Skull,
  Operation Monster 175.00
6 Seven Skulls of Magondi . . 150.00
7 Pit of the Damned 150.00
8 Formula for Death 150.00
9 Bondage cover 125.00
10 Cave of Death 125.00
11 Curse of Morgan Kilgane . . 100.00
12 Swamp Monster 100.00
13 The Lost Race 125.00
14 Down to Death 100.00
15 Nightmare of Doom 125.00
16 Cycle of Horror 125.00
17 Amnesia 125.00
18 Hair cut-Atom Bomb 150.00
19 Happy Anniversary 125.00
20 Shock is Struck 125.00
21 BP,Nose for News 160.00
22 Is Death the End? 125.00
23 BP,Heartline 125.00
24 BP,Bondage(c) 150.00
25 . . . . 75.00
26 HN,Captains Return 75.00
Becomes:

CHAMBER OF CLUES
27 BP,A:Kerry Drake 85.00
28 A:Kerry Drake 50.00

CHAMPION COMICS
Worth Publishing Co.
December, 1939

2 B:Champ, Blazing Scarab, Neptina,
  Liberty Lads, Jingleman . . 1,000.00
3 . . . . 500.00
4 Bailout(c) 550.00
5 Jungleman(c) 550.00
6 MNe 550.00
7 MNe,Human Meteor 575.00
8 . . . . 600.00
9 . . . . 600.00
10 Bondage cover 750.00
Becomes:

CHAMP COMICS
11 Human Meteor 650.00
12 Human Heteor 500.00
13 Dragon's Teeth 450.00
14 Liberty Lads 450.00
15 Liberty Lads 450.00
16 Liberty Lads 450.00
17 Liberty Lads 450.00
18 Liberty Lads 450.00
19 A:The Wasp 600.00
20 A:The Green Ghost 450.00
21 . . . . 350.00
22 A:White Mask 425.00
23 Flag cover 425.00
24 . . . . 350.00
25 . . . . 350.00
26 thru 29 . . . . 350.00

CHARLIE McCARTHY
Dell Publishing Co.
November, 1947

1 . . . . 150.00
2 . . . . 75.00
3 . . . . 75.00
1 . . . . 75.00
2 . . . . 75.00
3 . . . . 75.00
4 . . . . 75.00
5 . . . . 75.00
6 . . . . 75.00
7 . . . . 75.00
8 . . . . 75.00
9 . . . . 75.00

CHIEF, THE
Dell Publishing Co.
August, 1950

(1) *see Dell Four Color #290*
2 . . . . 30.00

CHILLING TALES
(see CAPTAIN SCIENCE)

CHUCKLE THE GIGGLY
BOOK OF COMIC ANIMALS
R. B. Leffing Well Co.
1944

1 . . . . 125.00

CINEMA COMICS
HERALD
Paramount/Universal/RKO/
20th Century Fox
Giveaways 1941-43

N# Mr. Bug Goes to Town 75.00
N# Bedtime Story 75.00
N# Lady for a Night,J.Wayne . 100.00

N# Reap the Wild Wind 75.00
N# Thunderbirds 75.00
N# They All Kissed Me 75.00
N# Bombardier 75.00
N# Crash Dive 75.00
N# Arabian Nights 75.00

CIRCUS THE
COMIC RIOT
Globe Syndicate
June, 1938

1 BKa,WE,BW 4,500.00
2 BKa,WE,BW 2,500.00
3 BKa,WE,BW, August, 1938 . 2,500.00

CISCO KID, THE
Dell Publishing Co.

(1) *See Dell Four Color #292*
2 January, 1951 . . . . 250.00
3 thru 5 . . . . @125.00
6 thru 10 . . . . @90.00
11 thru 20 . . . . @75.00
21 thru 36 . . . . @60.00
37 thru 41 Ph(c)'s . . . . @100.00

CLAIRE VOYANT
Leader Publ./Visual Ed./
Pentagon Publ.
1946-47

N# 400.00
2 JKa(c) 350.00
3 Case of the Kidnapped Bride 325.00
4 Bondage cover 375.00

CLOAK AND DAGGER
Approved Comics
(Ziff-Davis)
Fall, 1952

1 NS(c),Al Kennedy of the Secret
  Service 175.00

CLUE COMICS
Hillman Periodicals
January, 1943

1 O:Boy King,Nightmare,Micro-Face,
  Twilight,Zippo. 750.00
2 . . . . 325.00
3 Boy King V:The Crane 350.00
4 V:The Crane 275.00
5 V:The Crane 250.00
6 Hells Kitchen 175.00
7 V:Dr. Plasma,Torture(c) . . . 200.00
8 RP,A:The Gold Mummy King 250.00
9 I:Paris 175.00
10 O:Gun Master 175.00
11 A:Gun Master 125.00
12 O:Rackman 175.00
2-1 S&K,O:Nightro,A:Iron Lady 325.00
2-2 S&K,Bondage(c) 350.00
2-3 S&K 300.00
Becomes:

REAL CLUE
CRIME STORIES
2-4 DBw,S&K,True Story of
  Ma Barker 300.00
2-5 S&K, Newface surgery cover 250.00
2-6 S&K, Breakout cover 225.00
2-7 S&K, Stick up cover 225.00
2-8 Kidnapping cover 75.00
2-9 DBa,Boxing fix cover 75.00
2-10 DBa,Murder cover 75.00
2-11 Attempted bank

robbery cover 75.00
2-12 Murder cover 75.00
3-1 thru 3-12 . . . . @50.00
4-1 thru 4-12 . . . . @75.00
5-1 thru 5-12 . . . . @40.00
6-1 thru 6-12 . . . . @40.00
6-10 Bondage(c) 70.00
7-1 thru 7-12 . . . . @30.00
8-1 thru 8-4 . . . . @30.00
8-5 May, 1953 . . . . 30.00

C-M-O COMICS
Comic Corp. of America
(Centaur)
May, 1942
1 Invisible Terror 700.00
2 Super Ann 450.00

COCOMALT BIG BOOK
OF COMICS
Harry A. Chesler
1938
1 BoW,PGn,FG,JCo,(Give away)
Little Nemo 1,500.00

COLOSSUS COMICS
Sun Publications
March, 1940
1 A:Colossus 2,500.00

COLUMBIA COMICS
William H. Wise Co.
1944
1 Joe Palooka,Charlie Chan . 200.00

COMICS, THE
Dell Publishing Co.
March, 1937
1 I:Tom Mix & Arizona Kid . . 1,400.00
2 A:Tom Mix & Tom Beaty . . . 600.00
3 A:Alley Oop 500.00
4 same 500.00
5 same 500.00
6 thru 11 same . . . . @500.00

COMICS ON PARADE
United Features Syndicate
April 1938–Feb. 1955
1 B:Tarzan,Captain and the Kids,
Little Mary, Mixup,Abbie & Slats,
Broncho Bill,Li'l Abner . . . 3,000.00
2 Circus Parade of all 1,100.00
3 . . . . 800.00
4 On Rocket 750.00
5 All at the Store 750.00
6 All at Picnic 400.00
7 Li'l Abner(c) 400.00
8 same 400.00
9 same 400.00
10 same 400.00
11 same 350.00
12 same 350.00
13 same 350.00
14 Abbie n' Slats (c) 350.00
15 Li'l Abner(c) 350.00
16 Abbie n' Slats(c) 350.00
17 Tarzan,Abbie n' Slats(c) . . . 375.00
18 Li'l Abner(c) 350.00
19 same 350.00
20 same 350.00
21 Li'l Abner(c) 250.00
22 Tail Spin Tommy(c) 250.00

23 Abbie n' Slats(c) 250.00
24 Tail Spin Tommy(c) 250.00
25 Li'l Abner(c) 250.00
26 Abbie n' Slats(c) 250.00
27 Li'l Abner(c) 250.00
28 Tail Spin Tommy(c) 250.00
29 Abbie n' Slats(c) 250.00
30 Li'l Abner(c) 200.00
31 The Captain & the Kids(c) . . 175.00
32 Nancy and Fritzi Ritz(c) . . . 125.00
33 Li'l Abner(c) 150.00
34 The Captain & the Kids(c) . . 125.00
35 Nancy and Fritzi Ritz(c) . . . 110.00
36 Li'l Abner(c) 145.00
37 The Captain & the Kids(c) . . 110.00
38 Nancy and Fritzi Ritz(c) . . . 100.00
39 Li'l Abner(c) 135.00
40 The Captain & the Kids(c) . . 110.00
41 Nancy and Fritzi Ritz(c) 75.00
42 Li'l Abner(c) 125.00
43 The Captain & the Kids(c) . . 110.00
44 Nancy and Fritzi Ritz(c) 75.00
45 Li'l Abner(c) 110.00

Comics on Parade #9
© United Features Syndicate

46 The Captain & the Kids(c) . . . 90.00
47 Nancy and Fritzi Ritz(c) 75.00
48 Li'l Abner(c) 100.00
49 The Captain & the Kids(c) . . . 90.00
50 Nancy and Fritzi Ritz(c) 75.00
51 Li'l Abner(c) 100.00
52 The Captain & the Kids(c) . . . 75.00
53 Nancy and Fritzi Ritz(c) 75.00
54 Li'l Abner(c) 100.00
55 Nancy and Fritzi Ritz(c) 75.00
56 The Captain & the Kids(c) . . . 75.00
57 Nancy and Fritzi Ritz(c) 70.00
58 Li'l Abner(c) 100.00
59 The Captain & the Kids(c) . . . 70.00
60 Nancy and Fritzi Ritz(c) 55.00
61 thru 76 same . . . . @55.00
77 Nancy & Sluggo(c) 50.00
78 thru 104 same . . . . @50.00

COMPLETE BOOK OF
COMICS AND FUNNIES
William H. Wise & Co.
1945
1 Wonderman-Magnet 300.00

CONFESSIONS OF LOVE
Artful Publications
April, 1950
1 . . . . 200.00
2 July, 1950 . . . . 125.00

CONFESSIONS OF LOVE
Star Publications
July, 1952
11 AW,LbC(c)Intimate Secrets of
Daring Romance 75.00
12 AW,LbC(c),I Couldn't Say No 75.00
13 AW,LbC(c),Heart Break . . . 75.00
14 AW,LbC(c),My Fateful Love . 40.00
4 JyD,AW,LbC(c),The Longing
Heart 40.00
5 AW,LbC(c),I Wanted Love . . 40.00
6 AW,LbC(c),My Jealous Heart . 40.00
Becomes:
CONFESSIONS OF
ROMANCE
7 LbC(c)Too Good 75.00
8 AW,LbC(c),I Lied About Love 50.00
9 WW,AW,LbC(c),I Paid
Love's Price 100.00
10 JyD,AW,LbC(c),My Heart Cries
for Love 50.00
11 JyD,AW,LbC(c),Intimate
Confessions, November, 1954 50.00

CONFESSIONS OF
LOVELORN
(see LOVELORN)

CONQUEROR COMICS
Albrecht Publications
Winter, 1945
1 . . . . 100.00

CONTACT COMICS
Aviation Press
July, 1944
N# LbC(c),B:Black Venus,
Golden Eagle 350.00
2 LbC(c),Peace Jet 250.00
3 LbC(c),LbC,E:Flamingo . . . 225.00
4 LbC(c),LbC 225.00
5 LbC(c),A:Phantom Flyer . . . 250.00
6 LbC(c),HK 275.00
7 LbC(c),Flying Tigers 200.00
8 LbC(c),Peace Jet 200.00
9 LbC(c),LbC,A:Marine Flyers . 200.00
10 LbC(c),A:Bombers of the AAF 200.00
11 LbC(c),HK,AF,Salutes Naval
Aviation 300.00
12 LbC(c),A:Sky Rangers, Air Kids,
May, 1946 . . . . 225.00

COO COO COMICS
Nedor/Animated Cartoons
(Standard)
October, 1942
1 O&I:Super Mouse 200.00
2 . . . . 100.00
3 . . . . 50.00
4 . . . . 50.00
5 . . . . 50.00
6 . . . . 40.00
7 thru 10 . . . . @35.00
11 thru 33 . . . . @35.00
34 thru 40 FF illustration . . . . @50.00

41 FF	125.00
42 FF	125.00
43 FF illustration	75.00
44 FF illustration	75.00
45 FF illustration	75.00
46 FF illustration	45.00
47 FF	75.00
48 FF illustration	50.00
49 FF illustration	60.00
50 FF illustration	60.00
51 thru 61	@25.00
62 April, 1952	25.00

"COOKIE"
Michel Publ./Regis Publ.
(American Comics Group)
April, 1946

1	125.00
2	50.00
3	40.00
4	40.00
5	40.00
6 thru 20	@30.00
21 thru 30	@25.00
31 thru 54	@20.00
55 August, 1955	20.00

COSMO CAT
Fox Features Syndicate
July/August, 1946

1	150.00
2	75.00
3 O:Cosmo Cat	65.00
4 thru 10	@35.00

COURAGE COMICS
J. Edward Slavin
1945

1	50.00
2 Boxing cover	50.00
77 Naval rescue, PT99 cover	50.00

COWBOY COMICS
(see STAR RANGER)

COWBOYS 'N' INJUNS
Compix
(M.E. Enterprises)
1946-47

1 Funny Animal Western	40.00
2 thru 8	@25.00

COWBOY WESTERN
COMICS/HEROES
(see YELLOWJACKET
COMICS)

COWGIRL ROMANCES
Fiction House Magazine
1952

1 The Range of Singing Guns	225.00
2 The Lady of Lawless Range	125.00
3 Daughter of the Devil's Band	100.00
4 Bride Wore Buckskin	90.00
5 Taming of Lone-Star Lou	90.00
6 Rose of Mustang Mesa	85.00
7 Nobody Loves a Gun Man	85.00
8 Wild Beauty	85.00
9 Gun-Feud Sweethearts	85.00
10 JKa,AW,No Girl of Stampede Valley	90.00

11 Love is Where You Find It	85.00
12 December, 1952	85.00

COW PUNCHER
Avon Periodicals/
Realistic Publ.
January, 1947

1 JKu	275.00
2 JKu,JKa(c),Bondage cover	200.00
3 AU(c)	150.00
4	150.00
5	150.00
6 WJo(c),Drug story	175.00
7	150.00
1 JKu	150.00

Crack Comics #40
© Quality Comics Group

CRACK COMICS
Comic Magazines
(Quality Comics Group)
May, 1940

1 LF,O:Black Condor,Madame Fatal, Red Torpedo, Rock Bradden, Space Legion, B:The Clock,Wizard Wells	4,000.00
2 Black Condor cover	1,700.00
3 The Clock cover	1,200.00
4 Black Condor cover	1,000.00
5 LF,The Clock cover	800.00
6 PG,Black Condor cover	750.00
7 Clock cover	750.00
8 Black Condor cover	750.00
9 Clock cover	750.00
10 Black Condor cover	750.00
11 LF,PG,Clock cover	650.00
12 LF,PG,Black Condor cover	650.00
13 LF,PG,Clock cover	650.00
14 AMc,LF,PG,Clack Condor(c)	650.00
15 AMc,LF,PG,Clock cover	650.00
16 AMc,LF,PG,Black Condor(c)	650.00
17 FG,AMc,LF,PG,Clock cover	650.00
18 AMc,LF,PG,Black Condor(c)	650.00
19 AMc,LF,PG,Clock cover	650.00
20 AMc,LF,PG,Black Condor(c)	650.00
21 AMc,LF,PG,same	500.00
22 LF,PG,same	500.00
23 AMc,LF,PG,same	500.00
24 AMc,LF,PG,same	500.00

25 AMc,same	450.00
26 AMc,same	450.00
27 AMc,I&O:Captain Triumph	750.00
28 Captain Triumph cover	450.00
29 A:Spade the Ruthless	450.00
30 I:Biff	400.00
31 Helps Spade Dig His Own Grave	200.00
32 Newspaper cover	200.00
33 V:Men of Darkness	200.00
34	200.00
35 V:The Man Who Conquered Flame	200.00
36 Good Neighbor Tour	200.00
37 V:The Tyrant of Toar Valley	200.00
38 Castle of Shadows	200.00
39 V:Crime over the City	200.00
40 Thrilling Murder Mystery	125.00
41	125.00
42 All that Glitters is Not Gold	125.00
43 Smashes the Evil Spell of Silent	125.00
44 V:Silver Tip	125.00
45 V:King-The Jack of all Trades	125.00
46 V:Mr. Weary	125.00
47 V:Hypnotic Eyes Khor	135.00
48 Murder in the Sky	135.00
49	135.00
50 A Key to Trouble	135.00
51 V:Werewolf	135.00
52 V:Porcupine	135.00
53 V:Man Who Robbed the Dead	135.00
54 Shoulders the Troubles of the World	135.00
55 Brain against Brawn	135.00
56 Gossip leads to Murder	135.00
57 V:Sitok–Green God of Evil	135.00
58 V:Targets	125.00
59 A Cargo of Mystery	125.00
60 Trouble is no Picnic	125.00
61 V:Mr. Pointer-Finger of Fear	125.00
62 V:The Vanishing Vandals	125.00

Becomes:

CRACK WESTERN

63 PG, I&O:Two-Gun Lil, B:Frontier Marshal,Arizona Ames,	120.00
64 RC,Arizona AmesV:Two-Legged Coyote	90.00
65 RC,Ames Tramples on Trouble	90.00
66 Arizona Ames Arizona Raines, Tim Holt,Ph(c)	75.00
67 RC, Ph(c)	85.00
68	75.00
69 RC	75.00
70 O&I:Whip and Diablo	80.00
71 RC(c)	85.00
72 RC,Tim Holt,Ph(c)	72.00
73 Tim Holt,Ph(c)	55.00
74 RC(c)	60.00
75 RC(c)	60.00
76 RC(c),Stage Coach to Oblivion	60.00
77 RC(c),Comanche Terror	60.00
78 RC(c),Killers of Laurel Ridge	60.00
79 RC(c),Fires of Revenge	60.00
80 RC(c),Mexican Massacre	60.00
81 RC(c),Secrets of Terror Canyon	60.00
82 The Killer with a Thousand Faces	40.00
83 Battlesnake Pete's Revenge	40.00
84 PG(c),Revolt at Broke Creek May,1951	40.00

CRACKAJACK FUNNIES
Dell Publishing Co.
June, 1938
1 AMc,A:Dan Dunn,The Nebbs,
  Don Winslow 2,000.00
2 AMc,same 750.00
3 AMc,same 600.00
4 AMc,same 400.00
5 AMc,Naked Women(c) 450.00
6 AMc,same 350.00
7 AMc,same 350.00
8 AMc,same 350.00
9 AMc,A:Red Ryder 1,000.00
10 AMc,A:Red Ryder 350.00
11 AMc,A:Red Ryder 300.00
12 AMc,A:Red Ryder 300.00
13 AMc,A:Red Ryder 300.00
14 AMc,A:Red Ryder 300.00
15 AMc,A:Tarzan 350.00
16 AMc 250.00
17 AMc 250.00
18 AMc 250.00
19 AMc 250.00
20 AMc 250.00
21 AMc 250.00
22 AMc 250.00
23 AMc 250.00
24 AMc 250.00
25 AMc,I:The Owl 500.00
26 AMc 375.00
27 AMc 375.00
28 AMc,A:The Owl 375.00
29 AMc,A:Ellery Queen 375.00
30 AMc,A:Tarzan 375.00
31 AMc,A:Tarzan 375.00
32 AMc,O:Owl Girl 450.00
33 AMc,A:Tarzan 300.00
34 AMc,same 300.00
35 AMc,same 300.00
36 AMc,same 300.00
37 AMc 275.00
38 AMc 275.00
39 AMc,I:Andy Panada 400.00
40 AMc,A:Owl(c) 300.00
41 AMc 300.00
42 AMc 300.00
43 AMc,A:Owl(c) 250.00

CRASH COMICS
Tem Publishing Co.
May, 1940
1 S&K,O:Strongman, B:Blue Streak,
  Perfect Human, Shangra .. 2,200.00
2 S&K 1,100.00
3 S&K 1,000.00
4 S&K,O&I:Catman 1,900.00
5 S&K, November, 1940 .... 950.00

CRIME AND PUNISHMENT
Lev Gleason Publications
April, 1948
1 CBi(c),Mr.Crime(c) 200.00
2 CBi(c) 100.00
3 CBi(c),BF 125.00
4 CBi(c),BF 75.00
5 CBi(c) 75.00
6 thru 10 CBi(c) .... @55.00
11 thru 15 CBi(c) .... @50.00
16 thru 27 CBi(c) .... @40.00
28 thru 38 .... @35.00
39 Drug issue 60.00
40 thru 44 .... @35.00

Crime and Punishment #10
© Lev Gleason Publications

45 Drug issue 60.00
46 thru 73 .... @25.00
66 ATh 250.00
67 Drug Storm 200.00
68 ATh(c) 175.00
69 Drug issue 55.00
74 August, 1955 .... 25.00

CRIME DETECTIVE COMICS
Hillman Publications
March-April, 1948
1 BFc(c),A:Invisible 6 ... 150.00
2 Jewel Robbery cover 60.00
3 Stolen cash cover 50.00
4 Crime Boss Murder cover . 50.00
5 BK,Maestro cover 50.00
6 AMc,Gorilla cover 45.00
7 GMc,Wedding cover 45.00
8 .... 30.00
9 Safe Robbery cover
  (a classic) 200.00
10 .... 40.00
11 BP 40.00
12 BK 40.00
2-1 Bluebird captured 45.00
2-2 .... 30.00
2-3 .... 30.00
2-4 BK 40.00
2-5 .... 30.00
2-6 .... 30.00
2-7 BK,GMc 40.00
2-8 .... 30.00
2-9 .... 30.00
2-10 .... 30.00
2-11 .... 30.00
2-12 .... 30.00
3-1 Drug Story 30.00
3-2 thru 3-7 .... @30.00
3-8 May/June, 1953 ..... 25.00

CRIME DOES NOT PAY
(see SILVER STREAK COMICS)

CRIME ILLUSTRATED
E.C. Comics
November-December, 1955
1 Grl,RC,GE,JO 90.00
2 Grl,RC,JCr,JDa,JO 75.00

CRIME MUST STOP
Hillman Periodicals
October, 1952
1 BK 400.00

CRIME MYSTERIES
Ribage Publishing Corp.
May, 1952
1 Transvestism,Bondage(c) .. 375.00
2 A:Manhunter, Lance Storm,
  Drug 250.00
3 FF-one page, A:Dr. Foo .. 200.00
4 A:Queenie Star, Bondage Star 300.00
5 Claws of the Green Girl ... 150.00
6 .... 150.00
7 Sons of Satan 150.00
8 Death Stalks the Crown,
  Bondage(c) 175.00
9 You are the Murderer 150.00
10 The Hoax of the Death 150.00
11 The Strangler 150.00
12 Bondage(c) 175.00
13 AT,6 lives for one 175.00
14 Painted in Blood 150.00
15 Feast of the Dead,Acid Face 250.00
Becomes:
SECRET MYSTERIES
16 Hiding Place,Horror 135.00
17 The Deadly Diamond,Horror . 90.00
18 Horror 100.00
19 Horror,July, 1955 .... 100.00

CRIMES ON THE WATERFRONT
(see FAMOUS GANGSTERS)

INTERNATIONAL COMICS
E.C. Publ. Co.
Spring, 1947
1 KS,I:Manhattan's Files 600.00
2 KS,A: Van Manhattan &
  Madelon 450.00
3 KS,same 300.00
4 KS,same 300.00
5 I:International Crime-Busting
  Patrol 300.00
Becomes:
INTERNATIONAL CRIME PATROL
6 A:Moon Girl & The Prince .. 550.00
Becomes:
CRIME PATROL
7 SMo,A:Capt. Crime Jr.,Field
  Marshall of Murder 450.00
8 JCr,State Prison cover 400.00
9 AF,JCr,Bank Robbery 400.00
10 AF,JCr,Wanted:James Dore 400.00
11 AF,JCr 400.00
12 AF,Grl,JCr,Interrogation(c) . 400.00
13 AF,JCr 400.00
14 AF,JCr,Smugglers cover ... 400.00
15 AF,JCr,Crypt of Terror ... 1,800.00
16 AF,JCr,Crypt of Terror ... 1,400.00
Becomes:

GOLDEN AGE

CRYPT OF TERROR
E.C. Comics
April, 1950
17 JCr&(c),AF,'Werewolf
  Strikes Again' 2,000.00
18 JCr&(c),AF,WW,HK
  'The Living Corpse' 1,200.00
19 JCr&(c),AF,Grl,
  'Voodoo Drums' 1,200.00
Becomes:

TALES FROM THE CRYPT
October, 1950
20 JCr&(c),AF,GI,JKa
  'Day of Death' 900.00
21 AF&(c),WW,HK,GI,'Cooper
  Dies in the Electric Chair . 700.00
22 AF, JCr(c) 700.00
23 AF&(c),JCr,JDa(c),
  'Locked in a Mauseleum' . . 450.00
24 AF(c),WW,JDa,JCr,Grl
  'Danger...Quicksand' 450.00
25 AF(c),WW,JDa,JKa,Grl
  'Mataud Waxworks' 450.00
26 WW(c),JDa,Grl,
  'Scared Graveyard' 350.00
27 JKa, WW(c), Guillotine cover 350.00
28 AF&(c),JDa,JKa,Grl,JO
  'Buried Alive' 350.00
29 JDa&(c),JKa,Grl,JO
  'Coffin Burier' 350.00
30 JDa&(c),JO,JKa,Grl
  'Underwater Death' 350.00
31 JDa&(c),JKa,Grl,AW
  'Hand Chopper' 400.00
32 JDa&(c),GE,Grl,'Woman
  Crushed by Elephant' 300.00
33 JDa&(c),GE,JKa,Grl,'Lower
  Berth',O:Crypt Keeper 500.00
34 JDa&(c),JKa,GE,Grl,'Jack the
  Ripper,'Ray Bradbury adapt. 300.00
35 JDa&(c),JKa,JO,Grl,
  'Werewolf' 300.00
36 JDa&(c),JKa,GE,Grl, Ray
  Bradbury adaptation 300.00
37 JDa(c),JO,BE 300.00
38 JDa(c),BE,RC,Grl,'Axe Man' 300.00
39 JDa&(c),JKa,JO,Grl,'Children
  in the Graveyard' 300.00
40 JDa&(c),GE,BK,Grl,
  'Underwater Monster' 300.00
41 JDa&(c),JKa,GE,Grl,
  'Knife Thrower' 250.00
42 JDa(c),JO,Vampire cover . 250.00
43 JDa(c),JO,GE 250.00
44 JO,RC,Guillotine cover 250.00
45 JDa(c),JKa,BK,GI,'Rat
  Takes Over His Life' 250.00
46 JDa&(c),GE,JO,GI,'Werewolf
  man being hunted,Feb.1955 350.00

CRIME REPORTER
St. John Publishing Co.
August, 1948
1 Death Makes a Deadline . . 300.00
2 GT,MB(c),Matinee Murders . 500.00
3 GT,MB(c),December, 1948 . 250.00

CRIMES BY WOMEN
Fox Features Syndicate
June, 1948
1 Bonnie Parker 900.00
2 Vicious Female 500.00

---

3 Prison break cover 425.00
4 Murder cover 400.00
5 . . . . 400.00
6 Girl Fight cover 500.00
7 . . . . 400.00
8 . . . . 400.00
9 . . . . 400.00
10 . . . . 400.00
11 . . . . 400.00
12 . . . . 400.00
13 ACME jewelry robbery cover 400.00
14 Prison break cover 400.00
15 August, 1951 . . . . 400.00

CRIME SMASHER
Fawcett Publications
Summer, 1948
1 The Unlucky Rabbit's Foot . 300.00

CRIME SMASHERS
Ribage Publishing Corp.
October, 1950
1 Girl Rape 600.00
2 JKu,A:Sally the Sleuth, Dan Turner,
  Girl Friday, Rat Hale 300.00
3 MFa 200.00
4 Zak(c) 200.00
5 WW 250.00
6 . . . . 150.00
7 Bondage cover,Drugs 175.00
8 . . . . 150.00
9 Bondage cover 175.00
10 . . . . 150.00
11 . . . . 150.00
12 FF 175.00
13 . . . . 165.00
14 . . . . 150.00
15 . . . . 150.00

Crime Suspenstories #22
© *L.L. Publishing/E.C. Comics*

CRIME SUSPENSTORIES
L.L. Publishing Co.
(E.C. Comics)
October-November, 1950
1a JCr,Grl 1,000.00
1 JCr,WW,Grl 800.00
2 JCr,JKa,Grl 450.00

---

3 JCr,WW,Grl 350.00
4 JCr,Gln,Grl,JDa 325.00
5 JCr,JKa,Grl,JDa 300.00
6 JCr,JDa,Grl 250.00
7 JCr,Grl 250.00
8 JCr,Grl 250.00
9 JCr,Grl 250.00
10 JCr,Grl 250.00
11 JCr,Grl 200.00
12 JCr,Grl 200.00
13 JCr,AW 225.00
14 JCr 200.00
15 JCr 200.00
16 JCr,AW 225.00
17 JCr,FF,AW, Ray Bradbury . 250.00
18 JCr,RC,BE 200.00
19 JCr,RC,GE,AF(c) 200.00
20 RC,JCr, Hanging cover . . . 250.00
21 JCr 150.00
22 RC,JO,JCr(c),
  Severed head cover 175.00
23 JKa,RC,GE 175.00
24 BK,RC,JO 150.00
25 JKa,(c),RC 150.00
26 JKa,(c),RC,JO 150.00
27 JKa,(c),GE,Grl,March, 1955 150.00

CRIMINALS ON THE RUN
Premium Group of Comics
August, 1948
4-1 LbC(c) 175.00
4-2 LbC(c), A:Young King Cole 150.00
4-3 LbC(c), Rip Roaring Action
  in Alps 150.00
4-4 LbC(c), Shark cover 150.00
4-5 AMc 150.00
4-6 LbC 125.00
4-7 LbC 300.00
5-1 LbC 125.00
5-2 LbC 125.00
10 LbC 150.00
Becomes:

CRIME-FIGHTING DETECTIVE
11 LbC, Brodie Gang Captured 100.00
12 LbC(c), Jail Break Genius . 100.00
13 . . . . 50.00
14 LbC(c), A Night of Horror . . 75.00
15 LbC(c) 75.00
16 LbC(c), Wanton Murder . . . 75.00
17 LbC(c), The Framer
  was Framed 75.00
18 LbC(c), A Web of Evil 75.00
19 LbC(c), Lesson of the Law . . 75.00
Becomes:

SHOCK DETECTIVE CASE
20 LbC(c), The Strangler 100.00
21 LbC(c), Death Ride 100.00
Becomes:

SPOOK DETECTIVE CASES
22 Headless Horror 150.00
Becomes:

SPOOK SUSPENSE AND MYSTERY
23 LbC,Weird Picture of Murder 125.00
24 LbC(c),Mummy's Case 150.00
25 LbC(c),Horror Beyond Door 100.00
26 LbC(c),JyD,Face of Death . . 100.00

GOLDEN AGE

27 LbC(c),Ship of the Dead . . . 100.00
28 LbC(c),JyD,Creeping Death . . 100.00
29 LbC(c),Solo for Death 100.00
30 LbC(c),JyD,Nightmare,
   Oct.,1954 . . . . 100.00

CROWN COMICS
Golfing/McCombs Publ.
Winter 1944
1 Edgar Allen Poe adapt. 250.00
2 MB,I:Mickey Magic 125.00
3 MB,Jungle adventure cover . . 125.00
4 MB(c) 150.00
5 MB(c),Jungle adventure cover 150.00
6 MB(c),Jungle adventure cover 150.00
7 JKa,AF,MB(c),Race Car driving
   cover 150.00
8 MB 135.00
9 . . . . 85.00
10 Plane crash cover 85.00
11 LSt 75.00
12 LSt 75.00
13 LSt 75.00
14 . . . . 95.00
15 FBe 75.00
16 FBe,Jungle adventure(c) 75.00
17 FBe 75.00
18 FBe 75.00
19 BP,July, 1949 . . . . 75.00

CRUSADER FROM MARS
Approved Publ.
(Ziff-Davis)
January-March, 1952
1 Mission Thru Space, Death in
   the Sai 500.00
2 Beachhead on Saturn's Ring,
   Bondage(c),Fall, 1952 . . . . 400.00

CRYIN' LION, THE
William H. Wise Co.
Fall, 1944
1 . . . . 65.00
2 . . . . 40.00
3 Spring, 1945 . . . . 40.00

CRYPT OF TERROR
(see CRIME PATROL)

CYCLONE COMICS
Bibara Publ. Co.
June, 1940
1 O:Tornado Tom 1,000.00
2 . . . . 550.00
3 . . . . 500.00
4 Voltron 400.00
5 A: Mr. Q,October, 1940 . . . . 400.00

ALL GREAT COMICS
Fox Features Syndicate
October, 1947
12 A:Brenda Starr 275.00
13 JKa,O:Dagger, Desert Hawk 250.00
Becomes:
DAGAR, DESERT HAWK
14 JKa,Monster of Mura 550.00
15 JKa,Curse of the Lost
   Pharaoh 350.00
16 JKa,Wretched Antmen 300.00
19 Pyramid of Doom 275.00
20 . . . . 275.00
21 JKa(c),The Ghost of Fate . . 300.00

Dagar, Desert Hawk #20
© Fox Features Syndicate

22 . . . . 275.00
23 Bondage cover 300.00
Becomes:
CAPTAIN KIDD
24 Blackbeard the Pirate 85.00
25 Sorceress of the Deep 85.00
Becomes:
MY SECRET STORY
26 He Wanted More Than Love . 85.00
27 My Husband Hated Me 50.00
28 I Become a Marked Women . 50.00
29 My Forbidden Rapture,
   April, 1950 . . . . 50.00

DAFFY
Dell Publishing Co.
March, 1953
(1) see Dell Four Color #457
(2) see Dell Four Color #536
(3) see Dell Four Color #615
4 thru 7 . . . . @18.00
8 thru 11 . . . . @15.00
12 thru 17 . . . . @12.00
Becomes:
DAFFY DUCK
18 . . . . 12.00
19 . . . . 12.00
20 . . . . 12.00
21 thru 30 . . . . @8.00
Gold Key
31 thru 40 . . . . @7.00
41 thru 59 . . . . @5.00
60 B&A:Road Runner 3.00
61 thru 90 same . . . . @3.00
91 thru 127 . . . . @2.00
Whitman
128 thru 145 . . . . @2.00

DAGWOOD
Harvey Publications
September, 1950
1 . . . . 85.00
2 . . . . 50.00
3 thru 10 . . . . @35.00
11 thru 20 . . . . @30.00

21 thru 30 . . . . @20.00
31 thru 50 . . . . @15.00
51 thru 70 . . . . @10.00
71 thru 109 . . . . @8.00
110 thru 140 . . . . @7.00

DANGER AND ADVENTURE
(see THIS MAGAZINE IS HAUNTED)

DANGER IS OUR BUSINESS
Toby Press/
I.W. Enterprises
1953
1 AW,FF,Men who Defy Death
   for a Living 300.00
2 Death Crowds the Cockpit . . 75.00
3 Killer Mountain 60.00
4 . . . . 60.00
5 thru 9 . . . . @50.00
10 June, 1955 . . . . 60.00

DAREDEVIL COMICS
Lev Gleason Publications
July, 1941
1 Daredevil Battles Hitler, A:Silver
   Streak, Lance Hale, Dickey Dean,
   Cloud Curtis,V:The Claw,
   O:Hitler 9,000.00
2 I:The Pioneer, Champion of
   American,B:London,Pat
   Patriot,Pirate Prince 2,500.00
3 CBi(c),O:Thirteen 1,400.00
4 CBi(c),Death is the Refere . 1,200.00
5 CBi(c),I:Sniffer&Jinx, Claw
   V:Ghost,Lottery of Doom . . 1,000.00
6 CBi(c) 850.00
7 CBi(c), What Ghastly Sight Lies
   within the Mysterious Trunk . 750.00
8 V:Nazis cover, E:Nightro . . . 700.00
9 V:Double 700.00
10 America will Remember
   Pearl Harbor 700.00
11 Bondage cover, E:Pat
   Patriot, London 750.00
12 BW,CBi(c), O:The Law . . . 1,100.00
13 BW,I:Little Wise Guys . . . 1,000.00
14 BW,CBi(c) 500.00
15 BW,CBi(c), D:Meatball 700.00
16 BW,CBi(c) 475.00
17 BW,CBi(c), Into the Valley
   of Death 450.00
18 BW,CBi(c), O:Daredevil,
   double length story 1,000.00
19 BW,CBi(c), Buried Alive . . . 375.00
20 BW,CBi(c), Boxing cover . . 375.00
21 CBi(c), Can Little Wise Guys
   Survive Blast of Dynamite? . 650.00
22 CBi(c) 300.00
23 CBi(c), I:Pshyco 300.00
24 CBi(c), Punch and Judy
   Murders 300.00
25 CBi(c), baseball cover 325.00
26 CBi(c) 275.00
27 CBi(c), Bondage cover 300.00
28 CBi(c) 275.00
29 CBi(c) 275.00
30 CBi(c), Ann Hubbard White
   1922-1943 . . . . 275.00
31 CBi(c), D:The Claw 600.00
32 V:Blackmarketeers 200.00

GOLDEN AGE

GOLDEN AGE

33 CBi(c) 200.00
34 CBi(c) 200.00
35 B:Two Daredevil stories
   every issue 175.00
36 CBi(c) 175.00
37 CBi(c) 175.00
38 CBi(c), O:Daredevil 350.00
39 CBi(c) 175.00
40 CBi(c) 175.00
41 . . . . 150.00
42 thru 50 CBi(c) . . . . @150.00
51 CBi(c) 125.00
52 CBi(c),Football cover 150.00
53 thru 57 . . . . @125.00
58 Football cover 150.00
59 . . . . 125.00
60 . . . . 125.00
61 thru 68 . . . . @125.00
69 E:Daredevil 125.00
70 . . . . 100.00
71 thru 78 . . . . @75.00
79 B:Daredevil 85.00
80 . . . . 80.00

Daredevil #37
© Lev Gleason Publications

81 . . . . 55.00
82 . . . . 55.00
83 thru 99 . . . . @55.00
100 . . . . 75.00
101 thru 133 . . . . @50.00
134 September, 1956 . . . . 50.00

DARING CONFESSIONS
(see YOUTHFUL HEART)

DARING LOVE
(see YOUTHFUL ROMANCES)

DARK MYSTERIES
Merit Publications
June-July, 1951
1 WW, WW(c), Curse of the
   Sea Witch 650.00
2 WW, WW(c), Vampire Fangs
   of Doom 450.00
3 Terror of the Unwilling
   Witch 200.00
4 Corpse that Came Alive . . . 200.00

5 Horror of the Ghostly Crew . 150.00
6 If the Noose Fits Wear It! . . 150.00
7 Terror of the Cards of Death . 150.00
8 Terror of the Ghostly Trail . . 150.00
9 Witch's Feast at Dawn 150.00
10 Terror of the Burning Witch . 225.00
11 The River of Blood 125.00
12 Horror of the Talking Dead . 125.00
13 Terror of the Hungry Cats . . 125.00
14 Horror of the Fingers of Doom 135.00
15 Terror of the Vampires Teeth 125.00
16 Horror of the Walking Dead . 125.00
17 Terror of the Mask of Death . 125.00
18 Terror of the Burning Corpse 125.00
19 The Rack of Terror 150.00
20 Burning Executioner 135.00
21 The Sinister Secret 110.00
22 The Hand of Destiny 110.00
23 The Mardenburg Curse 100.00
24 Give A Man enough Rope,
   July, 1955 . . . . 100.00

DAVY CROCKETT
Avon Periodicals
1951
1 . . . . 125.00

DEAD END
CRIME STORIES
Kirby Publishing Co.
April, 1949
N# BP 400.00

DEAD-EYE
WESTERN COMICS
Hillman Periodicals
November-December, 1948
1 BK 100.00
2 . . . . 60.00
3 . . . . 50.00
4 thru 12 . . . . @35.00
2-1 . . . . 30.00
2-2 . . . . 30.00
2-3 . . . . 45.00
2-4 . . . . 45.00
2-5 thru 2-12 . . . . @25.00
3-1 . . . . 25.00

DEADWOOD GULCH
Dell Publishing Co.
1931
1 . . . . 125.00

DEAR BEATRICE
FAIRFAX
Best Books
(Standard Comics)
November, 1950
5 . . . . 40.00
6 thru 9 . . . . @25.00

DEAR LONELY HEART
Artful Publications
March, 1951
5 . . . . 75.00
6 . . . . 35.00
7 MB,Jungle Girl 75.00
8 . . . . 30.00
9 . . . . 30.00

DEAR LONELY HEARTS
Comic Media
August, 1953
1 Six Months to Live 38.00
2 Date Hungry, Price of Passion 22.00
3 thru 8 . . . . @22.00

DEARLY BELOVED
Approved Comics
(Ziff-Davis)
Fall, 1952
1 Ph(c) 75.00

DEBBIE DEAN,
CAREER GIRL
Civil Service Publishing
April, 1945
1 . . . . 75.00
2 . . . . 70.00

DELL GIANT EDITIONS
Dell Publishing Co.
1953-58
Abe Lincoln Life Story 125.00
Cadet Gray of West Point 100.00
Golden West Rodeo Treasury . 150.00
Life Stories of
   American Presidents 90.00
Lone Ranger Golden West . . . 300.00
Lone Ranger Movie Story 500.00
Lone Ranger Western
   Treasury('53) 275.00
Lone Ranger Western
   Treasury('54) 175.00
Moses & Ten Commandments . . 75.00
Nancy & Sluggo Travel Time . . 100.00
Pogo Parade 450.00
Raggedy Ann & Andy 275.00
Santa Claus Funnies 150.00
Tarzan's Jungle Annual #1 . . . 200.00
Tarzan's Jungle Annual #2 . . . 150.00
Tarzan's Jungle Annual #3 . . . 125.00
Tarzan's Jungle Annual #4 . . . 125.00
Tarzan's Jungle Annual #5 . . . 125.00
Tarzan's Jungle Annual #6 . . . 125.00
Tarzan's Jungle Annual #7 . . . 125.00
Treasury of Dogs 100.00
Treasury of Horses 100.00
Universal Presents-Dracula-
   The Mummy & Other Stories 300.00
Western Roundup #1 . . . . 300.00
Western Roundup #2 . . . . 200.00
Western Roundup #3 . . . . 150.00
Western Roundup #4 thru #5 @150.00
Western Roundup #6 thru #10 @140.00
Western Roundup #11 thru #17@135.00
Western Roundup #18 . . . . . . 125.00
Western Roundup #19 thru #25 125.00
Woody Woodpecker Back
   to School #1 . . . . 165.00
Woody Woodpecker Back
   to School #2 . . . . 120.00
Woody Woodpecker Back
   to School #3 . . . . 90.00
Woody Woodpecker Back
   to School #4 . . . . 90.00
Woody Woodpecker County
   Fair #5 . . . . 90.00
Woody Woodpecker Back
   to School #6 . . . . 80.00
Woody Woodpecker County
   Fair #2 . . . . 75.00
Also See:

Bugs Bunny
Marge's Little Lulu
Tom and Jerry, and
Walt Disney Dell Giant Editions

DELL GIANT COMICS
Dell Publishing Co.
September 1959

21 M.G.M. Tom & Jerry
  Picnic Time 200.00
22 W.Disney's Huey, Dewey & Louie
  Back to School (Oct 1959) . 135.00
23 Marge's Little Lulu &
  Tubby Halloween Fun 200.00
24 Woody Woodpeckers
  Family Fun 125.00
25 Tarzan's Jungle World . . . 175.00
26 W.Disney's Christmas
  Parade,CB 375.00
27 W.Disney's Man in
  Space (1960) 250.00
28 Bugs Bunny's Winter Fun . . 175.00
29 Marge's Little Lulu &
  Tubby in Hawaii 225.00

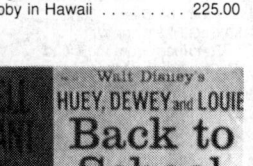

Dell Giant #22 © Dell Publishing Co.

30 W.Disney's DisneylandU.S.A. 200.00
31 Huckleberry Hound
  Summer Fun 225.00
32 Bugs Bunny Beach Party . . 100.00
33 W.Disney's Daisy Duck &
  Uncle Scrooge Picnic Time . 175.00
34 Nancy&SluggoSummerCamp 120.00
35 W.Disney's Huey, Dewey &
  Louie Back to School 150.00
36 Marge's Little Lulu & Witch
  Hazel Halloween Fun 220.00
37 Tarzan, King of the Jungle . 150.00
38 W.Disney's Uncle Donald and
  his Nephews Family Fun . . 125.00
39 W.Disney's Merry Christmas 125.00
40 Woody Woodpecker
  Christmas Parade 100.00
41 Yogi Bear's Winter Sports . . 225.00
42 Marge's Little Lulu &
  Tubby in Australia 100.00
43 Mighty Mouse in OuterSpace 400.00
44 Around the World with

Huckleberry & His Friends . 225.00
45 Nancy&SluggoSummerCamp 100.00
46 Bugs Bunny Beach Party . . 100.00
47 W.Disney's Mickey and
  Donald in Vacationland 175.00
48 The Flintstones #1
  (Bedrock Bedlam) 275.00
49 W.Disney's Huey, Dewey &
  Louie Back to School 105.00
50 Marge's Little Lulu &
  Witch Hazel Trick 'N' Treat . 225.00
51 Tarzan, King of the Jungle . 150.00
52 W.Disney's Uncle Donald &
  his Nephews Dude Ranch . 150.00
53 W.Disney's Donald Duck
  Merry Christmas 135.00
54 Woody Woodpecker
  Christmas Party 120.00
55 W.Disney's Daisy Duck & Uncle
  Scrooge Show Boat (1961) . 200.00

DELL JUNIOR TREASURY
Dell Publishing Co.
June, 1955

1 Alice in Wonderland 100.00
2 Aladdin 65.00
3 Gulliver's Travels 50.00
4 Adventures of Mr. Frog 55.00
5 Wizard of Oz 60.00
6 Heidi 65.00
7 Santa & the Angel 65.00
8 Raggedy Ann 65.00
9 Clementina the Flying Pig . . . 60.00
10 Adventures of Tom Sawyer . . 60.00

Dennis the Menace #100
© Fawcett Publications

DENNIS THE MENACE
Visual Editions/Literary Ent.
(Standard, Pines)
August, 1953

1 . . . . 425.00
2 . . . . 200.00
3 . . . . 90.00
4 . . . . 90.00
5 thru 10 . . . . @75.00
11 thru 20 . . . . @60.00
21 thru 31 . . . . @40.00
Hallden (Fawcett)

32 thru 40 . . . . @25.00
41 thru 50 . . . . @20.00
51 thru 60 . . . . @15.00
61 thru 70 . . . . @10.00
71 thru 90 . . . . @7.00
91 thru 140 . . . . @3.50
141 thru 166 . . . . @3.00

DESPERADO
Lev Gleason Publications
June, 1948

1 CBi(c) 75.00
2 CBi(c) 40.00
3 CBi(c) 30.00
4 CBi(c) 25.00
5 CBi(c) 25.00
6 CBi(c) 25.00
7 CBi(c) 25.00
8 CBi(c) 25.00
Becomes:

BLACK DIAMOND
WESTERN

9 CBi(c) 125.00
10 CBi(c) 60.00
11 CBi(c) 50.00
12 CBi(c) 50.00
13 CBi(c) 50.00
14 CBi(c) 50.00
15 CBi(c) 50.00
16 thru 28 BW,Big Bang Buster @65.00
29 thru 40 . . . . @30.00
41 thru 52 . . . . @25.00
53 3-D 60.00
54 3-D 50.00
55 thru 60 . . . . @25.00

DETECTIVE EYE
Centaur Publications
November, 1940

1 B:Air Man, The Eye Sees,
  A:Masked Marvel 1,500.00
2 O:Don Rance, Mysticape,
  December, 1940 . . . . 1,000.00

DETECTIVE
PICTURE STORIES
Comics Magazine Co.
December, 1936

1 The Phantom Killer 3,500.00
2 . . . . 1,500.00
3 . . . . 1,000.00
4 WE, Muss Em Up 900.00
5 Trouble, April, 1937 . . . . . 1,100.00

DEXTER COMICS
Dearfield Publications
Summer, 1948

1 . . . . 35.00
2 . . . . 25.00
3 . . . . 15.00
4 . . . . 15.00
5 July, 1949 . . . . 15.00

DIARY CONFESSIONS
(see TENDER ROMANCE)

DIARY LOVES
Comic Magazines
(Quality Comics Group)
September, 1949

1 BWa 100.00

GOLDEN AGE

2 BWa	80.00
3	30.00
4 RC	45.00
5	25.00
6	25.00
7	25.00
8 BWa	75.00
9 BWa	60.00
10 BWa	75.00
11	25.00
12	25.00
13	25.00
14	25.00
15 BWa	50.00
16 BWa	50.00
17	25.00
18	25.00
19	25.00
20	25.00
21 BWa	40.00
22 thru 93	@15.00

Becomes:

G.I. SWEETHEARTS

32 Love Under Fire	25.00
33	25.00
34	25.00
35	25.00
36 Lend Lease Love Affair	25.00
37 thru 45	@25.00

Becomes:

GIRLS IN LOVE

46 Somewhere I'll Find You	30.00
47 thru 56	@20.00
57 MB,MB(c), Can Love Really Change Him, Dec., 1956	40.00

DIARY SECRETS
(see TEEN-AGE DIARY SECRETS)

DICK COLE
Curtis Publ./ Star Publications
December-January, 1949

1 LbC(c),LbC(c),CS,All sports(c)	175.00
2 LbC	85.00
3 LbC, LbC(c)	100.00
4 LbC, LbC(c),Rowing cover	100.00
5 LbC,LbC(c)	100.00
6 LbC,LbC(c), Rodeo cover	100.00
7 LbC,LbC(c)	100.00
8 LbC,LbC(c), Football cover	100.00
9 LbC,LbC(c), Basketball cover	100.00
10 Joe Louis	100.00

Becomes:

SPORTS THRILLS

11 Ted Williams & Ty Cobb	250.00
12 LbC, Joe Dimaggio & Phil Rizzuto, Boxing cover	150.00
13 LbC(c),Basketball cover	150.00
14 LbC(c),Baseball cover	150.00
15 LbC(c),Baseball cover, November, 1951	150.00

DICKIE DARE
Eastern Color Printing Co.
1941

1 BEv(c)	250.00
2	175.00
3	175.00
4 1942	200.00

DICK TRACY MONTHLY
Dell Publishing Co.
January, 1948

1 ChG,Dick Tracy & the Mad Doctor'	450.00
2 ChG,A:MarySteele,BorisArson	250.00
3 ChG,A:Spaldoni,Big Boy	250.00
4 ChG,A:Alderman Zeld	200.00
5 ChG,A:Spaldoni,Mrs.Spaldoni	200.00
6 ChG,A:Steve the Tramp	200.00
7 ChG,A:Boris Arson,Mary Steele	200.00
8 ChG,A:Boris & Zora Arson	200.00
9 ChG,A:Chief Yellowpony	200.00
10 ChG,A:Cutie Diamond	200.00
11 ChG,A:Toby Townly, Bookie Joe	150.00
12 ChG,A:Toby Townly, Bookie Joe	150.00
13 ChG,A:Toby Townly, Blake	160.00
14 ChG,A:Mayor Waite Wright	150.00

Dick Tracy Monthly #5 © Dell Publ. Co.

15 ChG,A:Bowman Basil	150.00
16 ChG,A:Maw,'Muscle' & 'Cut' Famon	150.00
17 ChG,A:Jim Trailer, Mary Steele	150.00
18 ChG,A:Lips Manlis, Anthel Jones	150.00
19 'Golden Heart Mystery'	200.00
20 'Black Cat Mystery'	200.00
21 'Tracy Meets Number One'	200.00
22 'Tracy and the Alibi Maker'	150.00
23 'Dick Tracy Meets Jukebox'	150.00
24 'Dick Tracy and Bubbles'	150.00

Becomes:

DICK TRACY COMICS MONTHLY
Harvey

25 ChG,A:Flattop	175.00
26 ChG,A:Vitamin Flintheart	150.00
27 ChG,'Flattop Escapes Prision'	150.00
28 ChG,'Case o/t Torture Chamber'	160.00
29 ChG,A:Brow,Gravel Gertie	150.00
30 ChG,'Blackmail Racket'	150.00
31 ChG,A:Snowflake Falls	125.00
32 ChG,A:Shaky,Snowflake Falls	125.00
33 ChG,'Strange Case of Measles'	150.00
34 ChG,A:Measles,Paprika	125.00
35 ChG,'Case of Stolen $50,000'	125.00
36 ChG,'Case of the Runaway Blonde'	150.00
37 ChG,'Case of Stolen Money'	125.00
38 ChG,A:Breathless Mahoney	125.00
39 ChG,A:Itchy,B.O.Pleanty	125.00
40 ChG,'Case of Atomic Killer'	125.00
41 ChG,Pt.1'Murder by Mail'	100.00
42 ChG,Pt.2'Murder by Mail'	100.00
43 ChG,'Case of the Underworld Brat'	100.00
44 ChG,'Case of the Mouthwash Murder'	100.00
45 ChG,'Case of the Evil Eyes'	100.00
46 ChG,'Case of the Camera Killers'	100.00
47 ChG,'Case of the Bloodthirsty Blonde'	100.00
48 ChG,'Case of the Murderous Minstrel'	100.00
49 ChG,Pt.1'Killer Who Returned From the Dead	100.00
50 ChG,Pt.2'Killer Who Returned From the Dead'	100.00
51 ChG,'Case of the High Tension Hijackers'	75.00
52 ChG,'Case of the Pipe-Stem Killer	75.00
53 ChG,Pt.1'Dick Tracy Meets the Murderous Midget'	75.00
54 ChG,Pt.2'Dick Tracy Meets the Murderous Midget'	75.00
55 ChG,Pt.3'Dick Tracy Meets the Murderous Midget'	75.00
56 ChG,'Case of the Teleguard Terror'	75.00
57 ChG,Pt.1'Case of the Ice Cold Killer'	100.00
58 ChG,Pt.2'Case of the Ice Cold Killer'	75.00
59 ChG,Pt.1'Case of the Million Dollar Murder'	75.00
60 ChG,Pt.2'Case of the Million Dollar Murder'	60.00
61 ChG,'Case of the Murderers Mask'	60.00
62 ChG,Pt.1'Case of the White Rat Robbers'	60.00
63 ChG,Pt.2'Case of the White Rat Robbers'	60.00
64 ChG,Pt.1'Case of the Interrupted Honeymoon'	60.00
65 ChG,Pt.2'Case of the Interrupted Honeymoon'	60.00
66 ChG,Pt.1'Case of the Killer's Revenge'	60.00
67 ChG,Pt.2'Case of the Killer's Revenge'	60.00
68 ChG,Pt.1'Case of the TV Terror'	60.00
69 ChG,Pt.2'Case of the TV Terror'	60.00
70 ChG,Pt.3'Case of the TV Terror'	60.00
71 ChG,A:Mrs. Forchune,Opal	60.00
72 ChG,A:Empty Wiliams,Bonny	60.00
73 ChG,A:Bonny Braids	60.00
74 ChG,A:Mr. & Mrs. Fortson Knox	60.00
75 ChG,A:Crewy Lou, Sphinx	60.00
76 ChG,A:Diet Smith,Brainerd	60.00
77 ChG,A:Crewy Lou,	

Bonny Braids 60.00
78 ChG,A:Spinner Records 60.00
79 ChG,A:Model Jones,
   Larry Jones 60.00
80 ChG,A:Tonsils,Dot View 60.00
81 ChG,A:Edward Moppet,Tonsils 60.00
82 ChG,A:Dot View,Mr. Crime . . 60.00
83 ChG,A:Rifle Ruby,Newsuit Nan 60.00
84 ChG,A:Mr. Crime,Newsuit Nan 60.00
85 ChG,A:Newsuit Nan, Mrs.Lava 60.00
86 ChG,A:Mr. Crime, Odds Zonn 60.00
87 ChG,A:Odds Zonn,Wingy . . . 60.00
88 ChG,A:Odds Zonn,Wingy . . . 60.00
89 ChG,Pt.1'Canhead' 60.00
90 ChG,Pt.2'Canhead' 60.00
91 ChG,Pt.3'Canhead' 60.00
92 ChG,Pt.4'Canhead' 60.00
93 ChG,Pt.5'Canhead' 60.00
94 ChG,Pt.6'Canhead' 60.00
95 ChG,A:Mrs. Green,Dewdrop . 60.00
96 ChG,A:Dewdrop,Sticks 60.00
97 ChG,A:Dewdrop,Sticks 60.00
98 ChG,A:Open-Mind Monty,
   Sticks 60.00
99 ChG,A:Open-Mind Monty,
   Sticks 70.00
100 ChG,A:Half-Pint,Dewdrop . . 75.00
101 ChG,A:Open-Mind Monty . . 60.00
102 ChG,A:Rainbow Reiley,Wingy 60.00
103 ChG,A:Happy,Rughead 60.00
104 ChG,A:Rainbow Reiley,Happy 60.00
105 ChG,A:Happy,Rughead 60.00
106 ChG,A:Fence,Corny,Happy . 60.00
107 ChG,A:Rainbow Reiley 60.00
108 ChG,A:Rughead,Corny,Fence 60.00
109 ChG,A:Rughead,Mimi,Herky 60.00
110 ChG,A:Vitamin Flintheart . . . 60.00
111 ChG,A:Shoulders,Roach . . . 60.00
112 ChG,A:Brilliant,Diet Smith . . 60.00
113 ChG,A:Snowflake Falls 60.00
114 ChG,A:'Sketch'Paree, ... 60.00
115 ChG,A:Rod & Nylon Hoze . . 60.00
116 ChG,A:Empty Williams 60.00
117 ChG,A:Spinner Records . . . 60.00
118 ChG,A:Sleet 60.00
119 ChG,A:Coffyhead 60.00
120 ChG,'Case Against
   Mumbles Quartet' 50.00
121 ChG,'Case of the Wild Boys' 50.00
122 ChG,'Case of the
   Poisoned Pellet' 50.00
123 ChG,'Case of the Deadly
   Treasure Hunt' 50.00
124 ChG,'Case of Oodles
   Hears Only Evil 50.00
125 ChG,'Case of the Desparate
   Widow' 50.00
126 ChG,'Case of Oodles'
   Hideout' 50.00
127 ChG,'Case Against
   Joe Period' 50.00
128 ChG,'Case Against Juvenile
   Delinquent' 50.00
129 ChG,'Case of Son of Flattop' 50.00
130 ChG,'Case of Great
   Gang Roundup' 50.00
131 ChG,'Strange Case of
   Flattop's Conscience' 55.00
132 ChG,'Case of Flattop's
   Big Show' 55.00
133 ChG,'Dick Tracy Follows Trail
   of Jewel Thief Gang' 50.00
134 ChG,'Last Stand of
   Jewel Thieves' 50.00
135 ChG,'Case of the

Rooftop Sniper' 50.00
136 ChG,'Mystery of the
   Iron Room' 50.00
137 ChG,'Law Versus Dick Tracy' 50.00
138 ChG,'Mystery of Mary X' . . . 50.00
139 ChG,'Yogee the Merciless' . 50.00
140 ChG,'The Tunnel Trap' 50.00
141 ChG,'Case of Wormy &
   His Deadly Wagon 50.00
142 ChG,'Case of the
   Killer's Revenge' 50.00
143 ChG,'Strange Case of
   Measles' 50.00
144 ChG,'Strange Case of
   Shoulders' 50.00
145 ChG,'Case of the Feindish
   Photo-graphers';April, 1961 . . 50.00

DIME COMICS
Newsbook Publ. Corp.
1945
1 LbC,A:Silver Streak 300.00

DING DONG
Compix
(Magazine Enterprises)
1947
1 (fa) 75.00
2 (fa) 45.00
3 thru 5 (fa) . . . . @35.00

DINKY DUCK
St. John Publ. Co./Pines
November, 1951
1 . . . . 50.00
2 . . . . 30.00
3 thru 10 . . . . @20.00
11 thru 15 . . . . @15.00
16 thru 18 . . . . @10.00
19 Summer, 1958 . . . . 10.00

DIXIE DUGAN
Columbia Publ./
Publication Enterprises
July, 1942
1 Boxing cover,Joe Palooka . . 200.00
2 . . . . 125.00
3 . . . . 85.00
4 . . . . 60.00
5 . . . . 60.00
6 thru 12 . . . . @45.00
13 1949 . . . . 45.00

DIZZY DAMES
B&M Distribution Co.
(American Comics)
September-October, 1952
1 . . . . 60.00
2 . . . . 40.00
3 thru 6 July-Aug., 1953 . . . @25.00

DIZZY DON COMICS
Howard Publications/
Dizzy Dean Ent.
1943
1 B&W interior 45.00
2 B&W Interior 20.00
3 B&W Interior 15.00
4 B&W Interior 15.00
5 thru 21 . . . . @15.00
22 October, 1946 . . . . 40.00
1a thru 3a . . . . @30.00

DIZZY DUCK
(see BARNYARD COMICS)

DOC CARTER
V.D. COMICS
Health Publ. Inst.
1949
N# 150.00
N# 100.00

Doc Savage Comics #3
© *Street & Smith Publications*

DOC SAVAGE COMICS
Street & Smith Publications
May, 1940
1 B:Doc Savage, Capt. Fury, Danny
   Garrett, Mark Mallory, Whisperer,
   Capt. Death, Treasure
   Island, A: The Magician . . 3,800.00
2 O:Ajax,The Sun Man,E:The
   Whisperer 1,200.00
3 Artic Ice Wastes 900.00
4 E:Treasure Island, Saves
   U.S. Navy 750.00
5 O:Astron, the Crocodile
   Queen, Sacred Ruby 550.00
6 E: Capt. Fury, O:Red Falcon,
   Murderous Peace Clan . . . 450.00
7 V:Zoombas 450.00
8 Finds the Long Lost Treasure 450.00
9 Smashes Japan's Secret Oil
   Supply 450.00
10 O:Thunder Bolt, The Living
   Dead A:Lord Manhattan . . . 450.00
11 V:Giants of Destruction 400.00
12 Saves Merchant Fleet from
   Complete Destruction 400.00
2-1 The Living Evil 400.00
2-2 V:Beggar King 400.00
2-3 . . . . 400.00
2-4 Fight to Death 400.00
2-5 Saves Panama Canal from
   Blood Raider 400.00
2-6 . . . . 400.00
2-7 V:Black Knight 400.00
2-8 October, 1943 . . . . 400.00

GOLDEN AGE

All comics prices listed are for *Near Mint* condition.

DR. ANTHONY KING HOLLYWOOD LOVE DOCTOR
Harvey, Publ.
1952

1	75.00
2	40.00
3	40.00
4 BP,May, 1954	40.00

DOLL MAN
Comic Favorites (Quality Comics Group)
Fall, 1941

1 RC,B:Doll Man & Justine Wright	2,200.00
2 B:Dragon	900.00
3 Five stories	650.00
4 Dolls of Death, Wanted: The Doll Man	600.00
5 RC,Four stories	500.00
6 Buy War Stamps cover	450.00
7 Four stories	450.00
8 BWa,Three stories,A:Torchy	500.00
9	300.00
10 RC,V:Murder Marionettes, Grim, The Good Sport	250.00
11 Shocks Crime Square in the Eye	250.00
12	250.00
13 RC,Blows Crime Sky High	250.00
14 Spotlight on Comics	250.00
15 Faces Danger	250.00
16	250.00
17 Deals out Punishment for Crime	250.00
18 Redskins Scalp Crime	250.00
19 Fretted for a Cement Coffin	250.00
20 Destroys the Black Heart of Nemo Black	250.00
21 Problem of a Poison Pistol	200.00
22 V:Tom Thumb	200.00
23 V:Minstrel, musician of menace	200.00
24 V:Elixir of Youth	200.00
25 V:Thrawn, Lord of Lightning	200.00
26 V:Sultan of Satarr & Wonderous Runt	200.00
27 Space Conquest	200.00
28 V:The Flame	200.00
29 V:Queen MAB	200.00
30 V:Lord Damion	200.00
31 I:Elmo, the Wonder Dog	175.00
32 A:Jeb Rivers	175.00
33	175.00
34	175.00
35 Prophet of Doom	175.00
36 Death Trap in the Deep	175.00
37 V:The Skull,B:Doll Girl, Bondage(c)	250.00
38 The Cult of Death	175.00
39 V:The Death Drug	200.00
40 Giants of Crime	150.00
41 The Headless Horseman	150.00
42 Tale of the Mind Monster	150.00
43 The Thing that Kills	150.00
44 V:Radioactive Man	150.00
45 What was in the Doom Box?	150.00
46 Monster from Tomorrow	150.00
47 V:Mad Hypnotist, October, 1953	150.00

FAMOUS GANG, BOOK OF COMICS
Firestone Tire & Rubber Co.
1942

N#	750.00

Becomes:

DONALD AND MICKEY MERRY CHRISTMAS

N# (2),CB, 1943	700.00
N# (3),CB, 1944	700.00
N# (4),CB, 1945	950.00
N# (5),CB, 1946	750.00
N# (6),CB, 1947	650.00
N# (7),CB, 1948	650.00
N# (8),CB, 1949	675.00

DONALD DUCK
Whitman

W.Disney's Donald Duck ('35)	2,200.00
W.Disney's Donald Duck ('36)	2,000.00
W.Disney's Donald Duck ('38)	2,200.00

DONALD DUCK GIVEAWAYS

Donald Duck Surprise Party (Icy Frost Ice Cream 1948)WK	900.00
Donald Duck (Xmas Giveaway 1944)	350.00
Donald Duck Tells About Kites (P.G.&E., Florida 1954)	2,000.00
Donald Duck Tells About Kites (S.C.Edison 1954)	1,800.00
Donald Duck and the Boys (Whitman 1948)	125.00
Donald Ducks Atom Bomb (Cherrios 1947)	275.00

Donald Duck #46
© Dell Publishing Co.

(WALT DISNEY'S) DONALD DUCK
Dell Publishing Co.
November 1952
(#1-#25) See Dell Four Color

26 CB;"Trick or Treat" (1952)	350.00
27 CB(c);"Flying Horse"('53)	150.00
28 CB(c); Robert the Robot	125.00

29 CB(c)	125.00
30 CB(c)	125.00
31 thru 39	@65.00
40 thru 44	@60.00
45 CB	160.00
46 CB; "Secret of Hondorica"	250.00
47 thru 51	@60.00
52 CB; "Lost Peg-Leg Mine"	150.00
53	40.00
54 CB; "Forbidden Valley"	150.00
55 thru 59	@40.00
60 CB; "Donald Duck & the Titanic Ants"	150.00
61 thru 67	@40.00
68 CB	125.00
69 thru 78	@35.00
79 CB (1 page)	45.00
80	30.00
81 CB (1 page)	35.00
82	30.00
83	30.00
84	30.00

See: Independent Color Listings

DON FORTUNE MAGAZINE
Don Fortune Publ. Co.
August, 1946

1 CCB	125.00
2 CCB	75.00
3 CCB,Bondage(c)	60.00
4 CCB	50.00
5 CCB	50.00
6 CCB, January, 1947	50.00

DON NEWCOMBE
Fawcett Publications
1950

1 Baseball Star	300.00

DON WINSLOW OF THE NAVY
Fawcett Publ./ Charlton Comics
February, 1943

1 Captain Marvel cover	750.00
2 Nips the Nipponese in the Solomons	400.00
3 Single-Handed invasion of the Philippines	300.00
4 Undermines the Nazis!	200.00
5 Stolen Battleship Mystery	200.00
6 War Stamps for Victory cover	200.00
7 Coast Guard	150.00
8 U.S. Marines	150.00
9 Fighting Marines	150.00
10 Fighting Seabees	150.00
11	125.00
12 Tuned for Death	125.00
13 Hirohito's Hospitality	135.00
14 Catapults against the Axis	135.00
15 Fighting Merchant Marine	120.00
16 V:The Most Diabolical Villain of all Time	120.00
17 Buy War Stamps cover	120.00
18 The First Underwater Convoy	100.00
19 Bonape Excersion	100.00
20 The Nazi Prison Ship	100.00
21 Prisoner of the Nazis	90.00
22 Suicide Football	90.00
23 Peril on the High Seas	90.00
24 Adventures on the High Seas	90.00
25 Shanghaied Red Cross Ship	90.00

GOLDEN AGE

Don Winslow of the Navy #6
© Fawcett Publications

26 V:The Scorpion	90.00
27 Buy War Stamps	90.00
28	90.00
29 Invitation to Trouble	90.00
30	90.00
31 Man or Myth?	75.00
32 Return of the Renegade	75.00
33 Service Ribbons	75.00
34 Log Book	75.00
35	75.00
36	75.00
37 V: Sea Serpent	75.00
38 Climbs Mt. Everest	75.00
39 Scorpion's Death Ledger	75.00
40 Kick Off!	70.00
41 Rides the Skis!	65.00
42 Amazon Island	65.00
43 Ghastly Doll Murder Case	65.00
44 The Scorpions Web	65.00
45 V:Highwaymen of the Seas	65.00
46 Renegades Jailbreak	65.00
47 The Artic Expedition	65.00
48 Maelstrom of the Deep	65.00
49 The Vanishing Ship!	65.00
50 V:The Snake	65.00
51 A:Singapore Sal	55.00
52 Ghost of the Fishing Ships	55.00
53	55.00
54	55.00
55	55.00
56 Far East	55.00
57 A:Singapore Sal	55.00
58	55.00
59	55.00
60	55.00
61	55.00
62	55.00
63	55.00
64 MB	65.00
65 Ph(c)	75.00
66 Ph(c)	75.00
67 Ph(c)	75.00
68 Ph(c)	75.00
69 Ph(c), Jaws of Destruction	75.00
70	50.00
71	50.00
72	50.00
73 September, 1955	50.00

DOPEY DUCK
Non-Pareil Publ. Corp.
Fall, 1945

1 A:Krazy Krow,Casper Cat	100.00
2 same	75.00

Becomes:

WACKY DUCK

3	50.00
4	40.00
5	40.00
6 Summer, 1947	40.00

DOROTHY LAMOUR
(see JUNGLE LIL)

DOTTY DRIPPLE
Magazine Enterprises/
Harvey Publications
1946

1	50.00
2	25.00
3 thru 10	@15.00
11 thru 20	@10.00
21 thru 23	@8.00
24 June, 1952	8.00

Becomes:

HORACE &
DOTTY DRIPPLE

25 thru 42	@6.00
43 October, 1955	6.00

DOUBLE COMICS
Elliot Publications

1 ('40),Masked Marvel	1,600.00
2 ('41),Tornado Tim	1,200.00
3 ('42)	1,000.00
4 ('43)	750.00
5 ('44)	750.00

DOUBLE UP
Elliot Publications
1941

1	600.00

DOWN WITH CRIME
Fawcett Publications
November, 1951

1 A:Desarro	150.00
2 BP, A:Scanlon Gang	100.00
3 H-is for Heroin	75.00
4 BP, A:Desarro	60.00
5 No Jail Can Hold Me	75.00
6 The Puncture-Proof Assassin	60.00
7 The Payoff, November, 1952	60.00

DUDLEY
Prize Publications
November-December, 1952

1	85.00
2	50.00
3 March-April, 1950	45.00

DUMBO WEEKLY
The Walt Disney Co.
1942

1 Gas giveaways	400.00
2	125.00
3	125.00
4	125.00
5 thru 16	@125.00

DURANGO KID
Magazine Enterprises
October-November, 1949

1 FF, Charles Starrett photo cover B:Durango Kid & Raider	500.00
2 FF, Charles Starrett Ph(c)	300.00
3 FF, Charles Starrett Ph(c)	275.00
4 FF, Charles Starrett Ph(c), Two-Timing Guns	250.00
5 FF, Charles Starrett Ph(c), Tracks Across the Trail	250.00
6 FF	150.00
7 FF,Atomic(c)	165.00
8 FF thru 10	@150.00
11 FF	125.00
12 FF	125.00
13 FF	125.00
14 thru 16 FF	@125.00
17 O:Durango Kid	150.00
18 FMe,DAy(c)	75.00
19 FMe,FG	60.00
20 FMe,FG	60.00
21 FMe,FG	60.00
22 FMe,FG	65.00
23 FMe,FG,I:Red Scorpion	65.00
24 thru 30 FMe,FG	@65.00
31 FMe,FG	65.00
32 thru 40 FG	@60.00
41 FG,October, 1941	70.00

DYNAMIC COMICS
Dynamic Publications
(Harry 'A' Chesler)
October, 1941

1 EK,O:Major Victory, Dynamic Man, Hale the Magician, A:Black Cobra	1,200.00
2 O:Dynamic Boy & Lady Satan,I:Green Knight, Lance Cooper	600.00
3 GT	450.00
8 Horror cover	450.00
9 MRa,GT,B:Mr.E	500.00
10	350.00
11 GT	300.00
12 GT	275.00
13 GT	300.00
14	285.00
15	285.00
16 GT,Bondage(c),Marijuana	300.00
17	425.00
18 Ric	250.00
19 A:Dynamic Man	235.00
20 same,Nude Woman	275.00
21 same	225.00
22 same	225.00
23 A:Yankee Girl,1.0948	225.00

DYNAMITE
Comic Media/Allen Hardy Publ.
May, 1953

1 DH(c),A:Danger#6	120.00
2	50.00
3 PAM,PAM(c),B:Johnny Dynamite,Drug	60.00
4 PAM,PAM(c),Prostitution	90.00
5 PAM,PAM(c)	50.00
6 PAM,PAM(c)	50.00
7 PAM,PAM(c)	50.00
8 PAM,PAM(c)	50.00
9 PAM,PAM(c)	50.00

Becomes:

GOLDEN AGE

GOLDEN AGE

JOHNNY DYNAMITE
Charlton Comics
10 PAM(c) 35.00
11 . . . . 30.00
12 . . . . 35.00
Becomes:
FOREIGN INTRIGUES
13 A:Johnny Dynamite 30.00
14 same 25.00
15 same 25.00
Becomes:
BATTLEFIELD ACTION
16 . . . . 20.00
17 . . . . 10.00
18 . . . . 10.00
19 . . . . 10.00
20 . . . . 10.00
21 thru 30 . . . . @7.00
31 thru 70 . . . . @3.00
71 thru 84 October 1984 . . . . . @1.00

EAGLE, THE
Fox Features Syndicate
July, 1941
1 B:The Eagle,A:Rex Dexter
of Mars 1,400.00
2 B:Spider Queen 650.00
3 B:Joe Spook 550.00
4 January, 1942 . . . . 500.00

EAGLE
Rural Home Publ.
February-March, 1945
1 LbC 250.00
2 LbC,April-May, 1945 . . . . . 150.00

EAT RIGHT
TO WORK AND WIN
Swift Co.
1942
N# Flash Gordon,Popeye . . . 250.00

EDDIE STANKY
Fawcett Publications
1951
N# New York Giants 250.00

EERIE
Avon Periodicals
May-June, 1951–Aug.-Sept. 1954
1 JKa,Horror from the Pit,
Bondage(c) 2,000.00
2 WW,WW(c), Chamber
of Death 400.00
3 WW,WW(c),JKa,JO
Monster of the Storm 500.00
4 WW(c),Phantom of Reality . 400.00
5 WW(c), Operation Horror . . 350.00
6 Devil Keeps a Date 175.00
7 WW(c),JKa,JO,Blood for
the Vampire 300.00
8 EK, Song of the Undead . . 175.00
9 JKa, Hands of Death 200.00
10 Castle of Terror 175.00
11 Anatomical Monster 150.00
12 Dracula 225.00
13 . . . . 200.00
14 Master of the Dead 200.00
15 . . . . 125.00
16 WW, Chamber of Death . . 150.00
17 WW(c),JO,JKa, ... 175.00

Eerie #17 © Avon Periodicals

EERIE ADVENTURES
Approved Comics
(Ziff-Davis)
Winter, 1951
1 BP,JKa,Bondage 250.00

EGBERT
Arnold Publications/
Comic Magazine
Spring, 1946
1 I:Egbert & The Count 125.00
2 . . . . 50.00
3 . . . . 25.00
4 . . . . 25.00
5 . . . . 25.00
6 . . . . 50.00
7 . . . . 25.00
8 . . . . 25.00
9 . . . . 25.00
10 . . . . 25.00
11 thru 17 . . . . @20.00
18 1950 . . . . 20.00

EH!
Charlton Comics
December, 1953
1 DAy(c),DG 200.00
2 DAy(c) 125.00
3 DAy(c) 100.00
4 DAy(c) 100.00
5 DAy(c) 100.00
6 DAy(c) 100.00
7 DAy(c),November, 1954 . . . 100.00

EL BOMBO COMICS
Frances M. McQueeny
1945
1 . . . . 50.00

ELLERY QUEEN
Superior Comics
May–Nov., 1949
1 LbC(c),JKa,Horror 350.00
2 . . . . 250.00
3 Drug issue 275.00
4 The Crooked Mile 250.00

ELLERY QUEEN
Approved Comics
(Ziff-Davis)
January-March, 1952
1 NS(c),The Corpse the Killed 300.00
2 NS,Killer's Revenge,
Summer, 1952 . . . . 250.00

ELSIE THE COW
D.S. Publishing Co.
October-November, 1949
1 P(c) 150.00
2 Bondage(c) 175.00
3 July-August, 1950 . . . . 150.00

ENCHANTING LOVE
Kirby Publishing Co.
October, 1949
1 Branded Guilty, Ph(c) 75.00
2 Ph(c),BP 35.00
3 Ph(c),Utter Defeat was our
Victory; Jan.-Feb., 1950 . . . . 25.00

ETTA KETT
Best Books, Inc.
(Standard Comics)
December, 1948
11 . . . . 50.00
12 . . . . 30.00
13 . . . . 30.00
14 September, 1949 . . . . 30.00

ERNIE COMICS
(see SCREAM COMICS)

EXCITING COMICS
Better Publ./Visual Editions
(Standard Comics)
April, 1940
1 O:Mask, Jim Hatfield,
Dan Williams 2,500.00
2 B:Sphinx 1,100.00
3 V;Robot 750.00
4 V:Sea Monster 500.00
5 V:Gargoyle 500.00
6 . . . . 600.00
7 AS(c) 400.00
8 . . . . 400.00
9 O:Black Terror & Tim,
Bondage(c) 5,500.00
10 A:Black Terror 1,600.00
11 same 800.00
12 Bondage(c) 600.00
13 Bondage(c) 600.00
14 O:Sphinx 400.00
15 O:Liberator 425.00
16 Black Terror 350.00
17 same 350.00
18 same 350.00
19 same 350.00
20 E:Mask,Bondage(c) 375.00
21 A:Liberator 300.00
22 O:The Eaglet,B:American
Eagle 375.00
23 Black Terror 275.00
24 Black Terror 275.00
25 Bondage(c) 300.00
26 ASh(c) 275.00
27 ASh(c) 275.00
28 ASh(c) 350.00
29 ASh(c) 350.00
30 ASh(c),Bondage(c) 375.00

 All comics prices listed are for *Near Mint* condition.

Exciting Comics #4
© *Better Publ./Visual Editions*

31 ASh(c)	325.00
32 ASh(c)	325.00
33 ASh(c)	325.00
34 ASh(c)	325.00
35 ASh(c),E:Liberator	325.00
36 ASh(c)	325.00
37 ASh(c)	325.00
38 ASh(c)	325.00
39 ASh(c)O:Kara, Jungle Princess	400.00
40 ASh(c)	375.00
41 ASh(c)	375.00
42 ASh(c),B:Scarab	400.00
43 ASh(c)	375.00
44 ASh(c)	375.00
45 ASh(c),V:Robot	375.00
46 ASh(c)	375.00
47 ASh(c)	375.00
48 ASh(c)	375.00
49 ASh(c),E:Kara & American Eagle	375.00
50 ASh(c),E:American Eagle	375.00
51 ASh(c),B:Miss Masque	450.00
52 ASh(c),Miss Masque	350.00
53 ASh(c),Miss Masque	350.00
54 ASh(c),E:Miss Masque	350.00
55 ASh(c),O&B:Judy o/t Jungle	400.00
56 ASh(c)	375.00
57 ASh(c)	375.00
58 ASh(c)	375.00
59 ASh(c),FF,Bondage(c)	400.00
60 ASh(c),The Mystery Rider	325.00
61 ASh(c)	300.00
62 ASh(c)	300.00
63 thru 65 ASh(c)	@325.00
66	300.00
67 GT	300.00
68	300.00
69 September, 1949	300.00

EXCITING ROMANCES
Fawcett Publications
1949

1 Ph(c)	75.00
2 thru 3	@40.00
4 Ph(c)	45.00
5 thru 14	@30.00

EXOTIC ROMANCE
(see TRUE WAR ROMANCES)

EXPLORER JOE
Approved Comics
(Ziff-Davis)
Winter, 1951

1 NS,The Fire Opal of Madagscar	75.00
2 BK, October-November, 1952	85.00

EXPOSED
D.S. Publishing Co.
March-April, 1948

1 Corpses Cash and Carry	145.00
2 Giggling Killer	150.00
3 One Bloody Night	60.00
4 JO,Deadly Dummy	60.00
5 Body on the Beach	60.00
6 Grl,The Secret in the Snow	150.00
7 The Gypsy Baron, July-August, 1949	250.00

EXTRA
Magazine Enterprises
1947

1	400.00

EXTRA!
E.C. Comics
March-April, 1955

1 JCr,RC,JSe	125.00
2 JCr,RC,JSe	75.00
3 JCr,RC,JSe	75.00
4 JCr,RC,JSe	75.00
5 November-December, 1955	75.00

FACE, THE
Publication Enterprises
(Columbia Comics)
1942

1 MBi(c),The Face	550.00
2 MBi(c)	325.00

Becomes:

TONY TRENT

3 MBi,A:The Face	75.00
4 1949	55.00

FAIRY TALE PARADE
Dell Publishing Co.
1942

1 WK,Giant	1,400.00
2 WK,Flying Horse	600.00
3 WK	400.00
4 WK	375.00
5 WK	375.00
6 WK	300.00
7 WK	300.00
8 WK	300.00
9 WK	300.00

FAMOUS COMICS
Zain-Eppy Publ.

N# Joe Palooka	325.00

FAMOUS CRIMES
Fox Features Syndicate
June, 1948

1 Cold Blooded Killer	350.00
2 Near Nudity cover	250.00

3 Crime Never Pays	300.00
4	125.00
5	125.00
6	125.00
7 Drug issue	250.00
8 thru 19	@100.00
20 August, 1951	75.00
51 1952	50.00

FAMOUS FAIRY TALES
K.K. Publication Co.
1942

N# WK, Giveaway	325.00
N# WK, Giveaway	250.00
N# WK, Giveaway	250.00

FAMOUS FEATURE STORIES
Dell Publishing Co.
1938

1 A:Tarzan, Terry and the Pirates Dick Tracy,Smilin' Jack	550.00

FAMOUS FUNNIES
Eastern Color Printing Co.
1933

N# A Carnival of Comics	8,000.00
N# February, 1934, 1st 10¢ comic	20,000.00
1 July, 1934	15,000.00
2	2,700.00
3 B:Buck Rogers	3,500.00
4 Football cover	1,200.00
5	1,000.00
6	700.00
7	700.00
8	700.00
9	700.00
10	700.00
11 Four pages of Buck Rogers	600.00
12 Four pages of Buck Rogers	600.00
13	500.00
14	475.00
15 Football cover	475.00
16	475.00
17 Christmas cover	475.00
18 Four pages of Buck Rogers	600.00

Famous Funnies #22
© *Eastern Color Printing Co.*

GOLDEN AGE

GOLDEN AGE

19	475.00
20	475.00
21 Baseball	375.00
22 Buck Rogers	400.00
23	350.00
24 B: War on Crime	350.00
25	350.00
26	350.00
27 G-Men cover	350.00
28	350.00
29	350.00
30	350.00
31	250.00
32	250.00
33 A:Baby Face Nelson & John Dillinger	250.00
34	250.00
35 Buck Rogers	275.00
36	250.00
37	250.00
38 Portrait,Buck Rogers	275.00
39	250.00
40	250.00
41 thru 50	@200.00
51 thru 57	@175.00
58 Baseball cover	175.00
59	175.00
60	175.00
61	150.00
62	150.00
63	150.00
64	150.00
65 JK	150.00
66	150.00
67	150.00
68 JK	150.00
69	150.00
70	150.00
71 BEv	125.00
72 BEv,B:Speed Spaulding	125.00
73 BEv	125.00
74 BEv	125.00
75 BEv	125.00
76 BEv	125.00
77 BEv,Merry Christmas cover	125.00
78 BEv	125.00
79 BEv	125.00
80 BEv,Buck Rogers	125.00
81 O:Invisible Scarlet O'Neil	100.00
82 Buck Rogers cover	125.00
83 Dickie Dare	100.00
84 Scotty Smith	100.00
85 Eagle Scout,Roy Rogers	100.00
86 Moon Monsters	100.00
87 Scarlet O'Neil	100.00
88	100.00
89 O:Fearless Flint	100.00
90 Bondage cover	110.00
91	75.00
92	75.00
93	75.00
94 War Bonds	85.00
95 Invisible Scarlet O'Neil	75.00
96	75.00
97 War Bonds Promo	75.00
98	75.00
99	75.00
100 Anniversary issue	75.00
101 thru 110	@75.00
111 thru 130	@60.00
131 thru 150	@50.00
151 thru 162	@50.00
163 Valentine's Day cover	45.00
164	40.00
165	40.00

166	40.00
167	40.00
168	40.00
169 AW	75.00
170 AW	75.00
171 thru 190	@40.00
191 thru 203	@35.00
204 War cover	32.00
205 thru 208	@30.00
209 FF(c),Buck Rogers	550.00
210 FF(c),Buck Rogers	550.00
211 FF(c),Buck Rogers	550.00
212 FF(c),Buck Rogers	550.00
213 FF(c),Buck Rogers	550.00
214 FF(c),Buck Rogers	550.00
215 FF(c),Buck Rogers	550.00
216 FF(c),Buck Rogers	550.00
217	40.00
218 July, 1955	40.00

FAMOUS GANG, BOOK OF COMICS
(see DONALD AND MICKEY MERRY CHRISTMAS)

FAMOUS GANGSTERS
Avon Periodicals
April, 1951

1 Al Capone, Dillinger, Luciano & Shultz	250.00
2 WW(c),Dillinger Machine-Gun Killer	250.00
3 Lucky Luciano & Murder Inc.	250.00

Becomes:

CRIME ON THE WATERFRONT

4 Underworld Gangsters who Control the Shipment of Drugs!, May, 1952	200.00

FAMOUS STARS
Ziff-Davis Publ. Co.
August, 1950

1 OW,Shelley Winter,Susan Peters & Shirley Temple	200.00
2 BEv,Betty Hutton, Bing Crosby	150.00
3 OW,Judy Garland, Alan Ladd	165.00
4 RC,Jolson, Bob Mitchum	125.00
5 BK,Elizabeth Taylor, Esther Williams	150.00
6 Gene Kelly, Spring, 1952	125.00

FAMOUS STORIES
Dell Publishing Co.
1942

1 Treasure Island	200.00
2 Tom Sawyer	200.00

FAMOUS WESTERN BADMEN
(see REDSKIN)

FANTASTIC
(see CAPTAIN SCIENCE)

FANTASTIC COMICS
Fox Features Syndicate
December, 1939

1 LFc(c),I&O:Samson,B:Star Dust, Super Wizard, Space

Smith & Capt. Kid	3,500.00
2 BP,LFc(c),Samson destroyed the Battery and Routed the Foe	1,500.00
3 BP,LF(c),Slays the Iron Monster	3,000.00
4 GT,LFc(c),Demolishes the Closing Torture Walls	1,200.00
5 GT,LFc(c),Crumbles the Mighty War Machine	1,200.00
6 JSm(c),Bondage(c)	1,000.00
7 JSm(c)	1,000.00
8 GT,Destroys the Mask of Fire,Bondage(c)	700.00
9 Mighty Muscles saved the Drowning Girl	700.00
10 I&O:David	600.00
11 Wrecks the Torture Machine to save his fellow American	600.00
12 Heaved the Huge Ship high into the Air	600.00
13	600.00
14	600.00
15	600.00

Fantastic #11 © Fox Features Syndicate

16 E:Stardust	600.00
17	600.00
18 I:Black Fury & Chuck	650.00
19	600.00
20	600.00
21 B&I: The Banshee,Hitler(c)	625.00
22	500.00
23 O:The Gladiator, Nov., 1941	625.00

FARGO KID
(see JUSTICE TRAPS OF THE GUILTY)

FAST FICTION
Seaboard Publ./
Famous Author Illustrated
October, 1949

1 Scarlet Pimpernel	275.00
2 HcK,Captain Blood	250.00
3 She	350.00
4 The 39 Steps	200.00
5 HcK,Beau Geste	200.00

Becomes:

STORIES BY FAMOUS

AUTHORS ILLUSTRATED

1a Scarlet Pimpernel	250.00
2a Captain Blood	250.00
3a She	300.00
4a The 39 Steps	200.00
5a Beau Geste	175.00
6 HcK,MacBeth	200.00
7 HcK,Window	165.00
8 HcK,Hamlet	175.00
9 Nicholas Nickleby	150.00
10 HcK,Romeo & Juliet	150.00
11 GS,Ben Hur	165.00
12 GS,La Svengali	165.00
13 HcK,Scaramouche	165.00

FAWCETT FUNNY ANIMALS
Fawcett Publications
December, 1942

1 I:Hoppy the Marvel, Captain Marvel cover	350.00
2 X-Mas Issue	175.00
3 Spirit of '43	120.00
4 and 5	@120.00
6 Buy War Bonds and Stamps	80.00
7	80.00
8 Flag cover	75.00
9 and 10	@70.00
11 thru 20	@50.00
21 thru 30	@30.00
31 thru 40	@25.00
41 thru 83	@20.00

Charlton Comics

84	25.00
85 thru 91 Feb. 1956	@20.00

FAWCETT MOVIE COMICS
Fawcett Publications
1949

N# Dakota Lil	220.00
N#a Copper Canyon	200.00
N# Destination the Moon	600.00
N# Montana	175.00
N# Pioneer Marshal	175.00
N# Powder River Rustlers	200.00
N# Singing Guns	160.00
7 Gunmen of Abilene	175.00
8 King of the Bull Whip	275.00
9 BP,The Old Frontier	160.00
10 The Missourians	160.00
11 The Thundering Trail	225.00
12 Rustlers on Horseback	165.00
13 Warpath	125.00
14 Last Outpost,RonaldReagan	300.00
15 The Man from Planet-X	1,500.00
16 10 Tall Men	100.00
17 Rose Cimarron	55.00
18 The Brigand	65.00
19 Carbine Williams	75.00
20 Ivan hoe, December, 1952	125.00

FEATURE BOOKS
David McKay Publications
May, 1937

N# Dick Tracy	7,000.00
N# Popeye	7,000.00
1 Zane Grey's King of the Royal Mounted	650.00
2 Popeye	650.00
3 Popeye and the "Jeep"	600.00
4 Dick Tracy	1,000.00
5 Popeye and his Poppa	600.00

6 Dick Tracy	800.00
7 Little Orphan Annie	900.00
8 Secret Agent X-9	500.00
9 Tracy & the Famon Boys	800.00
10 Popeye & Susan	600.00
11 Annie Rooney	250.00
12 Blondie	600.00
13 Inspector Wade	200.00
14 Popeye in Wild Oats	700.00
15 Barney Baxter in the Air	250.00
16 Red Eagle	275.00
17 Gang Busters	500.00
18 Mandrake the Magician	400.00
19 Mandrake	400.00
20 The Phantom	750.00
21 Lone Ranger	600.00
22 The Phantom	600.00
23 Mandrake in Teibe Castle	400.00
24 Lone Ranger	600.00
25 Flash Gordon on the Planet Mongo	750.00
26 Prince Valiant	750.00
27 Blondie	125.00

Feature Books #2
© David McKay Publications

28 Blondie and Dagwood	100.00
29 Blondie at the Home Sweet Home	100.00
30 Katzenjammer Kids	125.00
31 Blondie Keeps the Home Fires Burning	100.00
32 Katzenjammer Kids	100.00
33 Romance of Flying	85.00
34 Blondie Home is Our Castle	90.00
35 Katzenjammer Kids	100.00
36 Blondie on the Home Front	100.00
37 Katzenjammer Kids	100.00
38 Blondie the ModelHomemaker	80.00
39 The Phantom	400.00
40 Blondie	80.00
41 Katzenjammer Kids	90.00
42 Blondie in Home-Spun Yarns	80.00
43 Blondie Home-Cooked Scraps	80.00
44 Katzenjammer Kids in Monkey Business	80.00
45 Blondie in Home of the Free and the Brave	75.00
46 Mandrake in Fire World	275.00
47 Blondie in Eaten out of House and Home	80.00

48 The Maltese Falcon	450.00
49 Perry Mason - The Case of the Lucky Legs	175.00
50 The Shoplifters Shoe, P. Mason	175.00
51 Rip Kirby - Mystery of the Mangler	250.00
52 Mandrake in the Land of X	275.00
53 Phantom in Safari Suspense	350.00
54 Rip Kirby - Case of the Master Menace	250.00
55 Mandrake in 5-numbers Treasue Hunt	275.00
56 Phantom Destroys the Sky Band	300.00
57 Phantom in the Blue Gang, 1948	300.00

FEATURE FUNNIES
Harry A. Chesler Publ./
Comic Favorites
October, 1937–May 1950

1 RuG,RuG(c),A:Joe Palooka, Mickey Finn, Bungles, Dixie Dugan, Big Top, Strange as It Seems, Off the Record	2,000.00
2 A: The Hawk	900.00
3 WE,Joe Palooka,The Clock	700.00
4 RuG,WE,RuG(c),Joe Palooka	500.00
5 WE, Joe Palooka drawing	500.00
6 WE, Joe Palooka cover	500.00
7 WE,LLe, Gallant Knight story by Vernon Henkel	400.00
8 WE	375.00
9 WE, Joe Palooka story	400.00
10 WE,Micky Finn(c)	375.00
11 WE,LLe,The Bungles(c)	375.00
12 WE, Joe Palooka(c)	400.00
13 WE,LLe, World Series(c)	450.00
14 WE,Ned Brant(c)	300.00
15 WE,Joe Palooka(c)	350.00
16 Mickey Finn(c)	300.00
17 WE	300.00
18 Joe Palooka cover	325.00
19 WE,LLe,Mickey Finn(c)	300.00
20 WE,LLe	300.00

Becomes:

FEATURE COMICS

21 Joe Palooka(c)	450.00
22 LLe(c),Mickey Finn(c)	300.00
23 B:Charlie Chan	325.00
24 AAr,Joe Palooka(c)	300.00
25 AAr,The Clock(c)	300.00
26 AAr,The Bundles(c)	300.00
27 WE,AAr,I:Doll Man	2,700.00
28 LF,AAr,The Clock(c)	1,200.00
29 LF,AAr,The Clock(c)	650.00
30 LF,AAr,Doll Man(c)	650.00
31 LF,AAr,Mickey Finn(c)	550.00
32 PGv,LF,GFx,Doll Man(c)	375.00
33 PGv,LF,GFx,Bundles(c)	350.00
34 PGv,LF,GFx,Doll Man(c)	375.00
35 PGv,LF,GFx,Bundles(c)	350.00
36 PGv,LF,GFx,Doll Man(c)	375.00
37 PGv,LF,GFx,Bundles(c)	350.00
38 PGv,GFx,Doll Man(c)	300.00
39 PGv,GFx,Bundles(c)	325.00
40 PGv,GFx,WE(c),Doll Man(c)	300.00
41 PGv,GFx,WE(c),Bundles(c)	325.00
42 GFx,Doll Man(c)	225.00
43 RC,GFx,Bundles(c)	200.00
44 RC,GFx,Doll Man(c)	325.00
45 RC,GFx,Bundles(c)	200.00
46 RC,PGv,GFx,Doll Man(c)	225.00

GOLDEN AGE

All comics prices listed are for _Near Mint_ condition.

GOLDEN AGE

47 RC,GFx,Bundles(c) 200.00
48 RC,GFx,Doll Man(c) 225.00
49 RC,GFx,Bundles(c) 200.00
50 RC,GFx,Doll Man(c) 225.00
51 RC,GFx,Bundles(c) 200.00
52 RC,GFx,Doll Man(c) 200.00
53 RC,GFx,Bundles(c) 175.00
54 RC,GFx,Bundles(c) 200.00
55 RC,GFx,Bundles(c) 175.00
56 RC,GFx,Bundles(c) 225.00
57 RC,GFx,Bundles(c) 175.00
58 RC,GFx,Doll Man cover 200.00
59 RC,GFx,Mickey Finn(c) 175.00
60 RC,GFx,Doll Man(c) 200.00
61 RC,GFx,Bundles(c) 185.00
62 RC,GFx,Doll Man(c) 190.00
63 RC,GFx,Bundles(c) 175.00
64 BP,GFx,Doll Man(c) 185.00
65 BP,GFx(c),Bundles(c) 175.00
66 BP,GFx,Doll Man(c) 175.00
67 BP 150.00
68 BP,Doll Man vs.BeardedLady 175.00
69 BP,GFx(c),Devil cover 165.00
70 BP,Doll Man(c) 175.00
71 BP,GFx(c) 125.00
72 BP,Doll Man(c) 125.00
73 BP,GFx(c),Bundles(c) 110.00
74 Doll Man(c) 125.00
75 GFx(c) 100.00
76 GFx(c) 100.00
77 Doll Man cover until #140 . . 110.00
78 Knows no Fear but the
   Knife Does 100.00
79 Little Luck God 100.00
80 . . . . 100.00
81 Wanted for Murder 100.00
82 V:Shawunkas the Shaman . . 90.00
83 V:Mechanical Man 90.00
84 V:Masked Rider, Death
   Goes to the Rodeo 90.00
85 V:King of Beasts 90.00
86 Is He A Killer? 90.00
87 The Maze of Murder 90.00
88 V:The Phantom Killer 90.00
89 Crook's Goose 90.00
90 V:Whispering Corpse 90.00
91 V:The Undertaker 90.00
92 V:The Image 90.00
93 . . . . 90.00
94 V:The Undertaker 90.00
95 Flatten's the Peacock's Pride 90.00
96 Doll Man Proves
   Justice is Blind 90.00
97 V:Peacock 90.00
98 V:Master Diablo 90.00
99 On the Warpath Again! 90.00
100 Crushes the City of Crime . 125.00
101 Land of the Midget Men! . . 75.00
102 The Angle 75.00
103 V:The Queen of Ants 75.00
104 V:The Botanist 75.00
105 Dream of Death 75.00
106 V:The Sword Fish 75.00
107 Hand of Horror! 75.00
108 V:Cateye 75.00
109 V:The Brain 75.00
110 V:Fat Cat 75.00
111 V:The Undertaker 75.00
112 I:Mr. Curio & His Miniatures 75.00
113 V:Highwayman 75.00
114 V:Tom Thumb 75.00
115 V:The Sphinx 75.00
116 V:Elbows 75.00
117 Polka Dot on the Spot 75.00
118 thru 144 . . . . @75.00

FEDERAL MEN COMICS
Gerard Publ. Co.
1942

2 S&S,Spanking 250.00

FELIX THE CAT
Dell Publishing Co.
Feb.-March 1948

1 . . . . 250.00
2 . . . . 150.00
3 . . . . 100.00
4 . . . . 100.00
5 . . . . 100.00
6 . . . . 75.00
7 . . . . 75.00
8 . . . . 75.00
9 . . . . 75.00
10 . . . . 75.00
11 thru 19 . . . . @65.00

Toby Press

20 thru 30 . . . . @125.00
31 . . . . 25.00

Felix the Cat #36
© Dell Publishing Co./Toby Press

32 . . . . 60.00
33 . . . . 60.00
34 . . . . 25.00
35 . . . . 25.00
36 thru 59 . . . . @60.00
60 . . . . 55.00
61 . . . . 55.00

Harvey

62 thru 80 . . . . @18.00
81 thru 99 . . . . @15.00
100 . . . . 20.00
101 thru 118 . . . . @12.00
Spec., 100 pgs, 1952 . . . . . . 175.00
Summer Ann., 100 pgs. 1953 . 150.00
Winter Ann.,#2 100 pgs, 1954. 125.00

FERDINAND THE BULL
Dell Publishing Co.
1938

1 . . . . 125.00

FIGHT AGAINST CRIME
Story Comics May, 1951
1 Scorpion of Crime Inspector

"Brains" Carroway 200.00
2 Ganglands Double Cross . . 100.00
3 Killer Dolan's Double Cross . 75.00
4 Hopped Up Killers - The
   Con's Slaughter,Drug issue . 80.00
5 Horror of the Avenging Corpse 75.00
6 Terror of the Crazy Killer . . . 75.00
7 . . . . 75.00
8 Killer with the Two-bladed
   Knife 65.00
9 Rats Die by Gas,Horror 175.00
10 Horror of the Con's Revenge 175.00
11 Case of the Crazy Killer . . . 175.00
12 Horror,Drug issue 200.00
13 The Bloodless Killer 175.00
14 Electric Chair cover 200.00
15 . . . . 150.00
16 RA,Bondage(c) 200.00
17 Knife in Neck(c) 200.00
18 Attempted hanging cover . . 225.00
19 Bondage(c) 225.00
20 Severed Head cover 300.00
21 . . . . 150.00
Becomes:

FIGHT AGAINST
THE GUILTY

22 RA,Electric Chair 150.00
23 March, 1955 . . . . 100.00

FIGHT COMICS
Fight Comics Inc.
(Fiction House Magazines)
January, 1940

1 LF,GT,WE(c),O:Spy Fighter 2,000.00
2 GT,WE(c),Joe Lewis 800.00
3 WE(c),GT,B:Rip Regan,
   The Powerman 600.00
4 GT,LF(c) 500.00
5 WE(c) 500.00
6 GT,BP(c) 400.00
7 GT,BP(c),Powerman-Blood
   Money 400.00
8 GT,Chip Collins-Lair of
   the Vulture 400.00
9 GT,Chip Collins-Prey of the
   War Eagle 400.00
10 GT,Wolves of the Yukon . . . 400.00
11 . . . . 350.00
12 RA,Powerman-Monster of
   Madness 350.00
13 Shark Broodie-Legion
   of Satan 350.00
14 Shark Broodie-Lagoon
   of Death 350.00
15 Super-American-Hordes of
   the Secret Dicator 450.00
16 B:Capt.Fight,SwastikaPlague 450.00
17 Super-American-Blaster of
   the Pig-Boat Pirates 400.00
18 Shark Broodie-Plague of
   the Yellow Devils 400.00
19 E:Capt. Fight 400.00
20 . . . . 300.00
21 Rip Carson-Hell's Sky-Riders 250.00
22 Rip Carson-Sky Devil's
   Mission 250.00
23 Rip Carson-Angels of
   Vengeance 250.00
24 Baynonets for the Banzai
   Breed! Bondage(c) 200.00
25 Rip Carson-Samurai
   Showdown 175.00
26 Rip Carson-Fury of

---

the Sky-Brigade 175.00
27 War-Loot for the Mikado,
   Bondage(c) 175.00
28 Rip Carson 175.00
29 Rip Carson-Charge of the
   Lost Region 175.00
30 Rip Carson-Jeep-Raiders of
   the Torture Jungle 175.00
31 Gangway for the Gyrenes,
   Decapitation cover 185.00
32 Vengeance of the Hun-
   Hunters,Bondage(c) 185.00
33 B:Tiger Girl 150.00
34 Bondage(c) 165.00
35 MB 150.00
36 MB 150.00
37 MB 150.00
38 MB,Bondage(c) 165.00
39 MB,Senorita Rio-Slave Brand
   of the Spider Cult 150.00
40 MB,Bondage cover 165.00
41 MB,Bondage cover 165.00
42 MB 150.00

Fight Comics #12
© Fiction House Magazines

43 MB,Senorita Rio-The Fire-Brides
   o/t Lost Atlantis,Bondage(c)   165.00
44 MB,R:Capt. Fight 150.00
45 MB,Tonight Don Diablo Rides 150.00
46 MB 150.00
47 MB,SenoritaRio-Horror's
   Hacienda 150.00
48 MB 150.00
49 MB,JKa,B:Tiger Girl(c) 150.00
50 MB 150.00
51 MB,O:Tiger Girl 250.00
52 MB,Winged Demons of Doom 125.00
53 MB,Shadowland Shrine . . . 125.00
54 MB,Flee the Cobra Fury . . . 125.00
55 MB,Jungle Juggernaut 125.00
56 MB 125.00
57 MB,Jewels of Jeopardy 125.00
58 MB 125.00
59 MB,Vampires of CrystalCavern125.00
60 MB,Kraal of Deadly Diamonds125.00
61 MB,Seekers of the Sphinx,
   O:Tiger Girl 150.00
62 MB,Graveyard if the
   Tree Tribe 110.00
63 MB 110.00

64 MB,DawnBeast from
   Karama-Zan! 110.00
65 Beware the Congo Girl 110.00
66 Man or Ape! 100.00
67 Head-Hunters of Taboo Trek 100.00
68 Fangs of Dr. Voodoo 100.00
69 Cage of the Congo Fury . . . 100.00
70 Kraal of Traitor Tusks 100.00
71 Captives for the Golden
   Crocodile 100.00
72 Land of the Lost Safaris . . . 100.00
73 War-Gods of the Jungle . . . 100.00
74 Advengers of the Jungle . . . 100.00
75 Perils of Momba-Kzar 100.00
76 Kraal of Zombi-Zaro 100.00
77 Slave-Queen of the Ape Man 100.00
78 Great Congo Diamond
   Robbery 125.00
79 A:Space Rangers 125.00
80 . . . . 100.00
81 E:Tiger Girl(c) 100.00
82 RipCarson-CommandoStrike 100.00
83 NobodyLoves a Minesweeper 100.00
84 Rip Carson-Suicide Patrol . . 100.00
85 . . . . 100.00
86 GE,Tigerman,Summer,1954 110.00

FIGHTING AMERICAN
Headline Publications
(Prize)
April-May, 1954
1 S&K,O:Fighting American &
   Speedboy 1,400.00
2 S&K,S&K(c) 600.00
3 S&K,S&K(c) 500.00
4 S&K,S&K(c) 500.00
5 S&K,S&K(c) 500.00
6 S&K,S&K(c),O:Fighting
   American 475.00
7 S&K,S&K(c), April-May, 1955 425.00

FIGHTING DAVY
CROCKETT
(see KIT CARSON)

FIGHTING INDIANS OF
THE WILD WEST
Avon Periodicals
March, 1952
1 EK,EL,Geronimo, Crazy Horse,
   Chief Victorio 75.00
2 EK,Same, November, 1952 . 45.00

FIGHTING
LEATHERNECKS
Toby Press
February, 1952
1 JkS,Duke's Diary 75.00
2 . . . . 65.00
3 . . . . 50.00
4 . . . . 50.00
5 . . . . 45.00
6 December, 1952 . . . . 40.00

FIGHTIN' TEXAN
(see TEXAN, THE)

FIGHTING YANK
Nedor Publ./Better Publ.
(Standard Comics) Sept., 1942
1 B:Fighting Yank, A:Wonder Man,

Mystico, Bondage cover . . 1,500.00
2 JaB 650.00
3 . . . . 500.00
4 AS(c) 400.00
5 AS(c) 400.00
6 AS(c) 400.00
7 AS(c),A:Fighting Yank 350.00
8 AS(c) 350.00
9 AS(c) 350.00
10 AS(c) 350.00
11 AS(c), A:Grim Reaper, Nazis
   bomb Washington cover . . 300.00
12 AS(c), Hirohito bondage cover300.00
13 AS(c) 275.00
14 AS(c) 275.00
15 AS(c) 275.00
16 AS(c) 275.00
17 AS(c) 275.00
18 AS(c), A:American Eagle . . 275.00
19 AS(c) 275.00
20 AS(c) 275.00
21 AS(c) A:Kara,Jungle
   Princess 300.00
22 AS(c) A:Miss Masque-
   cover story 325.00
23 AS(c) A:Klu Klux Klan
   parody cover 325.00
24 A:Miss Masque 300.00
25 JRo,MMe,A:Cavalier 350.00
26 JRo,MMe,A:Cavalier 300.00
27 JRo,MMe,A:Cavalier 300.00
28 JRo,MMe,AW,A:Cavalier . . 325.00
29 JRo,MMe,August, 1949 . . . 325.00

FILM STAR ROMANCES
Star Publications
January-February, 1950
1 LbC(c), Rudy Valentino story 275.00
2 Liz Taylor & Robert Taylor,
   photo cover 225.00
3 May-June, 1950, photo cover 150.00

FIREHAIR COMICS
Flying Stories, Inc.
(Fiction House Magazine)
Winter, 1948
1 I:Firehair, Riders on the
   Pony Express 400.00
2 Bride of the Outlaw Guns . . 175.00
3 Kiss of the Six-Gun Siren! . 125.00
4 . . . . 125.00
5 . . . . 125.00
6 . . . . 110.00
7 War Drums at Buffalo Bend 110.00
8 Raid on the Red Arrows . . . 110.00
9 French Flags and Tomahawks 110.00
10 Slave Maiden of the Crees . 110.00
11 Wolves of the Overland
   Trail,Spring, 1952 . . . . 110.00

FLAME, THE
Fox Feature Syndicate
Summer, 1940
1 LF,O:The Flame 2,500.00
2 GT,LF 1,000.00
3 BP 700.00
4 . . . . 650.00
5 GT 650.00
6 GT 650.00
7 A:The Yank 650.00
8 The Finger of the Frozen
   Death!, January, 1942 . . . . 650.00

All comics prices listed are for *Near Mint* condition. **CVA Page 323**

FLAMING LOVE
Comic Magazines
(Quality Comics Group)
December, 1949

1 BWa,BWa(c),The Temptress I Feared in His Arms	. . . .	225.00
2 Torrid Tales of Turbulent Passion	. . . .	100.00
3 BWa,RC,My Heart's at Sea		150.00
4 One Women who made a Mockery of Love, Ph(c)	. . . . .	75.00
5 Bridge of Longing, Ph(c)	. . . .	75.00
6 Men both Loved & Feared Me, October, 1950	. . . .	75.00

FLASH GORDON
Harvey Publications
October, 1950

1 AR,Bondage(c)	. . . .	175.00
2 AR		150.00
3 AR Bondage(c)	. . . .	165.00
4 AR, April, 1951	. . . .	150.00

FLIP
Harvey Publications
April, 1954

1 HN	. . . .	150.00
2 HN,BP,June, 1954	. . . .	150.00

FLY BOY
Approved Comics
(Ziff-Davis)
Spring, 1952

1 NS(c),Angels without Wings		125.00
2 NS(c),Flyboy's Flame-Out, October-November, 1952	. . .	75.00

THE FLYING A'S RANGE RIDER
Dell Publishing Co.
June-August, 1953

(1) = Dell Four Color #404		
2 Ph(c) all	. . . .	75.00
3		50.00
4		50.00
5		50.00
6		50.00
7		50.00
8		50.00
9		50.00
10		50.00
11		40.00
12		40.00
13		40.00
14		40.00
15		40.00
16		40.00
17 ATh		55.00
19		40.00
20		40.00
21		40.00
22		40.00
23		40.00
24		40.00

FOODINI
Continental Publications
March, 1950

1	. . . .	90.00
2		50.00
3		40.00
4 August, 1950	. . . .	40.00

FOOTBALL THRILLS
Approved Comics
(Ziff-Davis)
Fall-Winter, 1952

1 BP,NS(c),Red Grange story		200.00
2 NS(c),Bronko Nagurski, Spring,1952	. . . .	150.00

FORBIDDEN LOVE
Comic Magazine
(Quality Comics Group)
March, 1950

1 RC,Ph(c),Heartbreak Road	.	500.00
2 Ph(c),I loved a Gigolo	. . .	225.00
3 Kissless Bride	. . . .	225.00
4 BWa,Brimstone Kisses, September, 1950	. . . .	250.00

Forbidden Worlds #115
© American Comics Group

FORBIDDEN WORLDS
American Comics Group
July-August, 1951

1 AW,FF	. . . .	1,000.00
2		475.00
3 AW,WW,JD	. . . .	500.00
4 Werewolf cover	. . . .	250.00
5 AW		400.00
6 AW,King Kong cover	. . . . .	350.00
7		200.00
8		200.00
9 Atomic Bomb	. . . .	200.00
10 JyD		175.00
11 The Mummy's Treasure	. .	125.00
12 Chest of Death	. . . .	125.00
13 Invasion from Hades	. . . .	125.00
14 Million-Year Monster	. . . .	125.00
15 The Vampire Cat	. . . . . .	125.00
16 The Doll	. . . .	125.00
17		125.00
18 The Mummy	. . . .	125.00
19 Pirate and the Voodoo Queen		125.00
20 Terror Island	. . . .	125.00
21 The Ant Master	. . . .	100.00
22 The Cursed Casket	. . . . .	100.00
23 Nightmare for Two	. . . . . .	100.00
24		100.00
25 Hallahan's Head	. . . .	100.00

26 The Champ	. . . .	100.00
27 SMo,The Thing with the Golden Hair	. . . .	100.00
28 Portrait of Carlotta	. . . . . .	100.00
29 The Frogman	. . . .	100.00
30 The Things on the Beach	.	100.00
31 SMo,The Circle of the Doomed		80.00
32 The Invasion of the Dead Things	. . . .	80.00
33		80.00
34 Atomic Bomb	. . . .	110.00
35 Comics Code	. . . .	75.00
36 thru 62	. . . .	@50.00
63 AW		75.00
64		45.00
65		45.00
66		45.00
67		45.00
68 OW(c)		45.00
69 AW		75.00
70		45.00
71		45.00
72 OW,I:Herbie		150.00
73		45.00
74		45.00
75 JB		40.00
76 AW		60.00
77		40.00
78 AW,OW(c)		60.00
79 thru 85 JB	. . . .	@40.00
86 Flying Saucer	. . . .	50.00
87		40.00
88		40.00
89		40.00
90		40.00
91		40.00
92		40.00
93		40.00
94 OW(c),A:Herbie	. . . .	75.00
95		30.00
96 AW		50.00
97 thru 115	. . . .	@30.00
116 OW(c)A:Herbie	. . . . . .	35.00
117		30.00
118		30.00
119		30.00
120 thru 124	. . . .	@30.00
125 I:O:Magic Man	. . . .	35.00
126 A:Magic Man	. . . .	25.00
127 same	. . . .	25.00
128 same	. . . .	25.00
129 same	. . . .	25.00
130 same	. . . .	25.00
131 same	. . . .	25.00
132 same	. . . .	25.00
133 I:O:Dragona	. . . .	25.00
134 A:Magic Man	. . . .	25.00
135 A:Magic Man	. . . .	25.00
136 A:Nemesis	. . . .	25.00
137 A:Magic Man	. . . .	25.00
138 A:Magic Man	. . . .	25.00
139 A:Magic Man	. . . .	25.00
140 SD,A:Mark Midnight	. . . . .	25.00
141 thru 145	. . . .	@15.00

FOREIGN INTRIGUES
(see DYNAMITE)

FOUR COLOR
Dell Publishing Co.
1939

N# Dick Tracy	. . . .	7,000.00
N# Don Winslow of the Navy		1,400.00
N# Myra North	. . . .	800.00

GOLDEN AGE

Dell Four Color #21
© Dell Publishing Co.

68 PAGES IN FULL COLOR

4 Disney'sDonaldDuck(1940) 11,000.00
5 Smilin' Jack 600.00
6 Dick Tracy 1,500.00
7 Gang Busters 400.00
8 Dick Tracy 800.00
9 Terry and the Pirates 650.00
10 Smilin' Jack 600.00
11 Smitty 400.00
12 Little Orphan Annie 500.00
13 Walt Disney's Reluctant
   Dragon (1941) 1,500.00
14 Moon Mullins 400.00
15 Tillie the Toiler 400.00
16 W.Disney's Mickey Mouse Outwits
   the Phantom Blob (1941) . 9,000.00
17 W.Disney's Dumbo the Flying
   Elephant (1941) 2,000.00
18 Jiggs and Maggie 450.00
19 Barney Google and
   Snuffy Smith 450.00
20 Tiny Tim 350.00
21 Dick Tracy 675.00
22 Don Winslow 350.00
23 Gang Busters 300.00
24 Captain Easy 450.00
25 Popeye 750.00

[Second Series]

1 Little Joe 500.00
2 Harold Teen 300.00
3 Alley Oop 500.00
4 Smilin' Jack 475.00
5 Raggedy Ann and Andy .. 550.00
6 Smitty 250.00
7 Smokey Stover 350.00
8 Tillie the Toiler 250.00
9 Donald Duck finds Pirate
   Gold! 8,000.00
10 Flash Gordon 800.00
11 Wash Tubs 350.00
12 Bambi 600.00
13 Mr. District Attorney 350.00
14 Smilin' Jack 400.00
15 Felix the Cat 750.00
16 Porky Pig 850.00
17 Popeye 600.00
18 Little Orphan Annie's
   Junior Commandos 450.00
19 W.Disney's Thumper meets

the Seven Dwarfs 600.00
20 Barney Baxter 275.00
21 Oswald the Rabbit 550.00
22 Tillie the Toiler 225.00
23 Raggedy Ann and Andy ... 400.00
24 Gang Busters 300.00
25 Andy Panda 500.00
26 Popeye 600.00
27 Mickey Mouse and the
   Seven Colored Terror 1,000.00
28 Wash Tubbs 250.00
29 CB,Donald Duck and the
   Mummy's Ring 7,000.00
30 Bambi's Children 600.00
31 Moon Mullins 200.00
32 Smitty 175.00
33 Bugs Bunny 900.00
34 Dick Tracy 475.00
35 Smokey Stover 175.00
36 Smilin' Jack 250.00
37 Bringing Up Father 200.00
38 Roy Rogers 1,000.00
39 Oswald the Rabbit 400.00
40 Barney Google and Snuffy
   Smith 250.00
41 Mother Goose 225.00
42 Tiny Tim 175.00
43 Popeye 350.00
44 Terry and the Pirates 450.00
45 Raggedy Ann 350.00
46 Felix the Cat and the
   Haunted House 450.00
47 Gene Autry 450.00
48 CB,Porky Pig o/t Mounties 1,100.00
49 W.Disney's Snow White and
   the Seven Dwarfs 700.00
50 WK,Fairy Tale Parade ... 325.00
51 Bugs Bunny Finds the
   Lost Treasure 400.00
52 Little Orphan Annie 350.00
53 Wash Tubbs 150.00
54 Andy Panda 300.00
55 Tillie the Toiler 125.00
56 Dick Tracy 350.00
57 Gene Autry 375.00
58 Smilin' Jack 250.00
59 WK,Mother Goose 200.00
60 Tiny Folks Funnies 150.00
61 Santa Claus Funnies 250.00
62 CB,Donald Duck in
   Frozen Gold 2,300.00
63 Roy Rogers-photo cover ... 500.00
64 Smokey Stover 150.00
65 Smitty 125.00
66 Gene Autry 400.00
67 Oswald the Rabbit 200.00
68 WK,Mother Goose 225.00
69 WK,Fairy Tale Parade ... 275.00
70 Popeye and Wimpy 300.00
71 WK,Walt Disney's
   Three Caballeros 850.00
72 Raggedy Ann 250.00
73 The Grumps 125.00
74 Marge's Little Lulu 1,000.00
75 Gene Autry and the Wildcat 300.00
76 Little Orphan Annie 275.00
77 Felix the Cat 450.00
78 Porky Pig & the Bandit Twins 275.00
79 Mickey Mouse in the Riddle
   of the Red Hat 1,200.00
80 Smilin' Jack 175.00
81 Moon Mullins 125.00
82 Lone Ranger 450.00
83 Gene Autry in Outlaw Trail . 325.00
84 Flash Gordon 450.00

Dell Four Color #62
© Dell Publishing Co.

85 Andy Panda and the
   Mad Dog Mystery 175.00
86 Roy Rogers-photo cover . 350.00
87 WK,Fairy Tale Parade 275.00
88 Bugs Bunny 250.00
89 Tillie the Toiler 150.00
90 WK,Christmas with
   Mother Goose 200.00
91 WK,Santa Claus Funnies .. 200.00
92 WK,W.Disney's Pinocchio .. 700.00
93 Gene Autry 250.00
94 Winnie Winkle 125.00
95 Roy Rogers,Ph(c) 350.00
96 Dick Tracy 275.00
97 Marge's Little Lulu 500.00
98 Lone Ranger 325.00
99 Smitty 100.00
100 Gene Autry Comics-photo
   cover 275.00
101 Terry and the Pirates 300.00
102 WK,Oswald the Rabbit ... 175.00
103 WK,Easter with
   Mother Goose 200.00
104 WK,Fairy Tale Parade ... 225.00
105 WK,Albert the Aligator ... 700.00
106 Tillie the Toiler 100.00
107 Little Orphan Annie 250.00
108 Donald Duck in the
   Terror of the River 1,600.00
109 Roy Rogers Comics 275.00
110 Marge's Little Lulu 350.00
111 Captain Easy 150.00
112 Porky Pig's Adventure in
   Gopher Gulch 150.00
113 Popeye 150.00
114 WK,Fairy Tale Parade ... 200.00
115 Marge's Little Lulu 350.00
116 Mickey Mouse and the
   House of Many Mysteries .. 275.00
117 Roy Rogers Comics,
   Ph(c) 200.00
118 Lone Ranger 325.00
119 Felix the Cat 300.00
120 Marge's Little Lulu 300.00
121 Fairy Tale Parade 100.00
122 Henry 125.00
123 Bugs Bunny's Dangerous
   Venture 165.00

124 Roy Rogers Comics,Ph(c) . 200.00
125 Lone Ranger 225.00
126 WK,Christmas with
   Mother Goose 175.00
127 Popeye 150.00
128 WK,Santa Claus Funnies . 150.00
129 W.Disney's Uncle Remus
   and his tales of Brer Rabbit . 300.00
130 Andy Panda 100.00
131 Marge's Little Lulu 300.00
132 Tillie the Toiler 100.00
133 Dick Tracy 250.00
134 Tarzan and the Devil Ogre . 650.00
135 Felix the Cat 250.00
136 Lone Ranger 225.00
137 Roy Rogers Comics 200.00
138 Smitty 75.00
139 Marge's Little Lulu 275.00
140 WK,Easter with
   Mother Goose 175.00
141 Mickey Mouse and the
   Submarine Pirates 250.00
142 Bugs Bunny and the
   Haunted Mountain 175.00
143 Oswald the Rabbit & the
   Prehistoric Egg 100.00
144 Poy Rogers Comics,Ph(c) . 200.00
145 Popeye 150.00
146 Marge's Little Lulu 275.00
147 W.Disney's Donald Duck
   in Volcano Valley 1,100.00
148 WK,Albert the Aligator
   and Pogo Possum 650.00
149 Smilin' Jack 125.00
150 Tillie the Toiler 100.00
151 Lone Ranger 200.00
152 Little Orphan Annie 150.00
153 Roy Rogers Comics 175.00
154 Andy Panda 100.00
155 Henry 75.00
156 Porky Pig and the Phantom 100.00
157 W.Disney's Mickey Mouse
   and the Beanstalk 250.00
158 Marge's Little Lulu 275.00
159 CB,W.Disney's Donald Duck
   in the Ghost of the Grotto . . 900.00
160 Roy Rogers Comics,Ph(c) . 150.00
161 Tarzan and the Fires
   of Tohr 550.00
162 Felix the Cat 175.00
163 Dick Tracy 175.00
164 Bugs Bunny Finds the
   Frozen Kingdom 175.00
165 Marge's Little Lulu 275.00
166 Roy Rogers Comics,Ph(c) . 175.00
167 Lone Ranger 175.00
168 Popeye 150.00
169 Woody Woodpecker,Drug . 165.00
170 W.Disney's Mickey Mouse
   on Spook's Island 200.00
171 Charlie McCarthy 200.00
172 WK,Christmas with
   Mother Goose 150.00
173 Flash Gordon 150.00
174 Winnie Winkle 75.00
175 WK,Santa Claus Funnies . 150.00
176 Tillie the Toiler 75.00
177 Roy Rogers Comics,Ph(c) . 150.00
178 CB,W.Disney's Donald Duck
   Christmas on Bear Mountain1,400.00
179 WK,Uncle Wiggily 150.00
180 Ozark the Ike 85.00
181 W.Disney's Mickey Mouse
   in Jungle Magic 200.00
182 Porky Pig in Never-

Never Land 125.00
183 Oswald the Rabbit 75.00
184 Tillie the Toiler 75.00
185 WK,Easter with
   Mother Goose 150.00
186 W.Disney's Bambi 175.00
187 Bugs Bunny and the
   Dreadful Bunny 125.00
188 Woody Woodpecker 125.00
189 W.Disney's Donald Duck in
   The Old Castle's Secret . . . 800.00
190 Flash Gordon 150.00
191 Porky Pig to the Rescue . . 125.00
192 WK,The Brownies 135.00
193 Tom and Jerry 150.00
194 W.Disney's Mickey Mouse
   in the World Under the Sea . 200.00
195 Tillie the Toiler 50.00
196 Charlie McCarthy in The
   Haunted Hide-Out 150.00
197 Spirit of the Border 125.00
198 Andy Panda 100.00

Dell Four Color #130
© Dell Publishing Co.

199 W.Disney's Donald Duck in
   Sheriff of Bullet Valley 800.00
200 Bugs Bunny, Super Sleuth 125.00
201 WK,Christmas with
   Mother Goose 125.00
202 Woody Woodpecker 75.00
203 CB,W.Disney's Donald Duck in
   The Golden Christmas Tree 650.00
204 Flash Gordon 100.00
205 WK,Santa Claus Funnies . 125.00
206 Little Orphan Funnies 75.00
207 King of the Royal Mounted 175.00
208 W.Disney's Brer Rabbit
   Does It Again 125.00
209 Harold Teen 50.00
210 Tippe and Cap Stubbs . . . 45.00
211 Little Beaver 60.00
212 Dr. Bobbs 40.00
213 Tillie the Toiler 50.00
214 W.Disney's Mickey Mouse
   and his Sky Adventure 175.00
215 Sparkle Plenty 100.00
216 Andy Panda and the
   Police Pup 75.00
217 Bugs Bunny in Court Jester 125.00
218 W.Disney's 3 Little Pigs . . 150.00

219 Swee'pea 120.00
220 WK,Easter with
   Mother Goose 150.00
221 WK,Uncle Wiggly 125.00
222 West of the Pecos 75.00
223 CB,W.Disney's Donald Duck in
   Lost in the Andes 850.00
224 Little Iodine 75.00
225 Oswald the Rabbit 50.00
226 Porky Pig and Spoofy 75.00
227 W.Disney's Seven Dwarfs . 125.00
228 The Mark of Zorro 200.00
229 Smokey Stover 50.00
230 Sunset Press 60.00
231 W.Disney's Mickey Mouse
   and the Rajah's Treasure . . 150.00
232 Woody Woodpecker 75.00
233 Bugs Bunny 125.00
234 W.Disney's Dumbo in Sky
   Voyage 125.00
235 Tiny Tim 45.00
236 Heritage of the Desert . . . 75.00
237 Tillie the Toiler 50.00
238 CB,W.Disney's Donald Duck
   in Voodoo Hoodoo 600.00
239 Adventure Bound 50.00
240 Andy Panda 60.00
241 Porky Pig 75.00
242 Tippie and Cap Stubbs . . . 35.00
243 W.Disney's Thumper
   Follows His Nose 125.00
244 WK,The Brownies 125.00
245 Dick's Adventures in
   Dreamland 40.00
246 Thunder Mountain 45.00
247 Flash Gordon 125.00
248 W.Disney's Mickey Mouse
   and the Black Sorcerer . . . 150.00
249 Woody Woodpecker 65.00
250 Bugs Bunny in
   Diamond Daze 135.00
251 Hubert at Camp Moonbeam 50.00
252 W.Disney's Pinocchio 125.00
253 WK,Christmas with
   Mother Goose 140.00
254 WK,Santa Claus Funnies . 140.00
255 The Ranger 45.00
256 CB,W.Disney's Donald Duck in
   Luck of the North 450.00
257 Little Iodine 50.00
258 Andy Panda and the
   Ballon Bee 75.00
259 Santa and the Angel 50.00
260 Porky Pig, Hero of the
   Wild West 75.00
261 W.Disney's Mickey Mouse
   and the Missing Key 150.00
262 Raggedy Ann and Andy . . . 60.00
263 CB,W.Disney's Donald Duck in
   Land of the Totem Poles . . . 450.00
264 Woody Woodpecker in
   the Magic Lantern 50.00
265 King of the Royal Mountain . 85.00
266 Bugs Bunny on the Isle of
   Hercules 125.00
267 Little Beaver 40.00
268 W.Disney's Mickey Mouse's
   Surprise Visitor 150.00
269 Johnny Mack Brown,Ph(c) . 200.00
270 Drift Fence 40.00
271 Porky Pig 75.00
272 W.Disney's Cinderella 125.00
273 Oswald the Rabbit 45.00
274 Bugs Bunny 125.00
275 CB,W.Disney's Donald Duck

Dell Four Color #298
© Dell Publishing Co.

THIS IS AN ANIMATED COVER! TO MAKE IT MOVE, SEE THE BACK COVER.

in Ancient Persia 425.00
276 Uncle Wiggly 75.00
277 PorkyPig in DesertAdventure 75.00
278 Bill Elliot Comics,Ph(c) . . . 150.00
279 W.Disney's Mickey Mouse &
   Pluto Battle the Giant Ants . 125.00
280 Andy Panda in the Isle
   of the Mechanical Men 60.00
281 Bugs Bunny in The Great
   Circus Mystery 125.00
282 CB,W.Disney's Donald Duck in
   The Pixilated Parrot 450.00
283 King of the Royal Mounted   100.00
284 Porky Pig in the Kingdom
   of Nowhere 75.00
285 Bozo the Clown 200.00
286 W.Disney's Mickey Mouse
   and the Uninvited Guest . . . 125.00
287 Gene Autry's Champion in the
   Ghost of BlackMountain,Ph(c) 100.00
288 Woody Woodpecker 75.00
289 BugsBunny in IndianTrouble 120.00
290 The Chief 50.00
291 CB,W.Disney's Donald Duck in
   The Magic Hourglass 450.00
292 The Cisco Kid Comics 150.00
293 WK,The Brownies 125.00
294 Little Beaver 45.00
295 Porky Pig in President Pig . 75.00
296 W.Disney's Mickey Mouse
   Private Eye for Hire 125.00
297 Andy Panda in The
   Haunted Inn 50.00
298 Bugs Bunny in Sheik
   for a Day 125.00
299 Buck Jones & the Iron Trail 175.00
300 CB,W.Disney's Donald Duck in
   Big-Top Bedlam 450.00
301 The Mysterious Rider 40.00
302 Santa Claus Funnies 35.00
303 Porky Pig in The Land of
   the Monstrous Flies 65.00
304 W.Disney's Mickey Mouse
   in Tom-Tom Island 100.00
305 Woody Woodpecker 30.00
306 Raggedy Ann 35.00
307 Bugs Bunny in Lumber
   Jack Rabbit 85.00

308 CB,W.Disney's Donald Duck in
   Dangerous Disguise 375.00
309 Dollface and Her Gang 40.00
310 King of the Rotal Mounted . 55.00
311 Porky Pig in Midget Horses
   of Hidden Valley 45.00
312 Tonto 150.00
313 W.Disney's Mickey Mouse in
   the Mystery of the Double-
   Cross Ranch 125.00
314 Ambush 40.00
315 Oswald Rabbit 30.00
316 Rex Allen,Ph(c) 150.00
317 Bugs Bunny in Hare Today
   Gone Tomorrow 75.00
318 CB,W.Disney's Donald Duck in
   No Such Varmint 375.00
319 Gene Autry's Champion . . . 40.00
320 Uncle Wiggly 60.00
321 Little Scouts 30.00
322 Porky Pig in Roaring Rockies 50.00
323 Susie Q. Smith 30.00
324 I Met a Handsome Cowboy . 75.00
325 W.Disney's Mickey Mouse
   in the Haunted Castle 125.00
326 Andy Panda 35.00
327 Bugs Bunny and the
   Rajah's Treasure 100.00
328 CB,W.Disney's Donald Duck
   in Old California 400.00
329 Roy Roger's Trigger,Ph(c) . 100.00
330 Porky Pig meets the
   Bristled Bruiser 50.00
331 Disney's Alice in
   Wonderland 150.00
332 Little Beaver 35.00
333 Wilderness Trek 40.00
334 W.Disney's Mickey Mouse
   and Yukon Gold 120.00
335 Francis the Famous
   Talking Mule 75.00
336 Woody Woodpecker 35.00
337 The Brownies 35.00
338 Bugs Bunny and the
   Rocking Horse Thieves 90.00
339 W.Disney's Donald Duck
   and the Magic Fountain . . . 100.00
340 King of the Royal Mountain   65.00
341 W.Disney's Unbirthday Party
   with Alice in Wonderland . . . 150.00
342 Porky Pig the Lucky
   Peppermint Mine 45.00
343 W.Disney's Mickey Mouse in
   Ruby Eye of Homar-Guy-Am 100.00
344 Sergeant Preston from
   Challenge of the Yukon . . . 125.00
345 Andy Panda in Scotland Yard 35.00
346 Hideout 40.00
347 Bugs Bunny the Frigid Hare 75.00
348 CB,W.Disney's Donald Duck
   The Crocodile Collector . . . 250.00
349 Uncle Wiggly 60.00
350 Woody Woodpecker 35.00
351 Porky Pig and the Grand
   Canyon Giant 50.00
352 W.Disney's Mickey Mouse
   Mystery of Painted Valley . . . 85.00
353 CB(c),W.Disney'sDuckAlbum100.00
354 Raggedy Ann & Andy 45.00
355 Bugs Bunny Hot-Rod Hair . 75.00
356 CB(c),W.Disney's Donald
   Duck in Rags to Riches . . . 250.00
357 Comeback 35.00
358 Andy Panada 35.00
359 Frosty the Snowman 60.00

Dell Four Color #328
© Dell Publishing Co.

360 Porky Pig in Tree Fortune . 35.00
361 Santa Claus Funnies 35.00
362 W.Disney's Mickey Mouse &
   the Smuggled Diamonds . . . 100.00
363 King of the Royal Mounted . 60.00
364 Woody Woodpecker 30.00
365 The Brownies 30.00
366 Bugs Bunny Uncle
   Buckskin Comes to Town . . . 75.00
367 CB,W.Disney's Donald Duck in
   A Christmas for Shacktown . 375.00
368 Bob Clampett's
   Beany and Cecil 275.00
369 Lone Ranger's Famous
   Horse Hi-Yo Silver 75.00
370 Porky Pig in Trouble
   in the Big Trees 45.00
371 W.Disney's Mickey Mouse
   the Inca Idol Case 85.00
372 Riders of the Purple Sage . . 30.00
373 Sergeant Preston 75.00
374 Woody Woodpecker 30.00
375 John Carter of Mars 275.00
376 Bugs Bunny 75.00
377 Susie Q. Smith 30.00
378 Tom Corbett, Space Cadet 175.00
379 W.Disney's Donald Duck in
   Southern Hospitality 100.00
380 Raggedy Ann & Andy 40.00
381 Marge's Tubby 150.00
382 W.Disney's Show White and
   the Seven Dwarfs 150.00
383 Andy Panda 25.00
384 King of the Royal Mounted . 50.00
385 Porky Pig 35.00
386 CB,W.Disney's Uncle Scrooge
   in Only A Poor Old Man . . 1,000.00
387 W.Disney's Mickey Mouse
   in High Tibet 85.00
388 Oswald the Rabbit 35.00
389 Andy Hardy Comics 30.00
390 Woody Woodpecker 30.00
391 Uncle Wiggly 60.00
392 Hi-Yo Silver 40.00
393 Bugs Bunny 75.00
394 CB(c),W.Disney's Donald Duck
   in Malayalaya 250.00
395 Forlorn River 35.00

GOLDEN AGE

396 Tales of the Texas Rangers,
   Ph(c) 100.00
397 Sergeant Preston o/t Yukon 75.00
398 The Brownies 30.00
399 Porky Pig in the Lost
   Gold Mine 35.00
400 AMc,Tom Corbett 125.00
401 W.Disney's Mickey Mouse &
   Goofy's Mechanical Wizard . . 75.00
402 Mary Jane and Sniffles 75.00
403 W.Disney's Li'l Bad Wolf . . 100.00
404 The Ranger Rider,Ph(c) . . 100.00
405 Woody Woodpecker 30.00
406 Tweety and Sylvester 75.00
407 Bugs Bunny, Foreign-
   Legion Hare 65.00
408 CB,W.Disney's Donald Duck
   and the Golden Helmet 400.00
409 Andy Panda 25.00
410 Porky Pig in the
   Water Wizard 40.00
411 W.Disney's Mickey Mouse
   and the Old Sea Dog 75.00
412 Nevada 35.00
413 Disney's Robin Hood(movie),
   Ph(c) 125.00
414 Bob Clampett's Beany
   and Cecil 175.00
415 Rootie Kazootie 125.00
416 Woody Woodpecker 30.00
417 Double Trouble with Goober 25.00
418 Rusty Riley 40.00
419 Sergeant Preston 75.00
420 Bugs Bunny 55.00
421 AMc,Tom Corbett 125.00
422 CB,W.Disney's Donald Duck
   and the Gilded Man 375.00
423 Rhubarb 30.00
424 Flash Gordon 100.00
425 Zorro 140.00
426 Porky Pig 35.00
427 W.Disney's Mickey Mouse &
   the Wonderful Whizzix 65.00
428 Uncle Wiggily 35.00
429 W.Disney's Pluto in
   Why Dogs Leave Home . . . 100.00
430 Marge's Tubby 75.00
431 Woody Woodpecker 30.00
432 Bugs Bunny and the
   Rabbit Olympics 60.00
433 Wildfire 35.00
434 Rin Tin Tin,Ph(c) 165.00
435 Frosty the Snowman 35.00
436 The Brownies 30.00
437 John Carter of Mars 175.00
438 W.Disney's Annie
   Oakley (TV) 125.00
439 Little Hiawatha 50.00
440 Black Beauty 30.00
441 Fearless Fagan 25.00
442 W.Disney's Peter Pan 100.00
443 Ben Bowie and His
   Mountain Men 50.00
444 Marge's Tubby 75.00
445 Charlie McCarthy 40.00
446 Captain Hook and Peter Pan 100.00
447 Andy Hardy Comics 25.00
448 Beany and Cecil 175.00
449 Tappan's Burro 35.00
450 CB(c),W.Disney's DuckAlbum 75.00
451 Rusty Riley 30.00
452 Raggedy Ann and Andy . . 40.00
453 Susie Q. Smith 30.00
454 Krazy Kat Comics 35.00
455 Johnny Mack Brown Comics,

Ph(c) 50.00
456 W.Disney's Uncle Scrooge
   Back to the Klondike 600.00
457 Daffy 75.00
458 Oswald the Rabbit 25.00
459 Rootie Kazootie 75.00
460 Buck Jones 75.00
461 Marge's Tubby 75.00
462 Little Scouts 15.00
463 Petunia 30.00
464 Bozo 100.00
465 Francis the Talking Mule . . 50.00
466 Rhubarb, the Millionaire Cat 30.00
467 Desert Gold 30.00
468 W.Disney's Goofy 125.00
469 Beetle Bailey 75.00
470 Elmer Fudd 35.00
471 Double Trouble with Goober 20.00
472 Wild Bill Elliot,Ph(c) 55.00
473 W.Disney's Li'l Bad Wolf . . 65.00
474 Mary Jane and Sniffles . . . 70.00
475 M.G.M.'s the Two
   Mouseketeers 60.00

Dell Four Color #454
© Dell Publishing Co.

476 Rin Tin Tin,Ph(c) 60.00
477 Bob Clampett's Beany and
   Cecil 150.00
478 Charlie McCarthy 40.00
479 Queen o/t West Dale Evans 150.00
480 Andy Hardy Comics 25.00
481 Annie Oakley and Tagg . . . 65.00
482 Brownies 30.00
483 Little Beaver 30.00
484 River Feud 30.00
485 The Little People 40.00
486 Rusty Riley 35.00
487 Mowgli, the Jungle Book . . 35.00
488 John Carter of Mars 175.00
489 Tweety and Sylvester 30.00
490 Jungle Jim 50.00
491 EK,Silvertip 75.00
492 W.Disney's Duck Album . . . 65.00
493 Johnny Mack Brown,Ph(c) . 45.00
494 The Little King 110.00
495 CB, W.Disney's Uncle
   Scrooge 500.00
496 The Green Hornet 275.00
497 Zorro, (Sword of) 150.00
498 Bugs Bunny's Album 45.00

499 M.G.M.'s Spike and Tyke . . 25.00
500 Buck Jones 65.00
501 Francis the Famous
   Talking Mule 35.00
502 Rootie Kazootie 60.00
503 Uncle Wiggily 40.00
504 Krazy Kat 35.00
505 W.Disney's the Sword and
   the Rose (TV),Ph(c) 100.00
506 The Little Scouts 20.00
507 Oswald the Rabbit 25.00
508 Bozo 80.00
509 W.Disney's Pluto 65.00
510 Son of Black Beauty 35.00
511 EK,Outlaw Trail 40.00
512 Flash Gordon 60.00
513 Ben Bowie and His
   Mountain Men 30.00
514 Frosty the Snowman 30.00
515 Andy Hardy 25.00
516 Double Trouble With Goober 20.00
517 Walt Disney's Chip 'N' Dale 100.00
518 Rivets 25.00
519 Steve Canyon 100.00
520 Wild Bill Elliot,Ph(c) 50.00
521 Beetle Bailey 40.00
522 The Brownies 25.00
523 Rin Tin Tin,Ph(c) 75.00
524 Tweety and Sylvester 25.00
525 Santa Claus Funnies 30.00
526 Napoleon 20.00
527 Charlie McCarthy 35.00
528 Queen o/t West Dale Evans,
   Ph(c) 75.00
529 Little Beaver 25.00
530 Bob Clampett's Beany
   and Cecil 150.00
531 W.Disney's Duck Album . . . 55.00
532 The Rustlers 35.00
533 Raggedy Ann and Andy . . . 40.00
534 EK,Western Marshal 40.00
535 I Love Lucy,Ph(c) 500.00
536 Daffy 25.00
537 Stormy, the Thoroughbred . 25.00
538 EK,The Mask of Zorro . . . 150.00
539 Ben and Me 25.00
540 Knights of the Round Table,
   Ph(c) 75.00
541 Johnny Mack Brown,Ph(c) . 50.00
542 Super Circus Featuring
   Mary Hartline 50.00
543 Uncle Wiggly 35.00
544 W.Disney's Rob Roy(Movie),
   Ph(c) 100.00
545 The Wonderful Adventures
   of Pinocchio 100.00
546 Buck Jones 75.00
547 Francis the Famous
   Talking Mule 40.00
548 Krazy Kat 30.00
549 Oswald the Rabbit 25.00
550 The Little Scouts 15.00
551 Bozo 100.00
552 Beetle Bailey 40.00
553 Susie Q. Smith 30.00
554 Rusty Riley 30.00
555 Range War 30.00
556 Double Trouble with Goober 20.00
557 Ben Bowie and His
   Mountain Men 30.00
558 Elmer Fudd 30.00
559 I Love Lucy,Ph(c) 350.00
560 W.Disney's Duck Album . . . 60.00
561 Mr. Magoo 125.00
562 W.Disney's Goofy 85.00

GOLDEN AGE

563 Rhubarb, the Millionaire Cat 30.00
564 W.Disney's Li'l Bad Wolf . . . 60.00
565 Jungle Jim 30.00
566 Son of Black Beauty 30.00
567 BF,Prince Valiant,Ph(c) . . . 125.00
568 Gypsy Cat 35.00
569 Priscilla's Pop 25.00
570 Bob Clampett's Beany
   and Cecil 150.00
571 Charlie McCarthy 40.00
572 EK,Silvertip 40.00
573 The Little People 30.00
574 The Hand of Zorro 125.00
575 Annie and Oakley and Tagg,
   Ph(c) 60.00
576 Angel 25.00
577 M.G.M.'s Spike and Tyke . . 25.00
578 Steve Canyon 55.00
579 Francis the Talking Mule . . . 40.00
580 Six Gun Ranch 30.00
581 Chip 'N' Dale 55.00
582 Mowgli, the Jungle Book . . . 30.00
583 The Lost Wagon Train 35.00
584 Johnny Mack Brown,Ph(c) . 40.00
585 Bugs Bunny's Album 45.00
586 W.Disney's Duck Album . . . 55.00
587 The Little Scouts 15.00
588 MB,King Richard and the
   Crusaders,Ph(c) 125.00
589 Buck Jones 60.00
590 Hansel and Gretel 50.00
591 EK,Western Marshal 50.00
592 Super Circus 45.00
593 Oswald the Rabbit 25.00
594 Bozo 100.00
595 Pluto 50.00
596 Turok, Son of Stone 600.00
597 The Little King 75.00
598 Captain Davy Jones 30.00
599 Ben Bowie and His
   Mountain Men 25.00
600 Daisy Duck's Diary 65.00
601 Frosty the Snowman 30.00
602 Mr. Magoo and the Gerald
   McBoing-Boing 125.00
603 M.G.M.'s The Two
   Mouseketeers 30.00
604 Shadow on the Trail 35.00
605 The Brownies 25.00
606 Sir Lancelot 100.00
607 Santa Claus Funnies 30.00
608 EK,Silver Tip 40.00
609 The Littlest Outlaw,Ph(c) . . . 60.00
610 Drum Beat,Ph(c) 100.00
611 W.Disney's Duck Album . . . 60.00
612 Little Beaver 25.00
613 EK,Western Marshal 50.00
614 W.Disney's 20,000 Leagues
   Under the Sea (Movie) 100.00
615 Daffy 40.00
616 To The Last Man 30.00
617 The Quest of Zorro 125.00
618 Johnny Mack Brown,Ph(c) . 50.00
619 Krazy Kat 30.00
620 Mowgli, Jungle Book 30.00
621 Francis the Famous
   Talking Mule 35.00
622 Beetle Bailey 40.00
623 Oswald the Rabbit 20.00
624 Treasure Island,Ph(c) 100.00
625 Beaver Valley 75.00
626 Ben Bowie and His
   Mountain Men 30.00
627 Goofy 100.00
628 Elmer Fudd 25.00

629 Lady & The Tramp with Jock 75.00
630 Priscilla's Pop 30.00
631 W.Disney's Davy Crockett
   Indian Fighter (TV),Ph(c) . . . 150.00
632 Fighting Caravans 30.00
633 The Little People 25.00
634 Lady and the Tramp Album . 60.00
635 Bob Clampett's Beany
   and Cecil 150.00
636 Chip 'N' Dale 55.00
637 EK,Silvertip 45.00
638 M.G.M.'s Spike and Tyke . . 20.00
639 W.Disney's Davy Crockett
   at the Alamo (TV),Ph(c) . . . 125.00
640 EK,Western Marshal 50.00
641 Steve Canyon 75.00
642 M.G.M.'s The Two
   Mouseketeers 30.00
643 Wild Bill Elliott,Ph(c) 35.00
644 Sir Walter Raleigh,Ph(c) . . . 75.00
645 Johnny Mack Brown,Ph(c) . 50.00
646 Dotty Dripple and Taffy 30.00
647 Bugs Bunny's Album 45.00

Dell Four Color #666
© Dell Publishing Co.

648 Jace Pearson of the
   Texas Rangers,Ph(c) 50.00
649 Duck Album 60.00
650 BF,Prince Valiant 75.00
651 EK,King Colt 35.00
652 Buck Jones 45.00
653 Smokey the Bear 120.00
654 Pluto 50.00
655 Francis the Famous
   Talking Mule 35.00
656 Turok, Son of Stone 350.00
657 Ben Bowie and His
   Mountain Men 30.00
658 Goofy 75.00
659 Daisy Duck's Diary 60.00
660 Little Beaver 25.00
661 Frosty the Snowman 30.00
662 Zoo Parade 50.00
663 Winky Dink 60.00
664 W.Disney's Davy Crockett in
   the Great Keelboat
   Race (TV),Ph(c) 125.00
665 The African Lion 50.00
666 Santa Claus Funnies 35.00
667 EK,Silvertip and the Stolen

Stallion 40.00
668 W.Disney's Dumbo 100.00
668a W.Disney's Dumbo 75.00
669 W.Disney's Robin Hood
   (Movie),Ph(c) 60.00
670 M.G.M.'s Mouse Musketeers 25.00
671 W.Disney's Davey Crockett
   and the River Pirates(TV),
   Ph(c) 125.00
672 Quentin Durward,Ph(c) 60.00
673 Buffalo Bill Jr.,Ph(c) 60.00
674 The Little Rascals 75.00
675 EK,Steve Donovan,Ph(c) . . 60.00
676 Will-Yum! 30.00
677 Little King 75.00
678 The Last Hunt,Ph(c) 60.00
679 Gunsmoke 150.00
680 Out Our Way with the
   Worry Wart 25.00
681 Forever, Darling,Ph(c) 125.00
682 When Knighthood Was
   in Flower,Ph(c) 60.00
683 Hi and Lois 25.00
684 SB,Helen of Troy,Ph(c) . . . 125.00
685 Johnny Mack Brown,Ph(c) . 50.00
686 Duck Album 50.00
687 The Indian Fighter,Ph(c) . . . 50.00
688 SB,Alexander the Great,
   Ph(c) 75.00
689 Elmer Fudd 25.00
690 The Conqueror,
   John Wayne Ph(c) 150.00
691 Dotty Dripple and Taffy 25.00
692 The Little People 30.00
693 W.Disney's Brer Rabbit
   Song of the South 125.00
694 Super Circus,Ph(c) 50.00
695 Little Beaver 25.00
696 Krazy Kat 30.00
697 Oswald the Rabbit 20.00
698 Francis the Famous
   Talking Mule 30.00
699 BA,Prince Valiant 75.00
700 Water Birds and the
   Olympic Elk 50.00
701 Jimmy Cricket 100.00
702 The Goofy Success Story . 100.00
703 Scamp 100.00
704 Priscilla's Pop 30.00
705 Brave Eagle,Ph(c) 50.00
706 Bongo and Lumpjaw 40.00
707 Corky and White Shadow,
   Ph(c) 60.00
708 Smokey the Bear 60.00
709 The Searchers,John
   Wayne Ph(c) 250.00
710 Francis the Famous
   Talking Mule 30.00
711 M.G.M.'s Mouse Musketeers 25.00
712 The Great Locomotive
   Chase, Ph(c) 75.00
713 The Animal World 40.00
714 W.Disney's Spin
   & Marty (TV) 100.00
715 Timmy 30.00
716 Man in Space 100.00
717 Moby Dick,Ph(c) 75.00
718 Dotty Dripple and Taffy 25.00
719 BF,Prince Valiant 75.00
720 Gunsmoke,Ph(c) 100.00
721 Captain Kangaroo,Ph(c) . . . 150.00
722 Johnny Mack Brown,Ph(c) . 40.00
723 EK,Santiago 85.00
724 Bugs Bunny's Album 45.00

725 Elmer Fudd 20.00
726 Duck Album 40.00
727 The Nature of Things 60.00
728 M.G.M.'s Mouse Musketeers 20.00
729 Bob Son of Battle 30.00
730 Smokey Canyon 30.00
731 EK,Silvertip and The
    Fighting Four 40.00
732 Zorro, (the Challenge of) . . 125.00
733 Buck Rogers 35.00
734 Cheyenne,C.Walker Ph(c) . 150.00
735 Crusader Rabbit 325.00
736 Pluto 45.00
737 Steve Canyon 55.00
738 Westward Ho, the Wagons,
    Ph(c) 90.00
739 MD,Bounty Guns 30.00
740 Chilly Willy 30.00
741 The Fastest Gun Alive,Ph(c) 60.00
742 Buffalo Bill Jr.,Ph(c) 55.00
743 Daisy Duck's Diary 45.00
744 Little Beaver 25.00
745 Francis the Famous
    Talking Mule 30.00
746 Dotty Dripple and Taffy . . . 25.00
747 Goofy 90.00
748 Frosty the Snowman 30.00
749 Secrets of Life,Ph(c) 50.00
750 The Great Cat 50.00
751 Our Miss Brooks,Ph(c) 75.00
752 Mandrake, the Magician . . 125.00
753 Walt Scott's Little People . . 30.00
754 Smokey the Bear 60.00
755 The Littlest Snowman 30.00
756 Santa Claus Funnies 30.00
757 The True Story of
    Jesse James,Ph(c) 90.00
758 Bear Country 45.00
759 Circus Boy,Ph(c) 100.00
760 W.Disney's Hardy Boys(TV) 100.00
761 Howdy Doody 125.00
762 SB,The Sharkfighters,Ph(c) 100.00
763 GrandmaDuck'sFarmFriends 75.00
764 M.G.M.'s Mouse Musketeers 20.00
765 Will-Yum! 20.00
766 Buffalo Bill,Ph(c) 35.00
767 Spin and Marty 75.00
768 EK,Steve Donovan, Western
    Marshal,Ph(c) 45.00
769 Gunsmoke 75.00
770 Brave Eagle,Ph(c) 30.00
771 MD,Brand of Empire 30.00
772 Cheyenne,C.Walker Ph(c) . . 65.00
773 The Brave One,Ph(c) 35.00
774 Hi and Lois 25.00
775 SB,Sir Lancelot and
    Brian,Ph(c) 85.00
776 Johnny Mack Brown,Ph(c) . 40.00
777 Scamp 75.00
778 The Little Rascals 50.00
779 Lee Hunter, Indian Fighter . 40.00
780 Captain Kangaroo,Ph(c) . . 150.00
781 Fury,Ph(c) 75.00
782 Duck Album 50.00
783 Elmer Fudd 20.00
784 Around the World in 80
    Days,Ph(c) 75.00
785 Circus Boys,Ph(c) 100.00
786 Cinderella 50.00
787 Little Hiawatha 40.00
788 BF,Prince Valiant 75.00
789 EK,Silvertip-Valley Thieves . 45.00
790 ATh,The Wings of Eagles,
    J.Wayne Ph(c) 150.00
791 The 77th Bengal Lancers,

Ph(c) 65.00
792 Oswald the Rabbit 20.00
793 Morty Meekle 25.00
794 SB,The Count of Monte
    Cristo 85.00
795 Jiminy Cricket 65.00
796 Ludwig Bemelman's
    Madeleine and Genevieve . . . 30.00
797 Gunsmoke,Ph(c) 75.00
798 Buffalo Bill,Ph(c) 40.00
799 Priscilla's Pop 30.00
800 The Buccaneers,Ph(c) 50.00
801 Dotty Dripple and Taffy . . . 25.00
802 Goofy 75.00
803 Cheyenne,C.Walker Ph(c) . . 60.00
804 Steve Canyon 40.00
805 Crusader Rabbit 250.00
806 Scamp 65.00
807 MB,Savage Range 30.00
808 Spin and Marty,Ph(c) 75.00
809 The Little People 30.00
810 Francis the Famous
    Talking Mule 25.00

Dell Four Color #711
© *Dell Publishing Co.*

811 Howdy Doody 100.00
812 The Big Land,A.Ladd Ph(c) . 85.00
813 Circus Boy,Ph(c) 100.00
814 Covered Wagon,A:Mickey
    Mouse 80.00
815 Dragoon Wells Massacre . . 75.00
816 Brave Eagle,Ph(c) 30.00
817 Little Beaver 25.00
818 Smokey the Bear 60.00
819 Mickey Mouse in Magicland 45.00
820 The Oklahoman,Ph(c) 45.00
821 Wringle Wrangle,Ph(c) 75.00
822 ATh,W.Disney's Paul Revere's
    Ride (TV) 125.00
823 Timmy 25.00
824 The Pride and the Passion,
    Ph(c) 100.00
825 The Little Rascals 50.00
826 Spin and Marty and Annette,
    Ph(c) 150.00
827 Smokey Stover 30.00
828 Buffalo Bill, Jr,Ph(c) 35.00
829 Tales of the Pony Express,
    Ph(c) 40.00
830 The Hardy Boys,Ph(c) 85.00

831 No Sleep 'Til Dawn,Ph(c) . . 60.00
832 Lolly and Pepper 30.00
833 Scamp 75.00
834 Johnny Mack Brown,Ph(c) . 50.00
835 Silvertip- The Fake Rider . . 40.00
836 Man in Fight 60.00
837 All-American Athlete
    Cotton Woods 40.00
838 Bugs Bunny's Life
    Story Album 60.00
839 The Vigilantes 50.00
840 Duck Album 55.00
841 Elmer Fudd 20.00
842 The Nature of Things 70.00
843 The First Americans 85.00
844 Gunsmoke,Ph(c) 75.00
845 ATh,The Land Unknown . . 150.00
846 ATh,Gun Glory 125.00
847 Perri 65.00
848 Marauder's Moon 40.00
849 BF,Prince Valiant 75.00
850 Buck Jones 30.00
851 The Story of Mankind,
    V.Price Ph(c) 60.00
852 Chilly Willy 25.00
853 Pluto 50.00
854 Hunchback of Notre Dame,
    Ph(c) 125.00
855 Broken Arrow,Ph(c) 45.00
856 Buffalo Bill, Jr.,Ph(c) 40.00
857 The Goofy Adventure Story . 75.00
858 Daisy Duck's Diary 50.00
859 Topper and Neil 30.00
860 Wyatt Earp,Ph(c) 100.00
861 Frosty the Snowman 30.00
862 Truth About Mother Goose . 65.00
863 Francis the Famous
    Talking Mule 30.00
864 The Littlest Snowman 30.00
865 Andy Burnett,Ph(c) 75.00
866 Mars and Beyond 100.00
867 Santa Claus Funnies 30.00
868 The Little People 30.00
869 Old Yeller,Ph(c) 75.00
870 Little Beaver 25.00
871 Curly Kayoe 25.00
872 Captain Kangaroo,Ph(c) . . 150.00
873 Grandma Duck's
    Farm Friends 50.00
874 Old Ironsides 60.00
875 Trumpets West 30.00
876 Tales of Wells Fargo,Ph(c) . 75.00
877 ATh,Frontier Doctor,Ph(c) . 100.00
878 Peanuts 150.00
879 Brave Eagle,Ph(c) 30.00
880 MD,Steve Donovan,Ph(c) . . 40.00
881 The Captain and the Kids . . 25.00
882 ATh,W.DisneyPresentsZorro 175.00
883 The Little Rascals 50.00
884 Hawkeye and the Last
    of the Mohicans,Ph(c) 75.00
885 Fury,Ph(c) 60.00
886 Bongo and Lumpjaw 30.00
887 The Hardy Boys,Ph(c) 75.00
888 Elmer Fudd 20.00
889 ATh,W.Disney's Clint
    & Mac(TV),Ph(c) 100.00
890 Wyatt Earp,Ph(c) 60.00
891 Light in the Forest,
    C.Parker Ph(c) 75.00
892 Maverick,J.Garner Ph(c) . . 275.00
893 Jim Bowie,Ph(c) 50.00
894 Oswald the Rabbit 20.00
895 Wagon Train,Ph(c) 135.00
896 Adventures of Tinker Bell . . 60.00

GOLDEN AGE

897 Jiminy Cricket	50.00
898 EK,Silvertip	45.00
899 Goofy	60.00
900 BF,Prince Valiant	75.00
901 Little Hiawatha	60.00
902 Will-Yum!	25.00
903 Dotty Dripple and Taffy	25.00
904 Lee Hunter, Indian Fighter	30.00
905 W.Disney's Annette (TV), Ph(c)	250.00
906 Francis the Famous Talking Mule	30.00
907 Ath,Sugarfoot,Ph(c)	100.00
908 The Little People and the Giant	30.00
909 Smitty	25.00
910 ATh,The Vikings, K.Douglas Ph(c)	100.00
911 The Gray Ghost,Ph(c)	100.00
912 Leave it to Beaver,Ph(c)	200.00
913 The Left-Handed Gun, Paul Newman Ph(c)	100.00
914 ATh,No Time for Sergeants, Ph(c)	125.00
915 Casey Jones,Ph(c)	50.00
916 Red Ryder Ranch Comics	25.00
917 The Life of Riley,Ph(c)	125.00
918 Beep Beep, the Roadrunner	100.00
919 Boots and Saddles,Ph(c)	75.00
920 Ath,Zorro,Ph(c)	125.00
921 Wyatt Earp.Ph(c)	60.00
922 Johnny Mack Brown,Ph(c)	50.00
923 Timmy	20.00
924 Colt .45,Ph(c)	75.00
925 Last of the Fast Guns,Ph(c)	60.00
926 Peter Pan	35.00
927 SB,Top Gun	30.00
928 Sea Hunt,L.Bridges Ph(c)	125.00
929 Brave Eagle,Ph(c)	30.00
930 Maverick,J. Garner Ph(c)	125.00
931 Have Gun, Will Travel,Ph(c)	150.00
932 Smokey the Bear	60.00
933 ATh,W.Disney's Zorro	100.00
934 Restless Gun	100.00
935 King of the Royal Mounted	30.00
936 The Little Rascals	50.00
937 Ruff and Ready	125.00
938 Elmer Fudd	20.00
939 Steve Canyon	60.00
940 Lolly and Pepper	25.00
941 Pluto	40.00
942 Pony Express	40.00
943 White Wilderness	60.00
944 SB,7th Voyage of Sinbad	125.00
945 Maverick,J.Garner Ph(c)	125.00
946 The Big Country,Ph(c)	60.00
947 Broken Arrow,Ph(c)	40.00
948 Daisy Duck's Diary	50.00
949 High Adventure,Ph(c)	45.00
950 Frosty the Snowman	30.00
951 ATh,Lennon Sisters Life Story,Ph(c)	150.00
952 Goofy	60.00
953 Francis the Famous Talking Mule	30.00
954 Man in Space	75.00
955 Hi and Lois	25.00
956 Ricky Nelson,Ph(c)	225.00
957 Buffalo Bee	75.00
958 Santa Claus Funnies	30.00
959 Christmas Stories	30.00
960 ATh,W.Disney's Zorro	125.00
961 Jace Pearson's Tales of Texas Rangers,Ph(c)	40.00
962 Maverick,J.Garner Ph(c)	125.00

963 Johnny Mack Brown,Ph(c)	40.00
964 The Hardy Boys,Ph(c)	85.00
965 GrandmaDuck'sFarmFriends	55.00
966 Tonka,Ph(c)	75.00
967 Chilly Willy	25.00
968 Tales of Wells Fargo,Ph(c)	75.00
969 Peanuts	125.00
970 Lawman,Ph(c)	125.00
971 Wagon Train,Ph(c)	75.00
972 Tom Thumb	85.00
973 SleepingBeauty & the Prince	150.00
974 The Little Rascals	50.00
975 Fury,Ph(c)	50.00
976 ATh,W.Disney's Zorro,Ph(c)	125.00
977 Elmer Fudd	20.00
978 Lolly and Pepper	20.00
979 Oswald the Rabbit	20.00
980 Maverick,J.Garner Ph(c)	125.00
981 Ruff and Ready	100.00
982 The New Adventures of Tinker Bell	65.00
983 Have Gun, Will Travel,Ph(c)	100.00
984 Sleeping Beauty's Fairy	

Dell Four Color #938
© Dell Publishing Co.

Godmothers	75.00
985 Shaggy Dog,Ph(c)	75.00
986 Restless Gun,Ph(c)	75.00
987 Goofy	60.00
988 Little Hiawatha	30.00
989 Jimmy Cricket	30.00
990 Huckleberry Hound	125.00
991 Francis the Famous Talking Mule	30.00
992 ATh,Sugarfoot,Ph(c)	100.00
993 Jim Bowie,Ph(c)	50.00
994 Sea HuntL.Bridges Ph(c)	100.00
995 Donald Duck Album	55.00
996 Nevada	30.00
997 Walt Disney Presents,Ph(c)	65.00
998 Ricky Nelson,Ph(c)	225.00
999 Leave It To Beaver,Ph(c)	175.00
1000 The Gray Ghost,Ph(c)	100.00
1001 Lowell Thomas' High Adventure,Ph(c)	45.00
1002 Buffalo Bee	50.00
1003 ATh,W.Disney's Zorro,Ph(c)	125.00
1004 Colt .45,Ph(c)	60.00
1005 Maverick,J.Garner Ph(c)	125.00
1006 SB,Hercules	100.00

1007 John Paul Jones,Ph(c)	45.00
1008 Beep, Beep, the Road Runner	50.00
1009 CB,The Rifleman,Ph(c)	200.00
1010 Grandma Duck's Farm Friends	125.00
1011 Buckskin,Ph(c)	75.00
1012 Last Train from Gun Hill,Ph(c)	75.00
1013 Bat Masterson,Ph(c)	135.00
1014 ATh,The Lennon Sisters, Ph(c)	150.00
1015 Peanuts	100.00
1016 Smokey the Bear	50.00
1017 Chilly Willy	25.00
1018 Rio Bravo,J.Wayne Ph(c)	225.00
1019 Wagoon Train,Ph(c)	75.00
1020 Jungle	25.00
1021 Jace Pearson's Tales of the Texas Rangers,Ph(c)	45.00
1022 Timmy	25.00
1023 Tales of Wells Fargo,Ph(c)	75.00
1024 ATh,Darby O'Gill and the Little People,Ph(c)	100.00
1025 CB,W.Disney's Vacation in Disneyland	225.00
1026 Spin and Marty,Ph(c)	60.00
1027 The Texan,Ph(c)	60.00
1028 Rawhide, Clint Eastwood Ph(c)	235.00
1029 Boots and Saddles,Ph(c)	50.00
1030 Spanky and Alfalfa, the Little Rascals	50.00
1031 Fury,Ph(c)	60.00
1032 Elmer Fudd	20.00
1033 Steve Canyon,Ph(c)	60.00
1034 Nancy and Sluggo Summer Camp	25.00
1035 Lawman,Ph(c)	60.00
1036 The Big Circus,Ph(c)	60.00
1037 Zorro,Ph(c)	150.00
1038 Ruff and Ready	75.00
1039 Pluto	40.00
1040 Quick Draw McGraw	125.00
1041 ATh,Sea Hunt, L.Bridges Ph(c)	100.00
1042 The Three Chipmunks	40.00
1043 The Three Stooges,Ph(c)	200.00
1044 Have Gun,Will Travel,Ph(c)	100.00
1045 Restless Gun,Ph(c)	75.00
1046 Beep Beep, the Road Runner	50.00
1047 CB,W.Disney's GyroGearloose	200.00
1048 The Horse Soldiers J.Wayne Ph(c)	150.00
1049 Don't Give Up the Ship J.Lewis Ph(c)	60.00
1050 Huckleberry Hound	75.00
1051 Donald in Mathmagic Land	100.00
1052 RsM,Ben-Hur	125.00
1053 Goofy	60.00
1054 Huckleberry Hound Winter Fun	75.00
1055 CB,Daisy Duck's Diary	125.00
1056 Yellowstone Kelly, C.Walker Ph(c)	50.00
1057 Mickey Mouse Album	40.00
1058 Colt .45,Ph(c)	60.00
1059 Sugarfoot	75.00
1060 Journey to the Center of the Earth, P.Boone Ph(c)	125.00
1061 Buffalo Bill	50.00
1062 Christmas Stories	35.00
1063 Santa Claus Funnies	35.00

GOLDEN AGE

All comics prices listed are for *Near Mint* condition.

GOLDEN AGE

1064 Bugs Bunny's Merry
　Christmas 55.00
1065 Frosty the Snowman 30.00
1066 ATh,77 Sunset Strip,Ph(c) 125.00
1067 Yogi Bear 120.00
1068 Francis the Famous
　Talking Mule 30.00
1069 ATh,The FBI Story,Ph(c) . . 100.00
1070 Soloman and Sheba,Ph(c) 75.00
1071 ATh,TheRealMcCoys,Ph(c) 125.00
1072 Blythe 40.00
1073 CB,Grandma Duck's Farm
　Friends 150.00
1074 Chilly Willy 25.00
1075 Tales of Wells Fargo,Ph(c) 75.00
1076 MSy,The Rebel,Ph(c) . . . 125.00
1077 SB,The Deputy,
　H.Fonda Ph(c) 150.00
1078 The Three Stooges,Ph(c) 125.00
1079 The Little Rascals 50.00
1080 Fury,Ph(c) 60.00
1081 Elmer Fudd 20.00
1082 Spin and Marty 60.00
1083 Men into Space,Ph(c) . . . 75.00
1084 Speedy Gonzales 35.00
1085 ATh,The Time Machine . . 195.00
1086 Lolly and Pepper 25.00
1087 Peter Gunn,Ph(c) 110.00
1088 A Dog of Flanders,Ph(c) . 35.00
1089 Restless Gun,Ph(c) 70.00
1090 Francis the Famous
　Talking Mule 30.00
1091 Jacky's Diary 40.00
1092 Toby Tyler,Ph(c) 50.00
1093 MacKenzie's Raiders,Ph(c) 60.00
1094 Goofy 55.00
1095 CB,W.Disney's
　GyroGearloose 125.00
1096 The Texan,Ph(c) 60.00
1097 Rawhide,C.Eastwood Ph(c) 175.00
1098 Sugarfoot,Ph(c) 75.00
1099 CB(c),Donald Duck Album . 75.00
1100 W.Disney's Annette's
　Life Story (TV),Ph(c) . . . 225.00
1101 Robert Louis Stevenson's
　Kidnapped,Ph(c) 60.00
1102 Wanted: Dead or Alive,
　Ph(c) 135.00
1103 Leave It To Beaver,Ph(c) 175.00
1104 Yogi Bear Goes to College 75.00
1105 ATh,Gale Storm,Ph(c) . . . 125.00
1106 ATh,77 Sunset Strip,Ph(c) 125.00
1107 Buckskin,Ph(c) 60.00
1108 The Troubleshooters,Ph(c) 50.00
1109 This Is Your Life, Donald
　Duck,O:Donald Duck 175.00
1110 Bonanza,Ph(c) 375.00
1111 Shotgun Slade 50.00
1112 Pixie and Dixie
　and Mr. Jinks 60.00
1113 Tales of Wells Fargo,Ph(c) 75.00
1114 Huckleberry Finn,Ph(c) . . 40.00
1115 Ricky Nelson,Ph(c) 165.00
1116 Boots and Saddles,Ph(c) . . 50.00
1117 Boy and the Pirate,Ph(c) . . 50.00
1118 Sword and the Dragon,Ph(c) 60.00
1119 Smokey and the Bear
　Nature Stories 50.00
1120 Dinosaurus,Ph(c) 75.00
1121 RC,GE,HerculesUnchained 120.00
1122 Chilly Willy 25.00
1123 Tombstone Territory,Ph(c) . 75.00
1124 Whirlybirds,Ph(c) 60.00
1125 GK,RH,Laramie,Ph(c) 85.00
1126 Sundance,Ph(c) 75.00

Dell Four Color #1013
© Dell Publishing Co.

1127 The Three Stooges,Ph(c) 125.00
1128 Rocky and His Friends . . 335.00
1129 Pollyanna,H.Mills Ph(c) . . . 85.00
1130 SB,The Deputy,
　H.Fonda Ph(c) 125.00
1131 Elmer Fudd 20.00
1132 Space Mouse 30.00
1133 Fury,Ph(c) 50.00
1134 ATh,Real McCoys,Ph(c) . 110.00
1135 M.G.M.'s Mouse Musketeers 60.00
1136 Jungle Cat,Ph(c) 45.00
1137 The Little Rascals 50.00
1138 The Rebel,Ph(c) 100.00
1139 SB,Spartacus,Ph(c) 125.00
1140 Donald Duck Album 65.00
1141 Huckleberry Hound for
　President 75.00
1142 Johnny Ringo,Ph(c) 65.00
1143 Pluto 40.00
1144 The Story of Ruth,Ph(c) . 110.00
1145 GK,The Lost World,Ph(c) 125.00
1146 Restless Gun,Ph(c) 65.00
1147 Sugarfoot,Ph(c) 75.00
1148 I aim at the Stars,Ph(c) . . . 75.00
1149 Goofy 55.00
1150 CB,Daisy Duck's Diary . . 125.00
1151 Mickey Mouse Album 40.00
1152 Rocky and His Friends . . 275.00
1153 Frosty the Snowman 30.00
1154 Santa Claus Funnies 30.00
1155 North to Alaska 150.00
1156 Walt Disney Swiss
　Family Robinson 65.00
1157 Master of the World 50.00
1158 Three Worlds of Gulliver . . 50.00
1159 ATh,77 Sunset Strip 125.00
1160 Rawhide 175.00
1161 CB,Grandma Duck's
　Farm Friends 150.00
1162 Yogi Bera joins the Marines 75.00
1163 Daniel Boone 50.00
1164 Wanted: Dead or Alive . . 100.00
1165 Ellery Queen 125.00
1166 Rocky and His Friends . . 275.00
1167 Tales of Wells Fargo,Ph(c) 65.00
1168 The Detectives,
　R.Taylor Ph(c) 125.00
1169 New Adventures of

Sherlock Holmes 150.00
1170 The Three Stooges,Ph(c) 125.00
1171 Elmer Fudd 20.00
1172 Fury,Ph(c) 50.00
1173 The Twilight Zone 200.00
1174 The Little Rascals 40.00
1175 M.G.M.'s Mouse Musketeers 25.00
1176 Dondi,Ph(c) 45.00
1177 Chilly Willy 25.00
1178 Ten Who Dared 60.00
1179 The Swamp Fox,
　L.Nielson Ph(c) 75.00
1180 The Danny Thomas Show 150.00
1181 Texas John Slaughter,Ph(c) 60.00
1182 Donald Duck Album 45.00
1183 101 Dalmatians 125.00
1184 CB,W.Disney's
　Gyro Gearloose 125.00
1185 Sweetie Pie 30.00
1186 JDa,Yak Yak 75.00
1187 The Three Stooges,Ph(c) 125.00
1188 Atlantis the Lost
　Continent,Ph(c) 110.00
1189 Greyfriars Bobby,Ph(c) . . . 50.00
1190 CB(c),Donald and
　the Wheel 75.00
1191 Leave It to Beaver,Ph(c) . 175.00
1192 Rocky Nelson,Ph(c) 175.00
1193 The Real McCoys,Ph(c) . 100.00
1194 Pepe,Ph(c) 45.00
1195 National Velvet,Ph(c) 65.00
1196 Pixie and Dixie
　and Mr. Jinks 40.00
1197 The Aquanauts,Ph(c) 50.00
1198 Donald in Mathmagic Land 75.00
1199 Absent-Minded Professor,
　Ph(c) 75.00
1200 Hennessey,Ph(c) 60.00
1201 Goofy 55.00
1202 Rawhide,C.Eastwood Ph(c) 175.00
1203 Pinocchio 60.00
1204 Scamp 40.00
1205 David Goliath,Ph(c) 50.00
1206 Lolly and Pepper 25.00
1207 MSy,The Rebel,Ph(c) . . . 100.00
1208 Rocky and His Friends . . 275.00
1209 Sugarfoot,Ph(c) 75.00
1210 The Parent Trap,
　H.Mills Ph(c) 85.00
1211 RsM,77 Sunset Strip,Ph(c) 100.00
1212 Chilly Willy 25.00
1213 Mysterious Island,Ph(c) . . 150.00
1214 Smokey the Bear 50.00
1215 Tales of Wells Fargo,Ph(c) 65.00
1216 Whirlybirds,Ph(c) 75.00
1218 Fury,Ph(c) 50.00
1219 The Detectives,
　R Taylor Ph(c) 60.00
1220 Gunslinger,Ph(c) 75.00
1221 Bonanza,Ph(c) 200.00
1222 Elmer Fudd 20.00
1223 GK,Laramie,Ph(c) 50.00
1224 The Little Rascals 40.00
1225 The Deputy,H.Fonda Ph(c) 85.00
1226 Nikki, Wild Dog of the North 50.00
1227 Morgan the Pirate,Ph(c) . . 75.00
1229 Thief of Bagdad,Ph(c) 70.00
1230 Voyage to the Bottom
　of the Sea,Ph(c) 125.00
1231 Danger Man,Ph(c) 125.00
1232 On the Double 40.00
1233 Tammy Tell Me True 60.00
1234 The Phantom Planet 75.00
1235 Mister Magoo 100.00
1236 King of Kings,Ph(c) 75.00

1237 ATh,The Untouchables,
Ph(c) 250.00
1238 Deputy Dawg 125.00
1239 CB(c),Donald Duck Album . 65.00
1240 The Detectives,
R.Taylor Ph(c) 75.00
1241 Sweetie Pies 30.00
1242 King Leonardo and
His Short Subjects 150.00
1243 Ellery Queen 75.00
1244 Space Mouse 30.00
1245 New Adventures of
Sherlock Holmes 150.00
1246 Mickey Mouse Album 40.00
1247 Daisy Duck's Diary 45.00
1248 Pluto 40.00
1249 The Danny Thomas Show,
Ph(c) 175.00
1250 Four Horseman of the
Apocalypse,Ph(c) 75.00
1251 Everything's Ducky 60.00
1252 The Andy Griffith Show,
Ph(c) 250.00
1253 Spaceman 100.00
1254 "Diver Dan" 50.00
1255 The Wonders of Aladdin . . 50.00
1256 Kona, Monarch of
Monster Isle 50.00
1257 Car 54, Where Are You?,
Ph(c) 100.00
1258 GE,The Frogmen 60.00
1259 El Cid,Ph(c) 60.00
1260 The Horsemasters,Ph(c) . . 125.00
1261 Rawhide,C.Eastwood Ph(c) 175.00
1262 The Rebel,Ph(c) 100.00
1263 RsM,77 Sinset Strip,Ph(c) 100.00
1264 Pixie & Dixie & Mr.Jinks . . 40.00
1265 The Real McCoys,Ph(c) . . 100.00
1266 M.G.M.'s Spike and Tyke . . 15.00
1267 CB,GyroGearloose 75.00
1268 Oswald the Rabbit 20.00
1269 Rawhide,C.Eastwood Ph(c) 175.00
1270 Bullwinkle and Rocky . . . 200.00
1271 Yogi Bear Birthday Party . . 50.00
1272 Frosty the Snowman 25.00
1273 Hans Brinker,Ph(c) 60.00
1274 Santa Claus Funnies 30.00
1275 Rocky and His Friends . . 225.00
1276 Dondi 30.00
1278 King Leonardo and
His Short Subjects 125.00
1279 Grandma Duck's Farm
Friends 55.00
1280 Hennessey,Ph(c) 50.00
1281 Chilly Willy 25.00
1282 Babes in Toyland,Ph(c) . . 100.00
1283 Bonanza,Ph(c) 200.00
1284 RH,Laramie,Ph(c) 55.00
1285 Leave It to Beaver,Ph(c) . 175.00
1286 The Untouchables,Ph(c) . 175.00
1287 Man from Wells Fargo,Ph(c) 40.00
1288 RC,GE,The Twilight Zone 150.00
1289 Ellery Queen 75.00
1290 M.G.M.'s Mouse
Musketeers 25.00
1291 RsM,77 Sunset Strip,Ph(c) 100.00
1293 Elmer Fudd 15.00
1294 Ripcord 60.00
1295 Mr. Ed, the Talking Horse,
Ph(c) 100.00
1296 Fury,Ph(c) 50.00
1297 Spanky, Alfalfa and the
Little Rascals 40.00
1298 The Hathaways,Ph(c) 35.00
1299 Deputy Dawg 125.00

1300 The Comancheros 160.00
1301 Adventures in Paradise . . 40.00
1302 JohnnyJason,TeenReporter 25.00
1303 Lad: A Dog,Ph(c) 30.00
1304 Nellie the Nurse 75.00
1305 Mister Magoo 100.00
1306 Target: The Corruptors,
Ph(c) 55.00
1307 Margie 45.00
1308 Tales of the Wizard of Oz . 75.00
1309 BK,87th Precinct,Ph(c) . . 85.00
1310 Huck and Yogi Winter
Sports 75.00
1311 Rocky and His Friends . 275.00
1312 National Velvet,Ph(c) . . . 35.00
1313 Moon Pilot.Ph(c) 75.00
1328 GE,The Underwater
City,Ph(c) 60.00
1330 GK,Brain Boy 100.00
1332 Bachelor Father 75.00
1333 Short Ribs 40.00
1335 Aggie Mack 30.00
1336 On Stage 40.00
1337 Dr. Kildare,Ph(c) 75.00
1341 The Andy Griffith Show,
Ph(c) 250.00
1348 JDa,Yak Yak 80.00
1349 Yogi Berra Visits the U.N. 100.00
1350 Commanche,Ph(c) 50.00
1354 Calvin and the Colonel . . . 60.00

FOUR FAVORITES
Ace Magazines
September, 1941
1 B:Vulcan, Lash Lighting, Magno
the Magnetic Man, Raven,
Flag cover,Hitler 1,000.00
2 A: Black Ace 400.00
3 E:Vulcan 350.00
4 E:Raven,B:Unknown Soldiers 350.00
5 B:Captain Courageous 325.00
6 A: The Flag, B: Mr. Risk . . . 325.00
7 JM 300.00
8 . . . . 300.00
9 RP,HK 300.00
10 HK 350.00
11 HK,LbC,UnKnown Soldier . . 325.00
12 LbC 225.00
13 LbC 175.00
14 Fer 175.00
15 Fer 175.00
16 Bondage(c) 200.00
17 Magno Lighting 150.00
18 Magno Lighting 150.00
19 RP,RP(c) 150.00
20 RP,RP(c) 150.00
21 RP,RP(c) 125.00
22 RP(c) 125.00
23 RP(c) 125.00
24 RP(c) 125.00
25 RP(c) 125.00
26 RP(c) 125.00
27 RP(c) 110.00
28 . . . . 100.00
29 . . . . 100.00
30 . . . . 100.00
31 . . . . 100.00
32 . . . . 100.00

FRANKENSTEIN COMICS
Crestwood Publications
(Prize Publ.)
Summer, 1945
1 B:Frankenstein,DBr,DBr(c) . 750.00

2 DBr,DBr(c) 400.00
3 DBr,DBr(c) 275.00
4 DBr,DBr(c) 275.00
5 DBr,DBr(c) 275.00
6 DBr,DBr(c),S&K 200.00
7 DBr,DBr(c),S&K 200.00
8 DBr,DBr(c),S&K 200.00
9 DBr,DBr(c),S&K 200.00
10 DBr,DBr(c),S&K 200.00
11 DBr,DBr(c)A:Boris Karloff . 175.00
12 DBr,DBr(c) 175.00
13 DBr,DBr(c). 175.00
14 DBr,DBr(c) 175.00
15 DBr,DBr(c) 175.00
16 DBr,DBr(c) 175.00

Frankenstein #23
© Crestwood/Prize Publications

17 DBr,DBr(c) 175.00
18 B:Horror 185.00
19 . . . . 150.00
3-4 . . . . 135.00
3-5 . . . . 135.00
3-6 . . . . 135.00
4-1 thru 4-6 . . . . @135.00
5-1 thru 5-4 . . . . @135.00
5-5 October-November, 1954 . 135.00

FRISKY FABLES
Novelty Press/Premium Group
Spring, 1945
1 AFa 75.00
2 AFa 40.00
3 AFa 35.00
4 AFa 28.00
5 AFa 28.00
6 AFa 28.00
7 AFa,Flag (c) 30.00
2-1 AFa,Rainbow(c) 25.00
2-2 AFa 20.00
2-3 AFa 20.00
2-4 AFa 20.00
2-5 AFa 20.00
2-6 AFa 20.00
2-7 AFa 20.00
2-8 AFa,Halloween (c) 20.00
2-9 AFa,Thanksgiving(c) 18.00
2-10 AFa,Christman cover 20.00
2-11 AFa 20.00
2-12 AFa,Valentines Day cover . 18.00

GOLDEN AGE

All comics prices listed are for *Near Mint* condition.

GOLDEN AGE

3-1 AFa	15.00
3-2 AFa	15.00
3-3 AFa	18.00
3-4 AFa	15.00
3-5 AFa	15.00
3-6 AFa	15.00
3-7 AFa	15.00
3-8 AFa,Turkey (c)	15.00
3-9 AFa	15.00
3-10 AFa	15.00
3-11 AFa,1948(c)	15.00
3-12 AFa	15.00
4-1 thru 4-7 AFa	@15.00
5-1 AFa	15.00
5-2 AFa	15.00
5-3	15.00
5-4 Star Publications	15.00
39 LbC(c)	50.00
40 LbC(c)	50.00
41 LbC(c)	50.00
42 LbC(c)	50.00
43 LbC(c)	20.00

Becomes:

FRISKY ANIMALS
Star Publications

44 LbC	70.00
45 LbC	100.00
46 LbC,Baseball	60.00
47 LbC	60.00
48 LbC	60.00
49 LbC	60.00
50 LbC	60.00
51 LbC(c)	60.00
52 LbC(c)	75.00
53 LbC(c)	55.00
54 LbC(c),Supercat(c)	55.00
55 LbC(c),same	55.00
56 LbC(c),same	55.00
57 LbC(c),same	55.00
58 LbC(c),same,July, 1954	55.00

FRITZI RITZ
United Features Syndicate/
St. John Publications
Fall, 1948

N# Special issue	75.00
2	35.00
3	30.00
4 thru 7	@25.00
6 A:Abbie & Slats	27.00
8 thru 10	@18.00
11 1958	18.00

FROGMAN COMICS
Hillman Periodicals
Jan.-Feb., 1952–May 1953

1	75.00
2	40.00
3	40.00
4 MMe	30.00
5 BK,AT	40.00
6	25.00
7	25.00
8 thru 11	@25.00

FRONTIER ROMANCES
Avon Periodicals
November-December, 1949

1 She Learned to Ride and Shoot, and Kissing Came Natural	350.00
2 Bronc-Busters Sweetheart, January-February, 1950	225.00

FRONTLINE COMBAT
Tiny Tot Publications
(E.C. Comics)
July-August, 1951

1 HK(c),WW, JSe,JDa,Hanhung Changjn cover	500.00
2 HK(c),WW,Tank Battle cover	300.00
3 HK(c),WW,Naval Battleship fire cover	275.00
4 HK(c),WW, Bazooka cover	225.00
5 HK(c),JSe	200.00
6 HK(c),WW,JSe	175.00
7 HK(c),WW,JSe,Document of the Action at Iwo Jima	175.00
8 HK(c),WW,ATh	175.00
9 HK(c),WW,JSe,Civil War iss.	175.00
10 GE,HK(c),WW, Crying Child cover	225.00
11 GE	150.00
12 GE,Air Force issue	150.00
13 JSe,GE,WW(c), Bi-Planes cover	150.00
14 JKu,GE,WW(c)	150.00
15 JSe,GE,WW(c), Jan., 1954	150.00

FRONT PAGE COMIC BOOK
Front Page Comics
1945

1 JKu,BP,BF(c),I:Man in Black	250.00

FUGITIVES FROM JUSTICE
St. John Publishing Co.
February, 1952

1	125.00
2 MB, Killer Boomerang	150.00
3 GT	125.00
4	50.00
5 Bondage cover, October, 1952	70.00

FUNNIES, THE
(1ST SERIES)
Dell Publishing Co.
1929-30

1 B:Foxy Grandpa, Sniffy	600.00
2 thru 21	@250.00
N#(22)	225.00
N#(23) thru (36)	@200.00

FUNNIES, THE
(2ND SERIES)
Dell Publishing Co.
October, 1936

1 Tailspin Tommy,Mutt & Jeff, Capt. Easy,D.Dixon	2,000.00
2 Scribbly	850.00
3	700.00
4 Christmas issue	550.00
5	550.00
6 thru 22	@400.00
23 thru 29	@300.00
30 B:John Carter of Mars	750.00
31 inc. Dick Tracy	500.00
32	500.00
33	500.00
34	500.00
35 John Carter (c)	500.00
36 John Carter (c)	500.00
37 John Carter (c)	500.00
38 Rex King of the Deep (c)	500.00
39 Rex King (c)	500.00

Funnies #6 © Dell Publishing Co.

40 John Carter (c)	500.00
41 Sky Ranger (c)	500.00
42 Rex King (c)	500.00
43 Rex King (c)	500.00
44 Rex King (c)	500.00
45 I&O:Phantasmo:Master of the World	400.00
46 Phantasmo (c)	400.00
47 Phantasmo (c)	300.00
48 Phantasmo (c)	275.00
49 Phantasmo (c)	275.00
50 Phantasmo (c)	275.00
51 Phantasmo (c)	275.00
52 Phantasmo (c)	300.00
53 Phantasmo (c)	300.00
54 Phantasmo (c)	300.00
55 Phantasmo (c)	300.00
56 Phantasmo (c) E:John Carter	300.00
57 I&O:Captain Midnight	850.00
58 Captain Midnight (c)	350.00
59 Captain Midnight (c)	350.00
60 Captain Midnight (c)	350.00
61 Captain Midnight (c)	350.00
62 Captain Midnight (c)	350.00
63 Captain Midnight (c)	350.00
64 B: Woody Woodpecker	350.00

Becomes:

NEW FUNNIES
Dell Publishing Co.
July, 1942

65 Andy Panda, Ragady Ann & Andy, Peter Rabbit	650.00
66 same	350.00
67 Felix the Cat	350.00
68	350.00
69 WK, The Brownies	350.00
70	350.00
71	200.00
72 WK	200.00
73	200.00
74	200.00
75 WK,Brownies	200.00
76 CB,Andy Panda, Woody Woodpecker	900.00
77 same	200.00
78 Andy Panda	200.00
79	150.00
80	150.00

GOLDEN AGE

81	150.00
82 WK,Brownies	175.00
83 WK,Brownies	175.00
84 WK,Brownies	150.00
85 WK,Brownies	175.00
86	125.00
87 Woody Woodpecker	100.00
88 same	100.00
89 same	100.00
90 same	100.00
91 thru 99	@75.00
100	85.00
101 thru 110	@50.00
111 thru 118	@40.00
119 Christmas	35.00
120 thru 142	@30.00
143 Christmas cover	35.00
144 thru 149	@30.00
150 thru 154	@20.00
155 Christmas cover	22.00
156 thru 167	@20.00
168 Christmas cover	22.00
169 thru 181	@20.00
182 I&O:Knothead & Splinter	20.00
183 thru 200	@20.00
201 thru 240	@15.00
241 thru 288	@10.00

FUNNY BOOK
Funny Book Publ. Corp.
(Parents Magazine)
December, 1952

1 Alec, the Funny Bunny, Alice in Wonderland	100.00
2 Gulliver in Giant-Land	45.00
3	35.00
4 Adventures of Robin Hood	30.00
5	30.00
6	30.00
7	30.00
8	30.00
9	30.00

FUNNY FILMS
Best Syndicated Features
(American Comics Group)
September-October, 1949

1 B:Puss An' Boots, Blunderbunny	125.00
2	75.00
3	40.00
4	35.00
5	35.00
6	35.00
7	35.00
8	35.00
9	35.00
10	35.00
11 thru 20	@25.00
21 thru 28	@22.00
29 May-June, 1954	22.00

FUNNY FUNNIES
Nedor Publ. Co.
April, 1943

1 Funny Animals	135.00

FUNNYMAN
Magazine Enterprises of Canada
December, 1947

1 S&K,S&K(c)	300.00
2 S&K,S&K(c)	175.00

3 S&K,S&K(c)	150.00
4 S&K,S&K(c)	150.00
5 S&K,S&K(c)	150.00
6 S&K,S&K(c), August, 1948	150.00

FUTURE COMICS
David McKay Publications
June, 1940

1 Lone Ranger,Phantom	2,000.00
2 Lone Ranger	950.00
3 Lone Ranger	750.00
4 Lone Ranger,Sept., 1940	700.00

Future World Comics #2
© George W. Dougherty

FUTURE WORLD COMICS
George W. Dougherty
Summer, 1946

1	165.00
2 Fall, 1946	150.00

GABBY HAYES WESTERN
Fawcett Publ./Charlton Comics
November, 1948

1 Ph(c)	350.00
2 Ph(c)	150.00
3 The Rage of the Purple Sage, Ph(c)	100.00
4 Ph(c)	100.00
5 Ph(c)	85.00
6 Ph(c)	85.00
7 Ph(c)	75.00
8 Ph(c)	75.00
9 Ph(c),V:The Kangaroo Crook	75.00
10 Ph(c)	75.00
11 Ph(c), Chariot Race	75.00
12 V:Beaver Ben, The Biting Bandit, Ph(c)	65.00
13 thru 15	@65.00
16	50.00
17	50.00
18 thru 20	@50.00
21 thru 51	@35.00
51 thru 59 December, 1954	@20.00

GANGSTERS AND GUN MOLLS
Realistic Comics
(Avon)
September, 1951

1 WW,A:Big Jim Colosimo, Evelyn Ellis	325.00
2 JKa, A:Bonnie Parker, The Kissing Bandit	250.00
3 EK, A:Juanita Perez, Crimes Homicide Squad	225.00
4 A:Mara Hite, Elkins Boys, June, 1952	175.00

GANGSTERS CAN'T WIN
D.S. Publishing Co.
February-March, 1948

1 Shot Cop cover	200.00
2 A:Eddie Bentz	100.00
3 Twin Trouble Trigger Man	75.00
4 Suicide on SoundStageSeven	75.00
5 Trail of Terror	75.00
6 Mystery at the Circus	75.00
7 Talisman Trail	60.00
8	60.00
9 Suprise at Buoy 13, June-July, 1949	60.00

GANG WORLD
Literary Enterprises
(Standard Comics)
October, 1952

5 Bondage cover	100.00
6 Mob Payoff, January, 1953	75.00

GASOLINE ALLEY
Star Publications
October, 1950

1	150.00
2 LBc	90.00
3 LBc(c), April, 1950	125.00

GEM COMICS
Spotlight Publ.
April, 1945

1 A:Steve Strong,Bondage(c)	175.00

GENE AUTRY COMICS
Fawcett Publications
January, 1942

1 The Mark of Cloven Hoof	5,500.00
2	1,000.00
3 Secret of the Aztec Treasure	1,000.00
4	650.00
5 Mystery of PaintRockCanyon	700.00
6 Outlaw Round-up	650.00
7 Border Bullets	650.00
8 Blazing Guns	600.00
9 Range Robbers	600.00
10 Fightin' Buckaroo, Danger's Trail, Sept., 1943	600.00
11	625.00
12	600.00

GENE AUTRY COMICS
Dell Publishing Co.
May/June 1946

1	400.00
2 Ph(c)	225.00
3 Ph(c)	150.00
4 Ph(c),I:Flap Jack	150.00

GOLDEN AGE

5 Ph(c), all 135.00
6 thru 10 . . . . @125.00
11 thru 19 . . . . @100.00
20 . . . . 110.00
21 thru 29 . . . . @65.00
30 thru 40, B:Giants . . . . . . @70.00
41 thru 56 E:Giants . . . . @60.00
57 . . . . 35.00
58 Christmas cover 40.00
59 thru 66 . . . . @35.00
67 thru 80, B:Giant . . . . @40.00
81 thru 90, E:Giant . . . . @30.00
91 thru 93 . . . . @22.00
94 Christmas cover 25.00
95 thru 99 . . . . @22.00
100 . . . . 28.00
101 thru 111 . . . . @22.00
112 thru 121 . . . . @18.00

GENE AUTRY'S CHAMPION
Dell Publishing Co.
August, 1950
(1) see Dell Four Color #287
(2) see Dell Four Color #319
3 thru 19 . . . . @25.00

GEORGE PAL'S PUPPETOON'S
Fawcett Publications
December, 1945
1 Captain Marvel (c) 300.00
2 . . . . 150.00
3 . . . . 100.00
4 thru 17 . . . . @90.00
18 December, 1947 . . . . 90.00

GERALD McBOING-BOING AND THE NEARSIGHTED MR. MAGOO
Dell Publishing Co.
August-October, 1952
1 . . . . 100.00
2 . . . . 75.00
3 . . . . 75.00
4 . . . . 75.00
5 . . . . 75.00

GERONIMO
Avon Periodicals
1950
1 Massacre at San Pedro Pass 100.00
2 EK(c), Murderous Battle
  at Kiskayah 60.00
3 EK(c) 60.00
4 EK(c),Apache Death Trap,
  February, 1952 . . . . 60.00

GET LOST
Mikeross Publications
February-March, 1954
1 . . . . 175.00
2 . . . . 125.00
3 June-July, 1954 . . . . 100.00

GHOST
Fiction House Magazine
Winter, 1951
1 The Banshee Bells 450.00
2 I Woke In Terror 225.00
3 The Haunted Hand of X . . . 200.00

Ghost #3 © Fiction House Magazine

4 Flee the Mad Furies 200.00
5 The Hex of Ruby Eye 200.00
6 The Sleepers in the Crypt . . 225.00
7 When Dead Rogues Ride . . 225.00
8 Curse of the Mist-Thing . . . 225.00
9 It Crawls by Night,Bondage(c) 250.00
10 Halfway to Hades 200.00
11 GE, The Witch's Doll,
  Summer, 1954 . . . . 225.00

GHOST BREAKERS
Street & Smith Publications
September, 1948
1 BP,BP(c), A:Dr. Neff 250.00
2 BP,BP(c), Breaks the Voodoo
  Hoodoo,December, 1948 . . 200.00

GHOSTLY WEIRD STORIES
(see BLUE BOLT)

GIANT BOY BOOK OF COMICS
Newsbook Publ.
(Lev Gleason)
1945
1 A:Crime Buster & Young
  Robin Hood 700.00

GIANT COMICS EDITION
St. John Publ.
1948
1 Mighty Mouse 450.00
2 Abbie and Slats 200.00
3 Terry Toons 350.00
4 Crime Comics 500.00
5 MB, Police Case Book 500.00
6 MB,MB(c), Western
  Picture Story 475.00
7 May not exist
8 The Adventures of Mighty
  Mouse 300.00
9 JKu,MB,Romance & Confession
  Stories,Ph(c) 450.00
10 Terry Toons 300.00
11 MB,MB(c),JKu,Western

Picture Stories 450.00
12 MB,MB(c),Diary Secrets,
  Prostitute 750.00
13 MB,JKu, Romances 425.00
14 Mighty Mouse Album 350.00
15 MB(c),Romance 425.00
16 Little Audrey 300.00
N#, Mighty Mouse Album 300.00

GIANT COMICS EDITION
United Features Syndicate
1945
1 A:Abbie & Slats, Jim Hardy,
  Ella Cinders,Iron Vic 250.00
2 Elmo, Jim Hardy, Abbie &
  Slats, 1945 . . . . 200.00

G.I. COMBAT
Quality Comics Group
October, 1952
1 RC(c), Beyond the Call
  of Duty 400.00
2 RC(c), Operation Massacre . . 175.00
3 An Indestructible Marine . . . 165.00
4 Bridge to Blood Hill 165.00
5 Hell Breaks loose on
  Suicide Hill 165.00
6 Beachhead Inferno 150.00
7 Fire Power Assault 125.00
8 RC(c),Death-trap Hill 125.00
9 Devil Riders 125.00
10 RC(c), Two-Ton Booby Trap 150.00
11 Hell's Heroes 100.00
12 Hand Grenade Hero 100.00
13 Commando Assault 100.00
14 Spear Head Assault 100.00
15 Vengeance Assault 100.00
16 Trapped Under Fire 90.00
17 Attack on Death Mountain . . 90.00
18 Red Battle Ground 90.00
19 Death on Helicopter Hill . . . 90.00
20 Doomed Legion-Death Trap . 90.00
21 Red Sneak Attack 75.00
22 Vengeance Raid 75.00
23 No Grandstand in Hell 75.00
24 Operation Steel
  Trap,Comics Code 75.00
25 Charge of the CommieBrigade 70.00
26 Red Guerrilla Trap 70.00
27 Trapped Behind Commie Lines 70.00
28 Atomic Battleground 70.00
29 Patrol Ambush 70.00
30 Operation Booby Trap 70.00
31 Human Fly on Heartbreak Hill 70.00
32 Atomic Rocket Assault 90.00
33 Bridge to Oblivion 70.00
34 RC,Desperate Mission 85.00
35 Doom Patrol 70.00
36 Fire Power Assault 70.00
37 Attack at Dawn 70.00
38 Get That Tank 70.00
39 Mystery of No Man's Land . . 70.00
40 Maneuver Battleground . . . 70.00
41 Trumpet of Doom 70.00
42 March of Doom 70.00
43 Operation Showdown 70.00
  See DC Comics for 44-120

GIFT COMICS
Fawcett Publications
March, 1942
1 A:Captain Marvel, Bulletman,
  Golden Arrow,Ibis, the
  Invincible, Spy Smasher . . 2,200.00

2 . . . . 1,650.00
3 . . . . 1,000.00
4 A:Marvel Family, 1949 . . . . 650.00

GIGGLE COMICS
Creston Publ./
American Comics Group
October, 1943

1 (fa)same 175.00
2 KHu 90.00
3 KHu 55.00
4 KHu 50.00
5 KHu 50.00
6 KHu 45.00
7 KHu 45.00
8 KHu 45.00
9 I:Super Katt 50.00
10 KHu 45.00
11 thru 20 KHu . . . . @30.00
21 thru 30 KHu . . . . @25.00
31 thru 40 KHu . . . . @20.00
41 thru 94 KHu . . . . @18.00
95 A:Spencer Spook 20.00
96 KHu 18.00
97 KHu 18.00
98 KHu 18.00
99 KHu 18.00
100 and 101 March-April,1955 @18.00

G.I. JANE
Stanhall Publ.
May, 1953

1 . . . . 60.00
2 thru 6 . . . . @25.00
7 thru 9 . . . . @20.00
10 December, 1954 . . . . 18.00

G.I. JOE
Ziff-Davis Publication Co.
1950

10 NS(c),Red Devils of Korea,
  V:Seoul City Lou 65.00
11 NS(c),The Guerrilla's Lair . . . 40.00
12 NS(c) 40.00
13 NS(c),Attack at Dawn 40.00
14 NS(c), Temple of Terror,
  A:Peanuts the Great 35.00
2-6 It's a Foot Soldiers Job,
  I:Frankie of the Pump 35.00
2-7 BP,NS(c),The Rout at
  Sugar Creek 35.00
8 BP,NS(c),Waldo'sSqueezeBox 35.00
9 NS(c),Dear John 35.00
10 NS(c),Joe Flies the Payroll . 35.00
11 NS(c),For the Love of Benny . 35.00
12 NS(c),Patch work Quilt 35.00
13 NS(c) 35.00
14 NS(c),The Wedding Ring . . . 35.00
15 The Lacrosse Whoopee 35.00
16 Mamie's Mortar 35.00
17 A Time for Waiting 35.00
18 Giant 100.00
19 Old Army Game..Buck Passer 30.00
20 General Confusion 30.00
21 Save 'Im for Brooklyn 30.00
22 Portrait of a Lady 30.00
23 Take Care of My Little Wagon 30.00
24 Operation 'Operation' 30.00
25 The Two-Leaf Clover 30.00
26 NS(c),Nobody Flies Alone
  Mud & Wings 30.00
27 "Dear Son...Come Home" . . . 30.00
28 They Alway's Come Back
  Bondage cover 30.00

G.I. Joe #14
© *Ziff-Davis Publication Co.*

29 What a Picnic 28.00
30 NS(c),The One-Sleeved
  Kimono 28.00
31 NS(c),Get a Horse 25.00
32 thru 47 . . . . @25.00
48 Atom Bomb 28.00
49 thru 51 June, 1957 . . . . . . @25.00

GINGER
Close-Up Publ.
(Archie Publications)
January, 1951

1 GFs 75.00
2 . . . . 40.00
3 . . . . 30.00
4 . . . . 30.00
5 . . . . 25.00
6 . . . . 25.00
7 thru 9 . . . . @35.00
10 A:Katy Keene,Summer,1954 . 40.00

GIRLS IN LOVE
Fawcett Publications
May, 1950

1 . . . . 55.00
2 Ph(c),July, 1950 . . . . 50.00

GIRLS IN LOVE
(see DIARY LOVES)

G.I. SWEETHEARTS
(see DIARY LOVES)

G.I. WAR BRIDES
Superior Publ. Ltd.
April, 1954

1 . . . . 30.00
2 . . . . 25.00
3 thru 7 . . . . @15.00
8 June, 1955 . . . . 15.00

GOING STEADY
(see TEEN-AGE
TEMPTATIONS)

GOLDEN ARROW
Fawcett Publications
Spring, 1942

1 B:Golden Arrow 650.00
2 . . . . 300.00
3 . . . . 250.00
4 . . . . 200.00
5 Spring, 1947 . . . . 200.00
6 BK 250.00
6a 1944 Well Known Comics
  (Giveaway) 275.00

GOLDEN LAD
Spark Publications
July, 1945

1 MMe,MMe(c),A:Kid Wizards,
  Swift Arrow,B:Golden Ladd . 500.00
2 MMe,MMe(c) 250.00
3 MMe,MMe(c) 250.00
4 MMe,MMe(c), The Menace of
  the Minstrel 250.00
5 MMe,MMe(c),O:Golden Girl,
  June, 1946 . . . . 250.00

GOLDEN WEST LOVE
Kirby Publishing Co.
September-October, 1949

1 BP,I Rode Heartbreak Hill,
  Ph(c) 125.00
2 BP 85.00
3 BP,Ph(c) 85.00
4 BP,April, 1950 . . . . 85.00

GOLD MEDAL COMICS
Cambridge House
1945

N# Captain Truth 200.00

GOOFY COMICS
Nedor Publ. Co./
Animated Cartoons
(Standard Comics)
June, 1943

1 (fa) 125.00
2 . . . . 70.00
3 VP 45.00
4 VP 35.00
5 VP 35.00
6 thru 10 VP . . . . @35.00
11 thru 15 . . . . @30.00
15 thru 19 . . . . @25.00
20 thru 35 FF . . . . @40.00
36 thru 48 . . . . @25.00

GREAT AMERICAN
COMICS PRESENTS–
THE SECRET VOICE
4 Star Publ.
1944

1 Hitler,Secret Weapon 175.00

GREAT COMICS
Novak Publ. Co.
1945

1 LbC(c) 250.00

GREAT COMICS
Great Comics Publications
November, 1941

1 I:The Great Zorro 900.00
2 Buck Johnson 500.00

3 The Lost City, Jan., 1942 .. 850.00

GREAT LOVER ROMANCES
Toby Press
March, 1951
1 Jon Juan,A:Dr. King 100.00
2 Hollywood Girl 50.00
3 Love in a Taxi 30.00
4 The Experimental Kiss 30.00
5 After the Honeymoon 30.00
6 HK,The Kid Sister Falls
　in Love 50.00
7 Man Crazy 25.00
8 Stand-in Boyfriend 25.00
9 The Cheat 25.00
10 Heart Breaker 25.00
11 .... 25.00
12 .... 25.00
13 Powerhouse of Deciet 25.00
14 .... 25.00
15 Ph(c),Still Undecided,
　Liz Taylor 60.00
16 thru 21 .... @25.00
22 May, 1955 .... 25.00

GREEN GIANT COMICS
Pelican Publications
1941
1 Black Arrow, Dr. Nerod
　O:Colossus 8,500.00

Green Hornet #24
© Helnit Publ./Family Comics

GREEN HORNET COMICS
Helnit Publ. Co./ Family Comics (Harvey Publ.)
December, 1940
1 B:Green Hornet,P(c) 4,000.00
2 .... 1,200.00
3 BWh(c) 1,000.00
4 BWh(c) 750.00
5 BWh(c) 750.00
6 .... 750.00
7 BP, O:Zebra, B:Robin

Hood & Spirit of 76 .... 650.00
8 BP,Bondage cover 550.00
9 BP, Behind the Cover ... 525.00
10 BP 525.00
11 Who is Mr. Q? 525.00
12 BP,A:Mr.Q 525.00
13 Hitler cover 500.00
14 BP,Spirit of 76-Twinkle
　Twins, Bondage(c) 425.00
15 ASh(c),Nazi Ghost Ship ... 400.00
16 BP,Prisoner of War 400.00
17 BP,ASh(c),Nazis' Last Stand 400.00
18 BP,ASh(c),Jap's Treacherous
　Plot,Bondage cover 425.00
19 BP,ASh(c),Clash with the
　Rampaging Japs 400.00
20 BP,ASh(c),Tojo's
　Propaganda Hoax 425.00
21 BP,ASh(c),Unwelcome Cargo 350.00
22 ASh(c),Rendezvous with
　Jap Saboteurs 350.00
23 BF,ASh(c),Jap's Diabolical
　Plot #B2978 .... 350.00
24 BF,Science Fiction cover .. 375.00
25 thru 29 .... @350.00
30 BP,JKu 350.00
31 BP,JKu 375.00
32 BP,JKu 300.00
33 BP,JKu 300.00
34 BP,JKu 300.00
35 BP,JKu 300.00
36 BP,JKu,Bondage cover ... 300.00
37 BP,JKu 300.00
38 BP,JKu 300.00
39 S&K 300.00
40 thru 45 .... @225.00
46 Drug 250.00
47 September, 1949 .... 225.00

GREEN LAMA
Spark Publications/Prize Publ.
December, 1944
1 I:Green Lama, Lt. Hercules
　& Boy Champions 1,000.00
2 MRa,Forward to Victory
　in 1945 .... 600.00
3 MRa,The Riddles of Toys .. 500.00
4 MRa,Dive Bombs Japan ... 475.00
5 MRa,MRa(c),Fights for
　the Four Freedoms 475.00
6 MRa,Smashes a Plot
　against America 475.00
7 MRa,Merry X-Mas 400.00
8 MRa,Smashes Toy Master
　of Crime, March, 1946 ... 400.00

GREEN MASK, THE
Fox Features Syndicate
Summer, 1940
1 O:Green Mask & Domino . 2,700.00
2 A:Zanzibar 1,000.00
3 BP 600.00
4 B:Navy Jones 500.00
5 .... 350.00
6 B:Nightbird,E:Navy Jones,
　Bondage cover 300.00
7 B:Timothy Smith &
　The Tumbler 250.00
8 JSs 225.00
9 E:Nightbird, Death Wields
　a Scalpel! 250.00
10 .... 200.00
11 The Banshee of Dead
　Man's Hill 200.00

The Green Mask #11
© Fox Feature Syndicate

2-1 Election of Skulls 175.00
2-2 Pigeons of Death 175.00
2-3 Wandering Gold Brick ... 150.00
2-4 Time on His Hands 150.00
2-5 JFe,SFd 175.00
2-6 Adventure of the Disappearing
　Trains, Oct.-Nov., 1946 .... 175.00

GUMPS, THE
Dell Publishing Co.
1945
1 .... 100.00
2 .... 75.00
3 .... 50.00
4 .... 50.00
5 .... 50.00

GUNS AGAINST GANGSTERS
Curtis Publ./Novelty Press
September-October, 1948
1 LbC,LbC(c),B:Toni Gayle . 200.00
2 LbC,LbC(c) 150.00
3 LbC,LbC(c) 125.00
4 LbC,LbC(c) 125.00
5 LbC,LbC(c) 125.00
6 LbC,LbC(c),Shark 125.00
2-1 LbC,LbC(c),
　September-October, 1949 . 125.00

GUNSMOKE
Western Comics, Inc.
April-May, 1949
1 GRi,GRi(c),Gunsmoke & Masked
　Marvel,Bondage cover 300.00
2 GRi,GRi(c) 175.00
3 GRi,GRi(c) 150.00
4 GRi(c),Bondage(c) 125.00
5 GRi(c) 125.00
6 .... 65.00
7 .... 65.00
8 .... 65.00
9 .... 65.00
10 .... 65.00
11 thru 15 .... @50.00
16 Jan., 1952 .... 50.00

GOLDEN AGE

HA HA COMICS
Creston Publ.
(American Comics Group)
October, 1943

1 Funny Animal, all	175.00
2	75.00
3	55.00
4	55.00
5	55.00
6 thru 10	@40.00
11	30.00
12 thru 15 KHu	@30.00
16 thru 20 KHu	@28.00
21 thru 30 KHu	@25.00
31 thru 101	@20.00
102 February-March, 1955	20.00

MISTER RISK
Humor Publ.
(Ace Magazines)
October, 1950

1 (7) B:Mr. Risk	30.00
2	25.00

Becomes:
MEN AGAINST CRIME

3 A:Mr. Risk, Case of the Carnival Killer	60.00
4 Murder-And the Crowd Roars	30.00
5	30.00
6	30.00
7 Get Them!	30.00

Becomes:
HAND OF FATE
Ace Magazines

8	250.00
9 LC	175.00
10 LC	150.00
11 Genie(c)	125.00
12	125.00
13 Hanging(c)	135.00
14	125.00
15	125.00
16	100.00
17	100.00
18	100.00
19 Drug issue,Quicksand(c)	125.00
20	100.00
21 Drug issue	125.00
22	100.00
23 Graveyard(c)	100.00
24 LC,Electric Chair	175.00
25 November, 1954	75.00
25a December, 1954	100.00

HANGMAN COMICS
(see LAUGH COMICS)

HAP HAZARD COMICS
A.A. Wyn/Red Seal Publ./
Readers Research
Summer, 1944

1 Funny Teen	60.00
2 Dog Show	30.00
3 Sgr,	28.00
4 Sgr,	28.00
5 thru 10 Sgr,	@20.00
11 thru 13 Sgr,	@15.00
14 AF(c)	35.00
15	15.00
16 thru 24	@15.00

Becomes:

REAL LOVE

25 Dangerous Dates	50.00
26	25.00
27 LbC(c), Revenge Conquest	35.00
28 thru 40	@18.00
41 thru 66	@15.00
67 Comics code	12.00
68 thru 76, Nov. 1956	@12.00

HAPPY COMICS
Nedor Publications/
Animated Cartoons
(Standard Comics)
August, 1943

1 Funny Animal in all	125.00
2	75.00
3	45.00
4	40.00
5 thru 10	@40.00
11 thru 20	@35.00
21 thru 30	@30.00
31 and 32	@50.00
33 FF	125.00
34 thru 37 FF	@50.00
38 thru 40	@20.00

Becomes:
HAPPY RABBIT

41 Funny Animal in all	25.00
42 thru 50	@15.00

Becomes:
HARVEY COMIC HITS

51 Phantom	200.00
52 Steve Canyon's Air Power	85.00
53 Mandrake	150.00
54 Tim Tyler's Tales of Jungle Terror	75.00
55 Love Stories of Mary Worth	30.00
56 Phantom, Bondage cover	175.00
57 Kidnap Racket	110.00
58 Girls in White	25.00
59 Tales of the Invisible	60.00
60 Paramount Animated Comics	275.00
61 Casper the Friendly Ghost	300.00
62 Paramount Animated Comics, April, 1953	100.00

HAPPY HOULIHANS
(see SADDLE JUSTICE)

HAUNTED THRILLS
Four Star Publ.
(Ajax/Farrell)
June, 1952

1 Ellery Queen	275.00
2 LbC,Ellery Queen	175.00
3 Drug Story	150.00
4 Ghouls Castle	125.00
5 Fatal Scapel	125.00
6 Pit of Horror	100.00
7 Trail to a Tomb	100.00
8 Vanishing Skull	100.00
9 Madness of Terror	100.00
10	100.00
11 Nazi Concentration Camp	135.00
12 RWb	100.00
13	100.00
14 RWb	125.00
15 The Devil Collects	100.00
16	100.00
17 Mirror of Madness	100.00
18 No Place to Go, November-December, 1954	110.00

Haunted Thrills #16 © Four Star Publ.

HAUNT OF FEAR
Fables Publ.
(E.C. Comics)
May-June, 1950

15 JCr,JCr(c),AF,WW	2,000.00
16 JCr,JCr(c),AF,WW	850.00
17 JCr,JCr(c),AF,WW,O:Crypt of Terror,Vault of Horror & Haunt of Fear	850.00
4 AF(c),WW,JDa	600.00
5 JCr,JCr(c),WW,JDa,Eye Injury	500.00
6 JCr,JCr(c),WW,JDa	325.00
7 JCr,JCr(c),WW,JDa	325.00
8 AF(c),JKa,JDa, Shrunken Head	325.00
9 AF(c),JCr,JDa	325.00
10 AF(c),Grl,JDa	300.00
11 JKa,Grl,JDa	275.00
12 JCr,Grl,JDa	275.00
13 Grl,JDa	275.00
14 Grl,Grl(c),JDa,O:Old Witch	325.00
15 JDa	275.00
16 GRi(c),JDa,Ray Bradbury adaptation	275.00
17 JDa,Grl(c),Classic Ghastly (c)	275.00
18 JDa,Grl(c),JKa,Ray Bradbury adaptation	300.00
19 JDa,Guillotine (c), Bondage cover	300.00
20 RC,JDa,Grl,Grl(c)	250.00
21 JDa,Grl,Grl(c)	200.00
22 same	200.00
23 same	200.00
22 same	200.00
23 same	200.00
24 same	200.00
25 same	200.00
26 RC,same	250.00
27 same, Cannibalism	225.00
28 December, 1954	225.00

HAWK, THE
Approved Comics
(Ziff-Davis)
Winter, 1951

1 MA,The Law of the Colt,P(c)	150.00
2 JKu,Iron Caravan of the	

GOLDEN AGE

Mojave, P(c)	75.00
3 Leverett's Last Stand,P(c)	60.00
4 Killer's Town,P(c)	50.00
5	40.00
6	40.00
7	40.00
8 MB(c),Dry River Rampage	50.00
9 MB,MB(c),JKu	55.00
10 MB(c)	50.00
11 MB(c)	50.00
12 MB,MB(c), May, 1955	50.00

HEADLINE COMICS
American Boys Comics/
Headline Publ. (Prize Publ.)
February, 1943

1 B:Jr. Rangers	275.00
2 JaB,JaB(c)	125.00
3 JaB,JaB(c)	110.00
4	100.00
5 HcK	100.00
6 HcK	100.00
7 HcK,Jr. Rangers	100.00
8 HcK,Hitler cover	250.00
9 HcK	100.00
10 HcK,Hitler story,Wizard(c)	150.00
11	65.00
12 HcK,Heroes of Yesterday	65.00
13 HcK,A:Blue Streak	75.00
14 HcK,A:Blue Streak	75.00
15 HcK,A:Blue Streak	75.00
16 HcK,O:Atomic Man	175.00
17 Atomic Man(c)	100.00
18 Atomic Man(c)	100.00
19 S&K,Atomic Man(c)	175.00
20 Atomic Man(c)	100.00
21 E:Atomic Man	100.00
22 HcK	50.00
23 S&K,S&K(c),Valentines Day Massacre	150.00
24 S&K,S&K(c),You can't Forget a Killer	150.00
25 S&K,S&K(c),CrimeNeverPays	125.00
26 S&K,S&K(c),CrimeNeverPays	125.00
27 S&K,S&K(c),CrimeNeverPays	125.00
28 S&K,S&K(c),CrimeNeverPays	125.00
29 S&K,S&K(c),CrimeNeverPays	125.00
30 S&K,S&K(c),CrimeNeverPays	125.00
31 S&K,S&K(c),CrimeNeverPays	125.00
32 S&K,S&K(c),CrimeNeverPays	125.00
33 S&K,S&K(c),Police and FBI heroes	125.00
34 S&K,S&K(c),same	125.00
35 S&K,S&K(c),same	125.00
36 S&K,S&K(c),same,Ph(c)	100.00
37 S&K,S&K(c),MvS,same,Ph(c)	125.00
38 S&K,S&K(c),same,Ph(c)	30.00
39 S&K,S&K(c),same,Ph(c)	30.00
40 S&K,S&K(c),Ph(c)Violent Crime	30.00
41 Ph(c),J.Edgar Hoover(c)	30.00
42 Ph(c)	20.00
43 Ph(c)	20.00
44 MMe,MvS,WE,S&K	35.00
45 JK	22.00
46	18.00
47	18.00
48	18.00
49 MMe	18.00
50	18.00
51 JK	20.00
52	18.00
53	18.00
54	18.00
55	18.00

56 S&K	30.00
57	18.00
58	18.00
59	18.00
60 MvS(c)	18.00
61 MMe,MvS(c)	18.00
62 MMe,MMe(c)	18.00
63 MMe,MMe(c)	18.00
64 MMe,MMe(c)	18.00
65 MMe,MMe(c)	18.00
66 MMe,MMe(c)	18.00
67 MMe,MMe(c)	18.00
68 MMe,MMe(c)	18.00
69 MMe,MMe(c)	18.00
70 MMe,MMe(c)	18.00
71 MMe,MMe(c)	18.00
72 MMe,MMe(c)	18.00
73 MMe,MMe(c)	18.00
74 MMe,MMe(c)	18.00
75 MMe,MMe(c)	18.00
76 MMe,MMe(c)	18.00
77 MMe,MMe(c),October, 1956	18.00

HEART THROBS
Comics Magazines
(Quality)
August, 1949

1 BWa(c),PG,Spoiled Brat	275.00
2 BWa(c),PG,Siren of the Tropics	175.00
3 PG	50.00
4 BWa(c),Greed Turned Me into a Scheming Vixen,Ph(c)	100.00
5 Ph(c)	30.00
6 BWa	85.00
7	30.00
8 BWa	85.00
9 I Hated Men,Ph(c)	45.00
10 BWa,My Secret Fears	50.00
11	18.00
12	15.00
13	18.00
14 BWa	18.00
15 My Right to Happiness,Ph(c)	45.00
16	16.00
17	16.00
18	16.00
19	16.00
20	16.00
21 BWa	35.00
22 BWa	30.00
23 BWa	30.00
24 thru 30	@15.00
31 thru 33	@15.00
34 thru 39	@15.00
40 BWa	25.00
41	15.00
42	15.00
43 thru 45	@15.00

(Please see DC listings)

HECKLE AND JECKLE
St. John Publ./Pines
November, 1951

1 Blue Ribbon Comics	200.00
2 Blue Ribbon Comics	125.00
3	85.00
4	75.00
5	75.00
6	75.00
7	55.00
8	50.00
9	50.00
10	50.00

PAUL TERRY'S
HECKLE AND JECKLE
COMICS

In this issue
NAUTICAL
NONSENSE.

Heckle and Jeckle #17
© St. John Publications

11 thru 15	@40.00
16 thru 20	@35.00
21 thru 33	@30.00
34 June, 1959	32.00

HELLO PAL COMICS
Harvey Publications
January, 1943

1 B:Rocketman & Rocket Girl, Mickey Rooney cover, Ph(c) all	500.00
2 Charlie McCarthy cover	400.00
3 Bob Hope cover, May, 1943	375.00

HENRY
Dell Publishing Co.
October, 1946

1	100.00
2	50.00
3 thru 10	@35.00
11 thru 20	@25.00
21 thru 30	@20.00
31 thru 40	@15.00
41 thru 50	@12.00
51 thru 65	@10.00

HENRY ALDRICH COMICS
Dell Publishing Co.
August-September, 1950

1	90.00
2	45.00
3	30.00
4	30.00
5	30.00
6 thru 10	@25.00
11 thru 22	@20.00

HEROIC COMICS
Eastern Color Printing Co./
Famous Funnies
August, 1940

1 BEv,BEv(c),O:Hydroman,Purple Zombie, B:Man of India	1,200.00
2 BEv,BEv(c),B:Hydroman covers	600.00
3 BEv,BEv(c)	375.00

GOLDEN AGE

4 BEv,BEv(c)	350 00
5 BEv,BEv(c)	325.00
6 BEv,BEv(c)	300.00
7 BEv,BEv(c),O:Man O'Metal	350.00
8 BEv,BEv(c)	200.00
9 BEv	200.00
10 BEv	200.00
11 BEv,E:Hydroman covers	175.00
12 BEv,B&0:Music Master	200.00
13 BEv,RC,LF	175.00
14 BEv	200.00
15 BEv,I:Downbeat	200.00
16 BEv,CCB(c),A:Lieut Nininger, Major Heidger,Lieut Welch,B:P(c)	150.00
17 BEv,A:JohnJames Powers,Hewitt T.Wheless, Irving Strobing	150.00
18 HcK,BEv,Pass the Ammunition	150.00
19 HcK,BEv,A:Barney Ross	150.00
20 HcK,BEv	125.00
21 HcK,BEv	100.00
22 HcK,BEv,Howard Gilmore	100.00
23 HcK,BEv	100.00
24 HcK,BEv	100.00
25 HcK,BEv	100.00
26 HcK,BEv	100.00
27 HcK,BEv	100.00
28 HcK,BEv,E:Man O'Metal	100.00
29 HcK,BEv,E:Hydroman	100.00
30 BEv	90.00
31 BEv,CCB,Capt. Tootsie	25.00
32 ATh,CCB,WWII(c), Capt. Tootsie	35.00
33 ATh,	35.00
34 WWII(c)	20.00
35 Ath,B:Rescue(c)	35.00
36 HcK,ATh	35.00
37 same	35.00
38 ATh	35.00
39 HcK,ATh	35.00
40 ATh,Boxing	35.00
41 Grl(c),ATh	35.00
42 ATh	35.00
43 ATh	30.00
44 HcK,ATh	30.00
45 HcK	30.00
46 HcK	30.00
47 HcK	30.00
48 HcK	30.00
49 HcK	30.00
50 HcK	30.00
51 HcK,ATh,AW	32.00
52 HcK,AW	32.00
53 HcK	30.00
54	18.00
55 ATh	18.00
56 ATh(c)	28.00
57 ATh(c)	25.00
58 ATh(c)	25.00
59 ATh(c)	25.00
60 ATh(c)	25.00
61 BEv(c)	20.00
62 BEv(c)	20.00
63 BEv(c)	20.00
64 GE,BEv(c)	22.00
65 HcK(c),FF,ATh,AW,GE	50.00
66 HcK(c),FF	35.00
67 HcK(c),FF,Korean War(c)	35.00
68 HcK(c),Korean War(c)	35.00
69 HcK(c),FF	40.00
70 HcK(c),FF,B:Korean War(c)	35.00
71 HcK(c),FF	35.00
72 HcK(c),FF	40.00
73 HcK(c),FF	35.00
74 HcK(c)	35.00
75 HcK(c),FF	35.00
76 HcK,HcK(c)	12.00
77 same	12.00
78 same	12.00
79 same	12.00
80 same	12.00
81 FF,HcK(c)	15.00
82 FF,HcK(c)	15.00
83 FF,HcK(c)	15.00
84 HcK(c)	15.00
85 HcK(c)	15.00
86 FF,HcK(c)	20.00
87 FF,HcK(c)	20.00
88 HcK(c),E:Korean War covers	12.00
89 HcK(c)	12.00
90 HcK(c)	12.00
91 HcK(c)	12.00
92 HcK(c)	12.00
93 HcK(c)	12.00
94 HcK(c)	12.00
95 HcK(c)	12.00
96 HcK(c)	12.00
97 HcK(c),E:P(c),June, 1955	12.00

HICKORY
Comic Magazine
(Quality Comics Group)
October, 1949

1 ASa,	75.00
2 ASa,	35.00
3 ASa,	25.00
4 ASa,	25.00
5 ASa,	25.00
6 ASa,August, 1950	25.00

HI-HO COMICS
Four Star Publications
1946

1 LbC(c)	150.00
2 LbC(c)	85.00
3 1946	70.00

HI-JINX
B & I Publ. Co.
(American Comics Group)
July-August, 1947

1 (fa) all	100.00
2	60.00
3	50.00
4 thru 7	@40.00
N#	75.00

HI-LITE COMICS
E.R. Ross Publ.
Fall, 1945

1	75.00

HIT COMICS
Comics Magazine
(Quality Comics Group)
July, 1940

1 LF(c),O:Neon,Hercules,I:The Red Bee, B:Bob & Swab, Blaze Barton Strange Twins,X-5 Super Agent Casey Jones,Jack & Jill	5,000.00
2 GT,LF(c),B:Old Witch	2,000.00
3 GT,LF(c),E:Casey Jones	1,800.00
4 GT,LF(c),B:Super Agent & Betty Bates,E:X-5	1,500.00
5 GT,LF(c),B:Red Bee cover	4,000.00
6 GT,LF(c)	1,500.00
7 GT,LF(c),E:Red Bee cover	1,550.00
8 GT,LF(c),B:Neon cover	1,500.00
9 JCo,LF(c),E:Neon cover	1,500.00
10 JCo,RC,LF(c),B:Hercules(c)	1,500.00
11 JCo,RC,LF(c),A:Hercules	950.00
12 JCo,RC,LF(c),A:Hercules	950.00
13 JCo,RC,LF(c),A:Hercules	950.00
14 JCo,RC,LF(c),A:Hercules	950.00
15 JCo,RC,A:Hercules	900.00
16 JCo,RC,LF(c),A:Hercules	900.00
17 JCo,RC,LF(c),E:Hercules	900.00
18 JCo,RC,RC(c),O:Stormy Foster,B:Ghost of Flanders	1,000.00
19 JCo,RC(c),B:StormyFoster(c)	800.00
20 JCo,RC(c),A:Stormy Foster	800.00
21 JCo,RC(c)	750.00
22 JCo	750.00
23 JCo,RC,RC(c)	700.00
24 JCo,E:Stormy Foster cover	700.00
25 JCo,RP,O:Kid Eternity	1,200.00
26 JCo,RP,A:Black Hawk	800.00
27 JCo,RP,B:Kid Eternity covers	400.00

Hit Comics #39
© Quality Comics Group

28 JCo,RP,A:Her Highness	400.00
29 JCo,RP	400.00
30 JCo,RP,HK,V:Julius Caesar and his Legion of Warriors	350.00
31 JCo,RP	350.00
32 JCo,RP,V:Merlin the Wizard	200.00
33 JCo,RP	175.00
34 JCo,RP,E:Stormy Foster	175.00
35 JCo,Kid Eternity accused of Murder	175.00
36 JCo,The Witch's Curse	175.00
37 JCo,V:Mr. Silence	175.00
38 JCo	175.00
39 JCo,Runaway River Boat	175.00
40 PG,V:Monster from the Past	175.00
41 PG,Did Kid Eternity Lose His Power?	125.00
42 PG,Kid Eternity Loses Killer Cronson	125.00
43 JCo,PG,V:Modern Bluebeard	125.00
44 JCo,PG,Trips up the Shoe	125.00
45 JCo,PG,Pancho Villa against Don Pablo	125.00
46 JCo,V:Mr. Hardeel	125.00
47 A Polished Diamond can be	

GOLDEN AGE

Rough on Rats 125.00
48 EhH,A Treasure Chest
  of Trouble 125.00
49 EhH,V:Monsters from
  the Mirror 125.00
50 EhH,Heads for Trouble . . . 125.00
51 EhH,Enters the Forgotten
  World 100.00
52 EhH,Heroes out of the Past 100.00
53 EhH,V:Mr. Puny 100.00
54 V:Ghost Town Killer 100.00
55 V:The Brute 100.00
56 V:Big Odds 90.00
57 Solves the Picture in
  a Frame 90.00
58 Destroys Oppression! 90.00
59 Battles Tomorrow's Crimes
  Today! 90.00
60 E:Kid Eternity covers,
  V:The Mummy 90.00
61 RC,RC(c),I:Jeb Rivers 125.00
62 RC(c) 100.00
63 RC(c),A:Jeb Rivers 125.00
64 RC,A:Jeb Rivers 125.00
65 Bondage cover,RC,July, 1950 135.00

HOLIDAY COMICS
Fawcett Publ.
November, 1942
1 Captain Marvel (c) 1,400.00

HOLIDAY COMICS
Star Publ.
January, 1951
1 LbC(c),(fa),Christmas cover . 200.00
2 LbC(c),Parade(c) 250.00
3 LbC(c),July 4th(c) 150.00
4 LbC(c),Vacation(c) 150.00
5 LbC(c),Christmas(c) 150.00
6 LbC(c),Birthday(c) 150.00
7 LbC(c) 125.00
8 LbC(c),Christmas(c) 150.00

HOLLYWOOD COMICS
New Age Publishers
Winter, 1944
1 (fa) 125.00

HOLLYWOOD
CONFESSIONS
St. John Publ. Co.
October, 1949
1 JKu,JKu(c) 150.00
2 JKu,JKu(c), December, 1949 225.00

HOLLYWOOD DIARY
Comics Magazine
(Quality Comics)
December, 1949
1 . . . . 100.00
2 Photo cover 75.00
3 Photo cover 60.00
4 . . . . 60.00
5 Photo cover, August, 1950 . . 60.00

HOLLYWOOD FILM
STORIES
Feature Publications
(Prize)
April, 1950
1 June Allison,Ph(c) 125.00
2 Lizabeth Scott,Ph(c) 75.00

3 Barbara Stanwick,Ph(c) 75.00
4 Beth Hutton, August, 1950 . . 75.00

HOLLYWOOD SECRETS
Comics Magazine
(Quality Comics Group)
November, 1949
1 BWa,BWa(c) 200.00
2 BWa,BWa(c),RC 125.00
3 Ph(c) 60.00
4 Ph(c),May, 1950 . . . . 60.00
5 Ph(c) 60.00
6 Ph(c) 60.00

HOLYOKE ONE-SHOT
Tem Publ.
(Holyoke Publ. Co.)
1944
1 Grit Grady 75.00
2 Rusty Dugan 60.00
3 JK,Miss Victory,O:Cat Woman 150.00
4 Mr. Miracle 55.00
5 U.S. Border Patrol 50.00
6 Capt. Fearless 50.00
7 Strong Man 55.00
8 Blue Streak 50.00
9 S&K, Citizen Smith 80.00
10 S&K, Capt. Stone 75.00

HONEYMOON
ROMANCE
Artful Publications
(Digest Size)
April, 1950
1 . . . . 250.00
2 July, 1950 . . . . 225.00

HOODED HORSEMAN
(see OUT OF THE NIGHT)

HOPALONG CASSIDY
Fawcett Publications
February, 1943
1 B:Hopalong Cassidy & Topper,
  Captain Marvel cover 4,200.00
2 . . . . 600.00
3 Blazing Trails 275.00
4 5-full length story 250.00
5 Death in the Saddle, Ph(c) . 225.00
6 . . . . 200.00
7 . . . . 200.00
8 Phantom Stage Coach 200.00
9 The Last Stockade 200.00
10 4-spine tingling adventures . 200.00
11 Desperate Jetters! Ph(c) . . . 150.00
12 The Mysterious Message . . 150.00
13 The Human Target, Ph(c) . . 150.00
14 Land of the Lawless, Ph(c) . 150.00
15 Death holds the Reins, Ph(c) 150.00
16 Webfoot's Revenge, Ph(c) . 150.00
17 The Hangman's Noose, Ph(c) 150.00
18 The Ghost of Dude Ranch,
  Ph(c) 150.00
19 A:William Boyd,Ph(c) 150.00
20 The Notorious Nellie Blaine!,
  B:P(c) 125.00
21 V:Arizona Kid 125.00
22 V:Arizona Kid 125.00
23 Hayride Horror 125.00
24 Twin River Giant 125.00
25 On the Trails of the Wild
  and Wooly West 125.00

26 thru 30 . . . . @100.00
31 52 pages 50.00
32 36 pages 40.00
33 thru 35, 52 pages . . . . . . @50.00
36 36 pages 42.00
37 thru 40, 52 pages . . . . @50.00
40 36 pages 42.00
41 E:P(c) 40.00
42 B:Ph(c) 50.00
43 . . . . 50.00
44 . . . . 40.00
45 . . . . 50.00
46 thru 51 . . . . @40.00
52 . . . . 35.00
53 . . . . 40.00
54 . . . . 40.00
55 . . . . 35.00
56 . . . . 40.00
57 . . . . 40.00
58 thru 70 . . . . @35.00
71 thru 84 . . . . @25.00
85 E:Ph(c),January, 1954 . . . . 25.00
(Please see DC listings)

Hoppy the Marvel Bunny #3
© Fawcett Publications

HOPPY THE
MARVEL BUNNY
Fawcett Publications
December, 1945
1 A:Marvel Bunny 150.00
2 . . . . 75.00
3 . . . . 50.00
4 . . . . 50.00
5 . . . . 50.00
6 thru 14 . . . . @40.00
15 September, 1947 . . . . 40.00

HORRIFIC
Artful/Comic Media/
Harwell Publ./Mystery
September, 1952
1 Conductor in Flames(c) 250.00
2 Human Puppets(c) 125.00
3 DH(c),Bullet hole in
  head(c) 200.00
4 DH(c),head on a stick(c) . . 100.00
5 DH(c) 125.00

---

6 DH(c),Jack the Ripper 100 00
7 DH(c),Shrunken Skulls 75.00
8 DH(c),I:The Teller 100.00
9 DH(c),Claws of Horror, Wolves
of Midnight 75.00
10 DH(c),The Teller-four
eerie tales of Horror 75.00
11 DH(c),A:Gary Ghoul,Freddie,
Demon,Victor Vampire,
Walter Werewolf 65.00
12 DH(c),A:Gary Ghoul,Freddie
Demon,Victor Vampire,
Walter Werewolf 65.00
13 DH(c),A:Gary Ghoul,Freddie
Demom,Victor Vampire,
Walter Werewolf 65.00
Becomes:

TERRIFIC COMICS
14 .... 150.00
15 .... 100.00
16 B:Wonderboy 100.00
Becomes:

WONDERBOY
17 The Enemy's Enemy 175.00
18 Success is No Accident,
July, 1955 .... 150.00

HORROR FROM THE TOMB
(see MYSTERIOUS STORIES)

HORRORS, THE
Star Publications
January, 1953
11 LbC(c),JyD,of War 175.00
12 LbC(c),of War 150.00
13 LbC(c),of Mystery 125.00
14 LbC(c),of the Underworld .. 150.00
15 LbC(c),of the Underworld,
April, 1954 .... 150.00

HORSE FEATHER COMICS
Lev Gleason Publications
November, 1947
1 BW 135.00
2 .... 55.00
3 .... 50.00
4 Summer, 1948 .... 50.00

HOT ROD AND SPEEDWAY COMICS
Hillman Periodicals
February-March, 1952
1 .... 135.00
2 BK 100.00
3 .... 50.00
4 .... 50.00
5 April-May, 1953 .... 50.00

HOT ROD COMICS
Fawcett Publications
Feb., 1952–53
N# BP,BP(c),F:Clint Curtis ... 200.00
2 BP,BP(c),Safety comes First 125.00
3 BP,BP(c),The Racing Game 100.00
4 BP,BP(c),Bonneville National
Championships 100.00
5 BP,BP(c), ... 100.00
6 BP,BP(c),Race to Death ... 100.00

HOT ROD KING
**Approved Comics
(Ziff-Davis)
Fall, 1952**
1 P(c) 150.00

HOWDY DOODY
Dell Publishing Co.
January, 1950
1 Ph(c) 750.00
2 Ph(c) 325.00
3 Ph(c) 200.00
4 Ph(c) 200.00
5 Ph(c) 200.00
6 P(c) 150.00
7 .... 135.00
8 .... 135.00
9 .... 135.00
10 .... 135.00
11 .... 125.00
12 .... 125.00
13 Christmas (c) 125.00
14 thru 20 .... @125.00
21 thru 38 .... @100.00

Howdy Doody Comics #9
© Dell Publishing Co.

HOW STALIN HOPES WE WILL DESTROY AMERICA
Pictorial News
1951
N# (Giveaway) 400.00

HUMBUG
Harvey Kurtzman
1957
1 JDa,WW,WE,End of the World 175.00
2 JDa,WE,Radiator 100.00
3 JDa,WE 75.00
4 JDa,WE,Queen Victoria(c) ... 75.00
5 JDa,WE 75.00
6 JDa,WE 75.00
7 JDa,WE,Sputnik(c) 80.00
8 JDa,WE,Elvis/George
Washington(c) 75.00
9 JDa,WE 75.00

10 JDa,Magazine 100.00
11 JDw,WE,HK,Magazine 100.00

HUMDINGER
**Novelty Press/
Premium Service**
May-June, 1946
1 B:Jerkwater Line,Dink,
Mickey Starlight 200.00
2 .... 100.00
3 .... 75.00
4 .... 75.00
5 .... 75.00
6 .... 75.00
2-1 .... 60.00
2-2 July-August, 1947 ...... 60.00

HUMPHREY COMICS
Harvey Publications
October, 1948
1 BP,Joe Palooka 80.00
2 BP 35.00
3 BP 30.00
4 BP,A:Boy Heroes 40.00
5 BP 25.00
6 BP 25.00
7 BP,A:Little Dot 25.00
8 BP,O:Humphrey 30.00
9 BP 15.00
10 BP 15.00
11 thru 21 .... @15.00
22 April, 1952 .... 15.00

HYPER MYSTERY COMICS
Hyper Publications
May, 1940
1 B:Hyper 1,500.00
2 June, 1940 .... 800.00

IBIS, THE INVINCIBLE
Fawcett Publications
January, 1942
1 MRa(c),O:Ibis 1,400.00
2 Bondage cover 700.00
3 BW 600.00
4 BW,A:Mystic Snake People 400.00
5 BW,Bondage cover,The
Devil's Ibistick 425.00
6 BW, The Book of Evil,
Spring, 1948 .... 425.00

IDEAL ROMANCE
(see TENDER ROMANCE)

IF THE DEVIL WOULD TALK
Catechetical Guild
1950
N# Rare 550.00
N#, 1958 Very Rare 450.00

ILLUSTRATED STORIES OF THE OPERA
B. Bailey Publ. Co.
1943
N# Faust 500.00
N# Aida 450.00
N# Carman 450.00
N# Rigoletto 450.00

GOLDEN AGE

All comics prices listed are for *Near Mint* condition.

GOLDEN AGE

I LOVED
(see ZOOT COMICS)

I LOVE LUCY COMICS
Dell Publishing Co.
February, 1954
(1) *see Dell Four Color #535*
(2) *see Dell Four Color #559*
3 Lucile Ball Ph(c) all 225.00
4 . . . . 200.00
5 . . . . 200.00
6 thru 10 . . . . @175.00
11 thru 20 . . . . 125.00
21 thru 35 . . . . 100.00

IMPACT
E.C. Comics
March-April, 1955
1 RC,GE,BK,Grl 125.00
2 RC,JDu,Grl,BK,JO 100.00
3 JO,RC,JDU,Grl,JKa,BK 80.00
4 RC,JO,JDa,GE,Grl,BK 80.00
5 November-December, 1955 . 80.00

INCREDIBLE
SCIENCE FANTASY
(see WEIRD SCIENCE)

INCREDIBLE
SCIENCE FICTION
E.C. Comics
July-August, 1955
30 . . . . 250.00
31 . . . . 275.00
32 January-February, 1956 . . 275.00
33 . . . . 250.00

INDIAN CHIEF
Dell Publishing Co.
July-September, 1951
3 P(c) all 30.00
4 . . . . 15.00
5 . . . . 15.00
6 A:White Eagle 15.00
7 . . . . 15.00
8 . . . . 15.00
9 . . . . 15.00
10 . . . . 15.00
11 . . . . 15.00
12 I:White Eagle 25.00
13 thru 29 . . . . @10.00
30 SB 15.00
31 SB 15.00
32 SB 15.00
33 SB 15.00

INDIAN FIGHTER
Youthful Magazines
May, 1950
1 Revenge of Chief Crazy Horse 60.00
2 Bondage cover 35.00
3 . . . . 20.00
4 Cheyenne Warpath 20.00
5 . . . . 20.00
6 Davy Crockett in Death Stalks
the Alamo 20.00
7 Tom Horn-Bloodshed at
Massacre Valley 20.00
8 Tales of Wild Bill Hickory,
January, 1952 . . . . 20.00

INDIANS
Wings Publ. Co.
(Fiction House)
Spring, 1950
1 B:Long Bow, Manzar, White
Indian & Orphan 150.00
2 B:Starlight 75.00
3 Longbow(c) 60.00
4 Longbow(c) 50.00
5 Manzar(c) 60.00
6 Captive of the Semecas . . . 50.00
7 Longbow(c) 50.00
8 A:Long Bow 50.00
9 A:Long Bow 50.00
10 Manzar(c) 50.00
11 thru 16 . . . . @40.00
17 Spring, 1953,Longbow(c) . . . 40.00

Indians on the Warpath #1
© St. John Publishing Co.

INDIANS ON
THE WARPATH
St. John Publ. Co.
1950
N# MB(c) 200.00

INFORMER, THE
Feature Television
Productions
April, 1954
1 MSy,The Greatest Social
Menace of our Time! 65.00
2 MSy 35.00
3 MSy 30.00
4 MSy 30.00
5 December, 1954 . . . . 30.00

IN LOVE
Mainline/Charlton Comics
August, 1954
1 S&K,Bride of the Star 200.00
2 S&K,Marilyn's Men 125.00
3 S&K 100.00
4 S&K,Comics Code 50.00
5 S&K(c) 50.00
6 . . . . 20.00
Becomes:

I LOVE YOU
7 JK(c),BP 75.00
8 . . . . 25.00
9 . . . . 25.00
10 . . . . 25.00
11 thru 16 . . . . @20.00
17 . . . . 15.00
18 . . . . 10.00
19 . . . . 10.00
20 . . . . 10.00
21 thru 50 . . . . @7.00
51 thru 59 . . . . @5.00
60 Elvis 85.00
61 thru 100 . . . . @4.00
101 thru 130 . . . . @3.00

INTERNATIONAL COMICS
(see CRIME PATROL)

INTERNATIONAL
CRIME PATROL
(see CRIME PATROL)

INTIMATE
CONFESSIONS
Fawcett Publ./
Realistic Comics
1951
1a P(c) all, Unmarried Bride . 550.00
1 EK,EK(c),Days of Temptation...
Nights of Desire 150.00
2 Doomed to Silence 125.00
3 EK(c), The Only Man For Me 100.00
3a Robert Briffault 100.00
4 EK(c),Tormented Love 100.00
5 Her Secret Sin 100.00
6 Reckless Pick-up 100.00
7 A Love Like Ours,Spanking . 125.00
8 Fatal Woman, March, 1953 100.00

INTIMATE LOVE
Standard Magazines
January, 1950
5 Wings on My Heart,Ph(c) . . . 40.00
6 WE,JSe,Ph(c) 45.00
7 WE,JSe,Ph(c),I Toyed
with Love 45.00
8 WE,JSe,Ph(c) 45.00
9 Ph(c) 25.00
10 Ph(c),My Hopeless Heart . . . 35.00
11 . . . . 10.00
12 . . . . 10.00
13 thru 18 . . . . @10.00
19 ATh 35.00
20 . . . . 10.00
21 ATh 35.00
22 ATh 35.00
23 ATh 10.00
24 ATh 35.00
25 ATh 10.00
26 ATh 35.00
27 ATh 10.00
28 ATh,August, 1954 . . . . 10.00

INTIMATE SECRETS
OF ROMANCE
Star Publications
September, 1953
1 LbC(c) 75.00
2 LbC(c) 65.00

INVISIBLE SCARLET O'NEIL
Harvey Publications
December, 1950

1	100.00
2	75.00
3 April, 1951	75.00

IT REALLY HAPPENED
William H. Wise/ Visual Editions
1945

1 Benjamin Franklin, Kit Carson	120.00
2 The Terrible Tiddlers	60.00
3 Maid of the Margiris	35.00
4 Chaplain Albert J. Hoffman	30.00
5 AS(c),Monarchs of the Sea,Lou Gehrig, Amelia Earhart	80.00
6 AS(c),Ernie Pyle	30.00
7 FG,Teddy Roosevelt,Jefferson Davis, Story of the Helicopter	30.00
8 FG,Man O' War,Roy Rogers	90.00
9 AS(c),The Story of Old Ironsides	30.00
10 AS(c),Honus Wagner, The Story of Mark Twain	75.00
11 AS(c),MB,Queen of the Spanish Main, October, 1947	50.00

JACK ARMSTRONG
Parents' Institute
November, 1947

1 Artic Mystery	300.00
2 Den of the Golden Dragon	125.00
3 Lost Valley of Ice	100.00
4 Land of the Leopard Men	100.00
5 Fight against Racketeers of the Ring	100.00
6	75.00
7 Baffling Mystery on the Diamond	80.00
8	80.00
9 Mystery of the Midgets	80.00
10 Secret Cargo	80.00
11	75.00
12 Madman's Island	75.00
13 September, 1949	75.00

JACE PEARSON OF THE TEXAS RANGERS
Dell Publishing Co.
May, 1952

(1) see Dell Four Color #396	
2 Ph(c),Joel McRae	50.00
3 Ph(c),Joel McRae	50.00
4 Ph(c),Joel McRae	50.00
5 Ph(c),Joel McRae	50.00
6 Ph(c),Joel McRae	50.00
7 Ph(c),Joel McRae	50.00
8 Ph(c),Joel McRae	50.00
9 Ph(c),Joel McRae	50.00
(10) see Dell Four Color #648	

Becomes:

TALES OF JACE PEARSON OF THE TEXAS RANGERS

11	30.00
12	30.00
13	30.00
14	30.00
15 ATh	40.00

16 ATh	40.00
17	30.00
18	30.00
19	30.00
20	30.00

Jackie Gleason #4
© St. John Publishing Co.

JACKIE GLEASON
St. John Publishing Co.
September, 1955

1 Ph(c)	600.00
2	500.00
3	400.00
4 December, 1955	375.00

JACKIE ROBINSON
Fawcett Publications
May, 1950

N# Ph(c) all issues	700.00
2	500.00
3 thru 5	@400.00
6 May, 1952	350.00

JACK IN THE BOX
(see YELLOW JACKET COMICS)

JACKPOT COMICS
MLJ Magazines
Spring, 1941

1 CBi(c),B:Black Hood,Mr.Justice, Steel Sterling,Sgt.Boyle	2,200.00
2 SCp(c),	1,000.00
3 Bondage cover	750.00
4 First Archie	1,900.00
5 Hitler(c)	1,000.00
6 Son of the Skull v:Black Hood, Bondage(c)	850.00
7 Bondage (c)	850.00
8 Sal(c),	750.00
9 Sal(c),	800.00

Becomes:

JOLLY JINGLES

10 Super Duck,(fa)	250.00
11 Super Duck	135.00
12 Hitler parody cover,A:Woody	

Woodpecker	75.00
13 Super Duck	50.00
14 Super Duck	50.00
15 Super Duck	50.00
16 December, 1944	50.00

JACK THE GIANT KILLER
Bimfort & Co.
August-September, 1953

1 HcK,HcK(c)	135.00

JAMBOREE
Round Publishing Co.
February, 1946

1	125.00
2 March, 1946	75.00

JANE ARDEN
St. John Publ. Co.
March, 1948

1	120.00
2 June, 1948	70.00

JEEP COMICS
R.B. Leffingwell & Co.
Winter, 1944

1 B;Captain Power	275.00
2	200.00
3 LbC(c),March-April, 1948	250.00

JEFF JORDAN, U.S. AGENT
D.S. Publ. Co.
December, 1947

1	55.00

JESSE JAMES
Avon Periodicals/ Realistic Publ.
August, 1950

1 JKu,The San Antonio Stage Robbery	100.00
2 JKu,The Daring Liberty Bank Robbery	75.00
3 JKu,The California Stagecoach Robberies	65.00
4 EK(c),Deadliest Deed!	25.00
5 JKu,WW,Great Prison Break	65.00
6 JKu,Wanted Dead or Alive	65.00
7 JKu,Six-Gun Slaughter at San Romano!	55.00
8 EK,Daring Train Robbery!	40.00
9 EK	25.00
10 thru 14 {Do not exist}	
15	40.00
16	25.00
17	18.00
18 JKu	20.00
19 JKu	20.00
20 AW,FF,A:Chief Vic,Kit West	75.00
21	18.00
22	15.00
23	15.00
24 EK,B:New McCarty	18.00
25 EK	18.00
26 EK	18.00
27 EK,E:New McCarty	18.00
28	18.00
29 August, 1956	18.00

JEST
Harry 'A' Chesler
1944
10 J. Rebel,Yankee Boy 100.00
11 1944,Little Nemo 125.00

JET ACES
Real Adventure Publ. Co.
(Fiction House)
1952
1 Set 'em up in MIG Alley 75.00
2 Kiss-Off for Moscow Molly . . 40.00
3 Red Task Force Sighted 40.00
4 Death-Date at 40,000, 1953 . 40.00

JET FIGHTERS
Standard Magazines
November, 1953
5 ATh,Korean War Stories 60.00
6 Circus Pilot 25.00
7 ATh, Iron Curtains for Ivan,
  March, 1953 . . . . 45.00

JETTA OF THE
21st CENTURY
Standard Comics
December, 1952
5 Teen Stories 150.00
6 . . . . 75.00
7 April, 1953 . . . . 75.00

JIGGS AND MAGGIE
Best Books (Standard)/
Harvey Publ.
June, 1949
11 . . . . 60.00
12 thru 21 . . . . @30.00
22 thru 26 . . . . @22.00
27 February-March, 1954 . . . . . 22.00

JIM HARDY
Spotlight Publ.
1944
N# Dynamite Jim,Mirror Man . 275.00

JIM RAY'S AVIATION
SKETCH BOOK
Vital Publishers
February, 1946
1 Radar, the Invisible eye . . . 175.00
2 Gen.Hap Arnold, May, 1946 150.00

JINGLE JANGLE
COMICS
Eastern Color Printing Co.
February, 1942
1 B:Benny Bear,Pie Face Prince,
  Jingle Jangle Tales,Hortense 300.00
2 GCn 150.00
3 GCn 125.00
4 GCn,Pie Face cover 125.00
5 GCn,B:Pie Face 125.00
6 GCn, ... 100.00
7 . . . . 100.00
8 . . . . 100.00
9 . . . . 100.00
10 . . . . 100.00
11 thru 15 E:Pie Face . . . . . . @75.00
16 thru 20 . . . . @60.00
21 thru 25 . . . . @50.00

26 thru 30 . . . . @40.00
31 thru 41 . . . . @35.00
42 December, 1949 . . . . 40.00

JING PALS
Victory Publ. Corp.
February, 1946
1 Johnny Rabbit 60.00
2 . . . . 30.00
3 . . . . 30.00
4 August, 1948 . . . . 30.00

JOE COLLEGE
Hillman Periodicals
Fall, 1949
1 BP,DPr 45.00
2 BP, Winter, 1949 . . . . 40.00

JOE LOUIS
Fawcett Periodicals
September, 1950
1 Ph(c),Life Story 450.00
2 Ph(c),November, 1950 . . . . 300.00

JOE PALOOKA
Publication Enterprises
(Columbia Comics Group)
1943
1 Lost in the Desert 600.00
2 Hitler cover 400.00
3 KO's the Nazis! 250.00
4 Eiffel tower cover, 1944 . . . 225.00

Joe Palooka #38 © Harvey Comics

JOE PALOOKA
Harvey Publications
Nov., 1954–March 1961
1 Joe Tells How he became
  World Champ 350.00
2 Skiing cover 175.00
3 . . . . 100.00
4 Welcome Home Pals! 100.00
5 S&K,The Great Carnival
  Murder Mystery 150.00
6 Classic Joe Palooka (c) 90.00
7 BP,V:Grumpopski 90.00
8 BP,Mystery of the Ghost Ship 75.00
9 Drooten Island Mystery 75.00

10 BP 60.00
11 . . . . 50.00
12 BP,Boxing Course 50.00
13 . . . . 45.00
14 BP,Palooka's Toughest Fight 45.00
15 BP,O:Humphrey 100.00
16 BP,A:Humphrey 45.00
17 BP,A:Humphrey 45.00
18 . . . . 45.00
19 BP,Freedom Train(c) 50.00
20 Punch Out(c) 45.00
21 . . . . 40.00
22 V:Assassin 40.00
23 Big Bathing Beauty Issue . . . 40.00
24 . . . . 40.00
25 . . . . 40.00
26 BP,Big Prize Fight Robberies 40.00
27 BP,Mystery of Bal
  Eagle Cabin 40.00
28 BP,Fights out West 40.00
29 BP,Joe Busts Crime
  Wide Open 40.00
30 BP,V:Hoodlums 35.00
31 BP 35.00
32 BP,Fight Palooka was sure
  to Lose 35.00
33 BP,Joe finds Ann 35.00
34 BP,How to Box like a Champ 35.00
35 BP,More Adventures of Little
  Max 35.00
36 BP 35.00
37 BP,Joe as a Boy 35.00
38 BP 35.00
39 BP,Original Hillbillies with
  Big Leviticus 35.00
40 BP,Joe's Toughest Fight . . . 35.00
41 BP,Humphrey's Grudge Fight 35.00
42 BP 35.00
43 BP 35.00
44 BP,M:Ann Howe 40.00
45 BP 30.00
46 Champ of Champs 30.00
47 BreathtakingUnderwaterBattle 30.00
48 BP,Exciting Indian Adventure 30.00
49 BP 30.00
50 BP,Bondage(c) 30.00
51 BP 30.00
52 BP,V:Balonki 30.00
53 BP 30.00
54 V:Bad Man Trigger McGehee 30.00
55 . . . . 30.00
56 Foul Play on the High Seas . 30.00
57 Curtains for the Champ 30.00
58 V:The Man-Eating Swamp
  Terror 30.00
59 The Enemy Attacks 30.00
60 Joe Fights Escaped Convict . 30.00
61 . . . . 25.00
62 S&K 45.00
63 . . . . 25.00
64 . . . . 25.00
65 . . . . 25.00
66 . . . . 25.00
67 . . . . 25.00
68 . . . . 25.00
69 A Package from Home 25.00
70 BP 25.00
71 . . . . 25.00
72 . . . . 25.00
73 BP 25.00
74 thru 118 . . . . @25.00
Giant 1 Body Building 45.00
Giant 2 Fights His Way Back . . 125.00
Giant 3 Visits Lost City 60.00
Giant 4 All in Family 65.00

GOLDEN AGE

JOE YANK
Visual Editions
(Standard Comics)
March, 1952

5 ATh,WE,Korean Jackpot!	60.00
6 Bacon and Bullets, G.I.Renegade	40.00
7 Two-Man War,A:Sgt. Glamour	18.00
8 ATh(c),Miss Foxhole of 1952,	30.00
9 G.I.'s and Dolls,Colonel Blood	15.00
10 A Good Way to Die, A:General Joe	15.00
11	15.00
12 RA	15.00
13	15.00
14	15.00
15	15.00
16 July, 1954	15.00

JOHN HIX SCRAPBOOK
Eastern Color Printing Co.
1937

1 Strange as It Seems	250.00
2 Strange as It Seems	200.00

JOHNNY DANGER
Toby Press
August, 1954

1 Ph(c),Private Detective	100.00

JOHNNY DYNAMITE
(see DYNAMITE)

JOHNNY HAZARD
Best Books
(Standard Comics)
August, 1948

5 FR	100.00
6 FR,FR(c)	75.00
7 FR(c)	60.00
8 FR,FR(c), May, 1949	50.00

JOHNNY LAW, SKY RANGER
Good Comics (Lev Gleason)
April, 1955

1	35.00
2	20.00
3	20.00
4 November, 1955	20.00

JOHN WAYNE ADVENTURE COMICS
Toby Press
Winter, 1949

1 Ph(c),The Mysterious Valley of Violence	1,100.00
2 AW,FF,Ph(c)	500.00
3 AW,FF,Flying Sheriff	500.00
4 AW,FF,Double-Danger,Ph(c)	500.00
5 Volcano of Death,Ph(c)	450.00
6 AW,FF,Caravan of Doom, Ph(c)	450.00
7 AW,FF,Ph(c)	400.00
8 AW,FF,Duel of Death,Ph(c)	425.00
9 Ghost Guns,Ph(c)	300.00
10 Dangerous Journey,Ph(c)	250.00
11 Manhunt!,Ph(c)	250.00
12 HK,Joins the Marines,Ph(c)	275.00
13 V:Frank Stacy	225.00

14 Operation Peeping John	225.00
15 Bridge Head	250.00
16 AW,FF,Golden Double-Cross	250.00
17 Murderer's Music	250.00
18 AW,FF,Larson's Folly	275.00
19	200.00
20 Whale Cover	200.00
21	200.00
22 Flash Flood!	200.00
23 Death on Two Wheels	200.00
24 Desert	200.00
25 AW,FF,Hondo!,Ph(c)	275.00
26 Ph(c)	225.00
27 Ph(c)	225.00
28 Dead Man's Boots!	225.00
29 AW,FF,Ph(c),Crash in California Desert	275.00
30 The Wild One, Ph(c)	225.00
31 AW,FF,May, 1955	250.00

Jo-Jo #5 © Fox Feature Syndicate

JO-JO COMICS
Fox Features Syndicate
Spring, 1946

N# (fa)	50.00
2 (fa)	25.00
3 (fa)	25.00
4 (fa)	25.00
5 (fa)	25.00
6 (fa)	25.00
7 B:Jo-Jo Congo King	600.00
8 (7)B:Tanee,V:The Giant Queen	450.00
9 (8)The Mountain of Skulls	400.00
10 (9)Death of the Fanged Lady	375.00
11 (10)	375.00
12 (11)Bondage(c), Water Warriors	325.00
13 (12) Jade Juggernaut	300.00
14 The Leopards of Learda	300.00
15 The Flaming Fiend	300.00
16 Golden Gorilla,bondage(c)	300.00
17 Stark-Mad Thespian, bondage(c)	325.00
18 The Death Traveler	300.00
19 Gladiator of Gore	300.00
20	300.00
21	300.00
22	300.00
23	300.00

24	300.00
25 Bondage(c)	325.00
26	300.00
27	300.00
28	300.00
29 July, 1949	325.00

JOURNEY INTO FEAR
Superior Publications
May, 1951

1 MB,Preview of Chaos	400.00
2 Debt to the Devil	250.00
3 Midnight Prowler	225.00
4 Invisible Terror	200.00
5 Devil Cat	150.00
6 Partners in Blood	150.00
7 The Werewolf Lurks	150.00
8 Bells of the Damned	150.00
9 Masked Death	150.00
10 Gallery of the Dead	150.00
11 Beast of Bedlam	125.00
12 No Rest for the Dead	125.00
13 Cult of the Dead	125.00
14 Jury of the Undead	125.00
15 Corpse in Make-up	135.00
16 Death by Invitation	125.00
17 Deadline for Death	125.00
18 Here's to Horror	125.00
19 This Body is Mine!	125.00
20 Masters of the Dead	125.00
21 Horror in the Clock, September, 1954	125.00

JUDO JOE
Jay-Jay Corp.
August, 1952

1 Drug	35.00
2	25.00
3 Drug, December, 1953	25.00

JUDY CANOVA
Fox Features Syndicate
May, 1950

23 (1)WW,WW(c)	125.00
24 (2)WW,WW(c)	120.00
3 JO,WW,WW(c) September, 1950	135.00

JUKE BOX
Famous Funnies
March, 1948

1 ATh(c),Spike Jones	300.00
2 Dinah Shore,Transvestitism	200.00
3 Vic Damone	150.00
4 Jimmy Durante	150.00
5	125.00
6 January, 1949,Desi Arnaz	175.00

JUMBO COMICS
Real Adventure Publ. Co.
(Fiction House)
September, 1938

1 LF,BKa,JK,WE,WE(c),B:Sheena Queen of the Jungle,The Hawk The Hunchback	17,000.00
2 LF,JK,WE,BKa,BP, O:Sheena	5,500.00
3 JK,WE,WE(c),BP,LF,BKa	4,000.00
4 WE,WE(c),MMe,LF,BKa, O:The Hawk	3,500.00
5 WE,WE(c),BP,BKa	3,000.00
6 WE,WE(c),BP,BKa	2,700.00
7 WE,BKa,BP	2,600.00

GOLDEN AGE

GOLDEN AGE

8 LF(c),BP,BKa,World of
　Tommorow 2,600.00
9 LF(c),BP 2,400.00
10 WE,LF(c),BKa,Regular size
　issues begin 1,300.00
11 LF(c),WE&BP,War of the
　Emerald Gas 1,000.00
12 WE(c),WE&BP,Hawk in Buccaneer
　Vengeance,Bondage(c) . . . 1,100.00
13 WE(c),BP,Sheena in The
　Thundering Herds 1,000.00
14 WE(c),LF,BP,Hawk in Siege
　of Thunder Isle,B:Lightning 1,200.00
15 BP(c),BP,Sheena(c) 650.00
16 BP(c),BP,The Lightning
　Strikes Twice 750.00
17 BP(c), all Sheena covers
　and lead stories 650.00
18 BP 600.00
19 BP(c),BP,Warriors of
　the Bush 600.00
20 BP,BKa,Spoilers of
　the Wild 600.00
21 BP,BKa,Prey of the
　Giant Killers 500.00
22 BP,BKa,Victims of the
　Super-Ape,O:Hawk 550.00
23 BP,BKa,Swamp of the
　Green Terror 550.00
24 BP,BKa,Curse of the Black
　Venom 550.00
25 BP,BKa,Bait for the Beast . . 500.00
26 BP,BKa,Tiger-Man Terror . . 500.00
27 BP,BKa,Sabre-Tooth Terror 500.00
28 BKa,RWd,The Devil of
　the Congo 500.00
29 BKa,RWd,Elephant-Scourge 500.00
30 BKa,RWd,Slashing Fangs . 500.00
31 BKa,RWd,Voodoo Treasure
　of Black Slave Lake 450.00
32 BKa,RWd,AB,Captives of
　the Gorilla-Men 450.00
33 BKa,RWd,AB,Stampede
　Tusks 450.00
34 BKa,RWd,AB,Claws of the
　Devil-Cat 450.00
35 BKa,RWd,AB,Hostage of the
　Devil Apes 450.00
36 BKa,RWd,AB,Voodoo Flames 450.00
37 BKa,RWd,AB,Congo Terror . 450.00
38 BKa,RWd,ABDeath-Trap of
　the River Demons 450.00
39 BKa,RWd,AB,Cannibal Bait . 450.00
40 BKa,RWd,AB,
　Assagai Poison 450.00
41 BKa,RWd,AB,Killer's Kraal,
　Bondage(c) 350.00
42 BKa,RWd,AB,Plague of
　Spotted Killers 350.00
43 BKa,RWd,AB,Beasts of the
　Devil Queen 350.00
44 BKa,RWd,AB,Blood-Cult of
　K'Douma 350.00
45 BKa,RWd,AB,Fanged
　Keeper of the Fire-Gem . . . 350.00
46 BKa,RWd,AB,Lair of the
　Armored Monsters 350.00
47 BKa,RWd,AB,The Bantu
　Blood-Monster 350.00
48 BKa,RWd,AB,Red Meat for
　the Cat-Pack 350.00
49 BKa,RWd,AB,Empire of the
　Hairy Ones 350.00
50 BKa,RWd,AB,Eyrie of the
　Leopard Birds 350.00

51 BKa,RWd.AB,Monsters with
　Wings 275.00
52 BKa,RWd,AB,Man-Eaters
　Paradise 275.00
53 RWd,AB,Slaves of the
　Blood Moon 275.00
54 RWd,AB,Congo Kill 275.00
55 RWd,AB,Bait for the Silver
　King Cat 275.00
56 RWd,AB,Sabre Monsters of
　the Aba-Zanzi,Bondage(c) . . 275.00
57 RWd,AB,Arena of Beasts . . 275.00
58 RWd,AB,Sky-Atlas of the
　Thunder-Birds 275.00
59 RWd,AB,Kraal of Shrunken
　Heads 275.00
60 RWd,AB,Land of the
　Stalking Death 200.00
61 RWd,AB,King-Beast of
　the Masai 200.00
62 RWd,AB,Valley of Golden
　Death 200.00
63 RWd,AB,The Dwarf Makers 200.00

Jumbo Comics #27
© Real Adventure Publ./Fiction House

64 RWd,The Slave-Brand of Ibn
　Ben Satan,Male Bondage . . 200.00
65 RWd,The Man-Eaters of
　Linpopo 200.00
66 RWd,Valley of Monsters . . . 200.00
67 RWd,Land of Feathered Evil 200.00
68 RWd,Spear of Blood Ju-Ju . 200.00
69 RWd,AB,MB,Slaves for the
　White Sheik 200.00
70 RWd,AB,MB,The Rogue
　Beast's Prey 200.00
71 RWd,AB,MB,The Serpent-
　God Speaks 175.00
72 RWd,AB,MB,Curse of the
　Half-Dead 175.00
73 RWd,AB,MB,War Apes of
　the T'Kanis 175.00
74 RWd,AB,MB,Drums of the
　Voodoo God 175.00
75 RWd,AB,MB,Terror Trail of
　the Devil's Horn 175.00
76 RWd,AB,MB,Fire Gems of
　Skull Valley 175.00
77 RWd,AB,MB,Blood Dragons
　from Fire Valley 175.00

78 RWd,AB,MB,Veldt of the
　Vampire Apes 175.00
79 RWd,AB,MB,Dancing
　Skeletons 175.00
80 RWd,AB,MB,Banshee Cats 175.00
81 RWd,AB,MB,JKa,Heads for
　King' Hondo's Harem 160.00
82 RWd,MB,AB,JKa,Ghost Riders
　of the Golden Tuskers . . . 160.00
83 RWd,MB,AB,JKa,Charge of
　the Condo Juggernauts 160.00
84 RWd,MB,AB,JKa,Valley of
　the Whispering Fangs 160.00
85 RWd,MB,AB,JKa,Red Tusks
　of Zulu-Za'an 160.00
86 RWd,MB,AB,JKa,Witch-Maiden
　of the Burning Blade 160.00
87 RWd,AB,MB,JKa,Sargasso of
　Lost Safaris 160.00
88 RWd,AB,MB,JKa,Kill-Quest
　of the Ju-Ju Tusks 160.00
89 RWd,AB,MB,JKa,Ghost Slaves
　of Bwana Rojo 160.00
90 RWd,AB,MB,JKa,Death Kraal
　of the Mastadons 160.00
91 RWd,AB,MB,JKa,Spoor of
　the Sabre-Horn Tiger 150.00
92 RWd,MB,JKa,Pied Piper
　of the Congo 150.00
93 RWd,MB,JKa,The Beasts
　that Dawn Begot 150.00
94 RWd,MB,JKa,Wheel of a
　Thousand Deaths 150.00
95 RWd,MB,JKa,Flame Dance
　of the Ju-Ju Witch 150.00
96 RWd,MB,JKa,Ghost Safari . 150.00
97 RWd,MB,JKa,Banshee Wail
　of the Undead,Bondage(c) . 150.00
98 RWd,MB,JKa,Seekers of
　the Terror Fangs 150.00
99 RWd,MB,JKa,Shrine of
　the Seven Souls 150.00
100 RWd,MB,Slave Brand
　of Hassan Bey 175.00
101 RWd,MB,Quest of the
　Two-Face Ju Ju 135.00
102 RWd,MB,Viper Gods of
　Vengeance Veldt 135.00
103 RWd,MB,Blood for the
　Idol of Blades 135.00
104 RWd,MB,Valley of Eternal
　Sleep 135.00
105 RWd,MB,Man Cubs from
　Momba-Zu 200.00
106 RWd,MB,The River of
　No-Return 200.00
107 RWd,MB,Vandals of
　the Veldt 135.00
108 RWd,MB,The Orphan of
　Vengeance Vale 135.00
109 RWd,MB,The Pygmy's Hiss
　is Poison 135.00
110 RWd,MB,Death Guards the
　Congo Keep 135.00
111 RWd,MB,Beware of the
　Witch-Man's Brew 135.00
112 RWd,MB,The Blood-Mask
　from G'Shinis Grave 125.00
113 RWd,MB,The Mask's of
　Zombi-Zan 125.00
114 RWd,MB 125.00
115 RWd,MB,Svengali of
　the Apes 125.00
116 RWd,MB,The Vessel of
　Marbel Monsters 125.00

117 RWd,MB,Lair of the Half-
Man King 125.00
118 RWd,MB,Quest of the
Congo Dwarflings 125.00
119 RWd,MB,King Crocodile's
Domain 125.00
120 RWd,MB,The Beast-Pack
Howls the Moon 125.00
121 RWd,MB,The Kraal of
Evil Ivory 125.00
122 RWd,MB,Castaways of
the Congo 125.00
123 RWd,MB, ... 125.00
124 RWd,MB,The Voodoo Beasts
of Changra-Lo 125.00
125 RWd,MB,JKa(c),The Beast-
Pack Strikes at Dawn 125.00
126 RWd,MB,JKa(c),Lair of the
Swamp Beast 125.00
127 RWd,MB,JKa(c),The Phantom
of Lost Lagoon 125.00
128 RWd,MB,JKa(c),Mad Mistress
of the Congo-Tuskers 125.00
129 RWd,MB,JKa(c),Slaves of
King Simbas Kraal 125.00
130 RWd,MB,JKa(c),Quest of
the Pharaoh's Idol 125.00
131 RWd,JKa(c),Congo Giants
at Bay 125.00
132 RWd,JKa(c),The Doom of
the Devil's Gorge 125.00
133 RWd,JKa(c),Blaze the
Pitfall Trail 125.00
134 RWd,JKa(c),Catacombs of
the Jackal-Men 125.00
135 RWd,JKa(c),The 40 Thieves
of Ankar-Lo 125.00
136 RWd,JKa(c),The Perils of
Paradise Lost 125.00
137 RWd,JKa(c),The Kraal of
Missing Men 125.00
138 RWd,JKa(c),The Panthers
of Kajo-Kazar 125.00
139 RWd,JKa(c),Stampede of
the Congo Lancers 125.00
140 RWd,JKa(c),The Moon
Beasts from Vulture Valley . 125.00
141 RWd,JKa(c),B:Long Bow . . 135.00
142 RWd,JKa(c),Man-Eaters
of N'Gamba 135.00
143 RWd,JKa(c),The Curse of
the Cannibal Drum 135.00
144 RWd,JKa(c),The Secrets of
Killers Cave 135.00
145 RWd,JKa(c),Killers of
the Crypt 135.00
146 RWd,JKa(c),Sinbad of the
Lost Lagoon 135.00
147 RWd,JKa(c),The Wizard of
Gorilla Glade 135.00
148 RWd,JKa(c),Derelict of
the Slave King 135.00
149 RWd,JKa(c),Lash Lord of
the Elephants 135.00
150 RWd,JKa(c),Queen of
the Pharaoh's Idol 125.00
151 RWd,The Voodoo Claws
of Doomsday Trek 125.00
152 RWd,Red Blades of Africa 125.00
153 RWd,Lost Legions of the Nile 125.00
154 RWd,The Track of the
Black Devil 125.00
155 RWd,The Ghosts of
Blow- Gun Trail 125.00
156 RWd,The Slave-Runners

of Bambaru 125.00
157 RWd,Cave of the
Golden Skull 125.00
158 RWd,Gun Trek to
Panther Valley 125.00
159 RWd,A:Space Scout 110.00
160 RWd,Savage Cargo,
E:Sheena covers 110.00
161 RWd,Dawns of the Pit . . . 110.00
162 RWd,Hangman's Haunt . . 110.00
163 RWd,Cagliostro Cursed
Thee 110.00
164 RWd,Death Bars the Door 110.00
165 RWd,Day off from a Corpse 110.00
166 RWd,The Gallows Bird . . . 110.00
167 RWd,Cult of the Clawmen,
March, 1953 . . . . 110.00

Jungle Comics #30
© Glen Kel. Publ./Fiction House

JUNGLE COMICS
Glen Kel Publ./Fiction House
January, 1940

1 HcK,DBr,LF(c),O:The White
Panther,Kaanga,Tabu, B:The
Jungle Boy,Camilla, all
Kaanga covers & stories . . 3,500.00
2 HcK,DBr,WE(c),B:Fantomah 1,200.00
3 HcK,DBr,GT,The Crocodiles
of Death River 1,000.00
4 HcK,DBr,Wambi in
Thundering Herds 950.00
5 WE(c),GT,HcK,DBr,Empire
of the Ape Men 1,100.00
6 WE(c),GT,DBr,HcK,Tigress
of the Deep Jungle Swamp . 600.00
7 BP(c),DBr,GT,HcK,Live
Sacrifice,Bondage(c) 550.00
8 BP(c),GT,HcK,Safari into
Shadowland 550.00
9 GT,HcK,Captive of the
Voodoo Master 550.00
10 GT,HcK,BP,Lair of the
Renegade Killer 550.00
11 GT,HcK,V:Beasts of Africa's Ancient
Primieval Swamp Land 400.00
12 GT,HcK,The Devil's
Death-Trap 400.00
13 GT(c),GT,HcK,Stalker of

the Beasts 425.00
14 HcK,Vengeance of the
Gorilla Hordes 400.00
15 HcK,Terror of the Voodoo
Cauldron 400.00
16 HcK,Caveman Killers 400.00
17 HcK,Valley of the Killer-Birds 400.00
18 HcK,Trap of the Tawny
Killer, Bondage(c) 425.00
19 HcK,Revolt of the Man-Apes 400.00
20 HcK,One-offering to
Ju-Ju Demon 400.00
21 HcK,Monster of the Dismal
Swamp, Bondage(c) 375.00
22 HcK,Lair o/t Winged Fiend . 350.00
23 HcK,Man-Eater Jaws 350.00
24 HcK,Battle of the Beasts . . . 350.00
25 HcK,Kaghis the Blood God,
Bondage(c) 375.00
26 HcK,Gorillas of the
Witch-Queen 350.00
27 HcK,Spore o/t Gold-Raiders 350.00
28 HcK,Vengeance of the Flame
God, Bondage(c) 375.00
29 HcK,Juggernaut of Doom . . 350.00
30 HcK,Claws o/t Black Terror 350.00
31 HcK,Land of Shrunken Skulls 300.00
32 HcK,Curse of the King-Beast 300.00
33 HcK,Scaly Guardians of
Massacre Pool,Bondage(c) . 300.00
34 HcK,Bait of the Spotted
Fury,Bondage(c) 300.00
35 HcK,Stampede of the
Slave-Masters 300.00
36 HcK,GT,The Flame-Death of
Ju Ju Mountain 300.00
37 HcK,GT,Scaly Sentinel of
Taboo Swamp 300.00
38 HcK,GT,Duel of the Congo
Destroyers 300.00
39 HcK,Land of Laughing Bones 300.00
40 HcK,Killer Plague 300.00
41 Hck,The King Ape
Feeds at Dawn 225.00
42 Hck,RC,Master of the
Moon-Beasts 235.00
43 HcK,The White Shiek 225.00
44 HcK,Monster of the
Boiling Pool 225.00
45 HcK,The Bone-Grinders of
B'Zambi, Bondage(c) 235.00
46 HcK,Blood Raiders of
Tree Trail 200.00
47 HcK,GT,Monsters of the Man
Pool, Bondage(c) 225.00
48 HcK,GT,Strangest Congo
Adventure 200.00
49 HcK,GT,Lair of the King
-Serpent 200.00
50 HcK,GT,Juggernaut of
the Bush 200.00
51 HcK,GT,The Golden Lion of
Genghis Kahn 200.00
52 HcK,Feast for the River
Devils, Bondage(c) 225.00
53 HcK,GT,Slaves for Horrors
Harem 225.00
54 HcK,GT,Blood Bride of
the Crocodile 200.00
55 HcK,GT,The Tree Devil . . . 200.00
56 HcK,Bride for the
Rainmaker Raj 200.00
57 HcK,Fire Gems of T'ulaki . . 200.00
58 HcK,Land of the
Cannibal God 200.00

All comics prices listed are for *Near Mint* condition.

GOLDEN AGE

GOLDEN AGE

59 HcK,Dwellers of the Mist
Bondage(c) 225.00
60 HcK,Bush Devil's Spoor . . . 200.00
61 HcK,Curse of the Blood
Madness 200.00
62 Bondage(c) 210.00
63 HcK,Fire-Birds for the
Cliff Dwellers 175.00
64 Valley of the Ju-Ju Idols . . 175.00
65 Shrine of the Seven Ju Jus,
Bondage(c) 185.00
66 Spoor of the Purple Skulls . 175.00
67 Devil Beasts of the Golden
Temple 175.00
68 Satan's Safari 175.00
69 Brides for the Serpent King . 175.00
70 Brides for the King Beast,
Bondage(c) 185.00
71 Congo Prey,Bondage(c) . . . 185.00
72 Blood-Brand o/t Veldt Cats . 150.00
73 The Killer of M'omba Raj,
Bondage(c) 175.00
74 AgF,GoldenJaws,Bondage(c) 175.00
75 AgF,Congo Kill 150.00
76 AgF,Blood Thrist of the
Golden Tusk 150.00
77 AgF,The Golden Gourds
Shriek Blood,Bondage(c) . . 175.00
78 AgF,Bondage(c) 175.00
79 AgF,Death has a
Thousand Fangs 150.00
80 AgF,Salome of the
Devil-Cats Bondage(c) 175.00
81 AgF,Colossus of the Congo 150.00
82 AgF,Blood Jewels of the
Fire-Bird 150.00
83 AgF,Vampire Veldt,
Bondage(c) 175.00
84 AgF,Blood Spoor of the
Faceless Monster 150.00
85 AgF,Brides for the Man-Apes
Bondage(c) 175.00
86 AgF,Firegems of L'hama
Lost, Bondage(c) 175.00
87 AgF,Horror Kraal of the
Legless One,Bondage(c) . . . 150.00
88 AgF,Beyond the Ju-Ju Mists 165.00
89 AgF,Blood-Moon over the
Whispering Veldt 150.00
90 AgF,The Skulls for the
Altar of Doom,Bondage(c) . 165.00
91 AgF,Monsters from the Mist
Lands, Bondage(c) 165.00
92 AgF,Vendetta of the
Tree Tribes 150.00
93 AgF,Witch Queen of the
Hairy Ones 150.00
94 AgF,Terror Raid of
the Congo Caesar 150.00
95 Agf,Flame-Tongues of the
Sky Gods 150.00
96 Agf,Phantom Guardians of the
Enchanted Lake,Bondage(c) 135.00
97 AgF,Wizard of the Whirling
Doom,Bondage(c) 165.00
98 AgF,Ten Tusks of Zulu Ivory 175.00
99 AgF,Cannibal Caravan,
Bondage(c) 150.00
100 AgF,Hate has a
Thousand Claws 150.00
101 AgF,The Blade of
Buddha, Bondage(c) 150.00
102 AgF,Queen of the
Amazon Lancers 135.00
103 AgF,The Phantoms of

Lost Lagoon 135.00
104 AgF 135.00
105 AgF,The Red Witch
of Ubangi-Shan 135.00
106 AgF,Bondage(c) 150.00
107 Banshee Valley 150.00
108 HcK,Merchants of Murder . 150.00
109 HcK,Caravan of the
Golden Bones 135.00
110 HcK,Raid of the Fire-Fangs 135.00
111 HcK,The Trek of the
Terror-Paws 135.00
112 HcK,Morass of the
Mammoths 135.00
113 HcK,Two-Tusked Terror . . 135.00
114 HcK,Mad Jackals Hunt
by Night 135.00
115 HcK,Treasure Trove in
Vulture Sky 135.00
116 HcK,The Banshees of
Voodoo Veldt 135.00
117 HcK,The Fangs of the
Hooded Scorpion 135.00

Jungle Comics #34
© Glen Kel. Publ./Fiction House

118 HcK,The Muffled Drums
of Doom 135.00
119 HcK,Fury of the Golden
Doom 135.00
120 HcK,Killer King Domain . . 135.00
121 HcK,Wolves of the
Desert Night 135.00
122 HcK,The Veldt of
Phantom Fangs 135.00
123 HcK,The Ark of the
Mist-Maids 135.00
124 HcK,The Trail of the
Pharaoh's Eye 135.00
125 HcK,Skulls for Sale on
Dismal River 135.00
126 HcK,Safari Sinister 150.00
127 Hck,Bondage(c) 125.00
128 HcK,Dawn-Men of the Congo125.00
129 Hck,The Captives of
Crocodile Swamp 125.00
130 Hck,Phantoms of the Congo 125.00
131 HcK,Treasure-Tomb of the
Ape-King 125.00
132 HcK,Bondage(c) 150.00
133 HcK,Scourge of the Sudan

Bondage(c) 150.00
134 HcK,The Black Avengers of
Kaffir Pass 125.00
135 Hck 125.00
136 HcK,The Death Kraals
of Kongola 125.00
137 BWg(c),HcK,The Safari of
Golden Ghosts 125.00
138 BWg(c),HcK,Track of the
Black Terror Bondage(c) . . . 125.00
139 BWg(c),HcK,Captain Kidd
of the Congo 125.00
140 BWg(c),HcK,The Monsters
of Kilmanjaro 125.00
141 BWg(c)HcK,The Death Hunt
of the Man Cubs 125.00
142 BWg(c),HcK,Sheba of the
Terror Claws,Bondage(c) . . 150.00
143 BWg(c)Hck,The Moon of
Devil Drums 150.00
144 BWg(c)Hck,Quest of the
Dragon's Claw 150.00
145 BWg(c)Hck,Spawn of the
Devil's Moon 150.00
146 BWg(c),HcK,Orphans of
the Congo 150.00
147 BWG(c),HcK,The Treasure
of Tembo Wanculu 150.00
148 BWg(c),HcK,Caged Beasts
of Plunder-Men,Bondage(c) . 150.00
149 BWg(c),HcK 125.00
150 BWg(c),HcK,Rhino Rampage,
Bondage(c) 150.00
151 BWg(c),HcK 125.00
152 BWg(c),HcK,The Rogue of
Kopje Kull 125.00
153 BWg(c),Hck,The Wild Men
of N'Gara 125.00
154 BWg(c),HcK,The Fire Wizard125.00
155 BWg(c),HcK,Swamp of
the Shrieking Dead 125.00
156 BWg(c),HcK 125.00
157 BWg(c),HcK 125.00
158 BWg(c),HcK,A:Sheena . . . 125.00
159 BWg(c),HcK,The Blow-Gun
Kill 125.00
160 BWg,HcK,King Fang 125.00
161 BWg(c),HcK,The Barbarizi
Man-Eaters 125.00
162 BWg(c) 125.00
163 BWg(c),Jackals at the
Kill, Summer,1954 . . . . . . 125.00

JUNGLE JIM
Best Books
(Standard Comics)
January, 1949

11 . . . . 40.00
12 Mystery Island 25.00
13 Flowers of Peril 25.00
14 . . . . 25.00
15 . . . . 25.00
16 . . . . 25.00
17 . . . . 25.00
18 . . . . 25.00
19 . . . . 25.00
20 1951 . . . . 25.00

JUNGLE JIM
Dell Publishing Co.
August, 1953

(1) *see Dell Four Color #490*
(1) *see Dell Four Color #565*
3 P(c) all 30.00

4	25.00
5	25.00
6	20.00
7	20.00
8	20.00
9	20.00
10	20.00
11	20.00
12	20.00
13 'Mystery Island'	20.00
14 'Flowers of Peril'	20.00
15 thru 20	@20.00

JUNGLE JO
Hero Books
(Fox Features Syndicate)
March, 1950

N#	225.00
1 Mystery of Doc Jungle	275.00
2	200.00
3 The Secret of Youth, September, 1950	175.00

JUNGLE LIL
Hero Books
(Fox Features Syndicate)
April, 1950

1 Betrayer of the Kombe Dead	200.00

Becomes:
DOROTHY LAMOUR

2 WW,Ph(c)The Lost Safari	175.00
3 WW,Ph(c), August, 1950	125.00

JUNGLE THRILLS
(see TERRORS OF THE JUNGLE)

JUNIE PROM
Dearfield Publishing Co.
Winter, 1947

1 Teenage Stories	50.00
2	25.00
3	20.00
4	20.00
5	20.00
6 June, 1949	20.00

Junior Comics #15
© Fox Feature Syndicate

JUNIOR COMICS
Fox Features Syndicate
September, 1947

9 AF,AF(c) ,Teenage Stories	500.00
10 AF,AF(c)	450.00
11 AF,AF(c)	450.00
12 AF,AF(c)	450.00
13 AF,AF(c)	450.00
14 AF,AF(c)	450.00
15 AF,AF(c)	450.00
16 AF,AF(c),July,1948	450.00

JUNIOR HOOP COMICS
Stanmor Publications
January, 1952

1	40.00
2	20.00
3 July, 1952	20.00

JUSTICE TRAPS THE GUILTY
Headline Publications
(Prize)
October-November, 1947

2-1 S&K,S&K(c),Electric chair cover	375.00
2 S&K,S&K(c)	225.00
3 S&K,S&K(c)	200.00
4 S&K,S&K(c),True Confession of a Girl Gangleader	200.00
5 S&K,S&K(c)	200.00
6 S&K,S&K(c)	200.00
7 S&K,S&K(c)	200.00
8 S&K,S&K(c)	200.00
9 S&K,S&K(c)	200.00
10 S&K,S&K(c)	200.00
11 S&K,S&K(c)	75.00
12	35.00
13	50.00
14	35.00
15	35.00
16	35.00
17	50.00
18 S&K,S&K(c)	50.00
19 S&K,S&K(c)	50.00
20	30.00
21 S&K	40.00
22 S&K(c)	30.00
23 S&K(c)	30.00
24	20.00
25	25.00
26	20.00
27 S&K(c)	30.00
28	20.00
29	20.00
30 S&K	40.00
31 thru 50	@20.00
51	15.00
52	15.00
53	15.00
54	15.00
55	15.00
56	15.00
57	15.00
58 Drug	150.00
59 thru 92	@15.00

Becomes:
FARGO KID
Headline Publications
(Prize)

93 AW,JSe,O:Kid Fargo	120.00
94 JSe	75.00
95 June-July, 1958,JSe	75.00

KA'A'NGA COMICS
Glen-Kel Publ.
(Fiction House)
Spring, 1949

1 Phantoms of the Congo	400.00
2 V:The Jungle Octopus	175.00
3	150.00
4 The Wizard Apes of Inkosi-Khan	135.00
5	100.00
6 Captive of the Devil Apes	75.00
7 GT,Beast-Men of Mombassa	85.00
8 The Congo Kill-Cry	75.00
9	75.00
10 Stampede for Congo Gold	75.00
11 Claws of the Roaring Congo	60.00
12 Bondage(c)	75.00
13 Death Web of the Amazons	60.00
14 Slave Galley of the Lost Nile Bondage(c)	75.00
15 Crocodile Moon,Bondage(c)	75.00
16 Valley of Devil-Dwarfs	70.00
17 Tembu of the Elephants	50.00
18 The Red Claw of Vengeance	50.00
19 The Devil-Devil Trail	50.00
20 The Cult of the Killer Claws, Summer, 1954	50.00

KASCO COMICS
Kasco Grainfeed
(Giveaway)
1945

1 BWo	85.00
2 1949,BWo	75.00

KATHY
Standard Comics
September, 1949

1 Teen-Age Stories	40.00
2 ASh	22.00
3 thru 6	@15.00
7 thru 17	@12.00

KATY KEENE
Archie Publications/Close-Up
Radio Comics
1949

1 BWo	750.00
2 BWo	400.00
3 BWo	300.00
4 BWo	300.00
5 BWo	275.00
6 BWo	250.00
7 BWo	250.00
8 thru 12 BWo	@225.00
13 thru 20 BWo	@200.00
21 thru 29 BWo	@150.00
30 thru 38 BWo	@125.00
39 thru 62 BWo	@100.00
Ann.#1	375.00
Ann.#2 thru #6	225.00

KEEN DETECTIVE FUNNIES
Centaur Publications
July, 1938

1-8 B:The Clock,	1,500.00
1-9 WE	600.00
1-10	550.00
1-11 Dean Denton	550.00
2-1 The Eye Sees	500.00
2-2 JCo	500.00

GOLDEN AGE

2-3 TNT	500.00
2-4 Gabby Flynn	500.00
5	525.00
6	500.00
7 Masked Marvel	1,100.00
8 PGn,Gabby Flynn,Nudity Expanded 16 pages	550.00
9 Dean Denton	525.00
10	525.00
11 BEv,Sidekick	500.00
12 Masked Marvel(c)	650.00
3-1 Masked Marvel(c)	500.00
3-2 Masked Marvel(c)	500.00
3-3 BEv	500.00
16 BEv	500.00
17 JSm	500.00
18 The Eye Sees,Bondage(c)	550.00
19 LFe	500.00
20 BEv,The Eye Sees	500.00
21 Masked Marvel(c)	475.00
22 Masked Marvel(c)	475.00
23 B:Airman	600.00
24 Airman	600.00

KEEN KOMICS
Centaur Publications
May, 1939

1 Teenage Stories	700.00
2 PGn,JaB,CBu	450.00
3 JCo	450.00

KEEN TEENS
Life's Romances Publ./Leader/
Magazine Enterprises
1945

N# P(c)	175.00
N# Ph(c),Van Johnson	150.00
3 Ph(c),	50.00
4 Ph(c),Glenn Ford	50.00
5 Ph(c),Perry Como	50.00
6	50.00

KEN MAYNARD WESTERN
Fawcett Publications
September, 1950

1 B:Ken Maynard & Tarzan (horse) The Outlaw Treasure Trail	400.00
2 Invasion of the Badmen	250.00
3 Pied Piper of the West	200.00
4 Outlaw Hoax	200.00
5 Mystery of Badman City	200.00
6 Redwood Robbery	200.00
7 Seven Wonders of the West	200.00
8 Mighty Mountain Menace, Feb.,1952	200.00

KEN SHANNON
Quality Comics Group
October, 1951

1 RC, Evil Eye of Count Ducrie	250.00
2 RC, Cut Rate Corpses	200.00
3 RC, Corpse that Wouldn't Sleep	150.00
4 RC, Stone Hatchet Murder	125.00
5 RC, Case of the Carney Killer	125.00
6 Weird Vampire Mob	150.00
7 RC,Ugliest Man in the World	125.00
8 Chinatown Murders,Drug	150.00
9 RC, Necklace of Blood	100.00
10 RC, Shadow of the Chair, Apr. 1953	100.00

Ken Shannon #9
© Quality Comics Group

KERRY DRAKE DETECTIVE CASES
Life's Romances/M.E./
1944

(1) see N# A-1 Comics	175.00
2 A:The Faceless Horror	125.00
3	100.00
4 A:Squirrel, Dr. Zero, Caresse	100.00
5 Bondage cover	110.00

Harvey Publ.

6 A:Stitches	50.00
7 A:Shuteye	60.00
8 Bondage cover	65.00
9 Drug	100.00
10 BP,A:Meatball,Drug	100.00
11 BP,I:Kid Gloves	40.00
12 BP	40.00
13 BP,A:Torso	35.00
14 BP,Bullseye Murder Syndicate	35.00
15 BP,Fake Mystic Racket	35.00
16 BP,A:Vixen	30.00
17 BP,Case of the $50,000 Robbery	30.00
18 BP,A:Vixen	30.00
19 BP,Case of the Dope Smugglers	35.00
20 BP,Secret Treasury Agent	30.00
21 BP,Murder on Record	25.00
22 BP,Death Rides the Air Waves	25.00
23 BP,Blackmailer's Secret Weapon	25.00
24 Blackmailer's Trap	25.00
25 Pretty Boy Killer	25.00
26	25.00
27	25.00
28 BP	25.00
29 BP	25.00
30 Mystery Mine,Bondage(c)	35.00
31	25.00
32	25.00
33 August, 1952	25.00

KEWPIES
Will Eisner Publications
Spring, 1949

1	350.00

KEY COMICS
Consolidated Magazines
January, 1944

1 B:The Key, Will-O-The-Wisp	250.00
2	125.00
3	100.00
4 O:John Quincy,B:The Atom	110.00
5 HoK,August, 1946	100.00

KID COWBOY
Approved Comics/
St. John Publ. Co.
1950

1 B:Lucy Belle & Red Feather	65.00
2 Six-Gun Justice	35.00
3 Shadow on Hangman's Bridge	30.00
4 Red Feather V:Eagle of Doom	25.00
5 Killers on the Rampage	25.00
6 The Stovepipe Hat	25.00
7 Ghost Town of Twin Buttes	25.00
8 Thundering Hoofs	25.00
9 Terror on the Salt Flats	25.00
10 Valley of Death	25.00
11 Vanished Herds,Bondage(c)	35.00
12	25.00
13	25.00
14 1954	25.00

KIDDIE KARNIVAL
Approved Comics
1952

N#	250.00

KID ETERNITY
Comics Magazine
(Quality Comics Group)
Spring, 1946

1	600.00
2	300.00
3 Follow Him Out of This World	325.00
4 Great Heroes of the Past	175.00
5 Don't Kid with Crime	175.00
6 Busy Battling Crime	150.00
7 Protects the World	150.00
8 Fly to the Rescue	150.00
9 Swoop Down on Crime	150.00
10 Golden Touch from Mr. Midas	150.00
11 Aid the Living by Calling the Dead	125.00
12 Finds Death	125.00
13 Invades General Poschka	125.00
14 Battles Double	125.00
15 A: Master Man	125.00
16 Balance Scales of Justice	100.00
17 A:Baron Roxx	100.00
18 A:Man with Two Faces	100.00

Becomes:

BUCCANEERS

19 RC,Sword Fight(c)	400.00
20 RC,Treasure Chest	275.00
21 RC,Death Trap	325.00
22 A:Lady Dolores,Snuff, Bondage(c)	225.00
23 RC,V:Treasure Hungry Plunderers of the Sea	250.00
24 A:Adam Peril,Black Roger, Eric Falcon	175.00
25 V:Clews	175.00
26 V:Admiral Blood	175.00
27 RC,RC(c)May, 1951	275.00

All comics prices listed are for *Near Mint* condition.

KID ZOO COMICS
Street & Smith Publications
July, 1948
1 (fa) 125.00

KILLERS, THE
Magazine Enterprises
1947
1 LbC(c),Thou Shall Not Kill . . 650.00
2 Grl,OW,Assassins Mad Slayers
of the East,Hanging(c),Drug 650.00

KILROYS, THE
B&L Publishing Co./
American Comics
June-July, 1947
1 Three Girls in Love(c) 125.00
2 Flat Tire(c) 60.00
3 Right to Swear(c) 45.00
4 Kissing Booth(c) 45.00
5 Skiing(c) 45.00
6 Prom(c) 30.00
7 To School 30.00
8 . . . . 30.00
9 . . . . 30.00
10 B:Solid Jackson solo 30.00
11 . . . . 25.00
12 Life Guard(c) 25.00
13 thru 21 . . . . @25.00
22 thru 30 . . . . @20.00
31 thru 40 . . . . @18.00
41 thru 47 . . . . @15.00
48 3-D effect 100.00
49 3-D effect 100.00
50 thru 54, July 1954 . . . . . . @15.00

KING COMICS
David McKay Publications
April, 1936
(all have Popeye covers)
1 AR,EC,B:Popeye,Flash Gordon,B:
Henry,Mandrake 7,000.00
2 AR,EC,Flash Gordon 2,400.00
3 AR,EC,Flash Gordon 1,500.00
4 AR,EC,Flash Gordon 1,200.00
5 AR,EC,Flash Gordon 800.00
6 AR,EC,Flash Gordon 600.00
7 AR,EC,King Royal Mounties . 575.00
8 AR,EC,Thanksgiving(c) 550.00
9 AR,EC,Christmas(c) 550.00
10 AR,EC,Flash Gordon 550.00
11 AR,EC,Flash Gordon 475.00
12 AR,EC,Flash Gordon 475.00
13 AR,EC,Flash Gordon 475.00
14 AR,EC,Flash Gordon 475.00
15 AR,EC,Flash Gordon 475.00
16 AR,EC,Flash Gordon 475.00
17 AR,EC,Flash Gordon 450.00
18 AR,EC,Flash Gordon 450.00
Covers say: "Starring Popeye"
19 AR,EC,Flash Gordon 450.00
20 AR,EC,Football(c) 450.00
21 AR,EC,Flash Gordon 350.00
22 AR,EC,Flash Gordon 350.00
23 AR,EC,Flash Gordon 350.00
24 AR,EC,Flash Gordon 350.00
25 AR,EC,Flash Gordon 350.00
26 AR,EC,Flash Gordon 325.00
27 AR,EC,Flash Gordon 325.00
28 AR,EC,Flash Gordon 325.00
29 AR,EC,Flash Gordon 325.00
30 AR,EC,Flash Gordon 325.00
31 AR,EC,Flash Gordon 325.00

32 AR,EC,Flash Gordon 325.00
33 AR,EC,Skiing(c) 325.00
34 AR,Ping Pong(c) 275.00
35 AR,Flash Gordon 275.00
36 AR,Flash Gordon 275.00
37 AR,Flash Gordon 275.00
38 AR,Flash Gordon 275.00
39 AR,Baseball(c) 275.00
40 AR,Flash Gordon 275.00
41 AR,Flash Gordon 250.00
42 AR,Flash Gordon 250.00
43 AR,Flash Gordon 250.00
44 AR,Popeye golf(c) 250.00
45 AR,Flash Gordon 250.00
46 AR,B:Little Lulu 250.00
47 AR,Flash Gordon 250.00
48 AR,Flash Gordon 250.00
49 AR,Weather Vane 250.00
50 AR,B:Love Ranger 250.00
51 AR,Flash Gordon 250.00
52 AR,Flash Gordon 175.00
53 AR,Flash Gordon 175.00
54 AR,Flash Gordon 175.00

King Comics #43
© David McKay Publications

55 AR,Magic Carpet 175.00
56 AR,Flash Gordon 175.00
57 AR,Cows Over Moon(c) . . . 175.00
58 AR,Flash Gordon 175.00
59 AR,Flash Gordon 175.00
60 AR,Flash Gordon 175.00
61 AR,B:Phantom,Baseball(c) . 175.00
62 AR,Flash Gordon 175.00
63 AR,Flash Gordon 150.00
64 AR,Flash Gordon 150.00
65 AR,Flash Gordon 150.00
66 AR,Flash Gordon 150.00
67 AR,Sweet Pea 150.00
68 AR,Flash Gordon 150.00
69 AR,Flash Gordon 150.00
70 AR,Flash Gordon 150.00
71 AR,Flash Gordon 150.00
72 AR,Flash Gordon 125.00
73 AR,Flash Gordon 125.00
74 AR,Flash Godron 125.00
75 AR,Flash Gordon 125.00
76 AR,Flag(c) 135.00
77 AR,Flash Gordon 125.00
78 AR,Popeye,Olive Oil(c) 125.00
79 AR,Sweet Pea 125.00

80 AR,Wimpy(c) 125.00
81 AR,B:Blondie(c) 125.00
82 thru 91 AR . . . . @100.00
92 thru 98 AR . . . . @85.00
99 AR,Olive Oil(c) 100.00
100 . . . . 125.00
101 thru 116 AR . . . . @85.00
117 O:Phantom 75.00
118 Flash Gordon 85.00
119 Flash Gordon 75.00
120 Wimpy(c) 60.00
121 thru 140 . . . . @75.00
141 Flash Gordon 60.00
142 Flash Gordon 60.00
143 Flash Gordon 60.00
144 Flash Gordon 60.00
145 Prince Valiant 55.00
146 Prince Valiant 55.00
147 Prince Valiant 55.00
148 thru 154 . . . . @45.00
155 E:Flash Gordon 45.00
156 Baseball(c) 45.00
157 thru 159 . . . . @35.00

KING OF THE ROYAL MOUNTED
Dell Publishing Co.
Dec., 1948–1958
(1) *see Dell Four Color #207*
(2) *see Dell Four Color #265*
(3) *see Dell Four Color #283*
(4) *see Dell Four Color #310*
(5) *see Dell Four Color #340*
(6) *see Dell Four Color #363*
(7) *see Dell Four Color #384*
8 Zane Grey adapt. 40.00
9 . . . . 40.00
10 . . . . 40.00
11 thru 28 . . . . @30.00

KIT CARSON
Avon Periodicals
1950
N# EK(c) Indian Scout 75.00
2 EK(c),Kit Carson's Revenge,
Doom Trail 50.00
3 EK(c),V:Comanche Raiders . 35.00
4 . . . . 30.00
5 EK(c),Trail of Doom 30.00
6 EK(c) 30.00
7 EK(c) 35.00
8 EK(c) 30.00
Becomes:

FIGHTING DAVY CROCKETT
9 EK(c),October/Nov., 1955 . . . 35.00

KOKO AND KOLA
Compix/Magazine Enterprises
Fall, 1946
1 (fa) 40.00
2 X-Mas Issue 20.00
3 . . . . 15.00
4 . . . . 15.00
5 . . . . 15.00
6 May, 1947 . . . . 15.00

KO KOMICS
Gerona Publications
October, 1945
1 . . . . 400.00

All comics prices listed are for *Near Mint* condition.   **CVA Page 353**

KOMIK PAGES
Harry 'A' Chestler
April, 1945
1 JK,Duke of Darkness 375.00

KRAZY KAT COMICS
Dell Publishing Co.
May-June, 1951
1	50.00
2	35.00
3	35.00
4	35.00
5	35.00

KRAZY LIFE
(See PHANTOM LADY)

LABOR IS A PARTNER
Catechetical Guild
Educational Society
1949
1 .... 175.00

LAFFY-DAFFY COMICS
Rural Home Publ. Co.
February, 1945
1 (fa) 30.00
2 .... 30.00

LANCE O'CASEY
Fawcett
1946–47
1 High Seas Adventure
from Whiz comics 250.00
2 thru 4 .... @150.00

LAND OF THE LOST
EC Comics
July-Aug. 1946–Spring 1948
1 Radio show adapt. 225.00
2 .... 150.00
3 thru 9 .... @125.00

LARGE FEATURE COMICS
Dell Publishing Co.
1939
1 Dick Tracy vs. the Blank .. 1,500.00
2 Terry and the Pirates 700.00
3 Heigh-Yo Silver!
the Lone Ranger 900.00
4 Dick Tracy gets his man ... 700.00
5 Tarzan of the Apes 1,300.00
6 Terry and the Pirates 650.00
7 Lone Ranger to the rescue . 800.00
8 Dick Tracy, Racket Buster .. 675.00
9 King of the Royal Mounted . 450.00
10 Gang Busters 600.00
11 Dick Tracy, Mad Doc Hump 800.00
12 Smilin' Jack 550.00
13 Dick Tracy and Scottie
of Scotland Yard 800.00
14 Smilin' Jack helps G-Men .. 575.00
15 Dick Tracy and
the kidnapped princes 800.00
16 Donald Duck, 1st Daisy.. 5,500.00
17 Gang Busters 425.00
18 Phantasmo The Master
of the World 325.00
19 Walt Disney's Dumbo 2,400.00
20 Donald Duck 5,500.00

Large Feature Comics #13
© Dell Publishing Co.

21 Private Buck 100.00
22 Nuts and Jolts 100.00
23 The Nebbs 125.00
24 Popeye in 'Thimble Theatre' 450.00
25 Smilin'Jack 500.00
26 Smitty 225.00
27 Terry and the Pirates 550.00
28 Grin and Bear It 75.00
29 Moon Mullins 200.00
30 Tillie the Toiler 175.00
[Series 2]
1 Peter Rabbit 350.00
2 Winnie Winkle 150.00
3 Dick Tracy 600.00
4 Tiny Tim 250.00
5 Toots and Casper 100.00
6 Terry and the Pirates 550.00
7 Pluto saves the Ship 1,200.00
8 Bugs Bunny 750.00
9 Bringing Up Father 150.00
10 Popeye 400.00
11 Barney Google&SnuffySmith 200.00
12 Private Buck 100.00
13 1001 Hours of Fun 150.00

LARRY DOBY, BASEBALL HERO
Fawcett Publications
1950
1 Ph(c),BW 575.00

LARS OF MARS
Ziff-Davis Publishing Co.
April-May, 1951
10 MA,'Terror from the Sky' .. 600.00
11 GC, The Terror Weapon ... 500.00

LASH LARUE WESTERN
Fawcett Publications
Summer, 1949
1 Ph(c),The Fatal Roundups .. 750.00
2 Ph(c),Perfect Hide Out 325.00
3 Ph(c),The Suspect 275.00
4 Ph(c),Death on Stage 275.00
5 Ph(c),Rustler's Haven 275.00
6 Ph(c) 250.00

7 Ph(c),Shadow of the Noose . 200.00
8 Ph(c),Double Deadline 200.00
9 Ph(c),Generals Last Stand .. 200.00
10 Ph(c) 200.00
11 Ph(c) 175.00
12 thru 20 Ph(c) .... @125.00
21 thru 29 Ph(c) .... @100.00
30 thru 46 Ph(c) .... @75.00
46 Ph(c),Lost Chance 75.00

LASSIE
(& SEVERAL SPECIAL ISSUES)
Dell Publishing Co.
October-December, 1950
1 Ph(c) all 125.00
2	50.00
3	35.00
4	35.00
5	35.00
6	35.00
7	35.00
8	35.00
9	35.00
10	35.00
11	25.00
12 Rocky Langford	27.00
13	25.00
14	25.00
15 I:Timbu	27.00
16	25.00
17	25.00
18	25.00
19	25.00
20 MB	30.00
21 MB	30.00
22 MB	30.00
23 thru 38	@20.00
39 I:Timmy	22.00
40 thru 62	@18.00
63 E:Timmy	12.00
64 thru 70	@10.00

LATEST COMICS
Spotlight Publ./ Palace Promotions
March, 1945
1 Funny Animal-Super Duper .. 60.00
2 .... 40.00

SPECIAL COMICS
MLJ Magazines
(Archie Publ.)
Winter, 1941
1 O:Boy Buddies & Hangman,
D:The Comet 2,000.00
Becomes:

HANGMAN COMICS
2 B:Hangman & Boy Buddies 1,300.00
3 V:Nazis cover,Bondage(c) . 800.00
4 V:Nazis cover 750.00
5 Bondage cover 700.00
6 .... 675.00
7 BF,Graveyard cover 675.00
8 BF 675.00
Becomes:

BLACK HOOD
9 BF 750.00
10 BF,A:Dusty, the
Boy Detective 400.00
11 Here lies the Black Hood .. 300.00
12 .... 275.00
13 EK(c) 275.00

GOLDEN AGE

14 EK(c)	275.00
15 EK	275.00
16 EK(c)	275.00
17 Bondage cover	300.00
18	275.00
19 I.D. Revealed	400.00

Becomes:

LAUGH COMICS

20 BWo,B:Archie,Katy Keene	500.00
21 BWo	225.00
22 BWo	225.00
23 Bwo	225.00
24 BWo,JK,Pipsy	250.00
25 BWo	225.00
26 BWo	125.00
27 BWo	125.00
28 BWo	125.00
29 BWo	125.00
30 BWo	125.00
31 thru 40 BWo	@75.00
41 thru 50 BWo	@55.00
51 thru 60 BWo	@50.00
61 thru 80 BWo	@25.00
81 thru 99 BWo	@20.00
100 BWo	30.00
101 thru 126 BWo	@20.00
127 A:Jaguar	22.00
128 A:The Fly	22.00
129 A:The Fly	22.00
130 A:Jaguar	22.00
131 A:Jaguar	22.00
132 A:The Fly	22.00
133 A:Jaguar	22.00
134 A:The Fly	22.00
135 A:Jaguar	22.00
136 A:Fly Girl	22.00
137 A:Fly Girl	22.00
138 A:The Fly	22.00
139 A:The Fly	22.00
140 A:Jaguar	22.00
141 A:Jaguar	22.00
142 thru 144	@22.00
145 A:Josie	15.00
146 thru 165	@10.00
166 Beatles cover	15.00
167 thru 220	@5.00
221 thru 250	@2.50
251 thru 300	@2.00
301 thru 400	@1.00

LAUGH COMIX
(see TOP-NOTCH COMICS)

LAUREL AND HARDY
St. John Publishing Co.
March, 1949

1	500.00
2	275.00
3	200.00
26 Rep #1	100.00
27 Rep #2	100.00
28 Rep #3	100.00

LAWBREAKERS
Law & Order Magazines
(Charlton)
March, 1951

1	200.00
2	100.00
3	75.00
4 Drug	85.00
5	75.00
6 LM(c)	85.00
7 Drug	85.00
8	75.00
9 StC(c)	75.00

Becomes:

LAWBREAKERS SUSPENSE STORIES
January, 1953

10 StC(c)	175.00
11 LM(c),Negligee(c)	400.00
12 LM(c)	75.00
13 DG(c)	75.00
14 DG(c),Sharks	75.00
15 DG(c),Acid in Face(c)	250.00

Becomes:

STRANGE SUSPENSE STORIES

16 DG(c); January, 1954	150.00
17 DG(c)	125.00

Lawbreakers Suspense Stories #11
© Law & Order Magazines/Charlton

18 SD,SD(c)	200.00
19 SD,SD(c),Electric Chair	250.00
20 SD,SD(c)	200.00
21 SD,SD(c)	125.00
22 SD,SD(c)	175.00

Becomes:

THIS IS SUSPENSE

23 WW; February, 1955 Comics Code	135.00
24 GE,DG(c)	70.00
25 DG(c)	50.00
26 DG(c)	50.00

Becomes:

STRANGE SUSPENSE STORIES

27 October, 1955	50.00
28	35.00
29	35.00
30	35.00
31 SD	100.00
32 SD	100.00
33 SD	100.00
34 SD	100.00
35 SD	100.00
36 SD	100.00
37 SD	100.00
38	35.00
39 SD	120.00
40 SD	120.00
41 SD	120.00
42	30.00
43	30.00
44	30.00
45	30.00
46	30.00
47 SD	85.00
48 SD	85.00
49	30.00
50 SD	85.00
51 SD	85.00
52 SD	85.00
53 SD	85.00
54 thru 60	@25.00
61 thru 74	@15.00
75 SD,SD(c)	120.00
77 Oct 1965	35.00

LAWBREAKERS ALWAYS LOSE
Crime Bureau Stories
Spring, 1948

1 HK; FBI Reward Poster Photo	200.00
2	100.00
3	75.00
4 Vampire	100.00
5	75.00
6 Anti Wertham Edition	75.00
7 Drug	150.00
8	75.00
9 Ph(c)	75.00
10 Ph(c), October 1949	75.00

LAW-CRIME
Essenkay Publications
April, 1948

1 LbC,LbC-(c);Raymond Hamilton Dies In The Chair	450.00
2 LbC,LbC-(c);Strangled Beauty Puzzles Police	350.00
3 LbC,LbC-(c);Lipstick Slayer Sought; August '43	450.00

LEROY
Visual Editions
(Standard Comics)
November, 1949

1 FunniestTeenager of them All	25.00
2	20.00
3 thru 6	@15.00

LET'S PRETEND
D.S. Publishing Company
May-June, 1950

1 From Radio Nursery Tales	100.00
2	75.00
3 November, 1950	75.00

MISS LIBERTY
Burten/Green Publishing
Circa 1944

1 Reprints-Shield,Wizard	300.00

Becomes:

LIBERTY COMICS

10 Reprints,Hangman	125.00
11	90.00
12 Black Hood	90.00
14	90.00
15	75.00

GOLDEN AGE

LIBERTY GUARDS
Chicago Mail Order
(Comic Corp of America)
Circa 1942
1 PG(c),Liberty Scouts 225.00
Becomes:
LIBERTY SCOUTS
June, 1941
2 PG,PG(c)O:Fireman,Liberty
  Scouts 1,000.00
3 PG,PG(c) August,1941
  O:Sentinel 750.00

LIFE STORY
Fawcett Publications
April, 1949
1 Ph(c) 75.00
2 Ph(c) 35.00
3 Ph(c) 30.00
4 Ph(c) 30.00
5 Ph(c) 30.00
6 Ph(c) 30.00
7 Ph(c) 25.00
8 Ph(c) 25.00
9 Ph(c) 25.00
10 Ph(c) 25.00
11 . . . . 20.00
12 . . . . 20.00
13 WW,Drug 100.00
14 thru 21 . . . . @20.00
22 Drug 35.00
23 thru 35 . . . . @20.00
36 Drug 25.00
37 thru 42 . . . . @18.00
43 GE 25.00
44 . . . . 18.00
45 1952 . . . . 18.00

LIFE WITH
SNARKY PARKER
Fox Feature Syndicate
August, 1950
1 . . . . 150.00

LI'L ABNER
Harvey Publications
December, 1947
61 BP,BW,Sadie Hawkins Day . 225.00
62 . . . . 135.00
63 . . . . 135.00
64 . . . . 135.00
65 BP 135.00
66 . . . . 100.00
67 . . . . 100.00
68 FearlessFosdick V:Any Face 125.00
69 . . . . 100.00
70 . . . . 100.00
Toby Press
71 . . . . 80.00
72 . . . . 75.00
73 . . . . 75.00
74 . . . . 75.00
75 HK 100.00
76 . . . . 75.00
77 HK 100.00
78 HK 100.00
79 HK 100.00
80 . . . . 55.00
81 . . . . 55.00
82 . . . . 55.00
83 Baseball 60.00
84 . . . . 55.00

Li'l Abner #64 © Harvey Publications

85 . . . . 55.00
86 HK 100.00
87 . . . . 55.00
88 . . . . 55.00
89 . . . . 55.00
90 . . . . 55.00
91 Rep. #77 . . . . 60.00
92 . . . . 54.00
93 Rep. #71 . . . . 60.00
94 . . . . 55.00
95 Fearless Fosdick 75.00
96 . . . . 55.00
97 January, 1955 . . . . 55.00

LI'L GENIUS
Charlton Comics
1955
1 . . . . 35.00
2 . . . . 15.00
3 thru 15 . . . . @12.00
16 Giants 18.00
17 Giants 18.00
18 Giants,100 pages 22.00
19 thru 40 . . . . @8.00
41 thru 54 . . . . @5.00
55 1965 . . . . 5.00

LI'L PAN
Fox Features Syndicate
December-January, 1946-47
6 . . . . 35.00
7 . . . . 25.00
8 April-May, 1947 . . . . 25.00

LINDA
(see PHANTOM LADY)

LITTLE AUDREY
St. John Publ. Co./
Harvey Comics
April, 1948
1 . . . . 250.00
2 . . . . 125.00
3 thru 6 . . . . @75.00
7 thru 10 . . . . @40.00
11 thru 20 . . . . @25.00
21 thru 24 . . . . @18.00

Little Audrey #12 © Harvey Comics

25 B:Harvey Comics 55.00
26 A: Casper 25.00
27 A: Casper 25.00
28 A: Casper 25.00
29 thru 31 . . . . @20.00
32 A: Casper 25.00
33 A: Casper 25.00
34 A: Casper 25.00
35 A: Casper 25.00
36 thru 53 . . . . @12.00

LITTLE BIT
Jubilee Publishing Company
March, 1949
1 . . . . 20.00
2 June, 1949 . . . . 20.00

LITTLE DOT
Harvey Publications
September, 1953
1 I: Richie Rich & Little Lotta . 650.00
2 . . . . 300.00
3 . . . . 200.00
4 . . . . 150.00
5 O:Dots on Little Dot's Dress 200.00
6 1st Richie Rich(c) 175.00
7 . . . . 135.00
8 . . . . 75.00
9 . . . . 75.00
10 . . . . 75.00
11 thru 20 . . . . @60.00
21 thru 30 . . . . @30.00
31 thru 38 . . . . @25.00
39 . . . . 50.00
40 thru 50 . . . . @15.00
51 thru 60 . . . . @12.00
61 thru 70 . . . . @10.00
71 thru 80 . . . . @8.00
81 thru 100 . . . . @7.00
101 thru 130 . . . . @5.00
131 thru 140 . . . . @5.00
141 thru 145, 52 pages . . . . . @5.00
146 thru 163 . . . . @2.00

LITTLE EVA
St. John Publishing Co.
May, 1952
1 . . . . 60.00

2	30.00
3	18.00
4	18.00
5 thru 10	@12.00
11 thru 30	@10.00
31 November, 1956	10.00

LITTLE GIANT COMICS
Centaur Publications
July, 1938

1 PG, B&W with Color(c)	350.00
2 B&W with Color(c)	300.00
3 B&W with Color(c)	325.00
4 B&W with Color(c)	325.00

LITTLE GIANT DETECTIVE FUNNIES
Centaur Publications
October, 1938

1 B&W	450.00
2 B&W	400.00
3 B&W	400.00
4 January 1939	400.00

LITTLE GIANT MOVIE FUNNIES
Centaur Publications
August, 1938

1 Ed Wheelan-a	500.00
2 Ed Wheelan-a, Oct., 1938	400.00

LITTLE IKE
St. John Publishing Co.
April, 1953

1	50.00
2	25.00
3	20.00
4 October, 1953	20.00

LITTLE IODINE
Dell Publishing Co.
April, 1949

1	75.00
2	30.00
3	30.00
4	30.00
5	30.00
6 thru 10	@20.00
11 thru 30	@15.00
31 thru 50	@10.00
51 thru 56	@8.00

LITTLE JACK FROST
Avon Periodicals
1951

1	35.00

LITTLE LULU
(see MARGE'S LITTLE LULU)

LITTLE MAX COMICS
Harvey Publications
October, 1949

1 I: Little Dot,Joe Palooka	80.00
2 A: Little Dot	45.00
3 A: Little Dot,Joe Palooka(c)	30.00
4	20.00
5 C: Little Dot	20.00
6 thru 10	@18.00
11 thru 22	@15.00
23 A: Little Dot	10.00

24 thru 37	@8.00
38 Rep. #20	8.00
39 thru 72	@8.00
73 A: Richie Rich; Nov.'61	9.00

LITTLE MISS MUFFET
Best Books
(Standard Comics)
December, 1948

11 Strip Reprints	45.00
12 Strip Reprints	30.00
13 Strip Reprints; Mar.'49	30.00

LITTLE MISS SUNBEAM COMICS
Magazine Enterprises
June-July, 1950

1	60.00
2	30.00
3	30.00
4 December-January, 1951	30.00

LITTLE ORPHAN ANNIE
Dell Publishing Co.
1941

1	150.00
2 Orphan Annie and the Rescue	100.00
3	100.00

Little Roquefort #2
© St. John Publishing Co.

LITTLE ROQUEFORT
St. John Publishing Co.
June,1952

1	40.00
2	20.00
3 thru 9	@15.00

Pines

10 Summer 1958	18.00

LITTLE SCOUTS
Dell Publishing Co.
March, 1951

(1) see Dell Four Color #321	
2	20.00
3	20.00
4	20.00

5	20.00
6	20.00

LITTLEST SNOWMAN
Dell Publishing Co.
December, 1956

1	20.00

LIVING BIBLE, THE
Living Bible Corp.
Autumn, 1945

1 LbC-(c) Life of Paul	250.00
2 LbC-(c) Joseph &His Brethern	150.00
3 LbC-(c) Chaplains At War	250.00

LONE EAGLE
Ajax/Farrell
April-May, 1954

1	50.00
2	30.00
3 Bondage(c)	35.00
4 October-November, 1954	30.00

LONE RANGER
Dell Publishing Co.
January-February 1948

1 B:Lone Ranger & Tonto B:Strip Reprint	650.00
2	300.00
3	250.00
4	250.00
5	250.00
6	200.00
7	200.00
8 O:Retold	250.00
9	200.00
10	200.00
11 B:Young Hawk	125.00
12 thru 20	@125.00
21	100.00
22	100.00
23 O:Retold	125.00
24 thru 30	@100.00
31 (1st Mask Logo)	110.00
32 thru 36	@75.00
37 (E:Strip reprints)	75.00
38 thru 50	@60.00
51 thru 75	@50.00
76 thru 99	@45.00
100	75.00
101 thru 111	@40.00
112 B:Clayton Moore Ph(c)	135.00
113 thru 117	@75.00
118 O:Lone Ranger & Tonto retold, Anniv. issue	150.00
119 thru 144	@75.00
145 final issue,May/July 1962	75.00

THE LONE RANGER'S COMPANION TONTO
Dell Publishing Co.
January, 1951

(1) see Dell Four Color #312	
2 P(c) all	60.00
3	60.00
4	50.00
5	50.00
6 thru 10	@50.00
11 thru 20	@40.00
21 thru 25	@30.00
26 thru 33	@25.00

GOLDEN AGE

All comics prices listed are for *Near Mint* condition.

GOLDEN AGE

THE LONE RANGER'S FAMOUS HORSE HI-YO SILVER
Dell Publishing Co.
January, 1952

(1) *see Dell Four Color #369*	
(1) *see Dell Four Color #392*	
3 P(c) all	20.00
4	20.00
5	20.00
6 thru 10	@18.00
11 thru 36	@15.00

Lone Rider #1 © Superior Comics

LONE RIDER
Farrell
(Superior Comics)
April, 1951

1	125.00
2 I&O: Golden Arrow; 52 pgs.	60.00
3	50.00
4	50.00
5	50.00
6 E: Golden Arrow	60.00
7 G. Arrow Becomes Swift Arrow	65.00
8 O: Swift Arrow	70.00
9 thru 14	@30.00
15 O: Golden Arrow Rep. #2	35.00
16 thru 19	@25.00
20	20.00
21 3-D (c)	75.00
22	20.00
23 A: Apache Kid	25.00
24	20.00
25	20.00
26 July, 1955	20.00

LONG BOW
Real Adventures Publ.
(Fiction House)
Winter, 1950

1	100.00
2	50.00
3 "Red Arrows Means War"	45.00
4 "Trial of Tomahawk"	45.00
5	45.00
6 "Rattlesnake Raiders"	35.00
7	35.00

8	35.00
9 Spring, 1953	35.00

LOONEY TUNES AND MERRIE MELODIES
Dell Publishing Co.
1941

1 B:&1st Comic App. Bugs Bunny Daffy Duck,Elmer Fudd	10,000.00
2 Bugs/Porky(c)	1,500.00
3 Bugs/Porky(c) B:WK, Kandi the Cave	1,200.00
4 Bugs/Porky(c),WK	1,000.00
5 Bugs/Porky(c),WK, A:Super Rabbit	1,000.00
6 Bugs/Porky/Elmer(c),E:WK, Kandi the Cave	700.00
7 Bugs/Porky(c)	500.00
8 Bugs/Porky swimming(c),F:WK, Kandi the Cave	700.00
9 Porky/Elmer car painted(c)	500.00
10 Porky/Bugs/Elmer Parade(c)	500.00
11 Bugs/Porky(c),F:WK, Kandi the Cave	500.00
12 Bugs/Porky rollerskating(c)	400.00
13 Bugs/Porky(c)	400.00
14 Bugs/Porky(c)	400.00
15 Bugs/Porky X-Mas(c),F:WK Kandi the Cave	350.00
16 Bugs/Porky ice-skating(c)	350.00
17 Bugs/Petunia Valentines(c)	350.00
18 Sgt.Bugs Marine(c)	350.00
19 Bugs/Painting(c)	350.00
20 Bugs/Porky/ElmerWarBonds(c), B:WK,Pat,Patsy&Pete	350.00
21 Bugs/Porky 4th July(c)	300.00
22 Porky(c)	300.00
23 Bugs/Porky Fishing(c)	300.00
24 Bugs/Porky Football(c)	300.00
25 Bugs/Porky/Petunia Halloween(c),E:WK,Pat, Patsy & Pete	300.00
26 Bugs Thanksgiving(c)	250.00
27 Bugs/Porky New Years(c)	250.00
28 Bugs/Porky Ice-Skating(c)	250.00
29 Bugs Valentine(c)	250.00
30 Bugs(c)	250.00
31 Bugs(c)	200.00
32 Bugs/Porky Hot Dogs(c)	200.00
33 Bugs/Porky War Bonds(c)	210.00
34 Bugs/Porky Fishing(c)	200.00
35 Bugs/Porky Swimming(c)	200.00
36 Bugs/Porky(c)	200.00
37 Bugs Halloween(c)	200.00
38 Bugs Thanksgiving(c)	200.00
39 Bugs X-Mas(c)	200.00
40 Bugs(c)	200.00
41 Bugs Washington's Birthday(c)	150.00
42 Bugs Magician(c)	150.00
43 Bugs Dream(c)	150.00
44 Bugs/Porky(c)	150.00
45 Bugs War Bonds(c)	150.00
46 Bugs/Porky(c)	125.00
47 Bugs Beach(c)	125.00
48 Bugs/Porky Picnic(c)	125.00
49 Bugs(c)	125.00
50 Bugs(c)	125.00
51 thru 60	@90.00
61 thru 80	@75.00
81 thru 86	@45.00
87 Bugs X-Mas(c)	50.00
88 thru 99	@35.00
100	45.00

Looney Tunes & Merrie Melodies #1 © Dell Publ. Co.

101 thru 110	@30.00
111 thru 125	@25.00
126 thru 150	@20.00
151 thru 165	@18.00

Becomes:

LOONEY TUNES
August, 1955

166 thru 200	@15.00
201 thru 245	@12.00
246 final issue,Sept.1962	12.00

LOST WORLD
Literacy Enterprises (Standard Comics)
October, 1952

5 ATh, Alice in Terrorland	275.00
6 ATh	250.00

LOVE AND MARRIAGE
Superior Comics Ltd.
March, 1952

1	50.00
2	25.00
3	20.00
4	20.00
5	20.00
6	20.00
7	20.00
8 thru 15	@20.00
16 September, 1954	20.00

LOVE AT FIRST SIGHT
Periodical House (Ace Magazines)
October, 1949

1 P(c)	60.00
2 P(c)	25.00
3	15.00
4 P(c)	15.00
5 thru 10	@15.00
11 thru 33	@10.00
34 1st Edition Under Code	7.00
35 thru 41	@7.00
42 1956	7.00

GOLDEN AGE

LOVE CONFESSIONS
Comics Magazine
(Quality Comics Group)
October, 1949

1 PG,BWa(c)& Some-a	175.00
2 PG	65.00
3	40.00
4 RC	60.00
5 BWa	65.00
6 Ph(c)	20.00
7 Ph(c) Van Johnson	20.00
8 BWa	60.00
9 Ph(c)Jane Russell/Robert	
Mitchum	20.00
10 BWa	60.00
11 thru 18 Ph(c)	@35.00
19	18.00
20 BWa	60.00
21	12.00
22 BWa	15.00
23 thru 28	@12.00
29 BWa	35.00
30 thru 38	@10.00
39 MB	15.00
40	10.00
41	10.00
42	10.00
43 1st Edition Under Code	8.00
44 thru 46	@8.00
47 BWa(c)	20.00
48 thru 54 December, 1956 .	@8.00

LOVE DIARY
Our Publishing Co./Toytown
July, 1949

1 BK,Ph(c)	100.00
2 BK,Ph(c)	55.00
3 BK,Ph(c)	55.00
4 thru 9 Ph(c)	@20.00
10 BEv, Ph(c)	25.00
11 thru 24 Ph(c)	@15.00
25	12.00
26	12.00
27 Ph(c)	15.00
28	12.00
29 Ph(c)	15.00
30	12.00
31 JB(c)	15.00
32 thru 41	@12.00
42 MB(c)	12.00
43 thru 47	@12.00
48 1st Edition Under Code,	
Oct.'55	12.00

LOVE DIARY
Quality Comics Group
September, 1949

1 BWa(c)	175.00

LOVE LESSONS
Harvey Publications
October, 1949

1	65.00
2	30.00
3 Ph(c)	20.00
4	20.00
5 June, 1950	20.00

LOVE LETTERS
Comic Magazines
(Quality Comics Group)
November, 1949

1 PG,BWa(c)	150.00

2 PG,BWa(c)	125.00
3 PG	75.00
4 BWa	125.00
5	25.00
6	25.00
7	25.00
8	25.00
9 Ph(c) of Robert Mitchum . . .	35.00
10	25.00
11 BWa	45.00
12	18.00
13	18.00
14	18.00
15	18.00
16 Ph(c) of Anthony Quinn . . .	20.00
17 BWa, Ph(c) of Jane Russell .	20.00
18 thru 30	@12.00
31 BWa	25.00

Becomes:
LOVE SECRETS

32	32.00
33	15.00
34 BWa	35.00
35 thru 39	@15.00
40 MB(c)1st Edition Under Code	25.00
41 thru 50	@12.00
50 MB	12.00
51 MB(c)	12.00
52 thru 56	@10.00

LOVELORN
Best Syndicated/Michel Publ.
(American Comics Group)
August-September, 1949

1	75.00
2	35.00
3 thru 10	@25.00
11 thru 17	@18.00
18 2pgs. MD-a	15.00
19	12.00
20	12.00
21 Prostitution Story	30.00
22 thru 50	@12.00
51 July, 1954 3-D	75.00

Becomes:
CONFESSIONS OF LOVELORN

52 3-D	125.00
53	35.00
54 3-D	125.00
55	25.00
56 Communist Story	40.00
57 Comics Code	15.00
58 thru 90	@15.00
91 AW	35.00
92 thru 105	@10.00
106 P(c)	10.00
107 P(c)	10.00
108 thru 114	@10.00

LOVE MEMORIES
Fawcett Publications
Autumn, 1949

1 Ph(c)	50.00
2 Ph(c)	25.00
3 Ph(c)	25.00
4 Ph(c)	25.00

LOVE MYSTERY
Fawcett Publications
June, 1950

1 GE, Ph(c)	150.00

2 GE, Ph(c)	125.00
3 GE & BP, Ph(c); Oct., 1950 .	125.00

LOVE PROBLEMS AND ADVICE ILLUSTRATED
McCombs/Harvey Publications
Home Comics
June, 1949

1 BP	85.00
2 BP	35.00
3	25.00
4	25.00
5 L. Elias(c)	22.00
6	20.00
7 BP	20.00
8 BP	20.00
9 BP	20.00
10 BP	20.00
11 BP	18.00
12 BP	18.00
13 BP	18.00
14 BP	18.00
15	15.00

Love Problems & Advice #1
© McCombs/Harvey Publ.

16	15.00
17 thru 23 BP	@15.00
24 BP, Rape Scene	20.00
25 BP	12.00
26	12.00
27	12.00
28 BP	12.00
29 BP	12.00
30	12.00
31	12.00
32 Comics Code	8.00
33 BP	8.00
34	8.00
35	8.00
36	8.00
37	8.00
38 S&K (c)	8.00
39	8.00
40 BP	8.00
41 BP	8.00
42	8.00
43	8.00
44 March, 1957	8.00

LOVERS LANE
Lev Gleason Publications
October, 1949

1 CBi (c),FG-a	50.00
2 P(c)	35.00
3 P(c)	18.00
4 P(c)	18.00
5 P(c)	18.00
6 GT,P(c),	18.00
7 P(c)	18.00
8 P(c),	18.00
9 P(c),	18.00
10 P(c)	18.00
11 thru 19 P(c)	@15.00
20 Ph(c); FF 1 page Ad,	20.00
21 Ph(c)	10.00
22 Ph(c)	10.00
23	10.00
24	10.00
25	10.00
26 Ph(c)	10.00
27 Ph(c)	10.00
28 Ph(c)	10.00
29 thru 38	@10.00
39 Story Narrated by Frank Sinatra	30.00
40	9.00
41 June, 1954	9.00

LOVE SCANDALS
Comic Magazines
(Quality Comics Group)
February, 1950

1 BW(c)&a	175.00
2 PG-a, Ph(c)	50.00
3 PG-a, Ph(c)	50.00
4 BWa(c)&a 18Pgs.; GFx-a	135.00
5 Ph(c), October, 1950	50.00

LOVE STORIES OF MARY WORTH
Harvey Publications
September, 1949

1 Newspaper Reprints	40.00
2 Newspaper Reprints	25.00
3 Newspaper Reprints	20.00
4 Newspaper Reprints,	20.00
5 May, 1950	20.00

LUCKY COMICS
Consolidated Magazines
January, 1944

1 Lucky Star	125.00
2 Henry C. Kiefer(c)	75.00
3	75.00
4	75.00
5 Summer, 1946,Devil(c)	75.00

LUCKY DUCK
Standard Comics
(Literary Enterprises)
January, 1953

5 IS (c)&a	40.00
6 IS (c)&a	30.00
7 IS (c)&a	30.00
8 IS (c)&a, September, 1953	30.00

LUCKY FIGHTS IT THROUGH
Educational Comics
1949

N# HK-a, V.D. Prevention	1300.00

LUCKY "7" COMICS
Howard Publications
1944

1 Bondage(c) Pioneer	200.00

LUCKY STAR
Nationwide Publications
1950

1 JDa,B:52 pages western	75.00
2 JDa	40.00
3 JDa	40.00
4 JDa	35.00
5 JDa	35.00
6 JDa	35.00
7 JDa	35.00
8 thru 13	@25.00
14 1955,E:52 pages western	25.00

LUCY, THE REAL GONE GAL
St. John Publishing Co.
June, 1953

1 Negligee Panels,Teenage	65.00
2	35.00
3 MD-a	25.00
4 February, 1954	22.00

Becomes:

MEET MISS PEPPER
St. John Publishing Co.
April, 1954

5 JKu-a	100.00
6 JKu (c)&a, June,1954	90.00

MAD
E.C. Comics
October-November, 1952

1 JSe,HK(c),JDa,WW	5,000.00
2 JSe,JDa(c),JDa,WW	1,200.00
3 JSe,HK(c),JDa,WW	650.00
4 JSe,HK(c),JDa-Flob Was A Slob,JDa,WW	650.00
5 JSe,BE(c),JDa,WW	1,200.00
6 JSe,HK(c),Jda,WW	500.00
7 HK(c),JDa,WW	500.00
8 HK(c),JDa,WW	500.00
9 JSe,HK(c),JDa,WW	500.00
10 JSe,HK(c),JDa,WW	500.00
11 BW,BW(c),JDa,WW,Life(c)	500.00
12 BK,JDa,WW	400.00
13 HK(c),JDa,WW,Red(c)	400.00
14 RH,HK(c),JDa,WW, Mona Lisa(c)	400.00
15 JDa,WW,Alice in Wonderland(c)	400.00
16 HK(c),JDa,WW,Newspaper(c)	400.00
17 BK,BW,JDa,WW	400.00
18 HK(c),JDa,WW	400.00
19 JDa,WW,Racing Form(c)	300.00
20 JDa,WW,Composition(c)	300.00
21 JDa,WW,1st A.E.Neuman(c)	300.00
22 BE,JDa,WW,Picasso(c)	300.00
23 Last Comic Format Edition, JDa,WW Think(c)	300.00
24 BK,WW, HK Logo & Border; 1st Magazine Format	750.00
25 WW, Al Jaffee Sterts As Reg.	325.00
26 BK,WW,WW(c)	275.00
27 WWa,RH,JDa(c)	250.00
28 WW,BE(c),RH Back(c)	250.00
29 JKa,BW,WW,WW(c); 1st Don Martin Artwork	250.00
30 BE,WW,RC; 1st A.E.	

Neuman(c) By Mingo	400.00
31 JDa,WW,BW,Mingo(c)	200.00
32 MD,JO 1st as reg.;Mingo(c); WW-Back(c)	175.00
33 WWa,Mingo(c);JO-Back(c)	175.00
34 WWa,Mingo(c);1st Berg as Reg.	150.00
35 WW,RC,Mingo Wraparound(c)	150.00
36 WW,BW,Mingo(c),JO,MD	100.00
37 WW,Mingo(c)JO,MD	100.00
38 WW,JO,MD	80.00
39 WW,JO,MD	80.00
40 WW,BW,JO,MD	80.00
41 WW,JO,MD	75.00
42 WW,JO,MD	75.00
43 WW,JO,MD	75.00
44 WW,JO,MD	75.00
45 WW,JO,MD	75.00
46 JO,MD	75.00
47 JO,MD	75.00
48 JO,MD	75.00
49 JO,MD	75.00
50 JO,MD	75.00

Mad #9 © E.C. Comics

51 JO,MD	65.00
52 JO,MD	65.00
53 JO,MD	65.00
54 JO,MD	65.00
55 JO,MD	65.00
56 JO,MD	60.00
57 JO,MD	60.00
58 JO,MD	60.00
59 WW,JO,MD	65.00
60 JO,MD	60.00
61 JO,MD	60.00
62 JO,MD	50.00
63 JO,MD	50.00
64 JO,MD	50.00
65 JO,MD	50.00
66 JO,MD	45.00
67 JO,MD	45.00
68 Don Martin(c),JO,MD	45.00
69 JO,MD	45.00
70 JO,MD	45.00
71 JO,MD	45.00
72 JO,MD	45.00
73 JO,MD	45.00
74 JO,MD	45.00
75 Mingo(c),JO,MD	40.00
76 Mingo(c),SA,JO,MD	40.00

All comics prices listed are for *Near Mint* condition.

GOLDEN AGE

77 Mingo(c),SA,JO,MD	40.00	
78 Mingo(c),SA,JO,MD	40.00	
79 Mingo(c),SA,JO,MD	40.00	
80 Mingo(c),SA,JO,MD	40.00	
81 Mingo(c),SA,JO,MD	40.00	
82 BW,Mingo(c),SA,JO,MD	40.00	
83 Mingo(c),SA,JO,MD	40.00	
84 Mingo(c),SA,JO,MD	40.00	
85 Mingo(c)SA,JO,MD	40.00	
86 Mingo(c);1st Fold-in Back(c), SA,JO,MD	40.00	
87 Mingo(c),JO,MD	35.00	
88 Mingo(c),JO,MD	35.00	
89 WK,Mingo(c),JO,MD	40.00	
90 Mingo(c); FF-Back(c),JO,MD	35.00	
91 Mingo(c),JO,MD	30.00	
92 Mingo(c),JO,MD	30.00	
93 Mingo(c),JO,MD	30.00	
94 Mingo(c),JO,MD	30.00	
95 Mingo(c),JO,MD	30.00	
96 Mingo(c),JO,MD	30.00	
97 Mingo(c),JO,MD	30.00	
98 Mingo(c),JO,MD	30.00	
99 JDa,Mingo(c),JO,MD	40.00	
100 Mingo(c),JO,MD	30.00	
101 Infinity(c) by Mingo,JO,MD	25.00	
102 Mingo(c)JO,MD	25.00	
103 Mingo(c)JO,MD	25.00	
104 Mingo(c)JO,MD	25.00	
105 Mingo(c);Batman TV Spoof ,JO,MD	30.00	
106 Mingo(c);FF-Back(c),JO,MD	30.00	
107 Mingo(c),JO,MD	25.00	
108 Mingo(c),JO,MD	25.00	
109 Mingo(c),JO,MD	25.00	
110 Mingo(c),JO,MD	25.00	
111 Mingo(c),JO,MD	25.00	
112 JO,MD	25.00	
113 JO,MD	25.00	
114 JO,MD	25.00	
115 JO,MD	25.00	
116 JO,MD	25.00	
117 JO,MD	25.00	
118 JO,MD	25.00	
119 JO,MD	25.00	
120 JO,MD	25.00	
121 Beatles,JO,MD	25.00	
122 MD & Mingo(c),JO,MD, Reagan	20.00	
123 JO,MD	18.00	
124 JO,MD	18.00	
125 JO,MD	18.00	
126 JO,MD	18.00	
127 JO,MD	18.00	
128 Last JO;MD	18.00	
129 MD	18.00	
130 MD	18.00	
131 MD	18.00	
132 MD	18.00	
133 MD	18.00	
134 MD	18.00	
135 JDa(c),MD	17.00	
136 MD	15.00	
137 BW,MD	15.00	
138 MD	15.00	
139 JDa(c),MD	15.00	
140 thru 153 MD	@16.00	
154 Mineo(c),MD	16.00	
155	16.00	
156	16.00	
157	16.00	
158	16.00	
159	16.00	
160 Mingo(c),JDa,AT	16.00	
161	14.00	

162 Mingo(c),MD,AT	14.00	
163	14.00	
164 Mingo,PaperMoon(c),AT, MD,SA	14.00	
165 Don Martin(c),At,MD	14.00	
166	14.00	
167	14.00	
168 Mingo(c),AT,MD	14.00	
169 MD(c)	14.00	
170	14.00	
171 Mingo(c)	12.00	
172 Mingo(c)	12.00	
173 JDa(c)	12.00	
174	12.00	
175	12.00	
176 MD(c)	12.00	
177	12.00	
178 JDa(c)	12.00	
179	12.00	
180 Jaws(c),SA,MD,JDA,AT	12.00	
181 G.Washington(c),JDa	12.00	
182	12.00	
183 Mingo(c),AT,SA,MD	12.00	
184 Mingo(c),Md,AT	12.00	
185	12.00	
186 Star Trek Spoof	14.00	
187	12.00	
188	12.00	
189	12.00	
190	12.00	
191 Clark(c),JDa,MD,AT	12.00	
192	12.00	
193 Charlies Angels(c), Rickart,JDa,SA,MD	12.00	
194 Rocky(c),Rickart,AT,MD	12.00	
195	12.00	
196 Star Wars Spoof, Rickart,AT,JDa	18.00	
197	12.00	
198 UPC(c),AT,MD	12.00	
199 Jaffee(c),AT,JDa,SA,MD	12.00	
200 Rickart(c),Close Encounters	15.00	
201 Rickart(c),Sat.Night Fever	7.50	
202	7.50	
203 Star Wars Spoof,Rickart(c)	8.50	
204 Hulk TV Spoof,JawsII(c)	7.50	
205 Rickart(c),Grease	7.50	
206 Mingo,(c),AT,JDa,Md	7.50	
207 Jones(c),Animal House(c)	7.50	
208 Superman Movie Spoof, Rickart(c)	7.50	
209 Mingo(c),AT,MD	7.50	
210 Mingo,Lawn Mower,AT, JDa,MD	7.50	
211 Mingo(c)	7.50	
212 Jda(c),AT,MD	8.00	
213 JDa(c),SA,AT,JDa	8.00	
214	7.00	
215 Jones(c),MD,AT,JDa	7.00	
216	7.00	
217 Jaffee(c),For Pres,AT,MD	7.00	
218 Martin(c),AT,MD	7.00	
219 thru 250	@7.00	
251 thru 260	@5.00	
261 thru 299	@4.00	
300 thru 303	6.00	
304 thru 330	3.00	

MAGIC COMICS
David McKay Publications
August, 1939
1 Mandrake the Magician,
Henry,Popeye,Blondie,
Barney Baxter,Secret Agent
X-9, Bunky,Henry on(c) .. 1,800.00

2 Henry on(c)	700.00	
3 Henry on(c)	500.00	
4 Henry on(c),Mandrake-Logo	450.00	
5 Henry on(c),Mandrake-Logo	350.00	
6 Henry on(c),Mandrake-Logo	300.00	
7 Henry on(c),Mandrake-Logo	300.00	
8 B:Inspector Wade,Tippie	275.00	
9 Henry-Mandrake Interact(c)	275.00	
10 Henry-Mandrake Interact(c)	275.00	
11 Henry-Mandrake Interact(c)	225.00	
12 Mandrake on(c)	225.00	
13 Mandrake on(c)	225.00	
14 Mandrake on(c)	225.00	
15 Mandrake on(c)	225.00	
16 Mandrake on(c)	225.00	
17 B:Lone Ranger	250.00	
18 Mandrake/Robot on(c)	225.00	
19 Mandrake on(c)	225.00	
20 Mandrake on(c)	200.00	
21 Mandrake on(c)	175.00	
22 Mandrake on(c)	175.00	
23 Mandrake on(c)	175.00	
24 Mandrake on(c)	175.00	
25 B:Blondie; Mandrake in Logo for Duration	175.00	
26 Blondie (c)	150.00	
27 Blondie (c); High School Heroes	150.00	
28 Blondie (c); High School Heroes	150.00	
29 Blondie (c); High School Heroes	150.00	
30 Blondie (c)	150.00	
31 Blondie(c);High School Sports Page	125.00	
32 Blondie (c);Secret Agent X-9	125.00	
33 C.Knight's-Romance of Flying	125.00	
34 ClaytonKnight's-War in the Air	125.00	
35 Blondie (c)	125.00	
36 July'42; Patriotic-(c)	125.00	
37 Blondie (c)	125.00	
38 ClaytonKnight's-Flying Tigers	125.00	
39 Blondie (c)	125.00	
40 Jimmie Doolittle bombs Tokyo	125.00	
41 How German Became British Censor	90.00	
42 Joe Musial's-Dollar-a-Dither	90.00	
43 Clayton Knight's-War in the Air	90.00	
44 Flying Fortress in Action	90.00	
45 Clayton Knight's-Gremlins	90.00	
46 Adventures of Aladdin Jr.	90.00	

Magic Comics #7
© David McKay Publications

All comics prices listed are for *Near Mint* condition.

47 Secret Agent X-9 . . . . 90.00
48 General Arnold U.S.A.F. 90.00
49 Joe Musial's-Dollar-a-Dither . 90.00
50 The Lone Ranger 90.00
51 Joe Musial's-Dollar-a-Dither . 75.00
52 C. Knights-Heroes on Wings . 75.00
53 C. Knights-Heroes on Wings . 75.00
54 High School Heroes 75.00
55 Blondie (c) 80.00
56 High School Heroes 75.00
57 Joe Musial's-Dollar-a-Dither . 75.00
58 Private Breger Abroad 75.00
59 . . . . 75.00
60 . . . . 75.00
61 Joe Musial's-Dollar-a-Dither . 50.00
62 . . . . 50.00
63 B:Buz Sawyer, Naval Pilot . . 50.00
64 thru 70 . . . . @50.00
71 thru 80 . . . . @45.00
80 thru 90 . . . . @40.00
91 thru 99 . . . . @40.00
100 . . . . 50.00
101 thru 108 . . . . @35.00
108 Flash Gordon 40.00
109 Flash Gordon 40.00
110 thru 113 . . . . @30.00
114 The Lone Ranger 30.00
115 thru 119 . . . . @30.00
120 Secret Agent X-9 . . . . 35.00
121 Secret Agent X-9 . . . . 35.00
122 Secret Agent X-9 . . . . 35.00
123 Sec. Agent X-9;Nov-Dec.'49 35.00

MAJOR HOOPLE COMICS
Nedor Publications
1942
1 Mary Worth,Phantom Soldier;
Buy War Bonds On(c) 275.00

MAJOR VICTORY COMICS
H. Clay Glover Svcs./
Harry A. Chestler
1944
1 O:Major Victory,I:Spider
Woman 400.00
2 A: Dynamic Boy 275.00
3 A: Rocket Boy 225.00

MAN HUNT!
Magazine Enterprises
October, 1953
1 LbC,FG,OW(c);B:Red Fox,
Undercover Girl, Space Ace 350.00
2 LbC,FG,OW(c);
Electrocution(c) 250.00
3 LbC,FG,OW,OW(c) 225.00
4 LbC,FG,OW,OW(c) 225.00
5 LbC,FG,OW,OW(c) 200.00
6 LbC,OW,OW(c) 200.00
7 LbC,OW; E:Space Ace . . . 200.00
8 LbC,OW,FG(c);B:Trail Colt . 200.00
9 LbC,OW 200.00
10 LbC,OW,OW(c),Gwl 200.00
11 LbC,FF,OW;B:The Duke,
Scotland Yard 250.00
12 LbC,OW 150.00
13 LbC,FF,OW;Rep.Trail Colt #1 250.00
14 LbC,OW;Bondage,
Hypo-(c);1953 . . . . 225.00

MAN OF WAR
Comic Corp. of America
(Centaur Publ.)
November, 1941
1 PG,PG(c);Flag(c);B:The Fire-
Man,Man of War,The Sentinel,
Liberty Guards,Vapoman . 1,200.00
2 PG,PG(c);I: The Ferret . . . 1,000.00

MAN O'MARS
Fiction House/
I.W. Enterprises
1953
1 MA, Space Rangers 300.00
1 MA, Rep. Space Rangers . . . 50.00

March of Comics #22
© K.K. Publications/Western Publ.

MARCH OF COMICS
K.K. Publications/
Western Publ.
1946
(All were Giveaways)
N# WK back(c),Goldilocks . . . 300.00
N# WK,How Santa got His
Red Suit 300.00
N# WK,Our Gang 400.00
N# CB,Donald Duck;
"Maharajah Donald" 7,500.00
5 Andy Panda 150.00
6 WK,Fairy Tales 200.00
7 Oswald the Lucky Rabbit . . 150.00
8 Mickey Mouse 550.00
9 Gloomey Bunny 75.00
10 Santa Claus 65.00
11 Santa Claus 50.00
12 Santa's Toys 50.00
13 Santa's Suprise 50.00
14 Santa's Kitchen 50.00
15 Hip-It-Ty Hop 75.00
16 Woody Woodpecker 150.00
17 Roy Rogers 200.00
18 Fairy Tales 90.00
19 Uncle Wiggily 75.00
20 CB,Donald Duck 4,500.00
21 Tom and Jerry 100.00
22 Andy Panda 65.00
23 Raggedy Ann and Andy . . 125.00

24 Felix the Cat; By
Otto Messmer 200.00
25 Gene Autrey 200.00
26 Our Gang 200.00
27 Mickey Mouse 400.00
28 Gene Autrey 200.00
29 Easter 30.00
30 Santa 25.00
31 Santa 25.00
32 Does Not Exist
33 A Christmas Carol 25.00
34 Woody Woodpecker 75.00
35 Roy Rogers 200.00
36 Felix the Cat 175.00
37 Popeye 150.00
38 Oswald the Lucky Rabbit . . . 50.00
39 Gene Autrey 185.00
40 Andy and Woody 50.00
41 CB,DonaldDuck,SouthSeas 3,600.00
42 Porky Pig 60.00
43 Henry 40.00
44 Bugs Bunny 75.00
45 Mickey Mouse 300.00
46 Tom and Jerry 70.00
47 Roy Rogers 150.00
48 Santa 20.00
49 Santa 20.00
50 Santa 20.00
51 Felix the Cat 150.00
52 Popeye 125.00
53 Oswald the Lucky Rabbit . . . 50.00
54 Gene Autrey 150.00
55 Andy and Woody 45.00
56 CB back(c),Donald Duck . . . 275.00
57 Porky Pig 55.00
58 Henry 30.00
59 Bugs Bunny 70.00
60 Mickey Mouse 275.00
61 Tom and Jerry 50.00
62 Roy Rogers 150.00
63 Santa 20.00
64 Santa 20.00
65 Jingle Bells 20.00
66 Popeye 85.00
67 Oswald the Lucky Rabbit . . . 30.00
68 Roy Rogers 150.00
69 Donald Duck 250.00
70 Tom and Jerry 40.00
71 Porky Pig 55.00
72 Krazy Kat 50.00
73 Roy Rogers 100.00
74 Mickey Mouse 250.00
75 Bugs Bunny 65.00
76 Andy and Woody 35.00
77 Roy Rogers 100.00
78 Gene Autrey; last regular
sized issue 100.00
79 Andy Panda,5"x7" format . . . 25.00
80 Popeye 65.00
81 Oswald the Lucky Rabbit . . . 22.00
82 Tarzan 150.00
83 Bugs Bunny 50.00
84 Henry 20.00
85 Woody Woodpecker 22.00
86 Roy Rogers 80.00
87 Krazy Kat 25.00
88 Tom and Jerry 20.00
89 Porky Pig 25.00
90 Gene Autrey 90.00
91 Roy Rogers and Santa 90.00
92 Christmas w/Santa 15.00
93 Woody Woodpecker 20.00
94 Indian Chief 65.00
95 Oswald the Lucky Rabbit . . . 18.00
96 Popeye 60.00

GOLDEN AGE

March of Comics #36
© K.K. Publications/Western Publ.

97 Bugs Bunny 40.00
98 Tarzan,Lex Barker Ph(c) . . . 150.00
99 Porky Pig 25.00
100 Roy Rogers 75.00
101 Henry 15.00
102 Tom Corbet,P(c) 135.00
103 Tom and Jerry 15.00
104 Gene Autrey 75.00
105 Roy Rogers 75.00
106 Santa's Helpers 15.00
107 *Not Published*
108 Fun with Santa 15.00
109 Woody Woodpecker 18.00
110 Indian Chief 30.00
111 Oswald the Lucky Rabbit . . 15.00
112 Henry 12.00
113 Porky Pig 20.00
114 Tarzan,RsM 150.00
115 Bugs Bunny 40.00
116 Roy Rogers 65.00
117 Popeye 60.00
118 Flash Gordon, P(c) 120.00
119 Tom and Jerry 16.00
120 Gene Autrey 65.00
121 Roy Rogers 65.00
122 Santa's Suprise 12.00
123 Santa's Christmas Book . . . 12.00
124 Woody Woodpecker 15.00
125 Tarzan, Lex Barker Ph(c) . . 150.00
126 Oswald the Lucky Rabbit . . 12.00
127 Indian Chief 20.00
128 Tom and Jerry 15.00
129 Henry 12.00
130 Porky Pig 25.00
131 Roy Rogers 65.00
132 Bugs Bunny 30.00
133 Flash Gordon,Ph(c) 100.00
134 Popeye 45.00
135 Gene Autrey 60.00
136 Roy Rogers 60.00
137 Gifts from Santa 10.00
138 Fun at Christmas 10.00
139 Woody Woodpecker 15.00
140 Indian Chief 25.00
141 Oswald the Lucky Rabbit . . 12.00
142 Flash Gordon 80.00
143 Porky Pig 20.00
144 RsM,Ph(c),Tarzan 135.00

145 Tom and Jerry 15.00
146 Roy Rogers,Ph(c) 75.00
147 Henry 12.00
148 Popeye 35.00
149 Bugs Bunny 25.00
150 Gene Autrey 60.00
151 Roy Rogers 60.00
152 The Night Before Christmas 10.00
153 Merry Christmas 10.00
154 Tom and Jerry 15.00
155 Tarzan,Ph(c) 125.00
156 Oswald the Lucky Rabbit . . 12.00
157 Popeye 30.00
158 Woody Woodpecker 15.00
159 Indian Chief 20.00
160 Bugs Bunny 20.00
161 Roy Rogers 60.00
162 Henry 12.00
163 Rin Tin Tin 32.00
164 Porky Pig 15.00
165 The Lone Ranger 65.00
166 Santa & His Reindeer 10.00
167 Roy Rogers and Santa 60.00
168 Santa Claus' Workshop . . . 10.00
169 Popeye 30.00
170 Indian Chief 25.00
171 Oswald the Lucky Rabbit . . 20.00
172 Tarzan 100.00
173 Tom and Jerry 12.00
174 The Lone Ranger 60.00
175 Porky Pig 15.00
176 Roy Rogers 45.00
177 Woody Woodpecker 14.00
178 Henry 12.00
179 Bugs Bunny 20.00
180 Rin Tin Tin 25.00
181 Happy Holiday 10.00
182 Happi Tim 10.00
183 Welcome Santa 10.00
184 Woody Woodpecker 12.00
185 Tarzan, Ph(c) 100.00
186 Oswald the Lucky Rabbit . . 10.00
187 Indian Chief 25.00
188 Bugs Bunny 25.00
189 Henry 12.00
190 Tom and Jerry 13.00
191 Roy Rogers 45.00
192 Porky Pig 15.00
193 The Lone Ranger 50.00
194 Popeye 25.00
195 Rin Tin Tin 30.00
196 *Not Published*
197 Santa is Coming 10.00
198 Santa's Helper 10.00
199 Huckleberry Hound 50.00
200 Fury 30.00
201 Bugs Bunny 25.00
202 Space Explorer 50.00
203 Woody Woodpecker 10.00
204 Tarzan 55.00
205 Mighty Mouse 35.00
206 Roy Rogers,Ph(c) 45.00
207 Tom and Jerry 10.00
208 The Lone Ranger,Ph(c) . . . 90.00
209 Porky Pig 10.00
210 Lassie 30.00
211 *Not Published*
212 Christmas Eve 10.00
213 Here Comes Santa 10.00
214 Huckleberry Hound 50.00
215 Hi Yo Silver 35.00
216 Rocky & His Friends 75.00
217 Lassie 20.00
218 Porky Pig 15.00
219 Journey to the Sun 30.00

220 Bugs Bunny 20.00
221 Roy and Dale,Ph(c) 50.00
222 Woody Woodpecker 10.00
223 Tarzan 75.00
224 Tom and Jerry 10.00
225 The Lone Ranger 40.00
226 Christmas Treasury 10.00
227 *Not Published*
228 Letters to Santa 10.00
229 The Flintstones 100.00
230 Lassie 20.00
231 Bugs Bunny 20.00
232 The Three Stooges 75.00
233 Bullwinkle 75.00
234 Smokey the Bear 20.00
235 Huckleberry Hound 35.00
236 Roy and Dale 30.00
237 Mighty Mouse 20.00
238 The Lone Ranger 40.00
239 Woody Woodpecker 10.00
240 Tarzan 60.00
241 Santa Around the World . . . 10.00
242 Santa Toyland 10.00
243 The Flintstones 100.00
244 Mr.Ed,Ph(c) 25.00
245 Bugs Bunny 20.00
246 Popeye 20.00
247 Mighty Mouse 20.00
248 The Three Stooges 75.00
249 Woody Woodpecker 10.00
250 Roy and Dale 30.00
251 Little Lulu & Witch Hazel . . 100.00
252 P(c),Tarzan 45.00
253 Yogi Bear 25.00
254 Lassie 20.00
255 Santa's Christmas List 10.00
256 Christmas Party 10.00
257 Mighty Mouse 20.00
258 The Sword in the Stone
     (Disney Version) 50.00
259 Bugs Bunny 20.00
260 Mr. Ed 20.00
261 Woody Woodpecker 10.00
262 Tarzan 55.00
263 Donald Duck 75.00
264 Popeye 25.00
265 Yogi Bear 30.00
266 Lassie 18.00
267 Little Lulu 90.00
268 The Three Stooges 75.00
269 A Jolly Christmas 10.00
270 Santa's Little Helpers 10.00
271 The Flintstones 75.00
272 Tarzan 45.00
273 Bugs Bunny 20.00
274 Popeye 20.00
275 Little Lulu 75.00
276 The Jetsons 100.00
277 Daffy Duck 12.00
278 Lassie 18.00
279 Yogi Bear 30.00
280 Ph(c),The Three Stooges . . 75.00
281 Tom & Jerry 10.00
282 Mr. Ed 20.00
283 Santa's Visit 10.00
284 Christmas Parade 10.00
285 Astro Boy 25.00
286 Tarzan 40.00
287 Bugs Bunny 15.00
288 Daffy Duck 10.00
289 The Flintstones 65.00
290 Ph(c), Mr. Ed. 18.00
291 Yogi Bear 25.00
292 Ph(c), The Three Stooges . . 70.00
293 Little Lulu 55.00

294 Popeye 20.00	366 Tarzan 25.00	441 The Pink Panther 5.00
295 Tom & Jerry 10.00	367 Bugs Bunny & Porky Pig . . . 15.00	442 The Road Runner 5.00
296 Lassie 15.00	368 Scooby Doo 20.00	443 Baby Snoots 3.00
297 Christmas Bells 10.00	369 Little Lulu 20.00	444 Tom & Jerry 3.00
298 Santa's Sleigh 10.00	370 Ph(c), Lassie 10.00	445 Tweety & Sylvester 3.00
299 The Flintstones 60.00	371 Baby Snoots 9.00	446 Wacky Witch 2.00
300 Tarzan 40.00	372 Smokey The Bear 9.00	447 Mighty Mouse 3.00
301 Bugs Bunny 15.00	373 The Three Stooges 50.00	448 Cracky 2.00
302 Ph(c), Laurel & Hardy 30.00	374 Wacky Witch 8.00	449 The Pink Panther 3.00
303 Daffy Duck 10.00	375 Beep-Beep & Daffy Duck . . 10.00	450 Baby Snoots 3.00
304 Ph(c), The Three Stooges . . 70.00	376 The Pink Panther 15.00	451 Tom & Jerry 3.00
305 Tom & Jerry 10.00	377 Baby Snoots 9.00	452 Bugs Bunny 5.00
306 Ph(c), Daniel Boone 40.00	378 Turok, Son of Stone 95.00	453 Popeye 3.00
307 Little Lulu 45.00	379 Heckle & Jeckle 7.00	454 Woody Woodpecker 3.00
308 Ph(c), Lassie 15.00	380 Bugs Bunny & Yosemite Sam 15.00	455 The Road Runner 3.00
309 Yogi Bear 25.00	381 Lassie 9.00	456 Little Lulu 3.00
310 Ph(c) of Clayton Moore;	382 Scooby Doo 18.00	457 Tweety & Sylvester 3.00
The Lone Ranger 75.00	383 Smokey the Bear 7.00	458 Wacky Witch 2.00
311 Santa's Show 8.00	384 The Pink Panther 12.00	459 Mighty Mouse 3.00
312 Christmas Album 8.00	385 Little Lulu 15.00	460 Daffy Duck 3.00
313 Daffy Duck 9.00	386 Wacky Witch 7.00	461 The Pink Panther 3.00
314 Laurel & Hardy 25.00	387 Beep-Beep & Daffy Duck . . 8.00	462 Baby Snoots 2.00
315 Bugs Bunny 15.00	388 Tom & Jerry 8.00	463 Tom & Jerry 3.00
316 The Three Stooges 60.00	389 Little Lulu 15.00	464 Bugs Bunny 4.00
317 The Flintstones 30.00	390 The Pink Panther 12.00	465 Popeye 3.00
318 Tarzan 35.00	391 Scooby Doo 18.00	466 Woody Woodpecker 3.00
319 Yogi Bear 20.00	392 Bugs Bunny & Yosemite Sam 15.00	467 Underdog 8.00
320 Space Family Robinson . . 100.00	393 Heckle & Jeckle 6.00	468 Little Lulu 4.00
321 Tom & Jerry 9.00	394 Lassie 8.00	469 Tweety & Sylvester 3.00
322 The Lone Ranger 40.00	395 Woodsy the Owl 6.00	470 Wacky Witch 3.00
323 Little Lulu 30.00	396 Baby Snoots 6.00	471 Mighty Mouse 3.00
324 Ph(c), Lassie 12.00	397 Beep-Beep & Daffy Duck . . 7.00	472 Heckle & Jeckle 3.00
325 Fun With Santa 9.00	398 Wacky Witch 6.00	473 The Pink Panther 3.00
326 Christmas Story 9.00	399 Turok, Son of Stone 65.00	474 Baby Snoots 2.00
327 The Flintstones 55.00	400 Tom & Jerry 6.00	475 Little Lulu 3.00
328 Space Family Robinson . . . 55.00	401 Baby Snoots 6.00	476 Bugs Bunny 4.00
329 Bugs Bunny 15.00	402 Daffy Duck 6.00	477 Popeye 3.00
330 The Jetsons 75.00	403 Bugs Bunny 10.00	478 Woody Woodpecker 3.00
331 Daffy Duck 9.00	404 Space Family Robinson . . . 40.00	479 Underdog 7.00
332 Tarzan 35.00	405 Cracky 6.00	480 Tom & Jerry 8.00
333 Tom & Jerry 9.00	406 Little Lulu 15.00	481 Tweety & Sylvster 3.00
334 Lassie 10.00	407 Smokey the Bear 6.00	482 Wacky Witch 3.00
335 Little Lulu 25.00	408 Turok, Son of Stone 45.00	483 Mighty Mouse 3.00
336 The Three Stooges 55.00	409 The Pink Panther 10.00	484 Heckle & Jeckle 3.00
337 Yogi Bear 20.00	410 Wacky Witch 6.00	485 Baby Snoots 3.00
338 The Lone Ranger 35.00	411 Lassie 10.00	486 The Pink Panther 3.00
339 Not Published	412 New Terrytoons 4.00	487 Bugs Bunny 4.00
340 Here Comes Santa 9.00	413 Daffy Duck 4.00	488 April, 1982; Little Lulu 3.00
341 The Flintstones 55.00	414 Space Family Robinson . . . 35.00	
342 Tarzan 30.00	415 Bugs Bunny 10.00	
343 Bugs Bunny 15.00	416 The Road Runner 6.00	
344 Yogi Bear 23.00	417 Little Lulu 15.00	
345 Tom & Jerry 9.00	418 The Pink Panther 10.00	
346 Lassie 10.00	419 Baby Snoots 4.00	
347 Daffy Duck 9.00	420 Woody Woodpecker 4.00	
348 The Jetsons 65.00	421 Tweety & Sylvester 4.00	
349 Little Lulu 25.00	422 Wacky Witch 4.00	
350 The Lone Ranger 30.00	423 Little Monsters 4.00	
351 Beep-Beep, The	424 Cracky 4.00	
Road Runner 18.00	425 Daffy Duck 4.00	
352 Space Family Robinson . . . 75.00	426 Underdog 18.00	
353 Beep-Beep, The Road	427 Little Lulu 10.00	
Runner 18.00	428 Bugs Bunny 6.00	
354 Tarzan 25.00	429 The Pink Panther 6.00	
355 Little Lulu 25.00	430 The Road Runner 7.00	
356 Scooby Doo, Where Are You 22.00	431 Baby Snoots 4.00	
357 Daffy Duck & Porky Pig . . . 9.00	432 Lassie 5.00	
358 Lassie 10.00	433 Tweety & Sylvester 4.00	
359 Baby Snoots 10.00	434 Wacky Witch 4.00	
360 Ph(c), H.R. Pufnstuf 15.00	435 New Terrytoons 4.00	
361 Tom & Jerry 9.00	436 Cracky 4.00	
362 Smokey the Bear 11.00	437 Daffy Duck 4.00	
363 Bugs Bunny & Yosemite Sam 15.00	438 Underdog 10.00	
364 Ph(c), The Banana Splits . . 11.00	439 Little Lulu 10.00	
365 Tom & Jerry 9.00	440 Bugs Bunny 7.00	

Marge's Little Lulu #9
© Dell Publishing Co.

GOLDEN AGE

MARGE'S LITTLE LULU
Dell Publishing Co.
1 B:Lulu's Diary		600.00
2 I:Gloria,Miss Feeny		300.00
3		275.00
4		275.00
5		275.00
6		200.00
7 I:Annie,X-Mas Cover		200.00
8		200.00
9		200.00
10		200.00
11 thru 18		@175.00
19 I:Wilbur		175.00
20 I:Mr.McNabbem		175.00
21 thru 25		@150.00
26 rep.Four Color#110		150.00
27 thru 29		@150.00
30 Christmas cover		150.00
31 thru 34		@125.00
35 B:Mumday Story		125.00
36 thru 38		@125.00
39 I:Witch Hazel		150.00
40 Halloween Cover		125.00
41		125.00
42 Christmas Cover		125.00
43 Skiing Cover		125.00
44 Valentines Day Cover		125.00
45 2nd A:Witch Hazel		125.00
46 thru 60		@125.00
61		75.00
62		75.00
63 I:Chubby		75.00
64 thru 67		@75.00
68 I:Professor Cleff		75.00
69 thru 77		@75.00
78 Christmas Cover		75.00
79		75.00
80		75.00
81 thru 89		@60.00
90 Christmas Cover		60.00
91 thru 99		@60.00
100		75.00
101 thru 122		@60.00
123 I:Fifi		50.00
124 thru 164		@40.00
165 giant sized		150.00
166 giant sized		150.00
167 thru 169		@35.00
170		15.00
171		15.00
172		18.00
173		15.00
174		15.00
175		18.00
176		18.00
177		15.00
178 thru 196		@18.00
197		15.00
198 thru 200		@18.00
201		8.00
202		12.00
203		8.00
204		12.00
205		12.00
206		8.00

MARMADUKE MOUSE
Quality Comics Group
(Arnold Publications)
Spring, 1946
1 Funny Animal		75.00
2 Funny Animal		32.00
3 thru 8 Funny Animal		@25.00

9 Funny Animal		22.00
10 Funny Animal		22.00
11 thru 20 Funny Animal		@20.00
21 thru 30 Funny Animal		@18.00
31 thru 40 Funny Animal		@15.00
41 thru 50 Funny Animal		@12.00
51 thru 65 Funny Animal		@10.00

MARTIN KANE
Hero Books
(Fox Features syndicate)
June, 1950
1 WW,WW-(c)		200.00
2 WW,JO, Auguat, 1950		150.00

Marvel Family #9
© *Fawcett Publications*

MARVEL FAMILY, THE
Fawcett Publications
December, 1945
1 O:Captain Marvel,Captain Marvel Jr., Mary Marvel,Uncle Marvel; V:Black Adam		1,200.00
2		550.00
3		400.00
4 The Witch's Tale		325.00
5 Civilization of a Prehistoric Race		300.00
6		275.00
7 The Rock of Eternity		250.00
8 The Marvel Family Round Table		250.00
9 V: The Last Vikings		250.00
10 V: The Sivana Family		250.00
11 V: The Well of Evil		225.00
12 V: The Iron Horseman		225.00
13		225.00
14 Captain Marvel Invalid		225.00
15 V: Mr. Triangle		200.00
16 World's Mightiest Quarrell		200.00
17		200.00
18		200.00
19 V: The Monster Menace		200.00
20 The Marvel Family Feud		200.00
21 V: The Trio of Terror		160.00
22 V: The Triple Threat		160.00
23 March of Independence (c)		175.00
24 V: The Fighting Xergos		160.00
25 Trial of the Marvel Family		160.00

26 V: Mr. Power		150.00
27 V: The Amoeba Men		150.00
28		150.00
29 V: The Monarch of Money		150.00
30 A:World's Greatest Magician		150.00
31 V:Sivana & The Great Hunger		125.00
32 The Marvel Family Goes Into Buisness		125.00
33 I: The Hermit Family		125.00
34 V: Sivana's Miniature Menace		125.00
35 V: The Berzerk Machines		125.00
36 V: The Invaders From Infinity		125.00
37 V: The Earth Changer		125.00
38 V: Sivana's Instinct Exterminator Gun		125.00
39 The Legend of Atlantis		125.00
40 Seven Wonders of the Modern World		125.00
41 The Great Oxygen Theft		125.00
42 V: The Endless Menace		100.00
43		100.00
44 V: The Rust That Menaced the World		100.00
45 The Hoax City		100.00
46 The Day Civilization Vanished		100.00
47 V: The Interplanetary Thieves		150.00
48 V: The Four Horsemen		100.00
49 ...Proves Human Hardness		100.00
50 The Speech Scrambler Machine		100.00
51 The Living Statues		120.00
52 The School of Witches		100.00
53 V: The Man Who Changed the World		100.00
54		100.00
55		100.00
56 The World's Mightiest Project		100.00
57		100.00
58 The Triple Time Plot		100.00
59		100.00
60		100.00
61		90.00
62		90.00
63 V: The Pirate Planet		90.00
64		90.00
65		90.00
66 The Miracle Stone		90.00
67		90.00
68		90.00
69 V: The Menace of Old Age		90.00
70 V: The Crusade of Evil		90.00
71		90.00
72		90.00
73		90.00
74		90.00
75 The Great Space Struggle		90.00
76		125.00
77 Anti-Communist		150.00
78 V: The Red Vulture		125.00
79		90.00
80		90.00
81		90.00
82		90.00
83 V: The Flying Skull		90.00
84 thru 87		@90.00
88 Jokes of Jeopardy		90.00
89 And Then There Were None; January, 1954		90.00

MARVELS OF SCIENCE
Charlton Comics
March, 1946
1 1st Charlton Book; Atomic Bomb Story		125.00
2		75.00

3 . . . . 75.00
4 President Truman(c); Jun.'6 . 75.00

MARY MARVEL COMICS
Fawcett Publications/
Charlton Comics
December, 1945

1 Intro: Mary Marvel 1,300.00
2 . . . . 600.00
3 . . . . 400.00
4 On a Leave of Absence . . . 350.00
5 Butterfly (c) 250.00
6 A:Freckles,Teenager of
    Mischief 250.00
7 The Kingdom Undersea . . . 250.00
8 Holiday Special Issue 250.00
9 Air Race (c) 225.00
10 A: Freckles 225.00
11 A: The Sad Dryads 175.00
12 Red Cross Appeal on(c) . . . 175.00
13 Keep the Homefires Burning 175.00
14 Meets Ghosts (c) 175.00

Mary Marvel #15 © Fawcett
Publications/Charlton Comics

15 A: Freckles 175.00
16 The Jukebox Menace 150.00
17 Aunt Agatha's Adventures . . 150.00
18 . . . . 150.00
19 Witch (c) 150.00
20 . . . . 150.00
21 V: Dice Head 125.00
22 The Silver Slippers 125.00
23 The Pendulum Strikes 125.00
24 V: The Nightowl 125.00
25 A: Freckles 125.00
26 A:Freckles dressed as Clown 125.00
27 The Floating Oceanliner . . . 125.00
28 September, 1948 . . . . 125.00
Becomes:
MONTE HALE WESTERN
29 Ph(c),B:Monte Hale & His
    Horse Pardner 350.00
30 Ph(c),B:Big Bow-Little
    Arrow; CCB,Captain Tootsie 225.00
31 Ph(c),Giant 175.00
32 Ph(c),Giant 175.00
33 Ph(c),Giant 175.00
34 Ph(c),E:Big Bow-Little
    Arrow;B:Gabby Hayes,Giant 175.00

35 Ph(c),Gabby Hayes, Giant . 175.00
36 Ph(c),Gabby Hayes, Giant . 175.00
37 Ph(c),Gabby Hayes 125.00
38 Ph(c),Gabby Hayes, Giant . 150.00
39 Ph(c);CCB, Captain Tootsie;
    Gabby Hayes, Giant 150.00
40 Ph(c),Gabby Hayes, Giant . 150.00
41 Ph(c),Gabby Hayes 75.00
42 Ph(c),Gabby Hayes, Giant . 90.00
43 Ph(c),Gabby Hayes, Giant . 90.00
44 Ph(c),Gabby Hayes, Giant . 90.00
45 Ph(c),Gabby Hayes 75.00
46 Ph(c),Gabby Hayes, Giant . 75.00
47 Ph(c),A:Big Bow-Little Arrow;
    Gabby Hayes, Giant 75.00
48 Ph(c),Gabby Hayes, Giant . 75.00
49 Ph(c),Gabby Hayes 75.00
50 Ph(c),Gabby Hayes, Giant . 75.00
51 Ph(c),Gabby Hayes, Giant . 70.00
52 Ph(c),Gabby Hayes, Giant . 70.00
53 Ph(c),A:Slim Pickens;
    Gabby Hayes 50.00
54 Ph(c),Gabby Hayes, Giant . 70.00
55 Ph(c),Gabby Hayes, Giant . 70.00
56 Ph(c),Gabby Hayes, Giant . 70.00
57 Ph(c),Gabby Hayes 50.00
58 Ph(c),Gabby Hayes, Giant . 60.00
59 Ph(c),Gabby Hayes, Giant . 60.00
60 thru 79 Ph(c),Gabby Hayes @45.00
80 Ph(c),E: Gabby Hayes 45.00
81 Ph(c) 45.00
82 Final Ph(c), Last Fawcett
    Edition 45.00
83 1st Charlton Edition, R:G.
    Hayes Back B&W Ph(c) 45.00
84 . . . . 45.00
85 . . . . 42.00
86 E: Gabby Hayes 42.00
87 . . . . 42.00
88 January, 1956 . . . . 42.00

MASK COMICS
Rural Home Publications
February-March, 1945

1 LbC,LbC-(c), Evil (c) 1,800.00
2 LbC-(c),A:Black Rider,The
    Collector The Boy Magician;
    Apr-May'45, Devil (c) 1,100.00

MASKED MARVEL
Centaur Publications
September, 1940

1 I: The Masked Marvel . . . 1,300.00
2 PG, ... 900.00
3 December, 1940 . . . . 850.00

MASKED RANGER
Premier Magazines
April, 1954

1 FF,O&B:The Masked Ranger,
    Streak the Horse,The
    Crimson Avenger 250.00
2 . . . . 75.00
3 . . . . 75.00
4 B: Jessie James,Billy the Kid,
    Wild Bill Hickock,
    Jim Bowie's Life Story 90.00
5 . . . . 90.00
6 . . . . 90.00
7 . . . . 90.00
8 . . . . 90.00
9 AT,E:All Features; A:Wyatt
    Earp August, 1955 . . . . . 100.00

MASTER COMICS
Fawcett Publications
March, 1940
1-6 Oversized,7-Normal Format

1 O:Master Man; B:The Devil's
    Dagger, El Carin-Master of
    Magic, Rick O'Say, Morton
    Murch, White Rajah, Shipwreck
    Roberts, Frontier Marshall,
    Mr. Clue, Streak Sloan . . . 7,000.00
2 Master Man (c) 1,800.00
3 Master Man (c) Bondage . 1,500.00
4 Master Man (c) 1,400.00
5 Master Man (c) 1,400.00
6 E: All Above Features . . . 1,500.00
7 B:Bulletman,Zorro,The Mystery
    Man, Lee Granger, Jungle
    King,Buck Jones 2,200.00
8 B:The Red Gaucho,Captain
    Venture, Planet Princess . 1,200.00
9 Bulletman & Steam Roller . . 900.00
10 E: Lee Granger 900.00

Master Comics #7
© Fawcett Publications

11 O: Minute Man 2,000.00
12 Minute Man (c) 1,100.00
13 O:Bulletgirl; E:Red Gaucho 1,600.00
14 B: The Companions Three . 800.00
15 MRa, Bulletman & Girl (c) . . 800.00
16 MRa, Minute Man (c) 800.00
17 B:MRa on Bulletman 750.00
18 MRa, ... 750.00
19 MRa, Bulletman & Girl (c) . . 750.00
20 MRa,C:Cap.Marvel-Bulletman 750.00
21 MRa-(c),Capt. Marvel in
    Bulletman,I&O:CaptainNazi 4,500.00
22 MRa-(c),E:Mystery Man,Captain
    Venture; Bondage(c);Capt.
    Marvel Jr. X-Over In
    Bulletman; A:Capt. Nazi . 4,000.00
23 MRa,MRa(c),B:Capt.
    Marvel V:Capt. Nazi . . 2,200.00
24 MRa,MRa(c),Death By Radio 775.00
25 MRa,MRa(c),The Jap
    Invasion 775.00
26 MRa,MRa(c),Capt. Marvel Jr.
    Avenges Pearl Harbor 700.00
27 MRa.MRa(c),V For Victory(c) 700.00
28 MRa,MRa(c)Liberty Bell(c) . 700.00

29 MRa,MRa(c),Hitler &
  Hirohito(c) 700.00
30 MRa,MRa(c),Flag (c);Capt.
  Marvel Jr, V: Capt. Nazi . . . 700.00
31 MRa,MRa(c),E:Companions
  Three,Capt.Marvel Jr,
  V:Mad Dr. Macabre 500.00
32 MRa,MRa(c),E: Buck Jones;
  CMJr Strikes Terror Castle . 500.00
33 MRa,MRa(c),B:Balbo the Boy
  Magician, Hopalong Cassidy 500.00
34 MRa,MRa(c),Capt.Marvel Jr
  V: Capt.Nazi 500.00
35 MRa,MRa(c),CMJr Defies
  the Flame 500.00
36 MRa,MRa(c),Statue Of
  Liberty(c) 500.00
37 MRa,MRa(c),CMJr Blasts
  the Nazi Raiders 450.00
38 MRa,MRa(c),CMJr V:
  the Japs 450.00
39 MRa,MRa(c),CMJr Blasts
  Nazi Slave Ship 450.00
40 MRa,MRa(c),Flag (c) 450.00
41 MRa,MRa(c),Bulletman,Bulletgirl,
  CMJr X-Over In Minuteman . 500.00
42 MRa,MRa(c),CMJr V: Hitler's
  Dream Soldier 300.00
43 MRa(c),CMJr Battles For
  Stalingrad 300.00
44 MRa(c),CMJr In Crystal City
  of the Peculiar Penguins . . . 300.00
45 MRa(c), ... 300.00
46 MRa(c) 300.00
47 MRa(c),A:Hitler; E: Balbo . . 325.00
48 MRa(c),I:Bulletboy;Capt.
  Marvel A: in Minuteman . . . 350.00
49 MRa(c),E: Hopalong Cassidy,
  Minuteman 300.00
50 I&O: Radar,A:Capt. Marvel,
  B:Nyoka the Jungle Girl . . . 250.00
51 MRa(c),CMJr V: Japanese . 175.00
52 MRa(c),CMJr & Radar Pitch
  War Stamps on (c) 175.00
53 CMJR V: Dr. Sivana 175.00
54 MRa(c),Capt.Marvel Jr
  Your Pin-Up Buddy 175.00
55 . . . . 175.00
56 MRa(c) 150.00
57 CMJr V: Dr. Sivana 150.00
58 MRA,MRa(c), ... 150.00
59 MRa(c),A:The Upside
  Downies 165.00
60 MRa(c) 165.00
61 CMJr Meets Uncle Marvel . . 165.00
62 Uncle Sam on (c) 165.00
63 W/ Radar (c) 125.00
64 W/ Radar (c) 125.00
65 . . . . 125.00
66 CMJr & Secret Of the Sphinx 125.00
67 Knight (c) 125.00
68 CMJr in the Range of
  the Beasts 125.00
69 . . . . 125.00
70 . . . . 125.00
71 CMJr,V:Man in Metal Mask . 110.00
72 CMJr V: Sivana & The Whistle
  That Wouldn't Stop 110.00
73 CMJr V: The Ghost of Evil . 110.00
74 CMJr & The Fountain of Age 110.00
75 CMJr V: The Zombie Master 110.00
76 . . . . 110.00
77 Pirate Treasure (c) 110.00
78 CMJr in Death on the Scenic
  Railway 110.00

79 CMJr V: The Black Shroud . 110.00
80 CMJr-The Land of Backwards 110.00
81 CMJr & The Voyage 'Round
  the Horn 100.00
82 CMJr,IN,Death at the
  Launching 100.00
83 . . . . 100.00
84 CMJr V: The Human Magnet 100.00
85 CMJr-Crime on the Campus . 100.00
86 CMJr & The City of Machines 100.00
87 CMJr & The Root of Evil . . . 100.00
88 CMJr V: The Wreckers;
  B: Hopalong Cassidy 100.00
89 . . . . 100.00
90 CMJr V: The Caveman . . . 100.00
91 CMJr V: The Blockmen 100.00
92 CMJr V: The Space Slavers 100.00
93 BK,CMJr,V:TheGrowingGiant 125.00
94 E: Hopalong Cassidy 100.00
95 B: Tom Mix; CMJr Meets
  the Skyhawk 100.00
96 CMJr Meets the Worlds
  Mightiest Horse 100.00

Master Comics #32
© Fawcett Publications

97 CMJr Faces the Doubting
  Thomas 100.00
98 KKK Type 100.00
99 Witch (c) 100.00
100 CMJr V: The Ghost Ship . . 120.00
101 thru 105 . . . . @100.00
106 E: Bulletman 100.00
107 CMJr Faces the Disappearance
  of the Statue of Liberty 100.00
108 . . . . 80.00
109 . . . . 80.00
110 CMJr & The Hidden Death . 80.00
111 thru 122 . . . . @80.00
123 CMJr V: The Flying
  Desperado 80.00
124 . . . . 80.00
125 CMJr & The Bed of Mystery 80.00
126 thru 131 . . . . @80.00
132 V: Migs 90.00
133 E: Tom Mix; April, 1953 . . 100.00

MD
E.C. Comics
April 1955-Jan. 1956
1 RC,GE,Grl,JO,JCr(c) 90.00

2 RC,GE,Grl,JO,JCr(c) 75.00
3 RC,GE,Grl,JO,JCr(c) 75.00
4 RC,GE,Grl,JO,JCr(c) 75.00
5 RC,GE,Grl,JO,JCr(c) 75.00

MEDAL OF
HONOR COMICS
Stafford Publication
Spring, 1947
1 True Stories of Medal of Honor
  Recipants 55.00

MEET CORLISS
ARCHER
Fox Features Syndicate
March, 1948
1 AF,AF(c), Teenage 425.00
2 AF(c) 350.00
3 . . . . 275.00

My Life #10 © Fox Features Syndicate

Becomes:

MY LIFE
4 JKa,AF, ... 200.00
5 JKa, ... 125.00
6 JKa,AF, ... 125.00
7 Watercolor&Ink Drawing on(c) 75.00
8 . . . . 50.00
9 . . . . 50.00
10 WW, July, 1950 . . . . 85.00

MEET MERTON
Toby Press
December, 1953
1 Dave Berg-a,Teen Stories . . . 30.00
2 Dave Berg-a 15.00
3 Dave Berg-a 12.00
4 Dave Berg-a; June, 1954 . . . 12.00

MEET THE NEW
POST GAZETTE
SUNDAY FUNNIES
Pitsberg Post Gazette
N# One Shot Insert F: Several
  Syndicated Characters in Stories
  Exclusive to This Edition . . . 750.00

GOLDEN AGE

MEL ALLEN
SPORTS COMICS
Visual Editions
1949
1 GT 175.00
2 Lou Gehrig 125.00

MEN AGAINST CRIME
(see HAND OF FATE)

MERRY-GO-ROUND
COMICS
LaSalle/Croyden/
Rotary Litho.
1944
1 LaSalle Publications Edition . 100.00
1a 1946, Croyden Edition 35.00
1b Sept-Oct.'47,Rotary Litho Ed 50.00
2 . . . . 50.00

MERRY MOUSE
Avon Periodicals
June, 1953
1 (fa),F. Carin (c)&a 35.00
2 (fa),F. Carin (c)&a 20.00
3 (fa),F. Carin (c)&a 20.00
4 (fa),F. Carin (c)&a;Jan.'54 . . 20.00

METEOR COMICS
Croyden Publications
November, 1945
1 Captain Wizard & Baldy Bean 250.00

MICKEY FINN
Eastern Color/
Columbia Comics Group
1942
1 . . . . 225.00
2 . . . . 125.00
3 A: Charlie Chan 75.00
4 . . . . 60.00
5 thru 9 . . . . @40.00
10 thru 15 . . . . @30.00

(WALT DISNEY'S)
MICKEY MOUSE
Dell Publishing Co.
December 1952
#1-#27 Dell Four Color
28 . . . . 40.00
29 . . . . 35.00
30 . . . . 35.00
31 . . . . 35.00
32 thru 34 . . . . @35.00
35 thru 50 . . . . @25.00
51 thru 73 . . . . @15.00
74 . . . . 20.00
75 thru 99 . . . . @15.00
100 thru 105 rep. . . . . @20.00
106 thru 120 . . . . @15.00
121 thru 130 . . . . @10.00
131 thru 146 . . . . @10.00
147 rep,Phantom Fires 15.00
148 rep. 15.00
149 thru 158 . . . . @8.00
159 rep. 12.00
160 thru 170 . . . . @7.00
171 thru 199 . . . . @3.00
200 rep. 5.00
201 thru 218 . . . . @3.00
See: Independent Color Comics

MICKEY MOUSE MAGAZINE
Kay Kamen
1 (1933) scarce 3,200.00
2 . . . . 1,000.00
3 thru 8 . . . . @950.00
9 . . . . 900.00

MICKEY MOUSE MAGAZINE
Kay Kamen
1 digest size (1933) 1,200.00
2 dairy give-away promo(1933) 400.00
3 dairy give-away promo(1934) 350.00
4 dairy give-away promo(1934) 350.00
5 dairy give-away promo(1934) 350.00
6 dairy give-away promo(1934) 350.00
7 dairy give-away promo(1934) 350.00
8 dairy give-away promo(1934) 350.00
9 dairy give-away promo(1934) 350.00
10 dairy give-away promo(1934) 350.00
11 dairy give-awaypromo(1934) 350.00
12 dairy give-awaypromo(1934) 350.00
Volume II
1 dairy give-away promo(1934) 250.00
2 dairy give-away promo(1934) 250.00
3 dairy give-away promo(1935) 250.00
4 dairy give-away promo(1935) 250.00
5 dairy give-away promo(1935) 250.00
6 dairy give-away promo(1935) 250.00
7 dairy give-away promo(1935) 250.00
8 dairy give-away promo(1935) 250.00
9 dairy give-away promo(1935) 250.00
10 dairy give-awaypromo(1935) 250.00
11 dairy give-awaypromo(1935) 250.00
12 dairy give-awaypromo(1935) 250.00

Mickey Mouse Magazine #9
© Kay Kamen

MICKEY MOUSE MAGAZINE
K.K. Pub./Westen Pub
1 (1935) 13¼"x10¼" 12,000.00
2 . . . . 1100.00
3 . . . . 600.00
4 . . . . 600.00
5 (1936) Donald Duck solo . . . 700.00
6 Donald Duck editor 600.00
7 . . . . 600.00
8 Donald Duck solo 600.00
9 . . . . 600.00
10 . . . . 600.00
11 Mickey Mouse, editor 550.00

12 . . . . 550.00
Volume II
1 . . . . 550.00
2 . . . . 550.00
3 Christmas issue, 100pg . . . 2,500.00
4 (1937) Roy Ranger adv.strip 500.00
5 Ted True strip 400.00
6 Mickey Mouse cut-outs 375.00
7 Mickey Mouse cut-outs 375.00
8 Mickey Mouse cut-outs 375.00
9 Mickey Mouse cut-outs 375.00
10 Full color 550.00
11 . . . . 400.00
12 Hiawatha 400.00
13 . . . . 400.00
Volume III
2 Big Bad Wolf (c) 450.00
3 First Snow White 750.00
4 (1938) Snow White 600.00
5 Snow White (c) 700.00
6 Snow White ends 500.00
7 7 Dwarfs Easter (c) 375.00
8 . . . . 350.00
9 Dopey(c) 350.00
10 Goofy(c) 350.00
11 Mickey Mouse Sheriff 350.00
12 A:Snow White 350.00
Volume IV
1 Practile Pig 350.00
2 I:Huey,Louis & Dewey(c) . . . 400.00
3 Ferdinand the Bull 350.00
4 (1939),B:Spotty 325.00
5 Pluto solo 350.00
7 Ugly Duckling 325.00
7a Goofy & Wilber 350.00
8 Big Bad Wolf(c) 350.00
9 The Pointer 350.00
10 July 4th 450.00
11 . . . . 300.00
12 Donald's Penguin 400.00
Volume V
1 Black Pete 400.00
2 Goofy(c) 600.00
3 Pinochio 600.00
4 (1940) 350.00
5 Jimmy Crickett(c) 375.00
6 Tugboat Mickey 375.00
7 Huey, Louis & Dewey(c) . . . 400.00
8 Figaro & Cleo 375.00
9 Donald(c),J.Crickett 450.00
10 July 4th 425.00
11 Mickey's Tailor 450.00
12 Change of format 3,500.00
{becomes:
Walt Disney Comics & Stories}

MICKEY MOUSE
Whitman
904 W.Disney's Mickey Mouse
 and his friends (1934) 1,100.00
948 Disney'sMickeyMouse('34) 1,100.00

MIDGET COMICS
St. John Publishing Co.
February, 1950
1 MB(c),Fighting Indian Stories 80.00
2 April, 1950;Tex West-Cowboy
 Marshall 40.00

MIGHTY ATOM, THE
(see PIXIES)

MIGHTY MIDGET COMICS
Samuel E. Lowe & Co.
1942-43
4"x5" Format

1 Bulletman	125.00
2 Captain Marvel	125.00
3 Captain Marvel Jr.	100.00
4 Golden Arrow	100.00
5 Ibis the Invincible	100.00
6 Spy Smasher	100.00
7 Balbo, The Boy magician . . .	40.00
8 Bulletman	75.00
9 Commando Yank	50.00
10 Dr. Voltz, The Human Generator	40.00
11 Lance O'Casey	40.00
12 Leatherneck the Marine	40.00
13 Minute Man	75.00
14 Mister Q	40.00
15 Mr. Scarlet & Pinky	60.00
16 Pat Wilson & His Flying Fortress	40.00
17 Phantom Eagle	50.00
18 State Trooper Stops Crime . .	40.00
19 Tornado Tom	40.00

MIGHTY MOUSE
Fall, 1946
[1st Series]

1 Terytoons Presents	850.00
2	400.00
3	275.00
4 Summer, 1947	275.00

MIGHTY MOUSE
St. John Publishing
August, 1947

5	275.00
6 thru 10	@150.00
11 thru 20	@100.00
21 thru 25	@75.00
26 thru 30	@60.00
31 thru 34	@50.00
35 Flying Saucer	65.00
36	50.00
37	50.00
38 thru 45 Giant 100 pgs . . .	@150.00
46 thru 66	@40.00
67 P(c), ...	40.00

Pines

68 thru 81 Funny Animal	@25.00
82 Infinity (c)	25.00
83 June, 1959	25.00

MIGHTY MOUSE ADVENTURE STORIES
St. John Publishing Co.
1953

N# 384 Pages,Rebound	350.00

MIKE BARNETT, MAN AGAINST CRIME
Fawcett Publications
December, 1951

1 The Mint of Dionysosi	100.00
2 Mystery of the Blue Madonna	75.00
3 Revenge Holds the Torch . . .	50.00
4 Special Delivery	50.00
5 Market For Morphine	75.00
6 October, 1952	50.00

MILITARY COMICS
Comics Magazines
(Quality Comics Group)
August, 1941

1 JCo,CCu,FG,BP,WE(c),O:Blackhawk, Miss America, Death Patrol, Blue Tracer; B:X of the Underground, Yankee Eagle,Q-Boat, Shot & Shell, Archie Atkins, Loops & Banks	8,000.00
2 JCo,FG,BP,CCu,CCu(c),B: Secret War News	2,000.00
3 JCo,FG,BP,AMc,CCu,CCu(c), I&O:Chop Chop	1,800.00
4 FG,BP,AMc,CCu,CCu(c), .	1,400.00
5 FG,BP,AMc,CCu,CCu(c), B: The Sniper	1,200.00
6 FG,BP,AMc,CCu,CCu(c) . .	900.00
7 FG,BP,AMc,CCu,CCu(c) E:Death Patrol	900.00
8 FG,BP,AMc,CCu,CCu(c) . .	900.00
9 FG,BP,AMc,CCu,CCu(c), B: The Phantom Clipper . .	900.00
10 FG,BP,CCu,AMc,WE(c) . .	1,000.00
11 FG,BP,CCu,AMc, WE(c),Flag(c)	750.00
12 FG,BP,AMc,RC,RC(c) . . .	900.00
13 FG,BP,AMc,RC,RC(c),E:X of the Underground	700.00
14 FG,AMc,RC,RC(c),B:Private Dogtag	700.00
15 FG,AMc,RC,RC(c), ...	700.00
16 FG,AMc,RC,RC(c),E:The Phantom Clipper,Blue Tracer	600.00
17 FG,AMc,RC,RC(c), B:P.T. Boat	600.00
18 FG,AMc,RC,RC(c), V: The Thunderer	600.00
19 FG,RC,RC(c), V:King Cobra	600.00
20 GFx,RC,RC(c), Death Patrol	600.00
21 FG,GFx	550.00
22 FG,GFx	550.00
23 FG,GFx	550.00
24 FG,GFx,V: Man-Heavy Glasses	550.00
25 FG,GFx,V: Wang The Tiger	550.00
26 FG,GFx,V: Skull	500.00
27 FG,JCo,R:The Death Patrol	500.00
28 FG,JCo, Dungeon of Doom .	500.00
29 FG,JCo,V: Xanukhara	500.00
30 FG,JCo,BWa,BWa(c),B.Hwk V: Dr. Koro	500.00
31 FG,JCo,BWa,E:Death Patrol; I: Captain Hitsu . .	500.00
32 JCo,A: Captain Hitsu	450.00
33 W/ Civil War Veteran	450.00
34 A: Eve Rice	450.00
35 Shipwreck Island	450.00
36 Cult of the Wailing Tiger . .	450.00
37 Pass of Bloody Peace	450.00
38 B.Hwk Faces Bloody Death	450.00
39 A: Kwan Yin	450.00
40 V: Ratru	425.00
41 W/ Chop Chop (c)	425.00
42 V: Jap Mata Hari	425.00
43	425.00

Becomes:
MODERN COMICS

44 Duel of Honor	450.00
45 V: Sakyo the Madman	350.00
46 RC, Soldiers of Fortune . . .	350.00
47 RC,PG,V:Count Hokoy	350.00
48 RC,PG,V:Pirates of Perool .	350.00
49 RC,PG,I:Fear,Lady Adventuress	350.00
50 RC,PG	350.00
51 RC,PG, Ancient City of Evil .	300.00
52 PG,BWa,V: The Vulture . . .	300.00
53 PG,BWa,B: Torchy	350.00
54 PG,RC,RC/CCu,BWa	275.00
55 PG,RC,RC/CCu,BWa	275.00
56 PG,RC/CCu,BWa	275.00
57 PG,RC/CCu,BWa	275.00
58 PG,RC,RC/CCu,BWa, V:The Grabber	275.00
59 PG,RC/CCu,BWa	275.00
60 PG,RC/CCu,BWa,RC(c), V:Green Plague	275.00
61 PG,RC/CCu,BWa,RC(c) . . .	275.00
62 PG,RC/CCu,BWa,RC(c) . . .	275.00
63 PG,RC/CCu,BWa,RC(c) . . .	250.00
64 PG,RC/CCu,BWa,RC(c) . . .	250.00
65 PG,RC/CCu,BWa,RC(c) . . .	250.00
66 PG,RC/CCu,BWa	250.00
67 PG,RC/CCu,BWa,RC(c) . . .	250.00
68 PG,RC/CCu,BWa,RC(c); I:Madame Butterfly	250.00
69 PG,RC/CCu,BWa,RC(c) . . .	250.00
70 PG,RC/CCu,BWa,RC(c) . . .	250.00
71 PG,RC/CCu,BWa,RC(c) . . .	250.00
72 PG,RC/CCu,BWa,RC(c) . . .	225.00
73 PG,RC/CCu,BWa,RC(c) . . .	225.00
74 PG,RC/CCu,BWa,RC(c) . . .	225.00
75 PG,RC/CCu,BWa,RC(c) . . .	225.00
76 PG,RC/CCu,BWa,RC(c) . . .	225.00
77 PG,RC/CCu,BWa,RC(c) . . .	225.00
78 PG,RC/CCu,BWa,JCo,RC(c)	250.00
79 PG,RC/CCu,BWa,JCo,RC(c)	225.00
80 PG,RC/CCu,BWa,JCo,RC(c)	225.00
81 PG,RC/CCu,BWa,JCo,RC(c)	225.00
82 PG,RC/CCu,BWa,JCo,RC(c)	225.00
83 PG,RC/CCu,BWa,JCo,RC(c); E: Private Dogtag	225.00
84 PG,RC/CCu,BWa,RC(c) . . .	225.00
85 PG,RC/CCu,BWa,RC(c) . . .	225.00
86 PG,RC/CCu,BWa,RC(c) . . .	225.00
87 PG,RC/CCu,BWa,RC(c) . . .	225.00
88 PG,RC/CCu,BWa,RC(c) . . .	225.00
89 PG,RC/CCu,BWa,RC(c) . . .	225.00
90 PG,RC/CCu,GFx,RC(c) . . .	225.00
91 RC/CCu,GFx,RC(c)	225.00
92 RC/CCu,GFx,RC(c)	225.00

Modern Comics #57
© Quality Comics Group

GOLDEN AGE

GOLDEN AGE

93 RC/CCu,GFx,RC(c) 225.00
94 RC/CCu,GFx,RC(c) 225.00
95 RC/CCu,GFx,RC(c) 225.00
96 RC/CCu,GFx,RC/CCu(c) . . . 225.00
97 RC/CCu,GFx,RC/CCu(c) . . . 225.00
98 RC/CCu,GFx,RC/CCu(c) . . . 225.00
99 RC/CCu,GFx,JCo,RC/CCu(c) 225.00
100 GFx,JCo,RC/CCu(c) 225.00
101 GFx,JCo,RC/CCu(c) 225.00
102 GFx,JCo,WE,BWa,
    RC/CCu(c) 250.00

MILT GROSS FUNNIES
Milt Gross, Inc.
August, 1947
1 Gag Oriented Caricature 50.00
2 Gag Oriented Caricature . . . 45.00

MINUTE MAN
Fawcett Publications
Summer, 1941
1 V: The Nazis 1,200.00
2 V: The Mongol Horde 800.00
3 V: The Black Poet;Spr'42 . . 750.00

MIRACLE COMICS
Hillman Periodicals
February,1940
1 B:Sky Wizard,Master of Space,
    Dash Dixon,Man of Might,Dusty
    Doyle,Pinkie Parker, The Kid
    Cop,K-7 Secret Agent,Scorpion
    & Blandu,Jungle Queen . . 1,300.00
2 . . . . 600.00
3 B:Bill Colt,The Ghost Rider . 650.00
4 A:The Veiled Prophet,
    Bullet Bob; Mar'41 . . . . 600.00

MISS CAIRO JONES
Croyden Publishers
1944
1 BO,Rep. Newspaper Strip . 150.00

MR. ANTHONY'S
LOVE CLINIC
Hillman Periodicals
1945
1 Ph(c) 75.00
2 . . . . 50.00
3 . . . . 40.00
4 . . . . 40.00
5 Ph(c),Apr/May'50 . . . . 40.00

MR. MUSCLES
(see THING, THE)

MISTER MYSTERY
Media Publ./SPM Publ./
Aragon Publ.
September, 1951
1 HK,RA,Horror 550.00
2 RA,RA(c) 350.00
3 RA(c) 350.00
4 Bondage(c) 350.00
5 Lingerie(c) 300.00
6 Bondage(c) 350.00
7 BW,Bondage(c);The Brain
    Bats of Venus 750.00
8 Lingerie(c) 300.00
9 HN 275.00
10 . . . . 275.00
11 BW,Robot Woman 500.00

12 Flaming Object to Eye (c) . . 750.00
13 . . . . 200.00
14 . . . . 200.00
15 The Coffin & Medusa's Head 225.00
16 Bondage(c) 225.00
17 . . . . 200.00
18 BW,Bondage(c) 400.00

MISTER RISK
(see HAND OF FATE)

Mister Universe #1
© Mr. Publ./Media Publ.

MISTER UNIVERSE
Mr. Publ./Media Publ./
Stanmore
July, 1951
1 . . . . 120.00
2 RA(c);Jungle That time Forgot 100.00
3 Marijuana Story 80.00
4 Mr. Universe Goes to War . . . 45.00
5 Mr. Universe Goes to War;
    April, 1952 . . . . 45.00

MODERN COMICS
(see MILITARY COMICS)

MODERN LOVE
Tiny Tot Comics
(E.C. Comics)
June-July, 1949
1 Stolen Romance 450.00
2 JcR,AF(c),I Craved
    Excitement 350.00
3 AF(c);Our Families Clashed 300.00
4 AF(c);I Was a B Girl 400.00
5 AF(c);Saved From Shame . 400.00
6 AF(c);The Love That
    Might Have Been 400.00
7 AF(c);They Won't Let Me
    Love Him 300.00
8 AF(c);Aug-Sept'50 . . . . 300.00

MOE & SHMOE COMICS
O.S. Publishing Co.
Spring, 1948
1 Gag Oriented Caricature . . . 35.00

2 Gag Oriented Caricature . . . 25.00

MOLLY O'DAY
Avon Periodicals
February, 1945
1 GT;The Enchanted Dagger . 350.00

MONKEYSHINES COMICS
Publ. Specialists/Ace/
Summer, 1944
1 (fa),Several Short Features . . 50.00
2 (fa),Same Format Throughout
    Entire Run 25.00
3 thru 16 Funny Animal . . . . @20.00
Ace
17 Funny Animal 20.00
18 thru 21 . . . . @15.00
Unity Publ.
22 (fa) 15.00
23 (fa) 15.00
24 (fa),AFa,AFa(c) 15.00
25 (fa) 15.00
26 (fa) 15.00
27 (fa),July, 1949 . . . . 15.00

MONSTER
Fiction House Magazines
1953
1 Dr. Drew 350.00
2 . . . . 275.00

MONSTER CRIME
COMICS
Hillman Periodicals
October, 1952
1 52 Pgs,15 Cent Cover Price 650.00

MONTE HALL
WESTERN
(see MARY MARVEL COMICS)

MONTY HALL OF
THE U.S. MARINES
Toby Press
August, 1951
1 B:Monty Hall,Pin-Up Pete;
    (All Issues) 50.00
2 . . . . 30.00
3 thru 5 . . . . @25.00
6 . . . . 20.00
7 The Fireball Express 20.00
8 . . . . 20.00
9 . . . . 20.00
10 The Vial of Death 20.00
11 Monju Island Prison Break . . 20.00

MOON GIRL AND
THE PRINCE
E.C. Comics
Autumn, 1947
1 JCr(c),O:Moon Girl 650.00
2 JCr(c),Battle of the Congo . 350.00
3 . . . . 300.00
4 V: A Vampire 325.00
5 1st E.C. Horror-Zombie Terror 750.00
6 . . . . 400.00
7 O:Star;The Fient Who
    Fights With Fire 400.00
8 True Crime Feature 400.00
Becomes:

A MOON, A GIRL ...ROMANCE

9 AF,Grl,AF(c),C:Moon Girl;
Spanking Panels 500.00
10 AF,Grl,WW,AF(c),Suspicious
of His Intentions 450.00
11 AF,Grl,WW,AF(c),Hearts
Along the Ski Trail 450.00
12 AF,Grl,AF(c),
March-April, 1950 . . . . 550.00

MOPSY
St. John Publishing Co.
February, 1948

1 Paper Dolls Enclosed 100.00
2 . . . . 55.00
3 . . . . 50.00
4 Paper Dolls Enclosed 50.00
5 Paper Dolls Enclosed 50.00
6 Paper Dolls Enclosed 50.00
7 . . . . 40.00
8 Paper Dolls Enclosed;
Lingerie Panels 45.00
9 . . . . 40.00
10 . . . . 40.00

Mopsy #4 © St. John's Publishing Co.

11 . . . . 30.00
12 . . . . 30.00
13 Paper Dolls Enclosed 35.00
14 thru 18 . . . . @30.00
19 Lingerie(c);Paper
Dolls Enclosed 35.00

MORTIE
Magazine Publishers
December, 1952

1 ...Mazie's Friend 30.00
2 . . . . 18.00
3 . . . . 15.00

MOTION PICTURE COMICS
Fawcett Publications
November, 1950

101 Ph(c),Monte Hale's-
Vanishing Westerner 225.00
102 Ph(c),Rocky Lane's-Code
of the Silver Sage 200.00

103 Ph(c),Rocky Lane's-Covered
Wagon Raid 200.00
104 BP,Ph(c),Rocky Lane's-
Vigilante Hideout 200.00
105 BP,Ph(c),Audie Murphy's-
Red Badge of Courage 250.00
106 Ph(c),George Montgomery's-
The Texas Rangers 200.00
107 Ph(c),Rocky Lane's-Frisco
Tornado 200.00
108 Ph(c),John Derek's-Mask
of the Avenger 150.00
109 Ph(c),Rocky Lane's-Rough
Rider of Durango 200.00
110 GE,Ph(c), When Worlds
Collide 700.00
111 Ph(c),Lash LaRue's-The
Vanishing Outpost 225.00
112 Ph(c),Jay Silverheels'-
Brave Warrior 125.00
113 KS,Ph(c),George Murphy's-
Walk East on Beacon 100.00
114 Ph(c),George Montgomery's-
Cripple Creek;Jan, 1953 . . . 100.00

MOTION PICTURES FUNNIES WEEKLY
1st Funnies Incorporated
1939

1 BEv,1st Sub-Mariner . . . 18,000.00
2 Cover Only 250.00
3 Cover Only 250.00
4 Cover Only 250.00

MOVIE CLASSICS
(NO #S)
Dell Publishing Co.
January, 1953

1 Around the World Under
the Sea 30.00
2 Bambi 35.00
3 Battle of the Buldge 25.00
4 Ph(c),Beach Blanket Bingo . . 50.00
5 Ph(c),Bon Voyage 25.00
6 Castilian 30.00
7 Cat 20.00
8 Cheyenne Autumn 45.00
9 Ph(c),Circus World,
John Wayne (c) 100.00
10 Ph(c),Countdown,J.Caan(c) . 30.00
11 Creature 50.00
12 Ph(c),David Ladd's Life Story 75.00
13 Ph(c),Die Monster Die 50.00
14 Dirty Dozen 40.00
15 Ph(c),Dr. Who & the Daleks . 125.00
16 Dracula 40.00
17 El Dorado,J.WaynePh(c) . . . 125.00
18 Ensign Pulver 25.00
19 Frankenstein 40.00
20 Ph(c),Great Race 40.00
21 B.LancasterPh(c) 40.00
22 Hatari 65.00
23 Horizontal Lieutenant 25.00
24 Ph(c) Mr. Limpet 25.00
25 Jack the Giant Killer 60.00
26 Ph(c),Jason and the Argonauts 75.00
27 Lancelot & Guinevere 55.00
28 Lawrence 55.00
29 Lion of Sparta 25.00
30 Mad Monster Party 55.00
31 Magic Sword 45.00
32 Ph(c),Masque of Red Death . 40.00
33 Maya 35.00
34 McHale's Navy 40.00

35 Ph(c) Merrills' Marauders . . . 25.00
36 Ph(c),Mouse on the Moon . . . 20.00
37 Mummy 40.00
38 Music Man 30.00
39 Ph(c),Naked Prey 50.00
40 Ph(c),Night of the Grizzly . . . 35.00
41 None but the Brave 55.00
42 Ph(c),Operation Bikini 30.00
43 Operation Cross Bold 30.00
44 Prince & the Pauper 30.00
45 Raven,V.Price(c) 45.00
46 Ring of Bright Water 35.00
47 Runaway 20.00
48 Ph(c),Santa Claus Conquers
the Martians 65.00
49 Ph(c),Six Black Horses 30.00
50 Sky Party 35.00
51 Smoky 25.00
52 Ph(c),Sons of Katie Elder . . 125.00
53 GE,Tales of Terror 30.00
54 Ph(c),3 Stooges meet
Hercules 75.00
55 Tomb of Legeia 25.00
56 Treasure Island 25.00
57 Twice Told Tales(V.Price) . . . 35.00
58 Two on a Guillotine 25.00
59 Valley of Gwangi 45.00
60 War Gods of the Deep 20.00
61 War Wagon (John Wayne) . . . 85.00
62 Who's Minding the Mint 25.00
63 Wolfman 35.00
64 Ph(c),Zulu 30.00
65 . . . . 25.00

MOVIE COMICS
Fiction House Magazines
December, 1946

1 Big Town on(c) 400.00
2 MB,White Tie & Tails 300.00
3 MB,Andy Hardy Laugh Hit . 300.00
4 MB,Slave Girl 350.00

MOVIE LOVE
Famous Funnies Publications
February, 1950

1 Ph(c),Dick Powell(c) 75.00
2 Ph(c),Myrna Loy(c) 30.00
3 Ph(c),Cornell Wilde(c) 25.00
4 Ph(c),Paulette Goddard(c) . . 25.00
5 Ph(c),Joan Fontaine(c) 25.00
6 Ph(c),Ricardo Montalban(c) . 25.00
7 Ph(c),Fred Astaire(c) 30.00
8 AW,FF,Ph(c),Corinne
Calvert(c) 200.00
9 Ph(c),John Lund(c) 25.00
10 Ph(c),Mona Freeman(c) . . . 250.00
11 Ph(c),James Mason(c) 25.00
12 Ph(c),Jerry Lewis &
Dean Martin(c) 35.00
13 Ph(c),Ronald Reagan(c) . . . 125.00
14 Ph(c),Janet Leigh,Gene Kelly 35.00
15 Ph(c), ... 25.00
16 Ph(c),Angela Lansbury 50.00
17 FF,Ph(c),Leslie Caron 25.00
18 Ph(c),Cornel Wilde 25.00
19 Ph(c),John Derek 25.00
20 Ph(c),Debbie Reynolds 30.00
21 Ph(c),Patricia Medina 25.00
22 Ph(c),John Payne 25.00

MOVIE THRILLERS
Magazine Enterprises 1949

1 Ph(c),Burt Lancaster's-
Rope of Sand 200.00

All comics prices listed are for *Near Mint* condition.   **CVA Page 371**

GOLDEN AGE

MR. MUSCLES
(see THING!, THE)

MUGGY-DOO, BOY CAT
Stanhall Publications
July, 1953
1 . . . . 30.00
2 and 3 . . . . @20.00
4 January, 1954 . . . . 20.00

MURDER, INCORPORATED
Fox Features Incorporated
January, 1948
1 For Adults Only-on(c) 350.00
2 For Adults Only-on(c);Male
   Bondage(c),Electrocution sty 275.00
3 Dutch Schultz-Beast of Evil 150.00
4 The Ray Hamilton Case,
   Lingerie(c) 150.00
5 thru 8 . . . . @150.00
9 Bathrobe (c) 165.00
9a Lingerie (c) 175.00
10 . . . . 125.00
11 . . . . 110.00
12 . . . . 110.00
13 . . . . 125.00
14 Bill Hale-King o/t Murderers 110.00
15 . . . . 110.00
16(5),Second Series 90.00
17(2) 90.00
18(3), Bondage(c) w/Lingerie,
   August, 1951 . . . . 125.00

MURDEROUS GANGSTERS
Avon Periodicals/Realistic
July, 1951
1 WW,Pretty Boy Floyd,
   Leggs Diamond 300.00
2 WW,Baby Face Nelson,Mad
   Dog Esposito 200.00
3 P(c),Tony & Bud Fenner,
   Jed Hawkins 175.00
4 EK(c),Murder By Needle-
   Drug Story, June, 1952 . . . 200.00

MUTINY
Aragon Magazines
October, 1954
1 AH(c),Stormy Tales of the
   Seven Seas 100.00
2 AH(c) 75.00
3 Bondage(c),February, '55 . . . 75.00

MY CONFESSIONS
(see WESTERN TRUE CRIME)

MY DATE COMICS
Hillman Periodicals
July, 1944
1 S&K,S&K (c), Teenage 200.00
2 S&K,DB,S&K(c) 150.00
3 S&K,DB,S&K(c) 150.00
4 S&K,DB,S&K(c) 150.00

MY DESIRE
Fox Features Syndicate
October, 1949
1 Intimate Confessions 75.00
2 WW,They Called Me Wayward 60.00

3 I Hid My Lover 40.00
4 WW, April, 1950 . . . . 125.00

MY GREAT LOVE
Fox Features Syndicate
October, 1949
1 Reunion In a Shack 75.00
2 My Crazy Dreams 40.00
3 He Was Ashamed of Me . . . 35.00
4 My Two Wedding Rings;Apr'50 40.00

MY INTIMATE AFFAIR
Fox Features Syndicate
March, 1950
1 I Sold My Love 75.00
2 I Married a Jailbird;May'50 . . 45.00

MY LIFE
(see MEET CORLISS ARCHER)

I HAD MY HOUR • MY DREADFUL
SECRET • THEY SAID I WAS GUILTY

My Love Affair #2
© *Fox Features Syndicate*

MY LOVE AFFAIR
Fox Features Syndicate
July, 1949
1 Truck Driver's Sweetheart . . 75.00
2 My Dreadful Secret 50.00
3 WW,I'll Make Him Marry Me 100.00
4 WW,They Called Me Wild . 100.00
5 WW,Beauty Was My Bait . . 100.00
6 WW,The Man Downstairs . . 100.00

MY LOVE MEMORIES
(see WOMEN OUTLAWS)

MY LOVE LIFE
(see TEGRA, JUNGLE EMPRESS)

MY LOVE STORY
Fox Features Syndicate
September, 1949
1 Men Gave Me Jewels 75.00
2 He Dared Me 50.00
3 WW,I Made Love a Plaything 100.00
4 WW,I Tried to Be Good . . . 100.00

MY PAST CONFESSIONS
(see WESTERN THRILLERS)

MY PRIVATE LIFE
Fox Features Syndicate
February, 1950
16 My Friendship Club Affair . . . 75.00
17 My Guilty Kisses;April'50 . . . 50.00

MY SECRET
Superior Comics
August, 1949
1 True Love Stories 75.00
2 I Was Guilty of Being a
   Cheating Wife 50.00
3 Was I His Second Love?; . . . 50.00
Becomes:

OUR SECRET
4 JKa,She Loves Me,She Loves
   Me Not; November, 1949 . . 60.00
5 . . . . 40.00
6 . . . . 40.00
7 How Do You Fall In Love? . . . 45.00
8 His Kiss Tore At My
   Heart; June, 1950 . . . . 40.00

MY SECRET AFFAIR
Hero Books
(Fox Features Syndicate)
December, 1949
1 WW,SHn,My Stormy
   Love Affair 125.00
2 WW,I Loved a Weakling 75.00
3 WW, April, 1950 . . . . 100.00

MY SECRET LIFE
Fox Features Syndicate
July, 1949
22 WW,I Loved More Than Once 75.00
23 . . . . 100.00
24 Love Was a Habit 30.00
25 . . . . 30.00
Becomes:

ROMEO TUBBS
26 WW,That Lovable Teen-ager 100.00

MY SECRET LOVE
(see PHANTOM LADY)

MY SECRET MARRIAGE
Superior Comics
May, 1953
1 I Was a Cheat 55.00
2 . . . . 25.00
3 We Couldn't Wait 15.00
4 . . . . 15.00
5 . . . . 15.00
6 . . . . 15.00
7 thru 23 . . . . @15.00
24 1956 . . . . 15.00

MY SECRET ROMANCE
Hero Books
(Fox Features Syndicate)
January, 1950
1 WW,They Called Me 'That'
   Woman 85.00
2 WW,They Called Me Cheap . 75.00

MYSTERIES WEIRD AND STRANGE
Superior Comics/ Dynamic Publ.
May, 1953
1 The Stolen Brain 200.00
2 The Screaming Room,
  Atomic Bomb 125.00
3 The Avenging Corpse 100.00
4 Ghost on the Gallows 100.00
5 Horror a la Mode 100.00
6 Howling Horror 100.00
7 Demon in Disguise 100.00
8 The Devil's Birthmark 100.00
9 . . . . 100.00
10 . . . . 110.00
11 . . . . 100.00

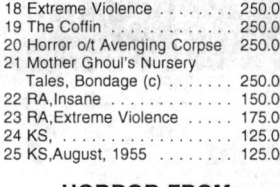

Mysterious Adventures #5
© Story Comics

MYSTERIOUS ADVENTURES
Story Comics
March, 1951
1 Wild Terror of the
  Vampire Flag 300.00
2 Terror of the Ghoul's Corpse . 175.00
3 Terror of the Witche's Curse . 150.00
4 The Little Coffin That Grew . 150.00
5 LC,Curse of the Jungle,
  Bondage(c) 165.00
6 LC,Ghostly Terror in the
  Cave 135.00
7 LC,Terror of the Ghostly
  Castle 250.00
8 Terror of the Flowers of Deat 250.00
9 The Ghostly Ghouls-
  Extreme Violence 200.00
10 Extreme Violence 150.00
11 The Trap of Terror 200.00
12 SHn,Vultures of Death-
  Extreme Violence 200.00
13 Extreme Violence 200.00
14 Horror of the Flame Thrower
  Extreme Violence 200.00
15 DW,Ghoul Crazy 250.00
16 Chilling Tales of Horror . . . 250.00
17 DW,Bride of the Dead 250.00

18 Extreme Violence 250.00
19 The Coffin 250.00
20 Horror o/t Avenging Corpse 250.00
21 Mother Ghoul's Nursery
  Tales, Bondage (c) 250.00
22 RA,Insane 150.00
23 RA,Extreme Violence 175.00
24 KS, ... 125.00
25 KS,August, 1955 . . . . 125.00

HORROR FROM THE TOMB
Premier Magazines
September, 1954
1 AT,GWb,The Corpse Returns 200.00
Becomes:
MYSTERIOUS STORIES
2 GWb(c),Eternal Life 250.00
3 GWb,The Witch Doctor . . . 175.00
4 That's the Spirit 150.00
5 King Barbarossa 150.00
6 GWb,Strangers in the Night . 175.00
7 KS,The Pipes of Pan;Dec'55. 150.00

MYSTERIOUS TRAVELER COMICS
Trans-World Publications
November, 1948
1 BP,BP(c),Five Miles Down . . 400.00

MYSTERY COMICS
William H. Wise & Co.
1944
1 AS(c),B:Brad Spencer-Wonderman,
  King of Futeria,The Magnet, Zudo-
  Jungle Boy,The Silver Knight 750.00
2 AS(c),Bondage (c) 550.00
3 AS(c),Robot(c),LanceLewis,B 500.00
4 AS(c),E:All Features,
  KKK Type(c) 500.00

MYSTERY MEN COMICS
Fox Features Syndicate
August, 1939
1 GT,DBr,LF(c),Bondage(c);I:Blue
  Beetle,Green Mask,Rex Dexter
  of Mars,Zanzibar,Lt.Drake,D-13
  Secret Agent,Chen Chang,
  Wing Turner,Capt. Denny 10,000.00
2 GT,BP,DBr,LF(c),
  Rex Dexter (c) 2,500.00
3 LF(c) 2,700.00
4 LF(c),B:Captain Savage . . 2,000.00
5 GT,BP,LF(c),Green Mask (c)2,000.00
6 GT,BP 1,800.00
7 GT,BP,Bondage(c),
  Blue Beetle(c) 2,000.00
8 GT,BP,LF(c),Bondage(c),
  Blue Beetle 1,800.00
9 GT,BP,DBr(c),B:The Moth . . 900.00
10 GT,BP,JSm(c),A:Wing
  Turner; Bondage(c) 800.00
11 GT,BP,JSm(c),I:The Domino 800.00
12 GT,BP,JSm(c),BlueBeetle(c) 800.00
13 GT,I:The Lynx & Blackie . . 525.00
14 GT,Male Bondage (c) 475.00
15 GT,Blue Beetle (c) 450.00
16 GT,Hypo(c),MaleBondage(c) 475.00
17 GT,BP,Blue Beetle (c) 450.00
18 GT,Blue Beetle (c) 450.00
19 GT,I&B:Miss X 500.00
20 GT,DBr,Blue Beetle (c) . . . 425.00

Mystery Men Comics #11
© Fox Features Syndicate

21 GT,E:Miss X 425.00
22 GT,CCu(c),Blue Beetle (c) . 425.00
23 GT,Blue Beetle (c) 425.00
24 GT,BP,DBr, Blue Beetle (c) . 425.00
25 GT,Bondage(c);
  A:Private O'Hara 450.00
26 GT,Bondage(c);B:The Wraith 450.00
27 GT,Bondage(c),BlueBeetle(c) 450.00
28 GT,Bondage(c);Satan's
  Private Needlewoman 450.00
29 GT,Bondage(c),Blue
  Beetle (c) 450.00
30 Holiday of Death 425.00
31 Bondage(c);Feb'42 . . . . . . 450.00

MY STORY
(see ZAGO, JUNGLE PRINCE)

NATIONAL COMICS
Comics Magazines
(Quality Comics Group)
July, 1940
1 GT,HcK,LF(c),B:Uncle Sam,Wonder
  Boy,Merlin the Magician,Cyclone,
  Kid Patrol,Sally O'Neil-Police-
  woman, Pen Miller,Prop
  Powers, Paul Bunyan . . . 4,500.00
2 WE,GT,HcK,LF&RC(c) 1,750.00
3 GT,HcK,WE&RC(c) 1,200.00
4 GT,HcK,LF&RC(c),E:Cyclone;
  Torpedo Islands of Death . 1,000.00
5 GT,LF&RC(c),B:Quicksilver;
  O:Uncle Sam 1,100.00
6 GT,LF&RC(c) 1,000.00
7 GT,LF&RC(c) 1,100.00
8 GT,LF&RC(c) 1,000.00
9 JCo,LF&RC(c) 1,000.00
10 RC,JCo,LF&RC(c) 1,000.00
11 RC,JCo,LF&RC(c) 1,000.00
12 RC,JCo,LF&RC(c) 750.00
13 RC,JCo,LF,LF&RC(c) 650.00
14 RC,JCo,LF,PG,LF&RC(c) . . 650.00
15 RC,JCo,LF,PG,LF&RC(c) . . 650.00
16 RC,JCo,LF,PG,LF&RC(c) . . 650.00
17 RC,JCo,LF,PG,LF&RC(c) . . 475.00
18 JCo,LF,PG,LF&RC(c),
  Pearl Harbor 850.00

19 JCo,LF,PG,RC(c),The Black
   Fog Mystery 475.00
20 JCo,LF,PG,LF&RC(c) 475.00
21 LF,JCo,PG,LF(c) 475.00
22 JCo,LF,PG,FG,GFx,LF(c),
   E:Jack & Jill,Pen Miller,
   Paul Bunyan 475.00
23 JCo,PG,FG,GFx,AMc,LF
   & GFx(c),B:The Unknown,
   Destroyer 171 . . . . 500.00
24 JCo,PG,RC,AMc,FG,
   GFx,RC(c) 475.00
25 AMc,RC,JCo,PG,FG,
   GFx,RC(c) 350.00
26 AMc,Jco,RC,PG,RC(c),
   E:Prop Powers,WonderBoy . 350.00
27 JCo,AMc 350.00
28 JCo,AMc 350.00
29 JCo,O:The Unknown;U.Sam
   V:Dr. Dirge 375.00
30 JCo,RC(c) 365.00
31 JCo,RC(c) 350.00
32 JCo,RC(c) 350.00
33 JCo,GFx,RC(c),B:Chic Carter;
   U.Sam V:Boss Spring 350.00
34 JCo,GFx,U.Sam V:Big John
   Fales 350.00
35 JCo,GFx,E:Kid Patrol 250.00
36 JCo 250.00
37 JCo,FG,A:The Vagabond . . 250.00
38 JCo,FG,Boat of the Dead . . 250.00
39 JCo,FG,Hitler(c);U.Sam
   V:The Black Market 250.00
40 JCo,FG,U.Sam V:The
   Syndicate of Crime 175.00
41 JCo,FG 175.00
42 JCo,FG,JCo(c),B:The Barker 150.00
43 JCo,FG,JCo(c) 150.00
44 JCo,FG 150.00
45 JCo,FG,E:Merlin the Magician 150.00
46 JCo,JCo(c),Murder is no Joke 150.00
47 JCo,JCo(c),E:Chic Carter . . 150.00
48 JCo,O:The Whistler 150.00
49 JCo,JCo(c),A Corpse
   for a Cannonball 150.00
50 JCo,JCo(c),V:Rocks Myzer 150.00
51 JCo,BWa,JCo(c),
   A:Sally O'Neil 200.00
52 JCo,A Carnival of Laughs . . 125.00
53 PG,V:Scramolo 125.00
54 PG,V:Raz-Ma-Taz 125.00
55 JCo,AMc,V:The Hawk 125.00
56 GFx,JCo,AMc,V:The Grifter . 125.00
57 GFX,JCo,AMc,V:Witch Doctor 125.00
58 GFz,JCo,AMc,Talking Animals 125.00
59 GFx,JCo,AMc,V:The Birdman 125.00
60 GFx,JCo,AMc,V:Big Ed Grew 125.00
61 GFx,AMc,Trouble Comes in
   Small Packages 90.00
62 GFx,AMc,V:Crocodile Man . . 90.00
63 GFx,AMc,V:Bearded Lady . . . 90.00
64 GFx,V:The Human Fly 90.00
65 GFx,GFx(c)V:The King 90.00
66 GFx,GFx(c)V:THe Man Who
   Hates the Circus 90.00
67 GFx,Gfx,A:Quicksilver;
   V:Ali Ben Riff Raff 90.00
68 GFx,GFx(c),V:Leo the LionMan 90.00
69 GFx,Gfx(c),A:Percy the
   Powerful 90.00
70 GFx,GFx(c),Barker Tires
   of the Big Top 90.00
71 PG,GFx,V:SpellbinderSmith 90.00
72 PG,GFx(c),The Oldest Man
   in the World 90.00

National Comics #59
© Comics Mag./Quality Comics Group

73 PG,GFx(c),V:A CountrySlicker 90.00
74 PG,GFx(c),V:Snake Oil Sam . 90.00
75 PG,GFx(c),Barker Breakes the
   Bank at Monte Marlo;Nov'49 . 90.00

NEBBS, THE
Dell Publishing Co.
1941
1 rep. 60.00

NEGRO ROMANCE
Fawcett Publications
June, 1950
1 GE,Ph(c), Love's Decoy . . . 800.00
2 GE,Ph(c), A Tragic Vow . . . 650.00
3 GE,Ph(c), My Love
   Betrayed Me 650.00
Charlton Comics
4 Rep.FawcettEd.#2;May,1955 500.00

NEW ROMANCES
Standard Comics
May, 1951
5 Ph(c), The Blame I Bore 55.00
6 Ph(c), No Wife Was I 30.00
7 Ph(c), My Runaway Heart,
   Ray Miland 25.00
8 Ph(c) 25.00
9 Ph(c) 25.00
10 ATh,Ph(c) 50.00
11 ATh,Ph(c) of Elizabeth Taylor 80.00
12 Ph(c) 20.00
13 Ph(c) 20.00
14 ATh,Ph(c) 35.00
15 Ph(c) 20.00
16 ATh,Ph(c) 35.00
17 Ath, ... 35.00
18 and 19 . . . . @20.00
20 GT, ... 25.00
21 April, 1954 . . . . 20.00

NICKEL COMICS
Dell Publishing Co.
1938
1 Bobby & Chip 500.00

NICKEL COMICS
Fawcett Publications
May, 1940
1 JaB(c),O&I: Bulletman . . . 3,000.00
2 JaB(c), ... 900.00
3 JaB(c), ... 700.00
4 JaB(c), B: Red Gaucho . . . 600.00
5 CCB(c),Bondage(c) 600.00
6 and 7 CCB(c) . . . . @550.00
8 CCB(c),August 23, 1940,
   World's Fair 600.00

NIGHTMARE
(see WEIRD HORRORS)

NIGHTMARE
Ziff-Davis Publishing Co.
1 EK,GT,P(c),The Corpse That
   Wouldn't Stay Dead 375.00
2 EK,P(c),Vampire Mermaid . 250.00
St. John Publishing Co.
3 EK,P(c),The Quivering Brain 200.00
4 P(c),1953 . . . . 175.00

NORTHWEST MOUNTIES
Jubilee Publications/
St. John Publ. Co.
October, 1948
1 MB,BLb(c),Rose of the Yukon 350.00
2 MB,BLb(c),A:Ventrilo 275.00
3 MB, Bondage(c) 250.00
4 MB(c),A:Blue Monk,July'49 . 250.00

NURSERY RHYMES
Ziff-Davis Publishing Co.
1950
1 How John Came Clean 75.00
2 The Old Woman Who
   Lived in a Shoe 50.00

NUTS!
Premere Comics Group
March, 1954
1 . . . . 200.00
2 . . . . 150.00
3 Mention of "Reefers" 165.00
4 . . . . 150.00
5 Captain Marvel Spoof;Nov.'54 150.00

NUTTY COMICS
Fawcett Publications
Winter, 1946
1 (fa),F:Capt. Kid,Richard Richard,
   Joe Miller...Among others . . 75.00

NUTTY LIFE
(see PHANTOM LADY)

NYOKA THE
JUNGLE GIRL
Fawcett Publications
Winter, 1945
1 Bondage(c);Partial Ph(c) of
   Kay Aldridge as Nyoka . . . 450.00
2 . . . . 225.00
3 . . . . 225.00
4 Bondage(c) 225.00
5 Barbacosi Madness;
   Bondage(c) 225.00
6 . . . . 175.00

Nyoka the Jungle Girl #13
© Fawcett Publications

7 North Pole Jungle;Bondage(c) 165.00
8 Bondage(c) 165.00
9 . . . . 150.00
10 . . . . 150.00
11 Danger! Death! in an
   Unexplored Jungle 125.00
12 . . . . 90.00
13 The Human Leopards 125.00
14 The Mad Witch Doctor;
   Bondage(c) 125.00
15 Sacred Goat of Kristan 100.00
16 BK,The Vultures of Kalahari . 110.00
17 BK 110.00
18 BK,The Art of Murder 110.00
19 The Elephant Battle 110.00
20 Explosive Volcano Action . . 110.00
21 . . . . 65.00
22 The Weird Monsters 65.00
23 Danger in Duplicate 65.00
24 The Human Jaguar;
   Bondage(c) 80.00
25 Hand Colored Ph(c) 60.00
26 A Jungle Stampede 60.00
27 Adventure Laden 60.00
28 The Human Statues of
   the Jungle 60.00
29 Ph(c) 60.00
30 Ph(c) 60.00
31 thru 40 Ph(c) . . . . @50.00
41 thru 50 Ph(c) . . . . @40.00
51 thru 59 Ph(c) . . . . @30.00
60 Ph(c) 25.00
61 Ph(c),The Sacred Sword of
   the Jungle 25.00
62 & 63 Ph(c) . . . . @25.00
64 Ph(c), The Jungle Idol 25.00
65 Ph(c) 25.00
66 Ph(c) 25.00
67 Ph(c), The Sky Man 25.00
68 thru 74 Ph(c) . . . . @25.00
75 Ph(c), The Jungle Myth
   of Terror 25.00
76 Ph(c) 25.00
77 Ph(c),The Phantoms of the
   Elephant Graveyard;Jun'53 . . 25.00

OAKY DOAKS
Eastern Color Printing Co.
July, 1942
1 Humor Oriented 225.00

OH, BROTHER!
Stanhall Publications
January, 1953
1 Bill Williams-a 25.00
2 thru 5 . . . . @15.00

OK COMICS
United Features Syndicate
July, 1940
1 B:Pal Peyton,Little Giant, Phantom
   Knight,Sunset Smith,Teller Twins,
   Don Ramon, Jerrry Sly,Kip Jaxon,
   Leatherneck,Ulysses 600.00
2 October, 1940 . . . . 575.00

100 PAGES OF COMICS
Dell Publishing Co.
1937
101 Alley Oop,OG,Wash Tubbs,
   Tom Mix,Dan Dunn 1,200.00

ON THE AIR
NBC Network Comics
1947
1 Giveaway, no cover 175.00

ON THE SPOT
Fawcett Publications
Autumn, 1948
N# Bondage(c),PrettyBoyFloyd 200.00

Operation Peril #4
© American Comics Group/Michel Publ.

OPERATION PERIL
**American Comics Group
(Michel Publ.)**
October-November, 1950
1 LSt,OW,OW(c),B:TyphoonTyler,
   DannyDanger,TimeTravellers 250.00
2 OW,OW(c) 150.00
3 OW,OW(c),Horror 125.00

4 OW,OW(c), Flying Saucers . 125.00
5 OW,OW(c), Science Fiction . 125.00
6 OW, Tyr. Rex 125.00
7 OW,OW(c) 100.00
8 OW,OW(c) 100.00
9 OW,OW(c) 100.00
10 OW,OW(c) 100.00
11 OW,OW(c), War 100.00
12 OW,OW(c),E:Time Travellers 100.00
13 OW,OW(c),War Stories 50.00
14 OW,OW(c),War Stories 50.00
15 OW,OW(c),War Stories 50.00
16 OW,OW(c),April-May,1953,
   War Stories 50.00

OUR FLAG COMICS
Ace Magazines
August, 1941
1 MA,JM,B:Capt.Victory,Unknown
   Soldier,The Three Cheers 1,600.00
2 JM,JM(c),O:The Flag 900.00
3 Tank Battle (c) 700.00
4 MA 700.00
5 I:Mr. Risk;April, 1942,
   Male Bondage 725.00

OUR GANG COMICS
Dell Publishing Co.
September-October, 1942
1 WK,Barney Bear, Tom & Jerry850.00
2 WK 450.00
3 WK,Benny Burro 300.00
4 WK 300.00
5 WK 300.00
6 WK 450.00
7 WK 225.00
8 WK,CB,Benny Burro 600.00
9 WK,CB,Benny Burro 550.00
10 WK,CB,Benny Burro 400.00
11 WK,I:Benny Bear 550.00
12 thru 20 WK . . . . @250.00
21 thru 29 WK . . . . @175.00
30 WK,Christmas(c) 125.00
31 thru 34 WK . . . . @100.00
35 WK,CB 100.00
36 WK,CB 100.00
37 thru 40 WK . . . . @60.00
41 thru 50 WK . . . . @50.00
51 thru 56 WK . . . . @35.00
57 . . . . 30.00
58 Our Gang 30.00
59 Our Gang 30.00
Becomes:

TOM AND JERRY
July, 1949
60 . . . . 60.00
61 . . . . 50.00
62 . . . . 45.00
63 . . . . 45.00
64 . . . . 45.00
65 . . . . 45.00
66 Christmas (c) 50.00
67 thru 70 . . . . @45.00
71 thru 76 . . . . @35.00
77 Christmas (c) 40.00
78 thru 80 . . . . @35.00
81 thru 89 . . . . @30.00
90 Christmas (c) 35.00
91 thru 99 . . . . @30.00
100 . . . . 35.00
101 thru 120 . . . . @25.00
121 thru 150 . . . . @20.00
151 thru 212 . . . . @12.00

GOLDEN AGE

OUR SECRET
(see MY SECRET)

OUTLAWS
D.S. Publishing Co.
February-March, 1948
1 HcK,Western Crime Stories . . 200.00
2 Grl,Doc Dawson's Dilema . . 185.00
3 Cougar City Cleanup 80.00
4 JO,Death Stakes A Claim . . 100.00
5 RJ,RJ(c),Man Who Wanted
   Mexico 75.00
6 AMc,RJ,RJ(c),The Ghosts of

Outlaws #1 © D.S. Publishing Co.

   Crackerbox Hill 75.00
7 Grl,Dynamite For Boss Cavitt 150.00
8 Grl,The Gun & the Pen . . . 150.00
9 FF,Shoot to Kill;June-
   July, 1949 . . . . 325.00

WHITE RIDER AND SUPER HORSE
Star Publications
September, 1950
1 LbC(c) 75.00
2 LbC(c) 30.00
3 LbC(c) 30.00
4 LbC(c) 35.00
5 LbC(c),Stampede of Hard
   Riding Thrills 35.00
6 LbC(c),Drums of the Sioux . . 35.00
Becomes:
INDIAN WARRIORS
7 LbC(c),Winter on the Great
   Plains 50.00
8 LbC(c) 30.00
Becomes:
WESTERN CRIME CASES
9 LbC(c),The Card Sharp Killer 60.00
Becomes:
OUTLAWS, THE
10 LbC(c),Federated Express . 75.00
11 LbC(c),Frontier Terror!!! . . . 50.00
12 LbC(c),Ruthless Killer!!! . . . 50.00
13 LbC(c),The Grim Avengers . . 50.00
14 AF,JKa,LbC(c),Trouble in

Dark Canyon,April'54 . . . . . . 50.00

OUT OF THE NIGHT
American Comics Group/ Best Synd. Feature
February-March, 1952
1 AW 450.00
2 AW 400.00
3 . . . . 175.00
4 AW 325.00
5 . . . . 175.00
6 The Ghoul's Revenge 175.00
7 . . . . 175.00
8 The Frozen Ghost 175.00
9 Death Has Wings,
   Science Fiction 175.00
10 Ship of Death 175.00
11 . . . . 125.00
12 Music for the Dead 125.00
13 HN,From the Bottom of
   the Well 125.00
14 Out of the Screen 125.00
15 The Little Furry Thing 100.00
16 Nightmare From the Past . . 100.00
17 The Terror of the Labyrinth . 100.00
Becomes:
HOODED HORSEMAN
18 B: The Hooded Horseman . . 75.00
19 The Horseman's Strangest
   Adventure 100.00
20 OW,O:Johnny Injun 65.00
21 OW,OW(c) 50.00
22 OW 50.00
23 . . . . 50.00
24 . . . . 50.00
25 . . . . 50.00
26 O&I:Cowboy Sahib 70.00
27 January-February, 1953 . . . 60.00

OUT OF THE SHADOWS
Visual Editions (Standard Comics)
July, 1952
5 ATh,GT,The Shoremouth
   Horror 300.00
6 ATh,JKz,Salesman of Death 225.00
7 JK,Plant of Death 150.00
8 Mask of Death 125.00
9 RC,Till Death Do Us Part . . 150.00
10 MS,We Vowed,Till Death
   Do Us Part 100.00
11 ATh,Fountain of Fear 150.00
12 ATh,Hand of Death 200.00
13 MS,The Cannibal 175.00
14 ATh,The Werewolf,
August, 1954 . . . . 185.00

OXYDOL-DREFT
Giveaways
1950
The Set is More Valuable if the
Original Envelope is Present
1 L'il Abner 75.00
2 Daisy Mae 75.00
3 Shmoo 80.00
4 AW&FF(c),John Wayne . . . 135.00
5 Archie 65.00
6 Terry Toons Comics 75.00

OZZIE AND BABS
Fawcett Publications
Winter, 1946
1 Humor Oriented, Teenage . . . 45.00

2 Humor Oriented 20.00
3 Humor Oriented 15.00
4 Humor Oriented 15.00
5 Humor Oriented 15.00
6 Humor Oriented 15.00
7 Humor Oriented 15.00
8 Humor Oriented 15.00
9 Humor Oriented 15.00
10 Humor Oriented 15.00
11 Humor Oriented 15.00
12 Humor Oriented 15.00
13 Humor Oriented;1949 . . . . . 15.00

PAGEANT OF COMICS
St. John Publishing Co.
September, 1947
1 Rep. Mopsy 75.00
2 Rep. Jane Arden,Crime
   Reporter 75.00

PANHANDLE PETE AND JENNIFER
J. Charles Lave Publishing Co.
July, 1951
1 (fa) 40.00
2 (fa) 30.00
3 (fa),November'51 . . . . 30.00

Panic #10 © E.C. Comics

PANIC
Tiny Tot Publications (E.C. Comics)
March, 1954
"Humor in a Jugular Vein"
1 BE,JKa,JO,JDa,AF(c) 175.00
2 BE,JO,WW,JDa,A:Bomb . . 125.00
3 BE,JO,BW,WW,JDa,AF(c) . 110.00
4 BE,JO,WW,JDa,BW(c),
   Infinity(c) 110.00
5 BE,JO,WW,JDa,AF(c) 90.00
6 BE,JO,WW,JDa,Blank (c) . . 90.00
7 BE,JO,WW,JDa 90.00
8 BE,JO,WW,JDa,Eye Chart (c) 90.00
9 BE,JO,WW,JDa,Ph(c),
   Confidential(c) 90.00
10 BE,JDa, Postal Package(c) . . 90.00
11 BE,WW,JDa,Wheaties parody

GOLDEN AGE

as Weedies (c) 90.00
12 BE,WW,JDa,JDa(c);
  December-January 1955-56 110.00

PARAMOUNT ANIMATED COMICS
Family Publications (Harvey Publ.)
June, 1953
1 (fa),B:Baby Herman & Katnip,
  Baby Huey,Buzzy the Crow 110.00
2 (fa) 60.00
3 (fa) 45.00
4 (fa) 45.00
5 (fa) 45.00
6 (fa) 45.00
7 (fa), Baby Huey (c) 120.00
8 (fa), Baby Huey (c) 50.00
9 (fa), Infinity(c),Baby Huey (c) . 50.00
10 thru 21 (fa),Baby Huey (c) @30.00
22 (fa), July, 1956, Baby Huey (c) 30.00

PAROLE BREAKERS
Avon Periodicals/Realistic
December, 1951
1 P(c),Hellen Willis,Gun
  Crazed Gun Moll 300.00
2 JKu,P(c),Vinnie Sherwood,
  The Racket King 200.00
3 EK(c),John "Slicer" Berry,
  Hatchetman of Crime;
  July,1952 . . . . 175.00

PATCHES
Rural Home Publ./ Patches Publ.
March-April, 1945
1 LbC(c),Imagination In Bed(c) 200.00
2 Dance (c) 75.00
3 Rocking Horse (c) 65.00
4 Music Band (c) 65.00
5 LbC(c),A:Danny Kaye,Football 100.00
6 A: Jackie Kelk 70.00
7 A: Hopalong Cassidy 100.00
8 A: Smiley Burnettte 70.00
9 BK,A: Senator Claghorn 70.00
10 A: Jack Carson 70.00
11 A: Red Skeleton; Dec'47 . . . . 75.00

PAWNEE BILL
Story Comics
Feb.–July, 1951
1 A:Bat Masterson,Wyatt Earp,
  Indian Massacre
  at Devil's Gulch 55.00
2 Blood in Coffin Canyon 35.00
3 LC,O:Golden Warrior,Fiery
  Arrows at Apache Pass; 35.00

PAY-OFF
D.S. Publishing Co.
July-Aug., 1948–March-April, 1949
1 . . . . 150.00
2 The Pennsylvania Blue-Beard 100.00
3 The Forgetful Forger 75.00
4 RJ(c),Lady and the Jewels . . 75.00
5 The Beautiful Embezzeler . . . 75.00

PEDRO
Fox Features Syndicate
January, 1950
1 WW,WW(c),Humor Oriented 165.00

2 August, 1950 . . . . 110.00

PENNY
Avon Publications
1947
1 The Slickest Chick of 'em All 60.00
2 . . . . 30.00
3 America's Teen-age
  Sweetheart 30.00
4 . . . . 30.00
5 . . . . 30.00
6 Perry Como Ph(c),September-
  October, 1949 . . . . 35.00

Pep Comics #42
© MJL Magazines/Archie Publ.

PEP COMICS
MJL Magazines/ Archie Publications
January, 1940
1 IN,JCo,MMe,IN(c),I:Shield,
  O:Comet,Queen of Diamonds,
  B:The Rocket,Press Guardian,
  Sergeant Boyle Chang,Bently
  of Scotland Yard 7,000.00
2 CBi,JCo,IN,IN(c),O:Rocket . 1,700.00
3 JCo,IN,IN(c),Shield (c) 1,200.00
4 Cbi,JCo,MMe,IN,IN(c),
  C:Wizard(not Gareb) 900.00
5 Cbi,JCo,MMe,IN,IN(c),
  C:Wizard 900.00
6 IN,IN(c), Shield (c) 750.00
7 IN,IN(c),Bondage(c),Shield(c) 750.00
8 JCo,IN, Shield (c) 700.00
9 IN, Shield (c) 700.00
10 IN,IN(c), Shield (c) 700.00
11 MMe,IN,IN(c),I:Dusty ,Boy
  Detective 700.00
12 IN,IN(c),O:Fireball Bondage(c),
  E:Rocket,Queen of Diamonds 900.00
13 IN,IN(c),Bondage(c) 625.00
14 IN,IN(c) 600.00
15 IN,Bondage(c) 625.00
16 IN,O:Madam Satan 900.00
17 IN,IN(c),O:Hangman,
  D:Comet 2,500.00
18 IN,IN(c),Bondage(c) 600.00
19 IN 575.00
20 IN,IN(c),E:Fireball 575.00

21 IN,IN(c),Bondage(c),
  E: Madam Satan 600.00
22 IN,IN(c)I:Archie,
  Jughead, Betty 8,500.00
23 IN,IN(c) 900.00
24 IN,IN(c) 800.00
25 IN,IN(c) 800.00
26 IN,IN(c),I:Veronica 1,100.00
27 IN,IN(c),Bill of Rights (c) . . . 650.00
28 IN,IN(c), V:Capt. Swastika . . 650.00
29 ASH (c) 650.00
30 B:Capt.Commando 650.00
31 Bondage(c) 650.00
32 Bondage(c) 550.00
33 . . . . 500.00
34 Bondage(c) 550.00
35 . . . . 500.00
36 1st Archie(c) 1,100.00
37 Bondage(c) 400.00
38 ASH(c) 375.00
39 ASH(c), Human Shield 375.00
40 . . . . 375.00
41 2nd Archie; I:Jughead 275.00
42 F:Archie & Jughead 250.00
43 F:Archie & Jughead 250.00
44 . . . . 250.00
45 . . . . 250.00
46 . . . . 225.00
47 E:Hangman,Infinity(c) 225.00
48 B:Black Hood 225.00
49 . . . . 225.00
50 . . . . 225.00
51 . . . . 200.00
52 B:Suzie 200.00
53 . . . . 200.00
54 E:Captain Commando 200.00
55 . . . . 200.00
56 thru 58 . . . . @175.00
59 E:Suzie 175.00
60 B:Katy Keene 175.00
61 . . . . 150.00

Pep Comics #50
© MJL Magazines/Archie Publ.

62 I L'il Jinx 150.00
63 . . . . 150.00
64 . . . . 150.00
65 E:Shield 150.00
66 thru 71 . . . . @100.00
72 thru 80 . . . . @85.00
81 thru 90 . . . . @65.00

All comics prices listed are for *Near Mint* condition.

GOLDEN AGE

GOLDEN AGE

91 thru 99	@50.00
100	85.00
101 thru 110	@40.00
111 thru 120	@35.00
121 thru 130	@30.00
131 thru 140	@25.00
141 thru 150	@20.00
151 thru 160,A:Super Heroes	@18.00
161 thru 200	@8.00
201 thru 250	@4.00
251 thru 300	@3.00
301 thru 350	@2.00
351 thru 411	@1.00

Perfect Crime #31
© Cross Publications

PERFECT CRIME, THE
Cross Publications
October, 1949

1 BP,DW	175.00
2 BP	100.00
3	75.00
4 BP	75.00
5 DW	75.00
6	75.00
7 B:Steve Duncan	75.00
8 Drug Story	85.00
9	75.00
10	75.00
11 Bondage (c)	100.00
12	50.00
13	50.00
14 Poisoning (c)	50.00
15 "The Most Terrible Menace", Drug	75.00
16	50.00
17	50.00
18 Drug (c)	125.00
19	50.00
20 thru 25	@50.00
26 Drug w/ Hypodermic (c)	150.00
27	50.00
28	50.00
29	50.00
30 E:Steve Duncan, Rope Strangulation (c)	125.00
31	50.00
32	50.00
33	50.00

PERFECT LOVE
Approved Comics(Ziff-Davis)/
St. John Publ. Co.
August-September, 1951

1 (10),P(c),Our Kiss was a Prelude to Love Adrift	125.00
2	75.00
3 P(c)	50.00
4	50.00
5	50.00
6	50.00
7	50.00
8 EK	55.00
9 EK,P(c)	40.00
10 Ph(c), Dec '53	40.00

PERSONAL LOVE
Famous Funnies
January, 1950

1 Ph(c) Are You in Love	100.00
2 Ph(c) Serenade for Suzette Mario Lanzo	50.00
3 Ph(c)	40.00
4 Ph(c)	40.00
5 Ph(c)	40.00
6 Ph(c) Be Mine Forever	45.00
7 Ph(c) You'll Always Be Mine, Robert Walker	45.00
8 EK,Ph(c),Esther Williams & Howard Keel	50.00
9 EK,Ph(c),Debra Paget & Louis Jordan	50.00
10 Ph(c),Loretta Young Joseph Cotton	45.00
11 ATh, Ph(c),Gene Tierney & Glenn Ford	75.00
12 Ph(c) Jane Greer & William Lundigan	40.00
13 Ph(c) Debra Paget & Louis Jordan	35.00
14 Ph(c) Kirk Douglas & Patrice Wymore	50.00
15 Ph(c) Dale Robertson & Joanne Dru	35.00
16 Ph(c) Take Back Your Love	35.00
17 Ph(c) My Cruel Deception	35.00
18 Ph(c) Gregory Peck & Susan Hayward	45.00
19 Ph(c) Anthony Quinn	45.00
20 Ph(c) The Couple in the Next Apartment, Bob Wagner	40.00
21 Ph(c) I'll Make You Care	35.00
22 Ph(c) Doorway To Heartbreak	35.00
23 Ph(c) SaveMe from that Man	35.00
24 FF, Ph(c) Tyrone Power	300.00
25 FF, Ph(c) The Dark Light	300.00
26 Ph(c) Love Needs A Break	35.00
27 FF, Ph(c) Champ or Chump?	300.00
28 FF, Ph(c) A Past to Forget	300.00
29 Ph(c) Charlton Heston	45.00
30 Ph(c) The Lady is Lost	35.00
31 Ph(c) Marlon Brando	60.00
32 FF, Ph(c) The Torment, Kirk Douglas	350.00
33 Ph(c) June ,1955	35.00

PETER COTTONTAIL
Key Publications
January, 1954

1 No 3-D (fa)	40.00
1 Feb '54 3-D (fa)	100.00
2 Rep of 3-D #1,not in 3-D	30.00

PETER PAUL'S 4 IN 1 JUMBO COMIC BOOK
Capitol Stories
1953

1 F: Racket Squad in Action, Space Adventures,Crime & Justice,Space Western	275.00

PETER PENNY AND HIS MAGIC DOLLAR
American Bakers Association
1947

1 History from Colonial America to the 1950's	125.00
2	50.00

PETER RABBIT
Avon Periodicals
1947

1 H. Cady art	225.00
2 H. Cady art	175.00
3 H. Cady art	150.00
4 H. Cady art	150.00
5 H. Cady art	150.00
6 H. Cady art	150.00
7 thru 10	@30.00
11	15.00

KRAZY LIFE
Fox Features Syndicate
1945

1 (fa)	55.00

Becomes:
NUTTY LIFE

2 (fa)	45.00

Becomes:
WOTALIFE
Fox Features Synd./
Green Publ.
August-September, 1946

3 (fa)B:L'il Pan,Cosmo Cat	35.00
4	25.00
5 thru 11	@20.00
12 July, 1947	20.00

Becomes:

Phantom Lady #17
© Fox Features Syndicate

PHANTOM LADY
Fox Features Syndicate
August, 1947

13(#1) MB,MB(c) Knights of the Crooked Cross	3,000.00
14(#2) MB,MB(c) Scoundrels and Scandals	1,700.00
15 MB,MB(c) The Meanest Crook In the World	1,600.00
16 MB,MB(c) Claa Peete The Beautiful Beast, Negligee	1,600.00
17 MB.MB(c) The Soda Mint Killer, Bondage (c)	4,000.00
18 MB,MB(c) The Case of Irene Shroeder	1,300.00
19 MB,MB(c) The Case of the Murderous Model	1,300.00
20 MB,MB(c) Ace of Spades	1,000.00
21 MB,MB(c)	1,000.00
22 MB,JKa	1,000.00
23 MB,JKa Bondage (c)	1,100.00

Becomes:

MY LOVE SECRET

24 JKa, My Love Was For Sale	90.00
25 Second Hand Love	50.00
26 WW I Wanted Both Men	100.00
27 I Was a Love Cheat	40.00
28 WW, I Gave Him Love	100.00
29	40.00
30 Ph(c)	40.00

LINDA
Ajax/Farrell
April-May, 1954

1	75.00
2 Lingerie section	55.00
3	40.00
4 October-November,1954	40.00

Becomes:

PHANTOM LADY

5(1) MB,Dec-Jan'54-55	750.00
2 Last Pre-Code Edition	600.00
3 Comics Code	500.00
4 Red Rocket,June, 1955	500.00

PHIL RIZZUTO
Fawcett Publications
1951

Ph(c) The Sensational Story of The American Leagues MVP   500.00

PICTORIAL CONFESSIONS
St. John Publishing Co.
September, 1949

1 MB,MB(c),I Threw Away My Reputation on a Worthless Love	175.00
2 MB,Ph(c) I Tried to be a Hollywood Glamour Girl	100.00
3 JKY,MB,MB(c),They Caught Me Cheating	100.00

Becomes:

PICTORIAL ROMANCES

4 Ph(c) MB, Trapped By Kisses I Couldn't Resist	175.00
5 MB,MB(c)	125.00
6 MB,MB(c) I Was Too Free With Boys	100.00
7 MB,MB(c)	100.00
8 MB,MB(c) I Made a Sinful Bargain	100.00
9 MB,MB(c) Dishonest Love	100.00

Pictorial Romances #14
© St. John Publishing Co.

10 MB,MB(c) I Was The Other Woman	75.00
11 MB,MB(c) The Worst Mistake A Wife Can Make	85.00
12 MB,MB(c) Love Urchin	60.00
13 MB,MB(c) Temptations of a Hatcheck Girl	60.00
14 MB,MB(c) I Was A Gamblers Wife	60.00
15 MB,MB(c) Wife Without Pride or Principles	60.00
16 MB,MB(c) The Truth of My Affair With a Farm Boy	60.00
17 MB,MB(c) True Confessions of a Girl in Love	175.00
18 MB,MB(c)	175.00
20 MB,MB(c)	175.00
21 MB,MB(c)	50.00
22 MB,MB(c)	50.00
23 MB,MB(c)	50.00
24 MB,MB(c) March,1954	50.00

PICTORIAL LOVE STORIES
St. John Publishing Co.
October, 1952

1 MB,MB(c) I Lost My Head, My Heart and My Resistance	150.00

PICTURE NEWS
299 Lafayette Street Corp.
January, 1946

1 Will The Atom Blow The World Apart	250.00
2 Meet America's 1st Girl Boxing Expert,Atomic Bomb	125.00
3 Hollywood's June Allison Shows You How to be Beautiful, Atomic Bomb	100.00
4 Amazing Marine Who Became King of 10,000 Voodoos, Atomic Bomb	125.00
5 G.I.Babies,Hank Greenberg	90.00
6 Joe Louis(c)	125.00
7 Lovely Lady, Englands Future Queen	80.00
8 Champion of them All	70.00

9 Bikini Atom Bomb, Joe DiMaggio	100.00
10 Dick Quick, Ace Reporter, Atomic Bomb January/February 1947	100.00

PICTURE STORIES FROM SCIENCE
Educational Comics
Spring, 1947

1 Understanding Air and Water	175.00
2 Fall '47 Amazing Discoveries About Food & Health	150.00

PICTURE STORIES FROM WORLD HISTORY
E.C. Comics
Spring, 1947

1 Ancient World to the Fall of Rome	200.00
2 Europes Struggle for Civilization	175.00

PINHEAD AND FOODINI
Fawcett Publications
July, 1951

1 Ph(c)	175.00
2 Ph(c)	100.00
3 Ph(c) Too Many Pinheads	60.00
4 Foodini's Talking Camel January, 1952	60.00

PIN-UP PETE
Minoan Magazine Publishers
1952

1 Loves of a GI Casanova	100.00

PIONEER PICTURE STORIES
Street & Smith Publications
December, 1941

1 Red Warriors in Blackface	200.00
2 Life Story Of Errol Flynn	100.00
3 Success Stories of Brain Muscle in Action	75.00
4 Legless Ace & Boy Commando Raid Occupied France	75.00
5 How to Tell Uniform and Rank of Any Navy Man	75.00
6 General Jimmy Doolittle	85.00
7 Life Story of Admiral Halsey	85.00
8 Life Story of Timoshenko	75.00
9 Dec. '43,Man Who Conquered The Wild Frozen North	75.00

PIRACY
E.C. Comics
October-November, 1954

1 WW,JDa,AW,WW(c),RC,AT	225.00
2 RC,JDa(c),WW,AW,AT	175.00
3 RC,GE, RC(c),Grl	150.00
4 RC,GE,RC(c),Grl	125.00
5 RC,GE,BK(c),Grl	125.00
6 JDa,RC,GE,BK(c),Grl	125.00
7 Oct Nov GE(c),RC,GE,Grl	125.00

PIRATE COMICS
Hillman Periodicals
February-March, 1950

1	150.00

All comics prices listed are for *Near Mint* condition.

GOLDEN AGE

2	120.00
3	100.00
4 Aug Sept 30	90.00

PIXIES, THE
Magazine Enterprises
Winter, 1946

1 Mighty Atom	45.00
2	25.00
3	20.00
4	20.00
5	25.00

Becomes:
MIGHTY ATOM, THE

6	25.00

Planet Comics #50
© *Fiction House Magazines*

PLANET COMICS
Love Romance Publ.
(Fiction House Magazines)
January, 1940

1 AB,DBR,HCk, Planet Comics, WE&LF,O:Aura,B:Flint Baker, Red Comet,Spurt Hammond, Capt. Nelson Cole	10,000.00
2 HcK,LF(c)	3,500.00
3 WE(c),HcK	2,500.00
4 HcK,B:Gale Allan and the Girl Squad	2,000.00
5 BP,HcK	1,900.00
6 BP,HcK,BP(c),The Ray Pirates of Venus	2,000.00
7 BP,AB,HcK,BP(c) B:Buzz Crandall Planet Payson	1,600.00
8 BP,AB HcK	1,500.00
9 BP,AB,GT,HcK,B:Don Granville Cosmo Corrigan	1,500.00
10 BP,AB,GT HcK	1,500.00
11 HcK, B:Crash Parker	1,500.00
12 Dri,B:Star Fighter	1,500.00
13 Dri,B:Reef Ryan	1,200.00
14 Dri B:Norge Benson	1,100.00
15 B: Mars,God of War	2,200.00
16 Invasion From The Void	1,100.00
17 Warrior Maid of Mercury	1,100.00
18 Bondage(c)	1,200.00
19 Monsters of the Inner World	1,100.00

20 RP, Winged Man Eaters of the Exile Star	1,100.00
21 RP,B:Lost World Hunt Bowman	1,200.00
22 Inferno on the Fifth Moon	1,100.00
23 GT,Lizard Tyrant of the Twilight World	1,000.00
24 GT,Grl Raiders From The Red Moon	1,000.00
25 Grl,B:Norge Benson	1,000.00
26 Grl,B:The Space Rangers Bondage(c)	1,100.00
27 Grl, The Fire Eaters of Asteroid Z	800.00
28 Grl, Bondage (c)	850.00
29 Grl,Dragon Raiders of Aztla	800.00
30 GT,Grl City of Lost Souls	800.00
31 Grl,Fire Priests of Orbit6X	675.00
32 Slaver's Planetoid	800.00
33 MA	675.00
34 MA,Bondage	850.00
35 MA B:Mysta of The Moon	700.00
36 MA Collosus of the Blood Moon	700.00
37 MA, Behemoths of the Purple Void	700.00
38 MA	600.00
39 MA. Death Webs Of Zenith 3	600.00
40 Chameleon Men from Galaxy 9	600.00
41 MA,Aaf,New O: Auro Bondage (c)	650.00
42 MA,AaF,E:Gale Allan	600.00
43 MA,AaF Death Rays From the Sun.	600.00
44 MA,Bbl,B:Futura	600.00
45 Ma,Bbl,Her Evilness from Xanado	600.00
46 MA,Bbl,GE The Mecho-Men From Mars	600.00
47 MA,Bbl,GE,The Great Green Spawn	550.00
48 MA,GE	550.00
49 MA,GE, Werewolves From Hydra Hell	550.00
50 MA,GE,The Things of Xeves	550.00
51 MA,GE, Mad Mute X-Adapts	500.00
52 GE,Mystery of the Time Chamber	500.00
53 MB,GE,Bondage(c) Dwarflings From Oceania	500.00
54 MB,GE,Robots From Inferno	500.00
55 MB,GE,Giants of the Golden Atom	500.00
56 MB,GE,Grl	450.00
57 MB,GE,Grl	450.00
58 MB,GE,Grl	450.00
59 MB,GE,Grl,LSe	450.00
60 GE,Grl,Vassals of Volta	450.00
61 GE,Grl, The Brute in the Bubble	350.00
62 GE,Musta,Moon Goddess	350.00
63 GE,Paradise or Inferno	350.00
64 GE,Monkeys From the Blue	350.00
65 The Lost World	350.00
66 The Plague of the Locust Men	350.00
67 The Nymphs of Neptune	350.00
68 Synthoids of the 9th Moon	350.00
69 The Mentalists of Mars	350.00
70 Cargo For Amazonia	350.00
71 Sandhogs of Mars	250.00
72 Last Ship to Paradise	250.00
73 The Martian Plague, Winter 1953	250.00

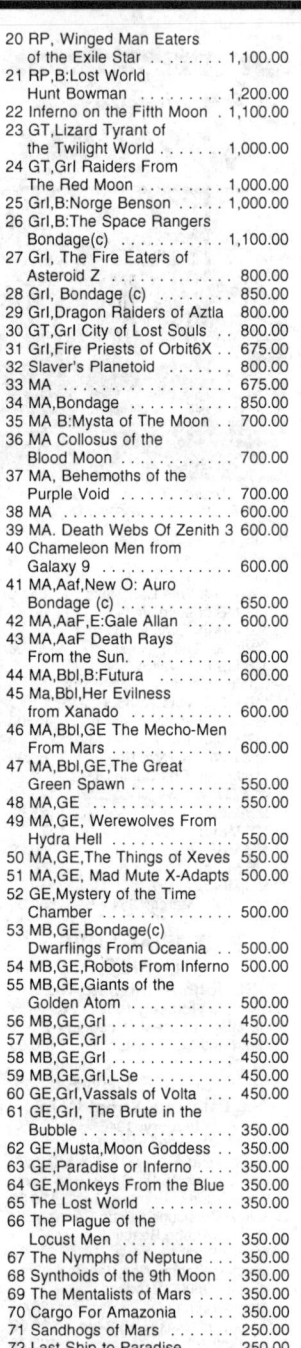

Plastic Man #29
© *Comics Magazines/Quality Comics*

PLASTIC MAN
Comics Magazines
(Quality Comics Group)
Summer, 1943

1 JCo,JCo(c)Game of Death	3,000.00
2 JCo,JCo(c)The Gay Nineties Nightmare	1,200.00
3 JCo,JCo(c)	750.00
4 JCo,JCo(c)	650.00
5 JCo,JCo(c)	550.00
6 JCo,JCo(c)	450.00
7 JCo,JCo(c)	450.00
8 JCo,JCo(c)	450.00
9 JCo,JCo(c)	450.00
10 JCo,JCo(c)	450.00
11 JCo,JCo(c)	400.00
12 JCo,JCo(c),V:Spadehead	400.00
13 JCo,JCo(c),V:Mr.Hazard	400.00
14 JCo,JCo(c),Words,Symbol of Crime	400.00
15 JCo,JCo(c),V:BeauBrummel	400.00
16 JCo,JCo(c),Money Means Trouble	400.00
17 JCo,JCo(c),A:The Last Man on Earth	400.00
18 JCo,JCo(c),Goes Back to the Farm	400.00
19 JCo,JCo(c),V:Prehistoric Plunder	400.00
20 JCo,JCo(c),A:Sadly,Sadly	400.00
21 JCo,JCo(c),V:Crime Minded Mind Reader	300.00
22 JCo,JCo(c), Which Twin is the Phony	300.00
23 JCo,JCo(c),The Fountain of Age	300.00
24 JCo,JCo(c),The Black Box of Terror	300.00
25 JCo,JCo(c),A:Angus MacWhangus	300.00
26 JCo,JCo(c),On the Wrong Side of the Law?	300.00
27 JCo,JCo(c),V:The Leader	300.00
28 JCo,JCo(c),V:Shasta	300.00
29 JCo,JCo(c),V:Tricky Toledo	300.00
30 JCo,JCo(c),V:Weightless Wiggins	300.00

31 JCo,JCo(c),V:Raka the
   Witch Doctor 225.00
32 JCo,JCo(c),V:Mr.Fission . . . 225.00
33 JCo,JCo(c),V:The Mad
   Professor 225.00
34 JCo,JCo(c),Smuggler'sHaven 225.00
35 JCo,JCo(c),V:The Hypnotist 225.00
36 JCo,JCo(c),The Uranium
   Underground 225.00
37 JCo,JCo(c),V:Gigantic Ants . 225.00
38 JCo,JCo(c),The Curse of
   Monk Mauley 225.00
39 JCo,JCo(c),The Stairway
   to Madness 225.00
40 JCo,JCo(c),The Ghoul of
   Ghost Swamp 225.00
41 JCo,JCo(c),The Beast with
   the Bloody Claws 200.00
42 JCo,JCo(c),The King of
   Thunderbolts 200.00
43 JCo,JCo(c),The Evil Terror . 200.00
44 JCo,JCo(c),The Magic Cup . 200.00
45 The Invisible Raiders 200.00
46 V:The Spider 200.00
47 The Fiend of a
   Thousand Faces 200.00
48 Killer Crossbones 200.00
49 JCo,The Weapon for Evil . . 200.00
50 V:Iron Fist 200.00
51 Incredible Sleep Weapon . . 175.00
52 V:Indestructible Wizard 185.00
53 V:Dazzia,Daughter of
   Darkness 185.00
54 V:Dr.Quomquat 185.00
55 The Man Below Zero 185.00
56 JCo, The Man Who Broke
   the Law of Gravity 185.00
57 The Chemist's Cauldron . . . 185.00
58 JCo,The Amazing
   Duplicating Machine 185.00
59 JCo,V:The Super Spy 185.00
60 The Man in the Fiery
   Disguise 175.00
61 V:King of the Thunderbolts . 175.00
62 V:The Smokeweapon 175.00
63 V:Reflecto 175.00
64 Nov'56 The Invisible
   Raiders 175.00

POCAHONTAS
Pocahontas Fuel Co.
October, 1941

N# 65.00
2 . . . . 50.00

POCKET COMICS
Harvey Publications
August, 1941

1 100 pages,O:Black Cat,Spirit
   of '76,Red Blazer Phantom
   Sphinx & Zebra,B:Phantom
   Ranger,British Agent #99,
   Spin Hawkins,Satan 700.00
2 . . . . 500.00
3 . . . . 400.00
4 Jan.'42,All Features End . . . 350.00

POGO POSSUM
Dell Publishing Co.

1 WK,A:Swamp Land Band . . 550.00
2 WK 400.00
3 WK 375.00
4 WK 375.00
5 WK 375.00

Pogo Possum #5 © Dell Publishing Co.

6 thru 10 WK . . . . @250.00
11 WK, Christmas cover . . . @300.00
12 thru 16 WK . . . . @200.00

POLICE COMICS
Comic Magazines
(Quality Comics Group)
August, 1941

1 GFx,JCo,WE.PGn,RC,FG,AB,
   GFx(c),B&O:Plastic Man
   The Human Bomb,#711,I&B,
   Chic Canter,The Firebrand
   Mouthpiece,Phantom Lady
   The Sword 6,500.00
2 JCo,GFx,PGn,WE,RC,FG,
   GFx(c) 2,200.00
3 JCo,GFx,PGn,WE,RC,FG,
   GFx(c) 1,500.00
4 JCo,GFx,PGn,WE,RC,FG,
   GFx&WEC(c) 1,400.00
5 JCo,GFx,PGn,WE,RC,FG,
   GFx(c) 1,300.00
6 JCo,GFx,PGn,WE,RC,FG,
   GFx(c) 1,200.00
7 JCo,GFx,PGn,WE,RC,FG,
   GFx(c) 1,100.00
8 JCo,GFx,PGn,WE,RC,FG,
   GFx(c),B&O:Manhunter . . 1,500.00
9 JCo,GFx,PGn,WE,RC,FG,
   GFx(c) 1,100.00
10 JCo,GFx,PGn,WE,RC,FG,
   GFx(c) 1,000.00
11 JCo,GFx,PGn,WE,RC,FG,
   GFx(c),B:Rep:Rep.Spirit
   Strips 1,600.00
12 JCo,GFX,PGn,WE,FG,AB,
   RC(c) I:Ebony 1,000.00
13 JCo,GFx,PGn,WE,FG,AB,RC(c)
   E:Firebrand,I:Woozy Winks 1,000.00
14 JCo,GFx,PGn,WE,Jku,GFX(c) 700.00
15 JCo,GFx,PGn,WE,Jku,GFX(c)
   E#711,B:Destiny 700.00
16 JCo,PGn,WE,JKu 700.00
17 JCo,PGn,WE,JKu,JCo(c) . . 700.00
18 JCo,PGn,WE,JCo(c) 700.00
19 JCo,PGn,WE,JCo(c) 700.00
20 JCo,PGn,WE,JCo(c),A:Jack
   Cole in Phantom Lady 700.00

21 JCo,PGn,WE,JCo(c) 600.00
22 JCo,PGn,WE,RP,JCo(c)
   The Eyes Have it 600.00
23 JCo,WE,RP,JCo(c),E:Phantom
   Lady 550.00
24 JCo,WE,HK,JCo(c),B:Flatfoot
   Burns 550.00
25 JCo,WE,HK,RP,JCo(c),The
   Bookstore Mysrery 550.00
26 JCo,WE,Hk,JCo,(c)E:Flatfoot
   Burns 550.00
27 JCo,WE,JCo(c) 550.00
28 JCo,WE,JCo(c) 550.00
29 JCo,WE,JCo(c) 550.00
30 JCo,WE,JCo(c),A Slippery
   Racket 550.00
31 JCo,WE,JCo(c),Is Plastic
   Man Washed Up? 350.00
32 JCo,WE,JCo(c),Fiesta Turns
   Into a Fracas 350.00
33 JCo,WE 350.00
34 JCo,WE,JCO(c) 350.00
35 JCo,WE,JCO(c) 350.00
36 JCo,WE,JCO(c),Rest
   In Peace 350.00
37 JCo,WE,PGn,JCo(c),Love
   Comes to Woozy 350.00
38 JCo,WE,PGn,JCo(c) 350.00
39 JCo,WE,PGn,JCo(c) 350.00
40 JCo,WE,PGn,JCo(c) 350.00
41 JCo,WE,PGn,JCo(c),E:Reps.
   of Spirit Strip 300.00
42 JCo,LF&WE,PGn,JCo(c),
   Woozy Cooks with Gas . . . 300.00
43 JCo,LF&WE,PGn,JCo(c) . . . 300.00
44 JCo,PGn,LF,JCo(c) 275.00
45 JCo,PGn,LF,JCo(c) 275.00
46 JCo,PGn,LF,JCo(c) 275.00
47 JCo,PGn,LF,JCo(c),
   V:Dr.Slicer 275.00
48 JCo,PGn,LF,JCo(c),V:Big
   Beaver 275.00
49 JCo,PGn,LF,JCo(c),V:Thelma
   Twittle 275.00
50 JCo,PGn,LF,JCo(c),V:The
   Granite Lady 200.00
52 JCo,PGn,LF,JCo(c) 200.00
53 JCo,PGn,LF,JCo(c),
   V:Dr.Erudite 200.00
54 JCo,PGn,LF,JCo(c) 200.00
55 JCo,PGn,LF,JCo(c),V:The
   Sleepy Eyes 200.00
56 JCo,PGn,LF,JCo(c),V:The
   Yes Man 200.00
57 JCo,PGn,LF,JCo(c),
   V:Mr.Misfit 200.00
58 JCo,PGn,LF,JCo(c),E:The
   Human Bomb 200.00
59 JCo,PGn,LF,JCo(c),A:Mr.
   Happiness 200.00
60 JCo,PGn,LF,JCo(c) 175.00
61 JCo,PGn,LF,JCo(c) 175.00
62 JCo,PGn,LF,JCo(c) 175.00
63 JCo,PGn,LF,JCo(c),
   V:The Crab 175.00
64 JCo,PGn,LF,HK,JCo(c) 175.00
65 JCo,PGn,LF,JCo(c) 175.00
66 JCo,PGn,LF,JCo(c) Love
   Can Mean Trouble 175.00
67 JCo,LF,JCo(c),
   V:The Gag Man 175.00
68 JCo,LF,JCo(c) 175.00
69 JCo,LF,JCo(c),V:Strecho . . 175.00
70 JCo,LF,JCo(c) 175.00

All comics prices listed are for *Near Mint* condition.

71 JCo,LF,JCo(c)	175.00
72 JCo,LF,JCo(c),V:Mr.Cat . . .	175.00
73 JCo,LF,JCo(c)	175.00
74 JCo,LF,JCo(c),V:Prof.Dimwit	175.00
75 JCo,LF,JCo(c)	175.00
76 JCo,LF,JCo(c),V:Mr.Morbid .	175.00
77 JCo,LF,JCo(c),V:Skull Face	
& Eloc	175.00
78 JCo,LF,JCo(c),A Hot Time In	
Dreamland	175.00
79 JCo,LF,JCo(c),V:Eaglebeak	175.00
80 JCo,LF,JCo(c),V:Penetro	175.00
81 JCo,LF,JCo(c),V:A Gorilla . .	175.00
82 JCo,LF,JCo(c)	175.00
83 JCo,LF,JCo(c)	175.00
84 JCo,LF,JCo(c)	175.00
85 JCo,LF,JCo(c),V:Lucky 7 . .	175.00
86 JCo,LF,JCo(c),V:The Baker	175.00
87 JCo,LF,JCo(c)	175.00
88 JCo,LF,JCo(c),V:The Seen .	175.00
89 JCo,JCo(c),V:The Vanishers	150.00
90 JCo,LF,JCo(c),V:Capt.Rivers	150.00
91 JCo,JCo(c),The	
Forest Primeval	160.00
92 JCo,LF,JCo(c),V:Closets	
Kennedy	160.00
93 JCo,JCo(c),V:The Twinning	
Terror	160.00
94 JCo,JCo(c),WE	225.00
95 JCo,JCo(c),WE,V:Scowls . .	225.00
96 JCo,JCo(c),WE,V:Black	
Widow	225.00
97 JCo,JCo(c),WE,V:The Mime	225.00
98 JCo,JCo(c),WE	225.00
99 JCo,JCo(c),WE	225.00
100 JCo,JCo(c)	250.00
101 JCo,JCo(c)	200.00
102 JCo,JCo(c),E:Plastic Man .	200.00
103 JCo,LF,B&I:Ken Shannon;	
Bondage(c)	150.00
104 The Handsome of Homocide	125.00
105 Invisible Hands of Murder .	125.00
106 Museum of Murder	125.00
107 Man with the ShrunkenHead	125.00
108 The Headless Horse Player	125.00
109 LF,Bondage(c),Blood on the	
Chinese Fan	135.00
110 Murder with a Bang	125.00
111 Diana, Homocidal Huntress	125.00
112 RC,The Corpse on the	
Sidewalk	125.00
113 RC,RC(c), The Dead Man	
with the Size 13 Shoe	125.00
114 The Terrifying Secret of	
the Black Bear	125.00
115 Don't Let Them Kill Me . . .	125.00
116 Stage Was Set For Murder	125.00
117 Bullet Riddled Bookkeeper	125.00
118 Case of the Absent Corpse	125.00
119 A Fast & Bloody Buck	125.00
120 Death & The Derelict	125.00
121 Curse of the Clawed Killer	125.00
122 The Lonely Hearts Killer . .	125.00
123 Death Came Screaming . . .	125.00
124 Masin Murder	125.00
125 Bondage(c),The Killer of	
King Arthur's Court	135.00
126 Hit & Run Murders	125.00
127 Oct'53,Death Drivers	125.00

POLICE LINE-UP
Avon Periodicals/
Realistic Comics
August, 1951

1 WW,P(c)	250.00

2 P(c),Drugs	175.00
3 JKu,EK,P(c)	125.00
4 July '52;EK	125.00

POLICE TRAP
Mainline Sept., 1954

1 S&K(c)	200.00
2 S&K(c)	100.00
3 S&K(c)	100.00
4 S&K(c)	100.00

Charlton Comics

5 S&K,S&K(c)	150.00
6 S&K,S&K(c)	150.00

Becomes:

PUBLIC DEFENDER
IN ACTION

7	50.00
8 thru 12, Oct. 1957	@40.00

POLLY PIGTAILS
Parents' Magazine Institute
January, 1946

1 Ph(c)	55.00
2 Ph(c)	25.00
3 Ph(c)	20.00
4 Ph(c)	20.00
5 Ph(c)	20.00
6 Ph(c)	20.00
7 Ph(c)	15.00
8	15.00
9	15.00
10	15.00
11 thru 22	@10.00
22 Ph(c)	10.00
23 Ph(c)	10.00
34 thru 43	@10.00

Popeye #10 © King Features

POPEYE
Dell Publishing Co.
1948

1	325.00
2	150.00
3 'Welcome to Ghost Island' . .	125.00
4	125.00
5	125.00
6	125.00
7	125.00

8	125.00
9	125.00
10	125.00
11	100.00
12	100.00
13	100.00
14 thru 20	@100.00
21 thru 30	@75.00
31 thru 40	@65.00
41 thru 45	@50.00
46 O:Sweat Pea	65.00
47 thru 50	@45.00
51 thru 60	@35.00
61 thru 65	@25.00

POPULAR COMICS
Dell Publishing Co.
February, 1936

1 Dick Tracy, Little Orphan	
Annie	3,500.00
2 Terry Pirates	1,200.00
3 Terry,Annie,Dick Tracy . . .	900.00
4	750.00
5 B:Tom Mix	750.00
6	600.00
7	600.00
8	600.00
9	600.00
10 Terry,Annie,Tracy	600.00
11 Terry,Annie,Tracy	500.00
12 Christmas(c)	500.00
13 Terry,Annie,Tracy	500.00
14 Terry,Annie,Tracy	500.00
15 same	500.00
16 same	500.00
17 same	500.00
18 same	500.00
19 same	500.00
20 same	500.00
21 same	400.00
22 same	400.00
23 same	400.00
24 same	400.00
25 same	400.00
26 same	400.00
27 E:Terry,Annie,Tracy	400.00
28 A:Gene Autry	300.00
29	300.00
30	300.00
31 A:Jim McCoy	300.00
32 A:Jim McCoy	300.00
33	300.00
34	300.00
35 Christmas(c),Tex Ritter . . .	300.00
36	300.00
37	300.00
38 B:Gang Busters	325.00
39	300.00
40	300.00
41	300.00
42	300.00
43 F:Gang Busters	325.00
44	200.00
45 Tarzan(c)	200.00
46 O:Martan the Marvel Man . .	300.00
47 F:Martan the Marvel Man . .	200.00
48 F:Martan the Marvel Man . .	200.00
49 F:Martan the Marvel Man . .	200.00
50	200.00
51 B&O:Voice	225.00
52 A:Voice	175.00
53 F:The Voice	175.00
54 F:Gang Busters,A:Voice . . .	175.00
55 F:Gang Busters	185.00
56 F:Gang Busters	175.00

All comics prices listed are for _Near Mint_ condition.

57 F:The Marvel Man 175.00
58 F:The Marvel Man 175.00
59 F:The Marvel Man 175.00
60 O:Prof. Supermind 185.00
61 Prof. Supermind & Son 150.00
62 Supermind & Son 150.00
63 B:Smilin' Jack 150.00
64 Smilin'Jack,Supermind 150.00
65 Professor Supermind 150.00
66 . . . . 150.00
67 Gasoline Alley 150.00
68 F:Smilin' Jack 150.00
69 F:Smilin' Jack 150.00
70 F:Smilin' Jack 150.00
71 F:Smilin' Jack 150.00
72 B:Owl,Terry & the Pirates . . 300.00
73 F:Terry and the Pirates 175.00
74 F:Smilin' Jack 175.00
75 F:Smilin'Jack,A:Owl 175.00
76 Captain Midnight 250.00
77 Captain Midnight 250.00
78 Captain Midnight 250.00
79 A:Owl 150.00

Popular Comics #78
© Dell Publishing Co.

80 F:Smilin' Jack,A:Owl 150.00
81 F: Terry&thePirates,A:Owl . . 150.00
82 F:Smilin' Jack,A:Owl 150.00
83 F:Smilin' Jack,A:Owl 150.00
84 F:Smilin' Jack,A:Owl 150.00
85 F:ThreeLittleGremlins,A:Owl 150.00
86 F:Three Little Gremlins 125.00
87 F:Smilin' Jack 125.00
88 F:Smilin' Jack 125.00
89 F:Smokey Stover 125.00
90 F:Terry and the Pirates 125.00
91 F:Smokey Stover 125.00
92 F:Terry and the Pirates 125.00
93 F:Smilin' Jack 125.00
94 F:Terry and the Pirates 125.00
95 F:Smilin' Jack 125.00
96 F:Gang Busters 125.00
97 F:Smilin' Jack 125.00
98 B:Felix Cat 135.00
99 F:Bang Busters 125.00
100 . . . . 150.00
101 thru 141 . . . . 75.00
142 E:Terry & the Pirates 70.00
143 . . . . 70.00
144 . . . . 70.00

145 F:Harold Teen 70.00

POPULAR ROMANCES
Better Publications
(Standard Comics)
December, 1949

5 B:Ph(c) 40.00
6 Ph(c) 25.00
7 RP 25.00
8 Ph(c) 25.00
9 Ph(c) 25.00
10 WW 40.00
11 thru 16 . . . . @20.00
17 WE 25.00
18 thru 21 . . . . @25.00
22 thru 27 ATh,Ph(c) . . . . . . @50.00

SCHOOL DAY ROMANCES
Star Publications
November-December, 1949

1 LbC(c),Teen-Age 125.00
2 LbC(c) 85.00
3 LbC(c),Ph(c) 85.00
4 LbC(c),JyD,RonaldReagan . 135.00
Becomes:
POPULAR TEEN-AGERS

5 LbC(c),Toni Gay,
   Eve Adams 175.00
6 LbC(c),Ginger Bunny,
   Midge Martin 150.00
7 LbC(c) 150.00
8 LbC(c) 150.00
9 LbC(c) 75.00
10 LbC(c) 75.00
11 LbC(c) 50.00
12 LbC(c) 50.00
13 LbC(c),JyD 50.00
14 LbC,WW,Spanking 125.00
15 LbC(c),JyD 40.00
16 . . . . 35.00
17 LbC(c),JyD 35.00
18 LbC(c) 35.00
19 LbC(c) 35.00
20 LbC(c),JyD 45.00
21 LbC(c),JyD 45.00
22 LbC(c) 30.00
23 LbC(c) 30.00

POWER COMICS
Holyoke/Narrative Publ.
1944

1 LbC(c) 1,000.00
2 B:Dr.Mephisto,Hitler(c) . . . 1,100.00
3 LbC(c) 1,100.00
4 LbC(c) 1,000.00

PRIDE OF THE YANKEES
Magazine Enterprises
1949

1 N#,OW,Ph(c),The Life
   of Lou Gehrig 600.00

PRISON BREAK
Avon Periodicals/Realistic
September, 1951

1 WW(c),WW 275.00
2 WW(c),WW,JKu 200.00
3 JD,JO 175.00
4 EK 150.00
5 EK,CI 150.00

PRIZE COMICS
Feature Publications
(Prize Publ.)
March, 1940

1 O&B:Power Nelson,Jupiter.
   B:Ted O'Neil,Jaxon of
   the Jungle,Bucky Brady,
   Storm Curtis, Rocket(c) . . 1,700.00
2 B:The Owl 750.00
3 Power Nelson(c) 650.00
4 Power Nelson(c) 650.00
5 A:Dr.Dekkar 600.00
6 A:Dr.Dekkar 600.00
7 S&K,DBr,JK(c),O&B DR Frost,
   Frankenstein,B:GreenLama,
   Capt Gallant,Voodini
   Twist Turner 1,400.00
8 S&K,DBr 750.00
9 S&K,DBr,Black Owl(c) 700.00
10 DBr,Black Owl(c) 600.00
11 DBr,O:Bulldog Denny 550.00
12 DBr 550.00

Prize Comics #44
© Feature Publications

13 DBR,O&B:Yank and
   Doodle,Bondage(c) 600.00
14 DBr,Black Owl(c) 550.00
15 DBr,Black Owl(c) 550.00
16 DBr,JaB,B:Spike Mason . . 550.00
17 DBr,Black Owl(c) 550.00
18 DBr,Black Owl(c) 550.00
19 DBr,Yank&Doodle(c) 550.00
20 DBr,Yank&Doodle(c) 550.00
21 DBr,JaB(c),Yank&Doodle(c) 350.00
22 DBr,Yank&Doodle(c) 350.00
23 DBr,Uncle Sam(c) 350.00
24 DBr,Abe Lincoln(c) 350.00
25 DBr,JaB,Yank&Doodle(c) . . 350.00
26 DBr,JaB,JaB(c),Liberty
   Bell(c) 350.00
27 DBr,Yank&Doodle(c) 225.00
28 DBr,Yank&Doodle(c) 200.00
29 DBr,JaB(c)Yank&Doodle(c) . 200.00
30 DBr,Yank&Doodle(c) 225.00
31 DBr,Yank&Doodle(c) 200.00
32 DBr,Yank&Doodle(c) 200.00
33 DBr,Bondage(c),Yank
   & Doodle 225.00
34 DBr,O:Airmale;New

GOLDEN AGE

Black Owl	225.00
35 DBr,B:Flying Fist & Bingo	125.00
36 DBr,Yank&Doodle(c)	125.00
37 DBr,I:Stampy,Hitler(c)	150.00
38 DBr,B.Owl,Yank&Doodle(c)	125.00
39 DBr,B.Owl,Yank&Doodle(c)	125.00
40 DBr,B.Owl,Yank&Doodle(c)	125.00
41 DBr,B.Owl,Yank&Doodle(c)	125.00
42 DBr,B.Owl,Yank&Doodle(c)	100.00
43 DBr,B.Owl,Yank&Doodle(c)	100.00
44 DBr, B&I:Boom Boom	
Brannigan	100.00
45 DBr	100.00
46 DBr	100.00
47 DBr	100.00
48 DBr,B:Prince Ra;Bondage(c)	125.00
49 DBr,Boom Boom(c)	90.00
50 DBr,Farnkenstein(c)	100.00
51 DBr	90.00
52 DBr, B:Sir Prize	90.00
53 DBr, The Man Who Could	
Read Features	100.00
54 DBr	90.00
55 DBr,Yank&Doodle(c)	90.00
56 DBr,Boom Boom (c)	90.00
57 DBr,Santa Claus(c)	90.00
58 DBr,The Poisoned Punch	90.00
59 DBr,Boom Boom(c)	90.00
60 DBr,Sir Prise(c)	90.00
61 DBr,The Man wih the	
Fighting Feet	90.00
62 DBr,Hck(c),Yank&Doodle(c)	90.00
63 DBr,S&K,S&K(c),Boom	
Boom(c)	100.00
64 DBr,Blackowl Retires	90.00
65 DBr,DBr(c),Frankenstein	90.00
66 DBr,DBr(c),Frankenstein	90.00
67 DBr,B:Brothers in Crime	90.00
68 DBr,RP(c)	90.00

Becomes:

PRIZE COMICS
WESTERN

69 ACa(c),B:Dusty Ballew	100.00
70 ACa(c)	75.00
71 ACa(c)	75.00
72 ACa(c),JSe	75.00
73 ACa(c)	75.00
74 ACa(c)	75.00
75 JSe,S&K(c),6-Gun Showdown	
at Rattlesnake Gulch	80.00
76 Ph(c),Randolph Scott	100.00
77 Ph(c),JSe,Streets of	
Laredo,movie	75.00
78 Ph(c),JSe,HK,Bullet	
Code, movie	120.00
79 Ph(c),JSe,Stage to	
China, movie	120.00
80 Ph(c),Gunsmoke Justice	75.00
81 Ph(c),The Man Who Shot	
Billy The Kid	75.00
82 Ph(c),MBi,JSe&BE,Death	
Draws a Circle	75.00
83 JSe,S&K(c)	70.00
84 JSe	50.00
85 JSe,B:American Eagle	150.00
86 JSe	60.00
87 JSe&BE	65.00
88 JSe&BE	65.00
89 JSe&Be	65.00
90 JSe&BE	65.00
91 JSe&BE,JSe&BE(c)	65.00
92 JSe,JSe&BE(c)	65.00
93 JSe,JSe&BE(c),	65.00
94 JSe&BE,JSe&BE(c)	65.00

Prize Comics Western #93
© Feature Publications

95 JSe,JSe&BE(c)	65.00
96 JSe,JSe&BE,JSe&BE(c)	65.00
97 JSe,JSe&BE,JSeBE(c)	65.00
98 JSe&BE,JSe&BE(c)	65.00
99 JSe&BE,JSe&BE(c)	65.00
100 JSe,JSe(c)	85.00
101 JSe	65.00
102 JSe	65.00
103 JSe	65.00
104 JSe	65.00
105 JSe	65.00
106 JSe	50.00
107 JSe	50.00
108 JSe	70.00
109 JSe&AW	80.00
110 JSe&BE	75.00
111 JSe&BE	75.00
112	50.00
113 AW&JSe	75.00
114 MMe,B:The Drifter	35.00
115 MMe	35.00
116 MMe	35.00
117 MMe	35.00
118 MMe,E:The Drifter	35.00
119 Nov/Dec'56	35.00

PSYCHOANALYSIS
E.C. Comics
March-April, 1955

1 JKa,JKa(c)	125.00
2 JKa,JKa(c)	100.00
3 JKa,JKa(c)	100.00
4 JKa(c) Sept.-Oct. 1955	100.00

PUBLIC ENEMIES
D.S. Publishing Co.
1948

1 AMc	150.00
2 AMc	150.00
3 AMc	75.00
4 AMc	75.00
5 AMc	75.00
6 AMc	75.00
7 AMc,Eye Injury	90.00
8	75.00
9	75.00

PUNCH AND JUDY
COMICS
Hillman Periodicals
1944

1 (fa)	100.00
2	50.00
3	40.00
4 thru 12	@35.00
2-1	30.00
2-2 JK	100.00
2-3	30.00
2-4	30.00
2-5	30.00
2-6	30.00
2-7	30.00
2-8	30.00
2-9	30.00
2-10 JK	100.00
2-11 JK	100.00
2-12 JK	100.00
3-1 JK	100.00
3-2	90.00
3-3	25.00
3-4	25.00
3-5	25.00
3-6	25.00
3-7	25.00
3-8	25.00
3-9	25.00

PUNCH COMICS
Harry 'A' Chesler
December, 1941

1 B:Mr.E,The Sky Chief,Hale	
the Magician,Kitty Kelly	900.00
2 A:Capt.Glory	600.00
3-8 Do Not Exist	
9 B:Rocket Man & Rocket	
girl,Master Ken	500.00
10 JCo,A:Sky Chief	400.00
11 JCo,O:Master Key,A:Little	
Nemo	400.00
12 A:Rocket Boy,Capt.Glory	500.00
13 Ric(c)	450.00
14 GT	400.00
15 FSm(c)	400.00
16	400.00
17	400.00
18 FSm(c),Bondage(c),Drug	500.00
19 FSm(c)	400.00
20 Women semi-nude(c)	550.00
21 Drug	400.00
22 I:Baxter,Little Nemo	200.00
23 A:Little Nemo	200.00

PUPPET COMICS
Dougherty, Co.
Spring, 1946

1 Funny Animal	35.00
2	30.00

PURPLE CLAW, THE
Minoan Publishing Co./
Toby Press
January, 1953

1 O:Purple Claw	200.00
2 and 3	@150.00

PUZZLE FUN COMICS
George W. Dougherty Co.
Spring, 1946

1 PGn	150.00

2 .... 125.00

QUEEN OF THE WEST, DALE EVANS
Dell Publishing Co.
July, 1953
(1) see Dell Four Color #479
(1) see Dell Four Color #528
3 ATh, Ph(c) all 75.00
4 ATh,RsM 65.00
5 RsM 45.00
6 RsM 45.00
7 RsM 45.00
8 RsM 45.00
9 RsM 45.00
10 RsM 45.00
11 .... 32.00
12 RsM 40.00
13 RsM 40.00
14 RsM 40.00
15 RsM 40.00
16 RsM 40.00
17 RsM 40.00
18 RsM 40.00
19 .... 30.00
20 RsM 40.00
21 .... 30.00
22 RsM 40.00

RACKET SQUAD IN ACTION
Capitol Stories/ Charlton Comics
May-June, 1952
1 Carnival(c) 175.00
2 .... 100.00
3 Roulette 100.00
4 FFr(c) 100.00
5 Just off the Boat 125.00
6 The Kidnap Racket 85.00
7 .... 75.00
8 .... 75.00
9 2 Fisted fix 75.00
10 .... 75.00
11 SD,SD(c),Racing(c) 175.00
12 JoS,SD(c),Explosion(c) .. 300.00
13 JoS(c),The Notorious Modelling
Agency Racket,Acid 75.00
14 DG(c),Drug 100.00
15 Photo Extortion Racket ... 60.00
16 thru 28 .... @60.00
29,March, 1958 .... 75.00

RAGGEDY ANN AND ANDY
Dell Publishing Co.
1942
1 Billy & Bonnie Bee 250.00
2 .... 125.00
3 DNo,B:Egbert Elephant ... 125.00
4 DNo,WK 150.00
5 DNo 100.00
6 DNo 100.00
7 Little Black Sambo 100.00
8 .... 100.00
9 .... 100.00
10 .... 100.00
11 .... 75.00
12 .... 75.00
13 .... 75.00
14 .... 75.00
15 .... 75.00
16 thru 20 .... @75.00

21 Alice in Wonderland 65.00
22 thru 27 .... @45.00
28 WK 50.00
29 thru 39 .... @45.00

RALPH KINER HOME RUN KING
Fawcett Publications
1950
1 N#, Life Story of the
Famous Pittsburgh Slugger . 450.00

RAMAR OF THE JUNGLE
Toby Press/ Charlton Comics
1954
1 Ph(c),TV Show 125.00
2 Ph(c) 75.00
3 .... 75.00
4 .... 75.00
5 Sept '56 .... 75.00

RANGE ROMANCES
Comics Magazines (Quality Comics)
December, 1949
1 PGn(c),PGn 150.00
2 RC(c),RC 175.00
3 RC,Ph(c) 125.00
4 RC,Ph(c) 125.00
5 RC,PGn,Ph(c) 125.00

RANGERS OF FREEDOM
Flying Stories, Inc. (Fiction House)
October, 1941
1 I:Ranger Girl & Rangers
of Freedom;V:Super-Brain . 1,600.00
2 V:Super -Brain 600.00
3 Bondage(c) The Headsman
of Hate 500.00
4 Hawaiian Inferno 450.00
5 RP,V:Super-Brain 450.00
6 RP,Bondage(c);Bugles
of the Damned 450.00
7 RP,Death to Tojo's
Butchers 400.00
Becomes:
RANGERS COMICS
8 RP,B:US Rangers 400.00
9 GT,BLb,Commando Steel
for Slant Eyes 400.00
10 BLb,Bondage (c) 425.00
11 Raiders of the
Purple Death 350.00
12 A:Commando Rangers 350.00
13 Grl,B:Commando Ranger .. 350.00
14 Grl,Bondage(c) 350.00
15 GT,Grl,Bondage(c) 350.00
16 Grl,GT;Burma Raid 375.00
17 GT,GT,Bondage(c),Raiders
of the Red Dawn 375.00
18 GT 375.00
19 GE,Blb,GT,Bondage(c) ... 300.00
20 GT 250.00
21 GT,Bondage(c) 300.00
22 GT,B&O:Firehair 225.00
23 GT,BLb,B:Kazanda 200.00
24 Bondage(c) 225.00
25 Bondage(c) 225.00
26 Angels From Hell 200.00

Rangers Comics #7 © Fiction House

27 Bondage(c) 225.00
28 BLb,E:Kazanda;B&O Tiger
Man 225.00
29 Bondage(c) 225.00
30 BLb,B:Crusoe Island 235.00
31 BLb,Bondage(c) 200.00
32 BLb 150.00
33 BLb,Drug 175.00
34 BLb 150.00
35 BLB,Bondage(c) 200.00
36 BLb,MB 150.00
37 BLb,Mb 150.00
38 BLb,MB,GE,Bondage(c) ... 200.00
39 BLb,GE 150.00
40 BLb,GE,BLb(c) 150.00
41 BLb,GE 150.00
42 BLb,GE 150.00
43 BLb,GE 150.00
44 BLb,GE 150.00
45 BLb,GEl 150.00
46 BLb,GE 135.00
47 BLb,JGr 135.00
48 BLb,JGr 135.00
49 BLb,JGr 135.00
50 BLb,JGr,Bondage(c) 150.00
51 BLb,JGr 135.00
52 BLb,JGr,Bondage(c) 150.00
53 BLb,JGr,Prisoners of
Devil Pass 135.00
54 JGr,When The Wild
Commanches Ride 135.00
55 JGr,Massacre Guns at
Pawnee Pass 135.00
56 JGr, Gun Smuggler of
Apache Mesa 135.00
57 JGr,Redskins to the
Rescue 135.00
58 JGr,Brides of the
Buffalo Men 135.00
59 JGr,Plunder Portage 135.00
60 JGr, Buzzards of
Bushwack Trail 135.00
61 BWh(c)Devil Smoke at
Apache Basin 100.00
62 BWh(c)B:Cowboy Bob 100.00
63 BWh(c) 100.00
64 BWh(c)B:Suicide Smith ... 100.00
65 BWh(c):Wolves of the
Overland Trail,Bondage(c) . 110.00

All comics prices listed are for *Near Mint* condition.   **CVA Page 385**

GOLDEN AGE

GOLDEN AGE

66 BWh(c) 100.00
67 BWh(c)B:Space Rangers .. 100.00
68 BWh(c);Cargo for Coje 100.00
69 BWh(c);Great Red Death
   Ray 100.00

REAL CLUE CRIME STORIES
(see CLUE COMICS)

REAL FUNNIES
Nedor Publishing Co.
January, 1943

1 (fa) 135.00
2 and 3 (fa) .... @65.00

REAL HEROES COMICS
Parents' Magazine Institiute
September, 1941

1 HcK,Franklin Roosevelt 225.00
2 J, Edgar Hoover 100.00
3 General Wavell 75.00
4 Chiang Kai Shek 75.00
5 Stonewall Jackson 90.00
6 Lou Gehrig 150.00
7 Chennault and his
   Flying Tigers 75.00
8 Admiral Nimitz 75.00
9 The Panda Man 60.00
10 Carl Akeley-Jungle
    Adventurer 60.00
11 Wild Jack Howard 55.00
12 General Robert L
    Eichelberger 50.00
13 HcK,Victory at Climback 50.00
14 Pete Gray 50.00
15 Alexander Mackenzie 50.00
16 Balto of Nome Oct '46 ..... 50.00

REAL LIFE STORY OF FESS PARKER
Dell Publishing Co.
1955

1 .... 75.00

REALISTIC ROMANCES
Avon Periodicals/
Realistic Comics
July-August, 1951

1 Ph(c) 125.00
2 Ph(c) 50.00
3 P(c) 35.00
4 P(c) 35.00
5 thru 14 .... @40.00
15 .... 30.00
16 Drug 55.00
17 .... 30.00

REAL LIFE COMICS
Visual Editions/Better/
Standard/Nedor
September, 1941

1 ASh(c),Lawrence of
   Arabia,Uncle Sam(c) ... 350.00
2 ASh(c),Liberty(c) 175.00
3 Adolph Hitler(c) 300.00
4 ASh(c)Robert Fulton,
   Charles DeGaulle 125.00
5 ASh(c)Alexander the Great . 125.00
6 ASh(c)John Paul Jones,CDR 100.00
7 ASh(c)Thomas Jefferson ... 100.00
8 Leonardo Da Vinci 100.00

9 US Coast Guard Issue ... 100.00
10 Sir Hubert Wilkens 100.00
11 Odyssey on a Raft 75.00
12 ImpossibleLeatherneck ... 75.00
13 ASh(c)The Eternal Yank 75.00
14 Sir Isaac Newton 75.00
15 William Tell 75.00
16 Marco Polo 75.00
17 Albert Einstein 85.00
18 Ponce De Leon 75.00
19 The Fighting Seabees 75.00
20 Joseph Pulitzer 75.00
21 Admiral Farragut 50.00
22 Thomas Paine 50.00
23 Pedro Menendez 50.00
24 Babe Ruth 125.00
25 Marcus Whitman 50.00
26 Benvenuto Cellini 50.00
27 A Bomb Story 125.00
28 Robert Blake 50.00
29 Daniel DeFoe 50.00
30 Baron Robert Clive 50.00
31 Anthony Wayne 50.00

Real Life Comics #30
© Visual Editions/Better/Standard

32 Frank Sinatra 75.00
33 Frederick Douglas 50.00
34 Paul Revere,Jimmy Stewart . 60.00
35 Rudyard Kipling 50.00
36 Story of the Automobile 50.00
37 Francis Manion 50.00
38 Richard Henry Dana 45.00
39 Samuel FB Morse 40.00
40 FG,ASh(c),Hans Christian
    Anderson 45.00
41 Abraham Lincoln,Jimmy Foxx 60.00
42 Joseph Conrad,Fred Allen . 50.00
43 Louis Braille,O.W.Holmes ... 45.00
44 Citizens of Tomorrow 45.00
45 ASh(c),Francois Villon 65.00
46 The Pony Express 65.00
47 ASh(c),Montezuma 45.00
48 .... 45.00
49 ASh(c),Gene Bearden,
    Baseball 50.00
50 FF,ASh(c),Lewis & Clark ... 175.00
51 GE,ASh(c),Sam Houston ... 125.00
52 GE,FF,ASh(c),JSe&BE
    Leif Erickson 160.00
53 JSe&BE,Henry Wells &

   William Fargo 65.00
54 GT,Alexander Graham Bell .. 65.00
55 ASh(c),JSe&BE, The James
    Brothers 65.00
56 JSe&BE 65.00
57 JSe&BE 65.00
58 JSe&BE,Jim Reaves 75.00
59 FF,JSe&BE,Battle Orphan
    Sept '52 .... 65.00

REAL LOVE
(see HAP HAZARD COMICS)

REAL WEST ROMANCES
Crestwoood Publishing Co./
Prize Publ.
April-May, 1949

1 S&K,Ph(c) 125.00
2 Ph(c),Spanking 90.00
3 JSe,BE,Ph(c) 40.00
4 S&K,JSe,BE,Ph(c) 75.00
5 S&K,MMe,JSe,Audie
   Murphy Ph(c) 65.00
6 S&K,JSe,BE,Ph(c) 50.00

RECORD BOOK OF FAMOUS POLICE CASES
St. John Publishing Co.
1949

1 N#,JKu,MB(c) 250.00

Red Arrow #1 © P.L. Publishing Co.

RED ARROW
P.L. Publishing Co.
May,1951

1 Bondage(c) 75.00
2 .... 50.00
3 P(c) 40.00

RED BAND COMICS
Enwil Associates
November, 1944

1 The Bogeyman 225.00
2 O:Bogeyman,same(c)as#1 .. 175.00
3 A:Captain Wizard 150.00
4 May '45,Repof#3,Same(c) .. 150.00

RED CIRCLE COMICS
Enwil Associates
(Rural Home Public)
January, 1945

1 B:Red Riot,The Prankster	200.00
2 LSt,A:The Judge	150.00
3 LSt,LSt(c)	125.00
4 LSt,LSt(c) covers of #4 stapled over other comics	125.00

TRAIL BLAZERS
Street & Smith Publications
January, 1942

1 Wright Brothers	225.00
2 Benjamin Franklin,Dodgers	150.00
3 Red Barber,Yankees	175.00
4 Famous War song	100.00

Becomes:

RED DRAGON COMICS

5 JaB(c),B&O:Red Rover: B:Capt.Jack Comkmando Rex King&Jet,Minute Man	750.00
6 O:Red Dragon	1,200.00
7 The Curse of the Boneless Men	800.00
8 China V:Japan	500.00
9 The Reducing Ray,Jan '44	500.00

November, 1947
(2nd Series)

1 B:Red Dragon	650.00
2 BP	500.00
3 BP,BP(c),I:Dr Neff	400.00
4 BP,BP(c)	550.00
5 BP,BP(c)	400.00
6 BP,BP(c)	400.00
7 BP,BP(c),May 49	400.00

RED MASK
(see TIM HOLT)

RED RABBIT
Dearfield/
J. Charles Lave Publ. Co.
January, 1941

1 (fa)	55.00
2	30.00
3 thru 10	@20.00
11 thru 22	@18.00

RED SEAL COMICS
Harry 'A' Chesler, Jr./Superior
October, 1945

14 GT,Bondage(c),Black Dwarf	450.00
15 GT,Torture	325.00
16 GT	450.00
17 GT,Lady Satan,Sky Chief	300.00
18 Lady Satan,Sky Chief	300.00
19 Lady Satan,Sky Chief	300.00
20 Lady Satan,Sky Chief	300.00
21 Lady Satan,Sky Chief	300.00
22 Rocketman	200.00

REDSKIN
Youthful Magazines
September, 1950

1 Redskin,Bondage(c)	75.00
2 Apache Dance of Death	45.00
3 Daniel Boone	35.00
4 Sitting Bull- Red Devil of the Black Hills	35.00
5	35.00
6 Geronimo- Terror of the	

Desert,Bondage	45.00
7 Firebrand of the Sioux	35.00
8	35.00
9	35.00
10 Dead Man's Magic	35.00
11	35.00
12 Quanah Parker,Bondage(c)	45.00

Becomes:

FAMOUS WESTERN BADMEN

13 Redskin- Last of the Comanches	40.00
14	25.00
15 The Dalton Boys Apr '52	25.00

REMEMBER PEARL HARBOR
Street & Smith Publications
1942

1 N# JaB,Battle of the Pacific,Uncle Sam(c)	300.00

RETURN OF THE OUTLAW
Minoan Publishing Co.
February, 1953

1 Billy The Kid	50.00
2	30.00
3 thru 11	@20.00

REVEALING ROMANCES
A.A. Wyn
(Ace Magazines)
September, 1949

1	40.00
2	20.00
3 thru 6	@15.00

REX ALLEN COMICS
Dell Publishing Co.
February, 1951

(1) see Dell Four Color #316	
2 Ph(c) all	75.00
3 thru 10	@60.00
11 thru 23	@40.00
24 ATh	50.00
25 thru 31	@40.00

REX DEXTER OF MARS
Fox Features Syndicate
Autumn, 1940

1 DBr,DBr(c) Battle ofKooba	1,500.00

RIBTICKLER
Fox Features Syndicate
1945

1	70.00
2	35.00
3 Cosmo Cat	25.00
4 thru 6	@20.00
7 Cosmo Cat	22.00
8 thru 9	@20.00

RIN TIN TIN
Dell Publishing Co.
November, 1952

(1) see Dell Four Color #434	
(1) see Dell Four Color #476	
(1) see Dell Four Color #523	
4 thru 10 Ph(c) all	@50.00

11 thru 20	@70.00

Rocket Comics #2 © Hillman Periodicals

ROCKET COMICS
Hillman Periodicals
March, 1940

1 O:Red Roberts;B:Rocket Riley,Phantom Ranger,Steel Shank,Buzzard Baynes,Lefty Larson,The Defender,Man with 1,000 Faces	1,700.00
2	600.00
3 May '40 E:All Features	900.00

ROCKET KELLY
Fox Features Syndicate
Autumn, 1945–Oct. Nov. 1946

N#	175.00
1	175.00
2 A:The Puppeteer	135.00
3 thru 6	@125.00

ROCKETMAN
Ajax/Farrell Publications
June, 1952

1 Space Stories of the Future	275.00

ROCKET SHIP X
Fox Features Syndicate
September, 1951

1	450.00
2 N# Variant of Original	300.00

ROCKY LANE WESTERN
Fawcett/Charlton Comics
May, 1949

1 Ph(c)B:Rocky Lane,Slim Pickins	750.00
2 Ph(c)	300.00
3 Ph(c)	200.00
4 Ph(c)CCB,Rail Riders Rampage,F Capt Tootsie	200.00
5 Ph(c)The Missing Stagecoaches	200.00
6 Ph(c)Ghost Town Showdown	150.00
7 Ph(c)The Border Revolt	175.00
8 Ph(c)The Sunset Feud	175.00
9 Ph(c)Hermit of the Hills	175.00

All comics prices listed are for *Near Mint* condition.

GOLDEN AGE

10 Ph(c)Badman's Reward	150.00
11 Ph(c)Fool's Gold Fiasco	125.00
12 Ph(c),CCB,Coyote Breed	
F:Capt Tootsie,Giant	125.00
13 Ph(c),Giant	125.00
14 Ph(c)	100.00
15 Ph(c)B:Black Jacks	
Hitching Post,Giant	110.00
16 Ph(c),Giant	100.00
17 Ph(c),Giant	100.00
18 Ph(c)	110.00
19 Ph(c),Giant	115.00
20 Ph(c)The Rodeo Rustler	
E:Slim Pickens	115.00
21 Ph(c)B: Dee Dickens	100.00
22 Ph(c)	90.00
23 thru 30	@100.00
31 thru 40	@90.00
41 thru 55	@90.00
56 thru 60	@65.00
61 thru 70	@60.00
71 thru 87	@50.00

ROD CAMERON WESTERN
Fawcett Publications
February, 1950

1 Ph(c)	400.00
2 Ph(c)	175.00
3 Ph(c),Seven Cities of Cipiola	150.00
4 Ph(c),Rip-Roaring Wild West	125.00
5 Ph(c),Six Gun Sabotage	125.00
6 Ph(c),Medicine Bead Murders	125.00
7 Ph(c),Wagon Train Of Death	125.00
8 Ph(c),Bayou Badman	125.00
9 Ph(c),Rustlers Ruse	125.00
10 Ph(c),White Buffalo Trail	125.00
11 Ph(c),Lead Poison	100.00
12 thru 19 Ph(c)	@100.00
20 Phc(c),Great Army Hoax	100.00

ROLY-POLY COMICS
Green Publishing Co.
1945

1 B:Red Rube&Steel Sterling	175.00
6 A:Blue Cycle	100.00

Roly-Poly Comics #15
© Green Publishing

10 A:Red Rube	100.00
11	100.00
12	100.00
13	100.00
14 A:Black Hood	100.00
15 A:Steel Fist;1946	225.00

ROMANCE AND CONFESSION STORIES
St. John Publishing Co.
1949

1 MB(c),MB	250.00

ROMANTIC LOVE
Avon Periodicals/Realistic
September-October, 1949

1 P(c)	135.00
2 P(c)	85.00
3 P(c)	75.00
4 Ph(c)	75.00
5 P(c)	75.00
6 Ph(c),Drug,Thrill Crazy	100.00
7 P(c)	75.00
8 P(c)	75.00
9 EK,P(c)	85.00
10 thru 11 P(c)	@80.00
12 EK	85.00
20	75.00
21	75.00
22 EK	75.00
23 EK	75.00

ROMANTIC MARRIAGE
Ziff-Davis/
St. John Publishing Co.
November-December, 1950

1 Ph(c),Selfish wife	125.00
2 P(c),Mother's Boy	60.00
3 P(c),Hen Peck House	50.00
4 P(c)	50.00
5 Ph(c)	50.00
6 Ph(c)	40.00
7 Ph(c)	40.00
8 P(c)	40.00
9 P(c)	40.00
10 P/PH(c)	100.00
11	40.00
12	40.00
13 Ph(c)	40.00
14 thru 20	@40.00
20 Ph(c)	40.00
21	40.00
22	40.00
23 MB	45.00
24	40.00

ROMANTIC PICTURE NOVELETTES
Magazine Enterprises
1946

1 Mary Wothr adventure	100.00

ROMANTIC SECRETS
Fawcett Publ./Charlton Comics
September, 1949

1 Ph(c)	100.00
2 MSy(c)	50.00
3 MSy(c)	50.00
4 GE	60.00
5 BP	55.00
6	25.00
7 BP	25.00

8	25.00
9 GE	35.00
10 BP	30.00
11	25.00
12 BP	30.00
13	25.00
14	25.00
15	25.00
16 BP,MSy	30.00
17 BP	30.00
18	25.00
19	25.00
20 BP.MBi	30.00
21	20.00
22	20.00
23	18.00
24 GE	40.00
25 MSy	18.00
26 BP,MSy	20.00
27 MSy	18.00
28	18.00
29 BP	20.00
30 thru 32	@18.00
33 MSy	20.00
34 BP	20.00
35	18.00
36 BP	20.00
37 BP	20.00
38 thru 52	@18.00

ROMANTIC STORY
Fawcett Publ./Charlton Comics
November, 1949

1 Ph(c)	75.00
2 Ph(c)	40.00
3 Ph(c)	30.00
4 Ph(c)	30.00
5 Ph(c)	30.00
6 Ph(c)	30.00
7 BP,Ph(c)	25.00
8 BP,Ph(c)	25.00
9 Ph(c)	22.00
10 Ph(c)	22.00
11 Ph(c)	22.00
12 Ph(c)	22.00
13 Ph(c)	22.00
14 Ph(c)	22.00
15 GE,Ph(c)	35.00
16 BP,Ph(c)	25.00
17 Ph(c)	20.00
18 Ph(c)	20.00
19 Ph(c)	20.00
20 BP,Ph(c)	22.00
22 ATh,Ph(c)	18.00

Charlton Comics

23	15.00
24 Ph(c)	15.00
25 thru 29	@15.00
30 BP	20.00
31 thru 39	@15.00

ROMANTIC WESTERN
Fawcett Publications
Winter, 1949

1 Ph(c)	125.00
2 Ph(c),AW,AMc	135.00
3 Ph(c)	100.00

ROMEO TUBBS
(see MY SECRET LIFE)

ROUNDUP
D.S. Publishing Co.
July-August, 1948
1 HcK	. . . .	125.00
2 Drug	. . . .	100.00
3	. . . .	75.00
4	. . . .	75.00
5 Male Bondage	. . . .	85.00

ROY CAMPANELLA, BASEBALL HERO
Fawcett Publications
1950
N# Ph(c),Life Story of the
Battling Dodgers Catcher . . 450.00

ROY ROGERS
Dell Publishing Co.
1 photo (c)	. . . .	750.00
2	. . . .	250.00
3	. . . .	175.00
4	. . . .	150.00
5	. . . .	150.00
6 thru 10	. . . .	@125.00
11 thru 20	. . . .	@100.00
21 thru 30	. . . .	@75.00
31 thru 46	. . . .	@60.00
47 thru 50	. . . .	@50.00
51 thru 56	. . . .	@45.00
57 Drug	. . . .	55.00
58 thru 70	. . . .	@40.00
71 thru 80	. . . .	@35.00
81 thru 91	. . . .	@30.00

Becomes:
ROY ROGERS AND TRIGGER
92 thru 99	. . . .	@30.00
100	. . . .	50.00
101 thru 118	. . . .	@30.00
119 thru 125 ATn	. . . .	@45.00
126 thru 131	. . . .	@35.00
132 thru 144 RsM	. . . .	@40.00
145	. . . .	45.00

ROY ROGER'S TRIGGER
Dell Publishing Co.
May, 1951
(1) see Dell Four Color #329
2 Ph(c)	. . . .	125.00
3 P(c)	. . . .	40.00
4 P(c)	. . . .	40.00
5 P(c)	. . . .	40.00
6 thru 17 P(c)	. . . .	@30.00

RULAH, JUNGLE GODDESS
(see ZOOT COMICS)

SAARI, THE JUNGLE GODDESS
P.L. Publishing Co.
November, 1951
1 The Bantu Blood Curse . . . 300.00

SABU, ELEPHANT BOY
Fox Features Syndicate
June, 1950
1(30) WW,Ph(c)	. . . .	150.00
2 JKa,Ph(c),August'50	. . . . . .	100.00

HAPPY HOULIHANS
Fables Publications (E.C. Comics)
Autumn, 1947
1 O:Moon Girl	. . . .	400.00
2	. . . .	250.00

Becomes:
SADDLE JUSTICE
3 HcK,JCr,AF	. . . .	300.00
4 AF,JCr	. . . .	275.00
5 AF,Grl,WI	. . . .	250.00
6 AF,Grl	. . . .	250.00
7 AF,Grl	. . . .	250.00
8 AF,Grl,WI	. . . .	250.00

Becomes:
SADDLE ROMANCES
9 Grl(c),Grl	. . . .	300.00
10 AF(c),WW	. . . .	325.00
11 AF(c),Grl	. . . .	275.00

SAD SACK
Harvey Publications
Sept. 1949
1 I:Little Dot	. . . .	400.00
2	. . . .	200.00
3	. . . .	100.00
4 thru 10	. . . .	@75.00
11 thru 21	. . . .	50.00
22 Back in the Army Again, The Specialist	. . . .	35.00
23 thru 50	. . . .	@20.00
51 thru 100	. . . .	@15.00
100 thru 150	. . . .	@7.50
151 thru 200	. . . .	@5.00
200 thru 287	. . . .	@4.00

See also Other Pub. (Color)

The Saint #1 © Avon Periodicals

SAINT, THE
Avon Periodicals
August, 1947
1 JKa,JKa(c),Bondage(c)	. . . .	500.00
2	. . . .	300.00
3 Rolled Stocking Leg(c)	. . . .	225.00
4 MB(c)	. . . .	200.00
5 Spanking Panel	. . . .	275.00
6 B:Miss Fury	. . . .	325.00

7 P(c),Detective Cases(c)	. . . .	175.00
8 P(c),Detective Cases"(c)	. . .	150.00
9 EK(c),The Notorious Murder Mob	. . . .	150.00
10 WW,P(c),V:The Communist Menace	. . . .	175.00
11 P(c),Wanted For Robbery	. .	100.00
12 P(c),The Blowpipe Murders March, 1952	. . . .	125.00

SAM HILL PRIVATE EYE
Close-Up Publications
1950
1 The Double Trouble Caper	.	100.00
2	. . . .	55.00
3	. . . .	50.00
4 Negligee panels	. . . .	65.00
5 thru 7	. . . .	@40.00

SAMSON
Fox Features Syndicate
Autumn, 1940
1 BP,GT,A:Wing Turner	. . .	1,500.00
2 BP,A:Dr. Fung	. . . .	600.00
3 JSh(c),A:Navy Jones	. . . .	500.00
4 WE,B:Yarko	. . . .	400.00
5 WE	. . . .	400.00
6 WE,O:The Topper;Sept'41	.	400.00

SAMSON
Ajax Farrell Publ (Four Star)
April, 1955
12 The Electric Curtain	. . . . .	175.00
13 Assignment Danger	. . . . .	150.00
14 The Red Raider;Aug'55	. . .	150.00

SANDS OF THE SOUTH PACIFIC
Toby Press
January, 1953
1 2-Fisted Romantic Adventure 125.00

SCHOOL DAY ROMANCES
(see POPULAR TEEN-AGERS)

SCIENCE COMICS
Fox Features Syndicate
February, 1940
1 GT,LF(c),O&B:Electro,Perisphere Payne,The Eagle,Navy Jones; B:Marga,Cosmic Carson, Dr. Doom; Bondage(c)	. . .	3,200.00
2 GT,LF(c)	. . . .	1,500.00
3 GT,LF(c),Dynamo	. . . . . .	1,300.00
4 JK,Cosmic Carson	. . . . .	1,100.00
5 Giant Comiscope Offer Eagle(c)	. . . .	700.00
6 Dynamop(c)	. . . .	700.00
7 Bondage(c),Dynamo	. . . .	700.00
8 September, 1940 Eagle(c)	. .	650.00

SCIENCE COMICS
Humor Publications
January, 1946
1 RP(c),Story of the A-Bomb	.	100.00
2 RP(c),How Museum Pieces Are Assembled	. . . .	45.00
3 AF,RP(c),How Underwater Tunnels Are Made	. . . . . .	75.00

GOLDEN AGE

GOLDEN AGE

4 RP(c),Behind the Scenes at
A TV Broadcast 30.00
5 The Story of the World's
Bridges; September, 1946 . . 35.00

SCIENCE COMICS
Ziff-Davis Publ. Co.
May, 1946
N# Used For A Mail Order
Test Market 250.00

SCIENCE COMICS
Export Publication Enterprises
March, 1951
1 How to resurrect a dead rat . . 50.00

SCOOP COMICS
Harry 'A' Chesler Jr.
November, 1941
1 I&B:Rocketman&Rocketgirl;B:Dan
Hastings;O&B:Master Key . 950.00
2 A:Rocketboy,Eye Injury 900.00
3 Partial rep. of #2 . . . . 500.00
4 thru 7 do not exist
8 1945 . . . . 300.00

SCREAM COMICS
Humor Publ./Current Books
(Ace Magazines)
Autumn, 1944
1 . . . . 100.00
2 . . . . 50.00
3 . . . . 40.00
4 thru 15 . . . . @40.00
16 I:Lily Belle 45.00
17 . . . . 30.00
18 Drug 40.00
19 . . . . 30.00
Becomes:
ANDY COMICS
20 Teenage 25.00
21 . . . . 25.00
Becomes:
ERNIE COMICS
22 Teenage 30.00
23 thru 25 . . . . @20.00
Becomes:
ALL LOVE ROMANCES
26 Ernie 25.00
27 LbC 32.00
28 thru 32 . . . . @15.00

(Capt. Silvers Log of...)
SEA HOUND, THE
Avon Periodicals
1945
N# The Esmeralda's Treasure . 90.00
2 Adventures in Brazil 70.00
3 Louie the Llama 70.00
4 In Greed & Vengence;
Jan-Feb, 1946 . . . . 70.00

SECRET LOVES
Comics Magazines
(Quality Comics)
November, 1949
1 BWa(c) 150.00
2 BWa(c),Lingerie(c) 125.00
3 RC 75.00
4 . . . . 50.00
5 Boom Town Babe 75.00

6 . . . . 50.00

SECRET MYSTERIES
(see CRIME MYSTERIES)

SELECT DETECTIVE
D.S. Publishing Co.
August-September, 1948
1 MB,Exciting New Mystery
Cases 150.00
2 MB,AMc,Dead Men 100.00
3 Face in theFrame;Dec-Jan'48 75.00

SERGEANT PRESTON
OF THE YUKON
Dell Publishing Co.
August, 1951
(1 thru 4) see Dell Four Color #344;
#373, 397, 419
5 thru 10 P(c) . . . . @65.00
11 P(c) 50.00
12 P(c) 50.00
13 P(c),O:Sergeant Preston . . . 50.00
14 thru 17 P(c) . . . . @50.00
18 P(c) 55.00
19 thru 29 Ph(c) . . . . @55.00

Seven Seas Comics #6 © Universal
Phoenix Features/Leader Publ

SEVEN SEAS COMICS
Universal Phoenix Features/
Leader Publ.
April, 1946
1 MB,RWb(c),B:South Sea
Girl, Captain Cutlass 550.00
2 MB,RWb(c) 500.00
3 MB,AF,MB(c) 400.00
4 MB,MB(c) 400.00
5 MB,MB(c),Hangman's Noose 400.00
6 MB,MB(c);1947 . . . . 400.00

SHADOW COMICS
Street & Smith Publications
March, 1940
1-1 P(c),B:Shadow,Doc Savage,
Bill Barnes,Nick Carter,
Frank Merriwell,Iron Munro 4,000.00

1-2 P(c),B: The Avenger 1,500.00
1-3 P(c),A: Norgill the
Magician 1,000.00
1-4 P(c),B:The Three
Musketeers 850.00
1-5 P(c),E: Doc Savage 850.00
1-6 A: Captain Fury 700.00
1-7 O&B: The Wasp 750.00
1-8 A:Doc Savage 700.00
1-9 A:Norgill the Magician . . . 700.00
1-10 O:Iron Ghost;B:The Dead
End Kids 650.00
1-11 O:Hooded Wasp 700.00
1-12 Crime Does Not pay 500.00
2-1 . . . . 500.00
2-2 Shadow Becomes Invisible 500.00
2-3 O&B:supersnipe;
F:Little Nemo 700.00
2-4 F:Little Nemo 500.00
2-5 V:The Ghost Faker 500.00
2-6 A:Blackstone the Magician 400.00
2-7 V:The White Dragon 400.00
2-8 A:Little Nemo 400.00
2-9 The Hand of Death 400.00
2-10 A:Beebo the WonderHorse 400.00
2-11 V:Devil Kyoti 400.00
2-12 V:Devil Kyoti 350.00
3-1 JaB(c),V:Devil Kyoti 350.00

Shadow Comics #65 (6/5)
© Street & Smith Publications

3-2 Red Skeleton Life Story . . 350.00
3-3 V:Monstrodamus 350.00
3-4 V:Monstrodamus 350.00
3-5 V:Monstrodamus 350.00
3-6 V:Devil's of the Deep 350.00
3-7 V: Monstrodamus 350.00
3-8 E: The Wasp 350.00
3-9 The Stolen Lighthouse . . . 350.00
3-10 A:Doc Savage 350.00
3-11 P(c),V: Thade 350.00
3-12 V: Thade 350.00
4-1 Red Cross Appeal on (c) . 350.00
4-2 V:The Brain of Nippon . . . 350.00
4-3 Little Men in Space 350.00
4-4 ...Mystifies Berlin 350.00
4-5 ...Brings Terror to Tokio . . 350.00
4-6 V:The Tarantula 350.00
4-7 Crypt of the Seven Skulls . 350.00
4-8 V:the Indigo Mob 350.00
4-9 Ghost Guarded Treasure

 All comics prices listed are for *Near Mint* condition.

of the Haunted Glen 350.00
4-10 V:The Hydra 350.00
4-11 V:The Seven Sinners 350.00
4-12 Club Curio 300.00
5-1 A:Flatty Foote 300.00
5-2 Bells of Doom 300.00
5-3 The Circle of Death 300.00
5-4 The Empty Safe Riddle ... 300.00
5-5 The Mighty Master Nomad . 300.00
5-6 ...Fights Piracy Among
   the Golden Isles 300.00
5-7 V:The Talon 300.00
5-8 V:The Talon 300.00
5-9 V:The Talon 300.00
5-10 V:The Crime Master 300.00
5-11 The Clutch of the Talon .. 300.00
5-12 Most Dangerous Criminal . 300.00
6-1 Double Z 300.00
6-2 Riddle of Prof.Mentalo ... 300.00
6-3 V:Judge Lawless 300.00
6-4 V:Dr. Zenith 300.00
6-5 .... 300.00
6-6 ...Invades the
   Crucible of Death 300.00
6-7 Four Panel Cover 300.00
6-8 Crime Among the Aztecs . 300.00
6-9 I:Shadow Jr. 350.00
6-10 Devil's Passage 300.00
6-11 The Black Pagoda 300.00
6-12 BP,BP(c),Atomic Bomb
   Secrets Stolen 325.00
7-1 The Yellow Band 325.00
7-2 A:Shadow Jr. 325.00
7-3 BP,BP(c),Crime Under
   the Border 350.00
7-4 BP,BP(c),One Tree Island,
   Atomic Bomb 375.00
7-5 A:Shadow Jr. 325.00
7-6 BP,BP(c),The Sacred Sword
   of Sanjorojo 350.00
7-7 Crime K.O. 350.00
7-8 ...Raids Crime Harbor 350.00
7-9 BP,BP(c),Kilroy Was Here   350.00
7-10 BP,BP(c),The Riddle of
   the Flying Saucer 400.00
7-11 BP,BP(c),Crime
   Doesn't Pay 350.00
7-12 BP,BP(c)Back From
   the Grave 350.00
8-1 BP,BP(c),Curse of the Cat 350.00
8-2 BP,BP(c),Decay,Vermin &
   Murder in the Bayou 350.00
8-3 BP,BP(c),The Spider Boy . 350.00
8-4 BP,BP(c),Death Rises
   Out of the Sea 350.00
8-5 BP,BP(c),Jekyll-
   Hyde Murders 350.00
8-6 Secret of Valhalla Hall ... 350.00
8-7 BP,BP(c),Shadow in Danger 350.00
8-8 BP,BP(c),...Solves a
   Twenty Year Old Crime ... 350.00
8-9 BP,BP(c),3-D Effect(c) 350.00
8-10 BP,BP(c),Up&Down(c) 350.00
8-11 BP,BP(c) 350.00
8-12 BP,BP(c),Arabs,Boat(c) .. 350.00
9-1 Airport(c) 350.00
9-2 BP,BP(c),Flying Cannon(c) 350.00
9-3 BP,BP(c),Shadow's Shadow 350.00
9-4 BP,BP(c) 350.00
9-5 Death in the Stars;Aug'49 . 350.00

SHARP COMICS
H.C. Blackerby
Winter, 1945
1 O:Planetarian(c) 275.00

2 O:The Pioneer 250.00

Sheena, Queen of the Jungle #9
© Real Adventures

SHEENA, QUEEN OF
THE JUNGLE
Real Adventures
(Fiction House)
Spring, 1942
1 Blood Hunger 1,800.00
2 Black Orchid of Death 800.00
3 Harem Shackles 600.00
4 The Zebra Raiders 400.00
5 War of the Golden Apes ... 350.00
6 .... 325.00
7 They Claw By Night 300.00
8 The Congo Colossus 300.00
9 and 10 .... @275.00
11 Red Fangs of the Tree Tribe 275.00
12 .... 225.00
13 Veldt o/t Voo Doo Lions ... 225.00
14 The Hoo Doo Beasts of
   Mozambique 225.00
15 .... 225.00
16 Black Ivory 225.00
17 Great Congo Treasure Trek 225.00
18 Doom of the Elephant Drum
   Winter, 1952 .... 225.00

SHIELD-WIZARD
COMICS
MLJ Magazines
Summer, 1940
1 IN,EA,O:Shield 3,200.00
2 O:Shield;I:Roy 1,400.00
3 Roy,Child Bondage(c) 850.00
4 Shield,Roy,Wizard 850.00
5 B:Dusty-Boy Dectective,Child
   Bondage 800.00
6 B:Roy the Super Boy,Child
   Bondage 750.00
7 Shield(c),Roy Bondage(c) .. 770.00
8 Bondage(c) 750.00
9 Shield/Roy(c) 600.00
10 Shield/Roy(c) 600.00
11 Shield/Roy(c) 600.00
12 Shield/Roy(c) 600.00
13 Bondage (c);Spring'44 .... 650.00

SHIP AHOY
Spotlight Publishers
November, 1944
1 LbC(c) 75.00

SHOCK DETECTIVE
CASE
(see CRIMINALS ON THE RUN)

SHOCK DETECTIVE
CASES
(see CRIMINALS ON THE RUN)

SHOCK SUSPENSTORIES
Tiny Tot Comics
(E.C. Comics)
February-March, 1952
1 JDa,JKa,AF(c),ElectricChair . 650.00
2 WW,JDa,Grl,JKa,WW(c) . . 350.00
3 WW,JDa,JKa,WW(c) 300.00
4 WW,JDa,JKa,WW(c) 300.00
5 WW,JDa,JKa,WW(c),Hanging 250.00
6 WW,AF,JKa,WW(c),
   Bondage(c) 300.00
7 JKa,WW,GE,AF(c),Face
   Melting 300.00
8 JKa,AF,AW,GE,WW,AF(c) . . 300.00
9 JKa,AF,RC,WW,AF(c) 300.00
10 JKa,WW,RC,JKa(c),Drug . . 300.00
11 JCr,JKa,WW,RC,JCr(c) 275.00
12 AF,JKa,WW,RC,AF(c)Drug(c) 300.00
13 JKa,WW,FF,JKa(c) 350.00
14 JKa,WW,BK,WW(c) 275.00
15 JKa,WW,RC,JDa(c)
   Strangulation 225.00
16 GE,RC,JKa,GE(c),Rape ... 225.00
17 GE,RC,JKa,GE(c) 200.00
18 GE,RC,JKa,GE(c);Jan'55 . . 200.00

SHOCKING MYSTERY
CASES
**(see THRILLING CRIME
CASES)**

SILVER STREAK
COMICS
**Your Guide/New Friday/
Comic House/Newsbrook
Publications/Lev Gleason**
December, 1939
1 JCo,JCo(c),I&B:The Claw,Red
   Reeves Capt.Fearless;B:Mr.
   Midnight,Wasp;A:Spiritman 10,000.00
2 JSm,JCo,JSm(c) 3,500.00
3 JaB(c),I&O:Silver Streak;
   B:Dickie Dean,Lance Hale,
   Ace Powers,Bill Wayne,
   Planet Patrol 2,800.00
4 JCo,JaB(c)B:Sky Wolf;
   N:Silver Streak,I:Lance
   Hale's Sidekick-Jackie ... 1,300.00
5 JCo,JCo(c),Dickie Dean
   V:The Raging Flood 1,500.00
6 JCo,JaB,JCo(c),O&I:Daredevil
   [Blue & Yellow Costume];
   R:The Claw 11,000.00
7 JCo,N: Daredevil 7,000.00
8 JCo,JCo(c) 2,200.00
9 JCo,BoW(c) 1,400.00
10 BoW,BoW(c) 1,200.00

All comics prices listed are for *Near Mint* condition.

GOLDEN AGE

Silver Streak #14
© Your Guide/New Friday

11 DRi(c) I:Mercury 900.00
12 DRi(c) 700.00
13 JaB,JaB(c),O:Thun-Dohr . . . 700.00
14 JaB,JaB(c),A:Nazi
　Skull Men 700.00
15 JaB,DBr,JaB(c),
　B:Bingham Boys 600.00
16 DBr,BoW(c),Hitler(c) 650.00
17 DBr,JaB(c),E:Daredevil 600.00
18 DBr,JaB(c),B:The Saint 500.00
19 DBr,EA 400.00
20 BW,BEv,EA 400.00
21 BW,BEv 400.00
Becomes:
CRIME DOES NOT PAY
22(23) CBi(c),The Mad Musician
　& Tunes of Doom 1,500.00
23 CBi(c),John Dillinger-One
　Man Underworld 900.00
24 CBi(c),The Mystery of the
　Indian Dick 700.00
25 CBi(c),Dutch Shultz-King
　of the Underworld 400.00
26 CBi(c),Lucky Luciano-The
　Deadliest of Crime Rats . . . 400.00
27 CBi(c),Pretty Boy Floyd . . . 400.00
28 CBi(c), ... 400.00
29 CBi(c),Two-Gun Crowley-The
　Bad Kid with the Itchy
　Trigger Finger 350.00
30 CBi(c),"Monk"Eastman
　V:Thompson's Mob 350.00
31 CBi(c) The Million Dollar
　Bank Robbery 250.00
32 CBi(c),Seniorita of Sin 250.00
33 CBi(c),Meat Cleaver Murder . 250.00
34 CBi(c),Elevator Shaft 250.00
35 CBi(c),Case o/t MissingToe . 250.00
36 CBi(c) 225.00
37 CBi(c) 225.00
38 CBi(c) 225.00
39 FG,CBi(c) 225.00
40 FG,CBi(c) 225.00
41 FG,RP,CBi(c),The Cocksure
　Counterfeiter 150.00
42 FG,RP,CBi(c) 175.00
43 FG,RP,CBi(c) 125.00

44 FG,CBi(c),The Most Shot
　At Gangster 125.00
45 FG,CBi(c) 125.00
46 FG,CBi(c),ChildKidnapping(c) 135.00
47 FG,CBi(c),ElectricChair 175.00
48 FG,CBi(c) 125.00
49 FG,CBi(c) 125.00
50 FG,CBi(c) 125.00
51 FG,GT,CBi(c),1st Monthly Iss.100.00
52 FG,GT,CBi(c) 100.00
53 FG,CBi(c) 100.00
54 FG,CBi(c) 100.00
55 FG,CBi(c) 100.00
56 FG,GT,CBi(c) 100.00
57 FG,CBi(c) 100.00
58 FG,CBi(c) 100.00
59 FG,Cbi(c) 100.00
60 FG,CBi(c) 100.00
61 FG,GT,CBi(c) 75.00
62 FG,CBi(c),Bondage(c) 100.00
63 FG,GT,CBi(c) 75.00
64 FG,GT,CBi(c) 75.00
65 FG,CBi(c) 75.00
66 FG,GT,CBi(c) 75.00
67 FG,GT,CBi(c) 75.00
68 FG,CBi(c) 75.00
69 FG,CBi(c) 75.00
70 FG,Cbi(c) 75.00
71 FG,CBi(c) 65.00
72 FG,CBi(c) 65.00
73 FG,CBi(c) 65.00
74 FG,CBi(c) 65.00
75 FG,CBi(c) 65.00
76 FG,CBi(c) 65.00
77 FG,CBi(c),The Electrified Safe 75.00
78 FG,CBi(c) 65.00
79 FG 65.00
80 FG 65.00
81 FG 65.00
82 FG 65.00
83 FG 65.00
84 FG 65.00
85 FG 65.00
86 FG 60.00
87 FG,P(c),The Rock-A-Bye
　Baby Murder 60.00
88 FG,P(c),Death Carries a Torch 60.00
89 FG,BF,BF P(c),The Escort
　Murder Case 60.00
90 FG,BF P(c),The Alhambra
　Club Murders 60.00
91 FG,AMc,BF P(c),Death
　Watches The Clock 60.00
92 BF,FG,BF P(c) 60.00
93 BF,FG,AMc,BF P(c) 60.00
94 BF,FG,BF P(c) 60.00
95 FG,AMc,BF P(c) 60.00
96 BF,FG,BF P(c),The Case of
　the Movie Star's Double . . . 60.00
97 FG,BF P(c) 60.00
98 BF,FG,BF P(c),Bondage(c) . 60.00
99 FG,BF,BF P(c) 60.00
100 FG,BF,AMc,P(c),The Case
　of the Jittery Patient 75.00
101 FG,BF,AMc,P(c) 50.00
102 FG,BF,AMc,BF P(c) 50.00
103 FG,BF,AMc,BF P(c) 50.00
104 thru 110 FG . . . . @50.00
111 thru 120 . . . . @50.00
121 thru 140 . . . . @45.00
141 JKu 40.00
142 JKu,CBi(c) 40.00
143 JKu,Comic Code 40.00
144 I Helped Capture"Fat Face"
　George Klinerz 30.00

145 RP,Double Barrelled Menace 30.00
146 BP,The Con & The Canary . 30.00
147 JKu,BP,A Long Shoe On the
Highway;July, 1955 . . . . 40.00

SINGLE SERIES
United Features Syndicate
1938
1 Captain & The Kids 550.00
2 Bronco Bill 300.00
3 Ella Cinders 250.00
4 Li'l Abner 500.00
5 Fritzi Ritz 175.00
6 Jim Hardy 225.00
7 Frankie Doodle 175.00
8 Peter Pat 175.00
9 Strange As it Seems 200.00
10 Little Mary Mixup 165.00
11 Mr. & Mrs. Beans 165.00
12 Joe Jinx 165.00
13 Looy Dot Dope 165.00
14 Billy Make Believe 165.00
15 How It Began 175.00
16 Illustrated Gags 125.00
17 Danny Dingle 125.00
18 Li'l Abner 400.00
19 Broncho Bill 225.00
20 Tarzan 1,200.00
21 Ella Cinders 200.00
22 Iron Vic 175.00
23 Tailspin Tommy 200.00
24 Alice In Wonderland 250.00
25 Abbie an' Slats 200.00
26 Little Mary Mixup 150.00
27 Jim Hardy 175.00
28 Ella Cinders & Abbie AN'
　Slats 1942 . . . . 175.00

SKELETON HAND
American Comics Group
September-October, 1952
1 . . . . 275.00
2 The Were-Serpent of Karnak 200.00
3 Waters of Doom 150.00
4 Black Dust 150.00
5 The Rise & Fall of the
　Bogey Man 150.00
6 July-August, 1953 . . . . 150.00

SKY BLAZERS
Hawley Publications
September, 1940
1 Flying Aces,Sky Pirates 375.00
2 November, 1940 . . . . 275.00

SKYMAN
Columbia Comics Group
1941
1 OW,OW(c),O:Skyman,Face . 700.00
2 OW,OW(c),Yankee Doodle . 400.00
3 OW,OW(c) 250.00
4 OW,OW(c),Statue of
　Liberty(c) 1948 . . . . 250.00

SKY PILOT
Ziff-Davis Publishing Co.
1950
10 NS P(c),Lumber Pirates 75.00
11 Ns P(c),The 2,00 Foot Drop;
　April-May, 1951 . . . . 65.00

　　All comics prices listed are for *Near Mint* condition.

SKY ROCKET
Home Guide Publ.
(Harry 'A' Chesler)
1944
1 Alias the Dragon,Skyrocket . 175.00

SKY SHERIFF
D.S. Publishing
Summer, 1948
1 I:Breeze Lawson & the Prowl
Plane Patrol 75.00

SLAM BANG COMICS
Fawcett Publications
January, 1940
1 B:Diamond Jack,Mark Swift,
Lee Granger,Jungle King . 1,500.00
2 F:Jim Dolan Two-Fisted
Crime Buster 600.00
3 A: Eric the Talking Lion . 750.00
4 F: Hurricane Hansen-Sea
Adventurer 500.00
5 . . . . 500.00
6 I: Zoro the Mystery Man;
Bondage(c) 550.00
7 Bondage(c);Sept., 1940 . . . 550.00

SLAPSTICK COMICS
Comic Magazine Distrib., Inc.
1945
N# Humorous Parody 150.00

SLAVE GIRL COMICS
Avon Periodicals
February, 1949
1 . . . . 600.00
2 April, 1949 . . . . 450.00

SLICK CHICK COMICS
Leader Enterprises, Inc.
1947
1 Teen-Aged Humor 65.00
2 Teen-Aged Humor 45.00
3 1947 . . . . 45.00

SMASH COMICS
Comics Magazine, Inc.
(Quality Comics Group)
August, 1939
1 WE,O&B:Hugh Hazard, Bozo
the Robot,Black X, Invisible
Justice: B:Wings Wendall,
Chic Carter 1,800.00
2 WE,A:Lone Star Rider 700.00
3 WE,B:Captain Cook,JohnLaw 450.00
4 WE,PGn,B:Flash Fulton . . 400.00
5 WE,PGn,Bozo Robot 400.00
6 WE,PGn,GFx,Black X(c) . . 400.00
7 WE,PGn,GFx,Wings
Wendell(c) 350.00
8 WE,PGn,GFx,Bozo Robot . . 350.00
9 WE,PGn,GFx,Black X(c) . . 350.00
10 WE,PGn,GFx,Bozo robot(c) 350.00
11 WE,PGn,GFx,BP,Black X(c) 350.00
12 WE,PGn,GFx,BP,Bozo(c) . . 350.00
13 WE,PGn,GFx,AB,BP,B:Mango,
Purple Trio,BlackX(c) 350.00
14 BP,LF,AB,PGn,I:The Ray . 2,000.00
15 BP,LF,AB,PGn,The Ram(c) . 900.00
16 BP,LF,AB,PGn,Bozo(c) 950.00
17 BP,LF,AB,PGn,JCo,
The Ram(c) 900.00

Smash Comics #38
© Comics Magazine/Quality Comics

18 BP,LF,AB,JCo,PGn,
B&O:Midnight 1,100.00
19 BP,LF,AB,JCo,PGn,Bozo(c) 600.00
20 BP,LF,AB,JCo,PGn,
The Ram(c) 600.00
21 BP,LF,AB,JCo,PGn 600.00
22 BP,LF,AB,JCo,PGn,
B:The Jester 600.00
23 BP,AB,JCo,RC,PGn,
The Ram(c) 500.00
24 BP,AB,JCo,RC,PGn,A:Sword,
E:ChicCarter,
N:WingsWendall 500.00
25 AB,JCo,RC,PGn,O:Wildfire . 600.00
26 AB,JCo,RC,PGn,Bozo(c) . . 450.00
27 AB,JCo,RC,PGn,The Ram(c) 450.00
28 AB,JCo,RC,PGn,
1st Midnight (c) 450.00
29 AB,JCo,Rc,PGn,B;Midnight(c) 425.00
30 AB,JCo,PGn 425.00
31 AB,JCo,PGn 350.00
32 AB,JCo,PGn 350.00
33 AB,JCo,PGn,O:Marksman . . 450.00
34 AB,JCo,PGn 350.00
35 AB,JCo,PGn 350.00
36 AB,JCo,RC,PGn,E:Midnight(c) 400.00
37 AB,JCo,RC,PGn,Doc
Wacky becomes Fastest
Human on Earth 350.00
38 JCo,RC,PGn,B:Yankee Eagle 375.00
39 PGn,B:Midnight(c) 325.00
40 PGn,E:Ray 325.00
41 PGn 200.00
42 PGn,B:Lady Luck 225.00
43 PGn 250.00
44 PGn 225.00
45 PGn,E:Midnight(c) 225.00
46 RC,Twelve Hours to Live . . 225.00
47 Wanted Midnight,
Dead or Alive 225.00
48 Midnight Meets the
Menace from Mars 225.00
49 PGn,FG,Mass of Muscle . . 225.00
50 I:Hyram the Hermit 225.00
51 A:Wild Bill Hiccup 150.00
52 PGn,FG,Did Ancient Rome Fall,
or was it Pushed? 150.00
53 Is ThereHonorAmongThieves 150.00

54 A:Smear-Faced Schmaltz . . 150.00
55 Never Trouble Trouble until
Trouble Troubles You 150.00
56 The Laughing Killer 150.00
57 A Dummy that Turns Into
A Curse 150.00
58 . . . . 150.00
59 A Corpse that Comes Alive . 150.00
60 The Swooner & the Trush . . 150.00
61 . . . . 125.00
62 V:The Lorelet 125.00
63 PGn 125.00
64 PGn,In Search of King Zoris 125.00
65 PGn,V:Cyanide Cindy 125.00
66 Under Circle's Spell 125.00
67 A Living Clue 125.00
68 JCo,Atomic Dice 125.00
69 JCo,V:Sir Nuts 125.00
70 . . . . 125.00
71 . . . . 100.00
72 JCo,Angela,the Beautiful
Bovine 100.00
73 . . . . 100.00
74 . . . . 100.00
75 The Revolution 100.00
76 Bowl Over Crime 100.00
77 Who is Lilli Dilli? 100.00
78 JCo,Win Over Crime 100.00
79 V:The Men From Mars 100.00
80 JCo,V:Big Hearted Bosco . . 100.00
81 V:Willie the Kid 100.00
82 V:Woodland Boy 100.00
83 JCo,Quizmaster 100.00
84 A Date With Father Time . . 100.00
85 JCo,A Singing Swindle 100.00

SMASH HITS SPORTS COMICS
Essankay Publications
January, 1949
1 LbC,LbC(c) 200.00

SMILEY BURNETTE WESTERN
Fawcett Publications
March, 1950
1 Ph(c),B:Red Eagle 325.00
2 Ph(c) 250.00
3 Ph(c) 250.00
4 Ph(c) 250.00

SMILIN' JACK
Dell Publishing Co.
1940
1 . . . . 125.00
2 . . . . 65.00
3 thru 8 . . . . @40.00

SMITTY
Dell Publishing Co.
1940
1 . . . . 100.00
2 . . . . 50.00
3 . . . . 40.00
4 thru 7 . . . . @30.00

SNAP
Harry 'A' Chesler Jr.
Publications
1944
N# Humorous 100.00

Smilin' Jack #1 © Dell Publishing Co.

SNAPPY COMICS
Cima Publications
(Prize)
1945
1 A:Animale 175.00

SNIFFY THE PUP
Animated Cartoons
(Standard Comics)
November, 1949
5 FF,Funny Animal 45.00
6 thru 9 Funny Animal . . . . @20.00
10 thru 17 Funny Animal . . . . @15.00
18 September, 1953 . . . . 15.00

SOLDIER COMICS
Fawcett Publications
January, 1952
1 Fighting Yanks on Flaming
  Battlefronts 70.00
2 Blazing Battles Exploding
  with Combat 35.00
3 . . . . 30.00
4 A Blow for Freedom 25.00
5 Only The Dead Are Free . . . 25.00
6 Blood & Guts 18.00
7 The Phantom Sub 18.00
8 More Plasma! 18.00
9 Red Artillery 18.00
10 . . . . 18.00
11 September, 1953 . . . . 18.00

SOLDIERS OF FORTUNE
Creston Publications
(American Comics Group)
February-March, 1952
1 OW(c),B:Ace Carter,
  Crossbones, Lance Larson   150.00
2 OW(c) 75.00
3 OW(c) 60.00
4 . . . . 60.00
5 OW(c) 60.00
6 OW(c),OW,Bondage(c) 65.00
7 . . . . 60.00
8 OW thru 10 . . . . @60.00
11 OW,Format Change to War . 30.00

12 . . . . 30.00
13 OW,February-March, 1953 . . 30.00

SON OF SINBAD
St. John Publishing Co.
February, 1950
1 JKu,JKu(c),The Curse of the
  Caliph's Dancer 275.00

SPACE ACTION
Junior Books
(Ace Magazines)
June, 1952
1 Invaders from a Lost Galaxy   500.00
2 The Silicon Monster from
  Galaxy X 400.00
3 Attack on Ishtar,
  October., 1952 . . . . 400.00

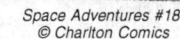

Space Adventures #18
© Charlton Comics

SPACE ADVENTURES
Capitol Stories/
Charlton Comics
July, 1952
1 AFa&LM(c) 300.00
2 . . . . 150.00
3 DG(c) 135.00
4 DG(c) 125.00
5 StC(c) 125.00
6 StC(c),Two Worlds 100.00
7 DG(c),Transformation 125.00
8 DG(c),All For Love 100.00
9 DG(c) 100.00
10 SD,SD(c) 250.00
11 SD,JoS 275.00
12 SD(c) 275.00
13 A:Blue Beetle 125.00
14 A:Blue Beetle 125.00
15 Ph(c) of Rocky Jones 125.00
16 BKa,A:Rocky Jones 150.00
17 A:Rocky Jones 125.00
18 A:Rocky Jones 125.00
19 . . . . 100.00
20 First Trip to the Moon 175.00
21 . . . . 100.00
22 Does Not Exist
23 SD,Space Trip to the Moon . 150.00

24 . . . . 125.00
25 Brontosaurus 125.00
26 SD,Flying Saucers 150.00
27 SD,Flying Saucers 150.00
28 Moon Trap 45.00
29 Captive From Space 45.00
30 Peril in the Sky 45.00
31 SD,SD(c),Enchanted Planet   125.00
32 SD,SD(c),Last Ship
  from Earth 125.00
33 Galactic Scourge,
  I&O:Captain Atom 300.00
34 SD,SD(c),A:Captain Atom . . 135.00
35 thru 40 SD,SD(c),
  A:Captain Atom . . . . @135.00
41 . . . . 25.00
42 SD,A:Captain Atom 25.00
43 . . . . 25.00
44 A:Mercury Man 25.00
45 A:Mercury Man 25.00
46 thru 58 . . . . @25.00
59 November, 1964 . . . . 25.00

SPACE BUSTERS
Ziff-Davis Publishing Co.
Spring, 1952
1 BK,NS(c),Ph(c),Charge of
  the Battle Women 600.00
2 EK,BK,MA,NS(c),
  Bondage(c),Ph(c) 500.00
3 Autumn, 1952 . . . . 450.00

SPACE COMICS
Avon Periodicals
March-April, 1954
4 (fa),F:Space Mouse 30.00
5 (fa),F:Space Mouse,
  May-June, 1954 . . . . 25.00

SPACE DETECTIVE
Avon Periodicals
July, 1951
1 WW,WW(c),Opium Smugglers
  of Venus 750.00
2 WW,WW(c),Batwomen of
  Mercury 500.00
3 EK(c),SeaNymphs ofNeptune 300.00
4 EK,Flame Women of Vulcan,
  Bondage(c) 325.00

SPACE MOUSE
Avon Periodicals
April, 1953
1 Funny Animal 45.00
2 Funny Animal 35.00
3 thru 5 Funny Animal . . . . . @20.00

SPACE PATROL
Approved Comics
(Ziff-Davis)
Summer, 1952
1 BK,NS,Ph(c), The Lady of
  Diamonds 600.00
2 BK,NS,Ph(c),Slave King of
  Pluto,Oct.-Nov., 1952 . . . . 450.00

SPACE THRILLERS
Avon Periodicals
1954
N# Contents May Vary 800.00

GOLDEN AGE

SPACE WESTERN COMICS
(see YELLOWJACKET COMICS)

SPARKLER COMICS
United Features Syndicate
July, 1940

1 Jim Handy		250.00
2 Frankie Doodle,August, 1940		200.00

Sparkler Comics #12
© United Features Syndicate

SPARKLER COMICS
United Features Syndicate
July, 1941

1 BHg,O:Sparkman;B:Tarzan,Captain
  & the Kids,Ella Cinders,Danny
  Dingle,Dynamite Dunn, Nancy,
  Abbie an' Slats, Frankie
  Doodle,Broncho Bill 1,600.00
2 BHg, The Case of Poisoned
  Fruit 600.00
3 BHg 450.00
4 BHg,Case of Sparkman &
  the Firefly 450.00
5 BHg,Sparkman,Natch 425.00
6 BHg,Case o/t Bronze Bees . 400.00
7 BHg,Case o/t Green Raiders 400.00
8 BHg,V:River Fiddler 400.00
9 BHg,N:Sparkman 400.00
10 BHg,B:Hap Hopper,
  Sparkman's ID revealed . . 400.00
11 BHg,V:Japanese 350.00
12 BHg,Another N:Sparkman . . 350.00
13 BHg,Hap Hopper Rides
  For Freedom 350.00
14 BHg,BHg(c),Tarzan
  V:Yellow Killer 400.00
15 BHg 350.00
16 BHg,Sparkman V:Japanese 350.00
17 BHg,Nancy(c) 350.00
18 BHg,Sparkman in Crete . . . 350.00
19 BHg,I&B:Race Riley,
  Commandos 350.00
20 BHg,Nancy(c) 350.00
21 BHg,Tarzan(c) 350.00
22 BHg,Nancy(c) 275.00

23 BHg,Capt&Kids(c) 275.00
24 BHg,Nancy(c) 275.00
25 BHg,BHg(c),Tarzan(c) 300.00
26 BHg,Capt&Kids(c) 275.00
27 BHg,Nancy(c) 275.00
28 BHg,BHg(c),Tarzan(c) 300.00
29 BHg,Capt&Kids(c) 275.00
30 BHg,Nancy(c) 275.00
31 BHg,BHg(c),Tarzan(c) 300.00
32 BHg,Capt&Kids(c) 125.00
33 BHg,Nancy(c) 125.00
34 BHg,BHg(c),Tarzan(c) 250.00
35 BHg,Capt&Kids(c) 125.00
36 BHg,Nancy(c) 125.00
37 BHg,BHg(c),Tarzan(c) 250.00
38 BHg,Capt&Kids(c) 125.00
39 BHg,BHg(c),Tarzan(c) 250.00
40 BHg,Nancy(c) 125.00
41 BHg,Capt&Kids(c) 100.00
42 BHg,BHg,Tarzan(c) 200.00
43 BHg,Nancy(c) 100.00
44 BHg,Tarzan(c) 200.00
45 BHg,Capt&Kids(c) 100.00
46 BHg,Nancy(c) 100.00
47 BHg,Tarzan(c) 200.00
48 BHg,Nancy(c) 95.00
49 BHg,Capt&Kids(c) 95.00
50 BHg,BHg(c),Tarzan(c) 165.00
51 BHg,Capt&Kids(c) 75.00
52 BHg,Nancy(c) 75.00
53 BHg,BHg(c),Tarzan(c) 150.00
54 BHg,Capt&Kids(c) 65.00
55 BHg,Nancy(c) 65.00
56 BHg,Capt&Kids(c) 65.00
57 BHg,F:Li'l Abner 60.00
58 BHg,A:Fearless Fosdick . . . 70.00
59 BHg,B:Li'l Abner 70.00
60 BHg,Nancy(c) 60.00
61 BHg,Capt&Kids(c) 60.00
62 BHg,Li'L Abner(c) 60.00
63 BHg,Capt&Kids(c) 60.00
64 BHg,Valentines (c) 60.00
65 BHg,Nancy(c) 60.00
66 BHg,Capt&Kids(c) 60.00
67 BHg,Nancy(c) 60.00
68 BHg, ... 60.00
69 BHg,B:Nancy (c) 60.00
70 BHg 60.00
71 thru 80 BHg . . . . @50.00
81 BHg,E:Nancy(c) 50.00
82 BHg 50.00
83 BHg,Tarzan(c) 40.00
84 BHg 40.00
85 BHg,E:Li'l Abner 40.00
86 BHg 40.00
87 BHg,Nancy(c) 40.00
88 thru 96 BHg . . . . @40.00
97 BHg,O:Lady Ruggles 75.00
98 BHg 40.00
99 BHg,Nancy(c) 40.00
100 BHg,Nancy(c) 50.00
101 thru 108 BHg . . . . @30.00
109 BHg,ATh 35.00
110 BHg 30.00
111 BHg 30.00
112 BHg 30.00
113 BHg,ATh 50.00
114 thru 120 BHg . . . . @30.00

SPARKLING STARS
Holyoke Publishing Co.
June, 1944

1 B:Hell's Angels,Ali Baba,FBI,
  Boxie Weaver,Petey & Pop . 100.00
2 . . . . 50.00

3 . . . . 40.00
4 thru 12 . . . . @30.00
13 O&I:Jungo, The Man-Beast . . 40.00
14 thru 19 . . . . @30.00
20 I:Fangs the Wolfboy 30.00
21 thru 28 . . . . @30.00
29 Bondage(c) 35.00
30 thru 32 . . . . @30.00
33 March, 1948 . . . . 30.00

SPARKMAN
Frances M. McQueeny
1944

1 O:Sparkman 200.00

SPARKY WATTS
Columbia Comics Group
1942

1 A:Skyman,Hitler(c) 300.00
2 . . . . 150.00
3 . . . . 125.00
4 O:Skyman 125.00
5 A:Skyman 100.00
6 . . . . 75.00
7 . . . . 75.00
8 . . . . 75.00
9 . . . . 75.00
10 1949 . . . . 75.00

[STEVE SAUNDERS] SPECIAL AGENT
Parents Magazine/
Commended Comics
December, 1947

1 J. Edgar Hoover, Ph(c) 60.00
2 . . . . 30.00
3 thru 7 . . . . @25.00
8 September, 1949 . . . . 25.00

SPECIAL COMICS
(see LAUGH COMICS)

SPECIAL EDITION COMICS
Fawcett Publications
August, 1940

1 CCB,CCB(c),F:Captain
  Marvel 8,500.00

SPEED COMICS
Brookwood/Speed Publ.
Harvey Publications
October, 1939

1 BP,B&O:Shock Gibson,B:Spike
  Marlin,Biff Bannon 2,500.00
2 BP ,B:Shock Gibson(c) 800.00
3 BP,GT 450.00
4 BP 400.00
5 BP,DBr 400.00
6 BP,GT 325.00
7 GT,JKu,B:Mars Mason . . . 325.00
8 JKu 300.00
9 JKu 300.00
10 JKu,E:Shock Gibson(c) . . . 300.00
11 JKu,E:Mars Mason 300.00
12 B:The Wasp 350.00
13 I:Captain Freedom;B:Girls
  Commandos,Pat Parker . . . 400.00
14 Pocket sized format-100pgs. 400.00
15 Pocket size 400.00
16 JKu,Pocket size 400.00
17 O:Black Cat 500.00

GOLDEN AGE

Speed Comics #9
© Brookwood/Speed Publ./Harvey Publ.

18 B:Capt.Freedom,Bondage(c)	425.00
19	400.00
20	400.00
21 JKu(c)	400.00
22 JKu(c)	400.00
23 JKu(c),O:Girl Commandos	425.00
24	275.00
25	250.00
26 Flag (c)	250.00
27	250.00
28 E:Capt Freedom	250.00
29 Case o/t Black Marketeers	250.00
30 POW Death Chambers	250.00
31 ASh(c),Nazi Thrashing(c)	325.00
32 ASh(c)	300.00
33 ASh(c)	300.00
34 ASh(c)	300.00
35 ASh(c),BlackCat'sDeathTrap	325.00
36 ASh(c)	300.00
37 RP(c)	300.00
38 RP(c),War Bond Plea with Iwo Jima flag allusion(c)	300.00
39 RP(c),B:Capt Freedom(c)	275.00
40 RP(c)	275.00
41 RP(c)	275.00
42 JKu,RP(c)	275.00
43 JKu,E:Capt Freedom(c)	275.00
44 BP,JKu,Four Kids on a raft, January-February, 1947	300.00

SPEED SMITH THE HOT ROD KING
Ziff-Davis Publishing Co.
Spring, 1952

1 INS,Ph(c),A:Roscoe the Rascal	125.00

SPIRIT, THE
Will Eisner
(Weekly Coverless Comic Book)
June, 1940

WE,O:SPirit	550.00
6/9/40 WE	250.00
6/16/40 WE,Black Queen	175.00
6/23/40 WE,Mr Mystic	150.00
6/30/40 WE	150.00
7/7/40 WE,Black Queen	150.00
7/14/40 WE	100.00
7/21/40 WE	100.00
7/28/40 WE	100.00
8/4/40 WE	100.00
7/7/40-11/24/40,WE	70.00
12/1/40 WE,Ellen Spanking(c)	125.00
12/8/40-12/29/40	60.00
1941 WE Each	50.00
3/16 WE I:Silk Satin	95.00
6/15 WE I Twilight	60.00
6/22 WE Hitler	60.00
1942 WE Each	40.00
2-1	60.00
2-15	45.00
2-23	65.00
1943 WE Each,LF,WE scripts	30.00
1944 JCo,LF	15.00
1945 LF Each,	15.00
1946 WE Each	30.00
1/13 WE,O:The Spirit	50.00
1/20 WE,Satin	50.00
3/17 WE,I:Nylon	50.00
4/21 WE,I:Mr.Carrion	55.00
7/7 WE,I:Dulcet Tone&Skinny	50.00
10/6 WE,I:F:Gell	60.00
1947 WE Each	30.00
7/13.,WE,Hansel &Gretel	45.00
7/20,WE,A:Bomb	50.00
9/28,WE,Flying Saucers	65.00
10/5 WE, Cinderella	32.00
12/7,WE,I:Power Puff	32.00
1948 WE Each	30.00
1/11,WE,Sparrow Fallon	35.00
1/25,WE,I:Last A Net	40.00
3/14,WE,A:Kretuama	35.00
4/4,WE,A:Wildrice	35.00
7/25,The Thing	60.00
8/22,Poe Tale,Horror	65.00
9/18, A:Lorelei	35.00
11/7,WE,A:Plaster of Paris	40.00
1949 WE Each	30.00
1/23 WE,I:Thorne	40.00
8/21 WE,I:Monica Veto	40.00
9/25 WE,A;Ice	40.00
12/4 WE,I:Flaxen	35.00
1950 WE Each	30.00
1/8 WE,I:Sand Saref	70.00
2/10, Horror Issue	35.00
1951 WE(Last WE 8/12/51)	@30.00
Non-Eisners	@12.00
1952 Non-Eisners	@12.00
7/27 WW,Denny Colt	350.00
8/3 WW,Moon	350.00
8/10 WW,Moon	350.00
8/17 WW,WE,Heart	300.00
8/24 WW,Rescue	300.00
8/31 WW,Last Man	300.00
9/7 WW,Man Moon	380.00
9/14 WE	80.00
9/21 WE Space	250.00
9/28 WE Moon	300.00
10/5 WE Last Story	125.00

SPIRIT, THE
Quality Comics Group/ Vital Publ.
1944

N# Wanted Dead or Alive!	500.00
N# ...in Crime Doesn't Pay	300.00
N# ...In Murder Runs Wild	225.00
4 ...Flirts with Death	200.00
5 ...Wanted Dead or Alive	175.00
6 ...Gives You Triple Value	150.00

The Spirit #19 © Quality Comics

7 ...Rocks the Underworld	150.00
8	150.00
9 ...Throws Fear Into the Heart of Crime	150.00
10 ...Stalks Crime	150.00
11 ...America's Greatest Crime Buster	150.00
12 WE(c),....The Famous Outlaw Who Smashes Crime	225.00
13 WE(c),...and Ebony Cleans Out the Underworld;Bondage(c)	225.00
14 WE(c)	225.00
15 WE(c),Bank Robber at Large	225.00
16 WE(c),The Caase of the Uncanny Cat	225.00
17 WE(c),The Organ Grinding Bank Robber	225.00
18 WE,WE(c),'The Bucket of Blood	275.00
19 WE,WE(c),'The Man Who Murdered the Spirit'	275.00
20 WE,WE(c),'The Vortex'	275.00
21 WE,WE(c),'P'Gell of Paris'	275.00
22 WE(c),TheOctopus,Aug.1950	400.00

SPIRIT, THE
Fiction House Magazines
1952

1 Curse of Claymore Castle	225.00
2 WE,WE(c),Who Says Crime Doesn't Pay	250.00
3 WE/JGr(c),League of Lions	150.00
4 WE&JGr(c),Last Prowl of Mr. Mephisto;Bondage (c)	225.00
5 WE,WE(c),Ph(c)1954	225.00

SPIRITMAN
Will Eisner
1944

1 3 Spirit Sections from 1944 Bound Together	150.00
2 LF, 2 Spirit Sections from 1944 Bound Together	125.00

SPITFIRE COMICS
Harvey Publ.
August, 1941

1 MKd(c), 100pgs., Pocket size	450.00

GOLDEN AGE

2 100 pgs.,Pocket size,
  October, 1941 . . . . 400.00

SPOOK COMICS
Baily Publications
1946
1 A:Mr. Lucifer 175.00

SPOOK DETECTIVE CASES
(see CRIMINALS ON THE RUN)

SPOOKY
Harvey Publications
November, 1955
1 Funny Apparition 200.00
2 same 100.00
3 thru 10 same . . . . @45.00
11 thru 20 same . . . . @25.00
21 thru 30 same . . . . @20.00
31 thru 40 same . . . . @15.00
41 thru 70 same . . . . @9.00
71 thru 90 same . . . . @5.00
91 thru 120 same . . . . @3.00
121 thru 160 same . . . . @2.50
161 same,September, 1980 . . . . 2.50

SPOOKY MYSTERIES
Your Guide Publishing Co.
1946
1 Rib-Tickling Horror 75.00

SPORT COMICS
(see TRUE SPORT PICTURE STORIES)

SPORTS THRILLS
(see DICK COLE)

SPOTLIGHT COMICS
Harry 'A' Chesler Jr. Publications
November, 1944
1 GT,GT(c),B:Veiled Avenger,
  Black Dwarf,Barry Kuda . . . 400.00
2 . . . . 350.00
3 1945,Eye Injury 375.00

SPUNKY
Standard Comics
April, 1949
1 FF,Adventures of a Junior
  Cowboy 40.00
2 FF 25.00
3 . . . . 20.00
4 . . . . 20.00
5 . . . . 20.00
6 . . . . 20.00
7 November, 1951 . . . . 20.00

SPY AND COUNTER SPY
Best Syndicated Features (American Comics Group)
August-September, 1949
1 I&O:Jonathan Kent 150.00
2 . . . . 100.00
Becomes:
SPY HUNTERS
3 Jonathan Kent 135.00

4 J.Kent 75.00
5 J.Kent 75.00
6 J.Kent 75.00
7 OW(c),J.Kent 75.00
8 OW(c),J.Kent 75.00
9 OW(c),J.Kent 75.00
10 OW(c),J.Kent 75.00
11 . . . . 50.00
12 OW(c),MD 50.00
13 and 14 . . . . @45.00
15 OW(c) 50.00
16 AW 100.00
17 . . . . 35.00
18 War (c) 45.00
19 and 20 . . . . @45.00
21 B:War Content 45.00
22 . . . . 45.00
23 Torture 125.00
24 'BlackmailBrigade',July,1953 . 45.00

SPY SMASHER
Fawcett Publications
Autumn, 1941
1 B;Spy Smasher 2,700.00
2 Mra(c) 1,200.00
3 Bondage (c) 800.00
4 . . . . 650.00
5 Mra,Mt. Rushmore(c) 800.00
6 Mra,Mra(c),V:The Sharks
  of Steel 750.00
7 Mra 750.00
8 AB 600.00
9 AB,Hitler,Tojo, Mussolini(c) . 650.00
10 AB,Did Spy Smasher
  Kill Hitler? 650.00
11 AB,February, 1943 . . . . . . 600.00

SQUEEKS
Lev Gleason Publications
October, 1953
1 CBi(c),(fa) 30.00
2 CBi(c),(fa) 15.00
3 CBi(c),(fa) 12.00
4 (fa) 12.00
5 (fa),January, 1954 . . . . 12.00

STAMP COMICS
Youthful Magazines/Stamp Comics, Inc.
October, 1951
1 HcK,Birth of Liberty 250.00
2 HcK,RP,Battle of White Plains 125.00
3 HcK,DW,RP,Iwo Jima 100.00
4 HcK,DW,RP 100.00
5 HcK,Von Hindenberg disaster 110.00
6 HcK,The Immortal Chaplains 100.00
7 HcK,RKr,RP,B&O:Railroad . 150.00
Becomes:
THRILLING ADVENTURES IN STAMPS
8 HcK, 100 Pgs.,Jan.,1953 . . 500.00

STAR COMICS
Comic Magazines/Ultem Publ./Chesler Centaur Publications
February, 1937
1 B:Dan Hastings 1,000.00
2 . . . . 500.00
3 . . . . 450.00
4 WMc(c) 475.00
5 WMc(c),A:Little Nemo 475.00

Star Comics #14
© Chester Centaur Publications

6 CBi(c),FG 425.00
7 FG 400.00
8 BoW,BoW(c),FG,A:Little
  Nemo,Horror 425.00
9 FG,CBi(c) 400.00
10 FG,CBi(c),BoW,A:Impyk . . 550.00
11 FG,BoW,JCo 450.00
12 FG,BoW,B:Riders of the
  Golden West 375.00
13 FG,BoW 350.00
14 FG,GFx(c) 350.00
15 CBu,B:The Last Pirate . . . 375.00
16 CBu,B:Phantom Rider . . . 375.00
2-1 CBu,B:Phantom Rider(c) . 375.00
2-2 CBu,A:Diana Deane 350.00
2-3 GFx(c),CBu 325.00
2-4 CBu 325.00
2-5 CBu 325.00
2-6 CBu,E:Phantom Rider . . . 325.00
2-7 CBu,August, 1939 . . . . . 325.00

STARLET O'HARA IN HOLLYWOOD
Standard Comics
December, 1948
1 The Terrific Tee-Age Comic . 100.00
2 Her Romantic Adventures in
  Movie land 75.00
3 and 4, Sept., 1949 . . . . . . @50.00

STAR RANGER
Comics Magazines/Ultem/Centaur Publ.
February, 1937
1 FG,I:Western Comic 1,100.00
2 . . . . 500.00
3 FG 450.00
4 . . . . 450.00
5 . . . . 375.00
6 FG 375.00
7 FG 350.00
8 GFx,FG,PGn,BoW 350.00
9 GFx,FG,PGn,BoW 350.00
10 JCo,GFx,FG, PGn,BoW . . . 600.00
11 . . . . 450.00
12 JCo,JCo(c),FG,PGn 450.00

All comics prices listed are for *Near Mint* condition.

GOLDEN AGE

Becomes:

COWBOY COMICS

13 FG,PGn	750.00
14 FG,PGn	600.00

Becomes:

STAR RANGER FUNNIES

15 WE,PGn	700.00
2-1(16) JCo,JCo(c)	500.00
2-2(17) PGn,JCo,A:Night Hawk	425.00
2-3(18) JCo,FG	400.00
2-4(19) A:Kit Carson	400.00
2-5(20) October, 1939	400.00

STARS AND STRIPES COMICS
Comic Corp of America
(Centaur Publications)
May, 1941

2 PGn,PGn(c),'Called to Colors', The Shark,The Voice	1,700.00
3 PGn,PGn(c),O:Dr.Synthe	1,000.00
4 PGn,PGn(c),I:The Stars & Stripes	875.00
5	600.00
6(5), December, 1941	600.00

STAR STUDDED
Cambridge House
1945
N# 25 cents (c) price;128 pgs.;

32 F:stories	200.00
N# The Cadet,Hoot Gibson, Blue Beetle	150.00

STARTLING COMICS
Better Publ./Nedor Publ.
June, 1940

1 WE,LF,B&O:Captain Future, Mystico, Wonder Man; B:Masked Rider	1,500.00
2 Captain Future(c)	650.00
3 same	500.00
4 same	400.00
5 same	325.00
6 same	325.00
7 same	325.00
8 ASh(c)	325.00
9 Bondage(c)	350.00
10 O:Fighting Yank	2,400.00
11 Fighting Yank(c)	725.00
12 Hitler,Mussolini,Tojo cover	500.00
13 JBi	350.00
14 JBi	350.00
15 Fighting Yank (c)	350.00
16 Bondage(c),O:FourComrades	425.00
17 Fighting Yank (c), E:Masked Rider	325.00
18 JBi,B&O:Pyroman	700.00
19 Pyroman(c)	325.00
20 Pyroman(c),B:Oracle	325.00
21 HcK,ASh(c)Bondage(c)O:Ape	325.00
22 HcK,ASh(c),Fighting Yank(c)	300.00
23 HcK,BEv,ASh(c),Pyroman(c)	300.00
24 HcK,BEv,ASh(c),Fighting Yank(c)	300.00
25 HcK,BEv,ASh(c),Pyroman(c)	300.00
26 BEv,ASh(c),Fighting Yank(c)	300.00
27 BEv,ASh(c),Pyroman(c)	300.00
28 BEv,ASh(c),Fighting Yank(c)	300.00
29 BEv,ASh(c),Pyroman(c)	300.00
30 ASh(c),Fighting Yank(c)	300.00

31 ASh(c),Pyroman(c)	300.00
32 ASh(c),Fighting Yank(c)	300.00
33 ASh(c),Pyroman(c)	300.00
34 ASh(c),Fighting Yank(c), O:Scarab	300.00
35 ASh(c),Pyroman(c)	325.00
36 ASh(c),Fighting Yank(c)	275.00
37 ASh(c),Bondage (c)	275.00
38 ASh(c),Bondage(c)	275.00
39 ASh(c),Pyroman(c)	275.00
40 ASh(c),E:Captain Future	275.00
41 ASh(c),Pyroman(c)	275.00
42 ASh(c),Fighting Yank(c)	275.00
43 ASh(c),Pyroman(c), E:Pyroman	275.00
44 Grl(c),Lance Lewis(c)	400.00
45 Grl(c),I:Tygra	400.00
46 Grl,Grl(c),Bondage(c)	400.00
47 ASh(c),Bondage(c)	400.00
48 ASh(c),Lance Lewis(c)	300.00
49 ASh(c),Bondage(c), E:Fighting Yank	1,000.00
50 ASh(c),Lance Lewis(c), Sea Eagle	300.00
51 ASh(c),Sea Eagle	300.00
52 ASh(c)	300.00
53 ASh(c),September, 1948	300.00

Startling Terror Tales #9
© Star Publications

STARTLING TERROR TALES
Star Publications
May, 1952

10 WW,LbC(c),The Story Starts	450.00
11 LbC(c),The Ghost Spider of Death	300.00
12 LbC(c),White Hand Horror	125.00
13 JyD,LbC(c),Love From a Gorgor	125.00
14 LbC(c),Trapped by the Color of Blood	125.00
4 LbC(c),Crime at the Carnival	100.00
5 LbC(c),The Gruesome Demon of Terror	100.00
6 LbC(c),Footprints of Death	100.00
7 LbC(c),The Case of the Strange Murder	125.00
8 RP,LbC(c),Phantom Brigade	125.00

9 LbC(c),The Forbidden Tomb	100.00
10 LbC(c),The Horrible Entity	125.00
11 RP,LbC(c),The Law Will Win, July, 1954	125.00

STEVE CANYON COMICS
Harvey Publications
February, 1948

1 MC,BP,O:Steve Canyon	150.00
2 MC,BP	100.00
3 MC,BP,Canyon's Crew	75.00
4 MC,BP,Chase of Death	75.00
5 MC,BP,A:Happy Easter	75.00
6 MC,BP,A:Madame Lynx, December, 1948	80.00

STEVE ROPER
Famous Funnies
April, 1948

1 Reprints newspaper strips	65.00
2	35.00
3 thru 4	@25.00
5 December, 1948	25.00

STORIES BY FAMOUS AUTHORS ILLUSTRATED
(see FAST FICTION)

STORY OF HARRY S. TRUMAN, THE
Democratic National Committee
1948

N# Giveaway-The Life of Our 33rd President	85.00

STRAIGHT ARROW
Magazine Enterprises
February-March, 1950

1 OW,B:Straight Arrow & his Horse Fury	275.00
2 BP,B&O:Red Hawk	125.00
3 BP,FF(c)	150.00
4 BP,Cave(c)	75.00
5 BP,StraightArrow'sGreatLeap	75.00
6 BP	60.00
7 BP,The Railroad Invades Comanche Country	60.00
8 BP	60.00
9 BP	60.00
10 BP	60.00
11 BP,The Valley of Time	70.00
12 thru 19 BP	@50.00
20 BP,Straight Arrow's Great War Shield	65.00
21 BP,O:Fury	75.00
22 BP,FF(c)	100.00
23 BP	45.00
24 BP,The Dragons of Doom	45.00
25 BP	45.00
26 BP	45.00
27 BP	45.00
28 BP,Red Hawk	40.00
29 thru 35 BP	@40.00
36 BP Drug	45.00
37 BP	35.00
38 BP	35.00
39 BP,The Canyon Beasts	30.00
40 BP,Secret of the Spanish Specters	30.00
41 BP	20.00

---

42 BP	20.00
43 BP,I:Blaze	25.00
44 BP	20.00
45 BP	20.00
46 thru 53 BP	@20.00
54 BP,March, 1956	20.00

STRANGE CONFESSIONS
Approved Publications
(Ziff-Davis)
Spring, 1952

1 EK,Ph(c)	300.00
2	200.00
3 EK,Ph(c),Girls reformatory	200.00
4 Girls reformatory	200.00

STRANGE FANTASY
Farrell Publications/
Ajax Comics
August, 1952

(2)1	250.00
2	200.00
3 The Dancing Ghost	200.00
4 Demon in the Dungeon, A:Rocketman	175.00
5 Visiting Corpse	125.00
6	125.00
7 A:Madam Satan	150.00
8 A:Black Cat	125.00
9 S&K,SD	175.00
10	125.00
11 Fearful Things Happen in a Lonely Place	125.00
12 The Undying Fiend	125.00
13 Terror in the Attic, Bondage(c)	175.00
14 Monster in the Building, October-November, 1954	125.00

UNKNOWN WORLD
Fawcett Publications
June, 1952

1 NS(c),Ph(c),Will You Venture to Meet the Unknown	250.00

Becomes:
STRANGE STORIES
FROM ANOTHER
WORLD

2 NS(c),Ph(c),Will You? Dare You	325.00
3 NS(c),Ph(c),The Dark Mirror	225.00
4 NS(c),Ph(c),Monsters of the Mind	225.00
5 NS(c),Ph(c),Dance of the Doomed February, 1953	225.00

STRANGE SUSPENSE
STORIES
Fawcett Publications
June, 1952

1 BP,MSy,MBi	500.00
2 MBi,GE	300.00
3 MBi,GE(c)	275.00
4 BP	275.00
5 MBi(c),Voodoo(c)	275.00
6 BEv	125.00
7 BEv	150.00
8 AW	150.00
9	125.00
10	150.00
11	100.00
12	100.00

Strange Suspense Stories #18
© Charlton Comics

13	100.00
14	125.00
15 AW,BEv	125.00

Charlton Comics

16	175.00
17	125.00
18 SD,SD(c)	225.00
19 SD,SD(c)	300.00
20 SD,SD(c)	225.00
21	125.00
22 SD(c)	200.00

Becomes:
THIS IS SUSPENSE!

23 WW	200.00
24	75.00
25	50.00
26	50.00

Becomes:
STRANGE SUSPENSE
STORIES

27	75.00
28	50.00
29	50.00
30	50.00
31 SD(c)	125.00
32 SD	125.00
33 SD	125.00
34 SD,SD(c)	125.00
35 SD	125.00
36 SD,SD(c)	125.00
37 SD	135.00
38	125.00
39 SD	150.00
40 SD	125.00
41 SD	125.00
42	35.00
43	35.00
44	35.00
45 SD	75.00
46	35.00
47 SD	75.00
48 SD	75.00
49	35.00
50 SD	90.00
51 thru 53 SD	@50.00
54 thru 60	@30.00
61 thru 74	@15.00

75	100.00
76	30.00
77	30.00

STRANGE SUSPENSE
STORIES
(see LAWBREAKERS)

STRANGE TERRORS
St. John Publishing Co.
June, 1952

1 The Ghost of Castle Karloff, Bondage(c)	300.00
2 UnshackledFlight intoNowhere	175.00
3 JKu,Ph(c),The Ghost Who Ruled Crazy Heights	235.00
4 JKu,Ph(c),Terror from the Tombs	275.00
5 JKu,Ph(c),No Escaping the Pool of Death	225.00
6 LC,PAM,Bondage(c),Giant	300.00
7 JKu,JKu(c),Cat's Death,Giant	325.00

STRANGE WORLD OF
YOUR DREAMS
Prize Group
August, 1952

1 S&K(c),What Do They Mean– Messages Rec'd in Sleep	450.00
2 MMe,S&K(c),Why did I Dream That I Was Being Married to a Man without a Face?	350.00
3 S&K(c)	300.00
4 MMe,S&K(c),The Story of a Man Who Dreamed a Murder that Happened	275.00

STRANGE WORLDS
Avon Periodicals
November, 1950

1 JKu,Spider God of Akka	600.00
2 WW,Dara of the Vikings	550.00
3 AW&FF,EK(c),WW,JO	1,100.00
4 JO,WW,WW(c),The Enchanted Dagger	550.00
5 WW,WW(c),JO,Bondage(c); Sirens of Space	375.00
6 EK,WW(c),JO,SC, Maid o/t Mist	275.00
7 EK, Sabotage on Space Station 1	200.00
8 JKu,EK,The Metal Murderer	200.00
9 The Radium Monsters	200.00
18 JKu	200.00
19 Astounding Super Science Fantasies	200.00
20 WW(c),Fighting War Stories	50.00
21 EK(c)	40.00
22 EK(c),Sept.-Oct., 1955	40.00

STRICTLY PRIVATE
Eastern Color Printing
July, 1942

1 You're in theArmyNow-Humor	150.00
2 F:Peter Plink, 1942	150.00

STUNTMAN COMICS
Harvey Publications
April-May, 1946

1 S&K,O:Stuntman	750.00
2 S&K,New Champ of Split- Second Action	500.00

GOLDEN AGE

All comics prices listed are for *Near Mint* condition.

3 S&K,Digest sized,Mail Order
Only, B&W interior,
October-November, 1946 .. 500.00

SUGAR BOWL COMICS
Famous Funnies
May, 1948
1 ATh,ATh(c),The Newest in
Teen Age! 80.00
2 .... 30.00
3 ATh 60.00
4 .... 30.00
5 January, 1949 .... 30.00

SUN FUN KOMIKS
Sun Publications
1939
1 F:Spineless Sam the
Sweetheart 200.00

SUNNY, AMERICA'S SWEETHEART
Fox Features Syndicate
December, 1947
11 AF,AF(c) 475.00
12 AF,AF(c) 400.00
13 AF,AF(c) 400.00
14 AF,AF(c) 400.00

SUNSET CARSON
Charlton Comics
February, 1951
1 Painted, Ph(c);Wyoming
Mail 650.00
2 Kit Carson-Pioneer 500.00
3 .... 375.00
4 Panhandle Trouble,
August, 1951 .... 375.00

SUPER BOOK OF COMICS
Western Publishing Co. 1943
N# Dick Tracy 300.00
1 Dick Tracy 250.00
2 Smitty,Magic Morro 80.00

Super Book of Comics #2
© Western Publishing Co.

3 Capt. Midnight 135.00
4 Red Ryder,Magic Morro 70.00
5 Don Winslow,Magic Morro ... 70.00
5 Dom Winslow,Stratosphere Jim 70.00
5 Terry & the Pirates 80.00
6 Don Winslow 75.00
7 Little Orphan Annie 70.00
8 Dick Tracy 100.00
9 Terry & the Pirates 100.00
10 Red Ryder, Magic Morro 70.00

SUPER-BOOK OF COMICS
Western Publishing Co.
1944
1 Dick Tracy (Omar) 135.00
1 Dick Tracy (Hancock) 100.00
2 Bugs Bunny (Omar) 40.00
2 Bugs Bunny (Hancock) 30.00
3 Terry & the Pirates (Omar) .. 75.00
3 Terry & the Pirates (Hancock) 65.00
4 Andy Panda (Omar) 35.00
4 Andy Panda (Hancock) 30.00
5 Smokey Stover (Omar) 30.00
5 Smokey Stover (Hancock) .. 20.00
6 Porky Pig (Omar) 35.00
6 Porky Pig (Hancock) 30.00
7 Smilin' Jack (Omar) 40.00
7 Smilin' Jack (Hancock) 35.00
8 Oswald the Rabbit (Omar) ... 30.00
8 Oswald the Rabbit (Hancock) 20.00
9 Alley Oop (Omar) 80.00
9 Alley Oop (Hancock) 70.00
10 Elmer Fudd (Omar) 30.00
10 Elmer Fudd (Hancock) 20.00
11 Little Orphan Annie (Omar) .. 45.00
11 Little Orphan Annie (Hancock) 35.00
12 Woody Woodpecker (Omar) . 35.00
12 WoodyWoodpecker(Hancock) 25.00
13 Dick Tracy (Omar) 80.00
13 Dick Tracy (Hancock) 75.00
14 Bugs Bunny (Omar) 30.00
14 Bugs Bunny (Hanock) 25.00
15 Andy Panda (Omar) 20.00
15 Andy Panda (Hancock) 15.00
16 Terry & the Pirates (Omar) .. 70.00
16 Terry & the Pirates (Hancock) 50.00
17 Smokey Stover (Omar) 30.00
17 Smokey Stover (Hancock) .. 30.00
18 Porky Pig (Omar) 25.00
18 Smokey Stover (Hancock) .. 20.00
19 Smilin' Jack (Omar) 35.00
N# Smilin' Jack (Hancock) 20.00
20 Oswald the Rabbit (Omar) .. 25.00
N# Oswald the Rabbit (Hancock) 15.00
21 Gasoline Alley (Omar) 45.00
N# Gasoline Alley (Hancock) ... 35.00
22 Elmer Fudd (Omar) 25.00
N# Elmer Fudd (Hancock) 30.00
23 Little Orphan Annie (Omar) .. 30.00
N# Little Orphan Annie (Hancock) 25.00
24 Woody Woodpecker (Omar) . 22.00
N# WoodyWoodpecker(Hancock) 18.00
25 Dick Tracy (Omar) 70.00
N# Dick Tracy (Hancock) 50.00
26 Bugs Bunny (Omar) 25.00
N# Bugs Bunny (Hancock) 20.00
27 Andy Panda (Omar) 20.00
27 Andy Panda (Hancock) 15.00
28 Terry & the Pirates (Omar) .. 70.00
28 Terry & the Pirates (Hancock) 50.00
29 Smokey Stover (Omar) 25.00
29 Smokey Stover (Hancock) .. 20.00
30 Porky Pig (Omar) 25.00

30 Porky Pig (Hancock) 20.00
N# Bugs Bunny (Hancock) 20.00

SUPER CIRCUS
Cross Publishing Co.
January, 1951
1 Partial Ph(c) 55.00
2 .... 40.00
3 .... 30.00
4 .... 30.00
5 1951 .... 30.00

SUPER COMICS
Dell Publishing Co.
May 1938
1 Dick Tracy,Terry and the
Pirates,Smilin'Jack,Smokey
Stover,Orphan Annie,etc. . 1,800.00
2 .... 700.00
3 .... 650.00
4 .... 550.00
5 Gumps(c) 500.00
6 .... 400.00
7 Smokey Stover(c) 400.00
8 Dick Tracy(c) 375.00
9 .... 375.00
10 Dick Tracy(c) 375.00
11 .... 325.00
12 .... 325.00
13 .... 325.00
14 .... 325.00
15 .... 325.00
16 Terry & the Pirates 300.00
17 Dick Tracy(c) 300.00
18 .... 300.00
19 .... 300.00
20 Smilin'Jack(c) 275.00
21 B:Magic Morro 250.00
22 Magic Morro(c) 265.00
23 all star(c) 250.00
24 Dick Tracy(c) 265.00
25 Magic Morro(c) 250.00
26 .... 200.00
27 Magic Morro(c) 250.00
28 Jim Ellis(c) 265.00
29 Smilin'Jack(c) 250.00
30 inc.The Sea Hawk 265.00
31 Dick Tracy(c) 200.00
32 Smilin' Jack(c) 210.00
33 Jim Ellis(c) 200.00
34 Magic Morro(c) 200.00
35 thru 40 Dick Tracy(c) ... @200.00
41 B:Lightning Jim 175.00
42 thru 50 Dick Tracy(c) ... @150.00
51 thru 54 Dick Tracy(c) ... @135.00
55 .... 125.00
56 .... 125.00
57 Dick Tracy(c) 125.00
58 Smitty(c) 125.00
59 .... 125.00
60 Dick Tracy(c) 150.00
61 .... 100.00
62 Flag(c) 125.00
63 Dick Tracy(c) 125.00
64 Smitty(c) 100.00
65 Dick Tracy(c) 125.00
66 Dick Tracy(c) 125.00
67 Christmas(c) 125.00
68 Dick Tracy(c) 125.00
69 Dick Tracy(c) 125.00
70 Dick Tracy(c) 125.00
71 Dick Tracy(c) 100.00
72 Dick Tracy(c) 100.00
73 Smitty(c) 100.00

---

74 War Bond(c)	100 00
75 Dick Tracy(c)	100.00
76 Dick Tracy(c)	100.00
77 Dick Tracy(c)	100.00
78 Smitty(c)	90.00
79 Dick Tracy(c)	90.00
80 Smitty(c)	90.00
81 Dick Tracy(c)	90.00
82 Dick Tracy(c)	90.00
83 Smitty(c)	85.00
84 Dick Tracy(c)	90.00
85 Smitty(c)	85.00
86 All on cover	90.00
87 All on cover	90.00
88 Dick Tracy(c)	90.00
89 Smitty(c)	75.00
90 Dick Tracy(c)	85.00
91 Smitty(c)	75.00
92 Dick Tracy(c)	85.00
93 Dick Tracy(c)	85.00
94 Dick Tracy(c)	85.00
95 thru 99	@75.00
100	90.00
101 thru 115	@50.00
116 Smokey Stover(c)	40.00
117 Gasoline Alley(c)	40.00
118 Smokey Stover(c)	40.00
119 Terry and the Pirates(c)	45.00
120	45.00
121	45.00

SUPER-DOOPER COMICS
Able Manufacturing Co.
1946

1 A:Gangbuster	125.00
2	75.00
3 & 4	@50.00
5 A:Captain Freedom,Shock Gibson	50.00
6 & 7 same	@50.00
8 A:Shock Gibson, 1946	50.00

SUPER DUCK COMICS
MLJ Magazines/Close-Up (Archie Publ.)
Autumn, 1944

1 O:Super Duck	300.00

Super Duck Comics #16
© MLJ Magazines

2	150.00
3 I:Mr. Monster	125.00
4 & 5	@100.00
6 thru 10	@75.00
11 thru 20	@50.00
21 thru 40	@40.00
41 thru 60	@30.00
61 thru 94	@25.00

Super Western Funnies #4
© Superior Comics Publishers

SUPER FUNNIES
Superior Comics Publishers
March, 1954

1 Dopey Duck	275.00
2 Out of the Booby-Hatch	50.00

Becomes:

SUPER WESTERN FUNNIES

3 F:Phantom Ranger	30.00
4 F:Phantom Ranger,Sept. 1954	30.00

SUPER MAGICIAN COMICS
Street & Smith Publications
May, 1941

1 B:The Mysterious Blackstone	400.00
2 V:Wild Tribes of Africa	275.00
3 V:Oriental Wizard	250.00
4 V:Quetzal Wizard,O:Transo	225.00
5 A:The Moylan Sisters	225.00
6 JaB,JaB(c),The Eddie Cantor story	225.00
7 In the House of Skulls	250.00
8 A:Abbott & Costello	250.00
9 V:Duneen the Man-Ape	250.00
10 V:Pirates o/t Sargasso Sea	250.00
11 JaB(c),V:Fire Wizards	250.00
12 V:Baal	225.00
2-1 A:The Shadow	225.00
2-2 In the Temple of the 10,00 Idols	100.00
2-3 Optical Illusion on (c)-Turn Jap into Monkey	100.00
2-4 V:Cannibal Killers	100.00
2-5 V:The Pygmies of Lemuria	100.00
2-6 V:Pirates & Indians	100.00
2-7 Can Blackstone Catch the	

Cannonball?	100.00
2-8 V:Marabout,B:Red Dragon	100.00
2-9	100.00
2-10 Pearl Dives Swallowed By Sea Demons	100.00
2-11 Blackstone Invades Pelican Islands	100.00
2-12 V:Bubbles of Death	100.00
3-1	100.00
3-2 Bondage(c),Midsummers Eve	90.00
3-3 The Enchanted Garden	90.00
3-4 Fabulous Aztec Treasure	90.00
3-5 A:Buffalo Bill	90.00
3-6 Magic Tricks to Mystify	90.00
3-7 V:Guy Fawkes	90.00
3-8 V:Hindu Spook Maker	90.00
3-9	90.00
3-10 V:The Water Wizards	90.00
3-11 V:The Green Goliath	90.00
3-12 Lady in White	90.00
4-1 Cannibal of Crime	85.00
4-2 The Devil's Castle	85.00
4-3 V:Demons of Golden River	85.00
4-4 V:Dr. Zero	85.00
4-5 Bondage(c)	85.00
4-6 V:A Terror Gang	85.00
4-7	85.00
4-8 Mystery of the Disappearing Horse	85.00
4-9 A Floating Light?	85.00
4-10 Levitation	85.00
4-11 Lost, Strange Land of Shangri	85.00
4-12 I:Nigel Elliman	85.00
5-1 V:Voodoo Wizards of the Everglades,Bondage (c)	90.00
5-2 Treasure of the Florida Keys; Bondage (c)	85.00
5-3 Elliman Battles Triple Crime	85.00
5-4 Can A Human Being Really Become Invisible	85.00
5-5 Mystery of the Twin Pools	85.00
5-6 A:Houdini	85.00
5-7 F:Red Dragon	85.00
5-8 F:Red Dragon, Feb.-March, 1947	85.00

SUPERMOUSE
Standard Comics/Pines
December, 1948

1 FF,(fa)	150.00
2 FF,(fa)	85.00
3 FF,(fa)	65.00
4 FF,(fa)	70.00
5 FF,(fa)	65.00
6 FF,(fa)	65.00
7 thru 10 (fa)	@25.00
11 thru 20 (fa)	@20.00
21 thru 44 (fa)	@15.00
45 (fa),Autumn, 1958	15.00

SUPER-MYSTERY COMICS
Periodical House (Ace Magazines)
July, 1940

1 B:Magno,Vulcan,Q-13,Flint of the Mountes	1,300.00
2 Bondage (c)	625.00
3 JaB,B:Black Spider	550.00
4 O:Davy;A:Captain Gallant	400.00
5 JaB,JM(c),I&B:The Clown	400.00
6 JM,JM(c),V:The Clown	350.00
2-1 JM,JM(c),O:Buckskin,	

GOLDEN AGE

Super-Mystery Comics #19 (4/1)
© Periodical House/Ace Magazines

Bondage(c) 350.00
2-2 JM,JM(c),V:The Clown . . . 300.00
2-3 JM,JM(c),V:The Clown . . . 300.00
2-4 JM,JM(c),V:The Nazis . . . 300.00
2-5 JM,JM(c),Bondage(c) 325.00
2-6 JM,JM(c),Bondage(c),
  'Foreign Correspondent' . . . 325.00
3-1 B:Black Ace 375.00
3-2 A:Mr. Risk, Bondage(c) . . 375.00
3-3 HK,HK(c),I:Lancer;B:Dr.
  Nemesis, The Sword 350.00
3-4 HK 350.00
3-5 HK,LbC,A:Mr. Risk 300.00
3-6 HK,LbC,A:Paul Revere Jr. 300.00
4-1 HK,LbC,A:Twin Must Die . 275.00
4-2 A:Mr. Risk 225.00
4-3 Mango out to Kill Davey! . 225.00
4-4 Danger Laughs at Mr. Risk 225.00
4-5 A:Mr. Risk 225.00
4-6 RP,A:Mr. Risk 225.00
5-1 RP 200.00
5-2 RP,RP(c),The Riddle of the
  Swamp-Land Spirit 200.00
5-3 RP,RP(c),The Case of the
  Whispering Death 200.00
5-4 RP,RP(c) 200.00
5-5 RP,Harry the Hack 200.00
5-6 . . . . 200.00
6-1 . . . . 175.00
6-2 RP,A:Mr. Risk 175.00
6-3 Bondage (c) 175.00
6-4 E:Mango;A:Mr. Risk 175.00
6-5 Bondage(c) 175.00
6-6 A:Mr. Risk 175.00
7-1 . . . . 175.00
7-2 KBa(c) 175.00
7-3 Bondage(c) 175.00
7-4 . . . . 175.00
7-5 . . . . 175.00
7-6 . . . . 175.00
8-1 The Riddle of the Rowboat 150.00
8-2 Death Meets a Train 150.00
8-3 The Man Who Couldn't Die 150.00
8-4 RP(c) 150.00
8-5 GT,MMe,Staged for Murder 150.00
8-6 Unlucky Seven,July, 1949 . 150.00

ARMY AND NAVY
COMICS
Street & Smith Publications
May, 1941
1 Hawaii is Calling You,Capt.
  Fury,Nick Carter 400.00
2 Private Rock V;Hitler 250.00
3 The Fighting Fourth 250.00
4 The Fighting Irish 250.00
5 I:Super Snipe 350.00
Becomes:
SUPERSNIPE COMICS
6 A "Comic" With A Sense
  of Humor 600.00
7 A:Wacky, Rex King 375.00
8 Axis Powers & Satan(c),
  Hitler(c) 400.00
9 Hitler Voodoo Doll (c) 500.00
10 Lighting (c) 350.00
11 A:Little Nemo 350.00
12 Football(c) 350.00
2-1 B:Huck Finn 250.00
2-2 Battles Shark 250.00
2-3 Battles Dinosaur 250.00
2-4 Baseball(c) 250.00
2-5 Battles Dinosaur 250.00
2-6 A:Pochontas 250.00
2-7 A:Wing Woo Woo 250.00
2-8 A:Huck Finn 250.00
2-9 Dotty Loves Trouble 250.00
2-10 Assists Farm Labor
  Shortage 250.00
2-11 Dotty & the Jelly Beans . . 250.00
2-12 Statue of Liberty 250.00
3-1 Ice Skating(c) 200.00
3-2 V:Pirates(c) 200.00
3-3 Baseball(c) 200.00
3-4 Jungle(c) 200.00
3-5 Learn Piglatin 200.00
3-6 Football Hero 200.00
3-7 Saves Girl From Grisley . . 200.00
3-8 Rides a Wild Horse 200.00
3-9 Powers Santa's Sleigh . . . 200.00
3-10 Plays Basketball 200.00
3-11 Is A Baseball Pitcher . . . 200.00
3-12 Flies with the Birds 200.00
4-1 Catches A Whale 150.00
4-2 Track & Field Athlete 150.00
4-3 Think Machine(c) 150.00
4-4 Alpine Skiier 150.00
4-5 Becomes a Boxer 150.00
4-6 Race Car Driver 150.00
4-7 Bomber(c) 150.00
4-8 Baseball Star 150.00
4-9 Football Hero 150.00
4-10 Christmas(c) 150.00
4-11 Artic Adventure 150.00
4-12 The Ghost Remover 150.00
5-1 August-September, 1949 . 150.00

SUPER SPY
Centaur Publications
Oct.–Nov., 1940
1 O:Sparkler 900.00
2 A:Night Hawk, Drew Ghost, Tim
  Blain, S.S. Swanson the Inner
  Circle, Duke Collins, Gentlemen
  of Misfortune 550.00

SUPER WESTERN
COMICS
Youthful Magazines Aug., 1950
1 BP,BP,(c),B:Buffalo Bill,Wyatt

Earp,CalamityJane,SamSlade 55.00
2 thru 4 March, 1951 . . . . . @35.00

SUPER WESTERN
FUNNIES
(see SUPER FUNNIES)

Superworld Comics #3
© Komos Publications

SUPERWORLD COMICS
Komos Publications
(Hugo Gernsback)
April, 1940
1 FP,FP(c),B:MilitaryPowers,BuzzAllen
  Smarty Artie, Alibi Alige . . 4,500.00
2 FP,FP(c),A:Mario 2,500.00
3 FP,FP(c),V:Vest Wearing
  Giant Grasshoppers 1,800.00

SUSPENSE COMICS
Et Es Go Mag. Inc.
(Continental Magazines)
December, 1945
1 LbC, Bondage(c),B:Grey
  Mask 2,800.00
2 DRi,I:The Mask 2,000.00
3 LbC,ASh(c),Bondage(c) . . 4,500.00
4 LbC,LbC(c),Bondage(c) . . 1,500.00
5 LbC,LbC(c) 1,500.00
6 LbC,LbC(c),The End of
  the Road 1,500.00
7 LbC,LbC(c) 1,200.00
8 LbC,LbC(c) 2,500.00
9 LbC,LbC(c) 1,200.00
10 RP,LbC,LbC(c) 1,200.00
11 RP,LbC,LbC(c),Satan(c) . . 2,500.00
12 LbC,LbC(c),Dec., 1946 . . . 1,200.00

SUSPENSE DETECTIVE
Fawcett Publications
June, 1952
1 GE,MBi,MBi(c),Death Poised
  to Strike 275.00
2 GE,MSy 150.00
3 A Furtive Footstep 135.00
4 MBi,MSy,Bondage(c),A Blood
  Chilling Scream 125.00

GOLDEN AGE

5 MSy,MSy(c),MBi,A Hair-Trigger
from Death, March, 1953 . . 140.00

SUZIE COMICS
(see TOP-NOTCH COMICS)

SWEENEY
Standard Comics
June, 1949
4 Buzz Sawyer's Pal 45.00
5 September, 1949 . . . . 40.00

SWEETHEART DIARY
Fawcett
Winter, 1949
1 . . . . 75.00
2 . . . . 40.00
3 and 4 WW . . . . @75.00
5 thru 10 . . . . @30.00
11 thru 14 . . . . @20.00

SWEETHEART DIARY
Charlton Comics
January 1953
32 . . . . 22.00
33 thru 40 . . . . @10.00
41 thru 65 . . . . @6.00

SWEET HEART
(see CAPTAIN MIDNIGHT)

SWEET LOVE
Harvey Publications
(Home Comics)
September, 1949
1 Ph(c) 35.00
2 Ph(c) 20.00
3 BP 20.00
4 Ph(c) 15.00
5 BP,JKa,Ph(c) 30.00

SWEET SIXTEEN
Parents' Magazine Group
August-September, 1946
1 Van Johnson story 125.00
2 Alan Ladd story 100.00
3 Rip Taylor 60.00
4 E:Taylor 60.00
5 Gregory Peck story (c) 55.00
6 Dick Hammes(c) 50.00
7 Ronald Reagan(c) 125.00
8 Shirley Jones(c) 50.00
9 William Holden(c) 50.00
10 James Stewart(c) 55.00
11 . . . . 50.00
12 Bob Cummings(c) 50.00
13 Robert Mitchum(c) 60.00

SWIFT ARROW
Farrell Publications(Ajax)
February-March, 1954
1 Lone Rider's Redskin Brother 60.00
2 . . . . 35.00
3 . . . . 30.00
4 . . . . 30.00
5 October-November, 1954 . . . 30.00
2nd Series
April, 1957
1 . . . . 30.00
2 B:Lone Rider 20.00
3 September, 1957 . . . . 20.00

TAFFY
Orbit Publications/Rural Home/
Taffy Publications
March-April, 1945
1 LbC(c),(fa),Bondage(c) 200.00
2 LbC(c),(fa) 100.00
3 (fa) 50.00
4 (fa) 45.00
5 LbC(c),A:Van Johnson 60.00
6 A:Perry Como 50.00
7 A:Dave Clark 55.00
8 A:Glen Ford 50.00
9 A:Lon McCallister 50.00
10 A:John Hodiak 50.00
11 A:Mickey Rooney 50.00
12 February, 1948 . . . . 50.00

TAILSPIN
Spotlight Publications
November, 1944
N# LbC(c),A:Firebird 150.00

TALES FROM
THE CRYPT
(see CRIME PATROL)

TALES FROM THE TOMB
(see Dell Giants)

TALES OF HORROR
Toby Press/Minoan Publ. Corp
June, 1952
1 Demons of the Underworld . 225.00
2 What was the Thing in
the Pool?,Torture 175.00
3 The Big Snake 100.00
4 The Curse of King Kala! . . . 100.00
5 Hand of Fate 100.00
6 The Fiend of Flame 100.00
7 Beast From The Deep 100.00
8 The Snake that Held A
City Captive 100.00
9 It Came From the Bottom
of the World 125.00
10 The Serpent Strikes 125.00
11 Death Flower? 125.00
12 Guaranteed to Make Your
Hair Stand on End 135.00
13 Ghost with a Torch;
October, 1954 . . . . 110.00

TALES OF TERROR
Toby Press
1952
1 Just A Bunch of Hokey
Hogwash 100.00

TALES OF TERROR
ANNUAL
E.C. 1951
N# AF 3,200.00
2 AF 1,500.00
3 . . . . 1,100.00

TALLY-HO COMICS
Baily Publishing Co.
December, 1944
N# FF,A:Snowman 225.00

Target Comics #9/9
© Funnies Inc./Novelty Publ.

TARGET COMICS
Funnnies Inc./Novelty Publ./
Premium Group/Curtis
Circulation Co./Star
Publications
February, 1940
1 BEv,JCo,CBu,JSm;B,O&I:Manowar,
White Streak,Bull's-Eye;B:City
Editor,High Grass Twins,T-Men,
Rip Rory,Fantastic Feature
Films, Calling 2-R 3,500.00
2 BEv,JSm,JCo,CBu,White
Streak(c) 1,800.00
3 BEv,JSm,JCo,CBu 1,000.00
4 JSm,JCo 1,000.00
5 CBu,BW,O:White Streak . 3,000.00
6 CBu,BW,White Streak(c) . 1,300.00
7 CBu,BW,BW(c),V:Planetoid
Stories,Space Hawk(c) . 3,500.00
8 CBu,BW,White Shark(c) . 1,000.00
9 CBu,BW,White Shark(c) . . 1,000.00
10 CBu,BW,JK(c),The
Target(c) 1,300.00
11 BW,The Target(c) 1,100.00
12 BW,same 1,000.00
2-1 BW,CBu 600.00
2-2 BW,BoW(c) 550.00
2-3 BW,BoW(c),The Target(c) . 450.00
2-4 BW,B:Cadet 450.00
2-5 BW,BoW(c),The Target(c) . 400.00
2-6 BW,The Target(c) 400.00
2-7 BW,The Cadet(c) 400.00
2-8 BW,same 400.00
2-9 BW,The Target(c) 400.00
2-10 BW,same 600.00
2-11 BW,The Cadet(c) 400.00
2-12 BW,same 400.00
3-1 BW,same 375.00
3-2 BW 375.00
3-3 BW,The Target(c) 375.00
3-4 BW,The Cadet(c) 375.00
3-5 BW 375.00
3-6 BW,War Bonds(c) 375.00
3-7 BW 375.00
3-8 BW,War Bonds(c) 375.00
3-9 BW 375.00
3-10 BW 375.00

GOLDEN AGE

3-11	90.00
3-12	90.00
4-1 JJo(c)	65.00
4-2 ERy(c)	65.00
4-3 AVi	65.00
4-4	65.00
4-5 API(c),Statue of Liberty(c)	75.00
4-6 BW	65.00
4-7 AVi	65.00
4-8,Christmas(c)	65.00
4-9	65.00
4-10	65.00
4-11	65.00
4-12	65.00
5-1	50.00
5-2 The Target	55.00
5-3 Savings Checkers(c)	50.00
5-4 War Bonds Ph(c)	50.00
5-5 thru 5-12	@50.00
6-1 The Target(c)	55.00
6-2	50.00
6-3 Red Cross(c)	45.00
6-4	45.00
6-5 Savings Bonds(c)	45.00
6-6 The Target(c)	50.00
6-7 The Cadet(c)	45.00
6-8 AFa	45.00
6-9 The Target(c)	50.00
6-10	45.00
6-11	45.00
6-12	50.00
7-1	45.00
7-2 Bondage(c)	50.00
7-3 The Target(c)	50.00
7-4 DRi,The Cadet(c)	45.00
7-5	45.00
7-6 DRi(c)	45.00
7-7 The Cadet(c)	45.00
7-8 DRi(c)	45.00
7-9 The Cadet(c)	45.00
7-10 DRi,DRi(c)	45.00
7-11	45.00
7-12 JH(c)	45.00
8-1	45.00
8-2 DRi,DRi(c),BK	50.00
8-3 DRi,The Cadet(c)	45.00
8-4 DRi,DRi(c)	45.00
8-5 DRi,The Cadet(c)	45.00
8-6 DRi,DRi(c)	45.00
8-7 BK,DRi,DRi(c)	50.00
8-8 DRi,The Cadet(c)	45.00
8-9 DRi,The Cadet(c)	45.00
8-10 DRi,KBa,LbC(c)	150.00
8-11 DRi,The Cadet	45.00
8-12 DRi,The Cadet	45.00
9-1 DRi,LbC(c)	150.00
9-2 DRi	45.00
9-3 DRi,Bondage(c),The Cadet(c)	50.00
9-4 DRi,LbC(c)	150.00
9-5 DRi,Baseball(c)	45.00
9-6 DRi,LbC(c)	150.00
9-7 DRi	45.00
9-8 DRi,LbC(c)	150.00
9-9 DRi,Football(c)	45.00
9-10 DRi,LbC(c)	150.00
9-11,The Cadet	45.00
9-12 LbC(c),Gems(c)	150.00
10-1,The Cadet	45.00
10-2 LbC(c)	150.00
10-3 LbC(c)	150.00

Becomes:

TARGET WESTERN ROMANCES
Star Publications

October-November, 1949

106 LbC(c),The Beauty Scar	200.00
107 LbC(c),The Brand Upon His Heart	175.00

Tarzan #7 © Dell Publishing Co.

TARZAN
Dell Publishing Co.
January-February 1948

1 V:White Savages of Vari	900.00
2 Captives of Thunder Valley	500.00
3 Dwarfs of Didona	350.00
4 The Lone Hunter	350.00
5 The Men of Greed	350.00
6 Outlwas of Pal-ul-Don	300.00
7 Valley of the Monsters	300.00
8 The White Pygmies	300.00
9 The Men of A-Lur	300.00
10 Treasure of the Bolgani	300.00
11 The Sable Lion	250.00
12 The Price of Peace	250.00
13 B:Lex Barker photo(c)	225.00
14	225.00
15	225.00
16	200.00
17	200.00
18	200.00
19	200.00
20	200.00
21 thru 30	@150.00
31 thru 54 E:L.Barker Ph(c)	@100.00
55 thru 70	@75.00
71 thru 79	@50.00
80 thru 90 B:ScottGordonPh(c)	@30.00
91 thru 99	@28.00
100	40.00
101 thru 110 E:S.GordonPh(c)	@25.00
111 thru 120	@20.00
121 thru 131	@15.00

TEEN-AGE DIARY SECRETS
St. John Publishing Co.
October, 1949

6 MB,PH(c)	75.00
7 MB,PH(c)	85.00
8 MB,PH(c)	75.00
9 MB,PH(c)	85.00

Becomes:

DIARY SECRETS

10 MB	65.00
11 MB	55.00
12 thru 19 MB	@50.00
20 MB,JKu	55.00
21 thru 28 MB	@30.00
29 MB,Comics Code	25.00
30 MB	25.00

TEEN-AGE ROMANCES
St. John Publishing Co.
January, 1949

1 MB(c),MB	225.00
2 MB(c),MB	125.00
3 MB(c),MB	150.00
4 Ph(c)	125.00
5 MB,Ph(c)	125.00
6 MB,Ph(c)	125.00
7 MB,Ph(c)	125.00
8 MB,Ph(c)	125.00
9 MB,MB(c),JKu	135.00
10 thru 27 MB,MB(c),JKu	@100.00
28 thru 30	@35.00
31 thru 34 MB(c)	@35.00
35 thru 42 MB(c),MB	@40.00
43 MB(c),MB,Comics Code	35.00
44 MB(c),MB	35.00
45 MB(c),MB	35.00

TEEN-AGE TEMPTATIONS
St. John Publishing Co.
October, 1952

1 MB(c),MB	275.00
2 MB(c),MB	100.00
3 MB(c),MB	125.00
4 MB(c),MB	125.00
5 MB(c),MB	125.00
6 MB(c),MB	125.00
7 MB(c),MB	125.00
8 MB(c),MB,Drug	135.00
9 MB(c),MB	120.00

Becomes:

GOING STEADY

10 MB(c),MB	85.00
11 MB(c),MB	60.00
12 MB(c),MB	60.00
13 MB(c),MB	60.00
14 MB(c),MB	60.00

TEENIE WEENIES, THE
Ziff-Davis Publishing Co.
1951

10	85.00
11	80.00

TEEN LIFE
(see YOUNG LIFE)

TEGRA, JUNGLE EMPRESS
(see ZEGRA, JUNGLE EMPRESS)

TELEVISION COMICS
Animated Cartoons
(Standard Comics)
February, 1950

5 Humorous Format,I:Willie Nilly	50.00
6	35.00
7	35.00
8 May, 1950	35.00

GOLDEN AGE

TELEVISION PUPPET SHOW
Avon Periodicals
1950
1 F:Sparky Smith,Spotty,
  Cheeta, Speedy 80.00
2 November, 1950 .... 75.00

TELL IT TO THE MARINES
Toby Press
March, 1952
1 I:Spike & Pat 125.00
2 A:Madame Cobra 60.00
3 Spike & Bat on a
  Commando Raid! 40.00
4 Veil Dancing(c) 42.00
5 .... 42.00
6 To Paris 35.00
7 Ph(c),The Chinese Bugle ... 30.00
8 Ph(c),V:Communists in
  South Korea 30.00
9 Ph(c) 30.00
10 .... 30.00
11 .... 30.00
12 .... 30.00
13 John Wayne Ph(c) 75.00
14 Ph(c) 30.00
15 Ph(c),July, 1955 .... 30.00

TENDER ROMANCE
Key Publications
December, 1953
1 .... 65.00
2 .... 35.00
Becomes:
IDEAL ROMANCE
3 .... 35.00
4 thru 8 .... @20.00
Becomes:
DIARY CONFESSIONS
9 .... 25.00
10 .... 15.00

TERRIFIC COMICS
(see HORRIFIC)

TERRIFIC COMICS
Et Es Go Mag. Inc./
Continental Magazines
January, 1944
1 LbC,DRi(c),F:Kid
  Terrific Drug 2,300.00
2 LcC,ASh(c),B:Boomerang,
  'Comics' McCormic 1,800.00
3 LbC,LbC(c) 1,500.00
4 LbC,RP(c) 1,800.00
5 LbC,BF,ASh(c),Bondage(c) 2,000.00
6 LbC,LbC(c),BF,Nov.,1944 . 1,500.00

TERROR ILLUSTRATED
E.C. Comics
November-December, 1955
1 JCr,GE,Grl,JO,RC(c) 75.00
2 Spring, 1956 .... 60.00

TERRIFYING TALES
Star Publications
January, 1953
11 LbC,LbC(c),'TyrantsofTerror' 300.00

---

12 LbC,LbC(c),'Bondage(c),
  'Jungle Mystery' 275.00
13 LbC(c),Bondage(c),'The
  Death-Fire,Devil Head(c) ... 350.00
14 LbC(c),Bondage(c),'The
  Weird Idol' 275.00
15 LbC(c),'The Grim Secret',
  April, 1954 .... 275.00
Becomes:
JUNGLE THRILLS
Star Publications
February, 1952
16 LbC(c),'Kingdom of Unseen
  Terror' 275.00
Becomes:

Terrors of the Jungle #6
© Star Publications

TERRORS OF THE JUNGLE
17 LbC(c),Bondage(c) 275.00
18 LbC(c),Strange Monsters .. 175.00
19 JyD,LbC(c),Bondage(c),The
  Golden Ghost Gorilla 175.00
20 JyD,LbC(c),The Creeping
  Scourge 175.00
21 LbC(c),Evil Eyes of Death! . 200.00
4 JyD,LbC(c),Morass of Death 150.00
5 JyD,LbC(c),Bondage(c),
  Savage Train 175.00
6 JyD,LbC(c),Revolt of the
  Jungle Monsters 165.00
7 JyD,LbC(c) 150.00
8 JyD,LbC(c),Death's Grim
  Reflection 150.00
9 JyD,LbC(c),Doom to
  Evil-Doers 150.00
10 JyD,LbC(c),Black Magic,
  September, 1954 .... 150.00

BOY EXPLORERS
1 S&K(c),S&K,The Cadet 650.00
2 S&K(c),S&K 750.00
Becomes:
TERRY AND THE PIRATES
3 S&K,MC(c),MC,Terry and
  Dragon Lady 300.00
4 S&K,MC(c),MC 175.00
5 S&K,MC(c),MC,BP,

  Chop-Chop(c) 100.00
6 S&K,.MC(c),MC 100.00
7 S&K,MC(c),MC,BP 100.00
8 S&K,MC(c),MC,BP 100.00
9 S&K,MC(c),MC,BP 100.00
10 S&K,MC(c),MC,BP 100.00
11 S&K,MC(c),MC,BP,
  A:Man in Black 75.00
12 S&K,MC(c),MC,BP 75.00
13 S&K,MC(c),MC,Belly Dancers 75.00
14 thru 20 S&K,MC(c),MC ... @60.00
22 thru 26 S&K,MC(c),MC ... @55.00
27 Charlton Comics 50.00
28 .... 50.00

TERRY-BEARS COMICS
St. John Publishing Co.
June, 1952
1 .... 20.00
2 & 3 .... @15.00

Terry-Toons Comics #38
© Select Comics/Timely Comics

TERRY-TOONS COMICS
Select,Timely,Marvel,St. Johns
1942
1 Paul Terry (fa) 1,200.00
2 .... 450.00
3 thru 6 .... @300.00
7 Hitler,Hirohito,Mussolini(c) .. 250.00
8 thru 20 .... @200.00
21 thru 37 .... @150.00
38 I&(c):Mighty Mouse 750.00
39 Mighty Mouse 225.00
40 thru 49 All Mighty Mouse @125.00
50 I:Heckle & Jeckle 250.00
51 thru 60 .... @75.00
61 thru 70 .... @55.00
71 thru 86 .... @50.00

TEXAN, THE
St. John Publishing Co.
August, 1948
1 GT,F:Buckskin Belle,The Gay
  Buckaroo,Mustang Jack 80.00
2 GT 40.00
3 BLb(c) 35.00
4 MB,MB(c) 60.00

GOLDEN AGE

---

5 MB,MB(c),Mystery Rustlers
　of the Rio Grande 60.00
6 MB(c),Death Valley
　Double-Cross 50.00
7 MB,MB(c),Comanche Justice
　Strikes at Midnight 60.00
8 MB,MB(c),Scalp Hunters
　Hide their Tracks 60.00
9 MB(c),Ghost Terror of
　the Blackfeet 60.00
10 MB,MB(c),Treason Rides
　the Warpath 50.00
11 MB,MB(c),Hawk Knife 60.00
12 MB 60.00
13 MB,Doublecross at Devil'sDen 60.00
14 MB,Ambush at Buffalo Trail . 60.00
15 MB,Twirling Blades Tame
　Treachery 60.00
Becomes:
FIGHTIN' TEXAN
16 GT,Wanted Dead or Alive .. 45.00
17 LC,LC(c);Killers Trail,
　December, 1952 .... 40.00

TEX FARRELL
D.S. Publishing Co.
March-April, 1948
1 Pride of the Wild West 75.00

TEX GRANGER
(see CALLING ALL BOYS)

TEX RITTER WESTERN
Fawcett Publications/
Charlton Comics
October, 1950
1 Ph(c),B:Tex Ritter, his Horse
　White Flash, his dog Fury, and
　his mom Nancy 500.00
2 Ph(c),Vanishing Varmints .. 250.00
3 Ph(c),Blazing Six-Guns ... 175.00
4 Ph(c),The Jaws of Terror .. 150.00
5 Ph(c),Bullet Trail 150.00
6 Ph(c),Killer Bait 150.00
7 Ph(c),Gunsmoke Revenge . 125.00
8 Ph(c),Lawless Furnace Valley 125.00
9 Ph(c),The Spider's Web ... 125.00
10 Ph(c),The Ghost Town ... 125.00
11 Ph(c),Saddle Conquest 125.00
12 Ph(c),Prairie Inferno 75.00
13 Ph(c) 75.00
14 Ph(c) 75.00
15 Ph(c) 75.00
16 thru 19 Ph(c) .... @75.00
20 Ph(c),Stagecoach To Danger 75.00
21 .... 75.00
22 Panic at Diamond B 60.00
23 A:Young Falcon 50.00
24 A:Young Falcon 50.00
25 A:Young Falcon 50.00
26 thru 38 .... @45.00
39 AW,AW(c) 45.00
40 thru 45 .... @40.00
46 May, 1959 .... 40.00

THING!, THE
Song Hits/Capitol Stories/
Charlton Comics
February, 1952
1 Horror 550.00
2 Crazy King(c) 350.00
3 .... 350.00
4 AFa(c),I Was A Zombie ... 300.00

5 LM(c),Severed Head(c) 325.00
6 .... 300.00
7 Fingenail to Eye(c) 450.00
8 .... 300.00
9 Severe 500.00
10 Devil(c) 300.00
11 SC,Cleaver 400.00
12 SD,SD(c),Neck Blood
　Sucking 550.00
13 SD,SD(c) 550.00
14 SD,SD(c) 550.00
15 SD,SD(c) 550.00
16 Eye Torture 350.00
17 BP,SD(c) 500.00
Becomes:
BLUE BEETLE
18 America's Fastest Moving
　Crusader Against Crime ... 125.00
19 JKa,Lightning Fast 150.00
20 JKa 150.00
21 The Invincible 100.00
Becomes:
MR. MUSCLES
22 World's Most Perfect Man ... 30.00
23 August, 1956 .... 20.00

THIS IS SUSPENSE
(see LAWBREAKERS)

THIS IS WAR
Standard Comics
July, 1952
5 ATh,Show Them How To Die 80.00
6 ATh,Make Him A Soldier ... 75.00
7 One Man For Himself 25.00
8 Miracle on Massacre Hill ... 25.00
9 ATh,May, 1953 .... 60.00

THIS IS SUSPENSE!
(see STRANGE SUSPENSE
STORIES)

THIS MAGAZINE IS
HAUNTED
Fawcett Publications/
Charlton Comics
October, 1951
1 MBi,F:Doctor Death 400.00
2 GE 250.00
3 MBi,Quest of the Vampire . 175.00
4 BP,The Blind, The Doomed
　and the Dead 175.00
5 BP,GE,The Slithering Horror
　of Skontong Swamp! 250.00
6 Secret of the Walking Dead . 125.00
7 The Man Who Saw Too Much 125.00
8 The House in the Web 125.00
9 The Witch of Tarlo 125.00
10 I Am Dr Death,
　Severed Head(c) 200.00
11 BP,Touch of Death 125.00
12 BP 125.00
13 BP,Severed Head(c) 200.00
14 BP,Horrors of the Damned . 125.00
15 DG(c) 100.00
16 SD(c) 250.00
17 SD,SD(c) 265.00
18 SD,SD(c) 265.00
19 SD(c) 225.00
20 SMz(c) 125.00
21 SD(c) 200.00
Becomes:

DANGER AND
ADVENTURE
22 The Viking King,F:Ibis the
　Invincible 50.00
23 F:Nyoka the Jungle Girl
　Comics Code 45.00
24 DG&AA(c) 35.00
25 thru 27 .... @30.00
Becomes:
ROBIN HOOD AND HIS
MERRY MEN
28 .... 40.00
29 thru 37 .... @30.00
38 SD,August, 1958 .... 75.00

3-D-ELL
Dell Publishing Co.
1953
1 Rootie Kazootie 300.00
2 Rootie Kazootie 250.00
3 Flunkey Louise 225.00

THREE RING COMICS
Spotlight Publishers
March, 1945
1 Funny Animal 50.00

THREE STOOGES
Jubilee Publ.
February, 1949
1 JKu,Infinity(c) 750.00
2 JKu,On the Set of
　'The Gorilla Girl' 600.00
St. John Publishing Co.
1 JKu,'Bell Bent for
　Treasure, Sept., 1953 ..... 500.00
2 JKu 350.00
3 JKu,3D 350.00
4 JKu,Medical Mayhem 250.00
5 JKu,Shempador-Matador
　Supreme 250.00
6 JKu, ... 250.00
7 JKu,Ocotober, 1954 ...... 250.00

Thrilling Comics #9
© Better Publ./Nedor/Standard Comics

THRILLING COMICS
Better Publ./Nedor/
Standard Comics
February, 1940

1 B&O:Doc Strange,B:Nickie Norton	1,800.00
2 B:Rio Kid,Woman in Red Pinocchio	800.00
3 B:Lone Eagle,The Ghost	500.00
4 Dr Strange(c)	450.00
5 Bondage(c)	400.00
6 Dr Strange(c)	400.00
7 Dr Strange(c)	400.00
8 V:Pirates	400.00
9 Bondage(c)	400.00
10 V:Nazis	400.00
11 ASh(c),V:Nazis	375.00
12 ASh(c)	350.00
13 ASh(c),Bondage(c)	400.00
14 ASh(c)	375.00
15 ASh(c),V:Nazis	375.00
16 Bondage(c)	400.00
17 Dr Strange(c)	400.00
18 Dr Strange(c)	400.00
19 I&O:American Crusader	425.00
20 Bondage(c)	400.00
21 American Crusader(c)	300.00
22 Bondage(c)	325.00
23 American Crusader	300.00
24 I:Mike in Doc Strange	300.00
25 DR Strange(c)	300.00
26 Dr Strange(c)	300.00
27 Bondage(c)	325.00
28 Bondage(c)	325.00
29 E:Rio Kid;Bondage(c)	325.00
30 Bondage(c)	325.00
31 Dr Strange(c)	300.00
32 Dr Strange(c)	250.00
33 Dr Strange(c)	250.00
34 Dr Strange(c)	250.00
35 Dr Strange	250.00
36 ASh(c),B:Commando	275.00
37 BO,ASh(c)	250.00
38 ASh(c)	250.00
39 ASh(c),E:American Crusader	250.00
40 ASh(c)	250.00
41 ASh(c),F:American Crusader	250.00
42 ASh(c)	200.00
43 ASh(c)	200.00
44 ASh(c),Hitler(c)	275.00
45 EK,ASh(c)	210.00
46 ASh(c)	210.00
47 ASh(c)	200.00
48 EK,ASh(c)	200.00
49 ASh(c)	200.00
50 ASh(c)	200.00
51 ASh(c)	200.00
52 ASh(c),E:Th Ghost; Peto-Bondage(c)	225.00
53 ASh(c),B:Phantom Detective	200.00
54 ASh(c),Bondage(c)	225.00
55 ASh(c),E:Lone Eagle	200.00
56 ASh(c),B:Princess Pantha	300.00
57 ASh(c)	250.00
58 ASh(c)	250.00
59 ASh(c)	250.00
60 ASh(c)	250.00
61 ASh(c),GRi,A:Lone Eagle	250.00
62 ASh(c)	250.00
63 ASh(c),GT	250.00
64 ASh(c)	250.00
65 ASh(c),E:Commando Cubs, Phantom Detective	250.00
66 ASh(c)	250.00
67 FF,ASh(c)	300.00
68 FF,ASh(c)	300.00
69 FF,ASh(c)	300.00
70 FF,ASh(c)	300.00
71 FF,ASh(c)	300.00
72 FF,ASh(c)	300.00
73 FF,ASh(c)	300.00
74 E:Princess Pantha; B:Buck Ranger	200.00
75 B:Western Front	75.00
76	75.00
77 ASh(c)	75.00
78 Bondage(c)	85.00
79 BK	75.00
80 JSe,BE,April, 1951	85.00

Thrilling Crime Cases #46
© Star Publications

THRILLING CRIME CASES
Star Publications
June-July, 1950

41 LbC(c),The Unknowns	150.00
42 LbC(c),The Gunmaster	125.00
43 LbC,LbC(c),The Chameleon	135.00
44 LbC(c),Sugar Bowl Murder	135.00
45 LbC(c),Maze of Murder	135.00
46 LbC,LbC(c),Modern Communications	100.00
47 LbC(c),The Careless Killer	100.00
48 LbC(c),Road Black	100.00
49 LbC(c),The Poisoner	225.00

Becomes:

SHOCKING MYSTERY CASES

50 JyD,LbC(c),Dead Man's Revenge	200.00
51 JyD,LbC(c),A Murderer's Reward	100.00
52 LbC(c),The Carnival Killer	100.00
53 LbC(c),The Long Shot of Evil	100.00
54 LbC(c),Double-Cross of Death	100.00
55 LbC(c),Return from Death	100.00
56 LbC(c),The Chase	150.00
57 LbC(c),Thrilling Cases	85.00
58 LbC(c),Killer at Large	85.00
59 LbC(c),Relentless Huntdown	85.00
60 LbC(c),Lesson of the Law, October, 1954	85.00

THRILLING ROMANCES
Standard Comics
December, 1949

5 Ph(c)	55.00
6 Ph(c)	25.00
7 Ph(c),JSe,BE	35.00
8 Ph(c)	25.00
9 Ph(c),GT	30.00
10 Ph(c),JSe,BE	30.00
11 Ph(c),JSe,BE	30.00
12 Ph(c),WW	45.00
13 Ph(c),JSe	25.00
14 Ph(c),Danny Kaye	18.00
15 Ph(c),Tony Martin,Ph(c)	18.00
16 Ph(c)	15.00
17 Ph(c)	15.00
18 Ph(c)	15.00
19 Ph(c)	15.00
20 Ph(c)	15.00
21 Ph(c)	15.00
22 Ph(c),ATn	35.00
23 Ph(c),ATn	35.00
24 Ph(c),ATn3	35.00
25 Ph(c),ATn	35.00

THRILLING TRUE STORY OF THE BASEBALL GIANTS
Fawcett Publications
1952

N# Partial Ph(c),Famous Giants of the Past	550.00
2 Yankees Ph(c),Joe DiMaggio, Yogi Berra,Mickey Mantle, Casey Stengel	500.00

TICK TOCK TALES
Magazine Enterprises
January, 1946

1 (fa) Koko & Kola	65.00
2 (fa) Calender	35.00
3 thru 10 (fa)	@25.00
11 thru 18 (fa)	@20.00
19 (fa),Flag(c)	20.00
20 (fa)	20.00
21 (fa)	15.00
22 (fa)	15.00
23 (fa),Mugsy Mouse	15.00
24 thru 33 (fa)	@15.00
34 (fa), 1951	15.00

TIM HOLT
Magazine Enterprises
January-February, 1949

4 FBe,Ph(c)	350.00
5 FBe,Ph(c)	200.00
6 FBe,Ph(c),I:Calico Kid	225.00
7 FBe,Ph(c),Man-Killer Mustang	175.00
8 FBe,Ph(c)	175.00
9 FBe,DAy(c),TerribleTenderfoot	175.00
10 FBe,DAy(c),The Devil Horse	175.00
11 FBe,DAy(c),O&I:Ghost Rider	275.00
12 FBe,DAy(c),Battle at Bullock Gap	80.00
13 FBe,DAy(c),Ph(c)	80.00
14 FBe,DAy(c),Ph(c),The Honest Bandits	80.00
15 FBe,DAy,Ph(c)	80.00
16 FBe,DAy,Ph(c)	80.00
17 FBe,DAy,Ph(c)	250.00
18 FBe,DAy,Ph(c)	75.00
19 FBe,DAy,They Dig By Night	60.00
20 FBe,DAy,O:Red Mask	90.00

GOLDEN AGE

21 FBe,DAy,FF(c) 225.00
22 FBe,DAy 55.00
23 FF,FBe,DAy 175.00
24 FBe,DAy,FBe(c) 55.00
25 FBe,DAy,FBe(c) 100.00
26 FBe,DAy,FBe(c) 50.00
27 FBe,DAy,FBe(c),V:Straw Man 50.00
28 FBe,DAy,FBe(c),Ph(c) 50.00
29 FBe,DAy,FBe,Ph(c), ... 50.00
30 FBe,DAy,FBe(c),Lady Doom
   & The Death Wheel 45.00
31 FBe,DAy,FBe(c) 45.00
32 FBe,DAy,FBe(c) 45.00
33 FBe,DAy,FBe(c) 45.00
34 FBe,DAy,FBe(c) 60.00
35 FBe,DAy,FBe(c) 60.00
36 FBe,DAy,FBe(c),Drugs 65.00
37 FBe,DAy,FBe(c) 65.00
38 FBe,DAy,FBe(c) 65.00
39 FBe,DAy,FBe(c),3D Effect . . 70.00
40 FBe,DAy,FBe(c) 70.00
41 FBe,DAy,FBe(c) 70.00
Becomes:

RED MASK

42 FBe,DAy,FBe(c),3D 125.00
43 FBe,DAy,FBe(c),3D 100.00
44 FBe,DAy,FBe(c),Death at
   Split Mesa,3D 90.00
45 FBe,DAy,FBe(c),V:False Red
   Mask 90.00
46 FBe,DAy,FBe(c) 90.00
47 FBe,DAy,FBe(c) 90.00
48 FBe,DAy,FBe(c),Comics Code 85.00
49 FBe,DAy,FBe(c) 85.00
50 FBe,DAy 85.00
51 FBe,DAy,The Magic of 'The
   Presto Kid' 85.00
52 FBe,DAy,O:Presto Kid 90.00
53 FBe,DAy 70.00
54 FBe,DAy,September, 1957 . . 90.00

TIM TYLER COWBOY
Standard Comics
November, 1948

11 . . . . 40.00
12 . . . . 30.00
13 The Doll Told the Secret 30.00
14 Danger at Devil's Acres 30.00
15 Secret Treasure 30.00
16 . . . . 30.00
17 . . . . 30.00
18 1950 . . . . 30.00

TINY TOTS COMICS
Dell Publishing Co.
1943

1 . . . . 250.00

TINY TOTS COMICS
E.C. Comics
March, 1946

N# Your First Comic Book
   B:Burton Geller(c) and art . . 225.00
2 . . . . 125.00
3 Celebrate the 4th 100.00
4 Go Back to School 120.00
5 Celebrate the Winter 100.00
6 Do Their Spring Gardening . . 90.00
7 On a Thrilling Ride 100.00
8 On a Summer Vacation 100.00
9 On a Plane Ride 100.00
10 Merry X-Mas Tiny Tots
   E:Burton Geller(c)and art . . 100.00

TIP TOP COMICS
United Features,St. John,Dell
1930

1 HF,Li'l Abner 5,800.00
2 HF 1,300.00
3 HF,Tarzan(c) 1,200.00
4 HF,Li'l Abner(c) 700.00
5 HF,Capt&Kids(c) 525.00
6 HF 500.00
7 HF 500.00
8 HF,Li'l Abner(c) 500.00
9 HF,Tarzan(c) 525.00
10 HF,Li'L Abner(c) 500.00
11 HF,Tarzan(c) 525.00
12 HF,Li'l Abner 500.00
13 HF,Tarzan(c) 525.00
14 HF,Li'L Abner(c) 500.00
15 HF,Capt&kids(c) 500.00
16 HF,Tarzan(c) 525.00
17 HF,Li'L Abner(c) 500.00
18 HF,Tarzan(c) 525.00
19 HF,Football(c) 400.00

Tip Top Comics #33
© United Features/St. John/Dell

20 HF,Capt&Kids(c) 400.00
21 HF,Tarzan(c) 400.00
22 HF,Li'l Abner(c) 350.00
23 HF,Capt&Kids(c) 350.00
24 HF,Tarzan(c) 400.00
25 HF,Capt&Kids(c) 350.00
26 HF,Li'L Abner(c) 350.00
27 HF,Tarzan(c) 400.00
28 HF,Li'l Abner(c) 350.00
29 HF,Capt&Kids(c) 350.00
30 HF,Tarzan(c) 400.00
31 HFCapt&Kids(c) 350.00
32 HF,Tarzan(c) 350.00
33 HF,Tarzan(c) 350.00
34 HF,Capt&Kids(c) 350.00
35 HF 275.00
36 HF,HK,Tarzan(c) 350.00
37 HF,Tarzan 350.00
38 HF 275.00
39 HF,Tarzan 300.00
40 HF 250.00
41 Tarzan(c) 300.00
42 . . . . 225.00
43 Tarzan(c) 300.00
44 HF 225.00

45 HF,Tarzan(c) 300.00
46 HF 225.00
47 HF,Tarzan(c) 300.00
48 HF 225.00
49 HF 200.00
50 HF,Tarzan(c) 275.00
51 . . . . 200.00
52 Tarzan(c) 275.00
53 . . . . 200.00
54 . . . . 250.00
55 . . . . 200.00
56 . . . . 200.00
57 BHg 250.00
58 . . . . 225.00
59 BHg 250.00
60 . . . . 200.00
61 and 62 BHg . . . . @250.00
63 thru 90 . . . . @125.00
91 thru 99 . . . . @75.00
100 . . . . 100.00
101 thru 150 . . . . @50.00
151 thru 188 . . . . @30.00
189 thru 225 . . . . @30.00

T-Man #22 © Quality Comics Group

T-MAN
Comics Magazines
(Quality Comics Group)
September, 1951

1 JCo,Pete Trask-the
   Treasury Man 275.00
2 RC(c),The Girl with Death
   in Her Hands 150.00
3 RC,RC(c),Death Trap in Iran 125.00
4 RC,RC(c),Panama Peril . . . 125.00
5 RC,RC(c),Violence in Venice 125.00
6 RC(c),The Man Who
   Could Be Hitler 125.00
7 RC(c),Mr. Murder & The
   Black Hand 125.00
8 RC(c),Red Ticket to Hell . . . 110.00
9 RC(c),Trial By Terror 110.00
10 . . . . 110.00
11 The Voice of Russia 75.00
12 Terror in Tokyo 75.00
13 Mind Assassins 75.00
14 Trouble in Bavaria 75.00
15 The Traitor,Bondage(c) 75.00
16 Hunt For a Hatcheman 75.00

17 Red Triggerman	75.00
18 Death Rides the Rails	75.00
19 Death Ambush	75.00
20 The Fantastic H-Bomb Plot	90.00
21 The Return of Mussolini	75.00
22 Propaganda for Doom	50.00
23 Red Intrigue in Parid,H-Bomb	75.00
24 Red Sabotage	50.00
25 RC,The Ingenious Red Trap	75.00
26 thru 37	@50.00
38 December, 1956	50.00

TNT COMICS
Charles Publishing Co.
February, 1946

1 FBI story,YellowJacket	175.00

TODAY'S BRIDES
Ajax/Farrell Publishing Co.
November, 1955

1	35.00
2	20.00
3	20.00
4 November, 1956	20.00

TODAY'S ROMANCE
Standard Comics
March, 1952

5	35.00
6 ATh	40.00
7	20.00
8	20.00

TOM AND JERRY
DELL GIANT EDITIONS
Dell Publishing Co.
1952–58

Back to School	200.00
Picnic Time	150.00
Summer Fun 1	250.00
Summer Fun 2	100.00
Winter Carnival 1	350.00
Winter Carnival 2	175.00
Winter Fun 3	100.00
Winter Fun 4	90.00
Winter Fun 5	80.00
Winter Fun 6	75.00
Winter Fun 7	75.00

TOMB OF TERROR
Harvey Publications
June, 1952

1 BP,The Thing From the Center of the Earth	250.00
2 RP,The Quagmire Beast	135.00
3 BP,RP,Caravan of the Doomed, Bondage(c)	150.00
4 RP,I'm Going to Kill You, Torture	135.00
5 RP	125.00
6 RP,Return From the Grave	125.00
7 RP,Shadow of Death	125.00
8 HN,The Hive	125.00
9 BP,HN,The Tunnel	125.00
10 BP,HN,The Trial	125.00
11 BP,HN,The Closet	125.00
12 BP,HN,Tale of Cain	135.00
13 BP,What Was Out There	150.00
14 BP,SC,End Result	150.00
15 BP,HN,Break-up	200.00
16 BP,Going,Going,Gone	150.00
Becomes:	

THRILLS OF TOMORROW

17 RP,BP,The World of Mr. Chatt	40.00
18 RP,BP,The Dead Awaken	30.00
19 S&K,S&K(c),A:Stuntman	250.00
20 S&K,S&K(c),A:Stuntman	200.00

Tom Corbett, Space Cadet #5
© Dell Publishing Co.

TOM CORBETT SPACE CADET
Dell Publishing Co.
Jan., 1952
See also Dell Four Color

4 based on TV show	100.00
5	75.00
6	70.00
7	60.00
8	50.00
9	50.00
10	50.00
11	50.00

TOM CORBETT SPACE CADET
Prize Publications
May-June, 1955

1	200.00
2	175.00
3 September-October, 1955	175.00

TOM MIX
Ralston-Purina Co.
September, 1940

1 O:Tom Mix	2,600.00
2	850.00
3	550.00
4 thru 9	@500.00
Becomes:	

TOM MIX COMMANDOS COMICS

10	400.00
11 Invisible Invaders	400.00
12 Terrible Talons Of Tokyo	400.00

Tom Mix Western #5
© Fawcett Publications

TOM MIX WESTERN
Fawcett Publications
January, 1948

1 Ph(c),Two-Fisted Adventures	750.00
2 Ph(c),Hair-Triggered Action	350.00
3 Ph(c),Double Barreled Action	250.00
4 Ph(c),Cowpunching	250.00
5 Ph(c),Two Gun Action	250.00
6 CCB,Most Famous Cowboy	200.00
7 CCB,A Tattoo of Thrills	200.00
8 EK,Ph(c),Gallant Guns	185.00
9 CCB,Song o/t Deadly Spurs	175.00
10 CCB,Crack Shot Western	175.00
11 CCB,EK(C),Triple Revenge	175.00
12 King of the Cowboys	150.00
13 Ph(c),Leather Burns	150.00
14 Ph(c),Brand of Death	150.00
15 Ph(c),Masked Treachery	150.00
16 Ph(c),Death Spurting Guns	150.00
17 Ph(c),Trail of Doom	150.00
18 Ph(c),Reign of Terror	150.00
19 Hand Colored Ph(c)	125.00
20 Ph(c),CCB,F:Capt Tootsie	100.00
21 Ph(c)	100.00
22 Ph(c),The Human Beast	100.00
23 Ph(c),Return of the Past	100.00
24 Hand Colored Ph(c), The Lawless City	100.00
25 Hand Colored Ph(c), The Signed Death Warrant	100.00
26 Hand Colored Ph(c), Dangerous Escape	100.00
27 Hand Colored Ph(c), Hero Without Glory	100.00
28 Ph(c),The Storm Kings	100.00
29 Hand Colored Ph(c),The Case of the Rustling Rose	100.00
30 Ph(c),Disappearance in the Hills	100.00
31 Ph(c)	80.00
32 Hand Colored Ph(c), Mystery of Tremble Mountain	75.00
33	75.00
34	65.00

All comics prices listed are for *Near Mint* condition.

GOLDEN AGE

35 Partial Ph(c),The Hanging
   at Hollow Creek 75.00
36 Ph(c) 75.00
37 Ph(c) 75.00
38 Ph(c),36 pages 65.00
39 Ph(c) 75.00
40 Ph(c) 75.00
41 Ph(c) 70.00
42 Ph(c) 75.00
43 Ph(c) 50.00
44 Ph(c) 50.00
45 Partial Ph(c),The Secret
   Letter 50.00
46 Ph(c) 50.00
47 Ph(c) 50.00
48 Ph(c) 50.00
49 Partial Ph(c),Blind Date
   With Death 50.00
50 Ph(c) 50.00
51 Ph(c) 50.00
52 Ph(c) 50.00
53 Ph(c) 50.00
54 Ph(c) 50.00
55 Ph(c) 50.00
56 Partial Ph(c),Deadly Spurs . . 50.00
57 Ph(c)5 . . . . 50.00
58 Ph(c) 50.00
59 Ph(c) 50.00
60 Ph(c) 50.00
61 Partial Ph(c),Lost in the
   Night,May 1953 . . . . 60.00

TOMMY OF THE
BIG TOP
King Features/
Standard Comics
1948
10 Thrilling Circus Adventures . . 30.00
11 . . . . 20.00
12 March, 1949 . . . . 20.00

TOM-TOM THE
JUNGLE BOY
Magazine Enterprises
1946
1 (fa) 40.00
2 (fa) 30.00
3 Winter 1947,(fa),X-mas issue . 15.00
1 . . . . 15.00

TONTO
(See LONE RANGER'S
COMPANION TONTO)

TONY TRENT
(see FACE, THE)

TOP FLIGHT COMICS
Four Star/St. John Publ. Co.
July, 1949
1 . . . . 60.00
1 Hector the Inspector 40.00

TOP LOVE STORIES
Star Publications
May, 1951
3 LbC(c) 125.00
4 LbC(c) 100.00
5 LbC(c) 100.00
6 LbC(c),WW 150.00
7 thru 16 LbC(c) . . . . @100.00
17 LbC(c),WW 125.00

18 LbC(c) 100.00
19 LbC(c),JyD 100.00

Top-Notch Comics #15
© MLJ Magazines

TOP-NOTCH COMICS
MLJ Magazines
December, 1939
1 JaB,JCo,B&O:The Wizard,
   B:Kandak,Swift of the Secret
   Service,The Westpointer,
   Mystic, Air Patrol,Scott
   Rand, Manhunter 4,500.00
2 JaB,JCo,B:Dick Storm,
   E:Mystic, B:Stacy Knight . . 1,700.00
3 JaB,JCo,EA(c),E:Swift of the
   Secret Service,Scott Rand 1,200.00
4 JCo,EA(c),MMe,O&I:Streak,
   Chandler 1,000.00
5 Ea(c),MMe,O&I:Galahad,
   B:Shanghai Sheridan 1,000.00
6 Ea(c),MMe,A:The Sheild . . . 900.00
7 Ea(c),MMe,N:The Wizard . 1,000.00
8 E:Dick Sorm,B&O:Roy The
   Super Boy,The Firefly . . . 1,000.00
9 O&I:Black Hood,
   B:Fran Frazier 4,000.00
10 . . . . 1,200.00
11 . . . . 700.00
12 . . . . 700.00
13 . . . . 700.00
14 Bondage(c) 750.00
15 MMe 650.00
16 . . . . 650.00
17 Bondage(c) 650.00
18 . . . . 600.00
19 Bondage(c) 650.00
20 . . . . 600.00
21 . . . . 500.00
22 . . . . 500.00
23 Bondage(c) 525.00
24 Black Hood Smashes
   Murder Ring 500.00
25 E:Bob Phantom 500.00
26 . . . . 500.00
27 E:The Firefly 500.00
28 B:Suzie,Pokey Okay,
   Gag Oriented 500.00
29 E:Kandak 500.00

30 . . . . 500.00
31 . . . . 300.00
32 . . . . 300.00
33 BWo,B:Dotty&Ditto 300.00
34 BWo 300.00
35 BWo 300.00
36 BWo 300.00
37 thru 40 BWo . . . . @300.00
41 . . . . 300.00
42 BWo 300.00
43 . . . . 300.00
44 EW:Black Hood,I:Suzie . . . 275.00
45 Suzie(c) 275.00
Becomes:
LAUGH COMIX
46 Suzie & Wilbur 100.00
47 Suzie & Wilbur 85.00
48 Suzie & Wilbur 85.00
Becomes:
SUZIE COMICS
49 B:Ginger 150.00
50 AFy(c) 90.00
51 AFy(c) 90.00
52 AFy(c) 90.00
53 AFy(c) 90.00
54 AFy(c) 100.00
55 AFy(c) 110.00
56 BWo,B;Katie Keene 65.00
57 thru 70 BWo . . . . @65.00
71 thru 79 BWo . . . . @55.00
80 thru 99 BWo . . . . @45.00
100 August, 1954, BWo 45.00

TOPS
Tops Mag. Inc.
(Lev Gleason)
July, 1949
1 RC&BLb,GT,DBa,CBi(c),I'll Buy
   That Girl,Our Explosive
   Children 800.00
2 FG,BF,CBi(c),RC&BLb 750.00

TOPS COMICS
Consolidated Book Publishers
1944
2000 Don on the Farm 200.00
2001 The Jack of Spades
   V:The Hawkman 100.00
2002 Rip Raiders 75.00
2003 Red Birch 20.00

TOP SECRET
Hillman Publications
January, 1952
1 The Tricks of the Secret
   Agent Revealed 125.00

TOP SECRETS
Street & Smith Publications
November, 1947
1 BP,BP(c),Of the Men Who
   Guard the U.S. Mail 225.00
2 BP,BP(c),True Story of Jim
   the Penman 150.00
3 BP,BP(c),Crime Solved by
   Mental Telepathy 125.00
4 Highway Pirates 125.00
5 BP,BP(c),Can Music Kill . . . 125.00
6 BP,BP(c),The Clue of the
   Forgotten Film 125.00
7 BP,BP(c),Train For Sale . . . 200.00
8 BP,BP(c) 100.00

All comics prices listed are for *Near Mint* condition.

9 BP,BP(c) 100.00
10 BP,BP(c),July-August, 1949 100.00

TOPS IN ADVENTURE
Approved Comics
(Ziff-Davis)
Autumn, 1952
1 BP,Crusaders From Mars . . 300.00

TOP SPOT COMICS
Top Spot Publishing Co.
1945
1 The Duke Of Darkness 175.00

TOPSY-TURVY
R.B. Leffingwell Publ.
April, 1945
1 I:Cookie 50.00

TOR
St. John Publishing Co.
September, 1953
1 JKu,JKu(c),O:Tor,One Million
   Years Ago 85.00
2 JKu,JKu(c),3-D Issue 75.00
3 JKu,JKu(c),ATh,historic Life . 80.00
4 JKu,JKu(c),ATh 80.00
5 JKu,JKu(c),ATh,October, 1954 80.00

Torchy #4 © Quality Comics Group

TORCHY
Quality Comics Group
November, 1949
1 GFx,BWa(c),The Blonde
   Bombshell 900.00
2 GFx,GFx(c),Beauty at
   its' Best 450.00
3 GFX,GFx(c),You Can't
   Beat Nature 450.00
4 GFx,GFx(c),The Girl to
   Keep Your Eye On 550.00
5 BWa,GFx,BWa(c),At the
   Masquerade Party 750.00
6 September, 1950,BWa,GFx,
   BWa(c),The Libido Driven
   Boy Scout 750.00

TORMENTED, THE
Sterling Comics
July, 1954
1 Buried Alive 150.00
2 September, 1954,The Devils
   Circus 100.00

TOYLAND COMICS
Fiction House Magazines
January, 1947
1 Wizard of the Moon 175.00
2 Buddy Bruin & Stu Rabbit . . 100.00
3 GT,The Candy Maker 125.00
4 July, 1947 . . . . 100.00

TOY TOWN COMICS
Toytown Publ./Orbit Publ.
February, 1945
1 LbC,LbC(c)(fa) 150.00
2 LbC,(fa) 100.00
3 LbC,LbC(c),(fa) 75.00
4 LbC,(fa) 75.00
5 LbC,(fa) 75.00
6 LbC,(fa) 75.00
7 LbC,(fa),May, 1947 . . . . 75.00

TRAIL BLAZERS
(see RED DRAGON COMICS)

TREASURE COMICS
Prize Comics Group
1943
1 S&K,Reprints of Prize Comics
   #7 through #11 . . . . 1,600.00

TREASURE COMICS
American Boys Comics
(Prize Publications)
June-July, 1945
1 HcK,B:PaulBunyan,MarcoPolo 200.00
2 HcK,HcK(c),B:Arabian Knight,
   Gorilla King,Dr.Styx 100.00
3 HcK 75.00
4 HcK 75.00
5 HcK,JK 125.00
6 HcK,BK,HcK(c) 100.00
7 HcK,FF,HcK(c) 225.00
8 HcK,FF 225.00
9 HcK,DBa 75.00
10 JK,DBa,JK(c) 175.00
11 BK,HcK,DBa,The Weird
   Adventures of Mr. Bottle . . . 125.00
12 DBa,DBa(c),Autumn, 1947 . . 90.00

TREASURY OF COMICS
St. John Publishing Co.
1947
1 RvB,RvB(c),Abbie an' Slats 125.00
2 Jim Hardy 75.00
3 Bill Bimlin 75.00
4 RvB,RvB(c),Abbie an' Slats . 75.00
5 Jim Hardy,January, 1948 . . . 70.00

TRIPLE THREAT
Gerona Publications
Winter, 1945
1 F:King O'Leary,The Duke of
   Darkness,Beau Brummell . . 125.00

TRUE AVIATION PICTURE STORIES
Parents' Institute/P.M.I.
August, 1942
1 How Jimmy Doolittle
   Bombed Tokyo 100.00
2 Knight of the Air Mail 50.00
3 The Amazing One-Man
   Air Force 40.00
4 Joe Foss America's No. 1
   Air Force 40.00
5 Bombs over Germany 40.00
6 Flight Lt. Richard
   Hillary R.A.F. 40.00
7 "Fatty" Chow China's
   Sky Champ 40.00
8 Blitz over Burma 40.00
9 Off the Beam 40.00
10 "Pappy" Boyington 40.00
11 Ph(c) 40.00
12 . . . . 40.00
13 Ph(c),Flying Facts 40.00
14 . . . . 40.00
15 . . . . 40.00

Becomes:

AVIATION AND MODEL BUILDING
16 . . . . 45.00
17 February, 1947 . . . . 50.00

True Comics #20
© True Comics/Parents' Magazine

TRUE COMICS
True Comics/
Parents' Magazine Press
April, 1941
1 My Greatest Adventure-by
   Lowell Thomas 225.00
2 BEv,The Story of the
   Red Cross 125.00
3 Baseball Hall of Fame 135.00
4 Danger in the Artic 100.00
5 Father Duffy-the Fighting
   Chaplin 120.00
6 The Capture of Aquinaldo . . 120.00
7 JKa,Wilderness Adventures of
   George Washington 120.00
8 U.S. Army Wings 60.00

All comics prices listed are for *Near Mint* condition.

GOLDEN AGE

9 A Pig that Made History	60.00
10 Adrift on an Ice Pan	60.00
11 Gen. Douglas MacArthur	65.00
12 Mackenzie-King of Cananda	60.00
13 The Real Robinson Crusoe	65.00
14 Australia war base of the South Pacific	65.00
15 The Story of West Point	75.00
16 How Jimmy Doolittle Bombed Tokyo	70.00
17 The Ghost of Captain Blig, B.Feller	75.00
18 Battling Bill of the Merchant Marine	80.00
19 Secret Message Codes	50.00
20 The Story of India	45.00
21 Timoshenko the Blitz Buster	50.00
22 Gen. Bernard L. Montgomery	45.00
23 The Story of Steel	45.00
24 Gen. Henri Giraud-Master of Escape	45.00
25 Medicine's Miracle Men	45.00
26 Hero of the Bismarck Sea	45.00
27 Leathernecks have Landed	50.00
28 The Story of Radar	40.00
29 The Fighting Seabees	40.00
30 Dr. Norman Bethune-Blood Bank Founder	40.00
31 Our Good Neighbor Bolivia, Red Grange	50.00
32 Men against the Desert	35.00
33 Gen. Clark and his Fighting 5th	40.00
34 Angel of the Battlefield	35.00
35 Carlson's Marine Raiders	35.00
36 Canada's Sub-Busters	35.00
37 Commander of the Crocodile Fleet	35.00
38 Oregon Trailblazer	35.00
39 Saved by Sub	35.00
40 Sea Furies	35.00
41 Cavalcade of England	30.00
42 Gen. Jaques Le Clerc-Hero of Paris	30.00
43 Unsinkable Ship	35.00
44 El Senor Goofy	30.00
45 Tokyo Express	25.00
46 The Magnificent Runt	30.00
47 Atoms Unleashed, Atomic Bomb	60.00
48 Pirate Patriot	30.00
49 Smiking Fists	30.00
50 Lumber Pirates	30.00
51 Exercise Musk-Ox	30.00
52 King of the Buckeneers	30.00
53 Baseline Booby	30.00
54 Santa Fe Sailor	30.00
55 Sea Going Santa	30.00
56 End of a Terror	30.00
57 Newfangled Machines	30.00
58 Leonardo da Vinci-500 years too Soon	30.00
59 Pursuit of the Pirates	35.00
60 Emmett Kelly-The World's Funniest Clown	30.00
61 Peter Le Grand-Bold Buckaneer	30.00
62 Sutter's Gold	30.00
63 Outbound Outcome	30.00
64 Man-Eater at Large	30.00
65 The Story of Scotland Yard	30.00
66 Easy Guide to Football Formations	35.00
67 The Changing Zebra	30.00
68 Admiral Byrd	25.00

69 FBI Special Agent Steve Saunders	35.00
70 The Case of the Seven Hunted Men	30.00
71 Story of Joe DiMaggio	150.00
72 FBI,Jackie Robinson	60.00
73 The 26 Mile Dash-Story of the Marathon	35.00
74 A Famous Coach's Special Football Tips	35.00
75 King of Reporters	35.00
76 The Story of a Buried Treasure	35.00
77 France's Greatest Detective	35.00
78 Cagliostro-Master Rogue	50.00
79 Ralph Bunche-Hero of Peace	35.00
80 Rocket Trip to the Moon	150.00
81 Red Grange	150.00
82 Marie Celeste Ship of Mystery	125.00
83 Bullfighter from Brooklyn	125.00
84 King of the Buckaneers, August, 1950	125.00

TRUE CONFIDENCES
Fawcett Publications
Autumn, 1949

1	75.00
2 and 3	@45.00
4 DP	45.00

True Crime Comics #3
© Magazine Village, Inc.

TRUE CRIME COMICS
Magazine Village, Inc.
May, 1947

2 JCo(c),JCo(c),James Kent-Crook,Murderer,Escaped Convict; Drug	1,000.00
3 JCo,JCo(c),Benny Dickson-Killer;Drug	750.00
4 JCo,JCo(c),Little Jake-Big Shot	650.00
5 JCo(c),The Rat & the Blond Gun Moll;Drug	450.00
6 Joseph Metley-Swindler, Jailbird, Killer	300.00
2-1(7) ATh,WW,Ph(c),Phil Coppolla,September, 1949	600.00

TRUE LIFE SECRETS
Romantic Love Stories/ Charlton Comics
March-April, 1951

1	70.00
2	40.00
3	30.00
4	30.00
5 thru 20	@30.00
21 thru 25	@20.00
26 Comics Code	15.00
27 thru 29	@15.00

TRUE LIFE ROMANCES
Ajax/Farrell Publications
December, 1955

1	50.00
2	30.00
3 August, 1956	35.00

TRUE LOVE PICTORIAL
St. John Publishing Co.
1952

1 Ph(c)	100.00
2 MB	65.00
3 MB(c),MB,JKu	200.00
4 MB(c),MB,JKu	200.00
5 MB(c),MB,JKu	200.00
6 MB(c)	100.00
7 MB(c)	100.00
8 MB(c)	75.00
9 MB(c)	75.00
10 MB(c),MB	75.00
11 MB(c),MB	75.00

TRUE MOVIE AND TELEVISION
Toby Press
August, 1950

1 Liz Taylor, Ph(c)	275.00
2 FF,Ph(c),John Wayne, L.Taylor	200.00
3 June Allyson,Ph(c)	175.00
4 Jane Powell,Ph(c),Jan.,1951	100.00

SPORT COMICS
Street & Smith Publications
October, 1940

1 F:Lou Gehrig	400.00
2 F:Gene Tunney	200.00
3 F:Phil Rizzuto	250.00
4 F:Frank Leahy	200.00

Becomes:

TRUE SPORT PICTURE STORIES

5 Joe DiMaggio	250.00
6 Billy Confidence	125.00
7 Mel Ott	150.00
8 Lou Ambers	125.00
9 Pete Reiser	125.00
10 Frankie Sinkwich	125.00
11 Marty Serfo	125.00
12 JaB(c),Jack Dempsey	135.00
2-1 JaB(c),Willie Pep	100.00
2-2 JaB(c)	100.00
2-3 JaB(c),Carl Hubbell	110.00
2-4 Advs. in Football & Battle	125.00
2-5 Don Hutson	100.00
2-6 Dixie Walker	125.00
2-7 Stan Musial	150.00

2-8 Famous Ring Champions	
of All Time	125.00
2-9 List of War Year Rookies .	150.00
2-10 Connie Mack	125.00
2-11 Winning Basketball Plays .	100.00
2-12 Eddie Gottlieb	100.00
3-1 Bill Conn	110.00
3-2 The Philadelphia Athletics ..	80.00
3-3 Leo Durocher	100.00
3-4 Rudy Dusek	85.00
3-5 Ernie Pyle	85.00
3-6 Bowling with Ned Day	85.00
3-7 Return of the Mighty (Home	
from War);Joe DiMaggio(c) .	250.00
3-8 Conn V:Louis	200.00
3-9 Reuben Shark	85.00
3-10 BP,BP(c),Don "Dopey"	
Dillock	75.00
3-11 BP,BP(c),Death	
Scores a Touchdown	85.00
3-12 Red Sox V:Senators	85.00
4-1 Spring Training in	
Full Spring	75.00
4-2 BP,BP(c),How to Pitch 'Em	
Where They Can't Hit 'Em .	75.00
4-3 BP,BP(c),1947 Super Stars	90.00
4-4 BP,BP(c),Get Ready for	
the Olympics	100.00
4-5 BP,BP,(c),Hugh Casey ...	75.00
4-6 BP,BP(c),Phantom Phil	
Hergesheimer	75.00
4-7 BP,BP(c),How to Bowl Better	70.00
4-8 Tips on the Big Fight	100.00
4-9 BP,BP(c),Bill McCahan	70.00
4-10 BP,BP(c),Great Football	
Plays	60.00
4-11 BP,BP(c),Football	60.00
4-12 BP,GE(c),Basketball	60.00
5-1 Satchel Paige	150.00
5-2 History of Boxing,	
July-August, 1949	75.00

TRUE SWEETHEART SECRETS
Fawcett Publications
May, 1950

1 Ph(c)	75.00
2 WW	125.00
3 BD	50.00
4 BD	50.00
5 BD	50.00
6 thru 11	@40.00

TRUE-TO-LIFE ROMANCES
Star Publications
November-December, 1949

3 LbC(c),GlennFord/JanetLeigh	125.00
4 LbC(c)	100.00
5 LbC(c)	100.00
6 LbC(c)	100.00
7 LbC(c)	100.00
8 LbC(c)	100.00
9 LbC(c)	100.00
10 LbC(c)	100.00
11 LbC(c)	100.00
12 LbC(c)	100.00
13 LbC(c),JyD	100.00
14 LbC(c),JyD	100.00
15 LbC(c),WW,JyD	125.00
16 LbC(c),WW,JyD	125.00
17 LbC(c),JyD	100.00
18 LbC(c),JyD	100.00
19 LbC(c),JyD	100.00

20 LbC(c),JyD	100.00
21 LbC(c),JyD	100.00
22 LbC(c)	90.00
23 LbC(c)	90.00

TRUE WAR ROMANCES
Comic Magazines, Inc.
(Quality Comics)
September, 1952

1 Ph(c)	75.00
2	40.00
3 thru 10	@20.00
11 thru 20	@15.00
21 Comics Code	15.00

Becomes:
EXOTIC ROMANCES

22	35.00
23 thru 26	@20.00
27 MB	35.00
28 MB	35.00
29	20.00
30 MB	35.00
31 MB	35.00

TUROK, SON OF STONE
Dell Publishing Co.
December, 1954

(1) see Dell Four Color #596	
(2) see Dell Four Color #656	
3	250.00
4 and 5	@225.00
6 thru 10	@150.00
11 thru 20	@90.00
21 thru 29	@60.00
See Other Color section	

TWEETY AND SYLVESTER
Dell Publishing Co.
June, 1952

(1) see Dell Four Color #406	
(2) see Dell Four Color #489	
(3) see Dell Four Color #524	
4 thru 20	@15.00
21 thru 37	@8.00

TWINKLE COMICS
Spotlight Publications
May, 1945

1 Humor Format	70.00

TWO-FISTED TALES
Fables Publications
(E.C. Comics)
November-December, 1950

18 HK,JCr,WW,JSe,HK(c)	750.00
19 HK,JCr,WW,JSe,HK(c)	500.00
20 JDa,HK,WW,JSe,HK(c)	300.00
21 JDa,HK,WW,JSe,HK(c)	250.00
22 JDa,HK,WW,JSe,HK(c)	250.00
23 JDa,HK,WW,JSe,HK(c)	225.00
24 JDa,HK,WW,JSe,HK(c)	200.00
25 JDa,HK,WW,JSe,HK(c)	200.00
26 JDa,JSe,HK(c),Action at	
the Changing Reservoir ...	150.00
27 JDa,JSe,HK(c)	150.00
28 JDa,JSe,HK(c)	150.00
29 JDa,JSe,HK(c)	200.00
30 JDa,JSe,JDa(c)	200.00
31 JDa,JSe,HK(c),Civil	
War Story	160.00
32 JDa,JKu,WW(c)	160.00
33 JDa,JKu,WW(c)	175.00

Two-Fisted Tales #36 © E.C. Comics

34 JDa,JSe,JDa(c)	160.00
35 JDa,JSe,JDa(c),Civil	
War Story	175.00
36 JDa,JSe,JSe(c),A	
Difference of Opinion	100.00
37 JSe,JSe(c),Bugles &	
Battle Cries	100.00
38 JSe,JSe(c)	100.00
39 JSe,JSe(c)	100.00
40 JDa,JSe,GE,GE(c)	150.00
41 JSe,GE,JDa(c),March, 1955	100.00

UNCLE CHARLIE'S FABLES
Lev Gleason Publications
January, 1952

1 CBi(c),Ph(c)	55.00
2 BF,CBi(c),Ph(c)	30.00
3 CBi(c),Ph(c)	35.00
4 CBi(c),Ph(c)	35.00
5 CBi,Ph(c),September, 1952 .	30.00

UNCLE SAM
(see BLACKHAWK)

UNCLE SCROOGE
Dell Publishing Co.
March, 1952

(1) see Dell Four Color #386	
(2) see Dell Four Color #456	
(3) see Dell Four Color #495	
4	400.00
5	300.00
6	250.00
7 CB	225.00
8	200.00
9	200.00
10	200.00
11 thru 20	@175.00
21 thru 30	@150.00
31 thru 39	@100.00
See Other Pub. section	

UNDERWORLD
D.S. Publishing Co.
February-March, 1948

1 SMo(c),Violence	275.00

GOLDEN AGE

GOLDEN AGE

2 SMo(c),Electrocution 275.00
3 AMc,AMc(c),The Ancient Club 250.00
4 Grl,The Beer Baron Murder . . 175.00
5 Grl,The Postal Clue 150.00
6 The Polka Dot Gang 100.00
7 Mono-The Master 100.00
8 The Double Tenth 100.00
9 Thrilling Stories of the Fight
  against Crime,June, 1953 . 100.00

UNDERWORLD CRIME
Fawcett Publications
June, 1952
1 The Crime Army 200.00
2 Jailbreak 125.00
3 Microscope Murder 100.00
4 Death on the Docks 100.00
5 River of Blood 100.00
6 The Sky Pirates 100.00
7 Bondage & Torture(c) 175.00
8 . . . . 100.00
9 June, 1953 . . . . 100.00

UNITED COMICS
United Features Syndicate
1950
8 thru 26 Bushmiller(c),
  Fritzi Ritz . . . . @25.00

UNITED STATES
FIGHTING AIR FORCE
Superior Comics, Ltd.
September, 1952
1 Coward's Courage 50.00
2 Clouds that Killed 25.00
3 Operation Decoy 15.00
4 thru 28 . . . . @15.00
29 October, 1959 . . . . 15.00

UNITED STATES
MARINES
Wm. H. Wise/Magazine Ent/
Toby Press
1943
N# MBi,MBi(c),Hellcat out
  of Heaven 50.00
2 MBi,Drama of Wake Island . . 35.00
3 A Leatherneck Flame Thrower 30.00
4 MBi 30.00
5 BP 25.00
6 BP 25.00
7 BP 20.00
8 thru 10 . . . . @20.00
11 1952 . . . . 20.00

UNKEPT PROMISE
Legion of Truth
1949
1 Anti:Alcoholic Drinking 50.00

UNKNOWN WORLDS
**(see STRANGE STORIES
FROM ANOTHER WORLD)**

UNSEEN, THE
Visual Editions
(Standard Comics)
1952
5 ATh,The Hungry Lodger . . . 250.00
6 JKa,MSy,Bayou Vengeance 175.00
7 JKz,MSy,Time is the Killer . 150.00

---

8 JKz,MSy,The Vengance Vat 150.00
9 JKz,MSy,Your Grave is Ready 150.00
10 JKz,MSy 150.00
11 JKz,MSy 150.00
12 ATh,GT,Till Death Do Us Part 175.00
13 . . . . 100.00
14 . . . . 100.00
15 ATh,The Curse of the
  Undead!, July, 1954 . . . . . . 175.00

UNTAMED LOVE
Comic Magazines
(Quality Comics Group)
January, 1950
1 BWa(c),PGn 150.00
2 Ph(c) 100.00
3 PGn 100.00
4 . . . . 100.00
5 PGn 100.00

USA IS READY
Dell Publishing Co.
1941
1 Propaganda WWII 275.00

U.S. JONES
Fox Features Syndicate
November, 1941
1 Death Over the Airways . . 1,000.00
2 January, 1942 . . . . 650.00

U.S. MARINES IN
ACTION!
Avon Periodicals
August, 1952
1 On Land,Sea & in the Air . . . 50.00
2 The Killer Patrol 20.00
3 EK(c),Death Ridge,
  December, 1952 . . . . 22.00

U.S. TANK
COMMANDOS
Avon Periodicals
June, 1952
1 EK(c),Fighting Daredevils
  of the USA 50.00
2 EK(c) 25.00
3 EK,EK(c),Robot Armanda . . 25.00
4 EK,EK(c),March, 1953 . . . . . 25.00

VALOR
E.C. Comics
March, 1955
1 AW,AT,WW,WW(c),Grl,BK . 250.00
2 AW(c),AW,WWGrl,BK 200.00
3 AW,RC,BK,JOc(c) 150.00
4 WW(c),RC,Grl,BK,JO 150.00
5 WW(c),WW,AW,GE,Grl,BK . 125.00

VARIETY COMICS
Rural Home Publ./
Croyden Publ. Co.
1944
1 MvS,MvS(c),O:Capt, Valiant 125.00
2 MvS,MvS(c) 75.00
3 MvS,MvS(c) 50.00
4 . . . . 50.00
5 1946 . . . . 50.00

VAULT OF HORROR
(see WAR AGAINST CRIME)

V...COMICS
Fox Features Syndicate
January, 1942
1 V:V-Man 900.00
2 The Horror of the
  Dungeons, March, 1942 . . . 750.00

VERI BEST SURE SHOT
COMICS
Holyoke Publishing Co. 1945
1 reprint Holyoke One-Shots . 250.00

VIC FLINT
St. John Publishing Co.
August, 1948
1 ...Crime Buster 60.00
2 . . . . 40.00
3 . . . . 35.00
4 . . . . 35.00
5 April, 1949 . . . . 35.00

VIC JORDAN
Civil Service Publications
April, 1945
1 Escape From a Nazi Prison . 75.00

VIC TORRY AND HIS
FLYING SAUCER
Fawcett Publications
1950
1 Ph(c),Revealed at Last 400.00

VICTORY COMICS
Hillman Periodicals
August, 1941
1 BEv,BEv(c),F:The Conqueror 2,200.00
2 BEv,BEv(c) 1,000.00
3 The Conqueror(c) 650.00
4 December, 1941 . . . . 600.00

VIC VERITY MAGAZINE
Vic Verity Publications
1945
1 CCB,CCB(c),B:Vic Verity,Hot-
  Shot Galvan, Tom Travis . . 125.00
2 CCB,CCB(c),Annual Classic

Vic Verity Magazine #1
© Vic Verity Publications

Dance Recital 60.00
3 CCB 50.00
4 CCB,I:Boomer Young;The
  Bee-U-TiFul Weekend 50.00
5 CCB,Championship Baseball
  Game 50.00
6 CCB,High School Hero 50.00
7 CCB,CCB(c),F:Rocket Rex .. 50.00

Voodoo #22
© Four Star Publ./Farrell/Ajax Comics

VOODOO
Four Star Publ./Farrell/
Ajax Comics May, 1952

1 MB,South Sea Girl 350.00
2 MB 275.00
3 Face Stabbing 200.00
4 MB,Rendezvous 200.00
5 Ghoul For A Day,Nazi 150.00
6 The Weird Dead,
  Severed Head 165.00
7 Goodbye World 150.00
8 MB, Revenge 200.00
9 Will this thing Never Stew? . 150.00
10 Land of Shadows & Screams 150.00
11 Human Harvest 150.00
12 The Wazen Taper 150.00
13 Bondage(c),Caskets to
   Fit Everybody 165.00
14 Death Judges the
   Beauty Contest 125.00
15 Loose their Heads 150.00
16 Fog Was Her Shroud 125.00
17 Apes Laughter,Electric Chair 150.00
18 Astounding Fantasy 125.00
19 MB,Bondage(c);
   Destination Congo 165.00
Ann.#1 .... 425.00
Becomes:
VOODA
20 MB,MB(c),Echoes of
   an A-Bomb 200.00
21 MB,MB(c),Trek of Danger .. 175.00
22 MB,MB(c),The Sun Blew
   Away, August, 1955 ...... 175.00

WACKY DUCK
(see DOPEY DUCK)

WALT DISNEY'S
COMICS & STORIES
Dell Publishing Co.
N# 1943 dpt.store giveway ... 400.00
N# 1945 X-mas giveaway 150.00

WALT DISNEY'S
COMICS & STORIES
Dell Publishing Co.
October, 1940
1 (1940)FG,Donald Duck &
  Mickey Mouse 17,000.00
2 .... 6,500.00
3 .... 2,000.00
4 Christmas(c) 1,400.00
4a Promo issue 1,500.00
5 .... 1,100.00
6 .... 900.00
7 .... 900.00
8 .... 900.00
9 .... 900.00
10 .... 900.00
11 1st Huey,Louie,Dewey 750.00
12 .... 800.00
13 .... 750.00
14 .... 750.00
15 3 Little Kittens 700.00
16 3 Little Pigs 650.00
17 The Ugly Ducklings 700.00
18 .... 550.00
19 .... 525.00
20 .... 525.00
21 .... 550.00
22 .... 500.00
23 .... 475.00
24 .... 475.00
25 .... 475.00
26 .... 475.00
27 .... 500.00
28 .... 475.00
29 .... 475.00
30 .... 475.00
31 CB; Donald Duck 3,000.00
32 CB 1,400.00
33 CB 1,000.00
34 CB;WK; Gremlins 800.00
35 CB;WK; Gremlins. 750.00
36 CB;WK; Gremlins 750.00
37 CB;WK; Gremlins 375.00
38 CB;WK; Gremlins 475.00
39 CB;WK; Gremlins 475.00
40 CB;WK; Gremlins 425.00
41 CB;WK; Gremlins 425.00
42 CB 425.00
43 CB 400.00
44 CB 400.00
45 CB 400.00
46 CB 400.00
47 CB 375.00
48 CB 375.00
49 CB 375.00
50 CB 375.00
51 CB 300.00
52 CB; Li'l Bad Wolf begins .. 300.00
53 CB 300.00
54 CB 300.00
55 CB 300.00
56 CB 300.00
57 CB 300.00
58 CB 300.00
59 CB 300.00
60 CB 300.00
61 CB; Dumbo 225.00
62 CB 225.00

63 CB; Pinocchio 225.00
64 CB; Pinocchio 225.00
65 CB; Pluto 225.00
66 CB 225.00
67 CB 225.00
68 CB 225.00
69 CB 225.00
70 CB 225.00
71 CB 175.00
72 CB 175.00
73 CB 175.00
74 CB 175.00
75 CB; Brer Rabbit 175.00
76 CB; Brer Rabbit 175.00
77 CB; Brer Rabbit 175.00
78 CB 175.00
79 CB 175.00
80 CB 175.00
81 CB 150.00
82 CB;Bongo 175.00
83 CB;Bongo 175.00
84 CB;Bongo 175.00
85 CB 175.00
86 CB;Goofy & Agnes 175.00
87 CB;Goofy & Agnes 150.00
88 CB;Goofy & Agnes,
   I:Gladstone Gander 175.00
89 CB;Goofy&Agnes,Chip'n'Dale 150.00
90 CB;Goofy & Agnes 150.00
91 CB 125.00
92 CB 125.00
93 CB 125.00
94 CB 125.00
95 .... 125.00
96 Little Toot 125.00
97 CB; Little Toot 125.00
98 CB; Uncle Scrooge 275.00
99 CB 125.00
100 CB 175.00
101 CB 125.00
102 CB 125.00
103 CB 110.00
104 .... 110.00
105 CB 125.00
106 CB 125.00
107 CB 125.00
108 .... 110.00
109 .... 110.00
110 CB 125.00
111 CB 125.00
112 CB; drugs 125.00
113 CB 125.00
114 CB 125.00
115 .... 40.00
116 .... 40.00
117 .... 40.00
118 .... 40.00
119 .... 40.00
120 .... 40.00
121 Grandma Duck begins ... 40.00
122 .... 40.00
123 .... 40.00
124 CB 110.00
125 CB;I:Junior Woodchucks .. 125.00
126 CB 75.00
127 CB 75.00
128 CB 75.00
129 CB 75.00
130 CB 75.00
131 CB 75.00
132 CB A:Grandma Duck 75.00
133 CB 75.00
134 I:The Beagle Boys 175.00
135 CB 75.00
136 CB 75.00

GOLDEN AGE

GOLDEN AGE

Walt Disney's Comics and Stories #102
© Dell Publ. Co.

137 CB 75.00
138 CB 75.00
139 CB 75.00
140 CB; I:Gyro Gearloose 175.00
141 CB 60.00
142 CB 60.00
143 CB; Little Hiawatha 60.00
144 CB; Little Hiawatha 60.00
145 CB; Little Hiawatha 60.00
146 CB; Little Hiawatha 60.00
147 CB; Little Hiawatha 60.00
148 CB; Little Hiawatha 60.00
149 CB; Little Hiawatha 60.00
150 CB; Little Hiawatha 60.00
151 CB; Little Hiawatha 60.00
152 thru 200 CB . . . . @50.00
201 CB 40.00
202 CB 40.00
203 CB 40.00
204 CB, Chip 'n' Dale & Scamp . 40.00
205 thru 240 CB . . . . @40.00
241 CB; Dumbo x-over 30.00
242 CB 30.00
243 CB 30.00
244 CB 30.00
245 CB 30.00
246 CB 30.00
247 thru 255 CB;GyroGearloose@30.00
256 thru 263 CB;Ludwig Von
    Drake & Gearloose . . . . . . @30.00
    See: Independent Color Comics

WALT DISNEY ANNUALS

Walt Disney's Autumn Adventure . 4.00
Walt Disney's Holiday Parade . . . 3.50
Walt Disney's Spring Fever 3.25
Walt Disney's Summer Fun 3.25

WALT DISNEY
DELL GIANT EDITIONS
Dell Publishing Co.

1 CB,W.Disney'sXmas
    Parade('49) 900.00
2 CB,W.Disney'sXmas
    Parade('50) 700.00
3 W.Disney'sXmas Parade('51) 225.00
4 W.Disney'sXmas Parade('52) 200.00

5 W.Disney'sXmas Parade('53) 200.00
6 W.Disney'sXmas Parade('54) 200.00
7 W.Disney'sXmas Parade('55) 200.00
8 CB,W.Disney'sXmas
    Parade('56) 350.00
9 CB,W.Disney'sXmas
    Parade('57) 300.00
1 CB,W.Disney's Christmas in
    Disneyland (1957) 400.00
1 CB,W.Disney's Disneyland
    Birthday Party (1958) 400.00
1 W.Disney's Donald and Mickey
    in Disneyland (1958) 175.00
1 W.Disney's Donald Duck
    Beach Party (1954) 225.00
2 W.Disney's Donald Duck
    Beach Party (1955) 175.00
3 W.Disney's Donald Duck
    Beach Party (1956) 175.00
4 W.Disney's Donald Duck
    Beach Party (1957) 175.00
5 W.Disney's Donald Duck
    Beach Party (1958) 175.00
6 W.Disney's Donald Duck
    Beach Party (1959) 175.00
1 W.Disney's Donald Duck
    Fun Book (1954) 600.00
2 W.Disney's Donald Duck
    Fun Book (1954) 550.00
1 W.Disney's Donald Duck
    in Disneyland (1955) 200.00
1 W.Disney's Huey, Dewey
    and Louie (1958) 150.00
1 W.Disney's DavyCrockett('55) 135.00
1 W.Disney's Lady and the
    Tramp (1955) 275.00
1 CB,W.Disney's Mickey Mouse
    Almanac (1957) 400.00
1 W.Disney's Mickey Mouse
    Birthday Party (1953) 500.00
1 W.Disney's Mickey Mouse
    Club Parade (1955) 400.00
1 W.Disney's Mickey Mouse
    in Fantasyland (1957) 200.00
1 W.Disney's Mickey Mouse
    in Frontierland (1956) 200.00
1 W.Disney's Summer Fun('58) 200.00
2 CB,W.Disney'sSummer
    Fun('59) 200.00
1 W.Disney's Peter Pan
    Treasure Chest (1953) . . 1,500.00
1 Disney Silly Symphonies('52) 450.00
2 Disney Silly Symphonies('53) 400.00
3 Disney Silly Symphonies('54) 350.00
4 Disney Silly Symphonies('54) 350.00
5 Disney Silly Symphonies('55) 300.00
6 Disney Silly Symphonies('56) 300.00
7 Disney Silly Symphonies('57) 300.00
8 Disney Silly Symphonies('58) 300.00
9 Disney Silly Symphonies('59) 300.00
1 Disney SleepingBeauty('59) . 450.00
1 CB,W.Disney's Uncle Scrooge
    Goes to Disneyland (1957) . 400.00
1 W.Disney's Vacation in
    Disneyland (1958) 175.00
1 CB,Disney's Vacation
    Parade('50) 1,300.00
2 Disney'sVacation Parade('51) 450.00
3 Disney'sVacation Parade('52) 225.00
4 Disney'sVacation Parade('53) 225.00
5 Disney'sVacation Parade('54) 225.00
6 Disney's Picnic Party (1955) 175.00
7 Disney's Picnic Party (1956) 175.00
8 CB,Disney's Picnic
    Party (1957) 350.00

DELL JUNIOR TREASURY

1 W.Disney's Alice in Wonderland
    (1955) 85.00

WALT DISNEY
PRESENTS
Dell Publishing Co.
June-August, 1952

1 Ph(c), Four Color 40.00
2 Ph(c) 25.00
3 Ph(c) 25.00
4 Ph(c) 25.00
5 and 6 Ph(c) . . . . @25.00

WAMBI
JUNGLE BOY
Fiction House Magazines
Spring, 1942

1 HcK,HcK(c),Vengence of
    the Beasts 700.00
2 HcK,HcK(c),Lair of the
    Killer Rajah 400.00
3 HcK,HcK(c) 250.00
4 HcK,HcK(c),The Valley of
    the Whispering Drums 150.00
5 HcK,HcK(c),Swampland Safari 150.00
6 Taming of the Tigress 100.00
7 Duel of the Congo Kings . . 100.00
8 AB(c),Friend of the Animals 100.00
9 Quest of the Devils Juju . . . 100.00
10 Friend of the Animals 75.00
11 . . . . 75.00
12 Curse of the Jungle Jewels . . 75.00
13 New Adventures of Wambi . . 75.00
14 . . . . 75.00
15 The Leopard Legions 75.00
16 . . . . 75.00
17 Beware Bwana! 75.00
18 Ogg the Great Bull Ape,
    Winter, 1952 . . . . 75.00

WANTED COMICS
Toytown Comics/
Orbit Publications
September-October, 1947

9 Victor Everhart 125.00
10 Carlo Banone 75.00
11 Dwight Band 75.00
12 Ralph Roe 80.00
13 James Spencer;Drug 80.00
14 John "Jiggs" Sullivan;Drug . . 80.00
15 Harry Dunlap;Drug 40.00
16 Jack Parisi;Drug 40.00
17 Herber Ayers;Drug 40.00
18 Satan's Cigarettes;Drug . . . 120.00
19 Jackson Stringer 35.00
20 George Morgan 35.00
21 BK,Paul Wilson 40.00
22 . . . . 35.00
23 George Elmo Wells 30.00
24 BK,Bruce Cornett;Drug . . . 50.00
25 Henry Anger 30.00
26 John Wormly 30.00
27 Death Always Knocks Twice . 30.00
28 Paul H. Payton 30.00
29 Hangmans Holiday 30.00
30 George Lee 30.00
31 M Consolo 30.00
32 William Davis 30.00
33 The Web of Davis 30.00
34 Dead End 30.00
35 Glen Roy Wright 50.00
36 SSh,SSh(c),Bernard Lee . . . .

Wanted #26 © Toytown Comics

Vault of Horror #29 © E.C. Comics

Thomas	30.00
37 SSh,SSh(c),Joseph M. Moore	30.00
38 SSh,SSh(c)	30.00
39 The Horror Weed;Drug	55.00
40	25.00
41	25.00
42	25.00
43	25.00
44	25.00
45 Killers on the Loose;Drug	45.00
46 Chalres Edward Crews	25.00
47	25.00
48 SSh,SSh(c)	25.00
49	25.00
50 JB(c),Make Way for Murder	55.00
51 JB(c),Dope Addict on a Holiday of Murder;Drug	35.00
52 The Cult of Killers; Classic Drug	35.00
53 April, 1953	25.00

WAR AGAINST CRIME
L.L. Publishing Co.
(E.C. Comics)
Spring, 1948

1 Grl	500.00
2 Grl,Guilty of Murder	300.00
3 JCr(c)	300.00
4 AF,JCr(c)	250.00
5 JCr(c)	250.00
6 AF,JCr(c)	250.00
7 AF,JCr(c)	250.00
8 AF,JCr(c)	250.00
9 AF,JCr(c),The Kid	250.00
10 JCr(c),I:Vault Keeper	1,500.00
11 JCr(c)	1,000.00

Becomes:
VAULT OF HORROR

12 AF,JCr,JCr(c),Wax Museum	3,600.00
13 AF,WW,JCr(c),Grl,Drug	800.00
14 AF,WW,JCr(c),Grl	750.00
15 AF,JCr,JCr(c),Grl,JKa	600.00
16 Grl,JKa,JCr,JCr(c)	550.00
17 JDa,Grl,JKa,JCr,JCr(c)	400.00
18 JDa,Grl,JKa,JCr,JCr(c)	400.00
19 JDa,Grl,JKa,JCr,JCr(c)	400.00
20 JDa,Grl,JKa,JCr,JCr(c)	275.00
21 JDa,Grl,JKa,JCr,JCr(c)	275.00

22 JDa,JKa,JCr,JCr(c)	275.00
23 JDa,Grl,JCr,JCr(c)	275.00
24 JDa,Grl,JO,JCr,JCr(c)	275.00
25 JDa,Grl,JKa,JCr,JCr(c)	275.00
26 JDa,Grl,JCr,JCr(c)	275.00
27 JDa,Grl,JCr,GE,JCr(c)	200.00
28 JDa,Grl,JCr,JCr(c)	200.00
29 JDa,Grl,JCr,JKa,JCr(c), JDa,Grl,JCr,JCr(c) Bradbury Adapt	200.00
30 JDa,Grl,JCr,JCr(c)	200.00
31 JDa,Grl,JCr,JCr(c), Bradbury Adapt	175.00
32 JDa,Grl,JCr,JCr(c)	175.00
33 JDa,Grl,RC,JCr(c)	175.00
34 JDa,Grl,JCr,RC,JCr(c)	175.00
35 JDa,Grl,JCr,JCr(c)	175.00
36 JDa,Grl,JCr,BK,JCr(c),Drug	175.00
37 JDa,Grl,JCr,AW,JCr(c) Hanging	175.00
38 JDa,Grl,JCr,BK,JCr(c)	175.00
39 GRi,JCr,BK,RC,JCr(c) Bondage(c)	200.00
40 January, 1955, Grl,JCr,BK,JO JCr(c)	175.00

WAR BATTLES
Harvey Publications
February, 1952

1 BP,Devils of the Deep	75.00
2 BP,A Present From Benny	40.00
3 BP	30.00
4	30.00
5	30.00
6 HN	30.00
7 BP	35.00
8	30.00
9 December, 1953	30.00

WAR BIRDS
Fiction House Magazines
1952

1 Willie the Washout	75.00
2 Mystery MIGs of Kwanjamu	45.00
3 thru 6	@40.00
7 Winter, 1953,Across the Wild Yalu	40.00

WAR COMICS
Dell Publishing Co.
May, 1940

1 AMc,Sky Hawk	400.00
2 O:Greg Gildam	250.00
3	150.00
4 O:Night Devils	200.00

WAR HEROES
Dell Publishing Co.
July-September, 1942

1 Gen. Douglas MacArthur (c)	175.00
2	75.00
3	50.00
4 A:Gremlins	100.00
5	45.00
6 thru 11	@40.00

WAR HEROES
Ace Magazines
May, 1952

1 Always Comin'	50.00
2 LC,The Last Red Tank	30.00
3 You Got it	20.00
4 A Red Patrol	20.00
5 Hustle it Up	20.00
6 LC,Hang on Pal	25.00
7	25.00
8 LC,April, 1953	25.00

WARPATH
Key Publications/
Stanmore
November, 1954

1 Red Men Raid	50.00
2 AH(c),Braves Battle	30.00
3 April, 1955	30.00

WARRIOR COMICS
H.C. Blackerby
1944

1 Ironman wing Brady	100.00

WAR SHIPS
Dell Publishing Co.
1942

1 AMc	75.00

WAR STORIES
Dell Publishing Co.
1942

5 O:The Whistler	175.00
6 A:Night Devils	125.00
7 A:Night Devils	125.00
8 A:Night Devils	125.00

WARTIME ROMANCES
St. John Publishing Co.
July, 1951

1 MB(c),MB	175.00
2 MB(c),MB	125.00
3 MB(c),MB	100.00
4 MB(c),MB	100.00
5 MB(c),MB	75.00
6 MB(c),MB	100.00
7 MB(c),MB	75.00
8 MB(c),MB	75.00
9 MB(c),MB	50.00
10 MB(c),MB	50.00
11 MB(c),MB	50.00

12 Mb(c),MB	50.00
13 MB(c)	40.00
14 MB(c)	40.00
15 MB(c)	40.00
16 MB(c),MB	40.00
17 MB(c)	40.00
18 MB(c),MB	40.00

WAR VICTORY COMICS
U.S. Treasury/War Victory/
Harvey Publ.
Summer, 1942

1 Savings Bond Promo with Top Syndicated Cartoonists, benefit USO	275.00

Becomes:

WAR VICTORY ADVENTURES

2 BP,2nd Front Comics	150.00
3 BP,F:Capt Cross of the Red Cross	125.00

Web of Evil #3
© Quality Comics Group

WEB OF EVIL
Comic Magazines, Inc.
(Quality Comics Group)
November, 1952

1 Custodian of the Dead	350.00
2 JCo,Hangmans Horror	250.00
3 JCo	250.00
4 JCo,JCo(c),Monsters of the Mist	250.00
5 JCo,JCo(c),The Man who Died Twice,Electric Chair(c)	275.00
6 JCo,JCo(c),Orgy of Death	250.00
7 JCo,JCo(c),The Strangling Hands	250.00
8 JCo,Flaming Vengeance	200.00
9 JCo,The Monster in Flesh	200.00
10 JCo,Brain that Wouldn't Die	200.00
11 JCo,Buried Alive	200.00
12 Phantom Killer	100.00
13 Demon Inferno	100.00
14 RC(c),The Monster Genie	100.00
15 Crypts of Horror	100.00
16 Hamlet of Horror	100.00
17 Terror in Chinatown	110.00

18 Scared to Death,Acid Face	125.00
19 Demon of the Pit	100.00
20 Man Made Terror	100.00
21 December, 1954, Death's Ambush	100.00

WEB OF MYSTERY
A.A. Wyn Publ.
(Ace Magazines)
February, 1951

1 MSy,Venom of the Vampires	300.00
2 MSy,Legacy of the Accursed	165.00
3 MSy,The Violin Curse	150.00
4 GC	150.00
5	150.00
6 LC	150.00
7 MSy	150.00
8 LC,LC(c),MSy,The Haunt of Death Lake	150.00
9 LC,LC(c)	150.00
10	150.00
11 MSy	150.00
12 LC	125.00
13 LC,LC(c)	125.00
14 MSy	125.00
15	125.00
16	125.00
17 LC,LC(c)	125.00
18 LC	125.00
19 LC	125.00
20 LC	125.00
21 MSy	125.00
22	125.00
23	125.00
24 LC	125.00
25 LC	125.00
26	125.00
27 LC	125.00
28 RP,1st Issue under Comics Code Authority	100.00
29 MSy,September, 1955	100.00

WEDDING BELLS
Quality Comics Group
February, 1954

1 OW	100.00
2	45.00
3	25.00
4	25.00
5	25.00
6	25.00
7	25.00
8	25.00
9 Comics Code	25.00
10 BWa	75.00
11	25.00
12	20.00
13	20.00
14	20.00
15 MB(c)	25.00
16 MB(c),MB	35.00
17	20.00
18 MB	25.00
19 MB	25.00

WEEKENDER, THE
Rucker Publishing Co.
September, 1945

3	125.00
4	100.00
2-1(5)JCo,WMc,January, 1946	145.00

WEIRD ADVENTURES
P.L. Publishing
May, 1951

1 MB,Missing Diamonds	300.00
2 Puppet Peril	250.00
3 Blood Vengeance, October 1951	225.00

WEIRD ADVENTURES
Approved Comics
(Ziff-Davis)
July-August, 1951

10 P(c),Seeker from Beyond	250.00

WEIRD CHILLS
Key Publications
July, 1954

1 MBi(c),BW	450.00
2 Eye Torture(c)	425.00
3 Bondage(c),November, 1954	250.00

WEIRD COMICS
Fox Features Syndicate
April, 1940

1 LF(c),Bondage(c),B:Birdman, Thor,Sorceress of Doom, BlastBennett,Typhon,Voodoo Man, Dr.Mortal	3,500.00
2 LF(c),Mummy(c)	1,500.00
3 JSm(c)	900.00
4 JSm(c)	900.00
5 Bondage(c),I:Dart,Ace;E:Thor	900.00
6 Dart & Ace(c)	750.00
7 Battle of Kooba	750.00
8 B:Panther Woman,Dynamo, The Eagle	750.00
9 V:Pirates	650.00
10 A:Navy Jones	650.00
11 Dart & Ace(c)	450.00
12 Dart & Ace(c)	450.00
13 Dart & Ace(c)	450.00
14 The Rage(c)	450.00
15 Dart & Ace (c)	450.00
16 Flag,The Encore(c)	450.00
17 O:Black Rider	475.00
18	450.00
19	450.00
20 January, 1941,I'm The Master of Life and Death	450.00

WEIRD FANTASY
I.C. Publishing Co.
(E.C. Comics)
May-June, 1950

13(1)AF,HK,JKa,WW,AF(c), Roger Harvey's Brain	1,500.00
14(2)AF,HK,JKa,WW,AF(c), Cosmic Ray Brain Explosion	600.00
15(3)AF,HK,JKa,WW,AF(c),Your Destination is the Moon	450.00
16(4)AF,HK,JKa,WW,AF(c)	450.00
17(5)AF,HK,JKa,WW,AF(c),Not Made by Human Hands	400.00
6 AF,HK,JKa,WW,AF(c)	300.00
7 AF,JKa,WW,AF(c)	300.00
8 AF,JKa,WW,AF(c)	300.00
9 AF,Jka,WW,JO,AF(c)	300.00
10 AF,JKa,WW,JO,AF(c)	350.00
11 AF,Jka,WW,JO,AF(c)	250.00
12 AF,Jka,WW,JO,AF(c)	250.00
13 AF,Jka,WW,JO,AF(c)	250.00
14 AF,JKa,WW,JO,AW&FF,AF(c)	350.00

15 AF,JKa,JO,AW&RKr,AF(c),
    Bondage(c) 250.00
16 AF,JKa,JO,AW&RKr,AF(c) . 200.00
17 AF,JOP,JKa,AF(c),Bradbury 200.00
18 AF,JO,JKa,AF(c),Bradbury . 200.00
19 JO,JKa,JO(c),Bradbury 200.00
20 JO,JKa,FF,AF(c) 225.00
21 JO,JKa,AW&FF(c) 350.00
22 JO,JKa,JO(c),Nov.,1953 ... 195.00

WEIRD HORRORS
St. John Publishing Co.
June, 1952
1 GT,Dungeon of the Doomed 300.00
2 Strangest Music Ever 175.00
3 PAM,Strange Fakir From
    the Orient 175.00
4 Murderers Knoll 150.00
5 Phantom Bowman 150.00
6 Monsters from Outer Space 250.00
7 LC,Deadly Double 275.00
8 JKu,JKu(c),Bloody Yesterday 225.00
9 JKu,JKu(c),Map Of Doom .. 225.00
Becomes:

NIGHTMARE
10 JKu(c),The Murderer's Mask 350.00
11 BK,Ph(c),Fangs of Death . 250.00
12 JKu(c),The Forgotten Mask . 225.00
13 BP,Princess of the Sea 200.00
Becomes:

AMAZING GHOST STORIES
14 EK,MB(c), ... 150.00
15 BP 125.00
16 February, 1955, EK,JKu ... 150.00

Weird Mysteries #3
© *Gilmore Publications*

WEIRD MYSTERIES
Gilmore Publications
October, 1952
1 BW(c) 450.00
2 BWi 650.00
3 Severed Heads(c) 350.00
4 BW,Human headed ants(c) . 550.00
5 BW,Brains From Head(c) .. 550.00
6 Severed Head(c) 300.00
7 Used in "Seduction" 500.00

8 The One That Got Away .. 300.00
9 Epitaph,Cyclops 300.00
10 The Ruby 250.00
11 Voodoo Dolls 250.00
12 September, 1954 .... 250.00

WEIRD SCIENCE
E.C. Comics
1950
1 AF(c),AF,JKu,HK,WW 1,400.00
2 AF(c),AF,JKu,HK,WW,Flying
    Saucers(c) 650.00
3 AF(c),AF,JKu,HK 600.00
4 AF(c),AF,JKu,HK 550.00
5 AF(c),AF,JKu,HK,WW,
    Atomic Bomb(c) 400.00
6 AF(c),AF,JKu,HK 350.00
7 AF(c),AF,JKu,HK,Classic(c) . 400.00
8 AF(c),AF,JKu 350.00
9 WW(c),JKu,Classic(c) 400.00
10 WW(c),JKu,JO,Classic(c) .. 400.00
11 AF,JKu,Space war 275.00
12 WW(c),JKu,JO,Classic(c) .. 275.00
13 WW(c),JKu,JO, ... 300.00
14 WW(c),WW,JO 300.00
15 WW(c),WW,JO,GRi,AW,
    RKr,JKa 300.00
16 WW(c),WW,JO,AW,RKr,JKa 300.00
17 WW(c),WW,JO,AW,RKr,JKa 300.00
18 WW(c),WW,JO,AW,RKr,
    JKa,Atomic Bomb 250.00
19 WW(c),WW,JO,AW,
    FF,Horror(c) 400.00
20 WW(c),WW,JO,AW,FF,JKa . 400.00
21 WW(c),WW,JO,AW,FF,JKa . 400.00
22 WW(c),WW,JO,AW,FF 400.00
Becomes:

WEIRD SCIENCE FANTASY
23 WW(c),WW,AW,BK 200.00
24 WW,AW,BK,Classic(c) 225.00
25 WW,AW,BK,Classic(c) 250.00
26 AF(c),WW,RC,
    Flying Saucer(c) 200.00
27 WW(c),WW,RC 200.00
28 AF(c),WW 250.00
29 AF(c),WW,Classic(c) 400.00
Becomes:

INCREDIBLE SCIENCE FANTASY
30 WW,JDa(c),BK,AW,RKr,JO 250.00
31 WW,JDa(c),BK,AW,RKr ... 300.00
32 JDa(c),BK,WW,JO 300.00
33 WW(c),BK,WW,JO 300.00

WEIRD TALES OF THE FUTURE
S.P.M. Publ./ Aragon Publications
March, 1952
1 RA 525.00
2 BW,BW(c) 800.00
3 BW,BW(c) 800.00
4 BW,BW(c) 525.00
5 BW,BW(c),Jumpin' Jupiter
    Lingerie(c) 800.00
6 Bondage(c) 350.00
7 BW,Devil(c) 500.00
8 July-August 1953 .... 300.00

WEIRD TERROR
Allen Hardy Associates (Comic Media)
September, 1952
1 RP,DH,DH(c),Dungeon of the
    Doomed;Hitler 300.00
2 HcK(c),PAM 200.00
3 PAM,DH,DH(c) 200.00
4 PAM,DH,DH(c) 250.00
5 PAM,DH,RP,DH(c),Hanging(c) 200.00
6 DH,RP,DH(c),Step into
    My Parlour 225.00
7 DH,PAM,DH(c),Blood o/t Bats 175.00
8 DH,RP,DH(c),Step into
    My Parlour 200.00
9 DH,PAM,DH(c),The Fleabite 175.00
10 DH,BP,RP,DH(c) 175.00
11 DH,DH(c),Satan's Love Call 200.00
12 DH,DH(c),King Whitey 150.00
13 DH,DH(c),September, 1954,
    Wings of Death 175.00

WEIRD THRILLERS
Approved Comics (Ziff-Davis)
September-October, 1951
1 Ph(c),Monsters & The Model 450.00
2 AW,P(c),The Last Man 350.00
3 AW,P(c),Princess o/t Sea .. 400.00
4 AW,P(c),The Widows Lover . 300.00
5 BP,October, 1952,AW,P(c),
    Wings of Death 275.00

WESTERN ACTION THRILLERS
Dell Publishing Co.
April, 1937
1 .... 600.00

WESTERN ADVENTURES COMICS
A.A. Wyn, Inc. (Ace Magazines)
October, 1948
N#(1)Injun Gun Bait 135.00
N#(2)Cross-Draw Kid 75.00
N#(3)Outlaw Mesa 75.00
4 Sheriff 50.00
5 .... 50.00
6 Rip Roaring Adventure 50.00
Becomes:

WESTERN LOVE TRAILS
7 .... 75.00
8 Maverick Love 50.00
9 March, 1950 .... 40.00

WESTERN BANDIT TRAILS
St. John Publishing Co.
January, 1949
1 GT,MB(c) 150.00
2 GT,MB(c) 100.00
3 GT,MB,MB(c),Gingham Fury 125.00

WESTERN CRIME-BUSTERS
Trojan Magazines
September, 1950
1 Gunslingin' Galoots 200.00
2 K-Bar Kate 100.00

All comics prices listed are for *Near Mint* condition.

GOLDEN AGE

3 Wilma West	100.00
4 Bob Dale	100.00
5 Six-Gun Smith	100.00
6 WW	200.00
7 WW,Wells Fargo Robbery	200.00
8	100.00
9 WW,Lariat Lucy	200.00
10 WW,April 1952;Tex Gordon	200.00

WESTERN CRIME CASES
(see WHITE RIDER)

WESTERNER, THE
Wanted Comics Group/
Toytown Publ.
June, 1948

14 F:Jack McCall	75.00
15 F:Bill Jamett	35.00
16 F:Tom McLowery	35.00
17 F:Black Bill Desmond	35.00
18 BK,F:Silver Dollar Dalton	50.00
19 MMe,F:Jess Meeton	30.00
20	25.00
21 BK,MMe	50.00
22 BK,MMe	50.00
23 BK,MMe	50.00
24 BK,MMe	50.00
25 O,I,B:Calamity Jane	50.00
26 BK,F:The Widowmaker	65.00
27	75.00
28 thru 31	@25.00
32 E:Calamity Jane	25.00
33 A:Quest	25.00
34	25.00
35 SSh(c)	25.00
36	25.00
37 Lobo-Wolf Boy	25.00
38	25.00
39	25.00
40 SSh(c)	25.00
41 December, 1951	25.00

WESTERN FIGHTERS
Hillman Periodicals
April-May, 1948

1 S&K(c)	250.00
2 BF(c)	60.00

Western Fighters #1
© Hillman Periodicals

3 BF(c)	50.00
4 BK,BF	55.00
5	35.00
6	34.00
7 BK	60.00
8	35.00
9	35.00
10 BK	60.00
11 AMC&FF	200.00
2-1 BK	60.00
2-2 BP	40.00
2-3 thru 2-12	@20.00
3-1 thru 3-11	@20.00
3-12 BK	40.00
4-1	20.00
4-2 BK	50.00
4-3 BK	50.00
4-4 BK	50.00
4-5 BK	50.00
4-6 BK	50.00
4-7 March-April 1953	20.00

WESTERN FRONTIER
P.L. Publishers
(Approved Comics)
May, 1951

1 Flaming Vengeance	75.00
2	35.00
3 Death Rides the Iron Horse	25.00
4 thru 6	@25.00
7 1952	25.00

WESTERN HEARTS
Standard Magazine, Inc.
December, 1949

1 Ph(c),JSe	125.00
2 Ph(c),AW,FF	150.00
3 Ph(c)	65.00
4 Ph(c),JSe,BE	65.00
5 Ph(c),JSe,BE	65.00
6 Ph(c),JSe,BE	65.00
7 Ph(c),JSe,BE	65.00
8 Ph(c)	75.00
9 Ph(c),JSe,BE	75.00
10 Ph(c),JSe,BE	50.00

WESTERN LOVE
Feature Publications
(Prize Comics Group)
July-August, 1949

1 S&K	200.00
2 S&K	150.00
3 JSE,BE	100.00
4 JSE,BE	100.00
5 JSE,BE	100.00

WESTERN PICTURE STORIES
Comics Magazine Co.
February, 1937

1 WE,Treachery Trail, 1st Western	1,400.00
2 WE,Weapons of the West	850.00
3 WE,Dragon Pass	650.00
4 June, 1937,CavemanCowboy	650.00

WESTERN THRILLERS
Fox Features Syndicate
August, 1948

1	350.00
2	125.00
3 GT,RH(c)	100.00

4	125.00
5	125.00
6 June, 1949	100.00

Becomes:
MY PAST CONFESSIONS

7	60.00
8	40.00
9	40.00
10	40.00
11	75.00
12	20.00

WESTERN TRUE CRIME
Fox Features Syndicate
August, 1948

1	175.00
2	150.00
3	125.00
4 JCr	150.00
5	100.00
6	100.00

Becomes:
MY CONFESSION

7 WW	150.00
8 WW,My Tarnished Reputation	125.00
9 I:Tormented Men	40.00
10 February, 1950,I Am Damaged Goods	40.00

WHACK
St. John Publishing Co.
December, 1953

1 Steve Crevice,Flush Jordan V:Bing(Crosby)The Merciful	200.00
2	125.00
3 F:Little Awful Fannie	125.00

WHAM COMICS
Centaur Publications
November, 1940

1 PG,The Sparkler & His Disappearing Suit	1,100.00
2 December, 1940,PG,PG(C), Men Turn into Icicles	750.00

WHIRLWIND COMICS
Nita Publications
June, 1940

1 F:The Cyclone	1,100.00
2 A:Scoops Hanlon,Cyclone(c)	750.00
3 September, 1940,A:Magic Mandarin,Cyclone(c)	700.00

WHITE PRINCESS OF THE JUNGLE
Avon Periodicals
July, 1951

1 EK(c),Terror Fangs	350.00
2 EK,EK(c),Jungle Vengeance	300.00
3 EK,EK(c),The Blue Gorilla	225.00
4 Fangs of the Swamp Beast	200.00
5 EK,Coils of the Tree Snake November, 1952	200.00

WHIZ COMICS
Fawcett Publications
February, 1940

1 O:Captain Marvel,B:Spy Smasher,Golden Arrow,Dan Dare, Scoop Smith,Ibis the Invincible, Sivana	65,000.00

2 . . . . 4,500.00	40 A:Three Lt. Marvels, The	103 . . . . 150.00
3 Make way for	Earth's 4 Corners 325.00	104 . . . . 150.00
Captain Marvel 3,500.00	41 Captain Marvel 1,000 years	105 . . . . 150.00
4 Captain Marvel	from Now 250.00	106 A:Bulletman 150.00
Crashes Through 2,200.00	42 Returns in Time Chair 250.00	107 The Great Experiment . . . 175.00
5 Captain Marvel	43 V:Sinister Spies,	108 thru 114 . . . . @150.00
Scores Again! 1,800.00	Spy Smasher(c) 250.00	115 The Marine Invasion 150.00
6 Circus of Death 1,500.00	44 Life Story of Captain Marvel 275.00	116 . . . . 150.00
7 B:Dr Voodoo,Squadron	45 Cures His Critics 250.00	117 V:Sivana 150.00
of Death 1,400.00	46 . . . . 250.00	118 . . . . 150.00
8 Saved by Captain Marvel! 1,200.00	47 Captain Marvel needs	119 . . . . 150.00
9 MRa,Captain Marvel	a Birthday 250.00	120 . . . . 150.00
on the Job 1,200.00	48 . . . . 250.00	121 . . . . 150.00
10 Battles the Winged Death . 1,200.00	49 Writes a Victory song 250.00	122 V:Sivana 150.00
11 Hurray for Captain Marvel . 1,000.00	50 Captain Marvel's most	123 . . . . 150.00
12 Captain Marvel rides	embarrassing moment 250.00	124 . . . . 150.00
the Engine of Doom 1,000.00	51 Judges the Ugly-	125 Olympic Games of the Gods 150.00
13 Worlds Most Powerful Man! 900.00	Beauty Contest 200.00	126 . . . . 150.00
14 Boomerangs the Torpedo . . 900.00	52 V:Sivana, Chooses	127 . . . . 150.00
15 O:Sivana 1,000.00	His Birthday 200.00	128 . . . . 150.00
16 . . . . 1,000.00	53 Captain Marvel fights	129 . . . . 150.00
17 Knocks out a Tank 1,000.00	Billy Batson 200.00	130 . . . . 150.00
18 V:Spy Smasher 1,000.00	54 Jack of all Trades 200.00	131 The Television Trap 150.00
	55 Family Tree 200.00	
	56 Tells what the Future Will Be 200.00	
	57 A:Spy Smasher,Golden Arrow,	

Whiz Comics #25
© Fawcett Publications

	Ibis 200.00	
	58 . . . . 200.00	
	59 V:Sivana's Twin 200.00	
	60 Missing Person's Machine . 200.00	
	61 Gets a first name 175.00	
	62 Plays in a Band 175.00	
	63 Great Indian Rope Trick . . . 175.00	
	64 Suspected of Murder 175.00	
	65 Lamp of Diogenes 175.00	
	66 The Trial of Mr. Morris! . . . 175.00	
	67 . . . . 175.00	
	68 Laugh Lotion, V:Sivana . . . 175.00	
	69 Mission to Mercury 175.00	
	70 Climbs the World's Mightiest	
	Mountain 175.00	
	71 Strange Magician 150.00	
	72 V:The Man of the Future . . . 150.00	
	73 In Ogre Land 150.00	*Whiz Comics #46*
	74 Old Man River 150.00	*© Fawcett Publications*
	75 The City Olympics 150.00	
	76 Spy Smasher become	132 thru 142 . . . . @150.00
	Crime Smasher 150.00	143 Mystery of the Flying Studio 150.00
19 Crushes the Tiger Shark . . 650.00	77 . . . . 150.00	144 V:The Disaster Master . . . 150.00
20 V:Sivana 650.00	78 . . . . 150.00	145 . . . . 150.00
21 O:Lt. Marvels 700.00	79 . . . . 150.00	146 . . . . 150.00
22 Mayan Temple 500.00	80 . . . . 150.00	147 . . . . 150.00
23 GT,A:Dr. Voodoo 500.00	81 . . . . 150.00	148 . . . . 150.00
24 . . . . 500.00	82 The Atomic Ship 150.00	149 . . . . 150.00
25 O&I:Captain Marvel Jr.,	83 Magic Locket 150.00	150 V:Bug Bombs 150.00
Stops the Turbine of Death 4,400.00	84 . . . . 150.00	151 . . . . 150.00
26 . . . . 475.00	85 The Clock of San Lojardo . . 150.00	152 . . . . 150.00
27 V:Death God of the Katonkas 500.00	86 V:Sinister Sivanas 150.00	153 V:The Death Horror 200.00
28 V:Mad Dervish of Ank-Har . 500.00	87 The War on Olympia 150.00	154 Horror Tale, I:Dr.Death . . . 200.00
29 Three Lt. Marvels (c), Pan	88 The Wonderful Magic Carpet 150.00	155 V:Legend Horror,Dr.Death . 225.00
American Olympics 500.00	89 Webs of Crime 150.00	
30 . . . . 450.00	90 . . . . 150.00	**WHODUNIT?**
31 Douglass MacArthur&Spy	91 Infinity (c) 150.00	**D.S. Publishing Co.**
Smasher(c) 400.00	92 . . . . 150.00	**August-September, 1948**
32 Spy Smasher(c) 400.00	93 Captain America become	1 MB,Weeping Widow 150.00
33 Spy Smasher(c) 450.00	a Hobo? 150.00	2 Diploma For Death 100.00
34 Three Lt. Marvels (c) 350.00	94 V:Sivana 150.00	3 December-January, 1949 . . 100.00
35 Capt. Marvel and the	95 Captain Marvel is grounded 150.00	
Three Fates 375.00	96 The Battle Between Buildings 150.00	
36 Haunted Hallowe'en Hotel . . 325.00	97 Visits Mirage City 150.00	
37 Return of the Trolls 325.00	98 . . . . 150.00	
38 Grand Steeplechase 325.00	99 V:Menace in the Mountains . 150.00	
39 A Nazi Utopia 325.00	100 . . . . 175.00	
	101 . . . . 150.00	
	102 A:Commando Yank 150.00	

GOLDEN AGE

GOLDEN AGE

WHO IS NEXT?
Standard Comics
January, 1953
5 ATh,RA,Don't Let Me Kill .. 125.00

WILD BILL ELLIOT
Dell Publishing Co.
May, 1950
(1) *see Dell Four Color #278*
2 .... 45.00
3 thru 5 .... @35.00
6 thru 10 .... @35.00
(11-12) *see Four Color #472, 520*
13 thru 17 .... @30.00

WILD BILL HICKOK
AND JINGLES
(see YELLOWJACKET
COMICS)

WILBUR COMICS
MLJ Magazines
(Archie Publications)
Summer, 1944
1 F:Wilbur Wilkin-America's Song
  of Fun 350.00
2 .... 200.00
3 .... 150.00
4 .... 125.00
5 I:Katy Keene 450.00
6 .... 125.00
7 .... 125.00
8 .... 125.00
9 .... 125.00
10 .... 125.00
11 thru 20 .... @75.00
21 thru 30 .... @45.00
31 thru 40 .... @35.00
41 thru 50 .... @25.00
51 thru 89 .... @20.00
90 October, 1965 .... 20.00

WILD BILL HICKOK
Avon Periodicals
September-October, 1949
1 GRl(c),Frontier Fighter 150.00
2 Ph(c),Gambler's Guns 60.00
3 Ph(c),Great Stage Robbery . 30.00
4 Ph(c),Guerilla Gunmen 30.00
5 Ph(c),Return of the Renegade 30.00
6 EK,EK(c),Along the Apache
  Trail 30.00
7 EK,EK(c)Outlaws of
  Hell's Bend 30.00
8 Ph(c),The Border Outlaws .. 30.00
9 PH(c),Killers From Texas ... 30.00
10 Ph(c) 30.00
11 EK,EK(c),The Hell Riders ... 30.00
12 EK,EK(c),The Lost Gold Mine 35.00
13 EK,EK(c),Bloody Canyon
  Massacre 35.00
14 .... 35.00
15 .... 20.00
16 JKa 30.00
17 thru 23 .... @25.00
24 EK,EK(c) 30.00
25 EK,EK(c) 30.00
26 EK,EK(c) 30.00
27 EK,EK(c) 30.00
28 EK,EK(c),May-June, 1956 ... 30.00

Wild Boy of the Congo #12
© Approved/Ziff-Davis/St. Johns

WILD BOY OF
THE CONGO
Approved(Ziff-Davis)/
St. John Publ. Co.
February-March, 1951
10(1)NS,PH(c),Bondage(c),The
  Gorilla God 125.00
11(2)NS,Ph(c),Star of the Jungle 75.00
12(3)NS,Ph(c),Ice-Age Men 75.00
4 NS.Ph(c),Tyrant of the Jungle 85.00
5 NS,Ph(c),The White Robe
  of Courage 50.00
6 NS,Ph(c) 50.00
7 MB,EK.Ph(c) 60.00
8 Ph(c),Man-Eater 50.00
9 Ph(c),Killer Leopard 50.00
10 .... 50.00
11 MB(c) 60.00
12 MB(c) 60.00
13 MB(c) 60.00
14 MB(c) 60.00
15 June, 1955 .... 40.00

WINGS COMICS
Wings Publ.
(Fiction House Magazines)
September, 1940
1 HcK,AB,GT,Ph(c),B:Skull Squad,
  Clipper Kirk,Suicide Smith,
  War Nurse,Phantom Falcons,
  Greasemonkey Griffin,Parachute
  Patrol,Powder Burns 1,600.00
2 HcK,AB,GT,Bomber Patrol . 750.00
3 HcK,AB,GT 500.00
4 HcK,AB,GT,B:Spitfire Ace .. 500.00
5 HcK,AB,GT,Torpedo Patrol . 500.00
6 HcK,AB,GT,Bombs for Berlin 425.00
7 HcK,AB 425.00
8 HcK,AB,The Wings of Doom . 425.00
9 Sky-Wolf 400.00
10 The Upside Down 400.00
11 .... 350.00
12 Fury of the fire Boards 350.00
13 Coffin Slugs For The
  Luftwaffe 350.00
14 Stuka Buster 350.00

15 Boomerang Blitz 350.00
16 O:Capt.Wings 400.00
17 Skyway to Death 300.00
18 Horsemen of the Sky 300.00
19 Nazi Spy Trap 300.00
20 The One Eyed Devil 300.00
21 Chute Troop Tornado 275.00
22 TNT for Tokyo 275.00
23 RP,Battling Eagles of Bataan 275.00
24 RP,The Death of a Hero ... 275.00
25 RP,Suicide Squeeze 275.00
26 Tojo's Eagle Trap 275.00
27 Blb,Mile High Gauntlet 275.00
28 Blb,Tail Gun Tornado 275.00
29 Blb,Buzzards from Berlin .. 275.00
30 Blb,Monsters of the
  Stratosphere 225.00
31 BLb,Sea Hawks away 225.00
32 BLb,Sky Mammoth 225.00
33 BLb,Roll Call of the Yankee
  Eagles 225.00
34 BLb,So Sorry,Mr Tojo 225.00
35 BLb,RWb,Hell's Lightning . 225.00
36 RWb,The Crash-Master ... 225.00
37 RWb,Sneak Blitz 225.00
38 RWb,Rescue Raid of the
  Yank Eagle 225.00
39 RWb,Sky Hell/Pigboat Patrol 225.00
40 RWb,Luftwaffe Gamble .. 225.00
41 RWb,.50 Caliber Justice ... 175.00
42 RWb,PanzerMeat forMosquito 175.00
43 RWb,Suicide Sentinels ... 175.00
44 RWb,Berlin Bombs Away .. 175.00
45 RWb,Hells Cargo 175.00
46 RWb,Sea-Hawk Patrol ... 175.00
47 RWb,Tojo's Tin Gibraltar ... 175.00
48 RWb 175.00
49 RWb,Rockets Away 175.00
50 RWb,Mission For a Madman 175.00
51 RWb,Toll for a Typhoon ... 150.00
52 MB,Madam Marauder 150.00
53 MB,Robot Death Over
  Manhattan 150.00
54 MB,Juggernauts of Death .. 150.00
55 MB 150.00
56 MB,Sea Raiders Grave ... 150.00
57 MB,Yankee Warbirds over
  Tokyo 150.00
58 MB 150.00
59 MB,Prey of the Night Hawks 150.00
60 MB,E:Skull Squad,
  Hell's Eyes 150.00
61 MB,Raiders o/t Purple Dawn 135.00
62 Twilight of the Gods 135.00
63 Hara Kiri Rides the Skyways 135.00
64 Taps For Tokyo 135.00
65 AB,Warhawk for the Kill ... 135.00
66 AB,B:Ghost Patrol 135.00
67 AB 125.00
68 AB,ClipperKirkBecomesPhantom
  Falcon;O:Phantom Falcon .. 125.00
69 AB,O:cont,Phantom Falcon . 125.00
70 AB,N:Phantom Falcon;
  O:Final Phantom Falcon ... 125.00
71 Ghost Patrol becomes
  Ghost Squadron 125.00
72 V:Capt. Kamikaze 125.00
73 Hell & Stormoviks 125.00
74 BLb(c),Loot is What She
  Lived For 125.00
75 BLb(c),The Sky Hag 125.00
76 BLb(c),Temple of the Dead . 125.00
77 BLb(c),Sky Express to Hell . 125.00
78 BLb(c),Loot Queen of
  Satan's Skyway 125.00

Wings Comics #27
© Fiction House Magazines

79 BLb(c),Buzzards of
   Plunder Sky 125.00
80 BLb(c),Port of Missing Pilots 125.00
81 BLb(c),Sky Trail of the
   Terror Tong 125.00
82 BLb(c),Bondage(c),Spider &
   The Fly Guy 135.00
83 BLb(c),GE,Deep Six For
   Capt. Wings 125.00
84 BLb(c),GE,Sky Sharks to
   the Kill 125.00
85 BLb(c),GE 125.00
86 BLb(c),GE,Moon Raiders .. 125.00
87 BLb(c),GE 125.00
88 BLb(c),GE,Madmans Mission 125.00
89 BLb(c),GE,Bondage(c),
   Rockets Away 135.00
90 BLb(c),GE,Bondage(c),The
   Radar Rocketeers 135.00
91 BLb(c),GE,Bondage(c),V-9 for
   Vengeance 135.00
92 BLb(c),GE,Death's red Rocket125.00
93 BLb(c),GE,Kidnap Cargo .. 125.00
94 BLb(c),GE,Bondage(c),Ace
   of the A-Bomb Patrol 135.00
95 BLb(c),GE,The Ace of
   the Assassins 125.00
96 BLb(c),GE 125.00
97 BLb(c),GE,The Sky Octopus 125.00
98 BLb(c),GE,The Witch Queen
   of Satan's Skyways 125.00
99 BLb(c),GE,The Spy Circus . 125.00
100 BLb(c),GE,King o/t Congo . 150.00
101 BLb(c),GE,Trator of
    the Cockpit 125.00
102 BLb(c),GE,Doves of Doom 125.00
103 BLb(c),GE 125.00
104 BLb(c),GE,Fireflies of Fury 125.00
105 BLb(c),GE 125.00
106 BLb(c),GE,Six Aces & A
    Firing Squad 125.00
107 BLb(c),GE,Operation Satan 125.00
108 BLb(c),GE,The Phantom
    of Berlin 125.00
109 GE,Vultures of
    Vengeance Sky 125.00
110 GE,The Red Ray Vortex .. 125.00
111 GE,E:Jane Martin 100.00

112 The Flight of the
    Silver Saucers 100.00
113 Suicide Skyways 100.00
114 D-Day for Death Rays ... 100.00
115 Ace of Space 100.00
116 Jet Aces of Korea 100.00
117 Reap the Red Wind 100.00
118 Vengeance Flies Blind ... 100.00
119 The Whistling Death 100.00
120 Doomsday Mission 100.00
121 Ace of the Spyways 100.00
122 Last Kill Korea 100.00
123 The Cat & the Canaries .. 100.00
124 Summer, 1954, Death
    Below Zero 100.00

WINNIE WINKLE
Dell Publishing Co.
1941

1 .... 45.00
2 .... 30.00
3 .... 20.00
4 thru 7 .... @20.00

WITCHCRAFT
Avon Periodicals
March-April, 1952

1 SC,JKu,Heritage of Horror . 450.00
2 SC,JKu,The Death Tattoo .. 350.00
3 EK,Better off Dead 225.00
4 Claws of the Cat,
  Boiling Humans 250.00
5 Ph(c),Where Zombies Walk 300.00
6 March, 1953 Mysteries of the
  Moaning Statue 225.00

Witches Tales #25
© Harvey Publications

WITCHES TALES
Harvey Publications
January, 1951

1 RP,Bondage(c),Weird Yarns
  of Unseen Terror 300.00
2 RP,We Dare You 150.00
3 RP,Bondage(c)Forest of
  Skeletons 100.00
4 BP 100.00
5 BP,Bondage(c),Share

My Coffin 110.00
6 BP,Bondage(c),Servants of
  the Tomb 110.00
7 BP,Screaming City 110.00
8 Bondage(c) 120.00
9 Fatal Steps 100.00
10 BP,.....,IT! 100.00
11 BP,Monster Maker 90.00
12 Bondage(c);The Web
   of the Spider 100.00
13 The Torture Jar 90.00
14 Transformation 100.00
15 Drooling Zombie 90.00
16 Revenge of a Witch 90.00
17 Dimension IV 110.00
18 HN,Bird of Prey 100.00
19 HN,The Pact 100.00
20 HN,Kiss & Tell 100.00
21 HN,The Invasion 100.00
22 HN,A Day of Panic 100.00
23 HN,The Wig Maker 100.00
24 HN,The Undertaker 100.00
25 What Happens at 8:30 PM?
   Severed Heads(c) 100.00
26 Up There 90.00
27 The Thing That Grew 90.00
28 Demon Flies 90.00
Becomes:

WITCHES WESTERN
TALES

29 S&K,S&K(c),F:Davy Crockett 125.00
30 S&K.S&K(c) 125.00
Becomes:

WESTERN TALES

31 S&K,S&K(c),F:Davy Crockett   90.00
32 S&K,S&K(c) 90.00
33 S&K,S&K(c),July-Sept.,1956 . 90.00

WITH THE MARINES
ON THE BATTLEFRONTS
OF THE WORLD
Toby Press
June, 1953

1 Ph(c),Flaming Soul 200.00
2 Ph(c),March, 1954 .... 50.00

WITTY COMICS
Irwin H. Rubin/Chicago Nite
Life News
1945

1 .... 100.00
2 1945 .... 50.00
3 thru 7 .... @40.00

WOMEN IN LOVE
Fox Features Synd./
Hero Books/
Ziff-Davis
August, 1949

1 .... 350.00

WOMEN OUTLAWS
Fox Features Syndicate
July, 1948

1 .... 500.00
2 .... 450.00
3 .... 450.00
4 .... 450.00
5 thru 8 .... @350.00
Becomes:

GOLDEN AGE

All comics prices listed are for *Near Mint* condition.

MY LOVE MEMORIES
9 .... 75.00
10 .... 35.00
11 .... 70.00
12 WW 75.00

WONDERBOY
(see HORRIFIC)

WONDER COMICS
Great Publ./Nedor/
Better Publications
May, 1944
1 SSh(c),B:Grim Reaper,
  Spectro Hitler(c) 800.00
2 ASh(c),O:Grim Reaper,B:Super
  Sleuths,Grim Reaper(c) ... 450.00
3 ASh(c),Grim Reaper(c) 425.00
4 ASh(c),Grim Reaper(c) 400.00
5 ASh(c),Grim Reaper(c) 400.00
6 ASh(c),Grim Reaper(c) 350.00
7 ASh(c),Grim Reaper(c) 350.00
8 ASh(c),E:Super Sleuths,
  Spectro 350.00
9 ASh(c),B:Wonderman 350.00
10 ASh(c),Wonderman(c) ... 350.00
11 Grl(c),B:Dick Devins 375.00
12 Grl(c),Bondage(c) 375.00
13 ASh(c),Bondage(c) 375.00
14 ASh(c),Bondage(c)
  E:Dick Devins 375.00
15 ASh(c),Bondage(c),B:Tara . 450.00
16 ASh(c),A:Spectro,
  E:Grim Reaper 375.00
17 FF,ASh(c),A:Super Sleuth .. 400.00
18 ASh(c),B:Silver Knight 375.00
19 ASh(c),FF 400.00
20 FF,October, 1948 .... 450.00

WONDERLAND COMICS
Feature Publications
(Prize Comics Group)
Summer, 1945
1 (fa),B:Alex in Wonderland ... 60.00
2 .... 35.00
3 thru 8 .... @25.00
9 1947 .... 25.00

WONDER COMICS
Fox Features Syndicate
May, 1930–Jan. 1942
1 BKa,WE,WE(c),B:Wonderman,
  DR.Kung,K-51 .... 15,000.00
2 WE,BKa,LF(c),B:Yarko the
  Great,A:Spark Stevens ... 4,500.00
Becomes:

WONDERWORLD
COMICS
3 WE,LF,BP,LF&WE,I:Flame 6,000.00
4 WE,LF,BP,LF(c) 2,400.00
5 WE,LF,BP,GT,LF(c),Flame 1,500.00
6 WE,LF,BP,GT,LF(c),Flame 1,300.00
7 WE,LF,BP,GT,LF(c),Flame 1,300.00
8 WE,LF,BP,GT,LF(c),Flame 1,400.00
9 WE,LF,BP,GT,LF(c),Flame 1,300.00
10 WE,LF,BP,LF(c),Flame .. 1,300.00
11 WE,LF,BP,LF(c),O:Flame . 1,100.00
12 BP,LF(c),Bondage(c),Flame 900.00
13 E:Dr Fung,Flame 850.00
14 JoS,Bondage(c),Flame 900.00
15 JoS&LF(c),Flame 800.00
16 Flame(c) 650.00

17 Flame(c) 650.00
18 Flame(c) 650.00
19 Male Bondage(c),Flame ... 675.00
20 Flame(c) 650.00
21 O:Black Club &Lion,Flame .. 600.00
22 Flame(c) 550.00
23 Flame(c) 500.00
24 Flame(c) 500.00
25 A:Dr Fung,Flame 500.00
26 Flame(c) 500.00
27 Flame(c) 450.00
28 Bondage(c)I&O:US Jones,
  B:Lu-nar,Flame 600.00
29 Bondage(c),Flame 400.00
30 O:Flame(c),Flame 700.00
31 Bondage(c),Flame 400.00
32 Hitler(c),Flame 425.00
33 Male Bondage(c) 400.00

WORLD FAMOUS
HEROES MAGAZINE
Comic Corp. of America
(Centaur)
October, 1941
1 BLb,Paul Revere 900.00
2 BLb,Andrew Jackson,V:
  Dickinson 400.00
3 BLb,Juarez-Mexican patriot 350.00
4 BLb,Canadian Mounties ... 350.00

WORLD'S GREATEST
STORIES
Jubilee Publications
January, 1949
1 F:Alice in Wonderland 175.00
2 F:Pinocchio 150.00

World War III #1 © Ace Periodicals

WORLD WAR III
Ace Periodicals
March–May, 1953
1 Atomic Bomb cover 400.00
2 The War That Will Never
  Happen 375.00

WOTALIFE COMICS
(see PHANTOM LADY)

WOW COMICS
David McKay/Henle Publ.
July, 1936
1 WE,DBr(c),Fu Manchu,
  Buck Jones, ... 2,000.00
2 WE,Little King 1,400.00
3 WE,WE(c) 1,400.00
4 WE,BKa,AR,DBr(c),Popeye,
  Flash Gordon,Nov.,1936 . 1,700.00

Wow Comics #36 © Fawcett Publ.

WOW COMICS
Fawcett Publications
Winter, 1940
N#(1)S&K,CCB(c),B&O:Mr Scarlett;
  B:Atom Blake,Jim Dolan,Rick
  O'Shay,Bondage(c) 14,000.00
2 B:Hunchback 1,800.00
3 V:Mummy Ray Gun 800.00
4 O:Pinky 900.00
5 F:Pinky the Whiz Kid 600.00
6 O:Phantom Eagle;
  B:Commando Yank 550.00
7 Spearhead of Invasion 500.00
8 All Three Heroes 500.00
9 A:Capt Marvel,Capt MarvelJr.
  Shazam,B:Mary Marvel 900.00
10 The Sinister Secret of
  Hotel Hideaway 450.00
11 .... 350.00
12 Rocketing adventures 350.00
13 Thrill Show 350.00
14 V:Mr Night 350.00
15 The Shazam Girl of America 300.00
16 Ride to the Moon 300.00
17 V:Mary Batson,Alter Ego
  Goes Berserk 300.00
18 I:Uncle Marvel,Infinity(c)
  V is For Victory 300.00
19 A Whirlwind Fantasy 300.00
20 Mary Marvel's Magic Carpet 300.00
21 Word That Shook the World 175.00
22 Come on Boys-
  Everybody Sing 175.00
23 Trapped by the Terror of
  the Future 175.00
24 Mary Marvel 175.00
25 Mary Marvel Crushes Crime 175.00
26 Smashing Star-

Studded Stories 150.00
27 War Stamp Plea(c) 150.00
28 . . . . 150.00
29 . . . . 150.00
30 In Mirror Land 150.00
31 Stars of Action 125.00
32 The Millinery Marauders . . . 125.00
33 Mary Marvel(c) 125.00
34 A:Uncle Marvel 125.00
35 I:Freckles Marvel 125.00
36 Secret of the Buried City . . . 125.00
37 7th War loan plea 125.00
38 Pictures That Came to Life . 125.00
39 The Perilous Packages 125.00
40 The Quarrel of the Gnomes . 125.00
41 Hazardous Adventures 100.00
42 . . . . 100.00
43 Curtain Time 100.00
44 Volcanic Adventure 100.00
45 . . . . 100.00
46 . . . . 100.00
47 . . . . 100.00
48 . . . . 100.00
49 . . . . 100.00
50 Mary Marvel/Commando Yank 100.00
51 . . . . 75.00
52 . . . . 75.00
53 Murder in the Tall Timbers . . 75.00
54 Flaming Adventure 75.00
55 Earthquake! 75.00
56 Sacred Pearls of Comatesh . 75.00
57 . . . . 75.00
58 E:Mary Marvel;The Curse
   of the Keys 75.00
59 B:Ozzie the Hilarious
   Teenager 75.00
60 thru 64 . . . . @75.00
65 A:Tom Mix 75.00
66 A:Tom Mix 75.00
67 A:Tom Mix 75.00
68 A:Tom Mix 75.00
69 A:Tom Mix,Baseball 75.00
Becomes:

REAL WESTERN HERO
70 It's Round-up Time 225.00
71 CCB,P(c),A Rip
   Roaring Rodeo 150.00
72 w/Gabby Hayes 150.00
73 thru 75 . . . . @150.00
Becomes:

WESTERN HERO
76 Partial Ph(c)&P(c) 200.00
77 Partial Ph(c)&P(c) 125.00
78 Partial Ph(c)&P(c) 125.00
79 Partial Ph(c)&P(c),
   Shadow of Death 100.00
80 Partial Ph(c)&P(c) 125.00
81 CCB,Partial Ph(c)&P(c),
   F:Tootsie 125.00
82 Partial Ph(c)&P(c),
   A:Hopalong Cassidy 125.00
83 Partial Ph(c)&P(c) 125.00
84 Ph(c) 100.00
85 Ph(c) 100.00
86 Ph(c),The Case of the
   Extra Buddy, giant 100.00
87 Ph(c),The Strange Lands . . 100.00
88 Ph(c),A:Senor Diablo 100.00
89 Ph(c),The Hypnotist 100.00
90 Ph(c),The Menace of
   the Cougar, giant 90.00
91 Ph(c),Song of Death 90.00
92 Ph(c),The Fatal Hide-out,
   giant 90.00

Western Hero #97 © Fawcett Publ.

93 Ph(c),Treachery at
   Triple T, giant 90.00
94 Ph(c),Bank Busters,giant . . . 90.00
95 Ph(c),Rampaging River 80.00
96 Ph(c),Range Robbers,giant . . 90.00
97 Ph(c),Death on the
   Hook,giant 90.00
98 Ph(c),Web of Death,giant . . . 90.00
99 Ph(c),The Hidden Evidence . 80.00
100 Ph(c),A:Red Eagle,Giant . . 90.00
101 Ph(c) 90.00
102 thru 111 Ph(c) . . . . @80.00
112 Ph(c),March, 1952 . . . . . . 100.00

YANKEE COMICS
**Chesler Publications
(Harry A. Chesler)
September, 1941**
1 F:Yankee Doodle Jones . . 1,000.00
2 The Spirit of '41 . . . . 500.00
3 Yankee Doodle Jones 400.00
4 JCo,Yankee Doodle Jones
   March, 1942 . . . . 400.00

YELLOWJACKET COMICS
**Levy Publ./Frank Comunale/
Charlton
September, 1944**
1 O&B:Yellowjackets,B:Diana
   the Huntress 400.00
2 Rosita &The Filipino Kid . . . 225.00
3 . . . . 175.00
4 Fall of the House of Usher . . 225.00
5 King of Beasts 200.00
6 . . . . 200.00
7 I:Diane Carter;The
   Lonely Guy 175.00
8 The Buzzing Bee Code . . . 175.00
9 . . . . 175.00
10 Capt Grim V:The Salvage
   Pirates 175.00
Becomes:

JACK IN THE BOX
11 Funny Animal,Yellow Jacket . 55.00
12 Funny Animal 25.00
13 BW,Funny Animal 80.00

14 thru 16 Funny Animal . . . . @30.00
Becomes:

COWBOY WESTERN COMICS
17 Annie Oakley,Jesse James . . 75.00
18 JO,JO(c) 50.00
19 JO,JO(c),Legends of Paul
   Bunyan 50.00
20 JO(c),Jesse James 35.00
21 Annie Oakley VisitsDryGulch . 35.00
22 Story of the Texas Rangers . 35.00
23 . . . . 35.00
24 Ph(c),F:James Craig 35.00
25 Ph(c),F:Sunset Carson 35.00
26 Ph(c) 65.00
27 Ph(c),Sunset Carson movie . 150.00
28 Ph(c),Sunset Carson movie . 100.00
29 Ph(c),Sunset Carson movie . 100.00
30 Ph(c),Sunset Carson movie . 150.00
31 Ph(c) 30.00
32 thru 34 Ph(c) . . . . @25.00
35 thru 37 Sunset Carson . . @75.00
38 and 39 . . . . @25.00
Becomes:

SPACE WESTERN COMICS
40 Spurs Jackson,V:The
   Saucer Men 400.00
41 StC(c),Space Vigilantes . . . 300.00
42 StC(c) 350.00
43 StC(c),Battle of
   Spacemans Gulch 300.00
44 StC(c),The Madman of Mars 300.00
45 StC(c),The Moon Bat 300.00
Becomes:

COWBOY WESTERN COMICS
46 . . . . 70.00
Becomes:

COWBOY WESTERN HEROES
47 . . . . 25.00
48 . . . . 25.00
Becomes:

COWBOY WESTERN
49 . . . . 25.00
50 F:Jesse James 20.00
51 thru 56 . . . . @20.00
58, giant 25.00
59 thru 66 . . . . @20.00
67 AW&AT 50.00
Becomes:

WILD BILL HICKOK AND JINGLES
68 AW 50.00
69 AW 35.00
70 AW 30.00
71 thru 73 . . . . @20.00
74 1960 . . . . 20.00

YOGI BERRA
**Fawcett
1957**
1 Ph(c) 500.00

YOUNG BRIDES
**Feature Publications
(Prize Comics) Sept.-Oct., 1952**
1 S&K,Ph(c) 150.00
2 S&K,Ph(c) 100.00

GOLDEN AGE

GOLDEN AGE

3 S&K,Ph(c)	75.00
4 S&K	75.00
5 S&K	75.00
6 S&K	75.00
2-1 S&K	50.00
2-2 S&K	35.00
2-3 S&K	40.00
2-4 S&K	40.00
2-5 S&K	40.00
2-6 S&K	40.00
2-7 S&K	40.00
2-8 S&K	25.00
2-9 S&K	25.00
2-10 S&K	40.00
2-11 S&K	40.00
2-12 S&K	40.00
3-1	15.00
3-2	18.00
3-3	18.00
3-4	18.00
3-5	18.00
3-6	18.00
4-1	18.00
4-2 S&K	50.00
4-3	18.00
4-4 S&K	40.00
4-5	18.00

YOUNG EAGLE
Fawcett Publications/
Charlton Comics
December, 1950

1 Ph(c)	125.00
2 Ph(c),Mystery of Thunder Canyon	60.00
3 Ph(c),Death at Dawn	50.00
4 Ph(c)	50.00
5 Ph(c),The Golden Flood	50.00
6 Ph(c),The Nightmare Empire	50.00
7 Ph(c),Vigilante Veangeance	50.00
8 Ph(c),The Rogues Rodeo	50.00
9 Ph(c),The Great Railroad Swindle	50.00
10 June, 1952, Ph(c),Thunder Rides the Trail,O:Thunder	30.00

YOUNG KING COLE
Novelty Press/Premium
Svcs. Co.
Autumn, 1945

1-1 Detective Toni Gayle	175.00
1-2	100.00
1-3	75.00
1-4	50.00
2-1	50.00
2-2	50.00
2-3	50.00
2-4	50.00
2-5	50.00
2-6	50.00
2-7	50.00
3-1	45.00
3-2 LbC	45.00
3-3 The Killer With The Hat	40.00
3-4 The Fierce Tiger	40.00
3-5 AMc	40.00
3-6	50.00
3-7 LbC(c),Case of the Devil's Twin	75.00
3-8	60.00
3-9 The Crime Fighting King	60.00
3-10 LbC(c)	75.00
3-11 LbC(c)	75.00
3-12 July, 1948,AMc(c)	40.00

YOUNG LIFE
New Age Publications
Summer, 1945

1 Partial Ph(c),Louis Palma	75.00
2 Partial Ph(c),Frank Sinatra	80.00

Teen Life #5 © New Age Publications

Becomes:
TEEN LIFE

3 Partial Ph(c),Croon without Tricks,June Allyson(c)	50.00
4 Partial Ph(c),Atom Smasher Blueprints,Duke Ellington(c)	45.00
5 Partial Ph(c), Build Your Own Pocket Radio, Jackie Robinson(c)	60.00

YOUNG LOVE
Feature Publ.
(Prize Comics Group)
February-March, 1949

1 S&K,S&K(c)	275.00
2 S&K,Ph(c)	125.00
3 S&K,JSe,BE,Ph(c)	100.00
4 S&K,Ph(c)	75.00
5 S&K,Ph(c)	75.00
2-1 S&K,Ph(c)	75.00
2-2 Ph(c)	40.00
2-3 Ph(c)	40.00
2-4 Ph(c)	40.00
2-5 Ph(c)	40.00
2-6 S&K(c)	75.00
2-7 S&K(c),S&K	75.00
2-8 S&K	75.00
2-9 S&K(c),S&K	75.00
2-10 S&K(c),S&K	75.00
2-11 S&K(c),S&K	75.00
2-12 S&K(c),S&K	75.00
3-1 S&K(c),S&K	75.00
3-2 S&K(c),S&K	75.00
3-3 S&K(c),S&K	75.00
3-4 S&K(c),S&K	75.00
3-5 Ph(c)	50.00
3-6 BP,Ph(c)	50.00
3-7 Ph(c)	50.00
3-8 Ph(c)	50.00
3-9 MMe,Ph(c)	50.00
3-10 Ph(c)	50.00
3-11 Ph(c)	50.00

3-12 Ph(c)	50.00
4-1 S&K	50.00
4-2 Ph(c)	40.00
4-3 Ph(c)	40.00
4-4 Ph(c)	40.00
4-5 Ph(c)	40.00
4-6 S&K,Ph(c)	40.00
4-7 thru 4-12 Ph(c)	@35.00
5-1 thru 5-12 Ph(c)	@25.00
6-1 thru 6-9	@20.00
6-10 thru 6-12	@20.00
7-1 thru 7-7	@15.00
7-8 thru 7-11	@15.00
7-12 thru 8-5	@15.00
8-6 thru 8-12	@20.00

YOUNG ROMANCE
COMICS
Feature Publ./Headline/
Prize Publ.
September-October, 1947

1 S&K(c),S&K	300.00
2 S&K(c),S&K	175.00
3 S&K(c),S&K	150.00
4 S&K(c),S&K	150.00
5 S&K(c),S&K	150.00
6 S&K(c),S&K	125.00
2-1 S&K(c),S&K	125.00
2-2 S&K(c),S&K	125.00
2-3 S&K(c),S&K	125.00
2-4 S&K(c),S&K	125.00
2-5 S&K(c),S&K	125.00
2-6 S&K(c),S&K	75.00
3-1 thru 3-12 S&K(c),S&K	@75.00
4-1 thru 4-12 S&K	@65.00
5-1 ATh,S&K	75.00
2	75.00
3	75.00
5-4 thru 5-12 S&K	@75.00
6-1 thru 6-3	@30.00

YOUR UNITED STATES
Lloyd Jacquet Studios
1946

1N# Teeming nation of Nations	175.00

YOUTHFUL HEART
Youthful Magazines
May, 1952

1 Frankie Lane(c)	100.00
2 Vic Damone	75.00
3 Johnnie Ray	75.00

Becomes:
DARING CONFESSIONS

4 DW,Tony Curtis	50.00
5	35.00
6 DW	40.00
7	35.00
8 DW	40.00

YOUTHFUL ROMANCES
Pix Parade/Ribage/
Trojan
August-September, 1949

1	135.00
2	75.00
3 Tex Beneke	50.00
4	50.00
5	35.00
6	35.00
7 Tony Martin(c)	40.00
8 WW(c)	125.00

9 thru 14 . . . . @ 35.00
Becomes:
DARLING LOVE
15 WD 40.00
16 . . . . 30.00
17 DW,Ph(c) 30.00

ZAGO, JUNGLE PRINCE
Fox Features Syndicate
September, 1948
1 A:Blue Beetle 400.00
2 JKa 300.00
3 JKa 250.00
4 MB(c) 250.00
Becomes:
MY STORY
5 JKa,Too Young To Fall in Love 75.00
6 I Was A She-Wolf 35.00
7 I Lost My Reputation 35.00
8 My Words Condemned Me . . 35.00
9 WW,Wayward Bride 85.00
10 WW,March, 1950,Second
    Rate Girl 85.00
11 . . . . 35.00
12 . . . . 35.00

TEGRA, JUNGLE EMPRESS
Fox Features Syndicate
August, 1948
1 Blue Bettle,Rocket Kelly . . . 325.00
Becomes:
ZEGRA, JUNGLE EMPRESS
2 JKa 300.00
3 . . . . 250.00
4 . . . . 250.00
5 . . . . 250.00
Becomes:
MY LOVE LIFE
6 I Put A Price Tag On Love . . 65.00
7 An Old Man's Fancy 35.00
8 My Forbidden Affair 35.00
9 I Loved too Often 35.00
10 My Secret Torture 35.00
11 I Broke My Own Heart 35.00
12 I Was An Untamed Filly . . . 35.00
13 I Can Never Marry You,
    August 1950 . . . . 30.00

ZIP COMICS
MLJ Magazines
February, 1940
1 MMe,O&B:Kalathar,The Scarlet
  Avenger,Steel Sterling,B:Mr
  Satan,Nevada Jones,War Eagle
  Captain Valor 3,500.00
2 MMe,CBi(c)B:Steel
  Sterling(c) 1,500.00
3 CBi,MMe,CBi(c) 1,100.00
4 CBi,MMe,CBi(c) 900.00
5 CBi,MMe,CBi(c) 900.00
6 CBi,MMe,CBi(c) 750.00
7 CBi,MMe,CBi(c) 700.00
8 CBi,MMe,CBi(c),Bondage(c) 750.00
9 CBi,MMe,CBi(c)E:Kalathar,
  Mr Satan;Bondage(c) 750.00
10 CBi,MMe,CBi(c),B:Inferno . . 800.00
11 CBi,MMe,CBi(c) 600.00
12 CBi,MMe,CBi(c),Bondage(c) 625.00
13 CBi,MMe,CBi(c)E:Inferno,

Bondage(c),Woman in
  Electric Chair 650.00
14 CBi,MMe,CBi(c),Bondage(c) 600.00
15 CBi,MMe,CBi(c),Bondage(c) 600.00
16 CBi,MMe,CBi(c),Bondage(c) 600.00
17 CBi,CBI(c),E:Scarlet
  Avenger Bondage(c) 625.00
18 IN(c),B:Wilbur 600.00
19 IN(c),Steel Sterling(c) 600.00
20 IN(c),O&I:Black Jack
  Hitler(c) 1,000.00
21 IN(c),V:Nazis 600.00
22 IN(c) 550.00
23 IN(c),Flying Fortress 550.00
24 IN(c),China Town Exploit . . 550.00
25 IN(c),E:Nevada Jones 550.00
26 IN(c),B:Black Witch,
  E:Capt Valor 575.00
27 IN(c),I:Web,V:Japanese . . . 950.00
28 IN(C),O:Web,Bondage(c) . 1,000.00
29 Steel Sterling & Web 450.00
30 V:Nazis 450.00
31 IN(c) 350.00

Zip Comics #13
© MLJ Magazines/Archie Comics

32 . . . . 350.00
33 Bondage(c) 375.00
34 I:Applejack;Bondage(c) . . . 375.00
35 E:Zambini 350.00
36 I:Senor Banana 350.00
37 . . . . 350.00
38 E:Web 350.00
39 O&B:Red Rule 350.00
40 . . . . 250.00
41 . . . . 250.00
42 . . . . 250.00
43 . . . . 250.00
45 E:Wilbur 250.00
46 . . . . 250.00
47 Crooks Can't Win,
  Summer, 1944 . . . . 250.00

ZIP-JET
St. John Publishing Co.
February, 1953
1 Rocketman 450.00
2 April,May, 1953, Assassin
  of the Airlanes 350.00

ZOOM COMICS
Carlton Publishing Co.
December, 1945
N# O:Captain Milksop 275.00

ZOOT COMICS
Fox Features Syndicate
Spring, 1946
N#(1)(fa) 100.00
2 A:Jaguar(fa) 85.00
3 (fa) 50.00
4 (fa) 50.00
5 (fa) 35.00

Zoot Comics #5
© Fox Features Syndicate

6 (fa) 35.00
7 B:Rulah 650.00
8 JKa(c),Fangs of Stone 450.00
9 JKa(c),Fangs of Black Fury . . 450.00
10 JKa(c),Inferno Land 450.00
11 JKa,The Purple Plague,
   Bondage(c) 475.00
12 JKa(c),The Thirsty Stone,
   Bondage(c) 325.00
13 Bloody Moon 300.00
14 Pearls of Pathos,Woman
   Carried off by Bird 400.00
15 Death Dancers 300.00
16 . . . . 300.00
Becomes:
RULAH, JUNGLE GODDESS
17 JKa(c),Wolf Doctor 600.00
18 JKa(c),Vampire Garden . . . 450.00
19 JKa(c) 425.00
20 . . . . 425.00
21 JKa(c) 425.00
22 JKa(c) 425.00
23 . . . . 350.00
24 . . . . 325.00
25 . . . . 325.00
26 . . . . 325.00
27 . . . . 350.00
Becomes:
I LOVED
28 . . . . 35.00
29 thru 31 . . . . @ 25.00
32 My Poison Love, March, 1950 25.00

GOLDEN AGE

ACCLAIM

Archer & Armstrong #1 © Valiant

ARCHER & ARMSTRONG
Valiant 1992
0 JiS(s),BWS,BL,I&O:Archer,
  I:Armstrong,The Sec 3.00
0 Gold Ed. 5 . . . . 7.00
1 FM(c),B:JiS(s),BWS,BL,Unity #3,
  A:Eternal Warrior 3.00
2 WS(c),E:JiS(s),BWS,BL,Unity
  #11,2nd A:Turok,A:X-O 3.00
3 B:BWS(a&s), BWi, V:Sect in
  Rome 2.50
4 BWS,BWi,V:Sect in Rome 2.50
5 BWS,BWi,I:Andromeda 2.50
6 BWS,BWi, A:Andromeda,
  V:Medoc 2.50
7 BWS,ANi,BWi,V:Sect in England 2.50
8 BWS,as Eternal Warrior #8,
  Three Musketeers,I:Ivan 2.50
9 BCh,BWi,in Britain 2.25
10 BWS,A:Ivar 2.25
11 BWS,A:Solar,Ivar 2.25
12 BWS,V:The Avenger 2.25
13 B:MBn(s),RgM,In Los Angeles 2.25
14 In Los Angeles 2.25
15 E:MBn(s),In LasVegas, I:Duerst 2.25
16 V:Sect 2.25
17 B:MBn(s),In Florida 2.25
18 MV,in Heaven 2.25
19 MV,V:MircoboticCult,D:Duerst . 2.25
20 MV,Chrismas Issue 2.25
21 MV,A:Shadowman,Master
  Darque 2.25
22 MV,A:Shadowman,Master
  Darque,w/Valiant Era card . . . 2.25
23 MV, ... 2.25
24 MV, ... 2.25
25 MV,A:Eternal Warrior 2.25
26 Chaos Effect-Gamma #4, A:Ivar,
  Et. Warrior 2.25

ARMED & DANGEROUS
Valiant (B&W) 1995
1 thru 4 . . . . @2.95

Spec.#1 . . . . 2.95

ARMED & DANGEROUS
Acclaim (B&W) 1996
1 BH,"Hell's Slaughterhouse" Pt.1 2.95
2 BH,"Hell's Slaughterhouse" Pt.2 2.95
3 BH,"Hell's Slaughterhouse" Pt.3 2.95
4 BH,"Hell's Slaughterhouse" Pt.4 2.95

ARMED & DANGEROUS
No. 2
Acclaim (B&W) Dec. 1996
1 BH,"When Irish Eyes are Dying,"
  pt.1 . . . . 2.95
2 BH,"When Irish Eyes are Dying,"
  pt.2 . . . . 2.95
3 BH,"When Irish Eyes are Dying,"
  pt.3 . . . . 2.95
4 BH,"When Irish Eyes are Dying,"
  pt.4 concl. 2.95

ARMORINES
Valiant 1994
0 (from X-O #25),Card Stock (c),
  Diamond Distributors "Fall Fling"
  Retailer Meeting 3.00
0a Gold Ed. 4.00
1 JGz(s),JCf,B:White Death 2.50
2 JGz(s),JCf,E:White Death 2.50
3 JGz(s),JCf,V:Spider Aliens . . . 2.50
4 JCf, V: Spider Aliens 2.25
5 JCf, Chaos Effect-Delta #2,
  A:H.A.R.D. Corp 2.25
6 Spider Alien Mothership 2.25
7 Rescue 2.25
8 Rescue in Iraq 2.25
9 . . . . 2.25
10 Protect Fidel Castro 2.25
11 V: Spider Super Suit 2.25
12 F: Sirot 2.25
Yearbook I:Linoff 2.95

BAD EGGS
Acclaim 1996
1 thru 4 BL,DP,"That Dirty Yellow
  Mustard" . . . . @2.95

BAR SINISTER
Windjammer 1995
1 From Shaman's Tears 2.50
2 V:SWAT Team 2.50
3 F: Animus Prime 2.50
4 MGe,RHo,V:Jabbersnatch . . . 2.50

BART SEARS'
X-O MANOWAR
Valiant 1995
HC Bart Sears' Artwork 17.95

BLOODSHOT
Valiant 1992
0 KVH(a&s),DG(i),Chromium (c),
  O:Bloodshot,A:Eternal Warrior . 3.00
0a Gold Ed.,w/Diamond "Fall Fling"
  logo 7.00
1 BWS(c),B:KVH(s),DP,BWi,I:Carbo

---

ni, V:Mafia,1st Chromium(c) . . 3.50
2 DP,I:Durkins,V:Ax 3.00
3 DP,V:The Mob 3.00
4 DP,A:Eternal Warrior 2.50
5 DP,A:Eternal Warrior,Rai 2.50

Bloodshot #6 © Valiant

6 DP,I:Ninjak (Not in Costume) . . 3.00
7 DP,JDx,A:Ninjak (1st appearance
  in costume) 2.50
8 DP,JDx,A:Geoff 2.50
9 DP,JDx,V:Slavery Ring 2.50
10 DP,JDx,V:Tunnel Rat 2.50
11 DP,JDx,V:Iwatsu 2.50
12 DP,JDx,Day Off 2.50
13 DP,JDx,V:Webnet 2.50
14 DP,JDx,V:Carboni 2.50
15 DP,JDx,V:Cinder 2.50
16 DP,JDx,w/Valiant Era Card . . . 2.50
17 DP,JDx,A:H.A.R.D.Corps 2.50
18 DP,KVH,After the Missile 2.50
19 DP,KVH,I:Uzzi the Clown 2.25
20 DP,KVH, Chaos Effect-Gamma
  #1, V:Immortal Enemy 2.25
21 DP,V: Immortal Enemy, Ax . . . 2.25
22 Immortal Enemy 2.25
23 Cinder 2.25
24 Geomancer, Immortal Enemy . 2.25
25 V:Uzzi the Clown 2.25
26 V:Uzzi the Clown 2.25
27 Rampage Pt. 1 . . . . 2.25
28 Rampage Pt. 3 . . . . 2.25
29 Rampage Conc. A:Ninjak 2.25
30 V:Shape Shifter 2.25
31 Nanite Killer 2.25
32 KVH,SCh,V: Vampires 2.25
33 KVH,SCh,V: Vampires 2.25
34 NBy,KVH,new villains spawned 2.50
35 NBY,KVH,attempts to control . 2.50
36 V:Voodoo Drug Dealer 2.50
37 V:Voodoo Drug Dealer 2.50
38 V:Rampage 2.50
39 V:Rampage 2.50
40 USA wants Bloodshot 2.50
41 F:Jillian Alcott 2.50
42 Virtual Nightmare 2.50

All comics prices listed are for *Near Mint* condition.

43 V:U.S. Troops 2.50
44 I:Deathangel, V:Speedshots . . 2.50
45 thru 51 . . . . @2.50
Yearbook #1 KVH,briefcase bomb 4.25
Yearbook 1995 Villagers 2.95
Spec.GN Last Stand 5.95

BLOODSHOT Series Two
Acclaim March 1997
1 LKa(s),SaV "Behold, a Pale
  Horseman" 2.50
1a variant cover 3.00
2 LKa(s),SaV "Dead Man Walking" 2.50
3 LKa(s),SaV "ChainsawMassacre" 2.50
4 LKa(s),SaV Search for Identity . 2.50
5 LKa(s),SaV V:Simon Oreck . . . 2.50

Captain Johner & The Aliens #1
© Valiant

CAPTAIN JOHNER
& THE ALIENS
Valiant May 1995
1 Rep. Magnus Robot Fighter #1–7
  (Gold Key 1963–64) 2.95

CHAOS EFFECT
Valiant 1994
Alpha DJ(c), BCh, JOy, A:All Valiant
  Characters 2.25
Alpha Red (c) 4.00
Omega DJ(c), BCh, JOy, A:All
  Valiant Characters 2.25
Omega Gold(c) 4.00
Epilogue pt.1 . . . . 2.95
Epilogue pt.2 . . . . 2.95

CITY KNIGHTS, THE
Windjammer 1995
1 I:Michael Walker 2.50
2 I:Herald 2.50
3 V:Herald 2.50
4 V:Herald 2.50

DEATHMATE
Valiant/Image 1993
Preview (Advanced Comics) 4.00

Preview (Previews) 4.00
Preview (Comic Defense Fund) . . 5.00
Prologue BL,JLe,RLd,Solar meets
  Void 3.25
Prologue Gold 5.00
Blue SCh, HSn, F:Solar, Magnus,
  Battlestone, Livewire, Stronghold,
  Impact, Striker, Harbinger,
  Brigade, Supreme 4.00
Blue Gold Ed. 5.00
Yellow BCh,MLe,DP,F:Armstrong,
  H.A.R.D.C.A.T.S.,Ninjak,Zealot,
  Shadowman,Grifter,Ivar 4.00
Yellow Gold Ed. 5.00
Black JLe,MS,F:Warblade,Ripclaw,
  Turok,X-O Manowar 5.25
Black Gold Ed. 8.00
Red RLd,JMs, ... 5.25
Red Gold Ed. 5.00
Epilogue 3.25
Epilogue Gold 5.00

DESTROYER
Valiant 1994
0 MM 41st Century 2.95

DR. TOMORROW
Acclaim May 1997
1 (of 12) BL,Bart Simms finds
  Angel Computer 2.50
2 BL,V:Teutonic Knight 2.50
3 BL,V:Teutonic Knight concl. . . 2.50

DISNEY'S ACTION CLUB
Acclaim Young Readers 1997
Spec. F: Buzz Lightyear, digest size 4.50
Spec. "My Fill of Phil" F:Hercules . 4.50

DISNEY'S
ENCHANTING STORIES
Acclaim Young Readers 1997
Spec. F: Beauty and the Beast,
  digest size 4.50
Spec. "A Torch For Meg," F:
  Hercules 4.50

ETERNAL WARRIOR
Valiant 1992
1 FM(c),JDx,Unity #2,O:Eternal
  Warrior,Armstrong 4.00
1a Gold Ed. 6.00
1b Gold Foil Logo 8.00
2 WS(c),JDx,Unity #10,A:Solar,
  Harbinger,Eternal Warrior of
  4001 . . . . 3.00
3 JDx,V:Armstrong,I:Astrea 2.50
4 JDx(i),I:Caldone, C:Bloodshot . 4.00
5 JDx,I:Bloodshot,V:Iwatsu's Men 3.00
6 BWS,JDx,V:Master Darque . . . 3.00
7 BWS,V:Master Darque, D:Uncle
  Buck 3.00
8 BWS,as Archer & Armstrong #8
  Three Musketeers,I:Ivar 3.00
9 MMo,JDx,B:Book of the
  Geomancer 3.00
10 JDx,E:Bk. o/t Geomancer . . . 3.00
11 B:KVH(s),JDx(i), V:Neo-Nazis . 3.00
12 JDx(i),V:Caldone 3.00
13 MMo,JDx(i),V:Caldone,
  A:Bloodshot 2.75
14 E:KVH(s),MMo,V:Caldone,
  A:Geoff 2.50
15 YG,A:Bloodshot,V:Tanaka . . . 2.50

16 YG,A:Bloodshot 2.50
17 A:Master Darque 2.50
18 C:Doctor Mirage 2.50
19 KVH(s),TeH,A:Doctor Mirage . 2.50
20 KVH(s),Access Denied 2.50
21 KVH(s),TeH,V:Dr. Steiner . . . 2.50
22 V:Master Darque,w/Valiant Era
  Card 2.50
23 KVH(s),TeH,Blind Fate 2.50
24 KVH(s),TeH,V:Immortal Enemy 2.50
25 MBn(s),A:Archer,Armstrong . . 2.50
26 Double(c), Chaos Effect-
  Gamma#4, A:Archer, Armstrong,
  Ivar 3.00
27 JOs(s) 2.25
28 War on Drugs 2.25
29 Immortal Enemy 2.25
30 Lt. Morgan 2.25
31 JD,JOs 2.25
32 . . . . 2.25
33 Mortal Kin Pt.1 . . . . 2.25
34 Mortal Kin Pt.2 . . . . 2.25
35 Mortal Kin Finale 2.50
36 Fenris League 2.50
37 Youthful Tale 2.50
38 V:Niala, The Dead Queen . . . 2.50
39 JOs,JG,PG(c),V:body thieves . 2.50
40 JOs,JG,PG(c),finds organ farm 2.50
41 War in Herznia 2.50
42 I: Brisbane 2.50
43 V:Neo Nazi 2.50
44 V:Neo Nazi 2.50
45 R:Fenris Society 2.50
46 V:Fenris Society 2.50
47 Jihad 2.50
48 Immortal Life in Danger 2.50
49 JOs,JG,Hallucinations 2.50
50 . . . . 2.50
Yearbook #1 . . . . 4.25
Yearbook #2 . . . . 4.00
Wings of Justice WWI 2.50
Quarterly
Time and Treachery 3.95
Digital Alchemy 3.95

FOX FUNHOUSE
Acclaim Young Readers 1997
Spec. "A World of Pain(t)" F: The
  Tick 4.50

GEOMANCER
Valiant 1994
1 RgM, I:Geomancer 3.50
2 RgM, Eternal Warrior 2.25
3 RgM, Darque Elementals 2.25
4 RgM 2.25
5 Riot Gear pt. 1 . . . . 2.25
6 Riot Gear pt. 2 . . . . 2.25
7 F:Zorn 2.25
8 v:Zorn 2.25

GRACKLE, THE
Acclaim (B&W) Sept. 1996
1 MBn,PG,"Double Cross" Pt.1 . . 2.95
2 MBn,PG,"Double Cross" Pt.2 . . 2.95
3 MBn,PG,"Double Cross" Pt.3 . . 2.95
4 MBn,PG,"Double Cross" Pt.4 . . 2.95

GRAVEDIGGERS
Acclaim (B&W) 1996
1 (of 4) 2.95
2 thru 4 . . . . @2.95

ACCLAIM

ACCLAIM

HARBINGER
Valiant 1992
0 DL,O:Sting,V:Harada, from TPB
  (Blue Bird Ed.) 5.00
0 from coupons 10.00
1 DL,JDx,I:Sting,Torque,
  Zeppelin,Flamingo,Kris 8.00
1a w/o coupon 1.00
2 DL,JDx,V:Harbinger Foundation,
  I:Dr.Heyward 5.00
2a w/o coupon 1.00
3 DL,JDx,I:Ax,Rexo, V:Spider
  Aliens 4.00
3a w/o coupon 1.00
4 DL,JDx,V:Ax,I:Fort,
  Spikeman,Dog,Bazooka 5.00
4a w/o coupon 1.00
5 DL,JDx,I:Puff,Thumper,
  A:Solar,V:Harada 3.00
5a w/o coupon 1.00
6 DL,D:Torque,A:Solar,
  V:Harada,Eggbreakers 3.00
6a w/o coupon 1.00
7 DL,Torque's Funeral 2.50
8 FM(c),DL,JDx,Unity#8,
  A:Magnus,Eternal Warrior 2.50
9 WS(c),DL,Unity #16,
  A:Magnus,Armstrong,Rai,
  Archer,Eternal Warrior 2.50
10 DL,I:H.A.R.D.Corps, Daryl,
  Shetiqua 3.00
11 DL,V:H.A.R.D.Corps 2.50
12 DL,F:Zeppelin,A:Elfquest . . . 2.50
13 Flamingo Vs. Rock 2.50
14 A:Magnus(Dream Sequence),
  C:Stronghold 3.00
15 I:Livewire,Stronghold 3.00
16 A:Livewire,Stronghold 2.50
17 HSn,I:Simon 2.00
18 HSn,I:Screen 2.00
19 HSn,I:Caliph 2.00
20 HSn,V:Caliph 2.00
21 I:Pete's Father 2.00
22 HSn,A:Archer & Armstrong . . 2.00
23 HSn,B:Twlight of the Eighth Day2.00
24 HSn,V:Eggbreakers 2.00
25 HSn,V:Harada,E:Twlight of the
  Eighth Day 2.50
26 SCh,AdW,I:Jolt,Amazon,
  Mircowave,Anvil,Sonix 2.00
27 SCh,AdW,Chrismas issue 2.00
28 SCh,AdW,O:Sonix,J:Tyger . . . 2.00
29 SCh,AdW,A:Livewire,Stronghold,
  w/Valiant Era card 2.00
30 SCh,AdW,A:Livewire,Stronghold 2.00
31 SCh,AdW,V:H.A.R.D.Corps . . . 2.00
32 SCh,AdW,A:Eternal Warrior . . 2.00
33 SCh, V:Dr. Eclipse 2.00
34 SCh,Chaos Effect-Delta#1, A:X-
  O, Dr. Eclipse 2.00
35 Zephyr 2.00
36 Zephyr, Magnus 2.00
37 Magnus, Harada 2.00
38 A:Spikeman 2.00
39 Zepplin vs. Harada 2.00
40 V:Harbinger 2.00
41 V:Harbinger 2.00
TPB w/#0,rep#1-4 . . . . 25.00
TPB 2nd Printing w/o #0 . . . . . 9.95
TPB #2, Rep. 6-7,10-11 . . . . . 9.95

HARBINGER FILES:
HARADA
Valiant 1994
1 BL,DC,O:Harada 2.75
2 Harada's ultimate weapon 2.50

H.A.R.D. Corps #11 © Valiant

H.A.R.D. CORPS
Valiant 1992
1 JLe(c),DL,BL,V:Harbinger
  Foundation, I:Flatline, D:Maniac 3.00
1a Gold Ed. 7.00
2 DL,BL,V:Harb.Foundation 2.50
3 DL,BL,J:Flatline 2.50
4 BL 2.50
5 BCh,BL(i),A:Bloodshot 2.50
5a Comic Defense System Ed. . . 2.50
6 MLe,A:Spider Aliens 2.50
7 MLe,V:Spider Aliens, I:Hotshot . 2.50
8 MLe,V:Harada,J:Hotshot 2.50
9 MLe,V:Harada,A:Turok 2.00
10 MLe,A:Turok,V:Dinosaurs 2.00
11 YG,I:Otherman 2.00
12 MLe,V:Otherman 2.00
13 YG,D:Superstar 2.50
14 DvM(s),YG,V:Edie Simkus . . . 2.00
15 DvM(s),YG,V:Edie Simkus . . . 2.00
16 DvM(s),YG, ... 2.00
17 DvM(s),RLe,V:Armorines 2.00
18 DvM(s),RLe,V:Armorines,
  w/Valiant Era card 2.00
19 RLe,A:Harada 2.00
20 RLe,V:Harbingers 2.00
21 RLe,New Direction 2.00
22 RLe,V:Midnight Earl 2.00
23 RLe,Chaos Effect-Delta #4,
  A:Armorines, X-O 2.00
24 Ironhead 2.00
25 Midnight Earl 2.00
26 Heydrich, Omen 2.00
27 Heydrich shows evil 2.00
28 New Hardcorps 2.00
29 V:New Guard 2.00
30 Final Issue 2.00

KILLER INSTINCT
1 thru 3 . . . . @2.50

Spec. Brothers by Art Holcomb . . 2.50

KNIGHTHAWK
Windjammer 1995
1 NA(c&a),I:Knighthawk the
  Protector,V:Nemo 2.75
2 NA(c&a),Birth of Nemo 2.50
3 NA,V:Nemo 2.50
4 NA,V:Nemo 2.50
5 I:Cannon, Brick 2.50
6 V:Cannon, Brick 2.50

MAGIC THE GATHERING:
ANTIQUITIES WAR
Armada 1995
1 Based on the Antiquities Set . . 2.75
2 F:Urza, Mishra 2.50
3 I:Tawnos, Ashod 2.50
4 The War Begins 2.50

MAGIC THE GATHERING:
ARABIAN KNIGHTS
Armada 1995
1 Based on Rare Card set 2.75
2 V:Queen Nailah 2.50

MAGIC THE GATHERING:
CONVOCATIONS
Armada 1995
1 Gallery of Art from Game 2.50

MAGIC THE GATHERING:
FALLEN EMPIRES
[Mini-series]
Armada
1 with pack of cards 2.75
2 F:Tymolin 2.50
TPB Rep. #1-#2 . . . . 4.95

MAGIC THE GATHERING:
HOMELANDS
Armada 1995
1 I:Feroz, Serra 5.95

MAGIC THE GATHERING:
ICE AGE
Armada 1995
1 Dominaia, from card game . . . 3.50
2 Ice Age Adventures 2.75
3 CV(c) Planeswalker battles . . . 2.50
4 final issue 2.50
TPB Rep. #1-#2 . . . . 4.95
TPB Rep. #3-#4 . . . . 4.95

MAGIC THE GATHERING:
SHADOW MAGE
Armada 1995
1 I:Jared 3.00
2 F:Hurloon the Minotaur 2.75
3 VMk(c&a),V:Juggernaut 2.50
4 Final issue 2.50
TPB Rep. #1-#2 . . . . 4.95
TPB Rep. #3-#4 . . . . 4.95

MAGIC THE GATHERING:
THE URZA-MISHRA WAR
Armada
1 & 2 with Ice Age II card 5.95

MAGIC THE GATHERING: WAYFARER
Armada 1995
1 R:Jared	2.75
2 I:New Land	2.50
3 R:Liana, Ravidel	2.50
4 I:Golthonor	2.50
5	2.50

MAGIC THE GATHERING: THE LEGENDS OF:
THE ELDER DRAGONS
1 & 2	@2.50

JEDIT OJANEN
1 & 2	@2.50

SHANDALAR
1 & 2	@2.50

[ON THE WORLD OF] MAGIC THE GATHERING
GN Serra Angel + card	5.95
GN Legend of the Fallen Angel + card	5.95
GN Dakkon Blackblade + card	5.95

MAGNUS: ROBOT FIGHTER
Valiant 1991
0 PCu,BL,"Emancipator",w/ BWS card	15.00
0a PCu,BL,w/o card	4.00
1 ANi,BL,B:Steel Nation	7.00
1a w/o coupon	1.00
2 ANi,BL,Steel Nation #2	5.00
2a w/o coupon	1.00
3 ANi,BL,Steel Nation #3	3.00
3a w/o coupon	1.00
4 ANi,BL,E:Steel Nation	3.00
4a w/o coupon	1.00
5 DL,BL(i),I:Rai(#1),V:Slagger Flipbook format	4.00
5a w/o coupon	1.00
6 DL,A:Solar,V:Grandmother	
A:Rai(#2)	3.00
6a w/o coupon	1.00
7 DL,EC,V:Rai(#3)	3.00
7a w/o coupon	1.00
8 DL,A:Rai(#4),Solar,X-O Armor.E:Flipbooks	2.50
8a w/o coupon	1.00
9 EC,V:Xyrkol,E-7	2.50
10 V:Xyrkol	2.50
11 V:Xyrkol.	2.50
12 I:Turok,V:Dr. Noel, I:Asylum,40pgs	12.00
13 EC,Asylum Pt 1	2.50
14 EC,Asylum Pt2	2.50
15 FM(c),EC,Unity#4,I:Eternal Warrior of 4001, O:Unity	2.50
16 WS(c),EC,Unity#12,A:Solar, Archer,Armstrong,Harbinger, X-O,Rai,Eternal Warrior	2.50
17 JaB,V:Talpa	2.50
18 SD,R:Mekman,V:E-7	2.50
19 SD,V:Mekmen	2.50
20 EC,Tale of Magnus' past	2.50
21 JaB,R:Malevalents, Grand-mother	3.00
21a Gold Ed.	6.00
22 JaB,D:Felina,V:Malevalents, Grandmother	2.50
23 V:Malevolents	2.50
24 V:Malevolents	2.50

Magnus: Robot Fighter #26
© *Voyager Communications, Inc.*

25 N:Magnus,R:1-A,silver-foil(c)	3.00
26 I:Young Wolves	2.50
27 V:Dr.Lazlo Noel	2.50
28 V:The Malevs	2.25
29 JCf,A:Eternal Warrior	2.25
30 JCf,V:The Malevs	2.25
31 JCf,V:The Malevs	2.25
32 JCf,Battle for South Am	2.25
33 B:JOs(s),JCf,A:Ivar	2.25
34 JCf,Captured	2.25
35 JCf,V:Mekman	2.25
36 JCf,w/Valiant Era Card	2.25
37 JCf,A:Starwatchers	2.25
38 JCf,	2.25
39 JCf,F:Torque	2.25
40 JCf,F:Torque, A:Rai	2.25
41 JCf,Chaos Effect-Epsilon#4 A:Solar, Psi-Lords,Rai	2.50
42 JCf, F:Torque,A:Takashi	2.25
43 JCf,F:Torque,Immortal E	2.25
44 JCf,F:Torque,Stagger	2.25
45 V:Immortal Enemy	2.25
46 V:Immortal Enemy	2.25
47 Cold Blooded,pt.1	2.25
48 Cold Blooded,pt.2	2.25
49 F:Slagger	2.25
50 V:Invisible Legion	2.25
51 KoK,RyR,Return of the Robots,pt.1	2.25
52 KoK,RyR,Return of the Robots,pt.2	2.25
53 KoK,RyR,Return of the Robots,pt.3	2.25
54 KoK,RyR,Return of the Robots,pt.4	2.25
55 KG,A:Rai	2.50
56 Magnus in Japan	2.50
57	2.50
58	2.50
59 V:Rai	2.50
60 R:The Malevs	2.50
61 Secrets of the Malevs	2.50
62 V:Leeja	2.50
63 R:Destroyer	2.50
64 Ultimatum, F:Destroyer	2.50
Yearbook #1	3.95
TPB 1-4	9.95

MAGNUS (ROBOT FIGHTER)
Acclaim Jan. 1997
1 Magnus back from the future	2.50
2 "Tomorrow Never Knows"	2.50
3 "Tomorrow Never Knows"	2.50
4 "Tomorrow Never Knows"	2.50
5 "Tomorrow Never Knows"	2.50
6 A:Janice Whitcraft	2.50
7 "When Titans Clash"	2.50

MAN OF THE ATOM
Valiant Heroes Special Project
Acclaim Jan 1997
Spec.	3.95

MUTANT CHRONICLES— GOLGOTHA
Valiant
1 thru 4 + game trading card	@2.95
TPB, Vol. 1 rep. Pt.#1–#4	10.95

NINJAK
Valiant 1994
0: O:Ninjak, Pt. 1	2.50
00: O:Ninjak, Pt.2	2.50
1 B:MMo(s),JQ,JP,Chromium(c), I:Dr.Silk,Webnet	3.00
1a Gold Ed	5.00
2 JQ,JP,V:Dr.Silk,Webnet	2.50
3 JQ,JP,I:Seventh Dragon	2.25
4 MMo(a&s),V:Seventh Dragon, w/Valiant Era card	2.25
5 MMo(a&s),A:X-O Manowar	2.25
6 MMo(a&s),A:X-O Manowar, V:Dr.Silk,Webnet	2.25
7 MMo(a&s),I:Rhaman	2.25
8 MMo(a&s),Chaos Effect-Gamma #3, A:Madame Noir	2.25
9 Dogs of War	2.00
10 Cantebury Tale #1	2.00
11 Cantebury Tale #2	2.00
12	2.00
13 Mad Dogs and English	2.00
14 Cry Wolf pt. 1	2.00
15 Cry Wolf pt. 2	2.25
16 Plague Pt. 1	2.25
17 Plague Pt. 2	2.25
18 Computer Virus	2.25
19 DAn,ALa,MM,Breaking the Web,pt.1	2.25
20 DAn,ALa,MM,Breaking the Web,pt.2	2.25
21 DAn,ALa,MM,Breaking the Web,pt.3	2.25
22 Bitter Wind	2.25
23 w/o arsenal	2.25
24 Unusual sidekick	2.25
25	2.25
26	2.25
27 Diamond Smugglers	2.25
28 F:Sister Gabriela	2.25
Yearbook #1, Dr. Silk	3.95

NINJAK
Acclaim 1996
1 KBb(s), Denny Meechum becomes Ninjak	2.50
2 KBb(s) video game spin-off	2.50
3 KBb(s) video game spin-off	2.50
4 KBb(s) video game spin-off	2.50
5 KBb(s) video game spin-off	2.50

ACCLAIM

6 KBk(s) "The World's Finest" . . . 2.50
7 KBk(s) video game spin-off . . 2.50
8 KBk(s) video game spin-off . . 2.50
9 KBk(s) video game spin-off . . 2.50

OPERATION: STORMBRINGER
Acclaim Special Event, April 1997
Spec. F:Teutonic Knight 3.95

ORIGINAL CAPTAIN JOHNAR AND THE ALIENS
Valiant 1995
1 Reprint from Magnus 2.95
2 Russ Manning rep. 2.95

ORIGINAL DR. SOLAR MAN OF THE ATOM
Valiant 1995
1 Reprint 2.95
2 Reprints 2.95
3 Reprints 2.95

ORIGINAL MAGNUS ROBOT FIGHTER
Valiant 1995
1 Reprint 2.95
2 Russ Manning Art 2.95
3 Russ Manning 2.95

ORIGINAL TUROK, SON OF STONE
Valiant 1995
1 Reprint 2.95
2 Alberto Gioletti art 2.95
3 Alberto Gioletti 2.95
4 Reprints 2.95

OUTCAST SPECIAL
Valiant 1995
1 R:The Outcast 2.50

PLANESWALKER WAR
Acclaim Aug. 1996
GN #1 Magic: The Gathering tie-in 5.95

PSI-LORDS: REIGN OF THE STARWATCHERS
Valiant 1994
1 MLe,DG,Chromium(c),Valiant
Vision,V:Spider Aliens 3.00
2 MLe,DG,V:Spider Aliens 2.25
3 MLe,DG,Chaos Effect-Epsilon#2,
A:Solar 2.25
becomes:

PSI-LORDS
4 V:Ravenrok 2.25
5 V:Ravenrok 2.25
6 . . . . 2.25
7 Micro-Invasion 2.25
8 A:Solar the Destroyer 2.25
9 Frozen Harbingers 2.25
10 F:Ravenrok 2.25

PUNX
Windjammer 1995
1 KG,I:Punx 2.50
2 KG,A:Harbinger 2.50

3 KG,F:P.M.S 2.50
4 KG,final issue 2.50
Spec.#1 . . . . 2.50

PUNX REDUX
1 thru 4 . . . . @2.50

PUNX
Acclaim Jan. 1997
One Shot Spec. F:Big Max 2.50

QUANTUM LEAP
Acclaim Jan. 1997
1 BML(s),"Into the Void," pt.1 . . . 2.50
2 BML(s),"Into the Void," pt.2 . . . 2.50
3 BML(s),"Into the Void," pt.3 . . . 2.50
Spec. "The Leaper Before 3.95

QUANTUM & WOODY
Acclaim Feb. 1997
1 CPr(s),MBr Woodrow Van
Chelton & Eric Henderson
become unlikely superhero team 2.50
2 CPr(s),MBr,World's worst
superhero team 2.50
3 CPr(s),MBr,Woody buys a goat 2.50
4 CPr(s),MBr 2.50
5 CPr(s),MBr 2.50
6 CPr(s),MBr 2.50

RAI
Valiant 1991
0 DL,O:Bloodshot,I:2nd Rai,D:X-O,
Archer,Shadowman,F:all Valiant
heroes,bridges Valiant Universe
1992-4001 . . . . 6.00
1 V:Grandmother 8.00
2 V:Icespike 6.00
3 V:Humanists,Makiko 7.00
4 V:Makiko,rarest Valiant 9.00
5 Rai leaves earth, C:Eternal
Warrior 3.00
6 FM(c),Unity#7,V:Pierce 2.50
7 WS(c),Unity#15,V:Pierce,
D:Rai,A:Magnus 2.50
8 Epilogue of Unity in 4001 . . . . 2.50
Becomes:

RAI AND THE FUTURE FORCE
Valiant 1993
9 F:Rai,E.Warrior of 4001,Tekla, X-
O Commander,Spylocke 2.50
9a Gold Ed. 4.00
10 Rai vs. Malev Emperor 2.25
11 SCh,V:Malevolents 2.25
12 V:Cyber Raiders 2.25
13 Spylocke Revealed 2.25
14 SCh,D:M'Ree 2.25
15 SCh,V:X-O 2.25
16 SCh,V:Malevs 2.25
17 . . . . 2.25
18 JOs(s),Spk,V:Malevs 2.25
19 JCf,V:Malves 2.25
20 JOs(s),DR,V:Malves,Spylocke
realed to be Spider Alien 2.25
21 DR,I:Starwatchers,b:Torque,
w/Valiant Era card 2.25
22 DR,D:2nd Rai, A:Starwatchers 2.25
23 DR,A:Starwatchers, ... 2.25
24 DR,in Tibet 2.00
25 DR,F:Spylocke 2.00
26 DR,Chaos Effect-Epsilon#3,

A:Solar Magnus,Psi-Lords 2.00

Rai #27 © Valiant

Becomes:

RAI
Valiant 1994
27 "Rising Son" 2.00
28 V:Takashi 2.00
29 A:Rentaro Nakadai 2.00
30 Splocke 2.00
31 Bad Penny pt. 1 . . . . 2.00
32 Bad Penny pt. 2, F:Axscan . . . 2.00
33 F:Spylocke, Rentaro 2.00
TPB #0-#4 . . . . 11.95
TPB Star System ed. 11.95

REVELATIONS
one-shot by Jim Krueger 3.95

SABAN POWERHOUSE
Young Readers
Acclaim 1997
Spec. F: Power Rangers Turbo,
digest size 4.50

SAMUREE
Windjammer 1995
1 I:Samuree 2.50
2 V: The Dragon 2.50
3 V: The Dragon 2.50

THE SECOND LIFE OF DR. MIRAGE
Valiant 1993
1 B:BL(s),BCh,V:Mast.Darque . . . 3.00
1a Gold Ed. 5.00
2 BCh,V:Master Darque 2.50
3 BCh 2.50
4 BCh,V:Bhrama 2.50
5 BCh,A:Shadowman,V:Master
Darque 2.50
6 BCh,V:Dr.Eclipse 2.50
7 BCh,V:Dr.Eclipse,w/card 2.50
8 BCh, ... 2.50
9 BCh,A:Otherman 2.50
10 BCh,V:Otherman 2.50
11 BCh,Chaos Effect-Beta#2, ... 2.50

ACCLAIM

12 BCh	2.25
13 BCh	2.25
14	2.25
15 Chaos Effect	2.25
16	2.25
17	2.25
18 F:Deathsmith	2.25
19 R:Walt Wiley	2.25

SECRETS OF THE VALIANT UNIVERSE
Valiant 1994
1 from Wizard 2.50
2 BH,Chaos Effect-Beta#4,A:Master
Darque,Dr.Mirage,Max St.James,
Dr. Eclipse 2.25

Secret Weapons #9
© Voyager Communications, Inc.

SECRET WEAPONS
Valiant 1993
1 JSP(a&s),BWi(i),I:Dr.Eclipse,
A:Master Darque,A:Geoff,
Livewire,Stronghold,Solar,X-O,
Bloodshot,Shadowman 2.75
1a Gold Ed. 5.00
2 JSP(a&s),V:Master Darque,
Dr.Eclipse 2.25
3 JSP(a&s),V:Speedshots 2.25
4 JSP(a&s),V:Scatterbrain 2.25
5 JSP(a&s),A:Ninjak 2.25
6 JPS(s),JPh(pl),TeH, V:Spider
Aliens 2.25
7 JPS(s),V:Spider Aliens 2.25
8 JSP(a&pl),V:Harbingers 2.25
9 JSP(a&s),V:Webnet, w/Valiant
Era card 2.25
10 JSP(a&s),V:Webnet 2.25
11 PGr,New Line-up 2.25
12 PGr,A:Bloodshot 2.25
13 PGr,Chaos Effect-Gamma#2 . . 2.25
14 PGr,F:Bloodshot 2.00
15 . . . . 2.00
16 . . . . 2.00
17 V:Dr. Silk 2.00
18 Gigo 2.00
19 A:Ninjak 2.00

20 Bloodshot Rampage Pt.2	2.00
21 Bloodshot Rampage Pt.4	2.00
22 I:Gestalt, Pyroclast	2.00
23 A:Bloodshot	2.00

SECRET WEAPONS: PLAYING WITH FIRE
Valiant
1 & 2 . . . . @2.50

SHADOW MAN
Valiant 1992
0 BH,TmR,Chromium (c),O:Maxim
St.James,Shadowman 3.00
0a Newstand ed. 2.50
0b Gold Ed. 5.00
1 DL,JRu,I&O:Shadowman 6.00
2 DL,V:Serial Killer 3.00
3 V:Emil Sosa 3.00
4 DL,FM(c),Unity#6,A:Solar 2.50
5 DL,WS(c),Unity#14, A:Archer &
Armstrong 2.50
6 SD,L:Lilora 2.50
7 DL,V:Creature 2.50
8 JDx(i),I:Master Darque 3.00
9 JDx(i),V:Darque's Minions 3.00
10 BH,I:Sandria 2.50
11 BH,N:Shadowman 2.50
12 BH,V:Master Darque 2.50
13 BH,V:Rev.Shadow Man 2.50
14 BH,JDx,V:Bikers 2.50
15 BH,JDx,V:JB,Fake Shadow
Man,C:Turok 2.50
16 BH,JDx,I:Dr.Mirage, Carmen . . 4.00
17 BH,JDx,A:Archer & Armstrong . 2.25
18 BH,JDx,A:Archer & Armstrong . 2.25
19 BH,A:Aerosmith 2.25
20 BH,A:Master Darque,
V:Shadowman's Father 2.25
21 BH,I:Maxim St.James (1895
Shadowman) 2.25
22 V:Master Darque 2.25
23 BH(a&s),A:Doctor Mirage,
V:Master Darque 2.25
24 BH(a&s),V:H.A.T.E. 2.25
25 RgM,w/Valiant Era card 2.25
26 w/Valiant Era card 2.50
27 BH,V:Drug Lord 2.25
28 BH,A:Master Darque 2.25
29 Chaos Effect-Beta#1,V:Master
Darque 2.25
30 R:Rotwak 2.25
31 thru 33 . . . . @2.25
34 Voodoo in Carribean 2.25
35 A:Ishmael 2.25
36 F:Ishmael 2.25
37 A:X-O, V:Blister 2.25
38 V:Ishmael, Blister 2.25
39 BH,TmR,Explores Powers 2.25
40 BH,TmR,I,Vampire! 2.25
41 A:Steve Massarsky 2.25
42 . . . . 2.25
43 V:Smilin Jack 2.25
TPB rep.#1-#3,#6 . . . . 9.95

SHADOWMAN
Acclaim Nov. 1996
1 GEn(s),"Deadside," pt.1 . . . . . . 2.50
2 GEn(s),"Deadside," pt.2 . . . . . . 2.50
3 GEn(s),"Deadside," pt.3 . . . . . . 2.50
4 GEn(s),"Deadside," pt.4 . . . . . . 2.50
5 JaD,CAd,"Nothing is True," pt.1 2.50
6 JaD,CAd,"Nothing is True," pt.2 2.50

7 JaD,CAd,"Nothing is True," pt.3	2.50
8 JaD,CAd,"Nothing is True," pt.4	2.50
9 JaD,CAd,"The Buzz," pt.1	2.50

SLIDERS
Valiant 1996
1 & 2 . . . . @2.50

SLIDERS: DARKEST HOUR
1 DGC,DG. 2.50
2 DGC,DG. 2.50
3 DGC,DG, Concl. 2.50
Spec. RgM, Montezuma IV rules the
world 3.95
Spec. #2 "Secrets" 3.95

SLIDERS: ULTIMATUM
Valiant 1996
1 & 2 . . . . @2.50

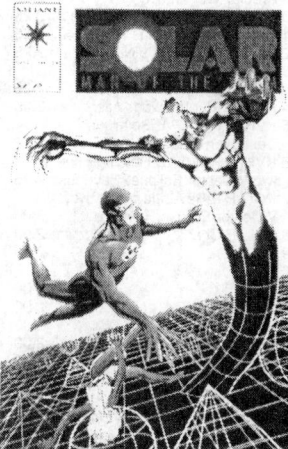

Solar: Man of the Atom #19,
© Voyager Communications, Inc.

SOLAR: MAN OF THE ATOM
Valiant 1991
1 BWS,DP,BL,B:2nd Death B:Alpha
& Omega 6.00
2 BWS,DP,BL,V:Dr Solar 4.00
3 BWS,DP,BL,V:Harada I:Harbinger
Foundation 6.00
4 BWS,DP,BL,E:2nd Death V:Dr
Solar 4.00
5 BWS,EC,V:Alien Armada 3.00
6 BWS,DP,SDr, V:Alien Armada X-
O Armor 2.50
7 BWS,DP,SDr, V:Alien Armada X-
O Armor 2.50
8 BWS,V:Dragon of Bangkok . . . 2.50
9 BWS,DP,SDr, V:Erica's Baby . . 2.50
10 BWS,DP,SDr,JDx,I:Eternal
Warrior,E:Alpha&Omega 10.00
10a 2nd printing 2.50
11 SDr,A:Eternal Warrior, Prequel
to Unity #0 . . . . 5.00
12 SDr,FM(c),Unity#9,O:Pierce,

ACCLAIM

Albert 2.50
13 DP,SDr,WS(c),Unity #17,
  V:Pierce 2.50
14 DP,SDr,I:Bender (becomes
  Dr.Eclipse) 4.00
15 SD,V:Bender 3.00
16 Solar moves to California 2.50
17 SDr(i),V:X-O Manowar 2.50
18 SDr(i),A:X-Manowar 2.50
19 SDr(i),V:Videogame 2.50
20 SDr(i),Dawn of the Malevolence 2.50
21 SDr(i),Master Darque 2.50
22 SDr(i),V:Master Darque,A:
  Bender(Dr.Eclipse) 2.50
23 SDr(i),JQ(c),V:Master
  Darque,I:Solar War God . . . 2.50
24 SDr(i),A:Solar War God 2.50
25 V:Dr.Eclpise 2.25
26 Phil and Gayle on vaction . . . 2.25
27 in Austrialia 2.25
28 A:Solar War God 2.25
29 KVH(s),JP(i),Valiant Vision,
  A:Solar War God 2.50
30 KVH(s),JP,V:Energy Parasite . 2.25
31 KVH(s),JP,Chrismas Issue . . . 2.25
32 KVH(s),JP,Parent's Night 2.25
33 KVH(s),PGr,JP,B:Solar the
  Destroyer,w/Valiant Era card . . 2.25
34 KVH(s),PGr,V:Spider Alien . . . 2.25
35 KVH(s),PGr,JP,E:Solar the
  Destroyer,Valiant Vision 2.25
36 KVH(s),PGr,JP,B:Revenge times
  two,V:Doctor Eclipse, Ravenus 2.25
37 PGr,JP,E:Revenge times two,
  V:Doctor Eclipse,Ravenus 2.00
38 PGr,JP,Chaos Effect-Epsilon#1 2.00
39 . . . . 2.00
40 . . . . 2.00
41 . . . . 2.00
42 Elements of Evil pt.1 . . . . . . 2.00
43 Elements of Evil pt.2 . . . . . . 2.00
44 I:New Character 2.00
45 Explores Powers 2.00
46 I:The Sentry 2.25
47 DJu,DG,Brave New World,pt.2 2.25
48 DJu,DG,Brave New World,pt.3 2.25
49 DJu,DG,Brave New World,pt.4 2.25
50 DJu,DG,Brave New World,pt.5 2.25
51 I:Aliens on the Moon 2.25
52 Solar Saves Earth 2.25
53 I:Marauder 2.25
54 V:Marauder 2.25
55 I:Black Star 2.25
56 V:Black Star 2.25
57 A:Armorines 2.25
58 I:Atman, The Inquisitor 2.25
59 and 60 KG . . . . @2.25
TPB #0 JiS,BWS,BL,Alpha and
  Omega rep. from Solar #1–#10 9.95
TPB #1 JiS,BWS,GL,V:Doctor Solar
  rep. from Solar #1–#4 . . . . . . 9.95

STARSLAYER DIRECTORS CUT
Windjammer 1995

1 R:Starslayer, Mike Grell 2.50
2 I:New Star Slayer 2.50
3 Jolly Rodger 2.50
4 V:Battle Droids 2.50
5 I:Baraka Kuhi 2.50
6 V:Valkyrie 2.50
7 MGr(c&a),Can Torin destroy? . 2.50
8 MGr(c&a),JAl, Can Torin live with
  his deeds?,final issue 2.50

STARWATCHERS
Valiant

1 MLe,DG,Chromium(c),Valiant
  Vision, ... 3.50

SUPER MARIO BROS.
Valiant 1991

1 thru 6 . . . . @1.95
Spec. #1 . . . . 1.95

TICK, THE

Spec. digest size 4.50

TIMEWALKER
Valiant 1994

0 BH,DP,O:3 Immortals 2.95
1 DP, BH 2.50
2 DP,BH 2.50
3 DP BH 2.50
4 Ten Commandments 2.50
5 DP,BH 2.50
6 Harbinger Wars Pt.1 . . . . 2.50
7 Harbinger Wars Pt.2 . . . . 2.50
8 Harbinger Wars Pt.3 . . . . 2.50
9 V:Jahk rt 2.50
10 Last God of Dura-Europus,pt.1
  time: 260 A.D. 2.50
11 Last God of Dura-Europus,pt.2 2.50
12 3RW,DP,Ashes to Ashes,pt.1 . 2.50
13 3RW,DP,Ashes to Ashes,pt.2 . 2.50
14 Meets Mozart 2.50
15 26th Century 2.50
Yearbook F:Harada 2.95
TPB F:Archer & Armstrong 9.95

TRINITY ANGELS
Acclaim March 1997

1 KM,DPs, Maria, Gianna &
  Theresa Barbella become Trinity
  Angels 2.50
2 KM,DPs, V:The 99 . . . . 2.50
3 KM,DPs, looking for a little head 2.50
4 KM,DPs, V:Flaming Queen . . . 2.50
5 KM, New costumes 2.50

TROUBLEMAKERS
Acclaim Dec. 1996

1 FaN(s) 2.50
2 FaN(s) go back in time 2.50
3 FaN(s) Jane has a big problem 2.50
4 FaN(s) Can Blur prevent parents
  divorce? 2.50
5 FaN(s) A:Ninjak 2.50
6 FaN(s) in outer space 2.50
7 FaN(s) I:The Rabble Rousers . . 2.50
8 FaN(s) Rabble Rousers, part
  deux 2.50

TUROK: DINOSAUR HUNTER
Valiant 1993

1 BS,Chromium(c),O:Turok
  retold,V:Monark 3.00
1a Gold Ed. 7.00
2 BS,V:Monark 2.75
3 BCh,V:Monark 2.75
4 TT(s),RgM,O:Turok 2.75
5 TT(s),RgM,V:Dinosaurs 2.75
6 TT(s),RgM,V:Longhunter 2.75
7 TT(a&s),B:People o/t Spider . . 2.75
8 TT(a&s),V:T-Rex 2.75
9 TT(a&s),E:People o/t Spider . . 2.75

10 MBn,RgM,A:Bile 2.75
11 MBn,RgM,V:Chun Yee,w/
  ValiantEra card 2.75
12 MBn,RgM,V:Dinosaur 2.75
13 B:TT(c&s),RgM, ... 2.75
14 V:Dino-Pirate 2.50
15 RgM,V:Dino-Pirate 2.25
16 Chaos Effect-Beta#3, V:Evil
  Shaman 2.75
17 V:C.I.A. 2.50
18 V:Bionosaurs 2.50
19 A:Manowar 2.50
20 Chichak 2.50
21 Ripsaw 2.50
22 . . . . 2.50
23 A:Longhunter 2.50
24 R:To The Lost Land 2.50
25 I:Warrior of Mother God 2.50
26 V:Overlord 2.50
27 TT,RgM,Lost Land,pt.4 . . . . . 2.50

Turok: Dinosaur Hunter #6 © Valiant

28 MBn,DEA hunts rogue T-Rex . 2.50
29 SFu,Manhunt,pt.1 . . . . 2.50
30 SFu,Manhunt,pt.2 . . . . 2.50
31 F:Darwin Challenger 2.50
32 V:Special Effects 2.50
33 V:Aliens 2.50
34 V:Alien Ooze 2.50
35 Early Years 2.50
36 Confronts Past 2.50
37 V:Nazi Women 2.50
38 V:Bigfoot 2.50
39 TT,Shainer Silver 2.50
40 A:Longhunter 2.50
41 Church of the Poison Mind . . . 2.50
42 Church of the Poison Mind . . . 2.50
43 thru 47 . . . . @2.50
Yearbook #1 MBn(s),DC, N&V:Mon
  Ark 4.25
Yearbook 1995 MGr,The Hunted . 2.95

TUROK: THE HUNTED
Valiant

1 & 2 . . . . 2.50

TUROK QUARTERLY— REDPATH

March 1997, FaN(s),"Spring Break

ACCLAIM

in the Lost Land" 3 95
June 1997, FaN(s), Killer loose in
   Oklahoma City 3.95

TUROK/SHAMAN'S TEARS
Valiant 1995
1 MGr,Ghost Dance Pt. 1 . . . . . . 2.50
2 MGr,JAl,White Buffalo
   kidnapped,V:Bar Sinister 2.50
3 V:Supremeists/Circle Sea 2.50

TUROK/TIMEWALKER
Acclaim 1997
1 of 2 FaN(s),"Seventh Sabbath" 2.50
2 of 2 FaN(s),"Seventh Sabbath" 2.50

UNITY
Valiant 1992
0 BWS,BL,Chapter#1,A:All Valiant
   Heroes,V:Erica Pierce 3.00
0a Red ed.,w/red logo 6.00
1 BWS,BL,Chapter#18,A:All Valiant
   Heroes,D:Erica Pierce 3.00
1a Gold logo 6.00
1b Platinum 6.00
TPB Previews Exclusive,Vol.I
   Chap.#1-9 . . . . 8.00
TPB Previews Exclusive,Vol.II
   Chap.#10-18 . . . . 8.00
TPB #1 rep Chapters #1-4 . . 10.95
TPB #2 rep Chapters #5-9 . . . . . 9.95
TPB #3 rep Chapters #10-14 . . . 9.95

VALERIA, THE SHE-BAT
Windjammer 1995
[Mini-series]
1 NA,Valeria & 'Rilla 2.50
2 NA,BSz, final issue 2.50

VALIANT ERA
Valiant
TPB rep.Magnus #12,Shadowman
   #8, Solar #10-11,Eternal
   Warrior#4-5 . . . . 13.95

VALIANT READER: GUIDE TO THE VALIANT UNIVERSE
1 O:Valiant Universe 1.00

VALIANT VISION STARTER KIT
Valiant
1 w/3-D Glasses 2.95
2 F:Starwatchers 2.95

VINTAGE MAGNUS ROBOT FIGHTER
Valiant
1 rep. Gold Key Magnus #22
   (which is #1) 6.00
2 rep. Gold Key Magnus #3 . . . 4.50
3 rep. Gold Key Magnus #13 . . . 3.50
4 rep. Gold Key Magnus #15 . . . 3.50

VISITOR
Valiant 1994
1 New Series 2.50
2 F:The Harbinger 2.50
3 The Bomb 2.50

4 V:F/X Specialists 2.50
5 R:Harbinger 2.50
6 KVH,BS(c),V:Men in Black 2.50
7 KVH,BS(c),V:Men in Black,pt.2 . 2.50
8 KVH,V:Harbinger identity 2.50
9 KVH,A:Harbinger,Flamingo . . 2.50
10 Weather Problems 2.50
11 V:Cannibals 2.50
12 V:Harada, Men in Black 2.50
13 Visitor is the Future Harbinger . 2.50

VISITOR VS. VALIANT
Valiant 1994
1 V:Solar 2.95
2 . . . . 2.95

WATERWORLD
Acclaim 1997
1 of 4 V:Leviathan 2.50
2 of 4 "Children of Leviathan" . . . 2.50
3 of 4 KoK 2.50
4 of 4 KoK "Children of Leviathan" 2.50

WWF BATTLEMANIA
Valiant
1 WWF Action 2.50
2 . . . . 2.50
3 . . . . 2.50
4 . . . . 2.50
5 . . . . 2.50

X-O MANOWAR
Valiant 1992
0 JQ,O:Aric,1st Full Chromium(c) 3.00
0a Gold Ed. 7.00
1 BL,BWS,I:Aric,Ken 8.00
2 BL(i),V:Lydia,Wolf-Class Armor 6.00
3 I:X-Caliber,A:Solar 6.00
4 MM,A:Harbinger,C:Shadowman
   (Jack Boniface) 6.00
5 BWS(c),V:AX 4.00
5a w/Pink logo 5.00
6 SD,V:Ax(X-O Armor) 4.00
7 FM(c),Unity#5,V:Pierce 3.50
8 WS(c),Unity#13,V:Pierce 3.50
9 Aric in Italy,408 A.D. 3.50
10 N:X-O Armor 3.50
11 V:Spider Aliens 2.50
12 A:Solar 2.50
13 V:Solar 2.50
14 BS,A:Turok,I:Randy Cartier . . 3.00
15 BS,A:Turok 2.50
15a Red Ed. 9.00
16 V:The Mob 2.50
17 BL 2.50
18 JCf,V:CIA,A:Randy,I:Paul . . . 2.50
19 JCf,V:US Government 2.50
20 A:Toyo Harada 2.50
21 V:Ax 2.50
22 Aria in S.America 2.50
23 Aria in S.America 2.50
24 Aria comes back 2.50
25 JCf,JGz,PaK,I:Armories,
   BU:Armories#0 . . . . 4.00
26 JGz(s),RLv,F:Ken 2.50
27 JGz,RLe,A:Turok,Geomancer,
   Stronghold,Livewire 2.50
28 JGz,RLe,D:X-O,V:Spider
   Aliens,w/Valiant Era card 2.75
29 JGz,RLe,A:Turok, V:Spider
   Aliens 2.50
30 JGz,RLe,A:Solar 2.50
31 JGz,RLe, ... 2.50

X-O Manowar #24
© *Voyager Communications, Inc.*

32 JGz,RLe,at Orb,Inc. 2.25
33 JGz,RLe,Chaos Effect-Delta#3,
   A:Armorines,H.A.R.D. Corps . . 2.25
34 . . . . 2.25
35 . . . . 2.25
36 . . . . 2.25
37 Wolfbridge Affair pt.1 . . . . . . 2.25
38 Wolfbridge Affair pt.2 . . . . . . 2.25
39 Wolfbridge Affair pt.3 . . . . . . 2.25
40 Wolfbridge Affair pt.4 . . . . . . 2.25
41 Aftermath 2.25
42 A:Shadowman Surprise 2.25
43 Chasitty's Boys 2.25
44 Bart Sears New Direction . . . 2.50
45 RMz,V:Crescendo 2.50
46 RMz,V:Crescendo 2.50
47 RMz,V:Crescendo 2.50
48 RMz,BS,A:Turok 2.50
49 RMz,loses control of armor . . . 2.50
50-X R:Paul, I:Alloy 2.50
50-O V:Alloy 2.50
51 V:Lummox 2.50
52 V:A Blast From the Past 2.50
53 Returns To Space 2.50
54 I:New Aliens 2.50
55 V:Aliens 2.50
56 V:Aliens 2.50
57 I:Gamin 2.50
58 I:Volt 2.50
59 thru 67 . . . . @2.50
TPB rep.#1-4,w/X-O Manual . . . 11.00

X-O MANOWAR
Series Two
Acclaim Oct. 1997
1 Rand Banion v. R.A.G.E. 2.50
2 v. R.A.G.E. 2.50
3 . . . . 2.50
4 R.A.G.E. is back 2.50
5 Donovan Wylie vs. Internaut . . 2.50
6 Internaut controls X-O suit . . . 2.50
7 SEa, Donovan wears his armor 2.50
8 SEa, V:Basilisk 2.50
9 SEa, A: new Hard Corps 2.50
10 SEa, R:Bravado 2.50

ACCLAIM

All comics prices listed are for *Near Mint* condition.

DARK HORSE

ABYSS, THE
1 MK,Movie Adaptation pt.1 . . . . 2.50
2 MK,Movie Adaptation pt.2 . . . . 2.50

Agents of Law #3 © Dark Horse Comics

ACCIDENT MAN
(B&W)
1 I:Accident Man 2.50
2 and 3 . . . . @2.50

ADVENTURES OF LUTHER ARKWRIGHT
Valkyrie Press/Dark Horse
(B&W) 1987–89
1 thru 9 . . . . @2.00
(B&W) 1990
1 thru 9 Rep. . . . . @1.95
TPB 14.95

ADVENTURES OF THE MASK
1996
1 thru 12 by Michael Eury & Marc
Campos, TV cartoon adapt. @2.50

AGENTS OF LAW
Comics' Greatest World 1995
1 KG, I:Law 2.50
2 A:Barb Wire 2.50
3 KG,DLw,The Judgment Gate . . 2.50
4 Open Golden City 2.50
5 Who is the Mystery figure 2.50
6 V:Predator 2.50

AGE OF REPTILES
1993–94
1 DRd,Story on Dinosaurs 3.00
2 DRd,Story on Dinosaurs 3.00
3 DRd,Story on Dinosaurs 3.00

4 DRd,Story on Dinosaurs 3.00
TPB Tribal Warfare 14.95

AGE OF REPTILES: THE HUNT
1996
1 thru 5 by Ricardo Delgado . . @2.95
TPB 17.95

ALIENS
(B&W) 1988
1 Movie Sequel,R:Hicks,Newt . . 25.00
1a 2nd printing 4.00
1b 3rd printing 3.00
1c 4th printing 2.50
2 Hicks raids Mental Hospital . . 15.00
2a 2nd printing 3.50
2a 3rd printing 3.00
3 Realize Queen is on Earth 6.00
3a 2nd printing 2.50
4 Queen is freed, Newton on Aliens
World 5.00
5 All out war on Aliens World . . . 4.00
6 Hicks & Newt return to Earth . . 4.00
TPB rep.#1–#6 & DHP #24 . . . . 11.00
TPB 2nd printing, DvD(c) 11.00
HC rep..#1–#6 & DHP #24 . . . . 25.00

Aliens: Colonial Marines #5
© Dark Horse Comics

ALIENS (II)
[Mini-Series] 1989
1 DB,Hicks,Newt hijack ship 6.00
1a 2nd Printing 3.00
2 DB,Crazed general trains aliens 4.00
2a 2nd Printing 3.00
3 DB,HicksV:General Spears . . . 3.00
3a 2nd Printing 2.50
4 DB,Heroes reclaim earth from
aliens 3.00
HC, 2,500 made 80.00
HC, 1,000 made 100.00

ALIENS: BERSERKER
1 I:Crew of the Nemesis 2.50
2 Terminall 949 . . . . 2.50
3 Traitor 2.50
4 Finale 2.50

ALIENS: COLONIAL MARINES
1 I: Lt. Joseph Henry 3.00
2 I: Pvt. Carmen Vasquez 2.75
3 V:Aliens 2.75
4 F:Lt.Henry 2.75
5 V:Aliens 2.75
6 F:Herk Mondo 2.75
7 A:Beliveau 2.75
8 F:Lt.Joseph Henry 2.75
9 F:Lt.Joseph Henry 2.75
10 final issue 2.50

ALIENS: EARTH ANGEL
1 JBy 3.00
HC rep. Earth Angel 21.00

ALIENS: EARTH WAR
1 SK,JBo(c),Alien's War renewed 6.00
1a 2nd Printing 2.50
2 SK,JBo(c),To trap the Queen . . 5.00
3 SK,JBo(c) Stranded on Alien's
planet 4.00
4 SK,JBo(c),Resolution,final 4.00
HC Earth War, rep. #1–#4, signed
and numbered edition 60.00

ALIENS: GENOCIDE
1 Aliens vs. Aliens 4.00
2 Alien Homeworld 3.50
3 Search for Alien Queen 3.00
4 Conclusion, inc. poster 3.00
TPB Genocide rep. #1–#4 . . . . . 13.95
TPB Vol. 4 Remastered 17.95

ALIENS: HIVE
1 KJo,I:Stanislaw Mayakovsky . . 4.00
2 KJo,A:Norbert 3.50
3 KJo,A:Julie,Gill 3.25
4 KJo,A:Stan,Final 3.00
TPB Hive rep. #1–#4 . . . . 14.00

ALIENS: HAVOC
1 (of 2) "over 40 creators" 2.95
2 . . . . 2.95

ALIENS: LABYRINTH
1 F:Captured Alien 3.00
2 . . . . 2.50
3 O:Dr.Church 2.50
4 D:Everyone 2.50
TPB rep. #1–#4 . . . . 17.95
TPB remastered 17.95

ALIENS: MONDO HEAT
1 I:Herk Mondo 2.50

ALIENS: MONDO PEST
one-shot 2.95

All comics prices listed are for *Near Mint* condition.

ALIENS: MUSIC OF THE SPEARS
1 I:Damon Eddington 3.00
2 TBd(c),A:Damon Eddington . . . 2.75
3 TBd(c),A:Damon Eddington . . . 2.75
4 TBd(c),last issue 2.75

ALIENS: NEWT'S TALE
1 How Newt Survived 5.50
2 JBo(c),Newt's point of view on how 'Aliens' ended 4.95

ALIENS: PIG
one-shot by Chuck Dixon and Flint Henry 2.95

ALIENS: ROGUE
1 F:Mr.Kay 3.00
2 V:Aliens 3.00
3 V:Aliens 3.00
4 V:Aliens King 3.00
TPB Nel(c),rep.#1–#4 . . . . 14.95
TPB Remastered 16.95

ALIENS: SACRIFICE
1 Rep.Aliens UK 4.95

ALIENS: SALVATION
1 MMi,F:Selkirk 4.95

ALIENS: STRONGHOLD
1 DoM,JP 2.50
2 DoM,JP 2.50
3 DoM,JP 2.50
4 DoM,JP 2.50
TPB 16.95

ALIENS: TRIBES
HC DvD(c) 24.95
TPB 11.95
HC SBi,DvD 24.95

ALIENS/PREDATOR: DEADLIEST OF THE SPECIES
1 B:CCI(s),JG,F:Caryn Delacroix . 3.75
2 JG,V:Predator 3.00
3 JG,F:Caryn Delacroix 3.00
4 JG,V:Predator 3.00
5 JG,Roadtrip 3.00
6 JG,in Space Station 3.00
7 JG,EB 2.50
8 JG,EB 2.50
9 JG,EB 2.50
10 CCI(s), Human Predators 2.50
11 CCI,EB,JBo(c),Delacroix vs. DeMatier 2.50
12 Caryn's Fate 2.50
TPB 29.95
Lim. Ed. hc 99.95

ALIENS VS. PREDATOR
0 PN,KS,Rep.DHP#34-36,(B&W) 11.00
1 Duel to the Death 8.00
1a 2nd Printing 3.00
2 Dr. Revna missing 6.00
3 Predators attack Aliens 5.00
4 CW,F:Machiko & Predator 4.00
TPB Rep.#1–#4 . . . . 19.95
TPB PN,KS,rep.DHP#34-36 . . . 19.95
HC PN,KS,rep.DHP#34-36 . . . . 79.95

ALIENS VS. PREDATOR: BOOTY
1-shot Rep. Diamond Previews . . 2.50

ALIENS VS. PREDATOR: DUEL
1 Trap, JS 2.50
2 War 2.50

ALIENS VS. PREDATOR: WAR
0 Prelude to New Series 2.50
1 RSd,MM,RCo(c) F:Machiko . . . 2.50
2 I:Machiko Naguchi 2.50
3 F:Machiko Naguchi 2.50
4 final issue 2.50
TPB 19.95

ALIEN 3
1 thru 3 Movie Adaptation . . . @2.50

AMERICAN, THE
(B&W)
1 CW,'Chinese Boxes,'D:Gleason 6.00
2 CW,'Nightmares 4.50
3 CW,Secrets of the American . . 4.00
4 CW,American vs.Kid America . . 4.00
5 A:Kiki the Gorilla 4.00
6 Rashomon-like plot 3.50
7 Pornography business issue . . 3.50
8 Deals with violence issue 3.50
9 American Falls into a cult 3.50

THE AMERICAN: LOST IN AMERICA
1 CMa, American joins a cult . . . 2.50
2 CMa, V:"Feel-Good" cult 2.50
3 CMa, "ApeMask" cult 2.50
4 CMa, Final issue 2.50
ColorSpec.#1 . . . . 2.95

AMERICAN SPLENDOR
1 Letterman 2.95
Spec. A Step Out of the Nest . . 2.95
One-shot On the Job 2.95

AMERICAN SPLENDOR: COMIC-CON COMICS
(B&W) 1996
1-shot JZe 2.95

AMERICAN SPLENDOR WINDFALL
(B&W) 1995
1 Windfall Gained,pt.1 . . . . 3.95
2 Windfall Lost 3.95

ANOTHER CHANCE TO GET IT RIGHT
1 B&W 14.95
TPB by Andrew Vachss 9.95

APPLESEED
(B&W)
by Masamune Shirow
TPB Book One: The Promethean Challenge 14.95
TPB Book Two: Prometheus Unbound 14.95

TPB Book Three: The Scales of Prometheus 14.95
TPB Book Four: The Promethean Balance 14.95

APPLESEED DATABOOK
1 Flip Book 7.50
1a 2nd printing 3.50
2 Flip Book 3.50
TPB Rep. #1–#2 . . . . 12.95

ARZACH
TPB by Moebius 6.95

A SMALL KILLING
GN by Alan Moore & Oscar Zarate 11.95

Atlas #2 © Dark Horse Comics

ATLAS
1 BZ,I:Atlas 2.75
2 BZ,V:Sh'en Chui 2.75
3 BZ,V:Sh'en Chui 2.50
4 BZ, final issue 2.50

BABE
Legend 1994
1 JBy(a&s) 3.00
2 thru 4 JBy(a&s) . . . . @2.50

BABE 2
Legend 1995
1 V:Shrewmanoid 2.50
2 A:Abe Sapien 2.50

BACCHUS COLOR SPECIAL
1 A:Thor 2.95
2 A:Abe Sapien 2.50

BADGER: SHATTERED MIRROR
1 R:Badger 2.50
2 R:Badger 2.50
3 Badger 2.50
4 Phantom, final issue 2.50

DARK HORSE

BADGER: ZEN POP FUNNY ANIMAL VERSION
1 MBn,R:Badger 2.50
2 Ham 2.50

BADLANDS
(B&W)
1 I:Connie Bremen 3.50
2 Anne Peck, C.I.A. 3.00
3 Assassination Rumor 2.50
4 Connie heads South 2.50
5 November 22, 1963, Dallas . . . 2.25
6 . . . . 2.25

Barb Wire #2 © Dark Horse Comics

BARB WIRE
Comics' Greatest World
1 Foil(c),I:Deathcard 2.25
2 DLw,I:Hurricane Max 2.25
3 V:Mace Blitzkrieg 2.00
4 Ghost pt.1 . . . . 2.00
5 Ghost pt.2 . . . . 2.00
6 Hardhide, Ignition 2.50
7 A:Motorhead 2.50
8 V:Ignition 2.50
9 A:Mecha, V:Ignition 2.50
Movie Spec. 3.95
TPB 8.95

BARB WIRE: ACE OF SPADES
1 thru 4 by CW, TBd & DoM . . @2.95

BARRY WINDSOR-SMITH: STORYTELLER
Oct. 1996
TPBs 1 thru 9 9"x12½" . . . . . . @4.95

BASEBALL GREATS
1 Jimmy Piersall story 3.25

BASIL WOLVERTON'S FANTASIC FABLES
(B&W)
1 BW 2.50

2 BW 2.50

BATMAN/ALIENS
Dark Horse/DC March 1997
1 (of 2) by Ron Marz and Bernie Wrightson 4.95
2 conclusion 4.95

BETTIE PAGE
1-shot, some nudity 3.95

BETTIE PAGE COMICS: SPICY ADVENTURE
one-shot by Jim Silke 2.95

BETTIE PAGE: QUEEN OF HEARTS
1 Movie adaptation 2.00
TPB 19.95

BIG
1 Movie Adaptation 2.00

BIG BLOWN BABY
(B&W) Aug. 1996
1 thru 4 by Bill Wray . . . . @2.95

BIG GUY AND RUSTY THE ROBOT BOY
1 V:Monster 4.95
2 V:Monster 4.95
TPB by Frank Miller and Geof Darrow 14.95

BILLI 99
(B&W)
1 'Pray for us Sinners' 4.50
2 'Trespasses' 4.00
3 'Daily Bread' 4.00

BLACK CROSS: DIRTY WORK
April 1997
one-shot by Chris Warner 2.95
Spec. #1 reoffer . . . .

BLACK DRAGON, THE
(B&W)
TPB Chris Claremont & John Bolton7.95

BLACK PEARL, THE
Sept. 1996
1 by Mark Hamill 2.95
2 thru 5 . . . . @2.95
TPB by Mark Hamill 16.95

BLADE OF THE IMMORTAL: BLOOD OF A THOUSAND
(B&W)
TPB by Hiroaki Samura 12.95

BLADE OF THE IMMORTAL: CONQUEST
(B&W)
1 by Hiroaki Samura 2.95
2 and 3 . . . . @2.95

BLADE OF THE IMMORTAL: CALL OF THE WORM
(B&W) April 1997
1 by Hiroaki Samura 3.95
2 . . . . 3.95
3 . . . . 3.95

BLADE OF THE IMMORTAL: DREAMSONG
(B&W)
1 (of 7) by Hiroaki Samura 2.95

BLADE OF THE IMMORTAL: FANATIC
(B&W)
1 by Hiroaki Samura 2.95
2 . . . . 2.95

BLADE OF THE IMMORTAL: GENIUS
(B&W) Oct. 1996
1 by Hiroaki Samura 2.95
2 . . . . 2.95

BLANCHE GOES TO NEW YORK
1 Turn of the Century N.Y. 2.95

BLUE LILY
1 thru 3 . . . . @4.00

BODY BAGS
Aug. 1996
1 (of 4) by Jason Pearson and Ken Bruzinak 2.95
2 & 3 . . . . @2.95
TPB 12.95

BOOK OF NIGHT
(B&W)
1 CV 2.50
2 CV 2.00
TPB Children of the Stars 12.95

BOOK OF NIGHT
1 thru 3 . . . . 3.95

BORIS THE BEAR
(B&W)
1 V:Funny Animals 3.00
1a 2nd printing 2.00
2 V:Robots 2.00
3 V:Super Heroes 2.00
4 Bear of Steel 2.00
5 Dump Thing 2.00
6 Bat Bear 2.00
7 Elves 2.00
8 LargeSize 2.50
9 Awol 2.00
10 thru 12 . . . . @2.00
See: B & W Pub. section

BORIS THE BEAR
Color Classics
1 thru 7 . . . . @1.95

BRAVE
March 1997
1 by Cully Hamner & Jason Martin 2.95

BUBBLE GUM CRISIS: GRAND MAL
1	2.75
2 and 3	@2.75
4 final issue	2.50
TPB Rep.#1–#4	14.95

BY BIZARRE HANDS
(B&W)
1 JLd(s)	2.50
2 JLd(s)	2.50
3 JLd(s)	2.50

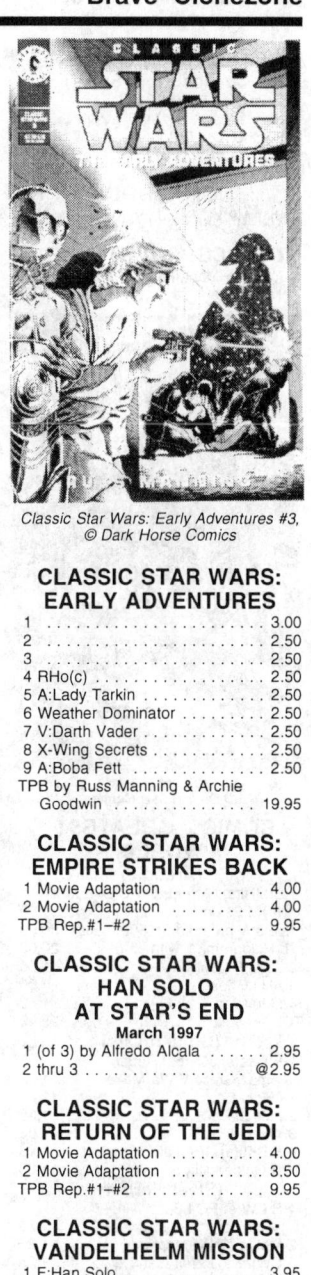

Caravan Kid (3rd Series) #3
© Dark Horse

CARAVAN KIDD
(B&W)
1 thru 10	@2.50
[2nd Series]	
1 thru 9 F:Miam	@2.50
10	2.50
TPB Rep. #1–#10	19.95
Holiday Spec.	2.50
Valentine's Day Spec.	2.50
[3rd Series]	
1 thru 8	@2.50
Christmas Special	2.50

CATALYST: AGENTS OF CHANGE
Comics' Greatest World
1 JPn(c),V:US Army	2.25
2 JPn(c),I:Grenade	2.25
3 JPn(c),Rebel vs. Titan	2.25
4 JPn(c),Titan vs. Grace	2.00
5 JPn(c),V:Ape	2.00
6 and 7	@2.00

CHEVAL NOIR
(B&W)
1 DSt(c)	4.00

2 thru 6	@3.50
7 DSt(c)	3.50
8	3.50
9	3.50
10 80 page	4.50
11 80 page	4.50
12 MM(c)	3.95
13 thru 15	@3.95
16 thru 19 with 2-card strip	@3.95
20'Great Power o/t Chninkel'	4.50
21'Great Power o/t Chninkel'	3.95
22'Great Power o/t Chninkel' concl.	4.50
23 inc."Rork','Forever War' concl.	3.95
24 'In Dreams' Pt.1	3.95
25 'In Dreams' Pt.2	3.95
26 'In Dreams' Pt.3	3.95
27 I:The Man From Ciguri (Airtight Garage Sequel) Dreams Pt.4	2.95
28 Ciguri cont.	2.95
29 Ciguri cont.	2.95
30 Ciguri,cont.	2.95
31 Angriest Dog in the World	2.95
32 thru 38	@2.95
39 In Search of Peter Pan	2.95
40	2.95
41 F:Demon	2.95
42 F:Demon	2.95
43 F:Demon	2.95
44 F:Demon	2.95
45	2.95
46	2.95
47	2.95
48 SwM(c)	2.95
49 F:Rork	2.95
50 F:Rork	2.95

CHRONOWAR
(B&W) Aug. 1996
1 (of 9) by Kazumasa Takayama	2.95
2 thru 9	@2.95

CLASSIC STAR WARS
1 AW,newspaper strip reps.	8.00
2 AW,newspaper strip reps.	4.00
3 AW,newspaper strip reps.	4.00
4 AW,newspaper strip reps.	4.00
5 AW,newspaper strip reps.	4.00
6 AW,newspaper strip reps.	4.00
7 AW,newspaper reps.	4.00
8 AW,newspaper reps. w/card	4.00
9 AW,newspaper reps.	3.50
10 AW,newspaper reps.	3.50
11 thru 19 AW,newspaper reps.	@3.00
20 AW,newspaper strip reps., with trading card, final issue	4.00
TPB Vol. 1, rep. #1–#7	15.99
TPB Vol. 1, rep. 2nd edition	16.95
TPB Vol. 2, rep. "Rebel Storm"	16.95
TPB Vol. 3, rep. "Escape to Hoth"	16.95

CLASSIC STAR WARS: A NEW HOPE
1 AAd(c), rep.	4.25
2 AAd(c), rep.	3.95
TPB Rep. #1–#2	9.95

CLASSIC STAR WARS: DEVILWORLDS
Aug. 1996
1 (of 2) by Alan Moore	2.50
2	2.50

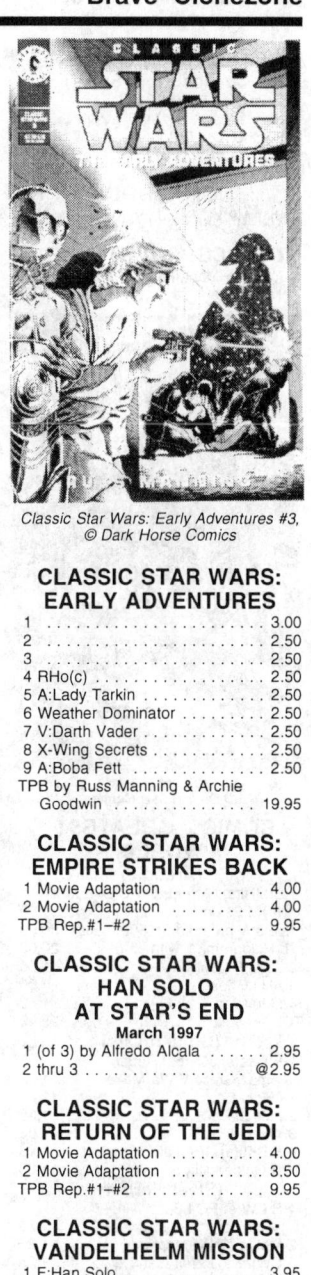

Classic Star Wars: Early Adventures #3,
© Dark Horse Comics

CLASSIC STAR WARS: EARLY ADVENTURES
1	3.00
2	2.50
3	2.50
4 RHo(c)	2.50
5 A:Lady Tarkin	2.50
6 Weather Dominator	2.50
7 V:Darth Vader	2.50
8 X-Wing Secrets	2.50
9 A:Boba Fett	2.50
TPB by Russ Manning & Archie Goodwin	19.95

CLASSIC STAR WARS: EMPIRE STRIKES BACK
1 Movie Adaptation	4.00
2 Movie Adaptation	4.00
TPB Rep.#1–#2	9.95

CLASSIC STAR WARS: HAN SOLO AT STAR'S END
March 1997
1 (of 3) by Alfredo Alcala	2.95
2 thru 3	@2.95

CLASSIC STAR WARS: RETURN OF THE JEDI
1 Movie Adaptation	4.00
2 Movie Adaptation	3.50
TPB Rep.#1–#2	9.95

CLASSIC STAR WARS: VANDELHELM MISSION
1 F:Han Solo	3.95

CLONEZONE
(B&W)
Spec #1	2.00

DARK HORSE

COLORS IN BLACK
Comics From Spike
1 B:Passion Play 2.95
2 Images 2.95
3 Back on the Bus 2.95
4 final issue 2.95

COMIC BOOK
1 thru 4 9"x12" by John Kricfalus@ 5.95

COMICS AND STORIES
4 (of 4) by Mark Martin & Tony
Millionaire 2.95

Arcadia #4 (Monster)
© Dark Horse Comics

COMICS' GREATEST WORLD
(Arcadia)
1 B:MRi(s),FM(c),B:LW,B:O:Vortex,
  F:X,I:Seekers 3.00
1a B&W proof ed. (1,500 made) 20.00
1b Hologram(c), with cards 20.00
2 JoP,I:Pit Bulls 1.50
3 AH,I:Ghost 7.00
4 I:Monster 1.50
TPB Arcadia 25.00

(Golden City)
1 B:BKs(s),JOy(c),I:Rebel,
  Amaz.Grace,V:WarMaker 1.25
1a Gold Ed. 12.00
2 I:Mecha 1.25
3 WS(c),I:Titan 1.25
4 E:BKs(s),GP(c),JD,I:Catalyst . 1.25
TPB Golden City 11.00

(Steel Harbor)
1 B:CW(s),PG,I:Barb Wire,
  V:Ignition 1.25
2 MMi(c),TNa,I:Machine 1.25
3 CW(a&s),I:Wolf Gang 1.25
4 E:CW(s),VGi,I:Motorhead . . . 1.25
TPB Steel Harbor 11.00

(Vortex)
1 B:RSd(s),LW,DoM,I:Division 13 1.25
2 I:Hero Zero 1.25
3 PC,I:King Tiger 1.25
4 B:RSd(s),E:MRi(s)BMc,E:LW,
  E:O:Vortex,C:Vortex 1.25

TPB Vortex 11.00
Sourcebook 10.00

CONCRETE
(B&W)
1 PC,R:Concrete, A Stone among
  Stones 14.00
1a 2nd printing 3.00
2 PC,'Transatlantic Swim' 7.00
3 PC 5.00
4 PC 4.00
5 PC,'An Armchair Stuffed with
  Dynamite' 4.00
6 PC,Concrete works on farm . . . 4.00
7 PC,Concrete grows horns 4.00
8 PC,Climbs Mount Everest 3.50
9 PC,Mount Everest Pt.2 . . . . . . 3.50
10 PC,last Issue 3.50
TPB 25.00

CONCRETE
1 PC,ColorSpec. 4.00
EarthDay Spec. PC,Moebius 4.00

CONCRETE: A NEW LIFE
1 . . . . 3.50
Spec.Land & Sea,rep. 3.25

CONCRETE CELEBRATES EARTH DAY 1990
one-shot 2.50

CONCRETE: ECLECTICA
1 PC,The Ugly Boy 3.25
2 PC 3.25

CONCRETE: FRAGILE CREATURE
1 PC,'Rulers o/t Omniverse'Pt.1 . 4.00
2 PC,'Rulers o/t Omniverse'Pt.2 . 3.00
3 PC,'Rulers o/t Omniverse'Pt.3 . 3.00
4 PC,'Rulers o/t Omniverse'Pt.3 . 3.00
TPB 15.95

CONCRETE: KILLER SMILE
Dark Horse-Legend 1994
1 PC 3.50
2 PC 2.95
3 PC 2.95
4 PC, final issue 2.95
TPB Rep.#1–#4 . . . . 16.95

CONCRETE: ODD JOBS
(B&W)
one-shot 3.50

CONCRETE: THINK LIKE A MOUNTAIN
1 thru 6 by Paul Chadwick . . . @2.95
TPB 17.95

CORMAC MAC ART
1 Robert E. Howard adapt. 2.25
2 . . . . 2.25
3 . . . . 2.25

COUTOO
1 Lt. Joe Kraft 3.50

CREEPY
(B&W)
1 KD,TS,GC,SL,Horror 3.95
2 TS,CI,DC,Demonic Baby 3.95
3 JM,TS,JG,V:Killer Clown 3.95
4 TS,Final issue 3.95

CREATURE FROM THE BLACK LAGOON
1 Movie Adaptation 4.95

CRITICAL ERROR
1 rep.Classic JBy story 2.75

[ANDREW VACHSS'] CROSS
0 I:Cross,Rhino,Princess 2.50
1 thru 7 . . . . @2.95

CUD COMICS
(B&W) 1995
1 thru 7 by Terry LaBan . . . . @2.95

CYBERANATICS
HC by Jerry Prosser & Rick Geary14.95

Danger Unlimited #3
© Dark Horse Comics

DANGER UNLIMITED
Dark Horse-Legend
1 JBy(a&s),KD,I:Danger Unlimited,
  B:BU:Torch of Liberty 2.50
2 JBy(a&s),KD,O:DangerUnlimited 2.25
3 JBy(a&s),KD,O:Torch of Liberty 2.25
4 JBy(a&s),KD,Final Issue 2.25
TPB rep. #1–#4 . . . . 14.95

DARK HORSE CLASSICS
(B&W)
1 Last of the Mohicans 3.95
2 20,000 Leagues Under the Sea 3.95

DARK HORSE CLASSICS: ALIENS VS. PREDATOR
Feb. 1997
1 thru 6 Rep. . . . . @2.95

DARK HORSE

DARK HORSE CLASSICS: PREDATOR: JUNGLE TALES
one-shot Rep. 2.95

DARK HORSE CLASSICS: STAR WARS— DARK EMPIRE
1 Rep. by Tom Veitch & Cam
Kennedy 2.95
2 thru 6 Rep. . . . . @2.95

DARK HORSE COMICS
1 RL,CW,F:Predator,Robocop,
I:Renegade,Time Cop,(double
gatefold cover) 4.00
2 RL,CW,F:Predator,Robocop,
Renegade,Time Cop 3.00
3 CW,F:Robocop,Time Cop,Aliens,
Indiana Jones 3.00
4 F:Predator,Aliens,Ind.Jones . . . 2.75
5 F:Predator,E:Aliens 2.75
6 F:Robocop,Predator, E:Indiana
Jones 2.75
7 F:Robocop,Predator,B:StarWars 12.00
8 B&I:X,Robocop 14.00
9 F:Robocop,E:Star Wars 8.00
10 E:X,B:Godzilla,Predator, James
Bond 5.50

Dark Horse Comics #1
© Dark Horse Comics

11 F:Godzilla,Predator,James
Bond,B:Aliens 2.75
12 F:Predator 2.75
13 F:Predator,B:Thing 2.75
14 MiB(s),B:The Mark 2.75
15 MiB(s),E:The Mark,B:Aliens . . 2.75
16 B:Predator,E:Thing,Aliens 2.75
17 B:Aliens,Star Wars:Droids 2.75
18 E:Predator 2.75
19 RL(c),B:X,E:Star Wars:Droids,
Aliens 2.75
20 B:Predator 2.75
21 F:Mecha 2.75
22 B:Aliens, E:Mecha 2.75

23 B:The Machine 2.50
24 The Machine 2.50
25 Final issue 2.50

DARK HORSE DOWNUNDER
(B&W)
1 F:Australian Writers 2.50
2 Australian Writers 2.50
3 Australian Writers, finale 2.50

DARK HORSE MONSTERS
Feb. 1997
one-shot 2.95

DARK HORSE PRESENTS
(B&W)
1 PC,I:Concrete 17.00
1a 2nd printing 3.00
2 PC,Concrete 10.00
3 Boris theBear,Concrete 8.00
4 PC,Concrete 7.00
5 PC,Concrete 6.00
6 PC,Concrete 5.00
7 I:MONQ 5.00
8 PC,Concrete 5.00
9 . . . . 5.00
10 PC,Concrete, I:Masque 15.00
11 Masque 12.00
12 PC,Concrete, Masque 10.00
13 Masque 10.00
14 PC,Concrete, Masque 10.00
15 Masque 10.00
16 PC,Concrete, Masque 10.00
17 . . . . 4.00
18 PC,Concrete, Mask 10.00
19 Masque 10.00
20 double,Flaming Carrot 12.00
21 Masque 10.00
22 . . . . 3.00
23 . . . . 3.00
24 PC,I:Aliens 20.00
25 thru 31 . . . . @3.00
32 . . . . 4.00

Dark Horse Presents #4
© Dark Horse Comics

33 . . . . 3.00
34 Aliens 6.00
35 Predator 6.00
36 Aliens vs.Predator 6.00
36a painted cover 9.00
37 . . . . 2.50
38 . . . . 2.50
39 . . . . 2.50
40 I:The Aerialist 2.50
41 . . . . 2.50
42 Aliens 5.00
43 Aliens 4.00
44 . . . . 2.50
45 . . . . 2.50
46 Predator 4.00
47 . . . . 2.50
48 with 2-card strip 2.50
49 with 2-card strip 2.50
50 inc.'Heartbreakers', with 2-card
strip 2.50
51 FM(c),inc.'Sin City' 9.00
52 FM,inc. 'Sin City' 6.00
53 FM,inc. 'Sin City' 6.00
54 FM,Sin City;JBy Preview of Next
Men Pt.1 . . . . 9.00
55 FM,Sin City;JBy Preview of Next
Men (JBy) Pt.2 . . . . 8.00
56 FM,Sin City,JBy,Next MenPt.3
Aliens Genocide(prologue) . . . 6.00
57 FM,SinCity;JBy Next Men Pt.4 6.00
58 FM,Sin City,Alien Fire 4.00
59 FM,Sin City,Alien Fire 4.00
60 FM,Sin City 4.00
61 FM,Sin City 3.00
62 FM,E:Sin City 3.00
63 Moe,Marie Dakar 2.50
64 MWg,R:The Aerialist 2.50
65 B:Accidental Death 2.50
66 PC,inc.Dr.Giggles 2.50
67 B:Predator story (lead in to
"Race War"),double size 3.95
68 F:Predator,Swimming Lessons
(Nestrobber tie-in) 2.50
69 F:Predator 2.50
70 F:Alec 2.50
71 F:Madwoman 2.50
72 F:Eudaemon 2.50
73 F:Eudaemon 2.50
74 . . . . 2.50
75 F:Chairman 2.50
76 F:Hermes Vs.the Eye,Ball Kid . 2.50
77 F:Hermes Vs.the Eye,Ball Kid . 2.50
78 F:Hermes Vs.the Eye,Ball Kid . 2.50
79 B:Shadow Empires Slaves . . . 2.50
80 AAd,I:Monkey Man & O'Brien . 6.00
81 B:Buoy 2.50
82 B:Just Folks 2.50
83 Last Impression 2.50
84 MBn,F:Nexus,E:Hermes Vs. the
Eye Ball Kid 2.50
85 Winner Circle 2.50
86 . . . . 2.50
87 F:Concrete 2.50
88 Hellboy 3.00
89 Hellboy 3.00
90 Hellboy 3.00
91 Blackheart, Baden 3.00
92 Too Much Coffee Man 7.00
93 Cud, Blackheart,Coffee Man . . 9.00
94 A:Eyeball Kid,Coffee Man 7.00
95 Too Much Coffee Man 8.00
96 Kabuli Kid 2.50
97 F:Kabuki Kid 2.50
98 Pot Full of Noodles 2.50
99 Anthology title 2.50

DARK HORSE

DARK HORSE

100–#1 Lance Blastoff 2.50
100–#2 Hellboy 2.50
100–#3 Concrete 2.50
100–#4 Black Cross 2.50
100–#5 Pan Fried Girl 2.50
101 BW,F:Aliens 2.50
102 F:Mr. Painter 2.50
103 F:The Pink Tornado 3.00
104 F:The Pink Tornado 3.00
105 F:The Pink Tornado 3.00
106 F:Godzilla 3.00
107 F:Rusty Razorclam 3.00
108 . . . . 2.95
109 . . . . 2.95
110 . . . . 2.95
111 . . . . 2.95
112 three stories, concl. 2.95
113 . . . . 2.95
114 F:Star Slammers 2.95
115 flip-book 2.95
116 . . . . 2.95
117 F:Aliens 2.95
118 . . . . 2.95
119 . . . . 2.95
120 "One Last Job" 2.95
121 F: Jack Zero 2.95
122 "Lords of Misrule" 2.95
123 F: Jack Zero 2.95
Fifth Anniv. Special DGi,PC,
 SBi,CW,MW,FM,Sin City,
 Aliens,Give Me Liberty 12.00
Milestone Ed.#1,rep.DHP#1 . . . . 2.25
TPB rep.Sin City 15.00
TPB Best of DHP #1–#20 . . . . . . 9.95
TPB Best of DHP #1–#20 2nd
 edition 9.95
TPB Best of DHP #21–#30 . . . . . 8.95
TPB Best of DHP #31–#50 . . . . . 8.95

DARK HORSE PRESENTS: ALIENS

1 Rep. 4.95
1a Platinum Edition 8.00

DEADFACE: DOING ISLANDS WITH BACCHUS
(B&W)

1 rep. Bacchus apps. 2.95
2 rep. inc.'Book-Keeper of Atlantis 2.95

DEADFACE: EARTH, WATER, AIR & FIRE
(B&W)

1 Bacchus & Simpson in Sicily . . 2.50
2 A:Don Skylla 2.50
3 Mafia/Kabeirol-War prep. 2.50
4 Last issue 2.50

DEAD IN THE WEST
(B&W)

1 TT,Joe Landsdale adapt. 5.00
2 TT,adapt. 5.00

DEAD IN THE WEST

1 TT(c) 3.95

DEADLINE USA
(B&W)

1 rep. Deadline UK,Inc. Tank Girl
 Johnny Nemo 9.95
2 inc. Tank Girl,Johnny Nemo . . . 9.95

DECADE OF DARK HORSE, A

1 (of 4) inc. Star Wars, Nexus,
 Ghost 2.95
2 thru 4 . . . . @2.95

DEVIL CHIEF

1 I:Devil Chief 2.50

DIRTY PAIR: A PLAGUE OF ANGELS

Book 3 . . . . 12.95

DIRTY PAIR: DANGEROUS ACQUAINTANCES

TPB by Toren Smith and Adam
 Warren 12.95

DIRTY PAIR: FATAL BUT NOT SERIOUS

1 R:Kei,Yuri 2.95
2 V:Kevin Sleet,Yuri 2.95
3 Anti Yuri 2.95
4 V:Terrorists 2.95
5 conclusion 2.95

DIRTY PAIR: SIM HELL

1 thru 4 . . . . @3.25
TPB rep. #1–#4 . . . . 13.95

DIVISION 13

1 . . . . 2.50
2 . . . . 2.50
3 A:Payback 2.50
4 Carnal Genesis 2.50

DOC SAVAGE: CURSE OF THE FIRE GOD

1 R:Man of Bronze 2.95
2 Exploding Plane 2.95
3 & 4 . . . . @2.95

DR. GIGGLES

1 Horror movie adapt. 2.50
2 Movie adapt.contd. 2.50

DOMINION
(B&W)

TPB 1 . . . . 15.00
TPB 2nd printing 14.95

DOMINION: CONFLICT 1 — NO MORE NOISE
(B&W) 1996

1 thru 6 by Masamune Shirow @2.95
TPB 14.95

DOMINION SPECIAL: PHANTOM OF THE AUDIENCE
(B&W)

one-shot by Masamune Shirow . . 2.50

DOMU: A CHILD'S DREAMS
(B&W) Manga

1 Psychic Warfare 5.95

2 Murders Continue 5.95
3 Psychic war conclusion 5.95
TPB by Katsuhiro Otomo 17.95

DRACULA

1 Movie Adaptation 4.95

DRAKUUN: RISE OF THE DRAGON PRINCESS
(B&W) Feb. 1997

1 by Johji Manabe 2.95
2 thru 6 (of 6) . . . . @2.95

EDGAR RICE BURROUGHS' RETURN OF TARZAN
April 1997

1 adapted by Thomas Yeates &
 John Totleben 2.95
2 thru 3 . . . . @2.95

EDGAR RICE BURROUGHS' TARZAN: THE LOST ADVENTURE

1 Lost Manuscript 2.95
2 V:Gorgo the Buffalo 2.95
3 V:Bandits 2.95
4 V:Bandits 2.95
HC 19.95

EDGAR RICE BURROUGHS' TARZAN: LE MONSTRE
June 1997

1 (of 2) 2.95
2 (of 2) Bernie Wrightson(c) 2.95

EDGAR RICE BURROUGHS' TARZAN: MUGAMBI

1 by Bruce Jones, Christopher
 Schenck & Thomas Yeates,
 Betrayed by 3 man-beasts . . . 2.95
2 "Tarzan's Jungle Fury" 2.95
3 "Tarzan's Jungle Fury" 2.95
4 vs. the Tara virus 2.95
5 Cure to the Tara virus 2.95
6 . . . . 2.95
7 by Allan Gross, Christopher
 Schenck, George Freeman,
 "Tarzan and the Legion of Hate".2.95
8 "Tarzan and the Legion of Hate"
 cont. 2.95
9 "Tarzan and the Legion of Hate"
 cont. 2.95
10 "Tarzan and the Legion of Hate"
 cont. 2.95

ELRIC: STORMBRINGER
Dark Horse/Topps 1996

1 by Michael Moorcock & PCR . . 2.95
2 thru 5 (of 7) . . . . @2.95

ENEMY

1 MZ(c),StG(s),I:Enemy 2.75
2 MZ(c),StG(s),F:Heller 2.75
3 MZ(c),StG(s),A:Heller 2.50
4 . . . . 2.50
5 final issue 2.95
TPB 14.95

DARK HORSE

Eudaemon #2 © Dark Horse Comics

EUDAEMON, THE
1 Nel,I:New Eudaemon	3.00
2 Nel,V:Mordare	2.75
3 Nel,V:Mordare	2.75

EVIL DEAD III: ARMY OF DARKNESS
1 JBo,Movie adaptation	4.00
2 JBo,Movie adaptation	3.50
3 JBo,Movie adaptation	3.00

EXOTICS, THE
TPB by Moebius	7.95

EYEBALL KID
(B&W)
1 I:Eyeball Kid	2.25
2 V:Stygian Leech	2.25
3 V:Telchines Brothers,last iss.	2.25

FAT DOG MENDOZA
(B&W)
1 I&O:Fat Dog Mendoza	2.50

FAX FROM SARAJEVO
Oct. 1996
GN by Joe Kubert	24.95

FLAMING CARROT
(B&W)
18	3.50
18a Ash-Can-Limited	5.00
19	2.00
20	2.00
21	2.00
22	2.00
23	2.00
24	3.00
25 F:TMNT,Mysterymen, with 2-card strip	4.00
26 A:TMNT	2.50
27 TM(c),A:TMNT conclusion	2.50
28	2.50
29 Man in the Moon,Iron City	2.50
30 V:Man in the Moon	2.50
31 A:Fat Fury	2.50

Ann. 1 by Bob Burden	5.00
TPB Man of Mystery, B&W	12.95

FLAXEN
1 Based on Model,w/poster	2.95

FLOATERS
(B&W)
1 thru 6 From Spike Lee	2.50

FOOT SOLDIERS, THE
1 thru 4	2.95

FRANKENSTEIN
1 Movie Adaptation	3.95

FREAKSHOW
1 JBo,DMc,KB, "Wanda the Worm Woman," "Lillie"	9.95

GAMERA
Aug. 1996
1 (of 4) by Dave Chipps & Mozart Couto	2.95
2 thru 4	@2.95

GHOST
Comics' Greatest World
Spec. AH(c)	3.95

Ghost #15 © Dark Horse

GHOST
1 by Eric Luke, R:Ghost	2.50
2 AH,MfM,Arcadia Nocturne,pt.2	2.50
3 Arcadia Nocturn,pt.3	2.50
4	2.50
5 V:Predator	2.50
6	2.50
7 Hell Night	2.50
8 thru 20	@2.50
21 Two heroes, one room	2.50
22 "The key is forever beyond your reach"	2.50
23 I: The Goblins	2.50
24 X is dead	2.50

25 double size	3.95
26 Fairytale version	2.95
27	2.95
TPB	8.95

GHOST/HELLBOY COLLECTION
TPB	4.95

GHOST: NOCTURNES
TPB	9.95

GHOST AND THE SHADOW
Spec. 1-shot	2.95

GHOST IN THE SHELL
1 Manga Style	3.95
2 Wetware Virus	3.95
3 Killer Robots	3.95
4 Rookie Cop Killed	3.95
5 F:Major Kusangi	3.95
6	3.95
7 Kusanagi in Jail	3.95
8 final issue	3.95
TPB by Masamune Shirow	24.95

G.I. JOE
1 by Mike Barr & Tatsuya Ishida	1.95
2 thru 4	@2.50

GIRL CRAZY
TPB by Gilbert Hernandez, rep.#1–#3	9.95

GIVE ME LIBERTY
1 FM/DGb, Homes & Gardens	9.00
2 FM/DGb	7.00
3 and 4 FM/DGb	@6.00
TPB	16.00

GODZILLA
(B&W) 1988
1 Japanese Manga	3.50
2 thru 6	@2.25
Spec #1	1.50
TPB 2nd printing	17.95

GODZILLA COLOR SPECIAL
1 AAd,R:Godzilla,V:Gekido-Jin	4.00

GODZILLA
0 RSd,The King of Monsters is back!	2.50
1 R:Godzill	2.50
2 V:Cybersaur	2.50
3 I:Bagorah the Bat Creature	2.50
4 V:Bagorah,Cybersaur	2.50
5 V:U.S. Army	2.50
6 thru 14	@2.50
15 "Thunder Downunder"	2.95
16 "Thunder in the Past"	2.95

GODZILLA VS. BARKLEY
1 MBn(s),JBt,DvD	3.50

GODZILLA VS. HERO ZERO
1 Tatsuya Ishida	2.50

DARK HORSE

DARK HORSE

GRENDEL CLASSICS
1 Rep.#18–#19 Comico series . . 3.95

GRENDEL CYCLE
1 Grendel History 5.95

GRENDEL: DEVIL BY THE DEED
1 MWg,RRa 3.95

GRENDEL: DEVIL'S LEGACY
Aug. 1996
1 (of 12) by Matt Wagner 2.75
2 thru 3 . . . . @2.75
TPB Devils and Deaths 16.95

GRENDEL: HOMECOMING
1 Babylon Crash 2.95
2 Babylon Crash pt. 2 . . . . 2.95
3 Too Dead To Die 2.95

GRENDEL: WAR CHILD
1 MWg 5.00
2 thru 9 MWg 3.00
10 MWg, final issue, dbl.size 4.00
TPB 18.95
HC signed and numbered 100.00

GRENDEL TALES: DEVILS AND DEATHS
1 . . . . 2.95
2 . . . . 2.95

GRENDEL TALES: DEVIL'S CHOICES
1 F:Goran 2.95
2 Marica 2.95
3 Marica vs. Goran 2.95
4 conclusion 2.95

GRENDEL TALES: FOUR DEVILS, ONE HELL
1 MWg(c),F:Four Grendels 3.50
2 MWg(c),F:Four Grendels 3.50
3 MWg(c),F:Four Grendels 3.50
4 MWg(c),F:Four Grendels 3.50
5 MWg(c),F:Four Grendels 3.50
6 MWg(c),last issue 3.25
TPB Rep. #1–#6 . . . . 17.95

GRENDEL TALES: THE DEVIL IN OUR MIDST
1 MWg(c) 3.50
2 MWg(c) 3.25
3 MWg(c) 2.95
4 & 5 . . . . @2.95

GRENDEL TALES: THE DEVIL MAY CARE
1 thru 6 mini-series 2.95

GRENDEL TALES: THE DEVIL'S HAMMER
1 MWg(a&s),I:Petrus Christus . . . 3.50
2 MWg(a&s),A:P.Christus 3.25
3 MWg(a&s),last issue 3.25

GRIFTER AND THE MASK
Sept. 1996
1 by Seagle, Lima & Pimentel . . . 2.50
2 . . . . 2.50

GUNSMITH CATS
(B&W)
1 I:Rally & Mini May 2.95
2 Revolver Freak 2.50
3 . . . . 2.95
4 V:Bonnie and Clyde 2.95
5 V:Bonnie and Clyde 2.95
6 Hostage Situation 2.95
7 & 8 (10 part series) 2.95

GUNSMITH CATS: BONNIE & CLYDE
TPB by Kenichi Sonoda 12.95

GUNSMITH CATS: SHADES OF GRAY
(B&W) May 1997
1 (of 5) by Kenichi Sonoda 2.95
2 (of 5) 2.95

GUNSMITH CATS: THE RETURN OF GRAY
(B&W) Aug. 1996
1 thru 7 by Kenichi Sonoda . . @2.95

HAMMER OF GOD: PENTATHLON
1 MiB(s),NV 2.50

HAMMER OF GOD: BUTCH
1 MBn 2.50
2 and 3 MBn . . . . @2.50

HAPPY BIRTHDAY MARTHA WASHINGTON
1 Frank Miller 2.95

HARD BOILED
1 . . . . 7.50
2 and 3 . . . . @7.00
TPB 14.95
HC 99.95

HARD LOOKS
(B&W)
1 thru 10 AVs Adaptations . . . @2.50
Book One 14.95
TPB by Andrew Vachss 17.95

HARLAN ELLISON'S DREAM CORRIDOR
1 Various stories 2.95
2 Various stories 2.95
3 JBy, I Have No Mouth and I Must
   Scream and other stories . . . 2.95
4 Catman 2.95
5 . . . . 2.95
6 Opposites Attract 2.95
Spec.#1 Various stories 4.95
TPB 18.95

HARLAN ELLISON'S DREAM CORRIDOR QUARTERLY
Aug. 1996
1 . . . . 5.95
2 . . . . 5.95

HEARTBREAKERS
1 . . . . 2.95

HELLBOY: ALMOST COLOSSUS
1 (of 2) by Mike Mignola, sequel to
   Wake the Devil 2.95
2 (of 2) 2.95

HELLBOY: SEEDS OF DESTRUCTION
Legend/Dark Horse
1 JBy,MMi,AAd,V:Vampire Frog,
   BU:Monkeyman & O'Brien . . . 4.00
2 MMi(c),JBy,AAd,BU:Monkeyman
   & O'Brien 3.00
3 MMi(c),JBy,AAd,BU:Monkeyman
   & O'Brien 3.00
4 MMi(c),JBy,AAd,BU:Monkeyman
   & O'Brien 3.00
TPB 17.95

HELLBOY: THE LOST ARMY
GN 14.95

HELLBOY: WAKE THE DEVIL
Legend
1 (of 5) by Mike Mignola 2.95
2 thru 5 . . . . @2.95
TPB 17.95

HELLHOUNDS
(B&W)
1 I:Hellhounds 2.50

Hellhounds #6,
© Dark Horse Comics

2 thru 6 A:Hellhounds ..... @2.50

HELLHOUNDS: PANZER CORPS
(B&W) 1994
1 thru 6 .... @2.95
TPB 14.95

HERBIE
1 JBy,reps.& new material 2.50
2 Reps.& new material 2.50

HERETIC, THE
Nov. 1996
1 (of 4) by Rich DiLeonardo, Joe
Phillips & Dexter Vines 2.95
2 thru 4 .... @2.95

HERMES VS. THE EYEBALL KID
1 thru 3 Symphony of Blood 2.95

HERO ZERO
1 First and last issue 2.50

H.P.'S ROCK CITY
TPB by Moebius 7.95

INDIANA JONES AND THE ARMS OF GOLD
1 In South America 2.75
2 In South America 2.75
3 V:Incan Gods 2.75
4 .... 2.50

Indiana Jones and the Fate of Atlantis #1 © Dark Horse Comics

INDIANA JONES AND THE FATE OF ATLANTIS
1 DBa,Search for S.Hapgood with
2-card strip 5.00
1a 2nd printing 3.00
2 DBa,Lost Dialogue of Plato with
2-card strip 3.00
3 Map Room of Atlantis 3.00

4 Atlantis, Last issue 3.00
TPB 13.95

INDIANA JONES AND THE GOLDEN FLEECE
1 SnW 2.75
2 SnW 2.50

INDIANA JONES AND THE IRON PHOENIX
1 .... 2.50
2 V:Nazis 2.50
3 A:Nadia Kirov 2.50
4 V:Undead 2.50

INDIANA JONES AND THE SARGASSO PIRATES
1 thru 4 .... @2.50

INDIANA JONES AND THE SHRINE OF THE SEA DEVIL
1 .... 2.50

INDIANA JONES AND THE SPEAR OF DESTINY
1 I:Spear T/Pierced Christ 2.50
2 DSp, with Henry Jones 2.50
3 Search for the Shaft 2.50

INDIANA JONES: THUNDER IN THE ORIENT
1 DBa(a&s),in Tripoli 2.75
2 DBa(a&s),Muzzad Ram 2.75
3 DBa(a&s),V:Sgt.Itaki 2.75
4 DBa(a&s),In Hindu Kush 2.75
5 DBa(a&s),V:Japanese Army 2.75
6 DBa(a&s),last issue 2.75

INSTANT PIANO
1 Offbeat humor 3.95
2 .... 3.95
3 Various stories 3.95
4 Devil Puppet 3.95

IRON HAND OF ALMURIC
(B&W)
1 Robert E. Howard adaption .. 2.00
2 A:Cairn,V:Yagas 2.25
3 V:Yasmeena,The Hive Queen .. 2.00
4 Conclusion 2.25
GN 10.95

JAMES BOND 007: QUASIMODO GAMBIT
1 I:Maximillion Quasimodo 3.95
2 V:Fanatical Soldiers 3.95
3 V:Steel 3.95

JAMES BOND 007: SERPENT'S TOOTH
1 PG,DgM,V:Indigo 5.50
2 PG,DgM,V:Indigo 5.00
3 PG,DgM 5.25
TPB 15.95

JAMES BOND 007: SHATTERED HELIX
1 V:Cerberus 2.50
2 V:Cerberus 2.50

JAMES BOND 007: A SILENT ARMAGEDDON
1 V:Troy 3.25
2 V:Omega 3.25
3 V:Omega 3.25

JOHNNY DYNAMITE
1 .... 2.95
2 .... 2.95
3 V:Faust 2.95
4 Last issue 2.95

JONNY DEMON
1 SL(c),KBk,NV 2.75
2 SL(c),KBk,NV 2.75
2 SL(c),KBk,NV, final issue 2.50

JUNIOR CARROT PATROL
(B&W)
1 .... 2.00
2 .... 2.00

KINGS OF THE NIGHT
1 .... 2.25
2 end Mini-Series 2.25

KING TIGER/MOTORHEAD
1 (of 2) by D.G. Chichester, Karl
Waller & Eric Shanower 2.95
2 .... 2.95

KLING KLANG KLATCH
GN 11.95

LAND OF NOD
(B&W) July 1997
1 (of 3) by Jay Stephens 2.95

THE LEGEND OF MOTHER SARAH
B&W, Manga
1 I:Mother Sarah 2.50
2 Sarah and Tsutsu 2.50
3 Firing Squad 2.50
4 F:Toki 2.50
5 Yunnel Town 2.50
6 Kill or Be Killed 2.95
7 Firing Squad 2.95
8 Conclusion 2.95
TPB The Tunnel Town 18.95

THE LEGEND OF MOTHER SARAH: CITY OF THE ANGELS
(B&W) Oct. 1996
1 (of 9) by Katsuhiro Otomo and
Takumi Nagayasu 3.95
2 thru 4 .... 3.95

THE LEGEND OF MOTHER SARAH: CITY OF THE CHILDREN
(B&W) 1995
1 thru 4 (7 part mini-series) .. @3.95

DARK HORSE

LORDS OF MISRULE
(B&W) Jan. 1997
1 by Dan Abnett, John Tomlinson,
Steve White & Peter Snejbjerg 2.95
2 thru 6 . . . . @2.95

THE LUCK IN THE HEAD
TPB 11.95

THE MACHINE
Comics Greatest World 1994
1 (a) The Barb Wire spin 2.50
2 V:Salvage 2.50
3 Freak Show 2.50
4 I:Skion 2.50

MADMAN
Legend 1994
1 MiA(s) 8.00
2 MiA(s) 5.00
3 MiA(s) 4.00
4 MiA(s),Muscleman 4.00
5 MiA(s),I:The Blast 4.00
6 MiA(s),A:Big Guy, Big Brain-o-
rama,pt.1 . . . . 4.00
7 MiA(s),FM,A:Big Guy, Big Brain-
o-rama,pt.2 . . . . 4.00
8 MiA(s) 3.50
9 Micro Madman 3.50
10 . . . . 3.50
11 . . . . 3.50
Yearbook '95 TPB 17.95
Yearbook '96 TPB 17.95
TPB Vol. 2 . . . . 17.95

MADWOMAN OF THE SACRED HEART, THE
(B&W)
TPB by Alexandro Jodorowsky and
Moebius 12.95

MAGNUS/NEXUS
Dark Horse/Valiant
1 MBn(s), SR 3.25
2 MBn(s), SR 3.25

MAN FROM THE CIGUIRI
TPB by Moebius 7.95

MARK, THE
1 LSn, in America 1.75
2 LSn 1.95
3 LSn 1.95
4 . . . . 1.95

MARK, THE
(B&W)
1 . . . . 1.95
2 thru 7 . . . . @1.75

MARK, THE
1 MiB(s),V:Archon 2.75
2 MiB(s),V:Archon 2.75
3 MiB(s),V:Archon,A:Pierce 2.75
4 MiB(s),last issue 2.75

MARK, THE
1 I:The Mark 2.50
2 V:Child Killer 2.50

MARSHALL LAW: CAPE FEAR
1 KON 2.95

MARSHALL LAW: SECRET TRIBUNAL
1 KON 2.95
2 KON 2.95

MARSHALL LAW: SUPER BABYLON
1 KON 4.95

Martha Washington Goes To War #3
© Dark Horse Comics

MARTHA WASHINGTON GOES TO WAR
Dark Horse-Legends
1 FM(s),DGb, V:Fat Boys Corp. . 3.25
2 FM(s),DGb, V:Fat Boys Corp. . 3.25
3 FM(s),DGb, V:Fat Boys Corp. . 3.25
4 FM(s),DGb, V:Fat Boys Corp. . 3.25
5 FM(s),DBb, final issue 3.25
TPB Rep.#1–#5 . . . . 17.95

MARTHA WASHINGTON STRANDED IN SPACE
1 . . . . 2.95

MASK, THE
0 . . . . 4.00
1 I:Lt.Kellaway Mask 11.00
2 V:Rapaz & Walter 9.00
3 O:Mask 8.00
4 final issue 7.50
TPB 14.95

MASK, THE
1 Movie Adaptation 3.00
2 Movie Adaptation 2.50

MASK, THE
(B&W)
0 'Who's Laughing Now' 6.00

MASK RETURNS, THE
1 inc.cut-out Mask 6.00
2 Mask's crime spree 4.00
3 . . . . 4.00
4 . . . . 4.00
TPB by John Arcudi & Doug
Mahnke 14.95

MASK STRIKES BACK, THE
[Mini-series]
1 Mask Strikes Back pt.1 . . . . . ,2.50
2 Mask Strikes Back pt.2 . . . . . . 2.50
3 Mask Strikes Back pt.3 . . . . . . 2.50
4 DoM,Mask Strikes Back pt.4 . . 2.50
5 Mask Strikes Back,pt.5 . . . . . . 2.50
TPB by John Arcudi, Doug Mahnke
& Keith Williams 14.95

MASK, THE: THE HUNT FOR GREEN OCTOBER
1 . . . . 2.50
2 Kellaway vs. Ray Tuttle 2.50
3 F:Emily Tuttle 2.50
4 final issue 2.50

MASK, THE: SOUTHERN DISCOMFORT
1 Mardi Gras time 2.50

MASK, THE: VIRTUAL SURREALITY
one-shot F: art by Mike Mignola and
Sergio Aragones 2.95

MASK, THE: WORLD TOUR
1 thru 4 . . . . @2.50

MAXIMUM OVERLOAD
1 Masque (Mask) 25.00
2 Mask 20.00
3 Mask 20.00
4 Mask 20.00

MAXIMUM OVERLOAD
1 thru 5 . . . . @3.95

MECHA
Comics Greatest World 1995
1 color 1.75
2 color 1.75
3 thru 6 B&W . . . . @1.75
Spec.(#1) CW(c),color 2.95

MEDAL OF HONOR
1 Ace of Aces 2.50
2 . . . . 2.50
3 Andrew's Raid 2.50
4 Frank Miller(c) 2.50
5 final issue 2.50

MEDAL OF HONOR SPECIAL
1 JKu 2.50

MEZZ GALACTIC TOUR
1 MBn,MV 2.50

THE MINOTAUR'S TALE
TPB by Al Davison 11.95

MR. MONSTER
(B&W)
1	3.50
2	2.50
3 Alan Moore story	2.50
4	2.50
5 I:Monster Boy	2.00
6	2.00
7	2.00
8 V:Vampires (giant size)	4.95

MONKEYMAN & O'BRIEN
Legend
1 by Arthur Adams	2.95
2 and 3	@2.95
Spec.	2.95
TPB	16.95

MOTORHEAD
Comics Greatest World 1995
1 V:Predator	2.50
2 Laughing Wolf Carnival	2.50
3 V:Jackboot	2.50

MOTORHEAD SPECIAL
1 JLe(c),V:Mace Blitzkrieg	3.95

NEW FRONTIER
(B&W)
1 From series in Heavy Metal . . .	2.75
2 Who Killed Ruby Fields?	2.75
3 Conclusion	2.75

NEW TWO FISTED TALES: VOL II
1 War stories	4.95

Next Men #11 © Dark Horse Comics

[JOHN BYRNE'S]
NEXT MEN
0 Rep Next Men from Dark Horse Presents	5.00
1 JBy,'Breakout'inc.trading card	

certificate	7.00
1a 2nd Printing Blue	3.00
2 JBy,World View	5.00
3 JBy,A:Sathanis	4.00
4 JBy,A:Sathanis	4.00
5 JBy,A:Sathanis	4.00
6 JBy,O:Senator Hilltop, Sathanis,Project Next Men . . .	3.50
7 JBy,I:M-4,Next Men Powers explained	3.50
8 JBy,I:Omega Project,A:M-4 . . .	3.00
9 JBy,A:Omega Project,A:M-4 . . .	3.00
10 JBy,V:OmegaProject,A:M-4 . . .	3.00
11 JBy,V:OmegaProject,A:M-4 . . .	3.00
12 JBy,V:Dr.Jorgenson	3.00
13 JBy,Nathan vs Jack	3.00
14 JBy,I:Speedboy	2.75
15 JBy,in New York	2.75
16 JBy,Jasmine's Pregnant	2.75
17 FM(c),JBy,Arrested	2.75
18 JBy,On Trial	2.75
TPB rep.#1-6	16.95
TPB Parallel Collection	16.95

NEXT MEN: FAITH
Dark Horse-Legend 1993
1 JBy(a&s),V:Dr.Trogg, Blue Dahlia	3.25
2 JBy,(a&s),F:Jack	2.75
3 MMi(c),JBy(a&s),I:Hellboy . . .	3.50
4 JBy(a&s),Last issue	2.75
TPB Book Four	14.95

NEXT MEN: LIES
Dark Horse-Legend 1994
1 JBy	2.50
2 JBy	2.50
3 JBy	2.50
4 JBy	2.50
Book 6 TPB Lies	16.95

NEXT MEN: POWER
Dark Horse-Legend 1994
1 JBy(a&s)	2.75
2 JBy(a&s)	2.75
3 JBy(a&s)	2.75
4 JBY(a&s), final issue	2.50

NEXUS: ALIEN JUSTICE
1	4.25
2	4.25
3	3.95
TPB	16.95

NEXUS: EXECUTIONER'S SONG
1 (of 4) by Mike Baron, Steve Rude & Gary Martin	2.95
2 thru 4	@2.95

NEXUS: GOD CON
April 1997
1 (of 2) by Mike Baron, Steve Rude & Gary Martin	2.95
2	2.95

NEXUS: THE LIBERATOR
1 "Waking Dreams"	2.75
2 Civil War,D:Gigo	2.75
3 Civil War contd.	2.75
4 Last issue	2.75

NEXUS MEETS MADMAN
One-shot 2.95

NEXUS: NIGHTMARE IN BLUE
(B&W) July 1997
1 (of 4) by Mike Baron, Steve Rude & Gary Martin	2.95

NEXUS: THE ORIGIN
1 SR,O:Nexus	4.95

NEXUS: OUT OF THE VORTEX
1 R:Nexus	2.50
2 Zolot & Nexus Together	2.50
3 O:Vortex	2.50

NEXUS: THE WAGES OF SIN
1 The Client	2.95
2 V:Munson	2.95
3 SR(c&a) Murders in New Eden	2.95

NIGHT BEFORE CHRISTMASK
1 Rick Geary	9.95

NINA'S NEW AND IMPROVED ALL-TIME GREATEST
1 Anthology: Nina Paley	2.50

NINTH GLAND, THE
(B&W) March 1997
one-shot by Renee French 3.95

NOSFERATU
(B&W)
1 The Last Vampire	3.95
2	2.95

OH MY GODDESS!
B&W, Manga
1	5.00
2 and 3	@3.50
4 thru 6	@3.00
Part 2	
1 F:Keiichi	4.00
2 thru 8	@3.00
Part 3	
1 Wishes are Granted	4.00
2 Love Potion Number Nine	3.50
3 thru 11	@3.00

OH MY GODDESS!: MARA STRIKES BACK
(B&W) May 1997
1 (of 3) by Kosuke Fujishima . . .	2.95
2 & 3	@2.95

OH MY GODDESS!: 1-555-GODDESS
(B&W) Nov. 1996
TPB 12.95

OH MY GODDESS!: TERRIBLE MASTER URD
(B&W)
1 (of 6) by Kosuke Fujishima . . . 2.95
2 thru 6 . . . . @2.95

OH MY GODDESS!: THE QUEEN OF VENGEANCE
(B&W) April 1997
one-shot 2.95

OH MY GODDESS!: THE TRIALS OF MORISATO
(B&W) Jan. 1997
1 thru 3 by Kosuke Fujishima . @2.95

OH MY GODDESS: VALENTINE RHAPSODY
(B&W)
1 thru 5 (8 part mini-series) . . @2.95

OKTANE
1 R:Oktane 2.50
2 V:God Zero 2.50
3 V:God Zero 2.50
4 conclusion 2.50

ONE BAD RAT
1 BT 2.95
2 thru 4 . . . . @2.95

ONE-TRICK RIP-OFF
TPB by Paul Pope 12.95

ORION
(B&W)
1 SF manga-Masamune Shirow . 2.50
2 F:Yamata Empire 2.95
TPB 15.95

OTIS GOES HOLLYWOOD
(B&W) April 1997
1 (of 2) by Bob Fingerman 2.95
2 . . . . 2.95

OUTLANDERS
(B&W)
1 . . . . 3.00
2 . . . . 2.50
3 thru 7 . . . . @2.00
8 thru 20 . . . . @2.25
21 Operation Phoenix 2.25
22 thru 24 . . . . @2.50
25 thru 29 with 2-card strip . . . @2.50
30 . . . . 2.50
31 Tetsua dying 2.50
32 D:The Emperor 2.50
33 Story finale 2.50
#0 The Key of Graciale 2.75
TPB Vol. 1 . . . . 13.95
TPB Vol. 2 . . . . 13.95
TPB Vol. 3 . . . . 13.95
TPB Vol. 4 . . . . 12.95

OUTLANDERS: EPILOGUE
(B&W)
1 . . . . 2.75

OUT OF THE VORTEX
Comics' Greatest World 1993
1 B:JOs(s),V:Seekers 2.25
2 MMi(c),DaW,A:Seekers 2.25

Out of the Vortex #10
© Dark Horse Comics

3 WS(c),E:JOs(s),DaW,A:Seeker, C:Hero Zero 2.25
4 DaW,A:Catalyst 2.25
5 V:Destroyers,A:Grace 2.25
6 V:Destroyers,A:Hero Zero 2.25
7 AAd(c),DaW,V:Destroyers, A:Mecha 2.25
8 DaW,A:Motorhead 2.25
9 DaW,V:Motorhead 2.25
10 MZ(c), A:Division 13 . . . . 2.25
11 V:Reaver Swarm 2.50
12 Final issue 2.50

OZ
by Eric Shanower
TPB The Blue Witch of Oz 9.95
TPB The Forgotten Forest of Oz . 8.95
TPB The Ice King of Oz 8.95
TPB The Secret Island of Oz . . . 8.95

PETE & MOE VISIT PROFESSOR SWIZZLE'S ROBOTS
HC 14.95

PREDATOR
1 CW,Mini Series 10.00
1a 2ndPrinting 3.00
1b 3rdPrinting 2.50
2 CW 6.00
2a 2ndPrinting 3.00
3 CW 4.00
3a 2ndPrinting 2.50
4 CW 3.00
4a 2ndPrinting 2.50

PREDATOR: BAD BLOOD
1 CW,I:John Pulnick 2.75
2 CW,V:Predator 2.75

3 CW,V:Predator,C.I.A. 2.75
4 Last issue 2.50

PREDATOR: BIG GAME
1 Corp.Nakai Meets Predator . . . 4.00
2 Army Base Destroyed, with 2-card strip 3.50
3 Corp.Nakai Arrested, with 2-card strip 3.50
4 Nakai vs. Predator 3.50
TPB rep. #1–#4 . . . . 13.95

PREDATOR: BLOODY SANDS OF TIME
1 DBa,CW,Predator in WWI 4.00
2 DBa,CW, WWII cont'd. 3.25

PREDATOR: COLD WAR
1 Predator in Siberia 4.00
2 U.S. Elite Squad in Siberia . . . 3.25
3 U.S. vs. USSR commandos . . . 3.25
4 U.S. vs. USSR in Siberia 3.00
TPB 13.95
TPB 2nd printing 13.95

PREDATOR: CONCRETE JUNGLE
TPB 14.95

PREDATOR: DARK RIVER
1 thru 4 by Verheiden,RoR,RM @2.95

PREDATOR: HELL & HOT WATER
1 thru 3 MSh, GC & GWt . . . . @2.95

PREDATOR: INVADERS FROM THE FOURTH DIMENSION
1 . . . . 3.95

PREDATOR JUNGLE TALES
1 Rite of Passage 2.95

PREDATOR: KINDRED
1 . . . . 2.50
2 thru 4 . . . . @2.95

PREDATOR: PRIMAL
1 (of 2) by Kevin J. Anderson, Scott Kolins & John Lowe 2.95

PREDATOR: RACE WAR
0 F:Serial Killer 2.75
1 V:Serial Killer 2.75
2 D:Serial Killer 2.75
3 in Prison 2.75
4 Last Issue 2.75

PREDATOR: STRANGE ROUX
one-shot 2.95

PREDATOR 2
1 DBy, Movie Adapt Pt1 . . . . . . 3.50
2 MBr, Movie Adapt. Pt2 with 2-card strip 3.00

DARK HORSE

PREDATOR VS. MAGNUS ROBOT FIGHTER
Valiant/Dark Horse 1992
1 LW,A:Tekla	5.00
1a Platinum Ed.	8.00
1b Gold Ed.	5.00
2 LW,Magnus Vs. Predator, with 2-card strip	4.00
TPB Rep. #1–#2	7.95

PRIMAL
1 Contd.from Primal:from the Cradle to the Grave	2.95
2 A:TJ Cyrus	2.50

PRIMAL FROM THE CRADLE TO THE GRAVE
GN	9.95

PROPELLER MAN
1 I:Propeller Man	2.95
2 O:Propeller Man,w/2 card strip	2.95
3 V:Manipulator	2.95
4 V:State Police,w/2 card strip	2.95
5 V:Manipulator	2.95
6 V:Thing, w/2 card strip	2.95
7	2.95
8 Last issue,w/2 card strip	2.95

PUMPKINHEAD
1 Based on the movie	2.50

RACE OF SCORPIONS
(B&W)
1 A:Argos,Dito,Alma,Ka	2.25

RACE OF SCORPIONS
Book 1 short stories	5.00
Book 2	4.95
Book 3	2.50
Book 4 Final issue	2.50

RACK & PAIN
1 GCa(c),I:Rack,Pain	2.50
2 GCa(c),V:Web	2.50
3 GCa(c),V:Web	2.50
4 GCa(c),Final Issue	2.50

RASCALS IN PARADISE
1 I:Spicy Sanders	3.95
2	3.95
3 last issue	3.95
TPB Rep.#1–#3	16.95

REAL ADVENTURES OF JONNY QUEST, THE
Sept. 1996
1	2.95
3 thru 10	@2.95

REBEL SWORD
1 B&W	2.50
2 B&W	2.50
3 B&W	2.50
4 V:Ruken	2.50
5 Choice of Jiro	2.50
6 R:Ruken	2.50

REDBLADE
1 V:Demons	2.50

2 V:Tull	2.50
3 Last Issue	2.50

RING OF ROSES
(B&W)
1 Alternate world,1991	2.50
2 Plague in London	2.50
3 Plague cont.A:Secret Brotherhood of the Rosy Cross	2.50
4 Conclusion	2.50

RIO AT BAY
1 F:Doug Wildey art	2.95
2 F:Doug Wildey art	2.95
TPB	6.95

ROACHMILL
(B&W)
1 thru 8	@3.50
9 and 10	@2.00

Robocop: Mortal Coils #2
© Dark Horse Comics

ROBOCOP: MORTAL COILS
1 V:Gangs	2.75
2 V:Gangs	2.75
3 V:Coffin,V:Gangs	2.75

ROBOCOP VERSUS TERMINATOR
1 FM(s),WS,w/Robocop cut-out	3.50
2 FM(s),WS,w/Terminator cut-out	3.00
3 FM(s),WS,w/cut-out	3.00
4 FM(s),WS,Conclusion	3.00

ROBOCOP: PRIME SUSPECT
1 Robocop framed	2.75
2 thru 4 V:ZED-309s	@2.50
Collected	13.95

ROBOCOP: ROULETTE
1 V:ED-309s	2.75
2 I:Philo Drut	2.75
3 V:Stealthbot	2.75
4 last issue	2.75

ROBOCOP 3
1 B:StG(s),Movie Adapt	2.75
2 V:Aliens,OCP	2.75
3 HNg,ANi(i)	2.75

ROCKETEER ADVENTURE MAGAZINE
1988–95
1 and 2	@4.00
3	2.95
TPB Cliff's New York Adventure by Dave Stevens	9.95

THE SAFEST PLACE
SC, SD	2.50

SECRET OF THE SALAMANDER
(B&W)
1 Jacquestardi, rep	2.95

SERGIO ARAGONES' LOUDER THAN WORDS
(B&W) July 1997
1	2.95

SEX WARRIORS
1 I:Dakini	2.50
2 V:Steroids	2.50

THE SHADOW
1 MK	2.75
2 MK	2.50

THE SHADOW AND DOC SAVAGE
1	2.95
2 The Shrieking Skeletons	2.95

THE SHADOW: HELL'S HEAT WAVE
1 Racial War	2.95
2 MK,V:Ghost	2.95
3 Final issue	2.95

THE SHADOW: IN THE COILS OF LEVIATHAN
1 MK,V:Monster	3.25
2 MK	3.25
3 MK,w/ GfD poster	3.25
4 MK,Final issue	3.25
TPB, reprints #1–#4	13.95

THE SHADOW AND THE MYSTERIOUS 3
1 Three stories	2.95

SHADOW EMPIRE: FAITH CONQURES
1 CsM	2.95
2 CsM,V:Vaylen	2.95
3 CsM	2.95
4 CsM, final issue	2.95

SIN CITY: A DAME TO KILL FOR
Dark Horse-Legend (B&W)
1 FM(a&s),I:Dwight,Ava	6.00

DARK HORSE

All comics prices listed are for *Near Mint* condition.

DARK HORSE

1a 2nd printing 3.25
2 FM(a&s),A:Ava 4.00
2a 2nd printing 3.25
3 FM(a&s),D:Ava's Husband 4.00
3a 2nd printing 2.95
4 FM(a&s) 3.50
5 FM(a&s) 3.50
6 FM(a&s),Final issue 3.00
TPB rep. #1–#6, new pages . . 15.00
HC rep. #1–#6, new pages 25.00
HC signed, limited 90.00

SIN CITY:
A SMALL KILLING
Dark Horse-Legend
1 GN 14.00

SIN CITY:
SEX AND VIOLENCE
(B&W)
one-shot by Frank Miller 3.00

SIN CITY:
THAT YELLOW BASTARD
(B&W)
1 F.Miller 5.00
2 . . . . 4.00
3 thru 6 . . . . @3.00
TPB by Frank Miller 15.00
HC 25.00

SIN CITY:
THE BABE WORE RED
Dark Horse-Legend 1994
1 PM 3.50

SIN CITY:
THE BABE WORE RED
AND OTHER STORIES
(B&W) 1996
1-shot, some nudity 3.00

SIN CITY:
THE BIG FAT KILL
Dark Horse-Legend 1994
1 FM 5.00
2 FM 4.00
3 FM, Dump the Stiffs 3.50
4 FM, Town Without Pity 3.50
5 FM, final issue 3.50
TPB 15.00
HC 25.00

SIN CITY: SILENT NIGHT
Dark Horse-Legend
(B&W) 1995
1-Shot 2.95

SIN CITY:
THAT YELLOW BASTARD
1 thru 3 Frank Miller . . . . @2.95

SOLO
1 and 2 . . . . @.50

SPACEHAWK
(B&W)
1 BW reps. 2.25

---

2 thru 4 BW . . . . @2.00
5 BW 2.50

SPACE USAGI
1 thru 3 Stan Sakai . . . . @2.95

SPECIES
1 Alien Human Hybrid 2.50
2 thru 4 SIL . . . . @2.50

SPECIES: HUMAN RACE
1 PhH 2.95
2 . . . . 2.95
3 SBi 2.95
4 (of 4) 2.95
TPB 11.95

SPIRIT OF WONDER
(B&W)
1 thru 5 by Kenji Tsuruia . . . . @2.95

STAN SHAW'S
BEAUTY & THE BEAST
1 Based on the book 4.95

STARSTRUCK:THE
EXPANDING UNIVERSE
(B&W)
1 Pt1 . . . . 2.95
2 Pt2, with 2-card strip 2.95

STAR WARS:
A NEW HOPE—
SPECIAL EDITION
Jan. 1997
1 EB, AW 2.95
2 thru 4 . . . . @2.95
TPB Rep. #1–#4 Hildebrandt(c) . 9.95

STAR WARS:
BOBA FETT—
BOUNTY ON BAR-KOODA
1-shot 48pg 3.95

STAR WARS:
BOBA FETT—
LADY SWINGS
Sept. 1996
1-shot by John Wagner & CK . . 3.95

STAR WARS:
BOBA FETT—
TWIN ENGINES
OF DESTRUCTION
Jan. 1997
1-shot 2.95

STAR WARS:
DARK EMPIRE
1 CK,Destiny of a Jedi 35.00
1a 2nd Printing 5.00
1b Gold Ed. 35.00
2 CK,Destroyer of worlds, very low
　 print run 30.00
2a 2nd Printing 5.00
2b Gold Ed. 35.00
3 CK,V:The Emperor 20.00
3a 2nd printing 4.00

3b Gold Ed. 20.00
4 CK,V:The Emperor 15.00
4a Gold Ed. 20.00
5 CK,V:The Emperor 15.00
5a Gold Ed. 20.00
6 CK,V:Emperor,last issue 10.00
6a Gold Ed. 18.00
TPB Preview 32pg. 99
TPB rep.#1–#6 . . . . 19.95
TPB CK & Tom Veitch 2nd ed. . 17.95

STAR WARS
DARK EMPIRE II
1 2nd chapter 7.50
2 F:Boba Fett 4.00
3 V:Darksiders 4.00
4 Luke Vs. Darksiders 3.50
5 Creatures 3.50
6 CK,DvD(c), save the twins . . . 3.50
TPB CK & Tom Veitch rep.#1–#6 17.95

STAR WARS:
DARK FORCE RISING
May 1997
1 thru 3 (of 6) MBn,TyD,KN . . @2.95

STAR WARS:
DARK FORCES—
SOLDIER FOR
THE EMPIRE
HC by William C. Dietz and Dean
　 Williams 24.95

STAR WARS: DROIDS
1 F:C-3PO,R2-D2 . . . . 3.50
2 V:Thieves 2.75
3 on the Hosk moon 2.75
4 . . . . 2.75
5 A meeting 2.50
6 final issue 2.50
Spec.#1 I:Olag Greck 2.50
2nd Series
1 Deputized Droids 3.00
2 Marooned on Nar Shaddaa . . . 2.50
3 C-3PO to the Rescue 2.50
4 . . . . 2.50
5 Caretaker virus 2.50
6 Revolution 2.50
7 & 8 . . . . @2.50
TPB 17.95

STAR WARS:
EMPIRE'S END
1 R:Emperor Palpatine 2.95
2 conclusion 2.95

STAR WARS:
HEIR TO THE EMPIRE
1 I:Grand Admiral Thrawn 2.95
2 thru 6 . . . . 2.95
TPB from novel by Timothy Zahn 19.95

STAR WARS:
JABBA THE HUTT
1 F:Jabba the Hutt 2.50

STAR WARS:
JABBA THE HUTT—
DYNASTY TRAP
1 V: Cabrool Nuumt 2.50

STAR WARS: JABBA THE HUTT—THE HUNGER OF PRINCESS NAMPI
1 Wheel and Deal 2.50

STAR WARS: RETURN OF THE JEDI—SPECIAL EDITION
TPB Hildebrandt(c) 9.95

STAR WARS: RIVER OF CHAOS
1 LSi,JBr,Emperor sends spies . . 2.50
2 Imperial in Allies Clothing 2.50
3 . . . . 2.50
4 F:Ranulf 2.50

STAR WARS: SHADOWS OF THE EMPIRE
1 (of 6) by John Wagner, Kilian
   Plunkett & P. Craig Russell . . 2.95
2 thru 6 . . . . @2.95
TPB 17.95

STAR WARS: SPLINTER OF THE MIND'S EYE
1 thru 4 A.D.Foster novel adapt. @2.95
TPB 14.95

STAR WARS: TALES FROM MOS EISLEY
1-shot, from Star Wars Galaxy Mag.
#2–#4 . . . . 2.95

STAR WARS: TALES OF THE JEDI
1 RV,I:Ulic Qel-Droma 7.00
2 RV,A:Ulic Qel-Droma 6.00
3 RV,D:Andur 4.00
4 RV,A:Jabba the Hut 3.50
5 RV,last issue 3.50
TPB 14.95
TPB 2nd printing 14.95

STAR WARS: TALES OF THE JEDI: DARK LORDS OF THE SITH
1 Bagged with card 3.00
2 . . . . 2.50
3 Krath Attack 2.50
4 F:Exar Kun 2.50
5 V:TehKrath 2.50
6 Final battle 2.50
TPB 17.95

STAR WARS: TALES OF THE JEDI: THE FREEDON NADD UPRISING
1 . . . . 2.75
2 . . . . 2.50

STAR WARS: TALES OF THE JEDI: THE SITH WAR
1 F:Exar Kun 2.50
2 F:Ulic Oel-Droma 2.50
3 F:Exar Kun 2.50
4 thru 6 (6 part mini-series) . . @2.50
TPB 17.95

STAR WARS: TALES OF THE JEDI—THE FALL OF THE SITH EMPIRE
June 1997
1 (of 5) 2.95
2 (of 5) 2.95

STAR WARS: TALES OF THE JEDI—THE GOLDEN AGE OF THE SITH
Oct. 1996
1 thru 5 . . . . @2.95
TPB 16.95

STAR WARS: THE EMPIRE STRIKES BACK
TPB Hildebrandt(c) 9.95

Star Wars: X-Wing Rogue Squadron: #4
© Dark Horse Comics

STAR WARS: X-WING ROGUE SQUADRON
1 F:Wedge 4.00
2 . . . . 3.00
3 F:Tycho Clehu 3.00
4 F:Tycho Clehu 3.00
5 thru 12 . . . . @3.00

STAR WARS: X-WING ROGUE SQUADRON— BATTLEGROUND: TATOOINE
1 thru 4 . . . . @3.00

STAR WARS: X-WING ROGUE SQUADRON— REQUIEM FOR A ROGUE
April 1997
1 . . . . 3.00
2 thru 4 concl. . . . . @3.00

STAR WARS: X-WING ROGUE SQUADRON: THE PHANTOM AFFAIR
1 thru 4 (4-part mini-series) . . @3.00

STAR WARS: X-WING ROGUE SQUADRON— THE WARRIOR PRINCESS
1 (of 4) 3.00
2 thru 4 . . . . @3.00

STARSHIP TROOPERS: INSECT TOUCH
1 by Warren Ellis & Paolo Parente 2.95
2 and 3 (of 3) . . . . @2.95

SUPERMAN/MADMAN HULLABALOO
June 1997
1 (of 3) by Mike Allred 2.95
2 (of 3) 2.95

SUPERMAN VS. ALIENS
DC/Dark Horse
1 DJu,KN 7.00
2 V:Queen Alien 6.00
TPB 14.95

TALE OF ONE BAD RAT
1 BT 2.95
2 thru 4 . . . . 2.95
TPB Rep.#1–#4 . . . . 14.95

TALES OF ORDINARY MADNESS
(B&W)
1 JBo(c),Paranoid 3.00
2 JBo(c),Mood 2.50
3 JBo(c),A Little Bit of Neurosis . 2.50

TALES TO OFFEND
July 1997
one-shot by Frank Miller 2.95

TANK GIRL
(B&W) 1991
1 Rep. from U.K.Deadline Mag. with
   2-card strip 5.00
2 V:Indiana Potato Jones 4.00
3 On the Run 3.00
4 . . . . 3.00
TPB colorized 14.95
[2nd Series]
1 . . . . 3.50
2 . . . . 3.00
3 and 4 . . . . @3.00

TANK GIRL
1 and 2 . . . . @3.00

TARZAN/JOHN CARTER: WARLORDS OF MARS
1 thru 4 E.R.Burroughs adapt. @2.50

TARZAN VS. PREDATOR AT THE EARTH'S CORE
1 Tarzan vs. Predator 2.50
2 V:Predator 2.50

DARK HORSE

---

3 Tarzan on the Hunt 2.50
4 . . . . 2.50

TERMINAL POINT
1 . . . . 2.50
2 . . . . 2.50

TERMINATOR
1 CW,Tempest 5.00
2 CW,Tempest 4.00
3 CW 3.00
4 CW, conclusion 3.00

Terminator: End Game #3
© Dark Horse Comics

TERMINATOR:
END GAME
1 JG,Final *Terminator* series . . 3.00
2 JG,Cont.last Term.story 2.75
3 JG,(Conclusion of Dark Horse
  Terminator stories) 2.75

TERMINATOR:
ENEMY WITHIN
1 cont. from Sec.Objectives . . . 4.00
2 C890.L.threat contd. 3.00
3 Secrets of Cyberdyne 3.00
4 Conclusion 3.00
SC rep #1–#4 . . . . 13.95

TERMINATOR: HUNTERS
& KILLERS
1 V:Russians 3.00
2 V:Russians 2.75
3 V:Russians 2.75

TERMINATOR:
ONE SHOT
1 MW,3-D const(c2,pop-up inside 7.00

TERMINATOR:
SECONDARY
OBJECTIVES
1 cont. 1st DH mini-series 4.00

2 PG,A:New Female Terminator . 3.00
3 PG,Terminators in L.A.&Mexico 3.00
4 PG,Terminator vs Terminator
  concl. 3.00

TEX AVERY'S DROOPY
1 Dr. Droopenstein 3.00
2 & 3 . . . . @2.50

TEX AVERY'S
SCREWBALL SQUIRREL
1 I:Screwball Squirrel 2.50
2 Cleaning House 2.50
3 School of Hard Rocks 2.50

THING, THE
1 JHi, Movie adaptation 5.00
2 JHi, Movie adaptation 3.50

THE THING: COLD FEAR
1 R:Thing 3.00
2 . . . . 2.75

THING FROM
ANOTHER WORLD:
CLIMATE OF FEAR
1 Argentinian Military Base
  (Bahiathetis) 2.75
2 Thing on Base 2.75
3 Thing/takeover 2.75
4 Conclusion 2.75
TPB 15.95

THING FROM
ANOTHER WORLD:
ETERNAL VOWS
1 PG,I:Sgt. Rowan 2.75
2 PG 2.75
3 PG,in New Zealand 2.75
4 PG,Last issue 2.75

THIRTEEN O'CLOCK
(B&W)
1 Mr.Murmer,from Deadline USA 2.95

3 X 3 EYES
(B&W)
1 I:Pai,Yakumo, (Manga) 2.95
2 & 3 (5-part mini-series) . . . . @2.95
TPB Curse of the Gesu, by Yuzo
  Takada 12.95

TIME COP
1 Movie Adaptation 2.75
2 Movie Adaptation 2.50

TITAN
Spec.#1 BS(c),I:Inhibitors 4.25

TONGUE*LASH
Aug. 1996
1 by Randy and Jean-Marc Lofficier
  & Dave Taylor 2.95
2 . . . . 2.95

TOO MUCH COFFEE MAN
(B&W) July 1997
one-shot by Shannon Wheeler . . . 2.95

TREKKER
(B&W)
1 thru 4 . . . . @1.50
5 thru 7 . . . . @1.75
8 O:Trekker 1.50
9 . . . . 1.50

TREKKER
1 . . . . 2.95

TRIPLE•X
(B&W)
TPB by Arnold & Jacob Pander . 24.95

TWO FISTED TALES
Spec. WW,WiS 4.95

2112
GN JBy,A:Next Men 2.00
2nd Printing 10.00
TPB GNv, JBy,A:Next Men . . . 17.00
2nd printing 9.95
3rd printing 9.95

[ANDREW VACHSS']
UNDERGROUND
(B&W)
1 AVs(s) 4.25
2 thru 4 AVs(s) . . . . @3.95

UNIVERSAL MONSTERS
1 AAd,Creature From The Black
  Lagoon 5.50
2 The Mummy 5.50

USAGI YOJIMBO
(B&W)
1 by Stan Sakai 2.95
2 thru 9 . . . . 2.95
10 with Sergio Aragones 2.95
11 "The Lord of Owls" 2.95
12 "Vampire Cat of the Geishu" . . 2.95

USAGI YOJIMBO
1996
1 SS,color spec 4.00
2 SS,color spec. 3.00
3 SS,color spec. 3.00
4 thru 6 . . . . @3.00

USAGI YOJIMBO
COLOR SPECIAL:
GREEN PERSIMMON
one-shot by Stan Sakai 2.95

VAMPIRELLA
(B&W)
1 'The Lion and the Lizard'Pt.1 . . 4.50
2 'The Lion and the Lizard'Pt.2 . . 3.95
3 'The Lion and the Lizard'Pt.3 . . 3.95
4 'The Lion and the Lizard'Pt.3 . . 3.95

VENUS WARS
(B&W)
1 Aphrodia V:Ishtar, with 2-card
  strip 3.00
2 I: Ken Seno 2.50
3 Aphrodia V:Ishtar 2.50
4 Seno Joins Hound Corps. 2.50
5 SenoV:Octopus Supertanks . . . 2.50

  All comics prices listed are for *Near Mint* condition.

DARK HORSE

6 Chaos in Aphrodia 2.50
7 All Out Ground War 2.50
8 Ishtar V:Aphrodia contd. 2.50
9 Ishtar V:Aphrodia contd. 2.50
10 Supertanks of Ishtar Advance . 2.50
11 Aphrodia Captured 2.50
12 A:Miranda,48pgs 2.75
13 Hound Brigade-Suicide Assault 2.25
14 V:Army 2.50
15 . . . . 2.50
TPB Vol. 1 . . . . 13.95

VENUS WARS II
1 V:Security Police 2.75
2 Political Unrest 2.25
3 Conspiracy 2.25
4 A:Lupica 2.25
5 Love Hotel 2.25
6 Terran Consulate 2.25
7 Doublecross 2.25
8 D:Lupisa 2.95
9 A:Matthew 2.95
10 A:Mad Scientist 2.95
11 thru 15 V:Troopers . . . . @2.95

VIRUS
1 MP(c),F:The Wan Xuan & the
   crew of the Electra 3.00
2 MP(c),V:Captian Powell 3.00
3 MP(c),V:Virus 3.00
4 MP(c),Last issue 3.00
TPB rep.#1–#4 . . . . 16.95

VERSION
(B&W)
1.1 thru 2.6 by H. Sakaguchi . . . 2.75
2.7 by H. Sakaguchi 2.50

VORTEX, THE
1 . . . . 2.00

WALTER:
CAMPAIGN OF TERROR
1 thru 3 . . . . @2.50

WARRIOR OF
WAVERLY STREET, THE
Nov. 1996
1 (of 2) by Manny Coto and John
   Stokes 2.95

WARRIOR OF WAVERLY
STREET, THE:
BROODSTORM
March 1997
1-shot Manny Coto & John Stokes 2.95

WARWORLD!
(B&W)
1 . . . . 1.75

WHAT'S MICHAEL?
(B&W)
TPB by Makoto Kobayashi 5.95

WHAT'S MICHAEL?—
LIVING TOGETHER
(B&W)
TPB by Makoto Kobayashi 5.95

WHITE LIKE SHE
(B&W)
1 thru 4 by Bob Fingerman 2.95

Will to Power #8 © Dark Horse Comics

WILL TO POWER
Comics' Greatest World 1994
1 BS, A:X 1.25
2 BS, A:X,Monster 1.25
3 BS, A:X 1.25
4 BS, In Steel Harbor 1.25
5 V:Wolfgang 1.00
6 V:Motorhead 1.00
7 JOy(c),V:Amazing Grace 1.00
8 V:Catalyst 1.00
9 Titan, Grace 1.00
10 Vortex alien, Grace 1.00
11 Vortex alien, King Titan 1.00
12 Vortex alien 1.00

WIZARD OF
FOURTH STREET
(B&W)
1 thru 4 . . . . @1.75

WOLF & RED
1 Looney Tunes 2.50
2 Watchdog Wolf 2.50
3 Red Hot Riding Hood 2.50

WOLVERTON IN SPACE
(B&W) April 1997
TPB by Basil Wolverton 16.95

X
Comics' Greatest World 1994
1 B:StG(s),DoM,JP,I:X-Killer 3.00
2 DoM,JP,V:X-Killer 2.25
3 DoM,JP,A:Pit Bulls 2.25
4 DoM,JP 2.25
5 DoM,JP,V:Chaos Riders 2.00
6 Cyberassassins 2.00
7 Alamout 2.00
8 A:Ghost 2.50
9 War for Arcadia 2.50
10 War for Arcadia 2.50
11 I:Coffin, War 2.50

X #4 © Dark Horse Comics

12 V:Coffin, A:Monster 2.50
13 D:X 2.50
14 conclusion to War 2.50
15 JS,SiG,war survivors 2.50
16 V:Headhunter 2.50
17 . . . . 2.50
18 V:Predator 2.50
19 V:Challenge 2.50
20 thru 24 . . . . @2.50

X: ONE SHOT
TO THE HEAD
1 . . . . 2.50

XXX
1 . . . . 3.95
2 V:Dr. Zemph 3.95
3 . . . . 3.95
4 V:Rhine Lords 3.95
5 I:Klaar 3.95
6 Klaar captured 4.95
7 Revolution Consequences 4.95

YOUNG CYNICS CLUB
(B&W)
1 . . . . 2.50

THE YOUNG INDIANA
JONES CHRONICLES
1 DBa,FS,TV Movie Adapt 3.25
2 DBa,TV Movie Adapt 2.75
3 thru 5 DBa,GM . . . . @2.75
6 BBa,GM,WW1,French Army . . 2.75
7 The Congo 2.75
8 Africa,A:A.Schweitzer 2.50
9 Vienna,Sophie-daughter of Arch-
   Duke Ferdinand 2.50
10 In Vienna continued 2.50
11 Far East 2.50
12 Fever Issue 2.50

YOU'RE UNDER ARREST!
(B&W) 1995–96
1 thru 8 (mini-series) . . . . . . @2.95

DARK HORSE

IMAGE

AARON STRIPS
Image April 1997
(B&W) by Aaron Warner
1 & 2 from Sunday comic strips @2.95

ADVENTURES OF AARON
Image March 1997
(B&W) by Aaron Warner
1 "Baby-sitter Gone Bad" 2.95
2 "Thunder Thighs of the
Terrordome" 2.95
100 Super Special 2.95

AGE OF HEROES, THE
Image/Halloween 1996
(B&W)
1 JHl & JRy 2.95
2 JHl & JRy 5.95
3 JHl & JRy,Luko,Trickster &
Aerwyn try to steal treasure of
the gods 2.95
4 JHl & JRy,Drake, the blind
swordsman returns 2.95
Spec. #1 rep. #1 & #2 . . . . 4.95

ALLEGRA
Image/Wildstorm 1996
1 ScC,SSe 2.50
2 thru 4 . . . . @2.50

ALLIANCE, THE
Image/Shadowline 1995
1 I:The Alliance 2.50
1a variant cover 2.50
2 Team Comes Together 2.50
2a variant cover 2.50
3 I:Slash C 2.50
3a variant cover 2.50
4 . . . . 2.50
4a variant cover 2.50

ALLIES, THE
Image/Extreme 1995
1 thru 4 mini-series . . . . @2.50

AMANDA AND GUNN
Image April 1997
(B&W)
1 JeR, Montana 2036 . . . . 2.95
2 (of 4) JeR 2.95

ANGELA
Image/TMP 1994–95
1 NGa(s),GCa,A:Spawn 10.00
2 NGa(s),GCa,Angela's trial . . 5.00
3 NGa(s),GCa,In Hell 4.00
Spec. Pirate Spawn(c) 20.00
Spec. Pirate Angela(c) 25.00
TPB Rep.#1–#3 . . . . 9.95

ANGELA/GLORY:
RAGE OF ANGELS
Image/TMP/Extreme 1996
1 x-over begins 2.50

ARCANUM
Image/Top Cow March 1997
Mini-series
1 BPe, from Medieval
Spawn/Witchblade 2.50
1a variant MS(s) (1:4) 2.50
2 BPe, Chi in Asylum 2.50
3 BPe, Ming Chang captive in
Atlantis 2.50
4 BPe, "The End?" 2.50

ART OF ERIK LARSEN
1 Sketchbook 4.95

ART OF
HOMAGE STUDIOS
1 Various Pin-ups,All Homage
Artists 4.95

Backlash #11 © Image/Wildstorm

BACKLASH
Image/Wildstorm 1994
1 Taboo, 2 diff. covers 5.00
1a variant edition, 2 covers 4.00
2 Savage Dragon 2.50
3 V:Savage Dragon 2.50
4 SRf,A:Wetworks 2.50
5 SRf,A:Dane 2.50
6 BBh,SRf,A:Wetworks 2.50
7 BBh,SRf,V:Bounty Hunters . . . 2.50
8 RMz,BBh,BWS(c),WildStorm
Rising,pt.8,w/2 cards 2.50
8a Newsstand ed. 1.95
9 F:Dingo,V:Chasers 2.50
10 I:Crimson 2.50
11 R:Bloodmoon 2.50
12 R:Taboo, Crimson's Costume . 3.00
13 Taboo to the Rescue 2.50
14 A:Deathblow 2.50
15 F:Cyberjack 2.50
16 thru 18 . . . . @2.50
19 Fire From Heaven,pt.2 . . . . . . 2.50
20 SRf,BBh 2.50

21 SRf,BBh 2.50
22 SRf,BBh 2.50
23 SRf,BBh 2.50
24 SRf,BBh,return of Dingo 2.50
25 SRf,BBh,56pg. special 4.00
26 SRf,BBh,Gramalkin identity
revealed 2.50
27 SRf,BBh, ... 2.50
28 SRf,BBh,Backlash leads PSI
team to Europe 2.50
29 SRf,BBh,Haroth raises the
remnants of Atlantis 2.50
30 SRf,BBh,Backlash confronts
Kherubim lords 2.50
31 SRf,BBh,team returns to PSI . . 2.50
32 SRf,BBh,earth-shattering final
issue 2.50
TPB Backlash/Spider-Man, Webs &
Whips, crossover 4.95

BACKLASH/SPIDER-MAN
Image/Wildstorm/Marvel 1996
1 . . . . 2.50
1a variant cover 3.00
2 . . . . 2.50

BADGER
Image May 1997
(B&W)
1 MBn, the Badger returns in
"Betelgeuse 2.95
2 MBn, "Beefalo don't like fences" 2.95
3 MBn, "Loose Eel" 2.95

BADROCK
Image/Extreme 1995
1a RLd(p),TM(c), A:Dragon 1.75
1b SPa(ic),A:Savage Dragon . . . 1.75
1c DF(ic) 1.75
2 RLd,ErS(s),V:Girth,A:Savage
Dragon 2.50
3 RLd,ErS,V:The Overlord 2.50
Ann.#1 I:Gunner 2.95
Super-Spec. #1 A:Grifter & The
Dragon 2.50

BADROCK
AND COMPANY
Image/Extreme 1994–95
1 KG(s), ... 2.50
1a San Diego Comic Con Ed. . . . 5.00
2 RLd(c),Fuji 2.50
3 Overtkill 2.50
4 TBm,MBm,TNu,A:Velocity . . . 2.50
5 A:Grifter 2.50
6 Finale, A:ShadowHawk 2.50

BALLISTIC
Image/Top Cow 1995
1 A:Wetworks 2.50
2 Jesters Transformation 2.50
3 final issue 2.50

BALLISTIC ACTION
Image/Top Cow 1996
1 MSi(c) pin-ups 2.95

BALLISTIC IMAGERY
Image/Top Cow 1995
1 anthology 2.50

BALLISTIC/WOLVERINE
Image/Top Cow 1996
1 Devil's Reign, pt.4 . . . . 4.00

BATTLESTONE
Image/Extreme 1994
1 New Series 2.50
1a variant cover 5.00
2 RLd,ErS,MMy,AV,I&D:Roarke,
finale 2.50

BEETLEBORGS
Image/Extreme Nov. 1996
1 from TV show 2.50

BERZERKERS
Image/Extreme 1995
1 From Youngblood #2 . . . . 2.50
2 Escape from Darkthorne 2.50
3 In the Darklands 2.50
4 final issue 2.50

BIG BANG COMICS
Image/Big Bang Studios 1996
(B&W) Prev. Caliber
1 F:Mighty Man 2.00
2 Silver Age Shadowhawk 2.00
3 . . . . 2.00
4 . . . . 2.50
5 Top Secret Origins 2.95
6 Round Table of America and
Knights of Justice meet, orig.
mini-series #3 (color) 2.95
7 . . . . 2.95
8 F:Mister U.S. 2.95
9 I:Peter Chefren 2.95
10 F:Galahad 2.95
11 Faulty Towers is destroying
Midway City 2.95
12 F:The Savage Dragon 2.95
13 by Jeff Weigel, 40pg spec. . . . 2.95

BLACK AND WHITE
Image/Hack Studios 1996
1 New heroes 1.95
2 ATi(p),apparent death 1.95
3 V:Chang 1.95
Ashcan 5.00

BLACK ANVIL
Image/Top Cow 1996
1 & 2 . . . . 2.50

BLACK FLAG
Image/Extreme 1994
1 B&W Preview 3.00

BLACK OPS
Image/Wildstorm 1996
1 thru 5 . . . . @2.50
TPB 14.95

BLINDSIDE
Image/Extreme Aug. 1996
1 MMy & AV, F:Nucgaek Jeno . . 2.50
2 MMy & AV, Origin continues . . 2.50

BLISS ALLEY
Image (B&W) July 1997
1 BML 2.95

BLOODHUNTER
Image/Extreme Nov. 1996
1 RV, Cabbot Stone rises from the
slab 2.95

BLOODPOOL
Image/Exteme 1995
1 I:Seoul,Rubbe,Wylder 2.50
1a variant cover 2.50
2 New Neighborhood 2.50
3 The Mummy's Curse 2.50
4 final issue 2.50
TPB Rep. #1-#4 . . . . 12.95
[Regular Series] 1996
1 thru 3 JDy . . . . @2.50

Bloodstrike #18 © Rob Liefeld

BLOODSTRIKE
Image/Extreme 1993
1 A:Brigade,Rub the Blood(c) . . . 3.50
2 V:Brigade,B:BU:Knight 2.50
3 B:ErS(s),ATi(c),V:Coldsnap . . . 2.25
4 ErS(s), ... 2.25
5 KG,A:Supreme, ... 2.25
6 KG(s),CAx,C&J:Chapel 2.25
7 KG,RHe,A:Badrock 2.25
8 RHe,A:Spawn 2.25
9 RHe,Extreme Prejudice #3,
I:Extreme Warrior,ATh,BU: Black
& White 2.25
10 V:Brigade, B:BU:Knight 1.95
25 I:Cabbot Bloodstrike 2.50
11 ErS(s),ATi(c),V:Coldsnap 1.95
12 ErS(s) 1.95
13 KG,A:Supreme 2.50
14 KG(s),CAx,C&J:Chapel 2.50
15 KG,RHe,A:Badrock 1.95
16 KG,RHe 1.95
17 KIA,V:The Horde 2.50
18 ExtremeSacrifice x-over,pt.2 . . 2.50
19 V:The Horde 2.50
20 R:Deadlock New Order 2.50
21 KA,V:Epiphany New Order . . . 2.50
22 V:The Horde, last issue 2.50

25 see above, after #10
Ashcan 5.00

BLOODSTRIKE: ASSASSIN
Image/Extreme 1995
0 R:Battlestone 2.50
1 Debut new series 2.50
1a alternate cover 2.50
2 V:M.D.K. Assassins 2.50
3 V:Persuasion 2.50

BLOODWULF
[Miniseries]
1 RLd,R:Bloodwulf 2.50
1b Run OJ Run 2.50
1c Alternate cover 2.50
1d Alternate cover 2.50
2 A:Hot Blood 2.50
3 Slippery When Wet 2.50
4 final issue 2.50
Spec.#1 V:Supreme Freeferall . . . 2.50

BODY COUNT
1 & 2 . . . . @2.50

BONE
(B & W)
[Previously by Cartoon Books]
21 thru 25 . . . . @2.95
26 The Turning 2.95
27 end of dragonslayer storyline . 2.95
Bone Sourcebook 25
HC#1 Out of Boneville, rep. 19.95
HC#2 The Great Cow Race, rep. 19.95
HC#3 Gran'ma's Story, rep. . . . 19.95
Image reprints with new covers
#1 thru 9 . . . . @2.95
10 rep. "Great Cow Race" 2.95
Image/Cartoon Books
11 Aftermath of the Great Cow
Race 2.95
12 . . . . 2.95
13 Thar she blows 2.95
14 . . . . 2.95
15 Double or nothing 2.95
16 hiding from the Rat Creatures . 2.95
17 with 5 new pages 2.95
18 Betrayed 2.95
19 three cheers for dragon-slayer
Phoney Bone 2.95
20 Phoney Bone vs. Lucius 2.95

BOOF
1 . . . . 1.95
2 Meathook 1.95
3 Joyride 1.95
4 Beach 1.95
5 Down on the Farm 1.95
6 V:Gangster Chimps 1.95

BOOF AND THE BRUISE CREW
1 thru 4 . . . . @1.95
5 Supermarket 1.95
6 I:Mortar, O:Bruise Crew 1.95

BRASS
Image/Wildstorm
1 Rib,AWa,Folio Edition 4.50
2 Rib,AWa, ... 2.50
3 Rib,AWa,concl. 2.50

Brigade #10 © Rob Liefeld

BRIGADE
Image/Extreme 1993
[1st Series]

1 RLd(s),MMy,I:Brigade	3.50
1a Gold Ed.	7.00
2 RLd(s),V:Genocide,w/coupon#4	5.00
2a w/o coupon	1.00
2b Gold Ed.	10.00
3 V:Genocide	2.00
4 CyP,Youngblood#5 flip	2.00

[2nd Series]

0 RLd(s),ATi(c),JMs,NRd,I:Warcry, A:Emp,V:Youngblood	2.25
1 V:Bloodstrike	2.75
1a Gold Ed.	6.00
2 C:Coldsnap	3.50
3 ErS(s),GP(c),MMy,NRd(i), V:Bloodstrike	2.25
4 Rip(s),MMy,RHe,I:Roman, BU:Lethal	2.25
5 Rip(s),MMy,	2.25
6 Rip(s),MMy,I:Coral,BU:Hackers Tale	2.25
7 Rip(s),MMy,V:Worlok	2.25
8 ErS(s),MMy,Extreme Prejudice #2,BU:Black & White	2.25
9 ErS(s),MMy,Extreme Prejudice #6,ATh,BU:Black & White	2.25
25 ErS(s),MMy,D:Kayo,Coldsnap, Thermal,	2.25
26 Images of Tomorrow	2.25
10 Extreme Prejudice	1.95
11 WildC.A.T.S	2.50
12 Battlestone	2.50
13 Thermal	1.95
14 Teamate deaths	1.95
15 MWm,R:Roman Birds of Prey	1.95
16 ExtremeSacrifice x-over,pt.3	2.50
17 MWn,I:New Team	2.50
18 I:The Shape New Order	2.50
19 MWn,F:Troll	2.50
20 MWn,alien cult saga,concl.	2.50
21 F:ShadowHawk	2.50
22 F:Brigade Team	2.50
23 & 24	@2.50
25 & 26 see above	
27 Extreme Babewatch	2.50
Sourcebook	2.95

CASUAL HEROES

1 thru 5	@2.50

CELESTINE
Image/Extreme 1996

1	2.50
2	2.50

CHAPEL
Image/Extreme 1995

1 BWn,F:Chapel	3.50
2 V:Colonel Black	3.00
2a variant cover	2.50

[Regular Series]

1 BWn,F:Chapel	2.50
1a variant cover	2.50
2 V:Giger	2.50
3 V:Giger	2.50
4 Extreme Babewatch	2.50
5 Hell on Earth,pt.1	2.50
6 Hell on Earth,pt.2	2.50
7 Shadowhunt x-over,pt.2	2.50

CODENAME: STYKE FORCE
Image/Top Cow 1994

1A MS(s),BPe,JRu(i),	3.50
1B Gold Embossed Cover	12.00
1C Blue Embossed Cover	18.00
2 MS(s),BPe,JRu(i),	2.50
3 MS(s),BPe,JRu(i),	2.50
4 MS(s),BPe,JRu(i),	2.50
5 MS(s),BPe,JRu(i),	2.50
6 MS(s),BPe,JRu(i),	2.25
7 MS(s),BPe,JRu(i),	2.25
8A Cyblade poster (Tucci)	4.00
8B Shi poster (Silvestri)	4.00
8C Tempest poster (Tan)	2.25
9 New Teamate	2.25
10 SvG, B:New Adventure	2.25
11 F:Bloodbow	1.95
12 F:Stryker	1.95
13 SvG(s),F:Strkyer	2.25
14 New Jobs	2.25
Spec.#0 O:Stryke Force	2.50
TPB Rep. Death's Angel Saga	9.95

Crush #1 © Motown Machineworks

COMBAT

1	2.50

CRUSH, THE
Image/Motown Jan. 1996

1 thru 5 mini-series	@2.50

CRYPT
Image/Extreme 1995

1 A:Prophet	2.50
1a Variant cover	2.50
2 A:Prophet	2.50

CURSE OF THE SPAWN
Image/TMP Sept. 1996

1 DT,DaM,F:Daniel Lianso	3.50
2 DT,DaM,Dark Future, Pt. 2: Blood Lust	2.50
3 DT,DaM,Dark Future, Pt. 3: Corpse Candles	1.95
4 DT,DaM,	1.95
5 DT,DaM,Sam & Twitch search for Gretchen Culver	1.95
6 DT,DaM,Sam & Twitch pursue Suture	1.95
7 DT,DaM,Suture is captured	1.95
8 DT,DaM,Suture escapes police custody	1.95
9 DT,DaM,Angela's secret origin	1.95
10 DT,DaM,Angela, Spawn Slayer	1.95
11 DT,DaM,Angela's story, concl.	1.95

CYBERFORCE
Image/Top Cow
[Limited Series] 1992–93

0 WS,O:Cyber Force	2.50
1 MS,I:Cyberforce,w/coupon#3	6.00
1a w/o coupon	3.00
2 MS,V:C.O.P.S.	3.50
3 MS	2.50
4 MS,V:C.O.P.S,BU:Codename Styke Force.	2.50
TPB Rep. mini-series	12.95

[Regular Series] 1993

1 EcS(s),MS,SW,	2.50
1B Gold Foil Logo	10.00
2 EcS(s),MS,SW,Killer Instinct #2,A:Warblade	2.25
2B Silver Embossed Cover	12.00
3 EcS(s),MS,SW,Killer Instinct #4, A:WildC.A.T.S.	2.25
3B Gold Embossed Cover	12.00
4 EcS(s),MS,Ballistic	2.00
5 EcS(s),MS	2.00
6 EcS(s),MS,Ballistic's Past	2.00
7 S.H.O.C.s	2.00
8	2.50
9 A:Huntsman	2.00
10 A:Huntsman	2.00
10 A Alternate Cover	4.00
10B Silver Seal Oz-Con 500c	20.00
11	2.00
12 T.I.M.M.I.E. goes wild	2.00
13 EcS,MS,O:Cyberdata	2.25
14 EcS,MSI,V:T.I.M.M.I.E.	2.25
15 New Cyberdata Threat	2.25
16 O:Ripclaw	2.25
17 Regrouping	2.25
18 thru 25	@2.50
26 KWo	2.50
27 F:Ash	2.50
27a variant cover by JQ&JP (1:4)	4.00

Top Cow 1996

IMAGE

28 A:Gabriel	2.50
29	2.50
30 ScL,"Devil's Reign" tie-in	2.50
31 The team in conflict	2.50
32 Cyblade leads rejuvenated team	2.50
33 KWo, Cheleene in midst of civil war	2.50
34 KWo,Royal Blood, pt.3	2.50
35	2.50
Ashcan 1 (San Diego)	8.00
Ashcan 1 (signed)	12.00
Sourcebook 1	2.50
Sourcebook 2 I:W.Zero	2.50
Ann.#1 O:Velocity	2.50
Ann.#2	2.95
TPB new art	12.95
TPB EcS,MS,SW,Assault with a Deadly Woman	9.95

CYBERFORCE/ CODENAME STRYKEFORCE: OPPOSING FORCES

1 V:Dangerous Threat	2.50
2 Team Vs. Team	2.50

CYBERFORCE ORIGINS
Image/Top Cow 1995

1 O:Cyblade	2.50
1B Gold Seal 1000c	12.00
2 O:Stryker	2.50
3 O:Impact	2.50
4 Misery	3.00

CYBERFORCE UNIVERSE SOURCEBOOK
Image/Top Cow 1994–95

1 and 2	@2.50

CYBERNARY
Image/Wildstorm 1995–96

1 thru 5 mini-series	@2.50

CYBERPUNX
Image/Extreme 1996

1 & 2	@2.50
3 RLe & Ching Lau,F:Drake	2.50

DAMNED
Image/Homage June 1997

1 (of 4) StG, MZ & DRo	2.50
2 StG, MZ & DRo	2.50

DARKCHYLD/GLORY
Image/Extreme

one-shot, four variant covers, by RLd, RQu, JDy & PtL	2.95

DARKCHYLDE
Image/TMP

1	8.00
1a remastered, RLd(c)	12.00
1b American Entertainment	8.00
2	5.00
2a Variant cover	5.00
3	4.00
4 RQu,Ariel & Kauldron's past	2.50
5 RQu,No one here gets out alive	2.50
TPB Rep. #1–#5	12.95

DARKCHYLDE: THE DIARY
Image May 1997

one-shot, RQu et al,diary excerpts	2.50

DARKER IMAGE

1 BML,BCi(s),RLd,SK,JLe,I:Blood Wulf,Deathblow,Maxx	4.00
1a Gold logo(c)	15.00
1b White(c)	10.00
Ashcan 1	4.00

DARKNESS, THE
Image/Top Cow

0 Preview Edition, B&W	8.00
1 GEn, MS	2.50
1a Dark cover	12.00
1b Platinum cover	12.00
2 GEn, MS	4.00
3 GEn,MS,Jackie pursued by many foes	2.50
4 GEn,MS,Jackie explores Darkness power	2.50
5 GEn,MS,New York gangs on verge of all-out war	2.50
6 GEn,MS,F:JackieEstacado,concl.	2.50
7 MS	2.50
GN rep. #1–#2	4.95

DART

1 thru 3	@2.50

Deadly Duo #4 © Erik Larsen

DEADLY DUO, THE
Image/Highbrow 1994–95

1 A:Kill-Cat	2.50
2 A:Pitt, O:Kid Avenger	2.50
3 A:Roman, O:Kill-Cat	2.50
[Second Series] 1995	
1 A:Spawn	2.50
2 A:Savage Dragon	2.50
3 A:Grunge, Gen¹³	2.50
4 Movie Mayhem	2.50

DEATHBLOW
Image/Wildstorm 1993

1 JLe,MN,I:Cybernary	3.00

2 JLe,BU:Cybernary	2.50
3 JLe(a&s),BU:Cybernary	5.00
4 JLe(s),TSe,BU:Cybernary	2.50
5 JLe(s),TSe,BU:Cybernary	2.50
5a different cover	9.00
6 Black Angel	2.00
7	2.00
8 Black Angel	2.00
9 The Four Horseman	2.00
10 Michael Cray, Sister Mary	2.00
11 A:Four Horseman	2.00
12 Final Battle	2.50
13 New Story Arc	2.50
14 A:Johnny Savoy	2.50
15 F:Michael Cray	2.50
16 TvS,BWS(c),WildStorm Rising,pt.6,w/2 cards	2.50
16a Newsstand ed.	2.00
17 V:Gammorran Hunter Killers	2.50
18 F:Cybernary	2.50
19 F:Cybernary	2.50
20 A:Gen 13	3.50
21 Brothers in Arms,pt.2,A:Gen13	3.50
22 Brothers in Arms,pt.3	2.50
23 Brothers in Arms,pt.4	2.50
24 Brothers in Arms,pt.5	3.00
25 Brothers in Arms,pt.6	2.50
26 Fire From Heaven prelude	2.50
27 Fire From Heaven,pt.8	3.00
28	2.50
29	2.50
Ashcan 1	8.00

DEATHBLOW/WOLVERINE
Image/Wildstorm

1 RiB, AWs,crossover, set in San Francisco's Chinatown	2.50
2 RiB, AWs,concl	2.50

DEFCON 4
Image/Wildstorm 1996

1 thru 4 mini-series	@2.50

A DISTANT SOIL
Image/Highbrow
(B&W) Prev: Warp Graphics

15 CDo	3.00
16 CDo,A:Bast, Avatar	3.00
17 CDo,D'mer & Bast conflict	3.00
18 CDo,"Ascension" finale	3.00
19 CDo,"Spires of Heaven" pt.1	3.00
20 CDo,Lord Merai's suicide weakens Hierachy	3.00
21 CDo,"Exile for D'mer?"	3.00
Images of A Distant Soil	3.00
Images of A Distant Soil, signed, limited	34.95

DOOM'S IV
Image/Extreme 1994

1 I:Doom's IV	2.50
1a Variant(c)	2.50
2 MECH-MAX	2.50
2a variant cover	2.50
3 Dr. Lychee, Brick	2.50
4 Dr. Lyche, Syber-idol	2.50
Sourcebook	2.50

DRAGON, THE

1 Rep. of Savage Dragon	0.99
2 Rep. of Savage Dragon	0.99

All comics prices listed are for *Near Mint* condition.

IMAGE

THE DRAGON: BLOOD AND GUTS
Image/Highbrow 1995
1 I:Grip	2.50
2 and 3 JPn,KIS	@2.50

DUSTY STAR
Image April 1997 (B&W)
0 sci-fi,western,adventure	2.95
1	2.95

DV8
Image/Wildstorm 1996
1 WEl(s),HuR	4.00
1a JLe(c)	8.00
1b Kevin Nowlan(c)	4.00
2 WEl(s),HuR,Gen-active serial killers are reported	3.00
3 WEl(s), Evo & Frostbite go for a walk	2.50
4 Ivana tries to tighten her control on Threshold	2.50
5 Ivana sends DV8 to Japan	2.50
6 idle hands are the devil's tools	2.50
7 Sideways Bob's bedtime story	2.50
8 Sublime, Evo & Frostbite abandoned	2.50
9 "Ivana Dead?!"	2.50
10 "A Team Divided," pt.2	2.50

ELEKTRA/CYBLADE
Image/Top Cow Jan 1997
one-shot "Devil's Reign" pt.7 (of 8)	2.95

ESPERS
Image April 1997 (B&W) Vol. 3
1 JHI,A:Brian Marx,V:Architects	2.95
2 JHI,	2.95

EXTREME ANTHOLOGY
1	2.50

EXTREME CHRISTMAS SPECIAL
Various artists, new work	2.95

EXTREME HERO
1	2.95

EXTREME PREJUDICE
0 Prelude to X-over	2.50

EXTREME SACRIFICE
Prelude A:Everyone + card	2.50
Epiloque, conclusion + card	2.50
TPB Rep. whole x-over series	16.95

EXTREME 3000
Prelude	2.50

EXTREME TOUR BOOK
Tour Book 1992	3.00
Tour Book 1994	25.00

EXTREMELY YOUNGBLOOD
Image/Extreme Sept 1997
1 TBm&MBm(s)	3.50

EXTREME ZERO
0 RLd,CYp,ATi(i),I:Cybrid, Law & Order, Risk, Code 9, Lancers, Black Flag	2.75
0a Variant cover	2.75

FIRE FROM HEAVEN
1 x-over	3.50

FIRSTMAN
Image April 1997
1 ASm,LukeHenry becomesApollo	2.50

Freak Force #7 © Highbrow

FREAK FORCE
Image/Highbrow 1993–95
1 EL(s),KG	2.25
2 EL(s),KG	2.25
3 EL(s),KG	2.25
4 EL(s),KG,A:Vanguard	2.25
5 EL(s),KG	2.25
6 EL(s),KG	2.25
7 EL(s),KG	2.25
8 EL(s),space ants	2.25
9 EL(s),Cyberforce	2.25
10 EL(s),Savage Dragon	2.25
11 EL(s),Invasion pt.1	2.50
12 EL(s),Invasion pt.2	2.50
13 EL(s),Invasion pt.3	2.50
14 EL(s),Team Defeated	2.50
15 EL(s),F:Barbaric	2.50
16 KG,EL(s),V:Chelsea Nirvana	2.50
17 EL,KG,major plots converge	2.50
18 Final Issue	2.50
TPB 448pg	29.95

Series Two
Image March 1997
1 EL,Star joins team,V:The Frightening Force	2.95
2 EL,Dart quits team	2.95
3 EL,"Lo there shall come..an ending"	2.95

FRIENDS OF MAXX
Image/I Before E
1 WML&SK	2.95
2 MHs&SK	2.95

GEN[13]
Image/Wildstorm
0 Individual Hero Stories	8.00
1 JLe(s),BCi(s),I:Fairchild,Grunge, Freefall,Burnout	40.00
1a 2nd printing	10.00
2 JLe(s),BCi(s),	35.00
3 JLe(s),BCi(s),A:Pitt	14.00
4 JLe(s),BCi(s)	10.00
5 Final issue	8.00
5a WP variant cover	17.00
TPB	12.95
HC 1,000 copies	40.00

Gen[13] #0 © Jim Lee

Regular Series 1995
1a BCi(s),V:Mercenaries	7.00
1b Common Cover 2	7.00
1c Heavy Metal Gen	20.00
1d Pulp Fiction Parody	25.00
1e Gen 13 Bunch	20.00
1f Lin-Gen-re	25.00
1g Lil Gen 13	20.00
1h Friendly Neighbor Grunge	20.00
1i Gen 13 Madison Ave	20.00
1j Gen-Et Jackson	20.00
1k Gen Dress Up cover	20.00
1l Verti-Gen	20.00
1m Do It Yourself Cover	20.00
2 BCi,BWS(c),WildStorm Rising, pt.4, w/2 cards	4.00
2a Newstand Edition	2.25
3 Coda Island	3.00
4 Coda Island	2.50
5 I:New Member	2.50
6 I:The Deviants	3.00
7 European Vacation,pt.2	3.00
8	2.50
9	2.50
10 Fire From Heaven, pt.3	2.50
11	2.50
12	2.50
13A, B & C	@1.30
14 back to school	2.50
15 Fraternity and Sorority rush	2.50
16	2.50
17 BCi,JSC,AGo,battle royale in Tower of Luv	2.50
18 BCi,JSC,AGo,V:Keepers	2.50
19 BCi,JSC,AGo,Lynch & kids flee	

IMAGE

to Antarctica	2.50
20 BCi,JSC,AGo,"Spaced Out"	2.50
21 BCi,JSC,AGo,V:Drahn	2.50
College Yearbook 1997	2.50
Ann. #1 WEI,SDi"London'sBrilliant"	2.95
TPB rep.1–#5 of original mini-series, 3rd printing	12.95
TPB Lost in Paradise, rep. #3–#5	6.95

GEN 13 BOOTLEG
Image/Wildstorm Nov. 1996

1 MFm&AD,lost in the "Linquist Fault"	2.50
2	2.50
3 On the banks of the River Plin	2.50
4 WS&LSi,F:Valaria	2.50
5 Fairchild looses 30 minutes of her life	2.50
6 Fairchild goes back in time,pt.2	2.50
7 Day before a big exam	2.50
8 Adam Warren, pt.1 (of 3)	2.50
9 Adam Warren, pt.2 (of 3)	2.50

GEN 13/ GENERATION X
Image/Wildstorm July 1997

1 BCi&AAd	2.95
1 variant cover by JSC	2.95

GEN¹³/MAXX

1	4.00

GEN¹³: ORDINARY HEROES

1	2.50
2	2.50

Glory #15 © Extreme

GLORY
Image/Extreme 1995

0 JDy	2.50
1 JDy,F:Glory	4.50
1a variant cover	5.00
2 JDy,V:Demon Father	3.00
3 JDy,A:Rumble & Vandal	2.50
4 Vandal vs. Demon Horde	2.50
4a JDy variant cover	4.00
5 F:Vandal	2.50
6 Drug Problem	2.50

7 F:Superpatriot	2.50
8 Extreme Babewatch	2.50
9 thru 11	@2.50
12 JDy, EBe & JSb	3.50
13 JDy, EBe & JSb	2.50
14 JDy, EBe & JSb	2.50
15 JDy, EBe & JSb, Out for vengeance	2.50
continued: see Color Comics section
| TPB Rep.#1-#4 | 9.95 |

GLORY/ANGELA HELL'S ANGELS

1	5.00

GLORY/AVENGELYNE

1 V:B'lial,I:Faith	5.00
1a no chrome (c)	4.00

GLORY/AVENGELYNE: THE GODYSSEY
Image/Extreme

1 RLd & JDy	3.00
1a photo (c)	4.00

GLORY/CELESTINE: DARK ANGEL
Image/Extreme Sept. 1996

1 (of 3) JDy,PtL,sequel to Rage of Angels, A:Maximage	2.50
2 JDy,PtL,"Doomsday+1"	2.50

GLORY & FRIENDS BIKINI FEST

1 Nuff said	2.50

GRIFTER
Image/Wildstorm 1995

1 BWS(c), WildStorm Rising,pt.5,w/2 cards	2.50
1a Newsstand Ed.	1.95
2 City of Angels,pt.1	2.50
3 City of Angels,pt.2	2.50
4 R:Forgotten Hero	2.50
5 Rampage of a Fallen Hero	2.50
6 V:Poerhouse	2.50
7 & 8	@2.50

GRIFTER/BADROCK

1 To Save Badrock's Mom	4.00
1a Variant cover	2.50
2	3.00
3 double size	3.50

GRIFTER-ONE SHOT

1 SS,DN	5.00

GRIFTER
Image/Wildstorm

1 StG	4.00
2 StG	3.00
3 StG,captured by MadJackPower	3.00
4 StG,vs. Condition Red	2.50
5 StG,Grifter gambles his soul	2.50
6 StG,	2.50
7 StG,MtB,I:Charlatan	2.50
8 StG,MtB,Zealot disappears,V:Soldier	2.50
9 StG,Zealot captured?, secret history of Quiet Men	2.50
10 StG,Grifter & Soldier go to	

rescue Zealot	2.50
11 StG, renegade former agent	2.50
12 StG,"Who is Tanager?"	2.50
13 StG,"Family Feud"	2.50

GRIFTER/SHI

1 & 2	3.00
HC	29.95
HC signed & numbered(Lee)	75.00
HC signed & numbered(Tucci)	75.00
HC signed & numbered(Charest)	65.00
HC signed & numbered(Hubbs)	50.00

GROO

1 SA	2.25
2 A:Arba, Dakarba	2.00
3 The Generals Hat	2.00
4 A Drink of Water	2.00
5 SA,A Simple Invasion	2.00
6 SA,A Little Invention	2.00
7 The Plight of the Drazils	2.00
8	2.25
9 I:Arfetto	2.25
10 The Sinkes	2.25
11 The Gamblers	2.25
12	2.25

HAZARD
Image/Wildstorm 1996

1 JMi,RMr	2.50
2 JMi,RMr	1.75
3 JMi,RMr	1.75
4 JMi,RMr	1.75
5 JMi,RMr,Hazard finds Dr. D'Oro	2.25
6 JMi,RMr	2.25
7 JMi,RMr,Hazard meets Prism	2.25

HEADHUNTERS
Image April 1997 **(B&W)**

1 ChM,V:Army of Wrath	2.95
2 ChM,V:undead militia	2.95
3 ChM,"Slaughterground"	2.95

HEARTBREAKERS VERSUS BIOVOC
Image

TPB "Bust Out"	9.95
TPB PGn	14.95

HELLSHOCK
Image 1994

1 I:Hellshock	3.50
2 Powers & Origin	3.50
3 New foe	3.50
4	3.50

HELLSHOCK
Image Jan. 1997

1 JaL,Something wrong with Daniel, 48pg.	3.00
2 JaL,Daniel learns to control powers	2.50
3 JaL,Daniel free of madness	2.50
4 JaL,Daniel searches for his mother, Jonakand plans escape from Hell	2.50
5 JaL,Jonakand and fallen angels tear hell apart	2.50
6 JaL,"The Milk of Paradise"	2.50
7 JaL,"A Mother's Story", double size	3.95

IMAGE

HOMAGE STUDIOS
Swimsuit Spec.#1 JLe,WPo, MS . 2.25

HONG ON THE RANGE
Image/Matinee Entertainment/Flypaper
1 (of 3) by William Wu & Jeff Lafferty 2.50

IMAGE ZERO
Image 1993
0 I:Troll,Deathtrap,Pin-ups,rep. Savage Dragon #4,O:Stryker, F:ShadowHawk 40.00

IMAGES OF SHADOWHAWK
Image 1993–94
1 KG,V:Trencher 2.25
2 thru 3 V:Trencher 2.25

IMMORTAL II
Image May 1997
(B&W)
1 MsM,F:Gaijin & Gabrielle 2.50
2 MsM 2.50
3 MsM 2.50

JINX
Image June 1997
(B&W)
1 by Brian Michael Bendis 2.95

KID SUPREME
Image/Supreme 1996–97
1 & 2 . . . . 2.50
3 DaF,ErS 2.50
4 DaF,ErS,Party time 2.50
5 DaF,ErS,"Birds of a Feather" . . 2.50
6 DaF,ErS,I: The Sensational Spinner 2.50
7 DaF,ErS,Everything falls apart . 2.50

KILLER INSTINCT TOUR BOOK
1 All Homage Artist,I:Crusade . . . 5.00
1a signed 45.00

KILLRAZOR SPECIAL
1 O:Killrazor 2.50

KINDRED
Image/Wildstorm 1994
1 JLe,BCi(s),BBh,I:Knidred 5.00
2 JLe,BCi(s),BBh,V:Kindred 3.50
3 JLe,BCi(s),BBh,V:Kindred 3.00
3a WPo(c),Alternate(c) 6.00
4 JLe,BCi(s),BBh,V:Kindred 3.00
TPB rep. #1–#4 . . . . 9.95

KISS: THE PSYCHO CIRCUS
Image/TMP July 1997
one-shot SvG,AMe 1.95

KNIGHTMARE
Image/Extreme 1995
0 O:Knightmare 2.50
1 I:Knightmare MMy 2.50

2 I:Caine 2.50
3 RLd,AV,The New Order, F:Detective Murtaugh 2.50
4 RLd,AV,MMy,I:Thrillkill 2.50
5 V:Thrillkill 2.50
6 Extreme Babewatch 2.50
7 . . . . 2.50
8 I:Acid 2.50

KURT BUSIEK'S ASTRO CITY
1 I:Samaritan 2.25
2 V:Shirak the Devourer 2.25
3 F:Jack in the Box 2.25
4 & 6 . . . . @2.25
TPB 19.95
HC 39.95

KURT BUSIEK'S ASTRO CITY VOL.2
Homage Comics 1996–97
1 KBk(s),BA 2.50
1 2nd printing 2.25
2 KBk(s),BA,F:Astra 2.50
3 KBk(s),BA, ... 2.50
Image/Homage Comics
4 KBk,BA,Teenager seeks to become teen sidekick, pt.1 (of 6)2.50
5 . . . . 2.50
6 V: creatures of Shadow Hill . . . 2.50
7 Aliens invade Astro City 2.50
8 The aliens are out there 2.50
9 Honor Guard versus Aliens finale2.50
10 meet the junkman 2.50
11 . . . . 2.50

LABMAN
1 . . . . 3.50
1a variant cover 3.50
2 and 3 . . . . @2.95

LADY SUPREME
Image/Extreme
1 TMr 2.50
2 TMr 2.50
3 TMr,V:Manassa 2.50
4 TMr,"Lady Supreme goes undercover" 2.50

LEAVE IT TO CHANCE
Homage Comics Sept. 1996
1 JeR,PS,I:Chance Falconer 2.50
2 . . . . 2.50
Image/Homage Comics
3 Chance and St. George race against time 2.50
4 . . . . 2.50
5 Halloween Night in Devil's Echo 2.50
6 Chance sent to private school . 2.50
7 Falconer's battle with Captain Hitch, pt.2 . . . . 2.50
8 "The Phantom of the Mall" 2.50
TPB rep. #1–#4 . . . . 9.95

LEGEND OF SUPREME
1 KG(s),JJ,DPs,Revelations pt.1 . 2.50
2 Revelations pt.2 . . . . 2.50
3 Conclusion 2.50

LETHAL
Image 1996
1 and 2 . . . . @2.50

LITTLE-GREYMAN
Image
(B&W)
TPB by C. Scott Morse 6.95

LYNCH
Image/Wildstorm June 1997
1 TVs,"Terror in the Jungle" 2.50

MAN AGAINST TIME
1 . . . . 2.50
2 . . . . 2.50

MAGE: THE HERO DEFINED
Image
1 MWg, F:Kevin Matchstick 2.50

Mars Attacks #1 © Image

MARS ATTACKS
Image 1996
1 KG,BSz(of 4) 2.50
2 . . . . 2.50
3 . . . . 2.50
4 End of their world as they knew it 2.50

MAXIMAGE
1 thru 8 . . . . @2.50
9 BML, Sex Slaves of Bomba Island 2.50
10 BML, The King of Emotion is back 2.50

MAXX
1/2 SK,from Wizard 8.00
1 SK,I:The Maxx 6.00
1a glow in the dark(c) 25.00
2 SK,V:Mr.Gone 6.00
3 SK,V:Mr.Gone 5.00
4 SK, ... 4.00
5 SK, ... 3.50
6 SK, ... 3.50
7 SK,A:Pitt 4.00
8 SK,V:Pitt 4.00
9 SK 3.00
10 SK 3.00

 All comics prices listed are for *Near Mint* condition.

IMAGE

11 SK	2.50
12 SK	2.50
13 Maxx Wanders in Dreams	2.50
14 R:Julie	2.50
15 Julia's Pregnant	2.50
16 SK,Is Maxx in Danger?	2.50
17 Gardener Maxx	2.25
18	1.95
19 V:Hooley	1.95
20 Questions are answered	2.25
21 AM story	1.95
22 SK	1.95
23 SK	1.95
24 SK	1.95
25 SK	1.95
26 SK	1.95
27 V:Iago the Killer Slug	1.95
28 Sara and Norberg look for Julie	1.95
29 Sara and Gone defeat Iago the Slug	1.95
30 Lil' Sara faces her fears	1.95
31 F:The Library girl	1.95
Spec. Friends of Maxx	2.95
TPB Rep. #1-#5	12.95
TPB Vol. 2	12.95

MEDIEVAL SPAWN/ WITCHBLADE

1	2.95
TPB collected	9.95

MIKE GRELL'S MAGGIE THE CAT

1 thru 4	@2.50

MISERY SPECIAL

1 Cyberforce Origins	2.95

MYSTERY, INC.

Ashcan 1	13.50

NAMELESS, THE
Image May 1997 (B&W)

1 PhH,I:The Nameless, protector of Mexico City's lost children	2.95
2	2.95
3	2.95

NEW FORCE

1 thru 4 mini-series	@2.50

THE NEW ORDER HANDBOOK

Various artists	1.50

NEW MAN

1 thru 3	@2.50
4 Shadowhunt x-over,pt.5	2.50

NEWMEN
Image/Extreme 1994

1 JMs	3.00
2 JMs,I:Girth	2.25
3 JMs,V:Girth,I:Ikonna	2.25
4 JMs,A:Ripclaw	1.95
5 JMs,Ripclaw,V:Ikonn	2.50
6 JMs	2.50
7 JMs	2.50
8 JMs,Team Youngblood	2.50
9 ErS(s),JMs,Kodiak Kidnapped	2.50

10 ExtremeSacrifice x-over,pt.4	2.50
11 F:Reign	2.50
12 R:Elemental	2.50
13 ErS,I:Bootleg	2.50
14 ErS,Dominion's Secret	2.50
15 I:Time Guild	2.50
16	2.50
16a variant cover	4.00
17 R:Girth	2.50
18 F:Byrd	2.50
19 I:Bordda Khan,Shepherd	2.50
20 Extreme Babewatch	2.50
21 ErS,CSp,(1 of 5)	2.50
22 ErS,CSp, Who Needs the Newmen?	2.50
23 ErS,CSp,Who are the Newmen?	2.50

NEW SHADOWHAWK, THE

1 I:New ShadowHawk	2.50
2 V:Mutants	2.50
3 I:Trophy	2.50
4 V:Blowfish	2.50
5 thru 7	@2.50

1963 #3 © Image

1963

1 AnM(s),RV,DGb,I:Mystery, Inc.	2.50
1a Gold Ed.	15.00
1b Bronze Ed.	15.00
2 RV,SBi,DGb,JV,I:The Fury	2.25
3 RV,SBi,I:U.S.A.	2.25
4 JV,SBi,I:N-Man, Johnny Beyond	2.25
5 JV,SBi,I:Horus	2.25
6 JV,SBi,I:Tommorrow Synicate, C:Shaft	2.25
Ashcan #1	8.00
Ashcan #2	7.00
Ashcan #4	5.00

NINE VOLT
Image/Top Cow

1 ACh	2.50
2 ACh	2.50

NORMAL MAN/ MEGATON MAN SPECIAL

1	2.50

OPERATION KNIGHTSTRIKE

1 RHe,A:Chapel,Bravo,Battlestone	2.50
2 In Afganistan	2.50
3 final issue	2.50

THE OTHERS

0 JV(s),From ShadowHawk	2.50
1 JV(s)V:Mongrel	2.50
2 JV,Mongrel takes weapons	2.50
3 War	2.50
4 O:Clone	2.50

PACT
Image 1994

1 JV(s),WMc,I:Pact, C:Youngblood	2.25
2 JV(s),V:Youngblood	1.95
3 JV(s),V:Atrocity	1.95

PHANTOM FORCE

1 RLd,JK,w/card	2.75
2 JK,V:Darkfire	1.95
See also Color Comics section	

PITT
Image/Top Cow 1993–95

1 DK,I:Pitt,Timmy	5.00
2 DK,V:Quagg	3.00
3 DK,V:Zoyvod	7.00
4 DK,V:Zoyvod	3.00
5 DK	2.50
6 DK	2.50
7 DK	2.50
8 Ransom	2.50
9 DK,Artic Adventures	2.00
Ashcan 1	9.00

POWER OF THE MARK

1 I:Ted Miller	2.50
2 V:The Fuse	2.50
3 TMB(s), The Mark	2.50
4 TMB,Mark's secrets revealed	2.50

POWER RANGERS ZEO
Image/Extreme Sept. 1997

1 thru 3 TBm&MBm(s),TNu,NRd	@2.50

POWER RANGERS ZEO YOUNGBLOOD
Image/Extreme Oct. 1997

1 thru 2 RLd,TBm,MBm	@2.95

PROPHET
Image/Extreme 1993–95

0 San Diego Comic-Con Ed.	7.00
1 RLd(s)DPs,O:Prophet	3.00
1a Gold Ed.	7.00
2 RLd(s),DPs,C:Bloodstrike	2.50
3 RLd(s),DPs, V:Bloodstrike, I:Judas	2.50
4 RLd(s),DPs,A:Judas	2.50
4a SPa(c),Limited Ed.	7.00
5 SPa	3.00
6 SPa	2.50
7 SPa War Games pt.1	2.25
8 SPa War Games pt.2	2.50
9 SPa,Extreme Sacrifice Prelude	2.50
10 ExtremeSacrifice x-over,pt.6	2.50
Sourcebook	2.95
Ashcan #1	7.00
Ashcan #2	7.00

IMAGE

[Regular Series]

1 SPI, New Series	2.75
2 SPI, New Direction	2.50
2a variant cover	2.50
3 True Nature	2.50
4 The Dying Factor	2.50
5 and 6	@2.50
7 CDi,SPa	2.50
8 and 9	@2.50
TPB	12.95
Ann.#1 Supreme Apocalypse	2.50
Spec.#1 Babewatch special	2.50

PROPHET/AVENGELYNE

1	3.00

Regulators #1 © Image

REGULATORS
June 1995

1 F:Blackjack,"Touch of Scandal"	2.50
2 F:Vortex	2.50
3 F:Arson	2.50
4 F:Scandal	2.50

REPLACEMENT GOD AND OTHER STORIES, THE
Image May 1997
(B&W)

1 Knute vs. King Ursus	2.95
2	2.95

RIPCLAW
Image/Top Cow 1995

1/2 Prelude to Series (Wizard)	3.00
1/2a Con versions	15.00
1 A:Killjoy, I:Shadowblade	3.00
2 Cyblade, Heatwave	2.50
3 EcS,BPe,AV,Alliance with	
S.H.O.C.s	2.50
4 conclusion	2.50
Spec.#1 I:Ripclaw's Brother	3.00
[1st Regular Series]	
1 thru 5	@2.50

RIPTIDE
Image 1995

1 O:Riptide	2.50

2 O:Riptide	2.50

SAVAGE DRAGON
Image/Highbrow

1 EL,I:Savage Dragon	4.00
2 EL,I:Superpatriot	3.00
3 EL,V:Bedrock,w'coupon#6	3.00
3a EL,w/o coupon	2.50
Spec. Savage Dragon Versus Savage	
Megaton Man #1 EL,DSm	2.50
Gold Ed.	12.00
TPB	9.95
[2nd Series] 1993	
1 EL,I:Freaks	3.00
2 EL,V:Teen.Mutant Ninja Turtles,	
Flip book Vanguard #0	2.50
3 EL,A:Freaks	2.25

Savage Dragon #28 © Erik Larsen

4 EL,A:Freaks	2.25
5 EL,Might Man flip book	2.25
6 EL,A:Freaks	2.25
7 EL,Overlord	2.25
8 EL,V:Cutthroat,Hellrazor	2.25
9 thru 10 EL,	2.25
11 EL,A:Overlord	1.95
12 EL	1.95
13 EL,Mighty Man,Star,I:Widow	
(appeared after issue #20)	2.50
13a Larsen version of 13	2.50
14 Possessed pt.1	2.50
15 Possessed pt.2	2.50
16 Possessed pt.3,V:Mace	2.50
17 V:Dragonslayer	2.50
18 R:The Fiend	2.50
19 V:The Fiend	2.50
20 Rematch with Ovrlord	2.50
21 V:Overlord	2.50
22 A:Teenage Mutant Turtles	2.50
23 Rapture vs. SheDragon	2.50
24 Gang War pt.1	2.50
25 Gang War,pt.2 double size	4.00
26	2.50
27	2.50
28	2.50
29	2.50
30	2.50
31 "The Dragon is trapped in Hell"	2.50
32 Kill-Cat vs. Justice	2.50
33 fatherhood	2.50
34 F:Hellboy, pt.1	3.00

35 F:Hellboy, pt.2	2.50
36 Dragon & Star try to rescue Peter	
Klaptin	2.50
37 mutants struggle in ruins of	
Chicago	2.50
38 Dragon vs. Cyberface	2.50
39 Dragon vs. Dung	2.50
40 "G-Man"	2.50
TPB A Talk With God	17.95

SAVAGE DRAGON DESTROYER DUCK
Image Comics

1 SvG,ChM,EL	3.95

SAVAGE DRAGON, THE: RED HORIZON
Image Comics Feb. 1997

1 MsM	2.50
2 MsM,Dragon in the ER,A:Freak	
Force	2.50
3 (of 3) MsM,Freak Force beaten	2.50

SAVAGE DRAGON: MARSHAL LAW
Image July 1997
(B&W)

1 (of 2) PMs,KON,F:Marshal Law	2.50

SAVAGE DRAGON: SEX & VIOLENCE
Image July 1997

1 (of 2) TBm,MBm	2.50

SAVANT GARDE
Image/Wildstorm March 1997

1 "A team without a rule book"	2.50
2 Between killer & killer cat	2.50
3 V: strange Tapestry	2.50
4 "Any super-villain can take over	
the world"	2.50
5 "The Final Showdown"	2.50

SHADOWHAWK
Image/Shadowline

1 JV,I:ShadowHawk,Black Foil(c),	
Pin-up of The Others,w/	
coupon#1	4.00
1a w/o coupon	2.00
2 JV,V:Arsenal,A:Spawn, I:Infiniti	3.00
3 JV,V:Arsenal,w/glow-in-the-	
dark(c)	2.50
4 V:Savage Dragon	2.50
TPB rep.#1-4	19.95
Ashcan #1	4.00
Ashcan #2	4.00
Ashcan #3	4.00
Ashcan #4	4.00
[2nd Series] 1993	
1 JV,Die Cut(c)	2.50
1a Gold Ed.	6.00
2 JV,ShadowHawk I.D.	2.50
2a Gold Ed.	4.00
3 Poster(c),JV,w/Ash Can	2.50
TPB	19.95
[3rd Series] 1993	
0 Zero issue	2.25
1 JV,CWf,V:Vortex,Hardedge, Red	
Foil(c)	2.50
1a Gold Ed.	4.00
2 JV,CWf,MA,I:Deadline, BU&I:US	

Male 2.50
3 JV(a&s),ShadowHawk has AIDS,
V:Hardedge,Blackjak 2.25
4 JV(a&s),V:Hardedge, ... 2.25
Note: #5 to #11 not used; #12 below
is the next issue, and the 12th
overall.
12 Monster Within, pt.1 . . . . 1.95
13 Monster Within, pt.2 . . . . 1.95
14 Monster Within, pt.3 . . . . 2.50
15 Monster Within, pt.4 . . . . 2.50
16 Monster Within, pt.5 . . . . 2.50
17 Monster Within, pt.6 . . . . 2.50
18 JV,D:ShadowHawk 2.50
Spec.#1 . . . . 3.50
Gallery#1 . . . . 1.95

SHADOWHAWK/ VAMPIRELLA
Book 2 V:Kaul 4.95
Book #1: see Vampi/ShadowHawk

SHADOWHUNT SPECIAL
1 Shadowhunt x-over, pt.1 . . . . . 2.50

SHAMAN'S TEARS
0 . . . . 2.50
1 MGr,I:Shaman,B:Origin 3.00
1a Siver Prism Ed. 10.00
2 MGr,Poster(c) 2.50
3 MGr,V:Bar Sinister 2.50
4 MGr,V:Bar Sinister,E:Origin . . . 1.95
5 MGr,R:Jon Sable 1.95
6 MGr,V:Jon Sable 1.95
7 MGr,V:Rabids 1.95
8 MGr,A:Sable 1.95
9 MGr,Becoming of Broadarrow . 1.95
10 Becoming of Broadarrow,pt.2 . 2.50
11 Becoming of Broadarrow,pt.3 . 2.50
12 Becoming of Broadarrow,pt.4 . 2.50
13 The Offspring,pt.1 . . . . 2.50

SHATTERED IMAGE
Image/Wildstorm
1 KBk,TnD,crossover 2.50
2 KBk,TnD, ... 2.50
3 KBk,TnD, ... 2.50
4 KBk,TnD,concl. 2.50

SIEGE
Image/Wildstorm Jan. 1997
1 JPe,AV,Nothing you believe is
real 2.50
2 JPe,AV,Omega goes to Hawaii
for funeral 2.50
3 JPe,AV,Zontarian Crab Ships vs.
Drop Ship 2.50
4 JPe,AV,Raid to rescue Omega
Squad 2.50

SIGMA
1 Fire From Heaven prelude 2.50
2 Fire From Heaven, pt.6 . . . . . . 2.50

SOULWIND
Image March 1997 (B&W)
1 quest for Soulwind begins 2.95
2 Nick becomes "Captain Crash" 2.95
3 Captain Crash & Poke pursue
Soulwind info 2.95
4 . . . . 2.95

SPARTAN: WARRIOR SPIRIT
1 thru 4 . . . . @2.95

SPAWN
Image/TMP 1992
1 TM,I:Spawn,w/GP,DK pinups . 18.00
2 TM,V:The Violator 13.00
3 TM,V:The Violator 12.00
4 TM,V:The Violator,+coupon #2 16.00
4a w/o coupon 3.50
5 TM,O:Billy Kincaid 9.00
6 TM,I:Overt-Kill 6.00
7 TM,V:Overt-Kill 6.00
8 TM,AMo(s),F:Billy Kincaid . . . 7.00

Spawn #10 © Rob Liefeld

9 NGa(s),TM,I:Angela 10.00
10 DS(s),TM,A:Cerebus 5.00
11 FM(s),TM 5.00
12 TM,Chapel killed Spawn 5.00
13 TM,A:Youngblood 4.50
14 TM,A:The Violator 4.50
15 TM 4.50
16 GCa,I:Anti-Spawn 4.50
17 GCa,V:Anti-Spawn 6.00
18 GCa,ATi,D:Anti-Spawn 15.00
19 & 20 see after #25
21 TM 14.00
22 TM 4.00
23 TM 4.00
24 TM 4.50
25 Image X Book 6.00
19 I:Houdini 5.00
20 J:Houdini 5.00
26 TM 4.00
27 I:The Curse 4.00
28 Faces Wanda 4.00
29 Returns From Angela 4.00
30 A:KKK 4.00
31 R:Redeemer 3.00
32 TM,GCa,New Costume 5.00
33 R:Violator 2.50
34 V:Violator 2.50
35 F:Sam & Twitch 2.50
36 Talks to Wanda 2.50
37 I:The Freak 2.50
38 & 39 . . . . @2.50
40 & 41 V:Curse . . . . @2.50
42 thru 49 . . . . @2.50

50 48pgs 5.00
51 and 52 . . . . @2.50
53 A:Malebolgia 2.50
54 return to New York, alliance with
Terry Fitzgerald 2.25
55 plans to defeat Jason Wynn . . 2.25
56 efforts to defeat Jason Wynn . 2.25
57 . . . . 2.25
58 sequel to Spawn #29 . . . . . . 2.00
59 . . . . 2.00
60 battle between Spawn and Clown
cont. 1.95
61 battle with Clown concl. 1.95
62 Spawn reverts to Al Simmons for
one day 1.95
63 Operation: Wynn fall, pt.1 . . . 1.95
64 Wynn falls, bagged with toy
catalog 1.95
TPB Capital Collection rep.#1-3
limited to 1,200 copies 300.00
TPB TM,rep.#1–#5 . . . . 9.95
TPB Spawn III rep. #12–#15 . . . 9.95
TPB Spawn IV rep. #16–#20 . . . 9.95

SPAWN/BATMAN
Image/DC
1 FM(s),TM, ... 5.00

SPAWN BLOOD FEUD
1 V:Vampires 2.25
2 . . . . 2.25
3 Hunted as a Vampire 2.25
4 V:Heartless John 2.25

SPAWN BIBLE
Image/TMP
1 TM,GCa 2.00

SPAWN THE IMPALER
Image/TMP Mini-series
1 (of 3) MGr, fully painted 3.50
2 and 3 MGr . . . . @3.00

SPAWN: BLOODFEUD
1 thru 4 reoffered 2.25

SPAWN/WILDC.A.T.S
1 thru 4 mini-series 2.50

SPLITTING IMAGE
1 DsM,A:Marginal Seven 2.25
2 DsM,A:Marginal Seven 2.25

STAR
1 F:Star from Savage Dragon . . . 2.50
2 Buried Alive 2.50
3 A:Savage Dragon,Rapture 2.50
4 A:Savage Dragon,Rapture 2.50

STARCHILD: MYTHOPOLIS
Image (B&W)
0 JOn, "Prologue" 2.95

STORMWATCH
Image/Wildstorm 1993
0 JSc(c),O:StormWatch,
V:Terrorists,w/card 2.50
1 JLe(c&s),ScC,TvS(i),
I:StormWatch 2.25

IMAGE

1a Gold Ed. 5.00
2 JLe(c&s),ScC,TvS(i),I:Cannon,
   Winter,Fahrenheit,Regent 2.25
3 JLe(c&s),ScC,TvS(i),V:Regent,
   I:Backlash 5.00
4 V:Daemonites 2.50
5 SRf(s),BBh,V:Daemonites 2.25
6 BCi,ScC,TC,A:Mercs 2.25
7 BCi,ScC,TC,A:Mercs 2.25
8 BCi,ScC,TC,A:Mercs 2.25
9 BCi,I:Defile 2.25
25 BCi,A:Spartan 2.50
10 V:Talos 2.00
10a variant (c) 7.00
11 the end? 2.00
12 V:Hellstrike 2.00
13 V:M.A.D.-1 . . . . 2.00
14 Despot 2.00
15 Batallion, Flashpoint 2.00
16 V:Defile 2.00
17 D:Batallion 2.00
18 R:Argos 2.50
19 R:M.A.D.-1,L:Winter 2.50

StormWatch #3 © Jim Lee

20 F:Cannon,Winter,Bendix 2.50
21 V:Wildcats 2.50
22 RMz,BWS(c),WildStorm
   Rising,pt.9,w/2 cards 2.50
22a Newsstand ed. 1.95
23 R:Despot,Warguard 2.50
24 V:Despot 2.50
25 BCi,A:Spartan 2.75
26 V:Despot 2.50
27 Rebuilding 2.50
28 New Adventures 2.50
29 Reorganization 2.50
30 . . . . 2.50
31 V:Middle Eastern Terrorists . . . 2.50
32 thru 34 . . . . @2.50
35 Fire From Heaven,pt.5 . . . . . . 2.50
36 Fire From Heaven 2.50
37 Double size 3.50
38 . . . . 2.50
39 . . . . 2.50
40 virus 2.50
41 . . . . 2.50
42 Weatherman discovers a
   conspiracy 2.50
43 . . . . 2.50
44 history of Jenny Sparks 2.50

45 Battalion visits his family 2.50
46 secrets and more secrets,
   prologue 2.50
47 WEl(s), JLe, SW, dangerous
   experiment gone awry 2.50
48 "Change or Die" pt.1 . . . . 2.50
49 "Change or Die" pt.2 . . . . 2.50
50 "Change or Die" concl.large size 4.50
Sourcebok JLe(s),DT 2.75
Spec.#1 RMz(s),DT, ... 4.25
Spec.#2 F:Fleshpoint 2.50
Ashcan 1 . . . . 5.00
TPB Change the World 9.95

STRANGERS IN PARADISE VOL. 3
Homage Comics (B&W) 1996
1 TMr 2.75
2 TMr 2.75
Image/Homage Comics
3 TMr,David & Katchoo fight 2.75
4 TMr,Katchoo makes startling
   discovery 2.75
5 TMr,Francine's college days . . 2.75
6 TMr,Katchoo searches for David 2.75
7 TMr, ... 2.75

STRIKEBACK!
1 thru 4 . . . . @2.50

SUPER-PATRIOT
1 N:Super-Patriot 2.25
2 KN(i),O:Super-Patriot 2.25
3 A:Youngblood 2.25
4 . . . . 1.95

SUPER-PATRIOT: LIBERTY AND JUSTICE
1 R:Covenant 2.50
2 Tokyo 2.50
3 Tokyo gets Trashed 2.50
4 Final issue 2.50

SUPREME
Image/Supreme 1992
0 O:Supreme 2.50
1 B:RLd(s&i),BrM, V:Youngblood 3.50
1a Gold Ed. 5.00
2 BrM,I:Heavy Mettle 2.50
3 thru 4 BrM 2.50
5 BrM(a&s),Clv(i),I:Thor,V:Chrome 2.50
6 BrM,Clv(i),I:Starguard,
   A:Thor,V:Chrome 2.50
7 Rip,ErS(s),SwM,A:Starguard,
   A:Thor, ... 2.50
8 Rip(s),SwM,V:Thor, ... 2.50
9 Rip&KtH(s),BrM,Clv(i),V:Thor . 2.50
10 KrH(s),BrM,JRu(i), BU:I:Black &
   White 2.50
11 I:Newmen 2.50
12 SPa(c),RLd(s),SwM, ... 2.25
25 SPa(c),RLd(s),SwM,V:Simple
   Simon,Images of Tomorrow . . 5.00
13 B:Supreme Madness 2.50
14 Supreme Madness, pt.2 . . . . . 2.50
15 RLd(s)A:Spawn 2.50
16 V:StormWatch 2.50
17 Supreme Madness, pt.5 . . . . . 2.50
18 E:Supreme Madness 2.50
19 V:The Underworld 2.50
20 V:The Unterworld 2.50
21 God Wars 2.50
22 RLd,CNn,God Wars, V:Thor . . 2.50

Supreme #23 © Image Comics

23 ExtremeSacrifice x-over,pt.1 . . 2.50
24 Identity Questions 2.50
#25, see above, after #12
26 F:Kid Supreme 2.50
27 Rising Son,I:Cortex 2.50
28 Supreme Apocalypse:Prelude . 2.50
29 Supreme Apocalypse,pt.1 . . . . 2.50
30 . . . . 2.50
31 V:Equinox 2.50
32 V:Cortex 2.50
33 Extreme Babewatch 2.50
34 She-Supreme 2.50
35 thru 38 . . . . @2.50
39 AMo 2.50
40 AMo 2.50
41 AMo 2.50
42 AMo,"Secret Origins" 2.50
43 AMo,"Secrets of the Citadel
   Supreme" 2.50
44 See Color Comics section
Ann.#1 TMB,CAd,KG,I:Vergessen 2.95
Ashcan #1 . . . . 7.00
Ashcan #2 . . . . 4.00

SUPREME: GLORY DAYS
1 Supreme in WWI 2.95
2 (of 2) BNa&KIA(s),DdW,GyM,
   A:Superpatriot 2.95

SWORD OF DAMOCLES
1 prelude to Fire From Heaven x-
   over 2.50

TALES OF THE WITCHBLADE
Image/Top Cow
1 . . . . 2.95
2 new tale of previous wielder of
   Witchblade 2.95

TEAM 1: STORMWATCH
1 I:First StormWatch Team 2.50
2 V:Helspont,D:Think Tank 2.50

TEAM 1: WILDCATS
1 I:First Wildcats Team 2.50
2 B:Cabal 2.50

IMAGE

TEAM 7
Image/Wildstorm 1994–95
1 New team 4.00
2 New powers 2.50
3 Members go insane 2.50
4 final issue,V:A Nuke 2.50
Ashcan 4.00
TPB 9.95

TEAM 7
OBJECTIVE: HELL
1 CDi,CW,BWS(c),WildStorm
  Rising,Prologue,w/2 cards 2.50
1a Newsstand ed. 1.95
2 Cambodia 2.50

TEAM 7 III:
DEAD REACONING
1 thru 4 . . . . @2.50

TEAM YOUNGBLOOD
Image/Extreme 1993
1 B:ErS(s),ATi(c),CYp,NRD(i),
  I:Masada,Dutch,V:Giger 2.50
2 ATi(c),CYp,NRd(i),V:Giger . . . 2.25
3 RLd(s),CYp,NRd(i),C:Spawn,
  V:Giger 2.25
4 ErS(s), ... 2.25
5 ErS(s),CNn,V:Lynx 2.25
6 ErS(s),N:Psi-Fire,
  BU:Black&White 2.25
7 ErS(s),CYp,ATh,Extreme
  Prejudice#1,I:Quantum, BU:Black
  & White 2.25
8 ErS(s),CYp,ATh,Extreme Pre-
  judice #5, V:Quantum, BU:B&W 2.25
9 RLd 4.00
10 ErS(s),CYp,ATh, ... 2.50
11 RLd,ErS,Cyp 2.00
12 RLd,ErS,Cyp 2.50
13 ErS,Cyp 2.50
14 RLd,ErS,Cya 2.50
15 New Blood 2.50
16 RLd,ErS,TNu,I:New Sentinel,
  A:Bloodpool 2.50
17 ExtremeSacrifice x-over,pt.5 . 2.50
18 MS, membership drive 2.50
19 R:Brahma 2.50
20 Contact,pt.1 1000 yr Badrock . 2.50
21 Contact,pt.2 . . . . 2.50
22 Shadowhunt x-over,pt.4 . . . . 2.50

TEENAGE MUTANT
NINJA TURTLES
Image/Highbrow
(B&W)
1 thru 3 . . . . @2.00
4 Donatello resurrected 2.00
5 FFo,Warlord Komodo uses
  Splinter as guinea pig 2.50
6 FFo 2.50
7 FFo,Raphael joins Foot Clan? . 2.50
8 FFo,Michelangelo tries to rescue
  Casey Jones' daughter 2.95
9 Enter: the Knight Watchman . . 2.95
10 "Enter: The Dragon" 2.95
TPB A New Beginning 9.95

TENTH, THE
Image Comics
1 BSt,TnD,Last stand against Hell
  on Earth 2.50

2 BSt,TnD,invasion of Darklon
  Corp. begins 2.50
3 BSt,TnD,Tenth & Espy team-up 2.50
4 BSt,TnD.confrontation with
  possible Armageddon 2.50

TOP COW/
BALLISTIC STUDIOS
Swimsuit Spec.#1 MS(c) 2.95

A TOUCH OF SILVER
Image Jan. 1997
(B&W)
1 JV,"Birthday" 2.95
2 JV,"Dance" 2.95
3 JV,"Bullies" 2.95
4 JV,"Separation" 2.95

TRENCHER
1 KG,I:Trencher 2.25
2 KG, ... 2.25
3 KG,V:Supreme 2.25
4 KG,V:Elvis 2.25

TRIBE
1 TJn(s),LSn,I:The Tribe 2.50
1a Ivory(White) Editon 25.00
2 . . . . 2.25
Ashcan 1 . . . . 8.00

TROLL
Image/Extreme Dec. 1993
1 RLd(s),JMs,I:Evangeliste,
  V:Katellan Command, ... 2.50
2 . . . . 2.50
Halloween Spec.#1 . . . . 2.50
X-Mas Stocking Stuffer #1 . . . . 2.95

Troll Once a Hero #1 © Image Comics

TROLL: ONCE A HERO
1 Troll in WWII 2.50

TROUBLEMAN
Image/Motown June 1996
1 and 2 . . . . @2.50

"21"
Image/Top Cow
1 thru 3 LWn,MDa, ... @2.50
4 LWn,MDa,"Time Bomb" pt.1 . . 2.50
5 LWn,MDa,"Time Bomb" pt.2 . . 2.50
6 LWn,MDa,"Time Bomb" pt.3
  "Detonation" 2.50

UNION
Image/Wildstorm
0 O:Union 2.50
0a WPo(c), ... 6.00
1 MT,I:Union,A:StormWatch . . . 2.75
2 MT 2.75
3 MT 2.75
4 MT,Good Intentions 2.75
Regular Series 1995
1 R:Union, Crusade 2.50
2 V:Crusade & Mnemo 2.50
3 A:Savage Dragon 2.50
4 JRo,BWS(c), WildStorm
  Rising,pt.3,w/2 cards 2.50
4a Newsstand ed. 1.95
5 V:Necros 2.50
6 V:Necros 2.50
7 Jill's Surprise 2.50
8 Regal Vengeance,pt.1 . . . . . 2.50
9 Regal Vengeance,pt.2 . . . . . 2.50
10 Regal Vengeance,pt.3 . . . . . 2.50

UNION
Image/Wildstorm 1996
1 MHs,RBn 2.50
2 MHs,RBn 2.50
3 MHs,RBn 1.75

VANGUARD
Image/Highbrow 1993–94
1 EL(s),BU:I:Vanguard 2.25
2 EL(s),Roxann 2.25
3 AMe, ... 2.25
4 AMe, ... 2.25
5 AMe,V:Aliens 2.25
6 V:Bank Robber 1.95

VANGUARD:
STRANGE VISITORS
by Gary Carlson, Scot Eaton & Bill
Anderson
1 (of 4) SEa,BAn,A:Amok 2.95
2 SEa,BAn, ... 2.95
3 SEa,BAn, ... 2.95
4 SEa,BAn,finale 2.95

VELOCITY
1 V:Morphing Opponent 2.50
2 V:Charnel 2.50
3 & 4 conclusion . . . . @2.50

VIOLATOR
1 AMo(s),BS,I:Admonisher 2.25
2 AMo(s),BS 1.95
3 AMo(s),BS,last issue 1.95

VIOLATOR/BADROCK
1 AMo(s),A:Celestine 2.50
2 V:Celestine 2.50
3 F:Dr. McAllister 2.50
4 Final issue 2.50
TPB Rep. 9.95

IMAGE

VOGUE
1 F:Vogue,I:Redbloods 2.50
2 & 3 conclusion 2.50

WARBLADE: ENDANGERED SPECIES
1 I:Pillar 2.95
2 V:Ripclaw 2.50
3 I:Skinner 2.50
4 final issue 2.50

WAY OF THE CODA: THE COLLECTED WILDC.A.T.S
TPB VOL.II 12.95

WEAPON ZERO
Image/Top Cow
T-Minus-4 WS 7.00
T-Minus-3 Alien Invasion 4.00
T-Minus-2 Formation of a Team .. 4.00
T-Minus-1 Alien Invasion 4.00
0 Whole Team Together 4.00
1 .... 3.50
2 .... 3.50
3 .... 3.50
4 WS,JBz 3.00
5 WS,JBz 3.00
6 WS,JBz 3.00
7 WS,JBz 3.00
8 WS,JBz 3.00
9 WS,JBz 3.00
10 WS,ScL,"Devil's Reign" tie-in . 3.00
11 WS,JBz,Weapon Zero & Lilith
  return to T'srii moonbase 3.00
12 WS,JBz, What's wrong with
  Jamie 3.00
13 WS,JBz,problems with Jamie . 3.00

WETWORKS
Image/Wildstorm 1994
1 WPo 5.00
2 WPo,BCi 4.00
3 WPo,BCi,V:Vampire 3.00
4 WPo,BCi,Dozer 2.50
5 WPo,BCi,Pilgrim's Turn 2.50
6 WPo,BCi,Civil War 2.50
7 WPo,BCi,F:Pilgrim 2.50
8 WPo,SW,BWS(c), Wildstorm
  Rising,pt.7,w/2 cards 2.50
8a Newsstand ed. 2.25
9 F:Jester,Pilgrim Dozer 2.50
10 R:Dozer to Action 2.50
11 Blood Queen Vs. Dane 2.50
12 V:Vampire Nation 2.50
13 Fire From Heaven,pt.1 ..... 2.50
14 Fire From Heaven,pt.2 ..... 2.50
15 Fire From Heaven,pt.3 ..... 2.50
16 Fire From Heaven,pt.4 ..... 2.50
17 FTa, ... 2.50
18 FTa, ... 2.50
19 FTa, ... 2.50
20 FTa, ... 2.50
21 FTa, ... 2.50
22 FTa,Dave vs.Bloodqueen concl. 2.50
23 FTa,Flattop & Crossbones,
  V:Lady Feign 2.50
24 FTa, ... 2.50
25 FTa,Can Pilgrim withstand the
  beast that lurks within her,
  double size 4.00
26 team parts ways with Armand

Waering 2.50
27 V:Craven, no rest for the weary 2.50
28 Vampire tracked in Pacific
  Northwest,A:Johnny Savoy ... 2.50
29 V:Soulbender 2.50
30 "Secret of the Symbiotes" 2.50
31 "Time of the Blood War" 2.50
Sourcebook 2.50
TPB Rebirth 9.95

WETWORKS/VAMPIRELLA
Image/Wildstorm
1 JMi & GK, x-over 2.95

WILDC.A.T.S.
Image/Wildstorm 1992
1 B:BCi(s),JLe, SW(i), I:Wild-
  C.A.T.S. 6.00
1a Gold Ed. 9.00
1b Gold and Signed 14.00
2 JLe,SW(i),V:Master Gnome,
  I:Wetworks, Prism foil(c),
  w/coupon#5 .... 8.00
2a w/o coupon 3.00
3 RLd(c),JLe,SW(i), V:Youngblood 4.00
4 E:BCi(s),JLe,LSn,SW(i),w/card,
  A:Youngblood,BU:Tribe 4.00
4a w/red card 9.00
5 BCi(s),JLe,SW,I:Misery 3.50
6 BCi(s),JLe,SW,Killer Instinct,
  A:Misery,C:Ripclaw 3.50
7 BCi(s),JLe,SW, A:Cyberforce . 4.00
8 BCi(s),JLe,SW, ... 4.00
9 BCi(s),JLe,SW, ... 3.50
10 CCi(s),JLe,SW,I:Huntsman . 2.50
11 CCi(s),JLe,SW,V:Triad,
  A:Huntsman 2.50
11a WPo(c) 10.00
12 JLe,CCi,A:Huntsman 3.00
13 JLe,CCi,A:Huntsman 2.50
14 X book 2.50
15 F:Black Razors 2.50
16 Black Razors 2.50
17 A:StormWatch 2.50
18 R:Hightower 2.50
19 V:Hightower 2.50
20 TC,JeR,BWS(c),WildStorm
  Rising,pt.2,w/2 cards 2.50
20a Newsstand ed. 2.00
21 Into Space Back Home 2.50
22 Space Adventures 2.50
23 F:Mr. Majestic's Team 2.50
24 O:Maul 2.50
25 double sized 5.00
28 .... 2.50
27 .... 2.50
28 .... 2.50
29 Fire From Heaven,pt.7 ..... 2.50
30 BKs 2.50
31 BKs 2.50
32 BKs 2.50
33 BKs,gang war rages on 2.50
34 AMo,MtB,New York seconds
  away from nuclear disaster ... 2.50
35 AMo,MtB,BKs,V:Crusade 2.50
36 AMo,MtB,BKs,V:Crusade,
  A:Union, pt.2 .... 2.50
37 BCi,JPe,MtB,WildC.A.T.s team
  divided 2.50
38 BCi,JPe,MtB,Puritans debut . 2.50
39 BCi,JPe,MtB,"C.A.T. Fight" .. 2.50
40 BCi,JPe,MtB,MtB(c) 2.50
40a variant cover by TC 2.50
TPB A Gathering of Eagles 9.95

Spec.#1 SrG(s),TC,SW,I:Destine,
  Pin-ups 3.50
Spec.#2 .... 2.50
TPB rep. #1-4,w/0 .... 11.00

WILDC.A.T.S ADVENTURES
Image/Wildstorm 1994
1 From animated TV series 2.50
2 Helspont,Troika 2.00
3 Caught in war 2.00
4 V:The President 2.50
5 I:Lonely 2.50
6 I:Majestics 2.50
7 .... 2.50
8 Betrayed 2.50
9 V:Black Razors 2.50
10 F:Voodoo 2.50
Sourcebook (JS(c) 2.95

WILDC.A.T.S/ CYBERFORCE: KILLER INSTINCT
Image/Wildstorm
TPB 16.95

WildCats Trilogy #2 © Jim Lee

WILDC.A.T.S. TRILOGY
1 BCi(s),JaL,V:Artemis 2.50
2 BCi(s),JaL,V:Artemis 2.25
3 BCi(s),JaL,V:Artemis 2.25

WILDC.A.T.S/X-MEN
Image/Wildstorm Feb. 1997
1 (of 4) SLo,TC, giant Marvel/Image
  crossover 4.50
1a alternate cover by JLe 4.50
2 & 4 see Marvel

WILDC.A.T.S/X-MEN: THE SILVER AGE
Image/Wildstorm June 1997
1 SLo, JLe & SW, cross over ... 4.50

WILDSTAR
1 JOy,AG,I:WildStar 2.25

IMAGE

1a Gold Ed.	4.00
2 JOy,AG	2.25
3 JOy,AG,V:Savage Dragon, D:WildStar	2.25
4 JOy,AG,Last Issue,Pin-ups	2.25
TPB	12.95

[Regular Series]

1 R:WildStar	2.00
2 V:Mighty Man	2.50
3	2.50
Ashcan	1.00
TPB WildStar Sky Zero	12.95

WILDSTORM!

1 F:Spartan,Black Razors	2.50
2 F:Deathblow	2.50
3 F:Taboo,Spartan	2.50
4	2.50
Winter Wonderfest Spec.#1	3.50

WILDSTORM CHAMBER OF HORRORS

1 Horror Anthology	3.50

WILDSTORM RISING
Image/Wildstorm

1 JeR,BWS(c&a) WildStorm Rising, pt.1:Tricked by Defile, w/2 cards	2.50
1a Newsstand ed.	1.95
2 RMz,BBo,BWS(c) WildStorm Rising,pt.10,w/2 cards	2.50
2a Newsstand ed.	1.95
Wildstorm Sourcebook #1	2.50
TPB Rep. Mini-series	16.95

WILDSTORM SPOTLIGHT
Image/Wildstorm Feb. 1997

1 AMo,F:Majestic, at the end of time	2.50
2 StG,RMr,Loner returns	2.50
3 StG,RMr,Secret past of original Loner	2.50
4 F:Hellstrike	2.50

WILDSTORM SWIMSUIT SPECIAL '97
Image/Wildstorm June 1997

1	2.50

WILDSTORM UNIVERSE '97
Image/Wildstorm Nov. 1997

Sourcebook #1 thru #3	@2.50

WITCHBLADE
Image/Top Cow 1995–96

1 I:Witchblade	25.00
1A Special retailer edition	25.00
1B Wizard Ace edition,acetate(c)	30.00
2	30.00
2 encore edition	4.00
3	18.00
4	12.00
5	9.00
6	5.00
7	5.00
8	4.00

Top Cow 1996

9	4.00
9A variant cover	5.00
10 I:Darkness	5.00

10a variant Darkness cover (1:4)	12.00
11	2.50
12 Connection between Lisa, Microwave Murderer and Kenneth Irons	2.50

Image/Top Cow 1997

13 Dannette Boucher's secret past	2.50
14 Sara searches for Microwave Murderer	2.50
15 "There is a war brewing..."	2.50
16 "Will Witchblade come between Sarah and Jake?"	2.50
Coll.Ed.Vol.#1	4.95
Coll.Ed.Vol.#2	4.95
Coll.Ed.Vol.#3	4.95
Coll.Ed.Vol.#4, rep. #7 & #8	4.95

WIZARDS TALE, THE
Image/Homage Comics

one-shot KBk,DWe	19.95
TPB	19.95

WOLVERINE/ WITCHBLADE
Image/Top Cow Jan. 1997

one-shot "Devil's Reign" pt.5 (of 8)	4.00

WYNONNA EARP
Image/Wildstorm

1 BSt,	2.50
2 BSt,The Law comes to San Diablo	2.50
3 BSt,desperate to stop Hemo from going nationwide	2.50
4 BSt,goes to New York, V:ancient evil	2.50
5 BSt,battle with Raduk—Eater of the Dead concl.	2.50

Youngblood #8 © Rob Liefeld

YOUNGBLOOD
Image/Extreme

0 RLd,O:Youngblood,w/coupon#7	3.00
0a without coupon	1.50
0b gold coupon	9.00
1 RLd,I:Youngblood(flipbook)	5.00
1a 2nd print.,gold border	2.50
1b RLD,Silent Edition	12.95

2 RLd,I:ShadowHawk	6.00
3 RLd,I:Supreme	3.00
4 RLd,DK,A:Prophet,BU:Pitt	3.00
5 RLd,Flip book,w/Brigade #4	2.50
6 RLd(a&s),J:Troll,Knight Sabre, 2nd Die Hard, Proposal to Girl friend	3.50
7 Badrock, V:Overkill	2.50
8 Chapel, V:Spawn	2.50
9	2.50
9a variant cover	5.00
10 Bravo, Badrock, Troll	2.50
Yr.Bk.#1 CYp,I:Tyrax	2.75
Ashcan #1	9.00
Ashcan #2	5.00
TPB rep. #1-#5	16.95

[Volume 2] 1995

1 New Roster	2.50
2 The Program Continues	2.50
3 Extreme Babewatch	2.50
4 thru 6	@2.50
7 Shadowhunt x-over,pt.3	2.50
8 thru 10, ErS,RCz	@2.50
TPB Baptism of Fire, F:Spawn	
See Color Pub. section	

YOUNGBLOOD BATTLEZONE

1 BrM	2.25
2	2.95

YOUNGBLOOD STRIKEFILE
Image/Extreme 1993

1 JaL,RLd,I:Allies,A:Al Simmons (Spawn)	3.00
1a Gold Ed.	5.00
2 JaL,RLd,V:Super Patriot, Giger	2.50
2a Gold Ed.	3.50
3 RLd,JaL,DaM(i), A:Super Partiot	2.50
4 I:Overtkill	2.25
5	3.00
6 flip book	3.00
7 flip book	3.00
8 Shaft	3.00
9 Knight Sabre	3.00
10 RLd,TNu,I:Bloodpool,Task, Psilence,Wylder,Rubble	3.50
11 O:Link Crypt	2.50
TPB rep.#1-#3,sketchbook	12.95
Ashcan	9.00

YOUNGBLOOD/X-FORCE
Image/Extreme/Marvel 1996

1-shot Mojo visits Image x-over	5.00
1-shot RLd variant cover	5.00

YOUNGBLOOD YEARBOOK

1 CYp,I:Tyrax	2.75

YOUNGBLOOD: YEAR ONE

1 KBk(s),RLd, the early years	2.50
2 KBk(s),RLd,V:Giger,Cybernet	2.50

ZEALOT
Image/Wildstorm 1995

1 O:Zealot	2.50
2 In Japan	2.50
3 V:Prometheus	2.50

IMAGE

MALIBU

AIRMAN
1 I:Thresher 1.95

ALL NEW EXILES
Ultraverse 1995–96
Infinity F:Juggernaut,Blaze 2.50
1 TKa,KeL,Beginning the Quest . 1.50
1a Computer painted cover (1:6) . 2.50
1b signed edition 5.00
2 I:Hellblade, Phoenix flip issue . 1.50
3 TKa,KeL,Phoenix Resurrection 1.50
4 . . . . 1.50
5 . . . . 1.50
6 I:Moloch 1.50
7 . . . . 1.50
8 I:Maxis 1.50
9 . . . . 1.50
10 "Aladdin Attacks" 1.50
11 V:Maxis,A:Ripfire 1.50

ANGEL OF DESTRUCTION
Oct. 1996
1 . . . . 2.50

ARROW
1 V:Dr.Sheldon,A:Man O'War . . . 1.95

BATTLETECH
Feb. 1995
0 . . . . 2.95

BATTLETECH: FALLOUT
Dec. 1994–Mar. 1995
1 3 tales, Based on FASA game . 2.95
1a gold foil limited edition 3.50
1b limited holographic editon . . . 5.00
2 V:Clan Jade Falcon 2.95
3 R:Lea 2.95
4 Conclusion 2.95

BLACK SEPTEMBER
Ultraverse 1995
Infinity End of Black September . . 2.95

BRAVURA
1995
0 Preview book, mail-in 5.00

BREAK-THRU
Ultraverse 1993–94
1 GJ(s),GP,AV(i),A:All Ultraverse
  Heroes 2.75
1a Foil Edition 7.50
2 GJ(s),GP,AV(i),A:All Ultraverse
  Heroes 2.75

'BREED
Bravura
[Limited Series] 1994
1 JSn(a&s),Black (c),I:Stoner . . 3.00
2 JSn(a&s),I:Rachel 2.75
3 JSn(a&s),V:Rachel 2.75
4 JSn(a&s),I:Stoner's Mom 2.75
5 JSn(a&s),V:Rachel 2.75
6 JSn(a&s),final issue 2.50
TPB Book of Genesis, rep.#1–#6 12.95

'BREED II
Bravura
[Limited Series] 1994–95
1 JSn,The Book of Revelation . . 2.95
1a gold foil edition 5.00
2 JSn,A:Rachel 2.95
3 JSn,V:Actual Demon 2.95
4 JSn,Language of Demons 2.95
5 JSn,R:Rachael 2.95
6 JSn,final issue 2.95

BRUCE LEE
1994
1 MBn(s), Stories of B.Lee 2.95
2 MBn(s) 2.95
3 MBn(s) 2.95
4 thru 6 . . . . @2.95

CODENAME: FIREARM
Ultraverse 1995
0 I:New Firearm 2.95
1 F:Alec Swan 2.95
2 Dual Identity 2.95
3 F:Hitch and Lopez 2.95
4 F:Hitch and Lopez 2.95
5 Working Together 2.95

CURSE OF RUNE
Ultraverse 1995
1A CU,Rune/Silver Surfer tie-in . . 2.50
1B CU, alternate cover 2.50
2 COntrol of the Soul Gem 2.50
3 F:Marvel's Adam Warlock 2.50
4 N:Adam Warlock 2.50

DEAD CLOWN
1 I:Force America 2.50
2 I:Sadistic Six 2.50
3 TMs(s),last issue 2.50

DINOSAURS FOR HIRE
1 3-D rep. B&W 3.00

Dinosaurs for Hire #3 © Malibu Comics

[2nd Series] 1993–94
1 B:TMs(s),A:Reese,Archie,
  Lorenzo 3.00
2 BU:Dinosaurs 2099 . . . . 2.50
3 A:Ex-Mutants 2.50
4 V:Poacher,Revenue 2.50
5 . . . . 2.50
6 V:Samantha 2.50
7 V:Turret 2.50
8 Genesis #2, with Skycap 2.50
9 Genesis #5 . . . . 2.50
10 Flip(c) 2.50
11 V:Tiny Lorenzo 2.50
12 I:Manhatten Bob 2.50
13 I:Lil' Billy Frankenstein 2.50
14 final issue 2.50

DREADSTAR
Bravura 1994–95
1 JSn(c),PDd(s),EC,I:New
  Dreadstar (Kalla),w/stamp . . 2.75
2 JSn(c),PDd(s),EC,w/stamp . . 2.50
3 JSn(c),PDd(s),EC,w/stamp . . 2.75
4 PDd,EC,Kalla's origin,w/stamp 2.50
5 PDd,F:Vanth,w/stamp 2.50
6 PDd,w/stamp 2.50

EDGE
Bravura 1994–95
1 GK,I:Edge 2.50
2 GK,STg,Gold Stamp 2.50
3 GK,The Ultimates 2.50
4 GK,V:Mr. Ultimate 2.50

ELIMINATOR
Ultraverse 1995
0 Man,DJa,MZ,Zothros tries to re-
  open passage to the Godwheel 2.95
1 MZ,Man,DRo, The Search for the
  Missing Infinity Gems,I:Siren . . 2.95
1a Black Cover ed. 3.95
2 MZ 2.50
3 MZ, Infinity Gem tie-in,finale . . 2.50

ELVEN
Ultraverse 1994
0 Rep.,A:Prime, double size 2.95
Mini-Series 1994–95
1 A:Prime, Primevil 2.50
2 AaL,R:Maxi-Man 2.50
3 AaL,V:Duey, Primevil 2.50
4 AaL,F:Primevil 2.50

ETERNITY TRIPLE ACTION
B&W
1 F:Gazonga 1.95
2 F:Gigantor 2.50

EXILES
Ultraverse 1993
1 TMs(s),PaP,I:Exiles 5.00
1a w/out card 2.25
1b Gold hologram ed. 20.00
1c Ultra-limited 25.00
2 V:Kort 3.00
3 BWS,Mastodon,BU:Rune 4.00

4 V:Kort 3.00

EX-MUTANTS
Nov. 1992–Apr. 1994
1 I&O:Ex-Mutants	2.25
2 V:El Motho,Beafcake,Brickhouse	2.25
3 A:Sliggo,Zygote	2.25
4	2.25
5 Piper Kidnapped	1.95
6 A:Dr.Kildare	1.95
7 V:Dr.Kildare	1.95
8 O:Gelson	1.95
9 F:Dillion	1.95
10 F:Sluggtown	1.95
11 Man(s),Genesis#1,w/card	2.25
12 ROM(s),Genesis#4	2.25
13 J:Gravestone,Arc	2.25
14 C:Eye	2.25
15 A:Arrow	2.50
16 A:Arrow,I:KillCorp	2.50
17 A:Arrow,V:KillCorp	2.50
18 A:Arrow,V:KillCorp	2.50

FERRET
1 (From Protectors),DZ,V:Purple Dragon Tong,A:Iron Skull	2.25

[Regular Series] 1992–93
1 thru 3	2.50
4 V:Toxin	2.50
4a Newstand Ed.	2.25
5 SEr,Genesis	2.25
6 SEr,Genesis crossover	2.25
7 V:Airman	2.25
8 I:Posse	2.25
9 DZ,R:Iron Skull,I:Deathsong	2.25
10 DZ	2.25
11	2.25

FIREARM
Ultraverse 1993–95
0 w/video,I:Duet	4.00
1 I:Firearm,Alec Swan	2.50
1 silver foil, limited edition	4.00
2 BWS,A:Hardcase,BU:Rune	2.75
3 V:Sportsmen	2.25
4 HC,Break-Thru x-over	2.25
5 O:Prime,I:Ellen	2.25
6 A:Prime	2.25
7 V:Killer	2.25
8 DIB(c)	2.25
9 at the Rose Bowl	1.95
10 The Lodge	1.95
11 Ultraverse Premier #5,BU:Prime	3.50
12 Rafferty Saga,pt.1	1.95
13 Rafferty Saga,pt.2	1.95
14 Swan	1.95
15 Rafferty Saga,pt.3	1.95
16 Rafferty Saga,pt.4	1.95
17 Rafferty Saga,pt.5	1.95
18 JeR,HC(c),Rafferty Saga,finale	2.50

FLOOD RELIEF
Ultraverse 1994
TPB Ultraverse Heroes 5.00

FOXFIRE
Ultraverse 1996
1 From Phoenix Resurrection	1.50
2 Fate of Mastodon revealed	1.50
3 & 4	@1.50

FRANKENSTEIN
1 thru 3 movie promo . . . . @2.50

JONES · HERERRA · CHRISTIAN

Freex #1 © Malibu Comics

FREEX
Ultraverse 1993–95
1 I:Freex w/Ultraverse card	3.00
1a Ultra-Limited	4.00
1b Full Hologram (c)	5.00
2 L:Valerie,I:Rush	3.00
3 A:Rush	3.00
4 GJ(s),DdW,BWS,BU:Rune	2.75
5 GJ(s),V:Master of the Hunt	2.50
6 GJ(s),BH,Break Thru x-over, A:Night Man	2.25
7 BHr,MZ,O:Hardcase	2.25
8 BHr,V:Lost Angel	2.25
9 BHr,A:Old Man	2.25
10 BHr,V:Ms. Contrary	2.25
11 BHr,E:Origins	2.25
12 GJ,Ultraforce	1.95
13 New look	1.95
14 R:Boomboy	1.95
15 Death of Teamate	3.50
16 Prelude to Godwheel	1.95
17 A:Rune	2.50
18 GJ,A:Contray, Cayman, Juice	2.50
Giant Size#1 A:Prime	2.50

GENESIS
0 GP,w/Pog,F:Widowmaker, A:Arrow	3.50
0a Gold Ed.	5.00

GODWHEEL
Ultraverse 1995
0 R:Argus to Godwheel	2.50
1 I:Primevil	2.50
2 Hardcase new costume	2.50
3 F:Lord Pumpkin	2.50
TPB Wheel of Thunder,rep.#0–#3	9.95

GRAVESTONE
July 1993–Feb. 1994
1 D:Gravestone,V:Wisecrack	2.25
1a Newstand Ed.	1.95
2 A:Eternal Man, V:Night Plague	2.25
2a Newstand Ed.	1.95
3 Genesis Tie in,w/skycap	2.25
4 Genesis	2.25
5 V:Scythe	2.25
6 V:Jug	1.95

7 R:Bogg	2.25
8	2.25
9	2.25

HARDCASE
Ultraverse 1993–95
1 I:Hardcase,D:The Squad	3.00
1a Ultra-Limited, silver foil	4.00
1b Full Hologram (c)	5.00
1c Platinum edition	3.50
2 w/Ultraverse card	3.00
3 Hard decisions	2.75
4 A:Strangers	2.75
5 BWS,V:Hardwire,BU:Rune	2.75
6 V:Hardwire	2.50
7 ScB,Break-Thru x-over, I:Nanotech,A:Solution	2.25
8 GP,O:Solitare	2.25
9 B:O:Choice,I:Turf	2.25
10 O:Choice	2.25
11 ScB,V:Aladdin	2.25
12 AV,A:Choice	1.95
13 A:Choice	2.25
14 A:Choice	2.25
15 Hardwires, NIM-E	1.95
16 NIM-E	3.50
17 Prime,NIM-E	1.95
18 V:Nim-E, Battle Royale	1.95
19 Prelude to Godwheel	1.95
20 R:Rex Mindi	2.50
21 Mundiquest prelude	2.50
22 Mundiquest.	2.50
23 A:Loki	2.50
24 Mundiquest,pt.3	2.50
25 Mundiquest,concl.	2.95
26 Time Gem Disaster	2.95

HOSTILE TAKEOVER
1 ashcan Ultraverse x-over 75

LITA FORD
Rock-It Comix
1 JBa 3.95

LORD PUMPKIN
Oct. 1994
0 Sludge 2.50

MAN CALLED A-X
Bravura 1994–95
[Limited Series]
0 1st Puzzle piece	2.95
1 MWn,SwM	2.95
1a Gold foil Edition	4.00
2 MWn,SwM,VLElectobot	2.95
3 MWn,SwM,Mercy Island	2.95
4 MWn,SwM,One Who Came Before	2.95
5 MWn,SwM,Climax	2.95

MAN OF WAR
1993–94
1 thru 3 V:Lift	2.50
1a thru 5a Newstand Ed.	1.95
4 w/poster	2.50
5 V:Killinger	2.50
6 KM,Genesis Crossover	2.50
7 DJu,Genesis Crossover	2.50
8 TMs(s),A:Rocket Ranger	2.25
9	2.25
10	2.25
11	2.25
12	2.25

MALIBU

All comics prices listed are for *Near Mint* condition.

MANTRA
Ultraverse 1993–95
1 AV,I:Mantra,w/Ultraverse card	3.00
1a Full Hologram (c)	7.00
1b Silver foil (c)	5.00
2 AV,V:Warstrike	2.50
3 AV,V:Kismet Deadly	2.50
4 BWS,Mantra's marriage, BU:Rune story	2.50
5 MiB(s),AV(i),V:Wiley Wolf	2.00
6 MiB(s),AV(i),Break Thru x-over	2.00
7 DJu,TA,A:Prime, O:Prototype	2.00
8 B:MiB(s),A:Warstrike	2.00
9 V:Iron Knight,Puppeteer	2.00
10 NBy(c),DaR,B:Archmage Quest, Flip/UltraversePremiere #2	3.00
11 MiB(s),V:Boneyard	2.00
12 MiB(s),A:Strangers	2.00
13 Topaz, Boneyard	2.00
14 Tradesmen, Boneyard	2.00
15 A:Prime, Doc Gross	2.00
16 A:Prime	2.00
17 A:Necromantra	2.00
18 Pregnancy	2.25
19 MiB,Pregnancy	2.25
20 Aftermath of Godwheel	2.25
21 TyD,MiB,Mantra goes bad	2.25
22 A:Marvel's Loki	2.25
23 I:Tremblor, A:Prime	2.25
24 V:Topaz	2.25
Giant Sized#1 GP(c),I:Topaz	2.25
Ashcan #1	2.00

MANTRA
Ultraverse 1995–96
Infinity N:Mantra	2.50
1 Mantra in all Female Body	1.50
1a Computer Painted Cover	1.50
2 Phoenix flip issue	1.50
3 Phoenix Resurrection	1.50
4	1.50
5	1.50
6 TMs,I:Tattoo,A:Rush	1.50
7	1.50

MANTRA: SPEAR OF DESTINY
Ultraverse 1995
1 Search for Artifact	2.50
2 MiB,Eden vs. Aladdin	2.50

MARVEL/ULTRAVERSE BATTLEZONES
Ultraverse 1996
1 DPs(c),The Battle of the Heroes	3.95

MEGADETH
Rock-it Comix
1	4.25

METALLICA
Rock-it Comix
1	4.25

METAPHYSIQUE
Bravura 1995
1 NBy,I:Metaphysique	2.95
1a Gold foil edition	4.00
2 NBy,Mandelbrot malfunctions	2.95
3 I:Harridas	2.95
4 D:Maj.Character,B:Superious	2.95

5 V:Astral Kid	2.95
6 Apocalyptic Armageddon, finale	2.95
Ashcan NBy,B&W	1.00

The Mighty Magnor #2 © Malibu Comics

MIGHTY MAGNOR, THE
1 thru 6 SA	@1.95

MONSTER POSSE
B&W
1 I:Monster Posse	2.50
2 I:P.O.N.E,Wack Mack Dwac's sister,D-Vicious	2.50

MORTAL KOMBAT
1994
0 Four stories	2.95
1 Based on the Video Game	2.95
1a Foil Ed	4.00
1b with new material	2.95
2	2.95
3	2.95
4	2.95
5 I:Mortal Kombat II	2.95
6 Climax	2.95
Spec. #1 Tournament edition	3.95
Spec. #2 Tournament edition II	3.95
TPB rep. #1–#6	14.95

MORTAL KOMBAT: BARAKA
1 V:Scorpion	2.95

MORTAL KOMBAT: BATTLEWAVE
1 New series	2.95
2 Action, Action, Action	2.95
3 The Gathering	2.95
4 F:Goro	2.95
5 F:Scorpion	2.95
6 final issue	2.95

MORTAL KOMBAT: GORO, PRINCE OF PAIN
1 Goro	2.95
1a Platinum Edition	6.25
2 Goro, V:Kombatant	2.95

3 Goro, V:God of Pain	2.95

MORTAL KOMBAT: KITANA & MILEENA
1 Secrets of Outworld	2.95

MORTAL KOMBAT: KUNG LAO
1 one-shot Battlewave tie-in	2.95

MORTAL KOMBAT: RAYDEN AND KANO
1 J:Rayden Kano	2.95
1a Deluxe Edition	4.95
2 A:Reptile	2.95
3 Kano, conclusion	2.95

MORTAL KOMBAT: U.S. SPECIAL FORCES
1 V:Black Dragon	3.50
2 V:Black Dragon	2.95

NECROMANTRA/ LORD PUMPKIN
Ultraverse 1995
1 A:Loki (from Marvel)	2.95
2 MiB,V:Godwheel, flipbook	2.95
3 O:Lord Pumpkin	2.95
4 Infinity Gem tie-in	2.95
4a variant cover	3.50

NECROSCOPE
1 Novel adapt., holo(c)	3.25
1a 2nd printing	2.95
2 thru 4 Adapt. cont.	@2.95
Book II	
1 thru 5	2.95

NIGHT MAN, THE
Ultraverse 1993–95
1 I:Night Man,Deathmask	2.75
1a Silver foil (c)	4.00
2 GeH,V:Mangle	2.25
3 SEt,GeH,A:Freex,Mangle	2.25
4 HC,I:Scrapyard,O:Firearm	2.25
5 SEt(s)	2.25
6 V:TNTNT	2.25
7 V:Nick	2.25
8 V:Werewolf	1.95
9 V:Werewolf	2.25
10	1.95
11	1.95
12	1.95
13	1.95
14 V:Rafferty	1.95
15 I:Rigoletto	1.95
16 I:Bloodfly	3.50
17 D:Playland	2.50
18 DZ,SEt,V:Bloodfly	2.50
19 DZ,SEt,V:Deathmask	2.50
20 DZ,V:Bloody fly	2.50
21 Identity Revealed	2.50
22 Infinity Gem tie-in,A:Loki	2.50
23 R:Rhianon	2.50
Ann.#1 V:Pilgrim, 64pg.	3.95

NIGHT MAN, THE
Ultraverse 1995
Infinity Night Man vs. Night Man	2.50
1 Discovers New powers	1.50
1a Computer Painted Cover	1.50

MALIBU

2 phoenix flip issue	1 50
3 Phoenix Resurrection	1.50
4 final issue	1.50

NIGHT MAN/GAMBIT
1996

1 thru 3	@2.50

NOCTURNALS
Bravura 1995

1 DIB,I:Nocturnals	2.95
1a Glow-in-the-Dark	4.00
2 DIB,I:Komodo, Mister Fane	2.95
3 DIB,F:Raccoon	2.95
4 DIB,I:The Old Wolf	2.95
5 Discovered by Police	2.95
6 DIB,	2.95

ORIGINS
Ultraverse

1 O:Ultraverse Heroes	1.25

OZZY OSBORNE
Rock-It Comix

1 w/guitar pick	3.95

PANTERA
Rock-it Comix

1	3.95
1a Gold Ed.	19.95

PHOENIX RESURRECTION
Ultraverse 1995–96

0 Intro to Phoenix Resurrection	1.95
Genesis, A:X-Men	3.95
Revelations, A:X-Men	3.95
Aftermath, A:X-Men	3.95

PLAN 9 FROM OUTER SPACE

GNv Movie Adapt.	4.95

POWER & GLORY
Bravura 1994

1A HC(a&s),I:American Powerhouse	3.00
1B alternate cover	3.00
1c Blue Foil (c)	5.00
1d w/seirgraph	5.00
1e Newsstand	3.00
2 HC(a&s), O:American Powerhouse	2.75
3 HC(a&s)	2.50
4 HC(a&s)	2.50
Winter Special	2.95
TPB Series reprint, w/stamp	12.95

POWER OF PRIME
Ultraverse 1995

1 O:Prime Powers,Godwheel tie-in	2.50
2 V:Doc Gross, Godwheel tie-in	2.50
3 F:Prime Phade	2.50
4 F:Elven,Turbocharge	2.50

PRIME
Ultraverse 1993–95

1 B:GJ(s),I:Prime	6.00
1a Ultra-Limited	8.00
1b Full Hologram (c)	8.00
2 V:Organism 8, with Ultraverse card	5.00

3 NBy,I:Prototype	3.00
4 NBy,V:Prototype	3.00
5 NBy,BWS,I:Maxi-Man, BU:Rune	3.00
6 NBy,A:Pres. Clinton	2.75
7 NBy,Break-Thru x-over	2.25
8 NBy,A:Mantra	2.25
9 NBy,Atomic Lies	2.25
10 NBy,A:Firearm,N:Prime	2.25
11 NBy	2.25

Prime #12 © Malibu Comics

12 NBy,(Ultraverse Premiere#3) I:Planet Class	3.50
13 NBy,V:Kutt,Planet Class	2.95
14 DaR,I:Voodoo Master	2.25
15 abused kids	1.95
16 I:Turbo	1.95
17 Atalon	1.95
18 Prime's new partner	1.95
19 Prime accused	1.95
20 GJ,LeS,A:Rafferty	2.50
21 GJ,LeS,World without Prime	2.50
22 GJ,LeS,F:Primevil	2.50
23 F:Prime's Mother	2.50
24 F:Prime's Mother	2.50
25 A:Chelsea Clinton	2.50
26 True Powers	2.50
Ashcan (first)	7.00
Ashcan #1 BV(c),B&W	.75
Ann.#1 R:Doc Gross	3.95
TPB Rep. #1-#4	9.95

PRIME
Ultraverse 1995–96

Infinty I:Spider-Prime	3.00
1 Spider-Prime vs. Lizard	1.50
1a Computer painted cover	2.00
2 Phoenix flip issue	1.50
3 Phoenix Resurrection	1.50
4	1.50
5	1.50
6 Prime on Drugs,pt.1,F:Solitaire	1.50
7 F:Solitaire, pt.2	1.50
8 F:Solitaire, pt.3	1.50
9 and 10	@1.50
11 "Absolute Power Corrupts? Absolutely!"	1.50
12 HuR,KG, pt.3 (of 3)	1.50
13 KG,Prime exposed, V:Colonel	

Rinaldo	1.50
14 KG, Return of Lord Pumpkin	1.50
15 Return of Lord Pumpkin	1.50

PRIME/CAPTAIN AMERICA
Ultraverse 1996

1 GJ,NBy	3.95

PRIME VS. HULK

0	10.00
0a signed premium edition	20.00

PROJECT A-KO

1 thru 4 Based on anime movie	@2.95

Protectors #1 © Malibu Comics

PROTECTORS
1992–94

1 I:Protectors, inc. JBi poster (direct)	3.00
1a thru 12a Newsstand	@1.95
2 V:Mr.Monday,w/poster	2.50
3 V:Steel Army,w/poster	2.50
4 V:Steel Army	2.50
5 Die Cut(c),V:Mr.Monday	2.50
6 V:Mr.Monday	2.50
7 A:Thresher	2.50
8 V:Wisecrack	1.95
9 V:Wisecrack	2.50
10 I:Mantoka	2.50
11 A:Ms.Fury,V:Black Fury	2.50
12 A:Arrow	2.50
13 RAJ(s),Genesis#3	2.25
14 RB(c),RAJ(s),Genesis#6	2.25
15 RAJ(s),J:Chalice	2.25
16 So Help Me God	2.25
17 L:Ferret	2.25
18 V:Regulators,BU:Mantako, R:Mr. Monday	2.25
19 A:Gravestone,Arc	2.50
20 V:Nowhere Man	2.50
Protectors Handbook	2.50

PROTOTYPE
Ultraverse 1993–95

1 V:Ultra-Tech,w/card	2.50
1a Ultra-lim. silver foil(c)	5.00
1b Hologram	6.00

All comics prices listed are for *Near Mint* condition.

MALIBU

2 I:Backstabber	2.50
3 LeS(s),DvA,JmP,BWS, V:Ultra-Tech,BU:Rune	2.50
4 TMs(s),V:Wrath	2.25
5 TMs(s),A:Strangers,Break-Thru x-over	2.25
6 TMs(s),Origins Month C:Arena	2.25
7 TMs(s),V:Arena	2.25
8 TMs(s),V:Arena	2.25
9 Prototype Unplugged	2.25
10 TMs(s),V:Prototype	1.95
11 TMs(s),R:Glare	2.25
12 V:Ultratech	1.95
13 Ultraverse Premiere #6	3.50
14 Jimmy Ruiz, new boss	1.95
15 Techuza, Donovan	1.95
16 New CEO for Terrordy	1.95
17 Ranger Vs. Engine	1.95
18 Turf War	2.50
G-Size, Hostile Takeover	2.50
Spec.#0 LeS,JQ/JP(c)	2.50

PROTOTYPE: TURF WAR
Ultraverse

1 LeS,V:Techuza	2.50
2 LeS,F:Ranger,Arena	2.50
3	2.50

RAFFERTY

1 Ashcan	1.00

Raver #3 © Malibu Comics

RAVER

1 Prism cover	3.00
1a Newsstand	2.25
2	1.95
3 Walter Koenig(s)	1.95
4 and 5	@1.95

RIPFIRE

0 Prequel to Ripfire Series	2.50

RUNE
Ultraverse 1994–95

0 BWS(a&s)	4.00
1 BWS(a&s),from Ultraverse	2.50
1a Foil cover	4.00

2 CU(s),BWS,V:Aladdin	2.25
3 DaR,BWS,(Ultraverse Premiere #1), Flip book	3.75
4 BWS,V:Twins	2.25
5 BWS	1.95
6 BWS	1.95
7 CU,JS	1.95
8 Rise of Gods,pt.2	1.95
9 Prelude to Godwheel	1.95
G-Size #1	2.50
TPB BWS(c&a),CU,The Awakening, rep.#1–#5	12.95

RUNE
Ultraverse 1995–96

Infinity V:Annihilus	2.50
1 A:Adam Warlock	1.50
1a Computer painted cover	1.50
2 Phoenix flip issue,A:Adam Warlock	1.50
3 Phoenix Resurrection	1.50
4	1.50
5	1.50
6 LKa,A:Warlock	1.50

RUNE: HEARTS OF DARKNESS
Ultraverse 1996

1 DgM(s),KHt,TBd, flip book	1.50
2 DgM,KHt,TBd, flip book	1.50
3 DgM,KHt,TBd, flip book	1.50

RUNE/SILVER SURFER
Ultravrse 1995

1 BWS(c),A:Adam Warlock	5.95
1a Lim. edition (5,000 made)	8.00
1b Standard ed.newsprint	2.95

RUNE VS. VENOM
Ultraverse 1996

1 one-shot x-over	1.95

RUST

1 O:Rust	2.95
2 V:Marion Labs	2.95
3 I:Ashe Sapphire,5th Anniv.	2.95
4 I:Rustmobile	2.95

SANTANA
Rock-it Comix

1 TT(c&s),TY	3.95

SIREN
Ultraverse 1995

Infinity V:War Machine	2.50
1 V:War Machine	1.50
1a Computer painted cover	1.50
2 Phoenix flip issue	1.50
3 Phoenix Resurrection	1.50
Spec. #1 O:Siren	1.95

SLUDGE
Ultraverse 1993–94

1 BWS,I:Sludge,BU:I:Rune	2.75
1a Ultra-Limited	6.00
2 AaL,I:Bloodstorm	2.25
3 AaL,V:River Men	2.50
4 AaL,Origins Month, V:Alligator	2.25
5 AaL,V:Garret Whale	2.25
6 AaL,A:Dragon Fang,Lord Pumpkin	2.25

Siren #3 © Malibu Comics

7 V:Frank Hoag	2.25
8 AaL,V:Monsters	2.25
9 AaL,O:Sludge	2.25
10 AaL,O:Sludge	1.95
11 AaL,V:Bash Brothers	1.95
12 AaL,V:Prime, w/flip book w/Ultraverse Premiere #8	3.50
13	1.95
Red X-Mas	2.50

SOLITAIRE
Ultraverse 1993–94

1 black baged edition with playing card: Ace of Clubs, Diamonds, Hearts or Spades	2.75
1d Newsstand edition,no card	2.25
2 GJ(s),JJ,Break-Thru x-over, V:Moon Man	2.25
3 Origins Month, I:Monkey-Woman	2.25
4 O:Solitaire	2.25
5 JJ,V:Djinn	2.25
6 JJ,V:Lone	1.95
7 JJ,I:Double Edge	2.25
8 GJ,I:Degenerate	1.95
9 GJ,Degenerate Rafferty	1.95
10 Hostile Takeover #2	1.95
11 V:Djinn	1.95
12 V:Anton Lowe	1.95

SOLUTION
Ultraverse 1993–95

0 DaR,O:Solution	5.00
1 DaR,I:Solution	2.50
1a foil cover	4.00
2 DaR,BWS,V:Rex Mundi,Quatro, BU:Rune	2.50
3 DaR,A:Hardcase,Choice	2.50
4 DaR,Break-Thru x-over, A:Hardcase,Choice	2.50
5 F:Dropkick	2.25
6 B:O:Solution	2.25
7 KM,O:Solution	2.25
8 KM(c),E:O:Solution	2.25
9 F:Shadowmage	2.25
10 V:Vyr	2.25
11 V:Vorlexx	2.25
12 JHi	1.95

MALIBU

13 Hostile Takeover pt.3	1.95
14 old foes	1.95
15 V:Casino	1.95
16 Flip/UltraverePremiere#10	3.50
17 F:Casino, Dragons Claws	2.50

SQUAD, THE

0-A Hardcase's old team	2.50
0-B	2.50
0-C L.A.Riots	2.50

STAR SLAMMERS
Bravura 1994

1 WS(a&s)	2.75
2 WS(a&s),F:Meredith	2.75
3 WS(a&s)	2.50
4 WS(a&s)	2.50
5 WS,Rojas Choice	2.50

STAR TREK: DEEP SPACE NINE

1 Direct ed.	3.25
1a Photo(c).	3.00
1b Gold foil	5.00
2 w/skycap	3.50
3 Murder on DS9	2.75
4 MiB(s),F:Bashir,Dax	2.75
5 MiB(s),V:Slaves	2.75
6 MiB(s),Three Stories	2.75
7 F:Kira	2.75
8 B:Requiem	2.75
9 E:Requiem	2.75
10 Descendants	2.50

Star Trek: Deep Space Nine #16
© Malibu Comics

11 A Short Fuse	2.75
12 Baby on Board	2.50
13 Problems with Odo	2.75
14 on Bejor	2.75
15 mythologic dilemma	2.75
16 Shangheid	2.50
17 Voyager preview	2.50
18 V:Gwyn	2.50
19 Wormhole Mystery	2.50
20 Sisko Injured	2.50
21 Smugglers attack DS9	2.50
22 Commander Quark	2.50

23 Secret of the Lost Orb,pt.1	2.50
24 Secret of the Lost Orb,pt.2	2.50
25 Secret of the Lost Orb,pt.3	2.50
26 Mudd's Pets, pt.1	2.50
27 Mudd's Pets, pt.2	2.50
28 F:Ensign Ro	2.50
29 F:Thomas Riker,Tuvok	2.50
30 F:Thomas Riker	2.50
31 thru 32	@2.50
Ann.#1 Looking Glass	3.95

STAR TREK: DEEP SPACE NINE CELEBRITY SERIES: BLOOD AND HONOR

1 Mark Lenard(s)	2.95
2 Rules of Diplomacy	2.95

STAR TREK: DEEP SPACE NINE: LIGHTSTORM

1 Direct ed.	3.50
1a Silver foil	8.00

STAR TREK: DEEP SPACE NINE: HEARTS AND MINDS
[Limited Series]

1	3.00
2	2.50
3 Into the Abyss,X-over preview	2.50
4 final issue	2.50

STAR TREK: DEEP SPACE NINE: THE MAQUIS
[Limited Series]

1 Federation Renegades	2.50
1a Newsstand, photo(c)	2.50
2 Garack	2.50
3 F:Quark, Bashir	2.50

STAR TREK: DEEP SPACE NINE/ THE NEXT GENERATION

1 Prophet & Losses, pt.2	2.50
2 Prophet & Losses, pt.4	2.50

STAR TREK: DEEP SPACE NINE: TEROK NOR

0 Fully painted by Goring	2.95

STAR TREK: DEEP SPACE NINE SPECIAL

1 Collision COurse	3.50

STAR TREK: VOYAGER

A V:Maquis	2.75
Aa Newsstand, photo(c)	2.50
B conclusion	2.75
Ba Newsstand, photo(c)	2.50

STRANGERS, THE
Ultraverse 1993–95

1 I:Strangers	3.00
1a Ultra-Limited	5.00
1b Full Hologram (c)	6.00
2 A:J.D.Hunt,w/Ultraverse card	3.00
3 I:TNTNT	2.50
4 A:Hardcase	2.50
5 BWS,BU:Rune	2.50

6 J:Yrial,I:Deathwish	2.25
7 Break-Thru x-over	2.25
8 RHo,ANi,O:Solution	2.25
9 AV(i),I:Ulta Pirates	2.25

The Strangers #9 © Malibu Comics

10 AV(i),V:Bastinado	2.25
11 in Alderson Disk	2.25
12 O:Yrial	2.25
13 (Ultraverse Premiere#4)	3.50
14	2.25
15 Zip-Zap, Yrail	1.95
16 Ultras, Teknight	1.95
17 Rafferty	1.95
18 Ultra Pirates	1.95
19 V:Pilgrim	1.95
20 Stranger Destroyed	1.95
21 A:Rex Mundi	2.50
22 SEt,V:Guy Hunt	2.50
23 SEt,RHo,V:Tabboo	2.50
24 RHo,SEt,V:Taboo	2.50
25 V:Godwheel Aliens	2.50
26 RHo,SEt,V:Aladdin	2.50
Ann.#1 Death	3.95
TPB rep. #1-#4	9.95
Ashcan 1 (signed)	8.00
Ashcan 1 (unsigned)	8.00

STREET FIGHTER

1 thru 3 Based on Video Game	@3.00

STRIKEBACK
Bravura 1994–95

1	2.95
2	2.95
3 V:Doberman	2.95
4 V:Dragonryder Island	2.95
Spec.#1 KM,JRu,V:Dragon	3.50

TARZAN: THE BECKONING

1 TY,I:The Spider Man	2.75
2 TY,Going back to Africa	2.50
3 thru 6	2.50

TARZAN THE WARRIOR

1 SBs(c),O:Tarzan	3.50
2	2.75

All comics prices listed are for *Near Mint* condition.

MALIBU

MALIBU

3 . . . . 2.75
4 Wom'cha's Ship 2.75
5 . . . . 2.75

TARZAN: LOVE, LIES, AND THE LOST CITY
1 MWg&WS(s),Short Stories 3.95
2 The lost city of Opar 2.50
3 Final issue 2.50

TERMINATOR 2: CYBERNETIC DAWN
1995–96
1 thru 4 . . . . @2.50
0 flip-book/T2 Nuclear Twilight . . 2.50

TERMINATOR 2: NUCLEAR TWILIGHT
1995–96
1 thru 4 . . . . @2.50
0 flip-book, see above

ULTRAFORCE
Ultraverse 1994–95
1 Prime, Prototype 2.50
2 . . . . 1.95
3 . . . . 1.95
4 . . . . 1.95
5 V:Atalon 1.95
6 V:Atalon 2.50
7 CU,GP(c),F:Ghoul 2.50
8 MWn,CV,GP,F:Black Knight . . . 2.50
9 A:Marvel's Black Knight 2.50
10 . . . . 2.50
Spec.#0 . . . . 2.50

UltraForce #3 © Malibu Comics

ULTRAFORCE
Ultraverse 1995–96
Infinity Fant. Ultraforce Four 2.50
1 George Perez cover 1.50
1a Computer painted cover 1.50
2 Phoenix flip issue,I:Lament . . . 1.50
3 . . . . 1.50
4 . . . . 1.50
5 . . . . 1.50

6 Smoke and Bone,pt.2 . . . . 1.50
7 . . . . 1.50
8 . . . . 1.50
9 . . . . 1.50
10 A:Sersi,Eliminator 1.50
11 . . . . 1.50
12 MD2,LWn, cont. from All-New
   Exiles #12 . . . . 1.50
13 LWn,MD2,new UltraForce lineup 1.50
14 LWn,MD2,Hardcase returns . . 1.50
15 LWn,MD2,Hardcase returns . . 1.50

ULTRAFORCE/AVENGERS
Ultraverse Aug. 1995
1 GP 3.95

ULTRAFORCE/ SPIDER-MAN
Ultraverse 1996
1 . . . . 3.95

ULTRAVERSE DOUBLE FEATURE
Ultraverse
1 F:Prime, Solitaire 3.95

ULTRAVERSE FUTURE SHOCK
Ultraverse 1996
1 one-shot,MPc,alternate futures . 2.50

ULTRAVERSE ORIGINS
Ultraverse
1 O:Ultraverse Heroes 1.25
1a Silver foil cover 12.50

ULTRAVERSE UNLIMITED
Ultraverse 1996
1 F:Warlock 1.50
2 LWn,KWe, A:All-New Exiles,V:Max 1.50

ULTRAVERSE: YEAR ZERO: THE DEATH OF THE SQUAD
Ultraverse 1995
0-A hardcase's old team 2.50
0-B 2.50
0-C L.A. Riots 2.50
1 JHl,A:Squad, Mantra 2.95
2 JHl,DaR(c) prequel to Prime#1 2.95
3 Cont. Year Zero Story 2.95
4 I:NM-E 2.95

ULTRAVERSE: YEAR ONE
Ultraverse 1995
1 Handbook, double size 4.95
2 Prime 1.95

ULTRAVERSE: YEAR TWO
Ultraverse 1996
1 Marvel/Ultraverse/Info 4.95

VIRTUA FIGHTER
Ultraverse 1996
1 New Video Game Comic 2.95

WARSTRIKE
Ultraverse 1994–95
1 HNg,TA,in South America 1.95
2 HNg,TA,Gatefold(c) 1.95

Warstrike #2 © Malibu Comics

3 in Brazil 1.95
4 HNg,TA,V:Blind Faith 1.95
5 . . . . 1.95
6 Rafferty 1.95
7 Origin 1.95

WARSTRIKE: PRELUDE TO GODWHEEL
Ultraverse 1994
1 Blind Faith/Lord Pumpkin 1.95

WORLD DOMINATION
1 . . . . 3.95
1a 3.95

WRATH
Ultraverse 1994–95
1 B:MiB(s),DvA,JmP,C:Mantra . . 2.25
1a Silver foil 4.00
2 DvA,JmP,V:Hellion 2.25
3 DvA,JmP,V:Radicals, I:Slayer . 2.25
4 DvA,JmP,V:Freex 2.25
5 DvA,JmP,V:Freex 1.95
6 DvA,JmP 2.25
7 DvA,JmP,I:Pierce,Ogre, Doc
   Virtual 1.95
8 . . . . 1.95
9 A:Prime 2.25
G-Size #1 . . . . 2.50

COLOR COMICS

ABBOTT AND COSTELLO
Charlton Comics 1968–71
1 .... 45.00
2 thru 9 .... @30.00
10 thru 21 .... @20.00
22 .... 18.00

ACCIDENT MAN: THE DEATH TOUCH
Apocalypse
One Shot rep.Toxic #10-#16 .... 3.95

ACME NOVELTY LIBRARY
Fantagraphics 1994–97
1 thru 5 .... @4.50
6 thru 9 Jimmy Corrigan Meets His
  Dad, pt. 1 – pt. 4 (of 8) .... @4.50

ADAM-12
Gold Key 1973–76
1 Photo(c), From TV show 50.00
2 thru 9 .... @25.00
10 .... 22.00

ADAPTERS, THE
1 and 2 .... @2.00

ADDAMS FAMILY
Gold Key 1974–75
1 TV cartoon adapt. 75.00
2 .... 35.00
3 .... 30.00

ADLAI STEVENSON
Dell Publishing Co. Dec., 1966
1 Political Life Story 25.00

ADVENTURES OF BARON MUNCHAUSEN
Now Comics 1989
1 thru 4 movie adapt. series .. @1.75

ADVENTURES OF CHRISSIE CLAUS, THE
Hero Graphics
1 Trouble in Toyland 2.95

ADVENTURES OF FELIX THE CAT
Harvey 1992
1 Short Stories 1.25

ADVENTURES OF KUNG FU PIG NINJA FLOUNDER AND 4-D MONKEY
1 thru 6 .... @1.80
7 thru 10 .... @2.00

ADVENTURES OF ROBIN HOOD
Gold Key 1974–75

1 From Disney cartoon 6.00
2 thru 7 .... @3.50

ADVENTURES OF ROGER WILCO
Adventure
1 Based on Space-Quest Computer
  games 2.95

Adventures of the Fly #14
© Archie Publications

ADVENTURES OF THE FLY
Archie Publications/ Radio Comics 1959–65
1 JSm/JK,O:Fly,I:SpiderSpry
  A:Lancelot Strong/Shield ... 550.00
2 JSm/JK,DAy,AW 300.00
3 Jack Davis Art, O:Fly 250.00
4 V:Dazzler NA panel 125.00
5 A:Spider Spry 75.00
6 V:Moon Men 75.00
7 A:Black Hood 75.00
8 A:Lancelot Strong/Shield ... 75.00
9 A:Lancelot Strong/Shield I:Cat
  Girl 75.00
10 A:Spider Spry 75.00
11 V:Rock Men 50.00
12 V:Brute Invaders 50.00
13 I:Kim Brand 55.00
14 I:Fly-Girl(Kim Brand) 75.00
15 A:Spider 50.00
16 A:Fly-Girl 50.00
17 A:Fly-Girl 50.00
18 A:Fly-Girl 50.00
19 A:Fly-Girl 50.00
20 O:Fly-Girl 55.00
21 A:Fly-Girl 40.00
22 A:Fly-Girl 40.00
23 A:Fly-Girl,Jaguar 40.00
24 A:Fly-Girl 40.00
25 A:Fly-Girl 40.00
26 A:Fly-Girl,Black Hood 40.00

27 A:Fly-Girl,Black Hood 40.00
28 A:Black Hood 40.00
29 A:Fly-Girl,Black Hood 40.00
30 A:Fly-Girl,R:Comet 50.00
31 A:Black Hood, Shield, Comet 55.00
Becomes: Flyman

ADVENTURES OF THE JAGUAR
Archie Publications/ Radio Comics 1961–63
1 I:Ralph Hardy/Jaguar 150.00
2 10 cent cover 65.00
3 Last 10 cent cover 60.00
4 A:Cat-Girl 45.00
5 A:Cat-Girl 45.00
6 A:Cat-Girl 38.00
7 .... 30.00
8 .... 30.00
9 .... 30.00
10 .... 30.00
11 .... 30.00
12 A:Black Hood 30.00
13 A:Cat-Girl,A:Black Hood 30.00
14 A:Black Hood 30.00
15 V:Human Octopus,last issue . 25.00

ADVENTURES OF YOUNG DR. MASTERS
Archie Comics 1964
1 .... 5.00
2 .... 5.00

AGAINST BLACKSHARD
Sirius Comics Aug., 1986
1 3-D 2.25

AIR FIGHTERS, SGT. STRIKE SPECIAL
Eclipse 1988
1 A:Airboy,Valkyrie 1.95

AIR WAR STORIES
Dell Publishing Co. 1964
1 .... 30.00
2 .... 20.00
3 thru 8 .... @15.00

AIRBOY
Eclipse 1986–89
1 TT/TY,D:Golden Age Airboy
  O:New Airboy 3.25
2 TT/TY,I:Marisa,R:SkyWolf 2.25
3 A:The Heap 2.50
4 A:Misery 2.50
5 DSt(c),R:Valkyrie 4.00
6 R:Iron Ace,I:Marlene 3.00
7 PG(c), ... 2.50
8 FH/TT(c) 2.50
9 R:Flying Fool, Riot, O'Hara
  Cocky, Judge & Turtle 1.75
10 I:Manic,D:Cocky, Judge & Turtle 1.50
11 O:Birdie 1.50
12 R:Flying Fool 1.50
13 I:New Bald Eagle 1.50
14 A:Sky Wolf, Iron Ace 1.50

All comics prices listed are for *Near Mint* condition.

15 A:Ku Klux Klan 1.50
16 D:Manic,A:Ku Klux Klan 1.50
17 A:HarryS.Truman,Misery 1.75
18 A:Gold.Age Black Angel 1.75
19 A:Gold.Age Rats 1.75
20 Rat storyline 1.75
21 I:Lester Mansfield (rel. of
  Gold.Age Rackman), Artic
  Deathzone #1 . . . . 1.75
22 DSp,Artic Deathzone #2 . . . . 1.75
23 A:Gold.Age Black Angle, Artic
  Deathzone #3 . . . . 1.75
24 A: Heap 1.75
25 TY,I:Manure Man,A:Heap 1.50
26 R:Flying Dutchman 1.50
27 A:Iron Ace, Heap 1.50
28 A:Heap 1.50
29 . . . . 1.50
30 A:Iron Ace; Sky Wolf story . . 1.50
31 A:Valkyrie; Sky Wolf story 1.75
32 Hostage Virus, ... 1.75
33 DSp,SkyWolf sty,A:Sgt.Strike . 1.75
34 DSp,A:La Lupina 1.75
35 DSp,A:La Lupina, Sky Wolf . . . 1.75
36 . . . . 1.75
37 DSp 1.75
38 CI, Heap story 1.75
39 CI, Heap story 1.75
40 CI, Heap story 1.75
41 V:Steel Fox, Golden Age rep.
  O:Valkyrie 1.75
42 A:Rackman 1.95
43 Sky Wolf sty, A:Flying Fool . . . 1.95
44 A:Rackman 1.95
45 . . . . 1.95
46 EC,Airboy Diary #1 . . . . 1.95
47 EC,Airboy Diary #2 . . . . 1.95
48 EC,Airboy Diary #3 . . . . 1.95
49 EC,Airboy Diary #4 . . . . 1.95
50 AKu/NKu,double-size 3.95
Spec. Meets the Prowler 1.95
Spec. Mr. Monster 1.75
Spec. Vs Airmaidens 1.95

AIRMAIDENS SPECIAL
Eclipse Comics 1987
1 A:Valkyrie 1.75

AKEMI
Brainstorm Comics 1997
1 . . . . 2.95

ALADDIN
Walt Disney
Prestige. Movie Adapt. 4.95

ALARMING ADVENTURES
Harvey Publications 1962–63
1 AW,RC,JSe 45.00
2 AW,BP,RC,JSe 30.00
3 JSe 30.00

ALARMING TALES
Harvey Publications 1957–58
1 JK,JK(c) 125.00
2 JK,JK(c) 100.00
3 JK 65.00
4 JK,BP 60.00
5 JK,AW 75.00
6 JK 50.00

ALBEDO, VOL. 3
Antartic Press 1994–95
Vol. 1 and II, See B&W
1 thru 4 Various Artists . . . . . . @2.95

ALIAS
Now Comics 1990
1 . . . . 2.00
2 thru 5 . . . . @1.75

ALIAS: STORMFRONT
Now Comics
1 . . . . 1.75
2 . . . . 1.75

Alien Encounters #1 © Eclipse Comics

ALIEN ENCOUNTERS
Eclipse Comics 1985–87
1 . . . . 3.50
2 . . . . 3.00
3 "I Shot the Last Martian" 3.00
4 JBo(c) 3.00
5 RCo,"Night of the Monkey" . . . 2.00
6 "Now You See It,""Freefall" 2.00
7 . . . . 2.00
8 TY,"Take One Capsule Every
  Million Years,M.Monroe(c) . . . 2.75
9 The Conquered 2.00
10 . . . . 2.00
11 TT,"Old Soldiers" 2.00
12 "What A Relief,""Eyes of the
  Sibyl" 2.00
13 GN,"The Light at the End" . . . 2.00
14 JRy,GN,TL,RT,"Still born" . . . 2.00

ALIEN TERROR
Eclipse 1986
3-D #1 "Standard Procedure" . . . 2.00

ALIEN WORLDS
Pacific 1982
1 AW,VM,NR 4.00
2 DSt 3.50
3 . . . . 3.00
4 DSt(i) 3.00
5 . . . . 3.00
6 . . . . 3.00

7 . . . . 3.00
3-D #1 AAd,DSt 5.50
Eclipse 1985
8 AW 2.50
9 . . . . 2.50

[CAPTAIN JOHNER AND] ALIENS, THE
Gold Key 1967
1 Rep. Magnus Robot Fighter . . 12.50

ALISTER THE SLAYER
Midnight Press 1995
1 I:Alister The Slayer 2.50
2 V:Lady Hate 2.50
3 JQ&JP(c) V:Subterranean
  Vampire Bikers 2.50

ALL AMERICAN SPORTS
Charlton 1967
1 . . . . 10.00

ALL HALLOWS EVE
Innovation 1991
1 . . . . 4.95

ALLEY OOP
Dell Publishing Co. 1962–63
1 . . . . 50.00
2 . . . . 45.00

ALPHA KORPS
Diversity Comics 1996
1 I:Alpha Korps 3.00
1 signed 4.95
2 "The Price of Freedom," pt.2 . . 2.50
2 signed 4.95
3 "The Price of Freedom," pt.3 . . 2.50
3 signed 4.95
4 "The Price of Freedom," pt.4 (of
  4) 2.50

ALPHA WAVE
Darkline 1987
1 . . . . 1.75

ALTER EGO
First 1986
1 . . . . 1.75
2 . . . . 1.50
3 . . . . 1.50
4 . . . . 1.25

ALVIN (& THE CHIPMUNKS)
Dell Publishing Co. 1962–73
1 . . . . 100.00
2 . . . . 65.00
3 . . . . 50.00
4 thru 10 . . . . @45.00
11 thru 20 . . . . @35.00
21 thru 28 . . . . @30.00
1 Alvin for President & his pals in
  Merry Christmas with Clyde
  Crashcup & Leonardo 25.00

AMAZING CHAN & THE CHAN CLAN
Gold Key 1973
1 . . . . 15.00

COLOR PUB.

2 . . . . 7.00
3 and 4 . . . . @6.00

AMAZING HEROES SWIMSUIT ANNUALS
Fantagraphics 1990–93
1990 Spec. A:Dawn 25.00
1990 2nd printing 15.00
1991 A: Dawn 20.00
1992 A: Dawn 20.00
1993 A: Dawn 20.00

AMAZON, THE
Comico 1989
1 . . . . 1.95
2 . . . . 1.95
3 end mini-series 1.95

AMERICAN FLAGG
First 1983–88
1 HC,I:American Flagg, Hard Times
  Pt.1 . . . . 3.50
2 HC,Hard Times Pt.2 . . . . 2.75
3 HC,Hard Times Pt.3 . . . . 2.75
4 HC,Southern Comfort Pt.1 . . . . 2.75

American Flagg #5 © First Comics

5 HC,Southern Comfort Pt.2 . . . . 2.75
6 HC,Southern Comfort Pt.3 . . . 2.75
7 HC,State o/t Union Pt.1 . . . . . . 2.50
8 HC,State o/t Union Pt.2 . . . . . . 2.50
9 HC,State o/t Union Pt.3 . . . . . . 2.50
10 HC,Solidarity-For Now Pt.1
  I:Luthor Ironheart 2.50
11 HC,Solidarity-ForNowPt.2 . . . 2.50
12 HC,Solidarity-ForNowPt.3 . . . 2.50
13 HC 2.25
14 PB 2.25
15 HC,AmericanFlagg A Complete
  story Pt.1 . . . . 2.25
16 HC,Complete Story Pt.2 . . . . . 2.00
17 HC,Complete Story Pt.3 . . . . . 2.00
18 HC,Complete Story Pt.4 . . . . . 2.00
19 HC,Bullets&BallotsPt.1 . . . . . . 2.00
20 HC,LSn,Bullets&BallotsPt.2 . . . 2.00
21 HC,LSn,Bullets&BallotsPt.3 Alan
  Moore sty. 2.00
22 HC,LSn,Bullets&BallotsPt.4 Alan
  Moore sty. 2.00

23 HC,LSn,England Swings Pt.1
  Alan Moore sty. 2.00
24 HC,England Swings Pt.2, Alan
  Moore sty. 2.00
25 HC,England Swings Pt.3, Alan
  Moore sty. 2.00
26 HC,England Swings Pt.4, Alan
  Moore sty. 2.00
27 Alan Moore sty. with Raul the
  Cat 2.00
28 BWg 1.50
29 JSon 1.50
30 JSon 1.50
31 JSon,O:Bob Violence 1.50
32 JSon,A:Bob Violence 1.50
33 A:Bob Violence 1.50
34 A:Bob Violence 1.50
35 A:Bob Violence 1.50
36 A:Bob Violence 1.50
37 A:Bob Violence 1.50
38 New Direction 1.50
39 JSon,A:Bob Violence 1.50
40 A:Bob Violence 1.50
41 . . . . 1.50
42 F:Luther Ironheart 1.50
43 . . . . 1.50
44 . . . . 1.50
45 . . . . 1.50
46 PS 1.75
47 PS 1.75
48 PS 1.75
49 . . . . 1.75
50 HC,last issue 1.75
Special #1 HC,I:Time[2] 2.50
See Also: Howard Chaykin's American Flagg

AMERICOMICS
AC Comics 1983
1 GP(c),O:Shade 3.00
2 . . . . 2.00
3 Blue Beetle 2.00
4 O:Dragonfly 2.00
5 and 6 . . . . @1.75
Spec.#1 Capt.Atom,BlueBeetle . . 1.50

ANDROMEDA
Andromeda
1 I:Andromeda 2.50
2 Andromeda vs. Elite Force . . . 2.50

ANGEL FIRE
Crusade Comics
1 BiT, from Shi #12, BiT(c) 2.95
1a with Roberto Flores cover . . . 2.95
1b with photo cover 2.95
2 (of 3) 2.95

ANIMAL MYSTIC: WATER WARS
Sirius 1996
1 DOe 5.00
2 DOe 4.00
3 DOe 3.00

ANYTHING GOES
Fantagraphics 1986
1 GK,FlamingCarot,Savage 3.50
2 S:AnM,JK,JSt,SK 3.50
3 DS,NA(c),A:Cerebus 3.00
4 . . . . 2.50
5 A:TMNTurtles 5.00

6 . . . . 2.00

APE NATION
Adventure Comics 1991
1 Aliens land on Planet of the
  Apes 4.00
2 General Ollo 3.00
3 V:Gen.Ollo,Danada 2.50
4 D:Danada 2.50

ARACHNAPHOBIA
Walt Disney 1990
1 Movie Adapt 5.95
1a Newsstand 2.95

ARAKNIS
Mushroom Comics 1995–96
1 I:Araknis, Shades of Evil pt.1 . . 3.50
2 Shades of Evil pt.2 . . . . 3.50
3 with pin-ups 2.50
4 . . . . 2.50

ARAKNIS
Mushroom Comics April 1996
0 Michael & Mario Ortiz 3.00
0 signed 5.00
1 . . . . 2.50
1 special edition 10.00
Mystic Comics
2 thru 6 . . . . @2.50

ARAKNIS: RETRIBUTION
Morning Star Productions 1997
1 (of 4) by Michael & Mario Ortiz 2.50
2 . . . . 2.50

ARAKNIS: SHADES OF EVIL
Morning Star Productions
1 thru 4 . . . .

ARCHANGELS: THE SAGA
Eternal Studios
1 I:Cameron 2.50
2 V:Demons 2.50
3 . . . . 2.75
4 . . . . 2.75
5 . . . . 2.50

ARCHIE
Archie Publications
1 thru 300 see Golden Age Section
301 thru 400 . . . . @1.50
401 thru 449 . . . . @1.50
450 thru 464 . . . . @1.50
Archie's Christmas Stocking #4 . . 2.00
Archie's Spring Break Spec.1 . . . 2.00
Archie's Spring Break Spec.2 . . . 2.00
Archie's Vacation Spec.#4 . . . . . 2.00
Archie's Vacation Spec.#5 . . . . . 2.00

ARCHIE AND FRIENDS
Archie Publications 1992–95
1 thru 10 . . . . @1.50
11 thru 20 . . . . @1.50
20 thru 25 . . . . @1.50

ARCHIE AND ME
Archie Publications 1964–87
1 . . . . 120.00

COLOR PUB.

2	60.00
3	25.00
4	20.00
5	20.00
6 thru 10	@15.00
11 thru 20	@5.00
21 thru 100	@3.00
101 thru 162	@1.50

ARCHIE AS PUREHEART THE POWERFUL
Archie Publications 1966–67

1 superhero parody	50.00
2	30.00
3 thru 6 Captain Pureheart	@20.00

ARCHIE AT RIVERDALE HIGH
Archie Publications 1972

1	35.00
2	15.00
3	8.00
4	6.00
5	6.00
6 thru 10	@2.50
11 thru 114	@1.00

ARCHIE COMICS DIGEST
Archie Comics Digest 1973

1	35.00
2	20.00
3	9.00
4	6.00
5 thru 10	@2.00
11 thru 88	@1.00

ARCHIE MEETS THE PUNISHER
Archie/Marvel 1994

one-shot crossover, same contents as Punisher meets Archie	3.00

ARCHIE'S MADHOUSE
Archie Publications 1959–69

1	200.00
2	85.00
3	60.00
4	60.00
5	60.00
6 thru 10	@35.00
11 thru 16	@25.00
17 thru 21	@10.00
22	40.00
23 thru 30	@10.00
31 thru 40	@3.50
41 thru 65	@1.00
66	1.00

ARCHIE'S PAL JUGHEAD
SEE: JUGHEAD

ARCHIE'S SUPERHERO SPECIAL DIGEST MAGAZINE
Archie Publications

1 JSm/SK,Rept.Double of Capt.Strong #1,FLy,Black Hood.	1.20
2 GM,NA/DG,AMc,I:'70's Black Hood, Superhero rept.	2.00

ARCHIE'S TV LAUGH-OUT
Archie Publications 1969–86

1	30.00
2	12.00
3	6.00
4	6.00
5	6.00
6 thru 10	@2.00
11 thru 106	@1.00

Archie 3000 #12 © Archie Publications

ARCHIE 3000
Archie Publications
May, 1989–July, 1991

1 thru 16	1.00

ARENA, THE
Alchemy

1	1.00
2	1.00

ARIANE & BLUEBEARD
Eclipse 1988

Spec. CR	3.95

ARISTOKITTENS, THE
Gold Key 1971–75

1 Disney	20.00
2	10.00
3	10.00
4 thru 9	@10.00

ARMAGEDDON FACTOR
AC Comics

1 Sentinels of Justice	1.95
2	1.95

ARMOR
Continuity 1985

1 TGr,NA,A:Silver Streak, Silver logo	7.00
1a 2nd printing,red logo	2.50
2 TGr,NA(c)	2.50
3 TGr,NA(c)	2.50
4 TGr,NA(c)	2.50
5 BS,NA(c)	2.50
6 TVE,NA(c)	2.50

7 NA(c)	2.50
8 FS,NA(c)	2.50
9 FS,NA&KN(c)	2.50
10 FS,NA&KN(c)	2.50
11 SDr(i),KN(c)	2.50
12 KN(c)	2.50
13 NA(c),direct sales	2.50
14 KN(c), newsstand	2.50

[2nd Series]

1 V:Hellbender,Trading Card	2.50

[3rd Series, Deathwatch 2000]

1 Deathwatch 2000 pt.3,w/card	4.00
2 Deathwatch 2000 pt.9,w/card	2.50
3 Deathwatch 2000 pt.15,w/card	2.50
4	2.50
5 Rise of Magic	2.50
6 Rise of Magic	@2.50

ARMORED TROOPER VOTOMS
CPM Comics

1 TEl	2.95
2 TEl	2.95
3 TEl	2.95
4 TEl	2.95
GN Supreme Survivor	16.95

ARMY ATTACK
Charlton 1964

1 SG	25.00
2 SG	10.00
3 SG	8.00
4 thru 47	@8.00

ARMY WAR HEROES
Charlton 1963–70

1	25.00
2	10.00
3 thru 21	@10.00
22 GS,O&I:Iron Corporal	12.00
23 thru 38	@8.00

ART OF ZEN INTER-GALACTIC NINJA
Entity Comics 1994

1 Various artists	2.95

ASH
Event Comics

1 JQ,JP,Fireman with powers	14.00
2 JQ,JP,V:Theresa	10.00
3 JQ,JP,Secret of Origin	4.50
4 I:Actor	2.75
5 I:New Character	2.50
6 V:Gabriel	2.50
0 Red Laser ed., Current Ash (c)	29.95
0 Red Laser ed., Future Ash (c)	29.95
TPB Vol. 1, JQ,JP,sgn. lim.	34.95

ASH: CINDER AND SMOKE
Event Comics 1997

1 MWa,BAu,HuR,JP	2.95
2 HuR(c)	2.95
2 JQ(c)	2.95
3 (of 6) JQ&JP(c)	2.95
3 variant JP&HuR(c)	2.95

ASH FILES, THE
Event Comics 1997

1 JQ,JP	2.95

All comics prices listed are for *Near Mint* condition.

COLOR PUB.

ASH: THE FIRE WITHIN
Event Comics
2 JQ,JP	2.95
3 JQ,JP, Ash Rooftop cover	2.95
3a JQ,JP, Ash Firefighter cover	2.95

ASH/22 BRIDES
Event Comics 1996
1 FaN,HuR,JP	2.95

ASSASSIN, INC.
Solson
1 thru 4	@1.95

ASTER
Entity Comics 1995
0 O:Aster the Celestial Knight	4.50
1 I:Celestial Knight	5.00
1b 2nd printing	3.00
2	3.50
3 V:Tolmek	3.25
3a Variant cover	7.00
4 Final Issue	3.00
TPB Rep.#1–#4 + pin-up gallery	12.95

ASTER THE LAST CELESTIAL KNIGHT
Entity Comics 1995
1 R:Aster Chromium Cover	3.75
1a Clear Chromium Edition	10.00
1b Holo Chrome Edition	15.00
2 World Defender	2.50

ASTRO BOY
Gold Key Aug., 1965
1 I:Astro Boy	300.00

ASTRO BOY
Now
Prev.	Original Astro Boy	
18		1.75
19		1.75
20		1.75

ASYLUM
Pendragon 1995
1	2.95
2	2.95
3 three stories	2.95

ASYLUM
Maximum Press Dec. 1995
1 Warchild, Beanworld, Avengelyne, Battlestar Galactica	3.00
2 I:Deathkiss	3.00
3	3.00
4 RLd,A:Cybrid	3.00
5 I:Black Seed	3.00
6 R:Steve Austin & Jaime Sommers	3.00
7 RLe,F:Bloodwulf	3.00
8 RLd	3.00
9 RLd	3.00
10	3.00
11	3.00
12 MMy,F:Blindside	3.00
13	3.00

ATOM ANT
Gold Key Jan., 1966
1	65.00

ATOM-AGE COMBAT
Fago Magazines 1958–59
1	150.00
2	125.00
3	100.00

ATOMIK ANGELS
Crusade Entertainment 1996
1 BiT	2.95
1 variant cover (1:25)	5.00
2 BiT	2.95
3 BiT	2.95
4 BiT, conclusion	2.95

ATOMIC RABBIT
Charlton Comics 1955–58
1	150.00
2	50.00
3 thru 10	@30.00
11	50.00
Becomes:
ATOMIC BUNNY
12	75.00
13 thru 18	@35.00
19 Dec., 1959	35.00

AVENGEBLADE
Maximum Press 1996
1 RLe	2.99
2 RLe	2.99

AVENGELYNE
Maximum Press 1995
1 RLd,I:Avengelyne Dir ed.	4.00
1a Newstand Edition	5.00
1b Holochrome Edition	10.00
1 gold edition	8.00
2 V:B'Lial	4.00
3 I:Magogi	3.00
3 variant cover, pin-up	4.00
TPB rep. #1–#3	9.95
Regular Series April 1996
0 RLd,O:Avengelyne	3.00
1 RLd,BNa,F:Devlin	2.95
1 variant photo cover	2.95
2 I:Darkchylde	2.95
2a variant photo cover	2.95
3	2.95
4 A:Cybrid	2.95
5 A:Cybrid,	3.00
6 RLd,F:Divinity	3.00
7 RLd,F:Divinity	3.00
8 RLd,	3.00
9 RLd,	3.00
10 BNa,"The Possession," pt.1	3.00
11 BNa,"The Possession," pt.2	3.00
12 BNa,"The Possession," pt.3	3.00
13 BNa,"The Possession," pt.4	3.00
14 A:Bloodwulf	3.00
15 A:Glory, Prophet	3.00
Swimsuit Edition	3.50
Swimsuit book, American Entertainment exclusive	7.50

AVENGELYNE: ARMAGEDDON
Maximum Press 1996–97
1 (of 3) RLd	3.00
2 RLd,	3.00
3 BNa,ScC, finale	3.00

AVENGELYNE BIBLE: REVELATIONS
Maximum Press
one-shot RLd,	3.50

AVENGELYNE: DEADLY SINS
Maximum Press 1996
1 RLd (c)	3.00
1 photo (c)	3.00
2 RLd(c)	3.00

AVENGELYNE/GLORY
Maximum Press 1995
1 V:B'Lial	3.95
1a variant cover	5.00
Swimsuit Spec. #1	2.95

Avengelyne/Glory Godyssey #1
© Maximum Press

AVENGELYNE/GLORY: THE GODYSSEY
Maximum Press 1996
1 RLd,BNa	2.99
2 RLd	2.99
3 RLd	2.99
4 RLd	2.99
5 RLd	2.99

AVENGELYNE/POWER
Maximum Press 1995–96
1 RLd,V:Hollywood	3.00
1 variant cover	3.50
2 RLd(c)	2.95
3	2.95
3a photo (c)	2.95

AVENGELYNE/PROPHET
Maximum Press April 1996
1 RLd,BNa,MD2	2.95

AVENGELYNE/ WARRIOR NUN AREALA
Maximum Press 1997
Spec.	2.99

COLOR PUB.

All comics prices listed are for *Near Mint* condition.

AVENGELYNE/ WARRIOR NUN AREALA II THE NAZARENE AFFAIR
Awesome Entertainment 1997
one-shot? 2.99

AVENGERS, THE
Gold Key Nov., 1968
1 . . . . 250.00

AXA
Eclipse 1987
1 "Axa the Adopted" 1.75
2 . . . . 1.75

AXEL PRESSBUTTON
Eclipse 1984
1 BB(c),Origin 1.75
2 . . . . 1.75
3 thru 4 . . . . @1.75
Becomes:
PRESSBUTTON

AXION
Icon Creations
1 I:Obsidion 2.50

AXIS ALPHA
Axis Comics
1 LSn,I:BEASTIES,Dethgrip,
Shelter,W 2.75

AZ
Comico
1 . . . . 4.00
2 . . . . 2.25

AZTEC ACE
Eclipse 1984
1 NR(i),I:AztecAce 4.00
2 NR(i) 3.50
3 NR(i) 3.00
4 NR(i) 3.00
5 NR(i) 3.00
6 NR(i) 3.00
7 NR(i) 3.00
8 NR(i) 3.00
9 NR(i) 3.00
10 NR(i) 2.00
11 . . . . 3.50
12 . . . . 2.50
13 . . . . 2.50
14 . . . . 2.50
15 F:Bridget 2.50

BABES OF BROADWAY
Broadway 1996
1 . . . . 2.95

BABY HUEY, THE BABY GIANT
Harvey Publications 1956–80
1 . . . . 300.00
2 . . . . 150.00
3 . . . . 100.00
4 . . . . 75.00
5 . . . . 75.00
6 thru 10 . . . . @35.00
11 thru 20 . . . . @25.00
21 thru 40 . . . . @20.00

41 thru 60 . . . . @10.00
61 thru 79 . . . . @8.00
80 . . . . 8.00
81 thru 95 . . . . @4.00
96 Giant size 5.00
97 Giant size 5.00
98 . . . . 2.50
99 . . . . 2.50

BABY HUEY AND PAPA
Harvey Publications 1962–68
1 . . . . 125.00
2 . . . . 50.00
3 . . . . 35.00
4 . . . . 35.00
5 . . . . 35.00
6 . . . . 15.00
7 . . . . 15.00
8 . . . . 15.00
9 . . . . 15.00
10 . . . . 15.00
11 thru 20 . . . . @5.00
21 thru 33 . . . . @3.50
33 . . . . 3.50

BABY HUEY DUCKLAND
Harvey Publications 1962–66
1 . . . . 90.00
2 . . . . 50.00
3 . . . . 50.00
4 . . . . 50.00
5 . . . . 50.00
6 thru 14 . . . . @15.00
15 . . . . 15.00

BACHELOR FATHER
Dell Publishing Co. 1962
1 . . . . 75.00
2 . . . . 60.00

BACK TO THE FUTURE
Harvey 1991
1 Chicago 1927 . . . . 1.25
2 Cretaceous Period 1.25
3 World War I 1.25
4 Doc Retires 1.25

BAD COMPANY
Quality 1988
1 thru 19 . . . . @1.50

BADGER
Capital 1983
1 JBt,I:Badger,Ham,Daisy Yak,Yeti 4.00
2 JBt,I:Riley,A:YakYeti 3.00
3 JBt,O:Badger,Ham 3.00
4 JBt,A'Ham 3.00
First
5 BR,DruidTree Pt1 . . . . 2.50
6 BR,DruidTree Pt2 . . . . 2.50
7 BR,I:Wonktendonk,Lord
Weterlackus 2.50
8 BR,V:Demon 2.50
9 BR,I:Connie,WOatesCbra 2.50
10 BR,A:Wonktendonk, I:Hodag
Meldrum 2.50
11 BR,V:Hodag,L.W'lackus 2.50
12 BR,V:Hodag,L.W'lackus 2.50
13 BR,A:L.W'lakus,Clonezone,
Judah 2.50
14 BR,I:HerbNg 2.50
15 BR,I:Wombat,JMoranIbob 2.50

Badger #4 © Capital Comics

16 BR,A:Yak,Yeti 2.50
17 JBt,I:Lamont 3.00
18 BR,I:SpudsGroganA:Cbra . . . 2.50
19 BR,I:Senator1,ClZone 2.50
20 BR,Billionaire'sPicnic 2.50
21 BR,I&O:Phantom 2.50
22 BR,I:Dr.Buick Riviera 2.50
23 I:BobDobb,A:Yeti 2.50
24 BR,A:Riley 2.50
25 BR,I:Killdozer 2.50
26 BR,I:RoachWranger 2.50
27 BR,O:RoachWranger 2.50
28 BR,A:Yeti 2.50
29 A:Clonezone,C:GrimJack 2.50
30 BR,I:Dorgan 2.00
31 BR,I:HopLingSung 2.00
32 BR,D:Dorgan,HopLingSng . . . 2.00
33 RLm/AN,I:KidKang 3.00
34 RLm,I:Count Kohler 3.00
35 RLm,I:Count Kohler 3.00
36 RLm,V:Dire Wolf 3.00
37 AMe,A:Lamont 2.50
38 Animal Band 2.00
39 I:Buddy McBride 2.00
40 RLm,I:Sister Twyster 3.50
41 RLm,D:Sister Twyster 3.50
42 RLm,A:Paul Bunyan 3.50
43 RLm,V:Vampires 3.50
44 RLm,V:Vampires 3.50
45 RLm,V:Dr.Buick Riviera 3.50
46 RLm,V:Lort Weterlackus 3.50
47 RLm,Hmds.Sacr.BloodI 3.50
48 RLm,Hmds.Sacr.BloodII 3.50
49 RLm,TRoof off SuckerI 3.50
50 RLm,TRoof off SuckerII 5.00
51 RLm,V:Demon 3.00
52 TV,Tinku 4.00
53 TV,I:Shaza,Badass 4.00
54 TV,D:Shaza 4.00
55 I:Morris Myer 2.00
56 I:Dominance 2.00
57 A:KKang,V:L.W'lackus 2.00
58 A:Lamont,W'bat,V:SpudsJack . 2.00
59 Bad Art Issue 2.25
60 I:ChisumBros 2.00
61 V:ChismBros 2.00
62 I:Shanks 2.00
63 V:Shanks 2.00
64 A:Mavis Sykes 2.25

COLOR PUB.

65 A:BruceLee 2.25
66 I:Joe Nappleseed 2.25
67 Babysitting 2.25
68 V:GiantFoot 2.25
69 O:Mavis 2.25
70 BR:Klaus(last monthly) 2.25
Graphic Nov.BR,I:Mazis
Sykes,D:Hodag 10.00
Badger Bedlam 4.95

BADGER GOES BERSERK
First 1989
1 I:Larry,Jessie 4.00
2 MZ,V:Larry,Jessie 3.50
3 JBt/MZ,V:Larry,Jessie 3.00
4 JBt/MZ,V:Larry,Jessie 3.00

BAD GIRLS
OF BLACKOUT
Blackout Comics 1995
0 . . . . 3.50
1 I:Ms. Cyanide, Ice 3.50
Ann.#1 Hari Kari, Lady Vampre . 3.50
Ann.#1 Commemorative ed. 9.95

BAKER STREET
1 . . . . 3.00
2 . . . . 2.50

BALLAD OF HALO JONES
Quality 1987
1 IG Alan Moore story 2.00
1a IG rep. 2.00
2 thru 12 . . . . @1.25

BAMM BAMM & PEBBLES
FLINTSTONE
Gold Key Oct., 1964
1 . . . . 40.00

BARBARIANS, THE
Atlas June, 1975
1 O: Andrax,F:Iron Jaw 1.75

BARBIE & KEN
Dell Publishing Co.
May-July, 1962
1 . . . . 350.00
2 . . . . 250.00
3 . . . . 250.00
4 . . . . 250.00
5 . . . . 275.00

THE BARBIE TWINS
ADVENTURES
Topps 1995
1 I:Shane, Sia 2.50

BARNEY AND
BETTY RUBBLE
Charlton Comics 1973–76
1 . . . . 25.00
2 . . . . 10.00
3 . . . . 10.00
4 . . . . 10.00
5 . . . . 10.00
6 thru 10 . . . . @8.00
11 thru 22 . . . . @6.00
23 . . . . 6.00

BARRY M. GOLDWATER
Dell Publishing Co. March, 1965
1 . . . . 30.00

BART-MAN
Bongo 1993
1 Foil(c),I:Bart-Man 4.00
2 I:Penalizer 2.25
3 When Bongos Collide,pt.3, with
card 2.25
4 Crime-Time,pt.1 . . . . 2.25
5 Bad Guys Strike Back 2.25

BART SIMPSONS
TREEHOUSE OF HORROR
Bongo Comics 1995
1 Bart People 2.95

BART SIMPSON'S
TREEHOUSE OF TERROR
Bongo Comics 1995
One-shot 2.50

Baseball #1 © Kitchen Sink

BASEBALL
Kitchen Sink 1991
1 WE (c) reprint of 1949 orig. . . . 3.95
2 Ray Gotto (c), w/4 BB cards . . 2.95

BAT, THE
Adventure
1 R:The Bat,inspiration for Batman
says Bob Kane 2.50

BATTLE FORCE
Blackthorne 1987
1 and 2 . . . . @1.50
3 . . . . 1.75

BATTLE OF
THE PLANETS
Gold Key June, 1979
1 TV Cartoon 3.50
2 . . . . 2.50
3 . . . . 2.50
4 . . . . 2.50

5 . . . . 2.50
Whitman
6 . . . . 1.50
7 thru 10 . . . . 1.50

BATTLESTAR GALACTICA
Maximum Press 1995
1 Finds Earth 2.50
2 Council of Twelve 2.50
3 R:Adama 2.50
4 Pyramid Secrets 2.50
Spec. Painted Book 3.00
Compendium #1 rep. stories from
Asylum 3.00

BATTLESTAR GLACTICA:
APOLLO'S JOURNEY
Maximum Press April 1996
1 story by Richard Hatch 2.95

BATTLESTAR GLACTICA:
JOURNEY'S END
Maximum Press 1996
1 (of 4) RLd 3.00
2 RLd 3.00
3 RLd, the end of Galactica? . . . 3.00
4 RLd, conclusion 3.00

BATTLETECH
Blackthorne 1987
1 . . . . 1.50
2 . . . . 1.50
3 . . . . 1.50
4 . . . . 1.75
5 . . . . 1.75
6 . . . . 1.75
(Changed to Black & White)
1 3-D 2.50
2 3-D 2.50

BEAGLE BOYS, THE
Gold Key 1964–79
1 . . . . 30.00
2 thru 5 . . . . @20.00
6 thru 10 . . . . @15.00
11 thru 20 . . . . @10.00
21 thru 46 . . . . @6.00
47 . . . . 6.00

BEANIE THE MEANIE
Fargo Publications 1958
1 thru 3 . . . . @25.00

B.E.A.S.T.I.E.S.
Axis Comics
1 JS(a&s),I:Beasties 2.25

THE BEATLES,
LIFE STORY
Dell Publishing Co. 1964
1 . . . . 500.00

BEAUTY AND THE BEAST
Innovation
1 From TV series 2.50
1a Deluxe 3.95
2 . . . . 2.50
3 . . . . 2.50
4 Siege 2.50
5 Siege 2.50

COLOR PUB.

6 Halloween 2.50
7 . . . . 2.50

BEAUTY AND THE BEAST PORTRAIT OF LOVE
First 1989–90
1 WP,TV tie in 12.00
2 . . . . 8.00
Book II:Night of Beauty 5.95

BEAUTY AND THE BEAST
Walt Disney 1992
Movie adapt.(Prestige) 4.95
Movie adapt.(newsstand) 2.50
mini-series
1 Bewitched 1.50
2 Elsewhere 1.50
3 A:Catherine 2.50

BEDLAM!
Eclipse 1985
1 SBi,RV,reprint horror 1.75
2 SBi,RV,reprint horror 1.75

BEETLE BAILEY
Harvey 1992
1 F:Mort Walker's B.Bailey 1.95
2 Beetle builds a bridge 1.25
3 thru 12 . . . . 1.25

BEETLEJUICE
Harvey 1991
1 EC,"This is your lice" 2.00
Holiday Special #1 . . . . 1.25

BEN CASEY
Dell Publishing Co.
June-July, 1962
1 Ph(c) 35.00
2 Ph(c) 25.00
3 Ph(c) 25.00
4 Drug, Ph(c) 28.00
5 Ph(c) 25.00
6 thru 10 Ph(c) . . . . @25.00

BERNI WRIGHTSON MASTER OF THE MACABRE
Pacific
1 BWr 5.25
2 BWr 3.75
3 BWr 3.50
4 BWr 3.50
Eclipse 1984
5 BWr 3.50

BEST FROM BOY'S LIFE
Gilberton Company Oct., 1957
1 . . . . 75.00
2 . . . . 40.00
3 . . . . 35.00
4 LbC 50.00
5 . . . . 35.00

BEST OF DONALD DUCK & UNCLE SCROOGE
Gold Key 1964–67
1 . . . . 75.00
2 . . . . 70.00

BEST OF DONALD DUCK
Gold Key Nov., 1965
1 . . . . 75.00

BEST OF BUGS BUNNY
Gold Key 1966–68
1 Both Giants 35.00
2 . . . . 25.00

BEST OF DENNIS THE MENACE, THE
Hallden/Fawcett Publ.
Summer, 1959
1 . . . . 35.00
2 thru 5 Spring, 1961 . . . . 20.00

BETTY
Archie Publications 1992
1 thru 39 . . . . @1.50
40 thru 54 . . . . @1.50

Betty and Me #3 © Archie Comics

BETTY AND ME
Archie Publications 1965–92
1 . . . . 100.00
2 . . . . 50.00
3 . . . . 30.00
4 . . . . 30.00
5 . . . . 30.00
6 thru 10 . . . . @15.00
11 thru 30 . . . . @8.00
31 thru 50 . . . . @4.00
51 thru 55 . . . . @3.00
56 thru 199 . . . . @2.00
200 . . . . 2.00

BETTY AND VERONICA
Archie Publications June, 1987
1 thru 100 . . . . @1.50
101 thru 104 . . . . @1.50
105 "The Ugly Truth" 1.50
106 "Hearing Aided" 1.50
107 two stories 1.50
108 "Visions of a Sugarplum" . . . 1.50
109 . . . . 1.50
110 "The Trophy" 1.50
111 "Now Weight A Minute" 1.50

112 "Archie's Choice" 1.50
113 "Attitudes" 1.50
114 "Heard the Word" 1.50
115 "Moving Line" 1.50
116 "Model Muddle" 1.50

BETTY & VERONICA SPECTACULAR
1 thru 22 . . . . @1.50
23 "Scent Of Humor" 1.50
24 "Life's No Picnic" 1.50
25 "Warrior Princess of Riverdale" 1.50

BEVERLY HILLBILLYS
Dell Publishing Co.
April-June, 1963
1 Ph(c) 150.00
2 Ph(c) 80.00
3 Ph(c) 50.00
4 . . . . 30.00
5 . . . . 50.00
6 . . . . 50.00
7 . . . . 50.00
8 Ph(c) 50.00
9 Ph(c) 50.00
10 Ph(c) 50.00
11 Ph(c) 50.00
12 Ph(c) 50.00
13 Ph(c) 50.00
14 Ph(c) 50.00
15 . . . . 30.00
16 . . . . 30.00
17 Ph(c) 30.00
18 Ph(c) 30.00
19 Ph(c) 30.00
20 Ph(c) 30.00
21 Ph(c) 30.00

BEWITCHED
Dell Publishing Co.
April-June, 1965
1 . . . . 135.00
2 . . . . 75.00
3 Ph(c) 50.00
4 Ph(c) 50.00
5 Ph(c) 50.00
6 Ph(c) 50.00
7 Ph(c) 50.00
8 Ph(c) 50.00
9 Ph(c) 50.00
10 Ph(c) 50.00
11 Ph(c) 50.00
12 Ph(c) 50.00
13 Ph(c) 50.00
14 . . . . 30.00

BEYOND THE GRAVE
Charlton Comics 1975–84
1 SD,TS(c),P(c) 7.00
2 thru 5 . . . . @3.00
6 thru 16 . . . . @2.00
17 . . . . 2.00

BIG BANG
Caliber Press
0 Whole Timeline inc. 2.95
1 . . . . 1.95
2 . . . . 1.95
3 . . . . 1.95
4 25 years after #3 . . . . 1.95

COLOR PUB.

BIG VALLEY, THE
Dell Publishing Co. June, 1966
1 Ph(c)	35.00
2	15.00
3	15.00
4	15.00
5	15.00
6	15.00

BILL BLACK'S FUN COMICS
AC Comics
1 Cpt.Paragon,B&W	2.50
2 and 3 B&W	@2.25
4 Color	2.25

BILL THE GALACTIC HERO
Topps
1 thru 3 Harry Harrison adapt.	@4.95

BILLY NGUYEN
Caliber
1	2.50

Billy the Kid #62 © Charlton Publications

BILLY THE KID
Charlton Publ. Co. 1957–83
9	40.00
10	25.00
11	22.00
12	20.00
13 AW,AT	30.00
14	20.00
15 AW,O:Billy the Kid	30.00
16 AW	30.00
17	20.00
18	20.00
19	20.00
20	30.00
21	30.00
22	30.00
23	10.00
24	30.00
25 JSe	30.00
26 JSe	30.00
27	10.00

28	10.00
29	10.00
30	10.00
31 thru 40	@7.00
41 thru 60	@5.00
61 thru 80	@2.00
81 thru 152	@1.00
153	1.00

BIONEERS
Mirage/Next
1 New Heroes	2.75
2	2.75
3 All-out War	2.75

BIONIC WOMAN, THE
Charlton
1 ... Oct, 1977, TV show adapt.	2.00
2	1.50
3	1.50
4	1.50
5	1.50

BIONIX
Maximum Press 1996
1 (of 3) RLd,F:Steve Austin & Jaime Sommers	3.00
2 RLd,	3.00

BIZARRE 3-D ZONE
Blackthorne
1	2.50

[ORIGINAL] BLACK CAT
1 Reprints	2.00
2 MA(c) rep.	2.00
3 rep.	2.00

BLACK DIAMOND
AC Comics
1 Colt B..U. story	3.00
2 PG(c)	2.00
3 PG(c)	2.00
4 PG(c)	2.00
5 PG(c)	2.00

BLACK ENCHANTRESS
Heroic Publishing
1 and 2 Date Rape issues	@1.95

BLACK FLAG
Maximum Press
1 Dan Fraga	3.00
2 I:New Character	2.50
3 V:Network, I:Glitz	2.50
4 V:Glitz, Network	2.50
5 I:Jammers	2.50
6 I:Alphabots	2.50

BLACK FURY
Charlton Comics May, 1955
1	30.00
2	15.00
3 thru 15	@6.00
16 SD	30.00
17 SD	30.00
18 SD	30.00
19 and 20	@3.50
21 thru 30	@1.50
31 thru 56	@2.00
57 March-April, 1966	2.00

BLACK HOLE, THE
Whitman 1980
1 & 2 movie adaptation	@1.50
3 & 4 new stories	@1.50

BLACK HOOD
Archie Publications
1 ATh,GM,DW	1.00
2 ATh,DSp,A:Fox	1.00
3 ATh,GM	1.00

BLACK JACK
Charlton Comics 1957–59
20	40.00
21	15.00
22	25.00
23 AW,AT	30.00
24 SD	25.00
25 SD	25.00
26 SD	25.00
27	12.00
28 SD	25.00
29	10.00
30	10.00

BLACKJACK
Dark Angel
1 (of 3) JoB, 1930s Adventure	2.95
2 KeL,"Blood and Honor," pt.2	2.95

BLACK PHANTOM
AC Comics
1 F:Red Mask	2.50
2 F:Red Mask	2.50

BLACK RAVEN
Mad Monkey Press 1996
1 Blueprints pt.1	2.95
2 Blueprints pt.2	2.95
3 V:Temple Assassins	2.95
4 Blueprints pt.4	2.95
GN#1 Blueprints	6.95

BLACK TERROR
Eclipse 1989–90
1	3.95
2	3.95
3	4.95

BLACK WEB
Inks Comics
1 thru 3 V:Seeker	@2.50

BLACKBALL COMICS
Blackball Comics
1 KG,A:Trencher	3.25

BLAST-OFF
Harvey Publications Oct., 1965
1 JK,AW	30.00

BLAZING COMBAT
Warren Publishing Co. 1965–66
1 FF(c)	90.00
2 FF(c)	20.00
3 and 4 FF(c)	@15.00

BLAZING SIX-GUNS
Skywald Comics 1971
1 F: Red Mask, Sundance Kid	4.00

COLOR PUB.

Blazing Six-Guns #1 © Skywald Comics
2 Jesse James 3.00

BLOOD & ROSES
Sky Comics
1 I:Blood,Rose 2.75

BLOOD SWORD DYNASTY
Jademan
1	2.25
2 thru 6	@1.50
7 thru 14 MB	@1.95
15 thru 18 MB	@1.25
19 Kim & Zeo Escape the Crips	1.25
20 Skeleton Executioners	1.25
21 Kim,Seeto	1.25
22 Infinite Wounded	1.25
23 Kim vs. Ask me not	1.25
24	1.25
25	1.25
26 V:Fiery Bird	1.25
27 A:Hero, Shou, Fiery Bird . .	1.25
28 Hero vs. Fiery Bird	1.25
29	1.25
30	1.25
31 V:Devil Child	1.25
32	1.25
33	1.25
34	1.25
35 Hero's ancestry	1.25
36 Hero & son in danger	1.25
37 A:Hell Clan,D:North Pole . .	1.25
38 Fiery Hawk Vs.Inf.Seeto . .	1.25
39 Hero vs.Infinite seeto	1.25
40 Kim Hung vs.Inf.Seeto . . .	1.25

BLOOD SWORD
Jademan
1	3.25
2	2.50
3 thru 5	@2.00
6 thru 9	@1.75
10 thru 21	@2.50
22 LW	1.95
23 LW,D:Poisonkiller	1.95
24 LW,A:Hero	1.95
25	1.95
26	1.95
27	1.95

28 V:DevilHeart	1.95
29	1.95
30 A:Purgatory	1.95
31	1.95
32 V:Mummy	1.95
33 V:Mummy	1.95
34	1.95
35	1.95
36 A:King Rat	1.95
37	1.95
38 Kim Hung in Danger	1.95
39 Masked Men to the Rescue . .	1.95
40	1.95
41	1.95
42	1.95
43 A:Russell School Pack	1.95
44 FirefoxV:Tyrant of Venom . . .	1.95
45 A:Yuen Mo	1.95
46 V:Cannibal	2.50
47	1.95
48 A:Clairvoyant Assassin	1.95
49 Prophecy of Hero's fate	1.95
50 D:Poison Entity	1.95
51	1.95
52 Hero vs.Cannibal	1.95
53 Hero vs.Cannibal	1.95

BLOODBATH
Samson Comics
1 I:Alien,V:Starguile 2.50

BLOODCHILDE
Millenium
0 O:Bloodchilde	2.95
1 Neil Gaiman, Vampires	2.95
1 signed (lim. to 500)	4.95
2 Neil Gaiman, Vampires	2.95
3 Neil Gaiman, Vampires	2.95
4	2.95
5 Talk Show Host	2.95

BLOODFIRE
Lightning Comics
0 O:Bloodfire	3.00
1 JZy(s),JJn, red foil	8.00
1a Platinum foil Ed.	8.00
1b B&W Promo Ed. Silver ink . . .	7.00
1c B&W Promo Ed. Gold ink . .	15.00
2 JZy(s),JJn,O:Bloodfire	5.00
3 JZy(s),JJn,I:Dreadwolf,	
Judgement Day,Overthrow . . .	4.00
4 JZy(s),JJn,A:Dreadwolf, ...	3.00
5 JZy(s),TLw,I:Bloodstorm, w/card	3.00
6 SZ(s),TLw,V:Storman	3.00
7 SZ(s),TLw,A:Pres.Clinton	3.00
8 SZ(s),TLw,O:Prodigal	3.00
9 SZ(s),TLw,I:Prodigal (in Costume)	3.00
10 SZ(s),TLw,B:Rampage,I:Thorpe	3.00
11	2.95
12	2.95

BLOODFIRE/HELLINA
Lightning Comics
1 V:Slaughterhouse	3.00
1a Nude Version	9.95

BLOODLORE
Brave New Worlds
1 Dreamweavers	1.95
2 A Blow to the Crown	1.95

BLOODSCENT
Comico
1 GC 2.00

BLUE BEETLE
Charlton Comics June, 1964
{1st S.A. Series}
1 O:Dan Garrett/BlueBeetle . . .	60.00
2	40.00
3 V:Mr.Thunderbolt	50.00
4 V:Praying Mantis Man	40.00
5 V:Red Knight	40.00

{2nd S.A. Series} July 1965
Previously: UNUSUAL TALES
50 V:Scorpion	50.00
51 V:Mentor	50.00
52 V:Magno	50.00
53 V:Praying Mantis Man	50.00
54 V:Eye of Horus	50.00

Becomes: GHOSTLY TALES
{3rd S.A. Series} 1967
1 SD,I:Question	75.00
2 SD,O:TedKord,D:DanGarrett .	35.00
3 SD,I:Madmen,A:Question . . .	25.00
4 SD,A:Question	25.00
5 SD,VicSage(Question) app. in	
Blue Beetle Story	25.00

BLUE BULLETEER
AC Comics
1 . . . . 2.25

BLUE PHANTOM, THE
Dell Publishing Co.
June-Aug., 1962
1 . . . . 35.00

BLUE RIBBON
Archie Publications
1 JK,AV,O:Fly rep.	1.50
2 TVe,Mr.Justice	1.50
3 EB/TD,O:Steel Sterling	1.50
4	1.00
5 S&K,Shield rep.	1.00
6 DAy/TD,Fox	1.00
7 TD,Fox	1.00
8 NA,GM,Blackhood	1.00
9 thru 11	@1.00
12 SD,ThunderAgents	1.00
13 Thunderbunny	1.00
14 Web & Jaguar	1.00

BOLD ADVENTURE
Pacific
1	2.00
2	1.50
3 JSe	1.50

BOLT & STARFORCE
AC Comics
1	1.75
Bolt Special #1	1.50

BOMBAST
Topps
1 V:Savage Dragon,Trading Card 3.25

BONANZA
Dell Publishing Co.
June-Aug., 1960
1 . . . . 200.00

COLOR PUB.

2	100.00
3 thru 10	@75.00
11 thru 20	@50.00
21 thru 37	@40.00

Boris Karloff Tales of Mystery
© *Gold Key Comics*

BORIS KARLOFF TALES OF MYSTERY
Gold Key 1963–80

1 (Thriller)	75.00
2 (Thriller)	50.00
3 thru 8	@25.00
9 WW	40.00
10	25.00
11 AW,JO	35.00
12 AT,AMc,JO	25.00
13 & 14	@20.00
15 RC,GE	25.00
16 thru 20	@20.00
21 JJ,Screaming Skull	40.00
22 thru 50	@15.00
51 thru 74	@10.00
75 thru 96	@8.00
97	8.00

BOZO
Innovation

1 1950's reprint stories	6.95

BOZO THE CLOWN
Blackthorne

1 3-D	2.50
2 3-D	2.50

BRADY BUNCH, THE
Dell Publishing Co. Feb., 1970

1	40.00
2	40.00

BRAIN BOY
Dell Publishing Co.
April–June, 1962

1	100.00
2	60.00
3	50.00
4	50.00

5	50.00
6	50.00

BREEDING GROUND
Samson Comics

1 I:Mazit, Zero	2.50

BRENDA LEE STORY, THE
Dell Publishing Co. Sept., 1962

1	65.00

BRENDA STARR REPORTER
Dell Publishing Co. Oct., 1963

1	150.00

BRIAN BOLLAND'S BLACK BOOK
Eclipse 1985

1 BB	2.50

BRIDES IN LOVE
Charlton Comics 1956–65

1	25.00
2	10.00
3 thru 10	@7.00
11 thru 30	@3.50
31 thru 44	@2.00
45	2.00

BRUTE, THE
Atlas Feb.–July 1975

1 thru 3	@1.00

BUCK ROGERS
Gold Key 1964

1 P(c)	45.00
2 AMc,FBe,P(c),movie adapt	8.00
3 AMc,FBe,P(c),movie adapt	8.00
4 FBe,P(c)	8.00
5 AMc,P(c)	4.00
6 AMc,P(c)	4.00

Whitman

7 thru 9 AMc,P(c)	@3.50
10 and 11 AMc,P(c)	@2.00
12 and 13 P(c)	2.00
14 thru 16	2.00

BUCK ROGERS
TSR

1 thru 10	@2.95

BUCKY O'HARE
Continuity

1 MGo	2.75
2 & 3	@2.00

BUFFALO BILL JR.
Dell Publishing Co. 1956

1	50.00
2	30.00
3	30.00
4	30.00
5	30.00
6	30.00
7	25.00
8	25.00
9	25.00
10	25.00
11 thru 13	@25.00

BUGGED-OUT ADVENTURES OF RALFY ROACH
Bugged Out Comics

1 I: Ralfy Roach	2.95

BULLWINKLE
Gold Key 1962

1 Bullwinkle & Rocky	200.00
2	125.00
3 thru 5	@60.00
6 and 7, rep.	@50.00
8 thru 11	60.00
12 rep.	35.00
13 and 14	@40.00
15 thru 19	@35.00
20 thru 24, rep.	@15.00
25	25.00

BULLWINKLE
Charlton Comics July, 1970

1	35.00

Becomes:

BULLWINKLE AND ROCKY
Charlton Comics 1970–71

2 thru 7	@20.00

BULLWINKLE & ROCKY
Eclipse

3-D	15.00

BULLWINKLE FOR PRESIDENT
Blackthorne

1 3-D Special	2.50

BURKE'S LAW
Dell Publishing Co. 1964

1	40.00
2	25.00
3	25.00

BUTCH CASSIDY
Skywald Comics 1971

1	2.00
2 & 3	1.50

CABBOT: BLOODHUNTER
Maximum Press 1997

1 thru 4 RV	@2.50

CADILLACS & DINOSAURS
Kitchen Sink

1 Rep. from Xenozoic Tales in 3-D	6.00

Topps
BLOOD & BONES

1 thru 3 rep. Xenozoic Tales, all covers	@2.50

MAN-EATER

1 thru 3, all covers	2.50

THE WILD ONES

1 thru 3, all covers	2.50

CAGES
Tundra

1 DMc	14.00

COLOR PUB.

All comics prices listed are for *Near Mint* condition.

2 DMc	11.00
3 DMc	7.50
4 DMc	7.50
5 thru 7 DMc	5.00

CAIN
Harris

1 B:DQ(s),I:Cain,Frenzy	5.00
2 BSz(c),HBk,V:Mortatira	3.25

CAIN'S HUNDRED
Dell Publishing Co.
May-July, 1962

1	15.00
2	12.00

CALIFORNIA RAISINS
Blackthorne

1 thru 4 3-D	@2.50
5 3-D,O:Calif.Raisins	2.50
6 thru 8 3-D	@2.50

CALVIN & THE COLONEL
Dell Publishing Co.
April-June, 1962

1	75.00
2	50.00

CAP'N QUICK & FOOZLE
Eclipse 1984–85

1	2.00
2 and 3	@2.50

CAPT. ELECTRON
Brick Computers Inc.

1	2.00
2	2.25

CAPTAIN ATOM
See STRANGE SUSPENSE STORIES

CAPTAIN CANUCK
Comely Comix 1975–81

1 I:Blue Fox	2.50
2 I:Red Coat	2.00
3 I:Heather	2.00
4 thru 14	1.00
Summer Spec. #1	1.00

CAPTAIN GLORY
Topps

1 A:Bombast,Night Glider, Trading Card	3.25

CAPTAIN HARLOCK: FALL OF THE EMPIRE
Eternity

1 R:Captain Harlock	2.50
2 V:Tadashi	2.50
3 Bomb on the Arcadia	2.50
4 Final issue	2.50

CAPTAIN MARVEL
M. F. Enterprises April, 1966

1	17.00
2	12.00
3 Fights The Bat	10.00

4	10.00
5 Captain Marvel Presents the Terrible Five	8.00

CAPTAIN NAUTICUS
Entity 1994

1 V:Fathom	2.95
2 V:Fathom's Henchman	2.95
3 Surf's Up	1.95

CAPTAIN NICE
Gold Key Nov., 1967

1 Ph(c)	45.00

CAPTAIN PARAGON
Americomics

1 thru 4	@2.00

CAPTAIN POWER
Continuity

1a NA,TVtie-in(direct sale)	2.00
1b NA,TVtie-in(newsstand)	2.00
2 NA	2.00

CAPTAIN STERN
Kitchen Sink Press

1 BWr,R:Captain Stern	5.25
2 BWr,Running Out of Time	4.95

CAPTAIN THUNDER AND BLUE BOLT
Hero Graphics

1 I:Capt.Thunder & Paul Fremont	1.95
2 Paul becomes Blue Bolt	1.95
3 O:Capt.Thunder	1.95
4 V:Iguana Boys	1.95
5 V:Ian Shriver, in Scotland	1.95
6 V:Krakatoa	1.95
7 V:Krakatoa	1.95
8 A:Sparkplug (from League of Champions)	1.95
9 A:Sparkplug	1.95
10 A:Sparkplug	1.95

CAPTAIN VENTURE & THE LAND BENEATH THE SEA
Gold Key Oct., 1968

1	40.00
2	35.00

CAPTAIN VICTORY AND THE GALACTIC RANGERS
Pacific 1982

1 JK	2.00
2 JK	1.50
3 JK,BU:NA,I:Ms.Mystic	1.75
4 JK	1.00
5 JK	1.00
6 JK,SD	1.00
7 thru 13 JK	@1.00
Spec.#1 JK	1.50

CAR 54, WHERE ARE YOU?
Dell Publishing Co.
March-May, 1962

1 Ph(c)	70.00
2 thru 7 Ph(c)	@40.00

Captain Victory #1 © Pacific Comic

CARCA JOU RENAISSANCE

1 and 2	@1.50

CARNOSAUR CARNAGE
Atomeka

TPB	4.95

CAROLINE KENNEDY
Charlton Comics 1961

1	50.00

CASEY JONES & RAPHAEL
Mirage

1 Family War	2.75
2 Johnny Woo Woo	2.75
3 V:Johnny Woo Woo	2.75
4 9mm Raphael	2.75

CASPER ENCHANTED TALES
Harvey

1 short stories	1.25

CASPER
Harvey

1 thru 7	@1.00
8 thru 14	@1.25
15 thru 28	@1.50

CASPER THE FRIENDLY GHOST
Blackthorne

1 3-D	2.50

CASPER & FRIENDS
Harvey

1 thru 4	@1.00
5 short stories, cont	1.25

CASPER GHOSTLAND
Harvey

1 short stories	1.25

All comics prices listed are for *Near Mint* condition.

Casper's Ghostland #3 © Harvey Publ.

CASPER'S GHOSTLAND
Harvey Publications
Winter, 1958-59
1	125.00
2	50.00
3 thru 10	@30.00
11 thru 20	@15.00
21 thru 40	@8.00
41 thru 61	@6.00
62 thru 77	@3.50
78 thru 97	@2.50
98 Dec., 1979	2.50

CASPER
THE FRIENDLY GHOST
Harvey 1990–91
Prev: The Friendly Ghost Casper
254 thru 260	@1.00

[Second Series] 1991–94
1 thru 14	@1.25
15 thru 28	@1.50

CAT TALES
Eternity
1 3-D	1.95

CAULDRON
Real Comics 1995
1 Movie Style Comic	2.95
1a Variat cover	2.95

CAVE GIRL
AC Comics
1	2.95

CAVE KIDS
Gold Key 1963
1	20.00
2	15.00
3	15.00
4	15.00
5	15.00
6	8.00
7 A:Pebbles & Bamm Bamm	10.00
8 thru 10	8.00
11 thru 16	8.00

CHAINS OF CHAOS
Harris
1 Vampirella, Rook	5.00
2 V:Chaoschild	3.25
3 Final issue	3.25

CHAMPIONS
Eclipse 1986–87
1 I:Flare,League of Champions Foxbat, Dr.Arcane	1.25
2 I:Dark Malice	1.50
3 I:Lady Arcane	1.25
4 O:Dark Malice	2.00
5 O:Flare	1.25
6 D:Giant Demonmaster	1.25

[New Series]
Hero Graphics
1 EL,I:Madame Synn,Galloping Galooper	5.00
2 I:Fat Man, Black Enchantress	2.25
3 I:Sparkplug&Icicle,O:Flare	2.25
4 I:Exo-Skeleton Man	2.25
5 A:Foxbat	2.25
6 I:Mechanon, C:Foxbat	1.95
7 A:Mechanon,J:Sparkplug,Icicle	1.95
8 O:Foxbat	1.95
9 Flare #0 (Flare preview)	1.95
10 Olympus Saga #1	1.95
11 Olympus Saga #2	1.95
12 Olympus Saga #3	1.95
Ann.#1 O:Giant & DarkMalice	2.75
Ann.#2	3.95

CHAMPIONS CLASSIC
Hero Graphics
1 GP(c),Rep.1st champions series	1.00

CHAOS BIBLE
Chaos! Comics
1 Character Profiles	3.50

CHAOS! GALLERY
Chaos! Comics 1997
1	2.95

CHAOS QUARTERLY
Harris Comics 1995
1 F:Lady Death	4.95
1a Premium Edition	10.95
1b Signed,limited edition	20.00

CHARLEMAGNE
Defiant
1 JiS(s),From Hero	2.00
2 JiS(s),I:Charles Smith	2.75
3 JiS(s),A:War Dancer	2.75
4 DGC(s),V:Dark Powers	2.75
5 Schism prequel	2.75
6 V:Wardancer	2.75
7 R:To Vietnam	2.75

CHARLIE CHAN
Dell Publishing Co.
Oct.-Dec., 1965
1	25.00
2	15.00

CHARLTON BULLSEYE
Spec. #1	2.00

CHARLTON
SPORT LIBRARY
Charlton 1970
1 Professional Football	15.00

CHASSIS
Millenium/Expand 1995
1 I:Chassis McBain, Aero Run	2.95
1 chrome cover	9.95
2	2.95
2a Amanda Conner cover	2.95
2b foil cover, signed	7.95

CHASTITY:
THEATRE OF PAIN
Chaos! Comics 1997
1 (of 3) BnP,	2.95
2	2.95
3	2.95

CHEAP SHODDY
ROBOT TOYS
Eclipse
1 A:Ronald Reagan	1.75

CHECKMATE
Gold Key Oct., 1962
1 Ph(c)	30.00
2 Ph(c)	25.00

CHEMICAL MAN
1	1.75

CHERYL BLOSSOM
Archie Comics April 1996
1 "Love Showdown"	1.50
2 "Inn Big Trouble"	1.50
3 "Home Um-Improvement"	1.50
4 "Radio Daze"	1.50
5 "Cheryl in the Morning"	1.50
6 "What a Disaster"	1.50

CHERYL BLOSSOM
GOES HOLLYWOOD
Archie Comics 1996
1 (of 3) by Dan Parent & Bill Golliher	1.50
2 and 3	@1.50

CHEYENNE
Dell Publishing Co. Oct., 1956
1 Ph(c) all	150.00
2	75.00
3	50.00
4 thru 12	@40.00
13 thru 25	@35.00

CHEYENNE KID
(see WILD FRONTIER)

CHILD'S PLAY 2
Innovation
1 Movie Adapt Pt 1	2.50
2 Adapt Pt 2	2.50
3 Adapt Pt 3	2.50

CHILD'S PLAY 3
Innovation
1 Movie Adapt Pt 1	2.50

2 Movie Adapt Pt.2 . . . . 2.50

CHILD'S PLAY: THE SERIES
Innovation
1 Chucky's Back 2.50
2 Straight Jacket Blues 2.50
3 M.A.R.K.E.D. 2.50
4 Chucky in Toys 4 You 2.50
5 Chucky in Hollywood 2.50

CHILDREN OF FIRE
Fantagor
1 RCo 2.00
2 RCo 2.00
3 RCo 2.00

CHILLING ADVENTURES IN SORCERY AS TOLD BY SABRINA
Archie 1972–74
1 . . . . 5.00
2 . . . . 3.00
3 thru 5 . . . . @3.00

CHIP 'N DALE RESCUE RANGERS
Walt Disney 1990
1 Rescue Rangers to the Rescue,
  pt.1 . . . . 3.50
2 Rescue Rangers to the Rescue,
  pt.2 . . . . 3.00
3 . . . . 2.50
4 . . . . 2.50
5 . . . . 2.50
6 . . . . 2.50
7 . . . . 2.50
8 Coast to Coast Pt 1 . . . . 2.00
9 Coast to Coast Pt 2 . . . . 2.00
10 Coast to Coast Pt 3 . . . . 2.00
11 Coast to Coast Pt 4 . . . . 2.00
12 "Showdown at Hoedown" 1.75
13 Raining Cats & Dogs 1.75
14 "Cobra Kadabra" 1.75
15 I:Techno-Rats,WaspPatrol
  Fearless Frogs Pt.1 . . . . 1.75
16 A:Techno-Rats,WaspPatrol,
  Fearless Frogs Pt.2 . . . . 1.75
17 "For the Love of Cheese" 1.75
18 "Ghastly Goat of Quiver Moore,
  Pt.1 . . . . 1.50

CHOO CHOO CHARLIE
Gold Key Dec., 1969
1 . . . . 50.00

CHOPPER: EARTH, WIND, AND FIRE
Fleetway
1 F:Chopper 2.95

CHOSEN, THE
Click Comics 1995
1 I:The Chosen 2.50
2 I:Herman Cortez 2.50

CHRISTIAN
Maximum Press 1996
1 (of 3) RLd 2.95
2 RLd 2.95

CHRISTMAS PARADE
Gladstone
1 GiantEdition 4.00
2 . . . . 3.50

CHROMA-TICK SPECIAL EDITION
New England Press
1 Rep.Tick#1,new stories 3.95
2 Rep.Tick#2,new stories 3.95
3 thru 8 Reps.& new stories . . @3.50

CHROME
Hot Comics
1 Machine Man 3.50
2 thru 4 . . . . @2.00

CHROMIUM MAN, THE
Triumphant Comics
0 Blue Logo 6.00
0 Regular 2.50
1 I:Chromium Man,Mr.Death . . . 3.50
2 I:Prince Vandal 3.00
3 I:Candi,Breaker,Coil 2.50
4 JnR(s),AdP,Unleashed 2.50
5 JnR(s),AdP,Unleashed 2.50
6 JnR(s),Courier,pt.1 . . . . 2.50
7 JnR(s),Courier,pt.2 . . . . 2.50
8 JnR(s),Chromium finds peace . 2.50
9 V:Tarsak 2.50
10 . . . . 2.50
11 Prince Vandal #8 . . . . 2.50
12 Prince Vandal #9 . . . . 2.50
13 V:Realm 2.50
14 A:Light 2.50
15 . . . . 2.50

CHROMIUM MAN: VIOLENT PAST
Triumphant Comics
1 JnR(s), ... 2.50
2 JnR(s), ... 2.50
3 JnR(s), ... 2.50
4 JnR(s), ... 2.50

Chronicles of Corum #1 © First

CHRONICLES OF CORUM
First 1987–88
1 Michael Moorcock adapt. 2.25
2 thru 12 . . . . @2.00

CICERO'S CAT
Dell Publishing Co.
July-Aug., 1959
1 . . . . 25.00
2 . . . . 20.00

CIMMARON STRIP
Dell Publishing Co. Jan., 1968
1 . . . . 30.00

CITY PERILOUS
Broadway Comics
1 GI,"I Remember the Future,"
  part #1 . . . . 2.95
2 GI,"I Remember the Future,"
  part #2 . . . . 2.95
Becomes:

KNIGHTS ON BROADWAY
3 GI,"I Remember the Future,"
  part #3 . . . . 2.95
4 GI,"I Remember the Future,"
  part #4 . . . . 2.95
5 GI,"I Remember the Future,"
  part #5 . . . . 2.95

CLASSICS ILLUSTRATED
See Also:
CLASSICS ILLUSTRATED SECTION

CLASSICS ILLUSTRATED
First
1 GW,The Raven 3.75
2 RG,Great Expectations 3.75
3 KB,Thru the Looking Glass . . . 3.75
4 BSz,Moby Dick 3.75
5 SG,TM,KE, Hamlet 3.75
6 PCr,JT, Scarlet Letter 3.75
7 DSp,Count of Monte Cristo . . . 3.75
8 Dr.Jekyll & Mr.Hyde 3.75
9 MP,Tom Sawyer 3.75
10 Call of the Wild 3.75
11 Rip Van Winkle 3.75
12 Dr. Moreau 3.75
13 Wuthering Heights 3.75
14 Fall of House of Usher 3.75
15 Gift of the Magi 3.75
16 A: Christmas Carol 3.75
17 Treasure Island 3.75
18 The Devils Dictionary 3.95
19 The Secret Agent 3.95
20 The Invisible Man 3.95
21 Cyrano de Bergerac 3.95
22 The Jungle Book 3.95
23 Swiss Family Robinson 3.95
24 Rime of Ancient Mariner 3.95
25 Ivanhoe 3.95
26 Aesop's Fables 3.95
27 The Jungle 3.95

CLIVE BARKER'S DREAD
Eclipse
Graphic Album 7.95

COLOR PUB.

CLIVE BARKER'S TAPPING THE VEIN
Eclipse
1	13.00
2	8.50
3	8.50
4	8.50
5 inc."How Spoilers Breed"	8.50

CLYDE CRASHCUP
Dell Publishing Co.
Aug.-Oct., 1963
1	65.00
2	50.00
3 thru 5	@50.00

COBALT 60
Innovation
1 reprints	4.95

COBALT BLUE
Innovation
Spec.#1	1.95
Spec.#2	1.95
1 and 2	@1.95

Codename: Danger #4 © Lodestone

CODENAME: DANGER
Lodestone
1 RB/BMc,I:Makor	2.50
2 KB,I:Capt.Energy	2.00
3 PS/RB	1.50
4 PG	1.50

CODE NAME: DOUBLE IMPACT
High Impact 1997
1 RCI	3.00
1 variant cover	10.00
1 signed holofoil cover	14.95

CODENAME: STRIKEFORCE
Spectrum
1	1.00

COLLECTOR'S DRACULA
Millennium
1	4.25

COLOSSAL SHOW, THE
Gold Key Oct., 1969
1	30.00

COLOUR OF MAGIC
Innovation
1 Terry Pratchet novel adapt	3.00
2 "The Sending of Eight"	2.50
3 "Lure of the Worm"	2.50
4 final issue	2.50

COLT .45
Dell Publishing Co. 1958
1 Ph(c) all	85.00
2	50.00
3	50.00
4	50.00
5	50.00
6 ATh	65.00
7	50.00
8	50.00
9	50.00

COLT SPECIAL
AC Comics
1	1.75
2	1.75
3	1.75

COMBAT
Dell Publishing Co. 1961
1 SG	35.00
2 SG	15.00
3 SG	15.00
4 JFK cover, Story 2-D	20.00
5 SG	15.00
6 SG	10.00
7 SG	10.00
8 SG	10.00
9 SG	10.00
10 SG	10.00
11 thru 27 SG	@7.00
28 thru 40 SG	@5.00

COMET
Red Circle/Archie Publications
1 CI,O:Comet	1.00
2 CI,D:Hangman	1.00

COMET, THE
Red Circle 1983
1 Alex Nino	1.50

COMIC ALBUM
Dell Publishing Co. 1958
March-May, 1958
1 Donald Duck	75.00
2 Bugs Bunny	30.00
3 Donald Duck	50.00
4 Tom & Jerry	30.00
5 Woody Woodpecker	30.00
6 Bugs Bunny	30.00
7 Popeye	35.00
8 Tom & Jerry	30.00
9 Woody Woodpecker	30.00
10 Bugs Bunny	30.00
11 Popeye	35.00
12 Tom & Jerry	25.00
13 Woody Woodpecker	25.00
14 Bugs Bunny	25.00
15 Popeye	35.00
16 Flintstones	60.00
17 Space Mouse	30.00
18 3 Stooges,Ph(c)	75.00

COMICO X-MAS SPECIAL
Comico
1 SR/AW/DSt(c)	1.50

COMIX INTERNATIONAL
Warren Magazines July, 1974
1	35.00
2 WW,BW	20.00
3	8.00
4 RC	10.00
5 Spring, 1977	5.00

COMMANDER BATTLE AND HIS ATOMIC SUB
#20 3-D	2.50

COMMANDOSAURS
1	3.50

CONSTRUCT
Mirage
1 I:Constructs	2.75
2 F:Sect.Eight, Armor	2.75
3 O:Constructs	2.75
4 Fist-O-God	2.75

CORBEN SPECIAL
Pacific
1 RCo	1.75

CORUM: THE BULL & THE SPEAR
First
1 thru 4 Michael Moorcock adapt	@1.95

COSMONEERS SPECIAL
1	1.95

COUGAR, THE
Atlas Apr.–July 1975
1 & 2	@1.00

COURTSHIP OF EDDIE'S FATHER
Dell Publishing Co. 1970
1 Ph(c)	25.00
2 Ph(c)	20.00

COVER GIRL
1	1.95

COWBOY IN AFRICA
Gold Key March, 1968
1 Chuck Conners,Ph(c)	25.00

CRACKED
Major Magazines
Feb.-March, 1958
1 AW	125.00

COLOR PUB.

2	50.00
3 thru 6	@30.00
7 thru 10	@18.00
11 thru 20	@10.00
21 thru 30	@7.00
31 thru 60	@3.00
61 thru 252	@2.50

[THE INCREDIBLE] CRASH DUMMIES
Harvey 1993

1 thru 3, from the toy series	@1.50

CRAZYMAN
Continuity
[1st Series]

1 Embossed(c),NA/RT(i), O:Crazyman	6.00
2 NA/BB(c)	2.50
3 DBa,V:Terrorists	2.50

[2nd Series]

1 Die Cut(c)	2.50
2 thru 3	2.50
4 In Demon World	2.50

CREED/TEENAGE MUTANT NINJA TURTLES
Lightning Comics April 1996

1	3.00
1 variant cover	3.00
1 platinum edition B&W	9.95

CREED: CRANIAL DISORDER
Lightning Comics

1 (of 3)	3.00
1a variant cover, *Previews* exclusive	3.00
1b Platinum edition	9.00
1c Platinum edition, autographed	16.00
2	3.00
2a variant cover	3.00

CRIME MACHINE
Skywald Publications Feb., 1971

1	20.00
2	15.00

CRIME SUSPENSE STORIES
Russ Cochran

1 Rep. C.S.S. #1 (1950)	1.75
2 Rep. C.S.S.	1.75
3 Rep. C.S.S.	1.75
4 thru 6 Rep. C.S.S	2.00
7 Rep. C.S.S	2.00
8 thru 15 Rep.	2.00

Gemstone

16 thru 20 EC comics reprint	@2.50

CRIMSON NUN
Antarctic Press 1997

1 (of 4)	2.95
2	2.95

CROSSFIRE
Eclipse 1984–86

1 DSp	3.00
2 DSp	2.50
3 DSp	1.50
4 DSp	1.50

5 DSp	1.50
6 DSp	1.50
7 DSp	2.50
8 DSp	2.50
9 DSp	1.75
10 DSp	1.75
11 DSp	1.75
12 DSp,DSt(c),M.Monroe cover & story	2.50
13 DSp	1.75
14 DSp	1.75
15 DSp,O:Crossfire	1.75
16 DSp,"The Comedy Place"	1.75
17 DSp,"Comedy Place" Pt.2	1.75

Crossfire & Rainbow #2
© Eclipse Comics

CROSSFIRE & RAINBOW
Eclipse 1986

1 DSp,V:Marx Brothers	1.75
2 DSp,PG(c),V:Marx Brothers	1.50
3 DSp,HC(c),A:Witness	1.50
4 DSp,DSt(c),"This Isn't Elvis"	3.50

CROSSROADS
First

1 Sable,Whisper	4.00
2 Sable,Badger	4.00
3 JSon,JAl,Badger/Luther Ironheart	4.00
4 Grimjack/Judah Macabee	4.00
5 LM,Grimjack/Dreadstar/Nexus	4.00

CROW, THE: CITY OF ANGELS
Kitchen Sink

1 thru 3 movie adaptation	@2.95
1 thru 3 movie adaptation, photo covers	@2.95

CRYING FREEMAN III
Viz

1 A:Dark Eyes,Oshu	6.00
2 A:Dark Eyes, V:Oshu	5.25
3 Freeman vs. Oshu	5.25
4 Freeman Defeated	5.25
5 Freeman clones, A:Nitta	5.25

6 V:Nitta	5.25
7	4.95
8	4.95
9	4.95

CRYING FREEMAN IV
Viz

1 B:The Pomegranate	4.95
2	2.75
3	2.75
4	2.75
5 thru 7	@2.75
8 E:The Pomegranate	2.75

[2nd Series]

1 The Festival	2.50

CRYPT OF DAWN
Sirius 1996

1 JLi	2.95

CYBER CITY: PART ONE
CPM Comics 1995

1 I:Oedo City	2.95
2 Sengoku	2.95

CYBER CITY: PART TWO
CPM Comics 1995

1 Based on Animated Movie	2.95

CYBERCRUSH: ROBOTS IN REVOLT
Fleetway/Quality

1 inc.Robo-Hunter,Ro-Busters	1.95
2 and 3	@1.95
4 and 5 V:Terraneks	@1.95

CYBERFROG
Harris 1995

0 O:Cyberfrog	2.95
0 AAd(c), signed	19.95
1	2.00
1a Signed,numbered	24.95
1b Ultra Violent Cover	49.95
2	2.95
3	2.95
4	2.95
4a alternate cover, signed & numbered (#300)	29.95

CYBERFROG: RESERVOIR FROG
Harris

1 Preview Ashcan, signed & numbered	24.95
1 EL(c),V:the Swarm, Mr. Skorpeone	2.95
1 Signed & numbered (#250)	19.95
2	2.95
1 & 2 Signed & numbered, in binder (#250)	39.95

CYBERHOOD
Entity Comics 1995

1 R:Cyberhood	2.50
1a with PC Game	6.95

CYBERPUNK
Innovation

1	1.95
2	1.95

Book 2,#1	2.25
Book 2,#2	2.25

CYBERPUNK:
THE SERAPHIM FILES
Innovation 1990

1	2.50
2	2.50

CYBERPUNX
Maximum Press 1997

1 MHw,	2.50

CYBERRAD
Continuity

1 NA layouts,I:Cyberran	3.00
2 NA I/o	2.50
3 NA I/o	2.50
4 NA I/o	2.50
5 NA I/o Glow in the Dark cov	5.00
6 NA I/o,Pullout poster	2.50
7 NA I/o,See-thru(c)	2.50
[2nd Series]	
1 Hologram cover	2.00
2 NA(c),"The Disassembled Man"	2.00
[3rd Series]	
1 Holo.(c).just say no	3.50
[4th Series, Deathwatch 2000]	
1 Deathwatch 2000 pt.8,w/card	2.50
2 Deathwatch 2000 pt. w/card	2.50

CYBRID
Maximum Press 1995

1 F:Cybrid, I:The Clan	2.95

CYBRID
Maximum Press 1997

0 RLd, 48pg	3.50
1 MsM,BNa	3.00
2 MsM,BNa	3.00

CYNDER
Immortelle Studios
1 thru 3: see B&W

Ann. #1	2.95
Series II 1997	
1 A:Nira X	2.95

CYNDER/NIRA X
Immortelle Studios 1996

1 x-over	2.95
1 variant cover	3.00
1 gold edition	10.00

DAEMONSTORM
Caliber 1997

1 TM(c),JMt	3.95
1 signed	3.95
1 gold edition	19.95

DAEMONSTORM:
DEADWORLD
Caliber

one-shot	3.95

DAEMONSTORM: OZ
Caliber 1997

1	3.95

DAGAR THE INVINCIBLE
Gold Key 1972–82

1 O:Daggar;I:Villians Olstellon & Scorpio	15.00
2	6.00
3 I:Graylon	5.00
4	5.00
5	5.00
6 1st Dark Gods story	4.00
7	4.00
8	4.00
9	4.00
10	4.00
11 thru 19	@2.00

DAI KAMIKAZE
Now

1 Speed Racer	7.00
1a 2nd printing	1.50
2	2.00
3	1.50
4	1.50
5	1.50
6 thru 12	@1.75

DAKTARI
Dell Publishing Co. July, 1967

1	20.00
2	15.00
3	15.00
4	15.00

DALGODA
Fantagraphics

1	3.50
2 KN,I:Grinwood'Daughter	3.00
3 KN	2.50
4 thru 8	@2.25

DANGER
Charlton Comics June, 1955

12	40.00
13	30.00
14	30.00
Becomes:	

JIM BOWIE

15	25.00
16	12.00
17	12.00
18	12.00
19 April, 1957	12.00

DANIEL BOONE
Gold Key 1965–69

1	75.00
2 thru 5	@30.00
6 thru 14	@20.00
15	15.00

DANNY BLAZE
Charlton Comics Aug., 1955

1	35.00
2	30.00
Becomes:	

NATURE BOY

3 JB,O:Blue Beetle	125.00
4	100.00
5 Feb., 1957	85.00

DARE
Fantagraphics

1 F:Dan Dare	2.75
2 F:Dan Dare	2.75
3 F:Dan Dare	2.50
4 F:Dan Dare	2.50

DARE THE IMPOSSIBLE
Fleetway/Quality

1 DGb,rep.Dan Dare from 2000AD	1.95
2 DGb, Dare on Waterworld	1.95
3 DGb	1.95
4 DGb	1.95
5 DGb,"The Garden of Eden"	1.95
6 DGb	1.95
7 DGb,V:Deadly Primitives	1.95
8 DGb,The Doomsday Machine	1.95
9 thru 14 DGb	@1.95

The Dark #3 © Continuüm Comics

DARK, THE
Continüm 1992

1 LSn(c),MBr,V:Futura	4.00
2 LSn,Shot by Futura	3.00
3 MBr,Dark has amnesia	3.00
4 GT(c),MBr,O:The Dark	3.00
Convention Book 1992 MBr,GP, MFm,MMi,VS,LSn,TV	5.00
Convention Book 1993 MBr,PC, ECh,BS,BWi,GP(c),Foil(c),	4.00
Aug. House	
1 BS(c),Red Foil(c),	3.00
1a BS(c),newstand ed.	3.00
1b BS(c),Blue foil	3.00
2	3.00
3 BS(c),Foil(c),	3.00
4 GP(c),Foil(c),w/cards	3.00
5 thru 9	@2.50
[2nd Series]	
1 Dark Regains Memory	3.00
1a Signed, Foil Cover	2.75
2 War on Crime	2.75
3 Geoffery Stockton	2.50
4 I:First Monster	2.50

DARK ADVENTURES

1 thru 3	@1.75

COLOR PUB.

DARK CHYLDE
Maximum Press June 1996
1 RQu		8.00
1 American Entertainment edition		5.00
1 variant cover		5.00
2 RQu		5.00
2 variant cover		5.00
3 RQu		4.00
3 variant cover		7.00
4 RQu		3.00
5 RQu,"No One Here Gets Out Alive"		3.00

DARK CHYLDE/ AVENGELYNE
Maximum Press
Spec. RLd,RQu,I:Witch Tower . . . 3.00

DARK CHYLDE/GLORY
Maximum Press
Spec. RQu, ... 3.00

Dark Dominion #3 © Defiant Comics

DARK DOMINION
Defiant
1 SD,I:Michael Alexander		3.25
2 LWn(s),SLi(i),		2.75
3 LWn(s),SLi(i),		2.75
4 LWn(s),B:Hoxhunt		3.00
5 LWn(s),I:Puritan,Judah		2.75
6 LWn(s),I:Lurk		2.75
7 LWn(s),V:Glimmer		2.75
8 LWn(s),V:Glimmer		2.50
9 LWn(s)V:Puritan		2.50
10 LWn(s),Schism Prequel		2.50
11 LWn(s), X-Over		2.50
12 LWn(s), V:Chasm		2.50

DARKNESS, THE
Top Cow 1996
Preview Edition, GEn,MS		10.00
½		12.00
½ variant cover		15.00
1 GEn,MS		7.50
1 variant cover		10.00
1b platinum edition		12.00
2		4.00
3		2.50

4	2.50

DARK ONE'S THIRD EYE
Sirius April 1996
one-shot DOe 4.95

DARK SHADOWS
Gold Key March, 1969
1 W/Poster,Ph(c)		250.00
2 Ph(c)		100.00
3 W/Poster,Ph(c)		125.00
4 thru 7,Ph(c)		@75.00
8 thru 10		@60.00
11 thru 20		@50.00
21 thru 35		@40.00

DARK SHADOWS
Innovation
1 Based on 1990's TV series	3.50
2 O:Victoria Winters	2.50
3 Barnabus Imprisoned	2.50
4 V: Redmond Swann	2.75

[2nd Series]
1 A:Nathan	2.75
2 thru 4	2.75
Dark Shadows:Resurrected	15.95

DARK SIDE
Maximum Press 1997
1 RLd,RQu 3.00

DARK TOWN
Mad Monkey Press
1 (of 13)	3.95
2 thru 6	@3.95

DARKLON THE MYSTIC
Pacific
1 JSn 1.50

DARKWING DUCK
Walt Disney
1 I:Darkwing Duck	1.75
2 V:Taurus Bulba	1.75
3 "Fowl Play"	1.75
4 "End o/t beginning,"final issue	1.75

DARKWOOD
Aircel
1 thru 5 . . . . @2.00

DAUGHTERS OF TIME
3-D
1 I:Kris,Cori,Lhana 3.95

FRONTIER FIGHTER
Charlton Comics Aug., 1955
1	40.00
2	20.00
Becomes:	

DAVY CROCKETT
3 thru 7	@15.00
8 Jan., 1957	10.00
Becomes:	

KID MONTANA
9	20.00
10	9.00
11	6.00
12	6.00
13	14.00

14 thru 20	@6.00
21 thru 35	@3.50
36 thru 49	@2.00
50 March, 1965	2.00

DAWN
Sirius 1995–97
½	15.00
½ variant	20.00
1 JLi,R:Dawn	13.00
1 white trash edition	40.00
1 black light edition	35.00
1 look sharp edition	45.00
2 JLi, Trip to Hell	7.50
2 variant cover	30.00
3 JLi	5.00
3 limited edition	30.00
4 JLi,"The Gauntlet"	4.00
4a variant cover	20.00
5 JLi,"Everybody Dies"	3.00
6 (of 6) JLi	3.00

DAZEY'S DIARY
Dell Publishing Co.
June-Aug., 1962
1 . . . . 25.00

DEAD BOYS: DEATH'S EMBRACE
London Night 1996
1 EHr	3.00
1 platinum edition	6.00

DEAMON DREAMS
Pacific
1	1.50
2	1.50

DEAR NANCY PARKER
Gold Key 1963
1 P(c)	18.00
2 P(c)	15.00

DEATHDEALER
Verotika 1995
1 FF(c), I:Deathdealer	10.00
2 thru 4 FF(c)	@7.50

DEATH OF HARI KARI
Blackout Comics 1997
0	2.95
0 super Sexy Kari Cover	9.95
0 3-D super Sexy Kari Cover	14.95

DEATHRACE 2020
Roger Corman Cosmic Comics
1 Pat Mills, Tony Skinner	2.50
2 V:Spyda, Sawmill Jones	2.50
3 O:Frankenstein	2.50
4 Deathrace cont.	2.50
5 F:Death Racers, D:Alchoholic	2.50
6 V:Indestructiman	2.50
7 Smallville Mall	2.50

DEATH OF LADY VAMPRE
Blackout Comics 1995
1 V:Baraclaw	2.95
1 Commemorative Issue	9.95

COLOR PUB.

DEATH RATTLE
Kitchen Sink 1985–88

1 thru 7	@2.00
8 I:Xenozoic Tales	5.00
9 thru 18	@2.00

DEFENDERS, THE
Dell Publishing Co.
Sept.-Nov., 1962

1	30.00
2	25.00

DEFIANT:
ORIGIN OF A UNIVERSE
Defiant

1 Giveaway	1.50

DELIVERER
Zion Comics

1 thru 3	1.95
4 F:Gabriel	1.95
5 V:Division	1.95

DEMONIC TOYS
Eternity

1 Based on 1992 movie	2.50
2 thru 4	2.50

DEMONIQUE
London Night 1996

0 Manga	3.00
0a nude cover variant	10.00
0a nude cover variant, signed	8.00
1 EHr	3.00
1a nude cover	6.00
1a nude cover, signed	8.00
2 (of 2)	3.00
2a nude cover	6.00

DEN
Fantagor

1 thru 10 RCo	@2.00

DEN SAGA
Tundra/Fantagor

1 RCo,O:Den begins	4.95

DENNIS THE MENACE
Fawcett 1960-61

Fun Book #1	50.00
And his Pal Joey #1	30.00
And his Dog Ruff #1	30.00
Television Special #1	40.00
Triple Feature #1	40.00
Television Special #2	25.00

DENNIS THE MENACE
AND HIS FRIENDS
[VARIOUS SUBTITLES]
Fawcett 1969–1980

1 thru 10 rep.	@4.00
11 thru 20 rep.	@3.50
21 thru 46 rep.	@3.00

DENNIS THE MENACE
GIANTS
[VARIOUS SUBTITLES]
Fawcett 1955–69

N# Vacation Special	100.00

Dennis the Menace and His Friends #35
© Fawcett Comics

N# Christmas	100.00
2 thru 10	75.00
11 thru 20	50.00
21 thru 30	25.00
31 thru 40	15.00
41 thru 75	10.00

Becomes:

DENNIS THE MENACE
BONUS MAGAZINE
[VARIOUS SUBTITLES]
Fawcett 1970–79

76 thru 100	@4.00
101 thru 120	@3.00
121 thru 185	@2.00
186 thru 196 Big Bonus Series	@2.00

Becomes:

DENNIS THE MENACE
Fawcett 1979–1980

#16 Fun Fest	2.00
#17 Fun Fest	2.00
#10 Big Bonus Series	2.00
#11 Big Bonus Series	2.00

DEPUTY DAWG
Gold Key Aug., 1965

1	100.00

DESTROYER DUCK
Eclipse 1982–84

1 JK,AA,SA,I:Groo	12.00
2 JK,AA,Starling	1.50
3 thru 5 JK	@1.50
6 thru 7 JK	@2.00

DESTRUCTOR, THE
Atlas Feb.–Aug. 1975

1 thru 4	@2.00

DETECTIVES, INC.
Eclipse 1985

1 MR,rep.GraphicNovel	3.00
2 MR	2.25

[2nd Series]

1 GC,"A Terror of Dying Dreams"	2.50
2 GC	2.25

3 GC,"Cut to the Bone"	1.50

DETONATOR
Chaos! Comics 1994–95

1 I:Detonator	2.95
2 V:Messiah & Mindbender	2.75

DEVIL KIDS
STARRING HOT STUFF
Harvey Publications 1962–81

1	80.00
2	40.00
3 thru 10	@20.00
11 thru 20	@15.00
21 thru 30	@10.00
31 thru 40	@7.00
41 thru 50 68 pgs.	@7.00
51 thru 55 62 pgs.	@5.00
56 thru 70	@3.00
71 thru 100	@2.00
101 thru 106	@1.00
107	1.00

DEVILMAN
Verotika 1995

1 Go Nagi	2.95
2 F:Devilman	2.95
3 Through History	2.95
4 French Revolution	2.95
5 Custer's Last Stand	2.95

DEVLIN
Maximum Press 1996

1 A:Avengelyne,3-part mini-series	2.50
2 (of 3) RLd,BNa,A:Avengelyne	2.50

DICK TRACY

1 3-D	2.50

DICK TRACY:
BIG CITY BLUES

1 Mini Series	3.95
2 Mini Series	5.95
3 Mini Series	5.95

DINO ISLAND
Mirage

1 thru 2	2.75

DINOSAUR REX
Upshot/Fantagraphics 1987

1 thru 3 by Jan Strand & Henry Mayo	@2.00

DINOSAURS
Walt Disney

1 Citizen Robbie(From TV)	2.95

DINOSAURS ATTACK
Eclipse

1 HT,Based on Topps cards	3.50
2 and 3 HT,Based on cards	@3.50

DISNEY ADVENTURES
Walt Disney

1	2.75
2	2.50
3 thru 6	@2.25
7 Joe Montana	2.25
8 Bronson Pinchot	2.25

All comics prices listed are for *Near Mint* condition.   **CVA Page 493**

9 Hulk Hogan 2.25
10 Mayim Bialik 2.25
11 . . . . 2.25
12 Monsters 2.25
13 A:Darkwing Duck (inc. work by
   DW) 2.25
14 inc. "Big Top, Big Shot" 1.95
15 . . . . 1.95
16 inc."Turnabout is Fowl Play" . . 1.95
17 inc."Kitty Kat Kaper" 1.95
18 Kitty Kat Kaper 1.95
19 The Voice of Wisdom 1.95
20 thru 28 . . . . @1.95

DISNEY COLOSSAL
COMICS COLLECTION
Walt Disney
1 inc.DuckTales, Chip'n'Dale . . . 2.25
2 inc.Tailspin,Duck Tales 1.95
3 inc.Duck Tales 1.95
4 O:Darkwing Duck 1.95
5 Tailspin,Duck Tales 1.95
6 Darkwing Duck,Goofy 1.95
7 inc.Darkwing Duck.Goofy 1.95
8 inc.Little Mermaid 1.95
9 inc.Duck Tales 1.95

DISNEY COMICS IN 3-D
Walt Disney
1 . . . . 2.95

DISNEY COMICS SPEC:
DONALD & SCROOGE
1 inc."Return to Xanadu" 8.95

DISNEYLAND BIRTHDAY
PARTY
Gladstone
1 . . . . 6.00

DIVER DAN
Dell Publishing Co.
Feb.-April, 1962
1 . . . . 35.00
2 . . . . 30.00

DIVINE MADNESS
Dark Moon
1 Human Flesh Artist 2.50
2 . . . . 2.50
3 Ancient Cult 2.50

DNAGENTS
Eclipse
1 O:DNAgents 4.00
2 . . . . 3.00
3 . . . . 2.50
4 . . . . 2.50
5 . . . . 2.50
6 . . . . 2.50
7 . . . . 2.50
8 . . . . 2.50
9 DSp 2.50
10 . . . . 2.00
11 . . . . 2.00
12 . . . . 2.50
13 . . . . 2.00
14 . . . . 2.00
15 . . . . 2.50
16 . . . . 2.50
17 thru 21 . . . . @2.00

22 . . . . 1.75
23 . . . . 1.75
24 DSt(c) 1.75
25 . . . . 1.75
See also: NEW DNAGENTS

DO YOU BELIEVE
IN NIGHTMARES?
St. John Publishing Co. 1957–58
1 SD 250.00
2 DAy 160.00

DOBER-MAN
1 . . . . 2.50

DOC SAVAGE
Millenium
1 V:Russians 2.50

DOC SAVAGE,
THE MAN OF BRONZE
Millenium
1 Monarch of Armageddon,pt.1 . . 3.00
2 Monarch of Armageddon,pt.2 . . 2.75
3 Monarch of Armageddon,pt.3 . . 2.75
4 Monarch of Armageddon,pt.4 . . 2.75

DOC SAVAGE:
THE DEVIL'S THOUGHTS
Millenium
1 V:Hanoi Shan 2.50
2 V:Hanoi Shan 2.50
3 Final issue 2.50

DOC SAVAGE:
DOOM DYNASTY
Millenium
1 and 2 . . . . @2.50

Doc Savage, Manual of Bronze #1
© Millenium Comics

DOC SAVAGE:
MANUAL OF BRONZE
Millenium
1 Fact File 2.50

DOC SAVAGE: REPEL
Innovation
1 DvD(c) 2.50

DOCTOR BOOGIE
Media Arts
1 . . . . 1.75
2 . . . . 1.75

DOCTOR CHAOS
Triumphant Comics 1993
1 JnR(s),I:Doctor Chaos 2.50
2 JnR(s), ... 2.50
3 JnR(s),The Coming of the
  Cry,pt.1,I:Cry 2.50
4 JnR(s),The Coming of the
  Cry,pt.2,b:Ky'Li 2.50
5 JnR(s),E:Coming of the
  Cry,pt.3,V:Cry 2.50
6 Recovery 2.50
7 w/coupon 2.50
8 w/coupon 2.50
9 V:Mirth 2.50
10 Co. X #3 . . . . 2.50
11 Co. X #4 . . . . 2.50
12 A:Charlotte 2.50

DOCTOR SOLAR
MAN OF THE ATOM
Gold Key
1 BF,I:Dr. Solar 300.00
2 BF,I:Prof.Harbinger 110.00
3 BF,The Hidden Hands 75.00
4 BF,The Deadly Sea 75.00
5 BF,I:Dr.Solar in costume 75.00
6 FBe,I:Nuro 50.00
7 FBe,Vanishing Oceans 50.00
8 FBe,Thought Controller 50.00
9 FBe,Transivac The Energy
  Consuming Computer 50.00
10 FBe,The Sun Giant 50.00
11 FBe,V:Nuro 35.00
12 FBe,The Mystery of the
   Vanishing Silver 35.00
13 FBe,The Meteor from 100 Million
   BC 35.00
14 FBe,Solar's Midas Touch . . . 35.00
15 FBe O:Dr.Solar 45.00
16 FBe,V:Nuro 35.00
17 FBe,The Fatal Foe 35.00
18 FBe,The Mind Master 35.00
19 FBe,SolarV:Solar 35.00
20 AMc,Atomic Nightmares 35.00
21 AMc,Challenge from Outer
   Space 25.00
22 AMc,Nuro,I:King Cybernoid . . 25.00
23 AMc,A:King Cybernoid 25.00
24 EC,The Deadly Trio 25.00
25 EC,The Lost Dimension 25.00
26 EC,When Dimensions Collide 25.00
27 (1969) The Ladder to Mars . . 25.00
28 (1981),1 pg AMc,The Dome of
   Mystery 12.00
29 DSp,FBe,Magnus 12.00
30 DSp,FBe,Magnus 12.00

DOGHEAD
Tundra
1 Al Columbia,"Poster Child" . . . 4.95

COLOR PUB.

DOGS OF WAR
Defiant
1 F:Shooter,Ironhead	2.75
2	2.50
3 Mouse Deserts	2.50
4 Schism Prequel	2.50
5 X-over	2.50
6 Aftermath	2.50

DOLLMAN
Eternity
1 Movie adapt. sequel	2.50
2 V:Sprug & Braindead Gang	2.50
3 Toni Costa Kidnapped	2.50
4	2.50

Donald Duck #203 © Gold Key

DONALD DUCK
Dell/Gold Key Dec. 1962
85 thru 97	35.00
98 rep. #46 CB	35.00
99	25.00
100	22.00
101	20.00
102 A:Super Goog	20.00
103 thru 111	@20.00
112 I:Moby Duck	20.00
113 thru 133	@20.00
134 CB rep.	20.00
135 CB rep.	20.00
136 thru 156	@18.00
157 CB rep.	15.00
158 thru 163	@12.00
164 CB rep.	12.00
165 thru 216	@5.00

Whitman
217	5.00
218	5.00
219 CB rep.	5.00
220 thru 245	@5.00

Gladstone
246 CB,Gilded Man	15.00
247 CB	10.00
248 CB,Forbidden Valley	10.00
249 CB	10.00
250 CB,Pirate Gold	15.00
251 CB,Donald's Best Xmas	4.00
252 CB,Trail o/t Unicorn	4.00

253 CB	3.50
254 CB, in old Calif	7.00
255 CB	3.50
256 CB,Volcano Valley	3.50
257 CB,Forest Fire	4.00
258 thru 260 CB	@3.00
261 thru 266 CB	@2.50
267 thru 277 CB	@2.00
278 CB	4.00
279 CB	4.00
280 thru 298 CB rep.	@1.50
299 "Life Guard Daze"	1.50
300 "Donald's 300th Triumph" 48pg	2.25
301 "The Gold Finder"	1.95
302 "Monkey Business"	1.95
303 "The Cantankerous Cat"	1.95
304 "Donald Duck Rants about Ants"	1.95

DONALD DUCK ADVENTURES
Gladstone
1 CB,Jungle Hi-Jinks	5.00
2 CB,Dangerous Disquise	4.00
3 CB,Lost in the Andes	5.00
4 CB,Frozen Gold	4.00
5 Rosa Art	3.50
6	2.50
7	2.50
8 Rosa	3.50
9	2.50
10	2.50
11	2.50
12 Giant size,Rosa	3.50
13 Rosa(c)	2.50
14	3.00
15 CB	2.00
16	2.00
17	2.00
18	2.00
19	4.00
20 Giant size	4.00
21 thru 30	@2.95
31 thru 40	@1.50
41 "Bruce McDuck"	1.50
42 "The Saga of Sourdough Sam"	1.50
43 "The Lost Charts of Columbus"	1.50
44 "The Kitchy-Kaw Diamond"	1.95
45 "The Red Duck"	1.95
46	1.95

DONALD DUCK ADVENTURES
Walt Disney 1990
1 Don Rosa, "The Money Pit"	5.00
2	3.00
3	2.50
4	2.50
5	2.50
6	2.50
7	2.00
8	2.00
9	2.00
10 "Run-Down Runner"	2.00
11 "Whats for Lunch-Supper"	2.00
12 "Head of Rama Putra"	2.00
13 "JustAHumble,BumblingDuck"	2.00
14 "DayGladstonesLuckRanOut"	1.75
15 "A Tuft Luck Tale"	1.75
16 "Magica's Missin'Magic"	1.75
17 "Secret of Atlantis"	1.75
18 "Crocodile Donald"	1.75
19 "Not So Silent Service"	1.75
20 "Ghost of Kamikaze Ridge"	1.50

21 "The Golden Christmas Tree"	1.50
22 "The Master Landscapist"	1.50
23 "The Lost Peg Leg Mine"	1.50
24 "On Stolen Time"	1.50
25 Sense of Humor	1.50
26 Race to the South Seas	1.50
27 Nap in Nature	1.50
28 Olympic Tryout	1.50
29 rep.March of Comics#20	1.50
30 A:The Vikings	1.50
31 The Sobbing Serpent of Loch McDuck	1.50
32 It Was No Occident	1.50
33 Crazy Christmas on Bear Mountain	1.50
34 Sup.Snooper Strikes Again	1.50
35 CB rep.	1.50
36 CB rep.	1.50
37 CB rep.	1.50

DONALD DUCK ALBUM
Dell Publishing Co.
May-July, 1959
1 CB(c)	50.00
2	30.00

DONATELLO
Mirage
1	10.00

DONNA MIA
Dark Fantasy Prod. 1995
1 I:Donna Mia	3.95
1a Deluxe Edition	4.95
1 signed & numbered (100 copies)	8.95

DOOMSDAY + 1
Charlton July, 1975
1 JBy,JBy(c),P(c)	8.00
2	6.00
3 JBy,JBy(c),P(c)	5.00
4 JBy,JBy(c),P(c),I:Lok	5.00
5 and 6 JBy,JBy(c),P(c)	@5.00
7 thru 12 JBy,JBy(c),P(c),rep	5.00

DOOMSDAY SQUAD
Fantagraphics
1 rep. JBy	2.00
2 rep. JBy	2.00
3 rep. SS,A:Usagi Yojimbo	4.00
4 thru 7, rep. JBy	@2.00

DOUBLE DARE ADVENTURES
Harvey Publications
1 I:B-man,Glowing Gladiator, Magicmaster	22.00
2 AW/RC rep. A:B-Man,Glowing Gladiator, Magicmaster	17.00

DOUBLE IMPACT
High Impact Studios 1995–96
1 RCI,I:China & Jazz, chrome(c)	7.00
1 holographic rainbow (c) with certificate	40.00
1 rainbow (c), no certificate	30.00
1 chromium variant (c)	15.00
2 RCI,V:Castillo	3.50
2 signed, with certificate	6.00
2 nude cover	10.00
2a China Exposed edition	10.00
2b signed by China	19.95
3 China on cover	3.00

COLOR PUB.

3 Jazzler on cover	3.00
3 Nikki on cover	3.00
3 "Blondage"	10.00
4 F:Mordred, The Rattler	2.95
4 "Phoenix" variant (c)	10.00
5 RCI	3.00
5a nude cover	10.00
6 "Buttshots"	5.00
6 Jazz (c)	3.00
6 signed	10.00
7 I:Nikki Blade	3.00
8	3.00
8a variant (c)	7.00
Gold edition, Lingerie special	3.00

Volume 2 1996–97

0 RCI	3.00
0 nude cover	10.00
1 RCI	3.00
1 deluxe edition	4.00
1 prism foil (c)	7.00
1 gold foil (c)	5.00
2 RCI	3.00
2a Swedish Erotica cover	10.00
2b Swedish Erotica cover, signed	15.00

DOUBLE IMPACT/ HELLINA
High Impact 1996

1-shot RCI	3.00
1a nude cover	9.95
1b Gold edition, nude cover	9.95
1c Spec. nude cover, signed	14.95

DOUBLE IMPACT/ LETHAL STRYKE: DOUBLE STRIKE
High Impact/London Night 1996

1-shot RCI	3.00
1a nude cover	9.95

DOUBLE IMPACT SUICIDE RUN
High Impact

1 RCI	3.00
1 gold edition	10.00
1 platinum edition	20.00

DOUBLE LIFE OF PRIVATE STRONG
Archie Publications

1 JSm/JK,I:Lancelot Strong/Shield The Fly	450.00
2 JSm/JK,GT A:Fly	300.00

DR. KILDARE
Dell Publishing Co.
April-June, 1962

1	50.00
2	40.00
3	40.00
4	40.00
5	40.00
6	40.00
7	40.00
8	40.00
9	40.00

DRACULA
Dell Publishing Co. Nov., 1966

2 O:Dracula	25.00
3	15.00

4	15.00
6	12.00
7	10.00
8	10.00

DRACULA
Topps

1 MMi,Movie adaptation (trading cards in each issue)	5.00
1a Red Foil Logo	12.00
1b 2nd Print	2.95
2 MMi,Movie adapt.contd.	4.00
3 MMi,Movie adapt.contd.	4.00
4 MMi,Movie adapt.concludes	4.00
TPB Collected Album	13.95

DRACULA CHRONICLES
Topps

1 True Story of Dracula	2.50
2 RTs,rep. Vlad #2	2.50
3 RTs,rep. Vlad #3	2.50

DRACULA VS. ZORRO
Topps

1 DMg(s),TY,Black(c),	3.25
2 DMg(s),TY,w/Zorro #0	2.95
TPB	5.95

DRACULA: VLAD THE IMPALER
Topps

1 EM,I:Vlad Dracua, w/cards	3.25
1a Red Foil	10.00
2 EM, w/cards	3.25

DRAGONCHIANG
Eclipse

1 TT	2.95

DRAGONFLIGHT
Eclipse 1991

1 Anne McCaffrey adapt.	4.95
2 novel adapt	4.95
3 novel adapt	4.95

DRAGONFLY
AC Comics

1	3.50
2 and 3	@2.00
4 thru 8	@1.75

DRAGONFORCE
Aircel

1 DK	7.50
2 thru 7 DK	@5.00
8 thru 12	@5.00
13	2.00

DRAGONRING
Aircel 1987–88
Vol. 2

1	3.50
2 O:Dragonring	2.50
3 thru 15	@2.00
See also: B&W	

DREADSTAR
First

27 JSn,from Epic,traitor	2.50
28 JSn	2.25

Dreadstar #51 © First

29 JSn,V:Lord Papal	2.25
30 JSn,D:Lord Papal	2.25
31 JSn,I:The Power	2.25
32 JSn	2.25
33	2.25
34 LM/VM,A:Malchek	2.25
35 LM/VM	2.25
36 LM/VM	2.25
37 LM/VM,A:Last Laugh	2.25
38 LM/VM	2.25
39 AMc,Crossroads tie-in	2.25
40 LM/VM	2.25
41 AMe	2.25
42 JSn,AMe,B.U.Pawns begins	2.25
43 JSn,AMe,Pawns,pt.2	2.25
44 JSn,AMe,Pawns,pt.3	2.25
45 JSn,AMe,Pawns,pt.4	2.25
46 JSn,AMe,Pawns,pt.5	2.25
47 JSn,AMe,Pawns,pt.6	2.25
48 JSn,AMe,Pawns,pt.7	2.25
49 JSn,AMe,Pawns,pt.8	2.25
50 JSn,AMe,Pawns,pt.9 prestige format	4.25
51 PDd,Woj,Pawns,pt.10, Paladox epic begins	2.25
52 AMe	2.25
53 AMe,"Messing with Peoples Minds"	2.25
54 JSn,AMe,Pawns ends	2.25
55 AMe,I:Iron Angel	2.25
56 AME,A:Iron Angel	2.25
57 A:Iron Angel	2.25
58 A:Iron Angel	2.25
59 A:Iron Angel	2.25
60 AMe,Paladox epic ends	2.25
61 AME,A:Iron Angel	2.25
62 O:Dreadstar,I:Youngscuz	2.25
63 AMe,A:Youngscuz	2.25
64 AMe,A:Youngscuz	2.25

DREDD RULES
Fleetway/Quality

1 SBs(c),JBy,Prev.unpubl. in USA	5.00
2 inc."Eldster Ninja Mud Wrestling Vigilantes"	3.50
3 inc."That Sweet Stuff"	3.50
4 Our Man in Hondo City	3.50
5	3.25
6 BKi,DBw	3.25

COLOR PUB.

7 "Banana City" 3 25
8 "Over the Top" 3.25
9 "Shooting Match" 3.25
10 SBs,inc.Mega-City primer . . . 3.25
11 SBs,Legend/Johnny Biker 3.25
12 SBs,Rock on Tommy Who . . . 3.25
13 BMy,The Ballad of Toad
    McFarlane 3.25
14 thru 15 . . . . @3.25
16 A:Russians 3.25
17 F:Young Giant 3.25
18 F:Jonny Cool 2.95
19 V:Hunter's Club 2.95

DRIFT MARLO
Dell Publishing Co.
May-July, 1962
1 . . . . 18.00
2 . . . . 15.00

DRUG WARS
Pioneer
1 . . . . 1.95
2 . . . . 1.95
3 . . . . 1.95

DRUNKEN FIST
Jademan
1 . . . . 3.25
2 . . . . 2.50
3 . . . . 2.00
4 . . . . 1.75
5 . . . . 1.75
6 thru 9 . . . . @1.75
10 thru 27 . . . . @1.95
28 D:Mack 1.95
29 . . . . 1.95
30 . . . . 1.95
31 . . . . 1.95
32 Wong Mo-Gei vs.Swordsman . 1.95
33 Mo-Gei commits suicide 1.95
34 . . . . 1.95
35 . . . . 1.95
36 D:Fire Oak 1.95
37 Iron Law Kills Elephant-Man . . 1.95
38 A:Wayne Chan 1.95
39 D:Wayne Chan 1.95
40 D:Toro Yamamoto 1.95
41 Lord Algol vs. Ghing Mob 1.95
42 . . . . 1.95
43 D:Yamamoto,Swordsman in USA1.95
44 "Cool Hand Wong" 1.95
45 "Black Cult Rising" 1.95
46 . . . . 1.95
47 . . . . 1.95
48 Evil Child 1.95
49 I:Hurricane Child 1.95
50 Lord Algol vs.Diabol.Ent. 1.95
51 F:Flying Thunder 1.95
52 Madcap vs.Yama 1.95
53 Swordsman vs.Catman 1.95

DUCKMAN
Topps
1 USA Cartoon 2.50
2 XXX Files 2.50
3 I:King Chicken 2.50
4 V:Toys 2.50
5 F:Cornfed 2.50
6 Star Trek Parody 2.50
7 rep. 1990 B&W 1st app., now in
    color 2.50

DUCKMAN: THE MOB FROG SAGA
Topps
1 I:Mob Frog 2.50
2 D:Mob Frog 2.50
3 In the Name of the Duck 2.50

DUCK TALES
Gladstone
1 CB(r)I:LaunchpadMcQuck 5.00
2 CB(r) 3.00
3 . . . . 2.50
4 CB(r) 2.50
5 thru 11 . . . . @2.25
12 . . . . 4.00
13 . . . . 4.00

DUCK TALES
Walt Disney
1 . . . . 4.00
2 . . . . 2.50
3 . . . . 2.25
4 . . . . 2.25
5 Scrooges'Quest 2.25
6 Scrooges'Quest 2.00
7 Return to Duckburg 2.00
8 . . . . 2.00
9 7 Sojourns of Scrooge 2.00
10 Moon of Gold 2.00
11 Once & Future Warlock 2.00
12 Lost Beyond the MilkyWay . . . 1.75
13 The Doomed of Sarras 1.75
14 Planet Blues 1.75
15 The Odyssey Ends 1.75
16 The Great Chase 1.75
17 Duck in Time Pt.1 . . . . 1.75
18 Duck in Time Pt.2 . . . . 1.75
19 Bail Out 1.75

DUDLEY DO-RIGHT
Charlton Comics 1970–71
1 . . . . 40.00
2 thru 7 . . . . @30.00

DUNC & LOO
Dell Publishing Co.
Oct.-Dec., 1961
1 . . . . 65.00
2 . . . . 50.00
3 thru 8 . . . . @30.00

DWIGHT D. EISENHOWER
Dell Publishing Co. Dec., 1969
1 . . . . 30.00

DYNAMO
Tower Comics Aug., 1966
1 WW,MSy,RC,SD,I:Andor . . . 40.00
2 WW,DA,GT,MSy,Weed solo story
    A:Iron Maiden 30.00
3 WW,GT,Weed solo story, A:Iron
    Maiden 30.00
4 WW,DA,A:Iron Maiden, June,
    1967 . . . . 30.00

DYNAMO JOE
First
1 . . . . 3.00
2 . . . . 2.00
3 thru 14 . . . . @1.50
Spec.#1 . . . . 1.25

EARLY DAYS OF SOUTHERN KNIGHTS
Vol. 2 Graphic Novel 5.00

EARTH 4
Continuity
[1st Series, Deathwatch 2000]
1 Deathwatch 2000 Pt.6,w/card . 2.50
2 Deathwatch 2000 Pt.11,w/card . 2.50
3 V:Hellbenders, w/card 2.50
[2nd Series]
1 WMc, ... 2.50
2 . . . . 2.50
3 . . . . 2.50

EAST MEETS WEST
Innovation
1 . . . . 2.50
2 . . . . 2.50
3 . . . . 2.50

EBONY WARRIOR
Africa Rising
1 I:Ebony Warrior 1.95

Echo of Futurepast #4 © Continuity

ECHO OF FUTUREPAST
Continuity
1 NA,MGo,I:Bucky O'Hare,
    Frankenstein 4.00
2 NA,MGo,A:Bucky O'Hare,
    Dracula, Werewolf 3.50
3 NA,MGo,A:Bucky 3.50
4 NA,MGo,A:Bucky 3.50
5 NA,MGo,A:Drawla&Bucky . . . 3.50
6 Ath,B:Torpedo 3.50
7 ATh 3.50
8 Ath, ... 3.25
9 Ath,Last issue 3.25

ECLIPSE GRAPHIC NOVELS
Eclipse
1 Axa 7.00
2 MR,I Am Coyote 7.00
3 DSt,Rocketeer 10.00

COLOR PUB.

3a hard cover	40.00
4 Silver Heels	9.00
4a hard cover	40.00
5 Sisterhood of Steel	10.00
6 Zorro in Old Calif.	8.00

ECLIPSE MONTHLY
Eclipse

1 SD,DW,I:Static&Rio	2.00
2 GC,DW	2.00
3 thru 8 DW	@1.50
9 DW	1.75
10 DW	1.75

EDGE OF CHAOS
Pacific

1 GM	2.00
2 GM	2.00
3 GM	2.00

87th PRECINCT
Dell Publishing Co.
April-June, 1962

1 BK	75.00
2	60.00

ELEMENTALS
Comico 1984–88

1 BWg,I:Destroyers	5.00
2 BWg	3.00
3 BWg	3.00
4 BWg	2.50
5 BWg	2.50
6 BWg	2.00
7 BWg	2.00
8 BWg	2.00
9 BWg	2.00
10 BWg	2.00
11 BWg	1.50
12 BWg	1.50
13 thru 22	@1.50
23 thru 29	@1.75
Spec.#1	1.75
Spec.#2	1.95

[Second Series] 1989–94

1	2.25
2 thru 4	@1.95

Elementals 2nd Series #21 © Comico

5 thru 28	@2.50
GN Death & Resurrection	12.95

[Third Series] 1995

1 R:Elementals	2.50
2 R:Original Monolith	2.50
3 Destroy the Shadowspear	2.50
4 Memoirs,pt.1	2.95
5 Memoirs,pt.2	2.95
GN Ghost of a Chance	5.95
Spec. "Babes," photo multimedia bikini special	3.95
Spec. Hot Bikini Valentine	3.95

ELEMENTALS:
HOW THE WAR WAS ONE
Comico 1996

1 thru 4	@2.95

ELEMENTALS: THE
VAMPIRE'S REVENGE
Comico 1996–97

1 thru 4	@2.95

ELEMENTALS VS.
THE CHARNEL PRIESTS
Comico 1996

Spec. 1 (of 2)	2.95
2	2.95

ELEVEN OR ONE
Sirius 1995

1 JLi	5.00

ELFLORD
Aircel 1986–88
Volume 1: *See B&W*
Volume II

1	3.50
2	2.50
3 thru 20	@2.00
21 double size	4.95
22 thru 24	@2.00
Spec.#1	2.00
25 thru 32, see B&W	

ELFQUEST: BLOOD OF
TEN CHIEFS
Warp Graphics 1993–95

1 WP	2.50
2 WP	2.25
3 WP,B:Swift Spear pt. 1	2.25
4 WP,B:Swift Spear pt. 2	2.25
5 V:Dinosaurs	2.25
6 Snowbeast	2.25
7	2.25
8 Spirit Quest	2.25
9 Shadow Shifter	2.25
10 Spheres pt. 1	2.25
11 Spheres pt. 2	2.25
12	2.25
13 Forest	2.25
14 F:Mantricker	2.25
15 F:Bearclaw	2.25
16 Scar Vs. Bearclaw	2.50
17 F:Eldolil,"Howl for Eldolil"	2.50
18 F:Finder	2.50
19 F:Cutter & Skywise	2.50
20 final issue	2.50

ELFQUEST:
HIDDEN YEARS
Warp Graphics

1 WP	3.00
2 WP, w/coupon promo.	2.75
3 WP, w/coupon promo.Cont.sty. previewed in Harbinger#11	3.25
4 WP,w/coupon	2.50
5 WP,O:Skywise	2.50
6 WP,F:Timmain	2.50
7 F:Timmain	2.50
8 Daughter's Day	2.50
9 WP(s),Enemy Face	2.50
9 1/2 WP,JBy,Holiday Spec.	3.50
10 thru 14 WP	@2.50
15 WP Wolfrider Tribe Splits	3.50
16 thru 18 WP	2.25
19 Mousehunt	2.25
20 F:Recognition	2.25
21 F:Teir, Messenger	2.50
22 F:Embu, Making a Point	2.50
23 Not Wolf And Teir	2.50
24 Magic Menace	2.50
25 B&W Wolfrider's Death	2.25
26 thru 29 B&W finale	@2.25

ELFQUEST: JINK
Warp Graphics 1994–96

1 Future	3.00
2 Future	2.25
3 Neverending Story	2.25
4 Neverending Story	2.25
5 V:True Sons, Hide and Seek	2.50
6 V:Truth Holder, Should Auld Acquaintance	2.50
7 F:Black Snakes	2.50
8 B&W V:Black Snakes	2.25
9 thru 12	2.50

ELFQUEST:
NEW BLOOD
Warp Graphics 1992–96

1 JBy,artists try Elfquest	5.00
2 Barry Blair story	3.50
3 thru 5	@2.25
6 thru 24	@2.25
25 Forevergreen pt. 13	2.25
26 V:Humans	2.25
27 V:Door	2.25
28 I:Windkin, Triompe and Defeat	2.50
29 F:Windkin	2.50
30 V:Door	2.50
31 F:The Wanderer	2.50
32 B&W Sorrow's End	2.25
33 thru 35 B&W	2.25
Summer Spec.1993	4.25

ELFQUEST: THE REBELS
Warp Graphics 1994–96

1 Aliens, set several hundred years in future	2.75
2 Escape	2.50
3 He That Goes	2.25
4 Reasons	2.25
5 V:Skyward	2.50
6 F:Shimmer, The Edge	2.50
7	2.50
8 Squatters & Defenders	2.50
9 B&W Brother vs. Brother	2.25
10	2.50
11	2.50
12	2.50

COLOR PUB.

ELFQUEST: SHARDS
Warp Graphics 1994–96
1 Division	2.25
2 thru 5	@2.25
6 F:Two-Edge	2.25
7 F:Shuma	2.25
8 WP,Turnabout,pt.1	2.25
9 WP,Turnabout,pt.2,V:Djun	2.50
10 Revelations,pt.1	2.50
11 V:Humans	2.50
12 B&W F:High One Timmain	2.25
13 thru 16 B&W finale	@2.25

ELFQUEST: WAVE DANCERS
Warp Graphics 1993–96
1 Foil enhanced	3.25
2 thru 6	@2.25
Spec. #1	3.00

ELIMINATOR COLOR SPECIAL
Eternity 1991
1 DDo(c) set in the future	2.95

ELRIC
Pacific 1983–84
1 CR	4.00
2 CR	3.00
3 thru 6 CR	@2.50

ELRIC
Topps April 1996
0 NGa,CPR, "One Life," based on Michael Moorcock character	2.95

ELRIC, BANE OF THE BLACK SWORD
First 1988–89
1 Michael Moorcock adapt.	1.75
2	1.75
3 thru 5	@1.95

Elric, Sailor on the Seas of Fate #4
© First Comics

ELRIC, SAILOR ON THE SEAS OF FATE
First 1985–86
1 Michael Moorcock adapt.	4.00
2	3.00
3 thru 7	@2.00

ELRIC–VANISHING TOWER
First 1987–88
1 Michael Moorcock adapt.	2.50
2 thru 6	@2.00

ELRIC, WEIRD OF THE WHITE WOLF
First 1986–87
1 Michael Moorcock adapt.	3.00
2 thru 5	@2.00
Graphic Novel CR	7.00

E-MAN
Charlton Comics 1973–75
1 JSon,O:E-Man	20.00
2 SD	8.00
3	8.00
4 SD	8.00
5 SD,Miss Liberty Belle	6.00
6 JBy,Rog 2000	8.00
7 JBy,Rog 2000	8.00
8 J:Nova	10.00
9 JBy,Rog 2000	8.00
10 JBy,Rog 2000	8.00

E-MAN
First
1 JSon,O:E-Man & Nova, A:Rog 2000, 1 pg. JBy	1.75
2 JSon,I:F-Men (X-Men satire) 1 page Mike Mist	1.25
3 JSon, V:F-Men	1.25
4 JSon,Michael Mauser solo	1.25
5 JSon,I:Psychobabbler,A:Omaha, The Cat Dancer	1.25
6 JSon,O:E-Man,V:Feeder	1.25
7 JSon,V:Feeder	1.25
8 JSon,V:HotWax,A:CuteyBunny	1.25
9 JSon,I:Tyger Lili	1.25
10 JSon,O:Nova Kane pt.1	1.25
11 JSon,O:Nova Kane pt.2	1.25
12 JSon,A:Tyger Lili	1.25
13 JSon,V:Warp'sPrinceChaos	1.25
14 JSon,V:Randarr	1.25
15 JSon,V:Samuel Boar	1.25
16 JSon,V:Samuel Boar	1.25
17 JSon,"Smeltquest" satire	1.25
18 JSon,"Rosemary..& Time"	1.25
19 JSon, "Hoodoo Blues"	1.25
20 JSon,A:Donald Duke	1.25
21 JSon,A:B-Team,(satire)	1.25
22 JSon,A:Teddy Q	1.25
23 JSon,A:TygerLili,B-Team	1.25
24 JSon,O:Michael Mauser	1.25
25 JSon,last issue	1.25
Spec. #1	2.75

E-MAN
Comico
1 JSon	2.75
2 JSon	2.50
3 JSon	2.50

E-MAN
Alpha Productions 1993
1 JSon	2.75

EMERGENCY
Charlton Comics 1976
1 JSon(c),JBy	10.00
2 JSon	3.00
3 Thru 4	2.00

ENGIN
Samson Comics
1 I:The Mesh	2.50

ENSIGN O'TOOLE
Dell Publishing Co.
Aug.-Oct., 1962
1	20.00
2	15.00

EPSILON WAVE
Independent
1	3.00
2	2.50
3	2.25
4	2.00

Elite Comics
5 thru 10	@2.00

ESC.<ESCAPE>
Comico 1996
1 SPr	2.95
2 SPr	2.95
3 SPr	2.95
4 SPr	2.95
TPB SPr Rep. #1–#4	14.95

ESC: NO EXIT
Comico 1997
1	2.95
1 medallion edition	9.95
2	2.95

ESPERS
Eclipse
1 I:ESPers	2.00

ESPers #1 © Eclipse Comics

All comics prices listed are for *Near Mint* condition.

2 JBo(c),V:Terrorists 1.50
3 V:Terrorists 1.50
4 Beirut 1.75
5 "The Liquidators" 1.75
6 V:Benito Giovanetti 1.75

ESPIONAGE
Dell Publishing Co.
May-July, 1964
1 . . . . 20.00
2 . . . . 18.00

ETERNITY SMITH
Hero
1 . . . . 1.50
2 . . . . 1.50
3 . . . . 1.50
4 Knightshade solo 1.50
5 Knightshade solo 1.50
6 . . . . 1.50
7 . . . . 1.95
8 I:Indigo 1.95
9 A:Walter Koenig 1.95
10 . . . . 1.95
Heroic Publishing
1 Man Vs. Machine 1.95
2 Man Vs. Machine 1.95

EVA THE IMP
Red Top Comic/Decker 1957
1 . . . . 15.00
2 . . . . 10.00

EVANGELINE
Comico 1984
1 Guns of Mars 4.00
2 . . . . 3.00
Lodestone
1 . . . . 2.50
2 . . . . 2.50
First
1 . . . . 3.00
2 thru 9 . . . . @1.75
10 . . . . 1.95
11 . . . . 1.95
12 . . . . 1.95

EVERYTHING'S ARCHIE
Archie Publications May, 1969
1 . . . . 55.00
2 . . . . 25.00
3 . . . . 15.00
4 . . . . 15.00
5 . . . . 15.00
6 . . . . 10.00
7 . . . . 10.00
8 thru 10 . . . . @10.00
11 thru 20 . . . . @5.00
21 thru 40 . . . . @3.00
41 thru 134 . . . . @3.00

EVIL ERNIE
Eternity 1991–92
See: B&W

EVIL ERNIE: DESTROYER
Chaos! Comics 1997
1 (of 9) BnP 2.95
2 BnP 2.95

EVIL ERNIE: REVENGE
Chaos! Comics 1994–95
1 SHu,BnP,A:LadyDeath,glow(c) 11.00
1a limited, glow-in-the-dark (c) . 50.00
1a Commemorative edition 30.00
2 SHu,BnP,Loses Smiley 7.00
3 SHu,BnP,V:Dr. Price 5.00
4 SHu,BnP,Final Issue 5.00
TPB Rep. #1-#4 . . . . 12.95

EVIL ERNIE: STRAIGHT TO HELL
Chaos! Comics 1995–96
1 Rampage in Hell, coffin(c) 5.00
1 limited, chromium edition 30.00
2 Cremator 4.00
3 . . . . 4.00
3a Chastity (c) 20.00
4 and 5 . . . . @4.00
Spec. 25.00

EVIL ERNIE: THE RESURRECTION
Chaos! Comics 1993–94
1 R:Evil Ernie 20.00
1a gold edition 50.00
2 Enhanced Cover 14.00
3 "Massive Mayhem" Lady Death
   poster 14.00
4 final issue, extra pages 14.00
TPB Rep. #1-#4 . . . . 14.95

EVIL ERNIE VS. THE MOVIE MONSTERS
Chaos! Comics
1 one-shot 2.95
1 omega edition 2.95

EVIL ERNIE VS. THE SUPER-HEROES
Chaos! Comics 1995
1 one-shot 3.50
1a foil (c) 30.00
1b limited 20.00

EVIL ERNIE'S BADDEST BATTLES
Chaos! Comics 1996
1-shot, imaginary battles 2.00

EXECUTIONER
Innovation
1 F:Mack Bolan 3.95
2 War against Mafia 2.75

EXEMPLARS
1 and 2 . . . . @1.95

EXODUS, THE
Conquest Comics
1 V:Aliens 2.50

EXO-SQUAD
Topps 1994
[Mini-Series]
0 . . . . 1.00
1 From Animated Series 2.50
2 F:Nara Burns 2.50
3 V:Neo-Sapiens 2.50

EXPLORERS
Explorer Press 1995
1 I:Explorers 2.95
2 The Cellar 2.95

EXTREME VIOLET
Blackout Comics
0 I:Violet 2.95
1 V:Drug Lords 2.95
Becomes:
EXTREMES OF VIOLET
2 A:Matt Chaney 2.95
Commemorative Issue, 5000c . . 9.95

EYE OF THE STORM
Rival Productions
1 I:Killian, Recon, Finesse, Stray 2.95
2 Conspiracy 2.95
3 3-D Comic Background 2.95
4 F:Recon 2.95
5 Sinclair & Rott 2.95

FALCON, THE
Aircel
Spec. #1 . . . . 2.00

FAMILY AFFAIR
Gold Key Feb., 1970
1 W/Poster,Ph(c) 25.00
2 . . . . 15.00
3 Ph(c) 15.00
4 Ph(c) 15.00

FAMOUS INDIAN TRIBES
Dell Publishing Co.
July-Sept., 1962
1 . . . . 12.00
2 . . . . 3.00

FANG
Sirius
1 V:Vampires, I:Fang 4.00
2 5 . . . . 3.25
3 V:The Master 2.95

FANTASTIC VOYAGES OF SINBAD, THE
Gold Key Oct., 1965
1 Ph(c) 25.00
2 June, 1967 . . . . 20.00

FANTASY FEATURES
AC
1 . . . . 1.75
2 . . . . 1.75

FASHION IN ACTION
Eclipse
Summer Special #1 . . . . 1.75
Winter Special #1 . . . . 2.00

FAT ALBERT
Gold Key 1974–79
1 . . . . 4.00
2 . . . . 2.00
3 thru 10 . . . . @1.50
11 thru 28 . . . . @1.00
29 . . . . 1.00

COLOR PUB.

Fatale #5 © Broadway Comics

FATALE
Broadway 1995

1 thru 6 JJo, "Inherit the Earth," pt.5	@2.95
7 Fatale now Queen of the World	2.95
8 "Crown of Thorns", pt.2	2.95
9 "Crown of Thorns," pt.3	2.95
TPB Inherit the Earth	14.95
HC Inherit the Earth	75.00

FATHOM
Comico

1 thru 3 From Elementals	@2.50

FATMAN, THE HUMAN FLYING SAUCER
Lightning Comics April, 1967

1 CCB,O:Fatman & Tin Man	45.00
2 CCB	30.00
3 CCB,(Scarce)	45.00

FAZE ONE
AC Comics

1	1.75

FAZE ONE FAZERS
AC Comics

1	5.00
2	3.00
3	2.00
4 thru 6	@1.75

FAZERS SKETCHBOOK

1	1.75

FEARBOOK
Eclipse

1 SBi,RV,"A Dead Ringer"	1.75

FELIX THE CAT
Harvey

1 thru 4	1.25
5 thru 7	1.50

FELIX'S NEPHEWS INKY & DINKY
Harvey Publications Sept., 1957

1	45.00
2 thru 7	@20.00

FEM 5
Entity 1995

1 thru 4 five-part series	@2.95
1 signed & numbered	12.95

FEMFORCE
AC Comics

1 O:Femforce	5.00
2 A:Captain Paragon	3.50
3 "Skin Game"	3.00
4 "Skin Game"	3.00
5 Back in the Past	3.00
6 EL,Back in the Past	3.00
7 HB,O:Captain Paragon	3.00
8 V:Shade	3.00
9 V:Dr.Rivits	3.00
10 V:Dr.Rivits	3.00
11 D:Haunted Horsemen	3.00
12 V:Dr.Rivits	3.00
13 V:She-Cat	3.00
14 V:Alizarin Crimson	3.00
15 V:Alizarin Crimson	3.00
16 thru 56 See Black & White Pub.	
57 V:Goat God	2.75
58 I:New Sentinels	2.75
59 I:Paragon	2.75
60 V:Sentinels	2.75
61 F:Tara	2.75
62 V:Valkyra	2.75
63 I:Rayda	2.75
64 thru 67	@2.75
68 "Spellbound"	2.75
69 "She-Cat Possessed"	2.75
70 "Island Out of Time"	2.75
71	2.75
72 w/Sentinels of Justice	4.00
72a no extras	3.00
73 w/Compact Comic	4.00
73a Regular edition	3.00
74 Daughter of Darkness	4.00
74a Regular edition	3.00
75 Gorby Poster	5.00
75a Regular edition	3.00
76 Daughters pt. 3, polybagged with Compact Comic	4.00
76a no bag or comic	3.00
77 V:Sea Monster	3.00
78 V:Gorgana, bagged with comic	5.00
78a no bag or comic	3.00
79 V:Iron Jaw, polybagged with Index	5.00
79a no bag or index	3.00
80 polybagged with Index	6.00
80a F:Mr. Brimstone, Rad	3.00
81 polybagged with Index	6.00
81a Valentines Day Spec.	3.00
82 polybagged with Index	6.00
82a F:Ms. Victory	3.00
83 F:Paragon	3.00
84 The Death of Joan Wayne polybagged with index #4B	6.00
84a no bag or index	3.00
85 Synn vs. Narett, polybagged with card	5.00
85a no bag or card	3.00
86 polybagged with index #5	5.00
86a unbagged, no suplements	3.00

87 Pandemonium in Paradise, polybagged with plate	10.00
87a unbagged, no plate	3.00
88 F:Garganta, polybagged with index #6	6.00
88a unbagged, no index	3.00
89 polybagged with index	6.00
89a unbagged, no index	3.00
90 polybagged with index	6.00
90a unbagged, no index	3.00
91 polybagged with index	6.00
91a unbagged, no index	3.00
92 polybagged with index	6.00
92a unbagged, no index	3.00
Spec.#1	1.50
Untold Origin Spec #1	4.95

FEMFORCE: UP CLOSE
AC Comics

1 F:Stardust	2.75
2 F:Stardust	2.75
3	2.75
4	2.75
5 with Sticker	3.95
5a Regular Edition	2.95
6 with Sticker	3.95
6a Regular Edition	2.95
7 with Sticker	3.95
7a Regular Edition	2.95
8 with Sticker	3.95
8a Regular Edition	2.95
9	2.95
10	2.95
11	2.95

FENRY
Raven Publications

1	6.95
1a Platinum Ed.	15.00

FIGHT THE ENEMY
Tower Comics Aug., 1966

1 BV,Lucky 7	25.00
2 AMc	15.00
3 WW,AMc	15.00

FIGHTING AMERICAN
Harvey

1 SK,Rep Fighting American from 1950's	17.50

FIRST ADVENTURES
First

1 thru 5	@1.25

FIRST GRAPHIC NOVELS
First

1 JBi,Beowolf	8.00
1a 2nd Printing	7.00
2 TT,Time Beavers	6.00
3 HC,American Flag Hard Times	12.00
4 Nexus,SR	8.00
5 Elric,CR	15.00
6 Enchanted Apples of Oz	6.00
7 Secret Island of Oz	8.00
8 HC,Time 2	28.00
9 TMNT	20.00
10 TMNT II	18.00
11 Sailor on the Sea	15.00
12 HC,American Flagg	12.00
13 Ice Ring	8.00

COLOR PUB.

14 TMNT III	14.00
15 Hex Breaker	8.00
16 Forgotten Forest	9.00
17 Mazinger	9.00
18 TMNT IV	13.00
19 O;Nexus	8.00
20 American Flagg	12.00

1st FOLIO
Pacific

1 Joe Kubert School	1.50

FISH POLICE
Comico

Vol 2 #6 thru #15 rep.	@2.50
Vol 2 #16 rep.	3.00
Vol 2 #17 rep.,AuA	3.00
1 Color Special	3.50

FITCH IN TIME

1 and 2	@1.50

FLARE
Hero Graphics

1 I:Darkon&Prof.Pomegranite	4.00
2 Blonde Bombshell,A:Galooper	3.00
3 I:Sky Marshall	3.00
Ann.#1	4.50

[2nd Series]

1 A:Galloping Galooper	3.00
2 A:Lady Arcane	3.00
3 I:Britannia	3.00
4 A:Indigo	2.50
5 R:Eternity Smith,O:Die Kriegerin	3.95
6 I:Tigress	3.50
7 V:The Enemies	3.95
8 Morrigan Wars#4,A:Icicle Dragon	3.50
9 Morrigan Wars Pt.7 (B&W)	3.50

FLARE ADVENTURES
Hero Graphics

1 rep.	2.95
2 flipbook w/Champions Classics	2.95
3 flipbook w/Champions Classics	2.95
Becomes B&W	

FLASH GORDON
Gold Key June, 1965

1	15.00

FLASH GORDON
King 1966–69

1 AW,DH,A:Mandrake	35.00
1a Comp. Army giveaway	50.00
2 FBe,A:Mandrake,R:Ming	25.00
3 RE,"Lost in the Land of The Lizardmen"	30.00
4 AW,B:Secret Agent X-9	32.00
5 AW	32.00
6 RC,On the Lost Continent of Mongo	30.00
7 MR, rep. "In the Human Forest"	30.00
8 RC,JAp	30.00
9 AR,rep	35.00
10 AR,rep	35.00
11 RC	25.00

Charlton 1969–70

12 RC	25.00
13 JJ	20.00
14	20.00
15	20.00
16	20.00

Flash Gordon #7 © King Comics

17 Brick Bradford story	20.00
18 MK,"Attack of the Locust Men"	20.00

Gold Key Oct.-Nov 1975

19 Flash returns to Mongo	6.00
20	5.00
21	5.00
22	5.00
23	5.00
24	5.00
25	5.00
26	5.00
27	5.00
28	5.00
29	5.00
30	5.00
31 AW movie adapt	3.00
32 AW movie adapt	3.00
33 AW movie adapt	3.00
34 AW movie adapt	3.00
35 AW movie adapt	3.00
36 AW movie adapt	3.00
37 AW movie adapt	3.00

FLATLINE COMICS
Flatline Comics

1 Three stories River Prarie	2.50

FLAXEN: ALTER EGO
Caliber

1 V:Dark Flaxen	2.95

FLESH AND BONES
Fantagraphics

1 Moore	2.50
2 thru 4 Moore	@2.00

FLINTSTONES
Harvey

1	1.25
2 Romeo and Juliet	1.25

FLINTSTONES
Archie 1995

1 thru 10	@1.50
11 thru 14	@1.50
15 "Frankenstone's Monster"	1.50
20 "An Heir-Raising Tale"	1.50

21 "King Fred The Last"	1.50
22 "Something Gruesome This Way Comes"	1.50

FLINTSTONES, THE
Dell Publishing Co.
Nov.-Dec., 1961

#1 see Dell Giant	
2	100.00
3	75.00
4	75.00
5 and 6	@60.00

Gold Key

7	60.00
8 A:Mr.& Mrs. J. Evil Scientists	50.00
9 A:Mr.& Mrs. J. Evil Scientists	50.00
10 A:Mr.& Mrs. J. Evil Scientists	50.00
11 I:Pebbles	60.00
12 "The Too-Old Cowhand"	40.00
13	40.00
14	40.00
15	40.00
16 I:Bamm-Bamm	50.00
17	40.00
18	40.00
19	40.00
20	40.00
21	25.00
22	25.00
23	25.00
24 I:Gruesomes	28.00
25 thru 29	@22.00
30 "Dude Ranch Roundup"	22.00
31 Christmas(c)	22.00
32	20.00
33 A:Dracula & Frankenstein	22.00
34 I:The Great Gazoo	30.00
35	20.00
36 "The Man Called Flintstone"	20.00
37 thru 40	@20.00
41 thru 60	@16.00

FLINTSTONES, THE
Charlton Comics 1970

1	40.00
2	22.00
3 thru 7	@15.00
8	18.00
9	15.00
10	15.00
11 thru 20	@12.00
21 thru 50	@10.00

FLINTSTONES IN 3-D
Blackthorne

1 thru 5	@2.50

FLIPPER
Gold Key April, 1966

1 Ph(c)	35.00
2 and 3 Ph(c)	@25.00

FLY IN MY EYE EXPOSED
Eclipse

1 JJo(c),"Our Visitor"	4.95

FLY, THE
Archie Publications

1 JSn,A:Mr.Justice	1.25
2 thru 9 RB,SD	@1.00

All comics prices listed are for *Near Mint* condition.

FLYING SAUCERS
Dell April, 1967
1	15.00
2 thru 5	10.00

FLYMAN
Archie Publications
{Prev: Adventures of the Fly}
31 I:Shield (Bill Higgins), A:Comet, Black Hood	35.00
32 I:Mighty Crusaders	30.00
33 A:Mighty Crusaders, R:Hangman Wizard	30.00
34 MSy,A:Black Hood,Shield,Comet Shield back-up story begins	20.00
35 O:Black Hood	20.00
36 O:Web,A:Hangman in Shield strip	20.00
37 A:Shield	20.00
38 A:Web	18.00
39 A:Steel Sterling	17.00

FOES
Ram Comics
1 TheMaster's Game	1.95
2 TheMaster's Game #2	1.95

FOODANG
Aug. House
1 I:Foodang	1.95
1a Signed, Foil cover	2.50
2 I:Maude	2.50
3 V:Undead Clown Man	2.50
4 V:Executioner	2.50

FOOTSOLDIERS
Maximum Press 1996
1 KJo,PhH,	2.75

FORBIDDEN PLANET
Innovation 1992
1 Movie Adapt	2.50
2 Movie adapt.contd.	2.50
3 Movie adapt.contd.	2.50
4 Movie adapt.concl.	2.50

FORCE OF THE BUDDHA'S PALM
Jademan
1	3.00
2	2.25
3 thru 10	@1.75
11 thru 24	@1.95
25 V:Maskman	1.95
26 V:Maskman	1.95
27 A:SmilingDemon	1.95
28 Maskman v 10 Demons	1.95
29 Giant Bat	1.95
30	1.95
31	1.95
32 "White Crane Villa"	1.95
33 Devilito defeats White Crane & Giant Bat	1.95
34 Samsun Vs. Devilito	1.95
35 Samsun Vs.Devilito	1.95
36 Samson vs. Devilito	1.95
37 D:Galacial Moon	1.95
38 Persian Elders, Iron Boy	1.95
39 V:Mad Gen.,White Crane, Iron Boy	1.95
40 D:Heaven & Earth Elders	1.95
41 thru 43	@1.95
44 D:White Crane	1.95
45 V:Iron Boy	1.95
46 thru 48	@1.95
49 Iron Boy vs Sainted Jade	1.95
50 Iron Boy & The Holy Blaze	1.95
51 D:Aquarius	1.95
52 V:Son o/t Gemini Lord	1.95
53 Nine Continent's return to full powers	1.95

4-D MONKEY
1 thru 3	@1.80

FOREVER WAR, THE
NBM
GN Vol. 1 Joe Haldeman adapt.	8.95
GN Vol. 2 Joe Haldeman adapt.	8.95
GN Vol. 3 Joe Haldeman adapt.	8.95

FRANK
Nemesis
1 thru 4 DGc(s),GgP	2.50

FRANK IN THE RIVER
Tundra
1 Avery/Jones style cartoons	2.95

FRANK MERRIWELL AT YALE
Charlton Comics 1955–56
1	25.00
2	15.00
3	15.00
4	15.00

FRANKENSTEIN
Dell Publishing Co. 1964
1	20.00
2	15.00
3	10.00
4	10.00

FRANKENSTEIN
Caliber
Novel Adaptation	2.95

FRANKENSTEIN DRACULA WAR
Topps
1 Frank Vs. Drac	2.50
2 F:Saint Germaine	2.50
3 Frank Vs. Drac	2.50

FREDDY
Dell Publishing Co. 1963
1	7.00
2	5.00
3	5.00

FREDDY'S DEAD
3-D	2.50
1 GN, Movie Adapt	6.95

FREDDY'S DEAD: THE FINAL NIGHTMARE
Innovation
1 Movie adaption, Pt.1	2.50
2 Movie adaption, Pt.2	2.50

FRIDAY FOSTER
Dell Publishing Co. Oct., 1972
1	12.00

The Friendly Ghost Casper #135
© Harvey Comics

FRIENDLY GHOST CASPER, THE
Harvey Publications 1958
1	200.00
2	100.00
3 thru 10	@50.00
11 thru 20	@35.00
21 thru 30	@25.00
31 thru 50	@20.00
51 thru 100	@10.00
101 thru 159	@5.00
160 thru 163 52 pgs.	@4.00
164 thru 253	@3.00
Becomes:	
CASPER THE FRIENDLY GHOST	

FRIGHT NIGHT
Now
1 thru 22	@1.75

FRIGHT NIGHT
Now
1 Dracula,w/3-D Glasses	2.95

FRIGHT NIGHT II
Now
Movie Adaptation	3.95

FRISKY ANIMALS ON PARADE
Ajax-Farrell Publ. Sept., 1957
1 LbC(c)	60.00
2	20.00
3 LbC(c)	40.00

FROGMEN, THE
Dell Publishing Co. 1962
1 GE,Ph(c)	45.00
2 GE,FF	50.00
3 GE,FF	50.00

COLOR PUB.

4	20.00
5 ATh	30.00
6 thru 11	@20.00

FROM HERE TO INSANITY
Charlton Comics Feb., 1955
8	100.00
9	75.00
10 SD(c)	125.00
11 JK	150.00
12 JK	150.00
3-1	250.00

FRONTLINE COMBAT
EC Comics 1995
1 thru 4 Rep.	@2.00

Gemstone
5 thru 9	@2.50

"Annuals"
TPB Vol. 1 rebinding of #1–#5 .. 10.95

F-TROOP
Dell Publishing Co. 1966
1 Ph(c)	75.00
2 Ph(c)	40.00
3 Ph(c)	40.00
4 Ph(c)	40.00
5 Ph(c)	40.00
6 Ph(c)	40.00
7 Ph(c)	40.00

FUN-IN
Gold Key 1970–74
1	20.00
2 thru 6	@10.00
7 thru 10	@7.00
11 thru 15	@6.00

FUNKY PHANTOM
Gold Key 1972–75
1	15.00
2 thru 5	@5.00
6 thru 13	@3.50

FUTURIANS
Lodestone
1 DC,I:Dr.Zeus	1.00
2 DC,I:MsMercury	1.00
3 DC	1.00
Eternity Graphic Novel, DC, Rep. +new material	9.95

GALL FORCE: ETERNAL STORY
CPM
1 F:Solnoids	2.95
2 V:Paranoid	2.95
3	2.95
4 Implant Secrets	2.95

GALLANT MEN, THE
Gold Key Oct., 1963
1 RsM	20.00

GALLEGHER BOY REPORTER
Gold Key May, 1965
1	10.00

GARRISON
Zion Comics
1 I:Wage, Garrison	2.50

GARRISON'S GORRILLAS
Dell Publishing Co. Jan., 1968
1 Ph(c)	25.00
2 thru 5 Ph(c)	@15.00

GASP!
American Comics Group March, 1967
1	25.00
2 thru 4, Aug. 1967	@15.00

G-8 & BATTLE ACES
1 based on '40's pulp characters 3.00

GENE RODDENBERRY'S LOST UNIVERSE
Teckno-Comics 1994
0 I:Sensua	2.50
1 Gene Roddenberry's	2.50
2 Grange Discovered	2.25
3 Secrets Revealed	1.95
4 F:Penultra	1.95
5 I:New Alien Race	1.95
6 Two Doctor Granges	1.95
7 F:Alaa Chi Tskare	1.95

GENE RODDENBERRY'S XANDER IN LOST UNIVERSE
Teckno-Comics 1995
1 V:Black Ghost	2.25
2 V:Walker	2.25
3 V:Lady Sensua	2.25
4	2.25
5	2.25
6	2.25
7	2.25
8 F:Lady Sensua	2.25

[Mini-Series]
Teckno-Comics 1995
1 RoR,F:L.Nimoy's Primortals	2.25

GENSAGA: ANCIENT WARRIOR
Entity Comics 1995
1 I:Gensaga	2.50
1a with Computer Games	2.50
2 V:Dinosaurs	2.50
3 V:Lord Abyss	2.50

GENTLE BEN
Dell Publishing Co. Feb., 1968
1 Ph(c)	25.00
2	15.00
3 thru 5	@15.00

GEORGE OF THE JUNGLE
Gold Key Feb., 1969
1	45.00
2	35.00

GET SMART
Dell Publishing Co. June, 1966
1 Ph(c) all	80.00
2 SD	50.00

3 SD	45.00
4	40.00
5	40.00
6	40.00
7	40.00
8	40.00

Ghostbusters #2 © First Comics

[FILMATION'S] GHOSTBUSTERS
First 1987
1 thru 4	@1.50

GHOST BUSTERS II
Now
1 Mini-series	1.95
2	1.95
3	1.95

GHOST STORIES
Dell Publishing Co. Sept.-Nov., 1962
1	40.00
2	20.00
3	15.00
4	15.00
5	15.00
6	15.00
7	15.00
8	15.00
9	15.00
10	15.00
11	10.00
12	10.00
13	10.00
14	10.00
15	10.00
16	10.00
17	10.00
18	10.00
19	10.00
20	10.00
21 thru 33	@5.00
34 rep	5.00
35 rep	8.00
36 rep	5.00
37 rep	5.00

GHOSTLY TALES
Charlton 1966
Previously: Blue Beetle
55 I&O Dr. Graves	10.00
56 thru 70	@5.00
71 thru 169	@4.00

GIANT COMICS
Charlton Comics Summer, 1957
1 A:Atomic Mouse,Hoppy	60.00
2 A:Atomic Mouse	40.00
3	40.00

GIDGET
Dell Publishing Co. April, 1966
1 Ph(c),Sally Field	45.00
2 Ph(c),Sally Field	40.00

GIFT, THE
First
Holiday Special	6.00

G.I. JOE 3-D
Blackthorne
1	3.00
2 thru 5	@2.50
Ann. #1	2.50

GIL THORPE
Dell Publishing Co. 1963
1	15.00

GINGER FOX
Comico
1 thru 4	@1.75

GIN-RYU
Believe In Yourself
1 F:Japanese Sword	2.75
2 Identity Revealed	2.75
3	2.75
4 Manhunt For Gin-Ryu	2.75
Ash Can	.75

G.I. R.A.M.B.O.T.
Wonder Color 1987
1	1.95
2	1.95
3	1.95

G.I. ROBOT
Eternity
1	1.80

GIRL FROM U.N.C.L.E.
Gold Key Jan., 1967
1 "The Fatal Accidents Affair"	45.00
2 "The Kid Commandos Caper"	25.00
3 "The Captain Kidd Affair"	25.00
4 "One-Way Tourist Affair"	25.00
5 "The harem-Scarem Affair"	25.00

GLOBAL FORCE
Silverline
1	1.95
2	1.95
3	1.95
4	1.95

GLORY
Maximum Press 1996
1–15 see Image
16 JDy	2.50
17 JDy	2.50
18 JDy	2.50
19 JDy,A:Demeter, Silverfall	2.50
20 JDy,A:Silverfall	2.50
21 JDy	2.50
22 JDy	2.50
23 A:Prophet	2.50
TPB Vol. 2, rep.	16.95

GLORY/ANGELA
Maximum Press
TPB RLd, JDy	16.95

GLORY/CELESTINE: DARK ANGEL
Maximum Press 1996
1 & 2 See: Image	
3 (of 3) JDy	2.50

G-MAN
Conquest Comics
1 I:Richard Glenn	2.50

GOBLIN LORD, THE
Goblin Studios 1996
1 (of 6) sci-fi/fantasy	2.50
2 signed & numbered	9.95
3	2.50
4	2.50
5	2.50

GO-GO
Charlton Comics June, 1966
1 Miss Bikini Luv	25.00
2 Beatles	35.00
3 Blooperman	15.00
4	15.00
5	10.00
6 JAp	15.00
7	15.00
8 JAp	15.00
9 Ph(c),Oct., 1965	15.00

Gods For Hire #2 © Hot Comics

GODS FOR HIRE
Hot Comics
1 thru 7	@1.75

GOLDEN COMICS DIGEST
Gold Key 1969–76
1 Tom & Jerry,Woody Woodpecker, Bugs Bunny	15.00
2 Hanna-Barbera TV Fun Favorites	20.00
3 Tom & Jerry,Woody Woodpecker	7.00
4 Tarzan	20.00
5 Tom & Jerry,Woody Woodpecker, Bugs Bunny	7.00
6 Bugs Bunny	7.00
7 Hanna-Barbera TV Fun Favorites	12.00
8 Tom & Jerry,Woody Woodpecker, Bugs Bunny	5.00
9 Tarzan	15.00
10 Bugs Bunny	6.00
11 Hanna-Barbera TV Fun Favorites	6.00
12 Tom & Jerry,Bugs Bunny	6.00
13 Tom & Jerry	6.00
14 Bugs Bunny Fun Packed Funnies	6.00
15 Tom & Jerry,Woody Woodpecker, Bugs Bunny	6.00
16 Woody Woodpecker	6.00
17 Bugs Bunny	6.00
18 Tom & Jerry,	6.00
19 Little Lulu	15.00
20 Woody Woodpecker	6.00
21 Bugs Bunny Showtime	6.00
22 Tom & Jerry Winter Wingding	6.00
23 Little Lulu & Tubby Fun Fling	14.00
24 Woody Woodpecker Fun Festival	6.00
25 Tom & Jerry	6.00
26 Bugs Bunny Halloween Hulla- Boo- Loo,Dr. Spektor article	6.00
27 Little Lulu & Tubby in Hawaii	12.00
28 Tom & Jerry	6.00
29 Little Lulu & Tubby	12.00
30 Bugs Bunny Vacation Funni	6.00
31 Turk, Son of Stone	15.00
32 Woody Woodpecker Summer Fun	6.00
33 Little Lulu & Tubby Halloween Fun	12.00
34 Bugs Bunny Winter Funnies	6.00
35 Tom & Jerry Snowtime Funtime	6.00
36 Little Lulu & Her Friends	14.00
37 WoodyWoodpecker County Fair	6.00
38 The Pink Panter	6.00
39 Bugs Bunny Summer Fun	6.00
40 Little Lulu	15.00
41 Tom & Jerry Winter Carnival	5.00
42 Bugs Bunny	5.00
43 Little Lulu in Paris	14.00
44 Woody Woodpecker Family Fun Festival	5.00
45 The Pink Panther	5.00
46 Little Lulu & Tubby	12.00
47 Bugs Bunny	5.00
48 The Lone Ranger	5.00

GOLDEN PICTURE STORY BOOK
Racine Press (Western)
Dec., 1961
1 Huckleberry Hound	150.00
2 Yogi Bear	150.00
3 Babes In Toy Land	225.00
4 Walt Disney	150.00

COLOR PUB.

GOMER PYLE
Gold Key July, 1966
1 Ph(c)	45.00
2	30.00
3	30.00

GOOD GUYS
Defiant
1 JiS(s),I:Good Guys	3.75
2 JiS(s),V:Mulchmorg	3.25
3 V:Chasm	2.75
4 Seduction of the Innocent	3.25
5 I:Truc	2.75
6 A:Charlemagne	2.75
7 JiS(s),V:Scourge	2.50
8	2.50
9	2.50
10	2.50
11	2.50

GOOFY ADVENTURES
Walt Disney 1990
1 "Balboa de Goofy"	2.50
2	2.00
3 thru 9	@1.75
10 Samurai	1.75
11 Goofis Khan	1.75
12 "Arizona Goof" Pt. 1	1.75
13 "Arizona Goof" Pt. 2	1.75
14 "Goofylution"	1.75
15 "Super Goof Vs.Cold Ray"	1.75
16 "Sheerluck Holmes"	1.50
17 GC,TP,"Tomb of Goofula"	1.50

GORGO
Charlton Comics 1961–65
1 SD	150.00
2 SD,SD(c)	75.00
3 SD,SD(c)	55.00
4 SD(c)	45.00
5 thru 10	@45.00
11	22.00
12	10.00
13 thru 15	@22.00
16 SD	22.00
17 thru 22	@10.00
23	10.00

GORGO'S REVENGE
Charlton Comics 1962
1	30.00

Becomes:
RETURN OF GORGO, THE
2	25.00
3	25.00

G.O.T.H.
Verotik 1995
1 thru 3 mini-series	@2.95

GRATEFUL DEAD COMIX
Kitchen Sink
1 TT,inc.DireWolf(large format)	5.50
2 TT,inc.Jack Straw	4.95
3 TT,inc. Sugaree	4.95
4 TT,inc. Sugaree	4.95
5 TT,Uncle John's Band	4.95
6 TT,Eagle Mall #1	4.95

GREAT AMERICAN WESTERN
AC Comics
1	1.75
2	2.95
3	2.95
4	3.50

GREAT EXPLOITS
Decker Publ./Red Top Oct., 1957
91 BK	50.00

GREEN HORNET, THE
Gold Key Feb., 1967
1 Bruce Lee,Ph(c)	175.00
2 Ph(c)	125.00
3 Ph(c)	125.00

GREEN HORNET
Now
1 O:40's Green Hornet	10.00
1a 2nd Printing	4.00
2 O:60's Green Hornet	6.00
3	4.00
4	4.00
5	4.00
6	3.00
7 BSz(c),I:New Kato	3.00
8	3.50
9	3.50
10	3.50
11	3.50
12	3.50
13 V:Ecoterrorists	3.50
14 V:Ecoterrorists	3.50
Spec.#1	2.50
Spec.#2	2.25

[2nd Series]
1 V:Johnny Dollar Pt.1	2.25
2 V:Johnny Dollar Pt.2	2.25
3 V:Johnny Dollar Pt.3	2.25
4 V:Ex-Con/Politician	1.95
5 V:Ex-Con/Politician	1.95
6 Arkansas Vigilante	1.95
7 thru 9 The Beast	@1.95
10 Green Hornet-prey	1.95
11 F:Crimson Wasp	1.95
12 Crimson Wasp/Johnny Dollar Pt.1,polybagged w/Button	2.50
13 TD(i),Wasp/Dollar Pt.2	2.50
14 TD(i),Wasp/Dollar Pt.3	2.50
15 TD(i),Secondsight	1.95
16 A:Commissioner Hamiliton	1.95
17 V:Gunslinger	1.95
18 V:Sister-Hood	1.95
19 V:Jewel Thief	1.95
20 F:Paul's Friend	1.95
21 V:Brick Arcade	1.95
22 V:Animal Testers, with Hologravure card	2.95
23 with Hologravure card	1.95
24 thru 25 Karate Wars	@1.95
26 B:City under Siege	1.95
27 with Hologravure card	1.95
28 V:Gangs	1.95
29 V:Gangs	1.95
30 thru 37	@1.95
38 R:Mei Li	2.50
39 Crimson Wasp	2.50
40	2.50
41	2.50
42 Baby Killer	2.50

Green Hornet Ann. #1 © Now Comics

43 Wedding Disasters	2.50
44 F:Amy Hamilton	2.50
45 Plane Hijacking	2.50
46 Airport Terrorists	2.50
Ann.#1 The Blue & the Green	2.50
1993 Ann	2.95

GREEN HORNET: DARK TOMORROW
Now
1 thru 3 Hornet Vs Kato	@2.50

GREEN HORNET: SOLITARY SENTINAL
Now
1 Strike Force	2.50
2 thru 3	2.50

GREENHAVEN
Aircel
1	3.00
2	2.50
3	2.00

GRENDEL
Comico
1	6.00
1a 2nd printing	2.00
2	5.00
3	4.00
4	3.00
5	3.00
6	3.00
7 MW	2.50
8	2.50
9	2.50
10	2.50
11	2.50
12	2.50
13 KSy(c)	2.50
14 KSy(c)	2.50
15 KSy(c)	2.50
16 Mage	4.50
17 and 18	@3.00
19 thru 32	@2.50
33	3.50
34 thru 39	@2.50

40	4.00

GREYLORE
Sirius
1 thru 5	@2.00

GRIMJACK
First
1 TT Teenage suicide story	3.00
2 TT A:Munden's Bar	2.50
3 TT A:Munden's Bar	2.00
4 TT A:Munden's Bar	2.00
5 TT,JSon,A:Munden's Bar	2.00
6 TT,SR,A:Munden's Bar	2.00
7 TT,A:Munden's Bar	2.00
8 TT,A:Munden's Bar	2.00
9 TT "My Sins Remembered"	2.00
10 TT,JOy,A:Munden's Bar	2.00
11 TT,A:Munden'sBar	1.75
12 TT,A:Munden'sBar	1.75
13 TT,A:Munden'sBar	1.75
14 TT,A:Munden'sBar	1.75
15 TT,A:Munden'sBar	1.75
16 TT,A:Munden'sBar	1.75
17 TT,A:Munden'sBar	1.75
18 TT,A:Munden'sBar	1.75
19 TT,A:Munden'sBar	1.75
20 TT,A:Munden'sBar	1.75
21 TS,A:Munden's Bar	1.75
22 A:Munden's Bar	1.75
23 TS,A:Munden's Bar	1.75
24 PS,TT,rep.Starslayer10-11	1.75
25 TS,A:Munden's Bar	1.75
26 1st color TMNTurtles	10.00
27 TS,A:Munden's Bar	1.50
28 TS,A:Munden's Bar	1.50
29 A:Munden's Bar	1.50
30 A:Munden's Bar	1.50
31 A:Munden's Bar	1.50
32 A:Spook	1.50
33 JSon,Munden'sBarChristmas Tale	1.50
34 V:Spook	1.50
35 A:Munden's Bar	1.50
36 3rd Anniv.IssueD:Grimjack	2.50
37 A:Munden's Bar	1.50
38 A:Munden's Bar	1.50
39 R.Grimjack	1.50
40	1.75
41 "Weeping Bride"	1.75
42 "Hardball"	1.75
43 "Beneath the Surface"	1.75
44 Shadow Wars	1.75
45 Shadow Wars	1.75
46 Shadow Wars	1.75
47 Shadow Wars,A:EddyCurrent	1.75
48 Shadow Wars	1.75
49 Shadow Wars	1.75
50 V:Dancer,ShadowWars ends	1.75
51 Crossroads tie-in,A:Judah Macabee	2.00
52	2.00
53 Time Story	2.00
54	2.50
55 FH	2.00
56 FH	2.00
57 FH	2.00
58 FH	2.00
59 FH	2.00
60 FH,Reunion Pt.1	2.00
61 FH,Reunion Pt.2	2.00
62 FH,Reunion Pt.3	2.00
63 FH,A:Justice Drok	2.00
64 FH,O:Multiverse	2.00

65 FH	2.00
66 FH(c),Demon Wars Pt.1	2.00
67 FH(c),Demon Wars Pt.2	2.00
68 Demon Wars Pt.3	2.00
69 Demon Wars Pt.4	2.00
70 FH,I:Youngblood	2.00
71 FH,A:Youngblood	2.00
72	2.00
73 FH(c)	2.00
74 FH(c)	2.00
75 FH,TS,V:The Major	2.00
76 FH,A:Youngblood	2.00
77 FH,A:Youngblood	2.25
78	2.25
79 FH,Family Business #1	2.25
80 FH,Family Business #2	2.25
81 FH,Family Business #3	2.25

GRIMJACK CASEFILE
First
1 thru 5 rep.	@1.95

GRIMM'S GHOST STORIES
Gold Key/Whitman 1972–82
1	7.00
2	4.00
3	4.00
4	4.00
5 AW	5.00
6	4.00
7	4.00
8 AW	5.00
9	3.00
10	3.00
11 thru 16	@2.00
17 RC	4.00
18 thru 60	@2.00

Groo #1 © Pacific Comics

GROO
Pacific
1 SA,I:Sage,Taranto	22.00
2 SA,A:Sage	12.00
3 SA,C:Taranto	10.00
4 SA,C:Sage	9.00
5 SA,I:Ahax	9.00
6 SA,I:Gratic	9.00

7 SA,I:Chakaal	9.00
8 SA,A:Chakaal	9.00
Eclipse	
Spec.#1 SA,O:Groo,rep Destroyer Duck #1	23.00

GROUND ZERO
1	1.35

GROUP LARUE
Innovation
1	1.95
2	1.95
3	1.95

GULLIVER'S TRAVELS
Dell Publishing Co.
Sept.-Nov., 1965
1	20.00
2 and 3	@15.00

GUMBY
Comico
1 AAd,Summer Fun Special	5.00
2 AAd,Winter Fun Special	3.50

GUMBY IN 3-D
Spec.#1	4.00
2 thru 7	@2.50

GUNSMOKE
Dell Publishing Co. Feb., 1956
1 J.Arness Ph(c) all	135.00
2	65.00
3	65.00
4	65.00
5	65.00
6	50.00
7	50.00
8	60.00
9	60.00
10 AW,RC	65.00
11	60.00
12 AW	65.00
13	50.00
14	50.00
15	50.00
16	50.00
17	50.00
18	50.00
19	50.00
20	50.00
21	50.00
22	50.00
23	50.00
24	50.00
25	50.00
26	50.00
27	50.00

GUY WITH A GUN: A ZOMBIE NIGHTMARE
Alpha Productions
1 V:Gracel, Zombies	2.75

HALL OF FAME
J.C. Productions
1 WW,GK,ThunderAgents	1.00
2 WW,GK,ThunderAgents	1.00
3 WW,Thunder Agents	1.00

HALLOWEEN HORROR
Eclipse 1987
1 .... 1.75

HALO:
AN ANGEL'S STORY
Sirius April 1996
1 thru 3 by Chris Knowles ... @2.95
TPB rep. #1–#3 .... 12.95

HAMMER OF GOD
First
1 thru 4 .... @1.95
Deluxe #1"Sword of Justice Bk#1" 4.95
Deluxe #2"Sword of Justice Bk#2" 4.95

HAMSTER VICE
10 .... 2.00
3-D #1 .... 2.50

HAND OF FATE
Eclipse
1 I:Artemus Fate 1.75
2 F:Artemis & Alexis 2.00
3 Mystery & Suspense 2.00

HANDS OF THE DRAGON
Atlas June 1975
1 .... 1.00

HANNA-BARBERA
ALL-STARS
Archie 1995
1 thru 5 .... 1.50

HANNA-BARBERA
BAND WAGON
Gold Key 1962–63
1 .... 65.00
2 .... 45.00
3 .... 40.00

HANNA-BARBERA
PARADE
Charlton Comics 1971–72
1 .... 60.00
2 thru 10 .... @30.00

HANNA-BARBERA
PRESENTS
Archie 1995
1 thru 15 .... @1.50

HANNA-BARBERA
SUPER TV HEROES
Gold Key April, 1968
1 B:Birdman,Herculiods,Moby Dick,
  Young Samson & Goliath ... 100.00
2 .... 85.00
3 thru 7 Oct. 1969 .... @75.00

HARDY BOYS, THE
Gold Key April, 1970
1 .... 10.00
2 .... 5.00
3 .... 5.00
4 .... 5.00

HARI KARI
Blackout Comics 1995
0 I:Hari Kari 2.95
1 .... 2.95
1a commemorative, variant(c) .. 10.00

HARI KARI: BLOODSHED
Blackout Comics 1996
1-shot 3.00
1a deluxe, variant(c) 10.00

HARI KARI:
LIVE & UNTAMED!
Blackout Comics 1996
1-shot 2.95

HARI KARI:
PASSION & DEATH
Blackout Comics 1997
1 .... 2.95
1 photo cover 9.95

HARI KARI:
POSSESSED BY EVIL
Blackout Comics 1997
1 .... 2.95

HARI KARI: REBIRTH
Blackout Comics 1996
1 .... 2.95

Hari Kari: The Beginning #1
© Blackout Comics

HARI KARI:
THE BEGINNING
Blackout Comics 1996
1 O:Kari 2.95
1 Commemorative, signed 9.95

HARI KARI:
THE DIARY OF KARI SUN
Blackout Comics 1997
½ 2.95
½ deluxe 9.95

HARI KARI:
THE SILENCE OF EVIL
Blackout Comics 1996
0 A:Saburi Saki 2.95
0 limited, foil stamped 12.95

HARLEM GLOBTROTTERS
Gold Key April, 1972
1 .... 8.00
2 thru 12, Jan. 1975 .... @3.00

HARLEY RIDER
1 GM,FS 2.00

HARRIERS
Entity 1995
1 I:Macedon Arsenal, Cardinal .. 2.95
1a with Video Game 6.95
2 .... 2.50
3 V:Kr'llyn 2.50

HARSH REALM
Harris
1 thru 6 JHi(s), ... @2.95

HARVEY HITS
Harvey Publications 1957–67
1 The Phantom 250.00
2 Rags Rabbit 15.00
3 Richie Rich 750.00
4 Little Dot's Uncles 100.00
5 Stevie Mazie's Boy Friend .. 10.00
6 JK(c),BP,The Phantom 150.00
7 Wendy the Witch 150.00
8 Sad Sack's Army Life 40.00
9 Richie Rich's Golden Deeds . 350.00
10 Little Lotta 75.00
11 Little Audrey Summer Fun . 50.00
12 The Phantom 125.00
13 Little Dot's Uncles 50.00
14 Herman & Katnip 15.00
15 The Phantom 125.00
16 Wendy the Witch 60.00
17 Sad Sack's Army Life 30.00
18 Buzzy & the Crow 15.00
19 Little Audrey 30.00
20 Casper & Spooky 40.00
21 Wendy the Witch 30.00
22 Sad Sack's Army Life 22.00
23 Wendy the Witch 30.00
24 Little Dot's Uncles 45.00
25 Herman & Katnip 10.00
26 The Phantom 100.00
27 Wendy the Good Little Witch . 25.00
28 Sad Sack's Army Life 12.00
29 Harvey-Toon 18.00
30 Wendy the Witch 20.00
31 Herman & Katnip 5.00
32 Sad Sack's Army Life 10.00
33 Wendy the Witch 25.00
34 Harvey-Toon 10.00
35 Funday Funnies 5.00
36 The Phantom 100.00
37 Casper & Nightmare 14.00
38 Harvey-Toon 9.00
39 Sad Sack's Army Life 6.00
40 Funday Funnies 7.00
41 Herman & Katnip 7.00
42 Harvey-Toon 7.00
43 Sad Sack's Army Life 7.00
44 The Phantom 75.00
45 Casper & Nightmare 12.00

COLOR PUB.

46 Harvey-Toon	7.00
47 Sad Sack's Army Life	7.00
48 The Phantom	75.00
49 Stumbo the Giant	50.00
50 Harvey-Toon	7.00
51 Sad Sack's Army Life	8.00
52 Casper & Nightmare	15.00
53 Harvey-Toons	7.00
54 Stumbo the Giant	25.00
55 Sad Sack's Army Life	7.00
56 Casper & Nightmare	12.00
57 Stumbo the Giant	25.00
58 Sad Sack's Army Life	7.00
59 Casper & Nightmare	12.00
60 Stumbo the Giant	25.00
61 Sad Sack's Army Life	7.00
62 Casper & Nightmare	12.00
63 Stumbo the Giant	22.00
64 Sad Sack's Army Life	7.00
65 Casper & Nightmare	10.00
66 Stumbo the Giant	22.00
67 Sad Sack's Army Life	7.00
68 Casper & Nightmare	10.00
69 Stumbo the Giant	22.00
70 Sad Sack's Army Life	7.00
71 Casper & Nightmare	6.00
72 Stumbo the Giant	22.00
73 Little Sad Sack	7.00
74 Sad Sack's Muttsy	7.00
75 Casper & Nightmare	7.00
76 Little Sad Sack	7.00
77 Sad Sack's Muttsy	7.00
78 Stumbo the Giant	20.00
79 Little Sad Sack	7.00
80 Sad Sack's Muttsy	7.00
81 Little Sad Sack	7.00
82 Sad Sack's Muttsy	7.00
83 Little Sad Sack	7.00
84 Sad Sack's Muttsy	7.00
85 Gabby Gob	7.00
86 G.I. Juniors	7.00
87 Sad Sack's Muttsy	7.00
88 Stumbo the Giant	20.00
89 Sad Sack's Muttsy	5.00
90 Gabby Goo	5.00
91 G.I. Juniors	5.00
92 Sad Sack's Muttsy	5.00
93 Sadie Sack	5.00
94 Gabby Goo	5.00
95 G.I. Juniors	5.00
96 Sad Sack's Muttsy	5.00
97 Gabby Goo	5.00
98 G.I. Juniors	5.00
99 Sad Sack's Muttsy	5.00
100 Gabby Goo	5.00
101 G.I. Juniors	4.00
102 Sad Sack's Muttsy	4.00
103 Gabby Goo	4.00
104 G.I. Juniors	4.00
105 Sad Sack's Muttsy	4.00
106 Gabby Goo	4.00
107 G.I. Juniors	4.00
108 Sad Sack's Muttsy	4.00
109 Gabby Goo	4.00
110 G.I. Juniors	4.00
111 Sad Sack's Muttsy	4.00
112 G.I. Juniors	4.00
113 Sad Sack's Muttsy	4.00
114 G.I. Juniors	4.00
115 Sad Sack's Muttsy	4.00
116 G.I. Juniors	4.00
117 Sad Sack's Muttsy	4.00
118 G.I. Juniors	4.00
119 Sad Sack's Muttsy	4.00
120 G.I. Juniors	4.00
121 Sad Sack's Muttsy	4.00
122 G.I. Juniors	4.00

Haunted #12 © Charlton Comics

HAUNTED
Charlton 1971–75

1	7.50
2	5.00
3 thru 5	@4.00
6 thru 10	@3.50
11 thru 20	@3.00

HAUNT OF FEAR
Gladstone

1 EC Rep. H of F #17,WS#28	3.00
2 EC Rep. H of F #5,WS #29	2.50

HAUNT OF FEAR
Russ Cochran 1991

1 EC Rep. H of F #15	1.50
2 thru 5 EC Rep. H of F	@1.50

Second Series 1992

1 EC Rep. H of F #14,WS#13	2.25
2 EC Rep. H of F #18,WF#14	2.00
3 EC Rep. H of F #19,WF#18	2.00
4 EC Rep. H of F #16,WF#15	2.00
5 EC Rep. H of F #5,WF#22	2.00
6 EC Rep. H of F	2.00
7 EC Rep. H of F	2.00
8 thru 15 Rep.	@2.00

Gemstone

16 thru 20 EC comics reprint	@2.50

"Annuals"

TPB Vol. 1 rebinding of #1–#5	8.95
TPB Vol. 2 rebinding of #6–#10	8.95
TPB Vol. 3 rebinding of #11–#15	8.95

HAVE GUN, WILL TRAVEL
Dell Publishing Co. Aug., 1958

1 Richard Boone Ph(c) all	150.00
2	100.00
3	100.00
4	75.00
5	75.00
6	75.00
7	75.00
8	75.00
9	75.00
10	75.00
11	75.00
12	75.00
13	75.00
14	75.00

HAWKMOON, COUNT BRASS
First

1 Michael Moorcock adapt.	1.95
2	1.95
3	1.95
4	1.95

HAWKMOON JEWEL IN THE SKULL
First

1 Michael Moorcock adapt.	3.00
2	2.50
3	2.00
4	2.00

HAWKMOON, MAD GOD'S AMULET
First

1 Michael Moorcock adapt.	2.00
2	1.75
3	1.75
4	1.75

HAWKMOON, SWORD OF THE DAWN
First

1 Michael Moorcock adapt.	2.00
2 thru 4	@1.75

HAWKMOON, THE RUNESTAFF
First

1 Michael Moorcock adapt.	2.00
2	2.00
3	1.95
4	1.95

HEADMAN
Innovation

1	2.50
2	2.50

HEARTSTOPPER
Millenium

1 V:Demons	2.95
2 V:Demons	2.95
3 F:Hellfire	2.95

HEAVY METAL MONSTERS
3-D-Zone

1 w/3-D glasses	3.95

HECTOR HEATHCOTE
Gold Key March, 1964

1	30.00

HELLINA
See Also B&W

COLOR PUB.

HELLINA/ DOUBLE IMPACT
Lightning 1996
1-shot JCy(c) 3.00
1-shot variant (c) 3.00
1-shot nude cover 9.95
1-shot platinum edition, nude cover 9.95
1-shot spec. nude cover, signed 12.00

HELLINA: HEART OF THORNS
Lightning Comics 1996
1 . . . . 3.00
1 nude cover editions 10.00
1 autographed edition 10.00
2 . . . . 3.00
2 variant cover 3.00
2 platinum edition 5.95
2 nude cover editions 10.00

HELLINA/NIRA X: ANGEL OF DEATH
Lightning 1996
1A cover A 3.00
1B cover B 3.00
1C Platinum cover 9.00
1D signed 9.00

HELLINA/NIRA X: CYBERANGEL
Lightning
1 autographed edition 9.95

HERBIE
American Comics Group April-May, 1964
1 . . . . 125.00
2 . . . . 65.00
3 . . . . 60.00
4 . . . . 60.00
5 A:Beatles,Dean Martin, Frank
  Sinatra 80.00
6 . . . . 50.00
7 . . . . 50.00
8 O:Fat Fury 60.00
9 . . . . 50.00
10 . . . . 50.00
11 . . . . 30.00
12 . . . . 30.00
13 . . . . 30.00
14 A:Nemesis,Magic Man 30.00
15 thru 22 . . . . @30.00
23 Feb., 1967 . . . . 30.00

HERCULES
Charlton Comics Oct., 1967
1 . . . . 10.00
2 thru 7 . . . . @5.00
8 scarce 20.00
9 thru 13 Sept. 1969 . . . . 4.00

HERCULES: THE LEGENDARY JOURNEYS
Topps 1996
1 & 2 . . . . @2.95
3 RTs,JBt,SeM,"The Shaper," pt.1 2.95
4 RTs,JBt,SeM,"The Shaper," pt.2 2.95
5 RTs,JBt,SeM,"The Shaper," pt.3 2.95

HERETICS
Iquana
1 . . . . 2.95

Hero Alliance #1 © Wonder Comics

HERO ALLIANCE
Wonder Color Comics 1987
1 . . . . 2.00
Innovation 1989–91
1 RLm,BS(c),R:HeroAlliance 6.00
2 RLm,BS(c),Victor vs.Rage 5.00
3 RLm,A:Stargrazers 4.00
4 . . . . 3.00
5 RLm(c) 2.50
6 BS(c),RLm pin-up 3.25
7 V:Magnetron 2.50
8 I:Vector 2.50
9 BS(c),V:Apostate 2.50
10 A:Sentry 2.25
11 . . . . 2.25
12 I:Bombshell 2.25
13 V:Bombshell 2.25
14 Kris Solo Story 2.25
15 JLA Parody Issue 2.25
16 V:Sepulchre 2.25
17 O:Victor,I&D:Misty 2.25
Annual #1 PS,BS,RLm 3.00

HERO ALLIANCE: THE END OF THE GOLDEN AGE
Pied Piper 1986
1 Bart Sears/Ron Lim 20.00
1a signed 25.00
1b 2nd printing 2.50
2 . . . . 12.00
3 . . . . 3.00
Graphic Novel 10.00
Innovation 1989
1 RLm 5.00
1A 2nd printing 2.50
2 RLm 4.00
3 RLm 3.00

HERO ALLIANCE & JUSTICE MACHINE: IDENTITY CRISES

Innovation
1 . . . . 2.50

HERO ALLIANCE QUARTERLY
Innovation
1 Hero Alliance stories 2.75
2 inc."Girl Happy" 2.75
3 inc."Child Engagement" 2.75
4 . . . . 2.75

HERO ALLIANCE SPECIAL
Innovation
1 Hero Alliance update 2.50

HI-SCHOOL ROMANCE DATE BOOK
Harvey Publications Nov., 1962
1 BP 18.00
2 . . . . 8.00
3 March, 1963 . . . . 8.00

HIGH CHAPPARAL
Gold Key Aug., 1968
1 . . . . 35.00

HIGH SCHOOL CONFIDENTIAL DIARY
Charlton Comics June, 1960
1 . . . . 15.00
2 thru 11 . . . . @6.00
Becomes:

CONFIDENTIAL DIARY
12 . . . . 5.00
13 thru 17 March, 1963 . . . . . . @3.00

HIGH VOLTAGE
Blackout 1996
O 2.95

HILLBILLY COMICS
Charlton Comics Aug., 1955
1 . . . . 25.00
2 thru 4 July 1956 . . . . @12.00

HIS NAME IS ROG... ROG 2000
A Plus Comics
1 . . . . 1.75

HOBBIT, THE
Eclipse
1 . . . . 8.00
1a 2ndPrinting 6.00
2 . . . . 7.00
2a 2ndPrinting 5.00
3 . . . . 6.00

HOGAN'S HEROES
Dell Publishing Co. June, 1966
1 Ph(c) 60.00
2 Ph(c) 35.00
3 JD,Ph(c) 35.00
4 thru 8 Ph(c) . . . . @25.00
8 and 9 . . . . @25.00

COLOR PUB.

HOMICIDE
Chaos! Comics 1997
1 .... 2.95

HONEY WEST
Gold Key Sept., 1966
1 .... 100.00

The Honeymooners #4 © Triad Comics

HONEYMOONERS
Lodestone
1 .... 4.00
5 Mag. 2.50
Triad
[2nd Series]
1 "They Know What They Like" . . 3.00
2 "The Life You Save" 2.50
3 X-mas special,inc.Art Carney
   interview 3.50
4 "In the Pink" 3.00
5 "Bang, Zoom, To the Moon" . . . 2.00
6 "Everyone Needs a Hero" inc.
   Will Eisner interview 2.00
7 .... 2.00
8 .... 2.00
9 Jack Davis(c) 4.50
10 thru 13 .... @2.00

HONG KONG
Blackout Comics 1996
0 A:Hari Kari 2.95
0 limited commemorative edition . 9.95

HOT COMICS PREMIERE
Hot Comics
1 F:Thunderkill, Jacknife 1.95

HOT ROD RACERS
Charlton Comics Dec., 1964
1 .... 35.00
2 thru 5 .... @20.00
6 thru 15 July 1967 .... @15.00

HOT STUFF,
THE LITTLE DEVIL
Harvey Publications Oct., 1967

1 .... 175.00
2 1st Stumbo the Giant 100.00
3 thru 5 .... @75.00
6 thru 10 .... @50.00
11 thru 20 .... @30.00
21 thru 40 .... @20.00
41 thru 60 .... @10.00
61 thru 100 .... @5.00
101 thru 105 .... @4.00
106 thru 112 52 pg Giants .... @5.00
113 thru 172 .... @2.00

HOT STUFF SIZZLERS
Harvey Publications July, 1960
1 B:68 pgs 75.00
2 thru 5 .... @30.00
6 thru 10 .... @15.00
11 thru 20 .... @12.00
21 thru 30 .... @10.00
31 thru 44 .... @5.00
45 E:68 pgs 4.00
46 thru 50 .... @3.00
51 thru 59 .... @2.50

HOTSHOTS
1 thru 4 .... @1.95

HOTSPUR
Eclipse
1 RT(i),I:Josef Quist 1.75
2 RT(i),Amulet of Kothique Stolen 1.75
3 RT(i),Curse of the SexGoddess 1.75

HOWARD CHAYKIN'S
AMERICAN FLAGG!
First
1 thru 9 .... @1.75
10 thru 12 .... @1.95

H.P.LOVECRAFT'S
CTHULHU
Millenium
1 I:Miskatonic Project,V:Mi-Go . . 2.50
2 Arkham, trading cards 2.50

HUCK & YOGI JAMBOREE
Dell Publishing Co. March, 1961
1 .... 65.00

HUCKLEBERRY HOUND
Charlton Nov., 1970
1 .... 15.00
2 thru 7 .... @7.50
3 Jan., 1972 .... 8.00

HUCKLEBERRY HOUND
Dell Publishing Co.
May-July, 1959
1 .... 100.00
2 .... 75.00
3 .... 60.00
4 .... 60.00
5 .... 60.00
6 .... 60.00
7 .... 60.00
8 .... 50.00
9 .... 50.00
10 .... 50.00
11 .... 35.00
12 .... 35.00
13 .... 35.00

14 .... 35.00
15 .... 35.00
16 .... 35.00
17 .... 35.00
Gold Key
18 Chuckleberry Tales 60.00
19 Chuckleberry Tales 50.00
20 Chuckleberry Tales 40.00
21 .... 20.00
22 .... 20.00
23 .... 20.00
24 .... 20.00
25 .... 20.00
26 .... 20.00
27 .... 20.00
28 .... 20.00
29 .... 20.00
30 .... 20.00
31 thru 43 .... @10.00

HUEY, DEWEY & LOUIE
JUNIOR WOODCHUCKS
Gold Key Aug., 1966
1 .... 50.00
2 thru 5 .... @30.00
6 thru 17 .... @25.00
18 .... 15.00
19 thru 25 .... @18.00
26 thru 30 .... @15.00
31 thru 57 .... @15.00
58 .... 12.00
59 .... 12.00
60 thru 80 .... @8.00
81 1984 .... 8.00

HYBRIDS
Continuity
1 .... 2.50

HYBRIDS
Continuity
0 Deathwatch 2000 prologue . . . 5.00
1 Deathwatch 2000 pt.4,w/card . . 2.50
2 Deathwatch 2000 pt.13,w/card . 2.50
3 Deathwatch 2000 w/card 2.50
4 A:Valeria 2.50
5 O:Valeria 2.50

HYBRIDS: ORIGIN
Continuity
1 thru 5 .... 2.50

HYDE-25
Harris
1 New Drug 2.95

I DREAM OF JEANNIE
Dell Publishing Co. April, 1965
1 Ph(c),B.Eden 60.00
2 Ph(c),B.Eden 55.00

I SPY
Gold Key Aug., 1966
1 Bill Cosby Ph(c) 250.00
2 Ph(c) 150.00
3 thru 4 AMc,Ph(c) .... @125.00
5 thru 6 Ph(c) Sept.1968 .. @125.00

I'M DICKENS –
HE'S FENSTER
Dell Publishing Co.

COLOR PUB.

May-July, 1963
1 Ph(c) 25.00
2 Ph(c) 25.00

I•BOTS
Big Comics 1996
1 F:Lady Justice 2.25
2 thru 4 . . . . @2.25
5 StG(s),PB 2.25
6 StG(s),PB 2.25
7 PB,"Rebirth," pt.1, triptych (c) . . 2.25
8 PB,"Rebirth," pt.2, triptych (c) . . 2.25
9 PB,"Rebirth," pt.3, Original I•Bots
   return, triptych (c) 2.25

ICICLE
Hero Graphics
1 A:Flare,Lady Arcane,
   V:Eraserhead 4.95

IMP
1 . . . . 2.25

INNER CIRCLE
Mushroom Comics 1995
1.1 I:Point Blank 2.50
1.2 V:Deathcom 2.50
1.3 V:Deathcom 2.50
1.4 V:Deathcom 2.50

INNOCENTS
Radical Comics 1995
1 I:Innocent 2.50

INNOVATORS
Dark Moon
1 I:Innovator, LeoShan 2.50
2 O:Mr. Void 2.50
3 I:Quill 2.50

INTERVIEW WITH
A VAMPIRE
Innovation
1 based on novel,preq.to Vampire
   Chronicles 3.50
2 . . . . 3.00
3 Death & Betrayal 3.00
4 . . . . 3.00
5 D:Lestat 2.50
6 Transylvania Revelation 2.50
7 Louis & Claudia in Paris 2.50
8 thru 10 . . . . @2.50
11 . . . . 2.50

INTERVIEW WITH
A VAMPIRE
Innovation
1 based on novel, preq. to Vampire
   Chronicles 3.50
2 . . . . 3.00
3 Death & Betrayal 3.00
4 . . . . 3.00
5 D:Lestat 2.50
6 Transylvania Revelation 2.50
7 Louis & Claudia in Paris 2.50

INTIMATE
Charlton Comics Dec., 1957
1 . . . . 8.00
2 and 3 . . . . @8.00

Becomes:
TEEN-AGE LOVE
4 . . . . 8.00
5 thru 9 . . . . @4.00
10 thru 35 . . . . @3.00
36 thru 96 . . . . @1.00

INTRUDER
TSR
1 thru 8 . . . . @2.95

INVADERS FROM HOME
Piranha Press
1 thru 6 . . . . @2.50

INVADERS, THE
Gold Key Oct., 1967
1 Ph(c),DSp 75.00
2 Ph(c),DSp 60.00
3 Ph(c),DSp 60.00
4 Ph(c),DSp 60.00

INVINCIBLE FOUR OF
KUNG FU & NINJA
Victory
1 . . . . 2.75
2 . . . . 2.50
3 . . . . 2.50
4 . . . . 1.80
5 thru 11 . . . . @2.00

IO
Invictus Studios
1 I:IO 2.25
2 . . . . 2.25
3 V:Major Damage 2.25

IRON HORSE
Dell Publishing Co. March, 1967
1 . . . . 12.00
2 . . . . 12.00

IRONJAW
Atlas Jan.–July , 1975
1 NA(c),MSy 2.00

Iron Jaw #2 © Atlas Comics

2 NA(c) 1.50
3 . . . . 1.25
4 O:IronJaw 1.25

IRON MARSHAL
Jademan
1 . . . . 2.00
2 . . . . 1.75
3 . . . . 1.75
4 . . . . 1.75
5 . . . . 1.75
6 V:Bloody Duke 1.75
7 . . . . 1.75
8 . . . . 1.75
9 The Unicorn Sword 1.75
10 The Great Thor 1.75
11 A:Exterminator 1.75
12 Bloody Duke vs. Exterminator . 1.75
13 Secret of Unicorn Supreme . . . 1.75
14 A:The Great Thor 1.75
15 A:The Great Thor 1.75
16 V:Tienway Champ 1.75
17 thru 20 . . . . 1.75
21 Bloody Duke wounded 1.75
22 A:Great Thor 1.75
23 . . . . 1.75
24 . . . . 1.75
25 . . . . 1.75
26 Iron Marshal Betrayed 1.75
27 . . . . 1.75
28 . . . . 1.75
29 . . . . 1.75
30 . . . . 1.75

IRREGULARS, THE:
BATTLETECH Miniseries
Blackthorne
1 . . . . 1.75
2 . . . . 1.75
3 B&W 1.75

IRUKASHI
1 . . . . 1.75

ISAAC ASIMOV'S I-BOTS
Tekno-Comix 1995
1 I:I-Bots 1.95
2 O:I-Bots 1.95
3 V:Black OP 2.25

IT! TERROR FROM
BEYOND SPACE
Millenium
1 . . . . 2.50
2 . . . . 2.50

IT'S ABOUT TIME
Gold Key Jan., 1967
1 Ph(c) 25.00

ITCHY & SCRATCHY
Bongo Comics
1 DaC(s), ... 2.25
2 DaC(s), ... 2.25

IVANHOE
Dell Publishing Co.
July-Sept., 1963
1 . . . . 25.00

COLOR PUB.

JACK
Med Systems Company
1 Anubis in the 90's 2.95
2 Modern Society 2.95

JACK HUNTER
Blackthorne
1 . . . . 1.25
2 . . . . 1.25
3 . . . . 1.25

JACKIE CHAN'S SPARTAN X
Topps 1997
1 "The Armor of Heaven," pt.1 . . 2.95
2 "The Armor of Heaven," pt.2 . . 2.95
3 (of 6) 2.95

JADEMAN COLLECTION
1 . . . . 4.50
2 . . . . 3.00
3 . . . . 2.50
4 . . . . 2.50
5 . . . . 2.50

JADEMAN KUNG FU SPECIAL
1 I:Oriental Heroes, Blood
Sword, Drunken Fist 5.00

JAGUAR GOD
Verotika 1995
1 Frazetta, I:Jaquar God 2.95
2 V:Yi-Cha 2.95
3 V:Yi-Cha 2.95
4 V:Yi-Cha 2.95
5 AOI 2.95
6 LSh,AOI 2.95
7 LSh,AOI 2.95
8 AOI 2.95

JAKE TRASH
Aircel
1 thru 3 . . . . @2.00

JAMES BOND 007
Eclipse
1 MGr,PerfectBound 5.50
2 MGr 5.00
3 MGr,end series 5.00
GN Licence to Kill, MGr l/o 8.00

JAMES BOND: GOLDENEYE
Topps 1995
1 Movie adaptation 2.95
2 thru 3 Movie adaptation . . . . @2.95

JAM SPECIAL
Comico
1 . . . . 2.50

JASON GOES TO HELL
Topps
1 Movie adapt.,w/3 cards 3.25
2 Movie adapt.,w/3 cards 3.25
3 Movie adapt.,w/3 cards 3.25

JASON VS. LEATHERFACE
Topps 1995
1 Jason Meets Leatherface 2.95
2 SBi(c) Leatherface's family . . . 2.95
3 SBi(c),conclusion 2.95

JAVERTZ
Firstlight
1 New Series 2.95
2 thru 5 Pieces of an Icon 2.95

JET DREAM
Gold Key June, 1968
1 . . . . 20.00

JETSONS, THE
Gold Key Jan., 1963
1 . . . . 200.00
2 . . . . 125.00
3 thru 10 . . . . @100.00
11 thru 20 . . . . @65.00
21 thru 36 Oct. 1970 . . . . . . @50.00

JETSONS, THE
Charlton Comics Nov., 1970
1 . . . . 55.00
2 . . . . 31.00
3 thru 10 . . . . @20.00
11 thru 20 Dec. 1973 . . . . . . @15.00

JETSONS, THE
Harvey Comics 1991–92
1 thru 5 . . . . @1.95

The Jetsons #1 © Archie Comics

JETSONS, THE
Archie 1995
1 thru 17 . . . . @1.50

JEZEBEL JADE
Comico
1 AKu,A:Race Bannon 2.00
2 AKu 2.00
3 AKu 2.00

JIGSAW
Harvey Publications Sept., 1966
1 . . . . 6.00
2 . . . . 3.50

JIMBO
Bongo Comics
1 R:Jimbo 2.95
2 thru 4 . . . . @2.95

JIMMY CORRIGAN
Fantagraphics
1 Chris Ware 3.95

J. N. WILLIAMSON'S MASQUES
Innovation
1 TV,From horror anthology 4.95
2 Olivia(c) inc.Better Than One . . 4.95

JOHN BOLTON, HALLS OF HORROR
Eclipse
1 JBo 1.75
2 JBo 1.75

JOHN F. KENNEDY LIFE STORY
(WITH 2 REPRINTS)
Dell Publishing Co.
Aug.-Oct., 1964
1 . . . . 35.00
2 . . . . 25.00
3 . . . . 25.00

JOHN JAKES MULLKON EMPIRE
Tekno Comix 1995
1 I:Mulkons 2.25
2 O:Mulkons 1.95
3 D:Company Man 1.95
4 Disposal Problems 1.95
5 F:Granny 1.95
6 Where's Karma 2.25

JOHN LAW
Eclipse 1983
1 WE 2.00

JOHNNY GAMBIT
1 . . . . 1.75

JOHNNY JASON TEEN REPORTER
Dell Publishing Co. 1962
1 . . . . 10.00
2 . . . . 10.00

JOHNNY NEMO
Eclipse 1985–86
1 I:Johnny Nemo 2.00
2 . . . . 2.00
3 F:Sindy Shade 2.50

JOHN STEELE SECRET AGENT
Gold Key Dec., 1964
1 . . . . 65.00

COLOR PUB.

JONNY QUEST
Gold Key Dec., 1964
1 TV show 150.00

JONNY QUEST
Comico June, 1986
1 DW,SR,A:Dr.Zin 4.50
2 WP/JSon,O:RaceBannon 3.50
3 DSt(c) 3.00
4 TY/AW,DSt(i) 2.50
5 DSt(c)A:JezebelJade 2.50
6 AKu 2.00
7 . . . . 2.00
8 KSy 2.00
9 MA 2.00
10 King Richard III 2.00
11 JSon,BSz(c) 1.50
12 DSp 1.50
12 DSp 1.50
13 CI 1.50
14 . . . . 1.50
15 thru 31 . . . . @1.75
Spec.#1 . . . . 1.75
Spec.#2 . . . . 1.75

JONNY QUEST CLASSICS
Comico
1 DW 2.00
2 DW,O:Hadji 2.00
3 DW 2.00

JON SABLE
First
1 MGr,A:President 4.50
2 MGr,Alcohol Issue 3.50
3 MGr,O:Jon Sable 3.00
4 MGr,O:Jon Sable 3.00
5 MGr,O:Jon Sable 3.00
6 MGr,O:Jon Sable 3.00
7 MGr,The Target 2.50
8 MGr,Nuclear Energy 2.50
9 MGr,Nuclear Energy 2.50
10 MGr,Tripitych 2.50
11 MGr,I:Maggie 2.50
12 MGr,Vietnam 2.50
13 MGr,Vietnam 2.50
14 MGr,East Germany 2.50
15 MGr,Nicaragua 2.50
16 MGr,A:Maggie 2.50
17 MGr,1984 Olympics 2.50
18 MGr,1984 Olympics 2.50
19 MGr,,The Widow 2.50
20 MGr,The Rookie 2.50
21 MGr,Africa 2.25
22 MGr,V:Sparrow 2.25
23 MGr,V:Sparrow 2.25
24 MGr,V:Sparrow 2.25
25 MGr,Shatter 3.00
26 MGr,Shatter 3.00
27 MGr,Shatter 3.00
28 MGr,Shatter 3.00
29 MGr,Shatter 3.00
30 MGr,Shatter 2.25
31 MGr,Nicaragua 2.00
32 MGr,Nicaragua 2.00
33 MGr,SA,Leprechauns 2.25
34 MGr,Indians 2.00
35 MGr,Indians 2.00
36 MGr,Africa 2.00
37 MGr,Africa 2.00
38 MGr,Africa 2.00
39 MGr,Africa 2.00

Jon Sable #14 © First Comics

40 MGr,1st Case 2.00
41 MGr,1st Case 2.00
42 MGr,V:Sparrow 2.00
43 MGr,V:Sparrow 2.00
44 Hard Way 2.00
45 Hard Way II 2.00
46 MM,The Tower pt.1 . . . . 2.00
47 MM,The Tower pt.2 . . . . 2.00
48 MM,Prince Charles 2.00
49 MM,Prince Charles 2.00
50 A:Maggie the Cat 2.00
51 Jon Sable,babysitter pt.1 . . . 2.00
52 Jon Sable,babysitter pt.2 . . . 2.00
53 MGr. 2.00
54 Jacklight pt.1 . . . . 2.00
55 Jacklight pt.2 . . . . 2.00
56 Jacklight pt.3 . . . . 2.00

JOSIE
Archie Publications Feb., 1963
1 . . . . 100.00
2 . . . . 50.00
3 . . . . 25.00
4 . . . . 20.00
5 . . . . 25.00
6 thru 10 . . . . @15.00
11 thru 20 . . . . @12.00
21 thru 30 . . . . @7.00
31 thru 40 . . . . @5.00
41 thru 54 . . . . @4.00
55 thru 74 . . . . @2.00
75 thru 105 . . . . @1.00
106 Oct., 1962 . . . . 1.00

JUDGE COLT
Gold Key Oct., 1969
1 . . . . 8.00
2 . . . . 5.00
3 . . . . 5.00
4 Sept., 1980 . . . . 5.00

JUDGE DREDD
Eagle 1983
1 BB,I:Judge Death(in USA) . . . 15.00
2 BB(c&a),The Oxygen Board . . 12.00
3 BB(c),Judge Dredd Lives 10.00
4 BB(c),V:Perps 10.00
5 BB(c),V:Perps 8.00

6 BB(c),V:Perps 8.00
7 BB(c),V:Perps 8.00
8 BB(c),V:Perps 8.00
9 BB(c),V:Perps 8.00
10 BB(c),V:Perps 8.00
11 BB(c) 5.00
12 BB(c) 5.00
13 BB(c), The Day the Law Died,
  pt.5 . . . . 5.00
14 BB(c),Dredd vs. Dredd 5.00
15 BB(c) 5.00
16 BB(c) 5.00
17 BB(c) 5.00
18 BB(c) 5.00
19 BB(c) 5.00
20 BB(c) 5.00
21 BB(c) 5.00
22 BB(c),V:Perps 4.00
23 BB(c),V:Perps 4.00
24 BB(c),V:Perps 4.00
25 BB(c),V:Perps 4.00
26 BB(c),V:Perps 4.00
27 BB(c),V:Perps 4.00
28 A:Judge Anderson,V:Megaman 5.00
29 A:Monty, the guinea pig 4.00
30 V:Perps 4.00
31 Destiny's Angel, Pt. 1 . . . . . . 4.00
32 Destiny's Angel, Pt. 2 . . . . . . 4.00
33 V:League of Fatties 4.00
34 V:Executioner 4.00

JUDGE DREDD
Quality
1 Cry of the Werewolf Pt.1 . . . . . 7.00
2 Cry of the Werewolf Pt.2 . . . . . 5.00
3 Anti-smoking 4.00
4 Wreckers 4.00
5 Highwayman 4.00
6 . . . . 3.00
7 . . . . 3.00
8 . . . . 3.00
9 . . . . 3.00
10 . . . . 3.00
11 . . . . 3.00
12 Starborn Thing, Pt.1 . . . . 3.00
13 Starborn Thing, Pt.2 . . . . 3.00
14 BB, V:50 foot woman 3.00
15 City of the Damned Pt.1 . . . . . 3.00
16 City of the Damned Pt.2 . . . . . 3.00
17 City of the Damned conc. 3.00
18 V:Mean Machine Angel 3.00
19 Dredd Angel 3.00
20 V:Perps 3.00
21 V:Perps 3.00
22/23 Booby Trap 3.00
24 Junk food fiasco 3.00
25/26 V:Perps 3.00
27 V:Perps 3.00
28 Dredd Syndrome 3.00
29 V:Perps 3.00
30 V:Perps 3.00
31 Hunt Pudge Dempsey's killer . 3.00
32 V:Mutated Sewer Alligator . . . 3.00
33 V:Perps 3.00
34 V:Executioner 3.00
35 V:Shojan 3.00
36 V:Shojan 3.00
37 V:Perps 3.00
38 V:Perps 3.00
39 V:Perps 3.00
40 V:Perps 3.00
41 V:Perps 3.00
42 V:Perps 3.00
43 V:Perps 3.00
44 V:Perps 3.00

COLOR PUB.

45 V:DNA Man	2.50
46 Genie lamp sty	2.50
47 V:Perps	2.50
48 Murder in Mega-City One	2.50
49 V:Perps	2.50
50 V:Perps	2.50
51 V:Perps	2.50
52 V:Perps	2.50
53 V:Perps	2.50
54 V:Perps	2.50
55 V:Perps	2.50
56 inc.JudgeDredd Postcards	2.50
57 V:Perps	2.50
58 V:370lb Maniac	2.50
59 V:Perps	2.50
60 Social Misfit	2.50
61 V:Perps	2.50

Becomes:

JUDGE DREDD CLASSICS

62	2.50
63 Mutants from the Radlands	2.50
64	2.50
65	2.50
66 Wit and wisdom of Dredd	2.50
67 V:Otto Sump	2.50
68 V:Otto Sump	2.50
69	2.50
70 Dinosaurs in Mega City 1	2.50
71	2.50
72 Pirates o/t Black Atlantic	2.50
73	2.50
74	2.50
75	2.50
76 Diary of a Mad Citizen	3.00
TPB:Democracy Now	10.95
TPB:Rapture	12.95
Judge Dredd Special #1	2.50

JUDGE DREDD: AMERICA
Fleetway

1 I:America	3.50

JUDGE DREDD: JUDGE CHILD QUEST
Eagle

1	3.00
2	3.00
3	3.00
4 BB(c)	3.00
5	3.00

JUDGE DREDD'S CRIME FILE
Eagle 1984

1 Ron Smith, "The Perp Runners"	2.50
2	2.50
3	2.50
4	2.50
5	2.50
6	2.50

Quality
(Prestige format)

1 A:Rogue Trooper	6.50
2 IG,V:Fatties, Energy Vampires & Super Fleas	5.95
3 Battles foes from dead A:Judge Anderson	5.95

JUDGE DREDD'S EARLY CASES

Eagle

1 Robot Wars, Pt.1	4.00
2 Robot Wars, Pt.2	3.00
3 V:Perps	3.00
4 IG, Judge Giant	3.00
5 V:Perps	3.00
6 V:Judge killing car Elvis	3.00

JUDGE DREDD'S HARDCASE PAPERS
Fleetway/Quality

1 V:The Tarantula	7.50
2 Junkies & Psychos	6.50
3 Crime Call Vid. Show	6.50
4 "Real Coffee",A:Johnny Alpha	6.50

JUDGE DREDD: THE MEGAZINE
Fleetway/Quality 1991

1 Midnite's Children Pt.1 A:Chopper, Young Death	5.25
2 Midnite's Children Pt.2	4.95
3	4.95
23 thru 27	@3.95

JUDGE PARKER
Argo Feb., 1956

1	20.00
2	11.00

JUDGMENT DAY
Lightning Comics

1 B:JZy(s),KIK,V:Razorr,Rift, Nightmare, red prism(c)	5.00
1a Gold Prism(c)	5.00
1b Purple Prism(c)	7.00
1c Misprint,Red Prism(c), Bloodfire Credits inside	8.00
1d Misprint,Gold Prism(c), Bloodfire Credits inside	8.00
1e Misprint,Green Prism(c), Bloodfire Credits inside	8.00
1f B&W promo ed. Gold ink	5.00
1g B&W promo ed. platinum ed.	7.00
2 TLw,I:War Party,BU:Perg, w/Perg card	4.00
3 ErP,O:X-Treme	3.25
4 ErP,In Hell	3.25
5 TLw,In Hell	3.25
6 TLw,I:Red Front,O:Salurio	3.25
7 O:Safeguard	3.25
8	2.95
9	2.95
10	2.95

JUDGMENT DAY
Maximum Press 1997

Alpha AMo(s)	2.50
Alpha variant cover	2.50
Omega AMo(s)	2.50
Omega variant cover	2.50
Final Judgment AMo(s)	2.50
Final Judgment variant cover	2.50

JUDOMASTER
Charlton Comics

(Special War Series #4) I:Judomaster	5.00
89 FMc,War stories begin	7.00
89 (90) FMc,A:Thunderbolt	6.00
91 FMc,DG,A:Sarge Steel	6.00
92 FMc,DG,A:Sarge Steel	6.00
93 FMc,DG,I:Tiger	6.00

94 FMc,DG,A:Sarge Steel	6.00
95 FMc,DG,A:Sarge Steel	5.00
96 FMc,DG,A:Sarge Steel	5.00
97 FMc,A:Sarge Steel	4.00
98 FMc,A:Sarge Steel	4.00

JUGHEAD
Archie Publications
Dec., 1965–June, 1987

127 thru 130	@12.00
131 thru 150	@10.00
151 thru 160	@8.00
161 thru 352	1.50

Jughead #45 © Archie Comics

JUGHEAD
Archie Publications
[2nd Series] Aug., 1987

1 thru 45	@1.25

Becomes:

ARCHIE'S PAL JUGHEAD
June, 1993

46 thru 50	@1.25
51 thru 70	@1.25
71 thru 97	@1.50

JUGHEAD AS CAPTAIN HERO
Archie Publications Oct., 1966

1	25.00
2	15.00
3 thru 7	@10.00

JUGHEAD'S FANTASY
Archie Publications Aug., 1960

1	80.00
2	60.00
3	45.00

JUGHEAD'S JOKES
Archie Publications Aug., 1967

1	26.00
2	14.00
3 thru 5	@7.00
6 thru 10	@5.00
11 thru 30	@2.00
31 thru 77	@1.00

COLOR PUB.

All comics prices listed are for *Near Mint* condition. CVA Page 515

78 Sept., 1982 . . . . 1.00

JUGHEAD WITH ARCHIE DIGEST
Archie Publications March, 1974
1 . . . . 8.00
2 . . . . 4.00
3 thru 10 . . . . @2.00
11 thru 91 . . . . 1.00
130 thru 136 . . . . @1.79

JUNGLE ADVENTURES
Skywald March–June 1971
1 F:Zangar,Jo-Jo,Blue Gorilla . . . 9.00
2 F:Sheena, Jo-Jo,Zangar 8.00
3 F:Zangar,Jo-Jo,White Princess 7.50

JUNGLE COMICS
Blackthorne
1 DSt(c) 2.00
2 . . . . 2.00
3 . . . . 2.00

JUNGLE TALES OF TARZAN
Charlton Comics Dec., 1964
1 . . . . 25.00
2 . . . . 20.00
3 . . . . 20.00
4 July, 1965 . . . . 20.00

JUNGLE WAR STORIES
Dell Publishing Co.
July-Sept., 1962
1 P(c) all 15.00
2 . . . . 8.00
3 . . . . 8.00
4 . . . . 8.00
5 . . . . 8.00
6 . . . . 8.00
7 . . . . 8.00
8 . . . . 8.00
9 . . . . 8.00
10 . . . . 8.00
11 . . . . 8.00
Becomes:
GUERRILLA WAR
12 . . . . 7.00
13 . . . . 7.00
14 . . . . 7.00

JUNIOR WOODCHUCKS
Walt Disney
1 CB,"Bubbleweight Champ" 2.00
2 CB,"Swamp of no Return" 2.00
3 "Rescue Run-Around" 2.00
4 "Cave Caper" 2.00

JURASSIC PARK
Topps
1 Movie Adapt.,w/card 5.00
1a Newsstand Ed. 4.00
2 Movie Adapt.,w/card 3.25
2a Newsstand Ed. 2.75
3 Movie Adapt.,w/card 3.25
3a Newsstand Ed. 2.75
4 Movie Adapt.,w/card 3.25
4a Newsstand Ed. 2.75
Ann.#1 Death Lizards 3.95

JURASSIC PARK: ADVENTURES
Topps
1 thru 10 reprints titles . . . . . @1.95

JURASSIC PARK: RAPTOR
Topps
1 SE w/Zorro #0 ashcan & cards . 3.25
2 w/3 cards 2.95

JURASSIC PARK: RAPTORS ATTACK
Topps
1 SEt(s), ... 2.75
2 SEt(s), ... 2.75
3 SEt(s), ... 2.75
4 SEt(s), ... 2.75

JURASSIC PARK: RAPTOR HIJACK
Topps
1 SEt(s), ... 2.50
2 SEt(s), ... 2.50
3 SEt(s), ... 2.50
4 SEt(s), ... 2.50

[JURASSIC PARK:] THE LOST WORLD
Topps 1997
1 (of 4) movie adapt 2.95
2 thru 4 . . . . @2.95

JUSTICE MACHINE
Noble Comics 1981–85
1 JBy(c) Mag size,B&W 30.00
2 MGu,Mag size,B&W 16.00
3 MGu,Mag size,B&W 10.00
4 MGu,Bluecobalt 8.00
5 MGu 7.00
Texas Comics
Ann.#1:BWG,I:Elementals, A:
Thunder Agents 5.00

Justice Machine #2 © Comico

JUSTICE MACHINE
[Featuring the Elementals]
Comico 1986
1 thru 4 . . . . @2.50

JUSTICE MACHINE
Comico 1987–89
1 MGu 2.50
2 MGu 2.00
3 thru 14 MGu . . . . @1.50
15 thru 27 MGu . . . . @1.75
28 MGu 1.95
29 MGu,IW 1.95
Ann.#1 . . . . 2.50
SummerSpectacular 1 . . . . 2.75
MINI SERIES 1990
1 thru 4 F:Elementals . . . . . . @1.95
Innovation 1990
1 . . . . 1.95
2 thru 4 The Ragnarok Portfilio @1.95
5 thru 7 Demon trilogy . . . . . . @1.95

JUSTICE MACHINE: CHIMERA CONSPIRACY
Millenium
1 AH,R&N:Justice Machine,
wraparound cover 2.50

JUST MARRIED
Charlton Comics Jan., 1958
1 . . . . 25.00
2 . . . . 15.00
3 thru 10 . . . . @10.00
11 thru 30 . . . . @8.00
31 thru 113 . . . . @4.00
114 Dec., 1976 . . . . 4.00

KABUKI COLOR GALLERY
Caliber Press
1 32 paintings 2.95

KABUKI COLOR SPECIAL
Caliber Press
1-shot inc. pin-up gallery 3.00

KABUKI FEAR THE REAPER
Caliber 1994
1-shot Female assassin 5.00

KABUKI: SKIN DEEP
Caliber
1 DMk 2.95
2 DMk(c) 2.95
2 AxR(c) 2.95
3 Origin issue 2.95
4 . . . . 2.95

KATO OF THE GREEN HORNET
Now
1 BA,1st Kato solo story 2.50
2 BA,Kato in China contd. 2.50
3 Kato in China contd 2.50
4 Final Issue 2.50

KATO II
Now
1 VM,JSh,A:Karthage 2.50

Kato II #1 © Now Comics

2 VM,JSh,V:Karthage 2.50
3 VM,JSh,V:Karthage 2.50

KATY KEENE FASHION BOOK MAGAZINE
Archie Publications
1955

1 . . . . 350.00
2 . . . . 200.00
3 thru 10 not published
11 thru 18 . . . . @150.00
19 . . . . 125.00
20 . . . . 125.00
21 . . . . 125.00
22 . . . . 125.00
23 Winter 1958-59 . . . . 125.00

KATY KEENE PINUP PARADE
Archie Publications
1955

1 . . . . 350.00
2 . . . . 200.00
3 . . . . 175.00
4 . . . . 175.00
5 . . . . 175.00
6 . . . . 150.00
7 . . . . 150.00
8 . . . . 150.00
9 . . . . 150.00
10 . . . . 150.00
11 Story on comics 200.00
12 . . . . 150.00
13 . . . . 150.00
14 . . . . 150.00
15 Sept., 1961 . . . . 300.00

KELLY GREEN
Eclipse

1 SDr,O:Kelly Green 2.50
2 SDr,"One,Two,Three" 2.00
3 SDr,"Million Dollar Hit" 2.00
4 SDr,Rare 4.00

KELVIN MACE
Vortex

1 . . . . 6.50

1a 2nd printing 1.75
2 . . . . 4.00

KILLER TALES
Eclipse 1985
1 Tim Truman 1.75

KING COMICS PRESENTS
King Comics
1 I:Rick Dees, Angel Lopez 1.95

KING LEONARDO AND HIS SHORT SUBJECTS
Dell Publishing Co.
Nov.-Jan., 1961-62
1 . . . . 100.00
2 . . . . 75.00
3 . . . . 75.00
4 . . . . 75.00

KING LOUIE & MOWGLI
Gold Key May, 1968
1 . . . . 18.00

KING OF DIAMONDS
Dell Publishing Co.
July-Sept., 1962
1 Ph(c) 30.00

KIT KARTER
Dell Publishing Co.
May-July, 1962
1 . . . . 15.00

KNIGHTS OF THE ROUND TABLE
Dell Publishing Co.
Nov.-Jan., 1963-4
1 P(c) 25.00

KNUCKLES
Archie Comics
4 Lost Paradise 1.50
5 . . . . 1.50
6 "Lost Paradise" 1.50

KNUCKLES: THE DARK LEGION
Archie Comics 1997
1 . . . . 1.50
2 . . . . 1.50
3 (of 3) 1.50

KOL MANIQUE RENAISSANCE
1 . . . . 1.50
2 . . . . 1.50

KOMAH
Anubis Press
1 Urban Decay Title 2.75

KONA
Dell Publishing Co.
Feb.-April, 1962
1 P(c) all,SG 45.00
2 SG 20.00
3 SG 20.00
4 SG,B:Anak 20.00

5 SG 20.00
6 SG 20.00
7 SG 20.00
8 SG 20.00
9 SG 20.00
10 SG 20.00
11 SG 15.00
12 SG 15.00
13 SG 15.00
14 SG 15.00
15 SG 15.00
16 SG 15.00
17 SG 15.00
18 SG 15.00
19 SG 15.00
20 SG 15.00
21 SG 15.00

KONGA
Charlton Comics 1960–65
1 SD,DG(c), movie adapt. . . . 200.00
2 DG(c) 100.00
3 SD 75.00
4 SD 75.00
5 SD 75.00
6 thru 15 SD . . . . @55.00
16 thru 23 . . . . @30.00

KONGA'S REVENGE
Charlton Comics
2 Summer, 1962 . . . . 30.00
3 SD,Fall, 1964 . . . . 40.00
1 Dec., 1968 . . . . 17.00

KOOKIE
Dell Publishing Co.
Feb.-April, 1962
1 . . . . 55.00
2 . . . . 50.00

KORAK, SON OF TARZAN
Gold Key Jan., 1964
1 . . . . 40.00
2 thru 11 . . . . @30.00
12 thru 21 . . . . @20.00
22 thru 30 . . . . @10.00
31 thru 40 . . . . @8.00
41 thru 44 . . . . @5.00
45 Jan., 1972 . . . . 5.00
Continued by DC

KRUSTY COMICS
Bongo Comics
1 Rise and Fall of Krustyland . . . 2.25
2 Rise and Fall of Krustyland . . . 2.25
3 Rise and Fall of Krustyland . . . 2.25

KULL IN 3-D
Blackthorne
1 . . . . 2.50
2 . . . . 2.50
3 . . . . 2.50

KUNG FU & NINJA
1 . . . . 1.80
2 . . . . 1.80
3 . . . . 1.80
4 . . . . 1.80

COLOR PUB.

LAD: A DOG
Dell Publishing Co. 1961
1	30.00
2	25.00

LADY ARCANE
Hero Graphics
1 A: Flare,BU:O:Giant	4.95
2 thru 3	2.95

LADY DEATH
Chaos! Comics
1 BnP, A:Evil Ernie	75.00
1a signed gold foil	110.00
2 BnP	50.00
3 BnP	28.00
HC Foil Stamped Rep. #1-#3	24.95
TPB Rep. #1-#3	6.95
TPB The Reconing	12.95
1 Swimsuit Edition	12.00
1a Velvet Edition	30.00
1 reprint with 8-page pin-up gallery	2.95

LADY DEATH: BETWEEN HEAVEN & HELL
Chaos! Comics
1 V:Purgatori	10.00
1a Limited Edition 5,000c	40.00
2 Lives As Hope	5.00
3 V:Purgatori	4.00
4 final issue	4.00

LADY DEATH: THE CRUCIBLE
Chaos! Comics 1996
1 (of 6) BnP,SHu,	3.50
1 leather limited edition	19.95
2 BnP,SHu,	3.50
3 BnP,SHu,	3.50
4 BnP,SHu,	3.50
5 BnP,SHu,	3.50

LADY DEATH IN LINGERIE
Chaos Comics
1 various artists	10.00

LADY DEATH: THE ODYSSEY
Chaos! Comics 1996
Sneak Peek Preview	1.50
1 embossed cover	7.50
1 SHu(c) premium edition	25.00
2	5.00
3	4.00
4	4.00
4a variant cover	20.00
TPB	9.95

LADY DEATH & THE WOMEN OF CHAOS! GALLERY
Chaos! Comics 1996
1 pin-up book	2.25

LADY PENDRAGON
Maximum Press 1996
1 mini-series	2.50
2	2.50
3 (of 3) MD2	2.50

LADY RAWHIDE
Topps 1995
1 All New Solo series	5.00
2 It Can't Happen Here,pt.2	3.50
3	3.00
4	3.00
5 conclusion	3.00
Spec.#1 Rep. Zorro #2-#3	6.50

LADY RAWHIDE
Topps
Mini-Series
1 DMG	4.00
1a DMG,signed, numbered	9.95
2 DMG	2.95
3 DMG	2.95
4 DMG, EM, "Intimate Wounds"	2.95
5 DMG, EM	2.95
6 DMG	2.95
7 DMG	2.95
TPB	10.95

LADY RAWHIDE: OTHER PEOPLE'S BLOOD
Topps 1996
Mini-Series
1 DMG,EM,"A Slice of Breast"	2.95

LADY VAMPRE
Blackout 1995
0 B&W	3.50
1	3.00

LANCELOT STRONG, THE SHIELD
Red Circle 1983
1 A:Steel Sterling	3.50
2 A:Steel Sterling	2.00
3 AN/EB,D:Lancelot Strong	2.00

LARS OF MARS
Eclipse 1987
1 3-D MA	2.50

LASER ERASER & PRESSBUTTON
Eclipse 1985–87
1 GL,R:Laser Eraser	1.75
2 GL	1.75
3 GL,CK,"Tsultrine"	1.75
4 MC,"Death"	1.75
5 MC,JRy,"Gates of Hell"	.95
6 "Corsairs of Illunium"	.95
3-D#1 MC,GL(c),"Triple Cross"	1.50

LASH LARUE WESTERN
AC Comics
1	3.50
Annual	2.95

LAST OF THE VIKING HEROES
Genesis West
1 JK	4.00
2 JK	3.50
3	3.00
4	2.50
5A sexy cover	3.00
5B mild cover	2.50
6	2.50

7 AA(c)	3.50
8	2.25
9 Great Battle of Nidhogger	2.50
10 "Death Among the Heroes"	2.50
Summer Spec.#1 FF,JK	3.50
Summer Spec.#2	3.00
Summer Spec.#3,A:TMNT	2.50

Laugh #26 © Archie Comics

LAUGH
Archie 1987–91
1 thru 29	@1.00

LAUREL AND HARDY
Dell Publishing Co. Oct., 1962
1	45.00
2	35.00
3	35.00
4	35.00

LAUREL & HARDY
Gold Key Jan., 1967
1	30.00
2 Oct., 1967	30.00

LAWMAN
Dell Publishing Co. Feb., 1959
1 Ph(c) all	100.00
2	65.00
3 ATh	70.00
4	40.00
5	40.00
6	40.00
7	40.00
8 thru 11	@40.00

LAW & ORDER
Maximum Press 1995
1 D:Law, I:New Law, Order	2.50
2 V:Max Spur	2.50
3 V:Law's Murderer	2.50

LAW OF DREDD
Quality
1 V:Perps	5.00
2 BB,Lunar Olympics	4.00
3 BB,V:Judge Death	3.00

All comics prices listed are for *Near Mint* condition.

COLOR PUB.

4 V:Father Earth 3.00
5 Cursed Earth 3.00
6 V:Perps 3.00
7 V:Perps 3.00

Fleetway

8 Blockmania 3.00
9 BB,DGi,Framed for murders . . 3.00
10 BB,Day the Law Died Pt.1 . . . 2.50
11 BB,Day the Law Died Pt.2 . . . 2.50
12 BB,V:Judge Cal 2.50
13 V:Judge Caligula 2.50
14 BB, V:Perps 2.50
15 Under investigation 2.50
16 V:Alien Mercenary 2.50
17 thru 24 . . . . @2.50
25 Ugly Clinic 2.50
26 Judge Dredd & Gavel? 2.50
27 Cycles,Lunatics & Graffiti
   Guerillas 2.50
28 Cadet Training Mission 2.50
29 "Guinea Pig that changed the
   world 2.50
30 Meka-City,V:Robot 2.50
31 Iso-Block 666 . . . . 2.50
32 Missing Game Show Hosts . . . 2.50
33 League of Fatties,final issue . . 3.00

LAZARUS CHURCHYARD
Tundra

1 From UK Blast anthology 4.50
2 Goodnight Ladies 4.50

League of Champions
© Hero Graphics

LEAGUE OF CHAMPIONS
Hero Graphics
{Cont. from Champions #12}

1 Olympus Saga #4 . . . . 2.95
2 Olympus Saga #5,O:Malice . . . 2.95
3 Olympus Saga ends 2.95

LEATHERFACE
North Star

1 . . . . 2.75
2 . . . . 2.75
3 . . . . 2.75

LEGACY
Majestic

0 platinum 12.50
1 I:Legacy 2.25
2 . . . . 2.25

LEGEND OF CUSTER, THE
Dell Publishing Co. Jan., 1968

1 Ph(c) 15.00

LEGEND OF SLEEPY HOLLOW
Tundra

One shot.BHa,W.Irving adapt. . . . 6.95

LEGENDS OF JESSE JAMES, THE
Gold Key Feb., 1966

1 . . . . 20.00

LEGENDS OF NASCAR
Vortex

1 HT,Bill Eliott ($1.50 cover Price)
   15,000 copies . . . . ±25.00
1a ($2.00 cover price) 45,000
   copies . . . . ±8.00
1b 3rd pr., 80,000 copies 5.00
2 Richard Petty 4.50
3 Ken Schroder 3.50
4 Bob Alison 3.00
5 Bill Elliott 2.50
6 Jr. Johnson 2.50
7 Sterling Marlin 2.25
8 . . . . 2.00
9 Rusty Wallace 2.00

LEGENDS OF THE STARGRAZERS
Innovation

1 . . . . 1.95
2 . . . . 1.95
3 . . . . 1.95
4 . . . . 1.95
5 . . . . 1.95

LEJENTIA

1 . . . . 1.95
2 . . . . 2.25

LEMONADE KID
AC Comics

1 . . . . 2.50

LEONARD NIMOY'S PRIMORTALS
Teckno-Comics 1994

1 I:Primortals 5.50
2 Zeerus Reveals Himself 4.00
3 Contact 2.50
4 Message Deciphered 2.25
5 Place & Time Announced 2.25
6 Zeerus Arrives on Earth 2.25
7 Zeerus Recieved 2.25
8 Hyperspace Escape 2.25
9 Pristar Lands on Earth 1.95
10 V:U.S. Army 1.95
11 V:U.S. Army 1.95
12 V:Zeerus 2.25
13 thru 15 . . . . @2.25

Big Entertainment April 1996

0 SEa,MKb 2.25
1 . . . . 2.25
2 KWo,ANi 2.25
3 KWo,ANi 2.25
4 KWo,ANi 2.25
5 KWo,ANi 2.25
6 KWo,"Scorched Earth," concl. . 2.25
7 PB,KWo&ANi(c),Zeerus & Narab
   together again 2.25

LEONARDO
Mirage

1 TMNT Character 5.00

LEOPARD
Millenium

1 I:Leopard 2.95
1a Gold Cover 3.95
2 O:Leopard,V:Razor's Edge . . . 2.95

LETHAL STRYKE
London Night Studios 1995

1 F:Stryke 3.00
2 O:Stryke 3.00
Ann. #1 EHr 3.00
Ann. #1 platinum edition 10.00

LETHAL STRIKE/ DOUBLE IMPACT: LETHAL IMPACT
London Night April 1996

1 by Jude Millien 3.00
1 limited 5.00
1 nude edition 6.00

LIBERTY PROJECT, THE
Eclipse 1987–88

1 I:Liberty Project 2.50
2 . . . . 1.75
3 V:Silver City Wranglers 1.75
4 . . . . 1.75
5 . . . . 1.75
6 F:Cimarron,"Misery and Gin" . . 1.75
7 I:Menace 1.75
8 V:Savage 1.75

LIDSVILLE
Gold Key Oct., 1972

1 . . . . 15.00
2 . . . . 7.00
3 and 4 . . . . @7.00
5 Oct., 1973 . . . . 7.00

LIEUTENANT, THE
Dell Publishing Co. April-June, 1962

1 Ph(c) 25.00

LIFE & ADVENTURES OF SANTA CLAUS
Tundra

GN MP,L.Frank Baum adapt. . . . 24.95

LIFE IN HELL
Blackthorne

1 3-D 2.50

LIFE WITH ARCHIE
Archie Publications Sept., 1958

1 . . . . 225.00

COLOR PUB.

2	100.00
3	60.00
4	60.00
5	60.00
6	30.00
7	30.00
8	30.00
9	30.00
10	30.00
11 thru 20	@20.00
21 thru 30	@15.00
31 thru 40	@10.00
41	7.00
42 B:Pureheart	5.00
43	5.00
44	5.00
45	5.00
46 O:Pureheart	15.00
47 thru 59	@3.50
60 thru 100	@2.50
101 thru 285	@1.00

The Light Fantastic #2
© Innovation

LIGHT FANTASTIC, THE
Innovation

1 Terry Pratchett adapt.	2.50
2 Adaptation continues	2.50
3 Adaptation continues	2.50
4 Adapt.conclusion	2.50

LIGHTNING COMICS PRESENTS
Lightning Comics

1 B&W Promo Ed.	3.50
1a B&W Promo Ed. Platinum	3.50
1b B&W Promo Ed. Gold	3.50

LILLITH: DEMON PRINCESS
Antarctic Press 1996

1 (of 3) from Warrior Nun Areala	2.95
2	2.95
3	2.95

LINDA LARK
Dell Publishing Co.
Oct.-Dec., 1961

1	15.00
2	8.00
3	8.00
4	8.00
5	8.00
6	8.00
7	8.00
8	8.00

LINUS, THE LIONHEARTED
Gold Key Sept., 1965

1	50.00

LIPPY THE LION AND HARDY HAR HAR
Gold Key March, 1963

1	50.00

LISA COMICS
Bongo Comics

1 F:Lisa Simpson	2.25

LITTLE AMBROSE
Archie Publications Sept., 1958

1	75.00

LITTLE ARCHIE
Archie Publications
1956

1	300.00
2	150.00
3	100.00
4	100.00
5	100.00
6 thru 10	@75.00
11 thru 20	@40.00
21 thru 30	@25.00
31 thru 40	@15.00
41 thru 60	@10.00
61 thru 80	@5.00
81 thru 100	@3.00
101 thru 180	@2.00

LITTLE ARCHIE MYSTERY
Archie Publications May, 1963

1	75.00
2 Oct., 1963	40.00

LITTLE AUDREY & MELVIN
Harvey Publications May, 1962

1	50.00
2 thru 5	@20.00
6 thru 10	@15.00
11 thru 20	@10.00
21 thru 40	@7.00
41 thru 50	@5.00
51 thru 53 52 pgs Giant size	@5.00
54 thru 60	@8.00
61 Dec., 1973	6.00

LITTLE AUDREY TV FUNTIME
Harvey Publications Sept., 1962

1 A:Richie Rich	35.00

2 same	20.00
3 same	15.00
4	15.00
5	15.00
6 thru 10	@6.00
11 thru 20	@5.00
21 thru 32	@3.50
33 Oct., 1971	3.50

LITTLE DOT DOTLAND
Harvey Publications July, 1962

1	50.00
2	25.00
3	22.00
4	18.00
5	18.00
6 thru 10	@10.00
11 thru 20	@7.00
21 thru 50	@3.50
51 thru 60	@2.50
61 Dec., 1973	2.50

LITTLE DOT'S UNCLES & AUNTS
Harvey Enterprises Oct., 1961

1	55.00
2	30.00
3	25.00
4	15.00
5	15.00
6 thru 10	@12.00
11 thru 20	@10.00
21 thru 40	@7.00
41 thru 51	@5.00
52 April, 1974	5.00

LITTLE LOTTA
Harvey Publications Nov., 1955

1 B:Richie Rich and Little Lotta	225.00
2	125.00
3	100.00
4	60.00
5	60.00
6	45.00
7	45.00
8	45.00
9	45.00
10	45.00
11 thru 20	@30.00
21 thru 40	@20.00
41 thru 60	@15.00
61 thru 80	@7.00
81 thru 99	@5.00
100 thru 103 52 pgs	@3.00
104 thru 120	@2.00
121 May, 1976	2.00

LITTLE LOTTA FOODLAND
Harvey Publications Sept., 1963

1 68 pgs	75.00
2	40.00
3	25.00
4	14.00
5	14.00
6 thru 10	@10.00
11 thru 20	@7.00
21 thru 26	@5.50
27	4.50
28	4.50
29 Oct., 1972	3.50

COLOR PUB.

LITTLE MERMAID
Walt Disney
1 based on movie	1.75
2 "Serpent Teen"	1.50
3 "Guppy Love"	1.50
4	1.50

The Little Monsters © Gold Key

LITTLE MONSTERS, THE
Gold Key Nov., 1964
1	20.00
2	10.00
3 thru 10	@7.00
11 thru 20	@3.00
21 thru 43	@2.00
44 Feb., 1978	2.00

LITTLE MONSTERS
Now
1 thru 6	@1.75

LITTLE REDBIRDS
1	2.50
2	2.50
3	2.50
4	2.50

LITTLE SAD SACK
Harvey Publications Oct., 1964
1 Richie Rich(c)	15.00
2	5.00
3	3.00
4	3.00
5	5.00
6 thru 19 Nov. 1967	@4.00

LITTLE STOOGES, THE
Gold Key Sept., 1972
1	10.00
2	5.00
3	5.00
4	5.00
5	5.00
6 and 7 March, 1974	@5.00

LLOYD LLEWELLYN
1	2.00

LOBO
Dell Publishing Co.
Dec., 1965
1	10.00
2	8.00

LOCKE
Blackthorne
1 PO.Jones	1.75
2 TD	2.25
3	1.25
4	1.25
5	1.25

LONE RANGER, THE
Gold Key Sept., 1964
1	30.00
2	15.00
3	10.00
4	10.00
5	10.00
6	8.00
7	8.00
8	8.00
9	8.00
10	8.00
11 thru 18	@7.00
18 thru 27	@5.00
28 March, 1977	5.00

LOST IN SPACE
Innovation
{based on TV series}
1 O:Jupiter II Project	3.00
2 "Cavern of IdyllicSummersLost"	2.75
2a Special Edition	2.50
3 Do Not Go Gently into that Good Night',Bill Mumy script	2.50
4 "People are Strange"	2.50
5 The Perils of Penelope	2.50
6 Time Warp	2.50
7 thru 9	@2.50
10 inc.Afterthought	2.50
11 F:Judy Robinson	2.50
12	2.95
13 Voyage to the Bottom of the Soul	2.95
14	2.50
15	2.50
16	2.50
Project Krell	2.50
Ann.#2	2.95
Special- Seduction of the Innocent	2.50
GN Strangers among Strangers	6.00

LOST PLANET
Eclipse 1987–88
1 BHa,I:Tyler FLynn	2.00
2 BHa,R:Amelia Earhart	1.75
3 BHa	1.25
4 BHa,"Devil's Eye"	1.25
5 BHa,A:Amelia Earhart	2.00
6	2.00

LOVECRAFT
Adventure Comics
1 "The Lurking Fear" adapt.	2.95
2 Beyond the Wall of Sleep	2.95
3	2.95
4	2.95

LOVE DIARY
Charlton Comics July, 1958
1	30.00
2	15.00
3	10.00
4	10.00
5	7.00
6	10.00
7 thru 10	@7.00
11 thru 15	@3.00
16 thru 20	@3.00
21 thru 40	@1.50
41 thru 101	@1.00
102 Dec., 1976	1.00

LUCY SHOW, THE
Gold Key June, 1963
1 Ph(c)	100.00
2 Ph(c)	60.00
3	50.00
4	50.00
5	50.00

LUDWIG VON DRAKE
Dell Publishing Co.
Nov.-Dec., 1961
1	25.00
2	15.00
3	15.00
4	15.00

LUGER
Eclipse 1986–87
1 TY,I:Luger,mini-series	2.00
2 TY	1.75
3 TY,BHa,V:Sharks	1.75

LUNATIC
1 and 2	@1.75

LUNATIC FRINGE
Innovation
1	1.95
2	1.75

LUNATIC FRINGE
Innovation
1	1.75

LYNCH MOB
Chaos! Comics
1 GCa(c), I:Mother Mayhem	3.00
2 Lynch Mob Loses	2.50
3 1994 Time Trip	2.50
3a Gold cover	3.00
4 Mother Mayhem at UN	2.50

LYNDON B. JOHNSON
Dell Publishing Co. March, 1965
1 Ph(c)	15.00

M
Eclipse 1990–91
1 thru 4 JMu	4.95

MACROSS
Comico
1	12.00

Becomes:
Robotech, The Macross Saga

COLOR PUB.

MAD FOLLIES
E.C. Comics
1963

(N#)	150.00
2 1964	100.00
3 1965	75.00
4 1966	85.00
5 1967	60.00
6 1968	50.00
7 1969	50.00

MAD HOUSE
Red Circle 1974–82

95 thru 97 Horror stories	@4.00
98 thru 130 Humor stories	@2.00
Annual #8 thru #11	@2.50

Madman 1 © Tundra

MADMAN
Tundra 1992

1	8.00
2	6.00
3	5.00

MADMAN ADVENTURES
Tundra 1992

1 R & N:Madman	4.50
2	3.50
3	3.25

MADRAVEN
HALLOWEEN SPECIAL
Hamilton Comics 1995

1 Song of the Silkies	2.95

MAD SPECIAL
E.C. Publications, Inc.
Fall, 1970

1	75.00
2	50.00
3	35.00
4 thru 8	@35.00
9 thru 13	@30.00
14	20.00
15	25.00
16	20.00
17	20.00

18	22.00
19 thru 21	@22.00
22 thru 31	@10.00
32	12.00
33 thru 58	@8.00

MAGE
Comico

1 MWg,I:Kevin Matchstick	13.00
2 MWg,I:Edsel	9.00
3 MWg,V:Umbra Sprite	5.00
4 MWg,V:Umbra Sprite	5.00
5 MWg,I:Sean (Spook)	5.00
6 MWg,Grendel begins	20.00
7 MWg,Grendel	9.00
8 MWg,Grendel	5.00
9 MWg,Grendel	5.00
10 MWg,Grendel,Styx	5.00
11 MWg,Grendel,Styx	5.00
12 MWg,D:Sean,Grendel	5.00
13 MWg,D:Edsel,Grendel	5.00
14 MWg,Grendel,O:Kevin	5.00
15 MWg,D:Umbra Sprite	5.00

MAGEBOOK
Comico

1 rep. Mage #1-4	8.95
2 rep. Mage #5-8	8.95

MAGIC FLUTE
Eclipse 1989

1 CR	4.95

MAGILLA GORILLA
Gold Key May, 1964

1	30.00
2 thru 10 Dec. 1968	@20.00

MAGILLA GORILLA
Charlton Comics Nov., 1970

1	50.00
2 thru 5	@25.00

MAGNUS:
ROBOT FIGHTER
Gold Key Feb., 1963

1 RM,I:Magnus,Teeja,A-1, I&B:Capt.Johner&aliens	250.00
2 RM,I:Sen.Zeremiah Clane	125.00
3 RM,I:Xyrkol	125.00
4 RM,I:Mekamn,Elzy	75.00
5 RM,The Immortal One	75.00
6 RM,I:Talpa	70.00
7 RM,I:Malev-6,ViXyrkol	85.00
8 RM,I:Outsiders(Chet, Horio, Toun, Malf)	70.00
9 RM, I:Madmot	70.00
10 RM,Mysterious Octo-Rob	70.00
11 RM,I:Danae,Neo-Animals	50.00
12 RM,The Volcano Makers	50.00
13 RM,I:Dr Lazlo Noel	55.00
14 RM,The Monster Robs	50.00
15 RM,I:Mogul Radur	50.00
16 RM,I:Gophs	50.00
17 RM,I:Zypex	50.00
18 RM,I:V'ril Trent	50.00
19 RM,Fear Unlimited	50.00
20 RM,I:Bunda the Great	50.00
21 RM, Space Spectre	50.00
22 Rep. #1	35.00
23 DSp,Mission Disaster	35.00
24 Pied Piper of North Am	35.00

25 The Micro Giants	35.00
26 The Venomous Vaper	35.00
27 Panic in Pacifica	35.00
28 Threats from the Depths	35.00
29 Rep. #7	16.00
30 Rep. #15	16.00
31 Rep. #14	16.00
32 Rep. #2	16.00
33 Rep. #21	16.00
34 Rep. #13	16.00
35 Rep. #6	16.00
36 Rep. #8	16.00
37 Rep. #11	16.00
38 Rep. #12	16.00
39 Rep. #16	16.00
40 Rep. #17	16.00
41 Rep. #18	16.00
42 Rep. #19	16.00
43 Rep. #20	16.00
44 Rep. #23	16.00
45 Rep. #24	16.00
46 Rep. #25	16.00

MAJOR DAMAGE
Invictus Studios

1 I:Major Damage	2.25
2 V:Godkin	2.25
3 First Contact Conclusion	2.25

MAKABRE
Apocalypse

1 Gangsters	3.95

MALICE
Heroic Publishing

1 I:Queen of the Dead	1.95

MANDRAKE
THE MAGICIAN
King Comics 1966

1	40.00
2	25.00
3	25.00
4 A:Girl Phantom	25.00
5 Cape Cod Caper	25.00
6	25.00
7 O:Lothar	25.00
8	30.00
9 A:Brick Bradford	25.00
10 A:Rip Kirby	30.00

MAN FROM PLANET X
Planet X Prod.

1	3.00

MAN FROM U.N.C.L.E.
Gold Key Feb., 1965

1 "The Explosive Affair"	150.00
2 "The Forthur Cookie Affair"	75.00
3 "The Deadly Devices Affair"	50.00
4 "The Rip Van Solo Affair"	50.00
5 "Ten Little Uncles Affair"	50.00
6 "The Three Blind Mice Affair"	50.00
7 "The Pixilated Puzzle Affair" I:Jet Dream (back-up begins)	55.00
8 "The Floating People Affair"	50.00
9 "Spirit of St.Louis Affair"	50.00
10 "The Trojan Horse Affair"	50.00
11 "Three-Story Giant Affair"	40.00
12 "Dead Man's Diary Affair"	40.00
13 "The Flying Clowns Affair"	40.00
14 "Great Brain Drain Affair"	40.00

COLOR PUB.

Man From U.N.C.L.E. #10 © Gold Key

15 "The Animal Agents Affair" . . 40.00
16 "Instant Disaster Affair" 40.00
17 "The Deadly Visions Affair" . . 40.00
18 "The Alien Affair" 40.00
19 "Knight in Shining Armor Affair" 40.00
20 "Deep Freeze Affair" 40.00
21 rep. #10 . . . . 35.00
22 rep. #7 . . . . 35.00

MAN FROM U.N.C.L.E.
Entertainment
1 thru 11 . . . . 1.50

MAN FROM U.N.C.L.E.
Millennium
1 The Birds of Prey Affair,pt.1 . . . 2.95
2 The Birds of Prey Affair,pt.2 . . . 2.95

MANGA SHI 2000
Crusade Entertainment 1997
1 (of 3) BiT, "Final Jihad" flip-book
   Shi: Heaven and Earth 2.95
2 BiT, flip-book Tomoe:
   Unforgettable Fire preview . . . 2.95
3 BiT, conclusion 2.95

MANGLE TANGLE TALES
Innovation
1 . . . . 2.95

MANIFEST DESTINY
1 . . . . 1.95

MAN IN BLACK
Harvey Publications Sept., 1957
1 . . . . 75.00
2 . . . . 45.00
3 . . . . 45.00
4 March, 1958 . . . . 45.00

MANIK
Millenium/Expand (1995)
1 I:Macedon, Arsenal,Cardinal . . 2.95

MAN OF WAR
Eclipse 1987–88
1 thru 3 . . . . @1.75

MARK RAND'S SKY TECHNOLOGIES INC.
Red Mercenary 1995
1 I:Jae,Elliot,Firnn 2.95

MARKSMAN, THE
Hero Graphics
1 O:Marksman, Pt.#1 . . . . 1.95
2 O:Marksman, Pt.#2 . . . . 1.95
3 O:Marksman ends.I:Basilisk . . . 1.95
4 A:Flare 1.95
5 I:Radar,Sonar 1.95
Ann. #1, A:Champions 1.95

MARRIED... WITH CHILDREN
Now
1 . . . . 6.00
1a 2nd printing 2.00
2 . . . . 4.00
3 . . . . 3.00
4 . . . . 2.50
5 . . . . 2.50
6 . . . . 2.00
7 . . . . 2.50

[2nd Series]
1 Peg-Host of Radio Show 2.25
2 The Bundy Invention 1.95
3 Psychodad,(photo cover) 1.95
4 Mother-In-Law,(photo cover) . . 1.95
5 Bundy the Crusader 1.95
6 Bundy J: The Order of the Mighty
   Warthog 1.95
7 Kelly the VJ 1.95
Spec. 1.95
3-D Spec. 2.50

MARRIED WITH CHILDREN: DYSFUNCTIONAL FAMILY
Now
1 I:The Bundies 2.50
2 TV Appearance 2.50
3 Morally Pure Bundys 2.50

MARRIED WITH CHILDREN: FLASHBACK SPECIAL
Now
1 Peg and Al's first date 1.95
2 and 3 . . . . @1.95

MARRIED WITH CHILDREN: KELLY BUNDY SPECIAL
Now
1 with poster 1.95
2 and 3 with poster . . . . @1.95

MARRIED... WITH CHILDREN: QUANTUM QUARTET
Now
1 thru 4 Fantastic Four parody   @1.95

Fall 1994 Spec., flip book 1.95

MARRIED WITH CHILDREN 2099
Mirage
1 thru 3 Cable Parody . . . . @2.50

MARS
First
1 thru 12 . . . . @1.25

MARS ATTACKS
Topps
1 KG(s) 6.00
2 . . . . 4.00
3 thru 6 KG(s) 4.00
[Series 2] 1995
1 Counterstrike 3.50
2 Counterstrike,pt.2 . . . . 2.95
3 Counterstrike,pt.3 . . . . 2.95
4 Counterstrike,pt.4 Convictions . 2.95
5 Counterstrike concl. 2.95
6 "The Rescue of Janice Brown,"
   pt. 1 . . . . 2.95
7 "The Rescue of Janice Brown,"
   pt. 2 . . . . 2.95
8 . . . . 2.95
Spec. Baseball 3.00

MARS ATTACKS HIGH SCHOOL
Topps 1997
Spec. #1 (of 2) BSz(c) 2.95
Spec. #2 . . . . 2.95

MARS ATTACKS THE SAVAGE DRAGON
Topps
1 . . . . 3.00
2 . . . . 3.00
3 . . . . 3.00
4 (of 4) 3.00

MARSHAL LAW: HATEFUL DEAD
Apocalypse
1 "Rise of the Zombies" 5.95

MARTIANS!!! IN 3-D
1 . . . . 2.00

MARY WORTH
ARGO March, 1956
1 . . . . 40.00

MASKED MAN
Eclipse 1985–88
1 . . . . 3.00
2 . . . . 2.00
3 . . . . 2.00
4 . . . . 2.00
5 . . . . 2.00
6 V:Roxie Lamada 2.00
7 . . . . 2.00
8 "Roxy" 1.75
9 W:Dick and Maggie 1.75
10 . . . . 2.00

COLOR PUB.

MASTERWORK SERIES
Seagate DC
1 FFrep.DC,ShiningKnight	1.50
2 FFrep.DC,ShiningKnight	1.50
3 BWr,Horror DC rep.	1.50

MAVERICK
Dell Publishing Co. April, 1958
1 Ph(c) all	275.00
2 Ph(c)	125.00
3 Ph(c)	125.00
4 Ph(c)	125.00
5 Ph(c)	125.00
6 Ph(c)	85.00
7 Ph(c)	85.00
8 Ph(c)	85.00
9 Ph(c)	85.00
10 Ph(c)	85.00
11 Ph(c)	85.00
12 Ph(c)	85.00
13 Ph(c)	85.00
14 Ph(c)	85.00
15 thru 19 Ph(c)	85.00

MAVERICK MARSHALL
Charlton Comics Nov., 1958
1	25.00
2	15.00
3	15.00
4	15.00
5	15.00
6	15.00
7 May, 1960	15.00

MAVERICKS
Dagger
1 PuD,RkL, I:Mavericks	2.50
2 PuD,RkL	2.50

MAXIMORTAL
King Hell/Tundra
1 RV,A:True-Man	4.50
2 Crack in the New World	4.25
3 RV,Secret of the Manhattan Project revealed	4.25
4	4.25
5 A:True Man	3.25
6 A:El Guano	3.25

MAYA
Gold Key March, 1968
1	15.00

MAZE AGENCY
Comico
1 O:Maze Agency	3.00
2	2.50
3	2.50
4	2.50
5	2.50
6	2.50
7	2.75
8	1.95
9	1.95
10	1.95
11	1.95
12	2.50
13 thru 15	@1.95
16 thru 23	@2.50
Spec. #1	2.75

McHALE'S NAVY
Dell Publishing Co.
May-July, 1963
1 Ph(c)	45.00
2 Ph(c)	30.00
3 Ph(c)	30.00

McKEEVER & THE COLONEL
Dell Publishing Co.
Feb.-April, 1963
1 Ph(c)	35.00
2 Ph(c)	25.00
3 Ph(c)	25.00

M.D. GEIST
CPM
1 Cartoon Adaptation	2.95
2 J:Army	2.95
3 V:Final Terminator	2.95

MECHANICS
Fantagraphics
1 HB,rep.Love & Rockets	3.00
2 HB,rep.Love & Rockets	2.50
3 HB,rep.Love & Rockets	2.50

MEDIA STARR
Innovation
1 thru 3	@1.95

MEGALITH
Continuity
1 MT	6.00
2 MT	4.00
3 MT, Painted issue	2.50
4 NA,TVE	2.50
5 NA,TVE	2.50
6 MN	2.50
7 MN	2.50
8	2.50
9 SDr(i)	2.50
10	2.50
[2nd Series, Deathwatch 2000]	
0 Deathwatch 2000 prologue	5.00
1 Deathwatch 2000 Pt.5,w/card	2.50
2 Deathwatch 2000 Pt.10,w/card	2.50
3 pt.16,Indestructible(c),w/card	2.50
4 and 5 Rise of Magic	@2.50
6 and 7	2.50

MEGATON
1	1.50

Entity Comics
Holiday Spec. w/card	2.95

MEGATON EXPLOSION
1 RLd,AMe,I:Youngblood preview	25.00

MEGATON MAN
Kitchen Sink
1 Don Simpson art, I:Megaton Man	6.00
1a rep. B&W	2.00
2	4.00
3 and 4	@3.00
5	2.50
6 Border Worlds	2.50
7 Border Worlds	2.50
8 Border Worlds	2.50
9 Border Worlds	2.50
10 final issue, 1986	2.50

MELTING POT
Kitchen Sink
1	4.00
2 and 3	@2.95
4	3.50

MELVIN MONSTER
Dell Publishing Co.
April-June, 1965
1	125.00
2	75.00
3	75.00
4	75.00
5	75.00
6	75.00
7	75.00
8	75.00
9	75.00
10	75.00

Memories #1 © Epic

[Katshuiro Otomo's] MEMORIES
Epic 1992
1	2.50

MEN FROM EARTH
Future Fun
1 based on Matt Mason toy	6.50

MERCENARY
NBM
The Voyage	10.95
The Black Globe	9.95
The Fortress	9.95

MERCHANTS OF DEATH
Eclipse 1988
1 King's Castle, The Hero	3.50
2 King's Castle,Soldiers of Fortune	3.50
3 Ransom, Soldier of Fortune	3.50
4 ATh(c),Ransom, Men o/t Legion	3.50
5 Ransom,New York City Blues	3.50

MERLIN REALM
Blackthorne
1 3-D	2.50

COLOR PUB.

META 4
First
1 IG	3.95
2 IG	2.25
3 IG/JSon,FinalMonthly	2.25

METAL MILITIA
Entity Comics 1995
1 I:Metal Militia	2.50
1a with Video Game	6.95
2 ICO	2.50
3 F:Detective Calahan	2.50
Ashcan	2.50

MICHAELANGELO
Mirage
1 TMNT Character	15.00

MICKEY & DONALD
Gladstone
1 1449 Firestone	8.00
2	4.00
3 Man of Tomorrow	3.00
4	2.50
5	2.50
6	2.50
7	2.50
8	2.50
9	2.50
10	2.00
11	2.00
12	2.00
13	2.00
14	2.00
15	2.00
16 giant-size	2.50
17	3.00
18	4.00

Becomes:
DONALD AND MICKEY
19 thru 26	@1.50

MICKEY MANTLE COMICS
Magnum
1 JSt,Rise to Big Leagues	1.75

MICKEY MOUSE
Gladstone
219 FG,Seven Ghosts	6.00
220 FG,Seven Ghosts	7.00
221 FG,Seven Ghosts	7.00
222 FG,Editor in Grief	5.00
223 FG,Editor in Grief	4.00
224 FG,Crazy Crime Wave	3.00
225 FG,Crazy Crime Wave	3.00
226 FG,Captive Castaways	3.00
227 FG,Captive Castaways	3.00
228 FG,Captive Castaways	3.00
229 FG,Bat Bandit	3.00
230 FG,Bat Bandit	2.50
231 FG,Bobo the Elephant	2.50
232 FG,Bobo the Elephant	2.50
233 FG,Pirate Submarine	2.50
234 FG,Pirate Submarine	2.50
235 FG,Photo Racer	2.50
236 FG,Photo Racer	2.50
237 FG,Race for Riches	2.50
238 FG,Race for Riches	2.50
239 FG,Race for Riches	2.50
240 FG,March of Comics	2.50
241 FG	4.00
242 FG	2.50
243 FG	2.50
244 FG,60th Anniv	5.00
245 FG	2.25
245 FG	2.25
246 FG	2.25
247 FG	2.25
248 FG	2.25
249 FG	5.00
250 FG	2.25
251 FG	2.25
252 FG	2.25
253 FG	2.25
254 FG	2.25
255 FG	4.00
256 FG	4.00

Mickey Mouse #1 © Walt Disney

MICKEY MOUSE
Walt Disney 1990
1 "The Phantom Gondolier"	3.50
2	3.00
3	2.50
4	2.50
5	2.50
6	2.00
7 Phantom Blot	2.00
8 Phantom Blot	2.00
9	2.00
10 Sky Adventure	2.00
11 When Mouston Freezes Over	2.00
12 Hail & Farewell	2.00
13 "What's Shakin'"	2.00
14 Mouseton,Eagle-Landing	2.00
15 "Lost Palace of Kashi"	2.00
16 "Scoundrels in Space"	2.00
17 "Sound of Blunder" Pt.1	1.75
18 "Sound of Blunder" Pt.2	1.75
19 50th Ann. Fantasia Celebration Sorcerer's Apprentice adapt	1.50

MICKEY SPILLANE'S MIKE DANGER
Tekno Comix 1995
1 I:Mike Danger	2.25
2 Underside of the City	1.95
3 Judicial System	1.95
4 Mike's First Job	1.95
5 Old New York	1.95
6 Sin Syndicate Leader	2.25

7 thru 11	@2.25

Big Entertainment 1996
1	2.25
2	2.25
3 MCn,PGr,TBe,EB	2.25
4	2.25
5 "Time Heels"	2.25
6 TBe,"Paradox Rule"	2.25
7 TBe,"Red Menace," pt.1	2.25
8 TBe,"Red Menace," pt.2	2.25
9 TBe,"Red Menace," pt.3.	2.25
10 TBe,"Red Menace," concl.	2.25

MICROBOTS, THE
Gold Key Dec., 1971
1	5.00

MIDNIGHT EYE: GOKU PRIVATE INVESTIGATOR
Viz
1 A.D. 2014: Tokyo city	5.25
2 V:Hakuryu,A:Yoko	4.95
3 A:Ryoko,Search for Ryu	4.95
4 Goku vs. Ryu	4.95
5 Leilah Abducted	4.95
6 Lisa's I.D. discovered	4.95

MIGHTY COMICS
{Prev: Flyman}
40 A:Web	12.00
41 A:Shield, Black Hood	10.00
42 A:Black Hood	10.00
43 A:Shield, Black Hood,Web	9.00
44 A:Black Hood, Steel Sterling Shield	9.00
45 Shield-Black Hood team-up O:Web	9.00
46 A:Steel Sterling, Black Hood, Web	9.00
47 A:Black Hood & Mr.Justice	9.00
48 A:Shield & Hangman	9.00
49 Steel Sterling-Black Hood team up, A:Fox	9.00

[ALL NEW ADVENTURES OF] THE MIGHTY CRUSADERS
Red Circle
[1st Series] 1983
1 O:Shield (Joe Higgins & Bill Higgins)	25.00
2 MSy,O:Comet	20.00
3 O:Fly-Man	15.00
4 A:Fireball,Jaguar,Web,Fox, Blackjack Hangman & more Golden Age Archie Heroes	18.00
5 I:Ultra-Men&TerrificThree	15.00

Archie Publications
6 V:Maestro,A:Steel Sterling	12.00
7 O:Fly-Girl,A:Steel Sterling	12.00

[2nd Series]
1 RB,R:Joe Higgins & Lancelot Strong as the SHIELD, Mighty Crusaders, A:Mr.Midnight	1.50
2 RB,V:Brain Emperor & Eterno	1.50
3 RB,I:Darkling	1.50
4 DAy,TD	1.50
5	1.00
6 DAy,TD,Shield	1.00
7	1.00
8	1.00
9 Trial of the Shield	1.00
10	1.00

COLOR PUB.

11 DAy,D:Gold Age Black Hood, I:
Riot Squad, series based on toy
lines 1.00
12 DAy,I:She-Fox 1.00
13 Last issue 1.00

MIGHTY HERCULES, THE
Gold Key July, 1963
1 . . . . 65.00
2 . . . . 60.00

MIGHTY MORPHIN POWER RANGERS
Hamilton
1 From TV Series 2.75
2 Switcheroo 2.50
3 . . . . 2.25
4 F:White Ranger 1.95
5 F:Pink Ranger 1.95
6 V:Garganturon 1.95
TPB Re. #1-#6 photo (c) 9.95
[Series 2]
1 Unstoppable Force 1.95
2 V:Mechanical Octopus 1.95
3 . . . . 1.95
4 Lost Ranger 1.95
[Series 3] 1995
1 O:Green Ranger 1.95
2 O:Green Ranger 1.95
3 I:New Megazords 1.95

MIGHTY MOUSE
Spotlight 1987
1 FMc,PC(c) 1.50
2 FMc,CS(c) 1.50
1 Holiday Special 1.75

MIGHTY MUTANIMALS
Archie Publications
[Mini-Series]
1 Cont.from TMNT Adventures#19,
A:Raphael, Man Ray,
Leatherhead, Mondo
Gecko,Deadman, Wingnut &
Screwloose 1.25
2 V:Mr.Null,Malinga,Soul and Bean
and the Malignoid Army 1.25
3 Alien Invasion help off, Raphael
returns to Earth 1.25
4 "Days of Future Past" 1.25
5 "Into the Sun" 1.25
6 V:Null & 4 Horsemen Pt#2 . . . 1.25
7 Jaws of Doom 1.50
Spec.#1 rep. all #1-3 +SBi pin-ups 2.95

MIGHTY MUTANIMALS
Archie
1 Quest for Jagwar's Mother . . . 1.25
2 V:Snake Eyes 1.25
3 . . . . 1.25
4 "Days of Future Past" 1.25
5 "Into the Sun" 1.25
6 V:Null & 4 Horsemen Pt#2 . . . 1.25
7 Jaws of Doom 1.50

MIGHTY SAMSON
Gold Key 1964–82
1 O:Mighty Samson 40.00
2 . . . . 15.00
3 . . . . 15.00
4 . . . . 15.00
5 . . . . 15.00

6 thru 10 . . . . @12.00
11 thru 20 . . . . @10.00
21 thru 32 . . . . @5.00

MIKE GRELL'S SABLE
First
1 thru 8 rep. . . . . @1.75
9 . . . . 1.75
10 Triptych 1.75

MIKE SHAYNE PRIVATE EYE
Dell Publishing Co.
Nov.-Jan., 1961-62
1 . . . . 25.00
2 . . . . 12.00
3 . . . . 12.00

MILLENNIUM INDEX
Independent Comics 1988
1 . . . . 2.00
2 . . . . 2.00

MILTON THE MONSTER & FEARLESS FLY
Gold Key May, 1966
1 . . . . 55.00

Miracleman #4 © Eclipse

MIRACLEMAN
Eclipse 1985–94
1 R:Miracleman 5.00
2 AD,Moore,V:Kid Miracleman . . 4.00
3 AD,Moore,V:Big Ben 4.00
4 AD,Moore,R:Dr.Gargunza . . . 4.00
5 AD,Moore,O:Miracleman 4.00
6 Moore,V:Miracledog, D:Evelyn
Cream 4.00
7 Moore,D:Dr.Gargunza 4.00
8 Moore 4.00
9 RV,Moore,Birth of Miraclebaby . 4.50
10 JRy,RV,Moore 4.00
11 JTo,Moore,Book III,
I:Miraclewoman 5.00
12 thru 14 Moore 5.00
15 Moore 12.00
16 thru 23 . . . . @4.00

24 BWS(c),NGa(s) 5.00
25 thru 28 . . . . @2.95
3-D Special #1 . . . . 2.75
Graphic Albums
HC Book 1 A Dream of Flying . . 29.95
TPB Book 1,A Dream of Flying . . 9.95
HC Book 2 The Red Kings
Syndrome 30.95
TPB Book 2 The Red Kings
Syndrome 9.95
HC Book 3 Olympus 30.95
TPB Book 3 Olympus 12.00

MIRACLEMAN APOCRYPHA
Eclipse 1991–92
1 inc."Rascal Prince" 2.50
2 Miracleman, Family Stories . . . 2.50
3 . . . . 2.50

MIRACLEMAN FAMILY
Eclipse 1988
1 British Rep.,A:Kid Miracleman . 1.95
2 Alan Moore (s) 1.95

MIRACLE SQUAD, THE
Upshot/Fantagraphics 1986
1 Hollywood 30's 2.00
2 . . . . 2.00
3 . . . . 2.00
4 . . . . 2.00

MISS FURY
Adventure Comics
1 O:Cat Suit 2.50
2 Miss Fury impersonator 2.50
3 A:Three Miss Fury's 2.50
4 conclusion 2.50

MISSION IMPOSSIBLE
Dell Publishing Co. May, 1967
1 Ph(c) 100.00
2 Ph(c) 60.00
3 Ph(c) 50.00
4 Ph(c) 50.00
5 Ph(c) 50.00

MISSIONS IN TIBET
Dimension Comics 1995
1 I:New Series 2.50
2 F:Orlando,Ting,Alex 2.50
3 Two Worlds Collide 2.50
4 V:Sada 2.50

MISS PEACH
(& SPECIAL ISSUES)
Dell Publishing Co. 1963
1 . . . . 50.00

MR. AND MRS. J. EVIL SCIENTIST
Gold Key Nov., 1963
1 . . . . 40.00
2 . . . . 25.00
3 . . . . 25.00
4 . . . . 25.00

MR. JIGSAW
Spec. #1 . . . . 1.75

COLOR PUB.

MR. MONSTER
Eclipse 1985–87
1 I:Mr. Monster	9.00
2 DSt(c)	5.00
3 V:Dr. NoZone	3.50
4 "Trapped in Dimension X"	3.00
5 V:Flesh-eating Amoebo	3.00
6 KG,SD,reprints	3.00
7	3.00
8 V:Monster in the Atomic Telling Machine	3.00
9 V:Giant Clams	3.00
10 R:Dr.No Zone, 3-D	2.00

MR. MONSTER ATTACKS
Tundra
1 DGb,SK,short stories	4.25
2 SK,short stories cont.	4.25
3 DGb,last issue	4.25

MR. MONSTER SUPERDUPER SPECIAL
Eclipse 1986–87
1	2.50
2	2.00
3	2.00
4	2.00
5	2.00
6	2.00
Hi-Voltage Super Science	2.00
3-D Spec. Hi-Octane Horror,JKu, "Touch of Death" reprint	1.75
Triple Treat	3.95

MR. MONSTER TRUE CRIME
Eclipse
1	1.75
2	1.75
3-D Spec. #1	2.00

MR. MUSCLES
Charlton Comics 1956
22	25.00
23	25.00

MR. MYSTIC
Eclipse
1	2.00
2	2.00
3	2.00

MR. T AND THE T FORCE
Now
1 NA,R:Mr.T,V:Street Gangs	2.50
1a Gold Ed.	10.00
2 NA,V:Demons	2.25
3 NBy,w/card	2.25
4 NBy,In Urban America	2.25
5 thru 10, with card	@2.25

MISTER X
Vortex
1 HB	8.00
2 HB	5.00
3 HB	3.50
4 HB	3.00
5	3.00
6 thru 10	@2.50
11 thru 13	@2.00

14	2.25

The Mod Squad #1 © Dell Publishing

MOD SQUAD
Dell Publishing Co. 1969–71
1	35.00
2	18.00
3	18.00
4	18.00
5 thru 8	@18.00

MOD WHEELS
Gold Key 1971–76
1	10.00
2 thru 18	@5.00
19	4.00

MONKEE'S, THE
Dell Publishing Co. 1967
1 Ph(c)	80.00
2 Ph(c)	40.00
3 Ph(c)	40.00
4 Ph(c)	40.00
5	30.00
6 Ph(c)	40.00
7 Ph(c)	40.00
8	30.00
9	30.00
10 Ph(c)	40.00
11 thru 17	30.00

MONOLITH
Comico
1 From Elementals	2.50
2 "Seven Levels of Hell"	2.50
3 "Fugue and Variation"	2.50
4 "Fugue and Variation"	2.50

MONROE'S, THE
Dell Publishing Co. April, 1967
1 Ph(c)	15.00

MONSTER MASSACRE
Atomeka
1 SBs, DBr,DGb	8.50
1a Black Edition	35.00

MOONWALKER IN 3-D
Blackthorne
1 thru 3	@2.50

MORBID ANGEL
London Night
½ Angel's Tear, signed	10.00

MORBID ANGEL: PENANCE
London Night
Revised Color Spec., double size	4.00

MORLOCK 2001
Atlas Feb.–July 1975
1 thru 3 F:Midnight Men	@1.00

MORNINGSTAR
Spec. #1	2.50

MOTORBIKE PUPPIES
Dark Zulu Lies
1 I:Motorbike Puppies	2.50

MOVIE COMICS
Gold Key/Whitman Oct., 1962
Alice in Wonderland	30.00
Aristocats	75.00
Bambi 1	30.00
Bambi 2	25.00
Beneath the Planet of the Apes	40.00
Big Red	25.00
Blackbeard's Ghost	25.00
Buck Rogers Giant Movie Edition	22.00
Bullwhip Griffin	35.00
Captain Sinbad	50.00
Chitty, Chitty Bang Bang	45.00
Cinderella	45.00
Darby O'Gill & the Little People	45.00
Dumbo	25.00
Emil & the Detectives	30.00
Escapade in Florence	75.00
Fall of the Roman Empire	30.00
Fantastic Voyage	45.00
55 Days at Peking	30.00
Fighting Prince of Donegal	25.00
First Men of the Moon	30.00
Gay Purr-ee	30.00
Gnome Mobile	25.00
Goodbye, Mr. Chips	30.00
Happiest Millionaire	25.00
Hey There, It's Yogi Bear	40.00
Horse Without a Head	20.00
How the West Was Won	35.00
In Search of the Castaways	60.00
Jungle Book, The	35.00
Kidnapped	25.00
King Kong	30.00
King Kong N#	10.00
Lady and the Tramp	30.00
Lady and the Tramp 1	45.00
Lady and the Tramp 2	20.00
Legend of Lobo, The	25.00
Lt. Robin Crusoe	20.00
Lion, The	25.00
Lord Jim	25.00
Love Bug, The	25.00
Mary Poppins	45.00
Mary Poppins 1	65.00
McLintock	100.00
Merlin Jones as the Monkey's Uncle	45.00

COLOR PUB.

Miracle of the White Stallions	25.00
Misadventures of Merlin Jones	45.00
Moon-Spinners, The	60.00
Mutiny on the Bounty	30.00
Nikki, Wild Dog of the North	20.00
Old Yeller	25.00
One Hundred & One Dalmations	25.00
Peter Pan 1	30.00
Peter Pan 2	25.00
P.T. 109	45.00
Rio Conchos	40.00
Robin Hood	25.00
Shaggy Dog & the Absent-Minded Professor	45.00
Snow White & the Seven Dwarfs	25.00
Son of Flubber	25.00
Summer Magic	55.00
Swiss Family Robinson	25.00
Sword in the Stone	50.00
That Darn Cat	50.00
Those Magnificent Men in Their Flying Machines	30.00
Three Stooges in Orbt	90.00
Tiger Walks, A	40.00
Toby Tyler	25.00
Treasure Island	25.00
20,000 Leagues Under the Sea	25.00
Wonderful Adventures of Pinocchio	25.00
X, the Man with the X-Ray Eyes	70.00
Yellow Submarine	225.00

MS. MYSTIC
Pacific
1 NA,Origin	8.00
2 NA,Origin,I:Urth 4	6.00

Continuity
1 NA,Origin rep.	2.00
2 NA,Origin,I:Urth 4 rep	2.00
3 NA,New material	2.00
4 TSh	2.00
5 DT	2.00
6	2.00
7	2.00
8 CH/Sdr,B:Love Story	2.00
9 DB	2.00
9a Newsstand(c)	2.00

[3rd Series]
1 O:Ms.Mystic	2.50
2 A:Hybrid	2.50
3	2.50
4	2.50

[4th Series, Deathwatch 2000]
1 Deathwatch 2000 pt.8,w/card	2.50
2 Deathwatch 2000 w/card	2.50
3 Indestructible cover, w/card	2.50

MS. TREE'S THRILLING DETECTIVE ADVENTURES
Eclipse 1983
1 Miller pin up	4.00
2	2.50
3	2.00

Becomes:
MS. TREE 1984–89
4 thru 6	@2.00
7	2.50
8	8.00
9	2.00

Aardvark–Vanaheim
10	2.00

Renegade
1 3-D	2.00

MS. VICTORY GOLDEN ANNIVERSARY
AC Comics
1 Ms.Victory celebration	5.00

MS. VICTORY SPECIAL
AC Comics
1	1.75

The Mummy, or Ramses the Damned #11 © Millennium

MUMMY, OR RAMSES THE DAMNED, THE
Millenium 1992
1 Anne Rice Adapt.	5.00
2 JM,"Mummy in Mayfair"	3.75
3 JM	3.25
4 JM, To Egypt	3.00
5 JM"The Mummy's Hand"	2.50
6 JM 20th Century Egypt	2.50
7 JM,More Ramses Past Revealed	2.50
8 JM,Hunt for Cleopatra	2.50
9 JM,Cleopatra's Wrath contd.	2.50
10 JM,Subterranian World	2.50
11 JM	2.50

MUMMY ARCHIVES
Millenium
1.JM,Features,articles	2.50

MUNDEN'S BAR ANNUAL
First
1 BB,JOy,JSn,SR	2.95

MUNSTERS, THE
Gold Key 1965–68
1	200.00
2	100.00
3 thru 5	@75.00
6 thru 16	@70.00

MUPPET BABIES
Harvey
1 Return of Muppet Babies	1.25

MUTANTS & MISFITS
Silverline
1 thru 4	@1.95

MY FAVORITE MARTIAN
Gold Key 1964–66
1	150.00
2	75.00
3 thru 9	@60.00

MY LITTLE MARGIE
Charlton Comics 1954–65
1 Ph(c)	175.00
2 Ph(c)	100.00
3	50.00
4	50.00
5	50.00
6	50.00
7	50.00
8	50.00
9	45.00
10	30.00
11	15.00
12	15.00
13	30.00
14 thru 19	@25.00
20	50.00
21 thru 35	@15.00
36 thru 53	@10.00
54 Beatles (c)	100.00

MYSTERIES OF UNEXPLORED WORLDS/ SON OF VULCAN
Charlton Comics 1956
1	200.00
2	75.00
3	125.00
4 SD	135.00
5 SD,SD(c)	150.00
6 SD	150.00
7	155.00
8 SD	150.00
9 SD	150.00
10 SD,SD(c)	155.00
11 SD,SD(c)	155.00
12	100.00
13 thru 18	@30.00
19 SD(c)	80.00
20	30.00
21 thru 24 SD	@90.00
25	20.00
26 SD	90.00
27 thru 30	@20.00
31 thru 45	@15.00
46 I:Son ofVulcan,Dr.Kong(1965)	20.00
47 V:King Midas	12.00
48 V:Captain Tuska	12.00

Becomes:
SON OF VULCAN
49 DC redesigns costume	6.00
50 V:Dr.Kong	5.00

MYSTERIOUS SUSPENSE
Charlton 1968
1 SD,F:Question	35.00

MYSTERY COMICS DIGEST
Gold Key March, 1972–75
1 WW	10.00

COLOR PUB.

2 WW	8.00
3	4.00
4 Ripleys Believe It or Not	3.00
5 Boris Karloff	3.50
6 Twilight Zone	3.00
7 thru 20	@3.00
21 thru 26	@2.00

MYSTIC ISLE
1	1.95

NANCY & SLUGGO
Dell Publishing Co. 1957
146 B:Peanuts	30.00
147	20.00
148	20.00
149	20.00
150 thru 161	20.00
162 thru 165	30.00
166 thru 176 A:OONA	35.00
177 thru 180	30.00
181 thru 187	15.00

NATIONAL VELVET
Dell Publishing Co.
May-July, 1961
1 Ph(c)	35.00
2 Ph(c)	30.00

NEAT STUFF
Fantagraphics
1	4.50
2	3.00
3 thru 5	@2.50
6	2.25
7	2.25

NECROPOLIS
Fleetway
1 SBs(c),CE,A:Dark Judges/ Sisters Of Death	2.95
2	2.95
3 thru 9	@2.95

NEIL GAIMAN'S LADY JUSTICE
Tekno Comix (1995)
1 I:Lady Justice	2.50
1a	6.00
2 V:Blood Pirate	1.95
3 V:Blood Pirate	1.95
4 New Story Arc	1.95
5 Street Gang War	1.95
6 Street Gang War	2.25
7 thru 11	@2.25
Big Entertainment April 1996	
1 thru 4	@2.25
5 DIB(s)	2.25
6 DIB(s),"Woman About Town," pt.1	2.25
7 DIB(s),"Woman About Town," pt.2	2.25
8 DIB(s),"Woman About Town," pt.3	2.25

NEIL GAIMAN'S MR. HERO THE NEWMATIC MAN
Tekno-Comics 1994
1 I:Mr. Hero, Tecknophage	2.50
2 A:Tecknophage	2.25
3 I:Adam Kaine	1.95
4 I:New Body	1.95
5 Earthquake	1.95

6 I:New Character	1.95
7 I:Deadbolt, Bloodboil	1.95
8 V:Avatar	1.95
9 in London	1.95
10 V:Demon	1.95
11 V:Monster	1.95
12 The Great Goward	2.25
13 thru 17	@2.25

NEIL GAIMAN'S PHAGE
Tekno-Comics 1996
1	2.25

NEIL GAIMAN'S PHAGE: SHADOW DEATH
Big Entertainment
1 thru 4	@2.25
5 O:Orlando Holmes,A:Lady Messalina	2.25
6 conclusion	2.25

NEIL GAIMAN'S TECKNOPHAGE
Teckno-Comics 1995
1 I:Kalighoul, Tom Vietch	1.95
1a Steel Edition	3.95
2 F:Mayor of New Yorick	1.95
3 Phange Building	1.95
4 Horde eevils	1.95
5 Middle Management	1.95
6 Escape from Phange	1.95
7 Mecca	2.25

NEIL GAIMAN'S WHEEL OF WORLDS
Teckno-Comics 1995
0 Deluxe Edition w/Posters	2.95
0a I:Lady Justice	1.95
1	3.25

NEMESIS THE WARLOCK
Eagle
1	2.00
2 thru 8	@1.50

NEW ADVENTURES OF FELIX THE CAT
Felix Comics,Inc
1 New stories	2.25
2 "The Magic Paint Brush"	2.25

NEW ADVENTURES OF PINNOCCIO
Dell Publishing Co. 1962
1	75.00
2 and 3	@60.00

NEW ADVENTURES OF SPEED RACER
Now
0 Premiere, 3-D cover	1.95
1 thru 11	@1.95

NEW AMERICA
Eclipse 1987-88
1 A:Scout	1.75
2 A:Scout	1.75

3 A:Roman Catholic Pope	1.75
4 A:Scout	1.75

NEW BREED
Pied Piper
1	2.75
2	2.25

NEW CHAMPIONS
1	2.95
2	2.95

New DNAgents #6 © Eclipse

NEW DNAGENTS, THE
Eclipse 1985-87
1 R:DNAgents	1.50
2 F:Tank	1.00
3 Repopulating the World	1.00
4 Major Catastrophe for Earth	1.00
5 "Last Place on Earth"	1.00
6 JOy(c),"Postscript"	1.00
7 V:Venimus	1.00
8 DSp,V:Venimus	1.00
9 V:Venimus,I:New Wave	1.00
10 I:New Airboy	1.00
11 Summer Fun Issue	1.25
12 V:Worm	1.25
13 EL,F:Tank	1.25
14 EL,Nudity,"Grounded"	1.25
15 thru 17	@1.25
3-D #1	2.50

NEW JUSTICE MACHINE
Innovation
1	1.95
2	1.95
3	2.50

NEWMEN
Maximum Press
1–22 see Image
23 ErS,CSp,AG,"Anthem," pt.3	2.50
24 ErS,CSp,AG,"Anthem," pt.4	2.50
25 ErS,CSp,AG,"Anthem," pt.5	2.50

NEW ORLEANS SAINTS
1 Playoff season(football team)	6.00

COLOR PUB.

NEW STATESMEN
Fleetway

1	4.50
2 thru 5	@3.95

NEWSTRALIA
Innovation

1	1.75
2	1.75
3	1.95

NEW TERRYTOONS
Dell Publishing Co. 1960–61

1	35.00
2 thru 8	@25.00

Gold Key 1962

1 F:Heckle & Jeckle	60.00
2	50.00
3 thru 10	@18.00
11 thru 20	@8.00
21 thru 30	@5.00
31 thru 40	@4.00
41 thru 54	@3.00

NEW WAVE, THE
Eclipse 1986–87

1 Error Pages	2.00
1a Correction	1.50
2	1.00
3 "Space Station Called Hell"	1.00
4 Birth of Megabyte	1.00
5 PG(c),O:Avalon	1.50
6 O:Megabyte	1.50
7 Avalon disappears	1.00
8 V:Heap,V:Druids	1.00
9	1.00
10 V:Heap Team	1.00
11	1.50
12	1.50
13 V:Volunteers	1.50
14 1/3 issue	2.00

NEW WAVE vs. THE VOLUNTEERS
Eclipse

1 3-D,V:Volunteers	2.50
2 3-D,V:Volunteers	2.50

NEXT MAN
Comico 1985

1 I&O:Next Man	2.50
2	1.75
3	1.75
4	1.50
5	1.50

NEXT NEXUS
First

1 SR	1.95
2 SR	1.95
3 SR	1.95
4 SR	1.95

NEXUS
Capital

1 SR,I:Judah Maccabee	9.00
2 SR,Origin,V:Bellows	5.50
3 SR,Sundra Captive	5.00
4 SR,V:Ziggurat	5.00
5 SR,"I'm Bored!"	5.00
6 SR,A:Badger,TrialogueTrilogy#1	4.00

Nexus #5 © Capital Comics

First

7 SR,A:Badger,TrialogueTrilogy#2	5.00
8 SR,A:Badger,TrialogueTrilogy#3	4.00
9 SR,Teen Angel	2.50
10 SR,BWg,Talking Heads	2.00
11 SR,V:Clausius	2.00
12 SR,V:The Old General	2.00
13 SR,Sundra Peale solo	2.00
14 SR,A:Clonezone,Hilariator	2.00
15 SR,A:Clonezone	2.00
16 SR,A:Clonezone	2.00
17 Judah vs. Jacque,the Anvil	2.00
18 SR,A:Clonezone	2.00
19 SR,A:Clonezone	2.00
20 SR,A:Clonezone	2.00
21 SR,A:Clonezone	2.00
22 KG,A:Badger	2.00
23 SR,A:Clonezone	2.00
24 SR,A:Clonezone	2.00
25 SR,A:Clonezone	2.00
26 SR,A:Clonezone	2.00
27 SR,A:Clonezone	2.00
28 MMi	2.00
29 A:Kreed & Sinclair	2.00
30 JL,C:Badger	2.50
31 Judah solo story	2.00
32 JG,Judah solo story	2.00
33 SR,A:Kreed & Sinclair	2.00
34 SR,Judah solo story	2.00
35 SR,Judah solo story	2.00
36 SR	2.00
37 PS	2.00
38	2.00
39 SR, The Boom Search	2.00
40 SR	2.00
41 SR	2.00
42 SR,Bowl-Shaped world	2.00
43 PS	2.00
44 PS	2.00
45 SR,A:Badger Pt.1	2.00
46 SR,A:Badger Pt.2	2.00
47 SR,A:Badger Pt.3	2.00
48 SR,A:Badger Pt.4	2.00
49 PS,A:Badger Pt.5	2.00
50 SF,double size,A:Badger Pt.6 Crossroads tie-in	3.50
51 PS	2.00
52 PS	2.00
53 PS	2.00

54 PS	2.00
55 PS	2.00
56	2.00
57 AH	2.00
58 Sr,I:Stanislaus Korivitsky as Nexus	2.00
59 SR	2.00
60 SR	2.00
61	2.00
62	2.00
63 V:Elvonic Order	2.00
64 V:Elvonic Order	2.00
65 V:Elvonic Order	2.00
66 V:Elvonic Order	2.00
67 V:Elvonic Order	2.00
68 LM	2.00
69	2.00
70	2.00
71 V:Bad Brains	2.00
72 V:Renegade heads	2.00
73 Horatio returns to Ylum	2.00
74 Horatio vs. Stan	2.00
75 Horatio vs. Stan	2.00
76	2.25
77	2.25
78 O:Nexus,Nexus Files Pt#1	2.25
79 Nexus Files Pt#2	2.25
80 Nexus.Files Pt#3,last iss.	2.25

NEXUS LEGENDS
First

1 thru 13 rep.Nexus	@1.50
14 rep.Nexus	1.75
15 rep.Nexus	1.75
16 rep.Nexus	1.75
17 rep.Nexus	1.75
18 rep.Nexus	1.95
19 rep.Nexus	1.95
20 SR,Sanctuary	1.95
21 thru 23 SR	@1.95

NICK HOLIDAY
Argo May, 1956

1 Strip reprints	30.00

NIGHT GLIDER
Topps

1 V:Bombast,C:Captain Glory, Trading Card	3.25

NIGHTMARE
Innovation

1	2.50

NIGHTMARE AND CASPER
Harvey Publications 1963

1	40.00
2	20.00
3	20.00
4	20.00
5	20.00

Becomes:

CASPER AND NIGHTMARE

6 B:68 pgs	15.00
7	7.00
8	7.00
9	7.00
10	7.00
11 thru 20	@3.50
21 thru 30	@2.50

COLOR PUB.

31	2.50
32 E:68 pgs	2.50
33 thru 45	@2.00
46 Aug., 1974	2.00

NIGHTMARE ON
ELM STREET
Blackthorne

1 3-D	2.50
2 3-D	2.50
3 3-D	2.50

NIGHTMARES ON
ELM STREET
Innovation

1 Yours Truly, Freddy Krueger Pt.1	3.00
2 Yours Truly ,Freddy Krueger Pt.2	2.50
3 Loose Ends Pt.1,Return to	
Springwood	2.50
4 Loose Ends Pt 2	2.50
5	2.50
6	2.50

NIGHTMARES
Eclipse 1985

1	2.50
2	2.00

NIGHT MUSIC
Eclipse 1984–88

1	2.50
2	2.50
3 CR, Jungle Bear	3.00
4 Pelias & Melisande	2.00
5 Pelias	2.00
6 same as Salome #1	
7 same as Red Dog #1	
Graphic Novel	8.00

NIGHTVEIL
AC Comics

1	3.50
2	2.50
3	2.25
4	2.25
5	2.25

Ninja High School #8 © Eternity

6	1.75
7	1.75
Spec.#1	1.95

NIGHT WALKER
Fleetway

1 thru 2	2.95

NIGHTWOLF

1	1.75
2	1.75

9 LIVES OF FELIX
Harvey

1 thru 4	@1.25

NINJA HIGH SCHOOL
Eternity

1 Reps.orig.N.H.S.in color	1.95
2 thru 13 reprints	@1.95

NINJA HIGH SCHOOL
FEATURING
SPEED RACER
Eternity 1993

1B	2.95
2B	2.95

NINJA STAR

1	1.95

NIRA X: ANIMÉ
Entity Comics 1997

1 BMs	2.95
1a deluxe, foil cover	3.50
2 BMs	2.95
2a deluxe, foil cover	3.50
Swimsuit #0	2.75
Swimsuit #0 Manga (c)	2.75

NIRA X:
CYBERANGEL
Entity 1994

1 From pages of Zen	2.95
1a 2nd printing	2.75
2 V:Parradox	2.50
3 In Hydro-Dams	2.50
4 final issue	2.50
4a with computer game	6.95
Ashcan	2.50
TPB Birth of an Angel	12.95
[Series 2] 1995	
1 R:Nira X	3.75
1a Clear Chromium Edition	8.00
1b Holo-Chrome edition	10.00
2 Alien Invasion	2.50
3 Mecha New York	2.50
4 Final Issue	2.50
[Series 3] 1996	
0	2.75
0a signed & numbered	8.00
1	2.50
1a gold edition, signed & numb.	5.00
2	2.50
3	3.00

NIRA X/CYNDER:
ENDANGERED SPECIES
Entity Comics 1996

1	3.00

1a gold ink enhanced, bagged	13.00

NOID IN 3-D
Blackthorne

1 thru 3	@2.50

NOMAN
Tower Comics 1966

1 GK,OW	40.00
2 OW,A:Dynamo	30.00

NOOGIE KOOTCH:
SECRET AGENT MAN
Hobo Comics

1 I:Noogie Kootch	2.75
2 F:Celutron CIty	2.75

NOSFERATU:
PLAGUE OF TERROR
Millenium

1 I:Orlock	2.50
2 19th Century India,A:Sir W.	
Longsword	2.50
3 WWI/WWII to Viet Nam	2.50
4 O:Orlock,V:Longsword,conc.	2.50

NO TIME
FOR SERGEANTS
Dell Publishing Co. July, 1958

1 Ph(c)	40.00
2 Ph(c)	30.00
3 Ph(c)	30.00

NOVA HUNTER
Ryal Comics

1 thru 3	@2.50
4 Climax	2.50
5 Death and Betrayal	2.50

NUBIAN KNIGHT
Samson Comics

1 I:Shandai	2.50

NURSES, THE
Gold Key April, 1963

1	20.00
2	15.00
3	15.00

NYOKA, JUNGLE GIRL
Charlton Comics 1955–57

14	40.00
15	25.00
16	25.00
17	25.00
18	25.00
19	25.00
20	25.00
21	25.00
22	25.00

NYOKA, THE
JUNGLE GIRL
AC Comics

1 and 2	@1.95

OBLIVION
Comico 1995

1 R:The Elementals	2.50

COLOR PUB.

2 I:Thunderboy, Lilith 2.50
3 I:Fen, Ferril 2.50
4 War 2.95
5 The Unholy Trilogy 2.95

OCCULT FILES OF DR. SPEKTOR
Gold Key April, 1973

1 I:Lakot 10.00
2 thru 5 . . . . 5.00
6 thru 10 . . . . 3.50
11 I:Spertor as Werewolf 4.00
12 and 13 . . . . 2.50
14 A:Dr. Solar 15.00
15 thru 24 . . . . 2.50

Whitman

25 rep 2.00

O.G. WHIZ
Gold Key 1971–79

1 . . . . 60.00
2 . . . . 35.00
3 . . . . 25.00
4 . . . . 25.00
5 . . . . 25.00
6 . . . . 25.00
7 . . . . 8.00
8 . . . . 8.00
9 . . . . 8.00
10 . . . . 8.00
11 . . . . 8.00

O'MALLEY AND THE ALLEY CATS
Gold Key 1971–74

1 . . . . 15.00
2 thru 9 . . . . @10.00

OMEGA 7
Omega 7

1 V:Exterminator X 3.95

OMEGA ELITE
Blackthorne

1 . . . . 1.50
2 . . . . 1.50

OMNI MEN
Blackthorne

1 . . . . 1.25
2 . . . . 1.25

ON A PALE HORSE
Innovation

1 Piers Anthony adapt 4.95
2 "Magician",I:Kronos 4.95
3 . . . . 4.95
4 VV, ... 4.95
5 . . . . 4.95
6 . . . . 4.95

ONE-ARM SWORDSMAN

1 . . . . 2.95
2 . . . . 2.95
3 . . . . 2.75
4 . . . . 1.80
5 . . . . 1.80
6 . . . . 1.80
7 . . . . 1.80
8 . . . . 1.80
9 . . . . 2.00
10 . . . . 2.00
11 . . . . 2.00

ORBIT
Eclipse 1990

1 DSt(c) 3.95
2 . . . . 3.95
3 . . . . 4.95

ORIENTAL HEROES
Jademan

1 . . . . 2.50
2 . . . . 2.00
3 thru 13 . . . . @1.50
14 thru 27 . . . . @1.95
28 V:Skeleton Secretary 1.95
29 Barbarian vs.Lone Kwoon 1.95
30 Barbarian vs.Lone Kwoon 1.95
31 SkeletonSecretaryUprisng 1.95
32 Uprising Continues 1.95
33 Jupiter Kills His Brother 1.95
34 Skeleton Sec. Suicide 1.95
35 Red Sect Vs. Global Cult 1.95
36 A:Tiger 1.95
37 Old Supreme 1.95
38 Tiger vs. 4 Hitmen 1.95
39 D:Infinite White, V:Red Sect. . 1.95
40 The Golden Buddhha Temple . 1.95
41 thru 43 . . . . 1.95
44 SilverChime rescue 1.95
45 Global Cult Battle 1.95
46 thru 48 . . . . @1.95
49 F:GoldDragon/SilverChime . . . 1.95
50 Return to Global Cult 1.95
51 Gang Of Three Vs.White Beau &
   Lone Kwoon-Tin 1.95
52 Global Cult vs Red Sect 1.95
53 Global Cult vs.Red Sect 1.95

ORIGINAL ASTRO BOY
Now

1 KSy 3.00
2 KSy 2.00
3 KSy 2.00
4 KSy 2.00
5 KSy 2.00
6 thru 17 KSy . . . . @1.75

On a Pale Horse #5 © Innovation

ORIGINAL DICK TRACY
Gladestone

1 rep.V:Mrs.Pruneface 1.95
2 rep.V:Influence 1.95
3 rep.V:TheMole 1.95
4 rep.V:ItchyOliver 1.95
5 rep.V:Shoulders 2.00

ORIGINAL E-MAN
First
{rep. Charlton stories}

1 JSon,O:E-Man & Nova 1.75
2 JSon,V:Battery,SamuelBoar . . . 1.75
3 JSon,"City in the Sand" 1.75
4 JSon,A:Brain from Sirius 1.75
5 JSon,V:T.V. Man 1.75
6 JSon,I:Teddy Q 1.75
7 JSon,Vamfire 1.75

ORIGINAL SHIELD
ABC

1 DAy/TD,O:Shield 1.00
2 DAy,O:Dusty 75
3 DAy 75
4 DAy 75

ORIGIN OF THE DEFIANT UNIVERSE
Defiant

1 O:Defiant Characters 1.50

OUTBREED 999
Blackout Comics

1 thru 4 . . . . @2.95
5 Search For Daige 2.95

OUTCASTS

1 . . . . 1.25

OUTER LIMITS, THE
Dell Publishing Co.
Jan.-March, 1964

1 P(c) 75.00
2 P(c) 50.00
3 P(c) 35.00
4 P(c) 35.00
5 P(c) 35.00
6 P(c) 35.00
7 P(c) 35.00
8 P(c) 35.00
9 P(c) 35.00
10 P(c) 35.00
11 thru 18 P(c) 30.00

OUTLAWS OF THE WEST
Charlton Comics 1956–80

11 . . . . 40.00
12 . . . . 20.00
13 . . . . 20.00
14 Giant 25.00
15 . . . . 20.00
16 . . . . 20.00
17 . . . . 20.00
18 SD 50.00
19 . . . . 15.00
20 . . . . 15.00
21 thru 30 . . . . @10.00
31 thru 50 . . . . @5.00
51 thru 70 . . . . @3.00
71 thru 88 . . . . @2.00

COLOR PUB.

OUT OF THIS WORLD
Charlton Comics 1956–59
1	150.00
2	75.00
3 SD	175.00
4 SD	175.00
5 SD	175.00
6 SD	175.00
7 SD,SD(c)	175.00
8 SD	150.00
9 SD	150.00
10 SD	150.00
11 SD	150.00
12 SD	150.00
13	50.00
14	50.00
15	50.00
16	135.00

OUTPOSTS
Blackthorne
1 thru 6	@1.25

OWL, THE
Gold Key April, 1967
1	25.00
2 April, 1968	20.00

PACIFIC PRESENTS
Pacific 1992
1 DSt,Rocketeer,(3rd App.)	16.00
2 DSt,Rocketeer,(4th App.)	14.00
3 SD,I:Vanity	2.50
4	2.00
5	2.00

P.A.C.
Artifacts Inc
1 I:P.A.C.	1.95

PAINKILLER JANE
Event Comics 1997
1 JQ(c)	2.95
1 RL(c)	2.95
2 JQ&JP(c)	2.95
2 JP&RL(c)	2.95

PAINKILLER JANE/ THE DARKNESS
Event Comics
signed, limited edition, JQ(c)	29.95

PAINKILLER JANE VS. THE DARKNESS: STRIPPER
Event Comics 1997
1 GEn,JP,x-over, Amanda Connor cover	2.95
1a Greg & Tim Hildebrandt	2.95
1b MS(c)	2.95
1c JQ(c)	2.95

PALADIN ALPHA
Firstlight
1 I:Paladin Alpha	2.95
2 V:Hellfire Triger	2.95

PARADAX
Eclipes
1	2.25

PARADIGM
Gauntlet
1 A:Predator	2.95

PARAGON DARK APOCALYPSE
AC 1993
1 thru 4, Fem Force crossover	2.95

PARANOIA
Adventure Comics
1 (based on video game)"Clone1"	3.25
2 King-R-Thr-2	2.95
3 R:Happy Jack,V:N3F	2.95
4 V:The Computer	2.95
5 V:The Computer	2.95
6 V:Lance-R-Lot,last issue	2.95

PARTRIDGE FAMILY, THE
Charlton Comics 1971–73
1	30.00
2 thru 4	@15.00
5 Summer Special	20.00
6 thru 21	@15.00

PASSOVER
Maximum Press
1 (of 2) BNa	3.00
2 BNa,A:Avengelyne	3.00

PATHWAYS TO FANTASY
Pacific
1 BS,JJ art	3.00

PAT SAVAGE: WOMAN OF BRONZE
Millenium
1 F:Doc Savage's cousin	2.50

PEACEMAKER
Charlton
1 A:Fightin' 5	5.00
2 A:Fightin' 5	3.00
3 A:Fightin' 5	3.00
4 O:Peacemaker,A:Fightin' 5	4.00
5 A:Fightin' 5	2.50

PEANUTS
Dell Publishing Co. 1958
1	100.00
2	75.00
3	75.00
4	50.00
5	35.00
6	35.00
7	35.00
8	35.00
9	35.00
10	35.00
11	35.00
12	35.00
13	35.00

PEANUTS
Gold Key May, 1963
1	50.00
2 thru 4	30.00

PEBBLES & BAMM BAMM
Charlton Comics 1972–76
1	35.00
2 thru 10	@15.00
11 thru 36	@10.00

PEBBLES FLINTSTONE
Gold Key Sept., 1963
1 "A Chip off the old block"	70.00

PELLESTAR
1	1.75

Perg #5 © Lightning Comics

PERG
Lightning Comics
1 Glow in the dark(c),JS(c), B:JZy(s),KIK,I:Perg	3.75
1a Platinum Ed.	5.00
1b Gold Ed.	7.00
1 gold edition, glow-in-the-dark flip cover	30.00
2 KIK,O:Perg	3.25
2a Platinum Ed.	5.00
3 Flip Book (c).	3.25
3a Platinum Ed	5.00
4 TLw,I:Helana	3.25
4a Platinum Ed	5.00
5 A:Helena	3.25
6 PIA,A:Helena	3.25
6 nude cover	9.00
7	3.00
8 V:Police	3.00

PERRY MASON MYSTERY MAGAZINE
Dell Publishing Co. 1964
1	25.00
2 Ray Burr Ph(c)	25.00

PETER PAN: RETURN TO NEVERNEVER LAND
1 Peter in Mass.	2.50
2 V:Tiger Lily	2.50

COLOR PUB.

PETER POTAMUS
Gold Key Jan., 1965
1 . . . . 50.00

PETTICOAT JUNCTION
Dell Publishing Co. 1964
1 Ph(c) 60.00
2 Ph(c) 45.00
3 Ph(c) 45.00
4 . . . . 45.00
5 Ph(c) 45.00

PHANTOM, THE
Gold Key 1962
1 RsM 125.00
2 B:King, Queen & Jack 75.00
3 . . . . 50.00
4 . . . . 50.00
5 . . . . 50.00
6 . . . . 50.00
7 "The Super Apes" 50.00
8 . . . . 50.00
9 . . . . 50.00
10 "The Sleeping Giant" 50.00
11 E:King,Queen and Jack 40.00
12 B:Track Hunter 40.00
13 . . . . 40.00
14 "The Historian" 40.00
15 . . . . 40.00
16 . . . . 40.00
17 "Samaris" 40.00
King Comics Sept. 1966
18 "The Treasure of the Skull
Cave;"BU:Flash Gordon 50.00
19 "The Astronaut & the Pirates" 30.00
20 A:GirlPhantom,E:FlashGordon 30.00
21 BU:Mandrake 30.00
22 "Secret of Magic Mountain" . . 30.00
23 . . . . 30.00
24 A:Girl Phantom 30.00
25 . . . . 30.00
26 . . . . 30.00
27 . . . . 30.00
28 . . . . 30.00
29 . . . . 30.00
Charlton Comics 1969–77
30 . . . . 20.00
31 JAp,"Phantom of Shang-Ri-La" 20.00
32 JAp,"The Pharaoh Phantom" . 20.00
33 . . . . 20.00
34 . . . . 20.00
35 . . . . 20.00
36 . . . . 20.00
37 . . . . 20.00
38 . . . . 20.00
39 . . . . 20.00
40 "The Ritual" 20.00
41 . . . . 15.00
42 . . . . 15.00
43 . . . . 15.00
44 "To Right A Wrong" 15.00
45 . . . . 15.00
46 I:Piranha 20.00
47 "The False Skull Cave" 15.00
48 . . . . 15.00
49 . . . . 15.00
50 . . . . 15.00
51 "A Broken Vow" 15.00
52 . . . . 15.00
53 . . . . 15.00
54 . . . . 15.00
55 . . . . 15.00
56 . . . . 15.00
57 NightmareMedicine in Bengali 15.00

The Phantom #64 © Charlton Comics

58 . . . . 15.00
59 . . . . 15.00
60 . . . . 15.00
61 "A Dead Man's Promise" 15.00
62 . . . . 15.00
63 . . . . 15.00
64 "Duel With Death" 15.00
65 . . . . 15.00
66 "Goldbeard the Pirate" 15.00
67 "Triumph of Evil" 15.00
68 . . . . 15.00
69 . . . . 15.00
70 . . . . 15.00
71 . . . . 10.00
72 "Man in the Shadows" 10.00
73 . . . . 10.00
74 . . . . 10.00

PHANTOM
Wolf Publishing 1992
1 Drug Runners 2.25
2 Mystery Child of the Sea 2.25
3 inc.feature pages on
Phantom/Merchandise 2.25
4 TV Jungle Crime Buster 2.25
5 Castle Vacula-Transylvania . . . 2.25
6 The Old West 2.25
7 Sercet of Colussus 2.75
8 Temple of the Sun God 2.75

PHANTOM BOLT, THE
Gold Key 1964–66
1 . . . . 40.00
2 . . . . 25.00
3 . . . . 15.00
4 . . . . 15.00
5 . . . . 15.00
6 . . . . 15.00
7 . . . . 15.00

PHANTOM FORCE
Genesis West
Previously: Image
0 JK/JLe(c) 2.75
3 thru 10 . . . . @2.50

PHAZE
Eclipse 1988
1 BSz(c),Takes place in future . . 2.25
2 PG(c),V:The Pentagon 1.95
3 Schwieger Vs. Mammoth 1.95

PHOENIX
Atlas 1975
1 thru 4 . . . . @1.00

PINK PANTHER, THE
Gold Key April, 1971
1 . . . . 30.00
2 thru 10 . . . . @12.00
11 thru 30 . . . . @8.00
31 thru 60 . . . . @5.00
61 thru 5.00

PINOCCHIO
1 . . . . 1.50

PIRATE CORP.
Eternity
1 thru 5 . . . . @1.95

P.I.'S, THE
First
1 JSon,Ms.Tree,M Mauser 1.50
2 JSon,Ms.Tree,M Mauser 1.25
3 JSon,Ms.Tree,M Mauser 1.25

PLANET COMICS
Blackthorne
1 DSt(c) 2.00
2 thru 4 . . . . @2.00

PLANET OF VAMPIRES
Atlas Feb.–July 1975
1 thru 3 . . . . @1.00

POGZ N SLAMMER
Blackout Comics 1995
1 I:Pogz N Slammer 1.95
2 Contact Other Schools 1.95

POIZON
London Night Studios 1995
0 . . . . 3.00
0 signed gothchik edition 15.00
1/2 O:Poizon 3.00
1 . . . . 3.00
1a Necro-Nude edition 5.95
1b Photo Nude Edition signed . 15.00
1c signed 10.00
2 EHr 3.00

POIZON: CADILLACS AND GREEN TOMATOES
London Night 1997
2 . . . . 3.00
2a deluxe nude cover 6.00
3 . . . . 3.00
6 deluxe 6.00

POIZON: LOST CHILD
London Night Studios 1996
1 mini series 3.00
1a Necro-Nude variat cover 5.95
1 signed 10.00

COLOR PUB.

POPEYE
Gold Key 1962
1-65 See Golden Age Section
66 . . . . 75.00
67 . . . . 50.00
68 thru 80 . . . . @20.00
King Comics 1966
81 thru 92 . . . . @15.00
Charlton 1969
94 thru 99 . . . . @12.50
100 . . . . 15.00
101 thru 138 . . . . @12.50
Gold Key 1978
139 thru 143 . . . . @6.00
144 50th Aniv. Spec. 7.50
155 . . . . @6.00
Whitman
156 thru 159 . . . . @4.00
162 thru 171 . . . . @4.00

POPEYE
Harvey Comics 1993–94
1 thru 7 . . . . @1.50
Summer Spec.#1 . . . . 2.25

POPEYE SPECIAL
Ocean 1987–88
1 . . . . 1.75
2 . . . . 2.00

POWER FACTOR
Wonder Color Comics 1986
1 . . . . 4.00
2 . . . . 3.00
3 . . . . 3.00

POWER FACTOR
Innovation
1 thru 4 . . . . @2.25

POWERKNIGHTS
Amara 1995
P I:Powerknights 1.50

POWER RANGERS ZEO/YOUNGBLOOD
Maximum Press 1997
1 TNu,NRd 3.00

POWERS THAT BE
Broadway Comics
Preview Editions Sept. 1995
1 thru 3 B&W . . . . @2.50
Regular Series Nov. 1995
1 thru 4 . . . . @2.95
5 "It's the End of the World As We
Know It" pt.1 . . . . 2.95
6 "It's the End of the World As We
Know It" pt.2 . . . . 2.95
Becomes:
STAR SEED
7 "It's the End of the World As We
Know It" pt.3 . . . . 2.95
8 "It's the End of the World As We
Know It" pt.4 . . . . 2.95
9 "It's the End of the World As We
Know It" pt.5 . . . . 2.95
10 JiS(s),JRs,"It's the End of the
World As We Know It" pt6. . . . 2.95
11 JiS(s),JRs,"It's the End of the

World As We Know It" pt7. . . . 2.95

PRESSBUTTON
Eclipse
(see Axel Pressbutton)
5 and 6 . . . . @1.75

PRIEST
Maximum Press 1996
1 RLd, F:Michael O'Bannon 3.00
2 RLd,BNa, ... 3.00
3 RLd 3.00

PRIMAL RAGE
Sirius 1996
1 TAr,from video game 2.95
2 TAr,DOe(c) 2.95

PRIMER
Comico 1982–84
1 . . . . 10.00
2 I:Grendel 85.00
3 . . . . 5.00
4 C:Maxx 7.00
5 I:Maxx 35.00
6 I:Evangelyne 14.00

Primus #6 © Charlton Comics

PRIMUS
Charlton Comics 1972
1 . . . . 5.00
2 thru 5 . . . . @5.00
6 thru 7 . . . . @4.00

PRINCESS SALLY
Archie Comics
1 thru 3 Sonic tie-in . . . . @

PRINCE VANDAL
Triumphant
1 JnR(s), ... 2.50
2 JnR(s), ... 2.50
3 JnR(s),ShG,I:Claire,V:Nicket,
Vandal goes to Boviden 2.50
4 JnR(s),ShG,Game's End 2.50
5 JnR(s),ShG,The Sickness, the rat
appears 2.50

---

6 JnR(s),ShG,B:Gothic 2.50

PRIORITY: WHITE HEAT
AC Comics 1986
1 thru 2 miniseries . . . . @1.75

PRISON SHIP
1 . . . . 1.75

PRIVATEERS
Vanguard Graphics
1 . . . . 1.50
2 . . . . 1.50

PROFESSIONAL: GOGOL 13
Viz
1 . . . . 4.95
2 and 3 . . . . @4.95

PROFESSOR OM
Innovation
1 I:Rock Warrior 2.50
2 Samurai Drama 2.50

PROJECT A-KO 0
Antarctic Press 1994
0 digest size 5.00
Continued by Malibu

PROJECT A-KO 2
CPM 1995
Previously Malibu
1 Space Saga 2.95
2 Space Saga 2.95
3 Queen Margarita 2.95

PROJECT A-KO: VERSUS THE UNIVERSE
CPM 1995
1 Based on Animation 2.95
2 strange magician 3.00
3 . . . . 3.00
4 (of 5) TEl 2.95

PROPHET/CABLE
Maximum 1997
1 (of 2) RLd x-over 3.50
2 RLd x-over,A:Domino, Kirby,
Blaquesmith 3.50

PROWLER
Eclipse 1987
1 I:Prowler 1.75
2 GN,A:Original Prowler 1.75
3 GN 1.75
4 GN 1.75
5 GN, adaption of "Vampire Bat" . 1.75
6 w/flexi-disk record 1.75

PROWLER IN "WHITE ZOMBIE", THE
Eclipse 1988
1 . . . . 1.75

PRUDENCE AND CAUTION
Defiant
1 CCI(s), ... 3.25

COLOR PUB.

1a Spanish Version 3.25
2 CCi(s), ... 2.50
2a Spanish Version 2.50
3 CCi(s), ... 2.50
3a Spanish Version 2.50
4 CCi(s), ... 2.50
4a Spanish Version 2.50
5 CCi(s), ... 2.50
5a Spanish Version 2.50

PSYCHO
Innovation
1 Hitchcock movie adapt 2.50
2 continued 2.50
3 continued 2.50

PSYCHOBLAST
First
1 thru 9 . . . . @1.75

PUBLIC DEFENDER
IN ACTION
Charlton Comics 1957
7 . . . . 50.00
8 and 9 . . . . @40.00
10 thru 12, ... @40.00

PUDGE PIG
Charlton Comics Sept., 1958
1 . . . . 8.00
2 . . . . 8.00

PUPPET MASTER
Eternity
1 Movie Adapt.Andre Toulon 2.50
2 Puppets Protecting Diary 2.50
3 R:Andre Toulon 2.50
4 . . . . 2.50

PUPPET MASTER:
CHILDREN OF THE
PUPPET MASTER
Eternity
1 Killer Puppets on the loose . . . 2.50
2 concl. 2.50

PURGATORI
Chaos! Comics
1-shot prelude 1.50
1-shot signed, limited + print . . . 25.00

PURGATORI:
THE DRACULA GAMBIT
Chaos! Comics 1997
1 DQ & Brian LeBlanc 2.95

PURGATORI:
THE VAMPIRES MYTH
Chaos! Comics
1 (of 3) 2.95
1 one-shot limited chromium edition 9.95
2 BnP,JBa 2.95
3 BnP,JBa, final issue 2.95
TPB rep. 9.95

QUANTUM LEAP
Innovation
{based on TV series}
1 1968 Memphis 3.50

1a Special Edition 2.50
2 Ohio 1962,"Freedom of the
Press" 3.00
3 1958 "The $50,000 Quest" 3.00
4 "Small Miracles" 2.50
5 . . . . 2.50
6 . . . . 2.50
7 Golf Pro,School Bus Driver . . . 2.50
8 1958,Bank Robber 2.50
9 NY 1969,Gay Rights 2.50
10 1960s' Stand-up Comic 2.50
11 1959,Dr.(LSD experiments) . . . 2.50
12 . . . . 2.50

Queen of the Damned #3
© Innovation

QUEEN OF THE
DAMNED
Innovation
1 Anne Rice Adapt."On the Road to
the Vampire Lestat" 3.50
2 Adapt. continued 2.50
3 The Devils Minion 2.50
4 Adapt.continued 2.50
5 Adapt.continued 2.50
6 Adapt.continued 2.50
7 Adapt.continued 2.50
8 Adapt.continued 2.50

QUICK-DRAW McGRAW
Charlton Comics 1970–72
1 TV Animated Cartoon 35.00
2 . . . . 20.00
3 . . . . 20.00
4 thru 8 . . . . @20.00

Q-UNIT
Harris
1 I:Q-Unit,w/card 3.25

RACE FOR THE MOON
Harvey Publications 1958
1 BP 100.00
2 JK,AW,JK/AW(c) 175.00
3 JK,AW,JK/AW(c) 175.00

RACER-X
Now
Premire Special 5.00
1 thru 3 . . . . @2.50
4 thru 11 . . . . @1.75
[2nd Series]
1 thru 10 . . . . @1.75

RACK & PAIN
Chaos! Comics
3 (of 4) BnP,LJi, ... 2.95
4 BnP,LJi, final issue 2.95

RACK & PAIN: KILLERS
Chaos! Comics
1 (of 4) JaL(c) 2.95
2 BnP,LJi,JaL(c) 2.95

RADICAL DREAMER
Blackball
0 . . . . 2.00
1 thru 5 V:Jorge Futran . . . . . . @2.50

RADIOACTIVE MAN
Bongo
1 I:Radioactive Man 3.25
1 80pg offered again . . . .
88 V:Lava Man 1.95
212 V:Hypno Head 1.95
412 V:Dr. Crab 2.25
679 with card 2.25
1000 Final issue 2.25

RAD PATROL
1 . . . . 1.95

RADRAX
1 and 2 . . . . @2.25

RAEL
Eclipse
Vol 1 . . . . 6.95

RAGAMUFFINS
Eclipse 1985
1 . . . . 3.00

RALPH SNART
ADVENTURES
Now
[Volumes 1 & 2]
see B&W
9 and 10, color 2.50
[Volume 3]
1 . . . . 4.00
2 thru 10 . . . . @3.00
11 thru 21 . . . . @2.00
22 thru 26 . . . . @1.75
TPB 9.95
[Volume 4]
1 thru 3, with 1 of 2 trading cards 2.50
[Volume 5]
1 thru 5, with 1 of 2 trading cards 2.50
3-D Spec.#1 with 3-D glasses and
12 trading cards 3.50

RAMAR OF THE JUNGLE
Toby Press 1954
1 Ph(c), John Hall 125.00

All comics prices listed are for *Near Mint* condition.

COLOR PUB.

Charlton

2	85.00
3	85.00
4	85.00
5 Sept., 1956	85.00

RAMPANT
Manifest Destiny Comics

1/2 Various Artists	2.50

RANDOM 5
Amara Inc. 1995

1 I:Random 5	1.50

RANGO
Dell Publishing Co. Aug., 1967

1 Tim Conway Ph(c)	18.00

RANMA 1/2
Viz 1992

1 I:Ranma	50.00
2 I:Upperclassmen Kuno	17.00
3 F:Upperclassmen Kuno	15.00
4 Confusion	5.00
5 A:Ryoga	5.00
6 Ryoga plots revenge	9.00
7 Conclusion	5.00
[Part 2]	
1	10.00
2	5.00
3 thru 7	@4.00
8	5.00
9	7.00
10 and 11	3.00

continued, see Other Pub. B&W

RAPHAEL
Mirage

1 TMNTurtle characters	15.00

RARE BREED
Dark Moon Productions 1995

1 V:Anarchy	2.50
2 V:Anarchy	2.50

RAT PATROL, THE
Dell Publishing Co. March, 1967

1 Ph(c)	60.00
2	40.00
3 thru 6 Ph(c)	@30.00

RAVEN
Renaissance Comics

1 I:Raven	2.50
2 V:Macallister	2.50
3 thru 5	@2.50
6 V:Nightmare Creatures	2.75

RAVENS AND RAINBOWS
Pacific

1	1.50

RAY BRADBURY CHRONICLES
Byron Press

1 short stories	10.00
2 short stories	10.00
3 short stories	10.00

Ravens & Rainbows #1
© Pacific Comics

Topps 1993

1 w/Trading Card	3.25
2 w/Trading Card	3.25
3 w/Trading Card	3.25
4 thru 5 w/Trading Card	3.25

R.A.Z.E.
Firstlight

1 I:R.A.Z.E., Secret Weapon	2.95
2 V:Exterminators	2.95

RAZOR
London Night Studios

0	40.00
0a second printing	4.00
1 I:Razor	40.00
1a second printing	8.00
2	25.00
2a limited ed., red & blue	50.00
2b platinum ed.	60.00
3	25.00
3a with poster	60.00
4	12.00
4a with poster	40.00
5	25.00
5a platinum ed.	40.00
6	22.00
7	20.00
8	8.00
9	6.00
10	15.00
11 B&W	5.00
12 B&W	5.00
Ann.#1 I:Shi	65.00
Ann.#2 O:Razor B&W	100.00

Becomes
RAZOR UNCUT
see B&W
Volume 2 1996

1 DQ,	4.00
1 holochrome edition	15.00
2 DQ	3.00
3	3.00
4	3.00
5	3.00
6	3.00
7	3.00

RAZOR AND SHI SPECIAL
London Night Studios 1994

1 Rep. Razor Ann.#1 + new art	13.00
1a platinum version	30.00

RAZOR ARCHIVES
London Night

1 & 2 see B&W

3 rep. Razor #10–12	7.00

RAZOR BURN
London Night Studios 1994

1 V:Styke	7.00
1a signed	12.00
2 Searching for Styke	5.00
2a Platinum	15.00
3 Stryke's War	4.00
4 D:Razor, bagged	3.00
5 Epilogue	3.00

RAZOR: CRY NO MORE
London Night Studios 1995

1-shot	4.00
1a variant	8.00

RAZOR/MORBID ANGEL: SOUL SEARCH
London Night

1 (of 3)	3.00
1 platinum edition	10.00
1 Chromium edition	15.00
2	3.00
3	3.00

RAZOR: THE SUFFERING
London Night Studios 1994

1	7.00
1a Director's cut	6.00
1b signed, limited	30.00
2	7.00
2a Director's cut	6.00
3 final chapter	3.00

RAZOR: TORTURE
London Night Studios 1995

0 Razor back from dead	4.00
0a signed edition	18.00
1	3.00
2	3.00
3 EHr	3.00
4	3.00
5 alt. cover, signed	10.00
6 alt. cover, signed	10.00
7	3.00

RAZOR SWIMSUIT SPECIAL
London Night Studios 1995

1 pin-ups	5.00
1a platinum version	15.00
1b commemorative edition	7.00

RAZOR/ WARRIOR NUN AREALA: FAITH
London Night

1 by Jude Millien	4.00
1a variant cover	8.00

COLOR PUB.

REAL GHOSTBUSTERS
Now
1 KSy(c) 4.50
2 thru 7 . . . . @2.50
8 thru 24 . . . . @1.75
[2nd Series]
1 Halloween Special 1.75
Ann. 3-D w/glasses & pinups 2.95

REALITY CHECK
Sirius 1996
1 by Tavicat 2.95
2 thru 10 . . . . @2.95

REAL WAR STORIES
Eclipse 1987–91
1 BB 3.00
1a 2nd printing 1.50
2 . . . . 4.95

RE-ANIMATOR
Adventure Comics
1 movie adaption 2.95
2 movie adaption 2.95

RE-ANIMATOR
Adventure
1 Prequel to Orig movie 2.50

RE-ANIMATOR: DAWN OF THE RE-ANIMATOR
Adventure
1 Prequel to movie 2.50
2 . . . . 2.50
3 . . . . 2.50
4 V:Erich Metler 2.50

RE-ANIMATOR: TALES OF HERBERT WEST
Adventure Comics
1 H.P.Lovecraft stories 4.95

RED DOG
Eclipse 1988
1 CR,Mowgli "Jungle Book" story 2.00

RED DRAGON
Comico 1995
1 I:Red Dragon 2.50
2 How Soon is Nau? 2.95

RED HEAT
1 3-D 2.50

RED SONJA in 3-D
Blackthorne
1 . . . . 2.50
2 . . . . 2.50
3 . . . . 2.50

REESE'S PIECES
Eclipse 1985
1 reprint from Web of Horror . . . 1.50
2 reprint from Web of Horror . . . 1.50

REGGIE
Archie Publications 1963–65
15 . . . . 40.00
16 . . . . 35.00

17 . . . . 35.00
18 . . . . 35.00
Becomes:
REGGIE AND ME
Archie Publications 1966–80
19 . . . . 15.00
20 thru 23 . . . . @7.00
24 thru 40 . . . . @2.50
41 thru 126 . . . . @1.00

REGGIE'S WISE GUY JOKES
Archie Publications April, 1968
1 . . . . 15.00
2 . . . . 6.00
3 . . . . 6.00
4 . . . . 6.00
5 . . . . 2.50
6 . . . . 2.50
7 . . . . 2.50
8 . . . . 2.50
9 . . . . 2.50
10 . . . . 2.50
11 thru 60, Jan. 1982 . . . . . . @1.00

REIVERS
Enigma
1 thru 3 Rock 'n' Roll 2.95

REPTILICUS
Charlton Comics Aug., 1961
1 . . . . 100.00
2 . . . . 60.00
Becomes:
REPTISAURUS
3 . . . . 40.00
4 . . . . 35.00
5 . . . . 35.00
6 . . . . 35.00
7 . . . . 35.00
8 Summer, 1963 . . . . 35.00

RETURN OF KONGA, THE
Charlton Comics 1962
N# 30.00

RETURN OF MEGATON MAN
Kitchen Sink
1 Don Simpson art (1988) 2.00
2 Don Simpson art 2.00
3 Don Simpson art 2.00

RETURN TO JURASSIC PARK
Topps 1995
1 R:Jurassic Park 2.50
2 V:Blosyn Team, Army 2.50
3 The Hunted 2.50
4 Army 2.50
5 Heirs to the Thunder,pt.1 . . . . 2.95
6 Heirs to the Thunder,pt.2 . . . . 2.95
7 Inquiring Minds,pt.1 . . . . 2.95
8 Photo Finish, concl. 2.95
9 Jurassic Jam issue 2.95

REVENGE OF THE PROWLER
Eclipse 1988
1 GN,R:Prowler 1.75

2 GN,A:Fighting Devil Dogs with Flexi-Disk 2.50
3 GN,A:Devil Dogs 1.75
4 GN,V:Pirahna 1.75

REVENGERS
Continuity
1 NA,O:Megalith,I:Crazyman 5.50
2 NA,Megalith meets Armor & Silver Streak,Origin Revengers#1 2.50
3 NA/NR,Origin Revengers #2 . . . 2.50
4 NA,Origin Revengers #3 . . . . . 2.50
5 NA,Origin Revengers #4 . . . . . 2.50
6 I:Hybrids 3.00
Spec. #1 F:Hybrids 4.95

RIBIT
Comico
1 FT,Mini-series 1.95
2 FT,Mini-series 1.95
3 FT,Mini-series 1.95
4 FT,Mini-series 1.95

Richie Rich #107 © Harvey Publications

RICHIE RICH
Harvey Publications 1960–91
1 . . . . 1,200.00
2 . . . . 400.00
3 . . . . 250.00
4 . . . . 250.00
5 . . . . 250.00
6 . . . . 150.00
7 . . . . 150.00
8 . . . . 150.00
9 . . . . 150.00
10 . . . . 150.00
11 thru 20 . . . . @100.00
21 thru 40 . . . . @75.00
41 thru 60 . . . . @50.00
61 thru 80 . . . . @20.00
81 thru 99 . . . . @10.00
100 . . . . 15.00
101 thru 111 . . . . @7.00
112 thru 116 52 pg Giants . . . @8.00
117 thru 120 . . . . @6.00
121 thru 140 . . . . @4.00
141 thru 160 . . . . @3.00
161 thru 180 . . . . @2.00
181 thru 254 . . . . @1.00

COLOR PUB.

RICHIE RICH
Harvey 1991

1 thru 15	@1.25
16 thru 28	@1.50

Richie Rich Bank Books #24
© Harvey Publications

RICHIE RICH
BANK BOOKS
Harvey 1972–82

1	25.00
2 thru 5	@15.00
6 thru 10	@7.50
11 thru 20	@5.00
21 thru 30	@2.50
31 thru 40	@2.00
41 thru 59	@1.50

RICHIE RICH
BILLIONS
Harvey 1974–82

1	12.50
2 thru 5	@7.50
6 thru 10	@5.00
11 thru 20	@4.00
21 thru 30	@2.00
31 thru 48	@1.50

RICHIE RICH
DIAMONDS
Harvey 1972–82

1	32.00
2 thru 5	@15.00
6 thru 10	@7.00
11 thru 20	@5.00
21 thru 30	@2.00
31 thru 59	@1.50

RICHIE RICH
DOLLARS & CENTS
Harvey Publications 1963–82

1	135.00
2	50.00
3 thru 5	@25.00
6 thru 10	@15.00
11 thru 20	@10.00

21 thru 30	@7.00
31 thru 43	@5.00
44 thru 60	@4.00
61 thru 70	@3.00
71 thru 109	@1.00

RICHIE RICH
FORTUNES
Harvey 1971–82

1	30.00
2 thru 5	@15.00
6 thru 10	@7.00
11 thru 20	@4.00
21 thru 30	@2.00
31 thru 63	@1.00

RICHIE RICH
GEMS
Harvey 1974–82

1	15.00
2 thru 5	@6.00
6 thru 10	@4.00
11 thru 20	@3.00
21 thru 30	@2.00
31 thru 43	@1.00

RICHIE RICH
JACKPOTS
Harvey 1974–82

1	25.00
2 thru 5	@7.00
6 thru 10	@5.00
11 thru 20	@3.00
21 thru 30	@2.00
31 thru 58	@1.00

RICHIE RICH MILLIONS
Harvey Publications 1961–82

1	150.00
2	75.00
3 thru 10	@60.00
11 thru 20	@40.00
21 thru 30	@20.00
31 thru 48	@8.00
49 thru 60	@6.00
61 thru 64	@4.00
65 thru 74	@3.00
75 thru 94	@2.50
95 thru 113	@1.00

RICHIE RICH
MONEY WORLD
Harvey 1972–82

1	25.00
2 thru 5	@7.00
6 thru 10	@5.00
11 thru 20	@3.00
21 thru 30	@2.00
31 thru 59	@1.00

RICHIE RICH
PROFITS
Harvey 1974–82

1	15.00
2 thru 5	@7.00
6 thru 10	@5.00
11 thru 20	@3.00
21 thru 30	@2.00
31 thru 47	@1.00

RICHIE RICH
RICHES
Harvey 1972–82

1	15.00
2 thru 5	@7.00
6 thru 10	@5.00
11 thru 20	@3.00
21 thru 30	@2.00
31 thru 59	@1.00

RICHIE RICH
SUCCESS STORIES
Harvey Publications 1964–82

1	100.00
2 thru 5	@50.00
6 thru 10	@25.00
11 thru 30	@15.00
31 thru 38	@10.00
39 thru 55	@5.00
56 thru 66	@3.00
67 thru 105	@1.00

RICHIE RICH
VAULT OF MYSTERY
Harvey 1974–82

1	10.00
2 thru 5	@5.00
6 thru 10	@4.00
11 thru 20	@3.00
21 thru 30	@2.00
31 thru 47	@1.00

RICHIE RICH
ZILLIONS
Harvey 1976–82

1	10.00
2 thru 5	@5.00
6 thru 10	@4.00
11 thru 20	@2.00
21 thru 33	@1.00

RIFLEMAN, THE
Dell Publishing Co. 1959

1 Chuck Connors Ph(c) all	250.00
2	125.00
3 ATh	100.00
4	85.00
5	85.00
6 ATh	110.00
7	85.00
8	85.00
9	85.00
10	85.00
11	75.00
12	75.00
13	75.00
14	75.00
15	75.00
16	75.00
17	75.00
18	75.00
19	75.00
20	75.00

RIOT GEAR
Triumphant

1 JnR(s),I:Riot Gear	2.50
2 JnR(s),I:Rabin	2.50
3 JnR(s),I:Surzar	2.50
4 JnR(s),D:Captain Tich	2.50
5 JnR(s),reactions	2.50

<table>
<tr><td>6 JnR(s),Tich avenged</td><td>2.50</td></tr>
<tr><td>7 JnR(s),Information Age</td><td>2.50</td></tr>
<tr><td>8 JnR(s),</td><td>2.50</td></tr>
</table>

RIOT GEAR: VIOLENT PAST
Triumphant

1 and 2 .... @2.50

R.I.P.
TSR

1 thru 8 .... @2.95

RIPLEY'S BELIEVE IT OR NOT!
Gold Key 1967–80

4 Ph(c),AMc	40.00
5 GE,JJ	25.00
6 AMc	25.00
7	15.00
8	25.00
9	15.00
10 GE	25.00
11	10.00
12	10.00
13	10.00
14	10.00
15 GE	12.00
16	10.00
17	10.00
18	10.00
19	10.00
20	10.00
21 thru 30	@8.00
31 thru 38	@5.00
39 RC	6.00
40 thru 50	@5.00
51 thru 94	@4.00

RISK
Maximum Press 1995

1 V:Furious 2.50

ROBIN HOOD
Eclipse 1991

1 TT,Historically accurate series . 2.75
2 and 3 TT .... @2.75

ROBO HUNTER
Eagle

1 .... 1.50
2 thru 5 .... @1.00

ROBOTECH
Antarctic Press 1997

1 by Fred Perry & BDn 2.95
2 .... 2.95
3 .... 2.95

ROBOTECH: GENESIS
The Legend of Zor
Eternity

1 O:Robotech w/cards 2.95
1a Limited Edition,extra pages with
   cards #1 & #2 .... 5.95
2 thru 6, each with cards .... @2.50

ROBOTECH IN 3-D
Comico

1 .... 2.50

Robotech: Genesis, The Legend of Zor #1 © Eternity

ROBOTECH, THE MACROSS SAGA
Comico 1985–89
(formerly Macross)

2	5.00
3	4.00
4	3.00
5	2.50
6 J:Rick Hunter	2.50
7 V:Zentraedi	2.00
8 A:Rick Hunter	2.00
9 V:Zentraedi	2.00
10 "Blind Game"	2.00
11 V:Zentraedi	2.00
12 V:Zentraedi	2.00
13 V:Zentraedi	2.00
14 "Gloval's Reports"	2.00
15 V:Zentraedi	2.00
16 V:Zentraedi	2.00
17 V:Zentraedi	2.00
18 D:Roy Fokker	2.00
19 V:Khyron	2.00
20 V:Zentraedi	2.00
21 "A New Dawn"	2.00
22 V:Zentraedi	2.00
23 "Reckless"	2.00
24 HB,V:Zentraedi	2.00
25 "Wedding Bells"	2.00
26 "The Messenger"	2.00
27 "Force of Arms"	2.00
28 "Reconstruction Blues"	2.00
29 "Robotech Masters"	2.00
30 "Viva Miriya"	2.00
31 "Khyron's Revenge"	2.00
32 "Broken Heart"	2.00
33 "A Rainy Night"	2.00
34 "Private Time"	2.00
35 "Season's Greetings"	2.00
36 last issue	2.00
Graphic Novel #1	6.00

ROBOTECH MASTERS
Comico 1985–88

1	4.00
2	3.00
3 Space Station Liberty	3.00
4 V:Bioroids	2.50

5 V:Flagship	2.50
6 "Prelude to Battle"	2.50
7 "The Trap"	2.50
8 F:Dana Sterling	2.50
9 "Star Dust"	2.50
10 V:Zor	2.50
11 A:De Ja Vu	2.00
12 2OR	2.00
13	2.00
14 "Clone Chamber,"V:Zor	2.00
15 "Love Song"	2.00
16 V:General Emerson	2.00
17 "Mind Games"	2.00
18 "Dana in Wonderland"	2.00
19	2.00
20 A:Zor,Musica	2.00
21 "Final Nightmare"	2.00
22 "The Invid Connection"	2.00
23 "Catastrophe," final issue	2.00

ROBOTECH: THE NEW GENERATION
Comico 1985–88

1	4.00
2 "The Lost City"	3.00
3 V:Yellow Dancer	3.00
4 A:Yellow Dancer	3.00
5 SK(i),A:Yellow Dancer	2.50
6 F:Rook Bartley	2.50
7 "Paper Hero"	2.00
8	2.00
9 KSy,"The Genesis Pit"	2.00
10 V:The Invid	2.00
11 F:Scott Bernard	2.00
12 V:The Invid	2.00
13 V:The Invid	2.00
14 "Annie"s Wedding"	2.00
15 "Seperate Ways"	2.00
16 "Metamorphosis"	2.00
17 "Midnight Sun"	2.00
18	2.00
19	2.00
20 "Birthday Blues"	2.00
21 "Hired Gun"	2.00
22 "The Big Apple"	2.00
23 Robotech Wars	2.00
24 Robotech Wars	2.00
25 V:Invid, last issue	2.00

ROBOTECH SPECIAL DANA"S STORY
Eclipse

1 .... 5.00

ROBOTECH II: THE SENTINELS
Eternity

Swimsuit Spec.#1 .... 2.95

ROCK & ROLL
Revolutionary
Prev: Black & White

15 Poison	3.50
16 Van Halen	1.95
17 Madonna	2.50
18 AliceCooper	1.95
19 Public Enemy, 2 Live Crew	2.50
20 Queensryche	1.95
21 Prince	1.95
22 AC/DC	1.95
23 Living Color	1.95
24 Anthrax	1.95

COLOR PUB.

25 Z.Z.Top	2.50
26 Doors	2.50
27 Doors	2.50
28 Ozzy Osbourne	2.50
29 The Cure	2.50
30	2.50
31 Vanilla Ice	2.50
32 Frank Zappa	2.50
33 Guns n" Roses	2.50
34 The Black Crowes	2.50
35 R.E.M.	2.50
36 Michael Jackson	2.50
37 Ice T	2.50
38 Rod Stewart	2.50
39	2.50
40 N.W.A./Ice Cube	2.50
41 Paula Abdul	2.50
42 Metallica II	2.50
43 Guns "N" Roses	2.50
44 Scorpions	2.50
45 Greatful Dead	3.00
46 Grateful Dead	3.00
47 Grateful Dead	3.00
48 (now b/w),Queen	2.50
49 Rush	2.50
50 Bob Dylan Pt.1	2.50
51 Bob Dylan Pt.2	2.50
52 Bob Dylan Pt.3	2.50
53 Bruce Springsteen	2.50
54 U2 Pt.1	2.50
55 U2 Pt.2	2.50
56 thru 72	@2.50

ROCK 'N' ROLL HIGH SCHOOL
Cosmic Comics 1995

1 Sequel to the movie	2.50

ROCKETEER
Walt Disney

1 DSt,(c)RH,MovieAdaptation	7.00
Newsstand Version	3.25

ROCKETEER ADVENTURE MAGAZINE
Comico

1 DSt,MK,Rocketeer(6thApp.)	12.00
2 DSt,MK,Rocketeer(7thApp.)	10.00

ROCKETEER SPECIAL
Eclipse 1984

1 DSt, Rocketeer(5th App.)	26.00

ROCKET MAN: KING OF THE ROCKET MEN
Innovation

1 Adapts movie series	2.50
2 Adapts movie series	2.50
3 Adapts movie series	2.50
4 Adapts movie series	2.50

ROCKET RANGER
Adventure Comics

1 Based on computer game	2.95

ROCKMEEZ
Jzink Comics

1 I:Rockmeez,V:Pyrites	2.50
2 V:Pyrites,Silv.Embos.(c)	2.50

ROCKY HORROR PICTURE SHOW
Calibre/Tome

1	6.00
1a 2nd printing	3.25
2	3.50
3 "The Conclusion"	3.25
Rocky Horror Collection reps.	4.95

ROG 2000
Pacific

1 One-Shot, JBy	2.00

Roger Rabbit #7 © Walt Disney

ROGER RABBIT
Walt Disney 1990

1 I:Rick Flint, "The Trouble with Toons"	5.50
2	3.50
3	2.50
4	2.50
5	2.50
6 thru 9	@2.50
10 "Tuned-in-toons"	2.50
11 "Who Framed Rick Flint"	2.00
12 "Somebunny to Love"	2.00
13 "Honey,I Stink with Kids"	2.00
14 "Who Fired Jessica Rabbit"	2.00
15 "The Great Toon Detective"	2.00
16 "See you later Aviator"	2.00
17 Flying Saucers over Toontown	2.00
18 "I Have Seen the Future"	2.00

ROGER RABBIT'S TOONTOWN
Walt Disney

1 (inc.Baby Herman,Jessica stories	2.00
2 "Pre-Hysterical Roger"	1.75
3 "Lumberjack of tomorrow"	1.75
4 "The Longest Daze"	1.75

ROGUE TROOPER
Fleetway/Quality

1 thru 5	@1.00
6	1.50
7 thru 21	@1.25
22/23	1.50

24	1.50
25/26	1.50
27 thru 35	@1.50
36	1.95
37	1.95
38 thru 40	@1.50
41 thru 43	@1.75

ROGUE TROOPER: THE FINAL WARRIOR
Fleetway

1 RS,Golden Rebellion,pt 1	2.95
2 thru 3	2.95
4 "Saharan Ice-Belt War"	2.95

ROMAN HOLIDAYS, THE
Gold Key 1973

1	15.00
2	10.00
3	10.00
4	10.00

ROOK, THE
Harris Comics 1995

0 O:Rook	2.95
1 N:Rook	2.95
2 I:Coffin	2.95
3 The Spider Obsidian	2.95

ROOM 222
Dell Publishing Co. Jan. 1970

1	25.00
2	20.00
3 Drug	25.00
4 Ph(c)	20.00

ROSWELL
Bongo Comics 1996

1 by Bill Morrison,"The Story of the Century"	2.95
2 "The Untold Story"	2.95
3 "The Untold Story," concl.	2.95
4 V:Mutato	2.95

ROY ROGERS WESTERN CLASSICS
AC Comics

1	2.95
2	2.95
3	2.95
4	3.95

RUFF AND READY
Dell Publishing Co. Sept., 1958

1	75.00
2	50.00
3	50.00
4	35.00
5	35.00
6	35.00
7	35.00
8	35.00
9	35.00
10 thru 12	@35.00

RUN, BUDDY, RUN
Gold Key June, 1967

1	15.00

COLOR PUB.

RUST
Now

1	4.00
2	3.00
3 thru 11	@2.00
12 I:Terminator	10.00
13 thru 15	@1.75

[Volume 2]

1 thru 10	@1.75

SABLE
First 1988–90

1 AIDS story	1.75
2 Sable in Iran	1.75
3 Pentathelon	1.75
4	1.75
5 DCw,V:Tong Gangs	1.75
6 In Atlantic City	1.75
7 V:EnvironmentalTerrorists	1.75
8 In Argentina	1.95
9 In Kenya Pt.1	1.95
10 In Kenya Pt.2	1.95
11 Jon Sable bodyguard	1.95
12 In Cambodia Pt.1	1.95
13 In Cambodia Pt.2	1.95
14 Christmas story	1.95
15 A:Ted Koppel	1.95
16 Sable as "B.B.Flemm" rev.	1.95
17 Turning point issue	1.95
18 Richard Rockwell(i)	1.95
19 A:Maggie the Cat	1.95
20 A:Gary Adler	1.95
21 Richard Rockwell(i)	1.95
22 A:Eden Kendall	1.95
23 TV cover	1.95
24 TV cover	1.95
25 TV cover	1.95
26 TV cover	1.95
27	1.95
28 last issue	1.95

SABRE
Eclipse 1982–85

1 PG	2.50
2 PG	3.00
3 thru 14	@2.00

SABRINA, THE TEENAGE WITCH
Archie Publications 1971–83

1	40.00
2	15.00
3	7.00
4	7.00
5	7.00
6 thru 10	@4.00
11 thru 20	@2.00
21 thru 77	@1.00

SABRINA THE TEENAGE WITCH
Archie Comics 1996

one-shot photo cover	1.50
1 photo cover	1.50
2 "Trouble in Time"	1.50
3 photo cover	1.50
4 photo cover	1.50
5 "Driver's License"	1.50
6 "Treasure Troubles"	1.50
Halloween Spooktacular #1	2.00
Halloween Spooktacular #2	2.00
Holiday Spectacular #3	2.00

SAD SACK AND THE SARGE
Harvey Publications 1957–82

1	135.00
2	50.00
3 thru 10	@40.00
11 thru 20	@25.00
21 thru 40	@15.00
41 thru 50	@12.00
51 thru 90	@5.00
91 thru 96 52 pg Giants	@6.00
97 thru 155	@3.00

SAD SACK'S ARMY LIFE
Harvey Publications 1963–76

1	50.00
2 thru 10	@25.00
11 thru 20	@12.00
21 thru 30	@8.00
31 thru 50	@3.00
51 thru 61	@2.00

SAD SACK'S FUNNY FRIENDS
Harvey Publications 1955–69

1	85.00
2 thru 10	@40.00
11 thru 20	@18.00
21 thru 30	@8.00
31 thru 40	@4.00
41 thru 75	@3.00

SAD SACK in 3-D
Blackthorne

1 and 2	@2.50

SALOME
Eclipse 1987

1 CR	2.00

SAM AND MAX, FREE-LANCE POLICE SPECIAL
Comico 1987–89

1	2.75

Sam Slade Robohunter #14 © Quality

SAM SLADE ROBOHUNTER
Quality 1986–89

1	1.00
2	1.00
3 Filby Case	1.00
4	1.00
5	1.00
6 Bax the Burner,Moore	1.00
7	1.00
8 thru 21	@1.25
22/23	1.50
24	1.50
25/26	1.50
27 thru 33	@1.50

SAMSONS
Samsons Comics

1/2 Various Artists	2.50

SAMURAI
Eclipse

1	2.00
2	2.00
3 thru 5	@2.00

SAMUREE
Continuity 1993–94

1 NA,A:Revengers	2.00
2 A:Revengers	2.00
3 NA,A:Revengers	2.00
4 A:Revengers	2.00
5 BSz(c),A:Revengers	2.00
6 A:Revengers	2.00
7	2.00
8 Drug story	2.00
9 Drug story	2.00

[2nd Series]

1 thru 3 Rise of Magic	2.50

SARGE STEEL/ SECRET AGENT
Charlton 1964–66

1 DG,I:SargeSteel & IvanChung	5.00
2 DG,I:Werner Von Hess	2.50
3 DG,V:Smiling Skull	2.50
4 DG,V:Lynx	2.50
5 FMc,V:Ivan Chung	2.50
6 FMc,A:Judomaster	2.50
7 DG	2.50
8 V:Talon	2.50

Becomes:

SECRET AGENT

9 DG,A:The Lynx	3.50
10 DG,JAp,A:Tiffany Sinn	3.00

SATANIKA
Verotik 1995

0	5.00
1 New ongoing series	6.00
2 Femininity	3.50
3	3.00
4	3.00
5	3.00
6 thru 8	@2.95
1-shot Satanika X (adult)	5.00

SATANIKA VS. SHILENE
Verotik April 1996

1-shot	9.95

COLOR PUB.

SATAN'S SIX
Topps 1993
1 F:Satan's Six,w/3 cards	3.25
2 V:Kalazarr,w/3 cards	2.95
3 w/3 cards	2.95
4 w/3 cards	2.95

SATURDAY KNIGHTS
Hot
1	1.50
2 thru 4	@1.50

SAURAUS FAMILY
Blackthorne
1 3-D	2.00

SAVAGE COMBAT TALES
Atlas Feb.–July, 1975
1 F:Sgt Strykers Death Squad	1.25
2 ATh,A:Warhawk	1.25
3 final issue	1.25

SAVAGE DRAGON/ TEENAGE MUTANT NINJA TURLES CROSSOVER
Mirage
1 EL(s)	2.75

SAVED BY THE BELL
Harvey
1 based on TV series	1.25

SCARY TALES
Charlton 1975
1	3.00
2 thru 11	@2.00
12 thru 46	@1.50

SCAVENGERS
Quality 1988–89
1 thru 7	@1.25
8 thru 14	@1.50

SCAVENGERS
Triumphant Comics 1993–94
0 Fso(c),JnR(s)	2.50
0a "Free Copy"	2.50
0b Red Logo	2.50
1 JnR(s),I:Scavengers,Ximos, C:Doctor Chaos	2.50
1a 2nd Printing	2.50
2 JnR(s)	2.50
3 JnR(s),I:Lurok	2.50
4 JnR(s)	2.50
5 Fso(c),JnR(s),D:Jack Hanal	2.50
6 JnR(s)	2.50
7 JnR(s),I:Zion	2.50
8 JnR(s),Nativity	2.50
9 JnR(s),The Challenge	2.50
10 JnR(s),Snowblind	2.50

SCHISM
Defiant
1 thru 4 Defiant's x-over	3.25

SCION
1 and 2	@2.00

Scooby Doo #1 © Charlton

SCOOBY DOO
Gold Key 1970–75
1	45.00
2	30.00
3	20.00
4	20.00
5	20.00
6	15.00
7	15.00
8	15.00
9	15.00
10	15.00
11 thru 20	@10.00
21 thru 30	@6.00

SCOOBY DOO
Charlton Comics 1975–76
1	18.00
2	7.00
3	7.00
4	7.00
5	7.00
6	5.00
7	5.00
8	5.00
9	5.00
10	5.00
11	5.00

SCOOBY DOO
Archie 1995
1 thru 10	@1.50
11 thru 13	@1.50
14 "The Balloon Busters"	1.50
15 "On the Boardwalk in Atlantic City"	1.50
16 "The Ghost of Central Park"	1.50
19 "Electric Monster"	1.50
20 "The Legend of Spooky Doo"	1.50
21 "Monster Park After Dark"	1.50

SCORCHED EARTH
Tundra 1991
1 Earth 2025,I:Dr.EliotGodwin	3.50
2 Hunt for Eliot	2.95
3 Mystical Transformation	2.95

SCORPION CORP.
Dagger 1993
1 PuD,JRI,CH,	2.75
2 PuD,JRI,CH,V:Victor Kyner	2.75
3 PuD,BlH,V:Victor Kyner	2.75

SCORPIO ROSE
Eclipse 1983
1 MR/TP,I:Dr.Orient	2.00
2 MR/TP	2.00

SCOUT
Eclipse 1985–87
1 TT,I:Scout,Fash.In Action	6.00
2 TT,V:Buffalo Monster	3.00
3 TT,V:President Grail	2.50
4 TT,V:President Grail	2.50
5 TT,"Killin' Floor"	2.50
6 TT,V:President Grail	2.50
7 TT,TY,Rosanna's Diary	2.50
8 TT,TY	2.50
9 TT,TY,A:Airboy	2.50
10 TT,TY,I:Proj.Mountain Fire	2.00
11 TT,FH,V:Rangers	2.00
12 TT,FH,"Me and the Devil"	2.00
13 TT,FH,Monday:Eliminator	2.00
14 TT,FH,Monday:Eliminator	2.00
15 TT,FH,Monday:Eliminator	2.00
16 TT,3-D issue,F:Santana	2.00
17 TT,A:Beanworld	2.00
18 TT,FH,V:Lex Lucifer	2.00
19 TT,w/Record,V:Lex Lucifer	3.00
20 TT,A:Monday:Eliminator	2.00
21 TT,A:Monday:Eliminator	1.75
22 TT,A:Swords of Texas	1.75
23 TT,A:Swords of Texas	1.75
24 TT,last Issue	1.75

SCOUT: WAR SHAMAN
Eclipse 1988–89
1 TT,R:Scout (now a father)	2.25
2 TT,I:Redwire	1.95
3 TT,V:Atuma Yuma	1.95
4 TT,"Rollin' on the River"	1.95
5 TT,Hopi Katchina dieties	1.95
6 TT,Scout vs. Rosa Winter	1.95
7 TT,R:Redwire	1.95
8 TT,R:Beau LaDuke	1.95
9 TT,V:Doodyists	1.95
10 TT,TY,V:Redwire	1.95
11 TT,V:Redwire	1.95
12 TT,V:Snow Leopards	1.95
13 TT,F:Beau LaDuke	1.95
14 TT,V:Redwire	1.95
15 TT,V:Redwire	1.95
16 TT,"Wall of Death,"last issue	1.95

SEADRAGON
Elite 1986–87
1	3.00
1a 2nd printing	1.75
2	2.00
3	2.00
4	2.00
5 thru 8	@1.75

SEA HUNT
Dell Publishing Co. 1958
1 L.BridgesPh(c) all	125.00
2	100.00
3 ATh	110.00
4 RsM	100.00

5 RsM	100.00
6 RsM	100.00
7	90.00
8 RsM	100.00
9 RsM	100.00
10 RsM	100.00
11 RsM	100.00
12	100.00
13 RsM	100.00

SEAQUEST
Nemesis 1994

1 HC(c),DGC,KP,AA,Based on TV Show	2.50

SEBASTIAN
Walt Disney

1 From Little Mermaid	1.50
2 "While da Crab's Away"	1.50

SECRET AGENT
Gold Key Nov., 1966

1	120.00
2	75.00

SECRET CITY SAGA
Topps 1993

0 JK	3.25
0 Gold Ed.	15.00
0 Red	10.00
1 w/3 cards	3.25
2 w/3 cards	3.25
3 w/3 cards	3.25
4 w/3 cards	3.25

SECRET SQUIRREL
Gold Key Oct., 1966

1	50.00

SEDUCTION OF THE INNOCENT
Eclipse 1985–86

1 ATh,"Hanged by the Neck" reps.	2.50
2	2.25
3 ATh,"The Crushed Gardenia"	2.00
4 ATh,NC,"World's Apart"	2.00
5 ATh,"The Phantom Ship"	2.00
6 ATh,RA,"Hands of Don Jose"	2.00
3-D #1 DSt(c)	2.25
3-D #2 ATh,MB,BWr,"Man Who Was Always on Time"	2.00

SEEKER: VENGEANCE
Sky Comics

1 JMt(s),I:Seeker	2.50

SENSEI
First

1 Mini-Series	2.75
2	2.75
3	2.75
4	2.75

SENTINELS OF JUSTICE
AC Comics

1 Capt.Paragon	1.75
2	1.75
3	1.75
4	1.75
5	1.75
6	1.75

7	1.75

SENTRY: SPECIAL
Innovation 1991

1	2.75

SERAPHIM
Innovation 1990

1 and 2	@2.50

SERINA
Antarctic 1996

1	2.95

77 SUNSET STRIP
**Dell Publishing Co.
Jan.-March, 1960**

1 Ph(c)	75.00
2 Ph(c),RsM	80.00

SHADE SPECIAL
AC Comics

1	1.50

SHADOW, THE
Archie Comics 1964–65

1	45.00
2	30.00
3	30.00
4	30.00
5	30.00
6 and 8	@25.00

SHADOW COMICS

1 Guardians of Justice & The O-Force	1.50

SHADOW OF THE TORTURER, THE
Innovation 1991

1 thru 6 Gene Wolfe adapt.	@1.95

SHADOW RAVEN
Poc-It Comics

1 I:Shadow Raven	2.95

SHADOW STATE
Preview Editions

1 and 2 B&W	2.50

Broadway 1995

1 thru 4 F:BloodS.C.R.E.A.M.	@2.50
5 JiS, "Image Isn't Everything," concl.	2.50
6 "Anger of Lovers" pt.1	2.50
7 "Anger of Lovers" pt.2	2.95

SHAFT
Maximum Press 1997

1 RLd	2.50

SHAIANA
Entity 1995

1 R:Shaiana from Aster	3.75
1a clear chromium	8.00
1b Holochrome	10.00
2 Guardians of Earth	2.50

SHANGHAI BREEZE

1	1.75

SHAOLIN
Black Tiger Press

1 I:Tiger	2.95
2 I:Crane	2.95

Shatter #2 © First Comics

SHATTER
First 1985–88

1	3.00
2	2.50
3	2.50
4 and 5	@2.00
6 thru 14	@1.75
Spec. #1 Computer Comic	5.00
#1a 2nd Printing	2.00

SHE-DEVILS ON WHEELS
Aircel

1 V:Man-Eaters	2.95
2 V:Man-Eaters	2.95
3 V:Man-Eaters	2.95

SHERIFF OF TOMBSTONE
Charlton Comics 1958–61

1 AW,JSe	50.00
2	30.00
3 thru 10	@20.00
11 thru 17	@20.00

SHI
Crusade Comics

1 BiT,HMo,I:Shi	40.00
2 BiT	20.00
2 BiT, reissue, new cover	2.95
3 BiT	15.00
4 BiT	8.00
5 V:Arashi	6.00
5a variant cover	15.00
6 V:Tomoe	6.00
7 V:Nara Warriors	5.00
8 New costume	4.00
9 thru 11	@4.00
12 "Way of the Warrior" concl, flip-book Angel Fire.	3.00
TPB Shi:Way of the Warrior	12.95

COLOR PUB.

Shi/Cyblade Spec.#1 Battle of the
  Independents 4.00
Spec.#1a variant cover 6.00
TPB Vol. 1 revised rep.JuB(c) . . 14.95
TPB Vol. II, rep. #5–#8 . . . . . . 14.95
TPB rep. Shi #9–#12 & Shi vs. Tomoe 14.95

SHI/CYBLADE
Crusade
Spec.#1 The Battle for
  Independents...Endgame 2.95

SHI VS. TOMOE
Crusade April 1996
Spec. #1 BiT, double size 3.95

SHI: HEAVEN AND EARTH
Crusade Entertainment 1997
1 (of 3) BiT 2.95
1 variant cover 2.95

SHI: REKISHI
Crusade Entertainment 1997
1 (of 2) BiT 2.95
2 BiT, conclusion 2.95

SHI-SENRYAKU
Crusade 1995
1 BiT,R:Shi 3.00
1a variant cover 8.00
1 (of 3) 2nd edition 2.50
2 BiT,Arts of Warfare 3.00
2 2nd edition 2.50
3 BiT 3.00
3 2nd edition 2.50
HC Rep.#1-#2 . . . . 24.95
TPB Rep.#1-#2 . . . . 12.95

SHOCK SUSPENSE STORIES
Russ Cochran Press 1992
1 reps.horror stories 1.50
2 inc.Kickback 1.50
3 thru 4 . . . . @2.00
5 thru 7 reps.horror stories 2.00
8 reps.horror stories 2.00
Gemstone
18 EC comics reprint 2.50

SHOCK THE MONKEY
Millenium/Expand 1995
1 Shock therapy 2.95

SHOGUNAUT
Firstlight
1 I:Shogunaut 2.95
2 V:Teckno Terror 2.95

SHOOTING STARS
1 . . . . 2.50

SHOTGUN MARY
Antarctic Press 1995
1 I:Shotgun Mary 2.95
1a with CD Soundtrack 8.95
1b Red Foil cover 8.00
2 . . . . 2.95
Shooting Gallery 2.95
Deviltown 2.95

SHOTGUN MARY: BLOOD LORE
Antarctic Press 1997
1 (of 4) by Herb Mallette & Neil
  Googe 2.95
2 . . . . 2.95
3 . . . . 2.95

SIEGEL & SHUSTER
Eclipse 1984–85
1 . . . . 1.50
2 . . . . 1.75

SILENT MOBIUS
Viz 1991–92
1 Katsumi 5.75
2 Katsumi vs. Spirit 5.25
3 Katsumi trapped within entity . . 4.95
4 Nami vs. Dragon 4.95
5 Kiddy vs. Wire 4.95
6 Search for Wire 4.95
GN 14.95

SILENT MOBIUS II
Viz
1 AMP Officers vs. Entities cont . 4.95
2 Entities in Amp H.Q. 4.95
3 V:Entity 4.95
4 The Esper Weapon 4.95
5 Last issue 4.95

SILENT MOBIUS III
Viz
1 F:Lebia/computer network 2.75
2 Lebia/computer link cont. 2.75
3 Lebia in danger 2.75
4 Return to Consciousness 2.75
5 Conclusion 2.75

SILVERBACK
Comico 1989–90
1 thru 3 . . . . @2.50

SILVERHEELS
Pacific 1983–84
1 . . . . 2.00
2 and 3 . . . . @1.50

SILVER STAR
Pacific 1983–84
1 JK 1.00
2 JK 1.00
3 JK 1.00
4 JK 1.00
5 JK 1.00
6 JK 1.00

SILVER STAR
Topps
1 w/Cards 2.95

SILVER STORM
1 . . . . 2.25
2 . . . . 1.95
3 . . . . 1.95
4 . . . . 1.95

SIMPSONS COMICS
Bongo Comics 1993
1 Colossal Horner 3.00

2 A:Sideshow Bob 2.00
3 F:Bart 2.00
4 F:Bart 2.25
5 A:Itchy & Scratchy 2.25
6 F:Lisa 2.25
7 Circus in Town 2.25
8 Mr. Burns Voyage 2.25
9 Autobiographies 2.25
10 Tales of the Kwik-E-Mart 2.25
11 Ned Flanders Public Enemy . . 2.25
12 In the Blodome 2.25
13 F:Bart & Millhouse 2.25
14 Homer owns beer company . . 2.25
15 Waltons parody 2.25
16 thru 18 . . . . @2.25
19 thru 23 . . . . @2.25
24 . . . . 2.25
25 . . . . 2.25
26 Bart: action hero! 2.25
27 . . . . 2.25
28 Krusty the Clown, tax protest . 2.25
29 Captain Slamtastic 2.25
30 Montgomery Burns clones
  Smithers 2.25
31 Radioactive Homer 2.25
TPB Rep.#1-#4 . . . . 10.00
TPB Wing Ding, 120pg 11.95
Comic Spectacular,Vol.1 Rep. . . 10.00
Comic Spectacular,Vol.2 Rep. . . 10.00

SIMPSONS COMICS & STORIES
Welsh Publishing 1993
1 with poster 4.00
1a without poster 2.50

Six Million Dollar Man #1
© Charlton Comics Group

SIX MILLION DOLLAR MAN, THE
Charlton June 1976
1 JSon,Lee Majors Ph(c) 3.00
2 NA(c),JSon,Ph(c) 3.00
3 Ph(c) 1.50
4 Ph(c) 1.50
5 Ph(c) 1.50
6 Ph(c) 1.50
7 Ph(c) 1.50

COLOR PUB.

8 Ph(c) 1.50
9 Ph(c) 1.50

666: MARK OF THE BEAST
Fleetway/Quality
1 I:Fludd, BU:Wolfie Smith 1.95
2 thru 18. . . . . @1.95

SKATEMAN
Pacific 1983
1 NA 1.50

SKY WOLF
Eclipse 1988
1 V:Baron Von Tundra 1.75
2 TL,V:Baron Von Tundra 1.75
3 TL,cont. in Airboy #41 . . . . . . 1.75

SLAINE THE BERSERKER
Quality 1987–89
1 thru 14 . . . . @1.25
15/16 . . . . 1.50
17 . . . . 1.50
18/19 . . . . 1.50
20 thru 28 . . . . @1.50
Becomes:

SLAINE THE KING
26 . . . . 1.50

SLAINE
Fleetway
1 thru 4 SBs,From 2000 AD . . @4.95

SLIMER
Now 1989
1 . . . . 2.50
2 thru 15 . . . . @1.75
Becomes:

SLIMER & REAL GHOSTBUSTERS
16 thru 18 . . . . @1.75

SNAGGLEPUSS
Gold Key 1962–63
1 . . . . 50.00
2 . . . . 35.00
3 . . . . 35.00
4 . . . . 35.00

SNOOPER AND BLABBER DETECTIVES
Gold Key 1962–63
1 . . . . 50.00
2 . . . . 35.00
3 . . . . 35.00

SNOW WHITE & SEVEN DWARVES GOLDEN ANNIVERSARY
Gladstone
1 w/poster & stickers 24.00

SO DARK THE ROSE
CFD 1995
1 Fully Painted 2.95

SOLDIERS OF FREEDOM
Americomics 1987
1 . . . . 1.75
2 . . . . 1.95

SOLOMON KANE
Blackthorne
1 3-D Special 2.50
2 3-D Special 2.50
1 thru 4 . . . . @2.50

SOMERSET HOLMES
Pacific 1983–84
1 BA,AW,I:Cliff Hanger &
Somerset Holmes 2.50
2 thru 4 BA,AW . . . . @2.00
Eclipse 1984
5 BA,AW 2.00
6 BA 2.00

SONG OF THE CID
Calibre/Tome
1 Story of El Cid 2.95
2 Story of El Cid concl. 2.95

SONIC THE HEDGEHOG
Archie Publications 1993
1 A:Mobius,V:Robotnik 1.50
2 thru 36 . . . . @1.50
40 thru 51 . . . . @1.50
Sonic Live Spec.#1 . . . . 2.00

SONIC QUEST: THE DEATH EGG SAGA
Archie Comics
1 (of 3) by Mike Gallagher & MaG,
cont. from Sonic the Hedgehog
#41 . . . . 1.50
2 and 3 . . . . @1.50

SONIC THE HEDGEHOG PRESENTS KNUCKLES CHASTIC
Archie Comics 1995
1 I:New Heroes 2.00
Sonic Versus Knuckles Battle Royal
Spec.#1 . . . . 2.00

SONIC THE HEDGEHOG PRESENTS TAILS
Archie Comics 1995
1 F:Tails 1.50
2 F:Tails 1.50

SONIC'S FRIENDLY NEMESIS: KNUCKLES
Archie 1996
1 . . . . 1.50

SON OF MUTANT WORLD
Fantagor 1990
1 BA 2.00
2 . . . . 2.00

SOULQUEST
Innovation 1989
1 BA 3.95

SOUPY SALES COMIC BOOK
Archie Publications 1965
1 . . . . 75.00

Space Adventures #5 © Charlton

SPACE ADVENTURES
Charlton 1967–79
Volume 3
1 (#60) O&I:Paul Mann & The
Saucers From the Future . . . 25.00
2 thru 8 (1968–69) . . . . @10.00
9 thru 13 (1978–79) . . . . @2.50

SPACE: ABOVE AND BEYOND
Topps 1995
1 thru 3 TV pilot adaptation . . @2.95

SPACE: ABOVE AND BEYOND—THE GAUNTLET
Topps 1996
1 . . . . 2.95
2 (of 2) 2.95

SPACE ARK
AC Comics 1985–87
1 . . . . 3.00
2 . . . . 2.00

SPACE FAMILY ROBINSON
Gold Key Dec., 1962–69
1 DSp 250.00
2 . . . . 125.00
3 . . . . 75.00
4 . . . . 75.00
5 . . . . 75.00
6 B:Captain Venture 75.00
7 . . . . 75.00
8 . . . . 75.00
9 . . . . 75.00
10 . . . . 75.00
11 thru 20 . . . . @50.00
21 thru 36 . . . . @25.00

COLOR PUB.

SPACE GHOST
Gold Key March, 1967
1 . . . . 6.00

SPACE GHOST
Comico 1987
1 SR,V:Robot Master 3.50

SPACE MAN
Dell Publishing Co. 1962–72
1 . . . . 75.00
2 . . . . 40.00
3 . . . . 40.00
4 . . . . 30.00
5 . . . . 30.00
6 . . . . 30.00
7 . . . . 30.00
8 . . . . 30.00
9 . . . . 30.00
10 . . . . 30.00

SPACE: 1999
Charlton 1975–76
1 . . . . 5.00
2 JSon,"Survival" 4.00
3 JBy,"Bring Them Back Alive" . . 3.50
4 JBy 3.50
5 JBy 3.50
6 JBy 3.50
7 . . . . 3.00
8 B&W 3.00

SPACE: 1999
A Plus Comics
1 GM,JBy 2.50

SPACE USAGI
Mirage 1993
1 thru 3 From TMNT . . . . @2.75

SPACE WAR
Charlton Comics Oct., 1959
1 . . . . 125.00
2 . . . . 65.00
3 . . . . 60.00
4 SD,SD(c) 125.00
5 SD,SD(c) 125.00
6 SD 125.00
7 . . . . 30.00
8 SD,SD(c) 125.00
9 . . . . 35.00
10 SD,SD(c) 125.00
11 . . . . 35.00
12 . . . . 35.00
13 thru 15 . . . . @35.00
16 thru 27 . . . . @30.00
Becomes:

FIGHTIN' FIVE
28 SD,SD(c) 35.00
29 SD,SD(c) 35.00
30 SD,SD(c) 40.00
31 SD,SD(c) 40.00
32 . . . . 5.00
33 SD,SD(c) 40.00
34 Sd,SD(c) 40.00

SPECTRUM COMICS PRESENTS
Spectrum
1 I:Survivors 3.50

SPEED RACER
Now 1987–90
1 . . . . 3.50
1a 2nd printing 1.50
2 thru 33 . . . . @2.00
34 thru 38 . . . . @1.75
Spec. #1 . . . . 2.50
#1 2nd printing 1.75
Spec. #2 . . . . 3.50
Classics, Vol #2 . . . . 3.95
Classics, Vol #3 . . . . 3.95
[2nd Series]
1 R:Speed Racer 1.95
2 . . . . 1.95
3 V:Giant Crab 1.95
4 . . . . 1.95
5 Racer-X 1.95
6 . . . . 1.95
7 . . . . 1.95

Spellbinders #1 © Quality Comics

SPELLBINDERS
Quality 1986–88
1 Nemesis the Warlock 1.25
2 Nemesis the Warlock 1.25
3 Nemesis the Warlock 1.25
4 Nemesis the Warlock 1.25
5 Nemesis the Warlock 1.25
6 Nemesis the Warlock 1.25
7 Nemesis the Warlock 1.25
8 Nemesis the Warlock 1.25
9 Nemesis the Warlock 1.25
1O Nemesis the Warlock 1.25
11 Nemesis the Warlock 1.25

SPIDER
Eclipse 1991
1 TT,"Blood Dance" 7.00
2 TT,"Blood Mark" 6.00
3 TT,The Spider Unmasked 5.50

SPIDER: REIGN OF THE VAMPIRE KING
Eclipse 1992
1 TT,I:Legion of Vermin 5.25
2 thru 4 TT . . . . @2.50

SPIDERFEMME
Personality
1 Rep. parody 2.50

SPIDER-MAN/BADROCK
Maximum Press
1 (of 2) DJu,MMy x-over 3.00
2 DJu,DaF x-over 3.00

SPIRAL PATH
Eclipse 1986
1 V:Tairngir 1.75
2 V:King Artuk 1.75

SPIRIT
Harvey 1966
1 WE,O:Spirit 50.00
2 WE,O:The Octopus 50.00

SPIRIT, THE
Kitchen Sink 1983–92
1 WE(c) (1983) 5.25
2 WE(c) 4.25
3 WE(c) (1984) 4.00
4 WE(c) 4.00
5 WE(c) 3.00
6 WE(c) 3.00
7 WE(c) 3.00
8 thru 11 WE(c) (1985) color . . . 3.00
See: B&W section

SPIRIT, THE: THE NEW ADVENTURES
Kitchen Sink 1997
1 AMo,DGb 3.95
2 Eisner/Stout cover 3.50
2a Eisner/Schultz cover 3.50

SPOOKY HAUNTED HOUSE
Harvey Publications 1972–75
1 . . . . 10.00
2 . . . . 5.00
3 thru 5 . . . . @5.00
6 thru 10 . . . . @2.50
11 thru 15 . . . . @1.00

SPOOKY SPOOKTOWN
Harvey Publications 1966–76
1 B:Casper,Spooky,68 pgs . . 85.00
2 . . . . 50.00
3 . . . . 35.00
4 . . . . 35.00
5 . . . . 35.00
6 thru 10 . . . . @20.00
11 thru 20 . . . . @15.00
21 thru 30 . . . . @15.00
31 thru 39 E:68 pgs . . . . @4.50
40 thru 45 . . . . @2.50
46 thru 66 . . . . @1.00

SPYMAN
1 GT,JSo,1st prof work, I:Spyman 15.00
2 DAy,JSo,V:Cyclops 10.00
3 . . . . 8.00

SQUALOR
First 1989
1 . . . . 2.75
2 . . . . 2.75

---

3 . . . . 2.75

STAINLESS STEEL RAT
Eagle 1986
1 Harry Harrison adapt. 2.25
2 thru 6 . . . . @1.50

STAR BLAZERS
Comico 1989
1 . . . . 3.00
2 . . . . 1.75
3 . . . . 1.75
4 . . . . 1.75

[2nd Series]
1 . . . . 1.95
2 . . . . 1.95
3 thru 5 . . . . @2.50

STARBLAZERS
Argo Press 1995
0 Battleship Yamato 2.95
1 F:Dereck Wildstar 2.95
2 After the Comet War 2.95
3 . . . . 2.95
4 TEI 2.95
5 . . . . 2.95
6 . . . . 2.95
7 Icarus, pt.2 . . . . 2.95
8 . . . . 2.95
9 . . . . 2.95
10 . . . . 2.95
11 . . . . 2.95
12 Nova captured 2.95

STARFORCE SIX SPECIAL
AC Comics
1 . . . . 1.50

STARGATE
Entity Comics 1996
1 . . . . 2.95
2 . . . . 2.95
3 . . . . 2.95
4 (of 4) 2.95
4a deluxe limited edition 3.50

STARGATE: DOOMSDAY WORLD
Entity Comics 1996
1 new crew explores 2nd StarGate 2.95
1 prism-foil edition 3.50
2 . . . . 2.95
3 . . . . 2.95
3 deluxe 3.50

STARLIGHT
1 . . . . 1.95

STAR MASTERS
AC Comics
1 . . . . 1.50

STAR REACH CLASSICS
Eclipse 1984
1 JSn,NA(r) 2.00
2 AN 2.00
3 HC 2.00
4 FB(r) 2.00
5 . . . . 2.00

6 . . . . 2.00

STARSLAYER
Pacific 1982–83
1 MGr,O:Starslayer 3.00
2 MGr,DSt,I:Rocketeer 12.00
3 DSt,MGr,A:Rocketeer(2ndApp.) 8.00
4 MGr,Baraka Kuhr 2.00
5 MGr,SA,A:Groo 10.00
6 MGr,conclusion story 2.00

Starslayer #7 © First

First
7 MGr layouts 2.00
8 MGr layouts, MG 1.50
9 MGr layouts, MG 2.25
10 TT,MG,I:Grimjack 4.00
11 TT,MG,A:Grimjack 2.00
12 TT,MG,A:Grimjack 2.00
13 TT,MG,A:Grimjack 2.00
14 TT,A:Grimjack 2.00
15 TT,A:Grimjack 2.00
16 TT,A:Grimjack 2.00
17 TT,A:Grimjack 2.00
18 TT,Grimjack x-over 2.00
19 TT,TS,A:Black Flame 1.25
20 TT,TS,A:Black Flame 1.25
21 TT,TS,A:Black Flame 1.25
22 TT,TS,A:Black Flame 1.25
23 TT,TS,A:Black Flame 1.25
24 TT,TS,A:Black Flame 1.25
25 TS,A:Black Flame 1.25
26 TS,Black Flame full story 1.25
27 A:Black Flame 1.25
28 A:Black Flame 1.25
29 TS,A:Black Flame 1.25
30 TS,A:Black Flame 1.25
31 2nd Anniversary Issue 1.25
32 TS,A:Black Flame 1.25
33 TS,A:Black Flame 1.25
34 last issue 1.25
Graphic Novel 9.95

STAR TREK
Gold Key 1967–79
1 Planet of No Return 500.00
2 Devil's Isle of Space 300.00
3 Invasion of City Builders . . . 200.00
4 Peril of Planet Quick Change 200.00
5 Ghost Planet 200.00

6 When Planets Collide 165.00
7 Voodoo Planet 175.00
8 Youth Trap 150.00
9 Legacy of Lazarus 150.00
10 Sceptre of the Sun 100.00
11 Brain Shockers 100.00
12 Flight of the Buccaneer 90.00
13 Dark Traveler 80.00
14 Enterprise Mutiny 80.00
15 Museum a/t End of Time . . . 80.00
16 Day of the Inquisitors 80.00
17 Cosmic Cavemen 80.00
18 The Hijacked Planet 80.00
19 The Haunted Asteroid 80.00
20 A World Gone Mad 80.00
21 The Mummies of Heitus VII . . 65.00
22 Siege in Superspace 65.00
23 Child's Play 65.00
24 The Trial of Capt. Kirk 65.00
25 Dwarf Planet 65.00
26 The Perfect Dream 65.00
27 Ice Journey 65.00
28 The Mimicking Menace 65.00
29 rep. Star Trek #1 . . . . 65.00
30 Death of a Star 50.00
31 "The Final Truth" 50.00
32 "The Animal People" 50.00
33 "The Choice" 50.00
34 "The Psychocrystals" 50.00
35 rep. Star Trek #4 . . . . 50.00
36 "A Bomb in Time" 50.00
37 rep. Star Trek #5 . . . . 35.00
38 "One of our Captains is Missing" 35.00
39 "Prophet of Peace" 35.00
40 AMc,Furlough to Fury, A:
   Barbara McCoy 35.00
41 AMc,The Evictors 35.00
42 "World Against Time" 35.00
43 "World Beneath the Waves" . 35.00
44 "Prince Traitor" 35.00
45 rep. Star Trek #7 . . . . 35.00
46 "Mr. Oracle" 35.00
47 AMc,"This Tree Bears Bitter
   Fruit" 35.00
48 AMc,Murder on Enterprise . . 35.00
49 AMc,"A Warp in Space" 35.00
50 AMc,"The Planet of No Life" . 35.00
51 AMc,DestinationAnnihilation 6 30.00
52 AMc,"And A Child Shall Lead
   Them" 30.00
53 AMc,"What Fools..Mortals Be" 30.00
54 AMc,"Sport of Knaves" 30.00
55 AMc,A World Against Itself . . 30.00
56 AMc,No Time Like The Past,
   A:Guardian of Forever 30.00
57 AMc,"Spore of the Devil" . . . 30.00
58 AMc,"Brain Damaged Planet" 30.00
59 AMc,"To Err is Vulcan" 30.00
60 AMc,"The Empire Man" 30.00
61 AMc,"Operation Con Game" . 30.00

STAR WARS IN 3-D
Blackthorne
1 thru 7 . . . . @2.50

STARWOLVES: JUPITER RUN
1 . . . . 1.95

S.T.A.T.
Majestic 1993
1 FdS(s),PhH,I:S.T.A.T. 2.50

COLOR PUB.

STEALTH SQUAD
Petra Comics 1993
1 I:Stealth Squad 2.50

STEED & MRS PEEL
Eclipse 1990
1 IG,The Golden Game 4.95
2 IG,The Golden Game 4.95
3 IG,The Golden Game 4.95

STEEL CLAW
Quality
1 H:Ken Bulmer 1.25
2 . . . . 1.00
3 . . . . 1.00
4 . . . . 1.00

STEEL STERLING
Archie Publications 1984
(formerly LANCELOT STRONG)
4 EB 1.00
5 EB 1.00
6 EB 1.00
7 EB 1.00

STEVE CANYON 3-D
Kitchen Sink 1986
Milton Caniff & Peter Poplaski(c),
w/glasses (1985) 2.00

STEVE ZODIAC
& THE FIREBALL XL-5
Gold Key Jan., 1964
1 . . . . 50.00

Sting of the Green Hornet #2
© *Now Comics*

STING OF THE
GREEN HORNET
Now 1992
1 Polybagged w/trading card . . . 2.75
2 inc.Full color poster 2.75
3 inc.Full color poster 2.75

STINGER
1 . . . . 1.75

STITCH
Samsons Comics
1 I:Stitch 2.50

STORMQUEST
Caliber 1994
1 I:Stormquest 1.95
2 Time Stone 1.95
3 BU:Seeker 1.95
4 F:Shalimar 1.95
5 Reunion 1.95
6 V:Samuroids 1.95

STRANGE DAYS
Eclipse 1984–85
1 . . . . 3.50
2 . . . . 2.50
3 . . . . 1.50

STRANGE SUSPENSE
STORIES/
CAPTAIN ATOM
Charlton Comics
75 SD,O:CaptainAtom,1960Rep. 125.00
76 SD, Capt.Atom,1960Rep. . . . 75.00
77 SD, Capt.Atom,1960Rep. . . . 75.00
Becomes:
CAPTAIN ATOM
Charlton Comics 1965–67
78 SD, new stories begin 100.00
79 SD,I:Dr.Spectro 65.00
80 SD 65.00
81 SD,V:Dr.Spectro 65.00
82 SD,I:Nightshade,Ghost 65.00
83 SD,I:Ted Kord/Blue Beetle . . 45.00
84 SD,N:Captain Atom 40.00
85 SD,A:Blue Beetle,I:Punch &
    Jewelee 40.00
86 SD,A:Ghost, Blue Beetle 40.00
87 SD,JAp,A:Nightshade 40.00
88 SD/FMc,JAp,A:Nightshade . . 40.00
89 SD/FMc,JAp,A:Nightshade,
    Ghost, last issue Dec.1967 . . 40.00

STRAW MEN
Innovation
1 & 2 . . . . @1.95

STREET FIGHTER
Ocean 1986–87
1 thru 3 . . . . @1.75

STREET SHARKS
Archie Comics 1995
1 & 2 Based on Cartoons . . . . @1.50

STRIKE!
Eclipse 1988
1 TL,RT,I&O:New Strike 1.75
2 TL,RT 1.25
3 TL,RT 1.25
4 TL,RT,V:Renegade CIA Agents 1.25
5 TL,RT,V:Alien Bugs 1.25
6 TL,RT,"Legacy of the Lost" . . . 1.75
Spec. #1 Strike vs. Sgt. Strike
    TL,RT,"The Man" 1.95

STRIKER
Viz
1 thru 2 . . . . 2.75

STRIKEFORCE AMERICA
Comico
1 SK(c),I:Strikeforce America . . . 2.50
2 V:Superior-prisoner 2.95
3 Breakout, pt.2 . . . . 2.95

STRONG MAN
AC Comics
1 . . . . 2.95

STRONTIUM DOG
Eagle 1985
1 . . . . 1.50
2 . . . . 1.25
3 . . . . 1.25
4 . . . . 1.25
5 . . . . 1.25
6 . . . . 1.25
Quality
7 . . . . 1.25
8 . . . . 1.25
9 . . . . 1.25
10 . . . . 1.25
11 . . . . 1.25
12 . . . . 1.25
13 . . . . 1.25
14 . . . . 1.25
15/16 . . . . 1.50
17 . . . . 1.50
18/19 . . . . 1.50
20 thru 29 . . . . @1.50
[2nd Series]
1 . . . . 1.25
Quality
Spec.#1 . . . . 1.50

STRYKE
London Night Studios 1995
0 I:Stryke 5.00
1 . . . . 4.00

STUMBO THE GIANT
Blackthorne
1 3-D 2.50

STUMBO TINYTOWN
Harvey Publications 1963–66
1 . . . . 110.00
2 . . . . 60.00
3 . . . . 40.00
4 . . . . 40.00
5 . . . . 40.00
6 thru 13 . . . . @25.00

STUPID HEROES
Next
1 PeL(s),w/ 2 card-strip 2.75
2 . . . . 2.75
3 F:Cinder 2.75

STURM THE TROOPER
1 . . . . 1.95
2 . . . . 1.95
3 . . . . 1.95

SUBSPECIES
Eternity 1991
1 Movie Adaptation 3.00
2 Movie Adaptation 2.50
3 Movie Adaptation 2.50
4 Movie Adaptation 2.50

COLOR PUB.

All comics prices listed are for *Near Mint* condition.   **CVA Page 549**

SUN GLASSES AFTER DARK
Verotik 1995
1		2.95
2		@2.95
3		@2.95

SUN-RUNNERS
Pacific 1984
1		2.50
2		2.00
3		2.00

Eclipse 1984–86
4		2.00
5		2.00
6 "Sins of the Father"		1.75
7 "Dark Side of Mark Dancer"		1.75
Summer Special #1		1.75

SUNSET CARSON
AC Comics
1 Based on Cowboy Star		5.00

SUPERBABES: FEMFORCE
AC Comics
1 Various Artists		5.00

SUPER CAR
Gold Key 1962–63
1		150.00
2		75.00
3		75.00
4		100.00

SUPERCOPS
Now 1990
1 thru 4		@1.75

SUPER COPS, THE
Red Circle 1974
1		1.00

SUPER GOOF
Gold Key 1965–82
1		15.00
2 thru 10		@8.00
11 thru 20		@5.00
21 thru 30		@4.00
31 thru 74		@2.00

SUPER HEROES VERSUS SUPERVILLIANS
Archie Publications July, 1966
1 A:Flyman,Black Hood,The Web, The Shield		45.00

SUPERHUMAN SAMURAI SYBER SQUAD
Hamilton Comics 1995
0 Based on TV Show		2.95

SUPREME
Maximum Press
#1–#43 see Image
44 AMo, JoB, A:Glory		2.50
45 AMo, JoB, A:Glory		2.50
46 AMo,Suprema		2.50
47 AMo		2.50

48 AMo		2.50
49 AMo		2.50
50 double size		3.95
Collected edition #1, rep.#1–#2		4.95
TPB Supreme Madness		14.95

Surge #3 © Eclipse

SURGE
Eclipse 1984
1 A:DNAgents		3.00
2 A:DNAgents		2.00
3 A:DNAgents		3.00
4 A:DNAgents		3.00

SURROGATE SAVIOR
Hot Brazer Comic Pub.
1 I:Ralph		2.50
2 Baggage		2.50

SURVIVORS
Spectrum
1 Mag. size		5.00
2		3.50
3 The Old One		2.50
4		2.50

SURVIVORS
Fantagraphics
1		2.50
2		2.50
3		2.50

SUSPIRA: THE GREAT WORKING
Chaos! Comics 1997
1 (of 4) PNa		2.95
2 PNa		2.95
3 PNa		2.95
4 PNa		2.95

SWORDS OF TEXAS
Eclipse 1987
1 FH,New America		2.00
2 FH,V:Baja Badlands		1.75
3 FH,TY(c),V:Dogs of Danger		1.75
4 FH,V:Samurai Master		1.75

SYMBOLS OF JUSTICE
High Impact Studios
1 I:Granger,Justice,Rayven		2.95
2 V:Devil's Brigade		2.95

SYPHONS
Now 1994
1		1.50
2 thru 7		@1.50

SYPHONS: COUNTDOWN
Now
1 F:Brigade		2.95
2 Led By Cross		2.95
3 Blown Cover		2.95
1995 Ann. Doomsday Device		2.95

SYPHONS: THE STARGATE STRATAGEM
Now
1 thru 3		@2.95

TALES CALCULATED TO DRIVE YOU BATS
Archie Publications 1961–62
1		75.00
2		50.00
3 thru 6		@35.00

TALES FROM THE CRYPT
Gladstone 1990–91
1 E.C.rep.AW/FF,GS		5.00
2 rep.		4.00
3 rep.		3.50
4 rep.		3.00
5 rep.TFTC #45		3.00
6 rep.TFTC #42		3.00

TALES FROM THE CRYPT
Russ Cochran Publ 1992
1 rep. TFTC #31,CSS#12		2.75
2 rep. TFTC #34,CSS#15		2.50
3 rep. TFTC, CSS		2.50
4 rep. TFTC #43,CSS#18		2.50
5 rep. TFTC,CSS#23		2.00
[2nd Series]
1 rep.horror stories		2.00
2 inc.The Maestro's Hand		2.00
3 thru 6		@2.00
7 thru 8		@2.00
Gemstone
16 thru 21 EC comics reprint		@2.50
"Annuals"
TPB Vol. 1 rebinding of #1–#5		8.95
TPB Vol. 2 rebinding of #5–#10		8.95
TPB Vol. 3 rebinding of #11–#15		8.95
TPB Vol. 4 rebinding of #16–#20		12.95

TALES OF EVIL
Atlas Comics 1975
1		2.00

TALES OF TERROR
Eclipse 1985–87
1		3.00
2 "Claustrophobia"		2.00
3 GM,"Eyes in the Darkness"		2.00
4 TT,TY,JBo(c),"The Slasher"		2.00

COLOR PUB.

5 "Back Forty,""Shoe Button Eyes" 2.00	
6 "Good Neighbors"	2.00
7 SBi,JBo,SK(i),"Video"	2.00
8 HB,"Revenant,""Food for Thought"	2.00
9	2.00
10	2.00
11 TT,JBo(c),"Black Cullen"	2.00
12 JBo,FH,"Last of the Vampires"	2.00
13	2.00

TALES OF THE GREEN BERET
Dell Publishing Co. Jan., 1967

1 SG	15.00
2	10.00
3	10.00
4	10.00
5	7.00

TALES OF THE GREEN HORNET
Now 1990

1 NA(c),O:Green Hornet Pt.1	3.00
2 O:Green Hornet Pt.2	2.50
3 Gun Metal Green	2.50
4 Targets	1.95

TALES OF THE MYSTERIOUS TRAVELER
Charlton Comics Aug., 1956

1 DG	275.00
2 SD	250.00
3 SD,SD(c)	250.00
4 SD,SD(c)	275.00
5 SD,SD(c)	275.00
6 SD,SD(c)	275.00
7 SD	225.00
8 SD	225.00
9 SD	225.00
10 SD,SD(c)	250.00
11 SD,SD(c)	250.00
12	100.00
13	100.00
14 (1985)	3.00
15 (1985)	3.00

TALES OF THE SUN RUNNERS
Sirius Comics 1986

1	1.50
2 and 3	@2.00

TALES OF THE WITCHBLADE
Top Cow 1996

1 TnD	5.00
1a TnD, variant cover (1:4)	10.00

TALESPIN
Walt Disney 1991
(Reg.-Series)

1 "Sky-Raker" Pt.1	2.50
2 "Sky-Raker" Pt.2	2.00
3 "Idiots Abroad"	1.75
4 "Contractual Desperation"	1.75
5 "The Oldman & the Sea Duck"	1.75
6 "F'reeze a Jolly Good Fellow"	1.75

TALESPIN
Walt Disney 1991
[Mini-Series]

1 Take-off Pt.1	3.00
2 Take-off Pt 2	3.00
3 Take-off Pt 3,Khan Job	2.00
4 Take-off pt 4	2.00

TARGET AIRBOY
Eclipse 1988

1 SK,A:Clint	1.95

TARGITT
Atlas March–July 1975

1 thru 3	@1.00

Tarzan of the Apes © ERB, Inc.

TARZAN OF THE APES
Gold Key 1962–72
prev. Dell (see Golden Age)

132	20.00
133	16.00
134	16.00
135	16.00
136	16.00
137	16.00
138	16.00
139 I:Korak	17.50
140	15.00
141	15.00
142	15.00
143	15.00
144	15.00
145	15.00
146	15.00
147	15.00
148	15.00
149	15.00
150	15.00
151	15.00
152	15.00
153	15.00
154	15.00
155 O:Tarzan	20.00
156	10.00
157 Banlu, Dog o/t Arande, Pt.1	10.00
158 Banlu, Dog o/t Arande, Pt.2	10.00
159 Banlu, Dog o/t Arande, Pt.3	10.00

160	10.00
161	10.00
162 TV photo (c)	15.00
163	10.00
164	10.00
165 TV photo (c)	15.00
166	10.00
167	10.00
168 TV photo (c)	15.00
169 A:Leopard Girl	10.00
170	10.00
171 TV photo (c)	15.00
172	9.00
173	9.00
174	9.00
175	9.00
176	9.00
177	9.00
178 O:Tarzan, rep. #155	9.00
179 A:Leopard Girl	9.00
180	9.00
181	9.00
182	9.00
183 Down Trails of Terror	9.00
184	9.00
185	9.00
186	9.00
187	9.00
188	9.00
189	9.00
190	9.00
191	9.00
192 Tarzan and the Foreign Legion adaptation	9.00
193 "Escape From Sumatra"	9.00
194	9.00
195	9.00
196	9.00
197	9.00
198	9.00
199	9.00
200	12.50
201	9.00
202	9.00
203	9.00
204	9.00
205	9.00
206 last issue	9.00

Continued by DC; see also Marvel

TASK FORCE ALPHA
Alpha Productions

1 Forged in Fire	3.50

TASMANIAN DEVIL & HIS TASTY FRIENDS
Gold Key Nov., 1962

1	90.00

TASTEE-FREEZ COMICS
Harvey Comics 1957

1 Little Dot	40.00
2 Rags Rabbit	15.00
3 Casper	30.00
4 Sad Sack	15.00
5 Mazie	15.00
6 Dick Tracy	35.00

TEAM ANARCHY
Anarchy 1993

1 I:Team Anarchy	2.75
2 thru 3	2.75
4 PuD,MaS,I:Primal	2.75

COLOR PUB.

TEAM YANKEE
First 1989

1 Harold Coyle novel adapt.	1.95
2 thru 6	@1.95
Trade Paperback	12.95

T.E.C.H. BOYZ HYPERACTIVE
Dynasty Comics

1 I:T.E.C.H. Boyz	2.95
2 Man vs. Nature	2.95

TEEN-AGE CONFIDENTIAL CONFESSIONS
Charlton Comics 1960–64

1	9.00
2 thru 5	@5.00
6 thru 10	@3.00
11 thru 22	@2.00

TEENAGE HOTRODDERS
Charlton Comics April, 1963

1	22.00
2 thru 5	@12.00
6 thru 10	@7.00
11 thru 23	@5.00
24	4.00

Becomes:

TOP ELIMINATOR

25 thru 29	@5.00

Becomes:

DRAG 'N' WHEELS

30	6.00
31 thru 58	@4.00
59 May, 1973	4.00

TEENAGE MUTANT NINJA TURTLES
First

1	6.00
2	4.50
Graphic Novel	17.00

TEENAGE MUTANT NINJA TURTLES
Archie
(From T.V. Series)

1 O:TMNT, April O'Neil, Shredder Krang	6.00
2 V:Shredder, O:Bebop & Rocksteady	4.00
3 V:Shredder & Krang	3.00

TEENAGE MUTANT NINJA TURTLES
Mirage 1993

1 A:Casey Jones	3.00
2 JmL(a&s)	3.00
3 thru 8	@2.75
9 V:Baxter Bot	2.75
10 Mr. Braunze	2.75
11 V:Raphael	2.75
12 V:Darpa	2.75
13 J:Triceraton	2.75

TEENAGE MUTANT NINJA TURTLES ADVENTURES
Archie 1988
[2nd Series]

1 Shredder, Bebop, Rocksteady return to earth	5.00
2 I:Baxter Stockman	3.00
3 "Three Fragments" #1	3.00
4 "Three Fragments" #2	2.50
5 Original adventures begin, I:Man Ray	2.50
6 I:Leatherhead, Mary Bones	2.50
7 I:Cuddley the Cowlick; Inter-Galactic wrestling issue	2.50
8 I:Wingnut & Screwloose	2.00
9 I:Chameleon	2.00
10 I:Scumbug, Wyrm	2.00
11 I:Rat King & Sons of Silence; Krang returns to earth	2.00
12 Final Conflict #1, A:Leatherhead Wingnut, Screwloose, Trap, I:Malinga	2.00
13 Final Conflict #2	2.00
14 Turtles go to Brazil; I:Jagwar Dreadman	2.00
15 I:Mr. Null	1.50
16 I&D:Bubbla, the Glubbab	1.50
17 Cap'n Mossback	1.25
18 'Man Who Sold World'	1.25
19 I: Mighty Mutanimals	1.25
20 V:Supersoldier, War.Dragon	1.25
21 V:Vid Vicious	1.25
22 GC,Donatello captured	1.50
23 V:Krang, I:Slash, Belly Bomb	1.50
24 V:Krang	1.25
25	1.50
26 I:T'Pau & Keeper	1.50
27 I:Nevermore, Nocturno & Hallocat	1.50
28 Turtle go to Spain, I:Nindar & Chein Klan	1.50
29 Warrior Dragon captured	1.50
30 TMNT/Fox Mutant Ninjara team-up	1.25
31 TMNT/Ninjara team-up cont	1.25
32 A:Sumo Wrestler Tatoo	1.25
33 The Karma of Katmandu	1.25
34 Search For Charlie Llama	1.25
35	1.25
36 V:Shredder	1.25
37 V:Shredder	1.25
38 V:Null & 4 Horsemen Pt.1	1.25
39 V:Null & 4 Horseman Pt.3	1.25
40 1492, A:The Other	1.25
41 And Deliver us from Evil	1.25
42 Time Tripping Trilogy #1	1.25
43 thru 51	@1.25
52 thru 54	@1.50
55 thru 57 Terracide	@1.50
58 thru 70	@1.50
1990 Movie adapt(direct)	5.50
1990 Movie adapt(newsstand)	2.50
1991 TMNT meet Archie	2.50
1991 Movie Adapt II	2.50
Spec.#2 Ghost of 13 Mile Island	2.50
Spec.#3 Night of the Monsterex	2.50
TMNT Mutant Universe Sourcebook	1.95

TEENAGE MUTANT NINJA TURTLES/ FLAMING CARROT
Mirage/Dark Horse

1 JmL	3.00
2 thru 3 JmL	3.00
4 JmL	3.00

TMNT PRESENTS: APRIL O'NEIL
Archie

1 A:Chien Khan, Vid Vicious	1.25
2 V:White Ninja, A:V.Vicious	1.25
3 V:Vhien Khan, concl.	1.25

TMNT: THE MALTESE TURTLE
Mirage

Spec. F:Raphael Detective	2.95

TMNT PRESENTS: DONATELLO AND LEATHERHEAD

1 thru 2	@1.25

Teenage Mutant Ninja Turtles Presents: Merdude vs. Ray Fillet #3 © Archie

TMNT PRESENTS: MERDUDE VS. RAY FILLET
Archie 1993

1 thru 3	1.25

TMNT: APRIL O'NEIL THE MAY EAST SAGA
Archie

1 A:TMNT	1.25

TMNT: YEAR OF THE TURTLE
Archie Comics 1995

1 All New Era	1.50

[JACK KIRBY'S] TEENAGENTS
Topps
[Mini-Series]

1 WS,AH,w/3 cards	2.95
2 NV,w/3 cards	2.95
3 NV,w/3 cards	2.95
4 NV,w/3 leftover? cards	2.95

COLOR PUB.

TEEN CONFESSIONS
Charlton Comics 1959–76
1	40.00
2	25.00
3	15.00
4	15.00
5	15.00
6	15.00
7	15.00
8	15.00
9	15.00
10	15.00
11 thru 30	@8.00
31 Beatles cover	40.00
32 thru 36	@3.00
37 Beatles cover,Fan Club story	35.00
38 thru 97	@2.50

TEEN SECRET DIARY
Charlton Comics 1959–61
1	25.00
2	20.00
3	10.00
4	10.00
5	10.00
6	10.00
7	10.00
8	10.00
9	10.00
10	10.00
11	10.00

TENSE SUSPENSE
Fargo Publications 1958–59
1	45.00
2	40.00

TERMINATOR, THE
Now 1988–89
1	10.00
2	5.00
3	4.00
4	3.50
5	3.50
6	3.50
7	3.50
8	3.50
9	3.50
10	3.50
11	3.50
12 I:JohnConnor($1.75,cov,dbl.sz)	3.50
13	3.50
14	3.50
15	3.50
16	3.50
17	3.50
Spec. #1	3.50

TERMINATOR:
ALL MY FUTURES PAST
Now 1990
1 Painted Art	3.00
2 Painted Art	3.00

TERMINATOR:
THE BURNING EARTH
Now 1990
1	3.00
2	3.00
3	2.50
4	2.50
5	2.50

Terraformers #1
© Wonder Color Comics

TERRAFORMERS
Wonder Comics 1987
1	1.00
2	1.00
3	1.00
4	1.00

TERRANAUTS
Fantasy General 1986
1	1.75
2	1.75

TESS
1	1.95

TEXAS RANGERS
IN ACTION
Charlton Comics 1956–70
5	40.00
6	25.00
7	25.00
8	25.00
9	25.00
10	25.00
11	40.00
12	15.00
13	35.00
14	15.00
15	15.00
16	15.00
17	15.00
18	15.00
19	15.00
20	15.00
21 thru 30	@10.00
31 thru 59	@5.00
60 B:Riley's Rangers	6.00
61 thru 79	@3.00

THAT WILKIN BOY
Archie Publications Jan., 1969
1	15.00
2	7.00
3	7.00
4	7.00

5	7.00
6	7.00
7	7.00
8	7.00
9	7.00
10	7.00
11 thru 20	@3.00
21 thru 26 E:Giant size	@2.00
27 thru 52	@2.00

THESPIAN
Dark Moon
1 I:Thespian	2.50
2 V:Lemming	2.50
3 Lord of Manhattan	2.50

THING: COLD FEAR
1 R:Thing	3.00
2	2.75

THIRD WORLD WAR
Fleetway 1990–91
1 HamburgerLady	2.50
2	2.50
3 The Killing Yields	2.50
4	2.50
5	2.50
6	2.50

13: ASSASSIN
TSR 1990–91
1	2.95
2	2.95
3	2.95
4	2.95
5	2.95
6	2.95
7	2.95
[Mini-series]	
1	2.95

THOSE ANNOYING
POST BROTHERS
Vortex
1	1.75
2	1.75
3	1.75
4	1.75
5	1.75
6	1.75

3-D ZONE PRESENTS
Renegade 1987–89
1 L.B.Cole(c)	2.00
2	2.00
3	2.00
4	2.00
5	2.00
12 3-D Presidents	2.50
13 Flash Gordon	2.50
14 Tyranostar	2.50
15 Tyranostar	2.50
16 SpaceVixen	2.50

3-D ZONE - 3 DEMENTIA
15	2.50

THREE FACES
OF GNATMAN
1	1.75

COLOR PUB.

All comics prices listed are for *Near Mint* condition.   **CVA Page 553**

Three Stooges #23 © Gold Key

THREE STOOGES
Dell Publishing Co.
Oct.-Dec., 1959
6 Ph(c),B:Prof. Putter	100.00
7 Ph(c)	100.00
8 Ph(c)	100.00
9 Ph(c)	100.00

Gold Key 1962
10 Ph(c)	100.00
11 Ph(c)	75.00
12 Ph(c)	75.00
13 Ph(c)	75.00
14 Ph(c)	75.00
15 Ph(c)	90.00
16 Ph(c),E:Prof. Putter	75.00
17 Ph(c),B:Little Monsters	75.00
18 Ph(c)	75.00
19 Ph(c)	75.00
20 Ph(c)	75.00
21 Ph(c)	75.00
22 Ph(c),Movie Scenes	75.00
23 Ph(c)	60.00
24 Ph(c)	60.00
25 Ph(c)	60.00
26 Ph(c)	60.00
27 Ph(c)	60.00
28 Ph(c)	60.00
29 Ph(c)	60.00
30 Ph(c)	60.00
31 Ph(c)	50.00
32 Ph(c)	50.00
33 Ph(c)	50.00
34 Ph(c)	50.00
35 Ph(c)	50.00
36 Ph(c)	50.00
37 Ph(c)	50.00
38 Ph(c)	50.00
39 Ph(c)	50.00
40 Ph(c)	50.00
41 Ph(c)	50.00
42 Ph(c)	50.00
43 Ph(c)	50.00
44 Ph(c)	50.00
45 Ph(c)	50.00
46 Ph(c)	50.00
47 Ph(c)	50.00
48 Ph(c)	50.00
49 Ph(c)	50.00
50 Ph(c)	50.00
51	40.00
52 Ph(c)	50.00
53 Ph(c)	50.00
54 Ph(c)	50.00
55 Ph(c)	50.00

THREE STOOGES 3-D
Eclipse 1991
1 thru 3 reprints from 1953	@2.50
4 reprints from 1953	3.50

THRILLING SCIENCE TALES
AC Comics 1989
1	3.50

THRILLOGY
Pacific 1984
1	1.50

THRILL-O-RAMA
Harvey Publications 1965–66
1 A:Man in Black(Fate),DW,AW	18.00
2 AW,A:Pirana,I:Clawfang, The Barbarian	15.00
3 A:Pirana, Fate	10.00

THUNDER AGENTS
Archie Publications 1965–69
1 WW,RC,GK,MSy,GT,I:Thunder Agents,IronMaiden,Warlord	125.00
2 WW,MSy,D:Egghead	75.00
3 WW,DA,MSy,V:Warlords	50.00
4 WW,MSy,RC,I:Lightning	20.00
5 WW,RC,GK,MSy	50.00
6 WW,SD,MSy,I:Warp Wizard	40.00
7 WW,MSy,SD,D:Menthor	40.00
8 WW,MSy,GT,DA,I:Raven	40.00
9 OW,WW,MSy,A:Andor	40.00
10 WW,MSy,OW,A:Andor	40.00
11 WW,DA,MSy	25.00
12 SD,WW,MSy	25.00
13 WW,OW,A:Undersea Agent	25.00
14 SD,WW,GK,N:Raven,A:Andor	25.00
15 WW,OW,GT,A:Andor	20.00
16 SD,GK,A:Andor	20.00
17 WW,OW,GT	20.00
18 SD,OW,RC	20.00
19 GT,I:Ghost	20.00
20 WW,RC,MSy,all reprints	10.00

T.H.U.N.D.E.R. AGENTS
J.C. Productions 1983
1 MA,Centerfold	2.00
2 I:Vulcan	2.00

T.H.U.N.D.E.R. AGENTS
Maximum 1995
1 & 2	@2.95

THUNDERBOLT
Charlton Comics 1966–67
1 PAM,O:Thuderbolt	15.00
Prev: Son of Vulcan	
51 PAM,V:Evila	7.00
52 PAM,V:Gore the Monster	4.00
53 PAM,V:The Tong	5.00
54 PAM,I:Sentinels	5.00
55 PAM,V:Sentinels	4.00
56 PAM,A:Sentinels	4.00
57 A:Sentinels	4.00
58 PAM,A:Sentinels	4.00
59 PAM,A:Sentinels	4.00
60 PAM,JAp,I:Prankster	5.00

TIGER GIRL
Gold Key Sept., 1968
1	25.00

TIGER-MAN
Atlas April–Sept. 1975
1 thru 3	@1.00

TIME TUNNEL, THE
Gold Key Feb., 1967
1	45.00
2	40.00

TIME TWISTERS
Quality 1987–89
1 Alan Moore ser.	1.25
2 Alan Moore ser.	1.25
3 Alan Moore ser.	1.25
4 Alan Moore ser.	1.25
5	1.25
6 Alan Moore ser.	1.25
7 Alan Moore ser.	1.25
8	1.25
9	1.25
10	1.25
11	1.25
12	1.25
13 thru 21	@1.50

TIME 2
1 Graphic Novel	8.00

TIPPY'S FRIENDS GO-GO & ANIMAL
Tower Comics 1966–69
1	10.00
2	4.50
3	4.50
4	4.50
5	4.50
6	4.50
7	4.50
8 Beatles on cover & back	18.00
9 thru 15	@4.50

TIPPY TEEN
Tower Comics Nov., 1965–70
1	8.00
2 thru 27	@3.50

TO DIE FOR
1 3-D	2.50

TOM MIX WESTERN
AC Comics 1988
1	2.95

TOMMY & THE MONSTERS
1	2.00

TOM TERRIFIC!
Pines Comics
Summer, 1957
1	150.00
2	100.00

COLOR PUB.

3	100.00
4	100.00
5	100.00
6 Fall, 1958	100.00

TOMMI-GUNN
London Night 1997

0	3.00
0 nude cover	6.00
½	3.00
½a photo nude edition	10.00
1 signed	15.00
2	3.00
2 photo nude edition	6.00
3	3.00
3 photo nude edition	6.00

TOMMI-GUNN: KILLER'S LUST
London Night 1997

1	3.00
1 Japanese Chromium edition	12.00
2	3.00
2 photo nude edition	6.00
2 photo nude edition, signed	15.00

TOMOE
Crusade Entertainment 1996

0 BiT,	3.00
1 BiT,Fan Appreciation Edition	3.00
2	3.00
TPB rep.	13.95

TOMOE/WITCHBLADE: FIRE SERMON
Crusade Entertainment 1996

1	5.00
1a Gold foil	10.00

TOMOE: UNFORGETTABLE FIRE
Crusade Entertainment 1997

1 (of 3)	2.95

TOOL AND DIE
Samson Comics

1 Autographed	4.95
1a Blue Edition	9.95

TOP CAT
Charlton Comics 1970–73

1	30.00
2 thru 10	@20.00
11 thru 20	@12.00

TOR IN 3-D
Eclipse 1986

1 JKu	3.00
1a B&W limited 100 sign	5.00
2 JKu	3.00

TORI-SHI-KITA
Relative Burn

1 Hunter Prey	2.50

TORMENTRESS: MISTRESS OF HELL
Blackout Comics 1977

0	2.95

0a nude variant	9.95

TOTAL ECLIPSE
Eclipse 1988–89

1 BHa,BSz(c),A:Airboy,Skywolf	3.95
2 BHa,BSz(c),A:New Wave, Liberty Project	3.95
3 BHa,BSz(c),A:Scout,Ms.Tree	3.95
4 BHa,BSz(c),A:Miracleman, Prowler	3.95
5 BHa,BSz(c),A:Miracleman, Aztec Ace	3.95

TOTAL ECLIPSE, THE SERAPHIM OBJECTIVE
Eclipse 1988

1 tie-in Total Eclipse #2	1.95

TOTAL WAR
Gold Key July, 1965

1	50.00
2	50.00

Becomes:
M.A.R.S. PATROL

3 WW	50.00
4	25.00
5	25.00
6	25.00
7	25.00
8	25.00
9	25.00
10	25.00

Toy Boy #1 © Continuity Comics

TOY BOY
Continuity 1986–91

1 NA,I&O:Toy Boy,A:Megalith	2.00
2 TVE	2.00
3 TVE	2.00
4 TVE	2.00
5 TVE	2.00
6 TVE	2.00
7 MG	2.00

TRANCERS: THE ADVENTURES OF JACK DETH
Eternity

1 I:Jack Deth	2.50
2 A:Whistler, final issue	2.50

TRANSFORMERS

1 Robotics	1.50
2	2.00
3	2.50

TRANSFORMERS in 3-D
Blackthorne

1 thru 5	@2.50

TRAVEL OF JAMIE McPHEETERS, THE
Gold Key Dec., 1963

1 Kurt Russell	25.00

TRAVELLER
Maximum Press 1996

1 (of 3) RLd,MHw,	3.00

TRIBE
Axis Comics 1993–94

1 see Image Comics section	
2 TJn(s),LSn,V:Alex	2.25
3 TJn(s),LSn,	1.95

Good Comics 1996

0 TJn,LSn	2.95
1 TJn,LSn,Choice and Responsibility	2.95
2 TJn,LSn,Choice and Responsibility	2.95

TROLL LORDS
Comico 1989–90

Spec. #1	1.75
1	1.75
2 and 3	@1.75
4	2.50

TROUBLE WITH GIRLS
Comico 1987–88

1	3.00
2	2.50
3	2.50
4	1.95

TRUE LOVE
Eclipse 1986

1 ATh,NC,DSt(c),reprints	2.00
2 ATh,NC,BA(c),reprints	1.50

TUFF GHOSTS STARRING SPOOKY
Harvey Publications 1962–72

1	50.00
2	30.00
3	30.00
4	30.00
5	30.00
6	20.00
7	20.00
8	20.00
9	20.00
10	20.00
11 thru 20	@10.00
21 thru 30	@7.00

COLOR PUB.

31 thru 39 . . . . @3.00	11 . . . . 50.00	86 rep 8.00
40 thru 42 52 pg. Giants . . . . . @3.00	12 AW 50.00	87 thru 91 . . . . @10.00
43 . . . . 3.00	13 AW,RC,FBe,AMc 40.00	

TUROK: SON OF STONE
1 thru 29 see Golden Age
Gold Key 1962

30 . . . . 55.00	14 RC,JO,RC,AT 40.00
31 thru 40 . . . . @40.00	15 RC,JO 40.00
41 thru 50 . . . . @30.00	16 . . . . 25.00
51 thru 60 . . . . @25.00	17 . . . . 25.00
61 thru 75 . . . . @20.00	18 . . . . 25.00
76 thru 91 . . . . @15.00	19 JO 25.00

Whitman

92 thru 130 . . . . @7.00	20 . . . . 20.00
Giant #1 . . . . 75.00	21 RC 25.00
	22 JO 25.00

TURTLE SOUP
Millenium 1991

1 Book 1, short stories 2.50	23 JO 25.00
2 thru 4 . . . . 2.50	24 . . . . 20.00
	25 GE,RC,ATh 20.00

TV CASPER & COMPANY
Harvey Publications 1963–74

1 B:68 pg. Giants 55.00	26 RC,GE 20.00
2 . . . . 30.00	27 GE 20.00
3 . . . . 30.00	28 . . . . 15.00
4 . . . . 30.00	29 . . . . 15.00
5 . . . . 30.00	30 . . . . 15.00
6 . . . . 25.00	31 . . . . 15.00
7 . . . . 25.00	32 GE 20.00
8 . . . . 25.00	33 . . . . 15.00
9 . . . . 25.00	34 . . . . 15.00
10 . . . . 25.00	35 . . . . 15.00
11 thru 20 . . . . @7.00	36 . . . . 15.00
21 thru 31 E:68 pg. Giants . . . @5.00	37 . . . . 15.00
32 thru 46 . . . . @2.00	38 . . . . 15.00
	39 WMc 15.00

The Twilight Zone #10 © Now Comics

TWEETY AND SYLVESTER
Gold Key 1963–84

1 . . . . 25.00	40 . . . . 12.00
2 thru 10 . . . . @10.00	41 . . . . 12.00
11 thru 30 . . . . @7.00	42 . . . . 12.00
31 thru 121 . . . . @3.00	43 RC 15.00

TWILIGHT ZONE
Now 1990

44 . . . . 12.00	1 NA,BSz(c) 8.00
45 . . . . 12.00	1a 2nd printing Prestige +Harlan
46 . . . . 12.00	Ellison sty 6.00

TWILIGHT AVENGER
Elite 1986

1 thru 4 . . . . @1.75	47 . . . . 12.00

[Volume 2]

48 . . . . 12.00	#1 "The Big Dry" (direct) 2.50
49 . . . . 12.00	#1a Newsstand 1.95

TWILIGHT MAN
First 1989

1 Mini-Series 2.75	50 FBe,WS 12.00	2 "Blind Alley" 1.95

1 Mini-Series 2.75	50 FBe,WS 12.00	2 "Blind Alley" 1.95
2 Mini-Series 2.75	51 AW 15.00	3 Extraterrestrial 1.95
3 Mini-Series 2.75	52 . . . . 12.00	4 The Mysterious Biker 1.95
4 Mini-Series 2.75	53 . . . . 12.00	5 Queen of the Void 1.95
	54 . . . . 12.00	6 Insecticide 1.95
	55 . . . . 12.00	7 The Outcasts,Ghost Horse . . . 1.95
	56 . . . . 12.00	8 Colonists on Alcor 1.95

TWILIGHT ZONE, THE
Gold Key
March-May, 1961

1 RC,FF,GE,P(c) all 100.00	57 FBe 12.00	9 Dirty Lyle's House of Fun (3-D
2 . . . . 75.00	58 . . . . 12.00	Holo) 2.95
3 ATh,MSy 55.00	59 FBe,AMc 15.00	10 Stairway to Heaven,Key to
4 ATh 55.00	60 . . . . 10.00	Paradise 1.95
5 . . . . 50.00	61 . . . . 10.00	11 TD(i),Partial Recall 1.95
6 . . . . 50.00	62 . . . . 10.00	3-D Spec. 2.50
7 . . . . 50.00	63 . . . . 10.00	Ann. #1 . . . . 2.75
8 . . . . 50.00	64 . . . . 10.00	**[Volume 3]**
9 ATh 60.00	65 . . . . 10.00	1 thru 2 . . . . 2.50
10 . . . . 50.00	66 . . . . 10.00	
	67 . . . . 10.00	## TWISTED TALES
	68 . . . . 10.00	### Pacific 1982–84
	69 . . . . 10.00	1 RCo. "Infected" 3.50
	70 . . . . 10.00	2 . . . . 2.00
	71 rep 8.00	3 . . . . 2.00
	72 . . . . 10.00	4 . . . . 2.00
	73 rep 8.00	5 . . . . 2.00
	74 . . . . 10.00	6 . . . . 2.00
	75 . . . . 10.00	7 . . . . 2.00
	76 . . . . 10.00	8 . . . . 2.00
	77 FBe 12.00	**Eclipse**
	78 FBe,AMc,The Missing Mirage 12.00	9 . . . . 2.00
	79 rep 8.00	10 GM,BWr 2.00
	80 FBe,AMc 12.00	
	81 . . . . 10.00	## TWISTED TALES OF BRUCE JONES
	82 AMc 12.00	### Eclipse 1982–84
	83 FBe,WS 12.00	1 . . . . 2.00
	84 FBe,AMc 12.00	2 . . . . 2.00
	85 . . . . 10.00	

COLOR PUB.

3 . . . . 2.00
4 . . . . 2.00

TWISTER
Harris
1 inc.Special newspaper/poster,
and trading cards 2.95

TWO FISTED TALES
Russ Cochran 1992
1 JSe,HK,WW,JCr,reps 1.50
2 Reps inc.War Story 1.50
3 rep. 1.50
4 thru 6 rep. 2.00
7 thru 8 rep. 2.00
Gemstone
17 EC comics reprint 2.50
18 EC comics reprint 2.50
19 EC comics reprint 2.50
20 EC comics reprint 2.50
"Annuals"
TPB Vol.#4 reprint #16–#20 . . . . 12.95

2000 A.D. Monthly #1 © Eagle Comics

2000 A.D. MONTHLY
Eagle 1985
1 A:JudgeDredd 4.00
2 A:JudgeDredd 30.00
3 A:JudgeDredd 1.25
4 A:JudgeDredd 1.25
5 . . . . 1.25
6 . . . . 1.25
[2nd Series]
1 . . . . 1.25
2 . . . . 1.25
3 . . . . 1.25
4 . . . . 1.25
Quality
5 . . . . 1.25
6 . . . . 1.25
7 thru 27 . . . . @1.25
28/29 . . . . 1.50
30 . . . . 1.50
31/32 . . . . 1.50
33 . . . . 1.50
34 . . . . 1.50
35 . . . . 1.50
36 . . . . 1.50

37 . . . . 1.50
Becomes:
2000 A.D. SHOWCASE
38 . . . . 1.50
39 . . . . 1.50
40 . . . . 1.50
41 . . . . 1.50
42 . . . . 1.95
43 . . . . 1.95
44 . . . . 1.95
45 . . . . 1.95
46 . . . . 1.50
47 . . . . 1.75
48 thru 54 . . . . @1.75
TPB:Killing Time 12.95

UFO FLYING SAUCERS
Gold Key Oct. 1968
1 . . . . 15.00
2 . . . . 10.00
3 thru 13 . . . . @6.00
Becomes:
UFO & OUTER SPACE
Gold Key June 1978
14 thru 25 . . . . @3.00

ULTRAMAN
Nemesis 1994
1 EC,O:Ultraman 2.25
2 . . . . 2.50
3 . . . . 2.50
4 V:Blue Ultraman 2.50

ULTRAMAN
Harvey/Ultracomics 1993
1 with 1 of 3 cards 2.50
2 with 1 of 3 cards & virgin cover 2.50
3 with 1 of 3 cards & virgin cover 2.50

UNCLE SCROOGE
Dell/Gold Key Dec. 1962
40 . . . . 125.00
41 . . . . 100.00
42 . . . . 100.00
43 . . . . 100.00
44 . . . . 100.00
45 . . . . 100.00
46 Lost Beneath the Sea 100.00
47 . . . . 100.00
48 . . . . 100.00
49 Loony Lunar Gold Rush . . . 100.00
50 Rug Riders in the Sky 100.00
51 How Green Was my Lettuce . 90.00
52 Great Wig Mystery 90.00
53 Interplanetary Postman 90.00
54 Billion-Dollar Safari! 90.00
55 McDuck of Arabia 90.00
56 Mystery of the Ghost Town
Railroad 90.00
57 Swamp of No Return 90.00
58 Giant Robot Robbers 90.00
59 North of the Yukon 90.00
60 Phantom of Notre Duck 90.00
61 So Far and No Safari 75.00
62 Queen of the Wild Dog Pack . 75.00
63 House of Haunts! 75.00
64 Treasure of Marco Polo! . . . 75.00
65 Micro-Ducks from OuterSpace 75.00
66 Heedless Horseman 75.00
67 CB rep. 75.00
68 Hall of the Mermaid Queen! . 75.00
69 Cattle King! 75.00

70 CB,The Doom Diamond! 75.00
71 . . . . 60.00
72 CB rep. 75.00
73 CB rep. 75.00
74 thru 110 . . . . @50.00
111 thru 148 . . . . @30.00
149 . . . . 20.00
150 thru 168 . . . . @15.00
169 thru 173 . . . . @10.00
Whitman
174 thru 182 . . . . @8.00
183 thru 200 . . . . @6.00
201 thru 209 . . . . @5.00
Gladstone
210 CB 15.00
211 CB,Prize of Pizzaro 15.00
212 CB,city-golden roofs 15.00
213 CB,city-golden roofs 15.00
214 CB 15.00
215 CB, a cold bargain 15.00
216 CB 15.00
217 CB,7 cities of Cibola 15.00
218 CB 15.00
219 Don Rosa,Son of Sun 25.00
220 CB,Don Rosa 5.00
221 CB,A:BeagleBoys 3.00
222 CB,Mysterious Island 3.00
223 CB 3.00
224 CB,Rosa,Cash Flow 6.00
225 CB 3.00
226 CB,Rosa 4.00
227 CB,Rosa 4.00
228 CB 3.00
229 CB 3.00
230 CB 5.00
231 CB,Rosa(c) 3.00
232 CB 3.00
233 CB 3.00
234 CB 3.00
235 Rosa 3.50
236 CB 3.00
237 CB 3.00
238 CB 3.00
239 CB 3.00
240 CB 3.00
241 CB,giant 5.00
242 CB,giant 4.00
Walt Disney 1990
243 CB,"Pie in the Sky" 3.50
244 . . . . 2.50
245 . . . . 2.50
246 . . . . 2.50
247 . . . . 2.50
248 . . . . 2.50
249 . . . . 2.50
250 CB 3.50
251 . . . . 2.50
252 "No Room For Human Error" . 2.50
253 "Fab.Philosophers Stone 2.50
254 The Filling Station 2.50
255 The Flying Dutchman 2.50
256 CB,"Status Seeker" 2.50
257 "Coffee,Louie or Me" 2.50
258 CB,"Swamp of no return" . . . 2.50
259 "The only way to Go" 2.50
260 The Waves Above, The Gold
Below 2.50
261 Rosa,"Return to Zanadu" Pt.1 2.50
262 Rosa,"Return to Zanadu" Pt.2 2.50
263 Rosa,"Treasure Under Glass" 2.50
264 Snobs Club 2.25
265 CB,Ten Cent Valentine 2.25
266 The Money Ocean,Pt.1 . . . . 2.25
267 The Money Ocean,Pt 2 . . . . 2.25
268 CB,Rosa,Island in the Sky . . 2.00

COLOR PUB.

Uncle Scrooge #259 © Walt Disney

269 The Flowers 2.25
270 V:Magica DeSpell 2.25
271 The Secret o/t Stone 2.25
272 Canute The Brute's Battle Axe 2.25
273 CB,Uncle Scrooge-Ghost . . . 2.00
274 CB,Hall of the Mermaid Queen 2.00
275 CB,Rosa,Christmas Cheers,inc.
    D.Rosa centerspread 2.50
276 Rosa, thru 277 . . . . @2.25
278 thru 280 . . . . @2.25
Gladstone
281 Rosa 5.00
282 thru 284 . . . . 2.50
285 Rosa, Life & Times 10.00
286 thru 293 Rosa, Life & Times @5.00
294 thru 299 . . . . @1.50
300 Rosa & Barks 3.00
301 "Statuesque Spendthrifts" . . 1.50
302 . . . . 1.50
303 "Rocks to Riches" 1.50
304 "My Private Eye" 1.95
305 "The Vigilante of Pizen Bluff" . 1.95
306 . . . . 1.95

UNCLE SCROOGE ADVENTURES
Gladstone
1 CB,McDuck of Arabia 9.00
2 translated from Danish 5.00
3 translated from Danish 5.00
4 CB 5.00
5 Rosa 5.00
6 CB 3.50
7 CB 3.00
8 CB 3.00
9 Rosa 3.50
10 CB 3.00
11 CB 3.00
12 CB 3.00
13 CB 3.00
14 Rosa 3.50
15 CB 3.00
16 CB 3.00
17 CB 3.00
18 CB 3.00
19 CB,Rosa(c) 3.50
20 CB,giant 4.00
21 CB,giant 4.00

22 Rosa(c) 5.00
23 CB,giant 4.00
24 thru 26 . . . . @2.00
27 Rosa,O:Jr. Woodchuck 4.00
28 giant 3.00
29 . . . . 1.50
30 giant 4.00
31 thru 32 . . . . @3.00
33 Barks 4.00
34 thru 40 . . . . @3.00
41 . . . . 2.00
42 "The Dragon's Amulet" 2.00
43 "Queen of the Wild Dog Pack" 2.00
44 . . . . 2.00
45 "The Secret of the Duckburg
    Triangle" 2.00
46 "The Tides Turn" 2.25
47 "The Menehune Mystery" . . . 2.25
48 "The Tenth Avatar" 2.25
49 "Dead-Eye Duck" 2.25
50 CB,"The Secret of Atlantis" . . 2.50
51 . . . . 1.95

UNCLE SCROOGE ADVENTURES: DON ROSA 1997 SPECIAL
Gladstone 1997
Spec.#1 (of 4) 10.95
Spec.#2 thru #4 . . . . @9.95

UNCLE SCROOGE & DONALD DUCK
Gold Key
1 rep. 75.00

UNCLE SCROOGE GOES TO DISNEYLAND
Gladstone 1985
1 CB,etc. 100pp 11.00

UNDERDOG
Spotlight 1987
1 FMc,PC(c),The Eredicator 1.50
2 FMc,CS(c), Prisoner of Love/ The
   Return of Fearo 1.50

UNDERDOG
Charlton July, 1970
1 Planet Zot 70.00
2 Simon Sez/The Molemen . . . 40.00
3 Whisler's Father 40.00
4 The Witch of Pycoon 40.00
5 The Snowmen 40.00
6 The Big Shrink 40.00
7 The Marbleheads 40.00
8 The Phoney Booths 40.00
9 Tin Man Alley 40.00
10 Be My Valentine (Jan. 1972) . 40.00

UNDERDOG
Gold Key March, 1975
1 The Big Boom 40.00
2 The Sock Singer Caper 20.00
3 The Ice Cream Scream 20.00
4 . . . . 20.00
5 . . . . 20.00
6 Head in a Cloud 20.00
7 The Cosmic Canine 20.00
8 . . . . 20.00
9 . . . . 20.00
10 Bouble Trouble Gum 20.00

11 The Private Life of Shoeshine
   Boy 15.00
12 The Deadly Fist of Fingers . . 15.00
13 . . . . 15.00
14 Shrink Shrank Shrunk 15.00
15 Polluter Palooka 15.00
16 The Soda Jerk 15.00
17 Flee For Your Life 15.00
18 Rain Rain Go Away...Okay . . 15.00
19 Journey To the Center of the
   Earth 15.00
20 The Six Million Dollar Dog . . 15.00
21 Smell of Success 15.00
22 Antlers Away 15.00
23 Wedding Bells In Outer Space
   (Feb.,1979) 15.00

UNDERDOG IN 3-D
Blackthorne
1 Wanted Dead or Alive 2.50

UNEARTHLY SPECTACULARS
1 DW,AT,I:Tiger Boy 20.00
2 WW,AW,GK,I:Earthman,Miracles,I
  nc. A:Clawfang,TigerBoy 35.00
3 RC,AW,JO,A:Miracles,Inc. . . . 30.00

U.N. FORCE
Gauntlet Comics
0 BDC(s) 2.95
1 B:BDC(s),I:U.N.Force 2.95
2 O:Indigo 2.95
3 . . . . 2.95
4 A:Predator 2.95
5 B:Critial Mass 2.95

U.N. FORCE FILES
Gauntlet Comics
1 KP(c),F:Hunter Seeker, Lotus . 2.95

UNIVERSAL SOLDIER
Now 1992
1 Based on Movie,Holo.(c) 2.75
2 Luc & Ronnie on the run from
  UniSols 2.50
2a Photo cover 1.95
3 Photo(c) 1.95

UNKNOWN WORLDS OF FRANK BRUNNER
Eclipse 1985
1 FB 2.50
2 FB 2.50

UNLEASHED!
Triumphant
0 JnR(s),I:Skyfire 2.50
1 JnR(s), ... 2.50

UNLV
1 Championship season (basketball
  based on college team) 3.00

UNTAMED LOVE
1 FF 2.00

UNUSUAL TALES
Charlton Comics 1955–65
1 . . . . 150.00

COLOR PUB.

2	75.00
3	50.00
4	50.00
5	50.00
6 SD,SD(c)	125.00
7 SD,SD(c)	125.00
8 SD,SD(c)	125.00
9 SD,SD(c)	150.00
10 SD,SD(c)	135.00
11 SD	135.00
12 SD	100.00
13	40.00
14 SD	100.00
15 SD,SD(c)	110.00
16	40.00
17	40.00
18	40.00
19	40.00
20	40.00
21	25.00
22 SD	75.00
23	25.00
24	25.00
25 SD	75.00
26 SD	75.00
27 SD	75.00
28	25.00
29 SD	75.00
30 thru 49	@25.00

URI-ON

1	1.50
2	1.50

URTH 4
Continuity 1990

1 TVE,NA(c)	2.00
2 TVE,NA	2.00
3 TVE,NA	2.00
4 NA,Last issue	2.00

USAGI YOJIMBO
Mirage 1993

1 A:TMNT	3.00
2	3.00
3	3.00
4	3.00
5 thru 16	@3.00
17	8.00

VALERIA THE SHE BAT
Continuity 1993

1 NA,I:Valeria	20.00
2 thru 4	[NOT RELEASED]
5 Rise of Magic	2.50

VALKYRIE
Eclipse 1988

1 PG,I:Steelfox,C:Airboy, Sky Wolf	3.00
2 PG,O:New Black Angel	2.50
3 PG	2.50

[2nd Series]

1 BA,V:Eurasian Slavers	2.00
2 BA,V:Cowgirl	2.00
3 BA,V:Cowgirl	2.00

VALLEY OF
THE DINOSAURS
Charlton 1975

1 Hanna-Barbera TV adapt.	3.00
2 thru 11	@2.00

Valley of the Dinosaurs #7
© Hanna-Barbera

VAMPEROTICA
Brainstorm

1–16 see B&W

17	3.00
17a signed	5.00
17 Holochrome cover	65.00
18 Blood of the Damned (color)	3.00
18a Blood of the Damned, nude cover	4.00
18b signed	5.00
18c nude cover, signed	10.00
19 "Hunter's Blood"	3.00
19a deluxe	3.00
20 "Vampire Quest"	3.00
20a nude edition	4.00
21 hunting & feeding	3.00
21a nude edition	4.00
21b nude luxury edition	10.00
21c nude deluxe luxury edition	15.00
22	3.00
22a nude edition	4.00
TPB Red Reign, rep.	12.95

VAMPIRE LESTAT
Innovation 1990–91

1 Anne Rice Adapt.	26.00
1a 2nd printing	4.00
1b 3rd printing	2.50
2	13.00
2a 2nd printing	4.00
2b 3rd printing	2.50
3	10.00
3a 2nd printing	2.50
4	8.00
4a 2nd printing	2.50
5	7.00
6	5.00
7	5.00
8	5.00
9 scarce	8.00
9a 2nd Printing	3.00
10	5.00
11 "Those Who Must Be Kept"	4.00
12 conclusion	4.00
Vampire Companion #1	4.00
Vampire Companion #2 (preview "Interview With The Vampire")	3.00

Vampire Companion #3	3.00
GN rep.#1-#12 (Innovation)	24.95
GN rep.#1-#12 (Ballantine)	25.00

VAMPIRELLA
Warren Publishing Co. 1969–83

1 NA,FF(c),I:Vampirella	350.00
2 B:Amazonia	100.00
3 Very scarce	250.00
4	75.00
5 FF(c)	75.00
6	75.00
7 FF(c)	100.00
8 B:horror	75.00
9 BWS,BV(c),WW	85.00
10 No Vampirella,WW	20.00
11 TS,FF(c)O&I Pendragon.	50.00
12 WW	50.00
13	40.00
14	40.00
15	40.00
16	40.00
17 B:Tomb of the Gods	40.00
18	40.00
19 WW,1973 Annual	50.00
20 thru 25	@40.00
26	35.00
27 1974 Annual	40.00
28 thru 30	@35.00
31 FF(c)	40.00
32 thru 36	@30.00
37 1975 Annual	40.00
38	30.00
39	30.00
40	30.00
41 thru 45	@25.00
46 O:Vampirella	30.00
47 thru 99	@25.00
100 Double Size	35.00
101 thru 110	@20.00
111 Giant Edition	30.00
112	25.00

VAMPIRELLA
Harris 1992

0 Dracula Wars	5.00
0a Blue version	50.00
1 V:Forces of Chaos, w/coupon for DSt poster	40.00
1a 2nd printing	15.00
2 AH(c)	40.00
3 A:Dracula	15.00
4 A:Dracula	10.00
5	8.00
TPB The Dracula War signed & numbered	39.95

Harris Comics 1996

0 gold foil signed & numbered	100.00
1 Commemorative Edition	3.00
1 Commemorative Edition, sgn & num.	17.00
25th Anniv. Spec., FF(c)	5.95
25th Anniv. Spec., lim.	6.95
25th Anniv. Spec., lim., signed,	49.95
Spec. Death of Vampirella, memorial, chromium cover	
Spec. Death of Vampirella, memorial, chromium cover, signed	29.95

VAMPIRELLA/CAIN
Harris 1996

1 flipbook	6.95

COLOR PUB.

All comics prices listed are for *Near Mint* condition.

VAMPIRELLA/WETWORKS
Harris 1997
1 StG,SSh,image x-over 2.95
1 signed & numbered 17.95

VAMPIRELLA:
BLOOD LUST
Harris 1997
1 (of 2) JeR & JJu 3.95

VAMPIRELLA CLASSIC
Harris Comics 1995
1 Dark Angel 3.50
2 V:Demogorgon 3.25
3 V:Were Beast 3.25
4 R:Papa Voodoo 3.25
5 . . . . 3.00

Vampirella: Death and Destruction #1
© Harris Comics

VAMPIRELLA: DEATH
AND DESTRUCTION
Harris
1 limited preview ash can 5.00
1 limited preview ash can, signed &
  numbered 35.00
1 "The Dying of the Light" 3.00
1 signed & numbered 3.00
1 satin edition 30.00
1 satin edition, signed & numb. . 60.00
2 "The Nature of the Beast" 3.00
3 (of 3) TSg,ACo,JP,JJu(c),Mistress
  Nyx kills Vampi 2.95
TPB 14.95

VAMPIRELLA LIVES
Harris
1 Linen Edition 15.00
1a Censored Photo cover edition 10.00
2 Vengeance edition 3.00
2 Model photo edition 3.00
2 alternate edition, AH(c) 10.00
2 alternate edition, AH(c) signed 30.00
3 WEi(s),ACo,JP,Graveyard edition,
  JSC(c) 3.00
3 WEi(s),ACo,JP,Model photo
  edition 3.00

VAMPIRELLA
OF DRAKULON
Harris Comics 1996
1 V:assassin 3.00
2 Dracula returns 3.00
2a signed & numbered 20.00
3 and 4 . . . . @3.00
5 SEt, ... 3.00

VAMPIRELLA
PINUP SPECIAL
Harris Comics 1995
1 Various Artists 3.50

VAMPIRELLA:
SAD WINGS OF DESTINY
Harris
1 DQ(s),JJu(c) 4.00
1 signed & numbered (#1,500) . 5.00
Gold Emblem Seal Edition 4.00
Gold Emblem Seal Edition, signed 25.00

VAMPIRELLA/
SHADOWHAWK:
CREATURES OF
THE NIGHT
Harris/Image 1995
1 Book One 5.50

VAMPIRELLA/SHI
Harris
Ash-Can #1, limited, 16pg 5.00

VAMPIRELLA STRIKES
Harris Comics 1995
1 The Prize,pt.1 . . . . 3.00
1a limited, signed & numbered . 30.00
1b full moon background 3.50
2 V:Dante Corp.,A:Passion 3.00
3 V:subway stalker 3.00
4 IEd,RN "Soul Food" 3.00
5 DQ,RN,F:Eudaemon 3.00
5 signed & numbered, (200) . . . 20.00
6 . . . . 3.00
6 signed, alternate cover 25.00
6 signed & numbered 40.00
7 silver special flip book 3.00
Ann. #1 new cover 10.00
Ann. #1 new cover, signed &
  numbered 25.00

VAMPIRELLA
VS. EUDAEMON
Harris 1996
1 . . . . 10.00
1 signed & numbered 25.00

VAMPIRELLA
VS. HEMORRHAGE
Harris 1997
1 IEd,MIB 3.50
1 signed & numbered 24.95
1 Linen edition, signed & numb. 39.95
2 IEd,MIB 3.50
3 (of 3) IEd,MIB 3.50

VAMPIRELLA VS. PANTHA
Harris 1997
Showcase #1 preview 2.00

1 MMr,MT, MT(c) Vampirella vs.
  Pantha 3.50
1 MMr,MT, MT(c) Pantha vs.
  Vampirella 3.50
1 MT(c) Vampirella vs. Pantha,
  signed 19.95
1 MT(c) Pantha vs. Vampirella,
  signed 19.95
1a MMr,MT, MT(c) 9.95
1a MMr,MT, MT(c) signed &
  numbered 29.95

VAMPRESS LUXURA, THE
Brainstorm 1996
1 . . . . 3.00
1a gold edition 10.00
2 . . . . 2.95
2a gold foil 10.00

VANGUARD
1 . . . . 1.50

VANGUARD
ILLUSTRATED
Pacific 1983
1 . . . . 1.50
2 DSt(c) 1.50
3 thru 5 SR . . . . @1.50
6 GI 1.50
7 GE,I:Mr.Monster 6.00

VANITY
Pacific 1984
1 and 2 . . . . @1.50

VAULT OF HORROR
Gladstone 1990–91
1 Rep.GS,WW 5.00
2 Rep.VoH #27 & HoF #18 . . . . 3.00
3 Rep.VoH #13 & HoF #22 . . . . 3.00
4 Rep.VoH #23 & HoF #13 . . . . 2.50
5 Rep.VoH #19 & HoF #5 . . . . . 2.50
6 Rep.VoH #32 & WF #6 . . . . . 2.50
7 Rep.VoH #26 & WS #7 . . . . . 2.50

VAULT OF HORROR
Russ Cochran Publ. 1991–92
1 Rep.VoH #28 & WS #18 . . . . 2.25
2 Rep.VoH #33 & WS #20 . . . . 2.25
3 Rep.VoH #26 & WS #7 . . . . . 2.25
4 Rep.VoH #35 & WS #15 . . . . 2.00
4 Rep.VoH #18 & WS #11 . . . . 2.00
5 Rep.VoH #18 & WS #11 . . . . 2.00
2nd Series
1 thru 7 Rep.VoH . . . . @1.50
8 . . . . 2.00
Gemstone
17 EC comics reprint 2.50
18 EC comics reprint 2.50
19 EC comics reprint 2.50
20 EC comics reprint 2.50
"Annuals"
TPB Vol. 1 rebinding of #1–#5 . . 8.95
TPB Vol. 2 rebinding of #6–#10 . 8.95
TPB Vol. 3 rebinding of #11–#15 10.95
TPB Vol. 4 rebinding of #16–#20 12.95

VECTOR
Now 1986
1 . . . . 2.50
2 thru 5 . . . . @1.75

COLOR PUB.

VEGAS KNIGHTS
Pioneer 1989
1	1.95
2	1.95
3	1.95

VENGEANCE OF VAMPIRELLA
Harris 1994
1 Hemmorage	30.00
1a Gold Edition	28.00
1 gold edition, signed, numbered	99.95
2 Dervish	17.00
3 On the Hunt	11.00
4 Teenage Vampries	8.00
5 Teenage Vampires	6.00
6	6.00
7	6.00
8 bagged w/card	6.00
9	6.00
10 Bad Jack Rising	5.00
11 Pits of Hell, w/card	5.00
12 V:Passion	4.00
13 V:Passion	4.00
14 Prelude to the Walk,pt.2	4.00
14a Buzz	20.00
15 The Mystery Walk,pt.1	3.25
15a Buzz	20.00
16 The Mystery Walk,pt.2	3.25
16a Buzz	20.00
17 The Mystery Walk,pt.3	3.25
17a Buzz	20.00
18 The Mystery Walk,pt.4	3.00
18a Buzz	20.00
19 The Mystery Walk,pt.5	3.00
19a Buzz	20.00
20 Mystery Walk epilog	3.00
21 thru 24	@3.00
25 "The End"	3.00
25 variant cover, signed & numbered	30.00
25 signed & numbered (2,500)	40.00
25 gold edition, signed & numb.	100.00
25 alternate cover, signed by Jae Lee & numbered (#1,500)	29.95
Mini-comic gold foil, signed	39.95
TPB 1-3 Bloodshed	6.95

VENTURE
AC Comics 1986
1	2.00
2 thru 4	@1.75

VERONICA
Archie Publications April, 1989
1 thru 50	@1.50
51 thru 65	@1.50
66 Down Argentine Way, pt.1	1.50
67 Down Argentine Way, pt.2	1.50
68	@1.50

VEROTIKA
Verotika 1995
1 thru 3 Jae Lee, Frazetta	@2.95
4 thru 9	@2.95

VESPERS
Mars Media Group
1 Tony Caputo	2.50
2 I:Dark Side	2.50

VIC FLINT
Argo Publ. Feb., 1956
1	35.00
2	30.00

Vicki #1 © Atlas

VICKI
Atlas Feb.–Aug. 1975
1 Rep.	1.50
2 thru 4	@1.00

VILLAINS & VIGILANTES
Eclipse 1986–87
1 A:Crusaders,Shadowman	2.00
2 A:Condor	2.00
3 V:Crushers	2.00
4 V:Crushers	2.00

VIOLENT CASES
Tundra
1 20's Chicago	11.00

VIRGINIAN, THE
Gold Key June, 1963
1	40.00

VOLTRON
Solson 1985
1 TV tie-in	2.00
2	1.50
3	1.50

VORTEX
Vortex 1982–88
1 Peter Hsu art	22.00
2 Mister X on cover	9.00
3	5.00
4	4.00
5	3.00
6 thru 8	@3.00
9 thru 13	@1.75

VORTEX
Comico 1991
1 from Elementals	2.50
2	2.50

VORTEX:
THE SECOND COMING
Entity 1996
1 (of 6)	2.95
1a variant cover	2.95
2	2.95

VOYAGE TO THE DEEP
Dell Publishing Co.
Sept.-Nov., 1962
1 P(c)	40.00
2 P(c)	30.00
3 P(c)	30.00
4 P(c)	30.00

WACKY ADVENTURES OF CRACKY
Gold Key 1972–75
1	10.00
2 thru 11	@5.00
12	3.00

WACKY WITCH
Gold Key 1971–75
1	18.00
2	10.00
3 thru 20	@6.00
21	4.00

WAGON TRAIN
Gold Key Jan.–Oct., 1964
1	50.00
2	35.00
3	35.00
4	35.00

WALLY
Gold Key 1962–63
1	20.00
2	15.00
3	15.00
4	15.00

WALLY WOOD'S THUNDER AGENTS
Delux 1984–86
1 GP,KG,DC,SD,I:New Menth	3.00
2 GP,KG,DC,SD,"The Raven"	2.50
3 KG,DC,SD	2.00
4 GP,KG,RB,DA	2.00
5 JOy,KG,A:CodenamDangr	2.00

WALT DISNEY ANNUALS
Walt Disney's Autumn Adventure	4.00
Walt Disney's Holiday Parade #1	3.50
Walt Disney's Spring Fever	3.25
Walt Disney's Summer Fun	3.25
Walt Disney's Holiday Parade #2	3.25

WALT DISNEY'S AUTUMN ADVENTURE
1 Rep. CB	4.00

WALT DISNEY'S COMICS AND STORIES
Dell/ Gold Key 1962
264 CB;Von Drake & Gearloose	30.00
265 CB; Von Drake & Gearloose	30.00

COLOR PUB.

266 CB; Von Drake & Gearloose	30.00	352a CB rep. without poster . . . 15.00	510 CB rep. 6.00
267 CB; Von Drake & Gearloose	30.00	353 CB rep. with poster 20.00	**Gladstone**
268 CB; Von Drake & Gearloose	30.00	353a CB rep. without poster . . 15.00	511 translation of Dutch 22.00
269 CB; Von Drake & Gearloose	30.00	354 CB rep. with poster 20.00	512 translation of Dutch 15.00
270 CB; Von Drake & Gearloose	30.00	354a CB rep. without poster . . 15.00	513 translation of Dutch 15.00
271 CB; Von Drake & Gearloose	30.00	355 CB rep. with poster 20.00	514 translation of Dutch 8.00
272 CB; Von Drake & Gearloose	30.00	355a CB rep. without poster . . 15.00	515 translation of Dutch 8.00
273 CB; Von Drake & Gearloose	30.00	356 CB rep. with poster 20.00	516 translation of Dutch 8.00
274 CB; Von Drake & Gearloose	30.00	356a CB rep. without poster . . 15.00	517 translation of Dutch 3.50
275 CB 25.00	357 CB rep. with poster 20.00	518 translation of Dutch 3.50
276 CB 25.00	357a CB rep. without poster . . 15.00	519 CB,Donald Duck 3.50
277 CB 25.00	358 CB rep. with poster 20.00	520 translation of Dutch, Rosa . . . 7.00
278 CB 25.00	358a CB rep. without poster . . 15.00	521 Walt Kelly 3.00
279 CB 25.00	359 CB rep. with poster 20.00	522 CB,WK,nephews 3.00
280 CB 25.00	359a CB rep. without poster . . 15.00	523 Rosa,Donald Duck 7.00
281 CB 25.00	360 CB rep. with poster 20.00	524 Rosa,Donald Duck 7.00
282 CB 25.00	360a CB rep. without poster . . 15.00	525 translation of Dutch 3.00
283 CB 25.00	361 thru 400 CB rep. . . . . . . @15.00	526 Rosa,Donald Duck 7.00
284 . . . . 15.00	401 thru 409 CB rep. . . . . . . @12.00	527 CB 3.00
285 . . . . 15.00	410 CB rep. Annette Funichello . 12.00	528 Rosa,Donald Duck 5.00
286 CB 25.00		529 CB 3.00
287 . . . . 15.00		530 Rosa,Donald Duck 5.00
288 CB 20.00		531 WK(c),Rosa,CB 5.00
289 CB 20.00		532 CB 2.50
290 . . . . 15.00		533 CB 2.50
291 CB 20.00		534 CB 2.50
292 CB 20.00		535 CB 2.50
293 CB; Grandma Duck's Farm		536 CB 2.50
Friends 20.00		537 CB 2.50
294 CB 20.00		538 CB 2.50
295 . . . . 15.00		539 CB 2.50
296 . . . . 15.00		540 CB new art 3.50
297 CB; Gyro Gearloose 20.00		541 double-size,WK(c) 3.00
298 CB; Daisy Duck's Dairy 20.00		542 CB 5.00
299 CB rep. 20.00		543 CB,WK(c) 2.50
300 CB rep. 20.00		544 CB,WK(c) 2.50
301 CB rep. 20.00		545 CB 2.50
302 CB rep. 20.00		546 CB,WK,giant 4.00
303 CB rep. 20.00		547 CB,WK,Rosa,giant 4.50
304 CB rep. 20.00		**Walt Disney 1990**
305 CB rep. Gyro Gearloose . . . 20.00		548 CB,WK,"Home is the Hero" . . 3.00
306 CB rep. 20.00		549 CB, ... 2.50
307 CB rep. 20.00		550 CB,prev.unpub.story! 3.50
308 CB 20.00		551 . . . . 2.25
309 CB 20.00	*Walt Disney's Comics and Stories #446*	552 . . . . 2.25
310 CB 20.00	*© Walt Disney*	553 . . . . 2.25
311 CB 20.00		554 . . . . 2.25
312 CB 20.00	411 thru 429 CB rep. . . . . . . @12.00	555 . . . . 2.25
313 thru 327 . . . . @15.00	430 . . . . 8.00	556 . . . . 2.25
328 CB rep. 20.00	431 CB rep. 10.00	557 . . . . 2.25
329 . . . . 12.00	432 CB rep. 10.00	558 "Donald's Fix-it Shop" 2.25
330 . . . . 12.00	433 . . . . 8.00	559 "Bugs" 2.25
331 . . . . 12.00	434 CB rep. 10.00	560 CB,April Fools Story 2.00
332 . . . . 12.00	435 CB rep. 10.00	561 CB,Donald the "Flipist" 2.00
333 . . . . 12.00	436 CB rep. 10.00	562 CB,"3DirtyLittleDucks" 2.00
334 . . . . 12.00	437 . . . . 5.00	563 CB,"Donald Camping" 2.00
335 CB rep. 15.00	438 . . . . 5.00	564 CB,"Dirk the Dinosaur" 2.00
336 . . . . 12.00	439 CB rep. 8.00	565 CB,DonaldDuck,TruantOfficer 2.00
337 . . . . 12.00	440 CB rep. 8.00	566 CB,"Will O' the Wisp" 2.00
338 . . . . 12.00	441 . . . . 5.00	567 CB,"Turkey Shoot" 2.00
339 . . . . 12.00	442 CB rep. 8.00	568 CB,"AChristmas Eve Story" . . 2.00
340 . . . . 12.00	443 CB rep. 8.00	569 CB, New Years Resolutions . 2.00
341 . . . . 12.00	444 . . . . 5.00	570 CB,Donald the Mailman +Poster2.00
342 CB rep. 15.00	445 . . . . 5.00	571 CB,"Atom Bomb" 4.50
343 CB rep. 15.00	446 thru 465 CB rep. . . . . . . @8.00	572 CB, April Fools 2.00
344 CB rep. 15.00	466 . . . . 8.00	573 TV Quiz Show 2.00
345 CB rep. 15.00	467 thru 473 CB rep. . . . . . . @8.00	574 Pinnochio,64pgs 3.50
346 CB rep. 15.00	**Whitman**	575 Olympic Torch Bearer, Li'l Bad
347 CB rep. 15.00	474 thru 493 CB rep. . . . . . . @6.00	Wolf,64 pgs. 3.50
348 CB rep. 15.00	494 CB rep.Uncle Scrooge 7.00	576 giant 3.50
349 CB rep. 15.00	495 thru 505 CB rep. . . . . . . @6.00	577 A:Truant Officers,64 pgs. . . . 3.50
350 CB rep. 15.00	506 . . . . 5.00	578 CB,Old Quacky Manor 2.00
351 CB rep. with poster 20.00	507 CB rep. 6.00	579 CB,Turkey Hunt 2.00
351a CB rep. without poster . . 15.00	508 CB rep. 6.00	580 CB,The Wise Little Red Hen,
352 CB rep. with poster12 . . . . 20.00	509 CB rep. 6.00	64 page-Sunday page format . . . 3.50

COLOR PUB.

581 CB,Duck Lake	2.00
582 giant	3.50
583 giant	3.50
584	1.75
585 CB, giant	3.00

Gladstone

586	2.00
587 thru 600	@2.00
601 thru 605 prestige format	@5.95
606 "Winging It"	6.95
607 "Number 401"	6.95
608 "Sleepless in Duckburg"	6.95
609	6.95
610 "Treasures Untold"	6.95
611 "Romance at a Glance"	6.95
612 "The Sod Couple"	6.95
613 "Another Fine Mess"	6.95
614 "Airheads"	6.95
615 "Backyard Battlers"	6.95
616	6.95

WALT DISNEY COMICS DIGEST
Gold Key 1968–76
[All done by Carl Barks]

1 Rep,Uncle Scrooge	40.00
2	25.00
3	25.00
4	25.00
5	45.00
6	20.00
7	20.00
8	20.00
9	20.00
10	20.00
11	20.00
12	20.00
13	20.00
14	10.00
15	10.00
16 rep.Donald Duck #26	20.00
17	15.00
18	15.00
19	15.00
20	15.00
21	18.00
22	18.00
23	18.00
24	18.00
25	18.00
26	18.00
27	18.00
28	18.00
29	18.00
30	18.00
31	18.00
32	8.00
33	18.00
34 rep.Four Color #318	15.00
35	15.00
36	15.00
37	15.00
38 rep.Disneyland#1	15.00
39	15.00
40	10.00
41	8.00
42	8.00
43	8.00
44 Rep. Four Color #29 & others	25.00
45	6.00
46 CB	8.00
47	6.00
48	6.00
49	6.00

50 CB	8.00
51 rep.Four Color #71	12.00
52 CB	8.00
53	6.00
54	6.00
55	6.00
56 CB,rep. Uncle Scrooge #32	10.00
57 CB	8.00

WALT DISNEY SHOWCASE
Gold Key 1970–80

1 Boatniks (photo cover)	20.00
2 Moby Duck	10.00
3 Bongo & Lumpjaw	8.00
4 Pluto	10.00
5 $1,000,000 Duck (photo cover)	15.00
6 Bedknobs & Broomsticks	12.00
7 Pluto	10.00
8 Daisy & Donald	10.00
9 101 Dalmatians rep.	14.00
10 Napoleon & Samantha	12.00
11 Moby Duck rep.	7.00
12 Dumbo rep.	8.00
13 Pluto rep.	8.00
14 World's Greatest Athlete	12.00
15 3 Little Pigs rep.	12.00
16 Aristocats rep.	12.00
17 Mary Poppins rep.	12.00
18 Gyro Gearloose rep.	12.00
19 That Darn Cat rep.	12.00
20 Pluto rep.	10.00
21 Li'l Bad Wolf & 3 Little Pigs	7.00
22 Unbirthday Party rep.	10.00
23 Pluto rep.	10.00
24 Herbie Rides Again rep.	8.00
25 Old Yeller rep.	8.00
26 Lt. Robin Crusoe USN rep.	7.00
27 Island at the Top of the World	7.00
28 Brer Rabbit, Bucky Bug rep.	10.00
29 Escape to Witch Mountain	8.00
30 Magica De Spell rep.	15.00
31 Bambi rep.	12.00
32 Spin & Marty rep.	10.00
33 Pluto rep.	10.00
34 Paul Revere's Ride rep.	7.00
35 Goofy rep.	7.00
36 Peter Pan rep.	7.00
37 Tinker Bell & Jiminy Cricket rep.	7.00
38 Mickey & the Sleuth, Pt. 1	8.00
39 Mickey & the Sleuth, Pt. 2	8.00
40 The Rescuers	8.00
41 Herbie Goes to Monte Carlo	10.00
42 Mickey & the Sleuth	7.00
43 Pete's Dragon	10.00
44 Return From Witch Mountain & In Search of the Castaways	12.00
45 The Jungle Book rep.	12.00
46 The Cat From Outer Space	7.00
47 Mickey Mouse Surprise Party	8.00
48 The Wonderful Adventures of Pinocchio	7.00
49 North Avenue Irregulars; Zorro	7.00
50 Bedknobs & Broomsticks rep.	6.00
51 101 Dalmatians	6.00
52 Unidentified Flying Oddball	6.00
53 The Scarecrow	6.00
54 The Black Hole	6.00

WALT KELLY'S CHRISTMAS CLASSICS
Eclipse 1987

1	2.00

WALT KELLY'S SPRINGTIME TALES
Eclipse 1988

1	2.50

WARCAT SPECIAL
Entity Press 1995

1 I:Warcat	2.95

WARCHILD
Maximum Press 1995

1 I:Sword, Stone	3.50
2 I:Morganna Lefay	3.00
3 V: The Black Knight	2.50
4 Rescue Merlyn	2.50

[2nd Series]

1	2.50

WAR DANCER
Defiant 1994

1 B:JiS(s),I:Ahrq Tsolmec	2.75
2 I:Massakur	2.75
3 V:Massakur	2.75
4 JiS(s),A:Nudge	3.25

WARHAWKS
TSR 1990–91

1 thru 10 From game	@2.95

WARHAWKS 2050
TSR

1 Pt.1	2.95

WAR HEROES
Charlton Comics 1963–67

1	3.50
2 thru 10	@2.00
11 thru 27	@1.00

WARLASH
CFD

1 Project Hardfire	2.95

WARMASTER

1 and 2	@3.95

Warp #2 © First

COLOR PUB.

All comics prices listed are for *Near Mint* condition.   CVA Page 563

WARP
First March, 1983
1 FB,JSon,I:Lord Cumulus & Prince Chaos, play adapt pt.1	2.00
2 FB,SD,play adapt pt.2	1.50
3 FB,SD,play adapt pt.3	1.50
4 FB,SD,I:Xander,play pt.4	1.50
5 FB, play adapt pt.5	1.50
6 FB/MG, play adapt pt.6	1.50
7 FB/MG, play adapt pt.7	1.50
8 FB/MG,BWg,play adapt pt.8	1.25
9 FB/MG,BWg,play adapt conc.	1.25
10 JBi/MG,BWg, Second Saga, I:Outrider	1.25
11 JBi/MG,A:Outrider	1.25
12 JBi/MG,A:Outrider	1.25
13 JBi/MG,A:Outrider	1.25
14 JBi/MG,A:Outrider	1.25
15 JBi/MG/BWg	1.25
16 BWg/MG,A:Outrider	1.25
17 JBi/MG,A:Outrider	1.25
18 JBi/MG,A:Outrider&Sargon	1.25
19 MG,last issue	1.25
Spec. #1 HC,O:Chaos	1.50
Spec. #2 MS/MG,V:Ylem	1.50
Spec. #3	1.50

Warrior Nun Areala Vs. Razor #1
© Antarctic

WARRIOR NUN AREALA
Antartic Press 1995
1 V:Lilith	4.00
1a limited edition	7.00
2 V:Lilith	3.00
3 V:Hellmaster	3.00
3 silver edition	12.00
TPB Rep.#1-#3	9.95
BOOK II
1 Land of Rising Sun	2.95
1 Red edition	12.00
1 signed	9.95
2 I:Cheetah	2.95
3 Iraq, 1989	2.95
4	2.95
5 Rituals,pt.5	2.95
6	2.95
Spec. Warrior Nun Portraits	3.95
BOOK III 1997
1 "The Hammer and the Holocaust"	2.95

TPB Vol. 1	9.95
TPB Vol. 1 reprint	9.95
HC Vol. 2, lim. to 1,000 copies	29.95
TPB Rituals	15.95

WARRIOR NUN AREALA VS. RAZOR
Antarctic Press 1996
1 BDn,JWf x-over	3.95

WARRIOR NUN AREALA: SCORPIO ROSE
Antarctic Press 1996
1 SEt & BDn	2.95
2 thru 4 (of 4)	@2.95

WARRIOR NUN DEI: AFTERTIME
Antarctic Press 1997
1 (of 3) by Patrick Thornton	2.95
2	2.95

WARRIORS OF PLASM
Defiant 1993–95
1 JiS(s),DL,A:Lorca	3.25
2 JiS(s),DL,Sedition Agenda	3.25
3 JiS(s),DL,Sedition Agenda	3.25
4 JiS(s),DL,Sedition Agenda	3.25
5 JiS(s),B:The Demons of Darkedge	2.75
6 JiS(s),The Demons of Darkedge,pt.2	2.75
7 JiS(s),DL,	2.75
8 JiS(s),DL,40pages	3.00
9 JiS(s),LWn(s),DL,40pages	3.00
10 DL,	2.50
GN Home for the Holidays	5.95

WART AND THE WIZARD
Gold Key Feb., 1964
1	14.00

WAVE WARRIORS
1	2.00
2	2.00

WAXWORK in 3-D
Blackthorne
1	2.50

WAYFARERS
Eternity
1	1.80
2	1.80

WEAPON ZERO
See: Image

WEB-MAN
Argosy
1 flip book with Time Warrior	2.50

WEB OF HORROR
Major Magazines Dec., 1969
1 JJ(c),Ph(c),BWr	45.00
2 JJ(c),Ph(c),BWr	30.00
3 BWr,April, 1970	30.00

WEIRD FANTASY
Russ Cochran 1992
1 Reps	2.00
2 Reps.inc.The Black Arts	2.00
3 thru 4 rep.	@2.00
5 thru 7 rep.	2.50
8	2.50
Gemstone
9 thru 20 EC comics reprint	@2.50
"Annuals"	
TPB Vol. #1 rebinding of #1–#5	8.95
TPB Vol. #2 rebinding of #6–#10	9.95
TPB Vol. #3 rebinding of #11–#14	8.95
TPB Vol. #4 rebinding of #15–#18	9.95

WEIRD SCIENCE
Gladstone 1990–91
1 Rep. #22 + Fantasy #1	4.00
2 Rep. #16 + Fantasy #17	3.50
3 Rep. #9 + Fantasy #14	3.50
4 Rep. #27 + Fantasy #11	2.00
Russ Cochran/Gemstone 1992
1 thru 21 EC comics reprint	@2.50
"Annuals"	
TPB Vol. #1 rebinding of #1–#5	8.95
TPB Vol. #2 rebinding of #6–#10	9.95
TPB Vol. #3 rebinding of #11–#15	8.95

WEIRD SCIENCE–FANTASY
Russ Cochran/Gemstone 1992
1 Rep. W.S.F. #23 (1954)	2.00
2 Rep. Flying Saucer Invasion	2.00
3 Rep.	2.00
4 thru 6 Rep.	2.00
7 rep #29	2.00
8	2.00
Gemstone
"Annuals"	
TPB Vol. #1 rebinding of #1–#5	8.95
TPB Vol. #2 rebinding of #6–#10	12.95

WEIRD SUSPENSE
Atlas Feb.–July 1975
1 thru 3 F:Tarantula	@2.00

WEIRD TALES ILLUSTRATED
Millenium 1992
1 KJo,JBo,PCr,short stories	4.95

WENDY
Blackthorne
1 3-D	2.50

WENDY, THE GOOD LITTLE WITCH
Harvey Publications 1960–76
1	125.00
2	50.00
3	30.00
4	30.00
5	30.00
6	25.00
7	25.00
8	25.00
9	25.00
10	25.00
11 thru 20	@15.00
21 thru 30	@8.00
31 thru 50	@5.00

COLOR PUB.

51 thru 69 . . . . @4.00
70 thru 74 52 pg Giants . . . . . @4.00
75 thru 93 . . . . @2.00

WENDY WITCH WORLD
Harvey Publications 1961–74
1 . . . . 75.00
2 . . . . 30.00
3 . . . . 30.00
4 . . . . 30.00
5 . . . . 30.00
6 . . . . 15.00
7 . . . . 15.00
8 . . . . 15.00
9 . . . . 15.00
10 . . . . 15.00
11 thru 20 . . . . @9.00
21 thru 30 . . . . @5.00
31 thru 39 . . . . @3.00
40 thru 50 . . . . @2.00
51 thru 53 . . . . @2.00

WEREWOLF
Blackthorne
1 3-D 3.50

WESTERN ACTION
Atlas Feb. 1975
1 F:Kid Cody,Comanche Kid 1.00

WESTWYND
Westwynd 1995
1 I:Sable,Shiva,Outcast,Tojo 2.50

WHAM
1 . . . . 1.75

WHISPER
Capital 1983–84
1 MG(c) 10.00
2 . . . . 8.00
First
1 . . . . 2.50
2 . . . . 2.00
3 . . . . 2.00
4 . . . . 1.50
5 . . . . 1.50
6 thru 12 . . . . @1.25
13 thru 19 . . . . @1.75
20 O:Whisper 1.95
21 thru 26 . . . . @1.95
27 Ghost Dance #2 . . . . 1.95
28 Ghost Dance #3 . . . . 1.95
29 thru 37 . . . . @1.95
Spec. #1 . . . . 4.00

WHITE FANG
Walt Disney 1990
1 Movie Adapt. 5.95

WHITE TRASH
Tundra
1 I:Elvis & Dean 3.95
2 Trip to Las Vegas contd. 3.95
3 V:Purple Heart Brigade 3.95

WHODUNNIT
Eclipse 1986–87
1 DSp,A:Jay Endicott 2.00
2 DSp,"Who Slew Kangaroo?" . . 2.00
3 DSp,"Who Offed Henry Croft" . 2.00

WIDOW MADE IN BRITAIN
N Studio
1 I:Widow 2.60
2 F:Widow 2.60
3 Rampage 2.60
4 In Jail 2.60

WIDOW METAL GYPSIES
London Night Studios 1995
1 I:Emma Drew 3.00
2 Father Love 3.00
3 Final issue 3.00

WILD ANIMALS
Pacific 1982
1 . . . . 1.50

WILD BILL PECOS
AC Comics 1989
1 . . . . 3.50

WILDFIRE
Zion Comics
1 thru 3 V:Mr. Reeves . . . . . . @1.95
4 Lord D'Rune 1.95

WILD FRONTIER
Charlton Comics Oct., 1955
1 Davy Crockett 50.00
2 same 30.00
3 same 30.00
4 same 30.00
5 same 30.00
6 same 30.00
7 O:Cheyenne Kid 30.00
Becomes:
CHEYENNE KID
8 . . . . 25.00
9 . . . . 15.00
10 . . . . 45.00
11 . . . . 45.00
12 . . . . 45.00
13 . . . . 30.00
14 . . . . 30.00
15 . . . . 15.00
16 . . . . 15.00
17 . . . . 15.00
18 . . . . 30.00
19 . . . . 15.00
20 . . . . 18.00
21 . . . . 18.00
22 . . . . 18.00
23 . . . . 8.00
24 . . . . 8.00
25 . . . . 15.00
26 . . . . 10.00
27 . . . . 8.00
28 . . . . 8.00
29 . . . . 8.00
30 . . . . 10.00
31 thru 59 . . . . @3.00
60 thru 98 . . . . @2.00
99 Nov., 1973 . . . . 2.00

WILD WEST C.O.W.-BOYS OF MOO MESA
Archie 1992–93
1 Based on TV cartoon 1.25
2 Cody kidnapped 1.25
3 Law of the Year Parade, last
  issue 1.25

(Regular series)
1 Valley o/t Thunder Lizard 1.25
2 Plains, Trains & Dirty Deals . . . 1.25

Wild Western Action #2 © Skywald

WILD WESTERN ACTION
Skywald 1971
1 thru 3 . . . . @2.00

WILD WILD WEST
Gold Key 1966–69
1 TV show tie-in 125.00
2 . . . . 100.00
3 . . . . 75.00
4 . . . . 75.00
5 . . . . 75.00
6 . . . . 75.00
7 . . . . 75.00

WILD WILD WEST
Millenium 1990–91
1 . . . . 2.95
2 thru 4 . . . . @2.95

WILL EISNER'S 3-D CLASSICS
Kitchen Sink
WE art, w/glasses (1985) 2.00

WIN A PRIZE COMICS
Charlton Comics Feb., 1955
1 S&K,Edgar Allen adapt. 200.00
2 S&K 150.00
Becomes:
TIMMY THE TIMID GHOST
3 . . . . 30.00
4 . . . . 20.00
5 . . . . 20.00
6 . . . . 10.00
7 . . . . 10.00
8 . . . . 10.00
9 . . . . 10.00
10 . . . . 10.00
11 . . . . 20.00
12 . . . . 20.00
13 thru 20 . . . . @5.00

All comics prices listed are for *Near Mint* condition.

21 thru 44 . . . . @4.00
45 1966 . . . . 2.00

WINDRAGE
1 and 2 . . . . @1.25

WINTERWORLD
Eclipse 1987–88
1 JZ,I:Scully, Wynn 1.75
2 JZ,V:Slave Farmers 1.75
3 JZ,V:Slave Farmers 1.75

WIREHEADS
Fleetway
1 . . . . 2.95

WITCHBLADE
See Image

WITCHING HOUR, THE
Millenium/Comico
1 Anne Rice adaptation 2.50
2 thru 5 . . . . 2.50

Woody Woodpecker #1
© Harvey Comics

WOODY WOODPECKER
Harvey 1991–93
1 thru 5 . . . . 1.25

WORLD OF ARCHIE
Archie 1994
1 thru 21 . . . . @1.50

WORLD OF WOOD
Eclipse 1986–87
1 WW 1.75
2 WW,DSt(i) 1.75
3 WW 1.75
4 WW 1.75

WULF THE BARBARIAN
Atlas Feb.–Sept., 1975
1 O:Wulf 2.00
2 NA,I:Berithe The Swordsman . . 1.50
3 & 4 . . . . @1.00

WYATT EARP
Dell Publishing Co. Nov., 1957
1 . . . . 125.00
2 . . . . 75.00
3 . . . . 60.00
4 . . . . 50.00
5 . . . . 50.00
6 . . . . 50.00
7 . . . . 50.00
8 . . . . 50.00
9 . . . . 50.00
10 . . . . 50.00
11 . . . . 40.00
12 . . . . 40.00
13 . . . . 40.00

XANADU
Eclipse 1988
1 . . . . 2.00

XENYA
Sanctuary Press 1994
1 Hildebrandt Brothers 4.00
2 . . . . 3.25
3 . . . . 3.25
4 conclusion, Homecoming 2.95

XENO MAN
1 . . . . 1.75

XENOTECH
Mirage 1993–94
1 I:Xenotech 2.75
2 . . . . 2.75
3 w/2 card strip 2.75

X-FILES
Topps 1994–97
1 From Fox TV Series 50.00
1a Newstand 40.00
2 Aliens Killing Witnesses 30.00
3 The Return 20.00
4 Firebird,pt.1 . . . . 15.00
5 Firebird,pt.2 . . . . 10.00
6 Firebird,pt.3 . . . . 8.00
7 Trepanning Opera 7.00
8 Silent Cities of the Mind,pt.1 . . 6.00
9 Silent Cities of the Mind,pt.2 . . 5.00
10 Feeling of Unreality,pt.1 . . . . . 5.00
11 Feeling of Unreality,pt.2 . . . . . 5.00
12 Feeling of Unreality,pt.3 . . . . . 5.00
13 A Boy and His Saucer 5.00
14 . . . . 4.00
15 Home of the Brave 4.00
16 Home of the Brave,pt.2 . . . . . 3.50
17 DgM,CAd 3.50
18 thru 21 . . . . @3.50
22 JRz,CAd,"The Kanishibari" . . . 3.00
23 JRz,CAd,"Donor" 3.00
24 JRz,"Silver Lining" 3.00
25 JRz,CAd,"Remote Control," pt.1
  (of 3) 3.00
26 JRz,CAd,"Remote Control," pt.2 3.00
27 JRz,CAd,"Remote Control," pt.3 3.00
28 JRz,"Be Prepared,"
  pt.1,V:Windigo 3.00
29 JRz,"Be Prepared," pt.2 . . . . . 3.00
30 JRz,"Surrounded," pt.1 . . . . . 3.00
31 JRz,"Surrounded," pt.2 (of 2) . . 3.00
32 . . . . 3.00
Ann.#1 Hollow Eve 5.00
Ann.#2 . . . . 4.50
Spec.#1 Rep. #1-#3 . . . . 6.00

Spec.#2 Rep. #4-#6 Firebird 5.00
Spec.#3 Rep. #7-#9 . . . . 5.00
Spec.#4 Rep. 5.00
TPB Vol. 2 . . . . 19.95
GN Afterflight 5.95

X-FILES DIGEST
Topps 1995
1 All New Series, 96pg. 3.50
2 and 3 . . . . 3.50

X-FILES, THE: SEASON ONE
Topps
1 . . . . 3.95
2 . . . . 3.95
3 RTs,SSc,"Conduit" 3.95
4 RTs,"The Jersey Devil" 3.95
5 RTs,"Shadows" 3.95
6 . . . . 3.95
7 RTs,JVF,"Ice" 3.95
8 RTs,"Space" 3.95

XIMOS: VIOLENT PAST
Triumphant 1994
1 JnR(s) 2.50
2 JnR(s) 2.50

XL
1 . . . . 1.25

YAKKY DOODLE & CHOPPER
Gold Key Dec., 1962
1 . . . . 35.00

YIN FEI
Leung's Publications 1988–90
5 . . . . 1.80
6 thru 11 . . . . @2.00

YOGI BEAR
Dell Feb.-March, 1962
#1 thru #6, See Dell Four Color
7 thru 9 . . . . 50.00
Gold Key
10 . . . . 50.00
11 Jellystone Follies 50.00
12 . . . . 35.00
13 Surprise Party 50.00
14 thru 19 . . . . @35.00
20 thru 29 . . . . @20.00
30 thru 42 . . . . @15.00

YOGI BEAR
Charlton Comics 1970–76
1 . . . . 25.00
2 thru 10 . . . . @15.00
11 thru 35 . . . . 10.00

YOGI BEAR
Archie Comics 1997
1 . . . . 1.50

YOSEMITE SAM
Gold Key/Whitman 1970–84
1 . . . . 15.00
2 thru 10 . . . . @6.00
11 thru 40 . . . . @3.00
41 thru 81 . . . . @2.00

COLOR PUB.

YOUNGBLOOD
Maximum Press/Extreme
Volume 2 1996
Vol. 1 and Vol. 2 #1–#10, see Image
11 RLd,RCz, ... 2.50
12 Rle, V:Lord Dredd,A:New
Man,double size 3.50
13 RLd,RCz,F:Die-Hard 2.50
14 RLd,RCz, ... 2.50
Super Spec.#1 ErS,CSp,AG 3.00

YOUNGBLOOD CLASSICS
Image/Extreme Sept. 1996
1 RLd,ErS,rewritten & redrawn, new
cover 2.25
2 RLd,ErS,rewritten & redrawn, new
cover 2.25
3 RLd,ErS,rewritten & redrawn, new
cover 2.25

ZAANAN
Mainstream Comics
1 The Collectio,I:Zaanan 2.50

Zen Intergalactic Ninja #3
© Archie Comics

ZEN INTERGALACTIC NINJA
Archie 1992
1 Rumble in the Rain Forest
prequel,inc.poster 1.25
2 Rumble in Rain Forest #1 . . . . 1.25
3 Rumble in Rain Forest #2 . . . . 1.25
Entity Comics 1994
0 Chromium (c),JaL(c) 4.00
1 Joe Orbeta 2.50
1a Platinum Edition 20.00
2 Deluxe Edition w/card 4.95
3 V:Rawhead 3.00
4 thru 7 . . . . 3.25
GN A Fire Upon The Earth 12.95
[2nd Series]
1 Joe Orbeta 4.95
2 . . . . 4.95
3 thru 5 . . . . @2.50

ZEN/NIRA X: HELLSPACE
Zen Comics
1 . . . . 2.95

ZEN: NOVELLA
Eternity Comics
1 thru 8 . . . . 2.95

ZEN SPECIALS
Eternity
Spring#1 V:Lord Contaminous . . . 2.50
April Fools#1 parody issue 2.50
Color Spec.#0 . . . . 3.50

ZEN: WARRIOR
Eternity Comics 1994
1 vicious video game 3.00

ZENITH PHASE II
Fleetway
1 thru 2 . . . . 1.95

ZERO PATROL
Continuity 1984–90
1 EM,NA,O&I:Megalith 2.50
2 EM,NA 1.95
3 EM,NA,I:Shaman 1.95
4 EM,NA 1.95
5 EM 1.95
6 thru 8 EM . . . . @2.00

ZERO TOLERANCE
First 1990–91
1 TV 3.50
2 TV 3.00
3 TV 2.25
4 TV 2.25

ZOONIVERSE
Eclipse 1986–87
1 I:Kren Patrol,wrap-around(c) . . 1.25
2 . . . . 1.25
3 . . . . 1.25
4 V:Wedge City 1.25
5 Spak vs. Agent Ty-rote 1.25
6 last issue 1.25

ZORRO
Dell Publ. Co. 1959–61
1 thru 8, see Dell 4-Color
8 . . . . 100.00
9 . . . . 85.00
10 . . . . 85.00
11 . . . . 85.00
12 ATh 100.00
13 . . . . 75.00
14 . . . . 75.00
15 . . . . 75.00

ZORRO
Gold Key 1966–68
1 Rep. 75.00
2 Rep. 50.00
3 Rep. 50.00
4 Rep. 50.00
5 Rep. 50.00
6 Rep. 50.00
7 Rep. 50.00
8 Rep. 50.00
9 Rep. 50.00

ZORRO
Topps Nov., 1993
0 BSf(c),DMG(s), came bagged
with Jurassic Park Raptor #1 and
Teenagents #4 . . . . 4.00
1 DMG(s),V:Machete 3.00
2 DMG(s) 5.00
3 DMG(s) I:Lady Rawhide 20.00
4 MGr(c),DMG(s),V:Moonstalker . 2.50
5 MGr,DMG(s),V:Moonstalker . . 2.50
6 A:Lady Rawhide 8.00
7 A:Lady Rawhide 7.00
8 MGr(c),DMG(s) 3.00
9 A: Lady Rawhide 4.00
10 A:Lady Rawhide 4.50
11 A:Lady Rawhide 8.00

ZOT!
Eclipse 1984–85
1 by Scott McCloud 7.00
2 . . . . 3.00
3 . . . . 3.00
4 . . . . 3.00
5 . . . . 3.00
6 . . . . 2.00
7 . . . . 2.50
8 . . . . 2.00
9 . . . . 2.50
10 . . . . 2.00
10a B&W 6.00
10b 2nd printing 2.50
Original Zot! Book 1 . . . . 9.95
Book One TPB 24.95
(Changed to B & W)

COLOR PUB.

B & W PUBLISHERS

A1
Atomeka Press 1989–92
1 BWs,A:Flaming Carrot,Mr.X. . 10.00
2 BWs 9.75
3 . . . . 9.75
4 . . . . 5.95
5 . . . . 6.95
6a 4.95

AARDWOLF
Aardwolf 1994
1 DC,GM(c) 2.95
1a Certificate ed. signed 15.95
2 World Toughest Milkman 2.95
3 R.Block(s),O:Aardwolf 2.95

A.B.C. WARRIORS
Fleetway/Quality
1 thru 8 . . . . @1.95

ABSOLUTE ZERO
Antarctic Press 1995
1 . . . . 2.95
2 Rooftop,Athena 2.95
3 Stan Sakai 3.50
4 3-D Man and Kirby 2.95
5 & 6 Super Powers . . . . @2.95

ABUNDI SPECIAL
1 . . . . 2.50

AC ANNUAL
Aircel 1990
1 . . . . 3.95
2 Based on 1940's heroes 5.00
3 F:GoldenAge Heroes 3.50
4 F:Sentinels of Justice 3.95

ACE COMICS PRESENTS
Ace 1987
1 thru 7 . . . . @1.75

ACES
Eclipse 1988
1 thru 5, mag. size . . . . @2.95

ACME
Fandom House
1 thru 9 . . . . @1.95

ACOLYTE CHRONICLES
Azure Press 1995
1 I:Korath 2.95
2 V:Korath 2.95

ACTION FORCE
Lightning 1987
1 . . . . 1.75

ACTION GIRL COMICS
Slave Labor Graphics 1994
1 thru 7 . . . . @2.75
8 thru 12 . . . . @2.95

ADAM AND EVE A.D.
Bam
1 . . . . 3.00
2 thru 10 . . . . @1.50

ADAM LOGAN
1 . . . . 1.50

ADOLESCENT RADIOACTIVE BLACK-BELT HAMSTERS
Eclipse
1 I:Bruce,Chuck,Jackie,Clint 2.50
1a 2nd printing 2.00
2 A parody of a parody 2.00
3 I:Bad Gerbil 2.00
4 A:Heap (3-D),Abusement Park . 1.50
5 Abusement Park #2 . . . . 1.50
6 SK,Abusement Park #3 . . . . . 2.00
7 SK,V:Toe-Jam Monsters 2.00
8 SK 2.00
9 All-Jam last issue 2.00
[2nd Series]
Parody Press
1 . . . . 2.50
2 Hamsters Go Hollywood 2.50

ADVENT
1 . . . . 1.75

ADVENTURES INTO THE UNKNOWN
A Plus Comics
1 AW 2.95
2 AW 2.95
3 AW 2.95
Halloween Spec. Reps. Charlton &
American Comics GroupHorror . . 2.50

ADVENTURES OF B.O.C.
1 . . . . 1.50
2 . . . . 1.50
3 . . . . 1.50

ADVENTURERS
Aircel/Adventure Publ.
0 Origin Issue 2.50
1 with Skeleton 8.00
1a Revised cover 3.00
1b 2nd printing 2.00
2 Peter Hsu (c) 2.50
3 Peter Hsu (c) 2.50
4 Peter Hsu (c) 2.00
5 Peter Hsu (c) 2.00
6 Peter Hsu (c) 2.00
7 . . . . 2.00
8 . . . . 2.00
9 . . . . 2.00

ADVENTURERS BOOK II
Adventure Publ.
0 O:Man Gods 1.95
1 . . . . 1.95
2 thru 9 . . . . @1.95

ADVENTURERS BOOK III
1A Lim.(c)Ian McCaig 2.25
1B Reg.(c)Mitch Foust 2.25
2 thru 6 . . . . @2.25

ADVENTURES IN MYSTWOOD
1 . . . . 3.00
2 and 3 . . . . @2.00

ADVENTURES OF CHRISSY CLAWS, THE
Heroic 1991
1 thru 2 . . . . @3.25

Adventures of Chuk the Barbaric #1
© White Wolf

ADVENTURES OF CHUK THE BARBARIC
White Wolf
1 & 2 . . . . @1.25

ADVENTURES OF LUTHER ARKWRIGHT
Valkyrie Press 1987–89
1 . . . . 2.25
2 . . . . 2.25
3 . . . . 2.25
4 . . . . 2.25
5 . . . . 2.25
6 . . . . 2.25
7 . . . . 2.25
8 . . . . 2.25
9 . . . . 2.25
See Also: Dark Horse seciton

ADVENTURES OF MR. CREAMPUFF
1 . . . . 1.75

ADVENTURES OF MR. PYRIDINE
Fantagraphics
1 . . . . 2.25

ADVENTURES OF THE AEROBIC DUO
Lost Cause Productions
1 thru 3 . . . . @2.25
4 Gopher Quest 2.25
5 V:Stupid Guy 2.25

Adventures of Theown #1
© Pyramid

ADVENTURES OF THEOWN
Pyramid 1986
1 thru 3, Limited series . . . . . @1.75

AESOP'S FABLES
Fantagraphics
1 Selection of Fables 2.25
2 Selection of Fables 2.25
3 inc. Boy who cried wolf 2.25

AETOS
Hall of Heroes Jan. 1997
1 by Dan Parsons 2.50
1 variant cover 4.00
2 . . . . 2.50

AETOS 2: CHILDREN OF THE GRAVES
Orpahn Underground 1995
1 A:Nightmare 2.50

AFTERMATH
1 Type a, Partial map 4.50
1a Type b, Full map 2.00

AGENT ORANGE
1 . . . . 1.75
2 . . . . 1.75
3 . . . . 1.75

AGENT UNKNOWN
Renegade
1 thru 3 . . . . @2.00

AGE OF HEROES
1 . . . . 1.25
2 . . . . 1.25
3 . . . . 1.25

AGE OF HEROES, THE
Halloween Comics 1996
1 JHI 2.95
1A signed 2.95
2 JHI 2.95
2A signed 2.95

AGONY ACRES
AA² Entertainment
1 thru 3 . . . . @2.50
4 and 5 . . . . @2.95

AIRCEL
1 Graphic Novel year 1 . . . . 6.95

AIRFIGHTERS CLASSICS
Eclipse
1 O:Airboy,rep.Air Fighters#2 . . . 3.00
2 rep.Old Airboy appearances . . 3.00
3 thru 6 . . . . @3.95

AIRMEN
Mansion Comics
1 I:Airmen 2.50

AIRWAVES
Caliber
1 Radio Security 2.50
2 A:Paisley,Ganja 2.50
3 Formation of Rebel Alliance . . . 2.50
4 Big Annie,Pt. 1 . . . . 2.50
5 Big Annie, Pt 2 . . . . 2.50

A.K.A.: OUTCAST
1 . . . . 1.75

AKIKO
Sirius 1996
1 MCi 3.50
2 MCi 3.00
3 thru 16 MCi . . . . @2.50
HC Vol. 1 . . . . 20.00
TPB Vol. 1 . . . . 14.95

ALBEDO
Thoughts & Images
0 white cover, yellow drawing table Blade Runner 75.00
0a white(c) 50.00
0b blue(c),1st ptg 40.00
0c blue(c),2nd ptg 30.00
0d blue(c),3rd ptg 6.00
0e Photo(c),4th ptg.,inc. extra pages 4.00
1 SS,I:Nilson Groundthumper, dull red cover 25.00
1a bright red cover 20.00
2 SS,I:Usagi Yojimbo 15.00
3 SS,Erma, Usagi 5.00
4 SS,Usagi 7.00
5 Nelson Groundthumper 6.00
6 Erma, High Orbit 5.00

7 . . . . 3.00
8 Erna Feldna 3.00
9 High Orbit,Harvest Venture . . . 2.00
10 . . . . 2.00
11 . . . . 2.00
12 . . . . 2.00
13 . . . . 2.00
14 . . . . 2.00

ALBEDO VOL II
Antartic Press 1991–93
1 New Erma Story 2.50
2 E.D.F. HQ 2.50
3 Birth of Erma's Child 2.50
4 Non action issue 2.50
5 The Outworlds 2.50
6 War preparations 2.50
7 Ekosiak in Anarchy 2.50
8 EDF High Command 2.50
Spec. Color 3.00

ALIEN DUCKLING
1 . . . . 2.00
2 thru 4 . . . . @1.75

ALIEN ENCOUNTERS
Fantagor
1 . . . . 1.25

ALIEN FIRE
Kitchen Sink Press 1987
1 Eric Vincent art 3.50
2 Eric Vincent art 2.50
3 Eric Vincent art 2.00

ALIEN MUTANT WAR
1 . . . . 2.25

ALIEN NATION: A BREED APART
Adventure Comics
1 . . . . 3.00
2 . . . . 2.50
3 The 'Vampires' Busted 2.50
4 Final Issue 2.50

ALIEN NATION: THE FIRSTCOMERS
Adventure Comics
1 New Mini-series 2.50
2 Assassin 2.50
3 Search for Saucer 2.50
4 Final Issue 2.50

ALIEN NATION: PUBLIC ENEMY
Adventure Comics
1 'Before the Fall' 2.50
2 Earth & Wehlnistrata 2.50
3 Killer on the Loose 2.50

ALIEN NATION: THE SKIN TRADE
Adventure Comics
1 'Case of the Missing Milksop' . . 2.50
2 'To Live And Die in L.A' 2.50
3 A:Dr. Jekyll 2.50
4 D.Methoraphan Exposed 2.50

B & W PUB.

ALIEN NATION: THE SPARTANS
Adventure Comics
1 JT/DPo,Yellow wrap	4.00
1a JT/DPo,Green wrap	4.00
1b JT/DPo,Pink wrap	4.00
1c JT/DPo,blue wrap	4.00
1d LTD collectors edition	7.00
2 JT,A:Ruth Lawrence	2.50
3 JT/SM,Spartians	2.50
4 JT/SM,conclusion	2.50

ALIEN4 STRIKE FORCE
1	1.95

ALL-PRO SPORTS
All Pro Sports
1 Unauthorized Bio-Bo Jackson	2.50
2 Unauthorized Bio-Joe Montana	2.50

ALLY
Ally Winsor Productions 1995
1 I&O: Ally	2.95
2 and 3	@2.95

ALPHA PREDATOR
1	2.00

ALTERNATE HEROES
Prelude Graphics
1 and 2	@1.95

Amazing Comics Premieres #4
© Amazing Comics

AMAZING COMICS PREMIERES
1 thru 9	@1.95

AMAZING CYNICALMAN
Eclipse
1	1.50

AMAZING WAHZOO
1 RB	2.50
2	1.75
3	1.75

AMAZON WARRIORS
1 rep.	2.50

AMAZONS, THE
1	2.95

AMAZONS GONZANGAS: BAD GIRLS OF THE JUNGLE
Academy Comics 1995
0 Rites of passage(Jason Waltrip)	3.50

AMERICAN ANNIHILATOR
Night Realm Publishing
0 V:Synthetic Assassin	1.85

AMERICAN PRIMITIVE
Spec. #1	2.50

AMERICAN SPLENDOR
Harvey Bekar 1976–90
1 thru 15	@3.25

Tundra 1991
16	3.95

AMUSING STORIES
Blackthorne
1 thru 3	@2.00

ANGEL GIRL
Angel Entertainment 1997
0 by David Campiti & Al Rio	2.95
0 deluxe	5.95
0 nude manga cover	5.00
0 nude platinum cover	15.00
1 by David Campiti & Richard Fraga	2.95
1 deluxe	5.95
1 Virgin nude cover	5.00
1 Nude Manga cover	5.00
1 Nude Platinum cover	15.00

ANGEL GIRL: HEAVEN SENT
Angel Entertainment 1997
0 by David Campiti & Al Rio	2.95
0 Virgin nude	5.00
0 nude platinum cover	15.00

ANGEL OF DEATH
Innovation
1 thru 4	@2.25

ANGRY SHADOWS
1	4.95

ANIMAL MYSTIC
Cry For Dawn/Sirus 1993–95
1 DOe	60.00
1a variant, signed	90.00
1b 2nd printing, new (c)	15.00
2 I:Klor	60.00
2a 2nd printing, new (c)	12.00
3	25.00
3a 2nd printing	7.00
4 last issue	10.00
4a special	15.00
TPB DOe	14.95

ANIMERICA
(Viz Comics)
1 F:Bubble Gum Crisis	2.95
2 F:Bubble Gum Crisis	2.95
3 F:Bubble Gum Crisis	2.95

ANIVERSE, THE
1 thru 3	@1.95

ANT BOY
1	1.75
1a 2nd Printing	1.75
2	1.75

ANTARES CIRCLE
Antarctic Press
1	1.75
2	1.75

ANUBIS
Unicorn Books
1 I:Anubis	2.50
2 F:Anubis	2.50
3	2.50

Didactic Chocolate Press
3 by Scott Berwanger	2.75
4 thru 6	@2.75
7 "Sandy's Plight"	2.75

A-OK
Antarctic Press
1 Ninja H.S. spin-off series	2.50
2 F:Paul,Moniko,James	2.50
3 Confrontation	2.50
4	2.50

APACHE DICK
1 thru 4	@2.25

APATHY KAT
Entity 1995
1	2.75
1 signed, numbered	9.95
1 2nd printing	2.75
2	2.75
2 2nd printing	2.75
3 & 4	2.75
TPB Kollection #1	7.95

APE CITY
Adventure Comics
1 Monkey Business	3.00
2 thru 4	@2.50

APEX PROJECT
1	1.00

APPARITION, THE
Caliber
1 thru 4	@2.95
5 "Black Clouds"	2.95

APPLESEED
Eclipse
1 MSh,rep. Japanese comic	15.00
2 MSh,arrival in Olympus City	7.00
3 MSh,Olympus City politics	4.00
4 MSh,V:Director	4.00
5 MSh,Deunan vs. Chiffon	4.00
Book Two	

B & W PUB.

1 MSh,AAd(c),Olympus City 3 50
2 MSh,AAd(c),Hitomi vs.EswatUnit 3.00
3 MSh,AAd(c),Deunan vs.Gaia . . 3.00
4 MSh,AAd(c),V:Robot Spiders . . 3.00
5 MSh,AAd(c),Hitome vs.Gaia . . 3.00
Book Three
1 MSh,Brigreos vs.Biodroid 5.00
2 MSh,V:Cuban Navy 3.00
3 MSh,'Benandanti' 3.00
4 MSh,V:Renegade biodroid 3.00
5 . . . . 3.00
Book Four
1 MSh,V:Munma Terrorists 3.50
2 MSh,V:Drug-crazed Munma . . . 3.50
3 Msh,V:Munma Drug Addicts . . 3.50
4 MSh,Deunan vs. Pani 3.50

ARAMIS WEEKLY
1 mini-series 1.95
2 . . . . 1.95
3 . . . . 1.95

AREA 88
Eclipse
1 I:Shin Kazama 3.00
1a 2nd printing 1.50
2 Dangerous Mission 2.00
2a 2nd printing 1.50
3 O:Shin,Paris '78 . . . . 2.00
4 thru 8 . . . . @2.00
9 thru 39 . . . . @1.50
40 . . . . 1.75
41 . . . . 1.75
42 . . . . 2.00

ARGONAUTS
Eternity
1 thru 5 . . . . @1.95

ARGOSY
Caliber
1 'Walker' vs. Myth Beasts 2.50

ARIK KHAN
A Plus Comics
1 I:Arik Khan 2.50
2 . . . . 2.50

A.R.M. #1 © Adventure Comics

ARISTOCRATIC EXTRA-
TERRESTRIAL TIME-
TRAVELING THIEVES
Fictioneer Books
1 V:IRS 3.00
2 V:Realty 1.75
3 V:MDM 1.75
4 thru 12 . . . . @1.75

A.R.M.
Adventure Comics 1990
1 Larry Niven adapt. Death by
   Ecstasy,pt.1 . . . . 2.50
2 Death by Ecstasy,pt.2 . . . . 2.50
3 Death by Ecstasy,pt.3 . . . . 2.50

ARMADILLO ANTHOLOGY
1 & 2 . . . . @1.50

ARSENAL
SOL
1 . . . . 2.00

ART D'ECCO
FAN
1 . . . . 2.50

ARTHUR:
KING OF BRITAIN
Tome Press
1 Saga of King Arthur Chronicled
   by Geoffrey of Monmouth 2.95

ASHES
Caliber
1 thru 5 . . . . @2.50

ASHLEY DUST
Knight Press 1995
1 thru 3 . . . . @2.50
4 V:Allister Crowley 2.50
5 Metaphysical Adventure 2.50

ASRIAL VS. CHEETAH
Antarctic Press 1995–96
1 & 2 Ninja High School Gold
   Digger x-over . . . . @2.95

ASSASSINETTE
Pocket Change Comics
1 thru 3 . . . . @2.50
4 Psychic Realm 2.50
5 V:Nemesis 2.50
6 The Second Coming,pt.2 . . . . . 2.50
7 The Second Coming,pt.3 . . . . . 2.50
8 V:Crazy Actor 2.50
9 . . . . 2.50
10 final issue. 2.50

ASSASSINETTE:
HARDCORE
Pocket Change Comics
1 By Shadow Slasher Team 2.50
2 V:Bolero 2.50

ASSASSINETTE RETURNS
Power Comics
Spec. 2.50

ASSASSINETTE
VIOLATED
Power Comics
Spec. . . . . , . . . 2.50
Deluxe 4.25

ASTONISH
1 thru 4 . . . . @1.25

ASTRON
1 . . . . 2.00

ASYLUM
1 . . . . 1.75
2 thru 4 . . . . @1.95

ATOMIC COMICS
1 . . . . 1.50
Becomes: MARK I

ATOMIC MAN
1 . . . . 3.00
2 . . . . 2.00
3 . . . . 1.75

ATOMIC MOUSE
A Plus Comics
1 A:Atomic Bunny 2.50

A TRAVELLER'S TALE
Antarctic Press
1 I:Goshin the Traveller 2.50
2 . . . . 2.50

ATOMIC CITY TALES
Kitchen Sink
1 thru 4 by Jay Stephens . . . . @3.50
TPB Vol. 1 Go Power 12.95
TPB Vol. 1 signed & numbered . 20.95

ATTACK OF THE
MUTANT MONSTERS
A Plus Comics
1 SD,rep.Gorgo(Kegor) 2.50

AURORA
Dreamer Comics
1 I:Canadian Heroes   2.35

AUTUMN
Caliber Press 1995
1 I:James Turell 2.95

AVALON
Harrier
1 thru 3 . . . . 1.50

AVANT GUARD
Day 1 Comics
1 thru 4 F:Feedback 2.50

AV IN 3D
Aardvark–Vanaheim
1 Color,A:FlamingCarot 6.00

AVENUE X
Innovation
1 Based on NY radio drama 2.50

B & W PUB.

Purple Spiral
3 signed & numbered 3.00

AWESOME COMICS
1 thru 3 . . . . @2.00

AXED FILES, THE
Entity Comics
1 X-Files Parody 2.50
1 3rd printing, parody 2.75

B-MOVIE PRESENTS
B-Movie Comics
1 . . . . 1.70
2 . . . . 1.70
3 Tasma, Queen of the Jungle . . 1.70
4 . . . . 1.70

BABY ANGEL X
Brainstorm 1996
1 . . . . 2.95
2 . . . . 2.95
3 gold edition 5.00
3a signed edition 10.00

BABY ANGEL X: SCORCHED EARTH
Brainstorm 1997
1 by Scott Harrison 2.95
1a nude cover 2.95
2 . . . . 2.95
2a nude cover 2.95

BABYLON CRUSH
Boneyard Press
1 I:Babylon Crush 2.95
2 V:A Gang 2.95
3 V:Mafiaso Brothers 2.95
4 & 5 . . . . @2.95
CFD
6 . . . . 3.95
7 . . . . 3.95

BACK TO BACK HORROR SPECIAL
1 . . . . 1.50

BAD APPLES
High Impact Jan. 1997
1 . . . . 2.95
1 Bad Candies cover 9.95
2 . . . . 2.95
2 deluxe 15.00
3 by Billy Patton 2.95
3 deluxe adult cover 10.00

BAD AXE
1 thru 3 . . . . @2.25

BADEBIKER
1 . . . . 2.50
2 . . . . 2.00
3 thru 5 . . . . @1.50

BAD MOON
1 . . . . 3.00

BAD NEWS
3 . . . . 2.95

BAKER STREET
(Prev. color)
Caliber
3 . . . . 3.25
4 . . . . 1.95
5 Children of the Night Pt.1 . . . . 1.95
6 Children of the Night Pt.2 . . . . 1.95
7 Children of the Night Pt.3 . . . . 2.50
8 Children of the Night Pt.4 . . . . 2.50
9 Children of the Night Pt.5 . . . . 2.50
10 Children of the Night Pt.6 . . . . 2.50

BAKER ST.: GRAPHITTI
Caliber
1 'Elemenary, My Dear' 2.50

BALANCE OF POWER
MU Press
1 thru 4 . . . . @2.50

BANDY MAN, THE
Caliber 1996
1 SPr,CAd 2.95
2 SPr,CAd,JIT 2.95
3 SPr,CAd,JIT, conclusion 2.95

BANETOWN
1 . . . . 1.50

BANYON OF THE HIGH FORTRESS
1 . . . . 1.95

Baoh #5 ©Viz Comics

BAOH
Viz 1990
1 thru 8 . . . . @2.95
GN V:Juda Laboratory 14.95

BARABBAS
Slave Labor
1 . . . . 4.50
2 thru 4 . . . . @1.50

BARBARIC FANTASY
1 . . . . 1.95

2 . . . . 1.95

BARBARIC TALES
Pyramid
1 . . . . 3.00
2 and 3 . . . . @1.70

BARNEY THE INVISIBLE TURTLE
1 . . . . 1.95

BASEBALL SUPERSTARS
Revolutionary
1 Nolan Ryan 2.50

BAT
1 . . . . 2.25

BATHING MACHINE
1 thru 3 . . . . @2.50
4 . . . . 1.50

BATTLE ANGEL ALITA
Viz 1992
1 I:Daisuka,Alita 9.00
2 Alita becomes warrior 5.00
3 A:Daiuke,V:Cyborg 4.00
4 Alita/Cyborg,A:Makaku 4.00
5 The Bounty Hunters Bar 4.00
6 Confrontation 4.00
7 Underground Sewers,A:Fang . . 2.75
8 & 9 . . . . @2.75
Part II 1993
1 V:Zapan 2.95
2 V:Zapan 2.95
3 F:Ido 2.75
4 thru 7 V:Zapan . . . . @2.75
TPB Killing Angel 15.95
Part Three 1993
1 thru 5 . . . . @2.75
6 . . . . 5.00
7 thru 13 . . . . @2.75
Part Four 1994
1 thru 7 . . . . @2.75
Part Five 1995
1 thru 6 . . . . @2.75
7 . . . . 2.95
Part Six
1 thru 8 YuK . . . . @2.95
TPB Angel of Chaos 15.95
Part Seven Oct. 1996
1 thru 8 YuK . . . . @2.95
Part Eight 1997
1 (of 9) YuK 2.95
2 . . . . 2.95
TPB Vol. 5 . . . . 15.95
TPB Vol. 6 . . . . 15.95

BATTLE ARMOR
Eternity
1 thru 4 . . . . @1.95

BATTLE AXE
1 . . . . 2.50
2 . . . . 2.95

BATTLE BEASTS
Blackthorne
1 thru 4 . . . . @1.50

B & W PUB.

BATTLEGROUND EARTH
Best Comics 1996
1	2.50
2	2.50
3 "Destiny Quest: The Vengeance" concl.	2.50
4 V:Conjura	2.50
5 "The Pit of Black Death"	2.50

BATTLE GROUP PEIPER
Caliber
1 Bio S.S.Lt.Col Peiper	2.95

BATTLETECH
(Prev. Color)
7 thru 12	@1.75
Ann.#1	4.50

BATTLE TO DEATH
1 thru 3	@1.80

BATTRON
NEC
1 WWII story	2.75
2 WWII contd.	2.75

BEACH PARTY
1	2.50

BEAST WARRIOR OF SHAOLIN
1 thru 5	@1.95

THE BEATLES EXPERIENCE
Revolutionary
1 Beatles 1960's	3.00
2 Beatles 1964-1966	2.50
3	2.50
4 Abbey Road, Let it be	2.50
5 The Solo Years	2.50
6 Paul McCartney & Wings	2.50
7 The Murder of John Lennon	2.50
8 To 1992, final issue	2.50

Berzerker #6 © Gauntlet

BECK AND CAUL
Gauntlet
1 I:Beck and Caul	2.95
2 thru 6	@2.95
Ann.#1 A Single Step	3.50

BELLS OF KONGUR
1	2.25

BERZERKER
Gauntlet (Caliber)
1 thru 6	@2.95

BESET BY DEMONS
Tundra
1 Short stories by M.McLester	3.50

BEST CELLARS
Out of the Cellar 1995
1 New Anthology Comic	2.50

BEYOND HUMAN
Battlezone Comics
0	3.50

BEYOND MARS
Blackthorne
1 thru 5	@2.00

BIG BLACK KISS
Vortex
3 HC some color	3.75

BIG EDSEL BAND
1 FMc	1.75

BIG NUMBERS
1 BSz	6.00
2 BSz	5.50

BIG PRIZE
Eternity
1	1.95

BILL AND MELVIN
Newcomers Publishing
1 O:Bill & Melvin	2.95

BILL THE BULL
Boneyard Press
1 I:Bill the Bull	2.95
2 & 3 For Hire	@2.95

BILLY NGUYEN PRIVATE EYE
1	2.00
1a 2nd Printing	2.00
2 thru 6	@2.00

BIO-BOOSTER ARMOR GUYVER
Viz
Part II
1 thru 3 F:Sho	@2.75
4 V:Enzyme II	2.75
5 Sho VS Enzyme II	2.75
6 Final Issue	2.75
Part III
1 Sho Unconscious	2.75
2 V:Zoanoids	2.75
3 F:Murahani	2.75
4	2.75
5	2.75
6 V:Commando Guyver	2.75
7 Sho to the rescue	2.75
TPB Revenge of Chronos	15.95
TPB Vol. 4 Escape From Chronos	15.95
Part Four
1 thru 7	@2.95
Part Five
1 thru 7	@2.95
Part Six Dec. 1996
1 thru 6 by Yoshiki Takaya	@2.95

BIRTHRIGHT
1 thru 3	@2.00

BIZARRE HEROES
Kitchen Sink
1 DonSimpson art,parody (1990)	2.50

BIZARRE HEROES
Fiasco Comics
1 DSs, reprint	2.95

BLACK BOW
1	1.95

[Original] BLACK CAT
4 rep..	2.00
5 A:Ted Parrish	2.00
6 50th Anniv. Issue	2.00
7 rep.	2.00

BLACK CROSS
Spec #1	2.00
1a 2nd Print	1.75

BLACKENED
Enigma
1 V:Killing Machine	2.95
2 V:Killing Machine	2.95
3 Flaming Altar	2.95

BLACK KISS
Vortex
1 HC,Adult	7.00
1a 2nd printing	4.00
1b 3rd printing	1.25
2 HC	6.00
2a 2nd printing	3.00
3 HC	5.00
4 HC	4.00
5 HC	2.00
6 HC	2.00
7 thru 12 HC	@1.50

BLACK MAGIC
1	3.50
2 thru 4	@2.75

BLACKMASK
Eastern Comics
1 thru 6	@1.75

BLACK MOON
1	2.50
2 thru 4	@1.50
5	2.00

B & W PUB.

All comics prices listed are for *Near Mint* condition.

BLACK PHANTOM
1 .... 2.50

BLACK SCORPION
Special Studio
1 Knight of Justice 2.75
2 A Game for Old Men 2.75
3 Blackmailer's Auction 2.75

BLACK STAR
1 thru 4 .... @1.80

BLACKTHORNE 3 in 1
1 and 2 .... @2.00

BLACK ZEPPLIN
Renegade
1 .... 2.50
2 thru 6 .... @2.00

BLADE OF SHURIKEN
Eternity
1 thru 8 .... @1.95

BLADESMAN
1 .... 2.00

BLANDMAN
Eclipse
1 Sandman parody 2.50

BLAZING WESTERN
1 rep. 2.50

BLIND FEAR
Eternity
1 thru 4 .... @1.95

BLIP AND THE C CADS
1 .... 1.95

BLOOD & ROSES ADVENTURES
Knight Press

Blood is the Harvest #1 © Eclipse

1 F:Time Agents 2.95
2 F:Time Agents 2.95
3 Search for Time Agents 2.95
4 Time Adventures 2.95

BLOOD 'N' GUTS
Aircel
1 .... 2.50
2 .... 2.50
3 .... 2.50

BLOODBROTHERS
Eternity
1 thru 4 .... @1.95

BLOOD IS THE HARVEST
Eclipse 1992
1 I:Nikita,Milo 4.50
2 V:M'Raud D:Nikita? 2.50
3 Milo captured 2.50
4 F:Nikita/Milo 2.50

BLOOD JUNKIES
Eternity
1 Vampires on Capitol Hill 2.50
2 final issue 2.50

BLOODLETTING
Fantaco
1 A Shilling for a Redcoat 2.95
2 .... 2.95
3 Flee 2.95
4 thru 10 (of 11) by Chynna
Clugston, ... @3.95

BLOOD MASTERS
Night Realm Publishing
1 I:Blood Masters 1.80

BLOOD OF DRACULA
1 thru 7 .... @1.75
8 thru 14 .... @1.95
15 +Record&Mask 3.50
16 .... 1.95
17 .... 2.25

BLOOD OF INNOCENT
Warp Graphics
1 thru 4 .... @2.50

BLOODSHED
Damage
1 Little Brother 2.95
1a Commemorative issue 4.00
2 Little Brother 2.95
3 O:Bloodshed 2.95
3 "The Wastelands," cont. 3.50
"M" 3.50
"M" deluxe 5.00
Spec. Lunatics Fringe 3.50

BLOODWING
Eternity
1 thru 5 .... @1.95

BLOODY BOHES & BLACK-EYED PEAS
Galaxy
1 .... 2.00

BLUDGEON
Aardwolf 1997
1 by JPi & David Chylsetk 2.95
2 "Alise in Wonderland" 2.95
3 "Seeing Red" 2.95

BOB POWELL'S TIMELESS TALES
Eclipse
1 .... 2.00

BODY COUNT
1 .... 2.25
2 and 3 .... @1.95
4 .... 2.25

BOFFO LAFFS
1 1st hologram 4.00
2 thru 7 .... @2.00

BOGIE MAN: CHINATOON
Atomeka
1 I:Francis Claine 2.95
2 F:Bogie Man 2.95
3 thr 4 F:Bogie Man 2.95

BOGIE MAN: MANHATTEN PROJECT
Apocalypse
One Shot. D.Quale Assassination Plot 2.95

BOMARC: GUARDIANS OF THE I.FS. ZONE
Spec. 1.95
Spec. 2 .... 1.95

BONAFIDE
Bonafide Productions
1 F:Doxie 'th Mutt 3.50
2 F:Doxie 'th Mutt 3.50
3 F:Doxie 'th Mutt 3.50

BONE
Cartoon Books
1 I:Bone 235.00
1a 2nd printing 40.00
1b 3rd Printing 20.00
1c 4th printing 7.00
1d thru 1f 5th-7th printing .... @4.00
2 .... 125.00
2a 2nd printing 15.00
2b thru 2e 3rd-6th printing ... @3.00
3 .... 100.00
3a 2nd printing 8.00
3b thru 3d 3rd-5th printing .. @3.00
4 .... 60.00
4a thru 4c 2nd-4th printing .. @3.00
5 .... 50.00
5a thru 5c 2nd-4th printing .. @3.00
6 .... 50.00
6a thru 6c 2nd-4th printing .. @3.00
7 .... 40.00
7a,7b 2nd,3rd printing ..... @3.00
8 .... 35.00
8a,8b 2nd,3rd printing ..... @4.00
9 .... 15.00
9a 2nd printing 4.00
10 .... 8.00
11 .... 7.00
12 .... 7.00
13 .... 5.00

14 thru 17	@3.25
18 V:Bar owner	3.25
19 F:Phoney Bone	3.25
20 Dragonslayer Phoney Bone	3.25
21 thru 27, see Image	
28 "Rockjaw: Master of the Eastern	
Border"	2.95
29	2.95
TPB rep.#1-4	14.00
TPB Vol. 1 Rep.1-#6	12.95
TPB Vol. 2 Rep.#7-#12	12.95
TPB Vol. 3 Eyes of the Storm	16.95
HC Vol. 3 Eyes of the Storm	24.95
TPB Vol.4 Dragonslayer	16.95
HC Vol. 4 Dragonslayer	24.95
TPB Bone Reader	9.95

BONES
1 thru 4	@1.95

BONESHAKER
Caliber Press
1 Suicidal Wrestler	3.50

BOOGIE MAN
1 thru 4	@1.95

BOOK OF BALLADS AND SAGAS
Green Man Press
1 False Knight in the Road	2.95

BOOK OF THE TAROT
Caliber
1 History/Development o/t Tarot	3.95

BOONDOGGLE
Knight Press 1995
1 Waffle War	2.95
2 Waffle War	2.95
3 Waffle War	2.95

BORDER GUARD
1 and 2	@2.00

BORDER WORLDS
Kitchen Sink
1 adult	2.00
2 thru 7	@2.00

BORDER WORLDS: MAROONED
1	2.00

BORIS' ADVENTURE MAGAZINE
Nicotat
1 and 2	@2.00
3 thru 6	@2.95

BORIS THE BEAR
Nikotat
1–12: See Dark Horse section
13 thru 29	@2.00
30 thru 34	@2.50

BORN TO BE WILD
Eclipse
one shot. Benefit P.E.T.A.	10.95

BORN TO KILL
Aircel
1	2.50
2	2.50
3	2.50

BOSTON BOMBERS
Caliber
1	1.95
2	2.50
Spec.#1	3.95
Note: other issues are flipbook with Oz #17; The Searchers #5; Raven Chronicles #12, LegendLore #6

BOUNTY
1 'Bounty,"Navarro' Pt.1	2.50
2 'Bounty,"Navarro' Pt.2	2.50
3 'Bounty,"Navarro' Pt.3	2.50

BOX OFFICE POISON
Antarctic Press 1996
1 by Alex Robinson	3.50
3	2.95
4	2.95
5	2.95
Big Super Spec.#1	4.95

BOY AND HIS BOT
1	2.00

BRAT PACK
King Hell Publications
1	7.00
1a 2nd printing	3.50
2 thru 4	@4.25
5	4.00
Brat Pack Collection	13.00

BRATPACK/MAXIMORTAL
King Hell
Super Spec.#1 RV	3.00
Super Spec.#2 RV	3.00

BREAKNECK BLVD
Slave Labor Graphics 1995–96
1 thru 3 Jhonen Vasques art	@2.95
4 by Timothy Markin	2.95
5	2.95
6	2.95

BRICKMAN
1	2.00

BRIKHAUSS
1	1.75

BRINGERS
Blackthorne
1	3.50

BROID
Eternity
1 thru 4	@2.25

BRONX
Aircel
1 A.Saichann Short Stories	2.50
2 to 3	@2.50

Broid #2 © Eternity

BRONX
Aircel
Reprint	2.95

BROTHER MAN
New City Comics
1	5.00
1a	2.00
2 thru 7	@2.00

BRUCE JONES: OUTER EDGE
Innovation
1 All reprints	2.00

BRUCE JONES: RAZORS EDGE
Innovation
1 All reprints	2.50
2 D:Grimm, Gritty	2.50

BRU-HEAD
Schism Comics
1 Blockhead	2.95
1a 2nd printing	2.75
2 Blockhead	2.95

BRYMWYCK THE IMP
Planet X Productions
1	1.50

BUCE-N-GAR
RAK
1	1.75
2	1.75
3	1.75

BUCK GODOT
Palliard Press
1 I:Buck Godot	2.95

BUCKWHEAT
1	2.00
2	2.00

All comics prices listed are for *Near Mint* condition.

BUFFALO WINGS
Antarctic Press

1 and 2 .... @2.50

BUG
Planet X Productions

1	.... 1.50
2	.... 1.50

BULLET CROW
Eclipse

1	.... 2.00
2	.... 2.00

BULWARK
Millenium 1995

1 I:Bulwark	.... 2.95
2 O:Bulwark	.... 2.95

BUMBERCOMIC

1	.... 1.00
2	.... 1.00

BURNING KISS

1 with poster 4.95

BUSHIDO
Eternity

1 thru 6 .... @1.95

BUSHIDO BLADE OF ZATSICHI WALRUS

1	.... 3.00
2	.... 2.00

BUZZ
Kitchen Sink

1 Mark Landman (c) (1990)	.... 2.95
2 Mark Landman (c) (1991)	...... 2.95
3 Mark Landman (c) (1991)	...... 2.95

CABLE TV
Parody Press

1 Cable Satire 2.50

CAGES

8 Dave McKean art (1993) 3.95

CALIBER PRESENTS
(Prev. High Caliber)

1 TV,I:Crow	.... 85.00
2 Deadworld	.... 10.00
3 Realm	.... 3.00
4 Baker Street	.... 3.00
5 TV,Heart of Darkness, Fugitive	.... 2.50
6 TV,Heart of Darkness, Fugitive	.... 2.50
7 TV,Heart of Darkness, Dragonfeast	.... 2.50
8 TV,Cuda,Fugitive	.... 2.50
9 Baker Street,Sting Inc.	...... 2.00
10 Fugitive, The Edge	.... 2.50
11 Ashes,Random Thoughts	.... 2.50
12 Fugitive,Random Thoughts	... 2.50
13 Random Thoughts,Synergist	. 2.50
14 Random Thoughts,Fugitive	.. 2.50
15 Fringe, F:The Crow	...... 22.00
16 Fugitive, The Verdict	...... 3.50
17 Deadworld, The Verdict	..... 3.50

18 Orlak,The Verdict	.... 3.50
19 Taken Under,Go-Man	...... 3.50
20 The Verdict,Go-Man	.... 3.50
21 The Verdict,Go-Man	.... 3.50
22 The Verdict,Go-Man	.... 3.50
23 Go-Man,Heat Seeker	...... 3.50
24 Heat Seeker,MacktheKnife	... 3.50
Christmas Spec A:Crow,Deadworld Realm,Baker Street	.... 25.00
Summer Spec. inc. the Silencers, Swords of Shar-Pei (preludes)	. 3.95
One Shot	.... 2.50

CALIBER PRESENTS
(One Shots)

Hybrid 2.50

CALIBER SPOTLIGHT
Caliber

1 F:Kabuki,Oz 2.95

CALIFORNIA GIRLS
Eclipse

1 thru 8 .... @2.00

CALIGARI 2050

1 Gothic Horror	.... 2.25
2 Gothic Horror	.... 2.25

CAMELOT ETERNAL
Caliber

1	.... 3.00
2	.... 2.50
3	.... 2.50
4	.... 2.50
5 Mordred Escapes	.... 2.50
6 MorganLeFay returns from dead	2.50
7 Revenge of Morgan	.... 2.50
8 Launcelot flees Camelot	..... 2.50

CANADIAN NINJA

1	.... 1.50
2	.... 1.50

CANCER, THE
Humanity

1 V:Catharsis 2.50

CAPTAIN CANUCK REBORN
Semple Comics 1995–96

1 thru 3 by Richard Comely .. @2.50

CAPT. CONFEDERACY

1 adult	.... 8.00
2	.... 2.50
3	.... 2.00
4	.... 2.00
4a	.... 1.50
5 thru 8	.... @2.00
9 thru 11	.... @1.75
12	.... 1.95

CAPT. CULT

1 .... 2.00

CAPT. ELECTRON
Brick Computers Inc.

1	.... 2.00
2	.... 2.25

CAPTAIN HARLOCK
Eternity

1	.... 3.00
1a 2nd printing	.... 2.50
2	.... 2.50
3	.... 2.50
4 thru 13	.... @1.95
Christmas special	.... 2.50

CAPTAIN HARLOCK DEATHSHADOW RISING
Eternity

1	.... 2.75
2	.... 2.50
3	.... 2.25
4 Harlock/Nevich Truce	.... 2.25
5 Reunited with Arcadia Crew	... 2.25
6	.... 2.95

CAPTAIN HARLOCK: THE MACHINE PEOPLE
Eternity

1 O:Captain Harlock 2.50

[ADVENTURES OF] CAPTAIN JACK
Fantagraphics

1	.... 4.00
2	.... 2.50
3	.... 2.50
4 thru 12	.... @2.00

CAPT. OBLIVION

1 .... 1.95

CAPTAIN PHIL
Steel Dragon

1 .... 1.50

CAPTAIN SENTINEL

1 .... 2.00

CAPTAIN STERNN: RUNNING OUT OF TIME
Kitchen Sink

1 BWr(c) (1993)	.... 4.95
2 BWr(c)	.... 4.95
3 BWr(c) (1994)	.... 4.95
4 BWr(c)	.... 4.95

CAPTAIN THUNDER AND BLUE BOLT
Hero Graphics

1 New stories	.... 3.50
2 Hard Targets	.... 3.50

CARNIGE

1 & 2 .... @1.95

CARTOON HISTORY OF THE UNIVERSE
Rip Off Press

1 Gonick art	.... 2.50
2 Sticks & Stones	.... 2.50
3 River Realms	.... 2.50
4 Old Testament	.... 2.50
5 Brains & Bronze	.... 2.50
6 These Athenians	.... 2.50
7 All about Athens	.... 2.50

B & W PUB.

CARTUNE LAND
Magic Carpet Comics
1 .... 1.50

CASES OF SHERLOCK HOLMES
Renegade
1 thru 18 .... @2.00
19 .... 2.25

CASEY LACE
1 .... 1.50

CAT & MOUSE
Aircel
1 .... 4.00
2 .... 3.00
3 thru 8 .... @2.25
9 Cat Reveals Identity 2.25
10 Tooth & Nail 2.25
11 Tooth & Nail 2.25
12 Tooth & Nail, Demon 2.25
13 'Good Times, Bad Times' 2.25
14 Mouse Alone 2.25
15 Champion ID revealed 2.25
16 Jerry Critically Ill 2.25
17 Kunoichi vs. Tooth 2.25
18 Search for Organ Donor 2.25
Graphic Novel 9.95

CAT CLAW
Eternity
1 O:Cat Claw 2.75
1a 2nd printing 2.50
2 thru 9 .... @2.50

CATFIGHT
Lightning Comics
1 V:Prince Nightmare 4.00
1a Gold Edition 8.00

CATFIGHT: DREAM WARRIOR
Lightning Comics
1 V:The Slasher 2.75

CATFIGHT: DREAM INTO ACTION
Lightning Comics
1 A:Creed 3.00
1a signed and numbered 10.00
1 nude cover edition 10.00

CATFIGHT: ESCAPE FROM LIMBO
Lightning Comics 1996
1 .... 2.75
1a variant cover 2.75
1b platinum cover 5.95
1c nude cover 9.95
1d variant nude cover 9.95

CATFIGHT: SWEET REVENGE
Lightning Comics March 1997
1 .... 2.95
1a variant cover 2.95
1b nude cover 9.95
1c nude variant cover 9.95

CAT-KIND
1 .... 2.00

CAT MAN
AC Comics
Ashcan #1 I:Catman & Kitten ... 5.95

CAVEWOMAN
Bacement/Caliber 1994–95
1 .... 75.00
1 by Budd Root 2nd printing 4.00
1 3rd printing, new cover 3.00
2 .... 40.00
2a 2nd printing 3.00
2 3rd printing, new cover 3.00
3 .... 30.00
4 .... 30.00
5 Cavewoman vs. Klyde, Round
Two 25.00
6 .... 25.00

CAVEWOMAN: RAIN
Caliber 1996
1 by Budd Root 7.00
1a 2nd printing 3.00
2 .... 4.00
2a 2nd printing 3.00
3 .... 4.00
3a 2nd edition, new cover 3.00
4 .... 4.00
4a 2nd edition, new cover 3.00
5 .... 3.50
5 2nd edition, new cover 3.00
6 and 7 .... @3.00

CELESTIAL MECHANICS
Innovation
1 thru 3 .... @2.25

CECIL KUNKLE
Darkline Comics 1987
1 .... 1.50

CEMENT SHOOZ
Horse Feathers 1991
1 with color pin-up 2.50

Cement Schooz #1 © Horse Feathers

CENOTAPH: CYBER GODDESS
Northstar
1 I:Cenotaph 3.95

CENTRIFUGAL BUMBLE-PUPPY
1 Adult 2.25
2 thru 6 .... @2.25
7 .... 2.50

CEREBUS
Aardvark–Vanaheim
0 .... 3.00
0a Gold Ed. 25.00
1 B:DS(s&a),I:Cerebus 275.00
1a Counterfeit 50.00
2 DS,V:Succubus 100.00
3 DS,I:Red Sophia 100.00
4 DS,I:Elrod 70.00
5 DS,A:The Pigs 60.00
6 DS,I:Jaka 60.00
7 DS,R:Elrod 60.00
8 DS,A:Conniptins 35.00
9 DS,I&V:K'cor 35.00
10 DS,R:Red Sophia 35.00
11 DS,I:The Cockroach 35.00
12 DS,R:Elrod 35.00
13 DS,I:Necross 30.00
14 DS,V:Shadow Crawler 30.00
15 DS,V: Shadow Crawler 30.00
16 DS, at the Masque 25.00
17 DS,"Champion" 25.00
18 DS,Fluroc 25.00
19 DS,I:Perce & Greet-a 25.00
20 DS,Mind Game 25.00
21 DS,A:CaptCockroach,rare ... 50.00
22 DS,D:Elrod 20.00
23 DS,DuFort's school 10.00
24 DS,IR:Prof.Clarmont 10.00
25 DS,A:Woman-thing 10.00
26 DS,High Society 10.00
27 DS,Kidnapping of an Avrdvark 10.00
28 DS,Mind Game!! 10.00
29 DS,Reprocussions 10.00
30 DS,Debts 8.00
31 DS,Chasing Cootie 8.00
32 DS 8.00
33 DS,DS,Friction 5.00
34 DS,Three Days Before 5.00
35 thru 50 DS .... @5.00
51 DS,(scarce) 17.00
52 DS 5.00
53 DS,C:Wolveroach 7.00
54 DS,I:Wolveroach 9.00
55 DS,A:Wolveroach 8.00
56 DS,A:Wolveroach 8.00
57 DS 5.00
58 DS 5.00
59 DS,Memories Pt.V 5.00
60 DS,more vignettes 5.00
61 DS,A:Flaming Carrot 6.00
62 DS,A:Flaming Carrot 6.00
63 DS,Mind Game VI 5.00
64 DS,Never Pray for Change ... 5.00
65 DS,Papal Speech 5.00
66 DS,Thrill of Agony 5.00
67 thru 70 DS .... @5.00
71 thru 74 DS .... @4.00
75 DS,Terrible Analogies 4.00
76 DS,D:Weisshaupt 4.00
77 DS,Surreal daydream 4.00
78 DS,Surreal daydream 4.00

B & W PUB.

79 DS,Spinning Straw 4.00
80 DS,V:Stone Tarim 4.00
81 DS,A:Sacred Wars Roach 4.00
82 DS,A:Tarim 3.50
83 DS,A:Michele 3.50
84 DS,Weisshaupt's Letter 3.50
85 DS,A:Mick Jagger 3.50
86 DS,A:Mick Jagger 3.50
87 DS,Tower Climb 3.50
88 DS,D:Stone Tarim 3.50
89 DS,A:Cute Elf 3.50
90 DS,Anti-Apartheid(c) 3.50
91 DS 3.50
92 DS,A:Bill & Seth 3.50
93 DS,Astoria in Prison 3.50
94 DS,Rape of Astoria 3.50
95 DS,Sophia-Astoria Dream 3.50
96 DS,Astoria in Prison 3.50
97 DS,Escape Planned 3.50
98 DS,Astoria's Trial 3.50
99 DS,Sorcery in Court 3.50
100 DS,A:Cirin 3.50
101 DS,The Gold Sphere 3.00
102 DS,The Final Ascension 3.00
103 DS,On the Tower 3.00
104 DS,A:Flaming Carrot 3.00
105 DS,V:Fred & Ethel 3.00
106 DS,D:Fred & Ethel 3.00
107 DS,Judge on the Moon 3.00
108 DS,All History 3.00
109 DS,O:Universe 3.00
110 DS,More Universe 3.00
111 DS,Cerebus' Fate 3.00
112 DS,Memories 3.00
113 DS,Memories 3.00
114 DS,I:Rick nash 3.00
115 DS,I:Pud Withers 3.00
116 DS,Rick Meets Cerebus 3.00
117 DS,Young Jaka Injured 3.00
118 DS,Cerebus Apologizes 3.00
119 DS,Jaka Opens Door 3.00
120 DS,I:Oscar 3.00
121 DS,Women Explained 3.00
122 DS,Iest History 3.00
123 DS,Each One's Dream 3.00
124 DS 3.00
125 DS,C:Lord Julius 3.00
126 DS,R:Old Vet'ran 2.50
127 DS,Jaka Dances 2.50
128 DS,L:Cerebus as Fred 2.50
129 DS,Jaka's Story 2.50
130 DS,D:Pud Withers 2.50
131 DS,Jaka Imprisoned 4.00
132 DS,A:Nurse 4.00
133 DS,I:Mrs. Thatcher 4.00
134 DS,Dancing Debate 4.00
135 DS,Jaka Signs 4.00
136 DS,L:Rick 4.00
137 DS,Like-a-Looks 4.00
138 DS,Maids'Gossip 4.00
139 A:Misogynist-roach 4.00
140 I:Old Oscar 4.00
141 A:Cerebus 4.00
142 C:Mick Jagger 4.00
143 DS,Oscars Forboding 4.00
144 DS,I:Doris 4.00
145 thru 146 DS . . . . @4.00
147 Neil Gaiman, DS 9.00
148 thru 150 DS 3.00
151 DS,B:Mothers & Daughters,
   Book 1: Flight pt.1 . . . . 4.00
151a 2nd printing 2.50
152 DS,Flight pt.2 . . . . 4.00
152a 2nd printing 2.50
153 DS,Flight pt.3 . . . . 4.00

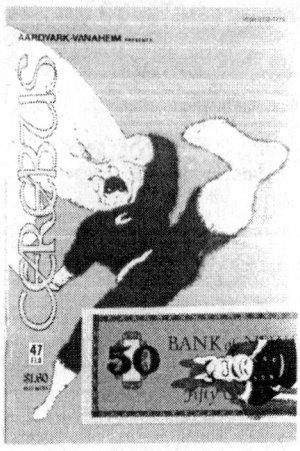

Cerebus #47 © Aardvark-Vanaheim

153a 2nd printing 2.50
154 DS,Flight pt.4 . . . . 4.00
155 DS,Flight pt.5 . . . . 4.00
156 DS,Flight pt.6 . . . . 3.00
157 DS,Flight pt.7 . . . . 3.00
158 DS,Flight pt.8 . . . . 3.00
159 DS,Flight pt.9 . . . . 3.00
160 DS,Flight pt.10 . . . . 3.00
161 DS,Flight pt.11, Bone story . . 10.00
162 DS,E:M&D,Bk.1:Flight pt.12 . 3.00
163 DS,B:Mothers & Daughters
   Book 2: Women pt.1 . . . . 2.75
164 DS,Women pt.2,inc. Tour
   Momentos 2.50
165 thru 174 Women pt.3–12 . . @2.50
175 DS,B:Mothers & Daughters,
   Book 3: Reads pt.1 . . . . 2.50
175 thru 186 Reads pt.1–12 . . @2.50
187 DS,B:Mothers & Daughters,
   Book 4:Minds pt.1 . . . . 2.50
188 thru 199 Minds pt.5–13 . . @2.25
200 . . . . 2.50
201 thru 219 Guys pt.1 to pt.19 . . 2.25
220 The Secret, pt.1 (of 12) 2.25
Cerebus rep.#1–#25 (500 pgs.) . . 25.00
High Society rep.#26–#50 . . . . . 25.00
Church & State I rep.#52–#85 . . . 30.00
Church & State II rep.#86–#111 . . 30.00
Jaka's Story rep.#114–#136 . . . . 25.00
Melmoth rep.#139–#150 . . . . . . 17.00
Flight rep.#151–#162 . . . . 17.00
Women rep.#163–#174 . . . . 17.00
Reads rep.#175–#186 . . . . 17.00
Reads 2nd printing 15.00
Reads, Signed, numbered ed. . . . 28.00
TPB Minds Rep.#175–#186 . . . . 16.00

CEREBUS
CHURCH & STATE
Aardvark–Vanaheim
1 DS rep.#51 . . . . 2.25
2 thru 30 DS rep.#52-#80 . . . @2.00

CEREBUS COMPANION
Aardvark–Vanaheim
1 . . . . 3.95

CEREBUS HIGH SOCIETY
Aardvark–Vanaheim
1 thru 14 DS (biweekly) . . . . . @1.70
15 thru 24 DS rep. . . . . @2.00
25 DS rep. #50, final 2.00

CEREBUSJAM
Aardvark–Vanaheim
1 MA,BHa,TA,WE,A:Spirit 15.00

CEREBUS REPRINTS
Aardvark–Vanaheim
1A thru 28A DS rep . . . . @1.25
See also: Church & State
See also: Swords of Cerebus

CHAINGANG
1 . . . . 2.50
2 . . . . 3.50

CHAINSAW VIGILANTE
New England Press
1 Tick Spinoff 3.25

CHAMPION, THE
1 . . . . 2.50

CHAMPIONS
1 . . . . 2.25

CHAMPION OF KITARA:
DUM DUM & DRAGONS
MU Press
1 Dragons Secret 2.95
2 Dragons Secret 2.95
3 Dragons Secret 2.95

CHARLIE CHAN
Eternity
1 thru 4 . . . . @1.95
5 and 6 . . . . @2.25

CHASER PLATOON
Aircel
1 Interstellar War 2.25
2 Ambush 2.25
3 New Weapon 2.25
4 Saringer Battle Robot 2.25
5 Behind Enemy Lines 2.25
6 . . . . 2.25

CHEERLEADERS
FROM HELL
1 and 2 . . . . @2.50

CHEMICAL FACTOR
1 . . . . 1.75

CHESTY SANCHEZ
Antarctic Press 1995
1 . . . . 2.95
2 . . . . 2.95

CHICAGO FOLLIES
1 . . . . 2.95

CHINA & JAZZ
CODE NAME
DOUBLE IMPACT
High Impact Oct. 1996

1	3.00
1a nude cover	9.95
2	2.95
2a nude RCI(c) cover	9.95

CHIPS & VANILLA
1 Spec. 1.75

CHIRON
Annurel Studio Graphics

1	2.50
1a 2nd printing	2.50
2 Transported to Doran	2.50
3 Transported to Doran	2.50
3a Gold Edition	4.00

CHRONOS CARNIVAL
Fleetway
1 reps. 200 AD stories 7.95

CHUCK CHICKEN
AND BRUIN BEAR
Jabberwocky
1 . . . . 3.00

CIRCLE WEAVE, THE
Indigo Bean Productions 1995

1 Apprentice to a God	2.00
2 Apprentice to a God,pt.2	2.00
3 Apprentice to a God,pt.3	2.00
4 Apprentice to a God,pt.4	2.00
5 Apprentice to a God,pt.5	2.50

CIRCUS WORLD
1 . . . . 2.50

CLANDE, INC.
Domain Publishing

1 I:Sam Davidson, Jeremy Clande	2.95
2 V:Dias	2.95

CLIFFHANGER COMICS
AC Comics

1 rep.	2.50
2 rep.	2.50

CLINT
1 Trigon comics 3.00

CLINT THE HAMSTER
Eclipse

1	2.50
2	1.50

COBALT BLUE
1 Gustovitch Art 77 . . . . 10.00

COBRA
Viz 1990–91

1 thru 6	@2.95
7	3.25
8 V:SnowHawks	3.25
9 Zados	3.25
10 thru 12	@3.25

CODA
1 . . . . 3.00

CODENAME NINJA
1 and 2 . . . . @2.00

COLD BLOODED
CHAMELEON
COMMANDOS
Blackthorne

1	2.00
2	1.50
3	1.50
4	1.75
5	1.75
6	2.00
7	2.00

COLD EDEN
Legacy 1995

1 Last City on Earth	2.35
2 V:Mutant Hunting Pack	2.35
3 D6 Tower	2.35

COLE BLACK

1 Vol.I	15.00
2 Vol.I	10.00
3 Vol.I	10.00
4 Vol.I	10.00
5 Vol.I	12.00
1 Vol.II	3.50
2 Vol.II	2.00
3 Vol.II	1.50

COLONEL KILGORE
Special Studios

1 WWII stories	2.50
2 Command Performance	2.50

COLT
K-Z Comics

1	5.00
2 pin-up by Laird	8.00
2 pin-up by Henbeck	2.00
3 thru 5	@1.00

COMICS EXPRESS

1 thru 4	@2.95
5 thru 11	@3.95

COMING OF APHRODITE
Hero Graphics
1 Aphrodite/modern day 3.95

COMMAND REVIEW
Thoughts & Images

1 rep. Albedo #1-4	6.00
2 rep. Albedo #5-8	4.00
3 rep. Albedo #9-13	4.00

COMPLETE FLUFFHEAD
1 . . . . 2.00

CONDOM-MAN
Aaaahh!! Comics

1 I:Condom Man	3.50
2 F:Condom Man	3.50
3 V:Alien Army	3.50
4 Brother bought back to life	3.50
5 O:Condom-Man (Chris Swafford)	3.50

Conqueror #6 © Harrier

CONQUEROR
Harrier 1984–86

1	3.50
2 thru 4	@2.00
5 thru 9	@1.75

CONQUEROR UNIVERSE
Harrier
1 . . . . 2.75

CONSPIRACY COMICS
Revolutionary

1 Marilyn Monroe	2.50
2 Who Killed JFK	2.50
3 Who Killed RFK	2.50

CONSTELLATION
GRAPHICS
STG
1 thru 4 . . . . @1.50

CONSTRUCT
Caliber "New Worlds"

1 (of 6) PJe,LDu, sci-fi,48pg	3.95
2 PJe,LDu	2.95
3 PJe,LDu	2.95
4 PJe,LDu	2.95
5 PJe,LDu	2.95
6 PJe,LDu, conclusion	2.95

CONTINUM

1	1.50
2	1.75

CONTRACTORS
Eclipse
1 . . . . 2.25

CORBO

1	1.75
2	1.75

CORMAC MAC ART
1 thru 4 R.E.Howard adapt. . . @1.95

B & W PUB.

All comics prices listed are for *Near Mint* condition. | **CVA Page 579**

B & W PUB.

COSMIC BOOK
1 . . . . 1.95

COSMIC HEROES
Eternity
1 Buck Rogers rep. 1.95
2 thru 6 Buck Rogers rep. . . . @1.95
7 thru 9 Buck Rogers rep. . . . @2.25
10 . . . . 3.50
11 . . . . 3.95

COSMIC STELLAR REBELERS
1 thru 4 . . . . @1.50

COSMOS
1 . . . . 1.70
2 . . . . 1.70

Counter Parts #2 © Tundra

COUNTER PARTS
Tundra
1 thru 3 . . . . @2.95

COVENTRY
Fantagraphics Oct. 1996
1 BWg, "The Frogs of God" 3.95
2 BWg, "Thirteen Dead Guys Named Bob" 3.95
3 BWg 3.95

CRAZY MEN GO WILD
1 . . . . 2.00

CREED
Hall of Heroes 1994
1 TKn,I:Mark Farley 30.00
1A Wizard Ace edition rep. 20.00
2 TKn,Camping 35.00

CREED
Lightning Comics 1995
1-shot TKn retelling of #1&#2 . . . 2.75
See also: *Color*

CREED THE VOID
TPB Collected edition 5.95
TPB Deluxe 9.95

CREED/TEENAGE MUTANT NINJA TURTLES
Lightning Comics 1996
1 TKn(c) 3.00
2 TKn(c) 3.00
1 Gold Collector's Edition 5.95
1 Platinum Edition 9.95

CREED: CRANIAL DISORDER
Lightning Comics
1 . . . . 3.00
1A Previews variant cover 3.00
1B Platinum Edition 9.00
1C signed platinum edition 15.00
2 . . . . 3.00
2b variant cover 2.95
3 . . . . 2.95
3b variant cover 2.95
3c limited edition 9.95

CREED: THE GOOD SHIP & THE NEW JOURNEY HOME
Lightning Comics
1 . . . . 2.95
1a variant cover 2.95
1b limited edition 9.95

CRIME BUSTER
AC Comics
0 from FemForce 2.95
1 Rep. From Boys Illustrated . . . 3.95

CRIME CLASSICS
Eternity
1 rep Shadow comicstrip 1.95
2 thru 11 . . . . @1.95
12 . . . . 2.25

CRIME SMASHERS
Special Edition
1 . . . . 1.80

CRIMSON DREAMS
Crimson
1 thru 11 . . . . @2.00

CRIMSON NUN
Antarctic Press 1997
1 (of 4) 2.95

CRITTER CORPS
1 . . . . 1.50
2 . . . . 1.50
3 . . . . 1.50

CRITTERS
Fantagraphics Books
1 SS,Usagi Yojimbo,Cutey . . . 7.00
2 Captain Jack,Birthright 4.50
3 SS,Usagi Yojimbo,Gnuff 4.50
4 Gnuff,Birthright 3.00
5 Birthright 3.00
6 SS,Usagi Yojimbo,Birthright . . . 3.00

7 SS,Usagi Yojimbo,Jack Bunny . 3.00
8 SK,Animal Graffiti,Lizards 2.50
9 Animal Graffiti 2.50
10 SS,Usagi Yojimbo 3.00
11 SS,Usagi Yojimbo, ... 4.00
12 Birthright II 2.00
13 Birthright II,Gnuff 2.00
14 SS,Usagi Yojimbo,BirthrightII . 2.50
15 Birthright II,CareBears 2.00
16 SS,Groundthumper,Gnuff 2.00
17 Birthright II,Lionheart 2.00
18 Dragon's 2.00
19 Gnuff,Dragon's 2.00
20 Gnuff 2.00
21 Gnuff 2.00
22 Watchdogs,Gnuff 2.00
23 Flexi-Disc,X-Mas Issue 4.00
24 Angst,Lizards,Gnuff 2.00
25 Lionheart,SBi,Gnuff 2.00
26 Angst,Gnuff 2.00
27 SS,Ground Thumper 2.00
28 Blue Beagle,Lionheart 2.00
29 Lionheart,Gnuff 2.00
30 Radical Dog,Gnuff 2.00
31 SBi,Gnuffs,Lizards 2.00
32 Lizards,Big Sneeze 2.00
33 Gnuff,Angst,Big Sneeze 2.00
34 Blue Beagle vs. Robohop 2.00
35 Lionheart,Fission Chicken 2.00
36 Blue Beagle,Fission Chicken . . 2.00
37 Fission Chicken 2.00
38 SS,double size,Usagi Yojimbo . 2.75
39 Fission Chicken 2.00
40 Gnuff 2.00
41 Duck'Bill Platypus 2.00
42 Glass Onion 2.00
43 Lionheart 2.00
44 Watchdogs 2.00
45 Ambrose the Frog 2.00
46 Lionheart 2.00
47 Birthright 2.00
48 Birthright 2.00
49 Birthright 2.00
50 SS,Neil the Horse, UsagiYojimbo 4.95
Spec.1 Albedo,rep+new 10pgStory 2.00

CROSSED SWORDS
1 and 2 . . . . @0.95

CROSSFIRE
Eclipse
18 thru 26 DSp . . . . @2.00

CROW, THE
Caliber
1 . . . . 75.00
1a 2nd Printing 5.00
1b 3rd Printing 3.00
2 . . . . 40.00
2a 2nd Printing 5.00
2b 3rd Printing 3.00
3 . . . . 30.00
3a 2nd Printing 3.00
4 . . . . 25.00
Tundra
1 reps. Crow #1, #2 . . . . 20.00
2 . . . . 15.00
3 . . . . 20.00
TPB 20.00

CROW, THE
Kitchen Sink
TPB Flesh & Blood Collection . . 10.95

All comics prices listed are for *Near Mint* condition.

TPB The Crow Collection, 7th
   printing 224pg 15.95

CROW, THE: DEAD TIME
Kitchen Sink
1 .... 5.00
2 .... 4.00
3 .... 3.00
TPB Collection rep. 10.95

CROW, THE: DEMON IN DISGUISE
Kitchen Sink 1997
1 (of 4) by John J. Miller & Dean
   Ormston 2.95
2 .... 2.95

CROW, THE: FLESH AND BLOOD
Kitchen Sink 1996
1 thru 3 .... @2.95

CROW, THE: WAKING NIGHTMARES
Kitchen Sink Jan. 1997
1 PhH 2.95
2 thru 4 PhH .... @2.95

CROW, THE: WILD JUSTICE
Kitchen Sink
1 thru 3 .... @2.95

CROW OF THE BEAR CLAN
Blackthorne
1 .... 2.25
2 thru 6 .... @1.75

CRUSADERS
Guild
1 Southern Knights 10.00

CRUSADERS
1 and 2 .... @1.50
3 and 4 .... @1.75

CRY FOR DAWN
1 .... 225.00
1a 2nd Printing 100.00
1b 3rd Printing 75.00
2 .... 125.00
2a 2nd Printing 25.00
3 .... 75.00
4 .... 50.00
5 .... 45.00
6 .... 45.00
7 Corporate Ladder, Rock A Bye
   Baby 25.00
8 Decay, This is the Enemy 25.00
9 .... 25.00

CRY FOR DAWN: SUBTLE VIOLENTS
one shot F:Ryder 3.00

CRYING FREEMAN
Viz
1 .... 6.50

2 .... 5.50
3 thru 5 .... @5.00
6 thru 8 .... @4.50

CRYING FREEMAN II
Viz
1 .... 4.75
2 .... 4.00
3 .... 4.00
4 thru 6 .... @4.25
7 V:Bugnug 4.00
8 Emu & The Samurai Sword ... 4.00
9 Final Issue 4.00

CRY FREEMAN V
Viz
1 Return to Japan 4.00
2 A:Tateoka-assassin 4.00
3 .... 4.00
4 A:Bagwana 4.00
5 V:Tsunaike 4.00
6 V:Aido Family 4.00
7 V:Tsunaike 4.00
GN:Taste of Revenge 14.95

CRYPT
1 .... 1.95

CRYPT OF DAWN
Sirius 1996
1 JLi(c) 2.95
1 variant cover 9.95
2 JLi(c) 2.95

CUDA
Rebel Studios
1 I:Cuda, Zora, V:Shanga Bai 2.00

CULTURAL JET LAG
Fantagraphics
1 .... 2.50

CURSE OF THE ATOMIC WRESTLING WOMEN
1 .... 1.95

Cyber 7 #6 © Rockland

CURSE OF THE SHE-CAT
1 .... 2.50

CUTEY BUNNY
1 .... 8.00
2 thru 4 .... @4.00
Eclipse
5 .... 3.00

CYBER 7
Eclipse
1 .... 2.50
2 thru 5 .... @2.00
Book 2   Rockland 1990
1 thru 7 .... @2.00
8 thru 10 .... @2.50

CYBERFROG
Hall of Heroes
1 I:Cyberfrog 15.00
1a 2nd printing 2.50
2 V:Ben Riley 2.50
2a 2nd printing 1.50

CYBERFROG
Harris Jan. 1997
1 3rd Anniv. Special 2.50
1a Walt Simonson(c) 6.00
1b signed & numbered 20.00
2 .... 3.50
2a variant cover 4.00
3 .... 3.50
4 .... 3.50
4a signed 30.00

CYBERFROG VS CREED
Harris 1997
1 .... 3.50

CYBERHAWKS
1 .... 1.85
2 thru 4 .... @1.80

CYBERZONE
Jet Black Graphics
1 thru 5 Never-never Land 2.50

CYBORG GERBELS
1 English comic 4.00

CYCLOPS
Blackthorne
1 Mini-series 1.95
2 .... 1.95
3 .... 1.95

CYGNUS X-1
Twisted Pearl Press
1 V:Yag'Nost 2.50
2 F:Rex and Bounty Hunters ... 2.50

CYNDER
Immortelle Studios
1 I:Cynder 5.00
2 .... 3.00
3 conclusion 2.50
Second Series
1 thru 3 .... 3.00

B & W PUB.

All comics prices listed are for *Near Mint* condition.

CYNDER/HELLINA
Immortelle Studios
Spec. 1 x-over 3.00

DAEMON MASK
1 . . . . 1.80
Mini-Series
1 . . . . 4.00

DAFFY QADDAFI
Comics Unlimited Ltd.
1 . . . . 2.00

DAIKAZU
1 . . . . 7.00
1a 2nd Printing 1.50
2 . . . . 3.00
2a 2nd Printing 1.50
3 . . . . 4.00
3a 2nd Printing 1.50
4 thru 7 . . . . @1.50
8 . . . . 1.75

DA'KOTA
Millennium Jan. 1997
1 by Pavlet & Petersen 2.95
1 signed 4.95
1 foil edition 9.95
2 . . . . 2.95
2 foil edition 4.95
3 foil deluxe edition 6.95
3 . . . . 2.95
3a variant cover 2.95

DAMLOG
1 . . . . 1.80
1a 2nd printing 1.00
2 thru 5 . . . . @1.80

DAMONSTREIK
Imperial Comics
1 I:Damonstreik 1.95
2 V:Sonix 1.95
3 V:Sonix 1.95
4 J:Ohm 1.95
5 V:Drakkus 1.95

DANGEROUS TIMES
1 MK 2.50
2 MA(c) 2.00
2a 2nd printing 1.75
3 MR(c) 1.95
3a 2nd printing 1.95
4 GP(c) 1.95

DANGERWORLD
1 . . . . 1.00
2 . . . . 1.00
3 . . . . 1.00

DAN TURNER
HOLLYWOOD DETECTIVE
Eternity
1 'Darkstar of Death' 2.50

DAN TURNER
HOMICIDE HUNCH
Eternity
1 Dan Turner Framed 2.50

DAN TURNER
THE STAR CHAMBER
Eternity
1 Death of Folly Hempstead 2.50

DARERAT
1 . . . . 1.95

DARK ADVENTURES
1 . . . . 1.25

DARK ANGEL SPECIAL
1 . . . . 1.75

DARK ASSASSIN
1 thru 3 . . . . @1.50
Vol. 2
1 thru 5 . . . . @2.00

DARK CITY ANGEL
Freak Pit Productions
1 I:Lt.Michelle Constello 3.50
2 . . . . 3.50
3 Sex Doll is Prime Suspect 3.50

DARK COMICS
1 . . . . 1.80
2 . . . . 1.80

DARK FORCE
Omega 7
1 A:Dark Force 2.00

DARK JUSTICE
IMP Press
1 I:Dark Justice 2.50

DARK LORD
RAK
1 thru 3 . . . . @1.75

DARK MUSE
Dark Muse Productions
1 with mini-comic 3.50
1a with mini-comic 5.00
2 . . . . 3.95
3 F:Coffin Joe 3.95

DARK REGIONS
1 . . . . 2.50
2 . . . . 2.50
3 Scarce 3.00
4 and 5 . . . . @1.50

DARK STAR
1 I:Ran 2.25
2 thru 3 . . . . @2.25

DARK VISIONS
Pyramid
1 I:Wasteland Man 1.70
2 thru 4 . . . . @1.70

DARK WOLF
Eternity
1 and 2 . . . . @1.95
Volume 2
1 thru 14 . . . . @1.95
Ann. #1 . . . . 2.25

DATA 6
1 . . . . 1.95
2 . . . . 1.95

DAZE & KNIGHT
1 . . . . 1.80

DAYS OF DARKNESS
Apple
1 From Pearl Harbor
to Midway 2.75
2 Pearl Harbor Attack,cont 2.75
3 Japanese Juggernaut 2.75
4 Bataan Peninsula 2.75
GN 14.95

Deadbeats #6 © Claypool Comics

DEADBEATS
Claypool Comics 1993
1 thru 13 . . . . @2.50
14 New Ways to Dream 2.50
15 thru 25 . . . . @2.50
TPB Rep. #1–#6 . . . . 12.95

DEADFACE
1 . . . . 3.00
2 . . . . 2.50
3 . . . . 1.95

DEADFISH BEDEVILED
1 . . . . 2.25

DEAD HEAT
1 . . . . 1.95

DEADKILLER
Caliber
1 Rep Deadworld 19 thru 21 . . . . 2.95

DEADTALES
Caliber
1 'When a Body Meets a Body' . . 2.95

DEADTIME STORIES
1 AAd,WS 1.75

B & W PUB.

DEADWORLD
Arrow
1 Arrow Pyb	. . . .	6.00
2	. . . .	4.00
3 V:King Zombie	. . . .	3.50
4 V:King Zombie	. . . .	3.50
5 Team Rests	. . . .	3.50
6 V:King Zombie	. . . .	3.50
7 F:KZ & Deake, Graphic(c)	. . . .	3.50
7a Tame cover	. . . .	2.00
8 V:Living Corpse, Graphic(c)	. . .	2.50
8a Tame cover	. . . .	2.00
9 V:Sadistic Punks, Graphic(c)	. .	2.50
9a Tame cover	. . . .	2.00
10 V:King Zombie, Graphic(c)	. . .	2.50
10a Tame cover	. . . .	2.00
11 V:King Zombie, Graphic(c)	. .	3.00
11a Tame cover	. . . .	2.50
12 I:Percy, Graphic(c)	. . . .	3.00
12a Tame cover	. . . .	2.50
13 V:King Zombie, Graphic(c)	. .	3.00
13a Tame cover	. . . .	2.50
14 V:Voodoo Cult,Graphic(c)	. . .	3.00
14a Tame cover	. . . .	2.50
15 Zombie stories,Graphic(c)	. . .	3.00
15a Tame cover	. . . .	2.50
16 V:'Civilized' Community	. . . .	2.50
17 V:King Zombie	. . . .	2.50
18 V:King Zombie	. . . .	2.50
19 V:Grakken	. . . .	2.50
20 V:King Zombie	. . . .	2.50
21 Dead Killer	. . . .	2.50
22 L:Dan & Joey	. . . .	2.50
23 V:King Zombie	. . . .	2.50
24	. . . .	2.50
25 (R:Vince Locke)	. . . .	2.50
26	. . . .	2.50

Caliber
1 thru 11	. . . .	@2.95
12 thru 14 Death Call	. . . . . .	@2.95
15 Death Call pt. 6	. . . .	2.95

DEADWORD ARCHIVES
Caliber
1 Rep.Deadworld series	. . . . 2.50

DEADWORLD:
BITS & PIECES
Caliber
1 Rep.1st Deadworld Story, Caliber presents #2&#8	. . . . 1.60

DEADWORLD: TO
KILL A KING
Caliber
1 R:Deadkiller	. . . . 2.95

DEATHBRINGER
1 thru 4	. . . . @1.60

DEATHDREAMS
OF DRACULA
Apple
1 Selection of short stories	. . . . . 2.50
2 short stories	. . . . 2.50
3 Inc. Rep. BWr,'Breathless'	. . . . 2.50
4 short stories	. . . . 2.50

DEATH HAWK
1 thru 6	. . . . @1.95

DEATH HUNT
Eternity
1	. . . .	1.95
2	. . . .	1.95

DEATHMARK
Lightning Comics
1 O:War Party	. . . . 2.75

DEATHQUEST
1	. . . . 1.50

DEATH RATTLE
Kitchen Sink
(Prev. Color)
4	. . . .	4.00
5	. . . .	3.00
6 Steve Bissette(c)	. . . .	2.00
7 Ed Gein	. . . .	2.00
8 I:Xenozoic Tales	. . . .	7.00
9 BW,rep.	. . . .	2.00
10 AW,rep.	. . . .	2.00
11 thru 15	. . . .	@2.00
16 BW,Spacehawk	. . . .	2.00
17 Rand Holmes(c)	. . . .	2.00
18 FMc	. . . .	2.00

DEATH'S HEAD
Crystal
1	. . . .	1.95
2	. . . .	1.95
3	. . . .	1.95

DEATH WATCH
1	. . . . 1.75

DEATHWORLD
Adventure Comics
1 Harry Harrison Adapt.	. . . . . .	2.50
2 thru 4	. . . .	@2.50

DEATHWORLD II
Adventure Comics
1 Harry Harrison Adapt.	. . . . . .	2.50
2 thru 4	. . . .	@2.50

Defenseless Dead #3
© Adventure Comics

DEATHWORLD III
Adventure Comics
1 H.Harrison Adapt.,colonization	.	2.50
2 Attack on the Lowlands	. . . . .	2.50
3 Attack on the Lowlands contd.	.	2.50
4 last issue	. . . .	2.50

DEFENSELESS DEAD
Adventure Comics 1991
1 Larry Niven adapt. A:Gil	. . . .	2.50
2 A:Organlegger	. . . .	2.50
3 A:Organlegger	. . . .	2.50

DELIRIUM
1	. . . .	2.00
2 KG	. . . .	2.00

DELTA SQUADRON
1	. . . .	2.00
2	. . . .	2.00

DELTA TENN
1 thru 11	. . . . @1.50

DEMON BLADE
1	. . . .	1.75
2	. . . .	1.95
3	. . . .	1.95

DEMONGATE
Sirius 1996–97
1 thru 12 by Bao Lin Hum	. . . @2.50

DEMON GUN
Crusade Entertainment
1 thru 3 GCh,KtH	. . . . @2.95

DEMON HUNTER
Aircel
1 thru 4	. . . . @1.95

DEMONIQUE
London Night Studios
1 by Membeila & Owens	. . . . . .	3.00
1a nude cover variant	. . . .	10.00
2 F:Viper	. . . .	3.00
3 Mayhem	. . . .	3.00
4 Final issue	. . . .	3.00

DEMON'S BLOOD
1	. . . .	1.70
2	. . . .	1.85

DEMON'S TAILS
Adventure
1	. . . .	2.50
2 A:Champion	. . . .	2.50
3 V:Champion	. . . .	2.50
4 V:Champion	. . . .	2.50

DEMON WARRIOR
1 thru 12	. . . .	@1.50
13	. . . .	1.75
14	. . . .	1.75

DENIZENS OF
DEEP CITY
Jabberwocky
1 thru 8	. . . . @2.00

B & W PUB.

DEPRESSOR
Humanity
1 I:Depressor 2.50

DERRECK WAYNE'S STRAPPED
Gothic Images
1 Confrontational Factor 2.25
2 Confrontational Factor 2.25

DESCENDING ANGELS
Millenium
1 I:3 Angels 2.00
2 F:Jim Johnson 2.95
3 F:Jim Johnson 2.95

DESERT PEACH
Thoughts & Images
1 thru 4 . . . . @2.00

DESTINY ANGEL
Dark Fantasy Productions 1996
1 (of 3) 3.95
1 2nd printing 3.95
1a deluxe 4.50
2 "Sunless Garden" 3.50
2a foil cover 3.95
2b photo cover 3.95

DESTROY
Eclipse
1 Large Size 4.95
2 Small Size,3-D 4.95

DEVIL JACK
Doom Theatre 1995
1 I:Devil Jack 2.95
1a Directors Cut 2.95
2 V:Belegosi 2.95

DEVIL'S WORKSHOP
Blue Comet Press 1995
1 Iron Cupcakes 2.95

DIATOM
Photographics
1 Dan Duto Photographic 4.95

DICK TRACY MAGAZINE
1 V:Little Face Finnyo 3.95

DICK TRACY MONTHLY
Blackthorne
1 thru 25 . . . . @2.00

DICK TRACY: THE EARLY YEARS
5 . . . . 2.95
6 . . . . 2.95
7 and 8 . . . . @3.50

DICK TRACY WEEKLY
26 thru 108 . . . . @2.00
Unprinted Stories #3 . . . . 2.95
1 3-D Special 3.00
Spec. #1 . . . . 2.95
Spec. #2 . . . . 2.95
Spec. #3 . . . . 2.95

DIGGERS, THE
C&T
3 . . . . 1.75

DILLINGER
Rip Off Press
1 Outlaw Dillinger 2.50

DINOSAUR REX
1 and 2 . . . . @2.00

DINOSAURS
Caliber
1 History of Dinosaurs 3.00

DINOSAURS FOR HIRE
Eternity
1 . . . . 3.00
1a Rep. 1.95
2 thru 9 . . . . @1.95
Fall Classic #1 . . . . 2.25
Malibu
#1 3-D special 3.50

DIRECTORY TO A NON-EXISTENT UNIVERSE
Eclipse
1 . . . . 1.95

DIRTY-NAIL
1 . . . . 2.00

DIRTY PAIR
1 . . . . 9.00
2 . . . . 6.00
3 . . . . 5.00
4 end mini-series 5.00
Eclipse
reprint 1-3 . . . . 5.00
Vol 2 #1 thru 5 . . . . @5.00

DIRTY PAIR: PLAGUE OF ANGELS
Eclipse
1 thru 5 . . . . @4.00

DIRTY PAIR: SIM EARTH
Eclipse
1 thru 4 . . . . 3.00

DISQUETTE
1 . . . . 2.50

A DISTANT SOIL
Warp Graphics
1 A:Panda Khan 15.00
2 . . . . 7.00
3 . . . . 7.00
4 . . . . 5.00
5 . . . . 5.00
6 thru 9 . . . . @5.00
Aria Press
1 . . . . 5.00
1a-2nd to 4th printing 2.50
2 . . . . 3.50
3 . . . . 3.00
4 . . . . 3.00
5 thru 8 . . . . 2.00
9 thru 11 . . . . 2.50

12 thru 14 . . . . @3.00
GN Knights of the Angel, deluxe 15.95
GN Immigrant Song rep.#1–#3 . . 6.95

DITKOS WORLD: STATIC
Renegade
1 thru 3 SD . . . . @1.70

DR. GORPON
Eternity
1 I:Dr.Gorpon,V:Demon 2.25
2 A:Doofus,V:ChocolateBunny . . 2.50
3 D:Dr.Gorpon 2.50

DR. RADIUM
Silverline
1 . . . . 3.00
2 . . . . 2.00
3 and 4 . . . . @1.50

DR. RADIUM: MAN OF SCIENCE
Slave Labor
1 And Baby makes 2, BU: Dr.
Radiums' Grim Future 2.50

DOC WEIRD'S THRILL BOOK
1 AW 1.75
2 . . . . 1.75
3 . . . . 1.75

DOCTOR WEIRD
Caliber Press
1 V:Charnogg 2.50
2 V:Charnogg 2.50

DODEKAIN
Antarctic Press
1 and 2 by Masayuki Fujihara . @2.95
3 Rampage Vs. Zogerians 2.95
4 V:Zogerians 2.95
5 F:Takuma 2.95
6 Dan vs. Takuma 2.75
7 V:Okizon 2.75
8 V:Okizon 2.95

Dogaroo #1 © Blackthorne

All comics prices listed are for *Near Mint* condition.

DOG
1 Military renegade 2.25

DOGAROO
Blackthorne 1988
1 . . . . 2.00

DOGS O'WAR, THE
Crusade Entertainment 1996
1 thru 3 (of 3) . . . . @2.95

DOLLS
Sirius
1-shot science fiction 2.95

DOMETRIUS KUIR
Newcomers Publishing
1 Walt Bayless 2.95

DOMINION
Eclipse
1 . . . . 3.00
2 thru 6 . . . . @2.00

DOMINO CHANCE
Chance
1 1,000 printed 10.00
1a 2nd printing 3.50
2 thru 6 . . . . @3.00
7 I:Gizmo 7.00
8 A:Gizmo 11.00
9 . . . . 2.50
[2nd Series]
1 . . . . 3.00
2 . . . . 1.95
3 . . . . 1.95

Donatello #1 © Mirage

DONATELLO
Mirage
1 A: Turtles 12.00

DON SIMPSON'S BIZARRE HEROES
Fiasco Comics
0 thru 7 . . . . 2.95

8 V:Darkcease 2.95
9 R:Yan Man 2.95
10 F:Mainstreamers 2.95
11 Search for Megaton Man 2.95
12 . . . . 2.95
13 House of Megaton Man 2.95
14 Cec Vs. Dark Cease 2.95
TPB Apocalypse Affiliation 12.95

DOUBLE EDGE DOUBLE
Double Edge
1 thru 3 . . . . 3.50
4 Heroes Inc. Rep.#1-#2 . . . . . . 2.95

DOUBLE IMPACT
High Impact Studios 1995–96
1 I: China & Jazz 7.00
1a Chromium (c) variant, signed 10.00
1b Rainbow (c) w/certificate . . . 35.00
1c Rainbow (c) w/o certificate . . 25.00
2 Castilo's Crime 4.00
2a nude cover variant 15.00
2b silver version 20.00
2c signed, w/certificate 7.00
3 . . . . 3.00
3a Bondage (c) 15.00
4 . . . . 3.00
4a Phoenix (c) 15.00
5 . . . . 3.00
5a nude cover 15.00
6 China cover 3.00
6a Jazz cover 3.00
6b signed China or Jazz(c) 15.00
6c bondage(c) 10.00
7 . . . . 3.00
8 . . . . 3.00
8a variant (c) 8.00
2nd Series 1996–97
0 . . . . 3.00
0a nude (c) 10.00
1 . . . . 3.00
1a chromium (c) 4.00
1b Christmas (c) 10.00
2 . . . . 3.00
2a Sweedish Erotica(c) 10.00

DOUBLE IMPACT/ LETHAL STRIKE: DOUBLE STRIKE
High Impact
1 x-over 3.00
1a nude RCI(c) cover 9.95

DOUBLE IMPACT: ASSASSINS FOR HIRE
High Impact April 1997
1 RCI,RkB 2.95
1 nude art cover 10.00
1 nude photo cover 15.00
2 . . . . 2.95
2 gold nude cover 10.00
2 signed nude cover 20.00

DRACULA
1 . . . . 3.75
1a 2nd printing 2.50
2 thru 4 . . . . @2.50

DRACULA IN HELL
Apple
1 O:Dracula 2.50
2 O:Dracula contd. 2.50

DRACULA: SUICIDE CLUB
Adventure
1 I:Suicide Club in UK 2.50
2 Dracula/Suicide Club cont. 2.50
3 Club raid,A:Insp.Harrison 2.50
4 Vision of Miss Fortune 2.50

DRACULA: THE LADY IN THE TOMB
Eternity
1 . . . . 2.50

DRACULA'S COZY COFFIN
Draculina Publishing 1995
1 thru 4 Halloween issue 2.95

DRAGONFORCE
Aircel (Prev. Color)
8 thru 13 DK . . . . @2.50

DRAGONFORCE CHRONICLES
Aircel
Vol. 1 thru Vol. 5 rep. . . . . @2.95

DRAGONMIST
Raised Brow Publications
1 I:Dragonmist 2.75
2 F:Assassin 2.75

DRAGON OF THE VALKYR
1 . . . . 1.75
2 thru 4 . . . . @2.00

DRAGON QUEST
1 TV 15.00
2 TV 7.50
3 TV 6.50

DRAGONRING
[1st Series]
1 B.Blair,rare 110.00
Aircel
1 . . . . 3.50
2 . . . . 2.00
3 thru 6 . . . . @1.75
See Also Independent Color

DRAGON'S STAR
1 and 2 . . . . @1.75
3 and 4 . . . . @2.00

DRAGON WEEKLY
1 Southern Knights 1.75
2 and 3 . . . . @1.75

DREAD OF NIGHT
Hamilton
1 Horror story collection 3.95
2 Json, inc.'Genocide' 3.95

DREAM ANGEL: THE QUANTUM DREAMER
Angel Entertainment 1997
0 Nude Manga cover 5.00
1 by Mort Castle & Adriana Melo 2.95

B & W PUB.

All comics prices listed are for *Near Mint* condition.

1 Virgin nude cover 5.00
1 Nude Platinum cover 15.00
2 . . . . 2.95
2 Virgin nude cover 5.00
2 Nude Platinum cover 15.00

DREAMGIRL
Angel Entertainment 1996
0 by David Campitti & Al Rio . . . 2.95
0 Virgin Nude cover 5.00
0 Lost in Heaven nude cover . . . 7.00
0 platinum edition, nude cover . 10.00
1 . . . . 2.95
1 deluxe 5.95
1 Manga cover 5.00
1 Nude Manga cover 5.00

DREAMERY
Eclipse
1 thru 13 . . . . @2.00

DREAMLANDS
Caliber "New Worlds" 1996
1 . . . . 2.95
2 flip book with Boston Bombers #3 2.95

DREAMTIME
Blind Rat
1 Young Deserter 2.95
2 Gypsy Trouble 2.50

DREAMWOLVES
Dramenon Studios
1 . . . . 3.00
2 . . . . 3.00
3 F:Desiree 3.00
4 V:Venefica 3.00
5 V:Venefica 3.00
6 R:Carnifax 3.00
7 . . . . 3.00
8 F:Wendy Bascum 3.00

DRIFTERS
Infinity Graphics 1986
1 . . . . 1.75

DRIFTERS AFAR
1 . . . . 1.70

DUCK & COVER
1 . . . . 2.00
2 . . . . 2.00

DUCKBOTS
1 . . . . 1.75
2 . . . . 1.75
3 . . . . 1.75

DUNGEONEERS
1 thru 8 . . . . @1.50

DURANGO KID
1 . . . . 2.50
2 . . . . 2.50

DUTCH DECKER
1 . . . . 1.95
2 . . . . 1.95
3 . . . . 1.95

DYNAMIC COMICS
1 . . . . 2.00
2 . . . . 2.00

Eagle #5 © Crystal

EAGLE
Crystal
1 . . . . 5.00
1a signed & limited 7.00
2 thru 5 . . . . @2.75
6 thru 11 . . . . @2.25
12 . . . . 2.50
13 thru 17 . . . . @2.00

Apple
18 thru 26 . . . . @1.95

EAGLE: DARK MIRROR
Comic Zone
1 A:Eagle, inc reps 2.75
2 In Japan, V:Lord Kagami 2.75
3 . . . . 2.95
4 . . . . 2.95

EAGLES DARE
Aager Comics
1 thru 4 . . . . 1.95
5 V:Dragon 1.95

EARTH LORE: LEGEND OF BEK LARSON
Eternity
1 . . . . 1.80

EARTH LORE: REIGN OF DRAGON LORD
1 . . . . 1.80
2 . . . . 1.75

EARTH WAR
Newcomers Publishing 1995
1 and 2 from Newcomers Illus. . . 2.95

EARTH: YEAR ZERO
Eclipse
1 thru 4 . . . . @2.00

EB'NN THE RAVEN
Now
1 . . . . 5.00
2 . . . . 3.00
3 . . . . 2.50
4 . . . . 2.00
5 thru 9 . . . . @1.50

EDDIE CAMPELL'S BACCHUS
Eddie Campell Comics 1995
1 V:Telchines 2.95
1 2nd printing 2.95
2 thru 10 V:Telchines 2.95
11 thru 26 ECa . . . . @2.95
GN Collected Bacchus, Vol. 1 . . . 9.95
TPB Collected Bacchus, Vol. 9 King
  Bacchus 12.95

EDDY CURRENT
1 thru 12 . . . . @2.00

EDGAR ALLAN POE
Tell Tale Heart 1.95
Pit & Pendulum 1.95
Masque of the Red Death 1.95
Murder in the Rue Morgue 1.95

EDGE
1 . . . . 3.00
Vol 2 #1 thru #3 . . . . @3.00
Vol 2 #4 thru #6 . . . . @2.00

EIGHTBALL
Fantagraphics
1 . . . . 10.00
1a 2nd to 6th printing 3.00
2 . . . . 7.00
2a 2nd to 5th printing 3.00
3 . . . . 6.00
3a 2nd to 4th printing 3.00
4 . . . . 5.00
4a 2nd to 4th printing 3.00
5 . . . . 4.00
5 3rd printing 3.50
6 thru 10 . . . . @4.00
11 A:Ghost World 3.50
12 F:Ghost World 3.25
13 thru 17 . . . . @3.00
18 . . . . 4.00
TPB Orgy Bound, rep. from #7–#14 4.95

ELECTRIC BALLET
Caliber
1 Revisionist History of Industrial
  Revolution 2.50

ELEGANT LADIES
1 . . . . 3.50

ELFLORD
[1st Series]
1 all rare 80.00
2 . . . . 65.00
3 . . . . 60.00
4 . . . . 50.00
5 . . . . 50.00
6 . . . . 80.00
7 . . . . 80.00
8 . . . . 80.00
9 thru 15 . . . . @50.00

B & W PUB.

 All comics prices listed are for *Near Mint* condition.

ELFLORD
Aircel 1986

1 I:Hawk	5.00
1a 2nd printing	3.50
2	3.00
2a 2nd printing	2.00
3 V:Doran	3.00
4 V:Doran	3.00
5 V:Doran	2.00
6 V:Nendo	2.00
Compilation Book	4.95

(Vol 2, #1 to #24, see Color)

25 thru 31	@1.95
32	2.50

ELFLORD
Warp Graphics Jan. 1997

1 (of 4) by Barry Blair & Colin Chan	2.95
2	2.95
3	2.95
4	2.95

ELFLORD CHRONICLES
Aircel

1 rep B.Blair	2.50
2 thru 8 rep	@2.50

ELFQUEST
Warp Graphics 1979–85

1 WP	45.00
1a WP,2nd printing	12.00
1b WP,3rd printing	5.00
1c WP,4th printing (1989)	4.00
2 WP	25.00
2a WP,2nd printing	4.00
2b WP,3rd printing	3.00
2c WP,4th printing (1989)	2.50
3 WP	20.00
3a WP,2nd printing	4.00
3b WP,3rd printing	3.00
3c WP,4th printing (1989)	2.50
4 WP	20.00
4a WP,2nd printing	4.00
4b WP,3rd printing	3.00
4c WP,4th printing (1989)	2.50
5 WP	20.00
5a WP,2nd printing	4.00
5b WP,3rd printing	3.00
6 WP	20.00
6a WP,2nd printing	4.00
6b WP,3rd printing	3.00
7 WP	15.00
7a WP,2nd printing	3.00
8 WP	15.00
8a WP,2nd printing	3.00
9 WP	15.00
9a WP,2nd printing	3.00
10 thru 15	@10.00
16 WP,I:DistantSoil	10.00
17 thru 21 WP	@10.00
TPB Gatherum	19.95

ELFQUEST
Warp Graphics

4 thru 14 ed. RPi	4.95
HC Wolfrider's Guide to the World of Elfquest	19.95

ELFQUEST: KAHVI
Warp Graphics 1995

1 thru 6 I:Kahvi	@2.25

ELFQUEST: KINGS OF THE BROKEN WHEEL
Warp Graphics 1990–92

1 WP	2.25
2 thru 9 WP	@2.25

ELFQUEST: METAMORPHOSIS
Warp Graphics April 1996

Spec.#1 WP,RPi	2.95

Elfquest: Seige at Blue Mountain #1
© Warp Graphics

ELFQUEST: SEIGE AT BLUE MOUNTAIN
Warp Graphics/Apple Comics 1987–88

1 WP,JSo	11.00
1a 2nd printing	3.00
2 WP	6.00
2a 2nd printing	3.00
3 WP	5.00
3a 2nd printing	2.00
4 thru 8 WP	@5.00

ELFQUEST: TWO SPEAR
Warp Graphics 1995

1 thru 3 (of 5) Two-Spears past	@2.25

ELFQUEST: WOLFRIDER
Warp Graphics

Spec.#1	2.95

ELFQUEST: WORLDPOOL
Warp Graphics

Spec.#1	2.95

ELFTHING
Eclipse

1	3.00

ELFTREK
Dimension

1 Elfquest's Star Trek parody	2.00
2	1.75

ELF WARRIOR

1	3.00
2	2.50
3 thru 5	@1.95

ELIMINATOR
Eternity

1 'Drugs in the Future'	2.50
2	2.50

ELVIRA, MISTRESS OF THE DARK
Claypool Comics

1 thru 35	@2.50
36 thru 51 photo covers	@2.50
TPB Elvira, Mistress of the Dark	12.95

ELVIRA
Eclipse

1 Rosalind Wyck	2.50

ELVIS: UNDERCOVER

1	2.00

EMERALDAS
Eternity

1 thru 4	@2.25

EMMA DAVENPORT
Lohamn Hill Press

1 I:Emma Davenport	2.75
2	2.75
3 O:Hammerin Jim	2.75
4 Cookie Woofer War	2.75

EMPIRE
Eternity

1 thru 4	@1.95

EMPIRE LANES
Comico

1	2.95

EMPTY BALLOONS

1	1.50
2	1.50

ENCHANTED VALLEY
Blackthorne

1	1.75
2	1.75

ENCHANTER
Eclipse

1 thru 3	@2.00

ENCHANTER: APOCALYPSE WIND NOVELLA
Entity

1 Foil Enhanced Cover	2.95

END, THE

1	1.95

ENEMY LINES SPECIAL

1	1.75

B & W PUB.

ENFORCERS
Dark Visions Publishing 1995
0 From Anthology Title 2.50

ENTROPY TALES
1 . . . . 2.00
2 Domino Chance 1.50
3 thru 5 . . . . @1.50

EPSILON WAVE
Elite
1 . . . . 3.00
2 . . . . 2.00
3 thru 5 . . . . @1.60

EQUINE THE UNCIVILIZED
Graphspress
1 . . . . 4.00
2 . . . . 2.50
3 thru 6 . . . . @2.00

EQUINOX CHRONICLES
Innovation
1 I:Team Equinox, Black Avatar . 2.25
2 Black Avatar Plans US conquest 2.25

EQUIS MORTIS
Crimson Studios
1 I:Carl Ragland (Equis Mortis) . . 2.50

ERADICATORS
1 RLm (1st Work) 5.00
1a 2nd printing 1.50
2 . . . . 2.50
3 Vigil 2.00
4 thru 8 . . . . @1.50

ERIC PRESTON IS THE FLAME
B-Movie Comics
1 Son of G.A.Flame 95

ERIN
1 . . . . 1.95

Escape Velocity #2
© *Escape Velocity Press*

ESCAPE TO THE STARS
Visionary
1 thru 7 . . . . @1.25
[2nd Series]
1 . . . . 1.25
2 . . . . 1.25

ESCAPE VELOCITY
Escape Velocity Press
1 and 2 . . . . @1.50

ESMERALDAS
Eternity
1 thru 4 . . . . 2.25

ESPERS
Halloween Comics April 1996
1 JHI, R:ESPers 2.95
1 JHI,signed 2.95
2 JHI,signed 2.95
3 JHI, ... 2.95
3 JHI,signed 2.95
4 thru 6 JHI, conclusion . . . . @2.95
Volume 2
1 "Undertow" 2.95
2 . . . . 2.95

ETERNAL THIRST
1 . . . . 2.00
2 . . . . 2.00

EVIL ERNIE
Eternity 1991–92
1 SHu,BnP,I&O:Evil Ernie, Lady
  Death 150.00
1a Spec. 1992 reprint, 16 extra
  pages 60.00
2 Death & Revival of Ernie, A:Lady
  Death, 1st (c) 125.00
3 Psycho Plague, A:Lady Death 100.00
4 A:Lady Death 75.00
5 A:Lady Death 60.00
TPB rep #1-5 . . . . 10.95

EVIL ERNIE
Chaos! Comics
1 thru 5 reprints . . . . @2.50
Spec. Youth Gone Wild, die-cut
  cover, Director's cut 5.00
TPB Youth Gone Wild 9.95

EVIL ERNIE
Chaos! Comics 1996
1 encore presentation 2.50
2 thru 5 encore presentation . . . 1.95

EXIT
Caliber 1995
1 I:New series 2.95
2 thru 4 "The Traitors," pt.2–pt.4 . 2.95
Epilogue 2.95
GN rep. 320 pages 19.95
GN rep. 160 pages 14.95

EX-MUTANTS
Amazing Comics
1 AC/RLm 5.00
1a 2nd printing 2.00
EC
2 . . . . 3.00

3 thru 5 . . . . @2.00
6 PP 1.95
7 . . . . 1.95
8 . . . . 1.95
Ann. #1 . . . . 1.95
Pin-Up Spec. #1 . . . . 1.95

EX-MUTANTS: THE SHATTERED EARTH CHRONICLES
Eternity
1 thru 3 . . . . @1.95
4 RLd(c) 2.75
5 RLd(c) 2.75
6 thru 14 . . . . @1.95
Winter Special #1 . . . . 1.95

EXILE
1 and 2 . . . . @2.00

EXTINCT
NEC
1 Rep Golden age stories 3.50

EXTREMELY SILLY
1 . . . . 4.00
1 Vol. II 1.25
2 Vol. II 1.25

EYE OF MONGOMBO
1 . . . . 3.00
2 thru 5 . . . . @2.00

FAERIE KING
Moordam Comics
1 In View of Man 2.50

FAILED UNIVERSE
1 . . . . 1.75

FAITH
Lightning Comics 1997
1 (of 2) 2.95
1a variant cover 2.95
1b Limited, cover A 9.95
1c Limited, cover B 9.95
1 signed & numbered 9.95

FANBOYS
Spec #1 . . . . 2.00

FANGS OF THE WIDOW
Ground Zero
1 I:Emma 2.50
London Night Studios 1995
1 O:The Widow 3.00
1a platinum edition 5.00
2 Body Count 3.00
3 Emma Revealed 3.00
Ground Zero
7 thru 9 "Metal Gypsies," pt.#1–#3 3.00
10 thru 13 rep. Widow: Bound by
  Blood #1–#4 + additional material 3.50
14 "Search and Destroy" pt.1 . . . 3.00
15 "Search and Destroy" pt.2 . . . 3.00
Ann. #1 Search and Destroy 5.95

FANTAESCAPE
1 . . . . 1.75
2 . . . . 1.75

FANTASCI
Warp Graphics-Apple
1	2.50
2	2.00
3	2.00
4	4.00
5 thru 8	@1.75
9 'Apple Turnover'	1.75

FANTASTIC ADVENTURES
1 thru 5	@1.75

FANTASTIC FABLES
Silver Wolf
1 and 2	@1.50

FANTASTIC PANIC
Antarctic 1993–94
1 thru 8 Ganbear	@2.75
[Volume 2]	
1 thru 4	@2.75
4 thru 9	@2.95
10 concl.	3.50

FANTASTIC WORLDS
Flashback Comics
1 Space Opera	2.95
2 F:Attu, Captain Courage	2.95

FANTASY QUARTERLY
1 1978 1st Elfquest	65.00

FART WARS:
SPECIAL EDITION
Entity Comics 1997
1 Star Wars trilogy parody,A:Nira X	2.75
1a Empire Attacks Back cover	2.75
1b Return of the One-Eye cover	2.75

FASTLANE ILLUSTRATED
Fastlane Studios
1 Super Powers & Hot Rods	2.50

FAT NINJA
1	2.50
2 Vigil	2.50
3 thru 8	@1.50

FAUNA REBELLION
1 thru 3	@2.00

FAUST
North Star
1 Vigil	42.00
1a Vigil,2nd Printing	5.00
1b Vigil,3rd Printing	2.00
1c Tour Edition	30.00
2 Vigil	32.00
2a Vigil,2nd Printing	3.00
2b Vigil,3rd Printing	2.50
3 Vigil	18.00
3a Vigil,2nd Printing	2.50
4 Vigil	15.00
5 Vigil	9.00
6 Vigil	9.00
Rebel Studios	
7 Vigil	5.00
8 TV	3.50
9 TV,Love of the Damned	3.50
10 E:DQ(s),TV,Love o/t Damned	3.50

FAUST VOL. II
REBEL
1 TV,Love of the Damned	2.50

FAUST PREMIERE
North Star
1 Vigil	45.00

FEM FANTASTIQUE
AC Comics
1	1.95

FEM FORCE
AC Comics
1 thru 15 See Color	
16 I:Thunder Fox	3.00
17 F:She-Cat,Ms.Victory, giant	3.00
18 double size	3.00
19	3.00
20 Giant,V:RipJaw, Black Commando	3.00
21 V:Dr.Pretorius	3.00
22 V:Dr.Pretorius	3.00
23 V:Rad	3.00
24 A:Teen Femforce	3.00
25 V:Madame Boa	3.00
26 V:Black Shroud	3.00
27 V:Black Shroud	3.00
28 A:Arsenio Hall	3.00
29 V:Black Shroud	3.00
30 V:Garganta	3.00
31 I:Kronon Captain Paragon	3.00
32 V:Garganta	3.00
33 Personal Lives of team	3.00
34 V:Black Shroud	2.75
35 V:Black Shroud	2.75
36 giant,V:Dragonfly,Shade	2.75
37 A:Blue Bulleteer,She-Cat	2.75
38 V:Lady Luger	2.75
39 F:She-Cat	2.75
40 V:Sehkmet	2.75
41 V:Captain Paragon	2.75
42 V:Alizarin Crimson	2.75
43 V:Glamazons of Galaxy G	2.75
44 V:Lady Luger,F:Garganta	2.75
45 Nightveil Rescued	2.75
46 V:Lady Luger	2.75
47 V:Alizarin Crimson	2.75
48	2.75
49 I:New Msw.Victory	2.75
50 Ms.Victory Vs.Rad,flexi-disc	2.95
51	2.75
52 V:Claw & Clawites	2.75
53 I:Bulldog Deni,V:(Dick Briefer's)Frightenstein	2.75
54 The Orb of Bliss	2.75
55 R:Nightveil	2.75
56 V:Alizarin Crimson	2.75
57 thru 92 See Color	
93 "Shattered Memories," pt.2	3.00
93a deluxe	5.90
94 "Shattered Memories," pt.3	3.00
94a deluxe	5.90
95	3.00
95a deluxe	5.90
96	3.00
96a deluxe	5.90
97	3.00
98 deluxe	5.90
98	3.00
98 deluxe	5.90
99	3.00
99 deluxe	5.90

100 Anniv. issue, with poster	.6.90
100A signed, with poster	12.00
100B no poster, not signed	4.00
Untold Origin of FemForce	4.95
GN The Capricorn Chronicles	12.50
GN Time Storm	9.95

FEMFORCE:
FRIGHTBOOK
AC Comics
1 Horror tales by Briefer,Ayers, Powell	2.95

FEMFORCE TIMELINES
AC Comics 1995
1 O:Femforce	2.95

FEMFORCE: THE
YESTERDAY SYNDROME
AC Comics 1997
1 sequal to Femforce #100	4.95
2 and 3	@4.95

FEMME NOIRE
1	2.00
2	2.00

FEVER, THE
Dark Vision Publishing
1 O:The Fever	2.50
2 Fever's Father	2.50

FIFTIES TERROR
Eternity
1 thru 6	@1.95

FIGMENTS
1	1.75
2	1.75

FINAL CYCLE
Sirius
Graphic Novel	4.00
1 thru 4	@1.50

FINAL MAN
1	1.50
2	1.75
3	1.75

FIRE TEAM
Aircel
1 thru 3	@2.50
4 V:Vietnamese Gangs	2.50
5 Cam in Vietnam	2.50
6	2.50

FISH POLICE
Fishwrap Productions
December 1985
1 1st printing	7.00
1a 2nd printing	3.00
2	5.00
3 thru 5	@4.00
Comico Publ.	
6 thru 12	@3.50
13 thru 17 see Color issues	
Apple Publ.	
18 thru 24	@2.50

B & W PUB.

FISH SHTICKS
Apple
1 and 2	@2.75
3 and 4	@2.50

FISSION CHICKEN
1 thru 5	@2.00

FIST OF GOD
Eternity
1 thru 4	@1.95

FIST OF THE NORTH STAR
Viz Select
1 thru 3	@3.25
4	1.95
5	3.25
6	2.95
7	2.95
TPB Vol. 2 Night of the Jackal, rep	16.95

Part Three
1 thru 5 by Buronson & Tetsuo Hara	@2.95

Part Four Dec. 1996
1 thru 7	@2.95
TPB Volume 2: Southern Cross	16.95

FITCH IN TIME
Renegade
1	1.50

FLAMING CARROT
Aardvark–Vanaheim
1 1981 Killian Barracks	75.00
1a 1984	40.00
2	35.00
3	30.00
4 thru 6	@25.00

Renegade
7	18.00
8	12.00
9	10.00
10	10.00
11	6.00
12	6.00
13	5.00
14	5.00
15	5.00
15a variant without cover price	10.00
16 and 17	@5.00
See: Dark Horse	

FLARE
Hero Graphics
1 thru 8	@3.95
9 F:Sparkplug	3.95
10 thru 12	2.95

FLARE ADVENTURES
Hero Graphics
1 Rep 1st issue Flare	1.00

Becomes:

FLARE ADVENTURES/ CHAMPIONS CLASSICS
2 thru 15	@3.95

FLARE VS. TIGRESS
Hero Graphics
1 and 2	@3.50

FLASH MARKS
Fantagraphics
1	2.95

FLOYD FARLAND
Eclipse
1	2.95

FLYIN RALPH COMICS
1	.75

FORBIDDEN KINGDOM
1 thru 11	@1.95

FORBIDDEN WORLDS
ACG 1996
1 SD,JAp,rep.	2.50

FORCE 10
Crow Comics
0 Ash Can Preview	.75
1 I:Force 10	2.50
2 Children of the Revolution,pt#2	2.50
3 Against all Odds	2.50

FOREVER NOW
1	1.50
2	1.50

FOREVER WARRIORS
Aardwolf 1996
1 (of 3) RTs,RB	2.95
2 RTs,RB	2.95
3 RTs,RB, concl.	2.95

FOREVER WARRIORS
CFD 1997
1 RB,RTs	2.95
2 RB,RTs,KN	2.95
3 RB,RTs, finale	2.95

FOTON EFFECT
1 thru 5	@1.50

FOX COMICS
1 Spec.	2.95
25	2.95
26	3.50

FRAGMENTS
1 thru 3	@1.75

FRAN AN' MAABL
1	2.50
2	2.50

FRANKENSTEIN
Eternity
1	1.95
2	1.95
3	1.95

FRANKIES FRIGHTMARES
1 Celebrates Frank 60th ann	1.95

FRANK THE UNICORN
Fish Warp
1 thru 7	@2.00

FREAK-OUT ON INFANT EARTHS
1 Don Chin	1.75
2 Don Chin	1.75

FREAKS
Monster Comics
1 Movie adapt	2.50
2 Movie adapt.cont.	2.50
3 thru 4 Movie adapt.	2.50

FREE FIRE ZONE
1 thru 3	@1.75

FREE LAUGHS
1	1.00

FRENCH ICE
Renegade Press
1 thru 15	@2.00

FRIENDS
1 thru 5	@2.00

FRIGHT
Eternity
1 thru 13	@1.95

FRINGE
1 thru 6	@2.50

FROM BEYOND
Studio Insidio
1 Short stories-horror	2.25
2 inc.Clara Mutilares	2.50
3 inc.The Experiment	2.50
4 inc.Positive Feedback	2.50

FROM HELL
Tundra
1	4.95

Kitchen Sink Volume Three
1 AMo(s)	3.95

FROM THE DARKNESS
Adventure Comics
1	30.00
2	35.00
3 and 4	@15.00

FROM THE DARKNESS II BLOODVOWS
Cry For Dawn
1 R:Ray Thorn,Desnoires	15.00
2 V:Desnoires	10.00
3	10.00

FROM THE VOID
1 1st B.Blair,1982	75.00

FROST
1 Heart of Darkness	1.95

FROST: THE DYING BREED
Caliber
1 thru 3 Vietnam Flashbacks	@2.95

F–III BANDIT
Antartic Press
1 F:Akira, Yoohoo 2.95
2 F:Yukio 2.95
3 F:Were-Women 2.95
4 . . . . 2.95
5 Romeo & Juliet story 2.95
6 thru 8 . . . . @2.95

FUGITOID
Mirage
1 TMNT Tie-in 12.00

FULL METAL FICTION
London Night Feb. 1997
1 EHr 3.95
1 Nun with a Gun edition 10.00
2 . . . . 3.95
3 "Hellborne" concl. 3.95

FURRLOUGH
Antartic Press 1991
1 Funny Animal Military stories . . 3.00
2 thru 10 . . . . @2.50
11 thru 20 . . . . @2.75
21 thru 33 . . . . @2.75
34 . . . . 2.95
35 48pg 4.00
36 thru 40 . . . . @2.95
41 thru 51 . . . . @2.95
Best of Furlough, Vol.1 . . . . 4.95
Best of Furlough, Vol.2 . . . . 4.95
Radio Comix
52 "Ninjara," pt.4 . . . . 2.95
53 "Bronze Age" 2.95
54 "Heebas" 2.95
55 "Star Run" cont. 2.95

FURY
Aircel
1 thru 3 . . . . @1.70

FURY OF HELLINA, THE
Lightning Comics 1995
1 V:Luciver 3.50
1a limited & signed 10.00
1b platinum 10.00

FUSION
Eclipse
1 . . . . 2.50
2 thru 17 . . . . @2.00

FUTURAMA
Slave Labor
1 thru 4 . . . . @1.75

FUTURE BEAT
1 thru 3 . . . . @1.50

FUTURE COURSE
1 thru 3 . . . . @1.75

FUTURE CRIME 98
1 . . . . 1.95

FUTURETECH
Mushroom Comics
1 Automotive Hi-Tech 3.50
2 Cyber Trucks 3.50

FUTURIANS
Aardwolf
0 DC R:Futurians 2.95

GAIJIN
1 thru 3 . . . . @1.95

GAJIT GANG
1 . . . . 1.95
2 . . . . 1.95

GAMBIT
1 . . . . 1.95
2 . . . . 1.95

GAMBIT & ASSOCIATES
1 thru 4 . . . . @1.75

GANTAR
1 thru 5 . . . . @1.75

Gatekeeper #1 © GK Publishing

GATEKEEPER
GK Publishing
1 . . . . 2.50
2 and 3 . . . . @2.95

GATES OF THE NIGHT
Jademan
1 thru 4 . . . . @3.50

GATEWAY TO HORROR
1 BW 1.75

GEMS OF THE SAMURAI
Newcomers Publishing
1 I:Master Samurai 2.95

GENOCYBER
Viz
1 I:Genocyber 2.75
2 . . . . 2.75
3 ToT 2.75
4 ToT 2.75
5 ToT 2.75

GERIATRIC GANGRENE JUJITSU GERBILS
Planet X Productions
1 . . . . 2.50
2 . . . . 1.50

GERIATRIC MAN
1 . . . . 1.75

GET LOST
1 . . . . 1.95
1a signed (1200 copies) 6.00
2 and 3 . . . . @1.95

GHOSTS OF DRACULA
Eternity
1 A:Dracula & Houdini 2.50
2 A:Sherlock Holmes 2.50
3 A:Houdini 2.50
4 Count Dracula's Castle 2.50
5 Houdini, Van Helsing, Dracula
team-up 2.50

GHOULS
1 . . . . 2.25

GIANT SIZE MINI COMICS
Eclipse
1 thru 4 . . . . @1.50

G.I. CAT
1 thru 3 . . . . @1.50

GI GOVERNMENT ISSUED
Paranoid Press
1 thru 7 F:Mac, Jack . . . . @2.00

G.I. MUTANTS
1 and 2 . . . . @1.95

GIDEON HAWK
Big Shot Comics
1 I:Gideon Hawk, Max 9471 . . . . 2.00
2 The Jewel of Shamboli,pt.2 . . . 2.00
3 The Jewel of Shamboli,pt.3 . . . 2.00
2 The Jewel of Shamboli,pt.4 . . . 2.50
3 The Jewel of Shamboli,pt.5 . . . 2.50

GIFT, THE
First
1 . . . . 5.95

GIZMO
Chance
1 . . . . 7.50
Mirage
1 . . . . 5.50
2 . . . . 2.50
3 . . . . 2.00
4 thru 7 . . . . @1.50

GIZMO & THE FUGITOID
1 and 2 . . . . @1.75

GNATRAT
Prelude
1 . . . . 5.00
2 Early Years 2.00

All comics prices listed are for *Near Mint* condition.

GNATRAT: THE MOVIE
1 .... 2.25

GNOSIS BRIDGE
1 .... 1.50

GOBBLEDYGOOK
Mirage
1 1st series, Rare 275.00
2 1st series, Rare 275.00
1 TMNT series reprint 12.00

GOD'S HAMMER
1 thru 3 .... @2.50

GOJIN
Antarctic Press 1995
1 F:Terran Defense Force 2.95
2 F:Terran Defense Force 2.95
3 V:Alien Monster 2.95
4 Aliens Bone 2.95
5 thru 8 .... @2.95

Gold Digger #14 © Antarctic Press

GOLD DIGGER
Antarctic Press
[Limited Series]
1 Geena & Cheetah in Peru 7.00
2 Adventures contd. 5.00
3 Adventures contd 5.00
4 Adventures contd 5.00
GN Rep. #1–#4 + new material . 9.95
[Volume 2]
1 by Fred Perry .... @10.00
2 and 3 Fred Perry .... @8.00
4 Fred Perry 7.00
5 misnumbered as #0 .... 6.00
6 thru 8 by Fred Perry ..... 4@.00
9 and 10 by Fred Perry ..... @3.50
11 thru 27 by Fred Perry .... @3.00
28 and 29 by Fred Perry ..... @2.75
30 .... 3.00
31 .... 3.00
32 Time Warp Part One 3.00
33 .... 3.00
34 .... 3.00
35 Time Warp Part Seven 3.00
36 .... 3.00

Ann.1995, 48pg 3.95
Ann.1996 .... 3.95
Collected Gold Digger,Vol.1 ..... 9.95
Coll. Vol. 1, 4th printing 9.95
Collected Gold Digger,Vol.2 ..... 9.95
Coll. Vol. 2, 3rd printing 9.95
Collected Gold Digger,Vol.3 ..... 9.95
Coll. Vol. 3, 2nd printing 9.95
Collected Gold Digger,Vol. 4 .... 9.95
Collected Gold Digger,Vol. 5 .... 9.95
Collected Gold Digger,Vol. 6 ... 10.95

GOLDEN FEATURES
1 thru 5 .... @2.00

GOLDEN GREATS
AC Comics 1995
Vol.#1 thru #6 40s and 50s ... @9.95

GOLDEN WARRIOR ICZER ONE
Antartic 1994
1 thru 5 .... @2.95

GOLDWYN 3-D
Blackthorne
1 .... 2.00

GOLGO 13
1 thru 5 .... @1.25

GO-MAN
1 thru 4 .... @1.50
Graphic Novel 'N' 9.95

GOOD GIRL COMICS
AC
1 F:Tara Fremont 3.95

GOOD GIRLS
Fantagraphics
1 adult 2.00
2 thru 4 .... @2.00

GOON PATROL
1 .... 1.75

GORE SHRIEK
Fantagor
1 .... 2.50
2 and 3 .... @1.50
4 +Mars Attacks 2.95
5 .... 2.95
6 .... 3.50
Vol 2 #1 .... 2.50

GRAPHIC STORY MONTHLY
1 thru 5 .... @2.95

GRAPHIQUE MUSIQUE
Slave Labor 1989–90
1 .... 50.00
2 .... 45.00
3 .... 40.00

GRAVE TALES
Hamilton
1 JSon,GM, mag. size 3.95

2 JSon,GM,short stories 3.95
3 JSon,GM, inc.'Stake Out' 3.95

GREMLIN TROUBLE
Anti-Ballistic Pixelation
1 & 2 Airstrike on Gremlin Home @2.95
3 thru 5 .... @2.95
6 "Fun with Electricity" 2.95
7 "Cypher in Fairyland" 2.95

GRENDEL
Comico
1 MW,Rare 75.00
2 MW,Rare 60.00
3 MW,Rare 55.00

GREY
Viz Select
Book 1 .... 5.00
Book 2 scarce 5.50
Book 3 .... 3.00
Book 4 .... 3.00
Book 5 .... 3.00
Book 6 thru Book 9 .... @2.50

GREYMATTER
Alaffinity Studios
1 thru 14 by Marcus Harwell . @2.95

GRIFFIN, THE
Slave Labor
1 .... 1.75
1a 2nd printing 1.75
2 thru 4 .... @1.75
5 .... 1.95

GRINGO
1 .... 1.95

GRIPS
Silver Wolf
1 Vigil 20.00
2 Vigil 16.00
3 Vigil 11.00
4 Vigil 9.00
Vol 1 #1 rep 2.50
Volume 2
1 .... 2.50
2 .... 2.50
3 thru 6 .... @2.00
7 .... 2.25
8 .... 2.25
9 thru 12 .... @2.50

GRIPS ADVENTURE
1 double-size 2.50
2 thru 5 .... @2.00

GROOTLOTE
1 .... 2.00

GROUND POUND
1 JohnPoundArt 2.00

GROUND ZERO
Eternity
1 Science Fiction mini-series ... 2.50
2 Alien Invasion Aftermath 2.50

B & W PUB.

GRUN

1 & 2 . . . . @1.95

GRUNTS

1 . . . . 1.50

GUERRILA GROUNDHOG
Eclipse

1 . . . . 1.50
2 . . . . 1.50

GUILLOTINE
Silver Wolf

1 and 2 . . . . @1.50

GUN FURY
Aircel

1 thru 10 . . . . @1.95

GUN FURY RETURNS
Aircel

1 . . . . 2.95
2 . . . . 2.95
3 V:The Yes Men 2.25
4 . . . . 2.25

GUNS OF SHAR-PEI
Caliber

1 The Good,the Bad & the Deadly 2.95

HADES
Domain Publishing 1995

1 F:Civil War Officer 3.00

HALL OF HEROES
Hall of Heroes 1993

1 I:Dead Bolt 20.00
2 and 3 . . . . @5.00

HALL OF HEROES PRESENTS
Hall of Heroes 1996–97

0 by Doug Brammer & Matt Roach,
"Slingers" by Matt Martin 2.50
1 . . . . 2.50
2 "The Last Days" 2.50
3 "The Power of the Golem" 2.50
4 F:Turaxx the Trobbit 2.50

HALLOWEEN TERROR
Eternity

1 . . . . 2.50

HALLOWIENERS
Mirage

1 . . . . 1.50
2 . . . . 1.50

HALO BROTHERS
Fantagraphics

Special #1 . . . . 2.25

HAMMER GIRL
Brainstorm April 1996

1 dinosaur, sci-fi adventure 2.95
2 . . . . 2.95
2a deluxe 5.00

HAMSTER VICE
Blackthorne

1 . . . . 3.50
2 . . . . 2.50
3 thru 11 . . . . @2.00
New Series
Eternity
1 and 2 . . . . @1.95

HAND SHADOWS

1 . . . . 2.00
2 . . . . 1.50

HARD-BOILED ANIMAL COMICS

1 . . . . 2.50

HARD ROCK COMICS
Revolutionary

1 Metallica-The Early Years 2.50

HAR HAR COMICS

1 . . . . 2.00

HARI KARI
Blackout 1995

1 . . . . 3.00
1a platinum 10.00

HARI KARI: POSSESSED BY EVIL
Blackout Comics 1997

1 Blackout Universe turns evil, with
evil alter-egos of Outbreed 999,
Lady Vampre & Black Lace . . . 2.95

HARTE OF HARKNESS
Eternity

1 I:Dennis Harte,Vampire private-
eye 2.50
2 V:Satan's Blitz St.Gang 2.50
3 Jack Grissom/Vampire 2.50
4 V:Jack Grissom, conc. 2.50

HARVEST

Spec. 3.00

HARVY FLIP BOOK
Blackthorne

1 . . . . 2.00
2 . . . . 2.00
3 . . . . 2.00

HATE
Fantagraphics

1 . . . . 20.00
2 . . . . 15.00
3 . . . . 10.00
4 . . . . 10.00
5 . . . . 8.00
6 . . . . 6.00
7 . . . . 7.00
8 thru 10 . . . . 5.00
11 and 12 . . . . 4.00
1a to 12a reprints . . . . @2.50
13 thru 15 . . . . 3.00

HEAD, THE

1 Old Airboy (1966) 2.00

HEADLESS HORSEMAN

1 . . . . 2.25
2 . . . . 2.25

HEARTBREAK COMICS
Eclipse

1 . . . . 1.50

HEAVY METAL MONSTERS
Revolutionary

1 'Up in Flames' 2.25

HE IS JUST A RAT
Exclaim Bound Comics

1 & 2 V:Jimmy and Billy Bob . . . 2.75

HELLBENDER

1 . . . . 2.25

HELL FOR LEATHER

1 and 2 . . . . @1.75

HELLGIRL
Knight Press

1 I:Jazzmine Grayce 2.95

HELLINA
Lightning Comics 1994

1-shot I&O:Hellina 5.00
1-shot commemorative 12.00
1-shot nude cover 8.00
1-shot 1996 rep. gold 5.00
1-shot 1996 rep nude (c) 15.00
TPB rep. Hellina appearances . . . 8.95
TPB rep. one-shots 12.95
Spec. 1997 Pin-up 3.50
Spec. 1997 Pin-up, cover B 3.50
Spec. 1997 Pin-up, cover A, nude 9.95
Spec. 1997 Pin-up, cover B, nude 9.95

HELLINA/CATFIGHT
Lightning Comics 1995

1-shot V:Prince of Sommia 2.75
1-shot gold 5.00
1-shot nude cover 10.00
1 two diff. mild covers, encore
edition 2.95
1 two diff. nude covers 9.95

HELLINA: GENESIS
Lightning Comics 1996

1-shot with poster 3.50
1-shot platinum edition 5.00
1-shot nude cover 10.00
1-shot platinum nude edition . . . 20.00

HELLINA: HEART OF THORNS
Lightning Comics

1 (of 2) 3.00
1a nude cover 9.00
1b autographed 9.00
2 . . . . 2.75
2a variant cover 2.75
2b platinum edition 5.95
2c nude cover 9.00
2d variant nude cover 9.00
2e platinum nude edition 19.00

B & W PUB.

HELLINA: HELL'S ANGEL
Lightning Comics Oct. 1996
1	2.75
1a platinum edition	10.00
1a platinum edition, signed	15.00
1b nude cover	10.00
1c nude platinum edition	30.00
2	2.75
2a platinum edition	10.00
2b nude cover	10.00
2c nude platinum edition	30.00

HELLINA: IN THE FLESH
Lightning Comics 1997
1 two diff. mild covers	2.95
1a two diff. nude covers	9.95

HELLINA: KISS OF DEATH
Lightning Comics 1995
1-shot A:Perg	4.00
1-shot nude cover	10.00
1-shot gold edition	20.00
1-shot Encore editions	3.00
1-shot Encore, nude cover	10.00

Lightning Feb. 1997
1A	2.95
1B variant cover	2.95
1A nude cover	9.95
1B nude cover	9.95
1 encore, signed & numbered	9.95

HELLINA: NAKED DESIRE
Lightning Comics April 1997
1	2.95
1 cover B	2.95
1 signed	2.95
1 nude cover A	9.95
1 nude cover B	9.95

HELLINA: THE RELIC
Lightning Comics
1 one-shot?	2.95
1a variant cover	2.95
1b nude cover	9.95
1c variant nude cover	9.95

HELLINA: TAKING BACK THE NIGHT
Lightning Comics 1995
1-shot V:Michael Naynar	3.00
1-shot nude cover	10.00

HELLINA: WICKED WAYS
Lightning Comics 1995
1-shot A:Perg	2.75
1-shot nude cover	10.00
1-shot Encore editions	3.00
1-shot Encore variant (c)	3.00
1-shot Encore, nude cover	10.00
1-shot Encore, nude variant (c)	10.00

HELLINA: X-MAS IN HELL
Lightning Comics 1996
1 two different covers	3.00
1 platinum edition	10.00
1 nude cover	10.00
1 nude variant cover	10.00
1 nude platinum edition	30.00

HELLSTALKER
1 thru 3	@2.25

HELLWARRIOR
1 and 2	@2.50
3 and 4	@1.95

HENRY V
Caliber
1 Play Adaptation	2.95

HEPCATS
Double Diamond
1	35.00
2	25.00
3 Snow Blind	15.00
4 thru 9	@10.00
10 thru 13	@3.50
14 Chapter 12	3.00
15 Snowblind Chp. 13	2.75

Antarctic Press
1 by Martin Wagner	3.00
2 "Trial by Intimacy"	3.00
3 Snowblind, pt.1	3.00
4 Snowblind, pt.2	3.00
5 Snowblind, pt.3	3.00
6 Snowblind, pt.4	3.00
7	3.00

HERALDS OF CANADA
1	1.50
2	1.50

HERCULES
A Plus Comics
1 Hercules Saga	2.50

Hercules Project # 1 © Monster Comics

HERCULES PROJECT
Monster Comics 1991
1 Origin issue,V:Mutants	1.95

HEROES
Blackbird
1	6.00
2	3.00
3	2.25
4 comic size	2.00
5 thru 7	@2.00

HEROES' BLOOD
1	1.95

HEROES FROM WORDSMITH
Special Studios
1 WWI,F:Hunter Hawke	2.50

HEROES INCORPORATED
Double Edge Publishing
1 I:Heroes, Inc.	2.95
2 Betrayal	2.95

HEROINES, INC.
1 thru 5	@1.75

HERO SANDWICH
Slave Labor
1 thru 4	@1.50
5 thru 8	@1.75
9	1.95
Graphic Novel	7.95

HEY, BOSS
1 and 2	@1.50

HIGH CALIBER
1	4.00
2	3.00
3 and 4	@2.50
Becomes:Caliber Presents

HIGH CALIBER
Caliber 1997
1 64pg	3.95
1 signed edition	3.95
2 64pg	3.95
3 48pg	3.95
4	3.95

HIGH SCHOOL AGENT
Sun Comics
1 I:Kohsuke Kanamori	2.50
2 Treasure Hunt at North Pole	2.50
3 and 4	@2.50

HIGH SHINING BRASS
Apple
1 thru 4	@2.75

HIGH SOCIETY
Aardvark–Vanaheim
1 DS,Cerebus	25.00

HILLY ROSE'S SPACE ADVENTURES
Astro Comics 1995
1 confronts Steeltrap	10.00
1 2nd & 3rd pr. by B.C. Boyer	3.00
2	5.00
2 2nd & 3rd printing	3.00
3	3.50
3 2nd printing	3.00
4 thru 9	@3.00
TPB Vol.1 Rocket Reporter	12.95

HIT THE BEACH
Antarctic 1993
1	2.95

B & W PUB.

1a deluxe edition 5.00
2 & 3 . . . . @2.95

HITOMI AND
HER GIRL COMMANDOS
Antarctic Press 1992
1 Shadowhunter,from Ninja HS . . 2.50
2 Synaptic Transducer 2.50
3 Shadowhunter in S.America . . . 2.50
4 V:Mr.Akuma,last issue 2.50
[Series II]
1 thru 10 . . . . @2.75

HOLIDAY OUT
1 thru 3 . . . . @2.00

The Holo Brothers #1
© Monster Comics

HOLO BROTHERS, THE
Monster Comics
1 thru 10 . . . . @1.95

HOLO BROTHERS, THE
Fantagraphics
Spec.#1 . . . . 2.25

HOLY KNIGHT
Pocket Change Comics
1 thru 3 . . . . @2.50
4 V:His Past 2.50
5 V:Souljoiner 2.50
6 V:Demon Priest 2.50
7 Silent Scream,pt.2 . . . . 2.50
8 "Dragon Quest," pt.1 . . . . 2.50
9 "Dragon Quest," pt.2 . . . . 2.50
10 "Dragon Quest," pt.3 . . . . 2.50
11 "Dragon Quest," pt.4 . . . . 2.50

HOMICIDE
1 . . . . 1.95

HONK
Fantagraphics
1 Don Martin 2.75
2 . . . . 2.75
3 . . . . 2.75

HONOR AMONG THIEVES
Gateway Grapnics
1 and 2 . . . . @1.50

HOODOO
Spec. 2.50

HOOHA COMICS
1 Mag. Size Animal
Anthology-500 print 15.00

HOON
Eenieweenie Comics
1 I:Hoon 2.50
2 Calazone Disaster 2.50
3 Reality Check 2.50
4 thru 8 . . . . @2.50

HOON, THE
Caliber Tapestry 1996
1 . . . . 2.95
2 . . . . 2.95
3 . . . . 2.95

HORDE
1 . . . . 2.00
2 . . . . 2.00

HORNET SPECIAL
1 . . . . 2.00

HOROBI
Viz
1 . . . . 4.00
2 thru 8 . . . . @3.75
Book 2
1 . . . . 3.50
2 D:Okado,Shoko Kidnapped . . . 4.25
3 Madoka Attacks Zen 4.25
4 D:Abbess Mitsuko 4.25
5 Catharsis! 4.25
6 Shuichi Vs. Zen 4.25
7 Shuichi vs. Zen, conc. 4.25

HORROR
1 . . . . 2.95
2 . . . . 2.95

HORROR IN THE DARK
Fantagor
1 RCo,Inc.Blood Birth 2.00
2 RCo,Inc.Bath of Blood 2.00
3 RCo 2.00
4 RCo,Inc.Tales o/tBlackDiamond 2.00

HORROR SHOW
Caliber
1 GD,1977-80 reprint horror . . . 3.50

HORSE
1 . . . . 2.95

HOT SHOTS
1 . . . . 1.95
2 . . . . 1.95

HOUSE OF
FRIGHTENSTEIN
AC Comics
1 . . . . 2.95

HOUSE OF HORROR
AC Comics
1 . . . . 2.50

HOWL
Eternity
1 . . . . 2.25
2 . . . . 2.25

HOW TO DRAW
ROBOTECH BOOK
1 . . . . 2.00
2 . . . . 2.00

HOW TO DRAW TEENAGE
MUTANT NINJA TURTLES
Solson
1 Lighter cover 15.00
1a Dark cover 5.00

HUGO
Fantagraphics
1 . . . . 4.00
2 . . . . 2.00
3 . . . . 2.00
4 . . . . 2.00

HUMAN GARGOYLES
Eternity
Book one 1.95
Book two 1.95
Book three 1.95
Book four 1.95

HUMAN HEAD
Caliber
1 Alice in Flames 2.50

HUMAN POWERHOUSE
1 and 2 . . . . @1.75
3 . . . . 2.00

HUNT AND
THE HUNTED, THE
Newcomers Publishing
1 I:Aramis Thiron 2.95
2 V:Werewolves 2.95
3 Rio De Janero 2.95
4 F:Aramis Thiron 2.95

HURRICANE GIRLS
Antarctic Press 1995
1 & 2 Tale of Dinon . . . . @3.50
3 thru 7 seven part series . . . . @2.95

HURRICANE LEROUX
Inferno Studios
1 I:Deja Vu Jones 2.50

HUZZAH
1 I:Albedo'sErmaFelna 60.00

HY-BREED
Division Publishing
1 thru 3 F:Cen Intel . . . . @2.25
4 thru 8 . . . . @2.50

B & W PUB.

HYPE
1 .... 2.00
2 .... 2.00

I.F.S. ZONE
1 thru 6 .... @1.25

I AM LEGEND
Eclipse
1 Novel Adaptation 5.95
2 Novel Adaptation Cont'd 5.95
3 Novel Adaptation Cont'd 5.95

IAN WARLOCKE
1 .... 1.50

ICARUS
1 thru 9 .... @1.70

ICON DEVIL
1 .... 2.00
2 .... 2.00
2nd Series
1 thru 5 .... @1.85

IDIOTLAND
Fantagraphic
1 .... 2.95

ILIAD II
1 .... 3.00
1a 2nd cover variation 3.00
2 .... 2.00
3 .... 2.00
4 .... 1.70

ILLUMINATUS
1 .... 2.00
2 .... 2.50
3 .... 2.50

IN-COUNTRY NAM
1 .... 1.75
2 .... 1.75
3 .... 1.75
4 .... 1.95
5 .... 1.95

INDEPENDENT COMIC BOOK SAMPLER
1 .... 1.50
2 .... 1.50

INFERNO
Caliber Press
1 I:City of Inferno 2.95
2 Search for Identity 2.95
3 V:Malateste 2.95
4 by MCy and Michael Gaydos .. 2.95
5 .... 2.95

INFINITE LINE COMICS PRESENTS
Infinite Line Comics
1 Arcone 1.00

INK COMICS
1 thru 3 .... @2.50

INSANE
1 .... 1.75
2 .... 1.75

INTERZONE
Brainstorm Comics
1 w/4 cards 2.50
2 w/4 cards 2.50

INVADERS FROM MARS
Eternity
1 .... 2.50
2 .... 2.50
3 .... 2.50
(Book II)
1 Sequel to '50's SF classic 2.50
2 Pact of Tsukus/Humans 2.50
3 Last issue 2.50

INVASION '55
Apple
1 .... 2.25
2 .... 2.25
3 .... 2.25

INVISIBLE PEOPLE
Kitchen Sink
1 WE,I:Peacus Pleatnik 2.95
2 WE,The Power 2.95
3 WE,Final issue 2.95

INVISIOWORLD
1 .... 1.95

IRON SAGA'S ANTHOLOGY
1 thru 3 .... @1.75

ISMET
1 Cartoon Dog 12.00
2 .... 5.00
3 Rare 5.00
4 .... 5.00

IS YOUR BOOGEY-MAN LOOSE?
1 .... 2.95

ITCHY PLANET
3 .... 2.25

IT'S SCIENCE WITH DR. RADIUM
1 thru 7 .... @1.50
8 .... 1.75
9 .... 1.95
Spec #1 .... 2.95

JACKAROO
Eternity
1 GCh 2.25
2 GCh 2.25
3 GCh 2.25

J.A.P.A.N.
1 .... 1.80

JACKFROST
1 .... 1.80

Jackaroo #1 © Eternity

2 .... 1.95
3 .... 1.95

JACK HUNTER
Blackthorne
1 .... 3.50
2 .... 3.50
3 .... 3.50

JACK OF NINES
1 .... 1.25
2 thru 4 .... @1.50
5 .... 2.00

JACK THE RIPPER
1 thru 4 .... @2.25

JAKE TRASH
1 .... 3.95

JAM, THE
Slave Labor
1 .... 2.00
2 .... 2.00
3 thru 5 .... @2.25
Dark Horse
6 thru 8 .... 2.50
Caliber
9 .... 2.95
9 signed edition 2.95
10 It's a Kafka Thing 2.95
11 thru 14 .... @2.95
15 "The Kinetic", pt.3 .... 2.95

JAM SPECIAL, THE
Matrix
1 .... 2.50

JANX
1 and 2 .... @1.00

JASON AND THE ARGONAUTS
Caliber
1 thru 5 .... @2.50

B & W PUB.

JAX AND THE HELL HOUND
1 thru 4 . . . . @1.75

JAZZ AGE CHRONICLES
1 thru 6 . . . . @1.50
7 . . . . 2.50

JCP FEATURES
1 1st MT;S&K,NA/DG rep.
  A:T.H.U.N.D.E.R.Agents,TheFly,
  Black Hood Mag.Size 4.50

JEREMIAH: BIRDS OF PREY
Adventure Comics
1 I: Jeremiah,A:Kurdy 2.50
2 conclusion 2.50

JEREMIAH: FIST FULL OF SAND
Adventure Comics
1 A:Captain Kenney 2.50
2 conclusion 2.50

JEREMIAH: THE HEIRS
Adventure Comics
1 Nathanial Bancroft estate 2.50
2 conclusion 2.50

JERRY IGERS FAMOUS FEATURES
Blackthorne
1 . . . . 3.00
2 thru 4 . . . . @2.00
Pacific
5 thru 8 . . . . @2.00

JIM
Fantagraphics 1987–90
1 . . . . 20.00
2 . . . . 15.00
3 and 4 . . . . @10.00
Second Series 1994
1 . . . . 4.00
1a 2nd printing 3.00
2 . . . . 3.50
2a 2nd printing 3.00
3 thru 5 . . . . @3.00

JOE SINN
Caliber
1 I:Joe Sinn,Nikki 2.95
2 . . . . 2.95

JOHNNY ATOMIC
Eternity
1 I:Johnny A.Tomick 2.50
2 Project X-contingency plan . . . 2.50
3 . . . . 2.50

JOHNNY DARK
Double Edge
1 V:Biker Gang 2.95

JOHNNY GAMBIT
4 . . . . 1.95

JOHNNY THE HOMICIDAL MANIAC
Slave Labor 1996
1 by Jhonen Vasquez 1.95
1 3rd printing 2.95
1 signed, limited 9.00
2 . . . . 2.95
2 3rd printing 2.95
3 . . . . 2.95
3 3rd printing 2.95
4 . . . . 2.95
4 2nd printing 2.95
5 . . . . 2.95
5 2nd printing 2.95
6 . . . . 2.95
7 . . . . 2.95
TPB 19.95
HC 29.95

JONTAR
1 thru 3 . . . . @1.75

JOURNEY
Aardvark–Vanaheim
1 . . . . 13.00
2 . . . . 9.00
3 . . . . 8.00
4 . . . . 5.00
5 thru 7 . . . . @3.00
8 thru 14 . . . . @2.50
Fantagraphics
15 . . . . 2.50
16 thru 28 . . . . @2.00

JR. JACKALOPE
1 orange cover,1981 . . . . 8.00
1a Yellow cover,1981 . . . . 15.00
2 . . . . 8.00

JUDO JOE
1 and 2 . . . . @1.75

JUNGLE COMICS
Blackthorne
4 thru 6 . . . . @2.00

JUNGLE GIRLS
AC Comics
1 incGold.Age reps. 1.95
2 . . . . 1.95
3 Greed,A:Tara 2.75
4 CaveGirl 2.75
5 Camilla 2.75
6 TigerGirl 2.75
7 CaveGirl 2.75
8 Sheena Queen o/t Jungle . . . 2.95
9 Wild Girl,Tiger Girl,Sheena . . . 2.95
10 F:Tara,Cave Girl,Nyoka 2.95
11 F:Sheena,Tiger Girl,Nyoka . . . 2.95
12 F:Sheena,Camilla,Tig.Girl 2.95
13 F:Tara, Tiger Girl 2.95

JURASSIC JANE
London Night 1997
1 by Sky Owens, F:Tira, elf
  princess of Atlantis 3.00
1 deluxe nude edition 6.00
1 deluxe nude edition, signed . . 10.00
2 . . . . 3.00
2 deluxe 6.00
3 . . . . 3.00
3 deluxe 6.00

JUSTICE
Newcomers Publishing 1995
1 I:Judiciary Urban Strike Team . 2.95

JUSTY
1 thru 9 . . . . @1.75

KABUKI: CIRCLE OF BLOOD
Caliber Press
1 R:Kabuki 7.00
2 Kabuki Goes Rogue 5.00
3 V:Noh Agents 5.00
4 V:Noh Agents 3.25
5 V:Kai 3.00
6 . . . . 3.00
TPB Rep.#1-#6 . . . . 16.95
TPB 2nd printing 16.95
HC DAv,rep.#1–#6 272pg. 100.00
TPB deluxe, signed, etc. 24.95

KABUKI: DANCE OF DEATH
London Night Studios
1 1st Full series 5.00

KABUKI: MASKS OF THE NOH
Caliber April 1996
1A JQ(c) 3.00
1B Mays/Mack(c) 3.00
1C Buzz(c) 3.00
2 . . . . 3.00
3 DMk 3.00
4 epilog 3.00

KAFKA
1 thru 5 . . . . @2.00
The Execution Spec. 2.25

KAMIKAZE CAT
1 . . . . 1.80
2 and 3 . . . . @1.95

KAMUI
Eclipse
1 Sanpei Shirato Art 4.00
1a 2nd printing 2.50
2 Mystery of Hanbie 1.50
2a 2nd printing 1.50
3 V:Ichijiro 2.00
3a 2nd printing 1.50
4 thru 15 . . . . @1.50
16 thru 19 . . . . @1.95
20 thru 37 . . . . @1.50

KAOS MOON
Caliber 1996
1 by DdB 3.50
1a 2nd edition 3.00
2 . . . . 3.00
2a 2nd edition, new cover 3.00
3 . . . . 3.00
4 Anubian Nights, Chapter 2 . . . . 3.00

KAPTAIN KEEN
1 thru 3 . . . . @1.75
4 and 5 . . . . @1.50
6 and 7 . . . . @1.75

B & W PUB.

KATMANDU
Antarctic Press
1 thru 3 . . . . @2.75
4 & 5 Woman of Honor 2.75
6 F:Laska 2.75
Med Systems
7 and 8 . . . . @1.95
Vision Comics
9 "When Warriors Die," pt.3(of 3) 1.95
10 "The Curse of the Blood," pt.1 . 2.50
11 "The Curse of the Blood," pt.2 . 2.50

KEIF LLAMA
1 thru 6 . . . . @2.00

KELLEY BELLE,
POLICE DETECTIVE
Newcomers Publishing
1 Debut issue 2.95
2 Case of the Jeweled Scarab . . 2.95
3 Case o/t Jeweled Scarab,pt.2 . 2.95
TPB #1 . . . . 8.95

KELLEY BELLE:
PERIL ON THE
HIGH SEAS
Atlantis Comics 1996
1 (of 6) 2.95

KELLY BELLE:
SEARCH FOR THE
GOLDEN MONKEY
Atlantis 1996
1 (of 2) by James Watson & Rob
Ewing 2.95

KENDOR THE
CREON WARRIOR
1 . . . . 1.50
2 . . . . 1.50

KID CANNIBAL
Eternity
1 I:Kid Cannibal 2.50
2 Hunt for Kid Cannibal 2.50
3 A:Janice 2.50
4 final issue 2.50

KID PHOENIX
1 . . . . 1.50

KI-GORR THE KILLER
AC
1 I:Ki-Gorr, Rae 2.95

KIKU SAN
Aircel
1 thru 6 . . . . @1.95

KILGORE
1 thru 5 . . . . @2.00

KILLER OF CROWS
one shot, story of John Johnson . 2.50

KILLING STROKE
Eternity
1 British horror tales 2.50

2 inc.'Blood calls to Blood' 2.50
3 and 4 . . . . @2.50

KILROY IS HERE
Caliber Press 1995
1 Kilroy Rescues Infant 2.95
2 Reflections,pt.2 . . . . 2.95
3 Reflections,pt.3 . . . . 2.95
4 Lincoln Memorial 2.95
5 thru 8 . . . . @2.95
9 and 10 . . . . @2.95
11 WEI,RPc,"Screen" 2.95
12 Khymer Rouge 2.95

KILROY: DAEMONSTORM
Caliber 1997
1 one-shot 2.95

KIMBER,
PRINCE OF FELONS
Antarctic Press
1 I:Kimber 2.50
2 V:Lord Tyrex 2.50

King Kong #1 © Monster Comics

KING KONG
Monster Comics 1991
1 thru 6 . . . . @2.50

KINGS IN DISGUISE
1 thru 5 . . . . @2.00
6 end Mini-series 2.00

KIRBY KING
OF THE SERIALS
Blackthorne
1 . . . . 2.00
2 . . . . 2.00
3 . . . . 2.00
4 . . . . 2.00

KITZ 'N' KATZ
1 . . . . 3.50
Eclipse
2 . . . . 2.00
3 . . . . 1.50

4 and 5 . . . . @2.00

KIWANNI
1 . . . . 2.25
2 . . . . 1.75

KLOWN SHOCK
North Star
1 Horror Stories 2.75

KNIGHTMARE
Antarctic Press
1 . . . . 2.75
2 . . . . 2.75
3 Wedding Knight pt.1 . . . . 2.75
4 Wedding Knight pt.2 . . . . 2.75
5 F:Dream Shadow 2.75
6 V:Razorblast 2.75

KNIGHT MASTERS
1 thru 7 . . . . @1.50

KNIGHT WATCHMAN
Caliber Press
1 Graveyard pt. 1 . . . . 2.95
2 Graveyard pt. 1 . . . . 2.95

KOMODO &
THE DEFIANTS
1 thru 6 . . . . @1.50

KUNG FU WARRIORS
(Prev. ROBOWARRIORS)
CFW
12 . . . . 1.95
13 thru 19 . . . . @2.25

KUNOICHI
Lightning Comics 1996
1 2 diff. mild covers 3.00
1 platinum edition 5.95
1 autographed edition 9.95

KURTZMAN KOMIX
1 . . . . 1.50

KWAR
1 . . . . 1.95

KYRA
1 thru 3 . . . . @1.75
4 . . . . 2.00
5 . . . . 1.75

KZ COMICS
1 I:Colt 1985 . . . . 1.95

L.A. RAPTOR
Morbid Graphics
1 Velocaraptor loose 2.95

L.F.S. ZONE
1 . . . . 1.25

L.I.F.E. BRIGADE
Blue Comet
1 A:Dr. Death 1.50
1a 2nd printing 1.50
2 . . . . 1.50

LABOR FORCE
Blackthorne
1 thru 4 . . . . @1.50
5 thru 8 . . . . @1.75

LACUNAE
CFD Producitons 1995
1 thru 4 F:Monkey Boys 2.50
5 thru 10 . . . . @2.50
11 HMo 2.50

LADY ARCANE
Heroic Publishing
1 thru 3 . . . . @3.50

LADY CRIME
AC Comics
1 Bob Powell reprints 2.75

LADY VAMPRÉ
Blackout Comics 1996
1 flip-book 2.95

LADY VAMPRÉ:
IN THE FLESH
Blackout Comics 1996
1 . . . . 2.95
1 photo sexy cover 9.95

LAFFIN GAS
Blackthorne
1 . . . . 2.50
2 thru 12 . . . . @2.00

LANCE STANTON
WAYWARD WARRIOR
1 and 2 . . . . @1.50

LANDER
Mermaid Producions
1 Power of the Dollar,pt.1 . . . . . . 2.25
2 Power of the Dollar,pt.2 . . . . . . 2.25
3 Power of the Dollar,pt.3 . . . . . . 2.25
Vol. 2
1 "By Whose Authority," pt.1 . . . . 2.75
2 "By Whose Authority," pt.2 . . . . 2.75

LANDRA
Polyventura Entertainment Group
1 . . . . 2.50

LAST DITCH
Edge Press
1 CCa(s),THa, ... 2.50

LAST GENERATION
Black Tie Studios
1 . . . . 6.00
2 . . . . 4.00
3 . . . . 2.25
4 . . . . 2.25
5 . . . . 2.25
Book One Rep. 6.95

LAST KISS, THE
Eclipse
Spec. 3.95

LATIGO KID WESTERN
AC Comics
1 . . . . 1.95

LAUGHING TARGET
1 . . . . 3.50
2 . . . . 3.50

LAUNCH
1 . . . . 1.75

LAUREL & HARDY
1 3-D 2.50

LAW
1 . . . . 1.75

LEAGUE OF CHAMPIONS
Hero Comics
(cont. from Innovation L.of C. #3)
1 GP,F:Sparkplug,Icestar 3.50
2 GP(i),F:Marksman,Flare,Icicle . 3.50
3 . . . . 3.50
4 F:Sparkplug,League 3.50
5 Morrigan Wars Pt.#1 . . . . 3.50
6 Morrigan Wars Pt.#3 . . . . 3.50
7 Morrigan Wars Pt.#6 . . . . 3.50
8 Morrigan Wars Conclusion 3.50
9 A:Gargoyle 3.50
10 A:Rose 3.50
11 thru 12 . . . . 3.95
13 V:Malice 3.95
14 V:Olympians 3.95
15 V:Olympians 2.95

LE FEMME VAMPRIQUE
Brainstorm 1997
1 . . . . 3.50

LEGEND LORE
1 and 2 . . . . @2.00
combined rep. 8.95

LEGENDLORE
Caliber "New Worlds"
1 JMt signed 2.95
3 JMt 2.95
4 JMt 2.95
5 JMt 2.95
6 flip book with Boston Bombers #4
. . . . 2.95
7 JMt 2.95
8 JMt 2.95
TPB Tainted Soul, rep. #1–#4 . . 12.95

LEGENDLORE:
REALM WARS
Caliber "New Worlds"
1 by Joe Martin & Philip Xavier,
  Fawn cover by Xavier 2.95
1 Falla cover by Boller 2.95
2 . . . . 2.95

LEGENDS OF LUXURA
Brainstorm 1996
1 platinum edition 5.00
2 gold edition 5.00
TPB #1 . . . . 12.95

LEGION OF
LUDICROUS HEROES
1 . . . . 2.00

LEGION X-I
1 McKinney 5.00
2 McKinney,rare 15.00
Volume 2
1 thru 4 . . . . @2.00

LEGION X-2
Vol 2 #1 . . . . 2.00
Vol 2 #2 . . . . 2.00
Vol 2 #3 . . . . 2.00
Vol 2 #4 . . . . 2.00

Lensman #2 © Eternity Comics

LENSMAN
Eternity
1 E.E.'Doc' Smith adapt. 2.25
2 . . . . 2.25
3 . . . . 2.25
4 . . . . 2.25
5 On Radelix 2.25
6 . . . . 2.25
Collectors Spec #1, 56 pgs. 3.95

LENSMAN:
GALACTIC PATROL
Eternity
1 thru 7 E.E. 'Doc' Smith adapt. @2.25

LENSMAN:
WAR OF THE GALAXIES
Eternity
1 thru 7 . . . . @2.25

LEONARDO
1 TMNT 13.00

LEVEL X
Caliber 1997
1 . . . . 2.95
2 32pg 2.95
3 48pg 3.95

B & W PUB.

LEVEL X:
THE NEXT REALITY
Caliber 1997
1 (of 2) by Dan Harbison & Randy
   Buccini, 64pg 3.95
2 48pg 3.95

LIBBY ELLIS
1 . . . . 1.95
2 . . . . 1.95
Eternity
1 thru 4 . . . . @1.95

LIBERATOR
Eternity
1 thru 6 . . . . @1.95

LIBRA
1 . . . . 1.95

LITERACY VOLUNTEERS
1 Word Warriors 1.50
2 Quest for 1.50

LITTLEST NINJA
1 . . . . 1.80
2 . . . . 1.80

Livingstone Mountain #3
© Adventure Comics

LIVINGSTONE MOUNTAIN
Adventure Comics
1 I:Scat,Dragon Rax 2.50
2 Scat & Rax Create Monsters . . 2.50
3 Rax rescue attempt 2.50
4 Final issue 2.50

LLOYD LLEWELLYN
Fantagraphics
1 Mag Size 4.00
2 Mag Size 2.25
3 Mag Size 2.25
4 Mag Size 2.25
5 Mag Size 2.25
6 Mag Size 2.25
7 Regular Size 2.25

LOCKE
1 . . . . 1.25
2 TD 1.25

LOCO VS. PULVERINE
Eclipse
1 Parody 2.50

LOGAN'S RUN
Adventure Comics
1 Novel Adapt 2.25
2 Novel Adapt 2.25
3 Novel Adapt 2.25
4 Novel Adapt 2.25
5 Novel Adapt 2.25
6 Novel Adapt 2.25

LOGAN'S WORLD
Adventure Comics
1 Seq. to Logan's Run 2.50
2 thru 6 . . . . @2.50

LOLLYMARS &
LIGHT LANCERS
1 . . . . 1.75

LONER
Fleetway
1 Pt. 1 of 7 . . . . 1.95
2 Pt. 2 . . . . 1.95
3 Pt. 3 . . . . 1.95
4 Pt. 4 . . . . 1.95
5 Pt. 5 . . . . 1.95
6 Pt. 6 . . . . 1.95

LONE WOLF & CUB
First
1 FM(c) 7.00
1a 2nd printing 2.50
1b 3rd printing 1.50
2 . . . . 4.00
2a 2nd printing 2.00
3 . . . . 3.50
4 thru 10 . . . . @3.00
11 thru 17 . . . . @2.75
18 thru 25 . . . . @2.50
26 thru 36 . . . . @2.95
37 and 38 . . . . @3.25
39 120 Page 5.95
40 . . . . 3.25
41 MP(c), 60 page 3.95
42 MP(c) 3.25
43 MP(c) 3.25
44 MP(c) 3.25
45 MP(c) 3.25

LORD OF THE DEAD
Conquest
1 R.E.Howard adapt. 2.95

LOST, THE
Caliber
1 . . . . 3.00
1a special ed. 7.00
1b signed 3.00
2 thru 4 . . . . @3.00

LOST ANGEL
Caliber
1 . . . . 3.50

LOST CONTINENT
Eclipse
1 thru 5 . . . . @3.50

LOST WORLD, THE
Millennium 1996
1 and 2 . . . . @2.95

LOTHAR
Powerhouse Graphics
1 I:Lothar,Galactic Bounty Hunter 2.50
2 I:Nightcap 2.50

LOVE AND ROCKETS
Fantagraphics
1 HB,B&W cover, adult 85.00
1a HB,Color cover 50.00
1b 2nd printing 4.00
2 HB 25.00
3 HB 15.00
4 HB 15.00
5 HB 15.00
6 HB 7.00
7 HB 9.00
8 HB 9.00
9 HB 7.00
10 HB 8.00
11 HB 5.00
12 HB 5.00
13 HB 5.00
14 HB 5.00
15 HB 5.00
16 thru 21 HB . . . . @4.00
22 thru 39 HB . . . . @3.50
40 thru 41 . . . . @3.50
Bonanza rep. 3.00
TPB Vol 9 Flies on the Ceiling, 2nd
   printing 16.95
HC Vol 10 Love & Rockets X . . . 35.00
HC Vol 10 deluxe 39.95
TPB Vol 10 . . . . 11.95
HC Vol 11 Wigwam Bam 35.00
HC Vol 11 deluxe 39.95
TPB Vol 11 . . . . 14.95
HC Vol 12 Poison River 35.00
HC Vol 12 deluxe 39.95
TPB Vol 12 . . . . 16.95
HC Vol 13 Chester Square 34.95
TPB Vol 14 Luba Conquers the
   World 14.95
HC Vol 14 Luba Conquers the
   World 34.95
HC Vol 14 , signed 39.95
TPB Vol 15 . . . . 14.95
HC Vol 15 . . . . 34.95
HC Vol 15 , signed 39.95

LOVE FANTASY
1 . . . . 2.00

LUGH, LORD OF LIGHT
1 . . . . 2.50
2 . . . . 1.75

LUM*URUSEI YATSURA
1 Art by Rumiko Takahashi 2.95
2 . . . . 2.95
3 . . . . 2.95
4 . . . . 2.95
5 . . . . 3.25
6 thru 8 . . . . @2.95

B & W PUB.

LUXURA
Brainstorm 1996
Convention Book 2 . . . . 2.95

LUXURA/BABY ANGEL X
Brainstorm 1996
Spec. x-over 2.95
Spec. deluxe 5.00
Luxury edition 10.00
Deluxe luxury edition 15.00

LUXURA LEATHER
Brainstorm
Platinum edition 5.00
Signed edition 10.00

LUXURA/WIDOW: BLOOD LUST
Brainstorm
Omega x-over pt.2 concl. 2.95
Omega Fusion cover 5.00
Luxury edition 10.00
Deluxe luxury edition 15.00
See: Widow/Luxura for pt.1

M.C. GRIFFIN
1 . . . . 1.95

MACABRE
1 thru 2.00

MACH 1
Fleetway
1 I:John Probe-Secret Agent 1.95

MACK THE KNIFE
1 . . . . 2.50

MACKENZIE QUEEN
1 thru 5 . . . . @3.75

MACROSS II
Viz
1 Macross Saga sequel 2.75
2 A:Ishtar 2.75
3 F:Reporter Hibiki,Ishtar 2.75
4 V:Feff,The Marduk 2.75
5 . . . . 2.75
6 . . . . 2.75
7 Sylvie Confesses 2.75
8 F:Ishtar 2.75
9 V:Marduk Fleet 2.75
10 . . . . 2.75

MACROSS II: THE MICRON CONSPIRACY
Viz 1994
1 Manga 2.75

MAD DOG MAGAZINE
1 thru 3 . . . . @1.75

MAD DOGS
Eclipse 1992
1 . . . . I:Mad Dogs(Cops)2.50
2 V:Chinatown Hood 2.50
3 . . . . 2.50

Mad Dogs #1 © Eclipse

MAD RACCOONS
MU Press
1 thru 5 Angst of an Artist . . . @2.95
6 & 7 by Cathy Hill . . . . @2.95

MAELSTROM
Aircel
1 thru 5 . . . . @1.70
6 thru 13 . . . . @1.50

MAGGOTS
1 JSon, mag size 3.95
2 JSon, mag size 3.95
3 GM/JSon,inc.'Some Kinda
   Beautiful' 3.95

MAGICAL MATES
Antarctic Press 1995
1 & 2 Manga, by Mio Odagi . . @2.95
3 thru 8 (of 8) . . . . @2.95

MAGNA-MAN: THE LAST SUPERHERO
1 . . . . 1.95
2 . . . . 1.95
3 . . . . 1.95

MAI, THE PSYCHIC GIRL
Eclipse
1 I:Mai,Alliance of 13 Sages 3.75
1a 2nd printing 2.00
2 V:Wisdom Alliance 2.00
2a 2nd printing 1.50
3 V:Kaieda,I:Ojii-San 2.00
4 . . . . 2.00
5 thru 19 . . . . @1.75
20 thru 28 . . . . @1.50

MAISON IKKOKU
Viz
1 thru 7 . . . . 2.95
[Part Two]
1 thru 6 . . . . 2.95
[Part Three]
1 thru 6 . . . . 2.95

[Part Four]
1 thru 6 F:Kyoko 2.95
7 thru 9 Plum Wine 2.95
10 Hickey on Yusaku 2.95
[Part Six] Aug. 1996
1 thru 11 by Rumiko Takahashi @3.50
TPB Vol. 4 Good Housekeeping 15.95
TPB Vol. 5 Empty Nest 15.95
TPB Vol. 6 Bedside Manners . . . 15.95
TPB Vol. 7 Intensive Care 15.95

MAN
1 . . . . 2.00
2 . . . . 2.00

MAN EATING COW
1 Spin-off from the Tick 3.25
2 O:Mr.Krinkles,A:Lt.Valentine . . 2.75
3 Final issue 2.75
Bonanza #1, 128pg. 4.95
Bonanza #2, 100pg. 4.95

MAN-ELF
3 A:Jerry Cornelius 2.25

MANDRAKE
1 . . . . 3.95
2 . . . . 3.95
3 . . . . 3.95
Ultimate Mandrake 14.95

MANDRAKE MONTHLY
1 . . . . 3.95
2 . . . . 3.95
3 . . . . 4.95
4 . . . . 4.95
5 . . . . 4.95
6 . . . . 6.95
Special #1 . . . . 6.95

MAN FROM U.N.C.L.E.
Entertainment Publ.
1 'Number One with a Bullet Affair 2.50
2 'Number One with a Bullet Affair 2.00
3 'The E-I-E-I-O Affair' 1.50
4 'The E-I-E-I-O Affair,' concl. . . 1.50
5 'The Wasp Affair' 1.50
6 'Lost City of THRUSH Affair' . . 1.50
7 'The Wildwater Affair' 1.50
8 'The Wilder West Affair' 1.50
9 'The Cahadian Lightning Affair' 1.75
10 'The Turncoat Affair' 1.75
11 'Craters of the Moon Affair' . . 1.75

MANGA MONTHLY
0 . . . . 3.00

MANGA VIZION
Viz
1 thru 8 Ogre Slayer 4.95

MANGAZINE
Antarctic Press
1 newsprint cover 7.00
1a reprint 3.00
2 . . . . 5.00
3 . . . . 4.00
4 . . . . 2.00
5 . . . . 1.50

New Series
1 . . . . 3.00

B & W PUB.

All comics prices listed are for *Near Mint* condition.

2	3.00
3	1.75
4	1.75
5 thru 7	@1.95
8 thru 13	@2.25
14 New Format	2.95
15	2.95
16	2.95
17	2.95

MANIMAL
| 1 EC,rep. | 1.70 |

MAN IN BLACK CALLED FATE
| 1 | 2.00 |

Man of Rust #1B © Blackthorne

MAN OF RUST
Blackthorne 1986
| 1 Cover A | 1.50 |
| 1 Cover B | 1.50 |

MANSLAUGHTER
Brainstorm 1996
| 1 | 2.95 |
| 1a gold foil edition | 5.00 |

MANTUS FILES
Eternity
1 Sidney Williams novel adapt	2.50
2 Vampiric Figures	2.50
3 Securas' Mansion	2.50
4 A:Secarus	2.50

MARAUDERS OF THE BLACK SUN
| 1 | 1.75 |
| 2 | 1.75 |

MARCANE
Eclipse
| 1 Book 1,JMu | 5.95 |

MARIONETTE
| 1 | .75 |

MARK I
(Prev.: Atomic Comics)
| 2 | 1.50 |

MARQUIS, THE
Caliber 1997
1 GyD	2.95
1 spec. double gatefold cover	6.95
2 Marquis cover by Vincent Locke	2.95
2a Marquis view of world GyD(c)	2.95

MARQUIS, THE: LES PRELUDES
Caliber 1996
| 1 GyD, prelude edition | 2.95 |
| 1 signed, prelude editon GyD | 2.95 |

MARTIANS
| 1 | 2.00 |

MARTIAN SUMMERS
| 1 | 1.75 |
| 2 | 1.75 |

MASKED MAN
Eclipse
| 12 | 2.00 |

MASKED WARRIOR X
Antarctic Press April 1996
1 (of 6) by Masayuki Fujihara	3.50
2	2.95
3 The Girls of Olympus," pt.2	2.95
4 "Protect the Silver Fortress"	2.95

MASQUERADE
Eclipse
1	1.50
2	1.95
3	1.95

MASTER
| 1 thru 4 | @1.95 |

MATAAK
K-Blamm 1995
| 1 I:Mataak | 2.50 |
| 2 Spirit of Peace | 2.50 |

MATT CHAMPION
| 1 EC | 2.00 |
| 2 EC | 2.00 |

MAX OF REGULATORS
1	5.00
2	3.50
3	3.50
4	3.50

MAX THE MAGNIFICENT
1	3.00
2	2.00
3	2.00

MAXWELL MOUSE FOLLIES
1 Large format (1981)	5.00
1a Comic Size(1986)	3.00
2 thru 6	@2.00

MAYHEM
| 1 thru 6 | @2.50 |

MECHANOIDS
Caliber
1	2.50
2	3.50
3	3.50

MECHARIDER: THE REGULAR SERIES
Castle
| 1 thru 3 F:Winter | 2.95 |
| Spec.#1 Limited Edition | 2.95 |

MECHOVERSE
| 1 | 1.80 |
| 2 | 1.50 |

MECHTHINGS
| 1 thru 5 | @2.00 |

MEDUSA
| 1 | 1.50 |

MEGATON
Megaton
1 JG(c),EL(1stProWork),GD,MG, A:Ultragirl,Vanguard	8.00
2 EL,JG(pin-up),A:Vanguard	5.00
3 MG,AMe,JG, EL, I:Savage Dragon	16.00
4 AMe,EL,2nd A:Savage Dragon (inc.EL profile)	12.00
5 AMe,RLd(inside front cover)	3.00
6 AMe,JG(inside back cover), EL(Back cover)	3.00
7 AMe	3.00
8 RLd,I:Youngblood(Preview)	18.00

MEGATON MAN
| 1 | 2.00 |

MEGATON MAN MEETS THE UNCATEGORIZABLE X-THEMS
Jabberwocky
| 1 | 2.00 |

MEGATON MAN VS. FORBIDDEN FRANKENSTEIN
Fiasco Comics April 1996
| 1 by Don Simpson & Anton Drek | 2.95 |

MELISSA MOORE: BODYGUARD
Draculina Publishing 1995
| 1 thru 3 V:Machine Gun Eddie | @2.95 |

MENAGERIE
| 1 and 2 | @1.95 |
| 3 | 2.00 |

MEN IN BLACK
Aircel
| 1 by Lowell Cunningham & Sandy Carruthers, basis of Movie | 2.25 |

B & W PUB.

2	2 25
3	2.25

(Book II)

1 thru 3	@2.50

MEN IN BLACK:
THE ROBORG INCIDENT
Castle

1 thru 3	@2.95

MEMORY MAN
Emergency Stop Press 1995

1 thru 2 Some of the Space Man	2.95

MERCHANTS OF DEATH
Eclipse

1 thru 5	@1.95

MERLIN
Adventure Comics

1 Merlin's Visions	2.50
2 V:Warlord Carados	2.50
3	2.50
4 Ninevah	2.50
5 D:Hagus	2.50
6 Final Issue	2.50

[2nd Series]

1 Journey of Rhiannon & Tryon	2.50
2 Conclusion	2.50

MERMAID'S GAZE
Viz

1 thru 3 V:Shingo	2.75
4 final issue	2.75

MESSENGER 29

1 and 2	@1.50

MESSIAH

1	1.50

METACOPS
Monster Comics

1 and 2	@1.95

METAPHYSIQUE
Eclipse

1 NB,Short Stories	2.50
2 NB,Short Stories	2.50

METAL MEN OF MARS

1	1.95

MIAMI MICE
Rip Off Press

1 1st printing	3.00
1a 2nd printing	2.00
3	2.00
4 Record,A:TMNT	3.00

MICHELANGELO
Mirage

1 TMNT	17.00
1a 2nd Printing	4.50

MICRA
Fictioneer

1	4.00
2	3.00

3	3.00
4	2.00
5 thru 7	@1.75
8	2.25

MIDNIGHT
Blackthorne

1 thru 4	@1.75

MIDNITE SKULKER

1 thru 7	@1.75

MIGHTY GUY
C&T

1 thru 6	@1.50
Summer Fun Spec #1	2.50

MIGHTY MITES
Continüm

1 I:X-Mites	1.95
2	1.95

MIGHTY MOUSE
ADVENTURE MAGAZINE

1	2.00

MIGHTY THUN'DA
KING OF THE CONGO

1	2.50

MIGHTY TINY

1 thru 4	@1.75
5	2.50
Mouse Marines Collection rep.	7.50

MIKE MIST
MINUTE MYSTERIES
Eclipse

1	3.00

MILK & CHEESE
Slave Labor 1991–97

1 EDo, Milk Products gone bad	90.00
1a 2nd thru 7th printing	3.00
2	40.00
2a 2nd thru 4th printing	3.00
3	30.00
3a 2nd thru 4th printing	3.00
4	20.00
4a 2nd & 3rd printing	3.00
5	20.00
5a 2nd & 3rd printing	3.00
6	15.00
6a 2nd printing	2.75
Other #1	2.75
Third #1	2.75
Fourth #1	2.75
First #2	2.75
Six Six Six #1	2.75
Six Six Six 2nd printing, EDo	2.75
Latest Thing	2.95

MINDLESS MADCAP MIS-
ADVENTURES OF THE
MANIAC MUTANT MACHO
MALLARD
Pocket Change Comics 1995

1 V:Toilet Paper Thieves	2.50

MIRACLE SQUAD
BLOOD & DUST
Apple

1 thru 3	@1.95

MISSING BEINGS

1 Special	2.25

MISSING LINK

1 and 2	@1.70

MISTER X
Vortex

Vol 2

1 thru 11	@2.00

MITES

1	2.50
1a	1.90
2B	1.80
3 and 4	@1.80

MODERN PULP
Special Studio

1 Rep.from January Midnight	2.75

MOEBIUS COMICS
Caliber 1996

1 Moe	2.95
2 Moe	2.95
3 Moe	2.95
4 Moe,MP	2.95
5 Moe,SL	2.95
6 Moe	2.95

MOGOBI DESERT RATS
Midnight Comics

1 I&O:Desert Rats 'Waste of the World'	2.25

MONNGA
Daikaiyu Enterprises 1995

1 & 2 Titanic Omega	3.95

Monsters From Outer Space #2
© Adventure Comics

B & W PUB.

All comics prices listed are for *Near Mint* condition.

MONSTER BOY
Monster Comics
1 A:Monster Boy 2.25

MONSTER FRAT HOUSE
Eternity
1 . . . . 2.25

MONSTER POSSE
Adventure
1 thru 3 . . . . 2.50

MONSTERS ATTACK
1 GM,JSe 2.00
2 GC 1.75
3 ATh,GC 1.50

MONSTERS FROM OUTER SPACE
Adventure 1992
1 thru 3 . . . . @2.50

MOONSTRUCK
1 . . . . 2.00

MOONTRAP
Special #1 . . . . 2.50

MORBID ANGEL: PENANCE
London Night Studios 1995
1 I:Brandon Watts 4.00

MORBID ANGEL: TO HELL AND BACK
London Night Oct. 1996
1 (of 3) EHr, ... 4.00
2 and 3 . . . . @3.00

MORPHS
1 thru 4 . . . . @2.00

MORTAL COIL
Mermaid
1 thru 3 . . . . @2.25
4 F:Red-Line,Gift 2.25
5 Pin-Up Issue 2.25

MORTAR MAN
Marshall Comics
1 I:Mortar Man 1.95
2 thru 3 . . . . @1.95

MORTY THE DOG
1 . . . . 2.00
1 digest size 3.95

MOSAIC
Oktober Black Press
1 F:Halo,Daeva 2.25
2 "Gun Metal Gray" 2.50
3 . . . . 2.50
4 Elf(c) 2.50
5 Wisps 2.50

MOUNTAIN WORLD
Newcomers Press 1995
1 I:Jeremiah Rainshadow 2.95

MR. CREAM PUFF
1 . . . . 1.75

MR. DOOM
1 and 2 . . . . @1.95

MR. FIXITT
Apple
1 and 2 . . . . @1.95

MR. MYSTIC
Eclipse
1 Will Eisner 2.50

MR. NIGHTMARE'S WONDERFUL WORLD
Moonstone 1995
1 Dreams So Real,pt.1 . . . . 2.95
2 Dreams So Real,pt.2 . . . . 2.95
3 Dreams So Real,pt.3 . . . . 2.95

MS. CHRIST
Draculina Publishing 1995
1 I:Ms. Christ 2.95

MS. TREE
Aardvark–Vanaheim
1-10 see Other Pub. (color)
11 thru 18 . . . . @2.00
Renegade
19 thru 49 . . . . @2.00
50 . . . . 4.50
1 3-D Classic 2.95

MUMMY, THE
Monster Comics
1 A:Dr.Clarke,Prof.Belmore 1.95
2 Mummy's Curse 1.95
3 A:Carloph 1.95
4 V:Carloph, conc. 1.95

MUMMY'S CURSE
Aircel
1 thru 4 . . . . @2.25

Murder #2 © Renegade

MURCIELAGA: SHE-BAT
Hero Graphics
1 Daerick Gross reps. 1.50
2 Reps. contd 2.95

MURDER
Renegade 1986
1 SD 1.70
2 CI(c) 1.70
3 SD 1.70

MURDER (2nd series)
1 . . . . 2.00

MUTANT FORCES
1 . . . . 1.50

MUTANT ZONE
Aircel
1 Future story 2.50
2 F.B.I. Drone Exterminators . . . 2.50
3 conclusion 2.50

MYRON MOOSE FUNNIES
1 thru 3 . . . . @1.75

MYSTERY MAN
Slave Labor
1 thru 5 . . . . @1.75

MYSTICAL NINJA
1 . . . . 1.50

MYTH ADVENTURES
Warp Graphics
1 Mag size 1.50
2 thru 4 . . . . @1.50
5 Comic size 1.50
6 thru 11 . . . . @1.50
12 . . . . 1.75

MYTH CONCEPTIONS
Apple
1 . . . . 1.75
2 . . . . 1.75
3 thru 8 . . . . @1.95

MYTHOGRAPHY
Bardic Press 1966
1 F:Poison Elves 3.95
2 fantasy stories 3.95
3 fantasy stories, inc. Elfquest . . 3.95
4 . . . . 4.25

MYTHOS
Wonder Comix
1 and 2 . . . . @1.50

NAIVE INTER-DIMENSIONAL COMMANDO KOALAS
Eclipse
1 . . . . 1.50

NATURE OF THE BEAST
Caliber
1 'The Beast' 2.95

NAUSICAÄ OF THE VALLEY OF WIND
Viz Select
Book One	4.50
Book Two	5.50
Book Three	4.00
Book Four	3.00
Book Five	2.50
Book Six	2.95
Book Seven	2.95

[Part 2]
#1 thru #4	@2.95

[Part 3]
#1 thru #3	@2.95

Nazrat #1 © Imperial

NAZRAT
Imperial 1986
1	2.50
2 thru 6	@2.00

NEAT STUFF
13	2.50

NEGATIVE BURN
Caliber
1 I:Matrix 7, Flaming Carrot	5.00
2	3.50
3 Bone preview	15.00
4 thru 12 various stories	@3.25
13 Strangers in Paradise	15.00
14 thru 18 various stories	@3.25
19 Flaming Carrot	5.00
20 In the Park	3.25
21 Trollords	3.00
22 Father the Dryad	3.00
23 I:The Creep	3.00
24 The Factor	3.00
25 The Factor	4.00
26 Very Vicki	3.00
27 Nancy Kate	3.00
28 Favorite Song	4.00
29 thru 33	3.00
34 thru 38	@4.00
39 "Iron Empires," pt. 4	4.00
40 "Suzi Romaine"	4.00
41 "Iron Empires," cont.	4.00
42	4.00

43 "Iron Empires," concl.	4.00
44 "Skeleton Key"	4.00
45 "Divine Winds"	4.00
46 "A Bullet For Me"	3.95
47	3.95
48 special 80 page issue	4.95
TPB Best of Year One	9.95
TPB Best of Year Two	9.95

NEIL AND BUZZ
1	2.00

NEIL THE HORSE
Aardvark–Vanaheim
1 Art:Arn Sara	6.00
1a 2nd printing	2.00
2	3.00
3	4.00
4	3.00
5 Video Warriors	2.00
6 Video Warriors	2.00
7 Video Warriors	2.00
8 Outer Space	2.00
9 Conan	2.00
10	2.00

Renegade
11 Fred Astair	1.70
12	1.70
13	1.70
14 Special	3.00
15	1.70

NEMESIS
Fleetway
1 thru 16	@1.95

NEO CANTON LEGACY
1	2.00

NEOMAN
1	1.75
2	1.75
3 double-size	3.50

NEON CITY
Innovation
1	2.25

NERVE
1	2.50
2	1.75
3 thru 5	@1.50

NERVOUS REX
1	3.00
1a 2nd printing	2.00
2	3.00
3	3.00
4	2.50
5 thru 10	@2.00
GraphicNovel	3.50

NETHERWORLDS
1	1.50
2	1.50
3	1.95
4	1.95

NEW BEGINNINGS
1 and 2	@1.75

NEWCOMERS ILLUSTRATED
Newcomers Publishing
1 thru 5 various artists	@2.95
6 Science Fiction	2.95
7 thru 8	@2.95
9 Shocking Machines	2.95
10	2.95
11 Hitman	2.95
12 final issue	2.95

NEW ENGLAND GOTHIC
3	2.00

NEW ERADICATORS
Vol 2 #1 NewBeginnings	2.00
Vol 2 #2 NewBeginnings	2.00
Vol 2 #3 NewFriends	2.00

NEW FRONTIERS
1 CS(c)	3.00
1a 2nd Printing	1.75

NEW FRONTIERS
Evolution
1 A:Action Master, Green Ghost	1.95

NEW GOLDEN AGE
1	1.50

NEW HERO COMICS
Pierce
1 and 2	@1.00

NEW HUMANS
Eternity
1	1.80
2 thru 15	@1.95
Ann. #1	2.95

NEW HUMANS
1 Shattered Earth Chron	1.95

NEW KIDS ON THE BLOCK
Harvey
1	1.25

NEW L.I.F.E. BRIGADE
1 thru 3	@1.80

NEW POWER STARS
1	2.00

NEW PULP ADVENTURES SPECIAL
Dunewadd Comics
1 I:Kawala	2.50

NEW REALITY
1 thru 6	@1.25

NEWSTRALIA
Innovation
(Prev. Color)
4	2.25
5	2.25

B & W PUB.

All comics prices listed are for *Near Mint* condition.

NEW TRIUMPH
Matrix Graphics
1 F:Northguard 3.00
1a 2nd printing 1.75
2 thru 4 . . . . @1.50

NEW WORLD DISORDER
Millenium 1995
1 I:King Skin Gang 2.95

NEW WORLD ORDER
Blazer Studios
1 thru 8 . . . . @2.50

NEW YORK CITY OUTLAWS
1 thru 5 . . . . @2.50

NEW YORK, YEAR ZERO
Eclipse
1 thru 4 . . . . @2.00

NEXUS
Capital
1 SR,I:Nexus,large size 30.00
2 SR,Mag size 15.00
3 SR,Mag size 7.00

NIGHT
Amaze Ink 1995
0 V:The Prince 1.50

NIGHT ANGEL
Substance Comics 1995
1 I:Night Angel 2.95

NIGHT CRY
CFD Productions 1995
1 Evil Ernie & Razor story 14.00
2 . . . . 7.00
3 . . . . 5.00
4 . . . . 4.00
4a platinum (c) 8.00
5 . . . . 4.00
6 . . . . 2.75
6a signed 8.00

NIGHT LIFE
Caliber
1 thru 7 . . . . @1.50

NIGHT MASTER
1 Vigil 5.50
2 Vigil 2.50
3 . . . . 1.50

NIGHT OF THE LIVING DEAD
Fantaco
0 prelude 1.75
1 based on cult classic movie . . . 4.95
2 Movie adapt,continued 4.95
3 Movie adapt,conclusion 4.95
5 . . . . 5.95
TPB London, Clive Barker's story 14.95

NIGHTSTAR
1 . . . . 2.50

NIGHT'S CHILDREN
Fantaco
1 . . . . 3.50
2 . . . . 3.50
3 . . . . 3.50

NIGHT'S CHILDREN: THE RIPPER
Millenium 1995
1 Klaus Wulfe 3.95

NIGHT'S CHILDREN: THE VAMPIRE
Millenium 1995
1 F:Klaus Wulfe 2.95
2 F:Klaus Wulfe 2.95

NIGHT STREETS
Arrow
1 . . . . 2.50
2 thru 4 . . . . @1.50

NIGHTVISION
London Night Nov. 1996
1 DQ,KHt, All About Eve 3.00
1 signed 12.95
1a erotica edition 10.00

NIGHT VISITORS
1 . . . . 1.95

NIGHT WOLF
1 thru 4 . . . . @1.75

NIGHTVEIL'S CAULDRON OF HORROR
1 . . . . 2.50

NIGHTWIND
1 . . . . 1.95
2 . . . . 1.95

NIGHT ZERO
Fleetway
1 thru 4 . . . . @1.95

NIKKI BLADE
High Impact 1997
0 . . . . 2.95
0a deluxe adult cover 10.00
0b gold edition variant cover . . . 14.95

NIKKI BLADE: FOREVER NIKKI
High Impact Feb. 1997
0 MIB(c) 2.95
0a deluxe RCI(c) 10.00

NINGA-BOTS
Prelude
1 . . . . 2.00

NINJA
Eternity
1 . . . . 3.00
2 thru 6 . . . . @1.80
7 thru 13 . . . . @1.95

NINJA ELITE
1 thru 5 . . . . @1.50
6 thru 8 . . . . @1.95

NINJA FUNNIES
Eternity
1 and 2 . . . . @1.80
3 thru 5 . . . . @1.95

NINJA HIGH SCHOOL
Eternity
1 . . . . 1.75
2 thru 4 . . . . @1.50
5 thru 22 . . . . @1.95
23 Zardon Assassin 2.25
24 . . . . 2.25
25 Return of the Zetramen 2.25
26 Stanley the Demon 2.25
27 Return of the Zetramen 2.25
28 Threat of the super computer . 2.25
29 V:Super Computer 2.25
30 I:Akaru 2.25
31 Jeremy V:Akaru 2.25
32 thru 34 V:Giant Monsters Pt.1
   thru Pt. 3 . . . . @2.50
35 thru 43 . . . . @2.50
44 Combat Cheerleaders 2.75
45 Cheerleader Competition 2.75
46 Monsters From Space 2.75
47 . . . . 2.75
48 F:Jeremy Feeple 2.75
49 thru 51 . . . . @2.95
52 thru 57 Time Warp, pt.4–pt.8 @2.95
Special #1 . . . . 2.95
Special #2 . . . . 2.95
Special #3 . . . . 2.95
Special #3 1/2 . . . . 2.25
Ann. 1989 . . . . 2.95
Ann.#3 . . . . 3.95
TPB Vol. 1 rep. #1–3 . . . . 12.00
TPB Vol. 2 rep. #4–7 . . . . 12.00
TPB Vol. 3 rep. #8–11 . . . . 9.00
TPB Vol. 4 rep. #12–15 . . . . . . 8.00
TPB Vol. 5 rep. #16–18 . . . . . . 7.95
TPB Vol. 6 rep. #19–21 . . . . . . 7.95
TPB Vol. 7 rep. #22–24 . . . . . . 7.95
TPB Vol. 8 rep. #25–27 . . . . . . 7.95
TPB Vol. 9 rep. #28–31 . . . . . 10.95
TPB Vol. 10 rep. #32–35 . . . . . 10.95
TPB Vol. 11 rep. #36–39 . . . . . 10.95
TPB Vol. 15 three stories 7.95
Yearbook 1994 . . . . 4.00
Yearbook 1995 . . . . 3.95
Yearbook 1996 . . . . 3.95

NINJA HIGH SCHOOL GIRLS
Antarctic Press
0 . . . . 2.75
1 and 2 rep. . . . . @2.75
3 thru 5 rep. 3.95
Yearbook 3.95

NINJA HIGH SCHOOL PERFECT MEMORY
Antarctic Press
1 thru 2, 96pg . . . . @4.95

NINJA HIGH SCHOOL SMALL BODIES
Antarctic Press
1 "Monopolize" 2.50

B & W PUB.

2 Omegadon Cannon	2.75
3 Omegadon Cannon	2.75
3a deluxe	4.50
4 Omegadon Cannon	2.75
5 Wrong Order	2.75
6 Chicken Rage	2.95
7	2.95

NIRA X/HELLINA: HEAVEN & HELL
Entity Comics

1 San Diego Con edition, BMs	5.00
1a foil	3.00

NIRA X: CYBERANGEL
Entity Comics April 1996

1	4.00
1a deluxe	8.00
2 BMs	4.00
3 and 4 BMs	@3.00
4a with PC Game	8.00
Ann.#1 BMs flip-cover	2.75

2nd Mini Series 1995

1	3.50
1a 2nd printing	2.50
2 thru 4	@2.50

3rd Mini Series 1995–96

1	2.50
1a Gold(c)	5.00
2	2.50
3	3.00

Regular Series

1	2.75
1a with game	7.00
2 thru 4	@2.75
4a with game	7.00

NIRA X: HEATWAVE
Entity Comics

1 encore special toy edition	2.50
1 encore special toy edition, signed & numbered	12.95

NIRA X: MEMOIRS
Entity 1997

1 BMs	2.75
1a deluxe	3.50

NIRA X: SOUL SKURGE
Entity Oct. 1996

1 (of 3) BMs, A:Vortex	2.75
2 BMs	2.75
3	2.75

NO COMICS

1	2.00
2	2.00

NO GUTS, NO GLORY
Fantaco

1 One Shot, K.Eastman's 1st solo work since TMNT	2.95

NOMADS OF ANTIQUITY

1 thru 6	@1.50

NO NEED FOR TENCHI
Viz Comics
Part One

1 thru 7 (of 7)	@2.95

Part Two Nov. 1996

1 thru 7 by Hitoshi Okuda	@2.95

Part Three 1997

1 (of 6) by Hitoshi Okuda	2.95
2	2.95
TPB	15.95

NORMAL MAN
Aardvark–Vanaheim

1	4.00
2 thru 9	@2.50

Renegade

10 thru 19	@1.70

NORTHERN EDGE
Northern Edge

1 New Anthology title	2.25

NORTHGUARD AND THE MANDES CONCLUSION

1 thru 3	@1.95

NOWHERESVILLE
Caliber March 1996

1 thru 3 by MRc	@2.95
Spec. The History of Cool	2.95

NULL PATROL

1 thru 2	@1.50

NYOKA THE JUNGLE GIRL
AC Comics

3	2.25
4	2.25
5	2.50

OCTOBERFEST
Now & Then

1 (1976) Dave Sim	15.00

OFFERINGS
Cry For Dawn

1 Sword & Sorcery stories	2.75

OFFICIAL BUZ SAWYER

1	2.00
2	2.00
3	2.00
4	1.50
5	2.00
6	2.00

OFFICIAL HOW TO DRAW G.I. JOE
Blackthorne

1 thru 5	@2.00

OFFICIAL HOW TO DRAW ROBOTECH
Blackthorne

12	2.95
13 thru 16	@2.00

OFFICIAL HOW TO DRAW TRANSFORMERS
Blackthorne

1 thru 7	@2.00

OFFICIAL JOHNNY HAZARD

1 thru 3	@2.00
4	1.50
5	2.00

OFFICIAL JUNGLE JIM

1 thru 5 AR,rep.	@2.00
6 AR,rep.	1.50
7 thru 10 AR,rep.	@2.00
11 thru 20 AR,rep.	@2.50
Ann.#1	2.00
Giant Size	3.95

OFFICIAL MANDRAKE

1 thru 5	@2.00
6	1.50
7 thru 10	@2.00
11	2.50
12	2.00
13 thru 17	@2.50
Ann. #1	3.95
King Size #1	3.95
Giant Size #1	3.95

international intrigue and danger

Official Modesty Blaise #1 © Pioneer

OFFICIAL MODESTY BLAISE
Pioneer 1988

1 thru 4	@2.00
5	1.50
6 thru 14	@2.00
Ann. #1	3.95
King Size #1	3.95

OFFICIAL PRINCE VALIANT

1 Hal Foster,rep.	2.00
2 Hal Foster,rep.	2.00
3 Hal Foster,rep.	2.00
4 Hal Foster,rep.	2.00
5 Hal Foster,rep.	2.00
6 Hal Foster,rep.	2.00
7	1.50
8 thru 14	@2.00
15 thru 24	@2.50
Ann. #1	3.95
King Size #1	3.95

B & W PUB.

OFFICIAL RIP KIRBY
1 thru 3 AR . . . . @2.00
4 AR 1.50
5 and 6 AR . . . . @2.00

OFFICIAL SECRET AGENT
Pioneer
1 thru 5 AW rep . . . . @2.00
6 AW 1.50
7 thru 9 AW . . . . @2.00

OFFWORLDERS' QUARTERLY
1 . . . . 1.50

OF MYTHS AND MEN
1 and 2 . . . . @1.75

OH..
B Publications
1 Tomboy Meets Agents street . . 2.95

OHM'S LAW
Imperial Comics
1 thru 2 . . . . @1.95
3 V:Men in Black 1.95
4 A:Damonstriek 1.95
5 F:Tryst 1.95

OKTOBERFEST
Now & Then
1 (1976) Dave Sim 20.00

OMEGA
North Star
1 1st pr by Rebel,rare 80.00
1a Vigil(Yellow Cov.) 27.00
2 . . . . 2.00

OMEN
North Star
1 . . . . 8.00
1a 2nd printing 2.00
2 thru 4 . . . . @3.50

OMICRON
1 and 2 . . . . @2.25
3 . . . . 2.50

OMNIMAN
1 . . . . 2.00

OMNIMEN
1 . . . . 3.50

ONE SHOT WESTERN
Calibur
One Shot F:Savage Sisters, Tornpath
Outlaw 2.50

ONLY A MATTER OF LIFE AND DEATH
1 . . . . 3.95

ON THE ROAD WITH GEORGE & BARBARA IN VACATIONLAND
1 . . . . 2.50

OPEN SEASON
Renegade
1 thru 7 . . . . @2.00

OPERATIVE SCORPIO
Blackthorne
1 . . . . 3.50

OPTIC NERVE
Adrian Tomine 1990
1 thru 5, mini-comic 18.00
6 . . . . 7.00
7 . . . . 5.00

OPTIC NERVE
Drawn & Quarterly 1995
1 Summer Job 3.00
1a 2nd printing 3.00
2 . . . . 5.00
3 and 4 . . . . @3.00

ORACLE PRESENTS
1 thru 4 . . . . @1.50

ORBIT
Eclipse
1 and 2 . . . . @3.95
3 . . . . 4.95

Original Tom Corbet #2 © Eternity

ORIGINAL TOM CORBET
Eternity 1990
1 thru 3 Rep. newspaper strips . @2.95

ORLAK: FLESH & STEEL
Caliber
1 '1991 A.D.' 2.50

ORLAK REDUX
Caliber
1 . . . . 3.95

OTHERS, THE
Cormac Publishing
1 . . . . 1.50

OUT OF THIS WORLD
1 . . . . 3.50

OUTLANDER
1 . . . . 4.50
2 . . . . 3.00
3 thru 5 . . . . @2.50
6 and 7 . . . . @1.95
8 . . . . 2.25

OUTLAW OVERDRIVE
Blue Comet Press
1 Red Edition I:Deathrow 2.95
1a Black Edition 2.95
1b Blue Edition 2.95

OVERLOAD
Eclipse
1 . . . . 1.50

OVERTURE
1 . . . . 2.25
2 . . . . 2.25

OZ
Imperial Comics
1 Land of Oz Gone Mad 12.00
2 Land of Oz Gone Mad 10.00
3 Land of Oz Gone Mad 6.00
4 Tin Woodsmen 6.00
5 F:Pumkinhead 6.00
6 Emerald City 6.00
7 V:Bane Wolves 4.00
8 V:Nome Hordes 4.00
9 Freedom Fighters Vs. Heroes . 4.00
10 thru 15 . . . . @4.00
16 . . . . 3.50
Spec.#1 . . . . 6.00
Spec. Scarecrow #1 . . . . 3.00
Spec. Lion #1 . . . . 3.00
Spec. Tin Man #1 . . . . 3.00
Spec. Freedom Fighters #1 . . . . 3.00
TPB Rep. #1-#4 . . . . 14.95
Caliber "New Worlds"
17 by Ralph Griffith, Stuart Kerr &
     Tim Holtrop 3.50
18 . . . . 3.00
19 . . . . 3.00
20 . . . . 3.00
21 "Witches War" pt.1 (of 5) 3.00
GN Heroes of Oz 14.95

OZ: ROMANCE IN RAGS
Caliber 1996
1 thru 3 . . . . @2.95

OZ SQUAD
Patchwork Press
1 thru 6 . . . . @2.95
7 Time Train Destroyed 2.95
8 Old West 2.75

OZ: STRAW AND SORCERY
Caliber "New Worlds" 1997
1 thru 3 . . . . @2.95

PAJAMA CHRONICLES
1 . . . . 1.50
2 . . . . 1.75
3 . . . . 1.75

B & W PUB.

PAKKINS' LAND
Caliber Tapestry 1996
1	2.95
1a signed edition	2.95
1a second edition, new cover	2.95
2	2.95
2a second edition, new cover	2.95
3 thru 6	@2.95

PALANTINE
Gryphon Rampant 1995
1 thru 5 V:Master of Basilisk	2.50

PANDA KHAN
1 thru 4	@2.00

PANDORA
Brainstorm 1996
1 (of 2)	3.00
1a nude cover	5.00

PANDORA
Avatar Press 1997
0	3.00
0 nude cover	4.95
1 signed	15.00
2 (of 2	3.00
2 deluxe	10.00

PANDORA PINUP
Avatar Press 1997
1	3.00
1 nude cover	4.95

PANDORA SPECIAL
Avatar Press 1997
1	3.00
1 nude cover	4.95
1 leather cover	25.00

PANDORA/WIDOW
Avatar Press 1997
1	3.95
1 nude cover	4.95
1 leather cover	25.00

PANDORA: DEMONOGRAPHY
Avatar Press 1997
1	3.00
1 nude cover	5.00
2 (of 3)	3.00
2 nude cover	4.95
3 (of 3)	3.00
3 nude cover	4.95

PAPER CUTS
1 E Starzer-1982	17.50
2 and 3	@2.50

PARTICLE DREAMS
Fantagraphics
1	3.00
2 thru 6	@2.25

PARTNERS IN PANDEMONIUM
Caliber
1 'Hell on Earth'	2.50

2 Sheldon&Murphy become mortal	2.50
3 A:Abra Cadaver	2.50

PARTS OF A HOLE
Caliber
1 Short Stories	2.50

PARTS UNKNOWN
Eclipse
1 I:Spurr,V:Aliens	2.50
2 Aliens on Earth cont.	2.50

PARTS UNKNOWN: DARK INTENTIONS
Knight Press
1 I:Prelude to limited Series	2.95
2 V:Luggnar	2.95
3 V:Luggnar	2.95
Super-Ann. #1	3.95

PATRICK RABBIT
1	2.00
2	2.00
3	2.00

PAUL THE SAMURAI
New England Comics
1 thru 3	@2.75

PELLESTAR
1 thru 3	@1.95

PENDULUM
Adventure
1 Big Hand,Little Hand	2.50
2 The Immortality Formula	2.50
3	2.50

PENGUIN AND PENCILGUIN
1 thru 6	@2.00

PENTACLE: SIGN OF 5
Eternity
1	2.25
2 Det.Sandler,H.Smitts	2.25
3 Det.Sandler => New Warlock	2.25
4 5 warlocks Vs. Kaji	2.50

PETER RISK, MONSTER MASHER
1 thru 4	@2.00
5	1.50

PHANTOM
1	5.95
2	5.95
3	5.95
4 and 5	@6.95

PHANTOM OF FEAR CITY
Claypool
1 thru 7	2.50

PHANTOM OF THE OPERA
Eternity
1	1.95

PHASE ONE
Victory
1	3.00
2	2.00
3 thru 5	@1.50

PHIGMENTS
Eternity
1	5.00
2	2.00
3	1.95

PHONEY PAGES
Renegade
1 and 2	@1.70

PIED PIPER OF HAMELIN
Tome
1	2.95

PINEAPPLE ARMY
1 thru 10	@1.75

PINK FLOYD EXPERIENCE
Revolutionary
1 based on rock group	2.50
2 Dark Side of the Moon	2.50
3 Dark Side of the Moon, Wish you were here	2.50
4 The Wall	2.50
5 A Momentary lapse of reason	2.50

PIRATE CORPS!
Eternity
6 and 7	@1.95
Spec. #1	1.95

PIRANHA! IS LOOSE
Special Studio
1 Drug Runners,F:Piranha	2.95
2 Expedition into Terror	2.95

PIXI JUNKET
Viz
1 thru 6	@2.75

P.J. WARLOCK
Eclipse
1 thru 3	@2.00

PLANET COMICS
Blackthorne (Prev. Color)
4 and 5	@2.00

PLANET OF TERROR
1 BW	1.75

PLANET OF THE APES
Adventure Comics 1990
1 WD,collect.ed.	7.00
1 2 covers	5.00
1a 2nd printing	2.50
1b 3rd printing	2.25
2	3.00
3	2.75
4	2.75
5 D:Alexander?	2.75
6 Welcome to Ape City	2.75

B & W PUB.

7 . . . . 2.75
8 Christmas Story 2.50
9 Swamp Ape Village 2.50
10 Swamp Apes in Forbidden City 2.50
11 Ape War continues 2.50
12 W.Alexander/Coure 2.50
13 Planet of Apes/Alien Nation/ Ape
    City x-over 2.50
14 Countdown to Zero Pt.1 . . . . . 2.50
15 Countdown to Zero Pt.2 . . . . . 2.50
16 Countdown to Zero Pt.3 . . . . . 2.50

Planet of the Apes #1 © Adventure

18 Ape City (after Ape Nation mini-
    series 2.50
19 1991 'Conquest..' tie-in 2.50
20 Return of the Ape Riders 2.50
21 The Terror Beneath,Pt.1 . . . . . 2.50
22 The Terror Beneath,Pt.2 . . . . . 2.50
23 The Terror Beneath,Pt.3 . . . . . 2.50
Ann #1,'Day on Planet o/t Apes' . 3.50
Lim.Ed. #1 . . . . 5.00

PLANET OF THE APES: BLOOD OF THE APES
Adventure Comics
1 A:Tonus the Butcher 3.00
2 Valia/Taylorite Connection 2.50
3 Ape Army in Phis 2.50
4 . . . . 2.50

PLANET OF THE APES: FORBIDDEN ZONE
Adventure
1 Battle for the Planet o/t Apes &
    Planet o/t Apes tie-in 2.50
2 A:Juilus 2.50

PLANET OF THE APES: SINS OF THE FATHER
Adventure Comics
1 Conquest Tie in 2.50

PLANET OF THE APES URCHAKS' FOLLY
Adventure Comics
1 . . . . 3.00

2 . . . . 2.50
3 'The Taylorites' 2.50
4 Conclusion 2.50

PLANET 29
Caliber
1 A Future Snarl Tale 2.50
2 A:Biff,Squakman 2.50

PLANET-X
Eternity
1 . . . . 2.50

PLAN 9 FROM OUTER SPACE
Eternity
1 . . . . 2.50
2 and 3 . . . . @2.25

PLASMA BABY
Caliber
1 'Strange New World' 2.50

PLASTRON CAFE
Mirage
1 RV,inc.North by Downeast 2.25

PLAYGROUND 1826
Caliber
1 . . . . 2.50

POINT BLANK
Eclipse
1 thru 5 . . . . @2.95

POISON ELVES
Mulehide Graphics 1993–95
Prev: I, Lusipher
8 DHa(c&a) 45.00
9 DHa 40.00
10 DHa 40.00
11 DHa, comic size 42.00
12 DHa 35.00
13 DHa 45.00
14 and 15 DHa . . . . @35.00
15a 2nd printing 10.00
16 and 17 DHa . . . . @30.00
17a 2nd printing 8.00
18 DHa 20.00
19 DHa 30.00
20 DHa 20.00
2nd Series, Sirius 1995–97
1 F:Lusipher 3.50
2 V:Assassins Guild 3.00
3 Sanctuary, pt.3 . . . . 2.50
4 Sanctuary, pt.4 . . . . 2.50
5 Sanctuary, pt.5 . . . . 2.50
6 I:Lester Gran 2.50
7 thru 24 . . . . @2.50
25 DHa 2.95
TPB Vol.1 Requiem for an Elf,rep 14.95
TPB Vol. 3, rep. #13–#18 . . . . 14.95

POLIS
Brave New World
1 I:Polis 2.50

POPCORN
Discovery 1993
1 . . . . 3.95

PORK KNIGHT
Silver Snail
1 . . . . 1.75

PORT
Silver Wolf
1 . . . . 1.50
2 . . . . 1.50

PORTABLE LOWLIFE
1 Real life Adventures 4.95

PORTIA PRINZ
Eclipse
1 thru 5 . . . . @2.00

POSSIBLE MAN
1 . . . . 1.75
2 . . . . 1.75

POST BROTHERS
Rip Off Press
15 thru 18 . . . . @2.00
19 . . . . 2.50
20 . . . . 2.50

POWER COMICS
1 Smart-Early Ardvaark 25.00
1a 2nd printing 8.00
2 I:Cobalt Blue 10.00
3 . . . . 3.00
4 . . . . 3.00
5 . . . . 4.00

POWER COMICS
Eclipse
1 BB,DGb,Powerbolt 2.00
2 BB,DGb 2.00
3 BB,DGb 2.00

POWER CORPS
1 . . . . 2.50
2 . . . . 2.50

POWER PLAYS
1 thru 3 . . . . @1.75

POWER PRINCIPLE
1 thru 3 . . . . @1.95

POWER STATION
1 . . . . 1.75

POWER UNLIMITED
1 . . . . 1.95

PRACTICE IN PAIN
Dramemon Studios
1 I:Queen of the Dead 3.00

PREMIERE
Diversity Comics 1995
1 F:Kolmec The Savage 2.75

PRETEEN DIRTY GENE KUNG FU KANGAROOS
Blackthorne
1 and 2 . . . . @1.50

PRETTY CITY ROXX
Mars Press
1 I:Roxx 3.50

PREY
Monster Comics
1 I:Prey,A:Andrina 2.25
2 V:Andrina 2.25
3 conclusion 2.25

PRICE, THE
1 Dreadstar mag. size 20.00

PRIMITIVES
Spartive Studios 1995
1 thru 3 On the Moon . . . . @2.50

PRIME CUTS
Fantagraphics
1 adult 3.50
2 thru 6 . . . . @3.50
7 thru 12 . . . . @3.95

PRIMER
Comico
1 . . . . 9.00
2 MW,I:Grendel 100.00
3 . . . . 5.00
4 . . . . 7.00
5 SK(1st work),I:Maxx 35.00
6 IN,Evangeline 18.00

PRIME SLIME TALES
Mirage
1 . . . . 5.00
2 . . . . 2.50
3 thru 6 . . . . @1.50

PRINCE VALIANT
1 thru 4 . . . . @4.95
Spec #1 . . . . 6.95

PRINCE VALIANT MONTHLY
1 thru 6 . . . . @3.95
6 . . . . 4.95
7 . . . . 4.95
8 . . . . 4.95
9 . . . . 6.95

PRIVATE EYES
Eternity
1 Saint rep. 1.95
2 . . . . 1.95
3 . . . . 1.95
4 . . . . 1.95
5 . . . . 1.95

PROBE
1 . . . . 1.80
2 . . . . 1.80

PROGENY
Spec 4.95

PROJECT: HERO
1 . . . . 1.50
2 . . . . 1.50
3 . . . . 1.50

PROTOTYPE
1 . . . . 1.75

PROWLER IN WHITE "WHITE ZOMBIE", THE
1 . . . . 2.00

PRYDERI TERRA
1 and 2 . . . . @1.75

PSI–JUDGE ANDERSON
1 thru 15 . . . . @1.95

PSYCHOMAN
Revolutionary
1 I:Psychoman 2.50

PUMA BLUES
Aardvark–Vanaheim
1 10,000 printed 4.50
1a 2nd printing 2.00
2 . . . . 3.00
3 . . . . 2.00
4 thru 19 . . . . @1.70
20 Special 2.25
Mirage
21 thru 24 . . . . @1.70
25 . . . . 1.50
26 thru 28 . . . . @1.75

PURGATORY USA
1 . . . . 1.75
2 . . . . 1.75
3 . . . . 1.95

PURGE
Amara
P V:Deadpoint 1.50

QUACK
Star Reach
1 . . . . 2.00
2 . . . . 2.00
3 . . . . 2.00
4 Dave Sim 3.00
5 Dave Sim 3.00
6 . . . . 2.00

QUADRO GANG
1 . . . . 1.25

QUAZAR
1 . . . . 2.00

QUEST PRESENTS
Quest
1 JD 1.75
2 JD 1.75
3 JD 1.75

RADICAL DREAMER
Mark's Giant Economy Sized Comics
1 thru 3 F:Max Wrighter 3.00
4 is Max the Devil? 3.00

RADIO BOY
Eclipse
1 . . . . 2.00

RADREX
1 thru 3 . . . . @2.25

RAGNAROK
Sun Comics
1 I:Ragnarok Guy,Honey 2.50
2 The Melder Foundation 2.50
3 Guy/Honey mission contd. 2.50
4 I:Big Gossage 2.50

RAIKA
Sun Comics
1 thru 12 . . . . @2.50

RALPH SNART
Now
1 . . . . 5.00
2 . . . . 4.00
3 . . . . 4.00
[Volume 2]
1 . . . . 3.00
2 thru 8 . . . . @1.50
Trade Paperback 2.95

RAMBO
Blackthorne
1 thru 5 . . . . @2.00

RAMBO III
Blackthorne
1 . . . . 2.00

Ramm #2 © Megaton Comics

RAMM
Megaton Comics 1987
1 and 2 . . . . @1.50

RAMPAGE ALLEY
1 . . . . 1.75
2 . . . . 1.75

RANMA 1/2
Viz 1993
Parts 1 & 2, see color
[Part 3]
1 thru 13 . . . . 2.75

All comics prices listed are for *Near Mint* condition.　　**CVA Page 611**

B & W PUB.

[Part 4]
1 thru 11 . . . . 2.75
[Part 5]
1 thru 9 . . . . 2.75
10 thru 12 . . . . @3.00
[Part Six] Dec. 1996
1 thru 8 (of 14) . . . . @3.00
TPB Vol. 6 . . . . 15.95
TPB Vol. 7 . . . . 15.95
TPB Vol. 8 . . . . 15.95
TPB Vol. 9 . . . . 15.95

RAPHAEL
1 TMNT 17.50
1a 2nd printing 7.50

RAPTUS
High Impact
1 . . . . 3.00
1 2nd printing, new cover 3.00
2 . . . . 3.00
3 . . . . 3.00

RAPTUS: DEAD OF NIGHT
High Impact
1 . . . . 2.95
2 . . . . 2.95

RAT FINK
World of Fandom
1 . . . . 2.50
2 . . . . 2.50

RAVEN CHRONICLES
Caliber Press
1 . . . . 2.95
1a Special Edition 5.95
2 Landing Zone 2.95
3 The Rain People 2.95
4 The Healer 2.95
5 thru 9 . . . . @2.95
Caliber "New Worlds"
10 by Scott Andrews, Laurence
   Campbell & Tim Perkins 2.95
11 "The Ghost of Alanzo Mann" . . 2.95
12 "The Compensators" flip book
   with Boston Bombers #1 . . . . . 2.95
13 48pg, bagged with back issue . 3.95
14 . . . . 2.95
GN 192pg rep. 16.95

RAVEN CHRONICLES: HEART OF THE DRAGON
Caliber "New Worlds"
1 . . . . 2.95

RAW CITY
Dramenon Studios
1 I:Dya,Gino 3.00
2 V:Crucifier 3.00
3 The Siren's Past 3.00

RAW MEDIA MAGS.
Reb
1 TV,SK,short stories 5.00

RAYNE
Wild Card Comics
1 I:Rayne 2.50

RAZOR: ARCHIVES
London Night 1997
1 EHr, rep #1–#4 . . . . 5.00
2 EHr, rep #5–#8 . . . . 5.00

RAZOR/DARK ANGEL: THE FINAL NAIL
Boneyard/London Night
1 X-over (Boneyard Press) 4.00
2 X-over concl.(London Night) . . 3.00

RAZOR UNCUT
London Night Studios
Prev. RAZOR (Ind. Color)
13 . . . . 3.00
14 V:Child Killer 3.00
15 Questions About Father 3.00
16 Nicole's Life,pt.1 . . . . 3.00
17 Nicole's Life,pt.2 . . . . 3.00
18 . . . . 3.00
19 & 20 Kiss from a Rose . . . . @3.00
21 "Kiss From a Rose," pt.3 . . . . 3.00
22 thru 24 . . . . @3.00
25 mild cover I:Knyfe 3.00
25a nude photo cover 10.00
25b signed 12.95
26 . . . . 3.00
27 A:Sade, pt.1 . . . . 3.00
28 A:Sade, pt.2 . . . . 3.00
29 . . . . 3.00
30 . . . . 3.00
31 "Strength by Numbers" 3.00
32 double sized 3.50
32a signed nude edition 3.00
33 "Let Us Prey," pt.2 . . . . 3.00
34 "Let Us Prey," pt.4 (of 4) 3.00
35 Let the battle begin 3.00
36 all-out war for Queen City . . . 3.00
37 "After the Fall" pt.1 . . . . 3.00

RAZORGUTS
Monster Comics 1992
1 thru 4 . . . . 2.25

REACTOMAN
B-Movie Comics
1 . . . . 1.50

Razorguts #4 © Monster Comics

1a signed,numbered 2.75
2 thru 4 . . . . @1.50
collection 4.95

REAGAN'S RAIDERS
1 thru 6 . . . . @2.50

REAL LIFE
1 . . . . 2.50

REALM
Arrow
1 Fantasy 7.50
2 . . . . 4.00
3 . . . . 3.00
4 TV,Deadworld 21.00
5 I:L.Kazan 2.00
6 thru 13 . . . . @1.50
14 thru 18 . . . . @1.95
19 . . . . 2.50

REAL STUFF
Fantagraphic
1 thru 12 . . . . @2.50

REAPER
Newcomers Publishing
1 V:The Chinde 2.95
2 . . . . 2.95
3 conclusion 2.95

REBELLION
Daikaiyu Enterprises 1995
1 I:Rebellion 2.50

RED FOX
Harrier
1 scarce 6.00
1a 2nd printing 2.50
2 rare 5.00
3 . . . . 3.00
4 I:White Fox 3.00
5 I:Red Snail 3.00
6 . . . . 1.75
7 Wbolton 1.75
8 . . . . 1.75
9 Demosblurth 1.75

RED & STUMPY
Parody Press
1 Ren & Stimpy parody 2.95

RED HEAT
Blackthorne
1 . . . . 2.00

REDLAW
Caliber
1 Preview Killer of Crows 2.50

RED SHETLAND
Blackthorne
1 . . . . 2.00

REID FLEMING
Blackbird-Eclipse
1 I:Reid Fleming 10.00
1a 2nd printing 5.50
1b 3rd printing 2.50
1b 4th printing 2.50

Volume 2
#1 Rogues to Riches Pt.1 . . . . . . 6.00
#2 Rogues to Riches Pt.2 . . . . . . 4.00
#3 Rogues to Riches Pt.3 . . . . . . 3.00
#3a LaterPrinting 2.50
#4 Rogues to Riches Pt.4 . . . . . . 3.00
#5 Rogues to Riches Pt.5 . . . . . . 2.50

REID FLEMING, WORLD'S TOUGHEST MILKMAN
Deep-Sea Comics
3 "Rogue to Riches," pt.2,4th pr . 2.95
4 "Rogue to Riches," pt.3,3rd pr . 2.95
5 "Rogue to Riches," pt.4,2nd pr . 2.95
6 "Rogue to Riches," pt.5,2nd pr . 2.95

REIGN OF THE DARK LORD
1 thru 3 . . . . @1.80
4 . . . . 1.95

REIVERS
Enigma
1 thru 2 Ch'tocc in Space 2.95

RELENTLESS PURSUIT
1 . . . . 2.00
2 . . . . 1.75
3 . . . . 1.95

RENEGADE
Rip Off Press
1 . . . . 2.50

RENEGADE RABBIT
1 and 2 . . . . @1.75

RENEGADE ROMANCE
1 . . . . 2.00
2 . . . . 3.50

RENEGADES OF JUSTICE
Blue Masque
1 I:Monarch,Bloodshadow 2.50
2 Madfire 2.50
3 Television Chronicles 2.50
4 R:Karen Styles 2.50

RENFIELD
Caliber
GN Conclusion of series 8.95

REPENTANCE
Advantage Graphics 1995
1 I:Repentance 1.95

REPLACEMENT GOD
Amaze Ink 1995
1 Child in The Land of Man 6.00
1a 2nd & 3rd printing 3.00
2 Eye of Knute 3.50
3 & 4 "Bravery" . . . . @3.50
5 thru 7 . . . . @3.00

RETALIATOR
Eclipse
1 I&O:Retaliator 2.50
2 O:Retaliator cont. 2.50

Retief #6 © Adventure Comics

RETIEF
Adventure 1990
1 thru 6 Keith Laumer adapt. . . @2.00
[New Series]
1 thru 6 . . . . @2.25

RETIEF OF THE CDT
1 Keith Laumer Novel Adapt. . . . 2.00
2 . . . . 2.00

RETIEF AND THE WARLORDS
Adventure Comics
1 Keith Laumer Novel Adapt. . . . 2.50
2 Haterakans 2.50
3 Retief Arrested for Treason . . . 2.50
4 Final Battle (last issue) 2.50

RETIEF: DIPLOMATIC IMMUNITY
Adventure Comics
1 Groaci Invasion. 2.50
2 Groaci story cont. 2.50

RETIEF: GARBAGE INVASION
Adventure Comics
1 . . . . 2.50

RETIEF: THE GIANT KILLER
Adventure Comics
1 V:Giant Dinasaur 2.50

RETIEF: GRIME & PUNISHMENT
Adventure Comics
1 Planet Slunch 2.50

RETRO-DEAD
Blazer Unlimited
1 Dimensional Rift 2.95

RETROGRADE
Eternity
1 thru 4 . . . . @1.95

RETURN OF HAPPY THE CLOWN
Caliber Press
1 & 2 V:Oni 2.95

RETURN OF THE SKYMAN
Ace Comics
1 SD 1.75

REVOLVER
Renegade
1 SD 1.70
2 thru 6 . . . . @1.70
Ann. #1 . . . . 2.00

REVOLVING DOORS
Blackthorne
1 . . . . 1.75
2 . . . . 1.75
3 . . . . 1.75
Graphic Novel 3.95

RHAJ
1 . . . . 2.00
2 . . . . 2.00

RHUDIPRRT PRINCE OF FUR
1 . . . . 2.00

RICK GEARY'S WONDERS & ODDITIES
1 . . . . 2.00

RICK RAYGUN
1 . . . . 2.00
2 thru 8 . . . . @1.75

RIO KID
Eternity
1 I:Rio Kid 2.50
2 V:Blow Torch Killer 2.50
3 . . . . 2.50

RION 2990
Rion
1 . . . . 2.75
2 . . . . 1.50

RIOT
Viz 1995
1 F:Riot,Axel 2.75
2 & 3 . . . . 2.75
4 final issue 2.75
TPB Rep. 15.95

RIOT ACT TWO
Viz Comics
1 thru 7 . . . . @2.95
TPB rep. 15.95

RIP IN TIME
Fantagor
1 RCo,Limited series 3.00

B & W PUB.

All comics prices listed are for *Near Mint* condition.

2 RCo 2.00
3 RCo 2.00
4 RCo 2.00
5 RCo,Last 2.00

RIPLASH: SWEET VENGEANCE
Pocket Change Comics
1 O:Riplash 2.95

RIPPER
1 thru 5 .... @2.50

RISING STARS
1 .... 1.95

RIVIT: COLD-BLOODED COMMANDO FROG
1 .... 1.75

ROACHMILL
1 .... 5.50
2 .... 3.00
3 .... 3.00
4 .... 3.00
See: Dark Horse

ROBIN HOOD
1 thru 4 .... @2.25

ROBIN RED
1 thru 3 .... @1.75

ROBO DEFENSE TEAM MECHA RIDER
Castle Comics
1 I:RDT Mecha Rider 2.95
2 Identity of Outlaw 2.95

R.O.B.O.T. BATTALION 2050
Eclipse
1 .... 2.00

ROBOT COMICS
1 .... 1.50

ROBO WARRIORS
CFW
1 thru 11 .... @1.95
Becomes:
KUNG FU WARRIORS

ROBOTECH
Academy Comics 1995
0 Robotech Information 2.50

ROBOTECH: ACADEMY BLUES
Academy Comics
0 Classroom Blues 3.50
1 F:Lisa 2.95
2 Bomb at the Academy 2.95
3 Roy's Drinking Buddy 2.95

ROBOTECH: AFTERMATH
Academy Comics
1 thru 10 R:Bruce Lewis ..... @2.95

11 Zentradi Traitor 2.95
12 and 13 .... @2.95

ROBOTECH: CLONE
Academy Comics
1 Dialect of Duality 2.95
2 V:Monte Yarrow 2.95
3 Ressurection 2.95
4 Ressurection 2.95
5 F:Bibi Ava 2.95

ROBOTECH: INVID WAR
Eternity 1993
1 No Man's Land 2.50
2 V:Defoliators 2.50
3 V:The Invid,Reflex Point ... 2.50
4 V:The Invid 2.50
5 Moonbase Aluce II 2.50
6 Moonbase-Zentraedi plot ... 2.50
7 Zentraedi plot contd. 2.50
8 A:Lancer 2.50
9 A:Johnathan Wolfe 2.50
10 .... 2.50
11 F:Rand 2.50
12 thru 15 .... 2.50

ROBOTECH: INVID WAR AFTERMATH
Eternity
1 thru 6 F:Rand 2.75

ROBOTECH: MACROSS TEMPEST
Academy Comics 1995
1 F:Roy Fokker, Tempest 2.95

ROBOTECH: MECH ANGEL
Academy Comics 1995
0 I:Mech Angel 2.95

ROBOTECH: MORDECAI
Academy Comics
1 .... 2.95
2 Annie meets her clone 2.95

ROBOTECH: RETURN TO MACROSS
Eternity 1993
1 thru 5 .... 2.50

ROBOTECH: RETURN TO MACROSS
Academy Comics
1 thru 17 Roy Fokker 2.75
18 F:The Faithful 2.75
19 F:Lisa 2.75
20 F:Lisa 2.75
21 V:Killer Robot 2.95
22 War of the Believers 2.95
23 War of the Believers,pt.2 .. 2.95
24 War of the Believers,pt.3 .. 2.95
25 War of the Believers,pt.4 ... 2.95
26 thru 30 .... @2.95
31 What is the Federalist Plan? .. 2.95
32 thru 34 .... @2.95
35 Typhoon threatens Macross
    Island 2.95
36 .... 2.95
37 round up of Federalist Agents . 2.95

Robotech: Return to Macross #20
© Academy

ROBOTECH ROMANCE
Academy Comics 1996
1 three stories 2.95

ROBOTECH: THE MISFITS
Academy Comics
1 Misfits from Sothern Cross
    transferred to Africa 2.95

ROBOTECH THE MOVIE
Academy Comics 1996
1 and 2 Benny R. Powell & Chi @2.95

ROBOTECH: THE THREADBARE HEART
Academy Comics
GN 9.95

ROBOTECH: UNTOLD STORIES
Eternity
1 .... 2.50

ROBOTECH: WARRIORS
Academy Comics
1 F:Breetai 2.95
2 F:Mirya 2.95
3 F:Mirya 2.95
GN The Terror Maker 9.95

ROBOTECH II THE SENTINELS
Eternity
1 .... 3.50
1a 2nd printing 1.95
2 .... 3.00
2a 2nd printing 1.95
3 .... 2.00
3a 2nd printing 1.95
4 thru 16 .... @1.95

Book 2
1 thru 12 .... @2.25
13 thru 20 .... @2.25
Wedding Special #1 .... 1.95

B & W PUB.

Wedding Special #2	1.95
Robotech II Handbook	2.50

Book Three

1 thru 8 V:Invid	2.50

Book Four
Academy Comics Dec. 1995

1 by Jason Waltrip	2.95
2 thru 13 F:Tesla	@2.75
14 V:Invid	2.75
15	2.75
16	2.75
17 V:Invid Mechas	2.75
18 F:"HIN"	2.95
19 V:Invid	2.95
20 Final Aplp. Invid Regiss	2.95
21 Predator and Prey	2.95
22 A Clockwork Planet	2.95

ROBOTECH II:
THE SENTINELS BOOK IV
Academy Comics

5 JWp,JWt,interior of Haydon IV	2.95
6 thru 8	@2.95
9 JWp,JWt,Breetai, Wolf & Vince return to Tirol	2.95
10 JWp,JWt,Ark Angel attacked by The Black Death Destroyers	2.95
11 JWp,JWt,Tirol, Wolff, Vince & Breetai on trial for treason	2.95
12 JWp,JWt,Dr. Lang exposes General Edwards' evil designs	2.95
Halloween Special JWp,JWt,	2.95

Robotech II: The Sentinels:
Cyberpirates #1 © Eternity

ROBOTECH II:
THE SENTINELS:
CYBERPIRATES
Eternity 1991

1 The Hard Wired Coffin	2.25
2 thru 4	@2.25

ROBOTECH: SENTINELS
STAR RUNNERS:
CARPENTER'S JOURNEY
Academy Comics 1996

1	2.95

ROBOTECH II:
THE SENTINELS:
THE MALCONTENT
UPRISING
Eternity

1 thru 12	@1.95

ROBOTECH WARRIORS:
THE TERROR MAKER
Academy Comics

GN	9.95

ROCITI'S REVENGE

1	1.95

ROCK & ROLL COMICS
Revolutionary

1 Guns & Roses	7.50
1a 2nd printing	3.50
1b 3rd printing	2.00
1c 4th-7th printing	2.00
2 Metalica	5.00
2a 2nd printing	3.00
2b 3rd-5th printing	2.00
3 Bon Jovi	3.50
4 Motley Crue	4.00
5 Def Leppard	2.50
6 RollingStones	5.00
6a 2nd-4th printing	2.00
7 The Who	3.50
7a 2nd-3rd printing	2.00
9 Kiss	8.00
9a 2nd-3rd Printing	2.00
10 Warrant/Whitesnake	2.50
10a 2nd Printing	2.00
11 Aerosmith	2.00
12 New Kids on Block	4.00
12a 2nd Printing	2.00
13 LedZeppelin	3.00
14 Sex Pistols	2.00

See Independent Color

ROCKET RANGERS
Adventure

1	2.95
2	2.95
3	2.95

ROCKHEADS

1	1.95

ROCKIN ROLLIN
MINER ANTS
Fate Comics

1 As seen in TMNT #40	2.25
1a Gold Variant copy	7.50
2 Elephant Hunting, A:Scorn,Blister	2.25
3 V:Scorn, Inc.,K.Eastman Ant pin-up	2.25
4 Animal Experiments,V:Loboto	2.25

ROCKOLA

1	1.50

ROLLING STONES: THE
SIXTIES
Personality

1 Regular Version	2.95
1a Deluxe Version,w/cards	6.95

ROSCOE THE DAWG

1 thru 4	@2.00

ROSE
Hero Graphics

1 From The Champions	3.50
2 A:Huntsman	3.50
3 thru 5	@2.95

ROSE AND GUNN
London Night

1	3.00
1a nude cover	6.00
1b signed	10.00
2	3.00
3	3.00

ROSE AND GUNN:
RECKONING
London Night

1 (of 2)	3.00

ROSE 'N GUNN
Bishop Pres 1995

1 Deadly Duo	5.00
2 V:Marilyn Monroe	3.00
3 Presidential Affairs	3.00
4 Without Each Other	3.00
5 V:Red	3.00
6 & 7	@3.00
Creator's Choice Rep. #1	2.95
Creator's Choice Rep. #2	2.95
Creator's Choice Rep. #3	2.95

ROTTWEILER

1	1.50
2	1.50

ROUGH RAIDERS

1	1.80
2	1.80
3	2.00

ROULETTE

1	2.50

ROVERS
Eternity

1 thru 7	@1.95

RUBES REVIVED
Fish Warp

1	2.00
2	2.00
3	2.00

RUK BUD WEBSTER
Fish Warp

1 thru 3	@1.70

SADE
Bishop Press

0 B:Adventures of Sade	3.00
1	3.00
1a variant	6.00
2	3.00

SADE
London Night

1	3.00

B & W PUB.

1a nude cover	10.00
2	3.00
3	3.00
4	3.00
5	3.00

SADE SPECIAL
Bishop Press

1 V:Razor	5.00
1a signed	7.00

SADE/ROSE AND GUNN
London Night Nov. 1996

1 Confederate Mist	3.00

SADE: TESTAMENTS OF PAIN
London Night Jan. 1997

1 (of 2)	3.00

SAGA OF THE MAN-ELF

1 thru 5	@2.25

SAGA OF THE VON ERICH WARRIORS

1	2.00

SAGE
Fantaco 1995

1 O:Sage	4.95

SAINT
Kick Ass Comics

1 & 2 V:Cerran	2.50

SALIMBA
Blackthorne

1	3.50

SAMURAI (1st series)

1	125.00
2	60.00
3	60.00
4	60.00
5	60.00

SAMURAI
Aircel

1 rare	9.00
1a 2nd printing	3.00
1b 3rd printing	2.00
2	6.00
2a 2nd printing	2.50
3	3.00
4	3.00
5 thru 12	@2.00
13 DK (1st art)	5.00
14 thru 16 DK	@4.00
17 thru 22	@2.00
[3rd series]	
#1 thru 3	@1.70
#4 thru 7	@1.95
Compilation Book	4.95

SAMURAI
Warp Graphics 1997

1	2.95
2	2.95
3	2.95

SAMURAI FUNNIES
Solson

1 thru 3	@2.00

SAMURAI PENGUIN
Solson

1	3.00
2 I:Dr.Radium	2.00
3	2.00
4	1.50
5 FC	1.50
6 color	2.25
7	2.25
8	1.75
9	1.75

SAMURAI 7
Gauntlet Comics

1 I: Samurai 7	2.50

SAMURAI, SON OF DEATH
Eclipse

1	3.95
1a 2nd printing	3.95

SANCTION 7

1	1.95
2	1.95

SANCTUARY
Viz

1 World of Yakuza	4.95
2 thru 4	@4.95
5 thru 9	@4.95
[Part Five] 1996	
7 thru 13 by Sho Fumimura & Ryoichi Ikegami	@3.50
GN rep. ½ of part 4 & ½ part 5	16.95
GN Vol. 5	17.95
GN Vol. 6	17.95

SANTA CLAWS
Eternity

1 'Deck the Mall with Blood and Corpses'	2.95

SAVAGE HENRY
Vortex

1 thru 13	@1.75
Rip Off Press	
14 thru 15	@2.00
16 thru 24	@2.50

SAVIOR

1 thru 5	@1.95

SAX AND COMPANY

1	1.50
2	1.50

SCARAMOUCH
Innovation

1	2.50

SCARLET IN GASLIGHT

1 A:SherlockHolmes	4.00
2	3.00
3	2.50
4	2.50

SCARLET KISS: THE VAMPIRE

1	2.95

SCARLET SCORPION/ DARKSIDE
AC Comics

1 & 2 Flipbooks	3.50

SCARLET THUNDER
Amaze Ink

1 thru 3	@2.50

SCIMIDAR
Eternity

1	4.25
1a 2nd Printing	2.50
2 and 3	@3.00
4 HotCover	3.50
4A MildCover	3.00

SCORN
SCC Entertainment 1996

Lingerie Spec.	2.95
Lingerie Spec. deluxe	9.95

SCORN: DEADLY REBELLION
SCC Entertainment

0	3.95
0a Birthday Suit cover	9.95
0b Celebrity photo cover	9.95

SCORN: FRACTURED
SCC Entertainment 1997

1 Fear cover	3.95
1 Rage cover	3.95
1a nude cover	9.95

SCORN: HEATWAVE
SCC Entertainment Jan. 1997

1 by Chris Crosby & Mike Morales	3.95
1a nude cover	9.95

SCORN: HOSTAGE
SCC Entertainment

1	3.95
1a nude cover	9.95

SCORN: NAKED TRUTH
SCC Entertainment April 1997

1	3.95
1a nude cover	9.95

SCOUT HANDBOOK
Eclipse

1	1.75

SCRATCH
Outside

1	3.00
2	2.00
3	1.75
4	1.75

SCREENPLAY

1	1.75
2 and 3	@1.95

B & W PUB.

SCRIMIDAR
CFD Productions 1995
1 I:Bloody Mary 2.75

SCROG SPECIAL
1 . . . . 2.50

SCUD: DISPOSABLE ASSASSIN
Fireman Press
1 I:Scud 15.00
1a 3rd printing 3.50
2 . . . . 12.00
3 . . . . 10.00
4 thru 6 F:Scud . . . . @6.00
7 Lupine Thoughts 5.00
8 Scud Looks for His Arm 5.00
9 Scud Looks for His Arm 5.00
10 thru 16 by Rob Schrab . . . . @3.50
TPB Rep.#1–#4 . . . . 12.95
TPB Programmed for Damage,
rep.#5–#9 . . . . 14.95

SEARCHERS
Caliber "New Worlds"
1A Red cover, signed 3.00
1B Blue cover, signed 3.00
3 . . . . 3.00
4 . . . . 3.00
5 flip book with Boston Bombers 3.00

SEARCHERS: APOSTLE OF MERCY
Caliber 1997
1 (of 2) 3.95
2 . . . . 3.95
Vol 2?
1 (of 4) 2.95
2 . . . . 2.95
3 (of 3) 48pg 3.95

SECRET DOORS
1 . . . . 6.00
1a 2nd printing 2.00

SECRET FILES
Angel Entertainment 1996
0 gold edition 8.00
0 nude cover 10.00
0 commemorative edition 2.95
0 nude commemorative edition . . 5.00
1 . . . . 2.95
1 spooky silver foil edition 5.95
1 nude signed 10.00
2 . . . . .2.95
2 deluxe 5.95
2 nude cover A 10.00
2 nude cover B 10.00

SECRET FILES: THE STRANGE CASE
Angel Entertainment 1996
0 by David Campitti & Al Rio . . . 2.95
0 Virgin nude cover 5.00
0 Slimy Wet Twins nude cover . . 7.00
0 nude manga cover 5.00
0 nude platinum cover 15.00
1 by David Campitti & Al Rio . . . 2.95
1 Virgin nude cover 5.00
1 nude manga cover 5.00
1 nude platinum cover 15.00

SECTION 8
Noir Press 1995
1 Anthology series 2.50
2 thru 6 . . . . @2.50
7 "Retribution," pt.1 . . . . 2.50
8 "Retribution," pt.2 . . . . 2.50
9 . . . . 2.50
10 "Chance" 2.50

SENTINEL
1 . . . . 1.95
2 thru 4 . . . . @1.95

SERAPHIN
Newcomers Press 1995
1 I:Roy Torres 2.95

SERIUS BOUNTY HUNTER
1 thru 4 . . . . @1.75

SERPENT RISING
Gauntlet Comics
1 . . . . 2.95

SHADES OF GRAY COMICS AND STORIES
Caliber Tapestry 1996
1 . . . . 2.95
2 . . . . 2.95
3 . . . . 2.95
4 . . . . 2.95
Super Summer Spec. rep. 3.95

SHADOWBLADE
1 . . . . 2.50
2 . . . . 2.50
3 . . . . 1.95
4 . . . . 1.95

SHADOW CROSS
Darkside Comics 1995
1 I:Shadow Cross 4.95
2 thru 7 . . . . @2.50

SHADOWLAND
1 . . . . 2.25
2 . . . . 2.25

SHADOWALKER
Aircel
1 thru 4 . . . . @1.70

SHADOW LORD
1 . . . . 1.50

SHADOWMEN
1 . . . . 2.25

SHADOW OF THE GROUND
1 Groundhog 1.25

SHADOWS FROM THE GRAVE
1 . . . . 2.00
2 . . . . 2.00

SHADOW SLASHER
Pocket Change Comics
1 I:Shadow Slasher 2.50
2 V:Riplash 2.50
3 F:Matt Baker 2.50
4 Evolution 2.50
5 F:Riplash 2.50
6 Next Victim 2.50
7 What Can Kill Him 2.50
8 . . . . 2.50
9 final issue 2.50

SHADOW SLAYER
0 . . . . 1.95

SHADOW WARRIOR
1 . . . . 1.60
2 . . . . 1.60

SHALOMAN
1 thru 5 . . . . @1.75

SHANDA [THE PANDA]
Antarctic Press
1 thru 11 . . . . @2.75
12 thru 14 . . . . @2.95

Med Systems
15 and 16 . . . . @1.95
Vision Comics
17 by Mike Curtis & Michelle Light 1.95
18 "Rocky Horror Picture Show" . 1.95
19 "Shine on Me, Cajun Moon" . . 2.50

SHANGHAIED
Eternity
1 . . . . 1.80
2 . . . . 1.80
3 . . . . 1.95
4 . . . . 1.95

SHAOLIN: 2000
1 . . . . 1.50

SHARDS
Acension Comics
1 I:Silver, Raptor, RIpple 2.50
2 F:Anomoly 2.50

SHATTERED EARTH
Eternity
1 thru 9 . . . . @1.95

SHATTERPOINT
Eternity
1 thru 4 Broid miniseries . . . . @2.25

SHE-CAT
AC Comics
1 thru 4 . . . . @2.50

SHE-DEVILS ON WHEELS
Aircel
1 thru 3 . . . . 2.95

SHIELA TRENT VAMPIRE HUNTER
Draculina Publishing
1 O:Sheild Trent 2.50

B & W PUB.

SHERLOCK HOLMES
Eternity
1 thru 22 . . . . @1.95

SHERLOCK HOLMES CASEBOOK
Eternity
1 and 2 . . . . @2.25

SHERLOCK HOLMES: CHRONICLES OF CRIME AND MYSTERY
Northstar
1 'The Speckled Band' 2.25

SHERLOCK HOLMES OF THE '30's
Eternity
1 thru 7 . . . . @2.95

SHERLOCK HOLMES: RETURN OF THE DEVIL
Adventure
1 V:Moriarty 2.50
2 V:Moriarty 2.50

SHERLOCK JUNIOR
Eternity
1 Rep.NewspaperStrips 1.95
2 Rep.NewspaperStrips 1.95
3 Rep.NewspaperStrips 1.95

SHI: KAIDAN
Crusade Entertainment
1 macabre 2.95

SHIP OF FOOLS
Caliber 1996
1 signed edition 3.00
2 "Dante's Compass" 3.00
3 The Great Escape begins 3.00
4 MiA 3.00
5 MiA 3.00
Spec. #1, Bon Voyage, Go to Hell,
  Mama Hades 3.95
continued: See Image Comics

SHOCK THE MONKEY
Millenium
1 & 2 Entering the Psychotic Mind 3.95

SHOCKWAVES
Knight Press
1 . . . . 2.95

SHRED
CFW
1 thru 10 . . . . @2.25

SHRIEK
1 . . . . 4.95
2 . . . . 4.95
3 . . . . 7.95

SHRIKE
1 thru 6 . . . . @1.50

SHURIKEN
Victory 1986
1 Reggi Byers 6.00
1a 2nd printing 1.50
2 . . . . 3.00
3 . . . . 2.00
4 . . . . 1.75
5 thru 13 . . . . @1.50
Graphic Nov. Reggie Byers . . . 8.00

SHURIKEN
Eternity
1 Shuriken vs. Slate 2.50
2 Neutralizer, Meguomo 2.50
3 R:Slate 2.50
4 Morgan's Bodyguard Serrate . . 2.50
5 Slate as Shuriken & Megumo . 2.50
6 Hunt for Bionauts, final issue . . 2.50

SHURIKEN: COLD STEEL
1 . . . . 1.95
2 . . . . 1.95
3 thru 6 . . . . @1.95

SHURIKEN TEAM-UP
1 thru 3 . . . . @1.95

SIAMESE TWIN COMICS
1 . . . . 2.50

SIDESHOW
7 . . . . 3.50

SIEGEL & SHUSTER
2 . . . . 1.70

SILBUSTER
Antarctic Press
1 thru 10 . . . . 3.50
11 I:Kizuki Sister 3.50
12 thru 14 . . . . @3.50
15 . . . . 3.95
16 thru 19 . . . . @3.50
TPB Rep. #1-#4 . . . . 10.95
TPB Vol.2 . . . . 10.95

Silver Storm #4 © Aircel

SILENT INVASION
Renegade
1 . . . . 4.00
2 thru 12, final issue . . . . @3.00

SILENT INVASION
Caliber
4 Red Shadows, pt.1 . . . . 3.00
5 Red Shadows, pt.2 . . . . 3.00

SILVER FAWN
1 . . . . 1.95

SILVER STORM
Aircel 1990
1 thru 4 . . . . 2.25

SILVER WING
1 . . . . 1.00

SIMON/KIRBY READER
1 . . . . 1.75

SINBAD
1 . . . . 2.25
2 . . . . 2.25
3 . . . . 2.25
4 . . . . 2.25

SINBAD: HOUSE OF GOD
Adventure Comics
1 Caliph's Wife Kidnapped 2.50
2 Magical Genie 2.50
3 Escape From Madhi 2.50
4 A:Genie 2.50

SINNAMON
Catfish Comics 1995
1 remastered 2.75
1a remastered deluxe 3.75
6 thru 8 . . . . @2.75
Mythic Comics
9 "Ashes to Ashes—The Pyre-Anna
  Saga," pt.2 . . . . 2.75
10 "Twas Beauty Bashed The
  Beast" 2.75
11 . . . . 2.75
Archives #1 . . . . 2.75

SINNER
4 . . . . 2.75
5 . . . . 2.95
6 . . . . 2.95

SISTER ARMAGEDDON
Dramenon Studios
1 & 2 Nun with a Gun 2.50
3 Mother Superior 2.50
4 V:Apoligon 2.95

SKELETON KEY
Amaze Ink 1995
1 1 I:Skeleton Key 1.50
1 2nd printing 1.75
2 F:Tansin 1.50
3 V:Japanese Burglar 1.50
4 V:Closet Monster 1.50
5 thru 10 . . . . @1.75
11 . . . . 1.75

12 .... 1.75
14 by Andi Watson 1.75
15 "The Celestial Calendar" 1.75
16 thru 24 .... @1.75

SKIN 13
Entity/Parody 1995
1/2a Grungie/Spider-Man 2.50
1/2b Heavy Metal 2.50
1/2c Gen-Et Jackson 2.50

SKROG
Comico
1 .... 3.00

SKULL
3 No price on cover 3.50

SKUNK, THE
Entity Comics April 1997
#Uno 2.75
5 BMs 2.75
6 BMs 2.75
Collection #1 rep. #1–#3 ..... 4.95
Collection #1a signed & numbered 9.95
Collection #2 rep. #4–#6 .... 4.95

SKUNK/FOODANG
FOODANG/SKUNK
Entity Comics
Spec. 1 BMs, BMs(c) 2.75
Spec. 1a BMs, Mike Duggan(c) .. 2.75

SKYNN & BONES: DEADLY ANGELS
Brainstorm April 1996
1 .... 2.95

SKYNN & BONES: FLESH FOR FANTASY
Brainstorm 1997
1 erotic missions 2.95
1a nude cover 2.95
2 erotic missions 2.95
2a nude cover 2.95

SLACK
Legacy Comics
1 Slacker Anthology 2.50
2 Loser 2.50

SLAUGHTERHOUSE
Caliber
1 Bizarre medical Operations ... 2.95
2 House of Death 2.95
3 House of Death 2.95
4 Dead Killer vs. Mosaic 2.95

SLAUGHTERMAN
1 and 2 .... @4.00

SLAVE GIRL
1 .... 2.25

SMALL PRESS SWIMSUIT SPECTACULAR
Allied Press
1 Supports Am. Cancer Assn. 2.95

SNAKE
Special Studio
1 .... 3.50

SNARF
Kitchen Sink
1 thru 10 .... @2.00
10 (c)BE 2.00
11 thru 13 .... @2.00

SNARL
1 and 3 .... @2.50

SNOWMAN
Hall of Heroes 1996
1 .... 10.00
1a variant (c) 25.00
1 3rd printing 2.75
1 San Diego Con. ed. 5.00
2 .... 7.00
2a 2nd printing 2.75
2b variant (c) 5.00
3 .... 3.75
3a variant (c) 6.00

SNOWMAN: 1994
Entity Oct. 1996
1 flip cover #0, by Matt Martin,
  O:Snowman 2.75
1 signed, numbered 10.00
3 .... 2.75
3 deluxe, variant, foil cover 3.50
4 .... 2.75
4 deluxe, variant, foil cover 3.50

SOB: SPECIAL OPERATIONS BRANCH
Promethean Studios 1994
1 I:SOB 2.50

SOCKETEER
Kardia
Rocketeer parody 2.25

SOLDIERS OF FORTUNE
1 .... 1.95

SOLD OUT
Fantagor
1 .... 1.75
2 .... 1.75

SOLO EX-MUTANTS
Eternity
1 thru 6 .... @1.95

SOLSON PREVIEW
Solson
1 .... 2.00

SONG OF THE SIRENS
Millennium
Earth 2.95
Earth, signed print edition 6.95
Fire 2.95
Fire, signed print edition 9.95
Wind 2.95
Wind collectors edition 4.95

SOUL
Samson Comics
1 thru 3 F:Sabbeth .... @2.50

SOULFIRE
Aircel
1 mini-series 1.70
2 .... 1.70
3 .... 1.70

Soulsearchers and Co. #6 © Claypool

SOULSEARCHERS AND CO.
Claypool 1993–95
1 thru 10 Peter David(s) ..... @3.00
11 thru 20 .... @2.50
21 thru 24 .... @2.50
TPB 12.95

SOUTHERN KNIGHTS
1 See Crusaders
2 .... 8.00
3 and 4 .... @5.00
5 thru 7 .... @4.00
Fictioneer
8 thru 11 .... @2.50
12 thru 33 .... @2.00
34 .... 2.25
35 The Morrigan Wars Pt.#2 .... 3.50
36 Morrigan Wars Pt.#5 .... 3.50
Ann. #1 .... 2.50
DreadHalloweenSpec #1 ...... 2.25
Primer #1 .... 2.25

SOUTHER SQUADRON
Aircel
1 .... 2.25
2 .... 2.25
3 .... 2.25
4 .... 2.25

SOUTHERN SQUADRON
Eternity
1 I:SQUAD 2.50
2 .... 2.25
3 .... 2.25
4 .... 2.25

SOUTHERN SQUADRON FREEDOM OF INFO. ACT.
Eternity

1 F.F.#1 Parody/Tribute cov.		2.50
2 A:Waitangi Rangers		2.50
3		2.50

SPACE ARK
Apple

1		2.75
2		2.50
3		1.75
4		1.75
5		1.75

SPACE BEAVER
Ten-Buck Comics

1		2.50
2		1.50
3 O&I:Stinger		1.50
4 A:Stinger		1.50
5		1.50
6 O:Rodent		1.50
7 thru 12		@1.50

SPACED

1 I:Zip; 800 printed		40.00
2		25.00
3 I:Dark Teddy		15.00
4		15.00
5 and 6		@5.00
7 and 8		@2.00

Eclipse

9		1.75
10		1.75
11 thru 13		@1.50

SPACE GUYS

1		2.25

SPACE PATROL
Adventure

1 thru 3		2.50

SPACE 34-24-34

1		4.50

SPACE USAGI
Mirage Studios

1 Stan Sakai,Future Usagi		2.00
2 Stan Sakai,Future Usagi		2.00
3 Stan Sakai,Future Usagi		2.00

SPACE WOLF
Antarctic Press

1 From Albedo,by Dan Flahive		2.50

SPARKPLUG
Hero Graphics

1 From League of Champions		2.95

SPARKPLUG SPECIAL
Heroic Publishing

1 V:Overman		2.50

SPARROW
Millenium

1 I:Sparrow		2.95
2		2.95
3 Valley of Fire		2.50

SPATTER

1		1.95
2		1.95
3		1.60
4		2.00

SPEED RACER

1		3.00
1a 2nd Printing		1.50

SPENCER SPOOK
A.C.E. Comics

1		1.95
2		1.95
3 thru 8		@1.75

SPICY TALES

1 thru 13		@1.95
14 thru 20		@2.25
Special #2		2.25

SPIDER KISS

1 Harlan Ellison		3.95

SPINELESS MAN
Parody Press

1 Spider-Man 2099 spoof		2.50

SPIRAL CAGE
Renegade

Special		3.00

SPIRIT, THE
Kitchen Sink

Note: #1 to #11 are in color

12 thru 86 WE,rep (1986–92)		@2.00

SPIRIT OF THE WIND

1		2.00

THE SPIRIT: ORIGIN YEARS
Kitchen Sink

1 I:Denny Colt,Ebony White		2.95
2 I:Commissioner&Ellen Dolan		2.95
3 WE,Palyachi,The Killer Clown		2.95
4 WE,Orphans,Orang t/Ape Man		2.95
5 WE		2.95
6 WE,Kiss of Death		2.95
7 thru 8 WE		2.95

SPIRIT OF THE DRAGON
Double Edge

0 Dragon Scheme		.75

SPIRITS
Mindwalker 1995

1 thru 3 Silver City		2.95
4 Caleb Escapes Zeus		2.95

SPITTING IMAGE
Eclipse

1 Marvel & Image parody		2.50

SPLAT

1 thru 4		@1.75

SPOTLIGHT

1		1.50

STAINLESS STEEL ARMIDILLO
Antartic Press

1 I:Saisni, Tania Badan		2.95
2 V:Mirage		2.95
3 V:Mirage		2.95
4 Spirit of Gaia		2.95
5 V:Giant		2.95
6 finale		2.95

STANLEY

1		1.50

STAR BLEECH THE GENERATION GAP
Parody Press

1 Parody		3.95

STARCHILD
Taliesin Press 1992–97

0		35.00
1		50.00
1a 2nd printing		4.00
2		50.00
2a 2nd printing		4.00
3		15.00
4		7.00
5		5.00
6		5.00
7		5.00
8		5.00
9		5.00
10 thru 13		5.00
14		3.00

STARGATE: ONE NATION UNDER RA
Entity March 1997

1		2.75
1a deluxe		3.50

STARGATE: REBELLION
Entity 1997

1 (of 3) from novel, sequel to movie		2.75
1 deluxe		3.50
2		2.75
2 deluxe		3.50
3 (of 3)		2.75
3 foil cover		3.50

STARGATE: UNDERWORLD
Entity April 1997

1		2.75
1a deluxe		3.50

STARGATORS

1		2.50
2		2.50
3		2.50

STAR JAM COMICS
Revolutionary

1 F:Hammer		2.50

STARJONGLEUR COLLECTION

1		2.50
2		2.50
3		2.50

B & W PUB.

STAR BIKERS
1	3.95
Special	2.00

STARK FUTURE
Aircel
1	2.50
2 thru 7	@1.75
8	2.00
9 thru 14	@1.70

STAR RANGERS
1 thru 3	@3.00
4	1.95
BOOK II
1	1.95
2	1.95

STAR REACH
Taliesin Press
1 HC,I:CodyStarbuck	8.00
2 DG,JSn	2.00
3 FB	2.00
4 HC	2.00
5 JSon	2.00
6 GD,Elric	2.00
7 DS	2.00
8 CR,KSy	2.00
9 KSy	2.00
10 KSy	2.00
11 GD	2.00
12 MN,SL	2.00
13 SL,KSy	2.00
14	2.00
15	2.00
16	2.00
17	2.00
18	2.00

STAR WOLF CONQUEROR
1	2.00
2	2.00

STARLIGHT
1	1.95
2	1.95

STARLIGHT AGENCY
Antartic Press
1 I:Starlight Agency	1.95
2 Anderson Kidnapped	1.95
3	1.50

STARLIGHT SQUADRON
Blackthorne
1	2.00

STATIC
1 SD	1.50
2 SD	1.50
3 SD	1.50

STEALTH FORCE
1 thru 8	@.95

STEALTH SQUAD
Petra Comics
0 O:Stealth Squad	2.50
1 I:Stealth Squad	2.50
2 I:New Member	2.50
Volume II	

1 F:Solar Blade	2.50
2 American Ranger Vs.Jericho	2.50

STECH
1 and 2	@1.50

STEEL DRAGON STORIES
Steel Dragon
1	1.50

STEELE DESTINES
Nightscapes
1 & 2 I:One Eyed Stranger	2.95
3 Kidnapped by Aliens	2.95

STEPHEN DARKLORD
1 thru 3	@1.75

STERN WHEELER
Spotlight
1 JA	1.75

STEVE CANYON
Kitchen Sink
1 thru 14	@5.00
3-D Spec. #1	6.00

STEVEN
1	4.00
1a 2ndPrinting	2.95
2	4.00
3	2.95
4 and 5	@3.50

STICKBOY
Revolutionary
1	2.00
2 thru 5	@2.50

STIG'S INFERNO
Vortex
1	6.00
2	3.50
3	3.00
4	3.00
5	2.00
Eclipse
6	1.75
7	1.75

STING
Artline
1	2.50

STINZ
Fantagraphics
1	4.00
2	4.00
3	4.00
4	4.00
[2nd series]
Brave New Words
1 thru 3	2.50

STORMBRINGER
Taliesin Press
1 thru 3	@2.00

STORMWATCHER
Eclipse
1 thru 4	@2.00

STRAND, THE
Trident
1	2.50

STRANGE BEHAVIOR
Twilite Tone Press
1 LSn,MBr,Short Stories	2.95

STRANGE BREW
Aardvark–Vanaheim
1	5.00

STRANGEHAVEN
Abiogenesis Press
1 Surrealistic Comic	2.95
2 Secret Brotherhood	2.95
3 thru 7 by Gary Spencer Millidge	@2.95

Strange Sports Stories #1
© Adventure

STRANGE SPORTS STORIES
Adventure 1992
1 w/2 card strip	2.50
2 The Pick-Up Game,w/cards	2.50
3 Spinning Wheels,w/cards	2.50
4 thru 6 w/cards	@2.50

STRANGE WORLDS
1	3.95
2 thru 4	@3.95

STRANGES IN PARADISE
Antarctic Press 1993–94
1 by Terry Moore, I:Katchoo	75.00
1a 2nd printing	75.00
2	50.00
3	38.00
Abstract Studio
1 TMr, Gold Logo edition	25.00
1a 2nd printing	5.00
2 and 3, Gold Logo edition	@15.00

B & W PUB.

All comics prices listed are for *Near Mint* condition.

4 . . . . 7.00
5 R:Mrs. Parker 7.00
6 . . . . 5.00
7 Darcey Uses Francine 5.00
8 thru 11 TMr . . . . @4.00

STRANGELOVE
Entity Comics 1995
1 I:Strangelove 2.50
2 V:Hyper Bullies 2.50
3 I:Bogie 2.50

STRATA
Renegade
1 . . . . 3.00
2 . . . . 2.50
3 . . . . 1.70
4 . . . . 1.70
5 . . . . 1.70
6 . . . . 2.00

STRAW MEN
1 thru 5 . . . . @1.95
6 thru 8 . . . . @2.25

STRAY BULLETS
El Capitan
1 . . . . 22.00
1a 2nd & 3rd printing 4.00
2 . . . . 17.00
2a 2nd printing 3.50
3 . . . . 15.00
4 . . . . 15.00
5 Dysfunctional Family 5.00
6 F:Amy Racecar 4.50
7 Virginias Freedom 4.50
8 DL,"Lucky to Have Her" 3.00
9 DL,"26 Guys Named Nick" 3.00
10 DL,"Here Comes the Circus" . . 3.00
11 DL,"How to Cheer Up Your Best
    Friend" 3.00
12 DL 3.00
13 DL "Selling Candy" 2.95
14 DL, 48pg 3.50

STREET FIGHTER
Ocean Comics
1 thru 4 limited series . . . . . . @1.75

STREET HEROES 2005
Eternity
1 thru 3 . . . . @1.95

STREET MUSIC
Fantagraphics
1 . . . . 2.75
2 . . . . 2.75
3 . . . . 2.95
4 . . . . 2.95
5 . . . . 2.50
6 . . . . 3.95

STREET POET RAY
Fantagraphics
1 . . . . 2.50
2 . . . . 2.00
3 . . . . 2.95
4 . . . . 2.95

STREET WOLF
1 limited series 2.00

2 and 3 . . . . @2.00
Graphic Novel 6.95

STRIKER: SECRET OF THE BERSERKER
Viz
1 & 2 V:The Berserker 2.75
3 F:Yu and Maia 2.75

STRIKER: THE ARMORED WARRIOR
Viz
1 Overture 2.75
2 V:Child Esper 2.75
3 Professor taken hostage 2.75

STYGMATA YEARBOOK
Entity
1 V:The Rodent 2.95
TPB Dragon Prophet 6.95

SUBTLE VIOLENTS
CFD Productions 1991
1 Linsner (c&a) 35.00
1a San Diego Con 100.00

SUBURBAN HIGH LIFE
1 thru 5 . . . . @1.75

SUBURBAN NIGHTMARES
1 thru 4 . . . . @2.00

SUGAR RAY FINHEAD
Wolf Press
1 I&O Sugar Ray Finhead 2.50
2 I:Bessie & Big-Foot Benny the Pit
   Bull Man 2.95
3 thru 7 Mardi Gras . . . . @2.95

SULTON
1 thru 3 . . . . @1.50

SULTRY TEENAGE SUPER-FOXES
Solson
1 thru 4 RB,Woj . . . . @2.00

SUNRISE
1 thru 4 . . . . @1.95

SUPERSWINE
Caliber
1 Parody, I:Superswine 2.50

SURF NEMO
Star Tiger 1995
1 Clone Wars 2.95

SURVIVALIST CHRONICLES
Survival Art
1 . . . . 6.50
2 . . . . 6.50
3 I:Bessie & Big Foot Benny 1.95

SWAN
Little Idylls
1 thru 3 Ghost of Lord Kaaren . . 2.95

4 V:Slake 2.95

SWEET CHILE BATTLE BOOK
Advantage Graphics 1995
1 I:Tasha Radcliffe 2.50

SWEET LUCY
Brainstorm Comics
1 w/4 cards 2.50
2 . . . . 2.50

SWERVE
Amaze Ink Dec. 1995
1 thru 3 by Kyle Hunter . . . . . @1.75

SWIFTSURE
Harrier Comics
1 . . . . 2.00
2 . . . . 2.00
3 thru 8 . . . . @1.75
9 . . . . 9.00
9a 2nd printing 1.75
10 . . . . 1.75
11 . . . . 1.95

SWORD OF VALOR
A Plus Comics
1 JAp,rep.Thane of Bagarth 2.50
2 JAp/MK rep 2.50

SWORDS AND SCIENCE
Pyramid
1 . . . . 1.70
2 . . . . 1.70
3 . . . . 1.70

SWORDS OF CEREBUS
Aardvark–Vanaheim
1 rep. Cerebus 1-4 . . . . 18.00
1a reprint editions 10.00
2 rep. Cerebus 5-8 . . . . 12.00
2a reprint editions 8.00
3 rep. Cerebus 9-12 . . . . 12.00
3a reprint editions 8.00
4 rep. Cerebus 13-16 . . . . 12.00
4a reprint editions 8.00
5 rep. Cerebus 17-20 . . . . 12.00
5a reprint editions 8.00
6 rep. Cerebus 21-25 . . . . 12.00
6a reprint editions 8.00

SWORDS OF SHAR-PAI
Caliber
1 Mutant Ninja Dog 2.50
2 Shar-Pei 2.50
3 Final issue 2.50

SWORDS OF VALORS: ROBIN HOOD
A Plus Comics
1 rep. of Charlton comics 2.50

SYSTEM SEVEN
Arrow
1 thru 4 . . . . @1.50

T-BIRD CHRONICLES
1 thru 3 . . . . @1.50

B & W PUB.

T-MINUS-ONE
1	....	2.00
2	....	2.00

TAKEN UNDER COMPENDIUM
Caliber
1 rep. Cal Presents #19-#22	...	2.95

TALES FROM DIMENSION X
Edge Publishing 1995
1 Dinosaur Mansion	....	3.95

TALES FROM THE ANIVERSE
Arrow
1 7,400 printed	....	10.00
2	....	4.00
3 10,000 printed	....	2.50
4	....	2.50

[2nd series]
Massive Comics Group
1 thru 3	....	1.50

TALES FROM THE HEART
1 thru 5	....	@1.75
6	....	1.95
7	....	1.95

TALES OF BEANWORLD
Eclipse
1	....	10.00
2	....	4.00
3	....	2.50
4 I:Beanish	....	1.50
5 thru 20	....	@2.00

TALE OF MYA ROM
Aircel
1	....	1.70

TALES OF PIRACY SAVING GRACE
1	....	1.95

TALES OF TEENAGE MUTANT NINJA TURTLES
1	....	13.00
1B 2nd printing	....	3.00
2	....	8.00
3	....	5.00
4	....	5.00
5	....	5.00
6 thru 9	....	@4.00

TALES OF THE FEHNRIK
Antarctic Press
1 I:Lady Zeista	....	2.95

TALES OF THE JACKALOPE
BF
1	....	5.00
2	....	3.00
3 and 4	....	@2.50
5 thru 9	....	@2.00

TALES OF THE NINJA WARRIORS
CFW
1 thru 14	....	@1.95
15 thru 19	....	@2.25

TALES OF THE PLAGUE
Eclipse
1 RCo	....	4.00

TALES THE STRIPED MAN KNEW
1 thru 4	....	@1.50

TALES TOO TERRIBLE TO TELL
1 thru 6 Pre-code horror stories	@3.50

TALONZ
1 and 2	....	@1.75

TAMMAS
1	....	1.50

TANTALIZING STORIES
Tundra
1 F:Frank & Montgomery Wart	..	2.25
2 Frank & Mont.stories cont.	....	2.25

TAOLAND
Sunitek
1 V:The Crocodile Warlord	.....	1.50
2 & 3 I:New Enemy	....	3.25

TASK FORCE ALPHA
Academy Comics
1 I:Task Force Alpha	....	3.50

TATTOOMAN SPECIAL
Fantagraphics
1	....	2.75

TEAM NIPPON
Aircel
1 thru 7	....	@1.95

TECHNOPHILIA
Brainstorm Comics
1 w/4 cards	....	2.50

TEDDY & JOE
1	....	1.50
2	....	1.75

TEENAGE MUTANT NINJA TURTLES*
Mirage Studios
Counterfeits Exist - Beware
1 I:Turtles	....	350.00
1a 2nd printing	....	50.00
1b 3rd printing	....	25.00
1c 4th printing	....	15.00
1d 5th printing	....	4.00
2	....	80.00
2a 2nd printing	....	18.00
2b 3rd printing	....	4.00
3	....	30.00
3a 2nd printing	....	3.50

Teenage Mutant Ninja Turtles #38
© Mirage Studios

3b Special printing,rare	......	75.00
4	....	15.00
4a 2nd printing	....	3.50
5 A:Fugitoid	....	12.00
5a 2nd printing	....	3.50
6 A:Fugitoid	....	11.00
6a 2nd printing	....	2.50
7 A:Fugitoid	....	13.00
7a 2nd printing	....	2.50
8 A:Cerebus	....	10.00
9	....	5.50
10 V:Shredder	....	5.50
11 A:Casey Jones	....	5.50
12 thru 18	....	@5.50
19 Return to NY	....	5.00
20 Return to NY	....	5.00
21 Return to NY,D:Shredder	....	5.00
22 thru 32	....	@5.00
33 color, Corben	....	3.25
34 Toytle Anxiety	....	3.25
35 Souls Withering	....	3.25
36 Souls Wake	....	3.25
37 Twilight of the Rings	......	3.25
38 Spaced Out Pt.1, A:President Bush		3.25
39 Spaced Out Pt.2	....	3.25
40 Spaced Out concl.,I:Rockin' Rollin' Miner Ants (B.U. story)	.	2.00
41 Turtle Dreams issue	....	2.00
42 Juliets Revenge	....	2.00
43 Halls of Lost Legends	......	2.00
44 V:Ninjas	....	2.00
45 A:Leatherhead	....	2.00
46 V:Samurai Dinosaur	......	2.00
47 Space Usagi	....	2.00
48 Shades of Grey Part 1	......	2.00
49 Shades of Grey Part 2	......	2.00
50 Eastman/Laird,new direction, inc.TM,EL,WS pin-ups	......	2.00
51 City at War #2	....	2.00
52 City at War #3	....	2.25
53 City at War #4	....	2.25
54 City at War #5	....	2.25
55 thru 65	....	@2.25
1990 Movie adaptation	....	6.50
Spec. The Haunted Pizza	......	2.25

Volume 2
1 thru 8	....	2.75

All comics prices listed are for *Near Mint* condition.   CVA Page 623

B & W PUB.

9 V:Baxter Bot 2.75
10 Mr. Braunze 2.75
11 F:Raphael 2.75
12 V:DARPA 2.75
13 J:Triceraton 2.75

TEENAGE MUTANT NINJA TURTLES TRAINING MANUAL
1 . . . . 5.00
2 thru 5 . . . . @3.00

TEKQ
Caliber
1 . . . . 2.95

TELL-TALE HEART & OTHER STORIES
1 . . . . 2.50

TEMPEST COMICS PRESENTS
Academy Comics
1 I:Steeple, Nemesis 2.50

TERROR ON THE PLANET OF THE APES
Adventure Comics
1 MP,collectors edition 2.50
2 MP, the Forbidden Zone 2.50
2 and 3 . . . . @2.50

TERROR TALES
Eternity
1 Short stories 2.50

TEX BENSON
Metro Comics
1 thru 3 . . . . @2.00

TEYKWA
1 . . . . 1.75

39 SCREAMS
1 thru 6 . . . . @2.00

THEY WERE 11
Viz
1 Galactic University 2.75
2 The Accident 2.75
3 Virus 2.75
4 V:Virus 2.75

THIEVES
1 thru 3 . . . . @1.50

THIEVES AND KINGS
I Box 1994–97
1 F:Ruebel The Intrepid 9.00
1a 2nd printing 2.50
2 . . . . 6.00
2a 2nd printing 2.50
3 . . . . 4.50
3a 2nd printing 2.50
4 . . . . 4.00
5 . . . . 4.00
6 V:Shadow Lady 4.00
7 V:Shadow Lady 2.50
8 thru 18 by Mark Oakley . . . . @2.50

TPB Vol. 1: rep.#1–#6 . . . . 12.00
TPB Vol. 2: The Green Book . . . 14.00

THIS MAGAZINE IS HAUNTED
A Plus Comics
1 . . . . 1.95

THISTLE
Fat Jar 1995
1 Three Policemen & Monk 2.00

THORR SUERD OR SWORD OF THOR
1 . . . . 3.00
1a 2nd printing 2.00
2 . . . . 1.75
3 . . . . 1.50

THREAT
1 . . . . 5.00
2 . . . . 3.00
3 and 4 . . . . @2.00
5 thru 10 . . . . @2.25

3 X 3 EYES
Innovation
1 Labyrinth o/t DemonsEyePt.1 . . 2.25
2 Labyrinth o/t DemonsEyePt.2 . . 2.25
3 Labyrinth o/t DemonsEyePt.3 . . 2.25
4 Labyrinth o/t DemonsEyePt.4 . . 2.25
5 Labyrinth o/t DemonsEye conc. 2.25

THREE IN ONE
1 . . . . 1.75

THREE MUSKETEERS
1 . . . . 1.95
2 . . . . 1.95
3 . . . . 1.95

THREE ROCKETEERS
Eclipse
1 JK,AW,rep. 2.00
2 JK,AW,rep. 2.00

THRESHOLD OF REALTY
1 5,000 printed 2.50
2 thru 4 . . . . @2.00

THRILLKILL
Caliber
1 rep. Cal.Presents #1-#4 . . . . . 2.50

THUNDERBIRD
Newcomers Publishing
1 & 2 2 Stories . . . . @2.95
3 . . . . 2.95
4 I:Mercer 2.95
5 R:Raven 2.95
6 & 7 . . . . 2.95
8 final issue 3.50
Ann.#1 The Great Escape 3.50

THUNDER BUNNY
1 O:Thunder Bunny 2.50
2 VO:Dr.Fog 2.00
3 I:GoldenMan 1.75
4 V:Keeper 1.75
5 I:Moon Mess 1.75

---

6 V:Mr.Endall 1.75
7 VI:Dr.Fog 1.75
8 . . . . 1.75
9 VS:Gen. Agents 1.75
10 thru 12 . . . . @1.75

THUNDER MACE
1 Proto type-blue & red very
rare:1,000 printed 15.00
1a four color cover 3.00
2 thru 5 . . . . @1.75
6 . . . . 2.00
7 . . . . 2.00
Graphic Novel, rep.1-4 . . . . 5.00

THUNDER SKULL
1 . . . . 1.95

Tick #7 © New England Comics

TICK
New England Comics
1 BEd 75.00
1a 2nd printing 35.00
1b 3rd printing 6.00
1c 4th printing 2.50
2 BEd 50.00
2a 2nd printing 25.00
2b 3rd printing 4.00
2c 4th printing 2.50
3 BEd 20.00
3a 2nd printing 2.50
4 BEd 15.00
4a 2nd printing 2.50
5 BEd 15.00
6 BEd 11.00
7 BEd,A:Chairface Chippendale 11.00
8 BEd 11.00
8a Spec.No Logo edition 20.00
9 BEd,A:Chainsaw Vigilante, Red
Eye 5.00
10 BEd 5.00
11 thru 12 BEd 4.00
Spec. Ed. #1, I:Tick 45.00
Spec. Ed. #2, 2nd App. Tick . . 40.00
Spec. #1 Reprise edition 5.95
TPB Omnibus #1 rep. #1–#6 . . . 17.95
TPB Omnibus #2 BEd,fifth printing 14.95
TPB Omnibus #3 BEd 10.95
TPB Omnibus #4 BEd 10.95

TICK: GIANT CIRCUS OF THE MIGHTY
New England Press
1 A-O	3.00
2 P-Z	3.00
3	3.00

TICK: KARMA TORNADO
New England Press
1	4.00
1 2nd printing	3.00
2	3.50
2 2nd printing	3.00
3 thru 9	3.50
3 thru 9 2nd printings	3.00
TPB #1 second edition	13.95

TICK OMNIBUS
New England Press
1 1 to 6 Rep.	14.95

TICK'S BACK, THE
New England Comics
0 by Eli Stone, V:Toy DeForce	2.95

TIC TOC TOM
Detonation Canada 1995
1 Various Artists	2.95

TIGERS OF TERRA
Mind-Visions
1 6,000 printed	4.50
1a Signed & Num.	14.00
2	2.00
2a Signed & Num.	11.00
5 thru 7	@3.50
8 thru 10	@3.75
Antarctic	
11 and 12	@3.95
[Vol. 2]	
0 thru 14	@2.75
15 Totenkopf Police,pt.2	2.75
16 Battleship Arizona,pt.3	2.75
17 thru 22	@2.95
23 "Trouble with Tigers" pt.3	2.95
24 48pg 10th Anniv.	3.95
25 "Battle for Terra" pt.1	2.95
TPB Book Two	9.95
TPB Book Three	9.95
TPB Book Four	9.95

TIGRESS
Hero Graphics
3 A:Lady Arcane	2.95
4 inc. B.U. Mudpie	2.95

TIGER-X
Eternity
Special #1	2.50
Spec. #1a 2nd printing	2.25
1 thru 3	@1.95
Book II	
1 thru 4	@1.95

TIME DRIFTERS
Innovation
1	2.25
2	2.25
3	2.25

TIME GATES
Double Edge
1 SF series,The Egg #1	1.95
2 The Egg #2	1.95
3 Spirit of the Dragon #1	1.95
4 Spirit of the Dragon #2	1.95
4a Var.cover	1.95

TIME JUMP WAR
Apple
1 thru 3	@1.95

TIME MACHINE
1 thru 3	@2.50

TIME OUT OF MIND
1 thru 4	@1.85

TIME TRIPPER
1	2.00

TIME WARRIORS
Fantasy General
1 rep.Alpha Track #1	1.50
1a Bi-Weekly	.75
2	.75
3	.75

TITANESS
Draculina Publishing 1995
1 I:Titaness,Tomboy	2.95

TO BE ANNOUNCED
1 thru 6	@1.50

TO DIE FOR
Blackthorne
1	2.00

TOM CORBETT SPACE CADET
Eternity
1	2.00
2	2.00
3	2.25
4	2.25

TOM CORBETT II
1	2.25
2	2.25
3	2.25
4	2.25

TOM MIX HOLIDAY ALBUM
Amazing Comics
1	3.50

TOM MIX WESTERN
AC Comics
1	2.50
2	2.50

TOMMI GUNN: KILLERS LUST
London Night Jan. 1997
1	3.00
1a nude cover	6.00
1 photo cover	6.00

TOMMY & THE MONSTERS
1 thru 3	@1.95

TOMORROW MAN
Antarctic
1 R:Tommorow Man	2.95
Spec.#1 48 pages	3.95

TONY BRAVADO
1 thru 3	@2.00
4	2.50

TOO MUCH COFFEE MAN
Adhesive Comics 1995
1 F:Too Much Coffee Man	20.00
1a 2nd printing	5.00
2 Wheeler (s&a)	10.00
3 Wheeler (s&a)	6.00
4 In love	5.00

TORG
Adventure
1 Based on Role Playing Game	2.50
2 thru 3 Based on Game	@2.50

TOR JOHNSON: HOLLYWOOD STAR
Monster Comics
1 Biographical story	2.50

TORRID AFFAIRS
1	2.25
2	2.25
3 thru 5, 60 pages	@2.95

TOTALLY ALIEN
1	17.00
2	12.00
3	8.00

TOUGH GUYS AND WILD WOMEN
Eternity
1	2.25
2	2.25

TRACKER
Blackthorne
1	2.00
2	1.75
3	2.00
4	2.00

TRANSIT
1	2.00
2 thru 6	@1.75

TRIAD
Blackthorne
1	1.75

TRIAL RUN
1	1.75

TRIARCH
Caliber
1	2.00

B & W PUB.

All comics prices listed are for *Near Mint* condition.

TRICKSTER
KING MONKEY
1 thru 5 . . . . @1.75

TRIDENT
1 thru 7 . . . . @3.50
8 . . . . 4.50

TRIO
1 . . . . 1.50

TRIMUVERATE
Mermaid Productions
1 I:Trimverate 2.25
2 & 3 Team captured 2.25
4 V:Ord,Ael 2.25

TROLLORDS
Tru Studios 1986
1 1st printing 6.00
1a 2nd printing 2.00
2 . . . . 3.00
3 . . . . 2.00
4 thru 15 . . . . @1.50
#1 special 1.75

TROLLORDS
Apple Comics 1989–90
1 thru 6 . . . . @2.50

TROLLORDS
Caliber Tapestry 1996
1 and 2 . . . . @2.95

TROLLORDS:
DEATH & KISSES
1 . . . . 1.95
2 thru 5 . . . . @2.25

TROPO
1 and 2 . . . . @2.00

TROUBLE SHOOTERS
Nightwolf
1 I:Trouble Shooters 2.50

The Trouble With Girls #10 © Eternity

2 V:Ifrit,Djin,Ghul 2.50
3 V:Morgath 2.50

TROUBLE WITH GIRLS
Eternity
1 . . . . 3.50
2 . . . . 2.50
3 thru 14 . . . . @1.95
15 thru 21 . . . . @2.25
22 Lester's Origin 2.25
Ann. #1 . . . . 2.95
Graphic Novel 7.95
Graphic Novel #2 . . . . 7.95
Xmas special 'World of Girls' . . . 2.95
NEW SERIES
1 thru 4 see color
5 thru 11 . . . . @1.95

TROUBLE WITH TIGERS
Antarctic Press
1 NinjaHighSchool/Tigers x-over . 2.00
2 . . . . 2.00

TRUE CRIME
Eclipse
1 thru 2 . . . . 2.95

TRUFAN ADVENTURES THEATRE
1 . . . . 8.00
2 3-D issue 5.00

TRYPTO THE ACID DOG
Renegade
1 . . . . 2.00

TUNESIA
1 . . . . 1.50

TURTLE SOUP
1 A:TMNT 6.00

TURTLES TEACH KARATE
Solson
1 . . . . 4.00
2 . . . . 3.50

TWILIGHT AVENGER
Eternity
1 thru 18 . . . . @1.95

TWILIGHT X QUARTERLY
Antarctic Press
1 thru 3 . . . . @2.95
4 Celebration 2.95

TWIST
Kitchen Sink
1 . . . . 1.95
2 and 3 . . . . @2.00

TWISTED TALES OF THE PURPLE SNIT
Blackthorne
1 . . . . 2.50
2 . . . . 2.00

2001 NIGHTS
Viz

1 . . . . 5.00
2 . . . . 4.00
3 thru 5 . . . . @3.75
6 thru 10 . . . . @4.25

TYLOR
Double Edge
0 The Egg 2.95

TYRANNY REX
Fleetway
GN reps. from 2000A.D. 7.95

ULTIMATE STRIKE
London Night 1996
1 . . . . 3.00
1 holochrome edition 15.00
1a nude commemorative edition . 5.00
2 thru 5 . . . . @3.00
6 sequel to Strike #0 . . . . 3.00
7 by Kevin Hill, "Stryke: Year One"
concl. 3.00

ULTRA KLUTZ
Onward Comics
1 . . . . 2.50
2 thru 18 . . . . @1.50
19 thru 24 . . . . @1.75
25 thru 30 . . . . @2.00

UNCANNY MAN-FROG
Mad Dog
1 . . . . 1.75
2 . . . . 1.75

UNCENSORED MOUSE
Eternity
1 Mickey Mouse 10.00
2 Mickey Mouse 11.00

UNDERGROUND
1 . . . . 1.70

UNDIE DOG
1 . . . . 1.50

UNFORGIVEN, THE
Trinity Comics Ministries
Mission of Tranquility
1 thru 6 V:Dormian Grath 1.95
7 I:Faith 1.95

UNICORN ISLE
Genesis West
1 . . . . 2.50
2 . . . . 1.50
3 . . . . 1.50
Apple
4 thru 6 . . . . @1.75

UNICORN KINGS
1 and 2 . . . . @1.00

UNION JACKS
1 thru 3 . . . . @2.00

UNLEASHED
Caliber Press
1 F:Carson Davis 2.95
2 V:North Harbor Crime 2.95

| **All comics prices listed are for *Near Mint* condition.**

UNSUPERVISED EXISTENCE
1	2.00
2 and 3	@2.50

UNTOLD ORIGIN OF MS. VICTORY
1	2.50

UNTOUCHABLES
1 thru 20	@.75

USAGI YOJIMBO
Fantagraphics 1987
1 SS	10.00
1a 2nd printing	5.00
2 SS,Samurai	8.00
3 SS,Samurai,A:Croakers	6.00
4 SS	5.00
5 thru 7 SS	@5.00
8 SS,A Mother's Love	5.00
8a 2nd printing	3.00
9 SS	4.00
10 SS,A:Turtles	5.00
10a 2nd printing	3.00
11 thru 18 SS	@4.00
19 SS,Frost & Fire,A:Nelson Groundthumper	3.50
20 thru 21 SS	@3.50
22 SS,A:Panda Khan	3.50
23 SS,V:Ninja Bats	3.50
24 SS	3.50
25 SS,A:Lionheart	3.50
26 SS,Gambling	3.50
27 SS	3.50
28 thru 31 SS,Circles Pt.1	@3.50
32	3.50
33 SS,Ritual Murder	3.50
34 thru 37	@3.50
Spec.#1 SS,SummerSpec,C:Groo	45.00
Radio Comix
Vol. 1 The Art of Usagi Yojimbo	3.95

VAGABONDS
1 thru 3	@1.75

VALENTINO
Renegade
1	1.70
2 and 3	@2.00

VALOR THUNDERSTAR
1 and 2	@1.75

VAMPEROTICA
Brainstorm Comics
1 I:Luxura	10.00
1a 2nd & 3rd printing	3.00
2	8.00
2 2nd printing	3.00
3	4.00
4 I:Blood Hunterq	4.00
5 Deadshot	4.00
6 Deadshot	4.00
7 Baptism	4.00
8 Pains,Peepers	4.00
9 thru 11	@4.00
12 thru 16	@3.00
17 thru 22 see: color	
23	3.00
23a nude edition	4.00
24	3.00

24a nude cover	4.00
25	3.00
25a deluxe, nude cover	4.00
26	3.00
26a nude cover	4.00
27	3.00
28 A:China & Jazz	3.00
28a nude cover	4.00
29 mild cover	3.00
Commemorative Edition	2.95
Lingerie Special #1	2.95
Spec. Lingerie, encore edition	2.95
Spec. Lingerie, deluxe	3.95
Spec. Swimsuit, encore edition	2.95
Spec. Swimsuit, deluxe nude cover	3.95

VAMPFIRE
Brainstorm 1996
1	2.95
1a nude cover	3.95
1 commemorative photo cover	10.00
2	2.95
2a nude cover	5.00
Pin-Up Spec.	2.95
Pin-Up Spec. deluxe	3.95
Tour Book #1	2.95
Tour Book #1 nude cover	2.95

VAMPFIRE: EROTIC ECHO
Brainstorm 1997
1 by Fauve	2.95
1a nude cover	2.95
1b photo cover	3.00
2	2.95
2a nude cover	2.95
2b photo cover	2.95

VAMPIRE BITES
Brainstorm
2	2.95
2a nude cover	2.95

VAMPIRE GIRLS EROTIQUE
Angel Entertainment 1996
1	2.95
1 nude cover	2.95

VAMPIRE GIRLS: BUBBLEGUM & BLOOD
Angel Entertainment 1996
1	2.95
1 deluxe edition	5.95
1 nude cover	10.00
2	2.95
2 deluxe edition	5.95
2 nude cover	10.00

VAMPIRELLA
Harris
1 DC,SL,Summer Nights,48page	3.95

VAMPIRELLA
Silver Anniversary Collection
Harris 1996
0 Vampirella of Darkulon, EM	2.95
1 good girl edition	2.50
1a bad girl edition	2.50
2 good girl edition	2.50
2a bad girl edition	2.50
3 good girl edition	2.50

3a bad girl edition	2.50
4 Silkie(c)	2.50
4a MBc(c)	2.50

VAMPIRELLA AND THE BLOOD RED QUEEN OF HEARTS
Harris
TPB rep. from Warren Vampirella, 96pg	9.95

VAMPIRELLA VS. HEMORRHAGE
Harris
1 Limited Preview Ashcan	5.00

Vampirella: Morning in America, Book 3
© Harris/Dark Horse

VAMPIRELLA: MORNING IN AMERICA
Harris/Dark Horse 1991–92
Book 1 thru 4	7.00
Book 2 thru 4	@5.00
TPB	25.00

VAMPIRE MIYU
Antarctica Press
1 I:Vampire Princess Miyu	2.95
2 thru 5	@3.95
6 48pg	4.95

VAMPRIE GIRLS: CALIFORNIA 1969
Angel Entertainment 1996
0 nude cover, signed	10.00
1 blood red foil deluxe edition	5.95
2	2.95
2 deluxe	5.95
2 nude cover A	10.00
2 nude cover B	10.00

VAMPRIE GIRLS: NEW YORK 1979
Angel Entertainment 1996
0	2.95

B & W PUB.

0 virgin nude cover 5.00
0 nude platinum cover 15.00
0 gold edition 8.00
1 .... 2.95
1 virgin nude cover 5.00
1 nude platinum cover 15.00

VAMPYRES
Eternity
1 thru 4 .... @2.25

VANGUARD: OUTPOST EARTH
1 and 2 .... @2.00

VARCEL'S VIXENS
1 thru 3 .... @2.50

VAULT OF DOOMNATION
B-Movie Comics
1 .... 1.70

VENGEANCE OF DREADWOLF
Lightning Comics
1 O:Dreadwolf 2.75

VERDICT
Eternity
1 thru 4 .... @1.95

VEROTIKA
Verotika 1995–97
1 Magical Times 16.00
2 .... 9.00
3 .... 6.00
4 thru 6 .... @4.00
7 thru 15 .... @3.00

VERY VICKY
Meet Danny Ocean
1 .... 3.50
1a 2nd printing 3.00

VERY VICKY: CALLING ALL HILLBILLIES
Meet Danny Ocean 1995
1 Pea Pickin Patty 2.50

VIC & BLOOD
Renegade
1 and 2 RCo,Ellison .... @2.00

VICKY VALENTINE
Renegade
1 thru 4 .... @1.70

VICTIMS
Silver Wolf
1 & 2 .... @1.50

VICTIMS
Eternity
1 thru 5 .... @1.95

VIDEO CLASSICS
1 Mighty Mouse 3.50

---

2 Mighty Mouse 3.50

VIETNAM JOURNAL
Apple Comics
1 .... 5.00
1a 2nd printing 3.00
2 .... 3.00
3 thru 5 .... @2.50
6 thru 13 .... @2.00
14 thru 16 .... @2.25

VIGIL: DESERT FOXES
Millenium
1 & 2 F:Grace Kimble 3.95

VIGIL: FALL FROM GRACE
Innovation
1 'State of Grace' 2.75
2 The Graceland Hunt 2.50

VINSON WATSON'S RAGE
Trinity Visuals
1 I:Rena Helen 3.00

VINSON WATSON'S SWEET CHILDE
Advantage Graphics Vol. 2
1 F:Spyder 1.95

VIOLET STING
ALTERNATE CONCEPTS
1 .... .95

VIRGIN: SLUMBER
Entity 1997
1 BMs 2.75
1 deluxe 3.50

VIRGIN: SURROUNDED
Entity 1997
1 BMs 2.75
1 deluxe 3.50

VIRGIN: TILL DEATH DO US PART
Entity April 1997
1 BMs 2.75
1 deluxe 3.50

VISION
1 I:Flaming Carrot 150.00
2 Flaming Carrot 50.00
3 Flaming Carrot 20.00
4 Flaming Carrot 15.00

VISUAL ASSAULT OMNIBUS
Visual Assault Comics 1995
1 thru 4 O:Dimensioner 3.00

VITAL-MAN
1 thru 3 .... @1.70

VITRUVIAM MAN
1 .... 2.50

VIXEN
Meteor Comics
1 & 2 Battle of the Vixens 2.95

VORTEX
Hall of Heroes
1 .... 18.00
1a commemorative 5.00
2 .... 10.00
3 thru 5 .... @3.00
6 V:The Reverend 3.00

Vox #1 © Apple Comics

VOX
Apple
1 JBy(c) 1.95
2 and 3 .... @1.95
4 and 5 .... @2.25

WABBIT WAMPAGE
Amazing Comics 1987
1 .... 2.00

WACKY SQUIRREL
1 thru 4 .... @1.75
Summer Fun Special #1 .... 2.00
Christmas Special #1 .... 1.75

WALKING DEAD
Aircel
1 thru 4 .... @2.25
Zombie Spec. 1 .... 2.25

WALK THROUGH OCTOBER
Caliber
1 I:Mr. Balloon 2.95
2 .... 2.95
3 All Hallow's Eve 2.95

WALT THE WILDCAT
Motion Comics 1995
1 I:Walt the Wildcat 2.50

WANDER
1 .... 1.75

B & W PUB.

    All comics prices listed are for *Near Mint* condition.

WANDERING STAR
Pen & Ink
1 I:Casandra Andrews	28.00
1a 2nd & 3rd printing	3.00
2	10.00
3 thru 7	3.00
8 and 9 F:Casandra Andrews	2.75
10 R:Mekron	2.75
11	2.75

Sirius 1995–97
12 thru 20 TWo	@2.50
21 TWo, final issue	2.50

WAR
A Plus Comics
1	2.50

WARCAT
Alliance Comics
1 thru 7 A:Ebonia	2.50

WARD: A BULLET SERIES
Liar Comics
1 Foresight,pt.1	2.50
2 Foresight,pt.2	2.50
3 Foresight,pt.3	2.50

WARDRUMS
1 Adult	1.75
2	1.75
3	1.75

WARLACE
K-Blamm 1995
1 I:Warlace	2.95

WARLOCK 5
Aircel
1	6.00
2	5.00
3	6.00
4	5.00
5	5.00
6 thru 11	@4.00
12	3.50
13	3.50
14 thru 16	@2.00
17	1.70
18	1.75
19 thru 22	@1.95
Book 2 #1 thru #7	@2.00

WARLOCKS
Aircel
1 thru 3	@1.70
4 thru 12	@1.95
Spec #1 Rep.	2.25

WAR OF THE WORLDS
Eternity
1 TV tie-in	1.95
2 thru 6	@1.95

WAR OF THE WORLDS, THE
Caliber "New Worlds" 1996
1 from H.G. Wells	2.95
1a signed	2.95
2 war for Kansas City	2.95
3	2.95

4	2.95
5	2.95

WAR PARTY VS. DEATHMARK
Lightning Comics
1 War Party vs. Deathmark	2.75

WARP WALKING
Caliber
1 'Quick and the Dead'	2.50

WARRIOR NUN: BLACK AND WHITE
Antarctic Press 1997
1	3.00
2	3.00
3	3.00

WARRIORS
1	2.50
2 thru 7	@1.95

WARZONE
Entity
1 I:Bella & Supra	2.95
2 F:Bladeback, Alloy, Granite	2.95
3 F:Bladeback	2.95

WATCHDOG
Hammerhead Comics
1 I:Watchdog	2.95

WAVE WARRIORS
1	2.00

WAXWORK
1	2.00

WAYWARD WARRIOR
1	2.00

WEAPON FIVE
Spec. #1	1.95

WEASEL PATROL
Eclipse
Spec. #1	2.00

WEIRDFALL
Antarctic Press 1995
1 I:Weirdfall	2.75
2 O:Weirdfall	2.75
3	2.75

WEIRD MACABRE THRILLERS
1	1.95

WEIRD ROMANCE
Eclipse
1	2.00

WEREWOLF
Blackthorne 1988–89
1 TV tie-in	2.00
2 thru 7	@2.00

Werewolf #2 © Blackthorne

WEREWOLF AT LARGE
1 thru 3	@2.25

WHAT IS THE FACE?
A.C.E. Comics
1 SD/FMc,I:New Face	1.95
2 SD/FMc	1.95
3 SD	1.75

WHISPERS & SHADOWS
1 8 1/2 x 11	2.00
1a Regular size	1.50
2 8 1/2 x 11	1.50
3 8 1/2 x 11	1.50
4 thru 9	@1.50

WHITE DEVIL
Eternity
1 thru 6 adult	2.50

WHITE RAVEN
Visionary Publications
1 Government Intrigue	2.95
2	2.95
3 Mystery Man Gets Wheels	2.95
4 Facility	2.95
5 V:Douglas	2.95
6	2.95
7	2.95

WICKED
Millenium
1 thru 4	2.50

WICKED: THE RECKONING
Millenium
1 R:Wicked	2.95
2 F:Rachel Blackstone	2.95

WIDOW
Ground Zero 1996
Cinegraphic Spec.#1: Daughter of Darkness	4.00

B & W PUB.

All comics prices listed are for _Near Mint_ condition.

WIDOW/LUXURA:
BLOOD LUST
Ground Zero 1996
Alpha x-over, pt.1 . . . . 3.50
see Luxura/Widow for pt. 2

WIDOW:
BOUND BY BLOOD
Ground Zero 1996
1 thru 5 by Mike Wolfer . . . . . @3.50

WIDOW: PROGENY
Ground Zero April 1997
1 by Mike Wolfer & Karl Moline . . 3.00
2 (of 3) 3.00

WIDOW:
THE COMPLETE WORKS
Ground Zero 1996
Vol.1 Flesh and Blood 10.95
Vol.1 deluxe 16.95
Vol.2 Kill Me Again 10.95
Vol.2 deluxe 16.95

WILD, THE
1 and 2 . . . . @1.50
3 thru 7 . . . . @1.75

WILD KNIGHTS
Eternity
1 thru 10 . . . . @1.95
Shattered Earth Chron. #1 . . . . . 1.95

WILDMAN
1 and 2 . . . . @1.50
3 thru 6 . . . . @1.85

WILD STARS
Vol 2 #1 . . . . 1.95

WILD THINGS
1 . . . . 2.00

WILD THINK
2 . . . . 2.00

WILLOW
Angel Entertainment 1996
0 commemorative edition 2.95
0 nude edition 5.00
1 . . . . 2.95
1 black magic foil edition 5.95
1 nude signed 10.00
2 . . . . 2.95
2 gold edition 8.00
2 Virgin nude cover 5.00
2 Virgin Sacrifice nude cover . . . 7.00
2 nude manga cover 5.00
2 nude platinum cover 15.00

WIMMINS' COMIX
13 and 14 . . . . @2.00

WIND BLADE
1 Elford 1st Blair 60.00

WINDRAVEN
Hero Graphics/Blue comet
1 The Healing,(see Rough Raiders)2.95

WINDRAVEN
Heroic
1 . . . . 2.95

WISHMASTER
Pocket Change Comics
1 I:Hell Bore 2.50

WITCH
Eternity
1 . . . . 1.95

WIZARDS OF
LAST RESORT
1 thru 3 . . . . @1.75
4 . . . . 2.00

WIZARD OF TIME
David House
1 . . . . 1.50
1a 2nd printing(blue) 1.50
2 and 3 . . . . @1.50

WOLF H
Blackthorne
1 and 2 . . . . @1.75

WORDSMITH
Renegade
1 . . . . 3.00
2 thru 6 . . . . @1.70
7 thru 12 . . . . @2.00

WORLD HARDBALL
LEAGUE
Titus Press
1 F:Big Bat 2.95
2 F:Big Bat 2.95
3 Mount Evrest 2.95
4 Juan Hernandez 2.95

WORLD OF ROBOTECH
Academy Comics 1995
GN Tales of Planets 12.95

WORLD OF WOOD
Eclipse
5 Flying Saucers 2.00

WORLD OF X-RAY
1 . . . . 1.80
2 . . . . 1.80

WORLDS OF FANTASY
Newcomers Publishing 1995
1 The Jenn Chronicles 2.95

WRAB
1 . . . . 2.95

WRAITH
Outlander
1 'Resurrected & the Damned' . . 1.75

WRONG COMIC
1 . . . . 1.70

WU WEI
Animus
1 "Debaser" 2.50
2 Blind Whisper 2.50

WYOMING TERRITORY
1 . . . . 1.95

XANADU
Thoughts & Images
1 thru 5 . . . . @2.00

XENA
Brown Study Comics
1 I:Xena 2.95

XENON
Eclipse
1 . . . . 3.00
2 thru 23 . . . . @1.50

Xenozoic Tales #3 © Kitchen Sink

XENOZOIC TALES
Kitchen Sink 1986
1 by Mark Schultz 11.00
1aRep. 2.00
2 . . . . 8.00
2a Rep. 2.00
3 . . . . 7.00
4 . . . . 6.00
5 thru 7 . . . . @4.00
8 thru 13 . . . . @3.00
14 MSh 2.95

X-BABES VS. JUSTICE
BABES
Personality
1 Spoof/parody 2.95

X-CONS
Parody Press
1 X-Men satire,flip cover 2.50

X-FARCE
Eclipse
One-Shot X-Force parody 3.00

B & W PUB.

XIOLA
Zion Comics
1 thru 3 F:Kantasia . . . . @1.95
4 Visitor 1.95

X-MAS WITH SUPERSWINE
Spec 2.00

XMEN
1 Parody 1.50

X-1999
Viz
1 I:Kamir Shiro 2.75
2 thru 5 F:Princess Hitane 2.75
6 Battle for X-1999 . . . . 2.75

X-THIEVES
1 . . . . 3.00
2 . . . . 1.75
3 . . . . 1.75

YAHOO
1 thru 3 . . . . @2.00

YAKUZA
Eternity
1 thru 5 . . . . @1.95

YARN MAN
1 . . . . 2.00

YAWN
Parody Press
1 Spawn parody 2.50
Enigma
1 Spawn parody rep.? 2.75

YIN-FEI
1 thru 4 . . . . @1.50

YOUNG HERO
1 . . . . 2.50
2 . . . . 2.50

YOUNG MASTERS
1 thru 10 . . . . @1.75

Z
Keystone Graphics
1 . . . . 2.75
2 House of Windsor-Yakonaral . . 2.75
3 House of Windsor-YakonaraII . 2.75

ZELL THE SWORDDANCER
1 Steve Gallacci 5.50
2 and 3 . . . . @2.00

ZEN ILLUSTRATED NOVELLA
Entity
1 thru 4 R:Bruce Lewis . . . . . . @2.95
5 Immortal Combat 2.95
6 Bubble Economy 2.95
7 Zen City 2.95
8 V:Assassins 2.95

ZEN, INTER-GALACTIC NINJA
Entity
1 . . . . 4.00
2 . . . . 3.00
3 thru 9 . . . . @3.00
X-mas Spec #1,V:Black Hole Bob 2.95
[2nd Series]
1 'Down to Earth' 2.50
2 RA, A:Jeremy Baker 2.50
2a polybagged, limited 5.00
3 thru 5 . . . . @2.50
[3rd Series]
0 . . . . 2.95
1 thru 3 A:Niro . . . . @2.95
Sourcebook #1 . . . . 3.50

ZEN INTERGALACTIC NINJA: STARQUEST
Entity
1 thru 6 V:Nolan the Destroyer @2.95
7 V:Dimensional 2.95
8 thru 9 I:New Team . . . . @2.95
10 In Deep Space 2.95
11 Dimensional Terrorists 2.95
TPB Rep. #1-#4 . . . . @6.95

ZEN INTERGALACTIC NINJA VS. MICHEAL JACK-ZEN
Entity
1 Cameos Galore 2.95

ZENISMS WIT AND WISDOMS
Entity
1 R:Bruce Lewis 2.95

ZEN: MISTRESS OF CHAOS
1 . . . . 2.95

ZENITH: PHASE II
Fleetway
1 GMo(s),SY,Rep.2000 AD 1.95

Zillion #2 © Eternity

ZERO & D.D.O.J.
1 . . . . 3.00

ZETRAMAN
Antarctic
1 thru 3 . . . . @1.95
[Vol. 2]
1 and 2 . . . . @2.75

ZETRAMAN: REVIVAL
Antarctic Press
1 thru 3 . . . . @2.75

ZIG ZAG
1 . . . . 1.25
2 . . . . 1.25

ZILLION
Eternity
1 thru 4 . . . . @2.50

ZOLASTRAYA AND THE BARD
1 thru 5 . . . . @1.70

ZOMBIE BOY
1 . . . . 1.50

ZOMBIE LOVE
1 . . . . 4.95

ZOMBIE WAR: EARTH MUST BE DESTROYED
Fantaco 1993
1 thru 3 Kevin Eastman 3.95

ZONE
1 . . . . 1.95

ZONE CONTINUUM
Caliber
1 Master of the Waves 2.95
2 . . . . 2.95

ZORANN: STAR WARRIOR
1 . . . . 2.00

ZOT!
Eclipse
(#1-#10 See: Color)
11 New Series 3.00
12 thru 15 . . . . @3.00
16 A:De-Evolutionaries 3.00
17 thru 36 . . . . @3.00

ZOOT!
Fantagraphics
1 thru 5 . . . . @2.50

B & W PUB.

Issued As Classic Comics
001-THE THREE MUSKETEERS
By Alexandre Dumas

10/41 (---) MKd,MKd(c),
Original,10¢ (c) Price 4,200.00
05/43 (10) MKd,MKd(c),
No(c)Price; rep 225.00
11/43 (15) MKd,MKd(c),Long
Island Independent Ed; 175.00
6/44 (18/20) MKd,MKd(c),
Sunrise Times Edition;rep . . . 125.00
7/44 (21) MKd,MKd(c),Richmond
Courrier Edition;rep 110.00
6/46 (28) MKd,MKd(c);rep 90.00
4/47 (36) MKd,MKd(c),
New CILogo;rep 40.00
6/49 (60) MKd,MKd(c),CI Logo;rep 25.00
10/49 (64) MKd,MKd(c),CI Logo;rep 25.00
12/50 (78) MKd,MKd(c),15¢(c)
Price; CI Logo 18.00
03/52 (93) MKd,MKd(c),
CI Logo;rep 16.00
11/53 (114) CI Logo;rep 12.00
09/56 (134) MKd,MKd(c),New
P(c),CI Logo,64 pgs;rep 12.00
03/58 (143) MKd,MKd(c),P(c),
CI Logo,64 pgs;rep 11.00
05/59 (150) GE&RC New Art,
P(c),CILogo;rep 11.00
03/61 (149) GE&RC,P(c),
CI Logo;rep 7.00
62-63 (167) GE&RC,P(c),
CI Logo;rep 7.00
04/64 (167) GE&RC,P(c),
CI Logo;rep 7.00
01/65 (167) GE&RC,P(c),
CI Logo;rep 7.00
03/66 (167) GE&RC,P(c),
CI Logo;rep 7.00
11/67 (166) GE&RC,P(c),
CI Logo;rep 7.00
Sp/69 (166) GE&RC,P(c),25¢(c)
Price,CILogo, Rigid(c);rep 7.00
Sp/71 (169) GE&RC,P(c),
CI Logo,Rigid(c);rep 7.00

002-IVANHOE
By Sir Walter Scott

1941 (---) EA,MKd(c),Original . 1,800.00
05/43 (1) EA,MKd(c),word "Presents"
Removed From(c);rep 200.00
11/43 (15) EA,MKd(c),Long Island
Independent Edition;rep 150.00
06/44 (18/20) EA,MKd(c),Sunrise
Times Edition;rep 125.00
07/44 (21) EA,MKd(c),Richmond
Courrier Edition;rep 110.00
06/46 (28) EA,MKd(c),rep 90.00
07/47 (36) EA,MKd(c),New
CI Logo; rep 50.00
06/49 (60) EA,MKd(c),CI Logo;rep 30.00
10/49 (64) EA,MKd(c),CI Logo;rep 25.00
12/50 (78) EA,MKd(c),15¢(c)
Price;CI Logo;rep 18.00
11/51 (89) EA,MKd(c),CI Logo;rep 16.00
04/53 (106) EA,MKd(c),CI
Logo;rep 14.00
07/54 (121) EA,MKd(c),CI
Logo;rep 12.00
01/57 (136) NN New Art,New
P(c),CI Logo;rep 14.00
01/58 (142) NN,P(c),CI Logo;rep . 6.00
11/59 (153) NN,P(c),CI Logo;rep . 6.00
03/61 (149) NN,P(c),CI Logo;rep . . 6.00

62/63 (167) NN,P(c),CI Logo;rep . 5.00
05/64 (167) NN,P(c),CI Logo;rep . . 6.00
01/65 (167) NN,P(c),CI Logo;rep . . 6.00
03/66 (167) NN,P(c),CI Logo;rep . . 6.00
09/67 (166) NN,P(c),CI Logo;rep . . 6.00
1968 (166) NN,P(c),CI Logo;rep . . 6.00
Wr/69 (169) NN,P(c),CI
Logo Rigid(c);rep 6.00
Wr/71 (169) NN,P(c),CI
Logo,Rigid(c);rep 6.00

*CI #4 Last of the Mohicans,
© Gilberton Publications*

003-THE COUNT OF MONTE CRISTO
By Alexandre Dumas

03/42 (---) ASm,ASm(c),Original 1,200.00
05/43 (10) ASm,ASm(c);rep . . . 200.00
11/43 (15) ASm,ASm(c),Long Island
Independent Edition;rep 150.00
06/44 (18/20) ASm,ASm(c),
Sunrise Times Edition;rep . . . 135.00
06/44 (20) ASm,ASm(c),Sunrise
Times Edition;rep 125.00
07/44 (21) ASm,ASm(c),Richmond
Courrier Edition;rep 110.00
06/46 (28) ASm,ASm(c);rep . . . 100.00
04/47 (36) ASm,ASm(c),New
CI Logo; rep 50.00
06/49 (60) ASm,ASm(c),CI
Logo;rep 35.00
08/49 (62) ASm,ASm(c),CI
Logo;rep 45.00
05/50 (71) ASm,ASm(c),CI
Logo;rep 25.00
09/51 (87) ASm,ASm(c),15¢(c)
Price, CI Logo;rep 18.00
11/53 (113) ASm,ASm(c),
CI Logo; rep 15.00
11/56 (---) LC New Art,New
P(c), CI Logo;rep 15.00
03/58 (135) LC,P(c),CI Logo;rep . . 6.00
11/59 (153) LC,P(c),CI Logo;rep . . 6.00
03/61 (161) LC,P(c),CI Logo;rep . . 6.00
62/63 (167) LC,P(c),CI Logo;rep . . 6.00
07/64 (167) LC,P(c),CI Logo;rep . . 6.00
07/65 (167) LC,P(c),CI Logo;rep . . 6.00
07/66 (167) LC,P(c),CI Logo;rep . . 6.00
1968 (166) LC,P(c),25¢(c)
Price, CI Logo;rep 6.00
Wn/69 (169) LC,P(c),CI Logo,
Rigid(c);rep 6.00

004-THE LAST OF THE MOHICANS
By James Fenimore Cooper

08/42 (---) RR,RR(c),Original . . 1,000.00
06/43 (12) RR,RR(c),Price
Balloon Deleted;rep 200.00
11/43 (15) RR,RR(c),Long Island
Independent Edition;rep 175.00
06/44 (20) RR,RR(c),Long Island
Independent Edition;rep 150.00
07/44 (21) RR,RR(c),Queens
Home News Edition;rep 125.00
06/46 (28) RR,RR(c);rep 100.00
04/47 (36) RR,RR(c),New
CI Logo; rep 50.00
06/49 (60) RR,RR(c),CI Logo;rep . 35.00
10/49 (64) RR,RR(c),CI Logo;rep . 25.00
12/50 (78) RR,RR(c),15¢(c)
Price,CI Logo rep 20.00
11/51 (89) RR,RR(c),CI Logo;rep . 18.00
03/54 (117) RR,RR(c),CI Logo;rep 15.00
11/56 (135) RR,New P(c),
CI Logo; rep 15.00
11/57 (141) RR,P(c),CI Logo;rep . 16.00
05/59 (150) JSe&StA New Art;
P(c), CI Logo;rep 15.00
03/61 (161) JSe&StA,P(c),CI
Logo; rep 6.00
62/63 (167) JSe&StA,P(c),CI
Logo; rep 6.00
06/64 (167) JSe&StA,P(c),CI
Logo; rep 6.00
08/65 (167) JSe&StA,P(c),CI
Logo; rep 6.00
08/66 (167) JSe&StA,P(c),CI
Logo; rep 6.00
1967 (166) JSe&StA,P(c),25¢(c)
Price, CI Logo; rep 6.00
Sp/69 (169) JSe&StA,P(c),CI
Logo, Rigid(c);rep 6.00

005-MOBY DICK
By Herman Melville

09/42 (---) LZ,LZ(c),Original . . 1,300.00
05/43 (10) LZ,LZ(c),Conray Products
Edition, No(c)Price; 225.00
11/43 (15) LZ,LZ(c),Long Island
Independent Edition;rep 175.00
06/44 (18/20) LZ,LZ(c),Sunrise
Times Edition;rep 150.00
07/44 (20) LZ,LZ(c),Sunrise
Times Edition;rep 135.00
07/44 (21) LZ,LZ(c),Sunrise
Times Edition;rep 125.00
06/46 (28) LZ,LZ(c),rep 100.00
04/47 (36) LZ,LZ(c),NewCILogo;rep 60.00
06/49 (60) LZ,LZ(c),CI Logo;rep . 35.00
08/49 (62) LZ,LZ(c),CI Logo;rep . 40.00
05/50 (71) LZ,LZ(c),CI Logo;rep . 25.00
09/51 (87) LZ,LZ(c),15¢(c)
Price, CI Logo;rep 20.00
04/54 (118) LZ,LZ(c),CI Logo;rep . 15.00
03/56 (131) NN New Art,New
P(c), CI Logo;rep 15.00
05/57 (138) NN,P(c),CI Logo;rep . . 6.00
01/59 (148) NN,P(c),CI Logo;rep . . 6.00
09/60 (158) NN,P(c),CI Logo;rep . . 6.00
62/63 (167) NN,P(c),CI Logo;rep . . 6.00
06/64 (167) NN,P(c),CI Logo;rep . . 6.00
07/65 (167) NN,P(c),CI Logo;rep . . 6.00
03/66 (167) NN,P(c),CI Logo;rep . . 6.00
09/67 (166) NN,P(c),CI Logo;rep . . 6.00
Wn/69 (166) NN,P(c),25¢(c) Price,
CI Logo, Rigid(c);rep 12.00
Wn/71 (169) NN,P(c),CI Logo;rep . 6.00

006-A TALE OF TWO CITIES
By Charles Dickens

11/42 (---) StM,StM(c),Original .	1,000.00
09/43 (14) StM,StM(c),No(c) Price; rep	200.00
03/44 (18) StM,StM(c),Long Island Independent Edition;rep	150.00
06/44 (20) StM,StM(c),Sunrise Times Edition;rep	135.00
06/46 (28) StM,StM(c);rep	90.00
09/48 (51) StM,StM(c),New Cl Logo; rep	50.00
10/49 (64) StM,StM(c),Cl Logo;rep	30.00
12/50 (78) StM,StM(c),15¢(c) Price, Cl Logo; rep	20.00
11/51 (89) StM,StM(c),Cl Logo;rep	18.00
03/54 (117) StM,StM(c),Cl Logo;rep	15.00
05/56 (132) JO New Art,New P(c), Cl Logo;rep	18.00
09/57 (140) JO,P(c),Cl Logo;rep	6.00
11/57 (147) JO,P(c),Cl Logo;rep	6.00
09/59 (152) JO,P(c),Cl Logo;rep	125.00
11/59 (153) JO,P(c),Cl Logo;rep	6.00
03/61 (149) JO,P(c),Cl Logo;rep	6.00
62/63 (167) JO,P(c),Cl Logo;rep	6.00
06/64 (167) JO,P(c),Cl Logo;rep	6.00
08/65 (167) JO,P(c),Cl Logo;rep	6.00
05/67 (166) JO,P(c),Cl Logo;rep	6.00
Fl/68 (166) JO,NN New P(c), 25¢(c)Price,Cl Logo;rep	15.00
Sr/70 (169) JO,NN P(c),Cl Logo, Rigid(c);rep	15.00

007-ROBIN HOOD
By Howard Pyle

12/42 (---) LZ,LZ(c),Original	800.00
06/43 (12) LZ,LZ(c),P.D.C. on(c) Deleted;rep	200.00
03/44 (18) LZ,LZ(c),Long Island Independent Edition;rep	150.00
06/44 (20) LZ,LZ(c),Nassau Bulletin Edition;rep	135.00
10/44 (22) LZ,LZ(c),Queens City Times Edition;rep	125.00
06/46 (28) LZ,LZ(c),rep	90.00
09/48 (51) LZ,LZ(c),New Cl Logo;rep	45.00
06/49 (60) LZ,LZ(c),Cl Logo;rep	25.00
10/49 (64) LZ,LZ(c),Cl Logo;rep	20.00
12/50 (78) LZ,LZ(c),Cl Logo;rep	20.00
07/52 (97) LZ,LZ(c),Cl Logo;rep	18.00
03/53 (106) LZ,LZ(c),Cl Logo;rep	15.00
07/54 (121) LZ,LZ(c),Cl Logo;rep	15.00
11/55 (129) LZ,New P(c), Cl Logo;rep	15.00
01/57 (136) JkS New Art,P(c);rep	6.00
03/58 (143) JkS,P(c),Cl Logo;rep	6.00
11/59 (153) JkS,P(c),Cl Logo;rep	6.00
10/61 (164) JkS,P(c),Cl Logo;rep	6.00
62/63 (167) JkS,P(c),Cl Logo;rep	6.00
06/64 (167) JkS,P(c),Cl Logo;rep	7.00
05/65 (167) JkS,P(c),Cl Logo;rep	6.00
07/66 (167) JkS,P(c),Cl Logo;rep	6.00
12/67 (166) JkS,P(c),Cl Logo;rep	7.00
Sr/69 (169) JkS,P(c),Cl Logo, Rigid(c);rep	6.00

008-ARABIAN KNIGHTS
By Antoine Galland

03/43 (---) LCh,LCh(c),Original	1,500.00
09/43 (14) LCh,LCh(c);rep	550.00
01/44 (17) LCh,LCh(c),Long Island	

Independent Edition;rep	600.00
06/44 (20) LCh,LCh(c),Nassau Bulletin Edition,64 pgs;rep	400.00
06/46 (28) LCh,LCh(c);rep	250.00
09/48 (51) LCh,LCh(c),New Cl Logo; rep	250.00
10/49 (64) LCh,LCh(c),Cl Logo;rep	200.00
12/50 (78) LCh,LCh(c),Cl Logo;rep	160.00
10/61 (164) ChB New Art,P(c), Cl Logo;rep	135.00

Cl #7 Robin Hood,
© Gilberton Publications

009-LES MISERABLES
By Victor Hugo

03/43 (---) RLv,RLv(c),Original	750.00
09/43 (14) RLv,RLv(c);rep	200.00
03/44 (18) RLv,RLv(c),Nassau Bulletin Edition;rep	175.00
06/44 (20) RLv,RLv(c),Richmond Courier Edition;rep	150.00
06/46 (28) RLv,RLv(c);rep	125.00
09/48 (51) RLv,RLv(c),New Cl Logo;rep	50.00
05/50 (71) RLv,RLv(c),Cl Logo;rep	40.00
09/51 (87) RLv,RLv(c),Cl Logo, 15¢(c)Price;rep	35.00
03/61 (161) NN New Art,GMc New P(c), Cl Logo;rep	30.00
09/63 (167) NN,GMc P(c),Cl Logo;rep	25.00
12/65 (167) NN,GMc P(c),Cl Logo; rep	25.00
1968 (166) NN,GMc P(c),25¢(c) Price, Cl Logo;rep	25.00

010-ROBINSON CRUSOE
By Daniel Defoe

04/43 (---) StM,StM(c),Original	650.00
09/43 (14) StM,StM(c);rep	225.00
03/44 (18) StM,StM(c),Nassau Bulletin Ed.,'Bill of Rights'Pge.64;rep	200.00
06/44 (20) StM,StM(c),Queens Home News Edition;rep	150.00
??/45 (23) StM,StM(c);rep	100.00
06/46 (28) StM,StM(c);rep	100.00
09/48 (51) StM,StM(c),New Cl Logo; rep	45.00
10/49 (64) StM,StM(c),Cl Logo;rep	30.00
12/50 (78) StM,StM(c),15¢(c) Price, Cl Logo;rep	25.00

07/52 (97) StM,StM(c),Cl Logo;rep	20.00
12/53 (114) StM,StM(c),Cl Logo;rep	20.00
01/56 (130) StM,New P(c),Cl Logo; rep	20.00
09/57 (140) SmC New Art,P(c), Cl Logo; rep	15.00
11/59 (153) SmC,P(c),Cl Logo;rep	6.00
10/61 (164) SmC,P(c),Cl Logo;rep	6.00
62/63 (167) SmC,P(c),Cl Logo;rep	9.00
07/64 (167) SmC,P(c),Cl Logo;rep	10.00
05/65 (167) SmC,P(c),Cl Logo;rep	6.00
06/66 (167) SmC,P(c),Cl Logo;rep	9.00
Fl/68 (166) SmC,P(c),Cl Logo, 25¢(c)Price;rep	8.00
1968 (166) SmC,P(c),Cl Logo,No Twin Circle Ad;rep	7.00
Sr/70 (169) SmC,P(c),Cl Logo, Rigid(c);rep	7.00

011-DON QUIXOTE
By Miguel de Cervantes Saavedra

05/43 (---) LZ,LZ(c),Original	700.00
03/44 (18) LZ,LZ(c),Nassau Bulletin Edition;rep	200.00
07/44 (21) LZ,LZ(c),Queens Home News Edition;rep	150.00
06/46 (28) LZ,LZ(c);rep	100.00
08/53 (110) LZ,TO New P(c),New Cl Logo;rep	25.00
05/60 (156) LZ,TO P(c),Pages Reduced to 48,Cl Logo;rep	15.00
1962 (165) LZ,TO P(c),Cl Logo;rep	8.00
01/64 (167) LZ,TO P(c),Cl Logo;rep	8.00
11/65 (167) LZ,TO P(c),Cl Logo;rep	8.00
1968 (166) LZ,TO P(c),Cl Logo, 25¢(c)Price;rep	20.00

012-RIP VAN WINKLE & THE HEADLESS HORSEMAN
By Washington Irving

06/43 (----) RLv,RLv(c),Original	675.00
11/43 (15) RLv,RLv(c),Long Island Independent Edition;rep	200.00
06/44 (20) RLv,RLv(c),Long Island Independent Edition;rep	150.00
10/44 (22) RLv,RLv(c),Queens City Times Edition;rep	135.00
06/46 (28) RLv,RLv(c);rep	100.00
06/49 (60) RLv,RLv(c),New Cl Logo;rep	40.00
08/49 (62) RLv,RLv(c),Cl Logo;rep	30.00
05/50 (71) RLv,RLv(c),Cl Logo;rep	25.00
11/51 (89) RLv,RLv(c),15¢(c) Price, Cl Logo;rep	15.00
04/54 (118) RLv,RLv(c),Cl Logo;rep	15.00
05/56 (132) RLv,New P(c), Cl Logo; rep	18.00
05/59 (150) NN New Art;P(c), Cl Logo; rep	18.00
09/60 (158) NN,P(c),Cl Logo;rep	6.00
62/63 (167) NN,P(c),Cl Logo;rep	6.00
12/63 (167) NN,P(c),Cl Logo;rep	6.00
04/65 (167) NN,P(c),Cl Logo;rep	7.00
04/66 (167) NN,P(c),Cl Logo;rep	6.00
1969 (166) NN,P(c),Cl Logo, 25¢(c)Price,Rigid(c);rep	12.00
Sr/70 (169) NN,P(c),Cl Logo, Rigid(c);rep	12.00

All comics prices listed are for *Near Mint* condition.

013-DR. JEKYLL AND MR.HYDE
By Robert Louis Stevenson
08/43 (---) AdH,AdH(c),Original . 950.00
11/43 (15) AdH,AdH(c),Long Island
Independent Edition;rep 250.00
06/44 (20) AdH,AdH(c),Long Island
Independent Edition;rep 175.00
06/46 (28) AdH,AdH(c),No(c)
Price; rep 125.00
06/49 (60) AdH,HcK New(c),New CI
Logo,Pgs.reduced to 48;rep . . . 40.00
08/49 (62) AdH,HcK(c),CI
Logo;rep 35.00
05/50 (71) AdH,HcK(c),CI
Logo;rep 25.00
09/51 (87) AdH,HcK(c),Erroneous Return
of Original Date,CI Logo;rep . . . 20.00
10/53 (112) LC New Art,New
P(c), CI Logo;rep 20.00
11/59 (153) LC,P(c),CI Logo;rep . . 7.00
03/61 (161) LC,P(c),CI Logo;rep . . 7.00
62/63 (167) LC,P(c),CI Logo;rep . . 7.00
08/64 (167) LC,P(c),CI Logo;rep . . 7.00
11/65 (167) LC,P(c),CI Logo;rep . . 7.00
1968 (166) LC,P(c),CI Logo,
25¢(c)Price;rep 8.00
Wr/69 (169) LC,P(c),CI Logo,
Rigid(c);rep 7.00

014-WESTWARD HO!
By Charles Kingsley
09/43 (---) ASm,ASm(c),Original 1,500.00
11/43 (15) ASm,ASm(c),Long Island
Independent Edition;rep 550.00
07/44 (21) ASm,ASm(c);rep . . . 400.00
06/46 (28) ASm,ASm(c),No(c)
Price; rep 300.00
11/48 (53) ASm,ASm(c),Pages reduced
to 48, New CI Logo;rep 275.00

015-UNCLE TOM'S CABIN
By Harriet Beecher Stowe
11/43 (---) RLv,RLv(c),Original . . 550.00
11/43 (15) RLv,RLv(c),Blank
Price Circle, Long Island
Independent Ed.;rep 200.00
07/44 (21) RLv,RLv(c),Nassau
Bulliten Edition;rep 150.00
06/46 (28) RLv,RLv(c),No(c)
Price; rep 100.00
11/48 (53) RLv,RLv(c),Pages Reduced
to 48, New CI Logo;rep 40.00
05/50 (71) RLv,RLv(c),CI Logo;rep 30.00
11/51 (89) RLv,RLv(c),15¢(c)
Price, CI Logo;rep 30.00
03/54 (117) RLv,New P(c),CI
Logo, Lettering Changes;rep . . 15.00
09/55 (128) RLv,P(c),"Picture
Progress"Promotion,CI Logo;rep 12.00
03/57 (137) RLv,P(c),CI Logo;rep . 6.00
09/58 (146) RLv,P(c),CI Logo;rep . 6.00
01/60 (154) RLv,P(c),CI Logo;rep . 6.00
03/61 (161) RLv,P(c),CI Logo;rep . 6.00
62/63 (167) RLv,P(c),CI Logo;rep . 6.00
06/64 (167) RLv,P(c),CI Logo;rep . 6.00
05/65 (167) RLv,P(c),CI Logo;rep . 6.00
05/67 (167) RLv,P(c),CI Logo;rep . 6.00
Wr/69 (166) RLv,P(c),CI
Logo, Rigid(c);rep 12.00
Sr/70 (169) RLv,P(c),CI
Logo, Rigid(c);rep 12.00

016-GULLIVER'S TRAVELS
By Johnathan Swift

12/43 (----) LCh,LCh(c),Original . 550.00
06/44 (18/20) LCh,LCh(c),Queen's Home
News Edition,No(c)Price;rep . . 175.00
10/44 (22) LCh, LCh(c),Queen's
Home News Editon;rep 135.00
06/46 (28) LCh,LCh(c);rep 100.00
06/49 (60) LCh,LCh(c),Pgs. Reduced
To 48, New CI Logo;rep 40.00
08/49 (62) LCh,LCh(c),CI Logo;rep 25.00
10/49 (64) LCh,LCh(c),CI Logo;rep 25.00
12/50 (78) LCh,LCh(c),15¢(c)
Price, CI Logo;rep 15.00
11/51 (89) LCh,LCh(c),CI Logo;rep 15.00
03/60 (155) LCh,New P(c),CI
Logo; rep 6.00
1962 (165) LCh,P(c),CI Logo;rep . 6.00
05/64 (167) LCh,P(c),CI Logo;rep . 6.00
11/65 (167) LCh,P(c),CI Logo;rep . 6.00
1968 (166) LCh,P(c),CI Logo,
25¢(c)Price;rep 6.00
Wr/69 (169) LCh,P(c),CI
Logo, Rigid(c);rep 6.00

CI #11 Don Quixote
© Gilberton Publications

017-THE DEERSLAYER
By James Fenimore Cooper
01/44 (----) LZ,LZ(c),Original . . 500.00
03/44 (18) LZ,LZ(c),No(c)Price;rep 175.00
10/44 (22) LZ,LZ(c),Queen's
City Times Edition;rep 150.00
06/46 (28) LZ,LZ(c);rep 100.00
06/49 (60) LZ,LZ(c),Pgs. Reduced
to 48,New CI Logo;rep 40.00
10/49 (64) LZ,LZ(c),CI Logo;rep . 25.00
07/51 (85) LZ,LZ(c),15¢(c)
Price, CI Logo;rep 20.00
04/54 (118) LZ,LZ(c),CI Logo;rep . 18.00
05/56 (132) LZ,LZ(c),CI Logo;rep . 15.00
11/66 (167) LZ,LZ(c),CI Logo;rep . 15.00
1968 (166) LZ,StA New P(c),CI
Logo, 25¢(c)Price;rep 20.00
Sg/71 (169) LZ,StA P(c),CI Logo,
Rigid(c), Letters From Parents
and Educators;rep 18.00

018-THE HUNCHBACK OF NOTRE DAME
By Victor Hugo
03/44 (----) ASm,ASm(c),Original
Gilberton Edition 700.00
03/44 (----) ASm,ASm(c),Original
Island Publications Edition . . . 525.00
06/44 (18/20) ASm, ASm(c),Queens

Home News Edition;rep 200.00
10/44 (22) ASm,ASm(c),Queens
City Times Edition;rep 150.00
06/46 (28) ASm,ASm(c);rep 125.00
06/49 (60) ASm,HcK New(c)8 Pgs.
Deleted, New CI Logo;rep 40.00
08/49 (62) ASm,HcK(c),CI
Logo;rep 25.00
12/50 (78) ASm,HcK(c),15¢(c)
Price; CI Logo;rep 20.00
11/51 (89) ASm,HcK(c),CI
Logo;rep 15.00
04/54 (118) ASm,HcK(c),CI
Logo;rep 25.00
09/57 (140) ASm,New P(c),CI
Logo; rep 20.00
09/58 (146) ASm,P(c),CI Logo;rep 20.00
09/60 (158) GE&RC New Art,GMc
New P(c),CI Logo;rep 7.00
1962 (165) GE&RC,GMc P(c),CI
Logo; rep 7.00
09/63 (167) GE&RC,GMc P(c),CI
Logo; rep 7.00
10/64 (167) GE&RC,GMc P(c),CI
Logo; rep 6.00
04/66 (167) GE&RC,GMc P(c),CI
Logo; rep 6.00
1968 (166) GE&RC,GMc P(c),CI
Logo, 25¢(c)Price;rep 6.00
Sr/70 (169) GE&RC,GMc P(c),CI
Logo, Rigid(c);rep 6.00

019-HUCKLEBERRY FINN
By Mark Twain
04/44 (----) LZ,LZ(c),Original
Gilberton Edition 400.00
04/44 (----) LZ,LZ(c),Original Island
Publications Company Edition 450.00
03/44 (18) LZ,LZ(c),Nassau
Bulliten Editon;rep 200.00
10/44 (22) LZ,LZ(c),Queens City
Times Edition;rep 150.00
06/46 (28) LZ,LZ(c);rep 100.00
06/49 (60) LZ,LZ(c),New CI Logo,
Pgs.Reduced to 48;rep 35.00
08/49 (62) LZ,LZ(c),CI Logo;rep . 25.00
12/50 (78) LZ,LZ(c),CI Logo;rep . 20.00
11/51 (89) LZ,LZ(c),CI Logo;rep . 18.00
03/54 (117) LZ,LZ(c),CI Logo;rep . 18.00
03/56 (131) FrG New Art,New
P(c), CI Logo: rep6.00
09/57 (140) FrG,P(c),CI Logo;rep . 6.00
05/59 (150) FrG,P(c),CI Logo;rep . 6.00
09/60 (158) FrG,P(c),CI Logo;rep . 6.00
1962 (165) FrG,P(c),CI Logo;rep . 6.00
62/63 (167) FrG,P(c),CI Logo;rep . 6.00
06/64 (167) FrG,P(c),CI Logo;rep . 6.00
06/65 (167) FrG,P(c),CI Logo;rep . 6.00
10/65 (167) FrG,P(c),CI Logo;rep . 6.00
09/67 (166) FrG,P(c),CI Logo;rep . 6.00
Wr/69 (166) FrG,P(c),CI Logo,
25¢(c)Price, Rigid(c);rep 5.00
Sr/70 (169) FrG,P(c),CI Logo,
Rigid(c);rep 5.00

020-THE CORSICAN BROTHERS
By Alexandre Dumas
06/44 (----) ASm,ASm(c),Original
Gilberton Edition 450.00
06/44 (----) ASm,ASm(c),Original
Courier Edition 400.00
06/44 (----) ASm,ASm(c),Original Long
Island Independent Edition . . . 400.00
10/44 (22) ASm,ASm(c),Queens

City Times Edition;rep 175.00
06/46 **(28)** ASm,ASm(c);rep . . . 150.00
06/49 **(60)** ASm,ASm(c),No(c)Price,
New CI Logo,Pgs. Reduced
to 48;rep 125.00
08/49 **(62)** ASm,ASm(c),CI
Logo;rep 115.00
12/50 **(78)** ASm,ASm(c),15¢(c)
Price, CI Logo;rep 100.00
07/52 **(97)** ASm,ASm(c),CI
Logo;rep 90.00

CI #17 The Deerslayer
© Gilberton Publications

021-FAMOUS MYSTERIES
By Sir Arthur Conan Doyle
Guy de Maupassant
& Edgar Allan Poe

07/44 **(---)** ASm,AdH,LZ,ASm(c),
Original Gilberton Edition 750.00
07/44 **(---)** ASm,AdH,LZ,ASm(c),
Original Island Publications
Edition; No Date or Indicia . . 775.00
07/44 **(---)** ASm,AdH,LZ,ASm(c),Original
Richmond Courier Edition 700.00
10/44 **(22)** ASm,AdH,LZ,ASm(c),
Nassau Bulliten Edition;rep . . . 275.00
09/46 **(30)** ASm,AdH,LZ,ASm(c);
rep 225.00
08/49 **(62)** ASm,AdH,LZ,ASm(c),
New CI Logo;rep 185.00
04/50 **(70)** ASm,AdH,LZ,ASm(c),
CI Logo;rep 175.00
07/51 **(85)** ASm,AdH,LZ,ASm(c),
15¢(c) Price,CI Logo;rep 150.00
12/53 **(114)** ASm,AdH,LZ,New
P(c), CI Logo;rep 150.00

022-THE PATHFINDER
By James Fenimore Cooper

10/44 **(---)** LZ,LZ(c),Original
Gilberton Edition 350.00
10/44 **(---)** LZ,LZ(c),Original
Island Publications Edition; . . . 300.00
10/44 **(---)** LZ,LZ(c),Original
Queens County Times Edition 300.00
09/46 **(30)** LZ,LZ(c),No(c)
Price;rep 100.00
06/49 **(60)** LZ,LZ(c),New CI Logo,
Pgs.Reduced To 48;rep 35.00
08/49 **(62)** LZ,LZ(c),CI Logo;rep . 28.00
04/50 **(70)** LZ,LZ(c),CI Logo;rep . 25.00
07/51 **(85)** LZ,LZ(c),15¢(c)

Price, CI Logo;rep 20.00
04/54 **(118)** LZ,LZ(c),CI Logo;rep . 15.00
05/56 **(132)** LZ,LZ(c),CI Logo;rep . 15.00
09/58 **(146)** LZ,LZ(c),CI Logo;rep . 25.00
11/63 **(167)** LZ,NN New P(c),CI
Logo; rep 20.00
12/65 **(167)** LZ,NN P(c),CI
Logo;rep 20.00
08/67 **(166)** LZ,NN P(c),CI
Logo;rep 20.00

023-OLIVER TWIST
By Charles Dickens
(First Classic produced by
the Iger shop)

07/45 **(---)** AdH,AdH(c),Original . 350.00
09/46 **(30)** AdH,AdH(c),Price
Circle is Blank;rep 250.00
06/49 **(60)** AdH,AdH(c),Pgs. Reduced
To 48, New CI Logo;rep 35.00
08/49 **(62)** AdH,AdH(c),CI
Logo;rep 25.00
05/50 **(71)** AdH,AdH(c),CI
Logo;rep 25.00
07/51 **(85)** AdH,AdH(c),15¢(c)
Price CI Logo;rep 20.00
04/52 **(94)** AdH,AdH(c),CI
Logo;rep 20.00
04/54 **(118)** AdH,AdH(c),CI
Logo;rep 15.00
01/57 **(136)** AdH,New P(c),CI
Logo; rep 15.00
05/59 **(150)** AdH,P(c),CI Logo;rep 12.00
1961 **(164)** AdH,P(c),CI Logo;rep . 12.00
10/61 **(164)** GE&RC New Art,P(c),
CI Logo;rep 20.00
62/63 **(167)** GE&RC,P(c),CI
Logo; rep 6.00
08/64 **(167)** GE&RC,P(c),CI
Logo; rep 6.00
12/65 **(167)** GE&RC,P(c),
CI Logo;rep 6.00
1968 **(166)** GE&RC,P(c),CI
Logo, 25¢(c)Price;rep 6.00
Wr/69 **(169)** GE&RC,P(c),CI
Logo, Rigid(c);rep 6.00

024-A CONNECTICUT
YANKEE IN KING
ARTHUR'S COURT
By Mark Twain

09/45 **(---)** JH,JH(c),Original . . . 300.00
09/46 **(30)** JH,JH(c),Price Circle
Blank;rep 100.00
06/49 **(60)** JH,JH(c),8 Pages
Deleted,New CI Logo;rep 30.00
08/49 **(62)** JH,JH(c),CI Logo;rep . 28.00
05/50 **(71)** JH,JH(c),CI Logo;rep . 20.00
09/51 **(87)** JH,JH(c),15¢(c) Price
CI Logo;rep 18.00
07/54 **(121)** JH,JH(c),CI Logo;rep 15.00
09/57 **(140)** JkS New Art,New
P(c),CI Logo; rep 15.00
11/59 **(153)** JkS,P(c),CI Logo;rep . 6.00
1961 **(164)** JkS,P(c),CI Logo;rep . 6.00
62/63 **(167)** JkS,P(c),CI Logo;rep . 6.00
07/64 **(167)** JkS,P(c),CI Logo;rep . 6.00
06/66 **(167)** JkS,P(c),CI Logo;rep . 6.00
1968 **(166)** JkS,P(c),CI logo,
25¢(c)Price;rep 6.00
Sg/71 **(169)** JkS,P(c),CI Logo,
Rigid(c);rep 6.00

025-TWO YEARS
BEFORE THE MAST
By Richard Henry Dana Jr.

10/45 **(---)** RWb,DvH,Original; . 300.00
09/46 **(30)** RWb,DvH,Price Circle
Blank;rep 100.00
06/49 **(60)** RWb,DvH,8 Pages
Deleted,New CI Logo;rep 35.00
08/49 **(62)** RWb,DvH,CI Logo;rep 30.00
05/50 **(71)** RWb,DvH,CI Logo;rep 20.00
07/51 **(85)** RWb,DvH,15¢(c) Price
CI Logo;rep 15.00
12/53 **(114)** RWb,DvH,CI Logo;rep 15.00
05/60 **(156)** RWb,DvH,New P(c),CI Logo,
3 Pgs. Replaced By Fillers;rep . 15.00
12/63 **(167)** RWb,DvH,P(c),CI
Logo; rep 6.00
12/65 **(167)** RWb,DvH,P(c),CI
Logo; rep 6.00
09/67 **(166)** RWb,DvH,P(c),CI
Logo; rep 6.00
Wr/69 **(169)** RWb,DvH,P(c),25¢(c)
Price, CI Logo,Rigid(c);rep 6.00

026-FRANKENSTEIN
By Mary Wollstonecraft Shelley

12/45 **(---)** RWb&ABr,RWb
& ABr(c), Original 750.00
09/46 **(30)** RWb&ABr,RWb &ABr(c),
Price Circle Blank;rep 225.00
06/49 **(60)** RWb&ABr,RWb&ABr(c),
New CI Logo;rep 65.00
08/49 **(62)** RWb&ABr,RWb
& ABr(c), CI Logo;rep 100.00
05/50 **(71)** RWb&ABr,RWb
& ABr(c), CI Logo;rep 45.00
04/51 **(82)** RWb&ABr,RWb &ABr(c),
15¢(c) Price,CI Logo;rep 30.00
03/54 **(117)** RWb&ABr,RWb
& ABr(c),CI Logo;rep 20.00
09/58 **(146)** RWb&ABr,NS
New P(c), CI Logo; rep 20.00
11/59 **(153)** RWb&ABr,NS
P(c),CI Logo; rep 35.00
01/61 **(160)** RWb&ABr,NS
P(c),CI Logo; rep 6.00
165 **(1962)** RWb&ABr,NS P(c),
CI Logo; rep 6.00
62/63 **(167)** RWb&ABr,NS P(c),
CI Logo; rep 6.00
06/64 **(167)** RWb&ABr,NS P(c),
CI logo; rep 6.00
06/65 **(167)** RWb&ABr,NS P(c),
CI Logo; rep 6.00
10/65 **(167)** RWb&ABr,NS P(c),
CI Logo; rep 6.00
09/67 **(166)** RWb&ABr,NS P(c),
CI Logo; rep 6.00
FI/69 **(169)** RWb&ABr,NS P(c),25¢(c)
Price,CI Logo,Rigid(c);rep 6.00
Sg/71 **(169)** RWb&ABr,NS P(c),
CI Logo, Rigid(c);rep 6.00

027-THE ADVENTURES
MARCO POLO
By Marco Polo & Donn Byrne

04/46 **(----)** HFI,HFI(c);Original . . 300.00
09/46 **(30)** HFI,HFI(c);rep 85.00
04/50 **(70)** HFI,HFI(c),8 Pages Deleted,
No(c) Price,New CI Logo;rep . . 25.00
09/51 **(87)** HFI,HFI(c),15¢(c)
Price,CI Logo;rep 20.00
03/54 **(117)** HFI,HFI(c),CILogo;rep 15.00
01/60 **(154)** HFI,New P(c),CI
Logo;rep 15.00

All comics prices listed are for *Near Mint* condition.　　　**CVA Page 635**

1962 **(165)** HFl,P(c),CI Logo;rep .. 6.00
04/64 **(167)** HFl,P(c),CI Logo;rep .. 6.00
06/66 **(167)** HFl,P(c),CI Logo;rep .. 6.00
Sg/69 **(169)** HFl,P(c),CI Logo,
25¢(c)Price,Rigid(c);rep 6.00

028-MICHAEL STROGOFF
By Jules Verne
06/46 **(---)** AdH,AdH(c),Original . 325.00
09/48 **(51)** AdH,AdH(c),8 Pages
Deleted,New CI Logo;rep 100.00
01/54 **(115)** AdH,New P(c),CI
Logo; rep 20.00
03/60 **(155)** AdH,P(c),CI Logo;rep 10.00
11/63 **(167)** AdH,P(c),CI Logo;rep 10.00
07/66 **(167)** AdH,P(c),CI Logo;rep 10.00
Sr/69 **(169)**AdH,NN,NewP(c),25¢(c)
Price, CI Logo,Rigid(c);rep 15.00

CI #24 A Connecticut Yankee in King
Arthur's Court © Gilberton Publications

029-THE PRINCE
AND THE PAUPER
By Mark Twain
07/46 **(---)** AdH,AdH(c),Original . 500.00
06/49 **(60)** AdH,New HcK(c),New CI
Logo,8 Pages Deleted;rep 35.00
08/49 **(62)** AdH,HcK(c),CILogo;rep 30.00
05/50 **(71)** AdH,HcK(c),CILogo;rep 25.00
03/52 **(93)** AdH,HcK(c),CILogo;rep 20.00
12/53 **(114)** AdH,HcK(c),CI
Logo;rep 15.00
09/55 **(128)** AdH,New P(c),CI
Logo; rep 15.00
05/57 **(138)** AdH,P(c),CI Logo;rep . 6.00
05/59 **(150)** AdH,P(c),CI Logo;rep . 6.00
1961 **(164)** AdH,P(c),CI Logo;rep .. 6.00
62/63 **(167)** AdH,P(c),CI Logo;rep . 6.00
07/64 **(167)** AdH,P(c),CI Logo;rep . 6.00
11/65 **(167)** AdH,P(c),CI Logo;rep . 6.00
1968 **(166)** AdH,P(c),CI Logo,
25¢(c)Price;rep 6.00
Sr/70 **(169)** AdH,P(c),CI Logo,
Rigid(c);rep 6.00

030-THE MOONSTONE
By William Wilkie Collins
09/46 **(---)** DRi,DRi(c),Original .. 300.00
06/49 **(60)** DRi,DRi(c),8 Pages
Deleted,New CI Logo;rep 40.00
04/50 **(70)** DRi,DRi(c),CI Logo;rep 35.00
03/60 **(155)** DRi,LbC New P(c),
CI Logo;rep 45.00

1962 **(165)** DRi,LbC P(c),CI Logo;
rep 20.00
01/64 **(167)** DRi,LbC P(c),CI Logo;
rep 15.00
09/65 **(167)** DRi,LbC P(c),CI Logo;
rep 10.00
1968 **(166)** DRi,LbC P(c),CI Logo,
25¢(c)Price;rep 8.00

031-THE BLACK ARROW
By Robert Louis Stevenson
10/46 **(---)** AdH,AdH(c),Original . 275.00
09/48 **(51)** AdH,AdH(c),8 Pages
Deleted,New CI Logo;rep 35.00
10/49 **(64)** AdH,AdH(c),CI
Logo;rep 20.00
09/51 **(87)** AdH,AdH(c),15¢(c)
Price;CI Logo;rep 17.00
06/53 **(108)** AdH,AdH(c),CI
Logo;rep 15.00
03/55 **(125)** AdH,AdH(c),CI
Logo;rep 14.00
03/56 **(131)** AdH,New P(c),CI
Logo; rep 12.00
09/57 **(140)** AdH,P(c),CI Logo;rep . 6.00
01/59 **(148)** AdH,P(c),CI Logo;rep . 6.00
03/61 **(161)** AdH,P(c),CI Logo;rep . 6.00
62/63 **(167)** AdH,P(c),CI Logo;rep . 6.00
07/64 **(167)** AdH,P(c),CI logo;rep . 6.00
11/65 **(167)** AdH,P(c),CI Logo;rep . 6.00
1968 **(166)** AdH,P(c),CI Logo,
25¢(c)Price;rep 6.00

032-LORNA DOONE
By Richard Doddridge Blackmore
12/46 **(---)** MB,MB(c),Original ... 300.00
10/49 **(53/64)** MB,MB(c),8 Pages
Deleted,New CI Logo;rep 40.00
07/51 **(85)** MB,MB(c),15¢(c)
Price, CI Logo;rep 30.00
04/54 **(118)** MB,MB(c),CI Logo;rep 20.00
05/57 **(138)** MB,New P(c); Old(c)
Becomes New Splash Pge.,CI
Logo;rep 20.00
05/59 **(150)** MB,P(c),CI Logo;rep . 6.00
1962 **(165)** MB,P(c),CI Logo;rep .. 6.00
01/64 **(167)** MB,P(c),CI Logo;rep . 6.00
11/65 **(167)** MB,P(c),CI Logo;rep . 6.00
1968 **(166)** MB,New P(c),CI Logo;
rep 15.00

033-THE ADVENTURES
OF SHERLOCK HOLMES
By Sir Arthur Conan Doyle
01/47 **(---)** LZ,HcK(c),Original . 1,000.00
11/48 **(53)** LZ,HcK(c),"A Study in Scarlet"
Deleted,New CI Logo;rep 350.00
05/50 **(71)** LZ,HcK(c),CI Logo;rep 275.00
11/51 **(89)** LZ,HcK(c),15¢(c)
Price,CI Logo;rep 225.00

034-MYSTERIOUS ISLAND
By Jules Verne
Last Classic Comic
02/47 **(---)** RWb&DvH,Original .. 325.00
06/49 **(60)** RWb&DvH,8 Pages
Deleted,New CI Logo;rep 35.00
08/49 **(62)** RWb&DvH,CI Logo;rep 25.00
05/50 **(71)** RWb&DvH,CI Logo;rep 40.00
12/50 **(78)** RWb&DvH,15¢(c) Price,
CI Logo;rep 20.00
02/52 **(92)** RWb&DvH,CI Logo;rep 20.00
03/54 **(117)** RWb&DvH,CI Logo;rep 20.00
09/57 **(140)** RWb&DvH,New P(c),CI
Logo;rep 20.00

05/60 **(156)** RWb&DvH,P(c),CI
Logo;rep 6.00
10/63 **(167)** RWb&DvH,P(c),CI
Logo;rep 6.00
05/64 **(167)** RWb&DvH,P(c),CI
Logo;rep 6.00
06/66 **(167)** RWb&DvH,P(c),CI
Logo;rep 6.00
1968 **(166)** RWb&DvH,P(c),CI Logo,
25¢(c)Price;rep 6.00

035-LAST DAYS
OF POMPEII
By Lord Edward Bulwer Lytton
First Classics Illustrated
03/47 **(---)** HcK,HcK(c),Original . 325.00
03/61 **(161)** JK,New P(c),
15¢(c)Price;rep 30.00
01/64 **(167)** JK,P(c);rep 15.00
07/66 **(167)** JK,P(c);rep 15.00
Sg/70 **(169)** JK,P(c),25¢(c)
Price, Rigid(c);rep 16.00

036-TYPEE
By Herman Melville
04/47 **(---)** EzW,EzW(c),Original . 175.00
10/49 **(64)** EzW,EzW(c),No(c)price,
8 pages deleted;rep 40.00
03/60 **(155)** EzW,GMc New
P(c);rep 15.00
09/63 **(167)** EzW,GMc P(c);rep .. 10.00
07/65 **(167)** EzW,GMc P(c);rep .. 10.00
Sr/69 **(169)** EzW,GMc P(c),25¢(c)
Price, Rigid(c);rep 10.00

037-THE PIONEERS
By James Fenimore Cooper
05/47 **(37)** RP,RP(c),Original ... 135.00
08/49 **(62)** RP,RP(c),8 Pages
Deleted;rep 30.00
04/50 **(70)** RP,RP(c);rep 25.00
02/52 **(92)** RP,RP(c),15¢(c)price;rep25.00
04/54 **(118)** RP,RP(c);rep 20.00
03/56 **(131)** RP,RP(c);rep 20.00
05/56 **(132)** RP,RP(c);rep 20.00
11/59 **(153)** RP,RP(c);rep 15.00
05/64 **(167)** RP,RP(c);rep 15.00
06/66 **(167)** RP,RP(c);rep 15.00
1968 **(166)** RP,TO New P(c),
25¢(c)Price;rep 25.00

038-ADVENTURES
OF CELLINI
By Benvenuto Cellini
06/47 **(---)** AgF,AgF(c),Original . 225.00
1961 **(164)** NN New Art,New P(c);
rep 20.00
12/63 **(167)** NN,P(c),rep 10.00
07/66 **(167)** NN,P(c);rep 10.00
Sg/70 **(169)** NN,P(c),25¢(c)
Price, Rigid(c);rep 12.00

039-JANE EYRE
By Charlotte Bronte
07/47 **(---)** HyG,HyG(c),Original . 225.00
06/49 **(60)** HyG,HyG(c),No(c)Price,
8 pages deleted;rep 35.00
08/49 **(62)** HyG,HyG(c);rep 30.00
05/50 **(71)** HyG,HyG(c);rep 25.00
02/52 **(92)** HyG,HyG(c),15¢(c)
Price; rep 20.00
04/54 **(118)** HyG,HyG(c);rep 20.00
01/58 **(142)** HyG,New P(c);rep .. 20.00
01/60 **(154)** HyG,P(c);rep 20.00

1962 **(165)** HjK New Art,P(c);rep . 20.00
12/63 **(167)** HjK,P(c);rep 20.00
04/65 **(167)** HjK,P(c);rep 20.00
08/66 **(167)** HjK,P(c);rep 20.00
1968 **(166)** HjK,NN New P(c);rep . 40.00

040-MYSTERIES
(The Pit & the Pendulum,
The Adventures of Hans Pfall,
Fall of the House of Usher)
By Edgar Allan Poe
08/47 **(---)** HcK,AgF,HyG,HcK(c),
Original 525.00
08/49 **(62)** HcK,AgF,HyG,HcK(c),
8 Pages deleted;rep 225.00
09/50 **(75)** HcK,AgF,HyG,
HcK(c);rep 200.00
02/52 **(92)** HcK,AgF,HyG,HcK(c)
15¢(c) Price;rep 150.00

041-TWENTY YEARS
AFTER
By Alexandre Dumas
09/47 **(---)** RBu,RBu(c),Original . 400.00
08/49 **(62)** RBu,HcK New(c),No(c)
Price, 8 Pages Deleted;rep 35.00
12/50 **(78)** RBu,HcK(c),15¢(c)
Price;rep 25.00
05/60 **(156)** RBu,DgR New P(c);rep 20.00
12/63 **(167)** RBu,DgR P(c);rep . . . 10.00
11/66 **(167)** RBu,DgR P(c);rep . . . 10.00
Sg/70 **(169)** RBu,DgR P(c),25¢(c)
Price,Rigid(c);rep 10.00

042-SWISS FAMILY
ROBINSON
By Johann Wyss
10/47 **(42)** HcK,HcK(c),Original . 150.00
08/49 **(62)** HcK,HcK(c),No(c)price,
8 Pages deleted,Not Every Issue
Has 'Gift Box' Ad;rep 35.00
09/50 **(75)** HcK,HcK(c);rep 25.00
03/52 **(93)** HcK,HcK(c);rep 20.00
03/54 **(117)** HcK,HcK(c);rep 15.00
03/56 **(131)** HcK,New P(c);rep . . . 15.00
03/57 **(137)** HcK,P(c);rep 15.00
11/57 **(141)** HcK,P(c);rep 15.00
09/59 **(152)** NN New art,P(c);rep . 15.00
09/60 **(158)** NN,P(c);rep 8.00
12/63 **(165)** NN,P(c);rep 15.00
12/63 **(167)** NN,P(c);rep 7.00
04/65 **(167)** NN,P(c);rep 7.00
05/66 **(167)** NN,P(c);rep 7.00
11/67 **(166)** NN,P(c);rep 6.00
Sg/69 **(169)** NN,P(c);rep 6.00

043-GREAT
EXPECTATIONS
By Charles Dickens
11/47 **(---)** HcK,HcK(c),Original . 700.00
08/49 **(62)** HcK,HcK(c),No(c)price;
8 pages deleted;rep 400.00

044-MYSTERIES
OF PARIS
By Eugene Sue
12/47 **(44)** HcK,HcK(c),Original . 550.00
08/47 **(62)** HcK,HcK(c),No(c)Price,
8 Pages Deleted,Not Every Issue
Has'Gift Box'Ad;rep 225.00
12/50 **(78)** HcK,HcK(c),15¢(c)
Price; rep 200.00

045-TOM BROWN'S
SCHOOL DAYS
By Thomas Hughes
01/48 **(44)** HFl,HFl(c),Original,
1st 48 Pge. Issue 125.00
10/49 **(64)** HFl,HFl(c),No(c)
Price;rep 40.00
03/61 **(161)** JTg New Art,GMc
New P(c);rep 15.00
02/64 **(167)** JTg,GMc P(c);rep . . . 12.00
08/66 **(167)** JTg,GMc P(c);rep . . . 12.00
1968 **(166)** JTg,GMc P(c),
25¢(c)Price;rep 12.00

046-KIDNAPPED
By Robert Louis Stevenson
04/48 **(47)** RWb,RWb(c),Original 100.00
08/49 **(62)** RWb,RWb(c),Red Circle
Either Blank or With 10¢;rep . . . 62.00
12/50 **(78)** RWb,RWb(c),15¢(c)
Price; rep 25.00
09/51 **(87)** RWb,RWb(c);rep 20.00
04/54 **(118)** RWb,RWb(c);rep 15.00
03/56 **(131)** RWb,New P(c);rep . . 15.00
09/57 **(140)** RWb,P(c);rep 6.00
05/59 **(150)** RWb,P(c);rep 6.00
05/60 **(156)** RWb,P(c);rep 6.00
1961 **(164)** RWb,P(c),Reduced Pge.
Width;rep 6.00
62/63 **(167)** RWb,P(c);rep 6.00
03/64 **(167)** RWb,P(c);rep 6.00
06/65 **(167)** RWb,P(c);rep 6.00
12/65 **(167)** RWb,P(c);rep 6.00
09/67 **(167)** RWb,P(c);rep 6.00
Wr/69 **(166)** RWb,P(c),25¢(c)
Price, Rigid(c);rep 6.00
Sr/70 **(169)** RWb,P(c),Rigid(c);rep . 6.00

047-TWENTY
THOUSAND LEAGUES
UNDER THE SEA
By Jules Verne
05/58 **(47)** HcK,HcK(c),Original . 100.00
10/49 **(64)** HcK,HcK(c),No(c)
Price; rep 30.00
12/50 **(78)** HcK,HcK(c),15¢(c)
Price; rep 25.00
04/52 **(94)** HcK,HcK(c);rep 25.00
04/54 **(118)** HcK,HcK(c);rep 20.00
09/55 **(128)** HcK,New P(c);rep . . . 15.00
07/56 **(133)** HcK,P(c);rep 15.00
09/57 **(140)** HcK,P(c);rep 6.00
01/59 **(148)** HcK,P(c);rep 6.00
05/60 **(156)** HcK,P(c);rep 6.00
62/63 **(165)** HcK,P(c);rep 6.00
05/48 **(167)** HcK,P(c);rep 6.00
03/64 **(167)** HcK,P(c);rep 6.00
08/65 **(167)** HcK,P(c);rep 6.00
10/66 **(167)** HcK,P(c);rep 6.00
1968 **(166)** HcK,NN New P(c),
25¢(c)Price;rep 12.00
Sg/70 **(169)** HcK,NN P(c),
Rigid(c);rep 12.00

048-DAVID
COPPERFIELD
By Charles Dickens
06/48 **(47)** HcK,HcK(c),Original . 100.00
10/49 **(64)** HcK,HcK(c),Price Circle
Replaced By Image of Boy
Reading;rep 30.00
09/51 **(87)** HcK,HcK(c),15¢(c)
Price; rep 25.00
07/54 **(121)** HcK,New P(c);rep . . . 15.00

10/56 **(130)** HcK,P(c);rep 7.00
09/57 **(140)** HcK,P(c);rep 7.00
01/59 **(148)** HcK,P(c);rep 7.00
05/60 **(156)** HcK,P(c);rep 7.00
62/63 **(167)** HcK,P(c);rep 6.00
04/64 **(167)** HcK,P(c);rep 6.00
06/65 **(167)** HcK,P(c);rep 6.00
05/67 **(166)** HcK,P(c);rep 6.00
R/67 **(166)** HcK,P(c);rep 11.00
Sg/69 **(166)** HcK,P(c),25¢(c)
Price, Rigid(c);rep 6.00
Wr/69 **(169)** HcK,P(c),Rigid(c);rep . 6.00

CI #31 The Black Arrow
© Gilberton Publications

049-ALICE IN
WONDERLAND
By Lewis Carroll
07/48 **(47)** AB,AB(c),Original . . . 135.00
10/49 **(64)** AB,AB(c),No(c)Price;rep 40.00
07/51 **(85)** AB,AB(c),15¢(c)Price;rep 30.00
03/60 **(155)** AB,New P(c);rep 30.00
1962 **(165)** AB,P(c);rep 25.00
03/64 **(167)** AB,P(c);rep 20.00
06/66 **(167)** AB,P(c);rep 20.00
Fl/68 **(166)** AB,TO New P(c),25¢(c)
Price, New Soft(c);rep 30.00
Fl/68 **(166)** AB,P(c),Both Soft &
Rigid(c)s;rep 50.00

050-ADVENTURES OF
TOM SAWYER
By Mark Twain
08/48 **(51)** ARu,ARu(c),Original . 125.00
09/48 **(51)** ARu,ARu(c),Original . 130.00
10/49 **(64)** ARu,ARu(c),No(c)
Price; rep 25.00
12/50 **(78)** ARu,ARu(c),15¢(c)
Price; rep 20.00
04/52 **(94)** ARu,ARu(c);rep 20.00
12/53 **(114)** ARu,ARu(c);rep 15.00
03/54 **(117)** ARu,ARu(c);rep 15.00
05/56 **(132)** ARu,ARu(c);rep 15.00
09/57 **(140)** ARu,New P(c);rep . . . 10.00
05/59 **(150)** ARu,P(c);rep 15.00
10/61 **(164)** ARu,New Art,P(c);rep 6.00
62/63 **(167)** P(c);rep 6.00
01/65 **(167)** P(c);rep 6.00
05/66 **(167)** P(c);rep 6.00
12/67 **(166)** P(c);rep 6.00
Fl/69 **(169)** P(c),25¢(c) Price,
Rigid(c);rep 6.00
Wr/71 **(169)** P(c);rep 6.00

All comics prices listed are for *Near Mint* condition.

051-THE SPY
By James Fenimore Cooper
09/48 **(51)** AdH,AdH(c),Original,
Maroon(c) 100.00
09/48 **(51)** AdH,AdH(c),Original,
Violet(c) 100.00
11/51 **(89)** AdH,AdH(c),15¢(c)
Price; rep 25.00
07/54 **(121)** AdH,AdH(c);rep 20.00
07/57 **(139)** AdH,New P(c);rep . . . 15.00
05/60 **(156)** AdH,P(c);rep 6.00
11/63 **(167)** AdH,P(c);rep 6.00
07/66 **(167)** AdH,P(c);rep 6.00
Wr/69 **(166)** AdH,P(c);rep,Price,
Both Soft & Rigid(c)s;rep 20.00

052-THE HOUSE OF SEVEN GABLES
By Nathaniel Hawthorne
10/48 **(53)** HyG,HyG(c),Original . 100.00
11/51 **(89)** HyG,HyG(c),15¢(c)
Price; rep 25.00
07/54 **(121)** HyG,HyG(c);rep 20.00
01/58 **(142)** GWb New Art,New
P(c); rep 15.00
05/60 **(156)** GWb,P(c);rep 6.00
1962 **(165)** GWb,P(c);rep 6.00
05/64 **(167)** GWb,P(c);rep 6.00
03/66 **(167)** GWb,P(c);rep 6.00
1968 **(166)** GWb,P(c),25¢(c)
Price; rep 6.00
Sg/70 **(169)** GWb,P(c),Rigid(c);rep . 6.00

053-A CHRISTMAS CAROL
By Charles Dickens
11/48 **(53)** HcK,HcK(c),Original . 125.00

054-MAN IN THE IRON MASK
By Alexandre Dumas
12/48 **(55)** AgF,HcK(c),Original . 100.00
03/52 **(93)** AgF,HcK(c),15¢(c)
Price; rep 25.00
09/53 **(111)** AgF,HcK(c);rep 35.00
01/58 **(142)** KBa New Art,New
P(c); rep 15.00
01/60 **(154)** KBa,P(c);rep 6.00
1962 **(165)** KBa,P(c);rep 6.00
05/64 **(167)** KBa,P(c);rep 6.00
04/66 **(167)** KBa,P(c);rep 6.00
Wr/69 **(166)** KBa,P(c),25¢(c)
Price, Rigid(c);rep 6.00

055-SILAS MARINER
By George Eliot
01/49 **(55)** AdH,HcK(c),Original . 100.00
09/50 **(75)** AdH,HcK(c),Price Circle
Blank,'Coming next'Ad(not
usually in reps.);rep 30.00
07/52 **(97)** AdH,HcK(c);rep 20.00
07/54 **(121)** AdH,New P(c);rep . . . 15.00
01/56 **(130)** AdH,P(c);rep 6.00
09/57 **(140)** AdH,P(c);rep 6.00
01/60 **(154)** AdH,P(c);rep 6.00
1962 **(165)** AdH,P(c);rep 6.00
05/64 **(167)** AdH,P(c);rep 6.00
06/65 **(167)** AdH,P(c);rep 6.00
05/67 **(166)** AdH,P(c);rep 6.00
Wr/69 **(166)** AdH,P(c),25¢(c) Price,
Rigid(c);rep,Soft & Stiff 16.00

056-THE TOILERS OF THE SEA
By Victor Hugo
02/49 **(55)** AgF,AgF(c),Original . 175.00
01/62 **(165)** AT New Art,New
P(c); rep. 30.00
03/64 **(167)** AT,P(c);rep. 20.00
10/66 **(167)** AT,P(c);rep. 20.00

057-THE SONG OF HIAWATHA
By Henry Wadsworth Longfellow
03/49 **(55)** AB,AB(c),Original . . . 100.00
09/50 **(75)** AB,AB(c),No(c)price,'
Coming Next'Ad(not usually
found in reps.);rep 30.00
04/52 **(94)** AB,AB(c),15¢(c)
Price;rep 20.00
04/54 **(118)** AB,AB(c);rep 20.00
09/56 **(134)** AB,New P(c);rep . . . 15.00
07/57 **(139)** AB,P(c);rep 6.00
01/60 **(154)** AB,P(c);rep 6.00
62/63 **(167)** AB,P(c),Erroneosly
Has Original Date;rep 6.00
09/64 **(167)** AB,P(c);rep 6.00
10/65 **(167)** AB,P(c);rep 6.00
Fl/68 **(166)** AB,P(c),25¢(c) Price;rep 6.00

CI #58 The Prairie
© Gilberton Publications

058-THE PRAIRIE
By James Fenimore Cooper
04/49 **(60)** RP,RP(c),Original . . . 100.00
08/49 **(62)** RP,RP(c),rep 45.00
12/50 **(78)** RP,RP(c),15¢(c) Price
In Double Circle;rep 25.00
12/53 **(114)** RP,RP(c),rep 20.00
03/56 **(131)** RP,RP(c),rep 15.00
05/56 **(132)** RP,RP(c),rep 15.00
09/58 **(146)** RP,New P(c);rep . . . 15.00
03/60 **(155)** RP,P(c);rep 6.00
05/64 **(167)** RP,P(c);rep 6.00
04/66 **(167)** RP,P(c);rep 6.00
Sr/69 **(169)** RP,P(c),25¢(c)
Price; Rigid(c);rep 6.00

059-WUTHERING HEIGHTS
By Emily Bronte
05/49 **(60)** HcK,HcK(c),Original . 110.00
07/51 **(85)** HcK,HcK(c),15¢(c)
Price; rep 35.00
05/60 **(156)** HcK,GB New P(c);rep 20.00
01/64 **(167)** HcK,GB P(c);rep 7.00

10/66 **(167)** HcK,GB P(c);rep 7.00
Sr/69 **(169)** HcK,GBP(c),25¢(c)
Price, Rigid(c);rep 6.00

060-BLACK BEAUTY
By Anna Sewell
06/49 **(62)** AgF,AgF(c),Original . 100.00
08/49 **(62)** AgF,AgF(c);rep 125.00
07/51 **(85)** AgF,AgF(c),15¢(c) Price;
rep 25.00
09/60 **(158)** LbC&NN&StA New
Art, LbC New P(c);rep 25.00
02/64 **(167)** LbC&NN&StA,LbC
P(c); rep 20.00
03/66 **(167)** LbC&NN&StA,LbC
P(c); rep 20.00
03/66 **(167)** LbC&NN&StA,LbC
P(c), 'Open Book'Blank;rep . . . 50.00
1968 **(166)** LbC&NN&StA,AIM New
P(c) 25¢(c) Price;rep 6.00

061-THE WOMAN IN WHITE
By William Wilke Collins
07/49 **(62)** AB,AB(c),Original,
Maroon & Violet(c)s 110.00
05/60 **(156)** AB,DgR New P(c);rep 25.00
01/64 **(167)** AB,DgR P(c);rep 20.00
1968 **(166)** AB,DgR P(c),
25¢(c)Price;rep 20.00

062-WESTERN STORIES
(The Luck of Roaring Camp & The Outcasts of Poker Flat)
By Bret Harte
08/49 **(62)** HcK,HcK(c),Original . . 90.00
11/51 **(89)** HcK,HcK(c),15¢(c)
Price; rep 25.00
07/54 **(121)** HcK,HcK(c);rep 20.00
03/57 **(137)** HcK,New P(c);rep . . . 15.00
09/59 **(152)** HcK,P(c);rep 7.00
10/63 **(167)** HcK,P(c);rep 7.00
06/64 **(167)** HcK,P(c);rep 6.00
11/66 **(167)** HcK,P(c);rep 6.00
1968 **(166)** HcK,TO New P(c),
25¢ Price;rep 20.00

063-THE MAN WITHOUT A COUNTRY
By Edward Everett Hale
09/49 **(62)** HcK,HcK(c),Original . 100.00
12/50 **(78)** HcK,HcK(c),15¢(c)Price
In Double Circles;rep 25.00
05/60 **(156)** HcK,GMc New P(c);rep 22.00
01/62 **(165)** AT New Art,GMc P(c),
Added Text Pages;rep 12.00
03/64 **(167)** AT,GMc P(c);rep 6.00
08/66 **(167)** AT,GMc P(c);rep 6.00
Sr/69 **(169)** AT,GMc P(c),25¢(c)
Price, Rigid(c);rep 6.00

064-TREASURE ISLAND
By Robert Louis Stevenson
10/49 **(62)** AB,AB(c),Original . . . 90.00
04/51 **(82)** AB,AB(c),15¢(c)
Price;rep 25.00
03/54 **(117)** AB,AB(c);rep 17.00
03/56 **(131)** AB,New P(c);rep 12.00
05/57 **(138)** AB,P(c);rep 6.00
09/58 **(146)** AB,P(c);rep 6.00
09/60 **(158)** AB,P(c);rep 6.00
1962 **(165)** AB,P(c);rep 6.00

62/63 **(167)** AB,P(c);rep 6.00	
06/64 **(167)** AB,P(c);rep 6.00	
12/65 **(167)** AB,P(c);rep 6.00	
10/67 **(166)** AB,P(c);rep 11.00	
10/67 **(166)** AB,P(c),GRIT Ad	
Stapled In Book;rep 64.00	
Sg/69 **(169)** AB,P(c),25¢(c)	
Price, Rigid(c);rep 6.00	

065-BENJAMIN FRANKLIN
By Benjamin Franklin

11/49 **(64)** AB,RtH,GS(Iger Shop),	
HcK(c),Original 100.00	
03/56 **(131)** AB,RtH,GS(Iger Shop),	
New P(c) ;rep 20.00	
01/60 **(154)** AB,RtH,GS(Iger Shop),	
P(c);rep 7.00	
02/64 **(167)** AB,RtH,GS(Iger Shop),	
P(c);rep 7.00	
04/66 **(167)** AB,RtH,GS(Iger Shop),	
P(c);rep 7.00	
Fl/69 **(169)** AB,RtH,GS(Iger Shop),	
P(c), 25¢(c)Price,Rigid(c);rep ... 6.00	

066-THE CLOISTER AND THE HEARTH
By Charles Reade

12/49 **(67)** HcK,HcK(c),Original . 200.00

067-THE SCOTTISH CHIEFS
By Jane Porter

01/50 **(67)** AB,AB(c),Original 90.00	
07/51 **(85)** AB,AB(c),15¢(c)	
Price;rep 25.00	
04/54 **(118)** AB,AB(c);rep 20.00	
01/57 **(136)** AB,New P(c);rep 15.00	
01/60 **(154)** AB,P(c);rep 10.00	
11/63 **(167)** AB,P(c);rep 10.00	
08/65 **(167)** AB,P(c);rep 10.00	

CI #68 Julius Caesar,
© Gilberton Publications

068-JULIUS CEASAR
By William Shakespeare

02/50 **(70)** HcK,HcK(c),Original .. 90.00	
07/51 **(85)** HcK,HcK(c),15¢(c)	
Price; rep 25.00	
06/53 **(108)** HcK,HcK(c);rep 20.00	
05/60 **(156)** HcK,LbC New P(c);rep 25.00	
1962 **(165)** GE&RC New Art,	
LbC P(c);rep 25.00	
02/64 **(167)** GE&RC,LbC P(c);rep . 6.00	

10/65 **(167)** GE&RC,LbC P(c),Tarzan	
Books Inside(c);rep 6.00	
1967 **(166)** GE&RC,LbC P(c);rep . 6.00	
Wr/69 **(169)** GE&RC,LbC P(c),	
Rigid(c);rep 6.00	

069-AROUND THE WORLD IN 80 DAYS
By Jules Verne

03/50 **(70)** HcK,HcK(c),Original .. 90.00	
09/51 **(87)** HcK,HcK(c),15¢(c)	
Price; rep 25.00	
03/55 **(125)** HcK,HcK(c);rep 20.00	
01/57 **(136)** HcK,New P(c);rep ... 15.00	
09/58 **(146)** HcK,P(c);rep 6.00	
09/59 **(152)** HcK,P(c);rep 6.00	
1961 **(164)** HcK,P(c);rep 6.00	
62/63 **(167)** HcK,P(c);rep 6.00	
07/64 **(167)** HcK,P(c);rep 6.00	
11/65 **(167)** HcK,P(c);rep 6.00	
07/67 **(166)** HcK,P(c);rep 6.00	
Sg/69 **(169)** HcK,P(c),25¢(c)	
Price, Rigid(c);rep 6.00	

070-THE PILOT
By James Fenimore Cooper

04/50 **(71)** AB,AB(c),Original 80.00	
10/50 **(75)** AB,AB(c),15¢(c)	
Price;rep 25.00	
02/52 **(92)** AB,AB(c);rep 20.00	
03/55 **(125)** AB,AB(c);rep 15.00	
05/60 **(156)** AB,GMc New P(c);rep . 8.00	
02/64 **(167)** AB,GMc P(c);rep 8.00	
05/66 **(167)** AB,GMc P(c);rep 8.00	

071-THE MAN WHO LAUGHS
By Victor Hugo

05/50 **(71)** AB,AB(c),Original ... 125.00	
01/62 **(165)** NN,NN New P(c);rep . 70.00	
04/64 **(167)** NN,NN P(c);rep 65.00	

072-THE OREGON TRAIL
By Francis Parkman

06/50 **(73)** HcK,HcK (c),Original .. 75.00	
11/51 **(89)** HcK,HcK (c),15¢(c)	
Price; rep 25.00	
07/54 **(121)** HcK,HcK (c);rep 20.00	
03/56 **(131)** HcK,New P(c);rep ... 15.00	
09/57 **(140)** HcK,P(c);rep 7.00	
05/59 **(150)** HcK,P(c);rep 6.00	
01/61 **(164)** HcK,P(c);rep 6.00	
62/63 **(167)** HcK,P(c);rep 6.00	
08/64 **(167)** HcK,P(c);rep 6.00	
10/65 **(167)** HcK,P(c);rep 6.00	
1968 **(166)** HcK,P(c),25¢(c)Price;rep 6.00	

073-THE BLACK TULIP
By Alexandre Dumas

07/50 **(75)** AB,AB(c),Original ... 225.00

074-MR. MIDSHIPMAN EASY
By Captain Frederick Marryat

08/50 **(75)** BbL,Original 225.00

075-THE LADY OF THE LAKE
By Sir Walter Scott

09/50 **(75)** HcK,HcK(c),Original .. 70.00	
07/51 **(85)** HcK,HcK(c),15¢(c)	
Price; rep 25.00	
04/54 **(118)** HcK,HcK(c);rep 20.00	

07/57 **(139)** HcK,New P(c);rep ... 15.00	
01/60 **(154)** HcK,P(c);rep 6.00	
1962 **(165)** HcK,P(c);rep 6.00	
04/64 **(167)** HcK,P(c);rep 6.00	
05/66 **(167)** HcK,P(c);rep 6.00	
Sg/69 **(169)** HcK,P(c),25¢(c)	
Price, Rigid(c);rep 6.00	

076-THE PRISONER OF ZENDA
By Anthony Hope Hawkins

10/50 **(75)** HcK,HcK(c),Original .. 65.00	
07/51 **(85)** HcK,HcK(c),15¢(c) Price;	
rep 25.00	
09/53 **(111)** HcK,HcK(c),rep 20.00	
09/55 **(128)** HcK,New P(c);rep ... 15.00	
09/59 **(152)** HcK,P(c);rep 6.00	
1962 **(165)** HcK,P(c);rep 6.00	
04/64 **(167)** HcK,P(c);rep 6.00	
09/66 **(167)** HcK,P(c);rep 6.00	
Fl/69 **(169)** HcK,P(c),25¢(c) Price,	
Rigid(c);rep 6.00	

077-THE ILLIAD
By Homer

11/50 **(78)** AB,AB(c),Original 70.00	
09/51 **(87)** AB,AB(c),15¢(c)	
Price;rep 25.00	
07/54 **(121)** AB,AB(c);rep 20.00	
07/57 **(139)** AB,New P(c);rep 15.00	
05/59 **(150)** AB,P(c);rep 6.00	
1962 **(165)** AB,P(c);rep 6.00	
10/63 **(167)** AB,P(c);rep 6.00	
07/64 **(167)** AB,P(c);rep 6.00	
05/66 **(167)** AB,P(c);rep 6.00	
1968 **(166)** AB,P(c),25¢(c)Price;rep 6.00	

078-JOAN OF ARC
By Frederick Shiller

12/50 **(78)** HcK,HcK(c),Original .. 70.00	
09/51 **(87)** HcK,HcK(c),15¢(c)	
Price; rep 25.00	
11/53 **(113)** HcK,HcK(c);rep 20.00	
09/55 **(128)** HcK,New P(c);rep ... 15.00	
09/57 **(140)** HcK,P(c);rep 6.00	
05/59 **(150)** HcK,P(c);rep 6.00	
11/60 **(159)** HcK,P(c);rep 6.00	
62/63 **(167)** HcK,P(c);rep 6.00	
12/63 **(167)** HcK,P(c);rep 6.00	
06/65 **(167)** HcK,P(c);rep 6.00	
06/67 **(166)** HcK,P(c);rep 6.00	
Wr/69 **(166)** HcK,TO New P(c),	
25¢(c)Price, Rigid(c);rep 14.00	

079-CYRANO DE BERGERAC
By Edmond Rostand

01/51 **(78)** AB,AB(c),Original,Movie	
Promo Inside Front(c) 70.00	
07/51 **(85)** AB,AB(c),15¢(c)	
Price;rep 25.00	
04/54 **(118)** AB,AB(c);rep 20.00	
07/56 **(133)** AB,New P(c);rep 20.00	
05/60 **(156)** AB,P(c);rep 15.00	
08/64 **(167)** AB,P(c);rep 15.00	

080-WHITE FANG
By Jack London
(Last Line Drawn (c)

02/51 **(79)** AB,AB(c),Original 70.00	
09/51 **(87)** AB,AB(c);rep 25.00	
03/55 **(125)** AB,AB(c);rep 20.00	
05/56 **(132)** AB,New P(c);rep 20.00	
09/57 **(140)** AB,P(c);rep 6.00	

All comics prices listed are for *Near Mint* condition.

11/59 **(153)** AB,P(c);rep 6.00
62/63 **(167)** AB,P(c);rep 6.00
09/64 **(167)** AB,P(c);rep 6.00
07/65 **(167)** AB,P(c);rep 6.00
06/67 **(166)** AB,P(c);rep 6.00
Fl/69 **(169)** AB,P(c),25¢(c)
Price, Rigid(c);rep 6.00

081-THE ODYSSEY
By Homer
(P(c)s From Now on)
03/51 **(82)** HyG,AB P(c),Original . 70.00
08/64 **(167)** HyG,AB P(c);rep 15.00
10/66 **(167)** HyG,AB P(c);rep 15.00
Sg/69 **(169)** HyG,TyT New P(c),
Rigid(c);rep 15.00

082-THE MASTER OF BALLANTRAE
By Robert Louis Stevenson
04/51 **(82)** LDr,AB P(c),Original .. 50.00
08/64 **(167)** LDr,AB P(c);rep 18.00
Fl/68 **(166)** LDr,Syk New P(c),
Rigid(c);rep 18.00

083-THE JUNGLE BOOK
By Rudyard Kipling
05/51 **(85)** WmB&AB,AB P(c),
Original 40.00
08/53 **(110)** WmB&AB,AB P(c);rep . 7.00
03/55 **(125)** WmB&AB,AB P(c);rep . 6.00
05/56 **(134)** WmB&AB,AB P(c);rep . 6.00
01/58 **(142)** WmB&AB,AB P(c);rep . 6.00
05/59 **(150)** WmB&AB,AB P(c);rep . 6.00
11/60 **(159)** WmB&AB,AB P(c);rep . 6.00
62/63 **(167)** WmB&AB,AB P(c);rep . 6.00
03/65 **(167)** WmB&AB,AB P(c);rep . 6.00
11/65 **(167)** WmB&AB,AB P(c);rep . 6.00
05/66 **(167)** WmB&AB,AB P(c);rep . 6.00
1968 **(166)** NN Art,NN New P(c),
Rigid(c);rep 12.00

084-THE GOLD BUG & OTHER STORIES
(The Gold Bug-The Telltale HeartThe Cask of Amontillado)
By Edgar Allan Poe
06/51 **(85)** AB,RP,JLv,AB P(c),
Original 90.00
07/64 **(167)** AB,RP,JLv,AB P(c);rep 58.00

085-THE SEA WOLF
By Jack London
08/51 **(85)** AB,AB P(c),Original .. 30.00
07/54 **(121)** AB,AB P(c);rep 5.00
05/56 **(132)** AB,AB P(c);rep 5.00
11/57 **(141)** AB,AB P(c);rep 5.00
03/61 **(161)** AB,AB P(c);rep 5.00
02/64 **(167)** AB,AB P(c);rep 5.00
11/65 **(167)** AB,AB P(c);rep 5.00
Fl/69 **(169)** AB,AB P(c),25¢(c)
Price, Rigid(c);rep 5.00

086-UNDER TWO FLAGS
By Oiuda
08/51 **(87)** MDb,AB P(c),Original . 30.00
03/54 **(117)** MDb,AB P(c);rep 6.00
07/57 **(139)** MDb,AB P(c);rep 6.00
09/60 **(158)** MDb,AB P(c);rep 6.00
02/64 **(167)** MDb,AB P(c);rep 6.00
08/66 **(167)** MDb,AB P(c);rep 6.00
Sr/69 **(169)** MDb,AB P(c),25¢(c)
Price, Rigid(c);rep 6.00

CI #77 The Iliad
© *Gilberton Publications*

087-A MIDSUMMER NIGHTS DREAM
By William Shakespeare
09/51 **(87)** AB,AB P(c),Original .. 30.00
03/61 **(161)** AB,AB P(c);rep 6.00
04/64 **(167)** AB,AB P(c);rep 5.00
05/66 **(169)** AB,AB P(c);rep 5.00
Sr/69 **(169)** AB,AB P(c),25¢(c)
Price; rep 5.00

088-MEN OF IRON
By Howard Pyle
10/51 **(89)** HD,LDr,GS,Original .. 35.00
01/60 **(154)** HD,LDr,GS,P(c);rep .. 6.00
01/64 **(167)** HD,LDr,GS,P(c);rep .. 6.00
1968 **(166)** HD,LDr,GS,P(c),
25¢(c)Price;rep 6.00

089-CRIME AND PUNISHMENT
By Fedor Dostoevsky
11/51 **(89)** RP,AB P(c),Original .. 35.00
09/59 **(152)** RP,AB P(c);rep 6.00
04/64 **(167)** RP,AB P(c);rep 6.00
05/66 **(167)** RP,AB P(c);rep 6.00
Fl/69 **(169)** RP,AB P(c),25¢(c)
Price, Rigid(c);rep 6.00

090-GREEN MANSIONS
By William Henry Hudson
12/51 **(89)** AB,AB P(c),Original .. 35.00
01/59 **(148)** AB,New LbC P(c);rep . 15.00
1962 **(165)** AB,LbC P(c);rep 5.00
04/64 **(167)** AB,LbC P(c);rep 5.00
09/66 **(167)** AB,LbC P(c);rep 5.00
Sr/69 **(169)** AB,LbC P(c),25¢(c)
Price, Rigid(c);rep 5.00

091-THE CALL OF THE WILD
By Jack London
01/52 **(92)** MDb,P(c),Original 30.00
10/53 **(112)** MDb,P(c);rep 6.00
03/55 **(125)**MDb,P(c),'PictureProgress'
Onn. Back(c);rep 5.00
09/56 **(134)** MDb,P(c);rep 5.00
03/58 **(143)** MDb,P(c);rep 5.00
1962 **(165)** MDb,P(c);rep 5.00
1962 **(167)** MDb,P(c);rep 5.00
04/65 **(167)** MDb,P(c);rep 5.00

03/66 **(167)** MDb,P(c);rep 5.00
03/66 **(167)** MDb,P(c),Record
Edition;rep 5.00
11/67 **(166)** MDb,P(c);rep 5.00
Sg/70 **(169)** MDb,P(c),25¢(c)
Price, Rigid(c);rep 5.00

092-THE COURTSHIP OF MILES STANDISH
By Henry Wadsworth Longfellow
02/52 **(92)** AB,AB P(c),Original .. 30.00
1962 **(165)** AB,AB P(c);rep 5.00
03/64 **(167)** AB,AB P(c);rep 5.00
05/67 **(166)** AB,AB P(c);rep 5.00
Wr/69 **(169)** AB,AB P(c),25¢(c)
Price, Rigid(c);rep 5.00

093-PUDD'NHEAD WILSON
By Mark Twain
03/52 **(94)** HcK,HcK P(c),Original . 32.00
1962 **(165)** HcK,GMc New P(c);rep . 8.00
03/64 **(167)** HcK,GMc P(c);rep ... 6.00
1968 **(166)** HcK,GMc P(c),25¢(c)
Price, Soft(c);rep 8.00

094-DAVID BALFOUR
By Robert Louis Stevenson
04/52 **(94)** RP,P(c),Original 32.00
05/64 **(167)** RP,P(c);rep 12.00
1968 **(166)** RP,P(c),25¢(c)Price;rep 12.00

095-ALL QUIET ON THE WESTERN FRONT
By Erich Maria Remarque
05/52 **(96)** MDb,P(c),Original 75.00
05/52 **(99)** MDb,P(c),Original 60.00
10/64 **(167)** MDb,P(c);rep 16.00
11/66 **(167)** MDb,P(c);rep 16.00

096-DANIEL BOONE
By John Bakeless
06/52 **(97)** AB,P(c),Original 30.00
03/54 **(117)** AB,P(c);rep 5.00
09/55 **(128)** AB,P(c);rep 5.00
05/56 **(132)** AB,P(c);rep 5.00
----- **(134)** AB,P(c),'Story of
Jesus'on Back(c);rep 5.00
09/60 **(158)** AB,P(c);rep 5.00
01/64 **(167)** AB,P(c);rep 5.00
05/65 **(167)** AB,P(c);rep 5.00
11/66 **(167)** AB,P(c);rep 5.00
Wr/69 **(166)** AB,P(c),25¢(c)
Price, Rigid(c);rep 12.00

097-KING SOLOMON'S MINES
By H. Rider Haggard
07/52 **(96)** HcK,P(c),Original 30.00
04/54 **(118)** HcK,P(c);rep 8.00
03/56 **(131)** HcK,P(c);rep 5.00
09/51 **(141)** HcK,P(c);rep 5.00
02/64 **(167)** HcK,P(c);rep 5.00
09/65 **(167)** HcK,P(c);rep 5.00
Sr/69 **(169)** HcK,P(c),25¢(c)
Price; Rigid(c);rep 6.00

098-THE RED BADGE OF COURAGE
By Stephen Crane
08/52 **(98)** MDb,GS,P(c),Original . 30.00
04/54 **(118)** MDb,GS,P(c);rep 5.00

All comics prices listed are for *Near Mint* condition.

05/56 **(132)** MDb,GS,P(c);rep 5 00
01/58 **(142)** MDb,GS,P(c);rep 5.00
09/59 **(152)** MDb,GS,P(c);rep 5.00
03/61 **(161)** MDb,GS,P(c);rep 5.00
62/63 **(167)** MDb,GS,P(c),Erroneously
  Has Original Date;rep 5.00
09/64 **(167)** MDb,GS,P(c);rep 5.00
10/65 **(167)** MDb,GS,P(c);rep 5.00
1968 **(166)** MDb,GS,P(c);25¢(c)
  Price, Rigid(c);rep 15.00

099-HAMLET
By William Shakespeare

09/52 **(98)** AB,P(c),Original 32.00
07/54 **(121)** AB,P(c);rep 5.00
11/57 **(141)** AB,P(c);rep 5.00
09/60 **(158)** AB,P(c);rep 5.00
62/63 **(167)** AB,P(c),Erroneously
  Has Original Date;rep 5.00
07/65 **(167)** AB,P(c);rep 5.00
04/67 **(166)** AB,P(c);rep 5.00
Sg/69 **(169)** AB,EdM New P(c),
  25¢(c)Price, Rigid(c);rep 12.00

100-MUTINY ON
THE BOUNTY
By Charrles Nordhoff

10/52 **(100)** MsW,HcK P(c),Original 28.00
03/54 **(117)** MsW,HcK P(c);rep ... 5.00
05/56 **(132)** MsW,HcK P(c);rep ... 5.00
01/58 **(142)** MsW,HcK P(c);rep ... 5.00
03/60 **(155)** MsW,HcK P(c);rep ... 5.00
62/63 **(167)** MsW,Herick P(c),Erroneusly
  Has Original Date;rep 5.00
05/64 **(167)** MsW,HcK P(c);rep ... 5.00
03/66 **(167)** MsW,HcK P(c),N#
  or Price;rep 10.00
Sg/70 **(169)** MsW,HcK P(c),
  Rigid(c); rep 4.00

101-WILLIAM TELL
By Frederick Schiller

11/52 **(101)** MDb,HcK P(c),Original 28.00
04/54 **(118)** MDb,HcK P(c);rep ... 5.00
11/57 **(141)** MDb,HcK P(c);rep ... 5.00
09/60 **(158)** MDb,HcK P(c);rep ... 5.00
62/63 **(167)** MDb,HcK P(c),Erroneously
  Has Original Date;rep 5.00
11/64 **(167)** MDb,HcK P(c);rep ... 5.00
04/67 **(166)** MDb,HcK P(c);rep ... 5.00
Wr/69 **(169)** MDb,HcK P(c)25¢(c)
  Price, Rigid(c);rep 5.00

102-THE WHITE
COMPANY
By Sir Arthur Conan Doyle

12/52 **(101)** AB,P(c),Original 65.00
1962 **(165)** AB,P(c);rep 25.00
04/64 **(167)** AB,P(c);rep 25.00

103-MEN AGAINST
THE SEA
By Charles Nordhoff

01/53 **(104)** RP,HcK P(c),Original 32.00
12/53 **(114)** RP,HcK P(c);rep ... 20.00
03/56 **(131)** RP,New P(c);rep ... 15.00
03/59 **(149)** RP,P(c);rep 15.00
09/60 **(158)** RP,P(c);rep 25.00
03/64 **(167)** RP,P(c);rep 10.00

104-BRING 'EM BACK
ALIVE
By Frank Buck & Edward Anthony

02/53 **(105)** HcK,HcK P(c)Original 27.00
04/54 **(118)** HcK,HcK P(c);rep ... 5.00
07/56 **(133)** HcK,HcK P(c);rep ... 5.00
05/59 **(150)** HcK,HcK P(c);rep ... 5.00
09/60 **(158)** HcK,HcK P(c);rep ... 5.00
10/63 **(167)** HcK,HcK P(c);rep ... 5.00
09/65 **(167)** HcK,HcK P(c);rep ... 5.00
Wr/69 **(169)** HcK,HcK P(c),25¢(c)
  Price, Rigid(c);rep 5.00

105-FROM THE EARTH
TO THE MOON
By Jules Verne

03/53 **(106)** AB,P(c),Original 28.00
04/54 **(118)** AB,P(c);rep 5.00
03/56 **(132)** AB,P(c);rep 5.00
11/57 **(141)** AB,P(c);rep 5.00
09/58 **(146)** AB,P(c);rep 5.00
05/60 **(156)** AB,P(c);rep 5.00
62/63 **(167)** AB,P(c),Erroneously
  Has Original Date;rep 5.00
05/64 **(167)** AB,P(c);rep 5.00
05/65 **(167)** AB,P(c);rep 5.00
10/67 **(166)** AB,P(c);rep 5.00
Sr/69 **(169)** AB,P(c),25¢(c)
  Price, Rigid(c);rep 5.00
Sg/71 **(169)** AB,P(c);rep 5.00

CI #81 The Odyssey
© Gilberton Publications

106-BUFFALO BILL
By William F. Cody

04/53 **(107)** MDb,P(c),Original 28.00
04/54 **(118)** MDb,P(c);rep 5.00
03/56 **(132)** MDb,P(c);rep 5.00
01/58 **(142)** MDb,P(c);rep 5.00
03/61 **(161)** MDb,P(c);rep 5.00
03/64 **(167)** MDb,P(c);rep 5.00
07/67 **(166)** MDb,P(c);rep 5.00
Fl/69 **(169)** MDb,P(c),Rigid(c);rep . 5.00

107-KING OF THE
KHYBER RIFLES
By Talbot Mundy

05/53 **(108)** SMz,P(c),Original ... 30.00
04/54 **(118)** SMz,P(c);rep 5.00
09/58 **(146)** SMz,P(c);rep 5.00
09/60 **(158)** SMz,P(c);rep 5.00
62/63 **(167)** SMz,P(c),Erroneously
  Has Original Date;rep 5.00
62/63 **(167)** SMz,P(c);rep 5.00
10/66 **(167)** SMz,P(c);rep 5.00

108-KNIGHTS OF THE
ROUND TABLE
By Howard Pyle?

06/53 **(108)** AB,P(c),Original 30.00
06/53 **(109)** AB,P(c),Original 36.00
03/54 **(117)** AB,P(c);rep 5.00
11/59 **(153)** AB,P(c);rep 5.00
1962 **(165)** AB,P(c);rep 5.00
04/64 **(167)** AB,P(c);rep 5.00
04/67 **(166)** AB,P(c);rep 5.00

109-PITCAIRN'S ISLAND
By Charles Nordhoff

07/53 **(110)** RP,P(c),Original 32.00
1962 **(165)** RP,P(c);rep 9.00
03/64 **(167)** RP,P(c);rep 9.00
06/67 **(166)** RP,P(c);rep 9.00

110-A STUDY IN
SCARLET
By Sir Arthur Conan Doyle

08/53 **(111)** SMz,P(c),Original .. 100.00
1962 **(165)** SMz,P(c);rep 60.00

111-THE TALISMAN
By Sir Walter Scott

09/53 **(112)** HcK,HcK P(c),Original 40.00
1962 **(165)** HcK,HcK P(c);rep 6.00
05/64 **(167)** HcK,HcK P(c);rep 6.00
Fl/68 **(166)** HcK,HcK P(c),
  25¢(c)Price;rep 6.00

112-ADVENTURES OF
KIT CARSON
By John S. C. Abbott

10/53 **(113)** RP,P(c),Original 40.00
11/55 **(129)** RP,P(c);rep 6.00
11/57 **(141)** RP,P(c);rep 6.00
09/59 **(152)** RP,P(c);rep 6.00
03/61 **(161)** RP,P(c);rep 6.00
62/63 **(167)** RP,P(c);rep 6.00
02/65 **(167)** RP,P(c);rep 6.00
05/66 **(167)** RP,P(c);rep 6.00
Wr/69 **(166)** RP,EdM New P(c),
  25¢(c)Price, Rigid(c);rep 12.00

113-THE FORTY-FIVE
GUARDSMEN
By Alexandre Dumas

11/53 **(114)** MDb,P(c),Original ... 60.00
07/67 **(166)** MDb,P(c);rep 25.00

114-THE RED ROVER
By James Fenimore Cooper

12/53 **(115)** PrC,JP P(c),Original . 60.00
07/67 **(166)** PrC,JP P(c);rep 25.00

115-HOW I FOUND
LIVINGSTONE
By Sir Henry Stanley

01/54 **(116)** SF&ST,P(c),Original . 65.00
01/67 **(167)** SF&ST,P(c);rep 30.00

116-THE BOTTLE IMP
By Robert Louis Stevenson

02/54 **(117)** LC,P(c),Original 70.00
01/67 **(167)** LC,P(c);rep 25.00

117-CAPTAINS
COURAGEOUS
By Rudyard Kipling

All comics prices listed are for *Near Mint* condition. **CVA Page 641**

03/54 **(118)** PrC,P(c),Original ... 55.00
02/67 **(167)** PrC,P(c);rep 20.00
Fl/69 **(169)** PrC,P(c),25¢(c)
Price, Rigid(c);rep 15.00

118-ROB ROY
By Sir Walter Scott
04/54 **(119)** RP,WIP,P(c),Original . 70.00
02/67 **(167)** RP,WIP,P(c);rep 35.00

119-SOLDERS OF FORTUNE
By Richard Harding Davis
05/54 **(120)** KS,P(c),Original 50.00
03/67 **(166)** KS,P(c);rep 20.00
Sg/70 **(169)** KS,P(c),25¢(c)
Price, Rigid(c);rep 15.00

120-THE HURRICANE
By Charles Nordhoff
1954 **(121)** LC,LC P(c),Original .. 50.00
03/67 **(166)** LC,LC P(c);rep 30.00

121-WILD BILL HICKOCK
Author Unknown
07/54 **(122)** MI,ST,P(c),Original .. 25.00
05/56 **(132)** MI,ST,P(c);rep 6.00
11/57 **(141)** MI,ST,P(c);rep 6.00
01/60 **(154)** MI,ST,P(c);rep 6.00
62/63 **(167)** MI,ST,P(c);rep 6.00
08/64 **(167)** MI,ST,P(c);rep 6.00
04/67 **(166)** MI,ST,P(c);rep 6.00
Wr/69 **(169)** MI,ST,P(c),Rigid(c);rep 6.00

122-THE MUTINEERS
By Charles Boardman Hawes
09/54 **(123)** PrC,P(c),Original ... 30.00
01/57 **(136)** PrC,P(c);rep 6.00
09/58 **(146)** PrC,P(c);rep 6.00
09/60 **(158)** PrC,P(c);rep 6.00
11/63 **(167)** PrC,P(c);rep 6.00
03/65 **(167)** PrC,P(c);rep 6.00
08/67 **(166)** PrC,P(c);rep 6.00

123-FANG AND CLAW
By Frank Buck
11/54 **(124)** LnS,P(c),Original ... 30.00
07/56 **(133)** LnS,P(c);rep 6.00
03/58 **(143)** LnS,P(c);rep 6.00
01/60 **(154)** LnS,P(c);rep 6.00
62/63 **(167)** LnS,P(c),Erroneously
Has Original Date;rep 6.00
09/65 **(167)** LnS,P(c);rep 6.00

124-THE WAR OF THE WORLDS
By H. G. Wells
01/55 **(125)** LC,LC P(c),Original .. 50.00
03/56 **(131)** LC,LC P(c);rep 6.00
11/57 **(141)** LC,LC P(c);rep 6.00
01/59 **(148)** LC,LC P(c);rep 6.00
05/60 **(156)** LC,LC P(c);rep 6.00
1962 **(165)** LC,LC P(c);rep 6.00
62/63 **(167)** LC,LC P(c);rep 6.00
11/64 **(167)** LC,LC P(c);rep 6.00
11/65 **(167)** LC,LC P(c);rep 6.00
1968 **(166)** LC,LC P(c),25¢(c)
Price;rep 6.00
Sr/70 **(169)** LC,LC P(c),Rigid(c);rep 6.00

125-THE OX BOW INCIDENT
By Walter Van Tilberg Clark
03/55 **(---)** NN,P(c),Original 25.00
03/58 **(143)** NN,P(c);rep 6.00
09/59 **(152)** NN,P(c);rep 6.00
03/61 **(149)** NN,P(c);rep 6.00
62/63 **(167)** NN,P(c);rep 6.00
11/64 **(167)** NN,P(c);rep 6.00
04/67 **(166)** NN,P(c);rep 6.00
Wr/69 **(169)** NN,P(c),25¢(c)
Price, Rigid(c);rep 6.00

126-THE DOWNFALL
By Emile Zola
05/55 **(---)** LC,LC P(c),Original,'Picture
Progress'Replaces Reorder List 30.00
08/64 **(167)** LC,LC P(c);rep 10.00
1968 **(166)** LC,LC P(c),25¢(c)
Price;rep 10.00

127-THE KING OF THE MOUNTAINS
By Edmond About
07/55 **(128)** NN,P(c),Original 30.00
06/64 **(167)** NN,P(c);rep 10.00
Fl/68 **(166)** NN,P(c),25¢(c)Price;rep 10.00

128-MACBETH
By William Shakespeare
09/55 **(128)** AB,P(c),Original 32.00
03/58 **(143)** AB,P(c);rep 6.00
09/60 **(158)** AB,P(c);rep 6.00
62/63 **(167)** AB,P(c);rep 6.00
06/64 **(167)** AB,P(c);rep 6.00
04/67 **(166)** AB,P(c);rep 6.00
1968 **(166)** AB,P(c),25¢(c)Price;rep 6.00
Sg/70 **(169)** AB,P(c),Rigid(c);rep .. 6.00

CI #125 The Ox Bow Incident
© Gilberton Publications

129-DAVY CROCKETT
Author Unknown
11/55 **(129)** LC,P(c),Original 75.00
09/66 **(167)** LC,P(c);rep 60.00

130-CAESAR'S CONQUESTS
By Julius Caesar
01/56 **(130)** JO,P(c),Original 40.00
01/58 **(142)** JO,P(c);rep 6.00
09/59 **(152)** JO,P(c);rep 6.00

03/61 **(149)** JO,P(c);rep 6.00
62/63 **(167)** JO,P(c);rep 6.00
10/64 **(167)** JO,P(c);rep 6.00
04/66 **(167)** JO,P(c);rep 6.00

131-THE COVERED WAGON
By Emerson Hough
03/56 **(131)** NN,P(c),Original 25.00
03/58 **(143)** NN,P(c);rep 6.00
09/59 **(152)** NN,P(c);rep 6.00
09/60 **(158)** NN,P(c);rep 6.00
62/63 **(167)** NN,P(c);rep 6.00
11/64 **(167)** NN,P(c);rep 6.00
04/66 **(167)** NN,P(c);rep 6.00
Wr/69 **(169)** NN,P(c),25¢(c)
Price, Rigid(c);rep 6.00

132-THE DARK FRIGATE
By Charles Boardman Hawes
05/56 **(132)** EW&RWb,P(c),Original 30.00
05/59 **(150)** EW&RWb,P(c);rep ... 9.00
01/64 **(167)** EW&RWb,P(c);rep ... 9.00
05/67 **(166)** EW&RWb,P(c);rep ... 9.00

133-THE TIME MACHINE
By H. G. Wells
07/56 **(132)** LC,P(c),Original 45.00
01/58 **(142)** LC,P(c);rep 8.00
09/59 **(152)** LC,P(c);rep 8.00
09/60 **(158)** LC,P(c);rep 8.00
62/63 **(167)** LC,P(c);rep 8.00
06/64 **(167)** LC,P(c);rep 8.00
03/66 **(167)** LC,P(c);rep 8.00
03/66 **(167)** LC,P(c),N# Or Price;rep 8.00
12/67 **(166)** LC,P(c);rep 8.00
Wr/71 **(169)** LC,P(c),25¢(c)
Price, Rigid(c);rep 8.00

134-ROMEO AND JULIET
By William Shakespeare
09/56 **(134)** GE,P(c),Original 30.00
03/61 **(161)** GE,P(c);rep 6.00
09/63 **(167)** GE,P(c);rep 6.00
05/65 **(167)** GE,P(c);rep 6.00
06/67 **(166)** GE,P(c);rep 6.00
Wr/69 **(166)** GE,EdM New P(c),
25¢(c)Price, Rigid(c);rep 21.00

135-WATERLOO
By Emile Erckmann & Alexandre Chatrian
11/56 **(135)** Grl,AB P(c),Original . 30.00
11/59 **(153)** Grl,AB P(c);rep 5.00
62/63 **(167)** Grl,AB P(c);rep 5.00
09/64 **(167)** Grl,AB P(c);rep 5.00
1968 **(166)** Grl,AB P(c),25¢(c)
Price; rep 5.00

136-LORD JIM
By Joseph Conrad
01/57 **(136)** GE,P(c),Original 30.00
62/63 **(165)** GE,P(c);rep 5.00
03/64 **(167)** GE,P(c);rep 5.00
09/66 **(167)** GE,P(c);rep 5.00
Sr/69 **(169)** GE,P(c),25¢(c)
Price, Rigid(c);rep 5.00

137-THE LITTLE SAVAGE
By Captain Frederick Marryat
03/57 **(136)** GE,P(c),Original 30.00
01/59 **(148)** GE,P(c);rep 5.00

All comics prices listed are for *Near Mint* condition.

05/60 **(156)** GE,P(c);rep 5.00
62/63 **(167)** GE,P(c);rep 5.00
10/64 **(167)** GE,P(c);rep 5.00
08/67 **(166)** GE,P(c);rep 5.00
Sg/70 **(169)** GE,P(c),25¢(c)
   Price, Rigid(c);rep 5.00

138-A JOURNEY TO THE CENTER OF THE EARTH
By Jules Verne
05/57 **(136)** NN,P(c),Original 45.00
09/58 **(146)** NN,P(c);rep 5.00
05/60 **(156)** NN,P(c);rep 5.00
09/60 **(158)** NN,P(c);rep 5.00
62/63 **(167)** NN,P(c);rep 5.00
06/64 **(167)** NN,P(c);rep 5.00
04/66 **(167)** NN,P(c);rep 5.00
1968 **(166)** NN,P(c),25¢(c)Price;rep 5.00

139-IN THE REIGN OF TERROR
By George Alfred Henty
07/57 **(139)** GE,P(c),Original 28.00
01/60 **(154)** GE,P(c);rep 5.00
62/63 **(167)** GE,P(c),Erroneously
  Has Original Date;rep 5.00
07/64 **(167)** GE,P(c);rep 5.00
1968 **(166)** GE,P(c),25¢(c)Price;rep 5.00

140-ON JUNGLE TRAILS
By Frank Buck
09/57 **(140)** NN,P(c),Original 25.00
05/59 **(150)** NN,P(c);rep 5.00
01/61 **(160)** NN,P(c);rep 5.00
09/63 **(167)** NN,P(c);rep 5.00
09/65 **(167)** NN,P(c);rep 5.00

141-CASTLE DANGEROUS
By Sir Walter Scott
11/57 **(141)** StC,P(c),Original 25.00
09/59 **(152)** STC,P(c);rep 7.00
62/63 **(167)** StC,P(c);rep 7.00
07/67 **(166)** StC,P(c);rep 7.00

142-ABRAHAM LINCOLN
By Benjamin Thomas
01/58 **(142)** NN,P(c),Original 35.00
01/60 **(154)** NN,P(c);rep 5.00
09/60 **(158)** NN,P(c);rep 5.00
10/63 **(167)** NN,P(c);rep 5.00
07/65 **(167)** NN,P(c);rep 5.00
11/67 **(166)** NN,P(c);rep 5.00
Fl/69 **(169)** NN,P(c),25¢(c) Price,
  Rigid(c);rep 5.00

143-KIM
By Rudyard Kipling
03/58 **(143)** JO,P(c)Original 30.00
62/63 **(165)** JO,P(c);rep 6.00
11/63 **(167)** JO,P(c);rep 6.00
08/65 **(167)** JO,P(c);rep 6.00
Wr/69 **(169)** JO,P(c),25¢(c) Price,
  Rigid(c);rep 6.00

144-THE FIRST MEN IN THE MOON
By H. G. Wells
05/58 **(143)** GWb,AW,AT,RKr,GMC
  P(c), Original 32.00
11/59 **(153)** GWb,AW,AT,RKr,GMC
  P(c); rep 6.00
03/61 **(161)** GWb,AW,AT,RKr,GMC

P(c); rep 6.00
62/63 **(167)** GWb,AW,AT,RKr,GMC
  P(c); rep 6.00
12/65 **(167)** GWb,AW,AT,RKr,GMC
  P(c); rep 6.00
Fl/68 **(166)** GWb,AW,AT,RKr,GMC P(c),
  25¢(c) Price,Rigid(c);rep 6.00
Wr/69 **(169)** GWb,AW,AT,RKr,GMC
  P(c), Rigid(c);rep 12.00

145-THE CRISIS
by Winston Churchill
07/58 **(143)** GE,P(c),Original 30.00
05/60 **(156)** GE,P(c);rep 6.00
10/63 **(167)** GE,P(c);rep 6.00
03/65 **(167)** GE,P(c);rep 6.00
1968 **(166)** GE,P(c),25¢(c)Price;rep 6.00

146-WITH FIRE AND SWORD
By Henryk Sienkiewicz
09/58 **(143)** GWb,P(c),Original . . . 35.00
05/60 **(156)** GWb,P(c);rep 9.00
11/63 **(167)** GWb,P(c);rep 9.00
03/65 **(167)** GWb,P(c);rep 9.00

147-BEN-HUR
By Lew Wallace
11/58 **(147)** JO,P(c),Original 30.00
11/59 **(153)** JO,P(c);rep 35.00
09/60 **(158)** JO,P(c);rep 6.00
62/63 **(167)** JO,P(c),Has the
  Original Date;rep 6.00
----- **(167)** JO,P(c);rep 6.00
02/65 **(167)** JO,P(c);rep 6.00
09/66 **(167)** JO,P(c);rep 6.00
Fl/68 **(166)** JO,P(c),25¢(c)Price,
  Both Rigid & Soft (c)s;rep 30.00

148-THE BUCKANEER
By Lyle Saxon
01/59 **(148)** GE&RJ,NS P(c),orig. 30.00
----- **(568)** GE&RJ,NS P(c),Juniors
  List Only;rep 10.00
62/63 **(167)** GE&RJ,NS P(c);rep . . 6.00
09/65 **(167)** GE&RJ,NS P(c);rep . . 6.00
Sr/69 **(169)** GE&RJ,NS P(c),25¢(c)
  Price, Rigid(c);rep 6.00

149-OFF ON A COMET
By Jules Verne
03/59 **(149)** GMc,P(c),Original . . . 25.00

Cl #144 Off on a Comet
© Gilberton Publications

03/60 **(155)** GMc,P(c);rep 6.00
03/61 **(149)** GMc,P(c);rep 6.00
12/63 **(167)** GMc,P(c);rep 6.00
02/65 **(167)** GMc,P(c);rep 6.00
10/66 **(167)** GMc,P(c);rep 6.00
Fl/68 **(166)** GMc,EdM New P(c),
  25¢(c)Price;rep 20.00

150-THE VIRGINIAN
By Owen Winster
05/59 **(150)** NN,DrG P(c),Original 40.00
1961 **(164)** NN,DrG P(c);rep 15.00
62/63 **(167)** NN,DrG P(c);rep 15.00
12/65 **(167)** NN,DrG P(c);rep 15.00

151-WON BY THE SWORD
By George Alfred Henty
07/59 **(150)** JTg,P(c),Original 40.00
1961 **(164)** JTg,P(c);rep 15.00
10/63 **(167)** JTg,P(c);rep 15.00
1963 **(167)** JTg,P(c);rep 15.00
07/67 **(167)** JTg,P(c);rep 15.00

152-WILD ANIMALS I HAVE KNOWN
By Ernest Thompson Seton
09/59 **(152)** LbC,LbC P(c),Original 40.00
03/61 **(149)** LbC,LbC P(c),P(c);rep . 6.00
09/63 **(167)** LbC,LbC P(c);rep 5.00
08/65 **(167)** LbC,LbC P(c);rep 5.00
fl/69 **(169)** LbC,LbC P(c),25¢(c)
  Price, Rigid(c);rep 5.00

153-THE INVISIBLE MAN
By H. G. Wells
11/59 **(153)** NN,GB P(c),Original . 45.00
03/61 **(149)** NN,GB P(c);rep 7.00
62/63 **(167)** NN,GB P(c);rep 6.00
02/65 **(167)** NN,GB P(c);rep 6.00
09/66 **(167)** NN,GB P(c);rep 6.00
Wr/69 **(166)** NN,GB P(c),25¢(c)
  Price, Rigid(c);rep 6.00
Sg/71 **(169)** NN,GB P(c),Rigid(c),
  Words Spelling'Invisible Man'
  Are' Solid'Not'Invisible';rep 6.00

154-THE CONSPIRACY OF PONTIAC
By Francis Parkman
01/60 **(154)** GMc,GMc P(c),Original 40.00
11/63 **(167)** GMc,GMc P(c);rep . . 15.00
07/64 **(167)** GMc,GMc P(c);rep . . 15.00
12/67 **(166)** GMc,GMc P(c);rep . . 15.00

155-THE LION OF THE NORTH
By George Alfred Henty
03/60 **(154)** NN,GMc P(c),Original 42.00
01/64 **(167)** NN,GMc P(c);rep . . . 15.00
1967 **(166)** NN,GMc P(c),25¢(c)
  Price; rep 12.00

156-THE CONQUEST OF MEXICO
By Bernal Diaz Del Castillo
05/60 **(156)** BPr,BPr P(c),Original 35.00
04/67 **(167)** BPr,BPr P(c);rep 10.00
08/67 **(166)** BPr,BPr P(c);rep 10.00
Sg/70 **(169)** BPr,BPr P(c),25¢(c)
  Price; Rigid(c);rep 9.00

All comics prices listed are for *Near Mint* condition.

157-LIVES OF THE HUNTED
By Ernest Thompson Seton
07/60 **(156)** NN,LbC P(c),Original 40.00
02/64 **(167)** NN,LbC P(c);rep 15.00
10/67 **(166)** NN,LbC P(c);rep 15.00

158-THE CONSPIRATORS
By Alexandre Dumas
09/60 **(156)** GMc,GMc P(c),Original 40.00
07/64 **(167)** GMc,GMc P(c);rep .. 15.00
10/67 **(166)** GMc,GMc P(c);rep .. 15.00

159-THE OCTOPUS
By Frank Norris
11/60 **(159)** GM&GE,LbC P(c),
Original 40.00
02/64 **(167)** GM&GE,LbC P(c);rep 15.00
166 **(1967)** GM&GE,LbC P(c),25¢(c)
Price;rep 15.00

160-THE FOOD OF THE GODS
By H.G. Wells
01/61 **(159)** TyT,GMc P(c),Original 40.00
01/61 **(160)** TyT,GMc P(c),Original;
Same Except For the HRN# ... 35.00
01/64 **(167)** TyT,GMc P(c);rep ... 15.00
06/67 **(166)** TyT,GMc P(c);rep ... 15.00

161-CLEOPATRA
By H. Rider Haggard
03/61 **(161)** NN,Pch P(c),Original . 45.00
01/64 **(167)** NN,Pch P(c);rep 20.00
08/67 **(166)** NN,Pch P(c);rep 20.00

162-ROBUR THE CONQUEROR
By Jules Verne
05/61 **(162)** GM&DPn,CJ P(c),
Original 40.00
07/64 **(167)** GM&DPn,CJ P(c);rep 15.00
08/67 **(166)** GM&DPn,CJ P(c);rep 15.00

163-MASTER OF THE WORLD
By Jules Verne
07/61 **(163)** GM,P(c),Original 40.00
01/65 **(167)** GM,P(c);rep 15.00
1968 GM,P(c),25¢(c)
Price;rep 15.00

164-THE COSSACK CHIEF
By Nicolai Gogol
1961 **(164)** SyM,P(c),Original ... 35.00
04/65 **(167)** SyM,P(c);rep 15.00
Fl/68 **(166)** SyM,P(c),25¢(c)
Price;rep 15.00

165-THE QUEEN'S NECKLACE
by Alexandre Dumas
01/62 **(164)** GM,P(c),Original 35.00
04/65 **(167)** GM,P(c);rep 15.00
Fl/68 **(166)** GM,P(c),25¢(c)
Price;rep 15.00

166-TIGERS AND TRAITORS
By Jules Verne
05/62 **(165)** NN,P(c),Original 65.00
02/64 **(167)** NN,P(c);rep 20.00
11/66 **(167)** NN,P(c);rep 20.00

167-FAUST
By Johann Wolfgang von Goethe
08/62 **(165)** NN,NN P(c),Original . 100.00
02/64 **(167)** NN,NN P(c);rep 50.00
06/67 **(166)** NN,NN P(c);rep 50.00

168-IN FREEDOM'S CAUSE
By George Alfred Henty
Wr/69 **(169)** GE&RC,P(c),
Original, Rigid (c) 100.00

169-NEGRO AMERICANS THE EARLY YEARS
AUTHOR UNKNOWN
Sg/69 **(166)** NN,NN P(c),
Original, Rigid(c) 80.00
Sg/69 **(169)** NN,NN P(c),
Rigid; rep 60.00

See Also:
Independent Color Listings

CLASSICS ILLUSTRATED GIANTS
An Illustrated Library of Great
Adventure Stories
-(reps. of Issues 6,7,8,10) .. 1,100.00
An Illustrated Library of Exciting
Mystery Stories
-(reps. of Issues 30,21,40,13) 1,200.00
An Illustrated Library of Great
Indian Stories
-(reps. of Issues 4,17,22,37) . 1,100.00

CLASSICS ILLUSTRATED JUNIOR
501-Snow White and the
Seven Dwarves 70.00
502-The Ugly Duckling 40.00
503-Cinderella 25.00
504-The Pied Piper 20.00
505-The Sleeping Beauty 20.00
506-The Three Little Pigs 20.00
507-Jack and the Beanstalk 20.00
508-Goldilocks and the Three
Bears 20.00
509-Beauty and the Beast 20.00
510-Little Red Riding Hood 20.00
511-Puss-N-Boots 20.00
512-Rumpelstilskin 20.00
513-Pinnochio 35.00
514-The Steadfast Tin Soldier .. 40.00
515-Johnny Appleseed 20.00
516-Alladin and His Lamp 25.00
517-The Emperor's New Clothes . 20.00
518-The Golden Goose 20.00
519-Paul Bunyan 20.00
520-Thumbelina 28.00
521-King of the golden River ... 20.00
522-The Nightingale 15.00
523-The Gallant Tailor 15.00
524-The Wild Swans 15.00
525-The Little Mermaid 20.00
526-The Frog Prince 18.00
527-The Golden-Haired Giant ... 15.00
528-The Penny Prince 15.00
529-The Magic Servants 15.00
530-The Golden Bird 15.00
531-Rapunzel 18.00
532-The Dancing Princesses ... 15.00
533-The Magic Fountain 15.00
534-The Golden Touch 15.00
535-The Wizard of Oz 35.00
536-The Chimney Sweep 15.00
537-The Three Faires 15.00
538-Silly Hans 15.00
539-The Enchanted Fish 30.00
540-The Tinder-Box 30.00
541-Snow White and Rose Red .. 20.00
542-The Donkey's Tail 20.00
543-The House in the Woods ... 15.00
544-The Golden Fleece 35.00
545-The Glass Mountain 20.00
546-The Elves and the Shoemaker 18.00
547-The Wishing Table 15.00
548-The Magic Pitcher 15.00
549-Simple Kate 15.00
550-The Singing Donkey 15.00
551-The Queen Bee 15.00
552-The Three Little Dwarves .. 20.00
553-King Thrushbeard 15.00
554-The Enchanted Deer 15.00
555-The Three Golden Apples ... 15.00
556-The Elf Mound 15.00
557-Silly Willy 30.00
558-The Magic Dish 30.00
559-The Japanese Lantern 30.00
560-The Doll Princess 30.00
561-Hans Humdrum 15.00
562-The Enchanted Pony 30.00
563-The Wishing Well 15.00
564-The Salt Mountain 15.00
565-The Silly Princess 15.00
566-Clumsy Hans 15.00
567-The Bearskin Soldier 15.00
568-The Happy Hedgehog 15.00
569-The Three Giants 15.00
570-The Pearl Princess 12.00
571-How Fire Came to the Indians 15.00
572-The Drummer Boy 18.00
573-The Crystal Ball 18.00
574-Brightboots 18.00
575-The Fearless Prince 20.00
576-The Princess Who Saw
Everything 30.00
577-The Runaway Dumpling 35.00

CLASSICS ILLLUSTRATED SPECIAL ISSUE
N# United Nations 250.00
129-The Story of Jesus 65.00
132A-The Story of America 45.00
135A-The Ten Commandments .. 50.00
138A-Adventures in Science ... 40.00
141A-The Rough Rider 40.00
144A-Blazing the Trails 40.00
147A-Crossing the Rockies 50.00
150A-Royal Canadian Police ... 45.00
153A-Men, Guns, and Cattle ... 45.00
156A-The Atomic Age 45.00
159A-Rockets, Jets and Missles . 45.00
162A-War Between the States .. 100.00
165A-To the Stars 50.00
166A-World War II 75.00
167A-Prehistoric World 80.00

AMAZING DOPE TALES
Greg Shaw
1 Untrimmed black and white pages,
out of order;artist unknown . 110.00
2 Trimmed and proper pages . . . 95.00

AMERICAN SPLENDOR
Harvey Pekar May, 1976
1 B:Harvey Pekar Stories,
HP,RCr,GDu,GBu 12.00
2 HP,RCr,GDu,GBu 6.50
3 HP,RCr,GDu,GBu 6.00
4 HP,RCr,GDu,GBu 5.50
5 HP,RCr,GDu,GBu 5.00
6 HP,RCr,GDu,GBu,GSh 4.50
7 HP,GSh,GDu,GBu 2.50
8 HP,GSh,GDu,GBu 2.00
9 and 10 HP,GSh,GDu,GBu . . @2.75
11 . . . . 3.00
12 . . . . 4.50
13 thru 19 . . . . @3.50
20 E:Harvey Pekar Stories 4.00

ANTHOLOGY OF SLOW DEATH
Wingnut Press/Last Gasp
1 140 pgs, RCr,RCo, GiS, DSh,
Harlan Ellison VB,RTu 37.00

APEX TREASURY OF UNDERGROUND COMICS, THE
Links Books Inc. Oct.,1974
1 . . . . 40.00

APEX TREASURY OF UNDERGROUND COMICS –BEST OF BIJOU FUNNIES
Quick Fox 1981
1 Paperback,comix,various artists 21.00

ARCADE THE COMICS REVUE
Print Mint Inc. Spring, 1975
1 ASp,BG,RCr,SRo,SCW 16.50
2 ASp,BG,RCr,SRo 12.00
3 ASp,BG,RCr,RW,SCW 8.50
4 ASp,BG,RCr,WBu,RW,SCW . . 8.50
5 thru 7 ASp,BG,SRo,RW,SCW @7.50

BABYFAT
Comix World/Clay Geerdes 1978
1 B:8pg news parodies, one page
comix by various artists 4.50
2 thru 9 same . . . . @3.00
10 thru 26 same . . . . @2.00

BATTLE OF THE TITANS
University of Illinois SF Society 1972
1 Sci-Fi;VB,JGa 50.00

BEST BUY COMICS
Last Gasp Eco-Funnies
1 Rep Whole Earth Review;RCr . . 3.50

BEST OF BIJOU FUNNIES, THE
Links Books Inc. 1975
1 164 pgs,paperback 235.00

BEST OF RIP-OFF PRESS
Rip Off Press Inc. 1973
1 132 pgs paperback,SCW,
RCr,SRo,RW 24.00
2 100 pgs,GS,FT 27.50
3 100 pgs,FS 10.75
4 132 pgs,GiS,DSh 13.00

BIG ASS
Rip Off Press 1969–71
1 28 pgs,RCr 75.00
2 RCr 42.00

BIJOU FUNNIES
Bijou Publishing Empire 1968
1 B:JLy,editor;RCr,GS SW . . . 285.00
2 RCr,GS,SW 100.00
3 RCr,SWi,JsG 52.00
4 SWi,JsG 30.00
5 SWi,JsG 33.50
6 E:JLy,editor,SWi,RCr,JsG . . . 27.00
7 and 8 . . . . @26.00

BINKY BROWN MEETS THE HOLY VIRGIN MARY
Last Gasp Eco-Funnies March, 1972
N# Autobiography about Growing up
w/a Catholic Neurosis,JsG . 22.50
2nd Printing:only text in
bottom left panel 12.00

BIZARRE SEX
Kitchen Sink Komix May, 1972
1 B:DKi,editor,various
artists 27.00
2 . . . . 22.00
3 . . . . 16.00
4 thru 6 . . . . @11.00
7 . . . . 4.00

Bizarre Sex #8
© Kitchen Sink

8 . . . . 3.50
9 Omaha the Cat Dancer,RW . 16.50

BLACK LAUGHTER
Black Laughter Pub. Co, Nov. 1972
1 James Dixon art 64.00

BLOOD FROM A STONE (GUIDE TO TAX REFORM)
New York Public Interest Research Group Inc. 1977
1 Tax reform proposals 8.50

BOBBY LONDON RETROSPECTIVE AND ART PORTFOLIO
Cartoonist Representatives
1 . . . . 19.50

BOBMAN AND TEDDY
Parrallax Comic Books Inc 1966
1 RFK & Ted Kennedy's struggle to
control Democratic party 35.50

BODE'S CARTOON CONCERT
Dell Sept., 1973
1 132 pgs; VB 27.50

BOGEYMAN COMICS
San Fransisco Comic Book Co., 1969
1 Horror,RHa 55.00
2 Horror,RHa 42.00
The Company & Sons
3 . . . . 31.00

BUFFALO RAG/THE DEAD CONCERT COMIX
Kenny Laramey Dec. 1973
1 Alice in Wonderland parody . 55.00

CAPTAIN GUTS
The Print Mint 1969
1 Super patriotV:Counter
culture 26.50
2 V:Black Panthers 19.00
3 V:Dope Smugglers 19.00

CAPTAIN STICKY
Captain Sticky 1974–75
1 Super lawyer V:SocialInjustice 17.50

CARTOON HISTORY OF THE UNIVERSE
Rip Off Press Sept., 1978
1 Evolution of Everything;
B:Larry Gonick 6.50
2 Sticks and Stones 6.50
3 River Realms-Sumer & Egypt . 6.50
4 Part of the Old Testament . . . 4.50
5 Brains and Bronze 4.50
6 Who are these Athenians 3.75

CASCADE COMIX MONTHLY
Everyman Studios March, 1978
1 Interviews,articles about
comix & comix artists 6.50

---

2 and 3 same	@6.50
4 thru 11	@3.00
12 thru 23	@2.25

CHECKERED DEMON
Last Gasp July, 1977

1 SCW	13.00
2 SCW	8.50
3 SCW	6.50

CHEECH WIZARD
**Office of Student Publications,
Syracuse U 1967**

n/n VB	120.00

CHICAGO MIRROR
**Jay Lynch/Mirror
Publishing Empire Autumn, 1967**

1 B:Bijou Funnies	45.00
2 same	35.00
3 same	115.00

COLLECTED CHEECH
WIZARD, THE
Company & Sons 1972

n/n VB	55.00

COLLECTED
TRASHMAN #1, THE
**Fat City & The Red Mountain
Tribe Productions**

n/n SRo	32.50

COMICS & COMIX
October, 1975

1	12.00

COMIX BOOK
**Magazine Management Co.
Oct., 1974**

1 Compilation for newsstand distribution	14.50
2 and 3	@9.00

Kitchen Sink Enterprises

4	14.50
5	8.50

*Comix Book #3
© Magazine Management Co.*

COMIX COLLECTOR, THE
Archival Press Inc. Dec., 1979

1 Fanzine	5.00
2 & 3 Fanzine	@4.00

COMMIES FROM MARS
Kitchen Sink March, 1973

1 TB	32.50

Last Gasp

2 thru 5 TB	@9.50

COMPLETE FRITZ
THE CAT
Belier Press 1978

n/n RCr,SRo,DSh	50.00

CONSPIRACY CAPERS
The Conspiracy 1969

1 Benefit Legal Defense of the Chicago-8	79.00

DAN O'NEIL'S COMICS
& STORIES
**VOL.1
Company & Sons**

1 B:Dan O'Neill	45.00
2 & 3	@30.00

1971 VOL.2

1	6.50
2 and E:Dan O'Neil	@4.50

DAS KAMPF
Vaughn Bode May, 1963

N# 100 Loose pgs.	750.00
2nd Printing 52pgs.-produced by Walter Bachner&Bagginer,1977	9.50

DEADBONE EROTICA
Bantam Books Inc. April, 1971

n/n 132 pgs VB	45.00

DEADCENTER CLEAVAGE
April, 1971

1 14 pgs	40.00

DEATH RATTLE
Kitchen Sink June, 1972

1 RCo,TB	25.00
2 TB	20.00
3 TB	16.00

DESPAIR
The Print Mint 1969

1 RCr	33.00

DIRTY DUCK BOOK, THE
Company & Sons March, 1972

1 Bobby London	25.00

DISNEY RAPES THE 1st
AMENDMENT
Dan O'Neil 1974

1 Benefit Air Pirates V:Disney Law suit; Dan O'Neill	8.50

DOPE COMIX
Kitchen Sink Feb., 1978

1 Drugs comix;various artists	7.50

2 same	5.75
3 & 4 LSD issue	@4.00

DOPIN DAN
Last Gasp Eco-Funnies April, 1972

1 TR	12.00
2 and 3 TR	@8.50
4 Todays Army,TR	7.50

DR. ATOMIC
Last Gasp Eco-Funnies Sept., 1972

1 B:Larry S. Todd	12.00
2 and 3	@10.00
4	7.50
5 E:Larry S. Todd	4.75

DR. ATOMIC'S
MARIJUANA MULTIPLIER
Kistone Press 1974

1 How to grow great pot	7.50

DRAWINGS BY
S. CLAY WILSON
San Francisco Graphics

1 28 pgs	185.00

DYING DOLPHIN
The Print Mint 1970

n/n	14.50

EBON
San Francisco Comic Book Company

1 Comix version; RCr	20.00
1 Tabloid version	18.00

EL PERFECTO COMICS
The Print Mint 1973

N# Benefit Timothy Leary	27.00
2nd Printing-1975	4.00

ETERNAL TRUTH
Sunday Funnies Comic Corp

1 Christian Comix	19.50

EVERMUCH WAVE
Atlantis Distributors

1 Nunzio the Narc; Adventures of God	60.00

FABULOUS FURRY
FREAK BROTHERS, THE
**COLLECTED ADVENTURES OF
Rip Off Press #1 Feb., 1971**

1 GiS	75.00

FURTHER ADVENTURES OF
Rip Off Press #2

1 GiS,DSh	47.50

A YEAR PASSES LIKE
NOTHING WITH
Rip Off Press #3

1 GiS	17.00

BROTHER CAN YOU
SPARE $.75 FOR
Rip Off Press #4

1 GiS,DSh	12.00

FABULOUS FURRY FREAK BROTHERS, THE
Rip Off Press #5
1 GiS,DSh 9.50

SIX SNAPPY SOCKERS FROM THE ARCHIVES OF
Rip Off Press #6
1 GiS 5.25

FANTAGOR
1970
1 (Corben), fanzine 100.00
1a (Last Gasp) 22.00
2 & 3 . . . . @20.00
4 . . . . 30.00

Fat Freddy's Cat #6 © Rip Off Press

THE ADVENTURES OF FAT FREDDY'S CAT,
Rip Off Press Feb., 1977
1 . . . . 14.00
2 . . . . 4.50
3 . . . . 6.00
4 . . . . 5.00
5 & 6 . . . . @2.50

FEDS 'N' HEADS
Gilbert Shelton/Print Mint 1968
N# I:Fabulous Furry Freak Bros.;
  Has no 'Print Mint' Address
  24 pgs. 350.00
2nd printing, 28 pgs. 55.00
3rd printing, May, 1969 . . . . . . 45.00
4th printing, Says 'Forth
  Printing' 17.50
5th-12th printings . . . . @8.00
13th printing 6.50
14th printing 4.75

FELCH
Keith Green
1 RW,SCW,RCr 40.00

FEVER PITCH
Kitchen Sink Enterprises July, 1976
1 RCo 20.00

Jabberwocky Graphix
2 250 signed & numbered 14.50
3 400 signed & numbered 13.50
4 . . . . 8.50

50'S FUNNIES
Kitchen Sink Enterprises 1980
1 Larry Shell, editor,various
  artists 5.00

FLAMING CARROT
Kilian Barracks Free Press 1981
1 Bob Budden,various artists . . 10.00

FLASH THEATRE
Oogle Productions 1970
1 44 pgs 37.50

FLESHAPOIDS FROM EARTH
Popular Culture Dec., 1974
1 36 pgs 33.00

THE COMPLETE FOO!
Bijou Publishing Sept., 1980
1 RCr, Charles Crumb, r:Crumb
  brothers fanzines 30.00

FRITZ BUGS OUT
Ballentine Books 1972
n/n RCr 50.50

FRITZ THE CAT
Ballentine Books 1969
n/n RCr 100.00

FRITZ THE NO-GOOD
Ballentine Books 1972
n/n RCr 45.00

FRITZ: SECRET AGENT FOR THE CIA
Ballentine Books 1972
n/n RCr 39.00

FUNNY AMINALS
Apex Novelties/Don Donahue 1972
1 RCr 50.00

GAY COMIX
Kitchen Sink Sept., 1981
1 36 pgs 7.50
2 36 pgs 5.00

GEN OF HIROSHIMA
Educomics/Leonard Rifas Jan., 1980
1 Antiwar comix by Hiroshima
  survivor Keiji Nakawaza 9.50
2 same 6.50

GHOST MOTHER COMICS
John "Mad" Peck 1969
1 SCw,JsG 47.50

GIMMEABREAK COMIX
Rhuta Press Feb., 1971
2 48 pgs, #0 & #1 were advertised,but
  may not have been printed . . 95.00

GIRLS & BOYS
Lynda J. Barry 1980
1 B:12 pgs with every other page
  blank, all Barry art 8.00
2 thru 10 same . . . . @6.50
11 thru 20 same . . . . @4.50
20 thru 25 same . . . . @3.50

GOD NOSE
**Jack Jackson/
Rip Off Press 1964**
N# 42 pgs. 995.00
2nd printing,Pinkish(c);44p 60.00
3rd printing,Blue Border(c) 30.00
4th printing,Red Border(c) 15.00

GOTHIC BLIMP WORKS LTD.
**East Village Other/
Peter Leggieri 1969**
1 VB,Editor,various artists . . . 185.00
2 same 145.00
3 KDe,editor 135.00
4 KDe,editor 130.00
5 thru 7 KDe,editor . . . . . . @125.00
8 various artists 185.00

GREASER COMICS
Half-Ass Press Sept. 1971
1 28 pgs, George DiCaprio 17.50
  Rip Off Press July 1972
2 George DiCaprio 10.00

GRIM WIT
Last Gasp 1972
1 RCo 35.00
2 RCo 25.00

HAROLD HEAD, THE COLLECTED ADVENTURES OF
Georgia Straight 1972
1 . . . . 45.00
2 . . . . 10.00

HARRY CHESS THAT MAN FROM A.U.N.T.I.E.
**The Uncensored Adventures
Trojan Book Service 1966**
N# 1st Comix By & For Gay
  Community 100.00

HEAR THE SOUND OF MY FEET WALKING....
Glide Urban Center 1969
1 Dan O'Neill, 128 pgs 65.00

HISTORY OF UNDERGROUND COMIX
Straight Arrow Books 1974
1 Book by Mark James Estren about
  Underground Comix 30.00

HOMEGROWN FUNNIES
Kitchen Sink 1971
1 RCr 39.00

HONKYTONK SUE, THE QUEEN OF COUNTRY SWING
Bob Boze Bell Feb., 1979
1 BBB 7.00
2 & 3 BBB . . . . @5.00

IKE LIVES
Warm Neck Funnies 1973
1 20 pgs,Mark Fisher 10.00

INSECT FEAR
Last Gasp 1970
1 SRo,GiS,RHa,JsG 75.00
Print Mint 1970–72
2 . . . . 30.00
3 . . . . 20.00

IT AIN'T ME BABE
Last Gasp Eco-Funnies July. 1970
n/n First all women comix
Womens Liberation theme . . 32.50

JAPANESE MONSTER
Carol Lay July, 1979
1 8pgs, Carol Lay 5.00

JESUS LOVES YOU
Zondervan Books/Craig Yoe 1972
1 Christian, RCr 29.50

THE NEW ADVENTURES OF JESUS
Rip Off Press Nov., 1971
1 44 pgs, FSt 50.00

JIZ
Apex Novelty 1969
1 36 pgs; RCr, SRo, VMo, SCW; hand
trimmed and unevenly stapled 45.00

JUNKWAFFEL
The Print Mint 1971
1 VB 30.00
2 and 3 VB . . . . @25.00
4 VB,JJ 18.00

KANNED KORN KOMIX
Canned Heat Fan Club 1969
1 20pgs 8.00

KAPTAIN AMERIKA KOMIX
Brief Candle Comix March 1970
1 anti U.S. involvement in Laos . 27.50

KING BEE
Apex/Don Donahue & Kerry Clark 1969
1 RCr,SCW 100.00

KURTZMAN COMIX
Kitchen Sink Sept., 1976
1 HK,RCr,GiS,DKi,WE 15.00

LAUGH IN THE DARK
Last Gasp
n/n KDe,RHa,SRo,SCW 14.00

LENNY OF LAVEDO
Sunbury Productions/Print Mint 1965
N# Green(c);1st Joel Beck-a . . 545.00
2nd printing, Orange(c) 390.00
3rd printing, White(c) 195.00

THE MACHINES
Office of Student Publications Syracuse University 1967
1 VB 125.00

THE MAN
Office of Student Publications Syracuse University 1966
1 VB 155.00

MAGGOTZINE
Charles Schneider May, 1981
1 Various Artists,conceptual
maggot stuff 3.50

MANTICORE
Joe Kubert School of Cartooning & Graphic Arts Inc. Autumn, 1976
1 Fanzine,various artists 7.50

MEAN BITCH THRILLS
The Print Mint 1971
1 SRO 7.00

MICKEY RAT
Los Angeles Comic Book Co. May, 1972
1 Robert Armstrong 32.50
2 same 29.00
3 same 9.50

MOM'S HOMEMADE COMICS
Kitchen Sink June 1969
1 DKi, RCr 125.00
The Print Mint
2 DKi 35.00
Kitchen Sink Enterprises
3 DKi,RCr 17.00

MONDAY FUNNIES, THE
Monday Funnies 1977
1 8pgs,various artists 6.50
2 16pgs,various artists 9.00
3 16pgs,various artists 6.50
4 16pgs,various artists 5.50

MONDAY FUNNIES, THE
Passtime Publ. July–Aug., 1980
1 thru 8 Marc L.Reed . . . . . . @4.00

MOUSE LIBERATION FRONT
COMMUNIQUE #2 August, 1979
1 SRo, SCW, VMo,DKi; Disney's sues
Dan O'Neil's Air Pirates 9.50

MOONCHILD COMICS
Nicola Cuti 1968
0 Nicola Cuti 27.00
2 Nicola Cuti 27.00
3 Nicola Cuti 75.00

MOONDOG
The Print Mint March, 1970
1 All George Metzer 11.00
2 same 6.50
3 and 4 same . . . . @3.75

MORE ADVENTURES OF FAT FREDDY'S CAT
Rip Off Press Jan., 1981
1 GiS 14.00

MOTOR CITY COMICS
Rip Off Press April, 1969
1 RCr 155.00
2 RCr 110.00

MR. NATURAL
San Fransisco Comic Book Co. August, 1970
1 RCr 85.00
2 RCr 40.00

Mr. Natural #3 © Robert Crumb

Kitchen Sink
3 RCr 10.00

NARD 'N' PAT, JAYZEY LYNCH'S
Cartoonists Cooperative Press March, 1974
1 Jay Lynch 7.00
2 Jay Lynch 4.50
Kitchen Sink Press 1972
3 . . . . 10.00

NEVERWHERE
Ariel Inc. Feb., 1978
1 RCo 17.50

NICKEL LIBRARY
Gary Arlington
1 1 pg heavy stock colored
paper, Reed Crandall 5.00
2 Kim Deitch 1.50
3 Harrison Cady 1.50
4 Frank Frazetta 4.00
5 Will Eisner 4.00
6 Justin Green 1.50

---

7 C.C. Beck	4.00
8 Wally Wood	4.00
9 Winsor McCay	1.50
10 Jim Osborne	1.50
11 Don Towlley	1.50
12 Frank Frazetta	4.00
13 Will Eisner	4.00
14 Bill Griffith	1.50
15 George Herriman	1.50
16 Cliff Sterrett	1.50
17 George Herriman	1.50
18 Rory Hayes & Simon Deitch	1.50
19 Disney Studios	2.00
20 Alex Toth	2.00
21 Will Eisner	2.00
22 Jack Davis	3.00
23 Alex Toth	2.00
24 Michele Brand	1.50
25 Roger Brand	1.50
26 Arnold Roth	1.50
27 Murphy Anderson	2.00
28 Wally Wood	3.00
29 Jack Kirby	4.00
30 Harvey Kurtzman	3.00
31 Jay Kinney	1.50
32 Bill Plimpton	1.50
33	1.50
34 Charles Dallas	1.50
35 thru 39	@1.50
40 Bill Edwards	1.50
41 Larry S. Todd	1.50
42 Charles Dallas	1.50
43 Jim Osborne	1.50
43 1/2 Larry S. Todd	1.50
44 Jack Jackson	1.50
45 Rick Griffin	1.50
46 Justin Green	1.50
47 and 48 Larry S. Todd	@1.50
49 Charles Dallas	1.50
50 Robert Crumb	3.00
51 Wally Wood	3.00
52 Charles Dallas	3.00
53 and 54 Larry S. Todd	@1.50
55 Charles Dallas	1.50
56 Jim Chase	1.50
57 Charles Dallas	1.50
58 Larry S. Todd	1.50
59 Dave Geiser	1.50
60 Charles Dallas	1.50

ODD WORLD OF RICHARD CORBEN
Warren Publishing 1977
1 84pgs paperback 20.00

O.K. COMICS
Kitchen Sink June, 1972
1 and 2 Bruce Walthers .... @7.00

O.K. COMICS
O.K. Comic Company 1972
1 Tabloid with comix, articles, reviews, nudie cuties photos . 27.50
2 thru 18 .... @18.75

ORACLE COMIX
Thru Black Holes
Comix Productions Oct., 1980
1 and 2 Michael Roden ..... @2.50

PENGUINS IN BONDAGE
Sorcerer Studio/
Wayne Gibson July, 1981
1 8pgs,Wayne Gibson 2.75

PHANTOM LADY
Randy Crawford June, 1978
1 Sex funnies 4.50

PHUCKED UP FUNNIES
Suny Binghamton 1969
1 ASp;insert bound in yearbook 400.00

PINK FLOYD, THE
October, 1974
1 sold at concerts 27.50

PLASTIC MAN
Randy Crawford May, 1977
1 Sex funnies,RandyCrawford .. 4.00

PORK
Co-op Press May, 1974
1 SCW 11.00

PORTFOLIO OF UNDERGROUND ART
Schanes & Schanes 1980
1 SRo,SCW,VMo,RW and many others 13 loose sheets in folder, 32pg book, 1200 signed & numb. . 75.00

POWERMAN AND POWER MOWER SAFETY
Frank Burgmeir, Co.
Outdoor Power Equipment
1 VB; educational comic about power mower safety 185.00

PROMETHIAN ENTERPRISES
Promethian Enterprises Memorial Day, 1969
1 B:Jim Vadeboncuor editor .. 72.00
2 same 60.00
3 thru 5 .... @25.00

PURE ART QUARTERLY
John A. Adams July, 1976
1 16pgs, All John A.Adams 8.50
2 thru 5 same .... @8.50
6 thru 10 same .... @5.00
11 thru 14 same .... @3.50

QUAGMIRE COMICS
Kitchen Sink Summer, 1970
1 DKi,Peter Poplaski 11.00

RAW
Raw Books 1980
1 36pgs,10pgs insert 310.00
2 36pgs,20pgs insert 185.00
3 52pgs,16pgs insert 155.00
4 44pgs,32pgs insert,Flexi disk record 125.00

R. CRUMB'S COMICS AND STORIES
Rip Off Press 1969
1 RCr 80.00

RAWARARAWAR
Rip Off Press 1969
1 GSh 55.00

RED SONJA & CONAN "HOT AND DRY"
Randy Crawford May, 1977
1 Sex funnies,Randy Crawford .. 3.50

REID FLEMING WORLD'S TOUGHEST MILKMAN
David E. Boswell Dec., 1980
1 .... 6.00

RIP OFF COMIX
Rip Off Press April, 1977
1 GiS,FSt,JsG,DSh 17.50
2 thru 5 GiS,FSt .... @6.00
6 thru 10 .... @4.25

ROWLF
Rip Off Press July, 1971
1 RCo 55.00

RUBBER DUCK TALES
The Print Mint March, 1971
1 Michael J Becker 12.00
2 Michael J Becker 11.00

S. CLAY WILSON TWENTY DRAWINGS
Abington Book Shop Inc. 1967
N# (a),Cowboy(c) 460.00
(b),Pirate(c) 460.00
(c),Motorcyclist(c) 460.00
(d),Demon(c) 460.00
(e),Deluxe with all 4 variations on same(c) with Gold Embossed Lettering 675.00

SAN FRANCISCO COMIC BOOK
San Francisco Comic Book Co. Jan.-Feb., 1970
1 .... 120.00
2 .... 20.00
3 .... 17.50
4 thru 6 .... @12.00

SAVAGE HUMOR
The Print Mint 1973
1 .... 4.00

SAY WHAT?
Loring Park Shelter Community Cartooning Workshop April, 1979
1 B:Charles T. Smith,editor, various artists 7.00
2 thru 6 same .... @6.50

All comics prices listed are for _Near Mint_ condition.

SCHIZOPHRENIA, CHEECH WIZARD
Last Gasp Eco-Funnies Jan., 1974
1 VB 30.00

SEX AND AFFECTION
C.P. Family Publishers 1974
1 Sex Education for Children . . . 5.50

SHORT ORDER COMIX
Head Press/Family Fun 1973
1 50 cents,36pgs. 8.50
2 75 cents,44pgs 2.25

SKULL COMICS
Last Gasp March, 1970
1 Horror,RHa 47.00
2 GiS,DSh,RCo 25.50
3 SRo,DSh,RCo 14.00
4 DSh,Lovecraft issue 14.00
5 SRo,RCo,Lovecraft issue . . . 14.00
6 RCo,Herman Hesse 14.00

SLOW DEATH FUNNIES
Last Gasp April 1970
1 Ecological Awarness & Red
 Border on (c) 47.00
2nd-4th Printings White
 Border(c) 10.00
2 Silver(c);1st edition' 34 pgs . . 85.00
2b Non Silver(c);Says 1st
 Edition, 34 pgs 20.00
2nd Amorphia Ad on pg 34 . . . . 6.75
3rd Yellow Skull on (c) 5.00
4th 'Mind Candy For the Masses'
 Ad on pg. 34 . . . . 5.00
5th $1.00(c) price 3.50
3 thru 5 . . . . @12.00
6 thru 10 . . . . 4.50

SMILE
Kitchen Sink Summer, 1970
1 Jim Mitchell 13.50
2 Jim Mitchell 12.00
3 Jim Mitchell 11.00

SNARF
Kitchen Sink Feb., 1972
1 DKi,editor,various artists 24.50
2 thru 5 same . . . . @15.00
6 thru 9 same . . . . @6.50

SNATCH COMICS
Apex Novelties 1968
1 RCr,SCW 295.00
2 RCr,SCW 145.00
3 RCr,SCW,RW 65.00

SNATCH SAMPLER
Keith Green 1979
n/n RCr,SCw,RW,RHa 32.00

SPACE INVADERS COMICS, DON CHIN'S
Comix World/Clay Geerdes April, 1972
1 8pgs 4.00

SPASM!
Last Gasp Eco-Funnies April, 1973
1 JJ 15.00

STONED PICTURE PARADE
San Francisco Comic Book Co., 1975
1 RCr,SRo,SCW,WE 20.00

SUBVERT COMICS
Rip Off Press Nov., 1970
1 SRo 25.00
2 SRo 20.00
3 SRo 12.00

TALES OF SEX & DEATH
Print Mint 1971
1 JsG,KDe.RHa,SRo 32.50
2 JsG,KDe.RHa,SRo 19.50

THRILLING MURDER COMICS
San Francisco Comic Book Co., 1971
1 SCW,KDe,RCr,SRo,Jim
 Arlington,editor 24.50

2 (TWO)
Keith Green Feb., 1975
1 SCW 7.00

VAMPIRELLA
Randy Crawford June, 1978
1 Sex Funnies 3.50

VAUGHN BODE THE PORTFOLIO
Northern Comfort Com. 1976
1 VB,16pgs 125.00

VAUGHN BODE PORTFOLIO #1
Vaughn Bode Productions 1978
1 VB,10 pgs 35.00

VAUGHN BODE'S CHEECH WIZARD, THE COLLECTED ADVENTURES OF THE CARTOON MESSIAH
Northern Comfort Com. 1976
1 VB,88pgs 55.00

VAUGHN BODE'S DEADBONE, THE FIRST TESTAMENT OF CHEECH WIZARD
Northern Comfort Com. 1975
1 VB 65.00

VIETNAM
N# 20pgs. Role of Blacks in
 the War,TG Lewis 125.00

WEIRDO
Last Gasp Eco-Funnies March, 1981
1 thru 3 RCr . . . . @10.00

WEIRDO, THE
Rodney Schroeter Oct., 1977
1 B:Rodney Schroezer,1pg 4.50
2 88pgs 4.50
3 44pgs 4.50

WIMMEN'S COMIX
Last Gasp Eco-Funnies Nov., 1972
1 All women artists&comix 10.75
2 thru 3 same . . . . @10.00
4 thru 7 same . . . . @6.75

WONDER WART-HOG AND THE NURDS OF NOVEMBER
Rip Off Press Sept., 1980
1 GiS 15.00

WONDER WART-HOG, CAPTAIN CRUD & OTHER SUPER STUFF
Fawcett Publications 1967
1 GiS,VB 22.00

YELLOW DOG
The Print Mint May, 1968
1 4pgs,RCr 30.00
2 and 3 8pgs,RCr . . . . @25.00
4 8pgs,RCr,SCW 25.00
5 8pgs,RCr,SCW,KDe 25.00
6 thru 12 . . . . @25.00
13/14 52pgs RCr,Jay Lynch . . . 12.00
15 Don Scheneker,editor 59.00
16 . . . . 55.00
17 thru 24 . . . . @15.00

YOUNG AND LUSTLESS
San Francisco Comic Book Co., 1972
1 BG 15.50

YOUNG LUST
Company & Sons Oct., 1970
1 BG,ASp 27.00
2 BG 15.00
3 BG,JsG,RCr,ASp 12.00
4 KDe,BG,SRo 10.50
5 BG,SRo 7.50
6 SRo,KDe 5.50

YOW
Last Gasp April, 1978
1 BG 5.75
2 BG 4.75
Becomes:

ZIPPY
3 BG 6.50

ZAP COMIX
Apex Novelties Oct., 1967
0 RCr 325.00
1 RCr 325.00
2 RCr,SCW 90.00
3 RCr,SCW,VMo,SRo 55.00
4 VMo,RW,RCr,SCW.SRo,GiS 55.00
5 RW,GiS,RCr,SCW,SRo 50.00
6 RW,GiS,RCr,SCW,SRo 25.00
7 RW,GiS,RCr,SCW,SRo 18.50
8 RW,GiS,RCr,SCW,SRo 10.00
9 RW,GiS,RCr,SCW,SRo 12.00

INDEX

CVA GRADING GUIDE

Grading comics is an objective art. This grading guide outlines the many conditions you should look for when purchasing comics, from the highest grade and top condition to the lowest collectible grade and condition. Your own comics will fall into one of these categories. A more complete description and our comments on comics grades can be found inside. We would like to point out, however, that no reader or advertiser is required to follow this or any other standard. All prices in Comics Values Annual are for comics in Near Mint condition. Happy collecting!

Mint: Perfect, pristine, devoid of any trace of wear or printing or handling flaws. Covers must be fully lustrous with sharply pointed corners. No color fading. Must be well centered. Many "rack" comics are not well centered. "Mint" even when new.

Near Mint: Almost perfect with virtually no wear. No significant printing flaws. Covers must be essentially lustrous with sharp corners. Spine is a light as new. In older comics, minimal color fading is acceptable, as is slight aging of the paper. Most price guides, including CVA, quote prices in this grade.

Very Fine: Well preserved, still pleasing in appearance. Small signs of wear, most particularly around the staples. Most luster is readily visible. Corners may no longer be sharp, but are not rounded. Typical of a comic read only a few times and then properly stored.

Fine: Clean, presentable, with noticeable signs of wear. Some white may show through enamel around staples, and moderate rounding of corners. No tape or writing damage. Book still lies flat.

Very Good: A well worn reading copy with some minor damage such as creasing, small tears or cover flaking. Some discoloration may be evident, with obvious wear around the staples. Little luster remains, and some rolling of the spine may be seen when comic is laid flat on the table.

Good: A fully intact comic with very heavy wear. Tears, cover creases and flaking, and rolled spine will all be evident. No tape repairs present. Only very scarce or valuable issues are collected in this state.

The adjoining price table shows the prices for the other collectible grades which correspond to any "near mint" price given in this book.

Mint	Near Mint	Very Fine	Fine	Very Good
$6,000	$5,000	$3,500	$2,000	$1,000
4,800	4,000	2,800	1,600	800
3,600	3,000	2,100	1,200	600
2,400	2,000	1,400	800	400
1,800	1,500	1,050	600	300
1,200	1,000	700	400	200
1,080	900	630	360	180
960	800	560	320	160
900	750	525	300	150
840	700	490	280	140
780	650	455	260	130
720	600	420	240	120
660	550	385	220	110
600	500	350	200	100
570	475	332	190	95
540	450	315	180	90
510	425	297	170	85
480	400	280	160	80
450	375	262	150	75
420	350	245	140	70
390	325	227	130	65
360	300	210	120	60
330	275	192	110	55
300	250	175	100	50
270	225	157	90	45
240	200	140	80	40
210	175	122	70	35
180	150	105	60	30
150	125	87	50	25
120	100	70	40	20
114	95	66	38	19
108	90	63	36	18
102	85	59	32	17
96	80	56	32	16
90	75	52	30	15
84	70	49	28	14
78	65	45	26	13
72	60	42	24	12
66	55	38	22	11
60	50	35	20	10
54	45	31	18	9
48	40	28	16	8
42	35	24	14	7
36	30	21	12	6
30	25	17	10	5
24	20	14	8	4
22	18	12	7	4
21	17	11	7	4
18	15	10	6	3
17	14	9	6	3
15	13	9	5	3
14	12	8	5	2
11	10	7	4	2
10	9	6	4	2
8	7	5	3	1
7	6	4	3	1
6	5	4	3	1
5	5	3	2	1
4	4	3	1	1
4	4	2	1	0
3	3	2	1	0
2	1	0	0	0

BIBLIOGRAPHY

Daniels, Les. *Comix: A History of Comic Books in America.* New York, NY: Bonanza Books, 1971.

Gerber, Ernst. *The Photo Journal Guide to Comic Books.* Minden, NV: Gerber Publishing, 1989. Vols. 1 & 2.

Gerber, Ernst. *The Photo Journal Guide to Marvel Comics.* Minden, NV: Gerber Publishing, 1991. Vols. 3 & 4.

Goulart, Ron. *The Adventurous Decade.* New Rochelle, NY: Arlington House, 1975.

Goulart, Ron. *The Encyclopedia of American Comics.* New York, NY. Facts on File Publications, 1990.

Goulart, Ron. *Over 50 Years of American Comic Books.* Lincolnwood, IL: Mallard Press, 1991.

Hegenburger, John. *Collectors Guide to Comic Books.* Radnor, PA: Wallace Homestead Book Company, 1990.

Kennedy, Jay. *The Official Underground and Newave Price Guide.* Cambridge, MA: Boatner Norton Press, 1982.

Malan, Dan. *The Complete Guide to Classics Collectibles.* St. Louis, MO: Malan Classical Enterprises, 1991.

O'Neil, Dennis. *Secret Origins of DC Super Heroes.* New York, NY: Warner Books, 1976.

Overstreet, Robert. *The Overstreet Comic Book Price Guide (27th Edition).* New York, NY. Avon Books, 1997

Rovin, Jeff. *The Encyclopedia of Super Heroes.* New York, NY: Facts on File Publications, 1985.

Rovin, Jeff. *The Encyclopedia of Super Villians.* New York, NY: Facts on File Publications, 1987.

Thompson, Don & Maggie. *The Golden Age of Comics, Summer 1982.* Tainpa, FL: New Media Publishing, 1982.

W9-CHW-676

Praise for
Diary of a Teenage Girl: Maya

"Maya is a fun character! It's not even possible to read *It's a Green Thing* and not relate to her questions, her challenges, and her struggles as a teen and Christian. *And* I found myself jotting down her awesome eco-friendly tips!"

—JENNY B. JONES, award-winning author of *In Between*
and *The Charmed Life* series

"As Maya Stark pours her heart out in her journal, readers are treated to an inside view of a life that is at times exotic and unfamiliar, and at other times hauntingly similar to our own. Maya's struggles become our struggles, her pain our pain, and her successes, therefore, even sweeter. *A Not-So-Simple Life* is another triumph for Melody Carlson."

—VIRGINIA SMITH, author of *Sincerely, Mayla* and
Stuck in the Middle

"Fantastic book! Maya is so easy to like—this is a hard story to put down!"

—ERYNN MANGUM, author of *Miss Match*

"Melody Carlson has proven her skill once again at writing gritty stories about characters in difficult situations. In *A Not-So-Simple Life*, Maya Stark seeks to escape life under the controlling hand of

her drug-addicted mother by acting on a plan for independence with admirable determination."

—MICHELLE BUCKMAN, author of *Maggie Come Lately* and *My Beautiful Disaster*

"I just finished Melody's book and loved it! The journal format makes the story, and Maya, so real and believable. Readers will easily be able to identify with the realistic approach to a prevalent situation."

—PATRICIA RUSHFORD, author of the Max & Me Mysteries

What Matters Most

Diary of a Teenage Girl

Maya book No. 3

What Matters Most

a novel

MELODY CARLSON

MULTNOMAH
BOOKS

WHAT MATTERS MOST
PUBLISHED BY MULTNOMAH BOOKS
12265 Oracle Boulevard, Suite 200
Colorado Springs, Colorado 80921

Scripture quotations are taken from the Contemporary English Version. Copyright ©
1991, 1992, 1995 by American Bible Society. Used by permission. Scripture quotation
on page 79 is from Matthew 10:34–39.

With the exception of Anna Gilbert, the characters and events in this book are fictional,
and any resemblance to actual persons or events is coincidental.

ISBN 978-1-60142-119-7
ISBN 978-1-60142-255-2 (electronic)

Copyright © 2009 by Carlson Management Co. Inc.

Lyrics of "Myself," "Give a Little," and "Having a Breakdown" copyright © 2007 by
Anna Gilbert. Used by permission.
Photo of Anna Gilbert by Kekoa Paakaula. Used by permission.

All rights reserved. No part of this book may be reproduced or transmitted in any form
or by any means, electronic or mechanical, including photocopying and recording, or
by any information storage and retrieval system, without permission in writing from
the publisher.

Published in the United States by WaterBrook Multnomah, an imprint of the Crown
Publishing Group, a division of Random House Inc., New York.

MULTNOMAH and its mountain colophon are registered trademarks of Random
House Inc.

Library of Congress Cataloging-in-Publication Data

Carlson, Melody.
    What matters most : a novel / Melody Carlson.—1st ed.
       p. cm.—(Diary of a teenage girl. Maya ; bk. #3)
    Summary: Sixteen-year-old Maya's commitment to live her life for God wavers
after she joins a Christian rock band.
    ISBN 978-1-60142-119-7—ISBN 978-1-60142-255-2 (electronic) [1. Christian
life—Fiction. 2. Interpersonal relations—Fiction. 3. Rock groups—Fiction. 4.
Diaries—Fiction.] I. Title.
    PZ7.C216637Wg 2009
    [Fic]—dc22
                                    2009015106

Printed in the United States of America
2009—First Edition

10 9 8 7 6 5 4 3 2 1

One

September 16

Is it possible that trouble just naturally follows some people? Or perhaps there's something about my "magnetic personality" that attracts negativity. Or as Caitlin would say, maybe God is at work on me. But seriously, sometimes a girl just needs a break.

Here's the deal. It's the third week of school, and I'm finally on fairly good terms with Brooke and Amanda, and Dominic and I are getting along okay, and my classes are going pretty well, and I've even made a few new friends. Things are looking up for Marissa, although she's still not out of the woods completely, but I'll get to that later.

So anyway, it almost seems like I can relax just a little—like maybe I can just breathe and enjoy a taste of the normal life (a life still fairly unfamiliar to me). And suddenly I find out that I've made an enemy. Not just any enemy either. The girl who's set her mean-girl sights on me is none other than Miss Popularity. Not that I'm into that kind of thing. But according to Brooke and Amanda, Vanessa Hartman is. And for whatever reason, Vanessa Hartman is also into making my life miserable. Yesterday I thought our little encounter was just an accident. I actually laughed when

she and her friends burst into the cafeteria with so much enthusiasm that they practically knocked me off my feet. Okay, I'll admit her apology sounded a little phony, and I thought I saw a glint of evil in her big blue eyes, but who am I to judge? Then today we had another "encounter." Only this one was a lot messier.

I was standing in the cashier's line, minding my own business and waiting to pay for my lunch, when something icy cold slid down my back. I jumped and turned around in time to see Vanessa looking surprised (maybe it was faux surprise).

"Oh, did I do that? I was trying to squeeze into line and lifted my tray up." She shook her head with dumb blond wonder. "And it just sort of tipped. Sorry."

Her friends were snickering, and I tried to shake ice off my back and pay for my lunch and get out of there as fast as possible to assess the damage.

"What's up with that girl?" I asked Brooke Marshall as I sat down next to her. I've been eating lunch with her and Amanda Groves lately. Although I'm sure we make a strange trio since both these girls are petite and preppy whereas I'm more into retro and almost a foot taller. "I mean, yesterday she practically knocked me down, and today she does this. I can't wait to see what's on tomorrow's agenda."

Brooke tried to blot the cold liquid out of my hoodie with a wad of napkins, but it was obvious I'd need to change. "It's okay," I told her. "I've got some work clothes in my car."

Brooke laughed as she tossed down the damp napkins. "It figures you'd keep your cool clothes in your car and dress like this for school."

"Well, Jacqueline's is known for stylish fashion, so I can't exactly show up in jeans." I peeled off my soggy hoodie. "And I can't go in wearing soda-soaked clothes either."

"I can't believe she really did that. And her apology…give me a break." Brooke rolled her eyes, then imitated Vanessa. "'It sort of tipped. Sorry.' I mean, how does something 'sort of' tip?"

"Conveniently down your back," added Amanda.

Now Dominic Walsh was joining us. I smiled up at him, thinking, not for the first time, that he has the dreamiest blue eyes— such a contrast to his dark hair. "Hi, ladies." He set down his tray and slid next to me.

"Did you see what Vanessa just did to Maya?" Amanda demanded.

He nodded. "And it was pretty low."

"Seriously, I wonder what's wrong with that girl?" Brooke asked.

"I know what's wrong." Dominic smiled knowingly.

"What?" I asked him. "What *is* her problem?"

"You mean besides being a little too full of herself?" He touched the back of my soggy shirt and made a face. "Yuck. That's sticky."

"It figures she spilled a soda with sugar in it," Amanda said. "I'll bet she normally drinks diet too."

"So you agree that it was premeditated?" I asked Dominic.

"That's my guess," he said.

"But why? I hardly even know her." I glanced over to where Vanessa was sitting with friends—a lot of friends. In a way, she reminded me of a queen holding court. "I mean, she's in a couple of my classes. In choir she even smiled at me. I actually thought she was kind of nice."

"That's what she *wants* you to think," Amanda said.

"That's what she wants *everyone* to think," Brooke said. "But beneath her nicey-nice veneer, she's really a witch."

"That's a little harsh," I countered. "I mean, the soda spill might've been an accident."

"I don't think so," Dominic said with a knowing look.

"Then tell me why."

"You know who Wyatt Cooper is, right?"

"Yeah. He's in my AP history. He seems like a nice guy."

"And he thinks the same about you."

"What's that supposed to mean?"

Dominic frowned slightly. "He thinks you're hot, Maya."

I just shrugged. "So?"

"So," declared Brooke, "*that* explains everything."

"How?"

Amanda nodded. "Mystery solved."

"Can someone please tell me what you guys are talking about?"

"Okay, let's bring her up to date," Brooke said. "Vanessa and Wyatt went together for the past couple of years."

"They were like the perfect couple," Amanda explained. "You know, the ones who act like they rule the entire school, like they think they should be called King Wyatt and Queen Vanessa—and they get crowned for homecoming or prom or wherever crowns are being handed out."

"Do you get it now?" Brooke asked with some impatience.

"Not exactly. But go on." Okay, I suppose I knew what they were suggesting. But it seemed a little presumptuous. I mean, can't a guy be nice just because he wants to be nice? Why does it have to mean something more? Why do people jump to the worst conclusions?

"The happy couple broke up this summer." Amanda glanced over to Vanessa's table. "And my guess is that Wyatt broke up with her."

"Not that we'll ever know," added Brooke.

"So now that Wyatt is into you, Vanessa probably wants you dead," declared Amanda.

"Great." I sighed.

"It might help your situation if they thought you and Dominic were still dating," Brooke suggested.

I gave Dominic a halfhearted smile. "Well, we're not, are we, Dominic?"

"That's right. We're just friends."

And that's what we've agreed to be. Just friends. Oh, I told Dominic that I'd consider going out with him again but only if we made some sort of agreement about our physical relationship

first. And I've been so distracted with school and visiting Marissa and my newspaper column ("It's a Green Thing") and the TV spot and occasionally working at Jacqueline's...well, I just haven't given the idea of dating Dominic that much thought. In fact, I like it better that we're just friends. I'm just not sure if he's happy about it. But Brooke or Amanda would love to date him. I'm not sure how I'd feel about that. Mostly I'm not thinking about it.

However, I did enjoy telling Marissa this whole story when I visited her at the hospital today. Although I don't think she quite got it (or maybe she did—it's hard to tell), she did seem to enjoy hearing it. Of course, she always seems happy to see me. She doesn't get that many visitors now. Part of the reason is because a lot of kids (like my cousin Kim) have gone off to college. But I think the rest of the reason is because it's hard seeing her like that.

As a result of the car wreck, Marissa suffered some fairly severe brain damage. She's doing a lot of therapy, and the doctor says her language skills will probably return eventually but she will never be the same person.

"Maybe it's for the best," Brooke said when I shared that news with youth group last Saturday night.

"What do you mean?" I demanded.

"Well, Marissa was pretty wild. Maybe this will settle her—"

"I can't believe you would say that!" I shot back at her.

Fortunately Caitlin intervened. A good thing, since I felt like smacking Brooke just then. I mean, I've been really trying to get along with her, but cracks like that... Well, I come kind of unglued.

Marissa was wild, and I know she made some incredibly stupid choices—like drinking and driving—but there was a part of her wild side that I actually liked. I enjoyed her wit and her sarcastic humor. I liked that she wasn't afraid to speak her mind or question Christians who weren't acting much like Christians. Those characteristics never really bothered me at all. And I always imagined her eventually finding God—on her terms...or maybe on His. I'm not even sure. But I always thought she'd make a cool Christian.

And now...well, I'm sure she'll still make a cool Christian. But she has changed. I miss the old Marissa. Still, I'm committed to being her friend, and I will continue to visit her. And who knows? Maybe the doctor is wrong. Maybe she'll get back her language skills and her personality too. Because really, why wouldn't God want Marissa to have her personality back? Anyway, that's what I'm praying for. Chloe and Caitlin and several others are praying for the same thing. We want Marissa back. But we also want her to give her heart to God. And we think it could happen.

September 18

Today I met with Mrs. King, the guidance counselor at Harrison High, to establish what year in school this should be for me. Because of my lack of transcripts from previous schooling—although I gave myself grades during my homeschooling era—my status as a student needs to be determined.

"Of course, you're aware," she began, "that you weren't even required to attend public school once you acquired your GED."

"I know…"

"But I'm glad you decided to come back here." She smiled. "I think Harrison High needs you."

I tried not to frown. "I'm not sure everyone agrees."

She looked surprised. "Why not?"

"Nothing—never mind." I waved my hand in dismissal. Why had I said that?

But she just chuckled. "Yes, I'm sure it won't be all smooth sailing, Maya. It never is. But like my dad used to tell me, what doesn't kill you will make you stronger."

I nodded. "Yes, I've heard that one."

"So…" She flipped through my file. "Based on the academic testing we did last year before you took the GED, you could easily make this your senior year. But based on your age"—she peered curiously at me—"this should be your junior year. Which do you want it to be?"

"It's my choice?"

"For the most part…since your case is rather exceptional. I assume you're still working on your emancipation?"

I gave her a quick update on my parents and how I was staying with my uncle for the time being. "My mother's appeal is at the end of the month," I said. "From what I've heard, there's a good chance she could be released. My dad said it wasn't so much due to her being proven innocent as to the overcrowded situation in California state prisons. And I suppose her attorney is pretty good too."

"So what does that mean for you, Maya?"

"I'm not totally sure. My dad hasn't had time to petition the courts for my custody yet. And to be honest, I don't really want him to. I mean, I've been taking care of myself for a while now. I think I'd like to continue that way. Plus he'll be out of the country for about six months anyway."

"Does your mother still have legal custody?"

"According to the law. But based on her criminal record, along with what I've managed to put together toward my emancipation, I think a judge would rule in my favor."

She nodded. "I think you're right, Maya. And if there's anything I can do to help your case, please feel free to ask."

I thanked her, and then we returned to the question of what year this should be for me.

"What do you really want, Maya?"

I thought carefully. "I'm not sure."

"I understand. But we should get this figured out, especially if you want to be a senior. You'll have to jump through certain hoops if you want to graduate in the spring—I mean, with a Harrison High School diploma and not just a GED or state degree."

So I asked her to explain the difference, and she told me that a diploma from Harrison would be much more impressive on my transcript than a GED or even a state diploma. "And I assume you will want to go to college?"

I nodded eagerly.

"And based on the testing we did last spring, I assume you'll want to go to a good college. I have a strong suspicion we can get some scholarship funds coming your way, which is just one more reason to determine whether this is your junior or senior year."

"What do you recommend?"

Her brow creased. "I think you're the only one who can answer that, Maya."

"Yes." I sighed. "I guess I should pray about it."

"That sounds wise. And if you could let me know by next week—especially if you want this to be your senior year—I would appreciate it."

I thanked her and left. But now I'm unsure. A part of me feels like I've barely gotten into a real school, like this is my first shot at a somewhat "normal" life. What if just one year isn't enough? But another part of me feels like maybe it will be more than enough. Like when I think about the juvenile games some high school kids play—like Vanessa Hartman plays. But I don't want to think about that right now. At the moment I'd rather think about whether I'm a junior or a senior this year. I've given myself the weekend to figure it out. I plan to e-mail Kim about it. And I'll talk to Caitlin on Saturday. Most importantly, I plan to pray about it. I want to know what God wants me to do. That's what matters most.

Maya's Green Tip for the Day

Even in September most people are still using air condi-tioning. I've mentioned before that it's a good idea to turn your AC up a couple of degrees and save a few bucks as well as some energy. But here's another way to keep your cool—and it doesn't involve electricity. You can cool yourself off internally by drinking cold tea, lemonade, or water. Not only will you conserve energy (since all the cooling power is directed straight at your body's core rather than at the air), but you'll stay hydrated as well.

Two

September 19

I agreed to go to the football game with Dominic tonight for three reasons. Reason number one was that I didn't want to go by myself, and I didn't really want to be stuck with Brooke and Amanda either. I mean, we're getting along okay, but sometimes their Christian-speak and evangelical ways get on my nerves. Like when they started to dis a girl I've recently been getting to know—a girl named Siobhan. She's in my art class, and her sense of humor reminds me of Marissa's. In fact, I was only partially shocked when she offered to pose nude for our class today. We were working on figure drawing, and Siobhan insisted that the wooden models were not "anatomically correct." Mr. Fenton said, "Thanks, but no thanks," and gave her a grim warning look. Everyone else just laughed.

"Why were you talking to *her*?" Amanda asked when I came over to sit with them at lunch.

"Huh? Who?"

"Siobhan Blakely."

"Oh." I shrugged. "Why not?"

"You were talking to *Siobhan Blakely*?" Brooke said.

"What's the big deal?" And now, despite the fact she'd turned me down, I was ready to go back to Siobhan and insist that she sit with us for lunch.

Then Brooke and Amanda proceeded to tell me that Siobhan had taken money in exchange for sex back when they were in middle school.

"And you know this for a fact?" I asked, then instantly regretted it as Brooke and Amanda took turns going into detail about how "everyone" knew it was true. Fortunately Dominic managed to derail the judgment train, which is actually one more reason I decided to go with him tonight.

But the second main reason I agreed to go with Dominic was because I want Vanessa to see me with him and assume we're dating and hopefully stop fretting over me stealing her ex-boyfriend. Like how is that even possible?

The third reason I agreed was because I made Dominic promise not to consider this a date. And he was okay with it.

"I need you as my friend," I told him. "And if you can't handle that, just be honest." Then I explained about how it was hard to hang with Brooke and Amanda all the time.

He laughed. "I've noticed."

"And I'm trying to love them, but when they said those things about Siobhan, I wanted to scream."

"I noticed the veins on your neck sticking out."

"And I appreciated you tossing the WWJD line at them."

I grinned. "At least it shut them up. God only knows if it made them think."

"Just for the record"—he lowered his voice—"what they said about Siobhan was true, Maya."

I raised my brows. "And you know about this from a *personal* point of view, do you?"

"No," he said quickly, "I didn't mean it like that. I mean I heard about it from sources—you know from *guy* sources. And—"

"And *your point is?*"

He shrugged. "I'm not sure. But I just thought you should know."

"Maybe I should throw the WWJD line at you now."

He grimaced, then held up his hands like he was surrendering. "Okay...okay, I mean, you're probably right."

"I'm not exactly inexperienced when it comes to being around people of questionable character, Dominic."

He looked uncomfortable. "I know. I guess I just feel kind of protective of you."

That actually made me laugh. Although it was kind of sweet, it was also slightly patronizing. "Thanks," I said crisply. "I'll let you know if I'm ever in need of protection."

The ironic thing is that later, this very afternoon, I almost wanted Dominic around to protect me. Although it had nothing to do with Siobhan—and everything to do with Wyatt and Vanessa. It's too bad those two can't get back together because I have a

feeling they belong together. I also have a feeling that I'm being used as a pawn in their relationship. But I could be wrong.

Anyway, I have AP U.S. History fifth period with Wyatt. And as I've already mentioned, Wyatt has been nice to me. Last week he asked to partner with me on a project, and since Vanessa hadn't come onto my radar screen at that time, I agreed. Wyatt is fairly intelligent, and he seemed sincere about the project, which is colonial history (something I'm fairly familiar with, thanks to the homeschool curriculum that I used to get online). So for the first few days, all seemed to be going well, and we were focused on the emergence of American cultural traits and their impact on contemporary culture. But the past couple of days, his interest in academics seems to have deteriorated. Instead of discussing puritanical principles, he's been questioning me about my personal life—about my dad and where I came from and how I got the TV and newspaper spots.

"What's the deal? Are you writing a biography on me or something?"

He smiled and looked into my eyes. "I just find you really interesting, Maya. Does that make you uncomfortable?"

Okay, I'll admit in my journal that his aqua blue eyes made me a little uncomfortable, but I didn't let it show. "No," I said coolly, "I just want to make sure we ace this project."

"We can work on it together this weekend."

"I plan to work on it this weekend."

"Why don't we work together?"

Fortunately, class ended just then. I smiled at him as I gathered my things and told him I'd think about it. Mostly it was a distraction tactic. Then as I was leaving the classroom, I realized he was sticking to me like superglue.

"So why don't you give me your number?" He opened his cell phone. "I'll give you a call."

I was literally cornered between the door and where the wall juts out, but I just smiled, acted like no big deal, and told him my number. I figured I could help him cool his jets later. But that's when I saw a blur of a cheerleader uniform lurking in a crowd of kids standing just behind him, and when I caught a glimpse of long blond hair, I suspected it might be Vanessa.

"I think someone wants to talk to you," I said, nodding toward where she was standing.

He turned, and I managed to slip out of my corner to see that it was indeed Vanessa, and she looked angry. "Well, it sure doesn't take some girls very long." She directed this to her red-headed friend, also in uniform. "I guess that's what my dad calls a fast girl." And they both laughed.

"I guess that's better than being a *slow* girl," I said lightly, then regretted it.

Vanessa took a step toward me, but Wyatt moved between us as if to break something up. "Ladies, ladies," he said in a cheerful but demeaning tone, "don't fight over me."

I stepped next to him and looked him directly in the eye. "Don't worry. I'm not."

He chuckled. "No, I doubt you need to fight for any guy, do you, Maya?" He winked at me. "I'll call you this weekend."

Vanessa looked daggers at me, then smiled a wicked smile. "You two deserve each other."

I couldn't think of a response for that, and maybe it was just as well. But I didn't like feeling that she'd gotten the last word. And I didn't like that everyone who witnessed this little scene probably assumed there really was something going on between Wyatt and me.

That's just one more reason I'm glad I agreed to go to the game with Dominic tonight. I hope he doesn't mind if I act like we really are a couple. Not that Wyatt will notice since he'll be on the football field. But hopefully Vanessa will look up from one of her cheerleader routines and see that Dominic and I are together and get the hint. Otherwise, I might just have to tell her straight out that I am not and never have been interested in her ex-boyfriend for anything beyond academics, and maybe not even for that.

September 20

Even before I met with Caitlin this morning, I knew I would have to tell her about last night…and how it went with Dominic. She's been mentoring me for a few months now, and I try to take her advice seriously—especially when it comes to dating and guys. But first I wanted to get her opinion about whether I should be a junior or a senior this year.

"What do you want to do?" Caitlin leaned forward slightly, watching me with that interest that always shows she genuinely cares. Although she's married to the youth pastor, Josh Miller, and she's also on staff at church, I never feel like a "project" as much as I feel like a friend.

So I told her I was kind of split. "I mean, this is my first real year in high school. I came so late in the year last year, and I wasn't really trying to fit in. And so it's kind of hard to want to give it all up after just one year."

She nodded. "But on the other hand?"

"Sometimes it all seems so childish."

Caitlin laughed. "Yes, I know exactly what you mean. That's kind of how I felt during my senior year too. Like I'd already outgrown high school. But good things came out of that year. My faith got pretty strong, and I made some cool connections with kids."

"So maybe I should go two years?"

"I can't tell you what's best for you. But I will tell you this."

"What?"

"God will lead you. Keep praying about it, and listen to your heart. And I know whichever way you choose, you'll be successful."

I took a sip of my coffee and thought about it. "You know, I think I know the answer to this already."

"What's that?"

"Well, it seems like the best relationships I have are with people who are older than me. Like you and my cousin Kim. And even Marissa...before the accident. And Chloe and Allie when

we've crossed paths at the hospital. Even Dominic is older. If I feel that high school is childish this year, how will I feel next year?"

She nodded. "Maybe you do know the answer."

"But I'll keep praying about it this weekend."

"Good." She leaned even closer to me. "Speaking of you and Dominic, I noticed you two at the game last night, and I could be wrong, but it almost seemed like you guys were a couple again."

I sighed loudly. "Yeah, that was my mistake."

"Your mistake?"

So I told her about Wyatt and Vanessa and how I wanted to make it look like Dominic and I really were a couple.

Caitlin frowned slightly. "So you were *using* Dominic?"

"That wasn't how it seemed at the time, but I suppose that's about right."

"But you said it was a mistake... What happened?"

Well, I was going there anyway, so I figured, *Why not just get it out in the open?* "I gave Dominic the wrong impression last night." Then I confessed how I'd been holding his hand and kind of snuggling up to him at the game, all to show Vanessa she had nothing to worry about. "And Dominic assumed we were really going back to our old relationship."

"Oh..." Caitlin shook her head.

I glanced around the Paradiso Café to be sure no one was within hearing distance. "So after the game and after we'd gotten a bite to eat, Dominic took me home, walked me to the door, and started to kiss me—just like old times."

"And?"

"And I had to push him away and tell him that he'd gotten the wrong idea."

"More like you'd given him the wrong idea."

I nodded. "That's more accurate."

"So, what now?"

"Now...I need to apologize to him."

"That's a switch, isn't it?"

"I guess." I looked over to the counter where Jill (one of the Paradiso owners) was taping a poster near the cash register. It had cool graphics with the image of an old guitar. The Paradiso was planning to have open-mike nights on Fridays again.

"So what are you going to say to him, Maya?"

"Just the truth—that I'm sorry, that I wanted to send a message to Vanessa and Wyatt."

"Wouldn't it have been easier to tell Vanessa and Wyatt the truth in the first place?"

"I guess I got caught up in the childish game-playing thing too."

She gave me a sympathetic smile. "It's an easy trap to fall into."

"But the problem is that I really do want to be friends with Dominic, and it had been going so well."

"Until you broke the rules."

I nodded. "I just hope I didn't ruin our friendship for good."

"So do you and Dominic have any shared interests, Maya, like some sort of hobby or something you can do together, that would

keep your friendship going without threatening to take off in the wrong direction?"

"Well, we're both into the green thing, and we talk about that sometimes. Plus we have our faith… That's a pretty big deal." I was still staring at the image of the guitar on the poster when something hit me. "And there's music."

"Music?" Caitlin looked confused. "I know Dominic plays guitar and bass for youth group, and I know about your dad's career. But are you musical too?"

I kind of shrugged. "Not that much."

"But?"

"My dad gave me an old acoustic guitar last year when I toured with him for a while. He probably thought it would keep me out of trouble. Anyway, it's a pretty cool instrument, and I've been playing around with it some."

"So you are musical?"

"I wouldn't go that far. But I like to write songs and play them just for my own entertainment. And I'm taking choir this year, and Mr. Thompson seems to think I have a decent voice."

Caitlin pointed to the poster. "Hey, maybe you could interest Dominic in doing open mike with you."

"With me?" I held up my hands. "I don't think so."

"But it would give you and Dominic a reason to be together, you know, something to do other than making out."

I rolled my eyes.

"Seriously, Maya. You should consider it. I mean, what if it's a God thing?"

I thought about this. "Yeah, I suppose it would be cool to play together. And Dominic could probably teach me some new chords and picking patterns. I'm kind of limited, and he's pretty talented."

Caitlin smiled. "And you'd be setting a good example for other kids in the youth group, Maya, by showing them that it's possible to hang with a guy and have fun without getting all physically involved."

"The question is whether or not Dominic is even speaking to me now."

Caitlin laughed. "Oh, I have a feeling he'll forgive you."

So after we said good-bye, I called Dominic, but his phone must've been turned off, because it went straight to voice mail.

"Hey, Dominic," I said quietly, "I just want to say I'm sorry for acting like such a jerk last night. You really deserve better. Anyway, I hope you can forgive me. If you want to talk, I'm working at Jacqueline's from noon until six, but I can take a break if you stop by. Or else I'll just see you at youth group tonight."

Okay, after I hung up, I wondered if my apology would be misunderstood. What if he thought I was apologizing for shoving him away when he wanted to kiss me? And that I wanted to reintroduce the whole romance thing again? I was tempted to call right back, just to clarify, but realized that might end up sounding even worse. Better to have this conversation face to face.

As it turned out, Dominic never came by to see me at work. He never called, and he wasn't at youth group tonight either. Even Josh wondered where Dominic was hiding out since he usually helps with worship time. Now, I don't want to be too narcissistic, but I'm afraid it might be my fault.

Maya's Green Tip for the Day

By now you know about storm drains (those grates in the gutters on the street) and how it's wrong, wrong, wrong to dump anything toxic or harmful into them because it can hurt fish and marine life. So what's the best way to wash a car? The most ecofriendly way to a sparkling car is to use automated car washes since they are federally regulated to protect the environment. But what if you are short of cash or don't have one of those places nearby? Here is an inexpensive and green way to wash your car at home. (1) Fill a spray bottle with water, and add about a ¼ cup of simple dishwashing soap (about an 8-to-1 ratio). (2) Get a high-pressure nozzle for your hose. (3) Use an old, recycled towel for a washrag. (4) Park your car on the grass (if your parents don't mind), because the soap runoff will be filtered through the soil. (5) Sparingly dampen your car, spray on the soap solution, scrub, and rinse.

Three

September 21

I started to get seriously worried when Dominic wasn't at church this morning. I had a hard time focusing on the sermon because I felt so certain he was skipping out on both youth group and the worship service just to avoid me. It turns out I was wrong. And now that kind of steams me...like I wasted a perfectly good sermon obsessing over whether or not I'd hurt Dominic's feelings.

As it turned out, he'd gone with his parents to a cousin's wedding. Sure, he could've called me, but I'm pretty sure he was punishing me. And now he'll probably punish me even more. The truth is, I'm so ticked at him right now that I almost don't care. Here's what happened.

I come home from church, and I'm feeling pretty worried and guilty about Dominic. So much so that I call again. This time his phone rings a few times, and I imagine him looking at it, seeing that it's me, and just ignoring it. When it goes to voice mail, I leave another message, saying that I missed him last night and this morning and that I hope everything's okay and that I'll be

hanging around the home front today if he wants to stop by and talk. Sweet and simple, right?

So I change clothes and get my guitar, and since it's one of those gorgeous September afternoons and my uncle is gone, I decide to just hang on the porch and play my guitar. Okay, I was hoping that Dominic would drive up and see me out there and we'd talk and I'd tell him about wanting to play guitar with him and all would be well again. But to my shock, a car pulls up, and out steps Wyatt Cooper!

"Hey, Maya," he calls as he comes up the walk. "That's sounding pretty good."

I stop playing and just stare at him. "What are you doing here?"

He puts his hand on his chest as if he's taken offense. "Are you saying I'm not welcome here?"

Now I feel guilty and force a weak smile. "No, I'm just surprised."

He smiles. "A good surprise?"

"Just surprised. I mean, how did you even know I live here?"

He nods to the house next door. "My older brother used to date Natalie a couple years ago. I remember being over here with him and that Kim Peterson lived next door."

"And?"

"And I heard that you're Kim's cousin and that you live here." He grins like he's so clever.

"So...what are you? Some kind of a detective?"

"Yeah, maybe so." He stands over me just looking down and making me feel more uncomfortable than ever. "Mind if I sit down?"

"Make yourself at home." I look down at my guitar with what I hope appears to be genuine disinterest in his presence. And for a couple of minutes I almost forget about him as I work on a tricky picking pattern my dad taught me last year.

"Hey, you really are good," he says.

I look up and blink. "Oh? Thanks."

"So why do you hate me so much, Maya Stark? Is it because you think you're so much better than me?"

"No," I say quickly, "not at all."

"What is it then? Not your type?"

"I don't have a type."

"What about Dominic?"

"What about him?"

"Well, I heard you guys are kind of a couple. Or that you were."

"We're friends." I frown now. "Or we were."

Wyatt smiles like I've just given him some kind of green light. "So what's the problem then, Maya? Why are you freezing me out?"

Now I look directly at him, remembering Caitlin's challenge to just be honest. "The truth is, I don't like being caught in the middle between you and Vanessa."

He frowns now. "Hey, that's so over with."

"Maybe for you. But she's not over it."

"So what am I supposed to do about it?"

I just shrug and go back to picking.

"Is it my fault if she's still into me?"

I look back up now. "I don't know. Is it?"

He shakes his head. "I don't see why. We broke up almost two months ago. She actually seemed to take it okay at the time. But then school starts, and she's acting like I'm this great big jerk. Is that fair?"

"I don't know." I continue to play.

"Seriously, Maya," he persists. "What am I supposed to do? I'm not into Vanessa anymore. It's like I've outgrown her."

I look back at him again, and I think he's actually being fairly sincere, but I'm also thinking, *Why is this my problem?* Still, I know it would be rude to say that. "Maybe it'll just take some time."

He nods. "I guess so. I mean, we did go together for a long time. Almost two years."

"Some marriages don't even last that long."

"Yeah, I guess that's true."

"So why don't you just cut her some slack? Give her some more time to get over it," I say in what I hope is a sympathetic tone. "Why jump into dating someone else already?"

"I guess I thought it might help Vanessa to move on."

Now this makes me laugh. "So very thoughtful of you."

"I know it sounds phony, but it's true. Even though I'm not in love with her, I still care about her. I wish she'd start dating some-one else."

"Have you tried telling her that?"

"Yeah." He slowly shakes his head. "That went over real well."

"Sorry." I sigh and wish there was a way to give him a gentle but firm hint. "I'm really not that experienced with relationships, you know. You should probably talk to someone with more expertise."

Now for some reason this seems to please him. And he reaches over and strokes my hair with his hand. "That's one of the things I really like about you, Maya. You're honest and straightforward and—"

But that's when I stand up because I notice that Dominic's car has pulled up behind Wyatt's, and he's sitting there staring at us like he's just caught us in the act of, well, whatever. And although I wave at him and start to walk toward his car, he just takes off. Without even saying a word, he drives away.

"What's his problem?" Wyatt asks as he comes over to join me on the sidewalk.

I turn and narrow my eyes at Wyatt now. "You."

He looks surprised. "Why me?"

"Okay," I admit, "and me too."

"I'm sorry, Maya." His expression actually looks sorry. "I shouldn't have come over here like this."

Now, what is it about a guy apologizing that makes a girl feel like she's to blame?

"No, I'm sorry, Wyatt. I haven't been very nice to you. And it's not like this thing with Dominic is your fault."

He nods. "Well, I'm going to get out of your hair." Then he sticks out his hand like he wants to shake. "Still friends?"

This makes me smile. "Sure. I'd like to be friends."

"Cool." He looks sincerely happy. "And I can just e-mail you about the history project, okay?"

"That'd be great."

Then he turns and walks away, and I feel totally confused. Like what just happened here?

So later, after I called Dominic about ten times, he finally answered and, in a grumpy tone, told me that he'd been out of town with his parents. "I was an usher in my cousin's wedding last night," he said stiffly. "I was going to tell you on Friday, but then you kind of blew me off, so I thought, why bother?"

"It would've been nice to know where you were."

"Yeah, that way you can schedule your time with Wyatt."

"That's not—"

"It's okay, Maya. I'm getting your message now, loud and clear." Then he hung up.

So I'm sitting here totally fuming now. What is going on? Oh, it's clear that I've hurt Dominic's feelings and that he's jealous of Wyatt. But what about that good old-fashioned honesty, like Caitlin encouraged? Why can't Dominic just be truthful?

This is what I learned today. Yes, I might only be sixteen (until my birthday in December), but I don't enjoy adolescent games like this. Yes, I do get pulled in, but I don't like it. And now more than ever I'm sure I want this to be my senior year

of high school, and that's exactly what I plan to tell Mrs. King tomorrow.

September 24

Dominic still hasn't spoken to me since our little falling-out last weekend. I wish I could say I don't care, but I really do. It makes me sad to see him by himself and looking so sad. And I especially miss him at lunchtime. Being stuck with Brooke and Amanda without Dominic to help balance things out just isn't much fun. I suppose this was the reason I agreed to eat lunch with Wyatt today. Well, that and because we needed to work out some final details of our AP history project.

"This certainly looks cozy," sniped Vanessa as she paused with her lunch tray.

"Hey, why don't you join us?" I smiled at her.

I could tell Wyatt was surprised, but he just nodded. "Yeah, sure, why not? The more the merrier."

Vanessa looked totally shocked, but then she actually sat down next to Wyatt and stared at me. "What's going on here?"

"We're just working on our AP history project." I stuck my fork in my salad. "But I think it's under control."

"So how's it going, Vanessa?" asked Wyatt.

It was obvious that we'd caught her off guard. With a suspicious expression, she looked from Wyatt to me and back at him again. "Okay, what's up? What kind of game are you two playing here?"

"We're not playing a game," I said. "We're just friends doing homework during lunchtime. Is there anything wrong with that?"

She scowled. "You guys are *just* friends? Yeah, right."

"It's true," I assured her. "I wish we could all be friends."

She laughed. "Oh, you mean *friends with benefits.*"

I frowned. "No, that's *not* what I mean."

"So why aren't you and Dominic together?"

"That's a good question. The truth is, I hurt his feelings, and he's not talking to me now."

Vanessa pointed a finger at Wyatt. "So is that your story too? You two are just friends?"

He nodded toward me and grinned. "What she said."

Vanessa seemed to be at a loss for words now.

"Look," I told her, "it's true. We are just friends. And Dominic and I were just friends too."

"Then why is he mad at you?"

I considered this. "I guess because it's hard to just be friends sometimes."

She glared at Wyatt now. "You got that right."

"But I think it'd be cool if we could." I attempted a smile at her.

She softened now. "Yeah, I guess it would be cool. But I'm not sure that it's possible."

Wyatt brightened now. "But why not give it a try?"

She narrowed her eyes at him. "You mean by being just friends with you?"

He shrugged. "Or with Maya...or whatever."

She looked at me now. "I don't know… I've seen you hanging with those two Bible thumpers, and I'm not really into that."

I kind of laughed. "To be honest, I'm not either. I mean, I am a Christian. But I don't always agree with everything Brooke and Amanda say." Then I told her about how they'd laid into me for being friends with Siobhan.

Vanessa laughed. "Well, I think I'd have to side with the Bible thumpers on that one."

"I don't see why," I countered. "Siobhan is an intelligent and interesting girl. Sure, she's no angel, but then who is?"

Vanessa's expression got serious. "Yeah, I guess that's true. Although Siobhan has a pretty slutty reputation."

"According to her, she made some bad choices a couple of years ago. But she says she's not into that now."

"She told you about it?" asked Wyatt with a little too much interest.

"Not the details," I said quickly, not really wanting to go there, mostly for Siobhan's sake. "Just that she wishes she hadn't done it."

"She said that?" Vanessa looked skeptical.

I nodded, then took another bite of salad. Siobhan and I have been talking a lot during art class, and she's pretty open about her life. I honestly don't think she'd mind if I straightened a few people out about her. Not that she seems to really care what people think. Or at least she acts like she doesn't. But underneath…I think maybe she does.

But here's the bizarre thing about lunch today. After we got over that initial awkward stage, the three of us (Vanessa, Wyatt, and me) actually had a pretty fun conversation. Oh sure, they gave me a bad time about being such a green freak. And now Vanessa calls me "Queen Green," but it's almost like we are friends. How weird is that? But here's the coolest part—Dominic was watching. He was trying to look like he was reading a book, but I could see him glance up occasionally, then quickly back down. I could tell that our strange little trio must've had him thinking. So now I'm determined to try— just one more time—to talk to him. And I have a plan.

After school I went to see Marissa again. It's not easy to go there, and I only go about two or three times a week now, but she looks forward to the visits. For that reason and because I care about her, I'll keep going. Still, I feel guilty for not being more thrilled about seeing her. I mean, her eyes light up, and she gets this big smile, kind of like a little kid at Christmas. That should make me feel good. But it makes me sad. And sometimes it makes me angry—like I want to shout at her and say, "Look what you did, Marissa! Look how you messed up your life by going to a stupid drinking party when people who loved you—people like me—warned you not to! How many times did we tell you that drinking and driving do not mix?!" But how can I do that? Especially when she's sitting there with her shaved head (from the surgery), looking rather pathetic with her scars and bruises still healing. And so I just sit down and talk to her like the therapist has encouraged us to do.

Today I told her about Wyatt and Vanessa and how I was eating lunch with them. She couldn't remember who they were, which is not so unusual. For that reason we keep some old yearbooks in her room. I found pictures of both of them, not hard to do since they're both so popular, but when I pointed them out, Marissa scowled.

She shook her head. "No," she said gruffly.

"Why?"

"Bad girl." She pointed to Vanessa's smiling face in the cheerleader photo.

"I know. She's a snob, and she can't be trusted, but if God loves her, so can I, right?"

Marissa frowned at me, then pointed at the photo again. "Bad girl, Maya. Not good."

I smiled. "Some people used to call you a bad girl, Marissa."

She gave me a lopsided grin. "I *good* bad girl."

"Maybe Vanessa will be a good bad girl too. People can change, you know."

"No," she said firmly. "Banana...no..." She looked confused now, and I had to think.

"You mean Vanessa?"

"Yes. Banessa."

I put my upper teeth against my lower lip to make a *V* sound. "Vanessa," I corrected her. This is something else we're encouraged to do.

She imitated me and said, "V-v-va-nessa."

"Good!"

"No. Bad. V-v-vanessa bad. Bad girl."

"Okay," I conceded. "Let me show you another bad girl who's one of my friends." I took the yearbook back and hunted until I found a photo of Siobhan. "Do you know her?" I asked Marissa.

"Yes."

"Siobhan." I said the name slowly.

"Shu-on," she tried.

"That's close," I told her and then repeated the name slowly. "SHUH–bon."

"Siobhan," she said perfectly.

"Good!"

"Siobhan good."

"Siobhan is a *good* girl?"

"Yes. Good girl. Good bad girl. Siobhan my friend."

I was surprised by this. I didn't recall Marissa hanging with Siobhan last year. But then I didn't even remember seeing Siobhan around. Perhaps more surprising was that Marissa not only had managed to get her name right and to string some words together but had remembered Siobhan in the first place.

"You and Siobhan were friends?" I persisted.

"Yes. Friend. Siobhan my friend." She pointed to me. "Maya my friend." Then she pointed over my shoulder. "Chloe my friend. Allie my friend."

I turned to see Chloe and Allie standing in the hallway. These girls have been friends with Marissa longer than I have. Even

before they started their rock band, Redemption. And when the band took off and they began recording and touring, they continued the friendship. Chloe, who looks like a real rocker chick with her spiky dark hair, pierced eyebrow, black leather skirt, and tall boots, waved to Marissa. "That's right," she said as the two of them came over to stand on the other side of Marissa's bed. "We're all friends, aren't we?"

"Siobhan friend," Marissa said again.

"Siobhan Blakely?" Allie glanced at me, but her blue eyes seemed slightly confused.

"Yeah," I said. "I was telling Marissa that Siobhan is my friend, and she said Siobhan was her friend too."

"That's cool," Chloe said in a way that reminded me of her sister-in-law, Caitlin. Both these girls are especially kind and gracious to everyone—no matter who they are.

At that point I was relieved to let Chloe and Allie take over the conversation. I just sat back and listened.

"Where Laura?" Marissa asked.

"Laura went to school," Allie said. "Remember?"

"School over." Marissa pointed to me. "Maya school over?"

"That's a different kind of school," Chloe clarified. "Laura went away to a college. Remember, college is where you go after high school."

"That's where Kim is too," I offered. "At college."

"Call..." Marissa tried.

"College," Allie said clearly. "College is *after* high school."

"College," Marissa said slowly. "College *after* high school."

"You're doing really great," Chloe said cheerfully. But there was sadness in her eyes. We all know that Marissa's chances of going to college are probably pretty slim now. Still, miracles can happen. And I'll keep praying.

In fact, I find myself praying for a number of miracles these days—like that somehow I'll patch things up with Dominic and that Wyatt and Vanessa will eventually figure out that they need God as much as I do. But first and foremost on my mind is Shannon. Oh, I try not to think about it, but I know her appeal is just a week away. So mostly I just pray about it. And it's not that I want God to keep my mother in prison. I mean, that's pretty harsh. But I just don't want her to make trouble for me. I don't want to be derailed by her...again.

Maya's Green Tip for the Day

We all enjoy our electronic devices, whether it's a cell phone, computer, DVD player, television, or MP3 player. But what do you do with those "old friends" when you upgrade to the latest and greatest? For starters, you might consider giving any usable item to a friend, or you might donate it to an organization that will repair, reuse, or recycle for profit. What you don't want to do is toss an electronic device into the garbage, where it will end up in a landfill. Most electronics contain hazardous materials that can threaten the environment. For more information on what to do with these items, check out this great recycling Web site: http://earth911.com. And you can donate functioning but outdated cell phones to women's shelters. (Any working cell phone can call 911 even without a wireless plan.)

Four

September 25

It seems that miracles still happen. Okay, it's not going to make the local news, but it feels miraculous just the same. My plan for getting Dominic back on speaking terms actually worked! Here's how it went down.

At lunch I found myself sitting with Wyatt and Vanessa once again. This time a couple of their friends joined us as well—I think out of curiosity more than anything. Like what were Wyatt and Vanessa doing hanging with the new girl? Then, as Dominic passed by, I slapped the seat next to me and called out to him. "Hey, Dominic, why don't you sit with us?"

Okay, he looked so stunned that I worried he would drop his lunch tray and totally humiliate himself. But being the cool dude that he is, he just turned around, nodded, and sat beside me.

"So, Dominic," said Wyatt all friendlylike. "What's up, buddy?"

Dominic's clear blue eyes flashed, like he wanted to lay into Wyatt. "Not much."

"Hey, Dominic," I began quickly, "I really need to ask you a huge favor."

His brow creased. "Like what?"

"Well, I wanted to do open mike at the Paradiso and—"

"No way," said Vanessa. "You'd actually *do* that, Maya?"

"Sure. Why not?" I nodded and tried to look more confident than I felt. The truth is, I hadn't even signed up to do open mike and hadn't been sure that I would. It wasn't until I opened my big mouth in front of everyone that I actually decided I would. Maybe it was my last-ditch effort to revive my friendship with Dominic and hopefully bury the hatchet for good.

"What are you going to *do* for open mike?" asked Vanessa's friend Becca Johnson.

"Just a song," I said.

"She plays guitar," Wyatt told them. "And she's pretty good too."

I saw Dominic's eyes flash again and knew I'd better jump back in. "So, here's the favor," I said quickly. "Will you perform with me for open mike?"

"What do you want me to do?"

"I know you're used to playing in front of people." I turned to the others now. "He's really good on guitar and bass. He plays for our youth group."

They looked at him with fresh interest, and he sort of shrugged.

"And I'm totally inexperienced…" I smiled hopefully at him. "So I thought if you were backing me up, just in case I really blow it, well, it wouldn't be quite so humiliating, you know?"

His countenance softened just a little. "I guess I could do that.

But we'll need to practice, and I'll have to learn your song. When were you planning to do it anyway?"

"Tomorrow." I smiled sheepishly.

"Tomorrow?"

"I know it's kind of sudden, but I also know you're good."

"Open mike's on Fridays?" Wyatt seemed truly disappointed.

I nodded. "That's what the poster at the Paradiso said."

"We have games on Fridays," Wyatt pointed out.

"Oh yeah." I nodded sadly. "Too bad."

Now everyone at the table actually looked bummed.

"Can't they change open mike to Saturdays?" suggested Vanessa.

"You'd have to talk to them about it at the Paradiso," I said, although I hoped she wouldn't since that would compete with youth group.

"It would've been cool to see you perform," Wyatt said more to me than Dominic.

"And Maya has a good voice," said Vanessa. "She sits behind me in choir, so I know."

I thanked her and pretended to be disappointed that they'd miss our performance, but I was hugely relieved. It's one thing to make a fool of yourself to preserve a friendship. It's another thing to make a fool of yourself in front of your new friends.

I think Dominic was relieved too. After school we went to the church to practice since his bass was already there. Dominic said

that Josh was totally okay with kids doing music in the youth room. And, he pointed out, it had pretty good acoustics.

So we met over there at four, and as we walked across the parking lot, I apologized again. "I know how it must've looked to you on Sunday," I began, "but honestly, there was nothing going on between Wyatt and me. He popped over unexpectedly. And we are just friends. That's all."

"That might be all it is to you, Maya," he warned me, "but I don't think you can speak for Wyatt."

"I know I can't control his feelings," I admitted, "any more than I can control yours. But I stand by what I said. *We are just friends.*"

"Well, I have to admit that it was kind of cool to see you were able to get Wyatt and Vanessa acting civilly to each other. And I'm impressed that you seem to have won Vanessa over as a friend. That couldn't have been easy."

I nodded. "I think God had more to do with it than me. I've really been praying for a breakthrough. I mean, it's probably good practice for me to love my enemies, but having Vanessa as a friend sure sounds a lot better."

"Even so," he said, "I wouldn't completely trust that girl if I were you, Maya. She could be up to something. She could be setting you up."

So I explained how I was the one to initiate the friendship and how it seemed to have caught her off guard. "It was obvious she wasn't happy. And I don't see how hating me was making her feel any better."

"Some girls seem to thrive on that sort of thing."

"Maybe on the outside." I glanced at him. "Don't you think it's possible for people to change?"

"Maybe…" He opened the door to the youth room for me. "But watch your back."

I kind of laughed as I set my guitar case on a chair. "I'm not worried, Dominic. In fact, I want to invite Vanessa and Wyatt and the others to youth group one of these days. Like if there's some kind of gathering or party or something where things don't feel too churchy or intimidating."

"They usually have a party around Halloween. Sometimes, if Chloe and the others are around, Redemption will do live music too. It's been kind of a cool event for bringing in a crowd."

"Maybe this year it will include Wyatt, Vanessa, and the others."

He chuckled. "I suppose that could happen, but it would be pretty amazing."

"Why?"

"Oh, you know…that crowd…they have their own kind of parties."

"Well, some of those parties end up in tragedies—like Marissa's."

He nodded as he picked up his bass and adjusted the strap. "So, what kind of music are you planning to do tomorrow night?" He gave me a knowing grin. "That is, if you're really serious about doing open mike."

"What do you mean?" I tuned a string.

He shrugged. "I don't know...but I sort of wondered if this wasn't just your way of forcing me to speak to you."

"And...what if it was? What if I really have no intention of doing open mike? What if I got you here under false pretenses?"

He laughed. "Then the joke's on you, Maya."

"What do you mean?"

"I mean, you and I are going to perform at open mike, whether you like it or not. Do you even *know* a whole song?"

Now that irked me. Of course I know a whole song. I actually know a bunch of whole songs. Not impressive songs. But just then an interesting one came to mind, and I began to sing it—with gusto!

Dominique-oh-Dominique,
Over the land he plods along...

To my surprise Dominic actually knew this funny old song. Soon we were singing it together, except that he knew all the lyrics, and I only knew the first few stanzas. We both ended it by messing up the lyrics and laughing so hard we were practically crying.

"How did you know that song?" he asked.

"My dad had that record. I used to listen to it when I was a kid."

"My mom taught it to me."

"Too funny."

"Maya, please tell me you don't plan to sing *that* at open mike."

"No..." I pulled a spiral notebook out of my guitar case and flipped to my latest song. "I had something more serious in mind."

"Let's hear it." He sat back on the stool and waited.

"Well, I don't know if it's any good, but—"

"Save the disclaimers for later."

"No, it's not a disclaimer. It's just that I'm not sure."

"What new musician is ever sure?"

"Well, it's about my mom."

He nodded with a serious expression. "Why don't you just play it? You know that you're safe with me."

"Yeah, I know. It's called 'Ode to Shannon,' but I suppose it could be 'Ode to My Mother.' Not that I think of her as a mother so much." And then, instead of rambling on like I wanted to do, I began to play the song I had written a few weeks ago, the song that got me playing my dad's guitar again.

Ode to Shannon
She lives in a box
Constructed of lies
Made it herself
Doesn't realize
It cannot conceal
Or hide her mistakes
It can only reveal
The life she fakes

Kick open that door
Break down that box
Let Jesus inside
Before all is lost

She lives in a box
Built of deceit
With pillars of shame
And walls of cheat
Broken promises layered
Upon warped floors
She locks herself
Behind closed doors

Kick open that door
Break down that box
Let Jesus inside
Before all is lost

She lives in a box
Made for privacy
But the walls are glass
And the whole world sees
The life she built
Is falling apart

She lives in a box
That will break her heart

Kick open that door
Break down that box
Let Jesus inside
Before all is lost

I stopped playing, and the room was quiet. Too quiet. I sus-pected he didn't like it. "I told you it wasn't very good," I said quickly. "I'm not ready for—"

"No," he cut me off. "It is good. It's really good, Maya. And the tune is catchy. I think I know what to do. Why don't you play it again, and I'll join in."

"Seriously?"

"Yeah." He nodded eagerly. "Go for it."

And so I played it again, and this time he played bass and even hummed along during the chorus. We played it several times, until I was sure he must be sick of it. "Want to try some-thing else?" I asked.

"Sure. Just for a break. Then we can come back to it."

Finally it was after six o'clock, and Dominic told me he had to get home. "My mom makes us sit down to dinner on Tues-days and Thursdays," he explained. "Be there or be on KP for the whole week."

"Yikes, you better run."

"But this was great," he told me as we headed out. "If you want, we can go through it a couple more times before open mike, but I think you're ready."

"We can figure that out tomorrow." Okay, everything in me wanted to hug him just then. It took all my self-control not to. But I knew it wouldn't be a good idea in light of my "just friends" position.

As we got into our separate but strikingly similar hybrid cars, I thought about how much we have in common and about how much I like this guy. Okay, this is my diary, and I can be honest. I love this guy. I love him on so many levels. I love his heart. I love his musical ability. I love that he's green. And it would be dishonest not to say I love his looks. And hey, I am only human—I have loved it when he's kissed me too. But that is probably the danger signal...the red flag.

Yet as I drive home, knowing that my uncle is probably working late and that I'll fix my own dinner like I usually do, I feel really lonely. I imagine Dominic going home and sitting at a table with his family, and I think about other families in this small town. Oh, I know not everyone sits down to eat together. But at least they have each other. And as much as I love my uncle and appreciate him allowing me to stay with him, it's not quite the same as having my own real family. It's times like this when I still feel like a misfit in this world. It's times like this when I really want to grab on to Dominic and just cling to him like Saran Wrap. I want

to make him my family, and I want to go home with him and sit at his table and laugh with his family. I want to take him home with me and play gin rummy with Uncle Allen. I want to belong to him, and I want him to belong to me.

And yet I know that's just really lame and pathetic. I always wince to see girls like that at school—the ones who can't let go of their boyfriends' hands even to carry their lunch trays. Or I think about the way Vanessa has acted toward Wyatt, like she thinks they really were married or like she wishes they were now. It's times like this when I question my commitment not to date Dominic. I ask myself, really, what would be wrong with that? But at the same time, I know the answer. It would ruin everything.

But seriously, if I didn't think that dating would totally mess up our relationship, I would be so into it. And I'm sure a lot of girls my age would say, why not go for it? And yet I know why not. I've seen *why not* in action, and it's not pretty. So I'm going to do what it takes to stick to my guns on this. I am not going to risk my friendship with Dominic by letting a physical relationship take over and destroy everything. God help me, I am not!

Maya's Green Tip for the Day

Too many beauty products still use petroleum products (a.k.a. petrolatum), and this is a nonrenewable resource. Plus, it's not that good for you. So take time to read the ingredients label on your next bottle of shampoo or conditioner or lip gloss. Opt for products that contain lubricating alternatives like coconut oil (which is great on my curly hair) or other natural products like beeswax, jojoba, or olive oil. For more good ideas, check out www.idealbite.com. This Web site's motto is "a sassier shade of green," and they're geared more to the feminine side of conservation.

September 26

D ominic and I spent a couple more hours practicing music this afternoon. Then shortly before eight we entered the Paradiso only to discover less than a dozen people there. And most of them had come to perform. Mike and Jill (the owners) seemed pleased that we'd come and were happy to put us on the open-mike list, but they apologized for the disappointing turnout.

"We really expected a bigger crowd," Jill admitted as I handed her back the clipboard. "But we forgot about football."

"We're hoping it'll pick up some after the game," Mike added.

"Yeah, I bet it will." I smiled like I hoped that would be the case, but to be honest, I was relieved. At least I wouldn't be making a fool of myself in front of a huge audience tonight. Then Dominic and I sat down with coffees and watched as three guys set up their sound system. It seemed to take forever before they finally began to play. By then a few more people had trickled in, but it was obvious they hadn't come for the music since they ordered their coffees to go and got out of there quickly. Can't say that I blame them because the music wasn't just too loud, but also not so great. Not that I consider myself some great music

critic, but Dominic wasn't liking it much either, and we were actually considering taking our names off the list and just leaving, but I didn't want to hurt Jill's feelings. She had seemed genuinely glad that we had signed up. And so we endured.

The next performer turned out to be a poet. My guess is that he was college age, and he was actually pretty good although his antiwar poem was incredibly long. Just the same, my ears enjoyed having a break from the music. After that was a flute solo by a girl who also seemed to be college age. At least I don't recall having seen her around school.

And then a surprising thing happened—the coffeehouse began to fill up. Apparently the football game had ended earlier than usual, the result of our team having been creamed. And so spirits were lagging as the flutist finished up her last piece—a melancholy number that seemed the perfect soundtrack to the gloomy crowd. But Dominic and I clapped with enthusiasm, probably because we'd be up there soon and desperately hoped that someone would clap for us. And then Jill announced that it was time for Dominic and me to perform. To say I was nervous is an understatement. My knees were actually shaking as I reached for my guitar.

Now, I'm sure that anyone who knows much about me assumes I have all this confidence and bravado. I mean, I've modeled professionally. I do my "green girl" TV spot as well as the newspaper column. And I suppose I even try to act like I'm not afraid of anything—an act I learned long ago while living with

Shannon. And maybe I am fairly confident...about most things. But not when it comes to music. I'm sure that's related to my dad. His standards have always been pretty high, and I've heard him critiquing others, and I imagine he'd probably do the same to me. Not that he has discouraged me necessarily...but more like he's been sort of ho-hum about my musical abilities. One time he told me it wasn't that he thought I lacked talent but that he never wanted me to get into a business where the industry can chew you up and spit you out faster than you can cash your first check. Anyway, as a result I felt pretty insecure as Dominic and I got ourselves set up on the little stage. As I did the final adjustment on my mike, I wondered what on earth I had gotten myself into...and why I didn't just stand up and make a run for it?

But then Dominic looked directly into my eyes and gave me that gorgeous smile, and I decided to simply pretend that the coffeehouse was still as empty as it had been more than an hour ago. Just Dominic and me. And we began to play. All I thought about was the words and the music, and before I knew it, we were done. Then I remembered where we were and realized that the room was pretty quiet...kind of like we'd just bombed. Then they began to clap, and the next thing I knew they were saying, "Encore."

"We didn't really plan any more songs," I told them. But the crowd kept urging us, and so we played a couple more tunes that we'd practiced some. When they begged for more, I winked at Dominic, then said to the crowd, "I'm pretty sure this song will shut us down for good." And so we played "Dominique," and

although some of them laughed, we still got applause before surrendering the stage to a guy who did a slightly amusing, albeit somewhat skanky, stand-up comic routine.

After that, to everyone's pleased surprise, Chloe and Allie stepped out of what seemed to be nowhere and took the stage. I could tell by Mike's and Jill's expressions that this was no surprise to them. Plus it seemed that their instruments were already up there and ready to go, so I'm pretty sure it was planned. Then, with Chloe on guitar and Allie on keyboard, they kept us entertained for about twenty minutes with some really great music. During that time I noticed that Wyatt and Vanessa and some of their friends were part of the crowd, and on my way back from picking up another mocha, I stopped by their table to say hey.

"You and Dominic were really good." The way Vanessa said this almost sounded as if she was surprised. But to be fair, so was I.

"You really were," added Becca.

"Seriously," said Wyatt, "your voice is amazing, Maya. You could go pro if you wanted."

"Well, that might be a stretch, but thanks anyway."

"Why don't you sit with us?" offered Wyatt.

"Thanks." I tipped my head in the direction of Dominic, sitting near the stage. "But I like that table better."

"Thanks a lot." Wyatt pretended to be hurt.

"It's closer to the music," I explained.

"Are you going to sing again tonight?" Wyatt looked hopeful.

"No, that was it."

"Tell Dominic he was good too," said Becca.

"And *hot*," added Vanessa with a wicked little smile.

I nodded. "I'll be sure to tell him you said so."

And I did, and he just laughed. Then we both focused our attention on Chloe and Allie—two extremely talented young women. After they finished their set, they came over to our table, and Allie asked to sit with us.

"Do you mind?" asked Chloe.

"Are you kidding?" Dominic jumped up, surrendering his seat to Chloe and grabbing an empty chair for Allie before he took off in search of another.

"We heard you and Dominic tonight." Chloe sat down across from me.

"Really? You guys were here then?"

"Yeah." Allie grinned. "We snuck in the back earlier, just kind of sat in the shadows until our turn."

"We didn't want to intimidate anyone," Chloe admitted.

"I appreciate that," I said. "I was pretty nervous already."

"You seemed totally cool," Allie said.

"You guys are really good," Chloe said as Dominic rejoined us.

"Thanks." He grinned. "Same back at you, only way more so."

Allie pointed at me now. "You have a really great voice, Maya."

"Thanks."

"And you're not bad either," Chloe told Dominic.

"Oh, I was just backup," he said.

"I was thinking we should jam together sometime," Chloe suggested. "If you want, that is."

"Bring it," teased Dominic.

"Hey, why not?" Allie stood up and waved her arms like she was trying to get attention. "All right, you guys!" she yelled out to the crowd. "Ya wanna hear some jamming tonight?" The response was loud and enthusiastic, and the next thing I knew the four of us were fumbling around for our instruments and back on the stage.

"My guitar's just an acoustic," I told Chloe.

"It's okay," she assured me, placing one of the mikes by my guitar and one by my mouth. Allie was already adjusting the sound. And suddenly we were playing. Okay, I wasn't sure if I'd be able to keep up with them, but to my surprise I didn't do too badly. And it was fun. Really fun!

Finally, it was past eleven, and we knew it was time to quit. Mike and Jill had already cleaned out the coffee machines and looked ready to call it a night. And although the crowd had thinned down some, they sounded disappointed when Chloe announced it would be our last number.

"Thanks for letting me jam with you guys," I told Chloe and Allie as we were putting our instruments away. "That was really incredible."

"We should do it again." Chloe closed her guitar case.

"For sure," I said. "How long will you guys be around before you start touring again?"

Allie frowned. "That's a good question."

"We're sort of on a hiatus," admitted Chloe.

"When Laura left for school, we became a *two-girl* band." Allie made a face. "Kind of small, doncha think?"

"But it's okay since we don't have any new recording contracts and we finished our concert tour." Chloe turned off some sound equipment. "Our manager had some ideas about replacing Laura, but we decided to take this opportunity to think and pray about where we need to be with our music. We all needed a break."

"I don't know." Allie pulled on her jacket. "I'm already getting antsy."

"You're always antsy," Chloe teased. "I'm enjoying this downtime. It's been a pretty wild ride these past couple of years."

"Not for me." Allie shook her head. "A few days off and I'm ready to rock and roll again."

We were all packed up now. "Well, anytime you want someone to jam with you," I assured them, "just call me, and I'll be there."

"Same goes for me." Dominic gave Chloe a cheesy smile. "Unless you're into the all-girl thing. In that case I could wear a dress and heels."

Chloe laughed. "We're gender neutral when it comes to jamming."

Then we all thanked Mike and Jill as we waited for them to unlock the door to let us out.

"Thank *you*!" called out Jill. "Thanks to you four, open-mike night was a hit."

"That's right." Mike patted me on the back. "You guys are welcome to play here any old time you like."

And so I'd have to say that all in all, tonight was a success. Oh, I don't have any false illusions that I've just launched my musical career. Not! But it was fun, and I didn't make a total fool of myself.

September 29

As usual, I checked my phone for messages during lunch break, and I was surprised to see that Chloe had called. And even more surprised that she was inviting me to come jam with them after school tomorrow. I called right back and told her "absolutely."

"Cool." She gave me directions to her house.

"Uh, what about Dominic?"

"Sure, bring him along too if you want."

"Okay." But as I hung up, I wondered about that. She hadn't sounded as enthusiastic about Dominic as I would've expected, but I knew I couldn't leave him out either. And of course, when I told him a few minutes later, he was totally jazzed.

"Very cool," he said as we sat down at the lunch table. "I get to jam with the chicks."

"The Dixie Chicks?" teased Becca.

So I explained that it was Chloe and Allie and decided to use the opportunity to bring up the subject of faith—or at least try. "So have you guys all heard their band play before, I mean, when they were still together?"

"Oh, sure," Becca said. "Everyone in town has heard Redemption by now."

"Whether or not they wanted to," added Vanessa in a slightly snooty tone.

"What's that supposed to mean?" I tried not to sound too defensive.

"You know...not everyone's into religion." She shrugged. "But I'll admit that their music, if you take away the God stuff, is okay."

"So you want to take away the God stuff?" I asked.

"I don't know. I guess it's not my cup of tea."

"I like Redemption," Becca admitted. "I mean, sure, their songs are about God, but it's not like they're real preachy, you know? Not like you think you're at church or something."

Dominic nodded. "Their music seems to be more about life and things that matter."

"Right," I agreed, "and if you happen to believe that God's a part of life, what's the big deal?"

"Let me guess," Vanessa said. "Now you're going to invite us to come to your church or Bible study or something?"

"No," I said quickly. "But would that offend you?"

"It wouldn't offend me," said Wyatt.

Okay, the whole table got pretty quiet then.

"Why should it?" he continued. "I believe in God. And sometimes I get worried that I might not be living my life, well, you know, like the Holy Book says to."

This made several of them laugh.

"You can say that again," Vanessa sniped.

"Hey, I never said I was an angel," he shot back at her. "I'm saying, yeah, maybe I do need a little bit more God in my life."

"Then consider yourself invited to our youth group," Dominic said.

Wyatt turned to me now. "Is that invitation from you too?"

"Of course."

Wyatt nodded. "Well, who knows, maybe I'll take you up on it."

"Seriously?" Vanessa looked skeptical.

"Absolutely." He pointed his fork at her. "It wouldn't hurt you to go either."

Now she made a sugary smile. "Sure, I'll go...if you want to take me."

Wyatt seemed to be considering this, but before he could answer, someone dropped a tray right behind him, making a huge crash. We all jumped at the sound and then, realizing what it was, just laughed it off. Soon they were teasing the poor guy who'd fumbled the tray and making jokes about the noise that could've been a gunshot, saying how they'd all be dead and standing before those locked pearly gates and wishing they'd gone to church a little more. But it was mostly a joke to them. I doubt that any of them took that whole pearly gate thing seriously. Still, maybe I would follow up the previous conversation with Wyatt...privately.

Maya's Green Tip for the Day

I don't know about where you live, but we have mosquitoes here. And since I like to garden, they can be real pests. Do yourself and your neighbors a favor by preventing mosquito breeding grounds. You can do this by eliminating sources of standing water such as wading pools, old tires, birdbaths, and watering cans. You can also keep mosquitoes out of your yard by using deterrents such as citronella candles or basil plants. And you might try spraying a solution of garlic powder mixed in water around your yard. It's not a huge problem in our country, but mosquitoes spread malaria and the West Nile virus, and although this pest is tiny, it's also one of the deadliest animals on the planet. Not to mention really irritating.

Six

September 30

I almost canceled jamming with Chloe and Allie today. By the time I drove to Chloe's house this afternoon, I was totally bummed. Now, most people would be glad to hear that their mother has been released from prison. But I'm not most people. Neither is Shannon.

School is over, and I've just gotten into my car, focusing on an afternoon of music and fun. The truth is, I've completely blocked what day this is and what's been going on in Los Angeles. But when I see the pay phone number on my caller ID, I have a strong suspicion who's on the other end. I almost don't answer.

"Hey, baby," she says in a smooth voice.

"Shannon," I say somberly. "What's up?"

"Good news, baby. I'm free!" Her voice has that little-girl sound to it. In the past it's always been a bad sign—a signal that she wants something from me or that she's done something wrong.

"That's great, Shannon." I feign enthusiasm and nearly ask her what she's going to do now, but thankfully I stop myself. I have no intention of getting pulled into her plans. No way. No how. "You must be really happy."

"I am totally happy, ecstatically happy. But then I realized that our house is gone, baby. The bank took it away from us. Can you believe that?"

I want to say, "Of course I believe it. You maxed out all your credit cards, you never paid your bills, the house was mortgaged beyond its worth. Crud, you even stole money from me. Why shouldn't the bank take it?" But I don't. I don't say anything. But I do pray. I ask God for self-control and to keep me from telling her what I really think.

"What are we going to do, baby? We don't have a house now. Where will we live?"

I'm still praying. I don't want to open my mouth. Don't want to say something ugly and horrible and something that, once it's out there, cannot be erased, rewound, or taken back. I bite into my lip so hard that I think I can taste blood.

"I miss you, baby. I need to see your beautiful face."

It feels as if my temperature has cooled by ten degrees. Okay, I realize that's highly unlikely since that would probably mean I was dead, but it's how I feel. Although it's sunny outside, I turn on my car's engine and crank up the heat.

"Are you there, baby? Can you hear me?"

"Yes, Shannon," I say quietly, "I can hear you." I watch as other kids get into their cars. I imagine them going home to houses where normal parents do normal things...so different from mine.

"I know I should have some sort of plan in place by now.

I should be able to put a roof over my baby's head, but I just don't know what to do. What should we do, baby?"

"Just take care of yourself," I say slowly. "Don't worry about me, Shannon. I'm fine. Really, I am."

"Oh, I know you're all happy and comfy living with Allen and Kim." The little-girl tone is evaporating now, and I can tell she's getting irked at me. "But don't forget, Maya. They are my family too. It was my sister's home, you know." She sighs loudly. "I sure miss Patty."

It's all I can do not to scream. *She misses Patty?* Give me a break. This is a woman who ran away and never lifted a finger to find her "beloved" sister. Even when Patricia was on her deathbed, Shannon chose to go shopping. By the time she got there, it was too late. And now she misses her? Tell me another one. Fortunately, I don't say any of this.

"So, what are you going to do, Shannon?" I ask calmly. "Is there someone in L.A. you can stay with for a while until you figure things out?"

"Lynnette got a new boyfriend." Shannon sounds like she's starting to cry now. "She said I can't stay with her."

"But there must be someone else."

"No one wants me, baby. Everyone has given up on me."

I want to say "including me." But again, I don't.

"All I have is you, baby. And I need you. I need to see your face...your pretty brown face. My little brown baby."

"Have you been drinking, Shannon?"

"Just a beer or two, baby. I had to celebrate my freedom."

"Shannon." My voice is icy now, and I'm just trying to breathe. "I'm sorry your life is a mess, but it's your mess, not mine. And if you're barely out of jail and already drinking, it seems to me that you plan to continue to make a mess."

"Why are you so mean, Maya? Why do you hate me?"

"I don't hate you, Shannon. I feel sorry for you. But I also feel sorry for me. And right now it's every woman for herself."

"Fine, if that's how you treat your mother."

Mother? I take in a sharp breath. "You know what you need, Shannon?"

"A rich man?" Now she laughs like that's so clever.

"No, Shannon, *you need God.* And until you figure that out, you'll probably keep going from one mess directly to another. And I'm sorry, I don't want to go there with you. The only thing I can offer you is my prayers. And if you really do need a place to stay, I'm sure there must be a mission or homeless center nearby that will take you in."

I'm not surprised when she hangs up on me. My hands are shaking as I close my phone and then turn it off. I can't handle any more calls from her. Not today. And as I drive over to Chloe's house, I question whether or not I handled that right. I mean, as a Christian. I'm supposed to love my enemies. I'm supposed to be kind, loving, generous, patient...all that good stuff. But how

am I supposed to be like that to Shannon? At least I'd been try-ing to forgive her. Anyway, I thought I had. But now I suspect it's going to take more time.

Later, as I parked my car and walked up to Chloe's house, I wasn't so sure. I tried to act like nothing was wrong, but as we started to jam, playing Christian songs about loving others and being changed to look more like God, I questioned myself even more. Finally, when we were having a break, Chloe looked directly at me and asked, "Maya, are you okay?" That's when I broke into tears and told Chloe, Allie, and Dominic the whole story about what I'd said to my mother less than an hour ago.

"I'm such a horrible Christian," I confessed. "I can't even love my own mother. I don't want to see her again. Not ever. I don't want her in my life. I can't stand her." My hands balled into fists, and I shook them. "I hate her! I honestly do hate her. What kind of a Christian hates her own mother?"

All three of them wrapped their arms around me. And then Chloe began to pray for me. I can't remember all that she prayed, but it wasn't like she was praying for God to make me a better Christian or to help me love my mother better. She was praying that God would hold me in His arms and that He would be my Father and that I would know how big His love for me was. And that was about it. And yet when she finished, I felt so much better.

"Thanks," I said as Chloe handed me a tissue. "Thanks, all you guys. I'm sorry I'm such a blubbering baby."

"Who can blame you?" Dominic just shook his head. "All you've been through and now this too. I can't believe your mom expects you to rescue her."

"And you shouldn't even think of trying to help her," Allie assured me. "That would be so codependent."

I nodded. "You're right. I mean, it never helped in the past. The more I did for her, the worse off she became. I know she needs to stand on her own two feet. But it's hard. I mean, I think about Jesus saying things like 'If someone hits you, just turn the other cheek' or 'If someone asks for your coat, give them your shirt too.' Stuff like that. And then I tell my own mother to stay out of my life, and I feel like a total hypocrite."

"But you're not," Chloe assured me. "God doesn't expect you to parent your mother, Maya."

I nodded. "Yeah...probably not."

So that's what I'm telling myself tonight. *God does not expect me to parent my mother.* It's like I need to say it over and over in my head just to get a firm hold on it. Because old habits die hard, and I spent a lot of time taking care of Shannon in the past, and I probably believed it was my job to do that. I mean, hey, I was a kid—how would I know better? In some ways Shannon stole my childhood from me and a chunk of my adolescence as well. But I don't have to let her steal anything else from me. Besides, I realize now that I can't help her. Not really. It's time for her to help herself, hopefully by turning to God and getting her life in order.

I know I need to keep forgiving her. (It's not like a one-time, it's-over-and-done-with sort of thing.) And I need to keep praying for her. And I need to obey God and love her too. But God will have to help me with some of these hurdles (or mountains), because the truth is, I can't do it on my own. I don't even want to.

October 8

Incredibly, a week has passed with no phone calls from Shannon. I feel like I should knock on wood or something. I also feel like I'm waiting for the other shoe to fall. But mostly I try not to think about it. I try to just focus on my life.

But speaking of bad mothers—okay, I know that sounds harsh—today I spoke to Marissa's dad, and after what he told me about his ex-wife (Marissa's mother), I really wanted to strangle that woman. What is wrong with some grownups? Why do they think it's okay to have children and then just abandon them? Because that is what Marissa's mom has done with her. Oh, it started a long time ago, and I suspect it has a lot to do with why Marissa has been so rebellious, although I used to think that had more to do with a cop dad who might've been overly strict. But now that I know him better and after some things Marissa told me before the accident, I think the missing mom is more to blame. But anyway, when it comes to winning the award for having the world's worst mother, Marissa and I might be tied. Or maybe she would win.

Because despite Shannon's faults, I think it's possible that if I were in a serious accident and needed her help, well, she might just be there for me. Or not. It's a hard call. And I have no plans to try it out to see.

But when Marissa's dad asked his ex if she could help with Marissa's recovery, since the doctor might release her from the hospital by the end of the week and thinks a home environment would be good for her, Marissa's mom said, "No way."

"I'm not that surprised she turned me down," Marissa's dad confided to me after I'd said good-bye to Marissa this evening. "But I'm just not sure what to do now. I can't afford to hire an in-home nurse, and my insurance won't cover it." He shook his head. "It's amazing all the things that insurance *doesn't* cover."

"That's got to be hard." I know for a fact that his finances have been a mess since the accident. The police force passed the hat around, and our church did a special collection for them, but I suspect those funds barely dented their bill pile.

"I think my only option is to put Marissa in a nursing home."

"A nursing home? Aren't those for old people?"

He nodded. "For the most part. But it's the best we can do in our town. And I don't like the idea of her being a hundred miles away."

"Oh..." I could tell he was bummed by this too, and I didn't want to make him feel worse. "But if she continues to recover,

well, maybe she wouldn't be there for long. And I'll bet that old people would enjoy having her around."

He brightened a little. "Let's hope so."

"And I'll keep visiting her, and I know others will too." Okay, even as I said this, I wasn't so sure. It seemed that it had only been Chloe and me visiting her this past week. Allie confessed that the whole hospital scene makes her want to climb the walls. And Eddie, still recovering from his own injury and guilty conscience since he was the drunk driver on the night of the accident, seems to have faded into the woodwork.

Marissa's dad nodded. "I really appreciate that, Maya. You kids have no idea what a comfort that is to me. Visits from her friends seem to be the best medicine my girl gets these days."

So my plan is to challenge our youth group on Saturday night. I'm going to bring a sign-up sheet and see if I can get anyone to commit to regularly visiting Marissa in the nursing home, hopefully spread out through the week. And maybe I can even come up with some ideas for them—ways to engage Marissa in conversations and help with her recovery.

October 10

Tonight was open mike again, and this time, after several fun jam sessions this past week, Chloe, Allie, Dominic, and I decided to debut a couple of Chloe's newest songs. And once again the response was pretty cool.

"Is this the new Redemption?" Mike asked us after closing time as we were putting our equipment away.

"I was just thinking the same thing," said Willy Johnson. That's Allie's stepdad, and he used to manage their band. "It's a different sound, but it's not bad."

"Not bad?" said Jill from behind the counter where she was cleaning out the coffee machine. "They're awesome!"

"I don't know." Willy scratched his chin. "Redemption was always known as a girls' band. Not sure their audience would welcome a fella." He grinned at Dominic. "No offense. I happen to think you have a lot of talent, young man. It's just that part of the charm of Redemption's persona was that it was all female. You know?"

Dominic nodded. "I offered to cross-dress, but they didn't like the idea."

Willie chuckled. "No, the Christian music industry probably isn't quite ready for cross-dressing." Now Willy turned to me. "But I could see you stepping into the band, Maya."

"Not seriously," I said.

He nodded. "Oh yeah, I mean seriously. You'd need to work on your playing skills and catch up some. But that voice of yours." He shook his head. "Well, it's a good one."

"Does that mean Laura has retired for good?" Mike asked as he set a chair upside down on a table.

"We don't know that for sure," Allie admitted. "She just wanted to do a term of college and think about it."

"And pray about it," Chloe added.

Okay, I was starting to feel pretty uneasy right then. I mean, just because I'd been jamming with Chloe and Allie didn't mean that I thought they were going to invite me to be part of their band. In fact, they *weren't* inviting me. And they both looked as uncomfortable about this little turn of events as I felt. I actually kind of resented the way Allie's stepdad had jumped the gun like that. I mean, he's not even their manager anymore. It seems out of line for him to start suggesting what they should do with their band. Fortunately, my guitar was already in its case, and I told them I needed to get home. I'm sure they knew that wasn't exactly true since my closer friends know that I sort of make my own rules while living at my uncle's. Oh, I try to be courteous and responsible, but I mostly come and go as I please. I don't bother Uncle Allen, and he doesn't bother me. It's not exactly a cozy family situation, but it's a safe place, and I know that Uncle Allen really does love me. I also know that his job as editor of the local paper is pretty demanding. And I understand that he doesn't want to parent me. The truth is, I wouldn't want him to anyway.

But I'll admit it's kind of a lonely way to live. Not that it's so much different from how it was with Shannon. But it's not what I'd imagined either...back in the days when I wanted to have my cousin Kim's "normal" life. I guess that normal doesn't really exist. Or maybe normal is simply different for everyone. My normal seems to be independence. Well, except for God. I am very dependent on Him.

Maya's Green Tip for the Day

Not everyone can afford to buy a gas-saving hybrid car, but here's a driving tip that might help you save some precious fuel. *Take a right.* Yes, turning right can conserve gasoline. Learn to plan your drive so that you make more right turns in city traffic. Waiting in left-turn lanes not only wastes time; it wastes gas. In fact, UPS has a policy to encourage drivers to use right turns, and in 2007 it saved them 2.5 million gallons of fuel. Okay, chances are you probably don't drive as much as the guy in the big brown truck, but you probably wouldn't complain over a few more bucks in your pocket either.

Seven

October 11

T hose are excellent ideas," Caitlin said. We met at the Paradiso this morning, and I'd just updated her on Marissa's situation. "A fund-raiser is always a fun way to bring people together. What exactly did you have in mind?"

"Well, because we were doing open mike last night, I suppose I was thinking music. I'm not sure exactly how or what it would be, but they could really use the help. Marissa's dad seemed pretty stressed this week."

"Did you ask Chloe and Allie about it?"

"No. I hadn't really thought of it until this morning."

"What about your dad, Maya? Would he be able to come?"

I considered this. "Probably not. He's touring in Europe until spring."

She nodded. "Right. Well, do you want me to talk to some people about this? To see if I can get the ball rolling?"

"Sure," I said eagerly. "And I'm willing to help, but I actually have a lot on my plate right now."

"I'm sure you do." She touched my arm. "Chloe told me about the phone call from your mother. I hope you don't mind."

"Not at all. Chloe knows I meet with you. And I had a little meltdown in front of her and Allie and Dominic this week."

"Sometimes we need to melt down. It allows friends to step in and help. And it reminds us of how weak we are so that we can invite God to make us strong."

"I actually felt a lot better after I told them about the whole thing," I admitted. "And it really helped when they prayed for me." I frowned slightly now.

"But?"

"But...I guess I still feel a little confused. I mean, if I think about it too much, and I try not to."

"Confused in what way?"

"Well, I want to live my life like a Christian even when it comes to my mom..."

"And?"

"And I feel kind of guilty right now. Like I know she's struggling, and she asked me to help her, and I turned her down."

"How did she want you to help her?"

"Oh, you know, a place to live, to be together...the happy little family."

"Meaning you'd be taking care of her again?"

I nodded. "But aren't we supposed to be like that? I mean, Jesus tells us to love everyone, even our enemies. And to feed the hungry and give to the needy. I feel selfish telling my mom she's on her own. And hypocritical."

"You're right. Jesus did say those things. And a lot more. But a lot of things in the Bible don't always make perfect sense. There's another thing that Jesus said that confuses a lot of people."

"What's that?"

She opened her Bible and read a pretty long section of Scripture.

Don't think that I came to bring peace to the earth! I came to bring trouble, not peace. I came to turn sons against their fathers, daughters against their mothers, and daughters-in-law against their mothers-in-law. Your worst enemies will be in your own family.

If you love your father or mother or even your sons and daughters more than me, you are not fit to be my disciples. And unless you are willing to take up your cross and come with me, you are not fit to be my disciples. If you try to save your life, you will lose it. But if you give it up for me, you will surely find it.

"Wow," I said, feeling overwhelmed. "What does that really mean?"

Caitlin closed her Bible and smiled. "To be honest, I don't know all that it's supposed to mean. But then there's a lot in the Bible that I don't get...yet. I guess what I want to say to you, Maya, is that the important thing is to *follow Jesus*. Follow Him

with your whole heart. And allow Him to lead you through this thing with your mother. Because He's the only one with all the answers."

"Did Chloe tell you that she told me I wasn't supposed to parent my mom?"

"She mentioned it."

"And that seemed right to me. I mean, when she said it, it's kind of like it clicked inside of me. Like it was the truth."

"It's possible God was using Chloe to speak to you, Maya. I have to say I agree with her on this. I don't think God does want you to parent your mother."

"And that verse about daughters turning against their mothers..." I thought about it for a moment. "Do you think that's because my mother has turned her heart against God?"

"That sounds right to me." Caitlin nodded. "I think it would be very difficult to align yourself with your parents' beliefs if their beliefs conflicted with your own."

"That pretty much describes Shannon and me. On top of illegal drugs and alcohol abuse, her whole moral standards and values are totally different than mine."

"So..." Caitlin sighed. "It's as if Jesus has already drawn a dividing line between you and your mother. I don't think you need to feel guilty about it, Maya. I could be wrong, but I don't think you have any responsibility to your mother, well, other than the responsibility we have for everyone that God brings into our lives.

To pray and love and forgive. Outside of that, I don't think you should feel guilty."

I was taking furious notes as she said all this because I knew what I was hearing was important.

"Does that make sense?" she finally asked.

I looked up. "It does...for the most part."

"The thing with any counseling or teaching or direction, Maya—whether it's from me or the pastor or even a radio show—is that you need to weigh it for yourself. You need to use discernment."

I nodded. "I know. You've told me that before."

She smiled. "Sorry. I didn't mean to be redundant."

I laughed. "That's okay. I'm sure I need to be reminded."

"So, tell me then, how do you weigh these things for yourself? Where do you get discernment?"

I tried not to feel like I was in first grade as I recited what she'd told me before. And the truth is, I'm glad she asks me questions like this. I appreciate her taking the time to mentor me. These things are important. "I compare what I've heard to what the Bible says. I pray about it. I talk to other Christians that I respect, and I listen to their advice. And then I try to hear that still small voice inside of me. Is there something I missed?"

"No, I'd give you an A+ in discernment."

"Thanks."

"But the proof of the pudding is in the eating."

I laughed. "I remember my grandmother saying that exact same thing when I was little, but what does it mean?"

"It means you can say that pudding looks yummy, but you don't really know that it is until you taste it."

"So I can say I know what discernment is, but until I actually use it, it's meaningless."

She nodded. "I wish all the high school girls I meet with were so smart." Now she frowned. "Sorry, I shouldn't have said that."

"It's okay."

"Speaking of high school, did you make a decision about graduation yet?"

"I told Mrs. King that I want this to be my senior year."

"I think that's a good choice."

We talked awhile longer, and then I remembered that I wanted to get over to see Marissa. She was moved to the nursing home yesterday, and I have a feeling it's not going to be easy for her.

My feeling turned out to be right. When I got to the nursing home, Marissa was sitting in a wheelchair facing a streaky window with a view of a cement wall and some trash cans. Not pretty.

"Hey, Marissa," I said as I turned her chair around. She's still recovering from some broken bones that make walking difficult, although she's not supposed to spend too much time in the wheelchair if she wants to recover more fully. "Want to go for a walk?"

"No." Her face looked dark and angry, almost like the old Marissa when she was in a foul mood, but different.

So I pulled a chair next to her and sat down. "How's it going?"

"Bad."

"Why?"

"Hate this."

"What do you hate?"

"Hate this…place."

I nodded. "Oh."

"Bad place. Hate this place."

At least her sentences were getting longer. "It's different than the hospital, isn't it?" I said. "Maybe it'll take getting used to it."

"Old people place."

I looked around the room. "Yeah. There are a lot of old people here, Marissa. Kind of like having a lot of grandparents." Then I told her about my own grandmother and how important she'd been in my life. Marissa actually seemed to be listening. Finally I asked her again if she'd like to walk.

"No."

And so I told her that the only way to get out of the old people place would be to keep working at getting well. I told her that her bones would heal better if she walked and that her brain would work better if she talked and did the other activities that her therapist had given to her.

"Video game?" she asked hopefully.

I nodded. "Yes. But we have to walk first, okay?"

"Walk first. Video game after?"

I smiled and reached for her hand. "It's a deal."

And so we walked and eventually, with the help of a nurse, made it to her room. We sat down and played a goofy video game that was designed for young children but is helping Marissa's brain to heal itself.

Finally it was nearly two o'clock. "I have to go now," I told her. As usual, this made her sad. Sometimes she cries when I leave. Sometimes I get lucky, and someone else comes along to distract her. But today she got mad.

"You bad!" she shouted. "Bad girl!"

"I love you, Marissa." I patted her shoulder. "And I'll be back to see you soon."

She continued to yell at me as I slipped out the door, trying not to feel guilty. I know that it's part of her brain recovering. The doctor told us that she's at Level 6, which means she has all kinds of emotions, gets mixed up, has a short attention span, and can act childish. I know this...and yet it hurts to experience it. I so want her to get well and be her old self again. And although I keep praying, I have to admit that my faith isn't as strong as I wish it was. I hope God understands.

Maya's Green Tip for the Day

Okay, based on some things I've observed lately, both at school and elsewhere, I think it's time to recycle some old conservation ideas. Now, I'm not naming names here, but you know who you are. (1) Turn off the lights when you leave a room. (2) If you're cold, don't automatically turn up the heat. Put on a sweater instead. (3) Don't turn on the tap and let it run and run and run. (4) Get a reusable water bottle. I may sound like Ralph Nader or some obsessive environmentalist, but it's worthwhile to remember the basics of conservation before you go out and waste a lot of time on expensive advanced techniques.

Eight

October 15

I wasn't consciously thinking that it had been more than two weeks since Shannon's release or that I hadn't heard from her since that first phone call, but when she called me this afternoon, I prepared myself for the worst. Enough time had passed for her to get into trouble. Was she using again? Had she linked up with some new questionable friends? Had she been rearrested?

All the negative scenarios raced through my mind, but I wasn't ready to hear her say that she'd gotten a job.

"A job?" I said warily. "What kind of job?" I know what Shannon's résumé looks like—a blank sheet. A short list of pathetic jobs flashed through my mind: flipping burgers, selling her blood...or maybe her body?

"Well, it's not very glamorous," she said slowly.

"Hey, a job is a job, Shannon. I think it's cool that you're working."

"My counselor helped me get it."

"Counselor?"

"Yeah, part of the judge's sentence included a treatment program."

"That's cool."

She groaned. "You should see the losers in my therapy group, Maya. It's definitely not cool. Not even close."

"I think it's cool that you're *doing* rehab, Shannon."

"Whatever."

We talked awhile longer—mostly she talked and I listened. She complained about her job, which turned out to be in fast food. She complained about her living conditions, which was group housing. She complained about my dad, which was ridiculous. And finally she complained about the L.A. area in general.

"I hate it here, Maya. It's such a rat race. And it gets worse every day." Then she actually complained about the fact that whites were a minority now and how that was so terrible.

I cleared my throat loudly. "Excuse me, Shannon," I said in a firm voice, "but if you're going to start insulting the nonwhite population, I might have to hang up."

"Oh, I didn't mean *you*, baby."

I didn't say anything.

"I'm talking about those Mexicans. They're taking over down here."

I still didn't say anything, but I did let out an exasperated sigh.

"Don't be so sensitive, Maya."

"I don't like that kind of talk."

"Don't go acting like I'm some kind of narrow-minded racist WASP, little girl. You know me better than that. Good grief, I married your father, didn't I?"

Okay, I've always wondered if she would've married a black man who wasn't famous and wealthy. But I knew better than to open my mouth just then. I didn't want to fight with her. There was a long pause, and I hoped that she'd hung up.

"I thought you'd be glad to hear that I'm doing okay, Maya."

"I am glad, Shannon." I tried to infuse warmth into my voice. "I really am. I think it's great that you got a job and are in a treatment program. Really great."

"Thank you." Her tone was still indignant.

I wanted to add that I hoped she'd keep it up—work and rehab—but I knew better than to say that. Shannon's been in treatment programs before, and they didn't usually last too long. Still, I know there's always a first time for the whole thing to kick into gear and really work. I hope and pray this is that time for her. We talked a bit more, and then I was relieved to hang up. I briefly considered changing my cell phone number. Not that it would matter since I'm sure she'd figure out how to track me down eventually.

Then instead of feeling sorry for myself, I headed my car over to Marissa's nursing home. Not that I was feeling particularly sorry for her. I mean, not any more than usual since I still struggle with balancing my irritation that she allowed such stupidity to waste her life against the fact that she is so pitiful and helpless now. To add insult to injury, if that's possible—and I think it is—it's depressing going to the nursing home to visit her.

It's like there's a spirit of hopelessness at that place. Like you're barely through the doors, and you just want to give up.

You see all these old people in varying stages of Alzheimer's and dementia, and it's like you can smell death—literally smell it. As Marissa says: "Bad place."

When Marissa was in the hospital, she had more people (nurses, therapists, doctors, etc.) to encourage her and work with her, and somehow it just made her recovery seem more positive and possible. Now her recovery is beginning to feel like a long shot. But according to what I've read, a brain injury takes at least six months to heal and sometimes as long as two years—depending on how much it's going to heal. On Monday, Marissa's dad told me that she's been elevated to Level 7, which is an improvement, but even so it's a long way to Level 10, which is considered normal. Still, it's only been a couple of months since the accident, so there's hope she can keep improving, working her way up the brain ladder.

But my hopes diminished as I entered the dreary building. As usual, it smelled like overcooked vegetables and Lysol...and other unpleasant things...and death. I always try to smile and look cheerful as I see wrinkled old people slumped in wheelchairs. One nearly bald woman smiled back at me today, and it seemed she wanted to talk. I said hello and asked how she was doing, but she got confused and frustrated when I wasn't who she thought I was, and then she shut down. I continued on to Marissa's room with a feeling of deep sadness, laced with anger. I need to get over it, but I still get mad when I think that none of this *had* to happen to Marissa, when I consider all the warnings we gave her—the ones

who loved her. How many times did we say she was risking too much? How many times did we caution her? Maybe we should've just locked her up until she turned thirty or until sensibility kicked in. She would be better off with a fully functioning brain in jail than the way she is in this place.

"Hey, Maya."

I turned to see Chloe coming down the hall behind me. "What are you doing here?" I asked.

"I know I didn't sign up for this time slot, but I just happened to be passing by the place and thought I'd pop in and say hi."

"Cool. It might be fun for Marissa to have more than one visitor for a change."

"And it's good timing too." We went down the hall toward Marissa's room. "Caitlin told me about the fund-raiser you suggested for Marissa."

"Oh yeah."

"She thinks we should do a concert in connection with the harvest party. Are you interested?"

"We, as in me too?"

"Yeah, we've been having so much fun jamming. Why don't we just put something together for the harvest party and see what kind of donations come in?"

"That's a great idea."

"And simpler than selling tickets."

"I like it."

She paused outside Marissa's room. "Do you think we should tell Marissa and her dad yet or just let it be a surprise?"

"Maybe a surprise. That way we won't get their hopes up in case it's not that lucrative."

"That's what I was thinking too."

"But maybe they'd like to come to the event. It might be fun for Marissa."

"Fun?" Marissa called from where she was sitting in the wheelchair. "Fun for Marissa?"

Chloe laughed. "Hey, you eavesdropper."

"Fun?"

I went into her room now. "Yeah, with both Chloe and me here to visit, you're going to have fun. Is that okay with you?"

"Yeah!"

As it turned out, we did have fun. The dynamics with three people (two normal and one trying) are a lot more lively and energetic. And I could tell Marissa was enjoying the double dose of attention too.

"So, Marissa," said Chloe, "did you hear that Maya is quite the musician?"

Marissa looked confused. "Music? Maya?"

I nodded. "I've been jamming with Chloe and Allie lately. Dominic's been playing too."

Her brow furrowed like she was trying to make sense of this. "Play music?"

"Yeah." Chloe did an air guitar and made some *twang-twang* sounds, and then I joined her.

"I play music?" asked Marissa with a hopeful expression.

"Hey, that's a great idea," said Chloe. "You should play music too."

Marissa smiled.

"Do you think there's an instrument Marissa could play?" I asked.

Chloe got thoughtful. "The first instrument I ever played was a recorder."

"I used to have a recorder too."

"Recorder?" Marissa looked confused.

Chloe put her hands up to pantomime a flutelike instrument and made some notes that sounded similar to a real recorder.

"Yes." Marissa put her hands up like Chloe and tried to make notes, but it didn't sound quite as good. Still, she was trying.

"Next time I come, I'll bring you a recorder," I promised her.

"Speaking of music..." Chloe lowered her voice and tipped her head toward the door. "I have to get going."

I nodded. "No problem. I'll stick around awhile longer."

"Thanks." Chloe had obviously experienced the tearful farewells too. So she said good-bye, and then I distracted Marissa as Chloe slipped out. We played video games for a while, and thankfully a nurse's aide came in to check on something, and I got my chance to say a quick good-bye and escape as well. Quicker is usually better.

I was barely out to my car when my phone rang again, and I hoped it wasn't Shannon. I wasn't sure I could take another conversation with her today. Fortunately it was Chloe.

"What's up?" I asked her.

"Our band manager, Bruce Glass, just called me. He's coming to town next week..." She sounded a little unsure or maybe just hesitant. "Anyway, I told him a little bit about you, and he wondered if it would be possible to hear you play with us."

"Seriously?"

"Totally."

"But what does that mean, Chloe?"

"I guess it's kind of like an audition."

"But to audition, I'd have to be interested in joining the band."

Now there was a long pause, and I wondered if I'd just insulted her. "I mean, it's not that I wouldn't be honored just to be considered. But it's not really something I've ever thought about. Not seriously."

"Meaning you're *not* interested?"

"I guess I don't really know."

"Because I wouldn't want to pressure you. It's just that I told Bruce you'd been jamming with us and that we need to rehearse for the harvest party fund-raiser anyway. I think Willy had talked to him before me. But if you're not into this, I can just tell him that—"

So I interrupted her and just dumped the stuff about my dad and how he never wanted me to get into music professionally,

and then I dumped about how I've never had a normal life and maybe this would be my only chance.

She laughed. "Take it from me, Maya—*normal* is highly over-rated. I lived normal for most of my life. I mean, you've seen my parents and their house. You know my brother, Josh. You live in our town. How much more normal does it get?"

"But it's cool too. Especially for someone who's missed out on that."

"Yeah, I can agree *now* that it's pretty cool. I appreciate our little town more after being gone on tour for a while. Still, for me, there's nothing quite like doing music, being on the road, performing in front of crowds. I mean, sure, it's tiring, but it's pretty cool too. I don't know if I'm ready to give that up for normal just yet."

The enthusiasm in her voice felt slightly contagious just then. "Well, is it okay if I pray about this and get back to you?"

She laughed really loud this time. "I wouldn't want it any other way."

"Thanks," I told her. "And honestly, I really am honored that you'd even consider me for this. And I'm slightly stunned too."

"Well, just so you don't get your hopes up, Bruce sounded rather skeptical. Despite Willy's two-thumbs-up, Bruce didn't think it was possible that we would find a replacement for Laura in our own hometown. And he's already got a couple of other girls in mind."

"Right...I understand."

"Cool."

And I do understand. I mean, seriously, what are the chances that a professional band would want someone like me to join them? And even if they did, would I want to? Beyond the flattery, I know what a professional musician's life is really like. I've been on the road with my dad. I've lived out of a suitcase before. I've woken in strange towns and wondered where I was. It's not for everyone. And yet...it was kind of fun too.

October 18

I've told only three people about my "audition" next week—Kim and Uncle Allen, and just this morning I told Caitlin as well.

"I'm not surprised at all," she said with enthusiasm. She and Josh had popped into Chloe's (also Josh's parents') house last week when we were jamming. They sat and listened to us for about fifteen minutes, then proclaimed us "Redemption Reinvented." Chloe also pointed out that Redemption was still a girl band and, as much as they've enjoyed Dominic, short of a sexchange operation (kidding), he wasn't going to make the cut. "Are you excited about it?" she asked.

"I'm just not sure," I admitted. "And it probably doesn't even matter, because I'm guessing their manager isn't going to like me."

"Don't be too sure."

"Both Kim and my uncle were really supportive of the idea." I was still trying to wrap my head around that one. I had imagined

that Kim (the academic) would say stay in school. I guess I assumed the same about Uncle Allen too. But both said it could be a huge opportunity.

"Did that surprise you?"

"A little. But then I got to thinking maybe it would be a way to get me out of their hair."

"Out of their hair?" Caitlin frowned. "They both love you, Maya."

"Oh, I know they do. But Uncle Allen didn't really want to raise another teenage girl."

"You're so independent, Maya. I'm sure he's not overly concerned."

"Maybe not...but you never know. Like I know he's got a woman friend. What if he wants to bring her home but not around his teenage niece?"

"He has a woman friend?"

I giggled. "Yes. Her name is Trina. I only met her once. She seems nice."

"Does Kim know?"

"I'm not sure. But I don't think it's any of my business."

Caitlin nodded. "You're right. So let's get back to your business. What are you going to do if your audition is a success and the next thing you know they're handing you a contract?"

"Good question."

"What do you *want* to do?"

I shrugged. "I'm not really sure. I mean, on one hand it does sound exciting. But then I weigh it against living the normal life that I'd always wanted."

"I hate to burst your bubble, Maya, but your life isn't exactly normal."

"I know." Then I told her about Shannon's last call. "I'm actually getting worried that she might try to come out here. I think I should go speak to a judge about my emancipation, just in case."

"Would joining Redemption help with that?"

I considered this. "Yeah, it might. But I think I'm making enough money now with my newspaper column, TV spot, and the few hours I get at Jacqueline's to convince a judge that I'm self-supporting."

"Have you talked to your dad about this?"

"Emancipation?"

"No, I meant the audition, but while we're on it, have you discussed emancipation with him?"

I nodded. "He's supportive. He said he'd do anything he could to help. But no, I haven't told him about the audition. I mean, chances are they won't want me, and that'll be the end of it. Why worry him?"

"So it would worry him?"

I explained his concerns over the music world at large.

"But at least you'd be in the Christian music business."

"I guess." I sighed. "Tell me what you think, Caitlin. If by some tiny chance they do invite me…what would you suggest?"

"Same as always, Maya."

"The rules of discernment?"

She nodded. "As well as to really listen to your heart. What do you really want?"

"I don't even know."

"Well, I know that God will show you. When the time is right. And not that my opinion matters, but I think it could be wonderful for you to be part of Redemption. Chloe and the others have grown so much as Christians. I know that for a fact because I was their chaperon for a while when Allie's mom needed a break. It's really an awesome opportunity. But only if it's the right thing for you."

Okay, I was actually starting to get excited. But then I realized I could be getting my hopes up for nothing. I told Caitlin I'd be praying and reading the Bible and all that. And I asked her to pray too.

"Count on it, Maya. And Josh will be praying too. And you can be certain that Chloe and Allie are."

And so that's what I'm doing. Chloe told me the audition will be on Thursday evening—and it'll also be a practice session for the fund-raiser the following week. We'll do it at the church in front of a small audience. Now all I need to do (besides figuring out what I really want to do) is tell Dominic. I think he deserves to know since he's been such a good friend, plus he's been having such a great time jamming with us. I hope he won't feel too left out.

It almost makes me wish he were a girl. Okay, not really. I pretty much like Dominic as a guy—as long as he keeps his distance, which he does a fairly good job of except for moments when I think we both are ready to toss away caution and commitment. Although I don't want to do that. I really don't want to go there. My commitment to God means more than anything to me. More than being with Dominic. More than being green. More than being in Chloe's band.

Seriously, when I think about Dominic and the ways we could go wrong, it almost seems like one more reason to consider joining the band. (I mean, *if* they even want me, which seems highly unlikely.) But if they did, and if I joined, it would put some space between Dominic and me. I'd want to stay in touch with him via e-mail and phone. But being on the road with Redemption might have some perks I haven't even considered. Still, I'd have to give up my TV news spot and working for Jacqueline. Although Uncle Allen said I could write my column on the road if I wanted. So much to consider...and pray about.

Maya's Green Tip for the Day

I know that as a kid I'm supposed to respect my elders. But what about when I see the guy across the street stashing an old car battery in his trash can? It will be picked up by the garbage truck and dumped in the local landfill. Being a good citizen of the planet, I went across the street and told him as politely as I could that his old battery contained harmful materials like lead and mercury and so it did not belong in the landfill because its poisons would contaminate the land and possibly the water for decades to come. I also reminded him that things like motor oil, leftover house paint, and other forms of HHW (household hazardous waste) must be handled and disposed of with care. You cannot simply toss them into the trash and think that's the end of it. If you're unclear on what products are HHW, here's a quick list: most automotive products, home-improvement products, household cleaners, and pesticides, as well as aerosols, batteries, pool chemicals, and a slew of other things. For more information on this, check out the U.S. Environmental Protection Agency Web site at www.epa.gov.

Nine

October 20

It was just before lunch when I checked my cell phone messages, which were numerous. I was surprised to see that the first one was from Uncle Allen.

"Uh, Maya?" he began as if uncertain. "Are you aware that your mother is in town? I have a strong suspicion you're not. So I thought I'd give you a little heads-up. *She is.*" He cleared his throat. "And she's been by my office and seems to be under the impression she's staying with us."

I actually shrieked, causing curious classmates to stop and stare. I kind of smiled and waved them off as I continued to listen to the message, which asked me to give him "a jingle ASAP."

Naturally, I did this immediately. "Uncle Allen," I said as soon as he answered, "I am so sorry. I had no idea she was in town. I *never* invited her, and I don't know what to—"

"It's okay, Maya. I actually got a co-worker with an empty guesthouse to offer her a place to stay for a few days."

"A few days?"

"Yes, apparently the guesthouse is going to be occupied by the end of the week."

"And then?"

"And then Shannon will have to figure something else out."

"But not with us—I mean, *you*, right?"

"It's your house too, Maya. I'm not throwing you out. It's just that I don't think I can handle, uh...well—"

"It's okay, Uncle Allen. I can't handle her either. And I'm so sorry she's crashing like this. Did you talk to her much? I mean, did she seem okay? Or should we—"

"She actually seemed all right—if you mean sober, which is my guess."

"Yeah."

"She wanted to see you, Maya. I told her you were in school."

"Well, there are a few messages on my phone. Probably from her."

As it turned out, some were from her, desperately begging for my attention, for me to meet with her, and for us to share a "home." How she thinks she's going to conjure up this home is a mystery to me. Although I can guess. She probably figures that with what I earn combined with Dad's child support, I should be able to take care of her again.

Fortunately, her calls had been from pay phones, so there was no point in returning them. But one of the calls was from Kim, so I decided to check in with her.

"Everything okay?" I asked after saying hello.

"That's what I wanted to ask you."

"Why?"

"Dad called."

"Oh. Did he tell you about Shannon?"

"Yes. He was a little unsure about what to do. After all, she is Mom's sister. He thought maybe that meant he should take her in."

"And what did you tell him?" Okay, this worried me since Kim has had a soft spot toward Shannon. She's the one who originally encouraged me to write to Shannon while she was in prison. And she'd been communicating with her off and on since Shannon's incarceration.

"I told him that Shannon should find someplace else to stay."

"Oh, good. I mean, Uncle Allen told me she was staying somewhere else, but I'm glad you agreed with that."

"Yes, for your sake and Dad's, I think it's for the best."

"I agree."

"So, are you going to be okay, Maya?"

"I don't know. I mean, it's going to be stressful; that's for sure. But if she only has a place to stay for a few days...well, what's she going to do?" Yet even as I said this, I realized I was talking about Shannon—the great manipulator.

"I don't know." Kim paused. "And I hate to cut you off, but I need to get to class right now."

"No problem. And don't worry. I can handle this thing with Shannon."

"Maybe you'll be invited to join Redemption," she said lightly, "and you can just get yourself outta Dodge."

I laughed. "Yeah, maybe so." Then we said good-bye, and I went into the cafeteria, where Dominic immediately knew that something was wrong. As we made our way through the lunch line, I gave him the short version of my messed-up mom's unexpected appearance in town. And he was very sympathetic. That's when I decided this might be my best chance to break the audition news to him.

"Seriously?" He seemed genuinely shocked as he put a garden burger on his tray. "A real audition?"

"Well, it's not like I'm being invited to join the band. It's just that Chloe told their manager about us jamming with them." I laughed. "I suspect if you were a girl, you'd be the one getting an audition."

"Yeah, right." He rolled his eyes.

"You're the one who plays bass, and that's what Laura played."

"But you've been picking it up pretty good too. And the sound with two guitars isn't bad either."

I smiled at him as I paid for my garden salad and drink. "Still, I feel bad. You've got way more talent than me. It seems unfair that just because you're a guy—"

"It's okay. The cool thing is that all that jamming's made me want to put together my own band. I already have a couple of guys in mind." He winked. "Not that this is going to be one of those sexually discriminative bands. I'm open to talented *females* too."

"I'll be sure to keep that in mind after I fall on my face at my audition."

"You won't fall on your face," he said as we found places at our regular table. We've continued sitting with Wyatt and Vanessa and the others. And it's like no one even questions this anymore. I have a feeling that both Becca and Vanessa are hoping Dominic will look their direction. And maybe he will. I suppose that might make me jealous, but since we're not really dating, I can't tell him not to.

"Fall on your face doing what?" asked Vanessa with too much interest. I tried to send Dominic a silent signal, but too late.

"Maya's going to audition for Redemption," he told them.

"That's so unfair," said Becca.

"Why?" asked Dominic.

"Maya gets to do everything. It's like she's this newcomer that came to town and took over. First the newspaper, then TV, and now she's going to be in the—"

"I'm not going to be in the band," I said quickly. "I'm just going to audition. The manager didn't even sound that interested."

"Oh, they'll want you," said Vanessa a little smugly. "And whatever will we do without you?" She looked directly at Wyatt now. "Who will you drool over if Maya's on the road playing gospel music with the girls' band?"

He pretended to dab his chin. "I didn't realize I was drooling."

Everyone laughed.

"And what about Dominic?" said Becca in a teasingly hopeful tone. "What will you do with no Maya to fixate over?"

"For your information," I said firmly, "I'm not planning on going anywhere. And Dominic is thinking about starting his own band, so I'm sure he'll have plenty to keep him busy."

Fortunately, this became the hot topic of conversation between Becca and Vanessa. But as Dominic bounced answers back at the two of them, I became aware that Wyatt really did seem to be staring at me. I suppose I've been deceiving myself that he and I really are only friends. I mean, we are just friends in my mind, but I should've realized by the little comments he makes and the way he sometimes touches me (not in a wrong way exactly but in a slightly intimate way) that he's still interested.

He confirmed this in history class. "Maya, Maya," he said like he was about five years old—or maybe eighty-five. "You can't leave us. School is going to be so dull without your pretty face around to look at."

I just laughed. "There are plenty of cute girls to hold your attention."

"Boring girls, you mean."

"Boring? That just sounds like you haven't taken time to get to know them."

"I've gone to school with most of them for years." He reached over and grabbed my hand. "Promise me that if you join that girls' gospel band, you'll go out with me just once, Maya?"

I laughed. "No way."

"Please."

"Don't beg, Wyatt."

"I'll beg you, Maya. Just say yes. If you're going to leave us, you could at least go out with me once. Please?"

I distracted myself with the computer we were sharing, trying to engage him in the research we were supposed to be doing. But he was relentless. He begged and begged until I told him to wait and see.

"Wait and see?" He looked slightly hopeful. "What does that mean?"

"It means if, and that's a big if, I get invited to join Redemption, then you can ask me."

"Meaning you'd consider it?"

"Meaning I want you to shut up about it, okay?"

"You heartbreaker, you." Of course, the twinkle in his eye told me that his dramatics were nothing more than that—dramatics. I know lots of girls think this is charming, but most of the time I think it's obnoxious, and I wish he'd save it for girls like Vanessa or Becca.

Somehow I made it to the end of the day without really thinking about Shannon. Then as I was leaving school, I realized I should probably turn my phone on. It was barely powered up before Shannon was on the other end, gushing about how she couldn't wait to see me.

"It's my day to visit Marissa," I said, as if she'd even know what I was talking about.

"Who is Marissa, and why is she more important than your very own mother?"

So I told her about Marissa's accident. I probably painted it more vividly than I would've if I'd been talking to anyone else. But I thought she needed to hear it. Shannon knows all about driving under the influence.

"I'm sorry to hear that your friend got hurt," Shannon said, "but I still don't see why that's more important than seeing me."

As a stall tactic, I asked her where she was, making it clear that she couldn't expect Uncle Allen to put her up in his home. But when I realized she was staying just a few blocks from the nursing home, I got an idea. "Tell you what," I said. "Why don't you come and visit Marissa with me?"

I knew by her response that she wasn't very excited about this, but she did agree. And I thought if nothing else, it would buy me time to figure this thing out. But I almost didn't recognize her when I stopped to pick her up. Or maybe I'd just forgotten what she really looked like. But she seemed older or perhaps simply her age (over fifty). And her hair, which had always been long and blond, was now shorter and mousy. Her lips, which she used to get puffed up with collagen, now looked thin and wrinkled, and her eyes, though clearer than I recalled, looked sad. I actually felt a small stab of pity. Even so, I was determined to hold my ground on keeping her safely at a distance. "I'm sorry you can't stay at Uncle Allen's," I said again. "I hope you understand."

"It's no big deal," she said defensively. "I have a place to stay."

"But only for a few days," I reminded her as I parked at the nursing home.

"I thought your friend was a teenager," she said as we went inside.

"She is."

"But this is an old folks' home."

I quietly explained the situation, smiling like usual to people who mostly didn't respond, as I led her down the corridor. When Marissa wasn't in her room, Shannon acted like that got us off the hook. "Guess we can go now. Want to get something to eat, or we could—"

"Not yet," I said. "Sometimes she's in the activity room."

As it turned out, she was in the activity room, along with her dad. "Hi, Mr. Phillips," I said as we joined them. "Hey, Marissa."

She grinned at me and said, "Hey." Then she frowned at Shannon, and I quickly introduced everyone, ending with, "Mr. Phillips, this is my mother, Shannon Stark."

He smiled and shook her hand. "But my friends call me Adam." He turned to me. "You should call me Adam too, Maya."

Now for some reason this caught me off guard. As did the way Mr. Phillips, make that *Adam,* was looking at Shannon. And then I realized that for a woman her age, which she lies about, she's not bad looking.

"Maya," Marissa commanded me. "Come here. You and I walk."

"Sure," I said, quickly going to her side so she could steady herself as needed. "Walking is good."

Soon we were out of earshot, and I could tell Marissa wanted to know about Shannon. "Your mom...Maya...your mom bad. Bad mom?"

I let out a big sigh. "Do you remember what I told you about my mom?" I asked, curious as to how much memory she really had.

"Your mom bad. My mom bad."

I kind of nodded. "My mom has made some bad choices."

"I made bad choices," she admitted.

I kind of laughed. "I guess we've all made some bad choices."

Now we were by her room, and she went right in. "Play video game," she commanded me.

"Sure." The truth is, I was relieved to be away from Shannon. However, I was curious as to what she might be saying to Marissa's dad. I was also curious as to why he was here. Since Marissa's accident he usually worked the day shift during the week and visited Marissa in the evenings. But today he wasn't even in uniform.

"Your dad's not working today?"

"Not today."

"That's right." He and Shannon came into Marissa's room. "I've changed to a four-day workweek."

"Oh?"

"I'm trying to figure out a way to bring Marissa home. If I only work four—"

"Marissa home!" she said with enthusiasm. "Marissa go home."

Just then I remembered the recorder that I'd bought for her

yesterday after church. So I explained I needed to get something from my car and hurried out. And here's the strangest thing. While I was gone for less than five minutes, Shannon offered to help care for Marissa in the Phillipses' home in exchange for room and board, and Marissa's dad had agreed! When I came in with the recorder, they all seemed quite pleased with themselves. Even Marissa, but then she's suffered brain damage.

"She won't be released from here for another couple of weeks," Adam explained to us. "But that will give you a chance to get to know her," he said to Shannon. And she just nodded like no big deal. Like she cares for brain-damaged teenage girls all the time. Like she has a clue...or is interested in anything beyond a roof over her head.

The only bright spot in all this was that Adam and Shannon decided to go get a bite to eat together, which struck me as totally bizarre. Even though they said it was to discuss this new "business arrangement," I couldn't help but feel skeptical. But at least I got to go home without her. Still, I can't help but wonder what is to come of all this. And what, if anything, should I tell Marissa's dad about Shannon's "little" problems? Should I warn him that this could, and likely will, blow up in all our faces? And don't I owe a warning to Marissa? On the other hand, Marissa's dad is a cop. Maybe he'll figure it out himself.

Maya's Green Tip for the Day

I've noticed something troubling in this town lately. School buses show up at the schools half-empty because grade-school kids are being transported by their parents. Not only does this cause traffic jams; it's unnecessarily wasteful. The same is true with the middle school and high school. Although I have a fuel-efficient car, I try not to use it too much. If the weather is good, I ride my bike to school. Now consider this: if every commuter would carpool, use public transportation, ride a bike, or even walk to school or work *just two days a week,* it would make an enormous difference in the environment. Not only would it conserve gas (a limited resource), it would also reduce the effect of greenhouse gas emissions. Plus, if you're biking or walking, you'll be in better shape. It's a win-win!

Ten

October 22

I'm not sure if I keep practicing my music because I want to be in Redemption, which is a ridiculous long shot, or because I need the distraction from Shannon. But the fact is, I've really been practicing both guitar and the bass that Dominic loaned me. I still haven't told my dad about this audition, but I did mention to him that I've been getting more into music lately.

"What do you mean *into* music?" he asked. He was in Portugal at the time, finally returning my call. I really wanted to discuss Shannon and what I should do about her, but I thought I'd soften up this prickly topic by mentioning music first.

"I've been playing your old acoustic guitar," I told him, "writing some songs, and even learning bass."

"Good for you, sweetie. I always knew you had natural talent. How's school?"

"Pretty good." I told him how I decided to be a senior.

"That makes sense to me too," he admitted. "You've always been mature for your age."

"And guess who's in town?"

His silence told me that he was either stumped or had guessed.

"Shannon."

"I'm sorry, Maya. I heard she'd been released. I was hoping she'd leave you alone."

"Me too, but that's not happening."

"She's not staying at the Petersons', is she?"

"Thankfully, Uncle Allen pulled in the welcome mat."

"Smart man."

"So what am I supposed to do about her, Dad?"

Another long silence.

"I mean, she's not my responsibility, is she?" Okay, I know the answer to this, but I was looking for validation.

"Of course not, sweetie. Shannon is a grown woman; it's about time she took care of herself."

So I told him about Marissa's dad and their clever plan for Shannon to play nurse to Marissa.

Dad groaned. "I met Adam at your dinner party last summer, Maya. He seemed like a sane person to me."

"I think he's desperate." So I explained about Marissa in the nursing home and how it's not the best situation for her recovery.

"And being cared for by Shannon will be an improvement?"

This time *I* groaned.

"Isn't Adam in law enforcement?"

"Yeah."

"And Shannon is aware of this?"

"Of course."

"And she's okay with it?" He chuckled.

"You think Adam will keep her in line?"

"I don't think anyone can keep your mother in line, Maya."

"You mean your ex-wife, Dad?"

"Yes."

"I mean, you're the one who chose her. I didn't really have a say in the matter."

"I know...and I'm sorry. But if I hadn't chosen her, I wouldn't have you, now would I?"

"I guess not."

"Here's what I think, sweetie. In regard to Shannon, just let her do her thing. It'll either fly or flop...and you know which scenario I'm putting my money on."

"So I shouldn't warn Marissa's dad or anything?"

"He's a cop. I bet he'll figure it out."

"But what about Marissa?"

"What's the worst thing Shannon can do in regard to Marissa?"

I considered this. Despite having no mothering skills whatsoever, Shannon wouldn't hurt anyone. Not intentionally. "She might neglect her."

"Hmm..."

"Maybe I should just give Adam a little heads-up," I said, "for Marissa's sake."

"Yes. You're probably right. For Marissa's sake."

We talked awhile longer, but I could tell he was tired, and it was really late over there. "Thanks for listening," I finally told him.

"Let me know how it goes."

"I'll e-mail you."

"Love you, sweetie!"

"Love you, Dad."

Then we hung up, and I prayed about the situation with Shannon and Marissa. I asked God to guide me and, if I need to say something to Marissa's dad, to show me how to do it without totally insulting my mother.

October 23

The audition is over—what a relief. And although Bruce Glass, the manager, seemed to like me and told me I was good, I don't think he was that impressed, and I don't think he's going to want me to replace Laura in the band.

"Thanks for playing for me," he said when we finished. "You have real talent. Chloe told me that your dad is Nick Stark."

I nodded as I unhooked my guitar strap.

"Your style is similar to his, but different."

I wasn't sure if that was a compliment or not. I just nodded and smiled. "Thanks for listening to me."

"We'll let you know our decision in a day or two."

I thanked him again and began gathering up my stuff.

"You were great," Chloe told me as I put my guitar away.

Allie grinned. "Yeah, I think Bruce likes you."

"But he still wants us to play with the other two girls that he's interested in," admitted Chloe. "That's probably why he's not saying much...yet."

"It's okay," I told them. "I understand. And I'm sure he's got a lot to think about."

But as I drove home and as I sit here tonight just thinking over this whole thing, I suddenly kind of want it. And that surprises me. To be honest, it might be that I want to escape Shannon. Or maybe avoid the calamity that I know she'll probably bring into Adam's and Marissa's lives. Or maybe I really do just want it. But the more I think I want it, the more convinced I am that it's not going to happen. And so I will simply pray about it. My prayer is that *if* this is God's will, He will open the door wide. And that if it's not His will, which seems most likely, He will slam the door shut and lock it tight. And having prayed this prayer, I know I can sleep easy tonight. God is in control.

October 27

It was just a regular Monday morning, and I was about to head out to my car to go to school, thinking how cool it is to have a normal life, when I saw Allie and Chloe at my door—and they had flowers and balloons in their hands.

"Hey, did someone just win the lottery?" I asked.

"Something like that." Allie laughed.

"Bruce wants you in the band!" Chloe thrust the roses at me and then hugged me. Allie hugged me too. And they both

seemed so genuinely happy that I actually started to cry. How weird is that?

"Really?" I sputtered. "I'm in the band?"

"If you want to be."

Now I considered this. I remembered my prayer about opened or closed doors, and I wondered if this really was God's work.

"Bruce suggested that you take a few days to think and pray about it," said Chloe, "to be really sure."

"And he'll bring a contract by." Allie frowned. "You'll need a parent or someone to sign it."

Now I frowned.

"Does your uncle have legal guardianship over you?"

"I'm not sure. He did represent me in the legal thing last summer, but it wasn't like he was officially signed over to be my guardian. I guess I better do some checking on it."

"Yeah." Chloe nodded. "Bruce is hoping you'll make a decision by the end of the week. He's already planning our new tour schedule, and he'd like to see us in concert by mid-November."

"Wow, that seems soon."

"It'll probably be kind of low key," Allie said. "Churches and conventions and small-time stuff."

"Until we get really used to playing together," Chloe explained.

"And until our audience gets used to us," Allie added.

"And it'll give you some experience before the real concert tour begins."

"So what do you think?" asked Allie. "Kind of freaky to think you could be hanging with us 24/7?"

"No," I said quickly, "that actually sounds cool."

"Allie snores," Chloe teased.

"Do not!"

I glanced at my watch. "I should probably get to school."

"Speaking of school," Chloe said as they walked me to my car, "they'll let you continue your classes on the road."

"Yeah," Allie chimed in. "Being in a professional band isn't a get-out-of-school-free card. They still expect you to graduate."

"Just talk to Mrs. King," said Chloe. "I mean, when you've decided."

"Pick us!" Allie cupped her hands in a beggar imitation. "Please, pick us!"

Chloe laughed. "Don't pressure her. She'll figure it out."

And that's what I'm hoping to do. I mostly think that I'm going to do this. But I want to be absolutely sure. This is a big decision, and it's not just about me either. Chloe and Allie have a lot at stake. If I do this thing, I need to be certain it's right.

Bruce dropped the contract by the house this evening. He met Uncle Allen, and we discussed my interesting custody situation. I even told him about Shannon and how she'd recently been doing time. "I don't want it to look like I've got any skeletons in my closet," I confessed.

He chuckled. "As long as you're open about it, I don't think it matters at all. In fact, it can be a strength—particularly when you're

giving a testimony, which is a fairly regular thing at concerts. I'm sure a lot of kids can relate to a parent who's less than perfect."

"That's an understatement when it comes to my mom." Then I told him about how I had everything pretty much ready for my emancipation.

"That might be the best way to go," Bruce said. "It would make it easier when you girls are on the road. Although I'll still recommend a chaperon since you're all under twenty-one."

Uncle Allen was browsing through the contract. "I'm sure you don't mind if Maya has an attorney go over this," he said.

"I'd be disappointed if she didn't."

After Bruce left, Uncle Allen congratulated me again. "Does Kim know about this?"

"I e-mailed her this afternoon."

"E-mail, she-mail—let's give her a call."

Then next thing I knew we were talking to Kim on the speaker phone. "That's so great," she said. "I hadn't checked my e-mail yet. I'm so happy for you, Maya!"

"Thanks. I have until Friday to make a final decision," I said.

"Meaning you're not completely sure?"

"I'm mostly sure, but I just want to be one hundred percent."

"That's right," said Uncle Allen. "It's a big decision and a big commitment. Not something you should do lightly."

"I'll have Robert Bernard go over the contract," I explained. "And I'll try to see about getting emancipated."

"Speaking of that..." Kim sounded concerned. "How are things with Shannon?"

I told Kim about the possibility of Shannon taking care of Marissa.

"You're kidding!" She sounded stunned.

"Yeah, pretty strange, huh?"

"I guess. But you never know, Maya. It could end up being a good thing."

"I'm not sure I want to be around to find out."

"When will Marissa get released?"

"In another week, I think."

"How's she doing?"

"She's still improving, but it's pretty slow going. And being in the nursing home is depressing, I can tell."

"Tell her I'm still praying for her."

"Absolutely."

"And I'll really be praying for you too, Maya, that God will direct this decision. But I think it sounds like a cool opportunity."

"Would you do it?" I asked suddenly. "I mean, if they'd asked you?"

She laughed. "I've jammed with them before, but they're not exactly a violin sort of band."

"But...if?" I persisted.

"I don't like hypothetical questions...but if I had the opportunity to, say, play violin with the philharmonic symphony orchestra,

well, I'm guessing I'd say yes." She chuckled. "I'll let you know when they call."

"It's not outside the realm of possibility, Kim." Her dad's voice was serious. "You are a very gifted violinist."

"That's right," I added.

"At the moment I have my hands full with college. I probably shouldn't have taken sixteen hours my first term."

"Well, if anyone can handle it, it's you," her dad said warmly.

"I agree!"

Then we hung up, and I took my contract to my room, where I read the whole thing twice through. And although it's hard to decipher all the legalese, I am pretty stunned at how much money I'd be making. That alone should make the emancipation judge stand up and pay attention. But I'm worried about the one-year commitment. A year is a long time. On the other hand, I'd make a lot of money. More than I can make with my three part-time jobs combined, which isn't bad. Still, I don't want money to be what's driving this decision. I want my choice to be God directed—and hopefully God blessed as well.

Maya's Green Tip for the Day

Plant a tree! Yes, I know it's not Arbor Day (that's in April), but have you heard that fall is a great time to plant trees too? Here are some good reasons to plant a tree (or two or three). (1) Trees improve the air quality by absorbing carbon dioxide. (2) Trees provide shade, which can provide natural cooling for a house. (3) Trees can offer protection to a house in the chill of winter. (4) The shade from trees helps to conserve water because irrigation doesn't evaporate as quickly. (5) Trees increase your property value. (6) Trees are nice to look at! To find out more about trees, what kind thrive in your area, and how to plant them safely, check out this Web site: www.arborday.org.

Eleven

October 29

Day three of my need-to-decide-my-future week—and only three days left. It's not helping that Dominic told all our friends that I've been invited to join Redemption. I know he did it because he's proud of me and thinks it's a great opportunity that I'd be foolish to pass up. But now everyone seems to have an opinion on it.

And even though I don't hang with Brooke and Amanda as much anymore (although I'm friendly to them), I'm not surprised that they want to put their two cents in as well.

"What's there to think about?" demanded Brooke after I informed her that I was still weighing the whole thing.

"A lot." I forced a smile.

"There wouldn't be for me," Amanda said. "If Redemption asked me to join up, my bags would be packed within the hour."

"Don't worry," Brooke told her. "Redemption is not asking you to join them. You can barely carry a tune."

"Thanks. Just the same, I'd go for it. Do you know that Redemption gets to do concerts with Iron Cross? And have you seen those guys? They are hot."

"I'm aware that they perform with Iron Cross." I glanced over to where Dominic was waiting for me to join him at the lunch table.

"And did you know that Chloe and Jeremy used to date?" asked Amanda. "He is so dreamy. I can't believe they broke up."

Now this is something I didn't actually know, but I didn't let on since it could just be gossip.

"Anyway," continued Brooke, "I just don't get why this is a hard choice for you, Maya. I mean, you'd be serving the Lord by singing and everything. What's the big deal?"

"The big deal is that I want to do what God wants me to do." I wanted to add "and it would be nice if everyone else kept out of it." But I'd already offended these two (they informed me a while ago) by not hanging with them so much anymore. I told them that part of my "outreach" plan was to share my faith with friends who aren't involved in church. Of course, they didn't really believe me. And Amanda reminded me that "darkness and light don't mix."

"That's because if there's a light," I told them a few weeks ago at youth group, "the darkness goes away."

"But that's not what that scripture means," Brooke said.

"How do you know?" I challenged.

"I'll ask Caitlin," Amanda said then.

I had simply nodded and tried not to appear smug, because I was pretty sure Caitlin agreed with me since she's the one who pointed this concept out to me in the first place. But I'm glad that

both Amanda and Brooke are meeting with Caitlin—they have been ever since that old lawsuit business went by the wayside.

Now if Amanda and Brooke putting their oars in wasn't bad enough, it got even worse when Vanessa and Becca chimed in. Naturally, they both think I should go. I'm sure there are two reasons for their enthusiasm—and not spiritual reasons either. Reason number one is Wyatt. Reason number two is Dominic. They think that with me out of the picture, touring the country for an entire year, they will immediately hook up with these two guys. I'm guessing they're already planning to double-date to the prom.

So there's another thing. I know it seems kind of shallow and silly, but I would like to go to prom—just once. And I might like to go to some of the other things and to graduate like I saw Kim do last spring. Oh, I know that I won't be the valedictorian (like her) since I haven't been in school long enough. But just the satisfaction of putting on that goofy hat and robe and being handed my diploma...well, I would never admit it out loud, but I think it'd be cool.

Cooler than being in a fairly well-known girls' gospel rock band? I'm not sure. How do you measure something like that?

The only one who seems to think I'd be making a mistake to join Redemption is Wyatt. But then his motives are pretty obvious and suspicious. However, I do wonder what my dad would say. And I'm getting worried that Shannon might find out since this is a small town. But I'm also proceeding with my emancipation

plan. I have a court date in two weeks (not like with a jury and everything, since I simply appear in front of a judge for a legal determination). But my boss's husband, Robert Bernard, has offered to go with me. Jacqueline already told him what was going on, and he refuses to let me pay him, although I plan to pay him for his legal advice regarding the contract, which he wants to speak to me about tomorrow after school. Hopefully his advice will help me decide. In the meantime I wish everyone else would just keep quiet.

Before I talk to Robert, I plan to talk to my dad. I'm expecting him to call early tomorrow morning. And although I know he probably won't be very happy to hear that I might be hitting the road as a "professional" musician, I hope he'll understand. And I hope he'll give me sound advice and not just some fatherly knee-jerk reaction.

October 30

First of all I have to say that my dad didn't surprise me much when I told him my "good news."

"Why on earth would you want to do that?" he demanded.

So I tried to explain that it was a huge opportunity.

"But no good can come of three young girls doing music out on the road. It's a formula for disaster."

When I tried to explain that we were a Christian band, meaning no drugs, no alcohol, no sex, he just didn't get it. He honestly thought there was no difference between a Christian band and

the kinds of people he deals with on an ongoing basis. I think he's jaded.

Finally we agreed to disagree. And he said that he was going to do some research on Redemption and that he planned to talk to some people and that he would get back to me. I almost reminded him that he doesn't actually have any kind of legal say in my life since he doesn't have custody of me and since in a couple of weeks I'll probably be emancipated anyway. Instead, I thanked him and reminded myself that the Bible says kids need to respect their parents. But it can sure be a challenge!

This was made crystal clear to me later in the day. After school it was my turn to visit Marissa, and I wasn't too surprised to see Shannon there. She called a few days ago to inform me that she was now volunteering at the nursing home. It had been Adam's idea, and although she hadn't seemed too thrilled about it, he must've convinced her since there she was, wearing one of those not-so-cute nurse jacket things. It was pink and blue with snaps. And not exactly something that Shannon (think designer-obsessed shopaholic) would have picked out for herself. And she had her hair in a ponytail. I don't know that I've ever seen her with her hair in a ponytail—well, not unless she was recovering from some wild binge. But to be out in public in a ponytail, well, that was different. It almost gave me hope.

But my hope was short-lived when I witnessed Shannon being unkind to one of the residents. She didn't know I was watching. It was in the activity room, and she was trying to get an old woman

named Lillian to do something—I have no idea what—but Lillian
wasn't interested. Her feet were planted on the floor, and Shannon
was trying to maneuver the wheelchair. Finally Shannon gave the
wheelchair such a jerk that poor old Lillian almost took a dive. It
must've scared her too, because she quit dragging her feet and
allowed Shannon to wheel her from the room. But Lillian was crying. And that just broke my heart.

"What's wrong?" I joined them, walking alongside Lillian.
"Why are you so sad?"

But Lillian wasn't talking now.

"Lillian is a stubborn woman," Shannon said like Lillian wasn't
listening, and maybe she wasn't. "But I showed her who's boss."

"Who *is* boss?" I asked Shannon.

She looked slightly stumped now.

"I mean, the residents here are the ones who pay the bills,
right? Shouldn't they be boss?"

"Oh, Maya." Shannon's voice grew condescending. "You can't
let the monkeys run the zoo."

And since I had no response to that, or at least nothing I
wanted to say in front of anyone, I headed on to Marissa's room.

I decided it was time to tell Marissa that I was considering
joining Chloe's band. I figured she might need a little heads-up,
especially if it somehow leaked to her that this was a possibility.
So I quickly told her about the audition and how I might actually
do this, and she seemed concerned.

"Chloe...Allie...Laura...and you?"

"No," I told her. "Laura isn't part of the band now."

"Why?"

I explained about school, and then she actually remembered this and nodded. "Yeah. Laura is in college," she said.

I smiled at her. "You're really getting better, aren't you?"

She got a frustrated expression. "Slow. I am so slow."

This was a sign that she was now in Level 7. The good news was that she could do more for herself. The bad news was that she was more aware of her impaired abilities and would get frustrated more easily. I suppose it kind of felt like one step forward and two steps back to her.

"You might feel like you're slow," I told her, "but you're actually becoming faster."

"Not fast enough."

"But you get to go home soon, right?"

She scrunched her forehead like she was trying to remember.

"I think I heard you get to go home this weekend."

"This weekend," she parroted. "Yes. This weekend."

I was tempted to mention the fund-raiser on Friday, but I didn't want to get her hopes up. The last time I mentioned the concert to her dad (without saying it was a fund-raiser), he had been cautious. The idea of taking her out is probably intimidating. Even though she can get around without the wheelchair, she's not that strong, and her balance is questionable. Still, I'm hoping and praying they'll both come.

"Shannon is mean," Marissa said suddenly.

"Really?" I waited.

"She pushes me."

"How?" I hoped she'd elaborate, because if Shannon was being abusive, which would've surprised me if I hadn't just seen her bossing Lillian, I wanted to know. And I'd have no problem informing Marissa's dad either.

"She pushes me...to do things...myself."

I considered this. "You mean like getting dressed and things like that?"

"Yes." Marissa had a defiant look now. "She's mean. She pushes me."

"Some kind of pushing is good," I told her. "I mean, the kind that encourages us to do new things and to grow and get better. Like playing your recorder. Have you been doing it?"

Marissa frowned. "They took it away."

"Who took it?"

"The nurse."

"Why?"

"Too much noise. She said too much noise."

"Oh." I nodded. I hadn't even thought about that. I suppose it would sound noisy to some of the residents. "Well, you can practice it at home."

"Home." She smiled now. "I want to go home."

"And how do you feel about Shannon being there to help you?"

Marissa looked unsure.

"Are you worried she'll be mean?"

She nodded slightly.

"And that she'll push you too hard?"

She nodded again.

"But you'll tell your dad, won't you?"

Now she looked confused.

"If Shannon is mean, Marissa, you have to tell your dad the truth."

She just sat there, and I wasn't sure if she actually understood me, but finally she nodded again. "I will tell."

"And if you can't tell your dad, you can tell me," I said suddenly.

"I will tell you."

But then I realized that I might not always be around for her to tell. I might be on tour. But maybe someone else would be there for her. Maybe I could talk to Caitlin about it. And I decided I'd better talk to Marissa's dad too.

We played video games until four, and then I told Marissa I had to go talk to my lawyer. To my surprise she seemed to get this.

"About Brooke?"

"No, but you're right. I did talk to my lawyer about Brooke. But that was last summer. This is something different. Something to do with the music business." I didn't want to go into much detail, so I just told her good-bye and that I hoped to see her again soon. "Maybe I'll see you in your house next time," I said as I left. I think that made her feel better.

Then I swung by Robert's law firm, and before long he was telling me the concerns he had about the contract. "A year seems

like a long time to commit to, Maya. Especially when you're only sixteen."

"Almost seventeen."

"Right. But just the same, a lot can happen in a year. For instance, what if you find you're incompatible with one of the band members? What then?"

"Is there a way to change the contract?"

"That's what I'm recommending. I think you should suggest a three-month trial, just to make sure you're happy with the situation."

"Yes," I said eagerly. "That sounds good to me too. Three months is a pretty long time to figure out if we really get along or not."

"And that will protect you from any financial risk," he pointed out. "Otherwise, if you broke your one-year contract, they could hold you liable for financial losses due to canceled concerts or record deals."

"I hadn't really considered that."

"I'll rewrite this contract to include the probationary period, with a full one-year contract to be renegotiated three months after signing. Does that sound acceptable to you?"

"Totally."

"Great. I should have it ready for you by tomorrow afternoon."

"Thanks."

"So, shall I assume this means you're going to join the band?" He made a face. "Because Jacqueline is not going to be happy.

She already told me she doesn't want to lose you. She might even blame me for helping you now."

I had to laugh. "Oh, Jackie will be fine without me. I'm only working about ten hours a week anyway."

"Just the same, she likes having you around." He winked. "But I don't blame you for taking this opportunity. It sounds like a lot of fun."

"That is unless we all decide we hate each other."

"In that case you'll be glad we added the probation clause."

"Absolutely."

And I can't even express what a relief it is to have that part of the contract changed. Not that I've made up my mind yet. But I do tend to be leaning that way. I just hope my dad's not too disappointed in me. Or maybe I'll just prove him wrong.

So anyway, I was coming out of the law office when I saw Marissa's dad heading for the coffee shop next door. "Hey, Mr. Phillips," I said. "Taking a break?"

He paused by the door. "No doughnut jokes, okay?"

"Right."

"And remember, you're supposed to call me Adam now."

"Have you got a minute, Adam?"

"Sure, want to join me for a cup of joe?"

I agreed, and soon we were seated at a table, and I just sat there, trying to decide where to begin.

"Something bothering you, Maya?" he finally asked.

"Sort of."

"Is it about your mom? Are you concerned that she might be getting in over her head?"

I nodded. "Actually I'm concerned for you as well. And Marissa too."

"It's a complicated setup. I'll give you that."

"But there's more to it..." I bit my lip and waited.

"How so?"

"Can I just cut to the chase?"

"I wish you would."

"Did my mom tell you that she was just released from prison?"

His dark brows arched slightly. "No. Do you want to explain?"

And so I did explain. I didn't tell him everything, but enough. "I'm sorry to be the one to dump all this on you, but it seemed like you deserve to know. And I'll admit that I'm worried for Marissa's sake."

"I guess I should've done some investigating on my own. I just figured that if she was your mom, well, she must be a decent person."

"Marissa told me a little about her mom, and I think our moms might be similar...if you know what I mean."

"Then why is Shannon so interested in helping me with Marissa?" He seemed to be asking this of himself as much as he was asking me.

"I don't know exactly why. I mean, it's pretty out of character for her to care about anyone. I know that sounds terrible, but it's true."

"Do you suppose she's changed?"

I didn't answer.

"Prison changes some people." He frowned. "Although statistics would tell a different story."

"I wish she had changed. But I've been disappointed so many times that I kind of gave up hope."

"I wonder what I should do."

I shook my head. "I don't know."

He looked so sad now, like I really had burst his balloon.

"I'm sorry."

"No, it's not your fault. I appreciate your honesty."

"Maybe I should've said something sooner."

"I'm sorry you had to say anything at all."

"I guess I thought this whole thing might've blown over by now. Like Shannon would've upped and gone, and you'd have seen what she's really like. In fact, I'm rather surprised she's still around and wanting to do this."

"She's been volunteering at the nursing home, you know."

"I know…"

He looked intently at me now. "What if she really has changed, Maya? Or what if she really wants to change?"

I shrugged.

"To be honest, I'm in a tough spot now. Marissa has her heart set on coming home. And the situation with Shannon working for room and board initially and possibly pay later on…well, it was like a gift from God."

I thought about the Trojan horse and how it appeared to be a gift too but was really just a diabolical trick.

"But now I suppose I should rethink that plan."

"I don't know…" I felt so guilty. "I mean, there's always the possibility that she's changed. I just don't know."

"Yes, this is something I'll have to figure out for myself."

"I just wanted you to know the truth…because I care about Marissa."

"I appreciate it."

"By the way, do you think you'll want to bring her to the harvest party tomorrow night?"

"I'm not sure. I'll do my best, but it might be a challenge since Marissa might be released to go home by then. I'm meeting with the doctor today."

I felt so sorry for him as I left the coffee shop. How hard would it be to deal with what's been put on his plate? A rotten marriage, followed by a rebellious daughter, and then the accident? I know my life hasn't been exactly a bed of roses, but at least I'm not responsible for a brain-damaged child. Then you add Shannon to this poor man's already messed-up life, and it gets really sad. Why did she have to get their hopes up like this?

Maya's Green Tip for the Day

Halloween might be fun, but thanks to increasing commercialism, it's quickly turning into one of the most environmentally wasteful holidays of the year. Here are some things you can do to help. (1) Recycle those jack-o'-lanterns! Even if you don't compost (and you should), you probably know someone with a compost maker. Pumpkin remains are great for composting, and while you're at it, throw in a bunch of those autumn leaves too. (2) Reuse Halloween decorations. Instead of throwing away all those ghoulish goodies, pack them in a well-marked plastic crate for next year. (3) Reduce wastefulness by recycling Halloween costumes, either by storing them for another year or donating them to Goodwill or the Salvation Army. (4) Give out ecofriendly treats. Did you know there are companies that make organic chocolate and lollipops? Not only are these kinder to the environment, but they're healthier too!

Twelve

October 31

It's been a long, crazy day, but for the most part it's been good. It started with another early-morning call from Dad. This time he did surprise me. It turned out that his investigative snooping into Redemption turned out better than he'd expected. "They sound like a legitimately healthy band," he told me.

"So you don't mind if I join them?"

"I'm not saying that I think a musician's life is great." He paused, and I could imagine him closing his eyes and tilting his head back like he does when he's thinking. "But I do trust your judgment, Maya. You have a good head on your shoulders. Where you got it from is a mystery." He chuckled. "Maybe Grandma Carolina passed some good DNA your way."

I thanked him for the compliment, and he asked if I had decided for sure that I was going to do it.

"I think so." Then I explained the trial-period addendum.

"That's a smart plan, Maya. Tell your attorney thank you from me."

"Some free concert tickets might be a nice thank-you," I teased. "Remember that Robert and Jackie are big Nick Stark fans."

"It's a done deal. But I won't be performing stateside until spring."

"I'm sure they won't complain."

Dad said he wished his European tour was shorter. "The life of a musician," he said with a sigh. "You don't get much say in where and when you play. You just thank your lucky stars that anyone wants to listen."

I wanted to say I'd rather thank God but didn't want to sound too preachy. Still, I might write something like that to him in an e-mail. I'm better at sharing my faith through the written word. I guess that's why I like to keep a journal and write my column... and, more recently, write songs.

"I wish I could hear you perform, Maya. Any chance you girls will make it across the pond?"

"I doubt it. At least not for a while. The first concerts are supposed to be pretty low key, kind of getting used to each other or getting fans used to us."

"That makes sense."

Then I told Dad about my court date and that I thought I had everything in order.

"I'm sure most parents wouldn't be happy to hear that kind of news, but in your case I feel nothing but relief. Have you told Shannon?"

"No. I thought I'd wait until after the fact."

"That's wise. You don't want her to do anything to slow it down."

"That's what Robert Bernard said too."

"So my little girl is in good hands."

"Yes...and in God's hands."

"That's a relief too."

Then we said good-bye, and I felt (more than ever) that I had already made my final decision to join Redemption. I almost called Chloe to tell her the good news but then decided to wait until the harvest party tonight.

So I was getting ready for what was starting to feel like my big debut concert, and I realized I was clueless about what to wear. I mean, I've learned how to dress fashionably for working at Jacqueline's (my modeling stint helped with that), and I know how to dress for my green spot on TV (don't wear white or black or stripes), but I have no idea how to dress for my new role as rocker chick. I seriously tried on about a dozen outfits before I finally settled on a brown turtleneck over a short plaid skirt, black leggings, and a pair of clunky Earth shoes. Now I realize this didn't exactly shout out "rocker chick," but it was the best I could do.

But when I got to the church sanctuary where everything was set up for our concert, I knew that my outfit wasn't quite right. Chloe and Allie both looked great—a cross between rocker, retro, and urban chic.

"I didn't know what to wear," I admitted.

"You're fine," Chloe assured me.

"For tonight anyway," said Allie.

"Have you decided—" Just then Chloe stopped talking and pointed to where Marissa and her dad and Shannon were approaching us.

"You came!" I ran over to hug Marissa.

She smiled shyly. "Yes. Dad brought me."

"Have you moved back home yet?" asked Chloe.

Marissa nodded. "Yes. Home."

"Is it great being back in your own bed?" asked Allie.

"Great." Marissa smiled even bigger now.

"Shannon is helping with Marissa." Adam said this more to me than to Chloe and Allie. I wondered if he'd talked to Shannon or had simply decided that he was too desperate to turn her out.

"Hi, Shannon," I said with hesitation. Then I realized I should introduce her to my friends. But I knew it would be awkward. So I did a stiff intro, telling them that she was my mom and trying to act perfectly natural, like she and I were on the best of terms. Naturally, she just played along, like she always does.

"Maya's doing music with us tonight," Chloe said.

"Really?" Shannon looked shocked by this.

"In fact, we should probably go do a sound test," Allie added quickly.

"That's right," Chloe said. "We need to make sure we're all set."

I wanted to thank and hug them both.

"And we'll get seats," said Adam. The sanctuary was starting to fill up. Plus there were lots of people down in the basement where the harvest party was already in high gear.

"In front?" asked Marissa. "To see Maya and Chloe and Allie?"

"Sure, wherever you want, princess." He smiled at her, and it was such a tender moment that I felt like crying. Until I noticed Shannon there too. That took all the sweetness out of the picture for me. But fortunately I didn't have to think about that then. I focused on our sound test and tuning my guitar and the music and anything besides my mother.

"Come with us," Chloe told me once it was pretty much set up. And we went to a small back room, and Allie closed the door.

"We always pray before a concert," Chloe explained.

I sighed in relief. "Thanks, I could use that."

And so the three of us joined hands and prayed. And I can't even write how cool it was—it's like God was right there with us. Amazing! We prayed that our music would bless people. They prayed for Shannon. And we all prayed that hearts would be generous toward Marissa tonight.

"I thought we could invite her onto the stage at the end," said Chloe. "Do you think she'd like that?"

"I think so," I told her. "I know she likes being with us. Too bad she didn't bring her recorder. She knows 'Twinkle, Twinkle, Little Star' now."

"I bet there's a recorder in the church somewhere," said Allie. "I'll ask Willy to look around."

"Do you think she'd really want to play it in front of all those people?" asked Chloe.

"We could sing with her," I suggested. "You know, just quietly and no instruments but so she doesn't feel too alone or scared."

"Cool!" Allie nodded. "That would be very cool."

I looked at my watch now. "Shouldn't we be out there by now?"

"Probably so." Allie reached for the door.

"But before we go out there..." Chloe had a questioning look in her eye. "Are you going to tell us your decision or—"

"Are you ready, ladies?" asked Willy. "Because your fans await."

Allie quickly told him about our need for a recorder, which he didn't even question, and the next thing I knew we were onstage, and Chloe's mike was on, and she was introducing us—to a packed house.

To say I had butterflies would be an understatement, but I just did what I always do when I'm in a situation like that. I block it all out. I pretend like no one is watching me and simply focus on what I'm doing and try to do my best. Fortunately, Chloe and Allie are old pros at this, and even if I had blown it, which I didn't, they would have carried on just fine without me.

But I actually think we sounded pretty good, because the crowd was very enthusiastic, and when we finished, we got a standing ovation (which Chloe and Allie had predicted). And so we played the final song, one that Chloe wrote—about generosity. Then after the applause finally died down, Chloe addressed the audience.

"Some of you are aware that tonight's concert, while free, was really meant to be a fund-raising event." She looked down at Marissa. "A very dear friend of ours, Marissa Phillips, was in a nearly fatal car accident last summer. She suffered a serious brain injury, and her recovery has been slow and painful—not only to Marissa but to the family budget as well. Our hope is that tonight's concert will encourage you guys to help out." Chloe motioned to Marissa now. "Can you come up here, Marissa?"

She immediately stood up and began to slowly approach the stage, stopping at the steps. Her dad, realizing her challenge, popped up and helped her up the two steps, and everyone clapped. Then Allie produced a recorder, and Marissa's eyes lit up.

"Want to play a song with us?" Allie asked.

Marissa nodded somberly as Chloe positioned her between us, explaining to the audience we'd be singing a song that Marissa had just learned. "You start it, Marissa."

She lifted the recorder to her lips and began to play the old children's song, and we joined her by quietly singing the lyrics. When we stopped, the room was silent for a few seconds, then to our relief erupted into huge applause, like that had been our best number of the night. Go figure.

"Tonight Marissa is our little star," said Chloe. "But tomorrow she'll be back working toward a full recovery. And that requires physical therapists and all kinds of things. Please bless the Phillips family as you leave. Baskets are by the doors."

"One more song," yelled someone from the back. Then everyone was clapping again. So with Marissa still on the stage, we did another song, and when it was over, I decided to speak up.

"While everyone is here," I began, looking directly at Shannon now, "I have a little announcement to make. Some of you may know that Redemption has been looking for a replacement for Laura Mitchell. What you may not know is that earlier this week, they offered the position to me. And tonight I want everyone to know that I've decided to accept it."

Allie and Chloe came over and hugged me, and everyone clapped. Even Shannon. Afterward, several of my friends came up to congratulate me, including Dominic. I could tell his was a happy-sad kind of congratulations. "Guess you won't be playing in my band then?"

"I'm sorry. It actually sounded like fun."

"Well, I don't blame you. You girls are great together, Maya."

Marissa, her dad, and Shannon came over to join us. With tears in his eyes, Adam hugged and thanked all of us. "You'll never know how much this has meant to me—to us."

"Thank you," said Marissa.

Shannon said nothing. For which I was thankful.

Then Bruce came over to shake my hand. "I think you made the right choice, Maya. But I have to admit you kept me on needles and pins, girl. I thought you were going to turn us down."

"I just wanted to be careful about the decision," I told him.

"And what about the changes that Robert Bernard made to the contract? Did you have a chance to read it yet?"

He nodded. "I did."

"Was that all right?"

"I think it was a brilliant idea. I'm cool with it."

"So this is really it?"

"Looks like our wheels are in motion now."

"Excuse me."

I turned to see that Shannon was standing nearby, within earshot.

Bruce gave her a slightly blank look.

"Uh, this is my mother," I told him, "Shannon Stark. Shannon, I'd like you to meet my new manager, Bruce Glass."

Shannon eyed him carefully. "It seems to me that a minor wouldn't be allowed to enter into a contract without parental permission, or am I wrong?"

He cleared his throat.

"And unless there's something I don't know, I'm still Maya's custodial parent. Her father gave up that right years ago."

Okay, that's not completely true, but I didn't want to go there just then. "Shannon, we can talk in private," I said quietly.

"Why?" Her voice actually got louder now.

"Perhaps your mother should consult with your attorney, Maya." Bruce gave me a look that suggested Robert Bernard might be just the guy to straighten my mother out.

"Yes," I said quickly, "that's an excellent idea." I pointed to where Robert and Jacqueline were still standing on the sidelines, chatting with Chloe's parents. "I can introduce you to him, and you guys can set up an appointment."

And that's exactly what I did. I can't say that Shannon was particularly pleased about it, but it really did seem the sane way to handle this. Now the big question is whether Robert will mention the emancipation or not. As much as I'd like to keep it from her, I don't really see any way around it. I just hope that Shannon doesn't flip out or do something to mess it all up.

Maya's Green Tip for the Day

Eat a peanut butter and jelly sandwich and save the world. Okay, that's a bit of an overstatement, but when you eat a plant-based lunch (foods like PB&J or veggie sandwiches or bean burritos) instead of something like a hamburger, grilled cheese, fish and chips, or chicken nuggets, you save water, preserve land, and help keep the planet green. Listen to these facts: Every time you choose a plant-based food over a hamburger, you save the equivalent of 2.5 pounds of carbon dioxide (which is almost as good as driving a hybrid car like mine). But eating peanut butter instead of burgers also saves water because plants grown for food use less water than animals. And it saves land because animal products use six to seventeen times as much land as plant products. So hey, why not a PB&J? For more information on this, check out http://environment.about.com.

Thirteen

November 3

After school I drive over to get Shannon. It was weird picking her up at Marissa's house. Like who would've thought (say, last summer) that my prison-inmate mother would be living with Marissa and her dad. Life is strange.

I would've visited with Marissa longer except that our appointment with Robert Bernard was at 3:45, and I didn't want to be late. I so appreciate all that he's doing for me, and his time is valuable. And after what went down today, I realize how valuable he is to me. I wonder how many other sixteen-year-olds need an attorney.

Anyway, Shannon and I are riding in my car, and all I want is to get there, get this over with, and be done with it. Naturally, it feels totally awkward. So I pray silently and then attempt some small talk about the weather and Harrison High's football game this week. But Shannon is having none of it.

"It seems you've done quite well for yourself, haven't you, Maya?"

I just shrug, keeping my eyes on the traffic.

"I never even asked you where you got your fancy little car."

"It's not fancy. It's economical."

"So where did you get it?"

"From a car dealership down—"

"You know that's not what I mean." Her tone is sharp.

"You mean *where* did I get the money to buy it?"

"Oh, don't be a moron, Maya. I can guess where you got the car. Your *dear old daddy,* right?" The way she says this sounds like such a put-down. So mean and nasty that I fall for it.

"You know, Shannon, I almost could've bought this car myself...if *someone* hadn't stolen my savings last year."

"Why do you go on and on about that?" She scowls as she digs through her purse like she's searching for lost treasure. "You know that was *our* money."

"*Our* money?" Okay, I feel like pulling over and really laying into her for what she did to me last year, but I don't. For one thing it would only complicate matters, and for another thing it would make us late for the appointment.

"You know good and well that the money was sent to us for your child support and that I was only—"

"Look, Shannon, I know good and well that you were probably high when you took it and that you were clueless and selfish and deceitful. But I assume you're not high now, are you?"

"Of course not!"

"You can try to rationalize what you did to me, Shannon, but

the fact is, *that was my money*—hard-earned money from working all summer—"

"Oh yes, I almost forgot your short-lived modeling career. Didn't that work out well for you?"

I manage to keep my mouth shut this time. Really, what's the use?

"I listened to the words of those sweet little Christian songs you were singing with the other sweet little Christian girls, Maya. Do you really believe all that crap?"

"It's not crap, and yes, I *do* believe it."

She smiles now, but her eyes are narrowed. "Oh, good. I was hoping you did. Because I'd hate to think you were a hypocrite. I've known some religious hypocrites in my time. I wouldn't want my only daughter to be one of them."

How is she so able to push my buttons like that? Is this some carefully calculated plan on her part—like, let's get Maya to fall apart right before we speak to the attorney? That way Shannon can act like she's the all-important mother, like I can't get along without her. Is that her game?

"By the way, I did some checking over the weekend, Maya, regarding the legal situation."

I will not say another word about this, I tell myself, not without my lawyer present!

"And I was right. A minor is not allowed to enter into a contract without parental permission, and that means a signature."

"What about a parent who's doing time in prison?" I say quietly. So much for keeping my mouth shut. "What about a parent whose logic is impaired by addiction, Shannon? What kind of parent is that anyway?"

She sniffs as if I've hit a soft spot, then returns to digging in her oversize bag like maybe she has a lace-trimmed hanky in there that she plans to dab her eyes with. "Yes, Maya, I can admit I've made some mistakes. But I'm not in prison now. And I am still your mother."

"What about your addiction problems?"

"I'm clean. I told you that already." She finally locates what she's looking for in her purse, a shabby-looking pack of cigarettes, but before she can light one, I speak up.

"Sorry, Shannon, no smoking in my car."

"I'll open a window," she snaps.

"No," I say firmly. "This is a *no-smoking* car. If you light up, I'll pull over, and you'll have to get out."

"It figures you'd throw your own mother out of your car."

"Look, we're almost there, Shannon. You can light up in about two minutes, okay?"

"That's so generous of you."

Now this just irks me. "And you're such an expert on generosity, Shannon? You have given me so much, haven't you?"

"Here's generosity," she says as I park. "I'd give anything to never have had you."

I blink but say nothing. I would think that after so many years, so much pain, that Shannon would be unable to hurt me anymore. But as usual when it comes to my mother, I am wrong.

"I'll be inside," I tell her as she lights up her beloved cancer stick.

"Oh no—no, you don't." She drops the unsmoked cigarette and grinds it under her heel, which leaves an ugly mess all over the sidewalk and just makes me want to scream. Then she hurries on ahead of me like she thinks this is a footrace and the first one there will win the best prize.

She goes straight to the receptionist. "I'm Shannon Stark, here to see Robert Bernard, please."

"Shannon Stark?" Cindy looks slightly confused, then spots me. "Oh, Maya, this must be your mother." She smiles. "Go on into Robert's office. You know the way."

This time I lead. And I try not to act too cocky as I push open the wide oak door. After all, I do know that scripture about pride coming before a fall. And at the rate this is going, I could be smacked down good at any given moment. Mostly, I just want to get this over with. I've been telling myself all weekend that if Shannon puts the brakes on everything, it could be that it's for the best—it could be God's will. Although the truth is, now that she's stuck her nose into my life, I want to be part of Redemption more than ever. I want my emancipation more than ever too. I just wish I'd taken care of it sooner.

To my surprise, Robert isn't alone in his office. Bruce Glass is here too. They both stand and politely shake our hands and offer us seats, and then we're all sitting around Robert's large mahogany desk, just like a happy little family.

"Let me cut right to the chase," Shannon begins. "I've done a little research on the situation, and I have discovered that because I have custodial rights over Maya, which her father surrendered some time ago, any contract she signs as a juvenile is worthless without my signature."

Robert nods somberly. "That's legally accurate."

"So do you plan to sign Maya's contract?" Bruce holds up the paperwork that I recently signed.

Shannon presses her lips together as if thinking this over. "Well, I must admit that seeing Maya perform with the band the other night helped me realize she does have some musical talent. I really wouldn't want to stand in her way. I suppose the right thing to do would be for me to allow her to pursue her dreams. And so I will sign the contract." She sighs as if this is a difficult decision.

Now Robert steps in. "I suppose you realize that if you sign the contract, it will mean that you, Mrs. Stark, as Maya's legal custodian, will be in charge of Maya's earnings."

She nods, then crosses one leg over the other and leans back.

"That's a large responsibility, Mrs. Stark. Are you absolutely certain you want to take that on? Are you prepared to handle the business side of Maya's musical career?"

Her brow creases slightly as if she's considering this. Then she slowly nods again. "As you may have heard, I was married to Nick Stark for a number of years. I'm fully aware of what's involved in handling the business side of a musician's career."

Now Robert peers at me with a sad expression. "How do you feel about this, Maya?"

I feel betrayed and angry and confused. And I'm sure I look like that proverbial deer caught in the headlights. How can this be happening? And what can I do to stop it? I am speechless.

"Maya is only sixteen," Shannon continues, like she's the expert on my life. "I'm sure this is all very overwhelming to her. She's had a rough year, and I'll admit that I played a small part in that. But I am much better now. I'm ready to step up to my responsibilities as her mother. And it's obvious that she needs a mother." She kind of laughs now. "Good grief, I remember what it felt like to be sixteen—barely able to drive and yet you think you rule the world." She gave the men a knowing look. "But time and age fix that, right?"

Bruce clears his throat and holds up the contract again. "Back to the contract."

"Yes, yes, I'm ready to sign it," she says quickly. "I won't waste any more of your time."

"And we won't waste any more of yours," says Robert. Then he nods to Bruce like they've just shared some kind of secret handshake. And the next thing I know Bruce slides the contract into a

paper shredder and pushes the button. After a growling noise my contract is transformed into a pile of thin white ribbons.

"What?" Shannon is on her feet now, pointing at the debris with a horrified expression.

I just sit there and try to make sense of this. Maybe Bruce changed his mind when he realized I was going to make things difficult for Redemption—or rather my mother was. Maybe he's got another girl all lined up now, one without the baggage that I bring. Who can blame him?

"*Why did you do that?*" Shannon demands.

"I think it's for the best." Bruce slowly shakes his head.

Shannon is staring at Bruce like he's nuts. "But I just told you that I'm happy to sign it. I'm perfectly fine with Maya being in a band. For Pete's sake, I married a musician. I know all about this kind of life."

Just then Robert winks at me. And suddenly I get it. At least I think I get it. I hope I get it. Still, I keep my mouth shut. I wouldn't be able to get a word in now anyway since Shannon is going on and on. Finally she's even sputtering as she begs Bruce to draw up another contract, promising him that he won't be sorry. But he folds his arms over his chest as if he's unmovable. And I want to applaud. Instead, I just sit there and stare at my lap.

"I'm sorry, Maya." Bruce looks sadly my way. "You have a lot of talent. But the timing is all wrong."

"I'm sorry too, Maya," Robert says. "But maybe it's for the best."

I just nod without speaking.

"You people have lost your freaking minds!" Shannon looks from Bruce to Robert and finally to me. "And you're not even going to fight this, Maya?"

I just shrug.

She grabs her bag and stomps out of the office, slamming the door loudly behind her.

Now I look to Bruce and Robert, hoping they'll shed some light on the situation—or else just put me out of my misery.

"I'll draw up a new contract," Bruce says quickly and quietly.

"Dated *after* your emancipation hearing," Robert says. "I told the judge about your situation, and she moved the court date to Wednesday of this week."

"After your emancipation is official, your mother won't have a legal leg to stand on," Bruce says. "After speaking to Robert, I got this sneaking suspicion that you wouldn't want her managing your money for you."

"Thank you so much," I say as I stand. "Thank you both so much!"

"You better hurry," Robert tells me. "You'll have to do damage control with your mother now."

And yes, I do have to do damage control. But ironically, our drive back to the Phillipses' house is much more pleasant than the one to the law firm.

"That Bruce Glass is certifiable, you know," she tells me once we're in the car.

"I think he was worried," I say.

"I think he's insane."

"Well, he's hired to look out for the best interests of the band, Shannon."

"I can't believe you're taking this so lightly."

"Like I told you, I'm a Christian, and I have to trust God with these things."

"So you're not upset?"

"Of course I'm upset. Who wouldn't be upset? One day you think you're about to embark on a music career, and the next day it's over." I make a forced-sounding laugh. "Although that's the exact thing Dad always told me. I guess he was right."

"Well, if you ask me, that Bruce Glass is a complete flipping nut case. I told him I'd sign the contract. Why was he so stubborn?"

"He's watching out for the band. And I wasn't the only girl they were considering to replace Laura."

Now there's a long silence, and finally Shannon speaks quietly. "Are you mad at me?"

"No more than usual."

"Well, you still have your other jobs, Maya. You've made quite the impression on this little hick town—what with being on the local news and in your uncle's paper."

"And I still have my job at Jacqueline's," I point out, although I hope I'll be giving Jackie notice by the weekend.

Shannon sighs as I pull into the driveway. "And you shouldn't complain either. Your jobs are a lot more glamorous than mine."

"Who's complaining?" I give her a small smile as she gets out of the car. I can tell she's eager to get away from me now. She probably thinks I want to kill her. "Tell Marissa I'll see her on Thursday."

And so, as I write this entry, I'm thinking, *God is good.* Really, really good. And He really does watch out for His children. I went over our conversation in the law office several times, and I'm convinced that none of us lied to Shannon. Not once. Not about anything. She simply believed what she wanted to believe. And Bruce and Robert protected me from her.

Oh, it's sad when a girl must be protected from her own mother. But I saw those dollar signs in Shannon's eyes as she offered to sign my contract. I could hear the eagerness in her voice when she volunteered to manage my earnings. And after all, hasn't she managed our money before? She managed to bankrupt my dad, and she managed to steal my savings. I am so very thankful for Bruce and Robert and the way they helped me avoid a train wreck today. And really, God does work in mysterious ways, doesn't He?

Maya's Green Tip for the Day

Cotton is cool, and it's green too, right? After all, it's a plant, and it's grown in fields. How much greener does it get? Most people assume that all cotton fabrics are organic, but that is not true! A lot of cotton is cultivated by using huge amounts of toxic insecticides, herbicides, and synthetic fertilizers. These chemicals aren't good for the soil or the water or even the person who ends up wearing the garment (since cancer-causing carcinogens are involved). That's why when you see a label that says Organic Cotton, you should buy it and wear it and feel good about it. Fortunately, organic cotton is becoming more available—and not just with the pricy, cool designers either. So when you can choose between organic and not organic, do yourself and the earth a great big favor by going green. Choose organic.

Fourteen

November 5

I'm so used to taking care of myself and depending on myself that I don't expect too much from anyone. And yet it seems people are always helping me. I believe it's a God thing (a phrase I picked up from Caitlin). Anyway, today was no different.

I had to leave school early to appear before the Honorable Judge Helen Anderson at 1:30 p.m. Robert told me that judges are sometimes in a better mood following lunch, and when he can, he tries to get those time slots. Although in this case he simply got lucky.

As he'd instructed me, I tried to put together a nice, neat outfit that looked "mature and responsible but not overly sophisticated"—a navy woolen skirt and navy hose, topped with a pale blue Ralph Lauren shirt and a tweed vest. I suppose it was kind of preppy looking, but I think it worked. And I arrived at the courthouse early—just to get acclimated…and to pray.

My biggest fear was that somehow, and I had no idea how, but that *somehow* Shannon was going to find out about it and turn the whole thing into a circus.

Robert Bernard met me in the lobby, then took me to a quiet room where he briefed me on what was about to happen. "I know I don't need to tell you to answer the questions honestly, Maya. But don't be afraid to explain some things to the judge. She's had the paperwork to examine, but judges are busy, and sometimes they skim over things. And remember, she doesn't really know you or Shannon. All she can work with is what she hears today."

I nodded and swallowed. "Okay."

"And I've got some witnesses lined up as well."

"Witnesses?"

"People like Jackie, who can testify to your maturity and conduct."

"Oh, good. Thanks."

"Are you ready?"

"I think so."

He grinned at me. "Let's do this."

He led me to the courtroom, and I was stunned to see quite a crowd when we walked in. But upon closer examination, I realized that they were all friends. Most of them were grown-up friends, but Chloe and Allie were there as well.

The procedure was actually rather simple. I was introduced to the judge, and with Robert's help I presented my case. Then Robert invited witnesses, one by one, to step up and speak on my behalf. And it was really amazing. From Uncle Allen to Suzy Richards (from Channel Five News) to Mrs. King (from school) to Jackie Bernard

(my boss and friend) to Caitlin and Bruce and Chloe and Allie and others, they all told Judge Anderson what they knew about me and why they thought I was capable of being emancipated from my parents. It was totally awesome…and humbling. I have never felt so thoroughly loved in my life. God really does take care of orphans. And okay, I know I'm not a real orphan, but there have been a lot of times when it felt like I was…or when it felt like I'd be better off as an orphan.

"This is all very impressive," Judge Anderson finally told me. "For a sixteen-year-old girl"—she glanced at her file—"who will turn seventeen next month, you've really worked hard to build yourself a respectable and worthwhile life that even an adult could be proud of."

"Thank you."

"At your attorney's suggestion I spoke to your father, Nick Stark, early this morning. Your father is completely supportive of your emancipation as well. He understands that his traveling schedule makes it impossible for him to perform the responsibilities of legal guardian to you. I've gone over your mother's arrest and court records, and after hearing all that I've heard today, I am in agreement, Miss Stark. You have certainly proven yourself ready to accept the responsibility of legal emancipation from your parents." She looked around the room. "And I must say it's reassuring to see that you have such a supportive circle of friends. You are a very fortunate girl."

I just nodded, trying not to tear up.

Then she signed and stamped the papers and congratulated me. And the room erupted into cheers and applause.

I thanked her again, and it seemed that we were done, but before we gathered our things to leave, the judge spoke up again. "By the way, Maya," she said, "I have enjoyed your green column in the newspaper as well as your spot on Channel Five News. I hope you'll continue your commitment to protecting our environment as you embark on your musical career."

"I plan on it," I told her.

"Good for you!"

And so I am free. Although I don't really feel any different. Well, besides relieved. *I am so relieved.* Robert pointed out that there's always the chance Shannon could challenge this. "But it's highly unlikely she'd succeed." And I decided I'm not going to worry about that. Then he told me that Bruce is drawing up a new contract that should be ready for me to sign on Friday.

"So how about if we practice this afternoon?" Chloe suggested as they walked out of the courthouse with me.

"I'd love to," I told her.

"Group hug," Allie said.

"We're your family now," Chloe told me.

And yes, they will be my family. But I realize I have a lot of other people in my family too. All the ones in the courtroom today plus some (like my dad and Kim and Dominic) who weren't

even there. Judge Anderson said I was fortunate, which is true, but I also think I've been blessed.

November 9

I took Marissa to church with me today. It was her idea to go (I think because she wanted to get out of the house—and probably wanted to get away from Shannon too). But I sure didn't argue with her. And I actually think she enjoyed the service, at least the music. But this made me think she might like youth group as well. So now I plan to get her going to some of these things, which means I need someone else to commit to taking her since Redemption hits the road next week. I'm pretty sure Shannon won't agree to do this since she made it perfectly clear when I picked up Marissa this morning that she has no desire to go to church—ever.

So I'm thinking of Dominic and Eddie. And maybe even Brooke and Amanda too. But I'd like to put some pressure on Eddie. He's been on such a guilt trip anyway...maybe he'd like to let some of it go by becoming Marissa's personal chauffeur. Just as long as he doesn't drink and drive this time. I'm pretty sure he has no intention of doing that again.

As I drove Marissa home, I explained to her that I wouldn't be around after next week but that I'd stay in touch through e-mail. She's just starting to read and write, so this will actually be good therapy for her.

"Where you going?" she asked with a furrowed brow.

"Remember the band Redemption?"

"Yes." She smiled. "The concert. I played my recorder."

"Well, I'm going to go on tour with them. We'll travel around in their big bus and do concerts all over the country. So I'll be gone quite a bit." Then I explained how I wanted to help her get rides to church things. I didn't mention Eddie, but I did mention Dominic, and this made her happy.

"Come inside," she said when I pulled into their driveway.

I started to make an excuse, but she started getting sad again. So I decided, why not? After all, her dad was home today, which meant Shannon (if she was even there) had to be on her best behavior. When Adam's around, Shannon acts almost like a different person. In some ways I think this could be good for her.

As it turned out, Adam wasn't there. "Where's Dad?" Marissa asked.

"Getting groceries," Shannon answered. She had on a pale blue jogging suit in need of laundering and was sitting by the open patio doors, smoking a cigarette and drinking coffee.

"Dad said no smoking in the house," Marissa chided her.

Shannon held out her packet, and to my surprise, Marissa took one and then joined her.

"When did you start smoking?" I asked Marissa.

"I always smoked." Marissa lit the cigarette and took a long drag, then blew it out. "Remember?"

Of course I remembered. I was just surprised that she remembered. But of course, Shannon had probably helped in that regard.

"How was church?" Shannon asked in a tone that suggested she really didn't care.

"Good music." Marissa pulled a kitchen chair close to the door and sat by Shannon.

"Church music," said Shannon with disdain.

"Maya makes good music," Marissa told her.

"Yeah...yeah..." Shannon took a disinterested sip of coffee.

"Maya and Chloe and Allie have a band," Marissa continued. For her that was a pretty long and cohesive sentence.

"They *had* a band," corrected Shannon. "Maya's out of it now. Remember?"

"No." Marissa shook her head as she took in another long draw of the cigarette.

Shannon just rolled her eyes.

"Actually...," I began, thinking, *Why not just get it out in the open?* "I am back in the band."

Shannon looked up at me with wide eyes. "Bruce Glass came to his senses?"

"Sort of."

"What are you saying?" Shannon stood up and ground out her cigarette in the bowl she was using for an ashtray. "Do they want you back or what?"

I nodded. "They want me back, but—"

"He's redrawn the contract?"

"Yes, but—"

"And they'll need me to sign it?"

She looked so hopeful that I really almost hated to burst her balloon.

"Well, what, Maya? Good grief, can't you even answer a simple question?"

"Don't yell at her," scolded Marissa.

"I can yell at her if I want to," Shannon shot back. *"She's my freaking daughter!"*

Marissa frowned. "Dad said no yelling. *Remember?"*

"Fine..." Shannon lowered her voice, but her eyes narrowed and locked on me. "Tell me what's going on, Maya. Does Bruce Glass need my signature or not?"

"Actually...*not.*"

"Then they don't really want you back."

"If you'd let me, I could explain."

"That's what I've been asking you to do, Maya. For a smart girl you can be awfully thick."

"Why don't you sit back down?" I said as I pulled up a chair for myself. I waited for her to sit and then light another cigarette. "Here's the deal, Shannon. You are no longer my legal guardian."

She laughed. "Tell me another one, Maya."

"It's true." So then I explained about Judge Anderson and my emancipation.

"That's impossible."

"No, it happened. If you don't believe me, you can call Robert Bernard, and he can—"

"You can't be emancipated without my permission!"

"No yelling," protested Marissa.

"I was never informed of this!"

"No yelling." Marissa stood and shook her finger at Shannon. "I'm telling Dad."

"Tell me how this happened," seethed Shannon in a quieter voice.

"I've been planning on doing it for a long time," I explained. "You know that. Remember when you got into my things back in Beverly Hills? You knew I was working on it even then."

Shannon didn't say anything now, just silently smoked.

"I didn't do it to hurt you, Shannon. I just need to have control of my life. I've known for a long time that you're not always around when I need you."

"But I'm here now, aren't I?" She turned and stared at me. "I came here for you, didn't I?"

I pressed my lips together. I wanted to say, "No, you came here for a handout," but thankfully I didn't.

"So...now you're free of me. I suppose you think Bruce Glass will offer you a new contract."

"He already has."

She didn't say anything, just looked out the back door to the gloomy gray day that loomed outside.

"We'll start touring the end of next week. I was just telling Marissa that I'll have to e-mail her, and I was hoping you could help her to—"

"I came to this town *for you*, Maya!" She stood up again—so quickly the chair fell down behind her with a crash. "And this is the thanks I get?"

I didn't know what to say.

"I thought you and I would have a chance here," she spat, "that we could finally live together again, like mother and daughter. But no, that's not good enough for you. You're too caught up in your own life. You have your own friends. Your own job. You think it's okay to just push me away."

"I haven't meant to push you—"

"You know what your problem is, Maya? *You are just plain selfish*. You're selfish and spoiled, and you think the whole flipping world revolves around you. Like you're the princess darling and everyone should bow down to you. Well, I have news for you, sweetheart. That ain't gonna happen. No one gives a flying fig about you. No one thinks you're special. And someday you're going to figure that out, and then you'll be sorry!" She marched off and slammed a door somewhere.

"Shannon's mad at you." Marissa's expression was serious.

"I think she's mad at herself too."

Marissa simply nodded, like she understood what I meant. And maybe she did. Sometimes I think she's taking in more than we give her credit for.

Maya's Green Tip for the Day

Now this might seem like a small thing, but it's something recyclers need to know. *Most plastic lids, tops, and caps are not recyclable.* The plastic in lids and caps is different from the plastic in the bottles. Recycling centers are set up to deal with the container but not the lids. In fact, you may be putting a recycling worker at risk if you don't remove the cap before you toss that disposable water bottle into the correct container. The caps can get caught in machinery or cause explosions as temperatures increase. So next time you're separating your recyclables, be sure to remove and dispose of those caps and lids.

Fifteen

November 20

We've been on the road for almost a week now. I'm barely past the totally overwhelmed stage and moving toward the "What am I doing here?" phase. Many people assume that being in a band like Redemption must be a lot of fun. And for sure, there's fun involved, but there's also a lot of hard work.

For starters, there is so much to learn. And I don't just mean the music, although I always feel like I'm trying to catch up with that. We practice daily and up to three times a day, depending on our concert schedule. Right now we perform twice a week, but we'll be up to four times a week by late December. Already it's pretty exhausting. Plus I'm still trying to keep up with my classes at school and my green column, as well as trying to e-mail Marissa and Dominic and my dad from time to time. Not that there's been much spare time. Unless you want to give up sleeping, and I've discovered that I actually need my sleep.

I honestly don't know how Allie and Chloe do it. They make it look so easy too. How do they keep up that kind of energy and enthusiasm? They hit the stage and just start rocking out like they've been doing it all their lives. And I suppose they've been

doing it for long enough that it might feel that way to them. They were totally jazzed to end their little hiatus, and I just hope they're not disappointed to be stuck with me. I hope I can keep up.

"You're doing just fine," Elise said yesterday. Elise is Allie's mom and our chaperon until we get to Nashville, where Caitlin's best friend, Beanie Jacobs, is going to join us so that Elise can fly home to be with her family. "Just give yourself time," she told me.

"Yeah, I'm trying to do that. But I feel like I'm barely keeping up," I confessed.

"I think it takes a couple of weeks to get in the groove."

"That's what Bruce said too."

"And the first week out is the hardest."

"That doesn't seem to be the case for Allie and Chloe."

She laughed. "Those two—they do seem to thrive on this. But trust me; they'll start feeling it in a couple of weeks."

"About the same time I'll be catching up?" I said hopefully.

"That's my best guess."

"I hope so." I let out a tired sigh. Elise is the only one I've felt free to be open with about how I'm feeling. Maybe it's because I know she'll be gone after another week. Or maybe it's because she's a good listener.

"I want to tell you something," she said in a lowered voice. Not that anyone was around to hear. We were alone on the bus while Allie and Chloe were on a junk-food scavenger hunt. "But I want to tell you in confidence, okay?"

"Sure." I waited.

"When Redemption first started, Laura felt a lot like you do now."

"Exhausted?"

She nodded. "At the time, Allie was still supposed to be taking medication for hyperactivity and attention deficit disorder."

I frowned. "I guess I didn't know about that."

"Well, that was the diagnosis the doctors gave us when Allie was about ten. Now I'm not so sure. She's obviously a live wire, but when she has something like music to throw her energy into, she seems just fine."

I nodded.

"So on our first road trip, I brought Allie's Ritalin along with us. She wasn't too pleased about it and said she didn't want to take it anymore, but I nagged her to stick with it because I was worried that her hyperactivity would drive all of us nuts. As you know, this bus is a rather confined space. Anyway, the tour continued, and I assumed that Allie was taking her meds."

"She wasn't?"

Elise shook her head. "But the pills were disappearing, so I just thought it was Allie."

"But it wasn't her?"

"No. It turned out to be Laura."

I blinked. "Really? Laura was taking Ritalin?"

"Yes. You might not know this, but Ritalin calms down people with ADD-ADHD, like Allie. But for a normal person—"

"It's a stimulant," I finished for her. "An upper."

She nodded, then peered curiously at me.

"My mother has used all kinds of things like that," I explained.

"So you know about addiction?"

"More than I'd like to know." I told her about my mother's arrest and subsequent prison sentence.

"I didn't know about that."

"So, are you telling me Laura's story as a warning?" I grinned at her. "Because I can assure you, I will never fall for something that dumb."

"Laura felt like that too."

"And I can understand that. But honestly, I cannot imagine ever doing that."

She smiled. "That's good to know."

"And you can trust me not to repeat Laura's story."

"Well, it's not that it's some deep, dark secret. Laura actually confessed her addiction problem to a packed-out concert. And the response was incredible. Still, I feel that it's her story to tell. Although I know she wouldn't mind that I told you."

Just then Allie and Chloe burst onto the bus with two bags of junk food. I guess that's their addiction, and I try not to pick on them for it.

"We did bring something for you, Maya." Chloe held up a bottle of my favorite brand of green tea.

Allie handed me a bag of Sun Chips. "It's kind of like junk food." Then she pulled out a bag of Cheetos for herself. "But it can't compare to these bad boys."

November 28

Yesterday was Thanksgiving, and I was reminded that I have so much to be thankful for. When I consider what my life was like just one year ago compared to what it is now…I am amazed and grateful. Last year at this time, I was still living with Shannon. I was working fiendishly and saving my money in the hope that I'd get away from my mother before her life turned into a real train wreck. Unfortunately I was too late. The train wrecked, and she took me down with her. But that wasn't the worst part. I know now that the worst part was going through all that crud without God. Without God I was so lost and alone and afraid. Of course, I was clueless at the time. But I know now that *with God* I can go through some pretty hard times and emerge stronger, healthier, and wiser. Right now I'm praying that God will strengthen me for this tour. And I'm trying to keep up a brave front for Chloe and Allie's sake.

"Are you doing okay?" Chloe asked me as we ate breakfast at a McDonald's about thirty miles out of Nashville (today's destination).

"Sure," I told her. "I'm fine."

"You seem tired," Allie said.

I forced what I hoped looked like an energetic smile. "I'm okay," I assured them.

"Tomorrow is Rendezvous." Allie poured more syrup over her pancakes.

I nodded. Rendezvous is big. It's this annual get-together of Christian rock bands, and Redemption has been one of the front-liners for the past couple of years. Also, according to Bruce,

"everyone who is anyone" will be there. I know that I need to be in top form. This could be a make-or-break for me.

"The good thing about Rendezvous," said Chloe as if sensing my concerns, "is that our performances are short."

"That's right," Allie said. "One twenty-minute set on both Saturday and Sunday, and then we're done."

"And then we have a couple days off," added Chloe.

"And then things speed up." Allie peered curiously at me now. "You're not sorry you joined us, are you?"

"No," I said quickly. "Not at all. You guys are amazing. I just don't want to be the weak link, you know?"

Chloe laughed. "That's exactly what Laura said when we first started touring."

"But she eventually got it together," said Allie.

"And you will too," Chloe assured me. "Don't be so hard on yourself."

"Totally," said Allie. "We think you're doing great. Bruce said we're sounding better than ever."

So I'm trying to think positively. And even though Chloe and Allie went to see a movie tonight, I opted to stay in, to catch up on e-mail and things. And to go to bed early. I want to be in top form tomorrow. I owe this to the band.

November 30

I am so relieved to say not only did I make it through Rendezvous—I did it with energy and enthusiasm that felt fairly

genuine. Maybe it was being around all those other musicians or being moved by some incredible talent, but I just felt like things were falling into place. Kind of like it was starting to click.

Our second concert was midafternoon today. After that we all just did our own thing. Chloe hung with Jeremy (from Iron Cross). Allie was pretty much all over the place. And I got acquainted with another musician whose music was totally inspiring. Her name is Anna Gilbert, and she's in her midtwenties, a few years older than Allie and Chloe but still relatively new to the music world.

"Your style is amazing," I told her as we met for coffee. "I bought your latest CD, and I can't wait to hear it."

"Thanks. And Redemption is sounding really good too."

"But different?" I queried.

"A little different."

"Good different?" Okay, my insecurities were showing.

"I think so." She paused as if considering her words. "They've always had a pretty vivacious kind of high-energy sound. But they seem a little mellower now." She smiled, and her eyes twinkled. "But I like that kind of sound."

"I know." I nodded. "I actually like a mellower kind of music too."

She looked surprised.

"You're probably wondering why I'm rocking out in Redemption."

"You seemed comfortable up there with them."

"The truth is, I don't really feel like I fit in that well. I mean, today was the best it's been. But I feel kind of like a fraud."

"A fraud?"

"Because I don't think I'm really a rocker chick at heart."

She laughed. "Well, you fooled the audience."

"I just hope I can keep up that act."

She looked thoughtful now. "Why?"

I considered this. "That's a good question... I guess for Chloe and Allie's sake. For the band."

"But if your heart's not in it?"

I didn't say anything.

"What kind of music do you love, Maya? I mean, really, really love. What kind of music speaks to you?"

"Well, your music for starters."

"Thanks. But besides that. What do you love to listen to? And sing?"

"I've always liked Norah Jones and Corinne Bailey Rae—kind of jazzy, bluesy, you know?"

"Totally."

"And Natalie Merchant and..." I began listing off a bunch of others. And she added some of her favorites to the list, and I could tell we had similar taste.

"Okay, I don't want to tell you what to do, Maya. But it seems to me that if God has really called you to be part of Redemption, your heart will be in it."

I swallowed my last sip of now lukewarm mocha, then nodded.

She was digging in her oversize bag now. "Here," she said as she slid a pale green CD across the table.

I read the title aloud: *"Falling in a Beautiful Place."*

"That's the first CD I ever made."

"I didn't see this on the sales table."

"It wasn't there. But I want you to have it."

"Thanks."

"Listen to the first song, okay?"

"I'll listen to the whole album," I assured her.

"But really listen to the first song. I think you'll relate to it."

"Okay."

"I know you're going to figure this out, Maya. And I'll be praying for you."

"Thanks. I appreciate that."

She glanced at her watch. "And now if I don't hurry, my sweet hubby will think I've forgotten him."

"You're married?"

She grinned. "Yeah, are you thinking I'm too young?"

I laughed. "Hey, I'm still just sixteen. I'd be the last person to tell anyone they were too young for anything."

We hugged, and Anna told me that she was going to open for Redemption in Atlanta next month. "So I'll see you in a few weeks," she called out as she left. And I took her CD up to the hotel room, popped it in the player, and listened to the whole CD.

Then I went back and listened to the first song with the lyric sheet open so I could sing along. And she was right. It was just what I needed to hear. And something I need to think and pray about.

Here is how it goes.

Myself

Verse 1:

I'm tired of deception

And secrecy

Behind closed doors

I am not me

I'm tired of living

I just lie to myself

I want authenticity

To be happy

To be Yours

With You in me

I just want to live

Totally

Myself

Chorus:

Life gets so shady

And blue

I want to be someone

More like You

I want to be free
To be totally
Myself

Verse 2:
All the impurities
Complexities
I want to move on
To the simple things
I want to discover
Entirely
Myself
I just want to rest at ease
And not people please
I want to be whole
With just You and me
We'd fit so perfectly
I'd be naturally
Myself

Maya's Green Tip for the Day

Have you seen the light yet? If not, it's time to start replacing your old-fashioned incandescent light bulbs with CFL (compact fluorescent light) bulbs. These bulbs cost a little more (in the short run), but they produce less heat and last a lot longer than regular bulbs. Just think, you'll never walk into your bedroom, flick on a switch, and be left in the dark (well, not until you go off to college anyway). Also, watch for the next-generation halogen bulbs. These will be more efficient, and the light they put out is much friendlier on the eyes. Either way you go, you'll save a lot of electricity and money in the long run.

Sixteen

December 2

Yesterday morning we dropped Elise at the Nashville airport, and then four hours later we picked up Beanie Jacobs, our new chaperon. Here is my first impression of Beanie: she looks kind of like Minnie Driver, and she is New York chic.

"Maya Stark," she said even before we were introduced. "I've been dying to meet you."

I suddenly felt tongue-tied.

She laughed. "Because of Caitlin. She's told me a lot about you."

"Oh." I smiled. "She's told me a lot about you too."

"Beanie's a famous fashion designer," Allie said as we waited for her bags.

"You mean *almost* famous." Beanie pushed a dark strand of hair away from her face and adjusted the strap of what looked like an authentic retro bag from the forties. "I was working with this awesome up-and-coming designer and feeling like I was on top of the world, and then, *wham, bam,* I got toppled by one of his assistants." She sighed. "But Caitlin probably told you the whole story."

"I heard some of it," admitted Chloe, "but not everything."

So Beanie proceeded to tell us about how she and the designer, Leo, were really working in sync and how much she was learning from him and how he was totally into green design and fair trade and recycled products (something I personally appreciate) and how they were just developing this new line when his assistant, Monica, began dating him. "Despite my assurances to Monica that my relationship with Leo was purely professional, she started getting jealous. I could've handled that, but when she started to use her romance with Leo as an excuse to push her design ideas onto me, I had to put my foot down." Beanie leaped forward to snag a cool tapestry bag from the carousel. "And finally I decided it just wasn't worth it. It seemed like God was trying to tell me something—like, get outta town, Beanie!"

"I think God was just telling you to come back to Redemption," Allie said.

"That's right," Chloe agreed. "We're in need of your fashion advice more than ever now."

"Wait'll you see my sketches," she called out as she nabbed a huge red duffel bag. "Well, that's all my bags."

"Man, I hope so." Chloe frowned at the enormous bag. "Don't forget we're traveling on the bus."

"If you knew what was in that bag, you'd offer to carry it for me." Beanie hoisted it onto the luggage cart.

As it turned out, her bag was full of fabrics and finds that she planned to use for us. And after just twenty-four hours, she's already got us looking way better than before. She's amazing. She just picks up a piece of fabric along with some interesting notions and then attaches them to a recycled T-shirt, and, voilà, it's a one-of-a-kind incredible creation. Not only are we dressing way better than before, but it's like she brings this whole new zest and energy to the band. And I feel like I'm fitting in better now. Like maybe I've made it over some kind of a hump or just turned a corner and this really is the right thing for me. It's possible I was just having the jitters before. But even as I write this down tonight, I'm not totally sure. And that bugs me. Still, I'm praying about it. I am committed to do all I can to be a highly functioning part of Redemption and do my very best. Really, what more can I do?

December 13

Yesterday I turned seventeen. A small step for most teenagers but a giant step for Maya Stark. For some reason seventeen feels so much older than sixteen to me. And it feels good.

"Sorry you can't have your birthday off," Chloe told me as we ate breakfast in the bus. We were on our way to Raleigh, North Carolina, where we were scheduled for three concerts. Last night our band performed alone. Tonight we'll perform with Iron Cross, which has got Chloe all charged up. She's been missing Jeremy a lot since Nashville. But back to yesterday...my birthday.

"Anyway," Allie said, "we decided that since it's your birthday, you can pick the closing song for tomorrow night's concert. So what'll it be?"

I just shrugged. "I don't know."

"What about one of the Anna Gilbert songs?" asked Chloe.

"You'd have to get permission," Beanie called out from where she was stitching something together.

"Bruce can do that," Chloe called back to her.

"But we haven't practiced her songs," I pointed out. Although I have to admit the idea of singing one of Anna's songs in a concert was appealing.

"I've heard you practicing them." Allie refilled her bowl with more Froot Loops. (I've already told her that Froot Loops are not real fruit, but she doesn't seem to care.)

"Not really practicing," I corrected. "I just like to play some of them sometimes. The lyrics connect with me."

Chloe spread peanut butter on her toast. "So why don't you pick one that you're comfortable with and do a solo, and we'll do backup."

"A solo?" I frowned at her. "I thought this was supposed to be a birthday present."

"You don't *want* to do a solo?" Allie shook her spoon at me. "*Everyone* wants to do a solo."

"Not everyone." Chloe made a face at Allie. "Some people are just better at backup."

Suddenly I realized I really did want to do a solo, especially if it could be an Anna song. "I think I'd like to do it."

"Great." Allie made a face at Chloe like she'd won this round.

"So which song will it be?" asked Chloe.

"Well, you've heard the CD, and you know that the songs aren't really Redemption sort of songs," I reminded them. "Anna's style is different."

"Just put the CD on, and we'll pick one," suggested Chloe.

So I put it in, and before long Allie and Chloe both wanted to do an upbeat song called "Give a Little."

"It sounds like a good birthday song to me," Chloe declared after we ran through it a couple of times.

And so last night I did my first solo with Redemption. And the response of the crowd was really positive. So much so that I think Chloe felt a little threatened afterward. Okay, *threatened* is not the right word. But I think she was a little concerned. And that surprised me.

"It's okay doing songs like that once in a while," she told me this morning. "But we need to remember that Redemption has its own unique sound. Like Willy used to say, 'Keep the cookies where the kiddies can reach 'em.'"

"What's that supposed to mean?" I asked.

"That we need to deliver what the audience wants," explained Allie. She kind of rolled her eyes then. "But to be honest, it sometimes feels like a sellout to me."

"The fact is, we're a girls' gospel rock band," continued Chloe. "And that's what works with our fans. It's why they buy Redemption concert tickets and CDs. It's what they want. We don't want to mess with it."

Okay, I know Chloe's not focused only on money, but her comments do make me wonder. It also made me want to sing the chorus of "Give a Little" to her again. Anyway, here's the song I sang for my birthday solo:

Give a Little
By Anna Gilbert

Verse 1:
Everybody's talking like they know just what to do
Everyone's saying that they have the key to truth
People buying lies that they see on the TV screen
People are believing that money is the only thing
But they don't realize that there's so much more to life

Chorus:
You gotta give a little
Step outta the middle
Holding on to everything
Will show no return, yeah
Take a stand for something
It's all or nothing.

You know you gotta be the change
That you want to see

Verse 2:
People are starting wars, calling brothers their enemies
People losing hope when they can't change what they see.
"Outta sight outta mind" is the worst lie to consume
Gotta try, gotta find a way to make some room
'Cause we don't realize that there's so much more to life.

December 16

We've been on the road for over a month now. In some ways it seems more like a year, and in some ways it seems like a week. But I'm starting to enjoy myself more, and at our manager's suggestion, I've even done a couple more solos. As a result it feels almost like I'm pulling my weight. And the fans seem to agree, because Redemption's popularity is as high as ever—at least that's what Bruce says. He also said that it's okay for Redemption "to evolve." He said this in response to Chloe's claim that Redemption needed to stay the same way it had been in the past.

I could tell by the look in her eyes that Bruce's comment might have hurt her feelings. And I felt kind of guilty, but at the same time, it's not like I can help what I am…or the way I do music…or even what the fans like. It's not like I'm trying to take over Redemption. I totally respect that Chloe started this band. I'm fully aware that I'm the newcomer. But it was kind of freeing to hear Bruce

say that. So when we did a joint concert with Iron Cross last night, it felt good to do another solo—this time with a song I'd written. And it felt good to hear the audience respond so positively to it.

Afterward we were having coffee in the hotel coffee shop with some of the guys from Iron Cross, and Jeremy mentioned my performance. "That was an awesome solo," he told me. "And the lyrics to that song were very cool. Who wrote it anyway?"

"Maya did," offered Allie.

"You're a songwriter too?" Jeremy seemed unduly impressed, and I suddenly felt Chloe watching me.

"I just dabble at it," I said quickly. "Chloe's the real songwriter of the band." I turned to her. "Like how many have you written by now? A couple hundred?"

She just shrugged.

"Did you guys know Maya's dad is Nick Stark?" Allie asked them.

"No way!" Now Jeremy looked even more impressed.

"That's crazy," said Michael, another member of Iron Cross. "Wasn't he popular in the seventies or eighties?"

I nodded. "I know. My dad's music is a little—"

"His music is great," Jeremy interrupted. "I kid you not. I've been a Nick Stark fan for years."

I had to laugh at that. "No way. My dad's music was way before your time."

"What Jeremy means is that our *parents* were fans," explained

Isaiah. He's Jeremy's younger brother. "But Jeremy was such a music geek that he'd listen to anything."

"Thanks, bro." He shook his head.

Isaiah grimaced now. "Hey, I'm sorry, Maya. I didn't mean to sound like your dad wasn't any—"

"It's okay," I assured him. "I tease Dad all the time about his geriatric music. I've even told him that he should cross-market his CDs with Depends."

This got a good laugh from the table.

"But seriously," Jeremy said again, "I was a Nick Stark fan. I used to sing along to his records."

"That's true," said Isaiah. "Back in grade school, he'd crank up the old vinyl and just rock out. I remember him pretending the TV remote was his mike." Isaiah continued to tease his older brother until we were all laughing so hard that I thought the manager of the coffee shop was about to throw us out. Then I noticed that Chloe wasn't really laughing. Oh, she kind of acted like she was, but her eyes were sad. And as we continued to joke around, I realized that Jeremy was paying too much attention to me. I had a feeling that was bothering Chloe, so I tried to put the spotlight back on her. "You guys should hear this new song that Chloe's working on. It's going to be really awesome."

But when they asked her about it, she just brushed them off and changed the subject.

"Okay, girls." Beanie came over to join us now. She'd been checking e-mail on her BlackBerry. "I hate to be the party pooper, but it's nearly midnight, and we have to hit the road to make it to Orlando by morning."

"And we'll catch up with you girls down there on Friday," Jeremy assured us.

So here I am at three in the morning, sitting in the front of the bus as we roll on down the highway. For some reason I couldn't sleep, which is why I'm writing in my diary as well as praying that things will be okay between Chloe and me. I know she's not mad at me or anything like that, but it does feel like she's treating me differently. Like maybe she wishes I hadn't been invited to join Redemption, like maybe she thinks I don't really fit in or that I'm changing something as far as the dynamics of the band...or that I might try to come between her and Jeremy, which is so not possible. Okay, maybe I'm just tired and a little paranoid. I'll pray about this and try to get some sleep. Tomorrow is another big day.

Maya's Green Tip for the Day

I'm dreaming of a green Christmas. And shouldn't we all? This will be my first Christmas as a Christian, and I've been comparing what I know about the first Christmas (Christ's birth) to what I see today. What a contrast! But why can't we be more like the first one—greener, simpler, happier? Here are some suggestions: (1) Recycle old Christmas cards by cutting them up and remaking them into new ones. Think collage, scrapbook, recycled paper, and voilà, you have some masterpieces to give to loved ones. (2) Use things like newspaper, craft paper, or even fabric to wrap gifts. (3) Instead of big glitzy bows on packages (which usually get tossed), why not decorate a gift with something natural like a snip of evergreen, twigs, pine cones, or whatever's available in your yard. (4) And speaking of gifts, make sure you're thinking green while you shop—meaning, why not consider reusable possibilities in thrift shops or create an art object from recycled materials? Not only will your gift be environmentally friendly, but it'll save you some money too.

Seventeen

December 19

Today was not a good day. Okay, there were some pretty cool things that happened. But all in all, not a good day. In some ways it was pretty disturbing. Thankfully, we're staying in a hotel tonight, which means there's a little more space. And believe me, I'm keeping some space between Chloe and me.

It all started during our rehearsal at Disney World this morning. The guys from Iron Cross had arrived, and Bruce decided that Redemption and Iron Cross should actually do a couple of numbers together—kind of share the stage during the transition from one band to the other tonight. And really, it wasn't a bad idea. Or so it seemed.

"I want to try Maya and Jeremy together on this song," suggested Larry (the manager of Iron Cross). "I think their voices would be good together."

Well, I was thinking no big deal. I mean, we're professionals, aren't we? Chloe's been in the biz long enough to know that this isn't personal, right? Wrong...wrong, wrong, wrong.

"That was superb," said Larry after Jeremy and I finished the first run-through. "Those kids sound so good together, we should

consider recording something." He said this more to Bruce than to us.

"I could get into that," said Jeremy with enthusiasm. "Doing an album with Nick Stark's daughter." He punched his brother in the arm. "Wait until the parents hear about this, eh?"

So we rehearsed some more. And I could tell that Chloe was kind of shutting down. Like she wasn't really herself. And it was showing in her music too.

"You feeling okay today?" Bruce asked her during a break.

"I'm fine," she snapped.

And so it went. Oh, she never said anything mean to me. She never did anything to offend anyone. But she was having a very off day. I felt certain that it was my fault. And that feels lousy.

"Okay, guys," said Jeremy as we finished up, "I don't know about everyone else, but I plan to hit MGM this afternoon."

"You mean Hollywood Studios," Isaiah corrected.

"Yeah, whatever." Jeremy grinned. "Rock 'n' Roller Coaster, here I come!"

"You girls coming too?" asked Michael hopefully.

"I'm in," said Allie.

"Sounds fun to me," called out Beanie from where she was sitting in the front row of the concert hall.

I glanced over at Chloe. With her back to me, she appeared to be absorbed in putting away her guitar, carefully snapping the case.

"How about it?" asked Jeremy. "Chloe and Maya? You girls brave enough to take on the Tower of Terror with us?"

"Come on." Isaiah nudged me with his elbow. "You know what they say about all work and no play, Maya."

"Okay," I agreed. The truth is, it sounded like fun. Besides that, I've never been to that park before. Not in California. And not here.

"Chloe?" Jeremy persisted. "Aren't you coming too?"

She stood up, turned around, and ran her hand through her hair. "I have a killer headache."

"I think Chloe needs to take it easy," said Bruce. "I recommend some Advil and a nice long nap," he told her. "You don't seem like yourself today. And we need you in top form tonight."

"I hope you're not coming down with something." Beanie came onto the stage and looked closely at Chloe, even putting her hand on her forehead. "It is flu season, you know."

"I'll just lay low this afternoon," Chloe said quietly. "You guys go ahead and have a good time."

"I'll stay with you," offered Beanie.

"No," Chloe said firmly. "Go ahead. I'll be fine."

"And if you get to feeling better, you could catch up with us," suggested Allie. "I'll have my cell phone on."

"Sure." Chloe nodded without enthusiasm.

So we took off. And I felt like I was about twelve years old as we did all the crazy rides and ate junk food and basically acted like middle-school kids. It was great.

"We have time for one more ride," Jeremy told the group. "I think I'll head for Tower of Terror again."

"Not me," said Beanie. "My stomach's still reeling from that last ride. I'll sit this one out."

"I'm with you," said Michael. "Besides, I need a hot dog."

"I want to ride the roller coaster once more." I looked at Allie. "Want to come with me?"

"I have to do Tower of Terror again," she admitted. "It's such a jolt."

"Me too," said Isaiah.

So we made a plan to meet up in thirty minutes, and I headed over to get in line for the Rock 'n' Roller Coaster. But to my surprise, Jeremy came along.

"I didn't think you should ride alone," he told me.

"That's okay," I assured him. "I'm fine. Go ahead and do the Tower of—"

"No, I think I'd rather do this one."

So I didn't argue. "This has been so fun," I told him. "I'm sure you guys have done stuff like this dozens of times. But it's actually a first for me."

He looked puzzled. "What do you mean? You've never been here before?"

"The last time I was in a theme park was Disneyland when I was about six."

"Seriously?"

I nodded. "It sounds lame, but it's true."

"I would've figured…you know, with your dad…that you'd have been everywhere and done everything."

So I explained how it really was. Oh, I didn't go into all the details. But I let him know that being the child of a professional musician wasn't exactly a walk in the park.

"I guess that makes sense," he admitted as we moved forward in the line. "I mean, I couldn't imagine doing what I do—being on the road so much—and having a wife and kids. It would be all wrong."

"It's kind of stressful on relationships."

Then he told me about his parents and how he was raised in a fairly normal, middle-class Christian home.

"That's what I used to dream of having," I told him as we were nearly to the front of the line. Then I told him about how much more normal my life became when I moved in with my cousin and uncle. "I don't think I'll ever have anything completely normal, but being part of a family felt pretty good." I also told him a little about Dominic and how I've sometimes envied his family.

"Is that your boyfriend?"

I smiled. "Well, if I was going to have a boyfriend, which isn't really my plan, I guess Dominic would be the guy."

"Lucky guy." He nodded. "But I think you're smart to keep that sort of thing at a distance for the time being. A lot of kids rush the romance, and it can really mess up a good relationship."

"I know exactly what you mean!" I exclaimed as we were directed to our seats on the ride. And then conversation became impossible because the roller coaster took off, and we were both holding on and listening to the screams of the other riders. Bruce

had made it clear to Allie and me that we were *not to scream* on the rides. "You could damage your vocal cords," he warned us. And I took him seriously.

"That was awesome!" I told Jeremy when we finally rolled to a stop. "Thanks for coming with me. It really does make it more fun to do it with a friend."

Then he put his arm around me and gave me a nice sideways squeeze. Like a brotherly hug. "I like having you for a friend," he told me.

Then as we were getting off, I noticed Chloe standing down below, watching us. And she did not look happy.

"Hey, Chloe," called out Jeremy with a big wave.

I smiled and waved too. But when we joined her, she was acting really stiff and formal.

"Are you feeling better?" Jeremy asked her.

"A little," she said. "I thought I'd come out and get some fresh air." She looked at me funny now. "I guess I made it just in time."

"Just in time to head back to the hotel with us." Jeremy gave her a sideways hug too, but then he kept his arm around her as they walked. Then I spotted Beanie and Michael and hurried over to join them.

On the shuttle back to the hotel, I sat with Beanie. And I'm sure I looked a little frustrated because she finally asked if something was wrong.

"I think Chloe is mad at me," I told her quietly. Not that there

was much chance of being heard since Chloe and the others were up in front and Beanie and I were clear in the back.

"Why's that?"

"Remember what you told us about your job in New York?"

She nodded.

"Well, I think Chloe might be worried I'm doing the same thing."

"Same thing?"

"When we were rehearsing earlier, I think it bothered her that I did a song with Jeremy. Then she saw me on the roller coaster with him. And he gave me a little hug—just a brotherly hug—and she might have read it wrong."

"But they're sitting together now."

I nodded. "Yes, but I'm afraid she might think I'm after him or something."

"Are you?"

I shook my head. "No, of course not."

"Well, that's a relief. I mean, he's a lot older than you and—"

"That has nothing to do with it," I clarified. "I'm just really not into him." Then I told her a little about Dominic and how much I missed him.

She smiled. "Maybe you need to let Chloe know that too."

"Okay...I'll try."

But when I tried to speak to her privately shortly before our performance, it only seemed to make matters worse.

"Do you think I'm jealous of you?" she asked me point-blank.

"No, I didn't mean it like that."

"What did you mean then?"

"I just meant to tell you that I'm not into Jeremy, okay?"

Her brows shot up. "Do you think you're too good for him?"

"No, nothing like that."

"Why are you telling me this then? Why is it so important for you to let me know that you really like Dominic?"

"I don't know... I guess I thought it would make you feel better."

"Because you think I'm jealous of you?" she said again.

"I don't know. Maybe it felt like you were mad at me. And I just wanted to make things better."

"Maybe I'm just having a bad day," she said.

"Yeah, maybe so. I hope it gets better."

But it did not get better. Chloe wasn't quite her vivacious self in our performance tonight. To make up for it, Allie and I both tried really hard to bring up the energy level. And maybe we succeeded. But all in all, I think our portion of the concert was just so-so.

However, the songs we did with Iron Cross did seem to raise the enthusiasm level of the crowd. And then when Jeremy and I did our duet, we got a standing ovation. He looked at me and asked if I wanted to do another. Fortunately, we know some of the same songs, so we just went for it. And once again the crowd was pleased. But I just bowed and made my way offstage, stepping into the shadows as I watched Iron Cross continuing their performance.

"I think Bruce is right," Chloe said to me.

I jumped because I hadn't even known she was standing there. "What?"

"You and Jeremy. You do make a good pair. And he certainly likes you. Maybe you two *should* consider doing an album together." Then she abruptly turned away and walked off. I felt like I'd been slapped. I started to say something to Allie, who was standing nearby, but she just gave me a questioning look and took off after Chloe.

Then I went over to join Beanie, who seemed to have witnessed the whole thing. "What do I do now?"

She just shrugged. "I don't know that there's much you can do. Maybe just wait until Chloe cools down."

I really didn't want to go back to our hotel room, so Beanie and I stuck around until the Iron Cross concert ended. But then I was ready to leave. I didn't want to take a chance of being seen by anyone while having any kind of interaction with Jeremy at all. Oh, Chloe's concerns were unfounded. But situations like this can get ugly quick. Maybe it was already ugly.

"I just want to get things straightened out with her," I told Beanie as we walked through the lobby to the elevators. "I want her to understand that I am not the least bit interested in Jeremy."

"It might be more complicated than that." Beanie paused by one of the big plush couches. "Want to sit down?"

I nodded.

"I don't think Chloe's *only* worried about Jeremy, Maya."

"What else then?"

"I think she feels threatened by you."

I let out a long sigh. "Because my style is different than hers?"

"That, and because you're talented, and because she's used to running the show with Redemption. I'm sure it's all pretty hard on her."

"It's hard on me too."

Beanie nodded. "It's a tough situation. Trust me, I know."

"So what can I do?"

"Besides pray about it?"

"I've been doing that."

Beanie smiled and patted my shoulder. "That might be about it for now. You might have to wait for Chloe to make the next move."

"Do you think I should quit the band?" I asked suddenly. "I mean, that's kind of what you did, right? In a similar situation... you left New York, right?"

"It was a similar situation but not exactly the same, Maya. You're under contract, remember?"

I nodded. "For almost two more months."

"It might be a long two months."

I could feel tears in my eyes now. I looked down at my lap and bit into my lip, hoping I could keep from crying.

"Let's pray about this," she suggested quietly. "I know that's what Caitlin would do right now."

I nodded and blinked back the tears.

"Dear Father God," she began. "Please help Maya through this rough spell with Chloe. Show Maya what she can do to make things better. And please help Chloe to see that Maya doesn't want to threaten her. Please send Your healing touch to their relationship so that they can minister through their music." Then she said, "Amen."

"Thanks." I wiped my wet cheeks.

"I suspect that God is going to use this." We headed for the elevators. "That's usually the case when we hit hard times."

"I sure hope so."

But when we got to our suite, Allie and Chloe were in their room. I could see the light beneath the door, and I could hear their voices, whispering in that way that makes me think they were talking about me. And they probably were.

"Don't worry," Beanie assured me. "It'll look better in the morning."

I nodded and tried to pretend like I believed her, but I was doubtful. Even so, I've been praying. I've decided that all I want is God's will. Just His perfect will. Nothing more. Nothing less.

Maya's Green Tip for the Day

'Tis the season to think about Christmas trees...and the environment. But what's the most green—fake trees, real trees, or live ones? Some people assume that fakes are the best option because they're reusable and prevent the wasteful harvesting of trees. But what consumers may not know is that most fakes are made in places like China, where environmental standards are minimal at best. Products like PVC (polyvinyl chloride) and other forms of nonrenewable, petroleum-based plastic are used to manufacture these fake "evergreens." Not only are carcinogens polluting the products, but they're endangering the workers in the factories that make them. So what about real Christmas trees from tree farms? Unfortunately, there are often chemicals involved (fertilizers and pesticides), and unless the used trees are recycled (by mulching them into compost), they ultimately become waste. However, some farmers are going green, and some states allow thoughtful harvesting from the forests. Plus, trees are a renewable resource. But the greenest trees (and also the most expensive) are live trees. Just remember that they're only good for about a week inside the house before the warm temperatures disturb their growth cycle.

Eighteen

December 21

Last night was our joint concert with Anna Gilbert. She opened for us, and then, once again for a transition, we did some songs together. Including one number with just Anna and me. And I have to say it felt the best of all the songs I have done. I felt like my most authentic self as I sang with her. The lyrics, the style…it all just seemed right. I wish that I could perform like that all the time.

After our concert ended, Chloe and Allie returned to our hotel suite. I suspected it was to get away from me. They're avoiding me. Not in a mean way—at least I don't think so—but more like an uncomfortable way. Or that's what I'm telling myself. That's what I'm hoping.

Anyway, I decided to hang with Anna for a while. She and Beanie and I decided to pig out on ice cream.

"You are one awesome performer," said Beanie as we sat down with our sundaes. "I think I've just become a huge fan."

"Thanks." Anna smiled as she dipped her spoon.

"And you know I'm already a fan," I told her.

"So how's it going with you?" she asked me. "Have things fallen into place for you with Redemption?"

So I told her about how the sound of the band has changed some. "And our manager is okay with that, but..."

"But?"

"It feels like I'm kind of rocking the boat."

Anna nodded like she understood.

"You are so lucky," I told her. "I mean, to be able to do what you're doing with the kind of freedom that you have."

"Blessed," she reminded me. "But I'm sure you could do it too...if you wanted it badly enough."

"I don't know." I frowned.

"What do you really want, Maya?" She asked this in an urgent way, as if I could simply decide what I want and then just go for it. And maybe I can. Or not.

"You know...if you'd asked me that same thing a few weeks ago, I might've given you a very specific answer in regard to my own music and where I'd like to be with it someday. But more recently...well, all I really want is just to do what God wants me to do. That's all. His will."

Her eyes twinkled like she got this. "Cool."

I sighed. "Now if I could just figure out what God's will for me is."

"He'll show you," Anna assured me, "in His timing."

"Thankfully, God doesn't throw it all at us at once." Beanie laughed. "I'm sure I'd be a basket case if He did."

Anna nodded. "For sure."

We talked some more about how we discern God's will for our lives, and Anna finally said, "I believe it's planted deep inside you, Maya—something that God put there like a mysterious kind of programming. Kind of like that scripture that says trust God, and He will give you the secret desires of your heart."

"That makes sense," agreed Beanie. "Like I love doing design— I always have. But sometimes I try to make my career happen in my own strength, and it falls apart. But when I trust God about it, I end up touring with an awesome Christian rock band and designing for some very cool girls." She grinned at me.

Anna continued. "And I think that sometimes we don't even know what the secret desires of our hearts are, especially if they're buried deep within us, but we can trust that God does. And the better we get to know Him, the easier it is for Him to reveal those desires along with His will to us. Does that make sense?"

I paused to let the words soak in. "Yeah...I think I get it."

"Man, Maya." Beanie gave me an odd look. "Does Anna remind you of anyone we know?"

I laughed. "You mean Caitlin?"

She nodded. "Do you think they could've been twins separated at birth?"

Now Anna laughed. "I think my mom would've told me about that."

"Well, I hope you and Caitlin get to meet someday," Beanie told her. "It would be like a family reunion."

Then it was time to say good night. I thanked Anna again, and we promised to stay in touch.

And today as we're heading back to Nashville for two pre-Christmas concerts followed by a short break back home, the bus is very quiet. I know Chloe is avoiding me, and I think Allie feels caught in the middle. They've been holed up in the master bedroom in back. Beanie's reading a novel. And I've been up here at the dining table just doing homework, writing my column, catching up on e-mail, and writing in my journal. I have no idea how this thing with Chloe is going to resolve. But I am trusting God for the outcome. I know He can handle it.

December 23

To my complete surprise, we had someone else join us in last night's concert. Laura, who is on winter break, flew to Nashville to perform with us. Everyone acted surprised, but I have a feeling that Chloe and Allie knew what was up. In fact, I was pretty sure they helped arrange it. Anyway, I was trying not to feel bad about this. Laura was in the band long before me. To be honest, not to mention insecure, I've sometimes wondered if the fact that Laura and I share the same African American heritage had something to do with me being picked to replace her. But Laura was friendly and cheerful, and I was actually relieved to have her here. I thought it might balance things out.

Plus it was nice not to play bass, which I've been doing off and on since this tour began. Instead, we had Laura on bass and

Chloe and me on guitar. Naturally, Chloe was *lead* guitar. I know I'm not ready for that. As we played, the band sounded more like it had been originally—before I came on board. I sort of stepped back a little and let the others take over. I told myself it was Laura's turn to shine. But the truth is…it hurt a little.

"You've gotten really good," Laura said to me afterward.

"Thanks. It was fun having you with us tonight." Okay, "fun" might've been an overstatement. But what was I going to say?

"It was fun for me too." Laura laughed. "Quite a change of pace after finals week, which I'm so glad is over with."

"Are you going to play with us tomorrow night too?" I tried to make this question sound more enthusiastic than I felt.

Laura glanced over at Bruce then. We were all sitting around a big table in the hotel restaurant having a late-night snack.

Bruce shrugged. "I don't see why not. The crowd seemed to like it well enough tonight. If you girls are happy, I'm happy."

At that point Laura, Allie, and Chloe began talking to each other in that enthused I-haven't-seen-you-for-so-long sort of way. They wanted to hear all about Laura's school, and she wanted to hear all about the tour—and the three of them were talking all at once. And I began to feel kind of out of it and displaced. I also felt tired. I wished Beanie were there, but she was in our suite, putting some finishing touches on tomorrow night's costumes.

"I think I'll call it a night," I told everyone, excusing myself. Then I went up to our suite and into my room, where I put on my nightgown, got into bed, and cried. I'm not even sure why I cried.

I just did. And in a way it felt good to cry—like a cleansing sort of cry. I told God, once again, that I only wanted His will. More than anything I want to be in His will. And before I went to sleep, I felt a sense of peace. I felt like I really was in His will…or that He would work His will through me. Whatever it was, I felt like it would be okay.

So this morning comes, and we're supposed to rehearse at ten, and I realize that Laura and Allie have already gone down. Beanie stays behind to work on some sketches for our outfits for the following year. "I want to make you guys really sizzle," she says as she continues to draw.

And Chloe, who's sitting on the couch, says nothing. In fact, she looks kind of like she's mad. And I suddenly just want to get away from her.

"I guess I'll go down to practice," I say to no one in particular.

"Wait." Chloe stands and looks at me.

And so I wait.

"I need to talk to you, Maya." Her tone and expression are serious.

"Okay…"

Then she asks me to sit down, and once we're both seated, I prepare myself for the worst.

"I need to apologize to you," she begins.

Okay, I have no idea what I should say or how to respond.

"Remember when I asked you if you thought I was jealous?"

I just nod.

"And I was acting all self-righteous and snooty?"

Okay, I am so not going there.

"The truth is...I was jealous." Her eyes get misty now. "And I'm really sorry. I know that comparison is sin. And I was comparing myself to you, and I felt like I was coming up short." She kind of smiles. "Well, I am short compared to you. But I mean short in other ways too."

"I don't see how that's possible," I say. "I mean, you are so talented, Chloe. You have so much more experience in the music business. And you're so—"

"Jealous." She just shakes her head. "That's what I am. Or was. I was just plain jealous. I'm ashamed to have to admit it, but I know that's exactly what I need to do. The Bible tells us to confess our sins to each other and to pray for each other so that we can be healed. And I want to be healed. So I need you to forgive me, Maya." She's crying now.

I feel tears coming to my eyes too. So I just nod again.

"Can we pray together?" She looks directly at me. "I mean, for real this time. Not the way I've prayed with you before our last several concerts. That was phony baloney, and I'm sorry about that too. I can't believe how pathetic I've been. God should've just smacked me across the side of the head."

"He seems to have gotten your attention without any smacking involved."

"So, I mean it, can we pray together?"

"Sure," I say. "But first you need to know that I do forgive you. I totally forgive you. And I should ask you to forgive me too."

"Why?"

"I've had some pretty negative thoughts about you, Chloe. Even if I didn't say them out loud, I know it was wrong. And it probably impacted the way I was around you."

"Well, I can't really blame you after the way I've treated you. You are totally forgiven, Maya. Now let's pray, okay?"

So we hold hands and begin to pray. Then, even before we're done, Beanie comes over and places both her hands on our heads, and she prays too. And I have to say, I'm still kind of stunned to think of how it went down. Like real Christian faith in action. The way people should act. It was very cool! But that's not the end of it. There's more to tell.

"Okay, we better go," Chloe says as she notices what time it is, "before Bruce sends up a search party."

Once we get down there, Chloe proceeds to tell everyone pretty much what she's told me. She confesses that she's been jealous and asks them all to forgive her, and then we all pray together, and everyone hugs. After that, we have the best practice we've had in weeks.

"You girls sound pretty strong," Bruce tells us when we finish up. "Tonight's concert should be good." Okay, it was meant to be praise, but I sense that he isn't completely pleased. Not that I want to go there. I don't. In fact, nothing in me wants to

rock this boat right now. But maybe someone else does... maybe God.

"So you really don't mind that I perform too?" Laura asks Bruce.

And he takes a deep breath and just presses his lips together as if he doesn't want to answer.

"Come on, Bruce," she urges him. "Be honest with me."

"Well, since Chloe's been confessing things, I guess I have a confession too."

Now he's got everyone's attention. We're all waiting and watching him, and he's looking pretty uncomfortable. Almost like he's squirming.

"Out with it, Bruce," commands Chloe. "What's up?"

"Okay." He gets a grim expression now. "The truth is, I wasn't too excited to hear that Laura wanted to perform with the band last night."

"And?" Chloe presses him.

"And I just figured it was a one-time thing. I hoped it was a one-time thing. I guess I'm a little surprised that Laura is going to play again tonight."

"But not good surprised?" Allie sets down her drumsticks and comes over to where we've now got Bruce surrounded.

Laura is nodding like she gets this, but her eyes are glistening, and I'm worried she's about to cry. Chloe reaches over and takes her hand. I take her other one.

"To be perfectly honest," Bruce continues, "I'm not sure it's a good idea. I know it's fun for you girls to have a little reunion

while you're on winter break, Laura. But the band was on a different track. Redemption's sound has changed with Maya on board. And I can't lie and say it hasn't been a good thing. It has."

Allie puts her arm around Laura's shoulders now. We all kind of huddle there around her, like we're holding her up. And she's really crying.

"I-I don't have to play tonight." Laura's voice trembles.

"We want you to play," Allie says quickly. "Don't we?"

"Yes," I add.

"Of course," Chloe agrees. "You're still a part of Redemption."

"But that's not how Bruce feels." Laura sniffs and looks down.

"I'm just being honest with you girls," he continues. "Keep in mind that's what I've been hired to do. It's okay with me if Laura plays tonight. But I just want to go on record as saying that I don't think it's a great idea. I don't think it's in the best interest of the band. And it might even confuse some of your fans."

That's when Laura sinks down to the platform on the stage and just breaks into sobs. We all gather around her, trying to comfort her. And I'm sure Bruce feels miserable, not to mention responsible, as he stands a few feet away with his arms folded across his chest and wearing a very grim expression.

"I wish I'd never quit," Laura sobs over and over. "I wish I'd never quit."

We try to comfort her, which is fairly useless. Finally Bruce walks over, fishes a handkerchief out of his sports jacket, and

hands it to Laura. "What's going on here, Laura?" he asks in a quiet voice.

She takes the handkerchief, wipes her face, and looks up at him. "I just wish I hadn't quit the band," she admits. "I've missed it so much. I know I said I wanted to go to college. At the time I thought that's what I wanted. I mean, I've always been so academic. It just seemed like the right thing for me. And really, school's been okay, but not what I expected. Then suddenly I started to realize that I could do school anytime." She looks at Chloe and Allie. "Just like you guys told me last year. Now I totally get that being a part of this...playing in Redemption...well, it means everything to me. And I-I can't believe I gave it up." She begins to cry again.

"You want back in the band?" Chloe quietly asks her.

Laura just nods and wipes her nose.

"You'd drop out of college?" Allie looks skeptical now. "What about your parents?"

"It's *my* choice." Laura sniffs and sits up straighter. "Not that I have a choice...anymore." She glances at me and then looks back down at her lap.

Okay, I'm not stupid. I know that I'm the one standing in her way. I'm Laura's replacement. And part of me is a little bit hurt... and yet another part of me is thinking.

"You seriously want back in the band?" I finally ask her.

She nods again. "But I know it's impossible."

I look at Bruce now. "What if I wanted out?" I ask him.

"What?" He looks alarmed.

"What if I wanted out of Redemption?" I say again. And suddenly I am crying too. I'm not sure if they're tears of relief or joy or what, but I am crying, and then I'm laughing—all at the same time. Kind of hysterical, like maybe someone should slap me or throw a bucket of water on my head. But everyone is just staring at me like I've lost my mind.

"I do!" I tell them. "I want out!"

"You want out of the band?" Allie looks stunned.

"You want to quit Redemption?" Chloe actually looks hurt.

"What are you saying?" demands Bruce. And Laura just stares at me with tears still running down her cheeks.

So I take in a long, deep breath and attempt to explain. "I've been praying and praying for God's will," I confess. "And the truth is, I haven't really fit in here—I'm not really like you guys. Oh, I've tried to make the best of it, but it's never really felt right to me."

"But we don't want to lose you," says Bruce.

"That's right," agrees Allie.

"For sure," adds Chloe.

"And I appreciate that. But what if—what *if* God is telling us that it's okay for me to go and for Laura to come back?" I smile at them. "What if I was going to quit the band anyway, you know, when my three months ended?"

"Were you?"

"I'd been thinking about it. But I felt guilty. Like I'd really be letting everyone down. I was really torn. But the truth is, I wanted out. I still want out."

"Seriously?" Allie looks genuinely shocked.

"Don't get me wrong," I say quickly. "Redemption is a great band, a really talented and amazing band. But it's just not me, you know? You guys are aware of the kind of music I love doing, right?"

They kind of nod and wait.

"So you have to know that it's not the same kind of music you guys love doing, right?"

"But you've made the adjustment," Bruce points out. "The crowds like you, and I have to say you girls sound great. Really, Maya, you've been doing a fabulous job."

"Not happily."

"Is this all my fault?" Chloe points to herself with a frown. "Is it because I was so jealous and all that crud? Because trust me, Maya, that's over and done with. I love having you in the band. And we'll be okay now. I promise!"

"No," I assure her. "It's a whole lot more than that." Then I explain what Anna said about being my authentic self and how God would lead me. "And that's just what happened. Don't you see?"

We all just stand there in silence for a short while. I can tell they're trying to take this in. In fact, so am I. It's not like I had this all planned out. I didn't. But I think God did.

Now Laura is just staring at me incredulously, like I've just handed her a winning lottery ticket. "Are you being totally honest, Maya? You really, truly want out of the band? You're not just saying and doing this for my sake?"

I firmly shake my head. "Not at all."

"Because it's not your fault that I stupidly quit the band. And you don't owe it to me to do—"

"Seriously," I tell her. "If you don't believe me, just ask Beanie. She knows how I've struggled with this." I turn to Chloe and Allie. "Honestly, I love you guys, and it's been so great getting to know you and just being with you. But you have no idea what a relief it would be for me to leave the band—especially without messing things up. I mean, with the concert tour picking up now and then the recording session that's scheduled for February, I so didn't want to leave you guys high and dry." I look hopefully at Laura now. "If it's possible that you're really coming back and that I can step down…well, it's like a huge gift to me. Like an early Christmas present."

"Seriously?" She still looks cautious, like maybe this is too good to be true.

"Absolutely seriously. Nothing would make me happier."

"And you're sure, Laura?" Bruce asks her. "You're not going to change your mind or anything?"

She nods her head firmly. "I'm positive. And I have no problem setting my parents straight on this too. I know they'll understand."

Bruce scratches his head now. "Well, if you really do want out, Maya, we should probably get it over with as soon as possible."

"What if we announce this change tonight?" I say suddenly. "Tell everyone that I'm leaving and Laura is coming and Merry Christmas?"

"And Happy New Year," adds Allie with a slightly confused expression, like she's still trying to wrap her head around this.

"Only if you do a solo," Chloe says suddenly. "You need to give the crowd something to remember you by."

"Not that you're going to be gone for long." Bruce winks at me. "I think we could launch you into a whole new—"

"No, thanks," I say. "At least not for a while. All I want right now, all I need, is to just have a normal life. To go home to my friends and family and finish high school and see how Marissa's doing and maybe even go to prom in the spring. Then we'll see."

So it was settled. I kind of sleepwalked through the rest of the day. To be honest, I experienced some doubts. Like, what was I doing? Was I a fool to give this up? And yet I felt a sense of peace too. When it was time for my solo, I sang another Anna Gilbert song. And it seemed to fit.

Having a Breakdown

Verse 1

Having a breakdown

And it never felt so good

The fences that I balanced on are gone

And I've fallen in a beautiful place
What mattered most to me I see
Shouldn't really matter at all

Chorus:
I let go of the want to fill the lack
Now I know there's more to life than that
Lost it all but now I can see
That having a breakdown
Never felt so good to me
Oh, it never felt so good...

Verse 2:
Having to slow down
And it never felt so good to me
The rush of days just weighed me down with chains
Now I'm resting in a beautiful Grace
What mattered most to me I see
Shouldn't really matter at all

Bridge:
Losing only made me see
And falling here left me in perfect peace
Now I release

Maya's Green Tip for the Day

Recycled fashion is one of the most fun ways to go green. And here's the trick: you take an item of clothing and imagine it in a whole new way. For instance, an over-size T-shirt might be cut down into a sun top. A pair of jeans could be transformed into a denim skirt. A sweater might turn into a vest. A bunch of old ties might become a dress. A blanket could make a poncho. Think of new ways of accessorizing these transformed creations—like beads, buttons, appliqués, buckles, stencils, ribbons. Your imagination is the only limit.

Nineteen

December 30

It's been a whirlwind this past week. Where to begin...

I'll start on the day after I quit the band. Bruce had booked me a flight "home" on Christmas Eve. We all decided it was for the best. But as I was flying over the Midwest, I began to totally question my decision to leave Redemption. I mean, at least I had some kind of an identity when I was with the band. It's like I finally fit in somewhere. In a way we were a family. Okay, sometimes we were a dysfunctional family, but we'd kind of gotten over some of those things too. And even though Laura wanted back in, I still could've stayed on. They all told me so.

And what about the money? I'd actually been earning some serious money. Now that was all over with. What kind of fool had I been? I could just imagine what people would say to me: *why did you give that up?* What would I tell them? Because I knew God had something better for me? What?

And so as the jet cruised along at thirty-five thousand feet, hurling me toward my destination, I honestly wondered if I'd just burned my one and only security blanket. And to return to what? Because that was the other thing worrying me just then. What

was I going home to—if I could even call it home? When I'd called Uncle Allen to say I was coming back, he'd sounded surprised and maybe even a little disappointed. Naturally, he said that he'd be glad to see me and that Kim would be pleased too...but I wondered. What right did I have to assume that they would welcome me back? That I could call their house home?

And then I thought about Shannon. It had been so good to have that distance between us. What would happen when we lived in the same town again? What if she expected me to give her money or to live with her? What if she was using again? Despite my emancipation, she is still my mother. What if I was supposed to help her?

Then I wondered about school. I'd had such a hard time getting people to accept me. Would it be even harder now that I'd been away? What about my friends? Or did I really have any friends? I'd sort of left Amanda and Brooke by the wayside. And Vanessa and Wyatt and the others...well, had they ever really been my friends in the first place? What if Vanessa saw me as a threat again? Would it be like starting over? In some ways I thought there was more to Vanessa than others saw. Maybe I'd get the chance to find out.

Then I thought about Siobhan and our last conversation before I left. She had been seriously bummed to see me go, like we'd barely gotten started in our friendship. Hopefully we'd be able to pick up where we left off. And really, if Siobhan turned

out to be my one and only friend, what would be so bad about that? Maybe I could take her with me to visit Marissa.

And then there was Dominic. I hadn't even had a chance to tell him I was coming home. Really, what made me think it was home? What if I had no home? All these questions were just pounding on me. So much so that all I could do was pray. And so I did. And that's when I realized I still had that sense of peace. I felt certain that, despite my mountain of doubts, I was right where God wanted me.

Kim picked me up at the airport. I can't even describe how good it felt to see her again. We hugged for a long time. And we were both crying.

"Welcome home!" she said as she helped me with my bags.

"Really?" I asked as we made our way toward the parking lot.

"What do you mean by 'really'?" She paused and stared at me.

So I confessed my insecurities, voicing my doubts as to whether I really even had a home anymore. Kim just laughed.

"You should've heard Dad." We made our way through the parking garage. "As soon as I got home from the grocery store, he told me you were coming home—and he was totally happy. We both were."

"Really?" I tried to absorb this. "He's not disappointed that I quit the band?"

"He said he was a little worried at first, but then he told me how you said it didn't feel right for you, and we both agreed

that you'd know best, Maya. And selfishly, we're glad to have you back."

"Seriously?"

"Absolutely. The truth is, I've worried about him being alone. And I know his housekeeping's not that great. Not that we expect you to—"

"I love helping out," I told her. And it was true. In fact, I was even looking forward to it.

She chuckled. "Dad was worried that you might not be pleased with the recycling center. He kind of let things go."

"I'll fix it for him," I assured her.

"That's what I told him."

It turned out that what Kim had said was true. To my pleasant surprise, Uncle Allen was truly happy to have me home again, and yes, the recycling center was a mess.

Another thing surprised me. Kim had already made plans for Christmas Day. She'd invited Marissa and her dad for Christmas dinner. "And Shannon too," she said quietly. "I hope you don't mind."

I sort of shrugged. "That was thoughtful of you," I said somewhat stiffly. "I'm sure they appreciate it."

"But I didn't know you were coming," she admitted. "And I can't exactly uninvite them."

"No, of course not," I said. "Really, it'll be great to see Marissa."

"She's doing pretty well," Kim assured me. "I was really impressed when I saw her at youth group last weekend."

"She's still going?"

"Absolutely." Kim grinned. "And Shannon is still going to church."

"Still?" This was news to me.

"Marissa kind of forced her to go at first. But according to Caitlin, all three of them have been going steadily. And..." Kim got a funny look. "Well, I'm not sure if I'm supposed to say anything. It was Marissa who told me...but your mom is getting counseling."

"Seriously?"

Kim nodded. "Now don't expect a miraculous transformation, Maya. But I do think she's changing some."

And I have to agree with my cousin. When I saw Shannon, after less than two months of being apart, she *did* seem different. Oh, she's still Shannon, for sure. And she still sticks her foot in her mouth (without even realizing it), and she's still self-centered. But something in her is different too. I noticed it most of all when I observed her interacting with Marissa on Christmas Day. And she didn't even know I was watching.

Marissa's hair has grown out some, but she doesn't like how it looks. Consequently, she had on an old ski hat that wasn't terribly becoming. I just happened to be going down the hallway when I noticed Shannon and Marissa in the bathroom with the door slightly ajar.

"If you're too hot, just take the hat off," Shannon was telling her. "No one cares what you look like."

"I care," Marissa shot back at her.

"Here," Shannon said. "Let me help you."

This is when I peeked in. To be honest, I imagined my mother snatching Marissa's knit hat and flushing it down the john. Extreme, I know, but then I also know Shannon. But to my surprise, Shannon began helping Marissa with her hair.

"I actually like your hair," she told Marissa as she used water to sculpt her short brown hair into kind of a spiky do. "How's that?"

Now Marissa smiled. "Okay."

"See, it's like I keep telling you," Shannon said. "You're a very pretty girl."

"Thanks."

"Not as pretty as me," Shannon teased. She pressed her way in front of the mirror and daubed on lipstick. Marissa just laughed.

Okay, I'll admit that I felt a tiny wave of jealousy to see my own mother acting more maternal toward Marissa than she's ever been toward me. But it also struck me that Marissa is a lot more needy (since her injury) than I have ever been in my whole life. And maybe if I hadn't been such a strong person...maybe Shannon would've tried harder to mother me. Or not. Mostly, I thank God that He made me like He did. I know it's what I needed to survive.

Here's what else I know. I know that the secret desire of my heart was to come home and live a somewhat normal life. I just needed that. I realize everyone's normal is different, but my normal includes family and friends, and I need them around me.

And I need to go to a regular school and do regular things—like attending ball games and dances and just hanging with friends. I also need to go to church and youth group and to meet with Caitlin. *I basically just need normal.*

Most of all I need God—and I realize now that God is what makes my life normal. He is my normal. And that's what matters most.

Maya's Green Tip for the Day

Once again I have to say that *God is the Great Recycler.* Not only has He salvaged my life, but I see His healing hand on others as well. And I'm finding that people I had almost given up on—people like Marissa and Shannon—can be renewed, reused, and recycled by God. He takes our messes and turns them into something usable. He salvages our wasted resources and recycles them into something full of life. And He wants to do the same for you. He wants to make you new and whole and useful. Just let Him!

Readers Group Guide

1. Early in the story Maya gets bullied by Vanessa. Have you ever been a victim of bullying? Or have you ever been a bully? Explain the circumstances.

2. Why do you think Vanessa feels so threatened by Maya? If you were Maya, how would you handle it?

3. In this book Maya begins to explore her musical talent. Do you have some hidden talent or something you want to try? Does something hold you back? Explain.

4. Maya continues to meet with and be mentored by Caitlin. Do you think mentoring is helpful? Describe why or why not.

5. A girl named Siobhan has a history that is put down by some of her peers, and yet Maya is determined to reach out to this girl. How would you react to a situation like this?

6. Maya's mother, Shannon, is back, and Maya knows that God wants her to respect her parents—but how is that possible? How would you advise someone in Maya's shoes?

7. Were you surprised when Maya was invited to replace Laura in Redemption? Do you think Maya made the right choice to join the band? Why or why not?

8. As leader of the band, Chloe really respects Maya's talents, and yet she becomes jealous. Why do you think that is? What do you do when you feel jealous? Explain.

9. More than anything, Maya decides she just wants a normal life. Explain what you think normal is and what you think Maya is really looking for. Would you describe your own life as normal?

10. What matters most to Maya is living her life for God. What matters most to you?

Dear Reader,

I hope you enjoyed this sixteenth and final book in the Diary of a Teenage Girl series. I've really enjoyed writing them—it's been fun getting to know the characters. And I have to admit it's a little sad to bring it to an end.

Because this was the last book, I did something a bit different. I decided to surprise you by introducing a character who is *not* fictional. Can you guess who it was?

Anna Gilbert is a real person! Not only is Anna the real deal, but she reminds me of some of the Diary characters. Like Caitlin (in the first Diaries), Anna has a tight relationship with God. And like Chloe and Maya, Anna is musically gifted. In fact, the lyrics I've used in this book are Anna's creation. And if you like her lyrics, you should hear the girl sing!

Anna is a singer and songwriter currently living in Nashville, where she's working on her third CD with Grammy Award–winning producer Charlie Peacock. (Peacock has produced Switchfoot, Warren Barfield, Sara Groves, Amy Grant, and many other great artists.) Her brand-new CD released in spring 2009 and is available for purchase online. Anna's first two CDs are titled *Falling in a Beautiful Place* and *God Sees*, and they are available on iTunes and http://cdbaby.com.

If you'd like to connect with Anna, you can find her at www.my space.com/annagilbert as well as on Facebook.com (just do a search for "Anna Gilbert"). She would love to hear from you!

On a final note, thanks for reading the Diary of a Teenage Girl series! If you want to find out more about what I'm doing, go to my Web site, http://melodycarlson.com, or look me up on Facebook.

Blessings!
Melody Carlson

Diary of a Teenage Girl series

Meet Caitlin, Chloe, Kim, and Maya

Experience the lives of four very different girls: Caitlin, Chloe, Kim, and Maya, through the pages of their diaries. Caitlin, the conservative Christian struggles to stand morally strong and pure; Chloe, the alternative rocker wants to be authentic to who she is and follow Christ; Kim, adopted from a Korean orphanage as a baby, searches out her true identity; and Maya, who has a glamorous life on the outside, but inside is desperately struggling to fit in after a series of tramatic events turns her world upside down. In each, you'll read a story for every girl longing to learn about who she is in Christ.

www.doatg.com

The Secret Life of Samantha McGregor series

A powerful gift requires a lot of responsibility...

Bad Connection

Kayla Henderson is missing, and everyone, including Samantha, assumes she ran away. But then Samantha has a vision... If Kayla really is in danger, then time is running out!

Beyond Reach

Garrett Pierson is one of those quiet, academic types. One day, Samantha has a vision of Garrett teetering on a railroad bridge - and then falling backwards, just beyond reach! What does this vision mean, and where is Garrett, anyway?

Playing with Fire

Samantha's brother, Zach, is finally home after a ninety-day rehab for his meth addiction. Then Samantha has a vision of a burning cabin, and a shooting. Convinced that Zach is involved somehow, Samantha must decide whether to risk getting Zach in trouble with the law—or ultimately risk his life.

Payback

Samantha is plunged into her biggest challenges yet, as she works against the clock to stop a mass murder, help a troubled youth, and save her mother from making a terrible mistake!